Halliwell's Who's Who in the Movies

Also available from HarperCollins*Publishers*

Halliwell's Film & Video Guide

HALLIWELL'S WHO'S WHO IN THE MOVIES

LESLIE HALLIWELL

14th Edition

Edited by JOHN WALKER

Harper Resource
An Imprint of HarperCollinsPublishers

This book is published in Great Britain by HarperCollins Publishers under the title
HALLIWELL WHO'S WHO IN THE MOVIES (Fourteenth Edition)

HALLIWELL WHO'S WHO IN THE MOVIES (Fourteenth Edition).
Copyright © 2001, 1999, 1997, 1995, 1993 by Ruth Halliwell and John Walker.
Copyright © 1988, 1984, 1980, 1977, 1976, 1974, 1970, 1967, 1965 by Leslie Halliwell.
All rights reserved.

HarperCollins books may be purchased for educational, business, or sales promotional use.
For information please write:
Special Markets Department, HarperCollins Publishers, Inc.,
10 East 53rd Street, New York, NY 10022.

First HarperPerennial edition published 1997
Formerly published in U.S. as Halliwell's Filmgoer's Companion

ISSN 1066-2912
ISBN 0-06-093507-3

01 02 03 04 05 10 9 8 7 6 5 4 3 2 1

Contents

Preface

Welcome to the second edition of a unique guide for movie lovers, one that explores the highways and byways of cinema. This is the latest revision of the venerable *Halliwell's Filmgoer's Companion*, updated and rearranged to make its contents easily accessible, and with more than 1,000 new entries to extend its coverage.

Here you will find information on not only the stars, but also the character actors, the directors and producers, writers, cinematographers, composers, editors, production and costume designers, who combine to film an art and an entertainment with a mass appeal.

Although the bulk of the book is concerned with concise biographies and filmographies, you will also find information on studios and production companies, on movie series, remakes, themes and genres, which also includes entries on many fictional and cartoon characters. There is a glossary of film terms, a brief history of the medium and a listing of some of the best movie books and periodicals. All cinematic life is here, apart from reviews of the films themselves. That information can be found in the annually updated *Halliwell's Film & Video Guide*.

It is now 36 years since Alfred Hitchcock welcomed the first edition of the *Filmgoer's Companion* as: 'obviously a good thing to have on a handy shelf'. I trust it remains so, even though now the internet offers much information on films and filming. Indeed, by the time you read this, Halliwell's itself should be available on the World Wide Web, as part of Coppernob's film coverage. But a book such as this continues to provide a quick and easy means of reference, and long may it complement newer ways of gaining information.

I am grateful for the helpful advice and comments of many readers and researchers, notably: William C. Clogston, Dr Robert Dassanowsky, Bill Edwards, Allan Fish, John Glynn, Alan Goble, David Hattenstone, Bob Mastrangelo, Don Minifie, Andrew Ross and John Thaxter. They have helped make my task easier and more enjoyable. I owe thanks, too, to the editorial skills of Val Hudson and Monica Chakraverty and the technical expertise of Graham Bell and Alan Trewartha at HarperCollins, and to my agents Gloria Ferris and Rivers Scott for their encouragement. My love goes to my wife Barbara, who makes the hard work worthwhile.

John Walker (e-mail: film@coppernob.net)

Explanatory Notes

Alphabetical order

The main section of this book (Section 1, Who's Who in the Movies) is an A–Z of actors, directors, producers, writers and other key personnel involved in the movies, where all entries are in alphabetical order, on normal dictionary lines. Mac and Mc are treated as one, although the spelling is of course left distinct. Names such as Von Stroheim come under 'V' and Cecil B. De Mille under 'D'. All names, whatever their nationality, are treated as if the last name were the surname, e.g. Zhang Yimou will be found under Yimou, Zhang. Fictional characters can be found in Section 2 (Movie Remakes, Series, Themes and Genres). They are listed under their complete names, so that Antoine Doinel is under 'A' and Sherlock Holmes is under 'S'.

Personal dates

The birth year of an actor or actress is often obscured beyond the powers of a crystal ball, and in some cases is impossible to discover in an industry that is averse to ageing. In general, the earliest date in print is the one preferred as most likely to be accurate.

Doubtful dates are prefaced by 'c.' (*circa*).

(*) indicates that the person has died, but the death is uncertain.

Film titles

The title by which the film is known in its English-speaking country of origin is given. Foreign-language titles are generally translated when the film has been released in English-speaking countries, with the original title following.

Film dates

It can be as difficult to ascertain the correct date of a film as it is to determine the personal dates of its stars. Some films sit on the shelf for several years before being released, while frequently more than 12 months can pass between an American film's release in its home country and in Britain. There is an undoubted area of confusion: *Casablanca*, for instance, was given a 50th-anniversary re-release in 1992, yet the film was not officially released until 1943, and also bears a 1943 copyright date. But it was shown to critics in November 1942, so it can also qualify as a movie from the earlier year. The aim here is to give wherever possible the date when the film was first publicly shown in its country of origin.

Filmographies

Complete filmographies are indicated by the symbol ■. A complete entry should not necessarily be taken as a sign of eminence or as a seal of approval. Some people simply made very few films or had compact typical careers which are worth detailing as instances of what goes on in the film industry: the gradual climb, the good cameo role, the star period, the two or three 'dogs' in a row, the gradual decline, the cheap exploitation movie. Filmographies cannot be completed for several major directors and stars because not all of their earlier films can be traced.

Incomplete lists normally end with 'etc.', which means that there may be up to as many films again as have been listed, while 'many others' indicates that the list has only scratched the surface. These lists usually include either the first film or the most significant role of the subject, and end up with his or her most recent work, with dates coming closest together over the most prolific and significant period.

A subject's most significant films are indicated by italics. The reader may interpret 'significant' as meaning commercial, artistic, critical or personal success.

Short films (less than 50 minutes or so) are not normally accounted for unless the subject worked chiefly in this field.

Almost every performer and director now works in TV as well as films, and many make their reputations these days on the small screen. For this reason, significant appearances in television series are also listed after the filmographies. The main lists also include some, but not all, of a subject's TV movies, made for any of its forms from cable to satellite, and are indicated by '(TV)' after the title. The majority of the TV movies listed have also been released on video-cassette.

Quotes
These are introduced by the symbol 66. Quotes by the subject are indicated by his or her initials; from other sources, by the person's name.

Rosettes (❂)
These are bestowed for significant work in a particular field over a sizeable period of film history, upon people with remarkable talents which are not easily duplicated. For rosette winners, one film is singled out in which the person concerned was at his or her peak.

Abbreviations
The main ones used are:

a	actor	m	musical score
ed	editor	md	musical director
AA	Academy Award, indicating	oa	original author
	the winning of a Hollywood	original sp	original screenplay
	Oscar, awarded annually by the	p	producer, which covers all the
	Academy of Motion Picture		many varieties of the breed,
	Arts and Sciences		from executive producer
AAN	indicates a nomination for an		to associate producer,
	Academy Award		co-producer, etc.
BFA	indicates the winning of a	d	director
	British Film Academy award,	pd	production designer
	awarded by the British	ph	cinematographer
	Academy of Film and	s	song(s)
	Television Arts	w	screenwriter
ch	choreographer	wd	writer and director
fx	special effects		

Where more than one person is involved in an activity, it is indicated by co-, so that co-w means that at least two writers scripted a film.

The symbol '&' means that the function abbreviated is in addition to that normally expected of the subject. In an actor's list, '& wd' would mean that he or she also wrote and directed.

Abbreviations for countries include:

Aus.	Australia	Gr.	Greece
Aust.	Austria	Hol.	Netherlands
Braz.	Brazil	Ire.	Ireland
Can.	Canada	It.	Italy
Den.	Denmark	Nor.	Norway
Fr.	France	Swe.	Sweden
GB	Great Britain	Swiss	Switzerland
Ger.	Germany	US	United States of America

Cross-References
People or organizations with their own significant entries are indicated by the use of SMALL CAPITALS.

1
Who's Who in the Movies
An A–Z of Personalities

A

Aakerú, Lee (1943–)
Child actor whose career faded in his early teens, when he quit the profession.

The Atomic City 52. Desperate Search 52. No Room for the Groom 52. My Son John 52. Jeopardy 52. Take Me to Town 53. Arena 53. Hondo 53. Rin Tin Tin, Hero of the West 55, etc.

TV series: Adventures of Rin Tin Tin 54–59.

Aames, Willie (1960–) (William Upton)
American leading actor, who began as a clean-cut teenager on television, but has found worthwhile adult roles harder to find. He runs his own TV and commercial production studio and produces and stars in *Bibleman*, a Christian video series for children.

Frankenstein (TV) 73. Scavenger Hunt 79. Paradise 82. Zapped! 82. Killing Machine (Sp.) 84. Cut and Run (It.) 85. Eight Is Enough: A Family Reunion (TV) 87. Eight Is Enough: Wedding (TV) 89, etc.

TV series: We'll Get By 75. Swiss Family Robinson 75–76. Eight Is Enough 77–81. We're Movin' 82. Charles in Charge 84–85.

Aaron, Caroline (1954–)
American actress.

Baby, It's You 82. The Brother from Another Planet 84. Heartburn 86. Crimes and Misdemeanors 89. Edward Scissorhands 90. Alice 90. This Is My Life 92. Mr 247 94. House Arrest 96. Big Night 96. A Modern Affair 96. Deconstructing Harry 97. Weapons of Mass Distraction (TV) 97. Primary Colors 98. There's No Fish Food in Heaven 98. Anywhere But Here 99. What Planet Are You From? 00, etc.

Aaron, Sidney
Pseudonym used by Paddy Chayefsky for his last film script, *Altered States* 80.

Abady, Temple (1903–1970)
British composer, from the theatre.

The Woman in the Hall 47. Miranda 48. Easy Money 48. All over the Town 49. Dear Mr Prohack 49. Folly to Be Wise 52. Miss Robin Hood 52. Never Look Back 52. The Oracle 52. Street Corner 53. Kill Me Tomorrow 57, etc.

Abatantuono, Diego (1955–)
Italian leading actor and screenwriter, born in Milan; he is frequently in the films of Gabriele Salvatores.

Attila 80. Il Tango Della Gelosia 81. Christmas Present/Regalo di Natale 86. Marrakech Express 88. On Tour/Turne 90. Mediterraneo 91. The Dark Continent/Nel Continente Nero 92. Puerto Escondido (& w) 93. The Bull/El Toro 95. The Best Man/Il Testimone dello Sposo 97, etc.

Abbott, Bud (1895–1974) (William Abbott)
American comedian, the brusque and slightly shifty 'straight man' half of Abbott and Costello, cross-talking vaudevillians of long standing who became Universal's top stars of the early 40s. Bud, seldom seen without his hat, was the bully who left the dirty work for his partner, never believed his tall but true stories of crooks and monsters, and usually avoided the pie in the face.

After a TV series (1953) using up all their old routines, the team split and Abbott retired. In 1975 there was published *Who's On First*, a selection of frame-by-frame routines, by Richard J. Anobile. Bob Thomas's biography, *Bud and Lou*, was published in 1977, and appeared in 1978 as a TV movie, with Harvey Korman and Buddy Hackett as Abbott.

All Abbott and Costello movies depended for their effectiveness on the number of old vaudeville routines included, such as the following: 'All Because You Don't Like Mustard' and 'Jonah and the Whale' (*One Night in the Tropics*); 'Drill' (*Buck Privates*); 'Bussing the Bee' and 'Seven Times Thirteen Is Twenty-Eight' (*In the Navy*); 'The Moving Candle' (*Hold That Ghost, Meet Frankenstein*); 'Don't Order Anything' (*Keep 'Em Flying*, borrowed from Laurel and Hardy's *Man o' War*); 'Poker Game' (*Ride 'Em Cowboy*); 'Ten Dollars You're Not There' (*Rio Rita*); 'The Poisoned Drink' (*Pardon My Sarong*); 'The Telephone Call' (*Who Done It*); 'Bagel Street' (*In Society*); 'The Magic Act' and 'Slowly I Turned' (*Lost in a Harem*); 'The Mirror' and 'Who's on First' (*The Naughty Nineties*); 'Hole in the Wall' (*The Noose Hangs High*); 'Identification' and 'Silver Ore' (*Mexican Hayride*); 'The Gorilla' (*Africa Screams*); 'The Shovel Is My Pick' (*Meet the Mummy*).

■ *One Night in the Tropics* (their only supporting roles) 40. *Buck Privates* 41. In The Navy 41. *Hold That Ghost* 41. Keep 'Em Flying 41. Ride 'Em Cowboy 41. Rio Rita 42. Pardon My Sarong 42. Who Done It? 42. It Ain't Hay 43. Hit the Ice 43. Lost In A Harem 44. *In Society* 44. Here Come the Co-Eds 45. *The Naughty Nineties* (featuring their famous 'Who's On First' routine) 45. Abbott and Costello in Hollywood 45. The Little Giant (a doomed attempt to work separately within the same film) 46. The Time of Their Lives (an interesting failure) 46. Buck Privates Come Home 46. The Wistful Widow of Wagon Gap 47. The Noose Hangs High 48. *Abbott and Costello Meet Frankenstein* 48. Mexican Hayride 48. Africa Screams 49. Abbott and Costello Meet the Killer, Boris Karloff 48. Abbott and Costello in the Foreign Legion 50. Abbott and Costello Meet the Invisible Man 51. Comin' Round the Mountain 51. Jack and the Beanstalk 52. Abbott and Costello Lost in Alaska 52. Abbott and Costello Meet Captain Kidd 52. Abbott and Costello Go to Mars 53. *Abbott and Costello Meet Dr Jekyll and Mr Hyde* 53. Abbott and Costello Meet the Keystone Kops 54. Abbott and Costello Meet the Mummy 55. Dance with Me Henry 56.

✪ For bringing authentic vaudeville to Hollywood in a few imperishable routines; and for cheering up a generation at war. *Abbott and Costello Meet Frankenstein*.

See Costello, Lou.

❝ Abbott and Costello's comedy depended on caricature and contrast: the fat and the thin, the nervous and the foolhardy, the stupid and the stupider. Their work falls into well-remembered routines and reactions. There is chubby, terrified Costello calling after his partner: 'Ch-ch-ch-ch-ch-i-ck!'

There is his shy admission: 'I'm a ba-a-a-ad boy!'

There is the old pantomime gag of his seeing something alarming and running to tell his partner; by the time the latter returns the thing has naturally disappeared. There are repetitive routines such as the 'Slowly I Turned' scene from *Lost in a Harem*, with its Laurel and Hardy-like inevitability. Most memorably there is skilful nightclub cross-talk, seen at its best in the 'Who's On First' sketch which first brought them to fame. Here is part of it: 'A: You know, these days they give ballplayers very peculiar names. Take the St Louis team: Who's on first, What's on second, I Don't Know is on third …

C: That's what I want to find out. I want you to tell me the names of the fellows on the St Louis team.

I'm telling you. Who's on first. What's on second, I Don't Know is on third.

– Who's playing first?

Yes.

– I mean, the fellow's name on first base.

Who.

– The fellow playing first base.

Who.

– The guy on first base.

Who is on first.

– Well, what are you asking me for?

I'm not asking you, I'm telling you. Who is on first.

– I'm asking you – who is on first?

That's the man's name.

– That's who's name?

Yes.

– Well, go ahead, tell me.

Who!

– All I'm trying to find out is, what's the guy's name on first base.

Oh no, What is on second.

– I'm not asking you who's on second.

Who's on first.

– That's what I'm trying to find out!

What's the guy's name on first base?

What's the guy's name on second base.

– I'm not asking who's on second.

Who's on first.

– I Don't Know.

He's on third …'

And so on, for another five minutes.

Abbott, Diahnne (1945–)
American actress. Her second husband (1976–78) was actor Robert De Niro.

Taxi Driver 76. New York New York 77. Welcome to L.A. 77. The King of Comedy 83. Love Streams 84. Jo Jo Dancer, Your Life Is Calling 86, etc.

Abbott, George (1887–1995)
American playwright and producer of lively commercial properties. He sporadically invaded Hollywood to supervise their filming, and stayed briefly to perform other services.

Autobiography: 1963, *Mister Abbott*.

as original author: Four Walls 28. Coquette 29. *Broadway* 29 (and 42). Lilly Turner 33. Heat Lightning 34. *Three Men on a Horse* 36. On Your Toes 39. The Boys from Syracuse 40. Where's Charley? 52. *The Pajama Game* (& co-d) 57. *Damn Yankees* (& co-d) 58, etc.

as producer: *Boy Meets Girl* 38. Room Service 38. The Primrose Path 40. *The Pajama Game* 57. *Damn Yankees* 58, etc.

as director: Why Bring That Up? 29. The Sea God 30. Stolen Heaven 31. Secrets of a Secretary 31. My Sin 31. Too Many Girls 40, etc.

❝ I must confess that one of my main defects as a director has always been an incurable impatience. – G.A.

Many great minds have made a botch of matters because their emotions fettered their thinking. – G.A.

Abbott, John (1905–1996)
British character actor, specializing in eccentric parts. Born in London, he began as a commercial artist, and made his professional debut on stage in 1934, before joining the Old Vic company to play Shakespearean roles, including Malvolio in *Twelfth Night*.

Mademoiselle Docteur 37. The Return of the Scarlet Pimpernel 37. The Saint in London 39. Ten Days in Paris 39. The Shanghai Gesture 41. Mrs Miniver 42. They Got Me Covered 42. The London Blackout Murders (lead) 42. The Gorilla Man 42. Jane Eyre 43. Saratoga Trunk 43. They Got Me Covered 43. Abroad with Two Yanks 44. The Falcon in Hollywood 44. The Mask of Dimitrios 44. Once Upon a Time 44. Secrets of Scotland Yard 44. Pursuit to Algiers 45.The Vampire's Ghost 45. The Bandit of Sherwood Forest 46. Deception 47. *The Woman in White* 48 (a memorable performance, as the grotesque invalid Frederick Fairlie). Madame Bovary 49. Crosswinds 51. Thunder on the Hill 51. The Merry Widow 52. Rogue's March 53. Sombrero 53. Public Pigeon Number One 57. Gigi 58. Who's Minding the Store? 63. Gambit 66. The Store 66. 2000 Years Later 69. The Black Bird 75. Slapstick 84. Lady Jane 85, many others.

Abbott, Philip (1923–1998)
American 'second lead' of the 50s.

Bachelor Party 57. Invisible Boy 57. *Sweet Bird of Youth* 62. The Spiral Road 62. Miracle of the White Stallions 63. Those Calloways 64. Tail Gunner Joe (TV) 77. Hangar 18 80. Savannah Smiles 82. The First Power 90, etc.

TV series: *The F.B.I.* 65–73. Rich Man, Poor Man – Book II 76–77.

Abdul-Jabbar, Kareem (1947–) (Lew Alcindor)
Lanky American actor, a former star basketball player.

Game of Death 78. The Fish that Saved Pittsburgh 79. Airplane! 80. Fletch 85. Purple People Eater 88. D2: The Mighty Ducks (as himself) 94. Slam Dunk Ernest 95, etc.

Abel, Alfred (1880–1937)
German character actor of weighty personality, in films from 1913.

Dr Mabuse 22. Phantom 22. Metropolis 26. Gold 28. Narkose (& d) 29. Congress Dances 31. Salon Dora Greene 33. Das Hofkonzert 36. Kater Lampe 36. Frau Sylvelin 38, etc.

Abel, Walter (1898–1987)
American character actor with stage experience. Made his Hollywood debut as D'Artagnan, but later settled enjoyably into variations on a single performance of harassment and nervousness, whether as father, friend of the family or professional man. Born in St Paul, Minnesota, he studied at the American Academy of Dramatic Art in New York, and began on stage and in vaudeville.

■ Liliom 30. *The Three Musketeers* 35. The Lady Consents 36. Two in the Dark 36. The Witness Chair 36. Fury 36. We Went to College 36. Second Wife 36. Portia on Trial 37. Wise Girl 37. Law of the Underworld 38. Racket Busters 38. Men with Wings 38. King of the Turf 39. Miracle on Main Street 40. Dance Girl Dance 40. *Arise My Love* (which provided him with a key line: 'I'm not happy. I'm not happy at all') 40. Michael Shayne Private Detective 40. Who Killed Aunt Maggie? 40. *Hold Back the Dawn* 41. Skylark 41. Glamour Boy 41. *Beyond the Blue Horizon* 42. *Star Spangled Rhythm* 42. *Holiday Inn* 42. Wake Island 42. So Proudly We Hail 43. Fired Wife 43. Follow the Boys 44. *Mr Skeffington* 44. An American Romance 44. *The Affairs of Susan* 45. Duffy's Tavern 45. *Kiss and Tell* 45. The Kid from Brooklyn 46. 13 Rue Madeleine 46. The Fabulous Joe 47. *Dream Girl* 48. That Lady in Ermine 48. Island in the Sky 53. So This is Love 53. Night People 54. The Indian Fighter 55. The Steel Jungle 56. *Bernardine* 57. Raintree County 57. Handle with Care 58. Mirage 65. Quick Let's Get Married 65. Zora 71. The Man without a Country (TV) 74. Silent Night, Bloody Night 74. The Ultimate Solution of Grace Quigley 84.

❝ Famous line *Arise My Love* 'I'm not happy. I'm not happy at all!'

Abraham, F(ahrid) Murray (1939–)
Intense American character actor, who has found effective film roles hard to come by, despite his Oscar. Born in Pittsburgh, Pennsylvania, of Italian and Syrian parents, he was brought up in El Paso, Texas, and educated at the University of Texas, beginning on stage in 1965. His finest performance remains that of Salieri in *Amadeus*.

They Might Be Giants 71. Serpico 73. The Sunshine Boys 75. All the President's Men 76. The Ritz 76. The Big Fix 78. Scarface 83. *Amadeus* (AA) 84. The Name of the Rose 86. Russicum 87. Personal Choice 88. Beyond the Stars 89. An Innocent Man 89. La Nuit du Serail 89. Slipstream 89. La Batalla de los Tres Reyes 90. Bonfire of the Vanities 90. Stockade 90. Mobsters

91. National Lampoon's Loaded Weapon 1 93. Sweet Killing 93. Last Action Hero 93. Surviving the Game 94. Jamila 94. L'Affaire (Fr.) 94. Nostradamus 94. Mighty Aphrodite 95. Children of the Revolution (as Stalin) 96. Looking for Richard 96. Larry McMurtry's Dead Man's Walk (TV) 96. Baby Face Nelson 97. Mimic 97. Falcone 98. Star Trek: Insurrection 98. Muppets from Space (voice) 99. Finding Forrester 00. The Knights of the Quest 01, etc.

Abrahams, Jim (1944–)
American director, screenwriter and actor, usually in collaboration with Jerry and David Zucker.
The Kentucky Fried Movie (a, co-w) 77. Airplane! (a, co-wd) 80. Top Secret! (co-wd) 84. Ruthless People (co-d) 86. The Naked Gun: From the Files of Police Squad (co-w) 88. Big Business (d) 88. Welcome Home Roxy Carmichael (d) 91. Hot Shots! (co-w, d) 91. Hot Shots! Part Deux (co-w, d) 93. First Do No Harm (TV) 97. Mafia!/Jane Austen's Mafia! 98, etc.

Abrams, Jeffrey
American scriptwriter.
Taking Care of Business/Filofax 90. Regarding Henry (& a) 91. Forever Young 92. Six Degrees of Separation (a) 93. Gone Fishin' 97, etc.

Abril, Victoria (1959–)
Spanish leading actress, who moved to France in the early 80s.
Mother, Dearly Loved/Mater Amatisima 79. The Beehive/La Colmena 81. The Moon in the Gutter/La Lune dans le Caniveau 83. On the Line/Rio Abajo 84. Our Father/Padre Nuestro 84. The Witching Hour/La Hora Bruja 85. Max, Mon Amour 86. Time of Silence/Tiempo de Silencio 86. Baton Rouge 88. Tie Me Up! Tie Me Down!/¡Atame! 89. Lovers/Amantes 91. High Heels/Tacones Lejanos 91. Wonderful Times/Une Epoque Formidable 91. Too Much Heart/Demasiado Corazón 92. Kika 93. Intruso 93. Jimmy Hollywood 94. French Twist/Gazon Maudit 95. Nobody Will Talk about Us When We're Dead/Nadie Hablará de Nosotros Cuando Haramos Muertos 95. Libertarias 96. Entre las Piernas 98, etc.

Abuladze, Tengiz (1924–1994)
Russian film director and screenwriter. Born in Georgia, he studied film in Moscow before returning to Georgia to work.
Magdana's Donkey/Magdanas Lurdzha (co-d) 55. Somebody Else's Children/Skhvisi Shvilebi 58. The Invocation/Vedreba 68. A Necklace for My Beloved/Samkauli Satr Posatvis 73. The Wishing Tree/Natvris Khe 76. *Repentance*/Monanieba 84, etc.

Achard, Marcel (1899–1974) (Marcel-Auguste Ferréol)
French dramatist, screenwriter and occasional director. Born in Ste-Foy-les-Lyon, and educated at the University of Lyon, he was active as a playwright of sentimental romances from the early 20s to the mid-60s.
The Merry Widow 34. Mayerling 36. Alibi (oa) 37. The Strange Monsieur Victor 38. Untel Père et Fils 40. Monsieur la Souris 43. The Paris Waltz (d only) 50. Madame De 53. La Garçonne 57. A Woman Like Satan 59. A Shot in the Dark (oa) 64.

Acheson, James
English costume designer, now in international films.
Time Bandits 81. Water 84. Brazil 85. Highlander 86. The Last Emperor (AA) 87. Dangerous Liaisons (AA) 88. The Sheltering Sky 90. Little Buddha 93. Mary Shelley's Frankenstein 94. Restoration (AA) 94, etc.

Acker, Jean (1893–1978)
American screen and stage actress, the first wife of Rudolph Valentino (1919–21).
Are You a Mason? 15. Arabian Knight 20. Brewster's Millions 21. The Woman in Chains 23. The Girl Habit 31. No More Ladies 35. My Favorite Wife 40. The Thin Man Goes Home 44. Spellbound 45. Something to Live For 52, etc.

Acker, Sharon (1935–)
Canadian leading lady.
Lucky Jim (GB) 57. Waiting For Caroline (Can.) 67. Point Blank 67. The First Time 68. Act of the Heart 70. A Clear and Present Danger (TV) 70. Hec Ramsey (TV) 72. The Stranger (TV) 73. The Hanged Man (TV) 74. Our Man Flint: Dead On Target (TV) 76. The Hostage Heart (TV) 77. The Murder That Wouldn't Die (TV) 79. Happy Birthday to Me 80.
TV series: The Senator 70-71. Perry Mason 73-74. Executive Suite 77.

Ackerman, Bettye (1928–)
American general purpose actress.
Face of Fire 59. Companions in Nightmare (TV) 68. Rascal 69. M*A*S*H. 70, etc.
TV series: *Ben Casey* 60–64.

Ackerman, Thomas
American cinematographer, a former camera operator. Born in Iowa, he was educated at the University of Iowa.
New Year's Evil 81. Roadhouse 66 84. Frankenweenie 84. Girls Just Want to Have Fun 85. Back to School 86. Beetlejuice 88. National Lampoon's Christmas Vacation 89. True Identity 91. Dennis the Menace/Dennis 93. Baby's Day Out 94. Jumanji 95. The Eighteenth Angel 97. George of the Jungle 97. My Favorite Martian 99. The Muse 99. The Adventures of Rocky and Bullwinkle 00, etc.

Ackland, Joss (1928–)
British actor of larger-than-life personality; much on TV. Born in London, he studied at the Central School of Dramatic Art and was on stage from 1946.
Autobiography: 1989, *I Must Be in There Somewhere*.
Seven Days to Noon 49. The Ghost Ship 53. Rasputin the Mad Monk 65. Crescendo 70. Mr Forbush and the Penguins 71. The House That Dripped Blood 71. Villain 71. England Made Me 72. The Happiness Cage (US) 72. Hitler: The Last Ten Days 73. Penny Gold 73. The Three Musketeers 73. The Black Windmill 74. S*P*Y*S. 74. Great Expectations 75. Royal Flash 75. Operation Daybreak 75. Silver Bears 78. Who is Killing the Great Chefs of Europe? 78. Saint Jack 79. The Apple 80. Rough Cut 80. Dangerous Davies (TV) 81. A Zed and Two Noughts 85. Lady Jane 86. White Mischief 87. It Couldn't Happen Here 88. Popielusko 88. Lethal Weapon 2 89. To Forget Palermo/Dimenticare Palermo 89. The Bridge 90. The Hunt for Red October 90. Tre Colonne in Cronaca 90. The Object of Beauty 91. Bill & Ted's Bogus Journey 91. Once Upon a Crime 92. The Mighty Ducks 92. The Princess and the Goblin (voice) 92. Nowhere to Run 92. Mad Dogs and Englishmen 95. Occhiopinocchio (It.) 95. Citizen X (US) 95. Daisies in December (TV) 95. Surviving Picasso 96. D3: Mighty Ducks (US) 96. To the Ends of Time (US) 96. Amy Foster/Swept from the Sea 97. Firelight 97. The Mumbo Jumbo 00, etc.
TV series: Kipling 64. Further Adventures of the Three Musketeers 67. The Crezz 76. Thicker Than Water 81. Ashenden 91.

Ackland, Rodney (1908–1991)
British writer, sporadically in films from 1930, usually in association with other scenarists.
Autobiography: 1954, *The Celluloid Mistress*.
Shadows 31. Number Seventeen 32. The Case of Gabriel Perry (a only) 35. Bank Holiday 38. Young Man's Fancy 39. 49th Parallel (co-w, AAN) 41. Dangerous Moonlight 41. Hatter's Castle 41. Thursday's Child (& d) 42. Wanted for Murder 46. Temptation Harbour 47. Queen of Spades 48, etc.

Ackland-Snow, Brian (1940–)
English production designer.
A Room with a View (AA, BFA) 85. Maurice 87. Without a Clue 88. Haunted 95, etc.

Ackroyd, Barry
English cinematographer, most closely associated with the films of director Ken Loach.
Riff-Raff 90. Raining Stones 93. Ladybird Ladybird 94. Land and Freedom 95. Carla's Song 96. Stella Does Tricks 96. Hillsborough (TV) 96. Under the Skin 97. My Name Is Joe 98. The Lost Son 99. Beautiful People 99. The Escort/Mauvaise Passe 99. Brad and Roses 00, etc.

Acord, Art (1890–1931)
Rugged American star of silent Westerns. Born in Stillwater, Oklahoma, he began as a stunt rider, noted for his roping skills, in rodeos and Wild West shows. Married actresses Edythe Sterling and Louise Lorraine. Sound, combined with a jail sentence for bootlegging, ended his career, and he died from cyanide poisoning, in Chihuahua, Mexico, a supposed suicide.
The Squaw Man 13. A Man Afraid of His Wardrobe 15. The Moon Riders 20. In the Days of Buffalo Bill 21. The Oregon Trail 23. The Call of Courage 25. Rustler's Ranch 26. Sky High Corral 26. Hard Fists 27. Loco Luck 27. Two Gun O'Brien 28. Bullets and Justice 29. Wyoming Tornado 29, etc.

Acosta, Rodolfo (1920–1974)
Cold-eyed Mexican-American character actor, a frequent western villain or henchman.
The Fugitive 48. One Way Street 50. Yankee Buccaneer 52. Hondo 54. Bandido 56. The Tijuana Story (leading role) 57. Flaming Star 60. How the West Was Won 62. Rio Conchos 64. Return of the Seven 66. Flap 70. The Great White Hope 70. The Magnificent Seven Ride 72, many others.
TV series: High Chaparral 67.

Acquanetta (1920–) (Burnu Davenport)
Exotic American leading lady of easterns and horrors in the early 40s.
Arabian Nights 42. Captive Wild Woman 43. Jungle Woman 44. Dead Man's Eyes 44. Tarzan and the Leopard Woman 46. The Lost Continent 51. The Sword of Monte Cristo 51. Grizzly Adams: The Legend Continues 90, etc.

Acres, Birt (1854–1918)
British cinematograph pioneer, American born, later projector manufacturer. Claimed to be the first producer of cinema films in Britain.
Haycart Crossing, Hadley 94. The Derby 95. Boxing Kangaroo 96. A Visit to the Zoo 96. Princess Maud's Wedding 96. An Unfriendly Call 97, etc.

Acuff, Eddie (1908–1956)
American supporting comedian, remembered as the postman in the 'Blondie' series.
Shipmates Forever 35. The Petrified Forest 36. The Boys from Syracuse 40. Hellzapoppin 41. Guadalcanal Diary 43. It Happened Tomorrow 44. The Flying Serpent 45. Blondie's Big Moment 47, many others.

Adair, Jean (1873–1953)
American stage actress best remembered by film fans as one of the sweetly murderous aunts in *Arsenic and Old Lace*.
■ In the Name of the Law 22. Advice to the Lovelorn 33. *Arsenic and Old Lace* 44. Something in the Wind 46. Living in a Big Way 47.

Adair, Robert (1900–1954)
English character actor, from the American stage. Born in San Francisco, he was educated at Harrow, made his screen debut as Captain Hardy in *Journey's End*, and spent his mid-career in Hollywood.
Journey's End 30. Raffles 32. King of the Jungle 33. Limehouse Blues 35. The Prince and the Pauper 37. Brilliant Marriage 38. Jamaica Inn 39. Man on the Run 49. The Gambler and the Lady 52. Meet Mr Callaghan 54, etc.

Adam, Alfred (1909–1982)
French character actor, usually of weak or villainous roles.
La Kermesse Héroïque 35. Carnet de Bal 37. Boule de Suif 45. La Ferme du Pendu 46. The Witches of Salem 56. Maigret Sets a Trap 57. Le Président 61. Vivre sa Vie 62. La Vie Conjugale 63. Les Fêtes Galantes 65. Que la Fête Commence 74, etc.

Adam, Ken (1921–) (Klaus Adam)
German-born art director, in films from 1947. Born in Berlin, he was in Britain from the mid-30s. The 60s were for him a period of spectacular inventiveness.
Books: 1999, Moonraker, Strangelove and other celluloid dreams: the visionary art of Ken Adam.
Queen of Spades 48. Around the World in Eighty Days (AAN) 56. The Trials of Oscar Wilde 60. *Dr Strangelove* 63. *Goldfinger* 64. The Ipcress File 65. Thunderball 65. Funeral in Berlin 66. *You Only Live Twice* 67. Chitty Chitty Bang Bang 68. Goodbye Mr Chips 69. The Owl and the Pussycat 70. Sleuth 72. Live and Let Die 73. Barry Lyndon (AA) 75. The Seven Per Cent Solution 76. The Spy Who Loved Me (AAN) 77. Moonraker 79. Pennies from Heaven 80. King David 84. Agnes of God 85. Crimes of the Heart 86. The Deceivers 88. Dead-Bang 89. The Freshman 90. The Doctor 91. Undercover Blues 93. Addams Family Values (AAN) 93. The Madness of King George (AA) 94. Bogus 96. In and Out 97, etc.

Adam, Ronald (1896–1979)
English character actor and playwright. Born in Worcestershire, he trained as a chartered accountant and began as a theatre manager in the mid-20s, turning to acting in the 30s. He specialized in well-bred but stuffy professional men. Married twice.
Autobiography: 1938, *Overture and Beginners*.
Inspector Hornleigh 36. Strange Boarders 38. The Drum 38. Escape to Danger 43. Journey Together 44. Take My Life 47. Bonnie Prince Charles 48. The Case of Charles Peace 49. Seven Days to Noon 50. My Daughter Joy 50. Laughter in Paradise 51. The Late Edwina Black 51. Hindle Wakes 52. Top Secret 52. Private's Progress 55. Reach for the Sky 56. Assignment Redhead 56. Carry On Admiral 57. The Golden Disc 58, etc.

Adams, Beverly (1945–)
Canadian-born leading lady in Hollywood films. Formerly married to hairdresser and businessman Vidal Sassoon. Retired to raise a family and write books on beauty.
Winter a GoGo 63. The New Interns 64. *The Silencers* 66. Birds Do It 66. Murderers' Row 66. The Torture Garden (GB) 67. The Ambushers 67, etc.

Adams, Brooke (1949–)
American leading lady of the *jolie laide* type; showed more promise than performance.
Shock Waves 77. Invasion of the Body Snatchers 78. *Days of Heaven* 78. The First Great Train Robbery 79. A Man, a Woman and a Bank 79. Cuba 79. Tell Me a Riddle 80. The Dead Zone 83. Almost You 84. Key Exchange 84. The Stuff 85. Man on Fire 87. The Unborn 91. Stephen King's Sometimes They Come Back 91. Gas Food Lodging 91. The Last Hit (TV) 93. The Baby-Sitters Club 95, etc.
TV series: O.K. Crackerby 65–66.

Adams, Casey (1917–2000)
See under Max Showalter (his real name, which he has recently used).

Adams, Claire (1900–1978)
Canadian-born leading lady of silent films. She retired early and in 1938 moved to Australia following her second marriage.
Riders of the Dawn 20. The Penalty 20. The Killer 21. Just Tony 22. Stepping Fast 23. Where the North Begins 23. Oh, You Tony! 24. The Fast Set 24. The Big Parade 25. The Sea Wolf 26. Married Alive 27, etc.

Adams, Don (1926–)
American comedian, from night-clubs and television, best known for his Emmy-winning performance as Maxwell Smart in the spy spoof *Get Smart*.
The Nude Bomb 80. Jimmy the Kid 82. Back to the Beach 87, etc.
TV series: Kraft Music Hall 61–63. Bill Dana Show 63–65. Get Smart 65–70. The Partners 71–72. Don Adams' Screen Test 75. Check It Out 85–88.

Adams, Dorothy (1900–1988)
American character actress, usually of timorous or sullen ladies.
Broadway Musketeers 38. The Flame of New Orleans 41. Laura 44. The Best Years of Our Lives 46. The Foxes of Harrow 48. Carrie 52. Three for Jamie Dawn 56. The Big Country 58. From the Terrace 60. Peeper 76, etc.

Adams, Edie (1927–) (Elizabeth Edith Enke)
Pert American singer-comedienne, widow of Ernie Kovacs.
■ *The Apartment* 60. Lover Come Back 61. Call Me Bwana 62. It's a Mad Mad Mad Mad World 63. Under the Yum Yum Tree 63. *Love with the Proper Stranger* 64. The Best Man 64. Made in Paris 66. The Oscar 66. *The Honey Pot* 66. Box Office 82. The Haunting of Harrington House 82. Shooting Stars 85. Adventures Beyond Belief 87.
TV series: Evil Roy Slade 71. The Return of Joe Forrester 75. Word Games/Mrs Columbo 79.

Adams, Ernie (1885–1947)
Short American character actor, from the stage, most often in westerns.

A Regular Girl 19. The Pony Express 25. The Main Event 27. The Tip-Off 31. Breed of the Border 33. Gun Lords of Stirrup Basin 37. Ridin' the Lone Trail 37. The Man Who Came to Dinner 41. The Perils of Pauline 47. Return of the Bad Men 48, etc.

Adams, Gerald Drayson (1904–1988)
Canadian screenwriter, former literary agent.
Dead Reckoning 47. The Big Steal 49. The Golden Horde 51. Flaming Feather 51. The Black Sleep 56. Kissing Cousins 64. Harum Scarum 65, many others.

Adams, Jane
American actress.
Vital Signs 90. Light Sleeper 91. Kansas City 95. Father of the Bride Part II 95. Happiness 98. Day at the Beach 98. Mumford 99. Wonder Boys 00, etc.

Adams, Jane (1921–)
American actress of the 40s.
House of Dracula 45. Gunman's Code 46. The Brute Man 46. Lost City of the Jungle 46. Smooth as Silk 46. Batman and Robin 49.

Adams, Jill (1930–)
Pert British leading lady, former model, who decorated a number of lightweight films in the 50s.
The Young Lovers 54. Doctor at Sea 55. Private's Progress 56. The Green Man 56. Brothers in Law 57. Carry On Constable 60. Doctor in Distress 63. Promise Her Anything 66, etc.

Adams, Joey Lauren (1971–)
American actress, in independent films, sometimes credited as Joey Adams. Born in Little Rock, Arkansas, she began her career in television. She has been romantically linked with director Kevin SMITH and actor Vince VAUGHN.
Dazed and Confused 93. Coneheads 93. The Program 93. SFW 94. Sleep with Me 94. Mallrats 95. Bio-Dome 96. Michael 96. Chasing Amy 97. A Cool Dry Place 98. Big Daddy 99. Beautiful 00, etc.
TV series: Top of the Heap 91. Vinnie and Bobby 92.

Adams, Julie (1926–) (formerly Julia, real name: Betty May Adams)
American leading lady in Hollywood from 1947. Her essentially soft and sympathetic nature made the slight change of first name seem especially apt.
Hollywood Story 51. Bright Victory 51. Bend of the River 52. Mississippi Gambler 53. The Creature from the Black Lagoon 54. One Desire 55. Away All Boats 56. Slaughter on Tenth Avenue 57. Raymie 60. Tickle Me 65. Valley of Mystery 67. The Last Movie 71. McQ 74. The McCullochs 75. Killer Force 76. The Killer Inside Me 76. Black Roses 88. Catchfire/Backtrack 89, etc.
TV series: Yancy Derringer 58–59. The Jimmy Stewart Show 71. Code Red 81.

Adams, Maud (Maude) (1945–) (Maud Wikstrom)
Persistently promising Swedish-American leading lady of the 70s.
The Boys in the Band 70. The Christian Licorice Store 71. Rollerball 74. The Man with the Golden Gun 74. Killer Force 76. Tattoo 80. Octopussy 83. Playing for Time (TV) 80. Nairobi Affair (TV) 85. Hell Hunters 86. The Women's Club 87. Jane and the Lost City 88. Deadly Intent 88. Ski School 89. Soda Cracker 89. The Kill Reflex 90. Initiation: Silent Night, Deadly Night 4 90, etc.
TV series: Chicago Story 82. Emerald Point N.A.S. 83–84.

Adams, Nick (1931–1968) (Nicholas Adamschock)
American leading man who usually played neurotic or aggressive types; never quite made the big time. Died of a drug overdose.
Somebody Loves Me (debut) 52. Mister Roberts 55. Our Miss Brooks 55. The Last Wagon 56. *No Time for Sergeants* 58. Sing, Boy, Sing 58. Teacher's Pet 58. The FBI Story 59. Pillow Talk 59. Hell is for Heroes 62. The Interns 62. The Hook 62. Twilight of Honor (AAN) 63. Young Dillinger 64. Monster of Terror (GB) 66. Frankenstein Conquers the World (Jap.) 66. Invasion of the Astro-Monsters (Jap.) 67, etc.
TV series: The Rebel 59–60. Saints and Sinners 62–63.

Adams, Richard (1920–)
British best-selling novelist who sees the world from the animals' point of view. His *Watership Down* and *The Plague Dogs* were somewhat unsatisfactorily turned into cartoon features.

Adams, Robert (1906–1965)
West Indian actor, former teacher, prominent in British films of the 40s.
Sanders of the River (debut) 35. King Solomon's Mines 37. Caesar and Cleopatra 45. Men of Two Worlds (leading role) 46. Old Mother Riley's Jungle Treasure 52. Man of Africa 52. Sapphire 59, etc.

Adams, Stanley (1915–1977)
American character actor. Committed suicide.
The Atomic Kid 54. Hell on Frisco Bay 56. Breakfast at Tiffany's 61. Nevada Smith 66. The Clones 74, etc.

Adams, Tom (1938–)
Burly British leading man whose career might have flourished better in the 50s.
The Great Escape 63. Licensed to Kill 65. Where the Bullets Fly 66. The Fighting Prince of Donegal 66. Fathom 67. Subterfuge 68. The Fast Kill 72. The Onedin Line (TV) 79. Mask of the Devil (TV) 84. The Pyrates (TV) 85.
TV series: Spy Trap 75.

Adamson, Al (1929–1995)
American director of exploitation movies noted for their high level of sex, violence and general incompetence, which gained a new audience following their release on video. Many exist in various versions under different titles. A former actor, known as Rick Adams, he was born in Hollywood, the son of silent western star, producer and director Denver DIXON. He turned to directing in the 60s, with films that tended to star actors past their prime, such as Lon CHANEY JNR and John CARRADINE. He was murdered.
AS ACTOR: Halfway to Hell 55.
AS DIRECTOR: Blood of Dracula's Castle/Dracula's Castle 69. Five Bloody Graves/The Gun Riders 69. Satan's Sadists 69. The Fakers 69. Vampire Men of the Lost Planet/Horror of the Blood Monsters 70. Dracula vs Frankenstein/Blood of Frankenstein 71. The Female Bunch (co-d) 71. Brain of Blood/The Creature's Revenge 71. Angels' Wild Women 72. Blood of Ghastly Horror 72. Man with the Synthetic Brain/Psycho a Go-Go 72. The Naughty Stewardesses 73. I Spit on Your Corpse 74. Jessie's Girls 75. Texas Layover 75. Blazing Stewardesses 75. Wanted Women 76. Nurse Sherri 77. Dr Dracula 77. Black Samurai 77. Cinderella 2000 77. Hospital of Terror 78. Sunset Cove 78. Carnival Magic 82, etc.

Adamson, Harold (1906–1980)
American lyricist, usually with Jimmy MCHUGH.
Dancing Lady 33. Kid Millions 34. Suzy 36. That Certain Age 38. Nob Hill 45. If You Knew Susie 48. Gentlemen Prefer Blondes 52. An Affair to Remember 57, many others.

Adamson, Joy (1910–1980)
Austrian-born wild-life expert who wrote *Born Free* and *Living Free*. A long-time resident of Kenya, she was mysteriously murdered. She was played by Honor BLACKMAN in the biopic *To Walk with Lions*, 99.
Biography: 1996, *Joy Adamson: Behind the Mask* by Caroline Cass.

Addams, Charles (1912–1988)
American cartoonist of ghoulish humour, much in the *New Yorker* from 1940. TV in 1964–65 ran *The Addams Family*, about creepy characters in a cobwebby house, which became the basis of successful feature films in the 90s. With regard to films he is best remembered for his remark on attending the premiere of *Cleopatra*: 'I only came to see the asp.'

Addams, Dawn (1930–1985)
Smart and glamorous British leading lady in international films. Films mainly unremarkable.
Night into Morning 51. Plymouth Adventure 52. The Robe 53. The Moon Is Blue 53. Khyber Patrol 54. A King in New York 57. The Silent Enemy 58. The Two Faces of Dr Jekyll 60. The Black Tulip 64. Ballad in Blue 65. Where the Bullets Fly 66. Vampire Lovers 70. Sappho 70. Vault of Horror 73, etc.
TV series: Star Maidens 77.

Addinsell, Richard (1904–1977)
British composer.
The Amateur Gentleman 36. Fire over England 37. Goodbye Mr Chips 39. Gaslight 40. *Dangerous Moonlight* (including 'Warsaw Concerto') 40. Love on the Dole 41. Blithe Spirit 45. Scrooge 51. Beau Brummell 54. The Prince and the Showgirl 57. The Admirable Crichton 57. The Waltz of the Toreadors 62, etc.

Addison, John (1920–1998)
British composer, in films from 1948. He studied at the Royal College of Music, where he also taught in the 50s, and began his film career through a friendship with producer-director Roy BOULTING, who admired his compositions. In the mid-70s, he moved to Los Angeles and scored many TV movies.
The Guinea Pig 49. Pool of London 50. Seven Days to Noon 50. Brandy for the Parson 51. High Treason 51. The Hour of Thirteen 52. Time Bomb 52. The Maggie 53. The Man Between 53. Red Beret 53. The Black Knight 54. The End of the Road 54. Make Me an Offer 54. One Good Turn 54. Cockleshell Heroes 55. Josephine and Men 55. That Lady 55. Touch and Go 55. It's Great to Be Young 56. Private's Progress 56. *Reach for the Sky* 56. Three Men in a Boat 56. Barnacle Bill 57. Lucky Jim 57. The Shiralee 57. Carlton-Browne of the FO 58. I Was Monty's Double 58. Look Back in Anger 59. The Entertainer 60. A French Mistress 60. School for Scoundrels 60. Go to Blazes 61. A Taste of Honey 61. The Loneliness of the Long Distance Runner 62. The Girl in the Headlines 63. Girl with Green Eyes 63. *Tom Jones* (AA) 63. Guns at Batasi 64. The Amorous Adventures of Moll Flanders 65. I Was Happy Here 65. The Loved One 65. Torn Curtain 66. A Fine Madness 66. The Honey Pot 66. Smashing Time 67. The Charge of the Light Brigade 68. Country Dance 69. Start the Revolution without Me 69. Mr Forbush and the Penguins 71. Sleuth 72. Luther 73. Dead Cert 74. Swashbuckler 76. The Seven Per Cent Solution 76. A Bridge Too Far 77. Joseph Andrews 77. Centennial (TV) 78. The Pilot 79. Pearl (TV) 80. Strange Invaders 83. The Ultimate Solution of Grace Quigley 84. Code Name: Emerald 85. Phantom of the Opera (TV) 90, etc.

Addy, Mark (1964–)
Chubby English actor, often in comic roles. Born in York, he studied at RADA and began in the theatre.
A Very Peculiar Practice (TV) 86. Band of Gold (TV) 95. The Full Monty 97. Jack Frost (US) 98. The Last Yellow 99. The Flintstones in Viva Rock Vegas (US) 99. Down to Earth (US) 01. In Shining Armour 01, etc.
TV series: The Thin Blue Line 96. Sunnyside Farm 97.

Addy, Wesley (1913–1996)
Thin American character actor, usually of humourless or sinister appearance. He married actress Celeste HOLM in 1966.
The First Legion 51. My Six Convicts 52. Kiss Me Deadly 55. The Big Knife 55. Timetable 57. The Garment Jungle 58. Ten Seconds to Hell 59. Whatever Happened to Baby Jane? 62. *Seconds* 66. Mister Buddwing 66. The Grissom Gang 71. Network 76. The Europeans 79. The Verdict 82. The Bostonians 84. Mr 247 94. Hiroshima (TV) 95. Before and After 96. A Modern Affair 96, etc.
TV series: Loving 83–91, 94–95.

Adefarasin, Remi
British cinematographer.
Truly, Madly, Deeply 90. Captives 94. Great Moments in Aviation 94. Hollow Reed 96. Elizabeth (AAN) 98. Onegin 98. House of Mirth 00, etc.

Adjani, Isabelle (1955–)
Franco-German leading lady of international films. She has a son by actor Daniel DAY-LEWIS.
Faustine 71. The Slap 74. *The Story of Adèle H* (AAN) 75. The Tenant 76. Barocco 77. The Driver 78. Nosferatu 78. The Brontë Sisters 79. Clara et les Chics Types 80. Possession 80. Quartet 81. One Deadly Summer 83. Subway 85. Maladie d'Amour 86. Ishtar 87. Camille Claudel (AAN) 88. La Reine Margot 94. Diabolique (US) 96, etc.

Adler, Buddy (1906–1960) (Maurice Adler)
American producer, with Columbia from 1948, Fox from 1954 (head of studio from 1956).
The Dark Past 48. No Sad Songs for Me 50. Salome 53. *From Here to Eternity* (AA) 53. Violent Saturday 55. *Love is a Many Splendored Thing* 55. The Left Hand of God 55. Bus Stop 56. Anastasia 56. A Hatful of Rain 57. South Pacific 58. *The Inn of the Sixth Happiness* 58, etc.

Adler, Gilbert
American director, screenwriter and producer.
Home Movies (p) 80. A Certain Fury (p) 85. Children of the Corn II: The Final Sacrifice (co-w) 93. Tales from the Crypt Presents Demon Knight (p) 95. Tales from the Crypt Presents Bordello of Blood (co-w, d) 96, etc.

Adler, Jay (1896–1978)
American character actor, brother of Luther ADLER; usually played hoboes, small-time gangsters, etc.
No Time to Marry 38. My Six Convicts 52. 99 River Street 54. The Big Combo 55. Sweet Smell of Success 57. The Brothers Karamazov 58. Seven Guns to Mesa 60. The Family Jewels 65, many others.

Adler, Larry (1914–)
American harmonica virtuoso and composer, in films usually as himself. Born in Baltimore, he has been resident in Britain since the 40s.
Autobiography: 1985, *It Ain't Necessarily So.*
Many Happy Returns (a) 34. The Big Broadcast of 1937 (a) 36. The Singing Marine (a) 37. St Martin's Lane (a) 38. Three Daring Daughters (a) 48. *Genevieve* (AAN,m) 53. Jumping for Joy (m) 55. A Cry from the Streets (m) 58. The Hellions (m) 61. The Hook (m) 62. The Great Chase (m) 63. King and Country (m) 64. A High Wind in Jamaica (m) 65, etc.

Adler, Luther (1903–1984) (Lutha Adler)
Heavy-featured American character actor, member of well-known theatrical family (brother Jay, sister Stella). Born in New York City, he was on-stage from the age of five. Married (1938-47) actress Sylvia SIDNEY.
■ Lancer Spy 37. Cornered 45. Saigon 48. The Loves of Carmen 48. *Wake of the Red Witch* 48. House of Strangers 49. D.O.A. 50. South Sea Sinner 50. Under My Skin 50. Kiss Tomorrow Goodbye 50. M 51. The Magic Face (as Hitler) 51. The Desert Fox 51. Hoodlum Empire 52. The Tall Texan 53. The Miami Story 54. Crashout 55. The Girl in the Red Velvet Swing 55. Hot Blood 56. The Last Angry Man 59. Cast a Giant Shadow 66. *The Brotherhood* 68. Crazy Joe 74. Murph the Surf 74. The Man in the Glass Booth 75. Mean Johnny Barrows 75. Voyage of the Damned 76. Absence of Malice 81.
TV series: The Psychiatrist 71. Also many guest appearances, especially in Naked City.

Adler, Richard (1921–)
American composer and lyricist who with his partner Jerry Ross (1926–55) (Jerold Rosenberg) wrote *The Pajama Game* and *Damn Yankees*.

Adler, Stella (1902–1992)
American stage actress, sister of Luther and Jay Adler. Known at one time as Stella Ardler.
Love on Toast 38. Shadow of the Thin Man 41. My Girl Tisa 48, etc.

Adler, Warren
American novelist and playwright of family tensions and relationships, a former journalist. He is making all his writings available via the Internet at his own site. So far ten of his books have been optioned for the movies, though only two have become feature films. He is the father of actor Michael Adler.
The War of the Roses 89. Random Hearts (&ex-p) 99, etc
❝ Having a book made into a movie with its original title is nothing short of a miracle. Having it become a hit and a long playing classic is beyond that…if there is such a condition. – *W.A.*

Adlon, Percy (1935–)
German producer-director and screenwriter. A former actor, broadcaster and documentary film-maker, he founded his own production company in 1978. His international success came in 1987 with *Bagdad Café*, which made a star of Marianne Sägebrecht and subsequently became the basis for a TV series starring Whoopi Goldberg.
Celeste 81. Five Last Days/Letz Funf Tage 82. The Swing/Die Schaukel 83. Sugar Baby/

Zuckerbaby 86. Bagdad Café 87. Rosalie Goes Shopping 89. Salmonberries 91. Younger and Younger 93, etc.

Adolfi, John G. (1888–1933)
American director at his peak in the transitional period between silent and sound. Began as an actor, but quickly turned to directing and found steady work. Three years before his death he formed an association with George Arliss and filmed the star's stage successes.
A Man and His Mate 15. The Sphinx 16. A Modern Cinderella 17. A Child of the Wild 17. Queen of the Sea 18. Who's Your Brother? 19. The Darling of the Rich 22. The Little Red Schoolhouse 23. Chalk Marks 24. The Phantom Express 25. The Checkered Flag 26. Husband Hunters 27. The Little Snob 28. Fancy Baggage 29. The Show of Shows 29. Dumbbells in Ermine 30. Sinner's Holiday 30. College Lovers 30. The Millionaire 31. Alexandra Hamilton 31. Compromised 31. The Man Who Played God 32. A Successful Calamity 32. Central Park 32. The King's Vacation 33. The Working Man 33. Voltaire 33, many others.

Adoree, Renee (1898–1933) (Jeanne de la Fonté)
French leading lady, former circus bareback rider, who became an exotic star of Hollywood films in the 20s but could not transfer to sound and died of tuberculosis. The first of her two husbands was actor Tom Moore (1921–24).
The Strongest 20. Made in Heaven 21. Monte Cristo 22. The Eternal Struggle 23. Women Who Give 24. The Bandolero 24. Man and Maid 25. Exchange of Wives 25. *The Big Parade* 25. La Bohème 26. The Exquisite Sinner 26. Tin Gods 26. The Flaming Forest 26. Heaven on Earth 27. Mr Wu 27. On ze Boulevard 27. Back to God's Country 27. The Cossacks 28. The Michigan Kid 28. The Mating Call 28. The Pagan 29. Tide of Empire 29. Redemption 30. Call of the Flesh 30.

Adorf, Mario (1930–)
Swiss actor in European films.
The Girl Rosemarie 59. Station Six Sahara 63. Major Dundee (US) 65. Ten Little Indians 66. The Red Tent 71. Journey to Vienna 73. Fedora 78. The Tin Drum 79. L'Empreinte des géants 80. Lola 81. Smiley's People (TV) 80. Marco Polo (TV) 81. The Holcroft Covenant 85. Momo 86. Quiet Days in Clichy 90. Money 91. Smilla's Sense of Snow/Smilla's Feeling for Snow 96, etc.

Adreon, Franklin (1902–1979)
American second feature director.
Canadian Mounties vs Atomic Invaders (serial) 53. The Man with the Steel Whip 54. Trader Tom of the China Seas 54. King of the Carnival 55. Panther Girl of the Congo 55. No Man's Woman 55. This Man Is Armed 56. Hell's Crossroads 57. The Steel Whip 58. The Nun and the Sergeant 62. Cyborg 2087 66. Dimension 5 66, etc.

Adrian (1903–1959) (Adrian Adolph Greenberg)
American costume designer, with MGM 1927–42 and credited with the authentic images of Garbo, Shearer, Harlow, etc. Married Janet Gaynor; quit films after being forced to create ordinary clothes for Garbo in *Two-Faced Woman*, a film that also ended Garbo's career. He opened his own successful fashion house and then retired to a ranch in Brazil, returning only to design the costumes for the stage version of *Camelot*. Committed suicide.
❝ If I'm copied, it's because of my clothes and Adrian does those. – *Joan Crawford*

Adrian, Iris (1912–1994) (I. A. Hostette)
American character actress, former Ziegfeld Follies dancer, familiar from the early 30s as wisecracking or tawdry blonde.
Paramount on Parade 30. Rumba 35. Our Relations 37. Professional Bride 41. The G-String Murders 42. Spotlight Scandals 44. I'm from Arkansas 45. Road to Alcatraz 46. The Paleface 48. G.I. Jane 51. Highway Dragnet 54. The Buccaneer 59. That Darn Cat 65. The Odd Couple 68. Scandalous John 71. The Shaggy D.A. 76. Murder Can Hurt You (TV) 78. Herbie Goes Bananas 80, many others.
TV series: The Ted Knight Show 78.

Adrian, Max (1903–1973) (Max Bor)
Irish stage actor of high camp personality; latterly a star of mischievous revue and an impersonator of Bernard Shaw. Too richly flavoured to star in films, but made occasional character appearances.
■ The Primrose Path 34. Eight Cylinder Love 34. A Touch of the Moon 36. To Catch a Thief 36. Nothing Like Publicity 36. The Happy Family 37. When the Devil Was Well 37. Why Pick on Me? 37. Macushla 38. Merely Mr Hawkins 38. *Kipps* 41. Penn of Pennsylvania 41. *The Young Mr Pitt* 42. Talk About Jacqueline 42. Henry V 45. Her Favorite Husband 50. Pool of London 51. The Pickwick Papers 52. *Dr Terror's House of Horrors* 65. *The Deadly Affair* 66. Funeral in Berlin 66. Julius Caesar 70. The Music Lovers 70. The Devils 71. *The Boy Friend* 71.

Affleck, Ben (1972–)
American leading actor and screenwriter. Born in Berkeley, California, and brought up in Cambridge, Massachusetts, he made a breakthrough to wide recognition in *Chasing Amy*, and by writing *Good Will Hunting* with his friend Matt Damon. He began acting on television at the age of eight. He has been romantically linked with actress Gwyneth Paltrow. Current asking price: around $12.5m.
Hands of a Stranger (TV) 87. School Ties 92. Dazed and Confused 93. Last Call 95. Mallrats 95. Glory Daze 96. Going All the Way 97. Chasing Amy 97. *Good Will Hunting* (& co-w) (AANw) 97. Armageddon 98. Shakespeare in Love 98. Phantoms 98. Dogma 98. Forces of Nature 99. Dogma 99. 200 Cigarettes 99. Boiler Room 00. Reindeer Games 00. Bounce 00. Daddy and Them 01. Pearl Harbor 01, etc.
TV series: Against the Grain 93-94.

Affleck, Casey (1975–)
American actor, the brother of Ben Affleck.
To Die For 95. Good Will Hunting 97. Desert Blue 98. 200 Cigarettes 99. Committed 99. Drowning Mona 00, etc.

Agar, John (1921–)
American leading man, once married to Shirley Temple; mainly in low-budgeters.
Fort Apache 48. Sands of Iwo Jima 49. The Magic Carpet 52. The Golden Mistress 53. Bait 54, Joe Butterfly 56. Daughter of Dr Jekyll 57. The Brain from Planet Arous 58. Journey to the Seventh Planet 61. Of Love and Desire 63. Cavalry Command 65. Waco 66. The St Valentine's Day Massacre 67. The Curse of the Swamp Creature 67. The Undefeated 69. Big Jake 71. King Kong 76. How's Your Love Life? 77. The Amazing Mr No-Legs 78. Perfect Victims 88. Miracle Mile 89. Fear 89. The Perfect Bride 91, etc.

Agate, James (1877–1947)
British drama critic with a passion for Sarah Bernhardt. He performed some reluctant stints of film reviewing, and the results are compiled in two volumes of *Around Cinema*. They show him as a highbrow waffler rather than a wit, and no real appreciation of the art of film comes through.
Autobiography: *Ego* (Vols 1–9, 1935–49).
Biography: 1986, *Agate* by James Harding.
❝ What I want in the cinema is something that can't possibly happen to me. – *J.A.*
The fact remains that if a young man has a good photogenic profile one picture will make him a star even if he hasn't enough acting talent to carry in the tea-things in a play at Kew. – *J.A.*
A professional is a man who can do his job when he doesn't feel like it. An amateur is a man who can't do his job when he does feel like it. – *J.A.*
James Agate, the dean of English critics, said in one of his early reviews, 'Charles Laughton is a genius.' Then, about a year later in a review, Agate said, 'This so-called genius …' And then, some time later he said, 'This self-styled genius …' – *Elsa Lanchester*

Agee, James (1909–1955)
One of America's most respected film critics, he also wrote novels and screenplays. A posthumous collection of his reviews was published under the title *Agee on Film*, and the screenplays followed. His novel *A Death in the Family* was filmed in 1963 as *All the Way Home*.
The African Queen (AAN) 51. Face to Face 52. The Night of the Hunter 55. All the Way Home 63, etc.
✪ For his brief, witty, incisive reviews which perfectly encapsulate hundreds of 40s films.

Ager, Cecelia (1898–1981)
American critic for various New York magazines in the 30s. Wrote a book of essays, *Let's Go to the Pictures*.

Ager, Milton (1893–1979)
American composer and former vaudeville accompanist who, with lyricist Jack Yellen, wrote the score for Sophie Tucker's first movie, *Honky Tonk* 29. The partnership's biggest hit was that movie's 'Happy Days Are Here Again', which has also turned up in *Beau James* 57, *This Earth Is Mine* 59, and *The Night of the Iguana* 64.
Chasing Rainbows (s) 30. King of Jazz (s) 30. They Learned about Women (s) 30, etc.

Aghayan, Ray (1934–)
Iranian-born costume designer, in America.
Father Goose 64. Do Not Disturb 65. The Glass Bottom Boat 66. Caprice 67. Doctor Dolittle 67. Gaily, Gaily (AAN) 69. Hannie Calder 72. Lady Sings the Blues (AAN) 72. Funny Lady (AAN) 75, etc.

Agland, Phil (1950–)
English director, from television documentaries. Born in Weymouth, he studied geography at Hull University.
China: Beyond the Clouds (doc) 94. The Woodlanders 97, etc.

Agnew, Robert (1899–1983)
American leading juvenile of silent pictures. Born in Louisville, Kentucky, he began on the stage and retired soon after the coming of sound to work at Warner Brothers as an assistant director.
The Valley of Doubt 20. The Passion Flower 21. Without Fear 22. The Spanish Dancer 23. Wine of Youth 24. The Great Love 25. She's My Baby 26. The Heart of Salome 27. The Heart of Broadway 28. Extravagance 30. The Naughty Flirt 31. Gold Diggers of 1933 33, etc.

Agostini, Philippe (1910–)
French director. Born in Paris, he was formerly a leading cinematographer of the 40s, who worked with such directors as Bresson, Carné and Ophuls. Married actress Odette Joyeux.
As cinematographer: Carnet de Bal (co-ph) 37. Les Anges du Péché 43. Les Dames du Bois de Boulogne 44. Les Portes de la Nuit 46. Pattes Blanches 48. Le Plaisir (co-ph) 51. Rififi 55, etc.
As director: Le Naif aux 40 Enfants 57. Tu es Pierre 58. Le Dialogue des Carmélites 59. La Soupe aux Poulets 63. La Petite Fille Qui Cherche le Printemps 71, etc.

Agren, Janet (1949–)
Swedish actress, best known internationally for appearances in Italian horror movies. Born in Landskrona, she won a beauty contest that took her to Italy, where she began her movie career in the late 60s. Now retired from acting, she works as an interior designer.
The Two Crusaders/I Due Crociati 68. Normal Young Man/Il Giovane Normale 69. Master of Love/Racconti Proibiti... Di Niente Vestiti 72. L'Erotomane 74. The Uranium Conspiracy/A Chi Tocca... Tocca! 78. The Perfect Crime/Indagine Su Un Delitto Perfetto 79. Gates of Hell/City of the Living Dead/La Paura 80. Emerald Jungle/Eaten Alive/Mangiati Vivi Dai Cannibali 80. Panic/Panico 80. Hands of Steel/Mani Di Pietra 85. Red Sonja (US) 85. Aladdin/Superfantagenio 86. Night of the Sharks/La Notte Degli Squali 87. Ratman 87. Silent Night/Magdalene 89, many more.

Agresti, Alejandro (1961–)
Argentinian director and screenwriter, a former cameraman, now based in Holland.
El Hombre que Ganó la Razón 86. Love is a Fat Woman/El Amor es una Mujer Gorda 88. Secret Wedding/Boda Secreta 89. City Life (co-d) 89. The Night of the Wild Donkeys/De Nacht de Wilde Ezels (a, p) 89. Luba 91. How to Survive a Broken Heart (a) 91. Modern Crimes (& a) 92. Just Good Friends 92. Pieces of Love 93. El Acto en Cuestión 93. Buenos Aires Vice Versa 96. Wind with the Gone/El Viento Se Llevó lo Que (wd) 98, etc.

Agutter, Jenny (1952–)
British actress who came to leading roles as a teenager.
East of Sudan 64. Gates to Paradise 67. Star! 68. I Start Counting 69. *The Railway Children* 70. Walkabout 70. The Snow Goose (TV) 71. A War of Children (TV) 72. Logan's Run 76. The Eagle Has Landed 76. Equus 77. Dominique 78. China 9, Liberty 37 78. The Riddle of the Sands 78. Sweet William 80. The Survivor 80. Amy 81. An American Werewolf in London 81. Secret Places 84. Silas Marner (TV) 85. Dark Tower 87. King of the Wind 89. Child's Play 2 90. Darkman 90. Freddie as FR07 (voice) 92. Blue Juice 95. The Buccaneers (TV) 95. A Respectable Trade (TV) 98. The Railway Children (TV) 00, etc.

Aherne, Brian (1902–1986)
Gentle-mannered British leading man of stage and screen; resident from 1933 in Hollywood and New York, where he became the American ideal of the charming Britisher. A child actor who trained under Italia Conti, he was on stage from the age of nine. His first wife (1939-44) was Joan Fontaine.
Autobiography: 1969, *A Proper Job*. Also published a memoir of George Sanders: 1979, *A Dreadful Man*.
■ The Eleventh Commandment 24. King of the Castle 25. The Squire of Long Hadley 26. Safety First 26. A Woman Redeemed 27. *Shooting Stars* 28. Underground 29. The W Plan 30. Madame Guillotine 31. *I Was A Spy* 33. *Song of Songs* 33. What Every Woman Knows 34. The Fountain 34. *The Constant Nymph* 34. Sylvia Scarlett 35. I Live My Life 35. *Beloved Enemy* 36. *The Great Garrick* 37. Merrily We Live 38. Captain Fury 39. *Juarez* (as Emperor Maximilian) (AAN) 39. Vigil in the Night 40. *The Lady In Question* 40. Hired Wife 40. *My Son My Son* 40. The Man Who Lost Himself 41. Skylark 41. Smilin' Through 41. My Sister Eileen 42. Forever and a Day 43. A Night to Remember 43. First Comes Courage 43. What a Woman! 43. The Locket 46. Smart Woman 48. Angel on the Amazon 48. *I Confess* 53. Titanic 53. Prince Valiant 54. A Bullet is Waiting 54. *The Swan* (first comic character role) 56. The Best of Everything 59. Susan Slade 61. *Lancelot and Guinevere* (as King Arthur) 63. The Waltz King 64. The Cavern 65. Rosie 67.

Aherne, Patrick (1901–1970)
Irish light actor, brother of Brian Aherne; in America from 1936. He was married to Renee Houston.
A Daughter in Revolt 25. Huntingtower 27. The Game Chicken 31. Trouble Ahead 36. Green Dolphin Street 47. The Paradine Case 48. Bwana Devil 52. The Court Jester 56, etc.

Ahlberg, Mac (1931–)
Swedish director who later worked as a cinematographer in America.
As director: I, a Woman 65. I, a Woman II 68. Nana/Take Me, Love Me 70. Flossie 74. Around the World with Fanny Hill 74. Justine and Juliet 75. Bel Ami 76. Sex in Sweden/Molly 77, etc.
As cinematographer: Nocturna 78. Hell Night 81. Parasite 82. My Tutor 82. Parasite 82. Young Warriors 83. The Dungeon Master 84. Ghoulies 85. Trancers 85. Re-Animator 85. Eliminators 86. House 86. From Beyond 86. House II 88. Deepstar Six 89. The Horror Show 89. Oscar 91. Innocent Blood 92. My Boyfriend's Back 93. Striking Distance 93. Beverly Hills Cop 3 94. The Brady Bunch Movie 95. A Very Brady Sequel 96. Space Truckers 96. Good Burger 97. Can't Stop Dancing 99, etc.

Ahlstedt, Börje (1939–)
Swedish character actor, best known internationally in the role of Uncle Carl in three films based on Ingmar Bergman's memories of his childhood.
I am Curious – Yellow/Jar Ar Nyfiken – Gul 67. I Am Curious – Blue/Jar Ar Nyfiken – Bla 68. Made in Sweden 69. Troll 71. A Lover and His Lass/En Kille Och En Tjej 75. Fanny and Alexander 82. Ronja Roverdatter 84. Amorosa 86. Emma's Shadow/Skyggen Af Emma 88. Fallgropen 89. The Best Intentions/Den Goda Viljan 92. Sunday's Children 92. Belma 95. Autumn in Paradise/Host I Paradiset 95. In the Presence of a Clown (TV) 97, etc.

Ahn, Philip (1911–1978)
American actor of Korean parentage, seen in Hollywood films as an assortment of Asiatic types.
The General Died at Dawn 36. Thank You Mr Moto 38. Charlie Chan in Honolulu 38. They Got Me Covered 42. China Sky 45. Rogues' Regiment 48. I was an American Spy 51. Love is a Many Splendored Thing 55. Never So Few 59. Diamond

Head 63. Thoroughly Modern Millie 67. The World's Greatest Athlete 73. Voodoo Heartbeat 75, many others.

TV series: Kung Fu 71–75.

Aidman, Charles (1925–1993)
American character actor, mostly on TV. He was narrator of the TV series *The Twilight Zone* 85–87.

The Hour of the Gun 67. Countdown 67. Kotch 72. Dirty Little Billy 72. Amelia Earhart (TV) 76. Twilight's Last Gleaming 77. Zoot Suit 81. Prime Suspect (TV) 81. Uncommon Valor 83, etc.

Aiello, Danny (1933–)
American actor, born in The Bronx, New York.

The Front 76. Fingers 77. Bloodbrothers 78. Fort Apache, the Bronx 80. Chu Chu and the Philly Flash 81. Old Enough 84. Once Upon a Time in America 84. The Purple Rose of Cairo 84. The Stuff 85. Man on Fire 87. Moonstruck 87. The Pick-Up Artist 87. Radio Days 87. Russicum 87. White Hot 88. Crack in the Mirror 88. Do the Right Thing (AAN) 89. Harlem Nights 89. The January Man 89. Jacob's Ladder 90. Once Around 91. Hudson Hawk 91. The Closer 91. Ruby 92. 29th Street 92. Mistress 92. The Cemetery Club 93. The Pickle 93. Me and the Kid 93. Leon/The Professional (Fr.) 94. Prêt-à-Porter/Ready to Wear 94. City Hall 96. 2 Days in the Valley 96. Two Much 96. Mojave Moon 96. The Last Don (TV) 97. Bring Me the Head of Mavis Davies 97. A Brooklyn State of Mind 97. The Last Don II (TV) 98. Wilbur Falls 98. Dinner Rush 00. The Prince of Central Park 00, etc.

TV series: Lady Blue 85–86. Dellaventura 97–98.

Aimée, Anouk (1932–) (Françoise Sorya Dreyfus)
Svelte French leading lady who captured many hearts in the days when she was known simply as 'Anouk'. She has subsequently lent her poise to many routine pictures. Married (1970-75) actor Albert Finney.

La Maison sous la Mer 47. *Les Amants de Vérone* 48. The Golden Salamander (GB) 49. The Crimson Curtain/Le Rideau Cramoisi 52. The Man Who Watched Trains Go By (GB) 52. Les Mauvaises Rencontres 55. Contraband Spain (GB) 55. Pot Bouille 56. Lovers of Montparnasse 58. La Tête Contre les Murs 58. Les Dragueurs 59. The Journey (US) 59. La Dolce Vita (It.) 60. *Lola* 60. Sodom and Gomorrah 63. Eight and a Half 63. La Fuga 65. *A Man and a Woman/Un Homme et une Femme* (AAN) 66. Justine (US) 69. The Model Shop (US) 69. The Appointment (US) 69. Si C'était à Refaire 76. Mon Premier Amour 78. The Tragedy of a Ridiculous Man 81. General of the Dead Army 83. Success is the Best Revenge 84. Long Live Life 84. A Man and a Woman: 20 Years Later 86. Arrivederci e Grazie 88. La Table Tournante 88. Bethune: The Making of a Hero 90. Il y a des Jours … et des Lunes 90. Ruptures 92. Les Marmottes 93. Prêt-à-Porter 94. Men Women: A User's Manual 96. LA without a Map (as herself) 98. 1999 Madeleine 99. One 4 All/Une Pour Toutes 99, etc.

Aimos, Raymond (1889–1944)
French general-purpose actor of the 30s; died from war injuries.

Vingt Ans Après 22. Quatorze Juillet 32. Le Dernier Milliardaire 34. Mayerling 36. Le Golem 36. La Belle Equipe 36. Quai des Brumes 38. De Mayerling à Sarajevo 40. Lumière d'Eté 42. Les Petites du Quai aux Fleurs 43, etc.

Ainley, Henry (1879–1945)
British stage actor in occasional films, a former accountant.

She Stoops to Conquer 14. The Prisoner of Zenda 15. Rupert of Hentzau 15. The Great Adventure 15. The Manxman 16. Quinneys 19. The Prince and the Beggarmaid 21. Sweet Lavender 23. The Good Companions 32. The First Mrs Fraser 32. As You Like It 36, etc.

Ainley, Richard (1910–1967)
British-born actor, son of Henry Ainley.

As You Like It 36. The Frog 37. A Stolen Life 39. Lady with Red Hair 40. The Smiling Ghost 41. White Cargo 42. Above Suspicion 43. Passage to Hong Kong 49, etc.

Aitken, Maria (1945–)
Lanky British comedy actress, popular on TV. Her second husband was actor Nigel Davenport (1972–80).

Some Girls Do 69. Mary, Queen of Scots 71. Half Moon Street 87. A Fish Called Wanda 88. The Grotesque/Gentlemen Don't Eat Poets/Grave Indiscretions 96. Jinnah (Pak.) 98, etc.

TV series: Company and Co. 80. Poor Little Rich Girls 84.

Aitken, Spottiswoode (1868–1933) (Frank Aitken)
Scottish-born character actor, usually as benign old men, in silent films in Hollywood, from the stage. He appeared in several of D. W. Griffith's films, including the role of Dr Cameron in *The Birth of a Nation*.

The Battle 11. The Avenging Conscience 14. The Birth of a Nation 15. Intolerance 15. Stage Struck 17. Her Kingdom of Dreams 19. Nomads of the North 20. The Unknown Wife 21. Manslaughter 22. The Young Rajah 22. Six Days 23. The Eagle 25. The Goose Woman 25. Roaring Fires 27, many others.

Aked, Muriel (1887–1955)
British character actress usually seen as comedy spinster or gossip.

A Sister to Assist 'Er 22 and 47. The Mayor's Nest 32. *Rome Express* 32. Friday the Thirteenth 33. Cottage to Let 41. Two Thousand Women 44. The Wicked Lady 45. *The Happiest Days of Your Life* 50. The Story of Gilbert and Sullivan 53, etc.

Akeley, Carl E. (1864–1926)
American taxidermist and photographer, inventor in the early 20s of a tripod camera which first made steady panning possible.

Akerman, Chantal (1950–)
Belgian director and screenwriter who learned her craft in New York in the early 70s.

Saute Ma Ville 68. La Chambre 72. News from Home 76. Dis Moi 80. L'Homme à la Valise 83. The Golden Eighties 86. Seven Women, Seven Sins (co-d) 87. Histoires d'Amérique 89. Night and Day/Nuit et Jour 91. Window Shopping 92. D'Est 93. A Couch in New York 96, etc.

Akins, Claude (1918–1994)
Solidly built American character actor who was usually cast as a western villain until it was realized that he could just as well play a burly middle-aged hero, Wallace Beery-style. In the late 70s he was much in demand as a TV star.

■ *From Here to Eternity* 53. Bitter Creek 54. The Caine Mutiny 54. The Raid 54. The Human Jungle 54. Down Three Dark Streets 54. Shield for Murder 54. The Sea Chase 55. Battle Stations 56. The Proud and Profane 56. Johnny Concho 56. The Burning Hills 56. The Sharkfighters 56. Hot Summer Night 57. The Kettles on Old Macdonald's Farm 57. The Lonely Man 57. Joe Dakota 57. The Defiant Ones 58. Onionhead 58. Rio Bravo 59. Don't Give Up the Ship 59. *Porgy and Bess* 59. Yellowstone Kelly 59. The Hound Dog Man 59. Comanche Station 60. Inherit the Wind 60. Claudelle Inglish 61. Merrill's Marauders 62. How the West Was Won 62. Black Gold 63. A Distant Trumpet 64. The Killers 64. Ride Beyond Vengeance 64. Return of the Seven 66. Incident at Phantom Hill 66. First to Fight 67. Waterhole Three 67. The Devil's Brigade 68. The Great Bank Robbery 69. Flap 70. A Man Called Sledge 71. The Night Stalker (TV) 71. Skyjacked 72. Battle for the Planet of the Apes 73. In Tandem (TV) 73. Timber Tramps 75. Tentacles 77. Tarantulas: The Deadly Cargo 77. Monster in the Closet 86. Sherlock Holmes: The Incident at Victoria Falls (TV) 91. Falling from Grace 92.

TV series: *Movin' On* 74–75. B.J. and the Bear 79. The Misadventures of Sheriff Lobo 79–81. Legmen 84.

Akins, Zoë (1886–1958)
American playwright and screenwriter. Born in Humansville, Missouri, she became a successful playwright in 1919 and remained one through the 20s, going to Hollywood in the 30s to write screenplays. By the end of the decade, her work no longer attracted much of an audience on stage or screen.

Daddy's Gone a-Hunting (oa) 25. Her Private Life (oa) 29. The Right to Love 30. Sarah and Son 30. Anybody's Woman 30. Once a Lady 31. *The Greeks Had a Word for Them* (oa) 32. Morning Glory (oa) 33. Christopher Strong 33. Outcast Lady 34. Lady of Secrets 36. Accused 36. Camille 37. The Toy Wife 38. Zaza 38. The Old Maid (oa) 39. Desire Me 47. How to Marry a Millionaire 53. Stage Struck (oa) 58, etc.

❝ A woman with a career is a tragedy. Women are not fitted for careers. I, who have one, say it! – Z.A.

Akkad, Moustapha
Syrian producer and director.

Mohammad, Messenger of God (p, d) 77. Lion of the Desert (p, d) 81. Appointment with Fear 85 (p). Free Ride 86. Halloween 5 (p) 89, etc.

Akst, Albert (c. 1890–1958)
American editor, long at MGM.

The Raven 35. Johnny Eager 42. Meet Me in St Louis 44. Ziegfeld Follies 46. Easter Parade 48. Annie Get Your Gun 50. Royal Wedding 52. The Band Wagon 53. Moonfleet 55. Somebody Up There Likes Me 56, many others.

Akst, Harry (1894–1963)
American composer and pianist. Born in New York, he worked in vaudeville and was staff pianist for Irving Berlin's publishing company before heading for Hollywood, where he wrote many songs for the studios, notably for Fox and Warner. He was also accompanist to Al Jolson. His best-known songs include 'Am I Blue?', 'Baby Face' and 'Dinah'.

The Squall 29. On with the Show 29. So Long, Letty 29. Song of the Flame 30. Leathernecking 30. Stand Up and Cheer 34. Bright Lights 35. Can This Be Dixie? 36. The Music Goes Round 36. Star for a Night 36. The Holy Terror 37. Sing and Be Happy 37. Rascals 38. Harvest Melody 43, etc.

Alazraki, Benito (1923–)
Mexican director best known abroad for his 1955 film of Indian life, *Roots*. Born in Mexico City, he moved to Spain in the early 60s, where he worked mainly in television, returning to Mexico in the early 70s. He began directing films again in the late 80s.

Roots/Raices 54. Los Amantes 57. Café Colon 58. Lost Souls/Infierno de Almas 58. The Karambazo Sisters/Las Hermanas Karambazo 59. Black Bull/Toro Negro 60. The Time and the Touch (US) 62. Los Jóvenes Amantes (Sp.) 70. Las Tres Perfectas Casadas (Sp.) 72. El Rey de los Taxistas 87. Objetos Sexuales 89, etc.

Alba, Jessica (1981–)
Sultry American actress. Born in Pomona, California, she began acting at the age of 12. She is best known for her role as Max in the TV series *Dark Angel*.

Never Been Kissed 99. Idle Hands 99. Paranoid 00. The Sleeping Dictionary 01, etc.

TV series: Flipper 95-97. Dark Angel 00- .

Alba, Maria (1905–) (Maria Casajuana)
Spanish actress and dancer, born in Barcelona, who was in American films of the late 20s and 30s.

Girl in Every Port 28. Hell's Heroes 30. Mr Robinson Crusoe 32. Chandu on the Magic Island 34. Return of Chandu 34, etc.

Albarn, Damon (1968–)
English pop singer, keyboard player and composer. Born in London, he was co-founder of the rock group Blur.

Face(a) 97. Ravenous (co-m) 99. Ordinary Decent Criminal (m) 00. 101 Reykjavik (co-m, Ice.) 00, etc.

Albee, Edward (1928–)
American playwright whose only significant contribution to cinema was *Who's Afraid of Virginia Woolf?* 66. *A Delicate Balance* however was filmed in 1973.

Biography: 1999, *Edward Albee: A Singular Journey* by Mel Gussow

❝ I have a fine sense of the ridiculous but no sense of humour. – *Quote from Who's Afraid of Virginia Woolf?*

Alberghetti, Anna Maria (1936–)
Italian-American operatic singer who came to films as a teenager and has made occasional appearances. Born in Pesaro, Italy, she retired from the screen in the early 60s. Married director Claudio Guzman.

Here Comes the Groom 51. The Stars Are Singing 53. The Medium 54. The Last Command 55. Ten Thousand Bedrooms 57. Cinderfella 60, etc.

Alberni, Luis (1887–1962)
Spanish-American character actor who played countless small film roles, usually featuring his mangled English.

Santa Fe Trail 30. Svengali 31. The Kid from Spain 32. Topaze 33. Flying Down to Rio 33. Roberta 35. Anthony Adverse 36. The Housekeeper's Daughter 39. That Hamilton Woman 42. Captain Carey USA 49. What Price Glory 52. The Ten Commandments 57, etc.

Albers, Hans (1892–1960)
Leading German actor with broad experience. Born in Hamburg, he began as a vaudeville comedian and dancer, and was in films from 1911. In the late 20s, he appeared in Max Reinhardt's stage productions and established himself as the leading German film actor of his time, gaining an international reputation with his performance in *The Blue Angel*.

Irene d'Or 23. A Midsummer Night's Dream 25. Rasputin 29. The Blue Angel 30. Drei Tage Liebe 31. FP 1 32. Gold 33. Peer Gynt 35. Casanova 36. Baron Munchausen 43. The White Hell of Pitz Palu 53. Der Greifer 58. Kein Engel ist so Rein 60, etc.

Albert, Eddie (1908–) (Eddie Albert Heimberger)
American character actor with radio and stage experience: for nearly forty years he has been playing honest Joes, nice guys and best friends, seldom winning the girl but allowing himself an occasional meaty role out of character.

■ *Brother Rat* 38. On Your Toes 39. *Four Wives* 39. Brother Rat and a Baby 40. An Angel from Texas 40. My Love Came Back 40. A Dispatch from Reuters 40. Four Mothers 41. The Wagons Roll at Night 41. Out of the Fog 41. Thieves Fall Out 41. The Great Mr Nobody 41. Treat 'Em Rough 42. Eagle Squadron 42. Ladies' Day 43. Lady Bodyguard 43. Bombardier 43. Strange Voyage 45. Rendezvous with Annie 46. The Perfect Marriage 46. *Smash Up* 47. Time out of Mind 47. Hit Parade of 1947 47. The Dude Goes West 48. You Gotta Stay Happy 48. The Fuller Brush Girl 50. Meet Me After the Show 51. You're in the Navy Now 51. Actors and Sin 52. *Carrie* 52. *Roman Holiday* (AAN) 53. The Girl Rush 55. *Oklahoma!* 55. *I'll Cry Tomorrow* 55. *Attack!* (his most serious role) 56. *The Teahouse of the August Moon* 56. The Sun Also Rises 57. The Joker is Wild 57. The Gun Runners 58. *The Roots of Heaven* 58. *Orders to Kill* (GB) 58. Beloved Infidel 59. The Young Doctors 61. The Two Little Bears 61. Madison Avenue 62. The Longest Day 62. Who's Got the Action? 62. The Party's Over (GB) 63. Miracle of the White Stallions 65. Captain Newman MD 63. Seven Women 65. See the Man Run (TV) 71. Fireball Forward (TV) 72. McQ 72. The Take 72. The Heartbreak Kid (AAN) 72. *The Longest Yard* 74. Escape to Witch Mountain 75. The Devil's Rain 75. Promise Him Anything (TV) 75. Hustle 76. Whiffs 76. Birch Interval 76. Moving Violation 76. The Word (TV) 78. Airport 80 The Concorde 79. Foolin' Around 80. How to Beat the High Cost of Living 80. Take This Job and Shove It 81. Yes Giorgio 82. Yesterday 80. This Time Forever 81. The Act 84. Dreamscape 84. Goliath Awaits (TV) 84. Head Office 85. Stitches 85. In Like Flynn (TV) 85. Turnaround 86. Head Office 86. The Big Picture 88. Brenda Starr 89. Return to Green Acres (TV) 90. The Girl from Mars 91. Brenda Starr 92.

TV series: *Leave It to Larry* 52. *Green Acres* 65–71. *Switch* 75–78. Falcon Crest 86. Beauty and The Beast 89–90.

Albert, Edward (1951–)
American light actor, son of Eddie Albert; his career to date has been somewhat disappointing.

The Fool Killer 65. Butterflies Are Free 72. Forty Carats 73. Midway 76. The Domino Principle 77. The Purple Taxi 77. The Greek Tycoon 78. The Word (TV) 78. Silent Victory (TV) 79. The Last Convertible (TV) 79. When Time Ran Out 80. Galaxy of Terror 81. Butterfly 81. The Squeeze 81. Blood Feud (TV) 81. The House Where Evil Dwells 82. Ellie 84. Getting Even 86. Distortions 87. Terminal Entry 87. The Underachievers 88. Fist Fighter 88. The Rescue 88. Mindgames 89. Wild Zone 89. Exiled in America 90. Body Language 92. Shootfighter: Fight to the Death 93. The Ice Runner 93. Guarding Tess 94. Space

And Mr Kelly graciously added: 'If I'm the Marlon Brando of dancing, he's Cary Grant.'

Graham Greene put it another way: 'The nearest we are ever likely to get to a human Mickey Mouse.'

C. A. Lejeune produced this analysis: 'I have never met anyone who did not like Fred Astaire. Somewhere in his sad monkey-sad face, his loose legs, his shy grin, or perhaps the anxious diffidence of his manner, he has found the secret of persuading the world.'

André Sennwald, in a review of *The Gay Divorcee*, was equally percipient: 'The audience meets Mr Astaire and the film at their best when he is adjusting his cravat to an elaborate dance routine or saying delicious things with his flashing feet that a lyricist would have difficulty putting into words.'

While Fred Astaire said in his 80s: 'When they review my shows, they don't say whether they're good or bad – they just write about how old I am.'

Asther, Nils (1897–1981)
Suave, exotic Swedish leading man in Hollywood from the mid-20s. He was married to Vivian DUNCAN.

Topsy and Eva 27. *Sorrell and Son* 27. The Blue Danube 28. Laugh Clown Laugh 28. The Cossacks 28. Loves of an Actress 28. The Cardboard Lover 28. *Our Dancing Daughters* 28. Dream of Love 28. Wild Orchids 29. *The Single Standard* 29. The Wrath of the Seas 29. Letty Lynton 32. The Washington Masquerade 32. *The Bitter Tea of General Yen* 32. Storm at Daybreak 33. The Right to Romance 33. *By Candlelight* 34. Madame Spy 34. The Crime Doctor 34. The Love Captive 34. *Abdul the Damned* (GB) 35. Make Up (GB) 37. Dr Kildare's Wedding Day 41. The Night Before the Divorce 41. The Night of January 16th 41. Sweater Girl 42. Night Monster 42. The Hour Before Dawn 44. *The Man in Half Moon Street* 44. Son of Lassie 45. Jealousy 45. The Feathered Serpent 49. That Man from Tangier 50. Vita Frun 62. Gudrun 63.

Astin, John (1930–)
American comic actor with stage experience. He was formerly married to actress Patty Duke.

West Side Story 61. That Touch of Mink 62. Candy 68. Viva Max 68. Evil Roy Slade (TV) 72. Get to Know Your Rabbit 72. The Brothers O'Toole 73. Freaky Friday 77. Body Slam 87. Gremlins 2: The New Batch 90. The Silence of the Hams (It.) 94. The Frighteners 96, etc.

TV series: I'm Dickens He's Fenster 63. The Addams Family 64. Operation Petticoat 77. Mary 85–86.

Astin, MacKenzie (1973–)
American actor, the son of John ASTIN and Patty DUKE and brother of Sean ASTIN.

The Garbage Pail Kids Movie 87. Iron Will 94. Wyatt Earp 94. Dream of an Insomniac 96. Evening Star 96. In Love and War 96. The Last Days of Disco 98. Stranger Than Fiction 99, etc.

TV series: The Facts of Life 85–88.

Astin, Sean (1971–)
American actor, the son of John ASTIN and Patty DUKE, who began as an adolescent.

The Goonies 85. Like Father Like Son 87. White Water Summer 87. Staying Together 89. The War of the Roses 89. Memphis Belle 90. Toy Soldiers 91. Encino Man/California Man 92. Where the Day Takes You 92. Rudy 93. Safe Passage 94. The Low Life 95. Harrison Bergeron (TV) 95. Courage under Fire 96. Bulworth 98. Dish Dogs 98. Deterrence 00, etc.

Astley, Edwin
Prolific British composer of the 50s and 60s, mainly of documentaries and 'B' features, many for the DANZIGER brothers.

Devil Girl from Mars 54. Star of My Night 54. To Paris with Love 54. What Every Woman Wants 54. The Gay Dog 54. The Crowded Day 54. The Happiness of Three Women 54. Alias John Preston 55. Fun at St Fanny's 55. Diamond Expert 55. Final Column 55. The Schemer 56. Stars in Your Eyes 56. At the Stroke of Nine 57. The Heart Within 57. Woman Eater 57. A Woman of Mystery 57. Three Sundays to Live 57. Kill Her Gently 57. Dublin Nightmare 58. The Man Who Liked Funerals 58. Innocent Meeting 58. A Woman Possessed 58. Three Crooked Men 58. The Day They Robbed the Bank of England 59. The Crowning Touch 59. In the Wake of a Stranger 59. The Great Van Robbery 59. The Mouse that Roared 59. Faces in the Dark 60. Let's Get Married 60. Visa to Canton/Passport to China 60. Follow That Man 61. The Last Rhino 61. A Matter of Who 61. The Phantom of the Opera 62. The World Ten Times Over 63. The Syndicate 67. All at Sea 69, etc.

Astor, Gertrude (1887–1977)
American silent screen actress, on stage from the age of 13.

Uncle Tom's Cabin 27. The Cat and the Canary 28. Camille 36. How Green Was My Valley 40. The Man Who Shot Liberty Valance 62, many others.

Astor, Mary (1906–1987) (Lucille Langehanke)
American leading lady who despite a stormy and well-publicized private life remained a star from the mid-20s to the mid-40s and remained in demand for character roles. Born in Quincy, Illinois, and a teenage beauty queen whose father was determined to get her into films, she found success when she appeared in *Beau Brummell* with John BARRYMORE, who became her lover. Her career not only survived a scandal in the mid-30s, when excerpts from her diary about her love affair with playwright George S. KAUFMAN were read out in divorce court and leaked to the press, but also her alcoholism in the 40s and 50s. She married four times, first in 1928 to director Kenneth Hawks, who died in a plane crash in 1930.

Autobiography: 1959, *My Story*. 1971, *A Life on Film*. Novels include: *Image of Kate* 1966. *A Place Called Saturday* 1969.

SILENT FILMS: *The Beggar Maid* 21. The Bright Shawl 23. Puritan Passions 23. *Beau Brummell* 24. Inez from Hollywood 25. *Don Q Son of Zorro* 25. *Don Juan* 26. Rose of the Golden West 27. Two Arabian Knights 27. Heart to Heart 28. Romance of the Underworld 29, etc.

■ SOUND: Ladies Love Brutes 30. The Runaway Bride 30. Holiday 30. The Lash 30. The Sin Ship 30. The Royal Bed 30. Other Men's Women 31. Behind Office Doors 31. White Shoulders 31. Smart Woman 31. Men of Chance 31. The Lost Squadron 32. A Successful Calamity 32. Those We Love 32. *Red Dust* 32. The Little Giant 33. Jennie Gerhardt 33. The Kennel Murder Case 33. Convention City 33. The World Changes 33. Easy to Love 34. The Man with Two Faces 34. Return of the Terror 34. Upper World 34. The Case of the Howling Dog 34. I am a Thief 34. Man of Iron 35. Red Hot Tires 35. Straight from the Heart 35. Dinky 35. Page Miss Glory 35. The Murder of Dr Harrigan 35. The Lady from Nowhere 36. And So They Were Married 36. *Dodsworth* 36. Trapped by Television 36. *The Prisoner of Zenda* 37. *The Hurricane* 37. Paradise for Three 38. No Time to Marry 38. There's Always a Woman 38. Woman against Woman 38. Listen Darling 39. *Midnight* 39. *Turnabout* 40. Brigham Young 40. *The Great Lie* (AA) (her most splendid bitchy performance) 41. *The Maltese Falcon* 41. *Across the Pacific* 42. *The Palm Beach Story* 42. Young Ideas 43. Thousands Cheer 43. *Meet Me in St Louis* 44. Blonde Fever 44. Claudia and David 46. Desert Fury 47. Cynthia 47. Fiesta 47. *Act of Violence* 49. Cass Timberlane 49. *Little Women* (as Marmee) 49. Any Number Can Play 49. A Kiss Before Dying 56. The Power and the Prize 56. The Devil's Hairpin 56. This Happy Feeling 58. Stranger in my Arms 59. *Return to Peyton Place* 61. *Youngblood Hawke* 64. Hush Hush Sweet Charlotte 64.

✪ For amiably sending herself up in half a dozen portraits of mature but fallible women between 1936 and 1942; and for sheer durability. *The Great Lie*.

❝ I was never totally involved in movies. I was making my father's dream come true. – M.A.

Famous line (*The Great Lie*) 'If I didn't think you meant so well, I'd feel like slapping your face.'

Astruc, Alexandre (1923–)
French director, former film critic.

The Crimson Curtain 51. Les Mauvaises Rencontres 54. Une Vie 56. La Proie Pour l'Ombre 61. L'Education Sentimentale 61. La Longue Marche 65. Flammes sur L'Adriatique 67. Charlotte/La Jeune Fille Assassinée 74. Sartre by Himself (doc) 76, etc.

❝ The fundamental problem of the cinema is how to express thought. – A.A.

Atchley, Hooper (1887–1943)
American character actor, from the stage. Committed suicide.

Love at First Sight 29. The Santa Fe Trail 30. Arizona Terror 31. Trouble in Paradise 32. Gun Justice 33. The Three Musketeers (serial) 34. Mystery Mountain (serial) 34. Law beyond the Range 35. Ace Drummond (serial) 36. A Day at the Races 37. Mr Wong, Detective 38. Pirates of the Skies 39. The Gay Caballero 40. Adventures of Red Ryder (serial) 40. Dick Tracy vs Crime, Inc (serial) 41. The Little Foxes 41. Gentleman Jim 42. Mission to Moscow 43. G-Men versus the Black Dragon (serial) 43. The Song of Bernadette 43, etc.

Ates, Roscoe (1892–1962)
Short, stuttering American character actor, on stage from 1915 and films from 1929. A former violinist and vaudeville performer, he played Eddie Dean's sidekick in many second-feature westerns.

South Sea Rose 29. Billy the Kid 30. Cimarron 31. Renegades of the West 33. Alice in Wonderland 33. Riders of the Black Hills 38. Gone with the Wind 39. Chad Hanna 40. Bad Men of Missouri 41. Sullivan's Travels 42. Stars over Texas 46. West to Glory 47. Black Hills 48. Thunder in the Pines 49. The Blazing Forest 52. The Stranger Wore a Gun 53. Abbott and Costello Meet the Keystone Cops 53. Meet Me in Las Vegas 56. The Birds and the Bees 57. The Ladies' Man 61, etc.

TV series: The Marshal of Gunsight Pass 50.

Atherton, William (1947–) (William Knight)
American actor with stage background.

The New Centurions 72. Class of '44 73. The Sugarland Express 74. The Day of the Locust 74. The Hindenburg 76. Looking for Mr Goodbar 77. Malibu (TV) 83. Ghostbusters 84. Real Genius 85. No Mercy 86. Intrigue 90. Die Hard 2 90. Oscar 91. Chrome Soldiers 92. The Pelican Brief 93. Saints and Sinners 95. Broken Trust (TV) 95. Bio-Dome 96. Mad City 97. The Crow: Salvation 00, etc.

Atkins, Christopher (1961–)
American actor who began by starring opposite Brooke SHIELDS in *The Blue Lagoon*.

The Blue Lagoon 80. The Pirate Movie 82. A Night in Heaven 83. Mortuary Academy 88. Listen to Me 89. Shakma 90. Exchange Lifeguards 93. Signal One (Aus) 95. It's My Party 96. The Little Unicorn 99, etc.

TV series: Dallas 83–84.

Atkins, Eileen (1934–)
British character actress, highly regarded on stage. She was co-creator of the TV series *Upstairs, Downstairs* and *The House of Elliott*. Formerly married to actor Julian GLOVER.

Inadmissible Evidence 68. I Don't Want to Be Born 75. Equus 77. She Fell Among Thieves (TV) 78. The Dresser 83. Let Him Have It 91. The Lost Language of Cranes (TV) 91. Wolf 94. Cold Comfort Farm (TV) 95. Jack & Sarah 95. Mrs Dalloway (w) 97. Vita and Virginia (& w) 97. The Avengers 98. Women Talking Dirty 00, etc.

Atkins, Robert (1886–1972)
English classical actor and stage director, in occasional films. Born in Dulwich, London, he studied at the Academy of Dramatic Art and was on stage from 1906. He staged and appeared in every one of Shakespeare's plays, notably at The Old Vic in the 20s, at the Stratford Memorial Theatre and with his own touring company.

Hamlet 13. Peg of Old Drury 35. The Cardinal 36. Everything is Thunder 36. He Found a Star 41. The Great Mr Handel 42. A Matter of Life and Death/Stairway to Heaven 46. Black Magic 49. That Dangerous Age/If This Be Sin 49. The House in the Square/I'll Never Forget You 51, etc.

❝ What actor has not tried to imitate his voice – the essence is there but never that idiosyncratic timbre wherein all his bass vowel sounds came through a cavern and down his nose. – *Donald Sinden*

Atkinson, Rowan (1955–)
English actor and comedian, best known as the hapless Mr Bean, which from 1990 to 1995 revived silent slapstick comedy on television. He studied electrical engineering at Newcastle University and then went to Oxford University, where he appeared in the Oxford Revue and then performed a one-man show before teaming with Mel SMITH and Griff Rhys JONES in the TV series *Not the Nine O'Clock News*. He runs his own production company Tiger Television. In 2000, *Broadcast* magazine estimated his financial worth at £40m.

Biography: 1999, *Rowan Atkinson* by Bruce Dessau.

Never Say Never Again 83. The Tall Guy 89. The Appointments of Dennis Jennings (short) 89. The Witches 90. Hot Shots! Part Deux 93. Four Weddings and a Funeral 94. The Lion King (voice of Zazu) 94. Bean (& co-w) 97, etc.

TV series: Not the Nine O'Clock News 81–82. Blackadder 83–84. Blackadder II 85. Blackadder III 87–88. Blackadder Goes Forth 89–90. The Thin Blue Line 95–96.

❝ It is better to make no films than bad films. I see the film world as a big bag of worry. – *R.A.*

Atsumi, Kiyoshi (1928–1996) (Yasuo Tadokoro)
Japanese leading comic actor, best known for playing Tora-san, an itinerant pedlar, in a long-running series which began on television in 1968 and encompassed 48 films from 1969 to 1995, mostly directed by Yoji YAMADA.

Attanasio, Paul (1959–)
American screenwriter who also created the mid-90s TV series *Homicide: Life on the Street*. Born in New York, he studied law at Harvard and, in the 1980s, was a film critic for the *Washington Post*.

Quiz Show (AAN) 94. Disclosure 94. Donnie Brasco 97. Sphere 98, etc.

❝ Films could return full circle to having just a lot of silent action and title cards – pure spectacle. It seems where the audience is going. – *P.A.*

Little guys aren't lovable. Chaplin's little tramp is not lovable. The little guy's usually mean and vindictive, because he's been made that way. – *P.A.*

Attenborough, Richard (1923–) (Lord Attenborough)
British character actor who escaped from early typecasting as a young coward, revealed an ambitious range of characterizations, and went on to produce and direct. He became a life peer in 1993. Married actress Sheila SIM in 1945.

In Which We Serve 42. Schweik's New Adventures 43. The Hundred Pound Window 43. Journey Together 44. A Matter of Life and Death 46. School for Secrets 46. The Man Within 47. Dancing with Crime 47. *Brighton Rock* 47. London Belongs to Me 48. *The Guinea Pig* (as a 13-year-old) 48. The Lost People 49. Boys in Brown 49. Morning Departure 50. Hell is Sold Out 51. The Magic Box 51. The Gift Horse 52. Father's Doing Fine 52. Eight O'Clock Walk 53. The Ship that Died of Shame 55. *Private's Progress* 56. The Baby and the Battleship 56. Brothers in Law 57. The Scamp 57. Dunkirk 58. *The Man Upstairs* 58. Danger Within 58. Sea of Sand 58. I'm All Right Jack 59. Jet Storm 59. SOS Pacific 59. *The Angry Silence* (& co-p) 60. *The League of Gentlemen* (& co-p) 60. All Night Long 61. Only Two Can Play 62. *Whistle Down the Wind* (p only) 62. The Dock Brief 62. *The Great Escape* (US) 63. *Seance on a Wet Afternoon* (& p) 64. The Third Secret 64. *Guns at Batasi* (BFA) 64. The Flight of the Phoenix (US) 65. The Sand Pebbles (US) 66. Doctor Dolittle 67. The Bliss of Mrs Blossom 68. Only When I Larf 68. *Oh What a Lovely War* (co-p and d only) 69. David Copperfield 69. The Last Grenade 69. The Magic Christian 69. A Severed Head 70. *Loot* 70. 10 Rillington Place 71. Young Winston (d only) 72. And Then There Were None 74. Conduct Unbecoming 75. Rosebud 75. Brannigan 75. A Bridge Too Far (d only) 77. The Chess Players (India) 77. Magic (d only) 78. The Human Factor 79. *Gandhi* (p, d only) (AA) 82. A Chorus Line (d only) 85. Cry Freedom (d only) 87. Chaplin (d) 92. Jurassic Park (a) 93. *Shadowlands* (p, d) 93. Miracle on 34th Street (a) 94. In Love and War (p, d) 96. Hamlet (a) 96. In Love and War (d) 97. Elizabeth (a) 98. Grey Owl (p, d) 98. The Railway Children (a, TV) 00, etc.

✪ For being a prime mover in most aspects of British entertainment for half a century and demonstrating in an age of hyperbole and bluster the effectiveness of understatement. *Shadowlands*.

Atterbury, Malcolm (1907–1992)
American character actor.

Dragnet 54. I Was a Teenage Werewolf 57. Blood of Dracula 57. Rio Bravo 59. The Birds 63. Seven Days in May 64. The Learning Tree 69. The Emperor of the North Pole 73. Day of Terror, Night of Fear (TV) 77, etc.

TV series: Thicker than Water 73. Apple's Way 74–75.

Atwater, Barry (1918–1978)
American character actor.
Nightmare 56. Pork Chop Hill 59. Sweet Bird of Youth 62. Return of the Gunfighter (TV) 66. The Night Stalker (TV) 72, etc.

Atwater, Edith (1911–1986)
American character actress, usually as a helpmeet – secretary, nurse or mother. Born in Chicago, Illinois, she was married to actors Joseph Allen, Jnr, Hugh Marlowe and Kent Smith.
We Went to College 36. The Body Snatcher 45. The Sweet Smell of Success 57. It Happened at the World's Fair 63. Strait Jacket 64. Strange Bedfellows 64. True Grit 69. Pieces of Dreams 70. Stand Up and Be Counted 71. Die Sister Die 74. Family Plot 76, etc.

Atwill, Lionel (1885–1946)
Incisive but rather stolid British actor who went to Hollywood in 1932 and stayed to play teutonic villians, mad doctors and burgomasters.
■ Eve's Daughter 18. For Sale 18. The Marriage Price 19. The Highest Bidder 21. Indiscretion 21. The Silent Witness 32. *Doctor X* 32. The Vampire Bat 33. The Secret of Madame Blanche 33. *The Mystery of the Wax Museum* 33. Murders in the Zoo 33. The Sphinx 33. Song of Songs 33. The Secret of the Blue Room 33. The Solitaire Man 33. *Nana* 34. Beggars in Ermine 34. Stamboul Quest 34. One More River 34. The Age of Innocence 34. The Firebird 34. The Man Who Reclaimed His Head 35. Mark of the Vampire 35. *The Devil is a Woman* 35. The Murder Man 35. Rendezvous 35. Captain Blood 35. Lady of Secrets 36. Absolute Quiet 36. Till We Meet Again 36. *The Road Back* 37. The High Command 37. Last Train from Madrid 37. The Great Garrick 37. Lancer Spy 37. Three Comrades 38. The Great Waltz 38. *Son of Frankenstein* (memorable as the one-armed police chief) 39. *The Three Musketeers* 39. *The Hound of the Baskervilles* 39. The Gorilla 39. The Sun Never Sets 39. Mr Moto Takes a Vacation 39. The Secret of Dr Kildare 39. Balalaika 39. Charlie Chan in Panama 39. The Mad Empress 40. Johnny Apollo 40. Charlie Chan's Murder Cruise 40. The Girl in 313 40. Boom Town 40. The Great Profile 40. *Man Made Monster* 41. The Mad Doctor of Market Street 42. *To Be Or Not To Be* 42. The Strange Case of Dr RX 42. The Ghost of Frankenstein 42. Pardon My Sarong 42. Cairo 42. Night Monster 42. Junior G-Men of the Air (serial) 42. *Sherlock Holmes and the Secret Weapon* (as Moriarty) 42. Frankenstein Meets the Wolf Man 43. House of Frankenstein 44. Captain America (serial) 44. Raiders of Ghost City (serial) 44. Lady in the Death House 44. Secrets of Scotland Yard 44. Fog Island 45. Genius at Work 45. Crime Incorporated 45. *House of Dracula* 45. Lost City of the Jungle (serial) 46.
❝ See, one side of my face is gentle and kind, incapable of anything but love of my fellow man. The other profile is cruel and predatory and evil, incapable of anything but lusts and dark passions. It all depends which side of my face is turned towards you – or the camera. – *L.A.*
One doesn't easily forget, Herr Baron, an arm torn out by the roots. – *L.A. in Son of Frankenstein*
My dear, why are you so pitifully afraid? Immortality has been the dream, the inspiration of mankind through the ages. And I am going to give you immortality! – *L.A. in The Mystery of the Wax Museum*

Atwood, Colleen
American costume designer; she began on *Ragtime* as an assistant to production designer Patrizia von Brandenstein.
Firstborn 84. Manhunter 86. The Pick-Up Artist 87. Someone to Watch Over Me 87. Married to the Mob 88. Torch Song Trilogy 88. Edward Scissorhands 90. Joe versus the Volcano 90. Hider in the House 91. Silence of the Lambs 91. Love Field 92. Rush 92. Lorenzo's Oil 92. Born Yesterday 93. Philadelphia 93. Cabin Boy 94. Ed Wood 94. Wyatt Earp 94. Little Women (AAN) 94. The Juror 96. Mars Attacks! 96. Gattaca 97. Head above Water 97. Fallen 98. Beloved (AAN) 98. Sleepy Hollow 99, etc.

Auberjonois, René (1940–)
American character actor.
M*A*S*H 70. Brewster McCloud 71. McCabe and Mrs Miller 71. Images 72. Pete 'n Tillie 72. Panache (TV) 76. The Hindenburg 76. King Kong 76. Eyes of Laura Mars 78. Where the Buffalo Roam 80. The Christmas Star (TV) 86. Walker 87. Police Academy 5: Assignment Miami Beach 88. The Little Mermaid (voice) 89. The Feud 90. The Lost Language of Cranes (TV) 91. The Player 92. The Ballad of Little Joe 93. Batman Forever 95. Los Locos 97. Inspector Gadget 99. The Patriot 00. We All Fall Down 00, etc.
TV series: Benson 80–85. Star Trek: Deep Space Nine 93–99 .

Aubert, Lenore (1913–1993) (Eleanore Maria Leisner)
Yugoslavian actress in Hollywood from the late 30s, usually in sinister roles.
Bluebeard's Eighth Wife 38. They Got Me Covered 43. Passport to Destiny 43. Action in Arabia 44. Catman of Paris 46. *Wife of Monte Cristo* 46. The Other Love 47. Return of the Whistler 48. *Abbott and Costello Meet Frankenstein* 48. Abbott and Costello Meet the Killer, Boris Karloff 48. Une Fille sur la Route 52, etc.

Aubrey, Anne (1937–)
British leading lady of a few comedies and adventures in the late 50s.
No Time To Die 58. The Man Inside 58. The Secret Man 58. The Bandit of Zhobe 59. Idle on Parade 59. Killers of Kilimanjaro 59. Jazzboat 60. In the Nick 60. Let's Get Married 60. The Hellions 61. Assignment Munich (TV) 72. The Carey Treatment 73.

Aubrey, James T. (1918–1994)
Production executive, nicknamed 'The Smiling Cobra'. He was president of CBS-TV at the height of its success (1959–65), and, from 1969–73, in charge of MGM, during which period he cut costs by cancelling movies and selling many of the studio's assets, including its wardrobe and props from its classic films. Then became an independent producer, mainly of TV movies. Married actress Phyllis Thaxter (1944–63).
Futureworld 76. The Hunger 83, etc.
❝ I don't want to hear any more bullshit about the old MGM. The old MGM is gone. – *J.T.A.*
Jim Aubrey doesn't know as much about film as a first-year cinema student. – *Blake Edwards*
No man in history ever had such a lock on such an enormous audience. – *Life magazine on Aubrey at CBS*

Aubrey, Jimmy (1887–1983)
English music-hall comedian and actor. Born in Liverpool, he was a member of Fred Karno's troupe that toured America and also included Charlie Chaplin and Stan Laurel. He starred in silent comedy shorts, with Oliver Hardy as the heavy, and had bit parts in a few Laurel and Hardy comedies before becoming a character actor in early talkies.
Footlights and Fakers 17. She Laughs Last 20. Their Purple Moment 28. That's My Wife 29. Courage in the North 35. Aces and Eights 36, etc.

Aubrey, Juliet (c. 1968–)
English leading actress. Born in Fleet, Hampshire, she studied archaeology at King's College, London, and acting at the Central School of Speech and Drama.
Jonah who Lived in the Whale/Jona Che Visse Nella Balena (It./Fr.) 92. Sherlock Holmes: The Last Vampyre (TV) 93. Middlemarch (BFA,TV) 94. Go Now (TV) 95. Food of Love 97. Welcome to Sarajevo 97. A Time to Love/Il Tempo Dell'Amore 99. Extremely Dangerous (TV) 99. For My Baby/Goodnight Vienna, etc.

Aubrey, Skye (1945–)
American leading lady of a few 70s films: daughter of James Aubrey, TV executive, and actress Phyllis Thaxter.
Vanished (TV) 71. The Carey Treatment 72. The Longest Night (TV) 72. The Phantom of Hollywood (TV) 73, etc.

Aubry, Cécile (1929–) (Anne-Marie-José Benard)
Petite French leading lady of the early 50s. Now a children's author.
Manon 49. The Black Rose 50. Bluebeard 51. La Ironia 54, etc.

Auclair, Michel (1922–1988) (Vladimir Vujovic)
French leading man.
La Belle et la Bête 46. Les Maudits 47. Manon 49. Justice Est Faite 50. Henriette 52. Funny Face (US) 56. The Fanatics 57. Rendezvous de Minuit 61. Symphony for a Massacre 64. The Day of the Jackal 73, etc.

Audiard, Jacques (1952–)
French screenwriter and director, the son of writer-director Michel Audiard, with whom he wrote his first scripts, *The Professional/Le Professionnel* 81 and *Mortel Randonnée* 82.
Vive le Sociale 83. La Cage aux Folles III (co-w) 85. Angel Dust/Poussière d'Ange 87. Australia (co-w) 89. Baxter (co-w) 89. Barjo (co-w) 93. See How They Fall/Regard les Hommes Tomber (wd) 94. *A Self-Made Hero*/Un Héro Très Discret (wd) 95, etc.

Audiard, Michel (1920–1985)
French writer-director.
Mr Peek-a-Boo (w) 51. Gas Oil (w) 55. Les Misérables (w) 57. Babette Goes to War (w) 60. A Monkey in Winter (w) 62. Mélodie en Sous-Sol (w) 63. Tendre Voyou (w) 66. Opération Léontine (wd) 68. Le Drapeau Noir (wd) 71. Tendre Poulet (wd) 78. Le Cavaleur (wd) 79, many others.

Audley, Maxine (1923–1992)
British stage actress who made occasional film appearances.
The Sleeping Tiger 54. The Barretts of Wimpole Street 57. The Vikings 58. Our Man in Havana 59. The Trials of Oscar Wilde 60. Hell Is a City 60. A Jolly Bad Fellow 64. Here We Go Round the Mulberry Bush 67. Frankenstein Must Be Destroyed 69, etc.

Audran, Stéphane (1933–)
Cool French leading actress, in international films. Married Jean-Louis Trintignant and Claude Chabrol.
La Bonne Tisane 58. Les Cousins 59. Les Bonnes Femmes 60. Les Godelureaux 61. Le Signe du Lion 62. Landru 63. Le Tigre Aime la Chair Fraîche 64. Paris vu Par 65. The Champagne Murders 67. *Les Biches* 68. La Femme Infidèle 69. The Lady in the Car with Glasses and a Gun 70. Just Before Nightfall 71. Without Apparent Motive 71. *The Discreet Charm of the Bourgeoisie* 72. Les Noces Rouges 73. Dead Pigeon on Beethoven Street 73. And Then There Were None 74. The Black Bird 75. Vincent, Paul, François and the Others 76. Folies Bourgeoises 76. Silver Bears 77. Violette Nozière 78. The Prisoner of Zenda 79. Eagle's Wing 79. Le Coeur à l'Envers 80. The Big Red One 80. Brideshead Revisited (TV) 80. Blood Relatives 81. Coup de Torchon 82. The Blood of Others 84. Cop au Vin 84. Mistral's Daughter (TV) 84. Les Plouffe 85. The Gypsy 85. Babette's Feast 87. Quiet Days in Clichy 90. Betty 92. Au Petit Marguery 95. Maximum Risk (US) 96, etc.

Audry, Jacqueline (1908–1977)
French director whose films were usually written by her husband, Pierre Laroche.
Gigi 49. L'Ingénue Libertine 50. *Olivia* 51. Huis Clos 54. In Six Easy Lessons 57. Mitsou 57. Les Petits Matins 62. Soledad 66. Le Lis de Mer 70, etc.

Audsley, Mick
British editor.
The Hit 85. Dance with a Stranger 85. My Beautiful Laundrette 86. Prick Up Your Ears 87. Sammy and Rosie Get Laid 87. Dangerous Liaisons 88. Soursweet 88. We're No Angels 89. The Grifters 90. Hero/Accidental Hero 92. Interview with the Vampire 94. 12 Monkeys 95. The Van 96. The Avengers 98. High Fidelity 00, etc.

Auer, John H. (1909–1975)
Hungarian-born American director, turning out 'B' films since the 30s.
Then to TV.
■ Frankie and Johnnie 35. The Crime of Dr Crespi 35. Rhythm in the Clouds 37. Circus Girl 37. A Man Betrayed 37. Outside of Paradise 38. Invisible Enemy 38. I Stand Accused 38. A Desperate Adventure 38. Orphans of the Street 38. Forged Passport 39. SOS Tidal Wave 39. Smuggled Cargo 39. Calling All Marines 39. Thou Shalt Not Kill 40. Women in War 40. Hit Parade of 1941 40. A Man Betrayed 41. The Devil Pays Off 41. Pardon My Stripes 42. Moonlight Masquerade 42. Johnny Doughboy 43. Tahiti Honey 43. *Gangway for Tomorrow* 43. Seven Days Ashore 44. Music in Manhattan 44. Pan Americana 45. Beat the Band 47. The Flame 47. I, Jane Doe 48. Angel on the Amazon 48. The Avengers 50. Hit Parade of 1951 50. Thunderbirds 52. *City that Never Sleeps* (& p) 53. Hell's Half Acre (& p) 53. The Eternal Sea (& p) 55. Johnny Trouble (& p) 56.

Auer, Mischa (1905–1967) (Mischa Ounskowsky)
Lanky Russian comedy actor with prominent eyes and wild gestures. Went to Broadway after the revolution, and in 1928 arrived in Hollywood; after several false starts found himself much in demand for noble idiot roles in broken English.
■ Something Always Happens 28. Marquis Preferred 28. The Benson Murder Case 30. Inside the Lines 30. Just Imagine 30. Women Love Once 30. The Unholy Garden 31. The Yellow Ticket 31. Delicious 31. The Midnight Patrol 32. No Greater Love 32. Mata Hari 32. Scarlet Dawn 32. The Monster Walks 32. Dangerously Yours 33. Sucker Money 33. Infernal Machine 33. Corruption 33. After Tonight 33. Cradle Song 33. Girl Without a Room 33. Wharf Angel 34. Bulldog Drummond Strikes Back 34. Stamboul Quest 34. I Dream too Much 34. The Crusades 35. Mystery Woman 35. Lives of a Bengal Lancer 35. Clive of India 35. Sons of Guns 36. Murder in the Fleet 36. The House of a Thousand Candles 36. One Rainy Afternoon 36. The Princess Comes Across 36. *My Man Godfrey* (in which his gorilla impersonation really put him on the map) (AAN) 36. *The Gay Desperado* 36. Winterset 36. That Girl from Paris 37. Three Smart Girls 37. Top of the Town 37. We Have Our Moments 37. Pick a Star 37. Marry the Girl 37. Vogues of 1938 37. *100 Men and a Girl* 37. Merry Go Round 37. It's All Yours 38. Rage of Paris 38. *You Can't Take It With You* 38. Service de Luxe 38. Little Tough Guys in Society 38. *Sweethearts* 38. *East Side of Heaven* 39. Unexpected Father 39. *Destry Rides Again* 39. Alias the Deacon 40. Sandy is a Lady 40. Public Deb Number One 40. *Spring Parade* 40. Seven Sinners 40. Trail of the Vigilantes 40. The Flame of New Orleans 41. Hold That Ghost 41. Moonlight in Hawaii 41. *Hellzapoppin* 41. Cracked Nuts 41. *Twin Beds* 42. Around the World 43. *Lady in the Dark* 44. *Up in Mabel's Room* 44. *A Royal Scandal* 45. Brewster's Millions 45. And Then There Were None 45. Sentimental Journey 46. She Wrote the Book 46. Sofia 48. The Sky is Red 52. Song of Paris 52. *Confidential Report* 55. Futures Vedettes 55. The Monte Carlo Story 58. Mam'zelle Pigalle 58. The Foxiest Girl in Paris 58. A Dog a Mouse and a Sputnik 60. We Joined the Navy 62. Ladies First 63. The Christmas that Almost Wasn't 66. Drop Dead Darling 66.
✪ For assuring the world that Russians could be fun. *Twin Beds*.
❝ Famous line (*Lady in the Dark*) 'This is the end! The absolute end!'

Auger, Claudine (1942–)
French leading lady, in occasional films abroad.
In the French Style 63. Thunderball 65. Triple Cross 66. Jeu de Massacre 67. The Devil in Love 67. The Bastard 68. The Crimebuster 77. Travels with Anita 79. Fantastica 80. Lovers and Liars 81. The Associate 82. Secret Places 84, etc.

August, Bille (1948–)
Danish director and screenwriter, a former cinematographer. He has won the Palme d'Or at the Cannes Film Festival with *Pelle the Conqueror* and *The Best Intentions*.
In My Life 78. Zappa (wd) 83. Twist and Shout (wd) 84. Buster's World (TV) 85. Pelle the Conqueror/Pelle Erobreren (wd) 88. The Best Intentions/Den Goda Viljan (d) 92. The House of the Spirits (wd) 93. Jerusalem (wd) 96. Smilla's Sense of Snow/Smilla's Feeling for Snow (d) 97. Les Misérables (d) (US) 98, etc.

August, Joseph (1890–1947)
Distinguished American cinematographer.
Selected silents: The Narrow Trail 17. Tiger Man 18. Square Deal Sanderson 19. Sand 20. O'Malley of the Mounted 21. *Travellin' On* 22. Madness of Youth 23. *Dante's Inferno* 24. *Tumbleweeds* 25. *The Road to Glory* 26. *The Beloved Rogue* 26. Fig Leaves 26. Two Arabian Knights 27. Honor Bound 28. The Black Watch 29.
■ Sound films: Men Without Women 30. Double Crossroads 30. On Your Back 30. Up the River 30. Seas Beneath 31. Mr Lemon of Orange 31. Quick Millions 31. The Brat 31. Heartbreak 31. Charlie Chan's Chance 31. Silent Witness 32. Mystery Ranch 32. Vanity Street 32. No More Orchids 32. That's My Boy 32. *Man's Castle* 33. Master of Men 33. As the Devil Commands 33. Cocktail Hour 33. Circus Queen Murder 33. The Captain Hates the Sea 34. Among the Missing 34.

The Defense Rests 34. Black Moon 34. Twentieth Century 34. No Greater Glory 34. Sylvia Scarlett 35. After the Dance 35. *The Informer* 35. I'll Love You Always 35. The Whole Town's Talking 35. The Plough and the Stars 36. *Mary of Scotland* 36. Every Saturday Night 36. A Damsel in Distress 37. Music for Madame 37. Super Sleuth 37. Fifty Roads to Town 37. *Michael Strogoff* 37. Sea Devils 37. Gun Law 37. This Marriage Business 38. The Saint in New York 38. *The Hunchback of Notre Dame* 39. *Gunga Din* 39. Nurse Edith Cavell 40. Man of Conquest 40. Melody Ranch 40. Primrose Path 40. *All that Money Can Buy* 41. They Were Expendable 45. *Portrait of Jennie* 48.
✪ For the imperishable visuals of his half-dozen melodramatic masterpieces. *Portrait of Jennie*.

August, Pernilla (1958–)
Swedish actress, best known internationally for playing Anakin Skywalker's mother in *Star Wars Episode 1: The Phanton Menace*. She was formerly married (1991-97) to director Bille August.
Giliap 75. Fanny and Alexander 82. The Best Intentions/Den Goda Viljan 92. Jerusalem 96. Private Confessions/Enskilda Samtal 97. The Last Contract/Sista Kontraktet 98. Where the Rainbow Ends/Dar Regnbagen Slutar 99. Mary, Mother of Jesus (TV) 99. Star Wars Episode l: The Phantom Menace 99, etc.

Auld, Georgie (1919–1990) (John Altwerger)
Jazz tenor saxophonist and occasional actor. Best known for his recordings with Benny Goodman in the 40s, he played a bandleader and dubbed Robert De Niro's saxophone playing in Martin Scorsese's *New York, New York* 77. He also dubbed fellow saxophonist Dexter Gordon's playing in *Unchained* 55.

Aulin, Ewa (1949–)
Scandinavian leading lady in international films.
Candy 68. Start the Revolution without Me 69. This Kind of Love 72, etc.

Ault, Marie (1870–1951) (Mary Cragg)
British character actress of stage and screen, usually in dialect comedy roles.
Woman to Woman 24. The Lodger 26. Hobson's Choice 31. *Major Barbara* 40. *Love on the Dole* 41. We Dive at Dawn 43. I See a Dark Stranger 46. Madness of the Heart 49, many others.

Aumont, Jean-Pierre (1909–2001) (J.-P. Salomons)
French leading man, in films from 1931, Hollywood from 1941. His three wives include actresses Maria Montez and Marisa Pavan. He was the father of actress Tina Aumont.
Autobiography: 1977, *Sun and Shadow*.
Jean de la Lune 32. Maria Chapdelaine 35. Drôle de Drame 36. *Hôtel du Nord* 38. The Cross of Lorraine 42. Assignment in Brittany 43. Heartbeat 46. Song of Scheherazade 48. The First Gentleman (GB) 48. Charge of the Lancers 53. *Lili* 53. Hilda Crane 56. The Seventh Sin 57. The Devil at Four O'Clock 61. Five Miles to Midnight 63. Castle Keep 69. *La Nuit Américaine* 73. The Happy Hooker 75. Catherine and Company 75. Seven Suspects for Murder 77. Nana 83. Shadow Dance 83. The Blood of Others 84. Sweet Country 86. Johnny Monroe 87. A Notre Regrettable Époux 88. Becoming Colette 92. Au Petit Marguery 95. Jefferson in Paris (US) 95. The Proprietor 96, etc.

Aumont, Tina (1946–)
French actress, the daughter of actors Jean-Pierre Aumont and Maria Montez. Married actor Christian Marquand, and was also credited as Tina Marquand in her early films.
Modestry Blaise (GB) 66. Texas Across the River (US) 66. L'Alibi (It.) 68. Satyricon (It.) 68. Corbari (It.) 70. Malizia (It.) 73. Illustrious Corpses/Cadaveri Eccellenti (It./Fr/) 75. Lifespan (Neth./Belg./US) 75. Casanova (It.) 76. A Matter of Time (US/GB) 76. Salon Kitty (It./Fr./Ger.) 78. Rebelote 83, etc.

Aurel, Jean (1925–)
French writer-director, originally of documentary shorts.
14–18 (d) 63. La Bataille de France (d) 64. De l'Amour (wd) 65. Manon 70 (wd) 68. Les Femmes (wd) 69. Comme un Pot de Fraises (wd) 74. The Woman Next Door 81. Vivement Dimanche (w) 83. Confidentially Yours (w) 84, etc.

Aurenche, Jean (1904–1992)
French writer who with Pierre Bost (1901–1975) wrote many well-known films.
Hôtel du Nord 38. Sylvie et le Fantôme 45. La Symphonie Pastorale 46. *Le Diable au Corps* 46. Occupe-Toi d'Amélie 49. Dieu A Besoin des Hommes 50. *The Red Inn* 51. *Les Jeux Interdits* 51. Ripening Seed 53. Gervaise 56. En Cas de Malheur 57. L'Affaire d'Une Nuit 60. The Clockmaker 76. De Guerre Lasse 87. Fucking Fernand 87. Le Palanquin des Larmes 88, etc. Aurenche worked alone on the screenplay of *Woman in White* 65.

Auric, Georges (1899–1983)
French composer who became director of the Paris Opéra.
Autobiography: 1974, *Quand J'étais Là*.
Le Sang d'un Poète 30. *à Nous la Liberté* 31. Lac aux Dames 34. L'Alibi 37. Orage 38. L'Eternel Retour 43. Dead of Night 45. Caesar and Cleopatra 45. La Belle et la Bête 46. It Always Rains on Sunday 47. Corridor of Mirrors 48. Passport to Pimlico 49. *Orphée* 49. *Belles de Nuit* 52. Roman Holiday 53. The Wages of Fear 53. Father Brown 54. Rififi 55. The Witches of Salem 56. Gervaise 56. The Picasso Mystery 56. Bonjour Tristesse 57. La Chambre Ardente 62. The Mind Benders 63. Thomas the Impostor 65. Therese and Isabelle 68. The Christmas Tree 69, many others.

Aurthur, Robert Alan (1922–1978)
American novelist and screenwriter.
Edge of the City 56. Warlock 59. For Love of Ivy 68. The Lost Man 70, etc.

Austen, Jane (1775–1817)
After years of being neglected by film-makers, the most delightful of English novelists enjoyed great popularity in the 90s, as part of the cycle of British period films, possibly in emulation of the successful films of Merchant-Ivory, who had turned the Edwardian novels of E. M. Forster into box-office successes.
Pride and Prejudice 40. *Clueless* (an update of Emma) 95. Persuasion 95. Pride and Prejudice (TV) 95. *Sense and Sensibilty* 95. Emma 96. Emma (TV) 96. Mansfield Park 99, etc.

Auster, Paul (1947–)
American minimalist novelist and screenwriter.
Autobiography: 1997, *Hand to Mouth: A Chronicle of Early Failure*.
The Music of Chance (oa) 93. Smoke (w) 95. Blue in the Face (co-w, co-d) 95. Lulu on the Bridge (wd) 98.

Austin, Albert (1882–1953)
English actor and director in Hollywood, from music hall. Born in Birmingham, he became a member of Fred Karno's group, touring America before making his film debut, working with Chaplin on his two-reel comedies for Mutual. He ended his career working for a decade as a studio guard at Warners.
The Floorwalker 16. The Fireman 16. The Vagabond 16. One a.m. 16. The Count 16. The Pawnshop 16. Behind the Screen 16. The Rink 16. Easy Street 17. The Cure 17. The Immigrant 17. The Adventurer 17. A Dog's Life 18. Shoulder Arms 18. A Day's Pleasure 19. The Kid 21. Pay Day 22. Trouble (d) 22. A Prince of a King (d) 23. The Gold Rush 25. City Lights 31, etc.

Austin, Charles (1878–1944)
English music-hall comedian who made a few films. He was on the halls from 1896, notably as cockney policeman Parker p.c.
Parker's Weekend 16. The Exploits of Parker 18. Hot Heir 31. It's a Cop (co-w) 34. School for Stars (story) 35, etc.

Austin, Charlotte (1933–)
American leading lady who moved from musicals to monsters in the 50s.
Sunny Side of the Street 51. The Farmer Takes a Wife 53. How to Marry a Millionaire 53. Gorilla at Large 54. Desirée 54. Daddy Long Legs 55. How to Be Very Very Popular 55. Bride of the Beast 58, etc.

Austin, Jerry (1892–1976)
Dwarf American actor.
Saratoga Trunk 43. Adventures of Don Juan 47, etc.

Austin, Ray (1932–)
British director, mostly of TV episodes, in America from the early 50s.
House of the Living Dead 73. Sword of Justice (TV) 79. Salvage I (TV) 79. Tales of the Gold Monkey (TV) 82. The Zany Adventures of Robin Hood (TV) 84. Return of the Six Million Dollar Man and the Bionic Woman (TV) 87. The New Zorro (TV) 92, etc.

Austin, Ron
American screenwriter.
The Happening 67. Harry in Your Pocket 73, etc.

Austin, William (1884–1975)
English character actor, mainly in Hollywood. Born in Georgetown, British Guiana, he trained in London but made his stage debut in Los Angeles in 1919.
Ruggles of Red Gap 21. Silk Stockings 24. Mysterious Dr Fu Manchu 29. Return of Dr Fu Manchu 31. High Society 32. Three Men in a Boat 33. Alice in Wonderland (as the Gryphon) 33. The Private Life of Henry VIII 33. The Gay Divorcee 35. Dr Rhythm 38. Sherlock Holmes 40. Charley's Aunt 41. Return of Monte Cristo 46. The Ghost & Mrs Muir 47. Batman 50, etc.

Autant-Lara, Claude (1903–2000)
French director, usually of stylish romantic dramas; former assistant to René Clair.
Ciboulette 33. L'Affaire du Courrier de Lyon 37. *Fric Frac* 39. Lettres d'Amour 42. Douce 43. Sylvie et le Fantôme 44. *Le Diable au Corps* 47. *Occupe-Toi d'Amélie* 49. *The Red Inn* 51. The Seven Deadly Sins 52. Ripening Seed 53. Le Rouge et le Noir 54. Marguerite de la Nuit 55. La Traversée de Paris 56. *En Cas de Malheur* 58. The Green Marc's Nest 59. Le Bois des Amants 60. The Count of Monte Cristo 61. Le Meurtrier 62. Thou Shalt Not Kill 62. The Woman in White 65. The Oldest Profession 67. Les Patates 69. Le Rouge et le Blanc 70. Gloria 77, etc.
❝ The director must consider himself surrounded by enemies; what I mean is that, in a business where the taste of one man must prevail, he is surrounded by people who want to do nothing but impose their own tastes. – C.A-L.

Auteuil, Daniel (1950–)
French leading actor, from the stage, where he played with the Théâtre National Populaire. His early parts tended to be comic, although since *Jean de Florette* brought him to international attention he has played more varied roles.
Le Sex Shop 73. Jean de Florette 87. *Manon des Sources* 87. Romuald et Juliette 89. *A Heart in Winter*/Un Coeur en Hiver 91. The Elegant Criminal/Lacenaire 92. My Favourite Season/Ma Saison Préférée 93. Queen Margot/La Reine Margot 94. Une Femme Française 95. According to Pereira 95. Thieves/Les Voleurs 96. The Eighth Day 96. On Guard! 97. The Lost Son (GB) 99. Sade 00 etc.

Autry, Gene (1907–1998)
Easy-going Texan who made innumerable minor westerns 1934–54 as singing cowboy, usually with his horse Champion. Beginning as a singer on radio, billed as 'Oklahoma's Yodeling Cowboy', he presented a clean-living image: he refused to hit anyone smaller than himself and would not smoke or drink on-screen. He made 56 features for Republic, often with his sidekick from radio, Lester 'Smiley' Burnette, or his later partner Pat Buttram. From 1937–42, he was the top western star, turning to TV in the 50s and retiring in 1960. Spin-offs he produced from his own TV series included *The Adventures of Champion* 55–56, and *Annie Oakley* 54–56, featuring his frequent movie co-star Gail Davis.
Autobiography: 1978, *Back in the Saddle Again*.
In Old Sante Fe 34. The Phantom Empire (serial) 35. Tumbling Tumbleweeds 35. The Big Show 36. Red River Valley 36. The Singing Cowboy 36. Boots and Saddles 37. Springtime in the Rockies 37. Rhythm of the Saddle 38. Home on the Range 39. Mexicali Rose 39. Shooting High 40. Melody Ranch 40. Back in the Saddle 41. The Singing Hills 41. Cowboy Serenade 42. Bells of Capistrano 42. Sioux City Sue 46. Robin Hood of Texas 47. The Strawberry Roan 48. Riders of the Whistling Pines 49. Riders in the Sky 49. Mule Train 50. Gene Autry and the Mounties 51. Valley of Fire 51. The Old West 52. On Top of Old Smoky 53. Last of the Pony Riders 53. Alias Jesse James 59, many others.
TV series: The Gene Autry Show 50–55.
❝ In my day, most people thought dance hall girls actually danced. – G.A.
Autry used to ride off into the sunset. Now he owns it. – *Pat Buttram*

Avakian, Aram (1926–1987)
American director.
■ Lad – a Dog 62. The End of the Road 69. Cops and Robbers 73. 11 Harrowhouse 74.

Avalon, Frankie (1939–) (Francis Avallone)
American light leading man and pop singer, former trumpeter.
Guns of the Timberland 60. The Alamo 60. Voyage to the Bottom of the Sea 62. Beach Blanket Bingo 65. I'll Take Sweden 65. Sergeant Deadhead 66. Fireball 500 66. Pajama Party in a Haunted House 66. How to Stuff a Wild Bikini 66. Skidoo 68. The Take 74. Grease 78. Back to the Beach 87. A Dream Is a Wish Your Heart Makes: The Annette Funicello Story (TV) (as himself) 95. Casino (as himself) 95, etc.

Avary, Roger (1965–)
American screenwriter and director.
Pulp Fiction (co-w) 94. Killing Zoe (wd) 94.

Avati, Pupi (1938–) (Giuseppe Avati)
Italian director. He is a former jazz musician and factory worker who decided to work in films after seeing Fellini's *81/2*.
Balsamus l'Uomo di Satana 68. Thomas the Possessed/Thomas … gli Indemoniati 69. La Mazurka del Barone 74. Bordella 75. Le Strelle nel Fosso 78. Zeder 83. Us Three/Noi Tre 84. Fiesta di Laurea 85. The Last Minute 87. Boys and Girls/ Storia di Ragazzi e Ragazze 89. Bix 91. Brothers and Sisters 92. Magnificat 93. Declarations of Love 94. The Arcane Enchanter 95. Festival 96. The Best Man/Il Testimone dello Sposo (AAN) 97. The Knights of the Quest 01, etc.

Avedon, Doe (1928–)
American leading lady who had a very short career before retiring to marry. She is the former wife of the director Don Siegel.
■ *The High and the Mighty* 54. Deep in My Heart 55. The Boss 56.
TV series: Big Town 55.

Averback, Hy (1925–1997)
American director with much TV experience, especially in comedy series.
Chamber of Horrors 66. Where Were You When the Lights Went Out? 68. *I Love You Alice B. Toklas* 68. The Great Bank Robbery 69. Suppose They Gave a War and Nobody Came 69. Where the Boys Are 84, etc.

Avery, Margaret
American character actress.
Magnum Force 73. Which Way Is Up? 77. The Fish that Saved Pittsburgh 79. The Lathe of Heaven 80. The Color Purple (AAN) 85. Blueberry Hill 88. Riverbend 89, etc.

Avery, Tex (1907–1980) (Fred Avery)
American animator, best known for MGM cartoons which combined savagery with hilarity. He created Droopy.
Biography: 1975, *Tex Avery: King of Cartoons* by Joe Adamson.

Avery, Val
American character actor.
King Creole 58. Too Late Blues 61. Hud 63. The Hallelujah Trail 65. The Pink Jungle 68. The Travelling Executioner 70. The Laughing Policeman 73. Let's Do It Again 75. Heroes 77. The Wanderers 79. Choices 81. Courage (TV) 86, etc.

Avildsen, John G. (1935–)
American director and screenwriter.
■ Turn on to Love 67. OK Bill 68. Guess What We Learned at School Today 69. *Joe* 70. Cry Uncle 71. Roger the Stoolie 72. Save the Tiger 73. WW and the Dixie Dance Kings 75. Foreplay (co-d) 75. *Rocky* (AA) 76. Slow Dancing in the Big City 78. The Formula 80. The President's Women 81. Neighbors 81. A Night in Heaven 83. The Karate Kid 84. The Karate Kid II 86. Happy New Year 87. For Keeps 88. The Karate Kid Part III 89. Lean on

Me 89. Rocky V 90. The Power of One 92. Lane Frost 93. 8 Seconds 94.

Avital, Mili (1972–)
Israeli actress, in Hollywood. After winning awards for her performances in Israeli films, she moved to the US in 1993, first working as a waitress before landing the role of Sha'uri in *Stargate*.

Me'Ever Layam 91. Stargate 94. Dead Man 96. Invasion of Privacy 96. The End of Violence (Ger.) 97. Kissing a Fool 98. Polish Wedding 98. Preston Tylk 00, etc.

Avnet, Jon (1949–)
American director, producer and screenwriter.
Outlaw Blues (p) 77. Risky Business (p) 83. Between Two Women (co-w, d) (TV) 86. Less than Zero (p) 87. Men Don't Leave (p, d) 90. Fried Green Tomatoes (p, co-w, d) 91. The Mighty Ducks (p) 92. D2: The Mighty Ducks (p) 94. When a Man Loves a Woman (p) 94. The War (p, d) 94. Up Close and Personal (p, d) 96. D3: The Mighty Ducks (p) 96. The Red Corner (co-p, d) 97, etc.

Axel, Gabriel (1918–)
French-born director and screenwriter who makes movies in Denmark. He mainly works as a stage actor and director in Denmark and France.
Guld Og Gronne Skove 59. Den Rode Kappe 67. Med Kaerlig Hilsen 71. Familien Gyldenkaal 75. *Babette's Feast* (AA) 87. Christian 89. Prince of Denmark (& co-w) 93, etc.

Axelrod, George (1922–)
American comedy writer.
■ Phffft 54. The Seven Year Itch (oa) 55. Bus Stop 56. Will Success Spoil Rock Hunter? (oa) 57. Breakfast at Tiffany's (AAN) 61. The Manchurian Candidate 62. Paris When It Sizzles 64. Goodbye Charlie 64. How to Murder Your Wife (& p) 65. Lord Love a Duck (& pd) 66. The Secret Life of an American Wife (& pd) 68. The Lady Vanishes 79. The Holcroft Covenant 85. The Fourth Protocol 87, etc.

Axt, Dr William (1888–1959)
American composer, almost entirely for MGM in the 30s.
Don Juan 26. Ben Hur 26. White Shadows of the South Seas 28. Smilin' Through 32. Dinner at Eight 33. The Thin Man 34. David Copperfield 35. Piccadilly Jim 36. Parnell 37. Yellow Jack 38. Stand Up and Fight 39, many others.

Axton, Hoyt (1938–1999)
American character actor, singer and songwriter.
The Black Stallion 79. Cloud Dancer 79. Endangered Species 82. Heart Like a Wheel 82. Liar's Moon 84. Gremlins 84. Dixie Lanes 88. Retribution 88. We're No Angels 89. Disorganised Crime 89. The Rousters (TV) 90. Season of Change 94. Number One Fan 94. King Cobra 98, etc.
TV series: The Rousters 83–84. Domestic Life 84.

Ayala, Fernando (1920–1997)
Argentinian producer, director and screenwriter. In the late 50s, together with Hector Olivera, he founded Aries, the country's most successful and longest-surviving production company. His early films dealt with social problems; his later ones concentrate more on entertainment.
Ayer Fue Primavera 55. El Jefe 58. El Candidato 59. Paula Cautiva 63. Primero Yo 64. Las Locas del Conventillo 65. La Fiaca 68. El Profesor Hippie 69. Argentisima (co-d) 71. Argentisima II (co-d) 72. Los Médicos 78. Plata Dulce 82. Sobredosis 86. Dios los Cria 91, etc.

Ayckbourn, Alan (1939–)
English playwright and theatre director whose work has been relatively neglected by the cinema. Born in London, he began as a stage manager and actor with Sir Donald WOLFIT, and became Britain's most commercially successful and performed dramatist, writing more than 50 plays, most of them increasingly dark, and technically complex, comedies of middle-class life.
Biography: 1981, *Conversations with Ayckbourn* by Ian Watson.
A Chorus of Disapproval 89. *Smoking/No Smoking* (Fr.) 93. The Revenger's Comedies 98.
66 All my characters seem to have this terrible disappointment, this terrible gap between what they meant to achieve and what they did achieve. – A.A.

Aykroyd, Dan (1952–)
Canadian revue comedian who made his name on *Saturday Night Live*. Married actress Donna DIXON, his second wife, in 1983.
1941 79. Mr Mike's Mondo Video 79. The Blues Brothers 80. Neighbours 81. Dr Detroit 82. Nothing Lasts Forever 82. Twilight Zone: The Movie 83. Trading Places 83. *Ghostbusters* 84. Into the Night 84. Nothing Lasts Forever 84. Spies Like Us 85. Dragnet 87. Caddyshack II 88. The Couch Trip 88. The Great Outdoors 88. My Stepmother Is an Alien 88. *Driving Miss Daisy* (AAN) 89. Ghostbusters II (& w) 89. Loose Cannons 90. Nothing but Trouble (& wd) 91. My Girl 91. This Is My Life 92. Chaplin 92. Sneakers 92. Coneheads (& co-w) 93. My Girl II 94. North 94. Exit to Eden 94. Canadian Bacon 95. Rainbow 95. Tommy Boy 95. Sgt Bilko 96. Getting Away with Murder 96. Celtic Pride 96. Feeling Minnesota 96. Rainbow 96. My Fellow Americans 96. Grosse Pointe Blank 97. Antz (voice) 98. Blues Brothers 2000 98. Susan's Plan 98. Stardom 00. Loser 00. The House of Mirth 00, etc.
TV series: Soul Man 97.
66 I have this kind of mild nice-guy exterior, but inside, my heart is like a steel trap. I'm really quite robotic. – D.A.
The entertainment business is not the be-all and end-all for me. – D.A.

Aylmer, Sir Felix (1889–1979) (Felix Edward Aylmer Jones)
Distinguished British stage character actor, a respected industry figure who from 1950 was president of Equity, the actors' trade union. In films he mainly played schoolmasters, bankers, bishops, etc. Born in Corsham, Wiltshire, he was educated at Exeter College, Oxford and studied for the stage under Rosina Filippi. He began on stage in 1911 and was in films from 1932.
The Wandering Jew 33. The Iron Duke 35. Tudor Rose 36. As You Like It 36. *Victoria the Great* 37. The Citadel 38. Saloon Bar 40. *The Ghost of St Michael's* 41. Mr Emmanuel 44. Henry V 44. The Ghost of Berkeley Square 47. *Hamlet* (as Polonius) 48. Edward My Son 49. Quo Vadis 51. Ivanhoe 52. The Master of Ballantrae 53. Knights of the Round Table 54. The Angel Who Pawned Her Harp 54. Saint Joan 57. *Separate Tables* 58. *Never Take Sweets from a Stranger* 60. The Chalk Garden 64. Becket 64. Decline and Fall 68. Hostile Witness 68, many others.

Aylward, Gladys (1901–1970)
British missionary whose exploits in China were fictionalized in *Inn of the Sixth Happiness*, in which she was played by Ingrid Bergman.

Ayres, Agnes (1898–1940) (Agnes Hinkle)
American leading lady of the silent screen.
Forbidden Fruit 19. The Affairs of Anatol 20. *The Sheik* 21. Racing Hearts 23. When a Girl Loves 24. Morals for Men 25. Her Market Value 26. Son of the Sheik 26. Eve's Love Letters 29, many others.

Ayres, Lew (1908–1996) (Lewis Ayer)
Boyish American leading man of the 30s; he occasionally got a chance to prove himself a comfortable and friendly actor, but his career suffered during World War II when he declared himself a conscientious objector. Born in Minneapolis, he studied medicine at the University of Arizona and became a singer and bandleader before entering films. The first two of his three wives were Lola Lane (1931–33) and Ginger ROGERS (1934–41). He enjoyed success in the 30s as Dr Kildare in a series of films.
■ *The Kiss* 29. The Sophomore 29. Many a Slip 30. *All Quiet on the Western Front* 30. Common Clay 30. East is West 30. Doorway to Hell 30. Iron Man 31. Up for Murder 31. The Spirit of Notre Dame 31. Heaven on Earth 31. The Impatient Maiden 32. Night World 32. Okay America 32. State Fair 33. Don't Bet On Love 33. My Weakness 33. Cross Country Cruise 34. She Learned About Sailors 34. Servants' Entrance 34. Let's Be Ritzy 34. Lottery Lover 35. The Silk Hat Kid 35. The Leathernecks have Landed 36. Panic on the Air 36. Shakedown 36. Lady be Careful 36. Murder with Pictures 36. The Crime Nobody Saw 36. *Last Train from Madrid* 37. Hold 'Em Navy 37. Scandal Street 38. King of the Newsboys 38. *Holiday* (a key performance as Katharine Hepburn's drunken brother) 38. Rich Man Poor Girl 38. *Young Dr Kildare* 38. Spring Madness 38. Ice Follies 39. Broadway Serenade 39. Calling Dr Kildare 39. These Glamour Girls 39. The Secret of Dr Kildare 39. Remember? 39. Dr Kildare's Strange Case 40. Dr Kildare Goes Home 40. The Golden Fleecing 40. Dr Kildare's Crisis 40. Maisie Was a Lady 41. The People vs Dr Kildare 41. Dr Kildare's Wedding Day 41. Fingers at the Window 42. Dr Kildare's Victory 42. *The Dark Mirror* 46. The Unfaithful 47. *Johnny Belinda* (AAN) 48. The Capture 50. New Mexico 51. No Escape 53. Donovan's Brain 54. *Advise and Consent* 61. *The Carpetbaggers* 64. Hawaii Five-O (TV pilot) 68. Marcus Welby MD (TV pilot) 68. Earth II (TV) 71. She Waits (TV) 72. The Man (TV) 72. The Biscuit Eater 72. The Stranger (TV) 72. The Questor Tapes (TV) 73. Battle For Planet of the Apes 73. Heatwave (TV) 74. Francis Gary Powers (TV) 76. End of the World 77. Greatest Heroes of the Bible (TV) (as Noah) 78. Damien-Omen II 78. Of Mice and Men (TV) 81. Cast the First Stone (TV) 89.
TV series: Hawkins 74. Lime Street 85.

Ayres, Robert (1914–1968)
Canadian actor of strong silent types, long resident in Britain.
They Were Not Divided 49. The Black Widow 51. To Have and To Hold 51. 13 East Street 52. Cosh Boy 52. The Wedding of Lilli Marlene 53. River Beat 54. Time Lock 57. Cat Girl 57. The Story of Esther Costello 57. First Men Into Space 59. Two and Two Make Six 62. The Sicilians 64. Lee Oswald–Assassin (TV) 66. Battle Beneath the Earth 67, many others.
TV series: The Cheaters 60-61.

Ayres, Rosalind (1944–)
English actress, born in Birmingham. Married actor Martin JARVIS.
The Lovers 73. That'll Be the Day 73. Stardust 74. Little Malcolm and His Struggle Against the Eunuchs 74. The Slipper and the Rose 76. Cry Wolf 80. Gods and Monsters 98. Beautiful People 99., etc.

Ayrton, Randle (1869–1940)
British character actor.
My Sweetheart. 18. The Wonderful Year 21. Chu Chin Chow 23. The Wonderful Year 21. Chu Chin Chow 23. Southern Love 24. Nell Gwynne 26. Passion Island 26. Glorious Youth 28. Comets 30. Dreyfus 31. Jew Süss 34. Me and Marlborough 35. Talk of the Devil 36, etc.

Azaria, Hank (1964–)
American stand-up comedian and actor. Married actress Helen HUNT in 1999 (separated 2000).
Pretty Woman 90. Quiz Show 94. Heat 95. If Not for You 95. The Birdcage 96. Anastasia (voice) 97. Grosse Point Blanke 97. Homegrown 98. Great Expectations 98. Godzilla 98. Celebrity 98. Mystery Men 99. The Cradle Will Rock 99. Mystery, Alaska 99. Fail Safe (TV) 00, etc.
TV series: The Simpsons (voices) 89. Herman's Head 91–94. Mad About You 93– .

Aznavour, Charles (1924–) (Shahnour Aznavurjan)
Armenian leading man of the small but rugged school, but better known as a singer-songwriter.
Autobiography: 1972, *Aznavour by Aznavour*.
La Tête Contre les Murs 58. *Shoot the Pianist* 60. Passage du Rhin 61. Cloportes 65. Candy 68. The Adventures 70. The Games 70. Un Beau Monstre 70. And Then There Were None 75. Sky Riders 76. Folies Bourgeoises 76. The Tin Drum 79. Les Fantômes du Chapelier 82. Der Zauberberg 82. Yiddish Connection (& w) 86. Migrations 88. Il Maestro 89. Les Années Campagne 91, etc.
66 Love now. Tomorrow, who knows? – C.A.

B

Baarova, Lida (1914–2000) (Ludmilla Babkova)
Czech actress who was a star in German films and gained some notoriety when she became the mistress of Nazi propaganda chief Josef Goebbels. Born in Prague, she began her career in Czechoslovakia before moving to Germany in the early 30s. Her two-year relationship with Goebbels, who wanted to divorce his wife and marry her, ended in 1938 at the insistence of Hitler. Her films were banned in Germany and she appeared in Italian movies for much of the 50s. She ended her career as a stage actress in Austria.
Barcarole 34. Die Fledermaus 37. Patriots/Patrioten 37. Virginity/Panenstv 37. Der Spieler 38. La Sua Strada (It.) 43. Spivs/I Vitelloni (It.) 53. Miedo (Sp.) 56, etc.

Babbitt, Art (1907–1992)
Leading animator, whose career began in the 20s. He worked for Disney, animating the Wicked Queen in *Snow White* and the dance of the mushrooms in *Fantasia*, for Warner's Looney Tunes, UPA and Hanna-Barbera. Married dancer Marjorie Belcher (later Marge Champion).
Snow White and the Seven Dwarfs 37. Pinocchio 40. Fantasia 40. The Thief and the Cobbler 93, etc.

Babcock, Barbara (1937–)
American character actress.
Heaven with a Gun 68. The Last Child (TV) 71. Bang the Drum Slowly 73. Chosen Survivors (TV) 74. Salem's Lot (TV) 79. The Lords of Discipline 82. Heart of Dixie 89. Happy Together 90. Far and Away 92, etc.
TV series: Dallas 78–82. Hill Street Blues 81–85. The Four Seasons 84. Mr Sunshine 86. Dr Quinn, Medicine Woman 93-98.

Babenco, Hector (1946–)
Argentinian-born director who worked in Brazil and then, declaring that Brazilian cinema was dead, moved to Hollywood.
Lucio Flavio 78. Pixote 81. Kiss of the Spider Woman (AAN) 85. Ironweed 87. At Play in the Fields of the Lord 91. Foolish Heart 98. The Venice Project (a) 99. Before Night Falls (a) 00, etc.

Baby Le Roy (1931–) (Le Roy Overacker)
American toddler who appeared to general delight in comedies of the early 30s. The story goes that W. C. Fields once spiked his orange juice with gin …
A Bedtime Story 33. Tillie and Gus 33. Miss Fane's Baby is Stolen 33. The Old Fashioned Way 34. The Lemon Drop Kid 34. It's a Gift 35. etc.

Baby Peggy (1917–) (Peggy Montgomery)
American child star of the 20s. Later appeared under her own name, and in the 70s published two books, *The Hollywood Posse* and *Hollywood Children*.
Peggy Behave 22. Captain January 23. The Law Forbids 24. The Speed Demon 25. April Fool 26. The Sonora Kid 27, etc.

Baby Sandy (1938–) (Sandra Henville)
American infant performer who made money for Universal in the early 40s.
■ East Side of Heaven 39. Unexpected Father 39. Little Accident 39. Sandy Is a Lady 40. Sandy Gets Her Man 40. Sandy Steps Out 41. Bachelor Daddy 41. Melody Lane 41. Johnny Doughboy 42.

Bacall, Lauren (1924–) (Betty Joan Perske)
Sultry American leading actress who after stage experience made her film debut opposite Humphrey Bogart ('If you want anything, just whistle …') and subsequently married him. Her image gradually changed to that of an astringent and resourceful woman of the world, and in 1970 she made a triumphant return to the Broadway stage in *Applause*. Her second husband was Jason Robards Jnr (1961–69).
Autobiography: 1978, *Lauren Bacall*.
Biography: 1976, *Bogey's Baby* by Howard Greenberger.
To Have and Have Not 45. Confidential Agent 45. *The Big Sleep* 46. Two Guys from Milwaukee (uncredited) 46. Dark Passage 47. Key Largo 48. *Young Man with a Horn* 50. Bright Leaf 50. *How to Marry a Millionaire* 53. Woman's World 54. The Cobweb 55. Blood Alley 55. Written on the Wind 56. Designing Woman 57. The Gift of Love 58. Northwest Frontier (GB) 59. Shock Treatment 64. Sex and the Single Girl 64. *Harper* 66. Murder on the Orient Express 74. The Shootist 76. Health 79. The Fan 81. Appointment with Death 88. Mr North 88. Misery 90. Dinner at Eight (TV) 90. Innocent Victim 90. Star for Two 91. All I Want For Christmas 91. The Portrait (TV) 93. A Foreign Field (TV) 93. Prêt-à-Porter 94. My Fellow Americans 96. *The Mirror Has Two Faces* (AAN) 96. The Day and the Night/Le Jour et la Nuit 97. The Venice Project 99. Presence of Mind/El Celo (Sp.) 00, etc.
❝ Slinky! Sultry! Sensational! – *1944 promotion for L.B.*
I used to tremble from nerves so badly that the only way I could hold my head steady was to lower my chin practically to my chest and look up at Bogie. That was the beginning of The Look. – *L.B.*
I was not a woman of the world. I'd lived with Mother all my life. – *L.B.*
What I learned from Mr Bogart I learned from a master, and that, God knows, has stood me in very good stead. – *L.B.*

Bacalov, Luis Enrique
Prolific Spanish-born composer and pianist, working in Italy. In the 60s he formed a guitar-dominated rock group, Luis Enrique and his Electronic Men.
La Banda del Buco 60. The Gospel According to St Matthew (AAN) 65. Django 66. A Bullet for the General/Quién Sabe? 66. L'Amica 69. Roma Bene 71. La Rosa Rossa 73. Le Maestro 79. City of Women 80. Entre Nous/Coupe de Foudre 83. Le Juge 83. Le Transfuge 85. The Postman/Il Postino (AA) 94. The Sky Will Fall/Il Cielo Cade 00, many others.

Baccaloni, Salvatore (1900–1969)
Italian opera singer who played some comedy roles in American films.
■ Full of Life 56. Merry Andrew 58. Rock a Bye Baby 58. Fanny 61. The Pigeon That Took Rome 62.

Bach, Barbara (1947–) (Barbara Goldbach)
American leading lady, first in Italian films, who played the female lead in *The Spy Who Loved Me* 77. Married former Beatle Ringo Starr.
Force Ten from Navarone 78. The Humanoid 79. Up the Academy 80. Caveman 81. The Unseen 81. Give My Regards to Broad Street 84, etc.

Bacharach, Burt (1929–)
American composer and songwriter (usually with lyricist Hal David), a former accompanist to Marlene Dietrich. The second of his three wives was actress Angie Dickinson.
Lizzie (s) 57. What's New Pussycat? (AANs) 65. Alfie (AANs) 66. Casino Royale (AANs, m) 67. *Butch Cassidy and the Sundance Kid* (AAs, m) 69. The April Fools (m) 69. Lost Horizon (s) 73. Together? 79. Arthur (AAs) 81. Night Shift 82. Best Defence 84. Arthur 2: On the Rocks 88, etc.
❝ The groovy thing about pop music is that it's wide open. Anything can happen. – *B.B.*

Bachelor, Stephanie (1924–)
American leading lady of 40s 'B' pictures.
Lady of Burlesque 43. Her Primitive Man 44. Lake Placid Serenade 44. Scotland Yard Investigator 45. I've Always Loved You 46. Blackmail 47. King of the Gamblers 48, etc.

Back, Frédéric
French-born animator who moved to Canada in the mid-40s.
Tout Rien 80. CRAC (AA) 81. The Man Who Planted Trees (AA) 87. The Mighty River/Le Fleuve aux Grandes Eaux 94, etc.

Backus, Jim (1913–1989)
Burly American character comedian, perhaps most famous as the voice of Mr Magoo in UPA cartoons of the 50s. Stock, vaudeville and radio experience.
Autobiography: 1958, *Rocks on the Roof*.
The Great Lover 49. Hollywood Story 51. His Kind of Woman 51. I Want You 51. Pat and Mike 52. Androcles and the Lion 53. *Rebel Without a Cause* 55. The Great Man 56. Man of a Thousand Faces 57. Macabre 58. Ice Palace 60. Boys' Night Out 62. *It's A Mad Mad Mad Mad World* 63. Advance to the Rear 64. Billie 65. Where Were You When the Lights Went Out? 68. Now You See Him Now You Don't 72. Pete's Dragon 77. There Goes the Bride 80, etc.
TV series: *I Married Joan* 52–56. Hot off the Wire 60. *Gilligan's Island* 64–66. Blondie 68.

Baclanova, Olga (1899–1974)
Russian actress who played leads in a few American films.
Street of Sin 27. Docks of New York 28. *Freaks* 32. Billion Dollar Scandal 32. Claudia 43, etc.

Bacon, Irving (1893–1965)
American character actor in films from 1920, often as not-so-dumb country type or perplexed official.
Street of Chance 30. Million Dollar Legs 32. Private Worlds 35. Sing You Sinners 38. Meet John Doe 41. Pin Up Girl 44. Monsieur Verdoux 47. Room for One More 52. A Star is Born 54. Fort Massacre 58, many others.

Bacon, Kevin (1958–)
American actor. Born in Philadelphia, Pennsylvania, he trained for the stage at Circle in the Square Theater in New York and the Manning Street Actors Theatre in Philadelphia. In the mid-90s he also formed a folk-rock group, the Bacon Brothers, with his brother Michael. Married actress Kyra Sedgwick.
National Lampoon's Animal House 78. Starting Over 79. Friday the 13th 80. Hero at Large 80. Only When I Laugh 81. Diner 82. Forty Deuce 82. Enormous Changes at the Last Minute 83. Footloose 84. Quicksilver 86. Planes, Trains and Automobiles 87. She's Having a Baby 88. The Big Picture 88. Criminal Law 89. Tremors 89. Flatliners 90. JFK 91. He Said, She Said 91. Pyrates 91. Queens Logic 91. A Few Good Men 92. The Air Up There 94. The River Wild 94. Apollo 13 95. Murder in the First 95. Balto (voice) 95. Losing Chase (d only, TV) 96. Sleepers 96. Telling Lies in America 97. Picture Perfect 97. Digging to China 98. Wild Things 98. Stir of Echoes 99. My Dog Skip 00. Hollow Man 00, etc.
❝ I've been a film star so long that I don't know what it would feel like not to be one. – *K.B.*

Bacon, Lloyd (1890–1955)
American director, long under contract to Warner. Born in San Jose, California, he began as a stage actor in 1911, later acting in silents before beginning to direct in the early 20s, working at Warner's from the mid-20s to the mid-40s, and then moving to Twentieth Century-Fox until the early 50s. Competent rather than brilliant, he nevertheless handled several memorable films among the mass of routine.
■ Private Izzy Murphy 26. Fingerprints 26. Broken Hearts of Hollywood 26. The Heart of Maryland 26. White Flannels 27. A Sailor's Sweetheart 27. Brass Knuckles 27. Pay As You Enter 28. The Lion and the Mouse 28. Women They Talk About 28. *The Singing Fool* 28. Stark Mad 29. Honky Tonk 29. No Defense 29. Say It with Songs 29. So Long Letty 30. She Couldn't Say No 30. A Notorious Affair 30. The Other Tomorrow 30. Moby Dick 30. The Office Wife 30. Kept Husbands 31. Sit Tight 31. Fifty Million Frenchmen 31. Gold Dust Gertie 31. Honor of the Family 31. Manhattan Parade 31. Fireman Save my Child 32. Alias the Doctor 32. The Famous Ferguson Case 32. *Miss Pinkerton* 32. Crooner 32. You Said a Mouthful 32. *42nd Street* 33. Footlight Parade 33. *Picture Snatcher* 33. Mary Stevens MD 33. Son of a Sailor 33. *Wonder Bar* 34. A Very Honorable Guy 34. He Was Her Man 34. Six Day Bike Rider 34. *Here Comes the Navy* 34. *Devil Dogs of the Air* 35. In Caliente 35. Broadway Gondolier 35. The Irish In Us 35. Frisco Kid 35. Sons of Guns 36. Cain and Mabel 36. Gold Diggers of 1937 36. *Marked Woman* 37. Ever Since Eve 37. *San Quentin* 37. Submarine D1 37. *A Slight Case of Murder* 38. Cowboy from Brooklyn 38. *Boy Meets Girl* 38. Racket Busters 38. Wings of the Navy 38. *The Oklahoma Kid* 39. Indianapolis Speedway 39. Espionage Agent 39. A Child Is Born 39. Invisible Stripes 39. Three Cheers for the Irish 40. *Brother Orchid* 40. Knute Rockne, All American 40. Honeymoon for Three 41. Footsteps in the Dark 41. Navy Blues 41. Affectionately Yours 41. Honeymoon for Three 41. Larceny Inc 42. Wings for the Eagle 42. Silver Queen 42. Action in the North Atlantic 43. The Sullivans 44. *Sunday Dinner for a Soldier* 44. Captain Eddie 45. Home Sweet Homicide 46. Wake Up and Dream 46. I Wonder Who's Kissing Her Now 47. You were Meant for Me 48. Give My Regards to Broadway 48. Don't Trust Your Husband 48. Mother Is a Freshman 48. It Happens Every Spring 49. Miss Grant Takes Richmond 49. Kill The Umpire 50. The Good Humor Man 50. The Fuller Brush Girl 50. Call Me Mister 51. Golden Girl 51. The Frogmen 51. The I Don't Care Girl 53. The Great Sioux Uprising 53. Walking My Baby Back Home 53. The French Line 53. She Couldn't Say No 54.

Bacon, Max (1904–1969)
Plump English character actor, usually in cockney roles. He was a former drummer and singer with Ambrose's Orchestra.
Soft Lights and Sweet Music 36. Calling All Stars 37. Kicking the Moon Around 38. King Arthur Was a Gentleman 42. Bees in Paradise 43. Pool of London 51. The Gambler and the Lady 52. Espresso Bongo 59. The Entertainer 60. Crooks in Cloisters 63. The Sandwich Man 66. Privilege 67. Chitty Chitty Bang Bang 68, etc.

Badalamenti, Angelo (1937–)
American composer.
Gordon's War 73. Law and Disorder 74. Across the Great Divide 76. Blue Velvet 86. Nightmare on Elm Street Part Three: Dream Warriors 87. Tough Guys Don't Dance 87. Weeds 87. Parents 88. Cousins 89. Twin Peaks 89. The Comfort of Strangers 90. Wild at Heart 90. Wait Until Spring, Bandini 90. Shattered 91. Other People's Money 91. Twin Peaks: Fire Walk with Me 92. Hotel Room (TV) 93. Naked in New York 93. Witch Hunt 94. City of Lost Children (Fr.) 95. Invasion of Privacy 96. Lost Highway 96. Arlington Road 99. The Straight Story 99. Holy Smoke 99. Forever Mine 99. The Beach 00. Birthday Girl 00, etc.

Baddeley, Angela (1904–1976)
British stage character actress, sister of Hermione Baddeley. Popular on TV as Mrs Bridges in *Upstairs Downstairs* 70–75. Married theatre director Glen Byam Shaw.
■ The Speckled Band 31. The Ghost Train 31. The Safe 32. Arms and the Man 32. Those Were the Days 34. The Citadel 38. Quartet 48. Zoo Baby 57. Tom Jones 63.

Baddeley, Hermione (1906–1986)
British character comedienne, adept at blowsy roles; long stage experience. Born in Broseley, Shropshire, she was performing from the age of 12 and at 16 was a star in the play *The Likes of 'Er*, going on to work in Cochran's revues in London's West End. Married twice. Her lovers included actor Laurence HARVEY.
Autobiography: 1984, *The Unsinkable Hermione Baddeley*.
■ A Daughter in Revolt 27. The Guns of Loos 27. Caste 30. Love Life and Laughter 34. Royal Cavalcade 35. Kipps 41. It Always Rains on Sunday 47. *Brighton Rock* 47. No Room at the Inn 48. Quartet 48. *Passport to Pimlico* 49. Dear Mr Prohack 49. The Woman in Question 49. There is Another Sun 51. Tom Brown's Schooldays 51. Hell is Sold Out 51. Scrooge 51. Song of Paris 52. Time Gentlemen Please 52. *The Pickwick Papers* 52. Cosh Boy 52. Counterspy 53. The Belles of St Trinian's 54. Women without Men 56. *Room at the Top* (AAN) 58. Jetstorm 59. Espresso Bongo 59. Let's Get Married 60. Midnight Lace 60. Information Received 61. Rag Doll 61. Mary Poppins 64. The Unsinkable Molly Brown 64. Do Not Disturb 65. Harlow 65. Marriage on the Rocks 65. Bullwhip Griffin 65. The Happiest Millionaire 67. Up the Front 72. The Black Windmill 74. Chomps 79. There Goes the Bride 80. The Secret of Nimh (voice) 82.
TV series: Camp Runamuck 65–66. The Good Life (US) 71. Maude 74–77.
❝ I have spent most of my life working in the theatre – which is always my greatest love, but the films and television were the providers of the little luxuries of life. – *H.B.*

Badel, Alan (1923–1982)
British stage and screen actor of considerable sensitivity, not easy to cast in leading roles. Born in Rusholme, Manchester, he studied at RADA and was on stage from 1940.
The Stranger Left No Card 52. Salome 53. *Three Cases of Murder* 54. Magic Fire 54. This Sporting Life 63. Children of the Damned 64. *Arabesque* 66. Otley 68. Where's Jack? 69. *The Adventurers* 70. The Day of the Jackal 73. Luther 73. Telefon 77. Force Ten From Navarone 78. The Riddle of the Sands 79. Nijinsky 80. Shogun (TV) 82, etc.

Baden-Semper, Nina (1945–)
West Indian leading lady, popular on British TV.
Kongi's Harvest 73. Love Thy Neighbour 73.

Badger, Clarence (1880–1964)
American director at his peak in the 20s.
Jubilo 19. Doubling for Romeo 21. Miss Brewster's Millions 26. *It* 27. Hot News 28. Three Weekends 28. No No Nanette 30. The Bad Man 32. Rangle River 39, etc.

Badham, John (1939–)
American director with a sharp visual style. Born in England, he is a graduate of Yale University and the Yale School of Drama.
The Impatient Heart (TV) 71. Isn't It Shocking? (TV) 73. The Godchild (TV) 74. *The Law* (TV) 74. The Gun (TV) 74. Reflections of Murder (TV) 74. The Keegans (TV) 76. The Bingo Long All Stars and Travelling Motor Kings 76. *Saturday Night Fever* 77. Dracula 79. Whose Life Is It Anyway? 81. War Games 83. Blue Thunder 83. American Flyers 85. Short Circuit 86. Stakeout 87. Bird on a Wire 90. The Hard Way 91. Point of No Return 93. Another Stakeout 93. Drop Zone 94. Nick of Time 95. Incognito 97. The Last Debate (TV) 00, etc.

Badham, Mary (1952–)
American teenage actress.
■ To Kill a Mockingbird (AAN) 62. This Property Is Condemned 66. Let's Kill Uncle 66.

Badiyi, Reza S. (1936–)
Iranian-born director in America, from TV, where he came to fame by devising the title sequence for Hawaii Five-O.
The Eyes of Charles Sand (TV) 72. Trader Horn 73. Of Mice and Men (TV) 81. Blade in Hong Kong (TV) 85, etc.

Baer, Buddy (1915–1986) (Jacob Henry Baer)
American heavyweight prizefighter, brother of Max.
Africa Screams 49. Quo Vadis 51. Jack and the Beanstalk 52. Slightly Scarlet 56. Snow White and the Three Stooges 61, etc.

Baer, John (1925–)
Boyish American actor, born in York, Pennsylvania.
Saturday's Hero 51. Arizona Manhunt 51. About Face 52. Indian Uprising 52. The Mississippi Gambler 53. The Miami Story 54. Riding Shotgun 54. We're No Angels 55. Huk! 56. Guns, Girls and Gangsters 58. Night of the Blood Beast 58. Tarawa Beachhead 58. The Cat Burglar 61. Fear No More 61. The Chapman Report 62. Bikini Paradise 64. The Late Liz 71, etc.

Baer, Max (1909–1959)
Former American world heavyweight champion who made several films.
The Prizefighter and the Lady 33. Riding High 50. The Iron Road 55. The Harder They Fall 56. Over She Goes 58, etc.

Baer Jnr, Max (1937–)
American actor who spent nine years playing Jethro in the TV sitcom *The Beverly Hillbillies*, then became an independent producer.
Macon County Line 73. The McCulloughs (& a, d) 75. Ode to Billy Joe (d only) 76. Hometown, USA (d only) 79, etc.

Baer, Parley
American character actor, usually as professional type.
Comanche Territory 50. Deadline USA 52. D-Day Sixth of June 56. Cash McCall 60. Gypsy 62. Fluffy 65. Counterpoint 67. Young Billy Young 69. Punch and Jody (TV) 74. The Amazing Dobermans 77. Rodeo Girl 80. White Dog 82, etc.
TV series: The Adventures of Ozzie and Harriet 55–61. The Andy Griffith Show 62–63. Double Life of Henry Phyfe 66.

Bagdadi, Maroun (1948–1993)
Lebanese director who studied film in Paris in the mid-70s.
Little Wars 82. L'Homme Voilé 87. Hors la Vie 91. *La Fille de l'Air* 92, etc.

Baggot, King (1874–1948) (aka King Baggott)
Tall, powerful American leading actor and director of silent adventure dramas. Made a few early talkies, then retired. Born in St. Louis, Missouri, he began in the theatre.
AS ACTOR: The Eternal Triangle 10. Lady Audley's Secret 12. Ivanhoe 13. Dr Jekyll and Mr Hyde 13. The Corsican Brothers 15. The Hawk's Trail (serial) 20. The Czar of Broadway 30. Once a Gentleman 30. Scareheads 32. Romance in the Rain 34. Mississippi 35. Come Live with Me 41. Abbott and Costello in Hollywood 45, many others.
AS DIRECTOR: Moonlight Follies 21. Tumbleweeds 25. Down the Stretch 27. The Notorious Lady 27. The House of Scandal 28. Romance of a Rogue 28, etc.

Baigelman, Steven (1961–)
Canadian director and screenwriter. Born in Toronto, he studied acting under Sanford MEISNER in New York and has also exhibited his paintings in the US and Europe.
Feeling Minnesota 96.

Bailey, John (1942–)
American cinematographer.
Welcome to L.A. 77. Boulevard Nights 79. American Gigolo 80. Ordinary People 80. Honky Tonk Freeway 81. Racing with the Moon 84. Silverado 85. Brighton Beach Memoirs 86. Crossroads 86. Swimming to Cambodia 87. The Accidental Tourist 88. My Blue Heaven 90. In the Line of Fire 93. Groundhog Day 93. China Moon (d) 94. Nobody's Fool 94. As Good as It Gets 97. Living Out Loud 98. The Out-of-Towners 99. Forever Mine 99, etc.

Bailey, Pearl (1918–1990)
American entertainer and Broadway star.
Autobiography: 1968, *The Raw Pearl*.
Variety Girl 47. Isn't It Romantic? 48. Carmen Jones 54. That Certain Feeling 56. St Louis Blues 58. Porgy and Bess 59. All the Fine Young Cannibals 60. The Landlord 70. Norman, Is That You? 76, etc.

Bailey, Raymond (1905–1980)
American small part actor, often a crook or lawyer.
Secret Service of the Air 39. Tidal Wave 40. I Want to Live 55. Picnic 56. The Incredible Shrinking Man 57. Vertigo 58. Al Capone 59. From the Terrace 60, many others.
TV series: My Sister Eileen 59. The Many Loves of Dobie Gillis 61–62. *The Beverly Hillbillies* (as Drysdale) 62–70.

Bailey, Robin (1919–1999)
British comedy character actor with a penchant for dialects as well as the extremes of 'Oxford English'. Born in Hucknall, Nottingham, he worked for the postal service and began as an amateur actor before turning professional in 1938. He became a television star in such series as *I Didn't Know You Cared*, and *Potter*.
School for Secrets 46. Private Angelo 49. Portrait of Clare 50. His Excellency 51. The Gift Horse 52. Glory at Sea 52. Single-Handed 53. Just My Luck 57. Hell Drivers 58. The Diplomatic Corpse 58. Catch Us If You Can 65. The Spy with the Cold Nose 66. You Only Live Twice 67. Blind Terror 71. The Four Feathers (TV) 78. Screamtime 83. Jane and the Lost City 88, etc.
TV series: I Didn't Know You Cared 75–79. Sorry I'm a Stranger Here Myself 81–82. Potter 83. Charters and Caldicott 85.

Bain, Barbara (1931–)
American leading lady, once married to Martin LANDAU. Best known on TV in series Mission Impossible (66–69). Space 1999 (75–76).
Murder Once Removed (TV) 71. Goodnight My Love 72. A Summer Without Boys (TV) 73. Destination Moonbase Alpha 75. Skinheads 88. Trust Me 89. Gideon 99., etc.

Bainbridge, Dame Beryl (1934–)
English novelist and playwright, a former actress. She became a Dame in 2000.
Adult Fun (a) 72. Sweet William (oa) 80. The Dressmaker (oa) 88. An Awfully Big Adventure (oa) 94.

Bainter, Fay (1892–1968)
American character actress who came to films from the stage in 1934 and specialized in stalwart but sympathetic matrons.
■ This Side of Heaven 34. *Quality Street* 37. The Soldier and the Lady 37. Make Way for Tomorrow 37. *Jezebel* (AA) 38. *White Banners* (AAN) 38. Mother Carey's Chickens 38. The Arkansas Traveller 38. The Shining Hour 38. Yes My Darling Daughter 39. The Lady and the Mob 39. Daughters Courageous 39. Our Neighbours the Carters 39. Young Tom Edison 40. *Our Town* 40. A Bill of Divorcement 40. Maryland 40. Babes on Broadway 41. Woman of the Year 42. *The War Against Mrs Hadley* 42. *Mrs Wiggs of the Cabbage Patch* 42. Journey for Margaret 43. *The Human Comedy* 43. Presenting Lily Mars 43. Salute to the Marines 43. Cry Havoc 43. The Heavenly Body 43. *Dark Waters* (rare villainous role) 44. Three is a Family 44. *State Fair* 45. The Virginian 46. The Kid from Brooklyn 46. *The Secret Life of Walter Mitty* 47. Deep Valley 47. Give My Regards to Broadway 48. *June Bride* 48. Close to My Heart 51. The President's Lady 53. *The Children's Hour* (AAN) 62. Bon Voyage 62.

Baio, Scott (1961–)
American actor who briefly became a star in his teens and is best remembered for the role of Chachi Arcola in the TV series *Happy Days*. Born in Brooklyn, New York, he began in commercials at the age of nine. He was once engaged to actress Pamela Anderson.
Bugsy Malone 76. Foxes 80. The Boy Who Drank Too Much (TV) 81. Something for Joey (TV) 81. Zapped! 82. Evil Laugh 88. Mixed Blessings (TV) 95. Detonator 97, etc.
TV series: Happy Days 77–84. Joanie Loves Chaci 82–83. Charles in Charge 84–85. Baby Talk 91. Diagnosis Murder 94–96.

Baird, Stuart (1948–)
Leading British editor, now working in Hollywood. He was a creative consultant at Warner 1989–92 after being called in to rescue *Tango and Cash*. He also worked uncredited on the final cuts of *Predator, New Jack City, Scrooged* and *Robin Hood: Prince of Thieves*.
Tommy 75. Lisztomania 75. The Omen 76. Valentino 77. Superman (AAN) 78. Superman II 80. Altered States 80. Outland 81. Five Days One Summer 82. Revolution 85. Ladyhawke 85. Lethal Weapon 87. Gorillas in the Mist (AAN) 88. Lethal Weapon II 89. Tango & Cash 89. Die Hard 2 90. Radio Flyer 92. *Demolition Man* 93. Maverick 94. Executive Decision 96. US Marshals 98, etc.
❝ If your megapic doesn't click, call Baird. – *Variety*

Baird, Teddy
British producer, in films from 1928 after journalistic experience.
The Browning Version 51. The Importance of Being Earnest 52. Carrington V.C. 56. Two Living One Dead 62, etc.

Bakaleinikoff, Constantin (1898–1966)
Russian-born musical director and composer, in Hollywood. Born in Moscow, he studied at the Moscow Conservatory of Music, and first worked in the USA with the Los Angeles Philharmonic Orchestra. He became musical director of the Grauman Theatre Corp., before working in a similar capacity for Paramount and MGM. In 1941, he became head of RKO's music department, staying until 1952.
Father and Son 29. A Date with the Falcon 41. The Big Street 42. The Tuttles of Tahiti 42. Here We Go Again 42. Cat People 43. Around the World 43. The Seventh Victim 43. I Walked with a Zombie 43. Tarzan Triumphs 43. Tarzan's Desert Mystery 43. Murder My Sweet 44. Step Lively 44. The Curse of the Cat People 44. Betrayal from the East 45. Isle of the Dead 45. Johnny Angel 45. The Falcon in San Francisco 45. Those Endearing Young Charms 45. The Body Snatcher 45. George White's Scandals 45. Deadline at Dawn 46. Sister Kenny 46. Notorious 46. Lady Luck 46. Bedlam 46. Magic Town 47. Mourning Becomes Electra 47. Blood on the Moon 48. Mr Blandings Builds His Dream House 48. If You Knew Susie 48. I Remember Mama 48. Caught 48. Adventure in Baltimore 49. She Wore a Yellow Ribbon 49. Easy Living 49. The Big Steal 49. Where Danger Lives 50. His Kind of Woman 51. At Sword's Point 52. The Big Sky 52. Androcles and the Lion – The Conqueror 56. The Bachelor Party 56, etc.

Bakaleinikoff, Mischa (1890–1960)
Russian-born musical director and composer, in Hollywood. Many of his own scores were for westerns and horror movies.
The Threat 42. One Mysterious Night 44. Cry of the Werewolf 44. Louisiana Hayride 44. Mysterious Intruder (serial) 46. Boston Blackie and the Law 46. The Lone Wolf in London 47. Bulldog Drummond Strikes Back 47. The Last of the Redmen 47. Devil Ship 47. The Prince of Thieves 48. My Dog Rusty 48. Riders in the Sky 49. Barbary Pirate 49. Ace Lucky 49. Prison Warden 49. Chinatown at Midnight 49. Batman and Robin (serial) 49. Blondie's Hero 50. Mule Train 50. Mark of the Gorilla 50. The Adventures of Sir Galahad 50. Captain Video (serial) 51. Harem Girl 51. Gasoline Alley 51. Jungle Manhunt 51. Smuggler's Gold 51. When the Redskins Rode 51. Night Stage to Galveston 52. Thief of Damascus 52. The Kid from Broken Gun 52. The Big Heat 53. Savage Mutiny 53. Serpent of the Nile 53. Prince of Pirates 53. Gun Fury 53. Conquest of Cochise 53. Cannibal Attack 54. It Came from Beneath the Sea 55. Devil Goddess 55. Women's Prison 55. Seminole Uprising 55. Creature with the Atom Brain 55. Earth vs the Flying Saucers 56. The Werewolf 56. Fury at Gunsight Pass 56. The Tall T 57. 20 Million Miles to Earth 57. The Tijuana Story 57. The Phantom Stagecoach 57. The Giant Claw 57. Hellcats of the Navy 57. Zombies of Mora-Tau 57. Screaming Mimi 58. The Lineup 58. Crash Landing 58. Apache Territory 58. The Flying Fontaines 59. The Enemy General 60. Comanche Station 60, many others.

Bakalyan, Richard (1941–)
American character actor, usually as villain.
The Brothers Rico 57. Up Periscope 59. Panic in Year Zero 62. Von Ryan's Express 65. The St Valentine's Day Massacre 67. Chinatown 74. Return from Witch Mountain 78, etc.

Baker, Art (1898–1966) (Arthur Shank)
American general-purpose actor.
Once Upon a Time 44. Spellbound 45. The Farmer's Daughter 47. *Cover Up* 48. Take One False Step 49. Cause for Alarm 51. Living It Up 54. Twelve Hours to Kill 60. Young Dillinger 65. The Wild Angels 66, etc.

Baker, Blanche (1956–)
American actress, the daughter of Carroll Baker.

The Seduction of Joe Tynan 79. French Postcards 79. Mary and Joseph: A Story of Faith (TV) 79. The Awakening of Candra (TV) 81. Cold Feet 84. Sixteen Candles 84. Raw Deal 86. Shakedown 88. The Handmaid's Tale 90, etc.

Baker, Buddy (1918–)
American composer for Walt Disney films.
Summer Magic 63. A Tiger Walks 64. The Gnome-Mobile 67. Napoleon and Samantha (AAN) 72. The Apple Dumpling Gang 75. The Shaggy D.A. 76. Hot Lead and Cold Feet 78. The Apple Dumpling Gang Rides Again 79. The Devil and Max Devlin 81. The Fox and the Hound 81, etc.

Baker, Carroll (1931–)
American leading lady who tried to vary her sex-symbol status via roles of melodramatic intensity. After her Hollywood career fizzled she made many exploitation pictures in Italy. Married director Jack Garfein (1955–69) and actor Donald Burton.
Autobiography: 1984, *Baby Doll*.
Easy to Love 53. *Giant* 56. *Baby Doll* (AAN) 56. The Big Country 58. The Miracle 59. But Not for Me 59. Something Wild 61. Bridge to the Sun 61. How the West Was Won 62. *The Carpetbaggers* 64. Station Six Sahara 64. Cheyenne Autumn 64. Sylvia 64. The Greatest Story Ever Told 65. Mr Moses 65. *Harlow* 65. Jack of Diamonds 67. The Sweet Body of Deborah 68. Paranoia 68. The Harem 68. The Spider 70. The Fourth Mrs Anderson 71. Captain Apache 71. Bloody Mary 72. Baba Yaga Devil Witch 74. Andy Warhol's Bad 76. The Devil Has Seven Faces 77. The World Is Full of Married Men 79. The Watcher in the Woods 80. Star 80 83. The Secret Diary of Sigmund Freud 84. Native Son 86. Ironweed 87. Blonde Fist 91. Cybereden (It.) 93. North Shore Fish 97. The Game 97. Heart Full of Rain (TV) 97, etc.
❝ More bomb than bombshell. – *Judith Crist*

Baker, Chet (1929–88) (Chesney H. Baker)
Cool American jazz trumpeter and singer who made his name playing with the Gerry Mulligan Quartet in the early 50s. His later career was hampered by his drug addiction and he moved to Europe in the 60s, dying after a fall from a hotel window in Amsterdam. He was the subject of a documentary, *Let's Get Lost* 89.
Autobiography: 1998: *As Though I Had Wings*.

Baker, Diane (1938–)
Demure-looking American leading actress who can also handle unsympathetic roles. Many TV guest appearances.
The Diary of Anne Frank 59. The Best of Everything 59. Journey to the Centre of the Earth 59. Tess of the Storm Country 60. Hemingway's Adventures of a Young Man 62. The 300 Spartans 62. Nine Hours to Rama 63. Stolen Hours 63. *Strait Jacket* 63. *The Prize* 63. Della (TV) 64. *Marnie* 64. *Mirage* 65. Sands of Beersheba 66. The Dangerous Days of Kiowa Jones (TV) 66. Krakatoa, East of Java 68. The Horse in the Grey Flannel Suit 69. Murder One (TV) 69. The Badge or the Cross (TV) 70. Do You Take This Stranger? (TV) 70. Wheeler and Murdoch (TV) 70. The Old Man Who Cried Wolf (TV) 70. A Little Game (TV) 71. Killer By Night (TV) 71. Congratulations, It's A Boy (TV) 71. A Tree Grows in Brooklyn (TV) 74. The Dream Makers (TV) 75. The Last Survivors (TV) 75. Baker's Hawk 76. The Summer of Sixty-Nine (TV) 77. Danger in the Skies 79. The Pilot 82. The Closer 90. The Silence of the Lambs 91. The Haunted (TV) 91. Twenty Bucks (TV) 93. The Joy Luck Club 93. Imaginary Crimes 94. The Net 95. The Cable Guy 96. Murder at 1600 97, etc.
TV series: *Here We Go Again* 73. The Blue and the Grey 82.

Baker, Eddie (1897–1968) (Edward King)
American comic actor, one of the original Keystone Kops.
Hold Your Breath 24. All at Sea 29. City Lights 31. Monkey Business 31. Babes in Toyland 34. Land of Fury 55, etc.

Baker, George (1929–)
British leading man, also on stage and TV; best known for his role as Inspector Wexford in the TV series *The Ruth Rendell Mysteries* 87–92.
The Intruder 52. The Dam Busters 55. A Hill in Korea 56. The Woman for Joe 56. *The Moonraker* 57. Tread Softly Stranger 58. No Time for Tears 59. Lancelot and Guinevere 62. Curse of the Fly 65. Mr Ten Per Cent 67. Justine 69. On Her Majesty's Secret Service 69. The Spy Who Loved Me 77. I, Claudius (TV) 77. Print Out (TV) 79. North Sea Hijack 79. Hopscotch 80. The Secret Adversary (TV) 82. Goodbye Mr Chips (TV) 84. A Woman of Substance (TV) 84. For Queen and Country 88. Simisola (TV) 96, etc.
TV series: Bowler 73. No Job for a Lady 90–91.

Baker, Graham
American director.
The Final Conflict 81. Impulse 84. Alien Nation 88. Born to Ride 91. Beowulf 99, etc.

Baker, Hylda (1908–1986)
English comedienne and character actress. Born in Bolton, she started on the music-halls at the age of ten. A dimunitive, dumpy figure, her act consisted of a one-sided conversation, full of malapropisms, with Cynthia, a tall, silent stooge, who was played by a man in drag. Her catchphrases included 'Be soon', and 'She knows, you know!'
■ Saturday Night and Sunday Morning 60. She Knows You Know 61. Up the Junction 67. Oliver! 68. Nearest and Dearest 73.
TV series: Be Soon 57-58. Our House 61-62. Best of Friends 63. Nearest and Dearest 68-73. Not on Your Nellie 74-75.

Baker, Ian
Australian cinematographer, associated with the films of Fred Schepisi.
Libido 73. The Devil's Playground 76. The Chant of Jimmy Blacksmith 78. Barbarosa 81. The Clinic 82. Iceman 84. Plenty 85. Roxanne 87. A Cry in the Dark 88. The Punisher 89. Everybody Wins 90. The Russia House 90. Six Degrees of Separation 93. I.Q. 94. The Chamber 96. Fierce Creatures 97, etc.

Baker, Joe Don (1936–)
Tough American leading man.
Cool Hand Luke 67. Guns of the Magnificent Seven 69. Adam at Six a.m. 70. Wild Rovers 71. Mongo's Back in Town (TV) 71. Welcome Home Soldier Boys 72. Junior Bonner 72. *Charley Varrick* 73. *Walking Tall* 73. The Outfit 74. Golden Needles 74. Mitchell 74. Framed 75. Crash 76. The Pack 77. To Kill a Cop (TV) 77. Power (TV) 79. Joysticks 83. The Natural 84. Fletch 85. Getting Even 85. The Killing Time 87. The Living Daylights 87. Criminal Law 89. The Children 90. Cape Fear 91. The Distinguished Gentleman 92. Ring of Steel 93. Reality Bites 94. Congo 95. The Underneath 95. Panther 95. The Grass Harp 95. GoldenEye 95. Congo 95. Mars Attacks! 96. Tomorrow Never Dies 97, etc.
TV series: Eischied/Chief of Detectives 79.

Baker, Josephine (1906–1975) (Josephine Carson)
American dancer, singer and actress. Born in the slums of St Louis, Missouri, she began in vaudeville, causing a sensation when she performed in Paris at the Folies Bergère. She became a French citizen in the early 40s and, in the 50s, established a home for children she had found on her various tours, though she was rarely free of financial difficulties. Married four times; her lovers included novelist Georges Simenon.
La Sirène des Tropiques 27. Zou Zou 34. Princesse Tam Tam 35. Moulin Rouge 44. The French Way 52. Ten on Every Finger/An Jedem Finger Zehn 54, etc.

Baker, Kathy (1950–)
American leading actress who began as a child and then spent time in France, studying Cordon Bleu cookery.
The Right Stuff 83. The Killing Affair 86. My Sister's Keeper 86. Street Smart (AAN) 87. Clean and Sober 88. Permanent Record 88. Dad 89. Jacknife 89. Edward Scissorhands 90. Article 99 92. Mad Dog and Glory 92. Lush Life 93. To Gillian on Her 37th Birthday 96. Inventing the Abbots 97. Weapons of Mass Distraction (TV) 97. The Cider House Rules 99, etc.
TV series: Picket Fences 92.

Baker, Kenny (1912–1985)
American crooner, popular in the late 30s but subsequently little heard of.
King of Burlesque 35. The Goldwyn Follies 38. The Mikado (GB: as Nanki Poo) 39. 52nd Street 39. At the Circus 39. Hit Parade of 1941 40. Silver Skates 42. Doughboys in Ireland 43. The Harvey Girls 46. That's Entertainment III 94, etc.

Baker, Lenny (1945–1982)
American actor of stage and screen. He died of cancer.
The Hospital 71. The Paper Chase 73. *Next Stop, Greenwich Village* 76, etc.

Baker, Phil (1896–1963)
American radio personality who appeared in a few films.
Gift of Gab 34. The Goldwyn Follies 38. The Gang's All Here 43. *Take It or Leave It* 44, etc.

Baker, Rick (1950–)
American make-up and special effects artist.
Octaman 71. Schlock 72. The Thing with Two Heads 72. It's Alive 74. King Kong 76. *Star Wars* 77. The Incredible Melting Man 77. *An American Werewolf in London* (AA) 81. Greystoke (AAN) 84. Teen Wolf 85. Harry and the Hendersons (AA) 87. Coming to America (AAN) 88. Gorillas in the Mist 88. Gremlins 2: The New Batch 90. Wolf 94. Ed Wood (AA) 94. Baby's Day Out 94. The Frighteners 96. Escape from L.A. 96. The Nutty Professor (AA) 96. Men in Black (AA) 97. Mighty Joe Young 98. Life (AAN) 99. Nutty Professor II: The Klumps 00. Dr Seuss' How the Grinch Stole Christmas (AA, BFA) 00, etc.

Baker, Robert S. (1916–)
British producer: co-founder with Monty Berman of Tempean Films, which since 1948 has produced many co-features, also *The Saint* and other TV series.
■ As director: Melody Club 49. Blackout 50. 13 East Street 52. The Steel Key 53. Passport to Treason 56. Jack the Ripper 58. The Siege of Sidney Street 60. The Hellfire Club 60. The Treasure of Monte Cristo 61.

Baker, Roy Ward (1916–)
Notable British director whose career declined in the 60s. Served apprenticeship at Gainsborough 1934–39, then war service.
The October Man 47. The Weaker Sex 48. *Morning Departure* 50. I'll Never Forget You (US) 51. *Inferno* (US) 52. Don't Bother to Knock (US) 52. Passage Home 54. Jacqueline 56. Tiger in the Smoke 56. *The One That Got Away* 57. *A Night to Remember* 58. The Singer Not the Song (& p) 60. Flame in the Streets (& p) 61. The Valiant 61. Two Left Feet 64. *Quatermass and the Pit* 67. The Anniversary 68. Moon Zero Two 69. The Vampire Lovers 70. Scars of Dracula 70. Dr Jekyll and Sister Hyde 71. Asylum 72. And Now the Screaming Starts 73. Vault of Horror 73. The Legend of the Seven Golden Vampires 74. The Monster Club 80. The Flame Trees of Thika (TV) 81, etc.

Baker, Sir Stanley (1927–1976)
Virile Welsh actor who rose from character roles to stardom, projecting honesty or villainy with equal ease.
Biography: 1977, *Portrait of an Actor* by Anthony Storey.
■ Undercover 41. All Over the Town 49. Obsession 49. Your Witness 50. The Rossiter Case 51. Cloudburst 51. Captain Horatio Hornblower 51. Home to Danger 51. Whispering Smith Hits London 52. Lili Marlene 52. *The Cruel Sea* 53. The Red Beret 53. Knights of the Round Table 53. *Hell Below Zero* 54. The Good Die Young 54. Beautiful Stranger 54. Helen of Troy 55. Alexander the Great 55. *Richard III* (as Henry Tudor) 55. Child in the House 56. A Hill in Korea 56. Checkpoint 56. *Campbell's Kingdom* 57. *Hell Drivers* 57. Violent Playground 58. Sea Fury 58. The Angry Hills 59. Hell Is a City 59. Blind Date 60. Jet Storm 60. Yesterday's Enemy 60. *The Criminal* 60. The Guns of Navarone 61. A Prize of Arms 61. Sodom and Gomorrah 62. The Man Who Finally Died 62. Eva 62. In the French Style 62. *Zulu* (& co-p) 64. Dingaka 65. Sands of the Kalahari (& co-p) 65. *Accident* 67. Robbery (& co-p) 67. Code Name: Heraclitus (TV) 67. Girl with Pistol 68. Where's Jack? 69. The Last Grenade 69. The Games 70. Perfect Friday 70. Popsy Pop 71. Schizoid 71. Who Killed Lamb? (TV) 72. Innocent Bystanders 72. Graceless Go I (TV) 74. Zorro 75.
TV series: How Green Was My Valley 76.

Baker, Tom (1936–)
British character actor with a larger-than-life air. On TV as Doctor Who 74–81. The second of his three wives was actress Lalla Ward.
Autobiography: 1997, *Who on Earth Is Tom Baker?*.
Nicholas and Alexandra (as Rasputin) 71. Luther 73. Vault of Horror 73. The Golden Voyage of Sinbad 73. The Mutations 74. Angels Die Hard 84. The Zany Adventures of Robin Hood 84, etc.
TV series: Medics 91–95.
❝ Doctor Who was the most wonderful part – I was a madman to give it up. They wouldn't give me the film, would they? They won't know how to do it. Popular films are tawdry, about images and not about thinking. – *T.B.*
The Doctor Who Society in America have conventions and I go among them and lay on hands. Middle-aged ladies stick their tongues in my ear under the pretext of listening. The odd thing is that after the age of 47 chunky little females have tongues like shrapnel. It makes me slightly deaf. A blessing in disguise in our business. – *T.B.*
I like the dead. They're so uncritical. – *T.B.*

Bakewell, William (1908–1993)
American general-purpose actor. Married actress Jennifer Holt.
The Heart Thief 27. All Quiet on the Western Front 30. Spirit of Notre Dame 31. Three Cornered Moon 33. Cheers for Miss Bishop 41. Davy Crockett 55, many others.
TV series: The Pinky Lee Show 50.

Bakshi, Ralph (1938–)
American director of animated features. Born in Palestine, he became a director of Terrytoons cartoons from 1964, including creating the *Sad Cat* series 65–68, directing a series of 17 James Hound cartoons 66–67, spoofing James Bond, and a series of 10 *The Mighty Heroes* 69–71, with such characters as Diaper Man and Cuckoo Man. He also directed for Famous Studios two of the *Go-Go Toons* series 67, and three of the *Fractured Fables* series 68. His first animated features featured sex and drugs, his later ones concentrated on sword and sorcery, while *Cool World* mixed animation and live action.
Books: 1989, *The Animated Art of Ralph Bakshi*.
Fritz the Cat (wd) 71. Heavy Traffic (wd) 73. Coonskin/Streetfight (wd) 75. Hey, Good Lookin' (p, wd) 75 (released 82). Wizards (d) 77. Lord of the Rings (d) 78. American Pop (d) 81. Fire and Ice (d) 83. Cool World 92, etc.

Bakula, Scott (1954–)
American leading actor, best known for his role as Dr Sam Beckett in the 90s TV series *Quantum Leap*.
The Last Fling (TV) 86. Sibling Rivalry 90. Necessary Roughness 91. Color of Night 94. A Passion to Kill 94. My Family/Mi Familia 95. Lord of Illusions 95. The Invaders (TV) 95. American Beauty 99, etc.
TV series: Gung Ho 86–87. Eisenhower & Lutz 88. Murphy Brown (occasionally) 93-96.

Balaban, Barney (1888–1971)
American executive, former exhibitor, president of Paramount 1936–64.

Balaban, Bob (1945–)
American character actor turned director.
Midnight Cowboy 69. Me Natalie 69. Girlfriends 78. Close Encounters of the Third Kind 78. Altered States 80. Prince of the City 81. Absence of Malice 81. Whose Life Is It Anyway? 81.2010 84. End of the Line 88. Parents (d) 88. Dead Bang 89. Bob Roberts 92. For Love or Money 93. Amos & Andrew 93. My Boyfriend's Back (d) 93. The Last Good Time (d) 94. Greedy/Greed 94. Pie in the Sky 95. The Late Shift (TV) 97. Deconstructing Harry 97. Jakob the Liar 99. The Cradle Will Rock 99. Best in Show 00, etc.

Balaban, Burt (1922–1965)
American director, son of Barney Balaban.
Stranger from Venus (GB) 54. Lady of Vengeance 57. High Hell 58. Murder Inc. 60. Mad Dog Coll 61. The Gentle Rain 66, etc.

Balanchine, George (1904–1983)
Distinguished Russian-born American choreographer who worked occasionally in Hollywood.
Dark Red Roses 29. The Goldwyn Follies 38. I Was an Adventuress 40. George Balanchine's The Nutcracker 93.

Balasko, Josiane (1952–)
French actress, screenwriter, dramatist and director, of Yugoslavian descent. She is best known internationally for her role as the plump and homely secretary for whom Gérard Depardieu's car dealer abandons his beautiful wife in *Too Beautiful for You*.

Le Locataire (a) 76. Une Fille Unique (a) 76. Dites-Lui que Je l'Aime (a) 77. Pardon Mon Affaire, Too/Nous Irons Tous au Paradis (a) 77. Les Bronzes Font du Ski (a) 78. L'Année Prochaine Si Tout Va Bien (co-w) 81. Clara et les Chics Types (a) 81. Hotel des Amériques (a) 81. Le Père Noel Est une Ordure (a) 82. P'tit Con (a) 84. La Vengeance du Serpent à Plumes (a) 84. Nuit d'Ivresse (a, w) 86. Les Keufs (a, wd) 87. *Too Beautiful for You*/Trop Belle pour Toi (a) 89. Ma Vie Est un Enfer (a, wd) 91. A Shadow of a Doubt/ L'Ombre du Doute (a) 93. Grosse Fatigue (a) 94. *French Twist*/Gauzon Maudit (a, wd) 95. A Great Shout of Love/Un Grand Cri d'Amour (a, wd) 98, etc.

Balazs, Bela (1884–1949) (Hubert Bauer)
Hungarian writer. Wrote book, *Theory of the Film*.
Die Dreigroschenoper 31. *The Blue Light* 31.

Balch, Antony (1937–1980)
British producer, director, screenwriter, editor and distributor, mainly of avant-garde films. His own short films featured writer William BURROUGHS, but his two commercial features stuck to the clichés of their genres while also parodying them. Died of cancer.

Towers Open Fire (short) 63. The Cut-Ups (short) 67. Secrets of Sex/Bizarre (co-w, p, d) 69. Bill & Tony (short) 72. Horror Hospital (co-w, d) 73.

Balchin, Nigel (1908–1970)
British novelist and screenwriter. Educated at Cambridge University, he was also a businessman and during the Second World War became Scientific Adviser to the Army Council. Married twice.

Fame Is the Spur 47. Mine Own Executioner (& oa) 47. The Small Back Room (& oa) 48. Mandy 52. Malta Story 53. Josephine and Men (& story) 55. The Man Who Never Was 55. 23 Paces to Baker Street (US) 56. The Blue Angel (US) 59. Circle of Deception 60. Suspect (& oa) 60. The Singer Not the Song 60. Barabbas (It.) 61, etc.

Balcon, Jill (1925–)
British actress, daughter of Sir Michael Balcon. She is the mother of Daniel Day-Lewis.

Nicholas Nickleby 47. Good Time Girl 48. Highly Dangerous 50. Edward II 91, etc.

Balcon, Sir Michael (1896–1977)
British executive producer. During a long and distinguished career he headed Gainsborough, Gaumont-British, MGM-British, Ealing, Bryanston and independent production companies, and was directly responsible for the planning and production of many famous films. He served as a model for the character of the mill-owner, played by Cecil Parker, in *The Man in the White Suit*.

Autobiography: 1969, *A Lifetime of Films*.

His more personal projects include: Woman to Woman 23. The Pleasure Garden 25. The Lodger 26. Easy Virtue 27. Man of Aran 33. The Man Who Knew Too Much 34. The 39 Steps 35. Sabotage 37. A Yank at Oxford 38. The Citadel 38. Goodbye Mr Chips 39. Convoy 40. The Next of Kin 42. The Bells Go Down 42. Champagne Charlie 44. Dead of Night 45. The Captive Heart 46. Hue and Cry 46. Nicholas Nickleby 47. It Always Rains on Sunday 48. Scott of the Antarctic 48. Kind Hearts and Coronets 49. Whisky Galore 49. Passport to Pimlico 49. The Blue Lamp 50. The Man in the White Suit 51. The Lavender Hill Mob 51. The Cruel Sea 53. The Ladykillers 55. Dunkirk 58. Saturday Night and Sunday Morning 60. Tom Jones 63.

✪ For steering his part of the British film industry in very much the right way, and for refusing to lower his standards. *Dead of Night*.

❝ I always look for people whose ideas coincide with mine, and then I'm ready to give them a chance to make a name for themselves. – M.B.

We made films at Ealing that were good, bad and indifferent, but they were indisputably British. They were rooted in the soil of the country. – M.B.

Balderston, John L. (1899–1954)
Anglo-American screenwriter and playwright, usually in collaboration, with a penchant for romantic and fantastic themes. Born in Philadelphia, and educated at Columbia University, he began as a war correspondent and journalist.

Frankenstein 31. Dracula (co-play) 31. *The Mummy* 32. *Berkeley Square* (oa) 33. Lives of a Bengal Lancer (AAN) 34. The Mystery of Edwin Drood 35. *Mad Love* 35. *Bride of Frankenstein* 35. Beloved Enemy 36. The Amazing Quest of Ernest Bliss 36. The Man Who Changed His Mind 36. The Last of the Mohicans 36. *The Prisoner of Zenda* 37. Victory 40. Scotland Yard 41. Smilin' Through 41. Tennessee Johnson 43. Stand by for Action 43. Gaslight (AAN) 44. The House in the Square 51. Red Planet Mars 52. The Prisoner of Zenda 52., etc.

Baldi, Ferdinando (1927–)
Italian director.

David and Goliath (co-d) 59. Duel of the Champions 71. Blindman 71. Get Mean 76. My Name Is Trinity 76. The Sicilian Connection 77. Comin' at Ya 81. Treasure of the Four Crowns 83. War Bus 86, etc.

Baldwin, Adam (1962–)
American actor.

My Bodyguard 80. Ordinary People 80. D.C. Cab 83. Reckless 84. Hadley's Rebellion 84. Love on the Run (TV) 85. Bad Guys 86. Full Metal Jacket 87. Cohen and Tate 88. Next of Kin 89. Internal Affairs 90. Predator 2 90. Radio Flyer 92. Bitter Harvest 93. Eight Hundred Leagues down the Amazon 93. Wyatt Earp 94. Lover's Knot 96. Independence Day 96. The Patriot 00, etc.

TV series: The Cape 96– .

Baldwin, Alec (1958–)
American leading actor. Born in New York, he studied at George Washington University, New York University, and New York's Lee Strasberg Institute. He is partner in the production company Eldorado Pictures. He is the brother of actors Daniel, Stephen and William BALDWIN. Formerly married to actress Kim BASINGER.

Forever Lulu 86. Beetlejuice 88. Married to the Mob 88. Talk Radio 88. Working Girl 88. Great Balls of Fire! 89. Alice 90. The Hunt for Red October 90. Miami Blues 90. The Marrying Man 91. Glengarry Glen Ross 92. Prelude to a Kiss 92. Malice 93. The Getaway 94. The Shadow 94. Ghosts of Mississippi 96. Heaven's Prisoners 96. The Juror 96. Looking for Richard 96. The Edge 97. Mercury Rising 98. Notting Hill 99. Outside Providence 99. Nuremberg (TV) (&ex-p) 00. Thomas and the Magic Railroad 00. State and Main 00, etc.

TV series: Cutter to Houston 83.

❝ I'm starting to feel I have to cure my addiction to Hollywood money, because while it's delightful, it's also insidious. – *A.B., 1997*

Baldwin, Daniel (1961–)
American actor, the brother of Alec BALDWIN.

The Heroes of Desert Storm 91. Nothing but Trouble 91. Harley Davidson and the Marlboro Man 91. Car 54, Where Are You? 94. Bodily Harm 95. Mulholland Falls 96. Trees Lounge 96. John Carpenter's Vampires 98. Love Kills 98. Desert Thunder 99, etc.

TV series: Homicide: Life on the Street 93-95.

Baldwin, Faith (1893–1978)
American novelist.

Scenario credits include: The Moon's Our Home 36. Men Are Such Fools 37. Apartment for Peggy 48. Queen for a Day 51.

Baldwin, Stephen (1966–)
American leading actor, the brother of Alec BALDWIN.

The Beast 88. Born on the Fourth of July 89. Bitter Harvest 93. Posse 93. Threesome 94. 8 Seconds 94. A Simple Twist of Fate 94. Mrs Parker and the Vicious Circle 94. Fall Time 94. The Usual Suspects 95. Dead Weekend 95. Bio-Dome 96. Crimetime 96. Fled 96. Half-Baked 97. One Tough Cop 98. Friends and Lovers 98. The Sex Monster 99. The Flinstones in Viva Rock Vegas 00, etc.

TV series: The Young Riders 89–92.

❝ If there's one thing I learned in the business, it's at least have your package looking good. – *S.B.*

Baldwin, Walter (1887–1977)
American character actor, often in owlish or countrified roles.

Angels Over Broadway 40. All That Money Can Buy 41. Kings Row 42. Happy Land 43. I'll Be Seeing You 44. The Lost Weekend 45. The Best Years of Our Lives 46. Mourning Becomes Electra 47. The Man from Colorado 48. Cheaper by the Dozen 50. Carrie 52. Scandal at Scourie 53. Glory 55. Cheyenne Autumn 64. Rosemary's Baby 68, many others.

Baldwin, William (1963–)
American actor, the brother of actor Alec BALDWIN.

Born on the Fourth of July 89. Internal Affairs 90. Flatliners 90. Backdraft 91. Three of Hearts 92. Sliver 93. A Pyromaniac's Love Story 95. Fair Game 95. Curdled 96. Shattered Image 98. Virus 99. Relative Values 00, etc.

Bale, Christian (1974–)
Welsh actor who made his screen debut as a teenager in the leading role in *Empire of the Sun*.

Empire of the Sun 87. Land of Faraway 88. Henry V 89. Treasure Island (TV) 90. Newsies/ News Boys 92. Swing Kids 93. Little Women 94. The Portrait of a Lady 96. Joseph Conrad's Secret Agent 96. Velvet Goldmine 98. All the Little Animals 98. William Shakespeare's A Midsummer Night's Dream 99. American Psycho 00. Shaft 00. Captain Corelli's Mandolin 01. Equilibrium 01, etc.

Balfour, Betty (1903–1978)
British comedienne of silent days, a popular favourite of the 20s as pert heroine of *Cinders*, *Love Life and Laughter* and the *Squibs* series.

The Brat 30. The Vagabond Queen 30. Paddy the Next Best Thing 33. Evergreen 34. Squibs (remake) 35. 29 Acacia Avenue 45, etc.

Balfour, Michael (1918–1997)
English character actor, frequently as a taxi-driver, serviceman or dumb gangster. Born in Kent, he began in repertory theatre in 1936, and from the mid-40s assumed an American identity as a Detroit-born former child actor to obtain a role in the London production of Garson KANIN's play *Born Yesterday*. He was also a sculptor and painter; from the late 70s to the mid-90s, he also worked as a circus clown.

Just William's Luck 47. The Front Page (TV) 48. No Orchids for Miss Blandish 48. Cosh Boy/The Slasher 52. Genevieve 53. Albert RN 53. The Sea Shall Not Have Them 54. Meet Mr Callaghan 54. The Belles of St Trinian's 54. Gentlemen Marry Brunettes 55. Reach for the Sky 56. Quatermass II/ Enemy from Space 57. Look Back in Anger 59. Carry On Constable 60. Sink the Bismarck! 60. The Hellfire Club 61. The Sicilians 64. Alfie 64. Fahrenheit 451 66. The Oblong Box 69. The Private Life of Sherlock Holmes 70. Macbeth 71. Joseph Andrews 76. Candleshoe 77. Prisoner of Zenda 79. The Holcroft Covenant 85. Revenge of Billy the Kid 91, many others.

TV series: Mark Saber 55–56. The Splendid Spur 60.

Balin, Ina (1937–1990) (Ina Rosenberg)
American leading lady, with stage experience.

Compulsion 58. The Black Orchid 58. The Comancheros 61. The Patsy 64. The Greatest Story Ever Told 65. Run Like a Thief 68. Charro 69. The Projectionist 71. The Don is Dead 73, etc.

Balin, Mireille (1909–1968)
French leading lady.

Don Quixote 33. Pépé le Moko 36. Gueule d'Amour 37, etc.

Balk, Fairuza (1974–)
American actress. Born in Point Reyes, California, she moved with her mother to England in the early 80s and studied at the Bush Davies Performing Arts School before appearing in *Return to Oz*, returning to live in Vancouver, Canada, in the late 80s.

Return to Oz (as Dorothy) 85. Valmont 89. Gas Food Lodging 91. Imaginary Crimes 94. Tollbooth 94. Things to Do in Denver When You're Dead 95. The Craft 96. What Is It? (voice) 96. The Island of Dr Moreau 96. The Maker 97. American Perfekt 97. American History X 98. The Waterboy 98. There's No Fish Food in Heaven 98. Great Sex 99. Almost Famous 00, etc.

Ball, Alan
American screenwriter.

American Beauty (AA) 99.

Ball, Angeline
British actress.

The Commitments 91. My Girl 2 (US) 94. Brothers in Trouble 96. The Gambler 97. Trojan Eddie 97. The The Gambler (GB/Hung.) 97 .General 98, etc.

TV series: Over the Rainbow 93.

Ball, Lucille (1911–1989)
American comedienne, a former Goldwyn girl who after a generally unrewarding youth in the movies, turned in middle age to TV and became known as one of the world's great female clowns and a highly competent production executive. She was formerly married to actor Desi ARNAZ. Their children were actors Desi ARNAZ Jnr and Lucie ARNAZ. Desilu, the production company she set up with Arnaz, was responsible not only for *I Love Lucy*, but also such series as *December Bride*, *The Untouchables* and *Mannix*. It was sold to Paramount in 1967 for some $20m. She was played by Frances Fisher in the TV movie *Lucy and Desi: Before the Laughter* 91.

Autobiography: 1996, *Love, Lucy*.

Biography: 1973, *Lucy: The Bittersweet Life of Lucille Ball* by Joe Morella and Edward Z. Epstein. 1994, *Lucille: The Life of Lucille Ball* by Kathleen Brady.

■ Broadway Thru a Keyhole 33. Blood Money 33. Roman Scandals 33. Moulin Rouge 33. Nana 34. Bottoms Up 34. Hold that Girl 34. Bulldog Drummond Strikes Back 34. The Affairs of Cellini 34. Kid Millions 34. Broadway Bill 34. Jealousy 34. Men of the Night 34. Fugitive Lady 34. Carnival (first billed role) 34. Roberta 35. Old Man Rhythm 35. Top Hat 35. The Three Musketeers 35. I Dream Too Much 35. Chatterbox 36. Follow the Fleet 36. The Farmer in the Dell 36. Bunker Bean 36. That Girl from Paris 36. Don't Tell the Wife 37. *Stage Door* 37. Joy of Living 38. Go Chase Yourself 38. Having A Wonderful Time 38. *The Affairs of Annabel* 38. Room Service 38. The Next Time I Marry 38. Annabel Takes a Tour 39. Beauty for the Asking 39. Twelve Crowded Hours 39. Panama Lady 39. *Five Came Back* 39. That's Right You're Wrong 39. The Marines Fly High 40. You Can't Fool Your Wife 40. Dance Girl Dance 40. Too Many Girls 40. A Guy, a Girl and Gob 40. Look Who's Laughing 41. Valley of the Sun 42. *The Big Street* (serious role) 42. Seven Days Leave 42. *Du Barry was a Lady* 43. Best Foot Forward 43. Thousands Cheer 43. Meet the People 44. *Without Love* 45. Abbott and Costello in Hollywood 45. Ziegfeld Follies 46. The Dark Corner 46. *Easy to Wed* 46. Two Smart People 46. Lover Come Back 46. Lured 47. *Her Husband's Affairs* 47. *Sorrowful Jones* 49. Easy Living 49. Miss Grant Takes Richmond 49. *Fancy Pants* 50. The Fuller Brush Girl 50. The Magic Carpet 51. *The Long Long Trailer* 54. Forever Darling 56. *The Facts of Life* 60. Critic's Choice 63. A Guide for the Married Man 67. *Yours Mine and Ours* 68. Mame 74. Stone Pillow (TV) 85.

TV series: *I Love Lucy* 51–55. *The Lucy Show* 62–68. *Here's Lucy* 68–73. Life with Lucy 86.

Ball, Suzan (1933–1955)
American leading lady of the early 50s.

Untamed Frontier 52. East of Sumatra 53. City Beneath the Sea 53. War Arrow 54. Chief Crazy Horse 54, etc.

Ball, Vincent (1924–)
Australian actor, in England for a time.

A Town Like Alice 56. Robbery under Arms 57. Danger Within 58. Identity Unknown 60. Where Eagles Dare 68. Oh What a Lovely War 69. Deadline (Aus) 81. Phar Lap (Aus) 83. The Year My Voice Broke (Aus) 87, etc.

Ballard, Carroll (1937–)
American director with a flair for wild life.

The Black Stallion 80. Never Cry Wolf 83. Nutcracker: The Motion Picture 86. Wind 92. Fly Away Home 96, etc.

Ballard, J. G. (1930–)
English writer, mainly of science fiction in an avant garde manner. Born in Shanghai, his childhood experiences in a Japanese prison camp during the Second World War formed the basis for his best-known novel, *Empire of the Sun*, which was filmed by Steven Spielberg. He studied medicine before becoming a full-time writer in 1962.

When Dinosaurs Ruled the Earth (treatment) 70. Empire of the Sun (oa) 87. Crash (oa) 96. The Atrocity Exhibition (oa) 00.

❝ I'm very proud that my first screen credit was for what is, without doubt, the worst film ever made. – *J.G.B.*

Film, for most of this century, has been a far more serious medium than the novel. – *J.G.B*

Ballard, Kay(e) (1926–) (Catherine Balotta)
American comedienne with stage experience.
The Girl Most Likely 58. A House is Not a Home 64. Freaky Friday 77. Falling in Love Again 80. Tiger Warshaw 87. Modern Love 90. Eternity 90, etc.
TV series: The Mothers-in-Law 67–68. The Doris Day Show 70–71.

Ballard, Lucien (1908–1988)
Distinguished American cinematographer. He was married (1945–49) to actress Merle OBERON.
Crime and Punishment 35. The King Steps Out 36. Craig's Wife 36. The Shadow 37. Penitentiary 38. *Blind Alley* 39. The Villain Still Pursued Her 40. Wild Geese Calling 41. The Undying Monster 42. Orchestra Wives 42. Holy Matrimony 43. *The Lodger* 44. *Laura* (co-ph) 44. This Love of Ours 45. Temptation 46. Night Song 47. Berlin Express 48. The House on Telegraph Hill 51. O. Henry's Full House 52. *Inferno* (3-D) 53. New Faces 54. White Feather 55. The Proud Ones 56. *The Killing* 56. Band of Angels 57. Murder by Contract 58. Al Capone 59. Pay or Die 60. The Parent Trap 61. Ride the High Country 62. *The Caretakers* (AAN) 63. The New Interns 64. Boeing Boeing 65. Nevada Smith 66. *Hour of the Gun* 67. Will Penny 68. *The Wild Bunch* 69. True Grit 69. The Ballad of Cable Hogue 70. The Hawaiians 70. What's the Matter with Helen? 71. Junior Bonner 72. The Getaway 72. Breakout 75. Breakheart Pass 76. St Ives 76, etc.

Ballhaus, Michael (1935–)
German cinematographer who worked on many of FASSBINDER's films before moving to Hollywood in the 80s.
Whity 70. Adele Spitzeder 72. The Bitter Tears of Petra von Kant/Die Bitteren Tränen der Petra von Kant 72. Adolf und Marlene 77. Despair 78. The Marriage of Maria Braun/Die Ehe der Maria Braun 79. Malou 81. Reckless 84. Heartbreakers 84. After Hours 85. The Color of Money 86. Under the Cherry Moon 86. Broadcast News (AAN) 87. The House on Carroll Street 88. Dirty Rotten Scoundrels 88. The Last Temptation of Christ 88. Working Girl 88. The Fabulous Baker Boys (AAN) 89. GoodFellas 90. Postcards from the Edge 90. Guilty by Suspicion 90. What about Bob? 91. The Mambo Kings 92. Bram Stoker's Dracula 92. The Age of Innocence 93. I'll Do Anything 94. Quiz Show 94. Outbreak 95. Sleepers 96. Air Force One 97. Primary Colors 98. Wild Wild West 99. What Planet Are You From? 00. The Legend of Bagger Vance 00, etc.

Ballin, Hugo (1879–1956)
American director and art director of silents. He studied in Rome and was a noted portrait and mural painter. Many of the films he directed starred his wife Mabel Ballin (1885–1958). Retired from films in the late 20s.
Baby Mine (co-d) 17. Jane Eyre 21. East Lynne 21. Vanity Fair 23. The Shining Adventure 25. *The Love of Sunya* (art d only) 27. The Princess and the Pirate (art consultant) 44, etc.

Balmain, Pierre (1914–1982)
French fashion designer who set up his own couture business in the 50s and worked on more than 70 films.
Sabrina (US) 54. Funny Face (US) 56. Bonsoir Paris 56. The Glass Tower/Der Glaserne Turm (Ger.) 57. Paris Holiday (US) 57. The Reluctant Debutante (US) 58. The Millionairess (GB) 60. The Roman Spring of Mrs Stone (GB) 61. Tender Is the Night (GB) 61. Two Weeks in Another Town (US) 62. Love Is a Funny Thing/Un Homme qui Me Plaît 69, etc.

Balsam, Martin (1919–1996)
American character actor of quiet and comfortable presence: range varies from executive to stagecoach driver.
■ On the Waterfront 54. *Twelve Angry Men* 57. *Time Limit* 57. Marjorie Morningstar 58. Al Capone 59. Middle of the Night 59. Everybody Go Home (It.) 60. *Psycho* (as the ill-fated private detective) 60. Ada 61. Breakfast at Tiffany's 61. Cape Fear 61. The Captive City 63. Who's Been Sleeping in My Bed? 63. *The Carpetbaggers* (as the Louis B. Mayer type studio chief) 64. Youngblood Hawke 64. *Seven Days in May* 64. Harlow 65. The Bedford Incident 65. *A Thousand Clowns* (AA) 65. After the Fox 66. Hombre 67. Me Natalie 69. Trilogy (TV) 69. *The Good Guys and the Bad Guys* 69. Tora! Tora! Tora! 70. Catch 22 70. Little Big Man 70. The Old Man Who Cried Wolf (TV) 70. Hunters Are for Killing (TV) 70. *The Anderson Tapes* 71. Confessions of a Police Commissioner (It.) 71. The Man (TV) 72. Night of Terror (TV) 72. *Summer Wishes Winter Dreams* 73. The Stone Killer 73. Six Million Dollar Man (TV) 73. Money to Burn (TV) 74. Trapped Beneath the Sea (TV) 74. The Taking of Pelham 123 74. Murder on the Orient Express 74. Miles to Go Before I Sleep (TV) 75. Corruption in the Halls of Justice (It.) 75. Mitchell 75. Death Among Friends (TV) 75. All the President's Men 76. Two Minute Warning 76. The Sentinel 76. Raid on Entebbe (TV) 77. Silver Bears 77. Rainbow (TV) 78. The Seeding of Sarah Burns (TV) 79. The House on Garibaldi Street (TV) 79. Aunt Mary (TV) 79. The Love Tapes (TV) 79. Cuba 79. There Goes the Bride 80. The Salamander 81. Little Gloria ... Happy at Last (TV) 82. The Goodbye People 84. St Elmo's Fire 85. Death Wish 3 85. Delta Force 86. Space (TV) 87. Queenie (TV) 87. Private Investigations 87. Two Evil Eyes/Due Occhi Diabolici 89. Cape Fear 91. Innocent Prey 92. The Silence of the Hams (It.) 94.
TV series: Archie Bunker's Place 79–81.

Balser, Ewald (1898–1978)
Austrian character actor in German films.
Rembrandt (title role) 42. The Last Act 48. Eroica (as Beethoven) 49. William Tell 56. Jedermann 62, many others.

Balto (1921–1933)
The lead husky in a sled team that brought an anti-diphtheria vaccine to the stricken town of Nome, Alaska, in 1925, he and the other dogs starred in a silent film, *Balto's Race to Nome*. They were briefly a vaudeville and sideshow attraction before spending the remainder of their lives at Cleveland Zoo. *Balto*, an animated feature in which he is depicted as a cross-breed between wolf and dog, was released in 1995, directed by Simon Wells. A commemorative statue to Balto stands in New York's Central Park.

Baluev, Alexander (1958–)
Russian leading actor, also in Hollywood movies. He studied at the Moscow Arts Theatre School and began on stage.
The Kerosene Seller's Wife 89. Richard the Lionheart/Richard Lvinoe Serdce 92. Rycar Kennet. The Muslim/Musul'manin 95. Ligne De Vie 96. The Peacemaker (US) 97. Deep Impact (US) 98. Mu-Mu 99. Moscow/Moskva 99. Proof of Life (US) 00, etc.

Bancroft, Anne (1931–) (Anna Maria Italiano)
Warm, ambitious and effective American leading actress who after TV experience went to Hollywood in 1952 and made inferior routine films; fled to Broadway stage and after triumph in *The Miracle Worker* returned to films as a star. She married Mel BROOKS in 1964.
Don't Bother to Knock 52. Treasure of the Golden Condor 52. Tonight We Sing 53. The Kid from Left Field 53. Demetrius and the Gladiators 54. The Raid 54. Gorilla at Large 54. A Life in the Balance 54. New York Confidential 55. The Naked Street 55. Walk the Proud Land 56. Nightfall 56. Savage Wilderness/The Last Frontier 56. The Restless Breed 57. The Girl in Black Stockings 57. So Soon to Die (TV) 57. *The Miracle Worker* (AA, BFA) 62. *The Pumpkin Eater* (AAN, BFA) 64. *The Slender Thread* 65. Seven Women 66. *The Graduate* (AAN) 67. *Young Winston* 72. The Prisoner of Second Avenue 75. The Hindenburg 76. Lipstick 76. Silent Movie 76. Jesus of Nazareth (TV) 77. *The Turning Point* (AAN) 77. The Elephant Man 80. Fatso (also directed) 80. Marco Polo (TV) 81. To Be or Not to Be 83. Garbo Talks 84. Agnes of God (AAN) 85. Night Mother 86. *84 Charing Cross Road* 86. Torch Song Trilogy 88. Bert Rigby, You're a Fool 89. Broadway Bound (TV) 91. Honeymoon in Vegas 92. Love Potion No. 9 92. Malice 93. Point of No Return 93. Mr Jones 93. Oldest Living Confederate Widow Tells All (TV) 94. How to Make an American Quilt 95. Home for the Holidays 95. Dracula: Dead and Loving It 95. The Sunchaser 96. Great Expectations 97. G.I. Jane 97. Critical Care 97. Antz (voice) 98. Keeping the Faith 00, etc.

Bancroft, George (1882–1956)
Burly American actor who after a period in the Navy became popular in Broadway musicals and straight plays. Went to Hollywood in the 20s and found his strong masculine personality much in demand for tough or villainous roles, almost always in run-of-the-mill films.
The Journey's End 21. *Driven* 21. *Pony Express* 25. *Code of the West* 25. *Old Ironsides* 26. *Underworld* 27. White Gold 27. Docks of New York 28. Thunderbolt (AAN) 29. Derelict 30. Ladies Love Brutes 30. Scandal Sheet 31. Lady and Gent 33. Blood Money 33. Mr Deeds Goes to Town 36. John Meade's Woman 37. Angels with Dirty Faces 38. *Stagecoach* 39. Each Dawn I Die 39. Young Tom Edison 40. Texas 41. Syncopation 41. Whistling in Dixie 42, many others.
❝ When words roll from his tongue, you expect them to be punctuated by lightning. – *N.Y. Times, 1929*

Band, Albert (1924–) (Alfredo Antonini)
Italian-born director and producer, in Hollywood since the 40s.
The Young Guns 56. I Bury the Living (& p) 57. Face of Fire 59. I Pascali Rossi 63. The Tramplers (& p) 66. A Minute to Pray, a Second to Die (p, co-w only) 68. Dracula's Dog 77. She Came to the Valley 79. Ghoulies II 88. Honey, I Blew Up the Kid (p) 92. Prehysteria (co-d) 93. Dragon World (co-p) 93, etc.

Band, Charles (1952–)
American producer and director of low-budget horror movies, many of them released direct to video. The son of Albert Band, he is founder of the production company Full Moon Entertainment.
AS PRODUCER: Ghoulies 85. Re-Animator 85. Crawlspace (ex p) 86. Troll (ex p) 86. Eliminators 86. Catacombs 87. Puppetmaster 89. Puppetmaster II 90. Puppetmaster III 91. Netherworld 91. Bad Channels 91. Demonic Toys 91. Arcade 92. Dragon World 93. Oblivion (& story) 94, etc.
AS DIRECTOR: Crash! 77. Parasite 82. Metalstorm: The Destruction of Jared-Syn 83. The Dungeonmaster (co-d) 85. Future Cop 85. Trancers 85. Pulsepounders 88. Meridian: Kiss of the Beast 90. Trancers II 91. Doctor Modrid (co-d) 91. Trancers III 92. Prehysteria (co-d) 93, etc.

Band, Richard H. (1953–)
American composer, the son of Albert Band.
Laserblast 78. The Day Time Ended 79. Dr Heckle and Mr Hype 80. Parasite 82. Time Walker 83. Ghoulies 85. Re-Animator 85. Eliminators 86. Terrorvision 86. Troll 86. Dolls 87. Prison 88. Puppet Master 89. Bride of Re-Animator 90. Doctor Mordrid: Master of the Unknown 90. Crash and Burn 90. The Resurrected 91. The Pit and the Pendulum 91. Remote 93. Doll vs Demonic Toys 93. Shrunken Heads 94. Dragonworld 94. Magic Island 95. Castle Freak 95. Head of the Family 96. Hideous 97, etc.

Banderas, Antonio (1960–)
Spanish leading actor, associated with the films of Pedro ALMODÓVAR. Married actress Melanie GRIFFITH in 1996 and began a career in Hollywood.
Labyrinth of Passion/Laberinto de Pasiones 82. The Stilts/Los Zancos 84. Matador 86. The Law of Desire/La Ley del Deseo 87. Baton Rouge 88. Women on the Verge of a Nervous Breakdown/ Mujeres al Borde de un Ataque de Nervios 88. Baton Rouge 88. Tie Me Up! Tie Me Down! / ¡Atame!90. Cuentos de Borges I 91. The Mambo Kings 92. A Woman in the Rain/Una Mujer bajo la Lluvia 92. Il Giovane Mussolini (as Mussolini) 93. ¡Dispara! 93. Philadelphia 93. Of Love and Shadows 94. Interview with the Vampire 94. Miami Rhapsody 95. Desperado 95. Four Rooms 95. Assassins 95. Never Talk to Strangers 95. Two Much 96. Evita (as Che Guevara) 96. The Mask of Zorro 98. The 13th Warrior 99. Crazy in Alabama 99. Play It To The Bone 99, etc.

Banerjee, Victor (1946–)
Indian leading actor, occasionally in international films.
The Chess Players/Shatranj Ke Khilari 77. Hullabaloo over Georgie and Bonnie's Pictures 78. A Passage to India 84. The Home and the World/ Ghare Baire 84. Foreign Body 86. World Within, World Without/Mahaprithivi 91. Bitter Moon 92, etc.

Bankhead, Tallulah (1903–1968)
Gravel-voiced, highly theatrical leading lady of American stage and screen. The daughter of an eminent politician, she titillated Broadway and London in the 20s by her extravagant performance on stage and off, and later tended to fritter away her considerable talents by living too dangerously. Films never managed to contain her. Married actor John Emery (1937–41).
Autobiography: 1952, *Tallulah*.
Biography: 1972, *Miss Tallulah Bankhead* by Lee Israel. 1972, *Tallulah, Darling of the Gods: An Intimate Portrait* by Kieran Tunney. 1979, *Tallulah: A Memory* by Eugenia Rawls. 1996, *A Scandalous Life* by David Bret.
■ When Men Betray 18. Thirty a Week 18. A Woman's Law 28. His House in Order 28. *Tarnished Lady* 31. My Sin 31. The Cheat 31. Thunder Below 32. The Devil and the Deep 32. Faithless 32. Make Me a Star 32. Stage Door Canteen 43. *Lifeboat* 43. *A Royal Scandal* 45. Main Street to Broadway 53. *Fanatic* (GB) 65.
❝ She said of herself: 'I'm as pure as the driven slush.'
What one remembers about Miss Bankhead is not her merit as a performer, which in her heyday was considerable, but rather her well-publicized lifestyle, which kept her in the headlines throughout the 20s and 30s. As Mrs Patrick Campbell said: 'Tallulah is always skating on thin ice. Everyone wants to be there when it breaks.'
The lady herself issued such statements as: 'Cocaine isn't habit-forming. I should know – I've been using it for years.'
As a result, in her later years: 'They used to photograph Shirley Temple through gauze. They should photograph me through linoleum.'
But it was more sad than funny when someone asked: 'Are you really the famous Tallulah?',
and got the answer: 'What's left of her.'
She concluded: 'The only thing I regret about my past is the length of it. If I had it to live over again I'd make the same mistakes, only sooner.'
Sooner or later she alienated most of her friends. Howard Dietz was the one who said: 'A day away from Tallulah is like a month in the country.'

Bankolé, Isaach de (1958–)
Ivory Coast-born actor and comedian.
Black and White/Noir et Blanc (Fr.) 86. Chocolate/Chocolat (Fr.) 88. How to Make Love to a Negro without Getting Tired/Comment Faire l'Amour avec un Nègre sans Se Fatiguer 89. S'en Fout la Mort (Fr.) 90. Night on Earth (US) 92. Heart of Darkness (US) (TV) 92. Down to Earth/ Casa de Lava 94. The Keeper (US) 96. Ghost Dog: The Way of the Samurai (US) 99, etc.

Banks, Don (1923–1981)
Australian composer in Britain.
Captain Clegg 62. The Punch and Judy Man 62. Hysteria 65. Die Monster Die 65. The Reptile 66. The Mummy's Shroud 67. The Torture Garden 68, etc.

Banks, Leslie (1890–1952)
Distinguished British stage actor who after unsuccessful experiments in home-grown silent films started his film career in Hollywood. His sophistication seemed to be enhanced by his war-scarred profile.
■ *The Most Dangerous Game* 32. Strange Evidence 32. The Fire-Raisers 33. I am Suzanne 33. Night of the Party 34. The Red Ensign 34. *The Man Who Knew Too Much* 34. The Tunnel 35. *Sanders of the River* 35. Debt of Honour 36. The Three Maxims 37. Fire over England 37. Farewell Again 37. Wings of the Morning 37. *Twenty-one Days* 37. Jamaica Inn 39. Dead Man's Shoes 39. The Arsenal Stadium 39. Sons of the Sea 39. Busman's Honeymoon 40. The Door with Seven Locks 40. Neutral Port 40. Ships with Wings 41. Cottage to Let 41. The Big Blockade 42. Went the Day Well? 42. *Henry V* (as Chorus) 44. Mrs Fitzherbert 47. The Small Back Room 49. Madeleine 49. Your Witness 50.

Banks, Lionel
American art director who worked for Columbia from the mid-30s.
Public Hero 35. Holiday (AAN) 38. Mr Smith Goes to Washington (AAN) 39. You Can't Take It with You 38. Golden Boy 39. Coast Guard 39. Before I Hang 40. Arizona (AAN) 40. Too Many

Husbands 40. Ladies in Retirement (AAN) 41. The Blonde from Singapore 41. The Devil Commands 41. You'll Never Get Rich 41. Cadets on Parade 42. Hello, Annapolis 42. The Talk of the Town (AAN) 42. A Night to Remember 42. You Were Never Lovelier 42. The Devil's Trail 43. Is Everybody Happy? 43. The Return of the Vampire 43. Address Unknown (AAN) 44. Cover Girl (AAN) 44. Guest Wife 45. So Goes My Love 46. Magic Town 47. Moonrise 48, etc.

Banks, Monty (1897–1950) (Mario Bianchi)
Italian comic dancer who appeared in many silent two-reel comedies of the 20s then moved to Britain and later turned director. He was married to Gracie Fields.
Atlantic 30. Weekend Wives 31. Almost a Honeymoon (d) 31. Tonight's the Night (d) 32. No Limit (d) 35. We're Going to be Rich (d) 38. Great Guns (US) (d) 41, etc.

Banks, Russell (1940–)
American novelist and academic. Born in Newton, Massachusetts, and brought up in New Hampshire, he graduated from the University of North Carolina.
The Sweet Hereafter (oa) 97. Affliction (oa) 98. Continental Drift (w, oa) 99, etc.

Banky, Vilma (1898–1991) (Vilma Lonchit)
Austro-Hungarian star of American silents, discovered by Sam Goldwyn during a European holiday. Popular in the 20s but could not make the transition to sound. Married Rod la Rocque.
■ Im Letzen Augenblick (Hung.) 20. Galathea (Hung.) 21. Tavaszi Szerelem (Hung.) 21. Veszelyben a Pokol (Hung.) 21. Kauft Mariett-Aktien (Ger.) 22. Das Auge des Toten (Ger.) 22. Schattenkinder des Glucks (Ger.) 22. Die Letzte Stinde (Ger.) 23. The Forbidden Land (Aust.) 24. Clown aus Liebe (Aust.) 24. The Lady from Paris (Ger.) 24. Das Bildnis (Aust.) 25. Sollman Heiraten (Ger.) 25. *The Dark Angel* 25. The Eagle 25. Son of the Sheik 26. The Winning of Barbara Worth 26. The Night of Love 27. The Magic Flame 27. Two Lovers 28. The Awakening 28. This Is Heaven 29. A Lady to Love 30. De Sehnsucht Jeder Frau (Ger.) 30. The Rebel (Ger.) 33.
❝ She spoke no English at all: for their love scenes in *The Dark Angel*, she spoke in her own language while co-star Ronald Colman chatted away about cricket. – *John Baxter, The Hollywood Exiles*

Bannen, Ian (1928–1999)
Scottish leading actor of stage, screen and TV. Died in a car crash.
Private's Progress 56. The Birthday Present 57. Behind the Mask 58. Carlton Browne of the F.O. 58. She Didn't Say No! 58. A Tale of Two Cities 58. Macbeth 59. *A French Mistress* 60. *Suspect* 60. On Friday at Eleven 60. Station Six Sahara 62. Psyche 59 64. Rotten to the Core 65. *The Hill* 65. The Flight of the Phoenix (AAN) 65. Mister Moses 65. Penelope 66. Sailor from Gibraltar 67. Lock Up Your Daughters 69. Too Late the Hero 69. The Deserter 70. Jane Eyre 70. Fright 71. Doomwatch 72. The Offence 72. From Beyond the Grave 73. The Mackintosh Man 73. Bite the Bullet 75. Sweeney! 76. Bastards Without Glory (It.) 78. The Watcher in the Woods 80. Eye of the Needle 81. Gandhi 82. Night Crossing 82. Gorky Park 83. Defence of the Realm 85. Lamb 86. Hope and Glory 87. The Courier 87. George's Island 89. Ghost Dad 90. The Big Man 90. Damage 92. A Pin for the Butterfly 94. The Politician's Wife (TV) 95. Braveheart 95. Something to Believe In 97. Waking Ned 98. To Walk with Lions 99. Best 99. The Testimony of Taliesin Jones 00, etc.
TV series: Doctor Finlay 93–96.

Banner, John (1910–1973)
American character actor of Polish origin; usually played explosive Europeans.
Once Upon a Honeymoon 42. The Fallen Sparrow 43. Black Angel 47. My Girl Tisa 48. The Juggler 53. The Rains of Ranchipur 56. The Story of Ruth 60. Hitler 63. Thirty-six Hours 64, etc.
TV series: *Hogan's Heroes* 65–70. Chicago Teddy Bears 71.

Bannerman, Celia (1944–)
English actress and theatre director.
The Tamarind Seed 74. Biddy (title role) 83. Little Dorrit 87. As You Like It 92, etc.

Bannon, Jim (1911–1984)
American actor with radio experience: played second feature leads in the 40s and starred in a western series as 'Red Ryder' in the 50s.
The Missing Juror 44. I Love a Mystery 45. The Thirteenth Hour 47. Daughter of the Jungle 49. The Man from Colorado 49. Rodeo 53. Chicago Confidential 58. Madame X 65, many others.
TV series: Adventures of Champion 55–56.

Banton, Travis (1894–1958)
American costume designer, long at Paramount, noted for dressing Mae West and Marlene Dietrich. Because of his heavy drinking, he was forced to leave the studio in 1938.
The Wild Party 29. Morocco 29. The Vagabond King 30. Dishonored 31. Shanghai Express 32. *The Scarlet Empress* 34. *The Devil Is a Woman* 35. The Crusades 35. Maid of Salem 37. Angel 37. Letter from an Unknown Woman 48, etc.

Bar, Jacques (1921–)
French producer, often in association with American companies.
Where the Hot Wind Blows 60. Vie Privée 61. A Monkey in Winter 62. Joy House 64. Once a Thief 65. The Guns of San Sebastian 67. The Mysterious Island of Captain Nemo 73, etc.

Bara, Nina (1925–1990)
Argentinian actress, best remembered for her role as Tonga in TV's children's series *Space Patrol* 51–52.
Missile to the Moon 58, etc.

Bara, Theda (1890–1955) (Theodosia Goodman)
American actress, the first to be called a 'vamp' (because of her absurdly vampirish, man-hungry screen personality). An extra in 1915, she was whisked to stardom on some highly imaginary publicity statistics (she was the daughter of an Eastern potentate, her name was an anagram of 'Arab death', etc.). *A Fool There Was* 15 is remembered for its classic sub-title, 'Kiss Me, My Fool!'; in 1919, her popularity waning, she forsook Hollywood for the Broadway stage, and when she returned in 1925 was forced to accept parts burlesquing her former glories, e.g. *Madame Mystery* 26. Wisely, she soon retired. Married director Charles Brabin in 1921.
Biography: 1998, *Vamp: The Rise and Fall of Theda Bara* by Eve Golden.
■ The Two Orphans 15. The Clemenceau Case 15. The Stain 15. Lady Audley's Secret 15. *A Fool There Was* 15. The Vixen 16. Sin 16. Carmen 16. Romeo and Juliet 16. The Light 16. Destruction 16. Gold and the Woman 16. The Serpent 16. Eternal Sappho 16. East Lynne 16. Her Double Life 16. *Cleopatra* 17. Madame Du Barry 17. Under Two Flags 17. Camille 17. Heart and Soul 17. The Tiger Woman 17. Salome 18. When a Woman Sins 18. The Forbidden Path 18. The She Devil 18. Rose of the Blood 18. Kathleen Mavourneen 19. La Belle Russe 19. When Men Desire 19. The Siren's Song 19. A Woman There Was 20. The Price of Silence 21. Her Greatest Love 21. The Hunchback of Notre Dame 23. The Unchastened Woman 25. Madame Mystery 26. The Dancer of Paris 26.
❝ She was divinely, hysterically, insanely malevolent. – *Bette Davis*
She made voluptuousness a common American commodity, as accessible as chewing gum. – *Lloyd Morris*

Baranski, Christine (1952–)
American actress, best known for her Emmy-winning role in the TV sitcom *Cybill*. Born in Buffalo, New York, she studied at the Juilliard School; married actor Matthew Cowles.
Crackers 83. Lovesick 83. $9\frac{1}{2}$ Weeks 84. Legal Eagles 86. House of Blue Leaves 87. Reversal of Fortune 90. The Night We Never Met 93. The Ref/Hostile Hostages 94. The War 94. New Jersey Drive 95. Jeffrey 95. The Birdcage 96. The Odd Couple II 98. Bulworth 98. Bowfinger 98. Cruel Intentions 99, etc.
TV series: Cybill 95–98.

Baratier, Jacques (1918–)
French director of shorts and occasional features, a former theatre critic.
Paris la Nuit 55. Goha 57. La Poupée 62. Dragées au Poivre 63. L'Or du Duc 65. Le Désordre à Vingt Ans 67. La Décharge 70, etc.

Barbara (1930–1997) (Monique Serf)
French cabaret singer and composer, and occasional actress. Born in Paris, the daughter of a Polish mother and a Russian father, she studied voice and piano at the Paris Conservatoire before working in Brussels and Paris as a singer, often performing her own songs, which were typically about the end of a love affair.
Franz 71. Das Ganze Leben (Swiss) 83. The Book (US) 90, etc.

Barbeau, Adrienne (1945–)
American leading actress, mostly on TV. Married (1979–84) director John Carpenter and producer and writer Billy Van Zandt.
Red Alert (TV) 77. Someone's Watching Me (TV) 78. The Disappearance of Flight 401 (TV) 79. The Fog 79. Escape from New York 81. Swamp Thing 81. Creep Show 82. The Next One 84. Seduced 85. Back to School 86. Two Evil Eyes/Due Occhi Diabolici 89. Cannibal Women in the Avocado Jungle of Death 89. Doublecrossed (TV) 91. Silk Degrees 94. Burial of the Rats (TV) 95, etc.
TV series: Maude 72–78.

Barber, Frances (1958–)
English actress, born in Wolverhampton, Staffordshire.
The Missionary 81. Zed and Two Noughts 85. Castaway 86. Prick Up Your Ears 87. Sammy and Rosie Get Laid 87. We Think the World of You 88. The Grasscutter 89. Secret Friends 91. Young Soul Rebels 91. Soft Top, Hard Shoulder 92. Germaine et Benjamin (Fr.) 94. Rhodes (TV) 97. The Ice House (TV) 97. Photographing Fairies 97. Still Crazy 98. Shiner 00, etc.

Barber, Glynis (1955–)
South African leading lady in Britain. Became popular on TV in Dempsey and Makepeace 85.
The Wicked Lady 83. Edge of Sanity 88. Déjà Vu (US) 97, etc.

Barbera, Joe (1911–)
American animator who with William Hanna created Tom and Jerry at MGM in 1937 and controlled the output until 1957: 'the cinema's purest representation of pure energy'. Later formed an independent company which produced dozens of 'semi-animated' cartoon series for TV, including the adventures of Yogi Bear, Huckleberry Hound, the Jetsons, the Flintstones, Magilla Gorilla, Scooby Doo and Snagglepuss.

Barbier, George (1864–1945)
American character actor remembered in talkies as a blustery but essentially kindly old man.
Monsieur Beaucaire 24. The Big Pond 30. The Sap from Syracuse 30. The Smiling Lieutenant 31. No Man of her Own 32. One Hour with You 32. Million Dollar Legs 32. The Big Broadcast 32. Mama Loves Papa 33. Tillie and Gus 34. Ladies Should Listen 34. *The Merry Widow* 34. The Crusades 35. The Cat's Paw 35. The Milky Way 36. The Princess Comes Across 36. *On the Avenue* 37. Hotel Haywire 37. Tarzan's Revenge 38. Little Miss Broadway 38. Sweethearts 38. News is Made at Night 39. The Return of Frank James 40. *The Man Who Came to Dinner* 41. Weekend in Havana 41. The Magnificent Dope 42. Song of the Islands 42. Hello Frisco Hello 43. Weekend Pass 44. Her Lucky Night 45, many others.

Barbieri, Gato (1934–) (Leandro Barbieri)
Argentinian jazz saxophonist and composer. Born in Rosario, he moved to Rome in the early 60s and worked in Europe for a decade before returning to Buenos Aires.
Before the Revolution (It.) 64. Last Tango in Paris (& a) (It.) 73. The Pig's War 75. Firepower (GB) 79. Stranger's Kiss (US) 83. Diario di un Vizio (It.) 93. Manhattan by Numbers 94. Calle 54 (Sp./Fr.) 00, etc.

Barclay, Don (1892–1975)
Chubby American character actor, on screen from 1914.
Frisco Kid 35. Man Hunt 36. I Cover the War 37. Outlaw Express 38. The Oklahoma Kid 39. The Falcon's Brother 42. Frankenstein Meets the Wolf Man 43. Shine On Harvest Moon 44. My Darling Clementine 46. Mr Perrin and Mr Traill 48. The Long Gray Line 55. A Hundred and One Dalmatians (voice) 61. Mary Poppins 64. Half a Sixpence 68, etc.

Barcroft, Roy (1902–1969) (Howard H. Ravenscroft)
American character actor, usually as a villain in westerns. Born in Crab Orchard, Nebraska, he worked in various jobs, as a soldier, sailor, truck driver and musician, before turning to acting in his thirties. He made more than 200 westerns as a heavy, mellowing into a crotchety bystander in his later movies. Died of cancer.
Mata Hari 32. Dick Tracy (serial) 37. The Frontiersmen 38. Renegade Trail 39. Ragtime Cowboy Joe 40. Flash Gordon Conquers the Universe (serial) 40. The Showdown 40. Jesse James at Bay 41. They Died with Their Boots On 41. Sunset Serenade 42. Sagebrush Law 43. Calling Wild Bill Elliott 43. Hoppy Serves a Writ 43. Cheyenne Wildcat 44. Wagon Wheels Westward 45. The Purple Monster Strikes (serial) 45. Alias Billy the Kid 46. My Pal Trigger 46. Stagecoach to Reno 47. Jesse James Rides Again (serial) 47. Son of Zorro (serial) 47. Sundown at Santa Fe 48. San Antone Ambush 49. North of the Great Divide 50. The Vanishing Westerner 50. Dakota Kid 51. Flying Disc Men from Mars (serial) 51. Oklahoma Annie 52. Marshall of Cedar Rock 53. Two Guns and a Badge 54. Man without a Star 55. The Last Hunt 56. Billy the Kid vs Dracula 65. Texas across the River 66. The Way West 67. Bandolero! 68. The Reivers 69. Gaily, Gaily 69, many others.
❝ I liked the roles best where I could be the dirtiest, meanest, unkempt individual possible. – *R.B.*

Bardem, Javier (1969–)
Spanish leading actor, in international films. He is the son of Spanish actress Pilar Bardem and nephew of director Juan-Antonio Bardem.
The Ages of Lulu/Las Edades de Lulú 90. High Heels/Tacones Lejanos 91.Jamón Jamón 92. Golden Balls/Huevos De Oro 93. The Tit and the Moon/La Teta i La Lluna 94. Mouth to Mouth/Boca a Boca 95. Ecstasy/Extasis 96. Live Flesh/Carne Tremula 97. Perdita Durango 97. Between Your Legs/Entre Las Piernas 99. Washington Wolves/ Los Lobos de Washington 99. Before Night Falls (US) (AAN) 00, etc.

Bardem, Juan-Antonio (1922–)
Spanish director and screenwriter, jailed in the 70s for political activities as a member of the Communist party; until the mid-80s he was unable to find work in Spain.
Welcome Mr Marshall (w) 52. *Death of a Cyclist* 54. Calle Mayor 56. Vengeance 57. Sonatas 59. Los Inocentes 62. Los Pianos Mecanicos 64. The Uninhibited 68. Variétés 71. Behind the Shutters 74. The Dog 77. Lorca, la Muerta de un Poeta 87, etc.

Bardette, Trevor (1902–1977)
American character actor, usually seen as western villain.
They Won't Forget 37. The Oklahoma Kid 39. Dark Command 40. The Moon Is Down 43. The Whistler 44. The Big Sleep 46. Song of India 49. The Texas Rangers 51. Lone Star 52. The Desert Song 53. Destry 54. The Man from Bitter Ridge 55. The Hard Man 57. The Mating Game 59. Papa's Delicate Condition 63. Mackenna's Gold 69, many others.

Bardot, Brigitte (1934–)
Pulchritudinous French pin-up girl who, given world publicity as a 'sex kitten', used her small but significant talents to make some routine movies very profitable. Her early career was orchestrated by her first husband, director Roger Vadim. Later she was often a reluctant star and attempted suicide on at least one occasion, becoming reclusive and, in 1986, setting up a foundation to care for the welfare of animals. (In 1997, she was fined 10,000 francs for inciting racial hatred, after criticizing the Muslim ritual slaughter of sheep.) Married actor Jacques Charrier, millionaire Gunter Sachs, and Bernard d'Ormale, who had connections with the right-wing National Front. Her lovers included singers Serge Gainsbourg and Sacha Distel and actor Jean-Louis Trintignant.
Biography: 1994, *Bardot: Two Lives* by Jeffrey Robinson.
Act of Love 54. Doctor at Sea (GB) 55. *The Light Across the Street* 55. Helen of Troy 55. *And God Created Woman* 57. Heaven Fell That Night 58. Une Parisienne 57. Please Mr Balzac 57. *En Cas de Malheur* 58. The Devil is a Woman 58. Mam'zelle Pigalle 58. Babette Goes to War 59.

Please Not Now 61. *The Truth* 61. *Vie Privée* 61. *Love on a Pillow* 62. *Contempt* 63. Dear Brigitte 65. *Viva Maria* 65. Two Weeks in September 67. Shalako 68. *The Novices* 70. The Legend of Frenchy King 72. Don Juan 73, etc.

❝ For twenty years I was cornered and hounded like an animal. I didn't throw myself off my balcony only because I knew people would photograph me lying dead. – *B.B.*

I started out as a lousy actress and have remained one. – *B.B.*

France's most ogled export. – *Time 1956*

It was the first time on the screen that a woman was shown as really free on a sexual level, with none of the guilt attached to nudity or carnal pleasure. – *Roger Vadim*

The cinema means nothing to me. I cannot remember it. – *BB in 1994*

Bare, Richard (1909–)
American director who moved into TV.
Smart Girls Don't Talk 48. Flaxy Martin 48. The House Across the Street 49. Return of the Frontiersman 50. This Side of the Law 51. Prisoners of the Casbah 53. Shoot-Out at Medicine Bend 57. This Rebel Breed 60. I Sailed to Tahiti with an All-Girl Crew 67. Wicked, Wicked 73, etc.

Bari, Lynn (1913–1989) (Marjorie Fisher; aka Marjorie Bitzer)
Pert American 'second lead', often in 'other woman' roles. A chorus graduate, she was given plenty of work in the 30s and 40s but almost all of it was routine.
Dancing Lady 33. Stand Up and Cheer 34. Thanks a Million 35. Sing Baby Sing 36. Wee Willie Winkie 37. Josette 38. Return of the Cisco Kid 39. Hollywood Cavalcade 39. Earthbound 40. *Sun Valley Serenade* 41. *Moon Over Her Shoulder* 41. *The Magnificent Dope* 42. *Orchestra Wives* 42. Hello Frisco Hello 43. *The Bridge of San Luis Rey* 44. Tampico 44. Captain Eddie 45. Shock 45. *Margie* 46. The Man from Texas 48. On the Loose 51. Has Anybody Seen My Gal? 52. Francis Joins the WACS 54. Women of Pitcairn Island 56. Damn Citizen 58. Trauma 64. The Young Runaways 68, many others.
TV series: Boss Lady 52.

Baring, Norah (1907–) (Norah Baker)
British leading lady.
Underground 28. Cottage on Dartmoor 29. At the Villa Rose 30. Escape from Dartmoor 30. Murder 30. The Lyons Mail 31. Strange Evidence 32. The House of Trent 33, etc.

Barker, Bradley (1883–1951)
American actor in silent films and animal impersonator who first supplied the roars for Leo, the MGM's trademark lion.
Erstwhile Susan 19. Adam and Eva 23. Into the Net (serial) 24. The Early Bird 25. The Brown Derby 26. The Potters 27. The Ape 28, etc.

Barker, Clive (1952–)
British horror author, screenwriter and director.
Underworld (co-w) 85. Rawhead Rex (oa) 87. Hellraiser (wd) 87. Transmutations (w) 88. Nightbreed (wd) 89. Sleepwalkers (a) 92. Candy Man (oa) 92. Hellraiser III: Hell on Earth (p) 92. Candyman: Farewell to the Flesh (ex p, story) 95. Lord of Illusions (wd) 95. Hellraiser: Bloodline (ex p) 96, etc.
TV series: Clive Barker's A–Z of Horror 97.

❝ True horror is seeing my stories turned into poor films. – *C.B.*

Barker, Eric (1912–1990)
British character comedian long popular on radio with his wife Pearl Hackney. A stroke in his early fifties brought his film career to an end.
Autobiography: 1956, *Steady Barker*.
Carry On London 37. Concert Party 37. On Velvet 38. *Brothers in Law* 57. Blue Murder at St Trinians 57.Happy Is the Bride 57. Bachelor of Hearts 58. Carry On Sergeant 58. Left Right and Centre 59. Carry On Constable 60. Dentist in the Chair 60. The Pure Hell of St Trinian's 60. Watch Your Stern 60. Dentist on the Job 61. Nearly a Nasty Accident 61. On the Fiddle 61. Raising the Wind 61. Carry On Cruising 62. The Bargee 64. Carry On Spying 64. Doctor in Clover 66. The Great St Trinian's Train Robbery 66. Maroc 7 67. Carry On Emmannuelle 78, etc.

Barker, Jess (1914–)
Lightweight American leading man of minor 40s films. He was married (1944-1954) to actress Susan Hayward.
Cover Girl 44. Keep Your Powder Dry 44. This Love of Ours 45. Take One False Step 49. Shack Out on 101 56. The Night Walker 65, etc.

Barker, Lex (1919–1973)
Blond, virile-looking American actor who in 1948 was signed to play Tarzan. After five films the role passed to another actor and Barker's stock slumped, but he continued to make routine action adventures. His five wives included actresses Arlene Dahl (1951–53) and Lana Turner (1953–57). Died of a heart attack.
Dick Tracy Meets Gruesome 47. Mr Blandings Builds His Dream House 48. Tarzan's Magic Fountain 49. Tarzan and the Slave Girl 50. Tarzan's Peril 51. Tarzan's Savage Fury 52. Battles of Chief Pontiac 53. Tarzan and the She-Devil 53. Thunder over the Plains 53. The Yellow Mountain 54. Duel on the Mississippi 55. The Man from Bitter Ridge 55. Away All Boats 56. The Price of Fear 56. The Girl in Black Stockings 57. The Girl in the Kremlin 57. Mission in Morocco 59. La Dolce Vita 60. Executioner of Venice 63. The Blood Demon 67. Woman Times Seven 67. Winnetou and Shatterhand 68, etc.

Barker, Ma (1880–1935) (Kate Barker)
Notorious American outlaw of the 30s, who with her four sons terrorized the central states before being shot in Florida. She was played by Jean Harvey in *Guns Don't Argue* 55, Lurene Tuttle in *Ma Barker's Killer Brood* 60, Shelley Winters in *Bloody Mama* 70, and Claire Trevor in an episode of *The Untouchables*. So-called fictional variants were played by Blanche Yurka in *Queen of the Mob* 40, Irene Dailey in *The Grissom Gang* 71 and Angie Dickinson in *Big Bad Mama* 74.

Barker, Mike
English director.
The Tenant of Wildfell Hall (TV) 96. The James Gang 97. Best Laid Plans (US) 99, etc.

Barker, Ronnie (1929–)
Portly but versatile British TV comedian, rarely seen in films; immensely popular in *The Two Ronnies* and *Porridge*. He retired in 1988.
Biography: 1998, *Ronnie Barker, the Authorized Biography* by Bob McCabe.
Doctor in Distress 63. The Bargee 64. The Man Outside 67. *Futtock's End* 70. Robin and Marian 76. Porridge 79, etc.

Barker, Sir Will G. (1867–1951)
Pioneer British producer of the cinema's fairground days. A former salesman and cameraman, he founded the original Ealing studio.
Henry VIII 11. Jim the Fireman 12. Sixty Years a Queen 13. Greater Love Hath No Man 13. The Fighting Parson 14. Jane Shore 15, many others.

Barkin, Ellen (1954–)
American leading actress, usually in sexy roles. Born in the Bronx, New York, she studied at Hunter College and began on stage. She was married (1988–94) to actor Gabriel Byrne.
Diner 82. Tender Mercies 82. Daniel 83. Eddie and the Cruisers 83. Enormous Changes at the Last Minute 83. The Adventures of Buckaroo Banzai Across the Eighth Dimension 84. Harry & Son 84. Terminal Choice 85. Desert Bloom 85. The Big Easy 86. Down by Law 86. Made in Heaven 87. Siesta 87. Clinton and Nadine/Blood Money (TV) 88. Johnny Handsome 89. Sea of Love 89. Switch 91. Into the West 92. Man Trouble 92. This Boy's Life 93. Bad Company 94. Wild Bill 95. The Fan 96. Mad Dog Time/Trigger Happy 96. Fear and Loathing in Las Vegas 98. Drop Dead Gorgeous 99. Mercy 00, etc.

Barks, Carl (1901–2000)
American animator and comic-book artist, credited with refining the appearance of Donald Duck. He also created the character of Scrooge McDuck for the Disney comic books that he drew from the early 40s. He joined Walt Disney as an animator in 1935 and worked on the feature films *Snow White*, *Bambi* and *Fantasia* as well as many shorts. After his retirement in the mid-60s, he turned to making oil paintings and prints of his cartoon characters. Married three times.

Barkworth, Peter (1929–)
Smooth British comedy actor, mostly on TV; very popular in diffident roles.
A Touch of Larceny 59. No Love for Johnnie 60. Play It Cool 62. Two a Penny 67. Where Eagles Dare 69. Escape from the Dark 76. International Velvet 78. Champions 83, etc.
TV series: *Telford's Change* 78.

Barnard, Ivor (1887–1953)
British character actor of stage and screen, often of henpecked or nosey parker types, on stage from 1908.
Waltz Time 33. The Wandering Jew 34. Storm in a Teacup 37. Pygmalion 38. The Saint's Vacation 41. Hotel Reserve 44. The Wicked Lady 45. Great Expectations 46. Oliver Twist 48. *Beat the Devil* (his last and best role, as a vicious killer) 53, many others.

Barnes, Barry K. (1906–1965) (Nelson Barnes)
Stylish British stage actor, in occasional films. Born in London, he worked in his father's store-fitting business before training for the stage at RADA. He was on stage from 1927 and in films from 1937. His second wife was actress Diana Churchill.
The Return of the Scarlet Pimpernel 37. Prison without Bars 38. *This Man Is News* 38. The Ware Case 38. Spies of the Air 39. This Man in Paris 39. The Girl in the News 40. Law and Disorder 40. Bedelia 46. Dancing with Crime 47, etc.
TV series: Silk, Satin, Cotton, Rags 52.

Barnes, Binnie (1905–1998) (Gitelle Barnes)
Self-confident British light actress who, after varied experience, made a few early British talkies, then went to Hollywood in 1934 and played mainly smart, wise-cracking ladies. Married Mike Frankovich.
Love Lies 31. Murder at Covent Garden 31. Heads We Go 33. *The Private Life of Henry VIII* (as Katherine Howard) 33. The Private Life of Don Juan 34. Diamond Jim 35. The Last of the Mohicans 35. The Magnificent Brute 36. *Three Smart Girls* 37. The Adventures of Marco Polo 38. Three Blind Mice 38. The Divorce of Lady X 38. *The Three Musketeers* 39. Till We Meet Again 40. Tight Shoes 41. Skylark 41. *Three Girls About Town* 41. The Man from Down Under 43. Barbary Coast Gent 44. *Up in Mabel's Room* 44. *It's in the Bag* 45. The Spanish Main 45. If Winter Comes 47. My Own True Love 48. Shadow of the Eagle 50. Fugitive Lady 51. Decameron Nights 53. *The Trouble with Angels* 66. Where Angels Go, Trouble Follows 68. Forty Carats 72, many others.

Barnes, George (c. 1880–1949)
American actor whose claim to fame was playing the outlaw who, in close-up, fired his revolver directly at the audience at the end (or, in some versions, the beginning) of *The Great Train Robbery* 03.

Barnes, George (1893–1953)
Distinguished American cinematographer. Married actress Joan Blondell (1933–35).
The Haunted Bedroom 19. Silk Hosiery 21. Hairpins 22. Dusk to Dawn 24. *The Eagle* 25. *Son of the Sheik* 26. Janice Meredith 27. Sadie Thompson 28. Our Dancing Daughters 28. *Bulldog Drummond* 29. The Trespasser 29. *Condemned* 29. Raffles 30. Five and Ten 31. The Unholy Garden 31. Street Scene 31. The Wet Parade 32. Sherlock Holmes 32. Peg O' My Heart 33. *Footlight Parade* 33. Massacre 34. *Dames* 34. Flirtation Walk 34. In Caliente 35. The Singing Kid 36. Black Legion 36. *Marked Woman* 37. Hollywood Hotel 37. Gold Diggers in Paris 38. *Jesse James* 39. *Rebecca* (AA) 40. Devil's Island 40. Hudson's Bay 40. *Meet John Doe* 41. *Ladies in Retirement* 41. Rings on Her Fingers 42. Once Upon a Honeymoon 42. Mr Lucky 43. *Frenchman's Creek* 44. *Jane Eyre* 44. None But the Lonely Heart 44. *Spellbound* 45. The Spanish Main 45. The Bells of St Mary's 45. *From This Day Forward* 46. Sinbad the Sailor 47. Mourning Becomes Electra 47. The Emperor Waltz 48. The Boy with Green Hair 48. *Force of Evil* 49. Let's Dance 50. Mr Music 50. Riding High 50. Here Comes the Groom 51. Something to Live For 52. *The War of the Worlds* 53. Little Boy Lost 53, etc.

Barnes, Joanna (1934–)
American actress occasionally seen in cool supporting roles. Also a novelist.
Home Before Dark 58. Spartacus 60. The Parent Trap 61. Goodbye Charlie 64. The War Wagon 67. B.S. I Love You 70. I Wonder Who's Killing Her Now? 76, etc.

Barnes, Peter (1931–)
British dramatist and screenwriter, a former film critic and story editor.
Offbeat 60. Ring of Spies/Ring of Treason 63. Not with My Wife, You Don't! 66. The Ruling Class 72. Nobody Here But Us Chickens (TV) 89. Spirit of Man (TV) 89. Revolutionary Witness (TV) 89. Enchanted April 91. Bye, Bye Columbus (TV) 92. Hard Times (TV) 94. Voices 95. Merlin (TV) 99. Alice in Wonderland (TV) 99. Noah's Ark (TV) 99. A Christmas Carol (TV) 99, etc.

Barnes, T. Roy (1880–1937)
English-born actor who went to America as a child. He spent 12 years in vaudeville in a comedy act with his wife, Bessie Crawford, and was on stage from 1914.
Scratch My Back 20. Adam and Eva 23. The Great White Way 24. Seven Chances 25. Body and Soul 27. Chicago 27. Dangerous Curves 29. Kansas City Princess 34. It's a Gift 34. The Virginia Judge 35, etc.

Barnet, Charlie (1913–1991)
American bandleader and jazz saxophonist, in films usually as himself. Born in New York, to a wealthy family, he resisted becoming a lawyer to lead a popular swing band in the 30s and 40s. He also made several shorts and soundies. Married many times.
Autobiography: 1984, *Those Swinging Years* (with Stanley Dance).
Love and Hisses (a) 37. Sally, Irene and Mary (a) 38. Juke Box Jenny 42. Syncopation 42. Jam Session (playing his hit recording of 'Cherokee') 44. Music in Manhattan 44. Freddie Steps Out 46. Idea Girl 46. The Fabulous Dorseys 47. A Song Is Born 48. Make Believe Ballroom 49. Bright and Breezy (short) 56. The Big Beat 57. The Swingin' Singin' Years (TV) 60, etc.

Barnett, Vince (1902–1977)
American character actor, usually of minor gangsters or downtrodden little men, from vaudeville. He was previously a professional insulter, hired to be be rude to people at parties. Born in Pittsburgh, Pennsylvania, he was educated at Duquesne University.
Her Man 30. *Scarface* 32. I Cover the Waterfront 33. Dancing Feet 36. A Star Is Born 37. Overland Trail 39. East Side Kids 40. A Dangerous Game 41. Baby Face Morgan 42. Kid Dynamite 43. The Killers 46. Big Town Scandal 48. Mule Train 50. Carson City 52. Springfield Rifle 52. The Quiet Gun 57. The Rookie 59. Dr Goldfoot and the Bikini Machine 65. The Big Mouth 67. Crazy Mama 75, many others.

Barnum, Phineas T. (1810–1891)
American showman who is alleged to have said 'There's one born every minute' of the people who flocked to see his freak shows. He became a multi-millionaire and co-founded the famous Barnum and Bailey Circus. He was played in *A Lady's Morals* 30 and *The Mighty Barnum* 35 by Wallace Beery; in *Rocket to the Moon* 67 by Burl Ives.

Baron, Auguste (1853–1938)
French inventor who patented a method of talking pictures (1896–99) and two multiscreen processes, Cinématorama in 1896 and Multirama in 1912, but failed to find backing for his ideas.

Baron Munchausen
There has been a longish line of movies about the tall story-teller. Méliès made a version in 1911; Emile Cole in 1913; Hans Albers starred in a German version in 1943. Karl Zeman made a semi-animated fantasy in 1962, and John Neville starred in Terry Gilliam's expensive version in 1989. The real Baron (1720–97) was a German army officer, but the collection of stories written by Rudolph Raspe, first published in English in 1785, included much material from other sources.

Baroncelli, Jacques de (1881–1951)
French director, a former journalist, who made more than 80 films in a career that ran from the silent era until the late 40s.
La Maison de l'Espoir 15. Le Père Goriot 21. La Femme et le Pantin 29. Michel Strogoff 37. La Duchesse de Langeais 42. Rocambole 48, etc.

Barr, Douglas (1931–)
English juvenile actor who also starred in the BBC's first radio comedy series aimed at teenagers, *It's Fine to Be Young* 48.
Hue and Cry 46. Fortune Lane 47. The Last Load 48. Dance Hall 50. Madeleine 50. One Good Turn 51, etc.

Barr, Jean-Marc (1960–)
French leading actor in international films. Bilingual, he has a French mother and an American father and trained as an actor in London. He directed his first film in 1999 according to the tenets of the Dogme group.
The Frog Prince 85. King David 85. Hope and Glory 87. The Big Blue/Le Grand Bleu 88. Le Brasier 90. Europa 91. The Plague/La Peste 92. Iron Horsemen 94. Les Faussaires 94. Breaking the Waves (Den.) 96. Close Shave 96. Preference 98. What I Did for Love 98. The Scarlet Tunic 98. Don't Let Me Die on a Sunday/J'Aimerais Pas Crever Un Dimanche 98. Lovers (p,co-w,d,ph) 99. Too Much Flesh (&co-d) 00, etc.

Barr, Patrick (1908–1985)
British stage, screen and TV actor who played solid, dependable types from the 30s.
Norah O'Neale 34. The Return of the Scarlet Pimpernel 37. The Frightened Lady 41. The Blue Lagoon 48. Robin Hood 52. Singlehanded 53. Crest of the Wave 54. Saint Joan 57. Next to No Time 60. The Longest Day 62. Billy Liar 63. Ring of Spies 64. House of Whipcord 74, many others.

Barr, Roseanne (1952–)
Plump, outspoken American actress, a former stand-up comic, who is a star on TV but not, so far, on film. Formerly married to actor Tom Arnold. She was played by Patrika Darbo in the made-for-TV biopic *Roseanne and Tom: Behind the Scenes* 95, concerned with the couple's brief and stormy marriage.
Autobiography: 1990, My *Life as a Woman*.
She Devil 89. Look Who's Talking Too (voice) 90.The Woman Who Loved Elvis (TV) 93. Even Cowgirls Get the Blues 94. Blue in the Face 95, etc.
TV series: Roseanne 88–97. The Roseanne Show 98– .

Barrat, Robert (1891–1970)
American character actor in films from silent days, usually as heavy western villain. In 1934 alone he appeared in 19 films.
Mayor of Hell 33. Wild Boys of the Road 33. Dark Hazard 34. Wonder Bar 34. Captain Blood 35. Dr Socrates 35. Trail of the Lonesome Pine 36. The Charge of the Light Brigade 36. The Life of Emile Zola 37. Souls at Sea 37. The Buccaneer 38. Union Pacific 39. Return of the Cisco Kid 39. Go West 40. Captain Caution 40. Riders of the Purple Sage 41. American Empire 42. They Came to Blow Up America 43. The Adventures of Mark Twain 44. Road to Utopia 45. They Were Expendable 45. The Time of Their Lives 46. Road to Rio 47. Joan of Arc 48. Canadian Pacific 49. The Baron of Arizona 50. Flight to Mars 51. Double Crossbones 51. Son of Ali Baba 52. Tall Man Riding 55, many others.

Barrault, Jean-Louis (1910–1994)
Celebrated French stage actor, in a few rewarding film roles. He was married to actress Madeleine Renaud.
Mademoiselle Docteur 36. *Drôle de Drame* 36. *La Symphonie Fantastique* 42. *Les Enfants du Paradis* 44. D'Homme à Hommes 48. La Ronde 50. Le Testament du Docteur Cordelier 59. The Longest Day 62. La Nuit de Varennes 83, etc.

Barrault, Marie-Christine (1944–)
French actress, best known for her work with Eric Rohmer. She is the niece of Jean-Louis Barrault.
My Night at Maud's/Ma Nuit Chez Maud 69. Lancelot of the Lake/Lancelot du Lac 74. Cousin Cousine (AAN) 75. Perceval 78. The Medusa Touch 78. Stardust Memories 80. Table for Five 83. A Love in Germany/Eine Liebe in Deutschland 83. Swann in Love/Un Amour de Swann 83. Table for Five 83. The Abyss/L'Oeuvre au Noir 88. The Silent Woman 89. Gallant Ladies/Dames Galantes 91. Necessary Love/L'Amore Necessario 91. La Prossima Volta Il Fuoco 93. Mad Love/Amour Fou 94. Obsession 97. Azzurro 00, etc.

Barreto, Bruno (1955–)
Brazilian director and screenwriter. The son of leading Brazilian producers Luis Carlos Barreto and Lucy Barreto, he began as a youth making experimental shorts before achieving an international success with *Dona Flor and Her Two Husbands*. He married actress Amy Irving and is now based in America.
Tati, a Garota 73. Dona Flor and Her Two Husbands/Dona Flor e Seus Dois Maridos 76. Amor Bandido 78. Lucia 81. Gabriela 83. Felizes para Sempre 84. A Show of Force 89. The Story of Fausta 92. Carried Away 95. Four Days in September (AAN) 97. One Tough Cop 98, etc.

Barreto, Lima (1905–1982)
Brazilian film director and screenwriter, a former actor and journalist. Born in Casa Branca, he became a documentary film-maker in the 40s and 50s before making his feature debut with the first Brazilian film to gain an international reputation.
The Bandit/O Cangaçeiro 53. A Primeira Missa 61, etc.

Barrett, Edith (1912–1977)
American character actress, usually in fey roles.
Ladies in Retirement 41. Jane Eyre 43. I Walked with a Zombie 43. The Song of Bernadette 43. The Swan 56, etc.

Barrett, James Lee (1929–1989)
American screenwriter. Born in Charlotte, North Carolina, he was educated at Penn State University and began as a writer working for Stanley Kramer and Universal.
The D.I. 58. The Greatest Story Ever Told (co-w) 65. The Truth About Spring 65. Shenandoah 65. Bandolero 68. The Green Berets 68. The Cheyenne Social Club (& p) 70. Smokey and the Bandit (co-w) 77, etc.

Barrett, Jane (1923–1969)
British leading actress. Born in London, she was on stage from 1938, and then worked for the BBC Repertory Company in the early 40s.
The Captive Heart 45. Eureka Stockade 48. Time Gentlemen Please 52. The Sword and the Rose 52, etc.

Barrett, Judith (1914–) (Lucille Kelly)
American leading lady of a few 30s films.
Flying Hostess 36. Let Them Live 37. Armored Car 37. Illegal Traffic 38. Television Spy 39. The Great Victor Herbert 39. Road to Singapore 40. Women without Names 40, etc.

Barrett, Ray (1926–)
Australian leading actor in British TV and films.
The Sundowners 60. Touch of Death 62. Jigsaw 63. The Reptile 65. Revenge 71. Waterfront 83. Where the Green Ants Dream 84. Rebel 86. Hotel Sorrento 94. Dad and Dave on Our Selection 95. Brilliant Lies 96. Heaven's Burning 97. In the Winter Dark 98, etc.
TV series: *The Troubleshooters* 66–71.

Barrett, Rona (1934–) (Rona Burnstein)
American gossip columnist who, centred in Hollywood for the television networks, has more or less inherited the mantle of Hedda and Louella.
Autobiography: 1974, *Miss Rona*.
❝ I'm not friends with the stars, because if I were I couldn't tell the truth about them. – *R.B.*
I'm really a pussycat – with an iron tail. – *R.B.*

Barrie, Amanda (1939–) (Amanda Broadbent)
British leading lady with TV experience. Born in Ashton-under-Lyne, Lancashire, she performed from infancy, trained as a ballet dancer and began as a chorus girl in London at the age of 14.
Doctor in Distress 63. Carry On Cabby 63. Carry On Cleo 64. I Gotta Horse 65. One of Our Dinosaurs Is Missing 75, etc.
TV series: Mood In 61. Bulldog Breed 62. It's Tarbuck! 64–65. The Reluctant Romeo 67. Time of My Life 80. Coronation Street 81. L for Lester 82. Coronation Street 89– .

Barrie, Barbara (1931–) (Barbara Berman)
Pert American character actress. Born in Chicago, Illinois.
One Potato Two Potato 64. Summer of My German Soldier (TV) 78. The Bell Jar 79. Breaking Away (AAN) 79. Private Benjamin 80. Real Men 87. End of the Line 88. Hercules (voice) 97. Judy Berlin 99, etc.
TV series: Diana 73–74. Barney Miller 75–76. Breaking Away 80–81. Tucker's Witch 82–83. Reggie 83. Double Trouble 84–85.

Barrie, Sir J. M. (1860–1937)
British playwright whose work usually had a recognizable fey quality, which even survived the film versions.
The Admirable Crichton 17. Peter Pan 24 Seven Days Leave (from *The Old Lady Shows Her Medals*) 29. The Little Minister 34. We're Not Dressing (from *The Admirable Crichton*) 34. What Every Woman Knows 34. Quality Street 37. Darling How Could You? (from *Alice Sit by the Fire*) 51. Peter Pan 53. Forever Female (from *Rosalind*) 53. The Admirable Crichton 57. Hook (from *Peter Pan*) 91, etc.

Barrie, John (1917–1980)
Heavily built British character actor with long repertory experience. Played *Sergeant Cork* on TV, and in the cinema is best remembered as the police inspector in *Victim* 63.

Barrie, Mona (1909–1964) (Mona Smith)
English actress, born in London, who began her career on stage in Australia, and was in Hollywood from the early 30s, playing second leads.
Carolina 34. The House of Connelly 34. A Message to Garcia 36. I Met Him in Paris 37. When Ladies Meet 41. Cairo 42. Storm over Lisbon 44. I Cover Big Town 47. Strange Fascination 52. Plunder of the Sun 53, many others.

Barrie, Wendy (1912–1978) (Wendy Jenkins)
Bright British leading lady who went to Hollywood in 1934 but found only mediocre roles. Had her own TV show in 1948, and was later active in local radio.
It's a Boy (GB) 32. *The Private Life of Henry VIII* (GB) 33. For Love or Money 34. A Feather in Her Hat 35. Love on a Bet 36. Dead End 37. I Am the Law 38. The Hound of the Baskervilles 39. Five Came Back 39. The Saint Takes Over 40. Who Killed Aunt Maggie? 40. The Gay Falcon 41. Eyes of the Underworld 42. Women in War 42. Forever and a Day 43. It Could Happen to You (guest appearance) 53. Summer Holiday 63. The Moving Finger 63, etc.

Barrier, Edgar (1907–1964)
American character actor with stage experience.
Escape 40. Arabian Nights 42. Phantom of the Opera 43. Flesh and Fantasy 44. *A Game of Death* 45. Macbeth 48. To the Ends of the Earth 48. Cyrano de Bergerac 50. Princess of the Nile 54. On the Double 61. Irma la Douce 63, many others.

Barron, Keith (1934–)
British leading actor of the angry young man type; mostly on TV.
Baby Love 69. Melody 70. The Fire Chasers 70. The Man Who Had Power Over Women 70. She'll Follow You Anywhere 71. Nothing but the Night 73. The Land that Time Forgot 75. Voyage of the Damned 76. The Elephant Man 80. Close Relations (TV) 98. This Could Be the Last Time (TV) 98, etc.
TV series: The Odd Man 62–63. It's Dark Outside 64–65. The New Adventures of Lucky Jim 67. Joint Account 69. My Good Woman 72. Brotherly Love 74. No Strings 74. Telford's Change 79. Leaving 84–85. Duty Free 84–86. Room at the Bottom 86–88. Late Expectations 87. Haggard 90–92. All Night Long 94.

Barron, Steve (1956–)
British director who began with pop videos. Born in Dublin, he worked in films from the early 70s. He is the son of Zelda Barron.
Electric Dreams 84. Bulldance 89. Teenage Mutant Ninja Turtles 90. Coneheads 93. The Adventures of Pinocchio 96. Merlin (TV) 98. Rat 00, etc.

Barron, Zelda
British director. She first worked in production and as a script supervisor.
Secret Places 84. Shag 88.

Barry, Don (1912–1980) (Donald Barry d'Acosta)
Rugged American actor, in Hollywood from 1939 after stage experience and immediately popular as hero of second-feature westerns. Sometimes known as Donald 'Red' Barry. Committed suicide.
Night Waitress 36. The Crowd Roars 38. Calling All Marines 39. Remember Pearl Harbor 42. The Chicago Kid 45. The Dalton Gang 49. Jesse James' Women (& d) 53. I'll Cry Tomorrow 55. Walk on the Wild Side 62. Fort Utah 66. Bandolero 68. Shalako 68. Dirty Dingus Magee 70. Junior Bonner 72. Hustle 75. Orca 77. The Swarm 78, etc.
TV series: Surfside Six 60. Mr Novak 63.

Barry, Gene (1921–) (Eugene Klass)
Poised and debonair American leading man who also does a song and dance act. Films routine, but TV has kept him busy. Married actress Betty Claire.
■ The Atomic City 52. The Girls of Pleasure Island 52. *The War of the Worlds* 53. Those Redheads from Seattle 53. Alaska Seas 54. *Red Garters* 54. *Naked Alibi* 54. Soldier of Fortune 55. The Purple Mask 55. The Houston Story 56. Back From Eternity 56. The 27th Day 57. China Gate 57. Ain't No Time for Glory (TV) 57. Forty Guns 57. Hong Kong Confidential 58. *Thunder Road* 58. Maroc 7 67. Prescription Murder (TV) 67. Istanbul Express (TV) 68. Subterfuge 69. Do You Take This Stranger? (TV) 70. The Devil and Miss Sarah (TV) 71. The Second Coming of Suzanne 73. Guyana, Crime of the Century 79. The Adventures of Nellie Bly (TV) 81. The Girl, The Gold Watch and Dynamite (TV) 81.
TV series: Our Miss Brooks 55. *Bat Masterson* 58–61. *Burke's Law* 63–66. *The Name of the Game* 68–71. The Adventurer 72. Aspen 77. Burke's Law 94–95.

Barry, Iris (1895–1969)
Founder-member of the London Film Society (1925); director of New York Museum of Modern Art Film Library from 1935; president of the International Federation of Film Archives 1946; author of books on the film.
❝ Film is a machine for seeing more than meets the eye. – *I.B.*

Barry, Joan (1903–1989)
British leading lady of the early 30s, chiefly known for dubbing Anny Ondra's voice in *Blackmail*.
The Card 22. The Rising Generation 28. The Outsider 31. Rich and Strange 31. Ebb Tide 32. Sally Bishop 32. Rome Express 32. Mrs Dane's Defence 34, etc.

Barry, John (1933–) (J. B. Prendergast)
British composer and musician, best known for writing the music to the James Bond movies and for his arrangement of the theme music. Born in York, the son of a cinema owner, he began by leading his own group, the John Barry Seven. Formerly married to actress Jane Birkin.
Biography: 1998, *John Barry: A Sixties Theme* by Eddi Fiegel; 1998, *John Barry–Bond and Beyond* by Geoff Leonard, Gareth Bramley and Pete Walker.
Beat Girl 59. Never Let Go 60. Dr No (md) 62. The Amorous Prawn 62. The L-shaped Room 62. *From Russia with Love* 63. Zulu 63. The Man in the Middle 64. Goldfinger 64. The Ipcress File 65. The Knack 65. Thunderball 65. King Rat 65. The Chase 66. *Born Free* (AA) 66. The Wrong Box 66. The Quiller Memorandum 66. Petulia 68. Boom 68. Deadfall 68. The Lion in Winter (AA) 68. Midnight Cowboy 69. Murphy's War 71. They Might Be Giants 71. Mary, Queen of Scots (AAN) 71. Diamonds Are Forever 72. The Tamarind Seed 73. The Man with the Golden Gun 74. King Kong 76. The Deep 77. The White Buffalo 77. The Betsy 78. Moonraker 79. The Black Hole 79. Raise the Titanic 80. Somewhere in Time 80. Body Heat 81. Hammett 82. Frances 82. Octopussy 83. Out of Africa (AA) 85. Jagged Edge 86. Peggy Sue got Married 86. The Living Daylights 87. Hearts of Fire 87. Masquerade 88. Dances with Wolves (AA) 90. Chaplin (AAN) 92. My Life 93. Indecent Proposal 93. Ruby Cairo 93. The Specialist 94. The Scarlet Letter 95. Swept from the Sea/Amy Foster 97. Mercury Rising 98. Playing By Heart 98, etc.

Barry, John (1935–1979)
Anglo-American production designer.
A Clockwork Orange 73. Phase IV 73. Lucky Lady 75. Star Wars 77. Superman 78. Superman 2 80. The Empire Strikes Back 80, etc.

Barry, Julian
American screenwriter.
Secret Agent Fireball 66. Rhinoceros 74. Lenny (AAN) 74. The River 84, etc.

Barry, Philip (1896–1949)
American playwright, several of whose sophisticated comedies have been filmed.
Holiday 30 and 38. The Animal Kingdom 32 (remade as One More Tomorrow 46). The Philadelphia Story 40. Without Love 45.

Barry, Tony (1941–)
Australian actor, usually in tough roles.
Break of Day 76. The Picture Show Man 77. Newsfront 78. Hard Knocks 80. Goodbye Pork Pie 81. We of the Never Never 82. With Prejudice 82. The Coca-Cola Kid 85. Two Friends 86. Never Say Die 88. Return to Snowy River 88. Deadly 90. Jack Be Nimble 92. The Last Tattoo 94. Country Life 94, etc.
TV series: Skippy 66.

Barry, Wesley (1907–1994)
American child actor, on screen from the age of six, who later became an assistant director of 'B' movies and retired in the 40s.
Rebecca of Sunnybrook Farm 13. The Country Kid 23. Battling Bunyon 24. Sunny Skies 30. Daddy Long Legs 31. Night Life of the Gods 35. The Plough and the Stars 36, etc.

Barrymore, Diana (1921–1960)
American actress, daughter of John Barrymore. She made a few mediocre films in the early 40s but was not a successful leading lady and later succumbed to alcoholism. Her autobiography *Too Much Too Soon* was filmed in 1958 with Dorothy Malone (and Errol Flynn as John Barrymore).
■ Eagle Squadron 42. *Between Us Girls* 42. Nightmare 42. Frontier Badmen 43. Fired Wife 43. *Ladies Courageous* 44.

Barrymore, Drew (1975–)
American leading actress who was in films from the age of five. Born in Los Angeles, the daughter of John Barrymore, Jnr, she first came to notice in *E.T. the Extra-Terrestrial*, but problems with drugs and alcohol derailed her career in her teens. She then wrote a book about her experiences, cleaned up her act, and began to make the transition to adult roles. She became engaged to actor and comic Tom Green in 2000.
Autobiography: 1989, *Little Girl Lost*, with Todd Gold.
E.T. The Extra-Terrestrial. 82. Firestarter 84. Irreconcilable Differences 84. Cat's Eye 85. A Conspiracy of Love (TV) 87. See You in the Morning 88. Far from Home 89. Guncrazy 92. Doppelganger 92. Motorama 92. Poison Ivy 92. Sketch Artist 92. Beyond Control: The Amy Fisher Story (TV) 93. Wayne's World 2 93. Bad Girls 94. Inside the Goldmine 94. Mad Love 95. Boys on the Side 95. Batman Forever 95. Scream 96. Everyone Says I Love You 96. The Wedding Singer 97. Best Men 97. Ever After: A Cinderella Story 98. Home Fries 98. Never Been Kissed 98. The Wedding Singer 98. Titan AE (voice) 00. Charlie's Angels 00. Skipped Parts 00, etc.
TV series: 2000 Malibu Road 92.
❝ I'm lucky. I grew up being famous, so I don't have any weird things about being famous. – *D.B.*

Barrymore, Ethel (1879–1959) (Edith Blythe)
Distinguished American actress of regal presence. The sister of Lionel and John, and daughter of leading stage actors Maurice Barrymore and Georgiana Drew Barrymore, she was born in Philadelphia and was on stage from 1893, becoming a Broadway star in 1901. She made a few silents but had contempt for Hollywood, alienating MGM when she went to work there in the 30s, when she was drinking heavily and had financial problems. She remained on Broadway until 1944, when she made her home in Hollywood. Her greatest role came after more than 40 years in the theatre: as Miss Moffat in Emlyn Williams's *The Corn Is Green*, a part that went to Bette Davis when it was filmed. Always conscious of her position as the most admired stage actress of her time, when a young actor pointed out that if he went where she directed him to stand he would be upstage of her, she replied, 'Oh, my dear, don't worry about me. Wherever I am is centre stage.' She was courted by Winston Churchill, engaged to actor Gerald Du Maurier, and had affairs, possibly platonic, with actors Conway Tearle and Henry Daniell. Married millionaire Russell Colt and had three children: Ethel (1912–1977), who became an opera singer and actress; the alcoholic John Drew (1913–1975); and Samuel (1910–1986). Both boys also occasionally acted, though without any particular distinction. She, her daughter, her brother John and her mother were satirized in George Kaufman and Edna Ferber's 1927 Broadway hit *The Royal Family*.
Autobiography: 1955, *Memories*.
Biography: 1964, *The Barrymores* by Hollis Alpert. 1981, *The Barrymores: The Royal Family in Hollywood* by James Kotsilibas-Davis. 1990, *The House of Barrymore* by Margot Peters.
■ The Nightingale 14. The Final Judgement 15. The Awakening of Helen Ritchie 16. Kiss of Hate 16. The White Raven 17. The Lifted Veil 17. The Eternal Mother 17. The American Widow 17. Life's Whirlpool 17. The Call of Her People 17. Our Miss McChesney 18. The Divorcee 19. Rasputin and the Empress (only film appearance with her brothers) 32. *None but the Lonely Heart* (AA) 44. The Spiral Staircase (AAN) 46. *The Farmer's Daughter* 47. Moss Rose 47. The Paradine Case (AAN) 48. Night Song 48. Moonrise 49. Portrait of Jennie 49. The Great Sinner 49. That Midnight Kiss 49. Pinky (AAN) 49. The Red Danube 49. The Secret of Convict Lake 51. *Kind Lady* 51. It's a Big Country 52. *Deadline* 52. Just for You 52. The Story of Three Loves 53. Main Street to Broadway 53. *Young at Heart* 54. Johnny Trouble 57.
✪ For spending her later years portraying Hollywood's idea of the indomitable old lady with a heart of gold. *The Farmer's Daughter*.
❝ That's all there is, there isn't any more! – *E.B.'s farewell line, delivered after her curtain calls*

Barrymore, John (1882–1942) (John Blythe)
Celebrated, self-destructive American stage and screen actor, the brother of Ethel and Lionel Barrymore, and son of leading stage actors Maurice Barrymore and Georgiana Drew Barrymore. Born in Philadelphia, he studied at the Slade School of Art and worked first as an illustrator and cartoonist before following the family occupation from 1900. An undisciplined talent, he quickly became bored with repeating his performances night after night and, after triumphing on Broadway and in London in *Hamlet* in the early 20s, he quit the stage when Warner Bros offered him a three-picture contract at $76,250 a picture plus plenty of perks. Plans to film his *Hamlet*, made at various times by Warner's, Selznick and Alexander Korda, went awry (though a colour test he later made in 1933 allegedly remains in New York's Museum of Modern Art). An irresistible matinee idol with a 'great profile', he became a romantic movie hero in the 20s, but thereafter abused his talent. When Warner's refused to renew his contract in the early 30s, he worked for MGM, though that studio also tired of him. Alcoholism often dampened his film performances and he became too erratic to employ. He was fired from the role of the drunken actor Norman Maine in the 1934 version of *A Star Is Born* and finished playing parodies of himself on stage (in *My Dear Children*) and screen (*The Great Profile*). His second wife was poet, playwright and occasional actress Michael Strange, by whom he had a daughter, Diana; his third, actress Dolores Costello, by whom he had a daughter and a son, John Drew, Jnr; his fourth, Elaine Barrie, briefly became an actress. His lovers included Evelyn Nesbit and Mary Astor. He was played by Errol Flynn in *Too Much, Too Soon* 58, based on the autobiography of his daughter Diana, and by Jack Cassidy in *W. C. Fields and Me* 76.
Autobiography: 1926, *Confessions of an Actor*.
Biography: 1941, *John Barrymore: The Legend and the Man* by Alma Power-Walters. 1943, *Goodnight, Sweet Prince* by Gene Fowler. 1964, *The Barrymores* by Hollis Alpert. 1977, *Damned in Paradise: The Life of John Barrymore* by John Kobler. 1981, *The Barrymores: The Royal Family in Hollywood* by James Kotsilibas-Davis. 1990, *The House of Barrymore* by Margot Peters.
Other books: 1980, *The Film Acting of John Barrymore* by Joseph Garton.
■ Are You a Mason? 13. An American Citizen 13. The Man from Mexico 14. The Dictator 15. The Incorrigible Dukane 16. The Lost Bridegroom 16. The Red Widow 16. *Raffles* 17. On the Quiet 18. Here Comes the Bride 18. Test of Honour 19. *Dr Jekyll and Mr Hyde* 20. The Lotus Eater 21. *Sherlock Holmes* 22. *Beau Brummell* 24. *The Sea Beast* 26. *Don Juan* 26. When a Man Loves 27. *The Beloved Rogue* 27. *Tempest* 28. Eternal Love 29. *Show of Shows* (first talkie: recites Richard III) 29. General Crack 29. The Man from Blankley's 30. *Moby Dick* 30. *Svengali* 31. The Mad Genius 31. *Arsène Lupin* 32. *Grand Hotel* 32. State's Attorney 32. *A Bill of Divorcement* 32. *Rasputin and the Empress* 32. *Topaze* 33. *Reunion In Vienna* 33. *Dinner at Eight* 33. Night Flight 33. *Counsellor at Law* 33. Long Lost Father 34. *Twentieth Century* 34. *Romeo and Juliet* (as Mercutio) 36. *Maytime* 37. *Bulldog Drummond Comes Back* (as the inspector) 37. Night Club Scandal 37. Bulldog Drummond's Revenge 37. Bulldog Drummond's Peril 37. *True Confession* 38. Romance in the Dark 38. *Marie Antoinette* 38. *Spawn of the North* 38. *Hold that Co-Ed* 38. *The Great Man Votes* 39. *Midnight* 39. The Great Profile 40. Invisible Woman 41. World Premiere 41. Playmates 42.
✪ For a few performances of fine swashbucking, for a few more of ripe ham, and as an awful warning of what can happen to a star who becomes too sure that the world is his oyster. *Twentieth Century*.
❝ I like to be introduced as America's foremost actor. It saves the necessity of further effort. – *J.B.*
My head is buried in the sands of tomorrow, while my tail feathers are singed by the hot sun of today. – *J.B.*
I'm fifty years old and I want to look like Jackie Cooper's grandson. – *J.B.*
If you stay in front of the movie camera long enough, it will show you not only what you had for breakfast but who your ancestors were. – *J.B.*
I've done everything three times. The fourth time around becomes monotonous. – *J.B.*
The good die young – because they see no point in living if you have to be good. – *J. B.*
Student to lecturer: Tell me, Mr Barrymore, in your view did Ophelia ever sleep with Hamlet?' J.B. to student, after much thought: 'Only in the Chicago company …'
Katharine Hepburn after finishing *A Bill of Divorcement*: 'Thank goodness I don't have to act with you any more!' J.B., sweetly: 'I didn't know you ever had, darling …'
J.B., flinging a fish at a coughing audience: 'Busy yourselves with that, you damned walruses, while the rest of us get on with the play!'
A producer's wife at a Hollywood party, finding J.B. relieving himself in a corner of the ladies' room: 'Mr Barrymore, this is for ladies!' J.B., turning around without buttoning up: 'So, madam, is this!'
'My memory is full of beauty: Hamlet's soliloquies, Queen Mab's speech, the Song of Solomon. Do you expect me to clutter up all that with this horse shit?' (When asked why he required idiot boards in the studio, having perfect recall elsewhere).,
He moved through a movie scene like an exquisite paper knife. – *Heywood Broun*
Die? I should say not, old fellow. No Barrymore would allow such a conventional thing to happen to him. – *J.B. during his last illness*
This is a man who went through all the genres, starting with vaudeville – he was a song and dance man – classical theatre, the great American Hamlet, the silent movies, straight through into talking pictures. Nobody else did all that. Nobody. – *Nicol Williamson*
What I really have in common with Jack Barrymore is a lack of vocation. He himself played the part of an actor because that was the role he'd been given. – *Orson Welles*
Unfortunately, he was dull when he hadn't had anything to drink. When he was a little tipsy, his eyes became sparkling and he began to look like Mephistopheles. – *Andrew Marton*
Perhaps the most cynical actor who ever rattled rafters. – *William Redfield*
Famous line (*Twentieth Century*) 'I close the iron door on you!'

Barrymore Jnr, John (1932–) (John Drew Barrymore)
American actor, son of John Barrymore and Dolores Costello. Usually plays weaklings. He is the father of actress Drew Barrymore.
The Sundowners 50. The Big Night 51. Thunderbirds 52. While the City Sleeps 56. Night of the Quarter Moon 59. The Boatmen 59. The Cossacks 60. Nights of Rasputin 61. War of the Zombies 63, etc.

Barrymore, Lionel (1878–1954) (Lionel Blythe)
Accomplished American character actor, the brother of Ethel and John Barrymore, and son of leading stage actors Maurice Barrymore and Georgiana Drew Barrymore. Born in Philadelphia, he first appeared on stage with his grandmother, the London-born actress Mrs John Drew, in 1893, and was a Broadway star by 1918, combining stage roles with screen appearances. Often reluctant to follow the family acting tradition, he preferred composing music and painting and etching, which he had studied in Paris, subsidized by Ethel. He turned his back on the stage to concentrate on movies after stage failures in the mid-20s. With the onset of sound, he also directed, including *Redemption* and *His Glorious Night*, the two films that destroyed the career of John Gilbert, and claimed to have invented the sound boom, by tying a microphone onto the end of a fishing rod. An addiction to morphine and cocaine hampered his screen career, as did his later confinement to a wheelchair, as the result of a fall or, possibly, syphilis. From the early 30s he was a familiar and well-loved member of the MGM galaxy, playing sentimental, crotchety grandpas, churlish millionaires and, in a long and successful series of films, Dr Gillespie. He was the author of a novel, *Mr Cantonwine, a Moral Tale*. Married actresses Doris Rankin and Irene Fenwick.
Autobiography: 1951, *We Barrymores*.
Biography: 1964, *The Barrymores* by Hollis Alpert. 1981, *The Barrymores: The Royal Family in Hollywood* by James Kotsilibas-Davis. 1990, *The House of Barrymore* by Margot Peters.
■ Friends 09. Fighting Blood 11. Judith of Bethulia 11. The New York Hat 12. The Seats of the Mighty 14. Under the Gaslight 14. Wildfire 15. A Modern Magdalen 15. The Curious Conduct 15. The Flaming Sword 15. Dora 15. A Yellow Streak 15. The Exploits of Elaine 15. Dorian's Divorce 16. The Quitter 16. The Upheaval 16. The Brand of Cowardice 16. His Father's Son 17. The End of the Tour 17. The Millionaire's Double 17. Life's Whirlpool 17. The Valley of Night 19. The Devil's Garden 20. The Copperhead 20. The Master Mind 20. Jim the Penman 21. The Great Adventure 21. Face in the Fog 22. Boomerang 22. Enemies of Women 23. Unseeing Eyes 23. The Eternal City 24. America 24. Meddling Women 24. The Iron Man 25. Children of the Whirlwind 25. The Girl Who Wouldn't Work 25. Fifty Fifty 25. I am the Man 25. The Wrongdoers 25. The Barrier 26. *The Bells* 26. The Splendid Road 26. The Temptress 26. Brooding Eyes 26. The Lucky Lady 26. Paris at Midnight 26. Women Love Diamonds 27. The Show 27. Body and Soul 27. The 13th Hour 27. Drums of Love 27. Love 27. *Sadie Thompson* 28. West of Zanzibar 28. Decameron Nights 28. The Lion and the Mouse 28. Roadhouse 28. The River Woman 28. Alias Jimmy Valentine (first talkie) 29. Mysterious Island 29. Hollywood Revue 29. Confession (d only) 29. Madame X (AAN d only) 29. His Glorious Night (d only) 29. The Unholy Night (d only) 29. The Rogue Song (d only) 30. Free and Easy 30. Ten Cents a Dance (d only) 31. *A Free Soul* (AA) 31. The Yellow Ticket 31. Guilty Hands 31. Mata Hari 31. *The Man I Killed* 32. *Arsène Lupin* 32. *Grand Hotel* 32. Washington Masquerade 32. *Rasputin and the Empress* (as Rasputin) 32. Sweepings 33. Looking Forward 33. The Stranger's Return 33. Dinner at Eight 33. One Man's Journey 33. Night Flight 33. Christopher Bean 33. Should Ladies Behave? 33. This Side of Heaven 34. Carolina 34. The Girl from Missouri 34. Treasure Island 34. David Copperfield 34. The Little Colonel 35. Mark of the Vampire 35. Public Hero Number One 35. The Return of Peter Grimm 35. *Ah Wilderness* 35. The Voice of Bugle Ann 36. The Road to Glory 36. *The Devil Doll* 36. The Gorgeous Hussy 36. *Camille* 37. *A Family Affair* (first of Hardy Family series) 37. Captains Courageous 37. Saratoga 37. Navy Blue and Gold 37. A Yank at Oxford 38. Test Pilot 38. *You Can't Take It With You* 38. *Young Dr Kildare* (start of series, as Dr Gillespie) 38. Let Freedom Ring 39. Calling Dr Kildare 39. *On Borrowed Time* 39. The Secret of Dr Kildare 39. Dr Kildare's Strange Case 40. Dr Kildare Goes Home 40. Dr Kildare's Crisis 40. The Bad Man 41. The Penalty 41. The People vs Dr Kildare 41. Dr Kildare's Wedding Day 41. Lady Be Good 41. Dr Kildare's Victory 41. *Calling Dr Gillespie* 42. Dr Gillespie's New Assistant 42. Tennessee Johnson 43. Dr Gillespie's Criminal Case 43. Thousands Cheer 43. A Guy Named Joe 43. Three Men in White 44. Since You Went Away 44. Between Two Women 45. The Valley of Decision 45. *Three Wise Fools* 46. *It's a Wonderful Life* 46. The Secret Heart 46. *Duel in the Sun* 46. Dark Delusion 47. *Key Largo* 48. Down to the Sea in Ships 49. Malaya 50. Right Cross 50. Bannerline 51. Lone Star 52. Main Street to Broadway 53.
✪ For having a go at everything in sight, even female impersonation; and for becoming

Hollywood's omnipresent crotchety grandpa. *You Can't Take It with You.*

66 I never played with him that I didn't envy his consummate art. – *Marie Dressler*

This is the age of insincerity. The movies had the misfortune to come along in the twentieth century, and because they appeal to the masses there can be no sincerity in them. Hollywood is tied hand and foot to the demands for artificiality of the masses all over the world. – *L.B.*

As my brother Lionel says in every single picture to some ingenue: 'You have spirit – I like that!' – *John Barrymore*

Barsacq, Léon (1906–1969)
Russian art director and set designer, long in France. He studied architecture and decorative arts in Paris before beginning work as an assistant designer, later collaborating with Alexandre TRAUNER and others.

La Marseillaise 38. Lumière d'Eté 43. *Les Enfants du Paradis* 44. L'Idiot 46. Le Silence est d'Or 47. *La Beauté du Diable* 50. Les Belles de Nuit 52. Les Diaboliques 55. Les Grandes Maneuvres 55. The Ambassador's Daughter (US) 56. Porte des Lilas 57. The Longest Day 62. The Visit 64. Phèdre 69, many others.

Barsi, Judith (1977–1988)
American child actress. Killed by her father.

Eye of the Tiger 86. Jaws: The Revenge 87. Slamdance 87. The Land before Time (voice) 88. All Dogs Go to Heaven (voice) 89, etc.

Barstow, Stan (1928–   )
British north country novelist whose *A Kind of Loving* was successfully filmed. Some of his other material has been adapted for television.

Bart (1978–2000)
American grizzly bear who gave fearsome performances in many films, frequently better than those of his co-stars. He stood 9 ft 6 ins tall and weighed 1480 lbs.

Clan of the Cave Bear 85. The Bear 89. White Fang 90. The Great Outdoors 88. Legends of the Fall 94. The Edge 97, etc.

Bart, Lionel (1930–1999) (Lionel Begleiter)
London-born lyricist and composer who could not read music but was phenomenally successful with West End musicals such as *Fings Ain't What They Used To Be, Oliver!, Blitz* and *Maggie May.*

The Tommy Steele Story (s) 57. The Duke Wore Jeans (story) 58. Tommy the Toreador (s) 59. In the Nick (s) 59. Sparrows Can't Sing (title s) 62. From Russia with Love (title s) 63. Man in the Middle (m) 63. Oliver! (oa) 68. Lock Up Your Daughters! (oa) 69. Black Beauty (m) 71, etc.

Bartel, Paul (1938–2000)
American actor and director. Born in Brooklyn, New York, he studied at UCLA and at Rome's Centro Sperimentale di Cinematografica. Latterly, he was more active as a character actor than as a director. Died from liver cancer.

Private Parts (d) 72. Death Race 2000 (d) 75. Eat My Dust (a) 76. Cannonball (adw) 76. Grand Theft Auto (a) 77. Hollywood Boulevard 77. Rock 'n' Roll High School 79.*Eating Raoul* (ad) 81. Lust in the Dust 84. Not for Publication 84. Longshot 85. Scenes from the Class Struggle in Beverly Hills 89. Gremlins 2: The New Batch (a) 89. The Pope Must Die/The Pope Must Diet (a) 91. Desire and Hell at Sunset Motel (a) 92. Shelf Life (a) 93. Acting on Impulse (a) 93. Grief (a) 94. The Usual Suspects (a) 95. Basquiat (a) 96. Lewis & Clark & George (a) 97. Billy's Hollywood Kiss (a) 98. Hamlet (a) 00, etc.

Barthelmess, Richard (1895–1963)
Presentable American leading man who went straight from college into silent films. Griffith used him memorably, and in 1921 he formed his own company and was popular until the advent of talkies, which made his innocent image seem old-fashioned and condemned him to insipid character roles.

■ Gloria's Romance 16. Camille 17. The Eternal Sin 17. The Moral Code 17. Rich Man Poor Man 18. The Hope Chest 19. Boots 19. The Girl Who Stayed Home 19. Three Men and a Girl 19. Peppy Polly 19. *Broken Blossoms* 19. I'll Get Him Yet 19. Scarlet Days 19. The Idol Dancer 20. The Love Flower 20. Way Down East 20. Experience 21. *Tol'able David* 21. The Seventh Day 22. Sonny 22. The Bond Boy 22. The Bright Shawl 23. The

Fighting Blade 23. Twenty One 24. *The Enchanted Cottage* 24. Classmates 24. New Toys 25. Soul Fire 25. Shore Leave 25. The Beautiful City 25. Just Suppose 26. Ranson's Folly 26. The Amateur Gentleman 26. The White Black Sheep 26. *The Patent Leather Kid* (AAN) 27. The Drop Kick 27. The Noose (AAN) 28. Kentucky Courage 28. Wheels of Chance 28. Out of the Ruins 28. Scarlet Seas 28. Weary River 29. Drag 29. Young Nowheres 29. Show of Shows 29. Son of the Gods 30. *The Dawn Patrol* 30. The Lash 31. Way Down East 31. The Finger Points 31. The Last Flight 31. Alias the Doctor 32. *The Cabin in the Cotton* 32. Central Airport 33. Heroes for Sale 33. Massacre 33. A Modern Hero 34. Midnight Alibi 34. Spy of Napoleon 35. Four Hours to Kill 35. *Only Angels Have Wings* 39. The Man Who Talked Too Much 40. The Mayor of 44th Street 42. *The Spoilers* 42.
66 He has the most beautiful face of any man who ever went before a camera. – *Lillian Gish*

Bartholomew, Freddie (1924–1992) (Frederick Llewellyn)
Impeccably well-bred British child actor whose success in Hollywood films of the 30s delighted elderly aunts the world over. His somewhat toffee-nosed image fell from favour during the war and as an adult he moved out of show business into advertising.

■ Fascination (GB) 30. Lily Christine (GB) 32. *David Copperfield* 35. Anna Karenina 35. Professional Soldier 35. *Little Lord Fauntleroy* 36. The Devil is a Sissy 36. Lloyds of London 36. *Captains Courageous* 37. *Kidnapped* 38. Lord Jeff 38. Listen Darling 38. Spirit of Culver 38. Two Bright Boys 39. *The Swiss Family Robinson* 40. *Tom Brown's Schooldays* 40. Naval Academy 41. Cadets on Parade 42. A Yank at Eton 42. The Town Went Wild 44. Sepia Cinderella 47. St Benny the Dip 51.

Bartkowiak, Andrzej (1950–   )
Polish-born cinematographer who studied at the Lodz Film School and emigrated to the US in 1972, where he first worked in commercials.

Deadly Hero 76. Prince of the City 81. Deathtrap 82. The Verdict 82. Daniel 83. Terms of Endearment 83. Prizzi's Honor 85. Power 86. Nuts 87. Twins 88. Q & A 90. Falling Down 92. A Good Man in Africa 94. Speed 94. Losing Isaiah 95. Species 95. The Mirror Has Two Faces 96. Dante's Peak 97. The Devil's Advocate 97, etc.

Bartlam, Dorothy (1908–   )
English leading actress and novelist, a former dancer who began in films as an extra in 1925. As a result of winning a beauty contest, she obtained leading roles with British Lion in the late 20s, retiring in the mid-30s, soon after her first novel, *Contrary-Wise,* was published.

The Flying Squad 29. The Ringer 31. Birds of a Feather 31. We Dine at Seven 31. The Fires of Fate 32. Call Me Mame 33. Up for the Derby 33. On Thin Ice 33, etc.

Bartlett, Hall (1922–1993)
American independent producer, director and screenwriter whose films seldom seem quite good enough to be independent about. Married Rhonda Fleming (1966–71).

■ *Navajo* 52. Unchained (& wd) 55. *Drango* (& wd) 56. Zero Hour (& d) 57. All the Young Men (& d) 60. *The Caretakers* (& d) 64. A Global Affair 64. Sol Madrid 68. Changes (d) 69. The Wild Pack (d) 72. Jonathan Livingston Seagull (& d, co-w) 73. The Children of Sanchez (d) 78. Leaving Home (d) 86.

Bartlett, Richard (1922–1994)
American director.

The Lonesome Trail 55. I've Lived Before 56. Rock Pretty Baby 56. Joe Dakota 57. Slim Carter 57. Money, Women and Guns 58. The Gentle People and the Quiet Land 71. A Christmas Story (TV) 88, etc.

Bartlett, Sy (1900–1978) (Sacha Baraniev)
American screenwriter and producer, a former journalist. Born in Kansas City, Missouri, and educated at Yale University, he began as a writer and later set up a production company with actor Gregory PECK, ending his career under contract to Twentieth Century-Fox.

The Big Brain (w) 33. Boulder Dam (w) 35. Coconut Grove 38. Road to Zanzibar (co-w) 41. Bullet Scars 42. The Princess and the Pirate 44. 13 Rue Madeleine 46. Down to the Sea in Ships 49.

Twelve O'Clock High (w) 49. That Lady (wp) 55. *The Big Country* (w) 57. A Gathering of Eagles (wp) 63. Che (p) 69, etc.

Bartok, Eva (1926–1998) (Eva Sjöke)
Glamorous Hungarian-born actress in international films. Born in Kecskemet, she came to England in the mid-40s and was put under contract by Alexander KORDA. In the early 50s, she moved to Europe and married actor Curt JURGENS, her fourth husband; after their divorce, she had a daughter by, she claimed, Frank SINATRA. She returned to England in the mid-80s, where she died, forgotten and penniless.
Autobiography: 1959, *Worth Living For.*

A Tale of Five Cities 51. Venetian Bird 52. The Crimson Pirate 52. Front Page Story 54. Ten Thousand Bedrooms 57. Operation Amsterdam 59. SOS Pacific 60. Beyond the Curtain 60. Blood and Black Lace 64, etc.
66 I have made a mess of my life. I have been a sentimental fool. – *E.B.*

Barton, Buzz (1914–1980)
American character actor, a child star in early westerns, from rodeo.

The Boy Rider 28. Apache Kid's Escape 30. The Lone Defender (serial) 32. Mystery Trooper 32. Powersmoke Range 35. The Tonto Kid 35. In the Heat of the Night 67. In Cold Blood 67, etc.

Barton, Charles (1902–1981)
Routine American director, long at Universal.
■ Wagon Wheels 34. Car 99 35. Rocky Mountain Mystery 35. The Last Outpost (co-d) 35. Timothy's Quest 36. And Sudden Death 36. Nevada 36. Rose Bowl 36. Murder with Pictures 36. The Crime Nobody Saw 37. Forlorn River 37. Thunder Train 37. Born to the West 38. Behind Prison Gates 39. Five Little Peppers and How They Grew 39. My Son is Guilty 40. Five Little Peppers at Home 40. Island of Doomed Men 40. Babies for Sale 40. Out West with the Peppers 40. Five Little Peppers in Trouble 40. Nobody's Children 40. The Phantom Submarine 40. The Big Boss 41. The Richest Man in Town 41. Harmon of Michigan 41. Two Latins from Manhattan 41. Sing for your Supper 41. Honolulu Lu 41. Shut My Big Mouth 42. Tramp Tramp Tramp 42. Hello Anapolis 42. Parachute Nurse 42. Sweetheart of the Fleet 42. A Man's World 42. Lucky Legs 42. The Spirit of Stanford 42. Laugh Your Blues Away 42. *Reveille with Beverly* 43. Let's Have Fun 43. She Has What It Takes 43. What's Buzzin Cousin 43. Is Everybody Happy 43. What a Woman 43. Beautiful but Broke 44. Hey Rookie 44. Jam Session 44. Louisiana Hayride 44. Men in her Diary 45. White Tie and Tails 45. *The Time of Their Lives* 46. Smooth as Silk 46. The Wistful Widow of Wagon Gap 47. Buck Privates Come Home 47. Mexican Hayride 48. *Abbott and Costello Meet Frankenstein* 48. The Noose Hangs High 48. Free for All 49. Africa Screams 49. Abbott and Costello Meet the Killer 49. The Milkman 50. Double Crossbones 50. Ma and Pa Kettle at the Fair 52. Dance with Me Henry 56. The Shaggy Dog 59. Toby Tyler 60. Swinging Along 62.

Barton, Dee
American composer.
Play Misty for Me 71. High Plains Drifter 73. Thunderbolt and Lightfoot 74, etc.

Barton, James (1890–1962)
Grizzled, good-humoured American character actor, a veteran of burlesque and Broadway.
Captain Hurricane 35. Shepherd of the Hills 41. *The Time of Your Life* 48. Yellow Sky 49. The Daughter of Rosie O'Grady 50. Wabash Avenue 50. Here Comes the Groom 51. Golden Girl 51. The Naked Hills 57. Quantez 57. *The Misfits* 61, etc.

Bartosch, Berthold (1893–1968)
Austro-Hungarian animator, best known for his symbolic *L'Idée* 34.

Barty, Billy (1924–2000) (William Bertanzetti)
American dwarf actor, 3 feet 9 inches high, in films from the age of three. Born in Millsboro, Pennsylvania, he came to notice in the 20s and 30s playing Mickey Rooney's brother in the *Mickey McGuire* comedy shorts. A former member of Spike Jones's City Slickers, he was noted for singing 'I'm in the Mood for Love', a parody of Liberace, complete with exploding candelabra, which he recorded with the band in 1954. In the late 50s, he

founded Little People of America, an advocacy group for those with dwarfism, and later The Billy Barty Foundation, with similar aims.

Gold Diggers of 1933 33. Mickey's Minstrels 34. Harum Scarum 65. Pufnstuf 70. The Day of the Locust 74. Won Ton Ton, The Dog Who Saved Hollywood 75. W. C. Fields and Me 76. Under the Rainbow 81. Legend 85. Masters of the Universe 87. Willow 88. Lobster Man from Mars 89. Life Stinks 91. Radioland Murders 94. An Alan Smithee Film: Burn Hollywood Burn 98, etc.

TV series: The Spike Jones Show 54. Circus Boy 56–58. The Spike Jones Show 57. Ace Crawford, Private Eye 82.

Barwood, Hal (1940–   )
American director and screenwriter, most recently involved in designing video games for George Lucas's software company LucasArts, including *Indiana Jones and the Fate of Atlantis.*

The Sugarland Express (co-w) 74. The Bingo Long Traveling All-Stars & Motor Kings (co-w) 76. MacArthur (co-w) 77. Corvette Summer (co-w) 78. Dragonslayer (co-w) 81. Warning Sign (co-w, d) 85, etc.

Baryshnikov, Mikhail (1948–   )
Latvian ballet dancer who made his American film debut in *The Turning Point* (AAN) 77 and consolidated this in *White Nights* 85, *Dancers* 87. The Cabinet of Dr Ramirez 91. Company Business 91.
66 I'm not the first straight dancer or the last. Anyway, it has nothing to do with art. – *M.B.*

Barzman, Ben (1911–1989)
Canadian screenwriter, a former journalist and novelist. Born in Toronto and educated at Reed College, he began working in Hollywood but was blacklisted in the early 50s. (He later said that he had been approached by lawyer Martin Gang, who told him that for a payment of $16,000 a congressman would prevent his name going on the list.) He moved to France and worked with other US exiles in Europe, including director Joseph LOSEY.

True to Life 42. The Boy with Green Hair 48. He Who Must Die 56. Time without Pity 57. Blind Date 59. The Ceremony 63. The Heroes of Telemark 65. The Blue Max 66, etc.

Base, Giulio (1964–   )
Italian actor, screenwriter and director. Born in Turin, he studied Literature and Philosophy in Rome and is studying for a degree in theology at the University of Vatican City. He studied acting in Rome under Vittorio Gassman and began on stage.

Crack (co-w, d, a) 91. Skinheads/Teste Rasate (a) 92. Lest (wd, a) 93. Dear Diary (a) 94. Cops/Poliziotti (co-w, d) 95. Lovest/The West (wd,a) 97. Once Upon a Time in Little Italy/La Bomba (co-w, d) 99, etc.

Basehart, Richard (1914–1984)
Thoughtful American leading actor who somehow never achieved his expected stardom; equally adept at honesty, villainy and mental disturbance. Many TV appearances. He was married to Valentina CORTESE.

■ Cry Wolf 47. Repeat Performance 47. *He Walked by Night* 48. Roseanna McCoy 49. *The Black Book* 49. Tension 49. Outside the Wall 50. *Fourteen Hours* 51. The House on Telegraph Hill 51. Fixed Bayonets 51. Decision Before Dawn 51. The Stranger's Hand 53. Titanic 53. La Strada 54. The Good Die Young 54. La Reprise de Justice 54. La Vena d'Oro 55. Cartouche 55. Canyon Crossroads 55. Il Bidone/The Swindlers 55. The Extra Day 56. Moby Dick 56. The Intimate Stranger 56. *Time Limit* 57. So Soon to Die (TV) 57. Arrivederci Dimas 57. *The Brothers Karamazov* 58. L'Ambiteuse 58. Jons und Erdme 59. Five Branded Women 60. Portrait in Black 60. For the Love of Mike 60. Passport to China 61. The Savage Guns 61. Tierra Brutal 62. Hitler (title role) 63. Kings of the Sun 63. The Satan Bug 65. The Sole Survivor (TV) 69. The Death of Me Yet (TV) 71. City Beneath the Sea/One Hour to Doomsday (TV) 71. Assignment Munich (TV) 72. The Bounty Man (TV) 72. Escape of the Birdmen (TV) 72. Chato's Land 72. Rage 72. Maneater (TV) 73. And Millions Will Die 73. How the West Was Won (TV) 75. Mansion of the Doomed 76. The Island of Dr Moreau 77. WEB (TV) 78. The Bastard (TV) 78. Being There 79. The Great Georgia Bank Hoax

79. Marilyn, the Untold Story (TV) 80. Knight Rider (TV) 82.
TV series: *Voyage to the Bottom of the Sea* 64–67.

Basevi, James (1890–1962)
Anglo-American art director and special effects wizard, at Fox from the mid-20s.
The Big Parade 25. The Hurricane 38. Wuthering Heights (AAN) 39. The Long Voyage Home 40. The Westerner (AAN) 40. Tobacco Road 41. The Ox-Bow Incident 43. The Gang's All Here (AAN) 43. The Song of Bernadette (AA) 43. Lifeboat 44. Jane Eyre 44. Spellbound 45. The Keys of the Kingdom (AAN) 45. Duel in the Sun 46. My Darling Clementine 46. Boomerang! 47. Fort Apache 48. Mighty Joe Young 49. She Wore a Yellow Ribbon 49. My Man and I 52. East of Eden 54. The Searchers 56, many others.

Basinger, Kim (1953–)
Sultry American leading actress, often in oversexed roles. Formerly married to actor Alec Baldwin.
Hard Country 81. Killjoy (TV) 81. Mother Lode 82. The Man Who Loved Women 83. Never Say Never Again 83. The Natural 84. Fool for Love 85. Nine and a Half Weeks 85. No Mercy 86. Blind Date 87. Nadine 87. My Stepmother Is an Alien 88. Batman 89. The Marrying Man/Too Hot to Handle 91. Final Analysis 92. The Real McCoy 93. Wayne's World 2 93. The Getaway 94. Prêt-à-Porter 94. *LA Confidential* (AA) 97. I Dreamed of Africa 00, etc.
TV series: Dog and Cat 79. From Here to Eternity 80.
❝ You have to be a little unreal to be in this business. – *K.B.*
I don't have any friends in this business at all. That Mafia guy John Gotti's best friend is the one who stabbed him in the back. Hollywood is a lot like that. It's like the Mafia. – *K.B.*

Baskett, James (1904–1948)
American character actor best known for his performance as Uncle Remus in *Song of the South* 48.

Basler, Marianne (1964–)
Blonde Swiss leading actress, in French and international films.
Alexina 85. La Soule 88. A Soldier's Tale 88. Dames Galantes 90. Overseas 90. Eline Vere 91. Blanc d'ébene 91. Farinelli the Castrato 94, etc.

Basquette, Lina (1907–1994)
American leading lady of the 20s, former child star and dancer. Her lively private life included seven husbands.
Autobiography: 1990, *Lina: DeMille's Godless Girl*.
Juvenile Dancer 16. Prince for a Day 17. Penrod 22. Ranger of the North 27. Wheel of Chance 28. Show Folks 28. *The Godless Girl* 29. Dude Wrangler 30. Hard Hombre 31. Morals for Women 31. Phantom Express 32. Ebb Tide 37. Four Men and a Prayer 38, etc.

Basquiat, Jean-Michael (1960–1988)
American artist, commemorated in the biopic *Basquiat*, directed by fellow-artist Julian Schnabel. Of middle-class Haitian and Puerto Rican descent, he first made his mark as a street graffiti artist, signing his work with the tag Samo (for Same old shit) before being promoted by influential dealers and galleries. He had a much-publicized affair with singer Madonna in the mid-80s. Died from a heroin overdose. In the biopic he is played by Jeffrey Wright, with David Bowie in the role of Andy Warhol and Gary Oldman as Schnabel. Basquiat's father refused permission for his paintings to be used, so those shown in the film were done by Schnabel.

Bass, Alfie (1920–1987)
Pint-sized British character comedian, adept at cockney/Jewish roles.
Johnny Frenchman 45. Holiday Camp 47. It Always Rains on Sunday 47. The Hasty Heart 49. *The Lavender Hill Mob* 51. *The Bespoke Overcoat* 55. A Kid for Two Farthings 55. A Tale of Two Cities 57. I Only Arsked 59. The Millionairess 60. Alfie 66. The Fearless Vampire Killers 67. The Magnificent Seven Deadly Sins 72. Moonraker 79, etc.
TV series: The Army Game 57–62. Bootsie and Snudge 60–63. Are You Being Served? 79.

Bass, Ronald
American screenwriter, a former attorney. He signed a six-picture deal worth $8m with Tri-Star Pictures in 1996, and includes in his contracts the clause that no one may rewrite his scripts.
Code Name: Emerald 85. Black Widow 87. Gardens of Stone 87. Rain Man (co-w, AA) 88. Sleeping with the Enemy 90. The Joy Luck Club (co-w) 93. When a Man Loves a Woman (co-w) 94. Dangerous Minds 95. My Best Friend's Wedding 97. How Stella Got Her Groove Back (co-w) 98. What Dreams May Come 98. Stepmom (co-w) 98, etc.
❝ He can turn out many more scripts than most of us can. He can fit the bill in terms of what the market is asking for. The studios aren't looking for a vision, they're looking for product. – *Robin Swicord*

Bass, Sam (1851–1878)
American western adventurer, played by Howard Duff in *Calamity Jane and Sam Bass*.

Bass, Saul (1921–1996)
American graphic designer and director, best known for creating title sequences for some 50 films, including many by Otto Preminger. He also designed the detailed storyboards for Hitchcock's *Psycho*, directed racing scenes for John Frankenheimer's *Grand Prix* and the final battle in *Spartacus*.
as director: Why Man Creates (short) (AA) 68. Phase IV 74, etc.
as title designer: Carmen Jones 54. The Shrike 55. The Man with the Golden Arm 55. The Seven Year Itch 55. Around the World in 80 Days (closing animated credit sequence) 56. Vertigo 58. The Big Country 58. Bonjour Tristesse 58. North by Northwest 59. Anatomy of a Murder 59. Psycho 60. Exodus 60. Ocean's Eleven 60. A Walk on the Wild Side 62. It's a Mad Mad Mad Mad World 63. Nine Hours to Rama 63. Bunny Lake Is Missing 65. The Human Factor 79. Broadcast News 87. Big 88. The War of the Roses 89. Cape Fear 91. The Age of Innocence 93, etc.

Bassani, Giorgio (1916–2000)
Italian poet and novelist, a former teacher. His novel *The Garden of Finzi-Continis*, published in 1962 and drawing on his youthful experiences during a time of fascism and anti-semitism, was filmed by Vittoria De Sica in 1970. As an publisher's editor, he was responsible for the publication of Lampedusa's novel *The Leopard*, which was filmed by Luchino Visconti in 1963.

Basserman, Albert (1867–1952)
Distinguished German stage actor who came to Hollywood as refugee in 1939 and played sympathetic roles.
■ Der Andere 13. Voruntersuchung 31. The Last Days Before the War 32. Kadetten 33. Ein Gewisser Herr Gran 33. Alraune 33. Letzte Liebe 38. Le Famille Lefrancois 39. Dr Ehrlich's Magic Bullet 40. *Foreign Correspondent* (AAN) 40. A Dispatch from Reuters 40. Moon Over Burma 40. Knute Rockne 40. Escape 40. *The Shanghai Gesture* 41. The Great Awakening 41. New Wine 41. A Woman's Face 41. The Moon and Sixpence 42. Invisible Agent 42. Once Upon a Honeymoon 42. Fly by Night 42. Desperate Journey 42. Good Luck Mr Yates 43. Passport to Heaven 43. Reunion in France 43. Madame Curie 44. Since You Went Away 44. *Rhapsody in Blue* 45. Strange Holiday 46. The Searching Wind 46. The Private Affairs of Bel Ami 47. Escape Me Never 47. *The Red Shoes* (GB) 48.
✪ For bringing to Hollywood a suggestion of the unique strength of the European theatre. *The Shanghai Gesture*.

Bassett, Angela (1958–)
American leading actress, from the stage. She played Tina Turner in the biopic *What's Love Got to Do with It?* Married actor Courtney B. Vance in 1997.
FX 86. Kindergarten Cop 90. Boyz N The Hood 91. Critters 4 92. Innocent Blood 92. Passion Fish 92. Malcolm X 92. *What's Love Got to Do with It?* (AAN) 93. Strange Days 95. Vampire in Brooklyn 95. Waiting to Exhale 95. Contact 97. How Stella Got Her Groove Back 98. Music of the Heart 99. Supernova 00. Whispers: An Elephant's Tale (voice) 00, etc.

Bassett, Linda
English stage actress in occasional films.
Waiting for the Moon (TV) 87. Paris by Night 88. News Hounds (TV) 90. Haunted 95. Loved Up (TV) 95. Mary Reilly 96. Oscar and Lucinda 97. Beautiful People 99. East is East 99, etc.

Bassey, Dame Shirley (1937–)
Torrid British-born cabaret singer whose film appearances have always been as a performer. She sang the title songs of the James Bond movies *Goldfinger* 64, *Diamonds Are Forever* 71, and *Moonraker* 79. She was made a Dame in the New Year's Honours of 1999.

Bassler, Robert (1903–1975)
American producer. Born in Washington, he was educated at George Washington University, and was in films from 1924, first in Paramount's research department and later as an editor. He became a literary agent in the early 30s, and was European story editor for Twentieth Century-Fox before becoming a producer from the 40s, and later working in television.
My Gal Sal 42. *The Black Swan* 43. The Lodger 44. Hangover Square 45. Thunder in the Valley 47. *The Snake Pit* 48. Thieves' Highway 49. Halls of Montezuma 50. Kangaroo 52. Beneath the Twelve-Mile Reef 53. Suddenly 54, etc.

Bassman, George (1914–)
American composer, working for MGM from the mid-30s and 40s.
A Day at the Races 37. Babes in Arms 39. Go West 40. Lady Be Good 41. The Big Store 41. The Canterville Ghost 44. The Clock 45. The Postman Always Rings Twice 46. Little Mister Jim 47. The Joe Louis Story 53. Ride the High Country 62. Mail Order Bride 63, etc.

Bastedo, Alexandra (1946–)
Leading lady of Canadian, Italian and English ancestry.
Thirteen Frightened Girls 63. Inside Daisy Clover 66. Casino Royale 67. The Ghoul 75. The Blood-Spattered Bride 80, etc.
TV series: *The Champions* 67.

Batchelor, Joy (1914–1991)
British animator, wife of John Halas and co-founder of Halas and Batchelor Cartoon Films.

Bate, Anthony (1929–)
Smooth English character actor, mostly on television. He trained at the Central School of Speech and Drama and was on stage from 1953.
Stopover Forever 64. Act of Murder 64. Ghost Story/Madhouse Mansion 74. Bismarck 76. Philby, Burgess and Maclean (TV) 80. Give My Regards to Broad Street 83. War and Remembrance 89. Eminent Domain 90. Prime Suspect 4: Inner Circles (TV) 95. Rebecca (TV) 97, etc.
TV series: Game, Set, and Match 88.

Bateman, Jason (1969–)
American actor, from television as a juvenile. He is the brother of Justine Bateman.
Can You Feel Me Dancing? 85. Teen Wolf Too 87. Breaking the Rules 92. A Taste for Killing 92. Love Stinks 99, etc.
TV series: Little House on the Prairie 81–82. Silver Spoons 82–84. It's Your Move 84–85. Valerie 86–87. The Hogan Family 88–91.

Bateman, Justine (1966–)
American actress, from television as a juvenile. She is the sister of Jason Bateman.
Can You Feel Me Dancing? 85. Satisfaction 88. The Fatal Image (TV) 90. The Closer 91. Primary Motive 92. Deadbolt 92. The Night We Never Met 93. God's Lonely Man 96. Kiss & Tell 96. Say You'll Be Mine 99, etc.
TV series: Family Ties 82–89. Men Behaving Badly 96-97.

Bates, Alan (1934–)
Leading British actor of stage and screen: tends to play thoughtful toughs with soft centres. Born in Allestree, Derbyshire, he trained at RADA and was on stage from 1955, first gaining fame in various roles at the Royal Court theatre.
■ The Entertainer 59. *A Kind of Loving* 62. *Whistle Down the Wind* 62. The Caretaker 63. The Running Man 63. *Nothing But the Best* 64. *Zorba the Greek* 65. Georgy Girl 66. King of Hearts 67. *Far from the Madding Crowd* 67. The Fixer (AAN) 68. *Women in Love* 69. Three Sisters 70. The Go-Between 70. *A Day in the Death of Joe Egg* 71. Impossible Object 73. Butley 73. In Celebration 74. Royal Flash 75. The Collection (TV) 76. An Unmarried Woman 77. The Shout 78. The Rose 79. Very Like a Whale (TV) 80. Nijinsky 80. Quartet 81. The Return of the Soldier 82. Britannia Hospital 82. An Englishman Abroad (TV) 83. A Voyage Around My Father (TV) 83. Dr Fischer of Geneva (TV) 83. Duet For One 86. A Prayer for the Dying 87. We Think the World of You 88. Force Majeure 89. 102 Boulevard Haussman (TV) 90. Docteur M. 90. Hamlet 90. Mister Frost 90. Secret Friends 91. Silent Tongue 93. The Grotesque/Gentlemen Don't Eat Poets/ Grave Indiscretions 96. St Patrick: The Irish Legend (TV) 00.

Bates, Barbara (1925–1969)
American leading lady, former model and ballet dancer. Committed suicide.
This Love of Ours 45. The Fabulous Joe 48. June Bride 48. *The Inspector General* 49. Cheaper by the Dozen 49. All About Eve 50. Belles on Her Toes 52. Rhapsody 54. House of Secrets (GB) 56. Town on Trial (GB) 57. Apache Territory 58, etc.
TV series: It's a Great Life 54–55

Bates, Florence (1888–1954) (Florence Rabe)
American character actress, adept at friendly or monstrous matrons. Born in San Antonio, Texas, she became the state's first woman lawyer in 1914, and was later a businesswoman. She trained at the Pasadena Playhouse in her late 40s, and was persuaded by Alfred Hitchcock to play the role of Mrs Van Hopper in *Rebecca*, for which she is best remembered; she remained in demand for the rest of her career.
■ The Man in Blue 37. *Rebecca* 40. Calling All Husbands 40. Son of Monte Cristo 40. Hudson's Bay 40. Kitty Foyle 40. Road Show 41. Love Crazy 41. The Chocolate Soldier 41. Strange Alibi 41. The Devil and Miss Jones 41. The Tuttles of Tahiti 42. *The Moon and Sixpence* 42. My Heart Belongs to Daddy 42. Mexican Spitfire at Sea 42. We Were Dancing 42. Slightly Dangerous 43. His Butler's Sister 43. They Got Me Covered 43. Mister Big 43. Heaven Can Wait 43. Mr Lucky 43. Since You Went Away 44. The Mask of Dimitrios 44. Kismet 44. Belle of the Yukon 44. The Racket Man 44. Saratoga Trunk 45. Tahiti Nights 45. *Tonight and Every Night* 45. Sanantonio 45. Out of This World 45. Claudia and David 46. Cluny Brown 46. The Diary of a Chambermaid 46. Whistle Stop 46. The Time the Place and the Girl 46. *The High Window* 47. Love and Learn 47. Desire Me 47. *The Secret Life of Walter Mitty* 47. Texas Brooklyn and Heaven 48. Winter Meeting 48. The Inside Story 48. River Lady 48. My Dear Secretary 48. Portrait of Jennie 48. *I Remember Mama* 48. A Letter to Three Wives 48. The Judge Steps Out 49. The Girl from Jones Beach 49. On the Town 49. Belle of Old Mexico 50. *County Fair* 50. The Second Woman 51. Lullaby of Broadway 51. The Tall Target 51. Havana Rose 51. Father Takes the Air 51. The Whistle at Eaton Falls 51. The San Francisco Story 52. Les Miserables 52. Paris Model 53. Main Street to Broadway 53.

Bates, Granville (1882–1940)
American general purpose supporting actor of the 30s: storekeepers, doctors and grandpas.
Jealousy 29. The Smiling Lieutenant 31. Woman Wanted 35. 13 Hours by Air 36. They Won't Forget 37. Nancy Steele is Missing 37. Wells Fargo 37. Go Chase Yourself 38. Gold is Where You Find It 38. The Great Man Votes 39. Pride of the Blue Grass 39. Of Mice and Men 39. Jesse James 39. My Favorite Wife 40. The Mortal Storm 40. Brother Orchid 40, many others.

Bates, H. E. (1905–1974)
British novelist who dabbled in the cinema. *The Darling Buds of May* was filmed as *The Mating Game* and formed the basis of a successful TV series from 1990.
The Loves of Joanna Godden (oa) 47. The Purple Plain (oa) 54. Summertime (co-w) 55. The Mating Game (oa) 58. Dulcima (oa) 71. Triple Echo (oa) 72. A Month by the Lake (oa) 94. Feast of July (oa) 95. Under the Sun/Under Solen (from *The Little Farm*) 99, etc.

Bates, Kathy (1948–)
American character actress, notable as the crazed fan in *Misery*. Born in Memphis, Tennessee, and educated at the Southern Methodist University, she first came to notice in the theatre.
Straight Time 78. Come Back to the Five and Dime, Jimmy Dean, Jimmy Dean 82. Summer Heat

87. Arthur 2: On the Rocks 88. High Stakes/Melanie Rose 89. Signs of Life 89. Men Don't Leave 90. Dick Tracy 90. White Palace 90. *Misery* (AA) 90. Fried Green Tomatoes at the Whistle Stop Café 91. The Road to Mecca 91. At Play in the Fields of the Lord 91. Shadows and Fog 92. Prelude to a Kiss 92. A Home of Our Own 93. North 94. Curse of the Starving Class 94. Angus 95. Diabolique 96. The War at Home 96. The Late Shift (TV) 96. Titanic 97. Amy Foster/Swept from the Sea 97. Primary Colors (AAN) 98. The Waterboy 98. A Civil Action 98. Dash and Lilly (d,TV) 99, etc.

Bates, Michael (1920–1978)
British character actor who specialized in stupid policemen and other caricatures.
Carrington VC 55. I'm All Right Jack 59. Bedazzled 67. *Here We Go Round the Mulberry Bush* 67. Don't Raise the Bridge Lower the River 67. Salt and Pepper 68. Hammerhead 68. Patton 69. The Rise and Rise of Michael Rimmer 70. A *Clockwork Orange* 71. No Sex Please, We're British 73. The Bawdy Adventures of Tom Jones 76, etc.
TV series: Mr John Jorrocks 66. Mr Digby, Darling 70-71. Turnbull's Finest Half-Hour 72. The Last of the Summer Wine 73-75. It Ain't Half Hot Mum 74–77.

Bates, Ralph (1940–1991)
Incisive British character actor who played Caligula on TV and took the natural step to Hammer horrors.
The Caesars (TV) 68. The Horror of Frankenstein 70. Lust for a Vampire 70. Dr Jekyll and Sister Hyde 71. Fear in the Night 73. Persecution 74. I Don't Want to be Born 75. Poldark (TV) 75. Penmaric (TV) 79. Letters to an Unknown Lover (TV) 84. King of the Wind (TV) 89, etc.
TV series: Broad and Narrow 65. Dear John 86-87.

Bath, Hubert (1883–1945)
British composer. Born in Barnstaple, Devon, he spent much of his career from the early 30s as a composer and arranger for Gaumont-British, where his work was frequently uncredited. His best-known composition was the concerto *Cornish Rhapsody* played by pianist Harriet Cohen, dubbing for Stewart Granger, in *Love Story*.
Kitty 29. Blackmail 29. The Plaything 29. Under the Greenwood Tree 29. Waltzes from Vienna 34. Chu Chin Chow (conductor) 34. The Thirty-Nine Steps 35. Rhodes of Africa 36. The Great Barrier 37. A Yank at Oxford 37. Yellow Sands 38. A Place of One's Own 44. *Love Story* 44, etc.

Báthory, Countess Elisabeth (1560–1614)
Hungarian aristocrat who is alleged to have killed more than 600 girls and women, and to have bathed in the blood of virgins to keep her skin white; though it is also claimed that these stories were inventions of her enemies at her trial, at which she was not present. Arrested in 1610, she was kept under house arrest until her death. So far, four films have been based on her legend, most notably Hammer's *Countess Dracula* 70.
Biography: 1997, *Countess Dracula: The Life and Times of Elisabeth Báthory the Blood Countess* by Tony Thorne.
Le Rouge aux Lèvres (Bel.) 71. Ceremonia Sangrienta (Sp./It.) 72. Immoral Tales/Contes Immoraux (Fr.) 74.

Batley, Ernest G. (1879–1916)
English director and actor of early silents. Married producer and director Ethyle Batley, in whose films he also appeared. Their daughter, Dorothy, starred in many of their films.

Batley, Ethyle (1879–1917)
English director of silents and occasional actress, one of the first woman producer and directors of fictional films, many of them starring her husband, Ernest G. *Batley*, or her daughter, Dorothy Batley (1902-1983).

Bators, Stiv (1950–1990) (Steve Bators)
American singer with the 70s punk group Dead Boys and occasional actor. Died after being hit by a car.
Polyester 81. Tapeheads 89.

Battle, John Tucker
American screenwriter.
Irish Eyes Are Smiling 44. Captain Eddie 45. So Dear to My Heart 48. The Frogmen 51. A Man Alone 55. Lisbon 56. Shootout at Medicine Bend 57, etc.

Bauchau, Patrick
Belgian leading actor; he quit the profession in the mid-60s for a time to continue a career as an artist.
Suzanne's Career/La Carrière de Suzanne 63. Paris Vu Par 64. The Collector/La Collectionneuse 66. Guns 80. Winter Journey/Le Voyage d'Hiver 82. The State of Things 82. Enigma 82. Entre Nous 83. Choose Me (US) 83. Coup de Foudre 83. Emmanuelle IV 84. Phenomena/Creepers 84. A View to a Kill (GB) 85. Cross 87. Comèdie d'Amour 89. The Rapture (US) 91. Double Identity 91. Chain of Desire (US) 92. Crystal Gazing (GB) 92. Acting on Impulse (US) 93. And the Band Played On (TV) 93. Every Breath (US) 93. The New Age (US) 94. The Dark Side of Genius (US) 94. Day of Reckoning (US) 94. Lisbon Story 95. Jenipapo 95. We Free Kings/I Magi Randagi 96. Twin Falls Idaho (US) 99. The Cell (US) 00, etc.

Bauchens, Anne (1882–1967)
American editor, almost always for De Mille.
The Squaw Man 18. Don't Change Your Husband 19. The Affairs of Anatol 21. The Ten Commandments 23. King of Kings 27. Dynamite 29. The Sign of the Cross 32. Cleopatra (AAN) 34. The Crusade 35. The Buccaneer 38. North West Mounted Police (AA) 40. Reap the Wild Wind 42. Love Letters 45. Unconquered 47. Samson and Delilah 49. The Greatest Show on Earth (AAN) 52. The Ten Commandments (AAN) 56, many others.

Bauer, Belinda (1956–)
Australian actress, a former model, in American films, usually in off-beat roles.
Winter Kills 79. Success 79. Fugitive from the Empire (TV) 81. Sins of Dorian Gray (TV) 82. Timerider 83. Flashdance 83. Samson and Delilah (TV) 84. The Rosary Murders 87. The Game of Love 87. UHF 89. Act of Piracy 90. Robocop 2 90. Necronomicon 93, etc.

Bauer, Steven (1956–) (Steven Echevarria)
Cuban character actor in Hollywood. Formerly married (1983–85) to actress Melanie Griffith.
Scarface 83. Thief of Hearts 84. Running Scared 86. Sword of Gideon 86. The Beast 88. Gleaming the Cube 89. A Row of Crows 90. Sweet Poison 91. False Arrest (TV) 91. Raising Caine 92. Snapdragon 93. Improper Conduct 94. Body Count 95. Primal Fear 96. Navajo Blues 97. Donald Cammell's Wild Side 00. Traffic 00, etc.

Baum, L. Frank (1856–1919)
American author of *The Wizard of Oz*, 1900, and other adventures set in the mythical kingdom. He brought out the book himself after every publisher turned it down, adapted it as a Broadway musical and financed early silent film versions, setting up the Oz Film Manufacturing Company in 1914 and briefly opening his own studio in Hollywood.
The Wizard of Oz 08. The Road to Oz 09. His Majesty the Tin Scarecrow of Oz 14. The Patchwork Girl of Oz 14. The Magic Cloak of Oz 14. The Wizard of Oz 25. The Wizard of Oz 39. The Wiz 78, etc.

Baum, Vicki (1896–1960)
Austrian novelist whose chief gift to Hollywood was the much-filmed and well imitated *Grand Hotel*, which she herself revamped as *Hotel Berlin*.
Autobiography: 1964, *It Was All Quite Different*.

Baur, Harry (1880–1943)
Celebrated French actor of stage and screen.
Shylock 10. La Voyante 23. David Golder 31. Poil de Carotte 32. Golgotha 34. Moscow Nights 35. Crime and Punishment 35. Taras Bulba 35. Un Carnet de Bal 37. The Rebel Son 38. Volpone 39. L'Assassinat du Père Noël 41. Symphonie eines Lebens 42, etc.

Bava, Lamberto (1944–)
Italian director of horror and action movies, the son of Mario Bava. Born in Rome, he began working as an assistant on his father's films, and later was an assistant director on Dario Argento's films in the early 80s.
Macabre/Macabro 80. Blastfighter 84. Monster Shark/Shark Rosso nell'Oceano 84. Demons/Demoni 85. Demons 2/Demoni 2 86. Le Foto di Gioia 87. Black Sabbath 89. Body Puzzle/Misteria 93, etc.

Bava, Mario (1914–1980)
Italian director, former photographer, of period muscleman epics and pseudo-British horror stories, revered by the *cognoscenti* for his tongue-in-cheek attitude towards some of them.
Black Sunday (wd, ph) 60. Hercules in the Centre of the Earth (wd, ph) 61. Erik the Conqueror (wd) 63. The Evil Eye (wd, ph) 63. *Black Sabbath* (wd) 63. *Blood and Black Lace* (wd, ph) 64. Planet of Blood (d) 65. Dr Goldfoot and the Girl Bombs (d) 66. Curse of the Dead (wd) 67. *Diabolik* (wd) 68. The Antecedent (d) 71, etc.

Bavier, Frances (1903–1989)
Motherly American actress, mainly on TV and best known for her Emmy award-winning performance as Aunt Bee on *The Andy Griffith Show* 60–68.
The Day the Earth Stood Still 51. The Lady Says No 51. Horizons West 52. Benji 74, etc.
TV series: It's a Great Life 54–56. The Eve Arden Show 57–58. Mayberry R.F.D. 68–70.

Bax, Sir Arnold (1883–1953)
British composer in a romantic style who scored occasional films. Born in London, he studied at the Royal Academy of Music. He was knighted in 1937 and became Master of the King's Music in 1942.
■ Malta GC 43. Oliver Twist 48. Journey into History 48.

Baxley, Barbara (1927–1990)
American character actress.
The Badlanders 58. The Savage Eye 60. All Fall Down 62. Countdown 67. No Way to Treat a Lady 68. The Impostor (TV) 74. Nashville 75. Norma Rae 79, etc.

Baxley, Craig R.
American director of action films.
Action Jackson 88. I Come in Peace/Dark Angel 91. Stone Cold 91, etc.

Baxt, George (1923–)
American author of mystery novels, dramatist and screenwriter, mainly of British movies. He has also written a series of mysery novels featuring screen actors, including *The William Powell and Myrna Loy Murder Case* and *The Mae West Murder Case*.
Circus of Horrors 60. City of the Dead 60. Payroll 61. Night of the Eagle 61. Payroll 61. Shadow of the Cat 61. Vampire Circus (story) 72. Tower of Evil/Horror of Snape Island (story) 72, etc.

Baxter, Alan (1908–1976)
Cold-eyed American second lead of the 40s; graduated to colonels and tough executives.
Mary Burns Fugitive 35. The Last Gangster 37. Gangs of New York 38. Each Dawn I Die 39. Santa Fe Trail 40. Saboteur 42. Submarine Base 43. Winged Victory 44. The Set Up 49. The Devil's Weed 49. End of the Line (in Britain) 56. The True Story of Jesse James 57. The Mountain Road 60. Judgment at Nuremburg 61. This Property is Condemned 66. Willard 71, etc.

Baxter, Anne (1923–1985)
American leading lady who usually played shy and innocent but proved equally at home as a schemer. Trained for the stage but was starring in Hollywood at seventeen. After 1960 found the going tough. The first of her three husbands was actor John Hodiak (1946–53).
Autobiography: 1977, *Intermission*.
■ Twenty Mule Team 40. The Great Profile 40. Charley's Aunt 41. Swamp Water 41. The Pied Piper 42. *The Magnificent Ambersons* 42. Crash Dive 43. *Five Graves to Cairo* 43. North Star 43. The Sullivans 44. The Eve of St Mark 44. Sunday Dinner for a Soldier 44. *Guest in the House* 45. A Royal Scandal 45. Smoky 46. Angel on My Shoulder 46. *The Razor's Edge* (AA) 46. Blaze of Noon 47. Homecoming 48. The Walls of Jericho 48. The Luck of the Irish 48. Yellow Sky 48. You're My Everything 49. A Ticket to Tomahawk 49. *All About Eve* (AAN) 50. Follow the Sun 51. The Outcasts of Poker Flat 52. My Wife's Best Friend 52. Full House 52. I Confess 53. The Blue Gardenia 53. Carnival Story 54. Bedevilled 55. One Desire 55. The Spoilers 55. The Come On 56. The Ten Commandments 56. Three Violent People 57. *Chase a Crooked Shadow* 57. Summer of the Seventeenth Doll 60. Mix Me a Person 61. Cimarron 61. A Walk on the Wild Side 62. The Family Jewels 65. Frontier Woman 66. The Busy Body 67. Companions in Nightmare (TV) 67. Stranger on the Run (TV) 68. The Challengers (TV) 68. The Tall Women 68. Marcus Welby MD (TV pilot) 69. Ritual of Evil 69. The Catcher (TV) 71. Fools Parade 71. The Late Liz 71. If Tomorrow Comes (TV) 71. Lisa Bright and Dark (TV) 72. The Moneychangers (TV) 76. Jane Austen in Manhattan 80. East of Eden (TV) 81.
TV series: Marcus Welby, MD 69–70. Hotel 83–85.

Baxter, Beryl (1926–) (Beryl Ivory)
British leading lady who was groomed for stardom but starred in only one film, and that notoriously poor *Idol of Paris* 46.
Subsequently: The Man with the Twisted Lip 51. Counterspy 53.

Baxter, Jane (1909–1996) (Feodora Forde)
Gentle-mannered British actress of stage and screen. Born in Germany, she studied drama with Italia Conti, and was on the London stage from 1925. Married twice.
Bed and Breakfast 30. The Constant Nymph 33 The Clairvoyant 34. Blossom Time 34. The Night of the Party 34. We Live Again (US) 34. Drake of England 35. Enchanted April 35. The Man Behind the Mask 36. Dusty Ermine 38. Second Best Bed 38. The Ware Case 38. The Chinese Bungalow 39. Ships with Wings 41. The Flemish Farm 43. Death of an Angel 52, etc.

Baxter, John (1896–1975)
Influential British producer-director of vigorous rough-and-ready dramas and comedies of the 30s and 40s which pointed the way to 50s realism and had an amiable style of their own.
Doss House 32. *Song of the Plough* 32. Lest We Forget 34. Music Hall 35. Say It with Flowers 36. Men of Yesterday 37. Crooks Tour 39. *Love on the Dole* 40. *The Common Touch* 41. *Let the People Sing* 42. *When We are Married* 43. The Shipbuilders 45. The Second Mate 50. Judgment Deferred 51. Ramsbottom Rides Again 56, many others including Old Mother Riley and Flanagan & Allen comedies.

Baxter, Les (1922–1996)
American composer and musical director. He began as a jazz saxophonist and singer, and was md for many Capitol Records albums from the 40s to the 60s.
Hot Blood 55. The Black Sleep 56. Macabre 58. Goliath and the Barbarians 59. *House of Usher* 60. The Pit and the Pendulum 61. Panic in Year Zero 62. Tales of Terror 62. *The Raven* 63. The Comedy of Terrors 63. Muscle Beach Party 64. Dr G and the Bikini Machine 65. Wild in the Streets 68. Flare Up 69. The Dunwich Horror 70. Cry of the Banshee 70. Frogs 72. I Escaped from Devil's Island 73. Savage Sisters 74. Born Again 78. The Beast Within 82, etc.

Baxter, Meredith
See Birney, Meredith Baxter.

Baxter, Stanley (1926–)
Rubber-faced Scottish comedian and impressionist of stage, screen and TV.
■ Geordie 55. *Very Important Person* 61. Crooks Anonymous 62. *The Fast Lady* 63. And Father Came Too 63. Joey Boy 65.
TV series: On the Bright Side 59–60. The Stanley Baxter Show 63, 67–68, 71. Baxter On … 64. The Stanley Baxter Picture Show 72. The Stanley Baxter Series 81.
❝ I'm the best known anonymity in the business. – *S.B.*

Baxter, Warner (1891–1951)
Distinguished-looking American leading man with stage experience. A popular hero of silent melodrama, he survived transition to talkies. Born in Columbus, Ohio, he worked as a salesman before turning to acting, and became a star in the late 20s playing the Cisco Kid in *Old Arizona*, a role he was to repeat in three more movies. After leaving Twentieth Century-Fox at the beginning of the 40s, he had a nervous breakdown and returned to make the 'B' picture series Crime Doctor for Columbia, which required no more than eight weeks' work a year. He suffered from severe arthritis and died of pneumonia following surgery.
■ Her Own Money 14. All Woman 18. Lombardi Ltd. 19. Cheated Hearts 21. First Love 21. The

Unfaithfully Yours 84. The Karate Kid 84. Mass Appeal 85. Nomads 85. Rocky IV 85. The Boss's Wife 86. F/X 86. The Karate Kid Part II 86. Broadcast News 87. Happy New Year 87. Cohen and Tate 88. A Night in the Life of Jimmy Reardon 88. The Karate Kid Part III 89. Lean on Me 89. Lock Up 89. The Fourth War 90. Rocky V 90. Year of the Gun 91. Necessary Roughness 91. Nails 92. The Adventures of Huck Finn 93. Blood In Blood Out 93. Rookie of the Year 93. 8 Seconds 94. The Next Karate Kid 94. The Scout 94. Bushwhacked 95. Spy Hard 96. Wrongfully Accused 98. Winchell (TV) 98, etc.

Conti, Tom (1941–)
Saturnine British actor, mostly on stage and TV.
Flame 74. Galileo 74. Eclipse 76. Full Circle 76. The Glittering Prizes (TV) 76. The Duellists 77. Blade on the Feather (TV) 80. The Wall (TV) 80. Merry Christmas Mr Lawrence 83. *Reuben Reuben* (AAN) 83. American Dreamer 84. Saving Grace 84. Miracles 85. Heavenly Pursuits 85. Nazi Hunter (TV) 86. Beyond Therapy 87. Shirley Valentine 89. That Summer of White Roses 89. Two Brothers Running 89. Shattered 90. Someone Else's America 95. Something to Believe In 97. Don't Go Breaking My Heart 98, etc.
TV series: The Wright Verdicts 95. Deadline 00.
❝ A film set is just a never-ending hell. – *T.C.*

Converse, Frank (1938–)
American general-purpose actor.
Hurry Sundown 67. Hour of the Gun 67. A Tattered Web (TV) 70. Dr Cook's Garden (TV) 73. The Rowdyman 73. Cruise into Terror (TV) 78. The Bushido Blade 79. Mystery at Fire Island 81. The Pilot 82. Spring Fever 83. Anne of Avonlea (TV) 87. Everybody Wins 90. Primary Motive 92, etc.
TV series: Coronet Blue 67. NYPD 67–68. *Movin' On* 74–75. The Family Tree 83.

Convertino, Michael
American composer and songwriter. Educated at Yale University and the Paris Conservatoire, he was also a singer with the rock group The Innocents.
Children of a Lesser God 86. The Hidden 87. Bull Durham 88. Queen of Hearts 89. The End of Innocence 90. Aspen Extreme 93. Bodies, Rest & Motion 93. Wrestling Ernest Hemingway 93. Guarding Tess 94. Milk Money 94. The Santa Clause 94. Things to Do in Denver When You're Dead 95. Bed of Roses 95. Mother Night 96. Jungle 2 Jungle 96. Pie in the Sky 96. The Last of the High Kings 96. Critical Care 97. Where's Marlowe 98, etc.

Conway, Gary (1936–) (Gareth Carmody)
American light leading man.
I was a Teenage Frankenstein (as the monster) 57. How to Make a Monster (as Frankenstein's Monster) 58. Young Guns of Texas 62. Black Gunn 72. Once is not Enough 75. The Farmer (& p) 77. American Ninja II (& co-w) 86. Liberty and Bash 90, etc.
TV series: *Burke's Law* 63–65. Land of the Giants 68–69.

Conway, Jack (1887–1952)
American action director, launched as acting member of D. W. Griffith's stock company; long with MGM.
■ The Old Armchair 12. Bond of Fear 18. Because of a Woman 18. Little Red Decides 18. Her Decision 18. You Can't Believe Everything 18. Diplomatic Mission 19. Desert Law 19. Riders of the Dawn 20. Lombardi Limited 20. Dwelling Place of Light 21. The Money Changers 21. The Spenders 21. The Kiss 21. A Daughter of the Law 21. Step On It 22. A Parisian Scandal 22. The Millionaire 22. Across the Deadline 22. Another Man's Shoes 22. Don't Shoot 22. The Long Chance 22. The Prisoner 23. Sawdust 23. Quicksands 23. What Wives Want 23. Trimmed in Scarlet 23. Lucretia Lombard 23. The Trouble Shooter 24. The Heart Buster 24. The Roughneck 25. The Hunted Woman 25. The Only Thing 25. Brown of Harvard 26. Soul Mates 26. The Understanding Heart 27. Twelve Miles Out 27. The Smart Set 28. Bringing Up Father 28. While the City Sleeps 28. Alias Jimmy Valentine 29. *Our Modern Maidens* 29. Untamed 29. They Learned about Women 30. *The Unholy Three* 30. New Moon 30. The Easiest Way 31. Just a Gigolo 31. *Arsène Lupin* 32. But the Flesh is Weak 32. Red-headed Woman 32. Hell Below 33. The Nuisance 33. The Solitaire Man 33. *Viva Villa* 34. The Girl from Missouri 34. The Gay Bride 34. One New York Night 35. *A Tale of Two Cities* 35. *Libeled Lady* 36. Saratoga 37. *A Yank at Oxford* 38. Too Hot to Handle 38. Let Freedom Ring 39. Lady of the Tropics 39. *Boom Town* 40. Love Crazy 40. Honky Tonk 40. Crossroads 42. Assignment in Brittany 43. Dragon Seed 44. High Barbaree 47. *The Hucksters* 47. Julia Misbehaves 48.

Conway, Morgan (1900–1981)
Tough-guy American actor of 40s 'B' pictures, chiefly notable as the screen's first Dick Tracy.
Looking for Trouble 34. Crime Ring 38. Blackwell's Island 39. Brother Orchid 40. Sing Your Worries Away 42. Jack London 44. *Dick Tracy* 45. Badman's Territory 46. Dick Tracy vs Cueball 46, many others.

Conway, Tim (1933–)
American television comic who found a niche in Disney films.
McHale's Navy 64. The World's Greatest Athlete 73. The Apple Dumpling Gang 75. Gus 76. The Billion Dollar Hobo 77. The Apple Dumpling Gang Rides Again 79. The Prize Fighter 79. The Private Eyes 80. The Long Shot 85. Dorf and the First Games of Mount Olympus 87. Dear God 96. Air Bud: Golden Receiver 98, etc.
TV series: McHale's Navy 62–65. The Tim Conway Show 70. Later with Carol Burnett. Ace Crawford 83.

Conway, Tom (1904–1967) (Thomas Sanders)
British light leading man, brother of George Sanders; well-liked as 'the Falcon' in the 40s, but his career declined very suddenly. He began drinking heavily and died in poverty.
Sky Murder 40. The Trial of Mary Dugan 41. Grand Central Murder 42. *The Falcon's Brother* 42. *Cat People* 42. I Walked with a Zombie 43. The Falcon Strikes Back 43. The Seventh Victim 43. The Falcon Out West 44 (and five other Falcon adventures ending in 1946). Criminal Court 46. Repeat Performance 47. One Touch of Venus 48. Confidence Girl 52. Park Plaza 505 (GB) 53. Barbados Quest (GB) 55. The Last Man to Hang (GB) 56. The She-Creature 56. Twelve to the Moon 60. What a Way to Go (unbilled) 64, many others.
TV series: Mark Saber 52–54. The Betty Hutton Show 59.

Conyers, Darcy (1919–1973)
British director, former actor.
Ha'penny Breeze (& p) 52. The Devil's Pass (& w, p) 56. The Night We Dropped a Clanger 60. Nothing Barred 61. In the Doghouse 62, etc.

Cooder, Ry (1947–)
American guitarist, singer and composer of blues-tinged scores.
Goin' South (s) 78. The Long Riders 80. Southern Comfort 81. The Border 81. Streets of Fire 84. Paris, Texas 84. Alamo Bay 85. Brewster's Millions 85. Crossroads 86. Blue City 86. Extreme Prejudice (md) 87. Johnny Handsome 90. Geronimo: An American Legend 93. Last Man Standing 96. The End of Violence 97. Primary Colors 98, etc.

Coogan, Jackie (1914–1984)
American child actor of the 20s who achieved outstanding star status but later reappeared as a less appealing adult in minor roles. Louis B. MAYER of MGM kept him out of films for six years after he refused to drop a law suit against his mother and stepfather who had squandered his earnings. He was married to actress Betty GRABLE (1937–39).
The Kid 20. *Peck's Bad Boy* 21. *Oliver Twist* 21. My Boy 22. Trouble 22. Daddy 23. Circus Days 23. Long Live the King 24. A Boy of Flanders 24. The Rag Man 24. Little Robinson Crusoe 25. Johnny Get Your Gun 25. Old Clothes 25. Johnny Get Your Hair Cut 26. The Bugle Call 27. Buttons 27. Tom Sawyer 30. Huckleberry Finn 31. Home on the Range 35. College Swing 38. Kilroy Was Here 47. Outlaw Women 52. Lost Women 56. High School Confidential 58. A Fine Madness 66. The Shakiest Gun in the West 68. Marlowe 69. Cahill 73. The Escape Artist 82, many others.
TV series: Cowboy G-Men 52. McKeever and the Colonel 62. *The Addams Family* (as Uncle Fester) 64–66, 73–74.

Coogan, Keith (1970–) (Keith Franklin)
Young American actor. He is the grandson of Jackie COOGAN.
Adventures in Babysitting 87. Hiding Out 87. Cheetah 89. Under the Boardwalk 89. Cousins 89. Book of Love 90. Toy Soldiers 91. Don't Tell Mom the Babysitter's Dead 91. In the Army Now 94. The Power Within 95. Downhill Willie 96. Ivory Tower 97, etc.

Cook, Clyde (1891–1984)
Australian clown and dancer who played in many Mack Sennett comedies and settled in California. Subsequently played character roles.
Soldiers of Fortune 19. Skirts 21. The Eskimo 22. He Who Gets Slapped 24. The Winning of Barbara Worth 26. Good Time Charley 27. The Spieler 28. The Taming of the Shrew 29. Sunny 30. Blondie of the Follies 32. Oliver Twist 33. Barbary Coast 35. Kidnapped 38. The Little Princess 39. The Sea Hawk 40. White Cargo 42. To Each His Own 46. Pride of Maryland 51, many others.

Cook, Donald (1900–1961)
American stage leading man who never quite made it in Hollywood.
The Mad Genius 31. The Public Enemy 31. The Conquerors 32. Heart of New York 32. The Man Who Played God 32. Penguin Pool Murder 32. The Trial of Vivienne Ware 32. Baby Face 33. The Circus Queen Murder 33. Fog 33. Frisco Jenny 33. Jennie Gerhardt 33. The World Changes 33. Jealousy 34. Long Lost Father 34. The Night Is Young 34. The Ninth Guest 34. Viva Villa! 34. Whirlpool 34. The Casino Murder Case 35. Confidential 35. Here Comes the Band 35. Ladies Love Danger 35. The Leavenworth Case 35. Murder in the Fleet 35. Can This Be Dixie? 36. Showboat 36. Bowery to Broadway 44. Murder in the Blue Room 44. Patrick the Great 44. Here Come the Coeds 45. Our Very Own 50, etc.
TV series: Too Young to Go Steady 59.

Cook Jnr, Elisha (1903–1995)
American character actor adept at cowards and neurotics.
Her Unborn Child 30. Two in a Crowd 36. Pigskin Parade 36. Love Is News 37. Breezing Home 37. Wife, Doctor and Nurse 37. Danger Love at Work 37. Life Begins in College 37. They Won't Forget 37. The Devil Is Driving 37. My Lucky Star 38. Submarine Patrol 38. Three Blind Mice 38. Grand Jury Secrets 39. Newsboy's Home 39. He Married His Wife 40. Stranger on the Third Floor 40. Public Deb Number One 40. Love Crazy 40. Tin Pan Alley 40. Man at Large 41. Sergeant York 41. Ball of Fire 41. *The Maltese Falcon* (as Wilmer the gunsel) 41. *I Wake Up Screaming* 41. A Gentleman at Heart 42. In This Our Life 42. Sleepytime Gal 42. A-Haunting We Will Go 42. Manila Calling 42. Hellzapoppin 42. Wildcat 42. Casanova Brown 44. *Phantom Lady* 44. Up in Arms 44. Dark Mountain 44. *Dark Waters* 44. Dillinger 44. Why Girls Leave Home 44. *The Big Sleep* 46. Blonde Alibi 46. Cinderella Jones 46. The Falcon's Alibi 46. Joe Palooka Champ 46. Two Smart People 46. Born to Kill 47. The Fall Guy 47. The Long Night 47. The Gangster 47. Flaxy Martin 49. The Great Gatsby 49. Behave Yourself 51. Don't Bother to Knock 51. I the Jury 53. Thunder over the Plains 53. *Shane* 53. The Outlaw's Daughter 54. Drum Beat 54. Timberjack 55. The Indian Fighter 55. Trial 55. *The Killing* 56. Accused of Murder 56. The Lonely Man 57. Voodoo Island 57. Baby Face Nelson 57. Plunder Road 57. Chicago Confidential 57. House on Haunted Hill 58. Day of the Outlaw 59. Platinum High School 60. College Confidential 60. One-Eyed Jacks 61. Papa's Delicate Condition 63. The Haunted Palace 63. Black Zoo 63. Johnny Cool 63. Blood on the Arrow 64. The Glass Cage 64. Welcome to Hard Times 67. Rosemary's Baby 68. The Great Bank Robbery 69. El Condor 70. The Movie Murderer (TV) 70. Night Chase (TV) 70. The Great Northfield Minnesota Raid 72. Blacula 72. The Night Stalker (TV) 72. Emperor of the North Pole 73. Electra Glide in Blue 73. The Outfit 73. The Black Bird 75. Messiah of Evil 75. Winterhawk 75. St Ives 76. Mad Bull (TV) 77. 1941 79. The Champ 79. Leave 'Em Laughing (TV) 80. Carny 80. Tom Horn 80. Harry's War 80. Salem's Lot 80. Hammett 82. This Girl for Hire 84. National Lampoon Goes to the Movies 84, etc.
❝ As he has grown older, the vulnerable look has congealed in his face so that his very presence has become an open invitation to destroy him. – *Ian Cameron*

Cook, Fielder (1923–)
American TV director who makes occasional films.
Patterns of Power 56. Home is the Hero (Eire) 59. *Big Hand for a Little Lady* 66. How to Save a Marriage 67. Prudence and the Pill 68. Teacher Teacher (TV) 69. Who Killed the Mysterious Mr Foster? (TV) 70. Goodbye Raggedy Ann (TV) 71. Eagle in a Cage 71. The Hands of Cormac Joyce (TV) 72. Miracle on 34th Street (TV) 73. From the Mixed Up Files of Mrs Basil E. Frankenweiler 73. This Is the West that Was (TV) 74. Judge Horton and the Scottsboro Boys (TV) 76. Beauty and the Beast (TV) 77. Too Far to Go (TV) 79. I Know Why the Caged Bird Sings (TV) 79. Family Reunion (TV) 81. Evergreen (TV) 85. A Special Friendship (TV) 87. The Member of the Wedding (TV) 97, etc.

Cook, Joe (1890–1959) (Joseph Lopez)
American comic in Broadway musicals and revues of the 20s, 30s and 40s, and star of the movie version of his 1928 stage success *Rain and Shine*, which was directed in 1930 by Frank Capra, who turned it into a drama without music. A comedian with a broad grin and an original line in nonsense patter, he was also a multi-instrumentalist, knife-thrower, expert shot, rope-spinner, juggler, slack-wire walker and acrobat, skills which he demonstrated in the film.

Cook, Peter (1937–1995)
English comic actor, writer and revue artist. Born in Torquay, Devon, and educated at Cambridge University, he found success early as a revue writer, and as a performer with Alan BENNETT, Jonathan MILLER and Dudley MOORE in the revue *Beyond the Fringe*. He founded the briefly fashionable nightclub The Establishment in the 60s and was the principal owner of the satirical magazine *Private Eye*. He formed a successful double-act with Dudley Moore, but boredom and heavy drinking hampered his later life. The second of his three wives was actress Judy Huxtable.
Biography: 1997, *Peter Cook* by Harry Thompson.
■ The Wrong Box 66. Bedazzled 67. A Dandy in Aspic 68. Monte Carlo or Bust 69. The Bed Sitting Room 69. The Rise and Rise of Michael Rimmer 70. The Adventures of Barry Mackenzie 72. The Hound of the Baskervilles 77. Yellowbeard 83. Supergirl 84. Whoops Apocalypse 86. Mr Jolly Lives Next Door 87. The Princess Bride 87. Without a Clue 88. Getting It Right 89. Great Balls of Fire 89. Black Beauty 94.
TV series: Not Only ... but Also 65–66. Goodbye Again 68–69. Not Only ... but Also 71.
❝ In him, morality is discovered far from its official haunts, the message of a character like Peter's being that a life of complete self-indulgence, if *led* with the whole heart, may also bring wisdom. – *Alan Bennett*

Cook, Rachael Leigh (1979–)
American actress. Born in Minneapolis, Minnesota, she began as a model from the age of ten.
The Babysitters Club 95. Tom and Huck 96. Carpool 96. The House of Yes 97. The Eighteenth Angel 97. Living Out Loud 98. The Naked Man 98. She's All That 99. Get Carter 00. Antitrust 01, etc.

Cook, Tommy (1930–)
American actor, in films from childhood; later became a tennis professional, concert promoter and producer.
The Tuttles from Tahiti 42. Tarzan and the Leopard Woman 45. Michael O'Halloran 48. American Guerilla in the Philippines 50. Panic in the Streets 50. Teen Age Crime Wave 55. Mohawk 56. Missile to the Moon 58. Roller Coaster (p) 77. Players (p) 79, etc.

Cool J, LL
see *LL Cool J*.

Coolidge, Martha (1946–)
American director and screenwriter. She trained as an actress and began as a documentary film-maker.
Not a Pretty Picture (& w) 76. Valley Girl 83. Joy of Sex 84. City Girl (& w) 84. Real Genius 85. Plain Clothes 88. That's Adequate (a) 90. Rambling Rose 91. Crazy in Love 92. Lost in

Yonkers 93. Angie 94. Three Wishes 95. Out to Sea 97, etc.

Coombe, Carol (1911–1966)
Blonde Australian leading actress who came to Britain in 1930 and starred in several films of the decade.
P.C. Josser 31. The Sport of Kings 31. Sally in Our Alley 31. The Ringer 31. Tilly of Bloomsbury 31. The Ghost Train 31. The Strangler 32. Double Bluff 33. The Man without a Face 35. Woman to Woman 46, etc.

Cooney, Ray (1932–)
English dramatist, screenwriter, director, producer and actor, mainly of farces, in occasional films. Born in London, he was on stage from the age of 14. A Hungarian version of his farce *Out of Order* became one of the most successful releases in that country in the late 90s.
The Hand (co-w, a) 60. The Night We Got the Bird (co-w) 60. Prize of Arms (a) 61. What a Carve Up! (co-w) 61. Not Now, Darling (co-d, a, oa) 72. Not Now, Comrade (w, co-d, a) 77. There Goes the Bride (p, co-w) 79. Why Not Stay for Breakfast? (ex p, co-w) 79. Whose Life Is It, Anyway? (ex p) 81, etc.
TV series: My Sister and I (a) 56. They Met in a City (a) 60–62. Norman (co-w) 70.

Coop, Denys (1920–1981)
British cameraman.
A Kind of Loving 61. Billy Liar 63. This Sporting Life 63. One Way Pendulum 64. King and Country 65. Bunny Lake Is Missing 65. The Double Man 67. My Side of the Mountain 68. 10 Rillington Place 70. Superman (AA visual effects) 78, etc.

Cooper, Ben (1930–)
American light juvenile lead, mainly in westerns.
The Woman They almost Lynched 52. Perilous Journey 53. Johnny Guitar 54. Jubilee Trail 54. The Eternal Sea 55. The Last Command 56. *The Rose Tattoo* 57. Chartroose Caboose 60. Gunfight at Comanche Creek 64. Arizona Raiders 65. Red Tomahawk 67. Support Your Local Gunfighter 71. One More Train to Rob 71. The Sky's the Limit 75. Lightning Jack 94, many others.

Cooper, Chris (1951–)
American character actor, often seen in the films of John Sayles.
Bad Timing 80. Matewan 87. Lonesome Dove (TV) 89. Guilty by Suspicion 90. City of Hope 91. Return to Lonesome Dove (TV) 93. This Boy's Life 93. Pharaoh's Army 95. Money Train 95. Lone Star 96. Great Expectations 98. The Horse Whisperer 98. American Beauty 99. October Sky 99. The Patriot 00. Me, Myself and Irene 00 etc.

Cooper, Frederick (1890–1945)
Ferrety-looking British character actor who managed a few choice roles.
Thunder Rock 42. The Great Mr Handel 42. Warn That Man 43. Henry V (as Nym) 44, etc.

Cooper, Gary (1901–1961) (Frank J. Cooper)
Slow-speaking, deep-thinking American leading man, a long-enduring Hollywood star who always projected honest determination. Born in Helena, Montana, of successful English immigrant parents, he was educated partly in England, before working unenthusiastically as an illustrator and cartoonist. Determined to break into films, he went to Hollywood, where he used his horse-riding skills, learned on the family ranch, as an extra and bit player in westerns, progressing to two-reelers before becoming a star in his first feature, *The Winning of Barbara Worth* 26. Thereafter, he remained one for 30 years, as an embodiment of a strong, silent man of integrity and honour. Special Academy Award 1960 'for his many memorable screen performances and for the international recognition he, as an individual, has gained for the film industry'. Married Veronica Balfe, who had a brief Hollywood career under the name of Sandra Shaw. His lovers included Clara Bow, Evelyn Brent, Lupe Velez, Ingrid Bergman and Patricia Neal; Cecil Beaton also claimed to have had an affair with him.
His defining roles were as The Virginian, in the film of the same name; Tom Brown, in *Morocco*; Lieutenant McGregor, in *The Lives of a Bengal Lancer*; Longfellow Deeds in *Mr Deeds Goes to Town*; Beau Geste, in the film of the same name; Long John Willoughby, in *Meet John Doe*; Alvin C. York, in *Sergeant York*; Lou Gehrig, in *Pride of the Yankees*; Robert Jordan, in *For Whom the Bell Tolls*; Howard Roark, in *The Fountainhead*; and Will Kane, in *High Noon*.
Biography: 1979, *Gary Cooper: An Intimate Biography* by Hector Arce. 1981, *The Last Hero* by Larry Swindell.
■ The Thundering Herd 25. Wild Horse Mesa 25. The Lucky Horseshoe 25. The Vanishing American 25. The Eagle 25. The Enchanted Hill 26. Watch Your Wife 26. The Winning of Barbara Worth 26. It 27. Children of Divorce 27. Arizona Bound 27. Wings 27. Nevada 27. The Last Outlaw 27. Beau Sabreur 28. Legion of the Condemned 28. Doomsday 28. Half a Bride 28. *Lilac Time* 28. The First Kiss 28. Shopworn Angel 28. Wolf Song 29. The Betrayal 29. The Virginian 29. Only the Brave 29. The Texan 29. Seven Days' Leave 30. A Man from Wyoming 30. Paramount on Parade 30. The Spoilers 30. Morocco 30. Fighting Caravans 31. I Take This Woman 31. His Woman 31. The Devil and the Deep 32. *A Farewell to Arms* 32. *City Streets* 32. If I Had a Million 32. One Sunday Afternoon 33. Alice in Wonderland (as the White Knight) 33. Today We Live 33. Design for Living 34. Peter Ibbetson 34. Operator Thirteen 34. The Wedding Night 35. *Lives of a Bengal Lancer* 35. Now and Forever 35. Desire 36. *Mr Deeds Goes to Town* (AAN) 36. The General Died at Dawn 36. *The Plainsman* 36. Souls at Sea 37. The Adventures of Marco Polo 38. Bluebeard's Eighth Wife 38. The Cowboy and the Lady 39. *Beau Geste* 39. The Real Glory 39. *The Westerner* 40. Northwest Mounted Police 40. *Meet John Doe* 41. *Sergeant York* (AA) 41. Ball of Fire 41. Pride of the Yankees (AAN) 42. *For Whom the Bell Tolls* (AAN) 43. The Story of Dr Wassell 44. Saratoga Trunk 44. Casanova Brown 44. Along Came Jones (& p) 45. Cloak and Dagger 46. Unconquered 47. Variety Girl 47 (cameo). Good Sam 48. The Fountainhead 49. Task Force 49. It's a Great Feeling 49 (cameo). Bright Leaf 50. Dallas 50. You're in the Navy Now 51. Distant Drums 51. Springfield Rifle 52. *High Noon* (AA) 52. Return to Paradise 52. Blowing Wild 53. Garden of Evil 54. *Vera Cruz* 54. The Court Martial of Billy Mitchell 55. Alias Jesse James 55 (cameo). Friendly Persuasion 56. Love in the Afternoon 56. *Ten North Frederick* 58. Man of the West 58. They Came to Cordura 59. The Hanging Tree 59. The Wreck of the Mary Deare 59. The Naked Edge (GB) 61.
✪ For his sheer domination of the Hollywood scene for the first twenty years of the talkies. *Mr Deeds Goes to Town*.
❝ The most underrated actor I ever worked with said Henry Hathaway.
Fred Zinnemann put it another way: 'He had magic. The only time he was in trouble was when he tried to act.',
He was a poet of the real –
said Clifford Odets. Whatever that means, it would have embarrassed Cooper. Perhaps Carl Sandburg put it another way: 'One of the most beloved illiterates this country has ever known.'
Cooper had no very high estimate of his own talent: 'People ask me how come you been around so long. Well, it's through playing the part of Mr Average Joe American.'
He had Mr Average Joe's reputed insularity: 'From what I hear about communism, I don't like it because it isn't on the level.'
He distrusted the socialism of plays like *Death of a Salesman*: 'Sure there are fellows like Willy Loman, but you don't have to write plays about them.'
He enjoyed his niche: 'Until I came along, all the leading men were handsome, but luckily they wrote a lot of stories about the fellow next door.'
For a man without acting training, he managed very well. King Vidor thought that: 'He got a reputation as a great actor just by thinking hard about the next line.'
Coop's own explanation was simpler: 'To get folks to like you, I figured you sort of had to be their ideal. I don't mean a handsome knight riding a white horse, but a fellow who answered the description of a right guy.'
Richard Arlen summed up: 'Coop just likes people, it's as simple as that.'
But Richard Zanuck latched on to another Cooper essential: he was part of the great outdoors: 'You could never put Coop in a small hat and get your money back.'
Famous line (*Sergeant York*) 'Folks back home used to say I could shoot a rifle before I was weaned. They was exaggerating some.'
Famous line (*The Virginian*) 'If you want to call me that, smile.'
Famous line (*For Whom the Bell Tolls*) 'A man fights for what he believes in, Fernando.'

Cooper, George A. (1916–)
British character actor of vengeful types.
Miracle in Soho 56. Violent Playground 58. Tom Jones 63. Nightmare 64. Life at the Top 65. The Strange Affair 68. Dracula Has Risen from the Grave 68. Start the Revolution without Me 70. Bless This House 72. The Black Windmill 74, etc.
TV series: Nice Work 89.

Cooper, Dame Gladys (1888–1971)
Distinguished, gracious British stage actress who essentially began her film career in Hollywood at the age of 52, subsequently airing her warm aristocratic personality in many unworthy roles and a few good ones.
Autobiography: 1931, *Gladys Cooper*.
Biography: 1953, *Without Veils* by Sewell Stokes.
■ Masks and Faces 17. The Sorrows of Satan 17. My Lady's Dress 18. The Bohemian Girl 22. Bonnie Prince Charles 23. Dandy Donovan 31. The Iron Duke 35. *Rebecca* 40. Kitty Foyle 40. That Hamilton Woman 41. The Black Cat 41. The Gay Falcon 41. This Above All 42. Eagle Squadron 42. *Now Voyager* (AAN) 42. Forever and a Day 43. Mr Lucky 43. Princess O'Rourke 43. The Song of Bernadette (AAN) 43. The White Cliffs of Dover 44. Mrs Parkington 44. The Valley of Decision 45. Love Letters 45. The Green Years 46. The Cockeyed Miracle 46. Green Dolphin Street 47. Beware of Pity 47. The Bishop's Wife 47. Homecoming 48. The Pirate 48. The Secret Garden 49. Madame Bovary 49. Thunder on the Hill 51. At Sword's Point 52. The Man Who Loved Redheads 54. *Separate Tables* 58. The List of Adrian Messenger 63. *My Fair Lady* (AAN) 64. The Happiest Millionaire 67. A Nice Girl Like Me 69.
TV series: *The Rogues* 64.

Cooper, Jackie (1921–)
'Little tough guy' American child actor who in adult life found roles getting rarer and became a powerful TV executive.
Autobiography: 1981, *Please Don't Shoot My Dog*.
■ *Our Gang* shorts 27–28. Movietone Follies 28. Sunny Side Up 29. *Skippy* (AAN) 31. Young Donovan's Kid 31. *The Champ* 31. Sooky 31. When a Feller Needs a Friend 32. Divorce in the Family 32. Broadway to Hollywood 33. *The Bowery* 33. *Treasure Island* 34. Peck's Bad Boy 34. Lone Cowboy 34. Dinky 35. O'Shaughnessy's Boy 35. Tough Guy 36. The Devil is a Sissy 36. Boy of the Streets 37. White Banners 38. That Certain Age 38. Gangster's Boy 38. Newsboys' Home 39. Scouts to the Rescue 39. Spirit of Culver 39. Streets of New York 39. Two Bright Boys 39. What a Life 39. The Big Guy 39. Seventeen 40. The Return of Frank James 40. Gallant Sons 40. Life with Henry 41. Ziegfeld Girl 41. Her First Beau 41. Glamour Boy 41. Syncopation 42. Men of Texas 42. The Navy Comes Through 42. Where are your Children? 44. Stork Bites Man 47. Kilroy Was Here 47. French Leave 48. Everything's Ducky 61. Shadow on the Land (TV) 68. The Astronaut (TV) 71. The Love Machine 71. Maybe I'll Come Home in the Spring (TV) 71. Stand Up and Be Counted (d only) 72. Chosen Survivors 74. The Day the Earth Moved (TV) 74. The Invisible Man (TV) 75. Mobile Two (TV) 75. Superman 78. Superman II 80. Superman III 83. Superman IV 87.
TV series: The People's Choice 56–58. Hennessey 59–71. Mobile One 75.

Cooper, James Fenimore (1789–1851)
American adventure novelist whose 'westerns' include *The Last of the Mohicans*, *The Pathfinder* and *The Deerslayer*, all frequently filmed.

Cooper, Melville (1896–1973)
British comedy character actor, long in Hollywood playing pompous upper-class idiots.
■ The Calendar 31. Black Coffee 31. Two White Arms 32. Forgin' Ahead 33. Leave It To Me 33. To Brighton with Gladys 33. The Private Life of Don Juan 34. The Scarlet Pimpernel 34. The Bishop Misbehaves (US from now on) 35. The Gorgeous Hussy 36. The Last of Mrs Cheyney 37. Thin Ice 37. The Great Garrick 37. Tovarich 37. Women Are Like That 37. *The Adventures of Robin Hood* (as Sheriff of Nottingham) 38. Gold Diggers in Paris 38. Four's a Crowd 38. Hard to Get 38. The Dawn Patrol 38. Comet over Broadway 38. Dramatic School 38. Garden of the Moon 38. I'm from Missouri 39. Blind Alley 39. The Sun Never Sets 39. Two Bright Boys 39. Rebecca 40. Too Many Husbands 40. *Pride and Prejudice* (his best role, as the pompous Mr Collins) 40. Murder over New York 40. Submarine Zone 40. The Flame of New Orleans 41. The Lady Eve 41. Scotland Yard 41. You Belong to Me 41. This Above All 42. The Affairs of Martha 42. Random Harvest 42. Life Begins at 8.30 42. The Immortal Sergeant 43. Hit Parade of 1943 43. Holy Matrimony 43. My Kingdom for a Cook 43. Heartbeat 46. 13 Rue Madeleine 46. The Imperfect Lady 47. Enchantment 48. The Red Danube 49. Love Happy 49. And Baby Makes Three 49. The Underworld Story 50. Father of the Bride 50. Let's Dance 50. The Petty Girl 50. It Should Happen to You 53. Moonfleet 55. The King's Thief 55. Diane 55. Bundle of Joy 56. Around the World in 80 Days 56. The Story of Mankind 57. From the Earth to the Moon 58.

Cooper, Merian C. (1893–1973)
American executive producer associated with many adventurous films. Special Academy Award 1952 'for his many innovations and contributions to the art of the motion picture'.
Grass 25. *Chang* 27. The Four Feathers 29. *King Kong* 33. The Last Days of Pompeii 35. The Toy Wife 38. Fort Apache 48. Mighty Joe Young 49. Rio Grande 50. The Quiet Man 52. *This is Cinerama* 52. The Searchers 56, etc.

Cooper, Miriam (1892–1976)
American silent screen actress who married Raoul Walsh.
Autobiography: 1978, *Dark Lady of the Silents*.
A Blot on the Scutcheon 11. When Fate Frowned 14. The Birth of a Nation 15. His Return 15. The Woman and the Law 18. Kindred of the Dust 22. Her Accidental Husband 23, many others.

Cooper, Richard (1893–1947)
English character actor, on stage from 1913 and notable in the title role of *Charley's Aunt*. In films from 1929, usually in muddle-headed roles.
At the Villa Rose 29. Enter the Queen 30. Black Coffee 31. The First Mrs Fraser 32. Home Sweet Home 33. Lord Edgware Dies 34. The Black Abbot 34. That's My Uncle 35. Shipyard Sally 39. Inspector Hornleigh Goes to It 41, etc.

Cooper, Stuart (1942–)
American director who got his first breaks in Britain.
Little Malcolm and his Struggle against the Eunuchs 74. Overlord 75. The Disappearance 77. A.D. (TV) 84. The Long Hot Summer (TV) 85. Christmas Eve (TV) 86. The Fortunate Pilgrim (TV) 88, etc.

Cooper, Violet Kemble (1886–1961)
British stage actress who appeared in a few Hollywood films in the 30s.
Our Betters 33. Vanessa 34. David Copperfield (as Miss Murdstone) 35. The Invisible Ray 36. Romeo and Juliet 36, etc.

Cooper, Wilkie (1911–)
British cinematographer, once a child actor.
The Rake's Progress 45. Green for Danger 46. Captain Boycott 47. London Belongs to Me 48. Stage Fright 50. The Admirable Crichton 57. Jason and the Argonauts 63. One Million Years BC 66, etc.

Coote, Robert (1909–1982)
British stage character actor who filmed mainly in Hollywood; familiar in amiable silly-ass roles.
Sally in Our Alley 31. *A Yank at Oxford* 38. Gunga Din (US) 39. You Can't Fool Your Wife 40. The Commandos Strike at Dawn 43. A Matter of Life and Death 46. The Ghost and Mrs Muir 47. Forever Amber 47. Bonnie Prince Charlie 48. The Three Musketeers 48. The Elusive Pimpernel 50. Rommel, Desert Fox 51. *The Prisoner of Zenda* 52. The Constant Husband 55. Othello (as Roderigo) 55. The Swan 56. Merry Andrew 58. The League of Gentlemen 59. The Golden Head 65. A Man Could Get Killed 66. The Swinger 66. Prudence and the Pill 68. Up the Front 72. Theatre of Blood 73. Institute for Revenge (TV) 79, etc.
TV series: *The Rogues* 64.

Cope, Kenneth (1931–)
British TV actor, usually of Liverpudlian types.
The Criminal 60. The Damned 62. Genghis Khan 65. Dateline Diamonds 65. She'll Follow You Anywhere 71, etc.
TV series: Coronation Street. Randall and Hopkirk (Deceased).

Copeland, Stewart (1952–)
American drummer and composer, in England as a child, and a founder of the rock band Police.
Rumble Fish 83. Out of Bounds 86. Wall Street 87. Talk Radio 88. She's Having a Baby 88. See No Evil, Hear No Evil 89. Hidden Agenda 90. The First Power 90. Highlander II: The Quickening 90. Men at Work 90. Riff-Raff 90. Taking Care of Business 90. Wide Sargasso Sea 92. Airborne 93. Bank Robber 93. Decadence 93. Raining Stones 93. Rapa Nui 94. Fresh 94. Surviving the Game 94. Silent Fall 94. Boys 96. The Pallbearer 96. Gridlock'd 97. Good Burger 97. Four Days in September 97. Pecker 98. Very Bad Things 98. West Beyrouth 98. She's All That 99. Simpatico 99. Skipped Parts 00, etc.

Copland, Aaron (1900–1990)
American composer. Born in Brooklyn, New York, the son of Russian immigrants, he studied in France and returned to the United States to make a reputation as an avante garde composer before writing more popular music that included his film scores. His lovers included composer Leonard Bernstein.
Biography: 2000, *Aaron Copland: The Life and Work of an Uncommon Man* by Howard Pollack.
■ *The City* 39. *Of Mice and Men* (AAN) 39. *Our Town* (AAN) 40. North Star (AAN) 43. Fiesta 47. *The Red Pony* 49. The Heiress (AA) 49. Something Wild 61. He Got Game 98.

Copley, Peter (1915–)
British stage actor who makes occasional film appearances, usually in quiet, downtrodden or slightly sinister roles. Born in Bushey, Hertfordshire, he studied acting at the Old Vic School, and was on stage from 1932. The first of his three wives was actress Pamela Brown.
The Golden Salamander 49. The Card 52. The Sword and the Rose 53. Foreign Intrigue 56. Victim 61. King and Country 64. Help! 65. The Knack 65. Quatermass and the Pit 67. The Shoes of the Fishermen 68. Frankenstein Must Be Destroyed 69. Jane Eyre 70. Hennessy 75. Shout at the Devil 76. Empire of the Sun 87. Second Best 94. Wives and Daughters (TV) 99, etc.

Coppel, Alec (1910–1972)
Australian playwright, screenwriter and novelist.
Over the Moon (w) 39. Obsession (oa) 46. Mr Denning Drives North (w) 51. The Captain's Paradise (AANw) 53. The Gazebo (oa) 59. Moment to Moment (w) 66. The Bliss of Mrs Blossom (w) 69, etc.

Coppola, Carmine (1910–1991)
American composer, musician and conductor, the father of Francis Ford Coppola and Talia Shire, and the grandfather of director Sofia Coppola and actor Nicolas Cage.
Tonight for Sure 61. Finian's Rainbow 68. The Godfather Part II (co-m) (AA) 74. Apocalypse Now 79. The Black Stallion 79. The Outsiders 83. Blood Red 86. Gardens of Stone 87. Tucker: The Man and His Dream 88. New York Stories 89. The Godfather Part III (AANs) 90, etc.
❝ My father had a slogan he always used to tell us – and it's a good slogan: Steal from the best. – *Francis Ford Coppola*

Coppola, Francis Ford (1939–)
American writer-director of overweening ambition, who began working for Roger Corman. After the deserved success of *The Godfather* he set up his own studio, American Zoetrope, but later ran into financial difficulties as the filming of *Apocalypse Now* went out of control. In the 90s, he reverted to being a director for hire. He also owns a California winery, sells food products including olive oil, sauces and pasta, publishes a short story magazine, and plans to start Internet companies. He is the father of director Sofia Coppola.
Biography: 1989, *Coppola* by Peter Cowie. 1995, *Whom God Wishes to Destroy: Coppola and the New Hollywood* by Jon Lewis. 2000, *Francis Ford Coppola: A Filmmaker's Life* by Michael Schumacher.
Other books: 1988, *Hollywood Auteur – Francis Coppola* by Jeffrey Chown.
■ Dementia 63. This Property Is Condemned (w) 65. Is Paris Burning? (w) 66. *You're a Big Boy Now* (wd) 67. Finian's Rainbow (d) 68. The Rain People (wd) 69. Patton (w only) (AA) 69. *The Godfather* (co-w) (AAN) 72. American Graffiti (p only) 73. The Great Gatsby (w only) 74. *The Conversation* (wd, p) (AANw) 74. The Godfather Part Two (wd, p) (AA) 74. Apocalypse Now (BFA, AAN) 79. One from the Heart (wd, p) 82. Hammett (p) 82. The Escape Artist (p) 82. The Outsiders 83. Rumble Fish 83. The Cotton Club (& co-2) 84. Peggy Sue Got Married 86. Gardens of Stone 87. Lionheart (p) 87. Tough Guys Don't Dance (p) 87. Powaqqatsi (p) 88. Tucker: The Man and His Dream (d) 88. New York Stories (co-d, co-w) 89. The Godfather Part III (wd, p) (AAN) 90. Bram Stoker's Dracula 92. The Secret Garden (p) 93. Mary Shelley's Frankenstein (p) 94. Jack (p, d) 96. John Grisham's The Rainmaker (wd) 97. The Third Miracle (ex-p) 99.
❝ I bring to my life a certain amount of mess. – *F.F.C.*
If you don't bet, you don't have a chance to win. – *F.F.C.*
Basically, both the Mafia and America feel they are benevolent organizations. And both the Mafia and America have their hands stained with blood from what it is necessary to do to protect their power and interests. – *F.F.C.*
I probably have genius. But no talent. – *F.F.C.*
Wall Street got interested in film and communications, and these are the people who brought you the Big Mac. In the past 12 years, I can't think of one classic they've made. – *F.F.C., 1996*
Lots of people have criticised my movies, but nobody has ever identified the real problem: I'm a sloppy filmmaker. – *F.F.C.*
He is his own worst enemy. If he directs a little romance, it has to be the biggest, most overdone little romance in movie history. – *Kenneth Turan*

Coppola, Sofia (1971–)
American actress and director, the daughter of director Francis Ford Coppola. Married director Spike Jonze.
Peggy Sue Got Married (a) 86. New York Stories (a) 89. The Godfather Part III (a) 90. Star Wars Episode I: The Phantom Menace (a) 99. The Virgin Suicides (d) 00, etc.

Coquillon, John
British cinematographer.
Witchfinder General 68. Scream and Scream Again 69. The Oblong Box 69. Triple Echo 72. Cross of Iron 77. The Four Feathers (TV) 78. The Thirty-Nine Steps 78. Final Assignment 80. The Changeling 80. The Amateur 82. The Osterman Weekend 83. Master of the Game (TV) 83. The Last Place on Earth (TV) 84. Clockwise 85. Absolution 88, etc.

Corbeil, Normand
Canadian composer
Screamers 96. Never Too Late 96. The Assignment 97. Les Boys 97. Double Jeopardy 99. The Art of War 00, etc.

Corbett, Glenn (1929–1993) (Glenn Rothenburg)
American second lead.
The Fireball 50. Man on a String 60. The Mountain Road 60. All the Young Men 60. Homicidal 61. Pirates of Blood River (GB) 61. Shenandoah 65. Big Jake 71. Dead Pigeon on Beethoven Street (Ger.) 72. The Stranger 73. Ride in a Pink Car 74. Nashville Girl 76, etc.
TV series: It's a Man's World 62–63. Route 66 63–64. The Road West 66–67. Dallas 83–84.

Corbett, Gretchen (1947–)
American character actress, mostly on TV.
Out of It 70. Let's Scare Jessica to Death 71. The Savage Bees (TV) 76. The Other Side of the Mountain Part Two 78. Secrets of Three Hungry Wives (TV) 78. Jaws of Satan 81. Change of Heart (TV) 98, etc.
TV series: The Rockford Files 74–80.

Corbett, Harry H. (1925–1982)
British stage actor who played tough guys, regional types and maniacs in an assortment of films before gaining great TV popularity in *Steptoe and Son;* subsequently starred in a number of unsatisfactory comedy vehicles.
Floods of Fear 57. Nowhere to Go 58. Cover Girl Killer 60. Sammy Going South 62. What a Crazy World 63. Ladies Who Do 63. The Bargee 64. Rattle of a Simple Man 64. Joey Boy 65. The Sandwich Man 66. Carry On Screaming 66. Crooks and Coronets 69. The Magnificent Seven Deadly Sins 71. Steptoe and Son 72, etc.

Corbett, Leonora (1907–1960)
British stage actress who made few films.
Love on Wheels 32. The Constant Nymph 33. Friday the Thirteenth 33. Warn London 34. Heart's Desire 35. Farewell Again 37. Under Your Hat 40, etc.

Corbett, Ronnie (1930–)
Pint-sized British TV comedian, one of the Two Ronnies.
Rockets Galore 58. Casino Royale 67. Some Will Some Won't 69. The Rise and Rise of Michael Rimmer 70. No Sex Please We're British 73. Fierce Creatures 97, etc.

Corbiau, Gérard (1941–)
Belgian director, from television, particularly of musical programmes.
The Music Teacher (AAN) 88. L'Année de l'éveil 91. Farinelli il Castrato (AAN) 95, etc.

Corbin, Barry (1940–)
American character actor in hearty, expansive roles. Born in Texas, he is best known as Maurice Minnifield in the TV sitcom *Northern Exposure* 90–95.
Urban Cowboy 80. Bitter Harvest (TV) 81. Prime Suspect (TV) 82. The Thorn Birds (TV) 83. My Science Project 85. Under Cover 87. Permanent Record 88. It Takes Two 88. Who's Harry Crumb? 89. Ghost Dad 90. Short Time 90. Career Opportunities 91. The Chase (TV) 91. Curdled 95. Solo 96. A Face to Kill For 99. Held Up 00, etc.
TV series: Boone 83–84. Spies 87.

Corbucci, Sergio (1927–1990)
Italian director.
Duel of the Titans 61. Son of Spartacus 62. The Slave 63. Minnesota Clay 64. Django 65. The Hellbenders 66. The Campanieros 71. Il Bestione 74. La Mazzetta 78. I Don't Understand You Anymore 80. I'm Getting Myself a Yacht 81. Super Fuzz 81. My Darling, My Dearest 82. Sing Sing 83. Sono un Fenomeno Paranormale 86. Rimini Rimini 87. Grazie Commissario 88, etc.

Corby, Ellen (1913–1999) (Ellen Hansen)
American character actress specializing in nosy neighbours and prim spinsters. She is best known for her early 70s role as Grandma in the TV series *The Waltons*, for which she won three Emmy awards as best supporting actress. Born in Racine, Wisconsin, and raised in Philadelphia, Pennsylvania, she first worked in Hollywood as a script girl from the early 30s, before becoming an actress in the 40s.
The Dark Corner 46. The Spiral Staircase 46. *I Remember Mama* (AAN) 48. Fighting Father Dunne 48. Caged 49. Captain China 49. Madame Bovary 49. On Moonlight Bay 51. Fearless Fagan 52. About Mrs Leslie 54. Illegal 55. The Seventh Sin 57. Macabre 58. Visit to a Small Planet 60. The Strangler 63. The Night of the Grizzly 66. The Gnome-Mobile 67. A Fine Pair 68. Support Your Local Gunfighter 71. Napoleon and Samantha 72. The Story of Pretty Boy Floyd (TV) 74. A Wedding on Waltons Mountain (TV) 82. A Walton Thanksgiving Reunion (TV) 93. A Walton Easter (TV) 97, many others.
TV series: Please Don't Eat the Daisies 65-67. *The Waltons* 72–79.

Corcoran, Donna (1942–)
American child actress of the 50s, the sister of Kevin Corcoran.
Angels in the Outfield 51. Don't Bother to Knock 52. Scandal at Scourie 53. Dangerous when Wet 53. Gypsy Colt 54. Violent Saturday 55, etc.

Corcoran, Kevin (1949–)
American child actor of the 50s and 60s who turned producer in the 70s.
Old Yeller 57. The Rabbit Trap 59. The Shaggy Dog 59. Toby Tyler 59. Pollyanna 60. The Swiss Family Robinson 60. Babes in Toyland 61. Savage Sam 62. A Tiger Walks 63, etc.

Cord, Alex (1931–) (Alexander Viespi)
Italian-American leading man.
Synanon 65. Stagecoach 66. The Brotherhood 68. Stiletto 69. Dead or Alive 69. The Last Grenade 69. The Dead Are Alive 72. Genesis II (TV) 73. Chosen Survivors 74. Sidewinder One 77. Greyeagle 77. Beggarman, Thief (TV) 79. Goliath Awaits (TV) 81. Jungle Warriors 84. A Girl to Kill For 90. Street Asylum 90. To Be the Best 93, etc.
TV series: W.E.B. 78. Cassie and Company 82. Airwolf 84–86.

Corda, Maria (c. 1902–1965) (Maria Farcas)
Hungarian actress, in films from 1921. She began as a dancer with the Royal Opera, Budapest, and was the first wife of producer and director Alexander Korda.
Dance Fever (Ger.) 21. A Modern Dubarry (Ger.) 21. The Last Days of Pompeii (It.) 26. The Guardsman (US) 27. The Private Life of Helen of Troy (US) 27. Tesha (GB) 28. Love and the Devil (US) 29, etc.

Corday, Mara (1932–) (Marilyn Watts)
American leading lady of the 50s, most notably when threatened by creatures from outer space or by giant insects mutated through atomic radiation. A former chorus girl and pin-up, she retired in the 60s after marrying actor Richard Long, returning to the screen in the late 70s in films starring Clint Eastwood.
Ready to Die 48. Sea Tiger 52. So This Is Paris 54. Drums across the River 54. Foxfire 55. Man without a Star 55. Tarantula 55. The Quiet Gun 56. The Giant Claw 57. Undersea Girl 57. The Black Scorpion 57. Girls on the Loose 58. The Gauntlet 77. Sudden Impact 83. Pink Cadillac 89. The Rookie 90, etc.

Corday, Paula (1924–1992) (Jeanne Paule Teipotemarga, aka Paule Croset and Rita Corday)
Anglo-Swiss leading lady who went to Hollywood in the 40s.
The Falcon Strikes Back 43. The Body Snatcher 45. The Exile 47. Sword of Monte Cristo 51. Because You're Mine 52. The French Line 54, etc.

Cordell, Frank (1918–1980)
British composer.
The Voice of Merrill 52. The Captain's Table 58. The Rebel 60. Flight from Ashiya (US) 63. Never Put It in Writing 63. The Bargee 64. Khartoum 66. Project Z 68. Mosquito Squadron 68. Hell Boats 69. Ring of Bright Water 69. *Cromwell* (AAN) 70. Trial by Combat/A Choice of Weapons 76. God Told Me To (US) 76, etc.

Cording, Harry (1891–1954)
British supporting actor in Hollywood, usually as tough, blunt types.
The Knockout 25. Captain of the Guard 30. Forgotten Commandments 33. The Crusades 35. Mutiny on the Bounty 35. Sutter's Gold 36. The Prince and the Pauper 37. The Adventures of Robin Hood 38. The Hound of the Baskervilles 39. The Wolf Man 41. Arabian Nights 42. Lost in a Harem 44. The House of Fear 45. Terror by Night 46. A Woman's Vengeance 48. Samson and Delilah 49. Mask of the Avenger 51. Road to Bali 52. Titanic 53. Demetrius and the Gladiators 54. East of Eden 55, many others.

Corduner, Allan (c. 1951–)
English actor, from the stage.
Yentl 83. Mandela (TV) 87. Shadow Makers/Fat Man and Little Boy 89. Edward II 91. Carry On Columbus 92. Heart of Darkness (TV) 94. Voices 95. Norma Jean & Marilyn (TV) 96. The Imposters 98. Topsy-Turvy 99. Joe Gould's Secret 00, etc.

Cordy, Raymond (1898–1956) (R. Cordiaux)
French comedy actor, especially seen in René Clair's films.
Le Million 31. à Nous la Liberté 31. Le Quatorze Juillet 33. Le Dernier Milliardaire 34. Ignace 37. Les Inconnus dans la Maison 42. Le Silence est d'Or 46. La Beauté du Diable 49. Les Belles de Nuit 52. Les Grandes Manoeuvres 55, etc.

Corenblith, Michael
American production designer.
Zandalee 91. He Said, She Said 91. Cool World 92. The Gun in Betty Lou's Handbag 92. Apollo 13 (AAN) 95. Down Periscope 96. Ransom 96.

Mighty Joe Young 98. EdTV 99. Dr Seuss' How the Grinch Stole Christmas (AAN) 00, etc.

Corey, Jeff (1914–)
Gaunt American supporting actor seen as farmer, gangster, junkie, wino, convict, cop, and even Wild Bill Hickok.
All that Money Can Buy 41. My Friend Flicka 43. The Killers 46. Brute Force 47. Home of the Brave 49. Bright Leaf 50. Rawhide 51. Red Mountain 52. The Balcony 63. Lady in a Cage 64. Mickey One 65. The Cincinnati Kid 65. *Seconds* 66. In Cold Blood 67. True Grit 69. *Little Big Man* 71. Catlow 72. Paper Tiger 75. Oh God 77. Butch and Sundance: The Early Days 79. Battle Beyond the Stars 80. The Sword and the Sorcerer 82. Conan the Destroyer 84. Creator 85. Bird on a Wire 90. Pay Off 91. Ruby Cairo 93. Surviving the Game 94. Color of Night 94, many others.
TV series: Hell Town 85.

Corey, Wendell (1914–1968)
American leading actor who usually played solid dependable types.
■ Desert Fury 47. I Walk Alone 47. The Search 48. Maneater of Kumaon 48. Sorry Wrong Number 48. The Accused 48. Any Number Can Play 49. The File on Thelma Jordon 49. Holiday Affair 49. No Sad Songs for Me 50. The Furies 50. Harriet Craig 50. The Great Missouri Raid 50. Rich Young and Pretty 51. The Wild Blue Yonder 51. The Wild North 52. Carbine Williams 52. My Man and I 52. Laughing Anne (GB) 53. Jamaica Run 53. Hell's Half Acre 54. Rear Window 54. The Big Knife 55. The Bold and the Brave 56. The Killer is Loose 56. The Rack 56. The Rainmaker 56. Loving You 57. The Light in the Forest 58. Alias Jesse James 59. Blood on the Arrow 64. Agent for Harm 66. Waco 66. Women of the Prehistoric Planet 66. Picture Mommy Dead 66. Red Tomahawk 67. Cyborg 2087 67. The Astro Zombies 68. Buckskin 68.
TV series: Harbor Command 57. Peck's Bad Girl 59. The Eleventh Hour 62.

Corfield, John (1893–)
British producer in films from 1929; co-founder of British National Films with Lady Yule and J. Arthur Rank.
Turn of the Tide 35. Laugh It Off 40. Gaslight 40. Headline 42. Bedelia 46. The White Unicorn 47. My Sister and I 48, etc.

Corigliano, John (1938–)
American composer, who writes the occasional film score.
Altered States (AAN) 80. Revolution 85. The Red Violin (AA) 98, etc.

Corman, Gene (1927–)
American producer, brother of Roger CORMAN.
Tower of London 62. The Secret Invasion 64. Tobruk 66. You Can't Win 'Em All 70, etc.

Corman, Roger (1926–)
American producer and director who during the 50s made a record number of grade Z horror films, then presented an interesting series of Poe adaptations; when he seemed poised for better things his career as a director slowed and he turned to producing low-budget exploitation movies and distributing foreign films. Among those who began their careers working for him are Martin Scorsese, Francis Ford Coppola, Peter Bogdanovich, Jack Nicholson, Monte Hellman, Jonathan Demme, Joe Dante, Jonathan Sayles, Ron Howard, Gale Anne Hurd and James Cameron. In 1994, he set up an Irish-based production company, New Concorde, which he sold three years later, as Concorde-New Horizons, to producer Elliott KASTNER for a reported $100m.
Autobiography: 1990, *How I Made a Hundred Movies in Hollywood and Never Lost a Dime.*
Biography: 1998, *Roger Corman: Best of the Cheap Acts* by Mark Thomas McGee. 2000, *Roger Corman* by Beverly Gray.
■ Five Guns West 55. Apache Woman 55. The Day the World Ended 56. Swamp Woman 56. The Gunslinger 56. Oklahoma Woman 56. It Conquered the World 56. Naked Paradise 57. Attack of the Crab Monsters 57. *Not of this Earth* 57. The Undead 57. Rock all Night 57. Carnival Rock 57. Teenage Doll 57. Sorority Girl 57. The Viking Women and the Sea Serpent 57. War of the Satellites 57. Machine Gun Kelly 58. Teenage Caveman 58. She-Gods of Shark Reef 58. I Mobster 59. Wasp Woman 59. *A Bucket of Blood* 59. Ski Troop Attack 60. *House of Usher* 60. The Little Shop of Horrors 60. The Last Woman on Earth 60. Creature from the Haunted Sea 60. Atlas 60. The Pit and the Pendulum 61. The Premature Burial 62. *The Intruder* 62. Tales of Terror 62. Tower of London 62. *The Raven* 63. The Young Racers 63. The Haunted Palace 63. The Terror 63. X – The Man with X-ray Eyes 63. *The Masque of the Red Death* 64. Secret Invasion 64. *The Tomb of Ligeia* 65. The Wild Angels 66. The St Valentine's Day Massacre 67. The Trip 67. Bloody Mama 70. Gas-s-s! 70. Von Richthofen and Brown 71. Boxcar Bertha (p only) 72. I Escaped from Devil's Island (co-p only) 73. Big Bad Mama (p only) 74. Cockfighter (p only) 74. Grand Theft Auto (p only) 77. Thunder and Lightning (p only) 77. Piranha (p only) 78. St Jack (p only) 78. Battle Beyond the Stars (p only) 80. Humanoids from the Deep (p only) 80. Smokey Bites the Dust (p only) 81. Forbidden World (p only) 82. Love Letters (p) 83. Space Raiders (p) 83. Suburbia (p) 83. The Warrior and the Sorceress (p) 83. Deathstalker (p) 84. Streetwalkin' (p) 85. Amazons (p) 87. Big Bad Mama II (p) 88. Daddy's Boys (p) 88. Dangerous Love (p) 88. The Drifter (p) 88. Nightfall (p) 88. Not of This Earth (p) 88. Watchers (p) 88. Andy Colby's Incredibly Awesome Adventure (p) 89. The Lawless Land (p) 89. The Masque of the Red Death (p) 89. Stripped to Kill II (p) 89. The Terror Within (p) 89. Time Trackers (p) 89. Two to Tango (p) 89. Wizards of the Lost Kingdom II (p) 89. Back to Back (p) 90. Bloodfist II (p) 90. A Cry in the Wild (p) 90. Full Fathom Five (p) 90. The Haunting of Morella (p) 90. Overexposed (p) 90. Primary Target (p) 90. Frankenstein Unbound (co-w, d) 90. Silk 2 (p) 90. Streets (p) 90. Transylvania Twist (p) 90. Watchers II (p) 90. Welcome to Oblivion (p) 90. Hollywood Boulevard II (p) 91. The Terror Within II (p) 91. Dracula Rising (p) 92. In the Heat of Passion (p) 92. Reflections on a Crime (p) 94. Cheyenne Warrior (p) 94.
❝ I've never made the film I wanted to make. No matter what happens, it never turns out exactly as I hoped. – *R.C.*
Poe writes the first reel or the last reel. Roger does the rest. – *James H. Nicholson*
All my films have been concerned simply with man as a social animal. – *R.C., 1970*
I think there is always a political undercurrent in my films. With the exception of *The Intruder*, I tried not to put it on the surface. – *R.C.*
To one degree or another, almost all films finally adhere to the Corman policy. So many of them do have an enormous amount of action; the sex is there; the laughs are there; and, sometimes, to some degree, the social statement is there as well. *The Godfather* films are the most expensive Roger Corman films ever made, and I think that everyone's trying to exploit that formula, one way or another. But most people are less candid about it than Roger is. – *Jonathan Demme*
He once said, 'Martin, what you have to get is a very good first reel because people want to know what's going on. Then you need a very good last reel because people want to hear how it all turns out. Everything else doesn't really matter.' Probably the best sense I have ever heard in the movies. – *Martin Scorsese*

Corneau, Alain (1943–)
French director and screenwriter, usually of thrillers. He trained at the national film school, IDHEC, before going to America to collaborate on a script with novelist Jim Thompson. He also worked as an assistant to Roger Corman, Marcel Camus and Costa-Gavras.
France S.A. 74. La Menace 77. Série Noire 79. Choice of Arms/Le Choix des Armes 81. Fort Saganne 84. Nocturne Indien 89. The New World 95, etc.

Cornelius, Henry (1913–1958)
British director with a subtle comedy touch.
■ It Always Rains on Sunday (co-w only) 47. *Passport to Pimlico* 48. The Galloping Major (& w) 51. *Genevieve* 53. I Am a Camera 55. Next to No Time 57. Law and Disorder 58.

Cornell, John (1941–)
Australian producer and director. A former journalist, he went on to work in television and discovered and managed comedian Paul Hogan.
Crocodile Dundee (p) 86. Crocodile Dundee II (p, d) 88. Almost an Angel (p) 90, etc.

Cornfield, Hubert (1929–)
American director.
■ Sudden Danger 56. Lure of the Swamp 57. Plunder Road 59. *The Third Voice* 59. Angel Baby (co-d) 61. Pressure Point 62. The Night of the Following Day 69. Les Grands Moyens 76.

Corraface, Georges (1953–)
French-born leading actor, of Greek parents. He studied law in Paris before becoming an actor.
Mahabharata 89. Impromptu 89. Not without My Daughter 91. Columbus: The Discovery 92. Pasiones Turcas 94. Muere Mi Vida (Sp.) 95. Escape from LA 96. Slaughter of the Cock 97. Preference (Fr./It./Sp.) 98. Algiers-Beirut: A Souvenir (Fr./Leb.) 98. Peppermint (Gr./Hung./Bulg.) 99. Standy-By 00, etc.

Corri, Adrienne (1930–) (Adrienne Riccoboni)
Tempestuous red-headed British leading lady of Italian descent.
The River 51. The Kidnappers 53. Devil Girl from Mars 54. *Lease of Life* 54. Make Me an Offer 54. The Feminine Touch 55. Three Men in a Boat 56. Corridors of Blood 58. The Rough and the Smooth 59. The Hellfire Club 61. The Tell-Tale Heart 61. A Study in Terror 65. Bunny Lake is Missing 65. The Viking Queen 67. Moon Zero Two 69. A Clockwork Orange 71. Vampire Circus 72. Madhouse 74, etc.
TV series: Sword of Freedom 57.

Corrigan, Douglas 'Wrong Way' (1907–1995)
American aviator who in 1939 left New York for Los Angeles and landed in Ireland, thus deserving the title Wrong Way Corrigan. In the same year he played himself in the film *The Flying Irishman*.

Corrigan, Lloyd (1900–1969)
Chubby American character actor, usually in jovial roles; also directed some films in the 30s.
The Splendid Crime 25. Daughter of the Dragon (d) 31. The Broken Wing (d) 32. Murder on a Honeymoon (d) 35. The Dancing Pirate (d) 36. Night Key (d) 37. Young Tom Edison 40. *The Ghost Breakers* 40. The Great Man's Lady 42. Since You Went Away 44. The Bandit of Sherwood Forest 45. Stallion Road 47. Cyrano de Bergerac 50. Son of Paleface 52. The Bowery Boys Meet the Monsters 54. Hidden Guns 57. The Manchurian Candidate 62, many others.
TV series: Willy 54–55. Happy 60–61. Hank 65–66.

Corrigan, Ray 'Crash' (1903–1976) (Ray Benard)
American leading man, hero of innumerable second-feature westerns, first for Republic as one of the THREE MESQUITEERS and then, for Monogram, as one of the three RANGE BUSTERS. He also appeared in jungle films as a gorilla and was the creature in *It! The Terror from beyond Space* 58. Retired to run Corriganville, a Californian location for western movies, which he later sold for several million dollars, becoming a property developer in Oregon.
The Three Mesquiteers 36. Wild Horse Rodeo 38. The Purple Vigilantes 38. Three Texas Steers 39. West of the Pinto Basin 40. Wrangler's Roost 41. Rock River Renegades 42. Bullets and Saddles 43. Arizona Stage Coach 46. The White Gorilla 46. Texas Trouble Shooters 47. Thunder River Feud 47. Zamba the Gorilla 49, many more.
TV series: Crash Corrigan's Ranch 50.

Cort, Bud (1950–) (Walter Edward Cox)
American actor with a tendency to play demented youths.
M*A*S*H 70. The Travelling Executioner 70. Brewster McCloud 70. Gas! or It Became Necessary to Destroy the World in Order to Save It 70. The Strawberry Statement 70. The Traveling Executioner 70. *Harold and Maude* 71. Why Shoot the Teacher 76. Hitler's Son 78. Die Laughing 80. She Dances Alone 82. Love Letters 83. Electric Dreams 84. Maria's Lovers 84. Invaders from Mars 86. Love at Stake 87. Out of the Dark 88. Brain Dead 89. Ted and Venus (& d) 91. And the Band Played On 93. Girl in the Cadillac 95. Theodore Rex 95. Dogma 99. The Million Dollar Hotel 99. Pollock 00, etc.

Cortese, Valentina (1924–)
Italian leading lady in international films. She was married to Richard Basehart.
The Glass Mountain 48. Thieves' Highway 49. Malaya 50. The House on Telegraph Hill 51. Les Misérables 52. The Barefoot Contessa 54. Le Amiche 55. Magic Fire 56. Calabuch 58. Barabbas 62. The Visit 64. Juliet of the Spirits 65. The Legend of Lylah Clare 68. Day for Night/La Nuit Américaine (AAN) 73. When Time Ran Out 80. The Adventures of Baron Munchhausen 89. Buster's Bedroom 91. Sparrow/Storia di una Capinera 93, etc.

Cortez, Ricardo (1899–1977) (Jake Kranz)
American leading man, groomed in the 20s as a Latin lover in the Valentino mould. Later developed outside interests and quit movies after a sojourn in routine roles.
Sixty Cents an Hour 23. Pony Express 24. *The Torrent* 26. *The Sorrows of Satan* 27. The Private Life of Helen of Troy 27. Behind Office Doors 28. Ten Cents a Dance 31. Melody of Life 32. The Phantom of Crestwood 33. *Wonder Bar* 34. Special Agent 35. The Walking Dead 36. Talk of the Devil (GB) 36. Mr Moto's Last Warning 38. City Girl (d only) 38. Free, Blonde and Twenty One (d only) 40. World Première 40. I Killed That Man 42. Make Your Own Bed 44. The Locket 46. Blackmail 47. The Last Hurrah 58, many others.

Cortez, Stanley (1908–1997) (Stanley Kranz)
American cinematographer, brother of Ricardo Cortez; in Hollywood from silent days.
■ Four Days Wonder 37. The Wildcatter 37. Armored Car 37. The Black Doll 38. Lady in the Morgue 38. Danger on the Air 38. Personal Secretary 38. The Last Express 38. For Love or Money 38. The Forgotten Woman 39. They Asked for It 39. Hawaiian Nights 39. Risky Business 39. Laugh It Off 39. Alias the Deacon 39. The Leatherpushers 40. Meet the Wildcat 40. Love Honor and Oh Baby 40. The Black Cat 40. A Dangerous Game 41. San Antonio Rose 41. Moonlight in Hawaii 41. Badlands of Dakota 41. Bombay Clipper 42. Eagle Squadron 42. *The Magnificent Ambersons* 42. Flesh and Fantasy 43. The Powers Girl 43. Since You Went Away (co-ph) 44. Smash-Up 47. The Secret Beyond the Door 48. Smart Woman 48. The Man on the Eiffel Tower 49. Underworld Story 50. The Admiral was a Lady 50. The Basketball Fix 51. Fort Defiance 51. Models Inc 52. Abbott and Costello Meet Captain Kidd 52. The Diamond Queen 53. Dragon's Gold 53. Shark River 53. Riders to the Stars 54. Black Tuesday 54. *The Night of the Hunter* 55. Man from Del Rio 56. Top Secret Affair 57. The Three Faces of Eve 57. Thunder in the Sun 59. Vice Raid 60. The Angry Red Planet 60. Dinosaurus 60. Back Street 61. Shock Corridor 63. The Candidate 64. Nightmare in the Sun 64. The Naked Kiss 65. The Navy vs the Night Monsters 66. The Ghost in the Invisible Bikini 66. Blue 68. The Bridge at Remagen 69. The Date 71. Do Not Fold, Spindle or Mutilate (TV) 72. Another Man, Another Chance (co-ph) 77.

Corti, Alex (1933–1993)
French-born director and screenwriter of Austrian descent, in international films.
The Refusal/Der Verweigerung 72. The Condemned/Totstellen 75. A Woman's Pale Blue Handwriting (& w) 84. God Does Not Believe in Us Anymore/An Uns Glaubt Gott Nicht Mehr 85. Sante Fe 85. Welcome in Vienna (& w) 86. The King's Whore (& w) 90, etc.

Cosby, Bill (1937–)
American leading man and TV personality.
To All My Friends on Shore (& p) (TV) 71. Hickey and Boggs 72. Uptown Saturday Night 74. Let's Do It Again 76. Mother, Jugs and Speed 76. A Piece of the Action 77. Top Secret (TV) 78. California Suite 79. Leonard Part 6 87. Ghost Dad 90. The Meteor Man 93. I Spy Returns (TV) 94. Jack 96, etc.
TV series: *I Spy* 66–68. The Bill Cosby Show 69–71, 72–73, 84–92. Fat Albert and the Cosby Kids 72. Cos 76. The Cosby Mysteries 94–95. Cosby 96– .

Coslow, Sam (1905–1982)
American producer, lyricist and composer. In collaboration with Arthur JOHNSTON, he wrote many songs for Paramount movies, including *Cocktails for Two, Just One More Chance, My Old Flame, Sing You Sinners*. Married actress Esther Muir.
Autobiography: 1977, *Cocktails for Two.*
AS PRODUCER: Dreaming Out Loud 40. Heavenly Music (short) (AA) 43. Out of This World 45. Copacabana 47, etc.

AS SONGWRITER: Dance of Life 29. Blonde Venus 32. College Coach 32. Too Much Harmony 33. Belle of the Nineties 34. Murder at the Vanities 34. All the King's Horses 35. Goin' to Town 35. It's Love Again 36. Mountain Music 37. This Way Please 37. You and Me 38. Out of This World 45. Copacabana 47, etc.

Cosma, Vladimir (1940–)
Romanian-born composer who has worked in France since the 60s.
Alexander 68. Maldonne 68. Le Distrait 70. The Tall Blond Man with One Black Shoe 72. Pleure pas la Bouche Pleine 73. Salut l'Artiste 73. The Mad Adventures of Rabbi Jacob 74. Lucky Pierre/La Moutarde me Monte au Nez 74. The Return of the Tall Blond Man with One Black Shoe 74. The Pink Telephone/Le Téléphone Rose 75. Dracula and Son 76. Pardon Mon Affaire/Un éléphant ça Trompe Enormément 76. Pardon Mon Affaire Too!/Nous Irons Tous au Paradis 77. Anne 78. The Getaway/La Déborade 79. La Boum 80. Diva 82. La Boum II 83. Just the Way You Are 84. Asterix vs Caesar 85. Judith Krantz's Till We Meet Again (TV) 89. The Jackpot/La Totale! 91. Cuisine et Dépendances 93. Le Mari de Léon 93. Cache Cash 94, etc.

Cosmatos, George Pan (1941–)
Greek director of international adventures.
Massacre in Rome 74. The Cassandra Crossing 77. Escape to Athena 79. Rambo: First Blood II 84. Cobra 85. Leviathan 89. Tombstone 93. Shadow Conspiracy 97, etc.
❝ My pictures appeal all round the world. I do slick American pictures with a European sensitivity. – *G.P.C.*

Cossart, Ernest (1876–1951)
Portly British actor, inevitably cast by Hollywood in butler roles. Born in Cheltenham, Gloucestershire, he was a former clerk and was on stage from 1896, going to America in 1908. He was on screen from 1935, but continued to act in the theatre in a wider variety of roles than Hollywood offered him. His daughter, Valerie Cossart, was a stage actress in America from the 30s.
The Scoundrel 35. Desire 36. The Great Ziegfeld 36. Angel 37. Zaza 39. The Light That Failed 39. Tom Brown's Schooldays 40. *Charley's Aunt* 41. Casanova Brown 44. Cluny Brown 46. John Loves Mary 49, many others.

Cossins, James (1933–1997)
British character actor, usually of pompous, flustered type.
The Anniversary 68. Lost Continent 68. Melody 70. Villain 71. Blood from the Mummy's Tomb 72. Deathline 72. The Man with the Golden Gun 74. The First Great Train Robbery 79. Gandhi 82. Sherlock Holmes and the Masks of Death (TV) 84. Grand Larceny 87. Immaculate Conception 92, etc.

Costa-Gavras (1933–) (Constantin Costa-Gavras)
Russo-Greek director, in France from childhood.
The Sleeping Car Murders 65. Un Homme de Trop 67. 'Z' (AAN) 68. L'Aveu 70. State of Siege 72. Special Section 75. *Missing* (AA co-w) 82. Hannah K 83. Conseil de Femme 86. Betrayed 88. Music Box 89. La Petite Apocalypse 93. A Propos de Nice, la Suite (Fr., co-d) 95. Mad City 97, etc.

Costello, Dolores (1905–1979)
Gentle American silent screen heroine, in films from 1911; married actor John BARRYMORE. Her lovers included producer Darryl ZANUCK and actor Conrad NAGEL.
Lawful Larceny 23. *The Sea Beast* 25. Bride of the Storm 26. When a Man Loves 27. Old San Francisco 27. Glorious Betsy 28. The Redeeming Sin 29. *Noah's Ark* 29. Show of Shows 29. Second Choice 30. Expensive Women 31. Little Lord Fauntleroy 36. King of the Turf 39. *The Magnificent Ambersons* 42. This is the Army 43, many others.

Costello, Helene (1903–1957)
American silent screen leading lady, sister of Dolores Costello, in films from 1912. Her first husband was actor Lowell Sherman.
The Man on the Box 25. Bobbed Hair 25. Don Juan 26. In Old Kentucky 27. *Lights of New York* 28. Midnight Taxi 28. The Circus Kid 28. Show of Shows 29. Riffraff 35, etc.

Costello, Lou (1906–1959) (Louis Cristillo)
Dumpy American comedian, the zanier half of Abbott and Costello. For films, see *Bud Abbott*. Costello finally made one on his own, *The Thirty-Foot Bride of Candy Rock* 59.

Costello, Maurice (1877–1950)
American matinée idol, the father of Dolores and Helena Costello, in films from 1907.
A Tale of Two Cities 11. The Night Before Christmas 12. Human Collateral 20. Conceit 21. Glimpses of the Moon 23. The Mad Marriage 25. Camille 27. Hollywood Boulevard 36. Lady from Louisiana 41, many others.

Costner, Kevin (1955–)
American leading actor who scored a big hit with his first attempt at directing.
Biography: 1991, *Kevin Costner* by Todd Keith. 1993, *Kevin Costner – A Life on Film* by Adrian Wright.
Sizzle Beach USA 74. Chasing Dreams 82. Night Shift 82. Table For Five 83. Stacy's Knights 83. Testament 83. Fandango 84. American Flyers 85. Silverado 85. Sizzle Beach 86. The Untouchables 87. No Way Out 87. Bull Durham 88. Field of Dreams 89. Revenge 89. Dances with Wolves (& d) (AAd, AANa) 90. Robin Hood: Prince of Thieves 91. JFK 91. The Bodyguard 92. A Perfect World 93. Rapa Nui (p) 94. Wyatt Earp (& p) 94. Waterworld (& p) 95. Tin Cup 96. The Postman (& p, d) 97. Message in a Bottle 98. For Love of the Game 99, etc.

Cottafavi, Vittorio (1914–1998)
Italian director, mainly of cut-rate spectaculars. Has won critical approval for stylish handling of some of them.
Revolt of the Gladiators 58. The Legions of Cleopatra 59. The Vengeance of Hercules 60. Hercules Conquers Atlantis 61, etc.

Cotten, Joseph (1905–1994)
Tall, quiet American leading man, former drama critic and Broadway stage star. His second wife was actress Patricia Medina.
Autobiography: 1987, *Vanity Will Get You Somewhere*.
■ *Citizen Kane* 41. Lydia 41. *The Magnificent Ambersons* 42. *Journey into Fear* 42. *Shadow of a Doubt* 43. Hers to Hold 43. Gaslight 44. Since You Went Away 44. Love Letters 45. *I'll Be Seeing You* 45. Duel in the Sun 46. The Farmer's Daughter 47. *Portrait of Jennie* 48. Under Capricorn 49. Beyond the Forest 49. *The Third Man* 49. Two Flags West 50. Walk Softly Stranger 50. September Affair 50. Half Angel 51. Man with a Cloak 51. Peking Express 52. Untamed Frontier 52. The Steel Trap 52. Niagara 52. Blueprint for Murder 53. Special Delivery 54. The Bottom of the Bottle 55. The Killer is Loose 56. The Halliday Brand 56. From the Earth to the Moon 58. Touch of Evil (uncredited cameo) 58. The Angel Wore Red 60. The Last Sunset 61. Hush Hush Sweet Charlotte 64. The Money Trap 65. The Great Sioux Massacre 65. The Tramplers 66. The Oscar 66. The Hell-benders 67. Jack of Diamonds 67. Brighty 67. Some May Live (TV) 67. Petulia 68. Days of Fire (It.) 68. Keene 69. Cutter's Trail (TV) 69. The Lonely Profession (TV) 69. Latitude Zero 69. The Grasshopper 70. Do You Take This Stranger (TV) 70. The Abominable Dr Phibes 71. City Beneath the Sea (TV) 71. Doomsday Voyage 71. Tora! Tora! Tora! 71. White Comanche 71. Lady Frankenstein 71. Baron Blood 72. Assault on the Wayne (TV) 72. The Screaming Woman (TV) 72. The Devil's Daughter (TV) 72. The Scientific Cardplayer 72. Soylent Green 73. A Delicate Balance 73. The Lindbergh Kidnapping Case (TV) 76. Twilight's Last Gleaming 76. Airport 77 77. Caravans 78. Churchill and the Generals (TV) 79. Island of Mutations 79. Guyana, Crime of the Century 79. The Survivor 80. Heaven's Gate 80. The Hearse 80. Delusion 81. The House Where Evil Dwells 82.
TV series: The 20th Century Fox Hour (as host) 55–56. The Joseph Cotten Show 56–57. Hollywood and the Stars 63–64.
❝ I didn't care about the movies, really. I was tall. I could talk. It was easy to do. – *J.C.*
I'm afraid you'll never make it as an actor. But as a star, I think you might well hit the jackpot. – *Orson Welles*

Cotton, Carolina (1926–1997) (Helen Hagstom)
Singing leading lady of westerns of the 40s and early 50s, opposite Ken Curtis and Gene Autry; she later worked as a school teacher.
Song of the Prairie 45. Singing on the Trail 46. Cowboy Blues/Beneath the Starry Skies 46. Blue Canadian Rockies 52. Apache Country 52, etc.

Cotton, Oliver (1944–)
Darkly brooding English character actor, mainly on stage, from 1965, and TV.
Here We Go Round the Mulberry Bush 67. Firefox 82. Eleni 85. The Sicilian 87. Hiding Out 87. Columbus: The Discovery 92. Son of the Pink Panther 93. The Innocent Sleep 95. Beowulf (US) 99, etc.
TV series: Robin of Sherwood 85–86. Westbeach 93.

Couffer, Jack (1922–)
American director with a penchant for natural history.
■ Nikki, Wild Dog of the North (co-d) 61. Ring of Bright Water 69. The Darwin Adventure 72. Jonathan Livingston Seagull (ph) 73. The Last Giraffe 79.

Coulouris, George (1903–1989)
British character actor, in America 1930–50; usually in explosive roles.
Christopher Bean 33. All This and Heaven Too 40. The Lady in Question 40. *Citizen Kane* 41. This Land is Mine 43. *Watch on the Rhine* 43. Between Two Worlds 44. The Master Race 44. Hotel Berlin 45. Confidential Agent 45. The Verdict 46. Sleep My Love 47. A Southern Yankee 48. *An Outcast of the Islands* 51. Doctor in the House 53. The Runaway Bus 54. I Accuse 57. Womaneater 59. Conspiracy of Hearts 60. King of Kings 61. The Skull 65. Arabesque 66. The Assassination Bureau 69. Blood from the Mummy's Tomb 71. Papillon 73. Mahler 74. Murder on the Orient Express 74. The Antichrist 75. The Ritz 76. The Long Good Friday 80, many others.

Coulter, Michael
English cinematographer, closely associated with director Bill FORSYTH.
That Sinking Feeling 79. Gregory's Girl 82. The Good Father 87. Housekeeping 87. The Dressmaker 88. Breaking In 89. Diamond Skulls/Dark Obsession 89. Bearskin: An Urban Fairytale 89. Monster in a Box 92. Being Human 94. The Neon Bible 95. Sense and Sensibility (AAN) 95. Fairytale: A True Story 97, etc.

Courant, Curt (1899–1968)
German cinematographer who did his best work elsewhere.
Quo Vadis 24. Woman in the Moon 29. Perfect Understanding (GB) 33. Amok 34. The Man Who Knew Too Much (GB) 34. The Iron Duke (GB) 35. Broken Blossoms (GB) 36. La Bête Humaine 38. Louise 39. Le Jour Se Lève 39. De Mayerling à Sarajevo 40. Monsieur Verdoux (US) 47. It Happened in Athens 61, etc.

Courau, Clotilde (1969–)
French actress in international films.
Le Petit Criminel 91. Map of the Human Heart (Aus./GB/Can.) 92. The Pickle (US) 93. Elisa 94. The Bait/L'Appat 95. Les Grands Ducs 96. Fred 97. Marthe 97. Foul Play/Hors Jeu 98. Milk (GB) 99. Deterrence (US) 99. En Face 00, etc.

Courcel, Nicole (1930–) (Nicole Andrieux)
French leading lady of warm personality.
La Marie du Port 49. Versailles 53. La Sorcière 55. The Case of Dr Laurent 56. Sundays and Cybele 62, etc.

Court, Hazel (1926–)
Red-headed British leading lady; moved into horror films and went to live in Hollywood.
Champagne Charlie 44. Dear Murderer 46. My Sister and I 48. It's Not Cricket 48. Bond Street 50. The Curse of Frankenstein 56. The Man Who Could Cheat Death 59. Doctor Blood's Coffin 60. The Premature Burial 62. The Masque of the Red Death 64, etc.
TV series: Dick and the Duchess 57.

Courtenay, Margaret (1923–1996)
British character actress, adept at playing grande dames. Born in Cardiff, she acted mainly on the stage, at the Old Vic and elsewhere, ranging from Shakespeare to musicals.
Hot Millions 68. Isadora 68. Under Milk Wood 71. Ooh … You Are Awful 72. Royal Flash 75. The Incredible Sarah 76. The Mirror Crack'd 80. Duet for One 86, etc.

Courtenay, Syd
British comic actor and screenwriter. A sketch writer from 1919 for Leslie FULLER, with whom he worked in revue, he began in films in 1930, writing, and appearing in, Fuller's low-budget comedies.
Not So Quiet on the Western Front (a, w) 30. Why Sailors Leave Home (a, story) 30. Kiss Me Sergeant (co-w) 30. Bill's Legacy (co-w) 31. Tonight's the Night (a, co-w) 31. What a Night (a, story) 31. Poor Old Bill (a, story) 31. Hawleys of High Street (co-w) 33. Pride of the Force (a, co-w) 33. Lost in the Legion (a, co-w) 34. Doctor's Orders (story) 34. Cotton Queen (a, co-w) 35. Captain Bill (co-w) 35. Everything Is Rhythm (co-w) 36. The Man behind the Mask 36. Boys Will Be Girls (a, co-w) 37. Darby and Joan (w) 37. Sing as You Swing (w) 37. The Reverse Be My Lot (w) 38, etc.

Courtenay, Sir Tom (1937–)
Lean British actor specializing in diffident, under-privileged roles. Born in Hull, Yorkshire, he studied at University College, London, and trained at RADA. On stage from 1960, he worked mainly in theatre in Manchester. He first made an impact in the cinema as the working-class athlete in *The Loneliness of the Long Distance Runner* and also repeated on film his stage success in the title role of *Billy Liar*, a part he took over from Albert FINNEY, an actor with whom he has formed an occasional, notable partnership. He was knighted in the New Year's Honours of 2001.
Autobiography: 2000, *Dear Tom: Letters from Home*.
Private Potter 62. *The Loneliness of the Long Distance Runner* 62. *Billy Liar* 63. King and Country 64. Operation Crossbow 65. King Rat 65. Doctor Zhivago (AAN) 65. The Night of the Generals 67. The Day the Fish Came Out 67. A Dandy in Aspic 68. *Otley* 68. One Day in the Life of Ivan Denisovich 71. Catch Me a Spy 71. *The Dresser* (AAN) 83. Happy New Year 87. Leonard Part 6 87. The Last Butterfly 90. Let Him Have It 91. The Old Curiosity Shop (as Quilp, TV) 95. The Boy from Mercury 96. A Rather English Marriage (TV) 98. Whatever Happened To Harold Smith? 99, etc.
❝ There just doesn't seem to be a market for something with aspiration any more. – *T.C.*
The film business is absurd. Stars don't last very long. It's much more interesting to be a proper actor. – *T.C.*
I don't want to peak too early. The worry is that you never know until it's all over whether you peaked at all – and then you're finished and it's too late. – *T.C.*

Courtland, Jerome (1926–)
Gangling young American lead of 40s comedies, now working as a producer.
Kiss and Tell 45. Man from Colorado 48. Battleground 49. The Barefoot Mailman 52. The Bamboo Prison 55. Tonka 59. O Sole Mio (It.) 60. Mary Read, Pirate (It.) 61. Thanis, Son of Attila (It.) 61. Black Spurs 65. Diamonds on Wheels (d only) 73. Pete's Dragon (co-p only) 77, etc.
TV series: Tales of the Vikings 60.

Courtneidge, Dame Cicely (1893–1980)
British comic actress. Born in Sydney, of a Scottish father and English mother – he was a producer, later successful in London's West End, she was an actress – during their tour of Australia. She was on stage from 1901 and also worked in music hall as a male impersonator. Her great vitality made her a favourite in musical comedy and revue, though during the 30s she abandoned the stage for the cinema, under contract to make two films a year. Married actor Jack HULBERT, with whom she often appeared on stage and screen.
Autobiography: 1953, *Cicely*.
Biography: 1975, *The Little Woman's Always Right* by Jack Hulbert.
■ Elstree Calling 30. *The Ghost Train* 31. *Jack's the Boy* 32. Happy Ever After 32. Aunt Sally 33. *Soldiers of the King* 33. Falling for You 33. Things are Looking Up 35. The Perfect Gentleman 35. Me and Marlborough 35. Everybody Dance 36. Take my Tip 37. *Under Your Hat* 40. Miss Tulip Stays the Night 56. The Spider's Web 60. *The L-Shaped Room* 62. Those Magnificent Men in their Flying

Machines 65. The Wrong Box 66. Not Now Darling 72.

❝ When I was in Delhi
I lay on my – hm, hm
In a flat-bottomed canoe.
They all called me barmy
But I know the army!
The nation depends on you! – *sung by* C.C. *in Under Your Hat*

Courtney, Inez (1908–1967)
American actress, singer and dancer, often seen as the waspish friend of the female star; retired in the early 40s when she married.

Suzy 26. Bright Lights 30. Big City Blues 31. Let's Sing Again 36. The Reckless Way 36. The Thirteenth Man 37. The Shop around the Corner 40. Turnabout 40. The Farmer's Daughter 40, etc.

Cousteau, Jacques-Yves (1910–1997)
French underwater explorer and documentarist.

The Silent World (AA) 56. *World without Sun* (AA) 64, etc.

Coutard, Raoul (1924–)
French cinematographer.

Ranuntcho 50. A Bout de Souffle 59. Shoot the Pianist 60. *Lola* 60. *Jules et Jim* 61. Vivre Sa Vie 61. Bay of Angels 62. Les Carabiniers 63. Silken Skin 63. Pierrot le Fou 65. Made in USA 66. Sailor from Gibraltar 66. The Bride Wore Black 67. 'Z' 68. L'Aveu 70. L'Explosion 70. Embassy 72. The Jerusalem File 72. A Pain in the A … 73. Le Crabe-Tambour 77. Le Légion Saute sur Kolwezi (d only) 80. Passion 82. SAS à San Salvador (d) 82. First Name: Carmen/Prénom Carmen 83. La Garce 84. Max, Mon Amour 86. Fuegos 87. Burning Beds/Brennende Betten 88. Bethune: The Making of a Hero 90. La Femme Fardée 90. Dien Bien Phu 91. La Naissance de l'Amour 93. Faut Pas Rire du Bonheur 94, etc.

Cowan, Jerome (1897–1972)
American character actor with an easy manner. In films from 1936 (*Beloved Enemy*: out of character as a fanatical Irishman). He played hundreds of supporting roles, typically in *The Maltese Falcon* 41 as the detective killed while searching for the mysterious Floyd Thursby; played the lead in *Crime by Night* 43, *Find The Blackmailer* 44. Latterly graduated from jealous rivals to executives, from lawyers to judges.

Claudia and David 46. The Unfaithful 47. Miracle on 34th Street 47. June Bride 48. The Fountainhead 49. Young Man with a Horn 50. Dallas 51. The System 53. Visit to a Small Planet 60. Frankie and Johnny 65. The Gnome-Mobile 67. The Comic 69, many others.

TV series: The Tab Hunter Show 60. Tycoon 64.

Cowan, Lester (1907–1990)
American producer from 1934.

My Little Chickadee 39. Ladies in Retirement 41. The Story of G.I. Joe 45. Love Happy 50. Main Street to Broadway 52, etc.

Cowan, Maurice (1891–1974)
British producer of mainly routine films.

Derby Day 52. Turn the Key Softly 55. The Gypsy and the Gentleman 57, etc.

Coward, Sir Noël (1899–1973)
British actor-writer-composer-director, the bright, sophisticated young man of international showbusiness in the 20s and 30s. On stage as a boy from 1911, he came to public attention by starring in his play *The Vortex* in 1924 and remained in the spotlight for the rest of his career. His best work dates from the 30s and 40s; from the 50s onwards, his performances, in occasional films and in cabaret, outshone his new plays and musicals. He was the model for Beverly Carlton in George Kaufman and Moss Hart's play *The Man Who Came to Dinner* (played by Reginald Gardiner in the 1941 film version), and was portrayed by Daniel Massey, his godson, in *Star!* 65, about the life of Gertrude Lawrence. His lovers included actors Louis Hayward and Alan Webb.

Autobiography: 1937, *Present Indicative*. 1944, *Middle East Diary*. 1954, *Future Indefinite*. 1986, *Past Conditional*. 1982, *The Noël Coward Diaries*.

Biography: 1969, *A Talent to Amuse* by Sheridan Morley. 1972, *Noël* by Charles Castle. 1976, *The Life of Noël Coward/Remembered Laughter* by Cole Lesley. 1995, *Noël Coward* by Philip Hoare.

Other books: 1982, *Noël Coward the Playwright* by John Lahr.

■ Hearts of the World (a) 18. Easy Virtue (oa) 27. Private Lives (oa) 31. Cavalcade (oa) 33. Tonight is Ours (oa) 33. Bitter Sweet (oa) 33 and 40. Design for Living (oa) 33. The Little Damozel (m) 33. *The Scoundrel* (a) 35. *In Which We Serve* (awpd) (AA special award, AANp, AANw) 42. We Were Dancing (oa) 42. *Blithe Spirit* (oa) 45. This Happy Breed (oa) 45. *Brief Encounter* (oa) 45. The Astonished Heart (a) 49. Meet Me Tonight (oa) 52. Around the World in Eighty Days (a) 56. *Our Man in Havana* (a) 59. Surprise Package (a) 60. The Grass Is Greener (m/l) 60. Paris When it Sizzles (a) 63. Bunny Lake is Missing (a) 65. Boom (a) 66. Pretty Polly (story) 67. The Italian Job (a) 69. Relative Values (oa) 00.

✪ For displaying, if only intermittently, a wholly professional talent to amuse. *In Which We Serve*.

❝ I don't think pornography is harmful, but it is terribly, terribly boring. – N.C.

There is nothing more old-fashioned than being up-to-date. – N.C.

Death seems to me as natural a process as birth; inevitable, absolute and final. If, when it happens to me, I find myself in a sort of Odeon ante-room queuing up for an interview with Our Lord, I shall be very surprised indeed. – N.C.

Destiny's tot. – *Alexander Woollcott*

He is simply a phenomenon, and one that is unlikely to occur ever again in theatre history. – *Terence Rattigan*

Coward invented the concept of cool, and may have had emotional reasons for doing so. – *Kenneth Tynan*

He wrote as he talked. I thought he was a lousy actor, personally. He was so mannered and unmanly. He was much better in cabaret, singing his own songs. But as an actor, he was a joke. – *Rex Harrison*

Cowen, William J. (1883–1964)
American director.

■ Kongo 32. Oliver Twist 33. Woman Unafraid 34.

Cowl, Jane (1884–1950)
American leading stage actress who made very few film appearances.

■ The Garden of Lies 15. The Spreading Dawn 17. Once More My Darling 49. No Man of Her Own 49. The Secret Fury 50. Payment on Demand 50.

Cox, Alex (1954–)
British director and screenwriter with a cult reputation. He studied law at Oxford and film at Bristol University before going to America for further film studies. He now lives and works in Mexico.

Repo Man (wd) 84. Sid and Nancy (wd) 86. Straight to Hell (wd) 87. Walker (d) 87. Highway Patrolman/El Patrullero (d) 92. Dead Beat (a) 94. The Queen of the Night 94. The Winner (d) 97. Fear and Loathing in Las Vegas (co-w) 98. Three Businessman (a, d) 98. Herod's Law/La Ley De Herodes (a, Mex) 99, etc.

❝ If you're a fascist in Hollywood, you work with great regularity. If you're not, you don't – so I don't. – A.C.

There is no place in Hollywood for certain directors. It has to do with the big corporations owning the studios and being tied into the military-industrial complex, or the Mafia. – A.C.

The movie business feels it must support war and encourage white yuppies to have babies. If you don't buy into that, you are ultimately excluded. – A.C.

Cox, Brian (1946–)
Scottish classical theatre actor and director, in occasional films.

Autobiography: 1989, *From Salem to Moscow: An Actor's Odyssey*. 1992, *The Lear Diaries*.

Nicholas and Alexandra 71. In Celebration 74. Manhunter 86. Shoot for the Sun 86. Hidden Agenda 90. The Lost Language of Cranes (TV) 91. Sharpe's Rifles (TV) 93. Sharpe's Eagle (TV) 93. Iron Will 94. Prince of Jutland 94. Rob Roy 95. Chain Reaction 96. The Glimmer Man 96. The Long Kiss Goodnight 96. The Boxer 97. Kiss the Girls 97. Food for Ravens (as Aneurin Bevan) (TV) 97. Desperate Measures 98. The Bixer 98. Rushmore 98. The Corruptor 99. Complicity 99. Nuremberg (as Hermann Goering) (TV) 00. Saltwater 00. Mad About Mambo 00, etc.

❝ Big audiences in Britain are mind-dead. The best British audience I ever played to was in Broadmoor asylum. – B.C.

Cox, Courteney (1964–)
American actress, best known for her role as Monica Geller in the TV sitcom *Friends*. Born in Birmingham, Alabama, she began as a model. In 2000, she signed a contract worth an estimated $40m to appear in *Friends* for the following two years. Married actor David Arquette in 1999, and announced three months later that henceforth she would be known as Courtney Cox Arquette. Current asking price: $1m.

Misfits of Science (TV) 85. Masters of the Universe 87. Cocoon: The Return 88. Down Twisted 89. The Prize Pulitzer (TV) 89. Curiosity Kills (TV) 90. Mr Destiny 90. Shaking the Tree 90. The Opposite Sex and How to Live with Them 93. Ace Ventura: Pet Detective 94. Sketch Artist II: Hands that See (TV) 95. Commandments 96. Scream 96. Scream 2 97. Commandments 97. The Runner 99. Scream 3 00, etc.

TV series: Family Ties 87–89. Misfits of Science 85–86. The Trouble with Larry 93. Friends 94– .

Cox, Jack (1896–1960) (John Jaffray Cox)
Distinguished British cinematographer who became a director of photography in 1920. His career ranged from being Alfred Hitchcock's cameraman on his early movies to photographing the popular comedies of Norman Wisdom in the late 50s.

A Romance of Wastdale 20. The Four Feathers 21. Guy Fawkes 23. The Ring 27. The Farmer's Wife 28. Champagne 28. The Manxman 29. Blackmail 29. Almost a Honeymoon 30. Juno and the Paycock 30. Murder! 30. The Skin Game 31. Number Seventeen 32. Arms and the Man 32. Rich and Strange/East of Shanghai 32. The Man Who Changed His Mind 36. Dr Syn 37. The Lady Vanishes 38. They Came by Night 39. The Ghost Train 41. We Dive at Dawn 43. Madonna of the Seven Moons 44. The Wicked Lady 45. Idol of Paris 48. The Cure for Love 49. Mr Drake's Duck 50. Jumping for Joy 55. Up in the World 56. The Big Money 56. Just My Luck 57. The Square Peg 58, etc.

Cox, Joel
American editor, associated with the films of Clint Eastwood.

Farewell My Lovely 75. The Enforcer (co-ed) 76. The Gauntlet (co-ed) 77. Every Which Way but Loose (co-ed) 78. Bronco Billy (co-ed) 80. Death Valley 82. Honkytonk Man (co-ed) 82. Sudden Impact 83. Tightrope 84. Pale Rider 85. Heartbreak Ridge 86. Ratboy 86. Bird 88. Pink Cadillac 89. White Hunter, Black Heart 90. The Rookie 90. Unforgiven 92. A Perfect World 93. The Bridges of Madison County 95. Absolute Power 97. Midnight in the Garden of Good and Evil 97, etc.

Cox, Paul (1940–)
Dutch-born director and screenwriter, a former photographer who settled in Australia in 1965. A *Journey with Paul Cox*, a Belgian documentary on his life, directed by Gerrit Messiaen and Robert Visser, was released in 1997.

Illuminations 76. Inside Looking Out 77. Kostas 79. Lonely Hearts 82. Man of Flowers 84. My First Wife 84. Death and Destiny 85. Cactus 86. Vincent: The Life and Death of Vincent van Gogh 87. Island 89. The Golden Braid 90. A Woman's Tale 91. Exile (wd, e) 94. Erotic Tales (co-d) 94. Lust and Revenge 96. Molokai 98. Innocence 00, etc.

Cox, Ronny (1938–)
American character actor with stage background.

The Happiness Cage 72. *Deliverance* 72. Bound for Glory 76. The Car 77. The Onion Field 79. Taps 81. The Beast Within 82. Robocop 87. Steele Justice 87. Loose Cannons 89. One Man Force 89. Captain America 90. Total Recall 90. Murder at 1600 97. Pride/Unmei No Toki (Jap.) 98. Forces of Nature 99, etc.

TV series: Apple's Way 74. Spencer 84–85. Cop Rock 90.

Cox, Tony
Diminutive (3 foot 6 inches tall) American actor, a former drummer.

Dr. Heckyl and Mr. Hype 80. Cheech & Chong's Nice Dreams 81. Under the Rainbow 81. Jekyll & Hyde… Together Again 82. The Ewok Adventure (TV) 84. Spaceballs 87. Beetlejuice 88.Willow 88. Bird 88. I'm Gonna Git You Sucka 88. Spaced Invaders 89. The Silence of the Hams 93. Leprechaun 2/One Weddings and Lots of Funerals 94. Blankman 94. Friday 95. Me, Myself & Irene 00, etc.

Cox, Vivian (1915–)
British producer.

Father Brown 54. The Prisoner 55. Bachelor of Hearts 58, etc.

Cox, Wally (1924–1973)
American comic actor, usually seen as the bespectacled, weedy character he played in the TV series *Mr Peepers*.

■ State Fair 62. Spencer's Mountain 63. Fate Is the Hunter 64. The Bedford Incident 65. Morituri 65. The Yellow Rolls-Royce 65. A Guide for the Married Man 67. The One and Only Genuine Original Family Band 68. The Barefoot Executive 70. The Boatniks 70. The Cockeyed Cowboys of Calico County 70. Up Your Teddy Bear 70. The Night Strangler (TV) 72.

TV series: Mr Peepers 52–55. The Adventures of Hirman Holiday 56–57. Underdog (voice) 64–73.

Coyote, Peter (1942–) (Peter Cohon)
American leading actor with stage experience.

Tell Me a Riddle 80. Die Laughing 80. Southern Comfort 81. The Pursuit of D. B. Cooper 81. E.T. – the Extraterrestrial 82. Endangered Species 82. Out 82. Cross Creek 83. Slayground 83. Heartbreakers 84. The Legend of Billie Jean 85. Jagged Edge 85. Man in Love 87. Outrageous Fortune 87. Season of Dreams/Stacking 87. Baja Oklahoma 88. Heart of Midnight 88. The Man Inside 90. Keeper of the City 91. Crooked Hearts 91. Exposure 91. Blind Judgement 91. Living a Lie 91. Bitter Moon 92. Kika 93. That Eye, the Sky 94. Buffalo Girls (TV) 95. Unforgettable 96. Top of the World 97. Two for Texas (TV) 98. Patch Adams 98. Sphere 98. Random Hearts 99. Erin Brockovich 00, etc.

Crabbe, Buster (1907–1983) (Clarence Linden Crabbe)
American Olympic athlete who became leading man of 'B' pictures.

King of the Jungle 33. Tarzan the Fearless 33. Nevada 36. *Flash Gordon's Trip to Mars* 38. Buck Rogers 39. Queen of Broadway 43. Caged Fury 48. Gunfighters of Abilene 59. Arizona Raiders 65, many others.

TV series: Captain Gallant 55–57.

Crabe, James (c. 1931–1989)
American cinematographer.

Zigzag 70. Save the Tiger 72. W.W. and the Dixie Dancekings 72. Rocky 76. Players 79. The China Syndrome 79. How to Beat the High Cost of Living 80. The Baltimore Bullet 80. The Formula (AAN) 80, etc.

Crabtree, Arthur (1900–1975)
British director, former cameraman.

Madonna of the Seven Moons 44. They Were Sisters 45. Dear Murderer 46. Caravan 46. The Calendar 48. Lili Marlene 50. Hindle Wakes 52. The Wedding of Lili Marlene 53. West of Suez 57. Morning Call 58. Horrors of the Black Museum 59, etc.

Craig, Alec (1878–1945)
Scottish character actor in Hollywood; often played misers, moneylenders and downtrodden roles.

Mutiny on the Bounty 35. Mary of Scotland 36. Winterset 36. Vivacious Lady 38. Tom Brown's Schooldays 40. Cat People 42. Holy Matrimony 43. Lassie Come Home 43. Spider Woman 44. Kitty 46, many others.

Craig, Daniel (1968–)
English actor. Born in Liverpool, he studied at the Guildhall School of Music and Drama.

The Power of One 92. A Kid in King Arthur's Court (US) 95. Moll Flanders (TV) 96. Obsession (Ger) 97. Love is the Devil 98. Elizabeth 98. The Trench 99. Shockers: The Visitor (TV) 99. Love and Rage 99. I Dreamed of Africa 00. Some Voices 00, etc.

TV series: Our Friends in the North 96.

Craig, Edward Gordon (1872–1966) (Henry Edward Wardell)
British stage designer, a former actor, the son of Ellen Terry and father of Edward Carrick. Although not directly employed in films, his theories, which stressed the visual aspect of theatre, and his designs, with their dramatic use of light and shade, influenced art directors such as

William Cameron MENZIES and Anton GROT. His lovers included dancer Isadora DUNCAN.
Autobiography: 1957, *Index to the Story of My Days 1872–1907*.
Other books: 1911, *On the Art of Theatre*. 1913, *Towards a New Theatre*.

Craig, H(arold) A. L. (1925–1978)
British scriptwriter, on historical themes.
Anzio (w) 68. Fräulein Doktor (co-w) (It./Yug.) 68. The Adventures of Gerard (w) 70. Waterloo (co-w) (It./USSR) 70. Mohammed, Messenger of God (w) (Leb.) 76. Foxtrot (co-w) (Mex.) 77. Lion of the Desert (w) (US) 80, etc.

Craig, James (1912–1985) (John Meador)
American leading man, usually the good-natured but tough outdoor type.
Thunder Trail 37. The Buccaneer 38. The Man They Could Not Hang 39. Zanzibar 40. Kitty Foyle 40. *All that Money Can Buy* (the 'Faust' role, and his best) 41. Valley of the Sun 41. The Omaha Trail 42. The Human Comedy 43. Lost Angel 43. Kismet 44. Our Vines Have Tender Grapes 45. Boys Ranch 45. Little Mister Jim 46. Northwest Stampede 48. Side Street 50. Drums in the Deep South 51. Hurricane Smith 52. Fort Vengeance 53. While the City Sleeps 56. Four Fast Guns 59. The Hired Gun 67, many others.
❝ I was out there in Hollywood on vacation, and I saw a lot of people making movies. If they could do it, why couldn't I? – *J.C.*

Craig, Michael (1929–) (Michael Gregson)
British light leading man, a former crowd artist groomed by the Rank Organization; later attempted more ambitious roles before settling in Australia.
Malta Story 53. The Love Lottery 54. Yield to the Night 56. House of Secrets 56. High Tide at Noon 57. Campbell's Kingdom 58. The Silent Enemy 58. Nor the Moon by Night 58. Sea of Sand 59. Sapphire 59. Upstairs and Downstairs 59. *The Angry Silence* (& w) 59. Cone of Silence 60. Doctor in Love 60. Mysterious Island 61. *Payroll* 61. A Pair of Briefs 62. Life for Ruth 62. The Iron Maiden 62. Stolen Hours 63. Of a Thousand Delights/Vaghe Stella dell'Orsa 65. Life at the Top 65. Modesty Blaise 66. Sandra (It.) 66. *Star!* 68. The Royal Hunt of the Sun 69. Twinky 69. Brotherly Love 70. A Town Called Bastard 71. Vault of Horror 73. The Emigrants (TV) 77. The Timeless Land (TV) 77. Turkey Shoot 82. Stanley 83, etc.

Craig, Stuart
English production designer.
Saturn 3 80. The Elephant Man (AAN) 80. Gandhi (AA) 82. Greystoke: The Legend of Tarzan, Lord of the Apes 84. Cal 84. The Mission (AAN) 86. Cry Freedom 87. Stars and Bars (co-pd) 88. Dangerous Liaisons (AA) 88. Chaplin (AAN) 92. The Secret Garden 93. Shadowlands 93. The English Patient (US) (AA) 96. Mary Reilly 96. In Love and War 97. The Avengers (US) 98. Notting Hill 99. The Legend of Bagger Vance (US) 00, etc.

Craig, Wendy (1934–)
British comedy actress, especially on TV in *Not in Front of the Children*, *And Mother Makes Three*, *Nanny*, etc.
The Mind Benders 63. The Servant 63. The Nanny 65. Just Like a Woman 66. I'll Never Forget What's 'Is Name 67. Joseph Andrews 77, etc.
TV series: Brighton Belles 93.

Craig, Yvonne (1937–)
American leading lady, now retired, who was best known for playing Batgirl on the TV series *Batman*.
The Young Land 60. By Love Possessed 61. Seven Women from Hell 62. Kissin' Cousins 64. One Spy Too Many 66. In Like Flint 67, etc.
TV series: Batman 67–68.

Craigie, Jill (1914–1999)
British documentary director.
The Flemish Farm 43. The Way We Live 46. Blue Scar 48. The Million Pound Note (w only) 53. Windom's Way (w only) 57, etc.

Crain, Jeanne (1925–)
American leading lady of the 40s; usually the personification of sweetness and light.
■ The Gang's All Here 43. Home in Indiana 44. In the Meantime Darling 44. Winged Victory 44. *State Fair* 45. Leave Her to Heaven 45. Centennial Summer 46. *Margie* 46. Apartment for Peggy 48. You Were Meant for Me 48. A Letter to Three Wives 49. The Fan 49. *Pinky* (AAN) 49. Cheaper by the Dozen 50. Take Care of My Little Girl 51. People Will Talk 51. The Model and the Marriage Broker 52. Belles on Their Toes 52. O'Henry's Full House 52. Dangerous Crossing 53. City of Bad Men 53. Vicki 53. Duel in the Jungle (GB) 54. Man Without a Star 55. Gentlemen Marry Brunettes 55. The Second Greatest Sex 55. The Fastest Gun Alive 56. The Tattered Dress 57. The Joker is Wild 58. Guns of the Timberland 60. Twenty Plus Two 61. Queen of the Nile (It.) 61. With Fire and Sword (It.) 61. Pontius Pilate (It.) 61. Madison Avenue 62. 52 Miles to Terror 64. The Night God Screamed 71. Skyjacked 72.

Cramer, Joey (1974–)
Canadian child actor of the 80s.
Runaway 84. I-Man (TV) 86. *Flight of the Navigator* 86. Clan of the Cave Bear 84. Stone Fox (TV) 87, etc.

Cramer, Rychard (1889–1960)
Malevolent-looking American character actor, a memorable foil for Laurel and Hardy in *Scram*, *Saps at Sea*, etc. He later played heavies in 'B' westerns.

Crane, Bob (1929–1978)
American light comic actor, popular in TV series *Hogan's Heroes*. He was murdered.
■ Return to Peyton Place 61. Mantrap 61. The Wicked Dreams of Paula Schultz 68. Superdad 74. Gus 76.

Crane, Richard (1919–1969)
American juvenile lead of the 40s.
Susan and God 40. This Time for Keeps 42. Happy Land 43. None Shall Escape 44. Captain Eddie 45. Behind Green Lights 46. Triple Threat 48. Dynamite 49. The Last Outpost 51. The Neanderthal Man 53. The Eternal Sea 55. The Deep Six 58. The Alligator People 59. House of the Damned 63. Surf Party 64, etc.
TV series: Surfside Six 61–62.

Crane, Stephen (1871–1900)
American novelist who crystallized aspects of the Civil War in *The Red Badge of Courage*.

Cranham, Kenneth (1944–)
British leading actor, mainly on stage and television.
Oliver! 68. All the Way Up 70. Brother Sun, Sister Moon 72. Joseph Andrews 77. Reilly, Ace of Spies (TV) 83. Hellbound: Hellraiser II 88. Stealing Heaven 88. Oranges Are Not the Only Fruit (TV) 90. Prospero's Books 91. Under Suspicion 91. Tale of a Vampire 92. Chimera (TV) 93. The Tenant of Wildfell Hall (TV) 96. The Boxer 97. Our Mutual Friend (TV) 98. The Last Yellow 99. Gangster No 1 00. Women Talking Dirty 00. without Motive (TV) 00, etc.
TV series: Shine on Harvey Moon 85–87.

Cravat, Nick (1911–1994)
Small, agile American actor, once Burt Lancaster's circus partner.
The Flame and the Arrow 50. The Crimson Pirate 52. King Richard and the Crusaders 54. Three-Ring Circus 55. Kiss Me Deadly 55. Davy Crockett 56. Run Silent, Run Deep 59. The Scalphunters 68. Ulzana's Raid 72. The Island of Dr Moreau 77, etc.

Craven, Frank (1875–1945)
American stage character actor who spent his later years in Hollywood; typically cast as kindly pipe-smoking philosopher.
■ We Americans 28. The Very Idea 29. State Fair 33. That's Gratitude 34. He Was Her Man 34. Let's Talk It Over 34. City Limits 34. Funny Thing Called Love 34. *Barbary Coast* 35. Car 99 35. Vagabond Lady 35. Small Town Girl 36. The Harvester 36. Penrod and Sam 37. Blossoms on Broadway 37. You're Only Young Once 37. Penrod and his Twin Brother 38. Our Neighbours the Carters 39. Miracles for Sale 39. Dreaming Out Loud 40. City for Conquest 40. *Our Town* (his stage role) 40. The Lady from Cheyenne 41. The Richest Man in Town 41. In This Our Life 41. *Thru Different Eyes* 42. Pittsburgh 42. Girl Trouble 42. Son of Dracula 43. Harrigan's Kid 43. Jack London 43. The Human Comedy 43. Keeper of the Flame 43. Destiny 44. My Best Gal 44. They Shall Have Faith 44. The Right to Live 45. Colonel Effingham's Raid 45.

Craven, Gemma (1950–)
Irish-born leading lady of the 70s.
■ *The Slipper and the Rose* 76. Why Not Stay for Breakfast 79. Wagner 83. Double X 91. The Mystery of Edwin Drood 93.
TV series: Pennies from Heaven 77.

Craven, Wes (1939–)
American director of horror movies, a former academic.
Books: 1998, *Screams and Nightmares: The Films of Wes Craven* by Brian J. Robb.
Summer of Fear 78. The Hills Have Eyes 79. Deadly Blessing 81. A Nightmare on Elm Street 84. Deadly Friend 86. Flowers in the Attic (w) 87. A Nightmare on Elm Street III: Dream Warriors (p, story) 87. The Serpent and the Rainbow (d) 88. Shocker (wd, a) 89. The People under the Stairs (wd) 91. Wes Craven's New Nightmare (wd, a) 94. The Fear (a) 95. Vampire in Brooklyn 95. Scream 96. Scream 2 97, etc.

Crawford, Andrew (1917–)
Scottish character actor.
The Brothers 46. Dear Murderer 47. London Belongs to Me 48. Morning Departure 50. Shadow of the Cat 61, etc.

Crawford, Anne (1920–1956) (Imelda Crawford)
British leading lady with gentle, humorous personality.
They Flew Alone (debut) 42. The Peterville Diamond 42. The Dark Tower 42. The Hundred-Pound Window 43. Millions Like Us 43. Two Thousand Women 44. They Were Sisters 45. Caravan 46. Bedelia 46. Master of Bankdam 47. Daughter of Darkness 48. The Blind Goddess 48. It's Hard To Be Good 49. Tony Draws a Horse 49. Thunder on the Hill (US) 50. Street Corner 52. Knights of the Round Table 53. Mad about Men 55, etc.

Crawford, Broderick (1911–1986)
Beefy American character actor, son of Helen Broderick; began by playing comic stooges and gangsters, with acting performances coming later; after a long spell in TV his popularity waned.
Woman Chases Man 37. The Real Glory 39. Eternally Yours 39. Beau Geste 39. Slightly Honorable 40. When the Daltons Rode 40. The Black Cat 41. Butch Minds the Baby 42. Broadway 42. Sin Town 42. *The Runaround* 46. Slave Girl 47. The Flame 47. The Time of Your Life 48. Anna Lucasta 49. *All the King's Men* (AA) 49. *Born Yesterday* 51. The Mob 51. Lone Star 52. Scandal Sheet 52. Last of the Comanches 52. Stop You're Killing Me 52. Night People 54. Human Desire 54. Down Three Dark Streets 54. New York Confidential 55. Il Bidone/The Swindlers 55. Not as a Stranger 55. The Fastest Gun Alive 56. The Decks Ran Red 58. Up from the Beach 65. The Oscar 66. The Texican 66. Red Tomahawk 66. The Vulture 67. Embassy 72. Terror in the Wax Museum 73. Smashing the Crime Syndicate 73. Mayday at 40,000 Feet (TV) 77. *The Private Files of J. Edgar Hoover* 78. A Little Romance 79. There Goes the Bride 80. Liar's Moon 82, etc.
TV series: *Highway Patrol* 55–58. King of Diamonds 61. The Interns 70.
❝ My trademarks are a hoarse, grating voice and the face of a retired pugilist: small narrowed eyes set in puffy features which look as though they might, years ago, have lost on points. – *B.C.*
A huge man with unlimited desire for trouble, he would often get into fights. The reason we didn't get hurt I can only attribute to the fact that Brod fought as a pro. Yet he could talk on most subjects as an erudite man. – *Don Siegel*

Crawford, Cindy (1966–)
American model and occasional actress, formerly married to Richard Gere.
Fair Game 95.

Crawford, Howard Marion
See MARION CRAWFORD, Howard.

Crawford, Joan (1904–1977) (Lucille le Sueur; known for a time as Billie Cassin)
American leading lady; one of Hollywood's most durable stars, first as a flapper of the jazz age and later as the personification of the career girl and the repressed older woman. Few of her films have been momentous, but she has always been 'box office', especially with women fans, who liked to watch her suffering in mink.
Autobiography: 1962, *A Portrait of Joan*.
In 1978 her adopted daughter Christine Crawford published *Mommie Dearest*, which painted her as a monster and caused a sensation. A film version of the book was released in 1981, with Faye Dunaway playing J.C.
■ Pretty Ladies 25. The Only Thing 25. Old Clothes 25. Sally, Irene and Mary 25. The Boob 25. Paris 25. Tramp Tramp Tramp 26. The Taxi Dancer 27. Winners of the Wilderness 27. The Understanding Heart 27. The Unknown 27. Twelve Miles Out 27. Spring Fever 27. West Point 28. Rose Marie 28. Across to Singapore 28. The Law of the Range 28. Four Walls 28. *Our Dancing Daughters* 28. Dream of Love 28. The Duke Steps Out 29. Our Modern Maidens 29. Hollywood Revue 29. Untamed 29. Montana Moon 30. Our Blushing Brides 30. Paid 30. Dance Fools Dance 31. Laughing Sinners 31. This Modern Age 31. Possessed 31. Letty Lynton 32. *Grand Hotel* 32. *Rain* 32. Today We Live 33. *Dancing Lady* 33. Sadie McKee 34. Chained 34. Forsaking All Others 34. No More Ladies 35. I Live My Life 35. *The Gorgeous Hussy* 36. Love on the Run 36. The Last of Mrs Cheyney 37. The Bride Wore Red 37. Mannequin 38. The Shining Hour 38. Ice Follies 39. *The Women* 39. Strange Cargo 40. Susan and God 40. *A Woman's Face* 41. When Ladies Meet 41. They All Kissed the Bride 42. Reunion in France 42. Above Suspicion 43. Hollywood Canteen 44. *Mildred Pierce* (AA) 45. *Humoresque* 46. *Possessed* (AAN) 47. Daisy Kenyon 47. Flamingo Road 49. The Damned Don't Cry 50. Harriet Craig 50. Goodbye My Fancy 51. This Woman is Dangerous 52. *Sudden Fear* (AAN) 52. Torch Song 53. Johnny Guitar 54. The Female on the Beach 55. Queen Bee 55. Autumn Leaves 56. The Story of Esther Costello (GB) 57. The Best of Everything 59. *Whatever Happened to Baby Jane?* 62. The Caretakers 63. Strait Jacket 64. Della (TV) 64. I Saw What You Did 65. The Karate Killers (TV) 67. Berserk (GB) 67. Night Gallery (TV pilot) 69. Trog 70.
✪ For sheer determination. *Mildred Pierce*.
❝ Everybody imitated my fuller mouth, my darker eyebrows. But I wouldn't copy anybody. If I can't be me, I don't want to be anybody. I was born that way. – *J.C.*
The most important thing a woman can have, next to her talent of course, is her hairdresser. – *J.C.*
Inactivity is one of the great indignities of life. The need to work is always there, bugging me. – *J.C.*
I never go out unless I look like Joan Crawford the movie star. If you want to see the girl next door, go next door. – *J.C.*
Whenever she came to the realisation that the men she loved simply didn't come back, she compensated by adopting children. – *Hedda Hopper*
The best time I ever had with her was when I pushed her downstairs in *Baby Jane*. – *Bette Davis*
With her emergence as a film star she dieted off her excess weight, lowered her voice range by several tones, was taught how to dress by Adrian and how to enter a room by Douglas Fairbanks Jnr. And she never let up in her quest for self-improvement. – *Radie Harris*
She was a mean, tipsy, powerful, rotten-egg lady. – *Mercedes McCambridge*
She's like that old joke about Philadelphia. First prize four years with Joan. Second, eight. – *Franchot Tone*
I tried to be a good listener. I decided that was what she wanted all along – not so much a friend as an audience. – *June Allyson*
Famous line (*The Female on the Beach*) 'I wouldn't have you if you were hung with diamonds – upside down!'

Crawford, John (1926–)
Forgettable American leading man.
Cyrano de Bergerac 50. Actors and Sin 52. Slaves of Babylon 53. Battle of Royne River 54. Orders to Kill 58. John Paul Jones 59. Floods of Fear 59. Hell is a City 60. The 300 Spartans 62. Captain Sinbad 63. The Americanization of Emily 64. The Greatest Story Ever Told 65. I Saw What You Did 65. J. W. Coop 71. Napoleon and Samantha 72. The Poseidon Adventure 72. The Towering Inferno 74. Night Moves 75. The Enforcer 76. Tilt 78. The Apple Dumpling Gang Rides Again 79. From Here to Eternity (TV) 79. The Boogens 81, etc.
TV series: The Waltons 72–81.

Crawford, Johnny (1946–)
American actor, mainly on television as a juvenile. He began as a child, was a Mickey Mouse Club Mousketeer in the mid-50s, and in the 60s made a few hit records during a spell of television fame, playing Chuck Connors' son in the series *The Rifleman* 58–63. From the mid-60s he worked in rodeos and now concentrates on his singing, leading his own big band and playing music from the 30s.
Courage of Black Beauty 57. Indian Paint 64. Village of the Giants 65. El Dorado 67. Outlaw Blues 77. The Great Texas Dynamite Chase 77. Kenny Rogers as The Gambler Part II: The Adventure Continues (TV) 83. The Gambler Returns: The Luck of the Draw (TV) 93, etc.

Crawford, Kathryn (1908–1980) (Kathryn Crawford Moran)
American leading actress and singer, from the Broadway stage, who quit films in the early 30s. She was married to Wesley Ruggles.
The Kid's Clever 29. King of the Rodeo 29. The Climax 30. Red Hot Rhythm 30. Hide Out 30. Safety in Numbers 30. King of Jazz 30. Flying High 31. Grand Hotel 32. New Morals for Old 32, etc.

Crawford, Michael (1942–) (Michael Dumble-Smith)
Lively British comedy lead, former child actor, now best known for stage musicals. In 1998, the *Sunday Times* estimated his wealth at £20m.
Autobiography: 1999, *Parcel Arrived Safely: Tied With String*.
Soap Box Derby 50. Blow Your Own Trumpet 54. Two Living One Dead 62. The War Lover 63. Two Left Feet 63. *The Knack* 65. A Funny Thing Happened on the Way to the Forum 66. *The Jokers* 66. How I Won the War 67. *Hello Dolly* 69. The Games 69. Hello Goodbye 70. Alice's Adventures in Wonderland 72. Condorman 81. Once Upon a Forest 93, etc.
TV series: Sir Francis Drake 62. *Some Mothers Do 'Ave 'Em* 74–79. Chalk and Cheese 79.

The Crazy Gang
Three pairs of British music hall comedians made up this famous group which was enormously popular on stage from 1935 till 1962. Bud Flanagan and Chesney Allen; Jimmy Nervo (James Holloway) and Teddy Knox; Charlie Naughton and Jimmy Gold. The group's success depended upon their spontaneity and ad-libbing, and their films failed to capture much of their appeal.
Books: 1986, *The Crazy Gang* by Maureen Owen.
■ OK for Sound 37. Alf's Button Afloat 38. The Frozen Limits 39. Gasbags 40. Life is a Circus 54.

Creasey, John (1908–1973)
British thriller writer, author under various pseudonyms of more than six hundred books. Creator of the Toff, the Baron and Gideon of Scotland Yard.
Salute the Toff 52. Hammer the Toff 52. Gideon's Day 58, etc.
TV series: Gideon's Way 64-65. The Baron 66-67.

Creber, William J.
American production designer.
Rio Conchos 64. The Greatest Story Ever Told 65. Caprice 67. Planet of the Apes 68. The Detective 68. Three in the Attic 68. Justine 69. Superdad 72. The Poseidon Adventure (AAN) 72. Towering Inferno (AAN) 72. Islands in the Stream 77. Any Which Way You Can 80. Yes, Giorgio 82. Twice in a Lifetime 85. Flight of the Navigator 86. Hot Pursuit 87. Mannequin 2: On the Move 91. Folks! 92. Spy Hard 96. Without Limits 97, etc.

Cregar, Laird (1916–1944)
Heavyweight American character actor who had a tragically brief but impressive career in a rich variety of roles.
■ Granny Get Your Gun 40. Oh Johnny How You Can Love 40. Hudson's Bay 40. Blood and Sand 41. *Charley's Aunt* 41. *I Wake Up Screaming* 41. Joan of Paris 42. Rings on Her Fingers 42. This Gun for Hire 42. *Ten Gentlemen from West Point* 42. *The Black Swan* 42. Hello Frisco Hello 43. *Heaven Can Wait* 43. Holy Matrimony 43. *The Lodger* 44. Hangover Square 44.
✪ For providing such a memorable gallery of middle-aged characters while still in his early 20s. *The Black Swan*.

Crehan, Joseph (1884–1966) (Charles Wilson)
American character actor, often as sheriff or cop.
Stolen Heaven 31. Before Midnight 33. Identity Parade 34. Boulder Dam 36. Happy Landing 38. Stanley and Livingstone 39. The Roaring Twenties 39. Brother Orchid 40. Texas 42. Phantom Lady 44. Deadline at Dawn 46. The Foxes of Harrow 48. Red Desert 54, many others.

Creme, Lol (1947–)
British director and musician. He was guitarist and vocalist with the 70s rock band 10CC, and also produces music videos.
The Lunatic 92.

Cremer, Bruno (1929–)
French leading actor.
The 317th Platoon/La 317ème Section 65. Is Paris Burning?/Paris Brûle-t-il? 68. Sorcerer (US) 77. A Simple Story/Histoire Simple 79. Josepha 82. Hail Mary/Je Vous Salue Marie 83. Tenue de Soirée/Menage) 86. Taxi de Nuit (Fr.) 94, etc.

Crenna, Richard (1927–)
American leading man, formerly boy actor on radio and TV. Born in Los Angeles, he was educated at the University of Southern California. He won an Emmy in 1985 for his performance in *The Rape of Richard Beck*.
Red Skies of Montana 52. It Grows on Trees 52. The Pride of St Louis 52. Our Miss Brooks 55. Over Exposed 56. John Goldfarb Please Come Home 65. Made in Paris 65. The Sand Pebbles 66. Wait until Dark 67. Star! 68. Marooned 69. Midas Run 69. The Deserter 70. Doctors' Wives 70. Red Sky at Morning 70. Thief (TV) 71. Catlow 71. Dirty Money (Fr.) 72. The Man Called Noon 73. Double Indemnity (TV) 73. Nightmare (TV) 75. Breakheart Pass 75. The Evil 78. Stone Cold Dead 79. Death Ship 80. Body Heat 81. First Blood 82. *Table for Five* 83. The Flamingo Kid 84. Rambo: First Blood 2 85. Summer Rental 85. Rambo III 88. Leviathan 89. And the Sea Will Tell (TV) 91. A Place to Be Loved (TV) 93. Hot Shots! Part Deux 93. A Pyromaniac's Love Story 95. Jade 95. Sabrina 95. Wrongfully Accused 98, etc.
TV series: Our Miss Brooks 52–55. The Real McCoys 57–62. Slattery's People 64–65. All's Fair 76-77. It Takes Two 82-83. Gabriel's Fire 91–92.

Crevenna, Alfredo B.
German-born director and screenwriter, in Mexico from the mid-30s and the most prolific of Mexican film-makers, directing more than 100 films of mainly escapist entertainment.
La Dama del Velo 48. Angelica 51. Rebellion of the Hanged 54. Invisible Man in Mexico 58. Red Blossoms 60. Aventura al Centro de la Tierra 64. Santo Faces Black Magic 74. El Centauro Negro 75. Five Nerds Take Las Vegas/5 Nacos Asaltan Las Vegas 86. Carrasco's Escape 87. Una Luz en la Escalera 94, many more.

Crews, Laura Hope (1880–1942)
American stage actress who played character parts in many films, usually as fluttery matron.
Charming Sinners 29. New Morals for Old 32. Escapade 35. *Camille* 36. Thanks for the Memory 38. *Gone with the Wind* (as Aunt Pittypat) 39. The Bluebird 40. The Flame of New Orleans 41. One Foot in Heaven 41, many others.

Crewson, Wendy (1956–)
Canadian actress, born in Hamilton, Ontario. Married actor Michael Murphy.
Skullduggery 83. Boat House 85. The Doctor 91. Folks! 92. The Good Son 93. Corrina, Corrina 94. The Santa Clause 95. To Gillian on Her 37th Birthday 96. Air Force One 97. Gang Related 97. The Eighteenth Angel 97. From the Earth to the Moon (TV) 98. Bicentennial Man 99. Summer's End (TV) 99. Better Than Chocolate 99. Escape Velocity 99. What Lies Beneath 00. Mercy 00, etc.

Cribbins, Bernard (1928–)
British comedy character actor and recording star. Played light support roles in several films.
Two Way Stretch 60. The Girl on the Boat 62. The Wrong Arm of the Law 62. Carry On Jack 63. Crooks in Cloisters 64. She 65. The Sandwich Man 66. Daleks Invasion Earth 2150 A.D. 66. The Railway Children 70. Frenzy 72. The Water Babies 78. Dangerous Davies (TV) 81. Carry On Columbus 92, etc.

Crichton, Charles (1910–1999)
British director, a former editor. Born in Wallasey, Cheshire, he was educated at New College, Oxford, and began in films in 1931 as a cutter. From 1940, he worked at Ealing Studios. Latterly directed TV episodes of such series as *Danger Man* and *The Avengers*.
As editor: Sanders of the River 35. Things to Come 36. Elephant Boy 37. Prison without Bars 38. Thief of Baghdad 40. Old Bill and Son 41.
As director: For Those in Peril 44. Dead of Night (part) 45. Painted Boats 45. *Hue and Cry* 46. Against the Wind 47. Another Shore 48. Train of Events 49. Dance Hall 50. *The Lavender Hill Mob* 51. Hunted 52. *The Titfield Thunderbolt* 52. The Love Lottery 53. The Divided Heart 54. The Man in the Sky 56. Law and Disorder 58. Floods of Fear (& w) 58. The Battle of the Sexes 60. The Boy Who Stole a Million 60. The Third Secret 64. He Who Rides a Tiger 65. A Fish Called Wanda (& story) (AAN) 88, etc.
TV series: Dick Turpin 78.

Crichton, Michael (1942–)
American novelist and screenwriter. He studied at Harvard and lectured in anthropology at Cambridge before qualifying as a doctor at the Harvard Medical School and then turning to writing. He was paid a record $10m for the screen rights to his novel *Airframe*.
The Andromeda Strain (oa) 71. The Carey Treatment (oa) 72. The Terminal Man (oa) 72. *Pursuit* (oa, d) (TV) 72. *Westworld* (wd) 73. Coma (d) 77. The Great Train Robbery (wd) 78. Looker (wd) 80. Runaway 84. Physical Evidence 88. Jurassic Park (co-w from his novel) 93. Rising Sun (co-w from his novel) 93. Disclosure (oa) 94. Congo (oa) 95. Twister (co-w) 96. The Lost World: Jurassic Park 97. Sphere (story) 98. The 13th Warrior (p,oa) 99, etc.
“ One of the definitions of intelligence is that you don't make the same mistake twice. – M.C.

Crisanti, Andrea
Italian art director, often for the films of Francesco Rossi and Giuseppe Tornatore.
Duck! You Sucker/Giu La Tester 71. The Mattei Affair/Il Caso Mattei 72. The Heroes/Gli Eroi 72. Lucky Luciano 73. Illustrious Corpses/Cadaveri Eccellenti 75. Christ Stopped at Eboli 79. Three Brothers/Tre Fratelli 80. Identification of a Woman 82. Chronicle of a Death Foretold 87. Cinema Paradiso 89. Everybody's Fine/Stanno Tutti Bene 90. The Stolen Children/Il Ladro di Bambini 92. A Simple Formality/Una Pura Formalita 94, etc.

Crisp, Donald (1880–1974)
Distinguished British screen actor, in Hollywood from 1906; worked with D. W. Griffith and directed some silents, but from 1930 settled on acting and played mainly stern character roles.
Home Sweet Home 14. The Birth of a Nation 15. Broken Blossoms 19. Why Smith Left Home (d) 19. The Bonnie Brier Bush (d) 21. The Mark of Zorro (d) 22. Ponjola (d) 23. *Don Q Son of Zorro* (ad) 25. The Black Pirate 26. Man Bait (d) 27. Stand and Deliver (d) 28. The Return of Sherlock Holmes 29. Runaway Bride (d) 30. Svengali 31. Red Dust 32. Crime Doctor 34. The Little Minister 34. Mutiny on the Bounty 35. Mary of Scotland 36. Beloved Enemy 36. Parnell 37. Jezebel 38. The Sisters 38. *The Dawn Patrol* 38. Wuthering Heights 39. The Old Maid 39. *Brother Orchid* 40. The Sea Hawk 40. Dr Jekyll and Mr Hyde 41. *How Green Was My Valley* (AA) 41. The Gay Sisters 42. Lassie Come Home 43. *The Uninvited* 44. National Velvet 44. Valley of Decision 45. Ramrod 47. Whispering Smith 49. Bright Leaf 50. Prince Valiant 54. The Man from Laramie 55. Saddle the Wind 58. The Last Hurrah 58. Pollyanna 60. Greyfriars Bobby 61. Spencer's Mountain 63, many others.

Crisp, Quentin (1909–1999) (Denis Pratt)
English eccentric and wit, artist's model, writer, film critic and occasional actor. He is the author of a best-selling autobiography, *The Naked Civil Servant*, which detailed his homosexuality and was turned into a successful TV drama in 1975. It led to his performing one-man shows in Britain and America.
Autobiography: 1996, *Resident Alien*.
Other books: 1989, *How to Go to the Movies: A Guide for the Perplexed*.
■ Hamlet (as Polonius) 77. An Evening with Quentin Crisp (TV) 83. The Bride 85. Orlando (as Queen Elizabeth I) 92. Naked in New York (as himself) 93. Philadelphia 93. The Celluloid Closet (doc) 95. Desolation Angels 95.
“ I took a friend to see *King Kong* (the first time around). During a dramatic episode in which a certain Miss Wray lay gibbering across Mr Kong's wrist, my friend, in a voice shrill with irritation, cried out, 'I can't think what he sees in her.' – Q.C.
What keeps a woman young and beautiful is not repeated surgery but perpetual praise. – Q.C.
If we go to the movies often enough and in a sufficiently reverent spirit, they will become more absorbing than the outer world, and the problems of reality will cease to burden us. – Q.C.
I believe it was Miss Cher who said that being in a film was like being asked to swallow broken glass, and I endorse that impression. – Q.C.
If Quentin Crisp had never existed, it is unlikely that anyone would have had the nerve to invent him. – *The Times*

Crispino, Armando (1925–)
Italian director and screenwriter of macabre thrillers. He began working in the early 50s as an assistant director and screenwriter, becoming a director in the mid-60s. In the mid-70s, he quit making films to work in television and commercials.
Le Piacevoli Notti 66. John, il Bastardo 67. Commandos 68. L'Etrusco Uccide Ancora 72. Autopsy/Macchie Solari 74. Frankenstein all'Italiana 75, etc.

Cristal, Linda (1934–) (Victoria Maya)
Argentinian leading lady, in Hollywood from 1956.
Comanche 56. The Fiend Who Walked the West 58. The Perfect Furlough 58. Cry Tough 59. The Alamo 60. Panic in the City 68. Mr Majestyk 74, etc.
TV series: The High Chaparral 67–71.

Cristaldi, Franco (1924–1992)
Italian producer of good reputation. He was formerly married to actress Claudia Cardinale.
La Pattuglia Sperduta 53. La Sfida 59. L'Assassino 60. Salvatore Giuliano 61. Divorce Italian Style 61. The Red Tent 69. In the Name of the Father/In Nome del Padre 71. Lady Caroline Lamb 72. Amarcord (AA) 73. Christ Stopped at Eboli/Cristo Si è Fermato a Eboli 79. Ratataplan 79. And the Ship Sails On/E la Nave Va 83. The Name of the Rose 86. Cinema Paradiso (AA) 88. Vanille Fraise 89. C'era un Castello con 40 Cani 90, etc.

Cristiani, Gabriella (1949–)
Italian film editor.
La Luna 79. The Tragedy of a Ridiculous Man 82. The Last Emperor (AA) 87. High Season 88. Francesco 89. The Sheltering Sky 90, etc.

Cristofer, Michael (1945–) (Michael Procaccino)
American playwright, screenwriter and actor.
Crime Club (a) 75. The Entertainer (TV) 76. An Enemy of the People (a) 77. Falling in Love (w) 84. The Little Drummer Girl (a) 84. The Witches of Eastwick (w) 87. The Bonfire of the Vanities (w) 90. Mr Jones (co-w) 93. Breaking Up 97. Gia (co-w, d) (TV) 98, etc.

Criswell (1907–1982) (Charles Criswell King)
Psychic of newspapers and television, best remembered for his portentous narration to Ed Wood's *Plan 9 from Outer Space* 58, intoning, 'My friends, can your hearts stand the shocking facts about grave robbers from outer space?'
Night of the Ghouls 59. Orgy of the Dead 65, etc.

Crocker, Barry (1935–)
Australian leading man.
Squeeze a Flower 69. The Adventures of Barry Mackenzie 72. Barry Mackenzie Holds His Own 74, etc.

Crockett, Davy (1786–1836)
American trapper and Indian scout who became a legendary hero and a politician before dying at the Alamo. He has been portrayed on film by George Montgomery (*Indian Scout*), Fess Parker (*Davy Crockett*, *Davy Crockett and the River Pirates*), Arthur Hunnicutt (*The Last Command*) and John Wayne (*The Alamo*), among others.

Crogan, Emma Jane (1972–)
Australian director and screenwriter.
Love and Other Catastrophes 96.

Crombie, Donald (1942–)
Australian director.
Caddie 76. The Irishman 78. Cathy's Child 79. The Killing of Angel Street 81. Kitty and the Bagman 82. Robbery under Arms (co-d) (TV) 85. Playing Beatie Bow 86. The Heroes (TV) 88. The Saint in Australia (TV) 89. The River Kings (TV) 91. Rough Diamonds 94, etc.

Crompton, Richmal (1890–1969)
British writer for children, author of the 'William' books which have been filmed from time to time.

Cromwell, James
Lean American character actor, born in Los Angeles. The son of director John CROMWELL and actress Kay JOHNSON, he came to notice as Archie Bunker's friend Stretch Cunningham in the TV sitcom *All in the Family*.
Murder by Death 76. The Deadly Game (TV) 77. The Girl in the Empty Grave (TV) 77. The Cheap Detective 78. The House of God 79. A Christmas without Snow (TV) 80. The Man with Two Brains 83. Spraggue (TV) 84. Revenge of the Nerds 84. Tank 84. Oh, God! You Devil 84. Explorers 85. A Fine Mess 86. Revenge of the Nerds II: Nerds in Paradise 87. The Rescue 88. Pink Cadillac 89. The Runnin' Kind 89. Miracle Landing (TV) 90. The Babe 92. Romeo Is Bleeding 93. The Shaggy Dog (TV) 94. *Babe* (AAN) 95. Star Trek: First Contact 96. The People vs Larry Flynt 96. Eraser 96. *LA Confidential* 97. The Education of Little Tree 97. Deep Impact 98. Species 2 98. Babe: Pig in the City 98. Fail Safe (TV) 00. Species II 98. The Green Mile 99. Snow Falling On Cedars 99. The General's Daughter 99. The Bachelor 99. Space Cowboys 00, etc.
TV series: All in the Family 74. Hot L Baltimore 75. The Nancy Walker Show 76. The Last Precinct 86. Easy Street 86–87.

Cromwell, John (1888–1979)
Distinguished American director with stage background. Formerly married to actresses Ruth NELSON and Kay JOHNSON. He and Johnson are the parents of actor James Cromwell.
■ The Dummy (a only) 29. The Mighty 29. The Dance of Life 29. Close Harmony 29. Street of Chance 30. Tom Sawyer 30. The Texan 30. For the Defense 30. Scandal Street 31. Rich Man's Folly 31. Vice Squad 31. Unfaithful 31. The World and the Flesh 31. Sweepings 33. The Silver Cord 33. Double Harness 33. Ann Vickers 33. Spitfire 34. This Man is Mine 34. *Of Human Bondage* 34. The Fountain 34. Jalna 35. Village Tale 35. I Dream Too Much 35. Little Lord Fauntleroy 36. To Mary With Love 36. Banjo on My Knee 36. *The Prisoner of Zenda* 37. *Algiers* 38. Made for Each Other 38. In Name Only 39. Abe Lincoln in Illinois 40. Victory 40. So Ends Our Night 41. Son of Fury 42. *Since You Went Away* 44. The Enchanted Cottage 45. *Anna and the King of Siam* 46. Dead Reckoning 47. Night Song 47. Caged 50. The Company She Keeps 51. The Racket 51. Top Secret Affair (a only) 57. The Goddess 58. The Scavengers 60. A Matter of Morals 61. *Three Women* (a only) 77. *A Wedding* (a only) 78.

Cromwell, Oliver (1599–1658)
The Puritan Protector of England during the Civil War has been shown on screen as a repressed rather than a heroic figure, as follows:
1937 *The Vicar of Bray*, George Merritt
1949 *Cardboard Cavalier*, Edmund Willard
1958 *The Moonraker*, John Le Mesurier
1968 *Witchfinder General*, Patrick Wymark
1970 *Cromwell*, Richard Harris

Cromwell, Richard (1910–1960) (Roy Radebaugh)
American leading man, gentle hero of early sound films. He was married to Angela Lansbury.
■ *Tol'able David* 30. Fifty Fathoms Deep 31. Shanghaied Love 31. Maker of Men 31. That's My Boy 32. Emma 32. The Strange Love of Molly Louvain 32. Age of Consent 32. Tom Brown of Culver 32. This Day and Age 33. Hoopla 33. Above the Clouds 34. Carolina 34. Among the Missing 34. Name the Woman 34. When Strangers Meet 34. Most Precious Thing in Life 34. *Lives of a Bengal Lancer* 35. McFadden's Flats 35. Life Begins at Forty 35. Men of the Hour 35. Unknown Woman 35. Annapolis Farewell 35. Poppy 36. Our Fighting Navy (GB) 37. The Road Back 37. The Wrong Road 37. Jezebel 38. Come On Leathernecks 38. Storm Over Bengal 38. Young Mr Lincoln 39. Enemy Agent 40. The Villain Still Pursued Her 40. Village Barn Dance 40. Parachute Battalion 41. Riot Squad 42. Baby Face Morgan 42. Bungalow 13 48.

Cronenberg, David (1943–)
Canadian director of outlandish and generally over-the-top horror films.
Autobiography: 1992, *Cronenberg on Cronenberg* (edited by Chris Radley).
Biography: 1994, *David Cronenberg: A Delicate Balance* by Peter Morris.
Crimes of the Future 70. Squirm 74. Shivers 75. Rabid 77. The Brood 80. Scanners 81. Videodrome 83. The Dead Zone 83. The Fly 86. Dead Ringers 88. Nightbreed (a only) 90. Naked Lunch 91. M. Butterfly 93. Blood & Donuts (a) 95. Extreme Measures (a) 96. Crash (wd) 97. Last Night (a) 98. eXistenZ 98. Resurrection (a) 99, etc.
❝ My dentist said to me the other day, I've enough problems in my life, so why should I see your films? – *D.C.*
A friend of mine saw *Videodrome*, said he really liked it, and added, you know someday they're going to lock you up. – *D.C.*
I don't have a moral plan. I'm a Canadian. – *D.C.*
Censorship is about control. It's not about morality at all. And it's about fear. I can't see how one adult citizen can control what another adult citizen can or cannot see. – *D.C.*
He works from his dreams. If he'd just dream a little more normally, I'd love to work with him again. – *James Woods*

Cronenweth, Jordan (c. 1935–1996)
American cinematographer.
Brewster McCloud 70. Play it as it Lays 72. Zandy's Bride 74. The Front Page 74. Handle With Care 77. Rolling Thunder 77. Altered States 80. Cutter's Way 81. Blade Runner 82. Best Friends 82. Peggy Sue Got Married (AAN) 86. Gardens of Stone 87. State of Grace 90. Get Back 91. Final Analysis 92, etc.

Cronin, A. J. (1896–1981)
British novelist, former doctor.
Grand Canary (US) 34. Once to Every Woman (US) 34. The Citadel 38. The Stars Look Down (&co-w) 39. Vigil in the Night (US) 40. Hatter's Castle 41. Shining Victory (US) 41. The Keys of the Kingdom (US) 44. The Green Years (US) 46. The Spanish Gardener 56. Beyond This Place 59. The Citadel (TV) 83, etc.
TV series: Dr Finlay's Casebook 59–66.

Cronjager, Edward (1904–1960)
American cinematographer.
The Quarterback 26. The Virginian 30. Cimarron 31. Roberta 35. The Gorilla 39. *Hot Spot* 41. *Heaven Can Wait* 43. Canyon Passage 46. The House by the River 50. Treasure of the Golden Condor 53. Beneath the Twelve-Mile Reef 53, many others.

Cronyn, Hume (1911–) (Hume Blake)
Canadian character actor of stage and screen; married Jessica Tandy.
Autobiography: 1991, *A Terrible Liar*.
■ *Shadow of a Doubt* 43. Phantom of the Opera 43. The Cross of Lorraine 43. *The Seventh Cross* (AAN) 44. Main Street After Dark 44. *Lifeboat* 44. A Letter for Evie 45. The Sailor Takes a Wife 45. The Green Years 46. The Postman Always Rings Twice 46. Ziegfeld Follies 46. The Beginning or the End 47. *Brute Force* 47. The Bride Goes Wild 48. Top o' the Morning 49. People Will Talk 51. Crowded Paradise 56. *Sunrise at Campobello* 60. Cleopatra 63. Hamlet 64. Gaily Gaily 69. The Arrangement 70. There Was a Crooked Man 70. The Parallax View 74. Conrack 74. Rollover 80. Honky Tonk Freeway 81. The World According to Garp 82. Brewster's Millions 84. Impulse 84. Cocoon 85. The Thrill of Genius 85. Batteries Not Included 87. Cocoon: The Return 88. To Dance with the White Dog (TV) 93. The Pelican Brief 93. Camilla 94.
❝ To act you must have a sense of truth and some degree of dedication. – *H.C.*

Cropper, Anna (1938–)
English actress, much on stage and television.
All Neat in Black Stockings 69. Cromwell 70. The Jewel in the Crown (TV) 84. Anna of the Five Towns (TV) 85, etc.
TV series: The Castles 95.

Crosbie, Annette (1934–)
Scottish character actress whose best roles have been on television as Catherine of Aragon in *The Six Wives of Henry VIII* 70, and as Queen Victoria in *Edward VII* 75. She is also known for the part of Margaret Meldrew in the TV sitcom *One Foot in the Grave*. Born in Gorebridge, she trained at the Bristol Old Vic Theatre School.
Sky West and Crooked 65. The Public Eye 72. The Slipper and the Rose 76. Hawk the Slayer 80. Ordeal by Innocence 85. Summer's Lease (TV) 89. Chernobyl: The Final Warning (TV) 91. The Pope Must Die/The Pope Must Diet 91. Leon the Pig Farmer 92. Solitaire for Two 94. Nervous Energy 95. P. D. James's An Unsuitable Job for a Woman (TV) 97. Shooting Fish 97. The Debt Collector 99. An Unsuitable Job for a Woman (TV) 99. Oliver Twist (TV) 99. Anchor Me (TV) 00, etc.
TV series: One Foot in the Grave 90–95, 00. Doctor Finlay 93–96. Underworld 96.

Crosby, Bing (1903–1977) (Harry Lillis Crosby)
Star American crooner of the 30s and 40s; former band singer, later an agreeable comedian, romantic lead and straight actor. His first wife was actress Dixie Lee and his sons Gary, Philip, Dennis and Lindsay CROSBY had show business careers.
Autobiography: 1953, *Call Me Lucky*.
Biography: 1982, *The Hollow Man* by Robert F. Slatzer.
■ King of Jazz 30. Check and Double Check 30. Reaching for the Moon 31. Confessions of a Co-Ed 31. The Big Broadcast 32. College Humor 33. Too Much Harmony 33. Going Hollywood 33. We're Not Dressing 34. She Loves Me Not 34. Here is My Heart 34. *Mississippi* 35. Two for Tonight 35. The Big Broadcast of 1936 36. *Anything Goes* 36. Rhythm on the Range 36. Pennies from Heaven 36. Waikiki Wedding 37. Double or Nothing 37. Dr Rhythm 38. *Sing You Sinners* 38. Paris Honeymoon 39. East Side of Heaven 39. The Star Maker 39. *Road to Singapore* 40. If I Had My Way 40. Rhythm on the River 40. Road to Zanzibar 41. Birth of the Blues 41. *Holiday Inn* 42. Road to Morocco 42. Star Spangled Rhythm 43. Dixie 43. *Going My Way* (AA) 44. Here Come The Waves 45. Duffy's Tavern 45. Road to Utopia 45. The Bells of St Mary's (AAN) 45. Out of This World (voice) 45. Blue Skies 46. Variety Girl 47. Welcome Stranger 47. Road to Rio 47. The Emperor Waltz 48. A Connecticut Yankee in King Arthur's Court 49. Top o' the Morning 49. Ichabod and Mr Toad (voice) 49. Riding High 50. Mr Music 50. Here Comes the Groom 51. Just for You 52. Road to Bali 52. Little Boy Lost 53. White Christmas 54. *The Country Girl* (AAN) 54. Anything Goes 56. High Society 56. Man on Fire 57. Say One for Me 59. High Time 60. Pepe 60. Road to Hong Kong 62. Robin and the Seven Hoods 64. Stagecoach 66. Dr Cook's Garden (TV) 70.
TV series: The Bing Crosby Show 64.
✪ For his songs; and for his acceptance as a member of everybody's family over a fifty-year career. *Holiday Inn*.
❝ Honestly, I think I've stretched a talent which is so thin it's almost transparent over a quite unbelievable term of years. – *B.C.*
He was an average guy who could carry a tune. – *B.C.'s own epitaph*
Once or twice I've been described as a light comedian. I consider this the most accurate description of my abilities I've ever seen. – *B.C.*

Crosby, Bob (1913–1993)
American bandleader, brother of Bing.
Let's Make Music 40. Reveille with Beverly 43. See Here Private Hargrove 44. Two Tickets to Broadway 51. The Five Pennies 59, etc.

Crosby, Denise (1957–)
American actress, the daughter of Dennis Crosby.
48 Hrs 82. Curse of the Pink Panther 83. Desert Hearts 85. Eliminators 86. Arizona Heat 87. Miracle Mile 89. Pet Sematary 89. Skin Deep 89. Red Shoe Diaries II: Double Dare 92. Desperate Crimes 93. Black Water 94. Max (Can.) 94. Mutant Species 95. Deep Impact 98, etc.

Crosby, Dennis (1934–1991)
American actor, singer and disc jockey, the son of Bing Crosby and Dixie Lee, twin brother of Philip and father of actress Denise Crosby. Committed suicide.
Duffy's Tavern 45. Sergeants 3 61, etc.

Crosby, Floyd (1899–1985)
American cinematographer who worked on everything from documentary to horror thrillers.
■ *Tabu* (AA) 31. *The River* (co-ph) 37. The Fight for Life 40. My Father's House 47. Of Men and Music 50. The Brave Bulls 51. *High Noon* 52. Man in the Dark 53. The Steel Lady 53. Man Crazy 53. Stormy 54. The Snow Creature 54. The Monster from the Ocean Floor 54. The Fast and the Furious 54. Five Guns West 55. The Naked Street 55. Shack out on 101 55. Hell's Horizon 55. Apache Woman 55. Naked Paradise 56. She Gods of Shark Reef 56. Attack of the Crab Monsters 56. Rock All Night 56. Reform School 57. Teenage Doll 57. Ride out for Revenge 57. Hell Canyon Outlaws 57. Carnival Rock 57. War of the Satellites 57. Suicide Battalion 58. Cry Baby Killer 58. Machine Gun Kelly 58. The Old Man and the Sea (co-ph) 58. Wolf Larsen 58. Hot Rod Gang 58. Teenage Caveman 58. I Mobster 59. Crime and Punishment USA 59. The Miracle of the Hills 59. The Wonderful Country 59. Blood and Steel 59. The Rookie 60. Twelve Hours to Kill 60. *House of Usher* 60. The High Powered Rifle 60. Walk Tall 60. Freckles 60. Operation Bottleneck 61. The Pit and the Pendulum 61. A Cold Wind in August 61. The Purple Hills 61. The Little Shepherd of Kingdom Come 61. The Gambler Wore a Gun 61. Seven Women from Hell 62. The Explosive Generation 62. Woman Hunt 62. The Premature Burial 62. The Two Little Bears 62. Tales of Terror 62. The Firebrand 62. The Broken Land 62. Terror at Black Falls 62. *The Raven* 63. Black Zoo 63. Yellow Canary 63. The Young Racers 63. X – the Man with X-ray Eyes 63. The Comedy of Terrors 64. Bikini Beach 64. Pajama Party 64. The Haunted Palace 64. Raiders from beneath the Sea 65. Beach Blanket Bingo 65. How to Stuff a Wild Bikini 65. Sergeant Deadhead 65. Sallah 65. Fireball 500 66. The Cool Ones 67.

Crosby, Gary (1933–1995)
American actor and singer, the eldest son of Bing Crosby and Dixie Lee. He began with appearances in his father's films and made a hit record in 1950 duetting with Bing, with whom he had an uneasy relationship (detailed in his 1983 autobiography *Going My Own Way*, written with Ross Firestone). He also performed in a musical act with his brothers Dennis, Philip and Lindsay. His career was disrupted by alcoholism and drug abuse.
Star Spangled Rhythm 42. Duffy's Tavern 45. Out of This World 45. Mardi Gras 58. Holiday for Lovers 59. A Private's Affair 59. Battle at Bloody Beach 61. Two Tickets to Paris 62. Girl Happy 65. Which Way to the Front? 70. The Night Stalker 87. Chill Factor 90, etc.
TV series: The Bill Dana Show 63–64. Adam 12 68–75. Chase 73–74.
❝ The way I saw it I only had two choices: manual labor or showbusiness. The more I thought about putting in ten hours a day busting my butt on someone's ranch the better showbusiness began to look. – *G.C.*
I did not make a lot of friends for myself on the set, not where it counted … Nor did the way I showed up for work totally wasted and bedraggled from the night before. I'd be popping bennies and juicing all morning just to stay up there enough to hit the mark and say the lines. – *G.C.*

Crosby, Lindsay (1938–1989)
American actor and singer, the son of Bing Crosby and Dixie Lee. Committed suicide.
Duffy's Tavern 45. Sergeants 3 61. The Glory Stompers 67. The Mechanic 72. Santee 72. Murph the Surf/Live a Little, Steal a Lot 74. Codename: Zebra 84, etc.

Crosby, Philip (1934–)
American actor and singer, the son of Bing Crosby and Dixie Lee.
Duffy's Tavern 45. Sergeants 3 61. Robin and the Seven Hoods 64. None but the Brave 65, etc.

Croset, Paule
See CORDAY, Paula.

Crosland, Alan (1894–1936)
Routine American director who happened to handle two innovative films. A former actor, he died of injuries sustained in a car crash. Married actress Natalie Moorhead.
Enemies of Women 23. Under the Red Robe 23. Three Weeks 24. Bobbed Hair 25. *Don Juan* (first film with synchronized music) 26. The Beloved Rogue 27. Old San Francisco 27. *The Jazz Singer*

(first film with talking sequences) 27. Glorious Betsy 28. General Crack 29. Song of the Flame 30. Captain Thunder 31. Weekends Only 32. The Case of the Howling Dog 34. Lady Tubbs 35. The Great Impersonation 35, many others.

Crosman, Henrietta (1861–1944)
American actress, a grande dame who made a few films. Born in Wheeling, West Virginia, she made her theatrical debut in 1883, becoming a star as Nell Gwyn in 1900, and acting on stage and in vaudeville thereafter.
■ The Unwelcome Mrs Hatch 14. How Molly Made Good 15. Broadway Broke 23. Wandering Fires 25. *The Royal Family of Broadway* 30. Pilgrimage 33. Three on a Honeymoon 34. Carolina 34. Such Women Are Dangerous 34. Among the Missing 34. The Curtain Falls 34. Menace 34. Elinor Norton 35. The Right to Live 35. *The Dark Angel* 35. Hitch Hike to Heaven 36. Charlie Chan's Secret 36. The Moon's Our Home 36. Girl of the Ozarks 36. Follow Your Heart 37. Personal Property 37.

Cross, Ben (1947–)
British leading man of somewhat lugubrious countenance.
Chariots of Fire 81. The Citadel (TV) 83. The Far Pavilions (TV) 83. The Assisi Underground 85. The Unholy 88. Steal the Sky 88. Paperhouse 89. Nightlife (TV) 89. Live Wire 92. Cold Sweat 93. Symphony 93. The Ascent 94. First Knight 95. The Invader 96. Turbulence 97. The Corporate Ladder 97. The Venice Project (US/Aus.) 99, etc.
TV series: Dark Shadows 91.

Cross, Eric (1902–)
British cinematographer.
The Bells 31. Song of Freedom 36. Cotton Queen 37. The Last Adventurers 37. Sporting Love 37. The Man at the Gate 41. Ships with Wings 41. The Flemish Farm 43. Don't Take it to Heart 44. Tawny Pipit 44. Quiet Weekend 46. Chance of a Lifetime 50. The Dark Man 50. Escape Route 52. Hunted 52. The Kidnappers 53. Escapade 55. Tiger by the Tail 55. Private's Progress 56. Three Men in a Boat 56. High Tide at Noon 57. The One that Got Away 57. Tiger Bay 59. Beyond the Curtain 60. Inn for Trouble 60, etc.

Crosse, Rupert (1927–1973)
American actor, born in New York City. Died of cancer.
Shadows 59. Too Late Blues 61. Ride in the Whirlwind 65. The Reivers (AAN) 69, etc.
TV series: The Partners 71-72.

Crossley, Syd (1885–1960)
British music-hall comedian who played comic supporting roles in many films. In US in 20s.
Keep Smiling 25. Fangs of the Wild 28. Atlantic 29. Tonight's the Night 31. Those were the Days 34. Dandy Dick 35. Music Hath Charms 36. The Ghost Goes West 36. Silver Blaze 37. Penny Paradise 38, many others.

Crothers, Rachel (1878–1958)
American playwright and occasional screenwriter. Born in Bloomington, Illinois, she began as an actress and also directed her own plays from 1903. In the late 20s to the late 30s, her comedies of manners, dealing with the problems of liberated women, proved attractive to film producers.
When Ladies Meet 33 and 41. As Husbands Go 34. Splendor (w, oa) 35. Susan and God/The Gay Mrs Trexel 40, etc.

Crothers, Scatman (1910–1986) (Sherman Crothers)
American character actor with a penchant for comedy.
Between Heaven and Hell 56. Lady in a Cage 64. Hello Dolly 69. The Great White Hope 70. Lady Sing the Blues 72. The Fortune 74. One Flew Over the Cuckoo's Nest 75. The Shootist 76. Silver Streak 77. Scavenger Hunt 79. Bronco Billy 80. The Shining 80. Twilight Zone 83. The Journey of Natty Gann 85, etc.
TV series: Chico and the Man 74–77. One of the Boys 82. Casablanca 83. Morning Star, Evening Star 86.

Crouse, Lindsay (1948–)
American leading lady, daughter of Russel Crouse. She was formerly married to director and writer David Mamet.
All the President's Men 76. Between the Lines 77. Slapshot 77. The Verdict 82. Iceman 82. Places in the Heart (AAN) 85. House of Games 87. Communion, a True Story 89. Desperate Hours 90. Chantilly Lace (TV) 93. Being Human 94. Parallel Lives (TV) 94. Bye Bye, Love 95. The Indian in the Cupboard 95. The Juror 96. The Arrival 96. Prefontaine 97. Progeny 98. The Insider 99, etc.

Crouse, Russel (1893–1966)
American librettist, usually with Howard Lindsay. Their musicals that have been filmed include *Anything Goes*, *Call Me Madam* and *The Sound of Music*. Non-musicals: *Life with Father*, *State of the Union*, etc.

Crowden, Graham (1922–)
Scottish character actor, often in querulous or eccentric roles. Born in Edinburgh, he first worked as a stage manager and in repertory and has been a member of the Royal National Theatre Company and the Royal Shakespeare Company.
Don't Bother to Knock 61. Nil Carborundum (TV) 62. One Way Pendulum 64. Morgan 66. If … 68. The Virgin Soldiers 69. Leo the Last 70. Up the Chastity Belt 71. The Ruling Class 72. O Lucky Man 73. Jabberwocky 77. For Your Eyes Only 81. Britannia Hospital 82. Company of Wolves 85. Out of Africa 85. The Innocent Sleep 95. Gulliver's Travels (TV) 96. I Want You 98, etc.
TV series: HMS Paradise 64. A Very Peculiar Practice 86–88. Waiting for God 90–93.

Crowe, Cameron (1957–)
American screenwriter and director, a former journalist.
Fast Times at Ridgemont High (w) 82. The Wild Life (w) 84. Say Anything (wd) 89. Singles (wd) 92. Sessions (wd) 92. *Jerry Maguire* (AANw,d) 96. Almost Famous (wd) (AAw, BFAw) 00, etc.

Crowe, Russell (1964–)
New Zealand-born leading actor who has lived most his life in Australia, now in international films. He began by playing guitar and singing with his own rock group. His role in *Gladiator* made him a bankable star. He was romantically involved with actress Meg Ryan.
Blood Oath 90. The Crossing 90. Proof 91. Spotswood/The Efficiency Expert 91. *Romper Stomper* 92. Love in Limbo 92. Hammers over the Anvil 93. The Silver Brumby 93. For the Moment (Can.) 94. The Sum of Us 94. The Quick and the Dead (US) 95. Virtuosity (US) 95. Rough Magic (Fr.) 95. Breaking Up (US) 96. No Way Back (US/Japan) 96. Heaven's Burning 97. LA Confidential (US) 97. *The Insider* (US, AAN) 99. *Gladiator* (US) (AA) 00. Proof of Life 00, etc.
❝ I'm a virtuoso in my job in that there's not an actor I can't go into a scene with and be absolutely confident that, whatever is required of my character, I can do it. – *R.C.*

Crowe, Sarah (1966–)
British blonde comic actress, best known as the greedy, giggling girl in TV advertisements for Philadelphia cheese.
Carry on Columbus 92. The Steal 95. Caught in the Act 96, etc.
TV series: Haggard 90–92. Roy's Raiders 91. Sometime Never 96.

Crowley, Pat (1929–)
American leading lady of the 50s.
Forever Female 53. Money from Home 54. Red Garters 54. There's Always Tomorrow 55. Hollywood or Bust 56. Key Witness 60. To Trap a Spy 64. A Family Upside Down (TV) 78, etc.
TV series: Please Don't Eat the Daisies 65–66. Joe Forrester 75. Dynasty 86.

Crowther, Bosley (1905–1981)
American film critic. Long with the *New York Times*.

Crudup, Billy (1968–)
American leading actor, from the theatre. Born in Long Island, New York, he was raised in Florida and Texas. He studied at the University of North Carolina, New York University and New York's Tisch School of the Arts. He has been romantically linked with actress Mary-Louise Parker.
Sleepers 96. Everyone Says I Love You 96. Inventing the Abbots 97. Snitch 98. Without Limits 98. The Hi-Lo Country 99. Princess Mononoke (voice) 99. Jesus' Son 99. Waking the Dead 00. Almost Famous 00, etc.
❝ When you do film, at the end of the day there's always a sort of emptiness, because your performance hasn't ended. It's lingering, and everything you did today you won't do again, so you can't learn from it. – *B.C.*
I don't want my own personality to become the role. – *B.C.*

Cruickshank, Andrew (1907–1988)
Scottish stage actor who appeared in a number of films, usually as doctor or judge. A national figure on TV as Dr Cameron in *Dr Finlay's Casebook* 59–66.
Auld Lang Syne 37. The Mark of Cain 47. Paper Orchid 49. Your Witness 50. The Cruel Sea 53. Richard III 56. Innocent Sinners 58. Kidnapped 60. *There Was a Crooked Man* 60. El Cid 61. Murder Most Foul 64, etc.

Cruise, Tom (1962–) (Thomas Cruise Mapother IV)
Leading American actor, the biggest attraction of the late 80s and early 90s. Born in Syracuse, New York, he is a high-school dropout who began acting in his late teens. His performance as a cocky jet pilot in *Top Gun* brought him stardom, and he proved he could also act in *Born on the Fourth of July*. He now runs his own production company, which starred him in the box-office hit *Mission: Impossible* and earned with a reported $70m; he then disappeared from view for more than a year, working on Stanley Kubrick's *Eyes Wide Shut*, while other, younger actors replaced him as box-office sensations. Married (1987–90) actress Mimi Rogers and, in 1990, actress Nicole Kidman.
Biography: 1997, *Tom Cruise* by Robert Sellers.
Endless Love 81. Taps 81. Losin' It 83. All the Right Moves 83. The Outsiders 83. Risky Business 84. Legend 84. *Top Gun* 85. *The Color of Money* 86. Cocktail 88. Rain Man 88. *Born on the Fourth of July* (AAN) 89. Days of Thunder 90. Far and Away 92. A Few Good Men 92. The Firm 93. Interview with the Vampire 94. Mission: Impossible 96. *Jerry Maguire* (AAN) 96. Without Limits (p only) 98. Eyes Wide Shut 99. Magnolia (AAN) 99. Mission: Impossible 2 00, etc.
❝ Hollywood didn't create Tom Cruise so that he could do *Rain Man* and *Born on the Fourth of July*. Hollywood created him to make twelve *Top Guns*, and it will replace him if he doesn't. – *Joe Queenan*
He's no more my Vampire Lestat than Edward G. Robinson is Rhett Butler. – *Anne Rice*
He has this light around him like he holds a little piece of the universe in his hands, and he has so much of it that he can afford to give a little bit to each person he encounters. – *Renee Zellweger*

Crumb, Robert (1943–)
American comic-book artist who emerged from underground publications of the 60s. He is the creator of Fritz the Cat, the randy hero of two animated features, *Fritz the Cat* 72, directed by Ralph Bakshi, and *The Nine Lives of Fritz the Cat* 74, directed by Robert Taylor. (Crumb disowned both movies.) A two-hour documentary on his life, *Crumb*, was released in 1994, directed by Terry Zwigoff.

Crutchley, Rosalie (1920–1997)
Striking, lean-featured British stage actress who makes occasional film appearances.
Take My Life 47. Give Us This Day 49. Quo Vadis 51. Make Me an Offer 55. The Spanish Gardener 56. *A Tale of Two Cities* (as Madame Lafarge) 58. Beyond This Place 59. Sons and Lovers 60. Freud 62. The Girl in the Headlines 63. Behold a Pale Horse 64. Jane Eyre (TV) 70. Blood from the Mummy's Tomb 71. Who Slew Auntie Roo? 71. Man of La Mancha 72. Mahler 74. Smiley's People (TV) 82. Eleni 85. Four Weddings and a Funeral 94, etc.

Cruttwell, Greg
English actor, born in London, from the theatre. He also began directing and writing in the 00s.
Naked 93. 2 Days in the Valley (US) 96. George of the Jungle (US) 97. Chunky Monkey (wd) 00, etc.

Cruz, Brandon (1962–)
American child actor of the 70s. Born in Bakersfield, California, he later fronted punk rock bands and worked as a film editor, including on the animated TV series *South Park* in the late 90s.
But I Don't Want to Get Married (TV) 70. The Going Up of David Lev (TV) 72. The Bad News Bears 76. The One and Only 78, etc.
TV series: *The Courtship of Eddie's Father* 69–72.

Cruz, Penélope (1974–) (Penélope Cruz Sanchez)
Smouldering Spanish leading actress, in international films. Born in Madrid, she trained as a dancer.
El Laberinto Griego 91. Jamon, Jamon 92. Belle Epoque 92. For Love, Only for Love/Per Amore, Solo per Amore 93. La Ribelle (It.) 93. It's All Lies/Todo Es Mentira 94. Allegro Ma No Troppo 95. The Man with Rain in His Shoes 98. Talk of Angels (US) 98. All About My Mother/Todo Sobre Mi Madre 99. The Naked Maja/Volavérunt 99. The Hi-Lo Country (US) 99. All the Pretty Horses (US) 00. Blow (US) 00. Woman on Top 01. Captain Corelli's Mandolin 01 etc.

Cruze, James (1884–1942) (Jens Cruz Bosen)
Danish-American silent screen actor who broke his leg and turned to direction.
As actor: A Boy of Revolution 11. She 11. The Star of Bethlehem 12. Joseph in the Land of Egypt 14. *The Million Dollar Mystery* (serial) 14. The Twenty Million Dollar Mystery (serial) 15. Nan of Music Mountain 17. Too Many Millions 18, etc.
As director: Too Many Millions 18. The Dollar a Year Man 21. One Glorious Day 22. The Dictator 22. *The Covered Wagon* 23. *Hollywood* 23. Ruggles of Red Gap 23. To the Ladies 23. Merton of the Movies 24. The Goose Hangs High 25. *Beggar on Horseback* 25. Pony Express 25. *Old Ironsides* 26. The Mating Call 27. The Great Gabbo 29. Salvation Nell 31. *Washington Merry Go Round* 32. I Cover the Waterfront 33. David Harum 34. Helldorado 34. *Sutter's Gold* 36. Prison Nurse 38. Gangs of New York 38, many others.

Cryer, Jon (1965–)
American actor. Born in New York, he studied acting at RADA and first came to notice as Duckie in *Pretty in Pink*. He began producing and writing independent movies with director Richard Schenkman in the late 90s.
No Small Affair 84. O. C. and Stiggs 85. Pretty in Pink 86. Dudes 87. Hiding Out 87. Morgan Stewart's Coming Home 87. Superman IV: The Quest for Peace 87. Hot Shots! 91. Heads 94. I'll Do Anything 94. The Pompatus of Love (& co-p, co-w) 96. Went to Coney Island on a Mission from God … Be Back by Five (& p, co-w) 98. Holy Man 98, etc.
TV series: The Famous Teddy Z 89-90. Partners 95-96. Getting Personal 98. The Trouble With Normal 00.

Crystal, Billy (1947–)
American stand-up comedian and writer turned light leading man. Born in Long Beach, New York, he went to Marshall University, West Virginia, on a baseball scholarship before switching to New York University, where he studied film and television direction. He worked as a teacher while honing his comic act. He first gained national attention in the role of the gay Jodie Dallas in the TV sitcom *Soap*. His movie career began inauspiciously as a pregnant man in *Rabbit Test*. He recovered with an Emmy-award-winning performance on *Saturday Night Live*, and star performances in *When Harry Met Sally* and *City Slickers*.
Rabbit Test 78. Animalympics (voice) 79. Enola Gay: The Men, the Mission, the Atomic Bomb (TV) 80. This Is Spinal Tap 83. Running Scared 86. The Princess Bride 87. Throw Momma from the Train 87. Memories of Me 88. When Harry Met Sally 89. City Slickers 91. Mr Saturday Night (& d) 92. City Slickers II: The Legend of Curly's Gold 94. Forget Paris (& co-w, d) 95. Hamlet 96. Deconstructing Harry 97. Father's Day 97. My Giant 98. Analyze This 99. The Adventures of Rocky and Bullwinkle 00, etc.
TV series: Soap 77–81.

Cuadrado, Luis (1934–1980) (Luis Cuadrado Encinar)
Spanish cinematographer, associated with the films of Carlos Saura, José Luis Borau and other directors of the New Spanish Cinema. Born in Toro, he studied at EOC (Escuela Oficial de Cinematografía). His career ended in 1975, when he went blind.

The Hunt/La Caza 65. Peppermint Frappé 67. Night Hair Child (GB) 71. Ana and the Wolves/ Ana y los Lobos 72. *The Spirit of the Beehive* 73. B. Must Die/Hay Que Matar a B. 73. Cousin Angelica 74. Poachers/Furtivos 75. Pascual Duarte 76, etc.

Cuaron, Alfonso (1961–)
Mexican director.
Tale of Love and Hysteria/Solo con Tu Pareja 91. *A Little Princess* (US) 95.

Cucciolla, Ricardo (1932–)
Italian leading actor.
Italia Brava Gente 65. Grand Slam 67. Sacco and Vanzetti 71, etc.

Cucinotta, Maria Grazia
Sultry Italian actress.
The Day of the Beast/Dia de la Bestia (Sp.) 95. I Laureati 95. The Postman/Il Postino 95. Italiani 96. A Brooklyn State of Mind (US) 97. The Second Wife/La Seconda Moglie 98. Ballad of the Nightingale (US) 98. The World Is Not Enough (US) 99, etc.

Cugat, Xavier (1900–1990)
Chubby, beaming Spanish-American bandleader and caricaturist, a feature of many MGM musicals of the 40s.
Autobiography: 1948, *Rumba Is My Life*.
You Were Never Lovelier 42. Two Girls and a Sailor 44. Holiday in Mexico 46. This Time for Keeps 47. A Date with Judy 48. Neptune's Daughter 49. Chicago Syndicate 55, etc.

Cukor, George (1899–1983)
American director, from the Broadway stage; proved to be one of Hollywood's most reliable handlers of high comedy and other literate material.
Biography: 1991, *A Double Life: Director George Cukor* by Patrick McGilligan.
■ Grumpy (co-d) 30. Virtuous Sin (co-d) 30. The Royal Family of Broadway 30. Tarnished Lady 30. Girls About Town 31. *One Hour with You* (with Lubitsch) 32. *What Price Hollywood?* 32. A Bill of Divorcement 32. Rockabye 32. Our Betters 33. *Dinner at Eight* 33. *Little Women* (AAN) 33. *David Copperfield* 34. Sylvia Scarlett 35. Romeo and Juliet 36. *Camille* 36. *Holiday* 38. Zaza 39. *The Women* 39. Susan and God 40. *The Philadelphia Story* (AAN) 40. A Woman's Face 41. Two-faced Woman 41. Her Cardboard Lover 42. *Keeper of the Flame* 43. Gaslight 44. Winged Victory 44. Desire Me (co-d) 47. A Double Life (AAN) 47. *Adam's Rib* 49. Edward My Son (GB) 49. A Life of Her Own 50. Born Yesterday (AAN) 50. The Model and the Marriage Broker 52. The Marrying Kind 52. Pat and Mike 52. The Actress 53. It Should Happen to You 53. *A Star is Born* 54. Bhowani Junction 56. Les Girls 57. Wild is the Wind 57. Heller in Pink Tights 59. Song Without End (part) 60. Let's Make Love 61. The Chapman Report 62. *My Fair Lady* (AA) 64. Justine 69. Travels with My Aunt 73. Love Among the Ruins (TV) 75. The Bluebird 76. The Corn Is Green (TV) 79. Rich and Famous 81.
✪ For adding to Hollywood a sense of light culture; and for his discretion in handling a score of the film colony's more temperamental ladies. *The Philadelphia Story*.
❝ His films vary drastically in their visual texture, their style reposing mainly in the theatrically accomplished handling of the actors. – *Charles Higham*
When a director has provided polished tasteful entertainments of a high order consistently over a period of thirty years, it is clear that said director is much more than a mere entertainer. – *Andrew Sarris*

Culkin, Kieran (1982–)
American juvenile actor, the brother of Macaulay CULKIN.
Father of the Bride 91. Home Alone II: Lost in New York 92. Nowhere to Run 93. It Runs in the Family 94. The Mighty 98. The Cider House Rules 99. Music of the Heart 99. She's All That 99, etc.

Culkin, Macaulay (1980–)
American juvenile actor who became a star with *Home Alone*, the most successful movie comedy yet made. He was reportedly paid $5 million and 5 per cent of the gross to appear in the sequel. Married actress Rachel Miner in 1998 (separated 2000).
Rocket Gibraltar 88. Uncle Buck 89. See You in the Morning 89. Home Alone 90. Jacob's Ladder (uncredited cameo) 90. My Girl 91. Only the Lonely 91. Home Alone 2: Lost in New York 92. The Good Son 93. George Balanchine's The Nutcracker 93. Getting Even with Dad 94. The Pagemaster 94. Richie Rich 94, etc.

Cullen, Max (1940–)
Australian leading actor.
You Can't See Round Corners 69. Stockade 71. Sunday Too Far Away 74. Summerfield 77. My Brilliant Career 79. Hard Knocks 80. Hoodwink 82. Running on Empty 82. Starstruck 82. Charley's Web 84. Boundaries of the Heart 88. Encounter at Raven's Gate 89. Garbo 90. Greenkeeping 91. Spider and Rosie 93. Lightning Jack 94. Rough Diamonds 94. Billy's Holiday 95. Kiss or Kill 97, etc.

Culp, Robert (1930–)
American leading man.
P.T. 109 62. The Raiders 63. Sunday in New York 64. Rhino! 64. *Bob and Carol and Ted and Alice* 69. Hannie Caulder 71. Hickey and Boggs (& d) 72. See the Man Run (TV) 72. The Castaway Cowboy 74. A Cry for Help (TV) 75. Inside Out 75. Sky Riders 76. The Great Scout and Cathouse Thursday 76. Breaking Point 76. Word Games (TV) 79. Goldengirl 79. Turk 182 84. The Blue Lightning (TV) 86. The Gladiator (TV) 86. Big Bad Mama II 87. Silent Night, Deadly Night 3: Better Watch Out! 89. Timebomb 91. The Pelican Brief 93. I Spy Returns (TV) 94. Mercenary 96. Most Wanted 97. Dark Summer (Can.) 99, etc.
TV series: Trackdown 57. *I Spy* 65–67. *The Greatest American Hero* 81–82.

Culver, Roland (1900–1984)
British stage actor of impeccable English types, usually comic. Born in London, he worked for an optical company before studying at RADA, and was on stage from 1924. In the late 40s he worked in Hollywood, under contract for two years to Paramount before returning to England. Married twice.
Autobiography: 1979, *Not Quite a Gentleman*.
77 Park Lane 32. Nell Gwyn 34. Paradise for Two 37. *French without Tears* (his stage role) 39. *Quiet Wedding* 40. Night Train to Munich 40. Talk about Jacqueline 42. *On Approval* 43. Dear Octopus 43. *Dead of Night* 45. Wanted for Murder 46. To Each His Own (US) 47. Down to Earth (US) 47. The Emperor Waltz (US) 48. Isn't It Romantic? 48. *Trio* (as Somerset Maugham) 50. The Holly and the Ivy 54. The Man Who Loved Redheads 55. Touch and Go 57. Bonjour Tristesse 58. The Yellow Rolls-Royce 64. A Man Could Get Killed 65. Fragment of Fear 70. Bequest to the Nation 73. The Word (TV) 78, many others.

Cumming, Alan (1965–)
Scottish actor.
Passing Glory (short) 86. Prague 91. Black Beauty 94. Second Best 94. Circle of Friends (Ire/US) 95. GoldenEye (US) 95. Emma 96. Buddy (US) 97. Romy and Michele's High School Reunion (US) 97. Spiceworld the Movie 97. Plunkett & Macleane 99. Eyes Wide Shut (US) 99. Annie (US,TV) 99. Titus (US) 99. The Flintstones in Viva Rock Vegas (US) 00. Company Man (US) 01, etc.

Cummings, Constance (1910–) (Constance Halverstadt)
American stage actress, long resident in England.
The Criminal Code (US) 31. The Guilty Generation (US) 31. Movie Crazy (US) 32. Channel Crossing 32. Broadway thro' a Keyhole (US) 33. Glamour 34. Looking for Trouble 34. Remember Last Night? (US) 35. Seven Sinners 36. *Busman's Honeymoon* 40. This England 41. The Foreman Went to France 42. *Blithe Spirit* 45. John and Julie 55. The Intimate Stranger 56. The Battle of the Sexes 59. Sammy Going South 62. In the Cool of the Day 63, etc.

Cummings, Irving (1888–1959)
American director, former actor; in films from 1909.
SELECTED SILENT FILMS: As Man Desires 25. The Johnstown Flood 26. The Brute 27, etc.
■ In Old Arizona (AAN) 29. Behind That Curtain 29. Cameo Kirby 30. On the Level 30. A Devil with Women 30. A Holy Terror 31. *The Cisco Kid* 31. Attorney for the Defense 32. Night Club Lady 32. Man Against Woman 32. Man Hunt 33. The Woman I Stole 33. The Mad Game 33. I Believed in You 34. Grand Canary 34. The White Parade 34. It's a Small World 35. Curly Top 35. Nobody's Fool 36. Poor Little Rich Girl 36. Girls Dormitory 36. White Hunter 36. Vogues of 1938 37. Merry go Round of 1938 37. Little Miss Broadway 38. Just Around the Corner 38. *The Story of Alexander Graham Bell* 39. *Hollywood Cavalcade* 39. Everything Happens at Night 39. *Lillian Russell* 40. Down Argentine Way 40. *That Night in Rio* 41. Belle Starr 41. Louisiana Purchase 41. My Gal Sal 42. Springtime in the Rockies 42. Sweet Rosie O'Grady 43. What a Woman 44. The Impatient Years 44. *The Dolly Sisters* 45. Double Dynamite 51.

Cummings, Jack (1900–1989)
American producer, especially of musicals; long with MGM.
The Winning Ticket 35. Born to Dance 36. Go West 40. Ship Ahoy 42. Bathing Beauty 44. Neptune's Daughter 49. Three Little Words 50. Lovely to Look At 52. Kiss Me Kate 53. Seven Brides for Seven Brothers 54. Many Rivers to Cross 55. The Teahouse of the August Moon 56. The Blue Angel 59. Can Can 60. Bachelor Flat 62. Viva Las Vegas 64, many others.

Cummings, Quinn (1967–)
American actress, from television, born in Hollywood.
Night Terror (TV) 76. The Goodbye Girl (AAN) 77. The Babysitter (TV) 80. Listen to Me 89, etc.
TV series: Big Eddie 75. Family 78–80. Hail to the Chief 85.

Cummings, Robert (1908–1990)
American light leading man of the 40s.
The Virginia Judge 35. Forgotten Faces 36. Last Train from Madrid 37. Souls at Sea 37. Three Smart Girls Grow Up 38. Rio 39. Spring Parade 40. The Devil and Miss Jones 41. Moon over Miami 41. *It Started with Eve* 41. *Kings Row* 41. *Saboteur* 42. Princess O'Rourke 43. You Came Along 45. The Bride Wore Boots 46. The Chase 46. Heaven Only Knows 47. The Lost Moment 47. Sleep My Love 48. The Accused 48. Paid in Full 50. For Heaven's Sake 50. The Barefoot Mailman 51. Marry Me Again 53. Lucky Me 54. Dial M for Murder 54. How to be Very Very Popular 55. My Geisha 62. Beach Party 63. What a Way to Go 64. *The Carpetbaggers* 64. Promise Her Anything 66. Stagecoach 66. 5 Golden Dragons 67. Partners in Crime (TV) 73, many others.
TV series: My Hero 52. *The Bob Cummings Show* 54–61. My Living Doll 64.

Cummins, Peggy (1925–) (Margaret Cummins)
Blonde Welsh leading actress, a former teenage star. Born in Prestatyn, she began on stage in Dublin in 1936 and in films from 1939. She went to Hollywood in the mid-40s before resuming her career in Britain from the 50s, retiring in the early 60s.
Dr O'Dowd 40. Salute John Citizen 42. English without Tears 44. Welcome Mr Washington 44. The Late George Apley (US) 46. Moss Rose (US) 47. Green Grass of Wyoming (US) 48. Escape 48. Gun Crazy (US) 49. That Dangerous Age 49. My Daughter Joy 50. Who Goes There? 52. The Love Lottery 53. Meet Mr Lucifer 53. Street Corner 53. Carry On Admiral 57. Hell Drivers 57. Night of the Demon 57. The Captain's Table 58. Dentist in the Chair 60. Your Money Or Your Wife 60. In the Doghouse 61, etc.

Cunard, Grace (1893–1967) (Harriet Jeffries)
American silent serial queen.
The Broken Coin 13. The Purple Mask 15. Peg o' the Ring 18. The Last Man on Earth 24. Untamed 29. Resurrection 31. Ladies They Talk About 33, many others.

Cundey, Dean
American cinematographer.
Bare Knuckles 78. Halloween 78. Roller Boogie 79. Rock 'n' Roll High School 79. The Fog 79. Galaxina 80. Without Warning 80. Halloween II 81. Escape from New York 81. Angels Brigade 81. The Thing 82. Halloween III: Season of the Witch 82. Separate Ways 83. Psycho II 83. Romancing the Stone 84. Back to the Future 85. Warning Sign 85. Big Trouble in Little China 86. Project X 87. Big Business 88. Who Framed Roger Rabbit (AAN) 88. Road House 89. Back to the Future Part II 89. Back to the Future Part III 90. Nothing but Trouble 91. Hook 91. Death Becomes Her 92. Jurassic Park 93. The Flintstones 94. Apollo 13 95. Casper 95. Flubber 97. The Parent Trap 98, etc.

Cundieff, Rusty
American director, screenwriter and actor, a former stand-up comedian.
Hollywood Shuffle (a) 87. House Party 2 (co-w) 91. *Fear of a Black Hat* (a, wd) 93. Tales from the Hood (a, co-w, d) 95. Sprung (co-w, d) 97, etc.

Cunningham, Cecil (1888–1959)
American character actress, usually in hard or wisecracking roles.
Their Own Desire 29. Monkey Business 31. Mata Hari 31. The Impatient Maiden 32. Blonde Venus 32. Baby Face 33. The Life of Vergie Winters 34. Come and Get It 36. Artists and Models 37. College Swing 38. Lady of the Tropics 39. Lillian Russell 40. New Moon 40. Back Street 41. Blossoms in the Dust 41. I Married an Angel 42. Twin Beds 42. The Hidden Hand 42. Du Barry Was a Lady 43. Wonder Man 45. Saratoga Trunk 45. My Reputation 46. The Bride Goes Wild 48, many others.

Cunningham, Sean S. (1941–)
American horror film director and producer.
Together 71. Here Come the Tigers 78. Manny's Orphans 79. Friday the 13th 80. A Stranger Is Watching 82. Spring Break 83. The New Kids (& p) 85. House (p) 86. House II (p) 87. Deepstar Six 89. My Boyfriend's Back (p) 93, etc.

Cuny, Alain (1908–1994)
Tall, imposing French actor, in occasional films. He directed his first film at the age of 83.
Les Visiteurs du Soir 42. Il Cristo Proibito 50. The Hunchback of Notre Dame 56. Les Amants 58. The Milky Way 68. Satyricon 69. Valparaiso Valparaiso 70. Emmanuelle 74. Il Contesto 75. Cadaveri Eccellenti 76. Christ Stopped at Eboli 79. Les Jeux de la Comtesse 80. Basileus Quartet 81. Camille Claudel 89. The Annunciation of Marie/ L'Annonce Faîte à Marie (& d) 91. Farewell Sweet War/Uova di Garofano 92, etc.

Cupito, Suzanne
See BRITTANY, Morgan.

Currie, Finlay (1878–1968) (Finlay Jefferson)
Veteran Scottish actor with stage and music-hall experience.
The Case of the Frightened Lady 32. Rome Express 32. Edge of the World 38. The Bells Go Down 42. *Great Expectations* (as Magwitch) 46. *Sleeping Car to Trieste* 48. *The History of Mr Polly* 49. Trio 50. Treasure Island 50. *The Mudlark* (as John Brown) 51. Quo Vadis 51. Kangaroo 51. *People Will Talk* (US) 52. Ivanhoe 52. Rob Roy 53. Treasure of the Golden Condor 53. Captain Lightfoot 54. Beau Brummell 54. The End of the Road (leading role) 54. Make Me an Offer 55. King's Rhapsody 56. Around the World in 80 Days 56. Saint Joan 57. Zarak 57. The Little Hut 57. Naked Earth 57. Dangerous Exile 57. Ben Hur (US) 59. Tempest 59. Solomon and Sheba 59. The Angel Wore Red 60. Huckleberry Finn 60. Kidnapped 60. Five Golden Hours 61. Francis of Assisi 61. The Inspector 62. Hand in Hand 62. The Amorous Prawn 62. Corridors of Blood 63. The Cracksman 63. West Eleven 63. The Three Lives of Thomasina 63. Billy Liar 63. The Fall of the Roman Empire 64. Who Was Maddox? (leading role) 64. The Battle of the Villa Fiorita 65. Bunny Lake is Missing 65, etc.

Curry, Tim (1946–)
English actor, hard to cast but with a wide range. Born in Cheshire, he first made his name in the theatre as Frankfurter in *The Rocky Horror Show*, a role he repeated on film.
The Rocky Horror Picture Show 74. Will Shakespeare (TV) (title role) 76. The Shout 77. Times Square 80. Oliver Twist (TV) 81. Annie 82. The Ploughman's Lunch 83. Baby 83. Legend 85. Clue 86. Pass the Ammo 87. The Hunt for Red October 90. Stephen King's It (TV) 91. Oscar 91. Passed Away 92. Home Alone 2: Lost in New York 92. Ferngully … The Last Rainforest (voice) 92. National Lampoon's Loaded Weapon 1 93. The Three Musketeers 93. The Shadow 94. Congo 95. The Pebble and the Penguin (voice) 95. Lover's Knot 96. Muppet Treasure Island (as Long John Silver) 96. Titanic (TV) 96. McHale's Navy 97. Doom Runners (TV) 97. Four Dogs Playing Poker 00. Sorted 00, etc.

TV series: Over the Top (& p) 97. The Net (voice) 98– . The Wild Thornberrys (voice) 98– .

Curtin, Valerie
American actress and screenwriter, formerly married to director Barry Levinson, with whom she has collaborated on scripts. She also wrote for the TV series *The Mary Tyler Moore Show* and *Phyllis*.
AS ACTRESS: Alice Doesn't Live Here Anymore 74. Silver Streak 76. Mother, Jugs and Speed 76. Silent Movie 76. All the President's Men 76. Different Story 78. A Christmas without Snow (TV) 80. Down and Out in Beverly Hills 85. Maxie 85. Big Trouble 86, etc.
AS WRITER: ... And Justice for All (AAN) 79. Inside Moves 80. Best Friends 82. Unfaithfully Yours 84. Toys 92.
TV series: 9 to 5 82–83, 86–88.

Curtis, Alan (1909–1953) (Harold Neberroth)
American leading man, and sometimes villain, of many 'B' pictures of the 40s. Married actresses Priscilla LAWSON and Ilona MASSEY.
Mannequin 37. The Duke of West Point 38. Good Girls Go to Paris 39. Hollywood Cavalcade 39. Sergeant Madden 39. Four Sons 40. Buck Privates 41. High Sierra 41. New Wine 41. Gung Ho! 43. Hitler's Madman 43. Two Tickets to London 43. Destiny 44. The Invisible Man's Revenge 44. Phantom Lady 44. The Daltons Ride Again 45. Frisco Sal 45. The Naughty Nineties 45. See My Lawyer 45. Shady Lady 45, etc.

Curtis, Dan (1928–)
American producer specializing in horror themes for TV.
Dark Shadows (serial) 66. The Night Strangler (TV) 72. *The Norliss Tapes* (TV) 73. Dracula (TV) (& d) 73. Kolchak, the Night Stalker (TV series) 74. Supertrain (TV) 79, etc.
AS DIRECTOR: House of Dark Shadows 70. Burnt Offerings 76. Melvin Purvis G-Man (TV) 77. The Raid on Coffeyville (TV) 79. *The Winds of War* (& p) 83. War and Remembrance (TV) 88–89. Me and the Kid 93.

Curtis, Dick (1902–1952) (Richard D. Dye)
Tall American character actor, often as a villain in 'B' westerns. Born in Newport, Kentucky, he began as an extra in silents in his teens.
The Unpardonable Sin 18. Shooting Straight 30. King Kong 33. Code of the Mounted 35. Racing Luck 35. Ghost Patrol 36. A Lawman Is Born 37. Rawhide 38. Valley of Terror 38. Mandrake the Magician (serial) 39. The Stranger from Texas 39. Trouble Finds Andy Clyde 39. Terry and the Pirates (serial) 40. Billy the Kid 41. Men of San Quentin 42. Pardon My Gun 43. Song of Prairie 45. Bandit of Sherwood Forest 46. Wymong 47. Covered Wagon Raid 50. The Red Badge of Courage 51. Lorna Doone 51. Rose of Cimmaron 52, many others.

Curtis, Jackie (1947–1985)
Transvestite actor, best known for roles in Andy Warhol's films. Born in New York, he was also a dramatist, providing Robert De Niro with a notable success in his off-Broadway play *Glamour, Glory and Gold* in 1968. Died of a drug overdose.
Flesh 68. WR: Mysteries of the Organism 71. Women in Revolt 72. Underground U.S.A. 80. Burroughs (doc) 84, etc.
❝ It's much easier to be a weird girl than a weird guy. – *J.C.*

Curtis, Jamie Lee (1958–) (Lady Haden-Guest)
American leading lady who seemed to get stuck in horrors. Daughter of Tony CURTIS and Janet LEIGH. She also writes children's books. She is married to Christopher GUEST, now Lord Haden-Guest.
Operation Petticoat (TV) 78. Halloween 79. The Fog 79. Prom Night 80. Terror Train 80. Halloween II 81. Road Games 81. Love Letters 83. Trading Places 83. Grandview USA 84. Perfect 85. Amazing Grace and Chuck 87. Un Homme Amoureux 87. Dominick and Eugene 88. A Fish Called Wanda 88. Blue Steel 89. Queen's Logic 91. My Girl 91. Forever Young 92. My Girl 2 94. Mother's Boys 94. True Lies 94. The Heidi Chronicles (TV) 95. House Arrest 96. Fierce Creatures 97. Halloween: H20 98. Homegrown 98. Virus 99. Drowning Mona 00. Daddy and Them 01, etc.
TV series: Operation Petticoat 78.

Curtis, Ken (1916–1991) (Curtis Gates)
American singing cowboy of the 40s and later a character actor, mainly in John Ford's westerns. He began as a singer with big bands, including those of Tommy Dorsey and Shep Fields.
Song of the Prairie 45. Lone Star Moonlight 46. Call of the Forest 49. Rio Grande 50. Don Daredevil Rides Again 51. Mr Roberts 55. The Searchers 56. The Wings of Eagles 57. The Last Hurrah 58. Escort West 59. Two Rode Together 61. Cheyenne Autumn 64. Pony Express Rider 76, many others.
TV series: Ripcord 61–63. Gunsmoke (as Festus Haggen) 64–75. The Yellow Rose 83–84.

Curtis, Richard
British comedy screenwriter, from television. He was co-writer of the *Blackadder* television series starring Rowan Atkinson and also wrote for *Not the Nine O'Clock News*.
The Tall Guy 89. *Four Weddings and a Funeral* (AAN) 94. Bean (co-w) 97. Notting Hill 99, etc.
❝ Whatever your script is like, no matter how much rewriting you do, if the punters don't want to sleep with the star, you may never be asked to write another one. – *R.C.*
I'm a great campaigner for light-hearted cinema. *The Sound of Music* gets called sentimental because it's about people who love children and hate Nazis. Whereas a TV play about a single mother raped by a schizophrenic black soldier would be called searingly realistic. – *R.C.*

Curtis, Tony (1925–) (Bernard Schwartz)
Bouncy American leading man of 50s actioners who constantly sought a wider range. Born in the Bronx, he studied acting at New York's Dramatic Workshop and began with a stock company before being signed by Universal. His five wives include (1951–62) actress Janet LEIGH (their daughter is actress Jamie Lee CURTIS) and actress (1963-67) Christine KAUFMANN. He is also a painter and sells prints of his work on the Internet.
Autobiography: 1994, *Tony Curtis* (with Barry Paris).
Other books: 1977, *Kid Andrew Cody and Julie Sparrow* (novel).
■ Criss Cross 49. City Across the River 49. The Lady Gambles 49. Johnny Stool Pigeon 49. Francis 49. I was a Shoplifter 50. Sierra 50. Kansas Raiders 50. Winchester 73 50. *The Prince Who Was a Thief* 51. Flesh and Fury 52. No Room for the Groom 52. Son of Ali Baba 52. *Houdini* 53. The All American 53. Forbidden 53. Beachhead 54. The Black Shield of Falworth 54. Johnny Dark 54. So This is Paris 54. The Purple Mask 54. Six Bridges to Cross 55. The Square Jungle 55. *Trapeze* 56. The Rawhide Years 56. Mister Cory 57. The Midnight Story 57. *Sweet Smell of Success* 57. *The Vikings* 58. Kings go Forth 58. *The Defiant Ones* (AAN) 58. The Perfect Furlough 58. *Some Like It Hot* 59. Operation Petticoat 59. Pepe 60. Who Was That Lady? 60. The Rat Race 60. *Spartacus* 60. The Great Imposter 60. The Outsider 61. Forty Pounds of Trouble 62. Taras Bulba 62. The List of Adrian Messenger 63. Captain Newman MD 63. Wild and Wonderful 64. Goodbye Charlie 64. Sex and the Single Girl 64. *The Great Race* 65. Boeing Boeing 65. Not With My Wife You Don't 66. Drop Dead Darling 67. Don't Make Waves 67. The Chastity Belt 68. *The Boston Strangler* 68. Those Daring Young Men in their Jaunty Jalopies 69. You Can't Win Them All 70. Suppose They Gave a War and Nobody Came 71. Third Girl from the Left (TV) 73. Lepke 75. Casanova 76. The Count of Monte Cristo (TV) 76. The Last Tycoon 76. The Manitou 78. Scarlett 78. The Bad News Bears Go to Japan 78. Little Miss Marker 80. The Mirror Crack'd 80. The Scarlett O'Hara Wars (TV) 81. Inmates (TV) 81. Portrait of a Showgirl (TV) 82. Brain Waves 83. Insignificance (TV) 85. King of the City 85. The Last of Philip Banter 86. Midnight 88. Welcome to Germany 88. Lobster Man from Mars 89. Walter and Carlo/Amerika 89. Prime Target 91. Center of the Web 92. Naked in New York 93. Last Action Hero (cameo) 93. The Immortals 95. The Continued Adventures of Reptile Man (and His Faithful Sidekick Tadpole) 96.
TV series: *The Persuaders* 71. McCoy 75. Vegas 78.
❝ I had to be careful where I went because I was a Jew, because I was young and because I was handsome. It made me wiry and erratic and paranoid, which is what I still am. Always on guard. – *T.C.*

Curtis-Hall, Vondie (1956–)
American actor, writer, director, and musician, born in Detroit. He is best known for his role as Dr Dennis Hancock in the TV series *Chicago Hope*. Married actress Kasi Lemmons.
Passion Fish (a) 92. Drop Squad (a) 94. Broken Arrow (a) 96. Heaven's Prisoners (a) 96. Gridlock'd 97 (wd). Turn It Up (a) 00, etc.
TV series: Chicagoo Hope 95-99.

Curtiz, Michael (1888–1962) (Mihaly Kertesz)
Hungarian director of more than 60 films in Europe before settling in Hollywood, where he made some of the smoothest spectacles and melodramas of the 30s and 40s and also became famous for his fractured English. Born in Budapest, and educated at Markoszy University and the city's Royal Academy of Art and Theatre, he began as an actor before directing Hungary's first feature film, leaving the country when the Communists nationalized the film industry in 1918. He moved to Hollywood in the mid-20s to work for Warner's, where he became noted for his on-set ruthlessness, enabling him to finish films on time and budget, and for his often acerbic working relationships with Bette DAVIS and Errol FLYNN, who both did much of their best work under his direction. Married actress Lucy Dorraine (1915–23) and screenwriter Bess MEREDYTH.
Books: 1995, *The Casablanca Man: The Cinema of Michael Curtiz* by James C. Robertson.
■ ENGLISH -SPEAKING FILMS: The Third Degree 26. A Million Bid 27. The Desired Woman 27. Good Time Charley 27. Tenderloin 28. *Noah's Ark* 28. Hearts in Exile 29. Glad Rag Doll 29. The Madonna of Avenue A 29. The Gamblers 29. *Mammy* 30. Under a Texas Moon 30. The Matrimonial Bed 30. Bright Lights 30. A Soldier's Plaything 30. River's End 30. God's Gift to Women 31. The Mad Genius 31. The Woman from Monte Carlo 32. Alias the Doctor 32. The Strange Love of Molly Louvain 32. *Doctor X* 32. Cabin in the Cotton 32. Twenty Thousand Years in Sing Sing 33. *The Mystery of the Wax Museum* 33. The Keyhole 33. Private Detective 33. Goodbye Again 33. The Kennel Murder Case 33. Female 33. Mandalay 34. *British Agent* 34. Jimmy the Gent 34. The Key 34. *Black Fury* 35. The Case of the Curious Bride 35. *Front Page Woman* 35. Little Big Shot 35. *Captain Blood* 35. The Walking Dead 36. *The Charge of the Light Brigade* 36. Mountain Justice 37. Stolen Holiday 37. Kid Galahad 37. The Perfect Specimen 37. Gold is Where You Find It 38. *The Adventures of Robin Hood* 38. *Four Daughters* (AAN) 38. Four's a Crowd 38. *Angels with Dirty Faces* (AAN) 38. Dodge City 39. Daughters Courageous 39. Four Wives 39. Elizabeth and Essex 39. Virginia City 40. *The Sea Hawk* 40. Santa Fe Trail 41. Dive Bomber 41. *The Sea Wolf* 41. Captains of the Clouds 42. *Yankee Doodle Dandy* 42. *Casablanca* (AA) 42. Mission to Moscow 43. This is the Army 43. Passage to Marseilles 44. Janie 44. Roughly Speaking 45. *Mildred Pierce* 45. Night and Day 46. Life with Father 47. The Unsuspected 47. Romance on the High Seas 48. My Dream is Yours 49. Flamingo Road 49. The Lady Takes a Sailor 49. Young Man with a Horn 50. Bright Leaf 50. The Breaking Point 51. Jim Thorpe – All American 51. Force of Arms 51. I'll See You in My Dreams 52. The Story of Will Rogers 52. The Jazz Singer 53. Trouble Along the Way 53. The Boy from Oklahoma 54. The Egyptian 54. White Christmas 54. We're No Angels 55. The Scarlet Hour 56. The Vagabond King 56. The Best Things in Life are Free 56. The Helen Morgan Story 57. The Proud Rebel 58. King Creole 58. The Hangman 59. The Man in the Net 59. The Adventures of Huckleberry Finn 60. A Breath of Scandal 60. Francis of Assisi 61. The Comancheros 62.
✪ For the striking Teutonic influence which he brought to a score of 30s melodramas; and for the apparent ease with which he handled top action films in a language which did not come easily to him. *Casablanca*.
❝ The next time I send a dumb sonofabitch to do something, I go myself – M.C.
So many times I have a speech ready but no dice. Always a bridesmaid, never a mother. – *M.C.'s Oscar acceptance speech for Casablanca*
When one speaks of a typical Warners film in the 30s and 40s, one is generally speaking of a typical Curtiz film of those periods. – *Andrew Sarris, 1968*
The only thing Curtiz has to say is 'Don't do it the way I showed you. Do it the way I mean.' – *James Cagney*
Bring on the empty horses! – *instruction attributed to* M.C.

Curwood, James Oliver (1878–1927)
American journalist and author of novels about the outdoor life.
River's End 40. The Gold Hunters (from Trail of the Yukon) 49. Kazan the Wolf Dog 49. The Wolf Hunters 49. Snow Dog 51. Back to God's Country 53. Northern Patrol 54. Nikki, Wild Dog of the North (from Nomads of the North) 62, etc.

Curzon, George (1896–1976)
British stage actor, in occasional films from early 30s, usually in aristocratic or sinister roles. Born in Amersham, Buckinghamshire, the grandson of the 3rd Earl Howe, he retired from the Royal Navy as a lieutenant-commander, made his stage debut at the age of 25, and was in films from 1931.
The Impassive Footman 32. Lorna Doone 35. *Young and Innocent* 37. Sexton Blake and the Hooded Terror 38. Uncle Silas 47. Harry Black 58, etc.

Cusack, Cyril (1910–1993)
Diminutive Irish actor with fourteen years' Abbey Theatre experience. Film debut as child in 1917.
Odd Man Out 47. The Blue Lagoon 48. The Elusive Pimpernel 50. The Blue Veil (US) 51. Soldiers Three (US) 51. The Man Who Never Was 56. *Jacqueline* 56. The Spanish Gardener 56. Ill Met by Moonlight 57. Floods of Fear 58. Shake Hands with the Devil 59. A Terrible Beauty 59. The Waltz of the Toreadors 62. Eighty Thousand Suspects 63. The Spy Who Came in from the Cold 65. I Was Happy Here 66. *Fahrenheit 451* 66. The Taming of the Shrew 67. Oedipus the King 67. Galileo (It.) 68. David Copperfield 69. King Lear 70. Harold and Maude (US) 71. The Day of the Jackal 73. The Homecoming 73. The Abdication 74. Execution Squad 76. An Eye for an Eye 78. Strumpet City (TV) 80. Tristam and Isolt 81. True Confessions 81. Little Dorrit 87. Menace Unseen (TV) 88. My Left Foot 89. The Fool 90. Memento Mori (TV) 92. Far and Away 92. As You Like It 92, many others.

Cusack, Joan (1962–)
American actress, often in comic roles. She is the sister of actor John Cusack.
My Bodyguard 80. Class 83. Grandview USA 84. Sixteen Candles 84. The Allnighter 87. Broadcast News 87. Married to the Mob 88. Stars and Bars 88. Working Girl (AAN) 88. Men Don't Leave 90. My Blue Heaven 90. The Cabinet of Dr Ramirez 91. Toys 92. Bram Stoker's Dracula 92. Addams Family Values 93. Corrina, Corrina 94. Nine Months 95. Mr Wrong 96. Two Much 96. *In & Out* (AAN) 97. Grosse Pointe Blank 97. A Smile Like Yours 97. Arlington Road 99. Runaway Bride 99. Toy Story 2 (voice) 99. The Cradle Will Rock 99. Where the Heart Is 00. High Fidelity 00, etc.

Cusack, John (1966–)
American leading actor. Born in Evanston, Illinois, he began as a child in theatre in Chicago and in commercials. He is co-founder of the production company New Crime.
Class 83. Grandview USA 84. Sixteen Candles 84. Stand by Me 86. Broadcast News 87. Eight Men Out 88. Fat Man and Little Boy/Shadow Makers 89. Say Anything 89. The Grifters 90. True Colors 91. Shadows and Fog 91. Roadside Prophets 92. Bob Roberts 92. Map of the Human Heart 92. Money for Nothing 93. Bullets over Broadway 94. Floundering 94. The Road to Wellville 94. City Hall 96. *Grosse Pointe Blank* (& co-w) 97. Con Air 97. Anastasia (voice) 98. The Thin Red Line 98. Chicago Cab 98. Being John Malkovich 99. Pushing Tin 99. The Cradle Will Rock 99. The Jack Bull (TV) 99. This is My Father 99. High Fidelity 00. America's Sweethearts 01, etc.
❝ I've been in Hollywood for ten years, and most of the dumb scripts that get made have passed my way. I haven't sold out so far, although I have made bad movies. By selling out, I mean crashing cars, pulling out guns, killing people – idiotic stories. – *J.C.*

Cusack, Sinead (1948–)
Irish leading lady, daughter of Cyril CUSACK. Married actor Jeremy IRONS in 1977.

David Copperfield 69. Alfred the Great 69. Hoffman 70. Revenge 71. Tam Ling 71. The Last Remake of Beau Geste 77. Bad Behaviour 93. The Cement Garden 93. Sparrow/Storia di una Capinera 93. Uncovered 94. Stealing Beauty 95. Have Your Cake and Eat It (TV) 97. Food for Ravens (TV) 97. The Nephew 98, etc.

Cushing, Peter (1913–1994)

British character actor of stage, TV and screen. His slightly fussy manner at first confined him to mild roles, but since allying himself with the Hammer horror school he has dealt firmly with monsters of all kinds.

Autobiography: 1986, *An Autobiography*. 1988, *Past Forgetting*.

■ The Man in the Iron Mask (US) 39. A Chump at Oxford (US) 39. Vigil in the Night (US) 40. Laddie (US) 40. They Dare Not Love (US) 41. Women in War (US) 42. *Hamlet* (as Osric) 47. Moulin Rouge 53. The Black Night 54. The End of the Affair 55. Magic Fire (US) 56. Time Without Pity 56. Alexander the Great 56. *The Curse of Frankenstein* 57. Violent Playground 57. The Abominable Snowman 57. *Dracula* 58. The Revenge of Frankenstein 58. Suspect 59. The Hound of the Baskervilles 59. John Paul Jones (US) 59. The Mummy 59. Cone of Silence 60. Brides of Dracula 60. The Hellfire Club 61. Fury at Smugglers Bay 61. The Flesh and the Fiends 61. Sword of Sherwood Forest 61. The Naked Edge 61. Captain Clegg 62. *Cash on Demand* 63. The Man Who Finally Died 63. The Gorgon 64. The Evil of Frankenstein 64. Dr Terror's House of Horrors 65. She 65. Dr Who and the Daleks 65. Island of Terror 66. Daleks Invasion Earth 66. The Skull 66. Frankenstein Created Woman 67. The Blood Beast Terror 67. Some May Live (TV) 67. Night of the Big Heat 67. The Torture Garden 67. Corruption 68. Frankenstein Must Be Destroyed 69. Scream and Scream Again 69. The House that Dripped Blood 70. The Vampire Lovers 70. One More Time 70. I Monster 70. Twins of Evil 71. Incense for the Damned 71. Dracula AD 1972 72. Dr Phibes Rises Again 72. Nothing But the Night 72. *Tales from the Crypt* 72. The Creeping Flesh 73. Asylum 73. Fear in the Night 73. The Satanic Rites of Dracula 73. Frankenstein and the Monster from Hell 73. From Beyond the Grave 74. The Beast Must Die 74. Horror Express 74. Shatter 74. The Legend of the Seven Golden Vampires 74. And Now the Screaming Starts 74. Madhouse 74. The Ghoul 75. Legend of the Werewolf 75. La Grande Trouille 75. Shock Waves 75. Trial by Combat 76. The Uncanny 76. The Devil's Men 76. At the Earth's Core 76. Battle Flag 77. Star Wars 77. The Great Houdinis (TV) 77. Hitler's Son 78. Arabian Adventure 79. A Touch of the Sun 79. Monster Island 81. The House of Long Shadows 83. The Masks of Death (TV) (as Sherlock Holmes) 85. Biggles 86.

66 If I played Hamlet, they'd call it a horror film. – P.C.

Custer, Bob (1898–1974) (Raymond Anthony Glenn)

American leading actor in westerns, a former engineer and cowboy.

Trigger Finger 24. The Dude Cowboy 26. Cactus Trails 27. Arizona Days 29. Riders of the Rio Grande 29. Code of the West 30. Riders of the North 31. Under Texas Skies 31. Mark of the Spur 32. The Law of the Wild (serial) 34. Ambush Valley 36, many others.

Custer, George Armstrong (1839–1876)

American major-general whose romantic eccentricities and foolish death at Little Big Horn have been favourite screen fodder. The screen Custers include Dustin Farnum in *Flaming Frontier* 26, Frank McGlynn in *Custer's Last Stand* 36, Ronald Reagan in *Santa Fe Trail* 40, Addison Richards in *Badlands of Dakota* 41, Errol Flynn in the large-scale Custer biopic *They Died with Their Boots On* 41, James Millican in *Warpath* 51, Sheb Wooley in *Bugles in the Afternoon* 52, Britt Lomond in *Tonka* 58, Phil Carey in *The Great Sioux Massacre* 65, Robert Shaw in *Custer of the West* 67, Leslie Nielsen in *The Plainsman* (TV) and Richard Mulligan in *Little Big Man* 70. There has also been a TV series, *The Legend of Custer*, with Wayne Maunder.

Cuthbertson, Allan (1920–1988)

Australian actor in Britain, adept at supercilious roles.

Carrington VC 54. Portrait of Alison 55. Room at the Top 58. The Stranglers of Bombay 60. Tunes of Glory 60. On the Double 61. The Boys 62. Tamahine 62. The Running Man 63. The Seventh Dawn 64. Life at the Top 65. Cast a Giant Shadow 66. Body Stealers 69. Captain Nemo and the Underwater City 69. Performance 70. The Sea Wolves 80, many others.

Cutts, Graham (1885–1958)

British director, eminent in silent days.

Woman to Woman 23. Looking on the Bright Side 31. The Sign of Four 32. Car of Dreams 35. Oh, Daddy! 35. Aren't Men Beasts! 37. Let's Make a Night of It 37. Over She Goes 37. Just William 39, etc.

Cutts, Patricia (1926–1974)

British child actress and leading lady. Daughter of Graham Cutts.

Self Made Lady 31. Just William's Luck 49. Your Witness 50. The Happiness of Three Women 54. The Man Who Loved Redheads 54. Merry Andrew 58. The Tingler (US) 59. Battle of the Coral Sea 59. Private Road 71, etc.

Cybulski, Zbigniew (1927–1967)

Handsome Polish leading actor, whose early death led him to be known as the 'James Dean of Poland', though his career was much longer than Dean's. Born in Katowice, Silesia, he studied at the Theatre School in Cracow. and began in the theatre He became a star with Wajda's *Ashes and Diamonds*; the director's *Everything for Sale* was a tribute to him, following his death from falling beneath a train.

A Generation 54. Ashes and Diamonds 58. The Eighth Day of the Week 59. Pociag 59. He, She or It 62. Love at Twenty 62. Silence 63. How to be Loved 63. To Love 64. Salto 65. *The Saragossa Manuscript* 65. Jowita 67, etc.

Czerny, Henry (1959–)

Canadian leading actor, from stage and television.

Buried on Sunday 92. *The Boys of St Vincent* 93. A Man in Uniform 93. Clear and Present Danger 94. Cold Sweat 94. When Night Is Falling 95. Notes from the Underground 95. Mission: Impossible 96. The Ice Storm 97. The Girl Next Door 98, etc.

TV series: Secret Service 92–93.

Czinner, Paul (1890–1972)

Hungarian producer-director, long in Britain: husband of Elisabeth Bergner. From 1955 he concentrated on films of opera and ballet, using multiple cameras.

Der Traumende Mund 32. Catherine the Great 33. Escape Me Never 35. As You Like It 36. Dreaming Lips 37. Stolen Life 39. The Bolshoi Ballet 55. The Royal Ballet 59. Der Rosenkavalier 61. Romeo and Juliet 66, etc.

D

Da Costa, Morton (1914–1989) (Morton Tecosky)
American director of stage musicals and three films.
■ Auntie Mame 58. *The Music Man* 62. Island of Love 64.

Da Silva, Howard (1909–1986) (Harold Silverblatt)
Tough, suspicious-looking American character actor with stage experience. Graduated from bit parts to a peak in the late 40s, then had McCarthy trouble.
Abe Lincoln in Illinois 40. The Sea Wolf 41. The Big Shot 43. *The Lost Weekend* 45. The Blue Dahlia 46. Blaze of Noon 47. Unconquered 47. They Live by Night 48. The Great Gatsby 49. Three Husbands 50. Fourteen Hours 51. M 51. David and Lisa 62. The Outrage 65. Nevada Smith 66. '1776' 72. The Great Gatsby 74. Mommie Dearest (as Louis B. Mayer) 81, etc.

D'Abo, Maryam (1960–)
London-born actress, of a Dutch mother and a Georgian father. Raised in Paris and Geneva, she returned to Britain in the early 80s.
Xtro 82. White Nights 85. The Living Daylights 97. Not a Penny More, Not a Penny Less (TV) 90. Tropical Heat 91. Leon the Pig Farmer 92. Red Shoe Diaries 3: Another Woman's Lipstick (TV) 93. The Browning Version 94. Double Obsession 94. Solitaire for Two 94. Savage Hearts 96. Timelock 96. Romance and Rejection 96. An American Affair 97. So This Is Romance? 98. The Sea Change 98, etc.

D'Abo, Olivia (1969–)
English actress in Hollywood. Born in London, she trained as a ballet dancer and appeared in television commercials as a teenager.
Conan the Destroyer 84. Mission Kill 85. Bullies 86. Flying 86. Into the Fire 87. Personal Choice 88. Beyond the Stars 89. The Spirit of 76 91. Point of No Return 93. Bank Robber 93. Wayne's World 2 93. Clean Slate 94. Greedy 94. The Last Good Time 94. The Big Green 95. Kicking and Screaming 95. Live Nude Girls 95. The Velocity of Gary 98. Soccer Dog: The Movie 98, etc.
TV series: The Wonder Years 88–92.

Dacascos, Mark (1964–)
Hawaiian-born karate expert and star of action movies.
American Samurai 92. Only the Strong 93. Double Dragon 94. Crying Freeman 95. Island of Dr Moreau 96. Redline 97. DNA 97. Boogie Boy 97. No Code of Conduct 98. The Base 99, etc.
TV series: The Crow: Stairway to Heaven 98– .

Dade, Frances (1910–1968)
Blonde American leading actress of the early 30s, on stage from the age of 16.
Grumpy 30. Raffles 30. Dracula 31. Seed 31. Mother's Millions 31. Pleasure 31. The She-Wolf 31. Daughter of the Dragon 31, etc.

Dade, Stephen (1909–)
British cinematographer, in films from 1927.
We'll Meet Again 42. Caravan 46. The Brothers 47. Snowbound 49. A Question of Adultery 57. Bluebeard's Ten Honeymoons 60. Zulu 64. City under the Sea 65. The Viking Queen 66, many others.

Dafoe, Willem (1955–)
American leading actor with powerful presence. Born in Appleton, Wisconsin, he studied for a time at the University of Wisconsin before joining a theatre group in Milwaukee, later becoming a founder-member of the Wooster Group, an experimental theatre company.
Heaven's Gate 80. The Loveless 81. New York Nights 82. The Hunger 83. Streets of Fire 84. Roadhouse 66 84. To Live and Die in L.A. 85. Platoon (AAN) 86. The Hitchhiker I (TV) 87. Off Limits/Saigon 88. The Last Temptation of Christ 88. Mississippi Burning 88. Born on the Fourth of July 89. Triumph of the Spirit 89. Cry-Baby 90. Wild at Heart 90. Flight of the Intruder 91. Light Sleeper 91. White Sands 92. Faraway, So Close!/In Weiter Ferne, So Nah 93. Body of Evidence 93. Tom and Viv 94. Night and the Moment 94. Clear and Present Danger 94. The English Patient 96. Basquiat 96. Speed 2: Cruise Control 97. Affliction 97. Lulu on the Bridge 98. New Rose Hotel 98. eXistenZ 99. American Psycho 00. Shadow of the Vampire (AAN) 00, etc.

D'Agostino, Albert S. (1893–1970)
American art director, in Hollywood from early silent days; with RKO 1936–58.
The Raven 35. The Werewolf of London 35. Dracula's Daughter 36. The Magnificent Brute (AAN) 36. The Magnificent Ambersons (AAN) 42. The 7th Victim 43. Flight for Freedom (AAN) 43. The Curse of the Cat People 44. Step Lively (AAN) 44. Experiment Perilous (AAN) 44. Isle of the Dead 45. Notorious 46. Bedlam 46. The Spiral Staircase 46. Mourning Becomes Electra 48. The Thing 51. Clash by Night 52. Androcles and the Lion 52. Run of the Arrow 57, many others.

Dagover, Lil (1897–1980) (Marta Maria Liletts)
Distinguished German actress.
The Cabinet of Dr Caligari 19. Destiny 21. Dr Mabuse Der Spieler 22. Chronicles of the Grey House 24. Tartuffe 26. Hungarian Rhapsody 27. The White Devil 30. Congress Dances 31. Kreutzer Sonata 35. Fredericus 39. Die Fussganger 73. Karl May 74, etc.

Daguerre, Louis (1787–1851)
French pioneer of photography; his original copper-plated prints were known as *daguerrotypes*.

Dahl, Arlene (1924–)
Red-haired American leading lady, former model; also beauty columnist.
■ Life with Father 47. *My Wild Irish Rose* 47. The Bride Goes Wild 48. A Southern Yankee 48. Reign of Terror 49. Scene of the Crime 49. Ambush 49. The Outriders 50. Three Little Words 50. Watch the Birdie 50. Inside Straight 51. No Questions Asked 51. Caribbean 52. Jamaica Run 53. Desert Legion 53. Sangaree 53. The Diamond Queen 53. Here Come the Girls 54. Woman's World 54. Bengal Brigade 54. Slightly Scarlet 56. Wicked as They Come (GB) 56. Fortune is a Woman (GB) 57. *Journey to the Centre of the Earth* 59. Kisses for My President 64. The Land Raiders 69. The Road to Khatmandu 69. Night of the Warrior 91.
TV series: One Life to Live 82. Night of the Warrior 91.
❝ With enthusiasm anything is possible. – *A.D.*
I considered the years in Hollywood nothing but an interim. What I always wanted was to be a musical comedy star. – *A.D.*

Dahl, John (1956–)
American director and screenwriter.
Kill Me Again (wd) 89. Red Rock West (wd) 93. *The Last Seduction* (d) 94. Unforgettable 96. Rounders 98, etc.
❝ Film noir is endlessly fascinating to me. I'm a movie buff, and I like to make films that movie fans like. – *J.D.*
It's only in the last thirty years that we've had all these Hollywood movies where they desperately want you to fall in love with the main character. I mean, who in a Shakespearean play did you ever want to take home and have dinner with? They were brooding, upset, frustrated, twisted, neurotic people. – *J.D.*

Dahl, Roald (1916–1990)
Norwegian writer of British adoption; switched from children's books to macabre short stories. He was married to actress Patricia Neal (1953–83).
You Only Live Twice 67. Chitty Chitty Bang Bang 69. Willy Wonka and the Chocolate Factory 70. Danny the Champion of the World (oa) 89. The Witches (oa) 90, etc.
TV series: *Roald Dahl's Tales of the Unexpected* 79 (introduced and w).

Dahlbeck, Eva (1920–)
Swedish actress, often in Ingmar Bergman's films.
Waiting Women 52. The Village (GB) 53. Smiles of a Summer Night 55. So Close to Life 61. Now About These Women 64. Loving Couples 64. Les Creatures 65. The Red Mantle 67. People Meet 69, etc.

Dahlquist, Åke (1901–1991)
Swedish cinematographer who helped Ingrid Bergman on her way to stardom by photographing her sympathetically in six of her early films. He also photographed the screen test that took Greta Garbo to Hollywood.
Swedenheilms 35. The Count of the Old Town/Munkbrogreven 35. Intermezzo 37. Dollar 38. A Woman's Face/En Kvinnas Ansikte 38. June Night/Juninatten 40. Ride Tonight!/Rid i Natt! 42. The Talisman/Galgmannen 45. The Song of the Scarlet Flower/Sangen Om Den Eldroda Blömman 56. The Doll 62. Carmilla 68. The Man from the Other Side/Mannen Fran Andra Sidan 72, many others.

Dailey, Dan (1914–1978)
Tall, affable American actor-dancer with wide experience in vaudeville and cabaret. Born in New York City, he began in minstrel shows as a child and was on Broadway in the mid-30s. He was at his most successful and popular in musicals, particularly when teamed with Betty GRABLE. In the early 50s various problems – a marital break-up, heavy drinking and transvestism – led to a breakdown, and he spent four months in a psychiatric hospital. He later enjoyed some success on television and returned to perform in the theatre and nightclubs. After a fall from a stage in the mid-70s left him slightly crippled, he retired and became reclusive and once more drank heavily. He was married and divorced four times and had one son, who committed suicide in 1975 at the age of 28.
The Mortal Storm 40. Dulcy 40. Ziegfeld Girl 41. Moon over Her Shoulder 41. Lady Be Good 41. Panama Hattie 42. Give Out Sisters 42. *Mother Wore Tights* 47. *Give My Regards to Broadway* 48. You Were Meant for Me 48. When My Baby Smiles at Me (AAN) 48. Chicken Every Sunday 49. My Blue Heaven 50. *When Willie Comes Marching Home* 50. A Ticket to Tomahawk 50. I Can Get It for You Wholesale 51. Call Me Mister 51. Pride of St Louis 51. What Price Glory? 52. Meet Me at The Fair 53. There's No Business Like Show Business 54. *It's Always Fair Weather* 55. Meet Me in Las Vegas 56. *The Best Things in Life are Free* 56. The Wings of Eagles 56. Oh Men, Oh Women 57. The Wayward Bus 57. Pepe 60. Hemingway's Adventures of a Young Man 62. The Private Files of J. Edgar Hoover 77, many others.
TV series: The Four Just Men 59. The Governor and J.J. 69. Faraday and Company 73.

Dainton, Patricia (1930–)
British leading lady who started as a teenager.
Don't Ever Leave Me 49. The Dancing Years 50. Castle in the Air 52. Operation Diplomat 54. The Passing Stranger 57. Witness in the Dark 60, etc.

Dalby, Amy (1888–1969)
British character actress who normally on screen played ageing spinsters.
The Wicked Lady 45. The Man Upstairs 57. The Lamp in Assassin Mews 62. *The Secret of My Success* 65. Who Killed the Cat? 66. The Spy with a Cold Nose 67, etc.

Daldry, Stephen (1960–)
English director, from the stage, where he was artistic director of the Royal Court theatre for much of the 90s, and was also noted for his production for the National Theatre of J.B. Priestley's *An Inspector Calls*. Born in Somerset, he studied English and drama at Sheffield University and then spent some time with an Italian circus.
Biography: 1997, *A Director Calls* by Wendy Lesser.
Billy Elliot (AAN, BFAp) 00, etc.

Dale, Charles (1881–1971) (Charles Marks)
American vaudevillian who, with Joe Smith (c. 1884–1981), made up Smith and Dale, the inspiration for *The Sunshine Boys*.
■ Manhattan Parade 31. The Heart of New York 32. Two Tickets to Broadway 51.

Dale, Esther (1885–1961)
American character actress usually a motherly soul, nurse or grandma.
Crime without Passion 34. Curly Top 35. Fury 36. Dead End 37. Prison Farm 38. Tell No Tales 39. The Mortal Storm 40. Back Street 41. North Star 43. Margie 44. Stolen Life 46. The Egg and I 47. Ma and Pa Kettle 49. No Man of Her Own 50. Ma and Pa Kettle at the Fair 52. The Oklahoman 57, many others.

Dale, Jim (1935–) (James Smith)
Cheerful English singer and songwriter turned light comedian and a member of the Carry On team. Born in Rothwell, Northamptonshire, he trained as a dancer, began as a comedian in the early 50s, and first came to notice on TV rock shows as a performer and host, with several hit records in the late 50s. He turned to acting in the 60s, enjoying his greatest success in the theatre, both with the National Theatre Company and notably in the acrobatic title role of the musical *Barnum*. He is now resident in the USA. He was nominated for an Oscar for writing the lyrics to the title tune for *Georgy Girl* 64.
Raising the Wind 62. Carry On Spying 64. Carry On Cleo 65. The Big Job 65. Carry On Cowboy 66. Carry On Screaming 66. Lock Up Your Daughters 69. *The National Health* 73. Digby 73. Joseph Andrews 77. *Pete's Dragon* 77. Bloodshy 79. The Spaceman and King Arthur 79. Scandalous 84. Adventures of Huckleberry Finn 85. Carry On Columbus 92. The Hunchback of Notre Dame (TV) 97, etc.

Dalen, Zale (1947–)
Canadian director, born in the Philippines.
Skip Tracer 77. Hounds of Nôtre Dame 80. Hollywood North 87. Terminal City Ricochet 90. Expect No Mercy 95, etc.

Daley, Cass (1915–1975) (Catherine Dailey)
American comedienne whose shouted songs and acrobatic contortions were a feature of several light musicals of the 40s.
The Fleet's In 41. Star Spangled Rhythm 42. Crazy House 43. Riding High 43. Out of This World 45. Ladies' Man 47. Here Comes the Groom 51. Red Garters 54. The Spirit Is Willing 67. Norwood 69., etc.

Dali, Salvador (1904–1989)
Spanish surrealist painter who collaborated with Luis Buñuel in making two controversial films: *Un Chien Andalou* 29 and *L'Age d'Or* 30. Later designed the dream sequence for *Spellbound* 45.
❝ His contribution to Mediterranean culture is as great as Warhol's to Anglo-Saxon culture. – *Bigas Luna*

Dalio, Marcel (1900–1983) (Israel Mosche Blauschild)
Dapper French comedy actor, frequently in Hollywood.

La Grande Illusion 37. Pépé le Moko 37. *La Règle du Jeu* 39. Unholy Partners 41. Casablanca 42. The Song of Bernadette 43. Temptation Harbour (GB) 46. On the Riviera 51. *The Happy Time* 52. The Snows of Kilimanjaro 52. Lucky Me 54. Sabrina 54. Miracle in the Rain 56. Pillow Talk 59. Can Can 59. Jessica 62. Wild and Wonderful 63. Lady L 65. The 25th Hour 67. How Sweet It Is 68. Catch 22 70. The Mad Adventures of Rabbi Jacob 73. L'Ombre de Château 76. Brigade Mondaine 80, many others.

Dall, Evelyn (c. 1914–)
American nightclub singer who appeared in some British film extravaganzas of the 40s.
He Found a Star 41. King Arthur Was a Gentleman 42. Miss London Ltd 43. Time Flies 44, etc.

Dall, John (1918–1971)
American stage leading man; played in occasional films. Died of a heart attack.
■ For the Love of Mary 45. *The Corn Is Green* (AAN). Something in the Wind 47. *Rope* 48. Another Part of the Forest 48. Gun Crazy 49. The Man Who Cheated Himself 50. Spartacus 60. Atlantis the Lost Continent 61.

Dalle, Béatrice (1965–)
French leading actress.
Betty Blue 86. Charlie Spencer 86. The Witches' Sabbath/La Visione del Sabba 88. Les Bois Noirs 89. Chimère 89. The Beautiful Story/La Belle Histoire 91. Night on Earth 91. La Fille de l'Air 92. I Can't Sleep/J'ai Pas Sommeil 94. Six Days Six Nights/A la Folie 94. Desire 96, etc.

Dallesandro, Joe (1948–)
American actor who gained fame as the object of desire in Andy WARHOL's films.
The Loves of Ondine 67. Flesh 68. Lonesome Cowboys 68. Trash 70. Heat 72. Andy Warhol's Frankenstein 73. Blood for Dracula 74. The Gardener 74. Black Moon 75. Seeds of Evil 76. Merry Go Round 83. The Cotton Club 84. Critical Condition 87. Sunset 88. Private War 89. The Hollywood Detective (TV) 89. Cry-Baby 90. Double Revenge 90. Wild Orchid II: Two Shades of Blue 92. Sugar Hill 93. LA without a Map (GB/ Fr./Fin.) 98. The Limey 99, etc.
❝ I don't know whether I'll ever become a household name in America, but my big thing is to land that television series that goes 50 episodes and you sit at home and collect the cheques. – *J.D. in 1993*

D'Almeida, Neville (1941–)
Brazilian director who spent some time studying film in the United States.
Jardin de Guerra 70. Lady on the Bus/A Dama de Lotaçao 78. Rio Babilonia 82, etc.

Dalrymple, Ian (1903–1989)
British screenwriter, producer and director. He was educated at Cambridge University and worked as an editor and supervising editor at Gaumont-British and Gainsborough Pictures from the late 20s to the mid-30s before becoming a screenwriter. In the 40s, he was a producer for the Crown Film Unit, producing wartime documentaries, then worked for MGM-Korda productions before setting up his own company, Wessex Productions, as part of Independent Producers, working at Pinewood Studios. Married twice.
The Good Companions (co-w) 33. Jury's Evidence (w) 35. South Riding (co-w) 37. Storm in a Teacup (wd) 37. Action for Slander (co-w) 37. *Pygmalion* (co-w) (AA) 38. The Citadel (co-w) 38. The Divorce of Lady X (co-w) 38. A Window in London (co-w) 39. Q Planes (co-w) 39. French without Tears (co-w) 39. *London Can Take It* (p) 40. Old Bill and Son (co-w, d) 41. Pimpernel Smith (co-w) 41. *Target for Tonight* (p) 41. *Coastal Command* (p) 42. The Woman in the Hall (p, co-w) 47. Esther Waters (p, d) 47. Once a Jolly Swagman (p) 48. Dear Mr Prohack (p, co-w) 49. All Over Town (p) 49. Family Portrait (p) 50. The Wooden Horse (p) 50. The Heart of the Matter (p, co-w) 53. Three Cases of Murder (p, co-w) 54. Raising a Riot (p, co-w) 55. A Hill in Korea (co-w) 56. The Admirable Crichton (p) 57. A Cry from the Streets (p) 58. Mix Me a Person (co-w) 61, etc.
❝ Ian is one of the great men of the British cinema. – *Michael Powell*

Dalton, Abby (1932–)
American actress, a former model who first appeared in low-budget teen movies in the late 50s.
Viking Woman and the Sea Serpent 57. Rock All Night 57. Stakeout on Dope Street 58. Cole Younger, Gunfighter 58. Girls on the Loose 58. The Plainsman 66. A Whale of a Tale 76. Roller Blade Warriors: Taken by Force 90. Cyber-Tracker 93. Buck and the Magic Bracelet 97, etc.
TV series: Hennesey 59–62. The Joey Bishop Show 62–65. Falcon Crest 81–86.

Dalton, Audrey (1934–)
British leading lady in Hollywood.
My Cousin Rachel 52. The Girls of Pleasure Island 53. Titanic 53. Casanova's Big Night 54. Drum Beat 54. Confession 55. The Prodigal 55. Hold Back the Night 56. The Monster that Challenged the World 57. Separate Tables 58. This Other Eden 60. Mr Sardonicus 61. Kitten with a Whip 64, etc.

Dalton, Dorothy (1894–1972)
American silent screen leading lady with stage experience.
The Disciple 14. Black is White 20. Moran of the Lady Letty 22. The Crimson Challenge 22. Fogbound 23. The Moral Sinner 24. The Lone Wolf 24, etc.

Dalton, Timothy (1944–)
Saturnine British stage actor in occasional films.
The Lion in Winter 68. *Wuthering Heights* 70. Cromwell 70. Mary Queen of Scots 71. Lady Caroline Lamb 72. Permission to Kill 75. Sextette 78. Agatha 79. Flash Gordon 80. Chanel Solitaire 81. Mistral's Daughter (TV) 84. Florence Nightingale (TV) 84. The Doctor and the Devils 85. Sins (TV) 85. *The Living Daylights* (as James Bond) 87. Hawks 88. Licence to Kill 89. Brenda Starr 90. The King's Whore 90. The Rocketeer 91. Naked in New York 93. Scarlett (TV) 94. The Beautician and the Beast 97. Made Men 99. Cleopatra (TV) 99, etc.

Daltrey, Roger (1944–)
British rock singer, composer, actor and producer. The lead singer with The Who, he was given dramatic roles by Ken Russell.
Tommy 74. Lisztomania 75. The Legacy 79. McVicar 80. Murder: Ultimate Grounds for Divorce 85. Mack the Knife 89. Buddy's Song (& p, m) 90. Teen Agent 91. Lightning Jack 94. Vampirella (TV) 96. Pirate Tales (TV) 97. Like It Is 98, etc.
❝ Of course, chicks keep popping up. When you're in a hotel, a pretty young lady makes life bearable. – *R.D.*

Daly, James (1918–1978)
American stage actor; film appearances rare.
■ The Court Martial of Billy Mitchell 55. Tender is the Night (TV) 55. The Young Stranger 57. I Aim at the Stars 60. Planet of the Apes 68. Code Named Red Roses/Rose Rosse Per Il Fuhrer (It.) 68. The Treasure of San Bosco Reef (TV) 68. The Big Bounce 69. The Five Man Army/Un Esercito Di 5 Uomini (It.) 69. U.M.C. (TV) 69. Wild in the Sky 71. The Resurrection of Zachary Wheeler (TV) 73. The Storyteller (TV) 77.
TV series: Foreign Intrigue 53–54. *Medical Center* 69–76.

Daly, John (1937–)
British independent producer and distributor, who moved to America in the 80s. A former journalist and actor, and David HEMMINGS's manager, he founded Hemdale Film Corporation, of which he was chairman, in 1967 with Hemmings, who sold his interest four years later. Hemdale went bankrupt in 1992, with debts of more than $130m. He now heads Global Entertainment Assets Corp., a company incorporated in Antigua, specializing in the entertainment industry. In 1998 he co-founded Greenhills Films, a European-based production company.
Melody 71. Where Does It Hurt? 71. Triple Echo 72. Images 72. The Amazing Mr Blunden 72. Cattle Annie and Little Britches 80. Race for the Yankee Zephyr 81. Carbon Copy 81. Yellowbeard 83. Terminator 84. Return of the Living Dead 85. Platoon (AA) 86. At Close Range 86. Salvador 86. Hoosiers 86. The Last Emperor (AA) 87. Buster 88. Miracle Mile 89. Out Cold 89. Chattahoochee 90. Hidden Agenda 90. Bright Angel 91, etc.

Daly, Mark (1887–1957)
British character actor, on stage from 1906, in films from 1930, often as cheerful tramp.
The Private Life of Henry VIII 33. A Cuckoo in the Nest 33. The Ghost Goes West 36. Wings of the Morning 37. Next of Kin 42. Bonnie Prince Charlie 49. Lease of Life 54. The Shiralee 57, many others.

Daly, Robert
Motion picture executive, in charge of Warner Bros from the early 80s until 1999 with Terry SEMEL. He was appointed president and chief operating officer of Warner in 1982, and became co-chief executive officer in 1994.

Daly, Timothy (1956–)
American actor, best known for his role as Joe Hackett in the TV sitcom *Wings*. He is the son of James DALY and brother of Tyne DALY.
Diner 82. I'll Take Manhattan 87. Made in Heaven 87. Spellbinder 88. Ambush in Waco (TV) 93. Dr Jekyll and Ms Hyde 95. Denise Calls Up 95. The Associate 96. The Object of My Affection 98, etc.
TV series: Ryan's Four 83. Almost Grown 88-89. Wings 90-97.

Daly, Tyne (1946–)
American leading lady. She is the daughter of James DALY.
John and Mary 69. Angel Unchained 70. Heat of Anger (TV) 71. Play It as It Lays 72. The Entertainer (TV) 75. The Enforcer 76. Telefon 77. Speedtrap 77. The Women's Room (TV) 80. Zoot Suit 82. Your Place or Mine (TV) 83. Movers and Shakers 85. The Aviator 85. Tricks 97. The Student Affair 97. Money Kings 98. Absence of the Good 99, etc.
TV series: Cagney and Lacey 82. Christy 94–95.

D'Amato, Joe (1936–1999) (Aristide Massaccesi)
Prolific Italian director of quickie exploitation movies that reach international audiences on video-cassette. His output, made under such pseudonyms as Steve Benson, Michael Wotruba, David Hills and Kevin Mancuso, ranges from horror to fantasy and soft-core pornography, including a *Black Emanuelle* series in the 70s.
Heroes in Hell/Eroi all'Inferno 67. Kneel Bastard/Inginocchiate 72. Black Emanuelle/ Emanuelle Nera 73. Emanuelle and the Last Cannibals/Emanuelle e gli Ultimi Cannibali/Trap Them and Kill Them 77. Beyond the Darkness/ Buio Omega 79. Grim Reaper/Anthropophagus 81. Ator the Fighting Eagle/Ator l'Invincibile 82. Ator the Invincible – the Return/Blade Master 83. 2020 Texas Gladiators/Texas 2000 84. Buried Alive 84. Quest for the Mighty Sword 90. Return from Death 91. Love Appurtenance 92, many others.
❝ I like to manipulate intestines, pieces of meat, vital organs. Is there a limit? Not at all! – *J. D'A.*
There's little doubt that sitting through one of Joe's efforts is as near to brain death as a film viewer can get. – *Stefan Jaworzyn, Shock Xpress*
His only fault, if you can call it that, is that he sees the cinema purely as a means of making money, and consequently he only puts so much effort into improving the quality of his products. – *Luigi Montefiori*

Damiani, Damiano (1922–)
Italian director.
The Empty Canvas 64. A Bullet for the General 66. Confessions of a Police Captain 71. The Tempter 74. The Genius 75. I Am Afraid 77. Goodbye and Amen 78. L'Ultimo Nome 79. Time of Jackals 80. Amityville II: The Possession 82. Attacco alla Piovra 85. The Inquiry/L'Inchiesta 87. Massacre Play/Gioco al Massacro (& co-w) 89. Angel of Death/L'Angelo con la Pistola 92, etc.

Damiano, Gerald
American director of hard-core porn movies.
Deep Throat 73. The Devil in Miss Jones 73. The Story of Joanna 75. Let My Puppets Come 77. Throat – 12 Years After 84, etc.

Damita, Lili (1901–1994) (Lilliane Carré)
French leading lady who made a few American films and married Errol Flynn (1935–42). Her death certificate gave her age as 85.
The Rescue 28. The Bridge of San Luis Rey 29. The Cockeyed World 29. The Match King 31. This Is the Night 32. Goldie Gets Along 33. The Frisco Kid 35. L'Escadrille de la Chance (Fr.) 36, etc.

Damon, Cathryn (1933–1987)
American comedy actress who played the slightly more sensible sister in TV's *Soap*.
Friendships, Secrets and Lies (TV) 80. How to Beat The High Cost of Living 80.

Damon, Mark (1933–) (Alan Mark Harris)
American leading man in routine films, now a producer in Europe.
Between Heaven and Hell 56. The Fall of the House of Usher 60. The Young Racers 63. Anzio 68. There Is No Thirteen 77. The Choirboys (co-p only) 77, etc.

Damon, Matt (1970–) (Matthew Paige Damon)
American leading actor and screenwriter. Born in Cambridge, Massachusetts, he was educated at Harvard, leaving to pursue his career as an actor. He became a star with *Good Will Hunting*, which he wrote for himself with fellow actor Ben AFFLECK. He has been romantically linked with actresses Claire DANES and Minnie DRIVER.
Mystic Pizza 88. The Good Mother 88. Rising Son (TV) 90. School Ties 92. Geronimo: An American Legend 93. The Good Old Boys 95. Courage under Fire 96. John Grisham's The Rainmaker 97. Chasing Amy 97. *Good Will Hunting* (AAw, AANa) 97. Saving Private Ryan 98. Rounders 98. The Talented Mr Ripley 99. Dogma 99. Titan AE (voice) 99. The Legend of Bagger Vance 00, etc.
❝ For the most part, young actors in Hollywood are actors by default. They're morons. – *M.D., 1994*

Damone, Vic (1928–) (Vito Farinola)
American light leading man and singer. He was married to actress Pier ANGELI (1955–59) and married singer Diahann CARROLL in 1987.
Rich, Young and Pretty 51. The Strip 51. Athena 54. Hit the Deck 55. Deep in My Heart 55. Kismet 55. Meet Me in Las Vegas 56. Hell to Eternity 60, etc.

Dampier, Claude (1879–1955) (Claude Cowan)
British comedian noted for nasal drawl and country yokel characterization. Long on stage and music hall.
Biography: 1978, *Claude Dampier, Mrs Gibson and Me* by Billie Carlyle (his wife and partner on the halls).
Radio Parade of 1935 34. Boys Will Be Boys 35. She Shall Have Music 35. Mr Stringfellow Says No 37. Riding High 39. Don't Take It to Heart 44. Meet Mr Malcolm 53, etc.

Damski, Mel (1946–)
American director, working mainly in television.
Yellowbeard 83. Mischief 85. Happy Together 90. Still Kicking: The Fabulous Palm Springs Follies (short) (AAN) 97, etc.

Dana, Bill (1924–)
American television comedian who used to play Mexicans.
Harrad Summer 74. Rossetti and Ryan (TV) 77. A Guide for the Married Woman 78. The Hungry Reunion 81. Lena's Holiday 91, etc.
TV series: The Bill Dana Show 62–65. No Soap Radio 82. Zorro and Son 83.

Dana, Leora (1923–1983)
American general-purpose actress.
3.10 to Yuma 57. Kings Go Forth 58. Some Came Running 58. Pollyanna 60. Change of Habit 69. Wild Rovers 71. Shoot the Moon 81. Baby It's You 82. Amityville 3-D 84, etc.

Dana, Viola (1897–1987) (Violet Flugrath)
American silent screen actress, usually in light comedy and fashionable drama.
Molly the Drummer Boy 14. Rosie O'Grady 17. A Chorus Girl's Romance 20. The Willow Tree 20. Open All Night 24. Merton of the Movies 24. Winds of Chance 25. Kosher Kitty Kelly 26. The Sisters 29, etc.

Dance, Charles (1946–)
British leading actor.
Saigon (TV) 83. *The Jewel in the Crown* (TV) 84. For Your Eyes Only 84. Plenty 86. Good Morning Babylon 86. Out on a Limb (TV) 87. The Golden Child 87. Hidden City 87. White Mischief 87. Pascali's Island 88. Alien^3 92. The Last Action Hero 93. Century 93. China Moon 94. Nanook/ Kabloonak 94. Shortcut to Paradise (Sp.) 94. Michael Collins 96. Rebecca (TV) 97. In the

Presence of Mine Enemies (TV) 97. Don't Go Breaking My Heart 98. Hilary and Jackie 98. Murder Rooms: The Dark Beginnings of Sherlock Holmes (TV) 200, etc.

Dancy, Hugh (1975–)
English actor, whose first professional experience was playing David Copperfield on TV. He studied at Oxford University.
David Copperfield (TV) 00. Young Blades 00. Madame Bovary (TV) 00. The Sleeping Dictionary 01, etc.

Dandridge, Dorothy (1922–1965)
American leading actress and singer whose career was one of unrealized potential. Born in Cleveland, she began in films as a child, but, apart from two charismatic performances in the musicals *Carmen Jones* and *Porgy and Bess*, was to find few roles as an adult that gave her the opportunity to display her talents. She died in poverty, of an overdose of drugs. The first of her two husbands was Harold Nicholas of the NICHOLAS BROTHERS. Her lovers included director Otto PREMINGER and actors Curt JURGENS and Peter LAWFORD. She was played by Halle BERRY in the TV biopic *Dorothy Dandridge* 99.
Autobiography: 1970, *Everything and Nothing*.
Biography: 1997, *Dorothy Dandridge* by Donald Bogle.
A Day at the Races 37. Bahama Passage 41. Lady from Louisiana 41. Sun Valley Serenade 41. Drums of the Congo 42. Hit Parade of 1943 43. Tarzan's Peril 51. Bright Road 53. Remains to Be Seen 53. *Carmen Jones* (AAN) 54. Island in the Sun 57. The Decks Ran Red 58. Porgy and Bess 59. Tamango 59. Moment of Danger 60, etc.

Dane, Karl (1886–1934) (Karl Daen)
Lanky Danish character actor who almost accidentally became a popular comedian at the end of the silent period, but could not survive sound. Committed suicide.
Lights of Old Broadway 25. *The Big Parade* 25. The Scarlet Letter 26. The Red Mill 27. *Rookies* 27. Baby Mine 28. Circus Rookies 28. Alias Jimmy Valentine 28. Speedway 29. Montana Moon 30. The Big House 30. Billy the Kid 30. Whispering Shadows 33, etc.

Daneman, Paul (1925–)
British light leading man, mainly on stage.
Time without Pity 57. The Clue of the New Pin 61. Zulu 64. How I Won the War 67. Oh What a Lovely War 69, etc.
TV series: Spy Trap.

Danes, Claire (1979–)
American actress, from the stage. Born in New York, she enrolled at the Lee Strasberg Theater Institute at the age of 10 and also studied at the Professional Performing Arts School. She made her television debut at the age of 11, and first gained fame as the troubled teenager Angela Chase in the TV series *My So-Called Life*. She is currently studying at Yale University.
Little Women 94. Home for the Holidays 95. How to Make an American Quilt 95. Romeo and Juliet 96. I Love You, I Love You Not 96. To Gillian on Her 37th Birthday 96. U-Turn 97. John Grisham's The Rainmaker 97. Les Misérables 98. Polish Wedding 98. The Cherry Orchard 98. Monterey Pop 98. The Mod Squad 99. Brokedown Palace 99. Princess Mononoke (voice) 99, etc.
TV series: My So-Called Life 94.

D'Angelo, Beverly (1953–)
American leading lady. Born in Columbia, Ohio, she began as a cartoonist for HANNA-BARBERA in Hollywood and also performed as a singer and with the rock group Elephant before turning to acting and making her Broadway debut in a musical, *Rockabye Hamlet*. She is romantically involved with actor Al PACINO.
First Love 77. Every Which Way but Loose 78. Hair 79. Coal Miner's Daughter 80. Paternity 81. Honky Tonk Freeway 81. Paternity 81. National Lampoon's Vacation 83. Big Trouble 84. Finders Keepers 84. Highpoint 84. National Lampoon's European Vacation 85. Maid to Order 87. The Woo Woo Kid 87. Aria 88. Trading Hearts 88. High Spirits 88. Cold Front 89. National Lampoon's Christmas Vacation 89. Pacific Heights 90. Daddy's Dyin', Who's Got the Will? 90. The Miracle 90. The Pope Must Die/The Pope Must Diet 91. Lonely Hearts 91. Man Trouble 92. Lightning Jack 94. Menendez: A Killing in Beverly Hills (TV) 94. Eye for an Eye 96. Pterodactyl Woman from Beverly Hills 96. Merchants of Venus 98. American History X 98. Lansky (TV) 99. Sugar Town 99, etc.

Dangerfield, Rodney (1921–) (Jacob Cohen)
American comedian and screenwriter.
The Projectionist 71. Caddyshack 80. Easy Money (& w) 83. Back to School (& story) 86. Moving 88. Rover Dangerfield 91. Ladybugs 92. Natural Born Killers 94. Meet Wally Sparks (& co-w) 97. The Godson 98. Little Nicky 00, etc.

Daniel, Rod
American director.
Teen Wolf 85. Stranded (TV) 86. Like Father Like Son 87. K-9 89. The Super 91. Ace Ventura: Pet Detective 92. Beethoven's 2nd 93, etc.

Daniell, Henry (1894–1963)
Incisive, cold-eyed British stage actor, a popular Hollywood villain of the 30s and 40s.
■ Jealousy 29. The Awful Truth 29. The Last of the Lone Wolf 30. Path of Glory 34. The Unguarded Hour 36. *Camille* 36. Under Cover of Night 37. The Thirteenth Chair 37. The Firefly 37. Madame X 37. Holiday 38. Marie Antoinette 38. The Private Lives of Elizabeth and Essex 39. We Are Not Alone 39. All This and Heaven Too 40. *The Sea Hawk* 40. The Great Dictator 40. *The Philadelphia Story* 40. A Woman's Face 41. Dressed to Kill 41. Four Jacks and a Jill 41. The Feminine Touch 41. Castle in the Desert 42. Random Harvest 42. Sherlock Holmes and the Voice of Terror 42. Reunion in France 42. The Great Impersonation 42. Nightmare 42. Mission to Moscow 43. *Sherlock Holmes in Washington* 43. Watch on the Rhine 43. Jane Eyre 43. *The Suspect* 44. The Chicago Kid 45. Hotel Berlin 45. The Woman in Green 45. *The Body Snatcher* 45. Captain Kidd 45. The Bandit of Sherwood Forest 46. Song of Love 47. The Exile 47. Siren of Atlantis 48. Wake of the Red Witch 48. The Secret of St Ives 49. Buccaneer's Girl 50. The Egyptian 54. The Prodigal 55. Diane 55. The Man in the Grey Flannel Suit 56. Lust for Life 56. Les Girls 57. The Story of Mankind 57. The Sun Also Rises 57. Witness for the Prosecution 57. Mr Cory 57. From the Earth to the Moon 58. The Four Skulls of Jonathan Drake 59. Voyage to the Bottom of the Sea 61. The Comancheros 61. Madison Avenue 62. The Notorious Landlady 62. Five Weeks in a Balloon 62. The Chapman Report 62. My Fair Lady 64.
❝ Famous line (*The Philadelphia Story*) "I understand we understand each other."

Daniels, Bebe (1901–1971) (Virginia Daniels)
American leading lady of the silent screen. Film debut at seven; played opposite Harold Lloyd and became a popular star; later married Ben Lyon, moved to Britain and appeared with their family on radio and TV.
Male and Female 19. Why Change Your Wife? 20. The Affairs of Anatol 21. Pink Gods 22. Unguarded Women 24. Monsieur Beaucaire 24. Campus Flirt 26. She's a Sheik 27. Rio Rita 29. Alias French Gertie 30. Reaching for the Moon 30. The Maltese Falcon 31. Forty-Second Street 33. Counsellor at Law 33. The Return of Carol Deane 35. Hi Gang (GB) 40. Life with the Lyons (GB) 53. The Lyons in Paris (GB) 55, etc.

Daniels, Gary
British-born actor in action movies.
Ring of Fire 91. Firepower 93. Knights 93. White Tiger 96. Fist of the North Star 96. American Streetfighter 96. Bloodmoon 97. American Streetfighter 2: The Full Impact 97. Cold Harvest 98. No Tomorrow 99, etc.

Daniels, Jeff (1955–)
Clean-cut American leading actor.
Ragtime 81. Terms of Endearment 83. The Purple Rose of Cairo 85. Something Wild 86. Radio Days 87. The House on Carroll Street 88. Love Hurts 89. Arachnophobia 90. Welcome Home, Roxy Carmichael 91. The Butcher's Wife 91. There Goes the Neighborhood/Paydirt 92. Gettysburg 93. Speed 94. Fly Away Home 96. 101 Dalmatians 96. 2 Days in the Valley 96. Trial and Error 97. Pleasantville 98. My Favorite Martian 99. The Crossing (TV) 00, etc.

Daniels, Mickey (1914–1970)
American actor, one of the original kids in the Our Gang comedies of the 20s. He retired in the early 40s to work as an engineer.
This Day and Age 33. Magnificent Obsession 35. The Great Ziegfeld 36, etc.

Daniels, Phil (1958–)
English character actor, best known for his role as a moody mod rebel in *Quadrophenia* 79.
The Class of Miss McMichael 78. Quadrophenia 79. Scum 79. Zulu Dawn 79. Breaking Glass 80. Meantime (TV) 81. Number One 84. Billy the Kid and the Green Baize Vampire 85. The Bride 85. Bad Behaviour 93. Sex and Chocolate (TV) 97. Still Crazy 98. Nasty Neighbours 99. Chicken Run (voice) 00, etc.
TV series: The Molly Wopsies 76. Four Idle Hands 76. Sunnyside Farm 97. Holding On 97. Sex, Chips and Rock 'n' Roll 99.

Daniels, William (1895–1970)
Distinguished American cinematographer, associated with the films of Greta Garbo.
■ Foolish Wives 21. Merry Go Round (co-ph) 23. Helen's Babies (co-ph) 24. *Greed* (co-ph) 25. Women and Gold 25. The Merry Widow (co-ph) 25. Bardelys the Magnificent 26. The Boob 26. Dance Madness (co-ph) 26. *Flesh and the Devil* 26. Money Talks 26. Monte Carlo 26. The Temptress (co-ph) 26. The Torrent 26. Altars of Desire 27. Captain Salvation 27. Love 27. On Ze Boulevard 27. Tillie the Toiler 27. The Actress 28. Bringing Up Father 28. Dream of Love 28. Lady of Chance 28. The Latest from Paris 28. The Mysterious Lady 28. Sally's Shoulders 28. A Woman of Affairs 28. *The Kiss* 29. The Last of Mrs Cheyney 29. Their Own Desire 29. The Trial of Mary Dugan 29. Wild Orchids 29. Wise Girls 29. Anna Christie 30. Montana Moon 30. Romance 30. Strictly Unconventional 30. Strangers May Kiss 31. The Great Meadow 31. Inspiration 31. A Free Soul 31. Susan Lenox 31. *Mata Hari* 32. Lovers Courageous 32. Grand Hotel 32. As You Desire Me 32. Skyscraper Souls 32. Rasputin and the Empress 33. The White Sister 33. Dinner at Eight 33. The Stranger's Return 33. Broadway to Hollywood 33. Christopher Bean 33. *Queen Christina* 33. The Barretts of Wimpole Street 34. The Painted Veil 34. Naughty Marietta 35. *Anna Karenina* 35. Rendezvous 35. Rose Marie 36. Romeo and Juliet 36. *Camille* 36. Personal Property 37. Broadway Melody of 1938 37. Double Wedding 37. The Last Gangster 37. Beg Borrow or Steal 37. Marie Antoinette 38. Three Loves Has Nancy 38. Dramatic School 38. Idiot's Delight 39. Stronger Than Desire 39. Ninotchka 39. Another Thin Man 39. The Shop Around the Corner 40. The Mortal Storm 40. New Moon 40. So Ends Our Night 41. Back Street 41. They Met in Bombay 41. Shadow of the Thin Man 41. Dr Kildare's Victory 41. *Keeper of the Flame* 42. Girl Crazy 42. Brute Force 47. Lured 47. *The Naked City* (AA) 48. For the Love of Mary 48. Family Honeymoon 48. The Life of Riley 49. Illegal Entry 49. Abandoned 49. The Gal who Took the West 49. Woman in Hiding 49. Winchester 73 50. Harvey 50. Deported 50. Thunder on the Hill 51. Bright Victory 51. The Lady Pays Off 51. When in Rome 52. Pat and Mike 52. Glory Alley 52. Plymouth Adventure 52. Never Wave at a WAC 53. Forbidden 53. Thunder Bay 53. *The Glenn Miller Story* 53. War Arrow 54. The Far Country 54. Six Bridges to Cross 55. Foxfire 55. The Shrike 55. Strategic Air Command 55. The Girl Rush 55. The Benny Goodman Story 55. Away All Boats (co-ph) 56. The Unguarded Moment 56. Istanbul 56. Night Passage 57. Interlude 57. My Man Godfrey 57. Voice in the Mirror 57. Cat on a Hot Tin Roof 58. Some Came Running 59. Stranger in My Arms 59. A Hole in the Head 60. Never So Few 60. Can Can 60. Ocean's Eleven 60. All the Fine Young Cannibals 60. Come September 61. Jumbo 62. How the West was Won (co-ph) 63. Come Blow Your Horn 63. The Prize 63. Robin and the Seven Hoods (& p) 64. Von Ryan's Express 65. Marriage on the Rocks 65. Assault on a Queen (& p) 66. In Like Flint 67. Valley of the Dolls 67. The Impossible Years 68. Marlowe 68. The Maltese Bippy 69. Move 70.
❝ We try to tell the story with light, and the director tells it with action. – *W.D.*

Daniels, William (1927–)
Dapper American actor, much on television. Born in Brooklyn, New York, he began working as a child with a family song-and-dance act and made his Broadway stage debut at the age of 16. He came to films and television in mid-career, where he was best known for his roles as heart surgeon Dr Mark Craig in *St Elsewhere*, for which he won two Emmys as best actor, and as the voice of the car in *Knight Rider*. Married actress Bonnie Bartlett.
Family Honeymoon 49. A Thousand Clowns 65. The President's Analyst 67. *The Graduate* 67. Two for the Road 67. Marlowe 69. *1776* (as John Adams) 72. The Parallax View 74. Black Sunday 77. The One and Only 78. Sunburn 79. The Blue Lagoon 80. All Night Long 81. Reds 81. Blind Date 87. Her Alibi 89. Magic Kid II 94. The Lottery (TV) 96, many others.
TV series: St Elsewhere 82–88. Knight Rider (voice of KITT) 82–86. Boy Meets World 93.

Daniely, Lisa (1930–)
Anglo-French leading lady.
Lili Marlene 50. Hindle Wakes 51. The Wedding of Lili Marlene 53. Tiger by the Tail 55. The Vicious Circle 57. An Honourable Murder 60. The Lamp in Assassin Mews 62. Goldeneye: The Secret Life of Ian Fleming (TV) 89, etc.

Danischewsky, Monja (1911–1994)
Russian writer-producer, in Britain since 20s. Publicist and writer for Ealing 1938–48. Produced *Whisky Galore* 48. *The Galloping Major* 50. *The Battle of the Sexes* 61, etc. Screenplays, *Topkapi* 64. *Mister Moses* 65.
Autobiography: 1966, *White Russian, Red Face*. 1972, *Out of My Mind*.

Dankworth, John (1927–)
British bandleader who has written scores. Married singer Dame Cleo Laine in 1958.
The Criminal 60. Saturday Night and Sunday Morning 60. The Servant 65. Darling 65. Return from the Ashes 65. Accident 67. The Last Grenade 69. Ten Rillington Place 70. The Engagement 70. Loser Take All 89. Gangster No 1 00, etc.

Danner, Blythe (1944–)
American leading actress of the 70s. Married director Bruce PALTROW. Their daughter is actress Gwyneth PALTROW.
Dr Cook's Garden (TV) 70. 1776 72. To Kill a Clown 72. Lovin' Molly 74. The Last of the Belles (TV) 74. Sidekicks (TV) 74. Hearts of the West 75. Futureworld 76. A Love Affair: The Eleanor and Lou Gehrig Story (TV) 78. Are You in the House Alone? (TV) 78. *Too Far to Go* (TV) 79. The Great Santini 80. Man, Woman and Child 83. Brighton Beach Memoirs 86. One Art 87. Another Woman 88. Alice 90. Mr & Mrs Bridge 90. The Prince of Tides 91. Husbands and Wives 92. Oldest Living Confederate Widow Tells All (TV) 94. Homage 95. The Myth of Fingerprints 97. Mad City 97. A Call to Remember (TV) 97. The X Files 98. No Looking Back 98. Murder She Purred: A Mrs Murphy Mystery (TV) 98. The Proposition 98. Forces of Nature 99. The Love Letter 99, etc.
TV series: Adam's Rib 73.

Danning, Sybil (1950–)
Blonde Austrian actress, in glamorous roles in forgettable films.
Swedish Love Games/Urlaubsreport 71. Bluebeard 72. The Three Musketeers 73. The Four Musketeers 74. The Prince and the Pauper 77. Meteor 79. Battle beyond the Stars 80. The Salamander 81. Jungle Warriors 84. The Seven Magnificent Gladiators 85. Howling II … Your Sister Is a Werewolf 86. Private Property/Young Lady Chatterley II 86. Reform School Girls 86. The Tomb 86. Warrior Queen 87. Amazon Women on the Moon 87. LA Bounty 89, etc.
❝ What I am is the new dream girl – one who has both body and intelligence. – *S.D.*

Dano, Royal (1922–1994)
American general-purpose supporting actor.
■ Undercover Girl 49. Under the Gun 50. *The Red Badge of Courage* (as The Tattered Man) 51. Flame of Araby 51. Bend of the River 52. Johnny Guitar 54. The Far Country 55. The Trouble with Harry 55. Tribute to a Bad Man 55. Santiago 56. Moby Dick 56. Tension at Table Rock 56. Crime of Passion 57. Trooper Hook 57. All Mine to Give 57. Man in the Shadow 57. Saddle the Wind 57. Handle with Care 58. Man of the West 58. Never Steal Anything Small 59. These Thousand Hills 59. Hound Dog Man 59. Face of Fire 59. Huckleberry Finn 60. Cimarron 60. Posse from Hell 61. King of Kings 61. Savage Sam 61. Seven Faces of Dr Lao 64. Gunpoint 66. The Dangerous Days of Kiowa Jones (TV) 66. Welcome to Hard

Times 67. The Last Challenge 67. Day of the Evil Gun 68. If He Hollers Let Him Go 68. The Undefeated 69. Backtrack (TV) 69. Run Simon Run (TV) 70. Moon of the Wolf (TV) 72. The Great Northfield Minnesota Raid 72. The Culpepper Cattle Company 72. Howzer 72. Ace Eli and Rodger of the Skies 73. Cahill 73. Electra Glide in Blue 73. Big Bad Mama 74. The Wild Party 75. Huckleberry Finn (TV) 75. Capone 75. Manhunter (TV) 76. Drum 76. Messiah of Evil 76. The Outlaw Josey Wales 76. The Killer Inside Me 76. Murder in Peyton Place (TV) 77. Donner Pass (TV) 78. Strangers (TV) 79. Take This Job and Shove It 81. Hammett 82. Something Wicked This Way Comes 83. The Right Stuff 83. Teachers 84. Red-Headed Stranger 86. Ghoulies II 88. Once Upon a Texas Train/Texas Guns 88. Cocaine Wars 89. Spaced Invaders 90. The Dark Half 91.

Danova, Cesare (1926–1992)
Italian leading man, often in Hollywood.
Crossed Swords 54. The Man Who Understood Women 59. Tarzan the Ape Man 59. Tender Is the Night 61. Cleopatra 63. Viva Las Vegas 64. Boy, Did I Get a Wrong Number 66. Chamber of Horrors 66. Che! 69. Tentacles 76. National Lampoon's Animal House 78., etc.
TV series: Garrison's Gorillas 67.

Danson, Ted (1947–)
Tall, craggy American leading man. Married actress Mary Steenburgen.
The Onion Field 79. Body Heat 81. Creepshow 82. Something about Amelia (TV) 84. Little Treasure 85. Just between Friends 85. A Fine Mess 86. Three Men and a Baby 87. Cousins 89. Dad 89. Three Men and a Little Lady 90. Made in America 93. Getting Even with Dad 94. Pontiac Moon 94. Gulliver's Travels (title role, TV) 96. Loch Ness 96. Homegrown 98. Jerry and Tom 98. Saving Private Ryan 98. Mumford 99, etc.
TV series: Somerset 74–76. *Cheers* 82–93. Ink 96–97. Becker 98– .

Dante, Joe (1946–)
American director, associated with Steven Spielberg. He is a former journalist who began his career cutting trailers for Roger Corman's movies.
Hollywood Boulevard (co-d) 76. Piranha 78. The Howling 80. Twilight Zone – the Movie (co-d) 83. *Gremlins* 84. Explorers 85. Amazon Women on the Moon (co-d) 87. Innerspace 87. The 'burbs 89. Gremlins II: The New Batch 90. Sleepwalkers (a) 92. *Matinee* 93. Picture Windows (TV) 95. The Second Civil War (TV) 97. Small Soldiers 98, etc.
❝ We did all kinds of things in trailers to help sell films. We had a famous exploding helicopter shot from one of those Filipino productions that we'd cut in every time a trailer was too dull because that was always exciting. – *J.D.*

Dante, Michael (1935–) (Ralph Vitti)
American 'second lead' with a screen tendency to villainy.
Fort Dobbs 58. Westbound 59. Seven Thieves 60. Kid Galahad 62. The Naked Kiss 64. Harlow 65. The Farmer 77. Cruise Missile 78. Beyond Evil 80. The Big Score 83. Cage 89. Crazy Horse and Custer – the Untold Story 90, etc.

Dantine, Helmut (1917–1982)
Lean good-looking Austrian actor, in US from 1938. Latterly an executive with the Joseph M. Schenck organization.
International Squadron 41. *Mrs Miniver* 41. Northern Pursuit 43. Passage to Marseilles 44. Hotel Berlin 45. Escape in the Desert 45. Shadow of a Woman 46. Whispering City 48. Call Me Madam 53. Stranger from Venus (GB) 54. War and Peace 56. Fraulein 57. Thundering Jets (d only) 58. Operation Crossbow 65. Garcia 74, etc.

Danton, Ray (1931–1992)
Tall, dark American leading man with radio experience.
Chief Crazy Horse 52. The Spoilers 55. I'll Cry Tomorrow 55. *Too Much Too Soon* 58. *The Rise and Fall of Legs Diamond* 59. Ice Palace 60. A Fever in the Blood 61. *The George Raft Story* 61. The Chapman Report 62. The Longest Day 62. Sandokan the Great (It.) 63. Tiger of Terror (It.) 64. The Spy Who Went into Hell (Ger.) 65. The Deathmaster (d only) 72. The Centrefold Girls 74, etc.
TV series: The Alaskans 59–60.

D'Antoni, Philip (1929–)
American producer for cinema and TV.
The French Connection (AA) 71. The Connection (TV) 73. Mr Inside Mr Outside (TV) 73. The Seven-Ups (& d) 74, etc.

Danvers-Walker, Bob (1907–1990)
A radio and television announcer, he was the distinctive voice of British Pathé newsreels from 1940–70.

The Danziger Brothers (Edward and Harry)
American producers who after making *Jigsaw* 46 and two or three other films came to England, set up New Elstree Studios and spent 15 years producing hundreds of second features and TV episodes, hardly any worth recalling. Their reputation in the industry was not high. When working on a film for the exploitation director-producer Harry Alan Towers, an actor was told to crouch down. Instructed to crouch lower, he protested that he was as low as he could get. Came the voice of the cameraman, 'You could be working for the Danzigers!'
❝ It would have been physically possible, if the spirit hadn't weakened, to make a hundred and twenty films in a year for Harry Lee and Edward J. Danziger, because any film they made that lasted more than three days began to run over budget. – *Christopher Lee*

Dapkunaité, Ingeborga
Lithuanian leading actress, in international films.
Night Whispers/Nochnye shyopoty 86. Thirteenth Apostle/Trinadtsatyj Apostol 88. Cynics/Tsiniki 91. Burnt by the Sun 94. Katia Ismailova 94. On Dangerous Ground (TV) 95. Mission: Impossible (US) 96. Seven Years in Tibet (US) 97, etc.
TV series: Alaska Kid 93.

Darabont, Frank (1959–)
American screenwriter and director.
A Nightmare on Elm Street 3: Dream Warriors (co-w) 87. The Blob (co-w) 88. The Fly II (co-w) 89. Buried Alive (d) (TV) 90. *The Shawshank Redemption* (wd) 94. Mary Shelley's Frankenstein (w) 94. The Green Mile (AANp,AANw,d) 99, etc.

D'Arbanville, Patty (1951–)
American actress, a former model, who began her career in one of Andy Warhol's underground films.
Flesh 68. Rancho Deluxe 75. Bilitis 77. Big Wednesday 78. Time after Time 79. The Main Event 79. The Fifth Floor 80. Hog Wild 80. Modern Problems 81. Real Genius 85. The Boys Next Door 85. Fresh Horses 88. Call Me 88. Wired 89. Frame-Up II: The Cover-Up 92. The Fan 96. New York Undercover 97. Archibald the Rainbow Painter 98. Celebrity 98 etc.

Darby, Ken (1909–1992)
American composer and arranger.
Song of the South 46. So Dear to My Heart 48. Rancho Notorious 52. The Robe 53. The Egyptian 54. Bus Stop (AAN) 56. The King and I (AA) 56. South Pacific (AAN) 58. Hound Dog Man 59. Porgy and Bess (AA) 59. Flower Drum Song (AAN) 61. How the West Was Won (AAN) 62. The Greatest Story Ever Told 65. Camelot (AA) 67, many others.

Darby, Kim (1947–) (Deborah Zerby)
American leading lady.
Bus Riley's Back in Town 65. A Time for Giving 69. *True Grit* 69. Norwood 69. The Grissom Gang 71. Rich Man Poor Man (TV) 76. The One and Only 78. The Pink Telephone 78. The Last Convertible (TV) 79. Better Off Dead 85. Teen Wolf Too 87. Halloween: The Curse of Michael Myers 95. The Last Best Sunday 99, etc.

Darc, Mireille (1938–) (M. Aigroz)
French leading lady.
Tonton Flingueurs 64. Galia 65. Du Rififi à Paname 66. Weekend 67. Jeff 68. Blonde from Peking 68. There was Once a Cop 72. The Tall Blond Man With One Black Shoe 74. The Pink Telephone/Le Téléphone Rose 75. Les Passagers 76. Man in a Hurry/L'Homme Pressé 77. Whirlpool/Pour la Peau d'un Flic 81. Si Elle Dit Oui … Je Ne Dis Pas Non 83, etc.

Darcel, Denise (1925–) (Denise Billecard)
French leading lady, in Hollywood from 1947.
To the Victor 48. Battleground 49. Tarzan and the Slave Girl 50. Westward the Women 51. Young Man with Ideas 52. Dangerous When Wet 53. Flame of Calcutta 53. Vera Cruz 53. Seven Women from Hell 62, etc.

D'Arcy, Alex (1908–1996) (Alexander Sarruf)
Egyptian light actor who has appeared in films of many nations.
Champagne 28. A Nous la Liberté 31. La Kermesse Héroique 35. The Prisoner of Zenda 37. Fifth Avenue Girl 39. Marriage Is a Private Affair 44. How to Marry a Millionaire 53. Soldier of Fortune 56. Way Way Out 66. The St Valentine's Day Massacre 67. Blood of Dracula's Castle (as Dracula) 69. The Seven Minutes 71, etc.

D'Arcy, Roy (1894–1969) (Roy F. Guisti)
American actor who hovered on the edge of stardom during the 20s and was in second features in the 30s, usually as a villain. Born in San Francisco, he was educated at the University of Jena, Germany, and worked in South America before becoming an actor in New York.
The Merry Widow 25. La Bohème 26. Trelawney of the Wells 26. King of the Khyber Rifles 26. The Gay Deceiver 26. Adam and Evil 27. The Actress 28. A Woman of Affairs 29. Romance 30. Sherlock Holmes 32. Whispering Shadows (serial) 33. Flying Down to Rio 33. Orient Express 34. Outlawed Guns 35. Revolt of the Zombies 36. Captain Calamity 36. Chasing Danger 39, etc.

Dard, Frederic (1921–2000)
Prolific and popular French thriller writer, dramatist and screenwriter, a former journalist. Best known for his many novels (more than 140) featuring policeman Superintendant San-Antonio, he wrote some 300 novels, which sold more than 270 million copies.
M'sieur La Calle 55. The Wicked Go To Hell/Les Salauds Vont En Enfer 55. Une Gueule Comme La Mienne (&d) 55. Back to the Wall/Le Dos Au Mur 58. Premeditation 59. La Menace 60. House of Sin/Les Menteurs 61. The Accident/L'Accident 63. The Old Lady Who Walked in the Sea/La Vieille Qui Marchait Dans La Mer 91. Leon's Husband/Le Mari de Léon, etc.

Darden, Severn (1929–1995)
American comedy character actor.
Dead Heat on a Merry-Go-Round 67. The President's Analyst 67. Luv 68. Pussycat Pussycat I Love You 70. Vanishing Point 71. The Hired Hand 71. Cisco Pike 71. The War Between Men and Women 72. Who Fears the Devil 74. In God We Trust 79. Why Would I Lie 80. Saturday the 14th 81. Real Genius 85. Back to School 86, etc.
TV series: Mary Hartman, Mary Hartman 77–78. Beyond Westworld 80. Take Five 87.

Dardenne, Jean-Pierre (1951–)
Belgian screenwriter and director, who works in collaboration with his brother Luc Dardenne. Born in Seraing, they began by making social documentaries on video. *Rosetta* won the Palme D'Or at the 1999 Cannes Film Festival.
Falsch 87. Je Pense a Vous. 92. The Promise/La Promesse 96. *Rosetta* 99, etc.
❝ We call our cinema 'realism' because it is inspired by the everyday world we live in. – *J-P. D.*

Dardenne, Luc (1954–)
Belgian screenwriter and director, in collaboration with his brother Jean-Pierre Dardenne.

Darien, Frank (1876–1955)
American character actor often seen as meek or downtrodden little man.
Five Star Final 31. The Miracle Man 32. Professional Sweetheart 33. Marie Galante 34. Brides are Like That 36. Love Finds Andy Hardy 38. At the Circus 39. *The Grapes of Wrath* 40. Hellzapoppin 42. Tales of Manhattan 42. The Outlaw 43. Bowery to Broadway 44. Kiss and Tell 45. Claudia and David 46. You Gotta Stay Happy 46. Merton of the Movies 47. The Flying Saucer 50, many others.

Darin, Bobby (1936–1973) (Walden Robert Cassotto)
American pop singer who alternated lightweight appearances with more serious roles. He was married to Sandra Dee.
Pepe 60. Come September 61. Too Late Blues 61. Hell Is for Heroes 62. If a Man Answers 62. *Pressure Point* 62. State Fair 62. Captain Newman MD (AAN) 63. That Funny Feeling 65. Gunfight in Abilene 67. The Happy Ending 69, etc.

Daring, Mason (1949–)
American composer, often for the films of John Sayles.
Return of the Secaucus Seven 80. The Brother from Another Planet 84. Matewan 87. Eight Men Out 88. The Laserman 88. Little Vegas 90. City of Hope 91. Wild Hearts Can't Be Broken 91. Passion Fish 92. The Secret of Roan Inish 94. Lone Star 96. Hidden in America (TV) 96. Prefontaine 97. Cold around the Heart 97. The Opposite of Sex 98. A Walk on the Moon 98. Music of the Heart 99. Limbo 99. Where the Heart Is 00, etc.

Darling, Candy (1946–1974) (James Hope Slattery)
Transvestite star, best known for roles in Andy Warhol's movies. Born in Massapequa, Long Island, he also appeared in European films and on stage. Died of leukaemia. He was played by Stephen Dorff in *I Shot Andy Warhol* 96.
Autobiography: 1992, *Candy Darling*.
Flesh 68. Der Tod der Maria Malibran (TV) 71. Women in Revolt 72. Silent Night, Bloody Night 73, etc.
❝ Candy didn't want to be a perfect woman – that would be too simple, and besides it would give her away. What she wanted was to be a woman with all the little problems that a woman has to deal with – runs in her stocking, runny mascara, men that left her. – *Andy Warhol*

Darling, William (1882–1963) (Wilhelm Sandorhazi)
Hungarian-American art director, long with Twentieth Century-Fox.
A Question of Honor 22. Seven Faces 29. Renegades 30. *Cavalcade* (AA) 33. In Old Kentucky 35. The Littlest Rebel 35. Under Two Flags 36. Lloyds of London 36. On the Avenue 37. *The Rains Came* 39. The Song of Bernadette (AA) 43. The Keys of the Kingdom 44. Anna and the King of Siam (AA) 46, etc.

Darnborough, Anthony (1913–2000)
British producer.
The Calendar 47. Quartet 48. The Astonished Heart 49. So Long at the Fair 50. The Net 52. To Paris with Love 55. The Baby and the Battleship 56, etc.

Darnell, Linda (1921–1965) (Monetta Eloisa Darnell)
Wide-eyed American leading lady of the 40s. Died in a fire.
■ Hotel for Women 39. Daytime Wife 39. Stardust 40. Brigham Young 40. The Mark of Zorro 40. Chad Hanna 40. Blood and Sand 41. Rise and Shine 41. The Loves of Edgar Allan Poe 42. The Song of Bernadette (as the Virgin Mary) 43. City Without Men 43. Buffalo Bill 44. *It Happened Tomorrow* 44. Summer Storm 44. Sweet and Lowdown 44. The Great John L 45. Fallen Angel 45. Hangover Square 45. Anna and the King of Siam 46. Centennial Summer 46. My Darling Clementine 46. Forever Amber 47. The Walls of Jericho 48. Unfaithfully Yours 48. A Letter to Three Wives 48. Slattery's Hurricane 49. Everybody Does It 49. No Way Out 50. Two Flags West 50. The Thirteenth Letter 51. The Lady Pays Off 51. The Guy who Came Back 51. Saturday Island 52. Night Without Sleep 52. Blackbeard the Pirate 52. Second Chance 53. This Is My Love 54. Forbidden Women (It.) 55. The Last Five Minutes (It.) 56. Dakota Incident 56. Zero Hour 57. Homeward Borne (TV) 57. Black Spurs 65.
❝ Linda Darnell, who you may remember as the star of Hollywood's 1947 romantic blockbuster *Forever Amber*, was a firm believer in moving her facial muscles as little as possible. It didn't do much for her acting, but when she died in her forties she had remarkably unlined skin. – *Joan Collins*

D'Arrast, Harry D'Abbabie (1893–1968)
American director of the 20s, with a reputation for style.
■ Service for Ladies 27. A Gentleman of Paris 27. Serenade 27. The Magnificent Flirt 28. Dry Martini 28. Raffles (part) 30. *Laughter* (AA co-story) 30. Topaze 33. It Happened in Spain 34.

Darren, James (1936–) (James Ercolani)
American leading man whose appeal seems to have waned with maturity although he is still seen occasionally on TV.
Rumble on the Docks 56. Operation Mad Ball 57. Gidget 59. Let No Man Write My Epitaph 60. *The Guns of Navarone* 61. Diamondhead 63. For Those Who Think Young 64. Venus in Furs 70. The Boss's Son 78, etc.
TV series: Time Tunnel 66. T. J. Hooker 83–86.

Darrieux, Danielle (1917–)
Vivacious French leading lady, in films since 1931.
Le Bal 32. *Mayerling* 35. *The Rage of Paris* (US) 38. *Battement de Coeur* 40. Premier Rendezvous 44. *Occupe-Toi d'Amélie* 49. La Ronde 50. Rich, Young and Pretty (US) 51. Five Fingers (US) 52. Le Plaisir 52. Adorables Créatures 52. *Madame De* 53. Le Rouge et le Noir 54. Lady Chatterley's Lover 55. Alexander the Great (US) 56. Marie Octobre 58. Murder at 45 RPM 61. The Greengage Summer (GB) 61. Landru 62. L'Or du Duc 65. Le Dimanche de la Vie 66. The Young Girls of Rochefort 67. L'Homme à la Buick 67. Birds Come to Die in Peru 68. The Lonely Woman 75. L'Année Sainte 76. Le Cavaleur 79. At the Top of the Stairs 83. The Scene of the Crime 86. Bille en Tête 89. Le Jour de Rois 90. Tomorrow's Another Day/Ca Ira Mieux Demain 00, many others.

Darro, Frankie (1917–1976) (Frank Johnson)
Tough-looking little American actor, former child and teenage player; star of many second features.
So Big 24. The Cowboy Cop 26. Long Pants 27. The Circus Kid 28. The Mad Genius 31. Wild Boys of the Road 33. Broadway Bill 34. Charlie Chan at the Race Track 36. Racing Blood 37. Chasing Trouble 39. Laughing at Danger 40. Freddie Steps Out 45. Heart of Virginia 48. Across the Wide Missouri 51. Operation Petticoat 59. Hook, Line and Sinker 68, many others.

Darrow, Clarence (1857–1938)
Celebrated American defence lawyer, impersonated by Orson Welles in *Compulsion* 58, and by Spencer Tracy in *Inherit the Wind* 60. In the 70s Henry Fonda played him in a one-man stage and TV show. In the 90s, Leslie Nielsen also played him in a one-man show.

Darrow, John (1907–1980) (Harry Simpson)
American light leading man of the 20s and 30s, who later became an agent.
High School Hero 27. Girls Gone Wild 29. Hell's Angels 30. The Lady Refuses 31. Ten Nights in a Bar-Room 31. The All American 32. Midshipman Jack 33. Monte Carlo Nights 34. A Notorious Gentleman 35. Crime over London (GB) 36, etc.

Darvi, Bella (1927–1971) (Bayla Wegier)
Polish-French leading lady, in a few Hollywood films after being discovered by Darryl Zanuck. Committed suicide.
■ Hell and High Water 54. The Egyptian 54. The Racers 55. Je Suis Un Sentimental 55. Sinners of Paris 59. Lipstick 65.

Darwell, Jane (1879–1967) (Patti Woodward)
American character actress, usually in warm-hearted motherly roles.
Rose of the Rancho 14. Brewster's Millions 20. Tom Sawyer 30. Back Street 32. Design for Living 34. Life Begins at Forty 35. Captain January 36. Slave Ship 37. Three Blind Mice 38. Jesse James 39. The Rains Came 39. Gone with the Wind 39. *The Grapes of Wrath* (AA: as the indomitable Ma Joad) 40. *All That Money Can Buy* 41. Private Nurse 41. The Ox Bow Incident 43. The Impatient Years 44. *Captain Tugboat Annie* (title role) 46. My Darling Clementine 46. Three Godfathers 48. Wagonmaster 50. Caged 50. The Lemon Drop Kid 51. Fourteen Hours 51. We're Not Married 52. The Sun Shines Bright 52. Hit the Deck 55. The Last Hurrah 58. Mary Poppins 64, many others.
✪ For the sheer maternal strength of her characterizations. *The Grapes of Wrath.*
❝ Famous line (*The Grapes of Wrath*) 'Can't nobody lick us, pa. We're the people.'

Dash, Stacey (1966–)
American actress who began in commercials as a child.
Enemy Territory 87. Moving 88. Tennessee Nights 89. Mo' Money 92. Renaissance Man 94. Clueless 95. Hoodlum 96. Cold around the Heart 97, etc.
TV series: TV 101 88–89.

Dassin, Jules (1911–)
American director, former radio writer and actor. Joined MGM 1941 to direct shorts (including a two-reel version of *The Tell-Tale Heart*); moved to features; left for Europe during the McCarthy witch hunt of the late 40s.
■ Nazi Agent 42. The Affairs of Martha 42. Reunion in France 42. Young Ideas 43. The Canterville Ghost 44. A Letter for Evie 44. Two Smart People 46. *Brute Force* 47. *Naked City* 48. *Thieves' Highway* (& a) 49. Night and the City (GB) 50. *Rififi* (also a, as Perlo Vita) 54. He Who Must Die 56. Where the Hot Wind Blows 58. *Never on Sunday* (also a) (AAN) 60. Phaedra 62. Topkapi 64. 10.30 p.m. Summer 66. Survival 68. Uptight 68. Promise at Dawn 70. Dream of Passion 78. Circle of Two 80.

Daugherty, Herschel (1909–1993)
American director, from TV.
The Light in the Forest 58. The Raiders 63. Winchester 73 (TV) 67. The Victim (TV) 72. Twice in a Lifetime (TV) 74, etc.

Dauphin, Claude (1903–1978) (Claude Franc-Nohain)
Dapper French actor of stage and screen: in films from 1930.
Entrée des Artistes 38. Battement de Coeur 39. Les Deux Timides 42. English Without Tears (GB) 44. Deported (US) 50. Le Plaisir 51. Casque d'Or 52. Little Boy Lost (US) 53. Innocents in Paris (GB) 54. Phantom of the Rue Morgue (US) 54. The Quiet American (US) 58. The Full Treatment 60. Lady L 65. Two for the Road 67. Hard Contract 69. Rosebud 75. The Tenant 76, many others.
TV series: Paris Precinct.

Davenport, A. Bromley (1867–1946)
Eton-educated English character actor who made his stage debut in Siberia in 1892 and was in films from 1920.
The Great Gay Road 20. Bonnie Prince Charlie 23. What the Butler Saw 24. Roses of Picardy 27. Too Many Crooks 30. Glamour 31. Mischief 32. Mr Bill the Conqueror 32. The Return of Raffles 32. A Shot in the Dark 33. The Warren Case 34. The Scarlet Pimpernel 34. The Cardinal 36. Owd Bob 38. Jamaica Inn 39. Love on the Dole 41. Old Mother Riley's Ghosts 41. The Young Mr Pitt 42. When We Are Married 43. The Way Ahead 44, etc.

Davenport, Doris (1915–1980)
American leading lady, formerly a Goldwyn Girl. Played several bit parts, but was prominent only in *Kid Millions* 35, *The Westerner* 40, *Behind the News* 40. Her career ended after she was injured in a car crash that left her with a limp.

Davenport, Dorothy (1895–1977) (aka Dorothy Reid)
Silent screen actress, often opposite her husband Wallace Reid, who turned to directing, writing and producing after his death in 1923.
Her Indian Hero 09. The Intruder 13. Fruit of Evil 14. The Fighting Chance 20. Every Woman's Problem 21. Human Wreckage 23. Broken Laws (& p) 24. The Earth Woman (p) 26. Linda (pd) 29. Sucker Money (d) 33. Road to Ruin (co-w, d) 34. Prison Break (w) 38. The Haunted House (w) 40. Redhead 41. Who Killed Doc Robbin? 48. Footsteps in the Fog 55, etc.

Davenport, Harry (1866–1949)
American character actor; long stage career, then in Hollywood as chucklesome, benevolent old man.
■ Her Unborn Child 30. My Sin 31. His Woman 32. Get That Venus 33. Three Cheers for Love 34. The Scoundrel 35. Three Men on a Horse 36. The Case of the Black Cat 36. King of Hockey 36. Fly Away Baby 36. The Life of Emile Zola 37. Under Cover of Night 37. Her Husband's Secretary 37. White Bondage 37. They Won't Forget 37. Mr Dodd Takes the Air 37. First Lady 37. The Perfect Specimen 37. Paradise Express 37. As Good as Married 37. Armored Car 37. Wells Fargo 37. Fit for a King 37. Gold is Where You Find It 38. Saleslady 38. The Sisters 38. The Long Shot 38. The First Hundred Years 38. Marie Antoinette 38. The Cowboy and the Lady 38. Reckless Living 38. The Rage of Paris 38. Tailspin 38. Young Fugitives 38. *You Can't Take It With You* 38. The Higgins Family 38. Orphans of the Street 38. Made for Each Other 39. My Wife's Relatives 39. Should Husbands Work 39. The Covered Trailer 39. Money to Burn 39. Exile Express 39. Death of a Champion 39. The Story of Alexander Graham Bell 39. Juarez 39. Gone with the Wind 39. *The Hunchback of Notre Dame* 39. Dr Ehrlich's Magic Bullet 40. Granny Get Your Gun 40. Too Many Husbands 40. Grandpa Goes to Town 40. Lucky Partners 40. I Want a Divorce 40. All This and Heaven Too 40. Foreign Correspondent 40. That Uncertain Feeling 41. I Wanted Wings 41. Hurricane Smith 41. The Bride Came COD 41. One Foot in Heaven 41. Kings Row 41. *Son of Fury* 42. Larceny Inc 42. Ten Gentlemen from West Point 42. Tales of Manhattan 42. Heading for God's Country 43. We've Never Been Licked 43. Riding High 43. *The Ox Bow Incident* 43. The Amazing Mrs Holliday 43. Gangway for Tomorrow 43. Government Girl 43. Jack London 43. Princess O'Rourke 43. *Meet Me In St Louis* 44. The Impatient Years 44. The Thin Man Goes Home 44. Kismet 44. Music for Millions 45. *The Enchanted Forest* 45. Too Young to Know 45. This Love of Ours 45. She Wouldn't Say Yes 45. Courage of Lassie 46. Blue Sierra 46. A Boy a Girl and a Dog 46. Faithful in My Fashion 46. Three Wise Fools 46. War Brides 46. Lady Luck 46. Claudia and David 46. Pardon My Past 46. Adventure 46. The Farmer's Daughter 47. That Hagen Girl 47. Stallion Road 47. Keeper of the Bees 47. Sport of Kings 47. The Fabulous Texan 47. *The Bachelor and the Bobbysoxer* 47. Three Daring Daughters 48. The Man from Texas 48. For the Love of Mary 48. That Lady in Ermine 48. The Decision of Christopher Blake 48. Down to the Sea in Ships 49. Little Women 49. Tell It To the Judge 49. *That Forsyte Woman* 49. Riding High 50.
✪ For being everybody's cheerful grandpa. *The Hunchback of Notre Dame.*

Davenport, Harry Bromley (1950–)
British director, screenwriter and composer of horror movies, a former special effects supervisor.
Whispers of Fear (d, m) 74. Full Circle/The Haunting of Julia (co-w) 76. Xtro (co-w, d, m) 82. Xtro II: The Second Encounter (d) 91. Life Amongst the Cannibals (d) 96, etc.

Davenport, Nigel (1928–)
Breezy, virile British actor, much on TV. His second wife (1972–80) was actress Maria Aitken.
Peeping Tom 59. Lunch Hour 62. In the Cool of the Day 63. A High Wind in Jamaica 65. Life at the Top 65. Sands of the Kalahari 65. Where the Spies Are 65. *A Man for All Seasons* 66. Red and Blue 67. Sebastian 68. Sinful Davey 68. *The Virgin Soldiers* 69. Play Dirty 69. The Royal Hunt of the Sun 69. The Last Valley 70. The Mind of Mr Soames 70. No Blade of Grass 70. Mary Queen of Scots 71. Villain 71. *Living Free* 72. Dracula (TV) (as Van Helsing) 73. Phase IV 73. The Island of Dr Moreau 77. Stand Up Virgin Soldiers 77. An Eye for an Eye 78. Zulu Dawn 79. Chariots of Fire 81. Nighthawks 81. Strata 82. Greystoke: The Legend of Tarzan, Lord of the Apes 84. Caravaggio 86. Without a Clue 88. The Return of El Coyote/La Vuelta de El Coyote (Sp.) 98. The Mumbo Jumbo 00, etc.
TV series: *Prince Regent* (as George III) 79.

Daves, Delmer (1904–1977)
American writer-producer-director with highly miscellaneous experience. Writer with MGM from 1933, writer-director with Warners from 1943.
Destination Tokyo (wd) 43. The Red House (wd) 47. *Dark Passage* (wd) 47. Broken Arrow (d) 50. Bird of Paradise (wd) 51. Never Let Me Go (d) 53. Demetrius and the Gladiators (d) 54. Jubal (wd) 56. The Last Wagon (wd) 56. *3.10 to Yuma* (d) 57. Cowboy (wd) 58. The Hanging Tree (d) 59. Parrish (wd) 61. Spencer's Mountain (wpd) 62. Youngblood Hawke (wd) 64. The Battle of the Villa Fiorita (wpd) 65, many others.
❝ He remains the property of those who can enjoy stylistic conviction in an intellectual vacuum. – *Andrew Sarris, 1968*

Davi, Robert (1953–)
Burly American actor, usually in menacing roles.
The Goonies 85. Wild Thing 87. Licence to Kill 89. Maniac Cop 2 90. Amazon 90. Predator 2 90. Legal Tender 90. Illicit Behaviour 91. The Taking of Beverly Hills 91. Center of the Web 92. Christopher Columbus: The Discovery 92. Wild Orchid 2: Two Shades of Blue 92. Maniac Cop 3: Badge of Silence 92. Night Trap/Mardi Gras for the Devil 93. Son of the Pink Panther 93. The November Men 93. Cops and Robbersons 94. Showgirls 95. An Occasional Hell 96. LA without a Map (GB/Fr./Fin.) (as himself) 98. My Little Assassin (TV) 99, etc.
TV series: The Gangster Chronicles 81.

Daviau, Allen (1942–)
American cinematographer.
E.T. – the Extraterrestrial (AAN) 82. Twilight Zone – the Movie 83. Harry Tracy 83. The Falcon and the Snowman 85. The Color Purple (AAN) 86. Harry and the Hendersons 87. Empire of the Sun (AAN) 87. Avalon (AAN) 90. Defending Your Life 91. Bugsy 91. Fearless 93. Congo 95. The Astronaut's Wife 99, etc.

David, Hal (1921–)
American lyricist and collaborator with Burt Bacharach (see entry for credits). He is the brother of Mack David.
Autobiography: 1968, *What The World Needs Now.*

David, Keith (1954–)
American actor. Born in New York, he studied at the High School for the Performing Arts and the Juilliard School, beginning in the theatre.
The Thing 82. Platoon 86. Bird 88. Stars and Bars 88. They Live 88. Always 89. Road House 89. Marked for Death 90. Article 99 92. The Last Outlaw 93. The Puppet Masters 94. Reality Bites 94. Blue in the Face 95. Clockers 95. Dead Presidents 95. The Quick and the Dead 95. Larger than Life 96. Johns 96. Loose Women 96. Volcano 97. Armageddon 98. There's Something about Mary 98. Dark Summer (Can.) 99. Pitch Black 00. Where the Heart Is 00, etc.

David, Mack (1912–1993)
American songwriter, in Hollywood from 1949, often in collaboration with Jerry Livingston. He is the brother of Hal David.
Cinderella (AAN) 49. At War with the Army 50. Sailor Beware 51. Jumping Jacks 52. Scared Stiff 53. The Hanging Tree (AAN) 59. Bachelor in Paradise (AAN) 61. Walk on the Wild Side (AAN) 62. It's a Mad, Mad, Mad, Mad World (AAN) 63. Hush, Hush Sweet Charlotte (AAN) 64. Cat Ballou (AAN) 65. Hawaii (AAN) 66, etc.

David, Saul (1921–1996)
American producer.
Autobiography: 1981, *The Industry.*
Von Ryan's Express 65. Our Man Flint 65. Fantastic Voyage 67. Skullduggery 69. The Black Bird 75. Logan's Run 76.

David, Thayer (1926–1978) (David Thayer Hersey)
American character actor.
A Time to Love and a Time to Die 58. Wolf Larsen 58. *Journey to the Center of the Earth* 59. The Story of Ruth 60. House of Dark Shadows 70. Night of Dark Shadows 71. Savages 72. Save the Tiger 73. The Werewolf of Washington 73. The Eiger Sanction 75. Peeper 75. The Duchess and the Dirtwater Fox 76. Rocky 76. House Calls 78, etc.

Davidovich, Lolita (1962–) (aka Lolita David)
Canadian actress of Yugoslavian descent.
Adventures in Babysitting 87. The Big Town 87. Blaze 89. Object of Beauty 91. The Inner Circle/El Proiezionista 91. Money Men 92. Raising Cain 92. Boiling Point 93. Younger and Younger 93. Intersection 94. Cobb 94. Now and Then 95. For Better or Worse (TV) 95. Touch 96. Jungle 2 Jungle 96. Dead Silence (TV) 96. Santa Fe 97. Gods & Monsters 98. Play It to the Bone 99. Touched (Can.) 99. Mystery, Alaska 99, etc.
❝ I'm Yugoslavian. They're passionate but not really ambitious. Life is eating and drinking and children. – *L.D.*

Davidson, Boaz (1943–)
Israeli director.
Azit the Paratrooper Dog 72. Lupo Goes to New York 77. Lemon Popsicle 81. Going Steady/Lemon Popsicle II 81. Hot Bubblegum/Lemon Popsicle III 82. The Last American Virgin 82. Private Popsicle/Lemon Popsicle IV 82. Dutch Treat 86. Going Bananas 87. Salsa 88. American Cyborg: Steel Warrior 94. Outside the Law 95, etc.

Davidson, Jaye (1968–)
American actor whose role as a transvestite surprised the hero, and the audience, of *The Crying Game*. Born in California, he moved to England as

a small child, returning to the United States to star in a million-dollar role in *Stargate*.

The Crying Game (AAN) 93. Stargate 94, etc.

Davidson, John (1886–1968)
American character actor, a piercing-eyed, white-haired villain of the 20s and 30s.

The Green Cloak 15. The Spurs of Sybil 18. The Bronze Bell 21. Under Two Flags 22. Monsieur Beaucaire 24. Kid Gloves 29. Arsène Lupin 32. Dinner at Eight 33. Hold That Girl 34. The Last Days of Pompeii 35. Mr Moto Takes a Vacation 38. Arrest Bulldog Drummond 38. Miracles for Sale 39. Captain Marvel 41. Captain America 44. The Purple Monster Strikes 45. Shock 46. Daisy Kenyon 47. A Letter to Three Wives 48. Oh You Beautiful Doll 49. A Gathering of Eagles 63, many others.

Davidson, John (1941–)
American light singer and leading man, mostly on television.

The Happiest Millionaire 67. The One and Only Genuine Original Family Band 68. Coffee, Tea or Me (TV) 73. The Mitera Targets (TV) 78. Shell Game (TV) 78. The Concorde – Airport '79 79. The Squeeze 87. Edward Scissorhands 90, etc.

TV series: The Entertainers 64–65. The Kraft Summer Music Hall 66. The John Davidson Show 69, 76. The Girl with Something Extra 73–74. That's Incredible 80–84.

Davidson, Max (1875–1950)
German-born slapstick comedian, in America from the 1890s and silents from 1913. Born in Berlin, he made a series of two-reelers for Hal ROACH in the late 20s, often with Walter 'Spec' O'DONNELL as his charmless son, which have been rediscovered and shown to acclaim in recent years. Later, he appeared as a character actor in small roles in the films of Cecil B. DE MILLE and others. He is featured in the compilation film *Laurel and Hardy's Laughing 20s* 65. He is also credited with suggesting to D. W. GRIFFITH, a fellow-actor in the late 1890s, that he should seek work in films.

Love in Armor 15. Intolerance 16. The Idle Rich 21. The Light that Failed 22. Untamed Youth 24. Hats Off (short) 27. *Call of the Cuckoos* (short) 27. *Don't Tell Everything* (short) 28. *Pass the Gravy* (short) 28. Jewish Prudence (short) 28. The Boy Friend (short) 28. Docks of San Francisco 32. The Cohens and Kellys in Trouble 33. Roamin' Wild 36. The Girl Said No 37. Union Pacific 39. Reap the Wild Wind 42, etc.

❝ Davidson is definitely and defiantly politically incorrect. He resurrects the Jewish comic stereotype that was already disreputable in his own time – apologetically shrugged shoulders, hands raised in palms-up supplication, clutching his cheeks, or stroking his beard. – *David Robinson*

Davidson, William B. (1888–1947)
American character actor, in hundreds of small roles, usually as pompous, lecherous or overbearing businessman.

A Modern Cinderella 17. The Capitol 19. Partners of the Night 20. Adam and Eva 23. Women and Gold 25. The Gaucho 28. For the Defense 30. Sky Devils 32. Fog over Frisco 34. Dangerous 35. Earthworm Tractors 36. Easy Living 37. Love on Toast 38. Indianapolis Speedway 39. Maryland 40. My Little Chickadee 40. Juke Girl 42. Up in Arms 44. See My Lawyer 45. My Darling Clementine 46. The Farmer's Daughter 47, many others.

Davidtz, Embeth (1966–)
South African-born actress in America. She is romantically involved with actor Ben CHAPLIN.

Army of Darkness 92. Deadly Matrimony (TV) 92. Schindler's List 93. Murder in the First 94. Feast of July 95. Matilda 96. The Gingerbread Man 97. The Garden of Redemption 97. Fallen 98. Simon Magus 99. Bicentennial Man 99. Mansfield Park 99, etc.

Davie, Cedric Thorpe (1913–1983)
British composer; he studied at the Royal College of Music under Ralph VAUGHAN WILLIAMS.

The Brothers 47. Snowbound 48. The Heart Is Highland (doc) 52. Rob Roy the Highland Rogue 53. The Dark Avenger/The Warriors 55. Jacqueline 56. The Green Man 56. The Kid from Canada 57. Rockets Galore/Mad Little Island 58. The Bridal Path 59. A Terrible Beauty/Night Fighters 60. Kidnapped 60, etc.

Davies, Andrew (1937–)
Welsh screenwriter and novelist, a former teacher, best known for adapting classic novels for television.

Time After Time 85. Consuming Passions 88. Mother Love (TV, BFA) 89. House of Cards (TV) 91. Middlemarch (TV) 94. Circle of Friends 95. Pride and Prejudice (TV) 95. The Fortunes and Misfortunes of Moll Flanders (TV) 96. Emma (TV) 97. Vanity Fair (TV) 98. B. Monkey (oa) 98. A Rather English Marriage (TV, BFA) 98. Wives and Daughters (TV) 99. Bridget Jones' Diary (co-w) 01, etc.

❝ My agent has taught me to be very philosophical about movies, saying: 'The film will probably never be made, you will probably be replaced as the writer and you have to accept these as normal things that happen. They will pay you a lot more money in compensation for the way they treat you.' – *A.D.*

Davies, Betty Ann (1910–1955)
British stage actress, usually in tense roles; occasional films from early 30s.

Chick 34. Kipps 41. It Always Rains on Sunday 47. The History of Mr Polly 49. *Trio* 50. Cosh Boy 52. Grand National Night 53. The Belles of St Trinian's 54, etc.

Davies, Jack (1913–1994)
British comedy scriptwriter, busy since 1932 on Will Hay and Norman Wisdom comedies, 'Doctor' series, etc. Father of John Howard DAVIES.

Laughter in Paradise 51. Top Secret 52. An Alligator Named Daisy 56. *Very Important Person* 61. *The Fast Lady* 62. Those Magnificent Men in Their Flying Machines (AAN) 65. Gambit 66. Monte Carlo 68. Doctor in Trouble 70. Paper Tiger 75, many others.

Davies, Jeremy (1969–)
American leading man in independent films, born in Rockford, Iowa.

Guncrazy 92. Spanking the Monkey 94. Nell 94. Twister 96. The Locusts 97. Going All the Way 97. Up at the Villa 98. Saving Private Ryan 98. The Million Dollar Hotel 99. Ravenous 99. Up at the Villa 00, etc.

TV series: General Hospital 92.

Davies, John Howard (1939–)
British child actor, who became a BBC TV director.

Oliver Twist 48. The Rocking-Horse Winner 49. The Magic Box 51. Tom Brown's Schooldays 51, etc.

Davies, Marion (1897–1961) (Marion Douras)
American leading lady famous less for her rather mediocre films than for being the protégée of William Randolph Hearst the newspaper magnate, who was determined to make a star out of her. She enjoyed moderate success 1917–36, then retired.

Autobiography: 1975, *The Times We Had*, collated by Pamela Pfau.

Biography: 1973, *Marion Davies* by Fred Lawrence Guiles.

■ Runaway Romany 17. Cecilia of the Pink Roses 18. The Burden of Proof 18. Getting Mary Married 19. The Cinema Murder 19. The Dark Star 19. The Belle of New York 19. The Restless Sex 20. April Folly 20. Enchantment 21. Buried Treasure 21. The Bride's Play 22. Beauty Worth 22. When Knighthood was in Flower 22. The Young Diana 22. Daughter of Luxury 22. Little Old New York 22. Adam and Eva 23. Janice Meredith 24. Yolanda 24. Lights of Old Broadway 25. Zander the Great 25. Beverly of Graustark 26. Quality Street 27. The Fair Co-ed 27. The Red Mill 27. Tillie the Toiler 27. The Cardboard Lover 28. The Patsy 28. *Show People* 28. Hollywood Revue 29. Marianne 29. The Gay Nineties 29. Not so Dumb 30. The Floradora Girl 30. It's a Wise Child 31. Five and Ten 31. Bachelor Father 31. Polly of the Circus 32. Blondie of the Follies 32. The Dark Horse 32. Peg O'My Heart 33. Operator 13 34. Going Hollywood 34. *Page Miss Glory* 35. Hearts Divided 36. Cain and Mabel 36. Ever Since Eve 37.

❝ Upon my honour
I saw a madonna
Sitting alone in a niche
Above the door
Of the glamorous whore
Of a prominent son-of-a-bitch.
Quote: – *attributed to Dorothy Parker on seeing the elaborate dressing room built by W. R. Hearst for M.D. at MGM*

With me it was 5 per cent talent and 95 per cent publicity. – *M.D.*

She was quite a comedian, and would have been a star in her own right without the cyclonic Hearst publicity. – *Charles Chaplin*

I have yet to encounter a single movie fan with the slightest respect for her ability – and yet the coal that has been used to keep her name flaming on the electric signs would probably run the city of Syracuse for a whole year. – *Robert Sherwood*

Davies, Rupert (1916–1976)
British character actor, formerly in small roles, then famous as TV's Maigret.

The Traitor 57. Sea Fury 58. Bobbikins 59. Devil's Bait 59. The Uncle 64. Five Golden Dragons 65. The Spy Who Came in from the Cold 65. The Brides of Fu Manchu 66. Curse of the Crimson Altar 68. Dracula Has Risen from the Grave 68. Witchfinder General 68. The Oblong Box 69. Waterloo 70. The Night Visitor 71. Zeppelin 71, etc.

TV series: Sailor of Fortune 56.

Davies, Terence (1945–)
British director of autobiographical films of working-class life in the 50s. He left school at 15 and worked as a clerk for 12 years before raising the money to make his first short.

Terence Davies Trilogy (The Children 76; Madonna and Child 80; Death and Transfiguration 83). Distant Voices, Still Lives 88. The Long Day Closes 92. The Neon Bible 95. The House of Mirth 00, etc.

❝ Cinema is not valid for me if it's just people talking their way through a plot. I couldn't get interested in all that. I just get bored, because that's not real cinema at all. It's talking pictures. – *T.D.*

The great thing in life is to be very beautiful and very stupid. – *T.D.*

Terry is a whirlwind of passion. He's a Tasmanian devil crossed with Doris Day. – *Eric Stloltz*

I believe Mr Davies went to film school – presumably not for long. – *Ken Russell*

Davies, Valentine (1905–1961)
American screenwriter.

Three Little Girls in Blue 46. *Miracle on 34th Street* (AA original story) 47. You Were Meant for Me 48. Chicken Every Sunday 48. It Happens Every Spring 49. On the Riviera 51. The Glenn Miller Story 53. *The Benny Goodman Story* (& d) 55. The Bridges at Toko-Ri 55. Strategic Air Command 55. Bachelor in Paradise 61, etc.

Davies, Windsor (1930–)
British comedy character actor, a former teacher, who rather overdoes the blustering sergeant-major act.

The Alphabet Murders 65. Hammerhead 67. Sex Clinic 71. Adolf Hitler – My Part in His Downfall 72. Mister Quilp 74. Carry on Behind 75. Carry On England 76. Confessions of a Driving Instructor 76. Not Now Comrade 77. Old Scores 91. Arabian Knight (voice) 95. Mosley (as Lloyd George) (TV) 98, etc.

TV series: It Ain't Half Hot, Mum 73–77. The New Statesman 85. Never the Twain 81–91.

Davion, Alexander (1929–)
Anglo-French leading man, mostly on stage and American TV.

Song without End (as Chopin) 60. Paranoiac 63. Valley of the Dolls 67. The Royal Hunt of the Sun 69. Incense for the Damned 71, etc.

TV series: Gideon's Way 64. The Man Who Never Was 66. Custer 67. Bloodsuckers 70, etc.

Davis, Andrew
American director and screenwriter, a former cinematographer.

Over the Edge (ph) 79. Stony Island (wd) 80. The Final Terror 83. Code of Silence 85. Above the Law (wd) 88. The Package 89. Under Siege 92. *The Fugitive* 93. Steal Big, Steal Little 95. Chain Reaction 96. A Perfect Murder 98, etc.

Davis, Bette (1908–1989) (Ruth Elizabeth Davis)
Inimitably intense American dramatic actress; a box-office queen for ten years from 1937, she later played eccentric roles. Her fourth, and last, husband was actor Gary Merrill (1940–50).

One story has it that she named the awards statuette Oscar because its backside resembled that of her first husband, Ham Oscar Nelson.

Autobiography: 1962, *The Lonely Life*. 1975, *Mother Goddam* (with Whitney Stine).

Biography: 1991, *No Guts, No Glory: Conversations with Bette Davis* by Whitney Stine. 1992, *Bette Davis* by Barbara Leaming.

■ Bad Sister 31. Seed 31. Waterloo Bridge 31. Way Back Home 31. The Menace 31. *The Man Who Played God* 32. Hell's House 32. So Big 32. The Rich are Always with Us 32. The Dark Horse 32. *The Cabin in the Cotton* 32. Three on a Match 32. 20,000 Years in Sing Sing 32. Parachute Jumper 32. The Working Man 33. Ex Lady 33. Bureau of Missing Persons 33. Fashions of 1934 34. The Big Shakedown 34. Jimmy the Gent 34. Fog over Frisco 34. *Of Human Bondage* 34. Housewife 34. Bordertown 34. The Girl from Tenth Avenue 35. *Front Page Woman* 35. Special Agent 35. *Dangerous* (AA) 35. The Petrified Forest 36. The Golden Arrow 36. Satan Met a Lady 36. Marked Woman 37. Kid Galahad 37. That Certain Woman 37. It's Love I'm After 37. *Jezebel* (AA) 38. The Sisters 38. *Dark Victory* (AAN) 39. Juarez 39. *The Old Maid* 39. *The Private Lives of Elizabeth and Essex* 39. All This and Heaven Too 40. *The Letter* (AAN) 40. *The Great Lie* 41. The Bride Came COD 41. *The Little Foxes* (AAN) 41. *The Man Who Came to Dinner* 41. In This Our Life 42. *Now Voyager* (AAN) 42. Watch on the Rhine 43. Thank Your Lucky Stars 43. Old Acquaintance 43. *Mr Skeffington* (AAN) 44. Hollywood Canteen 44. *The Corn is Green* 45. A Stolen Life 46. Deception 46. Winter Meeting 48. June Bride 48. Beyond the Forest 49. *All About Eve* (AAN) 50. Payment on Demand 51. Another Man's Poison 51. Phone Call from a Stranger 52. The Star (AAN) 52. The Virgin Queen 55. The Catered Affair 56. Storm Center 56. John Paul Jones 59. The Scapegoat 59. A Pocketful of Miracles 61. *Whatever Happened to Baby Jane?* (AAN) 62. Dead Ringer 64. The Empty Canvas 64. Where Love Has Gone 64. *Hush Hush Sweet Charlotte* 64. *The Nanny* 65. *The Anniversary* 68. Connecting Rooms 69. Bunny O'Hare 71. Madame Sin (TV) 71. The Scientific Cardplayer 72. The Judge and Jake Wyler (TV) 73. Scream Pretty Peggy (TV) 74. Burnt Offerings 76. The Disappearance of Aimée (TV) 76. The Dark Secret of Harvest Home (TV) 78. Return from Witch Mountain 78. Death on the Nile 78. Strangers (TV) 79. White Mama (TV) 79. The Watcher in the Woods 80. Skyward (TV) 81. Family Reunion (TV) 81. *Little Gloria ... Happy at Last* (TV) 82. *A Piano for Mrs Cimino* (TV) 82. Hotel (TV) 83. Right of Way (TV) 83. *The Whales of August* 87. Wicked Stepmother 89.

✪ For her ten-year domination of the 'woman's picture'. *The Great Lie*.

❝ For a girl with no looks, Bette Davis rose fast to the top and stayed there a long time. When she first arrived in Hollywood the official greeter missed her at the station, and his later excuse was: 'No one faintly like an actress got off the train.'

Carl Laemmle is credited with two waspish remarks about her: 'I can't imagine any guy giving her a tumble.'

And: 'She has as much sex appeal as Slim Summerville.'

She herself confesses: 'When I saw my first film test I ran from the projection room screaming.'

She finally settled for a career without glamour: 'Nobody knew what I looked like because I never looked the same way twice.'

Determination carried her through. As her later husband Gary Merrill said: 'Whatever Bette had chosen to do in life, she would have had to be the top or she couldn't have endured it.'

She admitted this herself: 'If Hollywood didn't work out I was all prepared to be the best secretary in the world.'

As David Zinman summarizes: 'All she had going for her was her talent.'

But by 1937 she was at the top of the tree, dishing out hell to those who had dished it out to her. Said her once co-star Brian Aherne: 'Surely no one but a mother could have loved Bette Davis at the height of her career.'

E. Arnot Robertson in 1935 had expressed a similar feeling in a different way: 'She would probably have been burned as a witch if she had lived two or three hundred years ago. She gives the curious feeling of being charged with power which can find no ordinary outlet.'

By the early 50s she was no longer a bankable star, and work was suddenly in short supply. She inserted a full-page ad in the Hollywood trade papers: 'MOTHER OF THREE: divorcee; American. Twenty years experience as an actress in motion pictures. Mobile still and more affable than rumour would have it. Wants steady employment in Hollywood. (Has had Broadway.) References upon request.'

She reflected bitterly on her career at the top: 'I was the only star they allowed to come out of the water looking wet.'

Jack L. Warner however remembered her with affection: 'An explosive little broad with a straight left.'

But despite all difficulties she persevered, and was still acting as she neared eighty. Vincent Canby said: 'Her career has been recycled more often than the average rubber tyre.'

Famous line (*The Cabin in the Cotton*) 'I'd like to kiss yuh, but I just washed my hair.'

Famous line (*All About Eve*) 'Fasten your seat belts, it's going to be a bumpy night.'

Famous line (*Old Acquaintance*) 'There comes a time in every woman's life when the only thing that helps is a glass of champagne.'

Famous line (*Now Voyager*) 'Oh, Jerry, don't let's ask for the moon: we have the stars.'

Davis, Brad (1949–1991)
American leading actor. Died of AIDS.

Midnight Express 77. A Small Circle of Friends 80. Chariots of Fire 81. Querelle 84. Chiefs (TV) 84. Robert Kennedy and his Times (TV) 84. Blood Ties 86. Cold Steel 87. Rosalie Goes Shopping 89. Hangfire 90. Child of Light (TV) 91, etc.

Davis, Carl (1936–)
American composer in Britain, best known for his silent film scores: *Napoleon*, *The Crowd*, Hollywood TV series, etc.

The Bofors Gun 68. Up Pompeii 71. Rentadick 72. Man Friday 75. The Sailor's Return 77. The French Lieutenant's Woman (BFA) 81. The Far Pavilions (TV) 81. King David 85. Scandal 89. The Rainbow 89. Frankenstein Unbound 90. The Trial 94. Widow's Peak 94. Coming Home (TV) 98. Topsy-Turvy 99, etc.

Davis, Desmond (1927–)
British director, former cameraman.

■ *Girl with Green Eyes* 64. The Uncle 65. *I Was Happy Here* 66. Smashing Time 67. A Nice Girl Like Me 69. Clash of the Titans 81. The Sign of Four (TV) 83. The Country Girls (TV) 83. Ordeal by Innocence 84. Camille (TV) 84. Freedom Fighter (TV) 88. The Man Who Lived at the Ritz (TV) 88.

Davis, Gail (1925–1997) (Betty Jeanne Grayson)
American leading lady of westerns, opposite Gene Autry in 15 films and many episodes of his TV show; she also had her own TV series, produced by Autry, and appeared with his rodeo.

Cow Town 50. Valley of Fire 51. Blue Canadian Rockies 52. Goldtown Ghost Riders 52. The Old West 52. On Top of Old Smoky 53. Winning of the West 53, etc.

TV series: Annie Oakley 53–56.

Davis, Geena (1957–)
Tall American leading actress, usually in off-beat roles. Born in Wareham, Massachusetts, she studied at Boston University and began as a model. She is also one of the best women archers in the US. Her career, which reached its peak so far with *Thelma and Louise*, seemed to lose its impetus in the films directed by her then third husband Renny Harlin (1992–97). Her second husband was actor Jeff Goldblum (1987–90).

Tootsie 82. Fletch 84. Transylvania 6–5000 84. The Fly 86. Beetlejuice 88. The Accidental Tourist (AA) 88. Earth Girls Are Easy 89. Quick Change 90. Thelma and Louise (AAN) 91. Hero 92. A League of Their Own 92. Speechless 94. Angie 94. CutThroat Island 95. The Long Kiss Goodnight 96. Stuart Little 99, etc.

TV series: Buffalo Bill 83–84. Sara 85. The Geena Davis Show 00- .

“ It seems that if a woman has a job in a movie now, she's cold and gets no sex – or if she does have sex, then she's either going to be punished for it or she's a psycho killer. – *G.D.*

A feminist spirit in the body of a goddess. – *Premiere*

Davis, Hope (1967?–)
American actress. Born in Tenafly, New Jersey, she studied cognitive science at Vassar.

Flatliners 90. Home Alone 90. Kiss of Death 95. Daytrippers 96. Mr Wrong 96. Guy 96. The Myth of Fingerprints 97. Next Stop, Wonderland 98. Arlington Road 99. Mumford 99. Joe Gould's Secret 00, etc.

TV series: Deadline 00.

Davis, James (Jim) (1915–1981)
Burly American actor who, despite star billing opposite Bette Davis, subsided quickly into second-feature westerns.

White Cargo 42. Swing Shift Maisie 43. Gallant Bess 46. The Fabulous Texan 47. *Winter Meeting* 48. Brimstone 49. Cavalry Scout 52. Woman of the North Country 52. The Fighting 7th 52. The Last Command 55. Timberjack 55. The Maverick Queen 56. Alias Jesse James 59. Fort Utah 66. Rio Lobo 70. Monte Walsh 70. Big Jake 71. The Honkers 72. Bad Company 72. The Deputies (TV) 76. The Choirboys 77. Comes a Horseman 78. The Day Time Ended 80, many others.

TV series: Stories of the Century. *Rescue 8*. *The Cowboys*. Dallas 78–80.

Davis, Joan (1907–1961)
Rubber-faced American comedienne, in show business from infancy, who enlivened many routine musicals of the 30s and 40s.

■ Millions in the Air 35. Bunker Bean 35. The Holy Terror 36. On the Avenue 37. Time Out for Romance 37. Wake Up and Live 37. Angel's Holiday 37. You Can't Have Everything 37. The Great Hospital Mystery 37. Sing and Be Happy 37. *Thin Ice* 37. Life Begins in College 37. Love and Kisses 37. Sally, Irene and Mary 38. Josette 38. My Lucky Star 38. *Hold that Coed* 38. Just Around the Corner 38. Tailspin 39. Daytime Wife 39. Too Busy to Work 39. Free, Blonde and Twenty One 40. Manhattan Heartbeat 40. Sailor's Lady 40. For Beauty's Sake 41. Sun Valley Serenade 41. *Hold that Ghost* 41. Two Latins from Manhattan 42. Yokel Boy 42. Sweetheart of the Fleet 42. He's My Guy 43. Two Señoritas from Chicago 43. Around the World 43. *Show Business* 44. Beautiful but Broke 44. Kansas City Kitty 44. She Gets Her Man 45. *George White's Scandals* 45. She Wrote the Book 46. If You Knew Susie 48. The Traveling Saleswoman 50. Love that Brute 50. The Groom Wore Spurs 51. Harem Girl 53.

TV series: I Married Joan 52–56.

Davis, Sir John (1906–1993)
British executive, a former accountant who became chairman of the Rank Organization. After the artistic extravagance of the mid-40s, he imposed financial stability; but subsequent film production was comparatively routine and in the late 60s dwindled to nothing as the group was diversified into other fields.

Davis, Johnny 'Scat' (1890–1983)
American character actor and singer in Warner's movies, who later beccame a bandleader.

Varsity Show 37. Brother Rat 38. Hollywood Hotel 38. Men Are Such Fools 38. Mr Chump 38. A Child is Born 40. Sarong Girl 43. Knickerbocker Holiday 44. You Can't Ration Love 44, etc.

Davis, Judy (1955–)
Australian leading actress, a former singer. Married actor Colin Friels.

My *Brilliant Career* (BFA) 79. Winter of Our Dreams 81. Hoodwink 81. Heatwave 82. Who Dares Wins 82. A Woman Called Golda (TV) 82. A Passage to India (AAN) 84. Kangaroo 86. High Tide 87. Georgia 88. Impromptu 89. Alice 90. Barton Fink 91. Where Angels Fear to Tread 91. Naked Lunch 91. *Husbands and Wives* (AAN) 92. The Ref 94. The New Age 94. Children of the Revolution 96. Blood & Wine 96. Deconstructing Harry 97. Absolute Power 97. Echo of Thunder (TV) 98. Celebrity 98, etc.. Dash and Lilly (TV) 99, etc.

“ She's the patron saint of modern emotions. – *Michael Tolkin*

Davis, Lilian Hall (1896–1933) (aka Lillian Hall-Davis)
Blonde English leading actress of the silent era and star of two of Hitchcock's early movies. Born in London, she was in films from childhood, but failed to make the transition to sound and committed suicide.

The Admirable Crichton 18. The Better 'Ole 18. The Honey Pot 20. The Game of Life 22. Brown Sugar 22. The Faithful Heart 22. A Royal Divorce 23. The Knock Out 23. Pagliacci 23. Should a Doctor Tell 23. Quo Vadis? 24. Roses of Picardy 27. The Ring 27. Blighty 27. The Farmer's Wife 28. Many Waters 31. Volga Volga 33, etc.

Davis, Marc (1913–2000)
American animator and designer for Walt Disney. He joined the studio in 1935 and was responsible for creating Bambi and Thumper for *Bambi*, Alice for *Alice in Wonderland*, *Tinker Bell* for Peter Pan, The princess and Maleficent for *Sleeping Beauty*, and Cruella De Vil for *101 Dalmatians*.

Davis, Martin S. (1927–1999)
American production executive. He resigned as chairman and chief executive of Paramount in April 1994.

Davis, Miles (1926–1991)
Innovative American jazz trumpeter, composer and actor. He was married to actress Cicely Tyson (1981–89).

Lift to the Scaffold/Ascenseur pour l'Echafaud (m) 57. Jack Johnson (m) 71. Siesta (m) 87. Dingo – Dog of the Desert (a, m) 91.

Davis, Nancy (1921–) (Anne Frances Robbins)
American leading lady of a few 50s films; married Ronald Reagan.

East Side West Side 49. Shadow on the Wall 49. The Next Voice You Hear 50. Night into Morning 51. Shadow in the Sky 51. It's a Big Country 52. Talk About a Stranger 52. Donovan's Brain 53. Hellcats of the Navy 57, etc.

Davis, Ossie (1917–)
American actor of massive presence.

No Way Out 50. The Joe Louis Story 53. Gone Are the Days (& w) 63. *The Hill* 65. *The Scalphunters* 68. Sam Whiskey 69. Slaves 69. Cotton Comes to Harlem (d only) 70. Kongi's Harvest (d only) 71. Black Girl (d only) 72. Malcolm X 72. Gordon's War (d only) 73. Let's Do It Again 75. Hot Stuff 79. Harry and Son 83. Avenging Angel 84. School Daze 88. Do the Right Thing 89. Joe versus the Volcano 90. Jungle Fever 91. Gladiator 92. Queen (TV) 93. Grumpy Old Men 93. Ray Alexander: A Taste for Justice (TV) 94. The Stand (TV) 94. The Client 94. I'm Not Rapaport 96. Get on the Bus 96. Twelve Angry Men (TV) 97. Miss Evers' Boys (TV) 97. Dr Dolittle 98. Dinosaur (voice) 00, etc.

Davis, Philip (1953–)
English actor, director and writer, usually in working-class roles and sometimes credited as Phil Davies. He began with the National Youth Theatre.

As actor: Quilp 74. Quadrophenia 79. Pink Floyd: The Wall 82. The Bounty 84. The Doctor and the Devils 85. Comrades 87. *High Hopes* 88. Howling V: The Rebirth 89. Blue Ice 92. Crimetime 96. Face 97. Photographing Fairies 97. Still Crazy 98, etc.

As director: i.d. 95.

TV series: Moving Story 94–95. North Square 00.

Davis, Sammi (1964–)
British actress.

Mona Lisa 86. Hope and Glory 87. Lionheart 87. A Prayer for the Dying 87. Consuming Passions 88. The Lair of the White Worm 88. The Rainbow 89. Chernobyl: The Final Warning (TV) 91. Shadow of China 91. Four Rooms (US) 95. Stand-Ins (US) 97. Woundings (US) 98, etc.

Davis Jnr, Sammy (1925–1990)
American singer and entertainer, a bundle of vitality who described himself as 'a one-eyed Jewish Negro'. His second wife was actress Mai Britt (1960–67).

Autobiography: 1966, *Yes I Can*. 1980, *Hollywood in a Suitcase*. 1989, *Why Me?*

Biography: 1996, *Sammy Davis Jnr, My Father* by Tracey Davis.

■ Rufus Jones for President (debut) 29. Season's Greetings 30. *Anna Lucasta* 58. *Porgy and Bess* 59. *Ocean's Eleven* 60. Pepe 60. A Raisin in the Sun 61. Sergeants Three 62. Convicts Four 62. Nightmare in the Sun 63. Johnny Cool 63. Robin and the Seven Hoods 64. The Threepenny Opera 65. A Man Called Adam 66. Salt and Pepper 68. Sweet Charity 68. Man without Mercy 69. Gone with the West 69. The Pigeon (TV) 70. One More Time 70. The Trackers (TV) 71. Diamonds Are Forever 71. Poor Devil (TV) 73. Cinderella at the Palace (TV) 78. Stop the World I Want to Get Off 78. Little Moon and Jud McGraw 78. The Cannonball Run 81. Heidi's Song 82. Cracking Up 83. Cannonball Run II 84. Moon over Parador 88. Tap 89.

Davis, Stringer (1896–1973)
Gentle-mannered British character actor who was usually to be found playing small roles in the films of his wife Margaret Rutherford.

The Happiest Days of Your Life 50. Curtain Up 53. Murder at the Gallop 63. Murder Most Foul 64. Murder Ahoy 64, etc.

Davis, Tamra (1962–)
American director, from rock videos.

Guncrazy 92. CB4 93. Billy Madison 95. Half-Baked 97. Half Baked 98. Skipped Parts 00, etc.

“ Most of Hollywood's so-called women's movies are based on men's fantasies. – *T.D.*

Davison, Bruce (1946–)
Slightly-built young American character actor.

Last Summer 69. The Strawberry Statement 70. *Willard* 71. The Jerusalem File 71. Ulzana's Raid 72. The Affair (TV) 73. Mame 74. Mother, Jugs and Speed 76. Short Eyes 77. Brass Target 78. High Risk 81. Crimes of Passion 84. Spies Like Us 85. The Ladies Club 86. The Misfit Brigade 86. Longtime Companion (AAN) 90. Steel and Lace 91. Oscar 91. An Ambush of Ghosts 93. Short Cuts 93. Six Degrees of Separation 93. Far from Home: The Adventures of Yellow Dog 94. Homage 95. The Cure 95. The Crucible 96. Grace of my Heart 96. It's My Party 96. Hidden in America (TV) 96. Lovelife 97. Apt Pupil 97. Paulie 98. Locked in Silence (TV) 99. At First Sight 99. Vendetta (TV) 99. X-Men 00, etc.

TV series: Hunter 85–86. Harry and the Hendersons 90–92.

D'Avril, Yola (1907–1984)
French actress and dancer who went to North America in the 20s, arriving in Hollywood in the mid-20s, where she first worked as an extra.

Lady Be Good 28. *All Quiet on the Western Front* 30. The Bad One 30. The Man from Yesterday 32. I Met Him in Paris 37. Little Boy Lost 53, etc.

Daw, Evelyn (1912–1970)
American leading lady of the 30s.

Something to Sing About 37. Panamint's Bad Man 38, etc.

Dawson, Anthony (1916–1992)
Lean-faced British character actor.

The Way to the Stars 45. The Queen of Spades 48. The Long Dark Hall 51. Valley of Eagles 51. Dial M For Murder 54. That Lady 55. Action of the Tiger 57. The Hour of Decision 57. Grip of the Strangler 58. The Snorkel 58. Libel 59. Tiger Bay 59. Midnight Lace 60. Offbeat 60. The Curse of the Werewolf 61. Doctor No 62. Seven Seas to Calais 62. Death Rides a Horse 67. Vengeance 68, etc.

Dawson, Anthony M.
See Margheriti, Antonio.

Dawson, Hal K. (1896–1987)
American character actor, usually in subservient roles.

Another Language 33. My American Wife 36. A Night at the Movies 37. Just Around the Corner 38. The Great Victor Herbert 39. Weekend in Havana 41. Baby Face Morgan 42. Song of the Islands 42. Coney Island 43. Guest Wife 45. The Shocking Miss Pilgrim 47. Wabash Avenue 50. Superman and the Mole Men 51. The Captive City 51. The Yellow Mountain 54. Cattle Empire 58. The Alligator People 59, many others.

Dawson, Marion (1889–1975)
English actress who began as an opera singer and switched to comedy when her voice failed. Her screen career faltered after she lost an eye in an accident with fireworks in 1932.

The Last Coupon 32. His Wife's Mother 32. The Love Nest 33. A Political Party 34. Save a Little Sunshine 38, etc.

Dawson, Ralph (1897–1962)
American editor.

Lady of the Night 25. The Singing Fool 28. Outward Bound 30. Girl Missing 33. The Story of Louis Pasteur 35. A Midsummer Night's Dream 35. Anthony Adverse 36. The Adventures of Robin Hood 38. Ivy 47. All My Sons 48. Undertow 49. Harvey 50. Island in the Sky 53. The High and the Mighty 54, many others.

Day, Clarence (1874–1935)
American humorist whose light pieces about his family were the basis for the apparently immortal play *Life with Father*, which was successfully filmed in 1947.

Day, Dennis (1921–1988) (Eugene Patrick McNulty)
American singer and light actor of the 40s and 50s, most familiar from Jack Benny's radio and TV show.
Buck Benny Rides Again 40. Music in Manhattan 44. One Sunday Afternoon 48. I'll Get By 50. Golden Girl 51. The Girl Next Door 53, etc.

Day, Doris (1924–) (Doris Kappelhoff)
Vivacious American dance-band singer who achieved instant star status in 1948 and preserved her eminence by transferring to a brand of innocent sex comedy which was all her own and pleased the 60s.
Biography: 1976, *Doris Day, Her Own Story* by A. E. Hotchner. 1992, *Doris Day* by Eric Braun.
■ *Romance on the High Seas* 48. My Dream is Yours 49. It's a Great Feeling 49. Young Man with a Horn 50. Tea for Two 50. West Point Story 50. *Storm Warning* 50. Lullaby of Broadway 51. *On Moonlight Bay* 51. I'll See You in My Dreams 51. Starlift 51. The Winning Team 52. April in Paris 52. By the Light of the Silvery Moon 53. *Calamity Jane* 53. Lucky Me 54. *Young at Heart* 55. Love Me or Leave Me 55. The Man Who Knew Too Much 56. Julie 56. *The Pajama Game* 57. Teacher's Pet 58. The Tunnel of Love 58. It Happened to Jane 59. *Pillow Talk* (AAN) 59. Please Don't Eat the Daisies 60. Midnight Lace 60. Lover Come Back 62. *That Touch of Mink* 62. Jumbo 62. The Thrill of It All 63. Move Over Darling 63. Send Me No Flowers 64. Do Not Disturb 65. The Glass Bottom Boat 66. Caprice 67. The Ballad of Josie 68. Where Were You When the Lights Went Out? 68. With Six You Get Egg Roll 68. That's Entertainment! III 94.
TV series: *The Doris Day Show* 68–72. Doris Day's Best Friends 85.
✪ For her box-office domination of 60s comedies by playing the perennial virgin. *That Touch of Mink*.
❝ I've been around so long I can remember Doris Day before she was a virgin. – *Groucho Marx*
She thinks she doesn't get old. She told me once it was her cameraman who was getting older. She was going to fire him. – *Joe Pasternak*
Just about the remotest person I know. – *Kirk Douglas*
No one guessed that under all those dirndls lurked one of the wildest asses in Hollywood. – *Ross Hunter*
My doctor won't let me watch Doris Day. I have a family history of diabetes. – *Marvin Kitman*
Underneath her wholesome exterior beat the heart of a true sex goddess and a very strong woman. – *Debbie Harry*

Day, Ernest (1927–)
British cinematographer and occasional director.
Running Scared 72. Visit to a Chief's Son 74. Ghost in a Noonday Sun 74. Made 75. The Song Remains the Same 76. The Revenge of the Pink Panther 78. Sphinx 80. Green Ice (co-d) 81. Waltz across Texas (d) 83. A Passage to India (AAN) 84. Superman IV: The Quest for Peace 87. Burning Secret 88. Parents 88, etc.

Day, Frances (1907–1984) (Frances Victoria Schenk)
American revue star, in London from 1925.
■ The Price of Divorce 27. OK Chief 30. Big Business 30. The First Mrs Frazer 32. Two Hearts in Waltztime 34. The Girl from Maxim's 34. Temptation 34. Oh Daddy 34. Public Nuisance No. 1 36. You Must Get Married 36. Dreams Come True 36. Who's Your Lady Friend? 37. The Girl in the Taxi 37. Kicking the Moon Around 38. Room for Two 40. *Fiddlers Three* (as Poppaea) 44. Tread Softly 52. There's Always a Thursday 57. Climb up the Wall 60.
❝ Little Day, you've had a busy man. – *Bud Flanagan, when F.D. turned up for rehearsals looking decidedly shaggy*

Day, Jill (1932–1990)
British pop singer and leading lady.
Always a Bride 54. All for Mary 55, etc.

Day, Josette (1914–1978) (J. Dagory)
French leading lady.
Allo Berlin, Ici Paris 32. La Fille du Puisatier 40. *La Belle et la Bête* 46. La Fille du Puisatier 46. Les Parents Terribles 48. Four Days' Leave 50, etc.

Day, Laraine (1917–) (Laraine Johnson)
American leading lady of the 40s, with stage experience.
Autobiography: 1952, *Day With The Giants*.
Stella Dallas 37. Scandal Street 38. Border G-Men 38. *Young Dr Kildare* (and others in the series) 39. My Son, My Son 40. *Foreign Correspondent* 40. *The Trial of Mary Dugan* 41. Unholy Partners 41. Fingers at the Window 41. Journey for Margaret 42. Mr Lucky 43. The Story of Dr Wassell 43. Bride by Mistake 44. Those Endearing Young Charms 45. Keep Your Powder Dry 45. *The Locket* 46. Tycoon 47. My Dear Secretary 48. I Married a Communist 49. Without Honour 49. The High and the Mighty 54. Toy Tiger 56. Three for Jamie Dawn 57. The Third Voice 59. Murder on Flight 502 (TV) 75. Return to Fantasy Island (TV) 78, etc.

Day, Matt
Australian actor, from the theatre.
Muriel's Wedding 94. Love and Other Catastrophes 96. Dating the Enemy 96. Kiss or Kill 97. Doing Time for Patsy Cline 97. Muggers 98, etc.
TV series: Water Rats 95–96.

Day, Richard (1896–1972)
Canadian-born production designer, in Hollywood from 1918.
Foolish Wives 22. Greed 24. The Merry Widow 25. The Student Prince 27. Queen Kelly 28. Whoopee (AAN) 30. The Front Page 31. Rain 32. Arrowsmith (AAN) 32. Moulin Rouge 34. The Affairs of Cellini (AAN) 34. *The Dark Angel* (AA) 35. *We Live Again* 35. Clive of India 35. *Dodsworth* (AA) 36. Dead End (AAN) 37. Goldwyn Follies (AAN) 38. Lillian Russell (AAN) 40. Down Argentine Way (AAN) 40. *How Green Was My Valley* (AA) 41. Tobacco Road 41. *The Little Foxes* 41. Blood and Sand (AAN) 41. This Above All (AA) 42. My Gal Sal (AA) 42. Orchestra Wives 42. The Razor's Edge (AAN) 46. Joan of Arc (AAN) 48. *A Streetcar Named Desire* (AA) 51. Hans Christian Andersen (AAN) 52. *On the Waterfront* (AA) 54. Solomon and Sheba 59. Exodus 60. The Chase 66. Valley of the Dolls 67. The Greatest Story Ever Told (AAN) 65. Tora! Tora! Tora! (AAN) 70, etc.

Day, Robert (1922–)
British director, former cameraman.
The Green Man 57. Grip of the Strangler 58. First Man into Space 58. Corridors of Blood 59. Bobbikins 59. Two-Way Stretch 60. The Rebel 61. Operation Snatch 62. Tarzan's Three Challenges 64. She 65. Tarzan and the Valley of Gold 66. Tarzan and the Great River 67. Ritual of Evil (TV) 69. The House on Greenapple Road (TV) 70. Banyon (TV) 71. In Broad Daylight (TV) 71. Mr and Mrs Bo Jo Jones (TV) 71. Death Stalk (TV) 75. Switch (TV) 75. Having Babies (TV) 76. Logan's Run (TV) 77. The Initiation of Sarah (TV) 77. The Grass Is Always Greener Over the Septic Tank (TV) 78. *Murder by Natural Causes* (TV) 79. Walking Through the Fire (TV) 79. The Man with Bogart's Face 80. Peter and Paul (TV) 81. Running Out (TV) 83. Hollywood Wives (TV) 85. Love, Mary (TV) 85. The Quick and the Dead (TV) 87. Higher Ground (TV) 88, etc.

Day, Vera (1939–)
Bubbly blonde British actress.
Dance Little Lady 52. A Kid for Two Farthings 55. It's a Great Day 56. Hell Drivers 57. Quatermass II 57. The Prince and the Showgirl 57. Up the Creek 58. I Was Monty's Double 58. Too Many Crooks 59. Watch It Sailor 61. Saturday Night Out 63, etc.

Day-Lewis, Daniel (1957–)
British leading actor. He is the son of Cecil Day-Lewis, poet laureate, and actress Jill Balcon.
Biography: 1995, *Daniel Day-Lewis* by Laura Jackson.
Gandhi 83. The Bounty 84. My Beautiful Laundrette 85. A Room with a View 85. Nanou 87. Stars and Bars 88. The Unbearable Lightness of Being 88. Eversmile, New Jersey 89. My Left Foot (AA) 89. The Last of the Mohicans 92. The Age of Innocence 93. *In the Name of the Father* (AAN) 93. The Crucible 96. The Boxer 97, etc.
❝ You always, in the end, believe you're a fraud. – *D.D-L.*

De Acosta, Mercedes (1893–1968)
American screenwriter and dramatist, the daughter of Spanish and Cuban parents, whose lasting claim to fame is that she was the lover of, among others, actresses Eva Le Gallienne, Ona Munson (Belle Watling in *Gone with the Wind*), Greta Garbo and Marlene Dietrich.
Autobiography: 1960, *Here Lies the Heart*.
Biography: 1994, *Loving Garbo* by Hugo Vickers.
❝ You can't dismiss Mercedes lightly. She has had two of the most important women in the United States – Garbo and Dietrich. – *Alice B. Toklas*

De Almeida, Joaquim (1957–)
Leading Portuguese actor, in international films.
The Honorary Consul/Beyond the Limit 83. Good Morning Babylon 87. Clear and Present Danger 94. Only You 94. According to Pereira 95. Desperado 95. Adam and Eve/Adao e Eva 96. Nostromo (TV) 96. Larry McMurtry's Dead Man's Walk (TV) 96. One Man's Hero 98. Vendetta (TV) 99. La Cucaracha 99. April Captains/Capitaes De Abril 00, etc.

De Anda, Peter (1940–)
American leading man of the 70s. In the 90s, he was working in a bookshop in Manhattan.
Cutter (TV) 72. Come Back Charleston Blue 72. The New Centurions 72. Beulah Land (TV) 80, etc.
TV series: One Life to Live 68–70.

De Angelis, Guido
Italian composer, in collaboration with Maurizio De Angelis.
They Call Me Trinity 70. Trinity Is Still My Name 71. All the Way Boys 73. Run Run Joe 74. Zorro 75. Keoma/The Violent Breed 76. Charleston 78. Killer Fish 79. Between Miracles 79. Safari Express 80. The Immortal Bachelor 80. Great White 82. Blue Paradise 82. Yor, the Hunter from the Future 83. Body Beat 89, etc.

De Angelis, Maurizio
Italian composer, in collaboration with Guido De Angelis (see entry for films).

De Antonio, Emile (1920–1989)
American experimental documentarist.
Point of Order 64. Rush to Judgment 67. America Is Hard to See 68. In the Year of the Pig 69. Milhouse 71. Painters Painting 73. Underground 76. In the King of Prussia 82. Mr Hoover and I 89, etc.

De Banzie, Brenda (1915–1981)
British character actress who got her big chance on the edge of middle age; later played flouncy matrons.
The Long Dark Hall 51. I Believe in You 52. *Hobson's Choice* 54. The Purple Plain 54. What Every Woman Wants 54. A Kid for Two Farthings 55. The Man Who Knew Too Much 56. The 39 Steps 59. *The Entertainer* 60. Flame in the Streets 61. The Mark 61. The Pink Panther 63. Pretty Polly 67, etc.

De Benning, Burr
American character actor.
Beach Red 67. Sweet November 69. City Beneath the Sea (TV) 71. St Ives 76. The Incredible Melting Man 77. Hanging by a Thread (TV) 79. A Nightmare on Elm Street 5: The Dream Child 89, etc.

De Bont, Jan (1943–)
Dutch cinematographer turned director, in Hollywood from the mid-80s. *Speed*, his first feature, was a success, his asking price as director rising to $4m. He followed it with *Twister*, another hit. He is co-founder of the production company Blue Tulip.
Turkish Delight/Turks Fruit 73. Katie's Passion/Keetje Tippel 75. Max Havelaar 76. Private Lessons 81. I'm Dancing as Fast as I Can 82. Cujo 83. All the Right Moves 83. The Fourth Man/De Vierde Man 83. Flesh and Blood 85. The Jewel of the Nile 85. Ruthless People 86. The Clan of the Cave Bear 86. Who's That Girl? 87. Leonard Part 6 87. Die Hard 88. Black Rain 89. Bert Rigby, You're a Fool 89. The Hunt for Red October 90. Flatliners 90. Basic Instinct 92. Shining Through 92. Lethal Weapon 3 92. *Speed* (d) 94. Twister (d) 96. Speed 2: Cruise Control (& co-w) 97, etc.

De Borba, Dorothy (1925–)
American child actress, in the Our Gang comedies 1930–35.

De Borman, John
British cinematographer.
Death Machine 94. The Passion of Darkly Noon 95. Small Faces 95. The Full Monty 97. Photographing Fairies 97. Trojan Eddie 97. Hideous Kinky 98. The Mighty (US) 98. Gregory's Two Girls 99. Saving Grace 00. Hamlet (US) 00. There's Only One Jimmy Grimble 00. New Year's Day 00, etc.

De Bray, Yvonne (1889–1954)
French character actress, in films from 1943.
Gigi 48. *Les Parents Terribles* 48. Olivia 50. Caroline Chérie 50. Nous Sommes Tous des Assassins 52, etc.

De Broca, Philippe (1933–)
French director and screenwriter who first worked as an assistant to François Truffaut and Claude Chabrol.
Les Jeux de l'Amour 60. Le Farceur 60. The Seven Deadly Sins (part) 61. L'Amant de Cinq Jours 61. Cartouche 62. *Les Veinards* (part) 63. *That Man from Rio* 63. Un Monsieur de Compagnie 64. Les Tribulations d'un Chinois en Chine 65. The Oldest Profession 67. King of Hearts 67. Devil by the Tail 68. Give Her the Moon 70. La Poudre d'Escampette 71. Chère Louise 72. Le Magnifique 73. Dear Inspector 77. Psy 80. On a Volé la Cuisse de Jupiter 80. Louisiana 84. The Gypsy 85. Chouans! 88. The 1001 Nights/Sheherazade (wd) 90. The Keys of Paradise/Les Clés du Paradis 91. Tales from the Zoo 95. On Guard! (co-w, d) 97, etc.

De Brulier, Nigel (1878–1948)
British actor in Hollywood: career waned with sound.
Intolerance 16. The Four Horsemen of the Apocalypse 21. The Three Musketeers (as Richelieu) 21. Salome 23. The Hunchback of Notre Dame 23. Ben Hur 26. Wings 27. Noah's Ark 29. The Iron Mask 29. Moby Dick 31. Rasputin and the Empress 32. Mary of Scotland 36. The Garden of Allah 36. The Hound of the Baskervilles 39. One Million B.C. 40. The Adventures of Captain Marvel 41, many others.

De Camp, Rosemary (1910–2001)
American character actress specializing in active motherly types. She was eleven years James Cagney's junior – but in *Yankee Doodle Dandy* she played his mother.
Cheers for Miss Bishop 41. Jungle Book 42. This is the Army 43. *The Merry Monahans* 44. *Rhapsody in Blue* 45. From this Day Forward 46. Nora Prentiss 47. Night unto Night 49. The Big Hangover 50. *On Moonlight Bay* 51. By the Light of the Silvery Moon 53. Many Rivers to Cross 55. Thirteen Ghosts 60. Blind Ambition (TV) 79. Saturday the 14th 81, etc.
TV series: The Life of Riley 49–50. *The Bob Cummings Show* 55–59. That Girl 66–70.

De Carlo, Yvonne (1922–) (Peggy Middleton)
Canadian leading lady, a star in the 40s of Hollywood's most outrageous easterns and westerns.
Salome Where She Danced 45. Frontier Gal 45. Song of Scheherezade 47. Brute Force 47. Slave Girl 47. Black Bart (as Lola Montez) 48. Casbah 48. River Lady 48. *Criss Cross* 49. Calamity Jane and Sam Bass 49. The Desert Hawk 50. Tomahawk 51. Hotel Sahara 51. Scarlet Angel 52. Sea Devils 52. Sombrero 53. The Captain's Paradise 53. Passion 54. Magic Fire 56. The Ten Commandments 56. Death of a Scoundrel 56. Band of Angels 57. McLintock 63. Law of the Lawless 64. Munster Go Home 66. The Power 68. The Seven Minutes 71. Guyana Cult of the Damned 80. The Man with Bogart's Face 80. Liar's Moon 82. Flesh and Bullets 85. A Masterpiece of Murder (TV) 86. American Gothic 88. Oscar 91, etc.
TV series: *The Munsters* 64–65.

De Casalis, Jeanne (1897–1966)
British revue comedienne and character actress, best known as radio's 'Mrs Feather' in dithery

telephone monologues. She was married to Colin Clive.

Autobiography: 1953, *Things I Don't Remember*.

Settled out of Court 25. The Arcadians 27. Nell Gwyn 34. Cottage to Let 41. Charley's Big Hearted Aunt 41. Those Kids from Town 42. Medal for the General 44. This Man Is Mine 46. Woman Hater 48, etc.

De Cordoba, Pedro (1881–1950)
American stage actor, lean and often sinister, in many silent and sound films.

Carmen 15. Maria Rosa 16. Runaway Romany 20. Young Diana 22. The Crusades 35. Anthony Adverse 36. The Light That Failed 39. The Ghost Breakers 40. The Mark of Zorro 40. Son of Fury 42. For Whom the Bell Tolls 43. The Beast with Five Fingers 47. When the Redskins Rode 50, etc.

De Cordova, Arturo (1908–1973) (Arturo Garcia)
Mexican leading man with flashing grin and impudent eyes. Popular in Mexico from 1935; made a few Hollywood films in the 40s.

For Whom the Bell Tolls 43. Hostages 43. *Frenchman's Creek* 44. Incendiary Blonde 44. A Medal for Benny 45. Masquerade in Mexico 45. The Flame 47. New Orleans 47. The Adventures of Casanova 48. *El* (Mex.) 51. Kill Him for Me 53, etc.

De Cordova, Frederick (1910–)
American director with stage and TV experience.

■ Too Young to Know 45. Her Kind of Man 46. That Way with Women 47. Love and Learn 47. Always Together 47. Wallflower 48. For the Love of Mary 48. The Countess of Monte Cristo 48. Illegal Entry 49. The Gal Who Took the West 49. Buccaneer's Girl 50. Peggy 50. The Desert Hawk 50. Bedtime for Bonzo 51. Katie Did It 51. Little Egypt 51. Finders Keepers 51. Here Come the Nelsons 52. Bonzo Goes to College 52. Yankee Buccaneer 53. Column South 53. I'll Take Sweden 65. Frankie and Johnny 66.

De Corsia, Ted (1904–1973)
American character actor with long vaudeville experience; usually played surly villains.

The Lady from Shanghai 48. The Naked City 48. It Happens Every Spring 49. Neptune's Daughter 49. Cargo to Capetown 50. The Enforcer 50. Three Secrets 50. Inside the Walls of Folsom Prison 51. Vengeance Valley 51. Captain Pirate 52. Man in the Dark 53. Crime Wave 54. Twenty Thousand Leagues under the Sea 54. The Big Combo 55. The Conqueror 55. The Killing 56. Mohawk 56. Slightly Scarlet 56. Baby Face Nelson 57. The Joker Is Wild 57. The Buccaneer 58. Enchanted Island 58. Blood on the Arrow 64. The Quick Gun 64. Nevada Smith 66. Five Card Stud 68, many others.

TV series: Steve Canyon 57–60.

De Courville, Albert (1887–1960)
British stage director who directed a few film comedies.

Wolves 30. The Midshipmaid 32. This is the Life 33. Things Are Looking Up 34. The Case of Gabriel Perry 35. Seven Sinners 36. Crackerjack 38. The Lambeth Walk 38. An Englishman's Home 39, etc.

DeCuir, John (1918–)
American production designer.

Naked City 48. The Snows of Kilimanjaro 51. Call Me Mister 52. The King and I 56. South Pacific 57. Cleopatra 63. The Agony and the Ecstasy 65. Hello Dolly 69. The Great White Hope 70. Once is not Enough 75. Raise the Titanic 80. Dead Men Don't Wear Plaid 82. Ghostbusters 84. Jo Jo Dancer, Your Life Is Calling 86. Legal Eagles 86, etc.

De Filippo, Eduardo (1900–1984) (Eduardo Passarelli)
Italian actor and director of many and varied talents.

Tre Uomini in Frac (a) 32. Il Capello a Tre Punte (a) 40. In Campagna e Caduta una Stella (w, d, a) 40. Il Sogno di Tutti (a) 40. La Vita Ricomincia (a) 45. Assunta Spina (w, a) 47. Napoli Milionaria (w, d, a) 50. Altri Tempi (a) 51. Filumena Marturano (w, d, a) 51. The Girls of the Spanish Steps (a) 52. Villa Borghese (a) 53. Napoletani a Milano (w, d, a) 53. Questi Fantasmi (w, d, a) 54. Fortunella (d, a) 58. Raw Wind in Eden (a) 58. Ghosts of Rome (a) 60. Shoot Loud, Louder, I Don't Understand (w, d, a) 66, many others.

DeFore, Don (1917–1993)
American second lead, the good guy or dumb hearty westerner of dozens of forgettable films in the 40s and 50s. Born in Cedar Rapids, Iowa, he studied acting at the Pasadena Community School Theater and was onstage from the mid 30s. He was also credited as Don Defore.

You Can't Escape Forever 42. A Guy Named Joe 43. Thirty Seconds Over Tokyo 44. The Affairs of Susan 45. You Came Along 45. Ramrod 47. Romance on the High Seas 48. Too Late for Tears 48. My Friend Irma 49. Dark City 50. The Guy Who Came Back 51. She's Working Her Way Through College 52. Battle Hymn 57. The Facts of Life 61. A Rare Breed (TV) 81, etc.

TV series: Ozzie and Harriet 52–58. Hazel 61–65.

De Forest, Lee (1873–1961)
American inventor, pioneer of many developments in wireless telegraphy, also the De Forest Phonofilm of the 20s, an early experiment in synchronized sound.

De Funès, Louis (1908–1983)
French character comedian.

The Seven Deadly Sins 52. Femmes de Paris 54. The Sheep Has Five Legs 54. Candide 60. Don't Look Now … We're Being Shot At! 66. Up a Tree 70. The Mad Adventures of Rabbi Jacob/Les Aventures de Rabbi Jacob 73. What's Cooking in Paris 77. Les Charlots 79. L'Avare 80, many others.

DeGeneres, Ellen (1958–)
American actress and stand-up comedian, best known for her title role in the TV sitcom *Ellen*. She caused a minor sensation in 1997 when she (as well as the character she plays in the sitcom) announced that she was a lesbian, and that her partner was actress Anne HECHE. Her sitcom was cancelled soon after the announcement. (The couple announced their separation in 2000.)

Coneheads 93. Mr Wrong 95. Goodbye, Lover 98. Doctor Dolittle (voice) 98. EdTV 99. The Love Letter 99. If These Walls Could Talk II (TV) 00, etc.

TV series: Open House 89–90. Ellen 92–98.

De' Giorgi, Elsa (1915–1997)
Leading Italian actress of the 30s and 40s, who turned in the 50s to writing novels and running an acting school. Her lovers included novelist Italo Calvino.

Autobiography: 1955, *I Coetantei*.

I'll Always Love You/T'Amero Sempre 33. Nini Falpala 33. Porto 35. Ma Non e Una Cosa Seria 36. La Mazurka di Papa 38. Il Fornaretto di Venezia 39. La Sposa dei Re 39. Capitan Fracassa 40. Fra Diavolo 42. La Locandiera 44. Manu, il Contrabbandiere 48. Salo, the 120 Days of Sodom 75, etc.

De Govia, Jackson
American production designer.

Boulevard Nights 79. Butch and Sundance, the Early Years 79. It's My Turn 80. My Bodyguard 80. Spacehunter: Adventures in the Forbidden Zone 83. Red Dawn 84. Remo Williams: The Adventure Begins 85. 'Night, Mother 86. Nobody's Fool 86. Roxanne 87. Punchline 88. Die Hard 88. In Country 89. Dad 89. Sister Act 92. Speed 94. Multiplicity 96. Volcano 97. My Giant 98, etc.

De Grasse, Robert (1900–1971)
American cinematographer, with RKO from 1934.

Three Pals 26. Fury of the Wild 29. Break of Hearts 35. *Stage Door* 37. The Story of Vernon and Irene Castle 39. Bachelor Mother 39. Kitty Foyle 40. Forever and a Day 43. Step Lively 44. *The Body Snatcher* 45. The Miracle of the Bells 48. Home of the Brave 49. The Men 50. Chicago Calling 52, many others.

De Grasse, Sam (1875–1953)
Canadian leading actor, often in villainous roles. In films from 1912.

Birth of a Nation 15. Intolerance 16. The Scarlet Car 17. Robin Hood (as Prince John) 22. The Spoilers 23. The Black Pirate 26. King of Kings 27. The Farmer's Daughter 28. Wall Street 29. Captain of the Guard 30, etc.

De Grunwald, Anatole (1910–1967)
British producer, in films since 1939.

French Without Tears (w) 39. Quiet Wedding (w) 40. The First of the Few (w) 42. The Demi-Paradise 42. The Way to the Stars 45. The Winslow Boy (& w) 48. The Holly and the Ivy (& w) 54. The Doctor's Dilemma 58. Libel (& w) 61. Come Fly with Me 62. The VIPs 63. The Yellow Rolls-Royce 64. Stranger in the House 67, many others.

De Grunwald, Dmitri (1914–1990)
British producer, brother of Anatole de Grunwald.

The Dock Brief 62. Perfect Friday 67. Connecting Rooms 69. The Last Grenade 69. Murphy's War 71. That Lucky Touch 75, etc.

De Haven, Carter (1887–1977)
American stage star who appeared in a few silent films. His son *Carter de Haven Jnr* (1910–1979) was a production manager, especially for Chaplin.

De Haven, Gloria (1924–)
American soubrette, films mostly light musicals of no enduring quality.

■ Modern Times 36. The Great Dictator 40. Susan and God 40. Keeping Company 41. Two Faced Woman 41. The Penalty 41. *Best Foot Forward* 43. Thousands Cheer 43. Broadway Rhythm 44. *Two Girls and a Sailor* 44. Step Lively 44. The Thin Man Goes Home 44. Between Two Women 45. Summer Holiday 48. Scene of the Crime 49. The Doctor and the Girl 49. Yes Sir That's My Baby 49. The Yellow Cab Man 50. Three Little Words 50. Summer Stock 50. I'll Get By 50. Two Tickets to Broadway 51. Down among the Sheltering Palms 53. So This Is Paris 55. The Girl Rush 55. Call Her Mom (TV) 72. Who Is the Black Dahlia? (TV) 75. Banjo Hackett (TV) 76. Sharon, Portrait of a Mistress 77. Evening in Byzantium (TV) 78. Bog 84. The Legend of O. B. Taggart 94. That's Entertainment! III 94. Out to Sea 97.

TV series: Ryan's Hope 75. Nakia 79.

De Havilland, Olivia (1916–)
British-born leading lady, sister of Joan Fontaine. In Hollywood from teenage as leading lady of comedy, romance and costume drama; later proved herself an actress.

Autobiography: 1960, *Every Frenchman Has One*.

■ *A Midsummer Night's Dream* 35. The Irish in Us 35. Alibi Ike 35. Captain Blood 35. Anthony Adverse 36. The Charge of the Light Brigade 36. Call It a Day 36. The Great Garrick 36. It's Love I'm After 37. Gold Is Where You Find It 37. Four's a Crowd 38. *The Adventures of Robin Hood* 38. Hard To Get 38. Wings of the Navy 39. Dodge City 39. *Gone with the Wind* (AAN) 39. Elizabeth and Essex 39. Raffles 40. My Love Came Back 40. Santa Fe Trail 40. Strawberry Blonde 41. Hold Back the Dawn (AAN) 41. They Died with Their Boots On 41. The Male Animal 42. In This Our Life 42. Government Girl 43. Thank Your Lucky Stars 43. Princess O'Rourke 43. The Well-Groomed Bride 45. *Devotion* (as Charlotte Brontë) 46. *The Dark Mirror* 46. *To Each His Own* (AA) 46. *The Snake Pit* (AAN) 47. *The Heiress* (AA) 49. My Cousin Rachel 52. That Lady 55. Not as a Stranger 55. The Ambassador's Daughter 56. The Proud Rebel 58. Libel (GB) 60. The Light in the Piazza 62. Lady in a Cage 64. *Hush Hush Sweet Charlotte* 64. The Adventurers 69. Pope Joan 72. The Screaming Woman (TV) 72. The Fifth Musketeer 77. Airport 77 77. The Swarm 78. Roots: The Next Generation (TV) 79. Murder Is Easy (TV) 82. Charles and Diana: A Royal Romance (TV) (as the Queen Mother) 82. The Woman He Loved (TV) 88.

✪ For her development from a charming leading lady to a star actress of some distinction. *The Dark Mirror*.

❝ Famous line (*The Heiress*) 'Yes, I can be very cruel. I have been taught by masters.'

De Heer, Rolf (1957–)
Dutch-born screenwriter and director, in Australia. He worked for the Australian Broadcasting Commission in a variety of jobs before studying at the Australian Film and TV School.

Tail of a Tiger 84. Incident at Raven's Gate 88. Dingo 91. *Bad Boy Bubby* 93. The Quiet Room (p, wd) 96. Dance Me to My Song (p, co-w, d) 98.

De Jesus, Luchi (1923–1984)
American composer and arranger.

Slaughter 72. A Time for Love 74. Black Belt Jones 74. Thieves 77, etc.

De Keyzer, Bruno (1949–)
French cinematographer in international films.

A Sunday in the Country/Un Dimanche à la Campagne 84. 'Round Midnight 86. Little Dorrit 87. Beatrice 88. Reunion/L'Ami Retrouvé 89. Impromptu 89. Life and Nothing But/La Vie et Rien d'Autre 89. December Bride (GB) 91. Impromptu (GB) 90. Afraid of the Dark 92. War of the Buttons (GB) 94. All Men Are Mortal 95. North Star 96. The Fifth Province 97. Mojo (GB) 97. The Commissioner 98. The Day the Ponies Come Back 00. About Adam (Ire./GB) 00, etc.

De La Iglesia, Alex (1965–)
Spanish director and screenwriter, born in Bilbao.

Acción Mutante (co-w, d) 93. The Day of the Beast (co-w, d) 95. Perdita Durango (d) 97. Dying of Laughter/Muertos de risa (co-w,d) 99. The Commonwealth/La Comunidad (co-w,d) 00, etc.

De La Iglesia, Eloy (1944–)
Spanish director and screenwriter, from the theatre. He studied film at IDHEC in Paris. His films, usually low-budget, tend to deal with social matters in a sensational manner. Problems with drugs slowed his career in the late 80s.

Glass Ceiling/Techo De Cristal 71. Cannibal Man/La Semana Del Asesino 72. Murder in a Blue World/Una Gota De Sangre Para Morir Amando 73. Hidden Pleasures/Los Placeres Ocultos 76. El Pico 83. El Pico II 84, etc.

De La Motte, Marguerite (1902–1950)
American leading actress in silent films. Born in Deluth, Minnesota, she trained as a dancer, studying under Pavlova, and had her greatest successes playing opposite Douglas FAIRBANKS. Married actor John Bowers, with whom she also starred in several films.

The Mark of Zorro 20. The Three Musketeers 21. When a Man's a Man 24. The Beloved Brute 24. Red Dice 26. The Unknown Soldier 26. The Iron Mask 29. Woman's Man 34. Reg'lar Fellers 42, etc.

De La Patellière, Denys (1921–)
French director.

Le Défroqué (w only) 52. Les Aristocrates 56. Retour de Manivelle 57. Les Grandes Familles 59. Marco the Magnificent 65. Du Rififi à Paname 66. Black Sun 66. Le Tatoué 68. Prêtres Interdits 73. Diamond Swords 95, etc.

De La Tour, Frances (1945–)
Angular British character actress who plays both comedy and drama.

Country Dance 69. Every Home Should Have One 70. Our Miss Fred 72. To the Devil a Daughter 76. Wombling Free 77. Rising Damp 80. Loser Takes All 90. Genghis Cohen (TV) 93. Tom Jones (TV) 97, etc.

TV series: Rising Damp 74–78. Every Silver Lining 93. Downwardly Mobile 94.

De Lane Lea, William (1900–1964)
British executive, pioneer of sound dubbing processes.

De Laurentiis, Dino (1919–)
Italian producer who made a stab at Hollywood in the 70s.

Bitter Rice 48. Ulysses 52. La Strada 54. Barabbas 62. The Bible 65. Kiss the Girls and Make Them Die 67. Anzio 68. Barbarella 68. Waterloo 69. Wild Horses 73. Death Wish 74. King Kong 76. The White Buffalo 77. King of The Gypsies 78. Hurricane 79. The Brinks Job 79. Flash Gordon 80. Ragtime 81. Conan the Barbarian 82. Fighting Back 82. The Bounty 84. Dune 85. Cat's Eye 85. Manhunter 86. Desperate Hours 90. Once Upon a Crime 92. Body of Evidence 93. Assassins 95. Solomon and Sheba (TV) 95. Unforgettable 96. Breakdown 97, etc.

De Leon, Gerardo (1913–1981)
American director of low-budget horror, made in the Phillipines.

Terror is a Man 59. The Lost Eden 61. The Walls of Hell 64. The Vampire People/The Blood Drinkers 66. Brides of the Beast/Brides of Blood 68. The Mad Doctor of Blood Island 69. Curse of the Vampires/Creatures of Evil 70. Women in Cages/ Bamboo Dolls House 71, etc.

De Luise, Dom (1933–)
Rotund American comedy star who became one of the Mel Brooks repertory company. He is also the

author of books, videos and a CD-ROM on the subject of cooking.

The Glass Bottom Boat 65. The Twelve Chairs 70. Blazing Saddles 73. Sherlock Holmes' Smarter Brother 75. Silent Movie 76. The World's Greatest Lover 78. The End 78. Hot Stuff (& d) 79. The Muppet Movie 79. Fatso 80. Smokey and the Bandit II 80. The Last Married Couple in America 80. Wholly Moses 80. The Cannonball Run 81. History of the World Part One 81. The Best Little Whorehouse in Texas 82. Happy (TV) 83. Johnny Dangerously 84. Haunted Honeymoon 86. Going Bananas 87. Spaceballs 87. Oliver and Company (voice) 88. All Dogs Go to Heaven (voice) 89. Loose Cannons 89. Happily Ever After 90. Driving Me Crazy 91. An American Tail: Fievel Goes West (voice) 91. Robin Hood: Men in Tights 93. Munchie Strikes Back 94. A Troll in Central Park (voice) 94. The Silence of the Hams (It.) 94. All Dogs Go to Heaven 2 (voice) 96. Boys Will Be Boys 97. The Godson 98. Baby Geniuses 98, etc.

TV series: Lotsa Luck 73. Burke's Law 94.

❝ I'm actually a thin serious person but I play fat and funny, but only for the movies. – *D. De L.*

De Marney, Derrick (1906–1978)
Good-looking British actor with stage experience.

Music Hall 35. Things to Come 36. *Young and Innocent* 37. Victoria the Great (as Disraeli) 37. Blonde Cheat (US) 38. The Spider 39. The Lion Has Wings 40. Dangerous Moonlight 40. The First of the Few 42. Latin Quarter (& co-p) 46. Uncle Silas 47. Sleeping Car to Trieste 48. She Shall Have Murder (& p) 50. Meet Mr Callaghan (& p) 54. Private's Progress 55. Doomsday at Eleven 62. The Projected Man 66, etc.

De Marney, Terence (1909–1971)
British actor with stage experience, brother of Derrick de Marney. Died after falling under a train.

The Mystery of the Marie Celeste 36. I Killed the Count 38. Dual Alibi 46. No Way Back 49. Uneasy Terms 49. The Silver Chalice (US) 55. Death Is a Woman 66. All Neat in Black Stockings 69, etc.

De Masi, Francesco (1930–)
Italian composer. Born in Rome, he studied composition in Naples.

Maciste il Gladiatore Piu Forte del Mondo 62. Il Leone di Tebe 64. Arizona Colt 66. Sette Dollari Sul Rosso 66. Ostia 69. Bawdy Tales 73. The Arena (US) 74. Private Vices, Public Virtues 76. Lone Wolf McQuade (US) 83. Thunder Warrior 83. Rush 84. The Manhunt 85. Escape from the Bronx 85. Formula for Murder 86, etc.

De Maupassant, Guy (1850–1893)
French short storywriter. Work filmed includes *Diary of a Madman*, *Une Vie*, *Le Rosier de Madame Husson*, and many versions of *Boule de Suif*.

De Medeiros, Maria (1965–) (Maria de Almeida)
Portuguese leading actress, in international films from the 90s, when she also turned to writing and directing.

Silvestre 80. Vertiges (Fr.) 84. 1871 (GB) 89. Henry and June (US) 90. L'Homme de Ma Vie (Fr./Can.) 92. Golden Balls/Huevos de Oro (Sp.) 93. Tous les Jours Dimanche (Fr.) 94. Des Feux Mal éteints (Fr.) 94. Two Brothers, My Sister/Tres Irmaos 94. Pulp Fiction (US) 94. Adam and Eve/Adao e Eva 96. Limited Edition/Tire à Part (Fr.) 96. The Lie Detector/Le Polygraphe (Can./Fr./Ger) 96. Spanish Fly (US) 98. April Captains/Capitaes De Abril (&co-w,d) 00, etc.

De Mille, Cecil B. (1881–1959)
American producer-director, one of Hollywood's pioneers and autocrats. Notable in the 20s for sex comedies, in the 30s and 40s for action adventures, then for biblical epics; all now seem very stolid, but were enormously successful in their day.

Autobiography: 1959.

■ *The Squaw Man* 13. The Virginian 14. The Call of the North 14. What's His Name 14. The Man from Home 14. Rose of the Rancho 14. The Girl of the Golden West 15. The Warrens of Virginia 15. The Unafraid 15. The Captive 15. Wild Goose Chase 15. The Arab 15. Chimmie Fadden 15. Kindling 15. Maria Rosa 15. Carmen 15. Temptation 15. Chimmie Fadden Out West 15. *The Cheat* 15. The Golden Chance 16. The Trail of the Lonesome Pine 16. Joan the Woman 16. The Heart of Nora Flynn 16. The Dream Girl 16. A Romance of the Redwoods 17. The Little American 17. The Woman God Forgot 17. The Devil Stone 17. The Whispering Chorus 18. Old Wives for New 18. We Can't Have Everything 18. Till I Come Back to You 18. The Squaw Man 18. Don't Change Your Husband 19. For Better for Worse 19. Male and Female 19. Why Change your Wife? 20. Something to Think About 20. Forbidden Fruit 21. *The Affairs of Anatol* 21. Fool's Paradise 22. Saturday Night 22. Manslaughter 22. Adam's Rib 23. *The Ten Commandments* 23. Triumph 24. Feet of Clay 24. The Golden Bed 25. The Road to Yesterday 25. The Volga Boatmen 26. *King of Kings* 27. The Godless Girl 28. Dynamite 29. Madam Satan 30. The Squaw Man 31. *The Sign of the Cross* 32. This Day and Age 33. Four Frightened People 34. Cleopatra 34. *The Crusades* 35. *The Plainsman* 36. The Buccaneer 38. *Union Pacific* 39. Northwest Mounted Police 40. *Reap The Wild Wind* 42. The Story of Dr Wassell 44. Unconquered 47. Variety Girl (a) 47. Samson and Delilah 49. Sunset Boulevard (a) 50. The Greatest Show on Earth (AAp, AANd) 52. The Ten Commandments 56. The Buccaneer (p only) 59.

✪ For making himself an unseen star by imposing the personality of an autocratic schoolmaster on a variety of somewhat dubious material. *The Sign of the Cross.*

❝ Ready when you are, Mr De Mille. It's the tag-line of a long shaggy dog story, the purpose of which is to establish de Mille as the producer of enormous, stagey biblical epics. Towards the end of his life he did submerge himself in this role, but his career embraced almost every kind of movie. Whatever the show, he made a success of it, and he was respected throughout Hollywood as a disciplinarian who always got his films out under budget. There was a joke during World War II: 'Anyone who leaves de Mille for the armed forces is a slacker.'

He is credited with sending back a writer's script and attaching a terrifying cover note: 'What I have crossed out I didn't like.

What I haven't crossed out I am dissatisfied with.'

He exercised supreme control over his stars, and once said to Paulette Goddard: 'Remember you are a star. Never go across the alley even to dump garbage unless you are dressed to the teeth.'

He told his staff: 'You are here to please me. Nothing else on earth matters.'

He went to extreme lengths to prove his authority. Arthur Miller thought: 'I never met such an egotist in my life.

Even if he was wrong and knew it, once he said it it had to be.'

His brother William was awed by his ambition and achievement: 'The trouble with Cecil is that he always bites off more than he can chew – and then chews it.'

The same William cast a wry eye on Cecil's first Bible picture in the 20s: 'Having attended to the underclothes, bathrooms and matrimonial irregularities of his fellow citizens, he now began to consider their salvation.'

Even when Cecil dealt with heavenly themes, he kept his feet on earth. He said to a scriptwriter: 'It's just a damn good hot tale, so don't get a lot of thees, thous and thums on your mind.'

His comparative ignorance of his favourite subject provoked a much-repeated clerihew: 'Cecil B. De Mille

Much against his will

Was persuaded to keep Moses

Out of the Wars of the Roses.'

He saw the Bible as a ready-made script factory: 'Give me any couple of pages of the Bible and I'll give you a picture.'

He took neither credit nor blame for his themes: 'I didn't write the Bible and didn't invent sin.'

He was also quite clear where his support lay: 'I make my pictures for people, not for critics.'

His approach to actresses was on similarly direct lines. In 1934, when he thought of Claudette Colbert as Cleopatra, he said to her: 'How would you like to be the wickedest woman in history?'

But he knew that what really mattered to a movie is not the star but the producer: 'A picture is made a success not on a set but over the drawing board.'

Action was another essential ingredient: 'I will trade you forty gorgeously beautiful Hawaiian sunsets for one good sock in the jaw.'

He chuckled at the result of his labours: 'Every time I make a picture the critics' estimate of American public taste goes down ten per cent.'

Typical reaction was Pauline Kael's: 'He made small-minded pictures on a big scale.'

Mitchell Leisen thought: 'He had no nuances. Everything was in neon lights six feet tall: *Lust, Revenge, Sex.*'

But Graham Greene had a soft spot for him: 'There has always been a touch of genius as well as absurdity in this warm-hearted sentimental salvationist.',

He remained true to the literary tradition of Cooper's Leatherstocking Tales and to the dramatic conventions of David Belasco. – *Andrew Sarris, 1968*

I learned an awful lot from him by doing the opposite. – *Howard Hawks*

He wore baldness like an expensive hat, as though it were out of the question for him to have hair like other men. – *Gloria Swanson*

He didn't make pictures for himself or for the critics. He made them for the public. – *Adolph Zukor*

De Mille, Katherine (1911–1995) (Katherine Lester)
American leading lady of the 30s. She was married to actor Anthony Quinn (1937–55).

Viva Villa 34. Call of the Wild 35. Ramona 36. Banjo on My Knee 37. Blockade 38. Reap the Wild Wind 42. The Story of Dr Wassell 44. Unconquered 47. The Gamblers 50, etc.

De Mille, William (1878–1955)
American director. Elder brother of Cecil B. De Mille, with theatrical background.

Nice People 22. Craig's Wife 28. Captain Fury (p only) 39, etc.

❝ William always brings his pictures in under budget and on schedule. The trouble is that we can't sell them. – *Cecil B. De Mille*

DeMornay, Rebecca (1962–)
American actress. She was educated in Austria and England (at Summerhill School). She had a daughter in 1997 by her partner Patrick O'Neal.

One from the Heart 82. Testament 83. Risky Business 84. The Trip to Bountiful 85. Runaway Train 85. The Slugger's Wife 85. The Murders in the rue Morgue (TV) 86. Beauty and the Beast 87 … And God Created Woman 87. Feds 88. Dealers 89. By Dawn's Early Light (TV) 90. An Inconvenient Woman (TV) 91. Backdraft 91. The Hand that Rocks the Cradle 91. Guilty as Sin 93. The Three Musketeers 93. Getting Out (TV) 94. Never Talk to Strangers 95. The Winner 96. The Con (TV) 98. Night Ride Home (TV) 99. Wicked Ways 99, etc.

❝ My mother told me: 'If you do not find a way of earning a living, a man will pay for the roof over your head and he's going to tell you what to do.' I've never forgotten that. I do not want anyone telling me how to live or saying what I can do or can't do or who I can or cannot see. – *R. DeM.*

In the best of all worlds and on the best of all days the last thing I like to do at night is feel the physical embrace of someone I love. – *R. DeM.*

DeMunn, Jeffrey (1947–)
American actor.

The Last Tenant (TV) 78. Christmas Evil 80. The First Deadly Sin 80. Resurrection 80. Windy City 84. The Hitcher 86. Warning Sign 85. Betrayed 88. Gore Vidal's Lincoln (TV) 88. Blaze 89. The Tender 89. The Shawshank Redemption 94. Hiroshima (TV) 95. Killer: A Journal of Murder 95. Phenomenon 96. Turbulence 97. Rocketman 97. The X-Files 98. Harvest 99. The Green Mile 99, etc.

De Niro, Robert (1943–)
Intense, brooding American leading actor whose best roles have been in the films of Martin Scorsese. Born in New York City, he studied acting with Stella Adler and Lee Strasberg and began in off-Broadway theatre. He founded the production facility TriBeCa Film Center, which houses his own production company, Tribeca Films, in New York in the late 80s, and is an occasional director. He married former flight attendant Grace Hightower in 1997. His first wife was actress Diahnne Abbott (1976–78), with whom he had a son, and he has a daughter by singer Helena Springs and twin sons with a former model, Toukie Smith.

His finest performances have been as Bruce Pearson in *Bang the Drum Slowly*, Johnny Boy in *Mean Streets*, Don Corleone in *The Godfather Part II*, Travis Bickle in *Taxi Driver*, Jake LaMotta in *Raging Bull*, and Al Capone in *The Untouchables*.

Biography: 1986, *Robert DeNiro: The Man Behind the Mask* by Keith McKay. 1995, *De Niro* by John Parker. 1997, *Untouchable: Robert De Niro* by Andy Dougan.

Greetings 68. Sam's Song 69. The Wedding Party 69. Hi, Mom! 69. Bloody Mama 69. Born to Win 71. The Gang that couldn't Shoot Straight 71. Jennifer on my Mind 71. *Bang the Drum Slowly* 73. *Mean Streets* 73. The Godfather Part Two (AA) 74. Taxi Driver (AAN) 76. The Last Tycoon 76. 1900 76. New York New York 77. *The Deer Hunter* (AAN) 78. *Raging Bull* (for which he became fifty pounds overweight) (AA) 80. True Confessions 81. King of Comedy 83. Once Upon a Time in America 84. Falling in Love 84. Brazil 85. The Mission 86. Angel Heart 87. The Untouchables 87. Midnight Run 88. Jacknife 88. We're No Angels 89. Stanley and Iris 89. Awakenings (AAN) 90. GoodFellas 90. Guilty by Suspicion 90. Backdraft 91. *Cape Fear* (AAN) 91. Mistress 92. Night and the City 92. This Boy's Life 93. A Bronx Tale (& p, d) 93. Mad Dog and Glory 93. Mary Shelley's Frankenstein (as the creature) 94. Casino 95. Heat 95. Sleepers 96. Marvin's Room 96. The Fan 96. Cop Land 97. Jackie Brown 97. Wag the Dog 97. Great Expectations 98. Ronin 98. Analyze This 99. Flawless 99. The Adventures of Rocky and Bullwinkle (&p) 00. Men of Honor 00, etc.

✪ For becoming the best film actor of his generation. *Raging Bull.*

❝ There is a mixture of anarchy and discipline in the way I work. – *R. deN.*

After my first movies, I gave interviews. Then I thought, what's so important about where I went to school, and hobbies … what does any of that have to do with acting, with my own head? – *R. deN.*

It's ridiculous for an actor that good to keep playing Las Vegas hoods – *Charlton Heston*

De Oliveira, Manoel (1908–)
Portuguese director of features and documentaries, a former racing driver, trapeze artist and businessman.

Aniki-Bobo 42. The Passion of Jesus/Acto de Primavera 63. Amor de Perdição (TV) 78. Francisca 81. The Satin Slipper (Fr.) 85. Mon Cas 86. The Cannibals/Os Canibais 88. The Divine Comedy/La Divina Comedia 91. The Day of Despair/O Dia do Desespero 92. Vale Abraao 93. Blindman's Buff/A Caixa 94. The Convent 95, etc.

De Ossorio, Amando (1925–1996)
Spanish director of horror movies, best known for his movies about the blind dead – corpses of the Knights Templar who rise from their graves to attack the living.

Fangs of the Living Dead/Malenka, la Nipote del Vampiro 68. Tomb of the Blind Dead/La Noche del Terror Ciego 71. Return of the Blind Dead/El Ataque de los Muertos sin Ojos 72. When the Screaming Stops/Las Garras de Lorelei 72. Horror of the Zombies/El Buqué Maldito 73. Night of the Sorcerers/La Noche de los Brujos 73. Night of the Death Cult/La Noche de las Gaviotas 74, etc.

De Palma, Brian (1940–)
American director who began in the satirical underground school, then graduated to glossy shock/horrors, usually in clever imitation of somebody else's style.

■ Murder à la Mode (& w) 68. *Greetings* 68. The Wedding Party 69. Dionysus 70. Hi Mom 70. Get to Know Your Rabbit 72. Sisters 73. Phantom of the Paradise (& w) 74. Obsession 76. *Carrie* 76. The Fury 78. Home Movies 79. Dressed to Kill 80. Blow Out 81. Scarface 83. Body Double 84. Wise Guys 86. *The Untouchables* 87. Casualties of War 89. Bonfire of the Vanities 90. Father's Day 92. Raising Cain 92. Carlito's Way 93. Mission: Impossible 96. Snake Eyes (& p, story) 98. Mission to Mars 00.

❝ A superb cinematic talent unable to do more than play doctor with his toy implements. – *Sunday Times, 1981*

My films deal with a stylized, expressionistic world that has a kind of grotesque beauty about it. – *B. de P.*

I don't see scary films. I certainly wouldn't go see my films. – *B. de P.*

De Palma, Rossy (1965–) (Rosy Garcia)
Tall, angular Spanish actress, known internationally for her appearances in the films of Pedro Almodóvar.

Women on the Verge of a Nervous Breakdown/Mujeres al Borde de un Ataque de Nervios 88. Tie Me Up! Tie Me Down!/¡Atame! 89. Don Juan, My

Darling Ghost/Don Juan, Mi Querido Fantasma 90. Sam Suffit (Fr.) 92. Kika 93. Prêt-à-Porter/Ready to Wear 94. The Next Worst Thing Is Death/ Peggio di Cosi Si Muore 95. The Flower of My Secret/La Flor de Mi Secreto 95. Body in the Wood 96. Foul Play/Hors Jeu (Fr.) 98. Talk of Angels (US) 98, etc.

De Putti, Lya (1901–1931) (Amalia Putty)
Hungarian star of silents in Germany, Britain and Hollywood. Died of pneumonia after an operation to remove a chicken bone from her throat.
Othello (Ger.) 22. Variety (Ger.) 25. Manon Lescaut (Ger.) 26. The Sorrows of Satan (US) 26. The Prince of Tempters (US) 26. Buck Privates (US) 28. The Scarlet Lady (US) 28. The Informer (GB) 29, etc.

De Rochemont, Louis (1899–1978)
American producer, from the world of newsreel. Devised *The March of Time* 34; later produced semi-documentaries like *The House on 92nd Street* 46 and *Boomerang* 47; and was involved in many ventures including Cinerama and Cinemiracle.

DeSalvo, Albert (1931–1973)
Serial killer known as The Boston Strangler who was the subject of a biopic of the same name starring Tony Curtis and directed by Richard Fleischer in 1968. DeSalvo raped and murdered at least 13 women (he claimed to have raped many hundreds) in the early 60s. He was committed to a mental institution in 1967 and was stabbed to death in his cell.

De Santis, Giuseppe (1917–1997)
Italian director and screenwriter, one of the leading figures in the neo-realism movement. Born in Fondi, he studied film at Rome's Centro Sperimentale di Cinematografia and began as a critic. He was one of the writers of Visconti's first film *Ossessione* 42, before becoming a director himself, usually writing his screenplays in collaboration with others.
Caccia Tragica 47. *Bitter Rice* (AANw) 49. *No Peace among the Olives* 50. Rome Eleven O'Clock 51. A Husband for Anna 53. Men and Wolves 56. La Garçonnière 60. Italiani Brava Gente 64. Un Apprezzato Professionista di Sicuro Avvenire 71, etc.

De Santis, Joe (1909–1989)
American character actor who often played Italianate gangsters.
Slattery's Hurricane 49. Man with a Cloak 51. The Last Hunt 56. Tension at Table Rock 57. And Now Miguel 66. The Professionals 66. Blue 68, etc.

De Santis, Pasqualino (1927–1996)
Italian cinematographer who worked with such directors as Robert Bresson, Luchino Visconti and Francesco Rosi.
Romeo and Juliet (AA) 68. The Damned/ Götterdämmerung (co-p) 69. *Death in Venice*/ Morte a Venezia 71. The Assassination of Trotsky 72. Lancelot du Lac 74. Conversation Piece/ Gruppo di Famiglia in un Interno 74. Illustrious Corpses/Cadaveri Eccellenti 75. L'Innocente 76. *Christ Stopped at Eboli* 79. Three Brothers 80. Bizet's Carmen 84. Sheena, Queen of the Jungle 84. Harem 85. Salome 86. *Chronicle of a Death Foretold*/Cronica di una Morte Annunciata 87. High Frequency 89. To Forget Palermo/ Dimenticare Palermo 89. Music for Old Animals/ Musica per Animali 90. A Month by the Lake 95, etc.

De Sarigny, Peter (1911–)
South African-born producer, in Britain from 1936.
The Malta Story 53. Simba 55. True as a Turtle 56. Never Let Go 61, etc.

De Seta, Vittorio (1923–)
Italian director, mainly of shorts until *Bandits at Orgosolo* 62.
Bandits at Orgosolo 62. Almost a Man/Uomo a Meta 66. The Uninvited/L'Invitata 69. Diary of a Teacher/Diario di un Maestro (TV) 73, etc.

De Sica, Vittorio (1901–1974)
Italian actor and director, in the latter respect an important and skilful realist. Well known in Italy in the 30s, but not elsewhere until after World War II.
as director: Teresa Venerdi (d) 41. I Bambini ci Guardino (d) 42. *Shoeshine* (AA) 46. *Bicycle Thieves* (AA) 48. *Miracle in Milan* 50. *Umberto D* 52. Stazione Termini/Indiscretion 52. Gold of Naples 54. Two Women 61. The Condemned of Altona 63. Yesterday, Today and Tomorrow (AA) 64. Marriage Italian Style 64. A New World 66. After the Fox 66. Woman Times Seven 67. A Place for Lovers 69. Sunflower 70. *The Garden of the Finzi-Continis* (AA) 71. The Voyage 73, etc.
as actor: *Madame De* 52. Bread, Love and Dreams 53. A Farewell to Arms (AAN) 57. Il Generale della Rovere 59. The Biggest Bundle of Them All 66. The Shoes of the Fisherman 68.
TV series (as actor): *The Four Just Men* (GB) 59.
For a half-dozen splendid films dotting a very variable career. *Miracle in Milan.*
“ A fine actor, a polished hack, and a flabby whore – not necessarily in that order. – *Stanley Kauffmann*

De Souza, Edward (1933–)
British leading man, mostly on stage.
The Roman Spring of Mrs Stone 61. The Phantom of the Opera 62. Kiss of the Vampire 64. The Spy Who Loved Me 77. The Return of the Soldier 82, etc.

De Souza, Steven E.
American screenwriter.
48 Hours 82. The Return of Captain Invincible 83. Commando 85. The Running Man 87. Seven Hours to Judgement 88. Die Hard 88. Bad Dreams 88. Die Hard 2 90. Hudson Hawk 91. Ricochet 92. The Flintstones (co-w) 94. Beverly Hills Cop III 94. Streetfighter (wd) 94. Judge Dredd 95. Knockoff 98, etc.

De Sylva, B. G. 'Buddy' (1895–1950) (George Gard De Sylva)
American lyricist, screenwriter and producer, notably in collaboration with Lew Brown and Ray Henderson, though he also worked with Naçio Herb Brown, George Gershwin, Jerome Kern and Vincent Youmans. Born in New York, he was in vaudeville from childhood and from the 20s was writing songs for Al Jolson. He became a producer, first of his Broadway shows and then in films for Fox, producing musicals for Shirley Temple, and, from 1939 to 1944, for Paramount, where he was production chief; later, he became an independent producer. He was also a co-founder of Capitol Records in the early 40s. In the biopic of De Sylva, Brown and Henderson, *The Best Things in Life Are Free* 56, he was played by Gordon MacRae; in *Star Spangled Rhythm* 42 he was caricatured by Walter Abel as G. B. de Soto. His best-known songs include 'April Showers', 'The Birth of the Blues', 'California Here I Come', 'If You Knew Susie', 'Look for the Silver Lining', and 'You're the Cream in My Coffee'.
The Singing Fool (s 'Sonny Boy') 28. Say It with Songs (s) 29. Sunny Side Up (co-w, s) 29. Good News (s) 30. Follow Thru (co-w, s) 30. Just Imagine (co-w, s) 30. Indiscreet (co-w, s) 31. My Weakness (s) 33. Take a Chance (co-w, s) 33. The Littlest Rebel (p) 35. The Birth of the Blues (p, s) 41. Caught in the Draft (p) 41. Louisiana Purchase (oa) 41. Lady in the Dark (p) 44. Frenchman's Creek (p) 44. The Stork Club (p, co-w) 45. Good News (s) 47. Jolson Sings Again (s) 49. The Eddie Cantor Story (s) 53, etc.

De Toth, André (1912–)
Hungarian-American director, mainly of routine actioners. Oddly enough, directed one of the first 3-D films; having only one eye, he could not see the effect.
Autobiography: 1994, *Fragments: Portraits from the Inside*.
Other books: 1997, *De Toth on De Toth: Putting the Drama in Front of the Camera*, ed. Anthony Slide.
■ Ot Ora forty (Hung.) 38. Ketlany Azultean (Hung.) 38. Har Het Bologsag (Hung.) 38. Semmelweis (Hung.) 38. Balalaika (Hung.) 39. Toprini Nasz (Hung.) 39. Passport to Suez 43. None Shall Escape 44. *Dark Waters* 44. Ramrod 47. The Other Love 47. Pitfall 48. Slattery's Hurricane 49. The Gunfighter (co-story only, AAN) 50. Man in the Saddle 51. Carson City 52. Springfield Rifle 52. Last of the Comanches 52. *House of Wax* 53. The Stranger Wore a Gun 53. Thunder Over the Plains 53. Crime Wave 54. Riding Shotgun 54. Tanganyika 54. The Bounty Hunter 54. The Indian Fighter 55. Monkey on My Back 57. Hidden Fear 57. The Two Headed Spy (GB) 59. Day of the Outlaw 59. Man on a String 60. Morgan the Pirate 61. The Mongols 62. Gold for the Caesars 64. Play Dirty (GB) 69.

DeTreaux, Tamara (1959–1990)
Tiny (31 ins) American actress who played E.T. in some scenes of the film.
Ghoulies 85. Rockula 90. The Linguini Incident 92, etc.

De Vinna, Clyde (1892–1953)
American cinematographer.
selected silents: The Raiders 16. Madam Who 18. Leave it to Me 20. Yellow Men and Gold 22. The Victor 23. Ben Hur (co-ph) 26. California 27. White Shadows in the South Seas (co-ph) (AA) 28. The Pagan 29.
■ sound films: *Trader Horn* 31. The Great Meadow (co-ph) 31. Shipmates 31. Politics 31. Tarzan the Ape Man (co-ph) 32. Bird of Paradise (co-ph) 32. Eskimo 33. Tarzan and His Mate (co-ph) 34. *Treasure Island* 34. West Point of the Air 35. The Last of the Pagans 35. Ah Wilderness 35. Old Hutch 36. Good Old Soak 36. Bad Man of Brimstone 38. Of Human Hearts 38. Fast Company 38. The Girl Downstairs 39. Bridal Suite 39. Blackmail 39. They All Come Out 39. 20 Mule Team 40. Phantom Raiders 40. Wyoming 40. The Bad Man 41. The People vs Dr Kildare 41. Barnacle Bill 41. Tarzan's Secret Treasure 41. The Bugle Sounds 41. Jackass Mail 41. Whistling in Dixie 42. The Immortal Sergeant 43. Within these Walls 45. The Caribbean Mystery 45. It's a Joke Son 47. Sword of the Avenger 48. The Jungle 52.

DeVito, Danny (1944–)
Diminutive and aggressive American character actor, often in venal roles, and producer, a former hairdresser. Born in Neptune, New Jersey, he studied acting at the American Academy of Dramatic Arts, and first came to public attention as Louie DiPalma in the TV series *Taxi*. He began directing in the late 80s. He also runs a production company, Jersey Films. Married actress Rhea Perlman.
Dreams of Glass 68. La Mortadella 72. Hurry Up, Or I'll Be 30 73. Scalawag 73. One Flew Over the Cuckoo's Nest 75. The Van 77. The World's Greatest Lover 77. Goin' South 78. Going Ape! 81. Terms of Endearment 83. Johnny Dangerously 84. The Ratings Game (& d) (TV) 84. Romancing the Stone 84. The Jewel of the Nile 85. Head Office 86. My Little Pony: The Movie 86. Ruthless People 86. Wise Guys 86. Throw Momma from the Train (& d) 87. Tin Men 87. Twins 88. Wars of the Roses (& d) 89. Other People's Money 91. Batman Returns 92. Hoffa (& d) 92. Jack the Bear 93. Look Who's Talking Now (voice) 93. Renaissance Man 94. Junior 94. Reality Bites (p) 94. Get Shorty (& p) 95. Sunset Park (p) 96. Matilda (& d) 96. Mars Attacks! (a) 96. Hercules (voice) 97. *John Grisham's The Rainmaker* (a) 97. *LA Confidential* (a) 97. Out of Sight (p) 98. Living Out Loud (a) 98. The Virgin Suicides 99. Man on the Moon 99. Screwed 00. The Big Kahuna 00. Drowning Mona 00. Erin Brockovich (AANp) 00, etc.
TV series: Taxi 78–83.
“ If you're my height and look the way I do and you don't have an abundance of ego and self-esteem, you become a basket case, one of life's prime losers, because height and looks and suave and all those qualities are worshipped. – *D. deV.*

De Vol, Frank (1911–1999)
American composer and occasional actor.
The Big Knife 55. Kiss Me Deadly 55. Attack 56. Johnny Trouble 56. The Ride Back 57. Pillow Talk (AAN) 59. Murder, Incorporated 60. Lover Come Back 61. The Parent Trap (a only) 61. Boys' Night Out 62. Whatever Happened to Baby Jane? 62. For Love or Money 63. McLintock 63. The Thrill of It All 63. Under the Yum Yum Tree 63. The Wheeler Dealers 63. Good Neighbour Sam 64. Hush Hush Sweet Charlotte (AAN) 64. Send Me No Flowers 64. Cat Ballou 65. The Flight of the Phoenix 65. What's So Bad about Feeling Good? 65. The Glass Bottom Boat 66. Texas across the River 66. The Ballad of Josie 67. Caprice 67. The Dirty Dozen 67. Guess Who's Coming to Dinner (AAN) 67. The Happening 67. The Big Mouth (a only) 67. Krakatoa, East of Java 68. The Legend of Lylah Clare 68. Ulzana's Raid 72. Emperor of the North Pole 73. The Longest Yard 74. Hustle 75. Herbie Goes to Monte Carlo 77. The Choirboys 78. The Frisco Kid (&a) 79. All the Marbles… 81, etc.

DeVore, Gary M. (1942–1997)
American screenwriter, mainly of action movies. Born in Los Angeles, he was a trucker for six years before beginning in television; he later worked as a script doctor on such films as *The Mean Season*, *The Relic* and *Passenger* 57. Died when his car ran off the road into an aqueduct, where his body lay undiscovered for a year. At the time of his death, he was planning to direct an updated remake of the 1949 movie *The Big Steal*. Married four times, including to Maria Cole, widow of Nat 'King' Cole, and actress Claudia Christian.
The Dogs of War (co-w) 80. Back Roads 81. Heart of Steel (TV) 83. Raw Deal (co-w) 86. Running Scared (co-w) 86. Traxx 88, etc.
“ He radiated testosterone. He wrote great street cop. – *Peter Hyams*

De Vorzon, Barry
American composer.
The Warriors 79. The Ninth Configuration 80. Xanadu 80. Looker 81. Tattoo 81. Tarzan, the Ape Man 82. Jekyll and Hyde … Together Again 82. Stick 85. Night of the Creeps 86. Exorcist III 90, etc.

De Wilde, Brandon (1942–1972)
American child actor, later juvenile lead. Died in a car accident.
■ *The Member of the Wedding* 52. *Shane* (AAN) 53. Goodbye My Lady 56. Night Passage 57. The Missouri Traveller 58. Blue Denim 59. All Fall Down 62. *Hud* 63. In Harm's Way 65. Those Calloways 65. The Deserter 70. Wild in the Sky 72.
TV series: Jamie 54.

De Wolfe, Billy (1907–1974) (William Andrew Jones)
Toothy, moustachioed American comedy actor, formerly dancer, with vaudeville and night club experience. (Famous act: a lady taking a bath.)
Dixie 43. Blue Skies 46. *Dear Ruth* 47. Dear Wife 50. Tea for Two 50. Lullaby of Broadway 51. *Call Me Madam* 53. Billie 65. The World's Greatest Athlete 73, etc.
TV series: The Pruitts of Southampton 67. Good Morning World 67. The Queen and I 69. The Debbie Reynolds Show 69. The Doris Day Show 70–71.

De Wolff, Francis (1913–1984)
Bearded, burly British character actor.
Adam and Evelyne 48. Under Capricorn 49. Treasure Island 50. Scrooge 51. Ivanhoe 53. The Master of Ballantrae 55. Geordie 55, many others.

De Young, Cliff (1945–)
American general-purpose actor.
Sunshine (TV) 73. Harry and Tonto 74. The Night that Panicked America (TV) 75. The Lindbergh Kidnapping Case (TV) (title role) 76. Blue Collar 78. King (TV) (as Bobby Kennedy) 78. Shock Treatment 81. The Hunger 83. Protocol 84. F/X 85. Flight of the Navigator 87. Crackdown 90. Nails 92. Revenge of the Red Baron 94. Infinity 95. The Substitute 96. The Craft 96. The Last Don (TV) 97, etc.
TV series: Sunshine 75. Centennial 78–79. Master of the Game 84.

Deacon, Brian (1949–)
British general-purpose actor.
Triple Echo 73. Vampire 74. Lillie (TV) 78. A Zed and Two Noughts 85, etc.

Deacon, Richard (1922–1984)
Bald, bespectacled American character actor who usually played comic snoops.
Abbott and Costello Meet the Mummy 55. The Power and the Prize 56. The Remarkable Mr Pennypacker 58. Dear Heart 64. Billie 65. Blackbeard's Ghost 67. The Gnome-Mobile 67. The King's Pirate 67. The One and Only Genuine Original Family Band 68. Piranha 78, many others.
TV series: Leave It to Beaver 57–63. *Dick Van Dyke* 61–66. Mothers-in-law 67–68.

Deakins, Roger (1949–)
British cinematographer.
Before Hindsight 77. Blue Suede Shoes 80. Another Time, Another Place 83. 1984 84. Return to Waterloo 85. Defence of the Realm 85. Shadey 85. Sid and Nancy 86. Kitchen Toto 87. Personal Services 87. White Mischief 87. Pascali's Island 88. Stormy Monday 88. Air America 90. Mountains of the Moon 90. The Long Walk Home 90. Barton

Fink 91. Homicide 91. Thunderheart 92. The Secret Garden 93. The Hudsucker Proxy 94. The Shawshank Redemption (AAN) 94. Rob Roy 95. Dead Man Walking 95. Fargo 96. Courage under Fire 96. *Fargo* (AAN) 96. *Kundun* (AAN) 97. The Big Lebowski 97. The Siege 98. Anywhere But Here 99. The Hurricane 99. O Brother, Where Art Thou? (AAN) 00, etc.

Dean, Basil (1888–1978)
British stage producer who also directed several important films for Associated Talking Pictures, which he founded. He was also responsible for the formation in wartime of the organization of travelling entertainers, ENSA, often known disrespectfully as Every Night Something Awful, but standing in fact for Entertainments National Service Association. Married actress Victoria Hopper.

Autobiography: 1973, *Mind's Eye*.

The Impassive Footman 32. The Constant Nymph (& co-w) 33. Java Head 34. Sing As We Go 34. Lorna Doone 35. 21 Days 39, etc.

Dean, Bill (1921–2000)
English character actor, a former stand-up comedian. He was best known for his role as the grumpy, busybody Harry Cross in the TV soap opera *Brookside*. Born in Everton, he worked in a variety of occupations before becoming an actor in the late 60s.

The Golden Vision 68. Kes 69. Roll on Four O'Clock (TV) 70. After a Lifetime (TV) 71. Family Life 71. The Rank and File (TV) 71. Gumshoe 72. Night Watch 73. Scum (TV) 77, etc.

TV series: The Wackers 75. Oh No – It's Selwyn Froggitt 76-77. Brookside 83-90. Bloomin' Marvellous 97.

Dean, Eddie (1907–1999) (Edgar D. Glossup)
American actor, singer and songwriter, in Westerns. Born in Posey, Texas, he began as a performer on radio shows, moving to Hollywood in the mid-30s and becoming one of the top Western stars of the mid-40s.

Renegade Trail 39. Sierra Sue 41. Romance of the West 47. Hawk of Powder River 50, many others.

TV series: The Marshal of Gunsight Pass 50.

Dean, Isabel (1918–1997) (Isabel Hodgkinson)
British stage actress, usually in upper-class roles: very occasional film appearances. She was at one time married to writer William Fairchild.

The Passionate Friends 47. 24 Hours of a Woman's Life 52. The Story of Gilbert and Sullivan 53. Out of the Clouds 55. Virgin Island 58. The Light in the Piazza 62. A High Wind in Jamaica 65. Inadmissible Evidence 68. Catch Me a Spy 71. Five Days One Summer 82. Weather in the Streets 84, etc.

Dean, James (1931–1955)
Moody young American actor who after a brief build-up in small roles was acclaimed as the image of the mid-50s; his tragic death in a car crash caused an astonishing world-wide outburst of emotional necrophilia. A biopic, *The James Dean Story*, was patched together in 1957.

Biography: 1956, *James Dean* by William Bast. 1974, *James Dean: The Mutant King* by David Dalton. 1975, *James Dean* by John Howlett. 1982, *James Dean: A Portrait* by Roy Schatt. 1994, *James Dean: Boulevard of Broken Dreams* by Paul Alexander. 1996, *Rebel: The Life and Legend of James Dean* by Donald Spoto. 1996, *James Dean* by Val Holley. 1997, *James Dean* by John Howlett.

■ Has Anybody Seen My Gal? 51. Sailor Beware 51. Fixed Bayonets 52. Trouble Along the Way 53. *East of Eden* (AAN) 55. *Rebel Without A Cause* 55. *Giant* (AAN) 56.

❝ Another dirty shirt-tail actor from New York. – *Hedda Hopper*

He was sad and sulky. You kept expecting him to cry. – *Elia Kazan*

Dean, Julia (1878–1952)
American stage actress who made a few movies after she retired to California.

How Molly Made Good 15. Curse of the Cat People 44. O.S.S. 46. Nightmare Alley 48. People Will Talk 51. Elopement 51, etc.

Dean, Loren (1969–)
American actor.

Plain Clothes 88. Say Anything 89. Billy Bathgate (title role) 91. 1492: Conquest of Paradise 92. JFK: Restless Youth (TV) 93. The Passion of Darkly Noon 95. How to Make an American Quilt 95. Apollo 13 95. Mrs Winterbourne 96. Gattaca 97. The End of Violence 97. Enemy of the State 98. Mumford 99. Space Cowboys 00, etc.

Dean, Man Mountain (1899–1963)
American wrestler who played comedy roles in a few films.

Reckless 35. The Gladiator 38. Surprise Package 60, etc.

Dean, Priscilla (1896–1987)
American star of silent films, on stage from the age of four and in films from the age of 12, notably for Universal.

Even as You and I 17. The Hand that Rocks the Cradle 17. She Hired a Husband 18. The Wicked Darling 19. The Exquisite Thief 19. Pretty Smooth 19. The Virgin of Stamboul 20. Outside the Law 21. Reputation 21. Under Two Flags 22. The Flame of Life 23. Drifting 23. The White Tiger 23. The Storm Daughter 24. Slipping Wives 26. Behind Stone Walls 32, etc.

Dear, William
American director.

Time Rider 83. Harry and the Hendersons 87. If Looks Could Kill 91. Angels in the Outfield 94. Wild America 97, etc.

Dearden, Basil (1911–1971)
British director, former editor. Began by co-directing Will Hay's last films for Ealing, then formed a writer-producer-director partnership with Michael Relph. Killed in a car crash.

■ The Black Sheep of Whitehall (co-d) 41. The Goose Steps Out (co-d) 42. The Bells Go Down 43. My Learned Friend (co-d) 43. The Halfway House 44. They Came to a City 44. Dead of Night (part) 45. *The Captive Heart* 46. Frieda 47. Saraband for Dead Lovers 48. Train of Events (co-d) 49. *The Blue Lamp* 50. Cage of Gold 50. Pool of London 51. I Believe in You (co-d) 52. The Gentle Gunman 52. The Square Ring 53. The Rainbow Jacket 54. Out of the Clouds (co-d) 55. The Ship That Died of Shame (co-d) 55. Who Done It (co-d) 56. The Smallest Show on Earth 57. Violent Playground 58. *Sapphire* 59. *The League of Gentlemen* 60. Man in the Moon 60. The Secret Partner 61. *Victim* 61. All Night Long (co-d) 62. Life for Ruth 62. The Mind Benders 63. A Place to Go 63. Woman of Straw 64. Masquerade 65. Khartoum 66. Only When I Larf 68. The Assassination Bureau 69. The Man Who Haunted Himself 70.

❝ He was a master film-maker. If we'd have had the right atmosphere in which he could have worked, he would have been a top one. – *Dirk Bogarde*

Dearden, James (1949–)
British director and screenwriter. He is the son of Basil Dearden.

Fatal Attraction (w) (AAN) 87. Pascali's Island 88. A Kiss before Dying, 91. Rogue Trader 99, etc.

Dearing, Edgar (1893–1974)
American character actor, often seen as tough cop.

Thanks for Everything 35. Swing Time 37. Miss Annie Rooney 42, many others.

D'Eaubonne, Jean (1903–1971)
French art director who studied painting and sculpture before entering films in the 30s. He also worked in Britain and the US.

Blood of a Poet/Le Sang d'un Poète 32. The Girl in the Taxi (GB) 37. La Chartreuse de Parme 47. Orphée 49. Black Magic (US) 49. La Ronde 50. Casque d'Or 52. Touchez Pas au Grisbi 54. Lola Montès 55. The Reluctant Debutante (US) 58. Crack in the Mirror (US) 60. Charade 63. Paris When It Sizzles (US) 64. Custer of the West (US) 66. The Girl on a Motorcycle 68, etc.

Debney, John (1956–)
American composer, from television.

The Further Adventures of Tennessee Buck 88. Jetsons: The Movie 90. Gunmen 92. Hocus Pocus 93. Little Giants 94. White Fang II: The Myth of the White Wolf 94. Cutthroat Island 95. Sudden Death 95. Getting Away with Murder 96. Carpool 96. I Know What You Did Last Summer 97. Liar, Liar 97. The Relic 97. I'll Be Home for Christmas 98. Paulie 98. My Favorite Martian 99. End of Days 99. Inspector Gadget 99. Komodo 99. Dick 99. The Replacements 00. Relative Values 00, etc.

Debucourt, Jean (1894–1958) (J. Pelisse)
French character actor with long stage experience.

Le Petit Chose 22. La Chute de la Maison Usher 28. Douce 43. Le Diable au Corps 46. Occupe-Toi d'Amélie 49, etc.

Decae, Henri (1915–1987)
Distinguished French cinematographer.

Le Silence de la Mer 49. Les Enfants Terribles 49. Crève-Coeur 52. Bob le Flambeur 55. Lift to the Scaffold 57. Le Beau Serge 58. A Double Tour 59. Les Quatre Cents Coups 59. Les Cousins 59. Plein Soleil 59. Les Bonnes Femmes 60. Léon Morin, Priest 61. Sundays and Cybele 62. Dragées au Poivre 63. Viva Maria 65. Weekend at Dunkirk 65. Night of the Generals 66. Le Voleur 67. The Comedians 67. Castle Keep 69. The Sicilian Clan 70. The Light at the Edge of the World 71. Bobby Deerfield 77. The Island 80. Exposed 83, etc.

Decker, Diana (1926–)
Bright, blonde, American leading lady, in Britain from 1939; became known through toothpaste commercials ('Irium, Miriam?').

Fiddlers Three 44. Meet Me at Dawn 48. Murder at the Windmill 49. Is Your Honeymoon Really Necessary? 53. Lolita 62. Devils of Darkness 65, etc.

TV series: Mark Saber 54

Deckers, Eugene (1917–1977)
French character actor who played Continental types in British films after 1946.

Sleeping Car to Trieste 48. The Elusive Pimpernel 50. The Lavender Hill Mob 51. Father Brown 54. Port Afrique 56. Northwest Frontier 59. Lady L 66. The Limbo Line 68, many others.

Decoin, Henri (1896–1969)
French director, in films since 1929.

Abus de Confiance 37. Les Inconnus dans la Maison 42. La Fille du Diable 46. Three Telegrams 50. The Truth about Bebe Donge 52. The Lovers of Toledo 53. Razzia sur la Chnouf 55. Charmants Garçons 57. The Face of the Cat 58. Outcasts of Glory 64, many others.

Dee, Frances (1907–) (Jean Dee)
American leading lady of the 30s, long married to Joel McCrea; a former extra, she was chosen by Chevalier to play opposite him in her first speaking role.

Playboy of Paris 30. An American Tragedy 31. Rich Man's Folly 32. King of the Jungle 33. Becky Sharp 35. If I Were King 38. So Ends Our Night 41. Meet the Stewarts 42. I Walked with a Zombie 43. Happy Land 43. Bel Ami 48. Four Faces West 48. Payment on Demand 51. Because of You 53. Mr Scoutmaster 53. Gypsy Colt 54, etc.

Dee, Ruby (1924–) (Ruby Ann Wallace)
American actress.

No Way Out 50. Tall Target 51. Go Man Go 53. Edge of the City 57. Take a Giant Step 59. *A Raisin in the Sun* 61. The Balcony 62. Buck and the Preacher 72. Black Girl 72. Cat People 82. Do the Right Thing 89. Jungle Fever 91. A Cop and a Half 93. The Stand (TV) 94. Just Cause 95. Mr & Mrs Loving 96. A Simple Wish 97. The Wall 98. Passing Glory (TV) 99, etc.

Dee, Sandra (1942–) (Alexandra Zuck)
Petite American leading lady, former model.

Until They Sail 57. The Reluctant Debutante 58. Gidget 59. *Imitation of Life* 59. A Summer Place 59. Portrait in Black 60. Romanoff and Juliet 61. Come September 62. Tammy and the Doctor 63. Take Her She's Mine 64. That Funny Feeling 65. A Man Could Get Killed 66. Doctor, You've Got to be Kidding 67. Rosie 68. The Dunwich Horror 70. The Daughters of Joshua Cabe (TV) 72. Houston We've Got a Problem (TV) 74. Manhunter (TV) 76. Fantasy Island (TV) 77, etc.

Deed, André (1884–1938) (Andre Chapuis)
French actor and director who was probably cinema's first comedian. A music-hall acrobat and singer, he entered films in 1905, when he was discovered by Charles Pathé, to become one of the screen's first stars, though hardly any of his films survive. He was known by different names in different countries: Boireau in France, Foolshead in Britain, Cretinetti in Italy, and Toribio in Spain. His popularity ending with the coming of sound, he became night-watchman at the Pathé studios and died forgotten.

Boireau Déménage 05. Cretinetti al Cinema 11. Boireau Domestique 13. Graine au Vent 28, etc.

Deeley, Michael (1932–)
British producer, a former EMI executive.

The Case of the Mukkinese Battlehorn 61. One Way Pendulum 64. Robbery 67. The Italian Job 69. Murphy's War 70. The Man Who Fell to Earth 75. Nickelodeon 76. The Deer Hunter 78, etc.

Deems, Barrett (1914–1998)
American jazz drummer and bandleader with a hyperactive style, in a few films as himself. Born in Springfield, Illinois, he is best known for playing with the Louis Armstrong All Stars in the 50s.

Rhythm Inn 51. High Society 56. Satchmo the Great 56, etc.

Defoe, Daniel (1659–1731)
English writer whose work included the oft-filmed *Robinson Crusoe;* also *Moll Flanders*, which the 1965 film resembled but slightly. A 1996 version also wandered far from the original.

Degermark, Pia (1949–)
Swedish leading lady in international films.

Elvira Madigan 67. The Looking Glass War 69, etc.

Degregorio, Eduardo (1942–)
Argentinian-born screenwriter and director who has lived in France since the mid-60s.

The Spider's Stratagem/La Strategia del Ragno (co-w) 70. Celine and Justine Go Boating/Celine et Justine Vont en Bateau (co-w) 74. Serail (d) 76, etc.

Dehlavi, Jamil
Pakistani director.

The Blood of Hussain 80. Immaculate Conception (GB) 92, etc.

Dehn, Paul (1912–1976)
British screenwriter, former film critic.

Seven Days to Noon (AA) 51. Orders to Kill 58. *Goldfinger* 64. The Spy Who Came in from the Cold 65. The Deadly Affair 66. The Taming of the Shrew 67. Beneath the Planet of the Apes (and two sequels) 67. Fragment of Fear (& p) 69. Murder on the Orient Express (AAN) 74, etc.

Dehner, John (1915–1992) (John Forkum)
American character actor, usually as sympathetic smart alec or dastardly villain, a former animator, from radio.

Captain Eddie 45. The Secret of St Ives 49. Last of the Buccaneers 50. Lorna Doone 51. Scaramouche 52. Apache 54. Carousel 56. The Left-handed Gun (as Pat Garrett) 58. Timbuktu 59. The Chapman Report 62. Critic's Choice 63. Youngblood Hawke 63. Stiletto 69. Support Your Local Gunfighter 71. Fun with Dick and Jane 77. The Boys from Brazil 78. The Right Stuff 83. Creator 84. Jagged Edge 85, etc.

TV series: The Westerner 60. The Roaring Twenties 60–62. The Baileys of Balboa 64–65. The Doris Day Show 71–73. Temperatures Rising 73–74. Big Hawaii 77. Young Maverick 79–80. Enos 80–81.

Deighton, Len (1929–)
British writer of convoluted spy thrillers.

The Ipcress File (oa) 65. Funeral in Berlin (oa) 66. Billion Dollar Brain (oa) 67. Only When I Larf (w) 68. Spy Story 76. Bullet to Beijing (oa) 95. Midnight in Saint Petersburg (oa) 95, etc.

Deitch, Donna (1945–)
American director who first attracted attention by making a lesbian affair a box-office success in *Desert Hearts*. She studied as an artist before attending film school and began by making documentaries. She appears in a documentary on women film-makers, *Calling the Shots* 88.

Woman to Woman (doc) 75. The Great Wall of Los Angeles (doc) 78. *Desert Hearts* 85. The Women of Brewster Place (TV) 89. Angel of Desire 94. Angel on My Shoulder (doc) 97, etc.

Dejczer, Maciej (1953–)
Polish director and screenwriter.

Dzieci-Smieci (wd) 86. Three Hundred Miles to Heaven/300 Mil Do Nieba (d) 89. The Brute/The Hoodlum (d) 96, etc.

Dekker, Albert (1904–1968)
Dutch-American stage actor of long experience; film career disappointing. Hanged himself.
■ The Great Garrick 37. Marie Antoinette 38. The Last Warning 38. She Married an Artist 38. The Lone Wolf in Paris 38. Extortion 38. Paris Honeymoon 39. Never Say Die 39. Hotel Imperial 39. Beau Geste 39. The Man in the Iron Mask 39. The Great Commandment 39. *Dr Cyclops* 40. Strange Cargo 40. Rangers of Fortune 40. Seven Sinners 40. You're the One 41. Blonde Inspiration 41. Reaching for the Sun 41. Buy Me That Town 41. Honky Tonk 41. *Among the Living* 41. Night in New Orleans 42. Wake Island 42. Once Upon a Honeymoon 42. Star Spangled Rhythm 42. The Lady Has Plans 42. In Old California 42. Yokel Boy 42. The Forest Rangers 42. Woman of the Town 43. War of the Wildcats 43. Buckskin Frontier 43. The Kansan 43. Experiment Perilous 44. Incendiary Blonde 45. Hold that Blonde 45. Salome Where She Danced 45. The French Key 46. *The Killers* 46. California 46. Suspense 46. The Pretender 47. Gentleman's Agreement 47. Wyoming 47. Cass Timberlane 47. Slave Girl 47. The Fabulous Texan 47. Fury at Furnace Creek 48. Lulu Belle 48. Search for Danger 49. Bride of Vengeance 49. Tarzan's Magic Fountain 49. The Kid from Texas 50. Destination Murder 50. The Furies 50. As Young as You Feel 51. Wait till the Sun Shines Nellie 52. The Silver Chalice 54. East of Eden 55. Kiss Me Deadly 55. Illegal 55. She Devil 57. These Thousand Hills 59. Middle of the Night 59. The Wonderful Country 59. Suddenly Last Summer 59. The Sound and the Fury 59. Come Spy with Me 67. The Wild Bunch 69.

Dekker, Fred (1959–)
American screenwriter and director.
Night of the Creeps 86. Monster Squad 87. Teen Agent (story) 91. Ricochet (story) 91. Robocop 3 (co-w, d) 93.

Del Carril, Hugo (1912–1989) (Piero Bruno Fontana)
Argentinian leading director and actor who first gained fame as a tango singer. The son of an Italian architect who spent his earliest years in France, he was in films from 1937, becoming a director in the late 40s. His greatest success came during the regime of Argentinian president Juan Perón, and his career declined with the president's departure in the mid-50s. When Perón returned to power in the early 70s, he became head of the National Film Institute, resigning on the death of the president in 1974.
Los Muchachos de Antes No Usaban Gomina (a only) 37. Madreselva (a only) 38. La Vida de Carlos Gardel (a only) 39. Historias del 900 49. *Dark River*/Las Aguas Bajan Turbias 52. La Quintrala 55. La Fille de Feu (Fr.) (a only) 58. Culpable 60. Amorina 61. Yo Maté a Facundo 75. The Tango Tells Its Story (a only) 78, etc.

Del Giudice, Filippo (1892–1961)
Exuberant Italian producer who settled in England and helped create some of the best British films of the 40s, persuading Noël Coward to write and star in *In Which We Serve* and Laurence Olivier to make *Henry V* (Olivier handed over the special Oscar he won for the film to Del Giudice in gratitude). Born in Trani, he became a lawyer, leaving Italy in the early 30s because of financial difficulties. In London, he first taught English to Italian waiters before finding financial backing to found Two Cities Films in 1937. After he lost control of the company to the Rank Organization in the mid-40s, when *Henry V* went over budget, he retired to a monastery and then founded Pilgrim Films, planning a series of religious epics. Later plans foundered for lack of finance, and he returned to Italy to die.
Books: 1997, *The Best of British* by Charles Drazin (contains a chapter on Del Giudice)
French without Tears 39. In Which We Serve 42. Henry V 44. The Way Ahead 44. Blithe Spirit 45. Odd Man Out 47. The Guinea Pig 48, many others.
❝ Everyman's image of the big-time movie producer – a cigar-chewing, language-fracturing executive, dumpy, pot-bellied and masked by the inevitable dark glasses. – *John Cottrell*
I know no one else in British films so kind, generous, imaginative and courageous. – *Laurence Olivier*

Del Prete, Duilio (c. 1937–1998)
Italian actor, singer and cabaret entertainer, from the stage.
I Sette Fratelli Cervi 68. Alfredo Alfredo 72. The Assassination of Trotsky 72. How Funny Can Sex Be? 73. Daisy Miller (US) 74. My Friends/Amici Miei 75. Divine Creature 75. At Long Last Love (US) 75. Nella Misura In Cui … 79. The Marseilles Connection 84. Carla 89. Voci dal Profundo 91, etc.

Del Rio, Dolores (1905–1983) (Dolores Asunsolo)
Mexican leading lady with aristocratic background; beautiful and popular star of the 20s and 30s. Her second husband was art director Cedric Gibbons.
Joanna (debut) 25. High Stepper 26. What Price Glory? 27. *The Loves of Carmen* 27. Resurrection 28. Evangeline 29. The Bad One 30. The Dove 31. Bird of Paradise 32. Flying Down to Rio 33. Wonder Bar 34. Madame Du Barry 34. Lancer Spy 37. *Journey into Fear* 42. Portrait of Maria 45. The Fugitive 47. *Cheyenne Autumn* 64. Once upon a Time 67, many others.

Del Ruth, Roy (1895–1961)
Very competent American director, former gag writer for Mack Sennett.
■ sound films: Conquest 29. The Desert Song 29. The Hottentot 29. Gold Diggers of Broadway 29. The Aviator 29. Hold Everything 30. The Second Floor Mystery 30. Three Faces East 30. The Life of the Party 30. My Past 31. Divorce Among Friends 31. *The Maltese Falcon* 31. Side Show 31. Blonde Crazy 31. Taxi 32. Beauty and the Boss 32. Winner Take All 32. *Blessed Event* 32. Employees Entrance 33. The Mind Reader 33. The Little Giant 33. Captured 33. Bureau of Missing Persons 33. *Lady Killer* 33. Bulldog Drummond Strikes Back 34. Upperworld 34. Kid Millions 34. *Folies Bergere* 35. Broadway Melody of 1936 35. *Thanks a Million* 35. It Had to Happen 36. Private Number 36. Born to Dance 36. *On the Avenue* 37. Broadway Melody of 1938. Happy Landing 38. My Lucky Star 38. Tail Spin 39. The Star Maker 39. Here I Am A Stranger 39. He Married His Wife 40. *Topper Returns* 41. The Chocolate Soldier 41. Maisie Gets Her Man 42. Dubarry was a Lady 43. Broadway Rhythm 44. Barbary Coast Gent 44. It Happened on Fifth Avenue 47. The Babe Ruth Story 48. The Red Light 49. Always Leave Them Laughing 49. West Point Story 50. On Moonlight Bay 51. Starlift 51. About Face 52. Stop You're Killing Me 52. Three Sailors and a Girl 53. Phantom of the Rue Morgue 54. The Alligator People 59. Why Must I Die 60.

Del Toro, Benicio (1967–)
American actor, from television. Born in Santurce, Puerto Rico, he was raised in Pennsylvania and studied at the University of California, planning to become a lawyer. Instead, he went on to study acting at New York's Circle in the Square Acting School, the Stella Adler Conservatory, and the Actors Circle Theater in Los Angeles.
Big Top Pee-wee 88. Licence to Kill 89. The Indian Runner 91. Christopher Columbus: The Discovery 92. Fearless 93. Money for Nothing 93. China Moon 94. Swimming with Sharks/The Buddy Factor 95. The Usual Suspects 95. Basquiat 96. The Fan 96. The Funeral 96. Excess Baggage 97. Fear & Loathing in Las Vegas 98. Che Guevara: A Revolutionary Life 99. Snatch 00. The Way of the Gun 00. Traffic (AA, BFA) 00, etc.
❝ It is possible for an actor to take his part too seriously. – *Terry Gilliam*

Del Toro, Guillermo (1965–)
Mexican director and screenwriter, from television, a former assistant to Jaime Humberto Hermosillo and a special effects and make-up expert, studying in the US under Dick Smith. He is also the author of a study of Alfred Hitchcock.
Invasion (TV) 90. Cronos 93. Mimic (co-w, d) 97, etc.

Delair, Suzy (1916–)
Vivacious French entertainer, in several films.
Quai des Orfèvres 47. Lady Paname 49. Robinson Crusoe Land 50. Gervaise 55. Rocco and his Brothers 60. Is Paris Burning? 66, etc.

Delaney, Shelagh (1939–)
British playwright whose chief contributions to the screen are *A Taste of Honey* and *Charlie Bubbles*.
The Railway Station Man 92.

Delannoy, Jean (1908–)
French director, formerly journalist and cutter.
La Symphonie Pastorale 40. *L'Eternel Retour* 43. Les Jeux Sont Faits 47. *Dieu a Besoin des Hommes* 49. Le Garçon Sauvage 51. The Moment of Truth 52. Marie Antoinette 56. Notre Dame de Paris 56. Maigret Sets a Trap 57. Le Soleil des Voyous 67. Only the Cool/La Peau de Torpedo 69. Bernadette 87, many others.

Delany, Dana (1956–)
American leading actress.
The Fan 81. Almost You 84. Where the River Runs Black 86. Moon over Parador 88. Patty Hearst 88. Light Sleeper 91. Housesitter 92. Tombstone 93. Batman: Mask of the Phantasm (voice) 94. *Exit to Eden* (as Mistress Lisa) 94. Live Nude Girls 95. Fly Away Home 96. Wide Awake 97. Dead Man's Curve/The Curve 98, etc.
TV series: China Beach (as Nurse Colleen McMurphy) 88–91.

Delderfield, Ronald Frederick (1912–1972)
English playwright and novelist of provincial domestic life, a former journalist.
Autobiography: 1951, *Nobody Shouted Author*. 1956, *Bird's Eye View*.
All Over Town (oa) 49. Worm's Eye View (w) 50. Glad Tidings (oa) 52. Where There's a Will (w) 53. Now and Forever (w) 56. On the Fiddle (oa) 61, etc.
TV series: The Adventures of Ben Gunn 56.

Delerue, Georges (1925–1992)
French composer.
Hiroshima Mon Amour 59. Les Jeux de L'Amour 60. Une Aussi Longue Absence 61. Shoot the Pianist 61. Jules et Jim 61. Silken Skin 63. The Pumpkin Eater 64. Viva Maria 65. A Man for All Seasons 66. The 25th Hour 67. Interlude 68. Women in Love 69. Anne of the Thousand Days (AAN) 69. The Conformist 70. The Horseman 70. The Day of the Dolphin (AAN) 73. The Slap 74. Julia (AAN) 77. Tendre Poulet 77. Get Out Your Handkerchiefs 78. A Little Romance (AA) 79. Love on the Run 79. True Confessions 81. Partners 82. The Escape Artist 82. Exposed 83. Agnes of God 85. Salvador 86. Platoon 86. The Lonely Passion of Judith Hearne 87. The House on Carroll Street 88. Biloxi Blues 88. Twins 88. Beaches 88. Steel Magnolias 89. Show of Force 90. Curly Sue 91. Black Robe 91. Dien Bien Phu 92. Memento Mori (TV) 92, many others.

Delevanti, Cyril (1887–1975)
British-born stage actor who played aged gentlemen for many years.
Red Barry 38. Man Hunt 41. Son of Dracula 43. Ministry of Fear 45. Forever Amber 47. Land of the Pharaohs 55. Bye Bye Birdie 63. Mary Poppins 64. *Night of the Iguana* 64. The Greatest Story Ever Told 65. Counterpoint 67. The Killing of Sister George 68. Bedknobs and Broomsticks 71. Black Eye 73, many others.

Delfont, Bernard (1910–1994) (Lord Delfont, formerly Barnet Winogradsky)
British show business entrepreneur, brother of Lord Grade; mainly involved in live entertainment until the 70s when he came to head the EMI entertainment complex.

Delgado, Roger (1918–1973)
English character actor, of Spanish and French parents, in aristocratic and villainous roles, best known as The Master in the TV series *Dr Who*. Educated at the London School of Economics, he began acting in regional repertory. Died in a car crash.
The Captain's Paradise 53. Star 53. Storm over the Nile 56. Battle of the River Plate 56. Sea Fury 58. First Man in Space 59. The Stranglers of Bombay 60. The Terror of the Tongs 61. The Singer Not the Song 61. The Road to Hong Kong 62. The Running Man 63. Masquerade 65. Khartoum 66. The Mummy's Shroud 67. The Assassination Bureau 69. Anthony and Cleopatra 73, etc.
TV series: Sir Francis Drake 62.

Delhomme, Benoit
French cinematographer, in international films.
The Scent of Green Papaya/Mui Du Du Xanh 93. Cyclo/Xich Lo 95. Un Air de Famille 96. When the Cat's Away/Chacun Cherche Con Chat 96. Artemisia 97. The Winslow Boy (US) 98. The Loss of Sexual Innocence (US) 98. With or Without You (GB) 99. Miss Julie (GB) 99. Sade 00, etc.

Dell, Dorothy (1915–1934) (Dorothy Goff)
American beauty queen whose film career was cut short by a car crash.
■ Wharf Angel 34. Little Miss Marker 34. Shoot the Works 34.

Dell, Gabriel (1920–1988) (Gabriel del Vecchio)
American actor, one of the original Dead End Kids who in the 60s emerged as a TV character actor.
Dead End 37. Crime School 38. Little Tough Guy 38. Hell's Kitchen 39. On Dress Parade 39. They Made Me a Criminal 39. Junior G-Men 40. Give Us Wings 41. Mob Town 41. Junior G-Men of the Air 42. Mug Town 42. Block Busters 44. Follow the Leader 44. Come Out Fighting 45. Who Is Harry Kellerman and Why Is He Saying These Terrible Things About Me? 71. Framed 74. The Escape Artist 82, etc.

Dell, Jeffrey (1904–1985)
British comedy writer, author in the 30s of *Nobody Ordered Wolves*, a satirical novel of the film industry.
Sanders of the River (co-w) 35. The Saint's Vacation 41. Thunder Rock (co-w) 42. *Don't Take it to Heart* (& d) 44. It's Hard to Be Good (& d) 48. The Dark Man (& d) 50. Brothers-in-Law (co-w) 56. Lucky Jim (co-w) 58. Carlton-Browne of the F.O. (& co-d) 59. A French Mistress (co-w) 61. Rotten to the Core (co-w) 65. The Family Way (co-w) 66, etc.

Dell, Myrna (1924–) (Marilyn Dunlap)
American supporting actress, with RKO in the 40s.
The Falcon in San Francisco 45. Step by Step 46. Nocturne 46. Fighting Father Dunne 48. The Judge Steps Out 49. The Bushwhackers 52. Last of the Desperados 55. Naked Hills 55. The Toughest Man Alive 55. Ma Barker's Killer Brood 60. Buddy Buddy 81, etc.

Delli Colli, Tonino (1923–)
Distinguished Italian cinematographer, noted for his work with Sergio Leone and Pier Paolo Pasolini.
Il Paese senza Pace 42. Toto a Colori 51. Le Rouge et le Noir 54. Accattone 61. Mama Roma 62. The Gospel According to St Matthew/Il Vangelo Secondo Matteo 64. The Hawks and the Sparrows/Uccellacci e Uccellini 66. The Good, the Bad and the Ugly 66. La Mandragola 66. Once Upon a Time in the West 68. Pigsty/Porcile 69. Pussycat, Pussycat I Love You 70. The Decameron 70. The Canterbury Tales 71. Lacombe, Lucien 73. Salo, or the 120 Days of Sodom 75. Seven Beauties 76. The Purple Taxi/Un Taxi Mauve 77. Viva Italia 78. Sunday Lovers 80. Tales of Ordinary Madness/Storie di Ordinaria Follia 81. Trenchcoat 83. Once Upon a Time in America 84. Ginger and Fred 86. The Name of the Rose 86. The Voice of the Moon/La Voce della Luna 90. The African/L'Africana 91. Bitter Moon 92. En Suivant la Comète 94. Death and the Maiden (GB/US/Fr.) 94. Life Is Beautiful 97, many others.

Delluc, Louis (1892–1924)
Pioneer French director of the 20s, associated with the impressionist school.
■ Fièvre 21. La Femme de Nulle Part 22. L'Inondation 24.

Delon, Alain (1935–)
Handsome, romantic-looking French leading actor, producer and occasional screenwriter. Born in the Paris suburb of Sceaux, after a disturbed childhood he joined the marines in his 'teens and later worked in various occupations before trying acting in 1957. He gained international recognition as the androgynous Tom Ripley in *Plein Soleil*, though he failed to make much of a mark in Hollywood. He maintained his European fame with a series of gangster movies from the 70s, and set up his own company, Adel Productions. The first of his two wives was actress Nathalie Delon (née Canovas). He was romantically involved with Romy Schneider and had a son with actress and singer Nico.
When a Woman Meddles/Quand La Femme S'en Mele 57. Christine 59. *Purple Noon/Plein Soleil* 60. Rocco and his Brothers (It./Fr.) 60. The Eclipse/L'Eclisse (It./Fr.) 62. The Leopard/Il Gattopardo (US/It.) 63. The Black Tulip/La Tulipe Noire 64. The Yellow Rolls-Royce (GB) 64. Joy

conceivable gadget; and when a scene, consisting of two lines and a movement to a door, has been played for the fortieth time, and is still not right, and it's hours over time and you've a headache like a load of bricks and an empty stomach, there was nothing, according to Gerald, which bore a greater similarity to unadulterated hell. – *Daphne du Maurier*

We really thought, looking at him, that it was easy; and for the first ten years of our life in the theatre, nobody could hear a word we said. We thought he was being really natural; of course, he was a genius of a technician giving that appearance, that's all. – *Sir Laurence Olivier*

Du Pré, Jacqueline (1945–1987)
English cellist, whose career was brought to an end in 1973 by multiple sclerosis. Married conductor Daniel Barenboim. She was played by Emily WATSON in the biopic *Hilary and Jackie* 98.

Biography: 1997, *A Genius in the Family* by Hilary and Piers du Pré. 1998, *Jacqueline du Pré* by Elizabeth Wilson.

Du Prez, John (1946–)
British composer.

Bullshot! 83. Monty Python's The Meaning of Life 83. A Private Function 84. She'll Be Wearing Pink Pajamas 84. Once Bitten 85. Personal Services 87. A Fish Called Wanda 88. A Chorus of Disapproval 89. Teenage Mutant Ninja Turtles 90. Teenage Mutant Ninja Turtles II: The Secret of the Ooze 91. Teenage Mutant Ninja Turtles III: The Turtles Are Back ... in Time 92, etc.

Dubbins, Don (1929–1991)
American second lead of the 50s.

From Here to Eternity 53. Tribute to a Bad Man 56. These Wilder Years 57. From the Earth to the Moon 58. The Enchanted Island 58. The Prize 63. The Illustrated Man 69, etc.

Dubov, Paul (c. 1917–1979)
American character actor and, with his wife Gwen Bagni, novelist and screenwriter; his best roles were in the films of Samuel FULLER.

Little Tough Guy 38. The Boss of Big Town 42. Bombay Clipper 42. Strange Holiday 45. Triple Trouble 50. High Noon 52. I, the Jury 53. Abbott and Costello Meet the Keystone Kops 55. The Day the World Ended 56. Shake, Rattle & Rock! 56. China Gate 57. Forty Guns 57. The Crimson Kimono 59. Verboten! 59. The Purple Gang 60. Underworld USA 61. Irma la Douce 63. Shock Corridor 63. With Six You Get Egg Roll (oa, co-w) 68, etc.

Dubroux, Danièle (1947–)
French director, screenwriter and actress, a former film critic.

The Heiress/Die Erbtochter (a, co-d) 82. Les Amants Terribles (a, w, co-d) 85. La Petite Allumeuse (co-w, d) 87. Border Line (a, wd) 91. Diary of a Seducer/Le Journal D'Un Seducteur (a, wd) 95. The School of Flesh/L'Ecole De La Chair (a) 98. Midnight Test/L'Examen De Minuit (a, wd) 98, etc.

Ducey, Caroline
French actress, who came to international notice in Catherine Breillat's movie *Romance*, which was a *succès de scandale*. She was acting from the age of 11, studied at the Marseille Conservatoire and began on stage.

Too Much Happiness/Trop de Bonheur 94. Innocent 98. Romance 99. La Chambre Obscure 00, etc.

Duchin, Eddy (1909–1951)
American pianist and bandleader, best remembered for being impersonated by Tyrone Power in *The Eddy Duchin Story*.

■ Mr Broadway 32. Coronado 35. Hit Parade 37.

Duchovny, David (1960–)
American leading actor, best known for playing FBI agent Fox Mulder in the TV series *The X Files*. Born in New York, he studied at Princeton and Yale, where he began acting to help pay for his studies. In the *X-Files'* eighth season, he was earning a reported $400,000 an episode. Married actress Tea LEONI in 1997.

Working Girl 88. New Year's Day 89. Julia Has Two Lovers 90. Bad Influence 90. The Rapture 91. Don't Tell Mom the Babysitter's Dead 91. Red Shoe Diaries (TV) 92. Ruby 92. Chaplin 92. Beethoven 92. Venice, Venice (It.) 92. Kalifornia 93. Playing God 97. Red Shoe Diaries 8: Night of Abandon 97. The X Files 98. Return to Me 00, etc.

TV series: Twin Peaks 90.

❝ I am the conduit through which America views the soft underbelly of women's erotic desires. – *D.D.*

Dudgeon, Elspeth (1871–1955)
British stage actress who made her first appearance on screen disguised as an old man.

The Old Dark House (as John Dudgeon) 32. The Moonstone 34. Becky Sharp 35. Camille 36. The Great Garrick 37. Mystery House 38. Pride and Prejudice 40. Random Harvest 42. The Canterville Ghost 44. If Winter Comes 47. The Paradine Case 48. The Great Sinner 49, etc.

Dudikoff, Michael (1954–)
American leading actor in action movies.

The Black Marble 77. Bloody Birthday 80. I Ought to Be in Pictures 82. Tron 82. Making Love 82. Bachelor Party 84. American Ninja 85. Avenging Force 86. Radioactive Dreams 86. American Ninja 2: The Confrontation 87. Platoon Leader 87. River of Death 90. American Ninja 4: The Annihilation 91. The Human Shield 92. Cyberjack/Virtual Assassin 95. Soldier Boyz 95. Chain of Command 95. Moving Target 96. Crash Drive 96. Bounty Hunters 96. Black Thunder 97. Freedom Strike 97. Hardball 97. Ringmaster 98, etc.

TV series: Cobra 93.

Dudley, Anne (1956–)
British composer and keyboard player, born in Chatham, Kent.

Hiding Out (US) 87. Buster 88. Wilt 89. The Mighty Quinn (US) 89. Say Anything (US) 89. The Miracle 90. The Pope Must Die/The Pope Must Diet 91. The Crying Game 92. Knight Moves (US/Ger.) 92. Felidae 94. When Saturday Comes 96. The Grotesque/Gentlemen Don't Eat Poets/ Grave Indiscretions 96. Hollow Reed 96. The Full Monty (AA) 97. American History X (US) 98, etc.

Dudley-Ward, Penelope (1919–1982)
British leading lady of the 40s.

The Case of the Frightened Lady 39. The Demi-Paradise 43. The Way Ahead 44, etc.

Duel, Pete (1940–1972) (Peter Deuel)
American leading man. Died of a gunshot wound, an apparent suicide.

A Time for Giving 69. Cannon for Cordoba 70. The Young Country (TV) 71, etc.

TV series: Gidget 65–66. Love on a Rooftop 66–67. *Alias Smith and Jones* 71–72.

Duff, Howard (1917–1990)
American actor with stage experience; usually played good-looking but shifty types.

Brute Force 47. *Naked City* 48. All My Sons 48. Calamity Jane and Sam Bass 50. Woman in Hiding 50. Shakedown 50. Steel Town 52. Women's Prison 54. While the City Sleeps 56. Boys' Night Out 62. Sardanapalus the Great (It.) 63. The Late Show 77. In the Glitter Palace (TV) 78. A Wedding 78. Kramer vs Kramer 79. Double Negative 80. Oh God Book Two 80. No Way Out 87, etc.

TV series: Mr Adams and Eve 56–57. Dante 60. The Felony Squad 66–68. Flamingo Road 80–81.

Duffell, Peter (1924–)
British director.

The House that Dripped Blood 71. England Made Me 72. Inside Out 75. The Far Pavilions (TV) 84. Letters to an Unknown Lover (TV) 85. Inspector Morse 88. Genghis Khan 92, etc.

Dugan, Dennis (1946–)
American director of lowbrow comedies, a former leading actor, usually in rather clumsy comic roles. He began acting while still at school and appeared in off-Broadway productions in the early 70s. Married actress Joyce VAN PATTEN.

AS ACTOR: The Day of the Locust 74. Smile 74. Norman ... Is That You? 76. Harry and Walter Go to New York 76. The Spaceman and King Arthur 79. The Howling 80. Water 85. Can't Buy Me Love 87. Parenthood 89, etc.

AS DIRECTOR: Problem Child 90. Brain Donors 92. Happy Gilmore 96. Beverly Hills Ninja 97. Big Daddy 99, etc.

TV series: Rich Man, Poor Man – Book 1 76. Richie Brockelman, Private Eye 78. Empire 84. Shadow Chasers 85–86.

Dugan, Tom (1889–1955)
American supporting comic actor, often seen as Irish cop or minor criminal.

Sharp Shooters 27. Lights of New York 28. Sonny Boy 29. Bright Lights 31. Doctor X 32. Grand Slam 33. Palooka 34. Princess O'Hara 35. Pick a Star 37. Four Daughters 38. The Housekeeper's Daughter 39. The Ghost Breakers 40. The Monster and the Girl 41. *To Be Or Not To Be* 42. Bataan 43. Up in Arms 44. Bringing Up Father 46. Good News 47. Take Me Out to the Ball Game 49. The Lemon Drop Kid 51, many others.

Duggan, Andrew (1923–1988)
American character actor of stalwart types.

Patterns 56. The Bravados 58. The Chapman Report 62. FBI Code 98 66. The Secret War of Harry Frigg 67. The Skin Game 71. Jigsaw (TV) 72. The Bears and I 74. It's Alive 77. The Private Files of J. Edgar Hoover 78, etc.

TV series: Bourbon Street Beat 59. Room for One More 61. Twelve O'Clock High 65–67. Lancer 68–69.

Duggan, Pat (1910–)
American producer, former performer and writer.

Red Garters 54. The Vagabond King 56. The Search for Bridey Murphy 57. The Young Savages 61, etc.

Duhamel, Antoine (1925–)
French composer.

Gala 62. Un Amour de Guerre 64. Pierrot le Fou 65. Fugue 66. Weekend 68. Stolen Kisses/Baisers Volés 68. Mississippi Mermaid/La Sirène du Mississippi 69. The Wild Child/L'Enfant Sauvage 69. Bed and Board/Domicile Conjugal 71. L'Acrobate 75. Twisted Obsession 90. These Foolish Things/Daddy Nostalgie 90. Age of Beauty/ Belle époque 92. Belmonte 95. Ridicule 96. The Good Life/La Buena Vida 96, etc.

Duigan, John (1949–)
English-born director and screenwriter, in Australia from the early 60s.

The Firm Man 75. The Trespassers 76. Mouth to Mouth (wd) 78. Dimboola 79. Winter of Our Dreams (wd) 81. Far East (wd) 82. One Night Stand 84. The Year My Voice Broke (wd) 87. Romero (d) 89. Flirting (wd) 89. Wide Sargasso Sea (co-w,d) 92. Sirens (wd) 94. The Journey of the August King (d) 95. The Leading Man (d) 96. Lawn Dogs (d) 97. Paranoid (wd) 99, etc.

Dukakis, Olympia (1931–)
American actress, mainly on the stage.

Lilith 64. Twice a Man 64. John and Mary 69. Death Wish 74. Rich Kids 79. The Wanderers 79. The Idolmaker 80. Flanagan 85. Walls of Glass 85. Moonstruck (AA) 87. Working Girl 88. Dad 89. Look Who's Talking 89. Steel Magnolias 89. In the Spirit 90. Look Who's Talking Too 90. Fire in the Dark 91. Over the Hill 93. The Cemetery Club 93. Look Who's Talking Now 93. Digger 93. I Love Trouble 94. Jeffrey 95. Mighty Aphrodite 95. Mr Holland's Opus 95. Jerusalem 96. Milk & Money 96. Picture Perfect 97. Mafia!/Jane Austen's Mafia 98. Armistead Maupin's More Tales of the City (TV) 98. Last of the Blonde Bombshells (TV) 00, etc.

TV series: Tales from the City 93.

Duke, Bill (1943–)
American director and actor, usually as a heavy, from television, where he also directed episodes of *Falcon Crest*, *Hill Street Blues* and *Miami Vice*.

An American Gigolo (a) 80. The Killing Floor (d) 84. Commando (a) 85. Predator (a) 87. No Man's Land (a) 87. Action Jackson (a) 88. Bird on a Wire (a) 91. A Rage in Harlem (d) 91. Deep Cover (d) 92. The Cemetery Club (d) 93. Menace II Society (a) 93. Sister Act 2 (d) 93. Hoods (d) 96. Hoodlum (d) 97. Susan's Plan (d) 98. Fever (a) 99. Payback (a) 99, etc.

TV series: Palmerstown, USA 80–81.

Duke, Daryl
Canadian director in Hollywood.

The Psychiatrist (TV) 70. Happiness Is a Warm Clue (TV) 73. The President's Plane Is Missing (TV) 73. I Heard the Owl Call My Name (TV) 73. Payday 73. A Cry for Help (TV) 75. *Griffin and Phoenix* (TV) 76. The Silent Partner 78. Hard Feelings 82. *The Thorn Birds* (TV) 83. Florence Nightingale (TV) 84. Tai-pan 86. Fatal Memories (TV) 92, etc.

Duke, Ivy (1895–)
Star of British silent screen; married to Guy Newall.

The Garden of Resurrection 18. The Lure of Crooning Water 20. The Persistent Lover 22. The Starlit Garden 23. The Great Prince Shan 24. A Knight in London 29, etc.

Duke, Patty (1946–)
American child actress who found difficulty in graceful adaptation to adult roles. Former wife of John Astin.

I'll Cry Tomorrow 55. Somebody Up There Likes Me 56. Country Music Holiday 57. The Goddess 58. Happy Anniversary 59. 4-D Man 59. The Power and the Glory (TV) 62. *The Miracle Worker* (AA) 62. Billie 65. Valley of the Dolls 67. Me Natalie 69. My Sweet Charlie (TV) 70. Two on a Bench (TV) 71. If Tomorrow Comes (TV) 71. She Waits (TV) 71. You'll Like My Mother 72. Deadly Harvest (TV) 72. Nightmare (TV) 73. Captains and the Kings (TV) 76. A Family Upside Down (TV) 78. The Swarm 78. Hanging by a Thread (TV) 79. The Miracle Worker (TV) 79. Before and After (TV) 80. Best Kept Secrets (TV) 84. Prelude to a Kiss 92. Harvest of Fire (TV) 95, etc.

TV series: *The Patty Duke Show* 63–65. It Takes Two 82. Hail to the Chief 85. Amazing Grace 95– .

Duke, Vernon (1903–1969) (Vladimir Dubelsky)
Russian-American song composer. Shows filmed include *Cabin in the Sky*, but he wrote mostly for revue.

Dukes, David (1945–2000)
American leading man. Died of heart failure.

The Wild Party 74. A Fire in the Sky (TV) 77. 79 Park Avenue (TV) 77. A Little Romance 79. The First Deadly Sin 80. Only When I Laugh 81. Without a Trace 83. The Winds of War (TV) 83. Space (TV) 85. The Men's Club 86. Catch the Heat 87. Rawhead Rex 87. Date with an Angel 87. See You in the Morning 89. Snow Kill 90. The Handmaid's Tale 90. She Woke Up 92. Me and the Kid 93. And the Band Played On 93. Norma Jean and Marilyn (TV) 95. Last Stand at Saber River (TV) 96. Fled 96. Gods and Monsters 98, etc.

TV series: Beacon Hill 75. Sisters 91. The Mommies 93-95. The Pauly Shore Show 97. Dawson's Creek 98.

Dulac, Germaine (1882–1942) (G. Saisset-Schneider)
French director with an interest in surrealism and the avant-garde. She began as a journalist, forming her own production company in 1915, becoming a member of the Impressionist school that also included Louis DELLUC. Many of her films no longer exist.

Ames de Fous 18. Le Diable dans la Ville 24. The Seashell and the Clergyman 26. Theme and Variations 30, etc.

Dullea, Keir (1936–)
American leading man, usually in roles of nervous tension.

The Hoodlum Priest 61. *David and Lisa* 62. Mail Order Bride 64. The Thin Red Line 64. Bunny Lake is Missing 65. Madame X 66. The Fox 68. De Sade 69. 2001: A Space Odyssey 69. Last of the Big Guns 73. Paperback Hero 73. Paul and Michelle 74. Black Christmas 75. Full Circle 77. Leopard in the Snow 78. Brave New World (TV) 79. Brain Waves 83. 2010 84. The Next One 85. Oh, What a Night 92, etc.

Dumas, Alexandre (1802–1870)
Highly industrious French novelist, mainly of swashbuckling adventures. Films resulting include several versions of *The Count of Monte Cristo* and *The Three Musketeers*, *The Man in the Iron Mask*, *The Fighting Guardsman* and *The Black Tulip*.

Dumas, Alexandre (1824–1895)
French novelist best known for *Camille*, which has been filmed several times.

Dumbrille, Douglass (1890–1974)
Canadian character actor, long in Hollywood and typecast as smooth, suave villain of many a 'B' picture and an admirable foil for many great comedians.

His Woman 31. That's My Boy 32. Elmer the Great 33. Voltaire 33. Lady Killer 34. Broadway Bill 34. Naughty Marietta 35. Crime and Punishment 35. Lives of a Bengal Lancer 35. *Mr Deeds Goes to Town* 36. *A Day at the Races* 37. The Firefly 37. Ali Baba Goes to Town 37. Mr Moto on Danger Island 38. The Three Musketeers 39. Charlie Chan at Treasure Island 39. *The Big Store* 41. Ride 'Em Cowboy 42. Lost in a Harem 44. The Frozen Ghost 45. *Road to Utopia* 45. The Cat Creeps 46. Christmas Eve 47. Alimony 49. Riding High 50. Son of Paleface 52. Jupiter's Darling 55. The Ten Commandments 56. The Buccaneer 58. Shock Treatment 63, many others.

TV series: China Smith 52–55. The Life of Riley 53–58. The Phil Silvers Show 63. Petticoat Junction 64–65.

Dumke, Ralph (1900–1964)
Heavily-built American supporting actor.

All the King's Men 49. Mystery Street 50. The Mob 51. Lili 53. Rails into Laramie 54. The Solid Gold Cadillac 56. The Buster Keaton Story 57, etc.

Dumont, Bruno (1985–)
French director and screenwriter of films dealing with relentlessly ordinary lives, a former philosophy teacher and journalist. His first two films used non-professional casts, two of whom, Emmanuel Schotté and Séverine Caneele, won best actor and actress awards at the Cannes Film Festival in 2000.

The Life of Jesus/La Vie de Jesus 97. Humanity/L'Humanité 99, etc.

“ What interests me is life, people, the small things. Cinema is for the body, for the emotions. – *B.D.*

I'm always looking for things to film that are drab, ordinary, and consequently it's why the crews on my movies get so bored: I'm forever filming boring, uninteresting things. When you shoot a beautiful landscape or a handsome actor, the camera has nothing to say. – *B.D.*

Dumont, Margaret (1889–1965) (Margaret Baker)
American character comedienne, the stately butt of many a comedian, notably Groucho Marx ('Ah, Mrs Rittenhouse, won't you … lie down?).

■ *The Coconuts* 29. *Animal Crackers* 30. The Girl Habit 30. *Duck Soup* 33. The Gridiron Flash 34. Fifteen Wives 34. Kentucky Kernels 34. *A Night at the Opera* 35. Orchids to You 35. Rendezvous 35. The Song and Dance Man 36. Anything Goes 36. *A Day at the Races* 37. The Life of the Party 37. High Flyers 37. Youth on Parole 37. Wise Girl 37. Dramatic School 39. *At the Circus* 39. *The Big Store* 41. Never Give a Sucker an Even Break 41. For Beauty's Sake 41. Born to Sing 41. Sing Your Worries Away 42. Rhythm Parade 42. About Face 42. The Dancing Masters 43. Bathing Beauty 44. Seven Days Ashore 44. Up in Arms 44. The Horn Blows at Midnight 45. Diamond Horseshoe 45. Sunset in El Dorado 45. The Little Giant 46. Susie Steps Out 46. Three for Bedroom C 52. Stop You're Killing Me 53. Shake Rattle and Rock 56. Auntie Mame 58. Zotz! 62. What a Way to Go 64.

TV series: My Friend Irma 52–54.

✪ For suffering beyond the call of comic duty. *A Day at the Races.*

Duna, Steffi (1913–1992) (Stephanie Berindey)
Hungarian dancer who appeared in some dramatic roles in the 30s.

The Indiscretions of Eve 31. La Cucaracha 35. The Dancing Pirate 36. Anthony Adverse 36. Pagliacci 37. Waterloo Bridge 40. River's End 41, etc.

Dunaway, Faye (1941–)
Blonde American leading actress. Born in Bascom, Florida, she studied drama at the University of Florida and at Boston University's School of Fine and Applied Arts, after which she made her debut on the New York stage, was soon contracted to producer Sam SPIEGEL and director Otto PREMINGER, and rapidly became a star with *Bonnie and Clyde*. She was romantically involved with comedian Lenny BRUCE, director Jerry SCHATZBERG and actors Marcello MASTROIANNI and Harris YULIN. Married rock singer Peter Wolf (1974–77) and photographer Terry O'Neill (divorced).

Evelyn Mulwray in *Chinatown* ; Diana Christensen in *Network*; her performance as Joan Crawford in *Mommie Dearest* has become a camp classic.

Autobiography: 1995, *Looking for Gatsby: My Life* (with Betsy Sharkey).

Biography: 1986, *Faye Dunaway* by Allan Hunter.

Hurry Sundown 67. The Happening 67. *Bonnie and Clyde* (AAN) 67. The Thomas Crown Affair 68. The Extraordinary Seaman 68. A Place for Lovers 69. The Arrangement 69. Little Big Man 70. Puzzle of a Downfall Child 70. Doc 71. The Deadly Trap 71. Oklahoma Crude 73. The Three Musketeers 73. Chinatown (AAN) 74. The Four Musketeers 74. The Towering Inferno 74. Three Days of the Condor 75. Voyage of the Dammed 76. *Network* (AA) 76. The Disappearance of Aimée (TV) 76. Eyes of Laura Mars 78. The Champ 79. The First Deadly Sin 80. Mommie Dearest 81. Evita Peron (TV) 82. The Wicked Lady 83. Christopher Columbus (TV) 84. Supergirl 84. Ordeal by Innocence 85. Barfly 87. Burning Secret 88. Midnight Crossing 88. The Gamble/La Partita 88. Crystal or Ash, Fire or Wind, as Long as It's Love/In una Notte di Chiaro di Luna 89. Wait until Spring, Bandini 89. The Handmaid's Tale 90. Silhouette 90. Christopher Columbus 91. Scorchers 91. Arizona Dream 91. The Temp 93. Don Juan DeMarco 95. Drunks 95. Dunston Checks In 96. Albino Alligator 96. Rebecca (TV) 97. The Twilight of the Golds (TV) 97. Gia (TV) 98. The Thomas Crown Affair 99. The Messenger: The Story Of Joan Of Arc 99. Stanley's Gig 00. The Yards 00, etc.

TV series: It Had to Be You 93.

“ A star today has to take charge of every aspect of her career. There are no studios left to do it for you. – *F.D.*

You could stand in the middle of the dirt road that ran in front of the house I was born in and look hard either way and see nothing but the long rows of peanuts snaking their way up to a stand of trees in the distance. – *F.D.*

Dunbar, Adrian (1958–)
Irish actor and screenwriter. He studied at the Guildhall School of Drama.

Sky Bandits/Gunbus 86. A World Apart 87. The Dawning 88. Dealers 89. My Left Foot 89. *Hear My Song* (& w) 91. Force of Duty (TV) 92. The Crying Game 92. The Playboys 92. A Woman's Guide to Adultery (TV) 93. Widow's Peak 93. Innocent Lies 95. The Near Room 95. Richard III 95. Melissa (TV) 97. The Jump (TV) 98. The General 98. The Wedding Tackle 99. Wild About Harry 00. Tough Love (TV) 00, etc.

Dunbar, Dixie (1915–1991) (Christina Dunbar)
American dancer and light lead, in films of the 30s.

George White's Scandals 34. King of Burlesque 36. Sing Baby Sing 36. Rebecca of Sunnybrook Farm 38. Alexander's Ragtime Band 38, etc.

Duncan, Archie (1914–1979)
Burly Scottish actor, the 'Little John' of TV's Robin Hood series.

Operation Diamond 47. The Bad Lord Byron 48. The Gorbals Story 51. Robin Hood 53. The Maggie 53. Laxdale Hall 54. Johnny on the Run 56. Harry Black 58. Lancelot and Guinevere 63. Ring of Bright Water 69, etc.

Duncan, Arletta (1914–1938)
American actress and singer, on the stage as a child, who was given a seven-year contract by Universal after winning a trip to Hollywood in a photographic contest. Committed suicide by jumping from the 'Hollywoodland' sign.

Frankenstein 31. Law and Order 32. Back Street 32. The Unexpected Father 32. Night World 32. Fast Companions 32, etc.

Duncan, David (1913–)
American screenwriter.

Sangaree 53. The Black Scorpion 57. The Thing that Couldn't Die 58. Monster on the Campus 58. The Leech Woman 60. The Time Machine 60.

Duncan, Isadora (1878–1927)
Flamboyant American dancer. Died when her scarf caught in the wheel of a car. She was the subject of a biopic, *Isadora/The Loves of Isadora* 58, directed by Karel Reisz and starring Vanessa Redgrave.

Duncan, Michael Clarke (1957–)
Massively-built American actor, born in Chicago.

Armageddon 98. The Green Mile (AAN) 99. The Whole Nine Yards 00, etc.

Duncan, Patrick (Patrick Sheane Duncan)
American screenwriter, director and producer.

The Beach Girls (co-w) 82. Charlie Mopic (wd) 89. A Home of Our Own (p, w) 93. The Pornographer (wd) 94. Nick of Time (w) 95. Mr Holland's Opus (w) 95. Courage under Fire (w) 96. The Wall (w) 98, etc.

Duncan, Peter
Australian director and screenwriter. Born in Sydney, he studied law at Sydney University before attending the Australian Film Television and Radio School.

Children of the Revolution (wd) 96. A Little Bit of Soul (wd) 98. Passion (d) 99, etc.

Duncan, Rosetta (1900–1959)
American vaudeville performer with her sister Vivian as the Duncan Sisters, who made only two films: an unsuccessful silent from their long-running stage show, based on *Uncle Tom's Cabin* (with Rosetta blacked up as Topsy), which they were still performing in the 40s, and one successful talkie.

Topsy and Eva 27. It's a Great Life 29.

Duncan, Sandy (1946–)
Tomboyish American leading lady.

■ Million Dollar Duck 71. *Star Spangled Girl* 71. Roots (TV) 77. The Cat from Outer Space 78. Rock-a-Doodle (voice) 90. The Swan Princess (voice) 94.

TV series: *Funny Face* 71.

Duncan, Todd (1903–1998)
American opera singer and actor, in occasional films. Born in Danville, Kentucky, he was educated at Butler University and Columbia University Teachers College, and also taught at Howard University and the Curtis Institute of Music in Philadelphia. A baritone, he was picked by GERSHWIN to originate the role of Porgy in *Porgy and Bess*.

Syncopation 42. Unchained 55.

Duncan, Vivian (1902–1986)
American vaudeville performer with her sister Rosetta DUNCAN. She was married to Nils Asther.

Duncan, William (1880–1961)
Scottish-born star, and writer-director of silent westerns. Born in Dundee, he was in the United States from childhood and began as a stage actor. He was in films from 1911, becoming Vitagraph's star serial actor-writer-director from 1916, noted for doing his own stunts. He joined Universal in 1922, heading his own serial production unit, where he ended his career in the mid-20s. Married Edith JOHNSON, his leading actress in many serials.

The Bully of Bingo Gulch 11. The Dynamiters (& d) 12. Gunfighter's On (& d) 13. The Servant Question Out West (& d) 14. The Navajo Ring 15. Dead Shot Baker (& d) 17. A Fight for Millions (serial, & d) 18. The Silent Avenger (serial, & d) 20. Where Men Are Men (& d) 21. Wolves of the North (serial, & d) 24, many others.

Dundas, David
English composer.

Withnail and I 87. How to Get Ahead in Advertising 89, etc.

Dunham, Duwayne
American editor turned director.

AS EDITOR: Return of the Jedi 83. The Mean Season 85. Blue Velvet 86. Mad House 90. Wild at Heart 90. Twin Peaks (TV) 90, etc.

AS DIRECTOR: Homeward Journey: The Incredible Journey 93.

Duning, George (1908–2000)
American music director and composer.

That's Right, You're Wrong 39. Around the World 43. Show Business 44. The Corpse Came COD 47. Her Husband's Affairs 47. The Dark Past 48. The Man from Colorado 48. The Return of October 48. Slightly French 48. To the Ends of the Earth 48. The Doolins of Oklahoma 49. Johnny Allegro 49. Jolson Sings Again (AAN) 49. Lust for Gold 49. Shockproof 49. Undercover Man 49. And Baby Makes Three 50. Between Midnight and Dawn 50. Convicted 50. The Flying Missile 50. Harriet Craig 50. No Sad Songs for Me (AAN) 50. The Petty Girl 50. The Barefoot Mailman 51. The Family Secret 51. The Lady and the Bandit 51. Lorna Doone 51. Man in the Saddle 51. Mask of the Avenger 51. The Mob 51. Two of a Kind 51. Affair in Trinidad 52. All Ashore 52. Assignment Paris 52. Captain Pirate 52. Paula 52. Scandal Sheet 52. Sound Off 52. From Here to Eternity (AAN) 53. The Last of the Comanches 53. Let's Do It Again 53. Miss Sadie Thompson 53. Salome 53. Count Three and Pray 55. Five Against the House 55. The Long Gray Line 55. The Man from Laramie 55. My Sister Eileen 55. *Picnic* (AAN) 55. Queen Bee 55. Three for the Show 55. Three Stripes in the Sun 55. The Eddy Duchin Story (AAN) 56. Full of Life 56. Nightfall 56. Storm Center 56. You Can't Run Away from It 56. The Brothers Rico 57. Jeanne Eagels 57. Operation Mad Ball 57. The Shadow on the Window 57. 3.10 to Yuma 57. Bell, Book and Candle 58. Cowboy 58. Gunman's Walk 58. Houseboat 58. Me and the Colonel 58. Gidget 59. It Happened to Jane 59. The Last Angry Man 59. The Wreck of the Mary Deare 59. All the Young Men 60. Let No Man Write My Epitaph 60. Man on a String 60. Strangers When We Meet 60. The Wackiest Ship in the Army 60. The World of Suzie Wong 60. Cry for Happy 61. The Devil at Four o'Clock 61. Sail a Crooked Ship 61. Two Rode Together 61. The Notorious Landlady 62. That Touch of Mink 62. 13 West Street 62. Who's Got the Action? 62. Critic's Choice 63. Island of Love 63. Toys in the Attic 63. Who's Been Sleeping in My Bed? 63. Ensign Pulver 64. Brainstorm 65. Dear Brigitte 65. My Blood Runs Cold 65. Any Wednesday 66. Yellow Submarine 68. Arnold 73. Terror in the Wax Museum 73. The Man with Bogart's Face 80. Goliath Awaits (TV) 81, etc.

Dunlap, Paul (1919–)
American composer, mainly for low-budget movies.

The Baron of Arizona 50. The Steel Helmet 50. Little Big Horn 51. Park Row 52. Loophole 54. Fort Yuma 55. The Broken Star 56. Dance with Me, Henry 56. Apache Warrior 57. I Was a Teenage Werewolf 57. I Was a Teenage Frankenstein 57. Blood of Dracula 57. Frankenstein – 1970 58. The Four Skulls of Jonathan Drake 59. The Rookie 59. The Angry Red Planet 60. Shock Corridor 63. The Naked Kiss 64. Castle of Evil 66. The Money Jungle 68, many others.

Dunn, Andrew
British cinematographer

Edge of Darkness (TV) 86. Strapless 88. Chattahoochee 89. L.A. Story 91. Blame It on the Bellboy 92. The Bodyguard 92. The Hawk 92. Clean Slate 94. The Madness of King George 94. A Simple Twist of Fate 94. The Crucible 96. The Grotesque/Gentlemen Don't Eat Poets 96. Addicted to Love 97. Ever After: A Cinderella Story 98. Hush 98. Practical Magic 98. Ordinary Decent Criminal 00. Liam 00, etc.

Dunn, Emma (1875–1966)
British character actress, long in Hollywood, typically as housekeeper.

Old Lady 31 20. Pied Piper Malone 23. Side Street 29. Bad Sister 31. Hard to Handle 33. The Glass Key 35. Mr Deeds Goes to Town 36. Thanks for the Memory 38. Son of Frankenstein 39. The Great Dictator 40. Ladies in Retirement 41. I Married a Witch 42. It Happened Tomorrow 44. Life with Father 47. The Woman in White 48, many others.

Dunn, James (1905–1967)
Genial American leading man of the 30s; later seized one good acting chance but slipped into low-budget westerns.

Bad Girl 31. Over the Hill 31. Sailor's Luck 33. Hold Me Tight 33. Stand Up and Cheer 34. Baby Take a Bow 34. Bright Eyes 34. The Daring Young Man 35. Don't Get Personal 36. Mysterious Crossing 37. Shadows over Shanghai 38. Government Girl 43. *A Tree Grows in Brooklyn* (AA) 45. That Brennan Girl 46. Killer McCoy 48. The Golden Gloves Story 50. The Bramble Bush 60. The Nine Lives of Elfego Baca 62. Hemingway's Adventures of a Young Man 62. The Oscar 66, etc.

TV series: It's A Great Life 54.

Dunn, Linwood Gale (1904–1998)
American visual effects cinematographer and photographic equipment designer. Born in Brooklyn, he was a projectionist and assistant cameraman before working for RKO as a visual effects cinematographer from 1929 to 1957. He was awarded an Oscar in 1944, together with associate

Cecil Love, for designing the Acme-Dunn Special Effects Optical Printer, and received the Academy's Outstanding Service and Dedication Award in 1979.

Cimarron 30. King Kong 33. Bringing Up Baby 38. Citizen Kane 41. The Thing 51. China Gate 57. West Side Story 61. It's a Mad, Mad, Mad, Mad World 63. My Fair Lady 64. Darling Lili 70. The Devil's Rain 75, etc.

Dunn, Michael (1935–1973) (Gary Neil Miller)
American dwarf actor. Found dead, a possible suicide, while filming *The Abdication*.

Ship of Fools 65. You're a Big Boy Now 67. No Way to Treat a Lady 68. Madigan 68. Boom 68. Justine 69. Murders in the Rue Morgue 71. Goodnight My Love (TV) 72. The Mutations 74, etc.

Dunne, Dominique (1959–1982)
American actress, the sister of Griffin Dunne. Killed by a former boyfriend.

Magic on Love Island 80. Poltergeist 82. The Shadow Riders (TV) 82. Haunting of Harrington House (TV) 82, etc.

Dunne, Griffin (1955–)
American leading actor who also produces and directs, the son of novelist and former TV and film producer Dominick Dunne.

AS ACTOR: An American Werewolf in London 81. Almost You 84. Johnny Dangerously 84. After Hours 85. Amazon Women on the Moon 87. Who's That Girl? 87. Me and Him 88. My Girl 91. Once Around 91. Big Girls Don't Cry ... They Get Even 92 Straight Talk 92. I Like It Like That 94. Quiz Show 94, etc.

AS PRODUCER: Chilly Scenes of Winter 79. Head over Heels 80. Baby, It's You 82. After Hours 85. Running on Empty 88. White Palace 90. Once Around 91, etc.

AS DIRECTOR: The Duke of Groove (short) (AAN) 95. Addicted to Love 97. Practical Magic 98, etc.

Dunne, Irene (1898–1990)
Gracious American leading lady of the 30s and 40s, usually in sensible well-bred roles.

■ Leathernecking 30. *Cimarron* (AAN) 31. The Great Lover 31. Consolation Marriage 31. Bachelor Apartment 31. *Back Street* 32. *Symphony of Six Million* 33. Thirteen Women 32. No Other Women 33. The Secret of Madame Blanche 33. The Silver Cord 33. *Ann Vickers* 33. If I Were Free 34. This Man is Mine 34. Stingaree 34. The Age of Innocence 34. Sweet Adeline 35. *Roberta* 35. *Magnificent Obsession* 35. *Show Boat* 36. *Theodora Goes Wild* (AAN) 36. *The Awful Truth* (AAN) 37. High Wide and Handsome 37. Joy of Living 38. *Love Affair* (AAN) 39. Invitation to Happiness 39. When Tomorrow Comes 39. *My Favourite Wife* 40. Penny Serenade 41. Unfinished Business 41. Lady in a Jam 42. A Guy Named Joe 43. The White Cliffs of Dover 44. Together Again 45. Over Twenty One 45. *Anna and the King of Siam* 46. *Life with Father* 47. *I Remember Mama* (AAN) 48. Never a Dull Moment 50. *The Mudlark* (as Queen Victoria) 51. It Grows on Trees 52.

✪ For epitomizing the American lady of a gentler, more romantic age than ours. *Love Affair*.

Dunne, John Gregory (1932–)
American screenwriter, novelist and essayist. He is also the author of *The Studio* (1970), a study of Twentieth Century Fox during the year it was making *Dr Dolittle* and *Star!* He is married to Joan DIDION, with whom he has collaborated on his film scripts.

Autobiography: 1997, *Monster: Up Close with a Screenplay*.

Panic in Needle Park (co-w) 71. Play It as It Lays (co-w) 71. A Star Is Born (co-w) 76. True Confessions (oa, co-w) 81. Broken Trust (co-w, TV) 95. Up Close and Personal (co-w) 96, etc.

❝ The truly absorbing aspect of the motion picture ethic, of course, is that it affects not only motion picture people but almost everyone alive in the United States today. By adolescence, children have been programmed with a set of responses and life lessons learned almost totally from motion pictures, television and the recording industry. – *J.G.D.*

Dunne, Philip (1908–1992)
American screenwriter and director.

Autobiography: 1980, *Take Two: A Life in Movies and Politics*.

Student Tour 34. The Last of the Mohicans 36. Lancer Spy 37. Suez 38. Stanley and Livingstone 39. The Rains Came 39. Swanee River 39. How Green was My Valley (AAN) 41. The Late George Apley 47. Forever Amber 47. The Luck of the Irish 48. Pinky 49. David and Bathsheba (AAN) 51. The Robe 53. Prince of Players (& pd) 55. Hilda Crane (& d) 56. Ten North Frederick (& d) 58. Blue Denim (& d) 59. Lisa (d only) 62. The Agony and the Ecstasy 65. Blindfold (& d) 66, many others.

Dunning, George (1920–1979)
Canadian animator whose main feature work was *The Yellow Submarine*.

Dunning, Ruth (1911–1983)
British character actress, mainly on TV.

Dunnock, Mildred (1904–1991)
American character actress specializing in motherly types.

The Corn is Green 45. Kiss of Death 47. *Death of a Salesman* (AAN) 51. Viva Zapata 52. The Jazz Singer 53. Love Me Tender 56. Baby Doll (AAN) 56. Peyton Place 57. The Nun's Story 57. Cat on a Hot Tin Roof 58. Butterfield 8 60. Something Wild 61. Sweet Bird of Youth 62. Behold a Pale Horse 64. Seven Women 66. Whatever Happened to Aunt Alice? 69. Murder or Mercy (TV) 74. The Spiral Staircase (GB) 75. The Pickup Artist 87, etc.

Dunst, Kirsten (1982–)
American actress, who began as a child.

Bonfire of the Vanities 90. Greedy/Greed 94. Interview with the Vampire 94. Little Women 94. Jumanji 95. Mother Night 96. Wag the Dog 97. Anastasia 97. Small Soldiers 98. Strike 98. Virgin Suicides 99. Dick 99. Drop Dead Gorgeous 99. The Crow: Salvation 00. Bring It On 00. Get Over It 01, etc.

❝ It's important to me that I don't get trapped in the whole teen scene because I feel you can get lost in those kind of movies, and they aren't really about the actors; they're about the selling of the concept, and how much money it makes. – *K.D.*

Dupont, E. A. (1891–1956) (Ewald André)
German director who moved with unhappy results to Britain and Hollywood.

Baruh 23. *Variety* 26. Love Me and the World Is Mine 27. Moulin Rouge 28. *Piccadilly* 29. Atlantic 30. Ladies Must Love 33. The Bishop Misbehaves 35. Forgotten Faces 36. Hell's Kitchen 39. The Scarf (& w) 50. The Neanderthal Man 53. Return to Treasure Island 54. Magic Fire (co-w only) 56, etc.

Dupontel, Albert (1964–)
French actor, screenwriter and director with a comic approach, from the stage. He studied acting with Antoine Vitez at the National Theatre School at Chaillot and first made a mark in a TV comedy series and with his one-man show in Paris.

Everyman for Yourself/Chacun Pour Toi (a) 93. A Self-Made Hero/Un Héros Très Discret (a) 95. Bernie (a, wd) 96. Serial Lover (a) 98. La Maladie de Sachs (a) 99. The Creator/Le Createur (wd, a) 99. Du Bleu Jusqu'en Amérique (a) 99, etc.

Dupree, Minnie (1873–1947)
American character actress seen infrequently as sweet old lady.

Night Club 29. *The Young in Heart* 38. Anne of Windy Poplars 40, etc.

Duprez, June (1918–1984)
British leading lady who moved to Hollywood in the 40s.

The Crimson Circle 36. The Spy in Black 38. The Four Feathers 39. The Thief of Baghdad 41. None But the Lonely Heart (US) 44. *And Then There Were None* (US) 45. Calcutta (US) 46. That Brennan Girl (US) 47. The Kinsey Report (US) 61, etc.

Dupuis, Paul (1916–1976)
French-Canadian leading man popular in British films in the late 40s.

Johnny Frenchman 45. The White Unicorn 47. Sleeping Car to Trieste 48. Passport to Pimlico 49. The Reluctant Widow 50, etc.

Durante, Jimmy 'Schnozzle' (1893–1980)
Long-nosed, well-loved American comedian with long career in vaudeville and nightclubs. Film appearances spasmodic, and most successful when involving his old routines: 'Umbriago', 'Ink-a-dink', etc.

Biography: 1951, *Schnozzola* by Gene Fowler. 1963, *Goodnight Mrs Calabash* by William Cahn.

■ Roadhouse Nights 30. The New Adventures of Get-Rich-Quick Wallingford 31. Cuban Love Song 31. The Passionate Plumber 32. The Wet Parade 32. Speak Easily 32. The Phantom President 33. Blondie of the Follies 33. Meet the Baron 33. What No Beer 33. Hell Below 33. Broadway to Hollywood 33. George White's Scandals 34. Hollywood Party 34. Joe Palooka 34. She Learned About Sailors 34. Strictly Dynamite 34. Student Tour 34. Carnival 35. Land without Music (GB) 36. Sally, Irene and Mary 38. Start Cheering 38. Little Miss Broadway 38. Melody Ranch 40. *You're in the Army Now* 40. *The Man who Came to Dinner* 41. Two Girls and a Sailor 44. Music for Millions 45. *Two Sisters from Boston* 46. It Happened in Brooklyn 47. This Time for Keeps 47. On an Island with You 48. The Great Rupert 50. The Milkman 50. Beau James 57. Pepe 60. The Last Judgment 61. *Jumbo* 62. It's a Mad Mad Mad Mad World (cameo) 63. That's Entertainment! III 94.

TV series: The Jimmy Durante Show 54–56.

❝ Everybody wants to get into de act! – *J.D., catchphrase*

Dere's a million good-looking guys in the world, but I'm a novelty. – *J.D.*

Goodnight, Mrs Calabash, wherever you are. – *J.D., closing words of music-hall act (Mrs Calabash was his pet name for his late wife)*

I don't split infinitives. When I go to work on 'em, I break 'em up into little pieces. – *J.D.*

Duras, Marguerite (1914–1996) (Marguerite Donnadieu)
French director, screenwriter, novelist and dramatist, born in French Indochina. Her award-winning autobiographical novel *L'Amant/The Lover* was turned into a hit movie in France in 1991.

The Sea Wall/Barrage contre le Pacifique (oa) 57. *Hiroshima Mon Amour* (AANw) 59. Moderato Cantabile (w) 60. The Long Absence/Une Aussi Longue Absence 61. 10.30 p.m. Summer (w) 66. La Musica (w, co-d) 66. The Sailor from Gibraltar (oa) 67. Destroy, She Said/Détruire, Dit-elle (wd) 69. Jaune de Soleil (wd) 71. Nathalie Granger (wd) 73. La Femmes du Gange (wd) 74. *India Song* (a, wd) 75. Entire Days in the Trees/Des Journées Entières dans les Arbres (wd) 77. Baxter, Vera Baxter (wd) 77. Le Navire Night (wd) 79. Aurelia Steiner (wd) 79. Les Enfants (w, co-d) 85, etc.

Durbin, Deanna (1921–) (Edna Mae Durbin)
Canadian girl-singer who won instant world-wide success as a teenage star; her career faltered after ten years when weight problems added to a change in musical fashion brought about her premature retirement. Special Academy Award 1938 'for bringing to the screen the spirit and personification of youth'. Long retired and living in France.

■ Every Sunday 36. *Three Smart Girls* 36. *One Hundred Men and a Girl* 37. *Mad about Music* 38. *That Certain Age* 38. Three Smart Girls Grow Up 38. First Love 39. It's a Date 39. Spring Parade 40. Nice Girl 40. *It Started with Eve* 41. The Amazing Mrs Holliday 42. Hers to Hold 43. His Butler's Sister 43. Christmas Holiday 44. *Can't Help Singing* 44. Lady on a Train 45. Because of Him 45. I'll Be Yours 46. Something in the Wind 47. Up in Central Park 47. For the Love of Mary 48.

✪ For pleasing world audiences by being the character she despised: 'Little Miss Fixit who bursts into song.' *That Certain Age*.

❝ Just as a Hollywood pin-up represents sex to dissatisfied erotics, so I represented the ideal daughter millions of fathers and mothers wished they had. – *D.D. in 1959*

She is one of those personalities whom the world will insist on regarding as its private property. – *Joe Pasternak, her producer*

Durfee, Minta (1897–1975)
American leading lady of knockabout comedies 1914–16, including some with Chaplin. Married Roscoe Arbuckle and retired, but much later played bit parts.

Durkin, Junior (1915–1935) (Trent Durkin)
American juvenile player who was Huck Finn in *Tom Sawyer* 30 and *Huckleberry Finn* 31. On stage from the age of two, he died in a car crash.

Durning, Charles (1933–)
Burly American TV actor who slowly gained a star footing in movies.

Harvey Middleman Fireman 65. Hi Mom! 69. I Walk the Line 70. Deadhead Miles 72. Dealing 72. Sisters 73. The Connection (TV) 73. The Sting 73. The Front Page 74. Dog Day Afternoon 75. The Hindenburg 75. The Trial of Chaplin Jensen (TV) 75. Queen of the Stardust Ballroom (TV) 75. Switch (TV) 75. Breakheart Pass 75. Captains and the Kings (TV) 76. Harry and Walter Go to New York 76. Twilight's Last Gleaming 77. An Enemy of the People 77. Special Olympics (TV) 78. *The Choirboys* 78. The Greek Tycoon 78. An Enemy of the People 78. The Fury 78. F.I.S.T. 79. Studs Lonigan (TV) 79. The Muppet Movie 79. North Dallas Forty 79. Tilt 79. Starting Over 79. When a Stranger Calls 79. Die Laughing 80. The Final Countdown 80. True Confessions 81. Sharky's Machine 81. *The Best Little Whorehouse in Texas* (AAN) 82. Tootsie 82. To Be or Not to Be (AAN) 83. Two of a Kind 83. Side by Side 83. Mass Appeal 84. Stick 85. The Man with One Red Shoe 85. Stand Alone 85. Private Conversations 85. Solar Warriors 86. Tough Guys 86. Where the River Runs Black 86. Happy New Year 87. A Tiger's Tale 87. The Rosary Murders 87. Cop 87. Far North 88. Cat Chaser 88. Brenda Starr 89. Etoile 89. Dick Tracy 90. Fatal Sky 90. Project: Alien 90. V.I. Warshawski 91. Brenda Starr 92. The Music of Chance 93. The Hudsucker Proxy 94. I.Q. 94. Home for the Holidays 95. The Grass Harp 95. Spy Hard 96. Mrs Santa Claus (TV) 96. The Last Supper 96. One Fine Day 96. Shelter 98. Hi-Life 98. Jerry and Tom 98. State and Main 00, etc.

TV series: Another World 64. The Cop and The Kid 75–76. Eye to Eye 85. Evening Shade 91–94.

Durrell, Lawrence (1912–1990)
English poet, novelist and occasional screenwriter. Born in India, he lived in England in his late teens before moving to France and several Mediterranean islands. The first part of *The Alexandria Quartet*, his celebrated sequence of novels on modern love, was filmed as *Justine* 69, directed by George CUKOR and starring Anouk AIMEE, Michael YORK, Dirk BOGARDE and Anna KARINA.

Biography: 1996, *Through the Dark Labyrinth: A Biography of Lawrence Durrell* by Gordon Bowker. 1998, *Lawrence Durrell: A Biography* by Ian MacNiven.

Cleopatra 63. Judith (story) 65, etc.

Dury, Ian (1942–2000)
British actor, singer and composer. He was leader of the rock bands Kilburn & The High Roads and The Blockheads in the 70s and 80s. Died of cancer.

AS ACTOR: Radio On 79. Number One 84. Pirates 86. Rocinante 86. Hearts of Fire 87. Red Ants 87. The Raggedy Rawney 87. The Cook, the Thief, His Wife and Her Lover 89. Bearskin 89. After Midnight 90. Split Second 91. Judge Dredd 95. The Crow: City of Angels 96. Different for Girls 96. Middleton's Changeling 97, etc.

AS SONGWRITER: Take It or Leave It 81. Real Genius 85. Brennende Betten 88, etc.

Duryea, Dan (1907–1968)
Laconic, long-faced American character actor often typecast as whining villain.

■ *The Little Foxes* 41. Ball of Fire 41. Pride of the Yankees 42. That Other Woman 42. Sahara 43. Man from Frisco 44. Ministry of Fear 44. None but the Lonely Heart 44. *The Woman in the Window* 44. Main Street After Dark 44. Mrs Parkington 45. The Great Flamarion 45. Lady on a Train 45. Scarlet Street 45. Along Came Jones 45. The Valley of Decision 45. *Black Angel* 46. White Tie and Tails 46. Black Bart 48. River Lady 48. *Another Part of the Forest* 48. Larceny 48. *Criss Cross* 49. Manhandled 49. Too Late for Tears 49. Johnny Stoolpigeon 50. One Way Street 50. The Underworld Story 50. Winchester 73 50. Al Jennings of Oklahoma 50. *Chicago Calling* 51. Sky Commando 53. Thunder Bay 53. 36 Hours 53. World for Ransom 54. Ride Clear of Diablo 54. Silver Lode 54. This is My Love 54. Rails Into Laramie 54. The Marauders 55. Foxfire 55. Storm Fear 56. Battle Hymn 57. The Burglar 57. Night Passage 57. Slaughter on Tenth Avenue 57. Kathy O 58. Platinum High School 60. Six Black Horses 62. He Rides Tall 64. Taggart 64. Walk a Tightrope 64. Do You Know This Voice? 64. The Bounty Killer 65. Incident at Phantom Hill 65. *The Flight of the Phoenix* 65. The Hills Run Red 67. Stranger on the Run (TV) 67. Five Golden Dragons 67. The Bamboo Saucer 68.

TV series: China Smith 58. Peyton Place 68.

66 The crime movie equivalent of an absolute bounder. – *Ian Cameron*

Duse, Eleonora (1858–1924)

Eminent Italian tragedienne whose one film appearance was in *Cenere* 16.

66 Something quite different is needed. I'm too old for it. Isn't it a pity. – *E.D. after making her film*

Dussollier, André (1946–   )

French leading actor.

And Now My Love 74. Perceval le Gallois 78. A Gorgeous Bird Like Me/Such a Gorgeous Kid Like Me/Une Belle Fille comme Moi 72. Le Beau Mariage 81. Three Men and a Cradle/Trois Hommes et un Couffin 85. Mélo 86. De Sable et de Sang/Blood and Sand 87. Un Coeur en Hiver 91. Les Marmottes 93. Montparnasse-Pondichery 94. Aux Petits Bonheurs 94. Le Colonel Chabert 94. The Story of a Poor Young Man (It.) 95. Same Old Song/On Connaît la Chanson 97. Ouch/Aïe 00, etc.

Dutronc, Jacques (1943–   )

French leading actor, singer and composer. Born in Paris, he began as a guitarist in local rock groups and became a record producer before turning to writing and performing, with his biggest hits coming in the 60s. Since the 70s he has turned more to acting. Married singer Françoise Hardy.

Antoine et Sebastien 73. The Good and the Bad/Les Bons Et Les Mechants 76. Mado 76. The Savage State/L'Etat Sauvage 78. An Adventure for Two/A Nous Deux 79. Every Man for Himself/Slow Motion/Sauve Qui Peut (La Vie) 80. Malevil 81. Sarah 82. Youth/Une Jeuness 83. Chambre a Part 89. *Van Gogh* 91. Les Victimes 96. Place Vendome 98. Nightcap/Merci Pour Le Chocolat 00, etc.

Dutta, Dulal (1925–   )

Indian editor, who worked on all of Satyajit Ray's films.

Pather Panchali 55. Aparajito 56. The Music Room/Jalsaghar 58. The World of Apu 59. Three Daughters/Teen Kanya 61. Kanchenjungha 62. Mahanagar 63. Nayak 66. Days and Nights in the Forest 69. Company Limited 71. Distant Thunder 73. The Middle Man 75. The Chess Players 77. Deliverance 81. The Home and the World 84. An Enemy of the People/Ganasatru 89. Target 95, etc.

Dutton, Charles S. (1951–   )

American character actor and occasional director.

No Mercy 86. Crocodile Dundee II 88. Runaway (TV) 89. An Unremarkable Life 89. Jacknife 89. Q & A 90. Alien³ 92. Mississippi Masala 92. Rudy 93. Surviving the Game 94. A Lowdown Dirty Shame 94. Foreign Student 94. Cry the Beloved Country 95. Nick of Time 95. A Time to Kill 96. Get on the Bus 95. Mimic 97. Blind Faith 98. Black Dog 98, *Cookie's Fortune* 99. Random Hearts 99. The Corner (d only, TV) 00. For Love and Country: The Arturo Sandoval Story (as Dizzy Gillespie, TV) 00, etc.

TV series: Roc 91–94.

Duvall, Robert (1930–   )

American character actor, often as a nervy outsider in early roles, later as an efficient, no-nonsense fixer. Born in San Diego, California, he studied under Sanford Meisner at the Neighborhood Playhouse in New York. After 13 years of trying to raise $5m for The Apostle, he decided to finance it himself.

Biography: 1985, *Robert Duvall: Hollywood Maverick* by Judith Slawson.

Captain Newman MD 63. To Kill a Mockingbird 63. The Chase 65. Bullitt 68. The Rain People 69. True Grit 69. M*A*S*H 70. Lawman 71. *The Godfather* (AAN) 72. The Great Northfield Minnesota Raid 72. Joe Kidd 72. The Godfather Part Two 74. The Outfit 74. Breakout 75. Killer Elite 76. Network 76. The Seven Per Cent Solution (as Dr Watson) 76. The Eagle Has Landed 76. The Greatest 77. The Betsy 78. Ike (TV) 79. Apocalypse Now (BFA, AAN) 79. The Great Santini (AAN) 80. True Confessions 81. The Pursuit of D. B. Cooper 81. Tender Mercies (AA) 83. The Stone Boy 84. The Natural 84. The Lightship 85. Hotel Colonial 87. Let's Get Harry 87. Colors 88. The Handmaid's Tale 89. Days of Thunder 90. A Show of Force 90. Rambling Rose 91. Newsies/The News Boys 92. *Falling Down* 92. Geronimo: An American Legend 93. Wrestling Ernest Hemingway 93. The Paper 94. The Stars Fell on Henrietta 95. Something to Talk About 95. The Scarlet Letter 95. A Family Thing 96. Phenomenon 96. The Man Who Captured Eichmann (TV) 96. The Gingerbread Man 97. *The Apostle* (& wd) (AANa) 97. Deep Impact 98. A Civil Action (AAN) 98, etc.

66 My theory is that no matter how many enemies you make, you can always work for their enemies. – *R.D.*

Being a star is an agent's dream, not an actor's. – *R.D.*

There are only two actors in America. One is Brando, who's done his best work, and the other is Robert Duvall. – *Sanford Meisner*

Famous line (as Lieutenant-Colonel Kilgore in *Apocalypse Now*) 'I love the smell of napalm in the morning … It smells like victory.'

Duvall, Shelley (1949–   )

American actress in off-centre roles. In the 80s, she became a producer for cable television.

Brewster McCloud 70. McCabe and Mrs Miller 71. Thieves Like Us 74. Nashville 75. Three Women 77. Annie Hall 77. The Shining 80. Popeye 80. Time Bandits 81. Roxanne 87. Suburban Commando 91. The Underneath 95. The Portrait of a Lady 96. Changing Habits 97. Home Fries 98. Teen Monster 99, etc.

Duvivier, Julien (1896–1967)

Celebrated French director of the 30s whose touch seemed to falter after a wartime sojourn in Hollywood. Born in Lille, he abandoned acting to become an assistant to directors Louis FEUILLADE and Marcel L'HERBIER before making his first feature in 1919. Among his regular collaborators were screenwriters Charles SPAAK and Henri JEANSON.

Hacadelma 19. Poil de Carotte 25 and 32. David Golder 30. Maria Chapdelaine 33. Le Golem 35. La Belle Equipe 36. *Pépé Le Moko* 37. Un Carnet de Bal 37. The Great Waltz (US) 38. *La Fin du Jour* 39. La Charrette Fantôme 39. Lydia (US) 41. Tales of Manhattan (US) 42. Flesh and Fantasy (US) 43. The Imposter (US) 44. *Panique* 46. Anna Karenina (GB) 48. Au Royaume des Cieux 49. Sous le Ciel de Paris 51. *Don Camillo* 52. La Fête à Henriette 54. L'Affaire Maurizius 54. Voici le Temps des Assassins 55. The Man in the Raincoat 57. Pot-Bouille 57. Marie Octobre 59. La Femme et le Pantin 59. La Grande Vie 61. La Chambre Ardente 62. Chair de Poule 63, etc.

66 He was a loner, too rich for his own good, who shot too many films, like others drink too much. The cinema was his drug. – *Charles Spaak*

If I were an architect and I had to build a monument to the cinema, I would place a statue of Duvivier over the entrance. – *Jean Renoir*

Dvorak, Ann (1912–1979) (Ann McKim)

Smart but sensitive American leading lady of the 30s.

Hollywood Revue 29. Way out West 30. The Guardsman 31. This Modern Age 31. The Crowd Roars 32. *Scarface* 32. The Strange Love of Molly Louvain 32. Three on a Match 32. The Way to Love 33. Heat Lightning 34. Housewife 34. I Sell Anything 34. G Men 35. Folies Bergère 35. *Dr Socrates* 35. We Who Are About to Die 36. Racing Lady 37. The Case of the Stuttering Bishop 37. Merrily We Live 38. Blind Alley 39. Café Hostess 40. Girls of the Road 40. Squadron Leader X (GB) 41. This Was Paris (GB) 42. Escape to Danger 44. Flame of the Barbary Coast 45. Abilene Town 46. The Long Night 47. The Walls of Jericho 48. A Life of Her Own 50. I Was an American Spy 51. The Secret of Convict Lake 51, etc.

Dwan, Allan (1885–1981)

Veteran American director, former writer; he competently handled commercial movies of every type.

Wildflower 14. The Good Bad Man 15. Manhattan Madness 16. A Modern Musketeer 18. Luck of the Irish 20. *Robin Hood* 22. Big Brother 23. Zaza 23. Manhandled 24. Stage Struck 25. *The Iron Mask* 29. Man to Man 31. Mayor of Hell 33. Human Cargo 36. Heidi 37. Suez 38. The Three Musketeers (Ritz Brothers version) 39. Trail of the Vigilantes 40. Rise and Shine 41. Abroad with Two Yanks 44. Up in Mabel's Room 44. Brewster's Millions 45. Getting Gertie's Garter 46. Angel in Exile 48. *Sands of Iwo Jima* 49. The Wild Blue Yonder 51. Montana Belle 52. The Woman They Almost Lynched 53. Silver Lode 54. Tennessee's Partner 55. Hold Back the Night 56. Slightly Scarlet 56. The River's Edge 56. The Most Dangerous Man Alive 61, many others.

66 If you get your head up above the mob, they try to knock it off. If you stay down, you last forever. – *A.D.*

Dwyer, Leslie (1906–1986)

Plump cockney character actor, in films from childhood.

The Fifth Form at St Dominic's 21. The Flag Lieutenant 31. The Goose Steps Out 41. The Way Ahead 44. Night Boat to Dublin 46. When the Bough Breaks 48. The Calendar 48. Midnight Episode 50. Laughter in Paradise 51. Hindle Wakes 52. Where There's a Will 53. Act of Love 54. Left, Right and Centre 59. I've Gotta Horse 64. Monster of Terror 65. Lionheart 68. Dominique 78, many others.

Dyall, Franklin (1874–1950)

British stage actor from 1894, in films from 1930. He was the father of Valentine Dyall.

Atlantic 30. The Ringer 32. The Private Life of Henry VIII 33. The Iron Duke 35. Fire Over England 36. Bonnie Prince Charlie 49, etc.

Dyall, Valentine (1908–1985)

Gaunt British actor with resounding voice, famous as radio's wartime 'Man in Black'. Son of stage actor Franklin Dyall. Film debut The Life and Death of Colonel Blimp 43; later in many supporting roles, notably Henry V 44. Caesar and Cleopatra 45. Brief Encounter 45. Vengeance Is Mine 48. City of the Dead 60. The Haunting 63. The Horror of It All 65, etc.

Dyer, Anson (1876–1962)

Pioneer British cartoonist: many entertainment shorts, also work for government departments.

Dykstra, John (1947–   )

Special effects expert. After working as an assistant to Douglas Trumbull, he founded Industrial Light and Magic with George Lucas before leaving to set up his own company, Apogee.

Silent Running 71. Star Wars (AA) 77. Avalanche Express 78. Star Trek: The Motion Picture (AAN) 79. Caddyshack 80. Firefox 82. Lifeforce 86. Invaders from Mars 87. My Stepmother Is an Alien 88. Spontaneous Combustion 89. Batman Forever 95. Batman & Robin 97. Stuart Little (AAN) 99, etc.

Dylan, Bob (1941–   ) (Robert Allen Zimmerman)

American singer in occasional films.

Don't Look Back 67. Pat Garrett and Billy the Kid 73. Renaldo and Clara 78. Hearts of Fire 87. Wonder Boys (AAN), etc.

Dyneley, Peter (1921–1977)

British character actor.

Beau Brummell 54. The Young Lovers 55. The Split 60. Call Me Bwana 63. Chato's Land 72, etc.

Dysart, Richard (1929–   )

American character actor.

Petulia 68. The Lost Man 69. The Hospital 71. The Terminal Man 74. The Hindenburg 75. Being There 79. Prophecy 79. Bitter Harvest 81. The Thing 82. The Falcon and the Snowman 85. Mask 85. Warning Sign 85. Pale Rider 85. Wall Street 87. Back to the Future Part III 90. Panther 95. Hard Rain 98, etc.

TV series: L.A. Law 86–93.

Dzundza, George (1945–   )

Burly American character actor.

The Deer Hunter 78. Brubaker 80. A Long Way Home 81. Honky Tonk Freeway 81. Streamers 83. Act of Passion 83. Best Defence 84. Brotherly Love (TV) 85. No Mercy 86. Glory Years (TV) 87. No Way Out 87. The Beast 88. White Hunter, Black Heart 89. Impulse 89. The Butcher's Wife 91. Basic Instinct 92. Crimson Tide 95. Dangerous Minds 95. That Darn Cat 97. Trading Favors 97. Species 2 98. Instinct 99, etc.

TV series: Jesse 98– .

E

Eady, David (1924–)
British director who turned to making mainly children's films in the 70s.
The Bridge of Time (doc) 52. Three Cases of Murder (one story) 55. In the Wake of a Stranger 58. Faces in the Dark 60. The Verdict 64. Operation Third Form 66. Anoop and the Elephant 72. Hide and Seek 72. The Laughing Girl Murder 73. The Hostages 75. Night Ferry 76. Deep Waters 78. Danger on Dartmoor 80, etc.

Eagels, Jeanne (1894–1929)
American leading lady of the 20s; her private life was highly publicized and Kim Novak played her in a 1957 biopic.
Biography: 1930, *The Rain Girl* by Edward Doherty.
■ The World and the Woman 16. Fires of Youth 17. Under False Colours 17. The Cross Bearer 18. Man, Woman and Sin 27. The Letter (AAN) 29. Jealousy 29.

Earle, Merie (1889–1984)
American character actress who began her career in her mid-70s.
Cat Ballou 65. Fitzwilly 67. Gaily, Gaily 69. Norwood 70. Crazy Mama 75. Fatso 80. Going Ape! 81, etc.
TV series: The Jerry Reed When You're Hot You're Hot Hour 72. The Waltons 73–79.

Earles, Harry (1902–1985)
German-American midget who appeared in *The Unholy Three* 25 and 30, Baby Mine 26, Do It Again 27, *Freaks* 32, *The Wizard of Oz* 39.

Earp, Wyatt (1848–1929)
American frontier marshal, the most famous lawman of the wild west. Screen impersonations of him include Walter Huston in *Law and Order* 31, George O'Brien in *Frontier Marshal* 35, Randolph Scott in *Frontier Marshal* 39, Richard Dix in *Tombstone* 42, Henry Fonda in *My Darling Clementine* 46, Joel McCrea in *Wichita* 55, Burt Lancaster in *Gunfight at the OK Corral* 57, James Stewart in *Cheyenne Autumn* 64, James Garner in *Hour of the Gun* 67, Harris Yulin in *Doc* 70, Kurt Russell in *Tombstone* 94, Kevin Costner in *Wyatt Earp* 94. There was also a long-running TV series starring Hugh O'Brian.
Biography: 1997, *Wyatt Earp: The Life behind the Legend* by Casey Tefertiller.
❝ Suppose, suppose ... – *W.E.'s last words*

Easdale, Brian (1909–1995)
English composer, associated with the films of Michael Powell and Emeric Pressburger. He studied at the Royal College of Music and began working on documentary films. After the failure of Powell's *Peeping Tom*, he wrote little for the screen. In the 90s, shortly before his death, his *Red Shoes Suite* was performed to acclaim.
GPO Film Unit shorts 34–38. Ferry Pilot 42. Black Narcissus 47. The Red Shoes (AA) 48. Gone to Earth 50. An Outcast of the Islands 51. The Battle of the River Plate 56. Peeping Tom 60, etc.

Eason, B. Reeves (1886–1956)
American action director, mostly of second features.
SELECTED SILENT FILMS: Moon Rider 20. *Ben Hur* (chariot race) 26.
■ SOUND FILMS: The Lariat Kid 29. Winged Horseman 29. Troopers Three 30. The Roaring Ranch 30. Trigger Tricks 30. Spurs 30. The Galloping Ghost 31. The Sunset Trail 32. Honor of the Press 32. The Heart Punch 32. Cornered 33. Behind Jury Doors 33. Alimony Madness 33. Revenge at Monte Carlo 33. Her Resale Value 33. Dance Hall Hostess 33. Red River Valley 36. Land Beyond the Law 37. Empty Holsters 37. Prairie Thunder 37. Sergeant Murphy 38. The Kid Comes Back 38. Daredevil Drivers 38. Call of the Yukon 38. Blue Montana Skies 39. Mountain Rhythm 39. Men with Steel Faces 40. Murder in the Big House 42. Spy Ship 42. Truck Busters 43. Rimfire 49.
Also directed action scenes in major films, notably *The Charge of the Light Brigade* 36.

Eastman, Carole
American screenwriter, a former dancer, who also used the pseudonym of Adrien Joyce. Born in Los Angeles, she became friendly with actor Jack NICHOLSON, for whom she wrote four films, when they attended the same acting classes. She stopped writing for a time after the failure of *The Fortune*; *Man Trouble* was originally written in the early 70s and gained a reputation as one of the best unproduced scripts in Hollywood – it, too, received a poor critical and commercial reception.
■ The Shooting 66. The Model Shop 69. Puzzle of a Downfall Child 70. Five Easy Pieces (AAN) 70. The Fortune 75. Man Trouble (& p) 92.

Eastman, George (1854–1932)
American pioneer of cinematography: invented the roll film, which made him a millionaire.

Eastwood, Clint (1930–)
American leading man who after TV success made his big screen name in Italian westerns, then returned to Hollywood and became one of the big action stars of the late 60s. From the 70s he also began to produce and direct. Married television reporter Dina Ruiz in 1996.
Biography: 1977, *Clint Eastwood, the Man behind the Myth* by Patrick Agan. 1983, *Clint Eastwood* by Gerald Cole and Peter Williams. 1992, *Clint Eastwood: Sexual Cowboy* by Douglas Thompson. 1996, *Clint Eastwood: a Biography* by Richard Schickel. 1999, *Clint: The Life and Legend* by Patrick McGilligan.
Other books: 1993, *Clint Eastwood, A Cultural Production* by Paul Smith.
Revenge of the Creature 55. Francis in the Navy 55. Lady Godiva 55. Tarantula 55. Never Say Goodbye 56. The First Travelling Saleslady 56. Star in the Dust 56. Escapade in Japan 57. Ambush at Cimarron Pass 58. Lafayette Escadrille 58. *A Fistful of Dollars* 64. *For a Few Dollars More* 65. *The Good the Bad and the Ugly* 66. The Witches 67. Hang 'em High 68. *Coogan's Bluff* 68. Where Eagles Dare 69. Paint Your Wagon 69. Kelly's Heroes 70. Two Mules for Sister Sara 70. The Beguiled 71. *Play Misty for Me* (& d) 71. *Dirty Harry* 71. Joe Kidd 72. Breezy (d only) 73. High Plains Drifter (& d) 73. Magnum Force 73. Thunderbolt and Lightfoot 74. The Eiger Sanction (& d) 75. The Outlaw Josey Wales (& d) 76. The Enforcer 76. The Gauntlet (& d) 77. Every Which Way but Loose 78. Escape from Alcatraz 79. Any Which Way You Can 80. Bronco Billy (& d) 80. Firefox 82. Honky Tonk Man 82. Sudden Impact 83. Tightrope 84. City Heat 84. Pale Rider 85. Heartbreak Ridge (& d) 86. Bird (p, d) 88. The Dead Pool (& p) 88. Thelonius Monk: Straight No Chaser (p) 88. Pink Cadillac 89. The Rookie (& d) 90. White Hunter, Black Heart (& p, d) 90. *Unforgiven* (& p, d) (AAp, d, AANa) 92. In the Line of Fire 93. A Perfect World (& d) 93. The Bridges of Madison County (a, d) 95. Absolute Power (a, p, d) 97. Absolute Power (a, p, d) 97. Midnight in the Garden of Good and Evil (p, d) 97. True Crime (a,p,d) 99. Space Cowboys (a,p,d) 00, etc.
TV series: *Rawhide* 58–65.
✪ For being the cynical tough guy the 70s seemed to want. *Dirty Harry*.
❝ I like to play the line and not wander too far to either side. If a guy has just had a bad day in the mines and wants to see a good shoot-'em-up, that's great. – *C.E.*
My involvement goes deeper than acting or directing. I love every aspect of the creation of motion pictures and I guess I'm committed to it for life. – *C.E.*
Whatever success I've had is due to a lot of instinct and a little luck. – *C.E.*
I've always had the ability to say to the audience, watch this if you like, and if you don't, take a hike. – *C.E.*
I try to approach film intellectually – how it moves me. If you start below the intellectual level, I think you're starting without the nucleus. – *C.E.*
I always cry when I watch myself on screen. – *C.E.*
I've actually had people come up to me and ask me to autograph their guns. – *C.E.*
I've never worked with a guy who was less conscious of his good image. – *Don Siegel of C.E.*

Eaton, Mary (1901–1948)
American leading lady whose brief teaming with Ziegfeld and the Marx Brothers makes her career a footnote at least to film history.
■ His Children's Children 23. Broadway after Dark 24. *Glorifying the American Girl* 29. *The Coconuts* 29.

Eaton, Shirley (1936–)
Pneumatic blonde British leading lady.
Doctor at Large 56. Sailor Beware 57. Carry on Sergeant 58. Carry on Nurse 59. What a Carve Up 62. The Girl Hunters 63. Goldfinger 64. Rhino 65. Ten Little Indians 65. Around the World Under the Sea 66. Eight on the Lam 67. Sumuru 68, many others.

Eatwell, Brian (1939–)
British art director and production designer.
Just Like a Woman 66. Here We Go round the Mulberry Bush 67. The Strange Affair 68. Walkabout (Aus.) 70. *The Abominable Dr Phibes* 71. Dr Phibes Rises Again 72. Godspell (US) 73. The Three Musketeers 73. The Four Musketeers 74. The Man Who Fell to Earth 76. Sgt Pepper's Lonely Hearts Club Band (US) 78. Butch and Sundance: The Early Days (US) 79. White Dog (US) 82. Exposed (US) 83. American Dreamer (US) 84. Morons from Outer Space 85. Wired (US) 89, etc.

Eberhardt, Thom
American director.
Sole Survivor 84. Night of the Comet 84. Without a Clue 88. Gross Anatomy 89. Captain Ron 92.

Eberhart, Mignon G. (1899–1996)
American detective novelist, several of whose works were filmed.
The White Cockatoo 35. While the Patient Slept 35. Murder by an Aristocrat 36. The Murder of Dr Harrigan 36. The Great Hospital Mystery 37. The Dark Stairway 38. Mystery House 38. The Patient in Room 18 38. Three's a Crowd 45, etc.

Ebsen, Buddy (1908–) (Christian Rudolf Ebsen)
American actor-dancer of the 30s, usually in 'countrified' parts; later emerged as a character actor and achieved his greatest success in a long-running TV series.
Ebsen was to have played the Tin Man in *The Wizard of Oz*, but was badly affected by the aluminium dust in the make-up.
Autobiography: 1993, *The Other Side of Oz*.
Broadway Melody 1936. Captain January 36. Born to Dance 36. Banjo on My Knee 36. The Girl of the Golden West 38. Four Girls in White 39. Parachute Battalion 41. Sing Your Worries Away 42. Thunder in God's Country 51. Night People 54. Red Garters 54. Davy Crockett 55. Attack 56. Breakfast at Tiffany's 61. The Interns 62. Mail Order Bride 64. The One and Only Genuine Original Family Band 68. The Daughters of Joshua Cabe (TV) 72. Horror at 37,000 Feet (TV) 72. The President's Plane is Missing (TV) 74. Smash-up on Interstate Five (TV) 77. Leave Yesterday Behind (TV) 78. The Bastard (TV) 78. *The Critical List* (TV) 81. The Return of the Beverly Hillbillies (TV) 81. The Beverly Hillbillies 93. That's Entertainment! III 94, etc.
TV series: Northwest Passage 57. *The Beverly Hillbillies* 62–70. Barnaby Jones 72–80. Matt Houston 85.

Eburne, Maude (1875–1960)
Diminutive American character actress who usually played frowning matrons and nosey neighbours.
The Bat Whispers 30. The Guardsman 31. The Vampire Bat 33. Lazy River 34. *Ruggles of Red Gap* 35. Champagne Waltz 37. Meet Doctor Christian 39. West Point Widow 41. Bowery to Broadway 44. The Suspect 45. Mother Wore Tights 47. Arson Inc. 50, many others.

Eccleston, Christopher (c. 1964–)
British leading actor. Born in Salford, he studied at the Central School of Speech and Drama.
Let Him Have It 91. Anchoress 93. *Shallow Grave* (as David Stephen) 94. Jude 96. A Price above Rubies 98. Elizabeth 98. Heart 98. eXistenZ 99. With or Without You 99. Gone In 60 Seconds 00, etc.
TV series: Cracker 93–94. Hearts and Minds 95. Our Friends in the North 96.
❝ The last of a dying breed within British acting: the committed working-class thirtysomething raised on a strain of homegrown, indigenous drama that is fast fading out. – *Xan Brooks*

Echevarria, Nicolas (1947–)
Mexican director and composer. Born in Tepic, he studied film in New York in the early 70s, and began by making documentaries.
Poetas Campesinos (doc) 80. Nino Fidencio, el Taumaturgo de Espinazo (doc) 81. Cabeza de Vaca 90, etc.

Eck, Johnnie (1909–1991)
American actor, born with a body that ended at the waist, and one of the stars of Tod Browning's *Freaks* 32. He also appeared in *Tarzan, the Ape Man* 32.

Eckhart, Aaron (1968–)
American actor, associated with the films of director Neil LABUTE. He studied at Brigham Young University.
In the Company of Men 97. Thursday 98. Your Friends & Neighbors 98. Molly 99. Any Given Sunday 99. Erin Brockovich 00. Nurse Betty 00, etc.

Ecoffey, Jean-Philippe
French leading actor.
L'Effrontée 85. No Man's Land (Swiss) 85. Nanou 87. L'Enfant de L'Hiver 88. The Possessed/Les Possédés 88. La Femme de Rose Hill 89. Henry and June (US) 90. Mina Tannenbaum 93. Sandra, C'est la Vie 94. Fiesta 95. L'Appartement 96. Portraits Chinois 96. Ma Vie en Rose 97. Le Ciel Est A Nous 97. Misfortunes of Beauty/Les Infortunes De La Beaute 99, etc.

Eddy, Helen Jerome (1897–1990)
American character actress who retired early. Always in high class films.
Rebecca of Sunnybrook Farm 16. The March Hare 21. The Country Kid 23. The Dark Angel 25. Camille 27. The Divine Lady 29. Skippy 31. Mata Hari 31. Madame Butterfly 32. The Bitter Tea of General Yen 33. Riptide 34. Keeper of the Bees 35. Stowaway 36. Winterset 36. The Garden of Allah 36. Outside the Law 38. Strike Up the Band 40, many others.

Eddy, Nelson (1901–1967)
Romantic American actor-singer with opera background; famous on screen for series of operettas with Jeanette MacDonald.

Eddy and MacDonald were rudely known in some quarters as The Singing Capon and The Iron Butterfly.
■ Broadway to Hollywood 31. Dancing Lady 33. Student Tour 34. *Naughty Marietta* 35. *Rose Marie* 36. *Maytime* 37. Rosalie 37. The Girl of the Golden West 38. *Sweethearts* 38. Let Freedom Ring 39. Balalaika 39. *New Moon* 40. Bitter Sweet 40. The Chocolate Soldier 41. I Married an Angel 43. Phantom of the Opera 43. Knickerbocker Holiday 44. Make Mine Music (voice only) 46. Northwest Outpost 47.

Edel, Uli (1947–) (Ulrich Edel)
German director.
The Little Soldier 70. Tommi Kehrt Zurück 72. Oisthalter 75. Christiane F. 81. *Last Exit to Brooklyn* 89. Body of Evidence 92. Tyson (TV) 95. Rasputin (TV) 96. The Little Vampire 00, etc.

Edelman, Herb (1930–1996)
Bald, lanky American character actor, usually in comic roles.
In Like Flint 67. Barefoot in the Park 67. The Odd Couple 68. The Front Page 74. The Yakuza 75. Charge of the Model-Ts 77. Smorgasbord 83, etc.
TV series: The Good Guys 68–70. Ladies' Man 80–81. Strike Force 81–82. 9 to 5 82–83.

Edelman, Louis F. (1901–1976)
American producer.
Once upon a Time 44. White Heat 48. I'll See You in My Dreams 52, etc.
TV series: *Wyatt Earp*, *The Big Valley*, etc.

Edelman, Randy (1947–)
American composer.
Outside In 72. Executive Action 73. Feds 88. Twins 88. Troop Beverly Hills 89. Ghostbusters II 89. Quick Change 90. Come See the Paradise 90. V.I. Warshawski 92. Shout 92. Drop Dead Fred 92. Dragon: The Bruce Lee Story 93. Gettysburg 93. Beethoven's 2nd 93. Angels in the Outfield (p) 94. The Mask 94. Billy Madison 95. While You Were Sleeping 95. The Indian in the Cupboard 95. Down Periscope 96. Diabolique 96. The Quest 96. Dragonheart 96. Anaconda 96. Daylight 96. Leave It to Beaver 97. Gone Fishin' 97. For Richer or Poorer 97. Six Days, Seven Nights 97. EdTV 99. The Whole Nine Yards 00. The Skulls 00. Shanghai Noon 00, etc.

Eden, Barbara (1934–) (Barbara Huffman)
American leading lady, former chorine.
Back from Eternity 56. Twelve Hours to Kill 60. Flaming Star 60. Voyage to the Bottom of the Sea 61. Five Weeks in a Balloon 62. The Wonderful World of the Brothers Grimm 63. The Brass Bottle 64. Seven Faces of Dr Lao 64. The Feminist and the Fuzz (TV) 71. The Woman Hunter (TV) 72. A Howling in the Woods (TV) 72. The Amazing Dobermans 76. Harper Valley PTA 78. Chattanooga Choo Choo 84. The Stepford Children (TV) 87. Her Wicked Ways (TV) 90, etc.
TV series: How to Marry a Millionaire 58. I Dream of Jeannie 65–70. Harper Valley PTA 81.

Edens, Roger (1905–1970)
American musical supervisor who moulded many MGM musicals, often as associate to producer Arthur Freed. Academy Awards for Easter Parade 48. On the Town 49. Annie Get Your Gun 50. Produced Deep in My Heart 55. Funny Face 56. Hello Dolly 69, etc.

Edeson, Arthur (1891–1970)
American cinematographer.
Wild and Woolly 17. *Robin Hood* 23. *The Thief of Baghdad* 24. *The Lost World* 25. The Bat 26. The Patent Leather Kid 27. In Old Arizona 28. *All Quiet on the Western Front* 30. *Frankenstein* 31. The Old Dark House 32. *The Invisible Man* 33. Mutiny on the Bounty 35. They Won't Forget 37. Each Dawn I Die 39. They Drive by Night 40. Sergeant York 41. *The Maltese Falcon* 41. *Casablanca* 42. Thank Your Lucky Stars 43. The Mask of Dimitrios 44. The Fighting O'Flynn 48, many others.

Edgar, Marriott (1880–1951)
British comedy scenarist, in films from 1935. Worked on many of the best vehicles of Will Hay and the Crazy Gang.
Good Morning Boys 36. Oh Mr Porter 38. Alf's Button Afloat 38. The Frozen Limits 39. The Ghost Train 41, many others; later on children's films. Also author of the 'Sam Small' and 'Albert' monologues made famous by Stanley Holloway.

Edgren, Gustav (1895–1954)
Swedish director, a former journalist; his early silent films tended towards slapstick comedy, while his later work dealt more with social problems.
Skeppargaten 25. The Ghost Baron 27. Tired Teodor 31. People of Värmland 32. Karl Fredrik Reigns 34. *Walpurgis Night* 35. *Katrin* 43. If Dew Falls Rain Follows (& co-w) 46, etc.

Edison, Thomas Alva (1847–1931)
American inventor of the phonograph and the incandescent lamp, among over a thousand other devices including the kinetoscope (a combined movie camera and projector), edge perforations and 35 mm gauge.
Biopics: *Young Tom Edison* 39 with Mickey Rooney; *Edison the Man* 40 with Spencer Tracy.

Edmondson, Adrian (1957–)
English comic actor, writer, director and novelist, best known for his partnership with actor Rik Mayall in anarchic and violent comedy. Born in Bradford, Yorkshire, he studied drama at Manchester University, where he first partnered Mayall. Married actress and writer Jennifer Saunders, with whom he runs the production company Mr amd Mrs Monsoon. In 2000, *Broadcast* magazine estimated their joint financial worth at £20m.
The Supergrass (a) 85. The Pope Must Die/The Pope Must Diet (a) 91. Guest House Paradiso (co-w,a,d) 99.
TV series: The Young Ones 82-84. Happy Families 85. Saturday Live 86-87. Filthy, Rich and Catflap 87. Snakes and Ladders 89. Bottom 91-92, 95. If You See God, Tell Him 93.

Edouart, Farciot (1895–1980)
American special effects man, with Paramount for many years.
Alice in Wonderland 33. Lives of a Bengal Lancer 35. Sullivan's Travels 41. Reap the Wild Wind 42. Unconquered 47. Ace in the Hole 51. The Mountain 56, many others.

Edson, Richard (1954–)
American actor and musican, usually in independent films. Born in New Rochelle, New York, he began as a drummer with such rock groups as Sonic Youth.
Stranger than Paradise 84. Howard the Duck 86. Platoon 86. Good Morning Vietnam 87. Do the Right Thing 89. Super Mario Brothers 93. Love, Cheat & Steal 94. Motorcycle Gang 94. Destiny Turns on the Radio 95. Strange Days 95. Jury Duty 95. The Winner 96. This World, Then the Fireworks 97. Lulu on the Bridge 98. The Shade 99. The Million Dollar Hotel 99. Timecode 00, etc.
TV series: Shannon's Deal 90-91.

Edwards, Anthony (1962–)
American leading actor. Born in Santa Barbara, California, he studied at the University of Southern California.
Fast Times at Ridgemont High 82. Heart Like a Wheel 82. Revenge of the Nerds 84. Gotcha! 85. The Sure Thing 85. Top Gun 86. Revenge of the Nerds II 87. Summer Heat 87. Mr North 88. Miracle Mile 89. How I Got into College 89. Hawks 89. Downtown 90. Landslide 92. Pet Sematary II 92. The Client 94. In Cold Blood (TV) 96. Don't Go Breaking My Heart 98. Playing by Heart 98, etc.
TV series: It Takes Two 82–83. Northern Exposure 92–93. ER 94– .

Edwards, Blake (1922–) (William Blake McEdwards)
American writer-producer-director with a leaning for all kinds of comedy. Married to Julie Andrews, who now appears mainly in his films, not always to her own advantage.
■ Panhandle (a, w) 47. All Ashore (w) 53. Cruising down the River (w) 53. Drive a Crooked Road (w) 54. Sound Off (w) 54. Bring Your Smile Along (wd) 55. My Sister Eileen (w) 55. He Laughed Last (wd) 55. Mr Cory (wd) 56. Operation Mad Ball (w) 57. This Happy Feeling (wd) 58. The Perfect Furlough (wd) 58. Operation Petticoat (d) 59. High Time (d) 60. Breakfast at Tiffany's (d) 61. Experiment in Terror (d) 62. Notorious Landlady (w) 62. *Days of Wine and Roses* (d) 62. The Pink Panther (wd) 63. A Shot in the Dark (wd, p) 64. *The Great Race* (wd, p) 64. Soldier in the Rain (w) 64. What Did You Do in the War, Daddy? (wd, p) 66. Waterhole 3 (p) 67. Gunn (d, p) 67. The Party (wd, p) 68. Darling Lili (wd, p) 69. Wild Rovers (wd, p) 71. The Carey Treatment (wd, p) 72. The Tamarind Seed (wd) 74. The Return of the Pink Panther (wd, p) 74. The Pink Panther Strikes Again (wd, p) 76. Revenge of the Pink Panther (wd, p) 78. '10' (wd, p) 79. S.O.B. (wd, p) 81. Trail of the Pink Panther (wd, p) 82. Victor/Victoria (wd, p) (AANw) 82. Curse of the Pink Panther (wd, p) 83. The Man Who Loved Women (wd) 83. Micki and Maude (d) 84. A Fine Mess (d) 86. That's Life! (d) 87. Blind Date (d) 87. Sunset (wd) 88. Skin Deep (wd) 89. Switch (wd) 91. Son of the Pink Panther (wd) 93.
TV series: Richard Diamond. Dante. Peter Gunn (all as creator).
❝ Make 'em redecorate your office. That's primary, to let them know where you stand. Then, when you're shooting interior sequences, use your own interior decorator and set dresser. That way, everything on the set will fit your house when you're finished. – *B.E.*

Edwards, Cliff (1895–1971)
Diminutive American entertainer known as 'Ukelele Ike'. Born in Hannibal, Missouri, he played Charles Starrett's sidekick in many westerns. A recording star in the 20s, he is best known for providing the voice of Jiminy Cricket in Disney's *Pinocchio*.
Hollywood Revue 29. Parlour Bedroom and Bath 31. Hell Divers 31. Flying Devils 33. Red Salute 35. Bad Guy 39. Pinocchio 40. The Monster and the Girl 41. The Falcon Strikes Back 43. She Couldn't Say No 45. The Avenging Rider 53, many others.

Edwards, Henry (1882–1952)
Gentlemanly British romantic lead of the 20s; later directed some films and came back to acting as amiable elderly man.
Broken Threads 18. The Amazing Quest of Ernest Bliss 22. A Lunatic at Large 23. *The Flag Lieutenant* 26. Fear 27. Three Kings 28. Call of the Sea 31. The Flag Lieutenant (talkie) 31. The Barton Mystery (d) 32. General John Regan 33. Discord Driven (d) 33. Scrooge (d) 35. Juggernaut (d) 37. Spring Meeting (d) 41. Green for Danger 46. Oliver Twist 48. London Belongs to Me 48. Madeleine 50. The Long Memory 52, many others.

Edwards, Hilton (1903–1982)
English stage actor, director and producer, in occasional films. With his partner Michael MacLiammoir, he founded the influential Gate Theatre, devoted to international drama, in Dublin in 1928, and gave Orson Welles his first engagement there as an actor in 1931.
Biography: 1994, *The Boys* by Christopher Fitz-Simon.
Return to Glennascaul (AAN, wd, short) 51. Othello 52. Cat & Mouse 58. She Didn't Say No 58. This Other Eden 59. A Terrible Beauty 60. Victim 61. The Quare Fellow 62. The Wrong Box 66, etc.

Edwards, J. Gordon (1867–1925)
American director of silent epics, especially for Theda Bara.
Anna Karenina 15. Under Two Flags 16. Cleopatra 17. Salome 18. The Queen of Sheba 21. Nero 22. The Shepherd King 23, many others.

Edwards, James (1922–1970)
American actor, on stage from 1945.
The Set-Up 49. *Home of the Brave* 49. The Member of the Wedding 52. The Caine Mutiny 54. The Phenix City Story 55. Men in War 57. The Sandpiper 65, etc.

Edwards, Jimmy (1920–1988)
Moustachioed British comedian of stage, radio and TV.
Autobiography: 1953, *Take It from Me*.
Murder at the Windmill 48. Treasure Hunt 52. Three Men in a Boat 55. Bottoms Up 60. Nearly a Nasty Accident 61. Rhubarb 70, etc.
TV series: *Whack-O!* 56–60. Seven Faces of Jim 61. Six More Faces of Jim 62. More Faces of Jim 63. Bold as Brass 64. Mr John Jorrocks 66. Blandings Castle 67. The Fossett Saga 69. Sir Yellow 73. The Glums 79.

Edwards, Meredith (1917–1999)
Balding Welsh character actor with stage experience.
A Run for Your Money 50. The Blue Lamp 50. Girdle of Gold 53. The Cruel Sea 53. The Long Arm 56. The Trials of Oscar Wilde 60. Only Two Can Play 61. This Is My Street 64. The Great St Trinian's Train Robbery 66. Fame Is the Spur (TV) 82, etc.

Edwards, Penny (1928–1998) (Millicent Edwards)
American light leading lady of the 40s.
Let's Face It 43. That Hagen Girl 47. Two Guys from Texas 48. The Wild Blue Yonder 51. Street Bandits 52. Powder River 53. Lady Beware 87, etc.

Edwards, Percy (1908–1996)
English animal impersonator who could imitate 600 species and provided many bird and animal sounds for films. A former plough-maker, he began in music hall in the 20s and was best known for his Psyche the dog in the long-running BBC radio sitcom *A Life of Bliss* in the 50s and 60s. His film work was not always credited.
The Rise and Rise of Michael Rimmer (bird impersonations) 70. The Belstone Fox 73. Orca – Killer Whale (title role) 77. The Dark Crystal (the voice of Fizzgig) 82. The Plague Dogs 82. The Labyrinth (the voice of Ambrosius) 86, etc.
TV series: Pet Pals 65. Hilary (as a myna bird) 84.

Edwards, Vince (1928–1996) (Vincento Eduardo Zoino)
American leading man of the tough/sincere kind; also a singer and director of TV series.
Mr Universe 51. Hiawatha 52. The Killing 56. City of Fear 58. *Murder by Contract* 59. The Victors 63. The Devil's Brigade 68. Hammerhead 68. The Desperadoes 69. The Mad Bomber 72. The Power and the Passion (TV) 79. Space Raiders 83. Cellar Dweller 87. The Gumshoe Kid 89. The Fear 95, etc.
TV series: *Ben Casey* 61–66. Matt Lincoln 70–71.

Edzard, Christine (1945–)
British director of meticulously researched historical films.
Stories from a Flying Trunk 79. Biddy 83. *Little Dorrit* (AANw) 87. The Fool 90. As You Like It 92, etc.

Egan, Eddie (1930–1995)
Burly American policeman whose exploits were the basis of *The French Connection*. He subsequently left the force and played small parts in films.
TV series: Joe Forrester 75. Eischied 79.

Egan, Peter (1946–)
British TV leading man who has sporadically appeared on stage and in films.
The Hireling 73. Callan 74. Hennessy 75. Chariots of Fire 81. A Woman of Substance (TV) 84. A Perfect Spy (TV) 87. Bean 97, etc.
TV series: Lillie (as Oscar Wilde) 78. Prince Regent 79. Ever Decreasing Circles 85–88. The Ambassador 98. Cry Wolf 99-00.

Egan, Richard (1921–1987)
Virile American leading man once thought likely successor to Clark Gable but who was mainly confined to westerns and action dramas.
The Damned Don't Cry 49. Undercover Girl 50. Split Second 52. Demetrius and the Gladiators 54. Wicked Woman 54. Gog 54. Underwater 55. Untamed 55. Violent Saturday 55. The View from Pompey's Head 55. Seven Cities of Gold 55. Love Me Tender 56. Tension at Table Rock 56. These Thousand Hills 58. A Summer Place 59. Pollyanna 60. Esther and the King 60. The 300 Spartans 62. The Destructors 66. Chubasco 68. The Big Cube 69. The Day of the Wolves (TV) 72. The Sweet Creek County War 79, etc.
TV series: Empire 62. Redigo 63.

Ege, Julie (1943–)
Decorative Norwegian leading lady in British films of the 70s. She retired from acting to return to Norway and became a nurse.
Every Home Should Have One 70. Up Pompeii 70. Creatures the World Forgot 71. The Magnificent Seven Deadly Sins 71. Rentadick 72. The Garnett Saga 72. Not Now Darling 73. Craze 73. The Mutations 74, etc.

Eggar, Samantha (1939–)
British leading lady, in international films.
The Wild and the Willing 62. Dr Crippen 63. Doctor in Distress 63. Psyche 59 63. *The Collector* (AAN) 65. Return from the Ashes 65. Walk Don't Run 66. Doctor Dolittle 67. The Molly Maguires 69. The Walking Stick 69. The Lady in the Car 70. The Light at the Edge of the World 71. The Dead Are Alive 72. A Name for Evil 72. Double Indemnity (TV) 73. All the Kind Strangers (TV) 74. The Seven Per Cent Solution 76. The Killer Who Wouldn't Die (TV) 76. Why Shoot the Teacher? 77. The Uncanny 77. Welcome to Blood City 77. Ziegfeld: The Man and His Women (TV) 78. Hagen (TV pilot) 79. The Brood 79. The Exterminator 80. Demonoid 81. Hot Touch 82. For the Term of His Natural Life 85. Ragin' Cajun 90. Dark Horse 92. Round Numbers 92. A Case for Murder (TV) 93. Inevitable Grace 94. The Phantom 96. Hercules (voice) 97. The Astronaut's Wife 99, etc.
TV series: *Anna and the King* 72.

Eggby, David
Australian cinematographer.
Mad Max 79. Kansas 88. The Salute of the Jugger 90. Quigley Down Under 90. Warlock 91. Harley Davidson and the Marlboro Man 91. The Paper 94. Dragonheart 96. Daylight 96, etc.

Eggleston, Colin
Australian director of adventure and horror movies.
Long Weekend 79. Bellamy 80. Sky Pirates 86. Cassandra 87. Innocent Prey 88. The Wicked 89, etc.

Egoyan, Atom (1960–)
Armenian director and screenwriter, in Canada. Born in Cairo, of Armenian parents, he moved to Canada as a child. Married actress Arsinee KHANJIAN.
Next of Kin 85. Family Viewing 87. Speaking Parts 89. Montreal Sextet (co-d) 91. The Adjuster 91. Calendar 93. Exotica 94. Sweet Hereafter (AAN) 97. Felicia's Journey 99, etc.
❝ The difference between a Hollywood film and what I do is this: in mainstream films, you're encouraged to forget that you're watching a movie, whereas in my films, you're always encouraged to remember that you're watching a collection of designed images. – *A.E.*

Ehle, Jennifer (c. 1970–)
Leading English actress, the daughter of Rosemary HARRIS and novelist John Ehle. Born in North Carolina, she studied at London's Central School of Speech and Drama.
The Camomile Lawn (TV) 91. Backbeat 93. Pride and Prejudice (TV) 95. Melissa (TV) 97. Paradise Road 97. Wilde 97. Bedrooms & Hallways 98. This Year's Love 99. Sunshine (Hun./Ger./Can./Au.) 99, etc.

Eichhorn, Lisa (1952–)
American actress who studied drama in Britain and works in both countries.
The Europeans 79. Yanks 79. Who Would I Lie? 80. Cutter's Way 81. The Weather in the Streets 83. Wildrose 84. Opposing Force 86. Grim Prairie Tales 90. Moon 44 90. The Vanishing 93. King of the Hill 93. A Modern Affair 95. First Kid 96. Spitfire Grill 96. Sticks and Stones 96. Judas Kiss 98, etc.

Eidelman, Cliff (1964–)
American composer and conductor.
Silent Night 88. To Die For 89. Triumph of the Spirit 89. Strike It Rich (co-w) 90. Crazy People 90. The Meteor Man 93. Untamed Heart 93. My Girl 2 94. Picture Bride 94. A Simple Twist of Fate 94. If These Walls Could Talk (TV) 96. The Beautician and the Beast 97. Free Willy 3: The Rescue 97. One True Thing 98, etc.

Eikenberry, Jill (1947–)
American leading lady of the early 80s.
The Deadliest Season (TV) 77. A Night Full of Rain 77. Butch and Sundance 79. Hide in Plain Sight 80. Arthur 81. Sessions 83. Manhattan Project 86. Cast the First Stone (TV) 89. Chantilly Lace (TV) 93. Parallel Lives (TV) 94. My Very Best Friend (TV) 97, etc.
TV series: Nurse 82. LA Law 86–94.

Eilbacher, Lisa (1947–)
American leading lady.
The War between Men and Women 72. Wheels (TV) 78. The Winds of War (TV) 83. Beverly Hills Cop 84. Monte Carlo (TV) 86. Leviathan 89. Living a Lie 91. Live Wire (TV) 92, etc.
TV series: The Texas Wheelers 74–75. The Hardy Boys Mysteries 77. Ryan's Four 83. Me and Mom 85.

Eilers, Sally (1908–1978)
Quiet-spoken American leading lady of the 30s. She was briefly married to cowboy star Hoot Gibson (1930–33).
The Goodbye Kiss 28. She Couldn't Say No 30. Quick Millions 31. The Black Camel 31. Over the Hill 31. State Fair 33. She Made Her Bed 34. Alias Mary Dow 34. Strike Me Pink 35. Talk of the Devil 36. Danger Patrol 37. Nurse from Brooklyn 38. They Made Her a Spy 39. Full Confession 39. I Was a Prisoner on Devil's Island 41. A Wave a WAC and a Marine 44. Coroner Creek 48. Stage to Tucson 50, many others.

Eisenberg, Hallie Kate (1992–)
American child actress, born in East Brunswick, New Jersey, who began in commercials.
Paulie 98. Bicentennial Man 99. The Insider 99. Beautiful 00. The Miracle Worker (as Helen Keller, TV) 00 , etc.

Eisenmann, Ike (1962–)
American child actor of the 70s.
Escape to Witch Mountain 74. Banjo Hackett (TV) 76. Return from Witch Mountain 78. The Hound of Hell (TV) 79, etc.
TV series: Fantastic Journey 77.

Eisenstein, Sergei (1898–1948)
Russian director, one of the cinema giants.
Biography: 1952, *Sergei Eisenstein* by Marie Seton. 1966, *Eisenstein* by Yon Barna. 1998, *Eisenstein: A Life in Conflict* by Ronald Bergan.
Other books: 1942, *The Film Sense*. 1948, *Notes of a Film Director*. 1949, *Film Form*.
■ *Strike* 24. *The Battleship Potemkin* 25. *October*/Ten Days That Shook the World 27. *The General Line* 28. *Que Viva Mexico* (unfinished: sections later released under this title and as *Time in the Sun*) 32. *Alexander Nevsky* 38. *Ivan the Terrible* 42–46.
✪ For virtually inventing montage, and for using the grammar of film-making more vividly and purposefully than almost anyone else. *Alexander Nevsky*.
❝ Which is the best picture I have ever seen? My answer always is *Battleship Potemkin*. – *Billy Wilder*

Eisinger, Jo
American screenwriter.
The Spider 45. Gilda 46. The Sleeping City 50. Night and the City 51. The System 53. Bedevilled 55. The Poppy is Also a Flower/Danger Grows Wild 66. The Jigsaw Man 84, many others.

Eisler, Hanns (1898–1962)
Austrian composer, who also collaborated with Brecht on plays and songs. Born in Leipzig, he studied music in Vienna under Arnold Schoenberg and left Germany in 1933, moving to the United States in the late 30s to lecture, teach, and to work in Hollywood. He fell foul of the Un-American Activities Committee in the late 40s and was deported, going to live and work in East Germany, where he wrote that country's national anthem.
Books: 1947, *Composing for Films*.
Kuhle Wampe (Ger.) 32. Song of Heroes (USSR) 32. New Earth (Netherlands) 34. Le Grand Jeu (Fr.) 34. Our Russian Front (co-m) 41. Hangmen Also Die 43. None but the Lonely Heart 43. Jealousy 45. The Spanish Main 45. Deadline at Dawn 46. A Scandal in Paris/Thieves' Holiday 46. Monsieur Verdoux 47. The Woman on the Beach 47. So Well Remembered 47. Herr Puntila and His Servant Matti/Herr Puntila und Sein Knecht Matti (Aus.) 55. Night and Fog/Nuit et Brouillard (Fr.) 55. Les Arrivistes (Fr.) 60, many others.
❝ Once or twice a year I write a motion picture. It interests me and I need the money – *H.E.*
Hanns Eisler is the Karl Marx of Communism in the musical field. – *Robert E. Stripling, chief investigator of the Un-American Activities Committee*

Eisley, Anthony (1925–)
American general-purpose actor.
The Naked Kiss 64. Frankie and Johnny 65. Journey to the Centre of Time 67. Star! 68. Blood of Frankenstein 70. The Doll Squad 73. Secrets (TV) 77, etc.
TV series: Hawaiian Eye 59–73. Capitol 82–84.

Eisner, Lotte H. (1896–1983)
German film historian.
Books: *The Haunted Screen*.

Eisner, Michael (1942–)
American production executive. He is chairman and chief executive officer of the Walt Disney Company.
Autobiography: 1998, *Work in Progress*.
Biography: 2000, *The Keys to the Kingdom: How Michael Eisner Lost His Grip* by Kim Masters.
❝ We have no obligation to make art. We have no obligation to make a statement. To make money is our only objective. – *M.E., 1981*

Ekberg, Anita (1931–)
Statuesque Swedish blonde who decorated a number of films in various countries.
The Golden Blade 53. Blood Alley 55. Artists and Models 55. Back from Eternity 56. War and Peace 56. Zarak 56. Interpol 57. Sign of the Gladiator 58. La Dolce Vita 59. The Mongols 60. Boccaccio 70 61. Summer is Short (Sw.) 62. Il Comandante (It.) 63. Call Me Bwana 63. Four for Texas 63. The Alphabet Murders 65. Who Wants to Sleep/Das Liebeskarussel 65. Way Way Out 66. The Glass Sphinx 67. If It's Tuesday, This Must Be Belgium 69. The Divorcee 70. The Clowns 70. Fangs of the Living Dead 73. Gold of the Amazon Women (TV) 79, etc.

Ekk, Nikolai (1902–1976)
Russian director.
The Road to Life 31. The Nightingale 36. A Night in May 41, etc.

Ekland, Britt (1942–) (Britt-Marie Eklund)
Swedish leading lady in international films. She was formerly married to Peter Sellers.
Too Many Thieves (TV) 66. After the Fox 66. The Bobo 67. The Double Man 68. The Night They Raided Minsky's 68. Stiletto 69. Percy 71. Get Carter 71. A Time for Loving 71. Night Hair Child 71. Baxter 72. Endless Night 72. Asylum 72. The Wicker Man 73. The Man with the Golden Gun 73. Royal Flash 74. The Ultimate Thrill 74. Casanova 77. High Velocity 77. King Solomon's Treasure 77. The Great Wallendas (TV) 77. Ring of Passion (TV) 79. Satan's Mistress 82. Moon in Scorpio 88. Scandal 89. The Children 90, etc.
❝ The ideal man doesn't exist. A husband is easier to find. – *B.E.*
I said I don't sleep with married men, but what I meant was I don't sleep with happily married men. – *B.E.*

Ekman, Gosta (1890–1948)
Swedish leading actor.
Charles XII 24. Faust 26. Intermezzo 36, etc.

Elam, Jack (1916–)
Laconic, swarthy American character actor, often seen as western villain or sinister comic relief.
Rawhide 50. Kansas City Confidential 52. The Moonlighter 53. Vera Cruz 54. Moonfleet 55. Kiss Me Deadly 55. *Gunfight at the OK Corral* 57. Baby Face Nelson 57. Edge of Eternity 59. The Comancheros 61. The Rare Breed 66. The Way West 67. Firecreek 67. Once Upon a Time in the West 69. Support Your Local Sheriff 69. Rio Lobo 70. Support Your Local Gunfighter 71. A Knife for the Ladies 74. Creature from Black Lake 76. Grayeagle 77. Lacy and the Mississippi Queen (TV) 78. The Villain 79. The Sacketts (TV) 79. The Cannonball Run 80. Jinxed! 82. Cannonball Run II 83. The Aurora Encounter 86. Hawken's Breed 89. Big Bad John 90. Suburban Commando 91. The Giant of Thunder Mountain 91. Uninvited 93. Shadow Force 93. Bonanza: The Return (TV) 93. Bonanza: Under Attack (TV) 95, etc.
TV series: *The Dakotas* 62. Temple Houston 63. The Texas Wheelers 77. Struck by Lightning (as the Frankenstein monster) 79.

Eldard, Ron (1964–)
American actor, best known as Ray 'Shep' Sheppard on the TV series *ER*. Born in New York, he studied at the drama department of the New York High School for the Performing Arts.
True Love 89. Drop Dead Fred 91. Captive 95. The Last Supper 96. Bastard out of Carolina (TV) 96. Sleepers 96. Deep Impact 98. Delivered 98. When Trumpets Fade 98. Mystery, Alaska 99, etc.
TV series: Arresting Behavior 92. Bakersfield P.D. 93-94. ER 95-96. Men Behaving Badly 96-97.

Eldredge, John (1917–1960)
Mild-looking American actor usually cast as weakling brother or bland schemer.
The Man with Two Faces 34. Persons in Hiding 38. Blossoms in the Dust 41. The French Key 47. Champagne for Caesar 50. Lonely Hearts Bandits 52. The First Travelling Saleslady 56, many others.

Eldridge, Florence (1901–1988) (Florence McKechnie)
Distinguished American stage actress, wife of Fredric March. Film appearances occasional.
Six Cylinder Love 23. The Studio Murder Mystery 29. The Matrimonial Bed 30. The Story of Temple Drake 33. Les Misérables 35. Mary of Scotland (as Elizabeth I) 36. *An Act of Murder* 48. *Another Part of the Forest* 48. Christopher Columbus 49. Inherit the Wind 60, etc.

Eldridge, John (1904–1961)
British documentary and feature director.
Waverley Steps 47. Three Dawns to Sydney 49. Brandy for the Parson 51. Laxdale Hall 53. Conflict of Wings 54, etc.

Eles, Sandor (1936–)
Hungarian leading man in Britain.
The Naked Edge 61. The Evil of Frankenstein 64. And Soon the Darkness 70. Countess Dracula 70. The Greek Tycoon 78, etc.

Elfand, Martin (1937–)
American producer.
Serpico 73. Dog Day Afternoon 75. It's My Turn 80. An Officer and a Gentleman 82. King David 85. Clara's Heart 86. A Talent for the Game 90, etc.

Elfman, Danny (1949–)
American musician, composer and singer with the rock band Oingo Boingo, who has scored the movies so far made by director Tim BURTON. He also composed the theme music for the TV series *The Simpsons*. He is the brother of director Richard ELFMAN.
Forbidden Zone 80. Pee-Wee's Big Adventure 85. Back to School 86. Wisdom 86. Summer School 87. Hot to Trot 88. Beetlejuice 88. Midnight Run 88. Big Top Pee-Wee 88. Scrooged 88. Batman 89. Nightbreed 90. Dick Tracy 90. Darkman 90. Edward Scissorhands 90. Article 99 92. Batman Returns 92. Sommersby 93. Tim Burton's The Nightmare before Christmas (& voice) 93. Black Beauty 94. To Die For 94. Dolores Claiborne 95. Dead Presidents 95. Freeway 96. The Frighteners 96. Mission: Impossible 96. Mars Attacks! 96. Extreme Measures 96. Mission: Impossible 96. *Men in Black* (AAN) 97. Flubber 97. *Good Will Hunting* (AAN) 97. A Simple Plan 98. Modern Vampires 98. Anywhere But Here 99. Instinct 99. Sleepy Hollow 99. The Family Man 00. Proof of Life 00, etc.

Elfman, Richard
American director of quirky exploitation movies with a cult reputation. A former percussionist, he founded in the 70s the avant garde performance group The Mystic Knights of the Oingo Boingo, which later became a rock group led by his brother, composer Danny ELFMAN. He is the father of actor Bodhi Elfman.
■ Forbidden Zone 84. Shrunken Heads 94. Modern Vampires/Revenant 98.

Elg, Taina (1931–)
Finnish leading lady in international films.
The Prodigal 55. Diane 56. Gaby 56. Les Girls 57. Imitation General 57. Watusi 58. The Thirty-Nine Steps 59, etc.

Elias, Michael (1940–)
American director and screenwriter, a former actor and comedian. He worked in television as a writer and producer on such shows as *The Mary Tyler Moore Show*, *All in the Family*, and *Head of the Class*.
The Jerk (co-w) 79. The Frisco Kid (co-w) 79. Serial (co-w) 80. Young Doctors in Love (co-w) 82. Lush Life (wd) 93.

Eliot, T. S. (1888–1965)
American poet who lived mainly in England. His play *Murder in the Cathedral* was his only work adapted for the cinema. A biopic about his first unhappy marriage, *Tom and Viv*, was released in 1994, with Willem Dafoe and Miranda Richardson in the title roles.

Eliscu, Edward (1902–1998)
American lyricist and screenwriter, a former actor. Born in New York, he studied science at the City College and made his Broadway stage debut in 1924 before turning to lyric writing, collaborating with such composers as Vincent Youmans, Gus Kahn and Vernon Duke. In the early 30s he worked as a writer and dialogue director for RKO. From the 50s, when he was blacklisted, he concentrated on television and the stage.
Professional Sweetheart (s) 33. Diplomaniacs (s) 33. *Flying Down to Rio* (s) 33. Silk Hat Kid (co-w) 35. Music Is Magic (co-w) 35. Paddy O'Day (co-w, s) 35. Every Saturday Night (w) 36. High Tension (co-w) 36. Little Miss Nobody (co-w) 36. Little Tough Guys in Society (w) 38. His Exciting Night (w) 38. Sis Hopkins (co-w) 41. Something to Shout About (co-w) 43. The Heat's On (s) 43. Hey, Rookie (co-w, s) 44. The Gay Senorita (w) 45, etc.

Elizabeth I
Queen of England (1533–1603), has been notably played by Sarah Bernhardt in *Queen Elizabeth* 12; by Flora Robson in *Fire Over England* 36 and *The Sea Hawk* 40; by Florence Eldridge in *Mary of Scotland* 36; by Bette Davis in *Elizabeth and Essex* 39 and *The Virgin Queen* 55; by Agnes Moorehead in *The Story of Mankind* 57; by Irene Worth in *Seven Seas to Calais* 63; by Catherine Lacey in *The Fighting Prince of Donegal* 65, and by Glenda Jackson in a 1971 TV series followed by *Mary Queen of Scots* 72; Jean Simmons played the young queen in *Young Bess* 53; Jean Kent had the role in the TV series *Sir Francis Drake*; Quentin Crisp played it in *Orlando* 92; Cate Blanchett played her as a far from virginal queen in *Elizabeth* 98.

Elizondo, Hector (1936–)
American character actor, mainly on stage.
Pocket Money 71, Stand Up and Be Counted 72. The Taking of Pelham One Two Three 74. Report to the Commissioner 75. Thieves 77. Cuba 79. American Gigolo 80. The Fan 81. Young Doctors in Love 82. The Flamingo Kid 84. Courage (TV) 86. Nothing in Common 86. Leviathan 89. Frankie and Johnny 91. Necessary Roughness 91. Lunatics: A Love Story 91. Final Approach 92. There Goes the Neighborhood/Paydirt 92. Samantha 92. Being Human 94. Exit to Eden 94. Beverly Hills Cop III 94. Getting Even with Dad 94. Dear God 96. Turbulence 97. Runaway Bride 99. The Other Sister 99, etc.
TV series: Freebie and the Bean 80. Casablanca 83. The Flamingo Kid/Pablo 84. Private Resort 85. Nothing in Common 86. Chicago Hope 94-99.

Ellenshaw, Peter (c. 1914–)
British special effects artist and production designer, with Disney from 1950.
Things to Come 36. Victoria the Great 37. The Drum 38. A Matter of Life and Death 45. The Red Shoes 48. Treasure Island 50. *20,000 Leagues Under the Sea* 54. Johnny Tremain 57. Darby O'Gill and the Little People 59. In Search of the Castaways 61. *Mary Poppins* 64. The Island at the Top of the World 74. *The Black Hole* 79, etc.

Ellington, Duke (1899–1974) (Edward Kennedy Ellington)
Celebrated American jazz bandleader, composer and pianist.
Hit Parade 37. New Faces 37. Reveille with Beverly 43. Anatomy of a Murder 59. Paris Blues 61. Change of Mind (m only) 69, etc.

Elliot, Laura (1929–)
American supporting actress.
Special Agent 49. Paid in Full 50. *Strangers on a Train* 51. When Worlds Collide 52. Jamaica Run 53. About Mrs Leslie 54, etc.

Elliot, Maxine
See Hicks, Maxine Elliott

Elliott, Alison (1969–)
American actress. Raised in San Francisco, she worked as a model until gaining a role in the TV sitcom *Living Dolls*.
Wyatt Earp 94. Monkey Trouble 94. The Underneath 95. The Buccaneers (TV) 95. The Spitfire Grill 97, etc.
TV series: Living Dolls 89.

Elliott, Denholm (1922–1992)
Incisive British actor of stage, screen and television, often of well-mannered, ineffectual types, latterly in more sophisticated roles. He trained briefly at RADA, then began acting in a German POW camp during the Second World War. The first of his two wives was actress Virginia McKenna (1954–57). Died of AIDS.
Biography: 1994, *Denholm Elliott – Quest for Love* by Susan Elliott with Barry Turner.
Dear Mr Prohack 49. The Sound Barrier 52. The Cruel Sea 53. The Heart of the Matter 53. They Who Dare 54. The Night My Number Came Up 55. Pacific Destiny 56. Scent of Mystery/Holiday in Spain 59. Station Six Sahara 63. *Nothing But the Best* 64. The High Bright Sun 65. You Must Be Joking 65. King Rat 65. Alfie 66. The Spy with a Cold Nose 67. Maroc 7 67. *Here We Go Round the Mulberry Bush* 67. The Night They Raided Minsky's 68. Too Late the Hero 69. The Rise and Rise of Michael Rimmer 70. Percy 70. Quest for Love 71. A Doll's House 73. Madame Sin 73. The Apprenticeship of Duddy Kravitz 75. Robin and Marian 75. Russian Roulette 76. A Bridge Too Far 77. The Boys from Brazil 78. Saint Jack 79. Cuba 79. Bad Timing 80. Sunday Lovers 80. Raiders of the Lost Ark 81. The Missionary 82. Brimstone and Treacle 82. Trading Places 83. The Razor's Edge 84. A Private Function (BFA) 84. A Room With a View (AAN) 85. Defence of the Realm (BFA) 85. Maurice 87. The Happy Valley (TV) 87. September 87. The Bourne Identity (TV) 88. Stealing Heaven 88. Indiana Jones and the Last Crusade 89. Killing Dad 89. Return to the River Kwai 89. Toy Soldiers 91. Scorchers 91. Noises Off 92, etc.
❝ I like actors – such as Margaret Rutherford and Peter Lorre – who aren't afraid to over-act like real people. When I take a job I can always come up with ten different ways of doing the part. But I'll always choose the flashiest one. You've got to dress the window a bit. – *D.E.*
He has a manner which suggests that he is about to preside with great dignity at a court martial, yet also to be cashiered in cringing disgrace at one and the same time, and that either pose is for him a matter both of raging disgust and total indifference. – *Dennis Potter*

Elliott, Robert (1879–1951)
Irish leading man of American silents.
Spirit of Lafayette 17. Resurrection 18. A Woman There Was 19. A Virgin Paradise 21. Man and Wife 23. Romance of the Underworld 28. Thunderbolt 29. The Divorcee 30. Five Star Final 31. Phantom of Crestwood 32. Crime of the Century 33. Girl of the Limberlost 34. Circumstantial Evidence 35. Trade Winds 38. Gone with the Wind 39. Captain Tugboat Annie 45, many others.

Elliott, Ross (1917–1999)
American character actor, best known for his role as Sheriff Abbott in the TV series *The Virginian*. He was also a regular in the TV soap opera *General Hospital* and had a recurring role in the '50s TV sitcom *I Love Lucy*. Born in New York, he began his acting career with Orson Welles' Mercury Theater.
Angel on the Amazon 48. Woman on the Run 50. Chicago Calling 51. Hot Lead 51. I Can Get It for You Wholesale 51. Woman in the Dark 52. The Beast from 20,000 Fathoms 53. Ma and Pa Kettle at Home 54. African Manhunt 55. Tarantula 55. D Day The Sixth of June 56. The Indestructible Man 56. Monster on the Campus 58. The Crawling Hand 63. Fargo 64. The Wild Seed 65. Kelly's Heroes 70. Paper Man (TV) 71. Linda 73. Scorpion 86, etc.
TV series: The Virginian 67-70.

Elliott, Sam (1944–)
American leading man of the 70s.
■ The Games 70. Frogs 72. Molly and Lawless John 72. The Blue Knight (TV) 73. I Will Fight No More Forever (TV) 75. Evel Knievel (TV) 75. Lifeguard 76. Once an Eagle (TV) 77. The Legacy 78. The Last Convertible (TV) 79. Aspen (TV) 79. The Sacketts (TV) 79. The Legacy 79. Wild Times (TV) 80. Murder in Texas (TV) 81. The Shadow Riders (TV) 82. Travis McGee (TV) 82. Mask 85. Fatal Beauty 87. Shakedown/Blue Jean Cop 88. Prancer 89. Road House 89. Sibling Rivalry 90. Rush 92. Gettysburg 93. Tombstone 93. The Desperate Trail (TV) 94. Woman Undone 94. Hole in the Sky (TV) 95. Buffalo Girls (TV) 95. Blue River (TV) 95. The Final Cut 96. Rough Riders (TV) 97. Dogwatch (TV) 97. The Big Lebowksi 98. The Hi-Lo Country 99. Fail Safe (TV) 00. The Contender 00.

Elliott, Stephan (1964–)
Australian director and screenwriter.
Frauds 93. *The Adventures of Priscilla, Queen of the Desert* 94. Welcome to Woop Woop 97, etc.

Elliott, Ted
American scriptwriter, usually in collaboration with Terry Rossio.
Little Monsters 89. Aladdin (& co-d) 92. Puppet Masters 94. Godzilla (story) 98. Small Soldiers 98. The Mask of Zorro (story) 98. Antz (story consultant) 98, etc.

Elliott, 'Wild Bill' (1904–1965) (Gordon Elliott)
Burly American leading man of the 20s who later appeared in many second feature westerns and mysteries.
The Private Life of Helen of Troy 27. Broadway Scandals 28. The Great Divide 31. Wonder Bar 34. False Evidence 40. Blue Clay 42. The Plainsman and the Lady 46. The Fabulous Texan 48. Hellfire 49. The Longhorn 51. Dial Red O 55. Chain of Evidence 57, etc.

Ellis, Don (1933–1978)
American composer, former jazz trumpeter.
Moon Zero Two 69. The French Connection 71. The Seven Ups 73. French Connection II 75. Ruby 77, etc.

Ellis, Edward (1872–1952)
American stage character actor who made a number of films in the 30s, usually as stern father or judge.
I Am a Fugitive from a Chain Gang 32. From Headquarters 33. The President Vanishes 34. The Return of Peter Grimm 35. Fury 36. Maid of Salem 37. *A Man to Remember* 38. Three Sons 39. A Man Betrayed 41. The Omaha Trail 42, etc.

Ellis, Mary (1897–) (Mary Elsas)
American leading lady and singer famous in British stage musicals, especially those of Ivor Novello.
Bella Donna 34. Paris Love Song 35. All the King's Horses 35. Paris in Spring 35. Fatal Lady 36. Glamorous Night 37. The Three Worlds of Gulliver 59, etc.

Ellis, Patricia (1916–1970) (Patricia Gene O'Brien)
American leading lady of the 30s.
Three on a Match 32. 42nd Street 33. Picture Snatcher 33. The St Louis Kid 34. The Case of the Lucky Legs 34. Boulder Dam 36. Melody for Two 37. Blockheads 38. Back Door to Heaven 39. Fugitive at Large 39, etc.

Ellis, Robert (1892–1974) (Robert Ellis Reel)
American leading actor, director of silents, and screenwriter. Born in Brooklyn, he worked in musical comedy and as a stuntman before entering films in 1913, working as an actor-director, and then acting in early talkies. In the mid-30s, he switched to screenwriting at Twentieth Century-Fox. Married actresses May Allison and Vera Reynolds, and screenwriter Helen Logan, with whom he wrote thrillers and musicals.
A Modern Jekyll and Hyde 13. The Apaches of Paris (& d) 15. Almost a Heroine (& d) 16. The Lurking Peril (& d) 16. The Lifted Veil 17. Louisiana 19. The Daughter Pays (& d) 20. Handcuffs or Kisses 21. A Divorce of Convenience (d only) 21. Chivalrous Charley (d only) 21. Anna Ascends 22. Wild Honey 22. Mark of the Beast 23. For Sale 24. Lady Robinhood 25. Ragtime 27. Restless Youth 28. Night Parade 29. The Deadline 31. The Good Bad Girl 31. The Fighting Fool 32. Reform Girl 33. A Girl of the Limberlost 34. Madame Spy 34, many others.
As writer, in collaboration with Helen Logan: Charlie Chan in Egypt 35. Charlie Chan in Shanghai 35. Charlie Chan's Secret 36. Charlie Chan at the Race Track 36. Charlie Chan on Broadway 37. Charlie Chan in the City of Darkness 39. Tin Pan Alley 40. Sun Valley Serenade 41. Iceland 42. Song of the Islands 42. Hello Frisco Hello 43. Pin Up Girl 44. Four Jills in a Jeep 44. Something for the Boys 44. Do You Love Me? 46. I'll Get By (story) 50, etc.

Ellis, Robert (1933–1973)
American actor who began in films at the age of five; he was known as Bobby Ellis in his juvenile roles. Died of kidney failure.
April Showers 48. The Green Promise 49. Walk Softly, Stranger 50. Call Me Mister 51. Retreat Hell! 52. The McConnell Story 55. Space Master X-7 58. Gidget 59, many others.
TV series: Meet Corliss Archer 51–52, 54–55. The Aldrich Family 52–53.

Ellis, Ruth (1927–1955)
The last woman to be hanged for murder in Britain has been the subject of two films: *Yield to the Night/Blonde Sinner* 56, starring Diana Dors, and *Dance with a Stranger* 85, starring Miranda Richardson.

Ellis, Vivian (1904–1996)
English composer and lyricist, a former concert pianist, who began writing for theatrical revues in 1922. 'Spread a Little Happiness' and 'This Is My Lovely Day' are his best-known songs, but most of his tinkly tunes were aired only on the London stage. He was also a novelist and wrote a series of humorous books (*How to Enjoy Your Operation*, *How to Bury Yourself in the Country*, etc.).
Autobiography: *Ellis in Wonderland*. 1953, *I'm on a See-Saw*.
Elstree Calling 30. Out of the Blue 31. Brother Alfred 32. Lord Babs 32. Jack's the Boy 32. The Water Gipsies 32. Falling for You 33. Mr Cinders 34. Over the Garden Wall 34. Public Nuisance No. 1 36. Who's Your Lady Friend 37. Under Your Hat 40, etc.

Ellis, Walter (1874– *)
English playwright, mainly of farces. Born in London, he was educated at Cambridge University; his plays were a mainstay of the London stage from 1911 until the mid-40s.
A Little Bit of Fluff 28. Almost a Honeymoon 30. Let Me Explain, Dear (from his play A Little Bit of Fluff) 32. Hawleys of High Street 33. Her Last Affaire 35. Almost a Honeymoon 38. Bedtime Story 38, etc.

Ellison, James (1910–1993) (James Ellison Smith)
Genial American leading man, mainly seen in routine westerns.
The Play Girl 32. Hopalong Cassidy 35. The Plainsman (as Buffalo Bill) 36. Vivacious Lady 38. Fifth Avenue Girl 39. Ice Capades 41. Charley's Aunt 41. The Undying Monster 42. I Walked with a Zombie 43. The Ghost Goes Wild 46. Calendar Girl 47. Last of the Wild Horses 48. Lone Star Lawman 50. Dead Man's Trail 52, etc.

Elmes, Frederick (1947–)
American cinematographer.
The Killing of a Chinese Bookie 76. Eraserhead 78. Opening Night 79. Valley Girl 83. Blue Velvet 86. Allan Quatermain and the Lost City of Gold 87. Heaven 87. River's Edge 87. Permanent Record 88. Moonwalker 89. Wild at Heart 90. Night on Earth 92. The Saint of Fort Washington 93. Trial by Jury 94. Reckless 95. The Empty Mirror 96. The Ice Storm 97, etc.

Elmes, Guy (1920–)
British writer.
The Planter's Wife (co-w) 51. The Stranger's Hand 53. Across the Bridge (co-w) 57. Swordsman of Siena 62. A Face in the Rain 63. El Greco 66. The Night Visitor 71, etc.

Elphick, Michael (1946–)
Heavy-set British character actor of all media.
Fraulein Doktor 67. Cry of the Banshee 69. Blind Terror 70. O Lucky Man 73. The Elephant Man 80. Privates on Parade 83. Gorky Park 83. Masada (TV) 83. Hitler's SS (TV) 84. Ordeal by Innocence 85. Supergrass 85. Little Dorrit 87. Buddy's Song 90. Let Him Have It 91. Ken Russell's Treasure Island (TV) 95, etc.
TV series: Boon 85–90. Three Up Two Down 85–87. Harry 93–95.

Elsom, Isobel (1893–1981) (Isobel Reed)
British stage actress who starred in over 60 early British romantic films; went to Hollywood in the late 30s and played innumerable great ladies.
A Debt of Honour 19. Dick Turpin's Ride to York 22. The Sign of Four 23. The Wandering Jew 23. The Love Story of Aliette Brunon 24. Stranglehold 30. Illegal 31. *Ladies in Retirement* 41. You Were Never Lovelier 42. Between Two Worlds 44. The Unseen 45. Of Human Bondage 46. Ivy 47. Love from a Stranger 47. Monsieur Verdoux 47. Desiree 54. 23 Paces to Baker Street 57. The Miracle 59. Who's Minding the Store? 63. My Fair Lady 64, many others.

Eltinge, Julian (1882–1941) (William J. Dalton)
American female impersonator who appeared in a few silent films.

The Countess Charming 17. Over the Rhine 18. Madame Behave 24, etc.

Elton, Sir Arthur (1906–1973)
British producer especially associated with documentary; GPO Film Unit 34–37, Ministry of Information 37–45, Shell Film Unit 45 on. Founder Film Centre, governor BFI, etc.

Elton, Ben (1959–)
English stand-up comedian, actor, writer, novelist and playwright. He studied drama at Manchester University and gained fame performing at London's Comedy Store, on television in *The Ben Elton Show*, and as co-writer of the popular TV series *The Young Ones* (1982–84) and *Blackadder* (1983–89), and writer of *Filthy Rich and Catflap* 87.

Stark (a, w from his novel) (TV) 93. Much Ado about Nothing (a) 93. Maybe Baby (wd, oa) 00, etc.

❝ I do feel sorry for my mum. For years she thought she had a fairly reasonable, moderately pleasant child, and it turns out she had a hypocritical, foul-mouthed, self-righteous wanker. – *B.E.*

His anxiety levels make Woody Allen look like a Zen Master. – *Guardian*

Elvey, Maurice (1887–1967) (William Folkard)
Veteran British director of over 300 features.

Maria Marten 12. Comradeship 18. Nelson 19. At the Villa Rose 20. The Elusive Pimpernel 20. The Hound of the Baskervilles 21. Dick Turpin's Ride to York 22. The Love Story of Aliette Brunon 24. The Flag Lieutenant 26. Hindle Wakes 27. Balaclava 28. High Treason 30. The School for Scandal 30. Sally in Our Alley 31. In a Monastery Garden 31. The Water Gypsies 32. The Lodger 32. The Wandering Jew 33. The Clairvoyant 34. *The Tunnel* 34. Heat Wave 35. The Return of the Frog 37. For Freedom 39. Room for Two 39. Under Your Hat 40. The Lamp Still Burns 43. The Gentle Sex (co-d) 43. Medal for the General 44. Salute John Citizen 44. *Beware of Pity* 46. The Third Visitor 51. My Wife's Lodger 52. Fun at St Fanny's 55. Dry Rot 56, many others.

Elwes, Cary (1962–)
British actor.

Another Country 84. The Bride 85. Lady Jane 86. The Princess Bride 87. Glory 89. Days of Thunder 90. Hot Shots! 91. Bram Stoker's Dracula 92. The Crush 93. Robin Hood: Men in Tights 93. The Chase 94. Rudyard Kipling's The Jungle Book 94. CutThroat Island 95. Twister 96. Liar Liar 96. Kiss the Girls 97. The Pentagon Wars (TV) 98. Quest for Camelot (voice) 98. The Cradle Will Rock (as John Houseman) 99, etc.

Ely, Ron (1938–) (Ronald Pierce)
American athlete who was television's Tarzan 1966–68.

The Fiend Who Walked the West 58. South Pacific 58. Night of the Grizzly 59. The Remarkable Mr Pennypacker 59. Once Before I Die 65. Mountains of the Moon 67. Doc Savage (title role) 75. Slavers 78, etc.

TV series: The Aquanauts 61.

Emerson, Eric (1946–1975)
Boyish American dancer, a star of Andy Warhol's films. He was found dead in a New York street, apparently the victim of a hit-and-run accident, though Warhol thought that he probably died of a drug overdose.

The Chelsea Girls 66. Lonesome Cowboys 68. Heat 72, etc.

Emerson, Faye (1917–1983)
American socialite leading lady popular for a time in the 40s following her marriage to Elliot Roosevelt, son of the President (1944–50). Retired to Majorca in the 60s.

Between Two Worlds 44. The Mask of Dimitrios 44. Hotel Berlin 45. Danger Signal 45. Nobody Lives Forever 46. Guilty Bystander 50. A Face in the Crowd 57, etc.

TV series: Faye Emerson Show 50. Faye Emerson's Wonderful Town 51–52.

Emerson, Hope (1897–1960)
Brawny 6 foot 2 inch American character actress, in films from early 30s.

Smiling Faces 32. Cry of the City 48. Adam's Rib 49. Caged (AAN) 50. Casanova's Big Night 54. The Day They Gave Babies Away 56. Rock a Bye Baby 58, many others.

TV series: Doc Corkle 52. Peter Gunn 58–60.

Emerson, Keith (1944–)
English composer and keyboard player, a former member of the rock groups Nice and Emerson, Lake and Palmer.

Inferno (US) 80. Nighthawks (US) 81. Best Revenge (Can.) 83. Murderock, Uccide a Passo di Danza (It.) 84, etc.

Emerton, Roy (1892–1944)
Long-nosed British character actor: an eminently hissable villain.

The Sign of Four 32. Java Head 34. Lorna Doone (as Carver) 35. Doctor Syn 38. The Drum 38. Busman's Honeymoon 40. The Thief of Baghdad 40. The Man in Grey 43. Henry V 44, etc.

Emery, Dick (1918–1983)
Chubby British TV comedian with a flair for disguise.

Autobiography: 1974, *In Character*.

Light Up the Sky 60. A Taste of Money 62. The Wrong Arm of the Law 63. Baby Love 69. *Ooh You Are Awful* 72, etc.

Emery, Gilbert (1875–1945) (Gilbert Emery Bensley Pottle)
British character actor long in Hollywood as police commissioners, lords of the manor, etc.

Behind that Curtain 29. The Royal Bed 30. A Farewell to Arms 32. The House of Rothschild 34. One More River 34. Clive of India 35. Magnificent Obsession 35. Dracula's Daughter 36. A Man to Remember 38. Nurse Edith Cavell 39. Raffles 39. Rage in Heaven 41. That Hamilton Woman 41. The Loves of Edgar Allan Poe 42. Between Two Worlds 44. The Brighton Strangler 45, many others.

Emery, John (1905–1964)
American stage and screen actor of suave and sometimes Mephistophelean types. Married actress Tallulah Bankhead (1937–41).

Here Comes Mr Jordan 41. Spellbound 45. Blood on the Sun 45. The Woman in White 48. The Gay Intruders 48. Let's Live Again 49. The Mad Magician 54. Ten North Frederick 57. Youngblood Hawke 64, many others.

Emhardt, Robert (1914–1994)
American character actor, short and tubby; once understudied Sydney Greenstreet.

The Iron Mistress 52. 3.10 to Yuma 57. Underworld USA 60. The Stranger 61. Kid Galahad 62. *The Group* 66. Where Were You When the Lights Went Out? 68. Lawman 71. Alex and the Gypsy 76, etc.

Emilfork, Daniel
Thin, beaky French character actor, usually in sinister roles.

The Hunchback of Notre Dame 57. What's New Pussycat? 65. Lady L 65. The Liquidator 66. Trans-Europ-Express 66. The Devil's Nightmare/Succubus 71. Travels with My Aunt 72. Kill 72. Who Is Killing the Great Chefs of Europe? 78. Pirates 86. The City of Lost Children/La Cité des Enfants Perdus 95, etc.

Emlyn, Endaf (1945–)
Welsh director and screenwriter, from television.

One Full Moon 91. Leaving Lenin 93.

Emmer, Luciano (1918–)
Italian director.

Domenica d'Agosto 50. The Girls of the Spanish Steps 52. The Bigamist 56, etc.

Emmerich, Roland (1955–)
German-born director of action and science-fiction films, in Hollywood. His special-effects-filled *Independence Day* was the surprise hit of 1996, breaking many box-office records.

Making Contact 85. Hollywood Monster 87. Moon 44 89. Universal Soldier 92. Stargate 94. *Independence Day* 96. Godzilla (US) 98, etc.

TV series: The Visitor (p, w) 97–98.

Emmett, E. V. H. (1902–1971)
Urgent-voiced commentator, film editor, screenwriter and producer, a former journalist. He was the voice of Gaumont-British News in the 30s until the mid-40s and Universal News in the 50s, and can also be heard as narrator in *Carry On Cleo* 64. He also produced features at Ealing from 1946–50.

Sabotage (co-w) 36. Young Man's Fancy (co-w) 39, etc.

Emney, Fred (1900–1980)
Heavyweight British comedian, characterized by a growl, a cigar, and a top hat.

Brewster's Millions 35. Yes Madam 39. Just William 40. Let the People Sing 42. Fun at St Fanny's 56. San Ferry Ann 65. The Sandwich Man 66. Lock Up Your Daughters 69, etc.

Ende, Michael (1929–1995)
German children's novelist, a former actor, whose bestseller *The Neverending Story*, about the power and importance of fantasy, was filmed by Wolfgang Petersen. He disliked the result, describing it as 'a gigantic melodrama of kitsch, commerce, plush and plastic'. Two lacklustre sequels followed.

The Neverending Story 84. Momo 85. The Neverending Story II 90. The Neverending Story III 94.

❝ In a world in which not just our own lives but nature itself is explained to us in terms of its usefulness, I think it is wonderful that there are creatures which have no use whatsoever. – *M.E.*

Endfield, Cy (1914–1995)
American director, in films since 1942. Made second features until 1951; thereafter resident in Britain.

Gentleman Joe Palooka 47. Stork Bites Man (& w) 47. The Argyle Secrets (& w) 48. Underworld Story 50. *The Sound of Fury* 51. Tarzan's Savage Fury 52. The Search 55. Child in the House 56. *Hell Drivers* 57. Sea Fury 58. Jet Storm 59. Mysterious Island 61. *Zulu* 63. Sands of the Kalahari 65. De Sade 69. Universal Soldier 71. Zulu Dawn (co-w) 79, etc.

Endore, Guy (1900–1970)
American screenwriter and novelist.

Mark of the Vampire 35. Mad Love 35. The Raven 35. The Devil Doll 36. The League of Frightened Men 37. Carefree 38. The Story of G.I. Joe (AAN) 45. Whirlpool (oa) 49. He Ran All the Way 51. Curse of the Werewolf (oa) 61. Captain Sinbad 63, etc.

Engel, Morris (1918–)
American producer-director of off-beat semi-professional features.

The Little Fugitive 53. Lovers and Lollipops 55. Weddings and Babies 58.

Engel, Samuel G. (1904–1984)
American producer, a former screenwriter.

Earthbound (w) 40. Scotland Yard (w) 41. My Darling Clementine 46. Sitting Pretty 48. Rawhide 50. Belles on Their Toes 52. Daddy Long Legs 55. Boy on a Dolphin 57. The Story of Ruth 60. The Lion 62, many others.

English, Arthur (1919–1995)
English stand-up comedian who became a sympathetic character actor, mainly on TV, from the 60s. A former painter and decorator, he began his career as a comic in 1949, when he was best known for his fast-talking (300 words a minute at its climax) act as a spiv in floor-length overcoat and wide, garish tie.

Catchphrase: Start the music – open the cage!

Autobiography: *Through the Mill and Beyond*.

The Hi-Jackers 63. Percy 71. For the Love of Ada 72. Love Thy Neighbour 73. Barry McKenzie Holds His Own 74. Are You Being Served? 77. The Boys in Blue 83, etc.

TV series: Are You Being Served? 73–85. How's Your Father? 74–75. The Ghosts of Motley Hall 76–78. In Sickness and in Health 86–91. Never Say Die 87.

English, John (1903–1969)
British director of second features, long in America; a specialist in serials.

Arizona Days 37. Drums of Fu Manchu 40. Captain Marvel 41. King of the Texas Rangers 41. Captain America 44. Don't Fence Me In 45. The Phantom Speaks 45. Murder in the Music Hall 46. Loaded Pistols 48. Riders in the Sky 49. Valley of Fire 51, many others.

Englund, George H. (1926–)
American producer-director.

The World, the Flesh and the Devil (p) 59. The Ugly American £ 62. Signpost to Murder (d) 64. Dark of the Sun (p) 67. Zachariah (d) 70. Snowjob (d) 71. A Christmas to Remember (d) (TV) 78. Dixie: Changing Habits (d) (TV) 83. The Vegas Strip War (d) (TV) 84, etc.

Englund, Ken (1914–1993)
American writer, in films from 1938.

Good Sam 47. The Secret Life of Walter Mitty 48. The Caddy 53. The Vagabond King 56, etc.

Englund, Robert (1949–)
American character actor who became a mild cult after playing the demoniacal Freddy in *Nightmare on Elm Street* and its sequels.

Buster and Billie 74. The Great Smokey Roadblock 76. St Ives 76. A Star Is Born 76. Blood Brothers 78. Galaxy of Terror 81. 976-EVIL (d) 88. The Phantom of the Opera 89. The Adventures of Ford Fairlane 90. Dance Macabre 91. Wes Craven's New Nightmare 94. Killer Tongue 96. Wishmaster 97. Perfect Target 98. Meet the Deedles 98. Urban Legend 98. Dee Snider's Strangeland 98, etc.

TV series: V 84–85. Downtown 86–87. Freddy's Nightmares (host) 88–90.

Engstead, John (1909–1983)
American portrait photographer in Hollywood. Born in Los Angeles and a graduate of Hollywood High School, he first worked at Paramount and, later, as a freelance, taking portraits of such stars as Humphrey Bogart, Lauren Bacall, Joan Crawford, James Stewart and Marlon Brando.

Ennis, Skinnay (1907–1963)
American bandleader and vocalist who appeared in such 30s films as *College Swing*, *Sleepytime Gal* and *Follow the Band*.

Eno, Brian (1948–)
English composer and keyboard player, a founder-member of Roxy Music.

Land of the Minotaur (co-m) 76. Dune (co-m) 84. For All Mankind (doc) 89, etc.

Enrico, Robert (1931–2001)
French director.

Incident at Owl Creek 64. Au Coeur de la Vie 65. La Belle Vie 65. Les Aventuriers 67. Zita 67. Ho! 68. Rum Runner 76. The Old Gun 76. L'Empreinte des Géants 80. For Those I Loved 83. Zone Rouge 86. The French Revolution (co-d) 89. Zone Rouge 90. East Wind/Vent d'Est 93, etc.

Enright, Nick
Australian dramatist and screenwriter.

Lorenzo's Oil (co-w) (AAN) 92. Blackrock (oa, w) 97, etc.

Enright, Ray (1896–1965)
American director, former editor and Sennett gagman. Films mostly routine.

Tracked by the Police 27. Dancing Sweeties 30. Havana Widows 33. Twenty Million Sweethearts 34. Dames 34. Alibi Ike 35. Miss Pacific Fleet 35. Earthworm Tractors 36. Slim 37. *Swing Your Lady* 37. Gold Diggers in Paris 38. Angels Wash Their Faces 39. On Your Toes 39.

Enyedi, Ildikó (1955–)
Hungarian director and screenwriter.

My Twentieth Century 90. Magic Hunter/Buvos Vadas (co-w, d) 94. Tamás és Juli 97, etc.

Ephron, Henry (1912–1992)
American screenwriter who invariably worked as a team with his wife Phoebe Ephron (1914–71). Their daughter is novelist and screenwriter Nora Ephron. He also produced a few films. Married former actress June Gale, the widow of pianist Oscar Levant, in 1978.

Bride by Mistake 44. Always Together 46. John Loves Mary 49. *The Jackpot* 50. On the Riviera 51. Belles on Their Toes 52. There's No Business Like Show Business 54. Daddy Long Legs 55. Carousel (& p) 56. The Best Things in Life Are Free (p only) 56. *Desk Set* 57. Take Her, She's Mine 63. Captain Newman MD (AAN) 63, etc.

Ephron, Nora (1941–)
American screenwriter and novelist, particularly witty on the traumas of marriage, who has now turned to directing. She is the daughter of screenwriters Phoebe and Henry Ephron, who wrote the plays *Three's a Family* about her childhood and *Take Her, She's Mine* about her life at college. Formerly married to writer Dan

Greenburg and journalist Carl Bernstein, she married screenwriter Nicholas Pileggi in 1987.

Silkwood (AAN) 83. Heartburn 86. Cookie 89. *When Harry Met Sally* (AAN) 89. My Blue Heaven 90. This Is My Life (wd) 92. *Sleepless in Seattle* (co-w, d) (AANw) 93. Mixed Nuts (co-w, d) 94. Michael (p, co-w, d) 96. You've Got Mail (wd) 98. Hanging Up (p, co-w) 00. Lucky Numbers (p, d) 00, etc.

❝ I know that people are afraid of me ... Sometimes it's helpful. The opposite of it is something I'm not interested in, which is that people think they can walk all over you – and when you're a screenwriter, people think that anyway. – *N.E.*

When you're a director, everyone wants a piece of you; they want to know what you think of the tablecloth. I loved nothing more than being asked 10,000 questions in one day. – *N.E.*

Epps Jnr, Jack
American screenwriter, often in collaboration with Jim Cash.

Top Gun (co-w) 86. Legal Eagles (co-w) 86. The Secret of My Success (co-w) 86. Turner & Hooch (co-w) 89, etc.

Epps, Omar (1973–)
American actor.

Juice 92. Bloodstream 93. The Program 93. Higher Learning 94. Major League II 94. The Mod Squad 99. The Wood 99. Brother (GB/Jap.) 00. Big Trouble 01, etc.

Epstein, Jean (1897–1953)
French director since 1922; also wrote books on film theory. His sister Marie Epstein (1899–1995) often worked with him, and herself directed La Maternelle 33. La Mort du Cygne 38, etc.

Cocur Fidèle 23. The Fall of the House of Usher 28. Finis Terrae 28. Mor Vran 30.

Epstein, Julius J. and Philip G. (1909–2000 and 1909–1952)
American twin screenwriters.

Four Daughters (AAN) 38. Four Wives 39. No Time for Comedy 40. Strawberry Blonde 41. The Man Who Came to Dinner 41. *Casablanca* (AA) 42. Mr Skeffington (& p) 44. Romance on the High Seas 48. My Foolish Heart 49. Forever Female 53. The Last Time I Saw Paris 54.

JULIUS ALONE: The Tender Trap 55. Tall Story 60. Take a Giant Step (& p) 61. Fanny 61. Send Me No Flowers 64. Any Wednesday (& p) 66. Pete 'n Tillie (& p) (AAN) 72. Reuben Reuben (AAN) 83, etc.

Erbe, Kathryn
American actress.

What about Bob? 91. Rich in Love 92. D2: The Mighty Ducks 94. The Addiction 95. Kiss of Death 95. Dream with the Fishes 97. Stir of Echoes 99, etc.

TV series: Chicken Soup 89.

Erdman, Richard (1925–)
American actor who began playing callow youths, later taking rather crustier roles; now a director for TV.

Thunder across the Pacific 44. Objective Burma 45. The Men 50. The Happy Time 52. Benghazi 55. Bernardine 57. Saddle the Wind 58. Namu the Killer Whale 66. The Brothers O'Toole (d only) 73. Heidi's Song 82. Tomboy 85. Trancers 85. Stewardess School 87. Valet Girls 87. The Pagemaster (voice) 94, etc.

TV series: The Tab Hunter Show 60.

Erice, Victor (1940–)
Spanish director.

Los Desafios 69. Spirit of the Beehive 73. El Sur 83. El Sol del Membrillo 92. The Promise of Shanghai 99, etc.

Erickson, Leif (1911–1986) (William Anderson)
American 'second lead', former singer. In unspectacular roles from 1935.

Wanderer of the Wasteland 35. College Holiday 36. Ride a Crooked Mile 38. Nothing But the Truth 41. Eagle Squadron 42. Sorry, Wrong Number 48. Fort Algiers 50. Carbine Williams 52. On the Waterfront 54. The Fastest Gun Alive 56. Tea and Sympathy 57. Straitjacket 63. Mirage 65. Twilight's Last Gleaming 76, many others.

TV series: High Chaparral 67–71.

Ericson, John (1926–) (Joseph Meibes)
German-born leading man, long in America.

Teresa (debut) 51. Rhapsody 54. Green Fire 54. Bad Day at Black Rock 54. The Return of Jack Slade 55. Forty Guns 57. Pretty Boy Floyd 59. Under Ten Flags 60. The Seven Faces of Dr Lao 64. The Destructors 66. Operation Bluebook 67. Bedknobs and Broomsticks 71. Hustler Squad 76. Crash 77. Zone of the Dead 78. Primary Target 89, etc.

TV series: Honey West 65.

Ermey, R. Lee (1944–)
American character actor.

The Boys in Company C 78. Purple Hearts 84. Full Metal Jacket 87. Mississippi Burning 88. Fletch Lives 89. The Rift/La Grieta 89. I'm Dangerous Tonight (TV) 90. Kid 90. Toy Soldiers 91. Bodysnatchers 93. Hexed 93. Sommersby 93. On Deadly Ground 94. Dead Man Walking 95. Leaving Las Vegas 95. Seven 95. Prefontaine 97. Switchback 97. Avalanche 99. Life 99. Skipped Parts 00, etc.

Errol, Leon (1881–1951)
Australian comedian who in 1910 left medicine for Broadway musical comedy and vaudeville, lately becoming familiar to filmgoers as twitchy, bald-pated, henpecked little man in innumerable 30s two-reelers and a number of features, mainly unworthy of his talents.

Paramount on Parade 30. Only Saps Work 30. One Heavenly Night 30. Alice in Wonderland 33. *We're Not Dressing* 34. Princess O'Hara 35. Make a Wish 37. *Mexican Spitfire* (first of a series with Lupe Velez in which Errol appeared as the drunken Lord Epping) 39. Pop Always Pays 40. Six Lessons from Madame la Zonga 41. Never Give a Sucker an Even Break 41. Higher and Higher 43. Hat Check Honey 44. The Invisible Man's Revenge 44. What a Blonde 45. Mama Loves Papa 45. Joe Palooka Champ (first of another series) 46. The Noose Hangs High 48, etc.

✪ For bringing a breath of inspired vaudeville to some pretty tired Hollywood formats, and for inventing Lord Epping. *Mexican Spitfire*.

Erskine, Chester (1905–1986)
American writer-producer-director.

Call it Murder £ 34. The Egg and I (wpd) 47. All My Sons (wp) 48. Take One False Step (co-wpd) 49. Androcles and the Lion (wd) 53. Witness to Murder (wp) 57. The Wonderful Country (p) 59, etc.

Erwin, Stuart (1903–1967)
American character comedian, who usually played Mr Average or the hero's faithful but slow-thinking friend.

The Cockeyed World 29. Love among the Millionaires 30. Men without Women 30. Playboy of Paris 30. Young Eagles 30. Up Pops the Devil 31. The Big Broadcast 32. Make Me a Star 32. The Misleading Lady 32. Strangers in Love 32. Before Dawn 33. Crime of the Century 33. Face in the Sky 33. Going Hollywood 33. Hold Your Man 33. International House 33. The Stranger's Return 33. The Band Plays On 34. Chained 34. Exclusive Story 34. Have a Heart 34. Palooka 34. Viva Villa! 34. After Office Hours 35. Ceiling Zero 35. Absolute Quiet 36. *Pigskin Parade* (AAN) 36. Checkers 37. I'll Take Romance 37. Second Honeymoon 37. Slim 37. Three Blind Mice 38. Back Door to Heaven 39. Hollywood Cavalcade 39. It Could Happen to You 39. A Little Bit of Heaven 40. Our Town 40. Sandy Gets Her Man 40. When the Daltons Rode 40. The Bride Came C.O.D. 41. The Adventures of Martin Eden 42. Pillow to Post 45. Heaven Only Knows 47. Father Is a Bachelor 50. For the Love of Mike 60. Son of Flubber 64. The Misadventures of Merlin Jones 64, etc.

TV series: *The Trouble with Father* 53. The Greatest Show on Earth 63. The Bing Crosby Show 65.

Escamilla, Teo (1940–1997)
Spanish cinematographer and occasional director, associated with the films of Carlos SAURA, with whom he worked in the late 70s and the 80s. He began as a camera operator to Luis CUADRADO. Died of a heart attack.

Raise Ravens 75. Mama Turns a Hundred 79. Blood Wedding 81. Carmen 83. You Alone/Tu Solo (d) 84. A Love Bewitched 86. Things I Left in Havana 97, etc.

Escoffier, Jean Yves
French cinematographer, a fixture on Leos CARAX's early films; he studied at the Louis Lumière Film School.

Trois Hommes et un Couffin 85. Bad Blood/Mauvais Sang 86. Les Amants du Pont Neuf 91. Charlie and the Doctor 93. Dream Lover (US) 94. Grace of My Heart (US) 96. The Crow: City of Angels (US) 96, etc.

Esmond, Carl (1906–) (Willy Eichberger)
Good-looking Austrian actor usually in haughty or arrogant roles, first in Britain and later in Hollywood.

Evensong 33. Invitation to the Waltz 37. Dawn Patrol 38. Thunder Afloat 39. Pacific Rendezvous 42. The Story of Dr Wassell 43. *Ministry of Fear* 44. *Address Unknown* 44. Without Love 45. This Love of Ours 45. Catman of Paris 46. Smash-Up 47. Walk a Crooked Mile 48. The Desert Hawk 50. Mystery Submarine 51. The World in His Arms 52. From the Earth to the Moon 58. Thunder in the Sun 59. Agent for H.A.R.M. 66. Morituri 66, etc.

Esmond, Jill (1908–1990)
British leading lady of the 30s, later in Hollywood. She was married to Laurence Olivier (1930–40).

The Skin Game 31. Ladies of the Jury 32. No Funny Business 32. This Above All 42. Random Harvest 42. The White Cliffs of Dover 44. The Bandit of Sherwood Forest 46. Escape 48. Night People 54. A Man Called Peter 55, etc.

Esposito, Giancarlo (1958–)
American actor.

Sweet Lorraine 87. School Daze 88. Do the Right Thing 89. King of New York 90. Mo' Better Blues 90. Night on Earth 91. Bob Roberts 92. Amos & Andrew 93. Fresh 94. Smoke 95. Blue in the Face 95. The Keeper 96. Loose Women 96. Twilight 98, etc.

TV series: Homicide: Life on the Street 98-99.

Esposito, Jennifer (1972–)
American actress, born in New York.

Kiss me, Guido 97. No Looking Back 98. I Still Know What You Did Last Summer 98. Just One Time 99. The Bachelor 99. Summer of Sam 99. Wes Craven Presents Dracula 2000 00. The Proposal 00, etc.

TV series: Spin City 97-99.

Esquivel, Laura (1950–)
Mexican screenwriter and novelist. She is married to actor and director Alfonso Arau.

Like Water for Chocolate/Como Agua para Chocolate (oa, w) 92. Estrellita Marinera 94.

Essex, David (1947–)
British pop singer.

■ Assault 70. Carry on Henry 71. All Coppers Are ... 71. That'll Be the Day 73. Stardust 74. Silver Dream Racer 80.

Essex, Harry (1910–1997)
American screenwriter and occasional director, often for television.

Boston Blackie and the Law 43. Desperate 47. Dragnet 47. He Walked by Night 48. The Killer that Stalked New York 50. The Fat Man 50. Undercover Girl 50. The Las Vegas Story 52. Kansas City Confidential 52. It Came from Outer Space 53. The Forty-Ninth Man 53. I the Jury (& d) 53. The Creature from the Black Lagoon 54. Raw Edge 56. The Lonely Man 57. The Sons of Katie Elder 65. Octaman (& d) 71. The Cremators (d only) 72, etc.

Estabrook, Howard (1884–1978)
American screenwriter.

The Four Feathers 28. Hell's Angels 30. *Cimarron* (AA) 31. A Bill of Divorcement 32. The Masquerader 33. David Copperfield 34. International Lady 39. The Bridge of San Luis Rey 44. The Human Comedy 45. The Girl from Manhattan 48. Lone Star 51. The Big Fisherman 59, many others.

Estevez, Emilio (1962–)
American leading man, son of Martin SHEEN.

Tex 82. Repo Man 84. The Breakfast Club 84. St Elmo's Fire 84. That was Then ... This is Now 85. Maximum Overdrive 86. Wisdom 86. Stakeout 87. Young Guns 88. Never on Tuesday 89. Men at Work (& wd) 90. Young Guns II 90. Freejack 92. The Mighty Ducks 92. National Lampoon's Loaded Weapon 1 93. Another Stakeout 93. Judgment Night 93. D2: The Mighty Ducks 94. Mission: Impossible 96. The War at Home (& p, d) 96. D3: The Mighty Ducks 96. The War at Home (& d) 97. Late Last Night 98. A Dollar for the Dead 99, etc.

Estrada, Erik (1949–)
American leading man of Puerto Rican descent.

The New Centurions 74. Trackdown 76. Fire! (TV) 77. Hour of the Assassin 87. Caged Fury 90. The Last Riders 90. Do or Die 91. The Divine Enforcer 91. National Lampoon's Loaded Weapon 1 93. Final Goal 94, etc.

TV series: *Chips* 77–82.

Estridge, Robin (1920–)
British screenwriter.

Above Us the Waves 54. The Young Lovers 54. Campbell's Kingdom 57. Northwest Frontier 59. Escape from Zahrain 62. Eye of the Devil 67, etc.

Eszterhas, Joe (1944–)
Hungarian-born American screenwriter. A former journalist, he writes scripts that tend to reflect current social concerns. He received a reported $3 million for his script for *Basic Instinct*.

Autobiography: 2000, *American Rhapsody*.

F.I.S.T. 78. Flashdance 83. Jagged Edge 85. Big Shots 87. Hearts of Fire 87. Betrayed 88. Checking Out 89. Music Box 89. Basic Instinct 92. Crossing the Line 92. Nowhere to Run (co-w) 93. Sliver 93. Showgirls 95. Jade 95. An Alan Smithee Film: Burn, Hollywood, Burn 97. Telling Lies in America 97, etc.

❝ I've always loved the notion of doing movies that provoke people, either move them in their hearts or disturb them, but when they leave the theater it sticks with them. – *J.E.*

He writes with a cattle prod. – *Janet Maslin*

Etaix, Pierre (1928–)
French mime comedian, former circus clown and assistant to Tati.

Rupture (short) 61. Happy Anniversary (short) 61. The Suitor 62. Yo Yo 65. As Long As You Have Your Health 67. Le Grand Amour 69. Henry and June 90, etc.

Etting, Ruth (1896–1978)
American popular singer of the 20s, a version of whose life was told in 1955 in *Love Me or Leave Me*. Very briefly on screen.

■ Roman Scandals 33. Hips Hips Hooray 33. Gift of Gab 34.

Ettlinger, Don (1914–2000)
American screenwriter. Born in Detroit, he studied at Stanford University and the University of Chicago, joining 20th Century Fox immediately after on the strength of a play written while he was an undergraduate. He worked in TV from the early 50s, becoming head writer of the soap opera *Love of Life* that began in 1951.

The Lady Escapes 37. Life Begins in College 37. Hold That Co-Ed 38. My Lucky Star 38. Rebecca of Sunnybrook Farm 38. Shipyard Sally 39. I Was an Adventuress 40. Young People 40. The Great American Broadcast 41, etc.

Eustache, Jean (1938–1981)
French director and screenwriter. A former film editor, he also acted in Godard's *Weekend* and Wender's *The American Friend*. He committed suicide.

Les Mauvaises Fréquentations 63. Le Père Noel a les Yeux Bleus 66. Le Cochon 70. Numéro Zéro 71. The Mother and the Whore/La Maman et la Putain 73. Mes Petites Amoureuses 74. Une Sale Histoire 77. Le Jardin des Délices de Jerome Bosch 79. Offre d'Emploi 80, etc.

Eustrel, Anthony (1903–1979)
British character actor.

The Silver Fleet 43. Caesar and Cleopatra 45. The Robe 53, etc.

Evans, Barry (1945–1997)
Youthful-looking English light leading man of the 70s, from the stage. He won a Gielgud scholarship to study at the Central School of Speech and Drama and found brief stardom with his first feature and TV sitcom. His career faltered in the 80s and at the time of his death he was working as a taxi driver. An 18-year-old man was charged with his attempted murder, but the prosecution offered no evidence at the trial and a verdict of not guilty was recorded.

Here We Go Round the Mulberry Bush 67. Alfred the Great 69. Die Screaming Marianne 70. Adventures of a Taxi Driver 75. Under the Doctor 76. Legacy of Murder (TV) 82. The Mystery of Edwin Drood 93, etc.

TV series: Doctor in the House 69–70. Doctor at Large 71. Mind Your Language 77–79, 86.

Evans, Clifford (1912–1985)
Welsh actor with stage experience. In films from 1936, at first as leading man and latterly as character actor.

Ourselves Alone 36. The Mutiny on the Elsinore 37. The Luck of the Navy 39. The Proud Valley 39. His Brother's Keeper 39. The Saint Meets the Tiger 40. *Love on the Dole* 41. Penn of Pennsylvania 41. Suspected Person 42. *The Foreman Went to France* 42; war service; The Silver Darlings 47. While I Live 48. Valley of Song 52. The Gilded Cage 55. Passport to Treason 56. Violent Playground 58. SOS Pacific 60. Curse of the Werewolf 62. Kiss of the Vampire 63. The Long Ships 64. Twist of Sand 69. One Brief Summer 70, etc.

TV series: Stryker of the Yard. The Power Game 65–67, etc.

Evans, Dale (1912–2001) (Frances Octavia Smith)
American leading lady of the 40s, former band singer; appeared frequently with Roy Rogers, and in 1947 married him.

Orchestra Wives 42. Swing Your Partner 43. Casanova in Burlesque 44. The Yellow Rose of Texas 44. Utah 45. Belles of Rosarita 45. My Pal Trigger 46. Apache Rose 47. Slippy McGee 48. Susanna Pass 49. Twilight in the Sierras 50. Trigger Jnr 51. Pals of the Golden West 51. Roy Rogers: King of the Cowboys (doc) 91, many others.

TV series: The Roy Rogers Show 51–56.

Evans, David Mickey
American screenwriter and director.

Radio Flyer (w) 92. Hocus Pocus (co-w) 93. Ed (w) 96. First Kid (d) 96, etc.

Evans, Dame Edith (1888–1976)
Distinguished British stage actress who made occasional films.

Biography: 1977, *Ned's Girl* by Bryan Forbes. *Edith Evans: A Personal Memoir* by Jean Batters.
■ A Welsh Singer 15. East is East 15. *The Queen of Spades* 48. *The Last Days of Dolwyn* 48. *The Importance of Being Earnest* 51. Look Back in Anger 59. The Nun's Story 59. Tom Jones (AAN) 63. The Chalk Garden (AAN) 64. Young Cassidy 65. *The Whisperers* (BFA, AAN) 67. Fitzwilly (US) 68. Prudence and the Pill 68. Crooks and Coronets 69. The Madwoman of Chaillot 69. David Copperfield 69. Scrooge 70. A Doll's House 73. Craze 73. QB VII (TV) 74. The Slipper and the Rose 76. Nasty Habits 76.

❝ As a young actress I always had a rule. If I didn't understand a line I always said it as though it were improper. – *E.E.*

Comedy, dear, is just like blowing powder puffs out of a cannon. – *E.E.*

Acting with her was heaven. It was like being in your mother's arms. – *Sir Michael Redgrave*

The dame, great actress though she was, resembled a gifted amateur. She didn't really know what she was doing. What she had was an infallible ear for the turn of a speech, or a line, and what she did was entirely instinctive, and executed without much thought, imagination, or guile. – *Robert Stephens*

Evans, Edward (1914–)
Welsh character actor, best known as Bob Grove in *The Grove Family*, Britain's first TV soap opera, 1954–57.

The Small Voice 48. Deadly Nightshade 53. Valley of Song 53. It's a Great Day! 56. Blind Corner 63. One More Time 70. Out of Season 75, etc.

Evans, Fred (1889–1951)
English comic actor and director, from music hall, who was one of the earliest stars of British cinema, notably in the character of 'Pimple' (renamed 'Flivver' in America). In films from 1910, he made his first Pimple short in 1912 and turned out between 10 and 30 a year until his last, *Pimple's Three Musketeers*, in 1922. In the 30s and 40s, he worked as an extra in films. He was the nephew of Will Evans and was a member of a famous family of music-hall performers and clowns.

Evans, Gene (1922–1998)
Stocky American actor in demand for heavy roles. Born in Holbrook, Arizona, and raised in Colton, California, he began acting as a GI in Europe in the late 40s. Retired in the 80s to farm in Tennessee.

Berlin Express 48. Park Row 52. Donovan's Brain 53. The Golden Blade 53. Hell and High Water 54. The Sad Sack 57. Operation Petticoat 59. Apache Uprising 65. Support Your Local Sheriff 69. The Ballad of Cable Hogue 70. Walking Tall 73. Devil Times Five 82, etc.

TV series: My Friend Flicka 57. Matt Helm 75. Spencer's Pilots 76.

Evans, Joan (1934–) (Joan Eunson)
American actress who played teenage roles in the early 50s, now working in education.

Our Very Own 50. On the Loose 51. Roseanna McCoy 51. Skirts Ahoy 52. Edge of Doom 54. The Fortune Hunter 54. No Name on the Bullet 59. The Flying Fontaines 60, etc.

Evans, Joe (1891–1967)
English music-hall performer who starred in many comedy shorts from 1912–18 and also appeared in the films of his brother Fred 'Pimple' Evans.

Evans, Josh (1971–)
American actor, director and writer, the son of producer Robert Evans and actress Ali McGraw.

Dream a Little Dream 89. Born on the Fourth of July 89. Ricochet 90. The Doors 90. The Killing Box 92. Inside the Goldmine (& co-w, d) 94. Glam (wd,co-m) 97, etc.

Evans, Lee (1965–)
English stand-up comedian and actor, in a style that owes something to Jerry Lewis and much to Norman Wisdom. He also runs a production company, Little Mo Films.

Funny Bones 95. The Fifth Element 97. *Mouse Hunt* 97, etc.

TV series: The World of Lee Evans 95.

❝ I don't think comedians are born. You have to find a way of surviving in this strange world and that tends to be with an exaggeration of your own personality. – *L.E.*

Evans, Linda (1942–) (Linda Evanstad)
Blonde American leading lady. Her first husband was actor-director John Derek.

Twilight of Honor 63. Those Calloways 64. Female Artillery (TV) 73. The Klansman 74. Mitchell 75. Nowhere to Run (TV) 78. Avalanche Express 79. The Gambler Part Two (TV) 83. *The Last Frontier* (TV) 86. She'll Take Romance 90. The Gambler Returns: The Luck of the Draw (TV) 93. The Stepsister (TV) 97, etc.

TV series: Bachelor Father 60. The Big Valley 65–69. Hunter 77. *Dynasty* 81–89.

Evans, Madge (1909–1981)
Blonde American actress, a child star of silent days and pretty heroine of mainly unremarkable films in the 30s. Born in New York City, she began in soap commercials at the age of two, and was a star at six. She made her last silent movie at the age of 15, and then acted on the stage before returning to films in her early 20s. Married playwright Sidney Kingsley.

The Sign of the Cross 14. The Burglar 16. Classmates 24. Son of India 29. Lovers Courageous 30. Guilty Hands 31. Sporting Blood 31. Are You Listening? 32. The Greeks Had a Word for Them 32. Huddle 32. Lovers Courageous 32. West of Broadway 32. Beauty for Sale 33. Broadway to Hollywood 33. Hallelujah I'm a Bum 33. Dinner at Eight 33. Hell Below 33. Made on Broadway 33. The Mayor of Hell 33. Grand Canary 34. David Copperfield 34. Death on the Diamond 34. Exclusive Story 34. Fugitive Lovers 34. Helldorado 34. Paris Interlude 34. The Show-Off 34. Stand Up and Cheer 34. What Every Woman Knows 34. Age of Indiscretion 35. Calm Yourself 35. Men without Names 35. The Tunnel (GB) 35. Pennies from Heaven 36. Piccadilly Jim 36. Espionage 37. The Thirteenth Chair 37. Army Girl 38. Sinners in Paradise 38, etc.

Evans, Maurice (1901–1989)
Eloquent English actor who, long in America, distinguished himself on the Broadway stage. Born in Dorchester, Dorset, he began performing as a boy singer and in amateur dramatics. He was on-stage from 1926, moving in the mid-30s to the US, where he was soon regarded as the best Shakespearean actor on the New York stage. He won an Emmy for his performance as Macbeth in 1961.

White Cargo 30. Raise the Roof 30. Wedding Rehearsal 32. Scrooge (GB) 35. Kind Lady 51. Androcles and the Lion (as Caesar) 52. The Story of Gilbert and Sullivan (as Sullivan) 53. Macbeth (title role) 59. The War Lord 65. Jack of Diamonds 67. Planet of the Apes 68. Rosemary's Baby 68. Beneath the Planet of the Apes 69. Body Stealers 69. Terror in the Wax Museum 73. The Jerk 79, etc.

TV series: Bewitched 68–71.

Evans, Norman (1901–1962)
British north-country music hall comedian famous for toothless characterization and female impersonation. Born in Rochdale, Lancashire, he began as a salesman and was discovered by singer and actress Gracie Fields.
■ Pathetone Parade of 1941 (short) 41. Demobbed 44. Under New Management 46. Over the Garden Wall 50.

Evans, Ray (1915–)
American songwriter, in Hollywood from 1945 in partnership with Jay Livingston. He wrote the theme to the TV series *Bonanza*.

Why Girls Leave Home (AANs 'The Cat and the Canary') 45. Smooth Sailing 47. *Paleface* (AAs 'Buttons and Bows') 48. The Great Lover 49. Captain Carey, USA (AAs 'Mona Lisa') 50. The Lemon Drop Kid 51. Aaron Slick from Punkin Crick 52. The Man Who Knew Too Much (AAs 'Whatever Will Be, Will Be') 56. Tammy and the Bachelor (AANs 'Tammy') 57. Houseboat (AANs 'Almost in Your Arms') 58. Dear Heart (AAN title s) 64, etc.

Evans, Rex (1903–1969)
British character actor in Hollywood, often as a stately butler. He ran an art gallery in his spare time.

Comets (GB) 30. Aunt Sally (GB) 33. Camille 37. The Wrong Road 37. The Philadelphia Story 40. Frankenstein Meets the Wolf Man 43. Dangerous Millions 46. It Should Happen to You 54. A Star is Born 54. The Birds and the Bees 56. Merry Andrew 58. The Matchmaker 58. On the Double 61, etc.

Evans, Robert (1930–)
Bland-faced American juvenile of the 50s; gave up acting to become a Paramount production executive, then went independent. He was formerly married to Ali McGraw. Married actress Catherine Oxenberg in July 1998; the couple agreed to annul their marriage the next month.

Autobiography: 1994, *The Kid Stays in the Picture*.

Lydia Bailey 52. *The Man of a Thousand Faces* (as Irving Thalberg) 57. The Sun Also Rises 57. The Fiend Who Walked the West (title role) 58. The Best of Everything 59. Desperate Hours 90, etc.

AS PRODUCER: Chinatown 74. The Great Gatsby 74. Marathon Man 76. Black Sunday 77. Players 79. Popeye 80. Urban Cowboy 80. The Cotton Club 84. The Two Jakes 90. Sliver 93. Jade 95. The Phantom 96. The Saint 97, etc.

Evans, Will (1867–1931)
English comic actor, notable pantomime dame at Drury Lane, and playwright, who filmed many of his classic music-hall slapstick sketches and appeared in the silent shorts of his nephew Fred Evans. He was the co-author of *Tons of Money*, the long-running and influential farce of the 20s which was filmed in 1930.

They Do Such Things at Brighton 1899. Will Evans the Living Catherine Wheel 1899. The Jockey 07. Harnessing a Horse 13. Whitewashing the Ceiling 14. Building a Chicken House 14. Moving a Piano 14. A Study in Skarlit 15, etc.

Eve, Trevor (1951–)
Slightly built English leading man who became popular as TV's radio station detective Eddie Shoestring. Born in Birmingham, he trained at RADA.

Dracula 79. Jamaica Inn (TV) 82. Lace (TV) 84. The Corsican Brothers (TV) 84. Scandal 88. A *Sense of Guilt* (TV) 90. A Doll's House (TV) 92. The President's Child (TV) 92. In the Name of the Father 93. Don't Get Me Started 94. The Politician's Wife (TV) 95. The Tribe (TV) 98. An Evil Streak (TV) 99, etc.

TV series: Shoestring 79-80. Shadow Chasers 85. Heat of the Sun 98. Waking the Dead 00- .

Evein, Bernard (1929–)
French art director.

Les Amants 57. Les Jeux de L'Amour 60. Zazie dans le Métro 61. Lola 61. Cléo de 5 à 7 62. La Baie des Anges 62. Le Feu Follet 63. The Umbrellas of Cherbourg 64. Do You Like Women? 64. Viva Maria 65. The Young Girls of Rochefort 67. Woman Times Seven 67. The Confession/L'Aveu 70. The Toy/Le Jouet 76. A Room in Town/Une Chambre en Ville 82. Separate Rooms/Notre Histoire 84. Thérèse 86, etc.

Evelyn, Judith (1913–1967) (J. E. Allen)
American stage actress; often played neurotic women.

The Egyptian 54. Rear Window 54. Hilda Crane 56. The Tingler 59, etc.

Everest, Barbara (1890–1968)
British stage actress who appeared in many films, latterly in motherly roles.

Lily Christine 31. The Wandering Jew 33. The Passing of the Third Floor Back 35. He Found a Star 40. Mission to Moscow (US) 43. Jane Eyre (US) 43. The Uninvited (US) 44. The Valley of Decision (US) 45. Wanted for Murder 46. Frieda 47. Madeleine 49. Tony Draws a Horse 51. The Man Who Finally Died 62, etc.

Everett, Chad (1936–) (Raymond Cramton)
Handsome American leading man of the 60s; films unremarkable.

Claudelle Inglish 61. The Chapman Report 62. Get Yourself a College Girl 65. The Singing Nun 66. First to Fight 67. The Last Challenge 67. The Firechasers (TV) 70. The French Atlantic Affair (TV) 79. Airplane 2: The Sequel 82. Fever Pitch 85. Heroes Stand Alone 89. Jigsaw Murders 89. The Rousters (TV) 90. Official Denial (TV) 93. When Time Expires 97, etc.

TV series: *Medical Center* 69–75. Hagen 79. The Rousters 83. McKenna 94–95. Manhattan, AZ 00- .

Everett, Francine (1917–1999)
American actress, dancer, and singer in soundies and independent black movies of the 30s and 40s. Born in North Carolina, she began as a chorus girl in her teens. Her second husband was actor Rex Ingram. She later worked as a clerk in a Harlem hospital.

Keep Punching 39. Paradise in Harlem 39. Big Timers 45. Tall, Tan and Terrific 46. Lost Boundaries 49. No Way Out 50, etc.

Everett, Rupert (1959–)
English leading actor, often in aristocratic or effete roles, and occasional singer. Born in Norfolk, he studied briefly at the Central School of Speech and Drama before working at Glasgow's Citizens' Theatre. He became a star with his first film, *Another Country*, but the roles that followed were less successful until his scene-stealing performance in *My Friend's Wedding*; his subsequent revelations about working as a male prostitute when young and penniless in London may not have helped his long-term career prospects. He has also modelled for Yves St Laurent's perfume advertisements and written two novels: *Hello Darling, Are You Working?* 93 and *The Hairdressers of St Tropez* 95. Current asking price: $4m a movie.

Princess Daisy (TV) 83. *Another Country* 84. Dance with a Stranger 85. The Right Hand Man 86. Duet for One 86. Hearts of Fire 87. Gli Occhiali d'Oro 87. Tolerance 89. The Comfort of Strangers 90. Dellamorte Dellamore (It.) 94. The Madness of King George 95. Dunston Checks In 96. *My Friend's Wedding* 97. B Monkey 98. An Ideal Husband 99. William Shakespeare's A Midsummer Night's Dream 99. Inspector Gadget 99. The Next Best Thing 00, etc.

❝ English actors are like immigrants – they're a gypsy race. They go where the work is and there's never been much work in England. They're treated very badly. – *R.E.*

One of the great things about getting older is that unemployment becomes more and more fun. – *R.E.*

He's clever, self-destructive, bright and brash at the same time. I must admit that I really like that mix. – *Rupert Graves*

What's most important about Rupert Everett is that aside from being talented, he's one of the first gay leading men who is sexy. – *Paul Rudnick*

towards roving, brawling, good-natured outdoor action films using a repertory of his favourite actors. His best films are milestones, but he disclaimed any artistic pretensions.

Biography: 1968, *John Ford* by Peter Bogdanovich. 1976, *The John Ford Movie Mystery* by Andrew Sarris. 1982, *The Unquiet Man* by Dan Ford (grandson). 2000, *Print the Legend: The Life and Times of John Ford* by Scott Eyman.

Other books: 1971, *The Cinema of John Ford* by John Baxter.

SELECTED SILENT FILMS: The Tornado 17. A Woman's Fool 18. Bare Fists 19. The Wallop 21. Silver Wings 22. The Face on the Bar Room Floor 23. *The Iron Horse* 24. Lightnin' 25. Three Bad Men 26. Four Sons 28. Mother Machree 28. Riley the Cop 28. Strong Boy 29.

■ SOUND FILMS: Black Watch 29. Salute 29. *Men Without Women* 30. Born Reckless 30. Up the River 30. The Seas Beneath 30. The Brat 31. *Arrowsmith* 31. Air Mail 32. Flesh 32. Pilgrimage 33. Doctor Bull 33. *The Lost Patrol* 34. The World Moves On 34. *Judge Priest* 34. *The Whole Town's Talking* 35. *The Informer* (AA) 35. *Steamboat Round the Bend* 35. Prisoner of Shark Island 36. Mary of Scotland 36. The Plough and the Stars 36. Wee Willie Winkie 37. *The Hurricane* 37. Four Men and a Prayer 38. Submarine Patrol 38. *Stagecoach* (AAN) 39. *Young Mr Lincoln* 39. *Drums Along the Mohawk* 39. *The Grapes of Wrath* (AA) 40. The Long Voyage Home 40. *Tobacco Road* 41. *How Green Was My Valley* (AA) 41. Why We Fight and other war documentaries 42–45. They Were Expendable 45. *My Darling Clementine* 46. The Fugitive 47. Fort Apache 48. Three Godfathers 48. *She Wore A Yellow Ribbon* 49. When Willie Comes Marching Home 50. Wagonmaster 50. Rio Grande 50. This is Korea 51. *The Quiet Man* (AA) 52. What Price Glory? 52. Mogambo 53. *The Sun Shines Bright* 54. The Long Gray Line 55. Mister Roberts (co-d) 55. *The Searchers* 56. The Wings of Eagles 57. The Rising of the Moon 57. *The Last Hurrah* 58. Gideon's Day 59. The Horse Soldiers 59. Sergeant Rutledge 60. Two Rode Together 61. The Man Who Shot Liberty Valance 62. How the West Was Won (part) 63. Donovan's Reef 63. Cheyenne Autumn 64. Young Cassidy (part) 64. Seven Women 66.

✪ For half-a-dozen simply marvellous films. *The Grapes of Wrath.*

❝ Anybody can direct a picture once they know the fundamentals. Directing is not a mystery, it's not an art. The main thing about directing is: photograph the people's eyes. – *J.F.*

It's no good asking me to talk about art. – *J.F.*

He developed his craft in the 20s, achieved dramatic force in the 30s, epic sweep in the 40s, and symbolic evocation in the 50s. – *Andrew Sarris, 1968*

He never once looked in the camera when we worked together. You see, the man had bad eyes, as long as I knew him, but he was a man whose veins ran with the business. – *Arthur Miller, photographer*

Knockabout comedy and tragedy co-exist with perfect ease in his work, which throughout a long career shows a clear development and progression. – *John M. Smith*

He had instinctively a beautiful eye for the camera. But he was also an egomaniac. – *Henry Fonda*

His films look entirely different one from another, the style emerging rather from a personal response to people: affectionate, warm, with a rural decency and intimacy. – *Charles Higham*

Ford, Paul (1901–1976) (Paul Ford Weaver)
American character actor best known on TV as the harassed colonel in the Bilko series and star of *The Baileys of Balboa.*

The House on 92nd Street 45. Lust for Gold 49. Perfect Strangers 50. *The Teahouse of the August Moon* 56. The Matchmaker 58. Advise and Consent 61. *The Music Man* 62. *Never Too Late* 65. Big Hand for a Little Lady 66. The Russians Are Coming, The Russians Are Coming 66. The Spy with a Cold Nose (GB) 67. The Comedians 67, etc.

Ford, Wallace (1898–1966) (Sam Grundy)
British general-purpose actor who went to Hollywood in the early 30s and after a few semi-leads settled into character roles.

Freaks 32. Lost Patrol 34. *The Informer* 35. OHMS (GB) 36. The Mummy's Hand 40. Inside the Law 42. Shadow of a Doubt 43. The Green Years 46. Embraceable You 48. *Harvey* 50. The Nebraskan 53. Destry 55. Johnny Concho 56. The Last Hurrah 58. A Patch of Blue 66, etc.

TV series: The Deputy 59.

Forde, Eugene (1898–1986)
American director of second features, former silent-screen actor.

Charlie Chan in London 33. Buy Me That Town 41. Berlin Correspondent 42. Jewels of Brandenberg 46. Invisible Wall 47, many others.

Forde, Florrie (1876–1940)
Australian actress and singer who became a top music-hall performer in Britain from the late 1890s with songs that featured a catchy chorus, including 'Down at the Old Bull and Bush' and 'It's a Long Way to Tipperary'.

Say It with Flowers 34. My Old Dutch 34. Royal Cavalcade 35, etc.

Forde, Walter (1897–1984) (Thomas Seymour)
British director, formerly a popular slapstick comedian of the silents: *Wait and See, Would You Believe It*, many shorts, one of which was featured in *Helter Skelter* 49. Directed some high-speed farces and several thrillers and melodramas. He had a habit of playing the piano after every take: excerpts from *HMS Pinafore* meant he was happy, anything from *Tosca* indicated that he was dissatisfied.

The Silent House 28. Lord Richard in the Pantry 30. *The Ghost Train* 31. Jack's the Boy 32. *Rome Express* 32. Orders Is Orders 33. Jack Ahoy 34. Chu Chin Chow 34. *Bulldog Jack* 35. King of the Damned 35. Land Without Music 36. The Gaunt Stranger 38. The Four Just Men 39. Inspector Hornleigh on Holiday 39. *Saloon Bar* 40. Sailors Three 40. The Ghost Train 41. Atlantic Ferry 41. Charley's Big-Hearted Aunt 41. *It's That Man Again* 42. Time Flies 44. Master of Bankdam 47. Cardboard Cavalier 48, many others.

Foreman, Carl (1914–1984)
American writer-producer-director, latterly resident in Britain after being blacklisted.

So This Is New York (w) 48. The Clay Pigeon (w) 49. Home of the Brave (w) 49. *Champion* (AANw) 49. The Men (AANw) 50. Cyrano de Bergerac (w) 50. *High Noon* (AANw) 52. *The Bridge on the River Kwai* (AAw) 57. The Key (wp) 58. *The Guns of Navarone* (wp) (AAN) 61. The Victors (wpd) 63. Born Free (p) 65. Mackenna's Gold (p) 68. The Virgin Soldiers (p) 69. Young Winston (wp) (AAN) 72. Force Ten from Navarone (p) 78. When Time Ran Out (co-w) 80.

❝ I think I was the only director who ever made a second film for Foreman. He was an excellent producer and an excellent, if lazy, writer but he did interfere with directors as well as being obsessive about credits. – *J. Lee-Thompson*

Foreman, John (1925–1992)
American producer, former agent.

WUSA 70. They Might Be Giants 71. The Effect of Gamma Rays on Man in the Moon Marigolds 72. The Life and Times of Judge Roy Bean 72. The Man Who Would Be King 75. The First Great Train Robbery 78. Prizzi's Honor 85, etc.

Forest, Jean-Claude (1930–1998)
French strip-cartoonist who created Barbarella, the sexy space adventurer, in the early 60s. She was played by Jane FONDA in *Barbarella*, 67, on which he worked as design supervisor. Born in Paris, he began as a magazine illustrator.

Forest, Mark (1933–) (Lou Degni)
American athlete and gymnast who appeared in many Italian muscle-man epics.

■ Goliath and the Dragon 60. Maciste the Mighty/Son of Samson 60. The Strongest Man in the World 61. Death in the Arena 62. Goliath and the Sins of Babylon 63. The Terror of Rome Against the Son of Hercules 63. Hercules Against the Sons of the Sun 64. The Lion of Thebes 64. Hercules Against the Barbarians 64. Hercules Against the Mongols 64. Kindar the Invulnerable 64.

Forester, C. S. (1899–1966)
British adventure novelist. Works filmed include *Captain Horatio Hornblower, The African Queen, Payment Deferred, The Pride and the Passion* ('The Gun').

Forman, Milos (1932–)
Czech-born director of realistic comedies, in Hollywood from the 70s.

Autobiography: 1994, *Turnaround – A Memoir* with Jan Novak.

Peter and Pavla 64. *A Blonde in Love* 65. The Fireman's Ball 68. *Taking Off* (US) 71. *One Flew Over the Cuckoo's Nest* (AA) 75. *Hair* 79. Ragtime 81. Amadeus (AA) 83. Valmont 89. The People vs Larry Flynt (AAN) 96, etc.

❝ One of the criteria of casting was that we couldn't afford to have a prick in the company. – *M.F., on One Flew Over the Cuckoo's Nest*

Formby, George (1904–1961) (George Booth)
British north-country comedian with a toothy grin and a ukelele, long popular in music halls. Born in Wigan, the son of music-hall performer George Formby (d.1921), he began as an apprentice jockey, and was on-stage from 1921. Married Beryl Ingham, a champion clog-dancer who appeared opposite him in his first film, *Boots, Boots*, and thereafter managed his career with an iron grip.

Biography: 1974, *George Formby* by Alan Randal and Ray Seaton.

■ Boots Boots (debut) 33. Off the Dole 34. *No Limit* 35. *Keep Your Seats Please* 36. Feather Your Nest 37. *Keep Fit* 37. I See Ice 38. *It's in the Air* 38. Trouble Brewing 39. Come On, George 39. *Let George Do It* 40. Spare a Copper 41. Turned Out Nice Again 41. South American George (dual role) 42. Much Too Shy 42. Get Cracking 43. Bell-Bottom George 43. He Snoops To Conquer 44. I Didn't Do It 45. George in Civvy Street 46.

Forrest, Frederic (1936–)
American leading man of the 70s.

■ Where the Legends Die 72. The Don Is Dead 74. The Conversation 74. The Gravy Train 74. Larry (TV) 74. Promise Him Anything (TV) 75. Permission to Kill 75. The Missouri Breaks 77. It Lives Again 79. Apocalypse Now 79. The Rose (AAN) 79. One from the Heart 82. Hammett 82. Saigon – Year of the Cat (TV) 83. Valley Girl 83. The Stone Boy 84. Best Kept Secrets (TV) 84. Return 85. Where are the Children? 85. Stacking 87. Valentino Returns 87. Quo Vadis 88. Tucker: The Man and His Dream 88. Cat Chaser 88. Music Box 89. The Two Jakes 90. Falling Down 92. Trauma 93. Against the Wall (TV) 94. Chasers 94. Hidden Fears 94. Before the Night 94. Lassie 94. One Night Stand 95. Andersonville (TV) 95. Crash Dive 96.

Forrest, George (1915–1999) (George Forrest Chichester Jnr)
American songwriter and lyricist, for Hollywood and Broadway, usually in collaboration with Robert WRIGHT. Their most successful collaboration was adding lyrics to, and adapting, the music of Borodin for the musical *Kismet*. Born in Brooklyn, he began in his 'teens as a pianist.

The Firefly (song, 'The Donkey Serenade') 37. Maytime (songs) 37. Mannequin (AANs 'Always and Always') 37. Sweethearts (songs) 38. Balalaika 39. Music in My Heart (AANs 'It's A Blue World') 40. Flying With Music (AANs 'Pennies for Peppino') 42. *Kismet* 55. Song of Norway 70, etc.

Forrest, Helen (1918–1999) (Helen Fogel)
American singer of the 40s, in occasional films. Born in Atlantic City, New Jersey, she sang with the big bands of Artie SHAW, Benny GOODMAN and Harry JAMES, to whom she was engaged before his marriage to Betty GRABLE. She made several hit recordings in the 40s and continued performing until the 1990s. Married three times, including to actor Paul Holahan.

Private Buckaroo 42. Springtime in the Rockies 42. Best Foot Forward 43. Two Girls and a Sailor 44. Bathing Beauty 44. Shine On Harvest Moon 44. You Came Along 45. Artie Shaw: Time Is All You've Got (doc) 86, etc.

Forrest, Sally (1928–) (Katharine Scully Feeney)
American leading lady of the early 50s.

Not Wanted 49. Mystery Street 50. Never Fear 50. Hard Fast and Beautiful 51. Excuse My Dust 51. The Strange Door 51. The Strip 51. Son of Sinbad 55. Ride the High Iron 56. While the City Sleeps 56, etc.

Forrest, Steve (1924–) (William Forrest Andrews)
American leading man, brother of Dana Andrews. The Bad and the Beautiful 52. Phantom of the Rue Morgue 54. Prisoner of War 54. Bedevilled 55. The Living Idol 57. Heller in Pink Tights 60. The Yellow Canary 63. Rascal 69. The Wild Country 71. Wanted the Sundance Woman (TV) 76. North Dallas Forty 79. The Manions of America (TV) 81. Malibu (TV) 83. Hollywood Wives (TV) 84. Spies Like Us 85. Amazon Women on the Moon 87. Killer: A Journal of Murder 95, etc.

TV series: The Baron 65. S.W.A.T. 75–76. Dallas 86.

Forst, Willi (1903–1980) (Wilhelm Frohs)
Austrian director and actor.

Maskerade (wd) 34. Bel Ami (a, wd) 39. Operette (a, wd) 40. Wiener Maedelin (a, w) 45. The Sinner (wd) 50. Vienna, City of My Dreams (d) 57, etc.

Forster, E. M. (1879–1970)
British novelist who stopped writing fiction in 1924. His novels, with the exception of *The Longest Journey*, have all been filmed in a mood of nostalgic Edwardiana.

A Passage to India (d David Lean) 84. A Room with a View (d James Ivory) 85. Maurice (d James Ivory) 87. Where Angels Fear to Tread (d Charles Sturridge) 91. Howards End (d James Ivory) 92.

Forster, Robert (1941–)
Sardonic-looking American leading man with echoes of John Garfield.

Reflections in a Golden Eye 67. The Stalking Moon 68. Justine 69. Medium Cool 69. Pieces of Dreams 70. Cover Me Babe 72. Death Squad (TV) 73. The Don Is Dead 73. Nakia (TV) 74. Stunts 77. Avalanche 78. Standing Tall 78. The Black Hole 79. Alligator 80. Vigilante 83. Goliath Awaits (TV) 84. Hollywood Harry (& pd) 85. Once a Hero 88. The Banker 89. Peacemaker 90. Satan's Princess 90. Jackie Brown (AAN) 97. Rear Window (TV) 98. Jackie Brown 97. American Perfekt 97. Me, Myself and Irene 00. Supernova 00, etc.

TV series: *Banyon* 71.

❝ Where have I been? I've had a five-year first act and a 25-year second act. I've been sliding quite a long time. – *R.F., 1998*

Forster, Rudolph (1884–1968)
German leading actor of heavy personality, seen abroad chiefly in *Die Dreigroschenoper/The Threepenny Opera* (as Macheath) 32.

Forsyth, Bill (1947–)
Scottish writer-director who met with instant success for his small local comedies. He moved to Hollywood in the late 80s, but failed to find a receptive audience for his pawky sense of humour. *Being Human*, made at a cost of $20m, was a box-office flop.

■ That Sinking Feeling 80. *Gregory's Girl* 81. Local Hero 83. Comfort and Joy 84. Housekeeping (US) 87. Breaking In (US) 89. Being Human (US) 94. Gregory's Two Girls (wd) 99.

❝ The thing about Hollywood is the mind-set that prevails. It works from the assumption that if you're in the movie business, you want all those people to like your film, you want to win an Oscar and you want to have a $100 million gross. That's what having a career in the industry means. – *B.F.*

The only ambitions I have for the films I make is that they're appreciated as poetical works. Either film is too crude a medium to handle that or else I can't make it do these things. If something doesn't work over a period of time you tend not to be so interested in it. In a way my perception of film has been reduced. – *B.F.*

My problem is that 40 per cent of me wants to make an entertaining film and 60 per cent of me wants to subvert the idea of movies. It's actually not a very happy way to work. – *B.F.*

Forsyth, Bruce (1927–) (Bruce Forsyth Johnson)
Bouncy, beaming, British TV comedian whose film appearances have been scant.

■ Star! 68. Hieronymus Merkin 69. The Magnificent Seven Deadly Sins 71. Bedknobs and Broomsticks 71.

❝ A tall, lean figure of inexhaustible energy, he wears down his audience by an aggressive humility, like Uriah Heep on speed. – *International Herald Tribune*

Forsyth, Frederick (1938–)
British writer of adventure thrillers, most of which have been picked up as screen material: *The Day of the Jackal, The Odessa File, The Dogs of War, The Fourth Protocol.*
❝ I've yet to be convinced that the film business is a profession for adults. – *F.F.*

Forsyth, Rosemary (1944–)
American leading actress.
Shenandoah (debut) 65. The War Lord 65. Texas Across the River 66. Where It's At 69. Whatever Happened to Aunt Alice? 69. How Do I Love Thee? 70. City Beneath the Sea (TV) 71. One Little Indian 73. Black Eye 74. Gray Lady Down 78. The Gladiator (TV) 86. A Friendship in Vienna (TV) 88. Disclosure 94. Daylight 96, etc.

Forsythe, John (1918–) (John Freund)
Smooth American leading man with Broadway experience.
Destination Tokyo 43. Captive City 52. Escape from Fort Bravo 53. The Trouble with Harry 56. *The Ambassador's Daughter* 56. See How They Run (TV) 64. Kitten with a Whip 65. Madame X 66. In Cold Blood 67. Topaz 69. The Happy Ending 69. Murder Once Removed (TV) 71. The Healers (TV) 75. The Feather and Father Gang (TV) 77. The Users (TV) 79. And Justice for All 79. Sizzle (TV) 81. Scrooged 88, etc.
TV series: Bachelor Father 57–61. The John Forsythe Show 65. To Rome with Love 69–70. Charlie's Angels (voice only) 76–80. *Dynasty* 81–86.
❝ I can't afford to bulge. Being a 64-year-old sex symbol is a hell of a weight to carry. – *J.F.*

Forsythe, William (1955–)
Burly American actor, often as a villain.
Cloak and Dagger 84. Once upon a Time in America 84. Savage Dawn 84. The Lightship 85. The Long Hot Summer (TV) 87. Raising Arizona 87. Extreme Prejudice 87. Weeds 87. Patty Hearst 88. Dead-Bang 89. Torrents of Spring (It./Fr.) 89. Dick Tracy 90. Career Opportunities 91. Out for Justice 91. Stone Cold 91. The Waterdance 91. The Gun in Betty Lou's Handbag 92. American Me 92. Stone Cold 92. Palookaville 95. Things to Do in Denver When You're Dead 95. Virtuosity 95. The Substitute 96. The Rock 96. Gotti (TV) 96. Palookaville 96. First Time Felon 97. Firestorm 98. Hell's Kitchen 98. Ambushed 98. Blue Streak 99. Deuce Bigalow: Male Gigolo 99, etc.
TV series: The Untouchables (as Al Capone) 92–93.

Fosse, Bob (1927–1987)
American dancer who became a Broadway director.
Biography: 1989, *Razzle Dazzle: The Life and Work of Bob Fosse* by Kevin Boyd Grubb.
■ Give a Girl a Break 52. The Affairs of Dobie Gillis 52. Kiss Me Kate 53. My Sister Eileen (& ch) 55. *The Pajama Game* (ch only) 57. Damn Yankees (ch only) 58. *Sweet Charity* (d, ch) 68. *Cabaret* (d, ch) (AA) 72. Lenny (AANd) 74. The Little Prince (a only) 75. *All That Jazz* (allegedly based on his life) (d, ch) (AAN) 79. Star 80 (wd) 83.

Fossey, Brigitte (1945–)
French actress.
Jeux Interdits 52. Le Grand Meaulnes 67. Adieu l'Ami 68. M comme Mathieu 71. Un Mauvais Fils 80. Enigma 82. The Last Butterfly 90. Les Enfants du Naufrageur 92, etc.

Foster, Barry (1931–)
British light actor, usually figuring as comic relief, but popular on TV as the Dutch detective Van der Valk.
Sea of Sand 56. Yesterday's Enemy 59. King and Country 64. The Family Way 66. Robbery 67. Twisted Nerve 68. Ryan's Daughter 70. Frenzy 72. Divorce His Divorce Hers (TV) 73. The Sweeney 77. The Three Hostages (TV) 78. The Wild Geese 78. Smiley's People (TV) 81. A Woman Called Golda (TV) 82. Heat and Dust 83, To Kill a King 84. The Whistle Blower 86, etc.

Foster, Ben (1980–)
American actor, born in Boston, Massachusetts.
Kounterfeit 96. Liberty Heights 99. Get Over It 01, etc.
TV series: Flash Forward 96. Freaks and Geeks 99.

Foster, David (1929–)
American producer, a former publicist. He is the father of producers Gary Foster, Greg Foster and Tim Foster.
McCabe and Mrs Miller 71. The Getaway 72. The Drowning Pool 75. Heroes 77. The Thing 82. Mass Appeal 84. The Mean Season 85. Short Circuit 86. Running Scared 86. Short Circuit II 88. Full Moon in Blue Water 88. The Getaway 93. The River Wild 94. The Mask of Zorro 98, etc.

Foster, Dianne (1928–) (D. Laruska)
Canadian leading lady who has made British and American films.
The Quiet Woman (GB) 51. Isn't Life Wonderful? (GB) 53. Drive a Crooked Road (US) 54. The Kentuckian (US) 55. The Brothers Rico (US) 57. Gideon's Day (GB) 58. The Last Hurrah (US) 58. King of the Roaring Twenties (US) 61. Who's Been Sleeping in My Bed (US) 63, etc.

Foster, Jodie (1962–)
Child actress in precocious roles who has matured successfully and become a director. She was in adverts from the age of three, including some as the Coppertone Girl for suntan lotion.
Biography: 1997, *Foster Child* by Buddy Foster. 1997, *Jodie* by Louis Chunovic.
Napoleon and Samantha 72. Kansas City Bomber 72. One Little Indian 73. Tom Sawyer 73. One Little Indian 73. *Alice Doesn't Live Here Any More* 74. *Bugsy Malone* 76. *Taxi Driver* (AAN) 76. The Little Girl Who Lives Down the Lane 76. Candleshoe 77. Freaky Friday 77. Carny 80. Foxes 80. O'Hara's Wife 81. Svengali (TV) 82. The Blood of Others 84. Hotel New Hampshire 84. Five Corners 87. Siesta 87. The Accused (AA) 88. Stealing Home 88. Catchfire/Backtrack 89. *Silence of the Lambs* (AA) 91. Little Man Tate (& d) 91. Shadows and Fog 91. Sommersby 93. Maverick 94. Nell (AAN) 94. Home for the Holidays (d) 95. Contact 97, etc.
TV series: Mayberry 69. Bob & Carol & Ted & Alice 73. Paper Moon 74–75.
❝ I believe women should be sexual. And why not? What a great thing to be: a sexual woman, coming of age and discovering sensuality and the intoxification of it. I've seen so many movies about women who don't like sex and really don't want to have sex, or have that posey stuff in Calvin Klein ads. Well, that's just not true and I'm sick of that myth being out there. What I'd like to do is develop movies that better reflect my generation of women. – *J.F.*
I don't talk about my private life, and that's probably why I'm sane. – *J.F.*

Foster, Julia (1941–)
British leading lady.
The Small World of Sammy Lee 63. Two Left Feet 63. The System 64. The Bargee 64. One-Way Pendulum 64. Alfie 66. Half a Sixpence 67. All Coppers Are 72. The Great McGonagall 74. F. Scott Fitzgerald in Hollywood (TV) 76. The Thirteenth Reunion 81, etc.

Foster, Lewis (1899–1974)
American director, former Hal Roach gag writer; won an Oscar in 1939 for the original story of *Mr Smith Goes to Washington.*
The Lucky Stiff (& w) 48. Manhandled (& w) 49. Captain China 49. The Eagle and the Hawk (& w) 49. Crosswinds 51. Those Redheads from Seattle (& w) 53. Top of the World 55. The Bold and the Brave 56. Tonka (& w) 58, etc.

Foster, Meg (1948–)
American leading lady with striking blue eyes.
The Death of Me Yet (TV) 71. Sunshine (TV) 73. Things in Their Season (TV) 74. James Dean (TV) 76. A Different Story 79. The Legend of Sleepy Hollow 79. Carny 80. Guyana Tragedy (TV) 81. Ticket to Heaven 81. The Osterman Weekend 83. The Emerald Forest 85. The Wind 87. Masters of the Universe 87. They Live 88. Tripwire 89. Blind Fury 89. Relentless 89. Stepfather II 89. Backstab 90. To Catch a Killer (TV) 92. Hidden Fears 94. Oblivion 94. Space Marines 96. The Man in the Iron Mask 97, etc.
TV series: Sunshine 73. Cagney and Lacey 82–84.

Foster, Norman (1900–1976) (Norman Hoeffer)
American leading man of the early 30s; became a director and had a rather patchy career. Married Claudette Colbert and Sally Blane.
Gentlemen of the Press 29. It Pays to Advertise 31. Reckless Living 31. Alias the Doctor 32. Skyscraper Souls 32. State Fair 33. Professional Sweetheart 33. Orient Express 34. Behind the Green Lights 35. High Tension 36. I Cover Chinatown (& d) 36.
■ directed only: Fair Warning 37. Think Fast Mr Moto 37. Thank You Mr Moto 37. Walking Down Broadway 38. Mysterious Mr Moto 38. Mr Moto Takes a Chance 38. Mr Moto's Last Warning 39. Charlie Chan in Reno 39. Mr Moto Takes a Vacation 39. *Charlie Chan at Treasure Island* 39. Charlie Chan in Panama 40. Viva Cisco Kid 40. Ride Kelly Ride 41. Scotland Yard 41. *Journey Into Fear* 42. Rachel and the Stranger 48. Kiss the Blood off My Hands 48. Tell It to the Judge 49. Father is a Bachelor 50. Woman on the Run 50. Navajo 52. Sky Full of Moon 52. Sombrero 53. Davy Crockett 55. Davy Crockett and the River Pirates 56. The Nine Lives of Elfego Baga 58. The Sign of Zorro 60. Indian Paint 66. Brighty 67.

Foster, Preston (1901–1970)
Handsome American leading man of the 30s, former clerk and singer.
Nothing But the Truth (debut) 30. Life Begins 31. *The Last Mile* 31. Wharf Angel 34. The Informer 35. The Last Days of Pompeii 35. Annie Oakley 36. The Plough and the Stars 37. First Lady 38. News Is Made at Night 38. Geronimo 39. Moon over Burma 40. Northwest Mounted Police 40. Unfinished Business 41. Secret Agent of Japan 42. My Friend Flicka 43. The Bermuda Mystery 44. The Valley of Decision 45. The Last Gangster 45. The Harvey Girls 46. Ramrod 47. Green Grass of Wyoming 48. Tomahawk 49. The Tougher They Come 51. The Big Night 52. Kansas City Confidential 53. I the Jury 55. Destination 60,000 58. Advance to the Rear 64. The Time Travellers 65. Chubasco 68, many others.
TV series: Waterfront 54–55. Gunslinger 60.

Foster, Stephen (1826–1864)
American songwriter of popular sentimental ballads: 'Old Folks at Home', 'Beautiful Dreamer', etc. Impersonated on screen by Douglass Montgomery in *Harmony Lane* 35, Don Ameche in *Swanee River* 39, and Bill Shirley in *I Dream of Jeannie* 52.

Foster, Susanna (1924–) (Suzan Larsen)
American operatic singer and heroine of several 40s films. She angered producers by turning down roles in order to study opera, and quit Hollywood to sing in operettas in the late 40s and early 50s with her husband, tenor Wilbur Evans (1948–56). After her divorce, she worked in a variety of low-paid office jobs.
The Great Victor Herbert 40. *There's Magic in Music* 41. The Hard Boiled Canary 42. Top Man 43. *Phantom of the Opera* 43. The Climax 44. Bowery to Broadway 44. This Is the Life 44. Frisco Sal 45. That Night with You 45, etc.

Fotopoulos, Vassilis (1934–)
Greek production designer, from the stage.
America America/The Anatolian Smile 63. Zorba the Greek (AA) 64. You're a Big Boy Now 67, etc.

Foulger, Byron (1900–1970)
American small-part actor, the prototype of the worried, bespectacled clerk.
The Prisoner of Zenda 37. Edison the Man 40. Sullivan's Travels 41. Since You Went Away 44. Champagne for Caesar 49. The Magnetic Monster 53. The Long Hot Summer 59. The Gnome-Mobile 67, many others.
TV series: Captain Nice 67. Petticoat Junction 68–70.

Fowlds, Derek (1937–)
British comedy character actor, usually in unassuming roles.
The Smashing Bird I Used to Know 69. Hotel Paradiso 66. Tower of Evil 71. Over the Hill 92, etc.
TV series: The Basil Brush Show 69–73. Yes Minister 80–85. Yes Prime Minister 86–90. Heartbeat 92– .

Fowler, Gene (1890–1960)
American journalist, author and screenwriter. Born in Denver, Colorado, he studied at the University of Colorado and worked as a reporter, sports editor and managing editor of New York newspapers while becoming a best-selling author. He went to Hollywood in the 30s, and was a biographer of Jimmy Durante, and chronicler and close friend of actor John Barrymore, who used to enjoy reciting his poem 'Testament of a Dying Ham'.
Autobiography: 1958, *Timberline.* 1961, *Skyline.*
The Roadhouse Murder 32. What Price Hollywood? 32. State's Attorney 32. The Way to Love 33. The Mighty Barnum 34. The Call of the Wild 35. Career Woman (story) 36. Professional Soldier 36. A Message to Garcia 36. Love under Fire 37. Nancy Steele Is Missing 37. Billy the Kid 41. Big Jack 49. Beau James (oa) 56, etc.
❝ What is success? It is a toy balloon among children armed with pins. – *G.F.*
You do not waste time; time wastes you. – *G.F.*

Fowler Jnr, Gene (1917–1998)
American editor and director, the son of Gene Fowler. He was also responsible for the technical direction of George S. Kaufman's one attempt at film direction, *The Senator Was Indiscreet* 48.
as editor: *The Oxbow Incident* 43. Philo Vance Returns 47. Captain Scarface 53. Main Street to Broadway 53. Naked Hills 55. Beyond a Reasonable Doubt 56. While the City Sleeps 56. China Gate 57. Forty Guns 57. Run of the Arrow 57. A Child Is Waiting 62. *It's a Mad, Mad, Mad World* (AAN) 63. Hang 'em High 68. A Death of Innocence 71. Smorgasbord 81, etc.
as writer: My Outlaw Brother 51. The Oregon Trail 59.

Fowler, Harry (1926–)
British cockney actor on screen since the early 40s, often in cameo roles.
Those Kids from Town 42. Champagne Charlie 44. Hue and Cry 46. For Them That Trespass 48. I Believe in You 52. Pickwick Papers 53. Home and Away 56. Idol on Parade 59. Ladies Who Do 63. Doctor in Clover 66. The Prince and the Pauper 77. Chicago Joe and the Showgirl 89, many others.
TV series: The Army Game, Our Man at St Mark's.

Fowler, Hugh (c. 1904–1975)
American editor.
Les Misérables 52. Gentlemen Prefer Blondes 53. The Last Wagon 56. Say One for Me 59. The Lost World 60. The List of Adrian Messenger 63. Stagecoach 66. Planet of the Apes 67. Patton (AA) 70. The Life and Times of Judge Roy Bean 72, many others.

Fowles, John (1926–)
British novelist whose slightly mystic themes have generally attracted film-makers, though not always with satisfactory results: *The Collector, The Magus, The French Lieutenant's Woman.*

Fowley, Douglas (1911–1998)
American character actor often seen as nervous or comic gangster.
Let's Talk it Over 34. Crash Donovan 36. Charlie Chan on Broadway 37. Mr Moto's Gamble 38. Dodge City 39. Ellery Queen Master Detective 40. Tanks a Million 41. Jitterbugs 42. The Kansan 43. One Body Too Many 44. The Hucksters 47. If You Knew Susie 48. Battleground 49. Edge of Doom 50. Criminal Lawyer 51. *Singin' in The Rain* (as the hysterical director) 52. The High and the Mighty 54. Macumba Love (p and d only) 59. Desire in the Dust 60. Barabbas 62. From Noon till Three 76. The White Buffalo 77, many others.
TV series: The Life and Legend of Wyatt Earp (as Doc Holliday) 56–61. Pistols and Petticoats 66. Gunsmoke 68–74.

Fox, Bernard (1927–)
British character actor in Hollywood: plays a rather stiff gent of the old school.
Soho Incident 56. The Safecracker 58. Honeymoon Hotel 64. Star 68. Big Jake 71. The Hound of the Baskervilles (TV) (as Dr Watson) 72. Herbie Goes to Monte Carlo 77. Alien Zone 78. The Private Eyes 80. Yellow Beard 83. Haunted Honeymoon 86. 18 Again 87. The Rescuers Down Under (voice) 90. Titanic 97. The Mummy 99, etc.
TV series: Bewitched 67–72.

Fox, Charles (1940–)
American composer.
Barbarella (co-m) 67. Goodbye Columbus 69. Star Spangled Girl 71. The Laughing Policeman 73. The Other Side of the Mountain 75. Foul Play 78. Nine to Five 80. Why Would I Lie 80. Zapped! 82. Love Child 82. Strange Brew 83. National Lampoon's European Vacation 85. Longshot 86.

Parent Trap 87. Love at Stake 88. Short Circuit II 88. The Gods Must Be Crazy II 89. It Had to Be You 89, etc.

TV series: Happy Days, The Love Boat, etc.

Fox, Edward (1937–)
Diffident British leading man of the 70s.

The Naked Runner 67. The Long Duel 67. Oh What a Lovely War 69. Skullduggery 69. The Breaking of Bumbo 70. The Go-Between 71. *The Day of the Jackal* 73. Doll's House 73. Galileo 74. The Squeeze 77. A Bridge Too Far 77. The Cat and the Canary 78. Force Ten From Navarone 78. *Edward and Mrs Simpson* (TV) 78. The Mirror Crack'd 80. Gandhi 82. Never Say Never Again 83. The Dresser 83. The Shooting Party 84. The Bounty 84. Wild Geese 2 85. Return to the River Kwai 88. They Never Slept 90. Robin Hood 91. A Feast at Midnight 95. Gulliver's Travels (TV) 96. A Dance to the Music of Time (TV) 97. Prince Valiant 97. Lost in Space 98, etc.

Fox, James (1939–)
British leading man, who usually plays a weakling. Once a child actor, notable in *The Magnet* 50 (as William Fox). Returned to acting in 1982 after a ten-year break in good works. Brother of Edward Fox, and very similar in style.

Autobiography: 1983, *Comeback*.

The Loneliness of the Long Distance Runner 62. Tamahine 62.The Servant 63. Those Magnificent Men in Their Flying Machines 65. King Rat 65. The Chase 66. Thoroughly Modern Millie 67. Duffy 68. Isadora 68. Arabella 69. Performance 70. Runners 83. A Passage to India 84. Greystoke: The Legend of Tarzan, Lord of the Apes 84. Absolute Beginners 86. The Whistle Blower 86. High Season 87. Comrades 87. White Mischief 87. Farewell to the King 88. She's Been Away 89. The Mighty Quinn 89. The Russia House 90. A Question of Attribution (TV) 91. Afraid of the Dark 92. As You Like It 92. Hostage 92. Patriot Games 92. The Remains of the Day 93. A Month by the Lake 94. Heart of Darkness (TV) 94. The Dwelling Place (TV) 94. Doomsday Gun (TV) 94. Clockwork Mice 95. The Old Curiosity Shop (TV) 95. Gulliver's Travels (TV) 96. Leo Tolstoy's Anna Karenina 97. Jinnah (Pak.) 98. Mickey Blue Eyes 99. Up at the Villa 00. The Golden Bowl 00. The Knights of the Quest 01, etc.

TV series: The Choir 95.

Fox, Kerry
New Zealand leading actress.

An Angel at My Table 90. The Last Days of Chez Nous 91. Friends 92. Taking Liberties 93. Country Life 94. The Last Tattoo 94. Shallow Grave (GB) 94. Black Tuesday (TV) 95. The Affair (TV) 95. Saigon Baby (TV) 96. Welcome to Sarajevo (GB/US) 97. The Hanging Garden (Can.) 97. The Wisdom of Crocodiles (GB) 98. The Darkest Light (GB) 99. To Walk With Lions (Can.) 99, etc.

Fox, Michael J. (1961–)
Canadian leading man in Hollywood who plays younger than his years. He won Emmy awards in 1987 and 1988 for his role as Alex P. Keaton in the TV sitcom *Family Ties*. Married actress Tracy Pollan. In 1998 he revealed that he had been suffering from Parkinson's disease for seven years. He quit the TV series *Spin City* in 2000 to spend more time with his family and help find a cure for Parkinson's Disease.

Midnight Madness 80. Class of 84 83. *Back to the Future* 85. Teen Wolf 85. Poison Ivy (TV) 85. The Secret of my Success 87. Light of Day 87. Bright Lights, Big City 88. Back to the Future II 89. Casualties of War 89. Back to the Future III 90. Doc Hollywood 91. The Hard Way 91. The Concierge 92. For Love or Money 93. Homeward Bound: The Incredible Journey (voice) 93. Where the Rivers Flow North 93. Life with Mikey 93. Greedy/Greed 94. Coldblooded 95. Blue in the Face 95. The American President 95. Homeward Bound II: Lost in San Francisco (voice) 96. The Frighteners 96. Mars Attacks! 96. Stuart Little (voice) 99. etc.

TV series: Palmerstown USA 80–81. *Family Ties* 82–89. Spin City (&p) 96-2000.

Fox, Sidney (1910–1942)
American leading lady of the early 30s.

Bad Sister 31. The Mouthpiece 32. Once In a Lifetime 32. Murders in the Rue Morgue 32. Midnight 34, etc.

Fox, Vivica A. (1964–)
American actress, a former model, from television. She was born in South Bend, Indiana, and raised in Indianapolis. According to her publicity, she was discovered by a producer while having lunch at a restaurant on Sunset Boulevard in the mid-80s.

Independence Day 96. Set It Off 96. Booty Call 96. Batman and Robin 97. Soul Food 97. Why Do Fools Fall in Love 98. Teaching Mrs Tingle 99., etc.

TV series: Getting Personal 98. City of Angels 2000- .

Fox, Wallace (1898–1958)
American director.

The Amazing Vagabond 29. Cannonball Express 32. Powdersmoke Range 35. The Last of the Mohicans (co-d) 36. Racing Lady 37. Pride of the Plains 40. Bowery Blitzkrieg 41. Kid Dynamite 43. Riders of the Santa Fe 44. Mr Muggs Rides Again 45. Gunman's Code 46. Docks of New York 48. Six Gun Mesa 50. Montana Desperado 51, many others.

Fox, William (1879–1952) (Wilhelm Fried)
Hungarian-American pioneer and executive, the Fox of Twentieth Century-Fox. Moved from the garment industry into exhibition, production and distribution.

Biography: 1933, *Upton Sinclair Presents William Fox*.

“ I always bragged of the fact that no second of those contained in the twenty-four hours ever passed but that the name of William Fox was on the screen, being exhibited in some theatre in some part of the world. – *W.F.*

Foxwell, Ivan (1914–)
British producer, in films since 1933.

No Room at the Inn 47. The Intruder 51. The Colditz Story 54. Manuela 56. A Touch of Larceny 59. Tiara Tahiti 62. The Quiller Memorandum 66. Decline and Fall (& w) 68, etc.

Foxworth, Robert (1941–)
American general-purpose actor.

The New Healers (TV) 72. Frankenstein (TV) 73. The Devil's Daughter (TV) 73. The Questor Tapes (TV) 74. Mrs Sundance (TV) 74. James Dean (TV) 76. Treasure of Matecumbe 76. It Happened at Lake Wood Manor (TV) 77. Death Moon (TV) 78. Damien: Omen II 78. Prophecy 79. The Black Marble 80. Double Standard (TV) 88. Beyond the Stars 89, etc.

TV series: Storefront Lawyers 70–71. Falcon Crest 81–89.

Foxx, Jamie (1967–)
American actor and comic who made his name on the TV show *In Living Color* and followed it with a successful sitcom.

Toys 92. The Great White Hype 96. The Truth about Cats & Dogs 96. Booty Call 97. The Players Club 98. Any Given Sunday 99. Bait 00, etc.

TV series: In Living Color 91-94. Roc 93-94. The Jamie Foxx Show 96- .

Foxx, Redd (1922–1991) (John Elroy Sanford)
American vaudevillian who became a 70s star in the long-running *Sanford and Son*.

Norman, Is That You? 76. Harlem Nights 89.

TV series: Sanford and Son 72–77. Redd Foxx 77–78. Sanford 80–81. The Redd Foxx Show 86.

Foy, Bryan (1895–1977)
American producer, mostly of low budgeters at Warner. Wrote song, 'Mr Gallagher & Mr Shean'; and was the oldest of the 'seven little Foys'.

The Home Towners (d) 28. Little Old New York (d) 28. The Gorilla (d) 31. Berlin Correspondent 42. Guadalcanal Diary 43. Doll Face 46. Trapped 49. Breakthrough 50. Inside the Walls of Folsom Prison 51. The Miracle of Fatima 52. *House of Wax* 53. The Mad Magician 54. Women's Prison 55. Blueprint for Robbery 61. PT 109 63, many others.

Foy Snr, Eddie (1854–1928) (Edward Fitzgerald)
Famous American vaudeville comedian who made few film appearances but was several times impersonated by Eddie Foy Jnr: in *Yankee Doodle Dandy, Wilson, Bowery to Broadway*, etc. Bob Hope played him in *The Seven Little Foys*. Films include A Favourite Fool 15.

Foy Jnr, Eddie (1905–1983)
American vaudeville entertainer, son of another and one of the 'seven little Foys'.

Fugitive from Justice 40. The Farmer Takes a Wife 53. Lucky Me 54. *The Pajama Game* 57. Bells Are Ringing 60. Thirty Is a Dangerous Age, Cynthia 67, etc.

TV series: Fair Exchange 63.

Frain, James (1969–)
English actor, born in Leeds, Yorkshire. He studied at the University of East Anglia and trained at the Central School of Speech and Drama.

Shadowlands 93. An Awfully Big Adventure 94. Loch Ness 95. Nothing Personal 95. Vigo: Passion for Life (as Vigo) 97. Elizabeth 98. Hilary and Jackie (as Daniel Barenboim) 98. Titus (US) 99. The Miracle Maker 99. Sunshine (Hung.) 99. Where the Heart Is (US) 00. Reindeer Games (US) 00, etc.

Fraker, William A. (1923–)
American cinematographer.

Games 67. The Fox 67. The President's Analyst 67. *Bullitt* 68. Rosemary's Baby 68. Paint Your Wagon 69. *Monte Walsh* (& d) 70. Day of the Dolphin 73. Lipstick 76. Exorcist II: The Heretic 77. Looking for Mr Goodbar (AAN) 77. American Hot Wax 78. Heaven Can Wait (AAN) 78. Hard Contract 78. 1941 (AAN) 79. Old Boyfriends 79. Hollywood Knights 80. Sharkey's Machine 81. The Legend of the Lone Ranger (d only) 81. The Best Little Whorehouse in Texas 82. War Games (AAN) 83. Protocol 84. Murphy's Romance (AAN) 85. Burglar 87. Baby Boom 87. Chances Are 89. An Innocent Man 89. The Freshman 90. Memoirs of an Invisible Man 92. There Goes My Baby 94. Street Fighter 94. Father of the Bride Part II 95. The Island of Dr Moreau 96. Vegas Vacation 97, etc.

Frakes, Jonathan (1952–)
American actor and director, born in Bethlehem, Pennsylvania, best known for his role as Commander William Riker in the TV series *Star Trek: The Next Generation*.

Beach Patrol (TV) 79. Nutcracker: Money, Madness and Murder (TV) 87. Star Trek: Generations 94. *Star Trek: First Contact* (& d) 96.

TV series: North and South Book 1 85.

France, C. V. (1868–1949)
British stage character actor, most typically seen in films as dry lawyer or ageing head of household.

Lord Edgware Dies 35. Scrooge 35. Victoria the Great 37. A Yank at Oxford 38. If I Were King (US) 39. Night Train to Munich 40. Breach of Promise 41. The Halfway House 44, etc.

Francen, Victor (1888–1977)
Belgian stage actor, occasionally in French films from 1921, but most familiar in Hollywood spy dramas during World War II.

Crépuscule d'Epouvante 21. Après l'Amour 31. Nuits de Feu 36. Le Roi 36. J'Accuse 38. Sacrifice d'Honneur 38. La Fin du Jour 39. Tales of Manhattan 42. Mission to Moscow 43. Devotion 43. The Mask of Dimitrios 44. The Conspirators 44. Passage to Marseilles 44. Confidential Agent 45. The Beast with Five Fingers 46. La Nuit s'achève 49. The Adventures of Captain Fabian 51. Hell and High Water 54. Bedevilled 55. A Farewell to Arms 58. Fanny 61. Top-Crack 66, many others.

Franciosa, Anthony (Tony) (1928–) (Anthony Papaleo)
Italian-American leading actor with lithe movement and ready grin. He was married to actress Shelley Winters (1957–60).

A Face in the Crowd (debut) 57. This Could Be the Night 57. *A Hatful of Rain* (his stage role) (AAN) 57. Wild Is the Wind 58. *The Long Hot Summer* 58. The Naked Maja 59. Career 59. The Story on Page One 59. Go Naked in the World 60. Period of Adjustment 62. Rio Conchos 64. The Pleasure Seekers 65. A Man Could Get Killed 65. Assault on a Queen 66. The Swinger 66. Fathom (GB) 67. The Sweet Ride 68. In Enemy Country 68. A Man Called Gannon 68. Across 110th Street 72. The Drowning Pool 75. The World Is Full of Married Men (GB) 79. Firepower 79. Death Wish II 82. Unsane/Tenebrae 82. Stagecoach (TV) 86. Death House 88. Ghostwriter 89. Backstreet Dreams 90. Double Threat 92. City Hall 96, etc.

TV series: Valentine's Day 64. *The Name of the Game* 68–70. Search 72. Matt Helm 75.

Franciosa, Massimo (1924–1998)
Italian screenwriter, director and novelist. Many of his 60 or so screenplays were written in collaboration with Pasquale Festa CAMPANILE, often for the films of Dino RISI. He turned to directing in the 60s, and later wrote mainly for television.

Wild Love 55. Poor but Beautiful 56. Beautiful but Poor 57. La Nonna Sabella 57. Venice, the Moon and You 58. Young Husbands 58. The Love Nakers 61. The Lady Killer of Rome 61. The Conjugal Bed 63. The Four Days of Naples (AAN) 63. Un Tentativo Sentimentale (& co-d) 63. White Voices/Le Voci Bianche (& co-d) 64. Extra Coniugale (co-d) 65. The Dreamer/Il Morbidone (d) 66. The Girl and the General 67. Pronto … C'e una Certa Giuliana per Te (d) 67. Quella Chiara Notte d'Ottobre (d) 70. The Voyage 74. Sono Fotogenico 80, etc.

Francis, Alec B. (1869–1934)
British-born character actor in Hollywood films as elderly gentleman.

Flame of the Desert 19. Smiling Through 22. Three Wise Fools 23. Charley's Aunt 25. Tramp Tramp Tramp 26. The Terror 28. Outward Bound 30. Arrowsmith 31. The Last Mile 32. Oliver Twist 33. Outcast Lady 34, many others.

Francis, Anne (1930–)
American leading lady of several 50s films: formerly model, with radio and TV experience.

Summer Holiday (debut) 48. So Young So Bad 50. Elopement 52. Lydia Bailey 52. Susan Slept Here 54. Bad Day at Black Rock 54. The Blackboard Jungle 55. Forbidden Planet 56. Don't Go Near the Water 57. Girl of the Night 60. The Satan Bug 65. Funny Girl 68. The Love God 69. More Dead than Alive 70. Pancho Villa 71. Haunts of the Very Rich (TV) 72. A Masterpiece of Murder (TV) 86. Little Vegas 92. The Double O Kid 93, etc.

TV series: Honey West 65. My Three Sons 71.

Francis, Arlene (1908–) (Arlene Kazanjian)
American TV personality who has appeared in a few films. Married actor Martin GABEL.

Stage Door Canteen 43. All My Sons 48. One Two Three 61. The Thrill of it All 63. Fedora 78, etc.

Francis, Connie (1938–) (Concetta Franconero)
American pop singer who had some light films built around her. She dubbed the singing voice of Freda Holloway in *Jamboree* 57, and Tuesday Weld in *Rock, Rock, Rock* 57.

Where the Boys Are 63. Follow the Boys 64. Looking for Love 65, etc.

Francis, Derek (1923–1984)
Portly British character actor, often in self-important roles.

Bitter Harvest 63. Ring of Spies 64. The Comedy Man 64. Carry on Camping 69. To the Devil a Daughter 75. Jabberwocky 77, etc.

Francis, Freddie (1917–)
British cinematographer who turned to direction with less distinguished results.

Mine Own Executioner 47. Time without Pity 57. Room at the Top 59. *Sons and Lovers* (AA) 60. The Innocents 61. The French Lieutenant's Woman 80. The Elephant Man 81. Dune 85. Code Name: Emerald 85. Dark Tower 87. Clara's Heart 88. Her Alibi 89. Brenda Starr 89. Glory (AA) 89. The Plot to Kill Hitler (TV) 90. Cape Fear 91. The Man in the Moon 91. School Ties 92. A Life in the Theatre 93. Princess Caraboo 94, etc.

AS DIRECTOR ONLY: Two and Two make Six 61. Vengeance 62. Paranoiac 63. Nightmare 63. The Evil of Frankenstein 64. Traitor's Gate 65. The Skull 65. The Deadly Bees 66. They Came from Beyond Space 66. The Torture Garden 67. Dracula has Risen from the Grave 68. Mumsy Nanny Sonny and Girlie 69. Tales from the Crypt 71. Asylum 72. Tales that Witness Madness 73. Legend of the Werewolf 74. The Doctor and the Devils 86. Dark Tower 87. Rainbow 95, etc.

Francis, Ivor (c. 1911–1986)
American character actor who played self-important or bumbling types.

I Love My Wife 70. The Late Liz 71. The World's Greatest Athlete 73. Superdad 74. The Prisoner of Second Avenue 75. The North Avenue Irregulars 78, etc.

TV series: Gilligan's Island 64–67. Dusty's Trail 73.

Francis, Karl (1943–)
Welsh director.
The Mouse and the Woman 81. Giro City 82. The Happy Alcoholic 84. Boy Soldier (TV) 86. Angry Earth (TV) 90. Rebecca's Daughters 91, etc.
TV series: Judas and the Gimp (p, wd) 93.

Francis, Kay (1899–1968) (Katherine Gibbs)
Ladylike, serious-faced American star of women's films in the 30s.
■ Gentlemen of the Press 29. The Coconuts 29. Dangerous Curves 29. Illusion 29. The Marriage Playground 29. Behind the Makeup 30. *Street of Chance* 30. Paramount on Parade 30. A Notorious Affair 30. Raffles 30. For the Defence 30. Let's Go Native 30. The Virtuous Sin 30. Passion Flower 30. Scandal Sheet 31. Ladies' Man 31. The Vice Squad 31. Transgression 31. Guilty Hands 31. Twenty-Four Hours 31. Girls about Town 31. The False Madonna 32. Strangers in Love 32. Man Wanted 32. Street of Women 32. Jewel Robbery 32. *One Way Passage* 32. *Trouble in Paradise* 32. *Cynara* 32. The Keyhole 33. Storm at Daybreak 33. Mary Stevens MD 33. I Loved a Woman 33. The House on 56th Street 33. Mandalay 34. Wonder Bar 34. Doctor Monica 34. British Agent 34. Stranded 34. The Goose and the Gander 35. Living on Velvet 35. I Found Stella Parish 35. *The White Angel* (as Florence Nightingale) 36. Give Me Your Heart 36. Stolen Holiday 37. Confession 37. Another Dawn 37. *First Lady* 37. Women Are Like That 38. My Bill 38. Secrets of an Actress 38. Comet over Broadway 38. King of the Underworld 39. Women in the Wind 39. In Name Only 39. It's a Date 40. Little Men 40. When the Daltons Rode 40. Play Girl 40. The Man Who Lost Himself 40. *Charley's Aunt* 41. The Feminine Touch 41. Always in My Heart 42. Between Us Girls 42. Four Jills in a Jeep 44. Divorce 45. Allotment Wives 45. Wife Wanted 46.

Francis, Raymond (1909–1987)
English character actor, best known for playing the precise, snuff-taking infallible detective Tom Lockhart in several TV crime series of the 50s and 60s. Born in Finchley, London, he began as a conjuror in his teens and worked in repertory for many years before succeeding on TV. He was the father of actor Clive Francis (1946–).
Mr Denning Drives North 51. Carrington VC 54. Storm over the Nile 55. Above Us the Waves 55. Reach for the Sky 56. Doublecross 56. Carve Her Name with Pride 58. It Shouldn't Happen to a Vet 76. The Case of Marcel Duchamp 83, etc.
TV series: Sherlock Holmes (as Dr Watson) 51. Murder Bag 57–59. Crime Sheet 59. No Hiding Place 59–67.

Francis, Robert (1930–1955)
American leading man whose budding career was cut short by an air crash.
The Caine Mutiny 54. The Long Gray Line 55, etc.

Franciscus, James (1933–1991)
American leading man.
Four Boys and a Gun 56. I Passed for White 60. The Outsider 61. The Miracle of the White Stallions 63. Youngblood Hawke 64. The Valley of Gwangi 69. Marooned 69. Beneath the Planet of the Apes 69. Cat O'Nine Tails 71. The Dream Makers (TV) 75. The Amazing Dobermans 76. The Greek Tycoon 78. When Time Ran Out 80. Jacqueline Bouvier Kennedy (TV) 81. Butterfly 81. The Great White 82. The Courageous 82. Secret Weapons (TV) 85, etc.
TV series: Naked City 58. Mr Novak 63–64. Longstreet 71. Hunter 77.

Francks, Don (1932–)
Canadian singer whose first notable film role was in *Finian's Rainbow* 68.
My Bloody Valentine 81. Terminal Choice 85. The Christmas Wife (TV) 88. Madonna: Innocence Lost 95. First Degree 95. Johnny Mnemonic 95. Harriet the Spy 96. Bogus 96. Summer of the Monkeys 98. Dinner at Fred's 98, etc.
TV series: La Femme Nikita 97.

Franco, Jess (Jesús)
Prolific Spanish director, mainly of exploitation and horror movies of extremely variable quality, usually ranging from bad to abysmal. He has made as many as eight features a year under several pseudonyms, including Jess Frank, Clifford Brown, and Frank Hollman, and was an assistant to Orson Welles on his unfinished *Don Quixote*.
Dr Orloff's Monster 64. The Diabolical Dr Z/Miss Muerte 65. Attack of the Robots 66. Succubus/Necronomicon 67. The Castle of Fu Manchu/El Castillo de Fu Manchu 68. Deadly Sanctuary 68. Kiss and Kill 68. 99 Women 69. Venus in Furs 69. Mrs Hyde/Sie Toetete in Extase 70. Lesbian Vampires/Vampyros Lesbos 70. De Sade 70 70. Bram Stoker's Count Dracula/Count Dracula/El Conde Dracula 70. Virgin among the Living Dead 71. Dracula Prisoner of Frankenstein/The Screaming Dead/Dracula contra Frankenstein 72. Jack the Ripper 76. Ilsa the Wicked Warden (& a) 78. Revenge in the House of Usher/El Hundimiento de la Casa Usher 83. Faceless 88, many others.

Franco, Ricardo (1949–1998)
Spanish director, the nephew of director Jesús Franco. Died of heart failure. He was part of Madrid's Independent Cinema, making films about life's dispossessed.
El Desastre de Anual (& a) 70. Pascal Duarte 75. The Remains from the Shipwreck/Los Restos del Naufragio (& a) 78. La Paloma Azul (a only) 80. In 'N' Out (US/Mex.) 84. The Dream of Tangiers/El Sueño de Tanger (d) 86. Berlin Blues 88. Blood and Sand (co-w) 89. Lucky Star 97. Black Tears/Lagrimas Negras (co-w,co-d) 99, etc.

Franju, Georges (1912–1987)
French director, former set designer. Co-founder of Cinémathèque Française. Best-known documentaries: *Le Sang des Bêtes* 49. *Hôtel des Invalides* 51. *Le Grand Méliès* 51. Features: *La Tête contre les Murs/The Keepers* 58. *Eyes without a Face* 59. Spotlight on a Murderer 61. Thérèse Desqueyroux 62. Judex 63. Thomas the Impostor 64. Les Rideaux Blancs 65.

Frank, A. Scott
American screenwriter.
Plain Clothes 88. Little Man Tate 91. Dead Again 91. Fallen Angels 2 (co-w) (TV) 93. Malice (co-w) 93. Get Shorty 95. Heaven's Prisoners (co-w) 95. Out of Sight (AAN) 98, etc.

Frank, Charles (1910–)
British director, former dubbing expert.
Uncle Silas 47. Intimate Relations 53, etc.

Frank, Christopher (1943–1993)
British-born director and screenwriter, based in France.
Josepha 81. The Year of the Jellyfish 84. Love in the Strangest Way/Elles N'Oublient Pas 94, etc.

Frank, Fredric M. (1911–1977)
American scriptwriter.
The Greatest Show on Earth (co-w, AA) 52. The Ten Commandments (co-w) 56. El Cid (co-w) 61, etc.

Frank, Gerold (1907–1998)
American 'ghost writer' who co-authored the autobiographies of such luminaries as Sheilah Graham, Lillian Roth and Diana Barrymore.

Frank, Harriet
See Ravetch, Irving.

Frank, Leo (1884–1915)
Jewish engineer who was lynched in Georgia after he had been found guilty of the murder of Mary Phagan, a 12-year-old girl, and his death sentence had been commuted to life imprisonment. No one was indicted for his murder. In 1985 he was posthumously pardoned by the State of Georgia. Two films have been based on his lynching, *Thou Shalt Not Kill*, 15, and *They Won't Forget*, 37, directed by Mervyn LeRoy. It has also been the inspiration of a TV mini-series, *The Murder of Mary Phagan*, 88, and a novel, *The Old Religion*, 97, by David Mamet.

Frank, Melvin (1913–1988)
American comedy scriptwriter and latterly producer/director.
with norman panama: *My Favourite Blonde* 42. Thank Your Lucky Stars 43. Road to Utopia (AAN) 45. Monsieur Beaucaire 46. *Mr Blanding Builds His Dream House* 48. The Reformer and the Redhead 50. Above and Beyond 52. Knock on Wood (AAN) 54. White Christmas 56. That Certain Feeling 56. Li'l Abner 59. *The Facts of Life* (AAN) 61. Road to Hong Kong 62. Strange Bedfellows 65, etc.
solo: A Funny Thing Happened on the Way to the Forum (wp) 66. Buona Sera Mrs Campbell (wpd) 68. A Touch of Class (wpd) (AANw) 72. The Prisoner of Second Avenue 75. The Duchess and the Dirtwater Fox (wpd) 76. Lost and Found (wpd) 79.

Frankau, Ronald (1894–1951)
British stage and radio comedian with an 'idle rich' characterization.
The Calendar 31. His Brother's Keeper 39. Double Alibi 46. The Ghosts of Berkeley Square 47, etc.
❝ To the pure *nothing* is pure. – *R.F.*

Franke, Christopher (1953–)
German-born composer in international movies. Born in Berlin, he studied at the Berlin Conservatory and was a founder-member of the electronic rock group Tangerine Dream. He left the group in the late 80s and moved to Los Angeles to work. In the early 90s he founded his own record label, Sonic Images.
with Tangerine Dream: Sorcerer 77. Thief 81. The Keep 83. Risky Business 83. Firestarter 84. Flashpoint 84. Heartbreakers 84. Near Dark 87. Shy People 87. Three O'Clock High 87. Catch Me If You Can 89. Miracle Mile 89, etc.
as solo composer: McBain 91. Universal Soldier 92. Exquisite Tenderness 94. Night of the Running Man 94. Public Enemies 96. Solo 96. Tarzan and the Lost City 98. Fortress 2: Re-entry 00. The Calling 00, etc.

Frankel, Benjamin (1906–1973)
British composer. Born in London, he studied at the Guildhall School of Music and began as a nightclub violinist and a musical director in the theatre. Scores include:
The Years Between 46. The Seventh Veil 46. Mine Own Executioner 47. Sleeping Car to Trieste 48. Appointment with Venus 51. The Importance of Being Earnest 52. A Kid For Two Farthings 55. Simon and Laura 55. Happy is the Bride 58. Libel 59. Guns of Darkness 62. Night of the Iguana 64. Battle of the Bulge 65, etc.

Frankel, Cyril (1921–)
British director, former documentarist with Crown Film Unit.
Devil on Horseback 54. Make Me an Offer 55. It's Great To Be Young 56. No Time for Tears 57. She Didn't Say No 58. Alive and Kicking 58. Never Take Sweets from a Stranger 61. Don't Bother To Knock 61. On the Fiddle 61. The Very Edge 63. The Witches/The Devil's Own 66. The Trygon Factor 67. Permission to Kill 75, etc.

Frankel, Mark (1962–1996)
English leading actor. Born in London, he acted from childhood and trained at the Webber Douglas Academy of Dramatic Art. Died in a motorcycle accident.
A Season of Giants (TV) 91. Leon the Pig Farmer 92. Solitaire for 2 94. The Ruth Rendell Mysteries: Vanity Dies Hard (TV) 95. Clare de Lune (TV) 95. Roseanna's Grave/For Roseanna 96, etc.
TV series: Sisters 92–93. Fortune Hunter 94. Kindred: The Embraced 96.

Frankenheimer, John (1930–)
Ebullient American director, formerly in TV.
The Young Stranger 57. The Young Savages 61. All Fall Down 61. *The Manchurian Candidate* 62. *Birdman of Alcatraz* 62. *Seven Days in May* 64. The Train 64. *Seconds* 66. Grand Prix 67. The Extraordinary Seaman 68. The Fixer 68. The Gypsy Moths 69. I Walk the Line 70. The Horsemen 71. Impossible Object 73. The Iceman Cometh 73. 99 44/100 Dead 74. French Connection II 75. Black Sunday 76. Prophecy 79. The Challenge 82. The Holcroft Covenant 85. 52 Pick-Up 86. Dead Bang 89. The Fourth War 90. Year of the Gun 91. Against the Wall (TV) 94. The Burning Season (TV) 94. The Island of Dr Moreau 96. The Long Rains 97. George Wallace (TV) 97. Ronin 98. The General's Daughter (a) 99. Reindeer Games/Deception 00, etc.

Franklin, Carl (1941–)
American director, a former actor on stage and television.
Nowhere to Run (d) 88. Eye of the Eagle II: Inside the Enemy (d) 89. Full Fathom Five (d) 90. Eye of the Eagle III (a) 91. *One False Move* (d) 91. Laurel Avenue (TV) 93. Devil in a Blue Dress (wd) 95. One True Thing (d) 98, etc.
TV series (as actor): Caribe 75. Fantastic Journey 77. McClain's Law 81–82.

Franklin, Howard
American screenwriter and director.
The Name of the Rose (co-w) 86. Someone to Watch Over Me (w) 87. Quick Change (w,co-d) 90. The Public Eye (wd) 92. Larger than Life (d) 96. The Man Who Knew Too Little (co-w) 97. Antitrust (w) 01, etc.

Franklin, Pamela (1949–)
British juvenile actress of the 60s.
The Innocents 61. The Lion 62. The Third Secret 64. The Nanny 65. Our Mother's House 67. The Night of the Following Day 68. *The Prime of Miss Jean Brodie* 69. Sinful Davey 69. David Copperfield 69. And Soon the Darkness 70. Necromancy 72. The Legend of Hell House 73. Food for the Gods 76, etc.

Franklin, Richard (1948–)
Australian director.
■ Belinda 72. Loveland 73. The True Story of Eskimo Nell/Dick Down Under 75. Fantasm 77. Patrick 78. Road Games 81. *Psycho II* 83. Cloak and Dagger 84. Link 86. FX/2: The Deadly Art of Illusion 91. Hotel Sorrento 95. Brilliant Lies 96.

Franklin, Sidney (1893–1972)
American producer-director, in Hollywood since leaving school. Academy Award 1942 'for consistent high achievement'.
Martha's Vindication (d) 16. Heart o' the Hills (d) 19. Dulcy (d) 23. Beverly of Graustark (d) 26. The Last of Mrs Cheyney (d) 29. Private Lives (d) 31. The Guardsman (d) 32. Smiling Through (d) 32. Reunion in Vienna (d) 33. The Barretts of Wimpole Street (d) 33. The Dark Angel (d) 35. The Good Earth (AANd) 37. On Borrowed Time (p) 39. Waterloo Bridge (p) 40. Mrs Miniver (p) 42. Random Harvest (p) 42. The White Cliffs of Dover (p) 44. The Yearling (p) 46. The Miniver Story (p) 50. Young Bess (p) 54. The Barretts of Wimpole Street (d) 57, many others.

Franklyn, Leo (1897–1975)
English character actor, mainly on the stage in musical comedy, revue and farce. In films from the early 30s in Australia. Father of actor William Franklyn.
Two Minutes Silence 34. I've Got a Horse 38. The Same to You 59. The Night We Dropped a Clanger 59. The Night We Got the Bird 60, etc.

Franklyn, William (1926–)
Smooth British character actor, popular on TV.
Quatermass II 57. Fury at Smugglers' Bay 58. Pit of Darkness 62. The Legend of Young Dick Turpin 64. The Intelligence Men 65. The Satanic Rites of Dracula 73. Splitting Heirs 93, etc.

Frankovich, Mike (1910–1992)
American producer, a former sports commentator and screenwriter. During the 50s he ran Columbia's British organization, and in the 60s became their head of world production, then turned independent again. He was the adopted son of Joe E. Brown and married to Binnie Barnes.
Fugitive Lady 51. Decameron Nights 53. Footsteps in the Fog 55. Joe Macbeth 56. Marooned 69. Bob and Carol and Ted and Alice 69. Cactus Flower 69. Butterflies are Free 72. Forty Carats 73. The Shootist 76, etc.

Franz, Arthur (1920–)
American leading man, latterly character actor; radio, stage and TV experience.
Jungle Patrol (debut) 48. Sands of Iwo Jima 49. Abbott and Costello Meet the Invisible Man 51. The Sniper 52. Eight Iron Men 52. The Caine Mutiny 54. The Unholy Wife 57. Running Target 58. Hellcats of the Navy 59. Alvarez Kelly 66. Anzio 68. Sisters of Death 77. That Championship Season 82, etc.

Franz, Dennis (1944–) (D. Schlachta)
American character actor, best known for his TV roles as a tough cop, from the stage. Born in Chicago, he studied at Southern Illinois University.

The Fury 78. Remember My Name 78. Dressed to Kill 80. Blow Out 81. Psycho 2 83. Body Double 84. Kiss Shot 89. The Package 89. Die Hard 2 90. The Player 92. American Buffalo 96. City of Angels 98, etc.

TV series: Chicago Story 82. Bay City Blues 83. Hill Street Blues 85–87. NYPD Blue 93– .

Franz, Eduard (1902–1983)
American character actor, often seen as foreign dignitary, Jewish elder, or psychiatrist.

The Iron Curtain 48. Francis 50. The Thing 51. The Jazz Singer 52. Dream Wife 53. Broken Lance 54. The Ten Commandments 56. Man Afraid 57. A Certain Smile 58. The Story of Ruth 60. Hatari 62. The President's Analyst 67, many others.

TV series: The Breaking Point 63. Zorro 78.

Fraser, Bill (1908–1987)
Burly Scottish comic character actor, with wide experience on stage and in revue, who found fame on television as the preening Sergeant Snudge in *The Army Game* and *Bootsie and Snudge*. He was in films from 1938, usually in small roles until the 50s. Born in Perth, he first worked as a bank clerk, and was on stage from the early 30s. Married actress Pamela Cundell.

Meet Me Tonight 52. The Americanization of Emily 65. Joey Boy 65. Masquerade 65. I've Gotta Horse 65. Up the Chastity Belt 71. That's Your Funeral 72, etc.

TV series: *The Army Game* (as Sgt Snudge) 57–59. Bootsie and Snudge 60–64, 74. Barney Is My Darling 65. Vacant Lot 67. That's Your Funeral 71. The Train Now Standing 72. Doctor's Daughters 80. The Secret Diary of Adrian Mole Aged 13¾ 85. The Growing Pains of Adrian Mole 87.

❝ What I do is play stuffy, pot-bellied, pompous old sods. Thank God England is full of them. – *B.F.*

Fraser, Brendan (1967–)
Versatile American leading actor, adept at action and comedy. The son of Canadian parents, he studied theatre at the Cornish College of the Arts in Seattle. Current asking price: around $13m.

Dogfight 91. Encino Man/California Man 92. School Ties 92. Twenty Bucks 93. With Honors 94. Airheads 94. The Scout 94. The Passion of Darkly Noon 95. Now and Then 95. Mrs Winterbourne 96. The Twilight of the Golds 97. George of the Jungle 97. Gods & Monsters 98. Blast from the Past 98. The Mummy 99. Dudley Do-Right 99. Bedazzled 00, etc.

Fraser, John (1931–)
British leading man with stage experience, sporadically in films.

The Good Beginning 53. Touch and Go 55. The Good Companions 57. Tunes of Glory 59. *The Trials of Oscar Wilde* (as Lord Alfred Douglas) 60. El Cid 61. Fury at Smugglers' Bay 61. The Waltz of the Toreadors 62. Repulsion 65. Operation Crossbow 65. Isadora 68. Schizo 77, etc.

Fraser, Laura (1976–)
Scottish actress, born in Glasgow.

Small Faces 95. Left Luggage (Neth./Belg./US) 97. Divorcing Jack 98. Whatever Happened To Harold Smith? 98. Cousin Bette 98. Titus 99. The Match 99. Virtual Sexuality 99. Kevin & Perry Go Large 00, etc.

Fraser, Liz (1933–)
British character actress, specializing in dumb cockney blondes.

Wonderful Things 58. I'm All Right Jack 59. The Night We Dropped a Clanger 59. Doctor in Love 60. The Night We Got the Bird 60. Two Way Stretch 60. Carry On Regardless 61. A Pair of Briefs 61. Raising the Wind 61. Watch It, Sailor 61. The Amorous Prawn 62. Carry On Cruising 62. Live Now, Pay Later 62. The Painted Smile 62. Carry On Cabby 63. The Americanization of Emily 64. The Family Way 66. Up the Junction 67. Dad's Army 71. Adventures of a Taxi Driver 75. Carry On Behind 75. Confessions of a Driving Instructor 76. Confessions from a Holiday Camp 77. Chicago Joe and the Showgirl 88, etc.

TV series: Citizen James 60. Turnbull's Finest Half Hour 72. Fairly Secret Army 84-86. Hardwicke House 87. Rude Health 88.

Fraser, Moyra (1923–)
Australian comedienne in British stage and TV.

Here We Go Round the Mulberry Bush 67. Prudence and the Pill 68. The Boy Friend 71, etc.

Fraser, Richard (1913–1971)
Scottish-born leading man of some American second features in the 40s.

How Green Was My Valley 41. The Picture of Dorian Gray 44. Fatal Witness 46. The Cobra Strikes 48. Alaska Patrol 51, etc.

Fraser, Ronald (1930–1997)
Stocky British character actor, in films and TV since 1954. Born in Ashton-under-Lyme, Lancashire, he studied at RADA and began on stage with Sir Donald Wolfit.

The Sundowners 59. The Pot Carriers 62. The Punch and Judy Man 63. Crooks in Cloisters 64. The Beauty Jungle 64. The Flight of the Phoenix 65. The Whisperers 67. The Killing of Sister George 68. Sinful Davey 69. Too Late the Hero 69. The Rise and Rise of Michael Rimmer 70. The Magnificent Seven Deadly Sins 71. Rentadick 72. Ooh You Are Awful 72. Swallows and Amazons 74. Paper Tiger 75. The Wild Geese 78. Trail of the Pink Panther 82. Absolute Beginners 86. Let Him Have It 91. The Mystery of Edwin Drood 93. P. G. Wodehouse's Heavy Weather (TV) 95, etc.

TV series: The Misfit 70–71. Spooner's Patch 79.

Frawley, James (1937–)
American director.

The Christian Licorice Store 70. Kid Blue 73. Delancey Street (TV) 75. The Eddie Capra Mysteries (pilot) (TV) 76. The Big Bus 76. The Muppet Movie 79. The Great American Traffic Jam (TV) 80. Fraternity Vacation 85. Assault and Matrimony (TV) 87. Spies, Lies and Naked Thighs 89. Sins of the Mind (TV) 97, etc.

Frawley, William (1887–1966)
Stocky, cigar-chewing American comedy character actor from vaudeville, in innumerable films as taxi driver, comic gangster, private detective or incompetent cop.

Moonlight and Pretzels 33. Crime Doctor 34. Alibi Ike 35. Desire 36. High Wide and Handsome 37. Professor Beware 38. Persons in Hiding 39. One Night in the Tropics 40. Footsteps in the Dark 42. *Roxie Hart* 42. Whistling in Brooklyn 43. Going My Way 44. Lady on a Train 45. The Crime Doctor's Manhunt 46. Miracle on 34th Street 47. The Babe Ruth Story 48. East Side West Side 49. Kill the Umpire 50. The Lemon Drop Kid 51. Rancho Notorious 52. Safe at Home 62, etc.

TV series: *I Love Lucy* 51–60. My Three Sons 60–63.

Frayn, Michael (1933–)
British dramatist, novelist and occasional screenwriter, a former journalist.

Clockwise 86. Noises Off (oa) 92.

Frazee, Jane (1918–1985) (Mary Jane Frehse)
Vivacious American singer and leading lady of minor musicals in the 40s.

Buck Privates 41. Moonlight in Havana 42. When Johnny Comes Marching Home 42. Practically Yours 44. Swing and Sway 44. Kansas City Kitty 45. Incident 48. Rhythm Inn (last appearance) 51, etc.

TV series: Beulah 52.

Frears, Stephen (1931–)
British director. Born in Leicester, he studied law at Cambridge University, worked at the Royal Court Theatre as assistant to Lindsay Anderson, and then joined the BBC, directing documentaries and drama before making his first feature in 1971.

■ Gumshoe 71. Saigon–Year of the Cat (TV) 83. Walter and June (TV) 83. The Hit 84. My *Beautiful Laundrette* 85. Prick Up Your Ears 87. Sammy and Rosie Get Laid 87. Dangerous Liaisons 88. *The Grifters* (AAN) 90. Hero/Accidental Hero 92. *The Snapper* (TV) 93. Mary Reilly 96. The Van 96. The Hi-Lo Country 99. High Fidelity 00. Fail Safe (TV) 00. Liam 00, etc.

❝ Having a big star skews the movie: you have to concentrate on this enormous investment. – *S.F.*

I was brought up to film what was in front of me, to concentrate on the people in hand rather than go on some interior journey or get into elaborate framings or effects. – *S.F.*

Being English drives you barmy. – *S.F.*

What happened to self-doubt? That was the basis of my generation – doubt mixed with confidence. – *S.F.*

Frechette, Mark (1947–1975)
American leading man of *Zabriskie Point*; subsequently died in prison.

Freda, Riccardo (1909–1999) (aka Robert Hampton, George Lincoln, Willy Pareto)
Egyptian-Italian director who brought some style to exploitation pictures. Born in Alexandria, he began began as a sculptor at the Centro Sperimentale in Rome, and also worked a a screenwriter, designer, editor and actor before becoming a director, frequently of costume films set in Rome's imperial past. Married actress Gianna Maria Canale, who starred in many of his films.

Les Misérables 46. Spartacus 52. Theodora, Slave Express 54. I Vampiri 57. Sign of the Gladiator 59. The Giant of Thessaly 61. The Terror of Dr Hitchcock 62. The Spectre 63. Le Due Orfanelle 66. Coplan FX18/Coplan, Secret Agent FX18 66. La Morte non Conta i Dollari 67. A Doppia Faccia 69. L'Iguana della Lingua di Fuoco 70. L'Ossessione che Uccide/Murder Obsession 80. D'Artagnan's Daughter (idea) 94, etc.

Frederick, Lynne (1953–1994)
British leading lady, widow of Peter Sellers. She was briefly married to David Frost.

No Blade of Grass 70. Vampire Circus 71. Henry VIII and His Six Wives 72. Schizo 76. Voyage of the Damned 76. The Prisoner of Zenda 79, etc.

Frederick, Pauline (1885–1938) (Pauline Libbey)
American leading lady of silent days.

Bella Donna 15. The Slave Island 16. Sleeping Fires 17. Her Final Reckoning 18. The Peace of Roaring River 19. *Madame X* 20. La Tosca 21. Married Flirts 24. Her Honour the Governor 26. Mumsie (GB) 27. On Trial 28. The Sacred Flame 29. This Modern Age 31. The Phantom of Crestwood 32. My Marriage 36. Thank You Mr Moto 38, etc.

Fredericks, Ellsworth
American cinematographer.

Invasion of the Body Snatchers 56. The Friendly Persuasion 56. Sayonara 57. High Time 60. Seven Days in May 64. Pistolero 66. The Power 67. Mister Buddwing 67, etc.

Freed, Alan (1922–1965)
American disc-jockey, the self-styled 'King of Rock 'n' Roll', which is a term he claimed to have coined. A tireless promoter of the music, he appeared as himself in several 50s films. His career was ruined at the end of that decade following accusations that he had accepted bribes to play records. Two movies have been made about his life: *Mister Rock and Roll*, in which he starred, and *American Hot Wax* 78, in which he was played by Tim McIntire.

■ Rock around the Clock 56. Don't Knock the Rock 56. Mister Rock and Roll 57. Rock Rock Rock 57. Go Johnny Go (& p) 58.

Freed, Arthur (1894–1973) (Arthur Grossman)
American producer, mainly of musicals for MGM, many of them featuring his own lyrics. He collaborated with Nacio Herb Brown on many songs, including 'All I Do Is Dream of You', 'I've Got a Feelin' You're Foolin'', 'Make 'Em Laugh', 'Pagan Love Song', 'Singin' in the Rain', 'You Are My Lucky Star' and 'You Were Meant for Me'.

Books: 1984, *The Movies' Greatest Musicals Produced in Hollywood USA by the Freed Unit* by Hugh Fordin.

Hold Your Man (ly only) 33. Hollywood Party (ly only) 34. Broadway Melody of 1936 (ly only). Broadway Melody of 1938 (ly only). *Babes In Arms* (& ly) 39. Strike Up the Band 40. Lady Be Good (& ly) 41. Cabin in the Sky 43. Meet Me in St Louis 44. Ziegfeld Follies 46. The Pirate 48. *On the Town* 49. Annie Get Your Gun 50. Showboat 51. *An American in Paris* 51. *Singin' in The Rain* (& ly) 52. *Band Wagon* 53. Kismet 55. Invitation to the Dance 56. *Gigi* 58. Bells are Ringing 60. The Light in the Piazza 62, many others.

❝ Frequently he would begin a sentence on, let us say, Wednesday and complete it on Friday. Yet this same man could look at me and say: 'Stop trying to be different. You don't have to be different to be good. To be good is different enough.' – *Alan Jay Lerner*

Freed, Bert (1919–1994)
Burly American character actor.

The Company She Keeps 50. Detective Story 51. Paths of Glory 57. The Goddess 58. The Gazebo 60. Invitation to a Gunfighter 64. Nevada Smith 65. Madigan 67. Hang 'Em High 68. Wild in the Streets 68. There Was a Crooked Man 70. Billy Jack 71. Norma Rae 79, etc.

Freed, Ralph (1907–1973)
American lyricist, the brother of Arthur Freed. His collaborators included Burton Lane, Sammy Fain and Jimmy McHugh.

She Married a Cop 39. Babes on Broadway (AANs, 'How About You') 41. Two Girls and a Sailor 44. No Leave, No Love 45. Holiday in Mexico 46. This Time for Keeps 47, etc.

Freedman, Jerrold (1919–)
American director.

Kansas City Bomber 72. Borderline 80. Native Son 86. The Comeback (TV) 89, etc.

Freeland, Thornton (1898–1987)
American director, former cameraman.

Three Live Ghosts 29. Whoopee 30. *Flying Down to Rio* 33. Brewster's Millions (GB) 35. The Amateur Gentleman (GB) 36. Jericho (GB) 37. The Gang's All Here (GB) 39. Over the Moon (GB) 39. Too Many Blondes 41. Meet Me at Dawn 47. The Brass Monkey/Lucky Mascot (GB) 48. Dear Mr Prohack (GB) 49, etc.

Freeman Jnr, Al (1934–)
American leading man, a regular on the daytime soap opera *One Life to Live*.

Black Like Me 64. Dutchman 67. The Detective 68. Finian's Rainbow 68. Castle Keep 69. The Lost Man 70. A Fable (& d) 71. Seven Hours to Judgment 88. The Defense Never Rests (TV) 90. Malcolm X 92. Once Upon a Time ... When We Were Colored 96. Down in the Delta 98, etc.

TV series: Hot L Baltimore 75. Roots 79.

Freeman, Everett (1911–1991)
American writer, usually in collaboration.

Larceny Inc. 42. Thank Your Lucky Stars 43. The Secret Life of Walter Mitty 47. Million Dollar Mermaid 52. My Man Godfrey 57. The Glass Bottom Boat 66. Where Were You When the Lights Went Out? (& co-p) 68. Zigzag 70, many others.

Freeman, Howard (1899–1967)
American character actor, usually in comic roles as businessman on the make.

Pilot Number Five 43. Once Upon a Time 44. Take One False Step 49. Scaramouche 52. Remains To Be Seen 53. Dear Brigitte 65, many others.

Freeman, Joan (1941–)
American general-purpose actress.

The Remarkable Mr Pennypacker 58. Come September 61. The Rounders 65. The Fastest Guitar Alive 66. The Reluctant Astronaut 67, etc.

Freeman, Kathleen (1919–)
American character actress.

Naked City 47. Lonely Heart Bandits 52. Bonzo Goes To College 52. Full House 52. Athena 54. The Fly 58. The Ladies' Man 61. The Disorderly Orderly 65. Three on a Couch 66. Support Your Local Gunfighter 71. Stand Up and Be Counted 72. The Blues Brothers 80. Innerspace 87. Gremlins 2: The New Batch 90. Dutch 91. FernGully: The Last Rainforest (voice) 92. Reckless Kelly 93. Hocus Pocus 93. Naked Gun $33\frac{1}{3}$: The Final Insult 94. At First Sight 95. Carpool 96. Hercules (voice) 97. Blues Brothers 2000 98, etc.

TV series: Topper 53. Mayor of the Town 54–55. It's about Time 66–67. The Beverly Hillbillies 69–71. Funny Face 71. Lotsa Luck 73–74.

Freeman, Leonard (1921–1974)
American TV producer best known for *Hawaii Five-O*.

Freeman, Mona (1926–) (Monica Freeman)
American leading lady, at her peak as a troublesome teenager in the 40s.

■ National Velvet 44. Our Hearts Were Young and Gay 44. Till We Meet Again 44. Here Come the Waves 44. Together Again 44. Roughly Speaking 45. Junior Miss 45. Danger Signal 45. Black Beauty 46. That Brennan Girl 46. Our Hearts Were Growing Up 46. Variety Girl 47. *Dear Ruth* 47. Mother Wore Tights 47. Isn't It Romantic? 48. Streets of Laredo 49. The Heiress 49. Dear Wife 49. Branded 50. Copper Canyon 50. I Was a Shoplifter 50. Dear Brat 51. Darling How Could

You? 51. The Lady from Texas 51. Flesh and Fury 52. Jumping Jacks 52. Angel Face 52. Thunderbirds 52. Battle Cry 55. The Road to Denver 55. The Way Out (GB) 56. Before I Wake (GB) 56. Hold Back the Night 56. Huk 56. Dragoon Wells Massacre 57. The World Was His Jury 58.

Freeman, Morgan (1937–)
American star character actor. Born in Memphis, Tennessee, he spent five years in the air force before studying acting in Los Angeles; he was on stage from 1968.
Brubaker 80. Eyewitness 80. Harry and Son 84. Teachers 84. Marie 85. That Was Then ... This Is Now 85. Street Smart (AAN) 87. Clean and Sober 88. Driving Miss Daisy (AAN) 89. Glory 89. Johnny Handsome 89. Lean on Me 89. The Bonfire of the Vanities 90. Robin Hood: Prince of Thieves 91. The Power of One 91. Unforgiven 92. The Positively True Adventures of the Alleged Texas Cheerleader-Murdering Mom (TV) 93. Bopha! (d) 93. The Shawshank Redemption (AAN) 94. Outbreak 95. The American President 95. *Seven* 95. Chain Reaction 96. Moll Flanders 96. Kiss the Girls 97. Amistad 97. Hard Rain 98. Deep Impact 98. Under Suspicion 00, etc.

Freeman, Morgan J(erome) (1969–)
American director and screenwriter of independent films.
Hurricane/Hurricane Streets 97. Desert Blue 99, etc.

Freeman, Paul (1943–)
British character actor, often as a villain.
The Long Good Friday 80. The Dogs of War 80. Raiders of the Lost Ark 81. The Sender 82. An Unsuitable Job for a Woman 82. Shanghai Surprise 86. A World Apart 87. Prisoner of Rio 88. Aces: Iron Eagle III 92. Just Like a Woman 92. Pretty Princess (It.) 93. Mighty Morphin Power Rangers: The Movie 95. Samson and Delilah (TV) 96. Call Girl/Squillo 96. Double Team 97. The Three Kings 00, etc.

Freeman, Robert (c. 1935–)
British director, former fashion director and title artist (*A Hard Day's Night, Help*).
The Touchables 68. World of Fashion (short) 68. L'Echelle Blanche 69. The Erotic Adventures of Zorro 72. Alexandra – Queen of Sex 83, etc.

Fregonese, Hugo (1908–1987)
Argentine-born director, former journalist, in Hollywood from 1945.
One-Way Street 50. Saddle Tramp 51. Apache Drums 51. Mark of the Renegade 52. My Six Convicts 52. The Raid 53. Decameron Nights 53. Blowing Wild 54. The Man in the Attic 54. Black Tuesday 54. Seven Thunders (GB) 57. Harry Black and the Tiger 58. Marco Polo 61. Apaches Last Battle/Old Shatterhand (Ger.) 64. Savage Pampas (Sp.) 66, etc.

Fréhel (1891–1951) (Marguérite Boulc'h)
French music-hall star who appeared in occasional films, usually playing a singer who has seen better days. Self-destructive and noted for her abandoned behaviour, she began performing in cafés at the age of five and was top of the bill in her teens, but died in alcoholic poverty. She was Maurice Chevalier's lover at the start of his career.
Coeur de Lilas 31. La Rue sans Nom 34. *Pépé le Moko* (as Tania) 37. La Rue sans Joie 38. L'Enfer des Anges 39. L'Homme Traque 46. Maya 49, etc.
❝ By the time she was forty, Fréhel had become so coarse and overweight, with hideous gaps in her blackened teeth, that it was difficult to imagine her earlier radiance. Her septum was so damaged by cocaine that she could do a frightening parlor trick, inserting a silk scarf up one nostril and exhaling it down the other. – *Edward Behr, Thank Heaven for Little Girls*

Freleng, Friz (1906–1995) (Isidore Freleng)
American director of cartoons whose creations include Speedy Gonzales, Yosemite Sam, and the Pink Panther. Born in Kansas City, he began working in animated films in 1924 and was among the first animators to work for Walt Disney, although the association was a brief one. In the 30s he became head animator and later a director at Warner, where he remained until the early 60s, apart from two unhappy years at MGM in the late 30s. With David De Patie, he set up his own cartoon production company, De Patie-Freleng Enterprises, before returning to Warner in 1980.
Wicked West 29. Bosko in Person 33. Bing Crosbyana 36. Sweet Sioux 37. A Star Is Hatched 38. Poultry Pirates 38. You Ought to Be in Pictures 40. Hiawatha's Rabbit Hunt (AAN) 41. Rhapsody in Rivets (AAN) 41. Pigs in a Polka (AAN) 42. Greetings Bait (AAN) 43. Life with Feathers (AAN) 45. Hare Trigger 45. Tweetie Pie (AA) 47. Sandy Claws (AAN) 54. Speedy Gonzales (AA) 55. Birds Anonymous (AA) 57. Show Biz Bugs 57. Knighty Knight Bugs (AA) 58. Mexicali Shmoes (AAN) 59. Mouse and Garden (AAN) 60. Pied Piper of Guadelupe (AANp) 61. The Pink Phink (AA) 64. The Pink Blueprint (AANp) 66. Friz Freleng's Looney Looney Bugs Bunny Movie (compilation) 81. Bugs Bunny's 3rd Movie: 1001 Rabbit Tales (compilation) 82. Daffy Duck's Movie: Fantastic Island (compilation) 83. Porky Pig in Hollywood (compilation, co-d) 86, many others.

French, Harold (1897–1997)
British stage actor and producer, in films since 1931.
Biography: 1970, *I Swore I Never Would*. 1972, *I Thought I Never Could*.
AS DIRECTOR: The House of the Arrow 39. Jeannie 41. Unpublished Story 42. The Day Will Dawn 42. Secret Mission 42. *Dear Octopus* 43. English Without Tears 44. Mr Emmanuel 44. Quiet Weekend 46. My Brother Jonathan 47. The Blind Goddess 48. Quartet (part) 48. The Dancing Years 49. Trio (part) 50. Encore (part) 51. The Hour of 13 52. Isn't Life Wonderful 53. Rob Roy 53. Forbidden Cargo 54. The Man Who Loved Redheads 55, etc.

French, Hugh (1910–1976)
English actor and singer, from the stage and music hall, who appeared in Hollywood movies of the 40s. Later, he became an agent and a producer. Born in London, he studied under Italia Conti and began as a chorus boy in 1927.
Simply Terrific 38. A Woman's Vengeance (US) 47. If Winter Comes (US) 47. The Countess of Monte Cristo (US) 48. Sword in the Desert (US) 49. Fancy Pants (US) 50. Shadow of the Eagle 50. I'll Get You For This/Lucky Mick Cain (GB/US) 51. La Rivale Dell'Imperatrice (It.) 51. Under Milk Wood (ex-p) 71, etc.

French, Leslie (1899–)
Diminutive British character player.
This England 41. *Orders to Kill* 58. The Leopard 63. More than a Miracle 67. Death in Venice 71. The Singing Detective (TV) 86. The Living Daylights 87, etc.

French, Valerie (1931–1990)
British actress, in occasional Hollywood films. Married screenwriter Michael Pertwee.
Jubal 56. Garment Center 57. Decision at Sundown 57. The Four Skulls of Jonathan Drake 59. Shalako 68, etc.

Frend, Charles (1909–1977)
British director.
AS EDITOR: Waltzes from Vienna 33. Secret Agent 36. Sabotage 37. Young and Innocent 37. The Citadel 38. Goodbye Mr Chips 39. Major Barbara 40, etc.
■ AS DIRECTOR: The Big Blockade 42. The Foreman Went to France 42. *San Demetrio London* (& w) 43. Johnny Frenchman 45. Return of the Vikings 45. The Loves of Joanna Godden 47. Scott of the Antarctic 48. A Run for Your Money 49. The Magnet 49. *The Cruel Sea* 53. Lease of Life 54. The Long Arm 56. Barnacle Bill 58. Cone of Silence 60. Girl on Approval 62. Torpedo Bay 62. The Shy Bike 67.

Fresnay, Pierre (1897–1975) (Pierre Laudenbach)
Distinguished French stage actor who made many films.
Marius (debut) 31. Fanny 32. César 34. The Man Who Knew Too Much (GB) 34. *La Grande Illusion* 37. Le Corbeau 43. *Monsieur Vincent* 47. *God Needs Men* 50. The Fanatics 57, many others.

Freud, Sigmund (1856–1939)
Viennese physician who became the virtual inventor of psychoanalysis and the discoverer of sexual inhibition as a mainspring of human behaviour; a gentleman, therefore, to whom Hollywood has every reason to be grateful. A biopic *Freud* 62 was directed by John Huston starring Montgomery Clift.

Freund, Karl (1890–1969)
Czech-born cinematographer, famous for his work in German silents like The Last Laugh 24. Metropolis 26. Variety 26. Berlin 27, etc.
SINCE IN USA: *The Mummy* (& d) 33. Moonlight and Pretzels (d only) 33. Madame Spy (d only) 33. Mad Love (d only) 35. Camille 36. *The Good Earth* (AA) 37. Marie Walewska 38. Pride and Prejudice 40. The Seventh Cross 44. Key Largo 48. Bright Leaf 50, many others.

Frewer, Matt (1958–)
American actor, best known for his role as Max Headroom on television.
Max Headroom (TV) 84. Supergirl 84. Speed Zone 88. Far from Home 89. Honey, I Shrunk the Kids 89. Short Time 90. The Taking of Beverly Hills 91. National Lampoon's Senior Trip 95. Lawnmower Man 2: Beyond Cyberspace 96. Kissinger and Nixon (TV) 97. Breast Men 98, etc.
TV series: Max Headroom 87.

Frey, Leonard (1938–1988)
American character actor. He died of AIDS.
The Magic Christian 70. Tell Me That You Love Me Junie Moon 70. *The Boys in the Band* 70. Fiddler on the Roof (AAN) 71. Shirts/Skins (TV) 73. Where the Buffalo Roam 80.
TV series: Best of the West 81.

Frey, Sami (1937–) (Samuel Frei)
French leading actor, in films from a teenager.
Cleo from 5 to 7 61. The Outsiders/Band of Outsiders/Bande à Part 64. César and Rosalie 72. Sweet Movie 75. Nea 78. The Little Drummer Girl 84. Blood and Sand/Sand and Blood/De Sable et de Sang 87. La Fille de D'Artagnan 94. Conjugal Duty 95, etc.

Fricker, Brenda (1944–)
Irish character actress.
My Left Foot (AA) 89. The Field 90. Utz (TV) 91. Home Alone 2: Lost in New York 92. So I Married an Axe Murderer 93. Seekers (TV) 93. Angels in the Outfield 94. Deadly Advice 94. A Man of No Importance 94. A Time to Kill 96. Moll Flanders 96. Swann 96, etc.
TV series: Casualty 86–90.

Friderici, Blanche (c. 1870–1933)
American character actress of stark, dour presence.
Trespassing 22. Sadie Thompson 28. Jazz Heaven 29. Billy the Kid 30. Kismet 30. Night Nurse 31. Murder by the Clock 31. Mata Hari 31. Love Me Tonight 32. A Farewell to Arms 32. If I Had a Million 32. Flying down to Rio 33. It Happened One Night 34, many others.

Fridriksson, Fridrick Thor (1954–)
Icelandic director and screenwriter, a former critic who founded and edited the country's first film magazine. He began as a documentary film-maker.
White Whales/Skytturnar 87. Sky without Limit/Flugthrá 89. Children of Nature (AAN) 91. Movie Days/Bíódagar 94. Cold Fever 95. Angel of the Universe 99, etc.

Fried, Gerald (1928–)
American composer, mainly for TV.
Killer's Kiss 55. Terror in a Texas Town 58. A Cold Wind in August 60. The Cabinet of Caligari 62. One Potato Two Potato 64. The Killing of Sister George 68. Too Late the Hero 69. The Grissom Gang 71. Soylent Green 73. Roots (TV) 76. Testimony of Two Men (TV) 77. Foul Play 78. Little Darlings 80. Nine to Five 80, many others.

Friedhofer, Hugo (1902–1981)
American composer.
The Adventures of Marco Polo 38. China Girl 42. The Lodger 44. The Woman in the Window 45. *The Best Years of Our Lives* (AA) 46. The Bishop's Wife 47. Joan of Arc 48. Broken Arrow 50. Ace in the Hole 51. Above and Beyond 52. Vera Cruz 54. The Rains of Ranchipur 55. The Harder They Fall 56. One-Eyed Jacks 59. The Secret Invasion 64. The Red Baron 71. Die Sister Die 78, etc.

Friedkin, William (1939–)
American director and screenwriter, from TV. Formerly married to actresses Jeanne Moreau and Lesley-Anne Down, subsequently to production executive Sherry Lansing.
Biography: 1990, *Hurricane Billy* by Nat Segaloff.
Good Times 67. The Birthday Party 68. The Night They Raided Minsky's 68. The Boys in the Band 70. *The French Connection* (AA) 71. *The Exorcist* (AAN) 73. Sorcerer 77. The Brinks Job 79. Cruising 80. Deal of the Century 84. To Live and Die in L.A. 85. Rampage 87. The Guardian 90. Blue Chips 94. Jade 95, etc.
❝ By the time a film of mine makes it into the theatres, I have a love-hate relationship with it. There is always something I could have done to make it better. – *W.F.*

Friedman, Seymour (1917–)
American second feature director.
Trapped by Boston Blackie 48. Prison Warden 49. Customs Agent 50. Criminal Lawyer 51. Son of Dr Jekyll 51. Escape Route (co-d) (GB) 53. Secret of Treasure Mountain 56, etc.

Friedman, Stephen (1937–1996)
American producer.
Loving Molly (& w) 73. Little Darlings 80. Hero at Large 80. Eye of the Needle 81. All of Me 84. Creator 85. Enemy Mine 85. The Big Easy 87. Miss Firecracker 89. There Goes the Neighborhood 92. Mother 96, etc.

Friel, Anna (1976–)
English actress, from television. Born in Rochdale, Lancashire, she began as a 13-year-old and was best known in the role of Beth Jordache on the TV soap opera *Brookside*.
GBH (TV) 91. Our Mutual Friend (TV) 98. The Tribe (TV) 98. The Land Girls 97. Rogue Trader 99. William Shakespeare's A Midsummer Night's Dream 99. Mad Cows 99, etc.
TV series: Brookside 93–95.

Friel, Brian (1929–)
Irish playwright. Born in Omagh, County Tyrone, he studied at St Patrick's College, Maynooth, and St Joseph's Training College, Belfast; he was a teacher for 10 years before becoming a writer in 1960.
Philadelphia, Here I Come (w, oa) 75. Dancing at Lughnasa (oa) 98.

Friels, Colin (1952–)
Scottish-born leading man, in Australia. Married actress Judy DAVIS.
Hoodwink 81. Monkey Grip 82. Buddies 83. Malcolm 86. Kangaroo 86. High Tide 87. Ground Zero 87. Warm Nights on a Slow Moving Train 87. Grievous Bodily Harm 88. Darkman 90. Dingo 90. Weekend with Kate 90. Class Action 91. The Nostradamus Kid 93. Stark (TV) 93. A Good Man in Africa 94. Angel Baby 95. Back of Beyond 95. Cosi 96. Mr Reliable: A True Story 96. Dark City 97, etc.

Friend, Philip (1915–1987)
British leading man with stage experience.
Pimpernel Smith 41. Next of Kin 42. The Flemish Farm 43. Great Day 45. My Own True Love (US) 48. Panthers' Moon (US) 50. The Highwayman (US) 51. Background 53. Son of Robin Hood 59. Strangehold 62, etc.

Friese-Greene, William (1855–1921)
Pioneer British inventor who built the first practical movie camera in 1889. Died penniless; his life was the subject of *The Magic Box* 51.
Biography: 1948, *Friese-Greene, Close-Up of an Inventor* by Ray Allister.

Friml, Rudolf (1879–1972)
Czech-American composer of operettas which were frequently filmed: *The Firefly, Rose Marie, The Vagabond King*, etc.

Frings, Ketti (1909–1981) (Catherine Frings)
American scenarist.
Hold Back the Dawn (& oa) 41. Guest in the House 44. The Accused 48. Dark City 50. Because of You 52. Come Back Little Sheba 53. Foxfire 55, etc.

Frinton, Freddie (1911–1968) (Frederick Hargate)
English comedian of stage, TV and films, best known for playing opposite Thora HIRD in the 60s TV series *Meet the Wife*. Born in Grimsby, he began as an amateur before turning professional at the age of 20. His 20-minute slapstick sketch, *Dinner for One*, in which, at a woman's 90th birthday party, he is a butler who assumes the roles of her dead friends while serving the dinner and becoming increasingly drunk, has been shown on German TV every New Year's Eve since the mid-1960s.

✪ For giving the appearance of culture and refinement while keeping his standards modest though irreproachable. *Wuthering Heights*.
❝ He was the archetypal movie mogul: the glove salesman from Minsk who became more American than apple pie and founded his credo on the family audience. His maxims included: 'Motion pictures should never embarrass a man when he brings his wife to the theatre',
and: 'I seriously object to seeing on the screen what belongs in the bedroom.'
He was proud of his art: 'The picture makers will inherit the earth.'
As an executive, he certainly knew his own mind: 'A producer shouldn't get ulcers: he should give them',
and: 'I was always an independent, even when I had partners',
and: 'In this business it's dog eat dog, and nobody's going to eat me.'
He was a great showman: 'What we want is a story that starts with an earthquake and works its way up to a climax ...'
But his logic was all his own: 'I don't care if it doesn't make a nickel. I just want every man, woman and child in America to see it!'
That was about *The Best Years of Our Lives*. He disdained subtlety. When a harassed publicist devised a campaign that began: 'The directing skill of Rouben Mamoulian, the radiance of Anna Sten and the genius of Samuel Goldwyn have combined to bring you the world's greatest entertainment ...'
Goldwyn nodded approval: 'That's the kind of advertising I like. Just the facts. No exaggeration ...'
He is said to have telegraphed Eisenstein as follows: 'Have seen your picture (*The Battleship Potemkin*) and enjoyed it very much. Should like you to do something of the same kind, but cheaper, for Ronald Colman.'
With this kind of gall, it is not surprising that intellectuals like Robert Sherwood continued to relish his company: 'I find I can live with Sam just as one lives with high blood pressure.'
Did he really coin all the famous Goldwynisms which have filled so many books? Not all of them, perhaps. One doubts the authenticity of: 'Directors are always biting the hand that lays the golden egg',
and: 'In two words: im-possible',
and: 'Tell me, how did you love the picture?',
and: 'We have all passed a lot of water since then.'
But I imagine Goldwyn probably did say, rather wittily: 'Gentlemen, kindly include me out',
and: 'Let's bring it up to date with some snappy nineteenth-century dialogue',
and: 'Anyone who goes to a psychiatrist should have his head examined',
and: 'I had a great idea this morning, but I didn't like it',
and: 'A verbal contract isn't worth the paper it's written on.'
His film appreciation was untutored but vivid, like his speaking style: 'When everybody's happy with the rushes, the picture's always a stinker',
he once said; and he can't have been alone among Hollywood producers in vowing: 'I'd hire the devil himself if he'd write me a good story.'
Lindsay Anderson summed him up in 1974: 'There are lucky ones whose great hearts, shallow and commonplace as bedpans, beat in instinctive tune with the great heart of the public, who laugh as it likes to laugh, weep the sweet and easy tears it likes to weep ... Goldwyn is blessed with that divine confidence in the rightness (moral, aesthetic, commercial) of his own intuition – and that I suppose is the chief reason for his success.'
Goldwyn had in fact summed up himself rather nicely: 'I am a rebel. I make a picture to please me. If it pleases me, there is a chance it will please others. But it has to please me first.'
And his son Samuel Goldwyn Jnr was taught the value of his legacy: 'With every picture he made, my father raised the money, paid back the bank, and kept control of the negative. He said, you be careful of these films: some people will tell you they're not worth anything, but don't you believe it.'

Goldwyn, Samuel, Jnr (1926–)
American producer, son of Samuel Goldwyn.
The Man with the Gun 55. Sharkfighters 56. The Proud Rebel 58. Huckleberry Finn 60. The Young Lovers (& d) 65. Cotton Comes to Harlem 70. Come Back Charleston Blue 72. The Golden Seal 83. A Prayer for the Dying 87. Mystic Pizza 88, etc.

Goldwyn, Tony (1960–)
American actor and director, the son of producer Samuel GOLDWYN Jnr. Married production designer Jane Musky.
Gaby – a True Story 87. Ghost 90. Traces of Red 92. The Pelican Brief 93. Doomsday Gun (TV) 94. A Woman of Independent Means (TV) 95. Reckless 95. The Substance of Fire 96. The Boys Next Door (TV) 96. Kiss the Girls 97. Kiss the Sky (d only) 98. Trouble on the Corner 98. The Lesser Evil 98. A Walk on the Moon (p, d) 98. Tarzan (voice) 99. Bounce 00, etc.

Golino, Valeria (1966–)
Italian leading actress, also in international films.
Blind Date 84. My Dearest Son/Figlio Mio Infinamente Caro 85. Dumb Dicks/Asilo di Polizia 86. Love Story/Storia d'Amore 86. Big Top Pee-Wee 88. Rain Man 88. Torrents of Spring 89. The King's Whore 90. Three Sisters/Paura e Amore 90. Hot Shots! 91. The Indian Runner 91. Year of the Gun 91. Tracce di Vita Amorosa 91. Hot Shots! Part Deux 93. Clean Slate 94. Come Due Coccodrilli 94. Immortal Beloved 94. Leaving Las Vegas 95. Four Rooms 95. Escape from LA 96. The Acrobats (It.) 97. Side Streets (US) 98. Shooting the Moon/L'Albero delle Pere 98. Harem Suare (It/Fr/Turk) 99. Ivansxtc (To Live and Die in Hollywood) (US) 00, etc.

Golitzen, Alexander (1907–)
Russian-born production designer, in Hollywood from the mid-30s, who spent most of his career at Universal Studios.
The Call of the Wild 35. Foreign Correspondent (AAN) 40. Sundown (AAN) 41. Arabian Nights (AAN) 42. The Phantom of the Opera (AA) 43. The Climax (AAN) 44. Letter from an Unknown Woman 48. Seminole 53. The Glenn Miller Story 54. The Far Country 55. The Incredible Shrinking Man 57. A Time to Love and a Time to Die 58. Imitation of Life 59. Spartacus (AA) 60. Flower Drum Song (AAN) 61. That Touch of Mink (AAN) 62. To Kill a Mockingbird (AA) 62. Gambit (AAN) 66. Coogan's Bluff 68. Sweet Charity (AAN) 69. Airport (AAN) 70. Play Misty for Me 71. Earthquake (AAN) 74, many others.

Gombell, Minna (1900–1973) (aka Winifred Lee and Nancy Carter)
American character actress of the 30s and 40s, usually in hard-boiled roles.
Doctors' Wives (debut) 31. The Thin Man 34. Babbitt 35. Banjo on My Knee 37. The Great Waltz 38. The Hunchback of Notre Dame 39. Boom Town 40. A Chip Off the Old Block 44. Man Alive 46. Pagan Love Song 51. I'll See You in My Dreams 52, etc.

Gomez, Nick (1963–)
American director, a former editor and musician.
Trust (e) 90. Laws of Gravity (d) 92. New Jersey Drive 95. Illtown 96, etc.

Gomez, Thomas (1905–1971)
Bulky American stage character actor who became a familiar villain or detective in Hollywood films.
■ Sherlock Holmes and the Voice of Terror 42. Arabian Nights 42. Pittsburgh 42. Who Done It 42. White Savage 43. Corvette K 225 43. Frontier Badmen 43. Crazy House 43. The Climax 44. Phantom Lady 44. Dead Man's Eyes 44. Follow the Boys 44. In Society 44. Bowery to Broadway 44. Can't Help Singing 45. Patrick the Great 45. I'll Tell the World 45. The Daltons Ride Again 45. Frisco Sal 45. A Night in Paradise 45. Swell Guy 46. *The Dark Mirror* 46. Singapore 47. *Ride the Pink Horse* (AAN) 47. Captain from Castile 47. Johnny O'Clock 47. Casbah 48. Angel in Exile 48. Key Largo 48. *Force of Evil* 48. Come to the Stable 49. Sorrowful Jones 49. That Midnight Kiss 49. The Woman on Pier 13 49. Kim 50. The Toast of New Orleans 50. The Eagle and the Hawk 50. The Furies 50. Anne of the Indies 51. The Harlem Globetrotters 51. The Sellout 51. The Merry Widow 52. Macao 52. Pony Soldier 52. Sombrero 53. The Gambler from Natchez 54. The Adventures of Hajji Baba 54. The Looters 55. The Magnificent Matador 55. Las Vegas Shakedown 55. Night Freight 55. Trapeze 56. The Conqueror 56. John Paul Jones 59. But Not for Me 59. Summer and Smoke 61. Stay Away Joe 68. Beneath the Planet of the Apes 70.
TV series: Life with Luigi 52.

Gonzalez, Myrtle (1891–1918)
American star of Vitagraph silents. Died of pneumonia.
The Spell 13. The Ebony Casket 15. The Secret of the Swamp 16. The End of the Rainbow 16. Captain Alvarez 17. Mutiny 17, etc.

Gooding, Jnr, Cuba (1968–)
American actor who made a breakthrough with his role in *Jerry Maguire*. Born in the Bronx, New York, and brought up in Los Angeles, he began in commercials. Current asking price: around $2m.
Boyz N The Hood 91. Gladiator 92. Bloodstream 93. Judgment Night 93. Lightning Jack 94. Outbreak 95. Losing Isaiah 95. The Tuskegee Airmen (TV) 95. Outbreak 95. *Jerry Maguire* (AA) 96. As Good as It Gets 97. What Dreams May Come 98. Instinct 99. Chill Factor 99. Men of Honor 00, etc.

Goodliffe, Michael (1914–1976)
British stage actor often cast as officer, professional man or diplomat.
The Small Back Room (debut) 48. The Wooden Horse 50. Rob Roy 53. The Adventures of Quentin Durward 55. The Battle of the River Plate 56. A Night To Remember 58. Sink the Bismarck 60. The Trials of Oscar Wilde 60. Jigsaw 62. The Seventh Dawn 64. The Man with the Golden Gun 73, many others.
TV series: *Sam* 73–75.

Goodman, Benny (1909–1986)
American clarinettist and bandleader, the 'King of Swing'.
Hollywood Hotel 38. Hello Beautiful 42. The Gang's All Here 44. Sweet and Lowdown 44. A Song Is Born 48, etc.
Provided the music for The Benny Goodman Story 55, in which he was portrayed by Steve Allen.

Goodman, David Zelag
American screenwriter.
Lovers and Other Strangers (AAN) 69. Monte Walsh 70. Straw Dogs 71. Man on a Swing 73. Farewell My Lovely 74. Logan's Run 76. March or Die 77. The Eyes of Laura Mars 78. Freedom Road (TV) 79. Fighting Back 82. Man, Woman and Child 83. Sheena 84, etc.

Goodman, John (1952–)
Heavyweight American actor, often in comic roles, from the stage.
Eddie Macon's Run 83. The Survivors 83. C. H. U. D. 84. Revenge of the Nerds 84. Maria's Lovers 85. Sweet Dreams 85. The Big Easy 86. True Stories 86. Burglar 87. Raising Arizona 87. Punchline 88. Everybody's All-American 88. The Wrong Guys 88. When I Fall in Love 88. Always 89. Sea of Love 89. Always 89. Arachnophobia 90. Stella 90. King Ralph 91. Barton Fink 91. The Babe 92. Born Yesterday 93. *Matinee* 93. Born Yesterday 93. We're Back! A Dinosaur's Story (voice) 93. The Flintstones 94. Kingfish (as Huey Long, TV) 95. Pie in the Sky 95. A Streetcar Named Desire (TV) 95. Mother Night 96. Fallen 97. The Borrowers 97. The Big Lebowski 98. Blues Brothers 2000 98. Rudolph the Red-Nosed Reindeer: The Movie (voice) 98. Fallen 98. Bringing Out the Dead 99. The Adventures of Rocky and Bullwinkle 00. What Planet Are You From? 00. O Brother, Where Art Thou? 00. Coyote Ugly 00. The Emperor's New Groove (voice) 00, etc.
TV series: Roseanne 88–97. Normal, Ohio 00.
❝ I'm not a major player. I just turn up and do my job. – J.G.

Goodman, Miles (1949–1996)
American composer. Died of a heart attack.
Skatetown USA 79. The Man Who Wasn't There 83. Table for Five (co-w) 83. Footloose 84. Teen Wolf 85. La Bamba (co-m) 86. Real Men 87. Like Father Like Son 87. Dirty Rotten Scoundrels 88. Vital Signs 90. Opportunity Knocks 90. Funny about Love 90. Problem Child 90. The Super 91. What about Bob? 91. He Said, She Said 91. Housesitter 92. Blankman 94. Getting Even with Dad 94. Dunston Checks In 95. Larger than Life 96, etc.

Goodrich, Frances (1891–1984)
American screenwriter, almost always in collaboration with her husband Albert HACKETT.
The Secret of Madame Blanche 33. *The Thin Man* (AAN) 34. Ah Wilderness 35. Naughty Marietta 35. After the Thin Man (AAN) 36. Another Thin Man 39. The Hitler Gang 44. Lady in the Dark 44. *It's a Wonderful Life* 46. The Pirate 48. Summer Holiday 48. Easter Parade 48. *Father of the Bride* (AAN) 50. Father's Little Dividend 51. The Long Long Trailer 54. Seven Brides for Seven Brothers (AAN) 55. The Diary of Anne Frank 60. Five Finger Exercise 62, etc.

Goodwin, Bill (1910–1958)
American character actor, usually of genial type in routine films.
Wake Island 42. So Proudly We Hail 43. Bathing Beauty 44. Spellbound 45. House of Horrors 46. *The Jolson Story* 46. Heaven Only Knows 47. Jolson Sings Again 49. Tea for Two 50. The Atomic Kid 54. The Big Heat 54. The Opposite Sex 56, etc.

Goodwin, Harold (1917–)
British character actor usually seen as cockney serviceman or small-time crook.
Dance Hall 50. The Card 52. The Cruel Sea 53. The Dam Busters 55. Sea of Sand 58. The Mummy 59. The Bulldog Breed 61. The Comedy Man 63. The Curse of the Mummy's Tomb 64. Frankenstein Must Be Destroyed 69, many others.

Goodwin, Ron (1929–)
English composer, arranger and orchestra leader. Born in Plymouth, Devon, he studied at the Guildhall School of Music.
I'm All Right Jack 59. The Trials of Oscar Wilde 60. Postman's Knock 62. Murder She Said 62. Lancelot and Guinevere 63. 633 Squadron 64. Operation Crossbow 65. Those Magnificent Men in Their Flying Machines 65. The Alphabet Murders 65. Where Eagles Dare 68. Battle of Britain 70. Frenzy 72. The Happy Prince 74. One of Our Dinosaurs Is Missing 75. Candleshoe 77. Force Ten from Navarone 78. Unidentified Flying Oddball 79. Clash of Loyalties 83. Valhalla 85, etc.

Goodwins, Leslie (1899–1969)
British-born director, in Hollywood for many years. Films mainly routine second features.
'Mexican Spitfire' series 39–44.
Glamour Boy 39. Pop Always Pays 40. Silver Skates 43. Murder in the Blue Room 44. What a Blonde 45. The Mummy's Curse 46. Gold Fever 52. Fireman Save My Child 54. Paris Follies of 1956 56.

Goolden, Richard (1895–1981)
British character actor, on stage and screen for many years, usually in henpecked or bewildered roles; created the radio character of Old Ebenezer the night watchman.
Whom the Gods Love 38. Meet Mr Penny 38. Mistaken Identity 43, etc.

Goorney, Howard (1921–)
English character actor, mainly on the stage. Born in Manchester, he left school at 14 and worked as a clerk before becoming a founder member of Theatre Workshop, later joining the National Theatre Company. He is the author of *The Theatre Workshop Story* 81.
Marriage of Convenience 60. The Evil of Frankenstein 64. The Hill 65. Bedazzled 67. Circus of Blood 67. Where's Jack? 69. Blood on Satan's Claw 70. Fiddler on the Roof (US) 71. The Offence 72. To the Devil a Daughter 76. Fanny Hill 83. Little Dorrit 87, etc.

Goorwitz, Allen
See GARFIELD, Allen.

Goosson, Stephen (1889–1973)
American art director, a former architect. In films from the early 20s, he worked for Mary Pickford and de Mille before going to Columbia in the 30s, where he became supervising art director.
Little Lord Fauntleroy 21. *The Hunchback of Notre Dame* 23. Skyscraper 28. Just Imagine (AAN) 30. American Madness 32. One Night of Love 34. It Happened One Night 34. The Black Room 35. *Lost Horizon* (AA) 37. Holiday (AAN) 38. The Little Foxes (AAN) 41. A Thousand and One Nights (AAN) 45. Gilda 46. The Lady from Shanghai 48, etc.

Gora, Claudio (1913–1998) (Emilio Giordana)
Italian actor, screenwriter and director. Born in Genoa, he was on-stage from 1937 and in films from 1939, appearing in 130 during his career, as

well as continuing his acting on stage and television. Married actress Marina Berti.

AS ACTOR: Trappola d'Amore 39. Amami, Alfredo 40. Amore Imperiale 41. Mater Dolorosa 43. Signorinette 43. Preludio d'Amore 46. La Poupée 58. Un Amore a Roma 60. Everybody Go Home! 60. A Difficult Life 61. An Easy Life 62. Gidget Goes to Rome (US) 63. Le Voci Bianche 64. Made in Italy 65. Diabolik 67. Confessions of a Police Captain 71. The Sunday Woman 75. Section Speciale 75. Amok 82. L'Amore che Non Sai 93, etc.

AS DIRECTOR: The Sky Is Red/Il Cielo e Rosso 50. *Eager to Live*/Febbre di Vivere 53. The Enchanting Enemy/L'Incantevole Nemica 53. La Grande Ombra 58. La Contessa Azzurra 60. Hate Is My God/L'Odio e il Mio Dio (& a) 69, etc.

Gorcey, Bernard (1888–1955)
American character actor and ex-vaudevillian, father of Leo Gorcey, with whom he often appeared in the Bowery Boys series.

Abie's Irish Rose 28. The Great Dictator 40. Out of the Fog 41. No Minor Vices 49. Pick-Up 51, many others.

Gorcey, Leo (1915–1969)
Pint-sized American second feature star, one of the original Dead End Kids; his screen personality was that of a tough, fast-talking, basically kindly Brooklyn layabout, and he developed this in scores of routine films, mostly under the Bowery Boys banner.

Dead End 37. Mannequin 38. Crime School 38. *Angels With Dirty Faces* 38. Hell's Kitchen 39. Angels Wash Their Faces 39. Invisible Stripes 40. Pride of the Bowery 40. Spooks Run Wild 41. Mr Wise Guy 42. Destroyer 43. Midnight Manhunt 45. Bowery Bombshell 46. Spook Busters 46. Hard Boiled Mahoney 47. Jinx Money 48. Angels in Disguise 49. Lucky Losers 50. Crazy over Horses 51. No Holds Barred 52. Loose in London 52. The Bowery Boys Meet the Monsters 54. Bowery to Bagdad 55. Crashing Las Vegas 56. The Phynx 69, many others.

Gordon, Bert (1898–1974)
American comedian. Known as The Mad Russian, he made a few films in the 40s. Born in New York City, he was on-stage from the age of 12, and made his name on radio with Eddie CANTOR.

She Gets Her Man 35. New Faces of 1937 37. Outside of Paradise 38. Sing for Your Supper 41. Laugh Your Blues Away 43. Let's Have Fun 43. Show Business 44. How Dooo You Do 45, etc.

Gordon, Bert I. (1922–)
American producer-director of small independent horror exploitation films.

The Beginning of the End 57. The Amazing Colossal Man 57. Cyclops 57. The Boy and the Pirates 60. The Magic Sword 62. Picture Mommy Dead 66. How to Succeed with Sex (wd only) 69. Necromancy (pd) 73. The Mad Bomber 75. Food of the Gods 76. Empire of the Ants 77. The Coming 81. Doing It 84. The Big Bet 86. Malediction 89. Satan's Princess 90, etc.

Gordon, Bruce (1919–)
American character actor, invariably a heavy.

Love Happy 50. The Buccaneer 58. Rider on a Dead Horse 61. Slow Run 68. Machismo 70. Piranha 78. Timerider 82, etc.

TV series: *The Untouchables* (as Frank Nitti) 59–62. Run Buddy Run 66.

Gordon, C. Henry (1882–1940)
American character actor, often seen as maniacally evil villain or Indian rajah.

Charlie Chan Carries On 31. Rasputin and the Empress 32. Mata Hari 32. Lives of a Bengal Lancer 35. *The Charge of the Light Brigade* 36. The Return of the Cisco Kid 38. Kit Carson 40. Charlie Chan at the Wax Museum 40, etc.

Gordon, Colin (1911–1972)
British light comedy actor, on stage from 1931; often seen as mildly cynical civil servant or schoolmaster.

Bond Street 47. The Winslow Boy 48. The Man in the White Suit 51. *Folly to Be Wise* 52. Escapade 55. The Safecracker 58. Please Turn Over 59. Night of the Eagle 62. The Pink Panther 63. The Family Way 66. Casino Royale 67, many others.

Gordon, Dexter (1923–1990)
Hard-blowing jazz tenor saxophonist and occasional actor. He played a musician somewhat like himself (though actually based on pianist Bud Powell) in *Round Midnight*. In *Unchained*, his music was dubbed by saxophonist Georgie Auld. Born in Los Angeles, he played with Lionel HAMPTON's band and led his own groups before moving to live in Europe in the 60s and most of the 70s, returning to the US in the late 70s. Alcoholism and heroin addiction bedevilled his career from the 50s. Died of kidney failure.

Unchained 55 (a). Round Midnight (AAN) (a, m) 86. Awakenings (a) 91.

Gordon, Gale (1905–1995) (Gaylord Aldrich)
Plump, fussy American comedy actor, best known on TV.

Here We Go Again 42. A Woman of Distinction 50. Don't Give Up the Ship 59. Visit to a Small Planet 60. Sergeant Deadhead 65. Speedway 68. The 'burbs 89, etc.

TV series: My Favorite Husband 53–54. Our Miss Brooks 52–56. The Brothers 57. Dennis the Menace 59–63. *The Lucy Show* 62–68. Life with Lucy 86.

Gordon, Gavin (1906–1970)
American general-purpose actor.

Romance (lead) 30. The Bitter Tea of General Yen 32. The Scarlet Empress 34. Bride of Frankenstein 35. Windjammer 38. Paper Bullets 41. Centennial Summer 46. Knock on Wood 54. The Bat 59, etc.

Gordon, Hal (1894–1946)
Hearty British comedy actor, often seen as good-natured foil to star comedian.

Adam's Apple 31. Happy 34. Captain Bill 36. Keep Fit 37. It's in the Air 38. Old Mother Riley, Detective 43. Give Me the Stars 45 (last appearance), etc.

Gordon, Irving (1915–1996)
American songwriter, best known for putting lyrics to the instrumental compositions of Duke ELLINGTON and for writing 'Unforgettable'. He also wrote vaudeville sketches, including ABBOTT AND COSTELLO's 'Who's on first' routine which was featured in *Buck Privates*/*Rookies*.

Gordon, Keith (1961–)
American actor, screenwriter, producer and director.

AS ACTOR: Home Movies 79. All That Jazz 79. Dressed to Kill 80. Kent State (TV) 81. Silent Rebellion 82. Single Bars, Single Women (TV) 84. Static (& co-w, p) 89. Christine 84. Legend of Billie Jean 85. Combat Academy 86. Back to School 86.

AS DIRECTOR: The Chocolate War (wd) 88. A Midnight Clear (wd) 92. Wild Palms (TV) (co-d) 93. Mother Night 96, etc.

Gordon, Lawrence (1934–)
American producer who veers between films and television (where he was the original producer of *Burke's Law*).

Dillinger 73. Hard Times 75. Rolling Thunder 77. Hooper 78. The Driver 78. The End 78. The Warriors 79. Xanadu 80. Paternity 81. 48 Hours 82. Streets of Fire 84. Brewster's Millions 85. Predator 87. Die Hard 88. Field of Dreams 89. Die Hard II 90. Predator 2 90. The Rocketeer 91, etc.

Gordon, Leo (1922–2000)
Thick-set American character actor, usually in tough-guy roles.

China Venture 53. Riot in Cell Block 11 53. Seven Angry Men 55. The Conqueror 55. The Man Who Knew Too Much 56. Cry Baby Killer (& w) 57. The Big Operator 59. The Stranger 62. The Terror (& w) 63. The Haunted Palace 64. Beau Geste 66. Tobruk (& w) 66. The St Valentine's Day Massacre 67. You Can't Win 'Em All 71. Rage 80. Bog 84. Maverick 94, etc.

TV series: Enos 81.

Gordon, Mack (1904–1959)
American lyricist.

Tin Pan Alley 40. Lillian Russell 40. Sun Valley Serenade ('Chattanooga Choo Choo') 41. Orchestra Wives ('Kalamazoo') 42. Mother Wore Tights 47. Wabash Avenue 50, etc.

Gordon, Mary (1882–1963)
Tiny Scottish character actress in Hollywood; best remembered as the perfect Mrs Hudson in many a Sherlock Holmes film.

The Home Maker 25. The Black Camel 31. The Little Minister 34. The Bride of Frankenstein 35. The Plough and the Stars 36. Kidnapped 38. The Hound of the Baskervilles 39. Tear Gas Squad 40. Appointment for Love 41. The Mummy's Tomb 42. Sherlock Holmes Faces Death 43. The Woman in Green 45. Little Giant 46. The Invisible Wall 47, many others.

Gordon, Michael (1909–1993)
American director with stage experience.

■ Boston Blackie Goes to Hollywood 42. Underground Agent 42. One Dangerous Night 43. Crime Doctor 43. *The Web* 47. Another Part of the Forest 48. An Act of Murder 48. The Lady Gambles 49. Woman in Hiding 49. Cyrano de Bergerac 50. I Can Get It for You Wholesale 51. The Secret of Convict Lake 51. Wherever She Goes 53. *Pillow Talk* 59. Portrait in Black 60. Boys' Night Out 62. For Love of Money 63. Move Over Darling 63. A Very Special Favor 65. Texas across the River 66. The Impossible Years 68. How Do I Love Thee? 70.

Gordon, Richard (1921–) (Gordon Ostlere)
British comic novelist whose accounts of hospital life were a staple of British comedy in the 50s and 60s and gave rise to the TV series *Doctor in the House* 70–73. The films were all directed by Ralph Thomas and the first established Dirk Bogarde as Britain's most popular actor.

Doctor in the House 54. Doctor at Sea 55. Doctor at Large 57. Doctor in Love 60. Doctor in Distress 63. Doctor in Clover 66. Doctor in Trouble 70.

Gordon, Ruth (1896–1985) (Ruth Gordon Jones)
Distinguished American stage actress who wrote several screenplays with her husband Garson Kanin, saw two of her own plays filmed, and had a long, sporadic career as film actress.

■ AS WRITER: Over 21 (oa/solo) 45. *A Double Life* 48. *Adam's Rib* (AAN) 49. The Marrying Kind 52. Pat and Mike (AAN) 52. The Actress (oa/solo) 53. Rosie (oa/solo) 58.

■ AS ACTRESS: Camille 15. The Wheel of Life 16. Abe Lincoln in Illinois 40. Dr Ehrlich's Magic Bullet 40. Two Faced Woman 41. Edge of Darkness 43. Action in the North Atlantic 43. Inside Daisy Clover (AAN) 66. Lord Love a Duck 66. *Rosemary's Baby* (AA) 68. Whatever Happened to Aunt Alice? 69. Where's Poppa? 70. *Harold and Maude* 72. Isn't It Shocking? (TV) 73. Panic 75. The Big Bus 76. The Great Houdinis (TV) 76. Look What Happened to Rosemary's Baby (TV) 76. Prince of Central Park (TV) 77. Boardwalk 78. Perfect Gentlemen (TV) 78. *Every Which Way but Loose* 78. My Bodyguard 80. Any Which Way You Can 80. Don't Go to Sleep (TV) 83. Jimmy the Kid 83. Maxie 85. Delta Pi 85.

Gordon, Steve (1938–1982)
American writer-director. Died of a heart attack.

The One and Only (co-p, w) 78. *Arthur* (wd) (AANw) 81.

Gordon, Stuart (1947–)
American director and screenwriter of horror films, from the theatre.

Re-Animator 85. From Beyond 86. Dolls 87. Daughter of Darkness (TV) 89. Robojox/Robot Jox 89. Honey, I Shrunk the Kids (co-w) 89. The Pit and the Pendulum 90. Chicago Cops 92. Honey, I Blew Up the Kid (p) 92. Fortress 93. Body Snatchers (co-w) 93. Castle Freak 95. The Wonderful Ice-Cream Suit 98, etc.

66 One of the great things about genre movies is that as long as you follow the rules of the genre you can do anything you want and say anything you want. There's a tremendous amount of freedom. – S.G.

Horror films are really the subconscious of the movies. – S.G.

Gore, Michael (1951–)
American composer.

Fame (AA) 80. Terms of Endearment (AAN) 83. Pretty in Pink 86. Don't Tell Her It's Me 90. The Butcher's Wife 91. Defending Your Life 91. Mr Wonderful 93, etc.

Goretta, Claude (1929–)
Swiss director.

The Invitation 73. *The Lacemaker* 77. La Provinciale/A Girl from Lorraine 80. La Mort de Mario Ricci 82. Si le Soleil ne Revenait pas 87. Le Rapport du Gendarme (TV) 87. Guillaume T – la Fouine 92, etc.

Goring, Marius (1912–1998)
British stage and screen actor adept at neurotic or fey roles.

Consider Your Verdict (debut) 36. Rembrandt 37. *The Case of the Frightened Lady* 38. *A Matter of Life and Death* 45. The Red Shoes 48. Mr Perrin and Mr Traill 49. So Little Time 52. *Ill Met by Moonlight* 57. Exodus 60. The Inspector/Lisa 62. Up From the Beach 65. Girl on a Motorcycle 68. Subterfuge 69. First Love 70. Zeppelin 71. Holocaust (TV) 78. Strike It Rich 89, etc.

TV series: The Scarlet Pimpernel 54. The Expert 68–70, 74.

Gorky, Maxim (1868–1936) (Alexei Maximovitch Peshkov)
Russian writer whose autobiography was filmed by Donskoi as *The Childhood of Maxim Gorky*, *Out in the World* and *My Universities*. Other filmed works include *The Lower Depths* (many times) and *The Mother*.

Gorman, Cliff (1936–)
American leading man of the 70s.

Justine 69. The Boys in the Band 70. Cops and Robbers 73. Rosebud 75. An Unmarried Woman 78. All That Jazz 79. Night of the Juggler 80. Angel 84. Internal Affairs 88. Murder Times Seven (TV) 90. Night and the City 92. Down Came a Blackbird (TV) 95. The 60s (TV) 99. Ghost Dog: The Way of the Samurai 99, etc.

Gorney, Karen Lynn (1945–)
American leading lady who was top-billed with Travolta in *Saturday Night Fever* 77.

The Hard Way 91. Ripe 97, etc.

Gorris, Marleen (1948–)
Dutch director and screenwriter of features with a feminist slant.

A Question of Silence/De Stilte Rond Christine M 82. Broken Mirrors/Gebrokene Spiegels 84. The Last Island 90. *Antonia's Line* (AA) 95. Mrs Dalloway 97. The Luzhin Defence (GB) 00, etc.

Gorshin, Frank (1933–)
Wiry American impressionist and character actor, popular as 'The Riddler' in TV's *Batman* series.

The True Story of Jesse James 57. Warlock 59. Studs Lonigan 60. Ring of Fire 61. The George Raft Story 61. Batman 65. Sky Heist (TV) 75. Underground Aces 81. Hot Resort 85. Hollywood Vice Squad 86. Upper Crust 88. Midnight 89. Sweet Justice 92. The Meteor Man 93. Amore! 93. Hail Caesar 94. Twelve Monkeys 95. The Big Story 95. Bloodmoon 97. Final Rinse 99, etc.

Gortner, Marjoe (1944–)
American evangelist turned actor (following a 1972 documentary on his life called *Marjoe*).

■ The Marcus Nelson Murders (TV) 73. Earthquake 74. The Gun and the Pulpit (TV) 74. Food of the Gods 76. Bobbie Joe and the Outlaw 76. Sidewinder One 77. Viva Knievel 77. Acapulco Gold 78. Starcrash 79. When You Comin' Back Red Ryder 79. Hellhole 85. American Ninja III 89. Fire, Ice and Dynamite 91. Wild Bill 95.

TV series: Falcon Crest 86–87.

Gorton, Assheton
British production designer.

The Knack ... and How to Get It 65. Blow Up 66. The Bliss of Mrs Blossom 68. The Bed Sitting Room 69. The Magic Christian 69. The Pied Piper 71. Zachariah 71. Get Carter 71. The French Lieutenant's Woman (AAN) 81. Legend 85. Revolution 85. Lost Angels 89. For the Boys 91. Rob Roy 95. 101 Dalmatians 96. 102 Dalmatians 00, etc.

Gosho, Heinosuke (1902–1981)
Japanese director and screenwriter who began as an assistant director and made his first film in 1925. He directed Japan's first talkie, *The Neighbour's Wife and Mine*, in 1931.

The Village Bride 28. Caress/Aibu 33. *Four Chimneys*/Entotsu No Mieru Basho 53. *Adolescence* 55. Yellow Crow/Kiiroi Karasu 57. The Fireflies/Hotarubi 58. When a Woman Loves/Waga Ai 60. Four Seasons of the Meiji Period/Meiji Haru Aki 68, etc.

Gossett, Lou (1936–) (aka Louis Gossett Jnr)
American character actor of striking presence.
Companions in Nightmare (TV) 68. The Landlord 70. The River Niger 72. It's Good to Be Alive (TV) 74. Sidekicks (TV) 74. Delancey Street (TV) 75. Roots (TV) 77. The Choirboys (TV) 77. The Deep (TV) 77. Little Ladies of the Night (TV) 78. To Kill a Cop (TV) 78. The Critical List (TV) 78. *The Lazarus Syndrome* (TV) (and series) 79. Backstairs at the White House (TV) 79. This Man Stands Alone (TV) 79. Don't Look Back (TV) 81. *An Officer and a Gentleman* (AA) 82. Sadat (TV) 83. Jaws 3-D 83. Finders Keepers 84. Enemy Mine 85. Iron Eagle 85. Firewalker 86. The Principal 87. Iron Eagle II 88. The Punisher 89. Cover Up 90. Toy Soldiers 91. Keeper of the City 91. Diggstown/Midnight Sting 92. Monolith 93. Blue Chips 94. Flashfire 94. Ray Alexander: A Taste for Justice (& p) (TV) 94. A Good Man in Africa 94. Curse of the Starving Class 94. Iron Eagle IV 95. Inside 96. Managua 97. In His Father's Shoes (TV) 97. Bram Stoker's The Mummy 97. The Highwayman 99, etc.
TV series: The Powers of Matthew Starr 82.

Gotell, Walter (1924–1997)
British character actor, often as Nazi or KGB menace.
Treasure of San Teresa 59. The Guns of Navarone 61. The Damned 61. Our Miss Fred 72. The Spy Who Loved Me 77. The Boys from Brazil 78. For Your Eyes Only 80. Basic Training 86. The Living Daylights 87. Puppet Master III (US) 90. Wings of Fame 90, etc.

Gottlieb, Carl (1938–)
American screenwriter, with TV comedy experience.
Jaws 75. Which Way Is Up 77. Jaws 2 78. The Jerk 79. Caveman (& d) 81. Doctor Detroit 83. Jaws 3-D 83. Amazon Women on the Moon (co-d) 87, etc.

Gottschalk, Ferdinand (1869–1944)
Bald-domed English character actor in Hollywood.
Zaza 26. Grand Hotel 32. The Sign of the Cross 32. Les Misérables 35. The Garden of Allah 36, many others.

Goudal, Jetta (1898–1985)
French leading lady of American silent films.
The Bright Shawl 24. Open All Night 24. Spanish Love 25. Road to Yesterday 25. The Coming of Amos 25. 3 Faces East 26. White Gold 27. Forbidden Woman 28. Her Cardboard Lover 28. Lady of the Pavements 30. Business and Pleasure 32, etc.

Gough, Michael (1917–)
Tall British stage (since 1936) and screen (since 1946) actor; has recently gone in for homicidal roles.
Blanche Fury (debut) 46. The Small Back Room 48. The Man in the White Suit 51. Richard III 56. Dracula 57. Horrors of the Black Museum 58. The Horse's Mouth 59. Konga 61. Black Zoo 63. Dr Terror's House of Horrors 65. Circus of Blood 67. Trog 70. The Corpse 70. The Go-Between 70. Henry VIII and His Six Wives 72. Horror Hospital 73. The Boys from Brazil 78. Suez 1956 (TV) (as Anthony Eden) 79. The Dresser 83. Memed My Hawk 83. Out of Africa 85. Let Him Have It 91. Batman Returns 92. Wittgenstein 93. The Age of Innocence 93. The Hour of the Pig 93. Nostradamus 94. Uncovered 94. Batman Forever 95. All for Love 98. The Cherry Orchard (Gr.) 98, many others.

Gould, Elliott (1938–) (Elliot Goldstein)
American actor whose very unhandsomeness made him the man for the early 70s. Formerly married to Barbra Streisand (1963–66).
The Confession 66. The Night They Raided Minsky's 68. *Bob and Carol and Ted and Alice* (AAN) 69. M*A*S*H 70. Getting Straight 70. Move 70. I Love My Wife 70. The Touch 70. Little Murders 71. The Long Goodbye 72. Busting 73. S.P.Y.S. 74. California Split 74. Who? 74. Nashville 74. Whiffs 76. I Will ... I Will ... for Now 76. Harry and Walter Go to New York 76. Mean Johnny Barrows 76. A Bridge Too Far 77. Matilda 78. The Silent Partner 78. Capricorn One 78. Escape to Athena 79. The Lady Vanishes 79. The Muppet Movie 79. Falling in Love Again 80. The Last Flight of Noah's Ark 80. Dirty Tricks 81. The Devil and Max Devlin 81. Rites of Marriage (TV) 82. The Muppets Take Manhattan 84. The Naked Face 84. Inside Out 86. I Miei Primi Quarant'Anni 87. Der Joker 87. Dangerous Love 88. The Telephone 88. The Lemon Sisters 89. Night Visitor 89. Scandalo Segreto 89. Massacre Play/Gioco al Massacro 89. Dead Men Don't Die 90. I Won't Disturb You/Tolgo il Disturbo 91. Bugsy 91. Exchange Lifeguards (Aus.) 93. The Glass Shield 94. White Man's Burden 94. A Boy Called Hate 95. Kicking and Screaming 95. Johns 96. The Feminine Touch 96. The Big Hit 98. American History X 98, etc.
TV series: E. R. 84. Together We Stand 86.
❝ Success didn't change me. I was distorted *before* I became a star. – *E.G.*

Gould, Harold (1923–)
American light character actor, a former drama teacher.
He and She 69. Where Does It Hurt? 71. Love and Death 75. Silent Movie 76. The Big Bus 76. *Washington: Behind Closed Doors* (TV) 77. The Feather and Father Gang 77. Seems Like Old Times 80. The Man in the Santa Claus Suit (TV) 80. Moviola (TV) 80. The Dream Chasers 84. The Fourth Wise Man 85. Romero 89. Killer: A Journal of Murder 95. My Giant 98, etc.
TV series: He & She 67–68. Rhoda 74–78. The Feather and Father Gang 77. Park Place 81. Foot in the Door 83. Under One Roof 85. Singer & Sons 90.

Gould, Heywood
American screenwriter and director.
Rolling Thunder (co-w) 77. The Boys from Brazil (w) 78. Fort Apache, the Bronx (w) 80. Streets of Gold (co-w) 86. Cocktail (w, oa) 88. One Good Cop (wd) 91. Trial by Jury (co-w, d) 94. Mistrial (wd) (TV) 96, etc.

Gould, Jason (1966–)
American actor, the son of Barbra Streisand and Elliott Gould.
The Big Picture 88. Listen to Me 89. The Prince of Tides 91, etc.

Gould, Morton (1913–1996)
American composer (and conductor).
Delightfully Dangerous 42. Cinerama Holiday 55. Holocaust (TV) 77.

Goulding, Alfred J. (1896–1972)
American director; active with Harold Lloyd in the 20s and later with Laurel and Hardy (*A Chump at Oxford*).

Goulding, Edmund (1891–1959)
English-born director, screenwriter, composer, playwright and novelist, in Hollywood, where he was a safe handler of female stars of the 30s and 40s. Born in London, he was on stage from 1904, emigrating to the US in 1915, where he began writing for the movies from the early 20s. In 1925, as a writer and director, he joined MGM, where he was protected from the consequences of several sexual scandals until Mayer fired him in 1936. He then worked for Warner's and Twentieth Century-Fox. He directed four of Bette DAVIS's films, but he is said to have faked a heart attack while arguing with her on the set of *Old Acquaintance* in order not to work with her again. Apart from his qualities as a director, he was noted for his ability to invent scenarios, design costumes and compose melodies, which he managed by whistling tunes to an arranger. 'Mam'selle', a ballad based on one of the themes he wrote for *The Razor's Edge*, was a hit in 1947.
■ Sun Up 25. Sally, Irene and Mary 25. Paris 26. Women Love Diamonds 26. Love 27. *The Trespasser* (& w) 29. The Devil's Holiday (& w) 30. Paramount on Parade (part) 30. Reaching for the Moon (& w) 30. The Night Angel (& w) 31. *Grand Hotel* 32. Blondie of the Follies 32. Riptide 34. The Flame Within (& wp) 35. That Certain Woman (& w) 37. White Banners 38. The Dawn Patrol 38. *Dark Victory* 39. *The Old Maid* 39. We Are Not Alone 39. Till We Meet Again 40. *The Great Lie* 41. Forever and a Day (co-d) 43. The Constant Nymph 43. *Claudia* 43. Of Human Bondage 46. *The Razor's Edge* 46. *Nightmare Alley* 47. Everybody Does It 49. Mister 880 50. We're Not Married 52. Down Among the Sheltering Palms 53. Teenage Rebel 56. Mardi Gras 58.
❝ Eddie was terribly inventive and full of ideas, but one of his peculiarities was that he could tell a story in the morning and forget everything about it by afternoon. – *Larry Weingarten*

Goulet, Robert (1933–) (Stanley Applebaum)
Canadian singer and leading man, with experience mainly on TV.
Honeymoon Hotel 63. I'd Rather Be Rich 64. Underground 70. Atlantic City USA 80. Scrooged 88. The Naked Gun $2\frac{1}{2}$: The Smell of Fear 91. Mr Wrong 96, etc.
TV series: The Blue Light 64.

Gowers, Patrick (1936–)
English composer.
The Virgin and the Gypsy 70. A Bigger Splash 75. Stevie 78. Smiley's People (TV) 82. Sorrel and Son (TV) 86. Whoops Apocalypse 86. The Hound of the Baskervilles (TV) 88, etc.

Gowland, Gibson (1872–1951)
English character actor in mainly American films.
The Promise 17. Blind Husbands 19. Ladies Must Love 21. Shifting Sands 23. *Greed* 24. The Phantom of the Opera 25. Don Juan 26. Topsy and Eva 27. Rose Marie 28. The Mysterious Island 29. The Sea Bat 30. Doomed Battalion 32. SOS Iceberg 33. The Secret of the Loch 34. The Mystery of the Marie Celeste 36. Cotton Queen 37, many others.

Goyer, David
American screenwriter. He graduated from the University of Southern California in 1988 with a degree in screenwriting.
Death Warrant 90. The Puppet Masters 94. The Crow: City of Angels 96. Ghost Rider 97. Venom 97. Dark City 97.

Gozzi, Patricia (1950–)
French juvenile actress of the 60s.
Sundays and Cybele 62. Rapture 65. Hung Up 68, etc.

Grable, Betty (1916–1973)
American leading lady who personified the peaches-and-cream appeal which was required in the 40s but which later seemed excessively bland. She performed efficiently in a series of light musicals and dramas, and was the most famous pin-up of World War II. Born in St Louis, she worked in vaudeville from childhood, encouraged by her mother, and began in films in blackface in the chorus line at the age of 13, also singing in her teens with the Ted Fio Rita orchestra. Her success began when Darryl ZANUCK signed her for Twentieth Century-Fox after Paramount had dropped her contract; she made an impact in the Broadway musical *Du Barry Was a Lady* and then replaced Alice FAYE in the film *Down Argentina Way*. By the mid-40s she was the highest-paid star in Hollywood and America's highest-paid woman, forming a successful musical partnership with Dan DAILEY. By the early 50s, Zanuck wanted to get rid of her, and she tore up her contract with the studio. In the mid-60s, she performed in theatres, returning to Broadway to replace Martha RAYE in *Hello Dolly*. Died from cancer. Married actor Jackie COOGAN (1937–40) and bandleader Harry JAMES (1943–65); she was romantically involved with bandleader Artie SHAW, singer Desi ARNAZ, and actor George RAFT.
Biography: 1982, *Betty Grable: The Reluctant Movie Queen* by Doug Warren.
■ Let's Go Places 30. New Movietone Follies of 1930 30. Whoopee 30. Kiki 31. Palmy Days 31. The Greeks had a Word for Them 32. The Kid from Spain 32. Child of Manhattan 32. Probation 32. Hold 'Em Jail 32. Cavalcade 33. What Price Innocence 33. Sweetheart of Sigma Chi 33. Melody Cruise 33. By Your Leave 34. Student Tour 34. *The Gay Divorcee* 34. The Nitwits 35. Old Man Rhythm 35. Collegiate 35. Follow the Fleet 36. Pigskin Parade 36. Don't Turn 'Em Loose 36. This Way Please 37. Thrill of a Lifetime 37. College Swing 38. Give Me a Sailor 38. Campus Confessions 38. Man About Town 39. Million Dollar Legs 39. The Day the Bookies Wept 39. *Down Argentine Way* 40. *Tin Pan Alley* 40. *Moon Over Miami* 41. A Yank in the RAF 41. *I Wake Up Screaming* 41. Footlight Serenade 42. Song of the Islands 42. Springtime in the Rockies 42. *Coney Island* 43. Sweet Rosie O'Grady 43. Four Jills in a Jeep 44. Pin Up Girl 44. Diamond Horseshoe 45. The Dolly Sisters 45. Do You Love Me (cameo) 46. The Shocking Miss Pilgrim 47. *Mother Wore Tights* 47. That Lady in Ermine 48. When My Baby Smiles at Me 48. The Beautiful Blonde from Bashful Bend 49. Wabash Avenue 50. My Blue Heaven 50. Call Me Mister 51. Meet Me After the Show 51. The Farmer Takes a Wife 53. *How To Marry A Millionaire* 53. Three for the Show 54. How to be Very Very Popular 55.
❝ There are two reasons why I'm in show business, and I'm standing on both of them. – *B.G.*
I'm strictly an enlisted man's girl. – *B.G.*
There's nothing mysterious about me. – *B.G.*
I don't think Betty would want an Oscar on her mantelpiece. She has every Tom, Dick and Harry at her feet. – *Nunnally Johnson*

Grace, Nickolas (1949–)
English character actor, mainly on stage. In films from 1974.
Sleepwalker 75. City of the Dead 78. Europe after the Rain 80. Heat and Dust 83. Salome's Last Dance 87. Just Ask for Diamond/Diamond's Edge 88. Dream Demon 88. Tom and Viv 94. Two Deaths 95. Shooting Fish 97, etc.

Grade, Lew (c. 1906–1998) (Lord Grade, born Lewis Winogradsky)
British impresario, brother of Lord Delfont, long in charge of Associated Television, latterly producing feature films for family audiences.
Autobiography: 1987, *Still Dancing*.
Biography: 1982, *My Fabulous Brothers* by Rita Grade Freeman. 1984, *The Grades* by Hunter Davies. 1987, *Last of a Kind: The Sinking of Lew Grade* by Quentin Falk and Dominic Prince.
Voyage of the Damned 76. March or Die 77. The Cassandra Crossing 77. The Boys from Brazil 78. Movie Movie 78. Firepower 79. Raise the Titanic 80. *On Golden Pond* 81. The Great Muppet Caper 81. Green Ice 81. The Legend of the Lone Ranger 81. Barbarosa 81. The Salamander 82. Sophie's Choice 82. The Dark Crystal 82, etc.
❝ All my shows are great. Some of them are bad, but they're all great. – *L.G.*
I intend to produce more feature films than any major studio in the world. I am only 68 and just beginning. By the time I am 70, British films will rule the world. – *L.G.*
It would have been cheaper to lower the Atlantic. – *L.G. on Raise the Titanic*
Lew Grade only did what everyone else did before him, which was to lose money on British films. People may not have liked the films he made. But he went out and slogged away and got money for hundreds and thousands of British actors, directors and technicians. I think the man should be applauded for that. – *Michael Winner*

Graetz, Paul (1901–1966)
Franco-Austrian independent producer.
Le Diable au Corps 46. Monsieur Ripois/Knave of Hearts 53. Is Paris Burning? 66, etc.

Graham, Heather (1970–)
American actress. Born in Milwaukee, Wisconsin, and brought up in California, she studied English at UCLA before leaving to begin her film career. She lhas been romantically linked with director Ed BURNS, actor James WOODS and director Stephen HOPKINS. Current asking price: $2m a movie.
License to Drive 87. Drugstore Cowboy 89. Shout 91. Diggstown/Midnight Sting 92. Twin Peaks: Firewalk with Me 92. Guilty as Charged 92. The Ballad of Little Jo 93. Six Degrees of Separation 93. Toughguy 94. Don't Do It 94. Desert Winds 95. Nowhere 96. Swingers 96. *Boogie Nights* 97. Two Girls and a Guy 98. Lost in Space 98. Bowfinger 98. Austin Powers: The Spy Who Shagged Me 99, etc.

Graham, Morland (1891–1949)
Stocky Scottish character actor, on stage and screen from 20s.
The Scarlet Pimpernel 34. Get Off My Foot 35. Twelve Good Men 36. Jamaica Inn 39. Old Bill and Son (as Old Bill) 41. Freedom Radio 41. The Ghost Train 41. This England 41. The Tower of Terror 41. Shipbuilders 43. Medal for the General 44. Gaiety George 46. Esther Waters 47. The Upturned Glass 47. Bonnie Prince Charlie 48. Whisky Galore 48, etc.

Graham, Ronny (1919–1999)
American comic actor and screenwriter.
New Faces (& w) 54. Dirty Little Billy 72. The World's Greatest Lover 77. To Be or Not to Be (co-w) 83. Finders Keepers 84. The Ratings Game (TV) 84. Spaceballs 87. The Substance of Fire 96, etc.

Graham, Sheilah (1904–1988) (Lilly Shiel)
British gossip columnist in America, companion of F. Scott Fitzgerald. Author of *Beloved Infidel*, *The Garden of Allah*, etc.
Biography: 1995, *Intimate Lies–F. Scott Fitzgerald and Sheilah Graham: Her Son's Story* by Robert Westbrook.
❝ One of her most striking qualities is honesty. She has never been a very exciting gossip columnist on account of her honesty and her freedom from malice. – *Edmund Wilson*

Graham, William (c. 1930–)
American director, from TV. (Sometimes billed as William A. Graham.)
The Doomsday Flight (TV) 66. Waterhole 3 67. Then Came Bronson (TV) 68. Submarine X1 68. Change of Habit 69. Thief (TV) 71. *Birds of Prey* (TV) 73. Get Christie Love (TV) 74. Trapped Beneath the Sea (TV) 74. 21 Hours at Munich (TV) 76. *Minstrel Man* (TV) 77. *The Amazing Howard Hughes* (TV) 77. Contract on Cherry Street (TV) 77. And I Alone Survived (TV) 78. Transplant (TV) 79. Guyana Tragedy (TV) 81. Harry Tracy 81. Mothers Against Drunk Drivers (TV) 82. Mussolini: The Untold Story (TV) 85. The Last Days of Frank and Jesse James (TV) 86. Proud Men 87. Street of Dreams 88. Return to the Blue Lagoon 91, etc.

Grahame, Gloria (1924–1981) (Gloria Hallward)
Blonde American leading lady, usually in off-beat roles.
■ Blonde Fever (debut) 44. Without Love 45. It's a Wonderful Life 46. It Happened in Brooklyn 47. Merton of the Movies 47. Song of the Thin Man 47. *Crossfire* (AAN) 47. Roughshod 48. A Woman's Secret 48. *In a Lonely Place* 50. *The Bad and the Beautiful* (AA) 52. Macao 52. Sudden Fear 52. The Glass Wall 53. Man on a Tightrope 53. Prisoners of the Casbah 53. The Greatest Show on Earth 53. Naked Alibi 54. *The Big Heat* 54. The Good Die Young (GB) 54. Human Desire 55. The Man Who Never Was (GB) 55. Not as a Stranger 55. The Cobweb 55. Oklahoma 56. Ride Out for Revenge 57. Odds Against Tomorrow 59. Ride Beyond Vengeance 66. The Todd Killings 70. Black Noon (TV) 71. Chandler 72. The Loners 72. Blood and Lace 72. Tarot 73. Mama's Dirty Girls 74. The Girl on the Late Late Show (TV) 75. Rich Man Poor Man (TV) 76. Mansion of the Doomed 76. Seventh Avenue (TV) 77. Head Over Heels 79. Melvin and Howard 80. A Nightingale Sang in Berkeley Square 80.

Grahame, Margot (1911–1982)
British leading lady of the 30s, with stage experience.
The Love Habit 30. Rookery Nook 30. Sorrell and Son 34. The Informer (US) 35. The Three Musketeers (US) 36. Michael Strogoff (US) 37. The Shipbuilders 44. Broken Journey 48. The Romantic Age 49. Venetian Bird 52. Orders Are Orders 55. Saint Joan 57, etc.

Grainer, Ron (1922–1981)
Australian composer in Britain.
A Kind of Loving 62. Nothing But the Best 64. To Sir with Love 67. Lock Up Your Daughters 68. In Search of Oregon 70. The Omega Man 71. Yellow Dog 73. I Don't Want to Be Born 75, many others.

Grainger, Edmund (1906–1981)
American producer and executive, long with RKO. Specialized in quality action pictures.
Diamond Jim 35. Sutter's Gold 36. International Squadron 41. Wake of the Red Witch 48. Sands of Iwo Jima 49. Flying Leathernecks 50. One Minute to Zero 52. Treasure of Pancho Villa 55. Green Mansions 59. Home from the Hill 60. Cimarron 61, many others.

Grammer, Kelsey (1955–)
American actor, best known for his role as Dr Frasier Crane in the 80s and 90s TV sitcoms *Cheers* and *Frasier*. He was reportedly earning $400,000 an episode for Frazier in 1999. Married his third wife, model Camille Donatucci, in 1997.
Autobiography: 1995, *So Far*.
Biography: 1995, *Kelsey Grammer* by Jeff Rovin.
Beyond Suspicion 93. Down Periscope 96. Anastasia (voice) 97. The Pentagon Wars (TV) 98. The Real Howard Spitz 98. Toy Story 2 (voice) 99. Animal Farm (voice, TV) 99, etc.
TV series: Cheers 82–93. Frasier 94–.

❝ I will always be foolhardy because, to me, the best fruit of life is the idea that you don't always play it safe. If you don't reach beyond where you're comfortable, you will not grow. – K.G.

Granach, Alexander (1890–1945)
Polish character actor who went to Hollywood in the late 30s.
Biography: 1945, *There Goes an Actor*.
Warning Shadows 23. Kameradschaft 31. *Ninotchka* 39. Hangmen Also Die 43. For Whom the Bell Tolls 43. The Hitler Gang 44. A Voice in the Wind 44. The Seventh Cross 44, etc.

Granger, Dorothy (1912–1995)
American actress, a foil to Laurel and Hardy, Charley Chase, and W. C. Fields, and Leon Errol's wife in a series of comedy shorts.
Hog Wild 30. The Laurel-Hardy Murder Case 30. One Good Turn 31. The Dentist 32. Crime Rave 39. When the Daltons Rode 40. Twin Husbands 46. Killer Dill 47. New York Confidential 55. Raintree Country 57, etc.

Granger, Farley (1925–)
American leading man who began his film career straight from school.
North Star (debut) 43. They Live By Night 47. *Rope* 48. *Strangers on a Train* 51. Hans Christian Andersen 52. Senso (It.) 53. The Girl in the Red Velvet Swing 55. Rogues' Gallery 68. Something Creeping in the Dark (It.) 71. The Serpent 72. Confessions of a Sex Maniac (It.) 72. They Call Me Trinity (It.) 72. The Man Called Noon 73. Arnold 75. Black Beauty (TV) 78. The Imagemaker 85. The Whoopee Boys 86, etc.

Granger, Stewart (1913–1993) (James Lablanche Stewart)
Darkly handsome English-born leading actor who gained fame in romantic melodramas of the 40s. Born in London, he studied acting at the Webber-Douglas School and started his career on the stage, beginning in films as an extra. He went to Hollywood, under contract to MGM, in 1950, and appeared in a series of swashbuckling roles. As his appeal declined, he returned to make films in Europe. He became an American citizen in 1956. The first two of his three wives were actresses Elspeth March (1938–48) and Jean SIMMONS (1950–60).
Autobiography: 1981, *Sparks Fly Upward*.
■ A Southern Maid 33. Give Her a Ring 34. So This Is London 38. Convoy 40. Secret Mission 42. Thursday's Child 43. *The Man in Grey* 43. The Lamp Still Burns 43. Fanny by Gaslight 43. *Waterloo Road* 44. *Love Story* 44. Madonna of the Seven Moons 44. *Caesar and Cleopatra* 45. Caravan 46. The Magic Bow (as Paganini) 46. *Captain Boycott* 47. Blanche Fury 48. Saraband for Dead Lovers (as Koenigsmark) 48. Woman Hater 49. Adam and Evelyne 49. *King Solomon's Mines* (US) 50. The Light Touch (US) 51. Soldiers Three 51. The Wild North 52. *Scaramouche* (US) 52. The Prisoner of Zenda (US) 52. Young Bess (US) 53. Salome (US) 53. All the Brothers Were Valiant (US) 54. *Beau Brummell* (US) 54. Green Fire (US) 55. Moonfleet (US) 55. Footsteps in the Fog 55. Bhowani Junction 56. The Last Hunt (US) 56. Gun Glory 57. The Little Hut 57. The Whole Truth 58. Harry Black and the Tiger 58. North to Alaska (US) 60. The Secret Partner 61. Sodom and Gomorrah 62. Swordsman of Siena (It.) 62. The Legion's Last Patrol (It.) 63. Among Vultures (Ger.) 64. The Secret Invasion 64. The Crooked Road 65. Der Oelprinz (Ger.) 65. Mission Hong Kong 65. Requiem for a Secret Agent 66. Glory City 66. Where Are You Taking that Woman? 66. The Trygon Factor 67. The Last Safari 67. The Flaming Frontier 68. The Hound of the Baskervilles (TV) (as Holmes) 71. The Wild Geese 77. The Royal Romance of Charles & Diana (TV) 82. Hell Hunters 88.
TV series: The Men from Shiloh 70.
❝ I've never done a film I'm proud of. – S.G.
The cinema world is not easy. It is full of envy from little people – heads of studios, for example, who hate people for their attractiveness. – S.G.
I was a good costume actor, but I shortened my career because I made the wrong choices. – S.G.

Grangier, Gilles (1911–1996)
French director. Born in Paris, he began as an extra and a stuntman, becoming an assistant director and emerging in the 50s as a commercially successful director, particularly with films starring Jean GABIN. He later worked in television.
Ademai Bandit d'Honneur 43. L'Aventure de Cabassou 46. L'Amant de Paille 51. L'Amour Madame 52. Gas-Oil 55. Le Sang à la Tête 56. Speaking of Murder/Le Rouge est Mis 57. Le Désordre et la Nuit 58. *The Magnificent Tramp*/Archmide le Clochard 59. The Old Guard/Les Vieux de la Ville 60. The Counterfeiters/Le Cave Se Rebiffe 61. *The Awkward Age*/L'Age Ingrat 61. Le Gentleman d'Epsom 62. La Cuisine au Beurre 63. Maigret Viot Rouge 63. Les Bons Vivants (co-d) 66. L'Homme à la Buick 67. Sous le Signe du Taureau 69. Un Cave 72. Le Locataire d'en Haut (TV) 84, etc.

Grant, Arthur (1915–1972)
British cinematographer.
Hell Is a City 60. Jigsaw 62. Eighty Thousand Suspects 63. The Tomb of Ligeia 64. Blood from the Mummy's Tomb 71, etc.

Grant, Cary (1904–1986) (Archibald Leach)
Debonair British-born leading man with a personality and accent all his own; varied theatrical experience before settling in Hollywood. Married five times, including to actresses Virginia CHERRILL (1934–35), Betsy DRAKE (1949–62) and Dyan CANNON (1965–68).
Biography: 1989, *Cary Grant: The Lonely Heart* by Charles Higham and Roy Moseley. 1991, *Evenings with Cary Grant* by Nancy Nelson. 1997, *Cary Grant: A Class Apart* by Graham McCann.
■ This Is the Night 32. Sinners in the Sun 32. Hot Saturday 32. Merrily We Go to Hell 32. The Devil and the Deep 32. Madame Butterfly 33. Blonde Venus 33. *She Done Him Wrong* 33. Alice in Wonderland (as the Mock Turtle) 33. The Eagle and the Hawk 33. Woman Accused 33. Gambling Ship 33. I'm No Angel 33. Thirty Day Princess 34. Born To Be Bad 34. Kiss and Make Up 34. Enter Madame 34. Ladies Should Listen 34. Wings in the Dark 35. The Last Outpost 35. Sylvia Scarlett 35. Big Brown Eyes 35. Suzy 36. Wedding Present 36. The Amazing Quest of Mr Ernest Bliss (GB) 36. When You're in Love 36. *The Awful Truth* 37. The Toast of New York 37. *Topper* 37. *Bringing Up Baby* 38. Holiday 38. *Gunga Din* 39. Only Angels Have Wings 39. In Name Only 39. *My Favorite Wife* 40. The Howards of Virginia 40. *His Girl Friday* 40. *The Philadelphia Story* 40. Penny Serenade (AAN) 41. Suspicion 41. Talk of the Town 42. Once upon a Honeymoon 42. Destination Tokyo 43. Mr Lucky 43. Once upon a Time 44. None But the Lonely Heart (AAN) 44. *Arsenic and Old Lace* 44. Night and Day (as Cole Porter) 45. Notorious 46. *The Bachelor and the Bobbysoxer* 47. The Bishop's Wife (as an angel) 48. Every Girl Should Be Married 48. *Mr Blandings Builds His Dream House* 48. I Was a Male War Bride 49. Crisis 50. People Will Talk 51. Room for One More 52. Monkey Business 52. Dream Wife 53. To Catch a Thief 55. The Pride and the Passion 57. *An Affair to Remember* 57. Kiss Them for Me 57. *Indiscreet* (GB) 58. Houseboat 58. *North by Northwest* 59. Operation Petticoat 59. The Grass Is Greener 60. That Touch of Mink 62. Charade 63. Father Goose 64. Walk Don't Run 66.
✪ For being the world's most admired sophisticated man for twenty-five years. *Mr Blandings Builds His Dream House*.
❝ When a journalist wired his agent 'How old Cary Grant?', Grant himself replied: 'Old Cary Grant fine. How you?',
Everyone tells me I've had such an interesting life, but sometimes I think it's been nothing but stomach disturbances and self-concern. – C.G.
I improve on misquotation. – C.G.
I think making love is the best form of exercise. – C.G.
I'd like to have made one of those big splashy Technicolor musicals with Rita Hayworth. – C.G.
Everyone wants to be Cary Grant, even I want to be Cary Grant. – C.G.
The drama in a Cary Grant movie is always seeing whether the star can be made to lose his wry, elegant and habitual aplomb. – *Richard Schickel*
A completely private person, totally reserved, and there is no way into him. – *Doris Day*
Cary's enthusiasm made him search for perfection in all things, particularly the three that meant most to him – film-making, physical fitness and women. – *David Niven*

Grant, Hugh (1960–)
Diffident-seeming English leading actor, often in foppish roles. Born in London and educated at Oxford University, he became a star with *Four Weddings and a Funeral*, and through his high-profile romance with actress Elizabeth HURLEY, who is also his partner in a production company. (Public interest in the couple was so strong that, in 1996, the mattress from their holiday home fetched £550 at auction.) In 1995, his career was threatened when he was arrested for committing a lewd act in a car on Sunset Boulevard with Divine Brown, a prostitute who subsequently appeared in a direct-to-video movie, *Taken for Granted*, featuring a Hugh Grant lookalike.
Biography: 1996, *Hugh Grant* by Jody Tresidder.
Maurice 87. White Mischief 87. The Dawning 88. The Lair of the White Worm 88. La Nuit Bengali 88. Impromptu 89. The Big Man 90. Bitter Moon 92. Night Train to Munich 92. The Remains of the Day 93. *Four Weddings and a Funeral* 94. *Sirens* 94. An Awfully Big Adventure 95. The Englishman Who Went up a Hill but Came Down a Mountain 95. Nine Months 95. Sense and Sensibility 95. Restoration 96. Extreme Measures 96. Notting Hill 99. Mickey Blue Eyes 99. Small Time Crooks 00, etc.
❝ He is a very bright man. He will not suffer fools gladly. – *Mike Newell*
He's found something that's gone from the movies: the intelligent comic leading man. – *Duncan Kenworthy*
From my personal experience, I think he is a self-important, boring, flash-in-the-pan Brit. – *Robert Downey Jnr*
The roles play into a certain fantasy of what people want English people to be, whereas half the time, as you know, we're vomiting beer and beating people up. I know I am. – H.G.
I never feel romantic in England. There's something in the air that switches off my libido. – H.G.

Grant, James Edward (1902–1966)
American writer.
Whipsaw 35. We're Going to Be Rich 38. Belle of the Yukon 44. The Great John L. 45. Angel and the Bad Man (& d) 46. Sands of Iwo Jima 49. Big Jim McLain 52. Hondo 54. Ring of Fear (co-w, d) 54. The Sheepman (AAN) 58. The Alamo 60. McLintock 63, etc.

Grant, Jennifer (1966?–)
American actress, the daughter of Cary GRANT and Dyan CANNON, from television.
The Evening Star 96, etc.

Grant, Kathryn (1933–) (Olive Grandstaff)
American leading lady who retired to marry Bing Crosby.
Arrowhead 53. Living it Up 54. The Phenix City Story 55. Mister Cory 56. Gunman's Walk 58. Operation Mad Ball 58. The Seventh Voyage of Sinbad 58. The Big Circus 60, etc.

Grant, Kirby (1914–1985) (K. G. Horn)
Dutch-Scottish-American leading man, former bandleader.
Red River Range 39. Ghost Catchers 44. The Lawless Breed 47. Trail of the Yukon 50. Snow Dog 51. Yukon Gold 52. The Court Martial of Billy Mitchell 55. Yukon Vengeance 55, etc.
TV series: Sky King 53–54.

Grant, Lawrence (1870–1952)
British character actor in American films.
The Great Impersonation 21. His Hour 24. The Grand Duchess and the Waiter 26. Doomsday 28. The Canary Murder Case 29. *Bulldog Drummond* 29. The Cat Creeps 30. Daughter of the Dragon 31. The Unholy Garden 31. Jewel Robbery 32. The Mask of Fu Manchu 32. Grand Hotel 32. Shanghai Express 32. Queen Christina 33. By Candlelight 34. Nana 34. Werewolf of London 34. The Devil is a Woman 35. Little Lord Fauntleroy 36. The Prisoner of Zenda 37. Bluebeard's Eighth Wife 38. Son of Frankenstein 39. Women in War 40. Dr Jekyll and Mr Hyde 41. Confidential Agent 45, many others.

Grant, Lee (1927–) (Lyova Rosenthal)
Dynamic American stage actress, sporadically seen in films. She turned to directing in the 80s. She is the mother of Dinah Manoff.
AS DIRECTOR: Tell Me a Riddle 80. A Matter of Sex (TV) 84. Nobody's Child (TV) 86. Staying Together 89. Women on Trial (TV) 92, etc.

■ AS ACTRESS: *Detective Story* (AAN) 51. Storm Fear 55. Middle of the Night 59. The Balcony 63. An Affair of the Skin 63. Terror in the City 66. Divorce American Style 67. In the Heat of the Night 67. Valley of the Dolls 67. Buona Sera Mrs Campbell 68. The Big Bounce 69. Perilous Voyage (TV) 69. Marooned 69. There Was a Crooked Man 70. *The Landlord* (AAN) 70. Night Slaves (TV) 70. Plaza Suite 71. *The Neon Ceiling* (TV) 71. Ransom for a Dead Man (TV) 71. Lt Schuster's Wife (TV) 72. Portnoy's Complaint 72. Partners in Crime (TV) 73. What Are Best Friends For (TV) 73. The Internecine Project 74. *Shampoo* (AA) 75. Voyage of the Damned (AAN) 76. Airport 77 77. The Spell (TV) 77. The Mafu Cage 77. The Swarm 78. Damien: Omen II 78. Backstairs at the White House (TV) 79. When You Comin' Back Red Ryder 79. You Can't Go Home Again (TV) 79. Tell Me a Riddle (d only) 80. Little Miss Marker 80. Charlie Chan and the Curse of the Dragon Queen 81. Visiting Hours 82. Will There Really Be a Morning? (TV) 83. Teachers 84. The Big Town 87. Calling the Shots 88. Staying Together (d) 89. Defending Your Life 91. Citizen Cohn (TV) 92. It's My Party 95. The Substance of Fire 96.

Grant, Richard E. (1957–) (Richard Grant Esterhuysen)
Lanky British leading actor and novelist. Born in Mbabane, Swaziland, he studied English and drama at the University of Cape Town, moving to London in the early 80s.
Autobiography: 1996, *With Nails – The Film Diaries of Richard E. Grant.*
Honest, Decent and True 85. Withnail and I 87. Hidden City 88. Warlock 88. How to Get Ahead in Advertising 88. Killing Dad 89. Mountains of the Moon 89. Henry and June 90. Hudson Hawk 91. L.A. Story 91. The Player 92. Bram Stoker's Dracula 92. Suddenly Last Summer (TV) 93. The Age of Innocence 93. Prêt-à-Porter/Ready to Wear 94. The Cold Light of Day 95. Jack and Sarah 95. Karaoke (TV) 96. A Royal Scandal (TV) 96. The Portrait of a Lady 96. Twelfth Night 96. The Serpent's Kiss 97. Food of Love 97. Spice World: The Movie 97. Keep the Aspidistra Flying 97. All for Love 98. Cash in Hand 98. The Match 99. Trial and Retribution (TV) 99. A Christmas Carol (TV) 99. The Miracle Maker (voice) 99. The Little Vampire 00, etc.
TV series: Scarlet Pimpernel 98-00.
❝ I defy anyone not to have their head turned by megastardom because it is a completely abnormal existence. You live a life of extreme fantasy: you're wonderful, you're paid millions, everyone thinks you're beautiful, brilliant, everyone's gagging to hear your every word, capture your every expression, and then the next day you learn you're ugly, you speak all wrong, you're not talented after all, your last three movies were shit, and you're gone. It's so fast and ruthless. – *R.E.G.*

Granville, Bonita (1923–1988)
American child actress of the 30s; adult career gradually petered out but she became a producer.
Westward Passage 32. Cradle Song 33. Ah Wilderness 35. *These Three* (AAN) 36. Maid of Salem 37. Call It a Day 37. Merrily We Live 38. Nancy Drew Detective (and subsequent series) 38. Angels Wash Their Faces 39. Escape 40. H.M. Pulham Esq. 41. The Glass Key 42. Now Voyager 42. *Hitler's Children* 43. Youth Runs Wild 44. Love Laughs at Andy Hardy 46. The Guilty 47. Treason 50. The Lone Ranger 56. Lassie's Greatest Adventure (p) 63, etc.
TV series: Lassie (p) 55–67.

Grapewin, Charley (1869–1956)
American character actor best remembered in movies for his range of grizzled old gentlemen.
Only Saps Work 30. The Night of June 13th 32. Heroes for Sale 33. Judge Priest 34. Ah Wilderness 35. Alice Adams 35. Libelled Lady 36. The Good Earth 37. Captains Courageous 37. Big City 37. Three Comrades 38. The Wizard of Oz 39. *The Grapes of Wrath* 40. Ellery Queen Master Detective 40. *Tobacco Road* (as Jeeter Lester) 41. They Died with Their Boots On 41. Crash Dive 42. The Impatient Years 44. Gunfighters 47. Sand 49. When I Grow Up 51, many others.

Grauman, Sid (1879–1950)
Flamboyant American showman and movie exhibitor. His family ran tent shows and movie houses in San Francisco, and he managed cinemas in various parts of the United States before opening in Los Angeles the Million Dollar Theater, the 3,600-seater Metropolitan, the Egyptian and, most famously, the Chinese Theater on Hollywood Boulevard in 1927. A notorious practical joker, he once gave a slight heart attack to director Ernst LUBITSCH, who was frightened of flying, by having two stuntmen dressed as pilots run down the aisle and parachute from the plane on which Lubitsch was travelling. He was given a special Oscar in 1948 for raising the standard of exhibition of motion pictures.

Grauman, Walter (1922–)
American director, from TV.
Lady in a Cage 63. 633 Squadron 64. A Rage to Live 65. I Deal in Danger 66. The Last Escape 69. Force Five (TV) 75. Most Wanted (TV) 76. Are You in the House Alone? (TV) 78. Pleasure Palace (TV) 80. Scene of the Crime (TV) 85. Shakedown on the Sunset Strip (TV) 88. Nightmare on the 13th Floor (TV) 90, etc.
TV series: The Untouchables, Naked City, Route 66, The Felony Squad, etc.

Graves, George (1876–1949)
English comic actor, in films of the 30s as an elderly bumbler. Born in London, he made his stage debut in 1896 and thereafter alternated between dramas, operetta, pantomime (often as a dame) and music hall.
Autobiography: 1931, *Gaieties and Gravities.*
The Crooked Lady 32. A Sister to Assist 'er 33. Those Were the Days 34. Royal Cavalcade 35. Wolf's Clothing 36. The Robber Symphony 36. A Star Fell from Heaven 36, etc.
❝ Nor must George Graves' dressing room be overlooked. Visitors going there found themselves in a sort of crazy chamber. Chairs collapsed when sat upon, cigarettes thrust upon them exploded, pencils refused to write and turned on those wielding them, coat hangers proffered for their coats shut up and threw the garments on the ground, and when the thoroughly startled visitor was offered a drink, he found the liquor pouring all over his waistcoat from cleverly concealed small holes in the chasing on the glass. Royal personages came, saw, even suffered, and laughed good naturedly. – *W. J. Macqueen-Pope, Theatre Royal, Drury Lane*

Graves, Peter (1911–1994)
British light leading man, tall and suave, usually in musical comedy.
Kipps (debut) 41. King Arthur Was a Gentleman 42. Bees in Paradise 44. I'll Be Your Sweetheart 44. Waltz Time 45. The Laughing Lady 46. Spring Song 47. Mrs Fitzherbert (as the Prince Regent) 47. Spring in Park Lane 48. Maytime in Mayfair 49. Derby Day 52. Lilacs in the Spring 54, etc. Latterly in cameo roles, e.g. The Wrong Box 66, The Slipper and the Rose 76.

Graves, Peter (1926–) (Peter Aurness)
American leading man, usually in 'B' action pictures: brother of James Arness.
Rogue River (debut) 50. Fort Defiance 52. Red Planet Mars 52. Stalag 17 53. Beneath the Twelve-Mile Reef 53. Black Tuesday 55. It Conquered the World 56. Wolf Larsen 59. A Rage to Live 65. The Ballad of Josie 67. The Five Man Army 68. Call to Danger (TV) 73. The President's Plane Is Missing (TV) 73. Scream of the Wolf (TV) 74. The Underground Man (TV) 74. Where Have All the People Gone (TV) 74. Dead Man on the Run (TV) 75. Disaster in the Sky (TV) 77. The Rebels (TV) 79. Airplane 80. Death Car on the Freeway (TV) 80. The Memory of Eva Ryker (TV) 81. Airplane 2: the Sequel 82. Savannah Smiles 82. The Winds of War (TV) 83. Number One with a Bullet 87, etc.
TV series: Fury 55–59. Whiplash 60. Court Martial/Counsellors at War 66. Mission Impossible 66–72.

Graves, Ralph (1901–1977)
American silent star of heroic roles. Later became writer and producer of minor films.
Talkies include: Submarine 28. Dirigible 30. Ladies of Leisure 30.

Graves, Rupert (1963–)
British actor usually in upper-class roles.
A Room with a View 85. Maurice 87. A Handful of Dust 88. The Children 90. Where Angels Fear to Tread 91. Damage 92. The Madness of King George 94. The Innocent Sleep 95. Intimate Relations 95. Different for Girls 96. The Tenant of Wildfell Hall (TV) 96. Mrs Dalloway 97. The Revenger's Comedies 97. Dreaming of Joseph Lees 99. Room to Rent 00. Take a Girl Like You (TV) 00, etc.

Graves, Teresa (1944–)
American leading lady.
Black Eye 73. That Man Bolt 73. Vampira 74.
TV series: Rowan and Martin's Laugh-In 69–70. Get Christie Love 74–75.

Gravey, Fernand (1904–1970) (Fernand Martens)
Debonair French leading man with some Hollywood experience.
Bitter Sweet 33. The Great Waltz 38. Fools for Scandal 38. Le Dernier Tournant 38. La Ronde 50. Short Head 53. How to Steal a Million 66. The Madwoman of Chaillot 69, etc.

Gray, Allan (1904– *)
Polish-born composer in Britain.
Emil and the Detectives (Ger.) 36. The Life and Death of Colonel Blimp 43. *A Matter of Life and Death* 45. Mr Perrin and Mr Traill 48. *The African Queen* 51. The Planter's Wife 52. Destination Milan 54. The Big Hunt 58, etc.

Gray, Billy (1938–)
American juvenile actor of the 50s, latterly working as a motorcycle racer.
Specter of the Rose 46. Fighting Father Dunne 49. *On Moonlight Bay* 52. The Day the Earth Stood Still 52. The Seven Little Foys 55. Two for the Seesaw 62. Werewolves on Wheels 71, etc.
TV series: Father Knows Best 54–60.

Gray, Carole (1940–)
South African leading lady in British films of the 60s.
The Young Ones 61. Curse of the Fly 64. Rattle of a Simple Man 64. Island of Terror 66, etc.

Gray, Charles (1928–2000) (Donald M. Gray)
British stage and TV actor usually seen in smooth, unsympathetic roles.
The Entertainer 60. The Man in the Moon 61. Masquerade 65. The Night of the Generals 66. The Secret War of Harry Frigg (US) 67. *The Devil Rides Out* 68. The File of the Golden Goose 69. Cromwell 69. *Diamonds Are Forever* 71. The Beast Must Die 74. Seven Nights in Japan 76. The Seven Per Cent Solution (as Mycroft Holmes) 76. Silver Bears 77. The Legacy 78. The Mirror Crack'd 80. The Jigsaw Man 84. An Englishman Abroad (TV) 84. Dreams Lost, Dreams Found (TV) 87. The Tichborne Claimant 98, etc.

Gray, Coleen (1922–) (Doris Jensen)
American leading lady of the 40s.
Kiss of Death 47. Nightmare Alley 47. Fury at Furnace Creek 48. *Red River* 48. Sand 49. Riding High 50. The Sleeping City 51. Kansas City Confidential 52. Sabre Jet 53. Arrow in the Dust 54. The Killing 56. Hell's Five Hours 57. The Leech Woman 60. Town Tamer 65. PJ 68. The Late Liz 71. Cry from the Mountain 86, etc.
TV series: Window on Main Street 61.

Gray, David Barry
American actor.
Blind Faith (TV) 90. Mr Wonderful 92. Cops and Robbersons 94. SFW 94. Soldier Boyz 95. Dead Presidents 95. John Grisham's The Client (TV) 95. Lawn Dogs 97, etc.
TV series: Dream Street 89.

Gray, Dolores (1924–)
Statuesque American singer-dancer, on stage in musical comedy (played *Annie Get Your Gun* in London).
■ It's Always Fair Weather 54. Kismet 55. The Opposite Sex 56. Designing Woman 57.

Gray, Donald (1914–1978) (Eldred Tidbury)
One-armed British leading man, former radio actor and announcer; best known as TV's Mark Saber.
Strange Experiment 37. The Four Feathers 39. Idol of Paris 48. Saturday Island/Island of Desire 52. Timeslip 55. Satellite in the Sky 56, etc.

Gray, Dulcie (1919–) (Dulcie Bailey)
Gentle-mannered British leading lady, married to Michael Denison.
A Place of One's Own 44. They Were Sisters 45. Mine Own Executioner 47. The Glass Mountain 48. Angels One Five 51. A Man Could Get Killed 65, etc.

Gray, Eddie (1898–1969) (Edward Earl Gray)
English comedian, eccentric juggler and conjuror, usually billed in theatres as 'Monsewer' Eddie Gray, because of the fractured French of his comic patter. Born in London, he was a performer from the age of nine and, later, was a frequent member of The CRAZY GANG. *European Nights* preserves part of his juggling act.
First a Girl 35. Skylarks 36. Keep Smiling 38. Don Chicago 45. Life Is a Circus 58. European Nights (It.) 59, etc.
❝ Je suis now is goin' to parlez Francais, and moi's goin' to do quelque-chose for vous that you 'ave never seen on any stage. As a matter of fact I goin' to take this 'ere pack of cards, and I'm goin' to ask Madame, or Mainsewer, to extract un card. Not deux. But un. – *E.G., on stage*

Gray, F. Gary (1969–)
American director, from music videos.
Friday 95. Set It Off 96. The Negotiator 98, etc.

Gray, Gary (1936–)
American boy actor of the 40s.
A Woman's Face 41. Address Unknown 44. The Great Lover 47. Rachel and the Stranger 48. Father Is a Bachelor 49. The Next Voice You Hear 50. The Painted Hills 51. The Party Crashers 58, many others.

Gray, Gilda (1901–1959) (Marianna Michalska)
Polish dancer who went to America and is credited with inventing the shimmy.
Aloma of the South Seas 26. The Devil Dancer 28. Rose Marie 36, etc.

Gray, Nadia (1923–1994) (Nadia Kujnir-Herescu)
Russian-Rumanian leading lady, in European and British films.
The Spider and the Fly 49. Night Without Stars 51. Valley of Eagles 51. Neapolitan Fantasy 54. Folies Bergères 56. The Captain's Table 58. Parisienne 59. La Dolce Vita 59. Maniac 63. Two for the Road 67. The Naked Runner 67, etc.

Gray, Sally (1916–) (Constance Stevens)
Popular British screen heroine of the 30s and 40s, with stage experience from 1925.
School for Scandal 30. Radio Pirates 35. Cheer Up! 36. The Saint in London 38. The Lambeth Walk 38. Dangerous Moonlight 40. Carnival 46. *Green for Danger* 46. They Made Me a Fugitive 47. The Mark of Cain 48. Silent Dust 49. Obsession 49. Escape Route 52, etc.

Gray, Simon (1936–)
British dramatist, novelist and screenwriter. He is also a university lecturer in English.
Butley 74. A Month in the Country 87. Common Pursuit (TV) 91. Running Late (TV) 93. Femme Fatale (TV) 93, etc.

Gray, Spalding (1941–)
American character actor and writer who turned a small part in *The Killing Fields* into a witty one-man show, *Swimming to Cambodia*, filmed by Jonathan Demme.
Heavy Petting 83. The Killing Fields 84. True Stories 86. Hard Choices 86. Swimming to Cambodia (&w) 87. Beaches 88. Clara's Heart 88. Stars and Bars 88. Monster in a Box (&w) 91. Straight Talk 92. Twenty Bucks 93. The Pickle 93. King of the Hill 93. The Paper 94. Bad Company 95. Beyond Rangoon 95. Drunks 95. Diabolique 96. Gray's Anatomy (& w) 97. Bliss 97. Coming Soon 99, etc.

Graysmark, John
British production designer.
Young Winston (AAN) 72. The Big Sleep 78. Flash Gordon 80. Ragtime (AAN) 81. The Lords of Discipline 83. The Bounty 84. Duet for One 87. Superman IV: The Quest for Peace 87. Gorillas in the Mist 88. White Hunter, Black Heart 90. Robin Hood: Prince of Thieves 91. White Sands 92. So I Married an Axe Murderer 93. Blown Away 94. Courage under Fire 96, etc.

Grayson, Godfrey
British second-feature director, especially for the Danzigers.
Room to Let 50. To Have and to Hold 51. The Fake 53. Black Ice 57. High Jump 59. Spider's Web

60. So Evil So Young 61. She Always Gets Their Man 62, etc.

Grayson, Kathryn (1922–) (Zelma Hedrick)
American singing star in Hollywood from 1941 (as one of Andy Hardy's dates).
■ Andy Hardy's Private Secretary 40. Andy Hardy's Spring Fever 41. The Vanishing Virginian 41. Rio Rita 42. Seven Sweethearts 42. Thousands Cheer 43. Anchors Aweigh 45. Two Sisters from Boston 46. Ziegfeld Follies 46. Till the Clouds Roll By 46. It Happened in Brooklyn 47. The Kissing Bandit 48. The Midnight Kiss 49. The Toast of New Orleans 50. Grounds for Marriage 50. *Show Boat* 51. Lovely to Look At 52. The Desert Song 53. So This Is Love (as Grace Moore) 53. *Kiss Me Kate* 53. The Vagabond King 56. That's Entertainment Two 76.

Grazer, Brian (1951–)
American producer, a former agent, now in partnership with director Ron Howard.
Night Shift 82. Splash 83. Real Genius 84. Spies Like Us 85. Armed and Dangerous (& story) 86. Like Father, Like Son 87. Parenthood 89. The Dream Team 89. Kindergarten Cop 90. Problem Child 90. Cry-Baby 90. Backdraft 91. Closet Land 91. My Girl 91. The Doors 91. Far and Away 91. Housesitter 92. Boomerang 92. For Love or Money 93. My Girl 2 94. The Cowboy Way 94. Greedy/Greed 94. The Paper 94. Apollo 13 95. Sgt Bilko 96. The Chamber 96. Fear 96. Ransom 96. The Nutty Professor 96. Liar Liar 97. Inventing the Abbotts 97. From the Earth to the Moon (TV) 98. Psycho 98, etc.

Graziano, Rocky (1921–1990) (Thomas Rocco Barbella)
World middleweight boxing champion whose 1955 autobiography, *Somebody Up There Likes Me*, was filmed in 1956 starring Paul Newman. He became a TV actor and a regular on variety shows in the 50s and 60s, and wrote another volume of autobiography, *Somebody Down Here Likes Me Too*, in 1981.
Mr Rock and Roll 57. Teenage Millionaire 61. Tony Rome 67, etc.
❝ I get a real belt out of this racket where I get paid because people laugh instead of stand up and scream for me to belt somebody. – *R.G.*

Greatrex, Richard
British cinematographer.
Knights and Emeralds 86. For Queen and Country 88. War Requiem 88. The Lunatic 92. Deadly Advice 94. Blue Juice 95. Mrs Brown 97. Shakespeare in Love (AAN) 98, etc.

Gréco, Juliette (1927–)
French singer who acted in several films both at home and abroad.
Au Royaume des Cieux 49. The Green Glove 52. *The Sun Also Rises* 57. Naked Earth 58. Roots of Heaven 59. Whirlpool 59. Crack in the Mirror 60. The Big Gamble (US) 61. Uncle Tom's Cabin 65. The Night of the Generals 66. Lily Aime-Moi 75, etc.

Green, Adolph (1915–)
American writer of books and lyrics for many Broadway shows and musical films, usually with Betty Comden.

Green, Alfred E. (1889–1960)
American director of mainly routine but generally competent films; in Hollywood from 1912.
Little Lord Fauntleroy 20. Ella Cinders 23. Through the Back Door 26. The Green Goddess 30. Old English 31. Smart Money 31. Disraeli 31. The Rich Are Always with Us 32. Parachute 33. Dangerous 35. Duke of West Point 38. South of Pago Pago 40. Badlands of Dakota 41. Meet the Stewarts 42. A Thousand and One Nights 44. *The Jolson Story* 46. The Fabulous Dorseys 47. They Passed This Way 48. Cover Up 49. Invasion USA 52. The Eddie Cantor Story 53, many others.

Green, Danny (1903–1973)
Heavyweight British character actor usually in cheerful – or sometimes menacing – cockney roles. Appeared in some American silents.
Crime over London 37. Fiddlers Three 44. The Man Within 47. No Orchids for Miss Blandish 48. Little Big Shot 52. A Kid for Two Farthings 55. The Lady Killers 55. Beyond This Place 59. The Old Dark House 62. A Stitch in Time 63. Smashing Time 67. The Fixer 68, etc.

Green, David (1948–)
British director, from television.
Car Trouble 86. Buster 88. Fire Birds 90. Wings of the Apache 90. Breathtaking 00, etc.

Green, Guy (1913–)
British cinematographer who became a useful director.
As cinematographer: In Which We Serve 42. The Way Ahead 44. *Great Expectations* (AA) 46. Take My Life 47. *Oliver Twist* 48. Captain Horatio Hornblower 51. The Beggar's Opera 52. Rob Roy 53, etc.
■ As director: River Beat 54. Portrait of Alison 55. Lost 56. House of Secrets 56. The Snorkel 58. Sea of Sand 58. SOS Pacific 59. *The Mark* 60. *The Angry Silence* 60. The Light in the Piazza 62. Diamond Head 63. A Patch of Blue 65. Pretty Polly 67. The Magus 68. A Walk in the Spring Rain 70. Luther 73. Once Is Not Enough 75. The Devil's Advocate 77. Strong Medicine (TV) 85.

Green, Harry (1892–1958)
American comedian, primarily on stage; former lawyer.
Close Harmony 31. Bottoms Up 34. The Cisco Kid and the Lady 37. Star Dust 40. Joe MacBeth (GB) 55. A King in New York (GB) 57, etc.

Green, Hughie (1920–1997)
Canadian actor in Britain, former juvenile, then popular TV quizmaster and talent scout. After his death it was revealed that he was the father of TV presenter and writer Paula Yates (1960-2000). His much-mocked catchphrase was, 'I mean this most sincerely, folks.'
Little Friend 34. Midshipman Easy 35. Tom Brown's Schooldays (US) 39. If Winter Comes (US) 48. Paper Orchid 49. What's Up Superdoc 78, etc.

Green, Jack N.
American cinematographer, mainly for Clint Eastwood's movies.
Heartbreak Ridge 86. Like Father, Like Son 87. The Dead Pool 88. Bird 88. Pink Cadillac 89. Race for Glory 89. White Hunter, Black Heart 90. The Rookie 90. Love Crimes 92. Rookie of the Year 93. A Perfect World 93. Trapped in Paradise 94. Bad Company 95. The Bridges of Madison County 95. The Net 95. The Amazing Panda Adventure 95. Twister 96. Absolute Power 97. Midnight in the Garden of Good and Evil 97. Speed 2: Cruise Control 97. Traveller (& d) 97, etc.

Green, Janet (1908–1993)
English screenwriter and playwright, a former actress. Born in London, she wrote her first play in 1945 and began working in films two years later, turning her story *The Clouded Yellow* into a screenplay. Her later scripts were written in collaboration with her husband, John McCormick.
The Clouded Yellow 50. The Good Beginning 53. Lost 55. Cast a Dark Shadow 55. The Long Arm 56. Eye Witness 56. Affair in Havana (US) 57. *Sapphire* 59. Midnight Lace (oa) (US) 60. *Victim* 61. Life for Ruth 62. 7 Women (US) 66, etc.

Green, Johnny (1908–1989)
American composer, songwriter, musical director and bandleader. Born in New York City, he studied at Harvard University and began as a rehearsal pianist and accompanist to Ethel Merman and Gertrude Lawrence. He worked for MGM in the early 40s, and then went to Warner before returning to MGM as general musical director in 1949, where he remained until 1958. He also produced some short films, winning an Oscar for *The Merry Wives of Windsor Overture* 53. His best-known songs include 'Body and Soul' and 'I Cover the Waterfront', which were both later used as the title themes for films. Married actresses Betty Furness and Bunny Waters.
Lost in a Harem 44. Bathing Beauty 44. Fiesta 47. *Easter Parade* (AA) 48. Up in Central Park 48. The Inspector General 49. Grounds for Marriage 50. Summer Stock 50. The Great Caruso 51. Royal Wedding/Wedding Bells 51. *An American in Paris* (AA) 51. Too Young to Kiss 51. Because You're Mine 52. Rhapsody 53. Brigadoon 54. I'll Cry Tomorrow 55. High Society 56. Meet Me in Las Vegas/Viva Las Vegas! 56. Raintree County 57. Pepe 60. West Side Story 61. This Rugged Land 62. Bye Bye Birdie 63. Twilight of Honor 63. Alvarez Kelly 66. *Oliver!* (GB) (AA) 68. *They Shoot Horses, Don't They?* (AAN) 69, etc.

Green, Joseph (1900–1996) (Joseph Greenberg)
American producer and director of Yiddish films, a former actor. Born in Poland, he went to America in the 20s, working as an extra in Hollywood, and began making films in Poland in the 30s for Yiddish-speaking audiences, a group that no longer existed by the end of the Second World War. His best-known *Yiddle with His Fiddle* starred Molly Picon.
■ Yiddle with His Fiddle 36. A Letter to Mama/A Brivele der Mamen 38. Mamele: Little Mothers 38. The Jester/Der Purimspieler 46.

Green, Martyn (1899–1975)
British light opera singer, with the D'Oyly Carte Company for many years; settled in America.
Autobiography: 1952, *Here's a How De Do*.
■ *The Mikado* 39. The Story of Gilbert and Sullivan 53. A Lovely Way to Die 68.

Green, Mitzi (1920–1969) (Elizabeth Keno)
American child performer of the 30s.
Honey 30. Tom Sawyer 30. Little Orphan Annie 32. Transatlantic Merry-Go-Round 34, etc.: later appeared in Lost in Alaska 52. Bloodhounds of Broadway 52.
TV series: So This is Hollywood 54.

Green, Nigel (1924–1972)
Dominant British character actor with stage experience.
Reach for the Sky 56. Bitter Victory 57. The Criminal 60. Jason and the Argonauts 63. *Zulu* 64. *The Ipcress File* 65. *The Face of Fu Manchu* 65. The Skull 66. Let's Kill Uncle (US) 66. *Deadlier than the Male* 66. *Tobruk* (US) 67. Africa Texas Style 67. Play Dirty 68. Wrecking Crew (US) 69. The Kremlin Letter 69. Countess Dracula 70. The Ruling Class 71, etc.
TV series: The Adventures of William Tell 58-59.

Green, Pamela
British actress and nude model, best known for her appearance in her then lover George Harrison Marks's film *Naked as Nature Intended* 61, which led to a long cycle of British films mixing sex and comedy in the 60s and 70s.
The Chimney Sweeps 63. The Naked World of Harrison Marks 67, etc.
❝ While the British film industry is brilliant at parochial comedy, drama and historical subjects, it has not so far produced one really good film featuring the nude. The naturist films were, in the main, made by people with very little imagination for titillating the raincoat brigade, in the hope of making a few bob at the end of it. – *P.G.*

Green, Philip (1911–1982)
Prolific English composer and musical director of the 50s and 60s. Born in London, he studied at the Trinity College of Music and first worked in the theatre as a conductor. At his busiest, he composed as many as 14 film scores a year.
Landfall 49. Murder without Crime 50. Elstree Story 52. Isn't Life Wonderful! 53. The March Hare 54. John and Julie 55. Man of the Moment 55. The Extra Day 56. Up in the World 56. The March Hare 56. Who Done It? 56. Carry On Admiral 57. Woman and the Hunter 57. The Violent Playground 57. Just My Luck 57. The Golden Disc 58. Rooney 58. Operation Amsterdam 58. Alive and Kicking 58. Innocent Sinners 58. Sea Fury 58. The Square Peg 58. Life Is a Circus 58. Life in Emergency Ward 10 58. Upstairs and Downstairs 59. Bobbikins 59. The Shakedown 59. Witness in the Dark 59. A Touch of Larceny 59. Sapphire 59. The League of Gentlemen 59. Operation Amsterdam 59. Follow a Star 59. Friends and Neighbours 59. Desert Mice 59. Don't Panic Chaps 59. The Bulldog Breed 60. Make Mine Mink 60. Piccadilly Third Stop 60. The Singer Not the Song 60. Your Money or Your Wife 60. Man in the Moon 60. And Women Shall Weep 60. All Night Long 61. Victim 61. The Secret Partner 61. Flame in the Streets 61. On the Beat 62. Victim 62. Tiara Tahiti 62. The Man Who Finally Died 62. The Devil's Agent 62. The Girl Hunters 63. Two Left Feet 63. A Stitch in Time 63. It's All Happening (& co-p) 63. The Intelligence Men 65. Joey Boy 65. Masquerade 65. The Yellow Hat 66, etc.

Green, S. C. (1928–1999) (aka Sid Green)
Prolific British comedy scriptwriter, mainly for television.
The Intelligence Men 65. That Riviera Touch 66. The Magnificent Two 67. The Boys in Blue 83, etc.

Green, Walon (1936–)
American screenwriter and director.
The Wild Bunch (AAN) 69. Sorcerer 77. The Brinks Job 78. The Secret Life of Plants (& d) 78. The Border 82. Solarbabies 86. Crusoe 88. Robocop 2 90. Eraser (co-w) 96. The Hi-Lo Country 99. Dinosaur (co-w) 00, etc.

Greenaway, Peter (1942–)
British director and screenwriter who has moved from the experimental to the near-mainstream without altering his style.
Books: 1996, *Being Naked Playing Dead: The Art of Peter Greenaway* by Alan Woods.
The Falls 80. Act of God 81. The Draughtsman's Contract 83. A Zed and Two Noughts 85. Drowning by Numbers 88. *The Cook, the Thief, His Wife and Her Lover* 89. A TV Dante (TV) 90. *Prospero's Books* 91. The Baby of Macon 93. The Pillow Book 95. 8&fr12; Women 99, etc.
❝ I do feel for me that cinema has somehow ceased to be a spectator sport. I get tremendous excitement out of making it rather than watching it. – *P.G.*
We live in a time of excess – excess population, excess information – *P.G.*
If you want to tell stories, be a writer, not a filmmaker. – *P.G.*
What is it about Greenaway's films that makes the flesh crawl? I think it's his apparent loathing of the human race. – *Ken Russell*
If Gucci handbags were still in fashion Greenaway would carry his scripts in them. – *Derek Jarman*

Greenberg, Adam
Polish cinematographer, working in Hollywood.
Diamonds 75. The Passover Plot 77. Operation Thunderbolt 77. The Big Red One 80. Lemon Popsicle 80. Teen Mothers/Seed of Innocence 80. Paradise 82. 10 to Midnight 83. The Terminator 84. The Ambassador 85. Once Bitten 85. Wisdom 86. Iron Eagle 86. La Bamba 87. Near Dark 87. Jocks 87. Three Men and a Baby 87. Spellbinder 88. Alien Nation 88. Turner & Hooch 89. Worth Winning 89. Love Hurts 90. Ghost 90. Three Men and a Little Lady 90. Terminator 2 91. Sister Act 92. Toys 92. Dave 93. Renaissance Man 94. North 94. First Knight 95. Eraser 96. Sphere 98. Rush Hour 98, etc.

Greenberg, Gerald (1936–)
American editor.
Bye Bye Braverman 68. The Boys in the Band 70. The French Connection (AA) 71. The Seven Ups 73. The Taking of Pelham One Two Three 75. The Missouri Breaks 76. Apocalypse Now (AAN) 79. Dressed to Kill 80. Heaven's Gate 80. Scarface 83. Body Double 84. Wise Guys 86. The Untouchables 87. The Accused 88. Awakenings 90. For the Boys 91. School Ties 92. Reach the Rock 98. American History X 98, etc.

Greenberg, Stanley R.
American screenwriter.
Welcome Home Johnny Bristol (TV) 72. Skyjacked 72. Soylent Green 73. The Missiles of October (TV) 73. The Silence (TV) 76. Blind Ambition (TV) 79. FDR, the Last Years (TV) 81, etc.

Greenbury, Christopher
American editor.
Some Kind of Hero 81. Smokey and the Bandit III 83. The Woman in Red 84. Haunted Honeymoon 86. Three for the Road 87. National Lampoon's Loaded Weapon 1 93. Dumb & Dumber 94. Bio-Dome 96. Kingpin 96. Booty Call 97. There's Something about Mary 98. American Beauty (AAN) 99, etc.

Greene, Clarence (1918–)
American writer-producer, usually in collaboration with Russel Rouse.
The Town Went Wild 45. D.O.A. 48. The Well (AAN) 51. New York Confidential 55. A House Is Not a Home 64. The Oscar 66. Caper of the Golden Bulls 67, etc.
TV series: Tightrope 57.

Greene, David (1921–)
British director, former small-part actor; became a TV director in Canada and the US.

The Shuttered Room 66. Sebastian 68. The Strange Affair 68. I Start Counting (& p) 69. The People Next Door 70. Madame Sin (TV) 72. *Godspell* 73. Ellery Queen (TV) 75. Rich Man Poor Man (TV) (co-d) 76. Roots (co-d) (TV) 77. Lucan (TV pilot) 77. The Man in the Iron Mask (TV) 77. Gray Lady Down 78. The Trial of Lee Harvey Oswald (TV) 78. Friendly Fire (TV) 79. A Vacation in Hell (TV) 80. Hard Country 81. World War III (TV) 81. Ghost Dancing (TV) 81. Prototype (TV) 83. The Guardian (TV) 84. Sweet Revenge (TV) 84. Fatal Vision (TV) 84. Guilty Conscience (TV) 85. Miles to Go (TV) 86. Vanishing Act (TV) 86. The Betty Ford Story (TV) 87. Night of the Hunter (TV) 91. Honor Thy Mother (TV) 92. Beyond Obsession (TV) 94, etc.

Greene, Graham (1904–1991)
Distinguished British novelist who provided material for many interesting films. His film criticisms have been collected in *The Pleasure Dome* (Oxford, 1980) and *Mornings in the Dark: The Graham Greene Film Reader* (Carcanet, 1993). He was romantically involved with actress Anita Bjork.

Books: 1990, *Travels in Greeneland: The Cinema of Graham Greene* by Quentin Falk.

Stamboul Train/Orient Express 34. This Gun for Hire 42. The Ministry of Fear 43. Confidential Agent 45. The Man Within 46. Brighton Rock 47. The Fugitive 48. The Fallen Idol (AAN) 48. The Third Man 49. The Heart of the Matter 53. The Stranger's Hand 54. The End of the Affair 55. The Quiet American 58. Our Man in Havana 59. The Comedians 67. Travels with My Aunt 73. The Human Factor 79. The Honorary Consul 83. The End of the Affair 99, etc.

Greene, Graham (1952–)
Native American actor.

Dances with Wolves (AAN) 90. Clearcut 91. Thunderheart 92. The Last of His Tribe 92. Medicine River 92. Benefit of the Doubt 93. Cooperstown (TV) 93. Huck and the King of Hearts 93. Camilla 94. Maverick 94. North 94. Die Hard with a Vengenace 95. Sabotage 96. Dead Innocent 96. The Education of Little Tree 97. Shattered Image 98. Heart of the Sun 98. Grey Owl 98. Misery Harbor 99. The Green Mile 99. Touched 99, etc.

Greene, Leon
Stalwart British supporting actor, former opera singer.

A Funny Thing Happened on the Way to the Forum 67. The Ritz 76. The Seven Per Cent Solution 76. Adventures of a Private Eye 77. Adventures of a Plumber's Mate 78. The Thief of Baghdad 78. Flash Gordon 80. The Return of the Musketeers 89, etc.

Greene, Lorne (1915–1987)
Solidly-built Canadian character actor, best known for his role as Ben Cartwright in the TV series *Bonanza* 59–73, and his similar role as Commander Adama in *Battlestar Galactica* 78–80.

The Silver Chalice 54. Tight Spot 55. Autumn Leaves 56. Peyton Place 57. The Gift of Love 58. The Trap 58. Legacy of a Spy (TV) 68. The Harness (TV) 71. Earthquake 74, etc.

TV series: Sailor of Fortune 56. *Bonanza* 59–73. Griff 73–74. Battlestar Galactica 78–80. Code Red 81–82.

Greene, Max (1896–1968) (Mutz Greenbaum)
German cinematographer, long in Britain.

The Stars Look Down 39. Hatter's Castle 41. Spring in Park Lane 48. Maytime in Mayfair 49. Night and the City 50, etc.

Greene, Richard (1918–1985)
Good-looking, lightweight British leading man with brief stage experience before 1938 film debut resulted in Hollywood contract. Born in Plymouth, Devon, he returned to England at the beginning of the Second World War to serve in the Army. From the mid-40s, he alternated between England and Hollywood, before gaining a new fame in the mid-50s as Robin Hood in the long-running TV series. He retired to Ireland in the 70s to breed horses.

■ *Four Men and a Prayer* 38. My Lucky Star 38. Submarine Patrol 38. Kentucky 38. The Little Princess 38. *The Hound of the Baskervilles* 39. Stanley and Livingstone 39. Here I Am a Stranger 39. Little Old New York 40. I Was an Adventuress 40. Unpublished Story 42. Flying Fortress 42. Yellow Canary 43. Don't Take It to Heart 45. Gaiety George 46. Forever Amber 47. The Fighting O'Flynn 48. The Fan 48. That Dangerous Age 49. Now Barabbas 49. The Desert Hawk 50. My Daughter Joy 50. Shadow of the Eagle 50. Lorna Doone 51. Black Castle 51. Rogue's March 53. Captain Scarlet 53. Bandits of Corsica 54. Contraband Spain 55. Beyond the Curtain 60. Sword of Sherwood Forest 61. Dangerous Island 67. Blood of Fu Manchu 68. Kiss and Kill 69. Tales from the Crypt 72.

TV series: *Robin Hood* 55–59.

Greene, W. Howard (1895–1956)
American colour cinematographer.

Trail of the Lonesome Pine 36. *The Garden of Allah* 36. *A Star is Born* 37. Nothing Sacred 37. *The Adventures of Robin Hood* 38. Jesse James 39. Elizabeth and Essex 39. Northwest Mounted Police 40. Blossoms in the Dust 41. The Jungle Book (AAN) 42. Arabian Nights 42. *Phantom of the Opera* (AA) 43. Ali Baba and the Forty Thieves 44. Can't Help Singing 44. Salome Where she Danced 45. A Night in Paradise 46. Tycoon 47. High Lonesome 50. Quebec 51. The Brigand 52. Gun Belt 53, etc.

Greene, Walter (1910–)
American composer and arranger, mainly of 'B' features and TV films.

Crime Inc 45. Why Girls Leave Home (AAN) 45. Return of the Lash 47. Mark of the Lash 48. The Dalton Gang 49. Hostile Country 50. Naked Gun 56. Jesse James' Women 54. Teenage Thunder 57. Teenage Monster 58. *The Brain from Planet Arous* 58. War of the Satellites 58. Carnival Rock 58. I Bombed Pearl Harbor 61. The Pique Poquette of Paris 66, etc.

Greenleaf, Raymond (1892–1963)
American character actor, usually seen as benevolent elderly man.

Storm Warning 51. Angel Face 53. Violent Saturday 54. *When Gangland Strikes* (leading role) 56. The Story on Page One 60, many others.

Greenstreet, Sydney (1879–1954)
Immense British stage actor long in America; a sensation in his first film, made at the age of 61, he became a major star of the 40s.

■ *The Maltese Falcon* (AAN) 41. They Died with Their Boots On 41. *Across the Pacific* 42. Casablanca 42. Background to Danger 42. Passage to Marseilles 44. *Between Two Worlds* 44. *The Mask of Dimitrios* 44. The Conspirators 44. Hollywood Canteen 44. Pillow to Post 45. Conflict 45. Christmas in Connecticut 45. *Three Strangers* 46. Devotion (as Thackeray) 46. The Verdict 46. That Way with Women 47. *The Hucksters* 47. *The Woman in White* 48. The Velvet Touch 48. Ruthless 48. Flamingo Road 49. It's a Great Feeling 49. Malaya 50.

✪ For his inimitable chuckle; and for the sheer improbability of his success. *The Maltese Falcon*.

❝ By gad, sir, you're a fellow worth knowing, a character. No telling what you'll say next, except that it'll be something astonishing. – *S.G. in The Maltese Falcon*

I distrust a man who says when. He's got to be careful not to drink too much, because he's not to be trusted when he does. Well, sir, here's to plain speaking and clear understanding. You're a close-mouthed man?

– No, I like to talk.

– Better and better. I distrust a close-mouthed man. He generally picks the wrong time to talk, and says the wrong things. Talking's something you can't do judiciously, unless you keep in practice. – *Ibid.*

Greenwald, Maggie (1955–)
American director, a former editor and dancer.

Home Remedy 87. The Kill Off 89. The Ballad of Little Joe 93.

Greenwood, Charlotte (1890–1978)
Tall American comedienne and eccentric dancer, on stage from 1905.

Autobiography: 1947, *Never Too Tall.*

Jane 18. Baby Mine 27. So Long Letty 30. Palmy Days 32. Down Argentine Way 40. Springtime in the Rockies 43. Up in Mabel's Room 44. Home in Indiana 47. Peggy 50. Dangerous when Wet 52. Glory 55. Oklahoma 56. The Opposite Sex 56, etc.

Greenwood, Jack (1919–)
British producer, responsible for second-feature crime series: Edgar Wallace, Scales of Justice, Scotland Yard, etc.

Greenwood, Joan (1921–1987)
Plummy-voiced British leading lady of the 40s. Born in London, she studied at RADA and was on-stage from 1938. Married actor André Morell.

■ John Smith Wakes Up 40. My Wife's Family 40. He Found a Star 41. *The Gentle Sex* 42. They Knew Mr Knight 44. Latin Quarter 44. A Girl in a Million 45. The Man Within 46. *The October Man* 47. The White Unicorn 47. *Saraband for Dead Lovers* 48. The Bad Lord Byron 48. Whisky Galore 49. *Kind Hearts and Coronets* 49. Flesh and Blood 50. The Man in the White Suit 50. Young Wives' Tale 51. Mr Peek-a-Boo 51. *The Importance of Being Earnest* 52. Knave of Hearts 54. *Father Brown* 54. Moonfleet (US) 55. Stage Struck (US) 57. Mysterious Island 62. The Amorous Prawn 62. Tom Jones 63. The Moon Spinners 64. Girl Stroke Boy 71. The Uncanny 77. The Hound of the Baskervilles 78. The Water Babies 78. Little Dorrit 87.

TV series: Girls on Top 85-86.

❝ She speaks her lines as though suspecting in them some hidden menace that she can't quite identify. – *Karel Reisz*

Greenwood, John (1889–1975)
English composer. Born in London, he studied at the Royal College of Music.

To What Red Hell? 30. The Constant Nymph 33. Elephant Boy 37. Pimpernel Smith 41. San Demetrio, London 44. Frieda 47. Quartet 48. The Last Days of Dolwyn 48. Trio 50. The Gentle Gunman 52, many others.

Greenwood, Walter (1903–1974)
British writer who chronicled industrial life, notably in *Love on the Dole.*

Greer, Dabs (1917–) (William Greer)
American character actor.

Affair with a Stranger 53. House of Wax 53. Riot in Cell Block 11 54. D-Day the Sixth of June 56. Baby Face Nelson 57. My Man Godfrey 57. It! The Terror from Beyond Space 58. The Lone Texan 59. The Cheyenne Social Club 70. White Lightning 73. Two-Moon Junction 88. Sundown 91. House 4: Home Deadly Home 92, etc.

TV series: Gunsmoke 55–60. Hank 65–66. Little House on the Prairie 74–83.

Greer, Howard (1886–1964)
American costume designer, in films from 1923 and chief designer at Paramount from 1924–27 before establishing his own salon in Hollywood.

Autobiography: 1949, *Designing Male.*

The Spanish Dancer 23. The Cheat 23. The Covered Wagon 23. The Ten Commandments 24. Coquette 29. Hell's Angels 30. The Animal Kingdom 32. Page Miss Glory 35. Bringing Up Baby 38. When Tomorrow Comes 39. Christmas Holiday 44. Spellbound 45. Holiday Affair 49. The French Line 54, etc.

❝ For every luscious bloom there's been a fat, sharp thorn. – H.G.

Greer, Jane (1924–) (Bettyjane Greer)
Cool American leading lady of the 40s; could play good-humoured dames, well-bred ladies or *femmes fatales*.

■ Pan Americana 45. Two o'Clock Courage 45. George White's Scandals 45. Dick Tracy 45. The Falcon's Alibi 46. Bamboo Blonde 46. Sunset Pass 46. Sinbad the Sailor 47. *They Won't Believe Me* 47. *Out of the Past* 47. Station West 48. *The Big Steal* 49. You're in the Navy Now 51. The Company She Keeps 51. The Prisoner of Zenda 52. Desperate Search 52. You for Me 52. The Clown 53. Down among the Sheltering Palms 53. *Run for the Sun* 56. *Man of a Thousand Faces* 57. Where Love Has Gone 64. Billie 65. The Outfit 74. The Shadow Riders (TV) 82. Against All Odds 84.

Gregg, Colin (1947–)
British director.

Remembrance 82. Lamb 85. We Think the World of You 88.

Gregg, Everley (1898–1959)
British character actress.

The Private Life of Henry VIII 33. The Ghost Goes West 36. Pygmalion 38. Brief Encounter 45, etc.

Gregg, Hubert (1914–)
British songwriter, screenwriter, and light actor, married to Pat Kirkwood. On stage from 1933, films from 1942.

In Which We Serve 42. 29 Acacia Avenue 45. Vote for Huggett 49. Robin Hood 52. The Maggie 54. Simon and Laura 55. Stars in My Eyes 57, etc.

Gregor, Nora (c. 1890–1949)
Austrian leading lady.

The Trial of Mary Dugan (US) 29. His Glorious Night (US) 30. *La Règle du Jeu* (Fr.) 39, etc.

Gregory, James (1911–)
American character actor with stage experience, a familiar Hollywood 'heavy' or senior cop.

Naked City 48. The Frogmen 51. The Scarlet Hour 56. The Young Stranger 57. Al Capone 59. Two Weeks in Another Town 62. *The Manchurian Candidate* 62. P.T. 109 63. A Distant Trumpet 64. The Sons of Katie Elder 65. A Rage To Live 65. *The Silencers* 66. Clambake 68. The Hawaiians 70. Million Dollar Duck 71. Shootout 71. The Main Event 79, etc.

TV series: The Lawless Years 59. Barney Miller 81.

Gregory, Paul (c. 1905–) (Jason Lenhart)
American impresario who teamed with Charles Laughton in the 40s to present dramatized readings: also produced *Night of the Hunter* 55, which Laughton directed, and *The Naked and the Dead* 58.

Gregson, John (1919–1975)
English leading man, a likeable and dependable star of British comedies and action dramas in the 50s.

■ Saraband for Dead Lovers 48. Scott of the Antarctic 48. Whisky Galore 49. The Hasty Heart 49. Train of Events 49. Treasure Island 50. Cairo Road 50. *The Lavender Hill Mob* 51. Angels One Five 51. *The Brave Don't Cry* 51. Venetian Bird 52. The Holly and the Ivy 52. The Titfield Thunderbolt 53. *Genevieve* 53. The Weak and the Wicked 53. Conflict of Wings 54. To Dorothy a Son 54. The Crowded Day 54. Above Us the Waves 55. Value for Money 55. Three Cases of Murder 55. *Jacqueline* 56. The Battle of the River Plate 56. True as a Turtle 56. Miracle in Soho 57. *Rooney* 57. Sea of Sand 58. *The Captain's Table* 58. SOS Pacific 59. Faces in the Dark 60. Hand in Hand 60. Treasure of Monte Cristo 61. Frightened City 61. *Live Now Pay Later* 62. Tomorrow at Ten 62. The Longest Day 62. The Night of the Generals 66. Fright 71.

TV series: Gideon's Way 64. Shirley's World 71.

Greig, Robert (1880–1958)
Australian character actor, long in Hollywood; the doyen of portly pompous butlers.

Animal Crackers 30. Tonight or Never 31. Love Me Tonight 32. Trouble in Paradise 32. Horse Feathers 32. Merrily We Go to Hell 33. Pleasure Cruise 33. Clive of India 35. Lloyds of London 36. Easy Living 37. Algiers 38. No Time for Comedy 40. The Lady Eve 41. Sullivan's Travels 42. *The Moon and Sixpence* 42. I Married a Witch 42. The Palm Beach Story 42. The Great Moment 44. The Picture of Dorian Gray 45. The Cheaters 45. Unfaithfully Yours 48, many others.

Greist, Kim (1958–)
American actress.

C.H.U.D. 84. Brazil 85. Manhunter 86. Throw Momma from the Train 87. Punchline 88. Why Me? 89. Payoff 91. Duplicates 92. Homeward Bound: The Incredible Journey 93. Homeward Bound II: Lost in San Francisco 96. The Hiding Place 00, etc.

Grémillon, Jean (1901–1959)
French director with limited but interesting output since 1929.

Remorques 39. Lumière d'Eté 42. Pattes Blanches 48, etc.

Grenfell, Joyce (1910–1979) (Joyce Phipps)
Angular British comedienne adept at refined gaucherie; a revue star and solo performer, on stage from 1939.

Autobiography: 1976, *Joyce Grenfell Requests the Pleasure*. 1979, *In Pleasant Places*. 1997, *Joyce and Ginnie – The Letters of Joyce Grenfell and Virginia Graham*, ed. Janie Hampton.

The Demi-Paradise 42. The Lamp Still Burns 43. While the Sun Shines 46. *The Happiest Days of*

Your Life 49. Stage Fright 50. *Laughter in Paradise* 51. Genevieve 53. The Million Pound Note 54. The Belles of St Trinian's 54. Happy Is the Bride 57. Blue Murder at St Trinian's 58. The Pure Hell of St Trinian's 60. The Old Dark House 63. The Americanization of Emily 64. The Yellow Rolls-Royce 64, etc.

Grenier, Adrian (1976–)
American actor, mainly in independent films.
Arresting Gena 97. Fishes Outta Water 98. Celebrity 98. Hurricane Streets 99. The Adventures of Sebastian Cole 99. Drive Me Crazy 99. Cecil B. Demented 00, etc.

Gréville, Edmond (1906–1966)
French director; assistant to Dupont on *Piccadilly* 29, to Clair on *Sous les Toits de Paris* 30.
Remous 34. Mademoiselle Docteur 37. L'Ile du Péché 39. Passionnelle 46. Noose (GB) 48. The Romantic Age (GB) 49. But Not in Vain (also w, p) (GB) 49. Port du Désir 56. Guilty (GB) 56. Beat Girl (GB) 60. The Hands of Orlac (GB) 61. Les Menteurs 61, etc.

Grey, Anne (1907–) (Aileen Ewing)
British leading actress of the late 20s and early 30s, a former journalist. Born in London, and educated at Lausanne and King's College, London, she moved to Hollywood in the mid-30s to make a few films there before retiring. Married actor Lester Matthews.
The Constant Nymph 27. The Warning 28. The School for Scandal 30. The Squeaker 30. Arms and the Man 32. The Faithful Heart 32. Leap Year 32. The Blarney Stone 32. The Fire Raisers 33. Just Smith 33. Colonel Blood 34. Bonnie Scotland (US) 35. Break of Hearts (US) 35. Just My Luck (US) 36. Dr Sin Fang 37. Chinatown Nights 38, etc.

Grey, Denise (1896–1996)
Leading French actress, most often seen in films in grandmotherly roles. She began her career at the Folies Bergère in 1915.
Bolero 41. Adieu Leonard 43. Devil in the Flesh/Le Diable au Corps 47. Carve Her Name with Pride (GB) 58. Sputnik/A Dog, a Mouse and a Sputnik 58. La Bonne Soupe 63. Hello-Goodbye (US) 70. La Venus de Milo 73. La Boum 80. La Boum II 82. Le Gaffeur 85. The Seasons of Pleasure/Les Saisons du Plaisir 87, etc.

Grey, Jennifer (1960–)
American actress, the daughter of Joel Grey.
Red Dawn 84. The Cotton Club 84. American Flyers 85. Ferris Bueller's Day Off 86. Dirty Dancing 87. Light Years 88. Bloodhounds of Broadway 89. The Sixth Family 90. Stroke of Midnight 91. A Case for Murder (TV) 93. The West Side Waltz (TV) 95. Lover's Knot 96. Bounce 00, etc.

Grey, Joel (1932–) (Joe Katz)
American singing entertainer who took a long time to hit stardom, managed it on the New York stage in *Cabaret*, but proved difficult to cast.
■ About Face 52. Come September 61. Man on a String (TV) 71. *Cabaret* (AA) 72. Man on a Swing 75. Buffalo Bill and the Indians 76. The Seven Per Cent Solution 76. Remo Williams ... the Adventure Begins 85. Kafka 91. The Music of Chance 93. The Empty Mirror (as Josef Goebbels) 96. My Friend Joe 96. A Christmas Carol (TV) 99. reaching Normal 99. Dancer in the Dark (Den.) 00. The Fantasticks (made 95) 00.

Grey, Lita (1908–1995) (Lillita MacMurray)
American juvenile actress of the 20s who appeared with Chaplin, became his child bride in 1924, and was the mother of Charles Chaplin Jnr (1925–68) and of actor Sydney Chaplin.
Autobiography: 1966, *My Life with Chaplin*.

Grey, Nan (1918–1993) (Eschal Miller)
American leading lady of the late 30s; married to singer Frankie Laine.
Dracula's Daughter 36. Three Smart Girls 36. Three Smart Girls Grow Up 38. Tower of London 39. The Invisible Man Returns 40. Sandy Is a Lady 41, etc.

Grey, Virginia (1917–)
American leading lady of minor films in the 30s and 40s.
Uncle Tom's Cabin (debut) 27. Misbehaving Ladies 31. Secrets 33. Dames 34. The Firebird 34. The Great Ziegfeld 36. Rosalie 37. Test Pilot 38. The Hardys Ride High 39. Hullaballoo 40. Blonde Inspiration 41. The Big Store 41. Grand Central Murder 42. Idaho 43. Strangers in the Night 44. Blonde Ransom 45. House of Horrors 46. Unconquered 47. Who Killed Doc Robbin? 48. Jungle Jim 49. Slaughter Trail 51. Desert Pursuit 52. Target Earth 54. The Last Command 55. Crime of Passion 56. The Restless Years 58. Portrait in Black 60. Back Street 61. Black Zoo 63. Love Has Many Faces 65. Madame X 66. Rosie 68. Airport 69, many others.

Grey, Zane (1875–1939)
American novelist whose western yarns provided the basis of hundreds of silent and sound movies. He lacked sophistication, but as late as 1960 TV had its *Zane Grey Theatre*. In 1996, Ed Harris and Amy Madigan starred in a TV film of his *Riders of the Purple Sage*, directed by Charles Haid.

Grey Owl
was the identity of an American Indian, adopted by Englishman Archie Belaney, who was born in Hastings, Sussex. After emigrating to North America in 1906, he lived in a log cabin in Canada, where he claimed to be the offspring of a Scottish father and an Apache mother. Through books and lecture tours, he campaigned for the preservation of forests and wildlife, particularly the Canadian beaver. His true identity was revealed only after his sudden death, from pneumonia. He was played by Pierce Brosnan in a biopic in 1999.

Greyson, John
Canadian director and screenwriter, of films on homosexual themes. *Zero Patience* was a musical about AIDS.
Kipling Meets the Cowboys (short) 85. Urinal 88. Zero Patience 93. Lilies 96, etc.

Grieco, Richard (1965–)
American leading actor in teen-oriented movies, from television.
If Looks Could Kill 91. Mobsters 91. Tomcat: Dangerous Desires 93. Born to Run (TV) 93. A Vow to Kill (TV) 94. Suspicious Agenda 94. The Demolitionist 95. Circuit Breaker 96. When Time Expires 97. A Night at the Roxbury 98, etc.
TV series: 21 Jump Street 88–89. Booker 89–90. Marker 95.

Griem, Helmut (1940–)
German leading man in international films.
The Damned 69. The Mackenzie Break 70. *Cabaret* 72. Ludwig 73. Voyage of the Damned 76. Sergeant Steiner 79. Children of Rage 82. Malou 83, etc.

Grier, David Alan (1955–)
American actor and comedian.
Streamers 83. A Soldier's Story 84. Beer 85. From the Hip 87. Off Limits 87. Saigon 88. Loose Cannons 90. Boomerang 92. In the Army Now 94. Blank Man 94. Tales from the Hood 95. Jumanji 95. McHale's Navy 97. Top of the World 97. Stuart Little 99. The 60s (TV) 99. The Adventures of Rocky and Bullwinkle 00. Return to Me 00, etc.
TV series: DAG 00.

Grier, Pam (1949–)
American leading lady, best known for her tough roles in blaxploitation movies of the 70s.
Beyond the Valley of the Dolls 70. The Big Doll House 71. Black Mama White Mama 72. Twilight People 72. Blacula 72. Hit Man 72. Coffy 73. The Arena 73. Scream, Blacula, Scream 73. Sheba Baby 75. Friday Foster 75. Drum 76. Greased Lightning 77. Fort Apache, the Bronx 80. Something Wicked This Way Comes 83. Tough Enough 83. Badge of the Assassin 85. Stand Alone 85. On the Edge 86. Naked Warriors 87. The Allnighter 87. Above the Law 88. The Package 89. Class of 1999 89. Bill & Ted's Bogus Journey 91. Posse 93. Original Gangstas 96. Escape from LA 96. Mars Attacks! 96. *Jackie Brown* 97. Holy Smoke 99. Snow Day 00. Fortress 2: Re-entry 00, etc.
TV series: Linc's 98– .

Grier, Roosevelt (1932–)
American footballer, cousin of Pam Grier; makes occasional showbiz appearances.
The Thing with Two Heads 72. Skyjacked 72. Evil in the Deep 76.

Grierson, John (1898–1972)
Distinguished British documentarist. Founded Empire Marketing Board Film Unit 30. GPO Film Unit 33; Canadian Film Commissioner 39–45, etc. Produced *Drifters* 29. *Industrial Britain* 33. *Song of Ceylon* 34. *Night Mail* 36, etc. In 1957–63 he had his own weekly TV show *This Wonderful World* showing excerpts from the world's best non-fiction films.

Gries, Tom (1922–1977)
American director (also co-writer and producer) with varied Hollywood experience from 1946 and much TV.
■ Hell's Horizon 55. The Girl in the Woods 58. *Will Penny* (& w) 68. 100 Rifles 69. Number One 69. The Hawaiians 70. Fools 71. Earth II (TV) 71. Call to Danger (TV) 72. The Glass House (TV) 72. Journey through Rosebud 72. Migrants (TV) 73. Lady Ice 73. QB VII (TV) 74. Breakout 75. Breakheart Pass 76. Helter Skelter (TV) 76. The Greatest 77.

Grifasi, Joe (1944–)
American character actor.
The Deer Hunter 78. On the Yard 78. Honky Tonk Freeway 81. Still of the Night 82. The Pope of Greenwich Village 84. Splash 84. Iron Weed 87. F/X 85. Presumed Innocent 90. City of Hope 91. Household Saints 93. Benny and Joon 93. Natural Born Killers 94. The Hudsucker Proxy 94. Money Train 95. Two Bits 96. One Fine Day 96. Sunday 97, etc.

Griffies, Ethel (1878–1975) (Ethel Woods)
Angular British character actress, in Hollywood for many years.
Waterloo Bridge 31. Love Me Tonight 32. The Mystery of Edwin Drood 35. Kathleen 37. We are Not Alone 39. Irene 40. Great Guns 41. *Time to Kill* 42. Jane Eyre 44. The Horn Blows at Midnight 45. Devotion 46. The Homestretch 47. The Birds 63. *Billy Liar* (GB) 63, many others.

Griffin, Josephine (1928–)
British leading lady.
The Weak and the Wicked 54. The Purple Plain 54. The Man Who Never Was 56. The Spanish Gardener (last to date) 56, etc.

Griffith, Andy (1926–)
Tall, slow-speaking American comic actor, adept at wily country-boy roles.
A Face in the Crowd (debut) 57. No Time for Sergeants 58. Onionhead 58. Winter Kill (TV) 73. Hearts of the West 75. *Washington: Behind Closed Doors* (TV) 76. The Girl in the Empty Grave (TV) 77. Deadly Game (TV) 77. Centennial (TV) 78. From Here to Eternity (TV) 79. Roots: The Next Generations (TV) 79. Fatal Vision (TV) 85. Spy Hard 96. Daddy and Them 01, etc.
TV series: The Andy Griffith Show 60–68. The Headmaster 70. Salvage 78. Matlock 86–92.

Griffith, Corinne (1898–1979)
American leading lady of the 20s.
The Yellow Girl 22. Six Days 23. Lilies of the Field 24. Love's Wilderness 24. The Marriage Whirl 25. Infatuation 25. Syncopating Sue 26. Three Hours 27. The Garden of Eden 28. The Divine Lady 29. Saturday's Children 29. Back Pay 30. Lily Christine 30. Papa's Delicate Condition (oa only) 52, etc.

Griffith, D. W. (1875–1948) (David Wark)
American film pioneer, the industry's first major producer-director; he improved the cinema's prestige, developed many aspects of technique, created a score of stars, and was only flawed by his sentimental Victorian outlook, which in the materialistic 20s put him prematurely out of vogue and in the 30s out of business. In 2000, the Director's Guild of America removed his name from their lifetime achievement award because of the racism of his *Birth of a Nation*.
Biography: 1969, *The Movies, Mr Griffith, and Me* by Lillian Gish. 1984, *D. W. Griffith and the Birth of Film* by Richard Schickel.
Selected early films: For the Love of Gold 08. The Song of the Shirt 08. Edgar Allan Poe 09. The Medicine Bottle 09. The Drunkard's Reformation 09. The Cricket on the Hearth 09. What Drink Did 09. The Violin Maker of Cremona 09. Pippa Passes 09. In the Watches of the Night 09. Lines of White on a Sullen Sea 09. Nursing a Viper 09. The Red Man's View 09. In Old California 10. Ramona 10. In the Season of Buds 10. The Face at the Window 10. The House with Closed Shutters 10. The Usurer 10. The Chink at Golden Gulch 10. Muggsy's First Sweetheart 10. The Italian Barber 10. The Manicure Lady 11. What Shall We Do with Our Old? 11. *The Lonedale Operator* 11. The Spanish Gypsy 11. Paradise Lost 11. Enoch Arden 11. Through Darkened Vales 11. The Revenue Man and the Girl 11. A Mender of Nets 12. The Goddess of Sagebrush Gulch 12. The Old Actor 12. *Man's Genesis* 12. The Sands of Dee 12. *The Musketeers of Pig Alley* 12. My Baby 12. *The New York Hat* 12. The God Within 12. The One She Loved 12. The Mothering Heart 13. The Sheriff's Baby 13. The Battle at Elderbush Gulch 13. *Judith of Bethulia* 13. The Escape 14. The Avenging Conscience 14. The Mother and the Law 14. Home Sweet Home 14, many others.
■ From 1915: *The Birth of a Nation* 15. *Intolerance* 16. *Hearts of the World* 18. The Great Love 18. The Greatest Thing in Life 18. A Romance of Happy Valley 19. *Broken Blossoms* 19. The Girl Who Stayed at Home 19. True Heart Susie 19. Scarlet Days 19. The Greatest Question 19. The Idol Dancer 20. The Love Flower 20. *Way Down East* 20. Dream Street 21. *One Exciting Night* 22. *Orphans of the Storm* 22. The White Rose 23. America 24. Isn't Life Wonderful 25. Sally of the Sawdust 26. That Royle Girl 26. *The Sorrows of Satan* 26. Drums of Love 28. The Battle of the Sexes 28. Lady of the Pavements 29. Abraham Lincoln 30. The Struggle 31. One Million Years BC (reputed contribution) 39.
✪ For enduring the fate of most monuments, and for deserving the tribute in the first place, despite being a personality with clearly unlikeable aspects. *Intolerance*.
❝ Remember how small the world was before I came along. I brought it all to life: I moved the whole world onto a 20-foot screen. – *D.W.G.*
He did what he did genuinely, and straight from the heart. His best films are passionate and tender, terrifying and pregnant, works of art certainly, and products too of an imagination far ahead of its time. – *Paul O'Dell*
It is time D. W. Griffith was rescued from the pedestal of an outmoded pioneer. The cinema of Griffith, after all, is no more outmoded than the drama of Aeschylus. – *Andrew Sarris, 1968*
Griffith's enormous success was due largely to the fact that his heroes and heroines firmly believed, and practised the belief, that babies are brought by the stork. The lowbrow who believed otherwise was always the Griffith villain. – *George Jean Nathan*
He was the first to photograph thought, said Cecil B. de Mille. It was quite a compliment. But Griffith was full of contradictions. His brain was progressive, his emotions Victorian. For a few years the two aspects were able to join in public favour, but he could not adapt himself to the brisker pace of the 20s, when he made many such blinkered and stubborn pronouncements as: 'We do not want now and we never shall want the human voice with our films.'
When the inevitable happened in 1928 he declared: 'We have taken beauty and exchanged it for stilted voices.'
He could be tactless too, as when in 1918 he commented: 'Viewed as drama, the war is somewhat disappointing.'
Yet this was the man of whom Gene Fowler could say: 'He articulated the mechanics of cinema and bent them to his flair.'
Lilian Gish, a great admirer of Griffith, said: 'He inspired in us his belief that we were working in a medium that was powerful enough to influence the whole world.'
To Mack Sennett: 'He was my day school, my adult education program, my university ... (but) he was an extremely difficult man to know.'
He said himself: 'The task I'm trying to achieve above all is to make you see ...'
He knew his own value, as many an actor found when asking for a rise: 'It's worth a lot more than money to be working for me!'
This was true enough up to the time of *The Birth of a Nation*, which President Wilson described as: 'Like writing history with lightning.'
But it became less so after the box-office flop of *Intolerance*, which Gene Fowler called: 'The greatest commercial anticlimax in film history.'
He became an embarrassment to Hollywood because his ideas seemed outmoded; in the 30s he scarcely worked at all. When he died in 1948 Hedda Hopper, recalling the marks made by stars in the wet cement at Hollywood's Chinese

Theater, said: 'Griffith's footprints were never asked for, yet no one has ever filled his shoes ...'

And James Agee added: 'There is not a man working in movies, nor a man who cares for them, who does not owe Griffith more than he owes anyone else.'

Ezra Goodman commented: 'At Griffith's funeral, the sacred cows of Hollywood gathered to pay him homage. A week before, he probably could not have gotten any of them on the telephone.'

It is said indeed that death had to come before such tributes as Frank Capra's: 'Since Griffith there has been no major improvement in the art of film direction.'

And Carmel Myers': 'He was the umbrella that shaded us all.'

And John Simon's: 'Griffith did for film what Sackville and Norton, the authors of *Gorboduc*, did for drama.'

Griffith, Edward H. (1894–1975)
American director.
Scrambled Wives 21. Unseeing Eyes 23. Bad Company 25. Afraid to Love 27. Paris Bound 29. Holiday 30. Rebound 31. The Animal Kingdom 32. Another Language 33. Biography of a Bachelor Girl 35. No More Ladies 35. Ladies in Love 36. Café Metropole 37. Café Society 39. Safari 40. Virginia 40. One Night in Lisbon 41. Bahama Passage 42. The Sky's the Limit 43. Perilous Holiday 46, etc.

Griffith, Hugh (1912–1980)
Flamboyant Welsh actor, former bank clerk.
Neutral Port (debut) 40; war service; The Three Weird Sisters 48. London Belongs to Me 48. The Last Days of Dolwyn 48. A Run for Your Money 49. Laughter in Paradise 51. The Galloping Major 51. The Beggar's Opera 52. *The Titfield Thunderbolt* 53. The Sleeping Tiger 54. Passage Home 55. *Lucky Jim* 57. *Ben Hur* (AA) 59. The Day They Robbed the Bank of England 60. Exodus 61. The Counterfeit Traitor 62. *Tom Jones* (AAN) 63. The Bargee 64. Moll Flanders 65. Oh Dad, Poor Dad 66. Sailor from Gibraltar 66. How to Steal a Million 66. The Chastity Belt 67. Oliver 68. The Fixer 68. Start the Revolution Without Me 69. Cry of the Banshee 70. Wuthering Heights 70. The Abominable Dr Phibes 71. Who Slew Auntie Roo? 72. What 72. Craze 73. Take Me High 73. Luther 75. Loving Cousins 76. Joseph Andrews 77. The Last Remake of Beau Geste 77. The Passover Plot 77, many others.

Griffith, James (1916–1993)
American general-purpose actor.
Bright Leaf 50. Rhubarb 51. The Law vs Billy the Kid (as Pat Garrett) 54. Anything Goes 56. The Big Fisherman 59. The Amazing Transparent Man 61. Advance to the Rear 63. A Big Hand for the Little Lady 66. Day of the Evil Gun 68. Vanishing Point 71. The Tooth of Crime 75. Speedtrap 78, etc.

Griffith, Kenneth (1921–)
Sharp-eyed Welsh actor of stage and screen, often the envious 'little man'.
Autobiography: 1994, *The Fool's Paradise*.
Love on the Dole 41. The Shop at Sly Corner 45. Bond Street 48. Forbidden 49. Waterfront 50. High Treason 51. The Green Buddha 54. The Prisoner 55. Private's Progress 56. Tiger in the Smoke 56. Blue Murder at St Trinians 57. Lucky Jim 57. The Man Upstairs 58. A Night to Remember 58. The Two-Headed Spy 58. I'm All Right, Jack 59. Circus of Horrors 60. A French Mistress 60. Rag Doll 60. Suspect 60. Frightened City 61. Payroll 61. *Only Two Can Play* 62. The Painted Smile 62. Rotten to the Core 65. The Bobo 67. The Assassination Bureau 68. Great Catherine 68. Jane Eyre 70. Revenge 71. The House in Nightmare Park 73. Callan 74. S*P*Y*S 74. Sky Riders 76. The Wild Geese 78. The Sea Wolves 80. Remembrance 82. Who Dares Wins 82. The Englishman Who Went up a Hill but Came Down a Mountain 95. Very Annie-Mary 99, etc.

Griffith, Melanie (1957–)
American leading actress, the daughter of Tippi Hedren. She entered hospital for treatment of a drug problem stemming from her use of a prescribed medication in 2000. She married actor Don Johnson (1976–77) and, following another divorce, remarried him in 1989. They were divorced again in 1995, and she subsequently married actor Antonio Banderas in 1996.
Night Moves 75. The Drowning Pool 76. Body Double 84. Fear City 85. Something Wild 86. The Milagro Beanfield War 88. Cherry 2000 88. Stormy Monday 88. Working Girl (AAN) 88. In the Spirit 90. The Bonfire of the Vanities 90. Pacific Heights 90. Paradise 91. Shining Through 92. Born Yesterday 93. Milk Money 94. Nobody's Fool 94. Buffalo Girls (TV) 95. Now and Then 96. Mulholland Falls 96. Lolita 97. Another Day in Paradise 98. Celebrity 98, etc.
TV series: Once an Eagle 76–77. Carter Country 78–79. Me and George 98– .
❝ There's a bit of a stripper in every woman. – M.G.
The instantly recognisable Griffith Girl: a trashy babe in black underpant and matching garter belt with a squeaky voice, a butt that is not to be trifled with, and a heart as wide as Asia. – *Joe Queenan*

Griffith, Raymond (1887–1957)
Dapper American comedian of the 20s, born in Boston, Massachusetts. Married actress Bertha Mann.
Fools First 22. The Eternal Three 23. Changing Husbands 24. Poisoned Paradise 24. Open All Night 24. Miss Bluebeard 24. A Regular Fellow 25. *Fine Clothes* 25. *Hands Up* 25. *Wet Paint* 26. You'd Be Surprised 27. Time to Love 27. Wedding Bills 27. *All Quiet on the Western Front* (as the dying soldier) 30, etc.

Griffith, Richard (1912–1969)
American film critic and curator of New York's Museum of Modern Art.

Griffith, Thomas Ian (1960–)
American actor, screenwriter and producer. Married actress Mary Page Keller.
Karate Kid Part III (a) 89. Ulterior Motives (a) 91. Night of the Warrior (p, w) 91. Excessive Force (p, a, w) 93. Crackerjack (a) 94. Blood of the Innocent (a) 94. Hollow Point (a) 95. Behind Enemy Lines (a) 96. Kull the Conqueror (a) 97. John Carpenter's Vampires (a) 97, etc.

Griffiths, Jane (1929–1975)
British leading lady of the 50s.
The Million Pound Note 54. The Green Scarf 54. Dead Man's Evidence 62. The Traitors 63, etc.

Griffiths, Linda
Canadian leading actress, dramatist and screenwriter.
Lianna 83. Overdrawn at the Memory Bank 83. Reno and the Doc 84. The Darling Family (& w) 94, etc.

Griffiths, Rachel
Australian leading actress.
Muriel's Wedding 94. Jude (GB) 96. My Best Friend's Wedding (US) 97. My Son the Fanatic 97. Welcome to Woop Woop 97. Among Giants (GB) 98. Divorcing Jack (GB) 98. Hilary and Jackie (GB, ANN) 98. *Me Myself I* 99, etc.

Griffiths, Richard (1947–)
Sizeable British actor, best known for his role as a police inspector-cum-restaurateur in the TV series *Pie in the Sky*. The son of deaf mute parents, he was for ten years a member of the Royal Shakespeare Company, where he was a notable Bottom in *A Midsummer Night's Dream*.
Greystoke 84. Gorky Park 84. A Private Function 85. Shanghai Surprise 86. Withnail and I 87. King Ralph 91. The Naked Gun $2\frac{1}{2}$: The Smell of Fear 91. Blame It on the Bellboy 92. Guarding Tess 94. Funny Bones 95. Sleepy Hollow 99. Gormenghast (TV) 2000, etc.
TV series: Bird of Prey 84. Nobody's Perfect 80–82. Ffizz 87–89. A Kind of Living 88–90. Pie in the Sky 94–95. Hope and Glory 00.
❝ I think of myself as the world's most intelligent ambulatory aubergine. – R.G.
No actor chooses to be in a film. In the real world you kick, scramble and stagger to get into the thing. I know actors who hold parties simply because they have an audition, which is tragic. – R.G.

Griggs, Loyal (1906–1978)
American cinematographer.
Shane (AA) 53. Elephant Walk 54. We're No Angels 55. The Ten Commandments 56. The Hangman 59. Walk Like a Dragon 60. The Slender Thread 66. Hurry Sundown 67. P. J. 68, many others.

Grimault, Paul (1905–1994)
French animator. *Le Petit Soldat* 47, many shorts.

Grimes, Gary (1955–)
American juvenile lead of the 70s.
■ *Summer of 42* 71. The Culpepper Cattle Co. 72. Class of 44 73. Cahill 73. The Spikes Gang 74. Once an Eagle (TV) 76. Gus 76.

Grimes, Stephen (1927–1988)
British production designer, particularly associated with the films of John Huston.
Heaven Knows Mr Allison 57. The Night of the Iguana 64. Reflections in a Golden Eye 67. Sinful Davey 68. Ryan's Daughter 70. Murder by Death 76. Bobby Deerfield 77. The Electric Horseman 79. Urban Cowboy 80. The Dresser 83. Krull 83. Never Say Never Again 83. Out of Africa (AA) 85. The Dead 87. Haunted Summer 88, etc.

Grimes, Tammy (1934–)
American comedy actress who never really made it in the movies. She is the mother of Amanda Plummer.
■ Three Bites of the Apple 67. Arthur Arthur 69. The Other Man (TV) 70. Play It As It Lays 72. The Borrowers (TV) 73. Horror at 37,000 Feet (TV) 73. Somebody Killed Her Husband 78. You Can't Go Home Again (TV) 79. The Runner Stumbles 79. Can't Stop the Music 80. America 86. Mr North 88. Mr 247 94.

Grimm, Jakob and Wilhelm (1785–1863 and 1786–1859)
German writers of philology and – especially – fairy tales. The latter are familiar throughout the world and have been the basis of many children's films by Walt Disney and others. A thin biopic, *The Wonderful World of the Brothers Grimm*, was made in 1962.

Grimm, Oliver (1948–)
German child actor of the 50s.
My Name is Nicki 52. Father Needs a Wife 52. My Father the Actor 56. Kleiner Mann – ganz gross 57. The Magnificent Rebel 60. Reach for Glory 61, etc.

Grinde, Nick (1891–1979)
American director.
Excuse Me 25. Upstage 26. Beyond the Sierra 28. *The Bishop Murder Case* 30. Good News 30. This Modern Age 31. Vanity Street 32. Ladies Crave Excitement 35. Public Enemy's Wife 36. White Bondage 37. King of Chinatown 39. The Man They Could Not Hang 39. Behind the Door 40. Hitler Dead or Alive 43. Road to Alcatraz 45, etc.

Grisham, John (1955–)
American best-selling novelist, a former lawyer. He was paid $2.25m for the film rights to *The Client* and a record $3.75m for the film rights to *The Chamber* before it was written. Film rights in his 1989 novel *A Time to Kill* were sold for around $6m in 1994. Screen rights to his novel *The Runaway Jury* were sold for $8m. In 1996, after a friend was killed by two teenagers who claimed to have been imitating the protagonists of *Natural Born Killers*, he suggested that the film's director Oliver Stone should be held legally accountable for it and other deaths – 'The "artist" should be required to share the responsibility along with the nut who actually pulled the trigger,' he wrote.
The Firm 92. The Pelican Brief 93. The Client 94. A Time to Kill 96. The Chamber 96. The Gingerbread Man 97. John Grisham's The Rainmaker 97.

Grizzard, George (1928–)
American stage actor, usually in sneaky roles in films.
From the Terrace 60. *Advise and Consent* 62. Warning Shot 66. Happy Birthday Wanda June 71. Travis Logan DA (TV) 71. Indict and Convict (TV) 74. The Stranger Within (TV) 74. Attack on Terror (TV) 75. The Lives of Jenny Dolan (TV) 75. Comes a Horseman 78. The Night Rider (TV) 79. Firepower 79. Seems Like Old Times 80. Wrong Is Right 82. Bachelor Party 84. Robert Kennedy and His Times (TV) 85. An Enemy of the People (TV) 90. Queen (TV) 93. Scarlett (TV) 94, etc.
TV series: Studio 5-B 89.

Grock (1880–1959) (Adrien Wettach)
Swiss clown who made a few silent films in Britain, and later in Germany. A biopic, *Farewell Mr Grock*, was made in 1954.

Grodin, Charles (1935–)
American leading man, usually in droll roles. He has also worked as a television talk show host and commentator.
■ Rosemary's Baby 68. Sex and the College Girl 70. Catch 22 70. *The Heartbreak Kid* 72. 11 Harrowhouse 74. King Kong 76. Thieves 77. Heaven Can Wait 78. Just Me and You (TV) 78. The Grass Is Always Greener Over the Septic Tank (TV) 78. Sunburn 79. Real Life 79. It's My Turn 80. Seems Like Old Times 80. The Great Muppet Caper 81. The Incredible Shrinking Woman 81. The Lonely Guy 83. Movers and Shakers 84. The Woman in Red 84. The Last Resort 86. Ishtar 87. The Couch Trip 88. Midnight Run 88. You Can't Hurry Love 88. Taking Care of Business 90. Clifford 91. Beethoven 92. Dave 93. So I Married an Axe Murderer 93. Beethoven's 2nd 93. Heart and Souls 93. Clifford 94. It Runs in the Family 94.
TV series: The Charles Grodin Show 94-98. 60 Minutes II 00
❝ He keeps threatening to be funny but he rarely makes it. – *Pauline Kael*

Gropman, David
American production designer.
Sweet Lorraine 87. Miles from Home 88. Slaves of New York 89. Mr & Mrs Bridge 90. Once Around 91. The Cutting Edge 92. Of Mice and Men 92. Searching for Bobby Fischer 93. Nobody's Fool 94. Waiting to Exhale 95. A Walk in the Clouds 95. Marvin's Room 96. One Fine Day 96. A Civil Action 98. Twilight 98. The Cider House Rules (AAN) 99, etc.

Grosbard, Ulu (1929–)
Belgian-American director, former diamond-cutter and Broadway director.
■ The Subject Was Roses 68. Who Is Harry Kellerman and Why Is He Saying Those Terrible Things About Me? 71. Straight Time 78. True Confessions 81. Falling in Love 84. Georgia 95.

Gross, Charles
American composer, mainly for TV movies.
The Group 65. Valdez Is Coming 71. Heartland 79. Sweet Dreams 85. Punchline 88. Turner & Hooch 89. Air America 90, etc.

Gross, Larry
American screenwriter.
Headin' for Broadway (co-w) 80. 48 Hrs (co-w) 82. Streets of Fire (co-w) 84. Another 48 Hrs (co-w) 90. Geronimo (co-w) 93. Rear Window (co-w) (TV) 98, etc.

Grossmith, George (1874–1935)
Elegant British musical comedy star who appeared in a few films. He was the son of author and actor George Grossmith (1847–1912), and brother of Lawrence Grossmith (1877–1944), who also appeared in some 30s films. He was the first chairman of Alexander Korda's London Films.
■ Women Everywhere 30. Service for Ladies 32. Wedding Rehearsal 32. The Girl from Maxim's 33. Princess Charming 34.

Grot, Anton (1884–1974) (Antocz Franziszek Groszewski)
Polish-born director in Hollywood, the driving force of Warner's 30s dream machine. He studied at the Cracow Academy of Arts and in Germany, emigrating to the United States in 1909. His paintings brought an offer of work in films with Lubin; he then designed for Vitagraph and Pathé, moving to Hollywood in the early 20s to work on Douglas Fairbanks's *Robin Hood*. He designed for Cecil B. De Mille before joining Warner's in 1927, where he stayed until he retired in 1948, designing 80 films, including many directed by Michael Curtiz. He was awarded a Technical Oscar in 1940 for his invention of a ripple machine used in *The Sea Hawk*. After he retired, he returned to his painting.
The Mouse and the Lion 13. Arms and the Woman 16. Pirate Gold 20. Tess of the Storm Country 22. *The Thief of Bagdad* 24. Don Q Son of Zorro 25. The Country Doctor 27. The King of Kings 27. The Blue Danube 28. Noah's Ark 29. *Little Caesar* 30. Hatchet Man 31. *Svengali* (AAN) 31. 20,000 Years in Sing Sing 32. Doctor X 32.

Baby Face 33. Footlight Parade 33. *The Mystery of the Wax Museum* 33. Gold Diggers of 1933 33. Gold Diggers of 1935 34. *A Midsummer Night's Dream* 35. Captain Blood 35. Dr Socrates 35. *Anthony Adverse* (AAN) 36. Tovarich 37. The Life of Emile Zola (AAN) 37. *The Private Lives of Elizabeth and Essex* (AAN) 39. They Made Me a Criminal 39. *Juarez* 39. *The Sea Hawk* (AAN) 40. *The Sea Wolf* 41. Thank Your Lucky Stars 43. The Conspirators 44. Rhapsody in Blue 45. Mildred Pierce 45. My Reputation 46. *The Unsuspected* 47. Possessed 47. One Sunday Afternoon 48, etc.

Gruault, Jean (1924–)
French screenwriter.
Jules et Jim 61. The Wild Child/L'Enfant Sauvage 70. The Story of Adele H. 75. Mon Oncle d'Amérique (AAN) 80. L'Amour à Mort 84. Life Is a Bed of Roses/La Vie Est un Roman 84. Les Années 80s (co-w) 85. The Mystery of Alexina (co-w) 85. Australia 89. Le Bateau de Mariage 93, etc.

Gruber, Frank (1904–1969)
American screenwriter.
Death of a Champion (oa) 39. The Kansan (oa) 43. *The Mask of Dimitrios* 44. Terror by Night 47. Fighting Man of the Plains 49. The Great Missouri Raid 51. Denver and Rio Grande 52. Hurricane Smith 52. Backlash (oa) 56. The Big Land (oa) 57. Town Tamer 65. Arizona Raiders (oa) 67, etc.
TV series (created): *Tales of Wells Fargo*.

Gruenberg, Louis (1884–1964)
Russian-American composer.
Stagecoach (co-m) 39. So Ends Our Night 40. Arch of Triumph 49. All the King's Men 49, etc.

Gruendgens, Gustav (1899–1963)
German stage actor and director; films occasional.
M (a) 31. Pygmalion (a) 35. Capriolen (d) 37. Friedemann Bach (a) 41. Faust (ad) 61.

Gruffudd, Ioan (1973–)
Welsh leading actor, best known for playing the title role in the TV seafaring series *Hornblower*. Born in Cardiff, he studied acting at RADA.
Poldark (TV) 96. Titanic 97. Wilde 97. Great Expectations (TV) 99. Solomon and Gaenor 98. Warriors (TV) 99. Another Life 00. Shooters 00. 102 Dalmatians 00, etc.

Grune, Karl (1890–1962)
Czech-Austrian director in German films.
The Street 23. At the Edge of the World 27. Waterloo 28. Abdul the Damned (GB) 35. Pagliacci (GB) 37, etc.

Gruner, Olivier (1960–)
French star of American action movies, a former marine and kick-boxing champion. Born in Paris, he worked as a model in TV commercials before moving to the USA.
Angel Town 89. Nemesis 93. Zero Hour 94. The Fighter 95. Savage 96. Mercenary 96. Mars 96. TNT 97, etc.

Grusin, Dave (1934–)
American composer.
Divorce American Style 67. The Graduate 67. Candy 68. The Mad Room 69. Tell them Willie Boy is Here 69. The Pursuit of Happiness 71. The Great Northfield Minnesota Raid 72. Bobby Deerfield 77. The Goodbye Girl 77. The Cheap Detective 78. Heaven Can Wait (AAN) 78. The Champ (AAN) 79. And Justice for All 79. The Electric Horseman 79. My Bodyguard 80. On Golden Pond (AAN) 81. Absence of Malice 81. Reds 81. The Little Drummer Girl 84. Falling in Love 84. The Goonies 85. Lucas 86. Ishtar 87. The Milagro Beanfield War (AA) 88. Tequila Sunrise 88. A Dry White Season 89. The Fabulous Baker Boys (AAN) 89. Bonfire of the Vanities 90. Look Who's Talking Too 90. Havana 90. For the Boys 91. The Firm (AAN) 93. The Cure 95. Mulholland Falls 96. Selena 96. In the Gloaming (TV) 97. Hope Floats 98, etc.

Guard, Dominic (1956–)
British juvenile actor of the 70s.
The Go-Between 70. The Hands of Cormac Joyce (TV) 72. Bequest to the Nation 73. The Count of Monte Cristo (TV) 74. Picnic at Hanging Rock 75. Gandhi 82. A Woman of Substance (TV) 84. Absolution 88. The Man Who Lost His Shadow 91, etc.

Guardino, Harry (1925–1995)
Leading American TV actor, in occasional films.
Houseboat 58. Pork Chop Hill 59. The Five Pennies 59. King of Kings 61. Hell is for Heroes 62. Rhino 64. Bullwhip Griffin 67. Madigan 68. Lovers and Other Strangers 69. Red Sky at Morning 71. Dirty Harry 71. Capone 75. St Ives 76. The Enforcer 76. Street Killing (TV) 76. Rollercoaster 77. Goldengirl (TV) 79. Any Which Way You Can 80. The Neon Empire 89, etc.
TV series: The Reporter 64. Monty Nash 71.

Guare, John (1938–)
American dramatist and screenwriter. Born in New York, he studied at the Yale School of Drama.
Taking Off (co-w) 71. Atlantic City (AANw) 81. Six Degrees of Separation (w, from his play) 93. The Venice Project (as himself) 99.

Guareschi, Giovanni (1908–1968)
Italian author of the 'Don Camillo' stories about a parish priest's comic struggles with a communist mayor. Several were filmed with Fernandel and Gino Cervi.

Guber, Peter (1939–)
Producer whose Guber-Peters production company, formed in partnership with Jon Peters, enjoyed success in the 80s. Head of Columbia 1989–94, following its takeover by Sony; now an independent producer.
Books: 1996, *Hit and Run: How Jon Peters and Peter Guber Took Sony for a Ride in Hollywood* by Nancy Griffin & Kim Masters.
The Deep 77. Midnight Express 78. An American Werewolf in London 81. Six Weeks 82. The Color Purple 85. The Clan of the Cave Bear 86. Innerspace 87. The Witches of Eastwick 87. Gorillas in the Mist 88. Rain Man 88. Batman 89. The Bonfire of the Vanities 90. Batman Returns 92. This Boy's Life 93. With Honors 94, etc.
❝ Failures are what teach you to be good. I've learned far more from those than from my successes. – P.G.

Guerman, Alexei (1938–) (aka Alexei Gherman)
Russian director and screenwriter, the son of writer Yuri Guerman, whose stories formed the basis of his film *My Friend Ivan Lapshin*. His career has been dogged by government censorship: *Trial on the Road*, about a Red Army sergeant who deserts from the German Army, was banned for 14 years, and his next film, dealing with the difference between the reality of the Battle of Stalingrad and a film director's recreation of it, was also withdrawn for several years.
The Seventh Satellite (co-d) 67. Trial on the Road/Proverka Na Dorogakh 71. Twenty Days without War/Dvadtsat Dnei Bez Voini 76. My *Friend Ivan Lapshin* 86. Happy Days 92. Khroustaliov, My Car! 98, etc.

Guerra, Ruy (1931–)
Brazilian director, playwright, actor and composer. Born in Mozambique and educated in France, he lived in Brazil from the late 50s to the mid-60s, leaving to settle in Mozambique, where he founded the National Institute of Cinema and made that country's first feature film in 1980.
Os Cafajestes 62. Os Fuzis 64. Sweet Hunters 69. Mueda, Memoria e Massacre 80. Erendira 82. Opera do Malandro 86. Kuarup 89, etc.

Guerra, Tonino (1920–)
Italian screenwriter and novelist who wrote five films for Antonioni.
La Notte 61. L'Avventura 61. Red Desert 65. Casanova '70 (AAN) 65. Blow-Up (AAN) 66. Zabriskie Point 70. Amarcord (AAN) 74. Un Papillon sur l'Epaule 78. The Night of the Shooting Stars/La Notte di San Lorenzo 82. And the Ship Sails On 83. Nostalgia 84. Henry IV 85. Ginger and Fred 86. Good Morning Babylon 86. The Beekeeper/O Melissokomos 86. Chronicle of a Death Foretold 87. To Forget Palermo/Dimenticare Palermo 89. The Dark Illness/Il Male Oscuro 89. Stanno Tutti Bene 90. Journey of Love/Viàggio d'Amore 91. Especially on Sundays/La Domenica Specialmente 91. The Petrified Garden 93. Beyond the Clouds 95, etc.

Guest, Christopher (1948–) (Lord Haden-Guest)
British actor and screenwriter turned director. He married actress Jamie Lee Curtis in 1984.
The Hot Rock (a) 72. Girlfriends (a) 78. The Long Riders (a) 80. Heartbeeps (a) 81. *This Is Spinal Tap* (w,a) 84. Beyond Therapy (a) 86. Little Shop of Horrors (a) 86. The Princess Bride (a) 87. Beyond Therapy (a) 87. Sticky Fingers (a) 88. The Big Picture (wd) 89. Attack of the 50 Ft Woman (d,TV) 93. Waiting for Guffman (co-w, d, a) 97. Best in Show (co-w,d,a) 00, etc.

Guest, Val (1911–) (Valmond Guest)
British writer-producer-director, former journalist. Worked on screenplays of 30s comedies for Will Hay, Arthur Askey, the Crazy Gang, etc. Married to Yolande Donlan.
SCREENPLAYS, mostly in collaboration: The Maid of the Mountains 32. Good Morning Boys 36. Okay for Sound 37. *Oh Mr Porter* 38. Convict 99 38. *Alf's Button Afloat* 38. Band Waggon 39. The Frozen Limits 39. Old Bones of the River 39. *Ask a Policeman* 40. Charley's Aunt 40. Gasbags 40. Inspector Hornleigh Goes to It 41. *The Ghost Train* 41. Back Room Boy 42. London Town 46. Paper Orchid 49 etc.
■ AS DIRECTOR (usually writer also): Miss London Ltd. 43. Bees in Paradise 44. Give Us the Moon 44. I'll Be Your Sweetheart 45. Just William's Luck 47. William Comes to Town 48. Murder at the Windmill 49. Miss Pilgrim's Progress 50. The Body Said No 50. *Mr Drake's Duck* 51. Penny Princess 52. *The Runaway Bus* 54. Life with the Lyons 54. Men of Sherwood Forest 54. Dance Little Lady 54. They Can't Hang Me 54. The Lyons in Paris 55. Break in the Circle 55. *The Quatermass Experiment* 55. It's A Wonderful World 55. The Weapon 56. Carry On Admiral 57. *Quatermass II* 57. The Abominable Snowman 57. Camp on Blood Island 58. Up the Creek 58. Life is a Circus 59. Yesterday's Enemy 59. *Expresso Bongo* 60. Further Up the Creek 60. Hell is a City 60. The Full Treatment 60. The Day the Earth Caught Fire 61. *Jigsaw* 63. 80,000 Suspects 63. The Beauty Jungle 64. Where the Spies are 65. Casino Royale (wd) 67. Assignment K 67. When Dinosaurs Ruled the World 68. Tomorrow 70. Au Pair Girls 72. Confessions of a Window Cleaner 74. The Diamond Mercenaries 76. Dangerous Davies (TV) 80. The Boys in Blue 83. Possession (TV) 84. The Scent of Fear (TV) 85.

Guétary, Georges (1915–1997) (Lambros Worloou)
Greek/Egpytian singer and actor in occasional films. Born in Alexandria, Egypt, he studied music in France and worked in music hall, first as a band guitarist from the mid-30s, and then becoming a protégé of Mistinguett. He became a star in London, in the musical *Bless the Bride*, appeared on Broadway and made his only American film, *An American in Paris* 51, before returning to France to star in many operettas. Among his stage successes was a musical, *La Polka des Lampions*, adapted from Billy Wilder's *Some Like It Hot*. He retired in the mid-80s.
Black Cavalier/Le Cavalier Noir 45. The Adventures of Casanova/Les Aventures de Casanova 46. *An American in Paris* 51. Une Fille sur la Route 52. Plume au Vent 53. The Road to Paradise/Le Chemin du Paradis 56. Une Nuit aux Baléares 57, etc.

Guevara, Che (1928–1967) (Ernesto Guevara)
Argentinian-born guerrilla leader who became a revolutionary icon in the 60s, after he had joined Fidel Castro to overthrow the regime of president Batista in Cuba. He was killed while attempting to lead a revolution in Bolivia. He was played by Francisco Rabal in the Italian biopic *El 'Che' Guevara* 68, Omar Sharif in *Che!* 69, and Antonio Banderas in the film version of the musical *Evita* 96.

Guffey, Burnett (1905–1983)
Distinguished American cinematographer.
Cover Girl 44. Johnny O'Clock 46. Gallant Journey 46. The Reckless Moment 48. *All the King's Men* 49. In a Lonely Place 50. The Sniper 52. *From Here to Eternity* (AA) 53. Human Desire 55. The Harder They Fall 56. Edge of Eternity 59. Birdman of Alcatraz 62. King Rat 65. *Bonnie and Clyde* (AA) 67. The Split 68. The Madwoman of Chaillot 69. The Great White Hope 70, etc.

Guffroy, Pierre (1926–)
French art director and production designer who worked on Buñuel's later films and also several by Roman Polanski. A documentary on his work, *Behind the Scenes: A Portrait of Pierre Guffroy*, was made in 1992.
Le Testament d'Orphée 59. Mouchette 67. The Bride Wore Black/La Mariée était en Noir 67. The Milky Way 68. Rider on the Rain 69. The Discreet Charm of the Bourgeoisie 72. Cesar and Rosalie 72. The Phantom of Liberty 74. The Tenant 76. That Obscure Object of Desire 77. Tess 79. L'Argent 83. Pirates 86. The Unbearable Lightness of Being 87. Mayrig 91. Giorgino 94. Death and the Maiden 95, etc.

Gugino, Carla (1971–)
American actress, a former model.
Son-in-Law 93. This Boy's Life 93. Miami Rhapsody 95. The Buccaneers (TV) 95. The War at Home 96. Wedding Bell Blues 97. Snake Eyes 98, etc.

Guild, Nancy (1925–1999)
American leading lady.
Somewhere in the Night 46. The Brasher Doubloon 46. The High Window 47. Give My Regards to Broadway 48. Abbott and Costello Meet the Invisible Man 51. Little Egypt 51. Francis Covers the Big Town 54. Such Good Friends 71, etc.

Guilfoyle, Paul (1902–1961)
American character actor usually in sly or sinister roles.
Special Agent 36. Blind Alibi 38. Time to Kill 42. Sweetheart of Sigma Chi 46. Miss Mink of 1949. Mighty Joe Young 50. Torch Song 52. Julius Caesar 53. Valley of Fury 55, many others.
AS DIRECTOR: Captain Scarface 53. A Life at Stake 54. Tess of the Storm Country 60.
TV series: CSI: Crime Scene Investigation 00- .

Guillaume, Robert (1927–) (Robert Williams)
Handsome American leading man and comedian, former opera singer.
Seems Like Old Times 80. The Kid with the Broken Halo (TV) 82. The Kid with the 200 I.Q. (TV) 83. Prince Jack 84. They Still Call Me Bruce 86. Wanted: Dead or Alive 86. Fire and Rain 89. Lean on Me 89. Death Warrant 90. The Meteor Man 93. The Lion King (voice) 94. First Kid 96. The Lion King II: Simba's Pride (voice) 98, etc.
TV series: *Soap* 77–80. *Benson* 79–86. Sports Night 98– .

Guillermin, John (1925–)
English director and screenwriter. Born in London of French parents, he was educated at Cambridge University and produced and directed documentaries in Paris before returning to England in the late 40s, moving to Los Angeles in the early 60s, after the success of *Waltz of the Toreadors*.
■ Torment 49. Smart Alec 50. Never Let Go (w) 50. Two on the Tiles 51. Four Days 51. Song of Paris 52. Miss Robin Hood 52. Operation Diplomat 53. Adventure in the Hopfields 54. The Crowded Day 54. Thunderstorm 55. Double Jeopardy 55. *Town on Trial* 56. The Whole Truth 57. *I Was Monty's Double* 58. Tarzan's Greatest Adventure 59. The Day They Robbed The Bank of England 60. Never Let Go (& w) 60. Waltz of the Toreadors 62. Tarzan Goes to India 62. Guns at Batasi 64. Rapture 65. *The Blue Max* 66. P.J. 68. House of Cards 68. The Bridge at Remagen 69. El Condor 70. Skyjacked 72. Shaft in Africa 74. The Towering Inferno (co-d) 74. King Kong 76. Death on the Nile 78. Mr Patman 80. Crossover 83. Sheena Queen of the Jungle 84. King Kong Lives 86.

Guinan, Texas (1884–1933) (Mary Louise Guinan)
Canadian star entertainer of 20s speakeasies: her catchphrase was 'Hello, sucker!', and she was one of Broadway's most prominent attractions. Betty Hutton played her in *Incendiary Blonde* 45.
■ The Gun Woman 18. Little Miss Deputy 19. I am the Woman 21. The Stampede 21. Queen of the Night Clubs 29. Glorifying the American Girl 29. Broadway through a Keyhole 33.

Guinness, Sir Alec (1914–2000)
Distinguished British stage actor, who in the late 40s started a spectacular film career, first as a master of disguise, then as a young hero and later as any character from an Arab king to Hitler. Honorary Oscar 1979 'for advancing the art of screen acting'.
Autobiography: 1985, *Blessings in Disguise*. 1996, *My Name Escapes Me: The Diary of a Retiring Actor*. 1999, *A Positively Final Appearance*.

Biography: 1994, *Master of Disguise* by Garry O'Connor.

■ Evensong 33. Great Expectations (as Herbert Pocket) 46. *Oliver Twist* (as Fagin) 48. *Kind Hearts and Coronets* (playing eight roles) 49. A Run for Your Money 49. Last Holiday 50. *The Mudlark* (as Disraeli) 50. *The Lavender Hill Mob* (AAN) 51. *The Man in the White Suit* 51. *The Card* 52. The Captain's Paradise 52. The Malta Story 53. *Father Brown* 54. To Paris with Love 54. The Prisoner 55. The Ladykillers 55. The Swan 56. Barnacle Bill 57. *The Bridge on the River Kwai* (AA, BFA) 57. The Scapegoat 58. The Horse's Mouth (& w) (AAN) 58. Our Man in Havana 59. *Tunes of Glory* 60. A Majority of One 61. HMS Defiant 62. Lawrence of Arabia 62. The Fall of the Roman Empire 64. Situation Hopeless but Not Serious 64. Doctor Zhivago 66. Hotel Paradiso 66. The Quiller Memorandum 66. The Comedians 67. Cromwell (as Charles I) 69. Scrooge 70. Hitler: The Last Ten Days (as Hitler) 73. Brother Sun and Sister Moon 73. Murder by Death 76. Star Wars (AAN) 77. Tinker Tailor Soldier Spy (TV) 79. The Empire Strikes Back 80. Raise the Titanic 80. Little Lord Fauntleroy (TV) 80. Smiley's People (TV) 82. Lovesick 83. A Passage to India 84. Monsignor Quixote (TV) 85. Little Dorrit (AAN) 87. A Handful of Dust 88. Kafka 91. A Foreign Field (TV) 93. Mute Witness 95. Eskimo Day (TV) 96.

✪ For a multitude of disguises in which he never allowed humanity to be swamped by dexterity. *Father Brown*.

❝ I gave my best performances, perhaps, during the war – trying to be an officer and a gentleman. – A.G.

I don't know what else I could do but pretend to be an actor. – A.G.

Once I've done a film, it's finished. I never look at it again. – A.G.

Getting to the theatre on the early side, usually about seven o'clock, changing into a dressing-gown, applying make-up, having a chat for a few minutes with other actors and then, quite unconsciously, beginning to assume another personality which would stay with me (but mostly tucked inside) until curtain down, was all I required of life. I thought it bliss. – A.G.

Personally, I have only one great regret–that I never *dared* enough. If at all. – A.G.

Guiol, Fred (1898–1964)
American director, mainly of second features; also worked as assistant on many of George Stevens's pictures.

Live and Learn 30. The Cohens and Kellys in Trouble 33. The Nitwits 35. Hayfoot 41. Here Comes Trouble 48. Giant (co-w, AAN) 56, many others.

Guitry, Sacha (1885–1957)
Distinguished French writer-director, in films occasionally over a long period.

Autobiography: 1956, *If Memory Serves*.

Biography: 1968, *The Last Boulevardier* by James Harding.

Ceux de Chez Nous 15. Les Deux Couverts 32. Bonne Chance 35. Le Roman d'un Tricheur 36. Quadrille 38. Ils Etaient Neuf Célibataires 39. Donne-moi tes yeux 43. Le Comédien 49. Deburau 51. Versailles 54. Napoleon 55. La Vie à Deux 57, etc.

Guizar, Tito (1908–1999) (Frederick Guizar)
Popular Mexican singer, guitarist and actor, in Hollywood from the mid-30s to the late 40s. Born in Mexico City, of Italian and French ancestry, he studied singing in Italy and worked with the Chicago Grand Opera in the early 30s. He became a star in Mexico with *Allá en el Rancho Grande* 36, which combined music and a narrative set on a ranch and established a popular genre, and was the first Mexican actor to gain an international reputation.

Big Broadcast of 1938 37. Tropic Holiday 38. Mis Dos Amores 38. St Louis Blues 39. The Singing Charro 39. The Llano Kid 39. Blondie Goes Latin 41. Brazil 44. Mexicana 45. The Thrill of Brazil 46. On the Old Spanish Trail 47. The Gay Ranchero 48. Tropical Masquerade 48. Música y Dinero 56, etc.

Gulager, Clu (1928–)
American leading man, mostly on TV.

The Killers (TV) 64. Winning 69. The Last Picture Show 71. The Glass House (TV) 72. Footsteps (TV) 72. Call to Danger (TV) 73. McQ 74. The Killer Who Wouldn't Die (TV) 76. The Other Side of Midnight 77. A Force of One 79. Touched by Love 80. The Return of the Living Dead 85. Hunter's Blood 86. The Offspring 86. Eddie Presley 93, etc.

TV series: The Tall Man 60–61. The Virginian 64–68. The Survivors 69. San Francisco International 70.

Gulpilil, David (1954–)
Australian actor, memorable as the aborigine youth in Nicolas Roeg's *Walkabout*. He is also head of an aboriginal dance company.

Walkabout 71. Mad Dog Morgan 76. Storm Boy 76. The Last Wave 77. Blue Fin 78. Long Weekend 78. Crocodile Dundee 86. Dark Age 88. Until the End of the World/Bis ans Ende der Welt 91, etc.

Güney, Yilmaz (1937–1984)
Leading Turkish actor and screenwriter who turned to directing after serving terms of imprisonment for his left-wing political activities. He supervised films in the mid-70s from his prison cell, escaped in 1981, lost his Turkish citizenship as a result, and died from cancer shortly afterwards.

My Name Is Kerim 67. Bride of the Earth 68. An Ugly Man 69. Hope 70. Tomorrow Is the Final Day 71. Pain 71. The Father 71. Anxiety (co-d) 74. The Poor Ones (co-d) 75. Yol (supervised direction by Serif Goren) 82. The Wall 83, etc.

Gunn, Gilbert (c. 1912–)
Scottish director and screenwriter, a former documentarist. Born in Glasgow and educated at Glasgow University, he was a playwright and theatre producer before entering films in the mid-30s as a screenwriter. He directed more than 50 documentaries for the Ministry of Information and the Central Office of Information.

The Door with Seven Locks (co-w) 40. Landfall (co-w) 49. The Elstree Story (p, d) 52. Valley of Song/Men Are Children Twice (d) 53. Strange World of Planet X (d) 57. Girls at Sea (co-w, d) 58. Operation Bullshine (co-w, d) 59. What a Whopper (d) 62, etc.

Gunn, Moses (1929–1993)
American actor.

The Great White Hope 70. Carter's Army (TV) 70. The Wild Rovers 71. Shaft 72. The Hot Rock 72. Haunts of the Very Rich (TV) 73. Rollerball 75. Remember My Name 78. The Ninth Configuration 80. Ragtime 81. Amityville II 82. Firestarter 84. Heartbreak Ridge 86.

TV series: The Cowboys 74. Roots 77. Good Times 77. The Contender 80. Father Murphy 80–81. A Man Called Hawk 89.

Gurie, Sigrid (1911–1969) (S. G. Haukelid)
American/Norwegian leading lady of the late 30s.

The Adventures of Marco Polo 38. Algiers 38. Rio 40. Three Faces West 40. Dark Streets of Cairo 41. A Voice in the Wind 44. Sword of the Avenger 48, etc.

Guthrie, A. B. (1901–1991)
American Western novelist and screenwriter, a former journalist, three of whose novels were filmed.

The Big Sky (oa) 52. Shane (AAN) 53. The Kentuckian 55. These Thousand Hills (oa) 59. The Way West (oa) 67.

Guthrie, Arlo (1947–)
American ballad singer, son of another (Woody Guthrie, whose story was told in *Bound for Glory*).

Alice's Restaurant 69. Roadside Prophets 92, etc.

Gutowski, Gene (1925–)
Polish producer with US TV experience.

Four Boys and a Gun 56. Station Six Sahara (GB) 63. Repulsion (GB) 65. Cul-de-Sac (GB) 66. The Fearless Vampire Killers (GB) 66. The Adventures of Gerard 70. Romance of a Horse Thief 71, etc.

Guttenberg, Steve (1958–)
American leading actor.

The Chicken Chronicles 77. Players 79. Diner 81. Police Academy 84. Police Academy II 85. Cocoon 85. Bad Medicine 85. Short Circuit 86. The Bedroom Window 86. Police Academy 4: Citizens on Parade 87. Surrender 87. Three Men and a Baby 87. Cocoon: The Return 88. High Spirits 88. Don't Tell Her It's Me 90. Three Men and a Little Lady 90. It Takes Two 95. The Big Green 95. Home for the Holidays 95. Zeus and Roxanne 96. Airborne (Can.) 97, etc.

TV series: Billy 79. No Soap, Radio 82.

❝ I'm not bragging but my movies have grossed well over a billion dollars. – S.G.

If you have a sister, you'd want her to marry Steve Guttenberg. He cooks, he gardens, he's kind to young children. – *Martha Frankel, Movieline*

Guy-Blaché, Alice (1873–1968)
French film director with claims to have been the world's first female director and possibly the world's first director. A secretary to Léon Gaumont, she began by making demonstration films for the company. With her cameraman-husband, Herbert Blaché, she went to America in 1910, set up her own companies and continued directing there until she returned to France in 1922. *The Lost Garden*, a documentary on her life and work directed by Marquise Lepage, was released in 1996.

Autobiography: 1997, *The Memoirs of Alice Guy-Blaché*, ed. Anthony Slide.

The Cabbage Fairy/La Fée aux Choux 1896. La Vie du Christ 06. Fra Diavolo 12. In the Year 2000 12. Michael Strogoff 14. Tarnished Reputations 20, many others.

Guyler, Deryck (1914–1999)
Deep-voiced English character actor, usually in comic roles and frequently as a pompous minor official; he was often on radio and television. Born in Wallasey, Cheshire, he began on stage with the Liverpool Repertory Company and first gained fame with the radio comedy series *ITMA* in the 40s. He also played the washboard.

The Fast Lady 62. It's Trad, Dad 62. Nurse on Wheels 63. Smokescreen 64. Ferry Cross the Mersey 64. A Hard Day's Night 64. The Big Job 65. The Magnificent Six and a Half 67. Carry On Doctor 67. Please Sir! 71. No Sex Please – We're British 73. Barry MacKenzie Holds His Own 74. One of Our Dinosaurs Is Missing 75, etc.

TV series: The Charlie Chester Show 51, 55. Emney Enterprises 54–57. Here's Harry 60. *Sykes* 60–65, 71–79 (as Corky the neighbourhood policeman). Three Live Wires 61–62. Room at the Bottom 67. Please Sir! 68–72.

Guzman, Pato (1933–1991)
American production designer.

I Love You Alice B. Toklas 68. Bob and Carol and Ted and Alice 69. Alex in Wonderland 70. Blume in Love 73. An Unmarried Woman 78. The In-Laws 79. Hide in Plain Sight 80. Willie and Phil 80. Tempest 82. Moscow on the Hudson 84. Down and Out in Beverly Hills 86. Enemies, a Love Story 89. Scenes from a Mall 91, etc.

Gwenn, Edmund (1875–1959)
Stocky English stage actor who in middle age became a Hollywood film star and gave memorable comedy portrayals into his 80s. Born in London, he was on stage from 1895. His brother was the stage and film actor Arthur Chesney (1882–1949).

■ SILENT FILMS: The Real Thing at Last 16. Unmarried 20. The Skin Game 20.

■ SOUND FILMS: How He Lied to Her Husband 31. Money for Nothing 31. Condemned to Death 31. Frail Women 31. Hindle Wakes 31. Tell Me Tonight 32. The Admiral's Secret 32. Love on Wheels 32. *The Skin Game* 32. *The Good Companions* 33. I Was a Spy 33. Early to Bed 33. Cash 33. Smithy 33. *Friday the Thirteenth* 33. Marooned 33. Java Head 34. Spring in the Air 34. Channel Crossing 34. Passing Shadows 34. Waltzes from Vienna 34. Father and Son 34. Warn London 34. The Bishop Misbehaves 35. Sylvia Scarlett 35. The Walking Dead 36. Anthony Adverse 36. All American Chump 36. Mad Holiday 36. *Laburnum Grove* 36. Parnell 37. A Yank at Oxford 38. *South Riding* 38. Penny Paradise 38. An Englishman's Home 38. Cheer Boys Cheer 39. The Earl of Chicago 40. Madmen of Europe 40. The Doctor Takes a Wife 40. *Pride and Prejudice* 40. *Foreign Correspondent* (rare villainous role) 40. Scotland Yard 41. Cheers for Miss Bishop 41. The Devil and Miss Jones 41. *Charley's Aunt* 41. One Night in Lisbon 41. A Yank at Eton 42. The Meanest Man in the World 43. Forever and a Day 43. *Lassie Come Home* 43. *Between Two Worlds* (his original 'Outward Bound' stage role) 44. The Keys of the Kingdom 45. Bewitched 45. Dangerous Partners 45. She Went to the Races 45. Of Human Bondage 46. Undercurrent 46. *Miracle on 34th Street* (AA) 47. Thunder in the Valley 47. Life with Father 47. Green Dolphin Street 47. Apartment for Peggy 48. Hills of Home 48. Challenge to Lassie 49. A Woman of Distinction 50. Louisa 50. *Pretty Baby* 50. *Mister 880* (AAN) 50. For Heaven's Sake 50. Peking Express 51. Sally and St Anne 52. Bonzo Goes to College 52. Les Misérables 52. Something for the Birds 52. Mister Scoutmaster 52. The Bigamist 53. *Them* 54. The Student Prince 54. *The Trouble with Harry* 55. It's a Dog's Life 55. Calabuch 57.

✪ For having the talent for remaining a star into his 80s, and the discretion not always to insist on star billing. *Pride and Prejudice*.

Gwynn, Michael (1916–1976)
British stage actor in occasional films.

The Runaway Bus 54. The Secret Place 57. The Revenge of Frankenstein (as the monster) 58. Village of the Damned 60. The Virgin Soldiers 69, etc.

Gwynne, Anne (1918–) (Marguerite Gwynne Trice)
American leading lady of the 40s, former model.

Sandy Takes a Bow 39. Jailhouse Blues 41. The Strange Case of Doctor RX 42. Weird Woman 44. House of Frankenstein 45. Fear 46. The Ghost Goes Wild 46. Dick Tracy Meets Gruesome 48. Call of the Klondike 51. Breakdown 52. The Meteor Monster 57, etc.

Gwynne, Fred (1926–1993)
Lanky, lugubrious American comic actor who appeared in On the Waterfront 54. Munster Go Home 66. Captains Courageous (TV) 77. La Luna 78. Simon 80. The Cotton Club 84. Fatal Attraction 87. Ironweed 87. The Secret of My Success 87. Disorganized Crime 89. Pet Sematary 89. Shadows and Fog 91. My Cousin Vinny 92, etc.

TV series: Car 54 Where Are You? 61–62 and The Munsters 64–65.

Gyllenhaal, Stephen (1949–)
American director, from TV.

A Certain Fury 85. The Abduction of Kari Swenson (TV) 87. Paris Trout 91. Waterland 92. A Dangerous Woman 93. Losing Isaiah 95. Homegrown (co-w, d) 97, etc.

Gynt, Greta (1916–2000) (Greta Woxholt)
Norwegian leading lady, popular in British films of the 40s. Born in Oslo, she settled in England in the mid-30s, and was put under contract by J. Arthur Rank. Tiring of being cast as a *femme fatale*, she retired in the mid-50s. Married four times.

Second Best Bed 38. Sexton Blake and the Hooded Terror 38. The Arsenal Stadium Mystery 39. Dark Eyes of London 39. Crooks' Tour 40. The Common Touch 41. Tomorrow We Live 42. It's That Man Again 42. Mr Emmanuel 44. London Town 46. Dear Murderer 47. Take My Life 47. The Calendar 48. Easy Money 48. Mr Perrin and Mr Traill 48. I'll Get You for This 50. Shadow of the Eagle 50. Soldiers Three (US) 51. Whispering Smith Hits London 51. The Ringer 52. Forbidden Cargo 54. The Blue Peter 55. See How They Run 55. Fortune Is a Woman 57. Bluebeard's Ten Honeymoons 60. The Runaway 66, etc.

Gyöngyössy, Imre (1930–1994)
Hungarian director, screenwriter, playwright and poet. Imprisoned in the early 50s, he later studied at the Budapest Academy of Film and Television and collaborated on films with his wife, the writer Katalin Petényi, and Barna Kabay, who co-wrote and co-directed their later work. In the late 70s, they moved to work from Munich.

Palm Sunday (wd) 69. You Are Naked 72. Sons of Fire 73. A Quite Ordinary Life (doc) 77. The Revolt of Job (AAN) 82. Homeless 90. Freedom of the Death/Holtak Szabadsaga 93. Death in Shallow Water/Halal A Sekely Vizben 94, etc.

H

Haanstra, Bert (1916–1997)
Dutch documentarist. Born in Holton, he studied to be a teacher and was first employed as a press photographer. He worked for a time with director Jacques TATI on *Traffic*, but left because of differences over Tati's style of directing.
Mirror of Holland 50. The Rival World 55. Rembrandt Painter of Man 56. Glass (AA) 58. Fanfare (feature) 58. Zoo 62. The Human Dutch (AAN) 64. The Voice of the Water 66. Traffic (co-d) 71. Ape and Super-Ape (AAN) 72. Doctor Pulder Sows Poppies 75. Mr Slotter's Jubilee 79. The World of Simon Carmiggelt 83, etc.

Haarman, Fritz (1879–1925)
German serial killer who raped and murdered at least 24 boys, though the body count was probably higher, and sold their flesh on the black market as pork. His character informed Fritz Lang's portrait of a mass murderer, M 31, starring Peter Lorre; his life was the basis of *The Tenderness of Wolves*, produced in 1973 by Rainer Werner FASSBINDER, directed by Ulli LOMMEL and written by Kurt RAAB, who also starred, and *The Deathmaker* 95, directed by Romauld Karmakar and starring Götz George.

Haas, Charles (1918–)
American director.
Star in the Dust 56. Screaming Eagles 56. Showdown at Abilene 56. Summer Love 58. Wild Heritage 58. The Beat Generation 59. The Big Operator 59. Girls' Town 59. Platinum High School 60, etc.

Haas, Dolly (1910–1994)
German leading lady of the 30s, in a few international films.
Dolly's Way to Stardom 30. Liebes-commando 32. Der Page vom Dalmasse Hotel 34. *Broken Blossoms* (GB) 36. Spy of Napoleon (GB) 37. I Confess (US) 53, etc.

Haas, Hugo (1901–1968)
Czech character actor, in Hollywood from the late 30s; later took to writing and directing low-budget melodramas as vehicles for himself.
Skeleton on Horseback 39. Summer Storm 44. A Bell for Adano 45. Dakota 45. Holiday in Mexico 46. The Foxes of Harrow 47. My Girl Tisa 48. King Solomon's Mines 50. Vendetta 50. The Girl on the Bridge (& wd) 51. Pickup (& wd) 51. Strange Fascination (& wd) 52. Thy Neighbour's Wife (& wd) 53. Hold Back Tomorrow (& wd) 55. The Other Woman (& wd) 55. Edge of Hell (& wd) 56. *Lizzie* (& wd) 57. Born to be Loved (& wd) 59. Night of the Quarter Moon (& wd) 59. Paradise Alley (& wd) 61, etc.

Haas, Lukas (1976–)
American juvenile actor.
Testament 83. Witness 85. Solarbabies 86. Lady in White 88. The Wizard of Loneliness 88. Music Box 89. See You in the Morning 89.Rambling Rose 91. Alan & Naomi 92. Leap of Faith 92. Johns 96. Mars Attacks! 96. Everyone Says I Love You 96. David and Lisa (TV) 98. The Thin Red Line 98, etc.

Haas, Philip (1944–)
American director and screenwriter who began as a maker of documentaries about artists.
The Music of Chance 93. Angels and Insects 95, etc.

Haas, Robert (1887–1962)
American art director, a former architect. In films from the early 20s, working for Warner Brothers from 1929.
Dr Jekyll and Mr Hyde 20. Sentimental Tommy 21. Fury 22. White Sister 23. Romola 24. Hell Harbor 30. Bureau of Missing Persons 33. The Key 34. The Story of Louis Pasteur 36. The Prince and the Pauper 37. Jezebel 38. Angels with Dirty Faces 38. Dark Victory 39. The Maltese Falcon 41. Now, Voyager 42. Devotion 46. Life with Father (AAN) 47. Johnny Belinda (AAN) 48. The Damned Don't Cry 50. The Glass Menagerie 50, etc.

Hack, Shelley (1948–)
American actress, a former teenage model. In the 90s, she became a TV producer.
Annie Hall 77. If I Ever See You Again 78. King of Comedy 83. Single Bars, Single Women (TV) 85. Troll 85. The Stepfather 85. Blind Fear 89. A Casualty of War (TV) 90. The Finishing Touch 92, etc.
TV series: Charlie's Angels 79–80. Cutter to Houston 83. Jack and Mike 86–87.

Hackathorne, George (1895–1940)
American light actor of the later silents.
The Last of the Mohicans 20. The Little Minister 21. Merry Go Round 23. Magnificent Obsession 35. Gone with the Wind 39, many others.

Hackett, Albert (1900–1995)
American writer, usually with his wife Frances GOODRICH. He began as an actor in silent films, together with his brother, Raymond Hackett.

Hackett, Buddy (1924–) (Leonard Hacker)
Tubby American comedian with vaudeville experience.
Walking My Baby Back Home 53. God's Little Acre 58. *The Music Man* 62. *It's a Mad Mad Mad Mad World* 63. The Golden Head 65. The Love Bug 69. The Good Guys and the Bad Guys 69. Bud and Lou (TV) 78. Scrooged 88. The Little Mermaid (voice) 89. Paulie 98, etc.
TV series: Stanley 56.

Hackett, Joan (1934–1983)
American leading lady usually seen in unglamorous roles. Died of cancer.
■ *The Group* 66. Will Penny 67. Support Your Local Sheriff 69. Assignment to Kill 69. The Other Man (TV) 70. How Awful About Allan (TV) 70. The Young Country (TV) 71. Five Desperate Women (TV) 71. The Rivals 73. The Last of Sheila 73. Class of 63 (TV) 73. Reflections of Murder (TV) 74. The Terminal Man 74. Mackintosh and T.J. 75. Treasure of Matecumbe 76. Stonestreet (TV) 77. The Possessed (TV) 77. Pleasure Cove (TV) 79. Mr Mike's Mondo Video 79. The North Avenue Irregulars 79. One Trick Pony 80. The Long Days of Summer (TV) 80. Only When I Laugh (AAN) 81. The Long Summer of George Adams (TV) 82. The Escape Artist 82.
TV series: The Defenders 61–62. Another Day 78.

Hackett, Raymond (1902–1958)
American leading man who had brief popularity during the changeover from silent to sound. Married actress Blanche Sweet.
The Loves of Sunya 28. Madame X 29. Our Blushing Brides 29. The Trial of Mary Dugan 30. The Sea Wolf 30. The Cat Creeps 31. Seed 31, etc.

Hackett, Walter (1876–1944)
American-born theatre manager and playwright, mainly of farces and light comedies, in England. Born in California, he came to London on his honeymoon in 1914 and stayed. Married actress Marion LORNE, who featured in many of his plays.
77 Park Lane 31. The Barton Mystery 32. Life Goes On 32. Freedom of the Seas 34. Road House 34. Their Big Moment 34. Hyde Park Corner 35. The Gay Adventure 36. Thunder in the City 37, etc.

Hackford, Taylor (1945–)
American director and producer who runs his own production company, New Visions Entertainment.
The Idolmaker 80. An Officer and a Gentleman 82. Against All Odds 83. White Nights 85. Hail! Hail! Rock 'n' Roll 87. La Bamba (p) 87. Everybody's All-American 88. Rooftops (p) 89. The Long Walk Home (p) 90. Mortal Thoughts (p) 91. Queen's Logic (p) 91. Sweet Talker (p) 91. Blood In, Blood Out (pd) 93. Dolores Claiborne 95. The Devil's Advocate 97. Proof of Life 00, etc.

Hackman, Gene (1930–)
Virile American character actor who unexpectedly became a star from the early 70s.
Biography: 1997, *Gene Hackman* by Michael Munn.
Mad Dog Coll 61. Lilith 64. Hawaii 66. A Covenant with Death 66. Banning 67. *Bonnie and Clyde* (AAN) 67. First to Fight 67. The Split 68. Shadow on the Land (TV) 68. Riot 68. Downhill Racer 69. *I Never Sang for My Father* (AAN) 69. The Gypsy Moths 69. Marooned 69. Doctors' Wives 70. The Hunting Party 71. *The French Connection* (AA) 71. Cisco Pike 71. Prime Cut 72. The Poseidon Adventure 72. Scarecrow 73. The Conversation 74. Zandy's Bride 74. Young Frankenstein 74. Bite the Bullet 75. French Connection II 75. Lucky Lady 75. Night Moves 75. The Domino Principle 77. A Bridge Too Far 77. March or Die 77. Superman 78. Superman 2 80. All Night Long 81. Reds 81. Eureka 82. Two of a Kind 83. Uncommon Valor 83. Under Fire 83. Misunderstood 84. Target 85. Twice in a Lifetime 85. Hoosiers 86. Power 86. No Way Out 87. Superman 4: The Quest for Peace 87. Another Woman 88. BAT 21 88. Full Moon in Blue Water 88. Split Decisions 88. Mississippi Burning (AAN) 88. The Package 89. Narrow Margin 90. Postcards from the Edge 90. Loose Cannons 90. Class Action 90. Company Business 91. Unforgiven (AA) 92. The Firm 93. Geronimo: An American Legend 94. Wyatt Earp 94. Crimson Tide 95. The Quick and the Dead 95. Get Shorty 95. The Bird Cage 96. Extreme Measures 96. The Chamber 96. Absolute Power 97. Twilight 98. Antz (voice) 98. Enemy of the State 98, etc.
❝ People in the street still call me Popeye, and *The French Connection* was 15 years ago. I wish I could have another hit and a new nickname. – G.H.
Each scene, I look for something not written down. – G.H.
The last honest man in America. – *Film Comment*

Hackney, Alan (1924–)
British comedy writer.
Private's Progress 55. I'm All Right, Jack 59. Two-way Stretch (co-w) 60. Swordsman of Siena 62. You Must Be Joking 65. Decline and Fall 68, etc.

Haddon, Peter (1898–1962) (Peter Tildsley)
British light actor, usually in silly-ass roles. Born in Rawtenstall, Lancashire, the son of a vicar, he studied medicine at Cambridge University, where he became a member of Footlights, and was on stage from 1920.
Death at Broadcasting House 34. The Silent Passenger (as Lord Peter Wimsey) 35. Kate Plus Ten 38. Helter Skelter 49. The Second Mrs Tanqueray 54, etc.

Haden, Sara (1897–1981)
American actress of quiet, well-spoken parts, best remembered as the spinster aunt of the Hardy family.
Spitfire (debut) 34. Magnificent Obsession 35. First Lady 38. H. M. Pulham Esquire 41. Lost Angel 43. Mr Ace 45. Our Vines Have Tender Grapes 45. She-Wolf of London (as villainess) 46. The Bishop's Wife 48. A Life of her Own 50. A Lion is in the Streets 53. Andy Hardy Comes Home 58, many others.

Hadjidakis, Manos (1925–1994)
Greek composer.
Stella 55. A Matter of Dignity 57. *Never on Sunday* (AA) 59. America America 63. Blue 68. The Martlet's Tale 70. The Pedestrian 74. Sweet Movie 75. Honeymoon 79, etc.

Hadley, Reed (1911–1974) (Reed Herring)
American 'second lead'.
Fugitive Lady 38. The Bank Dick 41. Guadalcanal Diary 43. Leave Her to Heaven 46. The Iron Curtain 48. Captain from Castile 49. Dallas 51. Big House USA 55. The St Valentine's Day Massacre 68, etc.
TV series: Racket Squad 51–53. Public Defender 53–54.

Hageman, Richard (1882–1966)
Dutch-American composer.
If I Were King (AAN) 38. Stagecoach (co-m, AA) 39. The Howards of Virginia (AAN) 40. The Long Voyage Home (AAN) 40. This Woman Is Mine (AAN) 41. The Shanghai Gesture (AAN) 42. Fort Apache 48. Three Godfathers 48. She Wore a Yellow Ribbon 49. Wagon Master 50, etc.

Hagen, Jean (1924–1977) (Jean Verhagen)
American comedy character actress, usually of Brooklynesque dames; also minor leading lady. Forced to retire in the mid-60s because of illness.
■ Side Street 49. *Adam's Rib* 49. Ambush 50. The Asphalt Jungle 50. A Life of Her Own 50. Night into Morning 50. No Questions Asked 51. *Singin' in the Rain* (a splendid performance as the silent star with the ghastly voice) (AAN) 52. Shadow in the Sky 52. Carbine Williams 52. Latin Lovers 53. Arena 53. Half a Hero 53. The Big Knife 55. Spring Reunion 57. The Shaggy Dog 59. Sunrise at Campobello 60. Panic in Year Zero 62. Dead Ringer 64.
TV series: The Danny Thomas Show 53–56.
❝ Famous line (*Singin' in the Rain*) 'If we bring a little joy into your humdrum lives, we feel all our hard work ain't been in vain for nothin'.'

Hagen, Julius (1884–1939)
British producer, a former actor, who founded Twickenham Film Studios and Real Art Productions in 1929, in partnership with director Leslie Hiscott, to turn out 'quota quickies' to meet the legal requirement of the time for exhibitors to show British films. Directors and writers spent a fortnight writing a script and a fortnight shooting it. He persuaded many leading British actors and some Hollywood ones to appear in his films, including Sydney HOWARD, Leslie FULLER, Henry KENDALL, Sir John MARTIN-HARVEY,Ivor NOVELLO, Gracie FIELDS, Sir Seymour HICKS, FLANAGAN and ALLEN, Edward Everett HORTON and Conrad VEIDT. He hired D.W. GRIFFITH to remake *Broken Blossoms* in sound, but Griffith walked out after a disagreement. He ran into trouble trying to make more expensive films and became bankrupt in 1938.
To What Red Hell 29. At the Villa Rose 30. Chin, Chin, Chinaman 31. Alibi 31. Bill's Legacy 31. The Lyons Mail 31. Condemned to Death 32. The Crooked Lady 32. The Lodger 32. Excess Baggage 33. This Week of Grace 33. The Wandering Jew 33. I Lived with You 33. The Black Abbot 34. Blind Justice 34. The Admiral's Secret 34. Bella Donna 34. Department Store 35. The Ace of Spades 35. A Fire Has Been Arranged 35. Scrooge 35. She Shall Have Music 35. The Triumph of Sherlock Holmes 35. The Last Journey 35. The Private Secretary 35. Broken Blossoms 36. Eliza Comes to Stay 36. Spy of Napoleon 36. Juggernaut 36. Beauty and the Barge 37. Silver Blaze 37. Clothes and the Woman 37. Underneath the Arches 37, etc.
❝ Hagen, who never read a script in his life, would edit a film in this fashion: for every day the director was behind schedule, Hagen would rip out five pages from the middle of his script. – *Bernard Vorhaus*

Hagerty, Julie (1955–)
American actress, a former model, usually in comic roles.
Airplane 80. Airplane II 82. A Midsummer Night's Sex Comedy 82. Bad Medicine 85. Goodbye New York 85. Lost in America 85. Aria 87. Beyond Therapy 87. Bloodhounds of Broadway 89. Rude Awakening 89. Reversal of Fortune 90. What About Bob? 91. Noises Off 92. The Wife 95. U-Turn 97. Boys Will Be Boys 97, etc.
TV series: Princesses 91. Reunited 98– .

Haggar, William (1851–1924)
British pioneer producer, a former fairground showman who made short sensational films featuring himself and his family.
The Maniac's Guillotine 02. The Wild Man of Borneo 02. Mirthful Mary 03. A Dash for Liberty 03. The Sign of the Cross 04. The Life of Charles Peace 05. Desperate Footpads 07. Maria Marten 08. The Dumb Man of Manchester 08, etc.

Haggard, Sir H. Rider (1856–1925)
British adventure novelist, whose most famous novel, *She*, has been filmed at least nine times. There have also been two versions of *King Solomon's Mines*, and two lightly disguised variants, *Watusi* and *King Solomon's Treasure*.

Haggard, Piers (1939–)
British director.
Wedding Night 69. Satan's Skin 70. Pennies from Heaven (TV) 78. The Fiendish Plot of Dr Fu Manchu 80. Venom 82. A Summer Story (TV) 88. I'll Take Romance (TV) 90. The Lifeforce Experiment (TV) 94. Conquest 98, etc.

Haggerty, Dan (1941–)
Hefty American leading man, notably on TV in *The Legend of Grizzly Adams*.
The Tender Warrior 70. Hex 73. When the North Wind Blows 74. Starbird and Sweet William 75. Frontier Freemont 76. Desperate Women (TV) 79. Condominium (TV) 80. Grizzly Adams: The Mark of the Bear 91. Ice Pawn 92. Cheyenne Warrior 94. Abducted 2: The Reunion 94. Grizzly Mountain 97, etc.

Hagman, Larry (1931–)
American comedy leading man, much on TV; son of Mary MARTIN.
Ensign Pulver 64. Fail Safe 64. In Harm's Way 65. The Group 65. Vanished (TV) 70. Up in the Cellar 70. Beware the Blob (TV) 71. A Howling in the Woods (TV) 72. The Alpha Caper (TV) 73. Stardust 74. Harry and Tonto 74. Mother Jugs and Speed 76. The Eagle Has Landed 76. Crash 77. The President's Mistress (TV) 78. Superman 78. SOB 81. Nixon 95. Primary Colors 98, etc.
TV series: *I Dream of Jeannie* 65–70. The Good Life 71. Here We Go Again 71. *Dallas* 78–88.
❝ People I meet really want me to be J.R., so it's hard to disappoint them. – *L.H.*
I was born with success. Lucky for me, I am able to handle it. Also, I damn well deserve it! – *L.H.*

Hagmann, Stuart (1939–)
American director who turned to making TV commercials after the failure of his second feature.
The Strawberry Statement 70. Believe in Me 71. Tarantulas: The Deadly Cargo 77, etc.

Hahn, Don
American producer of animated features, a former Walt Disney animator, who has worked at the studio since 1976. He was an assistant director on *The Fox and the Hound* and *Mickey's Christmas Carol*. He is the author of *Disney's Animation Magic: A Behind the Scenes Look at How an Animated Film Is Made*, 1996.
Beauty and the Beast 91. The Lion King 94. The Hunchback of Notre Dame 96, etc.

Haid, Charles (1943–)
American actor, producer and director.
AS ACTOR: The Choirboys 77. Oliver's Story 78. Who'll Stop the Rain/Dog Soldiers 78. Altered States 80. Twirl (TV) 81. Cop 88. Fire and Rain (TV) 89. Night Breed 90. Storyville 92. The Fire Next Time (TV) 93. Cooperstown (TV) 93. Broken Trust (TV) 95. The Third Miracle 99, etc.
AS DIRECTOR: Iron Will 94. Riders of the Purple Sage (TV) 96. Buffalo Soldiers 97, etc.
TV series (as actor): Kate McShane 75. Delvecchio 76–77. Hill Street Blues 81–87.

Haigh, Kenneth (1929–)
British stage actor, the original lead of *Look Back in Anger*, has tended to remain in angry young man roles.
My Teenage Daughter 56. High Flight 56. Saint Joan 57. Cleopatra 63. A Hard Day's Night 64. The Deadly Affair 66. A Lovely Way to Die (US) 68. Eagle in a Cage 71. Man at the Top 73. The Bitch 79. Wild Geese II 85. A State of Emergency 86. Shuttlecock 91, etc.
TV series: *Man at the Top* 71–73.

Hailey, Arthur (1920–)
English novelist who rigorously researches specific milieux and weaves a plot through them. Films of his work include *Hotel*, *Airport*, *The Moneychangers*, *Wheels*, *Flight into Danger* (which became *Zero Hour* and was parodied as *Airplane*).

Haim, Corey (1971–)
Canadian-born juvenile lead, in commercials from the age of 11.
Firstborn 84. Murphy's Romance 85. Secret Admirer 85. Silver Bullet 85. Lucas 86. The Lost Boys 87. License to Drive 88. Watchers 88. Dream a Little Dream 89. Dream Machine 90. Fast Getaway 91. Prayer of the Rollerboys 91. Oh, What a Night 92. Double O Kid 92. Fast Getaway II 94. National Lampoon's Last Resort 94. Demolition High 96, etc.

Haines, Connie (1922–) (Yvonne Marie Jamais)
Vivacious American singer in occasional films and soundies. Born in Savannah, Georgia, she was best known as a vocalist with the big band of Tommy DORSEY. She later became a church minister.
Ship Ahoy 42. Moon Over Las Vegas 44. Twilight on the Prairie 44. A Wave, a Wac and a Marine 44. Duchess of Idaho 50, etc.

Haines, Randa (1945–)
American director, from television.
Under This Sky (TV) 79. Something about Amelia (TV) 84. Children of a Lesser God 86. The Doctor 91. Wrestling Ernest Hemingway 93. Dance with Me 98, etc.

Haines, William (1900–1973)
American leading man of the silents.
Biography: 1998, *Wisecracker; The Life and Times of William Haines, Hollywood's First Openly Gay Star* by William J. Mann.
Three Wise Fools 23. Tower of Lies 24. Brown of Harvard 25. Tell It to the Marines 27. Alias Jimmy Valentine 28. Navy Blues 30. The Adventures of Get-Rich-Quick Wallingford 31. The Fast Life 33. The Marines Are Coming 35, etc.

Hajos, Karl (1889–1950)
Hungarian-born composer, in America from the 20s.
Morocco 30. Werewolf of London 35. Hitler's Hangman 43. Summer Storm (AAN) 44. Dangerous Intruder 45. Stars over Texas 46. Appointment with Murder 48. The Lovable Cheat 49. It's a Small World 50, etc.

Hakim, André (1915–)
Egyptian-born producer, long in US.
Mr Belvedere Rings the Bell 52. The Man Who Never Was 56. Sea Wife 56. Patate 64. Hello-Goodbye 70, etc.

Hakim, Robert and Raymond (1907– and 1909–1980)
Egyptian-born brothers who were in and out of film production from 1927.
Pépé Le Moko 36. La Bête Humaine 38. Le Jour Se Lève 39. The Southerner 44. Her Husband's Affairs 47. The Long Night 47. The Blue Veil 52. Belle de Jour 67. Isadora 68, many others.

Halas, John (1912–1995)
Hungarian-born animator, long in Britain producing in association with his wife Joy Batchelor (1914–1991) a stream of efficient short cartoons, many sponsored by official organizations.
FEATURES: *Animal Farm* 54. Ruddigore 67.

Hale, Alan (1892–1950) (Rufus Alan McKahan)
Jovial American actor, a hero of silent action films from 1911 and a familiar cheerful figure in scores of talkies.
The Cowboy and the Lady (debut) 11. The Four Horsemen of the Apocalypse 21. Robin Hood (as Little John) 22. The Covered Wagon 23. Main Street 24. She Got What She Wanted 27. The Rise of Helga 30. So Big 32. It Happened One Night 34. The Last Days of Pompeii 35. Jump for Glory (GB) 36. Stella Dallas 37. *The Adventures of Robin Hood* (as Little John) 38. Dodge City 39. The Man in the Iron Mask 40. The Sea Hawk 40. Tugboat Annie Sails Again 41. *Strawberry Blonde* 41. Manpower 41. *Desperate Journey* 42. Action in the North Atlantic 43. Destination Tokyo 44. Hotel Berlin 45. Escape in the Desert 45. Night and Day 45. My Wild Irish Rose 47. Pursued 48. The New Adventures of Don Juan 48. *My Girl Tisa* 49. Rogues of Sherwood Forest (as Little John) 50, many others.
✪ For innumerable stalwart performances, including three as Little John. *The Adventures of Robin Hood*.

Hale Jnr, Alan (1918–1990)
American character actor who bid fair to be his father's double.
To the Shores of Tripoli 42. One Sunday Afternoon 48. The Gunfighter 50. The Big Trees 52. Rogue Cop 54. Young at Heart 54. The Indian Fighter 55. The Killer is Loose 56, many others.
TV series: Biff Baker 52–53. *Casey Jones* 58. *Gilligan's Island* 64–67. The Good Guys 69.

Hale, Barbara (1922–)
Pleasant American leading lady of the 40s.
Higher and Higher 43. The Falcon in Hollywood 44. First Yank into Tokyo 45. Lady Luck 46. The Boy with Green Hair 48. The Window 48. *Jolson Sings Again* 49. The Jackpot 50. Lorna Doone 51. A Lion is in the Streets 53. Unchained 54. The Far Horizons 55. The Oklahoman 57. Airport 69. The Defence Never Rests (TV) 90, many others.
TV series: *Perry Mason* (as Della Street) 57–65.

Hale, Binnie (1899–1984) (Beatrice Mary Hale-Monro)
British actress and singer, the sister of Sonnie HALE, in occasional films. Born in Liverpool, she was on stage from 1916, appearing in revues, musicals and pantomimes.
This is the Life 34. The Phantom Light 35. Hyde Park Corner 36. Love from a Stranger 37. Take a Chance 37.
❝ The greatest woman caricaturist of the British stage. – *Charles B. Cochran*

Hale, Creighton (1882–1965) (Patrick Fitzgerald)
American leading man of the 20s, sometimes in meek-and-mild comedy roles.
The Exploits of Elaine 15. The Thirteenth Chair 19. Way Down East 20. Trilby (as Little Billee) 23. *The Marriage Circle* 24. The Circle 25. Beverly of Graustark 26. Annie Laurie 27. *The Cat and the Canary* 27. Rose Marie 28. Holiday 30. The Masquerader 33. Hollywood Boulevard 36. The Return of Dr X 39. The Gorilla Man 42. Bullet Scars 45. The Perils of Pauline 47, many others.

Hale, Georgia (1903–1985)
American leading lady of the 20s.
The Gold Rush 24. The Salvation Hunters 25. The Great Gatsby 26. The Last Moment 48, etc.

Hale, Georgina (1943–)
Generally strident British actress.
Eagle in a Cage 70. The Devils 71. Mahler 74. Sweeney 2 78. The World Is Full of Married Men 78. McVicar 80. The Watcher in the Woods 80. Castaway 86. Beyond Bedlam 94. Ken Russell's Treasure Island (TV) 95, etc.

Hale, Jonathan (1891–1966) (J. Hatley)
Canadian character actor, former consular attaché, in films from 1934, usually as mildly exasperated businessman or hero's boss. Committed suicide.
Lightning Strikes Twice 34. Alice Adams 35. Fury 36. The 'Blondie' series (as Mr Dithers) 38–50. Her Jungle Love 39. Johnny Apollo 40. Call Northside 777 48. The Steel Trap 52. The Night Holds Terror 56. Jaguar 58, many others.

Hale, Louise Closser (1872–1933)
American character actress with long stage experience.
The Hole in the Wall 29. Dangerous Nan McGrew 30. Platinum Blonde 31. Shanghai Express 32. Rasputin and the Empress 33. Today We Live 33. Dinner at Eight 33, etc.

Hale, Monte (1919–)
American western star of the 40s. Mostly with Republic.
Home on the Range 47. South of Rio 48. Rainbow Valley 49. The Missourians 50. Giant 56. The Chase 66. The Drifter 73. Guns of a Stranger 73, many others.

Hale, Richard (1893–1981)
American supporting actor.
The Other Love 47. All the King's Men 50. Scaramouche 52. Julius Caesar 53. Moonfleet 55. Pillars of the Sky 56. Ben Hur 59. Sergeants Three 62, etc.

Hale, Sonnie (1902–1959) (John Robert Hale-Monro)
English leading light comedian, director and writer, the brother of Binnie HALE. Born in London, he was on stage from 1921, becoming a star in revues and musicals. In the mid-30s, he quit the stage for five years to act in, and direct, films for Gaumont British. He starred in several with Jessie MATTHEWS, the second of his three wives, and directed her in her least successful, *Head over Heels*, and two others only marginally better, *Gangway* and *Sailing Along*. His film career faltered in 1938 when *Asking for Trouble*, a large-scale musical he had co-written for Matthews, was abandoned and Gaumont British did not renew his contract; instead Carol REED was hired to make a non-musical version of the story, retitled *Climbing High*. His first wife was actress Evelyn LAYE.
■ On with the Dance 27. The Parting of the Ways 27. Tell me Tonight 32. Happy Ever After 32. Friday the Thirteenth 33. Early to Bed 33. Evergreen 34. Wild Boy 34. My Song for You 34. My Heart is Calling 34. Are You a Mason? 34. Marry the Girl 35. First a Girl 35. It's Love Again 36. Head over Heels (d only) 37. Gangway (d only) 37. Sailing Along (wd only) 38. The Gaunt Stranger 38. Climbing High (co-w only) 38. Let's Be Famous 39. Fiddlers Three 44. London Town 46. A French Mistress (oa) 60.
❝ That excellent comedian. – *James Agate*
A gross, unfunny person offstage and someone, on the whole, to avoid. – *Robert Stephens*

Hale, William (1937–)
American director, from TV.
Gunfight in Abilene 66. Journey to Shiloh 67. Stalk the Wild Child (TV) 76. One Shoe Makes It Murder (TV) 82. Lace (TV) 84. Lace 2 (TV) 85. Liberace (TV) 88. Deadly Revenge 90. People Like Us 90, etc.

Haley, Bill (1926–1981)
American rock-and-roll musician and bandleader; Bill Haley and his Comets provided the title music for *The Blackboard Jungle* and starred in *Rock around the Clock*, which caused cinema riots in 1956. Also, *Don't Knock the Rock* 56.

Haley, Jack (1899–1979)
Diffident American light comedian, popular in the 30s and 40s.
Broadway Madness 27. Follow Thru 30. Sitting Pretty 33. The Girl Friend 35. *Poor Little Rich Girl* 36. Wake Up and Live 37. Pick a Star 37. Rebecca of Sunnybrook Farm 38. *Alexander's Ragtime Band* 38. Hold that Co-Ed 38. *The Wizard of Oz* (as the Tin Man) 39. Moon over Miami 41. Beyond the Blue Horizon 42. F Man 42. Higher and Higher 43. Scared Stiff 44. George White's Scandals 45. People are Funny 45. Vacation in Reno 47. Norwood 69, etc.

Haley Jnr, Jack (1934–)
American executive, best known for marrying Liza Minnelli and assembling *That's Entertainment* and *That's Dancing* 85. Directed *Norwood* 69 and *The Love Machine* 71.

Haley, Jackie Earle (1961–)
American juvenile of the 70s.
The Day of the Locust 74. Damnation Alley 75. The Bad News Bears 76. The Bad News Bears in Breaking Training 77. Breaking Away 79. The Zoo Gang 85. Maniac Cop 3: Badge of Silence 92, etc.
TV series: Wait Till Your Father Gets Home (voice) 72–74.

Hall, Alexander (1894–1968)
American director from 1932, previously on Broadway.
■ Sinners in the Sun 32. Madame Racketeer 32. The Girl in 419 33. Midnight Club 33. Torch Singer 33. Miss Fane's Baby is Stolen 34. Little Miss Marker 34. The Pursuit of Happiness 34. Limehouse Blues 34. Going to Town 35. Annapolis

Farewell 35. Give Us This Night 36. Yours for the Asking 36. Exclusive 37. There's Always a Woman 38. I am the Law 38. There's That Woman Again 38. The Lady's From Kentucky 39. Good Girls Go to Paris 39. The Amazing Mr Williams 39. The Doctor Takes a Wife 40. He Stayed for Breakfast 40. This Thing Called Love 40. *Here Comes Mr Jordan* (AAN) 41. Bedtime Story 41. They All Kissed the Bride 42. My Sister Eileen 42. The Heavenly Body 43. Once Upon a Time 44. She Wouldn't Say Yes 45. Down to Earth 47. The Great Lover 49. Love that Brute 50. Louisa 50. Up Front 51. Because You're Mine 52. Let's Do it Again 53. Forever Darling 56.

Hall, Anthony Michael (1968–)
American young leading actor, a former child actor on stage and TV.
Sixteen Candles 84. The Breakfast Club 85. Weird Science 85. Out of Bounds 86. Johnny Be Good 88. Edward Scissorhands 90. Into the Sun 92. Six Degrees of Separation 93. The Grave 96. Exit in Red 96. Hijacked: Flight 285 (TV) 96. Trojan War 97, etc.

Hall, Arsenio (1956–)
American comedian and actor, in occasional films. Born in Cleveland, Ohio, he studied at Kent State University and began as a standup comedian. He is best known for hosting a late-night TV talk show, *The Arsenio Hall Show*.
Biography: 1993, *The Prince of Late Night: An Unauthorized Biography* by Aileen Joyce.
Amazon Women on the Moon. Coming to America 88. Harlem Nights 89, etc.
TV series: The Half Hour Comedy Hour 83. Motown Revue 85. The Late Show 87. The Arsenio Hall Show 89-94. Arsenio 97. Martial Law 98-00.

Hall, Charles D. (1899–1968)
British-born production designer, long in Hollywood; a key craftsman of his time. Born in Norwich, he worked in an architect's office before designing stage sets for Fred KARNO. He emigrated to Canada, and then made his way to the United States and the film industry, working first as a scenic painter and finally becoming chief art director for Universal. In the late 30s he moved to the Hal ROACH studios, becoming a freelance from the mid-40s.
The Gold Rush 24. *The Phantom of the Opera* 25. The Cohens and the Kellys 26. *The Cat and the Canary* 27. The Man Who Laughs 28. The Circus 28. The Last Warning 29. *Broadway* 29. *All Quiet on the Western Front* 30. *Dracula* 30. *Frankenstein* 31. City Lights 32. *The Old Dark House* 32. *The Invisible Man* 33. By Candlelight 33. *The Bride of Frankenstein* 35. The Good Fairy 35. Showboat 36. *Modern Times* 36. My Man Godfrey 36. Captain Fury 39. Big House USA 55, etc.
✪ For bringing to Hollywood Gothic a mixture of English and German artistic sensibilities.

Hall, Charlie (1899–1959)
Rotund English music-hall comic and character actor. Born in Erdington, Birmingham (where there is now a pub named after him), he was a member of Fred KARNO's troupe. In America from the early 20s, he appeared in more than 40 movies as an irascible foil to LAUREL and HARDY.
Leave 'Em and Weep 27. College 27. Double Whoopee 28. Leave 'Em Laughing 28. Two Tars 28. Angora Love 29. The Bacon Grabbers 29. They Go Boom 29. Pardon Us 31. Come Clean 31. Laughing Gravy 31. Busy Bodies 33. Midnight Patrol 33. Twice Two 33. Sons of the Desert 34. Them Thar Hills 34. Tit for Tat 35. Thicker than Water 35. Swing Time 36. A Chump at Oxford 40. Saps at Sea 40. The Lodger 44. The Canterville Ghost 44. Hangover Square 45. Forever Amber 47. The Big Clock 48. The Vicious Years 51, many others.

Hall, Conrad L. (1926–)
American cinematographer.
Morituri (AAN) 65. Harper 66. The Professionals (AAN) 66. *Cool Hand Luke* 67. In Cold Blood (AAN) 67. Hell in the Pacific 69. *Butch Cassidy and the Sundance Kid* (AA) 69. Tell Them Willie Boy is Here 69. The Happy Ending 70. Fat City 72. The Day of the Locust (AAN) 74. Smile 75. Marathon Man 76. Black Widow 87. Tequila Sunrise (AAN) 88. Class Action 91. Jennifer 8 92. Searching for Bobby Fischer/ Innocent Moves (AAN) 93. Love Affair 94. Without Limits 98. A Civil Action (AAN) 98. *American Beauty* (AA) 99, etc.

Hall, Grayson (1927–1985)
American stage actress remembered for one film performance, in *Night of the Iguana* (AAN) 64.

Hall, Henry (1898–1989)
British bandleader of the 30s, popular on radio. Appeared in a few films including *Music Hath Charms* 36.
Autobiography: 1955, *Here's to the Next Time*.

Hall, Huntz (1920–1999) (Henry Hall)
Long-faced American character actor, the 'dumbbell' second lead of the original Dead End Kids and later of the Bowery Boys.
Dead End 37. Crime School 38. Angels with Dirty Faces 38. The Return of Doctor X 39. Give Us Wings 40. Spooks Run Wild 41. Private Buckaroo 42. Wonder Man 45. Bowery Bombshell 46. Bowery Buckaroos 47. Jinx Money 48. Angels in Disguise 49. Lucky Losers 50. Ghost Chasers 51. No Holds Barred 52. Loose in London 53. Paris Playboys 54. High Society 55. Dig That Uranium 56. Spook Chasers 57. In the Money 58. The Gentle Giant 67. The Love Bug Rides Again 73. The Escape Artist 82. Auntie Lee's Meat Pies 92, many others.
TV series: Chicago Teddy Bears 71.

Hall, James (1900–1940) (James Brown)
American leading man of the early talkie period.
The Campus Flirt 26. Stranded in Paris 27. Rolled Stockings 27. Four Sons 28. Smiling Irish Eyes 29. The Canary Murder Case 29. The Saturday Night Kid 29. Dangerous Nan McGrew 30. *Hell's Angels* 30. Millie 31. The Good Bad Girl 31. Divorce Among Friends 31. Manhattan Tower 33, etc.

Hall, Jon (1913–1979) (Charles Locher)
Athletic American leading man who became a star in his first year as an actor but whose roles gradually diminished in stature; he retired to a photography business. Committed suicide.
Charlie Chan in Shanghai 36. Mind Your Own Business 36. The Girl from Scotland Yard 37. *The Hurricane* 37. Kit Carson 40. South of Pago Pago 40. Aloma of the South Seas 41. Eagle Squadron 42. Invisible Agent 42. Arabian Nights 42. White Savage 43. Ali Baba and the Forty Thieves 44. Cobra Woman 44. The Invisible Man's Revenge 44. San Diego I Love You 45. Sudan 45. The Michigan Kid 47. Last of the Redmen 47. Prince of Thieves 48. Deputy Marshal 49. Hurricane Island 50. When the Redskins Rode 51. Last Train from Bombay 52. The Beachgirls and the Monster (& d) 65. Five the Hard Way (co-p & ph only) 69, etc.
TV series: Ramar of the Jungle 52–53.

Hall, Juanita (1901–1968)
American character actress and singer, best remembered in the stage and screen versions of *South Pacific* (as Bloody Mary) and *Flower Drum Song*.

Hall, Ken G. (1901–1994)
Australian producer, director and screenwriter, head of Cinesound Productions, which was the busiest company of the 30s and 40s, turning out low-budget movies reflecting Australian life, four of them based on the exploits of the Rudd family. The company was later part-owned by J. Arthur Rank and thereafter concentrated on distribution and exhibition. Hall began as a journalist and a film publicist and went on to run Australia's first television station in 1956.
Autobiography: 1977, *Directed by Ken G. Hall*. 1980, *Australian Film: The Inside Story*.
On Our Selection (co-w, d) 32. The Squatter's Daughter (p, d) 33. The Silence of Dean Maitland (p, d) 34. Grandad Rudd (p, d) 35. It Isn't Done (p, d) 37. Lovers and Luggers (p, d) 37. Tall Timbers (p, d) 37. Let George Do It/In the Nick of Time (p, d) 38. Dad and Dave Come to Town/The Rudd Family Goes to Town (p, story) 38. Gone to the Dogs (p, d) 39. Dad Rudd MP (p, d) 40. Kokoda Front Line (p) (AA doc) 42. Smithy/ Southern Cross/Pacific Adventure (co-w, d) 46, etc.

Hall, Kevin Peter (1955–1991)
American actor and stand-up comedian, 7 feet 2 inches tall, who was best known for playing the role of a Bigfoot in the film *Harry and the Hendersons* 87, and in the first season of the subsequent TV series 90–91.
Predator (as the alien) 87. Highway to Hell 92.
TV series: Misfits of Science 85–86.

Hall, Sir Peter (1930–)
British theatrical producer who ventured into films. His first wife was actress Leslie Caron (1956–65). In 1996, he became artistic director at London's Old Vic Theatre, staging productions of classic plays.
Autobiography: 1983, *Peter Hall's Diaries*. 1993, *Making an Exhibition of Myself*.
Biography: 1995, *Power Play – The Life and Times of Peter Hall* by Stephen Fay.
■ Work Is a Four-Letter Word 68. A Midsummer Night's Dream 68. Three Into Two Won't Go 69. Perfect Friday 70. The Homecoming 73. Akenfield 74. Never Talk to Strangers 95.

Hall, Philip Baker (1931–)
Craggy American character actor, usually as a weary, slightly crumpled authority figure. Born in Toledo, Ohio, he studied at the University of Toledo. He began acting in the 1970s.
The Last Reunion (TV) 80. Secret Honor (as Richard Nixon) 85. Three O'Clock High 87. Midnight Run 88. Ghostbusters II 89. Blue Desert 91. Kiss of Death 95. Hard Eight 96. Hit Me 96. Boogie Nights 97. Air Force One 97. Rush Hour 98. Sour Grapes 98. The Truman Show 98. Let the Devil Wear Black 98. The Talented Mr Ripley 99. The Insider 99. Magnolia 99. The Cradle Will Rock 99. Rules of Engagement 00. Jackie Bouvier Kennedy Onassis (TV, as Aristotle Onassis) 00. The Contender 00. Lost Souls 00, etc.
TV series: Mariah 87. Falcon Crest 89-90.

Hall, Porter (1888–1953)
Wry-faced American character actor with stage experience before settling in Hollywood.
■ *The Thin Man* 34. Murder in the Private Car 34. The Case of the Lucky Legs 35. The Story of Louis Pasteur 35. The Petrified Forest 36. Too Many Parents 36. The Princess Comes Across 36. And Sudden Death 36. *The General Died at Dawn* 36. Satan Met a Lady 36. The Plainsman 36. Snowed Under 36. Let's Make a Million 37. Bulldog Drummond Escapes 37. Souls at Sea 37. Make Way for Tomorrow 37. King of Gamblers 37. Hotel Haywire 37. This Way Please 37. True Confession 37. Wild Money 37. Wells Fargo 37. Scandal Street 38. Stolen Heaven 38. Dangerous to Know 38. Bulldog Drummond's Peril 38. Prison Farm 38. King of Alcatraz 38. The Arkansas Traveller 38. Men with Wings 38. Tom Sawyer Detective 38. Mr Smith Goes to Washington 39. Grand Jury Secrets 39. They Shall Have Music 39. His Girl Friday 40. Dark Command 40. Arizona 40. Trail of the Vigilantes 40. Sullivan's Travels 41. The Parson of Panamint 41. Mr and Mrs North 41. The Remarkable Andrew 42. Butch Minds the Baby 42. A Stranger in Town 43. The Desperadoes 43. Woman of the Town 43. The Miracle of Morgan's Creek 43. Standing Room Only 44. Going My Way 44. Double Indemnity 44. The Great Moment 44. Mark of the Whistler 44. Blood on the Sun 45. Bring on the Girls 45. Kiss and Tell 45. *Murder He Says* 45. Weekend at the Waldorf 45. Unconquered 47. Miracle on 34th Street 47. Singapore 47. You Gotta Stay Happy 48. That Wonderful Urge 48. The Beautiful Blonde from Bashful Bend 49. *Intruder in the Dust* 49. Chicken Every Sunday 49. *Ace in the Hole* 51. The Half Breed 52. Carbine Williams 52. Holiday for Sinners 52. Pony Express 53. Vice Squad 53. Return to Treasure Island 54.

Hall, Thurston (1883–1958)
American character actor adept at choleric executives. Long stage experience; ran his own touring companies.
Cleopatra (as Mark Antony) 18. Theodora Goes Wild 36. Professor Beware 38. The Great McGinty 40. He Hired the Boss 43. Brewster's Millions 45. The Secret Life of Walter Mitty 47. Affair in Reno 56, many others.
TV series: Topper 53–54.

Hall, Willis (1929–)
British playwright and screenwriter (in collaboration with Keith Waterhouse).
The Long and the Short and the Tall 61. Whistle Down the Wind 61. A Kind of Loving 62. Billy Liar 63. Lock Up Your Daughters! 69, etc.

Hall-Davis, Lillian
See DAVIS, Lilian Hall.

Hallahan, Charles (1943–1997)
American character actor of stage and screen, best known for his role as Captain Charlie Devane in the TV police series *Hunter*. Born in Philadelphia, he graduated from Rutgers University and began his acting career in the mid-70s. Died of a heart attack.
Twilight Zone: The Movie 76. American Hot Wax 77. Going in Style 79. Nightwing 79. Hide in Plain Sight 80. Skag 80. Margin for Murder (TV) 81. The Thing 82. Silkwood 83. Pale Rider 85. Vision Quest 85. A Winner Never Quits (TV) 86. True Believer 89. Nails 92. Body of Evidence 92. Warlock: Armageddon 93. Wild Palms 93. Dave 93. The Pest 96. The Rich Man's Wife 96. Executive Decision 96. The Fan 96. Dante's Peak 97, etc.
TV series: The Paper Chase 78–79. Hunter 86–91.

Hallatt, May (1882–1969)
British character actress, mainly on stage.
No Funny Business 33. The Lambeth Walk 39. Painted Boats 45. *Black Narcissus* 47. The Pickwick Papers 52. *Separate Tables* 58. Make Mine Mink 60, etc.

Haller, Daniel (1928–)
American director, former art director on Roger Corman's Poe films, etc.
Die Monster Die 67. The Devil's Angels 68. The Wild Racers 68. Paddy 70. The Dunwich Horror 70. Pieces of Dreams 70. The Desperate Miles (TV) 75. Sword of Justice (TV pilot) 78. Little Women (TV) 78. Little Mo (TV) 78. Buck Rogers in the 25th Century 78. Follow That Car 81. Welcome to Paradise 84, etc.

Haller, Ernest (1896–1970)
Distinguished American cinematographer.
Neglected Wives 20. Outcast 22. Stella Dallas 25. Weary River 29. The Dawn Patrol 31. The Emperor Jones 33. Dangerous 35. Jezebel 38. *Gone with the Wind* (AA) 39. Dark Victory 39. All This and Heaven Too 40. Saratoga Trunk 43. Mr Skeffington 44. *Mildred Pierce* 45. Humoresque 46. *My Girl Tisa* 47. The Flame and the Arrow 50. Rebel without a Cause 55. Back from the Dead 57. God's Little Acre 58. Man of the West 58. The Third Voice 59. Whatever Happened to Baby Jane? 62. Lilies of the Field 64. Dead Ringer 64, many others.

Halliday, John (1880–1947)
Suave and dapper Scottish actor, long in Hollywood.
■ The Woman Gives 20. East Side Sadie 29. Father's Sons 30. Recaptured Love 30. Scarlet Pages 30. Smart Women 31. Consolation Marriage 31. The Ruling Voice 31. Millie 31. Once a Sinner 31. Captain Applejack 31. Fifty Million Frenchmen 31. The Spy 31. Transatlantic 31. Men of Chance 32. The Impatient Maiden 32. The Age of Consent 32. Weekends Only 32. Bird of Paradise 32. Perfect Understanding 33. Terror Aboard 33. Bed of Roses 33. The House on 56th Street 33. Woman Accused 33. Return of the Terror 34. Housewife 34. A Woman's Man 34. Happiness Ahead 34. Registered Nurse 34. The Witching Hour 34. Desirable 34. Finishing School 34. Mystery Woman 35. The Dark Angel 35. The Melody Lingers On 35. Peter Ibbetson 35. *Desire* 36. Fatal Lady 36. Three Cheers for Love 36. *Hollywood Boulevard* 36. Arsène Lupin Returns 38. Blockade 38. That Certain Age 39. The Light that Failed 39. Hotel for Women 39. Intermezzo 39. *The Philadelphia Story* 40. Lydia 41. Escape to Glory 41.
❝ Famous line (*The Philadelphia Story*) 'What most wives fail to realize is that their husbands' philandering has nothing to do with them.'

Halliwell, Leslie (1929–1989)
British critic, author and creator of two of cinema's best-loved reference books, *Halliwell's Film Guide* (from 1977) and *Halliwell's Filmgoer's Companion* (from 1965). A former cinema manager and journalist, he was a film researcher for Britain's Granada TV, and went on to become programme buyer for the whole ITV network and, later, Channel 4. He wrote eleven other books, including *Halliwell's Hundred*, his choice of favourite films.
Autobiography: 1985, *Seats in All Parts*.

❝ It was an aroma compounded of soft plush and worn carpet and Devon violets and sweat. It was that scent, perhaps, which first made me a film fan; for it was to the Queen's in Bolton that I ventured on my first remembered visit to any cinema, one wet and windy afternoon in 1933, when I was four. – *L.H.*

Hallström, Lasse (1946–)
Swedish director who went to Hollywood in the 90s. Married actress Lena OLIN.
Abba – the Movie 77. Father to Be 79. The Rooster 81. Happy We 83. My Life as a Dog/Mitt Liv Som Hund (AAN) 85. A Lover and His Lass 85. The Children of Bullerby Village/Alla Vi Barn i Bullerby 86. More about the Children of Bullerby Village/Mer Om Oss Barn i Bullerbyn 87. Once Around 90. What's Eating Gilbert Grape? 93. Something to Talk About 95, etc.. The Cider House Rules (AAN) 99. Chocolat 00, etc.

Halop, Billy (1920–1976)
American actor, the erstwhile leader of the Dead End Kids; stardom failed to materialize, and he descended to bit parts.
Dead End 37. Crime School 38. Little Tough Guy 38. Angels with Dirty Faces 38. You Can't Get Away with Murder 39. Angels Wash Their Faces 39. Call a Messenger 39. Tom Brown's Schooldays 40. Hit the Road 41. Mob Town 41. Junior Army 43. Dangerous Years 47. Mister Buddwing 66. Fitzwilly 66, many others.
TV series: All in the Family 72–76.

Halperin, Victor (1895–1983)
American director.
Party Girl 29. Ex Flame 30. *White Zombie* 32. Supernatural 33. I Conquer the Sea 36. Revolt of the Zombies 36. Nation Aflame 37. Torture Ship 39. Buried Alive 40. Girls' Town 42.

Halsey, Brett (1933–) (Charles Hand)
American leading actor and novelist. Born in Santa Anna, California, he moved to Italy to make films in Europe from the 60s. From the mid-80s, he also worked in Hollywood as an acting teacher and coach.
The Glass Web 53. Ma and Pa Kettle at Home 54. Cry Baby Killer 58. The Best of Everything 59. Desire in the Dust 60. Return to Peyton Place 61. The Seventh Sword/Le Sette Spade Del Vendicatore (It.) 63. Twice Told Tales 63. Spy in Your Eye 65. A Day After August/Un Dia Despues De Agosto (Sp.) 66. Kill Johnny Ringo/Uccidete Johnny Ringo (It.) 66. Web of Violence/Tre Notti Violente (It./Sp.) 66. Bang Bang (Fr./It.) 67. Sartana (It./Ger.) 67. Roy Colt and Winchester Jack (It.) 70. Four Times That Night/Quante Volte... Quella Notte (It.) 72. Where Does It Hurt? 72. Ratboy 86. Dangerous Obsession/Il Miele Del Diavolo (It.) 87. Demonia (It.) 90. Desert Law 90. Search for Diana 93. First Degree 95, etc.
TV series: Follow the Sun 61–62.

Halton, Charles (1876–1959)
American character actor, inimitable as a sour-faced bank clerk, professor or lawyer.
Come and Get It 36. Penrod and Sam 37. Dead End 37. The Prisoner of Zenda 37. The Saint in New York 38. Room Service 38. Jesse James 39. Swanee River 39. Dodge City 39. Juarez 39. The Shop around the Corner 40. *Dr Cyclops* 40. Foreign Correspondent 40. Stranger on the Third Floor 40. The Westerner 40. Tobacco Road 41. The Smiling Ghost 41. *To Be or Not to Be* 42. Across the Pacific 42. Jitterbugs 43. Wilson 44. Rhapsody in Blue 45. The Best Years of Our Lives 46. Three Godfathers 48. The Nevadan 50. Here Comes the Groom 51. Carrie 52. Friendly Persuasion 56, many others.

Hambling, Gerry (1926–)
British film editor, a regular on the films of director Alan Parker, and a former sound editor.
The Whole Truth 58. The Bulldog Breed 60. The Early Bird 65. That Riviera Touch 68. Moses (TV) 75. Bugsy Malone 76. Midnight Express (AAN) 78. Fame (AAN) 80. Heartaches 82. Shoot the Moon 82. Pink Floyd the Wall 82. Another Country 84. Birdy 84. Invitation to the Wedding 85. Absolute Beginners 86. Leonard Part 6 87. Angel Heart 87. Mississippi Burning (AAN) 88. Lenny: Live and Unleashed 89. Come See the Paradise 90. The Commitments (AAN) 91. City of Joy 92. In the Name of the Father (AAN) 93. The Road to Wellville 94. White Squall 96. *Evita* (AAN) 96. The Boxer 97, etc.

Hamer, Gerald (1886–1973)
British character actor in Hollywood.
Swing Time 36. Bulldog Drummond's Bride 39. Sherlock Holmes Faces Death 43. The Scarlet Claw 44. The Sign of the Ram 48, etc.

Hamer, Robert (1911–1963)
British director, erratic but at his best impeccably stylish. Born in Kidderminster, Worcestershire, he graduated from Cambridge University, where he was sent down for a year because of a homosexual affair, and began as a clapper-boy at Gaumont Studios, later working as an editor, before becoming a producer and writer at Ealing Studios. His career was hampered by problems in getting backing for the dark-toned films he wanted to make, and by the alcoholism that finally made him unemployable. Married actress Joan Holt.
Books: 1998, *The Finest Years: British Cinema of the 1940s* by Charles Drazin (includes a chapter on Hamer).
■ San Demetrio London (w only) 43. Dead of Night (mirror sequence & w) 45. Pink String and Sealing Wax 45. *It Always Rains on Sunday* (& w) 47. *Kind Hearts and Coronets* (& w) 49. The Spider and the Fly 49. His Excellency (& w) 52. The Long Memory (& w) 52. *Father Brown* 54. To Paris With Love 54. The Scapegoat 59. *School for Scoundrels* 60. A Jolly Bad Fellow (w only) 63.
❝ No one can be satisifed with one death. I'd like to die like Charles XII, drowned in a butt of brandy, but I'd also like to die like Stefan George, poisoned by a rose-thorn. Bits of me have already died in these ways. – *R.H.*
He was a perfectionist, and knew more about acting for films than any director I know. He could be maddening over tiny details – he once had fifteen takes of a scene between Googie [Withers] and me, because he wanted Googie to give less emphasis to the 'k' in the word 'back'! – *John McCallum*

Hamill, Mark (1951–)
American leading man.
Sarah T (TV) 75. Delancey Street (TV) 75. Eric (TV) 75. Mallory (TV) 76. The City (TV) 77. *Star Wars* 77. Corvette Summer 78. The Big Red One 79. The Empire Strikes Back 80. The Night the Lights Went Out in Georgia 81. Return of the Jedi 83. Slipstream 89. Black Magic Woman 91. Sleepwalkers 92. Time Runner 93. Batman: Mask of the Phantasm (voice) 94. Village of the Damned 95. When Time Expires 97. Watchers Reborn 98. Hamilton (Swe.) 98, etc.
❝ I'm waiting for my body to catch up with my age. – *M.H.*
Acting in *Star Wars* I felt like a raisin in a giant fruit salad, and I didn't even know who the cantaloupes were. – *M.H.*

Hamilton, Ashley (1977–)
American teen actor, the son of George Hamilton.
Lost in Africa 94.

Hamilton, Bernie (1929–)
Burly American actor.
Let No Man Write My Epitaph 60. 13 West Street 62. Captain Sinbad 63. The Swimmer 67. The Lost Man 69. The Organization 71. Scream Blacula Scream 73. Bucktown 75, etc.
TV series: *Starsky and Hutch* 75–79.

Hamilton, Donald (1913–)
American thriller writer, creator of Matt Helm. The resulting films and TV series were undistinguished to say the least.

Hamilton, George (1939–)
American leading man, usually in serious roles.
Crime and Punishment USA (debut) 58. Home from the Hill 60. All the Fine Young Cannibals 60. Angel Baby 60. By Love Possessed 61. A Thunder of Drums 61. The Light in the Piazza 62. Two Weeks in Another Town 62. The Victors 63. *Act One* (as Moss Hart) 63. Your Cheatin' Heart 64. Viva Maria! 65. Doctor, You've Got To Be Kidding 67. The Long Ride Home 67. Jack of Diamonds 67. A Time for Killing 67. The Power 67. Evel Knievel 71. The Man Who Loved Cat Dancing 73. Once Is Not Enough 75. The Dead Don't Die (TV) 75. Roots (TV) 77. The Strange Possession of Mrs Oliver (TV) 77. Killer on Board (TV) 77. The Users (TV) 78. Institute for Revenge (TV) 79. Sextette 78. *Love at First Bite* (as Dracula) 79. Zorro the Gay Blade 81. Love at Second Bite 90. The Godfather Part III 90. Doc Hollywood 91. Once Upon a Crime 92. Danielle Steel's Vanished (TV) 95. 8 Heads in a Duffel Bag 97. Rough Riders (TV) 97. The Little Unicorn 99. Pets 99, etc.
TV series: The Survivors 69. Paris 7000 70: Dynasty 85. Spies 86.

Hamilton, Guy (1922–)
British director, former assistant to Carol Reed.
■ The Ringer 52. The Intruder 53. *An Inspector Calls* 54. The Colditz Story 54. Charley Moon 56. Manuela 57. The Devil's Disciple 58. A Touch of Larceny 59. The Best of Enemies 62. The Party's Over 63. The Man in the Middle 64. *Goldfinger* 64. Funeral in Berlin 66. The Battle of Britain 70. Diamonds are Forever 71. Live and Let Die 72. The Man with the Golden Gun 73. Force Ten from Navarone (also p) 78. The Mirror Crack'd 80. Evil under the Sun 82. Remo Williams ... the Adventure Begins 85. Try This One On for Size (Fr.) 89.

Hamilton, John (1886–1958)
Chubby American character actor, in hundreds of small parts as judge, cop, lawyer.
Rainbow Riley 26. White Cargo 30. Legion of Terror 37. Rose of Washington Square 39. The Maltese Falcon (as district attorney) 41. Meet Miss Bobby Socks 44. Law of the Golden West 49. The Pace that Thrills 52. On the Waterfront 54, many others.
TV series: Superman 51–57.

Hamilton, Josh (1969–)
American actor, from the stage and TV. Born in New York, he was a co-founder, with others including Ethan HAWKE, of the Malaparte Theater Company in 1993.
First Born 84. Old Enough 84. The Exchange Student (TV) 85. Another Woman 88. Abby, My Love (TV) 91. O Pioneers (TV) 92. Alive 93. With Honors 94. Kicking and Screaming 95. The Proprietor 96. Drive, She Said 97. The House of Yes 97. The 60s (TV) 99. Freak Talks About Sex 99, etc.

Hamilton, Linda (1956–)
American actress, born in Salisbury, Maryland. Formerly married (1997-1999) to director James CAMERON, her second husband.
Rape and Marriage: The Rideout Case (TV) 80. T.A.G. – the Assassination Game 82. The Terminator 84. Children of the Corn 84. Secret Weapons (TV) 85. King Kong Lives 86. Black Moon Rising 86. Mr Destiny 90. Terminator 2: Judgment Day 91. Silent Fall 94. Separate Lives 95. Dante's Peak 97. Shadow Conspiracy 97. On the Line (TV) 98. The Color of Courage 98. The Secret Life of Girls 99, etc.
TV series: Secrets of Midland Heights 81–82. King's Crossing 82. Beauty and the Beast 87–90.

Hamilton, Lloyd (1891–1935)
American silent slapstick comedian, in many two-reelers from 1914.

Hamilton, Margaret (1902–1985)
American character actress, a former kindergarten teacher who came to films via Broadway and usually played hatchet-faced spinsters or maids.
Another Language 33. These Three 36. Nothing Sacred 37. *The Wizard of Oz* 39. Invisible Woman 41. *Guest in the House* 44. Mad Wednesday 47. State of the Union 48. The Great Plane Robbery 50. Thirteen Ghosts 60. The Daydreamer 66. Rosie 67. The Anderson Tapes 71. Brewster McCloud 71, etc.

Hamilton, Murray (1923–1986)
American general-purpose actor.
Bright Victory 50. No Time for Sergeants 58. The FBI Story 59. Seconds 66. The Graduate 67. No Way to Treat a Lady 68. The Boston Strangler 68. If It's Tuesday This Must Be Belgium 69. The Way We Were 73. Jaws 75. Jaws 2 78. 1941 79. The Amityville Horror 79. Brubaker 80, etc.
TV series: Love and Marriage 59–60. The Man Who Never Was 66–67. Rich Man, Poor Man Book I 76. B.J. and the Bear 81. Hail to the Chief 85.

Hamilton, Neil (1899–1984)
Stalwart American leading man of silent days, a former model.
White Rose 23. America 24. Isn't Life Wonderful? 25. Beau Geste 26. The Great Gatsby 27. Why Be Good? 28. Keeper of the Bees 29. The Dawn Patrol 30. The Wet Parade 31. The Animal Kingdom 32. Tarzan the Ape Man 32. One Sunday Afternoon 33. Tarzan and His Mate 34. Federal Fugitives 41. The Little Shepherd of Kingdom Come 61. Madame X 66, many others.
TV series: Hollywood Screen Test 48–53. That Wonderful Guy 49–50. Batman 65–67.

Hamilton, Patrick (1904–1962)
British novelist and playwright whose work inspired a small but significant group of films.
■ *Gaslight* 39 and 44. Hangover Square 44. Rope 49.

Hamlin, Harry (1951–)
American light leading man. He has a son by Ursula ANDRESS.
Movie Movie 78. Studs Lonigan (TV) 79. Clash of the Titans 81. King of the Mountain 81. Dragonslayer 81. Making Love 82. Blue Skies Again 83. Maxie 85. Space (TV) 85. Laguna Heat 88. Dinner at Eight 89. Deceptions (TV) 90. Deadly Intentions ... Again (TV) 91. Tom Clancy's Op Center (TV) 95. Frogs for Snakes 98, etc.
TV series: L.A. Law 86–91.

Hamlisch, Marvin (1945–)
American composer and pianist.
The Swimmer 68. The April Fools 69. Flap 70. The Sting (AA) 73. The Way We Were (AAs, m) 73. The Prisoner of Second Avenue 75. The Spy Who Loved Me 77. Same Time Next Year 78. Ice Castles 79. Chapter Two 79. Starting Over 79. Ordinary People 80. Seems Like Old Times 80. Pennies from Heaven 81. The Fan 81. I Ought to Be in Pictures 82. Sophie's Choice (AAN) 82. Romantic Comedy 83. A Chorus Line 85. D.A.R.Y.L. 85. Three Men and a Baby 87. The January Man 88. Little Nikita 88. The Experts 89. Frankie and Johnny 91. The Mirror Has Two Faces (AANs 'I've Finally Found Someone') 96, etc.
❝ My whole life revolves around dessert. – *M.H.*
To put something on the earth that wasn't there yesterday, that's what I like. – *M.H.*

Hamm, Sam (1956–) (Gay Stewart Hamm)
American screenwriter, born Charlottesville, Virgina.
Never Cry Wolf (co-w) 83. Batman (co-w) 89. Batman Returns (co-story) 92, etc.

Hammer, Will (1887– *) (William Hinds)
British producer, one of the founders of Hammer Films.

Hammerstein II, Oscar (1895–1960)
Immensely successful American lyricist who wrote many stage musicals, usually with Richard RODGERS. The King and I, South Pacific, The Sound of Music, etc.

Hammett, Dashiell (1894–1961)
American writer of detective novels and occasional screenplays. He was played by Sam Shepard in the TV biopic *Dash and Lilly* 99, about his relationship with writer Lillian HELLMAN. Wim WENDERS' film *Hammett*, which appeared in 1982, was a pastiche in which the real Hammett became one of his own detective creations. In the vein of the Chandler movies, but less entertaining, it had minority appeal.
City Streets (& w) 31. The Maltese Falcon 31. The Thin Man 34. The Glass Key 35. The Maltese Falcon 41. The Glass Key 42. Watch on the Rhine (AANw) 43, etc.

Hammid, Alexander (c. 1910–) (Alexander Hackenschmied)
Czech documentarist in America.
Hymn of the Nations 46. Of Men and Music 51. To the Fair 65, etc.

Hammond, Kay (1909–1980) (Dorothy Standing)
Plummy-voiced English leading lady, mostly on the stage, the daughter of actor Sir Guy STANDING. Born in London, she studied at RADA and was on stage from 1927. Her best role, on stage and screen, was as Elvira in *Blithe Spirit*. Her second husband was actor Sir John CLEMENTS, and she was the mother of actor John STANDING.
Children of Chance 30. A Night in Montmartre 31. Out of the Blue 31. Almost a Divorce 32. A Night Like This 32. Sally Bishop 32. Yes Madam 33. Sleeping Car 33. Bitter Sweet 33. Two on a Doorstep 36. Jeannie 41. *Blithe Spirit* 45. Call of the Blood 47. Five Golden Hours 61, etc.

Hammond, Peter (1923–)
British juvenile player of the 40s; became a TV and film director.
They Knew Mr Knight 46. Holiday Camp 47. Fly Away Peter 48. Morning Departure 50. Vote for Huggett 50. The Adventurers 51. Spring and Port Wine (d only) 69, etc.
TV series: The Buccaneers 56–57.

Hampden, Walter (1879–1955) (Walter Hampden Dougherty)
American stage actor with a long career behind him when he came to Hollywood. Born in Brooklyn, the son of an attorney, he studied at Harvard University and in Paris, and was on stage, playing Shakespeare in England, from 1901.
■ Warfare of the Flesh 17. The Hunchback of Notre Dame 39. All This and Heaven Too 40. North West Mounted Police 40. They Died with Their Boots On 41. Reap the Wild Wind 42. The Adventures of Mark Twain 44. All About Eve 50. The First Legion 51. Five Fingers 52. Treasure of the Golden Condor 52. Sombrero 53. The Silver Chalice 54. Sabrina 54. Strange Lady in Town 55. The Prodigal 55. The Vagabond King 56.

Hampshire, Susan (1938–)
Talented British leading lady, somewhat handicapped by her own demureness.
Upstairs and Downstairs 59. Expresso Bongo 59. During One Night 61. The Long Shadow 61. The Three Lives of Thomasina 63. Night Must Fall 64. Wonderful Life 64. The Fighting Prince of Donegal 66. The Trygon Factor 67. Paris in August 67. Violent Enemy 69. Monte Carlo or Bust 69. David Copperfield (TV) 69. A Time for Loving 72. Living Free 72. Neither the Sea nor the Sand 72. Baffled (TV) 72. Malpertius 72. The Lonely Woman 76. The Barchester Chronicles (TV) 84. Nancherrow (TV) 99., etc.
TV series: The Andromeda Breakthrough 62. *The Forsyte Saga* (as Fleur) 68. *The Pallisers* 75. The Grand 97. Monarch of the Glen 00- .

Hampton, Christopher (1946–)
English dramatist and screenwriter.
A Doll's House 73. Tales from the Vienna Woods 81. Beyond the Limit 83. The Wolf at the Door 86. The Good Father 87. Dangerous Liaisons (AA) 88. Carrington (wd) 95. Total Eclipse (w) 95. Mary Reilly (w) 96. Joseph Conrad's Secret Agent (wd) 96, etc.

Hampton, Hope (1899–1982)
American leading lady of the silents.
The Bait 21. The Gold Diggers 23. Hollywood 23. The Truth about Women 24. Lover's Island 25. The Unfair Sex 26, etc.

Hampton, Lionel (1909–)
American jazz musician and bandleader, in films as himself. Born in Louisville, Kentucky, he was a drummer before first gaining fame playing vibraphone with Benny Goodman's trio and quartet in the mid-30s, later leading his own big band and small groups. He is caricatured in the Merrie Melodies cartoon *Hollywood Canine Canteen* 46.
Sing, Sinner, Sing 33. Pennies from Heaven 36. Hollywood Hotel 37. A Song Is Born 48. *The Benny Goodman Story* 55. Mister Rock and Roll 57. Force of Impulse 61. No Maps on My Taps (doc) 78. Cha Cha (doc) 80, etc.

Hampton, Louise (1881–1954)
British character actress.
Goodbye Mr Chips 39. Busman's Honeymoon 40. Bedelia 46, etc.

Hanbury, Victor (1897–1954)
English director and screenwriter. From the 1940s, he worked as a producer, notably until 1945 for RKO Radio British.
AS DIRECTOR: The Beggar Student 31. Dick Turpin 33. No Funny Business (& w) 33. Spring in the Air 34. The Crouching Beast 35. The Avenging Hand 36. Second Bureau 36. Return of a Stranger 37. Hotel Reserve (& p) 44, etc.
AS PRODUCER: They Flew Alone 41. Squadron Leader X 42. Great Day 45. Daughter of Darkness 47, etc.

Hancock, Herbie (1940–) (Herbert Jeffrey Hancock)
American composer and musician, a leading jazz keyboard player who turned to electronic music in the 70s, soon after he began writing for films.
Blow-Up 66. The Spook Who Sat by the Door 73. Death Wish 74. A Soldier's Story 84. Jo Jo Dancer, Your Life Is Calling 86. Round Midnight (& a) (AAm) 86. Action Jackson 88. Colors 88. Harlem Nights 89. Livin' Large 91, etc.

Hancock, John (1939–)
American director.
■ Let's Scare Jessica to Death 73. Bang the Drum Slowly 74. Baby Blue Marine 76. California Dreaming 78. Weeds 87. Prancer 89.

Hancock, Sheila (1933–)
British comic actress of stage and TV.
Light Up the Sky 58. The Girl on the Boat 61. Night Must Fall 63. The Anniversary 67. Take a Girl Like You 70. Three Men and a Little Lady 90. A Business Affair 94. Close Relations (TV) 98, etc.
TV series: The Rag Trade 61–63. The Bed-Sit Girl 65–66. Now Take My Wife ... 71. Gone to Seed 92. Brighton Belles 93.

Hancock, Tony (1924–1968)
Popular British radio and TV comedian. He committed suicide in Australia, leaving a note that said 'Things seemed to go wrong too many times'. He was the model for Lon Bracton, a self-destructive comedian, in J. B. Priestley's novel *London End*.
Biography: 1969, *Hancock* by Freddie Hancock and David Nathan. 1995, *Tony Hancock: When the Wind Changed* by Cliff Goodwin.
■ Orders are Orders 61. The Rebel 61. The Punch and Judy Man 62. Those Magnificent Men in their Flying Machines 65. The Wrong Box 66.
❝ A comedian with a touch of genius who had no enemy except himself. – *J. B. Priestley*
An indifferent performer saved by two of the most brilliant scriptwriters of the decade, Galton and Simpson, whom he rejected. Thereafter, it was all downhill. – *Kenneth Williams*

Hand, David (1900–1986)
American animator, formerly with Disney; came to Britain 1945 to found a cartoon unit for Rank with some pleasing results (*Musical Paintbox* series, etc.), but it was a financial failure and Hand returned to America in 1950.

Handke, Peter (1942–)
Austrian avant-garde dramatist, novelist, screenwriter and director.
The Goalkeeper's Fear of the Penalty Kick/Die Angst des Tormanns beim Elfmeter (w) 72. Wrong Move/Falsche Bewegung (w) 75. The Left-Handed Woman/Die Linkshändige Frau (wd) 77. Wings of Desire/Der Himmel über Berlin (w) 87, etc.

Handl, Irene (1902–1987)
Dumpy British character comedienne, frequently seen as maid or charlady; became a star in her later years. Born in London, the daughter of an Austrian banker and his aristocratic French wife, she studied at the Embassy School of Acting, and was on stage from 1937. She also wrote two novels, *The Sioux* 65 and *The Gold Tipped Phitzer* 66, noted for their originality and ornate literary style.
Missing Believed Married 37. The Girl in the News 41. Pimpernel Smith 41. Temptation Harbour 46. Silent Dust 48. One Wild Oat 51. The Belles of St Trinian's 54. A Kid for Two Farthings 56. Brothers in Law 57. *I'm All Right Jack* 59. Make Mine Mink 60. The Rebel 61. Heavens Above 63. Morgan 66. Smashing Time 67. On a Clear Day You Can See Forever 70. The Private Life of Sherlock Holmes 70. For the Love of Ada 72. Adventures of a Private Eye 76. Stand Up Virgin Soldiers 77, etc.
TV series: *For the Love of Ada* 70–72. Maggie and Her 78–79.

Handley, Tommy (1894–1949)
British radio comedian most famous for his long-running, morale-building *ITMA* series during World War II. Born in Liverpool, he began in concert parties and in a double-act with Jack Hylton. Died of a cerebral haemorrhage.
Elstree Calling 30. Two Men in a Box 38. *It's That Man Again* 42. Time Flies 43. Tom Tom Topia (short) 46.

Handy, W. C. (1873–1958) (William Christopher Handy)
Blind American blues pioneer; was impersonated by Nat King Cole in *St Louis Blues*.

Haneke, Michael (1942–)
German director and screenwriter. Born in Munich, he studied philosophy, psychology and theatre in Vienna before entering television as a scriptwriter, from 1967, and as a director, from 1974. He also works as a theatre director.
The Seventh Continent/Der Siebente Kontinent 88. Benny's Video 92. 71 Fragments of a Chronology of Chance/71 Fragmente Einer Chronologie des Zufalls 94. Age of the Wolves 95. The Castle 97. Funny Games 97. Code Unknown/Code Inconnu (Fr.) 00, etc.

Haney, Carol (1928–1964)
American dancer, former assistant to Gene Kelly.
■ Kiss Me Kate 53. Invitation to the Dance 54. *The Pajama Game* 57.

Hanff, Helene (1916–1997)
American writer and journalist. She was played by Anne Bancroft in her autobiographical *84 Charing Cross Road* 86, which was also turned into a TV, stage and radio play. Born in Philadelphia, she began by writing plays that were not performed and also read novels for Paramount, once adding $40 for 'mental torture' to her invoice after ploughing through J. R. R. Tolkien's *Lord of the Rings* trilogy.

Hani, Susumu (1926–)
Japanese 'new wave' director, a former journalist and maker of documentary shorts. Often uses non-professional actors. Married actress Sachiko Hidari.
Bad Boys/Furyo Shonen 60. He and She/Kanojo Ta Kare 63. Bwana Toshi 65. Bride of the Andes/Andesu No Hanayome 66. Nanami 68. Aido 69. Mio 72. Morning Schedule/Gozencho No Jikanwari 73. The Green Horizon/Afurika Monogatari 81, etc.

Hanks, Tom (1956–)
Versatile American leading actor, in sympathetic roles both in comedy and drama. Born in Concord, California, he studied at California State University and began his career on stage at the Great Lakes Shakespeare Festival in Ohio. A TV series followed in 1980 and gained him the beginnings of fame, though many of his subsequent films were second-rate at best, and not particularly successful until *Big* established his deftness in comedy. Forbes magazine estimated his 1999 earnings at $71.5m. Current asking price: around $25m. Married actresses Samantha Lewes (1980-87) and Rita Wilson. He is the father of actor Colin Hanks (1971-).
He Knows You're Alone 80. Bachelor Party 84. Splash! 84. The Man with One Red Shoe 85. Volunteers 85. The Money Pit 86. Nothing in Common 86. Every Time We Say Goodbye 86. Dragnet 87. Big (AAN) 88. Punchline 88. The 'burbs 88. Turner & Hooch 89. The Bonfire of the Vanities 90. Joe versus the Volcano 90. Radio Flyer 92. A League of Their Own 92. *Sleepless in Seattle* 93. *Philadelphia* (AA) 93. Forrest Gump (AA) 94. Toy Story (voice) 95. Apollo 13 95. That Thing You Do! (a, co-w, d) 96. *Saving Private Ryan* (AAN) 98. You've Got Mail 98. The Green Mile 99. Toy Story 2 (voice) 99. Cast Away (AAN) 00, etc.
TV series: Bosom Buddies 80–82.
❝ If you have to have a job in this world, a high-priced movie star is a pretty damned good gig. – *T.H.*
I think it's important that you still live up to your responsibilities as a professional. We work in a business where the structure is in place to allow you to be the biggest asshole you can be. – *T.H.*

Hanley, Jenny (1947–)
British light leading lady and television personality, daughter of Dinah Sheridan and Jimmy Hanley.
Joanna 68. On Her Majesty's Secret Service 69. Tam Lin 70. The Private Life of Sherlock Holmes 70. Scars of Dracula 72. Soft Beds Hard Battles 74. Alfie Darling 75, etc.

Hanley, Jimmy (1918–1970)
Former British child actor developed as 'the boy next door' type by Rank in the 40s. He was on stage from the age of 12 and a circus bareback rider at 14 before making his film debut when he was 16. In the mid-50s he was also presenter of a daily television programme, *Jolly Good Time*, and a consumer programme, *Jim's Inn*. The first of his two wives was actress Dinah Sheridan. Their daughter is actress Jenny Hanley and their son, Jeremy Hanley, MP, was chairman of the Conservative party in 1994–95.
Little Friend 34. Boys Will Be Boys 35. Night Ride 37. There Ain't No Justice 39. Salute John Citizen 42. For You Alone 44. The Way Ahead 44. Henry V 44. 29 Acacia Avenue 45. The Captive Heart 46. Master of Bankdam 47. It Always Rains on Sunday 48. It's Hard To Be Good 49. Here Come the Huggetts (and ensuing series) 49–52. The Blue Lamp 50. The Black Rider 54. The Deep Blue Sea 56. Lost Continent 68, etc.

Hanna, William (1910–2001)
American animator who with his partner Joe Barbera created Tom and Jerry for MGM, later founding their own successful company creating innumerable semi-animated series for TV: Huckleberry Hound, Yogi Bear, The Flintstones, The Jetsons, Wait Till Your Father Gets Home, etc.

Hannah, Daryl (1960–)
American leading lady.
The Fury 78. Hard Country 81. Blade Runner 82. The Pope of Greenwich Village 84. *Splash!* 84. Clan of the Cave Bear 86. Legal Eagles 86. Roxanne 87. Wall Street 87. High Spirits 88. Crimes and Misdemeanors 89. Steel Magnolias 89. At Play in the Fields of the Lord 91. Memoirs of an Invisible Man 92. Attack of the 50 Ft Woman (TV) 93. Grumpy Old Men 93. The Little Rascals 94. The Tie that Binds 95. Grumpier Old Men 95. Two Much 96. The Last Days of Frankie the Fly 96. The Last Don (TV) 97. The Gingerbread Man 97. Hi-Life 98. Rear Window (TV) 98. Enemy of My Enemy 99. My Favorite Martian 99. Hide and Seek 00, etc.

Hannah, John (1962–)
Scottish leading actor. Born in Glasgow, he trained as an electrician before studying at the Royal Scottish Academy of Drama.
Harbour Beat (Aus.) 90. Four Weddings and a Funeral 94. McCallum (TV) 95. Madagascar Skin 95. The James Gang 97. Resurrection Man 98. *Sliding Doors* 98. The Mummy 99. The Hurricane 99. Rebus (TV) 00. Circus 00. Pandaemonium (as William Wordsworth) 00, etc.
TV series: Out of the Blue 95. McCallum 97–98.

Hannam, Ken (1929–)
Australian director who moved to England in the late 60s to work as a television director.
Sunday Too Far Away 74. Break of Day 76. Summerfield 77. Dawn! 78.

Hannan, Peter (1941–)
Australian cinematographer, now working in Britain.
Eskimo Nell 71. Flame 74. The Haunting of Julia 77. The Stud 78. The Missionary 81. Brimstone and Treacle 82. Monty Python's Meaning of Life 83. The Razor's Edge 83. Blame It on Rio 83. Dance with a Stranger 84. Turtle Diary 85. Insignificance 85. Half Moon Street 85. Club Paradise 85. Withnail and I 87. The Lonely Passion of Judith Hearne 87. A Handful of Dust 88. How to Get Ahead in Advertising 89. Not without My Daughter 91, etc.

Hanray, Lawrence (1874–1947)
British stage character actor of great dignity. Born in London, he was on stage from 1892.
The Private Life of Henry VIII 33. That Night in London 33. Lorna Doone 34. The Scarlet Pimpernel 34. The Man Who Could Work Miracles 36. Knight without Armour 37. It's Never Too Late to Mend 37. On Approval 43, etc.

Hansberry, Lorraine (1930–1965)
American playwright, whose *A Raisin in the Sun* was filmed.

Hansen, Gunnar (1947–)
American actor, best known for playing the role of Leatherface in *The Texas Chainsaw Massacre* 74.
Scream of the Demon Lover 71. The Demon Lover 77. Hollywood Chainsaw Hookers 88. Mosquito 95. Freakshow 95, etc.

Hansen, Juanita (1895–1961)
American leading lady of the silents, especially in serials.
His Pride and Shame 16. Secret of the Submarine 16. Dangers of a Bride 17. The Brass Bullet 18. The Lost City 20. The Yellow Arm 21. Broadway Madonna 22. The Jungle Princess 23, etc.

Hansen, Peter (1922–)
American general-purpose actor.
Branded 50. When Worlds Collide 51. Darling How Could You 53. Three Violent People 56. The Deep Six 58. Harlow 65, etc.
TV series: Mr Parkson 64–65. General Hospital 65– .

Hanson, Curtis (1945–)
American director and screenwriter.
AS WRITER: The Silent Partner 78. White Dog 82. Never Cry Wolf 83, etc.
AS DIRECTOR: The Arousers 76. The Little Dragons 80. Losin' It 83. The Bedroom Window 86. Bad Influence 90. The Hand that Rocks the Cradle 91. The River Wild 94. *LA Confidential* (AANp, AAw, AANd) 97. Wonder Boys 00, etc.

Hanson, Lars (1887–1965)
Swedish stage actor who made silent films abroad but after the coming of sound remained in Sweden.
Ingeborg Holm (debut) 13. Dolken 16. Erotikon 19. The Atonement of Gosta Berling 24. The Scarlet Letter (US) 26. The Divine Woman (US) 27. The Wind (US) 28. The Informer (GB) 28, etc.

Harareet, Haya (1931–) (Haya Hararit)
Israeli leading lady. She is married to director Jack Clayton.
Hill 24 Does Not Answer 55. Ben Hur 59. The Secret Partner 61. The Lost Kingdom 61. The Interns 62. Our Mother's House (co-w only) 67, etc.

Harasimowicz, Cazary (1955–)
Polish screenwriter.
Sezon Na Bazanty 85. 300 Miles to Heaven/300 Mil Do Nieba 89. Seszele 90. Black Lights 91. Lazarus 94. The Brute/The Hoodlum 96, etc.

Harbach, Otto (1873–1963) (Otto Hauerbach)
American playwright and lyricist. Born in Salt Lake City, Utah, he was educated at Knox College, Galesburg, and Columbia University, and was for six years Professor of English at Whitman College, Washington, before working in advertising and journalism. The Broadway shows for which he wrote lyrics included *No, No, Nanette* and *The Desert Song*. His best-known lyrics include 'I Won't Dance', 'Indian Love Call', and 'Smoke Gets in Your Eyes'.
The Cat and Fiddle 34. Roberta 35. Rose Marie 36. Lovely to Look At 52. Rose Marie 54, etc.

Harburg, E. Y. (1896–1981) (Edgar 'Yip' Harburg)
American lyricist chiefly noted for the songs in *The Wizard of Oz*; also wrote 'Brother Can You Spare a Dime', 'Happiness Is a Thing Called Joe', 'Can't Help Singing', 'Lydia the Tattooed Lady', 'Last Night When We Were Young', 'April in Paris', 'How Are Things in Glocca Morra', etc.

Harcourt, James (1873–1951)
English character actor of stage and screen. Born in Headingly, Leeds, he was a cabinet-maker who began in amateur dramatics, and was on-stage from 1902, working for the Liverpool Repertory Company from 1919-31.
Hobson's Choice 31. Song of the Plough 33. The Old Curiosity Shop 34. Laburnum Grove 36. Wings Over Africa 36. Return of a Stranger 37. Penny Paradise 38. The House of the Arrow 40. Night Train to Munich 40. The Young Mr Pitt 42. He Snoops to Conquer 44. Johnny Frenchman 45. The Grand Escapade 46. Obsession 48, etc.

Harden, Marcia Gay (1959–)
American leading actress.
Miller's Crossing 90. Late for Dinner 91. Used People 92. Sinatra (TV) 92. Crush (NZ) 92. Used People 92. Safe Passage 94. The Spitfire Grill 96. Spy Hard 96. The First Wives Club 96. The Daytrippers 96. Flubber 97. Path to Paradise (TV) 97. Desperate Measures 98. Meet Joe Black 98. Pollock (AAN) 00, etc.

Hardin, Ty (1930–) (Orton Hungerford)
Muscular leading man, mostly on TV.
I Married a Monster from Outer Space 58. The Chapman Report 62. PT 109 63. Battle of the Bulge 65. Berserk (GB) 67. Custer of the West 68. The Last Rebel 71. Drums of Vengeance 77. Bad Jim 89. Born Killer 90, etc.
TV series: *Bronco* 58–61. Riptide 69.

“ I'm really a very humble man. Not a day passes that I don't thank God for my looks and my talent. – *T.H.*

Harding, Ann (1902–1981) (Dorothy Gatley)
Gentlewomanly American leading lady of 30s romances. Born in Fort Sam Houston, Texas, the daughter of an army officer who rose to be a general, she was briefly educated at Bryn Mawr and worked as a clerk and script-reader before beginning on stage in 1921. Married actor Harry Bannister (1926–32) and conductor and composer Werner Janssen (1937–62). She retired for a time after her second marriage before returning to the screen in the early 40s in more mature ladylike roles. Her best performances were as Linda Seton in *Holiday*, Daisy Sage in *The Animal Kingdom*, Marion in *Biography of a Bachelor Girl* and Carol Howard in *Love from a Stranger*.
■ Paris Bound 29. Her Private Affair 29. Condemned 29. *Holiday* (AAN) 30. Girl of the Golden West 30. East Lynne 31. Devotion 31. Prestige 31. Westward Passage 32. The Conquerors 32. *The Animal Kingdom* 32. When Ladies Meet 33. Double Harness 33. Right to Romance 33. Gallant Lady 33. The Life of Vergie Winters 34. The Fountain 34. *Biography of a Bachelor Girl* 35. Enchanted April 35. The Flame Within 35. Peter Ibbetson 35. The Lady Consents 36. The Witness Chair 36. *Love from a Stranger* (GB) 37. Eyes in the Night 42. Mission to Moscow 43. North Star 43. Janie 44. Nine Girls 44. Those Endearing Young Charms 45. Janie Gets Married 46. It Happened on Fifth Avenue 47. Christmas Eve 47. The Magnificent Yankee 50. Two Weeks with Love 50. The Unknown Man 51. The Man in the Grey Flannel Suit 56. I've Lived Before 56. Strange Intruder 56.

Harding, Gilbert (1907–1960)
Explosive British TV personality who appeared in a few films. Born in Hereford, he was educated at Queen's College, Cambridge, and worked as a policeman and teacher before joining the BBC. He appeared on numerous panel games from the mid-40s, where he became known for his irascibility.
The Gentle Gunman 52. The Oracle 52. Meet Mr Lucifer 53. As Long as They're Happy 55. An Alligator Named Daisy 55. Expresso Bongo 60, etc.

Harding, Lyn (1867–1952) (David Llewellyn Harding)
British stage actor who made a splendid 'heavy' in some films of the 20s and 30s.
The Barton Mystery 20. When Knighthood Was in Flower (as Henry VIII) 21. The Speckled Band (as Moriarty) 31. *The Triumph of Sherlock Holmes* (as Moriarty) 35. Spy of Napoleon 36. Fire Over England 36. Knight without Armour 37. *Goodbye Mr Chips* (as Chips' first headmaster) 39. The Prime Minister 40, etc.

Hardison, Kadeem (1965–)
American actor.
Rappin' 85. School Daze 88. I'm Gonna Git You Sucka 88. Dream Date (TV) 89. Def by Temptation 90. White Men Can't Jump 92. Mixed Nuts 94. Renaissance Man 94. Gunmen 94. Panther 95. Drive 96. The Sixth Man 97. Blind Faith 98, etc.
TV series: A Different World 87–92. Between Brothers 97– .

Hardwicke, Sir Cedric (1893–1964)
Leading English actor, from the stage, who moved to Hollywood in the late 30s, remaining there until the mid 40s. Born in Lye, Stourbridge, Worcestershire, he studied at the Academy of Dramatic Art and was on stage from 1912. He was knighted in the New Year's Honours of 1934. Married actresses Helena Pickard and Mary Scott. He was the father of actor Edward HARDWICKE.
Autobiography: 1932, *Let's Pretend*; 1961, *A Victorian in Orbit* (with James Brough).
■ Nelson 26. Dreyfus 31. Rome Express 32. Orders is Orders 33. The Ghoul 33. The Lady is Willing 33. *Nell Gwyn* (as Charles II) 34. Jew Süss 34.Belladonna 34. Peg of Old Drury 35. Les Misérables 35. King of Paris 35. *Becky Sharp* 35. Things to Come 36. Tudor Rose 36. Laburnum Grove 36. The Green Light 36. *King Solomon's Mines* (as Allan Quartermain) 37. *On Borrowed Time* (as Death) 39. *Stanley and Livingstone* (as Livingstone) 39. The Hunchback of Notre Dame (as Frollo) 39. The Invisible Man Returns 40. *Tom Brown's Schooldays* (as Dr Arnold) 40. The Howards of Virginia 40. *Victory* 40. Suspicion 41. Sundown 41. The Ghost of Frankenstein 42. Valley of the Sun 42. Invisible Agent 42. The Commandos Strike at Dawn 42. Forever and a Day 43. *The Moon is Down* 43. The Cross of Lorraine 44. The Lodger 44. Wing and a Prayer 44. Wilson 44. The Keys of the Kingdom 44. Sentimental Journey 46. Beware of Pity 46. The Imperfect Lady 46. Ivy 47. Lured 47. Song of My Heart 47. A Woman's Vengeance 47. *Nicholas Nickleby* 47. Tycoon 47. *I Remember Mama* 48. *The Winslow Boy* 48. Rope 48. A Connecticut Yankee in King Arthur's Court 49. Now Barabbas 49. The White Tower 50. Mr Imperium 51. The Desert Fox 51. The Green Glove 52. Caribbean 52. Botany Bay 52. The War of the Worlds (narrator) 53. Salome 53. Bait 54. *Richard III* 55. Helen of Troy 55. Diane 56. Gaby 56. The Vagabond King 56. The Power and the Prize 56. The Ten Commandments 56. Around the World in Eighty Days 56. The Story of Mankind 57. Baby Face Nelson 57. Five Weeks in a Balloon 62. The Pumpkin Eater 64.
TV series: Mrs G Goes to College 61.
“ An amateur acts for his own enjoyment, a professional for the enjoyment of others. – *C.H.*
I can't act. I have never acted. And I shall never act. What I can do is suspend my audience's power of judgment till I've finished. – *C.H.*
I had anticipated that Hollywood would be an actor's Eden. It proved to be a paradise only for the medical profession. – *C.H.*

Hardwicke, Edward (1932–)
English actor in occasional films, the son of Sir Cedric HARDWICKE. On stage from 1954, after training at RADA, he became a member of the National Theatre company in the 60s. On television, he has played Dr Watson to Jeremy BRETT's Sherlock Holmes.
Hell below Zero 53. Othello 65. Otley 68. A Flea in Her Ear 68. The Day of the Jackal 73. Venom 81. Shadowlands 93. The Scarlet Letter 95. Elizabeth 98, etc.
TV series: My Old Man 74–75.

Hardy, Forsyth (1910–1994)
Influential Scottish critic and writer. He was the first film critic of the *Scotsman* newspaper in 1929, one of the founders of *Film Quarterly* magazine in the 30s, and became the first director of the Edinburgh Film Festival, writing its history in *Slightly Mad and Full of Dangers* (1992). His other books include *Scotland in Film* (1990), and *John Grierson, A Documentary Biography*, and he also edited collections of GRIERSON's writings.

Hardy, Oliver (1892–1957)
Ample-figured American comedian, the fat half of the screen's finest comedy team, noted for his genteel pomposity, tie twiddle and long-suffering look at the camera.
Biography: 1961, *Mr Laurel and Mr Hardy* by John McCabe. 1989, *Babe – the Life of Oliver Hardy* by John McCabe.
SELECTED SOLO APPEARANCES: Outwitting Dad 13. Playmates 15. Lucky Dog 17. He Winked and Won 17. The Chief Cook 18. The Three Ages 23. Rex, King of the Wild Horses 24. The Wizard of Oz (as the Tin Man) 24. The Nicklehopper 25. Zenobia 39. The Fighting Kentuckian 49. Riding High 50, many others.
■ LAUREL AND HARDY FILMS: Slipping Wives 26. With Love and Hisses 27. Sailors Beware 27. Do Detectives Think? 27. Flying Elephants 27. Sugar Daddies 27. Call of the Cuckoo 27. The Rap 27. Duck Soup 27. Eve's Love Letters 27. Love 'em and Weep 27. Why Girls Love Sailors 27. Should Tall Men Marry? 27. Hats Off 27. Putting Pants on Philip 27. *The Battle of the Century* 27. Leave 'em Laughing 28. From Soup to Nuts 28. *The Finishing Touch* 28. *You're Darn Tootin'* 28. Their Purple Moment 28. Should Married Men Go Home? 28. Early to Bed 28. *Two Tars* 28. Habeas Corpus 28. We Faw Down 28. Liberty 28. Wrong Again 29. That's My Wife 29. *Big Business* 29. *Double Whoopee* 29. *Berth Marks* 29. *Men o'War* 29. *The Perfect Day* 29. They Go Boom 29. Bacon Grabbers 29. Angora Love 29. Unaccustomed as We Are 29. Hollywood Revue of 1929 29. The Hoosegow 29. Night Owls 30. Blotto 30. The Rogue Song (feature) 30. Brats 30. Be Big 30. Below Zero 30. The Laurel and Hardy Murder Case 30. *Hog Wild* 30. Another Fine Mess 30. Chickens Come Home 30. *Laughing Gravy* 31. Our Wife 31. *Come Clean* 31. Pardon Us (feature) 31. One Good Turn 31. Beau Hunks 31. *Helpmates* 31. Any Old Port 31. *The Music Box* (AA) 32. The Chimp 32. *County Hospital* 32. *Scram* 32. Pack Up Your Troubles (feature) 32. Their First Mistake 32. *Towed in a Hole* 33. Twice Two 33. Me and My Pal 33. *Fra Diavolo* (feature) 33. *The Midnight Patrol* 33. *Busy Bodies* 33. *Dirty Work* 33. *Sons of the Desert* (feature) 33. Oliver the Eighth 33. Hollywood Party (feature) 34. Going Bye Bye 34. *Them Thar Hills* 34. *Babes in Toyland* (feature) 34. The Live Ghost 34. *Tit for Tat* 35. The Fixer Uppers 35. Thicker than Water 35. Bonnie Scotland (feature) 35. The Bohemian Girl (feature) 36. *Our Relations* (feature) 36. *Way out West* (feature) 36. Pick a Star (feature) 37. Swiss Miss (feature) 38. *Blockheads* (feature) 38. *The Flying Deuces* (feature) 39. A *Chump at Oxford* (feature) 40. Saps at Sea (feature) 40. Great Guns (feature) 41. A Haunting We Will Go (feature) 42. Air Raid Wardens (feature) 43. Jitterbugs (feature) 43. The Dancing Masters (feature) 43. The Big Noise (feature) 44. Nothing but Trouble (feature) 44. The Bullfighters (feature) 45. Robinson Crusoeland/Atoll K (feature) 52.
■ COMPILATION FEATURES: The Golden Age of Comedy 58. When Comedy was King 60. Days of Thrills and Laughter 61. Thirty Years of Fun 62. MGM's Big Parade of Comedy 65. Laurel and Hardy's Laughing Twenties 65. The Crazy World of Laurel and Hardy 66. The Further Perils of Laurel and Hardy 69. Four Clowns 69. The Best of Laurel and Hardy 74.
✪ For his many unique qualities, seen to best advantage in his partnership with Stan Laurel. *Blockheads*.

Hardy, Robert (1925–)
British character actor, mostly on TV. He is also an authority on the longbow.
The Spy Who Came in from the Cold 65. How I Won the War 67. 10 Rillington Place 70. The Far Pavilions (TV) 84. The Shooting Party (TV) 84. Jenny's War (TV) 84. Middlemarch (TV) 94. Mary Shelley's Frankenstein 94. A Feast at Midnight 95. Sense and Sensibility 95. Gulliver's Travels (TV) 96. Mrs Dalloway 97. The Tichborne Claimant 98. The Barber of Siberia 99. Nancherrow (TV) 99, etc.
TV series: *Elizabeth R* 71. All Creatures Great and Small 77–79. *Churchill: the Wilderness Years* 81. Hot Metal 86–88. Bramwell 95.

Hardy, Robin (1929–)
British director.
The Wicker Man 75. The Fantasist 86.

Hardy, Thomas (1840–1928)
British novelist of dour country stories.
Far from the Madding Crowd 67. Tess 79. Day after the Fair 76. Jude 96.

Hare, Sir David (1947–)
British playwright, screenwriter and director. Born in Bexhill, Sussex, he was educated at Cambridge University.
Autobiography: 1999, *Acting Up*.
Licking Hitler (wd) 77. Saigon – Year of the Cat (w) 83. Wetherby (wd) 85. Plenty (w) 85. Paris by Night (wd) 88. Strapless (wd) 89. Heading Home (wd) 91. Damage (w) 92. The Secret Rapture (wd) 93. Designated Mourner (d) 96.

Hare, Doris (1905–2000)
Versatile English character actress and singer, who played in most forms of theatre, from music hall and revue to Shakespeare. She was best known for her role as Mrs Butler in the TV sitcom *On The Buses* and its movie spinoffs. Born in Bargoed, she began in her mother's repertory company at the age of three. She was the sister of stage actress and singer Betty Hare.
Halesapoppin! (TV) 48. Tiger by the Tail 55. The League of Gentlemen 60. A Place to Go 63. On the Buses 71. Holiday on the Buses 73. Confessions of a Pop Performer 75. Confessions of a Driving Instructor 76. Confessions from a Holiday Camp 77. Nuns on the Run 90. Second Best 94, etc.
TV series: On The Buses 69-73. The Secret Dairy of Adrian Mole 85. Comrade Dad 86. The Growing Pains of Adrian Mole 87.

Hare, Lumsden (1875–1964)
Irish character actor, long in Hollywood.
Charlie Chan Carries On 31. Clive of India 35. She 35. Gunga Din 39. Rebecca 40. The Lodger 44. Challenge to Lassie 49. Julius Caesar 53. The Four Skulls of Jonathan Drake 59, many others.

Hare, Robertson (1891–1979)
Bald-headed British comedian, the put-upon little man of the Aldwych farces of the 20s and 30s, transferred intact from stage to screen.
Autobiography: 1958, *Yours Indubitably*.
Rookery Nook 30. *A Cuckoo in the Nest* 33. *Thark* 33. *Fishing Stock* 35. *Aren't Men Beasts?* 38. *Banana Ridge* 41. *He Snoops To Conquer* 45. *Things Happen at Night* 48. One Wild Oat 51. *Our Girl Friday* 53. *Three Men in a Boat* 56. *The Young Ones* 61, *etc.*

Harewood, Dorian (1951–)
American actor.
Sparkle 75. Gray Lady Down 77. Looker 81. Against All Odds 83. The Falcon and the Snowman 84. Full Metal Jacket 87. Pacific Heights 90. Solar Crisis 90. Getting Up and Going Home 92. Shattered Image (TV) 93. Sudden Death 95. Twelve Angry Men (TV) 97, etc.
TV series: Roots: The Next Generation 79. Strike Force 81–82. Trauma Centre 83. Glitter 84–85. Trials of Rose O'Neill 91–92. Viper 93.

Hargreaves, John (1945–1996)
Australian leading actor, on screen from 1974. He won an Australian Film Institute award as best actor for *My First Wife*.
The Removalists 74. Don's Party 76. Mad Dog Morgan 76. Long Weekend 77. The Killing of Angel Street 81. *Careful He Might Hear You* 83. *My First Wife* 84. *Malcolm* 86. Sky Pirates 86. Comrades (GB) 86. Cry Freedom (GB) 87. Au Bout de l'Espoir (Fr.) 88. Sweet Revenge (US/Fr.) 90. Waiting 90. Rome Romeo (Fr.) 91. No Worries 93. The Lizard King (TV) 94. Country Life 94. Lust and Revenge 96, etc.

Hark, Tsui (1951–) (Xu Ke)
Vietnamese-born, Hong Kong-based director and producer.
The Butterfly Murders 79. We're Going to Eat You 80. Zu Warriors from the Magic Mountain 83. Shanghai Blues 84. Peking Opera Blues/Do Ma Dan 86. A Chinese Ghost Story/Qian Nu Youhun 87. A Better Tomorrow III 89. The Swordsman 90. A Chinese Ghost Story III 91. Once upon a Time in China/Wong Fei-hung 91. Swordsman II (co-w, p) 92. Once upon a Time in China II/Wong Fei-Hung II (wd) 92. Monkey King 93. The Iron Monkey (co-w, p) 93. Once Upon a Time in China III (wd) 93. Swordsman III (co-w, p) 93. The Lovers 95. The Blade 96. The Chinese Feast/ Gamyuk Muntong (co-w, d) 95. Double Team/The Colony (d) (US) 97. Knock Off (d) (US) 98, etc.
❝ The single most successful filmmaker in the history of Hong Kong cinema – Asia's answer to Howard Hawks, Irving Thalberg and Ben Hecht all rolled into one. – *Box Office*

Harker, Gordon (1885–1967)
English character actor of stage and screen, frequently in comic cockney roles. Born in London, into a well-known family of theatrical scenic artists, he was on stage from 1903 and in films from 1927.
The Ring 27. Champagne 28. The Farmer's Wife 28. The Crooked Billet 29. Elstree Calling 30. Escape 30. The W Plan 30. The Sport of Kings 31. Condemned to Death 32. The Frightened Lady 32. Love on Wheels 32. Rome Express 32. Friday the Thirteenth 33. Dirty Work 34. My Old Dutch 34. Road House 34. Boys Will Be Boys 35. Hyde Park Corner 35. The Lad 35. The Phantom Light 35. Squibs 35. The Amateur Gentleman 36. Millions 36. Two's Company 36. The Frog 37. Blondes for Danger 38. *Inspector Hornleigh* 38. No Parking 38. Inspector Hornleigh on Holiday 39. Inspector Hornleigh Goes to It 40. *Saloon Bar* 40. Once a Crook 41. Warn That Man 43. 29 Acacia Avenue 45. Her Favourite Husband 50. Derby Day 52. Bang, You're Dead 54. Out of the Clouds 54. A Touch of the Sun 56. Small Hotel 57. Left Right and Centre 59, etc.

Harlan, Kenneth (1895–1967)
American leading man of the silent screen.
Cheerful Givers 17. The Hoodlum 19. The Beautiful and the Damned 22. The Broken Wing 23. Bobbed Hair 24. Twinkletoes 26. San Francisco 36. Paper Bullets 41. The Underdog 44, many others.

Harlan, Otis (1865–1940)
Tubby American character actor with long stage experience.
What Happened to Jones? 25. Lightnin' 26. Man to Man 31. The Hawk 32. Married in Haste 34. Diamond Jim 35. A Midsummer Night's Dream 35. Mr Boggs Steps Out 38, many others.

Harlan, Russell (1903–1974)
American cinematographer, former stuntman.
Hopalong Rides Again 37. Stagecoach War 40. The Kansan 43. *A Walk in the Sun* 45. *Red River* 48. The Big Sky 52. *Riot in Cell Block Eleven* 54. The Blackboard Jungle 55. This Could Be the Night 57. Witness for the Prosecution 57. Run Silent Run Deep 58. King Creole 58. The Spiral Road 62. Hatari 62. To Kill a Mockingbird 62. Quick Before It Melts 65. Tobruk 66. Darling Lili 70, etc.

Harlan, Veit (1899–1964)
German director of Nazi propaganda.
Kreutzer Sonata 36. Jew Süss 40. Der Grosse Konig 41. Opfergang 43. Die Blaue Stunde 52. The Third Sex 57, etc.

Harlin, Renny (1959–) (Lauri Harjula)
Finnish director, now in Hollywood. Married actress Geena Davis in 1993.
Born American (& w) 86. A Nightmare on Elm Street Part 4: The Dream Master 88. Prison 88. The Adventures of Ford Fairlane 90. Die Hard II 90. Cliffhanger (& p) 93. CutThroat Island 95. The Long Kiss Goodnight 96. Deep Blue Sea 99, etc.
❝ In Europe, film-making is perceived as an art form with marginal business possibilities, and in the US, film-making is a business with marginal artistic possibilities. – *R.H.*

Harline, Leigh (1907–1969)
American screen composer.
Snow White and the Seven Dwarfs (s) 37. Pinocchio (s) (AA) 39. His Girl Friday 40. The Pride of the Yankees (AAN) 42. You Were Never Lovelier (AAN) 42. The Sky's the Limit (AAN) 43. Johnny Come Lately (AAN) 43. The More the Merrier 43. Road to Utopia 45. The Farmer's Daughter 47. The Big Steal 49. Monkey Business 52. Broken Lance 54. The Wayward Bus 57. Ten North Frederick 58. Warlock 60. The Wonderful World of the Brothers Grimm (AAN) 62. Seven Faces of Dr Lao 63. Strange Bedfellows 64, etc.

Harling, Robert
American director, screenwriter and playwright.
Steel Magnolias (w, oa) 89. Soapdish (co-w) 91. Evening Star (wd) 96.

Harling, W. Franke (1887–1958)
American composer.
One Hour with You 32. So Big 32. The Scarlet Empress 34. So Red the Rose 35. Souls at Sea 37. Stagecoach (co-m, AA) 39. Penny Serenade 41. The Lady Is Willing 42. Three Russian Girls (AAN) 44. The Bachelor's Daughter 46, etc.

Harlow, Jean (1911–1937) (Harlean Carpentier)
American leading lady and most sensational star of the early 30s, a wisecracking 'platinum blonde' with a private life to suit her public image. Her three husbands included MGM producer Paul Bern, who killed himself two months after their marriage in 1932, and cinematographer Hal Rosson (1933–35). Her lovers included actor William Powell.
Biography: 1937, *Hollywood Comet* by Dentner Davies. 1964, *Harlow* by Irving Shulman.
Last lines of *Dinner at Eight:*
■ Moran of the Marines 28. Double Whoopee (short) 29. The Unkissed Man 29. The Fugitive 29. Close Harmony 29. New York Nights 29. The Love Parade 29. Weak but Willing 29. Bacon Grabbers (short) 29. The Saturday Night Kid 29. The Love Parade 30. *Hell's Angels* 30. City Lights 31. The Secret Six 31. Iron Man 31. *Public Enemy* 31. Goldie 31. Platinum Blonde 31. Three Wise Girls 32. Beast of the City 32. *Red Headed Woman* 32. *Red Dust* 32. *Dinner at Eight* 33. Hold Your Man 33. *Bombshell* 33. The Girl from Missouri 34. Reckless 35. *China Seas* 35. Riffraff 35. Wife vs Secretary 35. Suzy 36. *Libelled Lady* 36. Personal Property 37. Saratoga 37.
✪ For combining a sophistication which she acted with an innocence which was her own. *Red Dust*.
❝ Would it shock you if I put on something more comfortable? – *Jean Harlow in Hell's Angels*
She didn't want to be famous. She wanted to be happy. – *Clark Gable*
A square shooter if ever there was one. – *Spencer Tracy*
She was not a good actress, not even by Hollywood standards, but she is delightful to watch today because the spirit of her era all but shines from her eyes. – *William Redfield*
Jean Harlow: 'You know, the other day I read a book. It said that machinery is going to take the place of every profession.'
Marie Dressler: 'Oh, my dear: that's something you'll *never* have to worry about!'

Harlow, John (1896–)
British writer-director, former music-hall performer.
Spellbound (d) 40. Candles at Nine (d) 43. Meet Sexton Blake (d) 44. The Agitator (d) 45. Appointment with Crime (wd) 46. Green Fingers (wd) 47. *While I Live*/Dream of Olwen (wd) 48. Old Mother Riley's New Venture (d) 49. Those People Next Door (d) 52. Dangerous Cargo 54, etc.

Harman, Hugh (1903–1982)
American animator who in the early 30s, with Rudolph Ising, formed Harman-Ising and made some brilliantly inventive cartoons for MGM. Later originated Merrie Melodies and Looney Tunes, and was cited by the Nobel Peace jury for *Peace on Earth* (1940).

Harmon, Mark (1951–)
Competent American leading man, difficult to distinguish from several others.
Eleanor and Franklin: the White House Years (TV) 77. Centennial 78. Comes a Horseman 78. Beyond the Poseidon Adventure 79. *The Dream Merchants* (TV) 80. Summer School 87. The Presidio 88. Worth Winning 89. Fourth Story (TV) 90. Till There Was You 91. Cold Heaven 92. Wyatt Earp 94. Magic in the Water 95. Casualties 97. Fear and Loathing in Las Vegas 98. Teen Monster 99, etc.
TV series: Flamingo Road 81–82.

Harmon, Robert (1953–)
American director.
The Hitcher 86. Nowhere to Run 93. Gotti (TV) 96, etc.

Harnett, Josh (1978–)
American actor, born in San Francisco and raised in St Paul, Minnesota. He began acting after an injury forced him to quit playing football at high school.
Debutante 97. Halloween: H20 98. The Faculty 98. Town and Country 99. The Virgin Suicides 99. O 99. Here on Earth 99. Blow Dry 00. Pearl Harbor 01, etc.
TV series: Cracker 97-98.

Harolde, Ralf (1899–1974) (R. H. Wigger)
American supporting actor often seen as thin-lipped crook.
Night Nurse 32. A Tale of Two Cities 35. Horror Island 41. Baby Face Morgan 42. Farewell My Lovely (as the doctor) 44. Alaska Patrol (last film) 51, many others.

Harper, Gerald (1929–)
Aristocratic-looking British actor familiar on TV as *Adam Adamant* and *Hadleigh*.
The Admirable Crichton 57. A Night to Remember 58. The League of Gentlemen 59. The Punch and Judy Man 62. The Lady Vanishes 79, etc.
TV series: Adam Adamant Lives! 66-67. Hadleigh 69-76.

Harper, Jessica (1949–)
American leading lady.
Inserts 76. Suspiria 77. The Evictors 79. Shock Treatment 81. Pennies from Heaven 81. My Favorite Year 82. Big Man on Campus 89. Safe 95, etc.

Harper, Tess (1950–) (Tessie Jean Washam)
American actress.
Amityville: The Demon/Amityville 3-D 83. Tender Mercies 83. Flashpoint 84. Crimes of the Heart (AAN) 86. Ishtar 87. Far North 88. Her Alibi 89. Criminal Law 89. Daddy's Dying … Who's Got the Will? 90. My Heroes Have Always Been Cowboys 91. The Man in the Moon 91. My New Gun 92. Christy (TV) 94. Children of Fury (TV) 94. The Road to Galveston (TV) 96. The Jackal 97, etc.

Harper, Valerie (1940–)
American leading comedy actress, a star of TV, a former dancer.
The Ones in Between 72. Freebie and the Bean 74. Thursday's Game (TV) 74. Night Terror (TV) 77. The Last Married Couple in America 79. Blame It on Rio 84. Drop-out Mother (TV) 88, etc.
TV series: *The Mary Tyler Moore Show* 70–73. *Rhoda* 74–78. Valerie 86–87.

Harrelson, Woody (1961–)
American leading actor, best known for his role as Woody Boyd in the TV series *Cheers*. He has been romantically linked with Penelope Ann Miller, Brooke Shields and Glenn Close. Married Laura Louie, with whom he has two daughters, in 1998.
Wildcats 86. Casualties of War 89. Doc Hollywood 91. Ted and Venus 91. White Men Can't Jump 92. Indecent Proposal 93. The Cowboy Way 94. *Natural Born Killers* 94. Money Train 95. The Sunchaser 96. Kingpin 96. *The People vs Larry Flynt* (AAN) 96. Welcome to Sarajevo 97. Wag the Dog 97. Palmetto 98. The Thin Red Line 98. EdTV 99. The Hi-Lo Country 99. Play It To The Bone 99, etc.
TV series: Cheers 85–92.

Harrer, Heinrich (1912–)
Austrian explorer and mountaineer, author of *Seven Years in Tibet*, telling how he escaped British internment to enter Tibet and reach the holy city of Lhasa in the late 40s. In the film of the book, directed by Jean-Jacques Annaud in 1997, he was played by Brad Pitt. Born in Hüttenberg, he was an Olympic skier, and later went on expeditions to the Amazon, the Himalayas and Africa. Revelations that he had also been a member of the Nazi Party came soon after the film's release.

Harrigan, William (1894–1966)
American actor, from the stage. Born in New York City, he was on stage from the age of five in his father's productions, and in films from 1929. Married three times.
On the Level 17. Cabaret 27. Nix on Dames 27. Born Reckless 30. Pick Up 33. The Invisible Man 33. 'G' Men 35. His Family Tree 35. The Silk Hat Kid 35. Whipsaw 35. Federal Bullets 37. Hawaii Calls 38. Back Door to Heaven 39. The Farmer's Daughter 47. Flying Leathernecks 51. Street of Sinners 55, etc.

Harrington, Curtis (1928–)
American director who made experimental shorts before graduating to features.
■ Night Tide 63. Voyage to a Prehistoric Planet 64. Queen of Blood 66. Games 67. How Awful About Allan (TV) 70. What's the Matter with Helen? 71. Who Slew Auntie Roo? 73. The Cat Creature (TV) 73. Killer Bees (TV) 74. The Dead Don't Die (TV) 74. The Killing Kind 76. Ruby 77. Devil Dog (TV) 78. Mata Hari 85.

Harris, Barbara (1935–)
American leading lady.
A Thousand Clowns 65. Oh Dad … 66. Plaza Suite 71. Who Is Harry Kellerman … ? (AAN) 71. The War between Men and Women 72. Family Plot 76. Freaky Friday 77. Movie Movie 78. The Seduction of Joe Tynan 79. Second Hand Hearts 80. Night Magic 85. Peggy Sue Got Married 86. Dirty Rotten Scoundrels 88. Grosse Pointe Blanke 97, etc.

Harris, Damian (1960–)
British director and screenwriter, the son of actor Richard Harris.
Otley (a) 68. The Rachel Papers (wd) 89. Deceived (d) 91. Bad Company 95.

Harris, Danielle (1976–)
American actress.
Halloween Four: The Return of Michael Myers 88. Halloween Five: The Revenge of Michael Myers 89. Marked for Death 90. The Last Boy Scout 91. Don't Tell Mom the Babysitter's Dead 91. City Slickers 91. Free Willy 93. Daylight 96. Back to Back 96, etc.
TV series: Roseanne 92–93.

Harris, Ed (1950–)
Dour American leading actor, from the stage. Born in Tenafly, New Jersey, he studied briefly at Columbia University and the University of Oklahoma, leaving to act; he then studied at the California Institute of the Arts, continuing to act

on stage and in some forgettable films until he broke through to wider acclaim with the role of John Glenn in *The Right Stuff*. Married actress Amy MADIGAN.

Coma 77. Zombies 80. Borderline 80. Knightriders 81. Dream On 81. Creepshow 82. *The Right Stuff* 83. Under Fire 83. Swing Shift 84. Places in the Heart 84. Sweet Dreams 85. Code Name: Emerald 85. Alamo Bay 85. A Flash of Green 85. The Last Innocent Man 87. Walker 87. To Kill a Priest 88. Jackknife 88. The Abyss 89. State of Grace 90. Paris Trout 91. Glengarry Glen Ross 92. The Firm 93. Needful Things 93. China Moon 94. Milk Money 94. Just Cause 95. Riders of the Purple Sage (TV) 96. Apollo 13 (AAN) 95. Nixon 95. Eye for an Eye 96. The Rock 96. Absolute Power 97. *The Truman Show* (AAN) 98. Stepmom 98. The Third Miracle 99. Pollock (&p,d) (d, a, AANa) 00. Enemy at the Gates 01, etc.

Harris, Edna Mae (1910–1997)
American actress and singer, mainly in movies made for black audiences of the 40s. Born in Harlem, she appeared on Broadway, sang with the bands of Noble Sissle, Benny CARTER and Lucky Millinder, was featured on some soundies, and was mistress of ceremonies at Harlem's Apollo Theater in the mid-40s.

The Green Pastures 36. Bullets or Ballots 36. The Garden of Allah 36. Spirit of Youth 38. Paradise in Harlem 39. The Notorious Elinor Lee 39. Murder on Lennox Avenue 41. Sunday Sinners 41. Tall, Tan and Terrific 46, etc.

Harris, Frank (1856–1931)
English journalist and writer, an influential editor of magazines and newspapers, but notorious for his boastful tales of his own life and many lovers. He was played by Jack LEMMON in *Cowboy*, a film based on *On the Trail*, an account of his time in America, where he lived in the 1870s.

Harris, Georgie (1898–1986)
Diminutive (4 ft 9 ins) English comic actor, from musical comedy and vaudeville. Born in Liverpool, he worked in America in the 20s, including a stint as a KEYSTONE KOP, before returning to Britain, where he quit films in the late 30s to become a successful businessman.

Lights of Old Broadway (US) 25. The Shamrock Handicap (US) 26. Three Bad Men (US) 26. The Floating College (US) 28. Don't Be a Dummy 32. I Adore You 33. Radio Parade of 1935 34. Captain Bill 35. Happy Days Are Here Again 36. Boys Will Be Girls 37. Saturday Night Revue 37. The Reverse Be My Lot 38, etc.

Harris, Hilary Tjader (1930–1999)
American experimental filmmaker. His short works ranged from a documentary of shipbuilding to films that exploited time-lapse photography.

Longhorns 51. Generation 56. Highway 58. Seawards the Great Ships (AA) 61. Nine Variations on a Dance Theme 66. Organism 75, etc.

Harris, Jack (1905–1971)
British editor.

The Sleeping Cardinal 31. The Wandering Jew 33. The Face at the Window 39. Let the People Sing 42. This Happy Breed 44. Blithe Spirit 45. Brief Encounter 45. Great Expectations 46. Oliver Twist 48. Where No Vultures Fly 51. The Crimson Pirate 53. Indiscreet 58. The Sundowners 60. Billy Budd 62. The Chalk Garden 64. Three Sisters 70, many others.

Harris, James B. (1928–)
American producer and director, associated with director Stanley KUBRICK.

The Killing 56. Paths of Glory 57. Lolita 62. The Bedford Incident (& d) 65. Some Call It Loving (& d) 71. Telefon 77. Fast Walking (& wd) 82. Cop (& wd) 88. Boiling Point (wd) 93, etc.

Harris, Jared (1961–)
British actor, the son of Richard HARRIS.

The Rachel Papers 89. The Public Eye 92. The Last of the Mohicans 92. Far and Away 92. Nadja 94. Natural Born Killers 94. Tall Tale: The Unbelievable Adventures of Pecos Bill 95. I Shot Andy Warhol (as Warhol) 96. Father's Day 96. Sunday 97. Lost in Space 98. B. Monkey 98. Happiness 98. Lulu on the Bridge 98, etc.

Harris, Jed (1900–1979) (Jacob Horowitz)
American theatrical impresario of the 30s and 40s, notorious for toughness and rudeness; lampooned in films *Twentieth Century* and *The Saxon Charm*. He was the model for both Walt Disney's Big Bad Wolf and Laurence Olivier's Richard III. Joseph Losey began as his assistant.

❝ The most loathsome man I'd ever met. – *Laurence Olivier*

Fresh as poison ivy. – *Edna Ferber*

When I die, I want to be cremated and have my ashes thrown in Jed Harris's face. – *George S. Kaufman*

Harris, Joel Chandler (1848–1908)
American journalist and story writer who created the characters of Uncle Remus and Brer Rabbit, filmed by Disney in *Song of the South*.

Harris, Jonathan (1914–)
American character actor, popular in prissy roles in TV series *The Third Man* 59–61, *The Bill Dana Show* 63–64, *Lost in Space* 65–68.

Botany Bay 54. The Big Fisherman 59. Pinocchio and the Emperor of the Night (voice) 87. Happily Ever After 90, etc.

Harris, Julie
British costume designer.

The Naked Edge 61. The Fast Lady 62. The Chalk Garden 64. Darling 65. The Wrong Box 65. Casino Royale 67. Goodbye Mr Chips 69. Live and Let Die 73. Rollerball 74. The Slipper and the Rose 76. Prostitute 80. The Hound of the Baskervilles 83, etc.

Harris, Julie (1925–)
American stage actress.

The Member of the Wedding (AAN) 53. East of Eden 55. I Am a Camera 56. The Truth about Women 56. Sally's Irish Rogue 60. Requiem for a Heavyweight 62. *The Haunting* 63. Harper 66. You're a Big Boy Now 66. *Reflections in a Golden Eye* 67. The Split 68. The House on Greenapple Road (TV) 69. How Awful about Allan (TV) 70. The People Next Door 70. Home for the Holidays (TV) 72. The Greatest Gift (TV) 74. The Hiding Place 75. Voyage of the Damned 76. The Bell Jar 79. Backstairs at the White House (TV) 79. Bronte 83. Leaving Home 86. Gorillas in the Mist 88. The Woman He Loved (TV) 88. Too Good to Be True (TV) 88. Single Women, Married Men (TV) 89. The Dark Half (TV) 91. Paris Trout 91. The Dark Half 91. Housesitter 92. When Love Kills (TV) 93. *Lucifer's Child* (TV) 95. Carried Away 96. Passaggio per il Paradiso 96, etc.

TV series: Thicker than Water 73. The Family Holvak 76. Knots Landing 81–87.

Harris, Julius W.
American character actor.

Slaves 69. Incident in San Francisco (TV) 71. Shaft's Big Score 73. A Cry for Help (TV) 75. King Kong 76. Rich Man Poor Man (TV) 76. Victory at Entebbe (as Idi Amin) (TV) 76. Islands in the Stream 77. Looking for Mr Goodbar 77. Ring of Passion (TV) 78. The First Family 80. Missing Pieces (TV) 83. Crimewave 85. Prayer of the Rollerboys 91. Harley Davidson and the Marlboro Man 91. Maniac Cop 3: Badge of Silence 92. Shrunken Heads 94, etc.

Harris, Mildred (1901–1944)
American leading lady of the silent era, first wife of Charles CHAPLIN. At the end of her career, she was working as an extra. Died from pneumonia after an operation.

Intolerance 15. Borrowed Clothes 18. Fool's Paradise 21. Fog 23. Unmarried Wives 24. My Neighbour's Wife 25. The Mystery Club 26. The Show Girl 27. Sea Fury 29. No No Nanette 30. Lady Tubbs 35. Reap the Wild Wind 42. The Story of Dr Wassell 44, etc.

Harris, Neil Patrick (1974–)
American actor, in films from his early teens, best known for his role as Doogie Howser in the TV sitcom *Doogie Howser, M.D.*

Clara's Heart 88. Purple People Eater 88. Home Fires Burning (TV) 89. The Cold Sassy Tree (TV) 89. Stranger in the Family (TV) 91. My Antonia (TV) 95. The Animal Room 95. Starship Troopers 97. The Proposition/Tempting Fate 98. The Next Best Thing 00, etc.

TV series: *Doogie Howser, M.D* 89–93. Stark Raving Mad 99-00.

Harris, Phil (1904–1995)
American bandleader and comic singer, best known for providing the voice of Baloo the bear in Disney's animated *The Jungle Book* 67. Married actress Alice Faye.

Melody Cruise 33. Man about Town 39. Buck Benny Rides Again 40. Here Comes the Groom 51. The Glenn Miller Story 54. The High and the Mighty 54. Anything Goes 56. The Wheeler Dealers 63. The Cool Ones 67. Robin Hood (voice) 73. Rock-a-Doodle (voice) 90, etc.

Harris, Richard (1932–)
Gaunt Irish leading actor. Usually cast as a rebel, he tries to match the part in real life.

Alive and Kicking 58. Shake Hands with the Devil 59. The Wreck of the Mary Deare 59. A Terrible Beauty 60. All Night Long 61. The Long the Short and the Tall 61. The Guns of Navarone 61. *Mutiny on the Bounty* 62. *This Sporting Life* (AAN) 63. The Red Desert 64. I Tre Volti 64. Major Dundee 65. The Heroes of Telemark 65. The Bible 66. Hawaii 66. Caprice 66. *Camelot* (as King Arthur) 67. The Molly Maguires 69. A Man Called Horse 69. Bloomfield (& d) 70. *Cromwell* (title role) 70. The Snow Goose (TV) 71. Man in the Wilderness 71. The Deadly Trackers 73. 99 44/100 Dead 74. Juggernaut 75. Robin and Marian 76. The Return of a Man Called Horse 76. Echoes of a Summer 76. Gulliver's Travels 76. The Cassandra Crossing 77. Orca – Killer Whale 77. Golden Rendezvous 77. The Wild Geese 78. Game for Vultures 79. The Last Word 79. The Revengers 79. Your Ticket Is No Longer Valid 79. Highpoint 80. Tarzan the Ape Man 81. Triumphs of a Man Called Horse 82. Martin's Day 84. The Return 88. Mack the Knife 89. King of the Wind 89. *The Field* (AAN) 90. Patriot Games 92. *Unforgiven* 92. Silent Tongue 93. The Bible: Abraham (TV) 93. Wrestling Ernest Hemingway 93. Cry the Beloved Country 95. Trojan Eddie 96. The Hunchback of Notre Dame (TV) 97. The Royal Way 97. The Barber of Siberia 98. To Walk with Lions 99. Gladiator 00, etc.

❝ He's something of a fuck-up, no question. – *Charlton Heston*

He hauls his surly carcass from movie to movie, being dismembered. I'd just as soon wait till he's finished. – *Pauline Kael*

Harris, Richard A.
American editor.

Downhill Racer 69. The Candidate (co-ed) 72. Catch My Soul 74. Smile 75. The Bad News Bears 76. Semi-Tough 77. The Bad News Bears Go to Japan 78. The Island 80. Mommie Dearest 81. The Chosen 81. The Survivors 83. Fletch 85. The Golden Child 86. The Couch Trip 88. Fletch Lives 89. My Boyfriend's Back (TV) 90. LA Story 91. The Bodyguard (co-ed) 92. True Lies 94. Titantic (AA) 97, etc.

Harris, Robert (1900–1995)
British classical actor who has played occasional film roles. Educated at Oxford University, he studied acting at RADA and was on stage from 1923.

How He Lied to Her Husband 31. The Life and Death of Colonel Blimp 43. The Bad Lord Byron 48. That Lady 55. Oscar Wilde 60. Decline and Fall 68, etc.

Harris, Robert H. (1911–1981)
American character actor, usually beaky, officious and unsympathetic.

Bundle of Joy 56. How to Make a Monster 58. America America 63. Mirage 65. Valley of the Dolls 67, etc.

TV series: The Goldbergs 56. Court of Last Resort 57–60.

Harris, Rosemary (1930–)
British leading actress, chiefly on stage.

Beau Brummell 54. The Shiralee 55. A Flea in Her Ear 68. Holocaust (TV) 77. The Boys from Brazil 78. The Chisholms (TV) 78. Crossing Delancey 88. The Bridge 91. Tom and Viv (AAN) 93. Hamlet 96. My Life So Far 99. Sunshine (Hun./Ger./Can./Aus.) 99., etc.

Harris, Theresa (1910–1985)
American actress.

Morocco 30. Blood Money 33. Morning Glory 33. Jezebel 38. Santa Fe Trail 40. Blossoms in the Dust 40. I Walked with a Zombie 43. Three Little Girls in Blue 46. Neptune's Daughter 49. And Baby Makes Three 50. The Company She Keeps 51, many others.

Harris, Thomas (1940–)
American thriller writer, a former journalist. Born in Jackson, Tennessee and raised in Rich, Mississippi, he studied at Baylor University before working as a reporter for Associated Press in New York. He received $10m for the screen rights to *Hannibal*, the third of his novels featuring serial killer Hannibal Lecter.

Black Sunday 77. Manhunter (from *Red Dragon*) 86. Silence of the Lambs 90. Hannibal 01, etc.

Harris, Vernon (c. 1910–)
British screenwriter. He also scripted the 1938 BBC radio series *Band Waggon* with Arthur Askey and Richard Murdoch.

Joy Ride (story) 35. Improper Duchess 36. Tropical Trouble 36. Albert RN (co-w) 53. The Sea Shall Not Have Them (co-w) 55. Reach for the Sky 56. Ferry to Hong Kong 57. The Admirable Crichton 57. Light up the Sky 61. Oliver! (AAN) 68. Paul and Michelle (co-w) 75, etc.

Harrison, Doane (c. 1894–1968)
American editor. Later associate producer for Billy Wilder.

Youth and Adventure 25. Celebrity 28. The Spieler 29. Her Man 30. 13 Hours by Air 36. Midnight 39. Hold Back the Dawn 41. The Major and the Minor 42. Five Graves to Cairo 43. The Uninvited 44. The Lost Weekend 45. A Foreign Affair 48. Branded 50, etc.

Harrison, George (1943–)
English composer, musician and producer. Formerly guitarist for The Beatles, he runs the British production company HandMade Films with Denis O'Brien. In 1997, *Business Age* estimated his personal fortune at £105m.

AS COMPOSER: Shanghai Surprise 86.

AS PERFORMER: A Hard Day's Night 64. Help 65. Magical Mystery Tour 67. The Concert for Bangladesh (concert) 72. The Rutles (TV) 78. Life of Brian 79, etc.

AS PRODUCER: Life of Brian 79. Time Bandits 81. Privates on Parade 83. Water 86. Withnail and I 87. Track 29 88. Powwow Highway 89. How to Get Ahead in Advertising 89. Cold Dog Soup 90. Nuns on the Run 90. The Raggedy Rawney 90, etc.

❝ I don't really think the film business is all it's cracked up to be … It's still much better being a guitar player. – G.H.

Harrison, Gregory (1950–)
American actor.

Trilogy of Terror (TV) 75. The Gathering (TV) 77. For Ladies Only 81. Razorback (Aus.) 84. Seduced (TV) 85. Oceans of Fire 86. The Hasty Heart 86. North Shore 87. Dangerous Pursuit 89. Bare Essentials (TV) 91. Body Chemistry II: Voice of a Stranger 91. Duplicates 92. Cadillac Girl 93. Hard Evidence 94. It's My Party 95, etc.

TV series: Logan's Run 77–78. Centennial 78–79. Trapper John, M.D. 79–86. Falcon Crest 89–90. The Family Man 90–91. True Detectives 90–91.

Harrison, Jim
American novelist, poet and screenwriter.

Revenge (oa, co-w) 89. Cold Feet 89. Legends of the Fall (oa) 94. Wolf (co-w) 94. Carried Away (from his novel *Farmer*) 95. Dalva (oa) (TV) 95, etc.

Harrison, Joan (1911–1994)
British writer-producer, assistant for many years to Alfred Hitchcock. She was married to author Eric Ambler.

Jamaica Inn (w) 39. Rebecca (co-w, AAN) 40. Foreign Correspondent (co-w, AAN) 40. Suspicion (w) 41. Saboteur (w) 42. Dark Waters (w) 44. Phantom Lady (p) 44. Uncle Harry (p) 45. Ride the Pink Horse (p) 47. Circle of Danger (p) 51, etc.

TV series: *Alfred Hitchcock Presents* (p) 55–63.

Harrison, Kathleen (1892–1995)
British character actress, usually seen as a cockney but born in Lancashire. On stage from 1926; films made her an amiable, slightly dithery but warm-hearted national figure.

Our Boys 15. Hobson's Choice 31. The Ghoul 33. Broken Blossoms 36. Night Must Fall (US) 37. *Bank Holiday* 38. The Outsider 39. *The Ghost Train*

41. Kipps 41. *In Which We Serve* 42. Dear Octopus 43. Great Day 45. *Holiday Camp* 47. *The Winslow Boy* 48. Bond Street 48. Oliver Twist 48. *Here Come the Huggetts* (and ensuing series) 49–52. Waterfront 50. Scrooge 51. Pickwick Papers 52. *Turn the Key Softly* 53. Cast a Dark Shadow 54. Where There's a Will 54. Lilacs in the Spring 54. *All for Mary* 55. Home and Away 56. A Cry from the Streets 58. Alive and Kicking 58. Mrs Gibbons' Boys 62. West Eleven 63. Lock Up Your Daughters 69, many others.

Harrison, Linda (1945–)
American leading lady, briefly evident at Twentieth Century-Fox: married Richard Zanuck.
Way Way Out 66. A Guide for the Married Man 67. Planet of the Apes 67. Airport 75 75.
TV series: Bracken's World 69–70.

Harrison, Philip
English production designer in Hollywood, associated with the films of John Badham. He studied at the Royal College of Art.
How I Won the War 67. The Ritz 76. Blue Thunder 83. Never Say Never Again 83. The Razor's Edge 84. Short Circuit 86. White Nights 85. 52 Pick Up 86. Stakeout 87. Mississippi Burning 88. Bird on a Wire 90. The Hard Way 91. Point of No Return 93. Timecop 94. Nick of Time 95. Sudden Death 95. The Relic 97. Spawn 97, etc.

Harrison, Sir Rex (1908–1990) (Reginald Carey Harrison)
Debonair British leading actor of pleasant if limited range, on stage since 1924; films only occasionally gave him the right material. Born in Huyton, Lancashire, he joined the Liverpool Repertory Company at the age of 16, began in films in 1929, and made his London stage debut in 1930. In 1936, after an unsuccessful screen test for Warner's, he was signed to an exclusive contract with Alexander Korda, following it with his stage performance in *French without Tears* which established him as a star and provided him with a type – elegant and charming – that he played for most of his career. In the mid-40s he went to Hollywood under contract to Twentieth Century-Fox, but his stay there came to a sudden end after a scandal resulting from his affair with actress Carole Landis, which ended with her suicide. His best screen performances were as Professor Henry Higgins in *My Fair Lady* (repeating his stage success), Adolphus Cusins in *Major Barbara*, Charles Condomine in *Blithe Spirit*, and Vivian Kenway in *The Rake's Progess*. His six wives included Lilli Palmer (1942–57), Kay Kendall (1957–59), whom he married knowing that she was dying from leukaemia, a fact he kept from her, and Rachel Roberts (1962–71). He was knighted in 1989.
Autobiography: 1974, *Rex*. 1991, *A Damned Serious Business: My Life in Comedy*.
Biography: 1985, *Rex Harrison* by Allen Eyles. 1991, *Rex Harrison* by Nicholas Wapshott. 1992, *Rex Harrison* by Alexander Walker. 1998, *The Incomparable Rex* by Patrick Garland.
■ The Great Game 30. The School for Scandal 30. All at Sea 34. Get Your Man 34. Leave It to Blanche 35. Men Are Not Gods 36. *Storm in a Teacup* 37. School for Husbands 37. St Martin's Lane 38. The Citadel 38. Over the Moon 39. The Silent Battle 39. Ten Days in Paris 39. *Night Train to Munich* 40. *Major Barbara* 40. I Live in Grosvenor Square 45. *Blithe Spirit* 45. *The Rake's Progress* 46. Anna and the King of Siam (US) 46. The Ghost and Mrs Muir (US) 47. The Foxes of Harrow (US) 47. Unfaithfully Yours (US) 48. Escape 48. The Long Dark Hall 51. The Fourposter (US) 52. King Richard and the Crusaders (as Saladin) (US) 54. The Constant Husband 55. The Reluctant Debutante (US) 58. Midnight Lace (US) 60. The Happy Thieves (US) 62. Cleopatra (US) (AAN) 62. *My Fair Lady* (AA) (US) 64. The Yellow Rolls-Royce 64. The Agony and the Ecstasy (US) (as a medieval pope) 65. The Honey Pot (US) 67. Doctor Dolittle (US) 67. A Flea in Her Ear (US/Fr.) 68. Staircase 69. Don Quixote (TV) 72. The Prince and the Pauper 77. The Fifth Musketeer 77. Ashanti 78. Shalimar 78. Crossed Swords 78. A Time to Die 79.
❝ I'm now at the age where I've got to prove that I'm just as good as I never was. – *R.H., 1980*
It takes a long time to learn to treat the camera as a friend and confidant, which finally you have to do if you're to become a good film actor. – *R.H.*
He exudes that combination of the aggressor and the injured, the schoolmaster and the truant, which adds up in Britain (and elsewhere) to erotic infallibility. – *Kenneth Tynan*
What has he ever done for England, except live abroad, refuse to pay his taxes, and call everyone a shit? – *Harold French*
If you weren't the finest light-comedy actor in the world next to me, you'd be good for only one thing – selling cars in Great Portland Street – *Noel Coward to R.H.*
A limited man, rather reppy, whose youthful good looks and some luck with the parts ensured a profitable career. – *Kenneth Williams*
Famous line (*Blithe Spirit*) 'If you're trying to compile an inventory of my sex life, I feel it only fair to warn you that you've omitted several episodes. I shall consult my diary and give you a complete list after lunch.'

Harrison, Richard
American strongman in Italian spectaculars.
Executioner on the High Seas 61. Invincible Gladiator 61. Perseus among the Monsters 63. Spy Killers 65. Adventures of the Bengal Lancers 65. Vengeance 68. Commando Attack 70. The Way of the Godfather 73. Thirty-Six Hours of Hell 77. Fireback 78. Blood Debts 83. His Name Was King 85. Ninja Commandments 87. Hands of Death 88. Ninja Strike Force 88. The Channeler 89. Ninja Powerforce 90. Rescue Force 90. The Alien Within 91. Highway to Hell 91. Angel Eyes 93, etc.

Harrison Marks, George (–1997)
English director of soft porn and limited talent, who deserves a footnote in the history of British cinema because of the ground-breaking success of his film *Naked as Nature Intended*, ostensibly about nudism but made as an exercise in exploitation, which ran for two years in London. A former music-hall comedian, he first specialized in air-brushed glamour photography for men's magazines. His still and moving pictures owed much to his mentor and lover, actress and nude model Pamela Green. Apart from his listed features, he made comedy shorts for children as well as several hundred shorts and, later, videos for the sex film market. From the mid-80s he specialized in producing a magazine, *Kane*, and videos devoted to spanking.
Naked as Nature Intended 61. The Naked World of Harrison Marks 65. Pattern of Evil 67. The Nine Ages of Nakedness 69. Come Play with Me 77.
❝ Marks actually led the kind of life that many assume to be concomitant with 'smut peddling': he was twice prosecuted for sending obscene materials through the post; he was bankrupted; and he survived four relationships (three marriages and an eight-year affair with his model Pamela Green) and five years of alcoholism. – *David McGillivray, Doing Rude Things*

Harrold, Kathryn (1950–)
American leading lady.
Yes Giorgio 82. The Sender 82. Into the Night 84. Raw Deal 86. Someone to Love 87. Deadly Desire 91. The Companion 94, etc.
TV series: MacGruder and Loud 85. The Bronx Zoo 87–88.

Harron, Mary
Canadian-born director and screenwriter. She was educated at Oxford University. A former rock journalist, she began by making documentaries for BBC TV. Married film director John C. Walsh. She is the daughter of Canadian actor and comedian Don Harron (1924-).
I Shot Andy Warhol (wd) 96. American Psycho (co-w,d) 00, etc.

Harron, Robert (Bobby) (1894–1920)
American juvenile lead who joined D. W. Griffith's company almost from school; died in shooting accident.
Dr Skinum 07. Bobby's Kodak 08. Man's Genesis 12. The Birth of a Nation 15. Intolerance 16. Hearts of the World 18. True Heart Susie 19. Darling Mine 21, many others.

Harrow, Lisa (1943–)
New Zealand leading actress.
The Devil Is a Woman (It.) 75. It Shouldn't Happen to a Vet (GB) 76. The Final Conflict (US) 81. Under Capricorn (Aus.) 82. Shaker Run 85. The Last Days of Chez Nous (Aus.) 92. That Eye, the Sky (Aus.) 94. Sunday 97. Country (Ire.) 00, etc.
TV series: Kavanagh QC 95–96.

Harry, Debbie (1954–) (Deborah Harry)
American actress and singer. She was the lead singer of the 70s rock band Blondie.
Roadie 80. Union City 81. Videodrome 83. The Foreigner 84. Forever Lulu 87. Hairspray 88. Satisfaction 88. New York Stories 89. Tales from the Darkside: The Movie 90. Intimate Stranger 91. After Midnight 93. Heavy 95. Drop Dead Rock 96. Six Ways to Sunday 98, etc.
❝ I am now a shopaholic and I shop 'til I drop. It's more expensive than taking drugs but it's legal and fun. – *D.H.*

Harryhausen, Ray (1920–)
American trick film specialist and model-maker; invented 'Superdynamation'.
Books: 1972, *Film Fantasy Scrapbook*.
Mighty Joe Young 49. It Came from Beneath the Sea 52. Twenty Million Miles to Earth 57. The Three Worlds of Gulliver 60. *Jason and the Argonauts* 63. The First Men in the Moon 64. One Million Years BC 66. The Valley of Gwangi 69. The Golden Voyage of Sinbad 73. Sinbad and the Eye of the Tiger 77, etc.

Hart, Dolores (1938–) (D. Hicks)
American lady of a few films in the late 50s. Retired to become a nun. She was among the singers from the Abbey of Regina Laudis in Bethlehem, Connecticut, whose CD of Gregorian chants, *Women in Chant*, was a best-seller in 1998. She was the daughter of actor Bert Hicks (1920-1965), who appeared in B movies of the 40s and 50s.
Loving You 57. Wild Is the Wind 57. King Creole 58. Lonelyhearts 58. The Plunderers 60. Where the Boys Are 60. Francis of Assisi 61. The Inspector 61. Sail a Crooked Ship 61. Come Fly with Me 62, etc.

Hart, Dorothy (1923–)
American second lead of the 50s.
Naked City 47. Take One False Step 49. Undertow 49. I Was a Communist for the FBI 51. Tarzan's Savage Fury 52, etc.

Hart, Harvey (1928–1989)
Canadian director, from TV, latterly in Hollywood.
■ Dark Intruder 65. Bus Riley's Back in Town 65. Sullivan's Empire 67. The Sweet Ride 68. The Young Lawyers (TV) 69. Fortune and Men's Eyes 71. The Pyx 73. Panic on the 5.22 (TV) 74. Can Ellen Be Saved? (TV) 74. Murder or Mercy? (TV) 74. Shoot 77. Goldenrod (TV) 77. Prince of Central Park (TV) 77. W.E.B. (TV) 78. Captains Courageous (TV) 78. Standing Tall (TV) 78. Like Normal People (TV) 79. The Aliens Are Coming (TV) 79. East of Eden (TV) 81. The High Country 81. Massarati and the Brain (TV) 82. Born Beautiful (TV) 82. Getting Even 83. Master of the Game (TV) 84. Reckless Disregard (TV) 85. Beverly Hills Madam (TV) 86. Stone Fox (TV) 87. Murder Sees the Light (TV) 87. Passion and Paradise (TV) 89.

Hart, Ian (1964–)
English leading actor.
No Surrender 85. The Hours and Times 91. Backbeat (as John Lennon) 93. The Englishman Who Went up a Hill but Came Down a Mountain 95. Clockwork Mice 95. *Land and Freedom* 95. Loved Up (TV) 95. Nothing Personal 95. Hollow Reed 96. Michael Collins 96. Mojo 97. Butcher Boy 97. Frogs for Snakes 98. B. Monkey 98. Snitch 98. Enemy of the State 98. This Year's Love 99. The End of the Affair 99. The Closer You Get 99. Best 99. Wonderland 99. Aberdeen 00. Born Romantic 00. Liam 00, etc.

Hart, Lorenz (1895–1943)
American lyricist, mostly with Richard Rodgers as composer. Shows filmed include *On Your Toes*, *Pal Joey*, *The Boys from Syracuse*. Played by Mickey Rooney in *Words and Music*.

Hart, Melissa Joan (1976–)
American actress who is best known for her title role in the TV sitcom *Sabrina, the Teenage Witch*, which is produced by Hartbreak Films, a production company she runs with her mother, Paula Hart. Born in Long Island, New York, she began in commercials from the age of 4.
Kane & Abel (TV) 85. Sabrina Down Under (TV) 99. Drive Me Crazy 99. The Specials 00, etc.
TV series: Clarissa Explains It All 91-94. Sabrina The Teenage Witch 96- .

Hart, Moss (1904–1961)
American playwright (usually in collaboration with George S. Kaufman) and theatrical producer. Wrote occasional screenplays. Married actress Kitty Carlisle.
Autobiography: 1958, *Act One* (filmed 1963).
Once in a Lifetime (oa) 32. You Can't Take It With You (oa) 38. *The Man Who Came to Dinner* (oa) 41. George Washington Slept Here (oa) 42. Lady in the Dark (oa) 44. Winged Victory (w) 44. *Gentleman's Agreement* (AANw) 47. Hans Christian Andersen (w) 52. A Star Is Born (w) 54. Prince of Players (w) 55, etc.

Hart, Richard (1915–1951)
American leading man with a very brief Hollywood career.
■ Green Dolphin Street 47. Desire Me 47. B.F.'s Daughter 48. The Black Book 49.

Hart, William S. (1870–1946)
Mature, solemn-faced hero of innumerable silent westerns; one of the key performers of the 20s. The initial 'S' is variously reputed to have stood for 'Shakespeare' and 'Surrey'.
Autobiography: 1929, *My Life East and West*.
The Disciple 15. The Captive God 16. The Return of Draw Egan 16. Hell's Hinges 17. Truthful Tolliver 17. Blue Blazes Rawden 18. Selfish Yates 18. Riddle Gawne 18. The Border Wireless 18. Wagon Tracks 18. The Poppy Girl's Husband 19. The Toll Gate 20. Sand 20. Cradle of Courage 20. O'Malley of the Mounted 21. White Oak 21. Travellin' On 22. Hollywood 23. Wild Bill Hickok 23. Singer Jim McKee 24. *Tumbleweeds* 25, many others.
❝ His frequently austere look breathed dedication to the West as a subject suited for all the artistic possibilities of cinema. – *Allen Eyles*

Harte, Bret (1836–1902) (Francis Brett Harte)
American short-story writer who wandered the old west. Works filmed include *The Outcasts of Poker Flat*, *Tennessee's Partner*.

Hartford-Davis, Robert (1923–1977)
British producer-director, in films from 1939.
That Kind of Girl 62. The Yellow Teddybears 63. Saturday Night Out 63. Black Torment 64. Gonks Go Beat 65. The Sandwich Man 66. Corruption 68. The Smashing Bird I Used to Know 69. The Fiend 71. Black Gunn (US) 72. The Take (US) 74, etc.

Hartl, Karl (1899–1978)
Austrian director.
The Doomed Battalion 31. F.P.1 32. Gold 34. The Gypsy Baron 35. The Man Who Was Sherlock Holmes 37. Whom the Gods Love 42. The Angel with the Trumpet 48. The Wonder Kid 51. Journey into the Past 54. Mozart 55. Love Is Red 57, many others. Also scenarist for many of the above.

Hartley, Hal (1959–)
American director, screenwriter and producer of quirky low-budget movies.
The Unbelievable Truth 90. Trust 91. Surviving Desire (TV) 92. Simple Men 92. Amateur 94. Flirt 95. Henry Fool 97, etc.

Hartley, L. P. (1895–1972) (Leslie Poles Hartley)
English novelist and short story writer of middle-class emotional repression. Born in Whittlesey, Cambridgeshire, he studied modern history at Oxford, and was a literary journalist before turning to fiction.
Biography: 1996, *Foreign Country: The Life of L. P. Hartley* by Adrian Wright.
The Go-Between (oa) 71. The Hireling (oa) 73.
❝ The past is another country. They do things differently there. – *L.P.H.*
After 70, it seems to me, there is no further need for self-discipline (e.g. avoiding the gin-bottle), or *any* form of self-improvement. – *L.P.H.*

Hartley, Mariette (1940–)
Under-used leading lady who makes an occasional impression.
Ride the High Country 62. Drums of Africa 63. Marooned 67. Barquero 70. The Return of Count Yorga 71. Earth II (TV) 71. Sandcastles (TV) 72. Genesis II (TV) 73. The Killer Who Wouldn't Die (TV) 76. The Last Hurrah (TV) 77. Improper Channels 81. No Place to Hide (TV) 82. 1969 89. Encino Man/California Man 92, etc.

TV series: Peyton Place 65. The Hero 66–67. Goodnight Beantown 83–84. WIOU 90–91.

Hartley, Richard
British composer.
Galileo 75. The Romantic Englishwoman 75. The Rocky Horror Picture Show 75. Aces High 76. The Lady Vanishes 79. Bad Timing 80. Bad Blood 81. Shock Treatment 82. The Trout 82. Sheena, Queen of the Jungle 84. Parker 84. Dance with a Stranger 85. Defence of the Realm 85. The Good Father 86. Soursweet 88. Consuming Passions 88. Tree of Hands 88. Dealers 89. She's Been Away 89. Afraid of the Dark 92. The Railway Station Man 92. The Secret Rapture 93. Princess Caraboo 94. An Awfully Big Adventure 95. Rough Magic 95. Stealing Beauty 95. The Van 96. The Brylcreem Boys 96. The Designated Mourner 97. Playing God 97. A Thousand Acres 97. All The Little Animals 98. Rogue Trader 98. When Brendan Met Rudy 00, etc.

Hartman, David (1937–)
Tall, gangling American leading man who after a few years, mostly in television, gained a permanent niche as anchorman for ABC's *Good Morning America.*
The Ballad of Josie 68. Nobody's Perfect 69. Ice Station Zebra 69. San Francisco International (TV) 70. The Feminist and the Fuzz (TV) 71. I Love a Mystery (TV) 73. You'll Never See Me Again (TV) 73. Miracle on 34th Street (TV) 74. The Island at the Top of the World 75, etc.
TV series: The Bold Ones 69–71. Lucas Tanner 76.

Hartman, Don (1901–1958) (Samuel Hartman)
American comedy screenwriter.
The Gay Deception (AAN) 35. The Princess Comes Across 35. Waikiki Wedding 37. Tropic Holiday 38. Paris Honeymoon 39. The Star Maker 39. *Road to Singapore* 40. Life with Henry 41. *Road to Zanzibar* 41. Nothing but the Truth 41. *Road to Morocco* (AAN) 42. True to Life 42. Up in Arms 44. The Princess and the Pirate 44. Down to Earth (& p) 47. It Had to be You (& d) 47. Every Girl Should Be Married (& pd) 48. Mr Imperium (& d) 51. Desire Under the Elms (p) 57. The Matchmaker (p) 58, many others.

Hartman, Elizabeth (1941–1987)
American leading actress. Committed suicide.
A Patch of Blue (AAN) 66. The Group 66. You're a Big Boy Now 67. The Fixer 68. The Beguiled 71. Walking Tall 73.

Hartman, Phil (1948–1998)
Canadian-born comic actor and writer. Born in Branford, Ontario, he was raised in Connecticut and Los Angeles, and first worked as a graphic designer, responsible for designing the logo for the rock group Crosby, Stills and Nash, before joining a Los Angeles comedy group in the mid-70s. He was noted for the brilliance of his impressions on NBC's *Saturday Night Live*, and for supplying many of the voices (including 'B'-movie star Troy McClure and sleazy lawyer Lionel Hutz) for the TV series *The Simpsons*. He was shot to death while sleeping by his wife, who committed suicide shortly after.
Cheech and Chong's Next Movie 80. Weekend Pass 84. Pee-Wee's Big Adventure (co-w only) 85. Jumpin' Jack Flash 86. Three Amigos 86. Blind Date 87. The Brave Little Toaster (voice) 87. Fletch Lives 89. Quick Change 90. Coneheads 93. So I Married an Axe Murderer 93. Greedy 94. Sgt Bilko 94. Jingle All the Way 96. Small Soldiers 98, etc.
TV series: Saturday Night Live 86–94. NewsRadio 95–98.

Hartnell, Sir Norman (1901–1979)
English couturier who designed costumes for British films of the 30s. Born in Streatham, London, he attended Cambridge University briefly before opening his own fashion business in the early 20s. He became a dressmaker to the British Royal Family from the mid-30s, and was knighted in 1977.
Autobiography: 1955, *Silver and Gold.*
Such Is the Law 30. Aunt Sally 33. That's a Good Girl 33. A Southern Maid 33. Give Her a Ring 34. Princess Charming 34. The Return of Bulldog Drummond 34. Brewster's Millions 35. Calling the Tune 36. Non-Stop New York 37. Sailing Along 38. A Clean Sweep 38, etc.

Hartnell, William (1908–1975)
Thin-lipped British character actor who rose briefly to star status in the 40s after playing many small-time crooks and tough sergeants. Popular on TV in the 60s as the first Dr Who.
Biography: 1996, *Who's There? – The Life and Career of William Hartnell* by Jessica Carney.
Follow the Lady 33. While Parents Sleep 35. Midnight at Madame Tussaud's 36. Farewell Again 37. They Drive by Night 39. Flying Fortress 40. Suspected Person 41. The Peterville Diamond 42. The Bells Go Down 43. Headline 43. *The Way Ahead* 44. The Agitator 44. Murder in Reverse 45. Strawberry Roan 46. Appointment with Crime 46. Odd Man Out 46. Temptation Harbour 47. *Brighton Rock* 47. Now Barabbas 49. The Lost People 49. The Dark Man 50. The Magic Box 51. The Holly and the Ivy 52. The Ringer 52. Will any Gentleman? 53. Footsteps in the Fog 54. Private's Progress 55. Hell Drivers 57. Carry on Sergeant 58. Piccadilly Third Stop 60. This Sporting Life 62. Heaven's Above 63, many others.
TV series: The Army Game 57–58.

Harvey, Anthony (1931–)
British editor, later director.
AS EDITOR: Private's Progress 56. Happy is the Bride 58. The Angry Silence 60. Lolita 62. Dr Strangelove 63. The Whisperers 67, etc.
■ AS DIRECTOR: Dutchman (& e) 66. The Lion in Winter (AAN) 68. They Might Be Giants 71. The Glass Menagerie (TV) 73. The Abdication 74. The Disappearance of Aimee (TV) 76. Players 79. Eagle's Wing 79. Richard's Things (TV) 81. Svengali (TV) 83. The Ultimate Solution of Grace Quigley 85.

Harvey, Forrester (1880–1945)
Irish character actor, long in Hollywood.
The Lilac Sunbonnet 22. The Flag Lieutenant 26. The Ring 27. The White Sheik 28. Sky Devils 32. Tarzan the Ape Man 32. Red Dust 33. The Invisible Man 33. The Painted Veil 34. The Mystery of Edwin Drood 35. Jalna 35. Lloyds of London 36. Personal Property 37. Kidnapped 38. Mysterious Mr Moto 38. Let Us Live 39. Rebecca 40. A Chump at Oxford 40. Little Nellie Kelly 40. The Wolf Man 41. Random Harvest 42. Scotland Yard Investigator 45, many others.

Harvey, Frank (1912–1981)
British playwright and screenwriter.
Saloon Bar (oa) 40. Things Happen at Night (oa) 48. Seven Days to Noon (w) 50. High Treason (w) 52. Private's Progress (w) 55. I'm All Right Jack (w) 59. Heaven's Above (w) 63. No My Darling Daughter (w) 63, etc.

Harvey, Laurence (1928–1973) (Larushka Mischa Skikne)
Lithuanian-born leading man who worked his way slowly from British second features to top Hollywood productions, but was only briefly in fashion. He was brought up in Johannesburg, South Africa, and studied at RADA. He became a protégé of James WOOLF, of Romulus Films, who made him a star. Married actress Margaret LEIGHTON (1957–60), Joan Cohn (1968–72), widow of film mogul Harry COHN, and, in 1969, model Paulene Stone. His lovers included Hermione BADDELEY. Died of cancer.
Biography: 1973, *The Prince* by Emmett and Des Hickey. 1975, *One Tear is Enough* by Paulene Stone.
House of Darkness 48. Man on the Run 48. The Dancing Years 48. The Man from Yesterday 49. Cairo Road 49. The Scarlet Thread 50. Landfall 50. The Black Rose 50. There is Another Sun 51. A Killer Walks 51. I Believe in You 52. Women of Twilight 52. Innocents in Paris 53. Romeo and Juliet 54. King Richard and the Crusaders 54. The Good Die Young 55. I Am a Camera 55. Storm over the Nile 56. Three Men in a Boat 57. After the Ball 57. The Truth About Women 58. The Silent Enemy 58. *Room at the Top* (AAN) 59. Expresso Bongo 59. The Alamo 60. Butterfield Eight 60. The Long and the Short and the Tall 61. Two Loves 61. Summer and Smoke 61. A Walk on the Wild Side 62. The Wonderful World of the Brothers Grimm 63. A Girl Named Tamiko 63. The Manchurian Candidate 63. The Running Man 63. The Ceremony (& pd) 64. Of Human Bondage 64. The Outrage 64. Darling 65. Life at the Top 65. The Spy with the Cold Nose 66. A Dandy in Aspic 67. The Winter's Tale 68. Rebus 68. Kampf um Rom 69. He and She 69. The Magic Christian 70. WUSA 71. Flight into the Sun 72. Night Watch 73. Welcome to Arrow Beach 73, etc.
❝ He demonstrated conclusively that it is possible to succeed without managing to evoke the least audience interest or sympathy and to go on succeeding despite unanimous critical antipathy and overwhelming public apathy. – *David Shipman*
Life with him was exciting and funny, but he was consumed with a hunger to have everything – fame, fortune, all the riches of life. It was as if he knew there was only so much time alloted to him. – *Hermione Baddeley*
Behind the public dandy, the pirouetting fop, hid a mature and sensitive artist. He simply believed it was slightly vulgar to let it be seen. – *Paulene Stone*
An appalling man and, even more unforgivably, an appalling actor. – *Robert Stephens*

Harvey, Lilian (1906–1968)
British leading lady who in the 30s became star of German films.
Biography: 1974, *The Lilian Harvey Story* by Hans Borgen.
Leidenschaft 25. Die Tolle Lola 227. Drei von der Tankstelle 30. *Congress Dances* 31. Happy Ever After 32. My Weakness (US) 33. I Am Suzanne (US) 34. Invitation to the Waltz (GB) 35. Capriccio 38. Serenade (Fr.) (last film) 39, etc.

Harvey, Paul (1884–1955)
American character actor who often played the choleric executive or kindly father.
Advice to the Lovelorn 34. Broadway Bill 34. Handy Andy 34. A Wicked Woman 34. The Plainsman 36. Private Number 36. High Flyers 37. Rebecca of Sunnybrook Farm 38. Algiers 38. Stanley and Livingstone 39. Meet Dr Christian 39. Arizona 40. You Can't Escape Forever 42. Pillow to Post 45. The Late George Apley 47. Father of the Bride 50. The Milkman 50. Side Street 50. The Yellow Cab Man 50. Dreamboat 52. The First Time 52. Calamity Jane 53. Three for the Show 55, many others.

Harvey, Rodney (1967–1998)
American actor, born in Philadelphia, Pennsylvania and best known for his role as the aggressive Sodapop Curtis in the TV series *The Outsiders*. His later career was hampered by his heroin addiction. Died of a drug overdose.
Mixed Blood 84. Initiation 87. Five Corners 88. Salsa: The Motion Picture 88. La Bocca (It.) 91. My Own Private Idaho 91. Guncrazy 92, etc.
TV series: The Outsiders 90.

Harwood, Ronald (1934–)
South African-born dramatist and screenwriter, in England since 1951. He was formerly an actor with Sir Donald Wolfit's company.
Private Potter 62. Eyewitness 70. One Day in the Life of Ivan Denisovich 71. Operation Daybreak 75. The Dresser (AAN) 83. The Doctor and the Devils 85. Tchin Tchin 91. The Browning Version 94. Cry the Beloved Country 95.

Has, Wojciech (1925–2000)
Polish director and screenwriter. Born in Cracow, he studied at that city's Film Institute and began in the late 40s making shorts and documentaries. He directed features from 1958, moving from narratives of individual lives to large-scale epics in his later films. He became director of the Lodz Film School in the early 80s.
The Noose (& co-w) 58. Goodbye to the Past 61. *The Saragossa Manuscript* 65. Lalka/The Doll (& w) 68. The Hourglass Sanatorium (& w) 73. Write and Flight 85. The Fabulous Journey of Balthazar Kober 88, etc.

Haskell, Jimmy
American composer, mainly for television movies since the 80s.
Love in a Goldfish Bowl 61. Wild on the Beach 65. Red Tomahawk 67. Zachariah 71. Night of the Lepus 72. Dirty Mary Crazy Larry 74. Joyride 77. Hard Country (co-m) 81. She's Back 89, etc.

Haskell, Peter (1934–)
American leading man.
The Ballad of Andy Crocker (TV) 69. The Eyes of Charles Sand (TV) 72. Phantom of Hollywood (TV) 74. Christina 74. The Night They Took Miss Beautiful (TV) 77. The Cracker Factory (TV) 79. Legend of Earl Durand 90. Child's Play 3 91, etc.
TV series: Bracken's World 69. Rich Man, Poor Man Book II 76–77. Rituals 84–85. The Law and Harry McGraw 87.

Haskin, Byron (1899–1984)
American director with a penchant for science fiction; some interesting films among the routine.
Cameraman and special effects expert through the 30s.
■ Matinée Ladies 27. Ginsberg the Great 27. Irish Hearts 27. The Siren 28. *I Walk Alone* 47. Maneater of Kumaon 48. Too Late for Tears 49. Treasure Island 50. Tarzan's Peril 51. Warpath 51. Silver City 51. Denver and Rio Grande 52. *The War of the Worlds* 53. His Majesty O'Keefe 53. The Naked Jungle 54. Long John Silver 55. Conquest of Space 55. The First Texan 56. The Boss 56. From the Earth to the Moon 58. The Little Savage 59. Jet over the Atlantic 59. September Storm 60. Armored Command 61. *Captain Sinbad* 63. *Robinson Crusoe on Mars* 64. The Power 67.

Hassall, Imogen (1942–1980)
Voluptuous English actress, a former dancer. Died of a drug overdose.
The Early Bird 65. The Long Duel 67. Mumsy, Nanny, Sonny and Girly 69. El Condor 70. The Virgin and the Gypsy 70. Tomorrow 70. When Dinosaurs Ruled the Earth 70. Carry on Loving 70. White Cargo 73. Licensed to Love and Kill 79, etc.

Hasse, O. E. (1903–1978)
German character actor: dubbed the voices of Spencer Tracy and Paul Muni.
Peer Gynt 34. Rembrandt 42. Berliner Ballade 48. Epilog 50. Decision Before Dawn (US) 51. I Confess (US) 53. Canaris 54. Mrs Warren's Profession 59. State of Siege 72. Ice Age 75, etc.

Hasselhoff, David (1952–)
American leading man, mainly on television.
Revenge of the Cheerleaders 76. Star Crash/Stella Star 78. Pleasure Cove (TV) 79. Cartier Affair (TV) 84. Terror at London Bridge (TV) 85. Witchery 88. The Final Alliance 89. Fire and Rain (TV) 89. Bail Out 90, etc.
TV series: The Young and the Restless 75–82. Semi-Tough 80. Knight Rider 82–86. Bay Watch 89– . Baywatch Nights 95– .

Hassett, Marilyn (1947–)
American leading lady.
Quarantined (TV) 70. They Shoot Horses Don't They? 72. *The Other Side of the Mountain* 76. Two Minute Warning 76. The Other Side of the Mountain: Part Two 77. The Bell Jar 79. Body Count 87. Messenger of Death 88, etc.

Hasso, Signe (1910–)
Swedish leading lady of the 40s, in Hollywood. Also a writer.
Assignment in Brittany 43. The Seventh Cross 44. *The House on 92nd Street* 45. Johnny Angel 45. A Scandal in Paris 46. Where There's Life 47. *To the Ends of the Earth* 48. A Double Life 48. Outside the Wall 50. Crisis 50. Picture Mommy Dead 66. Reflection of Fear 71. The Black Bird 75. I Never Promised You a Rose Garden 77, etc.

Hatcher, Teri (1964–)
American actress. She married actor Jon Tenney in 1994.
The Big Picture 89. Tango and Cash 89. Soapdish 91. Dead in the Water 91. Straight Talk 92. Brain Smasher 93. Heaven's Prisoners 96. 2 Days in the Valley 96. Tomorrow Never Dies 97. Fever 99, etc.
TV series: Lois & Clark: The New Adventures of Superman 93– .

Hatfield, Hurd (1918–1998)
American leading man whose coldly handsome face proved to be his misfortune.
■ Dragon Seed 44. *The Picture of Dorian Gray* 45. The Diary of a Chambermaid 46. The Beginning or the End 47. The Unsuspected 47. The Checkered Coat 48. Joan of Arc 48. Chinatown at Midnight 48. Tarzan and the Slave Girl 50. Destination Murder 51. The Left Handed Gun 58. King of Kings 61. El Cid 61. Mickey One 65. The Boston Strangler 68. Thief (TV) 70. Von Richthofen and Brown 71. The Norliss Tapes (TV) 73. The Word (TV) 78. You Can't Go Home Again (TV) 79. Crimes of the Heart 86. Her Alibi 88.

Hathaway, Henry (1898–1985)
American director, in films (as child actor) from 1907. Acted till 1932, then directed westerns. Later became known as a capable handler of big action adventures and thrillers.
■ Wild Horse Mesa 32. Heritage of the Desert 33. Under the Tonto Rim 33. Sunset Pass 33. Man of the Forest 33. To the Last Man 33. Come On Marines 34. The Last Round-Up 34. Thundering Herds 34. The Witching Hour 34. Now and Forever 34. *Lives of a Bengal Lancer* (AAN) 35. Peter Ibbetson 35. Trail of the Lonesome Pine 36. Go West Young Man 36. Souls at Sea 37. Spawn of the North 38. The Real Glory 39. Johnny Apollo 40. Brigham Young 40. Shepherd of the Hills 41. Sundown 41. Ten Gentlemen from West Point 42. China Girl 43. Home in Indiana 44. A Wing and a Prayer 44. Nob Hill 45. *The House on 92nd Street* 45. The Dark Corner 46. 13 Rue Madeleine 46. *Kiss of Death* 47. Call Northside 777 48. Down to the Sea in Ships 49. The Black Rose 50. You're in the Navy Now 51. Rawhide 51. Fourteen Hours 51. *Rommel, Desert Fox* 51. Diplomatic Courier 52. *Niagara* 52. White Witch Doctor 53. Prince Valiant 54. Garden of Evil 54. The Racers 54. The Bottom of the Bottle 55. 23 Paces to Baker Street 56. Legend of the Lost 57. From Hell to Texas 58. A Woman Obsessed 59. Seven Thieves 60. *North to Alaska* 60. How the West Was Won (part) 62. Circus World 64. The Sons of Katie Elder 65. Nevada Smith 66. The Last Safari 67. Five Card Stud 68. True Grit 69. Raid on Rommel 71. Shootout 72.
✪ For long-standing professionalism in handling all types of subject. *The House on 92nd Street*.
❝ Being educated is making the pictures themselves, if you make it your business to pay attention. – *H.H.*
To be a good director you've got to be a bastard. I'm a bastard and I know it. – *H.H.*
His charm consists of minor virtues uncorrupted by major pretensions. – *Andrew Sarris*

Hatley, Thomas Marvin (1905–1986)
American composer who was musical director at the Hal Roach Studio 1930–39, scoring several Laurel and Hardy movies. In the 40s he quit films to play the piano in cocktail lounges.
Hog Wild 30. The Music Box 31. Sons of the Desert (s, 'Honolulu Baby') 33. Way Out West (AAN) 37. Pick a Star 37. Block-Heads (AAN) 38. There Goes My Heart (AAN) 38. Captain Fury 39. Topper Takes a Trip 39. A Chump at Oxford 40, etc.

Hatosy, Shawn (1975–)
American actor. Born in Frederick, Maryland, he began acting at the age of 10.
Home for the Holidays 95. Double Jeopardy (TV) 96. Inventing the Abbots 97. All Over Me 97. In & Out 97. The Postman 97. The Faculty 98. Outside Providence 99. The Joyriders 99. Witness Protection (TV) 99. Simpatico 99. Anywhere But Here 99. Down to You 00. Borstal Boy (as Brendan Behan) 00, etc.

Hattie, Hilo (1901–1979)
Hawaiian entertainer who in 1942 made her only Hollywood musical: *Song of the Islands*.

Hatton, Raymond (1887–1971)
American character actor, the comic sidekick of a hundred minor westerns. Born in Bed Oak, Iowa, he first worked in carnivals and vaudeville, and was in Hollywood from 1911. He appeared with Buck Jones in the Rough Riders series in the late 30s before becoming one of The Three Mesquiteers in their later incarnation. He was comic relief to Johnny Mack Brown in more than 40 westerns, and formed a comedy team with Wallace Beery, 1926–29.
Oliver Twist 16. Whispering Chorus 18. Male and Female 19. Jes' Call Me Jim 20. The Affairs of Anatol 21. Ebb Tide 22. The Hunchback of Notre Dame 23. The Fighting American 24. In the Name of Love 25. Born to the West 26. *Behind the Front* 26. *We're In the Navy Now* 26. Fireman Save My Child 27. The Woman God Forgot 27. We're in the Air Now 27. Partners in Crime 28. Hell's Heroes 29. Midnight Mystery 30. Woman Hungry 31. The Squaw Man 31. Polly of the Circus 32. Terror Trail 33. Wagon Wheels 34. Laughing Irish Eyes 36. Roaring Timber 37. Love Finds Andy Hardy 38. Kit Carson 40. Tall in the Saddle 44. Black Gold 47. Operation Haylift 50. Shake Rattle and Rock 56. In Cold Blood 67, many others.

Hatton, Richard (1891–1931)
American star of silent westerns. Killed in a traffic accident.
Fearless Dick 22. Blood Test 23. Come On, Cowboys 24. 'Scar' Hanan 25. He-Man's Country 26. Saddle Jumpers 27. The Boss of Rustler's Roost 28. The Vanishing Legion (serial) 31, etc.
❝ Hatton was strictly a city man and our nickname for him was 'Fearless Richard' since he was actually afraid to go out at night unless someone was with him. – *Yakima Canutt*

Hatton, Rondo (1894–1946)
American actor who suffered from facial and bodily deformity as a result of acromegaly; he was rather tastelessly cast as a monstrous killer in several low-budget mysteries of the early 40s.
■ Hell Harbor 30. In Old Chicago 38. Alexander's Ragtime Band 38. The Hunchback of Notre Dame 39. Captain Fury 39. Chad Hanna 40. Moon over Burma 40. The Big Guy 40. The Cyclone Kid 42. The Moon and Sixpence 42. Sleepy Lagoon 43. The Ox Bow Incident 43. *The Pearl of Death* 44. Raiders of Ghost City 44. The Princess and the Pirate 44. Johnny Doesn't Live Here Any More 44. The Royal Mounted Rides Again 45. Jungle Captive 45. Spider Woman Strikes Back 46. House of Horrors 46. The Brute Man 46.

Hauer, Rutger (1944–)
Dutch leading actor, now in international films, associated with the early films of Paul Verhoeven.
Turkish Delight 73. Cold Blood 75. Keetje Tippel 75. Soldier of Orange 77. Spetters 80. Chanel Solitaire 81. Nighthawks 81. Blade Runner 82. Eureka 82. The Osterman Weekend 83. A Breed Apart 84. Ladyhawke 85. Flesh and Blood 85. The Hitcher 86. Wanted Dead or Alive 86. The Legend of the Holy Drinker/La Leggenda del Santo Bevitore 88. Bloodhounds of Broadway 89. Blind Fury 89. The Salute of the Jugger 89. In una Notte di Chiaro di Luna 89. Desert Law 90. The Blood of Heroes 90. Wedlock 91. Split Second 91. Past Midnight 91. Buffy the Vampire Slayer 92. Beyond Justice 92. Arctic Blue 93. Blind Side 93. Amelia Earhart: The Final Flight (TV) 94. Surviving the Game 94. Nostradamus 94. Fatherland (TV) 94. Forbidden Choices/The Beans of Egypt, Maine 94. Mr Stitch 95. Precious Find 96. Omega Doom 96. Blast 96. Crosswords 96. Armageddon 97. Redline 97. Hostile Waters 97. Merlin (TV) 98. Bone Daddy 98. Simon Magus 99, etc.
❝ He's both a genius and crazy at the same time. His entire approach to filmmaking is that he comes in, and he's like a gorilla, he comes in and his primary job, he feels, is to take everything out of focus. – *Roger Avary*

Hauser, Wings
Powerful American leading man of low-budget action films, who turned to directing in the 90s. He began in TV soap operas.
Who'll Stop the Rain/Dog Soldiers 78. Vice Squad 82. Homework 82. Deadly Force 83. Mutant 83. A Soldier's Story 84. The Long Hot Summer 86. Hostage 87. Tough Guys Don't Dance 87. The Wind 87. Nightmare at Noon 87. No Safe Haven 87. Dead Men Walking 88. Marked for Murder 89. Street Asylum 90. Reason to Die 90. Exiled 91. Pale Blood 91. Coldfire (& d) 91. Living to Die (& d) 91. In Between 92. Mind, Body and Soul 92. Frame-Up II: The Cover-Up 92. Tales from the Hood 95. Original Gangstas 96. Gang Boys 97, etc.
TV series: The Last Precinct 86. Lightning Force 91.

Havelock-Allan, Sir Anthony (1904–)
British producer. Born in Darlington, he first worked as an A&R manager in the record business and was in films from the mid-30s. Together with David Lean and Ronald Neame, he set up the production company Cineguild in the early 40s, to film works by Noël Coward and, later, Charles Dickens. He was formerly married to actress Valerie Hobson.
This Man Is News 38. In Which We Serve (associate) 42. Blithe Spirit 45. Brief Encounter (co-w, AAN) 46. Great Expectations 46. Oliver Twist 48. The Small Voice 49. Never Take No for an Answer 51. The Young Lovers 54. Orders to Kill 58. The Quare Fellow 61. An Evening with the Royal Ballet 64. Othello 65. The Mikado 67. Up the Junction 67. Romeo and Juliet 68. Ryan's Daughter 70, etc.

Haver, June (1926–) (June Stovenour)
American leading lady of the 40s, mostly in musicals; married Fred McMurray. Now retired.
■ The Gang's All Here 43. Home in Indiana 44. Irish Eyes Are Smiling 44. Where Do We Go from Here? 45. *The Dolly Sisters* 45. Three Little Girls in Blue 46. Wake Up and Dream 46. I Wonder Who's Kissing Her Now 47. Scudda Hoo Scudda Hay 48. Oh You Beautiful Doll 49. *Look for the Silver Lining* (as Marilyn Miller) 49. The Daughter of Rosie O'Grady 50. I'll Get By 50. Love Nest 51. The Girl Next Door 53.

Haver, Phyllis (1899–1960) (Phyllis O'Haver)
American leading lady of the silent screen, a former Sennett bathing beauty. Committed suicide.
Small Town Idol 20. Temple of Venus 23. Fig Leaves 25. Up in Mabel's Room 26. The Way of All Flesh 28. Hard Boiled 29. Hell's Kitchen 29, many others.

Havers, Nigel (1949–)
Elegant British actor. Born in London, the son of a former Attorney-General, he trained at the Arts Educational School and worked in the wine trade and as a researcher on radio before gaining success as an actor on television.
Chariots of Fire 81. A Passage to India 84. Burke and Wills 86. The Whistle Blower 86. Empire of the Sun 87. Farewell to the King 89. Quiet Days in Clichy 90. The Burning Season (TV) 94, etc.
TV series: Don't Wait Up 83–85. The Charmer 87. The Good Guys 92–93. Dangerfield 98– .

Havlick, Gene (c. 1895–1959)
American editor.
Beauty and Bullets 28. Madonna of the Streets 30. Shopworn 32. Broadway Bill 34. Mr Deeds Goes to Town 36. *Lost Horizon* (AA) 37. You Can't Take It with You 38. Mr Smith Goes to Washington 39. His Girl Friday 40. The Wife takes a Flyer 42. A Song to Remember 45. Relentless 48. Son of Dr Jekyll 51. Jungle Maneaters 54. Screaming Mimi 58, many others.

Havoc, June (1916–) (June Hovick)
American leading lady, former child actress; sister of Gypsy Rose Lee.
Autobiography: 1960, *Early Havoc*.
Four Jacks and a Jill 42. Brewster's Millions 45. The Story of Molly X 49. Once a Thief 50. A Lady Possessed 51. Three for Jamie Dawn 57. The Private Files of J. Edgar Hoover 78. Can't Stop the Music 80. A Return to Salem's Lot 87, etc.
TV series: Willy 54.

Hawk, Jeremy (1918–) (Cedric Lange)
Polished South African-born character actor in British films. Born in Johannesburg, he was educated at Harrow, studied at RADA and was on-stage from the late 30s, often as a straight man to comedians, including Arthur Askey, Norman Wisdom and Benny Hill. He also compered TV quiz shows. He was formerly married to actress Joan Heal.
The Goose Steps Out 42. In Which We Serve 42. Face the Music 54. Mask of Dust 54. The Stranger Came Home 54. Lucky Jim 57. Dentist in the Chair 60. Dentist on the Job 61. Mystery Submarine 63. Panic 65. The Trygon Factor 66. Eskimo Nell 74. Return of the Pink Panther 74. The Adventures of Little Lord Fauntleroy (TV) 82. Elizabeth 98, etc.
TV series: Criss Cross Quiz 57-62. Sid Caesar Invites You 58. Impromptu 67.

Hawke, Ethan (1970–)
American actor. He is also a novelist (1996, *The Hottest State*). Married actress Uma Thurman in 1998.
Explorers 85. Dead Poets Society 89. Dad 89. White Fang 90. A Midnight Clear 91. Mystery Date 91. Waterland 92. Alive 93. White Fang 2: Myth of the White Wolf 94. Reality Bites 94. Floundering 94. Before Sunrise 95. Search and Destroy 95. Great Expectations 98. Gattaca 98. The Velocity of Gary 98. The Newton Boys 98, etc.

Hawkins, Jack (1910–1973)
Dominant British actor; after long apprenticeship, became an international star in middle age, but in 1966 lost his voice after an operation; his subsequent minor appearances were dubbed. His first wife was Jessica Tandy.
Autobiography: 1974, *Anything for a Quiet Life*.
Birds of Prey 30. The Lodger 32. The Good Companions 32. The Lost Chord 33. I Lived with You 33. The Jewel 33. A Shot in the Dark 33. Autumn Crocus 34. Death at Broadcasting House 34. *Peg of Old Drury* 35. Beauty and the Barge 37. The Frog 37. Who Goes Next 38. A Royal Divorce 38. Murder Will Out 39. The Flying Squad 40. Next of Kin 42. *The Fallen Idol* 48. Bonnie Prince Charlie 48. The Small Back Room 48. *State Secret* 50. The Black Rose 50. The Elusive Pimpernel 50. The Adventurers 51. No Highway 51. Home at Seven 51. *Angels One Five* 52. The Planter's Wife 52. Mandy 52. *The Cruel Sea* 53. Twice Upon a Time 53. The Malta Story 53. The Intruder 53. Front Page Story 54. The Seekers 54. The Prisoner 55. Touch and Go 55. Land of the Pharaohs 55. The Long Arm 56. The Man in the Sky 56. Fortune is a Woman 57. *The Bridge on the River Kwai* 57. Gideon's Day 58. The Two-Headed Spy 58. *The League of Gentlemen* 59. *Ben Hur* (US) 59. Two Loves (US) 61. Five Finger Exercise (US) 62. *Lawrence of Arabia* 62. Lafayette 63. *Rampage* (US) 63. Zulu 63. The Third Secret 64. Guns at Batasi 64. Masquerade 65. Lord Jim 65. Judith 65. Great Catherine 67. Shalako 68. Oh What a Lovely War 69. Monte Carlo or Bust 69. Waterloo 70. The Adventures of Gerard 70. Nicholas and Alexandra 71. Kidnapped 72. Young Winston 72. Theatre of Blood 73. Tales that Witness Madness 73, etc.
TV series: *The Four Just Men* 59.
✪ For humorously perpetuating the image of the friendly World War II officer. *The League of Gentlemen*.

Hawkins, Screamin' Jay (1929–2000) (Jalacy Hawkins)
Exuberant and eccentric American rhythm and blues singer and actor. He was a former Golden Gloves middleweight boxing champion. His dying wish was that his children should meet one another. He put their number at around 75, and more than 30 have been traced so far.
American Hot Wax 78. Mystery Train 89. A Rage in Harlem 91. Perdita Durango 97, etc.

Hawks, Howard (1896–1977)
American director, at his best an incomparable provider of professional comedies and action dramas. Born in Goshen, Indiana, he studied mechanical engineering at Cornell University; he taught pilots to fly during the First World War and built the racing car that won the Indianapolis 500 in 1936. He began in films in 1917 as a prop boy, became an assistant director and, in the early 20s, ran Famous Players' story department. He began directing in 1926 for Fox, but after the success of *The Dawn Patrol* was able to work without signing a long-term contract with any studio. Awarded an honorary Oscar in 1974 as 'a master American filmmaker'. Died after a fall at his home. Married three times.
Biography: 1997: *Howard Hawks: The Grey Fox of Hollywood* by Todd McCarthy.
Other books: 1962, *The Cinema of Howard Hawks* by Peter Bogdanovich; 1977, *Howard Hawks* by Robin Wood; 1982, *Hawks on Hawks* (devised by Joe McBride); 1982, *Howard Hawks, Storyteller* by Gerald Mast.
■ Tiger Love (w only) 24. The Road to Glory (& w) 26. Fig Leaves (& w) 26. The Cradle Snatchers 27. Paid to Love 27. A Girl in Every Port (& w) 28. Fazil 28. The Air Circus 28. Trent's Last Case (& w) 29. *The Dawn Patrol* 30. The Criminal Code 31. The Crowd Roars 32. *Scarface* 32. Tiger Shark 32. Today We Live 33. *Twentieth Century* 34. Viva Villa (part) 34. *Barbary Coast* 35. Ceiling Zero 36. Road to Glory 36. Come and Get It (co-d) 36. *Bringing Up Baby* 38. Only Angels Have Wings 39. *His Girl Friday* 40. Sergeant York (AAN) 41. Ball of Fire 41. Air Force 42. Corvette K 225 (p only) 44. *To Have and Have Not* 44. *The Big Sleep* 46. A Song Is Born 48. *Red River* 48. I Was a Male War Bride 49. The Thing from Another World (p only) 52. The Big Sky 52. Monkey Business 52. O. Henry's Full House (one episode) 52. Gentlemen Prefer Blondes 53. Land of the Pharaohs 55. *Rio Bravo* 58. Hatari 62. Man's Favourite Sport 64. Red Line 7000 65. El Dorado 66. Rio Lobo 70.
✪ For the remarkably consistent vigour with which he presented a man's world invaded by a woman. *His Girl Friday*.
❝ For me the best drama is one that deals with a man in danger. – *H.H.*
He stamped his remarkably bitter view of life on adventure, gangster and private eye melodramas, the kind of thing Americans do best and appreciate least. – *Andrew Sarris, 1968*

Hawn, Goldie (1945–)
American leading lady who scored as blonde dimwit on TV's *Laugh-In*.
■ The One and Only Genuine Original Family Band 68. *Cactus Flower* (AA) 69. *There's a Girl in My Soup* 70. Butterflies are Free 72. Dollars 72. The Sugarland Express 73. The Girl from Petrovka 74. Shampoo 75. The Duchess and the Dirtwater Fox 76. Foul Play 78. Travels with Anita 79. Private Benjamin (AAN) 80. Seems Like Old Times 80. Best Friends 82. Protocol 84. Swing Shift 84. Wildcats 85. Overboard 87. Bird on the Wire 90. Deceived 91. Crisscross 92. Housesitter 92. Death Becomes Her 92. The First Wives Club 96. Everyone Says I Love You 96. Hope (TV) (d) 97.
TV series: Good Morning World 67.
❝ All I ever wanted to do was run a dance school and marry a Jewish dentist. – *G.H.*

Haworth, Jill (1945–)
British leading lady in Hollywood.
Exodus 60. In Harm's Way 65. It 66. Home for the Holidays (TV) 72. The Mutations 74.

Haworth, Ted (1917–1993)
American production designer.
Strangers on a Train 51. I Confess 53. Marty (AAN) 54. Invasion of the Body Snatchers 56. Friendly Persuasion 56. Sayonara (AA) 57. The Naked and the Dead 58. Some Like It Hot (AAN) 59. Pepe (AAN) 60. The Longest Day (AAN) 62. What a Way to Go (AAN) 64. Half a Sixpence 67. Villa Rides 68. The Kremlin Letter 70. The Getaway 72. Pat Garrett and Billy the Kid 73. Claudine 74. The Killer Elite 76. Cross of Iron 77. Bloodline 79. Rough Cut 80. Death Hunt 81. Blame It on the Night 84. Poltergeist II: The Other Side 86. Batteries Not Included 87, etc.

Hawthorne, Nathaniel (1804–1864)
American novelist and short-story writer, of oppressive Puritan attitudes in New England. His *The Scarlet Letter*, about a woman accused of adultery, has been filmed at least five times, notably in 1926 with Lillian Gish and 1934 with Colleen Moore. An updated version, starring Demi Moore, flopped at the box-office in 1995. *The House of Seven Gables* was transferred flatly to the screen in 1940, with a cast that included George Sanders, Margaret Lindsay and Vincent Price. His story 'Young Goodman Brown' was even less successfully filmed in 1993 by Peter George.

Hawthorne, Sir Nigel (1929–)
British star character actor.
A Tale of Two Cities (TV) 80. The Hunchback of Notre Dame (TV) 81. Firefox 82. Gandhi 82. Dream Child 84. Turtle Diary 84. Jenny's War (TV) 84. The Chain 86. A Handful of Time/En Handfull Tid 90. Demolition Man 93. *The Madness of King George* 95. Richard III 95. The Fragile Heart (TV) 96. Twelfth Night 96. Inside (TV) 96. Murder in Mind (US) 97. Amistad (US) 97. The Object of My Affection (US) 98. Madeline (US) 98. At Sachem Farm (US) 98. The Winslow Boy 98. Clandestine Marriage 99. Tarzan (voice) 99., etc.
TV series: *Yes, Minister* (as Sir Humphrey) 81–87.

Hawtrey, Charles (1914–1988) (George Hartree)
Spindle-shanked English comic actor, long cast as an ageing schoolboy in Will Hay's comedies. In the 60s, he was a familiar member of the Carry On team. Born in Hounslow, Middlesex, he trained at the Italia Conti School and was a boy soprano, on stage from 1925. His alcoholism brought to an end his association with the Carry On series in the early 70s. He retired to live in a cottage on the Kent coast in Deal, where the visiting Kenneth Williams reported, 'as we walked along the front, fishermen eyed us warily. Charlie was in orange trousers, blue shirt and silk scarf at the neck. He was carrying his umbrella as a parasol. The day was quite fine. The rest of us were trying to look anonymous. "Hello lads!"he kept calling out to men painting their boats. "They all adore me here," he told us, "brings a bit of glamour into their dull lives."'
Good Morning Boys 37. Where's That Fire 40. The Goose Steps Out 42. A Canterbury Tale 44. The Galloping Major 50. Brandy for the Parson 52. *You're Only Young Twice* 53. Carry On Jack 54. Carry On Sergeant 58. Carry On Nurse 59. Carry On Cowboy 67. Carry On at Your Convenience 71. Carry On Abroad 72, many others.
TV series: The Army Game 57–61. Our House 60. Best of Friends 63.

Hay, Alexandra (1944–1993)
American leading lady.
Skidoo 68. The Model Shop 69. The Love Machine 71. 1000 Convicts and a Woman 71. How Come Nobody's on Our Side 73, etc.

Hay, Will (1888–1949)
British character comedian, one of the screen's greats; after many years in the music halls, starred in several incomparable farces playing variations on his favourite role of an incompetent, seedy schoolmaster. Born in Stockton-on-Tees, he worked as a book-keeper before beginning in the music halls in a schoolmaster sketch in 1909, later joining Fred Karno's troupe and becoming a star attraction from the mid-20s. In private life, he was an expert amateur astronomer who built his own observatory and wrote a book on the subject (1935, *Through My Telescope*), a pilot and a linguist.
Biography: 1978, *Good Morning Boys* by Ray Seaton and Roy Martin.
■ Those Were the Days 34. Dandy Dick 34. Radio Parade 35. Boys will be Boys 35. Where There's a Will 36. Windbag the Sailor 36. *Good Morning Boys* 37. Convict 99 38. Hey Hey USA 38. *Old Bones of the River* 38. *Oh Mr Porter* 38. *Ask a Policeman* 39. Where's that Fire? 39. *The Ghost of St Michael's* 41. The Black Sheep of Whitehall 41. The Big Blockade 42. The Goose Steps Out 42. *My Learned Friend* 44.
✪ For developing an unforgettable comic persona which lives in the memory independently of his films; and for persuading us to root for that character despite its basically unsympathetic nature. *Oh Mr Porter.*
❝ A good comedy scenario is very near pathos. The character I play is really a very pathetic fellow. – *W.H.*
I've always found something funny in the idea of a hopelessly inefficient man blundering through a job he knows nothing about. – *W.H.*
For each one of us there comes a moment when death takes us by the hand and says: 'It is time to rest; you are tired; lie down and sleep; sleep well.' The day is gone and stars shine in the canopy of eternity. – *The last words Will Hay read before he died, which were inscribed at the foot of his grave*

Hayakawa, Sessue (1889–1973)
Japanese actor, a popular star of American silents; more recently in occasional character roles.
The Typhoon 14. *The Cheat* 15. Forbidden Paths 17. The Tong Man 19. Daughter of the Dragon 29. Tokyo Joe 49. Three Came Home 50. *The Bridge on the River Kwai* (AAN) 57. The Geisha Boy 59. The Swiss Family Robinson 60. Hell to Eternity 61, etc.

Hayasaka, Fumio (1914–1955)
Japanese composer, often for the films of Akira Kurosawa and Kenji Mizoguchi.
Drunken Angel/Yoidore Tenshi 48. Rashomon 50. Meshi 51. Ikiru 52. Ugetsu 53. Sansho the Bailiff/Sansho Dayu 54. Seven Samurai/Shichinin no Samurai 54. A Story from Chikamatsu/Chikamatsu Monogatari 54. I Live in Fear 55, etc.

Hayashi, Kaizo (1957–)
Japanese director and screenwriter.
Circus Boys/Ni Ju-Seiki Shonen Dokuhon 89. The Most Terrible Time in My Life/Waga Jinsei Saisuku no Toki 94. The Breath/Umihoozuki 95, etc.

Hayden, Harry (1884–1955)
Tubby American character actor who played scores of bankers, clergymen and unassuming family chaps.
I Married a Doctor 36. Black Legion 36. Ever Since Eve 37. Kentucky 38. Angels with Dirty Faces 38. Swanee River 39. Christmas in July 40. The Palm Beach Story 42. Up in Mabel's Room 44. The Killers 46. The Unfinished Dance 47. Intruder in the Dust 49. Double Dynamite 51. Army Bound 52, many others.

Hayden, Linda (1951–)
British leading lady; started by playing teenage sexpots.
Baby Love 69. Taste the Blood of Dracula 69. Satan's Skin 70. Something to Hide 72. Confessions of a Window Cleaner 74. Let's Get Laid 77. Confessions from a Holiday Camp 77. The Boys from Brazil 78, etc.

Hayden, Russell (1912–1981) (Pate Lucid)
American 'second string' leading man, for many years Hopalong Cassidy's faithful sidekick. Later produced TV westerns.
Hills of Old Wyoming (debut) 37. Range War 39. Lucky Legs 42. 'Neath Canadian Skies 46. Seven Were Saved 47. Silver City 49. Valley of Fire 51, many others.
TV series: Cowboy G-Men 52. Judge Roy Bean 55.

Hayden, Sterling (1916–1986) (Sterling Walter Relyea)
Rangy American leading man, part-time explorer and novelist. He began as a sailor and was a ship's captain before becoming an actor. His appearance before HUAC's investigation of Hollywood, in which he admitted to having been a Communist and named others, haunted him in later life, and after sailing his schooner to the South Seas in the late 50s, he showed only perfunctory interest in acting. The first of his three wives was actress Madeleine Carroll (1942-46).
Autobiography: 1963, *Wanderer*. 1978, *Voyage*.
Virginia 40. Bahama Passage 41. Blaze of Noon 47. Variety Girl 47. El Paso 49. Manhandled 49. *The Asphalt Jungle* 50. Flaming Feather 51. Journey into Light 51. Denver and Rio Grande 52. The Golden Hawk 52. The Star 52. Hellgate 52. So Big 53. Johnny Guitar 53. Fighter Attack 53. Prince Valiant 54. Arrow in the Dust 54. Take Me to Town 53. Battle Taxi 54. Shotgun 54. Crime Wave 54. Naked Alibi 54. Suddenly 54. Timberjack 54. The Eternal Sea 55. The Last Command 55. *The Killing* 56. Crime of Passion 56. The Come On 56. Five Steps to Danger 56. Zero Hour 57. Valerie 57. Terror in a Texas Town 58. Dr Strangelove 63. Hard Contract 69. Loving 70. The Godfather 72. The Long Goodbye 73. The Final Programme 73. Cobra 73. Deadly Strangers 74. Is It Any Wonder 75. 1900 76. King of the Gypsies 78. The Outsider 79. Winter Kills 79. Nine to Five 80. Venom 81. Lighthouse of Chaos 83. Voyager 84, etc.
❝ If I had the dough, I'd buy up the negative of every film I ever made … and start one hell of a fire. – *S.H.*
I don't think there are many other businesses where you can be paid good money and not know what you're doing. – *S.H.*
I started at the top and worked my way down. – *S.H.*

Haydn, Richard (1905–1985)
British revue star of the 30s, in Hollywood from 1941, usually in adenoidal character cameos. He performed in revue and on radio from the 30s as Professor Edwin Carp, the world's only fish mimic.
Ball of Fire (debut) 41. Charley's Aunt 41. Forever and a Day 43. And Then There Were None 45. *Cluny Brown* 46. *Sitting Pretty* 47. Miss Tatlock's Millions (& d) 48. Mr Music (& d) 50. Dear Wife (d only) 50. Jupiter's Darling 54. Please Don't Eat the Daisies 60. *The Lost World* 60. Mutiny on the Bounty 62. Five Weeks in a Balloon 62. The Sound of Music 65. Clarence the Cross-Eyed Lion 65. The Adventures of Bullwhip Griffin 66. Young Frankenstein 74, many others.

Haye, Helen (1874–1957) (Helen Hay)
Distinguished British stage actress (debut 1898), in occasional films, usually as kindly dowager.
Tilly of Bloomsbury 21. Atlantic 30. Congress Dances 31. *The Spy in Black* 39. Kipps 41. *Dear Octopus* 43. Anna Karenina 48. Richard III 56, many others.

Hayek, Salma (1969–)
Mexican leading actress, of Lebanese and Spanish parents. She has her own production company Ventanarosa. She has been romantically linked with English actor Edward Atterton.
Midaq Alley/El Callejón de los Milagros 95. Desperado 95. Four Rooms 95. From Dusk till Dawn 95. Fair Game 95. Fled 96. Fools Rush In 97. The Hunchback of Notre Dame (TV) 97. The Velocity of Gary 98. 54 98. The Faculty 98. Dogma 99. Wild Wild West 99. Timecode 00. Living It Up/La Gran Vida (Sp.) 00, etc.

Hayers, Sidney (1921–2000)
British director, in films since 1942. Former editor and second unit director.
■ Violent Moment 58. The White Trap 59. Circus of Horrors 59. Echo of Barbara 60. The Malpas Mystery 60. *Payroll* 61. *Night of the Eagle* 62. This Is My Street 63. Three Hats for Lisa 65. The Trap 66. Finders Keepers 66. The Southern Star 69. Mr Jerico 69. The Firechasers 70. Assault 71. Revenge 71. All Coppers Are … 72. Deadly Strangers 74. What Changed Charley Farthing 74. Diagnosis Murder (TV) 74. One Way 76. The Seekers (TV) 78. The Last Convertible (TV) 79. Condominium (TV) 80.

Hayes, Alfred (c. 1911–1985)
American screenwriter.
Paisa 46. Clash by Night 51. Teresa (co-w, AAN) 51. Act of Love 54. The Left Hand of God 55. The Double Man 67, etc.

Hayes, Allison (1930–1977) (Mary Jane Hayes)
American leading lady of a few films in the 50s.
Francis Joins the WACs 54. The Purple Mask 55. The Blackboard Jungle 55. Mohawk 56. The Zombies of Mora Tau 57. Attack of the Fifty-Foot Woman (title role) 58. Who's Been Sleeping in My Bed? 63. Tickle Me 65.
TV series: Acapulco 60.

Hayes, George 'Gabby' (1885–1969)
Bewhiskered American character comedian, in minor westerns from silent days. Born in Wellsville, New York, he began in theatre and vaudeville, becoming best known in the mid to late 30s as Hopalong Cassidy's sidekick Windy Halliday, before teaming up with 'Wild Bill' Elliott, and with Roy Rogers for much of the 40s.
The Rainbow Man 29. Beggars in Ermine 34. The Lost City 35. Three on the Trail 36. Mountain Music 37. Hopalong Rides Again 38. Gold is Where You Find It 38. Man of Conquest 39. Wagons Westward 40. Melody Ranch 41. In Old Oklahoma 43. Tall in the Saddle 44. Utah 45. My Pal Trigger 46. Wyoming 47. Return of the Badmen 48. El Paso 49. The Cariboo Trail 50, many others.
TV series: The Gabby Hayes Show 50.

Hayes, Helen (1900–1993) (Helen Hayes Brown)
Distinguished American stage actress who made a number of film appearances. She was married to writer Charles MacArthur.
Autobiography: 1965, *A Gift of Joy*. 1969, *On Reflection*. 1981, *Twice Over Lightly*.
Biography: 1985, *Helen Hayes – First Lady of the American Theatre* by Kenneth Barrow.
The Weavers of Life 17. *The Sin of Madelon Claudet* (AA) 31. Arrowsmith 31. *A Farewell to Arms* 32. The Son Daughter 33. The White Sister 33. Another Language 33. Night Flight 33. What Every Woman Knows 34. Crime without Passion (unbilled) 34. Vanessa 35. Stage Door Canteen 43. My Son John 51. Main Street to Broadway 53. *Anastasia* 56. Third Man on the Mountain (unbilled) 59. *Airport* (AA) 69. Do Not Fold Spindle or Mutilate (TV) 71. Herbie Rides Again 73. The Snoop Sisters (TV) 73 (and series). One of Our Dinosaurs Is Missing 75. Victory at Entebbe (TV) 76. Candleshoe 77. A Family Upside Down (TV) 78. The Moneychangers (TV) 79. Murder Is Easy (TV) 82. A Caribbean Mystery (TV) 83. Murder with Mirrors (TV) 84, etc.
TV series: The Snoop Sisters 73–74.
❝ An actor's life is so transitory. Suddenly you're a building. – *H.H. (on having a theatre named after her)*

Hayes, Isaac (1942–)
American composer, singer and actor.
Shaft (AAs, AANm) 71. Shaft's Big Score (co-m) 72. Wattstax (doc) 73. Save the Children (doc) 73. Three Tough Guys (a, m) 74. Truck Turner (a, m) 74. Escape from New York 81. I'm Gonna Git You Sucka 88. Guilty as Charged 91. Prime Target 91. Robin Hood: Men in Tights 93. Posse 93. Acting on Impulse 93. It Could Happen to You 94. Oblivion 94. Flipper 96. Six Ways to Sunday 98. South Park: Bigger Longer & Uncut (voice) 99. Ninth Street (&co-m) 99. Shaft (co-m) 00. Reindeer Games 00, etc.

Hayes, John Michael (1919–)
American screenwriter.
Rear Window (AAN) 54. To Catch a Thief 55. The Trouble with Harry 56. Peyton Place (AAN) 57. *The Carpetbaggers* 63. Where Love Has Gone 64. Harlow 65. Judith 66. Nevada Smith 66. Iron Will (co-w) 94, etc.

Hayes, Margaret (1915–1977)
American character actress, also in TV and public relations.

The Blackboard Jungle 55. Violent Saturday 55. Omar Khayyam 57. Fraulein 57. Damn Citizen 58, etc.

Hayes, Melvyn (1935–)
British comedy character actor, a former child star who was part of Cliff Richards' support in *The Young Ones*, *Summer Holiday*, etc; later became familiar on TV in *It Ain't Half Hot Mum*.

The Curse of Frankenstein 56. No Trees in the Street 58. The Young Ones 61. Summer Holiday 62. Wonderful Life 64. A Walk with Love and Death 69. Love Thy Neighbour 73. Carry on England 76. Santa Claus 85. King of the Wild 89, etc.

TV series: Here Come the Double Deckers 71. Sir Yellow 73. It Ain't Half Hot Mum (as Bombardier 'Gloria' Beaumont) 74–81. Potter's Picture Palace 76.

Hayes, Patricia (1909–1998)
British character actress, mainly in low-life comedy roles. Much on TV. She was the mother of actor Richard O'Callaghan (1945–).

Candles at Nine 44. Nicholas Nickleby 46. The Love Match 54. The Battle of the Sexes 59. Goodbye Mr Chips 69. Love Thy Neighbour 73. The Corn Is Green (TV) 79. The Never Ending Story 84. Little Dorrit 87. The Last Island 91. Blue Ice 92. The Steal 95, etc.

TV series: The Arthur Askey Show 61. Hugh and I 62–64. Till Death Us Do Part 81. Spooner's Patch 82. The Lady Is a Tramp 84. Marjorie and Men 85.

Hayes, Terry
Australian screenwriter and producer.

Mad Max II/The Road Warrior (co-w) 81. Mad Max beyond Thunderdrome (co-p, co-w) 85. Dead Calm (p, co-w) 89. Flirting (p) 89. The Saint (w) 97, etc.

Haygarth, Tony (1945–)
Bearded English character actor. Born in Liverpool, he worked as a psychiatric nurse before becoming an actor in the mid-60s.

Percy 70. Unman, Wittering and Zigo 71. Let's Get Laid 77. Dracula 79. The Human Factor 79. SOS Titanic (TV) 79. McVicar 80. A Private Function 84. A Month in the Country 87. The Dressmaker 88. Tree of Hands 88. London Kills Me 91. The Trial 92. Prince of Jutland 94. The Infiltrator (TV) 95. Amy Foster 97. The Woodlanders 97. Chicken Run (voice) 00, etc.

TV series: Rosie 75–81. Kinvig 81. Round and Round 84. Farrington of the FO 86–87. Hardwicke House 87. All Change 89–91. El CID 90–92. The Borrowers 93. Where the Heart Is 97– .

Hayles, Brian (1930–1978)
British scriptwriter, from TV.

Warlords of Atlantis 78. Arabian Adventure 79.

Hayman, David (1950–)
Scottish actor and director.

AS ACTOR: A Sense of Freedom (TV) 79. Sid and Nancy 86. Heavenly Pursuits 86. Hope and Glory 87. Venus Peter 89. Rob Roy 95. Regeneration 97. The Jackal 97. My Name Is Joe 98. The Match 99. Ordinary Decent Criminal 00. Unknown Things 00. Tough Love (TV) 00. Trial and Retribution IV (TV) 00. Vertical Limit (US) 00, etc.

AS DIRECTOR: Silent Scream 90. Black and Blue (TV) 92. The Hawk 93. A Woman's Guide to Adultery (TV) 93. The Near Room (& a) 95, etc.

Haymes, Dick (1918–1980)
High-living, heavy-drinking Argentine-born singer and actor. Born in Buenos Aires, he was one of the best crooners of the 40s, singing with the bands of Harry JAMES, Benny GOODMAN and Tommy DORSEY, and went on to make many hit recordings. Died of cancer. His seven wives included actress Joanne DRU (1941–49) and actress Rita HAYWORTH (1953–55).

Irish Eyes Are Smiling (debut) 44. Diamond Horseshoe 45. *State Fair* 45. Do You Love Me? 46. The Shocking Miss Pilgrim 47. Up in Central Park 48. One Touch of Venus 48. St Benny the Dip 51. All Ashore 53. Betrayal (TV) 74, etc.

Haynes, Todd (1961–)
American independent director and editor. He first attracted attention with *Superstar: The Karen Carpenter Story*, a short made in 1987 about the pop singer's life and anorexic death, in which he used Barbie dolls instead of live actors.

Poison 91. *Safe* 95. Office Killer (dialogue) 97. Velvet Goldmine 98, etc.

Hays, Robert (1947–)
American leading man of the early 80s.

The Young Pioneers (TV) 76. Delta County USA (TV) 78. The Initiation of Sarah (TV) 78. The Fall of the House of Usher (TV) 79. Airplane 80. Take This Job and Shove It 81. Airplane 2: The Sequel 82. Trenchcoat 83. Touched 83. Scandalous! 84. Cat's Eye 85. Murder by the Book 87. Honeymoon Academy 90. Fifty/Fifty 91. Homeward Bound II: Lost in San Francisco 96. Dr T & the Women 00, etc.

Hays, Will H. (1879–1954)
American executive, for many years (1922–45) president of the Motion Picture Producers and Distributors Association of America, and author of its high-toned Production Code (1930), which for many years put producers in fear of 'the Hays Office'.

Autobiography: 1955, *The Memoirs of Will Hays*.

❝ Good taste is good business. – *W.H. (1930)*

Haysbert, Dennis (1954–)
American actor

K 9000 89. Major League 89. Navy SEALS 90. Mr Baseball 92. Love Field 92. Return to Lonesome Dove (TV) 93. Suture 93. Major League II 94. Heat 95. Waiting to Exhale 95. Absolute Power 97. Stand Off 97. How to Make the Cruelest Month 98. Major League: Back to the Minors 98. Random Hearts 99. The Thirteenth Floor 99. Love & Basketball 00, etc.

TV series: Now and Again 99- .

Hayter, James (1907–1983)
Portly, jovial British character actor, on stage from 1925, films from 1936.

Sensation 36. Sailors Three 41. School for Secrets 46. *Nicholas Nickleby* (as the Cheeryble twins) 47. The Blue Lagoon 48. *Trio* 50. Tom Brown's Schooldays 51. Robin Hood (as Friar Tuck) 52. *Pickwick Papers* (title role) 53. The Great Game 53. A Day to Remember 54. Touch and Go 56. Port Afrique 58. The Thirty-Nine Steps 59. Stranger in the House 67. Oliver 68. David Copperfield 69. Song of Norway 70, many others.

TV series: Are You Being Served? 78.

Haythorne, Joan (1915–) (Joan Haythornthwaite)
British stage actress, usually in aristocratic roles.

School for Secrets 46. Jassy 47. Highly Dangerous 50. Svengali 54. The Weak and the Wicked 54. The Feminine Touch 56. Three Men in a Boat 56. Shakedown 59. So Evil So Young 61. The Battleaxe 62. Countess Dracula 70, etc.

Hayton, Lennie (1908–1971)
American composer.

The Bugle Sounds 41. Meet the People 43. Salute to the Marines 43. The Harvey Girls 45. Summer Holiday 46. The Hucksters 47. The Pirate 48. Battleground 49. On the Town (co-w) (AA) 49. Inside Straight 51. Singin' in the Rain 52. Battle Circus 53. Star! (AAN) 68. Hello Dolly (co-w) (AA) 69, etc.

Hayward, Leland (1902–1971)
American talent agent and stage producer. Also produced films. Born in Nebraska City, Nebraska, he began as a publicist for United Artists and a writer for First National before becoming a successful agent. His second wife was actress Margaret SULLAVAN (1936–48).

Mister Roberts 55. The Spirit of St Louis 57. The Old Man and the Sea 58, etc.

❝ Leland's disdain for movies earned him quickly the respect of the movie makers – particularly the front-office bosses who did the buying. They felt that a man so full of sneer for their product must be peddling a superior kind of wares. This wasn't true. All that Leland peddled was a superiority complex – and the same old plots. – *Ben Hecht*

Hayward, Louis (1909–1985) (Seafield Grant)
Mild-mannered, South African-born leading man with stage experience; in Hollywood from 1935. He was formerly married to Ida Lupino.

Chelsea Life (GB) 33. The Man Outside (GB) 33. I'll Stick to You (GB) 33. The Thirteenth Candle (GB) 33. The Love Test (GB) 34. *Sorrell and Son* (GB) 34. The Flame Within 35. Anthony Adverse 36. The Luckiest Girl in the World 36. Midnight Intruder 37. The Rage of Paris 38. *The Saint in New York* 38. *Duke of West Point* 39. *The Man in the Iron Mask* 39. My Son, My Son 40. Son of Monte Cristo 40. Ladies in Retirement 41. And Then There Were None 45. Monte Cristo's Revenge 47. Young Widow 47. Repeat Performance 47. The Black Arrow 48. Walk a Crooked Mile 48. Pirates of Capri 49. The Fortunes of Captain Blood 50. House by the River 50. Son of Dr Jekyll 51. The Lady and the Bandit 51. Lady in the Iron Mask 52. Captain Pirate 52. Royal African Rifles 53. The Saint's Return (GB) 53. Duffy of San Quentin 54. *The Search for Bridey Murphy* 56. Chuka 67. Terror in the Wax Museum 73, etc.

TV series: The Lone Wolf 53. The Pursuers 63. The Survivors 69.

Hayward, Susan (1918–1975) (Edythe Marrener)
Red-haired, vivacious American leading actress, often in aggressive roles. Born in Brooklyn, she began as a model before going to Hollywood to make a screen test for the role of Scarlett O'Hara in *Gone with the Wind*. She stayed to rid herself of her accent and to learn how to act, beginning with minor roles in Warner films. She was then signed to a seven-year contract by Paramount, whose executives found her difficult and retaliated by giving her poor parts to play. She tried Twentieth Century-Fox, who provided her mainly with a series of uninteresting roles. Her big breakthrough came with *I'll Cry Tomorrow*, about troubled singer Lillian ROTH: during the making of the film she attempted suicide. The first of her two husbands was actor Jess BARKER (1944–54); she was romantically involved with actors John Carroll and Don BARRY.

Biography: 1974, *Divine Bitch* by Doug McClelland. 1985, *Red: The Tempestuous Life of Susan Hayward* by Robert Laguardia and Gene Arceri.

■ Girls on Probation 38. Our Leading Citizen 39. $1000 A Touchdown 39. Beau Geste 39. Adam Had Four Sons 41. Sis Hopkins 41. Among the Living 41. Reap the Wild Wind 42. The Forest Rangers 42. I Married a Witch 42. Star Spangled Rhythm 42. Change of Heart 43. Jack London 43. Young and Willing 43. The Fighting Seabees 44. And Now Tomorrow 44. The Hairy Ape 44. Canyon Passage 45. Deadline at Dawn 46. Smash-Up (AAN) 47. They Won't Believe Me 47. The Lost Moment 47. Tap Roots 48. The Saxon Charm 48. *Tulsa* 49. *My Foolish Heart* (AAN) 49. House of Strangers 49. I'd Climb the Highest Mountain 50. *I Can Get It For You Wholesale* 51. Rawhide 51. David and Bathsheba 51. *With a Song in My Heart* (AAN) 52. The Lusty Men 52. The Snows of Kilimanjaro 52. The President's Lady 53. White Witch Doctor 53. Demetrius and the Gladiators 54. Garden of Evil 54. Untamed 55. Soldier of Fortune 55. The Conqueror 55. *I'll Cry Tomorrow* (as Lillian Roth) (AAN) 55. Top Secret Affair 57. *I Want to Live* (as Barbara Graham) (AA) 58. A Woman Obsessed 59. Thunder in the Sun 59. The Marriage-Go Round 60. Ada 61. Back Street 61. Stolen Hours (GB) 63. I Thank a Fool (GB) 63. Where Love Has Gone 64. The Honey Pot 67. Valley of the Dolls 67. Fitzgerald and Pride (TV) 71. Heat of Anger (TV) 71. The Revengers 72. Say Goodbye Maggie Cole (TV) 72.

Haywood, Chris (1949–)
English character actor, in Australia.

Newsfront 78. In Search of Anna 79. Kostas 79. The Clinic 82. Heatwave 82. The Return of Captain Invincible 82. Man of Flowers 83. Strikebound 84. Razorback 84. A Street to Die 85. Malcolm 85. Burke and Wills 85. Dogs in Space 87. Manifesto 88. The Tale of Ruby Rose 88. Emerald City 89. Island 89. Quigley Down Under 90. Golden Braid 91. Sweet Talker 91. A Woman's Tale 91. Alex 93. Exile 94. Erotic Tales 94. Muriel's Wedding 94. Shine 96. Lust and Revenge 96. Kiss or Kill 97. Blackrock 97. Molokai 98, etc.

TV series: The Boys from the Bush 91.

Hayworth, Rita (1918–1987) (Margarita Carmen Cansino)
Star American leading actress and dancer of the 40s, often in tempestuous roles, who became a sex symbol of the age with her performance in *Gilda*. Born in Brooklyn, New York, she was the daughter of an American mother and a Spanish gypsy father, whose dancing had topped the bill in vaudeville. She began as a 12-year-old, in a dance act with her sexually abusive father, before being briefly contracted to Fox as a replacement for Dolores DEL RIO. Columbia then signed her, but her success came only after her exploitative first husband made her lose weight, lighten her hair and raise her hairline. Often insecure with dialogue, she was at her best in roles that exploited her dancer's expressive movement: as Judy McPherson in *Only Angels Have Wings*; as Natalie Roguin in *The Lady in Question*; as Virgina Brush in *The Strawberry Blonde*; as Gilda Munson in *Gilda*; as Elsa Bannister in Orson Welles's *The Lady from Shanghai*; and as Sadie Thompson in *Miss Sadie Thompson*. Surprisingly, despite her ability, she was an uneasy partner for Fred Astaire in the two films they made together: *You'll Never Get Rich* and *You Were Never Lovelier*. She suffered from Alzheimer's disease from the early 70s, looked after by her daughter with Prince Aly Khan, Princess Yasmin, and was played by Lynda Carter in the 1983 TV movie, *Rita Hayworth: The Love Goddess*. Married Orson WELLES (1943–48), Aly Khan (1949–53), singer Dick HAYMES (1953–55), and producer James HILL (1958–61); she was romantically involved with actors Victor MATURE, David NIVEN and Gary MERRILL, singer Tony MARTIN, and producers Howard HUGHES and Charles FELDMAN.

Biography: 1983: *Rita: The Life of Rita Hayworth* by Edward J. Epstein and Joseph Morella. 1983, *Rita Hayworth: A Memoir* by James Hill. 1989, *If This Was Happiness: Rita Hayworth* by Barbara Leaming.

■ Dante's Inferno 35. Under the Pampas Moon 35. Charlie Chan in Egypt 35. Paddy O'Day 35. Human Cargo 36. A Message to Garcia 36. Meet Nero Wolfe 36. Rebellion 36. Old Louisiana 37. Hit the Saddle 37. Trouble in Texas 37. Criminals of the Air 37. Girls Can Play 37. The Game that Kills 37. Paid to Dance 37. The Shadow 37. Who Killed Gail Preston? 38. There's Always a Woman 38. Convicted 38. Juvenile Court 38. Homicide Bureau 38. The Lone Wolf's Spy Hunt 39. Renegade Ranger 39. *Only Angels Have Wings* 39. Special Inspector 39. Music in My Heart 40. Blondie on a Budget 40. Susan and God 40. *The Lady in Question* 40. Angels over Broadway 40. *The Strawberry Blonde* 41. Affectionately Yours 41. Blood and Sand 41. *You'll Never Get Rich* 41. My Gal Sal 42. Tales of Manhattan 42. You Were Never Lovelier 42. *Cover Girl* 44. Tonight and Every Night 45. *Gilda* 46. Down to Earth 47. *The Lady from Shanghai* 48. The Loves of Carmen 48. Affair in Trinidad 52. Salome 53. *Miss Sadie Thompson* 53. Fire Down Below 57. *Pal Joey* 57. *Separate Tables* 58. They Came to Cordura 59. The Story on Page One 59. The Happy Thieves 62. Circus World 64. The Money Trap 66. The Poppy is also a Flower 66. The Rover 68. Sons of Satan 68. The Road to Salina 70. The Naked Zoo 71. The Wrath of God 72.

✪ For supplying the kind of glamour the 40s needed, and for doing it with the saving grace of humour. *Gilda*.

❝ Every man I knew had fallen in love with Gilda and wakened with me. – *R.H.*

A girl is … a girl. It's nice to be told you're successful at it. – *R.H.*

I haven't had everything from life. I've had too much. – *R.H.*

I never really thought of myself as a sex symbol – more as a comedienne who could dance. – *R.H.*

Hazell, Hy (1920–1970) (Hyacinth Hazel O'Higgins)
British revue and musical comedy artist.

Meet Me at Dawn 46. Paper Orchid 49. Celia 49. The Lady Craved Excitement 50. The Night Won't Talk 52. Up in the World 56. The Whole Truth 58, etc.

Hazlehurst, Noni (1954–)
Australian leading actress.

The Getting of Wisdom 77. Fatty Finn 80. *Monkey Grip* 82. Waterfront (TV) 83. Fran 85. Australian Dream 85. True Colours 87. Waiting 90. Clowning Around 92, etc.

Head, Edith (1907–1981)
American dress designer, in Hollywood from the 20s. First solo credit *She Done Him Wrong* 33; later won Academy Awards for The Heiress 49. Samson and Delilah 51. A Place in the Sun 52, etc; worked on Olly Olly Oxen Free 78. Appeared in *The Oscar* 66.

Autobiography: 1940, *The Dress Doctor*.

Other books: 1983, *Edith Head's Hollywood* (with Paddy Calistro).

The Oregon Trail 59. Master of the World 61. The Fool Killer 64. The Chase 66, etc.

Hull, Josephine (1884–1957) (Josephine Sherwood)
Bubbly little American character actress who gave two memorable film performances, repeating her long-running stage roles. Born in Newtonville, Massachusetts, she began on stage in Boston in 1905.
Her best screen performances were as Abby Brewster in *Arsenic and Old Lace*; and Veta Louise Simmons in *Harvey*.
■ After Tomorrow 32. Careless Lady 32. *Arsenic and Old Lace* 44. *Harvey* (AA) 50. The Lady from Texas 51.
❝ Famous line (*Harvey*) 'Myrtle Mae, you have a lot to learn, and I hope you never learn it.'

Hull, Warren (1903–1974)
American leading man of many second features: also radio hero of such serials as *Mandrake the Magician* and *The Spider*. Born in Niagara Falls, New York, he began on stage in musicals.
Miss Pacific Fleet 35. Personal Maid's Secret 35. The Walking Dead 36. Night Key 37. Hawaii Calls 38. The Spider's Web 38. Mandrake the Magician 39. The Lone Wolf Meets a Lady 41. The Spider Returns 41, etc.

Hulme, Kathryn C. (1900–1981)
Author of *The Nun's Story*, which was filmed with Audrey Hepburn playing her.

Humberstone, H. Bruce (1903–1984)
American director, a competent craftsman of action films and musicals. Born in Buffalo, New York, he began as an actor.
If I Had a Million (part) 32. The Crooked Circle 32. Charlie Chan in Honolulu 37. Pack Up Your Troubles 39. Lucky Cisco Kid 40. Tall, Dark and Handsome 41. *Sun Valley Serenade* 41. Hot Spot 41. To the Shores of Tripoli 42. *Hello, Frisco Hello* 43. *Wonder Man* 45. Three Little Girls in Blue 46. *Fury at Furnace Creek* 48. East of Java 49. Happy Go Lovely (GB) 51. She's Working Her Way Through College 52. The Desert Song 53. The Purple mask 55. Tarzan and the Lost Safari 57. Madison Avenue 61, etc.
❝ He was known as Lucky Humberstone, for the very good reason he somehow continued to find work in Hollywood despite the fact that he had so small a talent. – *Milton Sperling*

Hume, Alan (1924–)
British cinematographer.
The Legend of Hell House 72. Carry on Girls 73. The Land that Time Forgot 74. Trial by Combat 76. Bear Island 80. The Eye of the Needle 81. For Your Eyes Only 81. Return of the Jedi 83. Octopussy 83. Supergirl 84. A View to a Kill 85. Lifeforce 85. Runaway Train 85. The Second Victory 87. Hearts of Fire 87. A Fish Called Wanda 88. Without a Clue 88. Shirley Valentine 89. Eve of Destruction 91. Just Like a Woman 95, etc.

Hume, Benita (1906–1967)
British leading actress of the 30s, who was in Hollywood from 1935. Born in London, she trained at RADA and was on stage from 1924. Retired to marry actor Ronald Colman, her second husband. Following his death she married actor George Sanders. Died of cancer.
The Constant Nymph 28. High Treason 29. Lord Camber's Ladies 32. Service for Ladies 32. Gambling Ship 33. The Little Damozel 33. Looking Forward 33. Only Yesterday 33. The Worst Woman in Paris 33. Jew Suss 34. The Private Life of Don Juan 34. The Gay Deception 35. Rainbow on the River 36. Suzy 36. Tarzan Escapes 36. The Last of Mrs Cheyney 37. Peck's Bad Boy with the Circus 38, etc.
TV series: Halls of Ivy 55.

Hume, Cyril (1900–1966)
British screenwriter and novelist in Hollywood. He is credited with suggesting Johnny Weismuller for the role of Tarzan. Married (1930-1934) actress Helen Chandler.
Wife of the Centaur (oa) 24. Daybreak 31. Tarzan the Ape Man 32. *Flying Down to Rio* 33. Affairs of a Gentleman 34. Limehouse Blues 34. The Jungle Princess 36. Tarzan Escapes 36. Bad Man of Brimstone 37. Live, Love and Learn 37. They Gave Him a Gun 37. Tarzan Finds a Son! 39. The Bugle Sounds 41. High Barbaree 47. Bride of Vengeance 48. Tokyo Joe 49. Branded 50. Tarzan's Savage Fury 52. Ransom 55. Bigger than Life 56. *Forbidden Planet* 56. Invisible Boy 57. The Killers of Kilimanjaro 59, etc.

Hume, Kenneth (1926–1967)
British producer, former editor.
Cheer the Brave (wpd) 50. Hot Ice (wd) 51. Sail into Danger (wd) 57. Mods and Rockers (d) 64. I've Gotta Horse (d) 65, etc.

Humphries, Barry (1934–)
Australian entertainer, aesthete and novelist, best known for his stage and television performances as his alter egos, Dame Edna Everage, Sir Les Patterson and Sandy Stone, characters that have not transferred happily to the big screen. His *Private Eye* comic strip, 'Barry McKenzie', was also the basis of a film.
Autobiography: 1992, *More Please*.
The Adventures of Barry McKenzie 72. Barry McKenzie Holds His Own 74. The Getting of Wisdom 77. Les Patterson Saves the World 87. The Leading Man 96, etc.

Hung, Sammo (1950–) (Hong Jinbao)
Hong Kong director, screenwriter and plump but agile leading actor of martial arts and comedy movies. *Painted Faces* is an autobiographical film based on his life from the age of seven to 17, training as a member of a traditional Chinese theatre group, where a fellow pupil was his frequent co-star Jackie Chan. Most recently, he starred in the TV series *Martial Law*.
Education of Love 61. Father and Son 63. The Fast Sword 70. The Valiant Ones 74. Iron Fisted Monk (& d) 77. Warriors Two 77. Enter the Fat Dragon 78. Spooky Encounters (& d) 80. Ghost against Ghost/Gui da Gui (& co-w, d) 81. The Prodigal Son 81. Carry On Pickpocket 82. Prodigal Son 83. Winners and Sinners (& d) 83. The Dead and the Deadly 83. Wheels on Meals (& d) 84. Project A 84. Twinkle, Twinkle, Lucky Stars (& d) 85. Eastern Condors 87. Dragons Forever 88. Painted Faces 89. Pantyhose Hero 91. The Prisoner 91. Moon Warriors 92. The Eagle Shooting Heroes: Dong Cheng Xi Jiu (action director) 93. Mr Nice Guy (d) 97, many others.
TV series: Martial Law 98– 00.

Hung, Tran Anh (1962–)
Vietnamese director, now resident in France.
Scent of Green Papaya (AAN) 93. Cyclo 95. At the Height of Summer/A La verticale de L'Ete 00.

Hunnicutt, Arthur (1911–1979)
American actor of slow-speaking country characters.
Wildcat 42. Lust for Gold 49. Broken Arrow 50. The Red Badge of Courage 51. The Big Sky (AAN) 52. The French Line 54. The Last Command 56. The Kettles in the Ozarks 56. Apache Uprising 65. Cat Ballou 65. El Dorado 66. Million Dollar Duck 71. The Revengers 72. Harry and Tonto 74. The Spikes Gang 74. Moonrunners 75, etc.

Hunnicutt, Gayle (1942–)
American leading lady of the 60s.
■ The Wild Angels 66. P.J. 68. Marlowe 69. Eye of the Cat 69. Fragment of Fear 70. Freelance 70. Scorpio 72. The Legend of Hell House 72. Running Scared 72. Voices 73. Nuits Rouges 73. The Spiral Staircase 75. Blazing Magnum 76. The Sellout 76. Once In Paris 78. A Man Called Intrepid (TV) 79. The Martian Chronicles (TV) 79. Kiss of Gold (TV) 80. The Return of the Man from UNCLE (TV) 83. The First Modern Olympics (TV) 84. A Woman of Substance (TV) 85. Target 85. Strong Medicine (TV) 86. Dream West (TV) 86. Turnaround 87. Hard to Be a God 87. Silence Like Glass 89.

Hunt, Bonnie (1964–)
American actress, screenwriter and director. Born in Chicago, Illinois, she began as a nurse before deciding to become an actress and working with Chicago's improvisational Second City troupe. She was the creator, writer and an executive producer of the TV sitcoms *The Building* and *The Bonnie Hunt Show*. MGM has signed her to direct further films following the success of her first, *Return to Me*.
Rain Man 88. Beethoven 92. Beethoven's 2nd 93. Only You 94. Jumanji 95. Getting Away with Murder 96. A Bug's Life (voice) 98. Kissing a Fool 98. The Green Mile 99. Random Hearts 99. Return to Me (& co-w, d) 00, etc.
TV series: Grand 90. Davis Rules 92. The Building 93. The Bonnie Hunt Show 95-96.

Hunt, Helen (1963–)
American leading actress who began on television as a child. In 1998 she earned $1m an episode for her TV series *Mad about You*, and also won her third consecutive Emmy as comedy actress. Married actor Hank Azaria in 1999 (separated 2000).
Trancers/Future Cop 85. Girls Just Want to Have Fun 85. Peggy Sue Got Married 86. Project X 87. Miles from Home 88. Stealing Home 88. Next of Kin 89. Trancers II 91. Into the Badlands (TV) 91. The Waterdance 91. Miles from Nowhere (TV) 92. Mr Saturday Night 92. Trancers III 92. Kiss of Death 95. Twister 96. *As Good as It Gets* (AA) 97. Dr T & the Women 00. Pay It Forward 00. Castaway 00. What Women Want 00, etc.
TV series: Amy Prentiss 74–75. Swiss Family Robinson 75–76. The Fitzpatricks 77–78. It Takes Two 82–83. Mad about You 92–99.

Hunt, Linda (1945–)
Diminutive American character actress.
The Year of Living Dangerously (AA) (as a man) 83. The Bostonians 84. Silverado 85. Eleni 85. Dune 85. Waiting for the Moon (as Alice B. Toklas) 87. She-Devil 89. Kindergarten Cop 90. Teen Agent 91. Younger and Younger 93. Twenty Bucks 93. Prêt-à-Porter/Ready to Wear 94. The Relic 96. Pocahontas II: Journey to a New World (voice) 98, etc.
TV series: Space Rangers 93.

Hunt, Marsha (1917–) (Marcia Hunt)
American leading lady who usually plays gentle characters. Married director Jerry Hoppert (1938–45) and writer Robert Presnell Jnr.
Virginia Judge (debut) 35. Hollywood Boulevard 36. The Hardys Ride High 38. These Glamour Girls 39. *Pride and Prejudice* 40. Blossoms in the Dust 41. Kid Glove Killer 42. Seven Sweethearts 42. The Human Comedy 43. *Lost Angel* 43. None Shall Escape 43. Cry Havoc 44. The Valley of Decision 45. A Letter for Evie 45. Carnegie Hall 46. Take One False Step 49. Mary Ryan, Detective 50. The Happy Time 52. No Place to Hide 56. Blue Denim 59. The Plunderers 60. Johnny Got His Gun 71. Rich and Famous 81, etc.
TV series: Peck's Bad Girl 59.

Hunt, Martita (1900–1969)
British stage and screen actress who graduated from nosy spinsters to *grandes dames*.
I Was a Spy (debut) 33. Spare a Copper 39. The Man in Grey 43. The Wicked Lady 45. *Great Expectations* (as Miss Havisham) 46. The Ghosts of Berkeley Square 47. My Sister and I 48. The Fan 49. *Treasure Hunt* 52. Melba 53. Three Men in a Boat 56. Anastasia 56. *Brides of Dracula* 60. The Unsinkable Molly Brown 64. Bunny Lake Is Missing 65, many others.

Hunt, Peter (1928–)
British director, former editor.
■ On Her Majesty's Secret Service 69. Gulliver's Travels 73. Gold 74. Shout at the Devil 76. The Beasts are on the Streets (TV) 78. Flying High (TV) 79. Death Hunt 80. Rendezvous Hotel (TV) 81. The Last Days of Pompeii (TV) 83. Wild Geese II 85. Hyper Sapien 86. Assassination 87.

Hunte, Otto (1883–1847)
German art director, associated with Fritz Lang's films of the 20s. He later worked on Nazi propaganda films, including the notorious *Jew Suess/Jud Süss* 40, and also designed the anti-Nazi *The Murderers Are among Us/Die Mörder Sind unter Uns* 46.
The Slave Ship/Die Spinnen 20. Dr Mabuse the Gambler/Dr Mabuse der Spieler 22. Die Niebelungen 24. Metropolis 26. The Woman in the Moon/Frau im Mond 29. The Blue Angel/Der Blaue Engel 30. Early to Bed 33. Gold 34. Razzia 47, etc.

Hunter, Bill (1940–)
Australian leading actor.
The Man from Hong Kong 75. Eliza Fraser 76. Backroads 77. Newsfront 77. Hard Knocks 80. Gallipoli 80. Heatwave 82. Far East 82. The Return of Captain Invincible 82. The Hit (GB) 84. Street Hero 84. An Indecent Obsession 85. Rebel 85. Death of a Soldier 86. Fever 88. The Last Days of Chez Nous 92. Strictly Ballroom 92. Broken Highway 93. The Custodian 93. The Adventures of Priscilla, Queen of the Desert 94. Muriel's Wedding 94. Everynight … Everynight 94. Race the Sun 96. River Street 96, etc.
TV series: The Dismissal 83.

Hunter, Evan (1926–) (Salvadore Lombino)
American novelist and screenwriter who also writes as Ed McBain.
The Blackboard Jungle (oa) 55. Strangers When We Meet (w) 60. The Young Savages (w) 61. The Birds (w) 63. Mister Buddwing (oa) 66. Walk Proud 79, etc.
TV series: 87th Precinct 61. The Chisholms 78.

Hunter, Glenn (1897–1945)
American leading man of the 20s.
The Case of Becky 21. The Country Flapper 22. Smilin' Through 22. Puritan Passions 23. *Merton of the Movies* 24. West of the Water Tower 24. The Pinch Hitter 25. For Beauty's Sake 41, etc.

Hunter, Holly (1958–)
American leading actress.
The Burning 81. Svengali (TV) 83. Swing Shift 84. Urge to Kill (TV) 84. The End of the Line 87. Crimes of the Heart 87. Raising Arizona 87. A Gathering of Old Men/Murder on the Bayou (TV) 87. Broadcast News (AAN) 87. Animal Behavior 89. Always 89. Roe vs Wade (TV) 89. Miss Firecracker 89. Once Around 90. Crazy in Love 92. The Positively True Adventures of the Alleged Texas Cheerleader-Murdering Mom (TV) 93. The Firm (AAN) 93. *The Piano* (AA) 93. Copycat 95. Home for the Holidays 95. Crash 96. A Life Less Ordinary 97. Living Out Loud 98. Jesus' Son 99. Things You Can Tell Just by Looking at Her 99. O Brother, Where Art Thou? 00. Timecode 00, etc.

Hunter, Ian (1900–1975)
British actor of dependable characters; on stage from 1919, films soon after.
Mr Oddy 22. Not for Sale 24. Confessions 25. The Ring 27. Something Always Happens 31. The Sign of Four (as Dr Watson) 32. Death at Broadcasting House 34. A Midsummer Night's Dream (US) 35. The White Angel (US) 36. Call It a Day (US) 37. *52nd Street* (US) 38. The Adventures of Robin Hood (as King Richard) (US) 38. Tower of London (US) 39. Strange Cargo (US) 40. Bitter Sweet (US) 40. Billy the Kid (US) 41. *Dr Jekyll and Mr Hyde* (as Lanyon) (US) 41. A Yank at Eton (US) 42. Bedelia 46. White Cradle Inn 47. The White Unicorn 48. *Edward My Son* 49. Appointment in London 52. Don't Blame the Stork 53. The Battle of the River Plate 56. Fortune Is a Woman 57. Northwest Frontier 59. The Bulldog Breed 60. Dr Blood's Coffin 61. Guns of Darkness 63, many others.

Hunter, Ian McLellan (1916–1991)
American screenwriter, often in collaboration with Ring Lardner Jnr. Blacklisted in the 50s he wrote for TV under pseudonyms and later taught screenwriting at New York University.
Fisherman's Wharf (co-w) 39. Meet Dr Christian (co-w) 39. Second Chorus (co-w) 40. Slightly Dangerous (co-w) 43. Young Ideas (co-w) 43. The Amazing Dr X/The Spiritualist (co-w) 48. Roman Holiday (AAstory, AANw) 53. The Outside Man (co-w Fr./It.) 72., etc.

Hunter, Jeffrey (1925–1969) (Henry H. McKinnies)
American leading man, in films from 1951 after radio experience. Born in New Orleans, Louisiana, he was educated at Northwestern Univesity and the University of California. Married actresses Barbara Rush (1950-55)., Dusty Bartlett (1957-67), and, in 1969, Emily McLaughlin. Died from injuries to his head after a fall at his home.
Fourteen Hours (debut) 51. Red Skies of Montana 52. Singlehanded 53. White Feather 55. The Searchers 56. A Kiss Before Dying 56. The True Story of Jesse James 57. No Down Payment 57. The Last Hurrah 57. Hell to Eternity 60. *King of Kings* (as Jesus) 61. The Longest Day 62. Vendetta 65. Brainstorm 65. Custer of the West 66. The Private Navy of Sgt O'Farrell 68, many others.
TV series: Temple Houston 63.

Hunter, Kim (1922–) (Janet Cole)
Pert, dependable American leading lady who after brief stage experience started a rather desultory film career, not helped by being blacklisted in the 50s.
The Seventh Victim 43. Tender Comrade 43. When Strangers Marry 44. You Came Along 45. A

Matter of Life and Death (GB) 46. *A Streetcar Named Desire* (AA) 51. *Deadline USA* 52. Anything Can Happen 52. Deadline USA 52. Bermuda Affair 56. Storm Center 56. The Young Stranger 57. Money Women and Guns 59. Lilith 64. Planet of the Apes 68. The Swimmer 68. Beneath the Planet of the Apes 69. Dial Hot Line (TV) 70. In Search of America (TV) 71. Escape from the Planet of the Apes 71. The Magician (TV) 73. Unwed Father (TV) 74. Born Innocent (TV) 74. Bad Ronald (TV) 74. Ellery Queen (TV) 75. The Dark Side of Innocence (TV) 76. Once an Eagle (TV) 76. Backstairs at the White House (TV) 79. The Kindred 87. Two Evil Eyes 89. Midnight in the Garden of Good and Evil 97. A Price Above Rubies 98. Out of the Cold 99. The Hiding Place 00, etc.

Hunter, Ross (1921–1996) (Martin Fuss)
American producer; a former actor, he has specialized in remakes of glossy dramas from Hollywood's golden age, and has seldom failed to make hot commercial properties of them.

AS ACTOR: A Guy a Gal and a Pal 45. Sweetheart of Sigma Chi 47, The Bandit of Sherwood Forest 47. The Groom Wore Spurs 51, etc.

AS PRODUCER: Take Me to Town 53. *Magnificent Obsession* 54. One Desire 55. The Spoilers 55. All that Heaven Allows 56. Battle Hymn 57. My Man Godfrey 57. *Pillow Talk* 58. *Imitation of Life* 59. Portrait in Black 60. Tammy Tell Me True 61. Back Street 61. Flower Drum Song 61. The Thrill of it All 63. The Chalk Garden 64. Madame X 66. The Pad 66. *Thoroughly Modern Millie* 67. *Airport* (AAN) 69. Lost Horizon 73. The Lives of Jenny Dolan (TV) 76. A Family Upside Down (TV) 78. The Best Place to Be (TV) 78. Suddenly Love (TV) 79, etc.

❝ The way life looks in my pictures is the way I want life to be. I don't want to hold a mirror up to life as it is. I just want to show the part which is attractive. – *R.H.*

Hunter, T. Hayes (1881–1944)
American director, in Britain in the 30s.

Desert Gold 19. Earthbound 20. The Triumph of the Scarlet Pimpernel 29. The Silver King 29. The Frightened Lady 32. Sally Bishop 33. *The Ghoul* 33. Warn London 34, etc.

Hunter, Tab (1931–) (Andrew Arthur Kelm)
Athletic American leading man, a teenage rave of the 50s.

The Lawless (debut) 48. Saturday Island 52. Gun Belt 53. Return to Treasure Island 53. *Track of the Cat* 54. Battle Cry 55. The Sea Chase 55. The Burning Hills 56. The Girl He Left Behind 57. Gunman's Walk 57. *Damn Yankees* 58. That Kind of Woman 59. The Pleasure of His Company 60. The Golden Arrow (It.) 62. City under the Sea 65. Birds Do It 66. Hostile Guns 67. Judge Roy Bean 72. The Timber Tramps 73. Grease II 82. Pandemonium 82. Polyester 82. Lust in the Dust 85. Cameron's Closet 87. Grotesque 88. Out of the Dark 88. Dark Horse 92, etc.

TV series: The Tab Hunter Show 60.

Hunter, Tim
American director.

Tex 82. Sylvester 85. River's Edge 87. Paint It Black 89. The Saint of Fort Washington 93, etc.

Huntington, Lawrence (1900–1968)
British director, mainly of routine thrillers.

Suspected Person (& w) 41. Night Boat to Dublin 41. *Wanted for Murder* 46. *The Upturned Glass* 47. When the Bough Breaks 48. *Mr Perrin and Mr Traill* 48. Man on the Run (& w) 49. The Franchise Affair (& w) 51. There Was a Young Lady (& w) 53. Contraband Spain (& w) 55. Stranglehold 62. The Fur Collar (& w, p) 63, etc.

Huntley, Raymond (1904–1990)
British character actor, often of supercilious types or self-satisfied businessmen; on stage from 1922, screen from 1934.

Rembrandt 37. *Night Train to Munich* 40. *The Ghost of St Michael's* 41. School for Secrets 45. Mr Perrin and Mr Traill 48. *Trio* 50. Room at the Top 59. Only Two Can Play 62. Rotten to the Core 65. Hostile Witness 67. Destiny of a Spy (TV) 69. *That's Your Funeral* 73, many others.

Huppert, Isabelle (1955–)
French leading lady in international films. Born in Paris, to a French father and English mother, she studied dramatic arts at the Conservatoire National and Russian at Paris University, and began acting in the city's café-theatres.

Faustine 71. Cesar and Rosalie 72. Les Valseuses 74. Rosebud 75. The Judge and the Assassin 76. *The Lacemaker* 77. *Violette Nozière* 78. Heaven's Gate 80. Sauve Qui Peut 80. Coup de Torchon 81. The Trout 82. Entre Nous/Coup de Foudre 83. My Best Friend's Girl/La Femme de Mon Pote 83. La Garce 84. Cactus 86. The Bedroom Window 87. Migrations 88. Malina 90. Madame Bovary 91. After Love/Après l'Amour 92. Amateur 94. The Flood/L'Inondation 94. A Judgment in Stone/La Cérémonie 95. Elective Affinities 96. Rien Ne Va Plus 97. The School of Flesh/L'école de la Chair 98. No Scandal/Pas De Scandale 99. Les Destinees Sentimentales 00. Son of Two Mothers/Fils De Deux Meres ou Comedie De L'Innocence 00, etc.

Hurd, Gale Anne (1955–)
American producer and screenwriter. She was married to director James CAMERON (1985–89).

The Terminator (& w) 84. Aliens 86. Alien Nation 88. Bad Dreams 88. The Abyss 89. Downtown 90. Tremors 90. Terminator 2: Judgement Day 91. The Waterdance 92. Raising Cain 92. No Escape 94. Safe Passage 94. Virus 99, etc.

❝ When I got to college I decided I was going to be a Marxist. My first B was in Marxist economics, so I decided to become a righteous capitalist. – *G.A.H.*

Hurley, Elizabeth (1966–)
English leading actress, from television. She studied dance at the London Studio and formed her own dance troupe before beginning in the theatre in 1986. She is partner in a production company with her former boyfriend, actor Hugh GRANT.

Rowing with the Wind 87. Aria 88. Passenger 57 92. Beyond Bedlam 94. Mad Dogs and Englishmen 95. Samson and Delilah (TV) 96. Extreme Measures (p) 96. Dangerous Ground 96. *Austin Powers: International Man of Mystery* 97. Permanent Midnight 98. EdTV 99. My Favorite Martian 99. Austin Powers: The Spy Who Shagged Me 99. Mickey Blue Eyes (p) 99. The Weight of Water 00. Bedazzled 00, etc.

❝ I would nationalise Elizabeth Hurley so each of us could claim our share. – *J. G. Ballard*

Hurndall, Richard (1910–1984)
Incisive British character actor.

Joanna 67. I Monster 71. Royal Flash 75. The Prince and the Pauper 77, etc.

Hurok, Sol (1889–1974)
Distinguished American impresario whose life in classical music was recounted in *Tonight We Sing* 53.

Hurrell, George (1904–1992)
Hollywood photographer whose flawless studio portraits of the stars of the 30s and 40s helped to create their images.

Books: 1997, *Hurrell's Hollywood Portraits – The Chapman Collection* by Mark Vieira.

❝ *Marlene Dietrich* (returning photographs to be retouched): You don't take pictures like you did fifteen years ago, George.
GH: But Marlene, I'm fifteen years older!

Hurst, Brandon (1866–1947)
British character actor in Hollywood; better roles in silents than sound films.

Legally Dead 23. *The Hunchback of Notre Dame* 23. He Who Gets Slapped 24. *The Thief of Baghdad* 24. The Grand Duchess and the Waiter 26. Love 27. Interference 29. A Connecticut Yankee 31. White Zombie 32. The Lost Patrol 34. The Charge of the Light Brigade 36. Mary of Scotland 36. If I Were King 38. Stanley and Livingstone 39. If I Had My Way 40. Dixie 43. Jane Eyre 44. House of Frankenstein 44. Devotion 46. Road to Rio 47, many others.

Hurst, Brian Desmond (1900–1986)
Irish director who made many kinds of film.

Sensation 36. Glamorous Night 37. Prison Without Bars 39. On the Night of the Fire 40. *Dangerous Moonlight* 41. Alibi 42. The Hundred Pound Window 43. Theirs Is the Glory 45. Hungry Hill 47. The Mark of Cain 48. Tom Brown's Schooldays (p only) 51. *Scrooge* 51. The Malta Story 53. Simba 55. The Black Tent 56. Dangerous Exile 57. Behind the Mask 58. His and Hers 60. The Playboy of the Western World 62, etc.

Hurst, David (1925–)
Austrian actor who played some comedy roles in British films.

The Perfect Woman 49. So Little Time 52. Mother Riley Meets the Vampire 52. As Long As They're Happy 53. The Intimate Stranger 56. After the Ball 57. Hello Dolly (US) 69. Kelly's Heroes (US) 70. The Boys from Brazil (US) 78, etc.

Hurst, Fannie (1889–1968)
American popular novelist, several of whose romantic novels, usually with a tragic finale, have been filmed more than once: *Humoresque*, *Imitation of Life*, *Back Street*, etc.

Hurst, Paul (1889–1953)
American character actor in hundreds of cameo roles from 1912, usually as gangster, bartender, outlaw or cop. Committed suicide.

The Red Raiders 27. Tugboat Annie 32. Riff Raff 34. Gone with the Wind 39. Caught in the Draft 41. Jack London 44. Yellow Sky 49. The Sun Shines Bright 53, many others.

Hurst, Veronica (1931–)
British light leading lady of the 50s.

Laughter in Paradise 51. Angels One Five 51. The Maze (US) 53. Will Any Gentleman? 53. The Yellow Balloon 54. Peeping Tom 59. Dead Man's Evidence 62. Licensed to Kill 64. The Boy Cried Murder 66, etc.

Hurt, John (1940–)
Off-beat British stage and film leading man.

The Wild and the Willing 62. This is my Street 63. *A Man for all Seasons* 66. The Sailor from Gibraltar 67. Before Winter Comes 69. Sinful Davey 69. In Search of Gregory 70. *10 Rillington Place* 71. Forbush and the Penguins 71. The Pied Piper 72. The Ghoul 74. Little Malcolm and His Struggle against the Eunuchs 74. *The Naked Civil Servant* (TV) 75. I Claudius (TV) 76. East of Elephant Rock 78. The Disappearance 78. The Shout 78. *Midnight Express* (AAN) 78. Spectre (TV) 78. Alien 79. Heaven's Gate 80. *The Elephant Man* (BFA, AAN) 80. Night Crossing 81. History of the World Part One 81. Partners 82. The Osterman Weekend 83. Champions 84. 1984 84. The Hit 84. Success is the Best Revenge 84. Sunset People 84. Jake Speed 86. Rocinante 86. From the Hip 87. Aria 87. Spaceballs 87. Vincent – the Life and Death of Vincent van Gogh 87. White Mischief 87. Little Sweetheart 88. La Nuit Bengali 88. Deadline 89. Scandal 89. Windprints 90. Frankenstein Unbound 90. The Field 90. Resident Alien 91. King Ralph 91. Lapse of Memory/Mémoire Traquée 91. I Dreamt I Woke Up 91. Dark at Noon/La Terreur de Midi 92. Even Cowgirls Get the Blues 93. Monolith 93. Thumbelina (voice) 94. Great Moments in Aviation 94. Second Best 94. Rob Roy 95. Wild Bill 95. Dead Man 95. Brute 96. Contact (US) 97. Love and Death on Long Island 98. All the Little Animals 98. You're Dead… 99. Night Train 99. Lost Souls 00. The Tigger Movie (voice) 00. Captain Corelli's Madolin 01, etc.

TV series: The Storyteller 87–88.

❝ America only makes children's pictures. – *J.H.*
Hollywood is simply geared to cheat you left, right and bloody centre. – *J.H.*

Hurt, Mary Beth (1948–) (Mary Supinger)
American leading lady.

Head over Heels 82. The World According to Garp 82. Compromising Positions 85. D.A.R.Y.L. 85. Parents 89. Slaves of New York 89. Light Sleeper 91. Defenseless 91. My Boyfriend's Back 93. The Age of Innocence 93. Six Degrees of Separation 93. Shimmer 93. From the Journals of Jean Seberg (as Jean Seberg) 95, etc.

Hurt, William (1950–)
American leading actor. With three children from his two marriages, he also has a daughter from a relationship with actress Sandrine BONNAIRE.

Altered States 80. Eyewitness 81. Body Heat 81. The Big Chill 83. Gorky Park 83. *Kiss of the Spider Woman* (AA, BFA) 85. Children of a Lesser God (AAN) 86. Broadcast News (AAN) 87. The Accidental Tourist 88. A Time of Destiny 88. Alice 90. I Love You to Death 90. The Doctor 91. Until the End of the World/Bis ans Ende der Welt 91. The Plague/La Peste 92. Mr Wonderful 93. Second Best 94. Trial by Jury 94. Confidences d'un Inconnu 95. Smoke 95. Secrets Shared with a Stranger 95. A Couch in New York (Fr.) 96. Jane Eyre (as Rochester) 96. Michael 96. Loved 96. Dark City 97. Lost in Space 98. The Proposition 98. One True Thing 98. The Miracle Maker (voice) 99. Sunshine 99 etc.

❝ I think what's taking something away from acting is not the inclusion of special effects, but what the studios have done to actors, which is to take away any rehearsal time. – *W.H.*
Film is not the innate art, theatre is. If all the film in the world burnt down today, you'd still have acting. – *W.H.*
William approaches every movie as if the studios and producers are commerce and he's art. – *Jesse Beaton, producer*

Hussein, Waris (1938–)
Anglo-Indian director, mostly for TV.

■ A Touch of Love 68. Quackser Fortune 69. Melody 71. The Possession of Joel Delaney 72. The Six Wives of Henry VIII 72. Divorce His, Divorce Hers (TV) 73. *The Glittering Prizes* (TV) 75. *Edward and Mrs Simpson* (TV) 78. *Little Gloria … Happy at Last* (TV) 82. Winter of our Discontent (TV) 83. Arch of Triumph (TV) 84. Surviving (TV) 85. Copacabana (TV) 86. When the Bough Breaks (TV) 86. Intimate Contact (TV) 87. Downpayment on Murder (TV) 87. The Richest Man in the World: The Aristotle Onassis Story (TV) 88. Those She Left Behind (TV) 89. She Woke Up 92. The Clothes in the Wardrobe/The Summer House (TV) 93.

Hussey, Olivia (1951–)
British leading lady, born in Argentina. She was married to actor Dean Paul MARTIN.

The Battle of the Villa Fiorita 65. Cup Fever 65. *Romeo and Juliet* 68. All the Right Noises 69. Summertime Killer 72. *Lost Horizon* 73. Black Christmas 75. Jesus of Nazareth (TV) 77. The Cat and the Canary 77. Death on the Nile 78. The Pirate (TV) 79. The Man with Bogart's Face 80. Turkey Shoot 81. Escape 2000 81. Virus 82. The Last Days of Pompeii (TV) 84. The Corsican Brothers (TV) 84. Distortions 87. The Goldsmith's Shop 87. The Undeclared War 90. Psycho IV: The Beginning 90. Save Me 93. Quest of the Delta Knights 93. Ice Cream Man 95, etc.

Hussey, Ruth (1914–) (Ruth Carol O'Rourke)
Smart, competent, sometimes wisecracking American leading lady of the early 40s.

■ Madame X 37. Big City 37. Judge Hardy's Children 38. Man Proof 38. Marie Antoinette 38. Hold that Kiss 38. Rich Man Poor Girl 38. Time Out for Murder 38. Spring Madness 38. Honolulu 39. Within the Law 39. Maisie 39. The Women 39. Another Thin Man 39. Blackmail 39. *Fast and Furious* 39. Northwest Passage 40. Susan and God 40. *The Philadelphia Story* (AAN) 40. Flight Command 40. Free and Easy 41. Our Wife 41. Married Bachelor 41. *H. M. Pulham Esq* 41. Pierre of the Plains 42. Tennessee Johnson 42. Tender Comrade 43. *The Uninvited* 44. Marine Raiders 44. Bedside Manner 45. I Jane Doe 48. The Great Gatsby 49. Louisa 50. Mr Music 50. That's My Boy 51. Woman of the North Country 52. Stars and Stripes Forever 52. The Lady Wants Mink 53. The Facts of Life 60. My Darling Daughter's Anniversary (TV) 72.

Huston, Anjelica (1952–)
American leading lady, daughter of John HUSTON. She was the partner of actor Jack NICHOLSON from the early 70s to 1990. Married sculptor Robert Graham in 1992.

Biography: 1992, *Anjelica Huston – The Lady and Her Legacy* by Martha Harris.

Sinful Davey 69. A Walk with Love and Death 69. The Last Tycoon 76. Swashbuckler 76. The Postman Always Rings Twice 81. Frances 82. The Ice Pirates 84. *Prizzi's Honor* (AA) 85. Good to Go 86. The Dead 87. Gardens of Stone 87. A Handful of Dust 88. Mr North 88. Enemies: A Love Story (AAN) 89. Crimes and Misdemeanors 89. The Grifters (AAN) 90. The Witches 90. The Addams Family 91. The Player 92. Family Pictures (TV) 93. Manhattan Murder Mystery 93. Addams Family Values 93. The Perez Family 95. Buffalo Girls (as Calamity Jane) 95. The Crossing Guard 95. Bastard out of Carolina (d only) 96. Buffalo '66 98. Ever After 98. Agnes Browne (&d) 99. The Golden Bowl 00, etc.

Huston, Danny (1962–)
American director and actor, the son of John Huston.
Bigfoot (d,TV) 87. Mr North (d) 88. Becoming Colette (d) 92. The Maddening (d) 95. Leo Tolstoy's Anna Karenina (a) 97. Ivansxtc (To Live and Die in Hollywood) (a) 00, etc.

Huston, John (1906–1987)
Unpredictable but occasionally splendid American director, son of Walter Huston.
Autobiography: 1981, *An Open Book*.
Biography: 1965, *King Rebel* by W. F. Nolan. 1990, *The Hustons* by Lawrence Grobel.
as screenwriter only: Murders in the Rue Morgue 32. The Amazing Dr Clitterhouse 38. Jezebel 38. High Sierra 40. Dr Ehrlich's Magic Bullet (co-w, AAN) 40. Sergeant York (AAN) 41. Three Strangers 46, etc.
■ as director: *The Maltese Falcon* (& w) 41. In This Our Life 42. Across the Pacific 42. Report from the Aleutians 43. Battle of San Pietro 45. Let There Be Light 45 (four other official war documentaries 44–45). *The Treasure of the Sierra Madre* (& w) (AA) 47. *Key Largo* (& w) 48. We Were Strangers 49. *The Asphalt Jungle* (& w) (AANw, d) 50. The Red Badge of Courage (& w) 51. *The African Queen* (& w) (AAN) 52. Moulin Rouge (& w) (AAN) 53. Beat the Devil (& w) 54. Moby Dick (& w) 56. Heaven Knows Mr Allison (& w) (AANw) 57. The Barbarian and the Geisha 58. The Roots of Heaven (& w) 58. The Unforgiven 60. The Misfits 60. *Freud* 62. The List of Adrian Messenger 63. *The Night of the Iguana* (& w) 64. The Bible 66. Casino Royale (part) 67. Reflections in a Golden Eye 67. Sinful Davey 69. A Walk with Love and Death 69. The Kremlin Letter 70. *Fat City* 72. Judge Roy Bean 72. The Mackintosh Man 73. The Man Who Would Be King (AANw) 75. Wise Blood 79. Phobia 80. Victory 81. Annie 82. Under the Volcano 84. *Prizzi's Honor* (AAN) 85. The Dead 87.
■ as actor: The Treasure of the Sierra Madre (uncredited) 47. The List of Adrian Messenger (uncredited) 63. *The Cardinal* (AAN) 63. *The Bible* (as Noah) 66. Casino Royale 67. Candy 68. A Walk with Love and Death 68. De Sade 69. The Kremlin Letter 70. The Bridge and the Jungle 70. Myra Breckinridge 70. The Deserter 70. Man in the Wilderness 71. Judge Roy Bean 72. Battle for the Planet of the Apes 73. Chinatown 74. Breakout 75. The Wind and the Lion 75. Tentacles 77. Sherlock Holmes in New York (TV) 77. The Word (TV) 78. Winter Kills 79. The Visitor 79. Jaguar Lives 79. Head On 80. Love Sick 83. Young Giants 83.
❝ I don't try to guess what a million people will like. It's hard enough to know what I like. – *J.H.*
I fail to see any continuity in my work from picture to picture. – *J.H.*
I completely storyboarded *The Maltese Falcon* because I didn't want to lose face with the crew: I wanted to give the impression that I knew what I was doing. – *J.H.*
Most of us go through life searching for the unobtainable and if we do get it, we find it's unacceptable. – *J.H.*
There is nothing more fascinating – and more fun – than making movies. Besides, I think I'm finally getting the hang of it. – *J.H. (1984)*

Huston, Walter (1884–1950) (W. Houghston)
Distinguished American character actor of stage and screen: latterly projected roguery and eccentricity with great vigour. He also played bit parts in his son John's first two films, as Captain Jacoby in *The Maltese Falcon* 41, and a bartender in *In This Our Life* 42. After his death his stage recording of 'September Song', played in *September Affair* 50, became a big hit.
Biography: 1998, *September Song* by John Weld.
■ Gentlemen of the Press 28. The Lady Lies 29. *The Virginian* 30. The Bad Man 30. The Virtuous Sin 30. *Abraham Lincoln* 30. The Criminal Code 31. Star Witness 31. The Ruling Voice 31. A Woman from Monte Carlo 31. A House Divided 32. *Law and Order* (as Wyatt Earp) 32. Beast of the City 32. The Wet Parade 32. Night Court 32. *American Madness* 32. Kongo 32. *Rain* 32. Hell Below 32. Gabriel over the White House 33. The Prizefighter and the Lady 33. Storm at Daybreak 33. Ann Vickers 33. Keep 'Em Rolling 33. The Tunnel (GB) 34. Rhodes of Africa (GB) 36. *Dodsworth* (AAN) 36. Of Human Hearts 38. The Light That Failed 39. *All that Money Can Buy* (as the devil) (AAN) 41. Swamp Water 41. The Shanghai Gesture 42. Always in My Heart 42. Yankee Doodle Dandy (AAN) 42. Mission to Moscow 42. Edge of Darkness 42. North Star 43. *The Outlaw* (as Doc Holliday) 43. Dragon Seed 44. *And Then There Were None* 45. Dragonwyck 46. Duel in the Sun 46. *The Treasure of the Sierra Madre* (AA) 47. Summer Holiday 47. The Great Sinner 49. The Furies 50.
✪ For star quality combined with acting ability; whatever the proportions, no audience could look away when he was on screen. *Dodsworth*.
❝ Son, give 'em a good show, and always travel first class. – *W.H.*
Hell, I ain't paid to make good lines sound good. I'm paid to make bad lines sound good. – *W.H.*
Famous line (*All that Money Can Buy*) 'A soul – a soul is nothing. Can you see it, smell it, touch it, no?'

Hutchence, Michael (1960–1997)
Australian rock singer, leader of the the band INXS, and occasional actor. Born in Sydney, he formed the Farris Brothers group with a school-friend in 1979, changing the name to INXS in 1980. He was romantically involved with singer and actress Kylie Minogue, model Helena Christensen, and had a daughter by English TV presenter and journalist Paula Yates. Committed suicide by hanging himself in a hotel room.
Dogs in Space 86. Frankenstein Unbound (as Shelley) (US) 90.

Hutcheson, David (1905–1976)
British light comedian who often played monocled silly-asses, mainly on stage.
This'll Make You Whistle 35. Sabotage at Sea 41. Convoy 42. School for Secrets 46. *Vice Versa* 48. Sleeping Car to Trieste 48. The Elusive Pimpernel 50. The Evil of Frankenstein 64. The National Health 73, etc.

Hutchins, Bobby 'Wheezer' (1920–1945)
American child actor in the Our Gang comedies of the late 20s and early 30s. Died in an accident.

Hutchins, Will (1932–)
Bland-faced American leading man who came to fame in 57–60 as TV's *Sugarfoot*.
No Time for Sergeants 58. Merrill's Marauders 62. The Shooting 66. Clambake 67. Slumber Party '57 77. The Happy Hooker Goes to Washington 77. Roar 81. Maverick 94, etc.

Hutchinson, Josephine (1903–1998)
American actress who usually played sweet or maternal types. Born in Seattle, she was on stage as a dancer from the age of seven, and made her film debut as a child in 1917 before returning to the stage until the 30s. The first of her three husbands was director Robert Bell.
The Little Princess 17. Happiness Ahead 34. The Story of Louis Pasteur 36. Son of Frankenstein 39. Somewhere in the Night 46. Ruby Gentry 52. Miracle in the Rain 56. North By Northwest 59. Huckleberry Finn 60. Baby the Rain Must Fall 64. Nevada Smith 66. Rabbit Run 70, etc.

Huth, Harold (1892–1967)
British light leading man of silent days; later became producer-director.
One of the Best 27. Balaclava 28. The Silver King 29. Leave it to Me 30. The Outsider 31. Sally Bishop 32. Rome Express 32. The Ghoul 33. The Camels are Coming 34. Take My Tip 37. Hell's Cargo (d) 39. East of Piccadilly (d) 40. Busman's Honeymoon (p) 40. Breach of Promise (d) 42. Love Story (p) 44. They Were Sisters (p) 45. Caravan (p) 46. Night Beat £ 47. My Sister and I £ 48. Look Before You Love £ 48. One Wild Oat (p) 51. Police Dog (p) 55. The Hostage (d) 56. Idol on Parade (p) 59. The Trials of Oscar Wilde (p) 60. The Hellions (p) 61, etc.

Hutton, Betty (1921–) (Betty Thornberg)
Blonde and bouncy American leading lady of many singing/dancing light entertainments of the 40s.
■ *The Fleet's In* 42. *Star Spangled Rhythm* 42. Happy Go Lucky 43. Let's Face It 43. *The Miracle of Morgan's Creek* 43. And the Angels Sing 44. Here Come the Waves 44. *Incendiary Blonde* (as Texas Guinan) 45. Duffy's Tavern 45. The Stork Club 45. Cross My Heart 46. *The Perils of Pauline* 47. Dream Girl 48. Red Hot and Blue 49. *Annie Get Your Gun* 50. Let's Dance 50. Somebody Loves Me 52. The Greatest Show on Earth 52. Spring Reunion 57.

Hutton, Brian G. (1935–)
American director.
■ Fargo 65. The Pad 66. Sol Madrid 67. *Where Eagles Dare* 68. Kelly's Heroes 70. Zee and Co 71. Night Watch 73. The First Deadly Sin 80. High Road to China 83. Ryder 89.

Hutton, Jim (1934–1979)
American leading man who usually played gangly types.
A Time to Love and a Time to Die 58. Bachelor in Paradise 61. The Horizontal Lieutenant 62. The Honeymoon Machine 62. Period of Adjustment 63. The Hallelujah Trail 65. Never Too Late 65. *Walk Don't Run* 66. Who's Minding the Mint 67. The Green Berets 68. Hellfighters 69, etc.
TV series: Ellery Queen 74.

Hutton, Lauren (1943–) (Mary Hutton)
American leading lady, a former model.
Little Fauss and Big Halsy 71. The Gambler 74. Welcome to L.A. 77. Viva Knievel 77. Someone's Watching Me! (TV) 78. A Wedding 78. American Gigolo 80. Zorro the Gay Blade 81. Paternity 81. Lassiter 83. Once Bitten 85. Flagrant Desire 85. Marathon 87. Malone 87. Forbidden Sun 88. Fear 89. Guilty As Charged 91. Billions/Miliardi 91. Missing Pieces 92. My Father, the Hero 94. A Rat's Tale 98. 54 98. Just a Little Harmless Sex 99. The Venice Project (as herself) 99, etc.
TV series: The Rhinemann Exchange 77. Paper Dolls 84. Central Park West 95– .

Hutton, Marion (1919–1987) (Marion Thornburg)
American singer, with the Glenn Miller band; appeared in a few 40s musicals. Sister of Betty Hutton.
Orchestra Wives 42. Crazy House 44. In Society 44. Babes on Swing Street 45. Love Happy 50, etc.

Hutton, Robert (1920–1994) (Robert Bruce Winne)
American leading man of the 40s.
Destination Tokyo 44. Janie 44. Too Young To Know 45. Time Out of Mind 47. Always Together 48. The Steel Helmet 51. Casanova's Big Night 54. Invisible Invaders 58. Cinderfella 60. The Slime People (& pd) 62. The Secret Man (GB) 64. Finders Keepers (GB) 66. They Came from Beyond Space (GB) 68. Can Hieronymus Merkin Ever Forget Mercy Humpe and Find True Happiness 68. Cry of the Banshee 70. Trog 70. Tales from the Crypt 72, etc.

Hutton, Timothy (1960–)
Leading young American actor of the early 80s, son of Jim Hutton. He was married to actress Debra Winger (1986–89).
Ordinary People (AA) 80. Taps 81. Daniel 83. Iceman 84. The Falcon and the Snowman 85. Turk 182 85. Made in Heaven 87. A Time of Destiny 87. Everybody's All American/When I Fall in Love 88. Torrents of Spring 89. Q & A 90. The Dark Half 91. The Temp 93. French Kiss 95. Beautiful Girls 96. The Substance of Fire 96. Digging to China (d) 97. Playing God 97. The General's Daughter 99, etc.

Huxley, Aldous (1894–1963)
Distinguished British novelist who spent some time in Hollywood and worked on the screenplays of *Pride and Prejudice* 40 and *Jane Eyre* 43.
Biography: 1989, *Huxley in Hollywood* by David King Dunaway.
❝ His erudition was staggering. I never discovered how many languages he knew, but one day I found him in his office at MGM reading Persian. – *Anita Loos*

Huyck, Willard
American screenwriter and director. He began as a reader for AIP.
American Graffiti (co-w only) 73. Lucky Lady (co-w only) 75. Messiah of Evil 75. French Postcards 79. Best Defence 84. Indiana Jones and the Temple of Doom (co-w only) 84. Howard the Duck 86. Radioland Murders (co-w) 94, etc.

Hyams, Leila (1905–1977)
Vivacious, blonde American leading lady of the 20s.
Sandra 24. Summer Bachelors 26. The Brute 27. The Wizard 27. Alias Jimmy Valentine 28. Spite Marriage 29. The Idle Rich 29. The Bishop Murder Case 30. The Big House 30. The Flirting Widow 30. Men Call It Love 31. The Phantom of Paris 31. Red Headed Woman 32. Freaks 32. Island of Lost Souls 32. Sing Sinner Sing 33. Affairs of a Gentleman 34. Ruggles of Red Gap 35. Yellow Dust 36, many others.

Hyams, Peter (1943–)
American director and cinematographer.
T.R. Baskin (w & p only) 71. The Rolling Man (TV) 72. *Goodnight My Love* (TV) 73. Busting (& w) 74. Our Time (& w) 74. Peeper 76. Telefon (co-w only) 77. Capricorn One (& w) 78. Hanover Street (& w) 79. The Hunter (& w) 80. Outland (& w) 81. The Star Chamber 83. 2010 84. Running Scared 86. The Presidio 88. Narrow Margin 90. Stay Tuned 92. Timecop 94. Sudden Death 95. The Relic 96, etc.

Hyde-White, Wilfrid (1903–1991)
Impeccably British character actor of stage and screen, mainly in comedy roles. Born in Bourton-on-the-Water, Gloucestershire, the son of a canon, he studied acting at RADA and was on stage from 1922. He moved to America in the 60s, at first to appear in *Let's Make Love*, a job that lasted eight months instead of the eight weeks planned because of its star, Marilyn Monroe. Married twice.
Murder by Rope 37. *The Third Man* 49. The Story of Gilbert and Sullivan 54. See How They Run 55. The Adventures of Quentin Durward 56. *North-West Frontier* 59. Carry On Nurse 59. Two-Way Stretch 61. *My Fair Lady* 64. John Goldfarb Please Come Home 64. You Must Be Joking 65. Ten Little Indians 65. The Liquidator 65. Our Man in Marrakesh 66. Chamber of Horrors 66. Skullduggery 69. Gaily Gaily 69. Fragment of Fear 70. A Brand New Life (TV) 73. The Great Houdinis (TV) 76. The Cat and the Canary 78. The Rebels (TV) 79. In God We Trust 80. Oh God Book Two 80. Damien: Leper Priest (TV) 80. The Toy 82, etc.
TV series: Peyton Place 67. The Associates 79–80. Buck Rogers in the 25th Century 81.
❝ I've owned 12 horses, seven Rolls-Royces, and I've had mistresses in Paris, London and New York – and it never made me happy. – *W.H-W.*

Hyer, Martha (1924–)
American light leading lady of the 50s, in mainly routine films.
The Locket 46. The Woman on the Beach 47. The Velvet Touch 48. The Clay Pigeon 49. The Lawless 50. Salt Lake Raiders 50. Abbott and Costello Go to Mars 52. So Big 53. Riders to the Stars 54. Sabrina 54. Francis in the Navy 55. Red Sundown 56. Battle Hymn 57. Mister Cory 57. My Man Godfrey 57. Paris Holiday 58. Houseboat 58. Some Came Running (AAN) 59. The Best of Everything 59. Ice Palace 60. The Last Time I Saw Archie 61. A Girl Named Tamiko 62. Wives and Lovers 63. The Carpetbaggers 64. The First Men in the Moon 64. The Sons of Katie Elder 65. The Chase 66. The Happening 67. Massacre at Fort Grant 68. Crossplot 69. Once You Kiss a Stranger 70, many others.

Hyland, Diana (1936–1977) (Diana Gentner)
American stage and TV actress. At her death she had just begun to star in the TV series *Eight is Enough*.
One Man's Way 64. The Chase 66. The Boy in the Plastic Bubble (TV) 76.

Hylands, Scott (1943–)
Canadian leading man.
Daddy's Gone A-Hunting 68. Fools 70. Earth II (TV) 71. Earthquake 74. Bittersweet Love 76. The Boys in Company C 77. With This Ring (TV) 78. Winds of Kitty Hawk (TV) 78. Tales of the Klondike: In a Far Country (TV) 81. A Savage Hunger 84. Coming Out Alive 84. Decoy 95. Titanic (TV) 96. The Halfback of Notre Dame (TV) 96, etc.
TV series: Night Heat 85–91.

Hylton, Jack (1892–1965)
British bandleader who appeared in two films: *She Shall Have Music* 35 and *Band Wagon* 40. Born in Bolton, Lancashire, he began his career in music hall at the age of 13, billed as 'The Singing Mill Boy', becoming a bandleader in the 30s and, from the 40s, an impresario.

Hylton, Jane (1926–1979)
British actress, in films after 1945.
When the Bough Breaks 47. Here Come the Huggetts 49. *It Started in Paradise* 52. The Weak and the Wicked 53. House of Mystery 59, many others.

Hylton, Richard (1921–1962)
American actor with stage experience.

Lost Boundaries 48. The Secret of Convict Lake 51. Fixed Bayonets 51. The Pride of St Louis 52, etc.

Hyman, Dick (1927–)
American composer and jazz pianist who has scored three of Woody Allen's films.

Scott Joplin 77. Zelig 83. Broadway Danny Rose 83. Radio Days 87. Leader of the Band 87. Moonstruck 87. Alan & Naomi 92. Everyone Says I Love You 96, etc.

Hyman, Eliot (1905–1980)
American entrepreneur who made a fortune from buying up Hollywood libraries for sale to television, notably Monogram and Warner. Formed Seven Arts, film financers and distributors.

Hyman, Kenneth (1928–)
American executive producer; formerly with Allied Artists and Seven Arts in Britain, now independent. Son of Eliot Hyman.

The Hound of the Baskervilles 59. The Roman Spring of Mrs Stone 61. Gigot 62. The Small World of Sammy Lee 63. The Hill 65. The Dirty Dozen 66, etc.

Hymer, Warren (1906–1948)
American character actor with stage experience; usually seen as dim-witted gangster.

Up the River 30. Charlie Chan Carries On 31. Twenty Thousand Years in Sing Sing 32. Kid Millions 35. San Francisco 36. Tainted Money 37. Destry Rides Again 39. Meet John Doe 41. Baby Face Morgan 42. Joe Palooka Champ 46, many others.

Hyson, Dorothy (1914–1996)
American-born leading lady of the 30s, in Britain. Born in Chicago, the daughter of Dorothy Dickson, she moved to England at the age of eight with her mother and was a noted beauty, on the West End stage from the age of 12. Married actor Robert DOUGLAS (1935–45) and retired soon after her second marriage, to Sir Anthony QUAYLE, in 1947.

Soldiers of the King 33. The Ghoul 33. Turkey Time 33. Sing As We Go 34. A Cup of Kindness 34. Spare a Copper 40, etc.
66 The most beautiful girl in the world. – *Cary Grant*

Without her I could have been nothing, done nothing. – *Sir Anthony Quayle*

Hytner, Nicholas (1957–)
British director, from the theatre, where he has worked for the Royal Shakespeare Company and the Royal National Theatre.

The Madness of King George 94. The Crucible 96. The Object of My Affection (US) 98, etc.

Hytten, Olaf (1888–1955)
Scottish character actor in American films.

It Is The Law 24. The Salvation Hunters 27. Daughter of the Dragon 31. Berkeley Square 33. Becky Sharp 35. The Good Earth 37. The Adventures of Robin Hood 38. Our Neighbours The Carters 40. The Black Swan 42. The Lodger 44. Three Strangers 46. Perils of the Jungle 53, etc.

I

Ibbetson, Arthur (1922–1997)
British cinematographer.
The Horse's Mouth 58. The Angry Silence 59. The League of Gentlemen 60. *Tunes of Glory* 61. Whistle Down the Wind 61. The Inspector 62. Nine Hours to Rama 63. I Could Go On Singing 63. The Chalk Garden 64. Sky West and Crooked 65. A Countess from Hong Kong 66. Inspector Clouseau 68. Where Eagles Dare 68. The Walking Stick 69. Anne of the Thousand Days (AAN) 70. The Railway Children 70. Willie Wonka and the Chocolate Factory 71. A Doll's House 73. Frankenstein: The True Story (TV) 73. 11 Harrowhouse 74. It Shouldn't Happen to a Vet 76. A Little Night Music 77. The Medusa Touch 77. The Prisoner of Zenda 79. Hopscotch 80. Little Lord Fauntleroy (TV) 80. Witness for the Prosecution 83. Master of the Game (TV) 83. The Bounty 84. Santa Claus 84.

Ibert, Jacques (1890–1962)
French composer.
The Italian Straw Hat 28. Don Quixote 34. Golgotha 35. La Charrette Fantôme 38. Panique 47. Macbeth 48. Invitation to the Dance 56, etc.

Ibsen, Henrik (1828–1906)
Norwegian dramatist who against great opposition brought social problems to the stage. Works filmed include *A Doll's House*, *An Enemy of the People*.

Ibuse, Masuji (1898–1993)
Distinguished Japanese novelist and short-story writer whose masterpiece *Black Rain/Kuroi Ame* was filmed in 1988 by Shohei Imamura.

Ice Cube (1969–) (O'Shea Jackson)
American rap performer, lyricist and actor. Born in Los Angeles, he trained as an architectural draughtsman before becoming a member of the group NWA (Niggaz Wit' Attitude) and went solo in 1990 with raps notorious for their misogyny and violence.
Boyz N The Hood 91. Trespass 93. The Glass Shield 94. Higher Learning 94. Friday (&ex-p, co-w) 95. Dangerous Ground 96. Anaconda 97. The Players Club (a, wd) 97. I Got the Hook-Up 98. Thicker Than Water 99. Three Kings 99. Next Friday (&p,w) 00, etc.

Ice-T (1958–) (Tracey Marrow)
Controversial American rap performer, lyricist and actor, notorious for his record 'Cop Killer'. Born in New Jersey, he was involved in crime before turning to performing.
Autobiography: 1994, *The Ice Opinion*.
Breakin' 84. Listen Up: The Lives of Quincy Jones 90. New Jack City 91. Ricochet 91. Who's the Man 93. Trespass 93. Surviving the Game 94. Johnny Mnemonic 95. Tank Girl 95. Mean Guns 96. The Deli 97. Body Count 97. Jacob Two Two Meets the Hooded Fang (Can.) 98, etc.
TV series: Players 97–98.
❝ Those criminal activities in my youth have got me where I am today, man. That's why people don't fuck with me. They know I'm real. – *I.T.*
America is a vicious killing machine based on rip-offs, lies, cheating and murder ... The pilgrims were some corrupt mothafuckas. – *I.T.*

Ichikawa, Kon (1915–)
Distinguished Japanese director and screenwriter.
The Heart 54. The Punishment Room 55. *The Burmese Harp* 55. Odd Obsessions 58. *Fires on the Plain* 59. The Sin 61. An Actor's Revenge 63. *Alone on the Pacific* 66. To Love Again 71. The Wanderers 73. I Am a Cat 75. The Inugami Family 76. Matababi 77. Queen Bee 78. The Devil's Island 78. The Phoenix 79. Actress 87. Taketori Monogatari 87. Noh Mask Murders/Tenkawa Densetsu Satsujin Jiken 91. 47 Ronin/Shiju Shichinin No Shikaku 94, etc.

Ichikawa, Raizo (1931–1969)
Brooding Japanese leading actor, sometimes compared to James Dean. He starred as wandering Eurasian samurai Kyoshiro Nemuri in eight films of the 60s.
Tales of the Taira Clan/Shin Heike Monogatari 55. Ambush at Iga Pass/Iga No Suigetsu 58. Conflagration/Flame of Torment/Enjo 58. The Lord and the Gambler/Nuregami Sandogasa 59. Bonchi 60. The Outcast/Hakai 61. Destiny's Son/Kiru 62. The Adventures of Kyoshiro Nemuri, Swordsman/Nemuri Kyoshiro Shobu 62. Band of Assassins/Shinobi No Mono 63. Sword Devil/Ken Ki 65. Nakano Army School/Rikugun Nakano Gakku 66. A Certain Killer/Aru Koroshiya 67. Castle Menagerie/Nemuri Kysoshiro Akujo-gari 69, etc.

Idle, Eric (1943–)
Comic actor and screenwriter, one of the members of Monty Python.
And Now for Something Completely Different 71. Monty Python and the Holy Grail 75. The Rutles (TV) (& d) 78. Monty Python's Life of Brian 79. Monty Python's The Meaning of Life 83. Yellowbeard 83. National Lampoon's European Vacation 85. Transformers – the Movie 86. The Adventures of Baron Munchausen 88. Nuns on the Run 90. Missing Pieces 92. Heirs and Graces 92. Mom and Dad Save the World 92. Splitting Heirs (a, w) 93. Casper 95. The Wind in the Willows 96. An Alan Smithee Film: Burn, Hollywood, Burn 97. Quest for Camelot (voice) 98. Rudolph the Red-Nosed Reindeer: The Movie (voice) 98. Dudley Do-Right 99. 102 Dalmatians (voice) 00, etc.

Idziak, Slawomir (1945–)
Polish cinematographer, frequently working with Krzysztof Zanussi and Krzysztof Kieslowski. He studied at the Lodz Film School.
The Balance Sheet 74. The Scar 76. The Conductor 79. The Constant Factor/Constans 80. The Contract/Kontrakt 80. Man from a Far Country 81. A Short Film about Killing 88. The Double Life of Veronique 91. Enak (wd) 92. Three Colours: Blue 93. The Journey of August King (US) 95. Gattaca (US) 97. Men with Guns (US) 97. I Want You (US) 98. Paranoid (GB) 99. he Last September (GB/Ire/Fr) 99. Proof of Life (US) 00, etc.

Ifans, Rhys
Gangling Welsh leading actor.
Street Life (TV) 95. August 96. Twin Town 97. Heart 97. Crime and Retribution (TV) 98. Dancing at Lughnasa 98. Notting Hill 99. Janice Beard 45 WPM 99. Love, Honour and Obey 99. You're Dead… 99. Rancid Aluminium 00. Kevin & Perry Go Large 00. Little Nicky (US) 00, etc.

Ifield, Frank (1937–)
British-born ballad singer who grew up in Australia.
Only film: *Up Jumped a Swagman* 65.

Ifukube, Akira (1914–)
Prolific Japanese composer, best known for scoring many of the Godzilla movies, and for creating the sound of the monster's roar and his footsteps. Born in Hokkaido, he was influenced by Japanese and Ainu folk music and taught at a music school before beginning to work in films. He was usually given less than a week to write his music for a film. His suite *Symphonic Fantasia* features many of the themes from his fantasy films.
The Quiet Duel 49. Children of Hiroshima 52. The Saga of Anatahan 53. Godzilla/Gojira 55. Rodan 56. The Burmese Harp 56. The Mysterians 57. Varan the Unbelievable 58. The Three Treasures 59. Battle in Outer Space 60. King Kong vs Godzilla 63. Godzilla vs Mothra 64. Frankenstein Conquers the World 65. Ghidrah, the Three Headed Monster 66. Return of Giant Majin 67. King Kong Escapes 68. Destroy All Monsters 68. Yog – the Monster from Space 70. Zatoichi Meets Yojimbo 70. Bokyo 75. Terror of Mechagodzilla 75. Love and Faith: Lady Ogin 79. Godzilla vs King Gidrah 91. Godzilla vs Mothra 92. Godzilla vs Mechagodzilla 93. Godzilla vs Destroyer 95, many others.

Ihnat, Steve (1934–1972)
Czech-born general-purpose actor in Hollywood, mostly in TV. Died of a heart attack.
The Chase 66. Countdown 67. The Hour of the Gun 67. Kona Coast 68. Madigan 69. Fuzz 72. *The Honkers* (wd only) 72, etc.

Ihnen, Wiard (1897–1979)
American art director, a former architect. In films from 1919, co-founding a short-lived production company in the late 20s, then at Paramount 1928–34, moving to Twentieth Century-Fox until the mid-40s. Married costume designer Edith Head.
Blonde Venus 32. Madame Butterfly 32. Duck Soup 33. Cradle Song 33. The Trumpet Blows 34. Becky Sharp 35. Go West Young Man 36. Every Day's a Holiday (AAN) 37. Hollywood Cavalcade 39. Jane Eyre 44. Wilson (AA) 44. Along Came Jones 45. Blood on the Sun (AA) 45. The Time of Your Life 48. I the Jury 53, etc.

Ikebe, Shinchiro
Japanese composer.
Kagemusha 80. The Ballad of Narayama 83. Zegen 87. Akira Kurosawa's Dreams 90, etc.

Iles, Francis (1893–1970)
British crime novelist who also wrote as Anthony Berkeley. *Before the Fact* formed the basis for Hitchcock's *Suspicion*; *Malice Aforethought* was filmed for television with Hywel Bennett.

Illing, Peter (1899–1966)
Austrian-born character actor, in British films since the 40s.
The End of the River 46. Eureka Stockade 48. I'll Get You for This 51. The Young Lovers 54. Zarak 56. Whirlpool 59. Sands of the Desert 60. The Twenty-fifth Hour 66, many others.

Image, Jean (1911–1989)
French animator, best known abroad for his cartoon feature *Johnny Lionheart/Jeannot l'Intrépide* 50.

Imai, Tadashi (1912–1991)
Japanese director, a controversial figure for his attacks on social injustice from a communist viewpoint. The son of a priest, he began as a screenwriter in 1934 and became a director in 1939; his best films were made in the 50s and 60s.
The Blue Mountains/Aoi Sanmyaku 49. Till We Meet Again/Mata au hi Made 50. And Yet We Live/Dokkoi Ikiteru 51. Troubled Waters/Nigorie 53. Monument of Star Lilies/Himeyuri no To 53. Darkness at Noon/Mahiru no Ankoku 56. Rice/Kome 57. Yoru no Tsuzumi/Night Drum 58. Kiku to Isamu 59. The Old Women's Paradise/Nippon no Obachan 62. Bushido: Samurai Saga/Bushido Zankoku Monogatari 63. A Story from Echigo/Echigo Tsutsuishi Oyashiraczu 64. A Woman Called En/En to iu Onna 71. The Life of a Communist Writer/Takiji Kobayashi 74. His Younger Sister/Ani Imoto 77. War and Youth/Senso to Seishun 91, etc.

Imamura, Shohei (1926–)
Japanese director, a former assistant to Ozu. He began as an amateur actor and playwright. During the 70s he worked mainly in television. In the 80s he founded his own film school, the Japan Academy of Visual Arts (Nihon Eiga Gakko) in Tokyo.
Stolen Desire/Nusumareta Yokubo 58. Endless Desire/Hateshi Naki Yokubo 58. Pigs and Battleships/Buta to Gunkan 61. The Insect Woman/Nippon Konchuki 63. The Pornographers/Jinruigaku Nyumon 66. The Profound Desire of the Gods/Kamigami no Fukaki Yokubo 68. Vengeance Is Mine/Fukushu Suru wa Ware ni Ari 79. The Ballad of Narayama/Narayamabushi 83. Zegen 87. Black Rain 89. Kanzo Sensei 98, etc.

Iman (1955–) (Iman Abdul Majid)
Tall, elegant Somalian model and actress, in occasional films. Born in Mogadishu, the daughter of the Somalian Ambassador to Saudi Arabia, she was discovered as a model in the mid-70s while studying at the University of Nairobi; she launched her own cosmetics company in the late 90s. Married singer David Bowie, her second husband, in 1992.
The Human Factor 79. Out of Africa 85. House Party 2 91. The Linguini Incident 92. Exit to Eden 94, etc.

Imi, Tony (1937–)
British cinematographer.
The Raging Moon 69. Dulcima 71. Universal Soldier 71. It's a 2'6" above the Ground World 72. Percy's Progress 74. House of Mortal Sin 75. The Likely Lads 76. The Slipper and the Rose 76. International Velvet 78. Brass Target 78. North Sea Hijack 79. Sergeant Steiner 79. The Sea Wolves 80. Inside the Third Reich (TV) 82. Little Gloria ... Happy at Last (TV) 82. Night Crossing 82. Savage Islands 83. Princess Daisy (TV) 83. Sakharov (TV) 84. A Christmas Carol (TV) 84. Reunion at Fairborough (TV) 85. Oceans of Fire 85. Enemy Mine 85. Not Quite Jerusalem 85. Queenie (TV) 87. Empire State 87. Buster 88. Wired 89. Options 89. Firebirds/Wings of the Apache 90. Fourth Story (TV) 91. Shopping 94. Downtime 97. Rancid Aluminium 00. The Testimony of Taliesin Jones 00, etc.

Imperioli, Michael (1966–)
American actor and screenwriter, born in Mount Vernon, New York. He is best known for his role as the quick-tempered Christopher Moltisanti in the TV gangster series *The Sopranos*.
Lean on Me 89. GoodFellas 90. Malcolm X 92. Household Saints 93. Postcards from America 94.The Addiction 95. Girl 6 96. Dead Presidents 95. I Shot Andy Warhol 96. Last Man Standing 96. Office Killer 97. Witness to the Mob (TV) 98. On the Run 98. Summer of Sam (&co-w) 99, etc.
TV series: The Sopranos 99- .

Imrie, Celia (1952–)
British character actress. Born in Guildford, Surrey, she began on stage and is much on television.
House of Whipcord 74. Death on the Nile 78. The Wicked Lady 83. Highlander 86. Oranges Are Not the Only Fruit (TV) 90. Blue Black Permanent 92. Dark-Adapted Eye (TV) 94. Mary Shelley's Frankenstein 94. In the Bleak Midwinter/A Midwinter's Tale 95. Black Hearts in Battersea (TV) 96. Hilary and Jackie 98. Gormenghast (TV) 00 etc.
TV series: Victoria Wood – As Seen on TV 85–86. Victoria Wood 89. Snakes and Ladders 89. The Riff Raff Element 93–94. Dinnerladies 98– .

Inagaki, Hiroshi (1905–1980)
Japanese director and screenwriter, a former actor, in films from the 1910s. He began as an assistant director and made his first film in 1928. His best-known work celebrates the way of the samurai, often starring Toshiro Mifune.
Peace on Earth 28. Travels under the Blue Sky/Tabi Wa Aozora 32. Miyamoto Musashi 40. The Last Days of Edo/Edo Saigo No Hi 41. Sword for Hire/Sengoku Burai 52. *Samurai* (a trilogy: Miyamoto Musashi (AA); Ichijoji No Ketto; Ketto Ganryujima) 54–55. The Rickshaw Man/Muhomatsu No Isso 58. Forty-Seven Ronin/Chushingura 62. Whirlwind/Dai Tatsumaki 64.

Kojiro 67. Samurai Banners/Furin Kazan 69. The Ambush 70, etc.

Ince, John (1887–1947)
American lead in silent films and a supporting actor in the 30s and 40s. On stage as a child, he was in films from 1913. The brother of Thomas and Ralph Ince, he also directed and produced some silent movies.
The Price of Victory (& d) 13. The House of Fear (& d) 14. The Urchin (d) 15. The Planter (& d) 17. Madame Sphinx 18. Old Lady 31 (d) 20. Hate 22. If Marriage Fails (d) 25. The Great Jewel Robbery (p, d) 26. Moby Dick 30. Passport to Paradise 32. Texas Terror 35. Way out West 36. Mr Smith Goes to Washington 39. Pride of the Yankees 42. Wilson 44. The Best Years of Our Lives 46. The Paradine Case 48, etc.

Ince, Ralph (1881–1937)
American leading man of the 20s who rather oddly ended his career in Britain directing quota quickies. He was killed in a car crash.
AS ACTOR: One Flag at Last 11. The Lady of the Lake 12. The Land of Opportunity 20. The Sea Wolf 25. Bigger than Barnum's 26. Wall Street 29. Little Caesar 30. The Big Gamble 31. The Hatchet Man 32. The Tenderfoot 32. Havana Widows 33, etc.
AS DIRECTOR: A Man's Home 21. Homeward Bound 23. A Moral Sinner 24. Smooth as Satin 25. Bigger than Barnum's 26. South Sea Love 28. Lucky Devils 33. What's in a Name? 34. Murder at Monte Carlo 34. Blue Smoke 35. It's You I Want 35. Hail and Farewell 36. The Vulture 36. The Man Who Made Diamonds 37, many others.

Ince, Thomas (1882–1924)
American director, a contemporary of D. W. Griffith and some say an equal innovator. On stage from the age of six, he began in films as an actor before becoming a director with Carl Laemmle's company. He systematized production methods, built his own studio and provided films of a high quality. Died suddenly at the end of a weekend aboard William Randolph Hearst's yacht, officially of a heart attack brought on by acute indigestion. There were rumours that he had been shot by Hearst, who suspected that Ince had seduced his mistress Marion Davies, that he died accidentally, hit by a shot intended for Charlie Chaplin, and that Louella Parsons owed her position as a columnist for Hearst's papers to not revealing the truth about the incident. He was the brother of John and Ralph INCE. Best remembered now for *Custer's Last Fight* 12. *Civilization* 15. *Human Wreckage* 23.

Inescort, Frieda (1900–1976) (Frieda Wightman)
Scottish-born actress of well bred roles, once secretary to Lady Astor; on stage from 1922. Went to Hollywood to begin film career.
If You Could Only Cook 35. Call it a Day 37. Beauty for the Asking 38. Woman Doctor 39. Pride and Prejudice 40. The Amazing Mrs Holliday 43. The Return of the Vampire 43. The Judge Steps Out 47. Foxfire 55. The Crowded Sky 60, etc.

Inge, William (1913–1973)
American playwright, most of whose work has been translated to the screen. Born in Independence, Kansas, and educated at the University of Kansas, he worked as a teacher, actor and drama critic before turning to writing in the late 40s. His early successes were followed in the late 50s and 60s by failures; a depressive and an alcoholic, he killed himself.
Biography: 1965, *William Inge* by Robert B. Shuman.
Come Back Little Sheba 52. Picnic 56. Bus Stop 56. The Dark at the Top of the Stairs 60. Splendor in the Grass (AAw) 61. The Stripper 63. Good Luck Miss Wycoff 79, etc.

Ingels, Marty (1936–)
American character comedian. He has been married to actress Shirley Jones since 1977.
Ladies' Man 60. Armored Command 61. The Horizontal Lieutenant 62. Wild and Wonderful 64. The Busy Body 67. For Singles Only 68. How to Seduce a Woman 74. Instant Karma 90. Round Numbers 92, etc.
TV series: *I'm Dickens He's Fenster* 62.

Ingham, Barrie (1934–)
British light leading man and general-purpose actor.
Tiara Tahiti 62. Invasion 66. Dr Who and the Daleks 66. A Challenge for Robin Hood (title role) 68. The Day of the Jackal 73. The Great Mouse Detective (voice) 86. Josh Kirby Timewarrior: Chapter 3, Trapped on Toyworld 95. Josh Kirby Timewarrior: Chapter 4, Eggs from 70 Million BC 95, etc.

Ingraham, Lloyd (1875–1956)
American director, screenwriter and leading actor of silent films, from 1912, who became a character actor in the sound era.
Aurora of the North (a) 14. The Missing Link (d) 15. Intolerance (a) 16. The Little Liar (d) 16. Wives and Other Wives (d) 18. The Girl in the Taxi 20. At the Sign of the Jack O'Lantern (wd) 21. A Front Page Story (a) 22. Going Up 23. Midnight Molly 25. Silver Comes Through (wd) 27. Jesse James (d) 27. Kit Carson (co-d) 28. Take the Heir (d) 30. Texas Gunfighter (a) 32. Sons of Steel (a) 35. Destry Rides Again (a) 39. Adventures of Red Ryder (a) (serial) 40. Never Give a Sucker an Even Break (a) 41. Blazing Guns (a) 43. Sudan (a) 45. Sister Kenny (a) 46. The Savage Horde (a) 50, etc.

Ingram, Jack (1902–1969)
American character actor, often as a villain in 'B' westerns and in more than 30 serials for Columbia. Born in Chicago, he studied law at the University of Texas, and began in a minstrel show. In the 40s and 50s, he ran a ranch used for movie and television locations, including many Roy ROGERS movies and episodes of the TV series *The Lone Ranger*, and later owned a yacht used for the TV series *Sea Hunt*. Died of a heart attack.
Rebellion 36. Whistling Bullets 36. Zorro Rides Again (serial) 37. Dick Tracy Returns (serial) 38. Outlaws of Sonora 38. Tumbleweeds 39. Terry and the Pirates (serial) 40. Young Bill Hickock 40. King of the Texas Rangers (serial) 41. The Lone Rider Ambushed 41. Billy the Kid Trapped 42. Lone Star Trail 43. Range Law 44. Devil Riders 45. Chick Carter, Detective (serial) 46. Ghost Town Renegades 47. Superman (serial) 48. Congo Bill (serial) 48. Whirlwind Riders 48. Son of a Badman 49. Bandit Queen 50. Fort Dodge Stampede 51. Fargo 52. Lost in Alaska 52. Cow Country 53. Five Guns West 55. Zorro Rides Again 59, many others.

Ingram, Rex (1892–1950) (Reginald Hitchcock)
Irishman who went to Hollywood and became first an actor and screenwriter, then a noted director of silent spectaculars. Married to Alice Terry.
Biography: 1980, *Rex Ingram* by Liam O'Leary.
AS ACTOR: The Great Problem 16. Reward of the Faithless 17. Under Crimson Skies 19. Trifling Women 22, etc.
AS DIRECTOR: *The Four Horsemen of the Apocalypse* 21. The Conquering Power 21. *The Prisoner of Zenda* 22. Where the Pavement Ends 23. *Scaramouche* 23. The Arab 24. *Mare Nostrum* 26. The Magician 26. The Garden of Allah 27. Baroud 31. Love in Morocco 33, etc.

Ingram, Rex (1895–1969)
Impressive actor, in films from 1929; former doctor. Married (1936-39) actress Francine EVERETT.
■ Hearts in Dixie 29. The Sign of the Cross 32. King Kong 33. The Emperor Jones 33. Harlem After Midnight 34. Captain Blood 35. *The Green Pastures* (as De Lawd) 36. *Huckleberry Finn* 39. *The Thief of Bagdad* 40. The Talk of the Town 42. Sahara 43. Cabin in the Sky 43. Fired Wife 43. Dark Waters 44. A Thousand and One Nights 45. Moonrise 48. King Solomon's Mines 50. Tarzan's Hidden Jungle 55. The Ten Commandments 56. Congo Crossing 56. Hell on Devil's Island 57. God's Little Acre 58. Anna Lucasta 59. Escort West 59. Watusi 59. Desire in the Dust 60. Elmer Gantry 60. Your Cheating Heart 64. Hurry Sundown 67. Journey to Shiloh 67.

Ingster, Boris (c. 1903–1978)
American writer-director.
The Last Days of Pompeii (co-w) 35. Happy Landing (w) 38. Stranger on the Third Floor (d) 40. Paris Underground (w) 45. The Judge Steps Out (wd) 49. Forgery (d) 50. Something for the Birds (co-w) 52. Abdulla the Great (co-w) 54. The Karate Killers (p) 67, etc.

Innes, Hammond (1913–1998)
English thriller writer, a former journalist.
Snowbound (oa) 48. Hell below Zero (oa) 53. Campbell's Kingdom (oa) 57. The Wreck of the Mary Deare (oa) 59, etc.

Ioseliani, Otar (1934–)
Georgian director and screenwriter. Born in Tbilisi, he studied at VGIK and began as a documentary filmmaker. Since the mid-80s he has been resident in Paris.
Falling Leaves/Listopad 68. Once Upon a Time There Was a Singing Blackbird/Zhil Pevchii Drozd 70. Pastoral 75. Favourites of the Moon/Les Favoris de la Lune 84. And Then There Was Light/Et La Lumière Fut 89. The Butterfly Hunt/La Chasse aux Papillons 92. Brigands, Chapter VII/Brigands: Chapitre VII 96. Farewell, Terra Firma!/Adieu, Plancher Des Vaches! 99, etc.

Ireland, Jill (1936–1990)
British leading lady of the 50s. She married David McCallum and, in 1968, Charles Bronson. She wrote *Life Wish*, detailing her battle against cancer, in 1987, and a further volume of autobiography: 1989, *Life Lines*.
Oh Rosalinda 55. Three Men in a Boat 55. Hell Drivers 57. Robbery under Arms 57. Carry On Nurse 59. Raising the Wind 61. Twice Round the Daffodils 62. Villa Rides (US) 68. Rider on the Rain (US) 70. The Mechanic (US) 72. Wild Horses (US) 73. The Valachi Papers (It.) 73. The Streetfighter 75. Breakheart Pass (US) 76. From Noon Till Three (US) 76. Death Wish II 82. Assassination 86, etc.
TV series: Shane 66.
❝ I'm in so many Charles Bronson films because no other actress will work with him. – *J.I.*

Ireland, John (1879–1962)
British composer whose only film score was *The Overlanders* (47).

Ireland, John (1914–1992)
Canadian leading man in Hollywood; a popular tough-cynical hero of the early 50s, he declined with unaccountable rapidity to bit parts and second features.
A Walk in the Sun 45. Behind Green Lights 46. The Gangster 47. Raw Deal 48. Red River 48. I Shot Jesse James 49. Anna Lucasta 49. The Doolins of Oklahoma 49. *All the King's Men* (AAN) 49. Cargo to Capetown 50. The Scarf 51. Red Mountain 51. Hurricane Smith 52. Outlaw Territory 53. Security Risk 54. *The Good Die Young* (GB) 54. Queen Bee 55. Gunfight at the OK Corral 57. Party Girl 58. No Place to Land 59. Spartacus 60. Brushfire 62. The Ceremony 63. The Fall of the Roman Empire 64. I Saw What You Did 65. Fort Utah 67. Caxambu 67. Arizona Bushwackers 68. One on Top of the Other 70. The House of the Seven Corpses 73. Welcome to Arrow Beach 75. The Swiss Conspiracy 76. Love and the Midnight Auto Supply 77. Madam Kitty 77. The Shape of Things to Come 79. Guyana 80. The Incubus 82, many others.
TV series: The Protectors 61.

Irene (1901–1962) (Irene Lenz-Gibbons)
American costume designer. Born in Brookings, South Dakota, she worked as an extra in Hollywood in the mid-20s before studying fashion design and opening her own dress shop on the UCLA campus. She was an established designer by the mid-30s, joining MGM in 1942, where she stayed, and later regretted it, for seven years before designing for a chain of boutiques, as well as creating clothes for many stars. Personal problems, allied to heavy drinking, led her to commit suicide.
The Animal Kingdom 32. Flying down to Rio 33. Mrs Parkington 44. Weekend at the Waldorf 45. The Postman Always Rings Twice 46. State of the Union 48. B.F.'s Daughter (AAN) 48. Key to the City 50. Midnight Lace (AAN) 60. A Gathering of Eagles 63, etc.
❝ So quiet she was – and expensive, Miss Don't-Melt-Ice-Cube. – *L. B. Mayer*

Iribé, Paul (1883–1935)
Paris fashion designer and artist who was brought to Hollywood by De Mille to create the costumes for Gloria Swanson in *Male and Female* 19 and went on to design several other of De Mille's films.
The Affairs of Anatol 20. The Ten Commandments 23. The Road to Yesterday 25. Madam Satan 30, etc.

Irons, Jeremy (1948–)
British leading man of the introspective type. Married actress Sinead CUSACK.
Nijinsky 80. *The French Lieutenant's Woman* 81. *Brideshead Revisited* (TV) 81. Moonlighting 82. The Captain's Doll (TV) 82. Betrayal 82. The Wild Duck 83. Swann in Love 84. The Mission 85. Dead Ringers 88. Australia 89. A Chorus of Disapproval 89. Reversal of Fortune (AA) 90. Kafka 91. Damage 92. Waterland 92. M. Butterfly 93. The House of the Spirits 94. *The Lion King* (voice) 94. Die Hard with a Vengeance 95. Stealing Beauty 95. Lolita 97. Chinese Box 97. The Man in the Iron Mask 98, etc.
❝ Actors often behave like children and so we're taken for children. I want to be grown-up. – *J.I.*
One of the things we have to do as artists is to stir things up. There is too little debate in our society. – *J.I.*
I have always believed that the afterlife is what you leave behind in other people. – *J.I.*

Ironside, Michael (1950–)
Canadian leading actor, in American movies from the mid-80s. Born in Toronto, he studied at the Ontario College of Art.
Scanners 80. Visiting Hours 81. Cross Country 83. Spacehunter: Adventures in the Forbidden Zone 83. The Falcon and the Snowman 85. Top Gun 86. Jo Jo Dancer, Your Life Is Calling 86. Nowhere to Hide 87. Extreme Prejudice 87. Watchers 88. Mindfield 89. Office Party 89. Total Recall 90. Highlander II – the Quickening 90. Deadly Surveillance 91. McBain 91. Neon City 91. Chaindance (& w, p) 91. Guncrazy 92. A Passion for Murder 92. The Vagrant 92. Black Ice 92. Night Trap/Mardi Gras for the Devil 93. Forced to Kill 93. Sweet Killing 93. Free Willy 93. Father Hood 93. The Next Karate Kid 94. Red Scorpion 2 94. Tokyo Cowboy 94. The Glass Shield 95. Major Payne 95. Kids of the Round Table 95. The Destiny of Marty Fine 96. Starship Troopers 97. Desert Blue 98. The Perfect Storm 00. Nuremberg (TV) 00, etc.
TV series: V 84–85. ER 95.

Irvin, John (1940–)
British director, from TV.
Tinker Tailor Soldier Spy (TV) 80. The Dogs of War 80. Ghost Story 81. Champions 83. Turtle Diary 85. Raw Deal 86. Hamburger Hill 87. Next of Kin 89. Robin Hood 91. Eminent Domain 91. Widow's Peak 93. Freefall 94. A Month by the Lake 94. Crazy Horse (TV) 96. City of Industry 96. Shiner 00, etc.

Irving, Amy (1953–)
American leading actress who trained in San Francisco and London. She is the former wife of director Steven SPIELBERG (1985–89) and is now married to director Bruno BARRETO.
Carrie 78. The Fury 79. Voices 79. Honeysuckle Rose 80. The Competition 81. Yentl (AAN) 83. Micki and Maude 84. Rumpelstiltskin 87. Crossing Delancey 88. Who Framed Roger Rabbit (voice) 88. A Show of Force 90. An American Tail: Fievel Goes West (voice) 91. Benefit of the Doubt 93. Kleptomania 93. Carried Away 95. I'm Not Rapaport 96. Deconstructing Harry 97. One Tough Cop 98. End of Innocence 99. The Rage: Carrie 2 99. Traffic 00, etc.

Irving, George (1874–1961)
American character actor, long on the Broadway stage, for some while a film director, and most memorable in middle-aged businessman roles.
The Jungle 14. Madonna of the Streets 24. Wild Horse Mesa 25. Craig's Wife 28. Thunderbolt 29. The Spoilers 30. Island of Lost Souls 32. Dangerous 35. Sutter's Gold 36. The Toast of New York 37. Bringing Up Baby 38. New Moon 40. Son of Dracula 43. Christmas Holiday 44. Magic Town 47, many others.

Irving, Sir Henry (1838–1905) (John Henry Broadribb)
Distinguished English actor-manager of Victorian theatre, the first actor to be knighted. He deserves a footnote to film history as the model for DRACULA, the character created by his secretary and aide Bram STOKER. His son H. B. Irving (1870–1919), who died by drowning, appeared in a few silent films.

Irving, John (1942–)
American novelist and screenwriter.
Autobiography: 1999, *My Movie Business: A Memoir*.
The World According to Garp (oa) 82. The Hotel New Hampshire (oa) 84. Simon Birch (oa) 98. The Cider House Rules (oa,AAw) 99, etc.
❝ There is less time for character development in a film than in a novel; a character's eccentricities

can easily become the character. – J.I.

In the world of would-be producers, you can meet some truly vile people. – J.I.

Irving, Laurence (1897–1988)
English art director and artist, the grandson of actor Sir Henry Irving, from the stage. He went to Hollywood in the late 20s to work for Douglas Fairbanks.

The Iron Mask (US) 29. The Taming of the Shrew (US) 29. Diamond Cut Diamond 32. Captain Blood 33. Moonlight Sonata 37. Pygmalion 38, etc.

Irving, Washington (1783–1859)
American humorist and storyteller whose *Rip Van Winkle* and *The Legend of Sleepy Hollow* have been filmed at various times and in various ways.

Irwin, Mark
Canadian cinematographer.

Starship Invasion 77. Blood and Guts 78. The Brood 79. Scanners 81. Night School 81. Videodrome 83. The Dead Zone 83. Spasms 83. The Protector 85. The Fly 86. Youngblood 86. The Blob 88. Love at Stake 88. I Come in Peace 90. Class of 1999 90. Paint It Black 90. Robocop 2 90. Passenger 57 92. Man's Best Friend 93. Slaughter of the Innocents 93. D2: The Mighty Ducks 94. Dumb and Dumber 94. Wes Craven's New Nightmare 94. The Net 95. Vampire in Brooklyn 95. Robin of Locksley 96. Kingpin 96. Scream 96. Steel 97. Misbegotten 97. Joe Torre: Curveballs along the Way (TV) 97. There's Something about Mary 98, etc.

Irwin, May (1862–1938)
American actress who appeared in one of the very first short films, *The Kiss* 96; her only other film was *Mrs Black Is Back* 14.

Isaak, Chris (1956–)
American singer, songwriter and actor.

Married to the Mob 88. The Silence of the Lambs 91. Twin Peaks: Fire Walk with Me 92. Little Buddha 93. That Thing You Do! 96. End of Innocence 99, etc.

Isham, Mark (1951–)
American composer and musician. Born in New York, he began by playing trumpet in the Oakland and San Francisco Symphony Orchestras and then joined the rock group Sons of Champlin, and also toured with singer Van Morrison before forming his own band, Group 87, in the late 70s.

Never Cry Wolf 83. Mrs Soffel 84. Trouble in Mind 85. The Hitcher 86. Made in Heaven 87. The Beast 88. The Moderns 88. Love at Large 90. Reversal of Fortune 90. Billy Bathgate 91. Little Man Tate 91. Mortal Thoughts 91. Point Break 91. Cool World 92. A Midnight Clear 92. Nowhere to Run 92. Of Mice and Men 92. The Public Eye 92. A River Runs through It 92. Sketch Artist 92. Fire

in the Sky 93. Short Cuts 93. Made in America 93. Romeo Is Bleeding 93. The Getaway 94. Mrs Parker and the Vicious Circle 94. Quiz Show 94. Nell 94. Timecop 94. Safe Passage 94. The Browning Version 94. Miami Rhapsody 95. Losing Isaiah 95. Home for the Holidays 95. Last Dance 96. Gotti (TV) 96. Fly Away Home 96. Kiss the Girls 97. Afterglow 97. Kiss the Girls 97. Night Falls on Manhattan 97. The Education of Little Tree 97. The Gingerbread Man 97. From the Earth to the Moon (TV) 98. Blade 98. At First Sight 99. Varsity Blues 99. October Sky 99. Body Shots 99. Men of Honor 00, etc.

Isherwood, Christopher (1904–1986)
English novelist and screenwriter, mainly in Hollywood. Born in Cheshire and briefly educated at Cambridge University, he was a member of the group of 30s left-wing writers clustered around poet W. H. Auden. An inveterate cinema-goer, he attempted to find work in British studios and first worked with visiting Hollywood director Berthold VIERTEL, a friendship he resumed after he and Auden moved to America in 1939. He lived in California, where he worked intermittently for Hollywood studios. *Goodbye to Berlin*, his book of stories, was dramatized by John VAN DRUTEN as *I Am a Camera*, which was subsequently filmed and later became the stage and screen musical *Cabaret*.

Autobiography: 1971, *Kathleen and Frank*. 1976, *Christopher and His Kind*. 1996, *Diaries, Volume One: 1939–1960*, ed. Katherine Bucknell. 2000, *Lost Years: A Memoir 1945-1951*, ed. Katherine Bucknell.

Biography: 1977, *Isherwood* by Jonathan Fryer. 1979, *Christopher Isherwood* by Brian Finney.

Little Friend (co-w) (GB) 34. Rage in Heaven (co-w) 41. Free and Easy (uncredited) 41. Forever and a Day (co-w) 43. The Woman in White (uncredited) 48. Adventure in Baltimore (co-w, story) 49. The Great Sinner (co-w) 49. I Am a Camera (oa) (GB) 55. Diane (w) 55. The Wayfarer (w) 57. The Loved One (co-w, a) 65. The Sailor from Gibraltar (co-w) (GB) 67. Cabaret (oa) 72. Frankenstein: The True Story (co-w) (TV) 73. Rich and Famous (a) 81, etc.

66 Screenwriting, to me, is the most absorbing of all games. – C.I.

I don't think that I bring very much to films. I think that films bring a great deal to me. By working in this medium, which is a medium of visualization primarily, I learned a great, great deal, which I could use in my books. I never really saw things before. – C.I.

I seem to have put my bad luck into film-writing and all my good luck into the rest of my life! It would be a bore to complain; but, really, the films I wrote have nearly all ended in disaster, mitigated or unmitigated. – C.I.

A good – because psychologically true – Hollywood story. A maid boasts to her friend – also a maid – about the house she works at: wonderful people – they entertain every night – and always

big celebrities, top stars. The friend is thrilled: 'And what do they talk about?' The maid: 'Us.' – C.I.

Ishii, Sogo (1957–)
Japanese director and screenwriter.

Gyakufunsha Kazoku 84. Angel Dust/Tenshi No Kuzu 94. August in the Water 96. Labyrinth of Dreams/Yume No Ginga 97. Gojoe 00, etc.

Itami, Juzo (1933–1997) (Yoshihiro Ikeuchi)
Japanese director and screenwriter, a former actor. He died in hospital after being found lying injured in the street outside his office, having fallen or jumped from the roof of the eight-floor building.

The Funeral 84. Tampopo 86. A Taxing Woman/Marusa no Onna 88. A Taxing Woman Too 89. The Gangster's Moll/Mimbo no Onna 92. Daibyonin 93. A Quiet Life/Shizukana Seikatsu 95. Supermarket Woman/Supa no Onna 96. Murutai no Onna 97, etc.

Ito, Daisuke (1898–1981)
Japanese director and screenwriter, one of the important early directors, usually of dramas in a period setting.

Jogoshima 24. *A Diary of Chuji's Travels*/Chuji Tabernikki 28. The Swordsman 38. King of Chess/Oosho 48. Lion's Dance 53. The Story of Shunkin/Shunkin Monogatari 54. The Conspirator/Hangyakuji 61. An Actor's Revenge/Yukinojo Henge (co-w only) 63, etc.

Iturbi, José (1895–1980)
Spanish pianist and conductor who made his American concert debut in 1929; in the 40s he appeared in a number of MGM musicals and helped to popularize classical music.

■ Thousands Cheer 43. Two Girls and a Sailor 44. Music for Millions 44. A Song to Remember (dubbed piano for Cornel Wilde; his recording of a Chopin Polonaise sold over one million copies) 44. Anchors Aweigh 45. Holiday in Mexico 46. Three Daring Daughters 48. That Midnight Kiss 49.

Ivan, Rosalind (1884–1959)
American character actress, mainly on stage.

The Suspect 44. The Corn Is Green 45. Three Strangers 46. Ivy 47. The Robe 53. Elephant Walk 54, etc.

Ivano, Paul (1900–1984)
American cinematographer.

The Dancers 25. No Other Woman 28. Atlantic Flight 37. The Shanghai Gesture 41. See My Lawyer 44. Spider Woman Strikes Back 46. Champagne for Caesar 50. For Men Only 52. Hold Back Tomorrow 55. Lizzie 57. Chubasco 68, many others, especially second unit shooting.

Ivens, Joris (1898–1989)
Dutch writer-director best known for documentaries.

Autobiography: 1969, *The Camera and I*.

Rain 29. Zuidersee 30. New Earth 34. Spanish Earth 37. The 400 Millions 39. The Power and the Land 40. Song of the Rivers 53. The Threatening Sky 66. Une Histoire de Vent 88, etc.

Ives, Burl (1909–1995) (Burl Icle Ivanhoe)
American actor and ballad-singer, once itinerant worker and professional footballer. His paunchy figure, beard and ready smile are equally adaptable to villainous or sympathetic parts.

Smoky (debut) 46. East of Eden 54. *Cat on a Hot Tin Roof* 57. Wind Across the Everglades 58. *The Big Country* (AA) 58. Our Man in Havana 59. The Brass Bottle 64. Rocket to the Moon 67. The McMasters 70. The Only Way Out is Dead 70. Baker's Hawk 76. Just You and Me, Kid 79. Earthbound (TV) 81. Uphill All the Way 84. Poor Little Rich Girl (TV) 88. Two Moon Junction 88, etc.

TV series: O.K. Crackerby 65. The Bold Ones 69.

Ivory, James (1928–)
American director who began by making films in India. A specialist in period drama, based on the works of such writers as Jane Austen, E. M. Forster and Henry James.

Books: 1992, *The Films of Merchant Ivory* by Robert Emmet Long.

■ The Householder 62. *Shakespeare Wallah* 65. The Guru 69. Bombay Talkie 70. Savages 72. The Wild Party 74. Autobiography of a Princess 75. Roseland 77. Hullaballoo over Bonnie and George's Pictures 78. The Europeans 79. Jane Austen in Manhattan 79. Quartet 81. *Heat and Dust* 82. The Bostonians 84. *A Room with a View* (AAN) 85. *Maurice* 87. Slaves of New York 89. Mr & Mrs Bridge 90. *Howards End* 92. The Remains of the Day (AAN) 93. Jefferson in Paris 95. Surviving Picasso 96. A Soldier's Daughter Never Cries 98. The Golden Bowl 00.

Iwerks, Ub (1900–1971)
American animator, long associated with Disney (he drew the first Mickey Mouse cartoon, *Plane Crazy*). Formed own company in 1930 to create Flip the Frog; went back to Disney 1940 as director of technical research. AA 1959 for improvements in optical printing, 1965 for advancing techniques of travelling matte. Iwerks did much of the complex trick-work for Hitchcock's *The Birds* (AAN).

Izzard, Eddie
English stand-up comedian and actor.

Joseph Conrad's Secret Agent 96. Lust for Glorious (& p, w) (TV) 97. The Avengers 98. Velvet Goldmine 98. Mystery Men 99. The Criminal 99. Circus 00, etc.

J

Jabor, Arnaldo (1940–)
Brazilian director, dramatist, poet and journalist.
Pindorama 70. Toda Nudez Será Castigada 72. Tudo Bem 78. I Love You/Eu Te Amo 81. Love Me for Ever or Never/Eu Sei Que Vou Te Amar 86, etc.

Jackley, Nat (1909–1988) (Nathaniel Jackley-Hirsch)
Skinny, lisping-voiced, rubber-necked English comedian in occasional films. Born in Sunderland, the son of comedian George Jackley, he was on-stage from childhood as a clog dancer with the Eight Lancashire Lads, an act that had earlier included Charlie CHAPLIN.
Demobbed 44. Under New Management 46. Stars in Your Eyes 57. Magical Mystery Tour (TV) 67. Mrs Brown, You've Got a Lovely Daughter 68. Yanks 79. The Ploughman's Lunch 83, etc.
TV series: Nat's in the Belfry 56.

Jackman, Hugh (1968–)
Australian actor and singer, from the stage. Born in Sydney, of English parents, He studied journalism at Sydney's University of Technology, and at the Western Australian Academy of Performing Arts. He came to notice in Britain as Curly in the National Theatre's production of *Oklahoma!*, followed by his performance as Wolverine in *X-Men* and its sequels. Married actress and director Deborra-Lee Furness in 1996.
Paperback Hero 98. Erskineville Kings 99. X-Men (US) 00. Animal Husbandry (US) 01, etc.

Jacks, Robert L. (1922–1987)
American producer, long with Fox.
Man on a Tightrope 53. White Feather 55. A Kiss Before Dying 56. Bandido 57. Roots of Heaven 59. Man in the Middle 64. Zorba the Greek 65. Bandolero 68, many others.

Jackson, Anne (1926–)
American actress, wife of Eli Wallach; films rare.
■ So Young So Bad 50. The Journey 58. Tall Story 60. The Tiger Makes Out 67. How to Save a Marriage 67. *The Secret Life of an American Wife* 68. Lovers and Other Strangers 70. Zigzag 70. Dirty Dingus Magee 70. The Angel Levine 70. Nasty Habits 76. The Bell Jar 79. The Shining 80. A Woman Called Golda (TV) 82. The Family Man 82. Blinded by the Light (TV) 82. Leave 'em Laughing (TV) 82. Sam's Son 84. Funny about Love 90. Folks! 92. Something Sweet 00.

Jackson, Freda (1909–1990)
British character actress with a penchant for melodrama; on stage from 1934, films from 1942.
A Canterbury Tale 44. Henry V 44. Beware of Pity 46. Great Expectations 46. *No Room at the Inn* 47. Women of Twilight 49. The Crowded Day 53. Brides of Dracula 60. The Third Secret 64. Monster of Terror 65, etc.

Jackson, Glenda (1936–)
British star actress. She announced her retirement from acting after being elected Labour MP for Hampstead and Highgate at the 1992 British general election.
Biography: 1999, *Glenda Jackson* by Chris Bryant.
■ This Sporting Life 63. The Marat/Sade 66. Tell Me Lies 67. Negatives 68. *Women in Love* (AA) 69. The Music Lovers 70. *Sunday Bloody Sunday* (AAN) 71. The Boy Friend (uncredited) 71. Mary Queen of Scots (as Queen Elizabeth) 71. A Touch of Class (AA) 72. The Triple Echo 72. A Bequest to the Nation 73. The Maids 74. The Tempter 74. The Romantic Englishwoman 75. Hedda (AAN) 76. The Incredible Sarah 76. Nasty Habits 76. House Calls 77. The Class of Miss MacMichael 78. Stevie 78. Lost and Found 79. Health 80. Hopscotch 80. The Patricia Neal Story (TV) 81. Return of the Soldier 82. Giro City (TV) 83. Sakharov (TV) 84. Turtle Diary 85. Business as Usual 87. Salome's Last Dance 88. The Rainbow 89. Doombeach 90.
TV series: *Elizabeth R* 71.
❝ I had no real ambition about acting, but I knew there had to be something better than the bloody chemist's shop. – *G.J.*
She's an absolute dreamboat, the epitome of professionalism, a splendid actress, and she has all the make-up of a fully rounded person. – *Walter Matthau*
If she went into politics she'd be prime minister; if she went into crime she'd be Jack the Ripper. – *Roy Hodge (her former husband)*

Jackson, Gordon (1923–1990)
Scottish actor whose rueful expression got him typecast as a weakling; maturity brought more interesting roles. He was best known for playing Hudson, the butler (a character he detested), in the TV series *Upstairs, Downstairs*. Born in Glasgow, he began as a draughtsman and apprentice engineer, and was on stage from the early 40s.
The Foreman Went to France (debut) 42. Millions Like Us 43. Nine Men 43. San Demetrio, London 44. Pink String and Sealing Wax 45. The Captive Heart 46. Against the Wind 47. Eureka Stockade 48. *Whisky Galore* 48. The Lady with a Lamp 51. Meet Mr Lucifer 54. Pacific Destiny 56. *Tunes of Glory* 60. The Great Escape (US) 62. *The Ipcress File* 65. Cast a Giant Shadow (US) 66. The Fighting Prince of Donegal 66. The Prime of Miss Jean Brodie 69. Run Wild Run Free 69. Kidnapped 72. Russian Roulette 75. Spectre (TV) 77. The Medusa Touch 77. The Last Giraffe (TV) 79. A Town Like Alice (TV) 80. The Shooting Party 84. The Masks of Death 85. The Whistle Blower 86. My Brother Tom (TV) 86. Beyond Therapy 87. The Lady and the Highwayman (TV) 89, many others.
TV series: *Upstairs Downstairs* 70–75. The Professionals 77–81.

Jackson, Janet (1966–)
American actress and singer, the sister of Michael Jackson, on stage with her family from the age of six.
Poetic Justice 93.
TV series: The Jacksons 76–77. Good Times 77–79. A New Kind of Family 79–80. Diff'rent Strokes 81–82. Fame 84–85.

Jackson, Kate (1948–)
American leading lady.
The Seven Minutes 70. Night of Dark Shadows 71. Limbo 72. Satan's School for Girls (TV) 73. Killer Bees (TV) 74. Death Cruise (TV) 74. Death Scream (TV) 75. Death at Love House (TV) 76. James at 15 (TV) 77. Thunder and Lightning 77. Topper (TV) 79. *Jacqueline Bouvier Kennedy* (TV) 81. Thin Ice (TV) 81. Dirty Tricks 81. Making Love 82. Listen to Your Heart (TV) 83. Rage of Angels (TV) 83. Loverboy 89. Adrift (TV) 93. Sweet Deception 99, etc.
TV series: Dark Shadows 67–71. The Rookies 71–74. *Charlie's Angels* 76–80. Scarecrow and Mrs King 83–87.

Jackson, Mary Ann (1923–)
American child actress, in the Our Gang comedies of the late 20s and early 30s.

Jackson, Michael (1958–)
Precocious American rock singer and songwriter, first as a member of the Jackson Five and then as a solo artist. Rich and reclusive, he has spent a fortune re-making his appearance with the aid of plastic surgeons. Promotional videos of his songs directed by, among others, John LANDIS and John SINGLETON have cost more than some feature films. He paid $1.5m in 1999 for the 'best picture' Oscar awarded to David Selznick for *Gone With The Wind*. The first of his two wives was Elvis Presley's daughter, Lisa Marie Presley (1994-1996).
Biography: 1994, *Michael Jackson Unauthorized* by Christopher Andersen.
Save the Children (concert) 73. The Wiz 78. Moonwalker 88.

Jackson, Mick (1943–)
British director, from television, now working in Hollywood.
Threads (TV) 85. Yuri Nosenk, KGB (TV) 86. A Very British Coup (TV) 88. Chattahoochee 90. L.A. Story 91. The Bodyguard 92. Clean Slate 94. Indictment: The McMartin Trial (TV) 95. Volcano 97, etc.

Jackson, Pat (1916–)
British director, a war documentarist whose later output has been disappointing.
Ferry Pilot 41. *Western Approaches* 44. The Shadow on the Wall (US) 48. *White Corridors* 50. Something Money Can't Buy 52. The Feminine Touch 55. Virgin Island 58. Snowball 60. What a Carve Up 62. Seven Keys 62. Don't Talk to Strange Men 62. Seventy Deadly Pills 64. Dead End Creek 65. On the Run 69, etc.

Jackson, Peter (1961–)
New Zealand director, screenwriter and producer whose low-budget visceral horror films have achieved cult status. He is currently filming a trilogy of films based on J. R. R. Tolkien's epic novel the *Lord of the Rings*.
Bad Taste 87. Meet the Feebles 89. Braindead 92. *Heavenly Creatures* 94. Forgotten Silver (a, co-w, co-d) 96. The Frighteners (co-p, co-w, d) 96, etc.

Jackson, Samuel L. (1948–)
Prolific American actor, from the stage. Born in Chattanooga, Tennessee, he studied drama at Morehouse College and began his career with the Negro Ensemble Company and at the New York Shakespeare Festival. His work rate slowed a little in the late 80s when he over-indulged on cocaine, but after rehabiliatation, he has averaged five films a year. Current asking price: around $8m a movie.
Ragtime 81. School Daze 88. Sea of Love 89. Do the Right Thing 89. GoodFellas 90. Def by Temptation 90. Jungle Fever 91. White Sands 92. Patriot Games 92. Juice 92. Amos & Andrew 93. National Lampoon's Loaded Weapon 1 93. Menace II Society 93. Jurassic Park 93. Against the Wall (TV) 94. Fresh 94. *Pulp Fiction* (AAN) 94. The New Age 94. Die Hard with a Vengeance 95. Losing Isaiah 95. Kiss of Death 95. The Great White Hype 96. A Time to Kill 96. The Search for One-Eyed Jimmy (made 93) 96. The Long Kiss Goodnight 96. Hard Eight 96. Trees Lounge 96. 187 97. Jackie Brown 97. Eve's Bayou 97. The Negotiator 98. The Red Violin 98. Sphere 98. Star Wars Episode 1: The Phantom Menace 99. Deep Blue Sea 99. Shaft 00. Unbreakable 00, etc.
❝ The golf course is the only place I can go dressed like a pimp and fit in perfectly. – *S.L.J.*
The phone stops ringing for everybody eventually: Gregory Peck, Sidney Poitier. Everybody. – *S.L.J.*

Jackson, Selmer (1888–1971)
American character actor who played hundreds of unobtrusive fathers, doctors, scientists and executives. In 1940 alone Jackson appeared in 20 films.
Dirigible 31. Doctor X 32. The Witching Hour 34. Front Page Woman 35. Grand Exit 35. The Westland Case 37. Stand Up and Fight 39. The Grapes of Wrath 40. It Started with Eve 41. It Ain't Hay 43. The Sullivans 44. The French Key 46. Mighty Joe Young 49. Elopement 51. Autumn Leaves 56. Atomic Submarine 59. The Gallant Hours 60, many others.

Jackson, Thomas E. (1886–1967)
Tough-looking American character actor, born in New York City, from the stage. He appeared in more than 200 movies, often as a police officer or reporter.
Broadway 29. *Little Caesar* 30. For the Defense 30. Doctor X 32. Terror Aboard 33. The Mystery of the Wax Museum 33. Manhattan Melodrama 34. Call of the Wild 35. Hollywood Boulevard 36. The Westland Case 37. Torchy Gets Her Man 38. Golden Gloves 40. Law of the Tropics 41. The Woman in the Window 44. The Big Sleep 46. Dead Reckoning 47. Stars and Stripes Forever 52. Attack of the Fifty Foot Woman 58. Synanon 65, many others.

Jacob, Irène (1966–)
Swiss actress in French and international films. Born in Geneva, she moved to live in Paris in the mid-80s.
Au Revoir les Enfants 87. La Bande des Quatre 89. *The Double Life of Veronique* 91. Claude 92. La Passion Van Gogh 93. The Secret Garden 93. *Three Colours: Red*/Trois Couleurs: Rouge 94. La Prédiction 94. Le Moulin de Daudet 94. Beyond the Clouds 95. All Men Are Mortal 95. Runaways 95. Othello (as Desdemona) 95. Incognito 97. Victory 98. American Cuisine/Cuisine Américaine 98. My Life So Far 99, etc.

Jacobi, Sir Derek (1938–)
British classical actor, in occasional films. A member of the National Youth Theatre, he made his professional debut in 1961, and acted with both the National Theatre and the Royal Shakespeare Company. He played the title role in the TV adaptation of Robert Graves's *I, Claudius* and also the medieval detective in the mid-90s TV series *Cadfael*.
Othello 65. The Three Sisters 70. The Day of the Jackal 73. Blue Blood 73. The Odessa File 74. Philby, Burgess and Maclean (TV) 77. The Medusa Touch 77. The Human Factor 79. The Secret of Nimh (voice) 82. The Hunchback of Notre Dame (as Frollo) (TV) 82. Inside the Third Reich (as Hitler) (TV) 82. Enigma 82. Mr Pye (TV) 86. Little Dorrit 87. Henry V 89. The Fool 90. Dead Again 91. The Vision Thing (TV) 93. Hamlet 96. Breaking the Code (TV) 97. *Love Is the Devil* 98. Molokai 98. Up at the Villa 00. Gladiator 00. Jason and the Argonauts (TV) 00, etc.

Jacobi, Lou (1913–)
Chubby Canadian character actor.
The Diary of Anne Frank 59. Song without End 60. Irma la Douce 63. Last of the Secret Agents 66. Penelope 66. Everything you Always Wanted to Know about Sex 72. Roseland 77. The Magician of Lublin 79. The Lucky Star 80. Arthur 81. My Favorite Year 82. Isaac Littlefeathers 85. The Boss's Wife 86. Amazon Women on the Moon 87. Avalon 90. I.Q. 94, etc.
TV series: Ivan the Terrible 76. Melba 86.

Jacobs, Arthur P. (1918–1973)
American independent producer, former publicist.
■ What a Way to Go 64. Dr Dolittle (AAN) 67. Planet of the Apes 68. The Chairman 69. Goodbye Mr Chips 69. Beneath the Planet of the Apes 69. Escape from the Planet of the Apes 71. Conquest of the Planet of the Apes 72. Tom Sawyer 73. Huckleberry Finn 73.

Jacobs, W(illiam) W(ymark) (1863–1943)
British short story writer and dramatist, whose output ran from seafaring humour to horror. His *The Monkey's Paw* has been filmed several times and its narrative has influenced many other horror writers. Born in Wapping, London, he worked as a clerk until the success of *Many Cargoes*, his first collection of stories published in 1896, enabled him to become a full-time writer.
Her Uncle 15. The Monkey's Paw 15. A Master of Craft 22. The Monkey's Paw 23. The Changeling 28. Beauty and the Barge 31. The Monkey's Paw (US) 33. Our Relations (US) 36.

The Monkey's Paw 48. Footsteps in the Fog 55. Espiritismo (Mex.) 61, etc.

Jacobsson, Ulla (1929–1982)
Leading Swedish actress.
One Summer of Happiness 51. Smiles of a Summer Night 55. Love is a Ball 63. Zulu 64. The Heroes of Telemark 65, etc.

Jacoby, Scott (1956–)
American juvenile lead.
Baxter 72. Rivals 73. Love and the Midnight Auto Supply 77. The Little Girl Who Lives Down the Lane 77. Our Winning Season 78. To Die For 89. To Die For II 91, etc.

Jacques, Hattie (1924–1980)
Oversized British comedienne, well known at the Players' Theatre and on TV. In most of the 'Carry On' films. Married John Le Mesurier.
Nicholas Nickleby 47. Oliver Twist 48. Trottie True 49. The Pickwick Papers 52. Make Mine Mink 61. In the Doghouse 62. The Bobo 67. Crooks and Coronets 69, etc.

Jaeckel, Richard (1926–1997)
American actor, former Fox mail-boy, who made a name playing frightened youths in war films.
Guadalcanal Diary 43. Jungle Patrol 48. Sands of Iwo Jima 49. The Gunfighter 50. Come Back Little Sheba 52. The Violent Men 55. Attack! 55. 3.10 to Yuma 57. The Gallant Hours 60. Town without Pity 61. Four for Texas 63. Town Tamer 65. The Dirty Dozen 67. The Devil's Brigade 68. The Green Slime 69. Chisum 70. Sometimes a Great Notion (AAN) 71. Chosen Survivors 74. Grizzly 76. Day of the Animals 77. *The Dark* 79. Herbie Goes Bananas 80. All the Marbles 81. The Awakening of Candra (TV) 81. The Fix 84. Starman 84. Pacific Inferno (TV) 85. Black Moon Rising 86. Ghetto Blaster 89. Delta Force II 90. King of the Kickboxers 91. Martial Outlaw 93, etc.
TV series: Frontier Circus 61. Banyon 70. Firehouse 74. Salvage 77. At Ease 83. Spenser: for Hire 85–87. Baywatch 91–92.

Jaeckin, Just (1940–)
French director and screenwriter of erotic movies that promise more than they deliver.
Emmanuelle 74. The Story of O 75. Madame Claude 79. The Last Romantic Lover/Le Dernier Amant Romantique 80. Lady Chatterley's Lover 82. The Perils of Gwendoline 84, etc.

Jaeger, Frederick (1928–)
Anglo-German general-purpose actor.
The Black Tent 56. I Was Monty's Double 59. The Looking Glass War 69. Scorpio 72. The Seven Percent Solution 76. The Passage 78. Nijinsky 80. Situation 81. Selling Hitler (TV) 91. Cold Comfort Farm (TV) 95, etc.

Jaffe, Carl (1902–1974)
Aristocratic-looking German actor, long in England.
Over the Moon 39. The Lion Has Wings 40. The Life and Death of Colonel Blimp 43. Gaiety George 46. Appointment in London 53. Operation Crossbow 65. The Double Man 67, many others.

Jaffe, Sam (1891–1984)
American character actor of eccentric appearance and sharp talent. On stage from 1916, films from 1933.
We Live Again 34. *The Scarlet Empress* 34. *Lost Horizon* (as the High Lama) 37. Gunga Din 39. Stage Door Canteen 43. 13 Rue Madeleine 46. Gentleman's Agreement 47. The Accused 48. Rope of Sand 49. *The Asphalt Jungle* (AAN) 50. Under the Gun 50. I Can Get It for You Wholesale 51. The Day the Earth Stood Still 51. All Mine to Give 57. Les Espions 57. The Barbarian and the Geisha 58. Ben Hur 59. A Guide for the Married Man 67. Guns for San Sebastian 68. The Great Bank Robbery 69. Night Gallery (TV) 69. Quarantined (TV) 70. The Kremlin Letter 70. The Old Man Who Cried Wolf (TV) 70. The Dunwich Horror 70. Who Killed the Mysterious Mr Foster? (TV) 71. Bedknobs and Broomsticks 71. QB VII (TV) 74. Battle Beyond the Stars 80. The End 81. Nothing Lasts Forever 82. On the Line 83, etc.
TV series: Ben Casey 60–64.

Jaffe, Stanley R. (1940–)
American producer. He is President and Chief Operating Officer of Paramount Communications.
Goodbye Columbus 69. Bad Company 72. The Bad News Bears 76. *Kramer vs Kramer* 78. Taps 81. Without a Trace (& d) 83. Racing with the Moon 84. Firstborn 84. Fatal Attraction (AAN) 87. The Accused 88. Black Rain 89. School Ties 92, etc.

Jaffrey, Madhur (1933–)
Indian actress, best known now for her books and television series on Indian cooking. She was formerly married to Saeed Jaffrey.
Shakespeare Wallah 65. The Guru 69. Autobiography of a Princess 75. Heat and Dust 82. The Assam Garden 85. The Perfect Murder 88. Vanya on 42nd Street 94, etc.
TV series: Firm Friends 93–94.

Jaffrey, Saeed
Exuberant Indian actor, in Britain. He studied at RADA, has acted with the National Theatre and also appeared in many Indian movies. He was formerly married to Madhur Jaffrey.
The Guru 69. The Man Who Would Be King 75. The Wilby Conspiracy 75. The Chess Players 77. Staying On (TV) 81. Gandhi 82. The Jewel in the Crown (TV) 83. The Razor's Edge 84. A Passage to India 84. My Beautiful Laundrette 85. The Deceivers 87. Masala 91. Guru in Seven 97. Second Generation 00, etc.
TV series: Tandoori Nights 85–87. Little Napoleons 94. Common as Muck 97.

Jagger, Dean (1903–1991) (Dean Jeffries)
American star character actor of the 40s, usually in sympathetic roles; later seen as colonels, fathers, town elders, etc.
Women from Hell 29. College Rhythm 34. Home on the Range 34. Men without Names 35. Revolt of the Zombies 36. Exiled to Shanghai 37. *Brigham Young* (title role) 40. Western Union 41. The Men in Her Life 41. The Omaha Trail 42. North Star 43. When Strangers Marry 44. I Live in Grosvenor Square (GB) 45. Sister Kenny 46. Pursued 47. *Twelve O'Clock High* (AA) 49. Dark City 50. Denver and Rio Grande 52. It Grows on Trees 52. The Robe 53. *Executive Suite* 54. Bad Day at Black Rock 55. The Great Man 56. X the Unknown (GB) 57. The Proud Rebel 58. The Nun's Story 59. Elmer Gantry 60. Parrish 61. The Honeymoon Machine 62. First to Fight 67. Firecreek 68. The Kremlin Letter 70. The Brotherhood of the Bell (TV) 70. Vanishing Point 71. The Glass House (TV) 72. God Bless Dr Shagetz 77. End of the World 77. Alligator 80. Evil Town 87, many others.
TV series: Mr Novak 63–65.

Jagger, Mick (1943–)
Heavy-faced British pop idol whose film career didn't get off the ground. He has his own production company, Jagged Films. In 1998, the *Sunday Times* estimated his fortune at £140m. After more than 22 years and four children together, he and model Jerry Hall in 1999 agreed a separation and an annulment of their marriage in 1990. She had previously sued for divorce on the grounds of his 'multiple adultery'.
Ned Kelly 69. Performance 70. Gimme Shelter 70. Burden of Dreams (doc) 82. The Nightingale (TV) 84. Freejack 92. Bent (a) 97. Tania (p) 97, etc.
❝ He sees all women as tarts. – *Bianca Jagger*
Mick's approach to acting was, once he discovered what it was about, he wasn't interested. – *James Fox*
Though fire and energy snake out of Mick like electricity in concert, he can't produce them cold as an actor. It's a problem with many rock performers. – *Tony Richardson*

Jaglom, Henry (1941–)
American writer-director of eccentric films.
■ A Safe Place 71. Tracks 76. Other People 79. Sitting Ducks (& a) 80. Can She Bake a Cherry Pie 83. Someone to Love 87. New Year's Day 89. Eating 90. Venice/Venice 92. Babyfever (co-w, d, e) 94. Last Summer in the Hamptons 95. Déjà Vu (co-w, d) 98.

Jakubowska, Wanda (1907–1998)
Polish director.
Soldier of Victory 43. The Last Stop 48. An Atlantic Story 54. Farewell to the Devil 56. Encounters in the Dark 60. The Hot Line 65. 150 Na Godzine 71. Bialy Mazur 73. Ludwik Warynski 78. Invitation to Dance 85, etc.

James, Brion (1945–1999)
Tall, lean American character actor, frequently in menacing roles, and best known for playing Leon, the replicant in Blade Runner. Born in Beaumont, California, he majored in theater at San Diego State College and studied acting with Stella ADLER in New York. Died of a heart attack.
Southern Comfort 81. Blade Runner 82. 48 Hours 82. A Breed Apart 84. Enemy Mine 85. Armed and Dangerous 85. Flesh and Blood 85. Crimewave 86. Steel Dawn 87. Nightmare at Noon 87. Dead Men Walking 88. Cherry 2000 88. Enid Is Sleeping 89. The Horror Show 89. Tango and Cash 89. Red Scorpion 89. Another 48 Hrs 90. Street Asylum 90. Mom 91. The Player 92. Black Magic (TV) 92. Time Runner 92. Future Shock 93. Nemesis 93. The Dark 93. Scanner Cop 93. Striking Distance 93. Cabin Boy 94. F.T.W. 94. Hatchet Man 94. Radioland Murders 94. Art Deco Detective 94. Cyberjack/Virtual Assassin 95. Pterodactyl Woman from Beverly Hills 96. American Strays 96. Bombshell 97. The Fifth Element 97. Brown's Requiem 98, etc.

James, Clifton (1893–1963)
British character actor who so resembled Field Marshal Montgomery that during World War II he was hired to impersonate him and hoodwink the Germans, as told in the subsequent book and film, *I Was Monty's Double*.

James, Clifton (1921–)
Corpulent American character actor.
David and Lisa 64. Cool Hand Luke 67. Tick Tick Tick 70. Live and Let Die 72. The Man with the Golden Gun 73. The Bank Shot 74. Silver Streak 76. The Bad News Bears in Breaking Training 77. Superman II 80. Talk to Me 82. Where Are the Children? 85. Eight Men Out 88. The Bonfire of the Vanities 90. Carolina Skeletons (TV) 91. Lone Star 96. The Summer of Ben Tyler 96, etc.
TV series: City of Angels 76. Lewis & Clark 81–82. All My Children 96–97.

James, Geraldine (1950–)
English leading actress, often on television. Born in Maidenhead, Kent, she trained at the Drama Centre.
Sweet William 80. Gandhi 82. *The Jewel in the Crown* (TV) 84. Blott on the Landscape (TV) 88. She's Been Away (TV) 89. The Wolves of Willoughby Chase 89. The Tall Guy 89. The Bridge 90. Beltenebros (Sp.) 91. Stanley and the Women (TV) 91. If Looks Could Kill/Teen Agent 91. Losing Track (TV) 92. No Worries (Aus.) 92. Words upon the Window Pane (Ire.) 94. The Healer (TV) 94. Moll Flanders 96. The Man Who Knew Too Little 97. Drover's Gold (TV) 97. Seesaw (TV) 98. The Luzhin Defence 00. The Testimony of Taliesin Jones 00, etc.
TV series: Band of Gold 95–96. Gold 97. The Sins 00.

James, Harry (1916–1983)
American band-leader and trumpeter who appeared in occasional films. He was married to Betty Grable (1943–65).
Biography: 00, *Trumpet Blues: The Life of Harry James* by Peter J. Levinson
Springtime in the Rockies 42. Best Foot Forward 43. Bathing Beauty 44. Do You Love Me 46. Carnegie Hall 47. I'll Get By 50. The Benny Goodman Story 56, etc.

James, Henry (1843–1916)
American novelist and playwright who lived for most of his life in Europe. Film-makers have been attracted by his supernatural story *The Turn of the Screw* and his novels dealing with Americans caught up in the more sophisticated and sometimes decadent society of Europe. He became a British citizen in 1915.
Autobiography: 1913, *A Small Boy and Others*. 1914, *Notes of a Son and Brother*. 1917, *The Middle Years*.
Berkeley Square (from *The Sense of the Past*) 33. The Lost Moment (from *The Aspern Papers*) 47. The Heiress (from *Washington Square*) 49. The Innocents (from *The Turn of the Screw*) 61. I'll Never Forget You (from *The Sense of the Past*) 51. The Nightcomers (a prequel to *The Turn of the Screw*) 72. Daisy Miller 74. The Green Room (Fr., from *The Altar of the Dead*) 78. The Europeans 79. Aspern (Port.) 81. The Bostonians 84. Los Papeles de Aspern (Sp.) 91. The Portrait of a Lady 96. The Pupil (Fr.) 96. Washington Square 97. The Wings of the Dove 97. The Golden Bowl 00. Presence of Mind/El Celo (from *The Turn of the Screw*) 00, etc.
❝ I've always been interested in people, but I've never liked them. – *H.J.*
Poor Henry James! He's spending eternity walking round and round a stately park and the fence is just too high for him to peep over and he's just too far away to hear what the countess is saying. – *Somerset Maugham*
One of the nicest old ladies I ever met. – *William Faulkner*

James, Jesse (1847–1882)
American wild west outlaw who has acquired the legend of a Robin Hood but in fact plundered ruthlessly as head of a gang which also included his sanctimonious elder brother *Frank James* (1843–1915). Among the many screen personifications of Jesse are Tyrone Power in *Jesse James* 39; Lawrence Tierney in *Badman's Territory* 46; Macdonald Carey in *The Great Missouri Raid* 52; Audie Murphy in *Kansas Raiders* 53; Willard Parker in *The Great Jesse James Raid* 53; Robert Wagner in *The True Story of Jesse James* 56; Dale Robertson in *Fighting Man of the Plains* 59; Ray Stricklyn in *Young Jesse James* 60; Chris Jones in a TV series *The Legend of Jesse James* 65; Robert Duvall in *The Great Northfield Minnesota Raid* 72; James Keach in *The Long Riders* 80 (brother Stacy was brother Frank); and Clayton Moore in several Republic serials. Henry Fonda was in *The Return of Frank James* 40.

James, M. R. (1862–1936)
English ghost-story writer, an academic with a splendid command of language. *The Night of the Demon* is a fairly satisfactory film version of *Casting the Runes*.

James, Peter (1946–)
Australian cinematographer, now resident in Canada.
Caddie 76. The Irishman 78. The Wild Duck 84. Rebel 85. The Right Hand Man 87. Echoes of Paradise 89. Driving Miss Daisy 89. Mr Johnson 90. Black Robe 91. My Life 93. Alive 93. Thing Called Love 93. Silent Fall 94. Last Dance 96. Diabolique 96. Paradise Road 97. Newton Boys 98. Double Jeopardy 99. Meet the Parents 00, etc.

James, Roderick
American editor, a psuedonym used by Ethan and Joel Cohen to disguise the fact that they edit the films they produce, write and direct between them.

James, Sid (1913–1976) (Sidney James Cohen)
Crumple-faced South African comedy actor, a former hairdresser, in London from 1946. He was a familiar face on TV and in scores of movies, including most of the Carry On series from 1958. Married three times. His lovers included actress Barbara Windsor. Died of a heart attack during a stage performance.
Black Memory 46. Once a Jolly Swagman 48. The Man in Black 49. The Lavender Hill Mob 51. The Titfield Thunderbolt 53. Joe Macbeth 55. The Silent Enemy 57. Too Many Crooks 58. Tommy the Toreador 59. Double Bunk 60. What a Carve Up 62. The Big Job 65. Don't Lose Your Head 67. Bless This House 73, many others.
TV series: Hancock's Half Hour 56–59. East End, West End 58. Citizen James 60. Taxi 63–64. George and the Dragon 66–68. Two in Clover 69–70. Bless This House 71–76.

James, Steve (1955–1993)
American star of martial arts movies. Born in New York City, he began in films as a stuntman. Died from leukaemia.
The Exterminator 80. The Brother from Another Planet 84. American Ninja 85. To Live and Die in LA 85. CAT Squad (TV) 86. Avenging Force 86. POW. The Escape 86. American Ninja 2: The Confrontation 87. Hero and the Terror 88. Johnny Be Good 88. CAT Squad: Python Wolf (TV) 88. American Ninja 3: Bloodhunt 89. I'm Gonna Get You Sucka 89. Riverbend 90. Street Hunter 90. McBain 91. Bloodfist V: Human Target 93. Weekend at Bernie's II 94. MANTIS (TV) 94, etc.

Jameson, Jerry
American director.
The Dirt Gang 72. The Bat People 74. The Elevator (TV) 74. The Secret Night Caller (TV) 74. *Heatwave* (TV) 74. Hurricane (TV) 74. Terror on the 40th Floor (TV) 75. The Deadly Tower

(TV) 75. The Invasion of Johnson County (TV) 76. Airport 77 77. A Fire in the Sky (TV) 77. High Noon Part Two (TV) 78. Raise the Titanic 80. The Cowboy and the Ballerina (TV) 84. Fire and Rain (TV) 89. Gunsmoke: To the Last Man (TV) 92. Bonanza: The Return (TV) 93. Gunsmoke: One Man's Justice (TV) 94, etc.

Jamison, Bud (1894–1944)
American character actor, a stock Columbia player who played the heavy in most of the Three Stooges two-reelers.

Jancso, Miklos (1921–)
Hungarian director.
Cantata 63. My Way Home 64. The Round Up 65. The Red and the White 67. Silence and Cry 68. Winter Wind 70. The Pacifist 71. Agnus Dei 71. Red Psalm 72. Electra 74. Private Vice and Public Virtue 76. Masterwork 77. Hungarian Rhapsody 79. Heart of a Tyrant 81. Huzsika (TV) 84. Omega, Omega 85. Budapest (doc) 85. Dawn 86. Season of Monsters 87. Jezus Krisztus Horoszkopia 89. The Blue Danube Waltz/Kek Duna Keringo 92, etc.

Janda, Krystyna (1952–)
Polish leading actress and occasional director. Born in Starachowice, she became a star on her debut, the first of several appearances in the films of director Andrezej WAJDA. She won a best actress award at the Cannes film Festival for her role in *Interrogation*.
Man of Marble/Czlowiek z Marmaru 78. The Beast/Bestia 78. The Conductor/Dyrygent 79. Man of Iron/Czlowiek z Zelaza 81. Bella Donna (Ger) 82. Interrogation 82 (released 90). Mephisto (Hung.) 81. Laputa (Ger.) 87. Ten Commandments, Part 2/Dekalog, Dwa 89. A Short Film About Killing/Krotki Film o Zabijaniu 89. Stan Posiadania 89. Zwolnieni z Zycia 91. Pestka (&d) 94, etc.

Jandl, Ivan (1941–1987)
Czech child actor whose sole performance as a war orphan in the tear-jerking *The Search*, opposite Montgomery Clift, won him an Academy Award for 'the outstanding juvenile performance of 1948'.

Jane, Thomas (1969–)
American actor, born in Baltimore, Maryland.
Buffy the Vampire Slayer 92. The Crow: City of Angels 96. The Last Time I Committed Suicide 97. Boogie Nights 97. The Thin Red Line 98. The Velocity of Gary 98. Deep Blue Sea 99. Magnolia 99. Molly 99. Under Suspicion 00. Original Sin 01, etc.

Janis, Conrad (1928–)
American character actor; began as a teenage player of the 40s.
Snafu 45. Margie 46. The High Window 46. Beyond Glory 48. Keep it Cool 58. The Duchess and the Dirtwater Fox 76. Roseland 77. Oh God Book Two 80. Brewster's Millions 84. Nothing in Common 86. Sonny Boy 90. The Feminine Touch (& d) 96, etc.
TV series: Quark 76. Mork and Mindy 78–80.

Janis, Elsie (1889–1956) (Elsie Bierbauer)
American musical comedy star who made a few silent movies such as *Betty in Search of a Thrill* and *A Regular Girl*; only talkie, *Women in War* 42.

Jankel, Annabel
British director who works in collaboration with Rocky Morton.
The Max Headroom Story (co-d) (TV) 85. D.O.A. (co-d) 88. Super Mario Bros (co-d) 93.

Janney, Leon (1917–1980)
American child actor, a member of the original Our Gang.
Doorway to Hell 30. Penrod and Sam 31. Should Ladies Behave 32, etc.

Janni, Joseph (1916–1994)
Italian producer, in England from 1939.
The Glass Mountain 48. Romeo and Juliet 53. *A Town Like Alice* 56. *A Kind of Loving* 62. Darling 65. Modesty Blaise 66. Far From the Madding Crowd 67. *Poor Cow* 68. *Sunday Bloody Sunday* (AAN) 71. Made 72. Yanks 79, etc.

Jannings, Emil (1882–1950) (Theodor Emil Janenz)
Distinguished German actor, on stage from ten years old. Entered films through his friend Ernst Lubitsch.
■ Im Banne der Leidenschaft 14. Passionels Tagebuch 14. Frau Eva 15. Vendetta 16. Wenn Vier Dasselbe Tun 17. Life Is a Dream 18. The Eyes of the Mummy 18. The Brothers Karamazov 18. Der Stier von Oliviera 18. Rose Bernd 18. *Madame Dubarry* 19. Anne Boleyn 20. Kohlhiesel's Daughter 21. Danton 21. The Wife of the Pharaoh 21. Tragedy of Love 22. Ratten 22. *Othello* 23. Peter the Great 24. All for Gold 24. *Quo Vadis* 24. Nju 24. *The Last Laugh* 24. Waxworks 24. Tartuffe 25. *Faust* 26. *Variety* 26. *The Way of All Flesh* (US) (AA) 27. *The Last Command* (US) (AA) 28. The Street of Sin (US) 28. The Patriot (US) 28. The Sins of the Fathers (US) 29. The Betrayal (US) 29. *The Blue Angel* 30. Darling of the Gods 31. The Tempest 31. Le Roi Pausaole 32. Der Schwarze Walfisch 34. *The Old and the Young King* 35. Traumulus 35. Der Herrscher 37. The Broken Jug 37. Robert Koch 39. Ohm Kruger 40. Die Entlassing 42. An Old Heart Becomes Young Again 42. Where Is Herr Belling 45.
✪ For being the last ham of the old school to become an international star. *The Blue Angel*.
❝ Nine people out of ten, if asked to say who is the greatest actor on the screen, would unhesitatingly reply Emil Jannings. – *Lionel Collier, Picturegoer, 1929*

Jansen, Pierre (1930–)
French composer who has scored many of the films of Claude Chabrol.
Les Bonnes Femmes 60. Les Sept Péchés Capitaux 62. Ophélia 62. Bluebeard/Landru 62. Les Plus Belles Escroqueries du Monde 64. Le Tigre Aime la Chair Fraîche 64. La 317 Section 65. La Ligne de Démarcation 66. The Champagne Murders/Le Scandale 67. La Route de Corinthe 67. Les Biches 68. The Unfaithful Wife/La Femme Infidèle 68. This Man Must Die/Que la Bête Meure 69. Le Boucher 69. La Rupture 70. Just before Nightfall/Juste avant la Nuit 71. High Heels/ Docteur Popaul 72. Wedding in Blood/Les Noces Rouges 73. Nada 74. Les Innocents aux Mains Sales 75. Nuit d'Or 76. The Lacemaker/La Dentellière 77. Violette 78. L'Etat Sauvage 78. Le Cheval d'Orgueil 80, etc.

Janssen, David (1930–1980) (David Meyer)
American leading man, very successful on TV; film roles routine, persona doggedly glum.
Yankee Buccaneer 52. Chief Crazy Horse 54. The Square Jungle 55. Toy Tiger 56. The Girl He Left Behind 56. *Hell to Eternity* 60. Ring of Fire 60. Mantrap 61. *King of the Roaring Twenties* (as Arnold Rothstein) 61. My Six Loves 63. Warning Shot 67. The Green Berets 68. The Shoes of the Fisherman 68. Where It's At 69. A Time for Giving 69. Macho Callahan 70. Birds of Prey (TV) 73. Fer de Lance (TV) 74. Once Is Not Enough 75. Stalk the Wild Child (TV) 76. The Swiss Conspiracy 76. Two Minute Warning 76. Mayday at 40,000 Feet 77. Warhead 77. The Word (TV) 78. The Golden Gate Murders (TV) 79. High Ice (TV) 79. City in Fear (TV) 79, etc.
TV series: *Richard Diamond* 59. *The Fugitive* 63–66. O'Hara US Treasury 71. Harry O 73–75.

Janssen, Eilene (1937–)
American child actress of the 40s.
The Green Years 46. About Mrs Leslie 54. The Search for Bridie Murphy 56. Beginning of the End 57. The Space Children 58. Escape from Red Rock 58. Black Zoo 63, etc.

Janssen, Famke (1964–)
Dutch-born actress and model who moved to the US in the mid-80s. Married director and screenwriter Todd Williams.
Fathers and Sons 92. Lord of Illusions 95. GoldenEye 95. City of Industry 96. The Gingerbread Man 97. Deep Rising 98. Celebrity 98. Monument Avenue 98. Rounders 98. Celebrity 98. The Faculty 98. Snitch 98. House on Haunted Hill 99. Circus 00. Love & Sex 00. X-Men 00, etc.

Janssen, Werner (1899–1990)
American composer. He was married to actress Ann Harding (1937–63).
The General Died at Dawn (AAN) 36. Blockade (AAN) 38. Eternally Yours (AAN) 39. Slightly Honorable 40. Guest in the House 44. The Southerner (AAN) 45. Captain Kidd (AAN) 45. A Night in Casablanca 46. Ruthless 48, etc.

Janus, Samantha (1974–)
Blonde English actress and singer, mainly on television. She trained at LAMDA and sang the British entry in the 1991 Eurovision Song Contest.
Jekyll and Hyde (TV) 90. A Murder of Quality (TV) 91. Breeders 97. Up 'n' Under 98, etc.
TV series: Demob 93. Pie in the Sky 95–96. Game On 95–98. Babes in the Wood 98. Liverpool One 98.

Jarman Jnr, Claude (1934–)
American boy actor of the 40s.
The Yearling (special AA) 46. High Barbaree 47. Intruder in the Dust 49. Rio Grande 51. Fair Wind to Java 53. The Great Locomotive Chase 56, etc.

Jarman, Derek (1942–1994)
British independent director and screenwriter, often on homosexual themes. He went to the Slade School of Fine Art and began as a painter, becoming a set and costume designer for ballet and opera. He started making short films in the early 70s and also directed pop videos in the 80s. He continued to work outside the mainstream, making low-budget films: *The Tempest* cost £150,000. Died of AIDS.
Autobiography: 1984, *Dancing Ledge*. 1991, *Modern Nature, the Journals of Derek Jarman*.
Biography: 1996, *Derek Jarman: Dreams of England* by Michael O'Pray.
■ The Devils (ad) 70. Savage Messiah (ad) 72. *Sebastiane* 76. Jubilee 78. The Tempest 79. In the Shadow of the Sun 72–80. Imagining October 84. The Angelic Conversation 85. Aria (co-d) 85. *Caravaggio* 86. The Last of England 86. War Requiem 89. The Garden 90. *Edward II* 91. *Wittgenstein* 93. Blue 93. Glitterbug 94.
❝ Most of the cinema is an enormous irrelevance, a medium that has crossed the boundaries of intelligence in very few hands. – *D.J.*

Jarmusch, Jim (1953–)
Off-beat, independent American director, screenwriter, musician and occasional actor.
Permanent Vacation 82. Stranger than Paradise 84. Down by Law 86. Mystery Train 89. Leningrad Cowboys Go America (a) 90. Night on Earth 91. In the Soup (a) 92. Iron Horsemen (a) 94. Blue in the Face (a) 95. Dead Man 95. Sling Blade (a) 96. Year of the Horse (wd, co-ph) 97, etc.
❝ If I had to make a film with some suit guys telling me how to make the damn thing, I think I'd go off my head and kneecap some executive. – *J.J.*

Jarre, Kevin
American screenwriter, the son of actress Laura Devon.
Rambo: First Blood Part II (story) 85. Glory 89. Tombstone 94. The Devil's Own 97, etc.

Jarre, Maurice (1924–)
French composer, conductor and timpanist whose best work has been for director David LEAN. Born in Lyon, he studied at the Paris Conservatoire of Music and first worked in the theatre with Jean-Louis BARRAULT and as director of music for the French National Theatre.
Hôtel des Invalides 52. La Tête contre les Murs 59. Eyes without a Face 59. Crack in the Mirror 60. *The Longest Day* 62. *Lawrence of Arabia* (AA) 62. Sundays and Cybele (AAN) 62. Weekend at Dunkirk 65. *Dr Zhivago* (AA) 65. Is Paris Burning? 66. The Professionals 66. The 25th Hour 67. Five Card Stud 68. Isadora 68. The Damned 69. *Ryan's Daughter* 70. Ash Wednesday 74. Great Expectations (TV) 76. The Last Tycoon 76. Jesus of Nazareth (TV) 76. March or Die 77. Mohammed, Messenger of God (GB/Leb.) (AAN) 77. Winter Kills 79. Resurrection 80. The Black Marble 80. Taps 81. Lion of the Desert 81. Young Doctors in Love 82. Firefox 82. The Year of Living Dangerously 83. A Passage to India (AA) 84. The Bride 84. Mistress (AAN, BFA) 84. Enemy Mine 85. Witness (AAN) 85. Mosquito Coast 86. Solarbabies 86. Tai-Pan 86. Fatal Attraction 87. No Way Out 87. Buster 88. Gorillas in the Mist (AAN) 88. Moon over Parador 88. Wildfire 88. Dead Poets Society 89. Enemies: A Love Story 89. Prancer 89. After Dark, My Sweet 90. Almost an Angel 90. Ghost 90. Jacob's Ladder 90. Solar Crisis 90. Only the Lonely 91. School Ties 92. Shadow of the Wolf (co-m) 93. Fearless 93. Mr Jones 94. A Walk in the Clouds 95. The Sunchaser 96. Sunshine 99, etc.

Jarrico, Paul (1915–1997) (Israel Shapiro)
American screenwriter who was blacklisted in the 50s. Born in Los Angeles, he graduated from the University of Southern California and went to work for Columbia Pictures, later moving to RKO. A Communist Party member, he refused to name names to HUAC in the early 50s and sued Howard HUGHES for refusing to give him a credit for writing *Las Vegas Story*. (He was later refused a credit on the remake of *Tom, Dick and Harry* as *The Girl Most Likely* 58.) After he was blacklisted, he moved to Europe for 20 years, writing under pseudonyms, and returning to Hollywood in the late 70s. Died in a car crash while returning from a ceremony marking the 50th anniversary of the beginning of blacklisting, at which the president of the Screen Writers' Guild had apologized for its past conniving in the denial of credits to blacklisted writers.
Little Adventuress (co-story) 38. No Time to Marry (co-w) 38. Beauty for the Asking (co-w) 39. *Tom, Dick and Harry* (AAN) 41. The Face behind the Mask (co-w) 41. Song of Russia (co-w) 44. Little Giant/On the Carpet (co-w) 46. The Search (co-w) 48. The White Tower 50. Las Vegas Story 52. *Salt of the Earth* (co-w) (Mex.) 53. Five Branded Women (It.) 60. All Night Long (co-w) (GB) 61. Treasure of the Aztecs (Ger.) 65. The Day the Hot Line Got Hot (Fr.) 68. The Day that Shook the World (Yug.) 76. Messenger of Death 88. Stalin (uncredited) (TV) 92, etc.

Jarrott, Charles (1927–)
British director, from TV.
■ Time to Remember 62. *Anne of the Thousand Days* 70. Mary Queen of Scots 72. Lost Horizon 73. The Dove 74. Escape from the Dark 76. The Other Side of Midnight 77. The Last Flight of Noah's Ark 79. Condorman 81. The Amateur 82. The Boy in Blue 85. Poor Little Rich Girl (TV) 87. The Women He Loved (TV) 88. Morning Glory (co-w) 93.

Jarvilaturi, Ilkka (1961–)
Finnish director, now in America.
Kotia Pänö 89. *Darkness in Tallinn*/Tallinnan Pimeys 93, etc.

Jarvis, Martin (1941–)
British leading man in all media.
The Last Escape 70. Taste the Blood of Dracula 70. Ike (TV) 79. The Bunker (TV) 81. Buster 88, etc.
TV series: Rings on their Fingers 78–80.

Jasny, Vojtech (1925–)
Czechoslovakian director and screenwriter, one of the leaders of the Czech new wave of the 50s. Born in Kelc, Moravia, he studied film at FAMU in Prague and began by directing documentaries. He went into exile after the Czech government banned *All My Good Countrymen*, which won the best director prize at the Cannes Film Festival in 1969, returning in 1998 to make *Return to Paradise Lost*.
Everything Ends Tonight (co-d) 54. September Nights (& co-w) 57. Desire (& co-w) 58. I Survived Certain Death 60. Pilgrimage to the Virgin Mary 61. When the Cat Comes (& co-w) 63. Pipes 65. All My Good Countrymen (& w) 68. The Clown (Aus.) 75. Attempt to Escape (Aus.) 76. The Maiden (Yug.) 80. The Suicide (Fin.) 84. The Great Land of Small (Can.) 87. Which Side Eden/Return to Paradise Lost 99, etc.

Jason, David (1940–) (David White)
British comedy character actor, mostly on radio and TV.
Under Milk Wood 73. Royal Flash 75. The Water Babies 78. The Odd Job 78. Porterhouse Blue (TV) 87. The Bullion Boys (TV) 93.
TV series: Open All Hours 76–85. A Sharp Intake of Breath 78–81. Only Fools and Horses 81–93. A Bit of a Do 88–90. The Darling Buds of May 91–93. A Touch of Frost 93–.

Jason, Leigh (1904–1979)
American director, mainly of second features.
The Price of Fear 28. Wolves of the City 29. High Gear 33. The Mad Miss Manton 38. Lady for a Night 39. Model Wife 41. Three Girls About Town 41. Nine Girls 44. Lost Honeymoon 46. Out of the Blue 48. Okinawa 52, etc.

Jason, Rick (1926–2000)
Tough American leading actor of the 50s, born in New York City. He was best known for his role as

Lt Gil Hanley in the TV series *Combat!*. He also had a recurring role on the daytime soap opera *The Young and the Restless*. Shot himself.

Sombrero 53. The Saracen Blade 54. This Is My Love 54. The Lieutenant Wore Skirts 55. The Wayward Bus 57. RX Murder 58. Colour Me Dead 70. Eagles Attack at Dawn 74. The Witch Who Came from the Sea 76. Partners 82. Around the World in 80 Days (TV) 89, etc.

TV series: The Case of the Dangerous Robin 60-61. *Combat* 62–67.

Jason, Sybil (1929–)
South African child actress of the 30s.

Barnacle Bill (GB) 35. Little Big Shot (GB) 36. The Singing Kid (US) 36. The Little Princess (US) 39. The Bluebird (US) 40, etc.

Jason, Will (1899–1970)
American second feature director.

The Soul of a Monster 44. Thief of Damascus 52, many others.

Jaubert, Maurice (1900–1940)
French composer.

L'Affaire Est dans le Sac 32. Le Quatorze Juillet 33. Zéro de Conduite 33. L'Atalante 34. Drôle de Drame 37. *Un Carnet de Bal* 37. *Quai des Brumes* 38. *Le Jour Se Lève* 39. La Fin du Jour 39, etc.

Jay, Ernest (1894–1957)
British stage character actor.

Tiger Bay 34. Broken Blossoms 36. Don't Take It to Heart 44. Vice Versa 47. The History of Mr Polly 49. Edward My Son 49. I Believe in You 52. Who Done It? 55. The Curse of Frankenstein 56.

Jay, Ricky (1948–)
American magician, historian and actor, often in the films of David Mamet. Born in Brooklyn, and raised in New Jersey, he began performing from childhood. He runs Deceptive Practices, a magic consultancy for films, theatre and TV.

Books: 1998, *Learned Pigs & Fireproof Women* by Ricky Jay; 2001, *Jay's Journal of Anomalies*.

House of Games 87. Things Change 88. Homicide 91. The Spanish Prisoner 97. Boogie Nights 91. Tomorrow Never Dies 97. Mystery Men 99. State and Main 00, etc.

Jayne, Jennifer (1932–)
British leading lady.

Once a Jolly Swagman 48. The Blue Lamp 50. It's a Grand Life 53. The Man Who Wouldn't Talk 57. The Trollenberg Terror 58. Raising the Wind 61. On the Beat 63. The Liquidator 65. The Medusa Touch 78. The Jigsaw Man 83. The Doctor and the Devils 85, etc.

TV series: The Adventures of William Tell 58–59.

Jayston, Michael (1935–) (Michael James)
British stage actor commanding reputable film roles.

Cromwell 70. *Nicholas and Alexandra* 71. Follow Me 72. Alice's Adventures in Wonderland 72. A Bequest to the Nation 73. Tales that Witness Madness 73. The Homecoming 73. Craze 73. The Internecine Project 74. She Fell Among Thieves (TV) 78. Tinker Tailor Soldier Spy (TV) 80. Dominique 78. Zulu Dawn 79. Highlander III: The Sorcerer 94. Element of Doubt 96. 20,000 Leagues under the Sea (TV) 97, etc.

Jeakins, Dorothy (1914–1995)
American costume designer.

Joan of Arc (AA) 48. Samson and Delilah (AA) 49. South Pacific 58. Let's Make Love 60. The Night of the Iguana (AA) 64. The Sound of Music (AAN) 65. The Hindenburg 75. The Way We Were (AAN) 73. The Betsy 78. On Golden Pond 81. The Dead (AAN) 87, etc.

Jean, Gloria (1927–) (Gloria Jean Schoonover)
Former American child singer, on screen from 1939 as second-feature rival to Deanna Durbin.

■ The Underpup 39. If I Had My Way 40. A Little Bit of Heaven 40. Never Give a Sucker an Even Break 41. What's Cookin'? 42. Get Hep to Love 42. It Comes Up Love 42. When Johnny Comes Marching Home 42. Mister Big 43. Moonlight in Vermont 43. Follow the Boys 44. Pardon My Rhythm 44. The Ghost Catchers 44. Reckless Age 44. Destiny 44. I'll Remember April 44. Easy to Look At 45. River Gang 45. Copacabana 47. I Surrender Dear 48. An Old Fashioned Girl 49. Manhattan Angel 49. There's a Girl in My Heart 50. Air Strike 55. The Ladies' Man 61.

Jean, Vadim (1966–)
British screenwriter and director.

Leon the Pig Farmer (co-d) 92. Beyond Bedlam (co-w, d) 94. Clockwork Mice (d) 95. The Real Howard Spitz 98, etc.

Jean Louis
see Louis, Jean.

Jean-Baptiste, Marianne (1967–)
English leading actress and singer. Born in London, she trained at RADA.

Secrets and Lies (as Hortense) (AAN) 95. Career Girls 97. Mr Jealousy 97. The 24-Hour Woman 98. New Year's Day 99. The Cell (US) 00, etc.

“ The old men running the industry just have not got a clue. They've got to come to terms with the fact that Britain is no longer a totally white place where people wear long frocks and drink tea. The national dish is no longer fish and chips, it's curry. – *M.J-B.*

Jeanmaire, Zizi (Renée) (1924–)
Leading lady and ballet dancer, in occasional films. Married choreographer Roland Petit.

Hans Christian Andersen 52. Anything Goes 56. Folies Bergère 56. Charmants Garçons 57. Black Tights 60, etc.

Jeans, Isabel (1891–1985)
British stage actress, invariably in aristocratic roles.

Tilly of Bloomsbury 21. The Rat 25. Downhill 27. Easy Virtue 28. Sally Bishop 33. *Tovarich* (US) 38. Suspicion (US) 41. Banana Ridge 41. Great Day 45. It Happened in Rome 57. *Gigi* 58. A Breath of Scandal 60. *Heavens Above* 63, etc.

Jeans, Ursula (1906–1973) (Ursula McMinn)
British stage actress, long married to Roger Livesey; in occasional films.

The Gypsy Cavalier (debut) 31. Cavalcade 33. Dark Journey 37. Mr Emmanuel 44. The Woman in the Hall 46. The Weaker Sex 48. The Dam Busters 55. Northwest Frontier 59. The Queen's Guards 61. The Battle of the Villa Fiorita 65, etc.

Jeanson, Henri (1900–1970)
French writer, a former actor and critic.

Pepe Le Moko 36. Life Dances On/Un Carnet de Bal 37. Hotel du Nord 38. The Curtain Rises/Entrée des Artistes 38. The Damned/Les Maudits 47. Lady Paname (& d) 50. Fanfan la Tulipe 51. Holiday for Henrietta/La Fête à Henrietta 52. Nana 55. The Lovers of Montparnasse/Modigliani of Montparnasse/Les Amants de Montparnasse 58. The Cow and I/La Vache et le Prisonnier 59. Madame/Madame Sans-Gêne 62. Paris in the Month of August/Paris au Mois d'Août 66, etc.

Jeayes, Allan (1885–1963)
British stage actor of dignified heavy presence; played supporting roles in many films.

The Ghost Train 31.The Impassive Footman 32. The Camels are Coming 34. The Scarlet Pimpernel 34. King of the Damned 35. His Lordship 36. Rembrandt 36. Seven Sinners 36. Elephant Boy 37. Man of Affairs 37. The Squeaker 37. They Drive by Night 38. The Four Feathers 39. The Good Old Days 39. The Proud Valley 39. The Spider 39. The Stars Look Down 39. Convoy 40. You Will Remember 40. The Thief of Bagdad 40. The Man Within 46. Saraband for Dead Lovers 48. Waterfront 50, many others.

Jefford, Barbara (1930–)
British stage actress, more recently in films.

Ulysses 67. The Bofors Gun 68. A Midsummer Night's Dream 68. The Shoes of the Fisherman 68. Lust for a Vampire 70. And the Ship Sails On 84. When the Whales Came 89. Where Angels Fear to Tread 91. The Saint 97. The Ruth Rendell Mysteries: Thornapple (TV) 97, etc.

Jeffrey, Peter (1929–1999)
British general-purpose actor. Died of cancer.

Becket 64. If 67. The Early Bird 65. The Fixer 68. Anne of the Thousand Days 69. Ring of Bright Water 69. Goodbye Gemini 70. The Horsemen 70. The Abominable Dr Phibes 71. The Horsemen 71. Countess Dracula 71. What Became of Jack and Jill? 71. Dr Phibes Rises Again 72. The Odessa File 74. Deadly Strangers 74. Midnight Express 78. The Return of the Pink Panther 74. Britannia Hospital 82. The Adventures of Baron Munchausen 89. Middlemarch (TV) 94. Rasputin 96. Our Friends in the North (TV) 96, etc.

Jeffreys, Anne (1923–) (Anne Carmichael)
American leading lady of the 40s, formerly in opera. She married actor Robert Sterling, her second husband, in 1956.

I Married an Angel 42. Step Lively 44. Dillinger 45. Riff Raff 47. Return of the Badmen 49. Boys Night Out 62. Panic in the City 68. Clifford 94, etc.

TV series: Topper 53. Love That Jill 58.

Jeffries, Fran (1939–) (Frances Makris)
American singer and actress, born in California. She appeared as a singer on the TV variety show *Spotlight* in 1967.

The Buccaneer 58. The Pink Panther 63. Sex and the Single Girl 64. A Talent for Loving 69, etc.

Jeffries, Lionel (1926–)
Bald British character comedian, who rose to co-star status, then turned to direction.

Stage Fright 50. Windfall 54. The Baby and the Battleship 55. Law and Disorder 57. The Nun's Story 58. Idol on Parade 59. *Two-Way Stretch* 60. *The Trials of Oscar Wilde* 60. The Hellions 61. The Notorious Landlady 61. The Wrong Arm of the Law 63. Call Me Bwana 63. The Long Ships 64. *The First Men in the Moon* 64. The Truth about Spring 65. The Secret of My Success 65. You Must Be Joking 65. Arrivederci Baby 66. *The Spy with a Cold Nose* 67. Rocket to the Moon 67. *Camelot* 67. Chitty Chitty Bang Bang 68. Eyewitness 70. Who Slew Auntie Roo 71. Royal Flash 75. The Prisoner of Zenda 79. Cream in My Coffee (TV) 80. Better Late than Never 81. A Chorus of Disapproval 88, etc.

■ as director: *The Railway Children* 70. The Amazing Mr Blunden 72. Baxter 72. The Water Babies 78. Wombling Free 78.

Jenkins, Allen (1900–1974) (Alfred McGonegal)
'Tough guy' American comic actor, a staple of Warners' repertory in the 30s.

The Girl Habit 31. Rackety Rax 32. Blessed Event 32. I am a Fugitive from a Chain Gang 32. Lawyer Man 32. Rackety Rax 32. Blondie Johnson 33. Bureau of Missing Persons 33. Employees' Entrance 33. 42nd Street 33. Hard to Handle 33. Havana Widows 33. The Keyhole 33. The Mayor of Hell 33. The Mind Reader 33. Professional Sweetheart 33. The Big Shakedown 34. The Case of the Howling Dog 34. Happiness Ahead 34. I've Got Your Number 34. Jimmy the Gent 34. The Merry Frinks 34. Sweet Music 34. Twenty Million Sweethearts 34. Whirlpool 34. Broadway Hostess 35. The Case of the Curious Bride 35. The Case of the Lucky Legs 35. I Live for Love 35. The Irish in Us 35. Page Miss Glory 35. Miss Pacific Fleet 35. While the Patient Slept 35. Cain and Mabel 36. Sing Me a Love Song 36. The Singing Kid 36. Three Men on a Horse 36. The Perfect Specimen 37. Dead End 37. Marked Woman 37. Marry the Girl 37. The Perfect Specimen 37. Ready Willing and Able 37. Sh! The Octopus 37. The Singing Marine 37. Swing Your Lady 37. *A Slight Case of Murder* 38. Fools for Scandal 38. Going Places 38. Gold Diggers in Paris 38. Hard to Get 38. Heart of the North 38. Racket Busters 38. The Amazing Dr Clitterhouse 38. Five Came Back 39. *Destry Rides Again* 39. Tin Pan Alley 40. Brother Orchid 40. Footsteps in the Dark 41. Ball of Fire 41. A Date with the Falcon 41. Dive Bomber 41. Maisie Gets Her Man 42. Eyes in the Night 42. The Falcon Takes Over 42. They All Kissed the Bride 42. Tortilla Flat 42. *Wonder Man* 45. Lady on a Train 45. Meet Me on Broadway 46. Easy Come, Easy Go 47. Fun on a Weekend 47. The Senator Was Indiscreet 47. Wild Harvest 47. The Big Wheel 49. Chained for Life 50. Behave Yourself 51. Pillow Talk 59. Robin and the Seven Hoods 64. For Those Who Think Young 64. Doctor You've Got to be Kidding 67. The Front Page 74, etc.

TV series: *Hey Jeannie* 56.

Jenkins, Charles Francis (1868–1934)
American inventor of the Phantascope, a camera using continuously moving film, which he patented in January 1894. He collaborated with Thomas Armat to demonstrate a Phantascope projector at the Cotton States Exposition at Atlanta, Georgia in October 1895. Armat improved the mechanism and patented it in February 1896 as the Vitascope, which was promoted under the aegis of Thomas Edison.

Jenkins, George (1914–)
American production designer.

The Best Years of Our Lives 46. The Secret Life of Walter Mitty 47. Roseanna McCoy 49. The Miracle Worker 62. Mickey One 65. Wait until Dark 67. Me Natalie 69. The Angel Levine.70. The Paper Chase 73. Night Moves 75. *All the President's Men* (AA) 76. Comes a Horseman 78. The China Syndrome (AAN) 79. Starting Over 79. The Postman Always Rings Twice 81. Rollover 81. Sophie's Choice 82. Dream Lover 86. Orphans 87. See You in the Morning 89. Presumed Innocent 90, etc.

Jenkins, Jackie 'Butch' (1937–)
Buck-toothed American child star of the 40s, son of Doris Dudley; retired because he developed a stutter.

■ *The Human Comedy* 43. National Velvet 44. An American Romance 44. Abbott and Costello in Hollywood 45. Our Vines Have Tender Grapes 45. Boys' Ranch 46. Little Mister Jim 46. My Brother Talks to Horses 46. Big City 48. The Bride Goes Wild 48. Summer Holiday 48.

Jenkins, Megs (1917–1998)
Plump British actress of kindly or motherly roles, on stage from 1933.

The Silent Battle 39. *Green for Danger* 46. The Brothers 47. The Monkey's Paw 48. *The History of Mr Polly* 49. White Corridors 51. Ivanhoe 52. The Cruel Sea 53. The Gay Dog 54. John and Julie 55. The Man in the Sky 56. Conspiracy of Hearts 59. *The Innocents* 61. The Barber of Stamford Hill 62. Bunny Lake Is Missing 65. Stranger in the House 67. Oliver 68. David Copperfield 69. The Amorous Milkman 74, etc.

Jenks, Frank (1902–1962)
American character comedian, usually seen as Runyonesque stooge, cop or valet.

When's Your Birthday? 37. You Can't Cheat an Honest Man 39. Dancing on a Dime 40. Rogues' Gallery 45. Loonies on Broadway 46. The She-Creature 56, many others.

TV series: Colonel Flack 53.

Jenks, Si (1876–1970) (Howard Jenkins)
American character actor, frequently a whiskery, comic sidekick in innumerable westerns. He worked in vaudeville and the circus before beginning his screen career in 1920.

Two Fisted Justice 31. Riders of Destiny 33. Charlie Chan's Courage 34. Rawhide Romance 34. The Outlaw Deputy 35. Fighting Shadows 35. Pigskin Parade 36. Captain January 36. Outcasts of Poker Flat 37. Topper 37. Rawhide 38. Stagecoach 39. Gone with the Wind 39. The Great Train Robbery 41. Sergeant York 41. It's a Great Life 43. Eve Knew Her Apples 45. Duel in the Sun 46. The Dark Horse 46. Son of Zorro (serial) 47. Kentucky Jubilee 51. Oklahoma Annie 52, etc.

Jennings, Al (1864–1961)
American outlaw of the old west who among other pursuits became a silent screen actor.

The Lady of the Dugout 18. Fighting Fury 24. The Sea Hawk 24. The Demon 26. Loco Luck 27. Land of Missing Men 30, etc.

Jennings, De Witt (1879–1937)
American character actor, stern and bulky.

The Warrens of Virginia 15. Three Sevens 21. The Enemy Sex 24. Exit Smiling 26. Alibi 29. The Big Trail 30. Min and Bill 30. Caught Plastered 31. Movie Crazy 32. Mystery of the Wax Museum 33. Little Man What Now 34. Mutiny on the Bounty 35. Sins of Man 36. Slave Ship 37, many others.

Jennings, Humphrey (1907–1950)
Distinguished British documentarist, with the GPO Film Unit from 1934. Responsible for a fine World War II series of sensitive film records of the moods of the time.

The First Days (co-d) 39. *London Can Take It* (co-d) 40. *Listen to Britain* 41. The Silent Village 43. *Fires Were Started* 43. *A Diary for Timothy* 45, etc. Also: The Cumberland Story 47. *Dim Little Island* 49. Family Portrait 50, etc.

✪ For his unbroken series of poetic and cinematic images of Britain at war. *Listen to Britain*.

Jennings, Talbot (1896–1985)
American screenwriter and playwright, usually in collaboration with other writers. Born in Shoshone, Idaho, he studied at Harvard and the Yale Drama School.

Mutiny on the Bounty (AAN) 35. Romeo and Juliet 36. The Good Earth 37. Spawn of the North 38. Rulers of the Sea 39. Northwest Passage 40. Edison the Man 40. So Ends Our Night 41. Frenchman's Creek 44. Anna and the King of Siam (AAN) 46. Landfall 49. The Black Rose 50. Across the Wide Missouri 51. Knights of the Round Table 53. Escape to Burma 55. Untamed 55, etc.

Jens, Salome (1935–)
American leading lady, in very occasional films.
■ *Angel Baby* 61. The Fool Killer 65. Seconds 66. Me Natalie 69. In the Glitter Palace (TV) 77. Sharon: Portrait of a Mistress (TV) 77. From Here to Eternity (TV) 79. Cloud Dancer 80. Harry's War 81. Clan of the Cave Bear 85. Just Between Friends 85.

Jergens, Adele (1922–)
American leading lady, mainly in second features. She was married to actor Glenn Langan.
A Thousand and One Nights 44. Ladies of the Chorus 48. Blonde Dynamite 50. Somebody Loves Me 52. The Cobweb 55. Girls in Prison 56. The Lonesome Trail 58, etc.

Jerome, Jerome K. (1859–1927)
British humorist and essayist. His *Three Men in a Boat* and *The Passing of the Third Floor Back* were filmed several times.

Jerrold, Mary (1877–1955) (Mary Allen)
British character actress, mainly on stage; in films, played mainly sweet old ladies.
Alibi 31. Friday the Thirteenth 33. The Man at the Gate 41. *The Way Ahead* 44. *The Queen of Spades* 48. Mr Perrin and Mr Traill 49. Top of the Form 52, etc.

Jessel, George (1898–1981)
American entertainer, in vaudeville from childhood. After making the mistake of turning down *The Jazz Singer*, he had a very spasmodic film career, but in the 50s he produced a number of musicals for Fox.
Autobiography: 1946, *So Help Me*. 1955, *This Way Miss*. 1975, *The World I Live In*.
AS ACTOR: The Other Man's Wife 19. Private Izzy Murphy 26. Lucky Boy/My Mother's Eyes 29. Love Live and Laugh 29. Stage Door Canteen 43. Four Jills in a Jeep 44. The I Don't Care Girl 53. The Busy Body 57. Hieronymus Merkin 69, etc.
AS PRODUCER: Do You Love Me 46. When My Baby Smiles at Me 48. Dancing in the Dark 49. Meet Me After the Show 51. Golden Girl 51. Wait Till the Sun Shines Nellie 52. The I Don't Care Girl 53. Tonight We Sing 53, etc.
❝ Did you ever catch him at a funeral? It's wonderful. All through the years he makes notes on his friends. He wants to be ready. – *Eddie Cantor*
That son of a bitch started his reminiscences when he was eight years old. – *Walter Winchell*

Jessel, Patricia (1920–1968)
British character actress, mostly on stage.
The Flesh Is Weak 57. The Man Upstairs 58. *City of the Dead* 61. A Jolly Bad Fellow 64. A Funny Thing Happened on the Way to the Forum 66, etc.

Jessua, Alain (1932–)
French writer-director of off-beat films.
Life Upside Down 63. Jeu de Massacre 67. Traitement de Choc 73. Armageddon 77. Les Chiens 79. Paradis pour Tous 82. Frankenstein 90 84. En Toute Innocence 88, etc.

Jeunet, Jean-Pierre (1955–)
French screenwriter and director, of a quirky style.
Delicatessen (co-w, co-d) 90. City of Lost Children (co-w, co-d) 95. Alien: Resurrection (d) (US) 97.

Jewell, Isabel (1913–1972)
Diminutive American leading lady of the 30s, a minor 'platinum blonde' who graduated to character parts.
Blessed Event 33. Counsellor at Law 33. Manhattan Melodrama 34. A Tale of Two Cities 35. The Man Who Lived Twice 37. Marked Woman 37. *Lost Horizon* 37. Gone with the Wind 39. The Leopard Man 43. The Bishop's Wife 48. The Story of Molly X 48. Bernardine 57, many others.

Jewison, Norman (1926–)
Canadian director and screenwriter, from TV.
■ Forty Pounds of Trouble 63. The Thrill of It All 63. Send Me No Flowers 64. The Art of Love 65. *The Cincinnati Kid* 65. *The Russians Are Coming, the Russians Are Coming* (& p) (AANp) 66. *In the Heat of the Night* (p, d) (AAp, AANd) 67. The Thomas Crown Affair (p, d) 68. The Landlord (p) 69. Gaily, Gaily (p, d) 69. Fiddler on the Roof (p, d) (AAN) 71. Jesus Christ Superstar (p, d) 73. Rollerball 75. And Justice for All (& co-p) 79. The Dogs of War (co-p only) 81. Best Friends (& p) 82. A Soldier's Story 84. Agnes of God 85. Moonstruck (AAN) 87. The January Man 88. In Country 89. Other People's Money 91. Only You 94. Bogus (p, d) 96.

Jhabvala, Ruth Prawer (1927–)
German-born screenwriter and novelist, mainly for the films of Merchant-Ivory.
The Householder/Gharbar 63. Shakespeare Wallah 65. The Guru 69. Bombay Talkie 70. Autobiography of a Princess 75. Roseland 77. Hullabaloo over Georgie and Bonnie's Pictures 78. The Europeans 79. Jane Austen in Manhattan 80. Quartet 81. Courtesans of Bombay 82. Heat and Dust 82. The Bostonians 84. *A Room with a View* (AAN) 85. Madame Sousatzka 88. Mr & Mrs Bridge 90. *Howards End* 92. The Remains of the Day 93. Jefferson in Paris 95. Surviving Picasso 96. A Soldier's Daughter Never Cries 98. The Golden Bowl 00, etc.

Jianxin, Huang (1954–)
Chinese director, a former photographer. He studied at the Beijing Film Academy, graduating in 1985.
The Black Cannon Incident/Haipao Shijan 85. The Stand-In/Cuowei 87. Samsara/Lunhui 88. The Wooden Man's Bridge/Wu Kui 93. Back to Back, Face to Face 94, etc.

Jimenez, Neal
American scriptwriter and director.
Where the River Runs Black (co-w) 86. River's Edge (w) 87: The Waterdance (w, co-d) 92. Sleep with Me (co-w) 94. Hideaway (co-w) 95, etc.

Jires, Jaromil (1935–)
Czech director, a graduate of the Prague Film School.
The Cry/Krick 63. *Valerie and Her Week of Wonders*/Valerie A Týden Divu 70. Payment in Kind/Causa Kralik 80. Helimadoe 94, etc.

Joan of Arc (c. 1412–1431)
The French heroine, martyr and saint, who persuaded the Dauphin that she had a divine mission to lead the French resistance to English occupation, was captured and sold to her enemies, tried for heresy and burned at the stake, and has defeated most film actresses who have tried to portray her. Carl Dreyer's silent *The Passion of Joan of Arc* 28 starred the remarkable Maria Falconetti in her only screen role; Ingrid Bergman took the role in Victor Fleming's dull *Joan of Arc* 48; Jean Seberg endured torments when directed by Otto Preminger in *Saint Joan* 57, based on Bernard Shaw's play; Hedy Lamarr popped up in the role in Irwin Allen's unintentionally hilarious *The Story of Mankind* 57; Robert Bresson's *The Trial of Joan of Arc* 62 had Florence Carrez as Joan; Jacques Rivette's four-hour *Jean La Pucelle* 94 starred Sandrine Bonnaire in a performance that came near to matching her subject.

Joanou, Phil (1961–)
American director.
Three O'Clock High 87. U2 Rattle and Hum (doc) 88. State of Grace 90. Final Analysis 92. Heaven's Prisoners 96, etc.

Jobert, Marlène (1943–)
French leading lady.
Masculin Féminin 66. Le Voleur 66. L'Astragale 68. Rider on the Rain 69. Last Known Address 70. Catch Me a Spy 72. Ten Days' Wonder 72. Juliette et Juliette 73. The Secret 74. Julie Pot de Colle 77. A Filthy Business 80. Souvenirs, Souvenirs 84. Les Cigognes n'en Font qu'à Leur Tête 89, etc.

Jodorowsky, Alexandro (1930–)
Chilean director, actor, writer and artist with surrealist tendencies.
Fando and Lis 70. El Topo 71. The Holy Mountain 74. Tusk 80. Santa Sangre 89, etc.

Joffe, Charles H.
American producer almost exclusively associated with the films of Woody Allen.
Take the Money and Run 69. Bananas 70. Everything You Always Wanted to Know about Sex 72. Sleeper 73. Love and Death 73. The Front 76. Annie Hall 77. Stardust Memories 80. A Midsummer Night's Sex Comedy 82. Zelig 83. Broadway Danny Rose 84. Hannah and Her Sisters 86. Radio Days 87. Alice 90. Shadows and Fog 92. Manhattan Murder Mystery 93. Bullets over Broadway 94. Mighty Aphrodite 95. Everyone Says I Love You 96. Deconstructing Harry 97. Celebrity 98, etc.

Joffe, Mark
Australian director.
Grievous Bodily Harm 88. Shadow of the Cobra (TV) 89. Spotswood/The Efficiency Expert 91. Cosi 96. The MatchMaker 97, etc.

Joffé, Roland (1945–)
British director and screenwriter with TV experience.
The Killing Fields (AAN) 84. The Mission (AAN) 85. Fat Man and Little Boy/The Shadowmakers 89. City of Joy 92. The Scarlet Letter 95. Goodbye, Lover (US) 98, etc.

Johann, Zita (1904–1993)
American leading lady of the early 30s.
The Struggle 31. Tiger Shark 32. *The Mummy* 32. Luxury Liner 33. Grand Canary 34. Raiders of the Living Dead 89, etc.

John, Sir Elton (1947–) (Reginald Dwight)
British pop singer. He heads his own production company Rocket Pictures. In 1997, *Business Age* estimated his personal fortune at £200m.
Friends (m) 71. Tommy (a) 75. The Lion King (AAs) 94. The Muse (m) 99. Women Talking Dirty (ex-p,m) 00, etc.

John, Gottfried (1942–)
German actor, associated with Rainer Werner FASSBINDER on stage and screen, in international films and television.
Carlos 71. Mother Kuster's Trip to Heaven/ Mutter Kusters Fahrt zum Himmel 75. 1982: Gutenbach 78. In a Year with 13 Moons/In einem Jahr mit 13 Monden 78. Fedora 78. The Marriage of Maria Braun/Die Ehe der Maria Braun 78. Berlin Alexanderplatz (TV) 79. Lili Marleen 80. Super 83. Chinese Boxes 84. Mata-Hari (US) 85. Of Pure Blood (TV) 86. Wings of Fame (Hol.) 90. Abraham (TV) 94. Institute Benjamenta (GB) 95. GoldenEye (US) 95. Am I Beautiful?/Bin Ich Schon? 98. Asterix and Obelix vs. Caesar/Astérix et Obélix (Fr.) 98. Proof of Life (US) 00, etc.

John, Rosamund (1913–1998) (Nora Jones)
Gentle-mannered British leading lady who turned in several pleasing performances in the 40s.
■ The Secret of the Loch 34. The First of the Few 42. *The Gentle Sex* 43. The Lamp Still Burns 43. Tawny Pipit 44. *The Way to the Stars* 45. Green for Danger 46. The Upturned Glass 47. Fame is the Spur 47. When the Bough Breaks 47. No Place for Jennifer 49. She Shall Have Murder 50. Never Look Back 52. Street Corner 53. Operation Murder 56.

Johns, Glynis (1923–)
Husky-voiced British actress, daughter of Mervyn Johns; on stage (as child) from 1935.
South Riding (debut) 36. Prison without Bars 38. 49th Parallel 41. Halfway House 44. *Perfect Strangers* 45. This Man Is Mine 46. Frieda 47. *Miranda* (as a mermaid) 47. An Ideal Husband 47. State Secret 50. Appointment with Venus 51. *The Card* 52. The Sword and the Rose 53. Personal Affair 53. Rob Roy 53. The Weak and the Wicked 54. The Beachcomber 55. Mad about Men 55. *The Court Jester* (US) 56. The Day They Gave Babies Away (US) 56. Shake Hands with the Devil 59. The Sundowners (AAN) 60. The Spider's Web 61. *The Chapman Report* (US) 62. Mary Poppins (US) 64. Dear Brigitte (US) 65. Don't Just Stand There (US) 68. Lock Up Your Daughters 69. Under Milk Wood 71. Vault of Horror 73. Little Gloria, Happy at Last (TV) 83. Zelly and Me 88. Nukie 89. The Ref/Hostile Hostages 94. While You Were Sleeping 95, etc.
TV series: Glynis 63.

Johns, Mervyn (1899–1992)
Welsh character actor, on stage from 1923; usually plays mild-mannered roles.
Lady in Danger (debut) 34. Jamaica Inn 39. *Saloon Bar* 40. *Next of Kin* 41. Went the Day Well? 42. My Learned Friend 44. *Dead of Night* 45. *Pink String and Sealing Wax* 45. Scrooge 51. The Intimate Stranger 56. No Love for Johnnie 61. 80,000 Suspects 63. The Heroes of Telemark 65. Who Killed the Cat? 66. The House of Mortal Sin 77, many others.

Johnson, Arch (1923–1997)
Burly American character actor.
Somebody Up There Likes Me 56. G.I. Blues 58. Twilight of Honor 63. Sullivan's Empire 67. Walking Tall 73. The Buddy Holly Story 77, many others.

Johnson, Arte (1934–)
Small-scale American comic actor.
Miracle in the Rain 56. The Subterraneans 60. The President's Analyst 67. Charge of the Model Ts 77. Love at First Bite 79. Bunco 83. The Raven Red Kiss-Off 90. Tax Season 90. Evil Spirits 91. Evil Toons 91, etc.
TV series: It's Always Jan 55–56. Sally 58. Hennessey 59–62. Don't Call Me Charlie 62–63. Rowan & Martin's Laugh-In 68–71. Games People Play 81–82. Glitter 84–85.

Johnson, Ben (1918–1996)
Leathery American character actor, a former cowboy and stunt rider. Born in Foreacre, Oklahoma, he began in movies after driving a herd of horses to California, where they had been ordered by Howard Hughes for *The Outlaw*. John Ford took him from the anonymity of stunt riding by giving him roles in his westerns, usually as a gruff but sympathetic companion to the hero. He went on to appear in around 300 films, with his finest moment coming in *The Last Picture Show* as Sam the Lion, proprietor of a failing cinema. He won a World Champion Cowboy title in 1953.
Three Godfathers 49. Mighty Joe Young 49. She Wore a Yellow Ribbon 49. *Wagonmaster* 50. Rio Grande 50. Fort Defiance 51. Shane 53. Slim Carter 57. Fort Bowie 60. One Eyed Jacks 61. Major Dundee 65. The Rare Breed 66. Will Penny 67. The Wild Bunch 69. The Undefeated 69. *The Last Picture Show* (AA) 71. Corky 72. Junior Bonner 72. Dillinger 73. The Sugarland Express 73. Bite the Bullet 75. Hustle 76. Breakheart Pass 76. The Greatest 77. The Town that Dreaded Sundown 77. The Swarm 78. Terror Train 80. The Hunter 80. Red Dawn 84. Cherry 2000 86. Let's Get Harry 86. Trespasses 86. Dark before Dawn 88. Back to Back 89. My Heroes Have Always Been Cowboys 91. Radio Flyer 92. The Legend of O. B. Taggart 94. Angels in the Outfield 94. Evening Star 96, many others.
TV series: The Monroes 66–67.

Johnson, Bumpy (1906–1968) (Ellsworth Johnson)
Gangster who controlled much of Harlem in the 20s and 30s, and was the subject of the biopic *Hoodlum* starring Laurence Fishburne in 1997. Fishburne also played Bumpy Rhodes, a character based on him, in *The Cotton Club* 84.

Johnson, Dame Celia (1908–1982)
Distinguished British actress, on stage from 1928, usually in well-bred roles: films rare.
Biography: 1991, *Celia Johnson* by Kate Fleming.
■ *In Which We Serve* (debut) 42. *Dear Octopus* 42. This Happy Breed 44. *Brief Encounter* (AAN) 46. The Astonished Heart 49. I Believe In You 52. The Captain's Paradise 53. The Holly and the Ivy 54. A Kid for Two Farthings 56. The Good Companions 57. The Prime of Miss Jean Brodie 69. Les Misérables (TV) 78. Staying On (TV) 79. The Hostage Tower (TV) 80.
❝ The only actress who thought acting was of secondary importance to living. – *Ronald Neame*

Johnson, Chic (1891–1962)
Portly American vaudeville comedian (with partner Ole Olsen).
■ Oh Sailor Behave 30. Fifty Million Frenchmen 31. Gold Dust Gertie 31. Country Gentlemen 36. All over Town 37. Hellzapoppin 41. Crazy House 43. Ghost Catchers 44. See My Lawyer 45, etc.

Johnson, Don (1949–)
American leading man; formerly twice married to Melanie GRIFFITH (1976–77, 1989–95).

Zachariah 70. The Harrad Experiment 73. Return to Macon County 75. Law of the Land (TV) 76. The City (TV) 77. Ski Lift to Death (TV) 78. Beulah Land (TV) 79. The Long Hot Summer (TV) 85. Sweet Hearts Dance 88. Dead Bang 89. The Hot Spot 90. Harley Davidson and the Marlboro Man 91. Paradise 91. Born Yesterday 93. Guilty as Sin 93. In Pursuit of Honor (TV) 95. Tin Cup 96. Goodbye, Lover 98, etc.

TV series: From Here to Eternity 79. *Miami Vice* 85–89. Nash Bridges 96– .

Johnson, Edith (1895–1969)
American silent film actress, in serials for Vitagraph and Universal. Married William JOHNSON, who starred opposite her in many of them.

The Flower of Faith 14. The Aunt 15. Behind the Lines 16. A Fight for Millions (serial) 18. The Man of Might (serial) 19. Smashing Barriers (serial 19. The Silent Avenger (serial) 20. Where Men Are Men 21. The Steel Trail (serial) 23. Wolves of the North (serial) 24, many others.

Johnson, Hugh
Irish cinematographer turned director, associated with the films of Ridley SCOTT, for whose commercials company he worked from the mid 80s.

AS CINEMATOGRAPHER: White Squall 96. GI Jane 97, etc.

AS DIRECTOR: Chill Factor 99.

Johnson, Jack (1878–1946)
American heavyweight boxer, world champion from 1908–15, who made a few films in the 20s. *The Great White Hope*, starring James Earl Jones, is a slightly fictionalized account of his life.

As the World Rolls On 21. For His Mother's Sake 22. Black Thunderbolt 22.

Johnson, Katie (1878–1957)
British character actress who became a star in her old age.

Jeannie 41. The Years Between 46. I Believe in You 52. *The Ladykillers* 55. How to Murder a Rich Uncle 56, many others.

Johnson, Kay (1904–1975) (Catherine Townsend)
American leading actress of the 30s. She was married to director John CROMWELL; their son is actor James CROMWELL.

■ *Dynamite* 29. The Ship from Shanghai 30. This Mad World 30. Billy the Kid 30. The Spoilers 30. Madam Satan 30. Passion Flower 30. The Single Sin 31. The Spy 31. American Madness 32. Thirteen Women 32. Eight Girls in a Boat 34. This Man Is Mine 34. Of Human Bondage 34. Their Big Moment 34. Village Tale 35. Jalna 35. White Banners 38. The Real Glory 39. Son of Fury 42. Mr Lucky 43. The Adventures of Mark Twain 44.

❝ Kay was a very talented lady from Broadway, and a lot of fun to work with, but she didn't quite set the screen on fire. – *Mitchell Leisen*

Johnson, Kyle (1952–)
American actor, in leading juvenile roles of the 60s.

Living between Two Worlds 63. *The Learning Tree* 69. The Sheriff (TV) 70. Man on the Run 74, etc.

Johnson, Lamont (1920–)
American director, from TV, a former actor.

Covenant with Death 67. Kona Coast (TV) 68. Deadlock (TV) 69. My Sweet Charlie (TV) 70. The Mackenzie Break 70. A Gunfight 71. That Certain Summer (TV) 72. The Groundstar Conspiracy 72. You'll Like My Mother 72. The Last American Hero 73. The Execution of Private Slovik (TV) 74. Fear on Trial (TV) 75. Lipstick 76. One On One 77. Somebody Killed Her Husband 78. Sunny Side 79. Foxes 80. Crisis at Central High (TV) 80. Off the Minnesota Strip 80. Escape from Iran (TV) 81. Cattle Annie and Little Britches 81. Spacehunter 83. Ernie Kovacs: Between the Laughter (TV) 84. Wallenberg: A Hero's Story (TV) 85. Unnatural Causes (TV) 86. Gore Vidal's Lincoln (TV) 88. The Kennedys of Massachusetts (TV) 89. Crash Landing: The Rescue of Flight 232 (TV) 92. Broken Chain 93, etc.

Johnson, Laurie (1927–)
British composer, mainly notable for themes of television's *The Avengers* and *The Professionals*.

The Good Companions 57. Tiger Bay 59. I Aim at the Stars 60. Dr Strangelove 63. First Men in the Moon 63. The Beauty Jungle 64. And Soon the Darkness 70. The Belstone Fox 74. Captain Kronos: Vampire Hunter 74. The Maids 75. Hedda 75. It Shouldn't Happen to a Vet 76. It's Alive II: It Lives Again 78. A Hazard of Hearts (TV) 87. The Lady and the Highwayman (TV) 89. A Ghost in Monte Carlo (TV) 90, etc.

Johnson, Lynn-Holly (1959–)
American leading lady, a former ice-skater.

Ice Castles 78. For Your Eyes Only 81. The Watcher in the Woods 81. The Sisterhood 88, etc.

Johnson, Martin and Osa (1884–1937 and 1894–1953)
American explorers who made several feature-length films. A Johnson Safari Museum is situated in Chanute, Kansas (Mrs Johnson's birthplace).

Jungle Adventure 21. Simba 28. Congorilla 32. Wings over Africa 34. Baboona 35. Borneo 38. I Married Adventure 40, etc.

Johnson, Noble (1881–1978)
American actor who played a multitude of fearsome native chiefs.

Robinson Crusoe (as Friday) 22. The Ten Commandments 23. The Navigator 24. Hands Up 26. Vanity 27. Redskin 28. The Four Feathers 29. Moby Dick 30. The Mummy 32. *King Kong* 33. She 35. Conquest 37. The Ghost Breakers 40. Jungle Book 42. A Game of Death 45. She Wore a Yellow Ribbon 49. North of the Great Divide 50, many others.

Johnson, Nunnally (1897–1977)
American screenwriter, producer and director.

■ AS WRITER: Rough House Rosie 27. A Bedtime Story (co-w) 33. Mama Loves Papa (co-w) 33. Moulin Rouge (co-w) 34. *The House of Rothschild* 34. *Bulldog Drummond Strikes Back* 34. Kid Millions (co-w) 35. Cardinal Richelieu (co-w) 35. Thanks a Million 35. The Man Who Broke the Bank at Monte Carlo (co-w) 35. *The Prisoner of Shark Island* (& p) 36. The Country Doctor (p only) 36. The Road to Glory (p only) 36. Dimples (p and original idea) 36. Banjo on My Knee (& p) 36. Nancy Steele Is Missing (p only) 37. Cafe Metropole (p only) 37. Slave Ship (p only) 37. Love under Fire (p only) 37. *Jesse James* (& p) 39. Wife, Husband and Friend (& p) 39. *Rose of Washington Square* (& p) 39. *The Grapes of Wrath* (& p) (AANw) 40. I Was an Adventuress (p only) 40. Chad Hanna (& p) 40. *Tobacco Road* 41. *Roxie Hart* (& p) 42. The Pied Piper (& p) 42. Life Begins at 8.30 (& p) 42. The Moon Is Down (& p) 43. Holy Matrimony (& p) (AANw) 43. Casanova Brown (& p) 44. *The Woman in the Window* (& p) 44. The Keys of the Kingdom (co-w) 44. Along Came Jones 45. *The Dark Mirror* (& p) 46. The Senator Was Indiscreet (p only) 47. Mr Peabody and the Mermaid (& p) 48. Everybody Does It (& p) 49. Three Came Home (& p) 49. The Gunfighter (co-w, p) 50. *The Mudlark* (& p) 50. The Long Dark Hall 51. *The Desert Fox* (& p) 51. Phone Call from a Stranger (& p) 52. We're Not Married (& p) 52. My Cousin Rachel (& p) 52. How to Marry a Millionaire (& p) 53. Night People (& pd) 53. Black Widow (& pd) 54. How to Be Very Very Popular (& pd) 55. The Man in the Grey Flannel Suit (& d) 56. Oh Men Oh Women (& pd) 56. *The Three Faces of Eve* (& p,d) 57. The Man Who Understood Women (& pd) 57. The Angel Wore Red (& d) 60. Flaming Star (co-d) 60. Mr Hobbs Takes a Vacation 62. Take Her She's Mine 63. The World of Henry Orient (co-d) 64. Dear Brigitte 65. The Dirty Dozen (co-w) 67.

✪ For being involved in so many of Hollywood's most intelligent pictures. *The Grapes of Wrath*.

❝ Movie actors wear dark glasses to funerals to conceal the fact that their eyes are not red from weeping. – *N.J.*

Johnson had been known to tell his bosses that he didn't want any producer 'pecking around' his work. 'It could delay me a month and if you don't like what I've written, it could upset me.' – *Fred Lawrence Guiles*

Johnson, Rafer (1935–)
American actor, formerly Olympic athlete.

The Fiercest Heart 61. The Sins of Rachel Cade 61. Wild in the Country 61. The Lion 63. None but the Brave 65. The Red, White and Black 70, etc.

Johnson, Richard (1927–)
British leading man of stage and screen.

Captain Horatio Hornblower 51. Never So Few (US) 59. Cairo (US) 62. *The Haunting* 63. Eighty Thousand Suspects 63. The Pumpkin Eater 64. Operation Crossbow 65. Moll Flanders 65. Khartoum 66. *Deadlier than the Male* (as Bulldog Drummond) 66. Danger Route 67. La Strega in Amore (It.) 67. Oedipus the King 68. A Twist of Sand 68. Lady Hamilton (as Nelson) (Ger.) 68. Some Girls Do 68. Julius Caesar 70. Hennessy 75. Aces High 76. The Four Feathers (TV) 78. Haywire (TV) 81. The Aerodrome (TV) 83. Turtle Diary (also p) 85. Lady Jane 86. Diving In 90. Crucifer of Blood (TV) 91. The Foreign Student 94. P. G. Wodehouse's Heavy Weather (TV) 95. Breaking the Code (TV) 97, etc.

Johnson, Rita (1912–1965)
American actress who usually played 'the other woman'.

Serenade 39. Edison the Man 40. Here Comes Mr Jordan 41. Thunderhead, Son of Flicka 44. They Won't Believe Me 47. Family Honeymoon 49. Susan Slept Here 54. Emergency Hospital 56. The Day They Gave Babies Away 57, etc.

Johnson, Tor (1903–1971)
Bald, menacing American character actor.

Ghost Catchers 44. Road to Rio 47. The Lemon Drop Kid 51. Bride of the Monster 55. Carousel 56. Plan 9 from Outer Space 56. Night of the Ghouls 59, etc.

Johnson, Van (1916–) (Charles Van Johnson)
American light leading man, in films since 1941 after stage experience.

Murder in the Big House (debut) 41. *Dr Gillespie's New Assistant* 42. The War against Mrs Hadley 42. Dr Gillespie's Criminal Case 43.The Human Comedy 43. Madame Curie 43. Pilot Number Five 43. A Guy Named Joe 44. The White Cliffs of Dover 44. Two Girls and a Sailor 44. Thirty Seconds over Tokyo 44. Thrill of a Romance 45. Weekend at the Waldorf 45. Easy to Wed 46. No Leave, No Love 46. Till the Clouds Roll By 46. High Barbaree 47. The Romance of Rosy Ridge 47. State of the Union 48. Mother Is a Freshman 48. The Bride Goes Wild 48. In the Good Old Summertime 49. Command Decision 49. *Battleground* 49. The Big Hangover 50. The Duchess of Idaho 50. Grounds for Marriage 50. Go for Broke 51. Three Guys Named Mike 51. Too Young to Kiss 51. Invitation 52. It's a Big Country 52. When in Rome 52. Washington Story 52. Plymouth Adventure 52. Confidentially Connie 53. Easy to Love 53. Remains to Be Seen 53 *The Caine Mutiny* 54. Brigadoon 54. The Last Time I Saw Paris 54. The End of the Affair (GB) 54. Men of the Fighting Lady 54. The Siege at Red River 54. *Miracle in the Rain* 55. The Bottom of the Bottle 56. Slander 56. Twenty-Three Paces to Baker Street 56. Kelly and Me 57. Action of the Tiger 57. Subway in the Sky (GB) 58. Beyond This Place (GB) 59. The Last Blitzkrieg 59. The Enemy General 60. Wives and Lovers 63. Divorce American Style 67. Where Angels Go Trouble Follows 68. Yours Mine and Ours 68. Battle Squadron (It.) 69. Company of Killers (TV) 70. Rich Man Poor Man (TV) 76. The Kidnapping of the President 80. Absurd! 81. The Purple Rose of Cairo 84. Down There in the Jungle 87. Killer Crocodile 88. Taxi Killer 88. Three Days to a Kill 92, etc.

TV series: Glitter 84.

Johnston, Arthur James (1898–1954)
American composer who began as an orchestrator for Irving BERLIN and went with him to Hollywood in 1929, where he wrote many songs for Bing CROSBY, usually with lyricist Sam Coslow. His hits include 'Just One More Chance' from *College Coach*, 'Cocktails for Two' from *Murder at the Vanities*, and the title song from *Pennies from Heaven*.

College Coach 32. College Humour 33. Too Much Harmony 33. Hello Everybody 33. Many Happy Returns 34. Belle of the Nineties 34. Murder at the Vanities 34. Thanks a Million 35. The Girl Friend 35. Go West Young Man 36. Pennies from Heaven 36. Sailing Along (GB) 37. Song of the South 47, etc.

Johnston, Eric A. (1895–1963)
American executive, successor to Will H. Hays as President of the MPAA (Motion Picture Association of America) (1945–63).

Johnston, Joe
American director, a former production designer.

Raiders of the Lost Ark (AA, visual effects) 81. Honey, I Shrunk the Kids 89. The Rocketeer 91. The Pagemaster (co-d) 94. Jumanji 95, etc.

Johnston, Margaret (1917–)
Australian actress who has made occasional British films, notably in mid-40s.

The Prime Minister (debut) 40. *The Rake's Progress* 45. A Man About the House 47. Portrait of Clare 50. The Magic Box 51. Knave of Hearts 53. Touch and Go 55. *Night of the Eagle* 62. Life at the Top 65. The Psychopath 66. Sebastian 67, etc.

Johnston, Oliver (1888–1966)
British character actor.

Room in the House 55. *A King in New York* 57. A Touch of Larceny 60. Dr Crippen 62. Cleopatra 63. A Countess from Hong Kong 67, etc.

Jolie, Angelina (1975–) (A. J. Voight)
American model turned actress, the daughter of actor Jon VOIGHT. Formerly married to actor Jonny Lee MILLER, she married actor-director Billy Bob THORNTON in 2000.

Cyborg II 93. Hackers 95. Without Evidence 96. Foxfire 96. Mojave Moon 96. Love Is All There Is 96. Playing God 97. True Women (TV) 97. George Wallace (TV) 97. Gia 97. Playing by Heart 98. The Bone Collector 99. Girl, Interrupted (AA) 99. Pushing Tin 99. Gone in 60 Seconds 00. Tomb Raider (as Lara Croft) 01, etc.

Jolley, I. Stanford (1900–1978)
American western character actor.

The Sombrero Kid 42. Frontier Fury 43. Lighting Raiders 45. Prairie Express 47. Waco 52. The Young Guns 56. 13 Fighting Men 60, many others.

Jolson, Al (1886–1950) (Asa Yoelson)
Celebrated Jewish-American singer and entertainer, of inimitable voice and electric presence. After years as a big Broadway attraction, he starred in the first talking picture and although his fortunes subsequently declined, a biopic using his voice made him a world celebrity again in his 60s.

Biography: 1962, *The Immortal Jolson* by Pearl Sieben. 1972, *Al Jolson* by Michael Friedland. 1975, *Sonny Boy* by Barrie Anderton.

■ *The Jazz Singer* 27. *The Singing Fool* 28. Sonny Boy 29. Say It with Songs 29. Mammy 30. Big Boy 30. Hallelujah I'm a Bum 33. Wonder Bar 34. Go into Your Dance 35. The Singing Kid 36. *Rose of Washington Square* 39. Hollywood Cavalcade 39. Swanee River 39. Rhapsody in Blue 45. *The Jolson Story* (voice only) 46. *Jolson Sings Again* (voice only) 49.

✪ For heralding an era, and for being a star again 20 years later without even being seen. *Rose of Washington Square*.

❝ It was easy enough to make Jolson happy at home. You just had to cheer him for breakfast, applaud wildly for lunch, and give him a standing ovation for dinner. – *George Burns*

He was more than just a singer or an actor. He was an experience. – *Eddie Cantor*

I'll tell you when I'm going to play the Palace. That's when Eddie Cantor and George Burns and Groucho Marx and Jack Benny are on the bill. I'm going to buy out the whole house, and sit in the middle of the orchestra and say: Slaves, entertain the king! – *A.J.*

Famous line (*The Jazz Singer*) 'You ain't heard nothin' yet!'

Jones, Allan (1907–1992)
American singing star of the 30s. Born in Old Forge, Pennsylvania, of Welsh parents, he worked as a miner before studying music at the University of Syracuse. The second of his four wives was actress Irene HERVEY; their son, Jack Jones, is a singer.

■ Reckless 35. *A Night at the Opera* 35. Rose Marie 36. The Great Ziegfeld (voice only, dubbing for Dennis Morgan) 36. Showboat 36. A Day at the Races 37. *The Firefly* 37. Everybody Sing 38. Honeymoon in Bali 39. The Great Victor Herbert 39. The Boys from Syracuse 40. One Night in the Tropics 40. There's Magic in Music 42. True to the Army 42. Moonlight in Havana 42. Rhythm of the Islands 43. Larceny with Music 43. Crazy House 43. You're a Lucky Fellow Mr Smith 43. When Johnny Comes Marching Home 43. Sing a Jingle 44. The Singing Sheriff 44. Señorita from the West

Devil and the Deep 32. Jewel Robbery 33. Imitation of Life 34. The Ghost Walks 34. The Case of the Curious Bride 34. Diamond Jim 35. Mad Love 35. The Last Days of Pompeii 35. The Black Room 35. Bullets or Ballots 36. Romeo and Juliet (as Friar Laurence) 36. Theodora Goes Wild 36. Conquest 37. Maid of Salem 37. The Cowboy and the Lady 38. *Holiday* 38. Union Pacific 39. The Real Glory 39. Grand Old Opry 40. A Woman's Face 41. Sarong Girl 43. Bluebeard 44. The Secret Life of Walter Mitty 47, many others.

Koller, Xavier (1944–)
Swiss director.
Black Tanner (AAN) 86. Journey of Hope/Reise der Hoffnung (AA) 90. Squanto: A Warrior's Tale (US) 94, etc.

Kolski, Jan Jakub (1956–)
Polish film director and screenwriter with a penchant for rural fantasy.
Burial of Potatoes/Pogrzeb Kartofla 91. Johnnie the Aquarius 93. Miraculous Place 94. The Man Who Reads Music from Plates 96, etc.

Koltai, Lajos (1946–)
Hungarian-born cinematographer, in America from the late 80s.
Mephisto 80. Angi Vera 81. Colonel Redl 85. Hanussen 88. Homer and Eddie 89. White Palace 90. Mobsters 91. Wrestling Ernest Hemingway 93. Born Yesterday 93. When a Man Loves a Woman 94. Just Cause 95. Home for the Holidays 95. Mother 96. Out to Sea 97. The Legend of 1900/The Legend of the Pianist on the Ocean (It.) 98. Sunshine 99. Malena (AAN) 00, etc.

Komai, Tetsu (1893–1970)
Japanese-American character actor.
Daughter of the Dragon 31. Island of Lost Souls 33. Tokyo Joe 49. Japanese War Bride 52. The Night Walker 64, etc.

Komeda, Krystof (1931–1969) (Krzysztof Trzcinski)
Polish composer and jazz musician, associated with the films of Roman Polanski.
Two Men and a Wardrobe/Dwaj Ludzie z Szafa 58. See You Tomorrow/Do Widzenia Do Jutra 60. Innocent Sorcerers/Niewinni Czarodzieje 60. The Glass Mountain/Szklana Gora 60. The Chain/Lancuch 60. Knife in the Water/Noz w Wodzie 60. Epilogue/Hvad Med Os? (Den.) 63. The Cats/Kattorna (Swe.) 64. The Penguin/Pingwin 64. The Barrier/Bariera 65. Cul-de-Sac (GB) 66. Le Départ (Bel.) 66. Hunger/Sult (Den./Swe./Nor.) 66. The Fearless Vampire Killers (GB) 67. Rosemary's Baby (US) 68, etc.

Konchalovsky, Andrei (1937–)
Russian director in the West.
Maria's Lovers 85. Runaway Train 85. Duet for One 86. Shy People 87. Homer and Eddie 89. Tango and Cash 89. The Inner Circle 91. Ryaba My Chicken/Riaba Ma Poule 93. The Odyssey (TV) 97, etc.

Konstam, Phyllis (1907–1976)
British stage actress who occasionally played film heroines.
Autobiography: 1969, *A Mixed Double* (with her husband Bunny Austin).
■ Champagne 28. Blackmail 29. Murder 30. Escape 30. Compromising Daphne 30. The Skin Game 31. Tilly of Bloomsbury 31. A Gentleman of Paris 31. The Forgotten Factor 52. Jotham Valley 52. The Crowning Experience 59. Voice of the Hurricane 60.

Kopelson, Arnold (1935–)
American producer and lawyer.
The Legacy 79. Lost and Found 79. Foolin' Around 80. Dirty Tricks 80. Platoon (AA) 86. Warlock 88. Triumph of the Spirit 89. Falling Down 92. The Fugitive 93. Outbreak 95. The Devil's Advocate 97. US Marshals 98. A Perfect Murder 98, etc.

Kopple, Barbara
American director, mainly of documentaries. Born in Scarsdale, New York, she studied clinical psychology and political science at Northeastern University and began by working for Albert and David Maysles.
Harlan County USA 76. Keeping On (TV) 82. American Dream 90. Beyond JFK: The Question of Conspiracy 92. Wild Man Blues 98, etc.

Korda, Sir Alexander (1893–1956) (Sandor Corda)
Hungarian producer-director who worked in Paris, Berlin and Hollywood before settling in London 1930. More than any other man the saviour of the British film industry. Formed London Films and sealed its success with *The Private Life of Henry VIII* 32; built Denham Studios. He was married to actresses Maria Corda and Merle Oberon (1939–45).
Other projects announced at various times by Korda include The Field of the Cloth of Gold, Marco Polo, Nijinsky, Hamlet, Zorro, Joseph and His Brothers, Young Mr Disraeli, Marlborough, King of the Jews, Franz Liszt, Lawrence of Arabia, Nelson, Precious Bane, Cyrano de Bergerac, Charles II, War and Peace, Burmese Silver, Elizabeth of Austria, Pocahontas, Manon Lescaut, New Wine, The Hardy Family in England, Greenmantle, The Old Wives' Tale, Mr Chips' Boys, The Pickwick Papers, The Wrecker, Around the World in Eighty Days, Gibraltar, The Eternal City, The King's General, Carmen, Salome, Faust, Arms and the Man, Macbeth, The Iliad.
Biography: 1956, *Alexander Korda* by Paul Tabori. 1975, *Alexander Korda* by Karol Kulik, 1980, *Charmed Lives* by Michael Korda.
■ The Duped Journalist (d) 14. Tutyu and Totyo (d) 14. Lea Lyon (d) 15. The Officer's Swordknot (d) 15. Fedora (d) 16. The Grandmother (d) 16. Tales of the Typewriter (d) 16. The Man with Two Hearts (d) 16. The Million Pound Note (d) 16. Cyclamen (d) 16. Struggling Hearts (d) 16. Laughing Saskia (d) 16. Miska the Magnate (d) 16. St Peter's Umbrella (d) 17. The Stork Caliph (d) 17. Magic (d) 17. Harrison and Barrison (d) 17. Faun (d) 18. The Man with the Golden Touch (d) 18. Mary Ann (d) 18. Hail Caesar (d) 19. White Rose (d) 19. Yamata (d) 19. Neither In Nor Out (d) 19. Number 111 (d) 19. The Prince and the Pauper (d) 20. Masters of the Sea (d) 22. A Vanished World (d) 22. Samson and Delilah (d) 22. The Unknown Tomorrow (d) 23. Everybody's Woman (d) 24. Mayerling (d) 24. Dancing Mad (d) 25. Madame Wants No Children (d) 26. A Modern Dubarry (d) 27. (All previous titles in Hungary, France and Germany; now Hollywood.) The Stolen Bride (d) 27. *The Private Life of Helen of Troy* (d) 27. Yellow Lily (d) 28. Night Watch (d) 28. Love and the Devil (d) 29. The Squall (d) 29. Her Private Life (d) 29. Lilies of the Field (d) 30. Women Everywhere (d) 30. The Princess and the Plumber (d) 31. (Now Paris.) Laughter (d) 31. *Marius* (d) 31. (Now London.) Service for Ladies (p, d) 32. Wedding Rehearsal (p, d) 32. That Night in London (p) 33. Strange Evidence (p) 33. Counsel's Opinion (p) 33. Cash (p) 33. Men of Tomorrow (p) 33. *The Private Life of Henry VIII* (p, d) 33. The Girl from Maxim's (p, d) 33. *The Rise of Catherine the Great* (p) 34. The Private Life of Don Juan (p, d) 34. *The Scarlet Pimpernel* (p, some d) 34. *Sanders of the River* (p) 35. *The Ghost Goes West* (p) 35. *Things to Come* (p) 36. Moscow Nights (ep) 36. Men Are Not Gods (p). 36. Forget Me Not (p) 36. *Rembrandt* (p, d) 36. *The Man Who Could Work Miracles* (p) 37. Fire over England (ep) 37. I Claudius (unfinished) (p) 37. Dark Journey (p) 37. Elephant Boy (p) 37. Farewell Again (ep) 37. Storm in a Teacup (ep) 37. Action for Slander (ep) 37. *Knight without Armour* (p) 37. The Squeaker (p) 37. The Return of the Scarlet Pimpernel (ep) 37. Paradise for Two (ep) 37. The Divorce of Lady X (p) 38. The Drum (p) 38. South Riding (ep) 38. The Challenge (ep) 38. Prison without Bars (ep) 38. Q Planes (ep) 39. *The Four Feathers* (p) 39. The Rebel Son (ep) 39. The Spy in Black (ep) 39. The Lion Has Wings (p) 39. Over the Moon (p) 40 (shot 1938). Twenty-one Days (p) 40 (shot 37). Conquest of the Air (p) 40. *The Thief of Baghdad* (p) 40. Old Bill and Son (ep) 41. *That Hamilton Woman* (in US) (p, d) 41. Lydia (in US) (p) 41. *To Be or Not to Be* (in US) (ep) 42. Jungle Book (in US) (p) 42. *Perfect Strangers* (p) 45. The Shop at Sly Corner (ep) 47. A Man about the House (ep) 47. Mine Own Executioner (ep) 47. An Ideal Husband (p, d) 47. Night Beat (ep) 48. *Anna Karenina* (p) 48. The Winslow Boy (ep) 48. The Fallen Idol (ep) 48. Bonnie Prince Charlie (ep) 48. The Small Back Room (ep) 49. That Dangerous Age (ep) 49. The Last Days of Dolwyn (ep) 49. Saints and Sinners (ep) 49. *The Third Man* (ep) 49. The Cure for Love (ep) 50. The Angel with the Trumpet (ep) 50. My Daughter Joy (ep) 50. State Secret (ep) 50. Seven Days to Noon (ep) 50. Gone to Earth (ep) 50. The Elusive Pimpernel (ep) 51. Tales of Hoffman (ep) 51. Lady Godiva Rides Again (ep) 51. The Wonder Kid (ep) 51. Mr Denning Drives North (ep) 52. An Outcast of the Islands (ep) 52. Home at Seven (ep) 52. Who Goes There? (ep) 52. Cry the Beloved Country (ep) 52. *The Sound Barrier* (ep) 52. The Holly and the Ivy (ep) 52. The Ringer (ep) 53. Folly to Be Wise (ep) 53. Twice Upon a Time (ep) 53. The Captain's Paradise (ep) 53. The Story of Gilbert and Sullivan (ep) 53. The Man Between (ep) 53. The Heart of the Matter (ep) 54. Hobson's Choice (ep) 54. The Belles of St Trinian's (ep) 54. The Teckman Mystery (ep) 54. The Man Who Loved Redheads (ep) 55. Three Cases of Murder (ep) 55. The Constant Husband (ep) 55. A Kid for Two Farthings (ep) 55. The Deep Blue Sea (ep) 55. Summer Madness (ep) 55. Storm over the Nile (ep) 55. *Richard III* (ep) 56. Smiley (ep) 56.
In the above list the abbreviation ep (executive producer) is meant to imply a considerable distancing by Korda from the product, as sponsor, or financier, or head of London Films.
✪ For reviving Britain's flagging film industry and making half-a-dozen imperishable classics. *Rembrandt*.
❝ The art of film-making is to come to the brink of bankruptcy and stare it in the face. – *A.K.*
Anyone who gets a raw deal in a film studio is no more deserving of pity than someone who gets beaten up in a brothel. A gentleman has no business in either place. – *A.K.*
When my friends and I were young in Hungary, we all dreamed of being poets. And what did we become? We became politicians and advertisement men and film producers. – *A.K.*
He represented, and indeed virtually created, the tradition of quality in the British cinema. – *Andrew Sarris*
His engaging personality and charm of manner must be resisted. His promises, even when they are sincere, are worthless. A very dominant man and very dangerous to converse with owing to (among other things) his powers of persuasion. – *Internal memo of the Prudential Assurance Company, which backed Korda*
His human wisdom was always greater than his film wisdom. – *Graham Greene*

Korda, Vincent (1896–1979)
Hungarian art director who usually worked on the films of his brothers Alexander and Zoltan.
The Private Life of Henry VIII 33. Sanders of the River 35. *Things to Come* 36. The Four Feathers 39. *The Thief of Baghdad* (AA) 40. To Be or Not to Be 42. The Fallen Idol 48. The Third Man 49. The Sound Barrier 52. The Deep Blue Sea 55. Summer Madness 56, etc.

Korda, Zoltan (1895–1961)
Hungarian director, brother of Alexander Korda; spent most of his career in Britain and Hollywood.
Cash 32. Sanders of the River 35. The Drum 38. *The Four Feathers* 39. Jungle Book 42. Sahara 43. Counterattack 43. *The Macomber Affair* 47. A Woman's Vengeance 48. Cry the Beloved Country 51, etc.

Korine, Harmony (1974–)
American screenwriter, director and novelist.
Kids (w) 96. Gummo (wd) 97.

Korjus, Miliza (1900–1980)
Polish operatic soprano who settled in America but did not pursue what looked like being a popular film career.
■ *The Great Waltz* (AAN) 38. Imperial Cavalry (Mex.) 42.

Korman, Harvey (1927–)
American character comedian, often as loud-mouthed show-off. On TV with Danny Kaye and Carol Burnett.
Lord Love a Duck 66. Don't Just Stand There 67. The April Fools 68. Blazing Saddles 74. High Anxiety 78. First Family 80. Herbie Goes Bananas 80. History of the World Part One 81. Trail of the Pink Panther 82. The Long Shot 85. Crash Course (TV) 88. The Flintstones 94. The Radioland Murders 94. Dracula: Dead and Loving It 95. Jingle All the Way 96. Gideon 99. The Flintstones in Viva Rock Vegas 00, etc.
TV series: The Danny Kaye Show 64–67. The Carol Burnett Show 67–77. The Tim Conway Show 80–81. Mama's Family 83–84. Leo & Liz in Beverly Hills 86.

Korngold, Erich Wolfgang (1897–1957)
Czech composer-conductor, a child prodigy. To Hollywood in 1935 with Warners.
Biography: 1997, *Erich Wolfgang Korngold* by Jessica Duchen.
■ Captain Blood 35. *Anthony Adverse* (AA) 36. The Green Pastures 36. A Midsummer Night's Dream 36. The Story of Louis Pasteur 36. Another Dawn 37. The Prince and the Pauper 37. *The Adventures of Robin Hood* (AA) 38. Juarez 39. Elizabeth and Essex (AAN) 39. *The Sea Hawk* (AAN) 40. The Sea Wolf 41. *Kings Row* 41. The Constant Nymph 43. Between Two Worlds 44. Devotion 44. Deception 46. Of Human Bondage 46. Escape Me Never 47. Magic Fire 56.
✪ For stirring romantic themes of a finer texture than anyone else in Hollywood could accomplish. *Kings Row*.

Kornman, Mary (1917–1973)
American actress, the only girl in the original Our Gang comedies of the 20s, on screen from the age of five. As a teenager she acted in Hal Roach's *The Boy Friends* series of shorts and later appeared in some features before retiring in 1940. The first of her two husbands was cinematographer Leo Tover.
Are These Our Children? 31. Flying Down to Rio 33. The Adventurous Knights 35. Desert Trail 35. Queen of the Jungle 35. Swing It Professor 37. On the Spot 40, etc.

Korris, Harry (1888–1971) (Henry Corris)
British music-hall comedian who became popular on radio as Mr Lovejoy in the 40s show *Happidrome* and made several slapdash film farces.
Somewhere in England 40. Somewhere in Camp 41. Happidrome 43, etc.

Korsmo, Charlie (1978–)
American juvenile actor.
Men Don't Leave 89. Dick Tracy 89. What about Bob? 91. Hook 91. The Doctor 91. Can't Hardly Wait 98, etc.

Kortner, Fritz (1892–1970) (Fritz Nathan Kohn)
Austrian character actor, in films of many nations, and director.
Autobiography: 1959, *The Evening of All Days*.
Police No. 1111 (debut) 16. Satanas 20. The Brothers Karamazov 20. The Hands of Orlac 24. Beethoven 26. Warning Shadows 27. Mata Hari 27. *Pandora's Box* 28. The Murder of Dimitri Karamazov 30. Dreyfus 30. Chu Chin Chow 34. Evensong 34. Abdul the Damned 35. The Crouching Beast 36. The Strange Death of Adolf Hitler 43. The Hitler Gang 44. Somewhere in the Night 46. The Brasher Doubloon 47. Berlin Express 48, many others.
■ As director: Der Brave Suender 31. So Ein Maedel Vergisst Man Nicht 33. Der Ruf 49. Die Stadt ist Voller Geheimnisse 55. Sarajevo 55. Lysistrata 61.

Korty, John (1941–)
American director.
The Crazy Quilt 65. Funnyman 67. Riverrun 68. The People (TV) 72. Class of 63 (TV) 73. Go Ask Alice (TV) 73. The Autobiography of Miss Jane Pittman (TV) 73. Silence 74. Alex and the Gypsy 76. Farewell to Manzanar (TV) 76. Who Are the De Bolts 77. Forever (TV) 78. Oliver's Story (& w) 78. A Christmas without Snow (TV) 80. Twice upon a Time (co-d) 83. The Haunting Passion (TV) 83. Second Sight: A Love Story (TV) 84. The Ewok Adventure (TV) 84. A Deadly Business (TV) 86. Resting Place (TV) 86. Baby Girl Scott (TV) 87. Eye on the Sparrow (TV) 87. Winnie (TV) 88. Long Road Home (TV) 91. They (TV) 93. Getting Out (TV) 94. Redwood Curtain (TV) 95, etc.

Korvin, Charles (1907–1998) (Geza Korvin Karpathi)
Hungarian-born leading actor, in Hollywood. Born in Piestany, he studied at the Sorbonne in Paris, working as a photographer and director of documentaries before moving to America in the late 30s. There he worked as a radio and stage actor before being put under contract by Universal. He was blacklisted in the early 50s, working in Europe until the mid-60s. Married three times.
Enter Arsène Lupin 44. This Love of Ours 45. Temptation 47. The Killer That Stalked New York 50. Lydia Bailey 52. Sangaree 53. Zorro the Avenger 60. Ship of Fools 65. The Man Who Had Power over Women 70. Inside Out 75, etc.
TV series: Interpol Calling 59.

Koscina, Sylva (1933–1994)
Yugoslavian leading lady in international films.

Hercules Unchained 60. Jessica 62. Hot Enough for June (GB) 63. Juliet of the Spirits (It.) 65. Three Bites of the Apple (US) 66. Deadlier Than the Male (GB) 67. A Lovely Way to Die 68. The Battle for Neretva 70. Hornet's Nest 70. Crimes of the Black Cat 72. The Slasher 74. Dracula in Brianza 75. Casanova and Co./The Rise and Rise of Casanova 77. Sunday Lovers 80. Cinderella '80 84. Deadly Sanctuary 86. Rimini Rimini 87, etc.

Kosleck, Martin (1907–1994) (Nicolai Yoshkin)
Russian character actor with experience on the German stage; in America from mid-30s.
Confessions of a Nazi Spy (as Goebbels) 39. Nurse Edith Cavell 39. A Date with Destiny 40. Foreign Correspondent 40. North Star 43. *The Hitler Gang* (as Goebbels) 44. The Frozen Ghost 44. The Mummy's Curse 45. House of Horrors 46. Hitler (as Goebbels) 61. Something Wild 62. Thirty-Six Hours 64. Morituri 65. The Flesh Eaters 67. Which Way to the Front? 70, etc.

Kosma, Joseph (1905–1969)
Hungarian composer, in France from 1933.
La Grande Illusion 37. *La Bête Humaine* 38. *Partie de Campagne* 38. La Règle du Jeu 39. *Les Enfants du Paradis* 44. Les Portes de la Nuit 45. Les Amants de Vérone 48. The Green Glove 52. Huis Clos 54. Calle Mayor 56. The Doctor's Dilemma 59. Lunch on the Grass 59. La Poupée 62. In the French Style 64. The Little Theatre of Jean Renoir 69, etc.

Kossoff, David (1919–)
British character actor and stage monologuist.
The Good Beginning 50. The Young Lovers 55. *A Kid for Two Farthings* 56. *The Bespoke Overcoat* 57. The Journey 59. Freud 62. Ring of Spies 64. Three for All 74. The London Connection 79. Staggered 94, etc.
TV series: The Larkins. A Little Big Business.

Kostal, Irwin (1911–1994)
American musical supervisor.
West Side Story (AA) 61. Mary Poppins (AAN) 64. *The Sound of Music* (AA) 65. Bedknobs and Broomsticks (AAN) 71. The Blue Bird 76. Pete's Dragon (AAN) 77, etc.

Koster, Henry (1905–1988) (Hermann Kosterlitz)
German director, in Hollywood from mid-30s, adept at sentimental comedy.
■ Thea Roland (Ger.) 32. Peter (Ger.) 33. Little Mother (Ger.) 33. Peter (Hung.) 35. Marie Bashkirtzeff (Ger.) 36. *Three Smart Girls* 36. *One Hundred Men and a Girl* 37. The Rage of Paris 38. Three Smart Girls Grow Up 38. First Love 39. Spring Parade 40. *It Started with Eve* 41. Between Us Girls 42. Music for Millions 44. Two Sisters from Boston 45. The Unfinished Dance 47. *The Bishop's Wife* (AAN) 47. The Luck of the Irish 47. Come to the Stable 49. *The Inspector General* 49. Wabash Avenue 50. My Blue Heaven 50. *Harvey* 50. No Highway (GB) 51. Mr Belvedere Rings the Bell 52. Elopement 52. Stars and Stripes Forever 52. My Cousin Rachel 52. *The Robe* 53. Désirée 54. A Man Called Peter 55. The Virgin Queen 55. Good Morning, Miss Dove 55. D-Day the Sixth of June 56. The Power and the Prize 56. My Man Godfrey 57. Fraulein 58. The Naked Maja 59. The Story of Ruth 60. Flower Drum Song 60. Mr Hobbs Takes a Vacation 62. Take Her She's Mine 63. Dear Brigitte 65. The Singing Nun 66.

Kosugi, Sho (1947–)
Japanese star of Hong Kong and US martial arts movies, a former karate champion. Born in Tokyo, he was educated in America.
Shaolin Temple Strikes Back (HK) 72. Master Ninja 78. The Bad News Bears Go to Japan 78. Enter the Ninja 82. Eagle Claws Champion (HK) 82. Revenge of the Ninja 84. Ninja III: The Domination 84. Nine Deaths of the Ninja 85. Pray for Death 85. Hanauma Bay 85. Rage of Honor 86. Aloha Summer 88. Black Eagle 88. Blind Fury 90, etc.
TV series: The Master 84.

Kotcheff, Ted (1931–)
Canadian director.
■ Tiara Tahiti 62. *Life at the Top* 65. Two Gentlemen Sharing 70. Outback 71. Billy Two Hats 73. The Apprenticeship of Duddy Kravitz 74. Fun with Dick and Jane 77. Someone Is Killing the Great Chefs of Europe 78. North Dallas Forty 79. First Blood 82. Split Image 83. Uncommon Valor 83. Joshua Then and Now 85. Switching Channels 88. Weekend at Bernie's 89. The Winter People 89. Hot and Cold 89. Folks! 92. The Shooter 95. The Populist 97.

Koteas, Elias (1961–)
Canadian actor, working in Hollywood.
One Magic Christmas 85. Gardens of Stone 87. Some Kind of Wonderful 87. Full Moon in Blue Water 88. Tucker: The Man and His Dream 88. Friends, Lovers and Lunatics 89. Desperate Hours 90. Teenage Mutant Ninja Turtles 90. Backstreet Dreams 90. Almost an Angel 90. The Adjuster 91. Teenage Mutant Ninja Turtles III 93. God's Army 93. Camilla 93. Exotica 94. God's Army 95. Sugartime (TV) 96. Crash 96. Gattaca 97. Fallen 97. Apt Pupil 98. Living Out Loud 98. The Thin Red Line 98. Lost Souls 99, etc.
❝ I would think I'd accomplished it all if I could get to play Quasimodo. – *E.K.*

Kotto, Yaphet (1937–)
American actor.
The Thomas Crown Affair 68. The Liberation of L. B. Jones 70. Across 110th Street 72. *Live and Let Die* 73. Truck Turner 74. Report to the Commissioner 74. Drum 76. Monkey Hustle 76. Blue Collar 78. Alien 79. Brubaker 80. The Star Chamber 83. Warning Sign 85. Prettykill 87. The Running Man 87. Midnight Run 88. Nightmares of the Devil (d only) 88. Ministry of Vengeance 89. After the Shock 90. Freddy's Dead: The Final Nightmare 91. Extreme Justice 93. Two If by Sea/Stolen Hearts 96, etc.
TV series: For Love and Honor 83. Homicide: Life on the Street 93–99.

Kovack, Nancy (1935–)
American leading lady with stage and TV experience. Married conductor Zubin Mehta.
Strangers When We Meet 60. Diary of a Madman 62. Jason and the Argonauts 63. The Outlaws Is Coming 65. Frankie and Johnny 66. The Silencers 66. Tarzan and the Valley of Gold 66. Marooned 69, etc.

Kovacs, Ernie (1919–1962)
Big, cigar-smoking American comedian and TV personality. Died in a car crash. Married to Edie Adams.
Biography: 1976, *Nothing in Moderation* by David G. Walley.
■ *Operation Mad Ball* 57. Bell, Book and Candle 58. It Happened to Jane 58. *Our Man in Havana* 59. Wake Me When It's Over 60. Strangers When We Meet 60. North to Alaska 60. Pepe 60. Five Golden Hours 61. Sail a Crooked Ship 62.

Kovacs, Laszlo (1932–)
American cinematographer given to experimentation which does not always please the eye.
Targets 68. The Savage Seven 68. Easy Rider 69. Getting Straight 70. Five Easy Pieces 70. Alex in Wonderland 70. The Last Movie 71. Marriage of a Young Stockbroker 71. Pocket Money 72. What's Up Doc? 72. Paper Moon 73. Freebie and the Bean 74. Shampoo 75. At Long Last Love 75. Nickelodeon 76. New York New York 77. Close Encounters of the Third Kind (co-ph) 77. The Last Waltz 78. Butch and Sundance 79. Heartbeat 79. The Legend of the Lone Ranger 81. The Toy 82. Frances 82. Crackers 84. Ghostbusters 84. Mask 85. Legal Eagles 86. Little Nikita 88. Say Anything 89. Shattered 91. Radio Flyer 92. Ruby Cairo 93. The Next Karate Kid 94. The Scout 94. Free Willy 2: The Adventure Begins 95. Multiplicity 96. My Best Friend's Wedding 97, etc.

Kove, Kenneth (1893–1965)
English character actor, in silly-ass roles, from Aldwych farces.
Murder 30. Fascination 31. Two White Arms 32. Pyjamas Preferred 32. Dora 33. Song of the Plough 33. Crazy People 34. Radio Pirates 35. Look Up and Laugh 35. Talking Feet 37. Asking for Trouble 42. Innocents in Paris 53. Dr Terror's House of Horrors 65, etc.

Kowalski, Bernard (1929–)
American director, from TV.
Hot Car Girl 58. Attack of the Giant Leeches 58. Night of the Blood Beast 58. Blood and Steel 59. Krakatoa East of Java 69. Stiletto 70. Macho Callahan 70. Ssss 73. The Nativity (TV) 78. B.A.D. Cats (TV) 80. Miracle at Beekman's Place (TV) 88. Nashville Beat 89, etc.

Kozak, Harley Jane (1953–) (Susan Jane Kozak)
Leading American actress.
Hair 79. The World according to Garp 82. When Harry Met Sally 89. Parenthood 89. Side Out 90. Arachnophobia 90. Necessary Roughness 91. All I Want for Christmas 91. The Taking of Beverly Hills 91. Beyond Control: The Amy Fisher Story (TV) 93. The Favor 94. Magic in the Water 95. Titanic (TV) 96. Dark Planet 97, etc.
TV series: The Secret Life of Men 98– .

Kozintsev, Grigori (1905–1973)
Russian director, in films from 1924.
The Youth of Maxim 35. *Don Quixote* 57. *Hamlet* 64. King Lear 69, etc.

Kozlowski, Linda (1958–)
American leading actress. She is married to actor Paul Hogan.
Crocodile Dundee 86. Pass the Ammo 88. Crocodile Dundee II 88. Almost an Angel 90. The Neighbor 93. Zorn (Swe.) 94. Village of the Damned 95, etc.

Krabbé, Jeroen (1944–)
Dutch leading actor in international films.
The Little Ark 72. Alicia 74. Soldier of Orange 79. Spetters 80. A Flight of Rainbirds 81. The Fourth Man 83. Turtle Diary 85. Jumpin' Jack Flash 86. No Mercy 86. The Living Daylights 87. A World Apart 87. Crossing Delancey 88. Scandal 89. The Punisher 89. Till There Was You 90. Murder East/Murder West 90. The Prince of Tides 91. Robin Hood 91. Kafka 91. For a Lost Soldier/Voor Een Verloren Soldaat 92. King of the Hill 93. Going Home/Oeroeg 93. The Fugitive 93. Immortal Beloved 94. Farinelli il Castrato (as Handel) 94. The Disappearance of Garcia Lorca 96. The Odyssey (TV) 97. Left Luggage (& d) 97. Dangerous Beauty 98. Ever After 98. An Ideal Husband 99. The Sky Will Fall/Il Cielo Cade (It.) 00. Jesus (as Satan) (TV) 00, etc.

Kragh-Jacobsen, Soren (1947–)
Danish director and screenwriter. He trained as an electrical engineer before studying film in Prague and working in Danish TV on children's programmes. Mifune. the film that brought him international acclaim, was made according to the precepts of DOGME.
Will You See My Beautiful Navel?/Vil Du Se Min Smukke Navle? 78. Rubber Tarzan/Gummi-Tarzan 81. Icebirds/Isfugle 83. The Shadow of Emma/Skyggen Af Emma 88. The Boys from St Petri/Drengene Fra Sankt Petri 91. Mifune 99, etc.

Kraly, Hans (1885–1950)
German screenwriter, associated with the early films of director Ernst LUBITSCH, whom he followed to the United States. Their friendship and working relationship came to an end in the early 30s when Kraly began an affair with Lubitsch's first wife, former actress Helene Sonnet, that ended their marriage. His career suffered as a result. In his first seven years on Hollywood, he had been credited as a writer on 23 films. He was credited on only seven more films until his death, with his last coming in 1943 with *The Mad Ghoul*.
The Blouse King/Der Blusenkonig 17. Carmen 18. Madame Dubarry 19. The Oyster Princess/Die Austernprinzessin 19. Romeo und Julia im Schnee 20. Forbidden Paradise (US) 24. The Duchess of Buffalo (US) 26. The Garden of Eden (US) 28. The Kiss (US) 29. Betrayal (US) 29. Devil-May-Care (US) 29. Eternal Love (US) 29. By Candlelight (US) 33. One Hundred Men and a Girl 37. It Started with Eve (US) 41. The Mad Ghoul (US) 43, etc.

Kramer, Larry (1935–)
American screenwriter and dramatist.
Women in Love (& p) (AANw) 69. Lost Horizon 72, etc.
❝ Writing movies is exceptionally boring, especially when you're good at it, and for some reason, it comes very easily to me. But if you're a serious writer, you shouldn't write movies; movies are simply not a first-rate art form. – *L.K.*

Kramer, Stanley (1913–2001)
American producer and director of clean-cut, well-intentioned films which sometimes fall short on inspiration.
Autobiography: 1998, *A Mad, Mad, Mad World – A Life in Hollywood* (with Thomas M. Coffey).
■ So Ends Our Night 41. *The Moon and Sixpence* 42. So This Is New York 48. Champion 49. Home of the Brave 49. *The Men* 50. Cyrano de Bergerac 50. *Death of a Salesman* 51. *High Noon* 52. The Sniper 52. The Happy Time 52. My Six Convicts 52. The Member of the Wedding 52. Eight Iron Men 52. The Fourposter 53. The Juggler 53. The 5000 Fingers of Dr T 53. The Wild One 54. *The Caine Mutiny* 54. Not as a Stranger (& d) 55. The Pride and the Passion (& d) 57. The Defiant Ones (& d) (AAN) 58. *On the Beach* (& d) 59. *Inherit the Wind* (& d) 60. Judgment at Nuremberg (& d) (AAN) 61. Pressure Point 62. A Child is Waiting 62. It's a Mad Mad Mad Mad World (& d) 63. Invitation to a Gunfighter 64. *Ship of Fools* (& d) 65. *Guess Who's Coming to Dinner* (& d) (AAN) 67. The Secret of Santa Vittoria (& d) 69 R.P.M. (& d) 71. Bless the Beasts and Children (& d) 71. *Oklahoma Crude* (& d) 73. The Domino Principle (& d) 77. The Runner Stumbles (& d) 79.
✪ For trying. *Inherit the Wind.*
❝ I'm always pursuing the next dream, hunting for the next truth. – *S.K.*
He will never be a natural, but time has proved that he is not a fake. – *Andrew Sarris, 1968*
He's the kind of man who invariably says he saves other people's films in the cutting room. – *Fred Zinnemann*

Krampf, Gunter (1899–1957*)
German cinematographer, in Britain from 1931.
The Student of Prague 24. The Hands of Orlac 24. *Pandora's Box* 28. Rome Express 32. Little Friend 34. Latin Quarter 45. Fame is the Spur 46. Portrait of Clare 50. The Franchise Affair 52, many others.

Krasker, Robert (1913–1981)
Australian cinematographer, long in Britain.
Dangerous Moonlight 40. *Henry V* 44. Caesar and Cleopatra 45. *Brief Encounter* 46. *Odd Man Out* 47. *The Third Man* (AA) 49. Romeo and Juliet 53. Trapeze 56. The Quiet American 58. The Criminal 60. El Cid 61. Billy Budd 62. The Running Man 63. The Fall of the Roman Empire 64. The Heroes of Telemark 65, many others.

Krasna, Norman (1909–1984)
American playwright who worked on many films from 1932, including adaptations of his own plays.
The Richest Girl in the World (AAN) 34. *Fury* (AAN) 36. *Bachelor Mother* 39. The Flame of New Orleans 41. The Devil and Miss Jones (AAN) 41. *Princess O'Rourke* (AA) (& d) 43. The Big Hangover (& pd) 50. The Ambassador's Daughter (& d) 56. *Indiscreet* 58. Who Was That Lady? (& d) 60. Let's Make Love 61. Sunday in New York 64, many others.

Krasner, Milton (1901–1988)
American cinematographer.
I Love That Man 33. The Crime of Dr Hallet 36. The House of the Seven Gables 40. *The Woman in the Window* 44. Scarlet Street 45. *The Dark Mirror* 46. The Farmer's Daughter 47. *The Set Up* 49. Rawhide 50. *All About Eve* 50. Monkey Business 51. *Three Coins in the Fountain* (AA) 54. The Rains of Ranchipur 55. Bus Stop 56. An Affair to Remember 57. The Four Horsemen of the Apocalypse 62. Two Weeks in Another Town 62. Love with the Proper Stranger 64. The Sandpiper 65. The Singing Nun 66. Hurry Sundown 67. The Epic of Josie 67. The St Valentine's Day Massacre 68. The Sterile Cuckoo 69. Beneath the Planet of the Apes 70, many others.

Kraushaar, Raoul (1908–)
American composer.
Melody Ranch 40. Stardust on the Sage 42. Stork Bites Man 47. Bride of the Gorilla 51. The Blue Gardenia 53. Mohawk 56. Mustang 59. Billy the Kid vs Dracula 65. Jesse James Meets Frankenstein's Daughter 65. An Eye for an Eye 66. Thriller – a Cruel Story (Swe.) 72, etc.

Krauss, Werner (1884–1959)
Distinguished German actor.
ETA Hoffman (debut) 16. *The Cabinet of Dr Caligari* 19. The Brothers Karamazov 20. Othello 22. Nathan the Wise 23. *Waxworks* 24. The Student of Prague 25. A Midsummer Night's Dream 25. Secrets of a Soul 26. Tartuffe 26. Jew Süss 40. John Ohne Heimat 55, etc.

The Krays (Ronald, 1933-1995, and Reginald, 1933-2000)
Twin brothers who were the most feared gangsters in the East End of London in the 1950s and 60s. They organised a gang of thugs known as The Firm and became minor celebrities, mixing with showbusiness stars. In 1969 they were both jailed for life for murder: Ronnie for shooting fellow gangster George Cornell in 1966, and Reggie for stabbing a crook called Jack 'The Hat' McVitie in 1967. In the biopic *The Krays*, 90, they were played by Gary and Martin KEMP.
Autobiography: 90, *Born Fighter* by Reggie Kray.
Biography: 70, *The Profession of Violence* by John Pearson.

Kress, Harold F. (1913–1999)
American editor and occasional director. Born in Pittsburgh, Pennsylvania and educated at UCLA, he spent most of his life working for Columbia and MGM.
Bitter Sweet 40. Dr Jekyll and Mr Hyde 41. Mrs Miniver 42. Dragon Seed 44. Command Decision 49. Green Fire 54. The Cobweb 55. Silk Stockings 57. King of Kings 61. How the West Was Won (AA) 63. Alvarez Kelly 66. I Walk the Line 70. The Poseidon Adventure 72. The Towering Inferno (AA) 74. Viva Knievel 77. The Swarm 78, etc.
■ AS DIRECTOR: Purity Squad 45. No Questions Asked 51. The Painted Hills 51. Apache War Smoke 52. Cromwell (2nd unit) 70.

Kreuger, Kurt (1917–)
Swiss actor, former ski instructor, who appeared in many Hollywood films as smooth continental heartthrob or menace.
Sahara 43. The Moon is Down 43. Mademoiselle Fifi 44. Madame Pimpernel 45. Unfaithfully Yours 48. The Enemy Below 58. What Did You Do in the War, Daddy? 66. The St Valentine's Day Massacre 67, etc.

Krige, Alice (1955–)
South African leading lady in international films.
Chariots of Fire 81. Ghost Story 81. A Tale of Two Cities (TV) 81. Ellis Island (TV) 84. King David 85. Dream West (TV) 85. Barfly 87. Haunted Summer 88. See You in the Morning 88. Sleepwalkers 92. Scarlet and Black (TV) 93. The Institute Benjamenta 95. Joseph (TV) 95. Star Trek: First Contact 96. Hidden in America (TV) 96. Habitat 97. Molokai 98. Close Relations (TV) 98. The Little Vampire 00, etc.

Krish, John (1923–)
British director who began in sponsored documentary field.
Unearthly Stranger 61. The Wild Affair 65. Decline and Fall 68. The Man Who Had Power over Women 70. Jesus (co-d) 79. Out of the Darkness 85, etc.

Krishnamma, Suri
English director, from television.
O Mary This London (TV) 94. A Man of No Importance 94. A Respectable Trade (TV) 98. New Year's Day 00, etc.

Kristel, Sylvia (1952–)
Dutch-born leading lady who became famous in the nude in the title role of *Emmanuelle* and its sequels.
Emmanuelle 74. La Marge 76. Réne La Canne 77. The Fifth Musketeer 78. The Concorde – Airport 79 79. The Nude Bomb 80. Private Lessons 81. Lady Chatterley's Lover 81. Private Lessons 81. Mata Hari 85. Casanova (TV) 87. Emmanuelle 7 92, etc.

Kristofferson, Kris (1936–)
American leading man of the 70s, former folk singer and musician.
The Last Movie 70. Cisco Pike 72. Blume in Love 73. Pat Garrett and Billy the Kid 73. Bring Me the Head of Alfredo Garcia 74. Alice Doesn't Live Here Any More 75. The Sailor who Fell from Grace with the Sea 76. A Star Is Born 76. Vigilante Force 76. Semi-Tough 78. Convoy 78. Heaven's Gate 80. Rollover 81. Flashpoint 84. Songwriter 84. Trouble in Mind 85. Blood and Orchids (TV) 86. The Last Days of Frank and Jesse James (TV) 86. Stagecoach (TV) 86. Amerika (TV) 87. Big Top Pee-Wee 88. Millennium 89. Welcome Home 89. Pair of Aces (TV) 90. Another Pair of Aces: Three of a Kind (TV) 91. Miracle in the Wilderness (TV) 91. Paper Hearts 93. Sodbusters (TV) 94. Pharaoh's Army 95. Lone Star 96. Fire Down Below 97. Dance with Me 98. Two for Texas (TV) 98. Blade 98. A Soldier's Daughter Never Cries 98. Girls' Night (GB) 98. Molokai 98. Father Damien 99. Payback 99. Limbo 99, etc.

Kruger, Alma (1868–1960)
American stage actress who made many films in later life and is specially remembered as the head nurse in the Dr Kildare series.
These Three 36. One Hundred Men and a Girl 37. Marie Antoinette 38. Balalaika 39. Saboteur 42. A Royal Scandal 46. Forever Amber (last film) 47, etc.

Kruger, Hardy (1928–)
Blond German leading man who has filmed internationally.
Junge Adler (debut) 43. Insel Ohne Moral 50. Solange 53. Alibi 55. *The One That Got Away* 57. Bachelor of Hearts 58. Blind Date 59. The Rest Is Silence 59. Sundays and Cybèle 62. Hatari 62. The Flight of the Phoenix 65. The Defector 66. The Secret of Santa Vittoria 69. The Red Tent 70. Night Hair Child 71. Paper Tiger 75. Barry Lyndon 75. A Bridge Too Far 77. The Wild Geese 78. Blue Fin 79. Society Limited 81. Wrong Is Right 82. The Inside Man 84. L'Atlantide 92, etc.

Kruger, Otto (1885–1974)
Suave American actor with long stage experience.
When the Call Came 15. Under the Red Robe 23. Beauty for Sale 33. The Prizefigher and the Lady 33. *Chained* 34. Springtime for Henry 34. Treasure Island 35. *Dracula's Daughter* 36. They Won't Forget 37. *The Housemaster* (GB) 38. Thanks for the Memory 38. Dr Ehrlich's Magic Bullet 40. This Man Reuter 40. The Big Boss 41. *Saboteur* 42. *Murder My Sweet* 44. Escape in the Fog 45. Duel in the Sun 46. Smart Woman 48. Payment on Demand 51. High Noon 52. Magnificent Obsession 54. The Last Command 56. The Wonderful World of the Brothers Grimm 63. Sex and the Single Girl 64, many others.

Krupa, Gene (1909–1973)
American jazz drummer and bandleader who rose to fame with the Benny Goodman orchestra in the 30s to become the first star of his instrument. In films usually as himself. In the biopic *The Gene Krupa Story* 59, he was played by Sal Mineo, though the drumming was his own.
Big Broadcast of 1937 36. Some Like It Hot/ Rhythm Romance 39. Ball of Fire 41. George White's Scandals 45. Beat the Band 46. Glamour Girl 48. Make Believe Ballroom 49. The Glenn Miller Story 54. The Benny Goodman Story 55, etc.

Kruschen, Jack (1922–)
American character comedian of stage and TV.
Red Hot and Blue 49. The Last Voyage 60. The Apartment (AAN) 60. Lover Come Back 62. The Unsinkable Molly Brown 64. Harlow (TV) (as Louis B. Mayer) 66. Million Dollar Duck 71. Freebie and the Bean 74. Sunburn 79. Under the Rainbow 81. Legend of the Wild 81. Penny Ante 90, etc.

Kubik, Gail (1914–1984)
American composer.
The World at War (doc) 42. The Memphis Belle (doc) 43. Thunderbolt (doc) 45. C-Man 45. Gerald McBoing Boing 50. The Desperate Hours 55. I Thank a Fool 62, etc.

Kubrick, Stanley (1928–1999)
American writer-producer-director, in whose psyche independence seems equated with excess. Born in New York, he was hired as a staff photographer by *Look* magazine at the age of 17. He moved to Britain to make *Lolita* and remained. His last film, *Eyes Wide Shut*, began shooting in 1996, and continued for some 18 months, with both Harvey KEITEL and Jennifer Jason LEIGH having to be replaced because of other commitments.
Biography: 1971, *Stanley Kubrick Directs* by Alexander Walker. 1982, *Kubrick, Inside a Film Artist's Maze* by T. A. Nelson. 1997, *Stanley Kubrick: A Biography* by Vincent LoBrutto. 1997, *Stanley Kubrick* by John Baxter. 1999, *Eyes Wide Open: A Memoir of Stanley Kubrick and Eyes Wide Shut* by Frederic Raphael.
■ Fear and Desire (wdph) 53. Killer's Kiss (wd) 55. *The Killing* (wd) 56. *Paths of Glory* (wd) 58. Spartacus (d) 60. Lolita (d) 62. *Dr Strangelove* (wdp) (AAN) 63. *2001: A Space Odyssey* (wdp) (AAN) 69. A Clockwork Orange (wdp) (AAN) 71. Barry Lyndon (AANp, AANw, AANd) 75. The Shining 79. Full Metal Jacket 87. Eyes Wide Shut 99.
✪ For managing to sustain a career on his own terms. *Dr Strangelove*.
❝ Man in the twentieth century has been cast adrift in a rudderless boat on an uncharted sea. The very meaninglessness of life forces man to create his own meaning. If it can be written or thought, it can be filmed. – *S.K.*
He gives new meaning to the word meticulous. – *Jack Nicholson*
Stanley Kubrick is a talented shit. – *Kirk Douglas*
His tragedy may have been that he was hailed as a great artist before he had become a competent craftsman. However, it is more likely that he has chosen to exploit the giddiness of middlebrow audiences on the satiric level of *Mad* magazine. – *Andrew Sarris, 1968*

Kudoh, Youki (1971–)
Japanese actress and singer in international films. Born in Tokyo, she began performing as a twelve-year-old.
Taifu Club 84. Mystery Train (US) 89. *War and Youth/Senso to Seishin* 91. Picture Bride (US/Jap.) 95. Heaven's Burning (Au.) 97. Snow Falling On Cedars 99, etc.

Kudrow, Lisa (1963–)
American actress who is best known for her role as the animal-loving, vegetarian folk singer Phoebe Buffay in the TV sitcom *Friends*, having played Phoebe's twin sister Ursula in the TV sitcom *Mad about You*. Born in Encino, California, she studied biology at Vassar, and began as a scientific researcher before switching to performing, first with the Los Angeles improvisational group The Groundlings. In 2000, she signed a contract worth an estimated $40m to appear in *Friends* for the following two years.
The Unborn 91. In the Heat of Passion 92. In the Heat of Passion 2: Unfaithful 94. Mother 96. Hacks 97. Romy and Michele's High School Reunion 97. Clockwatchers 97. The Opposite of Sex 98. Analyze This 99. Hanging Up 00. Lucky Numbers 00, etc.
TV series: Bob 92–94.

Kuei, Yuen
See YUEN, Corey.

Kuleshov, Lev (1899–1970)
Influential and precocious Russian director, screenwriter and theorist. Born in Tambov, he studied painting at the Fine Arts School in Moscow, worked as a set designer from 1916 and began publishing theoretical articles on film from his late teens. He demonstrated the possibilities of manipulating an audience's reaction through editing, by juxtaposing the same shot of an actor with different objects to suggest various emotions. This 'Kuleshov effect', and his theories of montage, influenced Eisenstein and other directors. He was involved in the establishment of the First National Film School in Moscow, where he also taught. After many controversies, he stopped directing for a time from the early 30s. In the mid-40s he was appointed director of the State Institute of Cinematography in Moscow. Married actress Alexandra Khokhlova. His books include *Art of the Cinema*, published in 1929, and *Fundamentals of Film Direction*, published in 1941.
Books: 1997, *Lev Kuleshov: Fifty Years in Film*, ed. Ekaterina Khokhlova.
The Project of Engineer Prite/Proyekt Inzhenera (& ad) 18. The Extraordinary Adventures of Mr West in the Land of the Bolsheviks 24. The Death Ray/Luch Smerti (& a) 25. 40 Hearts 31. Horizon (& co-w) 32. The Siberians 40. Incident in a Volcano (co-d) 41. Timur's Oath 42. We Are from the Urals (co-d) 44, etc.
❝ An actor's play reaches the spectator just as the editor requires it to, because the spectator himself completes the connected shots and sees in it what has been suggested to him by the montage. – *L.K.*
Kuleshov maintained that film art does not begin when the artists act and the various scenes are shot – this is only the preparation of the material. Film art begins from the moment when the director begins to combine and join together the various pieces of film. – *Vsevolod Pudovkin*

Kulik, Buzz (1923–1999) (Seymour Kulik)
American director, from TV.
The Explosive Generation 61. The Yellow Canary 63. Ready for the People 64. Warning Shot (& p) 66. Villa Rides 68. Riot 68. Vanished (TV) 71. Brian's Song (TV) 71. Owen Marshall (TV) 71. To Find a Man 72. Incident in a Dark Street (TV) 72. Shamus 73. Pioneer Woman (TV) 73. Remember When (TV) 74. Bad Ronald (TV) 74. Cage without a Key (TV) 75. Babe (TV) 75. Matt Helm (TV) 75. Feather and Father (TV) 76. The Lindbergh Kidnapping Case (TV) 76. Corey for the People (TV) 77. Kill Me If You Can (TV) 77. Ziegfeld: The Man and His Women (TV) 78. From Here to Eternity (TV) 79. The Pursuit of D. B. Cooper 81. Rage of Angels (TV) 83. George Washington (TV) 84. Kane & Abel (TV) 85. Women of Valor (TV) 86. Her Secret Life (TV) 87. Too Young the Hero (TV) 88. Around the World in 80 Days (TV) 89. Miles from Nowhere 92, etc.

Kulle, Jarl (1927–1997)
Distinguished Swedish leading actor and occasional director. Born in Angleholm, he spent much of his career on the stage and was best known to international audiences for his roles in five films for Ingmar Bergman. A notable performer at the Royal Dramatic Theatre of Stockholm from the 50s, he also played Professor Higgins in a Scandinavian version of *My Fair Lady*.
Waiting Women 52. Barabbas 53. Karin Mansdotter 54. Smiles of a Summer Night 55. The Devil's Eye 60. The Girl and the Press Photographer (& d) 62. Now about These Women 64. Wedding – Swedish Style 64. The Bookseller Who Gave Up Bathing (& d) 69. Ministern (& d) 71. Mats-Peter (d) 72. Fanny and Alexander 82. Babette's Feast 87. Herman 90. Zorn 94. Alfred 95, etc.

Kulp, Nancy (1921–1991)
American comedy actress, famous for TV portrayals.
The Model and the Marriage Broker 52. Shane 53. Five Gates to Hell 59. The Parent Trap 61. The Patsy 64. The Return of the Beverly Hillbillies (TV) 81, etc.
TV series: The Bob Cummings Show 55–59. *The Beverly Hillbillies* 62–71. The Brian Keith Show 73–74.

Kumashiro, Tatsumi (1927–1995)
Japanese director of ROMAN PORNO.
Front Row/Kaburitsukiu Jinsei 68. Following Desire/Nureto Yokujo 72. Paper Doors of a Secret Room/Yojohan Fusuma No Urabari 73. Kagi 74. Mr, Mrs and Miss Lonely 81. Appasionata 83. Koibumi 85. Like a Rolling Stone/Bo No Kanashimi 94, etc.

Kumel, Harry (1940–)
Belgian director and screenwriter.
Rag to a Red Rose (w) 59. Princess (w) 69. Daughters of Darkness 71. Malpertius 73. De Komst Van Joachim Stiller 76. Het Verloren Paradijs 78. The Secrets of Love 86. Eline Vere 91, etc.

Kureishi, Hanif (1954–)
British screenwriter, director and novelist, of Pakistani descent.
My Beautiful Laundrette (w) (AAN) 85. Sammy and Rosie Get Laid (w) 87. London Kills Me (wd) 91. The Buddha of Suburbia (co-w from novel) (TV) 93.

Kurnitz, Harry (1907–1968)
American screenwriter and novelist. Born in New York City and educated at the University of Pennsylvania, he was a journalist before joining MGM in 1938 when the studio bought his detective novel *Fast Company*, written under the pseudonym Marco Page. Blacklisted in the 50s, he left Hollywood to work in Europe.
Fast and Furious 38. The Thin Man Goes Home 44. What Next, Corporal Hargrove (AAN) 45. The Web 47. A Kiss in the Dark (& p) 48. Pretty Baby 49. The Inspector General 49. Melba 53. The Man Between 53. Land of the Pharaohs 55. *Witness for the Prosecution* 57. Goodbye Charlie 64. How to Steal a Million 66, many others.

Kurosawa, Akira (1910–1998)
Distinguished Japanese film director and screenwriter who revealed the splendours of Japanese cinema to the West when his *Rashomon*

was shown at the Cannes Film Festival. Born in Tokyo, he planned to be a painter before, in the mid-30s, joining as an assistant director what was to become Toho studios. There he also wrote scripts before getting the opportunity to direct in the early 40s. His postwar films were to make an international star of actor Toshiro MIFUNE and also featured notable collaborations with composer Fumio HAYASAKA and, later, Masura SATO. His samurai epics, especially *Yojimbo* and *The Seven Samurai*, were copied by Hollywood and the Italian directors of spaghetti westerns. Noted for his meticulous and painstaking approach to writing, production and rehearsals, he found it hard to get the necessary financial backing from the mid-60s and attempted suicide in 1971. His later films depended on finance from outside Japan.

Autobiography: 1982, *Something Like an Autobiography*.

Other books: 1985, *The Films of Akira Kurosawa* by Donald Richie.

■ Sanshiro Sugata (& w) 43. The Most Beautiful (& w) 44. Sanshiro Sugata II (& w) 44. Tora-no-o (& w) 45. Those Who Make Tomorrow (co-d) 46. No Regrets for Our Youth 46. Wonderful Sunday 47. Drunken Angel 48. A Quiet Duel 49. Stray Dog 49. Scandal 50. *Rashomon* 50. The Idiot 51. *Ikuru* 52. *The Seven Samurai* 54. I Live in Fear 55. *Throne of Blood* 56. *The Lower Depths* 57. *The Hidden Fortress* 58. The Bad Sleep Well 60. *Yojimbo* 61. Sanjuro 62. High and Low 63. Redbeard 65. Dodeska-den 70. Dersu Uzala (AA) 75. *The Shadow Warrior* 81. *Ran* (AAN) 85. Kurosawa's Dreams 90. Rhapsody in August/Hachigatsu-no Kyoshikyoku 91. Madadayo 93. After the Rain/ Ame Agaru (w) 99.

✪ For his brilliance as a maker of historical films with a universal appeal. *The Seven Samurai*.

Kurten, Peter (1883–1931)
German murderer who was the model for Fritz Lang's M 31 and its 1951 remake by Joseph Losey, and *The Vampire of Düsseldorf* 64.

Kurtz, Swoosie (1944–)
American leading actress with stage background. She won an Emmy in 1989 for her guest performance in the TV sitcom *Carol & Company*.

First Love 77. Slap Shot 77. Oliver's Story 78. Marriage Is Alive and Well (TV) 80. Walking

through the Fire 80. The Mating Season 81. The World According to Garp 82. Against All Odds 83. A Time to Live (TV) 85. True Stories 86. Wildcats 86. Baja Oklahoma (TV) 87. Bright Lights, Big City 88. Dangerous Liaisons 88. Vice Versa 88. The Image (TV) 89. A Shock to the System 90. Stanley and Iris 90. The Positively True Adventures of the Alleged Texas Cheerleader-Murdering Mom (TV) 93. And the Band Played On (TV) 93. Reality Bites 94. Story Book 94. Precious 96. Liar Liar 97. Citizen Ruth 96. Armistead Maupin's More Tales of the City (TV) 98. Outside Ozona 98. Cruel Intentions 99, etc.

TV series: Love, Sidney 81–83. Party Girl 96. Sisters 91-96. Suddenly Susan 96-98.

Kurys, Diane (1948–)
French director and screenwriter of films that have an autobiographical basis. She was formerly an actress, working in theatre and playing small parts in movies.

Peppermint Soda/Diablo Menthe 77. Cocktail Molotov 79. Entre Nous/Coup de Foudre (AAN) 83. A Man in Love/Un Homme Amoureux 87. C'est la Vie/La Baule-les-pins 90. After Love/Après l'Amour 92. Six Days, Six Nights/à la Folie 94, etc.

Kusturica, Emir (1955–)
Yugoslavian director and screenwriter, from TV. He is now a French citizen.

Do You Remember Dolly Bell? 81. When Father Was Away on Business/Otac Na Sluzbenom Putu (AAN) 85. Time of the Gypsies/Dom Za Vesanje 89. Arizona Dream 91. Underground 95. Black Cat, White Cat 98, etc.

Kutcher, Ashton (1978–)
American actor, a former model. Born in Cedar Rapids, Iowa, he is best known for his role as Michael Kelso in the TV sitcom *That '70s Show*.

Coming Soon 99. Down to You 00. Reindeer Games/Deception 00. Dude, Where's My Car? 00. Texas Rangers 01, etc.

TV series: That 70s Show 98- .

Kutz, Kazimierz (1929–)
Polish director and screenwriter, born in Silesia, who began as an assistant to Andrzej Wajda on *A Generation* 55. His films reflect his experience of

the region during times of war, particularly in his Silesian trilogy, 1969–79.

Cross of War/Krzyz Walecznych 59. The Silence/ Milczenie 63. Whoever May Know/Ktokolwiek Wie 66. Salt of the Black Country/Sol Ziemi Czarnej 69. Pearl in the Crown/Perla w Koronie 72. The Beads from a Rosary/Paciorki Jednego Rozanca 79. I Shall Always Stand Guard/Na Strazy Swej Stac Bede 84. Death as a Slice of Bread/ Smierc Jak Kromka Chleba 94. Colonel Kwiatkowski 96, etc.

Kwan, Nancy (1939–)
Chinese-English leading lady.

The World of Suzie Wong 60. Flower Drum Song 61. Tamahine 63. Fate Is the Hunter 64. The Wild Affair 65. Lt Robin Crusoe 65. Arrivederci Baby 66. Nobody's Perfect 67. The Wrecking Crew 68. The Girl Who Knew Too Much 69. The McMasters 70. Wonder Woman (TV) 73. Project: Kill 76. Night Creature 78. Streets of Hong Kong 79. Walking the Edge 83. Night Children 88. Cold Dog Soup 89. Dragon: The Bruce Lee Story 93, etc.

Kwan, Stanley (1957–) (Guan Jinpeng)
Hong Kong director, from television.

Love unto Waste 86. Rouge/Yanzhi Kou 88. Full Moon in New York/Yan Tsoi Nau Yeuk 89. Center Stage/Yun Ling-Yuk 92. Red Rose, White Rose 95. Hold You Tight/Yue Kuai Le, Yue Duo Luo 98. Love Will Tear Us Apart/Tianshang Renjian (p) 99, etc.

Kwang-Su, Park (1955–)
South Korean director. He studied sculpture at the Nation University in Seoul, founded the Seoul Film Group, the focus of the country's independent film movement, and studied at the ESEC Film School in Paris.

Chilsu and Mansu 89. The Black Republic 91. Berlin Report 92. To the Starry Island 94. A Single Spark 95, etc.

Kwapis, Ken (1958–)
American director.

The Beniker Gang (TV) 83. Follow That Bird 85. Vibes 88. He Said, She Said (co-d) 91. *Dunston Checks In* 95. The Beautician and the Beast 97, etc.

Kwon-Taek, Im (1936–)
Leading South Korean film director with a growing reputation in the West.

Testimony/Jungon 74. The Family Tree Book/ Jokbo 78. The Hidden Hero/Gitbal Obnun Gisu 79. *Mandala* 81. Village in the Mist/Angemaeul 83. Gilsodom 85. Ticket 86. Surrogate Woman 86. Diary of Yonsan/Yonsan Ilgi 87. Son of a General 91. Son of a General II 92. Taebaek Sanmaek 95, etc.

Kwouk, Burt (1930–)
Chinese-English character actor.

Goldfinger 64. You Only Live Twice 68. The Most Dangerous Man in the World 69. Deep End 71. The Return of the Pink Panther 75. The Last Remake of Beau Geste 77. The Fiendish Plot of Dr Fu Manchu 81. Trail of the Pink Panther 82. Plenty 85. Empire of the Sun 87. Air America 90. Son of the Pink Panther 93. Bullet to Beijing 95, etc.

Kydd, Sam (1917–1982)
British character comedian whose sharp features were seen in many films from 1945.

The Captive Heart 45. The Small Back Room 48. Treasure Island 50. The Cruel Sea 53. The Quatermass Experiment 55. I'm All Right Jack 59. Follow That Horse 60. Island of Terror 66, etc.

Kyo, Machiko (1924–) (Motoko Yamo)
Japanese actress.

Rashomon 50. Gate of Hell 52. The Teahouse of the August Moon 56. Ugetsu Monogatari 58. Floating Weeds 59. The Great Wall 62. Thousand Cranes 69. The Family 70. Kesho 85, etc.

Kyser, Kay (1897–1985)
Mild-mannered American bandleader who made a number of comedy films in the early 40s, then retired to become an active Christian Scientist.

■ That's Right You're Wrong 39. You'll Find Out 40. Playmates 41. My Favorite Spy 42. Around the World 43. Swing Fever 44. Carolina Blues 44.

L

La Bern, Arthur
British novelist whose low-life novels brought some realism into films of the 40s, although they cannot now stand comparison with such films of the 60s as *Saturday Night and Sunday Morning*.
Good-Timer Girl (from *Night Darkens the Streets*) 47. It Always Rains on Sundays 47. Paper Orchid 49. Dead Man's Evidence (w) 62. Freedom to Die (w) 62. Incident at Midnight (w) 63. Frenzy (from *Goodbye Piccadilly, Farewell Leicester Square*) 71.

La Cava, Gregory (1892–1952)
American director, former cartoonist and writer; a delicate talent for comedy usually struggled against unsatisfactory vehicles. He was impersonated by Allan Arbus in *W. C. Fields and Me*.
His Nibs 22. The New Schoolteacher 24. Womanhandled 25. Running Wild 27. Feel My Pulse 28. Laugh and Get Rich 31. Symphony of Six Million 32. The Half-Naked Truth 32. Gabriel over the White House 32. Affairs of Cellini 34. What Every Woman Knows 34. Private Worlds 35. She Married Her Boss 35. *My Man Godfrey* (AAN) 36. *Stage Door* (AAN) 37. Fifth Avenue Girl 39. The Primrose Path 40. Unfinished Business 41. Lady in a Jam 42. Living in a Big Way 47. One Touch of Venus 48, etc.

La Frenais, Ian (c. 1938–)
British comedy writer who works in conjunction with Dick CLEMENT.

La Marr, Barbara (1896–1926) (Reatha Watson)
Sultry American leading lady of silent movies, a former dancer. She married five times, once bigamously, and was romantically linked with producer Paul BERN, who helped her by writing *The Girl from Montmartre* for her after her career faltered in the mid-20s, following a nervous breakdown. Died from an overdose of sleeping pills.
The Prisoner of Zenda 22. The Eternal City 23. Thy Name Is Woman 24. The Shooting of Dan McGrew 24. The Girl from Montmartre 26, etc.

La Planche, Rosemary (1923–1979)
American leading lady of the 40s.
Mad about Music 38. The Falcon in Danger 43. Prairie Chickens 43. Devil Bat's Daughter 46, etc.

La Plante, Laura (1904–1996)
Blonde American leading lady of Universal pictures in the 20s.
Burning Words 23. The Ramblin' Kidd 23. Sporting Youth 24. The Dangerous Blonde 24. Smouldering Fires 25. Skinner's Dress Suit 26. The Beautiful Cheat 26. Silk Stockings 27. The Cat and the Canary 27. The Last Warning 28. Show Boat 29. The Love Trap 29. Captain of the Guard 30. Little Mister Jim 46. Spring Reunion 56, etc.

La Rocque, Rod (1896–1969) (Roderick la Rocque de la Rour)
Popular American leading man of the silent screen, in Hollywood from 1914 after circus experience. He was married to actress Vilma Banky.
The Snow Man 14. The Lightbearer 16. Efficiency Edgar's Courtship 17. The Venus Model 18. The Ten Commandments 23. Forbidden Paradise 25. Resurrection 26. Our Modern Maidens 28. Let Us Be Gay 29. One Romantic Night 30. SOS Iceberg 33. Till We Meet Again 36. The Hunchback of Notre Dame 40. Dr Christian Meets the Women 41. Meet John Doe 41, many others.

La Rue, Danny (1927–) (Daniel Patrick Carroll)
British revue star and female impersonator.
■ Our Miss Fred 72.

La Rue, Jack (1903–1984) (Gaspare Biondolillo)
Grim-faced American actor, typed as gangster from the early 30s.
Lady Killer 34. Captains Courageous 37. Paper Bullets 41. Gentleman from Dixie (a rare sympathetic part) 41. Machine Gun Mama 44. No Orchids for Miss Blandish (GB) (as the maniacal Slim Grisson) 48. Robin Hood of Monterey 49. Ride the Man Down 53. Robin and the Seven Hoods 64. Won Ton Ton 76, many others.

La Rue, Lash (c. 1915–1996) (Alfred La Rue)
American star of low-budget westerns of the 40s, noted for dressing in black and for his way with a 15-foot bullwhip. After the vogue for westerns passed, he worked in carnivals as the King of the Bullwhip, later became an evangelist, was arrested on charges of vagrancy and possessing marijuana, attempted suicide and died poor. He claimed to have been married 10 times.
Song of Old Wyoming 45. The Caravan Trail 46. Wild West 46. Return of the Lash 47. Law of the Lash 47. Ghost Town Renegades 47. Stage to Mesa City 48. Mark of the Lash 49. The Son of Billy the Kid 49. Dead Man's Gold 49. The Dalton's Women 50. King of the Bullwhip 50. Black Lash 51. The Dark Power 85. Stagecoach (TV) 86. Pair of Aces (TV) 90, etc.
TV series: Lash of the West 52–53.

La Shelle, Joseph (1903–1989)
American cinematographer.
Happy Land 43. *Laura* (AA) 44. *Hangover Square* 44. The Foxes of Harrow 47. Come to the Stable 49. Mister 880 50. Les Misérables 52. Marty 55. Storm Fear 55. *The Bachelor Party* 57. I Was a Teenage Werewolf 57. No Down Payment 57 The Naked and the Dead 58. The Apartment 60. Irma la Douce 63. The Fortune Cookie 66. The Chase 66. Barefoot in the Park 67. Kona Coast 68. Eighty Steps to Jonah 69, many others.

Laage, Barbara (1925–) (Claire Colombat)
French leading lady of several 50s films.
La Putain Respectueuse 52. L'Esclave Blanche 54. Act of Love 54. Un Homme à Vendre 58. Paris Blues 61. Domicile Conjugal 71. Private Projection 76, etc.

LaBruce, Bruce (1969–)
Canadian actor, director and writer of independent films, on homosexual themes. He studied at Ryerson University in Toronto.
No Skin off My Ass 92. Super 8½ 94. Hustler White 96.

LaBute, Neil (1963–)
American director, screenwriter and playwright, born in Detroit, Michigan. A Mormon, he studied at Brigham Young University, the University of Kansas and New York University, and is a former teacher of drama.
In the Company of Men 97. Your Friends & Neighbors 98.
❝ I tend to be one of those writers who taps the glass, gets the scorpions angry, but sits at a safe distance and watches. – *N.L.*

Lacey, Catherine (1904–1979)
British stage and screen actress, adept at sympathetic spinsters and eccentric types.
The Lady Vanishes (debut) 38. Cottage to Let 41. I Know Where I'm Going 45. *The October Man* 47. Whisky Galore 49. Rockets Galore 56. Crack in the Mirror 60. The Fighting Prince of Donegal (as Queen Elizabeth I) 66. The Sorcerers 67, etc.

Lacey, Ronald (1935–1991)
Solidly built British character actor.
The Boys 62. Of Human Bondage 64. How I Won the War 67. Crucible of Terror 71. Zulu Dawn 79. Nijinsky 80. Raiders of the Lost Ark 81. Firefox 82. Trenchcoat 83. Sahara 84. Sword of the Valiant 84. Flesh & Blood 85. Invitation to the Wedding 85. Red Sonja 85. Sky Bandits 86. Manifesto 88. Valmont 89, etc.
TV series: The Adventures of Don Quick 70.

Lachman, Ed(ward) (1946–)
American cinematographer.
The Lords of Flatbush 74. Stroszek 77. Lightning over Water 80. Union City 80. Say Amen, Somebody 83. Desperately Seeking Susan 85. True Stories 86. Making Mr Right 87. Less than Zero 87. Catchfire 90. Mississippi Masala 91. London Kills Me 91. Light Sleeper 91. My New Gun 92. My Family/Mia Familia 95. Selena 97. Touch 97. Why Do Fools Fall in Love 98. The Virgin Suicides 98, etc.

Lachman, Harry (1886–1975)
Anglo-American director, at his best in the 30s.
Weekend Wives 28. Under the Greenwood Tree 29. The Yellow Mask 30. The Outsider 30. The Compulsory Husband 30. Aren't We All 32. Insult 32. Paddy the Next Best Thing 33. Baby Take a Bow 34. *Dante's Inferno* 35. Charlie Chan at the Circus 36. *Our Relations* 36. The Devil Is Driving 37. No Time to Marry 38. They Came by Night 40. Dead Men Talk 41. The Loves of Edgar Allan Poe 42, etc.

Lackteen, Frank (1894–1968)
American character actor of Russian origin; his sharp features were adaptable to many ethnic roles.
Less Than the Dust 16. The Avenging Arrow 21. The Virgin 24. Hawk of the Hills 27. Hell's Valley 31. Escape from Devil's Island 35. Anthony Adverse 36. Suez 38. Juarez 39. Moon over Burma 40. The Sea Wolf 41. Chetniks 43. Can't Help Singing 44. Frontier Gal 45. Maneater of Kumaon 48. Daughter of the Jungle 49. King of the Khyber Rifles 53. Bengal Brigade 54. Devil Goddess 55. Requiem for a Gunfighter 65, many others.

Ladd, Alan (1913–1964)
Unsmiling, pint-sized tough-guy American star who proved to be just the kind of hero the 40s wanted. Born in Hot Springs, Arkansas, he worked in a variety of jobs, including as a grip on the Warner lot, before beginning to get small roles on stage and in films. Handicapped by his size – he was 5 feet 5 inches tall – and his lack of expression, he nevertheless became a star with *This Gun for Hire*, in which he played, for the first of several times, opposite Veronica LAKE; by 1947 he was among the top ten stars. He never displayed much interest in the techniques of acting. According to Robert Emmett Dolan, one of Ladd's friends met him and said that he'd noticed the star was about to start a new picture. Ladd replied that he'd yet to read the script. 'That must be kind of disturbing,' said his friend. 'Sure is,' said Ladd. 'I don't know what I'm going to wear.' His career declined from the early 50s, a slump exacerbated by his heavy drinking. He died as the result of an overdose of sleeping pills combined with a high level of alcohol, a probable suicide. His career owed much to his second wife, agent and former actress Sue Carol. He was the father of producer Alan LADD, Jnr.
Ladd is said to have turned down both the James Dean role in *Giant* and the Spencer Tracy role in *Bad Day at Black Rock*.
Biography: 1979, *Ladd* by Beverly Linet.
■ Once in a Lifetime 32. Pigskin Parade 36. Last Train from Madrid 37. Souls at Sea 37. Born to the West 37. Hold 'em Navy 37. The Goldwyn Follies 38. Come on Leathernecks 38. The Green Hornet 39. Rulers of the Sea 39. Beast of Berlin 39. Light of Western Stars 40. Gangs of Chicago 40. Her First Romance (reissued as The Right Man) 40. In Old Missouri 40. The Howards of Virginia 40. Those Were the Days 40. Captain Caution 40. Wildcat Bus 40. Meet the Missus 40. Great Guns 41. Citizen Kane 41. Cadet Girl 41. Petticoat Politics 41. The Black Cat 41. The Reluctant Dragon 41. Paper Bullets 41. Joan of Paris 42. *This Gun for Hire* 42. *The Glass Key* 42. Lucky Jordan 42. Star Spangled Rhythm 42. China 43. And Now Tomorrow 44. Salty O'Rourke 45. Duffy's Tavern 45. *The Blue Dahlia* 46. O.S.S. 46. Two Years Before the Mast 46. Calcutta 47. Variety Girl 47. Wild Harvest 47. My Favourite Brunette 47 (cameo). Saigon 48. Beyond Glory 48. Whispering Smith 48. *The Great Gatsby* 49. Chicago Deadline 49. Captain Carey USA 50. Branded 51. Appointment with Danger 51. Red Mountain 52. The Iron Mistress 53. Thunder in the East 53. Desert Legion 53. *Shane* 53. Botany Bay 53. The Red Beret (GB) 53. Saskatchewan 54. Hell Below Zero (GB) 54. The Black Knight (GB) 54. Drum Beat 54. The McConnell Story 55. Hell on Frisco Bay 55. Santiago 56. The Big Land 57. Boy on a Dolphin 57. The Deep Six 58. The Proud Rebel 58. The Badlanders 58. The Man in the Net 58. Guns of the Timberland 60. All the Young Men 60. One Foot in Hell 60. Duel of the Champions (It.) 61. 13 West Street 62. *The Carpetbaggers* 64.
❝ I have the face of an ageing choirboy and the build of an undernourished featherweight. If you can figure out my success on the screen you're a better man than I. – *A.L.*
A small boy's idea of a tough guy. – *Raymond Chandler*
That man had stature even if he was short. – *Stewart Granger*
He succeeded in reducing murder to an act as casual as crossing the street. – *Richard Schickel*
Nobody ever pretended he could act. He got to the top, therefore, by a combination of determination and luck. – *David Shipman*

Ladd Jnr, Alan (1937–)
American producer and production executive, a former agent, the son of actor Alan LADD. He became president of Fox in the mid-70s before leaving to found The Ladd Company. From the mid-80s he had an on-and-off relationship in charge of the troubled MGM/UA, finally resigning from the companies in 1993 to join Paramount.
The Night Comes 71. Fear Is the Key 72. Divine Madness 80. Outland 81. Chariots of Fire 81. Blade Runner 82. Five Days One Summer 82. Lovesick 83. Twice upon a Time 83. Braveheart 95. A Very Brady Sequel 96. The Phantom 96. The Man in the Iron Mask 98, etc.

Ladd, Cheryl (1951–) (Cheryl Stoppelmoor)
American leading lady who became familiar on TV as one of *Charlie's Angels* 78–81.
Satan's School for Girls 73. Evil in the Deep 76. Now and Forever 82. Grace Kelly (TV) 83. Purple Hearts 84. Romance on the Orient Express (TV) 85. Millennium 89. Lisa 90. Poison Ivy 92. Dancing with Danger (TV) 94. Permanent Midnight 98. A Dog of Flanders 99, etc.
TV series: One West Waikiki 94.

Ladd, David (1947–)
American child actor, the son of actor Alan LADD. He later became a producer.
The Big Land 57. The Proud Rebel 58. A Dog of Flanders 59. Misty 61. Catlow 71. Death Line/Raw Meat (GB) 72. The Klansman 74. The Wild Geese (GB) 78. Beyond the Universe 81, etc.

Ladd, Diane (1932–) (Diane Ladner)
American character actress, born in Meridian, Mississippi. She was formerly married to actor Bruce DERN, and is the mother of actress Laura DERN.
White Lightning 73. Chinatown 74. *Alice Doesn't Live Here Any More* (AAN) 75. Thaddeus Rose and Eddie (TV) 78. Willa 79. Cattle Annie and Little Britches 80. Guyana Tragedy (TV) 80. All Night Long 81. Grace Kelly (TV) 83. Something Wicked This Way Comes 83. Wild at Heart (AAN) 90. A Kiss before Dying 91. Rambling Rose (AAN) 91. The Cemetery Club 93. Carnosaur 93. Father Hood 93. Mrs Munck (& wd) 95. Raging Angels 95. Nixon 95. Precious 96. Citizen Ruth (uncredited) 96. Family of Cops II: Breach of Faith 97. Primary Colors 98. Daddy and Them 01, etc.
TV series: Alice 80–81.

Laemmle, Carl (1867–1939)
German-American pioneer, in films from 1906; produced *Hiawatha* 09, founded Universal Pictures 1912.
Biography: 1931, *The Life and Adventures of Carl Laemmle* by John Drinkwater.
❝ Uncle Carl Laemmle
Had a very large faemmle. – *Ogden Nash, satirizing the number of Laemmle relations who were found jobs at Universal Studios*
I hope I didn't make a mistake coming out here. – *C.L., Hollywood, 1915*
The prototype of the slightly mad movie mogul – impulsive, quixotic, intrepid, unorthodox, unpredictable. – *Norman Zierold*

Laemmle Jnr, Carl (1908–1979)
Son of Carl Laemmle; executive producer at Universal for many years. Credited with the success of *Frankenstein*, *Dracula*, and *All Quiet on the Western Front*.

Laffan, Patricia (1919–)
British stage actress.
The Rake's Progress 45. Caravan 46. Quo Vadis (as Poppea) 51. Devil Girl from Mars 54. Twenty-Three Paces to Baker Street 56. Crooks in Cloisters 64, etc.

Lafont, Bernadette (1938–)
Busy French leading actress, a former dancer, who has made more than 90 films. Formerly married to actor Gérard BLAIN.
Le Beau Serge 58. Web of Passion 59. Les Bonnes Femmes 60. Compartiment Tueurs/The Sleeping Car Murder 65. Le Voleur/The Thief 67. Catch Me a Spy 71. Une Belle Fille Comme Moi 72. Tendre Dracula 74. La Tortue sur le Dos 78. Il Ladrone 79. Le Roi des Cons 81. Cap Canaille 83. Inspector Lavardin 86. Waiting for the Moon 87. L'Air de Rien 89. Le Bonheur 94. Personne Ne M'Aime 94. Nine Months/Neuf Mois 94. Zadoc et le Bonheur 95, etc.

LaGarde, Jocelyn (1922–1979)
Tahitian-born actress who was nominated for a Best Supporting Actress Oscar for her only film, *Hawaii* 66.

Lagercrantz, Marika (1954–)
Swedish leading actress, best known internationally for the role of a teacher who has an affair with a 15-year-old boy in *Love Lessons*.
The Dive/Dykket 89. Hotell Cansino 91. Grandpa's Journey/Morfars Resa 92. Black Harvest/Sort Host 93. Against the Odds/Alskar, Alskar Inte 95. Love Lessons/All Things Fair/Lust och Fägring Stor 95. Vendetta 95. Nu är pappa trött igen! 96. Lithivm 98, etc.

LaGravenese, Richard (1959–)
American screenwriter turned director.
Rude Awakening 89. The Fisher King (AAN) 91. The Ref/Hostile Hostages 94. *The Bridges of Madison County* 95. A Little Princess 95. The Mirror Has Two Faces (w) 96. The Horse Whisperer (co-w) 98. Beloved (co-w) 98. Living Out Loud (wd) 98, etc.

Lahr, Bert (1895–1967) (Irving Lahrheim)
Wry-faced American vaudeville comedian who made occasional film appearances.
Biography: 1969, *Notes on a Cowardly Lion* by John Lahr (his son).
Faint Heart 31. Flying High 31. Love and Hisses 37. Josette 38. Just around the Corner 38. Zaza 39. *The Wizard of Oz* 39. Ship Ahoy 42. Meet the People 44. Always Leave Them Laughing 49. Mr Universe 51. Rose Marie 54. The Second Greatest Sex 56. The Night They Raided Minsky's 68, etc.
❝ After *The Wizard of Oz* I was typecast as a lion, and there aren't all that many parts for lions. – *B.L.*
The last and the most marvellous of the American clowns cradled by burlesque. – *Alastair Cooke*

Lahti, Christine (1950–)
American character actress, often in off-beat roles. Married director Thomas SCHLAMME in 1984.
... And Justice for All 79. The Henderson Monster (TV) 80. Whose Life Is It, Anyway? 81. The Executioner's Song (TV) 82. Ladies and Gentlemen, the Fabulous Stains 82. Swing Shift (AAN) 84. Single Bars, Single Women (TV) 84. Love Lives On (TV) 85. Just between Friends 86. Stacking 87. Housekeeping 87. Running on Empty 88. Gross Anatomy 89. Miss Firecracker 89. No Place Like Home (TV) 89. Funny about Love 90. The Doctor 91. Leaving Normal 92. The Fear Inside 92. Hideaway 95. Pie in the Sky 95. Liberman in Love (co-d, short) (AA) 96. A Weekend in the Country (TV) 96. Hope (TV) 97, etc.
TV series: Chicago Hope 95–99.

Lai, Francis (1932–)
French film composer.
Un Homme et une Femme 66. Mayerling 68. House of Cards 68. Rider on the Rain 70. *Love Story* (AA) 71. Le Petit Matin 71. Emmanuelle 75. Seven Suspects for Murder 77. International Velvet 78. Oliver's Story 78. Second Chance 80. Beyond the Reef 81. Edith and Marcel 83. My New Partner/Les Ripoux 84. Marie 85. A Man and a Woman: 20 Years Later 86. Dark Eyes/Ocie Ciornie 87. Keys to Freedom 89. Too Beautiful for You/Trop Belle pour Toi 89. My New Partner 2/Ripoux contre Ripoux 90. The Beautiful Story/La Belle Histoire 91. Stranger in the House/L'Inconnu dans la Maison 92. Tout ça ... Pour ça ... ! 93. Chance or Coincidence/Hasards ou Coincidences (co-m) 98. One 4 All/Une Pour Toutes 99, etc.

Laine, Frankie (1913–) (Frank Paul Lo Vecchio)
American pop singer who made several light musicals in the 50s. He also sang the title song in *Gunfight at the O.K. Corral* and for the TV series *Rawhide*.
When You're Smiling 50. Make Believe Ballroom 50. The Sunny Side of the Street 51. Rainbow round My Shoulder 52. Bring Your Smile Along 55. He Laughed Last 56. Meet Me in Las Vegas 56, etc.

Laine, Jimmy
See FERRARA, Abel.

Laird, Jenny (1917–)
British character actress.
Just William 39. The Lamp Still Burns 43. Black Narcissus 47. *Painted Boats* 47. The Long Dark Hall 51. Conspiracy of Hearts 60. The Horse without a Head 63, etc.

Lake, Arthur (1905–1987) (Arthur Silverlake)
Harrassed, crumple-faced American light comedy actor, best remembered as Dagwood Bumstead in the 'Blondie' series of 28 films in twelve years.
Jack and the Beanstalk 17. Skinner's Dress Suit 26. The Irresistible Lover 27. *Harold Teen* 28. On with the Show 29. Indiscreet 31. Midshipman Jack 33. Orchids to You 35. Topper 37. *Blondie* (and subsequent series) 38. Three is a Family 44. Sixteen Fathoms Deep 48, many others.
TV series: Blondie 54.

Lake, Florence (1904–1980)
American character comedienne best remembered as Edgar Kennedy's bird-brained wife in many of his two-reelers.

Lake, Lew (1874–1939)
British actor, from the theatre, who appeared in some popular 30s concert party films. His successful melodrama *The Bloomsbury Burglars*, performed in music halls in the early 1900s, gave the English language the nickname 'Jerry' to describe Germans in both the First and Second World Wars.
The Bloomsbury Burglars 12. Splinters 29. The Great Game 30. Splinters in the Navy 31. Splinters in the Air 37.

Lake, Ricki (1968–)
American actress, often in John Waters' films, and a successful television chat show hostess.
Hairspray 88. Working Girl 88. Cookie 89. Babycakes (TV) 89. Cry-Baby 90. Last Exit to Brooklyn 90. Where the Day Takes You 92. Cabin Boy 94. Serial Mom 94. Mrs Winterbourne 96, etc.

Lake, Veronica (1919–1973) (Constance Ockleman)
Petite American leading lady who now, with her limited acting ability and her 'peek a boo bang' (long blonde hair obscuring one eye), seems an appropriately artificial image for the Hollywood of the early 40s. Her second husband was André de Toth (1944–52).
Autobiography: 1968, *Veronica*.
■ All Women Have Secrets 39. Sorority House 39. Forty Little Mothers 40. *I Wanted Wings* 41. *Sullivan's Travels* 41. *This Gun for Hire* 42. The Glass Key 42. *I Married a Witch* 42. Star Spangled Rhythm 42. So Proudly We Hail 43. The Hour before the Dawn 44. Bring on the Girls 45. Out of this World 45. Duffy's Tavern 45. Hold That Blonde 45. Miss Susie Slagle's 45. *The Blue Dahlia* 46. Ramrod 47. Variety Girl 47. The Sainted Sisters 48. Saigon 48. Isn't It Romantic? 48. Slattery's Hurricane 49. Stronghold 52. Footsteps in the Snow 66. Flesh Feast 70.
❝ You could put all the talent I had into your left eye and still not suffer from impaired vision. – *V.L.*

LaLoggia, Frank (1955–)
American independent director, screenwriter, composer and occasional actor.
Fear No Evil (wd, m) 81. The Wizard of Speed and Time (a) 88. Lady in White (wd, m) 88. Mother (d) 94, etc.

Lam, Ringo (1954–)
Hong Kong-born director, screenwriter and producer, from television. He moved to Canada in the late 70s to study and became a Canadian citizen before returning to Hong Kong to make films. *City on Fire* was an influence on Quentin Tarantino's *Reservoir Dogs*.
Cupid One 85. Aces Go Places IV 86. *City on Fire* 87. Prison on Fire 87. School on Fire 88. Wild Search 90. Twin Dragons (co-d) 93. Full Contact 93. The Exchange (US) 96. Full Alert 97, etc.

Lamarque, Libertad (1908–2000)
Argentinian actress and singer, one of the most popular stars in Latin America, on stage and screen from childhood. She went to work in Mexico in the 50s because of a feud with Evita Perón, the president's wife and appeared in several Mexican TV soap operas.
Tango! 33. Magic Kisses/Besos Brujos 37. The Law They Forgot 38. Una Vez en la Vida 41. Gran Casino 46. Soledad (Mex.) 47. La Loca (Mex.) 51. Rostros Olvidados (Mex.) 53. La Sonrisa de Mama (Mex.) 71. Black Is a Beautiful Colour (Mex.) 74, etc.

Lamarr, Hedy (1914–2000) (Hedwig Kiesler)
Austrian leading lady of the 30s and 40s, in Hollywood from 1937 after creating a sensation by appearing nude in the Czech film *Extase* 33. She became a household word for glamour, but lacked the spark of personality. The third of her six husbands was actor John LODER (1943–47).
Autobiography: 1966, *Ecstasy and Me*.
■ AMERICAN FILMS: *Algiers* 38. Lady of the Tropics 39. I Take This Woman 40. Boom Town 40. Comrade X 40. Come Live with Me 41. Ziegfeld Girl 41. H.M. Pulham Esq. 41. Tortilla Flat 42. Crossroads 42. *White Cargo* (as Tondelayo) 42. The Heavenly Body 43. The Conspirators 44. Experiment Perilous 44. Her Highness and the Bellboy 45. The Strange Woman 46. Dishonoured Lady 47. Let's Live a Little 48. *Samson and Delilah* 49. A Lady without Passport 50. Copper Canyon 50. My Favorite Spy 51. The Face that Launched a Thousand Ships 54. The Story of Mankind 57. The Female Animal 57.
❝ Any girl can be glamorous: all you have to do is stand still and look stupid. – *H.L.*
When she spoke one did not listen, one just watched her mouth moving and marvelled at the exquisite shapes made by her lips. – *George Sanders*
She married a European multimillionaire, Fritz Mandl, and was terribly unhappy in the marriage. She went to the opera with him one night, loaded down with a fortune in jewels. He kept these in his safe and only gave them to her to wear on important occasions. Halfway through the performance she told him that she was sick. 'I don't want to spoil your evening,' she said. 'I'll go home, but you stay and see the rest.' She convinced him, went home alone, took the suitcases she had packed and her jewels and took off. Eventually she ended up in Hollywood – *Paul Henreid*

Lamas, Fernando (1915–1982)
Argentinian leading man, in Hollywood from 1950 in routine musicals and comedies. He was married to actresses Arlene Dahl (1954–60) and Esther Williams.
Rich, Young and Pretty 51. The Law and the Lady 51. The Merry Widow 52. The Girl Who Had Everything 53. Sangaree 53. Rose Marie 54. The Girl Rush 55. The Lost World 60. The Violent Ones (& d) 67. 100 Rifles 69. Powder Keg 71. The Cheap Detective 78, etc.

Lamas, Lorenzo (1958–)
American leading man of action films. He is the son of actors Fernando Lamas and Arlene Dahl, and is married to actress Kathleen Kinmont.
100 Rifles 69. Grease 78. Tilt 78. Take Down 79. Body Rock 84. SnakeEater 89. SnakeEater 2: The Drug Buster 89. Final Impact 91. Killing Streets 91. Night of the Warrior 91. SnakeEater 3: His Law 92. Bounty Tracker 93. CIA Codename: Alexa 93. CIA 2: Target Alexa 94. Gladiator Cop: The Swordsman II 95. Blood for Blood 95. The Rage 96. Mask of Death 97, etc.
TV series: California Fever 79. Secrets of Midland Heights 80–81. Falcon Crest 81–90. Renegade 92–94.

Lamb, Gil (1906–1995)
Rubber-boned American comic, seen in many 40s musicals.
The Fleet's In (debut) 42. Rainbow Island 44. Practically Yours 44. Humphrey Takes a Chance 50. Terror in a Texas Town 58. Blackbeard's Ghost 67. Day of the Animals 77, etc.

Lambert, Christopher (1957–) (aka Christophe Lambert)
Franco-American leading man. He is married to actress Diane LANE.
Le Bar du Téléphone 80. Legitimate Violence 80. Greystoke: The Legend of Tarzan, Lord of the Apes 84. Love Songs/Paroles et Musique 84. Subway 85. Highlander 86. I Love You 86. The Sicilian 87. Love Dream 88. To Kill a Priest 88. Un Plan d'Enfer 89. Why Me? 89. Highlander II – the Quickening 90. Knight Moves 92. Gunmen 92. Fortress 93. Highlander III: The Sorcerer 94. Nine Months (Fr.) 94. The Hunted 95. Don't Forget You're Going to Die 95. Mortal Kombat 95. Mean Guns 96. North Star 96. Nirvana 97. Beowulf 99. Gideon (&p) 99. Fortress 2: Re-entry 00. Highlander: Endgame 00, etc.
❝ Christophe has a beguiling innocence, a lot of energy and great charm. His only weakness is that when he kisses you on the cheek I think he assumes that you will never wash your cheek again. – *Joss Ackland*

Lambert, Constant (1905–1951)
British conductor whose one film score was *Anna Karenina* 47.

Lambert, Gavin (1924–)
British critic and novelist, in Hollywood since 1956. Stories about Hollywood: *The Slide Area*.
AS SCRIPTWRITER: Bitter Victory 57. Sons and Lovers (AAN) 60. The Roman Spring of Mrs Stone 61. Inside Daisy Clover 65. I Never Promised You a Rose Garden (AAN) 77, etc.

Lambert, Jack (1899–1976)
Scottish character actor.
The Ghost Goes West 36. Nine Men 43. Hue and Cry 46. Eureka Stockade 47. The Brothers 47. The Lost Hours 50. The Sea Shall Not Have Them 54. Storm over the Nile 56. Reach for the Sky 56. Greyfriars Bobby 60. Modesty Blaise 66. Neither the Sea Nor the Sand 72, many others.

Lambert, Jack (1920–)
American character actor, usually an evil-eyed heavy.
The Cross of Lorraine 43. The Killers 46. The Unsuspected 47. The Enforcer 51. Scared Stiff 53. Kiss Me Deadly 55. Machine Gun Kelly 57. The George Raft Story 61. Four for Texas 63, many others.

Lambert, Mary
American director.
Siesta 87. Pet Sematary 89. Pet Sematary II 92. Grand Isle 92. The Last Mardi Gras 92. The In Crowd 00, etc.

Lambert, Paul (1922–1997)
American character actor, much on TV; born in El Paso, Texas.
Spartacus 60. Planet of the Apes 68. All the Loving Couples 69. A Gunfight 70. Where Does It Hurt 72. The Execution of Private Slovik 74. All the President's Men 76. Death Wish II 81. Blue Thunder 82. A Soldier's Revenge 84, etc.
TV series: Executive Suite 76–77.

Lamble, Lloyd (1914–)
Australian light actor who has been in many British films as detective, official, or other man.

The Story of Gilbert and Sullivan 53. The Belles of St Trinian's 54. The Man Who Never Was 56. Quatermass II 57. Blue Murder at St Trinian's 58. No Trees in the Street 59. The Trials of Oscar Wilde 60. Term of Trial 62. Joey Boy 65. No Sex Please – We're British 73. And Now the Screaming Starts! 73. Eskimo Nell 74, etc.

Lamont, Charles (1898–1993)
American director, in Hollywood from silent days. With Universal from mid-30s, making comedies featuring Abbott and Costello; the Kettles, etc.
Love, Honour and Oh Baby 41. The Merry Monahans 44. Bowery to Broadway 44. Frontier Gal 45. The Runaround 46. Slave Girl 47. Baghdad 49. Flame of Araby 51. Abbott and Costello Meet Dr Jekyll and Mr Hyde 53. Ma and Pa Kettle in Paris 53. Untamed Heiress 54. Abbott and Costello Meet the Mummy 55. Francis in the Haunted House 56. The Kettles in the Ozarks 56, many others.

Lamont, Duncan (1918–1978)
Scottish character actor with stage experience., in films since World War II.
The Lost Hours 52. The Golden Coach 53. The Quatermass Experiment (TV) 53. The End of the Road 54. The Teckman Mystery 54. Passage Home 55. *Quentin Durward* 55. The Thirty-Nine Steps 59. A Touch of Larceny 59. Circle of Deception 60. The Queen's Guards 60. Mutiny on the Bounty 62. Murder at the Gallop 63. The Scarlet Blade 63. Devil Ship Pirates 64. The Evil of Frankenstein 64. The Brigand of Kandahar 65. Frankenstein Created Woman 66. Quatermass and the Pit 67. The Creeping Flesh 72, etc.
TV series: The Texan 59-60.

Lamont, Peter
British art director and production designer, associated with the James Bond films. He began as a draughtsman on *Goldfinger*, later working as a set decorator and art director on the films before becoming the production designer of *For Your Eyes Only* and subsequent Bonds.
Fiddler on the Roof (AAN) 71. The Dove (US) 74. Inside Out 75. The Spy Who Loved Me (AAN) 77. For Your Eyes Only 81. Octopussy 83. On the Third Day 83. A View to a Kill 85. Aliens (US) (AAN) 86. The Living Daylights 87. Licence to Kill 89. The Taking of Beverly Hills (US) 91. True Lies (US) 94. GoldenEye 95. Titanic (AA) 97, etc.

Lamorisse, Albert (1922–1970)
French director known for short fantasy films.
Bim 49. *Crin Blanc* 52. *The Red Balloon* (AAw) 55. Stowaway in the Sky 61. Fifi La Plume 64, etc.

Lamour, Dorothy (1914–1996) (Dorothy Kaumeyer)
Good-humoured American leading lady of the 30s and 40s: became typed in sarong roles, and happily guyed her own image.
Autobiography: 1981, *Dorothy Lamour*, with Dick McInnes.
■ *The Jungle Princess* 36. Thrill of a Lifetime 37. Swing High Swing Low 37. Last Train from Madrid 37. High Wide and Handsome 37. *The Hurricane* 37. The Big Broadcast of 1938. Her Jungle Love 38. Spawn of the North 38. Tropic Holiday 38. St Louis Blues 39. Man About Town 39. Disputed Passage 39. Johnny Apollo 40. Typhoon 40. *Road to Singapore* 40. Moon Over Burma 40. Chad Hanna 40. Road to Zanzibar 41. Caught in the Draft 41. Aloma of the South Seas 41. The Fleet's In 42. Beyond the Blue Horizon 42. Road to Morocco 42. Star Spangled Rhythm 42. They Got Me Covered 43. Dixie 43. Riding High 43. And the Angels Sing 43. Rainbow Island 44. Road to Utopia 45. A Medal for Benny 45. Duffy's Tavern 45. Masquerade in Mexico 45. My Favorite Brunette 47. Road to Rio 47. Wild Harvest 47. Variety Girl 47. On Our Merry Way 48. Lulu Belle 48. The Girl from Manhattan 48. Slightly French 48. Manhandled 48. The Lucky Stiff 49. Here Comes the Groom 51. The Greatest Show on Earth 52. Road to Bali 52. Road to Hong Kong 62. Donovan's Reef 63. Pajama Party 64. The Phynx 70. Won Ton Ton 75. Death of Love House (TV) 76. Creepshow 2 87. Entertaining the Troops (doc) 88.
❝ Dottie's one of the smartest gals I've ever known, but she gives off a fairly dumb quality on the screen that you have to cash in on. – *Mitchell Leisen*

L'Amour, Louis (1908–1988)
Best-selling American writer of western novels, many of which have been filmed.
Hondo 53. Four Guns to the Border 54. Stranger on Horseback 54. The Burning Hills 56. The Tall Stranger 57. Apache Territory 58. Guns of the Timberland 59. Heller in Pink Tights 60. Taggart 64. Shalako 68. Catlow 71. The Man Called Noon 73, etc.

Lampedusa, Giuseppe (1896–1957)
Italian novelist, a nobleman whose *The Leopard* was filmed and gave a picture of 19th-century Sicily.

Lampert, Zohra (1936–)
American TV actress.
Splendour in the Grass 60. Pay or Die 60. A Fine Madness 66. Opening Night 77. Alphabet City 84. Teachers 84. Stanley and Iris 89, etc.

Lancaster, Burt (1913–1994)
Athletic American leading man and latterly distinguished actor. Former circus acrobat; acted and danced in soldier shows during World War II.
Biography: 1995, *Against Type: The Biography of Burt Lancaster* by Larry Fishgall.
■ *The Killers* 46. Desert Fury 47. I Walk Alone 47. *Brute Force* 47. Variety Girl (cameo) 47. Sorry, Wrong Number 48. Kiss the Blood Off My Hands 48. All My Sons 48. Criss Cross 49. Rope of Sand 49. Mister 880 50. *The Flame and the Arrow* 50. Vengeance Valley 51. Ten Tall Men 51. Jim Thorpe All-American 51. The Crimson Pirate 52. *Come Back Little Sheba* 53. South Sea Woman 53. From Here to Eternity (AAN) 53. His Majesty O'Keefe 54. Apache 54. *Vera Cruz* 54. The Kentuckian (& d) 55. The Rose Tattoo 55. Trapeze 56. The Rainmaker 57. *Gunfight at the OK Corral* (as Wyatt Earp) 57. Sweet Smell of Success 57. Separate Tables 58. Run Silent Run Deep 58. The Devil's Disciple (GB) 59. The Unforgiven 59. *Elmer Gantry* (AA) 60. The Young Savages 61. Judgment at Nuremberg 61. *Birdman of Alcatraz* (AAN) 62. A Child is Waiting 62. The Leopard 63. The List of Adrian Messenger 63. Seven Days in May 64. The Train 64. The Hallelujah Trail 65. *The Professionals* 66. *The Swimmer* 67. The Scalphunters 68. Castle Keep 69. The Gypsy Moths 69. Airport 69. Lawman 70. Valdez is Coming 71. Ulzana's Raid 72. Scorpio 73. Executive Action 73. The Midnight Man (& co-p, co-d) 74. Conversation Piece 75. Moses (TV) 75. Buffalo Bill and the Indians 76. *1900* 76. Twilight's Last Gleaming 76. Victory at Entebbe (TV) 76. The Cassandra Crossing 77. The Island of Dr Moreau 77. Go Tell the Spartans 78. Zulu Dawn 79. Atlantic City USA (BFA, AAN) 80. Cattle Annie and Little Britches 80. Marco Polo (TV) 81. Local Hero 83. The Osterman Weekend 83. Scandal Sheet (TV) 85. Little Treasure 85. On Wings of Eagles (TV) 85. Tough Guys 86. Barnum (TV) 86. Rocket Gibraltar 88. Field of Dreams 89. Phantom of the Opera (TV) 90.
✪ For enthusiasm, shrewdness and agility. *The Flame and the Arrow*.
❝ Life is to be lived within the limits of your knowledge and within the concept of what you would like to see yourself to be. – *B.L.*
If I'm working with frightened people, I do tend to dominate them. I'm no doll, that's for sure. – *B.L.*
Most people seem to think I'm the kind of guy who shaves with a blowtorch. Actually I'm bookish and worrisome. – *B.L.*
Before he can pick up an ashtray he discusses his motivation for a couple of hours. You want to tell him to pick up the ashtray and shut up. – *Jeanne Moreau*

Lanchester, Elsa (1902–1986) (Elizabeth Sullivan)
British character actress married to Charles Laughton. On stage and screen in Britain before settling in Hollywood in 1940.
Autobiography: 1938, *Charles Laughton and I*; 1983, *Elsa Lanchester Herself*.
Bluebottles 28. *The Private Life of Henry VIII* 33. David Copperfield 35. *The Bride of Frankenstein* 35. The Ghost Goes West 36. *Rembrandt* 37. Vessel of Wrath 38. Ladies in Retirement 41. Tales of Manhattan 42. The Spiral Staircase 45. End of the Rainbow 47. The Inspector-General 49. Come to the Stable (AAN) 49. Androcles and the Lion 53. Bell, Book and Candle 57. *Witness for the Prosecution* (AAN) 57. Mary Poppins 64. Blackbeard's Ghost 67. Me, Natalie 69. Willard 71. Terror in the Wax Museum 73. *Murder by Death* 76, many others.
TV series: The John Forsythe Show 65.

Lanci, Giuseppe (1942–)
Italian cinematographer, frequently for the films of Marco Bellocchio, the Taviani brothers and Nanni Moretti.
Strange Occasion/Quelle Strane Occasioni 76. Those Eyes, That Mouth/Gli Occhi, La Bocca 82. Nostalgia 83. Kaos 84. Camorra: the Naples Connection/Un Complicato Intrigo Di Donne, Vicoli e Delitti 85. Every Time We Say Goodbye 86. Good Morning Babylon 87. Three Sisters/Paura e Amore 87. C'est la Vie/La Baule-les-Pins 90. Night Sun/Il Sole Anche di Notte 90. Johnny Stecchino 91. Fiorile 93. Dear Diary/Caro Diario 94. The Prince of Homburg/Il Principe Di Homburg 96. Aprile 98. You Laugh/Tu Ridi 98, etc.

Landau, David (1878–1935)
American character actor, familiar in early talkies as crook or roughneck.
I Take This Woman 31. Street Scene 31. Taxi 32. Polly of the Circus 32. Horse Feathers 32. I Am a Fugitive from a Chain Gang 32. She Done Him Wrong 33. One Man's Journey 33. Wharf Angel 34. Judge Priest 34, etc.

Landau, Ely (1920–1993)
American producer, former distributor.
Long Day's Journey into Night 62. The Pawnbroker 64. All productions of the American Film Theatre 72–74. Hopscotch 80. The Holcroft Covenant 85, etc.

Landau, Martin (1928–)
Gaunt American actor often in sinister roles. Born in New York City, he began as a newspaper cartoonist before studying at the Actors Studio. Married actress Barbara Bain.
North by Northwest 59. The Gazebo 59. Cleopatra 62. The Hallelujah Trail 65. Nevada Smith 66. They Call Me Mr Tibbs 70. Savage (TV) 72. Black Gunn 72. Blazing Magnum 76. Meteor 79. Without Warning 80. Alone in the Dark 82. Sweet Revenge 87. W.A.R. Women Against Rape 87. Empire State 87. *Tucker: The Man and His Dream* (AAN) 88. *Crimes and Misdemeanors* (AAN) 89. Neon Empire 89. Paint It Black 90. Real Bullets 90. The Color of Evening 91. Ganglands 91. Treasure Island 91. Mistress 92. Sliver 93. Intersection 94. Time Is Money 94. Eye of the Stranger 94. *Ed Wood* (as Bela Lugosi) (AA) 94. City Hall 96. The Adventures of Pinocchio 96. BAPS 97. The X Files 98. EdTV 99. Ready to Rumble 00. Shiner (GB) 00, etc.
TV series: Mission Impossible 66–68. Space 1999 75–76.

Landen, Dinsdale (1931–)
British stage actor who makes occasional films.
Operation Snatch 62. Rasputin the Mad Monk 66. Every Home Should Have One 70. Digby 71. International Velvet 78. Morons from Outer Space 85. The Steal 95, etc.
TV series: Devenish 77–78. Pig in the Middle 80–83.

Landers, Lew (1901–1962) (Lewis Friedlander)
American director of 'B' pictures, especially westerns, from silent days.
The Raven 35. The Man Who Found Himself 37. Canal Zone 39. Pacific Liner 39. The Boogie Man Will Get You 42. Return of the Vampire 43. The Enchanted Forest 46. State Penitentiary 49. Man in the Dark (in 3-D) 53. Captain Kidd and the Slave Girl 53. Hot Rod Gang 58. Terrified 62, many others.

Landeta, Matilde (1910–)
Mexican director. Born in San Luis Posi, she began as a continuity girl in the 30s and turned to directing in the late 40s, but prejudice made it difficult for her to continue her career, and she turned to writing and making short films. She was the subject of a 30-minute TV documentary, *Matilde Landeta – My Film-making, My Life* (GB) 90, directed by Patricia Diaz.
Lola Casanova 48. La Negra Augustias 49. Trotacalles 51. Islas Revillagigedo (doc) 90. Nocturno a Rosario (p, wd) 92, etc.

Landi, Elissa (1904–1948) (Elizabeth Kuhnelt)
Austrian-Italian leading lady, in international films of the 30s.
Underground 29. Children of Chance 30. Always Goodbye 31. The Yellow Ticket 31. Passport to Hell 32. *The Sign of the Cross* 32. The Masquerader 33. The Warrior's Husband 33. By Candlelight 34. Sisters under the Skin 34. *The Count of Monte Cristo* 34. Without Regret 35. Enter Madame 35. The Amateur Gentleman 36. After the Thin Man 36. The Thirteenth Chair 37. Corregidor 43, etc.

Landi, Marla (c. 1937–)
Italian leading lady and model, in British films.
Across the Bridge 57. First Man into Space 58. The Hound of the Baskervilles 59. Pirates of Blood River 61. The Murder Game 65, etc.

Landis, Carole (1919–1948) (Frances Ridste)
Uninhibited blonde American leading actress. Born in Fairchild, Wisconsin, she was working as a singer and dancer in nightclubs in her mid-teens, and was in films from the age of 18, first attracting attention clad in animal skins in *One Million BC*. Her best role was as herself in *Four Jills in a Jeep*, about her tour with Martha Raye, Kay Francis and Mitzi Mayfair, entertaining troops during the Second World War. Married four times, the first at the age of 15, she committed suicide over a failing love affair with actor Rex Harrison, which coincided with a decline in her career, as her unconventional attitudes alienated studio heads. Her lovers included Busby Berkeley, Darryl Zanuck and Jacqueline Susann, who used her as the model for the character Jennifer in her novel *Valley of the Dolls*.
Man and His Mate/One Million BC 40. *Turnabout* 40. Road Show 41. Topper Returns 41. Hot Spot 41. Orchestra Wives 42. Wintertime 43. Having Wonderful Crime 44. Behind Green Lights 45. It Shouldn't Happen to a Dog 46. A Scandal in Paris 46. Out of the Blue 47. The Brass Monkey (GB) 48. Noose (GB) 48, etc.
❝ I think I've always been a sucker. By sucker I mean someone who is very vulnerable, who wears her heart on her sleeve, who is easily hurt, who, in fact, almost asks to be hurt. – *C.L.*
I don't say she was a talented actress, but she was a beautiful girl, and full of life, and could certainly have fitted into many parts. – *Rex Harrison*

Landis, Cullen (1896–1975)
American silent screen hero.
Who Is Number One 17. Beware of Blondes 18. Almost a Husband 19. Born Rich 24, many others.

Landis, Jessie Royce (1904–1972) (Jessie Royce Medbury)
American character actress of long stage experience; usually in fluttery comedy roles.
Autobiography: 1954, *You Won't Be So Pretty*.
■ Derelict 30. Mr Belvedere Goes to College 49. It Happens Every Spring 49. My Foolish Heart 49. Mother Didn't Tell Me 50. Meet Me Tonight (GB) 51. *To Catch a Thief* 55. The Swan 56. The Girl He Left Behind 56. My Man Godfrey 57. I Married a Woman 58. *North by Northwest* 59. A Private's Affair 59. Goodbye Again 61. Bon Voyage 62. Boys' Night Out 62. Critic's Choice 63. Gidget Goes To Rome 63. Airport 69. Mr and Mrs Bo Jo Jones (TV) 71.
❝ Famous line (*North by Northwest*) 'You gentlemen are not really trying to murder my son, are you?'

Landis, John (1950–)
American director.
Schlock 76. Kentucky Fried Movie 77. National Lampoon's Animal House 78. The Blues Brothers 80. *An American Werewolf in London* 81. Twilight Zone 83. Trading Places 83. The Muppets Take Manhattan (cameo) 84. Into the Night 85. Spies Like Us 85. Three Amigos 86. Amazon Women on the Moon (co-d) 87. Coming to America 88. Darkman (a) 90. Oscar 91. Sleepwalkers (a) 92. Innocent Blood 92. Beverly Hills Cop III 94. The Stand (TV) (a) 94. The Stupids 96. Mad City (a) 97. Quicksilver Highway (a) (TV) 97. Blues Brothers 2000 (co-w, d) 98. Susan's Plan (wd) 98, etc.
❝ When *Animal House* turned out the way it did, they all rushed to me with barrels of money begging me to make them rich. – *J.L.*

Landon, Michael (1937–1991) (Eugene Orowitz)
American leading man best known as Little Joe in TV series *Bonanza* 59–73. He also wrote and directed many episodes of the series. Born in Long Island, New York, he went to the University of

California on an athletic scholarship, but dropped out to work in various occupations and to study acting briefly before finding work in television. Married three times, he had nine children. Died of cancer.

A TV movie about Landon's young manhood, *Sam's Son*, was released in 1984.

I Was a Teenage Werewolf 57. God's Little Acre 58. The Legend of Tom Dooley 59, etc.

TV series: Little House on the Prairie 74–82. Highway to Heaven 84–89.

Landone, Avice (1910–1976)
British stage actress, usually in cool, unruffled roles.
My Brother Jonathan 48. The Franchise Affair 51. An Alligator Named Daisy 55. Reach for the Sky 56. Carve Her Name with Pride 58. Operation Cupid 60, etc.

Landres, Paul (1912–)
American director, former editor.
Oregon Passage 57. The Vampire 57. The Miracle of the Hills 58. The Flame Barrier 58. The Return of Dracula 58. Son of a Gunfighter 65, etc.

Landru, Henri Désiré (1869–1922)
The story of the French murderer who killed 10 women for their money has been told several times on film, usually in a fictional guise and most notably by Charlie Chaplin in *Monsieur Verdoux* 47, and also in *Bluebeard's Ten Honeymoons* 60, starring George Sanders, and Claude Chabrol's *Landru* 62. Other films that draw on the story, and also on the folk-tale of Bluebeard, include Edward Dmytryk's *Bluebeard* 72, starring Richard Burton, and Sam Wood's *Bluebeard* 23, with Huntley Gordon and Gloria Swanson, which was remade by Ernst Lubitsch in 1938, starring Gary Cooper and Claudette Colbert.

Lane, Allan 'Rocky' (1900–1973) (Harry Albershart)
American cowboy star of the 30s, former athlete.
Night Nurse 32. Maid's Night Out 38. The Dancing Masters 44. Trail of Robin Hood 51. The Saga of Hemp Brown 58. Hell Bent for Leather 60, many second features.
TV series: Mister Ed (voice) 62–64.

Lane, Burton (1912–1997) (Burton Levy)
American composer and screenwriter. Born in New York, he began writing songs in his teens, then went to work for MGM in the 30s, where his lyricists included Harold ADAMSON, Frank LOESSER and Ralph FREED. His collaboration with E. Y. 'Yip' HARBURG led to the Broadway musical *Finian's Rainbow* 47, filmed in 1968. His other Broadway hit, *On a Clear Day You Can See Forever* 65, written with Alan Jay LERNER, was filmed in 1970. He also wrote the Broadway musical *Carmelina* 78, based on the film *Buona Sera Mrs Campbell*.
Dancing Lady 33. Cocoanut Grove 38. St Louis Blues 39. Babes on Broadway (AANs 'How About You') 41. Ship Ahoy 42. Rainbow Island 44. Royal Wedding (AANs 'Too Late Now') 51. Give a Girl a Break 53. Jupiter's Darling 54. Affair in Havana (co-w) 57. The Adventures of Huckleberry Finn 60. Heidi's Song 82, etc.

Lane, Charles (1905–) (Charles Levison)
American character actor seen since early 30s as comedy snoop, salesman or tax inspector; at the age of 80, he was vigorously playing a judge in *Soap*.
Mr Deeds Goes to Town 36. In Old Chicago 38. You Can't Take It with You 38. The Cat and the Canary 39. Hot Spot 41. Arsenic and Old Lace 44. Intrigue 49. The Juggler 53. Teacher's Pet 58. The Gnome-Mobile 67. What's So Bad about Feeling Good? 68. The Little Dragons 80. Strange Invaders 83. Murphy's Romance 85. When the Bough Breaks (TV) 86. Date with an Angel 87. War and Remembrance (TV) 89, etc.
TV series: Dear Phoebe 54–55. The Lucy Show 62–63. Petticoat Junction 63–68. The Pruitts of Southampton 66–67. Karen 75.

Lane, Diane (1965–)
American actress, in theatre as a child. She is married to actor Christopher LAMBERT.
A Little Romance 79. Touched by Love 79. Cattle Annie and Little Britches 80. Ladies and Gentlemen: The Fabulous Stains 81. Child Bride of Short Creek (TV) 81. National Lampoon's Movie Madness 81. Miss All-American Beauty (TV) 82. Six Pack 82. The Outsiders 83. Rumble Fish 83. Streets of Fire 84. The Cotton Club 84. The Big Town 87. Lady Beware 87. Love Dream 88. Vital Signs 90. Priceless Beauty 90. Descending Angel 91. Chaplin 92. Knight Moves 92. My New Gun 92. Indian Summer 93. Oldest Living Confederate Widow Tells All (TV) 94. Judge Dredd 95. Wild Bill 95. A Streetcar Named Desire (TV) 95. Jack 96. Mad Dog Time/Trigger Happy 96. Murder at 1600 97. The Blouse Man 98. Kiss the Sky 98. A Walk on the Moon 98. The Perfect Storm 00. My Dog Skip 00, etc.

Lane, Jackie (1937–) (Jocelyn Bolton)
Sultry Austrian actress and dancer, mainly in British films of the 50s. She was later credited as Jocelyn Lane. She was the sister of actress Mara LANE.
The Gamma People 56. These Dangerous Years 57. The Truth About Women 58. Wonderful Things! 58. The Angry Hills 59. Jet Storm 59. Goodbye Again 61. Two and Two Make Six 61. Operation Snatch 62. Tickle Me (US) 65. A Bullet for Pretty Boy (US) 70. Land Raiders (US) 70, etc.

Lane, Jocelyn
see Lane, Jackie

Lane, Lupino (1892–1959) (Henry George Lupino)
Diminutive, dapper British stage comedian and master of the pratfall, member of a family who had been clowns for generations. His American two-reelers of the 20s were little masterpieces of timing and hair-raising stunts, but he failed to develop a personality for sound. On his return to Britain from Hollywood, he directed one of the first British musicals, *No Lady*, and went to work at Elstree for British International Pictures as a director, before returning to his first love, the stage, climaxing in the long-running musical *Me and My Girl* featuring his singing of 'The Lambeth Walk'.
Biography: 1957, *Born to Star* by James Dillon White.
The Reporter 22. Isn't Life Wonderful? 24. The Love Parade 29. Bride of the Regiment 30. The Golden Mask 30.
GB FILMS: No Lady (& d) 31. The Love Race (d) 31. Love Lies (d) 31. Innocents of Chicago (d) 32. The Maid of the Mountains (d) 32. A Southern Maid (& d) 33. Letting in the Sunshine (d) 33. The Deputy Drummer 35. Hot News 36. Me and My Girl 39, etc.

Lane, Mara (1930–)
Austrian-born actress in international films. Born in Vienna, she was the sister of actress Jackie LANE.
Hell Is Sold Out (GB) 51. It Started in Paradise (GB) 52. Treasure Hunt (GB) 52. Decameron Nights (GB) 53. Casanova (It.) 54. Susan Slept Here (US) 54. Angela (It./US) 55. Love from Paris/Montpi (Ger.) 57. Sailor's Paradise/Paradies Der Matrosen (Ger.) 59. The Old Testament/Il Vecchio Testamento (It.) 63, etc.

Lane, Nathan (1956–)
American leading actor, mainly on Broadway and in occasional films in comic roles.
Ironweed 87. Frankie and Johnny 91. He Said, She Said 91. Addams Family Values 93. Life with Mikey 93. The Lion King (voice) 94. Jeffrey 95. *The Birdcage* 96. The Boys Next Door (TV) 96. Mousehunt 97. The Lion King II: Simba's Pride (voice) 98. At First Sight 99. Stuart Little (voice) 99. Love's Labours Lost 00. Titan A.E. 00. Isn't She Great 00, etc.
TV series: One of the Boys 82. Encore! Encore! 98-99.

Lane, Richard (1900–1982)
American supporting player, formerly and latterly sports announcer; frequently seen in the 40s as reporter, tough cop, or exasperated executive.
The Outcasts of Poker Flat 37. Union Pacific 39. Hellzapoppin 41. Meet Boston Blackie 41. What a Blonde 45. Gentleman Joe Palooka 46. Take Me Out to the Ball Game 48. I Can Get It For You Wholesale 51, etc.

The Lane Sisters
American leading ladies, real name Mullican. Three of the five sisters (all actresses) had sizeable roles in Hollywood films: *Lola* (1909–1981), *Rosemary* (1913–1974) and *Priscilla* (1917–1995).
TOGETHER: Four Daughters 38. Daughters Courageous 39. Four Wives 39. Four Mothers 40.
OTHER APPEARANCES FOR LOLA: Speakeasy 29. Death from a Distance 35. Marked Woman 37. Zanzibar 40. Why Girls Leave Home 36.
ROSEMARY: Hollywood Hotel 38. The Oklahoma Kid 38. The Return of Dr X 40. Time Out for Rhythm 42. The Fortune Hunter 45.
PRISCILLA: Brother Rat 39. Dust Be My Destiny 39. Yes My Darling Daughter 39. The Roaring Twenties 40. Blues in the Night 41. Saboteur 42. Arsenic and Old Lace 44. Fun on a Weekend 46. Bodyguard 48, etc.

Lanfield, Sidney (1900–1972)
American director from 1932; former jazz musician. Married actress Shirley Mason.
Hat Check Girl 32. Moulin Rouge 34. Sing Baby Sing 36. *The Hound of the Baskervilles* 39. Swanee River 39. You'll Never Get Rich 41. The Lady Has Plans 41. *My Favorite Blonde* 42. The Meanest Man in the World 42. Let's Face It 43. Standing Room Only 44. Bring on the Girls 45. The Well-Groomed Bride 45. Stations West 47. The Lemon Drop Kid 50. Follow the Sun 51. Skirts Ahoy 52, etc.

Lang, Charles (1902–1998)
Distinguished American cinematographer.
Shopworn Angel 29. *A Farewell to Arms* (AA) 33. Death Takes a Holiday 34. Lives of a Bengal Lancer 35. *Desire* 36. *The Cat and the Canary* 39. Nothing but the Truth 41. Practically Yours 44. The Uninvited 44. The Ghost and Mrs Muir 47. A Foreign Affair 47. *Ace in the Hole* 51. Sudden Fear 52. The Big Heat 53. The Female on the Beach 55. The Man from Laramie 55. Autumn Leaves 56. The Solid Gold Cadillac 56. Gunfight at the OK Corral 57. Some Like It Hot (AAN) 59. One-Eyed Jacks 59. The Facts of Life 60. The Magnificent Seven 60. Blue Hawaii 61. A Girl Named Tamiko 62. *Charade* 63. Inside Daisy Clover 65. How to Steal a Million 66. Not with My Wife You Don't 66. Hotel 67. The Flim Flam Man 67. Wait Until Dark 67. A Flea in Her Ear 68. Cactus Flower 69. Bob and Carol and Ted and Alice (AAN) 70. The Love Machine 71. Butterflies Are Free (AAN) 72, many others.

Lang, Charles (1915–)
American writer.
Killer Shark 50. Call of the Klondike 50. Captain Scarface 53. The Magnificent Matador 55. Buchanan Rides Alone 58. Desire in the Dust 60. Tess of the Storm Country 60, etc.

Lang, Fritz (1890–1976)
German director of distinguished silent films. Went to Hollywood 1934 and tended thereafter to make commercial though rather heavy-handed thrillers.
Biography: 1974, *Fritz Lang* by Lotte Eisner. 1997, *Fritz Lang: The Nature of the Beast* by Patrick McGilligan.
■ Helbblut 19. Der Herr der Liebe 19. Die Spinnen 19. Hara Kiri 19. Vier um die Frau 20. Das Wandernde Bild 21. *Destiny* 21. Das Brillanten Schiff 21. Der Müde Tod 21. *Dr Mabuse der Spieler* 22. Inferno 22. *Siegfried* 23. Krimhild's Revenge 24. *Metropolis* 26. *The Spy* 27. Frau im Mond 28. M 31. The Testament of Dr Mabuse 32. Liliom 33. *Fury* 36. *You Only Live Once* 37. You and Me 38. The Return of Frank James 40. Western Union 41. Man Hunt 41. Confirm or Deny (part) 42. Hangmen Also Die 43. *The Woman in the Window* 44. Ministry of Fear 44. Scarlet Street 45. Cloak and Dagger 46. The Secret beyond the Door 48. House by the River 49. An American Guerrilla in the Philippines 51. Rancho Notorious 52. Clash by Night 52. The Blue Gardenia 52. *The Big Heat* 53. Human Desire 54. Moonfleet 55. While the City Sleeps 55. Beyond a Reasonable Doubt 56. Der Tiger von Ischnapur (Ger.) 58. Das Indische Grabmal (Ger.) 58. The Thousand Eyes of Dr Mabuse (Ger.) 60. Contempt (a only) 63.
✪ For spinning out his well-deserved German reputation through an American career of dwindling talent. *Fury*.
❝ His cinema is that of the nightmare, the fable, and the philosophical dissertation. – *Andrew Sarris, 1968*
Lang makes you want to puke. Nobody in the whole world is as important as he imagines himself to be. I completely understand why he is so hated everywhere. – *Kurt Weill*

Lang, Harold (1923–1971)
Blond English general-purpose actor and drama teacher, often in shady roles, from the stage. Born in London, he studied at RADA.
Floodtide 49. Cairo Road 50. The Franchise Affair 51. Wings of Danger 52. The Intruder 53. Dance Little Lady 54. The Quatermass Experiment 55. It's a Wonderful World 56. Carve Her Name with Pride 58. Ben Hur 59. Dr Terror's House of Horrors 64. The Nanny 65. Two Gentlemen Sharing 69, etc.

Lang, Jennings (1915–1996)
American executive, long near the top of MCA TV and latterly executive producer of many Universal films. A lawyer and former agent, he was involved in the development of many successful TV series of the 50s and 60s, including *The Virginian*, *McHale's Navy* and *Wagon Train*. He also developed Sensurround, a sound system that helped make *Earthquake* a hit in 1975. In 1951, when he was agent of actress Joan Bennett, he was shot in the groin by Bennett's husband, producer Walter Wanger.
AS PRODUCER OR EXECUTIVE PRODUCER: Coogan's Bluff 68. Winning 69. Tell Them Willie Boy Is Here 69. The Beguiled 71. Play Misty for Me 71. Pete 'n' Tillie 72. Airport 1975 75. The Front Page 75. Airport '77 77. The Concorde: Airport '79/aka Airport 80: The Concorde (& story) 79, etc.

Lang, June (1915–) (June Vlasek)
American leading lady, former dancer.
Chandu the Magician 32. Bonnie Scotland 35. Ali Baba Goes to Town 38. Redhead 41. Flesh and Fantasy 44. Lighthouse 48, etc.

Lang, Matheson (1879–1948)
Tall, handsome Scottish-Canadian stage actor-manager and dramatist, a London matinée idol of the 20s who made occasional films. Born in Montreal, he was educated at St Andrew's University and was on-stage from 1897. He was on the London stage from 1900 and was playing the great Shakespearean roles there from 1907. Many of his films, such as *Mr Wu*, *Carnival*, *The Wandering Jew* and *The Chinese Bungalow* were based on his theatrical successes. Married stage actress Hutin Britton (1876-1965), who co-starred with him in the film of *The Wandering Jew*.
Autobiography: 1940, *Mr Wu Looks Back*.
Mr Wu 21. Carnival (& oa) 21. Dick Turpin's Ride to York 22. The Wandering Jew 23. The Chinese Bungalow (& oa) 25. Beyond the Veil 25. Island of Despair 26. The Triumph of the Scarlet Pimpernel 29. The Chinese Bungalow (& oa) 30. Carnival (& oa) 31. Channel Crossing 33. Little Friend 34. Drake of England 35. Royal Cavalcade 35. The Cardinal 36, etc.

Lang, Otto (1908–)
Austrian-born producer and director in Hollywood, a former ski instructor to Darryl Zanuck.
Call Northside 777 (p) 48. Five Fingers (p) 52. White Witch Doctor (p) 53. Vesuvius Express (AANp, short) 53. Jet Carrier (AANp, short) 54. Tora! Tora! Tora! (p) 69, etc.

Lang, Robert (1934–)
British character actor, mainly on stage.
Othello 65. Dance of Death 69. The Mackintosh Man 73. Night Watch 73. Savage Messiah 73. Shout at the Devil 76. The First Great Train Robbery 79. Runners 83. Hawks 88. The Trial 93. Four Weddings and a Funeral 94. Some Mother's Son 96. Rasputin (TV) 96. Wilde 97. Our Mutual Friend (TV) 98, etc.
TV series: The Old Boy Network 91. Under the Hammer 94.

Lang, Walter (1898–1972)
American director of competent but seldom outstanding entertainments.
The Satin Woman 27. The College Hero 27. Brothers 30. Hell Bound 30. Women Go On for Ever 31. No More Orchids 32. The Warrior's Husband 33. Meet the Baron 33. Whom the Gods Destroy 34. The Mighty Barnum 34. Carnival 35. Hooray for Love 35. Love Before Breakfast 36. *Wife, Doctor and Nurse* 37. Second Honeymoon 37. The Baroness and the Butler 38. I'll Give a Million 38. The Little Princess 39. *The Bluebird* 40. Star Dust 40. The Great Profile 40. *Tin Pan Alley* 40. Moon over Miami 41. Weekend in Havana 41. Song of the Islands 42. The Magnificent Dope 42.

Coney Island 43. Greenwich Village 44. *State Fair* 45. Sentimental Journey 46. Claudia and David 46. Mother Wore Tights 47. *Sitting Pretty* 48. When My Baby Smiles at Me 48. You're My Everything 49. Cheaper by the Dozen 50. The Jackpot 50. On the Riviera 51. *With a Song in My Heart* 51. *Call Me Madam* 53. There's No Business like Show Business 54. *The King and I* (AAN) 56. The Desk Set 57. But Not for Me 59. Can Can 60. The Marriage Go Round 61. Snow White and the Three Stooges 61, many others.

Langan, Glenn (1917–1991)
American light leading man, in films from the early 40s after stage experience.
Four Jills in a Jeep 44. *Margie* 46. Forever Amber 47. The Snake Pit 48. Treasure of Monte Cristo 49. Rapture (Swe.) 50. Hangman's Knot 52. 99 River Street 54. The Amazing Colossal Man 57, etc.

Langdon, Harry (1884–1944)
Baby-faced, melancholy American clown who was a great hit in the 20s but could not reconcile his unusual image with sound.
Picking Peaches 23. *Tramp Tramp Tramp* 26. *The Strong Man* 26. *Long Pants* 26. His First Flame 27. Three's a Crowd 27. The Chaser (& d) 28. See America Thirst 30. A Soldier's Plaything 31. Hallelujah I'm a Bum 33. My Weakness 33. There Goes My Heart 38. *Zenobia* 39. Misbehaving Husbands 40. House of Errors 42. Spotlight Scandals 44, etc.
❝ He was a quaint artist who had no business in business. – *Mack Sennett*

Langdon, Sue Ane (1936–)
American leading lady and comedienne.
The Outsider 61. The Rounders 65. A Fine Madness 66. A Guide for the Married Man 67. The Cheyenne Social Club 70. Without Warning 80. Zapped! 82, etc.
TV series: Bachelor Father 58–61. The Jackie Gleason Show 62–63. Arnie 70–72. Grandpa Goes to Washington 78–79. When the Whistle Blows 80.

Lange, Arthur (1889–1956)
American composer.
Hollywood Revue 29. Marie Galante 34. Banjo on My Knee 36. This Is My Affair 37. Kidnapped 38. Lady of Burlesque 43. The Woman in the Window 45. Woman on the Run 50. The Mad Magician 54, many others.

Lange, Hope (1931–)
American leading lady of the 50s who developed into a mature and pleasing comedienne. Born in Redding Ridge, Connecticut, she was on stage at the age of 12, and later was a dancer on *The Jackie Gleason Show*.
Bus Stop 56. The True Story of Jesse James 57. Peyton Place (AAN) 57. The Young Lions 58. In Love and War 58. The Best of Everything 59. Wild in the Country 61. Pocketful of Miracles 61. Love Is a Ball 63. Jigsaw (TV) 68. Crowhaven Farm (TV) 70. That Certain Summer (TV) 72. The 500 Pound Jerk (TV) 72. Death Wish 74. I Love You Goodbye (TV) 74. Fer de Lance (TV) 74. The Secret Night Caller (TV) 75. Like Normal People (TV) 79. The Day Christ Died (TV) 80. I Am The Cheese 83. The Prodigal 83. Nightmare on Elm Street II 85. Blue Velvet 86. Tune in Tomorrow/Aunt Julia and the Scriptwriter 90. Dead before Dawn (TV) 93. Message from 'Nam (TV) 93. Coopertown (TV) 93. Clear and Present Danger 94. Just Cause 95, etc.
TV series: The Ghost and Mrs Muir 68–70. The New Dick Van Dyke Show 71–74.

Lange, Jessica (1949–)
American leading lady who developed into an actress. She has a daughter by actor and dancer Mikhail BARYSHNIKOV and a son and a daughter by actor and dramatist Sam SHEPARD.
King Kong 76. All That Jazz 79. How to Beat the High Cost of Living 80. The Postman Always Rings Twice 81. *Frances* (AAN) 82. Tootsie (AA) 82. Country (AAN) 84. Sweet Dreams (AAN) 85. Crimes of the Heart 86. Everybody's All-American 88. Far North 88. Music Box (AAN) 89. Men Don't Leave 90. Cape Fear 91. Night and the City 92. Blue Sky (made 91) (AA) 94. Rob Roy 95. Losing Isaiah 95. A Streetcar Named Desire (TV) 95. Cousin Bette 97. A Thousand Acres 97. Hush 98. Titus 99, etc.

Langella, Frank (1940–)
American leading man of the 70s.
The Twelve Chairs 70. Diary of a Mad Housewife 70. The Deadly Trap 71. The Wrath of God 72. The Mark of Zorro (TV) 74. *Dracula* (title role) 79. Those Lips Those Eyes 80. Sphinx 80. The Men's Club 86. Masters of the Universe 87. And God Created Woman 87. True Identity 91. 1492: Conquest of Paradise 92. Body of Evidence 92. Dave 93. Doomsday Gun (TV) 94. Bad Company 94. Junior 94. Brainscan 94. Bad Company 95. CutThroat Island 95. Eddie 96. Lolita 97. Small Soldiers 98. Alegria (Can/Fr/Neth) 99. Dark Summer (Can., uncredited) 99. The Ninth Gate 99. Jason and the Argonauts (TV) 00. Stardom 00, etc.

Langenkamp, Heather (1964–)
American leading actress of horror movies.
The Outsiders 83. Rumble Fish 83. A Nightmare on Elm Street 84. Nickel Mountain 85. A Nightmare on Elm Street 3: Dream Warriors 87. Shocker 89. Wes Craven's New Nightmare 94. Tonya & Nancy: The Inside Story (TV) 94. The Demolitionist 95, etc.

Langford, Frances (1914–)
American band singer, popular in the 40s, mainly in guest spots. Appeared mainly in light musicals. Her first husband was actor Jon HALL (1938–55).
Every Night at Eight 35. Broadway Melody 36. Hollywood Hotel 37. Too Many Girls 40. Swing It, Soldier 41. The Girl Rush 44. The Bamboo Blonde 45. Beat the Band 46. No Time For Tears 52. The Glenn Miller Story 54, etc.

Langley, Noel (1911–1980)
South African playwright and screenwriter, in Britain and Hollywood.
Maytime (co-w) 38. The Wizard of Oz (co-w) 39. They Made Me a Fugitive 47. Tom Brown's Schooldays 51. Scrooge 52. The Pickwick Papers (& d) 53. Our Girl Friday (& d) 53. The Search for Bridey Murphy (& d) 56, many others.

Langlois, Henri (1914–1977)
Idiosyncratic French archivist, instigator of the Cinémathèque Française. His methods annoyed some, but his good intentions were never in question. Received Special Academy Award in 1974. A documentary on his life, *Citizen Langlois*, directed by Edgardo Cozarinsky, was released in 1995.
Biography: 1983, *A Passion for Films* by Richard Roud.

Langton, David (1912–1994)
English actor of stage and screen, best known for playing Richard Bellamy, the head of the household, in the TV series *Upstairs, Downstairs* (1970–75).
The Ship that Died of Shame 55. Saint Joan 57. Seven Waves Away 57. A Hard Day's Night 64. The Pumpkin Eater 64. The Incredible Sarah 76. The Whistle Blower 86, etc.

Langton, Simon (1941–)
British director, in TV from 1964.
The Whistle Blower 86. Laguna Heat 87. The Cinder Path (TV) 94. Pride and Prejudice (TV) 95, etc.

Langtry, Lillie (1853–1929) (Emilie Charlotte Le Breton)
British light actress who charmed, among others, Judge Roy Bean and Edward VII. Sole film appearance *His Neighbour's Wife* 13. Ava Gardner played her in *The Life and Times of Judge Roy Bean*.

Lanoux, Victor (1936–)
French leading actor. He left school at 14 and worked in cabaret before making his cinema debut in 1965.
La Vieille Dame Indigne 65. La Ville Normale 67. L'Affaire Dominici 73. Deux Hommes dans la Ville 73. Folle à Tuer 75. Cousin Cousine 75. Pardon Mon Affaire/Un éléphant ça Trompe Enormément 76. Servant et Maîtresse 77. One Wild Moment/Un Moment d'Egarement 77. Pardon Mon Affaire Too!/We Will All Meet in Paradise 78. Un Si Joli Village 79. Retour en Force 80. Dog Day/Canicule 83. Un Dimanche de Flics 83. Louisiana 84. National Lampoon's European Vacation 85. Scene of the Crime/Le Lieu du Crime 87. L'Invité Surprise 89. Le Bal des Casse-Pieds 92, etc.

Lansbury, Angela (1925–)
British character actress who has always seemed older than her years. Evacuated to Hollywood during World War II, she played a long succession of unsympathetic parts, but in the 60s became a Broadway musical star. She is best known as amateur detective Jessica Fletcher in the long-running TV series *Murder She Wrote*. Her first husband was actor Richard Cromwell (1945–46).
■ Gaslight (AAN) 44. National Velvet 44. *The Picture of Dorian Gray* (AAN) 45. The Harvey Girls 46. The Hoodlum Saint 46. The Private Affairs of Bel Ami 47. Till the Clouds Roll By 47. If Winter Comes 47. Tenth Avenue Angel 48. State of the Union 48. The Three Musketeers 48. The Red Danube 49. Samson and Delilah 49. Kind Lady 51. Mutiny 52. Remains to Be Seen 53. A Lawless Street 55. A Life at Stake 55. The Purple Mask 55. Please Murder Me 56. The Court Jester 56. The Reluctant Debutante 58. The Long Hot Summer 58. *The Dark at the Top of the Stairs* 60. A Breath of Scandal 61. Blue Hawaii 61. Summer of the Seventeenth Doll 61. All Fall Down 62. *The Manchurian Candidate* (AAN) 62. In the Cool of the Day 63. The World of Henry Orient 64. Dear Heart 64. The Greatest Story Ever Told 65. Harlow 65. Moll Flanders 65. Mister Buddwing 66. Something for Everyone 70. *Bedknobs and Broomsticks* 71. Death on the Nile 78. The Lady Vanishes 79. The Mirror Crack'd 80. Little Gloria … Happy at Last (TV) 82. The Pirates of Penzance 83. Lace (TV) 84. Company of Wolves 84. Rage of Angels: The Story Continues (TV) 86. Shootdown (TV) 88. The Shell Seekers (TV) 90. The Love She Sought (TV) 90. Beauty and the Beast (voice) 92. Mrs 'Arris Goes to Paris (TV) 92. Mrs Santa Claus (TV) 96. Beauty and the Beast: The Enchanted Christmas (voice) 97. Murder, She Wrote: South by Southwest (TV) 97. Anastasia (voice) 97.
TV series: Murder She Wrote 84–96.

Lansing, Joi (1928–1972) (Joyce Wassmansdoff)
American leading lady who played a few sharp blondes and left a pleasant impression.
■ The Counterfeiters 48. The Girl from Jones Beach 49. Hot Cars 56. The Brave One 56. Hot Shots 56. A Hole in the Head 59. It Started with a Kiss 59. The Atomic Submarine 59. Who Was That Lady? 59. Marriage on the Rocks 65. Bigfoot 71.
TV series: Love That Bob 56–59. Klondike 60–61.

Lansing, Robert (1929–1994) (Robert H. Brown)
Cold-eyed, virile American leading man of the 60s.
The 4-D Man 59. A Gathering of Eagles 63. Under the Yum Yum Tree 64. The Grissom Gang 71. Wild in the Sky 72. Bittersweet Love 76. Empire of the Ants 77. False Face 77. Island Claws/Night of the Claw 80. The Equalizer (TV) 87. The Nest 88. Blind Vengeance (TV) 90, etc.
TV series: 87th Precinct 61. 12 O'Clock High 64. The Man Who Never Was 66. Automan 83–84. The Equaliser 85–89.

Lansing, Sherry (1944–)
American producer, a former actress and one-time president of Twentieth Century-Fox, 1980–83, who is now chairman of the Motion Picture Group of Paramount Pictures. Married director William Friedkin.
Racing with the Moon 84. Firstborn 84. Fatal Attraction (AAN) 87. The Accused 88. Black Rain 89. School Ties 91. Indecent Proposal 93, etc.

Lantieri, Michael
American visual effects expert and director.
AS DIRECTOR: Komodo (Aus.) 99, etc.
VISUAL FX: The Last Starfighter 84. Poltergeist II 86. The Witches of Eastwick (BFA) 87. Indiana Jones and the Last Crusade 89. Back to the Future Part II (AAN, BFA) 89. Back to the Future Part III 90. Hook (AAN) 91. Death Becomes Her (BFA) 92. Bram Stoker's Dracula 92. Jurassic Park (AA, BFA) 93.The Flintstones 94. Casper 95. Congo 95. The Indian in the Cupboard 95. Mars Attacks! 96. The Lost World: Jurassic Park (AAN) 97. Mouse Hunt 97. Paulie 98. Deep Impact 98. Wild Wild West 99. The Astronaut's Wife 99. The 6th Day 00, etc.

Lantz, Walter (1900–1994)
American animator, in charge of Universal cartoons since 1928 and the creator of Woody Woodpecker. Special AA 1978 'for bringing joy and laughter to every part of the world'. His wife Grace (1904–1992) supplied Woody's laugh.
Biography: 1985, *The Walter Lantz Story* by Joe Adamson.

Lanza, Mario (1921–1959) (Alfredo Cocozza)
American opera singer, popular in MGM musicals until overcome by weight problem.
Biography: 1991, *Mario Lanza – A Biography* by Derek Mannering.
■ That Midnight Kiss 49. The Toast of New Orleans 50. *The Great Caruso* 51. Because You're Mine 52. The Student Prince (voice only) 54. Serenade 56. Seven Hills of Rome 58. For the First Time 58.
❝ That idiot Lanza! He had the greatest opportunities in the world, but he just couldn't handle success. – *Joseph Ruttenberg*
Mario, you doll, you sing like a son of a bitch. – *M.L.*

LaPaglia, Anthony (1959–)
Australian-born actor, working in America. Married actress Gia CARIDES.
Betsy's Wedding 90. Criminal Justice (TV) 90. Mortal Sins 90. Dangerous Obsession 90. One Good Cop 91. He Said, She Said 91. Keeper of the City 91. 29th Street 91. Innocent Blood 92. Whispers in the Dark 92. So I Married an Axe Murderer 93. The Custodian 93. Bulletproof Heart 94. The Client 94. Killer 94. Lucky Break (Aus.) 94. Empire Records 95. Mixed Nuts 95. Never Give Up: The Jimmy V. Story (TV) 96. Brilliant Lies 96. Trees Lounge 96. Paperback Romance 96. Commandments 97. The Garden of Redemption 97. Phoenix 98. Sweet and Lowdown 99. Summer of Sam 99. The House of Mirth 00. Company Man 01, etc.
TV series: Murder One 96.

Lapotaire, Jane (1944–)
Anglo-French stage actress in occasional films.
Crescendo 70. Antony and Cleopatra 72. The Asphyx 72. One of Our Dinosaurs Is Missing 75. Eureka 82. Lady Jane 86. Surviving Picasso 96. Shooting Fish 97. There's Only One Jimmy Gribble 00, etc.

Larch, John (1924–)
American character actor, often in crooked roles; born in Salem, Massachusetts.
Bitter Creek 54. Behind the High Wall 56. The Killer is Loose 56. Seven Men from Now 56. Quantez 57. Man in the Shadow 57. The Saga of Hemp Brown 58. The Wrecking Crew 68. Hail, Hero! 69. The Great Bank Robbery 69. Move 70. Dirty Harry 71. Play Misty for Me 71. Santee 72. Framed 74. The Amityville Horror 79. Airplane II: The Sequel 82, etc.
TV series: Arrest and Trial 63-64. Convoy 65. Dallas 90.

Lardner, Ring W. (1885–1933) (Ringgold Wilmer Lardner)
Sardonic American humorist, dramatist and sports writer. Born in Niles, Michigan, he became a leading journalist in Chicago and New York, and one of the quieter wits of the ALGONQUIN ROUND TABLE; also making a reputation as a short-story writer, in tales about boxers, baseball players and small town residents. He contracted tuberculosis in the late 20s and died of a heart attack. He was the father of screenwriter Ring LARDNER Jnr.
Biography: 1965, *Ring Lardner* by Otto Friedrich; 1977, *Ring: A Biography of Ring Lardner* by Jonathan Yardley; 1979, *Ring Lardner* by Elizabeth Evans.
Glorifying the American Girl (a) 29. June Moon (co-oa) 31. Elmer the Great (co-oa) 33. Alibi Ike (oa) 35. Blonde Trouble (co-oa, from *June Moon*) 37. The Cowboy Quarterback (co-oa, from *Elmer the Great*) 39. So This is New York (oa) 48. Champion (oa) 49. The Golden Honeymoon (oa ,TV) 77, etc.
❝ He was one of those forlorn, gifted creatures who could not submit to any faith or hope in mankind. – *Pat O'Brien*
He just doesn't like people. I believe he hates himself; most certainly he hates his characters; and most clearly of all, his characters hate each other. – *Clifton Fadiman*
'Shut up,' he explained. – *R.W.L.*

Lardner Jnr, Ring (1915–2000) (Ringgold Wilmer Lardner Jnr)
American screenwriter and novelist, the son of writer and humorist Ring LARDNER. He was one of the 'Hollywood Ten' jailed for refusing to disclose political affiliations to the House Un-American Activities Committee in 1947. He had been named to HUAC as a Communist by fellow writer Budd SCHULBERG, the man who had persuaded him to join the Communist Party in the 30s. Asked by HUAC if he had been a member of the party, Lardner replied, 'I could answer the way you want, but I'd hate myself in the morning.' Born in Chicago, he began as a journalist, later becoming a publicist for David SELZNICK. Following his appearance before HUAC, he was sacked by Fox and blacklisted. An alcoholic like his father, he worked uncredited or in Europe until the mid-60s, including writing for the British TV series *The Adventures of Robin Hood, The Adventures of Sir Lancelot*, and *The Buccaneers*. He won his second Oscar for his screenplay for *M*A*S*H*, though he turned down an offer to write the pilot and become head writer for the TV series because he thought it would not succeed.

Autobiography: 1976, *The Lardners: My Family Remembered*.; 2000, *I'd Hate Myself in the Morning: A Memoir*.

Meet Dr Christian 39. *Woman of the Year* (AA) 42. The Cross of Lorraine 44. Tomorrow the World 44. Cloak and Dagger 46. Forever Amber 47. Britannia Mews 48. The Cincinnati Kid 65. M*A*S*H (AA) 70. The Greatest 77, etc.

❝ Conscience is the only reliable guide to behavior. I disobeyed mine only once: when I failed to resign the day Ring Lardner was fired... my own inglorious Day of the Chicken. – *Philip Dunne*

Larkin, Peter
American production designer, from the Broadway stage.

Nighthawks 81. Neighbors 81. Tootsie 82. Reuben, Reuben 82. Compromising Positions 85. The Secret of My Success 87. Three Men and a Baby 87. Life Stinks 91. Night and the City 92. The Concierge/For Love or Money 93. House of Cards 93. Guarding Tess 94. Major Payne 95. Get Shorty 95. The First Wives Club 96. Bean 97, etc.

Larner, Jeremy (1937–)
American screenwriter and novelist. He is a former journalist and speechwriter to 60s presidential candidate Senator Eugene McCarthy. Since winning an Oscar, he has worked on films that are yet to be produced.

Drive He Said (co-w, from his novel) 71. The Candidate (AA) 72.

Laroche, Pierre (1902–1962)
French screenwriter, mainly for films directed by his wife, Jacqueline Audry.

Les Visiteurs du Soir (co-w) 42. Lumière d'été (co-w) 43. Les Malheurs de Sophie 45. Gigi 49. Minne 50. Huis Clos 54. La Garçonne 57, etc.

Larraz, José Ramón (1928–)
Spanish director of horror and erotic movies, sometimes combining both themes in movies featuring lesbian vampires. Born in Barcelona, he worked in Paris as a comic-book illustrator and fashion photographer before making his first film in Britain, where he continued to work until the mid-70s, when he was known as Joseph Larraz. *Symptoms* was a British entry at the Cannes Film Festival in 1974. He then returned to direct films in Spain and also worked under the pseudonym of Joseph Braunstein for the US video market.

Whirlpool/She Died with Her Boots On 69. Scream ... and Die! 73. Symptoms/The Blood Virgin; The House that Vanished 74. Vampyres – Daughters of Dracula 74. The Violation of the Bitch/La Visita del Vicio 78. Golden Lady 79. The National Mummy/La Momia Nacional 81. Estigma 81. Los Ritos Sexuales del Diábolo 82. Rest in Pieces (as Joseph Braunstein) 87. Edge of the Axe (as Joseph Braunstein) 89. Deadly Manor 90. Sevilla Connection 92, etc.

❝ I've never had a proper understanding producer, only philistine money-men telling me what to do. – *J.R.L.*

Larroquette, John (1947–)
American leading actor.

The Texas Chainsaw Massacre (uncredited narrator) 74. Heart Beat 80. Altered States 80. Stripes 81. Green Ice 81. Cat People 82. Meatballs 2 84. Star Trek III: The Search for Spock 84. Choose Me 84. Convicted (TV) 86. Blind Date 87. Second Sight 89. Madhouse 90. Tune in Tomorrow/Aunt Julia and the Scriptwriter 90. Richie Rich 94. Isn't She Great 00, etc.

TV series: Doctor's Hospital 75–76. Baa Baa Black Sheep 76. Night Court 84–92. The John Larroquette Show 93–96. Payne 99.

Larsen, Keith (1925–)
American second-string leading man. He was married to Vera Miles (1960–73).

Flat Top 52. Hiawatha 52. Arrow in the Dust 54. Wichita 55. Dial Red O 56. Fury River 61. Caxambu 67. The Trap on Cougar Mountain 76. White-Water Sam (wd) 78, etc.

TV series: The Hunter 54. Brave Eagle 55. Northwest Passage 57. The Aquanaut 60.

Larsen, Tambi (1914–2001)
Danish-born art director and production designer. He studied at the Yale Drama School in the mid-30s and first worked on Broadway as a scenic artist, entering films at Paramount Studios in the mid-40s.

Artists and Models 55. The Rose Tattoo (AA) 55. The Five Pennies 59. The Rat Race 60. Hud (AAN) 63. The Spy Who Came in from the Cold (AAN) 65. Nevada Smith 66. *The Molly Maguires* (AAN) 70. Thunderbolt and Lightfoot 74. The Outlaw Josey Wales 76. The White Buffalo 77. Heaven's Gate (AAN) 80, etc.

Larson, Eric (1905–1988)
Pioneer animator with Walt Disney, who worked on every full-length Disney animated film from *Snow White and the Seven Dwarfs* 37 to *The Great Mouse Detective* 86.

LaRue
See *La Rue*.

LaSalle, Eriq (1962–)
American actor and director, mainly on TV. Born in Hartford, Connecticut, he has a degree in theater arts from New York University and began on stage. He is best known for his role as Dr Peter Benton in the TV series *ER*. In 1999 he signed a three year contract for $27m to continue in the part.

Cut and Run/Inferno in Diretta (It) 85. Rappin' 85. Where are the Children 86. Coming to America 88. What Price Victory 88. Jacob's Ladder 90. That Magic Moment 90. Color of Night 94. Drop Squad 94. Rebound: The Legend of Earl 'The Goat' Manigault (TV, d) 96. Mind Prey (& co-p, TV) 99, etc.

TV series: The Human Factor 92. ER 94- .

Lasker, Lawrence (1949–)
American producer and screenwriter, a former art director.

War Games (co-w, AAN) 83. Project X (p, story) 87. Awakenings (AANp) 90. Sneakers (p, co-w) 92, etc.

Lasky, Jesse (1880–1958)
American pioneer. Formed his first production company in 1914 and had a big hit with *The Squaw Man*; in 1916 gained control of Famous Players and later Paramount. Later produced for Fox, Warner, RKO.

Autobiography: 1958, *I Blow My Own Horn*.

Sergeant York 41. The Adventures of Mark Twain 44. Rhapsody in Blue 45. The Miracle of the Bells 49. The Great Caruso 51, many others.

Lasky Jnr, Jesse (1910–1988)
American screenwriter, son of Jesse Lasky.

Autobiography: 1974, *Whatever Happened to Hollywood?*.

Union Pacific (co-w) 39. Reap the Wild Wind (co-w) 42. Unconquered (co-w) 48. Samson and Delilah (co-w) 49. The Thief of Venice 50. The Brigand 52. The Ten Commandments (co-w) 56. Seven Women from Hell (co-w) 61. Land Raiders 69. An Ace up My Sleeve 75. Crime and Passion 76, etc.

Lassally, Walter (1926–)
German cinematographer, long in Britain, and often on the films of Michael CACOYANNIS. Born in Berlin, the son of a maker of industrial films, he moved to Britain in 1939. He worked as a photographer before beginning in documentary films and moving to features as a clapper boy at Riverside Studios. He became involved with director Lindsay ANDERSON and Free Cinema.

Autobiography: 1987, *Itinerant Cameraman*.

We Are the Lambeth Boys 58. *A Taste of Honey* 61. The Loneliness of the Long-Distance Runner 62. *Tom Jones* 63. *Zorba the Greek* (AA) 65. The Day the Fish Came Out 67. Oedipus the King 67. Joanna 68. Turnkey 70. Something for Everyone 72. Malachi's Cove 74. Too Far to Go (TV) 77. Gauguin the Savage (TV) 80. Memoirs of a Survivor 82. Heat and Dust 83. Private School 83. The Bostonians 84. Indian Summer 87. The Deceivers 88. The Perfect Murder 88. Fragment of Isabella 89. The Ballad of the Sad Café 90, etc.

❝ Even quite hardened professionals often seem unable to separate the photography from other qualities (or lack of them) in a film, and it certainly pays to show prospective employers smash hits, if at all possible. – *W.L.*

Lasser, Louise (1939–)
American TV actress popular in the serial *Mary Hartman, Mary Hartman* 76. She was married to Woody ALLEN (1966–71).

Bananas 71. Such Good Friends 71. Everything You Always Wanted to Know about Sex 72. Coffee, Tea or Me? (TV) 73. Isn't It Shocking? (TV) 73. Slither 73. Just Me and You (TV) 78. In God We Trust 80. Stardust Memories (uncredited) 80. Blood Rage 83. Crimewave 85. Surrender 87. Sing 89. Rude Awakening 89. Frankenhooker 90. Modern Love 90. Sudden Manhattan 96. Layin' Low 96. Happiness 98, etc.

TV series: Mary Hartman, Mary Hartman 76–77. It's a Living 81–82.

Lasseter, John (1957–)
American director of computer-generated animated films, a former animator with Walt Disney. He was awarded an Oscar for special achievement for *Toy Story*.

Tin Toy (AA, short) 88. *Toy Story* 95. A Bug's Life 98, etc.

Lastfogel, Abe (1898–1984)
American talent agent, head of the William Morris Organization, which he joined in 1912 as an office boy.

Laszlo, Andrew (1926–)
Hungarian-American cinematographer.

You're a Big Boy Now 67. The Night They Raided Minsky's 68. Popi 69. Teacher Teacher 70. The Out of Towners 70. Lovers and other Strangers 71. The Owl and the Pussycat 71. Class of 44 73. The Man without a Country (TV) 74. Countdown at Kusini 76. The Warriors 79. Shogun (TV) 80. Southern Comfort 81. First Blood 82. Thief of Hearts 84. Remo Williams, the Adventure Begins 85. Poltergeist II 86. Innerspace 87. Star Trek V: The Final Frontier 89. Ghost Dad 90. Newsies 92, etc.

Laszlo, Ernest (1905–1984)
Hungarian-American cinematographer.

The Hitler Gang 44. Two Years Before the Mast 44. The Girl from Manhattan 48. Dead on Arrival 49. The Steel Trap 52. The Star 52. Stalag 17 53. *Vera Cruz* 54. The Big Knife 55. Judgment at Nuremberg 60. *Inherit the Wind* (AAN) 60. *It's a Mad Mad Mad Mad World* (AAN) 63. *Ship of Fools* (AA) 65. Fantastic Voyage (AAN) 66. Star! (AAN) 68. The First Time 69. Daddy's Gone A-Hunting 69. *Airport* (AAN) 69. Showdown 73. Logan's Run (AAN) 76. The Domino Principle (co-ph) 77, many others.

Latell, Lyle (1905–1967) (Lyle Zeiem)
Beefy American character actor in comic parts, best known for his role as Pat Patton, Dick Tracy's sidekick in the 'B' features of the 40s. Married actress Mary Foy (1903–1987), of vaudeville act 'Eddie Foy and the Seven Little Foys'.

Texas 41. In the Navy 41. Happy Go Lucky 43. One Mysterious Night 44. Hold That Blonde 45. Dick Tracy vs Cueball 45. Dick Tracy's Dilemma 47. Dick Tracy and Gruesome 47. Buck Privates Come Home/Rookies Come Home 47. The Noose Hangs High 48. Sky Dragon 49. A Street Car Named Desire 51. The Girl Rush 55, etc.

Latham, Louise
American actress.

Marnie 64. Firecreek 67. Adam at 6 AM 70. Making It 71. White Lightning 73. The Sugarland Express 74. 92 in the Shade 75. The Awakening Land (TV) 78. Pray TV (TV) 82. Mass Appeal 84. Love Lives On (TV) 85. Toughlove (TV) 85. Fresno (TV) 86. Crazy from the Heart 91. Paradise 91. Love Field 92. In Cold Blood (TV) 96. Mary & Tim 96, etc.

TV series: Sara 76. The Contender 80. Scruples 80.

Lathrop, Philip (1916–1995)
American cinematographer.

The Monster of Piedras Blancas 57. Experiment in Terror 62. *Lonely Are the Brave* 62. Days of Wine and Roses 63. The Pink Panther 63. The Americanization of Emily 64. Thirty-Six Hours 65. The Cincinnati Kid 65. What Did You Do in the War Daddy? 66. The Russians are Coming 66. The Happening 67. Point Blank 68. *Finian's Rainbow* 69. The Gypsy Moths 69. The Illustrated Man 69. They Shoot Horses Don't They? 69. Von Richthofen and Brown 71. Airport 77 77. The Driver 78. Little Miss Marker 80. Loving Couples 80. All Night Long 81. Jekyll and Hyde Together Again 82. Hammett 82. National Lampoon's Class Reunion 82. Deadly Friend 86, etc.

Latifah, Queen (1970–) (Dana Owens)
American actress and rap performer; her production company, Flavor Unit Entertainment, also embraces a music label and an artist management firm.

Set It Off 96. Living Out Loud 98, etc.

TV series: Living Single 93–98. Latifah 99– .

Latimer, Jonathan (1906–1983)
American thriller writer.

Topper Returns 41. They Won't Believe Me 47. Alias Nick Beal 49. Plunder of the Sun 51. Botany Bay 54. The Unholy Wife 57, etc.

Latimore, Frank (1925–) (Frank Kline)
American leading man with stage experience.

In the Meantime, Darling 44. Three Little Girls in Blue 46. Black Magic 49. Three Forbidden Stories (It.) 50. John Paul Jones 59. The Sergeant 68. All the President's Men 76, etc.

Lattuada, Alberto (1914–)
Italian director.

The Mill on the Po 48. Without Pity 48. Lights of Variety (co-d) 50. Il Capotto 52. The Wolf 53. The Beach 53. Guendalina 56. Tempest 58. The Adolescents 61. La Steppa 62. The Mandrake 65. The Betrayal 68. A Dog's Heart 75. Stay As You Are 78. A Thorn in the Heart 85. Christopher Columbus (TV) 85. Amori (co-d) 89, etc.

Lau, Andy (1961–) (Lau Tak Wah)
Leading Hong Kong actor, often in action films.

Boat People 82. Rich and Famous 87. As Tears Go By 88. Dragon Family 89. Moment of Romance 90. The Prisoner 90. God of Gamblers II 91. Days of Being Wild 91. Moon Warriors 92. Saviour of the Soul 92. Full Throttle 96, etc.

Lau, Jeffrey (1956–)
Hong Kong director and producer.

Haunted Cop Shop 87. Haunted Cop Shop II 88. Thunder Cops II 89. Mortuary Blues 90. Fury Fist 91. 92 *The Legendary La Rose Noire*/92 Hak Muigwai Dui Hak Mauigwai 92. Rose Rose I Love You 93. The Eagle Shooting Heroes: Dong Cheng Xi Jiu 93, etc.

Lauder, Sir Harry (1870–1950)
Scottish music-hall entertainer, a former miner who was knighted in 1919. He became a star in 1900 and made some silent shorts from 1907.

Autobiography: 1928, *Roamin' in the Gloamin'*.

Biography: 1968, *Great Scot!* by Gordon Irving.

■ Huntingtower 27. Happy Days 29. Auld Lang Syne 33. End of the Road 36. Song of the Road 40.

❝ He has the great artist's overweening conceit of himself. He emerges from the wings like a sun from base clouds. He irradiates his world, flattering stalls and gallery with sovereign eye. That a creature like ourselves should glow with such intensity of self-appreciation warms the cockles of the most sceptical heart. – *James Agate*

Laughlin, Tom (1938–)
American independent director, producer and actor who enjoyed a cult success as Billy Jack, a violent hero on the side of the disadvantaged, in the early 70s. His most recent film, *The Return of Billy Jack* 86, has never been completed. He sometimes used the pseudonym T.C. Frank as director.

■ Tea and Sympathy 56. South Pacific 58. Gidget (a) 59. Tall Story (a) 60. The Proper Time (a, d) 60. The Young Sinners (d) 65. Born Losers (a, p, d) 67. Billy Jack (a, p, wd) 73. The Trial of Billy Jack (a, p) 74. The Master Gunfighter (a, p) 75. Billy Jack Goes to Washington (a, p, d) 78.

Laughton, Charles (1899–1962)
Distinguished British character actor, whose plump wry face was one of the most popular on screen in the 30s. His later Hollywood roles showed a regrettable tendency to ham, but he was always worth watching.

Biography: 1938, *Charles Laughton and I* by his wife Elsa Lanchester. 1952, *The Charles Laughton Story* by Kurt Singer. 1976, *Charles Laughton* by Charles Higham. 1987, *Charles Laughton – a Difficult Actor* by Simon Callow.

■ Wolves 27. Bluebottles 28. Daydreams 28. Piccadilly 29. Comets 30. Down River 30. *The Old Dark House* 32. The Devil and the Deep 32. Payment Deferred 32. *The Sign of the Cross* (as Nero) 32. If I Had a Million 32. Island of Lost Souls 32. *The Private Life of Henry VIII* (AA) 33. White Woman 33. *The Barretts of Wimpole Street* 34. *Ruggles of Red Gap* 35. *Les Misérables* 35. *Mutiny on the Bounty* (as Captain Bligh) (AAN) 35. *Rembrandt* 36. *I Claudius* (unfinished) 37. Vessel of Wrath 37. St Martin's Lane 38. Jamaica Inn 39. *The Hunchback of Notre Dame* 39. They Knew What They Wanted 40. It Started with Eve 41. The Tuttles of Tahiti 42. Tales of Manhattan 42. Stand by for Action 43. Forever and a Day 43. This Land is Mine 43. The Man from Down Under 43. The Canterville Ghost 44. *The Suspect* 44. Captain Kidd 45. Because of Him 46. The Paradine Case 48. The Big Clock 48. Arch of Triumph 48. The Girl from Manhattan 49. The Bribe 49. The Man on the Eiffel Tower (as Maigret) 49. The Blue Veil 51. The Strange Door 51. Full House 52. Abbott and Costello Meet Captain Kidd 52. Salome 53. Young Bess 53. *Hobson's Choice* 54. *Witness for the Prosecution* (AAN) 57. Under Ten Flags 60. Spartacus 60. *Advise and Consent* 62.

AS DIRECTOR: *Night of the Hunter* 55.

✪ For a dozen splendid performances, unassailable by the self-doubt which later turned him into a ham. *Rembrandt*.

❝ They can't censor the gleam in my eye. – *C.L., when told that his performance as Mr Moulton-Barrett must not indicate incestuous love*

I have a face like the behind of an elephant. – *C.L.*

It's got so that every time I walk into a restaurant I get not only soup but an impersonation of Captain Bligh. – *C.L.*

You can't direct a Laughton picture. The best you can hope for is to referee. – *Alfred Hitchcock*

With him acting was an act of childbirth. What he needed was not so much a director as a midwife. – *Alexander Korda*

A great man who only accidentally became an actor. – *Alva Johnson*

You can tell how good an actor is by looking at his script. If he's no good, the script will be neat as a pin. Charles Laughton's was so filthy it looked like a herring had been wrapped in it. – *Billy Wilder*

The greatest actor that ever lived–everything you can dream of, times ten. – *Billy Wilder*

Everybody thought he was a genius. I didn't. I thought he was more of a show-off, really. – *Rex Harrison*

Famous line (*Mutiny on the Bounty*) 'I'll live to see you – all of you – hung from the highest yardarm in the British fleet!'

Famous line (*The Private Life of Henry VIII*) 'Am I a king or a breeding bull?'

Famous line (*The Private Life of Henry VIII*) 'There's no delicacy nowadays. No consideration for others. Refinement's a thing of the past!'

Launder, Frank (1907–1997)
English director and scriptwriter, often in a memorable partnership with Sidney GILLIAT. Born in Hitchin, Hertfordshire, he began as a title writer at Elstree in the late 20s, later working at Gaumont British and Gainsborough Pictures. He began his collaboration with Gilliat in the mid-30s: they first worked as writers, then, from the mid-40s with their own production company, as producers and directors; the pair were, in the late 50s, also directors of British Lion. Their comedies included the St Trinian's series, based on the books by Ronald Searle. His second wife was actress Bernadette O'FARRELL.

Biography: 1977, *Launder and Gilliat* by Geoff Brown.

Under the Greenwood Tree 29. The W Plan 30. Children of Chance 30. After Office Hours 31. Josser in the Army 31. Facing the Music 33. Those Were the Days 34. Emil and the Detectives 35. Seven Sinners 36. Educated Evans 36. *Oh Mr Porter* 38. *The Lady Vanishes* 38. A Girl Must Live 39. They Came by Night 40. *Night Train to Munich* 40. Kipps 41. The Young Mr Pitt 42. Millions Like Us (& d) 43. 2000 Women (& d) 43. *I See a Dark Stranger* (& d) 45. Captain Boycott (& d) 47. The Blue Lagoon (& d) 48. *The Happiest Days of Your Life* (& d) 50. Lady Godiva Rides Again (& d) 51. *The Belles of St Trinian's* (& d) 54. Geordie (& d) 55. The Bridal Path (& d) 59. Joey Boy (& d) 65. The Great St Trinian's Train Robbery (& d) 66. The Wildcats of St Trinian's (wd) 80, etc.

Launer, Dale (1953–)
American screenwriter turned director.

Ruthless People 86. Blind Date 87. Dirty Rotten Scoundrels 88. My Cousin Vinny 92. Love Potion 9 (wd) 92, etc.

Laurel, Stan (1890–1965) (Arthur Stanley Jefferson)
British-born comedian, the thin half and gag deviser of the Laurel and Hardy team. Went to USA with Fred Karno's troupe, was in short comedies from 1915, teamed with Hardy 1926. He had director credit on some of their films and virtually directed many others. Special Academy Award 1960 'for his creative pioneering in the field of cinema comedy'.

For list of films see *Oliver Hardy*.

✪ For his genius in the invention of comic gags, and for finding his perfect niche in partnership with Oliver Hardy. *Way Out West*.

❝ They were visual comedians, of course. But they successfully transferred to sound by the use of minimum sound, mainly in the form of carefully scattered catch phrases which arose naturally out of their characters as every child's foolish uncles. When disaster struck, as it inevitably did, who could resist the sight of Olly among the debris, gazing reprovingly at the unharmed Stan and saying: 'Here's another nice mess you've gotten me into.'

Or: 'Why don't you do something to HELP me?'

Or simply: 'I have NOTHING to say.'

Such results are Olly's reward for listening to Stan's suggestions earlier on. Stan's meaning is always unclear to begin with, so that Olly has to say: 'Tell me that again.'

But he finally gets the drift and agrees: 'That's a *good* idea.'

Olly of course was always shy, especially with women. When introduced, he was apt to twiddle his tie and observe: 'A lot of weather we've been having lately.'

His great asset was his courtly manner, preserved even when mistaking an open can of milk for the telephone receiver: 'Pardon me for a moment, my ear is full of milk.'

Stan, having no catch phrases, relied on lively non sequiturs. When asked: 'You never met my wife, did you?'

He would reply: 'Yes, I never did.'

His speciality was putting his foot in it, as when he visits Olly in hospital and announces: 'I brought you some hard-boiled eggs and some nuts.'

Not surprisingly, he eats them himself, having thoughtfully brought salt and pepper canisters in his pocket. Then there was the time in a bar when they could afford only one beer, ordered by Olly with his usual majesty. Stan did rather ruin the effect by calling after the waiter: 'And two clean straws that haven't been used …'

But he was capable of saying the right thing, as when Olly prepared a mundane repast of coffee and beans. Stan liked it: 'Boy, you sure know how to plan a meal!'

Behind the scenes, Stan was the producer. Olly was ready to admit: 'I have never really worked hard in the creation department.'

But he astutely saw the secret of their success: 'Those two fellows we created, they were nice, very nice people. They never get anywhere because they are both so dumb, but they don't know they're dumb. One of the reasons why people like us, I guess, is because they feel superior to us.'

That was put another way in the opening title to one of their silent films: 'Neither Mr Laurel nor Mr Hardy had any thoughts of getting married. In fact, they had no thoughts of any kind …'

And the opening of *Come Clean* summed up their best comedy style very neatly: 'Mr Hardy holds that a man should always tell his wife the whole truth. Mr Laurel is crazy too.'

Mr Laurel had his own philosophy: 'We were doing a very simple thing, giving some people some laughs, and that's all we were trying to do.'

Lauren, S. K. (1892–1979)
American screenwriter.

An American Tragedy 32. Bond Venus 34. Crime and Punishment 35. One Night of Love 36. Mother Carey's Chickens 39. Flight for Freedom 43, etc.

Laurenson, James (1935–)
New Zealand actor in British and Australian TV, especially series *Boney*.

The Magic Christian 69. Assault 70. The Monster Club 80. Pink Floyd the Wall 82. Heartbreakers 84. The Man Who Fell to Earth (TV) 87. A House in the Hills 93. The Cold Light of Day 94. Prime Suspect 4: Inner Circles (TV) 95. Sharpe's Siege (TV) 96. Sharpe's Mission (TV) 96. Sharpe's Revenge (TV) 97. The Vanishing Man (TV) 98, etc.

Laurents, Arthur (1918–)
American playwright, screenwriter and theatre director. Born in Brooklyn, he was educated at Cornell University. His first play, *Home of the Brave*, was also filmed, but he enjoyed his greatest success as the librettist for the musicals *West Side Story* and *Gypsy*. His lovers included actor Farley GRANGER.

Autobiography: 2000, Original Story By: A Memoir of Broadway and Hollywood.

Caught (w) 48. Rope (w) 48. Anna Lucasta (co-w) 49. Home of the Brave (oa) 49. Summertime (oa) 55. Anastasia (w) 56. Bonjour Tristesse (w) 57. West Side Story (oa) 61. Gypsy (oa) 62. The Way We Were (w,oa) 73. The Turning Point (AAN, w) 77. Anastasia (oa) 97.

Laurie, Hugh (1959–)
English comic actor and writer, most frequently seen partnering Stephen FRY in TV series and advertisements. He was educated at Eton and Cambridge University, where he was a rowing Blue and was a member of the losing crew in the Oxford and Cambridge Boat Race in 1980. He first partnered Fry in a Cambridge Footlights revue in 1981.

Blackadder's Christmas Carol (TV) 88. Strapless 88. Peter's Friends 92. A Pin for the Butterfly 94. *Sense and Sensibility* 95. 101 Dalmatians 96. Cousin Bette 97. The Borrowers 97. The Man in the Iron Mask 98. Stuart Little 99. Maybe Baby 00, etc.

TV series: Blackadder 84. Blackadder II 86. Blackadder the Third 87. Blackadder Goes Forth 89. A Bit of Fry and Laurie 89–92. Jeeves and Wooster 90–93.

Laurie, John (1897–1980)
Scottish character actor, often in dour roles. On stage from 1921.

Juno and the Paycock 30. Red Ensign 34. *The Thirty-Nine Steps* 35. Tudor Rose 36. As You Like It 36. Farewell Again 37. Edge of the World 38. Q Planes 39. Sailors Three 40. *The Ghost of St Michael's* 41. Old Mother Riley's Ghosts 41. The Gentle Sex 43. Fanny by Gaslight 43. *The Way Ahead* 44. *Henry V* 44. I Know Where I'm Going 45. Caesar and Cleopatra 45. The Brothers 47. Uncle Silas 47. Bonnie Prince Charlie 48. Hamlet 48. Trio 50. Laughter in Paradise 51. The Fake 53. Hobson's Choice 54. The Black Knight 55. Campbell's Kingdom 57. Kidnapped 60. Siege of the Saxons 63. Mr Ten Per Cent 66. Dad's Army 71. The Prisoner of Zenda 79, etc.

Laurie, Piper (1932–) (Rosetta Jacobs)
Pert American leading lady of 50s costume charades; later a notable character actress.

■ Louisa 50. The Milkman 50. Francis Goes to the Races 51. The Prince Who Was a Thief 51. No Room for the Groom 52. Has Anybody Seen My Gal 52. Son of Ali Baba 52. Mississippi Gambler 53. The Golden Blade 53. Dangerous Mission 54. Johnny Dark 54. Dawn at Socorro 54. Smoke Signal 55. Ain't Misbehavin' 55. Kelly and Me 57. Until They Sail 59. *The Hustler* (AAN) 61. *Carrie* (AAN) 76. Ruby 78. Tim 79. Skag (TV) 80. The Bunker (TV) 81. Mae West (TV) 82. The Thorn Birds (TV) 82. Toughlove (TV) 85. Return to Oz 85. Tender Is the Night (TV) 85. Children of a Lesser God (AAN) 86. Distortions 87. Appointment with Death 88. Tiger Warsaw 88. Dream a Little Dream 89. Other People's Money 91. Storyville 92. Trauma 93. Wrestling Ernest Hemingway 93. The Crossing Guard 95. The Grass Harp 95. Fighting for My Daughter (TV) 95. In the Blink of an Eye (TV) 96. Road to Galveston (TV) 96. St Patrick's Day 97. Alone (TV) 97. A Christmas Memory (TV) 97. Intensity (TV) 97. The Faculty 98. The Mao Game 99.

TV series: Twin Peaks 90.

Lauter, Ed (1940–)
American general-purpose actor.

The Last American Hero 73. Executive Action 73. Lolly Madonna XXX 74. The Longest Yard 75. Last Hours before Morning (TV) 75. King Kong 76. The Chicken Chronicles 77. Eureka 83. The Big Score 83. Cujo 83. Lassiter 83. Finders Keepers 84. Death Wish 3 85. Youngblood 85. Raw Deal 86. The Last Days of Patton (TV) 86. Tennessee Waltz 88. Gleaming the Cube 89. Tennessee Nights 89. The Rocketeer 91. School Ties 92. Wagons East! 94. Trial by Jury 94. Girl in the Cadillac 95. Mulholland Falls 96. A Bright Shining Lie (TV) 98, etc.

TV series: B.J. and the Bear 79–80.

Lauter, Harry (1920–1990)
American supporting actor.

The Gay Intruders 48. Tucson 49. Whirlwind 51. The Sea Tiger 52. Dragonfly Squadron 54. The Crooked Web 55. Hellcats of the Navy 57. Gunfight at Dodge City 59. Posse from Hell 61. Ambush Bay 66. More Dead than Alive 68, many others.

Lauzon, Jean-Claude (1953–1997)
French-Canadian director and screenwriter. Died in a plane crash.

Night Zoo/Un Zoo la Nuit 87. Léolo (wd) 92.

Laven, Arnold (1922–)
American director, former dialogue coach. From the 60s to the 80s, he directed episodes of such TV series as *Planet of the Apes*, *Fantasy Island* and *Hill Street Blues*.

Without Warning 52. Down Three Dark Streets 54. The Rack 56. The Monster that Challenged the World 57. Slaughter on Tenth Avenue 58. Anna Lucasta 58. Geronimo (& p) 62. The Glory Guys 66. Rough Night in Jericho 67. Sam Whiskey 68. The Scalphunters (p only) 68, etc.

Laverick, June (1932–)
British leading lady, groomed for stardom by the Rank charm school of the 50s.

Doctor at Large 56. The Gypsy and the Gentleman 57. Son of Robin Hood 58. Follow a Star 59, etc.

Lavery, Emmet (1902–1986)
American screenwriter.

Hitler's Children 43. Behind the Rising Sun 43. The First Legion (orig sp) 51. The Magnificent Yankee (orig sp) 52. The Court Martial of Billy Mitchell 55, etc.

Lavery Jnr, Emmet (1927–)
American TV executive producer, mainly with Paramount.

Delaney Street 75. Serpico (and series) 76. Nero Wolfe 77, etc.

Lavi, Daliah (1940–) (D. Levenbuch)
Israeli leading lady in international films.

Il Demonio (It.) 63. Old Shatterhand (Ger.) 64. Lord Jim 65. Ten Little Indians 65. The Silencers 66. The Spy with a Cold Nose 67. Some Girls Do 67. Nobody Runs Forever 68. Catlow 72, etc.

Law, Clara
Hong Kong film director and screenwriter. *Autumn Moon* was winner of the Golden Leopard at the Locarno Film Festival in 1992. She is now resident in Australia.

The Reincarnation of Golden Lotus 89. Farewell China 90. Fruit Punch 91. Autumn Moon 92. Erotique (co-d) 94. Floating Life (Aus.) 96. The Goddess of 1967 (Aus.) 00, etc.

Law, John Phillip (1937–)
American leading man.

The Russians Are Coming, the Russians Are Coming 66. Hurry Sundown 67. Barbarella 68. Skidoo 68. The Sergeant 68. Danger: Diabolik 68. The Hawaiians 70. Von Richthofen and Brown 71. The Love Machine 71. The Last Movie 71. The

Golden Voyage of Sinbad 73. Your Heaven, My Hell 76. The Cassandra Crossing 77. Tarzan the Ape Man 81. Going Straight 82. Night Train to Terror 84. L.A. Bad 85. American Commandos 85. Moon in Scorpio 86. Space Mutiny 88. Blood Delirium 88. Thunder Warrior III 88. Alienator 89. Cold Heat 90. Day of the Pig 92. Hindsight 97. Ghost Dog/My Magic Dog 97, etc.

TV series: The Young and the Restless 89–90.

Law, Jude (1972–)
English actor, from the theatre. He joined the National Youth Music Theatre before playing in the Granada TV soap opera *Families* and working for the Royal Shakespeare Company and Royal National Theatre. Married actress Sadie FROST in 1997. He is a founder member of the production company Natural Nylon.

Shopping 94. Bent 96. I Love You, I Love You Not 96. Wilde (as Lord Alfred Douglas) 97. Gattaca (US) 97. Midnight in the Garden of Good and Evil (US) 97. The Wisdom of Crocodiles 98. Final Cut 98. eXistenZ (US) 99. *The Talented Mr Ripley* (US, AAN) 99. Love, Honour and Obey 99. Enemy at the Gates 01, etc.

Law, Phyllida (1932–)
English actress, the mother of Emma Thompson.

Otley 68. Hitler: The Last Ten Days 73. Tree of Hands 88. Peter's Friends 92. Much Ado about Nothing 93. Emma 96. Winter Guest 96, etc.

Lawford, Peter (1923–1984)
British light leading man, former child actor, in Hollywood from 1938.

Biography: 1991, *Peter Lawford: The Man Who Kept Secrets* by James Spada.

Poor Old Bill 31. The Boy from Barnardo's 38. Mrs Miniver 42. The White Cliffs of Dover 44. Cluny Brown 46. It Happened in Brooklyn 47. Easter Parade 48. Little Women 49. Royal Wedding 52. Exodus 60. Advise and Consent 61. Sylvia 65. Harlow 65. Dead Run (Austria) 67. Salt and Pepper (GB) 68. Buona Sera Mrs Campbell 68. The April Fools 69. One More Time 70. Don't Look behind You (TV) 71. Phantom of Hollywood (TV) 74. Rosebud 75, etc.

TV series: Dear Phoebe 54. The Thin Man 58.

Lawrance, Jody (1930–1986) (Josephine Lawrence Goddard)
American leading lady.

Mask of the Avenger 51. Son of Dr Jekyll 51. The Brigand 52. Captain John Smith and Pocahontas 53. The Scarlet Hour 55. Stagecoach to Dancer's Rock 62.

Lawrence, Barbara (1928–)
American comedy actress, usually seen as wise-cracking friend of the heroine.

Biography: 1977, *Hollywood Starlet: The Career of Barbara Lawrence* by Jim Connor.

Margie 46. You Were Meant for Me 47. Thieves' Highway 49. Two Tickets to Broadway 51. Jesse James Versus the Daltons 54. *Oklahoma* 55. Joe Dakota 57, etc.

Lawrence, Bruno (1949–1995)
British-born actor and musician, in New Zealand from childhood, who became that country's leading film actor. He first gained a reputation as an anarchic performer and drummer with his band Blerta, and played with trumpeter Geoff MURPHY, who went on to direct him in three films. He also worked in Australia. Died of cancer. A documentary on his life, *Numero Bruno*, directed by Steve La Hood was released in 00.

Wild Man 76. Goodbye Pork Pie 80. Beyond Reasonable Doubt 80. Battletruck 81. *Smash Palace* 81. Race to the Yankee Zephyr 81. Utu 83. Heart of the Stag 83. The Quiet Earth 85. Bridge to Nowhere 85. As Time Goes By 87. Grievous Bodily Harm 88. Rikky and Pete 88. The Delinquents 89. Spotswood 91. Jack Be Nimble 92. Gino 94, etc.

Lawrence, D. H. (1885–1930)
Introspective British novelist whose novels have been adapted with varying success for the screen.

Lady Chatterley's Lover was filmed again in 1980 and on TV in 1993, and in 1981 Ian McKellen played Lawrence in *Priest of Love*.

The Rocking Horse Winner 49. Lady Chatterley's Lover 58. Sons and Lovers 60. The Fox 68. Women in Love 69. The Virgin and the Gypsy 70. The Rainbow 88, etc.

Lawrence, Delphi (1926–)
Anglo-Hungarian actress, in British films.

Blood Orange 54. Barbados Quest 55. It's Never Too Late 56. Too Many Crooks 59. Cone of Silence 60. Farewell Performance 63. Pistolero (US) 67. Cops and Robbers 73, many others.

Lawrence, Florence (1886–1938)
American leading lady of the silent screen; one of the industry's chief stars, she was known at first as 'the Biograph Girl'. Retired in the early 20s. Committed suicide.

Miss Jones Entertains 09. Resurrection 10. A Singular Cynic 14. The Enfoldment 20, many others.

Lawrence, Gertrude (1898–1952) (Alexandra Dagmar Lawrence-Klasen)
Vivacious British revue star of the 20s, especially associated with Noel Coward. Despite sporadic attempts, her quality never came across on the screen. She was impersonated by Julie Andrews in *Star!* 68. She was also unflatteringly portrayed as self-centred actress Lorraine Sheldon in *The Man Who Came to Dinner*.

Autobiography: 1949, *A Star Danced*.

■ The Battle of Paris 29. No Funny Business 32. Aren't We All 32. Lord Camber's Ladies 32. No Funny Business 33. Mimi 35. Rembrandt 36. Men are Not Gods 36. Stage Door Canteen 43. *The Glass Menagerie* 50.

Lawrence, Jerome (1915–)
American dramatist and screenwriter, in collaboration with Robert E. Lee.

Auntie Mame (from their play) 58. Inherit the Wind 60. First Monday in October 81.

Lawrence, Marc (1910–) (Max Goldsmith)
American character actor, former opera singer; usually seen as Italian gangster.

Autobiography: 1994, *Long Time, No See*.

White Woman 33. Dr Socrates 35. Penitentiary 38. The Housekeeper's Daughter 39. Johnny Apollo 40. The Monster and the Girl 41. Hold That Ghost 42. Dillinger 45. I Walk Alone 47. The Asphalt Jungle 50. My Favorite Spy 51. Helen of Troy 55. Kill Her Gently 58. Johnny Cool 64. Nightmare in the Sun (wd only) 64. Savage Pampas 66. Custer of the West 67. Krakatoa East of Java 69. Marathon Man 76. The Big Easy 86. Ruby 92. Life with Mikey 93. Four Rooms 95. From Dusk till Dawn 96, etc.

Lawrence, Marjorie (1902–1979)
Australian opera star crippled by polio; portrayed in 1955 by Eleanor Parker in *Interrupted Melody*.

Lawrence, Martin (1965–)
American stand-up comedian, actor, writer and director. He has also released the comedy albums *Talkin' Shit* and *Funk It*. He was paid $10m to star in *Big Moma's House*. Current asking price: $16.5m.

Do the Right Thing 89. House Party 90. House Party II 91. Boomerang 92. Bad Boys 95. You So Crazy (concert) 95. A Thin Line between Love and Hate (a, co-w, d) 96. Nothing to Lose 97. Blue Streak 99. Life 99. Big Momma's House 00, etc.

TV series: What's Happening Now!! 87–88. Martin 92–97.

Lawrence, Peter Lee (1943–1973) (Karl Hirenbach)
German-born leading actor, frequently in spaghetti westerns. Committed suicide.

For a Few Dollars More 65. Days of Violence 67. The Man Who Shot Billy the Kid 67. Killer Calibre 32 67. Killer Adios 68. A Pistol for a Hundred Coffins 68. They Paid with Bullets: Chicago 1929 68. Special Forces/Hell in Normandy 68. Garringo 69. Manos Torpes/When Satan Grips the Colt 69. Viva Sabata! 70. Black Beauty (GB) 71. Four Gunmen of the Holy Trinity 71. God in Heaven, Arizona on Earth 72. Il Bacio di una Morta 74, etc.

Lawrence, Quentin (c. 1920–1979)
British director, from TV.

The Trollenberg Terror 55. Cash on Demand 62. The Man Who Finally Died 63. The Secret of Blood Island 65, etc.

Lawrence, T. E. (1888–1935)
British adventurer and soldier whose book *Seven Pillars of Wisdom* made him a cult and remotely inspired the film *Lawrence of Arabia*.

Lawrence, Viola (1894–1973)
American editor, long with Columbia.

An Alabaster Box 17. Fighting the Flames 21. Bulldog Drummond 29. Man's Castle 33. Craig's Wife 36. Penitentiary 38. Here Comes Mr Jordan 41. My Sister Eileen 42. Cover Girl 44. Hit the Hay 46. The Dark Past 48. Tokyo Joe 49. Sirocco 51. Miss Sadie Thompson 53. Queen Bee 55. Pal Joey 57. Who Was That Lady 60, many others.

Lawson, John Howard (1886–1977)
American writer with Marxist affiliations.

Heart of Spain 37. Algiers 38. *Blockade* (AAN) 38. *Five Came Back* 39. *Sahara* 43. Counter-Attack 43. Smash-Up 47, etc.

Lawson, Leigh (1944–)
British light leading man of the 70s. Married actress and model TWIGGY.

Ghost Story 74. Percy's Progress 74. Love among the Ruins (TV) 75. Golden Rendezvous 77. The Devil's Advocate 78. Tess 80. Why Didn't They Ask Evans? (TV) 81. Murder Is Easy (TV) 81. Lace (TV) 84. Sword of the Valiant (TV) 85. Queenie (TV) 87. Madame Sousatzka 88. O Pioneers! (TV) 92. Battling for Baby (TV) 92, etc.

TV series: Kinsey 92.

Lawson, Priscilla (1915–) (Priscilla Shortridge)
American actress, a former model, best known for her role of Princess Aura in Flash Gordon. Married actor Alan Curtis. Her career was ended when she lost a leg in a car crash.

Flash Gordon 36. Spaceship to the Unknown 36. Girl of the Golden West 38. Heroes of the Hills 38. Test Pilot 38. Hero of the Hills 38. The Women 39, etc.

Lawson, Sarah (1928–)
British leading lady of the 50s.

The Browning Version 50. Street Corner 52. Blue Peter 54. It's Never Too Late 55. Night of the Big Heat/Island of the Burning Doomed 67. Battle of Britain 69. The Stud 78, etc.

Lawson, Wilfrid (1900–1966) (Wilfrid Worsnop)
British character actor, on stage from 1916; revelled in eccentric parts.

■ East Lynne on the Western Front 31. Strike it Rich 33. Turn of the Tide 35. The Man Who Made Diamonds 37. Bank Holiday 38. The Terror 38. Yellow Sands 38. The Gaunt Stranger 38. *Pygmalion* 38. Stolen Life 39. Dead Man's Shoes 39. *Pastor Hall* 40. Gentleman of Venture 40. The Man at the Gate 41. Danny Boy 41. Jeannie 41. The Farmer's Wife 41. Tower of Terror 41. *Hard Steel* 42. The Night Has Eyes 42. *The Great Mr Handel* 42. Thursday's Child 43. Fanny by Gaslight 44. The Turners of Prospect Road 47. Make Me an Offer 55. The Prisoner 55. An Alligator Named Daisy 55. Now and Forever 56. The Naked Truth 57. Hell Drivers 57. Tread Softly Stranger 59. Room at the Top 59. Expresso Bongo 60. The Naked Edge 61. Nothing Barred 61. Over the Odds 61. Go to Blazes 62. Postman's Knock 62. Tom Jones 63. Becket 64. *The Wrong Box* 66. The Viking Queen 66.

❝ The king of the dramatic pause, which sometimes left the other actors in agony, wondering if he had forgotten his lines (he seldom had). – *Walter Lassally*

Lawton Jnr, Charles (1904–1965)
American cinematographer.

My Dear Miss Aldrich 36. Miracles for Sale 39. Gold Rush Maisie 41. Fingers at the Window 42. Abroad with Two Yanks 44. The Thrill of Brazil 46. *The Lady from Shanghai* 48. Shockproof 49. Rogues of Sherwood Forest 50. Mask of the Avenger 51. *The Happy Time* 52. Miss Sadie Thompson 53. Drive a Crooked Road 54. The Long Gray Line 55. Jubal 56. *3.10 to Yuma* 57. The Last Hurrah 58. It Happened to Jane 59. Two Rode Together 61. 13 West Street 62. Spencer's Mountain 63. Youngblood Hawke 64. A Rage to Live 65, many others.

Lawton, Frank (1904–1969)
Charming but undynamic British leading man of the 30s, husband of Evelyn Laye; in British and American films.

Young Woodley 28. Birds of Prey 30. The Skin Game 31. The Outsider 31. Michael and Mary 31. After Office Hours 32. Cavalcade 33. Heads We Go 33. Friday the Thirteenth 33. One More River 34. *David Copperfield* (title role) 34. The Invisible Ray 36. The Devil Doll 36. The Mill on the Floss 37. The Four Just Men 39. Went the Day Well? 42. The Winslow Boy 48. Rough Shoot 52. The Rising of the Moon 57. A Night to Remember 57. Gideon's Day 57, etc.

Lay, Jnr, Beirne (1909–1982)
American screenwriter.

I Wanted Wings 41. Twelve O'Clock High 49. Above and Beyond 50. The Atomic City (AAN) 52. Strategic Air Command 54. Toward the Unknown 56, etc.

Laydu, Claude (1927–)
Undernourished-looking French leading actor.

Diary of a Country Priest 50. Nous Sommes Tous des Assassins 52. Symphonie d'Amour 55. Le Dialogue des Carmélites 59, etc.

Laye, Evelyn (1900–1996) (Elsie Evelyn Lay)
British musical comedy star of the 20s and 30s; films rare. Married Frank Lawton.

Autobiography: 1958, *Boo to My Friends*.

■ Luck of the Navy 27. Queen of Scandal 30. One Heavenly Night (US) 31. Waltz Time 33. Princess Charming 33. *Evensong* 34. The Night is Young 34. I'll Turn to You 46. Make Mine a Million 59. Theatre of Death 66. Say Hello to Yesterday 70. Within and Without (It.) 70. Second Star to the Right 80.

Lazar, Irving (1907–1993)
Prominent American agent, nicknamed 'Swifty' by Humphrey Bogart for making five movie deals for him in a day. He was noted for his skill in deals and was in part responsible for the growing importance and power of the agent in movie-making in Hollywood.

Lazenby, George (1939–)
Australian leading man who made the big jump from TV commercials to playing James Bond – once. In the 70s and 80s he raced motorcycles and in the 90s backed a restaurant chain, the Spy House.

On Her Majesty's Secret Service 69. Universal Soldier 71. Who Saw Her Die? 72. The Man from Hong Kong 75. Cover Girls (TV) 77. Evening in Byzantium (TV) 78. Saint Jack 79. Never Too Young to Die 86. Hell Hunters 87. Eyes of the Beholder 91. Fatally Yours 95. Twinsitters 95. Four Dogs Playing Poker 00, etc.

TV series: Rituals 84–85.

Le Borg, Reginald (1902–1989)
Austrian-born director, in Hollywood from 1937, at first as shorts director. Output mainly routine with occasional flashes of talent.

Books: 1992, *The Films of Reginald Le Borg* by Wheeler Winston Dixon.

She's for Me 42. The Mummy's Ghost 44. Calling Dr Death 44. *San Diego I Love You* 45. Joe Palooka, Champ 46. Young Daniel Boone 47. Wyoming Trail 49. Bad Blonde 51. Sins of Jezebel 53. The Black Sleep 56. The Dalton Girls 57. The Flight that Disappeared 61. The Diary of a Madman 62, many others.

Le Breton, Auguste (1915–1991)
French writer.

Razzia sur la Chnouf 54. Rififi 55. Bob le Flambeur 55. Rafles sur la Ville 57. Riff Raff Girls 59. Rififi in Paris 66. The Sicilian Clan 68, etc.

Le Brock, Kelly (1960–)
American leading lady. Formerly married to actor Steven Seagal.

The Woman in Red 84. Weird Science 85. Hard to Kill 90. Betrayal of the Dove 92. Hard Bounty 94. Tracks of a Killer 95. Wrongfully Accused 98, etc.

Le Carré, John (1931–) (David John Moore Cornwell)
British spy novelist, whose works have been eagerly filmed, though they centre on the more depressing aspects of espionage.

The Spy Who Came in from the Cold 66. The Deadly Affair (Call for the Dead) 67. The Looking Glass War 70. Tinker Tailor Soldier Spy (TV) 79. Smiley's People 82. The Little Drummer Girl 84. A Perfect Spy (TV) 87.

❝ If you live in secrecy, you think in secrecy. It is the very nature of the life you lead as an intelligence officer in a secret room that the ordinary winds of common sense don't blow through it. You are constantly looking to relate to your enemy in intellectual, adversarial and conspiratorial terms. – *J.L.C.*

Where I kick myself is where I think I actually contributed to the myth of the intelligence services being very good. – *J.L.C.*

Le Chanois, Jean-Paul (1909–1985) (J.-P. Dreyfus)
French director.

L'école Buissonnière 48. La Belle Que Voilà 51. Papa, Mama, the Maid and I 54. The Case of Dr Laurent 56. Les Misérables 58. Monsieur 64. Le Jardinier d'Argenteuil 66, etc.

Le Fanu, J. Sheridan (1814–1873)
Irish novelist specializing in mystery and the occult. His story *Carmilla*, about lesbian vampires, has been filmed as *Blood and Roses* and *The Vampire Lovers*; *Uncle Silas* was filmed in 1949.

Le Gallienne, Eva (1899–1991)
Distinguished American stage actress.
■ Prince of Players 54. The Devil's Disciple 59. Resurrection (AAN) 80.

Le Mat, Paul (1945–)
American leading man.

American Graffiti 73. Firehouse (TV) 74. Aloha Bobby and Rose 75. Citizen's Band 77. More American Graffiti 79. Melvin and Howard 80. Death Valley 81. Jimmy the Kid 82. Strange Invaders 83. The Hanoi Hilton 87. Private Investigations 87. Easy Wheels 89. Blind Witness (TV) 89. Puppet Master 89. Deuce Coupe 92. Wishman 93. Caroline at Midnight 94. Deep Down 94. Sensation 94. American History X 98, etc.

Le May, Alan (1899–1964)
American writer.

Reap the Wild Wind 42. The Adventures of Mark Twain 44. Tap Roots 48. High Lonesome (& d) 50. Thunder in the Dust 51. I Dream of Jeannie 53. The Searchers (oa) 56, etc.

Le Mesurier, John (1912–1983)
British character actor. Usually played bewildered professional men; a favourite for cameo roles from 1946. Married Hattie Jacques.

Autobiography: 1983, *A Jobbing Actor*.

Death in the Hand 48. Beautiful Stranger 54. Private's Progress 55. *Happy Is the Bride* 57. I Was Monty's Double 58. *School for Scoundrels* 60. *Only Two Can Play* 61. Invasion Quartet 62. The Pink Panther 63. The Moonspinners 64. Masquerade 65. Where the Spies Are 65. The Wrong Box 66. The Midas Run 69. *The Magic Christian* 70. Dad's Army 71. The Garnett Saga 72. Confessions of a Window Cleaner 75. Stand Up Virgin Soldiers 77. The Spaceman and King Arthur 79. The Fiendish Plot of Dr Fu Manchu 80. A Married Man (TV) 83, many others.

TV series: *Dad's Army* 67–77.

Le Roy, Mervyn (1900–1987)
American director, former actor, in Hollywood from 1924.

Autobiography: 1975, *Take One*.

Hot Stuff 27. Top Speed 28. Broken Dishes 29. *Little Caesar* 30. Broadminded 31. *Five Star Final* 32. Three on a Match 32. *I Am a Fugitive from a Chain Gang* 32. Two Seconds 32. *Tugboat Annie* 32. Gold Diggers of 1933. Hi Nellie 33. Oil for the Lamps of China 33. Hot to Handle 33. Sweet Adeline 34. Page Miss Glory 34. I Found Stella Parish 35. Anthony Adverse 36. Three Men on a Horse 36. *They Won't Forget* 37. Fools for Scandal 38. Stand Up and Fight (p only) 38. The Wizard of Oz (p only) 39. At the Circus (p only) 39. *Waterloo Bridge* 40. Escape 40. Blossoms in the Dust 41. Unholy Partners 41. Johnny Eager 41. *Random Harvest* (AAN) 42. Madame Curie 43. Thirty Seconds over Tokyo 44; war service; Without Reservations 47. Homecoming 48. Little Women 49. Any Number Can Play 49. East Side West Side 50. Quo Vadis 51. Lovely To Look At 52. Million Dollar Mermaid 53. Rose Marie 54. Mister Roberts (co-d) 55. Strange Lady in Town (& p) 55. The Bad Seed (& p) 56. Toward the Unknown (& p) 56. No Time for Sergeants (& p) 58. Home Before Dark (& p) 59. The FBI Story (& p) 59. A Majority of One (& p) 60. The Devil at Four O'Clock 61. Gypsy (& p) 62. Mary Mary (& p) 63. Moment to Moment (& p) 65, etc.

Leach, Rosemary (1935–)
British character actress, mostly on TV.

Brief Encounter (TV) 74. That'll Be the Day 74. SOS Titanic 79. The Jewel in the Crown (TV) 82. The Bride 84. Turtle Diary 85. A Room with a View 85. The Children 90. The Mystery of Edwin Drood 93. The Hawk 93. The Buccaneers (TV) 95, etc.

TV series: Berkeley Square 98.

Leachman, Cloris (1926–)
American character actress, mostly on TV.

Kiss Me Deadly 54. The Rack 56. The Chapman Report 62. Butch Cassidy and the Sundance Kid 69. WUSA 70. *The Last Picture Show* (AA) 71. Haunts of the Very Rich (TV) 72. Dillinger 73. Charley and the Angel 74. Daisy Miller 74. Hitch Hike (TV) 74. Crazy Mama 75. A Girl Named Sooner (TV) 75. Death Sentence (TV) 75. Young Frankenstein 75. Run Stranger Run 76. High Anxiety 78. SOS Titanic (TV) 79. The North Avenue Irregulars 79. Backstairs at the White House (TV) 79. Willa (TV) 79. Herbie Goes Bananas 80. History of the World Part One 81. Hansel and Gretel 87. Walk Like a Man 87. The Victory 88. Love Hurts 89. Prancer 89. Texasville 90. Miracle Child (TV) 93. My Boyfriend's Back 93. The Beverly Hillbillies 93. A Troll in Central Park (voice) 94. Double Double Toil and Trouble (TV) 94. Now and Then 95, etc.

TV series: Lassie (50s). The Mary Tyler Moore Show 70–73. *Phyllis* 75–76. The Facts of Life 86–88.

Leacock, Philip (1917–1990)
British director, noted for his way with children; latterly worked in American television.
■ *The Brave Don't Cry* 52. Appointment in London 52. *The Kidnappers* 53. Escapade 55. The Spanish Gardener 56. High Tide at Noon 57. Innocent Sinners 58. The Rabbit Trap 58. Let No Man Write My Epitaph 59. Hand in Hand 60. Take a Giant Step 61. Reach for Glory 61. 13 West Street 62. The War Lover 63. Tamahine 63. Adam's Woman 70. The Birdmen (TV) 71. The Great Man's Whiskers (TV) 72. When Michael Calls (TV) 72. Key West (TV) 72. The Daughters of Joshua Cabe (TV) 72. Baffled (TV) 72. Dying Room Only (TV) 73. Killer on Board (TV) 77. Wild and Wooly (TV) 78. The Curse of King Tut's Tomb (TV) 80. Angel City (TV) 80.

Leacock, Richard (1921–)
British-born cameraman and director, brother of Philip Leacock. Worked with Flaherty and became associated with the 'cinema vérité' school.

Primary 60. The Chair 62. Quints 63. Chiefs 68. Maidstone 70. Tread (d) 72. Elliott Carter 80. Lulu in Berlin (d) 84. Dance Black America 85. Girltalk 88, etc.

Lean, Sir David (1908–1991)
Distinguished British director whose work gradually took on epic proportions. Born in Croydon to a Quaker family, after working as a clerk he began as a runner at Gaumont Studios, where he was employed in various capacities before becoming an editor, eventually gaining the reputation as the best in Britain. He worked as co-director with Noël Coward on *In Which We Serve* and then became co-founder of the production company Cineguild, which began by filming Coward's plays. His six wives included actresses Kay Walsh and Ann Todd. His lovers included costume designer Margaret Furse.

Biography: 1989, *David Lean* by Stephen M. Silverman. 1996, *David Lean* by Kevin Brownlow.
■ In Which We Serve (co-d) 42. This Happy Breed 44. *Blithe Spirit* 45. *Brief Encounter* (AAN) 46. *Great Expectations* (AAN) 46. *Oliver Twist* 48. The Passionate Friends 48. Madeleine 49. *The Sound Barrier* (& p) 51. *Hobson's Choice* (& p) 54. *Summertime*/Summer Madness (AAN) 55. *The Bridge on the River Kwai* (AA) 57. *Lawrence of Arabia* (AA) 62. *Dr Zhivago* (AAN) 65. *Ryan's Daughter* 70. A Passage to India (AANd, AANw, AANed) 84.

✪ For his understanding of the art of cinema, despite his final submergence of his sensitive talent in pretentious but empty spectaculars. *Great Expectations*.

❝ I hope the money men don't find out that I'd pay them to let me do this. – *D.L.*

I wouldn't take the advice of a lot of so-called critics on how to shoot a close-up of a teapot. – *D.L.*

Actors can be a terrible bore on the set, though I enjoy having dinner with them. – *D.L.*

Inside every Lean film there is a fat film screaming to get out. – *Anon*

There was a touch of the bully about him – he'd take it out on the people who were weakest and most dependent. – *Judy Davis*

He played cruel games with us actors, did David. Not respecting actors too much, finding their breaking point gave him a kick. – *Sarah Miles*

He thought about film as a Jesuit thinks about his vocation. – *Anthony Havelock-Allan*

Lear, Norman (1926–)
American producer, former comedy writer.

Divorce American Style 67. The Night They Raided Minsky's 68. Start the Revolution without Me 69. Cold Turkey 71. The Princess Bride 87, etc.

TV series: *All in the Family* 71. *Maude* 72. Sanford and Son 72–78. One Day at a Time 75–84. Mary Hartman, Mary Hartman 76, etc.

Learned, Michael (1939–)
Motherly American character actress who scored on TV in *The Waltons* 72–81 and briefly in *Nurse* 82.

Hurricane (TV) 74. It Couldn't Happen to a Nicer Guy (TV) 74. Widow (TV) 76. Little Mo (TV) 78. Touched by Love 80. Power 86. All My Sons (TV) 86. Deadly Business (TV) 86. Roots: The Gift (TV) 88. Murder in New Hampshire: The Pamela Smart Story (TV) 91. Dragon: The Bruce Lee Story 93, etc.

Leary, Denis (1958–)
Aggressive American stand-up comedian and actor. He is co-founder of the production company Apostle Pictures.

The Sandlot/The Sandlot Kids 93. Gunmen 93. National Lampoon's Loaded Weapon 93. Who's the Man 93. Demolition Man 93. Judgment Night 93. The Ref 94. The Neon Bible 95. Operation Dumbo Drop 95. Two If by Sea/Stolen Hearts (& co-w) 96. Underworld 96. Subway Stories: Tales from the Underground (TV) 97. The Second Civil War (TV) 97. The Matchmaker 97. Wag the Dog 97. The Real Blonde 97. Suicide Kings 98. Small Soldiers 98. A Bug's Life (voice) 98. Snitch 98. True Crime 99. The Thomas Crown Affair 99. Jesus' Son 99. Company Man 01, etc.

Leasor, James (1923–)
British thriller writer whose Dr Jason Love was brought to the screen in 1964 in *Where the Spies Are*.

Léaud, Jean-Pierre (1944–)
French leading actor who began as a boy star.

Les Quatre Cents Coups 59. Love at Twenty 61. Masculin-Féminin 66. La Chinoise 67. Stolen Kisses 68. Pigsty 69. Last Tango in Paris 72. Day for Night 73. Love on the Run 79. Detective 84. Treasure Island 85. With All Hands 86. 36 Fillette 88. Bunker Palace Hotel 89. I Hired a Contract Killer 90. Zone 91. Bohemian Life/La Vie de Bohème 92. La Naissance de l'Amour 93. Personne Ne M'Aime 94. Nine Months/Neuf Mois 94. Irma Vep 96, etc.

Leavitt, Sam (1904–1984)
American cinematographer.

The Thief 52. *A Star is Born* 54. Carmen Jones 54. The Man with the Golden Arm 55. *The Defiant Ones* (AA) 58. Anatomy of a Murder (AAN) 59. Exodus (AAN) 60. Advise and Consent 62. Two on a Guillotine 64. Major Dundee 65. Brainstorm 65. An American Dream 66. Guess Who's Coming to Dinner 67. The Desperados 68. The Grasshopper 70. Star Spangled Girl 71. The Man in the Glass Booth 75, etc.

Lebedeff, Ivan (1899–1953)
Russian character actor, former diplomat, in US from 1925.

The Sorrows of Satan 27. Midnight Mystery 30. Blonde Bombshell 33. China Seas 35. History Is Made at Night 37. Hotel for Women 39. The Shanghai Gesture 41. They Are Guilty 45. The Snows of Kilimanjaro 52, many others.

LeBlanc, Matt (1967–)
American actor, best known for his role in the TV sitcom *Friends*. In 2000, he signed a contract worth an estimated $40m to appear in Friends for the following two years.

Anything to Survive (TV) 90. Red Shoe Diaries 3: Another Woman's Lipstick 93. Ed 96. Lost in Space 98. Charlie's Angels 00, etc.

Leclerc, Ginette (1912–1992)
Sulky-looking French stage and screen actress.

Prison sans Barreaux 38. *La Femme du Boulanger* 38. *Le Corbeau* 43. Le Plaisir 51. Les Amants du Tage 54. Gas-Oil 55. Le Cave Se Rebiffe 61. Goto, Island of Love 68. Tropic of Cancer 69, etc.

Leconte, Patrice (1947–)
French director and screenwriter, a former comic-book writer and artist, who switched from making local comedies to dramas with an international appeal.

Monsieur Hire 90. The Hairdresser's Husband/Le Mari de la Coiffeuse (co-w, d) 91. *Tango* 93. Le Parfum d'Yvonne 94. The Grand Dukes 95. Ridicule (AAN) 96, etc.

Ledebur, Friedrich (c. 1908–)
Austrian actor of eccentric roles.

Moby Dick 56. Roots of Heaven 58. The Blue Max 66. Alfred the Great 69. Juliet of the Spirits 69. Slaughterhouse Five 72. Ginger and Fred 86, etc.

Leder, Mimi (c. 1952–)
American director, from television, where she directed many of the episodes of *ER*, winning two Emmy awards, and was also nominated for directing episodes of *China Beach*, the medical drama set in Vietnam. So far, her features have been action movies. She graduated as a cinematographer from the American Film Institute's graduate film programme in the mid-70s and worked in television as a script supervisor. She is the daughter of independent director Paul Leder. Married actor and writer Gary Werntz.

A Little Piece of Heaven 91. House of Secrets (TV) 93. The Innocent (TV) 94. The Peacemaker 97. Deep Impact 98. Pay It Forward 00, etc.

Leder, Paul (1926–1996)
American director, writer and producer of independent low-budget movies, a former singer and dancer on the Broadway stage.

As actor: The Grass Eater 61. Five Minutes to Love 63. How to Succeed with Girls 64.

As director: Marigold Man 70. I Dismember Mama 72. Ape 76. My Friends Need Killing 76. Sketches of a Strangler 78. I'm Going to Be Famous 83. Vultures 84. Body Count 88. Goin' to Chicago 90. The Abduction of Alison Tate 92. The Baby Doll Murders 93. Killing Obsession 94. The Wacky Adventures of Dr Boris and Nurse Shirley 95, etc.

Lederer, Charles (1906–1976)
High-spirited American screenwriter and, later, director, in Hollywood from 1931. The nephew of actress Marion Davies, he was born in New York City and was a former journalist. He worked for writers Ben Hecht and Charles MacArthur when they set up their own unsuccessful production company, and spent a short period in the mid-30s as assistant to Irving Thalberg at MGM. Frequently off-hand in his attitude to work, and often mocking of studio bosses, he was also producer and co-author of the Broadway musical *Kismet*, which he helped adapt for the screen.

The Front Page 31. Topaze 33. Comrade X 40. His Girl Friday 40. Ride the Pink Horse 47. *Kiss of Death* 47. The Thing 52. It Started with a Kiss 58. The Spirit of St Louis 58. Can Can 59. Ocean's Eleven 61. Mutiny on the Bounty 62, many others.
■ As director: Fingers at the Window 42. On the Loose 51. Never Steal Anything Small (& w) 58, etc.

Lederer, Francis (1899–2000)
Czech-born leading man, in Hollywood from 1933, after European stage and film experience.

Pandora's Box (Ger.) 28. Atlantic (Ger.) 30. The Bracelet (Ger.) 32. The Pursuit of Happiness 34. It's All Yours 36. The Lone Wolf in Paris 37. Midnight 38. *Confessions of a Nazi Spy* 39. The Man I Married 40. The Bridge of San Luis Rey 44. A Voice in the Wind 45. The Diary of a Chambermaid 45. Million Dollar Weekend 48. Captain Carey USA 49. A Woman of Distinction 50. Stolen Identity 53. Lisbon 56. The Return of Dracula 58. Terror Is a Man 59, etc.

Lederman, D. Ross (1895–1972)
American director, former prop man for Mack Sennett.

Man Hunter 30. Riding Tornado 32. Glamour for Sale 40. The Body Disappears 41. Strange Alibi 41. Shadows on the Stairs 43. Key Witness 47, etc.

Ledger, Heath (1979–)
Australian leading actor, who began in the theatre as a child. Born in Perth, he moved to the United States at the age of 19.
Paws 97. Blackrock 97. Two Hands 98. 10 Things I Hate about You (US) 99. The Patriot (US) 00. In Shining Armour (US) 01, etc.
TV series: Sweat 96. Roar 97.

Ledoux, Fernand (1897–1993)
Belgian-born actor who had a long and distinguished stage and film career in France, working in more than 800 plays and movies. He was a member of the Comédie Française for more than 20 years.
Le Carnaval des Vérités 19. L'Homme à la Barbiche 32. Le Vagabond Bien-aimé 36. The Human Beast/La Bête Humaine 38. The Devil's Envoys/Les Visiteurs du Soir 42. Devil's Daughter/La Fille du Diable 46. An Act of Love/Un Acte d'Amour 54. Les Misérables 58. The Truth/La Verité 60. The Big Gamble (US) 61. The Longest Day (US) 62. The Trial 62. Up from the Beach (US) 65. Donkey Skin/Peau d'Ane 71. A Trillion Dollars/Mille Milliards de Dollars 82, etc.

Ledoyen, Virginie (1976–)
Leading French actress, who began in commercials from the age of 3.
Mimi 91. Le Voleur D'Enfants 91. L'Eau Froide 94. A Judgement in Stone/La Cérémonie 95. La Fille Seule 95. Majiang 96. Heroines 98. Jeanne Et La Garcon Formidable 98. A Soldier's Daughter Never Cries 98. Late August, Early September 99. The Beach (US) 00. Les Miserables (TV) 00. Cecilia 00, etc.

Leduc, Paul (1942–)
Mexican director and a pioneer of the country's 'New Cinema' movement. He studied architecture and theatre before becoming a film critic and worked in French TV before returning to Mexico, where he first produced and directed documentaries.
Reed: Mexico Insurgente 73. Etnocido: Notas sobre el Mezquital 78. Historias Prohibidas de Pulgarcito 79. La Cabeza de la Hidra (TV) 81. Frida 86. Barocco 89. Latino Bar 91. Dollar Mambo 93, etc.

Lee, Ang (1954–)
US-based Taiwanese director who studied at the University of Illinois and New York University.
Pushing Hands 91. The Wedding Banquet (AAN) 93. Eat Drink Man Woman (AAN) 94. *Sense and Sensibility* 95. *The Ice Storm* 97. Ride with the Devil 99. Crouching Tiger, Hidden Dragon (AANp, AANd, BFAp, BFAd) 00, etc.

Lee, Anna (1914–) (Joanna Winnifrith)
Blonde English leading actress, who went to Hollywood to play supporting roles. Born in Igtham, Kent, she began in films as an extra. She moved to the US with her then husband, director Robert STEVENSON and appeared in several of director John Ford's films. She was later a regular on the soap opera *General Hospital*. Her third husband (1970-85) was author and screenwriter Robert NATHAN. She was the mother of 60s actress Venetia Stevenson and actor Jeffrey Byron.
The Camels are Coming 34. First a Girl 35. The Passing of the Third Floor Back 35. The Man Who Changed His Mind 36. O.H.M.S. 36. King Solomon's Mines 37. Non Stop New York 37. The Four Just Men 39. Young Man's Fancy 39. Return to Yesterday 40. Seven Sinners 40. How Green Was My Valley 41. My Life with Caroline 41. The Commandos Strike at Dawn 42. Flying Tigers 42. Hangmen Also Die! 43. Summer Storm 44. Bedlam 46. The Ghost and Mrs Muir 47. High Conquest 47. Fort Apache 48. Gideon's Day 58. Jet over the Atlantic 58. The Last Hurrah 58. The Crimson Kimono 59. This Earth Is Mine 59. Whatever Happened to Baby Jane? 62. The Sound of Music 65. Seven Women 66. In Like Flint 67. Scruples (TV) 80. The Right Hand Man 87. Beverly Hills Brats 89. Listen to Me 89. What Can I Do? 94, etc.

Lee, Belinda (1935–1961)
Blonde British starlet trained for stardom by Rank but given poor material: appeared in Continental semi-spectaculars and died in car crash.
The Runaway Bus 54. Life with the Lyons 54. Meet Mr Callaghan 54. Man of the Moment 55. No Smoking 55. The Big Money 56. Eye Witness 56. The Feminine Touch 56. Who Done It? 56. Dangerous Exile 57. Miracle in Soho 57. Nor the Moon By Night 58. The Nights of Lucretia Borgia 59, etc.

Lee, Bernard (1908–1981)
British character actor with solid, friendly personality, on stage from 1926. In films, often a sergeant or a superintendent … or 'M' in the James Bond films.
The River House Mystery 35. The Terror 37. Spare a Copper 40. Once a Crook 41; war service; The Courtneys of Curzon Street 47. *The Fallen Idol* 48. Quartet 48. *The Third Man* 49. The Blue Lamp 50. Appointment with Venus 51. The Gift Horse 52. The Purple Plain 54. *Father Brown* 54. The Battle of the River Plate 56. Dunkirk 58. Danger Within 59. The Angry Silence 59. The Secret Partner 60. Whistle Down the Wind 61. *Dr No* 62. Two Left Feet 63. From Russia with Love 63. Ring of Spies 63. Goldfinger 64. The Legend of Young Dick Turpin 65. Thunderball 65. The Spy Who Came In from the Cold 65. You Only Live Twice 66. The Raging Moon 70. Dulcima 71. Frankenstein and the Monster from Hell 73. The Man with the Golden Gun 74. Beauty and the Beast 76. The Spy who Loved Me 77. Moonraker 79, many others.

Lee, Bert (1880–1947)
English screenwriter and songwriter, mainly in collaboration with R. P. WESTON.
Up For The Cup 31. No Lady 31. The Flag Lieutenant 32. Lucky Girl 32. The Mayor's Nest 32. This Is The Life 33. Trouble 33. Up For The Derby 33. Doctor's Orders 34. Girls Please! 34. It's a Cop 34. Where's George? 35. Squibs 35. Fame 36. Yes, Madam 38. She Couldn't Say No 39. Up for the Cup 50, etc.

Lee, Bill (1928–)
American composer and musician, for the films of his son, Spike LEE.
She's Gotta Have It 86. School Daze 88. Do the Right Thing 89. Mo' Better Blues (s) 90, etc.

Lee, Billy (1930–1989)
American child star of the 30s.
Wagon Wheels 34. Coconut Grove 38. *The Biscuit Eater* 40. Hold Back the Dawn 41. Mrs Wiggs of the Cabbage Patch 42, etc.

Lee, Brandon (1965–1993)
American action film star, the son of Bruce LEE. Born in Oakland, California, he was brought up in Hong Kong, where he was taught martial arts from an early age by his father. He died following a shooting accident while filming *The Crow*, a film about a rock musician who returns from the dead.
Kung Fu: The Next Generation (TV) 85. Legacy of Rage 86. Lazer Mission 87. Showdown in Little Tokyo 91. Rapid Fire 92. The Crow 94, etc.
❝ None of my friends would come over to the house when I was a kid because they were all scared to death. There would always be six or seven grown men in the backyard screaming and throwing each other around. – *B.L.*

Lee, Bruce (1940–1973) (Lee Yenn Kam)
Diminutive Chinese-American leading man and practitioner of the martial arts. After comparative failure in Hollywood (a bit part in *Marlowe* 69, a supporting role in a TV series *The Green Hornet* 68), he went to Hong Kong and became a sensation in 'chop socky' movies. A biopic of his life, *Dragon*, starring Jason Scott Lee, was released in 1993. He was the father of Brandon LEE.
Biography: 1997, *The Unseen Bruce Lee* by Louis Chunovic.
Fist of Fury 72. The Big Boss 72. Enter the Dragon 73. The Way of the Dragon 73. Game of Death (posthumously re-edited) 79, etc.
❝ Bruce Lee had bad eyesight and one leg that was shorter than the other. But he had a mental image of what he wanted, and he became the quintessential martial artist and the first Chinese superstar in American films. – *Chuck Norris*

Lee, Canada (1907–1952) (Lionel Canegata)
American actor.
■ Lifeboat 43. Body and Soul 47. Lost Boundaries 49. Cry the Beloved Country 52.

Lee, Christopher (1922–)
Gaunt, tall English actor whose personality lends itself best to sinister or horrific parts. Seems to have made more films than any other living actor, and has certainly played most of the known monsters. Born in London, the son of an army officer and the Contessa Carandini, he began work as a clerk and, after service in the Second World War, was one of many would-be actors signed to a seven-year contract to train in Rank's Charm School. He played small roles until cast as Dracula in one of the early Hammer horrors.
Autobiography: 1977, *Tall, Dark and Gruesome*.
Corridor of Mirrors 47. Hamlet 48. They Were Not Divided 49. Prelude to Fame 50. Valley of Eagles 51. The Crimson Pirate 52. Moulin Rouge 53. The Dark Avenger 54. Private's Progress 55. Alias John Preston 56. Moby Dick 56. *The Curse of Frankenstein* (as the monster) 56. Ill Met by Moonlight 57. The Traitor 57. A Tale of Two Cities 57. *Dracula* (title role) 58. Corridors of Blood 58. The Hound of the Baskervilles (as Sir Henry) 59. The Man Who Could Cheat Death 59. *The Mummy* (title role) 59. Beat Girl 60. City of the Dead 60. The Hands of Orlac 60. Taste of Fear 61. The Terror of the Tongs 61. The Devil's Daffodil 62. Pirates of Blood River 62. Sherlock Holmes and the Deadly Necklace (Ger.) 62. The Gorgon 63. Dr Terror's House of Horrors 63. She 65. The Face of Fu Manchu 65. The Skull 65. Dracula Prince of Darkness 65. Rasputin the Mad Monk 65. Theatre of Death 66. Night of the Big Heat 67. The Devil Rides Out 68. Curse of the Crimson Altar 68. Julius Caesar 70. I Monster 71. Dracula AD 1972 72. The Wicker Man 73. The Satanic Rites of Dracula 73. The Three Musketeers 74. The Man with the Golden Gun 74. Diagnosis Murder 75. To the Devil a Daughter 75. The Wicker Man 75. Killer Force 75. Airport 77 77. Return from Witch Mountain 78. The Silent Flute 78. The Pirate (TV) 78. Starship Invasions 78. The Passage 78. Arabian Adventure 79. Circle of Iron 79. 1941 79. Serial 80. The Salamander 80. An Eye for an Eye 81. Safari 3000 82. The House of Long Shadows 83. The Return of Captain Invincible 83. Howling II 85. The Rosebud Beach Hotel 85. Jocks 86. Dark Mission 88. Mask of Murder 89. The Return of the Musketeers 89. The Miser/L'Avaro 89. Panga 90. Gremlins 2: The New Batch 90. Honeymoon Academy 90. Sherlock Holmes and the Leading Lady (TV) 91. Curse III: Blood Sacrifice 91. Cybereden (It.) 93. Police Academy 7: Mission to Moscow 94. Funny Man 94. The Stupids 96. Ivanhoe (TV) 97. Jinnah (title role) (Pak.) 98. Sleepy Hollow 99. Gormenghast (TV) 00, etc.
❝ I stopped appearing as Dracula in 1972 because in my opinion the presentation of the character had deteriorated to such an extent, particularly bringing him into the contemporary day and age, that it really no longer had any meaning. – *C.L.*
As Boris Karloff told me, 'You have to make your mark in something other actors cannot, or will not, do and if it's a success you'll not be forgotten. The name of the game is survival.' – *C.L.*
Acting has been good to me. It has taken me to play golf all over the world. – *C.L.*

Lee, Davey (1925–)
American child actor of the early talkies.
The Singing Fool 28. Sonny Boy 29. The Squealer 30, etc.

Lee, Dixie (1911–1952) (Wilma Wyatt)
American leading lady, wife of Bing Crosby. She later had problems with alcoholism. Died of cancer. Dorothy Parker drew on her life for the story of *Smash-Up, the Story of a Woman* 47, which dealt with an alcoholic.
Not for Sale 24. Movietone Follies 29. The Big Party 30. No Limit 31. Manhattan Love Song 34. Love in Bloom 35, etc.
❝ Once I discovered that the old man wasn't the pillar of virtue he pretended to be, and that her insinuations weren't the half-crazed ramblings of a drunk, I stopped being afraid of her. She became more of a person to me, and I started to feel some sympathy for her drinking. – *Gary Crosby, her eldest son*

Lee, Dorothy (1911–1999) (Marjorie Millsap)
American leading lady of the 30s, especially associated with WHEELER and WOLSEY.
Syncopation 29. Rio Rita 29. The Cuckoos 30. Dixiana 30. Hook Line and Sinker 30. Half Shot at Sunrise 30. Cracked Nuts 31. Caught Plastered 31. Laugh and Get Rich 31. Peach O'Reno 31. Girl Crazy 32. Take a Chance 33. Cockeyed Cavaliers 34. Hips Hips Hooray 34. The Rainmakers 35. Silly Billies 36. Twelve Crowded Hours 39, etc.

Lee, Eugene (1933–)
American child actor who played 'Porky' in many of the Our Gang comedies of the mid to late 30s. Born in Fort Worth, Texas, he later became a teacher.

Lee, Gypsy Rose (1913–1970) (Louise Hovick)
American burlesque artiste, on stage from six years old: her early life, glamorized, is recounted in *Gypsy* 62, based on her 1957 book. She was the sister of actress June HAVOC. The second of her three husbands was actor Alexander Kirkland, and she had a son by director Otto PREMINGER.
■ You Can't Have Everything 37. Ali Baba Goes to Town 38. My Lucky Star 39. Belle of the Yukon 44. Babes in Baghdad 52. Screaming Mimi 57. Wind Across the Everglades 58. The Stripper 62. The Trouble with Angels 66.
TV series: The Pruitts of Southampton 66.
❝ Royalties are all very well, but shaking the beads brings in the money quicker. – *G.R.L.*
God is love, but get it in writing. – *G.R.L.*

Lee, Jack (1913–)
British director, originally in documentaries. Moved to work in Australia in the mid-50s.
Close Quarters 44. Children on Trial 46. The Woman in the Hall 47. *The Wooden Horse* (co-d) 50. Turn the Key Softly 53. *A Town Like Alice* 56. Robbery under Arms 57. The Captain's Table 58. Circle of Deception 61. From the Tropics to the Snow (doc) 64, etc.

Lee, Jason (1971–)
American actor in independent films, a former professional skateboarder.
My Crazy Life/Mi Vida Loca 93. Mallrats 95. Drawing Flies 96. A Better Place 97. Chasing Amy 97. Weapons of Mass Distraction (TV) 97. Dogma 98. Mumford 98. Kissing a Fool 98. Enemy of the State 98. American Cuisine (Fr.) 98. Kissing a Fool 98. Dogma 99. Mumford 99. Almost Famous 00. Big Trouble 01, etc.

Lee, Jason Scott (1966–)
American leading actor. Born in Los Angeles, to a third-generation Chinese-Hawaiian family, and raised on the Hawaiian island of Oahu, he returned to Los Angeles at the age of 19, beginning with bit parts on television and in films.
Dragon: The Bruce Lee Story 93. Map of the Human Heart 93. Rapa Nui 94. The Jungle Book 95. Murder in Mind 97. Soldier 98, etc.

Lee, Jet
See LI, Jet.

Lee, Lila (1902–1973) (Augusta Apple)
Demure American leading lady of the 20s.
The Cruise of the Make Believes 18. Male and Female 19. Terror Island 20. Blood and Sand 22. Million Dollar Mystery 25. Queen of the Night Clubs 29, etc.

Lee, Margaret (1943–)
English leading actress in European films, usually in sexy roles.
Colossus of the Stone Age/Fire Monsters against the Son of Hercules (It.) 62. Casanova 70 65. Five Golden Dragons 65. Circus of Fear 66. Dick Smart 2007 (It.) 66. Our Man in Marrakesh 66. The Action Man (Fr.) 66. Djurado (Sp.) 66. Devil's Garden (It.) 67. Five Golden Dragons 67. The Violent Four (It.) 68. Sons of Satan (It.) 68. House of Pleasure (Ger.) 68. Venus in Furs 69. Viva America! (Sp.) 69. Dorian Gray (Ger.) 70. Cold Blooded Beast/La Bestia Uccide a Sangue Freddo (It.) 71. Stangata Napoletana (It.) 82, etc.

Lee, Michele (1942–) (Michele Dusiak)
American leading lady and singer, with stage experience.
How to Succeed in Business 67. The Love Bug 69. The Comic 69. Dark Victory (TV) 76. Bud and Lou (TV) 78. Single Women, Married Men (TV) 89, etc.
TV series: Knots Landing 79–86.

Lee, Norman (1898– *)
British director and screenwriter, often of low-budget comedies. A former actor and playwright, he directed silent films in South Africa in the 20s, including a version of *The Blue Lagoon*. He was a theatre director and writer of revues in Britain before beginning to direct films at Elstree in 1929. After 1943, he concentrated on writing screenplays and novels.

Autobiography: 1945, *A Film Is Born*. 1947, *My Personal Log*. 1949, *Log of a Film Director*.
The Song of London 29. Lure of the Atlantic 29. Strip Strip Hooray! Dr Josser K.C. (& co-w) 31. Money Talks (& co-w) 32. The Strangler (& w) 32. Josser Joins the Navy 32. Josser on the River (& co-w) 32. Pride of the Force (& co-w) 32. Doctor's Orders 34. The Outcast 34. A Political Party 34. Royal Cavalcade (co-d) 35. Don't Rush Me 36. Kathleen Mavourneen 37. French Leave 37. Knights for a Day 37. Luck of the Navy 38. Mr Reeder in Room 13 38. Yes, Madam? 38. Murder in Soho 39. The Farmer's Wife (co-w, co-d) 40. This Man Is Mine (co-w) 46. The Monkey's Paw 48. Idol of Paris (co-w) 48. The Case of Charles Peace (& co-w) 49. The Girl Who Couldn't Quite 50, etc.
❝ The director is still a Big Shot but he shares his authority with others. He is no longer the man he was. The money kings have now got him by the short hairs. – *N.L.*

Lee, Pamela Anderson
Blonde and busty Canadian-born leading actress. Born in Vancouver, she began as a model, becoming the 'Blue Zone girl' in an advertising campaign for Labatt's beer and appearing in *Playboy* magazine. She appeared on television as Liza, The Tool Time Girl in the sitcom *Home Improvement* and as C. J. Parker in the series *Baywatch*. Married rock drummer Tommy Lee.
Snapdragon 94. Good Cop, Bad Cop 94. Barb Wire 96. Deader than Ever (TV) 96, etc.

Lee, Peggy (1920–) (Norma Egstrom)
American singer and songwriter, in occasional films. One of the great interpreters of popular song, she sang with the Benny Goodman orchestra in the early 40s and wrote many of the songs, and also sang them in Walt Disney's animated film *The Lady and the Tramp* 55.
Stage Door Canteen 43. Mr Music 50. The Jazz Singer 53. Johnny Guitar (title song) 54. Pete Kelly's Blues (AAN) 55. The Russians Are Coming! The Russians Are Coming! (s) 66, etc.

Lee, Robert E. (1918–1994)
American dramatist and screenwriter, in collaboration with Jerome Lawrence.
Auntie Mame (from their play) 58. Inherit the Wind 60. First Monday in October 81.

Lee, Rowland V. (1891–1975)
American director, in films from 1918.
Alice Adams 26. Barbed Wire 26. The Mysterious Dr Fu Manchu 29. *Zoo in Budapest* 33. *The Count of Monte Cristo* 34. Cardinal Richelieu 35. The Three Musketeers 35. Service de Luxe 38. *Son of Frankenstein* 39. Tower of London 39. Son of Monte Cristo 41. The Bridge of San Luis Rey 44. Captain Kidd 45. The Big Fisherman (p only) 59, etc.

Lee, Sheryl (1966–)
American actress who gained fame through the TV series *Twin Peaks* 90.
Wild at Heart 90. I Love You to Death 90. Twin Peaks: Fire Walk with Me 92. The Distinguished Gentleman 92. Backbeat 94. Don't Do It 94. Fall Time 95. Homage 95. Follow the River 95. Mother Night 96. Bliss 96. This World, Then the Fireworks 97. Angel's Dance 98. John Carpenter's Vampires 98, etc.
TV series: LA Doctors 98– .

Lee, Spike (1957–) (Shelton Jackson Lee)
American director, screenwriter and actor. He has his own production company, Forty Acres & A Mule Filmworks.
Autobiography: 1997, *Best Seat in the House* (with Ralph Wiley).
Biography: 1992, *Spike Lee* by Alex Patterson.
She's Gotta Have It 86. School Daze 88. Do the Right Thing (AANw) 89. Mo' Better Blues 90. Jungle Fever 91. Malcolm X 92. Crooklyn (co-w, a, d) 94. Clockers (co-w, d) 95. Girl 6 96. 4 Little Girls (TV, doc) (AAN) 97. He Got Game (co-p, wd) 98, etc.
❝ I remember trying to join the boy scouts and they told me I couldn't join because I wasn't Catholic. You can't help growing up thinking something is amiss. – *S.L.*

Lee-Thompson, J. (1914–)
Scottish director, screenwriter and playwright, a former actor. He had his first play produced in London at the age of 18, and went to work as a screenwriter for British International Pictures in 1935, turning director with a screen version of his second play.
■ The Middle Watch (w) 36. For Them that Trespass (w) 48. Murder without Crime (wd) 50. *The Yellow Balloon* (wd) 52. The Weak and the Wicked (wd) 53. As Long as They're Happy (d) 54. For Better for Worse (d) 54. An Alligator Named Daisy (d) 55. Yield to the Night (d) 56. The Good Companions (co-p, co-d) 57. No Trees in the Street (d) 58. Woman in a Dressing Gown (d) 59. Tiger Bay (d) 59. Northwest Frontier (d) 59. Ice Cold in Alex (d) 60. I Aim at the Stars (d) (US) 60. *The Guns of Navarone* (AANd) 61. Cape Fear (d) (US) 61. Taras Bulba (d) (US) 62. Kings of the Sun (d) (US) 63. What a Way to Go (d) (US) 64. John Goldfarb Please Come Home (d) (US) 65. Return from the Ashes (p, d) 65. Eye of the Devil (d) 66. Mackenna's Gold (d) (US) 68. Before Winter Comes (d) 68. The Chairman (d) 69. Country Dance (d) 70. Conquest of the Planet of the Apes (d) (US) 72. A Great American Tragedy (TV) 72. Huckleberry Finn (d) (US) 74. The Reincarnation of Peter Proud (d) (US) 74. The Blue Knight (TV) (d) 75. St Ives (d) 75. Widow (TV) (d) 76. The White Buffalo (d) (US) 77. The Greek Tycoon 78. The Passage 78. Cabo Blanco 79. Happy Birthday to Me 81. Ten to Midnight 83. The Ambassador 84. King Solomon's Mines 85. Murphy's Law 86. Firewalker 86. Death Wish IV: The Crackdown 88. Messenger of Death 88. Kinjite/Forbidden Subjects 89.

Leech, Richard (1922–) (Richard McClelland)
British character actor, often as army or air force officer.
The Dam Busters 55. A Night to Remember 57. The Good Companions 57. Ice Cold in Alex 59. The Horse's Mouth 59. Tunes of Glory 60. The Wild and the Willing 62. I Thank a Fool 63. The Fighting Prince of Donegal 66. Young Winston 72. Gandhi 82. The Shooting Party 84. A Woman of Substance (TV) 85. A Handful of Dust 87, etc.

Leeds, Andrea (1914–1984) (Antoinette Lees)
American leading lady of the late 30s.
Come and Get It 36. *Stage Door* (AAN) 37. The Goldwyn Follies 39. Letter of Introduction 39. Swanee River 39, etc.

Leeds, Herbert I. (*c.* 1900–1954) (Herbert I. Levy)
American director of second features, former editor.
Mr Moto in Danger Island 38. Island in the Sky 38. The Cisco Kid and the Lady 39. Manila Calling 42. *Time to Kill* 43. It Shouldn't Happen to a Dog 46. Let's Live Again 48. Father's Wild Game 51, etc.

Leeves, Jane (1962–)
English actress, in Hollywood, best known for her role as Daphne Moon in the TV sitcom *Frasier*. Born in London, and brought up in East Grinstead, Sussex, she is a former model and dancer who began on television in the early 80s as one of 'Hill's Angels', the girls that featured in comedian Benny Hill's TV series. Married TV executive Marshall Cohen in 1996.
Monty Python's The Meaning of Life 83. The Hunger 83. To Live and Die in LA 85. Mr Write (US) 92. Miracle on 34th Street (US) 94. James and the Giant Peach (voice) 96. Pandora's Clock (TV) 96. Us Begins with You 98, etc.
TV series: Throb 86–88. Murphy Brown 89–93. Frasier 93– .

Legg, Stuart (1910–1988)
British documentarist and administrator. From 1932 with GPO Film Unit and Empire Marketing Board. 1939–45: National Film Board of Canada. 1953–88: director of Film Centre Ltd.

Leggatt, Alison (1904–1990)
British character actress, mainly on stage.
Nine Till Six 32. This Happy Breed 44. Waterloo Road 45. Marry Me 47. The Card 52. Touch and Go 55. Never Take Sweets from a Stranger 60. Nothing but the Best 64. The Seven Per Cent Solution 76, etc.

Legrand, Michel (1931–)
French composer.
Lola 61. Eva 62. Vivre sa Vie 62. La Baie des Anges 63. *The Umbrellas of Cherbourg* (AAN) 64. Bande à Part 64. Une Femme Mariée 65. Les Demoiselles de Rochefort 67. Ice Station Zebra 68. Peau d'Ane 70. *Summer of 42* (AA) 71. A Time for Loving (& a) 71. One is a Lonely Number 72. Portnoy's Complaint 72. Cops and Robbers 73. The Three Musketeers 74. Ode to Billy Joe 75. The Other Side of Midnight 77. Atlantic City USA 80. Falling in Love Again 80. The Hunter 80. The Mountain Men 80. Best Friends 82. Yentl (AA) 83. Palace 84. Secret Places 85. Switching Channels 88. Eternity 90. The Pickle 93. Prêt-à-Porter/Ready to Wear 94. Madeline 98. Season's Beatings/La Buche 99, etc.

LeGros, James (1962–)
American leading actor.
Phantasm 79. Near Dark 87. Phantasm II 88. Drugstore Cowboy 89. Hollywood Heartbreak 89. The Rapture 91. Singles 92. Guncrazy 92. My New Gun 92. Where the Day Takes You 92. Bad Girls 94. Don't Do It 94. Mrs Parker and the Vicious Circle 94. Living in Oblivion 95. The Low Life 95. Destiny Turns on the Radio 95. Safe 95. The Destiny of Marty Fine 96. Marshal Law 96. Countdown 96. Boys 96. Wishful Thinking 97. The Myth of Fingerprints 97. Thursday 98. LA without a Map (GB/Fr./Fin.) 98. There's No Fish Food in Heaven 98. Enemy of the State 98, etc.

Leguizamo, John (1965–)
American actor and comedian. Born in Bogotá, Colombia, he studied drama at New York University.
Casualties of War 89. Mambo Mouth 90. Street Hunter 90. Hangin' with the Homeboys 91. Regarding Henry 91. Super Mario Bros 93. Night Owl 93. Carlito's Way 93. To Wong Foo, Thanks for Everything, Julie Newmar 95. A Pyromaniac's Love Story 95. Executive Decision 96. The Fan 96. Romeo and Juliet 96. The Pest 97. Spawn 97. Body Count 97. Dr Dolittle (voice) 98, etc.
TV series: House of Buggin' 95.

Lehman, Ernest (1920–)
American screenwriter. Honorary Oscar 2001.
Inside Story 48. Executive Suite 54. Sabrina (AAN) 54. *The Sweet Smell of Success* 57. *North by Northwest* (AAN) 59. West Side Story (AAN) 61. *The Prize* 63. The Sound of Music 65. Who's Afraid of Virginia Woolf? (& p) (AAN) 66. Hello Dolly (& p) (AAN) 69. Portnoy's Complaint (& p, d) 72. Family Plot 76. Black Sunday 77, etc.

Lehmann, Beatrix (1898–1979)
British character actress, often of withdrawn eccentrics; film appearances few. On stage from 1924.
The Passing of the Third Floor Back 36. Black Limelight 38. The Rat 38. The Key 58. Psyche 59 64. The Spy Who Came in from the Cold 66. Staircase 69, etc.

Lehmann, Carla (1917–1990)
Canadian leading lady, in British films of the 40s.
So This Is London 39. Cottage to Let 41. Talk about Jacqueline 42. Candlelight in Algeria 44. 29 Acacia Avenue 45. Fame Is the Spur 47, etc.

Lehmann, Michael (1957–)
American director and screenwriter.
Heathers (d) 88. Meet the Applegates (co-w, d) 89. Hudson Hawk (d) 91. Airheads (d) 94. The Truth about Cats and Dogs 96. My Giant 98, etc.

Lehrman, Henry 'Pathé' (1883–1946)
Austrian-born director and actor of silents in Hollywood who made Charlie CHAPLIN's earliest films for Keystone; later a screenwriter. His nickname was given to him by D. W. GRIFFITH and derived from the fact that he claimed to have worked for the Pathé company in France. Born in Vienna, he emigrated in his late teens, working first as a tram conductor, and began in films as an extra and bit-part player before joining Keystone as a director and actor. Chaplin disliked working with him, complaining that he ruined his best jokes. He later founded his own company, L-KO (for Lehrman-Knock Out), using a former Fred KARNO performer, Scotsman Billy Ritchie (1874–1921), as a comic in the Chaplin style, and then turned out comedies for Fox. After the arrival of sound, he had a brief career as a screenwriter, but was bankrupt by the early 40s. He was the lover of Virginia Rappe, the starlet for whose death Fatty ARBUCKLE was blamed, and was the chief prosecution witness at the subsequent trial that ended Arbuckle's career.
AS DIRECTOR: Between Showers 14. Kid Auto Races at Venice, California 14. Mabel's Strange Predicament 14. Making a Living 14. Double Dealing 23. Fighting Blood 23. For Ladies Only 27. Chicken à la King 28, etc.
AS WRITER: The Poor Millionaire (co-w) 30. Moulin Rouge (co-w) 34. Bulldog Drummond Strikes Back (co-w) 34. Show Them No Mercy (co-w) 35, etc.
❝ He used to say that he didn't need personalities, that he got all his laughs from mechanical effects and film-cutting. – *Charlie Chaplin*

Lehto, Pekka
Finnish director and producer, a former sound engineer, who began by working in collaboration with director Pirjo Honkasalo.
Their Age (short, co-d) 76. Flame Top/Tulipää (co-d) 80. Da Capo (co-d) 85. The Well (d) 91, etc.

Leiber, Fritz (1883–1949)
American Shakespearean actor who played many supporting roles in films.
A Tale of Two Cities 35. Anthony Adverse 36. The Hunchback of Notre Dame 40. Phantom of the Opera 43. Humoresque 46. Another Part of the Forest 48, etc.

Leibman, Ron (1937–)
American character actor of the 70s.
The Hot Rock 72. Slaughterhouse Five 72. The Super Cops 73. Your Three Minutes Are Up 74. The Art of Crime (TV) 75. Won Ton Ton 76. A Question of Guilt (TV) 78. Norma Rae 79. Up the Academy 80. Rivkin, Bounty Hunter (TV) 81. Zorro the Gay Blade 81, Romantic Comedy 83. Rhinestone 84. Seven Hours to Judgement 88. Night Falls on Manhattan 96. Don King: Only in America (TV) 97, etc.
TV series: *Kaz* 78.

Leigh, Janet (1927–) (Jeanette Morrison)
Capable American leading lady of the 50s and 60s; began as a peaches-and-cream heroine but graduated to sharper roles. Her third husband was Tony CURTIS (1951–62). She is the mother of actress Jamie Lee CURTIS.
■ The Romance of Rosy Ridge 47. If Winter Comes 47. Hills of Home 47. Words and Music 48. Act of Violence 48. Little Women 49. *That Forsyte Woman* 49. The Doctor and the Girl 49. The Red Danube 49. Holiday Affair 49. Strictly Dishonourable 51. Angels in the Outfield 51. Two Tickets to Broadway 51. It's a Big Country 51. Just This Once 52. Scaramouche 52. Fearless Fagan 52. The Naked Spur 53. Confidentially Connie 53. *Houdini* 53. Walking My Baby Back Home 54. Prince Valiant 54. Living It Up 54. The Black Shield of Falworth 54. Rogue Cop 54. Pete Kelly's Blues 55. My *Sister Eileen* 55. Safari (GB) 56. Jet Pilot 57. Touch of Evil 58. The Vikings 58. The Perfect Furlough 58. Who Was That Lady? 60. *Psycho* (AAN) 60. Pepe 60. The Manchurian Candidate 62. Bye Bye Birdie 62. Wives and Lovers 63. Three on a Couch 66. Harper 66. Kid Rodelo 66. An American Dream 66. Hello Down There 68. The Spy in the Green Hat 68. Grand Slam 68. Honeymoon with a Stranger (TV) 69. The House on Greenapple Road (TV) 70. The Monk (TV) 70. The Deadly Dream (TV) 71. One Is a Lonely Number 72. Night of the Lepus 72. Murdock's Gang (TV) 73. Murder at the World Series (TV) 77. Telethon (TV) 77. Boardwalk 79. The Fog 80. The Thrill of Genius 85. Halloween: H20 98.

Leigh, Jennifer Jason (1962–)
American actress, the daughter of actor Vic MORROW.
Eyes of a Stranger 80. The Best Little Girl in the World (TV) 81. The Killing of Randy Webster 81. Fast Times at Ridgemont High 82. Wrong Is Right 82. Death Ride to Osaka (TV) 83. Easy Money 83. Just Like Us (TV) 83. Grandview USA 84. Flesh and Blood 85. The Hitcher 86. The Men's Club 86. Sister, Sister 87. Heart of Midnight 88. The Big Picture 88. Last Exit to Brooklyn 89. Miami Blues 90. Crooked Hearts 91. Backdraft 91. Rush 92. Single White Female 92. Short Cuts 93. The Hudsucker Proxy 94. Mrs Parker and the Vicious Circle (as Dorothy Parker) 94. Dolores Claiborne 95. Georgia 95. Kansas City 96. Bastard out of Carolina 96. Washington Square 97. A Thousand Acres 97. eXistenZ 99. Skipped Parts 00, etc.

Leigh, Mike (1943–)
British director and screenwriter, also active in theatre and TV as a writer-director noted for creating scripts out of sessions of improvisation

with his actors. He trained at RADA and was an assistant director with the Royal Shakespeare Company 1967–68. Formerly married to actress Alison STEADMAN.

Bleak Moments 71. High Hopes 88. Life Is Sweet 90. Naked 93. *Secrets and Lies* (AANw, AANd) 95. Career Girls 97. *Topsy-Turvy* (AANw) 99, etc.

❝ Given the choice of Hollywood or poking steel pins into my eyes, I'd prefer steel pins. – *M.L.*

Leigh, Suzanna (1945–)
British leading lady.

Boeing Boeing 66. Paradise Hawaiian Style 66. Deadlier Than the Male 67. Lost Continent 68. Lust for a Vampire 70. The Fiend 71, etc.

Leigh, Vivien (1913–1967) (Vivian Hartley)
Distinguished British leading lady whose stage and screen career was limited by delicate health; for many years the wife of Laurence Olivier.

Biography: 1973, *Light of a Star* by Gwen Robyns. 1977, *Vivien Leigh* by Anne Edwards. 1987, *Vivien* by Alexander Walker.

■ Things Are Looking Up 34. The Village Squire 35. Gentleman's Agreement 35. Look Up and Laugh 35. Fire Over England 36. *Dark Journey* 37. Storm in a Teacup 37. St Martin's Lane 38. Twenty-One Days 38. *A Yank at Oxford* 38. *Gone with the Wind* (AA: as Scarlett O'Hara) (US) 39. Waterloo Bridge (US) 40. *Lady Hamilton* (US) 41. *Caesar and Cleopatra* 45. Anna Karenina 48. *A Streetcar Named Desire* (AA) (US) 51. The Deep Blue Sea 55. The Roman Spring of Mrs Stone 61. Ship of Fools (US) 65.

✪ For one performance which made each of her later ones an event to be savoured. *Gone with the Wind.*

Leigh-Hunt, Barbara (1935–)
British character actress.

Frenzy 72. Henry VIII and His Six Wives 72. A Bequest to the Nation 73. O Heavenly Dog 80. Paper Mask 90. Pride and Prejudice (TV) 95. Wives and Daughters (TV) 99, etc.

Leigh-Hunt, Ronald (1916–)
Smooth British supporting actor.

Tiger by the Tail 53. Shadow of a Man 55. A Touch of Larceny 59. Sink the Bismarck 60. Piccadilly Third Stop 61. The Truth about Spring 65. Hostile Witness 67. Le Mans 71. The Omen 76. Frankenstein (TV) 93, many others.

TV series: Sir Lancelot (as King Arthur) 56.

Leighton, Margaret (1922–1976)
Elegant English leading actress, mainly in the theatre. Born in Barnt Green, Worcestershire, she was on stage from the age of 16 and first gained notice acting with the Old Vic Company in the late 40s. Married three times: her second husband was actor Laurence HARVEY (1957–60) and her third Michael WILDING, whom she married in 1960. Her lovers included actor Robert STEPHENS.

■ Bonnie Prince Charlie 47. *The Winslow Boy* 48. Under Capricorn 49. The Astonished Heart 50. The Elusive Pimpernel 50. Calling Bulldog Drummond 51. Home at Seven 52. The Holly and the Ivy 52. The Good Die Young 54. Carrington VC 54. The Teckman Mystery 54. The Constant Husband 55. The Passionate Stranger 57. The Sound and the Fury 58. The Second Man (TV) 59. The Waltz of the Toreadors 62. The Third Secret 63. The Best Man 64. Seven Women 65. The Loved One 65. The Madwoman of Chaillot 69. The Go-Between (AAN) 70. Zee and Co 71. Lady Caroline Lamb 72. Bequest to the Nation 73. Frankenstein: The True Story (TV) 73. From Beyond the Grave 73. Galileo 74. Great Expectations 75. Trial by Combat 76.

Leisen, Mitchell (1898–1972)
American director, a former costume and set designer and art director; his films are mostly romantic trifles, but many have considerable pictorial values. Born in Menominee, Michigan, he studied architecture and commercial art at the Church School of Fine and Applied Arts in Chicago before moving to California. There he began designing costumes for Cecil B. DEMILLE and sets for William DEMILLE before becoming a director at Paramount. His career faltered in the 50s when he worked for other studios on movies that did not engage his attention. He directed some episodes of such TV series as *The Twilight Zone*, *Markham* and *The Girl From U.N.C.L.E.* before retiring. Married opera singer Stella Yeager. His lovers included actress Marguerite DE LA MOTTE, costume designer Natalie Visart and dancer and choreographer Billy Daniels.

Biography: 1972 (revised 1995), *Hollywood Director* by David Chierichetti.

AS COSTUME DESIGNER: Male and Female 19. Robin Hood 22. Rosita 23. The Courtship of Miles Standish 23. The Thief of Bagdad 24. Dorothy Vernon of Haddon Hall 24, etc.

AS ART DIRECTOR: His Dog 27. The Fighting Eagle 27. The Wise Wife 27. The King of Kings 27. Celebrity 28. The Godless Girl 29. The Squaw Man 31. The Sign of the Cross 32, etc.

■ AS DIRECTOR: *Cradle Song* 33. *Death Takes a Holiday* 34. Murder at the Vanities 34. Behold My Wife 35. Four Hours to Kill 35. Hands across the Table 35. Thirteen Hours by Air 36. The Big Broadcast of 1937. Swing High Swing Low 37. *Easy Living* 37. The Big Broadcast of 1938 37. Artists and Models Abroad 38. *Midnight* 39. Remember the Night 40. *Arise My Love* 40. I Wanted Wings 41. *Hold Back the Dawn* 41. The Lady Is Willing 42. Take a Letter Darling 42. No Time for Love (& p) 43. *Lady in the Dark* (also co-w) 44. *Frenchman's Creek* 44. Practically Yours (& p) 44. *Kitty* 45. Masquerade in Mexico 45. To Each His Own 46. Suddenly It's Spring 46. Golden Earrings 47. Dream Girl 48. Bride of Vengeance 49. Song of Surrender 49. Captain Carey USA 50. No Man of Her Own (& w) 50. The Mating Season 51. Darling How Could You? 51. Young Man with Ideas 52. Tonight We Sing 53. Bedevilled 55. The Girl Most Likely 57.

✪ For adding style to comedies and dramas that badly needed it. *Kitty.*

❝ The camera never moves arbitrarily in any of my films. It follows somebody across the room or some kind of action; therefore you are not particularly conscious of the camera moving. Unnecessary camera movement destroys the concentration of the audience. – *M. L.*

He found himself in the unenviable position of a diamond cutter working with lumpy coal. – *Andrew Sarris, 1968*

Leiser, Erwin (1923–1996)
Swedish documentarist.

Mein Kampf/Blodige Tiden 59. Murder by Signature/Eichmann and the Third Reich 61. Choose Life 62. Germany Awake 66. Women of the Third World 75. Hans Richter: Artist and Filmmaker 79. Following the Fuhrer 85. Berenice Abbott: American Photographer 92. Everyone Was a 'Pimpf' 93, etc.

Leister, Frederick (1885–1970)
British character actor, on stage from 1906, screen from 20s. Usually played distinguished and kindly professional men.

Dreyfus 30. The Iron Duke 35. Goodbye Mr Chips 39. The Prime Minister 41. *Dear Octopus* 43. *The Hundred Pound Window* 43. The Captive Heart 46. Quartet 48. The End of the Affair 54. Left, Right and Centre 59. A French Mistress 63, many others.

Leitao, Joaquim (1956–)
Portuguese director and screenwriter whose comedy *Adam and Eve* was that country's most successful local film.

One Marginal S/Um S Marginal (a, w) 83. Play … Boy/Uma Vez por Todas (wd) 87. To the Bitter End (Ger./Port.) 89. L'Amour Extreme (Fr./Port.) (wd) 90. Adios Princesa (co-w) 92. *Adam and Eve/Adao e Eva* (wd) 96, etc.

Leitch, Donovan (1968–)
Hollywood-born actor, the son of singer-songwriter DONOVAN and brother of actress Ione SKYE.

The In Crowd 87. And God Created Woman 87. The Blob 89. Glory 89. Gas Food Lodgings 91. Dark Horse 92. I Shot Andy Warhol 96. One Night Stand 97. Love Kills 98, etc.

Leith, Virginia (1932–)
American leading lady of the 50s.

Black Widow 54. Violent Saturday 55. White Feather 55. A Kiss Before Dying 56. On the Threshold of Space 56. The Beast That Wouldn't Die 63. First Love 77, etc.

Lejeune, C. A. (1897–1973)
British film critic whose work now tends to seem blithe but facetious. Collections of reviews were published in 1947 as *Chestnuts in My Lap* and in 1991 as *The C. A. Lejeune Film Reader*.

Leland, David (1947–)
British director and screenwriter, a former actor.

Mona Lisa (w) 86. Personal Services (w) 87. Wish You Were Here (wd) 87. Checking Out (d) 88. The Big Man (d) 90. When Saturday Comes (a) 96. The Land Girls (wd) 97, etc.

Lelouch, Claude (1937–)
French director and screenwriter with lush visual style; internationally fashionable in the mid-60s, but overreached himself.

Le Propre de l'Homme 60. Une Fille et des Fusils 63. Avec des Si 64. Secret Paris 64. *Un Homme et une Femme* (AAw, AANd) 66. *Vivre pour Vivre* 67. Challenge in the Snow 68. Far from Vietnam 69. A Man I Like 69. Life Love Death 69. Le Rose et le Noir 70. The Crook 71. Smic, Smac, Smoc 71. Adventure Is Adventure 72. *La Bonne Année* 73. And Now My Love (AANw) 75. Seven Suspects for Murder 77. Another Man, Another Chance 77. The Good and the Bad 77. A Nous Deux 79. Les Uns et les Autres 80. Edith and Marcel 83. Long Live Life 84. Departure, Return 85. A Man and a Woman: 20 Years Later 86. Attention Bandits 87. Itinéraire d'un Enfant Gâté 88. Il y a des Jours et des Lunes 90. The Beautiful Story/La Belle Histoire 92. Tout ça … pour ça 93. Les Misérables du XXème Siècle 95. Hommes, Femmes: Mode d'Emploi 96. Luck or Coincidence/Hasards ou Coincidences (p, wd) 98. One 4 All/Une Pour Toutes (co-w,p,d,ph) 99, etc.

❝ Film-making is like spermatozoa: only one in a million makes it. – *C.L.*

One day I'll make a film for the critics, when I have money to lose. – *C.L.*

Lelouch, Salomé (1984–)
French child actress, the daughter of director Claude LELOUCH and actress Evelyne Bouix.

When I Was Five I Killed Myself 94. Les Misérables 95, etc.

LeMaire, Charles (1897–1985)
American costume designer. Born in Chicago, Illinois, he worked in vaudeville as an actor before designing for the theatre and beginning his own couture business. In the early 40s he ran the wardrobe department at Twentieth Century-Fox, often working in collaboration with other designers, including Edith HEAD and Mary WILLS.

Boomerang! 47. The Ghost and Mrs Muir 47. All about Eve (AA) 50. The Model and the Marriage Broker (AAN) 51. David and Bathsheba (AAN) 51. My Cousin Rachel (AAN) 52. With a Song in My Heart (AAN) 52. The President's Lady (AAN) 53. The Robe (AA) 53. Gentlemen Prefer Blondes 53. How to Marry a Millionaire (AAN) 53. Desiree (AAN) 54. There's No Business Like Showbusiness (AAN) 54. Love Is a Many Splendored Thing (AA) 55. Teenage Rebel (AAN) 56. An Affair to Remember (AAN) 57. Forty Guns 57. A Certain Smile (AAN) 58. The Young Lions 58. The Diary of Anne Frank (AAN) 59. The Marriage-Go-Round 60. Walk on the Wild Side 62, etc.

Lembeck, Harvey (1925–1982)
American character actor, born in Brooklyn, New York, and best known for playing Corporal Rocco Barbella in *The Phil Silvers Show*. Died of a heart attack. His son Michael Lembeck (1948–) is also an actor.

The Frogmen 51. You're In the Navy Now 53. Back at the Front 53. Stalag 17 54. Life after Dark 55. Sail a Crooked Ship 62. Bikini Beach 65. There is No Thirteen 77, etc.

TV series: The Phil Silvers Show 55–59. The Hathaways 61–62. Ensign O'Toole 62–63.

Lemmon, Chris (1954–)
American actor, the son of Jack LEMMON.

Just before Dawn 80. C.O.D. 83. Swing Shift 84. Weekend Warriors 86. That's Life! 86. Going Undercover 88. Dad 89. Firehead 90. Lena's Holiday 90. Corporate Affairs 90. Lena's Holiday 91. Land of the Free 97. Wishmaster 97, etc.

TV series: Brothers and Sisters 79. Knots Landing 90. Thunder in Paradise 94.

Lemmon, Jack (1925–)
American light comedy leading actor with Broadway experience; sometimes typed in mildly lecherous or otherwise sex-fraught roles.

Biography: 1975, *Lemmon* by Don Widener. 1977, *The Films of Jack Lemmon* by Joe Baltake.

It Should Happen to You 53. Three for the Show 53. Phffft 54. My Sister Eileen 55. *Mister Roberts* (AA) 55. You Can't Run Away from It 56. Cowboy 57. Fire Down Below 57. Operation Mad Ball 57. Bell, Book and Candle 58. It Happened to Jane 58. *Some Like It Hot* (AAN) 59. The Wackiest Ship in the Army 60. *The Apartment* (AAN) 60. The Notorious Landlady 62. Days of Wine and Roses (AAN) 62. *Irma la Douce* 63. Under the Yum Yum Tree 64. Good Neighbour Sam 64. How to Murder Your Wife 65. *The Great Race* 65. The Fortune Cookie 66. Luv 67. *The Odd Couple* 68. The April Fools 69. The Out-of-Towners 69. *Kotch* (d only) 71. The War between Men and Women 72. Avanti 72. Save the Tiger (AA) 73. The Front Page 74. The Prisoner of Second Avenue 75. The Entertainer 75. Alex and the Gypsy 76. Airport 77 77. *The China Syndrome* (AAN, BFA) 79. Tribute (AAN) 80. Buddy Buddy 81. *Missing* (AAN) 82. Mass Appeal 84. Macaroni 85. That's Life! 86. Dad 89. JFK 91. Glengarry Glen Ross 92. Short Cuts 93. A Life in the Theatre 93. Grumpy Old Men 93. The Grass Harp 95. Grumpier Old Men 95. Getting Away with Murder 96. My Fellow Americans 96. The Odd Couple II 98. The Legend of Bagger Vance 00, etc.

TV series: That Wonderful Guy 49–50. Heaven for Betsy 52. Alcoa Theatre 57–58.

❝ The worst part about being me is when people want me to make them laugh. – *J.L.*

Every time when I said, 'Action', Jack would mutter under his breath, 'Magic time', as a little mantra to himself. – *Kenneth Branagh*

Famous line (*Mister Roberts*) 'Now, what's all this crud about no movie tonight?'

Lemont, John (1914–)
British director.

The Green Buddha 54. And Women Shall Weep (& co-w) 59. The Shakedown (& co-w) 59. Konga 60. Frightened City (& co-w) 61. Deep Waters (p) 78. A Horse Called Jester (p) 79, etc.

Lemper, Ute (1963–)
German actress and singer, noted for her interpretations of the songs of Kurt Weill.

L'Autrichienne 89. Prospero's Books 91. Prêt-à-Porter/Ready to Wear 94. Bogus 96. Wild Games/Combat de Fauves 97, etc.

Leni, Paul (1885–1929)
German director, former set designer; died in Hollywood.

Waxworks 24. *The Cat and the Canary* 27. The Man Who Laughs 28. The Chinese Parrot 28. The Last Warning 29, etc.

Lenica, Jan (1928–)
Polish animator.

Dom 58. Monsieur Tete 59. Janko the Musician 60. Rhinoceros 63. A 64. Adam 2 70. Ubu et la Grande Gidouille 87, etc.

Lenin (1870–1924) (Vladimir Ilyich Ulyanov)
Russian statesman, the power behind the Revolution. Little footage of him exists, but he has been played by various actors in such politically-based semi-fictions as *Lenin in October*, *Lenin in 1918* and *Lenin in Poland*. Michael Bryant played him in *Nicholas and Alexandra*; Roger Sloman in *Reds*; while Ben Kingsley played him in the TV film *The Train*.

Lennart, Isobel (1915–1971)
American screenwriter.

Lost Angel 44. Anchors Aweigh 45. East Side West Side 49. Skirts Ahoy 52. Latin Lovers 54. Love Me or Leave Me (AAN) 55. Inn of the Sixth Happiness 58. The Sundowners (AAN) 60. Period of Adjustment 62. Funny Girl 68, many others.

Lenoir, Denis
French cinematographer.

Monsieur Hire 89. Daddy Nostalgie 90. Decadence 93. Cold Water/L'Eau Froide 94. Carrington (GB) 95. Joseph Conrad's Secret Agent (GB) 96. Thursday (US) 98. Early September/Fin Août, Debut Septembre 98, etc.

Lenska, Rula (1947–)
Polish born, British leading lady, much on TV.

Soft Beds Hard Battles 73. Alfie Darling 75. The Deadly Females 76, etc.

Lenya, Lotte (1899–1981) (Caroline Blamauer)
Austrian character actress; also inimitable singer of her husband Kurt Weill's songs.

Die Dreigroschenoper 31. The Roman Spring of Mrs Stone (AAN) 61. *From Russia with Love* 63. The Appointment 69. Semi-Tough 77, etc.

Lenz, Kay (1953–)
American leading actress, born in Los Angeles, California. Married actor and singer David Cassidy (1977–81).
Breezy 73. Lisa Bright and Dark (TV) 73. White Line Fever 75. The Great Scout and Cathouse Thursday 76. Rich Man Poor Man (TV) 76. The Passage 79. House 86. Death Wish IV: The Crackdown 87. Stripped to Kill 87. Smoke 88. Physical Evidence 89. Headhunter 90. Souvenirs 91. Falling from Grace 92. Trapped in Space 94. Gunfighter's Moon 96. A Gun, a Car, a Blonde 97, etc.

Lenz, Rick (1939–)
American actor.
Cactus Flower 70. Where Does It Hurt? 72. The Shootist 76. Melvin and Howard 80. Little Dragons 80. Malice in Wonderland (TV) 85. Spooner (TV) 89. Perry Mason: The Case of the Telltale Talk Show Host (TV) 93, etc.
TV series: Hec Ramsey 72–74.

Lenzi, Umberto (1931–)
Italian director of exploitation movies, specializing in macabre thrillers; a former journalist and law graduate.
Pirates of the Seven Seas/Sandokan, la Tigre di Mompracem 63. Messalina vs the Son of Hercules/Gladiatore di Messalina 63. Kriminal 66. Paranoia/Orgasmo 68. Battle of the Commandos/La Brigada de los Condenados 69. A Quiet Place to Kill/Paranoia 70. Sacrifice/Il Paese del Sesso Selvaggio 72. Eyeball/Gatti Rossi in un Labirinto di Vetro 74. Battleforce/Il Grande Attacco 78. From Hell to Victory 79. City of the Walking Dead/Incubo sulla Citta Contaminata 80. Emerald Jungle/Cannibal Ferox 81. The Wild Team 85. Wartime/Tempo di Guerra 86. Ghosthouse/La Casa 3 87. Hell's Gate/Le Porte dell'Inferno (& w) 89. Cop Target 90. Black Demon/Demoni 3 90, etc.

Leon, Valerie (1945–)
British leading lady.
Smashing Time 67. Carry On up the Jungle 70. *Blood from the Mummy's Tomb* 71. Carry On Matron 72. The Spy Who Loved Me 77. Revenge of the Pink Panther 78, etc.

Leon de Aranoa, Fernando (c. 1968–)
Spanish director and screenwriter.
Los Hombres Siempre Mienten (w) 94. ¡Por fin solos! (w) 94. Familia (wd) 97. Barrio (d) 98, etc.

Leonard, Brett
American director.
The Dead Pit (co-w, d) 89. The Lawnmower Man 92. Hideaway 95. Virtuosity 95, etc.

Leonard, Elmore (1925–)
American western and crime novelist and screenwriter, who also adapts his thrillers into movies.
Hombre 66. Big Bounce 68. The Moonshine War (w) 70. Valdez Is Coming 71. Mr Majestyk 74. Stick 85. 52 Pick-Up 86. The Rosary Murders 87. Cat Chaser 88. Get Shorty (oa) 95. Jackie Brown (from Rum Punch) 97. Pronto (TV) 97. Elmore Leonard's Gold Coast (TV) 97. Last Stand at Saber River (TV) 97. Touch 97. Out of Sight 98, etc.
❝ In my books characters are more important than the plot, but Hollywood movies are based on plot. So when they make movies about the books they become much too theatrical. And Hollywood wants heroes who are major stars. My hero isn't a major star, he's just a guy. The films lose the feeling of the books completely. – *E.L.*
Donald Westlake wrote me a letter and asked: 'Why do you keep hoping to see a good movie made? The books are ours, everything else is virgins thrown in the volcano. Be happy if the check is good.' – *E.L.*

Leonard, Herbert B. (1922–)
American independent TV producer; best-known series include *Rin Tin Tin*, *Circus Boy*, *Naked City*, *Route 66*.

Leonard, Hugh (1926–) (John Keyes Byrne)
Irish playwright and occasional screenwriter.
Broth of a Boy (oa) 58. Interlude (co-w) 68. Great Catherine 68. Percy 71. Our Miss Fred 72. Da (from his play) 88. Widow's Peak 94.

Leonard, Murray (1898–1970)
American burlesque comedian who played small parts in films, notably with Abbott and Costello, who worked up several of his old routines.
Lost in a Harem 44. A Thousand and One Nights 45. Bring Your Smile Along 55, etc.

Leonard, Robert Sean (1969–)
American leading actor.
Bluffing It (TV) 87. My Best Friend Is a Vampire 88. Dead Poets Society 89. Mr & Mrs Bridge 91. Much Ado about Nothing 93. Married to It 93. Swing Kids 93. The Age of Innocence 93. Safe Passage 94. Killer: A Journal of Murder 96. The Boys Next Door (TV) 96. Standoff 97. In the Gloaming (TV) 97. I Love You, I Love You Not 97. The Last Days of Disco 98, etc.

Leonard, Robert Z. (1889–1968)
American director (former actor), in Hollywood from 1915. Showed care but not much imagination.
The Waning Sex 27. The Demi-Bride 27. Adam and Evil 28. Tea for Three 29. The Divorcee (AAN) 30. Susan Lenox 31. *Strange Interval* 32. *Dancing Lady* 33. Peg O' My Heart 33. Outcast Lady 34. *The Great Ziegfeld* (AAN) 36. Piccadilly Jim 37. Escapade 37. *Maytime* 38. The Firefly 38. New Moon (& p) 40. *Pride and Prejudice* 40. Ziegfeld Girl 41. When Ladies Meet (& p) 41. We Were Dancing 42. Stand By for Action 42. The Man from Down Under 43. Marriage Is a Private Affair 44. Weekend at the Waldorf 45. The Secret Heart 46. B.F.'s Daughter 48. The Bride 48. In the Good Old Summertime 49. Nancy Goes to Rio 49. Duchess of Idaho 50. Everything I Have Is Yours 52. The Clown 53. The King's Thief 55. Kelly and Me 56. Beautiful But Dangerous (It.) 56, many others.

Leonard, Sheldon (1907–1997) (Sheldon Bershad)
American character actor who played Runyonesque gangsters for years; finally quit to produce TV series.
Another Thin Man 39. Buy Me That Town 41. Street of Chance 42. *Lucky Jordon* 42. To Have and Have Not 44. Zombies on Broadway 45. Somewhere in the Night 46. Violence 47. The Gangster 47. Take One False Step 49. Behave Yourself 51. *Stop You're Killing Me* 52. Money from Home 54. Guys and Dolls 55. Pocketful of Miracles 61. The Brink's Job 78, many others.
TV series: The Duke 54. Danny Thomas 59–61. Big Eddie 75.

Leone, Sergio (1922–1989)
Italian director who came to the fore internationally via his savage westerns on the American pattern, making a star of Clint Eastwood in the process.
Biography: 1997, *Sergio Leone: The Great Italian Dream of Legendary America* by Oreste de Fornari. 2000, *Sergio Leone: Something to Do with Death* by Christopher Frayling.
The Colossus of Rhodes 61. *A Fistful of Dollars* 64. For a Few Dollars More 65. The Good the Bad and the Ugly 67. *Once upon a Time in the West* 69. A Fistful of Dynamite 72. *Once upon a Time in America* 84, etc.

Leonetti, Matthew F.
American cinematographer.
Mr Billion 77. Breaking Away 79. Raise the Titanic 80. Eyewitness 81. Poltergeist 82. Fast Times at Ridgemont High 82. The Ice Pirates 84. Fast Forward 85. Weird Science 85. Jagged Edge 85. Commando 85. Jumpin' Jack Flash 86. Dragnet 87. Extreme Prejudice 87. Red Heat 88. Johnny Handsome 89. Hard to Kill 90. Another 48 Hrs 90. Dead Again 91. Angels in the Outfield 94. Low Down, Dirty Shame 94. Strange Days 95. Fled 96. Star Trek: First Contact 96. Mortal Kombat: Annihilation 97. Species 2 98. Star Trek: Insurrection 98, etc.

Leoni, Tea (1966–) (Tea Pantleoni)
American actress, best known for her role as photo-journalist Nora Wilde in the TV sitcom *The Naked Truth*. Born in New York, she studied anthropology and psychology at Sarah Lawrence College. Married actor David Duchovny, her second husband, in 1998.
A League of Their Own 92. The Counterfeit Contessa (TV) 94. Wyatt Earp 94. Bad Boys 95. Flirting with Disaster 96. Deep Impact 98. There's No Fish Food in Heaven 98, etc.

TV series: Flying Blind 92. The Naked Truth 95– .

Leontovich, Eugenie (1900–1993)
Russian stage actress in occasional American films. She was formerly married to actor and director Gregory Ratoff.
Four Sons 40. The Men in Her Life 41. Anything Can Happen 52. The World in His Arms 53. Homicidal 61, etc.

Lepage, Robert (1957–)
Canadian director and actor, from the theatre.
Jesus of Montreal (a) 89. Le Confessional (wd) 95. The Polygraph (wd) 96. Nô (co-w, d) 98. Stardom (a) 98, etc.

Lerner, Alan Jay (1918–1986)
American lyricist, screenwriter and producer, at his best in collaboration with Frederick (Fritz) Loewe. Born in New York City, he was sent to school in England before studying at Harvard. He began as a writer for radio shows, then worked with Loewe for 18 years from 1942; their collaboration was renewed in the 70s. Their first hit came in 1947 with *Brigadoon*. His eight wives included actress Nancy Olsen.
Autobiography: 1978, *The Street Where I Live*.
An American in Paris (w) (AA) 51. Brigadoon (w, m in collaboration) 54. Gigi (m) (AA) 58. My Fair Lady (w, m in collaboration) (AA) 64. Camelot (w, m in collaboration) 67. Paint Your Wagon 69. On a Clear Day You Can See Forever (& p) 70. The Little Prince 74, many others.
❝ I have always made it a policy never to judge anyone by his behaviour with money and the opposite sex. – *A.J.L.*

Lerner, Carl (c. 1905–1975)
American editor.
Cry Murder 50. On the Bowery 56. *Twelve Angry Men* 57. The Fugitive Kind 59. Something Wild 61. All the Way Home 63. The Swimmer 68. The Angel Levine 70. Klute 72, etc.
DIRECTED: Black Like Me 64.

Lerner, Irving (1909–1976)
American director, former cameraman and documentarist.
■ Muscle Beach 46. Man Crazy 54. Edge of Fury 58. *Murder by Contract* 58. City of Fear 59. Studs Lonigan 60. Cry of Battle 63. The Royal Hunt of the Sun 69.

Lerner, Michael (1941–)
American character actor.
Alex in Wonderland 70. The Candidate 72. Busting 74. St Ives 76. Outlaw Blues 77. Borderline 80. Coast to Coast 80. The Baltimore Bullet 80. The Postman Always Rings Twice 81. National Lampoon's Class Reunion 82. Strange Invaders 83. Rita Hayworth: The Love Goddess (as Harry Cohn) 83. Movers and Shakers 84. Vibes 88. Eight Men Out 88. Harlem Nights 89. Maniac Cop 2 90. Omen IV: The Awakening 91. *Barton Fink* (AAN) 91. Newsies/The News Boys 92. Amos & Andrew 93. Blank Check 94. No Escape 94. The Road to Wellville 94. Radioland Murders 94. Girl in the Cadillac 95. A Pyromaniac's Love Story 95. No Way Back 96. For Richer or Poorer (TV) 97. The Beautician and the Beast 97. Godzilla 98. Celebrity 98, etc.
TV series: Love Story 73–74. Starsky and Hutch 75–79. Hart to Hart 79–84. Hollywood Beat 85.

Lesley, Carole (1935–1974) (Maureen Rippingdale)
British leading lady briefly groomed for stardom.
These Dangerous Years 57. Woman in a Dressing-Gown 57. No Trees in the Street 59. Doctor in Love 60. What a Whopper 62. The Pot Carriers 62, etc.

Leslie, Bethel (1929–1999)
American leading actress, mainly on TV. She began on the Broadway stage at the age of 15.
The Rabbit Trap 58. Captain Newman 63. A Rage to Live 65. The Molly Maguires 70. Old Boyfriends 78. Ironweed 87. Terror on Track 9 (TV) 92. Kansas (TV) 95. In Cold Blood (TV) 96. Message in a Bottle 99, etc.
TV series: The Girls 50. The Richard Boone Show 63. The Doctors 66.

Leslie, Joan (1925–) (Joan Brodel)
Pert, pretty American leading lady of the 40s; in vaudeville from childhood. Born in Detroit, Michigan, she began as a singer and dancer with her sisters as The Three Brodels and worked as a model before going to Hollywood.
Camille (debut) 36. Men with Wings 38. Foreign Correspondent 40. High Sierra 41. *Sergeant York* 41. The Male Animal 42. Yankee Doodle Dandy 42. The Hard Way 42. This Is the Army 43. Thank Your Lucky Stars 43. Hollywood Canteen 44. *Rhapsody in Blue* 45. Where Do We Go From Here? 45. Too Young to Know 45. Cinderella Jones 46. Royal Flush 46. Repeat Performance 47. Northwest Stampede 48. Born to Be Bad 51. The Toughest Man in Arizona 52. The Woman They Almost Lynched 53. Jubilee Trail 54. The Revolt of Mamie Stover 57. The Keegans (TV) 76. Charley Hannah (TV) 86. Fire in the Dark (TV) 91, etc.

Lesser, Sol (1890–1980)
American pioneer exhibitor of silent days, later producer: many Tarzan films.
Thunder Over Mexico 33. Our Town 40. Kon-Tiki 52, etc.

Lester, Bruce (1912–) (Bruce Lister)
South African leading man who made some British and American films; now plays support roles.
Death at Broadcasting House 34. Crime over London 37. If I Were King 39. Pride and Prejudice 40. Above Suspicion 43. Golden Earrings 47. King Richard and the Crusaders 54, etc.

Lester, Dick (Richard) (1932–)
American director who found his spurt to fame in Britain doing zany comedies full of fast fragmented action. As soon as commercial backing was available his style went way over the top.
■ It's Trad Dad 61. The Mouse on the Moon 63. *A Hard Day's Night* 64. *The Knack* 65. Help 65. A Funny Thing Happened on the Way to the Forum 66. How I Won the War 67. Petulia 68. The Bed Sitting Room 69. The Three Musketeers 73. Juggernaut 74. The Four Musketeers 75. Royal Flash 75. Robin and Marian 76. The Ritz 76. Butch and Sundance: The Early Days 79. Cuba 79. Superman II 80. Superman III 83. Finders Keepers 84. Return of the Musketeers 89. Get Back (doc) 91.

Lester, Mark (1958–)
Innocent-looking British child star of the 60s. Now an osteopath.
Allez France 64. Spaceflight IC/1 65. Our Mother's House 67. *Oliver* (title role) 68. Run Wild Run Free 69. Eye Witness 70. Melody 71. Black Beauty 71. Night Hair Child 71. Who Slew Auntie Roo? 72. Scalawag 73. Little Adventurer 75. The Prince and the Pauper/Crossed Swords 77, etc.

Lester, Mark L. (1946–)
American director.
Tricia's Wedding 71. Truck Stop Women 74. Bobbie Jo and the Outlaw 75. Stunts 77. Gold of the Amazon Women 77. Roller Boogie 79. Class of 84 82. Firestarter 84. Commando 85. Armed and Dangerous 86. Class of 1999 89. Showdown in Little Tokyo 91. The Fraternity 94. The Ex 96. Double Take 97. Misbegotten 98, etc.

Leterrier, François (1929–)
French director.
Les Mauvais Coups 61. Un Roi sans Divertissement 63. La Chasse Royale 68. Projection Privée 73. Goodbye Emmanuelle 77. The Rat Race 80. The Bodyguard 84. Slice of Life 85. Le Fils du Mekong 91, etc.

Leto, Jared (1972–)
American leading actor, best known for his role as Jordan Catalano in the TV series *My So-Called Life*. Born in Louisiania, he studied painting at the University of Arts in Philadelphia and the School of Visual Arts in New York. He has been romantically linked with actress Cameron Diaz.
How to Make an American Quilt 95. Last of the High Kings 96. Switchback/Going West in America 97. Prefontaine (title role) 97. Summer Fling 98. The Thin Red Line 98. Urban Legend 98. Fight Club 99. Girl, Interrupted 99. Black and White 99. American Psycho 00. Requiem for a Dream 00, etc.

Lettieri, Al (1927–1975)
American character actor. Died of alcoholism.
The Bobo 68. The Godfather 72. Getaway 73. Mr Majestyk 74. Deadly Trackers 75, etc.

Leung, Tony (Tony Leung Kar-fai)
Hong Kong leading actor who found an international audience from the late 80s.
The Last Emperor 88. The Laserman 90. *The Lover*/L'Amant 92. The Legendary La Rose Noire/Hak Muigwai Dui Hak Mauigwai 92. Evening Liaison 95. Love Will Tear Us Apart/Tianshang Renjian (&p) 99, etc.

Leung, Tony (1962–) (Tony Leung Chiu Wai)
Chinese leading actor, best known in the west for his performances in the films of Wong KAR-WAI.
People's Hero 87. Roboforce 89. City of Sadness/Beiqing Chengsi 89. Bullet in the Head 90. Days of Being Wild 91. Chung King Express 94. Cyclo/Xich Lo 95. War of the Underworld 96. Happy Together 97. Chinese Midnight Express 98, many others.

Levant, Brian (1952–)
American director.
Problem Child II 91. Beethoven 92. The Flintstones 94. Jingle All the Way 96.

Levant, Oscar (1906–1972)
American pianist, composer, songwriter, occasional screenwriter and master of insult, who appeared in several films as his grouchy, neurotic self. Born in Pittsburgh, the son of Russian immigrants, he was a child prodigy; in later life his career as the highest-paid concert pianist of his time was limited mainly to playing the work of his friend, George GERSHWIN. He first went to Hollywood to appear in a film of his Broadway success and stayed to provide songs and music for RKO, MGM and Twentieth Century Fox. His self-destructive personality provided the basis for John GARFIELD's star-making performance as Mickey Borden in the film *Four Daughters* 38. Married actresses Barbara Wooddell and June GALE. His lovers included actresses Nancy CARROLL, Virginia CHERRILL, and Jean ARTHUR.
Autobiography: 1944, *A Smattering of Ignorance*. 1965, *Memoirs of an Amnesiac*. 1968, *The Unimportance of Being Oscar*.
Biography: 1994, *A Talent For Genius: The Life and Times of Oscar Levant* by Sam Kashner and Nancy Schoenberger.
■ My Man (songs) 28. Street Girl (songs) 29. Tanned Legs (songs) 29. The Dance of Life (a) 29. Side Street (song) 29. The Delightful Rogue (song) 29. Half Marriage (songs) 29. Jazz Heaven (song) 29. Leathernecking/Present Arms (m) 30. Love Comes Along (songs) 30. Orient Express (co-w) 34. Crime without Passion (m) 34. Black Sheep (song) 35. Steamboat 'Round the Bend (title song) 35. Music is Magic (songs) 35. In Person (songs) 35. Charlie Chan at the Opera (opera selections) 36. Nothing Sacred (songs) 37. Made for Each Other (theme) 38. Rhythm on the River (a) 40. Kiss the Boys Goodbye (a) 41. *Rhapsody in Blue* (a) 45. *Humoresque* (a) 46. You Were Meant for Me (a) 47. Romance on the High Seas (a) 48. The Barkleys of Broadway (a) 49. *An American in Paris* (a) 51. O. Henry's Full House/Full House (a) 52. *The Band Wagon* (a) 53. The I Don't Care Girl (a) 53. *The Cobweb* (a) 55. Funny Lady (song) 75. That's Entertainment Part Two (a) 76.
❝ In some situations I was difficult, in odd moments impossible, in rare moments loathsome, but at my best unapproachably great. – *O.L.*
Strip the phoney tinsel off Hollywood and you'll find the real tinsel underneath. – *O.L.*
I'm a controversial figure. My friends either dislike me or hate me. – *O.L.*
I hate cold showers. They stimulate me, and then I don't know what to do. – *O.L.*
I played an unsympathetic part – myself. – *O.L. on his role in Humoresque*
I envy people who drink. At least they have something to blame everything on. – *O.L. in Humoresque*
It's not a pretty face, but underneath this flabby exterior is an enormous lack of character. – *O.L. of himself in An American in Paris*
There is absolutely nothing wrong with Oscar Levant that a miracle can't fix. – *Alexander Woollcott*
A tortured man who sprayed his loathing on anyone within range. – *Shelley Winters*
Oscar has mellowed – like an old pistol. – *Billy Rose*

Leven, Boris (1900–1986)
Russian-born production designer, long in US. Born in Moscow, he studied architecture at the University of Southern California and began at Paramount as a sketch artist.
Alexander's Ragtime Band (AAN) 38. *The Shanghai Gesture* (AAN) 41. Mr Peabody and the Mermaid 48. Sudden Fear 52. *Giant* (AAN) 56. Anatomy of a Murder 59. *West Side Story* (AA) 61. The Sound of Music (AAN) 65. The Sand Pebbles (AAN) 67. Star! (AAN) 68. The Andromeda Strain (AAN) 70. Jonathan Livingston Seagull 73. Mandingo 75. New York, New York 77. The Last Waltz 78. The King of Comedy 82. Fletch 85. The Color of Money (AAN) 86, many others.

Levene, Sam (1905–1980)
American stage actor, often in Runyonesque film roles.
Three Men on a Horse (debut) 36. Golden Boy 39. The Purple Heart 44. *Crossfire* 47. Boomerang 47. Guilty Bystander 50. Three Sailors and a Girl 53. Sweet Smell of Success 57. Act One 63. A Dream of Kings 69. Such Good Friends 71. Demon 77. Last Embrace 79. And Justice for All 79.

LeVien, Jack (1918–1999)
American documentarist responsible for several distinguished compilation films.
Black Fox 62. The Finest Hours 64. A King's Story 67.
TV series: *The Valiant Years* 60, on Churchill.

Levien, Sonya (1888–1960)
Russian-born writer, in the US from childhood. She studied at New York University and was briefly a lawyer before turning to journalism and fiction, and was story editor at various times for Fox, MGM, and Paramount. Married screenwriter Carl Hovey.
Behind That Curtain 29. Daddy Longlegs 31. Delicious 31. Surrender 31. After Tomorrow 32. Rebecca of Sunnybrook Farm 32. She Wanted a Millionaire 32. Tess of the Storm Country 32. *State Fair* (AAN) 33. *Berkeley Square* 33. The Warrior's Husband 33. As Husbands Go 34. Change of Heart 34. The White Parade 34. Navy Wife 35. Paddy O'Day 35. The Country Doctor 36. Reunion 36. In Old Chicago 37. The Cowboy and the Lady 38. Four Men and a Prayer 38. Kidnapped 38. Drums Along the Mohawk 39. *The Hunchback of Notre Dame* 39. Ziegfeld Girl 41. Rhapsody in Blue 45. The Valley of Decision 45. The Green Years 46. Three Daring Daughters 48. Cass Timberlane 48. The Great Caruso 51. Quo Vadis 51. The Merry Widow 52. The Student Prince 54. Hit the Deck 55. *Interrupted Melody* (AA) 55. Oklahoma! 55. Bhowani Junction 56. *Jeanne Eagels* 57, etc.

Levin, Henry (1909–1980)
American director, in Hollywood from 1943 after stage experience.
Cry of the Werewolf 44. I Love a Mystery 45. The Guilt of Janet Ames 47. The Mating of Millie 48. Jolson Sings Again 49. The Petty Girl 50. Convicted 50. Belles on Their Toes 52. The President's Lady 52. Mister Scoutmaster 53. Gambler from Natchez 54. The Lonely Man 57. Bernardine 57. Let's Be Happy (GB) 57. The Remarkable Mr Pennypacker 58. Holidays for Lovers 59. *Journey to the Centre of the Earth* 59. Where the Boys Are 60. The Wonderful World of the Brothers Grimm 62. Come Fly with Me 63. Honeymoon Hotel 64. Genghis Khan 65. Kiss the Girls and Make Them Die 66. Murderers' Row 67. The Desperados 70. That Man Bolt 73. The Thoroughbreds 77, many others.

Levin, Ira (1929–)
American thriller writer with a sharp edge.
A Kiss before Dying 56. Rosemary's Baby 68. The Stepford Wives 75. The Boys from Brazil 78. Death Trap 82. A Kiss before Dying 91. Sliver 93.

Levin, Meyer (1905–1981)
American author, the original writer of *Compulsion*, which was filmed in 1959.

Levine, Joseph E. (1905–1987)
American production executive and showman, former theatre owner. Formed Embassy Pictures in late 50s, originally to exploit cheap European spectacles; also set up finance for films like *Eight and a Half*, *Divorce Italian Style*, *Boccaccio*.
AS PRODUCER: The Carpetbaggers 63. Where Love Has Gone 64. Harlow 65. A Bridge Too Far 77. Magic 78, etc.
❝ You can fool all the people all the time if the advice is right and the budget is big enough. – *J.E.L.*
When I grew up, we were so poor that you had to go down the hall to the bathroom for a breath of fresh air. – *J.E.L.*
Everyone told me to make family films. So I made eight of them. Even my own family didn't go see them. – *J.E.L.*

Levinson, Barry (1942–)
American director and screenwriter. He began as a comedy writer and stand-up comedian. His first wife was actress and screenwriter Valerie CURTIN.
Autobiography: 1993, *Levinson on Levinson*.
Catholics (TV) 73. First Love 77. And Justice for All (AAN) 80. Inside Moves 81. *Diner* (& d) (AANw) 82. Best Friends 82. The Natural (d only) 84. Young Sherlock Holmes (d only) 85. Tin Men (wd) 87. Good Morning Vietnam (d) 87. *Rain Man* (d) (AA) 88. Avalon (wd, AAN) 90. Bugsy (d) (AAN) 91. Toys (co-w, d) 92. Jimmy Hollywood (wd) 94. Quiz Show (a) 94. Disclosure 94. Sleepers 96. Wag the Dog 97. Home Fries (co-p) 98, etc.

Levring, Kristian
Danish director, one of the signatories to the Dogme 95 manifesto, who has worked mostly on shooting commercials.
Shot from the Heart/Desertoren 86. The King is Alive 00, etc.

Levy, Eugene (1946–)
Canadian-born actor, usually in comic roles; also a director and screenwriter. Born in Hamilton, Ontario, he studied at McMaster University.
Cannibal Girls (a) 72. Running (a) 79. Heavy Metal (voice) 81. Splash! (a) 84. Armed and Dangerous (a) 85. Club Paradise (a) 86. Speed Zone (a) 89. Once Upon a Crime (d) 92. Sodbusters (wd, TV) 94. Multiplicity 96. Waiting for Guffman (co-w, a) 96. American Pie (a) 99. Best in Show (co-w, a) 00. Down to Earth 01, etc.
TV series: Second City TV 77-81. SCTV Network 90 81-83. Hiller and Diller 97-98.

Levy, Jefery (1958–)
American director.
Drive 92. Inside Monkey Zetterland 93. S.F.W. 94.

Levy, Jules (1923–1975)
American independent producer, of Levy-Gardner-Laven. See Arthur Gardner for credits.

Levy, Louis (1893–1957)
British musical director and composer, in films from 1916. Scored *Nanook of the North* 20. With Gaumont and Gainsborough 1928–47, supervising all musical productions.
Jack's the Boy 32. It's a Boy! 33. Falling for You 33. Friday the Thirteenth 33. The Good Companions 33. A Cuckoo in the Nest 33. Man of Aran 34. The Man Who Knew Too Much 34. The Camels Are Coming 34. Chu-Chin-Chow 34. Boys Will Be Boys 35. Bulldog Jack 35. The 39 Steps 35. Rhodes of Africa 36. King Solomon's Mines 37. Pygmalion 38. The Citadel 38. The Lambeth Walk 39. An Englishman's Home 39. The Young Mr Pitt 42. Dear Octopus 43. The Man in Grey 43. Madonna of the Seven Moons 44. Waterloo Road 44. The Wicked Lady 45. Under Capricorn 49. The Hasty Heart 49. Murder without Crime 50. Stage Fright 50. Where's Charley? 52. His Majesty O'Keefe 53. Woman in a Dressing Gown 57, many others.

Levy, Ralph (1919–)
American director, in TV from 1947.
Bedtime Story 64. Do Not Disturb 65.

Lévy, Raoul (1922–1966)
French producer.
Les Orgueilleux 53. And God Created Woman (& w) 56. Heaven Fell That Night 57. En Cas de Malheur 58. Babette Goes to War (& co-w) 59. Moderato Cantabile 60. The Truth 60. The Defector (& wd) 66, etc.

Lewin, Albert (1895–1968)
American writer-producer-director with something of an Omar Khayyam fixation. Production executive 1931–41.
■ *The Moon and Sixpence* (wd) 42. *The Picture of Dorian Gray* (wd) 44. The Private Affairs of Bel Ami (wd, p) 47. *Pandora and the Flying Dutchman* (wd, p) 51. Saadia (wd, p) 54. The Living Idol (wd, p) 57.
❝ A most intriguing little man. He completely checked out of his executive office at MGM every year or so when he wanted a year off to make one of his own pictures. – *James Mason*
Would that there were more room for accident in his clogged literary narrations and his naive conception of refinement in the cinema. – *Andrew Sarris, 1968*

Lewin, Ben (1946–)
Polish-born director, in Australia.
The Dunera Boys (TV) 85. Georgia 89. The Favour, the Watch and the Very Big Fish 91. Lucky Break 94. Paperback Romance (wd) 94, etc.

Lewis, Albert E. (1884–1978)
Polish-American producer and Broadway impresario who was associated with several films.
International House 32. Torch Singer 35. Mutiny on the Bounty 35. Cabin in the Sky 43, etc.

Lewis, Cecil (1898–1997)
English novelist, screenwriter, director and producer, activities that were almost sideshows in a varied, adventurous life. An aviator in the First World War, shooting down six enemy planes, he helped form the Chinese air force in the 1920s, and was also the first deputy director of the BBC, the author of a classic novel of war, *Sagittarius Rising*, a farmer and journalist. He began directing through the efforts of George Bernard Shaw, who stipulated it on the first films made from his plays. In the late 30s, he worked briefly for Paramount as a writer.
Autobiography: 1974, *Never Look Back*. 1993, *All My Yesterdays*.
How He Lied to Her Husband (co-w, d) 30. Carmen/Gipsy Blood (co-w, d) 32. Indiscretions of Eve (wd) 32. Arms and the Man (co-w, d) 32. Leave It to Me (co-w) 33. Café Mascot (oa) 36. Pygmalion (co-w) (AA) 38. Aces High (oa) 77, etc.

Lewis, Charlotte (1967–)
London-born actress, in international and American movies.
Pirates (Fr.) 86. The Golden Child 86. Dial Help (It.) 88. Tripwire 90. Bare Essentials (TV) 91. Storyville 92. Sketch Artist 92. Excessive Force 93. Men of War 94. Red Shoe Diaries 6: How I Met My Husband 95. Embrace of the Vampire 95. Decoy 95. The Glass Cage 96. Navajo Blues 97, etc.
TV series: Broken Badges 90–91.

Lewis, David (1903–1987) (David Levy)
American producer and associate producer, a former theatre actor, story editor, and personal assistant to Irving THALBERG at MGM. He worked at Warner for Hal B. WALLIS before becoming a fully fledged producer. He was also the lover of director James WHALE. Born in Trinidad, Columbia, he was educated at the University of Washington.
Crossfire 33. Where Sinners Meet 34. Camille 36. All This and Heaven Too 40. Kings Row 41. The Sisters 42. Frenchman's Creek 44. The Other Love 47. Arch of Triumph 48. The Seventh Sin 57. Raintree Country 57, etc.

Lewis, Diana (1919–1997)
American leading lady of the late 30s; retired when she married William Powell.
It's a Gift 34. Forty Little Mothers 39. Bitter Sweet 40. Johnny Eager 41. Seven Sweethearts 42. Cry Havoc 43, etc.

Lewis, Fiona (1946–)
British leading lady.
The Fearless Vampire Killers 67. Where's Jack? 69. Villain 71. Dracula (TV) 73. Lisztomania 75. The Fury 78. Strange Invaders 83. Innerspace 87, etc.

Lewis, Gary
Scottish character actor, born in Glasgow.
Shallow Grave 94. Carla's Song 96. Postmortem 97. My Name Is Joe 98. Orphans 99. East is East 99. The Match 99. Gregory's Two Girls 99. Billy Elliot 00, etc.

Lewis, Gena (1888–1979)
American screenwriter.
Sin Town 42. The Climax 44. Cobra Woman 45. Trail Street 49. Lonely Heart Bandits 51, etc.

Lewis, Geoffrey (1935–)
American character actor, often in harassed roles. He is the father of actress Juliette LEWIS.

Culpepper Cattle Company 72. Macon County Line 73. My Name Is Nobody 73. Thunderbolt and Lightfoot 74. The Great Waldo Pepper 75. The Wind and the Lion 75. Lucky Lady 75. Smile 75. Return of a Man Called Horse 76. Every Which Way but Loose 78. Any Which Way You Can 80. Bronco Billy 80. I the Jury 82. 10 to Midnight 83. Lust in the Dust 84. Night of the Comet 84. Out of the Dark 88. Pink Cadillac 89. Fletch Lives 89. Tango & Cash 89. Double Impact 91. The Lawnmower Man 92. Point of No Return 93. Only the Strong 93. The Man without a Face 93. Joshua Tree 93. White Fang II: Myth of the White Wolf 94. Maverick 94. Kansas 95. Rough Riders (TV) 97. American Perfekt 97. Midnight in the Garden of Good and Evil 97. The Way of the Gun 00, etc.

TV series: Flo 80–81. Gun Shy 83. Land's End 95.

Lewis, Herschell Gordon (1926–)
American director of exploitation films.

The Living Venus 61. Goldilocks and the Three Bares 63. Blood Feast 63. Monster a Go Go 65. The Gruesome Twosome 67. A Taste of Blood 67. The Ecstasies of Women 69. The Wizard of Gore 70. Stick It in Your Ear 72. Black Love 72. The Gore-Gore Girls 72, many others.

❝ In my movies I went for intensive rather than extensive gore, and the rationale is quite simple: I didn't have any budget. – *H.G.L.*

Lewis, Jay (1914–1969)
British producer, in films from 1933.

Morning Departure 50. The Gift Horse 52, etc.
AS DIRECTOR: The Baby and the Battleship 55. Invasion Quartet 61. Live Now Pay Later 62. A Home of Your Own 65, etc.

Lewis, Jerry (1926–) (Joseph Levitch)
Goonish American comedian whose style is a mixture of exaggerated mugging and sticky sentiment. Until 1956 he formed a popular partnership with Dean Martin, but his increasingly indulgent solo films since then have gradually reduced his once-fervent band of admirers.

Biography: 1996, *King of Comedy* by Shawn Levy.

My Friend Irma 49. My Friend Irma Goes West 50. At War with the Army 51. That's My Boy 51. Sailor Beware 52. Jumping Jacks 52. The Stooge 53. Scared Stiff 53. The Caddy 53. Money from Home 54. Living It Up 54. Three Ring Circus 54. You're Never Too Young 54. Artists and Models 55. Pardners 56. Hollywood or Bust 56. The Delicate Delinquent 57. The Sad Sack 58. Rock a Bye Baby 58. The Geisha Boy 58. Don't Give up the Ship 59. Visit to a Small Planet 60. *The Bellboy* 60. Cinderfella 60. Ladies' Man 61. The Errand Boy 61. It's Only Money 62. The Nutty Professor 63. Who's Minding the Store? 64. The Patsy 64. The Disorderly Orderly 64. The Family Jewels 65. Boeing-Boeing 65. Three on a Couch 66. Way Way Out 66. The Big Mouth 67. Don't Raise the Bridge, Lower the River 68. Hook Line and Sinker 69. Which Way to the Front? 70. One More Time (d only) 71. Hardly Working (& d) 79. Slapstick of the Fourth Kind 82. King of Comedy 83. Smorgasbord (& co-w, d) 83. Cookie 89. The Arrowtooth Waltz 92. Arizona Dream 92. Funny Bones 95, etc.

Gag appearance: It's a Mad Mad Mad Mad World 63.

❝ When the light goes on in the refrigerator, I do twenty minutes. – *J.L.*

At some point he said to himself, I'm extraordinary, like Chaplin. From then on nobody could tell him anything. He knew it all. – *Dean Martin*

Lewis, Jerry Lee (1935–)
American country-rock singer whose turbulent life was filmed as *Great Balls of Fire* 89, in which he was played by Dennis Quaid.

AS HIMSELF: Jamboree/Disc Jockey Jamboree 57. High School Confidential 58. American Hot Wax 76. Chuck Berry Hail! Hail! Rock 'n' Roll 87, etc.

Lewis, Joe E. (1901–1971) (Joseph Kleevan)
American night-club comedian, played by Frank Sinatra in *The Joker is Wild*

■ Too Many Husbands 31. Private Buckaroo 42. Lady in Cement 69.

Lewis, Joseph H. (1900–2000)
American director, mainly of second features, some of them well above average. Born in New York City, he began working for MGM as a camera assistant in the early 20s, later becoming a film editor with Republic and a second-unit director. He became a director for Universal in 1937 and later worked for Columbia. With the disappearance of second features in the late 50s he worked in TV, directing episodes of such series as *Gunsmoke* and *The Rifleman*.

Courage of the West 37. Two-Fisted Rangers 40. The Mad Doctor of Market Street 41. The Invisible Ghost 41. Pride of the Bowery 41. Bombs over Burma 42. The Mad Doctor of Market Street 42. Minstrel Man 44. The Falcon in San Francisco 45. *My Name Is Julia Ross* 45. *So Dark the Night* 46. *The Jolson Story* (musical numbers only) 46. The Swordsman 47. The Return of October 48. *Gun Crazy* 49. *The Undercover Man* 49. A Lady without Passport 50.Retreat, Hell! 52. Cry of the Hunted 53. The Big Combo 55. A Lawless Street 55. Seventh Cavalry 56. The Halliday Brand 56. *Terror in a Texas Town* 58, etc.

Lewis, Juliette (1973–)
American leading actress. She is the daughter of actor Geoffrey LEWIS.

My Stepmother Is an Alien 88. Life on the Edge 89. National Lampoon's Christmas Vacation 89. Cape Fear (AAN) 91. Crooked Hearts 91. Husbands and Wives 92. That Night 92. Kalifornia 93. Romeo Is Bleeding 93. What's Eating Gilbert Grape? 93. Natural Born Killers 94. Strange Days 95. Mixed Nuts 95. The Basketball Diaries 95. From Dusk till Dawn 95. The Evening Star 96. The Other Sister 99. Room to Rent (GB) 00. The Way of the Gun 00, etc.

TV series: Home Fires 87. I Married Dora 87–88. A Family for Joe 90.

Lewis, Michael J. (1939–)
British composer.

The Madwoman of Chaillot 69. The Man Who Haunted Himself 70. Unman Wittering and Zigo 72. Theatre of Blood 73. 11 Harrowhouse 74. Russian Roulette 75. The Medusa Touch 78. The Stick Up/Mud 78. The Passage 79. The Legacy 79. North Seas Hijack/ffolkes 80. The Unseen 81. Sphinx 81. Yes, Giorgio 82. The Naked Face 85. The Rose and the Jackal (TV) 90, etc.

Lewis, Ralph (1872–1937)
American character actor, often in villainous roles, in films from 1912. He played the abolitionist senator Austin Stoneman in *The Birth of a Nation* 15.

The Escape 14. Intolerance 16. Eyes of Youth 19. Flesh and Blood 22. Desire 23. Dante's Inferno 24. Casey Jones 27. The Girl in the Glass Cage 29. Abraham Lincoln 30. Riot Squad 33. Mystery Liner 34. Behind the Green Light 35, etc.

Lewis, Richard (1947–)
American stand-up comedian, and actor.

Diary of a Young Comic (& co-w) (TV) 79. The Wrong Guys 88. That's Adequate 90. Once upon a Crime 92. Robin Hood: Men in Tights 93. Wagons East! 94. Leaving Las Vegas 95. Danger of Love (TV) 95. A Weekend in the Country (TV) 96. Drunks 96. Hugo Pool 97, etc.

TV series: Harry 87. Anything but Love 89–91. Rude Awakening 98– .

Lewis, Robert (1909–1997)
American theatre director, teacher and occasional actor. He was a founding member of the GROUP THEATER of the 30s, and co-founder of the ACTORS' STUDIO, leaving after a disagreement with Elia KAZAN in 1948 to continue his career elsewhere as a director and teacher. Born in Brooklyn, he was educated at the Juilliard School, working in Hollywood as an actor in the 40s.

AS ACTOR: Paris after Dark 43. Tonight We Raid Calais 43. Dragon Seed 44. The Hidden Eye 45. Son of Lassie 45. Ziegfeld Follies 46. Monsieur Verdoux 47. The Lost Volcano 50, etc.

Lewis, Ronald (1928–1982)
British leading man, in films from 1953. Committed suicide.

The Prisoner 55. Storm over the Nile 55. A Hill in Korea 56. Bachelor of Hearts 59. The Full Treatment 61. Twice Round the Daffodils 62. Mr Sardonicus 62. The Brigand of Kandahar 65. Friends 71. Paul and Michelle 74, etc.

Lewis, Sheldon (1868–1958)
American character actor of stage and screen.

The Exploits of Elaine 15. Dr Jekyll and Mr Hyde (title role) 16. Orphans of the Storm 21. The Red Kimono 26. Black Magic 29. The Monster Walks 32. The Cattle Thief (last film) 36, many others.

Lewis, Sinclair (1885–1951)
American novelist. Works filmed include:

Arrowsmith 31. Ann Vickers 33. Babbitt 34. Dodsworth 36. Untamed 40. Cass Timberlane 47. Elmer Gantry 60.

Lewis, Stephen (1936–)
Lugubrious English comic actor and writer, best known as the put-upon Inspector Blake in the TV sitcom *On the Buses*. He also had recurring, occasional roles in the TV sitcoms *Last of the Summer Wine*, *One Foot in the Grave* and *2Point4 Children*. Born in London and a former bricklayer, he began on stage with THEATRE WORKSHOP.

A Prize of Arms 61. Sparrows Can't Sing (& co-w, oa) 62. Negatives 68. Staircase 69. Some Will, Some Won't 70. On the Buses 71. Mutiny on the Buses 72. Holiday on the Buses 73. Adventures of a Taxi Driver 75. Adventures of a Plumber's Mate 78. Personal Services 87, etc.

TV series: On the Buses 69–73. Don't Drink the Water 74–75. Rep 82. The All New Alexei Sayle Show 95. Oh, Doctor Beeching! 95–97.

Lewis, Ted (1891–1971) (Theodore Friedman)
American bandleader and entertainer ('Me and My Shadow') who appeared in a few movies.

■ Is Everybody Happy? 28. Show of Shows 29. Here Comes the Band 35. Manhattan Merry Go Round 37. Hold That Ghost 42. Follow the Boys 44.

Lewton, Val (1904–1951) (Vladimir Leventon)
American producer, remembered for a group of low-budget, high quality horror films made for RKO in the 40s.

Under the pseudonym Carlos Keith, Lewton contributed to the screenplays of *The Body Snatchers* and *Bedlam*.

Biography: 1973, *The Reality of Terror* by Joel E. Siegel.

■ *Cat People* 42. I Walked with a Zombie 43. The Leopard Man 43. The Seventh Victim 43. The Ghost Ship 43. Mademoiselle Fifi 44. Curse of the Cat People 44. Youth Runs Wild 44. *The Body Snatcher* 45. Isle of the Dead 45. Bedlam 46. My Own True Love 49. Please Believe Me 50. Apache Drums 51.

Lexy, Edward (1897–1970) (Edward Gerald Little)
British character actor in films from 1936, usually as sergeant-major, police inspector or irascible father.

Farewell Again 37. South Riding 38. Laugh It Off 40. Spare a Copper 40. Piccadilly Incident 46. It's Not Cricket 48. Miss Robin Hood 52. Orders Are Orders 55. The Man Who Wouldn't Talk 58, many others.

Leyton, John (1939–)
British pop singer who transferred to dramatic roles.

The Great Escape 63. Von Ryan's Express 65. Krakatoa 68. Schizo 77. Dangerous Davies – the Last Detective 80, etc.

TV series: Jericho 66.

L'Herbier, Marcel (1888–1979)
French director, an avant-garde leader in silent days.

Autobiography: 1979, *La Tête Qui Tourne*.

Rose France 19. Eldorado 22. The Late Mathias Pascal 25. L'Epervier 33. Nuits de Feu 37. La Nuit Fantastique 42. The Last Days of Pompeii 49. Le Père de Mademoiselle 53, etc.

Lhermitte, Thierry
French leading actor.

L'An 01 72. Next Year If All Goes Well 83. My Best Friend's Girl/La Femme de Mon Pote 83. Les Ripoux 84. Until September (US) 84. Tango 93. L'Honneur de la Tribu 93. Elles N'Oublient Jamais 94. Seven Sundays 94. Un Indien dans la Ville (& co-w) 95. My Woman Is Leaving Me 96. Fallait Pas! 96. Comme des Rois 97. An American Werewolf in Paris 97. Marquise (as Louis XIV) 97, etc.

Lhomme, Pierre (1930–)
French cinematographer.

St Tropez Blues 60. A Matter of Resistance/La Vie de Château 66. King of Hearts/Le Roi de Coeur 66. La Chamade 68. Mister Freedom 69. Four Nights of a Dreamer/Quatre Nuits d'un Rêveur 71. Sweet Movie 74. The Savage State/ L'Etat Sauvage 78. Quartet 81. My Little Girl 87. Maurice 87. *Cyrano de Bergerac* 90. Voyager 91. Premier Amour 92. Summer Strolls/Promenades d'Eté 92. Toxic Affair 93. Dieu que les Femmes Sont Amoureuses 94. Jefferson in Paris 95. My Man 96. Stolen Life/Voleur de Vie 98, etc.

Li, Bruce (Ho Chung Tao, aka Li Shaolung)
Taiwanese-born star of kung fu movies and occasional director, one of the many who attempted to take the place of Bruce Lee. Retired in the mid-80s to teach martial arts.

Return of the Tiger 73. Dragon Dies Hard 76. Exit the Dragon Enter the Tiger 76. Fists of Fury 2 76. Enter the Panther 79. Bruce Li the Invincible 80. Enter Three Dragons 81. Story of the Dragon/ Bruce Lee's Secret 82. Iron Dragon Strikes Back 84. Counter Attack (& d) 84. Chinese Connection 2 84. Kung Fu Avengers 85, etc.

Li, Gong (1966–)
Leading Chinese actress and drama teacher, closely associated with the work of director Zhang Yimou. In 1994, the Chinese government told her that she could no longer attend festivals in the West or give interviews to foreign journalists.

Red Sorghum/Hong Gaoliang 87. Ju Dou 90. The Terra-Cotta Warrior 90. *Raise the Red Lantern/ Dahong Denglong Gaogao Gua* 91. *The Story of Qui Ju* 92. Mary from Beijing/Mungsing Sifan 93. Farewell My Concubine/Bawang Bie Ji 93. To Live 94. The Great Conqueror's Concubine/Xi Chu Bawang 94. La Peintre/Hua Hun 94. Shanghai Triad 95. Temptress Moon 96, etc.

Li, Jet (1963–) (Li Lian Jie)
Chinese star of martial arts movies, and occasional director and producer. Born in Beijing, he was Chinese Wu Shu (a form of martial arts) champion from 1974 to 1979. He moved to America for a time before settling in Hong Kong in the early 90s.

Shaolin Temple 82. Shaolin Temple 2: Kids from Shaolin 84. Born to Defence (& d) 86. Martial Arts of Shaolin 86. *Once Upon a Time in China* 90. Once Upon a Time in China 2 91. The Master 92. Shaolin Cult Master 93. Once Upon a Time in China 3: Dance of the Lion King 93. Fong Sai Yuk 93. Fong Sai Yuk II 93. Last Hero in China/Wong Fei-Hung Tsi Titgai Dau Nggung 93. Fist of Legend 94. My Father Is a Hero 95. High Risk 95. The New Legend of Shaolin (& p) 95. Black Mask 96. Once Upon a Time in China & America 97. Lethal Weapon 4 (US) 98. Kiss of the Dragon 01, etc.

Liberace (1919–1987) (Wladziu Valentino Liberace)
American pianist-showman of stage, nightclubs and TV. Starred in his only major appearance, *Sincerely Yours* 55; also seen as a pianist in *East of Java* 49 and as a coffin salesman in *The Loved One* 65. Died of AIDS.

Autobiography: 1977, *The Things I Love*.

❝ You know that bank I used to cry all the way to? I bought it. – *L.*

Of course, I couldn't go out in the street in clothes like this, I'd get picked up. Come to think of it, it might be fun. – *L.*

Gee, you've been such a wonderful audience that I don't like to take your money. But I will! – *L.*

Some day that boy may take my place. – *Paderewski, on hearing the seven-year-old Liberace play*

This deadly, winking, sniggering, snuggling, chromium-plated, scent-impregnated, luminous, quivering, giggling, fruit-flavoured, mincing, ice-covered heap of mother-love. – *Cassandra (William Connor), Daily Mirror*

Licht, Daniel
Composer

Bad Moon 96.

Licudi, Gabriella (1943–)
Italian leading lady in international films.

The Liquidators 65. The Jokers 66. Casino Royale 66. The Last Safari 67. Soft Beds, Hard Battles 73, many others.

Lieven, Albert (1906–1971)
German actor in films from 1933, including many British productions. Married actress Valerie White.
Victoria the Great 37. Night Train to Munich 40. *Jeannie* 40. Yellow Canary 43. *The Seventh Veil* 45. *Beware of Pity* 46. Frieda 47. *Sleeping Car to Trieste* 48. Hotel Sahara 50. Conspiracy of Hearts 60. Foxhole in Cairo 61. The Victors 63. Traitor's Gate 65, many others.

Lightner, Winnie (1901–1971) (Winifred Hanson)
American vaudeville comedienne who appeared in several early talkies.
Gold Diggers of Broadway 30. Playgirl 32. Dancing Lady 32. I'll Fix It 34, etc.

Lillie, Beatrice (1898–1989) (Constance Sylvia Munston, later Lady Peel)
Sharp-faced, mischievous British revue star of the 20s and 30s who graced only a few films with her wit. Born in Toronto, she moved to England in her early teens and was appearing in musical hall from the age of 16.
Autobiography: 1973, *Every Other Inch a Lady*.
■ *Exit Smiling* 26. Show of Shows 29. Are You There? 30. Dr Rhythm 38. *On Approval* 43. Around the World in Eighty Days 56. Thoroughly Modern Millie 67.

Lima Jnr, Walter (1938–)
Brazilian director, a former journalist, who also worked as assistant to Glauber Rocha.
Menino do Engenho 65. Brasil, Anno 2000 69. Taim 77. Xico Rei 82. Dolphin 87. The Oyster and the Wind 97, etc.

Liman, Doug (c. 1967–)
American director and cinematographer. Born in New York, the son of a lawyer and of a writer and artist, he studied at Brown University and at the International Centre for Photography.
Getting In 93. Swingers 96. Go 99, etc.

Lincoln, Abbey (1930–) (Anna Marie Woolridge)
American character actress.
The Girl Can't Help It 56. Nothing but a Man 64. For Love of Ivy 68. Mo' Better Blues 90, etc.

Lincoln, Abraham (1809–1865)
Sixteenth American president, a familiar screen figure with his stovepipe hat, bushy whiskers, and his assassination during a performance of *Our American Cousin*. More or less full-length screen portraits include *Abraham Lincoln's Clemency* 10; *Lincoln the Lover* 13; Joseph Henabery in *Birth of a Nation* 14; Frank McGlynn in *The Life of Abraham Lincoln* 15; George A. Billings in *Abraham Lincoln* 25; Walter Huston in *Abraham Lincoln* 30; John Carradine in *Of Human Hearts* 38; Henry Fonda in *Young Mr Lincoln* 39; Raymond Massey in *Abe Lincoln in Illinois* 39.

Lincoln, Caryl (1908–1983)
American actress. Born in Oakland, California, she was a dancer from childhood and later a model. In films from 1926, she spent much of her career in Westerns. Married actor Byron Stevens.
Wolf Fangs 27. Wild West Romance 28. The Cyclone King 31. The Man from New Mexico 32. Man of Action 33. War of the Range 33, etc.

Lincoln, Elmo (1889–1952) (Otto Elmo Linkenhelter)
American silent actor who became famous as the first *Tarzan of the Apes* 18, and played small roles up to his death.
Birth of a Nation 14. Elmo the Mighty 19, etc.

Linda, Boguslaw (1952–)
Polish leading actor, who also directed one film.
No Trespassing/Droga Powrotna 72. Wierne Blizny 81. Man of Iron/Czlowiek z Zelaza 81. Shivers/Dreszcze 81. Danton/L'Affaire Danton 82. The Mother of Kings/Matka Krolow 82 (released 87). Lost Illusions/Elveszett Illuziok 83. Funeral Ceremony/Ceremonia Pogrzebowa 84. Cheap Money/Tanie Pieniadze 85. The Right Man for a Delicate Job/Megfelelö Ember Kényes Feladatra 85. Maskarada 86. Blind Chance/Przypadek 87. Suspended/W Zawieszeniu 87. Zabij Kill Me, Cop/ Mnie, Glino 87. The Road Home/Cienie 88. Potyautasok/Stowaways 89. En Verden Til Forskel/ A World of Difference 89. Seszele/Seychelles (d) 90. Jancio Wodnik/Johnnie the Aquarius 93. All the Most Important/Wszystko, Co Najwazniejsze 93. The Stranger Must Fly/Obcy Musi Fruwac 94. A Time for Witches/Pora na Czarownice 94. Psy 2/ Ostatnia Krew 94. Szamanka 96, etc.

Lindblom, Gunnel (1935–)
Leading Swedish actress who became a director and screenwriter from the 70s.
The Seventh Seal 56. Wild Strawberries 57. The Virgin Spring 60. Winter Light 62. *The Silence* 63. Rapture 65. Loving Couples 66. Sult 67. Flickorna 68. The Father 69. Brother Carl 71. Scenes from a Marriage 74. Summer Paradise/Paradistorg (wd) 77. Bomsalva 78. Sally Och Friheten (d) 81. Bakom Jalusin 84. Summer Nights/Sommarkvallar (wd) 87, etc.

Linden, Eric (1909–1994)
Swedish-American juvenile lead of the 30s. Disliked Hollywood and quit acting in the early 40s.
Are These Our Children? 32. The Silver Cord 33. Girl of the Limberlost 34. The Voice of Bugle Ann 36. Gone with the Wind 39. Criminals Within 41, etc.

Linden, Hal (1931–) (Harold Lipshitz)
American character actor, best known as TV's *Barney Miller*.
When You Comin' Back, Red Ryder? 79. Father Figure (TV) 80. My Wicked, Wicked Ways: The Legend of Errol Flynn (TV) 85. A New Life 88. The Colony 95. Out to Sea 97. Killers in the House (TV) 98, etc.
TV series: Jack's Place 92. The Boys Are Back 94.

Linden, Jennie (1939–)
British leading actress.
Nightmare 63. Dr Who and the Daleks 66. *Women in Love* 69. A Severed Head 70. Hedda 75. Valentino 77. Charlie Muffin 79, etc.
TV series: Lillie 77.

Linder, Cec (1921–1992)
Canadian character actor, long in British films.
Crack in the Mirror 59. Jetstorm 59. Too Young to Love 60. SOS Pacific 60. Goldfinger 64. Explosion 71. A Touch of Class 73. Sunday in the Country 74. Lost and Found 79. Atlantic City 80, many others.

Linder, Max (1883–1925) (Gabriel Leuvielle)
Dapper French silent comedian, a likely source for Chaplin. Between 1906 and 1925 he scripted and directed most of his own films, from 1917 in Hollywood. Committed suicide, together with his wife.
The Skater's Debut 07. Max Takes a Bath 07. Max and His Mother-in-Law's False Teeth 08. Max's New Landlord 08. Max in a Dilemma 10. Max Is Absent-Minded 10. How Max Went Around the World 11. Max, Victim of Quinquina 11. Max Teaches the Tango 11. Max Is Forced to Work 12. Max Toreador 12. Max Virtuoso 12. Who Killed Max? 13. Max's Hat 14. Max and Jane Make a Dessert 14. Max and the Clutching Hand 15. Max Comes Across 17. Max Wants a Divorce 17. Max and His Taxi 17. The Little Café 19. Seven Years Bad Luck* 20. Be My Wife* 20. The Three Must-Get-Theres* 22. Help! 24. King of the Circus 25, many others.
*These films formed the basis of a compilation, *Laugh with Max Linder*, which was issued in 1963.

Lindfors, Viveca (1920–1995) (Elsa Torstendotter)
Swedish actress, in films from 1941, Hollywood from 1946. She trained at Stockholm's Royal Theatre and gave her best performances on the stage. Married director Don Siegel (1948–53) and writer George Tabori.
Autobiography: 1981, *Viveka ... Viveca*.
To the Victor 47. Night Unto Night 48. The New Adventures of Don Juan 48. No Sad Songs for Me 50. Dark City 50. The Flying Missile 51. Four in a Jeep 51. The Raiders 52. Run for Cover 55. Moonfleet 55. I Accuse 57. Tempest 58. King of Kings 61. Sylvia 65. Brainstorm 65. The Way We Were 73. Welcome to L.A. 77. Girlfriends 78. A Wedding 78. Natural Enemies 79. Voices 79. The Hand 82. Creepshow 82. Silent Madness 83. The Sure Thing 85. Frankenstein's Aunt 86. Unfinished Business (& wd) 87. Rachel River 88. The Ann Jillian Story (TV) 88. Forced March 89. Zandalee 90. Luba 90. Exorcist III 90. Exiled 91. The Linguini Incident 92. Stargate 94. Last Summer in the Hamptons 95, many others.

Lindgren, Lars Magnus (1922–)
Swedish director.
Do You Believe in Angels? 60. Dear John 64. The Coffin/The Sadist 66. The Black Palm Trees 68. The Lion and the Virgin 74, etc.

Lindley, Audra (1913–1997)
American character actress, best known for her role as the lovelorn landlady Helen Roper in *Three's Company* and the spin-off series *The Ropers*.
The Heartbreak Kid 72. Pearl (TV) 79. When You Comin' Back Red Ryder 79. Moviola (TV) 80. Cannery Row 82. Desert Hearts 85. Spellbinder 88. Troop Beverly Hills 89. The New Age 94. Sudden Death 95, etc.
TV series: Bridget Loves Bernie 72–73. Fay 75–76. Doc 76. Three's Company 77–79. The Ropers 79–80.

Lindley, John (1952–)
American cinematographer.
The Goodbye People 84. Lily in Love 85. Killer Party 86. Home of the Brave 86. The Stepfather 87. In the Mood 87. The Serpent and the Rainbow 87. Shakedown/Blue Jean Cop 87. True Believer 89. Field of Dreams 89. Immediate Family 89. Vital Signs 90. Sleeping with the Enemy 91. Sneakers 92. The Good Son 93. I Love Trouble 94. Money Train 95. Michael 96. Pleasantville 98. You've Got Mail 98. Lucky Numbers 00, etc.

Lindo, Delroy (1952–)
London-born actor, of Jamaican parents, in America. He trained at the American Conservatory Theatre in San Francisco.
More American Graffiti 79. The Salute of the Jugger 89. Mountains of the Moon 89. Bright Angel 90. The Hard Way 91. Malcolm X 92. Blood In, Blood Out 93. Mr Jones 94. Crooklyn 94. Clockers 95. Get Shorty 95. Broken Arrow 96. Feeling Minnesota 96. Ransom 96, etc.

Lindo, Olga (1898–1968)
Anglo-Norwegian character actress, on British stage and screen.
The Shadow Between 32. The Last Journey 35. *When We Are Married* 42. Bedelia 46. Train of Events 49. *An Inspector Calls* 54. Woman in a Dressing Gown 57. Sapphire 59, etc.

Lindon, Lionel (1905–1971)
American cinematographer.
Going My Way 44. A Medal for Benny 45. Road to Utopia 46. *Alias Nick Beal* 49. Destination Moon 50. Conquest of Space 55. *Around the World in Eighty Days* (AA) 56. The Lonely Man 57. The Black Scorpion 57. Too Late Blues 61. *The Manchurian Candidate* 62. The Trouble with Angels 66. Boy Did I Get a Wrong Number 66. *Grand Prix* 66. Generation 69, etc.

Lindsay, Howard (1889–1968)
American actor-playwright-stage director. With Russel Crouse wrote *Life with Father and State of the Union*, both filmed. Acted in and directed *Dulcy* 21, co-authored *She's My Weakness* 31.

Lindsay, Margaret (1910–1981) (Margaret Kies)
American leading lady of the 30s, with stage experience; in Hollywood from 1931.
West of Singapore 32. Lady Killer 34. Bordertown 35. G-Men 35. The Green Light 37. Jezebel 38. The House of Seven Gables 40. There's Magic in Music 41. A Close Call for Ellery Queen 42. No Place for a Lady 43. Crime Doctor 43. Alaska 44. Club Havana 45. Scarlet Street 45. Her Sister's Secret 47. Cass Timberlane 47. Emergency Hospital 56. Jet over the Atlantic 59. Tammy and the Doctor 63, many others.

Lindsay, Robert (1949–)
English leading actor, from the stage.
Adventures of a Taxi Driver 75. Bert Rigby, You're a Fool 89. Strike It Rich/Loser Takes All 90. Fierce Creatures 96. Hornblower (TV) 98. Divorcing Jack 98. Oliver Twist (TV) 99, etc.
TV series: Citizen Smith 73–77. Jake's Progess 95. My Family 00.

Lindsay-Hogg, Michael (1940–)
British director and screenwriter. He is the son of actress Geraldine Fitzgerald.
Let It Be 70. Nasty Habits 77. Brideshead Revisited (co-d) (TV) 81. Master Harold and the Boys 84. As Is 86. The Object of Beauty (wd) 91. Frankie Starlight 95. Guy 96. Alone (TV) 97, etc.

Lindtberg, Leopold (1902–1984)
Austrian director, a former actor, who was a theatre director in Germany before moving to Switzerland in the early 40s, after the rise of the Nazis, to become an influential director of film and theatre there.
Jasoo (co-d) 35. Die Missbrauchten Liebesbriefe 40. Marie-Louise 44. The Last Chance/Die Letzte Chance 45. Four in a Jeep/Die Vier im Jeep 51. Daughter of the Storm 54, etc.

Linklater, Richard (1962–)
American actor, director and producer of independent films.
Slacker (a, wd) 91. Dazed and Confused (a, p, co-w) 93. Before Sunrise (co-w, d) 95. SubUrbia 97, etc.
❝ You need age and maturity to make a good film. – *R.L.*

Linn-Baker, Mark (1954–)
American actor.
My Favorite Year 82. Ghostwriter 84. Me and Him/Ich und Er (Ger.) 89. Bare Essentials 91. Noises Off 92, etc.
TV series: Perfect Strangers 86–93.

Linney, Laura (1964–)
American actress, from the theatre. Born in New York, she studied at Brown University, the Juilliard School, and at Moscow's Arts Theater School.
Class of '61 (TV) 92. Lorenzo's Oil 92. Searching for Bobby Fischer/Innocent Moves 93. Tales of the City (TV) 93. Dave 93. A Simple Twist of Fate 94. Congo 95. Primal Fear 96. Absolute Power 97. More Tales of the City (TV) 98. The Truman Show 98. You Can Count On Me (AAN) 00. The House of Mirth 00. Maze 00, etc.

Linson, Art (1942–)
American producer and occasional director. He is the author of *A Pound of Flesh: Perilous Tales of How to Produce Movies in Hollywood*, published in 1994.
Rafferty and the Gold Dust Twins 75. American Hot Wax 78. Melvin and Harold 80. Where the Buffalo Roam (& d) 80. Fast Times at Ridgmount High 82. The Wild Life (& d) 84. The Untouchables 87. Scrooged 88. Casualties of War 89. We're No Angels 89. Dick Tracy 90. Singles 92. Point of No Return 93. This Boy's Life 93, etc.

Linz, Alex D. (1989–)
American child star, born in Santa Barbara, California.
The Cable Guy 96. One Fine Day 96. Home Alone 3 97. Tarzan (voice) 99. Bounce 00, etc.

Liotta, Ray (1955–)
American actor from TV.
The Lonely Lady 83. Something Wild 86. Dominick and Eugene 88. Field of Dreams 89. GoodFellas 90. Article 99 92. Unlawful Entry 92. Judgment Night 93. No Escape 94. Corrina, Corrina 94. Operation Dumbo Drop 95. Unforgettable 96. Turbulence 97. Cop Land 97. The Rat Pack (TV) 98. Muppets from Space (voice) 99. Forever Mine 99, etc.
TV series: Casablanca 83. Our Family Honor 85–86.

Lipman, Jerzy (1922–1983)
Polish cinematographer.
A Generation 54. Kanal 57. The Eighth Day of the Week 58. Lotna 59. Knife in the Water 62. No More Divorces 63. Ashes 65. Zozya 67. Colonel Wolodyjowski 69. Dead Pigeon on Beethoven Street 72. The Martyr 75, etc.

Lipman, Maureen (1946–)
English character actress, often in comic roles. Married to writer Jack Rosenthal.
The Smashing Bird I Used to Know 61. Up the Junction 67. Gumshoe 71. The Wildcats of St Trinian's 80. Educating Rita 83. Water 85. Carry On Columbus 92. Eskimo Day (TV) 96. Captain Jack 98, etc.
TV series: A Soft Touch 78. Agony 79–81. All at Number 20 86.

Lippert, Robert L. (1909–1976)
American exhibitor, latterly head of company making second features for Twentieth Century-

Fox, many of them produced by his son Robert L. Lippert Jnr (1928–).

Lipscomb, W. P. (1887–1958)
British screenwriter who spent some years in Hollywood.
French Leave 27. The Good Companions 32. I Was a Spy 33. Clive of India (co-w) 34. A Tale of Two Cities 35. The Garden of Allah 36. Pygmalion (co-w) 38. A Town Like Alice 56. Dunkirk (co-w) 58, many others.

Lipstadt, Aaron (1952–)
American director.
■ Android 82. City Limits 85. Police Story: Monster Manor (TV) 88. Pair of Aces (TV) 90. The People 97.

Lisi, Virna (1937–) (Virna Pieralisi)
Voluptuous Italian leading lady who after starring in innumerable local spectaculars came on to the international market. She won the best actress award at the Cannes Film Festival for *La Reine Margot*.
The Black Tulip 63. Eva 63. How to Murder Your Wife (US) 65. Casanova 70 65. Signore e Signori 65. Assault on a Queen (US) 66. Not with My Wife You Don't (US) 66. The Girl and the General 67. The Twenty-fifth Hour 67. Arabella 68. The Secret of Santa Vittoria 69. Un Beau Monstre 70. The Statue 71. The Serpent 72. Bluebeard 72. White Fang 74. Challenge to White Fang 75. Cocktails for Three 78. Ernesto 78. La Cicala 80. Miss Right 81. I Love N.Y. 87. Merry Christmas, Happy New Year/Buon Natale, Buon Anno 89. Queen Margot/La Reine Margot 94. Follow Your Heart 96, etc.

Lister, Eve (1913–1997)
English actress and singer, from the musical theatre. Born in Brighton, Sussex, of a theatrical family, and on-stage from childhood, she appeared mainly in musicals in the 30s before returning to the theatre, retiring in the 50s.
■ A Glimpse of Paradise 34. Hyde Park 34. The Girl in the Crowd 34. City of Beautiful Nonsense 35. Cock o' the North 35. Birds of a Feather 35. Sunshine Ahead 36. Sweeney Todd, the Demon Barber of Fleet Street 36. Here and There 36. Servants All 36. Men of Yesterday 36.

Lister, Francis (1899–1951)
Suave British character actor, mainly on stage. Married actress Nora SWINBURNE.
Comin' Thro' the Rye 24. Atlantic 30. Jack's the Boy 32. Clive of India 35. The Return of the Scarlet Pimpernel 37. Henry V 44. The Wicked Lady 45. Home to Danger 51, etc.

Lister, Moira (1923–)
South African leading lady and character actress, in British films.
My Ain Folk 44. Uneasy Terms 48. Another Shore 48. *A Run for Your Money* 49. Grand National Night 53. John and Julie 55. Seven Waves Away 57. The Yellow Rolls-Royce 64. Stranger in the House 67. Ten Little Indians 89, etc.

Litel, John (1895–1972)
American character actor, in films from 1929; often seen as judge, lawyer or stern father.
Marked Woman 37. The Life of Emile Zola 37. Virginia City 40. Men Without Souls 40. They Died with Their Boots On 41. Sealed Lips 41. Boss of Big Town 43. Kiss Tomorrow Goodbye 50. Houseboat 58. A Pocketful of Miracles 61. The Sons of Katie Elder 65, many others.
TV series: My Hero 52.

Lithgow, John (1945–)
American character actor, a semi-star of the 80s. A graduate of Harvard University, he studied for the stage at LAMDA and is also a theatre director. He is best known for the role of Dick Solomons in the TV sitcom *3rd Rock from the Sun*.
Obsession 76. All that Jazz 79. Blow Out 81. The World According to Garp (AAN) 82. Twilight Zone: The Movie 83. Terms of Endearment (AAN) 83. Buckaroo Banzai 84. 2010 84. Santa Claus 84. Footloose 84. Mesmerized 84. The Manhattan Project 86. Bigfoot and the Hendersons 87. Distant Thunder 88. Out Cold 88. Traveling Man (TV) 89. Memphis Belle 90. Ivory Hunters (TV) 90. At Play in the Fields of the Lord 91. L.A. Story 91. Ricochet 91. Raising Cain 92. The Wrong Man 93. Cliffhanger 93. The Pelican Brief 93. A Good Man in Africa 94. Love, Cheat & Steal 94. Princess Caraboo 94. Silent Fall 94. My Brother's Keeper (TV) 95. The Tuskegee Airmen (TV) 95. Redwood Curtain (TV) 95. Hollow Point 96. Homegrown 97. Johnny Skidmarks 98. A Civil Action 98, etc.
TV series: 3rd Rock from the Sun 96– .

Littin, Miguel (1942–)
Chilean film director, a former actor and television director. He went into exile following the overthrow of President Allende to work mainly in Mexico.
El Chacal de Nahueltoro 70. Letters from Marusia/Actas de Marusia (AAN) 75. La Viuda de Montiel 80. Alsino and the Condor/Alsino y el Cóndor 82. Sandino 90. The Shipwrecked/Los Naufragos 94, etc.

Little, Cleavon (1939–1992)
American comedy actor.
What's So Bad About Feeling Good 68. Cotton Comes to Harlem 70. Vanishing Point 71. *Blazing Saddles* 74. Greased Lightning 77. Scavenger Hunt 79. High Risk 81. The Gig 85. Fletch Lives 89. Hearts of Fire 92, etc.
TV series: *Temperatures Rising* 72.

Little, Dwight H.
American director of action and horror movies. He also directed *Ground Zero Texas*, a computer game on CD-ROM which claims to be the first 'interactive movie'.
Lethal/KGB – The Secret War 86. Getting Even 86. Bloodstone 88. Halloween 4: The Return of Michael Myers 88. The Phantom of the Opera 89. Marked for Death 90. Rapid Fire 92. Free Willy 2: The Adventure Home 95. Murder at 1600 97, etc.

Little, Mark
Australian actor and stand-up comedian, more recently working as a television presenter in Britain.
An Indecent Obsession 85. Willis and Burke 86. A Cry in the Dark 88. The Passion and the Glory 89. Golden Braid 90. Nirvana Street Murders 90. Greenkeeping 91. Amnesty International's Big 30 (TV) 91, etc.
TV series: Neighbours 88–91.

Littlefield, Lucien (1895–1960)
American character actor, in Hollywood from 1913 in supporting roles.
The Sheik 22. Miss Pinkerton 32. Ruggles of Red Gap 34. Rose Marie 36. The Great American Broadcast 40. Scared Stiff 44. Susanna Pass 51. Pop Girl 56, etc.

Littlewood, Joan (1914–)
British stage director whose only film to date is *Sparrows Can't Sing* 63. Created London's 'Theatre Workshop', where she staged *Oh, What a Lovely War!*, which was later filmed by Richard Attenborough.
Autobiography: 1994, *Joan's Book*.

Litvak, Anatole (1902–1974)
Russian-born director in Germany and France from 1927, Hollywood from 1937. Married actress Miriam HOPKINS. His lovers included Bette DAVIS and Paulette GODDARD.
■ Dolly Gets Ahead (Ger.) 31. Nie Wieder Liebe (Ger.) 32. Coeur de Lilas (Fr.) 32. Be Mine Tonight (Ger.) 33. Sleeping Car (GB) 33. Cette Vieille Canaille (Fr.) 35. L'Equipage (Fr.) 36. *Mayerling* (Fr.) 36. *The Woman I Love* 37. Tovarich 38. The Amazing Dr Clitterhouse 38. The Sisters 38. Castle on the Hudson 39. *Confessions of a Nazi Spy* 39. All This and Heaven Too 40. *City for Conquest* 40. Out of the Fog 41. Blues in the Night 41. This Above All 42. The Long Night 47. Sorry Wrong Number 48. *The Snake Pit* (AAN) 48. Decision Before Dawn 52. Act of Love 53. The Deep Blue Sea 55. Anastasia 56. The Journey 59. Goodbye Again 61. Five Miles to Midnight 63. The Night of the Generals 67. The Lady in the Car 70.

Liu, Lucy (1968–)
American actress, born in Queens, New York. She studied at the University of Michigan at Ann Arbor and is best known for her role as Ling Woo on the TV series *Ally McBeal*.
Jerry Maguire 96. Flypaper 97. Gridlock'd 97. City of Industry 97. Molly 99. Payback 99. True Crime 99.The Mating Habits of the Earthbound Human 99. Play it to the Bone 99. Shanghai Noon 00. Charlie's Angels 00, etc.
TV series: Ally McBeal 98- .

Livesey, Jack (1901–1961)
British actor, brother of Roger Livesey.
The Wandering Jew 33. The Passing of the Third Floor Back 35. Old Bill and Son 40. The First Gentleman 47. Paul Temple's Triumph 51, etc.

Livesey, Roger (1906–1976)
Husky-voiced, often roguish British character star who divided his time between stage and screen.
■ The Old Curiosity Shop 20. Where the Rainbow Ends 21. The Four Feathers 21. Married Love 23. East Lynne on the Western Front 31. A Veteran of Waterloo 33. A Cuckoo in the Nest 33. Blind Justice 34. The Price of Wisdom 35. Lorna Doone 35. Midshipman Easy 35. *Rembrandt* 36. *The Drum* 38. Keep Smiling 38. Spies of the Air 39. The Rebel Son 39. The Girl in the News 40. 49th Parallel 41. *The Life and Death of Colonel Blimp* 43. *I Know Where I'm Going* 45. *A Matter of Life and Death* 46. *Vice Versa* 47. That Dangerous Age 49. Green Grow the Rushes 50. The Master of Ballantrae 53. The Intimate Stranger 56. The League of Gentlemen 59. The Entertainer 60. No My Darling Daughter 61. Of Human Bondage 64. Moll Flanders 65. Oedipus the King 68. Hamlet 69. Futtock's End 70.

Livesey, Sam (1873–1936)
British actor, father of Jack and Roger LIVESEY.
Young Woodley 30. The Flag Lieutenant 32. The Private Life of Henry VIII 33. Jew Süss 34. Turn of the Tide 36. Dark Journey 37, etc.

Livingston, Jay (1915–) (Jacob Harold Levison)
American composer who, with his partner Ray Evans, was under contract to Paramount 1945–55, turning out a succession of hit songs.
The Stork Club 45. The Cat and the Canary (AAN) 45. Golden Earrings 47. The Paleface (AA for 'Buttons and Bows') 48. My Friend Irma 49. My Friend Irma Goes West 50. Captain Carey (AA for 'Mona Lisa') 50. Fancy Pants 50. The Lemon Drop Kid 51. Aaron Slick from Punkin Crick 51. Son of Paleface 52. Here Come the Girls 53. Red Garters 54. The Man Who Knew Too Much (AA for 'Que Sera, Sera') 56. Tammy and the Bachelor (AAN) 57. Houseboat (AAN) 58. Dear Heart (AAN) 64, etc.
TV series: Bonanza. Mr Ed (themes).

Livingston, Jerry (1909–1987) (Jerome Levinson)
American composer and songwriter, usually in collaboration with lyricist Mack David. In Hollywood from 1949, moving to television in the late 50s. A former bandleader.
Cinderella (AAN) 49. At War with the Army 50. Sailor Beware 51. Jumping Jacks 52. Scared Stiff 53. The Hanging Tree (AAN) 59. Cat Ballou (AAN) 65, etc.

Livingston, Margaret (1895–1984)
American silent-screen leading lady.
Within the Cup 18. Lying Lips 21. Divorce 23. Butterfly 24. Havoc 25. A Trip to Chinatown 26. Married Alive 27. Streets of Shanghai 28. The Last Warning 29. Seven Keys to Baldpate 30. Kiki 31. Call Her Savage 32. Social Register 34, many others.

Livingston, Robert (1908–1988) (Robert Randall)
Tough star of westerns, best known for his role as Stony Brooke, one of the THREE MESQUITEERS, in the popular series of the 30s and 40s. He also played the title role in the serial *The Lone Ranger Rides Again* 38 and was Zorro in *The Bold Caballero* 36.
The Three Mesquiteers 36. The Mounties Are Coming 37. Arson Racket Squad 38. Orphans of the Street 39. Brazil 44. Lake Placid Serenade 44. The Big Bonanza 45. The Undercover Woman 46. Daredevils of the Clouds 48. Riders in the Sky 50. Winning of the West 52. The Naughty Stewardesses 73. Girls for Rent 74, etc.

Livingston, Ron (1970–)
American actor. He has a B.A. in theater studies and English Literature from Yale University.
The Low Life 93. Campfire Tales 96. Swingers 96. That's Life 98. Office Space 99. Body Shots 99. The Big Brass Ring 99. Buying the Cow 00, etc.
TV series: Townies 96. That's Life 98. Band of Brothers 01.

Lizzani, Carlo (1917–)
Italian director.
Caccia Tragica (co-w only) 47. Bitter Rice (co-w only, AAw) 49. Achtung Banditi 51. Ai Margini della Metropoli 54. The Great Wall 58. Hunchback of Rome 60. The Hills Run Red 66. The Violent Four 68. Crazy Joe 73. The Last Days of Mussolini 74. Kleinhoff Hotel 77. Fontamara 80. Nucleo Zero 84. Mamma Ebe 85. Selina 89. Wicked 91. Il Caso Dozier 93. Celluloide 95, etc.

LL Cool J (1968–) (James Todd Smith)
American rap performer and actor. Born in Queens, New York, he made his first record at the age of 16. His professional name is an acronym for 'Ladies Love Cool James'.
The Hard Way 91. Toys 92. The Right to Remain Silent 95. Out of Sync 95. Woo 98. Caught Up 98. Halloween: H20 98. Woo 98. Deep Blue Sea 99. Any Given Sunday 99. In Too Deep 99. Charlie's Angels 00, etc.
TV series: In the House 95.

Llewellyn, Richard (1906–1983) (Vivian Lloyd)
English playwright, screenwriter and best-selling novelist, famous for *How Green Was My Valley*. Born in Hendon, London, of Welsh parentage, he re-invented himself as a Welshman, claiming to have been a former miner and the son of a miner, born in St David's, Dyfed.
Catch as Catch Can/Atlantic Episode (w) 37. Inspector Hornleigh (co-w) 38. Englishmen's Home/Madmen of Europe (co-w) 39. Poison Pen (oa) 39. How Green Was My Valley (oa) 41. None But the Lonely Heart (oa) 44. Noose/The Silk Noose (w,oa) 48. How Green Was My Valley (TV,oa) 76, etc.

Llewelyn, Desmond (1914–1999)
Welsh character actor, best known for playing 'Q' in the James Bond films. Died in a car crash.
They Were Not Divided 50. The Lavender Hill Mob 51. A Night to Remember 55. The Pirates of Blood River 61. Cleopatra 62. Goldfinger 64. Thunderball 65. You Only Live Twice 67. Chitty Chitty Bang Bang 68. On Her Majesty's Secret Service 69. Diamonds Are Forever 71. Live and Let Die 73. The Man with the Golden Gun 74. The Spy Who Loved Me 77. Moonraker 79. The Golden Lady 79. Dr Jekyll and Mr Hyde 80. For Your Eyes Only 81. Octopussy 83. A View to a Kill 85. The Living Daylights 87. Prisoner of Rio 88. GoldenEye 95. Tomorrow Never Dies 97. The World Is Not Enough 99, etc.

Llosa, Luis
Peruvian-born director in Hollywood.
Hour of the Assassin 87. Crime Zone 89. Eight Hundred Leagues down the Amazon 93. Sniper 93. The Specialist 94. Anaconda 97, etc.

Lloyd, Christopher (1938–)
American character actor, often in crazed or comic roles.
One Flew over the Cuckoo's Nest 75. Goin' South 78. The Onion Field 79. The Black Marble 79. The Lady in Red 79. Schizoid 80. The Legend of the Lone Ranger 81. Mr Mom 83. To Be or Not To Be 83. Star Trek III: The Search for Spock 84. The Adventures of Buckaroo Banzai across the Eighth Dimension 84. Miracles 84. Clue 85. Back to the Future 85. Eight Men Out 88. Who Framed Roger Rabbit? 88. Dream Team 89. Back to the Future II 89. Back to the Future III 90. The Addams Family 91. Suburban Commando 91. T Bone 'n' Weasel (TV) 92. Dennis the Menace/Dennis 93. Twenty Bucks 93. Addams Family Values 93. Angels in the Outfield 94. Camp Nowhere 94. The Radioland Murders 94. The Pagemaster 94. Things to Do in Denver When You're Dead 95. Cadillac Ranch 96. Changing Habits 97. The Real Blonde 97. Angels in the Endzone (TV) 98. Convergence 98. My Favorite Martian 99. Alice in Wonderland (TV) 99. Wit 01, etc.
TV series: The Addams Chronicles 76. Taxi 79–83. Avonlea 90.

Lloyd, Doris (1899–1968)
British actress with repertory experience; in Hollywood from the 20s.
Charley's Aunt (as Donna Lucia) 30. Disraeli 30. Tarzan the Ape Man 32. Oliver Twist 33. Clive of India 35. Vigil in the Night 39. Phantom Lady

44. The Secret Life of Walter Mitty 47. A Man Called Peter 55. The Time Machine 60. The Notorious Landlady 62. Rosie 67, etc.

Lloyd, Emily (1970–)
British actress, now working in Hollywood. She is the daughter of actor Roger Lloyd-Pack and the granddaughter of actor Charles Lloyd-Pack.
Wish You Were Here 87. Cookie 89. In Country 89. Chicago Joe and the Showgirl 90. A River Runs Through It 92. Livers Ain't Cheap 96. When Saturday Comes 96. Welcome to Sarajevo 97. The Real Thing 97. Woundings 98, etc.

Lloyd, Euan (1923–)
British independent producer, former publicist.
Genghis Khan 65. Murderers' Row 66. Shalako 68. Catlow 71. The Man Called Noon 73. Paper Tiger 75. The Wild Geese 78. The Sea Wolves 80. Who Dares Wins 82. Wild Geese II 85, etc.

Lloyd, Frank (1889–1960)
Scottish-born director, in Hollywood from 1913 after acting experience.
Les Misérables 18. Madame X 20. Oliver Twist 22. The Eternal Flame 23. The Sea Hawk 24. Dark Streets 26. *The Divine Lady* (AA) 29. East Lynne 30. Sin Flood 31. Passport to Hell 32. *Cavalcade* (AA) 33. *Berkeley Square* 33. *Mutiny on the Bounty* (AAN) 35. Under Two Flags 36. Maid of Salem 37. Wells Fargo 37. If I Were King (& p) 38. Rulers of the Sea 39. The Tree of Liberty (& d) 40. The Lady from Cheyenne (& p) 41. This Woman Is Mine 41. *Blood on the Sun* 45. The Shanghai Story (& p) 54. The Last Command (& p) 55, many others.

Lloyd, Harold (1893–1971)
American silent comedian, famous for his timid bespectacled 'nice boy' character and for thrill-comedy situations involving dangerous stunts. In hundreds of two-reelers from 1916. He began as a stage actor before finding work first as a film extra and then as a Chaplin imitator in his Lucky Luke series of two-reelers. He first presented what was to become his world-famous quiet, bespectacled persona in *Over the Fence* in 1917. His career was interrupted in 1919 when a prop bomb turned out to be real and exploded in his face, removing a finger and thumb from his right hand. He recovered, signed a new contract with Hal Roach and by the beginning of the 20s was making big money: *Bumping into Broadway*, which cost $17,000 to make, took more than $150,000 in three years, bringing him a personal profit of more than $30,000. By 1922 his popularity rivalled Chaplin's. *Grandma's Boy*, his first feature, grossed nearly a million dollars and *Safety Last* more than $1.5m. He left Roach to run his own company in 1923. His career dwindled with the coming of sound and he spent time on his hobbies, which included stereoscopic photography. He married Mildred Davis, who starred with him in several of his films. A collection of his 3-D photographs, *Harold Lloyd's Hollywood*, was published in 1992. He was given a special Academy Award in 1952 as 'master comedian and good citizen'.
Autobiography: 1928, *An American Comedy*.
Biography: 1976, *Harold Lloyd* by Richard Schickel. 1983, *Harold Lloyd: The Man on the Clock* by Tom Dardis.
■ A Sailor-Made Man 21. *Grandma's Boy* 22. Dr Jack 22. *Safety Last* 23. Why Worry? 23. Girl Shy 24. Hot Water 24. *The Freshman* 25. For Heaven's Sake 26. *The Kid Brother* 27. Speedy 28. Welcome Danger 29. *Feet First* 30. *Movie Crazy* 32. The Catspaw 34. The Milky Way 36. Professor Beware 38. Mad Wednesday/The Sins of Harold Diddlebock 47.
Later produced two compilations of his comedy highlights: *World of Comedy* and *Funny Side of Life*.
✪ For skill, daring and ingenuity. *The Kid Brother*.
❝ Comedy comes from inside. It comes from your face. It comes from your body. – *H.L.*
I do not believe the public will want spoken comedy. Motion pictures and the spoken arts are two distinct arts. – *H.L.*
Basically he had not a funny bone in his body, but he was such a good actor that if you gave him a good script, he could play it to the best advantages for laughs. – *Hal Roach*
Lloyd was outstanding even among the master craftsmen at setting up a gag clearly, culminating and getting out of it deftly, and linking it smoothly to the next. – *James Agee*

Lloyd, Hugh (1923–)
British comic character actor, usually as a put-upon little man; in films and TV since 1955, often as a foil to Tony Hancock and Terry Scott.
She'll Have to Go 61. The Punch and Judy Man 62. Go to Blazes 62. The Mouse on the Moon 63. Intimate Games 76. Quadrophenia 79. Venom 81. August 96, etc.
TV series: Hugh and I 62–66. Hugh and I Spy 68. Lollipop Loves Mr Mole 71. Lollipop 72. The Clairvoyant 86.

Lloyd, Jake (1989–)
American child actor. Born in Fort Collins, Colorado, he is best known for playing Annakin Skywalker (the young Darth Vader) in *Star Wars Episode One: The Phantom Menace*.
Jingle All the Way 96. Unhook the Stars 96. Apollo II (TV) 96. Star Wars Episode l: The Phantom Menace 99. Crown of Blood 00. Madison 00. Ender's Game 00, etc.

Lloyd, Jeremy (1932–)
Lanky British comic actor and scriptwriter, frequently as an upper-class ass. He was co-creator of the television sit-coms *Are You Being Served?* 74–85, *O Happy Band!* 80, and *'Allo 'Allo!* 84–92. He was formerly married to actress Joanna Lumley.
Man in the Moon 61. Two and Two Make Six 62. Death Drums along the River 63. Doctor in Clover 65. Those Magnificent Men in Their Flying Machines 65. The Wrong Box 66. Salt and Pepper 68. Goodbye Mr Chips 69. The Magic Christian 70. Murder on the Orient Express 74. Are You Being Served? (co-w) 77, etc.

Lloyd, Norman (1914–)
British character actor in Hollywood, usually in mean or weak roles; gave up acting to become TV producer, mainly for Alfred Hitchcock but made an acting comeback in his 60s.
Autobiography: 1990, *Stages*.
Saboteur (as the villain who fell from the statue of Liberty) 42. A Letter for Evie 45. The Unseen 45. The Southerner 45. Spellbound 45. A Walk in the Sun 46. The Green Years 46. The Beginning or the End 47. No Minor Vices 48. Calamity Jane and Sam Bass 49. Scene of the Crime 49. The Flame and the Arrow 50. He Ran All the Way 51. The Light Touch 51. M 51. Limelight 52. Audrey Rose 77. The Nude Bomb 80. Dead Poets Society 89. Shogun Warrior 91. The Age of Innocence 93. Fail Safe (TV) 00. The Adventures of Rocky and Bullwinkle 00, etc.
TV series: St Elsewhere 82. 7 Days 98.

Lloyd, Russell (1916–)
British editor.
The Squeaker 37. Over the Moon 39. School for Secrets 46. Anna Karenina 48. Decameron Nights 52. The Sea Shall Not Have Them 54. Moby Dick 56. Roots of Heaven 58. The Unforgiven 60. Of Human Bondage 64. Reflections in a Golden Eye 67. The Kremlin Letter 70. The Mackintosh Man 73. The Man Who Would Be King 75. The Lady Vanishes 79. The Fiendish Plot of Dr Fu Manchu 80. Absolute Beginners 86, etc.

Lloyd, Sue (1939–)
British leading lady of the 60s.
The Ipcress File 66. Where's Jack? 68. Percy 71. The Bitch 79. UFO: The Movie 93. Bullet to Beijing 95, etc.
TV series: *The Baron* 66–67.

Lloyd, Walt
American cinematographer.
Dangerously Close 86. The Wash 88. sex, lies and videotape 89. To Sleep with Anger 90. Pump Up the Volume 90. Kakfa 91. There Goes the Neighborhood/Paydirt 92. Short Cuts 93. The Santa Clause 94. Empire Records 95. Feeling Minnesota 96. Private Parts 97. Dark Harbor 98, etc.

Lloyd Webber, Sir Andrew (1948–)
British composer, mainly of long-running stage musicals. He became Lord Lloyd Webber of Sydmonton in the New Year's Honours of 1996. In 1998, the *Sunday Times* estimated his fortune at £480m.
Biography: 1999, *Cats on a Chandelier: The Andrew Lloyd Webber Story* by Michael Coveney.
Gumshoe 71. Jesus Christ Superstar 73. The Odessa File 74. Evita (AAs 'You Must Love Me') 96.

Lloyd-Pack, Charles (1902–1983)
British character actor of stage and screen, usually in self-effacing roles: butlers, etc.
High Treason 51. *The Importance of Being Earnest* 52. The Constant Husband 55. Night of the Demon 57. Dracula 58. *Victim* 62. If 68. Song of Norway 70. Madame Sin 72. The Mirror Crack'd 80, etc.

Lloyd-Pack, Roger (1944–)
Lugubrious British character actor, the son of Charles Lloyd -Pack and the father of Emily Lloyd. He had a recurring role in the long-running TV sitcom *Only Fools and Horses* as the dim-witted Trigger.
The Magus 68. The Virgin Soldiers 69. The Go-Between 70. Figures in a Landscape 70. Fiddler on the Roof 71. Fright 71. 1984 84. Prick Up Your Ears 87. The Cook, the Thief, His Wife and Her Lover 89. Wilt 89. Hamlet 91. The Object of Beauty 91. American Friends 91. The Trial 92. Princess Caraboo 94. The Young Poisoner's Handbook 95. Hollow Reed 96. Preaching to the Perverted 97. Tom Jones (TV) 97, etc.
TV series: Spyder's Web 72. Moving 85. Health and Efficiency 93–95. The Vicar of Dibley 94–98.

Lo Bianco, Tony (1936–)
American character actor.
The Honeymoon Killers 69. The French Connection 71. The Seven Ups 73. God Told Me To 76. Jesus of Nazareth (TV) 77. Demon 77. Magee and the Lady (TV) 78. Bloodbrothers 78. F.I.S.T. 78. Separate Ways 81. City Heat 84. The Ann Jillian Story (TV) 88. City of Hope 91. Too Scared to Scream (d) 85. Boiling Point 93. Ascent 95. Tyson (TV) 95. Nixon 95. The Juror 96. Jane Austen's Mafia!/Mafia! 98. The Day the Ponies come Back 00, etc.
TV series: Jessie 84.

Loach, Ken (1936–)
English director and screenwriter, noted for the realism of his films, frequently dealing with working-class life, which often use little-known or non-professional actors. Born in Nuneaton, he studied law at Oxford University and worked in BBC-TV where he formed a notable partnership with producer Tony Garnett on the series *The Wednesday Play* and later in films. His *Cathy Come Home* 66, written by Jeremy Sandford, was one of the most controversial and memorable TV plays of its time. In the 80s, he made *Questions of Leadership*, four TV documentaries on the role of the embattled trades unions which were banned, and turned to making commercials for a time. He is also a director of Bath City Football Club, following a takeover by its fans.
Up the Junction 67. *Poor Cow* 67. *Kes* 69. *Family Life* 72. Days of Hope (TV) 75. Black Jack 79. The Gamekeeper 80. Auditions (TV) 80. Looks and Smiles 81. Fatherland 86. Hidden Agenda 90. *Riff-Raff* 90. *Raining Stones* 93. *Ladybird, Ladybird* 94. *Land and Freedom* 95. Carla's Song 96. My Name Is Joe 98. Bread and Roses 00, etc.
❝ We wanted to make plays or films that got the same responses as when you saw the news. We wanted to be seen as almost a part of the news, as reports from the front line. – *K.L. on his TV work*
There are two sorts of acting: theatre acting and film acting, which can be something different; where somebody can be taken through a story and experience the story and put themselves in that position, and respond as they would respond, so that you're really experiencing that person in that story. – *K.L.*
He's totally round the bend. You don't rehearse. Everything is a take. – *Ricky Tomlinson*
He reminds you always that you shouldn't become a film maker unless you have something to say. – *Alan Parker*

Locane, Amy (1971–)
American actress, from television. Born in Trenton, New Jersey, she began acting as a teenager.
Lost Angels 89. The Road Home 89. Cry-Baby 90. No Secrets 91. Blue Sky 92 (released 94). School Ties 92. Airheads 94. Carried Away 95. Prefontaine 96. Going All the Way 97. Love to Kill 97. Bram Stoker's The Mummy 97. Route 9 98, etc.
TV series: Spencer 84–85. Melrose Place 92–93.

Locke, Joseph (1918–1999) (Joseph McLaughlin)
Irish tenor, in occasional films with comedian Frank Randle. Born in Londonderry, he trained as an opera singer but became a regular on the British music-hall and variety stages. He fled to Ireland over income tax difficulties, and fear of arrest made it difficult for him to perform in Britain, a subject that formed the basis for the film comedy *Hear My Song* 92.
Holidays With Pay 48. Somewhere in Politics 49. What a Carry On! 49, etc.

Locke, Sondra (1947–)
American leading actress and occasional director.
Autobiography: 1997, *The Good, the Bad and the Very Ugly: A Hollywood Journey*.
The Heart Is a Lonely Hunter (AAN) 68. Willard 71. A Reflection of Fear 73. The Outlaw Josey Wales 76. Death Game 76. The Gauntlet 77. Seducers 77. Shadow of Chikara 77. Every Which Way but Loose 78. Any Which Way You Can 80. Bronco Billy 80. Suzanne 80. Sudden Impact 83. Ratboy (& d) 86. Impulse (d) 90. Death in Small Doses (d) 92, etc.

Lockhart, Calvin (1934–)
West Indian leading man.
A Dandy in Aspic 68. Joanna 68. Nobody Runs Forever 68. Leo the Last 70. Myra Breckinridge 70. Cotton Comes to Harlem 71. Melinda 72. The Beast Must Die 74. Uptown Saturday Night 74. Let's Do It Again 75. Three Days in Beirut 83. Wild at Heart 90. Predator 2 90, etc.

Lockhart, Gene (1891–1957)
Canadian character actor at home in genial or shifty parts. Also writer: in films since 1922.
■ Smilin' Through 22. The Gay Bride 34. Ah Wilderness 35. I've Been Around 35. Captain Hurricane 35. Star of Midnight 35. Thunder in the Night 35. Storm over the Andes 35. Crime and Punishment 35. Brides Are Like That 35. Times Square Playboy 36. Earthworm Tractors 36. The First Baby 36. Career Woman 36. The Garden Murder Case 36. The Gorgeous Hussy 36. The Devil Is a Sissy 36. Wedding Present 36. Mind Your Own Business 36. Come Closer Folks 36. Mama Steps Out 37. Too Many Wives 37. Make Way for Tomorrow 37. The Sheik Steps Out 37. Something to Sing About 37. Of Human Hearts 38. Listen Darling 38. A Christmas Carol 38. Sweethearts 38. Penrod's Double Trouble 38. Men Are Such Fools 38. Blondie 38. *Algiers* (AAN) 38. Sinners in Paradise 38. Meet the Girls 38. I'm from Missouri 39. Hotel Imperial 39. Our Leading Citizen 39. Geronimo 39. Tell No Tales 39. Bridal Suite 39. Blackmail 39. The Story of Alexander Graham Bell 39. Edison the Man 40. Dr Kildare Goes Home 40. We Who Are Young 40. South of Pago Pago 40. A Dispatch from Reuters 40. *His Girl Friday* 40. Abe Lincoln in Illinois 40. Billy the Kid 41. Keeping Company 41. Meet John Doe 41. All That Money Can Buy 41. The Sea Wolf 41. One Foot in Heaven 41. Steel Against the Sky 41. International Lady 41. They Died with Their Boots On 41. Juke Girl 42. The Gay Sisters 42. You Can't Escape Forever 42. Forever and a Day 43. Mission to Moscow 43. Hangmen Also Die 43. Find the Blackmailer 43. The Desert Song 43. Madame Curie 43. Northern Pursuit 43. The White Cliffs of Dover 44. *Going My Way* 44. Action in Arabia 44. The Man from Frisco 44. *The House on 92nd Street* 45. Leave Her to Heaven 45. That's the Spirit 45. Meet Me on Broadway 46. A Scandal in Paris 46. She Wolf of London 46. The Strange Woman 46. The Shocking Miss Pilgrim 47. Miracle on 34th Street 47. The Foxes of Harrow 47. Cynthia 47. Honeymoon 47. Her Husband's Affairs 47. Joan of Arc 48. Inside Story 48. That Wonderful Urge 48. Apartment for Peggy 48. I Jane Doe 48. Down to the Sea in Ships 49. Madame Bovary 49. The Red Light 49. The Inspector General 49. Riding High 50. The Big Hangover 50. The Sickle and the Cross 51. I'd Climb the Highest Mountain 51. Rhubarb 51. The Lady from Texas 51. Hoodlum Empire 52. A Girl in Every Port 52. Face to Face 52. Bonzo Goes to College 52. Androcles and the Lion 52. Apache War Smoke 52. Francis Covers the Big Town 53. Down Among the Sheltering Palms 53. Confidentially Connie 53. The Lady Wants Mink 53. World for Ransom 54. The Vanishing American 55. Carousel 56. The Man in the Grey Flannel Suit 56. Jeanne Eagels 57.

Lockhart, June (1925–)
American supporting actress, daughter of Gene Lockhart.
All This and Heaven Too 40. Meet Me in St Louis 44. Keep Your Powder Dry 45. Bury Me Dead 47. Time Limit 47. Lassie's Greatest Adventure 63.

Death Valley Days (TV) 65. Lost in Space (TV) 65. Curse of the Black Widow (TV) 77. The Gift of Love (TV) 78. Walking through the Fire (TV) 79. Deadly Games 80. Strange Invaders 83. Troll 86. A Whisper Kills (TV) 88. Rented Lips 88. The Big Picture 89. Sleep with Me 92. Out There (TV) 95. The Colony 95. Lost in Space 98, etc.

TV series: Lassie 55–64. Lost in Space 65–68. Petticoat Junction 68–70.

Lockhart, Kathleen (1893–1978)
American character actress, widow of Gene Lockhart; known previously as Kathleen Arthur.

The Devil is a Sissy 36. Sweethearts 38. All This and Heaven Too 41. Gentleman's Agreement 47. Plymouth Adventure 52. The Glenn Miller Story 54, many others.

Locklear, Heather (1961–)
American actress, born in Los Angeles. She began in commercials while studying at UCLA, and came to notice in the role of Sammy Jo in the TV soap opera *Dynasty*.

Twirl (TV) 81. City Killer (TV) 84. Firestarter 84. The Return of the Swamp Thing 89. The Great American Sex Scandal (TV) 89. The Big Slice 91. Fade to Black 93. The First Wives Club 96. Double Tap 97. Money Talks 97, etc.

TV series: Dynasty 81-89. T.J. Hooker 82-87. Going Places 90-91. Melrose Place 93-99. Spin City 99- .

Lockwood, Gary (1937–) (John Gary Yusolfsky)
American leading man of the 60s, mostly on TV.

Splendour in the Grass 61. Wild in the Country 61. It Happened at the World's Fair 63. Firecreek 67. 2001: A Space Odyssey 68. The Model Shop 69. RPM 70. Stand Up and Be Counted 72. Bad Georgia Road 77. Survival Zone 84. The Wild Pair 87. Terror in Paradise 90. Night of the Scarecrow 95, etc.

TV series: *Follow the Sun* 61. *The Lieutenant* 63.

Lockwood, Harold (1887–1918)
American romantic lead of early silents, most often opposite May Allison. He made more than 100 films before his early death from pneumonia.

Lockwood, Julia (1941–)
British leading lady, daughter of Margaret Lockwood.

My Teenage Daughter 56. Please Turn Over 59. No Kidding 60, etc.

Lockwood, Margaret (1916–1990) (Margaret Day)
Durable, indomitable British leading lady who was an appealing ingénue in the 30s, a rather boring star villainess in the 40s, and later a likeable character actress of stage and TV.

Autobiography: 1955, *Lucky Star*.

Biography: 1989, *Once a Wicked Lady* by Hilton Tims.

■ Lorna Doone 35. The Case of Gabriel Perry 35. Some Day 35. Honours Easy 35. Man of the Moment 35. Midshipman Easy 35. Jury's Evidence 36. The Amateur Gentleman 36. The Beloved Vagabond 36. Irish for Luck 36. The Street Singer 37. Who's Your Lady Friend? 37. Dr Syn 37. Melody and Romance 37. Owd Bob 38. Bank Holiday 38. *The Lady Vanishes* 38. A Girl Must Live 39. The Stars Look Down 39. Susannah of the Mounties (US) 39. Rulers of the Sea (US) 39. *Night Train to Munich* 40. The Girl in the News 40. Quiet Wedding 41. Alibi 42. *The Man in Grey* 43. Dear Octopus 43. Give Us the Moon 44. Love Story 44. A Place of One's Own 45. I'll Be Your Sweetheart 45. *The Wicked Lady* 45. Bedelia 46. Hungry Hill 46. Jassy 47. The White Unicorn 47. Look Before You Love 48. Cardboard Cavalier 49. Madness of the Heart 49. Highly Dangerous 50. Trent's Last Case 52. Laughing Anne 53. Trouble in the Glen 54. *Cast a Dark Shadow* 57. The Slipper and the Rose 76.

Lockwood, Preston (1912–1996)
Lean English character actor, often as a lawyer or cleric; he was much featured in radio drama, and best known for his role as Dennis the Dachshund in Children's Hour's *Toytown*.

Julius Caesar 70. Lady Caroline Lamb 72. The Black Windmill 74. The Prince and the Pauper 77. Absolution 78. Time Bandits 81. The Pirates of Penzance 82. The Fool 90, etc.

Loden, Barbara (1932–1980)
American general-purpose actress. She was married to director Elia Kazan.

Wild River 60. Splendor in the Grass 60, etc.

As director: Wanda 72.

Loder, John (1898–1988) (John Lowe)
Handsome British leading man, in international films from 1927 after varied experience. Educated at Eton and Sandhurst, he was first a cavalry officer. He started as an extra in German films before being invited to Hollywood by Jesse Lasky of Paramount Pictures. His third wife was actress Hedy Lamarr. In the late 50s he became a cattle-rancher in Argentina.

Autobiography: 1977, *Hollywood Hussar*.

The First Born 29. Java Head 34. Lorna Doone 35. Murder Will Out 38. Meet Maxwell Archer 39. How Green Was My Valley 41. *Now Voyager* 42. Gentleman Jim 42. The Gorilla Man 42. Old Acquaintance 43. The Hairy Ape 44. The Brighton Strangler 45. A Game of Death 46. Wife of Monte Cristo 46. Dishonoured Lady 47. Woman and the Hunter 57. Gideon's Day 58, etc.

❝ Why is it that I'm not able
to get the roles they give Clark Gable?
They always say 'You have no name
But when you have one, come again.'
By that time I'll be old and stiff
A kind of poor man's Aubrey Smith. – *J.L., 1940s*

John Loder played the king as though he was afraid someone would play the ace at any moment. – *Hannen Swaffer on Sing As We Go*

Lodge, David (1921–)
British character actor, with music-hall and stage experience.

Autobiography: 1986, *Up the Ladder to Obscurity*.

Private's Progress 56. Two Way Stretch 60. The Dock Brief 61. Yesterday's Enemy 61. The Long Ships 63. Guns at Batasi 64. Catch Us If You Can 65. Press For Time 66. Corruption 69. Doctors Wear Scarlet 70. The Railway Children 71. Go For a Take 72. The Amazing Mr Blunden 72. The Return of the Pink Panther 74. The Revenge of the Pink Panther 78. Sahara 82. Edge of Sanity 88, etc.

TV series: Potter's Picture Palace 76. Lovely Couple 79.

Lodge, John (1903–1985)
American leading man of the 30s, mainly European films. Retired to take up politics.

A Woman Accused (debut) 32. Little Women 33. The Scarlet Empress 34. Koenigsmark 35. Sensation 36. The Tenth Man 36. Bulldog Drummond at Bay 37. Bank Holiday 38. L'Esclave Blanche 39.

❝ Mr John Lodge continues to suffer from a kind of lockjaw, an inability to move the tight muscles of his mouth, to do anything but glare with the dumbness and glossiness of an injured seal. – *Graham Greene reviewing The Tenth Man*

LoDuca, Joseph
American composer, best known for his work for such TV series as *Hercules: The Legendary Journeys* and *Xena, Warrior Princess*.

The Evil Dead 83. Evil Dead 2 87. Army of Darkness 92. Necronomicon 93, etc.

Loeb, Philip (1894–1955)
American character actor, usually of smart types. Committed suicide after he was blacklisted and was unable to find work.

Room Service 38. A Double Life 48. Molly 51, etc.

Loesser, Frank (1910–1969)
American songwriter, in films since 1930. He began as a lyricist; from 1947 he wrote both words and music.

College Swing 38. St Louis Blues 39. Destry Rides Again 39. Seven Sinners 40. Kiss the Boys Goodbye 41. Thank Your Lucky Stars 43. The Perils of Pauline 47. Neptune's Daughter 49. Let's Dance 50. Where's Charley? 52. Hans Christian Andersen 52. Guys and Dolls 55. How to Succeed in Business without Really Trying 66, etc.

Loew, Marcus (1870–1927)
Austrian-American exhibitor and distributor, co-founder and controller of MGM, which is still run by Loews Inc.

Loewe, Frederick (1901–1988)
Austrian composer, in America from the early 20s. Born in Berlin of Austrian parents, he was a concert pianist at the age of 14. His father, an actor and singer, died while rehearsing a show in New York, stranding the young Loewe and his mother. He then worked as a cowboy, boxer and pianist before becoming a composer, notably in collaboration with Alan Jay Lerner from 1942.

Brigadoon 54. Gigi 58. My Fair Lady 64. Camelot 67. Paint Your Wagon 69. The Little Prince 74.

Loft, Arthur (1897–1947)
American supporting actor with a slightly bewildered face, often seen as businessman.

Prisoner of Shark Island 36. The Woman in the Window 45. Blood on the Sun 46. Scarlet Street 47, many others.

Lofting, Hugh (1886–1947)
English children's author, creator of the Doctor Dolittle stories, filmed as a musical starring Rex Harrison in 1967. In 1998, Eddie Murphy starred as Dr Dolittle in a non-musical version, and a new stage musical based on the stories also ran in London.

Loftus, Cecilia (1876–1943)
British character actress who went to Hollywood with a Shakespearean company in 1895, and stayed.

East Lynne 31. The Old Maid 39. The Bluebird 40. Lucky Partners 40. The Black Cat 41, etc.

Logan, Joshua (1908–1988)
American stage director whose occasional films tended towards stodginess.

Autobiography: 1976, *Josh, My Up and Down, In and Out Life*. 1978, *Movie Stars, Real People and Me*.

■ I Met My Love Again 38. *Picnic* (AAN) 56. *Bus Stop* 56. *Sayonara* (AAN) 57. South Pacific 58. Tall Story 60. Fanny 61. Ensign Pulver 64. *Camelot* 67. Paint Your Wagon 69.

Logan, Phyllis (1956–)
Scottish-born actress, probably best known for her role as Lady Jane in the TV series *Lovejoy*.

Another Time, Another Place (BFA) 83. 1984 84. The Chain 85. The McGuffin 85. The Inquiry 87. The Kitchen Toto 87. Freddie as F.R.0.7 (voice) 92. Soft Top, Hard Shoulder 92. Silent Cries (TV) 93. Love and Reason (TV) 93. Secrets and Lies 95. Shooting Fish 97, etc.

TV series: Hope and Glory 00.

Logan, Robert F. (1941–)
Brawny hero of American family films.

The Bridge at Remagen 69. The Wilderness Family 75. Across the Great Divide 76. The Wilderness Family Part Two 77. Snowbeast (TV) 77. The Sea Gypsies 78. Death Ray 2000 81. Man Outside 88, etc.

Loggia, Robert (1930–)
American leading man.

Somebody Up There Likes Me 56. Cop Hater 58. The Nine Lives of Elfego Baca (TV) 59. Cattle King 63. Che! 69. The Moneychangers (TV) 75. First Love 77. The Ninth Configuration 80. S.O.B. 81. An Officer and a Gentleman 82. Trail of the Pink Panther 82. A Woman Called Golda (TV) 82. Curse of the Pink Panther 83. Scarface 83. Jagged Edge (AAN) 85. The Believers 87. Over the Top 87. Hot Pursuit 87. Big 88. Relentless 89. Triumph of the Spirit 89. Opportunity Knocks 90. The Marrying Man/Too Hot to Handle 91. Necessary Roughness 91. Innocent Blood 92. Gladiator 93. Bad Girls 94. White Mile (TV) 94. I Love Trouble 94. The Last Tattoo 94. Coldblooded 95. Man with a Gun 95. Independence Day 96. Mistrial (TV) 96. Wide Awake 97. National Lampoon's The Don's Analyst 97. Holy Man 98. The Proposition 98, etc.

TV series: T.H.E. Cat 66–67. Emerald Point N.A.S. 83–84. Mancuso F.B.I. 89. Wild Palms 93.

Lohmann, Dietrich (1943–1997)
German cinematographer, associated with the films of Rainer Werner Fassbinder and other leading directors of the New German Cinema. Born in Berlin, he studied at the Berlin Film School, moving to the USA in the mid-80s. Died from leukaemia.

Signs of Life (co-ph) 67. Last Words (co-ph) 68. Precautions against Fanatics (co-ph) 68. Love Is Colder than Death 69. Katzelmacher 69. Gods of the Plague 70. Why Does Herr R. Run Amok 70. Rio das Mortes 70. The Niklashausen Journey 70. The American Soldier 70. Recruits in Ingolstadt 70. The Merchant of Four Seasons 71. Wildwechsel 72. Eight Hours Are Not a Day 72. Ludwig – Requiem for a Virgin King 72. Bremen Freedom (& co-d) 72. Effi Briest 74. Karl May 74. Baker's Bread 76. Hitler: A Film from Germany 77. The Serpent's Egg 77. Germany in Autumn (co-ph) 78. Strawanzer 83. War and Remembrance (TV) (US) 88. Silence Like Glass (US) 90. The Serbian Girl 91. Ted and Venus (US) 91. Wedlock (US) 91. Knight Moves (US/Fr.) 92. Salt on Our Skin (Ger./Fr./Can.) 92. The Innocent (GB/Ger.) 93. Me and the Kid (US) 93. La Machine (Fr./Ger.) 94. Color of Night (US) 94. The Peacemaker (US) 97. Deep Impact (US) 98, etc.

Lohr, Marie (1890–1975)
Distinguished Australian stage actress, on London stage from 1901; since 1930 in dowager roles.

Aren't We All? (debut) 32. *Pygmalion* 38. *Major Barbara* 40. The Winslow Boy 48. A Town Like Alice 56, many others.

Lollobrigida, Gina (1927–)
Italian glamour girl and international leading lady, in films since 1947.

Pagliacci 47. Fanfan la Tulipe 51. *Belles de Nuit* 52. The Wayward Wife 52. *Bread, Love and Dreams* 53. Beat the Devil 54. Le Grand Jeu 54. Trapeze 56. Where the Hot Wind Blows 58. Solomon and Sheba 59. Come September 61. Woman of Straw 64. Strange Bedfellows 65. Four Kinds of Love/Bambole 65. Hotel Paradiso 66. Buona Sera, Mrs Campbell 68. Bad Man's River 71. King Queen Knave 72. The Lonely Woman 76. La Romana 88, many others.

TV series: Falcon Crest 84.

Lom, Herbert (1917–) (Herbert Charles Angelo Kuchacevich ze Schluderpacheru)
Czech actor whose personality adapts itself equally well to villainy or kindliness; in Britain from 1939.

Mein Kampf 40. The Young Mr Pitt (as Napoleon) 41. The Dark Tower 43. Hotel Reserve 44. *The Seventh Veil* 46. Night Boat to Dublin 46. *Dual Alibi* 47. Good Time Girl 48. The Golden Salamander 49. *State Secret* 50. The Black Rose 50. Hell Is Sold Out 51. The Ringer 52. The Net 53. The Love Lottery 54. *The Ladykillers* 55. War and Peace (as Napoleon) 56. Chase a Crooked Shadow 57. Hell Drivers 57. No Trees in the Street 58. Roots of Heaven 58. Northwest Frontier 59. I Aim at the Stars (US) 59. Mysterious Island 61. El Cid 61. Phantom of the Opera (title role) 62. A Shot in the Dark 64. Return from the Ashes 65. Uncle Tom's Cabin (Ger.) 65. Gambit 66. Assignment to Kill 67. Villa Rides 68. Doppelgänger 69. The Hot Death (Ger.) 69. Murders in the Rue Morgue 71. Asylum 72. And Now the Screaming Starts 73. The Return of the Pink Panther 74. And Then There Were None 75. The Pink Panther Strikes Again 77. Revenge of the Pink Panther 78. Charleston 78. The Lady Vanishes 79. Hopscotch 80. The Man with Bogart's Face 80. Trail of the Pink Panther 82. Curse of the Pink Panther 83. The Dead Zone 83. Memed My Hawk 84. King Solomon's Mines 85. Whoops Apocalypse 86. Scoop (TV) 87. The Crystal Eye 88. River of Death 89. Ten Little Indians 89. The Sect 91. The Pope Must Die/The Pope Must Diet 91. Son of the Pink Panther 93, etc.

TV series: *The Human Jungle*.

Lomas, Herbert (1887–1961)
Gaunt, hollow-voiced British stage actor.

The Sign of Four 32. Lorna Doone 35. Rembrandt 36. Jamaica Inn 39. Ask a Policeman 39. *The Ghost Train* 41. I Know Where I'm Going 45. Bonnie Prince Charlie 48. The Net 53, etc.

Lombard, Carole (1908–1942) (Jane Peters)
American leading lady of the 30s, a fine comedienne with an inimitable rangy style. Married Clark Gable. Died in a plane crash.

Biography: 1976, *Screwball* by Larry Swindell.

■ A Perfect Crime 21. Hearts and Spurs 25. Marriage in Transit 25. Me Gangster 28. Power 28. Show Folks 28. Ned McCobb's Daughter 29. High Voltage 29. Big News 29. The Racketeer 29. The Arizona Kid 30. Safety in Numbers 30. Fast and Loose 30. It Pays to Advertise 31. Man of the World 31. Ladies' Man 31. Up Pops the Devil 31. I Take This Woman 31. No One Man 32. Sinners in the Sun 32. Virtue 32. No More Orchids 32. *No Man of Her Own* 32. From Heaven to Hell 33.

Supernatural 33. The Eagle and the Hawk 33. Brief Moment 33. White Woman 33. *Bolero* 34. We're Not Dressing 34. *Twentieth Century* 34. Now and Forever 34. Lady by Choice 34. The Gay Bride 34. *Rumba* 34. Hands across the Table 35. Love before Breakfast 36. *My Man Godfrey* (AAN) 36. The Princess Comes Across 36. Swing High Swing Low 37. True Confession 37. *Nothing Sacred* 37. Fools for Scandal 38. Made for Each Other 38. In Name Only 39. Vigil in the Night 40. *They Knew What They Wanted* 40. *Mr and Mrs Smith* 41. *To Be or Not To Be* 42.

✪ For daring to be wacky while glamorous. *Nothing Sacred*.

❝ I live by a man's code designed to fit a man's world, yet at the same time I never forget that a woman's first job is to choose the right shade of lipstick. – *C.L.*

Carole was the first woman I ever met who used four-letter words like a truck driver. – *Radie Harris*

Lombard, Karina (1969–)
Sultry American actress, of Lakota Indian and Russian descent.
Wide Sargasso Sea 92. The Firm 93. Legends of the Fall 94. Last Man Standing 96, etc.

Lombardi, Francisco José (1950–)
Leading Peruvian director, producer and screenwriter of films on social and political themes, a former movie critic.
Muerte al Amanecer 77. Maruja en el Infierno 83. *The City and the Dogs*/La Ciudad y los Perros 85. The Lion's Den/La Boca del Lobo 88. Fallen from the Sky/Caidos del Cielo (& co-w) 90. Traces from Paradise/Huellas del Paraiso (& co-w) 92. Sin Compasión 94. Don't Tell Anyone/No Se Lo Digas a Nadie 98. Red Ink/Tinto Roja 00, etc.

Lombardo, Louis (1933–)
American film editor and occasional director.
The Wild Bunch 69. The Ballad of Cable Hogue 69. Brewster McCloud 70. McCabe and Mrs Miller 71. Thieves Like Us 73. The Long Goodbye 73. California Split 74. The Black Bird 75. Russian Roulette (d) 75. All the President's Men 76. The Late Show 77. The Changeling 78. Just One of the Guys 85. P.K and the Kid (d) 87. Moonstruck 87. January Man 89. Uncle Buck 89. Defenceless 90. Other People's Money 91, etc.

Lommel, Ulli (1944–)
German-born director, screenwriter and cinematographer who began by working as an actor with Rainer Werner Fassbinder, remade Fritz Lang's M with Fassbinder producing, and then went to America to direct low-budget gore-filled horror movies.
Whity (a) 70. The American Soldier/Der Amerikanische Soldat (a) 70. The Tenderness of Wolves/Die Zartlickeit der Wolfe (d) 73. Fontane Effi Briest (a) 74. Chinesisches Roulette (a) 76. Satan's Brew/Satansbraten (a) 76. Adolf und Marlene (wd) 77. Cocaine Cowboys 79. The Boogey Man (a, d) 80. A Taste of Sin (co-w, d, ph) 83. Brainwaves (& ph) 83. The Demonsville Terror (co-w, d, ph) 83. Defense Play 86. Overkill 86. Warbirds (co-w, d) 88. Natural Instinct (p,d) 91. The Big Sweat 91, etc.

Loncraine, Richard (1946–)
British director.
Flame 74. Full Circle 76. Blade on the Feather (TV) 80. Brimstone and Treacle 82. The Missionary 84. Bellman and True 87. The Wedding Gift (TV) 94. *Richard III* 95, etc.

London, Jack (1876–1916)
American adventure novelist, whose most-filmed stories include *The Sea Wolf*, *Adventures of Martin Eden*, *Call of the Wild* and *White Fang*.

London, Jason (1972–)
American actor, born in San Diego, California. Married actress Charly Spradling. His twin brother Jeremy is also an actor.
The Man in the Moon 91. Dazed and Confused 93. Fall Time 94. Safe Passage 94. To Wong Foo, Thanks for Everything, Julie Newmar 95. Mixed Signals 97. Broken Vessels 98. The Rage: Carrie 2 99. Jason and the Argonauts (TV) 00. Spent 00, etc.

London, Julie (1926–2000) (Julie Peck)
Husky-voiced American singer and actress, who first came to notice with her recording of CRY ME A RIVER in the mid-50s. Born in Santa Rosa, California into a vaudeville family, she began singing as a child and was in films from the age of eighteen. Married (1945–53) actor and director Jack WEBB and musician and songwriter Bobby Troup.
On Stage Everybody 45. The Red House 47. Tap Roots 48. Task Force 49. The Fat Man 50. Return of the Frontiersman 50. The Girl Can't Help It 56. The Great Man 56. Drango 57. Man of the West 58. A Question of Adultery 58. Saddle the Wind 58. The Voice in the Mirror 58. The Third Voice 59. The Wonderful Country 59. The George Raft Story 61. The Helicopter Spies 67, etc.
TV series: *Emergency* 72–77.

London, Roy (1943–1993)
American director, screenwriter, playwright and actor who was also a noted acting coach.
Hardcore (a) 79. Jake Speed (a) 86. Rampage (a) 87. Tiger Warsaw (w) 88. Diary of a Hitman (d) 92, etc.

Lone, John (1952–)
Hong Kong-born leading actor, in America, who also makes pop records aimed at the Asian market.
Iceman 84. Year of the Dragon 85. Echoes of Paradise/Shadows of the Peacock 86. The Last Emperor 87. The Moderns 88. Shadow of China 91. M. Butterfly 93. The Shadow 94. The Hunted 95, etc.

❝ I don't want to stand behind someone and look important and inscrutable. I don't do Fu Manchu. – *J.L.*

Lonergan, Arthur (1906–1989)
American art director, a former architect, in films from 1938, first as an illustrator.
Intrigue 48. The Actress 53. *Forbidden Planet* 56. Robinson Crusoe on Mars 64. The Oscar (AAN) 66. Che! 69. M*A*S*H 70. Beyond the Valley of the Dolls 70. Plaza Suite 71, etc.

Long, Audrey (1924–)
American leading lady of the 40s.
A Night of Adventure 44. Pan Americana 45. Song of My Heart 47. The Petty Girl 50. Indian Uprising 52, etc.

Long, Howie (1960–)
American actor, a former professional footballer, born in Charlestown, Massachusetts.
Broken Arrow 96. Firestorm 97, etc.

Long, Huey (1893–1935)
American politician, governor of Louisiana and US senator with presidential ambitions, who was assassinated. He was the model for Willie Stark, the corrupt Southern protagonist of Robert Penn Warren's novel *All the King's Men*, which was filmed with Broderick Crawford in the leading role. *Kingfish*, a film of his life made for cable TV, starred John Goodman in 1995. He was the brother of Earl Long, governor of Louisiana in the 50s, whose affair with a stripper was commemorated in the movie *Blaze* 89, starring Paul Newman.

Long, Nia (1970–)
American actress, born in Brooklyn, New York, who began as a teenager.
The B.R.A.T. Patrol 86. Boyz N The Hood 91. Buried Alive 91. Made in America 93. Friday 95. Love Jones 97. Soul Food 97. The Secret Laughter of Women 98. Stigmata 99. In Too Deep 99. The Best Man 99. Boiler Room 00. Big Momma's House 00, etc.
TV series: Fresh Prince of Bel Air 94-95. Live Shot 95-96.

Long, Richard (1927–1974)
American leading man, mainly in second features. Married actress Mara Corday.
Tomorrow Is Forever 44. The Stranger 45. The Egg and I 47. Criss Cross 49. Saskatchewan 54. Cult of the Cobra 55. Home from the Hills 59. The Tenderfoot 64, etc.
TV series: *77 Sunset Strip* 58–60. *Bourbon Street Beat* 59. *The Big Valley* 65–68. *Nanny and the Professor* 69–71. Thicker Than Water 73.

Long, Shelley (1949–)
American leading lady.
A Small Circle of Friends 80. Night Shift 82. Irreconcilable Differences 84. The Money Pit 86. Outrageous Fortune 87. Hello Again 87. Troop Beverly Hills 89. Don't Tell Her It's Me 90. Frozen Assets 92. The Brady Bunch Movie 95. Freaky Friday (TV) 95. A Very Brady Sequel 96. Dr T & the Women 00, etc.
TV series: Cheers 82–87. Good Advice 93–94. Kelly Kelly 98.

Long, Walter (1879–1952)
Tough-looking American character actor, usually as a villain, in films from 1909. He was a regular in D. W. Griffith's films and blacked up to play the rapist who chases Mae Marsh to her death in *The Birth of a Nation*. He appeared in several Laurel and Hardy films, notably as a convict in *Pardon Us*, ending his career opposite Ken Maynard and William Boyd in westerns and, in *Man's Country*, playing twin baddies.
The Birth of a Nation 15. Intolerance 16. Joan the Woman 17. The Little American 17. Scarlet Days 18. The Sheik 21. Blood and Sand 22. Moran of the Lady Letty 22. The Call of the Wild 23. Little Church round the Corner 23. Raffles 25. Soul-Fire 25. Yankee Clipper 27. Me, Gangster 28. Moby Dick 30. The Maltese Falcon 31. Sea Devils 31. Pardon Us 31. Any Old Port 32. I Am a Fugitive from a Chain Gang 32. The Thin Man 34. The Live Ghost 34. Going Bye-Bye! 34. Naughty Marietta 35. North of the Rio Grande 37. The Painted Trail 38. Man's Country 38. Six Shootin' Sheriff 38. Union Pacific 39. Flaming Lead 39. Silver Stallion 41. Wabash Avenue 50, etc.

Longden, John (1900–1971)
British leading man of the early 30s; later graduated to character roles.
Blackmail 30. Atlantic 30. The Ringer 31. Born Lucky 33. French Leave 37. The Gaunt Stranger 38. The Lion Has Wings 39. The Common Touch 41. The Silver Fleet 43. Bonnie Prince Charlie 48. The Man with the Twisted Lip (as Sherlock Homes) 51. Quatermass II 56. An Honourable Murder 60, many others.

Longden, Terence (1922–)
British actor, in secondary roles.
Never Look Back 52. Simon and Laura 55. Doctor at Large 57. Carry On Sergeant 58. Ben Hur 59. The Return of Mr Moto 65. The Wild Geese 78. The Sea Wolves 80, etc.

Longo, Robert
American director and artist.
Johnny Mnemonic 95.

Longstreet, Stephen (1907–)
American screenwriter.
The Jolson Story 46. The Greatest Show on Earth (co-w) 52. The First Traveling Saleslady 55. The Helen Morgan Story 57, etc.

Lonsdale, Frederick (1881–1954) (Lionel Frederick Leonard)
Fashionable English playwright and screenwriter of the 20s and early 30s. Born in Jersey, the son of a tobacconist, he wrote sophisticated comedies of life in high society, and attempted to live in a similar manner. He signed a contract to work for MGM in 1930 but soon tired of Hollywood and returned to England, going back in 1936 to write a film for Ernst Lubitsch, which he abandoned after three weeks; he spent much of the remainder of his life in the United States.
Biography: 1957, *Freddy Lonsdale* by Frances Donaldson.
The Fast Set (US) 24. The Fake (oa, co-w) 27. The Last of Mrs Cheyney (US) 29. Canaries Sometimes Sing (oa, co-w) 30. On Approval 30. Lady of Scandal (US) 30. The Devil to Pay (US) (w) 30. Aren't We All 32. The Maid of the Mountains 32. Women Who Play 32. Lovers Courageous (US) (w) 32. Just Smith 33. The Private Life of Don Juan (co-w) 34. The Last of Mrs Cheyney (US) 37. On Approval 44. The Law and the Lady (US) 51, etc.

❝ I could never live in a film city because there is no conversation. – *F.L.*

Lonsdale, Michel (1931–) (sometimes Michael)
Chubby French character actor, in some international roles.
La Main Chaude 60. The Trial 62. Behold a Pale Horse 64. The Bride Wore Black 68. Stolen Kisses 68. Souffle au Coeur 71. *The Day of the Jackal* 73. Stavisky 74. Caravan to Vaccares 74. The Phantom of Liberty 74. The Romantic Englishwoman 75. The Pink Telephone 75. Mr Klein 76. The Passage 78. Moonraker 79. Les Jeux de la Comtesse 80. Enigma 82. The Name of the Rose 86. Souvenir 88. The Remains of the Day 93. Jefferson in Paris (as Louis XVI) 95. Nelly and M. Arnaud 95. Ronin (US) 98, many others.

Loo, Richard (1903–1983)
Hawaiian-Chinese actor who turned to films after business depression. Played hundreds of oriental roles.
Dirigible 31. The Good Earth 37. The Keys of the Kingdom 44. Rogues' Regiment 48. Love is a Many-Splendored Thing 54. The Quiet American 58. The Sand Pebbles 66. One More Time 71, etc.

Loos, Anita (1891–1981)
Witty American writer who spent 18 years with MGM. A former actress, she began by writing scenarios for D. W. Griffiths, progressing to subtitles for Douglas Fairbanks's films under the influence of director John Emerson, whom she married in 1919, though the liaison was a mostly unhappy one. She remains best known for her novel *Gentlemen Prefer Blondes*, inspired by writer H. L. Mencken's flirtation with a dumb blonde, which was turned into a film, a play and two musicals, one of which was also filmed as a vehicle for Marilyn Monroe.
Autobiography: 1966, *A Girl Like I*. 1974, *Kiss Hollywood Goodbye*. 1977, *Cast of Thousands*. Also wrote *The Talmadge Girls* (1977).
Biography: 1988, *Anita Loos* by Gary Carey.
Intolerance (subtitles) 16. Let's Get a Divorce (w) 18. A Temperamental Wife (oa) 19. Mama's Affair (d) 20. In Search of a Sinner (p) 20. Red Hot Romance (w) 22. Learning to Love (w) 25. Gentlemen Prefer Blondes (oa) 28. Midnight Mary (oa) 33. *San Francisco* (w) 36. Saratoga (w) 37. The Women (w) 39. When Ladies Meet (oa) 41. *Gentlemen Prefer Blondes* (oa) 53, etc.

❝ Kissing your hand may make you feel very, very good but a diamond and sapphire bracelet lasts forever. – *A.L.*, *Gentlemen Prefer Blondes*

Today, much as girls *look* like boys, they flunk out on the solicitude men are developing for each other. Less and less do men need women. More and more do gentlemen prefer gentlemen. – *A.L., 1974*

Lopez, Jennifer (1970–)
Sultry American actress and singer, a former dancer. Born in the Bronx, New York, to Puerto Rican parents, she began as one of the Fly Girls on the TV series *In Living Color*. She was briefly married (1997–98) to Cuban Ojani Noa. Current asking price: $8m.
Nurses on the Line (TV) 93. My Family/Mia Familia 95. Money Train 95. Jack 96. Blood & Wine 96. Selena 97. Anaconda 97. U-Turn 97. Out of Sight 98. Antz (voice) 98. The Cell 00. Angel Eyes 01, etc.
TV series: Malibu Road 92. Second Chances 93–94. South Central 94.

Lopez, Sergi (1965–)
Spanish actor, often in French movies. Born near Barcelona, he studied acting in Paris.
Western 97. Lisboa 99. An Intimate Affair/Un Liaison Pornographique 99. Harry, He's Here To Help/Harry, Un Ami Qui Vous Veut Du Bien, 00.

Lopez, Trini (1937–)
American character actor, ex-bandleader.
Marriage on the Rocks 66. The Dirty Dozen 67. Antonio 73, etc.

Loquasto, Santo (1944–)
American production designer, from the stage, often on Woody Allen's films.
Rancho Deluxe 75. Stardust Memories 80. The Fan 81. So Fine 81. Falling in Love 84. Desperately Seeking Susan 85. Radio Days (AAN) 87. September 87. Big 88. Another Woman 88. Bright Lights, Big City 88. New York Stories 89. Crimes and Misdemeanors 89. She-Devil 89. Alice 90. Shadows and Fog 92. Manhattan Murder Mystery 93. Bullets over Broadway (AAN) 94. Everyone Says I Love You 96. Deconstructing Harry 97. Celebrity 98, etc.

Lord, Del (1895–1970)
American second-feature director who handled most of the THREE STOOGES shorts.
Barnum Was Right 29. Trapped by Television 36. It Always Happens 39. She's a Sweetheart 44. I Love a Bandleader 45. Hit the Hay 45. Blonde from Brooklyn 45. Rough, Tough and Ready 45. Singin' in the Corn 46. It's Great to Be Young 46. In Fast Company 46, etc.

Lord, Jack (1920–1998) (John Joseph Ryan)
Craggy-faced American leading man who found his greatest success in television. Born in Brooklyn, he trained as a merchant marine officer, held a second mate's licence, and became interested in acting through involvement in maritime training films. He was also a painter.

Cry Murder 51. The Court Martial of Billy Mitchell 55. God's Little Acre 58. Walk Like a Dragon 60. Doctor No 62. The Road to Hangman's Tree 67. The Name of the Game Is Kill 68. M Station: Hawaii (d) (TV) 80, etc.

TV series: *Stoney Burke* 62–63. *Hawaii Five-O* 68–80.

Lord, Jean-Claude (1943–)
Canadian director.

■ Eclair au Chocolat 79. Visiting Hours 82. Dreamworld 83. Covergirl 84. The Vindicator/Frankenstein '88 85. Toby McTeague 85. Tadpole and the Whale 88. Mindfield 89. Eddie and the Cruisers: Eddie Lives! 89. Landslide 92.

Lord, Marjorie (1922–)
American leading lady of minor films in the 40s, later on TV as Danny Thomas' wife in comedy series. She is the mother of Anne Archer.

Forty Naughty Girls 38. Timber 42. Sherlock Holmes in Washington 42. Flesh and Fantasy 44. The Argyle Secrets 48. New Orleans 49. Port of Hell 55. Boy Did I Get a Wrong Number 66. Side by Side (TV) 88, etc.

TV series: Make Room for Daddy 53–57. Make Room for Granddaddy 70.

Lord, Pauline (1890–1950)
American stage actress who made only two films.

■ Mrs Wiggs of the Cabbage Patch 35. A Feather in Her Hat 36.

Lord, Robert (1900–1976)
American writer and producer associated with Warner Brothers throughout the 30s and 40s; later joined Humphrey Bogart in Santana Productions.

AS WRITER: The Johnstown Flood 26. A Reno Divorce 27. My Man 28. Five and Ten Cent Annie 28. On with the Show 29. Gold Diggers of Broadway 29. Hold Everything 30. Fireman Save My Child 32. One Way Passage (AA) 32. 20,000 Years in Sing Sing 32. The Little Giant 33. Dames 34. Page Miss Glory 35, etc.

AS PRODUCER: Wonder Bar 34. Oil for the Lamps of China 35. Black Legion 37. Tovarich 37. Brother Rat 38. The Dawn Patrol 38. Dodge City 39. Confessions of a Nazi Spy 39. The Letter 40. Dive Bomber 41. High Wall 47. Tokyo Joe 49. In a Lonely Place 50. Sirocco 51, etc.

Lords, Traci (1968–) (Nora Louise Kuzma)
American actress, a former star of pornographic films who made the transition to low-budget features in the late 80s.

Not of This Earth 88. Fast Food 89. Shock 'Em Dead 90. Cry-Baby 90. Raw Nerve 91. A Time to Die 91. Laser Moon 92. Skinner 93. The Tommyknockers (TV) 93. Ice 94. Serial Mom 94. Plughead Rewired: Circuitry Man II 94. The Nutt House 95. As Good as Dead 95. Blade 98, etc.

Loren, Sophia (1934–) (Sofia Scicolone)
Statuesque Italian leading lady, latterly an accomplished international actress. In films from 1950 (as extra). Married producer Carlo Ponti.

Autobiography: 1979, *Sophia: Living and Loving* (with A. E. Hotchner).

Biography: 1975, *Sophia* by Donald Zec. 1998, *Sophia Loren* by Warren G. Harris.

Aida 53. The Sign of Venus 53. Tempi Nostri 54. Attila 54. The Gold of Naples 54. *Woman of the River* 55. Too Bad She's Bad 55. The Miller's Wife 55. Scandal in Sorrento 55. Lucky To Be a Woman 56. The Pride and the Passion 57. *Boy on a Dolphin* 57. Legend of the Lost 57. Desire under the Elms 58. *The Key* 58. Houseboat 58. Black Orchid 59. That Kind of Woman 59. Heller in Pink Tights 60. A Breath of Scandal 61. *Two Women* (AA, BFA) 61. *The Millionairess* 61. El Cid 61. Boccaccio 70 61. The Condemned of Altona 62. Madame Sans Gêne 62. Five Miles to Midnight 62. Yesterday, Today and Tomorrow 63. The Fall of the Roman Empire 64. Marriage Italian Style (AAN) 64. Operation Crossbow 65. Judith 65. Arabesque 66. Lady L 66. A Countess from Hong Kong 66. Ghosts Italian Style 68. More Than a Miracle 69. Sunflower 70. Man of La Mancha 72. Lady Liberty 74. Brief Encounter (TV) 74. The Voyage 75. The Cassandra Crossing 77. A Special Day 77. Brass Target 78. Firepower 79. Angela 80. Sophia Loren (TV) 80. Aurora (TV) 84. Courage (TV) 86. The Fortunate Pilgrim (TV) 88. Running Away 89. Saturday, Sunday and Monday/Sabato, Domenica e Lunedi 90. Prêt-à-Porter/Ready to Wear 94. Grumpier Old Men 95, etc.

“ Everything you see, I owe to spaghetti. – *S.L.*

Sex appeal is fifty per cent what you've got and fifty per cent what people think you've got. – *S.L.*

I'm not ashamed of my bare-bottomed beginnings. – *S.L.*

In a restaurant or at a function I just walk straight in and it's an eternity. When I'm sitting, it's OK, but then I have to start thinking of a short cut out. – *S.L.*

All the natural mistakes of beauty fall together in her to create a magnificent accident. – *Rex Reed*

Working with her is like being bombed by watermelons. – *Alan Ladd*

Lorentz, Pare (1905–1992)
American documentarist and film critic.

The Plow that Broke the Plains 36. *The River* 37. The Fight for Life 40. The Nuremberg Trials 46.

Lorenz, Juliane (1957–)
German editor, associated with the films of Fassbinder from the mid-70s to the early 80s.

Chinese Roulette 76. Despair 78. The Third Generation/Die Dritte Generation 79. Berlin Alexanderplatz (TV) 80. The Marriage of Maria Braun 79. Querelle 82. The Rose King 86. The Night of the Mareten 87. Malina 90, etc.

Lorimer, Glennis (1913–)
English actress of the stage and screen in the 30s who impersonated Thomas Gainsborough's portrait of actress Sarah Siddons in the trademark of Gainsborough Pictures, a company co-owned by her father, Henry Ostrer.

The Ringer 31. There Goes the Bride 32. Britannia of Billingsgate 33. My Old Dutch 34. Rhodes of Africa 36. Alf's Button Afloat 38. Ask a Policeman 39, etc.

Lorne, Marion (1886–1968) (Marion Lorne MacDougal)
American character actress who came to films in older roles. Born in Wilkes Barre, Pennsylvania, she spent much of her career in England, appearing in the farces and comedies of her husband, playwright and theatre manager Walter HACKETT. After his death in 1944, she returned to the United States, where she was best known for playing the dithery Aunt Clara in the TV sitcom *Bewitched*.

■ Strangers on a Train 51. The Girl Rush 55. The Graduate 67.

TV series: Mr Peepers 52–55. Sally 57–58. The Garry Moore Show 58–62. Bewitched 64–68.

Lorre, Peter (1904–1964) (Laszlo Loewenstein)
Highly individual Hungarian character actor who filmed in Germany and Britain before settling in Hollywood. His rolling eyes, timid manner and mysterious personality could adapt to either sympathetic or sinister roles; a weight problem restricted his later appearances.

■ Frühlings Erwachen 29. Der Weisse Teufel 30. Die Koffer des Herrn O.F. 30. M 30. Bomben auf Monte Carlo 31. Fünf von der Jazzband 32. Schuss im Morgengrauen 32. Der Weisse Dämon 32. F.P.I. 32. Was Frauen Träumen 33. Unsichtbare Gegner 33. De Haut en Bas 34. *The Man Who Knew Too Much* 34. *Mad Love* 35. *Crime and Punishment* (as Raskolnikov) 35. *The Secret Agent* 36. Crack Up 36. Nancy Steele is Missing 37. Lancer Spy 37. Think Fast Mr Moto 37. Thank You Mr Moto 37. Mr Moto's Gamble 38. I'll Give a Million 38. Mr Moto Takes a Chance 38. Mysterious Mr Moto 38. Mr Moto on Danger Island 39. Mr Moto Takes a Vacation 39. Mr Moto's Last Warning 39. Strange Cargo 40. I Was an Adventuress 40. Island of Doomed Men 40. Stranger on the Third Floor 40. You'll Find Out 40. Mr District Attorney 41. *The Face Behind the Mask* 41. They Met in Bombay 41. *The Maltese Falcon* 41. All through the Night 42. Invisible Agent 42. The Boogie Man Will Get You 42. Casablanca 42. Background to Danger 43. The Cross of Lorraine 43. The Constant Nymph 43. Passage to Marseilles 44. *The Mask of Dimitrios* 44. Arsenic and Old Lace 44. The Conspirators 44. Hollywood Canteen 44. Hotel Berlin 45. Confidential Agent 45. Three Strangers 46. Black Angel 46. The Chase 46. The Verdict 46. *The Beast with Five Fingers* 46. My Favorite Brunette 47. Casbah 48. Rope of Sand 49. Quicksand 50. Double Confession 50. Der Verlorene (& d) 50. Beat the Devil 53. 20,000 Leagues under the Sea 54. *Congo Crossing* 56. Around the World in Eighty Days 56. The Buster Keaton Story 56. Silk Stockings 57. The Story of Mankind (as Nero) 57. Hell Ship Mutiny 57. The Sad Sack 58. The Big Circus 59. Scent of Mystery 59. Voyage to the Bottom of the Sea 61. *Tales of Terror* 62. Five Weeks in a Balloon 62. *The Raven* 63. The Comedy of Terrors 63. The Patsy 64.

✪ For the diffidence of his dark deeds and for his inimitable voice, still enthusiastically parodied by cartoon villains. *The Mask of Dimitrios*.

“ Those marbly pupils in the pasty spherical face are like the eye pieces of a microscope through which you can see laid flat on the slide the entangled mind of a man: love and lust, nobility and perversity, hatred of itself, and despair jumping up at you from the jelly. – *Graham Greene*

Lorring, Joan (1926–) (Magdalen Ellis)
English-Russian actress, evacuated to US in 1939; played some nasty teenagers.

Girls under Twenty-One 41. Song of Russia 44. The Bridge of San Luis Rey 44. The Corn Is Green (AAN) 45. The Verdict 46. The Lost Moment 47. Good Sam 49. Stranger on the Prowl 53. The Midnight Man 74, etc.

TV series: Norby 54.

Losch, Tilly (1901–1975)
Austrian exotic dancer, in Hollywood in the 30s and 40s.

■ The Garden of Allah 36. The Good Earth 37. Duel in the Sun 46.

Losey, Joseph (1909–1984)
American director of somewhat pretentious movies, in Britain from 1952 after the communist witch-hunt.

Biography: 1991, *Joseph Losey* by Edith Rham. 1994, *Joseph Losey: A Revenge on Life* by David Caute.

■ The Boy with Green Hair 48. The Lawless 50. *The Prowler* 50. M 51. The Big Night 51. Stranger on the Prowl 53. The Sleeping Tiger 54. The Intimate Stranger 56. Time without Pity 57. The Gypsy and the Gentleman 57. Blind Date 59. The Criminal 60. *The Damned* 61. Eva 62. *The Servant* 63. King and Country 64. Modesty Blaise 66. *Accident* 67. Boom 68. Secret Ceremony 68. Figures in a Landscape 70. The Go-Between 71. The Assassination of Trotsky 72. A Doll's House 73. Galileo 74. The Romantic Englishwoman 75. Mr Klein 76. Don Giovanni 79. The Trout 82. Steaming 84.

“ Films can illustrate our existence … they can distress, disturb and provoke people into thinking about themselves and certain problems. But NOT give the answers. – *J.L.*

Lotinga, Ernie (1876–1951)
British vaudeville comedian who began his career as a comic vocalist under the name of Dan Roe in 1898. During the early 1900s he was a member of the Six Brothers Luck in music hall before creating the slapstick character Jimmy Josser that made him a star until the mid-20s. He continued the character in some broadly comic movies that had their followers in the 30s. He was married to music-hall performer and male impersonator Hetty King.

Joining Up 28. Nap 28. The Raw Recruit 28. Dr Josser, K.C. (& co-w) 31. P.C. Josser 31. Josser Joins the Navy 32. Josser in the Army 32. Josser on the River 32. Josser on the Farm 34. Smith's Wives (& story) 35. Love up the Pole 36, etc.

Louis, Jean (1907–1997) (Jean-Louis Berthault)
Paris-born costume designer, in the US from the mid-30s and Hollywood from the mid-40s, working first at Columbia Pictures for 15 years as chief designer. In the 60s he worked at Universal and later opened his own couture house in Los Angeles. Among his best-known creations were the strapless black satin dress worn by Rita HAYWORTH as she sang 'Put the Blame on Mame' in *Gilda*, Marlene DIETRICH's elaborate, sculpted gowns for her cabaret performances, and the sequinned body-stocking Marilyn MONROE wore when she sang 'Happy Birthday' to President Kennedy at Madison Square Garden in 1962. The dress, which cost $12,000, was sold at auction in 1999 for $1,267,500. Married actress Loretta YOUNG, his second wife, in 1993.

Strange Affair 44. *Gilda* 46. The Jolson Story 46. The Lady from Shanghai 48. Jolson Sings Again 49. Born Yesterday (AAN) 50. Affair in Trinidad (AAN) 52. *Salome* 53. From Here to Eternity (AAN) 53. It Should Happen to You (AAN) 54. A Star Is Born (AAN) 54. The Caine Mutiny 54. Queen Bee (AAN) 55. Picnic 55. *The Solid Gold Cadillac* (AA) 56. Pal Joey (AAN) 57. The Story of Esther Costello 57. Bell, Book and Candle (AAN) 58. Imitation of Life 59. Song without End 60. Back Street (AAN) 61. Judgment at Nuremberg (AAN) 61. Ship of Fools (AAN) 65. Gambit (AAN) 66. Thoroughly Modern Millie (AAN) 67. Guess Who's Coming to Dinner 67. Lost Horizon 73, etc.

“ Jean Louis's creations metamorphosed me into a perfect, ethereal being, the most seductive that ever was. – *Marlene Dietrich*

Louis-Dreyfus, Julia (1960–)
American actress, from television's *Saturday Night Live*. Best known for her role as Elaine Benes in the TV sitcom *Seinfeld*, for which she was reportedly paid $600,000 an episode.

Soul Man 86. Hannah and Her Sisters 86. National Lampoon's Christmas Vacation 89. Jack the Bear 93. North 94. London Suite (TV) 96. Deconstructing Harry 97. Father's Day 97. A Bug's Life (voice) 98. Animal Farm (voice,TV) 99, etc.

TV series: Day by Day 88–89. Seinfeld 90–98.

Louise, Anita (1915–1970) (Anita Louise Fremault)
American leading lady, usually in gentle roles. Played child parts from 1924.

What a Man 30. A Midsummer Night's Dream 35. The Story of Louis Pasteur 35. Anthony Adverse 36. The Green Light 37. Marie Antoinette 38. The Sisters 39. Phantom Submarine 41. The Fighting Guardsman 45. The Bandit of Sherwood Forest 46. Retreat, Hell! 52.

TV series: *My Friend Flicka* 56.

“ As cold as a stepmother's kiss. – *Hal Wallis*

Louise, Tina (1934–) (Tina Blacker)
Statuesque American leading lady of routine films.

God's Little Acre 58. Day of the Outlaw 59. Armored Command 61. For Those Who Think Young 64. Wrecking Crew 68. The Good Guys and the Bad Guys 69. How to Commit Marriage 70. The Stepford Wives 75. Mean Dog Blues 78. The Day the Women Got Even 80. Hellriders 84. Evils of the Night 85. O.C. & Stiggs 87. Dixie Lanes 88. Johnny Suede 91, etc.

TV series: *Gilligan's Island* 64–66. Dallas 78. Rituals 84–85.

Lourié, Eugène (1905–1991)
Russian-born French production and visual effects designer, who also directed some monster movies in the 50s. Born in Kharkov, he moved to Paris in his 'teens and worked with director Jean RENOIR, accompanying him in the early 40s to Hollywood, where he stayed. Married costume designer Laure de Zarata (1911-2001).

AS DESIGNER: Les Bas Fonds 36. *La Grande Illusion* 37. La Règle du Jeu 39. This Land Is Mine (US) 42. *The Southerner* (US) 44. The House of Fear 44. The River 51. Flight from Ashiya 63. Shock Corridor 63. Crack in the World 64. The Naked Kiss 64. Krakatoa, East of Java (AANsp) 69. What's the Matter with Helen? 71. Burnt Offerings 76. The Amazing Captain Nemo 78. Bronco Billy 80, etc.

AS DIRECTOR: *The Beast from Twenty Thousand Fathoms* 53. The Colossus of New York 58. Behemoth, the Sea Monster/The Giant Behemoth (GB, & w) 59. Gorgo (GB) 60, etc.

Love, Bessie (1898–1986) (Juanita Horton)
Vivacious, petite American leading lady of the 20s. In films from childhood; from the mid-30s resident in London, playing occasional cameo parts.

Autobiography: 1977, *From Hollywood with Love*.

Intolerance 15. The Aryan 16. A Sister of Six 17. The Dawn of Understanding 18. The Purple Dawn 20. The Vermilion Pencil 21. Human Wreckage 23. Dynamite Smith 24. The Lost World 25. Lovey Mary 26. Sally of the Scandals 27. Broadway Melody (AAN) 28. Chasing Rainbows 30. Morals for Women 31. Conspiracy 32. Atlantic Ferry 42. Journey Together 45. Touch and Go 55. The Wild Affair 64. Isadora 68. Sunday Bloody Sunday 71. Mousey (TV) 74. The Ritz 76, many others.

Love, Courtney (1965–)
American rock singer and occasional actress. Widow of rock singer Kurt Cobain.

Biography: 1997, *Courtney Love: The Real Story* by Poppy Z. Brite.

Sid and Nancy 86. Straight to Hell 86. Feeling Minnesota 96. Basquiat 96. The People vs Larry Flynt 96. 200 Cigarettes 98, etc.

Love, Darlene (1938–) (Darlene Wright)
American character actress and singer. Born in Los Angeles, she sang with The Blossoms and was lead vocalist on 'He's a Rebel' and other hit singles made by Phil Spector in the 60s. On film, she is familiar as Danny Glover's wife in the *Lethal Weapon* series.

Lethal Weapon 88. Lethal Weapon 2 89. Lethal Weapon 3 92. Lethal Weapon 4 98, etc.

Love, Montagu (1877–1943)
Heavily built British character actor, long in Hollywood, latterly as stern fathers.

Bought and Paid For 16. The Gilded Cage 19. The Case of Becky 21. A Son of the Sahara 24. Son of the Sheik 26. Don Juan 26. King of Kings 27. Jesse James 27. The Haunted House 28. The Divine Lady 29. Bulldog Drummond 29. Outward Bound 30. The Cat Creeps 30. Midnight Lady 32. Clive of India 35. The White Angel 36. The Prince and the Pauper (as Henry VIII) 37. The Adventures of Robin Hood 38. Gunga Din 39. All This and Heaven Too 40. Shining Victory 41. The Constant Nymph 43. Devotion 44, many others.

Lovecraft, H. P. (1890–1937)
American horror writer, most of whose books were published posthumously. His stories featuring his invented Cthulhu mythology of ancient demonic forces attempting to return to Earth have become increasingly influential among makers of low-budget horror movies. The following all show the Lovecraft influence, though it is not always acknowledged by their makers:

The Haunted Palace (from *The Case of Charles Dexter Ward*) 63. Monster of Terror (from *Colour out of Space*) 65. Dunwich Horror (from *The Shuttered Room*) 69. Re-Animator (from *Herbert West – Re-Animator*) 85. From Beyond 86. The Farm 87. The Gate 87. Re-Animator 2 89. Gate 2 92. Cthulhu Mansion 92. The Unnameable Returns (from *The Statement of Randolph Carter*) 92. The Resurrected (from *The Case of Charles Dexter Ward*) 92. Necronomicon 93, a movie compendium, featured two Lovecraft stories, *Cool Air* and *The Whisperer in the Darkness*, with Jeffrey Combs appearing in the role of Lovecraft. In the Mouth of Madness 94. Lurking Fear 94, etc.

Lovejoy, Frank (1912–1962)
American actor of tough roles, with stage and radio experience.

Black Bart 48. Home of the Brave 49. In a Lonely Place 50. *The Sound of Fury* 51. I Was a Communist for the FBI 51. Force of Arms 51. The Hitch Hiker 52. Retreat Hell 52. The System 53. House of Wax 53. The Charge at Feather River 54. Beachhead 54. The Americano 55. Top of the World 55. Strategic Air Command 55. The Crooked Web 56. Cole Younger Gunfighter 58, etc.

TV series: Man against Crime 54. *Meet McGraw* 57–58.

Lovejoy, Ray
English film editor.

2001: A Space Odyssey 68. A Day in the Death of Joe Egg 72. The Ruling Class 72. The Shining 80. The Dresser 83. Aliens (AAN) 86. The House on Carroll Street 88. Batman 89. Mr Frost 90. Let Him Have It 91. The Year of the Comet 92. A Far Off Place 93. Monkey Trouble 94. Rainbow 95. Mrs Munck 95. The Last of the High Kings 96. Inventing the Abbotts 97. Lost in Space 98, etc.

Lovelace, Linda (1952–)
American female lead of *Deep Throat* and other porno films.

Lovell, Raymond (1900–1953)
Canadian stage actor long in Britain: often in pompous or sinister roles.

Warn London 34. Contraband 40. 49th Parallel 41. *Alibi* 42. Warn That Man 43. The Way Ahead 44. *Caesar and Cleopatra* 45. The Three Weird Sisters 48. Time Gentleman Please 52. The Steel Key 53, etc.

Lovett, Lyle (1958–)
American country singer and occasional actor. Briefly married to actress Julia Roberts.

The Player (a) 92. Short Cuts (a) 93. Prêt-à-Porter/Ready to Wear (a) 94. Bastard out of California (a) 96. Fear and Loathing in Las Vegas (a) 98. The Opposite of Sex (a) 98. Cookie's Fortune (a) 99. Dr T & the Women (m) 00, etc.

Lovitz, Jon (1957–)
American character actor.

Jumpin' Jack Flash 86. Three Amigos 86. Last Resort 86. Big 88. My Stepmother Was an Alien 88. Mr Destiny 90. An American Tail: Fievel Goes West 91. A League of Their Own 92. Mom and Dad Save the World 92. National Lampoon's Loaded Weapon 1 93. North 94. City Slickers II: The Legend of Curly's Gold 94. Trapped in Paradise 94. The Great White Hype 96. High School High 96. Matilda 96. The Wedding Singer 98. Happiness 98. Lost and Found 99. Small Time Crooks 00, etc.

TV series: Saturday Night Live 85–90. Foley Square 85–86. NewsRadio 98– .

Low, Warren (1905–1989)
American editor.

Dr Socrates 35. Anthony Adverse 36. The Great Garrick 37. The Life of Emile Zola 37. Juarez 39. *The Letter* 40. The Gay Sisters 42. Now Voyager 42. The Searching Wind 46. Sorry Wrong Number 48. September Affair 50. The Stooge 52. About Mrs Leslie 54. The Bad Seed 56. Gunfight at the OK Corral 57. Summer and Smoke 61. Boeing Boeing 65. Will Penny 68. True Grit 69. Willard 71, many others.

Lowe, Arthur (1915–1982)
Portly British character actor who achieved star status on television, and was best known for the role of the pompous Captain Mainwaring in the sitcom *Dad's Army*. In the 60s he played Leonard Swindley, the lay preacher and draper in the TV soap opera *Coronation Street*, and remains the only character so far to have had a spin-off series, *Pardon the Expression* 65–66. Born in Hayfield, Derbyshire, he worked in an aircraft factory and began in amateur drama during his service in the Second World War, making his first professional appearance at the age of 30. Married actress Joan Cooper. His best film roles were as Tucker, the anarchist butler in *The Ruling Class* 72, and as Duff, Johnson and Munda in *O Lucky Man!* 73.

Stormy Crossing 48. Kind Hearts and Coronets 49. This Sporting Life 63. The Rise and Rise of Michael Rimmer 70. *Dad's Army* 71. *The Ruling Class* 71. Theatre of Blood 73. *O Lucky Man* 73. *No Sex Please, We're British* 73. The Bawdy Adventures of Tom Jones 76. The Lady Vanishes 79. Britannia Hospital 82, etc.

TV series: Turn Out the Light 67. *Dad's Army* 68–77. Doctor at Large 71. Potter 79–80. Bless Me Father 78–81. A. J. Wentworth, BA 82.

Lowe, Chad (1968–)
American actor, the brother of Rob Lowe. Married actress Hilary Swank.

Silence of the Heart 84. Apprentice to Murder 88. True Blood 89. Nobody's Perfect 90. An Inconvenient Woman (TV) 91. Highway to Hell 92. Siringo 94. In the Presence of Mine Enemies (TV) 97, etc.

Lowe, Edmund (1890–1971)
Suave American leading man of the 20s and 30s who did not manage to age into a character actor.

The Spreading Dawn 17. The Devil 20. Peacock Alley 21. The Silent Command 23. The Fool 25. *What Price Glory?* 26. Is Zat So? 27. Dressed to Kill 28. In Old Arizona 29. The Cockeyed World 29. Scotland Yard 30. Transatlantic 31. *Chandu the Magician* 32. *Dinner at Eight* 33. Gift of Gab 34. Mr Dynamite 35. The Great Impersonation 35. Seven Sinners (GB) 36. The Squeaker (GB) 37. Secrets of a Nurse 38. Our Neighbours the Carters 39. Wolf of New York 40. Call out the Marines 41. Murder in Times Square 43. Dillinger 45. Good Sam 48. Around the World in Eighty Days 56. The Wings of Eagles 57. Heller in Pink Tights 60, etc.

TV series: *Front Page Detective* 52.

Lowe, Edward T. (1890–1973)
American screenwriter, notably of early horror and thriller movies. Born in Nashville, Tennessee, he contributed to the *Charlie Chan*, *Bulldog Drummond* and *Sherlock Holmes* series.

The Hunchback of Notre Dame 23. Lonesome 28. Tenderloin 28. The Vampire Bat 32. The Ghost Walks 34. Scattergood Baines 41. Sherlock Holmes and the Secret Weapon 42. Tarzan's Desert Mystery 43. House of Frankenstein 44. House of Dracula 45. Rough, Tough and Ready 45, etc.

Lowe, Rob (1964–)
American leading actor, born in Charlottesville, Virginia, and raised in Dayton, Ohio. A child model, he began acting in his teens, reaching starring roles in the 80s. His career came momentarily unstuck in the late 80s, when a videotape of his sexual exploits was made public and caused a minor scandal. He is the brother of actor Chad Lowe.

The Outsiders 83. Class 83. Oxford Blues 84. The Hotel New Hampshire 84. St Elmo's Fire 85. Youngblood 85. About Last Night 86. Square Dance 86. Masquerade 88. Illegally Yours 88. Bad Influence 90. Desert Shield 91. Stroke of Midnight 91. The Dark Backward 91. Wayne's World 92. The Finest Hour 92. Suddenly Last Summer (TV) 93. The Stand (TV) 94. Eye of the Storm 95. Midnight Man (TV) 95. On Dangerous Ground (TV) 95. First Degree 95. Tommy Boy 95. Mulholland Falls (uncredited) 96. For Hire 97. Living in Peril 97. Contact 97. Hostile Intent 97. Atomic Train (TV) 98. Outrage (TV) 98. One Hell of a Guy 98. Austin Powers: The Spy Who Shagged Me 99, etc.

TV series: A New Kind of Family 79–80. West Wing 99- .

Lowell, Carey (1961–)
American actress and model, born in New York. She is best known for her role as Pam Bouvier in the James Bond film *Licence to Kill*. She was formerly married to actor-director Griffin Dunne and has been romantically linked with actor Richard Gere.

Club Paradise 86. Dangerously Close/Choice Kill 86. Down Twisted 87. Me and Him/Ich und Er 88. Licence to Kill 89. The Guardian 90. Road to Ruin 92. Sleepless in Seattle 93. Fierce Creatures 97, etc.

TV series: A League of Their Own 93. Law and Order 96-98.

Löwensohn, Elina
Romanian-born actress in America.

Schindler's List 93. Amateur 94. Nadja 95. Basquiat 96. I'm Not Rappaport 96. Six Ways to Sunday 98. The Wisdom of Crocodiles 98. Sombre (Fr.) 98, etc.

Lowenstein, Richard (1960–)
Australian director and writer, also a director of rock videos.

Strikebound 84. White City 85. Dogs in Space 86. Say a Little Prayer 93.

Lowery, Robert (1916–1971) (R. L. Hanks)
American leading man of the 40s, mainly in routine films.

Wake Up and Live 37. Young Mr Lincoln 39. Lure of the Islands 42. A Scream in the Dark 44. Prison Ship 45. The Mummy's Ghost 46. Death Valley 48. Batman and Robin (serial) (as Batman) 50. Crosswinds 51. Cow Country 53. The Rise and Fall of Legs Diamond 60. Johnny Reno 66, many others.

TV series: Circus Boy 56–57.

Lowry, Malcolm (1905–1957)
English novelist of works based on his own life, which was characterized by heavy drinking and travelling. His second wife was American actress Margerie Bonner. His masterpiece, *Under the Volcano*, in which the central character of the alcoholic ex-British consul is a self-portrait, was filmed by John Huston with Albert Finney in the role.

Biography: 1973, *Malcolm Lowry* by Douglas Day. 1993, *Pursued by Furies: A Life of Malcolm Lowry* by Gordon Bowker.

Lowry, Morton (1908–1987)
British character actor in Hollywood.

The Dawn Patrol 38. The Hound of the Baskervilles 39. Tarzan Finds a Son! 39. Hudson's Bay 40. Charley's Aunt/Charley's American Aunt 41. How Green Was My Valley 41. This Above All 42. The Loves of Edgar Allan Poe 42. Immortal Sergeant 43. No Time for Love 43. The Man in Half Moon Street 44. Pursuit to Algiers 45. The Picture of Dorian Gray 45. The Verdict 46. Calcutta 47. Too Hot to Handle 59, etc.

Loy, Myrna (1905–1993) (Myrna Williams)
Likeable American leading lady of the 30s; began her career in villainous oriental roles but later showed a great flair for sophisticated comedy and warm domestic drama. She was awarded an Oscar for lifetime achievements in 1991.

Autobiography: 1987, *Myrna Loy: Being and Becoming*.

SELECTED SILENT FILMS: The Cave Man 26. Don Juan 26. The Climbers 27. Beware of Married Men 28. State Street Sadie 28. The Midnight Taxi 28. Noah's Ark 29, etc.

■ SOUND FILMS: The Jazz Singer 27. The Desert Song 29. The Squall 29. Black Watch 29. Hard Boiled Rose 29. Evidence 29. Show of Shows 29. The Great Divide 30. The Jazz Cinderella 30. Cameo Kirby 30. Isle of Escape 30. Under a Texas Moon 30. Cock of the Walk 30. Bride of the Regiment 30. Last of the Duanes 30. The Truth about Youth 30. Renegades 30. Rogue of the Rio Grande 30. The Devil to Pay 30. The Naughty Flirt 31. Body and Soul 31. A Connecticut Yankee 31. Hush Money 31. Transatlantic 31. Rebound 31. Skyline 31. Consolation Marriage 31. Arrowsmith 31. Emma 32. The Wet Parade 32. Vanity Fair 32. The Woman in Room 13 32. New Morals for Old 32. *Love Me Tonight* 32. Thirteen Women 32. *The Mask of Fu Manchu* 32. The Animal Kingdom 32. Topaze 33. The Barbarian 33. The Prizefighter and the Lady 33. *When Ladies Meet* 33. Penthouse 33. Night Flight 33. Men in White 34. Manhattan Melodrama 34. *The Thin Man* 34. Stamboul Quest 34. Evelyn Prentice 34. *Broadway Bill* 34. Wings in the Dark 35. Whipsaw 35. Wife versus Secretary 36. Petticoat Fever 36. The Great Ziegfeld 36. To Mary with Love 36. Libeled Lady 36. After the Thin Man 36. Parnell 37. *Double Wedding* 37. Man Proof 38. Test Pilot 38. Too Hot to Handle 38. Lucky Night 39. *The Rains Came* 39. Third Finger Left Hand 39. Another Thin Man 39. I Love You Again 40. Love Crazy 41. Shadow of the Thin Man 41. The Thin Man Goes Home 44. So Goes My Love 46. *The Best Years of Our Lives* 46. *The Bachelor and the Bobby Soxer* 47. Song of the Thin Man 47. *Mr Blandings Builds His Dream House* 48. The Red Pony 49. That Dangerous Age 49. *Cheaper by the Dozen* 50. Belles on Their Toes 52. The Ambassador's Daughter 56. Lonelyhearts 58. From the Terrace 60. Midnight Lace 60. The April Fools 69. Death Takes a Holiday (TV) 70. Do Not Fold Spindle or Mutilate (TV) 71. The Couple Takes a Wife (TV) 72. Indict and Convict (TV) 73. The Elevator (TV) 73. Airport 75 74. It Happened at Lakewood Manor (TV) 77. The End 79. Just Tell Me What You Want 80. Summer Solstice (TV) 81.

Gag appearance: The Senator Was Indiscreet 49.

✪ For the wit and elegance with which she lived up to her 30s title of 'Queen of Hollywood'. *The Thin Man*.

Loy, Nanni (1925–1995)
Italian director of the neo-realist school, a former assistant to Luigi Zampa.

Parola di Ladra 56. The Four Days of Naples (AAN) 62. Made in Italy 65. Head of the Family 67. Why 71. Insieme 79. Café Express 80. Where's Picone?/Mi Manda Picone 84. Amici Miei III 85. Gioco di Società 88. Scugnizzi 89. Pacco, Doppio Pacc e Contropaccotto 93, etc.

Lualdi, Antonella (1931–) (Antoinetta de Pasquale)
Italian leading lady of the 50s and 60s.

Three Forbidden Stories 52. Le Rouge et le Noir 54. Wild Love 55. Young Girls Beware 57. Run with the Devil 60. The Mongols 61. My Son the Hero 62. Let's Talk about Women 64. How to Seduce a Playboy 66. Vincent Francois Paul and the Others 75. Cross Shot/La Legge Violenta della Squadra Anticrimine 76. Una Spina nel Cuore 86. Diritto di Vivere 89, etc.

Lubezki, Emmanuel
Mexican cinematographer.

The Long Road to Tijuana/El Camino Larga a Tijuana 89. Bandits/Bandidos 91. Like Water for Chocolate/Como Agua para Chocolate 92. Miroslava 92. Twenty Bucks (US) 93. Reality Bites (US) 94. Ambar 94. A Little Princess (AAN) 95. A Walk in the Clouds (US) 95. The Birdcage (US) 96. Meet Joe Black 98. Great Expectations 98. Sleepy Hollow (AAN) 99. Things You Can Tell Just by Looking at Her 99, etc.

Lubin, Arthur (1899–1995)
American director from 1934, mainly of light comedy, and with a penchant for eccentric animals.
■ A Successful Failure 34. The Great God Gold 35. Honeymoon Limited 35. Two Sinners 35. Frisco Waterfront 35. The House of a Thousand Candles 36. Yellowstone 37. Mysterious Crossing 37. *California Straight Ahead* 37. I Cover the War 37. Idol of the Crowds 37. Adventure's End 37. Midnight Intruder 38. Beloved Brat 38. Prison Break 38. Secrets of a Nurse 38. Risky Business 38. Big Town Czar 39. Mickey the Kid 39. Called a Messenger 39. The Big Guy 40. *Black Friday* 40. Gangs of Chicago 40. I'm Nobody's Sweetheart Now 40. Meet the Wildcat 40. Who Killed Aunt Maggie? 40. San Francisco Docks 41. Where Did You Get That Girl? 41. *Buck Privates* 41. In the Navy 41. Hold That Ghost 41. Keep 'Em Flying 41. Ride 'Em Cowboy 42. Eagle Squadron 42. White Savage 43. *Phantom of the Opera* 43. Ali Baba and the Forty Thieves 44. Delightfully Dangerous 45. Spider Woman Strikes Back 46. A Night in Paradise 46. New Orleans 47. Impact 49. *Francis* 50. Queen for a Day 51. Francis Goes to the Races 51. *Rhubarb* 51. Francis Goes to West Point 52. It Grows on Trees 52. South Sea Woman 53, Francis Covers Big Town 53. Francis Joins the WACs 54. Francis in the Navy 55. Footsteps in the Fog 55. Lady Godiva 55. Star of India 56. The First Travelling Saleslady 56. Escapade in Japan 57. Thief of Baghdad 61. The Incredible Mr Limpet 64. Hold On 66. Rain for a Dusty Summer 71.
TV series: *Mister Ed* 60–65.

Lubitsch, Ernst (1892–1947)
German director, once a comic actor, in a series of silent farces starring him as 'Meyer'. After a variety of subjects he settled for a kind of sophisticated sex comedy that became unmistakably his: the 'Lubitsch touch' was a form of visual innuendo, spicy without ever being vulgar. His greatest period came after 1922, when he settled in Hollywood and became Paramount's leading producer. Early films include many shorts. Awarded special Oscar 1946 'for his distinguished contributions to the art of the motion picture'. Married actress Helene (Leni) Sonnet and his lovers included actresses Ona MUNSON and Natalie SCHAFER.
Biography: 1968, *The Lubitsch Touch* by Herman G. Weinberg. 1994, *Ernst Lubitsch, Laughter in Paradise* by Scott Eyman.
SELECTED EUROPEAN FILMS: Carmen 18. Madame du Barry 19. Sumurun 20. Anne Boleyn 20. Pharaoh's Wife 21. The Flame 21, etc.
■ AMERICAN FILMS: Rosita 23. *The Marriage Circle* 24. Three Women 24. *Forbidden Paradise* 24. Kiss Me Again 25. Lady Windermere's Fan 25. So This Is Paris 26. The Student Prince 27. The Patriot (AAN) 28. Eternal Love 29. *The Love Parade* (first sound film) (AAN) 29. Paramount on Parade (Chevalier sequences) 30. Monte Carlo 30. The Smiling Lieutenant 31. The Man I Killed 32. *One Hour With You* 32. *Trouble in Paradise* 32. If I Had a Million (Laughton sequence) 32. Design for Living 33. The Merry Widow 34. *Desire* (p only) 36. Angel 37. Bluebeard's Eighth Wife 38. *Ninotchka* 39. *The Shop Around the Corner* 40. That Uncertain Feeling 41. *To Be or Not To Be* 42. *Heaven Can Wait* (AAN) 43. A Royal Scandal (p only) 45. Cluny Brown 46. That Lady in Ermine (finished by Otto Preminger) 48.
✪ For extending the period of elegant comedy which is now a part of history. *Trouble in Paradise*.
❝ It's the Lubitsch touch that means so much –
piped the posters. 'He was the only director in Hollywood who had his own signature',
said S. N. Behrman. These were two ways of saying that Lubitsch was a master of cinematic innuendo. 'I let the audience use their imaginations. Can I help it if they misconstrue my suggestions?',
he asked archly. In fact he delighted in naughtiness, and carried it off with great delicacy, though he admitted his lapses: 'I sometimes make pictures which are not up to my standard, but then it can only be said of a mediocrity that all his work is up to his standard.'
And he gave in finally to the American way: 'I've been to Paris France and I've been to Paris Paramount. Paris Paramount is better.'
Some people, Mary Pickford for instance, failed to perceive his talents: 'I parted company with him as soon as I could. I thought him a very uninspired director. He was a director of doors.'
According to Andrew Sarris (1968): 'He was the last of the genuine Continentals let loose on the American continent, and we shall never see his like again because the world he celebrated had died – even before he did – everywhere except in his own memory.'

Lucan, Arthur (1887–1954) (Arthur Towle)
British music-hall comedian famous for his impersonation of Old Mother Riley, a comic Irish washerwoman. Made fourteen films featuring her, usually with his wife Kitty McShane (1898–1964) playing his daughter. Born in Boston, Lincolnshire, he developed the character of Old Mother Riley in the 20s. His on-stage partnership with his wife ended in 1951, after a stormy off-stage relationship. Died while waiting to make his entrance at the Tivoli Theatre, Hull.
■ Stars on Parade 35. Kathleen Mavourneen 36. Old Mother Riley 37. Old Mother Riley in Paris 38. Old Mother Riley MP 39. Old Mother Riley Joins Up 39. Old Mother Riley in Business 40. Old Mother Riley's Ghosts 41. Old Mother Riley's Circus 41. Old Mother Riley Detective 43. Old Mother Riley Overseas 44. Old Mother Riley at Home 45. Old Mother Riley's New Venture 49. Old Mother Riley Headmistress 50. Old Mother Riley's Jungle Treasure 51. Mother Riley Meets the Vampire 52.

Lucas, George (1944–)
American director and producer, one of the most commercially successful of contemporary film-makers. He also established Industrial Light and Magic, specializing in special effects, and, through his company Lucasfilm, is involved in the development of computer games software and interactive entertainment.
Biography: 1983, *Skywalking: The Life and Films of George Lucas* by Dale Pollock.
THX 1138 (wd, ed) 73. *American Graffiti* (wd, p) (AAN) 73. *Star Wars* (wd) (AAN) 77. More American Graffiti (p) 79. The Empire Strikes Back (w, p) 80. Raiders of the Lost Ark (p, story) 81. Return of the Jedi (w, p) 83. Twice upon a Time (p) 83. Indiana Jones and the Temple of Doom (p, story) 84. Mishima: A Life in Four Chapters (p) 85. Captain Eo (p) 86. Howard the Duck (p) 86. Labyrinth (p) 86. The Land before Time (p) 88. Powaqqatsi (p) 88. Tucker: The Man and His Dream (p) 88. Willow (p, story) 88. Indiana Jones and the Last Crusade (p, story) 89. Radioland Murders (p, story) 94. Star Wars Episode 1: The Phantom Menace (p, wd) 99, etc.
❝ He reminded me a little of Walt Disney's version of a mad scientist. – *Steven Spielberg*
It's not what you say, or what people think of you, it's what you do that counts. – *G.L.*
Making movies is like the construction business. You are fighting all possible odds and everyone is seemingly against you. – *G.L.*

Lucas, Leighton (1903–1982)
British composer and musical director; former ballet dancer.
Target for Tonight 41. Portrait of Clare 50. Stage Fright 50. Talk of a Million 51. The Third Visitor 51. The Weak and the Wicked 53. The Dam Busters 55. Yangtse Incident 56. A King in New York 57. Ice Cold in Alex 58. Son of Robin Hood 58. Serious Charge 59. The Millionairess 61, etc.

Lucas, Wilfred (1871–1940)
Canadian character actor in Hollywood, best remembered as a foil for Laurel and Hardy.
The Barbarian 08. The Spanish Gypsy 11. Cohen's Outing 13. Acquitted 16. The Westerners 18. The Barnstormer 22. The Fatal Mistake 24. Her Sacrifice 26. Just Imagine 30. *Pardon Us* 31. Fra Diavolo 33. The Count of Monte Cristo 34. Modern Times 36. The Baroness and the Butler 38. Zenobia 39. A Chump at Oxford 40. The Sea Wolf 41, many others.

Lucas, William (1926–)
British leading man of stage, TV and occasional films.
Timeslip 55. X the Unknown 56. Breakout 59. Sons and Lovers 60. The Devil's Daffodil 61. Calculated Risk 63. Night of the Big Heat/Isle of the Burning Doomed 67. Scramble 70. Tower of Evil 72. Operation Daybreak 75. The Plague Dogs (voice) 82, etc.
TV series: The Adventures of Black Beauty 72–74. Eldorado 92–93.

Luchaire, Corinne (1921–1950)
French actress who was a big hit in *Prison Without Bars* 38. After World War II was convicted as a collaborator and died in poverty.

Luchini, Fabrice (1948–)
French leading actor of stage and screen. Born in Paris, he began as a hairdresser at the age of 14, a trade to which he had to return in the late 70s when he could not find work.
Don't Be Blue/Tout Peut Arriver 69. Claire's Knee/Le Genou de Claire 70. Immoral Tales/Contes Immoraux 74. Violette Nozière 77. Perceval le Gallois 78. The Aviator's Wife/La Femme de l'Aviateur 80. Full Moon in Paris 84. Emmanuelle 4 84. 4 Aventures de Reinette et Mirabelle 86. Hotel du Paradis 86. The Colour of the Wind/La Couleur du Vent 88. Uranus 90. Casanova's Return/Le Retour de Casanova 92. Toxic Affair 93. Le Colonel Chabert 94. Beaumarchais 96. Un Air Si Pur 97. Le Bossu 97, etc.

Luckinbill, Laurence (1934–)
American leading man.
The Boys in the Band 70. Such Good Friends 71. The Delphi Bureau (TV) 72 (and short series). Death Sentence (TV) 74. Panic on the 5.22 (TV) 74. Winner Take All (TV) 75. The Lindbergh Kidnapping Case (TV) 76. Ike (TV) 79. The Promise (TV) 80. Messenger of Death 88. Star Trek V: The Final Frontier 89, etc.

Lucking, Bill
Sturdy American supporting actor.
Hell's Babies 69. Wild Rovers 71. Oklahoma Crude 73. The Return of a Man Called Horse 76. Power (TV) 79. Coast to Coast 80. The Mountain Men 80. Stripes 81. Rescue Me 93. Extreme Justice 93. The River Wild 94. Sleepstalker 95. The Trigger Effect 96, etc.
TV series: Big Hawaii 77. Shannon 81–82. The Blue and the Grey 82. The A-Team 83–84. Jessie 84.

Ludlow, Patrick (1903–1996)
Elegant English actor, on stage as a child from 1915 and still acting in the late 80s.
Autobiography: *Bloody Ludlow*.
Afraid of Love 25. Love on the Spot 32. Bitter Sweet 33. The Private Life of Henry VIII 33. Evergreen 34. Jury's Evidence 36. Old Mother Riley 37. Old Mother Riley MP 39. Goodbye Mr Chips 39. We'll Smile Again 42. The Great St Trinian's Train Robbery 66. Modesty Blaise 66, etc.

Ludwig, Edward (1899–1982)
American director, from 1932.
They Just Had To Get Married 33. Friends of Mr Sweeney 34. *The Man Who Reclaimed His Head* 34. Age of Indiscretion 36. That Certain Age 38. The Last Gangster 39. The Swiss Family Robinson 40. The Man Who Lost Himself 41. They Came to Blow Up America 43. The Fighting Seabees 44. Three's a Family 45. The Fabulous Texan 47. *Wake of the Red Witch* 48. Smuggler's Island 51. Big Jim McLain 52. Sangaree 53. Flame of the Islands 56. The Black Scorpion 57. The Gun Hawk 63, etc.

Ludwig, William (1912–)
American writer.
The *Hardy Family* films 38–44. Challenge to Lassie 49. Shadow on the Wall 50. The Great Caruso 51. *Interrupted Melody* (AA) 55. Back Street 61, etc.

Lugosi, Bela (1882–1956) (Bela Ferenc Blasko; known professionally for a time as Ariztid Olt)
Hungarian stage actor of chilling presence and voice; became famous in films as Dracula, but his accent was a handicap for normal roles and he became typecast in inferior horror films. He was played by Martin Landau in the 1994 biopic *Ed Wood*.
Biography: 1974, *The Count* by Arthur Lennig. 1976, *Lugosi, the Man behind the Cape* by Robert Cremer. 1997, *Lugosi* by Barry Don Rhodes.
The Silent Command 23. The Rejected Woman 24. The Thirteenth Chair 29. Renegades 30. Oh For a Man 30. *Dracula* 30. Broad Minded 31. The Black Camel 31. *The Murders in the Rue Morgue* 31. *White Zombie* 32. *Chandu the Magician* 32. Island of Lost Souls 33. The Death Kiss 33. *The Black Cat* 34. Mysterious Mr Wong 35. The Mystery of the Marie Celeste (GB) 35. Mark of the Vampire 35. The Raven 35. The Invisible Ray 35. Postal Inspector 36. Dark Eyes of London (GB) 38. The Phantom Creeps 39. *Son of Frankenstein* (as Igor) 39. The Saint's Double Trouble 40. Black Friday 40. The Wolf Man 41. Spooks Run Wild 41. Night Monster 42. The Ghost of Frankenstein 42. The Ape Man 43. Frankenstein Meets the Wolf Man (as the monster) 43. The Return of the Vampire 43. One Body Too Many 44. Zombies on Broadway 45. The Body Snatcher 45. Scared to Death 47. *Abbott and Costello Meet Frankenstein* (as Dracula) 48. Bela Lugosi Meets a Brooklyn Gorilla 52. Mother Riley Meets the Vampire (GB) 52. Bride of the Monster 56. Plan 9 from Outer Space 56, etc.
✪ For bringing a touch of European mystery to a succession of rudimentary melodramas. *Son of Frankenstein*.
❝ For some people he was the embodiment of all mysterious forces, a harbinger of evil from the world of shadow. For others he was merely a ham actor appearing in a type of film unsuitable for children and often unfit for adults. – *Arthur Lennig*
Famous line (*Dracula*) 'Listen to them – children of the night! What music they make!'

Luhrmann, Baz (1962–)
Australian director, a former actor, from the theatre.
Winter of Our Dreams (a) 81. Southern Cross (a) 82. Kids of the Cross (d) (TV) 92. *Strictly Ballroom* (d) 92. Romeo and Juliet (d) 96. Moulin Rouge (d) 01, etc.

Lukas, Paul (1887–1971) (Pal Lukacs)
Suave Hungarian leading actor, in Hollywood from the late 20s, first as a romantic figure, then as a smooth villain, finally as a kindly old man.
Two Lovers 28. Three Sinners 28. Manhattan Cocktail 28. Half Way to Heaven 29. Slightly Scarlet 30. The Benson Murder Case 30. Slightly Dishonorable 31. City Streets 31. Thunder Below 32. Rockabye 32. The Kiss Before the Mirror 33. The Secret of the Blue Room 33. *Little Women* 33. By Candlelight 33. Affairs of a Gentleman 34. I Give My Love 34. The Fountain 34. The Casino Murder Case 34. The Three Musketeers 35. I Found Stella Parish 35. *Dodsworth* 36. Dinner at the Ritz (GB) 37. *The Lady Vanishes* (GB) 38. The Chinese Bungalow (GB) 38. *Confessions of a Nazi Spy* 39. Strange Cargo 40. The Ghost Breakers 40. They Dare Not Love 41. Lady in Distress 42. *Watch on the Rhine* (AA) 43. Hostages 43. Uncertain Glory 44. *Address Unknown* 44. *Experiment Perilous* 44. Deadline at Dawn 46. Berlin Express 48. Kim 50. 20,000 Leagues Under the Sea 54. Roots of Heaven 58. Tender is the Night 61. 55 Days at Peking 63. Lord Jim 65. Sol Madrid 68, etc.
✪ For being such a gentleman. *The Lady Vanishes*.

Luke, Keye (1904–1991)
Chinese-American actor who was popular in the 30s as Charlie Chan's number-two son.
Charlie Chan in Paris 34. Oil for the Lamps of China 35. King of Burlesque 36. Charlie Chan at the Opera 36. Charlie Chan on Broadway 37. International Settlement 38. Mr Moto's Gamble 38. Disputed Passage 39. Bowery Blitzkrieg 41. Invisible Agent 42. Salute to the Marines 43. Three Men in White 44. First Yank into Tokyo 45. Sleep My Love 47. Hell's Half Acre 54. Battle Hell 57. Yangtse Incident (GB) 57. Nobody's Perfect 67. The Chairman (GB) 69. The Amsterdam Kill 78. Gremlins 84. A Fine Mess 86, many others.
TV series: Kentucky Jones 64–65. *Anna and the King* 72. *Kung Fu* 72–74. Harry-O 76. Sidekicks 86–87.

Lulli, Folco (1912–1970)
Italian character actor.
The Bandit 47. Caccia Tragica 48. Without Pity 49. Flight into France 49. No Peace Under the Olives 50. Infidelity 52. *The Wages of Fear* 54. An Eye for an Eye 60. Lafayette 63. Marco the Magnificent 66, many others.

Lulu (1948–) (Marie Lawrie)
British pop singer.
■ Gonks Go Beat 65. To Sir With Love 67. The Cherry Picker 72. Whatever Happened to Harold Smith 99, etc.

Lum and Abner (1902–1980) (Chester Lauk, 1902–1980, and Norris Goff, 1906–1978)
American comedy actors of hillbilly characters.
Dreaming Out Loud 40. Bashful Bachelors 42, etc.

Madison, Guy (1922–1996) (Robert Moseley)
Rugged American leading man, in films since 1944 after a naval career. In the 60s, he went to Italy to make spaghetti westerns and action movies. His first wife (1949-54) was actress Gail Russell.
Since You Went Away (debut) 44. Till the End of Time 46. Honeymoon 47. Texas, Brooklyn and Heaven 48. Drums in the Deep South 51. The Charge at Feather River 53. The Command 54. Five Against the House 55. On the Threshold of Space 56. The Beast of Hollow Mountain 56. The Last Frontier 56. Hilda Crane 56. Savage Wilderness 56. Jet over the Atlantic 58. La Schiava di Roma 60. Executioner of Venice (it.) 63. Sandokan against the Leopard of Sarawak (It.) 64. Sandokan Fights Back (It.) 64. Gunmen of the Rio Grande (it.) 65. The Mystery of Thug Island (It.) 66. The Last Panzer Battalion (it.) 68. This Man Can't Die (It.) 70. Where's Willie? 78. Red River (TV) 88, etc.
TV series: *Wild Bill Hickok* 51–54.

Madison, Noel (1898–1975) (Nathaniel Moscovitch)
American actor of sinister roles, especially gangsters. Formerly known as Nat Madison; son of actor Maurice Moscovitch.
Sinners' Holiday 30. Manhattan Melodrama 34. G-Men 35. The Man Who Made Diamonds 37. Crackerjack (GB) 39. Footsteps in the Dark 41. Jitterbugs 43. Gentleman from Nowhere 49, etc.

Madonna (1958–) (Madonna Louise Veronica Ciccone)
Raucous and raunchy pop-singer who courts controversy. Her film roles so far have won her few new fans. In 1992 she signed a $60 million deal with Time Warner to form Maverick, a joint production company covering records, music publishing, films, television and books. She was played by Terumi Matthews in the TV biopic *Madonna: Innocence Lost* 95. Married director Guy Ritchie in 2000.
A Certain Sacrifice 79. Desperately Seeking Susan 85. Shanghai Surprise 86. Who's That Girl? 87. Bloodhounds of Broadway 89. Dick Tracy 90. Truth or Dare/In Bed with Madonna 91. Shadows and Fog 91. A League of Their Own 92. Body of Evidence 92. Snake Eyes 93. Blue in the Face 95. Four Rooms 95. Girl 6 96. Evita 96. The Next Best Thing 00, etc.
❝ I lost my virginity as a career move. – M.
Every decade has its star and Madonna was it in the 80s. But the 80s are over. – *Courtney Love*

Madsen, Michael (1958–)
Burly American actor, often in tough-guy roles. He is the brother of actress Virginia Madsen.
War Games 83. Racing with the Moon 84. The Natural 84. The Killing Time 87. Shadows in the Storm 88. Blood Red 89. Kill Me Again 89. The End of Innocence 90. The Doors 91. Thelma & Louise 91. Fatal Instinct 92. Straight Talk 92. Reservoir Dogs 92. A House in the Hills 93. Free Willy 93. Money for Nothing 93. Trouble Bound 93. The Getaway 93. Season of Change 94. Wyatt Earp 94. Final Combination 94. Species 95. Free Willy 2: The Adventure Home 95. God's Army 95. Man with a Gun 95. Mulholland Falls 96. The Maker 97. Executive Target 97. Diary of a Serial Killer 97. Species 2 98. The Sender 98. Ballad of the Nightingale 98, etc.
TV series: Our Family Honor 85–86. Vengeance Unlimited 98– .

Madsen, Virginia (1963–)
American actress. She is married to director Danny Huston.
Class 83. Electric Dreams 84. Dune 84. Modern Girls 86. Slam Dance 87. Hot to Trot 88. Mr North 88. The Hot Spot 90. Highlander II: The Quickening 91. Candy Man 92. A Murderous Affair: The Carolyn Warmus Story (TV) 92. Blue Tiger 94. Bitter Vengeance (TV) 94. The Prophecy 95. Just Your Luck 96. Ghosts of Mississippi 96. John Grisham's The Rainmaker 97. Ballad of the Nightingale 98, etc.

Maeterlinck, Maurice (1862–1949)
Belgian writer whose fantasy play *The Blue Bird* was filmed several times, never with success.

Maffia, Roma
American actress, from the stage.
Smithereens 82. Married to the Mob 88. American Blue Note 91. The Paper 94. Disclosure 94. The Heidi Chronicles (TV) 95. Nick of Time 95. Eraser 96. Kiss the Girls 97. Double Jeopardy 99, etc.
TV series: Chicago Hope 94–95. Profiler 96.

Magee, Patrick (1924–1982)
British general-purpose actor, often in sinister roles.
The Criminal 60. The Servant 63. Zulu 64. Masque of the Red Death 64. The Skull 65. *The Marat/Sade* 67. *The Birthday Party* 68. King Lear 70. You Can't Win 'Em All 71. The Fiend 71. A Clockwork Orange 71. Demons of the Mind 72. Asylum 72. Rough Cut 80, etc.

Magnani, Anna (1907–1973)
Volatile Italian star actress (Egyptian-born).
The Blind Woman of Sorrento 34. Tempo Massimo 36. *Open City* 45. Angelina 47. *The Miracle* 50. Volcano 53. The Golden Coach 54. Bellissima 54. *The Rose Tattoo* (AA) 55. Wild is the Wind (AAN) 57. The Fugitive Kind 59. Mamma Roma 62. Made in Italy 67. The Secret of Santa Vittoria 69, etc.
❝ Anna Magnani could act anybody off the stage or screen. – *Shelley Winters*

Magne, Michel (1930–1984)
French composer and arranger.
Le Pain Vivant 54. Les Bricoleurs 61. Gigot (AAN) 62. Any Number Can Win 63. Germinal 63. La Ronde 64. Fantomas 64. The Sleeping Car Murders 66. Two Weeks in September 67. Belle de Jour 67. Manon 70 70. Le Complot 75. Emmanuelle 4 84, etc.

Maguire, Tobey (1975–) (Tobias Vincent Maguire)
American actor, from television, born in Santa Monica, California. He began in commercials from his early teens. He was chosen in mid-2000 to play Spiderman in an upcoming feature.
This Boy's Life 93. SFW 94. A Child's Cry for Help (TV) 94. Empire Records 95. Don's Plum 95. Joyride 96. The Ice Storm 97. Deconstructing Harry 98. Fear and Loathing in Las Vegas 98. Pleasantville 98. Ride with the Devil 99. The Cider House Rules 99. Wonder Boys 00, etc.
TV series: Great Scott! 92.
❝ I think fame is a real test of what kind of person you are and if you can stay intact. – *T.M.*

Maharis, George (1928–)
Intense-looking American leading man who has been most successful on TV.
■ Exodus 60. Sylvia 65. Quick Before it Melts 65. The Satan Bug 65. Covenant with Death 67. The Happening 67. The Land Raiders 69. The Monk (TV) 69. The Desperadoes 69. The Last Day of the War 69. The Victim (TV) 72. Rich Man Poor Man (TV) 76. Look What Happened to Rosemary's Baby (TV) 76. Death Flight (TV) 77. Return to Fantasy Island (TV) 78. Crash (TV) 78. The Sword and the Sorcerer 82.
TV series: *Route 66* 60–63. The Most Deadly Game 70.

Mahin, John Lee (1902–1984)
American scriptwriter.
Scarface 32. *Red Dust* 32. *Bombshell* 33. Naughty Marietta 35. Captains Courageous (AAN) 37. Too Hot to Handle 38. Dr Jekyll and Mr Hyde 41. Tortilla Flat 42. Down to the Sea in Ships 49. Quo Vadis? 51. Elephant Walk 54. Heaven Knows Mr Allison (AAN) 57. The Horse Soldiers (& p) 59. The Spiral Road 62. Moment to Moment 66, many others.

Mahoney, Jock (1919–1989) (Jacques O'Mahoney)
Athletic American leading man who, apart from playing Tarzan, was confined to routine roles. Former stuntman for Gene Autry and Charles Starrett.
The Doolins of Oklahoma 49. A Day of Fury 55. Away All Boats 56. I've Lived Before 56. A Time to Love and a Time to Die 58. The Land Unknown 58. Tarzan the Magnificent 60. Tarzan Goes to India 62. Tarzan's Three Challenges 64. The Walls of Hell 66. The Bad Bunch 76. The End 78, etc.
TV series: The Range Rider 51–52. Yancey Derringer 58.

Mahoney, John (1940–)
English-born actor in America, best known for playing Martin Crane in the TV sitcom *Frasier*.
Code of Silence 85. The Manhattan Project 86. Trapped in Silence 86. Tin Men 87. Moonstruck 87. Frantic 88. The Image 89. Say Anything 89. The Russia House 90. Barton Fink 91. Love Hurts 91. Article 99 92. In the Line of Fire 93. Striking Distance 93. The Hudsucker Proxy 94. Reality Bites 94. The American President 95. She's the One 96. Primal Fear 96. Antz (voice) 98, etc.
TV series: H.E.L.P. 90. Frasier 94– .

Maibaum, Richard (1909–1991)
American scriptwriter who wrote 13 Bond movies.
They Gave Him a Gun 37. Ten Gentlemen from West Point 40. O.S.S. 46. *The Great Gatsby* 49. Cockleshell Heroes 55. Zarak 57. The Day They Robbed the Bank of England 60. Dr No 62. From Russia with Love 63. Goldfinger 64. Thunderball 65. On Her Majesty's Secret Service 69. Diamonds Are Forever 71. The Man with the Golden Gun 74. The Spy Who Loved Me 77. For Your Eyes Only 81. Octopussy 83. A View to a Kill 85. The Living Daylights 87. Licence to Kill 89, etc.

Mailer, Norman (1923–)
Combative American novelist and occasional, unsuccessful scriptwriter, director and actor.
The Naked and the Dead (oa) 58. An American Dream (oa) 66. Beyond the Law (wd) 68. Wild 90 (wd) 69. Maidstone (wd) 70. Town Bloody Hall (a) 79. Ragtime (a) 81. Tough Guys Don't Dance (wd) 87. King Lear (a) 87, etc.

Main, Marjorie (1890–1975) (Mary Tomlinson)
American character actress, probably best remembered as Ma Kettle in the long-running hillbilly series.
Take a Chance (debut) 33. *Dead End* 37. Stella Dallas 37. Test Pilot 38. Angels Wash Their Faces 39. The Women 39. Turnabout 40. Bad Man of Wyoming 40. A Woman's Face 41. Honky Tonk 41. Jackass Mail 42. Tish 42. Heaven Can Wait 43. Rationing 43. *Meet Me in St Louis* 44. *Murder He Says* 44. The Harvey Girls 45. Bad Bascomb 45. Undercurrent 46. *The Egg and I* (AAN) 47. The Wistful Widow of Wagon Gap 47. *Ma and Pa Kettle* 49. Ma and Pa Kettle Go to Town 50 (then one Kettle film a year till 56). Mrs O'Malley and Mr Malone 50. The Belle of New York 52. Rose Marie 54. Friendly Persuasion 56, many others.

Mainwaring, Daniel (1902–1977) (aka Geoffrey Homes)
American screenwriter and novelist.
No Hands on the Clock 41. Dangerous Passage 44. Tokyo Rose 45. They Made Me a Killer 46. Out of the Past 47. The Big Steal 49. The Eagle and the Hawk 50. Bugles in the Afternoon 52. This Woman Is Dangerous 52. The Desperado 54. Invasion of the Body Snatchers 56. Baby Face Nelson 57. The Gun Runners 58. Walk Like a Dragon 60. The George Raft Story 61. Convict Stage 65, etc.

Maitland, Marne (1916–1991)
Anglo-Indian actor in British films; adept at sinister orientals.
Cairo Road 50. Father Brown 54. Bhowani Junction 56. The Camp on Blood Island 58. The Stranglers of Bombay 59. Sands of the Desert 60. Nine Hours to Rama 62. Lord Jim 65. The Reptile 65. Khartoum 66. The Pink Panther Strikes Again 76. The Black Stallion 79. Memed My Hawk 87. And the Violins Stopped Playing 89. The King's Whore 90, etc.

Majidi, Majid (1959–)
Iranian film director, screenwriter and actor.
as director and screenwriter: Baduk 92. The Father/Pedar 96. Children of Heaven/Bacheha-ye Aseman (AAN) 97. The Colour of Paradise/Rang-e Khoda 99, etc.

Majorino, Tina (1985–)
American child actor.
When a Man Loves a Woman 94. Corrina, Corrina 94. André 94. Waterworld 95. True Women (TV) 97. Santa Fe 97, etc.

Majors, Lee (1940–) (Harvey Lee Yeary II)
American leading man. Formerly married to actress Farrah Fawcett.
Will Penny 67. The Ballad of Andy Crocker (TV) 68. The Liberation of L.B. Jones 70. Weekend of Terror (TV) 73. The Six Million Dollar Man (TV) 73. Gary Francis Powers (TV) 76. Just a Little Inconvenience (TV) 78. The Norseman 78. Killer Fish 78. Steel 80. The Naked Sun 80. Agency 80. Sharks 80. The Fall Guy (TV) 81. Starflight One (TV) 83. The Cowboy and the Ballerina (TV) 84. Return of the Six Million Dollar Man and the Bionic Woman (TV) 87. Danger Down Under (TV) 88. Scrooged 88. Bionic Showdown (TV) 89. Keaton's Cop 90. Fire! Trapped on the 37th Floor (TV) 91. The Cover Girl Murders 93, etc.
TV series: *The Big Valley* 65–68. The Men from Shiloh 70. Owen Marshall 71–72. *Six Million Dollar Man* 73–78. The Fall Guy 81–86.

Makavejev, Dusan (1932–)
Yugoslavian director.
■ *The Switchboard Operator* 67. Innocence Unprotected 68. *WR: Mysteries of the Organism* 71. Sweet Movie 74. Montenegro 80. The Coca Cola Kid 84. Manifesto 88. Gorilla Bathes at Noon 93. A Hole in the Soul (doc) 95.

Makeham, Eliot (1882–1956)
British character actor of stage and screen, former accountant. For years played bespectacled little bank clerks who sometimes surprised by standing up for themselves.
Rome Express 32. Orders Is Orders 32. Lorna Doone 35. Dark Journey 37. Farewell Again 37. Saloon Bar 40. *Night Train to Munich* 40. The Common Touch 42. The Halfway House 44. Jassy 47. Trio 50. Scrooge 51. Doctor in the House 53. Sailor Beware 56, etc.

Makhmalbaf, Mohsen (1952–)
Iranian director, screenwriter, editor, author and playwright. Born in Teheran, he was a member of an Islamic militant group and was imprisoned for several years for his political activities. After the revolution of 1979, he began writing plays and became head of the Bureau of Islamic Arts and Thought. Some of his more recent films have run into censorship problems in Iran. He is the father of director Samirah Makhmalbaf.
Dasforush 87. The Cyclist 89. Close Up (a only) 90. Once upon a Time, the Movies 93. The Actor (& ed) 93. Gabbeh (AAN) 95. Bread and Flower 96. The Silence/Le Silence 98, etc.

Makhmalbaf, Samira (1980–)
Iranian director, the daughter of director Mohsen Makhmalbaf.
The Apple 98. Blackboards/Takhte Siah 00, etc.

Makk, Károly (1925–)
Hungarian director and screenwriter. He studied at the Academy of Film and Theatre Art.
Liliomfi 54. The House under the Rocks/Haz a Sziklak Alatt 58. Bolondas Vakacio 67. Love/Szerelem 71. A Very Moral Night/Egy Erkolcsos 78. Another Way/Olelkezo Tekintetek (wd) 82. Jatsani Kell 85. Hungarian Requiem/Magyar Rekviem 90. The Gambler 97, etc.

Mako (1933–) (Makoto Iwamatsu)
Japanese-American character actor.
The Sand Pebbles (AAN) 66. Hawaii 67. The Island at the Top of the World 74. The Big Brawl 80. The Bushido Blade 80. Under the Rainbow 81. Testament 83. Conan the Destroyer 84. Armed Response 86. Tucker: The Man and His Dream 88. The Wash 88. Fatal Mission 89. An Unremarkable Life 89. Pacific Heights 90. The Perfect Weapon 91. Rising Sun 93. Robocop 3 93. Cultivating Charlie 94. Highlander III: The Sorcerer 94. Crying Freeman 95. Blood for Blood 95. Riot in the Streets 96. Balance of Power 96. Seven Years in Tibet 97, etc.
TV series: Hawaiian Heat 84.

Mala (1906–1952) (Ray Wise)
Eskimo actor who was popular in a few American films of the 30s.
Igloo 32. Eskimo 33. Hawk of the Wilderness 35. The Tuttles of Tahiti 42. Red Snow 52, etc.

Mala, Ray (1906–1952) (R. Wise, aka Chee-ak)
Alaskan Eskimo cinematographer, writer and actor. Born in Candle Alaska, the son of an Inupiaq mother and an American father, he was cameraman for Danish explorer Knud Rasmussen's film *Teddy Bear* 23. He went to Hollywood to work as cameraman on *Iceberg* and *Frozen Justice* 30, and co-wrote and starred in *Igloo* 32, set in the Arctic, for Universal, but it failed at the box-office.
Books: 1995, *Freeze Frame: Alaska Eskimos in the Movies* by Ann Fienup-Riordan.
Igloo (&co-w) 32. Eskimo 33. Last of the Pagans 35. The Jungle Princess 36. Robinson Crusoe of

Clipper Island (serial) 36. Hawk of the Wilderness (serial) 38. Call of the Yukon 38. Green Hell 40. The Girl from Alaska 42. The Tuttles of Tahiti 42. The Mad Doctor of Market Street 42. Red Snow 52, etc.

Malahide, Patrick (1945–)
Gaunt English leading actor, mainly on television and best known as Inspector Alleyn in the TV series. He began as a stage manager before working in repertory as an actor and is also a television playwright.
The Killing Fields 84. Comfort and Joy 87. The Singing Detective (TV) 87. A Month in the Country 87. December Bride 90. Smack and Thistle 90. *Middlemarch* (TV) 94. A Man of No Importance 94. Two Deaths 95. CutThroat Island (US) 95. Deacon Brodie (TV) 96. The Long Kiss Goodnight (US) 96. 'Til There Was You (US) 97. The Beautician and the Beast (US) 97. Heaven (NZ) 98. Captain Jack 98. Ordinary Decent Criminal 00. The Fortress 2: Re-entry (US) 00. Quills (US) 00, etc.
TV series: Minder 79–85. The Inspector Alleyn Mysteries 93–94.

Malandrinos, Andrea (1896–1970)
Greek-born character actor in British films, from music hall.
Raise the Roof 30. The Lodger 32. The Admiral's Secret 34. Midshipman Easy 35. Limelight 36. Tropical Trouble 37. Thunder Rock 42. Champagne Charlie 44. My Brother Jonathan 48. The Lavender Hill Mob 51. Cockleshell Heroes 55. The Prince and the Showgirl 57. Tommy the Toreador 59. The Yellow Rolls-Royce 64. The Mummy's Shroud 67. The Oblong Box 69. Hell Boats 70, many more.

Malden, Karl (1912–) (Mladen Sekulovich)
Respected American stage actor whose film career has been generally disappointing because Hollywood has not seemed to know what to do with him.
Autobiography: 1997, *When Do I Start?* (with Carla Malden).
■ They Knew What They Wanted 40. Winged Victory 44. 13 Rue Madeleine 46. Boomerang 47. Kiss of Death 47. The Gunfighter 50. Where the Sidewalk Ends 50. Halls of Montezuma 50. *A Streetcar Named Desire* (AA) 52. Decision Before Dawn 52. Diplomatic Courier 52. Operation Secret 52. Ruby Gentry 52. I Confess 53. Take the High Ground 53. Phantom of the Rue Morgue 54. *On the Waterfront* (AAN) 54. *Baby Doll* 56. Fear Strikes Out 57. Time Limit (d only) 57. Bombers B52 57. The Hanging Tree 59. Pollyanna 60. The Great Imposter 60. Parrish 61. One Eyed Jacks 61. All Fall Down 62. Bird Man of Alcatraz 62. Gypsy 62. How the West Was Won 63. Come Fly with Me 63. Dead Ringer 64. Cheyenne Autumn 64. The Cincinnati Kid 65. Nevada Smith 66. The Silencers 66. Murderers Row 66. *Hotel* 67. The Adventures of Bullwhip Griffin 67. Billion Dollar Brain 67. Blue 68. Hot Millions 68. Patton 69. Cat O'Nine Tails 69. Wild Rovers 71. Captains Courageous (TV) 78. Meteor 79. Beyond the Poseidon Adventure 79. *Word of Honor* (TV) 81. The Sting II 82. Summertime Killer 82. Twilight Time 83. *Fatal Vision* (TV) 84. Billy Galvin 86. Nuts 87.
TV series: *Streets of San Francisco* 72–76. Skag 80.

Malick, Terrence (1945–)
Reclusive American director.
■ Pocket Money (w only) 72. *Badlands* (&w, p) 73. The Gravy Train (w only) 74. *Days of Heaven* (& w, p) 79. *The Thin Red Line* (AANw, AANd) 98.

Malik, Art (1953–)
Pakistani actor who grew up in Britain and made his reputation on TV.
Arabian Adventure 79. The Jewel in the Crown (TV) 84. A Passage to India 84. The Living Daylights 87. City of Joy 92. The Year of the Comet 92. Hostage 92. Turtle Beach 92. Uncovered 94. True Lies 94. A Kid in King Arthur's Court (US) 95. Booty Call (US) 96. Path to Paradise (TV) 97. Side Streets (US) 98, etc.
TV series: Hothouse 89. Life Support 99.

Malinger, Ross (1984–)
American child actor.
Kindergarten Cop 90. Eve of Destruction 91. Sleepless in Seattle 93. Bye Bye, Love 95. Sudden Death 95. Little Bigfoot 96. Toothless 97. Frog and Wombat 98, etc.
TV series: Good Advice 93–94.

Malkovich, John (1953–)
American leading actor of icy demeanour, from the stage. Born in Benton, Illinois, and educated at Illinois State University, he was a co-founder, with Gary Sinise, of the Steppenwolf Theatre Company in Chicago.
The Killing Fields 84. Places in the Heart (AAN) 84. Eleni 85. Private Conversations 85. Making Mr Right 87. The Glass Menagerie 87. Empire of the Sun 87. Miles from Home 88. Dangerous Liaisons 88. The Sheltering Sky 90. Object of Beauty 91. Shadows and Fog 91. Queen's Logic 91. Of Mice and Men 92. Jennifer 8 92. In the Line of Fire (AAN) 93. Heart of Darkness (TV) 93. Mary Reilly 95. Beyond the Clouds 95. The Convent (Port.) 95. Mulholland Falls 96. The Portrait of a Lady 96. The Ogre 96. Con Air 97. The Man in the Iron Mask 98. Rounders 98. Joan of Arc (Fr.) 99. Shadow of the Vampire 00, etc.
❝ In movies you're a product. And if I'm a product, I'm a Tabasco sauce. I'm not a sort of shepherd's pie, and that's the way it is. – *J.M.*
The movie business flattens everything in its wake like an ancient dead tree falling from an immense height into a particularly soft spot of moist, dumb green grass. It must be said, of course, that the public plays no small part in the movie business, greedily consuming the worst that movies have to offer. – *J.M.*

Malle, Louis (1932–1995)
French 'new wave' director, former assistant to Robert Bresson. Married Candice Bergen.
Books: 1993, *Malle on Malle* by Philip French.
World of Silence (co-d) 56. Lift to the Scaffold 57. *The Lovers* 58. *Zazie dans le Métro* 61. *Le Feu Follet* 63. Viva Maria 65. Le Voleur 67. *Souffle au Coeur* (AANw) 71. Lacombe Lucien 75. Black Moon 75. Pretty Baby 78. Atlantic City (BFA, AAN) 80. My Dinner with André 81. Crackers 84. Alamo Bay 85. *Au Revoir, les Enfants* (AAN) 87. *May Fools*/Milou en Mai 90. Bohemian Life/La Vie de Bohème (a) 92. Damage 92. Vanya on 42nd Street 94, etc.
❝ You see the world much better through a camera. – *L.M.*

Malleson, Miles (1888–1969)
British playwright, screen writer and actor whose credits read like a potted history of the British cinema.
as writer: *Nell Gwyn* 34. Peg of Old Drury 35. Rhodes of Africa 36. *Victoria the Great* 37. The Thief of Bagdad 40. The First of the Few 42. They Flew Alone 43. Mr Emmanuel 44, etc.
as actor: City of Song 31. The Sign of Four 32. Bitter Sweet 33. Nell Gwyn 34. Tudor Rose 36. Knight without Armour 37. The Thief of Bagdad (as the sultan) 40. Major Barbara 41. They Flew Alone 42. Dead of Night 45. While the Sun Shines 47. Saraband for Dead Lovers 48. *Kind Hearts and Coronets* (as the hangman) 49. The Perfect Woman 49. Stage Fright 50. The Man in the White Suit 51. The Magic Box 51. *The Importance of Being Earnest* (as Canon Chasuble) 52. Folly to Be Wise 52. The Captain's Paradise 53. Private's Progress 56. *Brothers in Law* 57. The Naked Truth 57. *Dracula* 58. The Captain's Table 58. The Hound of the Baskervilles 59. I'm All Right Jack 59. Brides of Dracula 60. The Hellfire Club 61. Heavens Above 63. First Men in the Moon 64. You Must Be Joking 65, many others.

Mallory, Boots (1913–1958) (Patricia Mallory)
American leading lady of the 30s; married William Cagney and Herbert Marshall.
Handle with Care 32. Hello Sister 33. Sing Sing Nights 35. Here's Flash Casey 37, etc.

Malo, Gina (1909–1963) (Janet Flynn)
Irish-German-American leading lady of the 30s, usually in tempestuous roles. Filmed in Britain; married Romney Brent.
In a Monastery Garden 32. Good Night Vienna 32. Waltz Time 33. The Private Life of Don Juan 34. Jack of All Trades 36. Over She Goes 38. The Door with Seven Locks 40, etc.

Malone, Dorothy (1925–) (Dorothy Maloney)
American leading lady of the 50s, often in sultry roles.
■ The Falcon and the Co-Eds 43. One Mysterious Night 44. Show Business 44. Seven Days Ashore 44. Hollywood Canteen 44. Too Young to Know 45. Janie Gets Married 46. *The Big Sleep* 46. Night and Day 48. To the Victor 48. Two Guys from Texas 48. One Sunday Afternoon 48. Flaxy Martin 49. South of St Louis 49. Colorado Territory 49. The Nevadan 50. Convicted 50. Mrs O'Malley and Mr Malone 50. The Killer that Stalked New York 50. Saddle Legion 51. The Bushwhackers 52. Scared Stiff 53. Torpedo Alley 53. Law and Order 54. Jack Slade 54. Loophole 54. Pushover 54. The Fast and Furious 54. Private Hell 36 54. Young at Heart 54. The Lone Gun 54. Five Guns West 55. Battle Cry 55. Tall Man Riding 55. Sincerely Yours 55. Artists and Models 55. At Gunpoint 55. Pillars of the Sky 56. Tension at Table Rock 56. *Written on the Wind* (AA) 56. Quantez 57. *Man of a Thousand Faces* 57. *The Tarnished Angels* 57. Tip on a Dead Jockey 57. *Too Much Too Soon* (as Diana Barrymore) 58. Warlock 59. The Last Voyage 60. The Last Sunset 61. Beach Party 63. Fate Is the Hunter 64. The Pigeon (TV) 69. Exzess (Ger.) 70. The Man Who Would Not Die 75. Rich Man Poor Man (TV) 76. Little Ladies of the Night (TV) 77. Murder in Peyton Place (TV) 77. Katie: Portrait of a Centerfold (TV) 78. Good Luck Miss Wyckoff 79. Winter Kills 79. Condominium (TV) 80. The Being 83. Peyton Place, the Next Generation (TV) 85. Basic Instinct 92.
TV series: *Peyton Place* 64–68.

Malone, Jena (1984–)
American actress, born in Sparks, Nevada. She made news In 1999 when she sued her mother for mismanagement of her earnings, which reportedly had reached more than $1m.
Bastard Out of Carolina (TV) 96. Contact 97. Hope (TV) 97. Ellen Foster (TV) 97. Stepmom 98. For Love of the Game 99, etc.

Malone, Mark
American screenwriter who turned to directing in the mid-90s.
Dead of Winter (co-w) 87. Signs of Life (w) 89. Killer/Bulletproof Heart (d) 94.

Malone, William
American director and screenwriter, mainly of horror movies.
Scared to Death (wd) 80. Creature(wd) 85. Universal Soldier: The Return (co-w) House on Haunted Hill (d) 99. Supernova (story) 00, etc.

Maloney, Michael (1957–)
English actor, from the stage, including leading roles with the Royal Shakespeare Company.
Sharma and Beyond (TV) 84. Henry V 89. Hamlet 90. Truly Madly Deeply 91. Love on a Branch Line (TV) 93. In the Bleak Midwinter 95. Othello 95. Looking for Richard 96. Hamlet 96. Sex and Chocolate (TV) 97. Painted Lady (TV) 97. A Christmas Carol (TV) 00, etc.

Malraux, André (1901–1976)
French author and politician, finally Minister of Culture; the leading spirit behind the 1937 documentary of the Spanish Civil War, *Days of Hope*.

Maltby, Henry Francis (1880–1963)
Prolific British comedy playwright and screenwriter, and actor of choleric characters. Born in Ceres, South Africa, he was first a bank clerk, and made his stage debut in 1899. He was the author of more than 50 plays from 1905 onwards.
Autobiography: 1950, *Ring Up the Curtain*.
as writer: For the Love of Mike (oa) 32. Just My Luck (oa) 33. The Laughter of Fools (oa) 33. The Love Nest (co-w) 33. Over the Garden Wall (co-w) 34. The Right Age to Marry (co-w, oa) 35. Department Store (co-w) 35. Busman's Holiday (co-w) 36. The Howard Case (oa) 36. Queen of Hearts (co-w) 36. It's Never Too Late to Mend 37. His Lordship Regrets (co-w, oa) 38. His Lordship Goes to Press (co-w) 38. Blind Folly 39. Crimes at the Dark House (co-w) 39, etc.
as actor: The Rotters (& w) 21. Facing the Music 33. Home Sweet Home 33. Those Were the Days 34. Josser on the Farm 34. Emil and the Detectives 35. Sweeney Todd 36. The Crimes of Stephen Hawke 36. Boys Will Be Girls 37. The Ticket of Leave Man 37. Pygmalion 38. A Yank at Oxford 38. Old Mother Riley Joins Up 39. Under Your Hat 40. Gert and Daisy's Weekend 41. The Great Mr Handel 42. A Canterbury Tale 44. Caesar and Cleopatra 45. The Trojan Brothers 46, many others.

Maltz, Albert (1908–1985)
American screenwriter who suffered from the anti-communist witch-hunt as one of the 'Hollywood Ten'.
Afraid to Talk 32. This Gun for Hire 42. Destination Tokyo 43. The Man in Half Moon Street 44. Pride of the Marines (AAN) 45. Cloak and Dagger 46. *Naked City* 48. The Robe 53. Broken Arrow 60. Two Mules for Sister Sara 70. Scalawag 73, etc.

Malyon, Eily (1879–1961)
English character actress in Hollywood, a familiar supporting face from *His Greatest Gamble* 34 to *The Secret Heart* 46, typically as the acidulous aunt in *On Borrowed Time* 38.

Mambéty, Djibril Diop (1945–1998)
Senegalese director, screenwriter and actor. Born in Dakar, he studied drama at the Daniel Sorano Theatre, where he worked as an actor and director, going on to make his first film with a camera he borrowed from the local Institut Français. Died of cancer.
■ Contras' City (short) 69. Badou Boy 70. Hyena's Progress/Touki-Bouki 73. Parlons Grandmère (short) 89. Hyenas/Hyènes 92. Le Franc 95. La Petite Vendeuse de Soleil 99.

Mamet, David (1947–)
American dramatist, director and screenwriter. He set up a film production company, Films of Atlantic, in 1998, with William H. Macy.
The Postman Always Rings Twice (w) 81. *The Verdict* (AANw) 82. About Last Night (oa) 86. Black Widow (a, w) 87. *House of Games* (wd) 87. *The Untouchables* (w) 87. Things Change (wd) 88. We're No Angels (w) 89. Homicide (wd) 91. Hoffa (w) 92. *Glengarry Glen Ross* (w) 92. The Water Engine (w) (TV) 92. A Life in the Theatre (w) 93. Vanya on 42nd Street (w) 94. Oleanna (wd) 94. American Buffalo (w) 96. The Edge (co-w) 97. Wag the Dog (co-w) (AAN) 97. The Spanish Prisoner (wd) 97. Ronin (co-w) 98. The Winslow Boy (wd) 98. Lansky (w, TV) 99. State and Main (wd) 00, etc.
❝ I've always been more comfortable sinking while clutching a good theory than swimming with an ugly fact. – *D.M.*
If Eisenstein would have lived longer and spent more time in Hollywood, he might have talked less about the Theory of Montage, and more about healthy eating, and what to have on the Craft Service Table. – *D.M.*
Working as a screenwriter-for-hire, one is in the employ *not* of the eventual consumers (the audience, whose interests the honest writer must have at heart), but of speculators, whose ambition, many times, is not to please the eventual consumer, but to extort from him as much money as possible as quickly as possible. – *D.M.*
The movies are a momentary and beautiful aberration of a technological society in the last stages of decay. – *D.M.*
I have always thought that in the motion picture business the real violence was not what people do on screen, but what we do to raise the money. – *D.M.*

Mamoulian, Rouben (1897–1987)
American stage director of Armenian origin. Over the years he made a number of films which vary in quality but at their best show a fluent command of the medium.
Began work on *Cleopatra* 62 but was replaced.
■ *Applause* 29. *City Streets* 31. *Dr Jekyll and Mr Hyde* 32. *Love Me Tonight* 32. Song of Songs 33. *Queen Christina* 33. We Live Again 34. *Becky Sharp* 35. *The Gay Desperado* 36. High, Wide and Handsome 37. Golden Boy 39. *The Mark of Zorro* 40. Blood and Sand 41. Rings on Her Fingers 42. Summer Holiday 48. Silk Stockings 57.
❝ His tragedy is that of the innovator who runs out of innovations. – *Andrew Sarris, 1968*

Mancina, Mark (1957–)
American composer.
Where Sleeping Dogs Lie 91. Speed 94. Monkey Trouble 94. Man of the House 95. Bad Boys 95. Money Train 95. Assassins 95. Fair Game 95. Twister 96. Moll Flanders 96. Speed 2: Cruise Control 97. Con Air 97. Return to Paradise 98. Tarzan 99. Bait 00, etc.

Mancini, Henry (1924–1994) (Enrico Mancini)
American composer and songwriter. Educated at the Juilliard School of Music, he was an arranger

and pianist with the post-war Glenn Miller orchestra before working at Universal, 1952–58. Apart from films, he also worked in television, notably for the *Peter Gunn* series 58. His best-known song was 'Moon River', written with lyricist Johnny Mercer, for *Breakfast at Tiffany's*.

Academy Award songs: 'Moon River', 'Days of Wine and Roses'.

AS ARRANGER: The Glenn Miller Story (AAN) 53. The Benny Goodman Story 56, etc.

AS COMPOSER: Touch of Evil 58. High Time 60. *Breakfast at Tiffany's* (AA) 61. Bachelor in Paradise 61. Days of Wine and Roses 62. *Hatari* 62. *The Pink Panther* (AAN) 63. Charade 63. A Shot in the Dark 64. Dear Heart 65. What Did You Do in the War, Daddy? 66. Two for the Road 67. Darling Lili 69. The White Dawn 73. The Return of the Pink Panther 75. Once is Not Enough 76. Silver Streak 76. W. C. Fields and Me 76. House Calls 78. Who is Killing the Great Chefs of Europe? 78. Nightwing 79. 10 (AAN) 79. Little Miss Marker 80. Back Roads 81. Mommie Dearest 81. Victor/Victoria (AA) 82. Harry and Son 84. Lifeforce 85. Santa Claus: The Movie 85. That's Dancing! 85. A Fine Mess 86. That's Life! (AAN) 86. Blind Date 87. The Glass Menagerie 87. Heavy Petting 88. Physical Evidence 88. Sunset 88. Without a Clue 88. Welcome Home 89. Ghost Dad 90. Switch 91. Married to It 91. Son of the Pink Panther 93, etc.

Mancuso, Frank (1928–)
American production executive, appointed head of MGM/UA in 1993, and a former chairman and CEO of Paramount. He remained in charge of the studio following a management buyout in 1996, financed by Kirk Kerkorian and the Australian television company Seven Network.

Mancuso, Kevin
see D'AMATO, Joe.

Mancuso, Nick (1949–)
Italian-born leading man who moved to Canada as a child.

Dr Scorpion (TV) 78. The House on Garibaldi Street (TV) 79. Torn between Two Lovers (TV) 80. Nightwing 80. The Kidnapping of the President 80. Scruples (TV) 81. Ticket to Heaven 81. Mother Lode 82. The Legend of Walks Far Woman (TV) 83. Heartbreakers 84. Night Magic 85. Death of an Angel 85. King of Love (TV) 87. Lena's Holiday 91. Double Identity 91. Rapid Fire 92. Danielle Steel's Message from 'Nam (TV) 93. Flinch 94. Young Ivanhoe 95. A Young Connecticut Yankee in King Arthur's Court 95. The Invader 96. The Ex 96. Marquis de Sade 97. Past Perfect 98. Misbegotten 98, etc.

Mandel, Babaloo (c. 1949–) (Mark Mandel)
American screenwriter and television producer, usually in collaboration with Lowell Ganz.

Night Shift 82. Splash 84. Spies Like Us 85. Gung Ho 86. Vibes 88. Parenthood 89. City Slickers (AAN) 91. Mr Saturday Night 92. A League of Their Own 92. City Slickers II: The Legend of Curly's Gold 94. Greedy/Greed 94. Forget Paris 95. Multiplicity 96. Fathers' Day 97, etc.

TV series: Hiller & Diller (p, co-w) 97.

Mandel, Johnny (1935–)
American composer, trumpeter and trombonist. His song 'The Shadow of Your Smile' (lyrics by Paul Francis Webster), the love theme from *The Sandpiper*, was an Oscar-winner in 1965.

I Want to Live 58. The Third Voice 59. The Americanization of Emily 64. The Sandpiper (AAs) 65. Point Blank 67. M*A*S*H 70. The Last Detail 73. Freaky Friday 76. Agatha 79. Being There 79. The Baltimore Bullet 80. Deathtrap 82. The Verdict 82. Staying Alive 83. Brenda Starr 89, etc.

Mandell, Daniel (1895–1987)
American editor.

The Turmoil 24. Showboat 29. Counsellor at Law 33. Diamond Jim 35. Dodsworth 36. Dead End 37. Wuthering Heights 39. The Little Foxes 41. Arsenic and Old Lace 44. Wonder Man 45. The Best Years of Our Lives (AA) 46. My Foolish Heart 49. Valentino 52. Guys and Dolls 55. Witness for the Prosecution 57. The Apartment (AA) 60. Irma la Douce 63. The Fortune Cookie 66, many others.

Mander, Miles (1888–1946) (Lionel Mander)
British character actor, a former theatre manager with long experience of all kinds of stage work. Later settled in Hollywood.

The Pleasure Garden 26. *The First Born* (& wd) 28. Loose Ends (wd only) 30. The Missing Rembrandt (wd only) 31. The Private Life of Henry VIII 33. Loyalties 33. The Morals of Marcus (d only) 35, etc.

In Hollywood as actor: *The Three Musketeers* (as Richelieu) 36. Lloyds of London 37. Slave Ship 37. Suez 38. The Three Musketeers (musical version; as Richelieu again) 39. *Wuthering Heights* 39. Tower of London 39. Lady Hamilton 41. *Five Graves to Cairo* 43. *Farewell My Lovely* 44. The Scarlet Claw 44. Pearl of Death 44. The Bandit of Sherwood Forest 46. The Walls Came Tumbling Down 46, many others.

Mandoki, Luis
Mexican-born director in Hollywood.

Motel 83. Gaby – A True Story 87. White Palace 90. Born Yesterday 93. When a Man Loves a Woman 94, etc.

Manfredi, Nino (1921–)
Italian leading actor, screenwriter and occasional director, from the stage.

Torna a Napoli 49. Viva il Cinema! 53. Gli Inamorati 55. Camping (a, w) 57. I Ragazzi dei Parioli 58. L'Impiegato (a, w) 59. Crimen 60. Wayward Love/L'Amore Difficile (a, d) 62. The Dolls/Le Bambole 65. A Rose for Everyone/Una Rosa per Tutti 67. Per Grazia Ricevuta (a, wd) 71. Il Conte de Monte Cristo 77. La Mazzetta 78. Café Express (a, w) 80. I Picari 87. Alberto Express 90. Mima 91. The Flying Dutchman 94, etc.

Manfredini, Harry
American composer, mainly for horror movies.

Here Come the Tigers 78. Friday the 13th 80. Friday the 13th Part 2 81. Friday the 13th Part 3 82. Swamp Thing 82. The Returning 83. Friday the 13th: The Final Chapter 84. The Hills Have Eyes Part II 84. Friday the 13th: A New Beginning 85. House 86. Friday the 13th Part VI: Jason Lives 86. House II: The Second Story 87. Friday the 13th Part VII: The New Blood (co-m) 88. Deep Star Six 89. Double Revenge 89. Aces: Iron Eagle III 92. My Boyfriend's Back 93. Jason Goes to Hell: The Final Friday 93. Dead on Sight 94. Wishmaster 97, etc.

Mangano, Silvana (1930–1989)
Italian actress, wife of producer Dino de Laurentiis. Former model.

L'Elisir d'Amore 49. Bitter Rice 51. Anna 51. Mambo 53. Ulysses 54. The Wolves 56. The Sea Wall 57. Tempest 59. Five Branded Women 61. Barabbas 62. Theorem 68. The Decameron 70. Death in Venice 71. Ludwig 72. Conversation Piece 76. Dune 84, etc.

Mangold, James (c. 1964–)
American screenwriter and director.

Heavy 96. Cop Land (wd) 97.

Mankiewicz, Don (1922–)
American scriptwriter and novelist, son of Herman MANKIEWICZ.

Trial 55. House of Numbers 57. I Want to Live (AAN) 58.

Mankiewicz, Francis (1944–1993)
Canadian film director. Born in Shanghai, he studied at the London School of Film Technique. *Good Riddance* is one of the most admired of Canadian films. Died of cancer.

Valentin (TV) 73. Le Temps d'une Chasse 73. *Good Riddance*/Les Bons Debarras 81. Les Beaux Souvenirs 82. And Then You Die (TV) 87. Les Portes Tournantes 88. Conspiracy of Silence (TV) 92, etc.

Mankiewicz, Herman (1897–1953)
American screenwriter, playwright and wit. Born in New York, the son of a Columbia University professor, he studied at Columbia University and the University of Berlin and began as a journalist, including a period as drama critic of the *New Yorker*. Self-destructive, and a compulsive gambler, he often wasted his considerable talents, eventually moving from one studio to another as he lost jobs through non-attendance or indiscretions. An alcoholic, he once threw up at a dinner given by producer Arthur HORNBLOW, Jnr, and remarked, 'It's all right. The white wine came up with the fish.' He lost his job at Columbia after the studio head, Harry COHN, explained that he could tell if a film was good or bad according to whether his fanny squirmed or not. 'Imagine,' said Mankiewicz, 'the whole world wired to Harry Cohn's ass!' He died of uremic poisoning. He was the brother of Joseph L. MANKIEWICZ; his son, Don MANKIEWICZ, was a novelist and screenwriter.

Road to Mandalay (co-w) 26. Stranded in Paris (w) 26. Abie's Irish Rose (co-w) 28. The Dummy (w) 29. Thunderbolt (co-w) 29. Men Are Like That (co-w) 29. The Vagabond King (w) 30. True to the Navy (co-w) 30. Honey (w) 30. The Royal Family of Broadway (co-w) 30. Ladies Love Brutes (co-w) 30. Ladies' Man (w) 31. Man of the World (w) 31. Dancers in the Dark (co-w) 32. Girl Crazy (co-w) 32. The Lost Squadron (co-w) 32. Dinner at Eight (co-w) 33. Another Language (co-w) 33. Meet the Baron (co-w) 33. The Show-Off (w) 34. Stamboul Quest (w) 34. Escapade (w) 35. After Office Hours (w) 35. Love in Exile (co-w) 36. John Meade's Woman (co-w) 37. The Emperor's Candlesticks (co-w) 37. The Three Maxims (w) (GB) 37. My Dear Miss Aldrich (w) 37. It's a Wonderful World (co-w) 39. *Citizen Kane* (contribution disputed; some say he wrote most of it) (AA) 41. Rise and Shine (w) 41. Pride of the Yankees (co-w) (AAN) 42. Goodfellows (oa) 43. Stand By for Action (co-w) 43. Christmas Holiday (w) 44. The Spanish Main (co-w) 45. The Enchanted Cottage (co-w) 45. A Woman's Secret (w) 49. The Pride of St Louis (w) 52, etc.

❝ Will you accept 300 per week to work for Paramount Pictures? All expenses paid. 300 is peanuts. Millions are to be grabbed out here and your only competition is idiots. Don't let this get around. – *H.M.'s wire to Ben Hecht, 1926*

Tell me, do you know any 75-dollar-a-week writers? – *Anon*

I know lots of them, but they're all making 1500 dollars a week. – *H.M.*

In a novel the hero can lay ten girls and marry a virgin for the finish. In a movie this is not allowed. The villain can lay anybody he wants, have as much fun as he wants cheating and stealing, getting rich and whipping the servants. But you have to shoot him in the end. When he falls with a bullet in the forehead, it is advisable that he clutch at the Gobelin tapestry on the wall and bring it down over his head like a symbolic shroud. Also, covered by such a tapestry, the actor does not have to hold his breath while being photographed as a dead man. – *H.M.*

Barbara Stanwyck is my favorite. My God, I could just sit and dream of being married to her, having a little cottage out in the hills, vines around the door. I'd come home from the office tired and weary, and I'd be met by Barbara, walking through the door holding an apple pie she had cooked herself. And wearing no drawers. – *H.M.*

I don't know how it is that you start working at something you don't like, and before you know it you're an old man. – *H.M.*

A greater phenomenon than Herman's wit was the fact that his victims employed him, at large sums, to write movies he despised for bosses he ridiculed. – *Ben Hecht*

Famous line (*Citizen Kane*) 'If I hadn't been so rich, I might have been a really great man.'

Mankiewicz, Joseph L. (1909–1993)
American film creator of many talents.

Biography: 1977, *Pictures Will Talk* by Kenneth Geist.

AS WRITER: The Mysterious Dr Fu Manchu 29. Skippy (AAN) 31. Million Dollar Legs 32. Forsaking All Others 34. The Keys of the Kingdom 44, etc.

AS PRODUCER: Fury 36. The Bride Wore Red 37. Three Comrades 38. Huckleberry Finn 39. Strange Cargo 40. The Philadelphia Story 40. Woman of the Year 42. The Keys of the Kingdom 44, etc.

■ AS WRITER -DIRECTOR: Dragonwyck 46. Somewhere in the Night 46. The Late George Apley 47. The Ghost and Mrs Muir 47. Escape 48. *A Letter for Three Wives* (AA script, AAd) 49. House of Strangers (d only) 50. No Way Out (AAN) 50. *All About Eve* (AA script, AAd) 50. People Will Talk 51. Five Fingers (d only) (AAN) 52. Julius Caesar 53. *The Barefoot Contessa* (AANw) 54. Guys and Dolls 55. The Quiet American (& p) 57. Suddenly Last Summer (d only) 59. Cleopatra 63. The Honey Pot 67. There Was a Crooked Man 70. Sleuth (d only) (AAN) 72.

❝ I got a job at Metro and went in to see Louis Mayer, who told me he wanted me to be a producer. I said I wanted to write and direct. He said, 'No, you have to produce first, you have to crawl before you can walk.' Which is as good a definition of producing as I ever heard. – *J.L.M.*

I felt the urge to direct because I couldn't stomach what was being done with what I wrote. – *J.L.M*

Every screenwriter worthy of the name has already directed his film when he has written his script. – *J.L.M*

There were always financial crises. Someone would come out from the East and announce that the business was in deep trouble, and what would happen was that they'd reduce the number of matzo balls in Louie Mayer's chicken soup from three to two. Then they'd fire a couple of secretaries and feel virtuous. – *J.L.M.*

The toughest three pictures I ever made. It was shot in a state of emergency, shot in confusion, and wound up in blind panic. – *J.L.M. on Cleopatra*

A cinema of intelligence rather than inspiration… his wit scratches more than it bites. – *Andrew Sarris, 1968*

Mankiewicz, Tom (1942–)
American screenwriter, son of Joseph L. MANKIEWICZ.

Live and Let Die 72. The Man with the Golden Gun 73. Mother, Jugs and Speed 76. The Cassandra Crossing 77. The Eagle Has Landed 77. Ladyhawke 85. Dragnet (co-w, d) 87. Delirious (d) 91, etc.

Mankowitz, Wolf (1924–1998)
British novelist and screenwriter.

A Kid for Two Farthings 56. Expresso Bongo 59. The Day the Earth Caught Fire 61. Waltz of the Toreadors 62. Where the Spies Are 65. Casino Royale 66. Dr Faustus 67. The 25th Hour 67. Bloomfield 71. The Hireling 73, etc.

Mann, Abby (1927–)
American playwright and screenwriter.

Judgment at Nuremberg (oa, w) (AA) 61. A Child Is Waiting (w) 63. The Condemned of Altona (w) 63. Ship of Fools (w) (AAN) 65. The Detective (w) 68. The Marcus Nelson Murders (TV) 73. King (TV) (& d) 80. Skag (TV) 80. The Atlanta Child Murders (& d) (TV) 85. Murderers among Us: The Simon Wiesenthal Story (TV) 89. Indictment: The McMartin Trial (TV) 95, etc.

Mann, Anthony (1906–1967) (Emil Bundesmann)
American director, usually of outdoor films; his best work was concerned with the use of violence by thoughtful men.

■ Dr Broadway 42. Moonlight in Havana 42. Nobody's Darling 43. My Best Gal 44. Strangers in the Night 44. The Great Flamarion 45. Two O'Clock Courage 45. Sing Your Way Home 45. Strange Impersonation 46. The Bamboo Blonde 46. Desperate 47. Railroaded 47. T-Men 47. Raw Deal 48. The Black Book 49. Border Incident 49. Side Street 49. Devil's Doorway 50. The Furies 50. *Winchester 73* 50. The Tall Target 51. *Bend of the River* 51. The Naked Spur 52. Thunder Bay 53. *The Glenn Miller Story* 54. The Far Country 55. Strategic Air Command 55. *The Man from Laramie* 55. The Last Frontier 56. Serenade 56. Men in War 57. The Tin Star 57. God's Little Acre 58. Man of the West 58. Cimarron 60. El Cid 61. The Fall of the Roman Empire 64. The Heroes of Telemark 65. A Dandy in Aspic (completed by Laurence Harvey) 68.

Mann, Barry (1942–)
American composer, singer and songwriter, often in collaboration with his wife Cynthia Weill, whose songs have featured in many films since a move from New York to Los Angeles in the 70s.

Wild in the Streets (s) 68. I Never Sang for My Father (co-m) 69. An American Tail (s) 86. Summer Heat (s) 87. Harry and the Hendersons (s) 87. Million Dollar Mystery (s) 87. Oliver and Company (s) 88. National Lampoon's Christmas Vacation 89. Sibling Rivalry 90. Muppet Treasure Island (s) 96. All Dogs Go to Heaven 2 (s) 96, etc.

Mann, Daniel (1912–1991) (Daniel Chugerman)
American director, ex stage and TV.

■ *Come Back Little Sheba* 52. About Mrs Leslie 54. The Rose Tattoo 55. I'll Cry Tomorrow 55. The Teahouse of the August Moon 56. Hot Spell 58. The Last Angry Man 59. The Mountain Road 60.

Butterfield 8 60. Ada 61. Who's Got the Action? 62. Five Finger Exercise 62. Who's Been Sleeping in My Bed? 63. Judith 65. Our Man Flint 66. For Love of Ivy 68. A Dream of Kings 69. Willard 71. The Harness (TV) 71. The Revengers 72. Maurie 73. Interval 73. Lost in the Stars 73. Journey into Fear 75. Matilda 78. Playing for Time (TV) 80. The Incredible Mr Chadwick 80. The Day the Loving Stopped (TV) 81. The Man Who Broke 1,000 Chains (TV) 87.

Mann, Delbert (1920–)
American director, ex TV.
■ *Marty* (AA) 55. *The Bachelor Party* 57. Desire Under the Elms 58. Separate Tables 58. Middle of the Night 59. *The Dark at the Top of the Stairs* 60. Lover Come Back 61. The Outsider 62. That Touch of Mink 62. A Gathering of Eagles 63. Dear Heart 65. Quick Before it Melts 65. Mister Buddwing 66. Fitzwilly 67. The Pink Jungle 68. Heidi (TV) 68. David Copperfield (TV) 69. She Waits (TV) 71. No Place to Run (TV) 72. Kidnapped 72. Jane Eyre (TV) 72. Man Without a Country (TV) 73. A Girl Named Sooner (TV) 75. Birch Interval 76. Francis Gary Powers (TV) 76. Tell Me My Name (TV) 77. Breaking Up (TV) 78. Love's Dark Ride (TV) 78. Home to Stay (TV) 78. Thou Shalt Not Commit Adultery (TV) 78. Torn Between Two Lovers (TV) 79. All Quiet on the Western Front (TV) 80. To Find My Son (TV) 81. Night Crossing 81. Love Leads the Way (TV) 84. A Death in California (TV) 84. The Last Days of Patton (TV) 86. The Ted Kennedy Jnr Story (TV) 86. April Morning (TV) 88. Incident in a Small Town (p, d) (TV) 94. Lily in Winter 94.

Mann, Hank (1887–1971) (David Liebermann)
Gargantuan American supporting player of silent days, especially with Chaplin; one of the Keystone Kops.
Modern Times 36. Hollywood Cavalcade 39. The Great Dictator 40, etc.

Mann, Heinrich (1871–1950)
German novelist. His story 'Professor Unrath', published in 1905, was filmed as *The Blue Angel*. Brother of Thomas Mann.

Mann, Hummie (1955–)
Canadian composer. Born in Montreal, he studied at Boston's Berklee College of Music, moving to in Los Angeles in the early 80s.
City Slickers 91. Year of the Comet 92. Benefit of the Doubt 93. Robin Hood: Men in Tights 93. Fall Time 94. Dracula: Dead and Loving It 95. Thomas and the Magic Railroad 00, etc.

Mann, Leslie (1972–)
American actress, from television, born in San Francisco.
The Cable Guy 96. She's the One 96. Last Man Standing 96. George of the Jungle 97. Big Daddy 99., etc.
TV series: Birdland 94.

Mann, Michael (1943–)
American director and screenwriter, from TV, where he produced *Miami Vice* 84–89 and *Crime Story* 86–88. *Heat* was a remake of *L.A. Takedown* 89, the pilot for a TV series that never materialized.
The Jericho Mile (TV) 79. Thief (wd) 81. The Keep (wd) 83. Manhunter (wd) 86. Last of the Mohicans (co-w, d) 92. *Heat* (wd) 95. The Insider (AANp, AANco-w, AANd) 99, etc.

Mann, Ned (1893–1967)
American special-effects director, a one-time professional roller-skater who entered films in 1920 as an actor. Best remembered for his long association with Alexander Korda.
Dirigible 30. *The Man Who Could Work Miracles* 35. *The Ghost Goes West* 36. *Things to Come* 36. *The Thief of Baghdad* 40. Anna Karenina 47. Bonnie Prince Charlie 48. Around the World in Eighty Days 56.

Mann, Stanley (1928–)
American screenwriter.
The Mouse That Roared 59. The Mark 61. Woman of Straw 64. Rapture 65. A High Wind in Jamaica 65. The Collector (AAN) 65. The Naked Runner 67. The Strange Affair 68. Russian Roulette 75. Sky Riders 76. Breaking Point 76. The Silent Flute 78. Damien – Omen II 78. Meteor 79. Circle of Iron 79. Eye of the Needle 81. Firestarter 84. Conan the Destroyer 84. Tai-Pan 86. Hanna's War 88, etc.

Mann, Thomas (1875–1955)
German novelist who spent his latter years in California. Brother of Heinrich Mann. *Buddenbrooks* became a TV serial (Germany, 1982), as did *The Confessions of Felix Krull* (Germany, 1981); *Death in Venice* was filmed to general acclaim.

Manners, David (1901–1998) (Rauff de Ryther Duan Acklom)
Canadian leading man of Hollywood films in the 30s; claimed to be descended from William the Conqueror.
■ *Journey's End* 30. He Knew Women 30. Sweet Mama 30. Kismet 30. Mother's Cry 30. The Truth About Youth 30. The Right to Love 30. Dracula 30. The Millionaire 31. *The Last Flight* 31. The Miracle Woman 31. The Ruling Voice 31. The Greeks Had a Word for Them 31. Lady with a Past 32. Beauty and the Boss 32. Stranger in Town 32. Crooner 32. Man Wanted 32. A Bill of Divorcement 32. They Call It Sin 32. The Mummy 32. The Death Kiss 32. From Hell to Heaven 33. The Warrior's Husband 33. The Girl in 419 33. The Devil in Love 33. Torch Singer 33. Roman Scandals 33. The Black Cat 34. The Luck of a Sailor 34. The Great Flirtation 34. The Moonstone 34. The Perfect Clue 35. The Mystery of Edwin Drood 35. Jalna 35. Hearts in Bondage 36. A Woman Rebels 36.

Manners, J. Hartley (1870–1928)
English-born actor and dramatist in America who enjoyed his greatest success with his play *Peg o' My Heart*, which starred his wife Laurette TAYLOR, as did all his subsequent works. This sentimental drama opened in 1912 and ran for 603 performances on Broadway, then the longest run of a non-musical play, and for 710 performances in London from 1914. It has been filmed twice: as a silent in 1922, directed by King VIDOR and starring Laurette Taylor, and in 1931, directed by Robert Z. LEONARD and starring Marion DAVIES. Born in London, of somewhat mysterious origins, he began as an actor in the late 1890s, and moved to the US in the early 1900s. Died of cancer.
Happiness (oa) 24. One Night in Rome (oa) 24.
❝ Alas, poor Hartley! Only the audiences liked his plays. – *Ethel Barrymore*

Mannheim, Lucie (1895–1976)
German-born character actress, married to Marius Goring.
The Thirty-Nine Steps (as the mysterious victim) 35. The High Command 37. Yellow Canary 43. Hotel Reserve 44. So Little Time 52. Beyond the Curtain 60. Bunny Lake Is Missing 65, etc.

Manni, Ettori (1927–1979)
Italian actor.
Girls Marked Danger 52. La Lupa 53. Two Nights with Cleopatra 54. Ulysses 54. Attila the Hun 54. Le Amiche 55. Revolt of the Gladiators 58. Legions of the Nile 59. Revolt of the Slaves 60. Hercules and the Captive Women 61. The Valiant 62. Gold for the Caesars 63. The Battle of the Villa Fiorita 65. The Devil in Love 66. The Battle of El Alamein 69. Street People 76, many others.

Manning, Irene (1917–) (Inez Harvuot)
American leading lady of the 40s, former café singer.
Two Wise Maids 37. The Big Shot 42. Yankee Doodle Dandy 42. The Desert Song 44. Shine On, Harvest Moon 44. Escape in the Desert 45. Bonnie Prince Charlie (GB) 48, etc.

Manoff, Dinah (1958–)
American actress, the daughter of actress and director Lee Grant.
The Possessed (TV) 77. Ordinary People 80. For Ladies Only (TV) 81. I Ought to Be in Pictures 82. Backfire 88. Child's Play 88. Bloodhounds of Broadway 89. Welcome Home Roxy Carmichael 90, etc.
TV series: Soap 78–79.

Manone, Joseph 'Wingy' (1900–1982)
American jazz trumpeter, singer and bandleader, in occasional films. Born in New Orleans, Louisiana, as a child he lost his right arm in a streetcar accident and learned to play left-handed. He moved to Hollywood in the early 40s, staying there until the mid-50s, appearing on Bing CROSBY's radio shows. Some performances feature his 'rhyming jive talk', which was novel at the time but now sounds merely dated.
Autobiography: 1948, *Trumpet on the Wing* (with Paul Vandervoort II).
Rhythm on the River 40. Juke Box Jenny 42. Hi-Ya Sailor 43. Sarge Goes to College 47. Rhythm Inn 51, etc.
❝ I figured while I ain't blowin' and singin' I might be able to snatch me a picture or two, doin' this sort of stuff. A hang-around guy to break it up between intervals, like Rags Ragland or Phil Silvers did. – *W.M.*

Mansfield, Duncan (1897–1971)
American editor and occasional director.
AS EDITOR: The Bond Boy 22. Fury 23. Embarrassing Moments 30. The Front Page 31. I'd Give My Life 36. So This Is Washington 43. A Walk in the Sun 45. Arch of Triumph 48, etc.
AS DIRECTOR: Along Came Love 36. Girl Loves Boy 37. Sweetheart of the Navy 37, etc.

Mansfield, Jayne (1932–1967) (Vera Jane Palmer)
Amply proportioned American leading lady whose superstructure became the butt of many jokes. She began as a beauty queen, Miss Photoflash 1952, and became a star on Broadway, after Warner had dropped her contract, in *Will Success Spoil Rock Hunter?* Her second husband, Mickey Hargitay, was a former Mr Universe and occasional actor, and her third was director Matt Cimber (aka Matteo Ottaviano). Her stardom was short-lived and she was performing in a night-club act at the time of her death in a car crash. Loni Anderson played her in a TV movie, *The Jayne Mansfield Story* 80. She was the mother of actress Mariska Hargitay (1964-).
Biography: 1973, *Jayne Mansfield* by May Mann. 1986, *Pink Goddess: The Jayne Mansfield Story* by Michael Feeney Callan.
The Female Jungle 55. Illegal 56. Pete Kelly's Blues 56. The Burglar 57. The Girl Can't Help It 57. The Wayward Bus 57. Will Success Spoil Rock Hunter? 57. Kiss Them For Me 57. The Sheriff of Fractured Jaw 59. Too Hot to Handle (GB) 60. The Challenge (GB) 60. It Happened in Athens 62. Panic Button 64. Country Music USA 65. The Fat Spy 66. A Guide for the Married Man 67, etc.
❝ Men are those creatures with two legs and eight hands. – *J.M.*
I always felt all my life that people who didn't grow up to be movie stars ... well, there was something wrong with them. – *J.M.*
You gotta have a body. – *J.M.*
Dramatic art in her opinion is knowing how to fill a sweater. – *Bette Davis*
Miss United Dairies herself. – *David Niven*
She was not strictly an exhibitionist, but she liked an audience. – *May Mann*

Mansfield, Martha (1900–1923)
American leading actress of silent films, from Broadway musicals. She died from burns after her dress caught fire during the filming of *The Warrens of Virginia*.
Broadway Bill 18. Dr Jekyll and Mr Hyde 20. Fogbound 23. The Woman in Chains 23. The Warrens of Virginia 24, etc.

Mantee, Paul (1936–) (Paul Marianetti)
American general-purpose actor.
Robinson Crusoe on Mars (leading role) 64. An American Dream 66. They Shoot Horses Don't They 69. W. C. Fields and Me 76. The Day of the Animals 77. The Great Santini 80. First Strike 87. Lurking Fear 94, etc.

Mantegna, Joe (1947–)
American character actor, associated on stage and screen with the work of writer and director David MAMET.
Who Stole My Wheels?/Towing 78. Second Thoughts 83. Compromising Positions 85. The Money Pit 86. Offbeat 86. Three Amigos! 86. Critical Condition 87. House of Games 87. Weeds 87. Suspect 87. Things Change 88. Wait until Spring, Bandini 90. Alice 90. Queen's Logic 90. The Godfather Part III 90. Homicide 91. Bugsy (as George Raft) 91. Body of Evidence 93. Family Prayers 93. Searching for Bobby Fischer/Innocent Moves 93. State of Emergency (TV) 94. Baby's Day Out 94. Airheads 94. Forget Paris 95. Eye for an Eye 95. Up Close and Personal 96. Underworld 96. Albino Alligator 96. Stephen King's Thinner 96. The Last Don (TV) 96. Face Down 96. A Call to Remember (TV) 97. The Wonderful Ice Cream Suit 97. The Rat Pack (TV) 98. Celebrity 98. Boy Meets Girl 98. The Runner 99. Liberty Heights 99, etc.

Mantell Joe (1920–)
American character actor.
Barbary Pirate 49. Marty (AAN) 55. Storm Centre 56. The Sad Sack 57. Beau James 57. Onionhead 58. The Crowded Sky 60. The Scarface Mob (TV) 62. The Birds 63. Mister Buddwing 66. Chinatown 74. They Only Come Out at Night (TV) 75. Blind Ambition (TV) 79. The Two Jakes 90, etc.

Mantle, Anthony Dod (1955–)
British-born cinematographer, who has worked in Denamrk, particularly on several Dogme 95 films.
The Birthday Trip 90. The Beast Within/ Menneskedyret 95. Operation Cobra 95. Festen 98. Mifune/Mifunes Sidste Sang 99. Julien Donkey-Boy (US) 99, etc.

Mantz, Paul (1903–1965)
American stunt pilot who died in a crash during the filming of *The Flight of the Phoenix*.
Biography: 1967, *Hollywood Pilot* by Don D. Wiggins.

Manvell, Roger (1909–1987)
British film historian. Director of the British Film Academy from 1947 and author of many books on cinema, the most influential being the Penguin *Film* 44.

Manville, Lesley (1956–)
English leading actress. Born in Brighton, Sussex, she was formerly married to actor Gary OLDHAM.
Dance with a Stranger 85. High Season 87. Sammy and Rosie Get Laid 87. High Hopes 88. The Firm (TV) 89. O Mary This London 94. Secrets and Lies 96. Topsy-Turvy 99, etc.

Manx, Kate (1930–1964)
American leading lady.
■ Private Property 60. Hero's Island 62.

Manz, Linda (1961–)
American leading lady.
Days of Heaven 78. King of the Gypsies 78. Boardwalk 79. Orphan Train (TV) 80. Out of the Blue 80. Gummo 97, etc.

Manzano, Lucas
Venezuelan director who directed, with Enrique Zimmerman, that country's first feature film, *La Dama de las Cayenas* 13, a version of Alexander Dumas's *Camille*.

Mapplethorpe, Robert (1946–1989)
American artist and photographer whose elegant photographs of sado-masochistic homosexual acts excited much controversy. He was the star of a once-celebrated underground film, *Robert Having His Nipple Pierced*, made by Sandy Daley and given its premiere at New York's Museum of Modern Art in 1971. Died of AIDS.
Biography: 1995, *Mapplethorpe* by Patricia Morrisroe.
❝ Sex is the only thing worth living for. – *R.M.*
My theory about creativity is that the more money one has, the more creative one can be. – *R.M.*

Mara, Adele (1923–) (Adelaida Delgado)
Spanish-American dancer who played leads in Hollywood co-features of the 40s.
Alias Boston Blackie 42. Bells of Rosarita 45. Tiger Woman 46. Diary of a Bride 48. The Sea Hornet 51. Back from Eternity 56. Curse of the Faceless Man 58. The Big Circus 59. Wheels (TV) 78, etc.
TV series: Cool Million 72–73.

Marais, Jean (1913–1998) (Jean Marais-Villain)
French romantic actor well remembered in several Cocteau films. Later films less notable; recently in cloak-and-sword epics, also playing 'The Saint', 'Fantomas' and various secret agents.
Autobiography: 1975, *Histoires de Ma Vie*.
L'Eternel Retour 43. La Belle et la Bête 45. L'Aigle à Deux Têtes 47. Les Parents Terribles 48. Orphée 49. Nez de Cuir 51. Les Amants de Minuit 53. Julietta 53. Le Comte de Monte Cristo 54. Napoléon 54. Paris Does Strange Things/Eléna et les Hommes 56. White Nights/Le Notti Bianche

57. *The Testament of Orpheus*/Le Testament d'Orphée 59. Austerlitz 60. Patate 64. Thomas l'Imposteur 65. Train d'Enfer 65. Le Paria 68. Peau d'Ane 70. Erimou 82. Parking 85. Les Misérables du XXème Siècle 95. Stealing Beauty 95, etc.

Marceau, Sophie (1967–) (Sophie Mapuis)
French leading actress, in films from the age of 13. She has a son by her partner, Polish director Andrzej ZULAWSKI.
La Boum 80. Police 85. Mes Nuits Sont Plus Belles que Vos Jours 89. Pacific Palisades 90. Fanfan 93. La Fille de D'Artagnan 94. Braveheart 95. Beyond the Clouds 95. Leo Tolstoy's Anna Karenina (US) 97. Firelight (GB/Fr.) 97. Marquise 97, etc.

Marcel, Terry (1942–)
British director and screenwriter.
Why Not Stay for Breakfast? 79. There Goes the Bride 80. Hawk the Slayer 80. Prisoners of the Lost Universe 83. Jane and the Lost City 87. Heartbeat (TV) 93, etc.

March, Alex (1920–1989)
American director and producer, a former stage actor and television script editor.
Paper Lion 68. The Big Bounce 68. Mastermind 69 (released 76). Firehouse (TV) 72. The Amazing Captain Nemo 78, etc.

March, Elspeth (1912–1999) (Elspeth Mackenzie)
English stage actress in occasional films. Born in London, she studied acting at the Central School of Dramatic Art and the Webber-Douglas School and was on-stage from 1932. In the early 40s she left the theatre for four years to work as an ambulance driver for the American Red Cross. Married (1938-48) actor Stewart GRANGER.
Mr Emmanuel 44. Which Will You Have? 49. Quo Vadis? 51. His Excellency 51. Follow That Man 61. Dr Crippen 62. The Playboy of the Western World 62. Woman Times Seven (US/It./Fr.) 67. Goodbye Mr Chips 69. The Rise and Rise of Michael Rimmer 70. Promise at Dawn/La Promesse De L'Aube (Fr.) 70, etc.

March, Fredric (1897–1975) (Frederick McIntyre Bickel)
One of America's most respected stage and screen actors, who always projected intelligence and integrity and during the 30s and 40s was at times an agreeable light comedian. Long married to Florence Eldridge.
■ The Dummy 29. The Wild Party 29. The Studio Murder Mystery 29. Paris Bound 29. Jealousy 29. Footlights and Fools 29. The Marriage Playground 29. Sarah and Son 30. Ladies Love Brutes 30. Paramount on Parade 30. True to the Navy 30. Manslaughter 30. Laughter 30. *The Royal Family of Broadway* (AAN) 30. Honor among Lovers 30. Night Angel 31. My Sin 31. Merrily We Go to Hell 32. *Dr Jekyll and Mr Hyde* (AA) 32. Smiling Through 32. Make Me a Star 32. Strangers in Love 32. The Sign of the Cross 33. Tonight Is Ours 33. The Eagle and the Hawk 33. The Affairs of Cellini 34. All of Me 34. Good Dame 34. Design for Living 34. *Death takes a Holiday* 34. The Barretts of Wimpole Street (as Robert Browning) 34. We Live Again 34. *Les Misérables* 35. The Dark Angel 35. Anna Karenina 35. Mary of Scotland 36. Anthony Adverse 36. The Road to Glory 36. *A Star Is Born* (AAN) 37. *Nothing Sacred* 37. The Buccaneer 38. There Goes My Heart 38. Trade Winds 39. Susan and God 40. Victory 40. So Ends Our Night 41. *One Foot in Heaven* 41. Bedtime Story 42. *I Married a Witch* 42. Tomorrow the World 44. *The Adventures of Mark Twain* 44. *The Best Years of Our Lives* (AA) 46. Another Part of the Forest 48. An Act of Murder 48. Christopher Columbus (GB) 49. It's a Big Country 51. *Death of a Salesman* (AAN) 52. Man on a Tightrope 53. *Executive Suite* 54. The Bridges at Toko Ri 54. The Desperate Hours 55. Alexander the Great 55. The Man in the Grey Flannel Suit 56. Middle of the Night 59. *Inherit the Wind* 60. The Young Doctors 62. The Condemned of Altona 63. *Seven Days in May* 64. Hombre 67. Tick Tick Tick 70. The Iceman Cometh 73.
✪ For the diligence with which he undertook every role, and for the satisfying success of most of the results. *A Star Is Born.*
❝ He was able to do a very emotional scene with tears in his eyes, and pinch my fanny at the same time. – *Shelley Winters*

March, Hal (1920–1970)
American comic actor who never quite made it.
Outrage 50. Yankee Pasha 54. My Sister Eileen 55. *Hear Me Good* 57. Send Me No Flowers 64, etc.

March, Jane (1975–)
British actress, a former model.
The Lover/L'Amant 91. Color of Night 94. Provocateur 96. Tarzan and the Lost City 98, etc.

Marchal, Georges (1920–1997) (Georges-Louis Lucot)
French leading actor, usually in heroic or swashbuckling roles. Born in Nancy, he was on-screen from his late teens. Married actress Dany ROBIN.
The French Way/Fausse Alerte 40. Première Rendez-Vous 41. Lumière d'été 42. Blondine 43. Vautrin 43. Pamela 44. Torrents 46. Bethsabée 47. The Last Days of Pompeii 48. Au Grand Balcon 49. Robinson Crusoe 50. Messalina 51. La Castiglione 53. The Three Musketeers (as D'Artagnan) 53. Theodora, Slave Empress 54. Si Versailles M'était Conte 54. Gil Blas 55. When the Sun Rises/Celà S'Appelle l'Aurore 55. Evil Eden/La Mort en Ce Jardin 56. Filles de Nuit 58. Spartan Gladiators/La Rivolta dei Gladiatori 58. Austerlitz 59. Legions of the Nile (as Mark Antony) 60. The Colossus of Rhodes 61. The Dirty Game/Guerre Secrète 65. Belle de Jour 67. The Milky Way/La Voie Lactée 69. Faustine 71. The Closet Children/Les Enfants du Placard 77, etc.

Marchand, Colette
French actress who was nominated for an Oscar as best supporting actress in *Moulin Rouge* 52, her only international film.

Marchand, Corinne (1937–)
French leading lady of the 60s.
Cléo de 5 à 7 62. Seven Deadly Sins 63. The Milky Way 69. Rider on the Rain 70. Borsalino 70. Travels with My Aunt 72. Crime and Punishment 83. Attention Bandits 87. Le Parfum d'Yvonne 94, etc.

Marchand, Henri (1889–1959)
French comedy actor.
A Nous la Liberté 31. Je Vous Aimerai Toujours 33. Volga en Flammes 35. Les Deux Combinards 38. L'Ennemi sans Visage 46. La Sorcière 50. Operation Magali 53. Till Eulenspiegel 56, many others.

Marchand, Nancy (1928–2000)
American character actress of stage, screen and TV. Born in Buffalo, New York, she won four Emmys for best supporting actress for her role as Margaret Pynchon in the TV drama series *Lou Grant*.. In the 90s she was known for her role as Livia, the mother of Tony Soprano in the TV series *The Sopranos*. She also appeared on daytime TV soap operas, including *Love of Life*.
Marty (TV) 53. The Bachelor Party 57. Ladybug, Ladybug 63. Me, Natalie 69. Tell Me That You Love Me, Junie Moon 69. The Hospital 71. The Bostonians 84. From the Hip 87. The Naked Gun: From the Files of Police Squad 88. Regarding Henry 91. Brain Donors 92. Jefferson in Paris 95. Sabrina 95. Dear God 96, etc.
TV series: Beacon Hill 75. *Lou Grant* 77-82. The Sopranos 99-2000.

Marcus, Lawrence B.
American screenwriter.
Petulia 68. Justine 69. Alex and the Gypsy 76. The Stunt Man (AAN) 80.

Marcus, Mike (1945–)
American production executive, a former agent, who became president of MGM in 1993.

Marcuse, Theodore (1920–1967)
Shaven-pated American character actor, usually in sinister roles.
The Glass Bottom Boat 65. The Cincinnati Kid 65. Last of the Secret Agents 66. The Wicked Dreams of Paula Schultz 67, etc.

Margetson, Arthur (1897–1951)
British stage actor, former stockbroker's clerk, who went to Hollywood in 1940 and played supporting roles.
Other People's Sins 31. His Grace Gives Notice 33. Little Friend 34. Broken Blossoms 36. Juggernaut 37. Action for Slander 38. Return to Yesterday 40. Random Harvest 43. Sherlock Holmes Faces Death 44, etc.

Margheriti, Antonio (1930–) (aka Anthony M. Dawson)
Italian director of horror and exploitation movies. Born in Rome, he studied engineering at university and worked in the 50s as an assistant editor and scriptwriter; he is also a special effects expert, specializing in model-making and optical effects.
Space-Men 60. The Golden Arrow 62. Lightning Bolt 65. Wild, Wild Planet 66. The Young, the Evil and the Savage 68. Decameron 3 73. Blood Money 74. The House of 1,000 Pleasures 77. Killer Fish 78. Cannibals in the Streets 80. Car Crash 81. Yor, the Hunter from the Future 83. Ark of the Sun God 84. Codename: Wildgeese 84. The Commander 88. Indio 89. Indio 2: The Revolt 91, many others.
❝ Sometimes when I do pictures I really need the money, so I just read the agreement and not the script, before I say OK. You do it because you want the house in town, the house in the country, you want this, that, maybe a beautiful girl … – A.M.

Margo (1918–1985) (Maria Marguerita Guadelupe Boldao Castilla y O'Donnell)
Mexican actress and dancer, once with Xavier Cugat's band, long married to Eddie Albert, in occasional Hollywood films from 1933.
Crime without Passion 34. Winterset 36. Lost Horizon 37. The Leopard Man 43. Behind the Rising Sun 43. Gangway for Tomorrow 44. Viva Zapata 52. I'll Cry Tomorrow 57. Who's Got the Action? 63, etc.

Margolin, Janet (1943–1993)
American leading lady.
David and Lisa 62. Bus Riley's Back in Town 65. The Greatest Story Ever Told 65. The Saboteur 65. Nevada Smith 66. Enter Laughing 67. Buona Sera Mrs Campbell 68. Take the Money and Run 70. The Last Child (TV) 71. Family Flight (TV) 72. Pray for the Wildcats (TV) 74. Planet Earth (TV) 74. Lanigan's Rabbi (TV) 76. Annie Hall 77. Murder in Peyton Place (TV) 77. The Triangle Factory Fire Scandal (TV) 79. Last Embrace 79. Ghostbusters II 89, etc.

Margolin, Stuart (c. 1940–)
American character actor and occasional director, born in Davenport, Iowa.
Limbo 72. The Stone Killer 73. Death Wish 74. Lanigan's Rabbi (TV) 76. The Big Bus 76. Futureworld 76. S.O.B. 81. Class 83. A Fine Mess 86. Iron Eagle II 88. Bye Bye Blues 90. Guilty by Suspicion 91. To Grandmother's House We Go (TV) 94. The Student Affair 97, etc.
AS DIRECTOR: A Shining Season (TV) 79. The Glitter Dome (TV) 84. Paramedics (TV) 88. Vendetta (& w) 90. Medicine River 94. How the West Was Fun (TV) 95, etc.
TV series: Occasional Wife 66–67. Love, American Style 69–72. Nichols 71–72. The Rockford Files 74–80. Bret Maverick 81–82. Mr Smith 83.

Margolyes, Miriam (1941–)
Plump British character actress, often in fussy roles.
A Nice Girl Like Me 69. Stand Up Virgin Soldiers 77. The Awakening 80. Reds 81. Scrubbers 82. Yentl 83. Morons from Outer Space 85. The Good Father 86. Little Shop of Horrors 86. Little Dorrit 88. Pacific Heights 90. The Fool 91. Dead Again 91. The Butcher's Wife 91. As You Like It 92. Ed and His Dead Mother 93. The Age of Innocence (US) 93. Immortal Beloved (GB/US) 94. Babe (US, voice) 95. Cold Comfort Farm (TV) 95. Balto (US/GB) 95. Different for Girls 96. James and the Giant Peach (US) 96. William Shakespeare's Romeo and Juliet (as The Nurse) (US) 96. Left Luggage (Hol.) 98. Pi (US) 98. Vanity Fair (TV) 98. Mulan (US, voice) 98. End of Days (US) 99. Dreaming of Joseph Lees 99. House! 99. Sunshine 99, etc.
TV series: Frannie's Turn 92.
❝ I'm not the sort of woman men boast of having slept with. – M.M.

Margulies, Julianna (1966–)
American actress, best known for her role as Nurse Hathaway in the TV series *ER*. Born in Spring Valley, New York, she was educated in part in France and England and studied at Sarah Lawrence College.
Out for Justice 91. Paradise Lost 97. The Newton Boys 98. A Price above Rubies 98 Dinosaur 00 (voice) 00, etc.
TV series: ER 94–00.

Marie, Lisa
American actress and model.
Dead and Buried 81. Alice 90. Ed Wood (as Vampira) 94. Mars Attacks! 96. Breast Men (TV) 97. Frogs for Snakes 98, etc.

Marielle, Jean-Pierre (1932–)
French leading actor.
Peau de Banane 63. Que la Fête Commence 75. Calmos 76. One Wild Moment 78. Coup de Torchon 81. Evening Dress/Tenue de Soirée 86. Uranus 91. The Smile/Le Sourire 94. Le Parfum d'Yvonne 94. Les Milles 95. The Grand Dukes 95. One 4 All/Une Pour Toutes 99, etc.

Marin, Edwin L. (1901–1951)
American director.
The Death Kiss 32. A Study in Scarlet 33. Paris Interlude 34. The Casino Murder Case 35. I'd Give My Life 36. Everybody Sing 38. A Christmas Carol 38. Fast and Loose 39. Maisie 39. Florian 40. A Gentleman After Dark 42. *Show Business* 44. Tall in the Saddle 44. Johnny Angel 45. The Young Widow 46. Nocturne 46. Christmas Eve 47. Race Street 48. Canadian Pacific 49. Fighting Man of the Plains 49. The Cariboo Trail 50. Fort Worth 51, etc.

Marin, Jacques (1919–)
French character actor.
The Enemy General 60. Tiara Tahiti 62. Charade 63. The Train 64. How to Steal a Million 66. Lost Command 66. The Girl on the Motorcycle 68. The Night of the Following Day 68. Darling Lili 69. The Madwoman of Chaillot 69. Shaft in Africa 73. The Island at the Top of the World 74. Marathon Man 76. Herbie Goes to Monte Carlo 77. Who Is Killing the Great Chefs of Europe? 78. Les Minipouss 86. A Star for Two 90, etc.

Marin, Richard 'Cheech' (1946–)
American actor, musician and screenwriter. One half of a coarse comic double-act with Thomas CHONG featuring two druggy hippies, which began on record albums and enjoyed a high popularity in the early 80s. The act split up in 1985.
Up in Smoke (a, w) 79. Cheech & Chong's Next Movie (a, w) 80. Cheech & Chong's Nice Dreams (a, w) 81. Things Are Tough All Over (a, w) 82. Cheech & Chong: Still Smokin' (a, w) 83. Yellowbeard (a) 83. Cheech & Chong's The Corsican Brothers (a, w) 84. After Hours (a) 85. Echo Park (a) 86. Born in East L.A. (a, d) 87. Rude Awakening (a) 89. Troop Beverly Hills (a) 89. Boyfriend from Hell/The Shrimp on the Barbie (a) 90. Ferngully … the Last Rainforest (voice) 92. The Cisco Kid (TV) 94. Desperado 95. From Dusk till Dawn 95. The Great White Hype 96. Tin Cup 96. Paulie 98. The Venice Project (as himself) 99, etc.
TV series: Nash Bridges 96– .

Marins, José Mojica (c. 1934–)
Brazilian director and actor. His films from the mid-60s, in which he also played the role of a murderous, long finger-nailed gravedigger known as Ze Do Caixao or Coffin Joe, gained him a cult reputation.
Sentenca De Deus 58. A Sina Do Adventureiro 59. Meu Destino Em Tuas Manos 62. At Midnight I Will Steal Your Soul 64. Tonight I Will Possess Your Corpse/Esta Noite Encarnarei No Tue Cadaver 66. The Strange World of Coffin Joe/O Estrano Mundo Ze Do Caixao 68. The Awkening of the Beast/O Despertar Da Bestia 69. When the Gods Fall Asleep/Quando Os Deuses Adormecem 72. Encarnacao De Demonio 81, etc.

Marion, Frances (1888–1973) (Frances Marion Owens)
American screenwriter. Married actor Fred THOMSON and director George HILL.
Autobiography: 1972, *Off with Their Heads*.
Other books: 1997, *Frances Marion and the Powerful Women of Early Hollywood* by Cari Beauchamp.
Daughter of the Sea 16. Humoresque 22. Stella Dallas 25. The Winning of Barbara Worth 26. The Scarlet Letter 27. *Love* 27. The Wind 28. *The Big House* (AA) 30. *The Champ* (AA) 32. The Prizefighter and the Lady (AAN) 33. *Dinner at Eight* 33. Riff Raff 36. *Knight without Armour* 37. Green Hell 40, etc.

Marion-Crawford, Howard (1914–1969)
British actor often seen in Watsonian roles or as jovial, beefy, sporting types.
Forever England 32. Freedom Radio 40. The Rake's Progress 45. The Hasty Heart 49. The Man in the White Suit 51. Where's Charley? 52. Reach for the Sky 56. Virgin Island 58. The Brides of Fu Manchu 66, etc.
TV series: Sherlock Holmes 55.

Maris, Mona (1903–1991) (Maria Capdevielle)
Franco-Argentinian 'second lead' in Hollywood films.
Romance of the Rio Grande 29. Secrets 33. Law of the Tropics 41. Tampico 44. Heartbeat 46. The Avengers 50, etc.

Maritza, Sari (1910–1987) (Patricia Nathan)
Anglo-Austrian leading lady, a short-lived sensation of the early 30s.
Monte Carlo Madness 31. Forgotten Commandments 32. Evenings for Sale 32. International House 33. Crimson Romance 34, etc.

Marken, Jane (1895–1976) (J. Krab)
French character actress with long stage experience.
Fioritures 15. Camille 34. *Partie de Campagne* 37. Hôtel du Nord 38. *Lumière d'été* 42. Les Enfants du Paradis 44. L'Idiot 46. Clochemerle 47. Une Si Jolie Petite Plage 48. Manèges 49. Ma Pomme 50. Les Compagnes de la Nuit 52. Marie Antoinette 55. And God Created Woman 56. Pot Bouille 57. The Mirror Has Two Faces 58, etc.

Marker, Chris (1921–) (Christian Bouche-Villeneuve)
French documentary director. Leader of the modernist 'left bank' school.
Olympia 52. Toute la Mémoire du Monde 56. Letter from Siberia 58. Description d'un Combat 60. Cuba Si 61. Le Joli Mai 62. *La Jetée* 63. If I Had Four Dromedaries 66. Le Fond de l'Air est Rouge 77. Sans Soleil 82. A.K. 85. L'Héritage de la Chouette 89. The Last Bolshevik 93, etc.

Markey, Enid (1896–1981)
American character actress. In 1918 she was the first screen Jane, to Elmo Lincoln's Tarzan.
Civilisation 16. Tarzan of the Apes 18. The Romance of Tarzan 18. Snafu 46. The Naked City 48. The Boston Strangler 68, etc.
TV series: Bringing Up Buddy 60–61.

Markey, Gene (1895–1980)
American screenwriter, producer, playwright and novelist. He was the second husband of Joan Bennett (1932–37), and of Hedy Lamarr (1939–40, the divorce court judge suggesting that in future she should not marry a man she had known for only four weeks), and the third of Myrna Loy (1946–51).
Stepping High (oa) 28. The Battle of Paris 29. The Florodora Girl 30. As You Desire Me 32. Midnight Mary 33. Fashions 34. A Modern Hero 34. Let's Live Tonight 35. King of Burlesque 36. Private Number 36. *On the Avenue* 37, etc.
AS PRODUCER ONLY: Wee Willie Winkie 37. The Little Princess 39. The Hound of the Baskervilles 39. The Blue Bird 40. Lillian Russell 40. Moss Rose 47.

Markham, Kika
English leading actress. Married Corin Redgrave.
Bunny Lake Is Missing 65. Futtocks End 69. Anne and Muriel (Fr.) 71. Operation: Daybreak (US) 75. Noriot (Fr.) 76. Outland 81. The Innocent 84, etc.

Markham, Monte (1935–)
American leading man, mostly on TV.
Hour of the Gun 67. Project X 68. Guns of the Magnificent Seven 69. Death Takes a Holiday (TV) 71. One is a Lonely Number 72. Midway 76. Airport 77 77. Hotline 82. Off the Wall 83. Hot Pursuit 87. Defense Play (& d) 88. Neon City (d) 91. Piranha 95, etc.
TV series: The Second Hundred Years 67. Mr Deeds Goes to Town 69. The New Perry Mason 73. Dallas 81. Rituals 84–85. Baywatch 89–.

Markle, Fletcher (1921–1991)
Canadian director, briefly in Hollywood. Married to Mercedes McCambridge (1950–62).
■ Jigsaw 49. Night into Morning 51. The Man with a Cloak 51. The Incredible Journey 63.

Markle, Peter (1946–)
American director.
The Personals 82. Youngblood 86. Bat-21 88. El Diablo (TV) 90. Through the Eyes of a Killer (TV) 92. Wagons East 94. White Dwarf 95. The Last Days of Frankie the Fly 96, etc.

Markopoulos, Gregory (1928–1992)
American avant garde filmmaker.
The Dead Ones 48. Psyche 48. Flowers Of Asphalt 51. Eldora 52. Serenity 61. Twice A Man 63. Galaxie 66. Himself As Herself 66. Ming Green 66. Eros, O Basileus 67. Bliss 67. The Illiac Passion 67. Mysteries 68. Political Portraits 69. Genius 70. 35, Boulevard General Koenig 71. Hagiographia 71, etc.

Marks, Alfred (1921–1996) (Alfred Touchinsky)
Bald-pated British comedian and singer, in films from 1950 but more usually seen on TV and stage. Born in London, he studied singing in Italy for three years and began as a stand-up comedian at London's Windmill Theatre. Married comedienne Paddie O'Neil.
Penny Points to Paradise 51. Desert Mice 59. There Was a Crooked Man 60. Frightened City 61. Weekend with Lulu 62. She'll Have to Go 62. Scream and Scream Again 69. Our Miss Fred 72. Valentino 77, etc.
TV series: Don't Look Now 50. Alfred Marks Time 56-61. Fire Crackers 64-65. Albert and Victoria 70-71. The All New Alexei Sayle Show 95.

Marks, Richard (1943–)
American film editor.
Little Big Man 70. Parades 72. Bang the Drum Slowly 73. Serpico 73. The Godfather Part II 74. Lies My Father Told Me 75. The Last Tycoon 76. Apocalypse Now (AAN) 79. The Hand 81. Pennies from Heaven 81. Terms of Endearment (AAN) 83. The Adventures of Buckaroo Banzai across the Eighth Dimension 84. St Elmo's Fire 85. Pretty in Pink 86. Firewalker 86. Broadcast News (AAN) 87. Say Anything 89. Dick Tracy 90. One Good Cop 91. I'll Do Anything 94. Assassins 95. Things to Do in Denver When You're Dead 95. 'Til There Was You 97. As Good as It Gets 97. You've Got Mail 98, etc.

Marky Mark
see WAHLBERG, Mark.

Marley, J. Peverell (1899–1964)
American cinematographer who worked on de Mille's silent epics.
The Ten Commandments 23. The Volga Boatmen 25. *King of Kings* 27. House of Rothschild 34. Clive of India 35. *Alexander's Ragtime Band* 38. *The Hound of the Baskervilles* 39. Night and Day 46. Life with Father 47. The Greatest Show on Earth 52. House of Wax 53. Serenade 56. The Left-Handed Gun 58. A Fever in the Blood 61, many others.

Marley, John (1907–1984)
American character actor.
My Six Convicts 52. Timetable 56. I Want to Live 58. America America 65. Cat Ballou 65. Faces 68. *Love Story* (AAN) 70. A Man Called Sledge 70. The Godfather 72. Blade 73. W. C. Fields and Me 76. The Car 77. The Greatest 77. Hooper 78. Tribute 80, etc.

Marlowe, Hugh (1911–1982) (Hugh Hipple)
American actor, former radio announcer, in films from 1937. His wives included actresses Edith Atwater and K. T. STEVENS; he was romantically linked with Eva GABOR.
Mrs Parkington 44. Meet Me In St Louis 44. *Twelve O'Clock High* 50. *All about Eve* 50. The Day the Earth Stood Still 51. Monkey Business 52. Garden of Evil 54. Earth Versus the Flying Saucers 56. Thirteen Frightened Girls 64. Castle of Evil 66. The Last Shot You Hear 68, etc.
TV series: Ellery Queen 54.

Marlowe, June (1903–1984)
American actress who was mainly a leading lady to Rin-Tin-Tin and later became the schoolteacher Miss Crabtree in the Our Gang shorts of the 30s.
Find Your Man 24. Clash of the Wolves 25. Night Cry 26. Don Juan 26. Life of Riley 27. Code of the Air 28. Pardon Us/Jail Birds 31. The Lone Defender (serial) 32. Riddle Ranch 36, etc.

Marlowe, Scott (1932–2001)
American juvenile actor of the late 50s.
Men in War 57. Young Guns 57. The Subterraneans 60. *A Cold Wind in August* 61. No Place Like Home (TV) 89. Lightning in a Bottle 93. Following Her Heart (TV) 94, etc.

Marly, Florence (1918–1978) (Hana Smekalova)
Franco-Czech leading lady, married to Pierre Chenal. Made a few films in Hollywood.
Sealed Verdict 48. Tokyo Joe 49. Tokyo File 212 51. Gobs and Gals 52. The Idol (Chilean) 52. Confession at Dawn (Chilean) 53. Undersea Girl 58. Queen of Blood 65. Games 67. Doctor Death 73, etc.

Marmont, Percy (1883–1977)
Veteran British romantic actor of silent era, in films since 1913.
SILENT FILMS: The Silver King (GB) 24. Lord Jim (US) 25. Mantrap (US) 26. Rich and Strange (GB) 27, etc.
SOUND FILMS: The Silver Greyhound 32. Secret Agent 36. Action for Slander 38. I'll Walk Beside You 41. Loyal Heart 45. No Orchids for Miss Blandish 48. Lisbon 56, many others.

Marquand, Christian (1927–2000)
French leading actor and occasional director. Born in Marseilles, the son of a Spanish father and an Arab mother, he was in films from 1946. His career ended in the early 80s, due to the onset of Alzheimer's disease. Formerly married to actress Tina AUMONT, he had a son by actress Dominique SANDA. His brother Serge Marquand (1930-) was also an actor, and his sister Nadine Trintignant (1934-), who married actor Jean-Louis TRINTIGNANT, was a director.
Beauty and the Beast/La Belle et La Bête 46. Senso (It.) 53. And God Created Woman 57. The Longest Day (US) 62. Of Flesh and Blood/Les Grand Chemins (d) 63. Behold a Pale Horse (US/Fr.) 64. The Flight of the Phoenix (US) 65. Lord Jim (GB/US) 65. The Peking Medallion (It./Ger./Fr.) 66. La Route de Corinthe 67. Candy (d) 68. Victory at Entebbe (TV) 76. The Other Side of Midnight (US) 77. Choice of Arms/Les Choix Des Armes 81. I Love All of You/Je Vous Aime 81. Emmanuelle IV 84, etc.

Marquand, John P. (1893–1960)
American novelist who wrote solid popular books about middle-aged men regretting their lost youth; also the Mr Moto series (filmed in the late 30s with Peter Lorre).
H.M. Pulham Esquire 41. The Late George Apley 47. B. F.'s Daughter 49. Top Secret Affair/Melville Goodwin USA 56. Stopover Tokyo 57, etc.

Marquand, Richard (1938–1987)
British director.
The Search for the Nile (TV) 75. The Legacy 78. Eye of the Needle 81. Return of the Jedi 83. Until September 84. *Jagged Edge* 85. Hearts of Fire 87.

Marriott, Moore (1885–1949) (George Thomas Moore-Marriott)
British leading man of silents who became a character comedian specializing in hoary rustics, chiefly beloved as the ancient but resilient old Harbottle of the Will Hay comedies: *Convict 99* 36, *Oh Mr Porter* 38, *Ask a Policeman* 39, *Where's That Fire?* 40, etc. Also notable with the Crazy Gang in *The Frozen Limits* 39, and *Gasbags* 40. Made over 300 films in all.
Dick Turpin 08. Passion Island 26. The Lyons Mail 31. The Water Gypsies 32. As You Like It 36. Millions Like Us 43. Time Flies 44. Green for Danger 46. The History of Mr Polly 49. High Jinks in Society 49.

Mars, Kenneth (1936–)
American character comedian who is usually way over the top.
The Producers 67. Desperate Characters 71. What's Up Doc? 72. Paper Moon 73. The Parallax View 74. Young Frankenstein 74. Night Moves 75. The Apple Dumpling Gang Rides Again 79. Radio Days 87. For Keeps 88. Police Academy 6: City under Siege 89. The Little Mermaid (voice) 89. Shadows and Fog 91. We're Back! A Dinosaur's Story (voice) 93. Precious 96. Citizen Ruth 96, etc.

Marsh, Carol (1926–) (Norma Simpson)
British leading lady whose career faltered when she outgrew *ingénue* roles.
■ *Brighton Rock* 47. Marry Me 49. Helter Skelter 50. Alice in Wonderland (French puppet version) 50. The Romantic Age 50. Scrooge 51. Salute the Toff 51. Private Information 51. Dracula 58. Man Accused 59.

Marsh, Garry (1902–1981) (Leslie March Geraghty)
Robust, balding British character actor; in films from 1930, usually as harassed father, perplexed policeman or explosive officer.
Night Birds 30. Dreyfus 30. Number Seventeen 32. The Maid of the Mountains 32. Scrooge 35. When Knights Were Bold 36. Bank Holiday 38. It's in the Air 38. The Four Just Men 39. Hoots Mon 40. I'll Be Your Sweetheart 45. The Rake's Progress 45. Dancing with Crime 46. Just William's Luck 48. Murder at the Windmill 49. Worm's Eye View 51. Mr Drake's Duck 53. Who Done It? 55. Where the Bullets Fly 66, many others.

Marsh, Jean (1934–)
British character actress who became internationally known as the maid in TV's *Upstairs Downstairs*, which she created with actress Eileen ATKINS. Also co-creator of the 90s TV series *The House of Elliott*. Married to actor Jon PERTWEE (1955–60).
The Tales of Hoffman 51. Cleopatra 63. Face of a Stranger 64. Unearthly Stranger 64. Frenzy 72. Dark Places 74. The Eagle Has Landed 76. Master of the Game (TV) 84. Return to Oz 85. Willow 88. A Connecticut Yankee in King Arthur's Court (TV) 89. Adam Bede (TV) 91. Fatherland (TV) 94, etc.
TV series: 9 to 5 82–83.

Marsh, Joan (1913–2000) (Nancy Ann Rosher)
American leading actress of the 30s, the daughter of cinematographer Charles ROSHER. On screen as a child, under the name Dorothy Rosher, she returned as a blonde in *The King of Jazz* 30. The first of her two husbands was screenwriter Charles BELDEN. Retired in the 40s.
The Little Princess 17. Daddy Longlegs 19. Little Lord Fauntleroy 21. All Quiet on the Western Front 30. Little Accident 30. Three Girls Lost 31. Bachelor's Affairs 31. Dance Fools Dance 31. The Man Who Dared 33. Three-Cornered Moon 33. We're Rich Again 34. Many Happy Returns 34. You're Telling Me 34. Anna Karenina 35. Hot Water 37. Fast and Loose 39. Road to Zanzibar 41. Secret Service in Darkest Africa 43. Follow the Leader 44, etc.

Marsh, Mae (1895–1968) (Mary Warne Marsh)
American leading lady of the silent screen; later played small character roles.
Man's Genesis 12. The Birth of a Nation 15. Intolerance 16. Polly of the Circus 17. Spotlight Sadie 18. The Little 'Fraid Lady 20. Flames of Passion 22. The White Rose 23. Daddies 24. The Rat (GB) 25. Tides of Passion 26. Over the Hill 32. Little Man What Now 34. Jane Eyre 43. A Tree Grows in Brooklyn 44. The Robe 53. Sergeant Rutledge 60, many others.

Marsh, Marian (1913–) (Violet Krauth)
American leading lady of English, German, French and Irish descent. Began in Hollywood as an extra; chosen by John Barrymore to play Trilby to his *Svengali* 31.
The Mad Genius 32. Five Star Final 32. The Eleventh Commandment 33. Love at Second Sight (GB) 34. The Black Room 35. When's Your Birthday 37. Missing Daughters 40. House of Errors 42, etc.

Marsh, Oliver H. T. (1893–1941)
American cinematographer.
The Floor Below 18. Good References 19. Lessons in Love 21. Jazzmania 23. The Dove 27. The Divine Woman 28. Not So Dumb 30. The Sin of Madelon Claudet 31. Arsene Lupin 32. Today We Live 33. The Merry Widow 34. *David Copperfield* 35. *A Tale of Two Cities* 35. The Great Ziegfeld 36. His Brother's Wife 36. After the Thin Man 36. Maytime 37. The Firefly 37. Sweethearts 38. It's a Wonderful World 39. Bitter Sweet 40. Rage in Heaven 41. Lady Be Good 41, many others.

Marsh, Terence (1931–)
British production designer.
Dr Zhivago (AA) 65. A Man for All Seasons 66. Oliver (AA) 68. The Looking Glass War 70.

Perfect Friday 70. Scrooge (AAN) 70. Mary, Queen of Scots (AAN) 71. A Touch of Class 73. The Mackintosh Man 73. Juggernaut 74. The Adventures of Sherlock Holmes' Smarter Brother 75. Royal Flash 76. A Bridge Too Far 77. Magic 78. The Frisco Kid 79. Absence of Malice 81. To Be or Not To Be 83. Haunted Honeymoon 86. Spaceballs 87. Bert Rigby, You're a Fool 89. The Hunt for Red October 90. Havana 90. Basic Instinct 92. Clear and Present Danger 94. The Shawshank Redemption 94. Forget Paris 95. Executive Decision 96, etc.

Marshal, Alan (1909–1961)
Australian-born actor of light romantic leads; came to films in 1936 after New York stage experience.
The Garden of Allah 36. Night Must Fall 38. The Hunchback of Notre Dame 40. Tom, Dick and Harry 40. *Lydia* 41. The White Cliffs of Dover 43. The Barkleys of Broadway 48. The Opposite Sex 56. The House on Haunted Hill 59, etc.

Marshall, Alan (1938–)
British producer associated with the films of Alan Parker.
Bugsy Malone 76. Midnight Express (AAN) 78. Fame 80. Shoot the Moon 81. Pink Floyd the Wall 82. Another Country 84. Birdy 84. Angel Heart 87. Leonard, Part 6 87. Homeboy 88. Jacob's Ladder 90. Basic Instinct 92. Cliffhanger 93, etc.

Marshall, Brenda (1915–1992) (Ardis Ankerson Gaines)
American leading lady who married William Holden and retired.
Espionage Agent 39. The Sea Hawk 40. Footsteps in the Dark 41. Singapore Woman 41. Background to Danger 43. The Constant Nymph 44. Strange Impersonation 45. Whispering Smith 49. The Tomahawk Trail 50, etc.

Marshall, Connie (1938–)
American child actress of the 40s.
Sunday Dinner for a Soldier 44. *Sentimental Journey* 45. Dragonwyck 46. Home Sweet Homicide 47. Mother Wore Tights 48. Kill the Umpire 50. Sagmaw Trail 53, etc.

Marshall, E(verett) G. (1910–1998)
American character actor, usually in authoritarian roles. Born in Owatonna, Minnesota, of Norwegian parents, he was educated at the University of Minnesota. He began acting in touring companies and later studied at the Actors' Studio in the 40s. He was much on the Broadway stage in the 40s and frequently on television from the 50s. Married twice.
■ The House on 92nd Street 45. 13 rue Madeleine 46. Untamed Fury 47. Call Northside 777 48. The Caine Mutiny 54. Pushover 54. The Bamboo Prison 54. Broken Lance 54. The Silver Chalice 54. The Left Hand of God 55. The Scarlet Hour 56. The Mountain 56. *Twelve Angry Men* 57. *The Bachelor Party* 57. Man on Fire 57. The Buccaneer 58. The Journey 59. Compulsion 59. Cash McCall 59. Town without Pity 61. The Chase 66. Is Paris Burning? 66. The Poppy Is Also a Flower (TV) 66. The Bridge at Remagen 69. A Clear and Present Danger (TV) 70. Tora! Tora! Tora! 70. The Pursuit of Happiness 71. Vanished (TV) 71. The City (TV) 71. Don't Look behind You (TV) 71. Pursuit (TV) 72. Money to Burn (TV) 73. The Abduction of St Anne (TV) 75. Collision Course (TV) 76. Interiors 78. The Private Files of J. Edgar Hoover 78. The Lazarus Syndrome (TV) 79. Superman II 80. Creepshow 82. Kennedy (as Joseph Kennedy) (TV) 83. Saigon – Year of the Cat (TV) 83. The Winter of our Discontent (TV) 84. Power 85. At Mother's Request (TV) 87. The Hijacking of the Achille Lauro (TV) 89. Consenting Adults 92. The Tommyknockers (TV) 93. Oldest Living Confederate Widow Tells All (TV) 94. Nixon 95.
TV series: The Defenders 61–65. The New Doctors 69–73. Chicago Hope 94-95.

Marshall, Frank (1947–)
American producer turned director. A former actor, he founded the production company Amblin Entertainment with Steven Spielberg and his wife Kathleen Kennedy. Now heads Kennedy/Marshall Productions.
AS PRODUCER: The Other Side of the Wind 75. The Warriors 78. Raiders of the Lost Ark (AAN) 81. Poltergeist 82. Indiana Jones and the Temple of Doom 84. Fandango 84. The Goonies 85. The Color Purple (AAN) 85. Back to the Future 85. The Money Pit 86. Innerspace 86. Who Framed Roger Rabbit? 88. The Land before Time 88. Back to the Future II 89. Indiana Jones and the Last Crusade 89. Hook 91. Swing Kids 93. The Indian in the Cupboard 95. Snow Falling on Cedars 98. The Sixth Sense (AAN) 99. A Map of the World 99, etc.
AS DIRECTOR: Arachnophobia 89. Alive 93. Milk Money 94. Congo 95, etc.

Marshall, Garry (1934–) (Gary Masciarelli)
American film director, screenwriter, producer and occasional actor, who started his career writing and producing TV sitcoms (*The Dick Van Dyke Show*, *Happy Days*, etc.). He is the brother of actress and director Penny Marshall.
How Sweet It Is (w, p) 68. The Grasshopper (w, p) 70. Young Doctors in Love (p, d) 82. The Flamingo Kid (wd) 84. Lost in America (a) 85. Nothing in Common (d) 86. Overboard (d) 87. Beaches (d) 88. Pretty Woman (d) 90. Frankie and Johnny (d) 91. Soapdish (a) 91. A League of Their Own (a) 92. Exit to Eden (d) 94. Dear God 96. The Twilight of the Golds (a) 97. Never Been Kissed 98. Runaway Bride (d) 99. This Space Between Us (a) 99. The Other Sister 99 (co-w,d), etc.

Marshall, George (1891–1975)
American director with over 400 features to his credit. Entered films 1912 as an extra; graduated to feature roles in early serials and comedies; began directing 1917 with a series of Harry Carey westerns.
Pack Up Your Troubles 32. A Message to Garcia 34. The Crime of Dr Forbes 37. In Old Kentucky 38. The Goldwyn Follies 38. You Can't Cheat an Honest Man 39. *Destry Rides Again* 39. *The Ghost Breakers* 40. When the Daltons Rode 40. The Forest Rangers 42. Star Spangled Rhythm 43. And the Angels Sing 43. *Murder He Says* 44. Incendiary Blonde 45. Hold That Blonde 45. The Blue Dahlia 46. The Perils of Pauline 47. Tap Roots 48. *Fancy Pants* 50. The Savage 52. Scared Stiff 53. *Red Garters* 54. The Second Greatest Sex 55. Beyond Mombasa (GB) 56. The Sad Sack 57. The Sheepman 58. Imitation General 58. The Gazebo 59. Cry for Happy 61. How the West Was Won (part) 62. Advance to the Rear 64. Boy, Did I Get a Wrong Number 66. Eight on the Lam 67. Hook Line and Sinker 69, many others.

Marshall, Herbert (1890–1966)
Urbane British actor who despite the loss of a leg in World War I invariably played smooth, sometimes diffident but always gentlemanly roles. In Hollywood from early 30s.
■ Mumsie 27. The Letter 29. Murder 30. The Calendar 31. Secrets of a Secretary 31. *Michael and Mary* 32. The Faithful Heart 32. Blonde Venus 32. *Trouble in Paradise* 32. Evenings for Sale 32. The Solitaire Man 33. I Was a Spy 33. Four Frightened People 34. Outcast Lady 34. The Painted Veil 34. Riptide 34. The Good Fairy 35. The Flame Within 35. Accent on Youth 35. *The Dark Angel* 35. If You Could Only Cook 35. The Lady Consents 36. Forgotten Faces 36. Till We Meet Again 36. Girls' Dormitory 36. A Woman Rebels 36. Make Way for a Lady 36. *Angel* 37. Breakfast for Two 37. Mad About Music 38. Always Goodbye 38. Woman against Woman 38. Zaza 39. A Bill of Divorcement 40. *Foreign Correspondent* 40. *The Letter* 40. When Ladies Meet 41. *The Little Foxes* 41. Kathleen 41. Adventure in Washington 41. *The Moon and Sixpence* (as Somerset Maugham) 42. Young Ideas 43. Forever and a Day 43. Flight for Freedom 43. Andy Hardy's Blonde Trouble 44. The Unseen 45. *The Enchanted Cottage* 45. Crack up 46. *The Razor's Edge* (as Somerset Maugham) 46. Duel in the Sun 46. High Wall 47. Ivy 47. The Secret Garden 49. The Underworld Story 50. Anne of the Indies 51. Black Jack 52. Angel Face 53. The Black Shield of Falworth 54. Gog 54. Riders to the Stars 54. The Virgin Queen 55. Wicked as They Come 56. The Weapon 56. *Stage Struck* 57. The Fly 58. A Fever in the Blood 60. Midnight Lace 60. Five Weeks in a Balloon 62. The List of Adrian Messenger 63. The Third Day 65.
✪ For his comforting upper class presence over thirty-five years of talkies. *Trouble in Paradise*.
❝ Fantasy droops before Mr Herbert Marshall, so intractably British in the American scene. He does, I suppose, represent some genuinely national characteristics, if not those one wishes to see exported: a kind of tobacco, a kind of tweed, a kind of pipe; or in terms of dog, something large, sentimental and moulting, something which confirms our preference for cats. – *Graham Greene, reviewing If You Could Only Cook*

Marshall, Herbert (1900–1991)
British documentarist, married to Fredda Brilliant. Associate of John Grierson; worked on English dubbing of Russian films. Produced and directed feature, *Tinker* 49.

Marshall, James (1967–)
American actor.
Twin Peaks: Fire Walk with Me 92. Gladiator 92. A Few Good Men 92. Don't Do It 94. Hits! 94. The Ticket (TV) 97, etc.
TV series: Twin Peaks 90.
❝ Hollywood is just full of people who want the quick buck and the quick fame, and they get burned out. – *J.M.*

Marshall, Penny (1942–) (Carole Penny Marsciarelli)
American director, a former comedy actress, known from TV. She is the sister of director Garry Marshall. Formerly married to actor and director Rob Reiner.
AS ACTRESS: How Sweet It Is 68. 1941 79. Movers and Shakers 84. Jumpin' Jack Flash 86. The Hard Way 91, etc.
AS DIRECTOR: Big 88. Awakenings 90. A League of Their Own 92. Renaissance Man 94. The Preacher's Wife 96, etc.
TV series: The Odd Couple 71–75. The Bob Newhart Show 72–73. Paul Sand in Friends and Lovers 74–75. *Laverne and Shirley* 76–83.

Marshall, Trudy (1922–)
American leading lady of minor films in the 40s.
Secret Agent of Japan 42. Girl Trouble 44. Sentimental Journey 46. Disaster 48. Mark of the Gorilla 50. The President's Lady 53. Once Is Not Enough 75, etc.

Marshall, Tully (1864–1943) (William Phillips)
American silent screen actor; stage experience from boyhood.
Intolerance 15. Oliver Twist (as Fagin) 16. Joan the Woman 16. The Slim Princess 20. The Hunchback of Notre Dame 23. The Merry Widow 25. The Red Mill 27. The Cat and the Canary 28. Trail of '98 29. Show of Shows 29. The Unholy Garden 31. Scarface 32. Grand Hotel 33. Diamond Jim 35. Souls at Sea 37. A Yank at Oxford 38. Brigham Young 40. Chad Hanna 41. This Gun for Hire 42, many others.

Marshall, William (1924–)
American character actor.
Lydia Bailey 52. Something of Value 57. The Boston Strangler 68. Blacula 72. Scream Blacula Scream 73. Twilight's Last Gleaming 77. Vasectomy – a Delicate Matter 86. Maverick 94, etc.

Marshall, Zena (1926–)
British leading lady with French ancestry; stage experience.
Caesar and Cleopatra (debut) 45. Good Time Girl 47. Miranda 48. Sleeping Car to Trieste 48. Marry Me 49. Hell Is Sold Out 51. The Embezzler 54. My Wife's Family 56. The Story of David 61. Dr No 62. Those Magnificent Men in Their Flying Machines 65. The Terronauts 67, etc.

Martelli, Carlo
English composer, mainly for horror movies of the 60s.
The Curse of the Mummy's Tomb 64. Catacombs 64. Witchcraft 64. The Murder Game 66. Who Killed the Cat? 66. Slave Girls/Prehistoric Women 68, etc.

Martelli, Otello (1903–2000)
Distinguished Italian cinematographer, associated with the early films of Roberto Rossellini and Federico Fellini. Born in Rome, he worked in silent films as an assistant cameraman from the age of 14, and later worked as a newsreel cameraman before switching to features from the early 30s.
Il Cardinale Lambertini 34. Old Guard/Vecchia Guardia 35. Arma Bianca 36. La Contessa Di Parma 37. Who is Happier Than I/Chi E Piu Felice Di Me? 38. Kean 40. Don Giovanni 42. Paisà 46. The Tragic Pursuit/Caccia Tragica 47. Amore 48. Bitter Rice/Riso Amaro 49. The Glass Mountain (GB/It.) 49. The Golden Madonna (GB) 49. Stromboli/Stromboli, Terra Di Dio 49. Francis, God's Jester/The Flowers of St Francis/Francesco, Giullare di Dio 50. Lights of Variety/Luci del Varieta 50. Anna 51. Honeymoon Deferred (GB, co-ph) 51. We, The Women/Siamo Donne (co-ph) 53. Spivs/The Young and Passionate/I Vitelloni 53. The Road/La Strada 54. Gold of Naples/L'Oro di Napoli 55. The Swindlers/Il Bidone 55. Woman of the River/La Donna del Fiume 55. Lucky To Be A Woman/La Fortuna Di Essere Donna 56. Nights of Cabiria/Le Notti Di Cabiria (co-ph) 57. Where the Hot Wind Blows/La Loi 58. The Sea Wall 58. La Dolce Vita 60. Boccaccio '70 (co-ph) 62. La Mia Signora 64. Three Faces/I Tre Volti 65. Death Walks in Laredo/Tre Pistole Contro Cesare 67, etc.

Martin, Chris-Pin (1894–1953)
Rotund Yaqui Indian actor who provided comic relief in many a western.
Four Frightened People 34. The Gay Desperado 36. The Return of the Cisco Kid 39 (and ensuing series). The Mark of Zorro 41. Weekend in Havana 42. Mexican Hayride 49. Ride the Man Down 53, etc.

Martin, Darnell (1965–)
American director and screenwriter, a former assistant camera operator.
I Like It Like That (wd) 94.

Martin, Dean (1917–1995) (Dino Crocetti)
Heavy-lidded, self-spoofing American leading man and singer. Teamed with Jerry Lewis until 1956, then enjoyed spectacular solo success in 60s.
Biography: 1976, *Everybody Loves Somebody Sometime* by Arthur Marx (of Martin and Lewis). 1992, *Dino: Living High in the Dirty Business of Dreams* by Nick Tosches.
■ My Friend Irma 49. My Friend Irma Goes West 50. At War with the Army 51. That's My Boy 51. Sailor Beware 51. Jumping Jacks 52. The Stooge 52. Scared Stiff 53. The Caddy 53. Money from Home 53. Living It Up 54. Three Ring Circus 54. You're Never Too Young 55. Artists and Models 55. Pardners 56. Hollywood or Bust 56. Ten Thousand Bedrooms 57. *The Young Lions* 58. Some Came Running 58. *Rio Bravo* 59. Career 59. Who Was That Lady? 60. Bells are Ringing 60. Ocean's Eleven 60. All in a Night's Work 61. Ada 61. Sergeants Three 62. Who's Got the Action? 62. Toys in the Attic 63. Who's Been Sleeping in My Bed? 63. Four For Texas 64. What a Way to Go 64. Robin and the Seven Hoods 64. *Kiss Me Stupid* 64. The Sons of Katie Elder 65. Marriage on the Rocks 65. *The Silencers* 66. Texas Across the River 66. Murderers' Row 67. Rough Night in Jericho 67. The Ambushers 67. Bandolero 68. How to Save a Marriage 68. Five Card Stud 68. Wrecking Crew 68. Airport 69. Something Big 71. Showdown 73. Mr Ricco 75. Angels in Vegas (TV) 78. The Cannonball Run 80. Cannonball Run II 83.
❝ I'd hate to be a teetotaller. Imagine getting up in the morning and knowing that's as good as you're going to feel all day. – *D.M.*
I can't stand an actor or actress who tells me acting is hard work. It's easy work. Anyone who says it isn't never had to stand on his feet all day dealing blackjack. – *D.M.*
Motivation is a lotta crap. – *D.M.*
Without any doubt the most conscientious actor I have ever worked with. – *Andrew V. McLaglen*
King Leer. – *Life magazine*

Martin, Dean Paul (1951–1987)
American actor, son of Dean Martin. He died when the aircraft he was piloting crashed. Married to actress Olivia Hussey.
Players 79. Heart Like a Wheel 82. Backfire 87.

Martin, Dewey (1923–)
American leading man.
Knock on Any Door (debut) 49. Kansas Raiders 50. The Thing 52. The Big Sky 52. Tennessee Champ 54. Prisoner of War 54. Land of the Pharaohs 55. The Desperate Hours 55. Ten Thousand Bedrooms 57. Wheeler and Murdoch (TV) 72. Seven Alone 75, etc.

Martin, Dick (1923–)
Married actress Dolly Read.
The Glass Bottom Boat 66. Carbon Copy 81. Air Bud: Golden Receiver 98, etc.
See also Rowan, Dan.

Martin, D'Urville (1939–1984)
American character actor, often in blaxploitation movies.
A Time to Sing 68. Watermelon Man 70. Book of Numbers 72. Hammer 72. The Legend of Nigger

Charley 73. Black Caesar 73. Hell up in Harlem 73. The Soul of Nigger Charley 73. Boss Nigger 74. Dolemite (& d) 75. Death Journey 76. The Big Score 83. The Bear 84, etc.

Martin, Edie (1880–1964)
The frail, tiny old lady of many British films. On stage from 1886, films from 1932.
■ Farewell Again 37. Under the Red Robe 37. The Demi-Paradise 42. A Place of One's Own 45. Oliver Twist 48. The History of Mr Polly 49. The Lavender Hill Mob 51. *The Man in the White Suit* 51. Time Gentlemen Please 52. The Titfield Thunderbolt 52. The End of the Road 54. Lease of Life 54. As Long as They're Happy 55. The Lady Killers 55. My Teenage Daughter 56. Too Many Crooks 59. Weekend with Lulu 61. Sparrows Can't Sing 63.

Martin, Hugh (1914–)
American composer and lyricist, generally in collaboration with Ralph Blane.
Best Foot Forward 41. Meet Me in St Louis 44. Athena 54. The Girl Rush 55. The Girl Most Likely 57. Hans Brinker (TV) 58, etc.

Martin, Marion (1916–1985)
American leading lady of 'B' pictures, a statuesque blonde who graduated from the Ziegfeld chorus.
Boom Town 40. Mexican Spitfire at Sea 41. The Big Store 41. They Got Me Covered 42. Abbot and Costello in Hollywood 45. Queen of Burlesque 47. Oh You Beautiful Doll 50. Thunder in the Pines 54, etc.

Martin, Mary (1913–1990)
American musical comedy star; her film career did not seem satisfactory. She was the mother of actor Larry Hagman.
Autobiography: 1976, *My Heart Belongs*.
■ The Rage of Paris 38. The Great Victor Herbert 39. Rhythm on the River 40. Love Thy Neighbour 40. Kiss the Boys Goodbye 41. New York Town 41. *Birth of the Blues* 41. Star Spangled Rhythm 42. Happy Go Lucky 42. True to Life 43. Night and Day 46. Main Street to Broadway 53. Valentine (TV) 79.
❝ She's OK, if you like talent. – *Ethel Merman*

Martin, Millicent (1934–)
British songstress of stage and TV.
The Horsemasters 60. The Girl on the Boat 62. Nothing But the Best 64. Those Magnificent Men in Their Flying Machines 65. Alfie 66. Stop the World I Want To Get Off 66, etc.
TV series: From a Bird's Eye View 69. Downtown 86–87.

Martin, Pamela Sue (1953–)
American leading lady who became familiar on TV (1977–78) as Nancy Drew the teenage detective.
To Find a Man 71. The Poseidon Adventure 72. Buster and Billie 73. The Girls of Huntington House (TV) 73. The Gun and the Pulpit (TV) 74. The Lady in Red 79. Torchlight 84. Flicks 87. A Cry in the Wild 90, etc.

Martin, Richard (1917–1994)
Tall, dark American actor, best remembered as Chito Rafferty, the half-Mexican, half-Irish sidekick to Tim Holt in many of his RKO westerns. He quit movies in the early 50s to become an insurance salesman.
Bombardier 43. Tender Comrade 43. Marine Raiders 44. Arizona Ranger 48. Guns of Hate 48. Mysterious Desperado 49. Riders of the Range 49. Rider from Tucson 50. Storm over Wyoming 50. Gun Play 51. Hot Lead 51. Road Agent 52. Target 52. Desert Passage 53. Four Fast Guns 59, etc.

Martin, Ross (1920–1981) (Martin Rosenblatt)
Polish-American character actor: film appearances sporadic.
Conquest of Space 55. The Colossus of New York 58. Experiment in Terror 62. The Ceremony 64. The Great Race 65. Charlie Chan: Happiness is a Warm Clue (TV: title role) 70.
TV series: *The Wild Wild West* 65–68.

Martin, Skip
English dwarf actor, mainly in horror movies.
The Hellfire Club 60. Masque of the Red Death 64. Whom the Gods Wish to Destroy/Die Nibelungen 66. Circus of Fear 66. The Sandwich Man 66. Where's Jack? 69. Vampire Circus 71. Horror Hospital 73, etc.

Martin, Steve (1945–)
American nightclub comic who turned comic actor and even goes straight occasionally. Formerly married to actress Victoria TENNANT, he was romantically linked with Anne HECHE. He is also a screenwriter, essayist, novelist and dramatist: his play *Picasso at the Lapin Agile* was staged in New York in 1996.
The Kids Are Alright 78. Sgt Pepper's Lonely Hearts Club Band 78. The Jerk 79. The Muppet Movie 79. Pennies from Heaven 81. Dead Men Don't Wear Plaid 82. The Man with Two Brains 83. The Lonely Guy 83. All of Me 84. Movers and Shakers 84. Three Amigos 86. The Little Shop of Horrors 86. Roxanne 87. Planes, Trains and Automobiles 87. Dirty Rotten Scoundrels 88. Parenthood 89. My Blue Heaven 90. L.A. Story 91. Father of the Bride 91. Grand Canyon 91. Housesitter 92. Leap of Faith 92. A Simple Twist of Fate (&w) 94. Mixed Nuts 94. Father of the Bride Part II 95. Sgt Bilko 96. The Spanish Prisoner 97. Bowfinger (&w) 99. The Venice Project (as himself) 99. The Out-of-Towners 99. Fantasia 2000 (host) 00, etc.
TV series: Leo & Liz in Beverly Hills (creator, co-p, wd) 86.
❝ As you get older, it's harder to be silly on the screen. – S.M.

Martin, Strother (1920–1980)
American character actor, often in grizzled western roles.
The Asphalt Jungle 50. Storm over Tibet 52. The Big Knife 55. The Shaggy Dog 59. The Deadly Companions 61. The Man Who Shot Liberty Valance 62. The Sons of Katie Elder 65. Harper 66. *Cool Hand Luke* 67. True Grit 69. Butch Cassidy and the Sundance Kid 69. The Wild Bunch 69. The Ballad of Cable Hogue 70. The Brotherhood of Satan 70. Fool's Parade 71. Pocket Money 72. Sssss 73. Rooster Cogburn 75. Hard Times 75. The Great Scout and Cathouse Thursday 76. Slap Shot 77. The End 78. Up in Smoke 78. The Villain 79, many others.
❝ Famous line (*Cool Hand Luke*) 'What we've got here is a failure to communicate.'

Martin, Tony (1912–) (Alfred Norris)
American cabaret singer and leading man, in Hollywood from 1936 after years of touring with dance bands. He married actress Cyd Charisse in 1948.
Autobiography: 1976, *The Two of Us*.
Sing, Baby, Sing 36. Banjo on My Knee 37. Ali Baba Goes to Town 38. Music in My Heart 40. The Big Store 41. Ziegfeld Girl 41. Till the Clouds Roll By 46. Casbah 48. Two Tickets to Broadway 51. Here Come the Girls 53. Deep in My Heart 54. Hit the Deck 55. Let's Be Happy (GB) 57, etc.

Martin-Harvey, Sir John (1863–1944)
British actor manager of the old school who appeared in a film or two.
Scaramouche 12. A Tale of Two Cities 13. The Cigarette Maker's Romance 13. The Only Way/A Tale of Two Cities (as Sydney Carton, his greatest stage success) 26. The Lyons Mail 31, etc.

Martinelli, Elsa (1933–)
Italian leading lady, in films from 1950.
The Indian Fighter (US) 55. Manuela (GB) 57. The Boatmen 60. Hatari (US) 62. The Trial 63. Marco the Magnificent 65. De l'Amour 65. The Tenth Victim 65. Candy 68. Once Upon a Crime 92, etc.

Martinez, Cliff (1954–)
American composer and musician, born in the Bronx, New York. A former rock drummer, who played with the Red Hot Chili Peppers and Captain Beefheart, he is associated with the films of director Steven SODERBERGH.
sex, lies and videotape 89. Pump Up The Volume 90. Kafka 91. King of the Hill 93. Underneath 95. Gray's Anatomy 96. Out of Sight 98. The Limey 99. Traffic 00, etc.

Martini, Nino (1904–1976)
Italian actor-singer, who made a few English-speaking films.
Here's to Romance (US) 35. The Gay Desperado (US) 36. One Night With You (GB) 48, etc.

Martino, Sergio (1938–)
Italian director, mainly known for horror films.
Mondo Sex/Wages of Sin/Mille Peccati ... Nessuna Virtù 69. The Strange Vice of Mrs Ward/Lo Strano Vizio della Signora Ward 70. They're Coming to Get You/Demons of the Dead/Tutti i Colori del Buio 72. Torso 73. Sex with a Smile 76. Slave of the Cannibal God/Prisoner of the Cannibal God/La Montagna del Dio Cannibale 76. Island of Mutations/Screamers/L'Isola degli Uomini Pesce 79. Caiman/The Great Alligator 79. Casablanca Express 89, etc.

Martins, Orlando (1899–1985)
West African actor in British films.
Sanders of the River 35. Jericho 37. The Man from Morocco 44. Men of Two Worlds (as the witch doctor) 46. End of the River 47. Where No Vultures Fly 52. Simba 55. Sapphire 59. Mister Moses 65, etc.

Martinson, Leslie H.
American director, from TV.
PT 109 62. For Those Who Think Young 64. Batman 66. Fathom 67. Mrs Pollifax – Spy 70. Escape from Angola 76. Cruise Missile 78. The Kid with the Broken Halo (TV) 82. The Kid with the 200 I.Q. (TV) 83. The Fantastic World of D.C. Collins (TV) 84, etc.

Marton, Andrew (1904–1992)
Hungarian-born director, in Hollywood from 1923; settled there after return visits to Europe. Co-directed *King Solomon's Mines* 50; directed the chariot race in *Ben Hur*.
Books: 1992, *Andrew Marton* interviewed by Joanne d'Antonio.
Two o'Clock in the Morning 29. SOS Iceberg 32. The Demon of the Himalayas 34. Wolf's Clothing (GB) 37. Secrets of Stamboul (GB) 37. Gentle Annie 45. The Wild North 52. Prisoner of War 54. Green Fire 55. The Thin Red Line 64. *Crack in the World* 65. Around the World under the Sea 65, etc.
AS SECOND-UNIT DIRECTOR: *The Red Badge of Courage* 51. A Farewell to Arms 57. *Ben Hur* 59. 55 Days at Peking 62. *The Longest Day* 62. Cleopatra 62, etc.

Marvin, Lee (1924–1987)
Ruthless-looking American actor who latterly switched from unpleasant villains to unsympathetic heroes.
Biography: 1997, *Lee: A Romance* by Pamela Marvin.
You're in the Navy Now 51. Duel at Silver Creek 52. The Big Heat 53. The Wild One 54. Gorilla at Large 54. The Caine Mutiny 54. Bad Day at Black Rock 54. Violent Saturday 55. Not as a Stranger 55. Pete Kelly's Blues 55. Shack Out on 101 55. I Died a Thousand Times 56. Seven Men from Now 57. *Attack* 57. Raintree County 57. The Missouri Traveller 58. The Comancheros 61. The Man Who Shot Liberty Valance 62. Donovan's Reef 63. *The Killers* 64. *Cat Ballou* (AA) 65. Ship of Fools 65. The Professionals 66. The Dirty Dozen 67. Point Blank 67. Hell in the Pacific 68. Paint Your Wagon 69. Monte Walsh 70. Prime Cut 72. Emperor of the North Pole 73. The Iceman Cometh 73. The Spikes Gang 75. The Klansman 75. Shout at the Devil 76. The Great Scout and Cathouse Thursday 76. The Big Red One 79. Avalanche Express 79. Death Hunt 81. Gorky Park 83. Dirty Dozen, the Next Mission (TV) 85. Delta Force 86, etc.
TV series: M Squad 57–59. Lawbreaker 63.

The Marx Brothers
A family of Jewish-American comics whose zany humour convulsed minority audiences in its time and influenced later comedy writing to an enormous extent. *Chico* (1886–1961) (Leonard Marx) played the piano eccentrically and spoke with an impossible Italian accent; *Harpo* (1888–1964) (Adolph Marx) was a child-like mute who also played the harp; *Groucho* (1890–1977) (Julius Marx) had a painted moustache, a cigar, a loping walk and the lion's share of the wisecracks. In vaudeville from childhood, they came to films after Broadway success. Originally there were two other brothers: *Gummo* (1893–1977) (Milton Marx), who left the act early on, and *Zeppo* (1901–79) (Herbert Marx), who didn't fit in with the craziness and left them after playing romantic relief in their first five films. These first five films contain much of their best work: later their concentrated anarchy was dissipated by musical and romantic relief.
Autobiography: 1961, *Harpo Speaks!* Among Groucho's semi-autobiographical works are *Groucho and Me* (1959), *Memoirs of a Mangy Lover* (1964) and *The Groucho Letters* (1967).
Biography: 1952, *Life with Groucho* by Arthur Marx; 1972, *Son of Groucho* by Arthur Marx. 1978; *Hello, I Must Be Going* (a rather depressing account of Groucho's last years) by Charlotte Chandler; 1999, Monkey Business: The Lives and Legends of the Marx Brothers by Simon Louvish. 2000, *Groucho: The Life and Times of Julius Henry Marx* by Stefan Kanfer.
Other books: 1974, *The Marx Brothers Scrapbook* by Richard Anobile and Groucho. The films are examined in detail in *The Marx Brothers at the Movies* by Paul D. Zimmerman and Burt Goldblatt.
■ The Cocoanuts 29. *Animal Crackers* 30. *Monkey Business* 31. *Horse Feathers* 32. *Duck Soup* 33. *A Night at the Opera* 35. *A Day at the Races* 37. Room Service 38. *At the Circus* 39. Go West 40. The Big Store 41. *A Night in Casablanca* 46. Love Happy (a curious and unhappy failure) 50. The Story of Mankind (guest appearances) 57.
GROUCHO ALONE: Copacabana 47. Mr Music 50. Double Dynamite 51. A Girl in Every Port 52. Will Success Spoil Rock Hunter? (gag appearance) 57. You Bet Your Life (TV series) 56–61. Skiddo 68.
✪ For shattering all our illusions, and making us love it. *Duck Soup*.
❝ The leader wore a large painted moustache and affected a cigar, and his three henchmen impersonated respectively a mute harpist afflicted with satyriasis, a larcenous Italian, and a jaunty cox-comb, who carried the love interest. – *S. J. Perelman*
Lines written by or for the Marx Brothers would fill a book in themselves. This is a selection of personal favourites, arranged chronologically and attributed to the authors of the films concerned.
1929: *The Cocoanuts* (George S. Kaufman, Morrie Ryskind) 'Ah, Mrs Rittenhouse, won't you ... lie down?
I'll wrestle anybody in the crowd for five dollars.
Be free, my friends. One for all and all for me – me for you and three for five and six for a quarter.
Do you know that this is the biggest development since Sophie Tucker?
Your eyes shine like the pants of my blue serge suit.'
1930: *Animal Crackers* (George S. Kaufman and Morrie Ryskind) 'You're the most beautiful woman I've ever seen, which doesn't say much for you.
What do you get an hour?
– For playing, we get ten dollars an hour.
What do you get for not playing?
– Twelve dollars an hour. Now for rehearsing, we make a special rate – fifteen dollars an hour.
And what do you get for not rehearsing?
– You couldn't afford it. You see, if we don't rehearse, we don't play. And if we don't play, that runs into money.
How much would you want to run into an open manhole?
– Just the cover charge.
Well, drop in some time.
– Sewer.
Well, I guess we cleaned that up.
You go Uruguay and I'll go mine.
One morning I shot an elephant in my pajamas. How he got into my pajamas I'll never know.'
1931: *Monkey Business* (S. J. Perelman, Will B. Johnstone, Arthur Sheekman) 'Do you want your nails trimmed long?
– Oh, about an hour and a half. I got nothing to do.
Look at me: I worked my way up from nothing to a state of extreme poverty.
I want to register a complaint. Do you know who sneaked into my room at three o'clock this morning?
– Who?
– Nobody, and that's my complaint.
Do you suppose I could buy back my introduction to you?
Sir, you have the advantage of me.
– Not yet I haven't, but wait till I get you outside.'
1932: *Horse Feathers* (Bert Kalmar, Harry Ruby, S. J. Perelman, Will B. Johnstone) 'Why don't you bore a hole in yourself and let the sap run out?
There's a man outside with a big black moustache.
– Tell him I've got one.
The dean is furious. He's waxing wroth.
– Is Roth out there too? Tell Roth to wax the dean for a while.

You're a disgrace to our family name of Wagstaff, if such a thing is possible.
You've got the brain of a four-year-old boy, and I bet he was glad to get rid of it.
What a day! Spring in the air!
– Who, me? I should spring in the air and fall in the lake?'
1933: *Duck Soup* (Bert Kalmar, Harry Ruby, Arthur Sheekman, Nat Perrin) 'Take a card. You can keep it: I've got fifty-one left.
My husband is dead.
– I'll bet he's just using that as an excuse.
I was with him to the end.
– No wonder he passed away.
I held him in my arms and kissed him.
– So it was murder!
This is a gala day for you.
– That's plenty. I don't think I could manage more than one gal a day.
What is it that has four pairs of pants, lives in Philadelphia, and it never rains but it pours?
I could dance with you till the cows come home. On second thoughts I'll dance with the cows and you come home.
Excuse me while I brush the crumbs out of my bed. I'm expecting company.'
1935: *A Night at the Opera* (George S. Kaufman, Morrie Ryskind, Al Boasberg) 'Do they allow tipping on the boat?
– Yes, sir.
Have you got two fives?
– Oh, yes, sir.
Then you won't need the ten cents I was going to give you.
Let joy be unconfined. Let there be dancing in the streets, drinking in the saloons, and necking in the park.'
1937: *A Day at the Races* (George Seaton, Robert Pirosh, George Oppenheimer) 'She looks like the healthiest woman I ever met.
– You look like you never met a healthy woman.
Don't point that beard at me, it might go off.
Closer … hold me closer …
– If I hold you any closer I'll be in back of you!
Marry me and I'll never look at another horse.
Isn't that awfully large for a pill?
– Well, it was too small for a basketball and I didn't know what to do with it.
One dollar and you remember me all your life.
– That's the most nauseating proposition I've ever had.'
1939: *At the Circus* (Irving Brecher) 'If you hadn't sent for me, I'd be at home now in a comfortable bed with a hot toddy.
– That's a drink!
I bet your father spent the first year of your life throwing rocks at the stork.'
1945: *A Night in Casablanca* (Joseph Fields, Roland Kibbee, Frank Tashlin) 'The first thing we're going to do is change all the numbers on all the doors.
– But sir, think of the confusion …
Yeah, but think of the fun.
Hey boss, you got a woman in there?
– If I haven't, I've been wasting thirty minutes of valuable time.
I'm Beatrice Ryner. I stop at the hotel.
– I'm Ronald Kornblow. I stop at nothing.'
Groucho himself later proved to be sometimes as funny as his scripts. He wrote to resign from a club: 'I don't care to belong to any social organization which would accept me as a member.'
And he wrote a threatening letter to *Confidential* magazine: 'Dear Sir: If you continue to publish slanderous pieces about me I shall feel compelled to cancel my subscription.'
His wit did not fail him with age: 'I've been around so long I can remember Doris Day before she was a virgin.'
His influence was international; an example of Paris graffiti in 1968 read: 'Je suis Marxiste, tendance Groucho.'
But life with the Marxes was seldom peaceful. Herman Mankiewicz said: 'I never knew what bicarbonate of soda was until I wrote a Marx Brothers picture.'
Groucho once removed Greta Garbo's hat and said: 'Excuse me, I thought you were a fellow I once knew in Pittsburgh.'
George F. Kaufman had soon had enough of them: '*Cocoanuts* was a comedy; the Marx Brothers are comics; meeting them was a tragedy.'
Groucho was perhaps too fearless a critic, as when giving his opinion of *Samson and Delilah*, starring Victor Mature and Hedy Lamarr: 'First picture I've seen in which the male lead has bigger tits than the female.'
And on the nudist musical *Hair*: 'Why should I pay ten dollars for something I can see in the bathroom for nothing?'
Harpo could be bitchy too. His appraisal of *Abie's Irish Rose* has lingered down the decades: 'No worse than a bad cold.'
And he was witty when refusing Alexander Woollcott's invitation to share a holiday on the French riviera: 'I can think of forty better places to spend the summer, all of them on Long Island in a hammock.'
Groucho even aspired to be a political thinker: 'Military intelligence is a contradiction in terms …'
A final thought from Groucho: 'If you want to see a comic strip you should see me in a shower.'
Well, one more from Groucho for luck: 'They say a man is as old as the woman he feels.'

Masamura, Yazuso (1924–1986)
Japanese director, an influence on the country's 'New Wave' directors of the late 50s. He studied film at the Centro Sperimentale in Rome and was influenced by NEO-REALISM.
Kisses/Kuchizuke 57. Warm Current/Donryu 57. Giants and Toys/The Build/Kyojin To Gangu 58. A Man Blown by the Wind/Karakkaze Yaro 60. All Mixed Up/Manji 62. The Black Test Car/Kuro No Tesuto Ka 62. The Hoodlum Soldier/Heitai Yakuza 65. Tatoo/Shishei 66. Red Angel/Akai Tenshi 66. Love for an Idiot/Chijin No Ai 67, etc.

Maschwitz, Eric (1901–1969)
English screenwriter, playwright and songwriter, whose lyrics include 'These Foolish Things' and 'A Nightingale Sang in Berkeley Square'. Born in Birmingham, he was educated at Cambridge University and worked for the BBC as a commentator, scriptwriter, editor of the *Radio Times*, and the first director of variety programmes from 1933–37. In 1937 he went to Hollywood under contract to MGM, returning to Britain at the outbreak of the Second World War, and becoming head of Light Entertainment for BBC-TV in the mid-50s. He was married briefly to Hermione GINGOLD.
Autobiography: 1957, *No Chip on My Shoulder*.
Goodnight Vienna/Magic Night (co-w, oa) 32. Death at Broadcasting House (co-w) 34. Royal Cavalcade (co-w) 35. Land without Music (co-story) 36. Café Colette (co-w from radio programme) 37. Goodbye Mr Chips (co-w) 39. Balalaika (oa) 39. Carnival (w) 46. Queen of Song (w) 47, etc.

Masina, Giulietta (1920–1994)
Italian gamin-like actress, married to Federico Fellini. In films since 1941.
Senza Pietà 47. *Lights of Variety* 48. *La Strada* 54. Il Bidone 55. *Nights of Cabiria* 57. Juliet of the Spirits 65. The Madwoman of Chaillot 69. Ginger and Fred 85. Aujourd'hui Peut-être 91. La Nonna 92, etc.

Maskell, Virginia (1936–1968)
British leading lady with attractively soulful eyes. Committed suicide.
■ Happy is the Bride 57. Our Virgin Island 58. The Man Upstairs 59. Jet Storm 59. Suspect 60. Doctor in Love 60. The Wild and the Willing 62. *Only Two Can Play* 62. Interlude 68.

Mason, A. E. W. (1865–1948)
British novelist whose *The House of the Arrow* and *The Four Feathers* have been filmed several times. *Fire Over England* and *At the Villa Rose* also came to the screen.

Mason, Elliott (1897–1949)
Scottish character actress with repertory experience. The Ghost Goes West 36. Owd Bob 38. The Ghost of St Michael's 41. The Gentle Sex 43. The Captive Heart 46, etc.

Mason, Herbert (1891–1960)
British director.
His Lordship 36. Strange Boarders 38. Back Room Boy 41. Flight from Folly 45, etc.

Mason, Jackie (1930–) (Yacov Moshe Maza)
Acerbic American comedian, in occasional films. Born in Sheboygan, Wisconsin, he was brought up in New York and studied at the City College, planning to become a rabbi before he discovered his talent as a comic.
Operation Delilah 67. The Stoolie 72. The Jerk 79. History of the World Part 1 81. Caddyshack 2 88. In the Aftermath 88, etc.
❝ I was nearly drafted. It's not that I mind fighting for my country, but they called me at a ridiculous time: in the middle of a war! – J.M.

Mason, James (1909–1984)
Leading British and international actor who became a star at home in saturnine roles during World War II, went to Hollywood and initially had a thin time but during the 50s became a respected interpreter of varied and interesting characters. Married Pamela KELLINO.
Autobiography: 1982, *Before I Forget*.
Biography: 1989, *James Mason: Odd Man Out* by Sheridan Morley. 1989, *James Mason – a Personal Biography* by Diana de Rosso.
■ Late Extra 35. Twice Branded 36. Troubled Waters 36. Prison Breaker 36. Blind Man's Bluff 36. The Secret of Stamboul 36. Fire Over England 36. The Mill on the Floss 37. The High Command 37. Catch as Catch Can 37. The Return of the Scarlet Pimpernel 37. *I Met a Murderer* 39. This Man Is Dangerous/The Patient Vanishes 41. Hatter's Castle 42. *The Night Has Eyes* 42. Alibi 42. Secret Mission 42. Thunder Rock 43. The Bells Go Down 43. *The Man in Grey* (a key role as an 18th-century villain) 43. They Met in the Dark 43. Candlelight in Algeria 44. Fanny by Gaslight 44. Hotel Reserve 44. A Place of One's Own 45. They Were Sisters 45. *The Seventh Veil* 45. *The Wicked Lady* 46. *Odd Man Out* 46. The Upturned Glass 47. Caught 49. Madame Bovary 49. The Reckless Moment 49. East Side West Side 49. One Way Street 50. *Pandora and the Flying Dutchman* 51. *The Desert Fox* (as Rommel) 51. Lady Possessed 52. *Five Fingers* 52. The Prisoner of Zenda (as Rupert) 52. Face to Face 52. The Desert Rats 53. *Julius Caesar* (as Brutus) 53. The Story of Three Loves 53. Botany Bay 53. The Man Between 53. Charade 53. Prince Valiant 54. *20,000 Leagues under the Sea* (as Captain Nemo) 54. *A Star Is Born* (AAN) 54. Forever Darling 56. Bigger Than Life (& p) 56. Island in the Sun 57. Cry Terror 58. The Decks Ran Red 58. North by Northwest 59. *Journey to the Center of the Earth* 59. A Touch of Larceny 60. The Trials of Oscar Wilde 60. The Marriage Go Round 61. The Land We Love/Hero's Island 62. Escape from Zahrain 62. Tiara Tahiti 62. *Lolita* (as Humbert) 62. The Fall of the Roman Empire 64. Torpedo Bay 64. *The Pumpkin Eater* 64. Lord Jim 65. The Player Pianos 65. Genghis Khan 65. *The Blue Max* 66. Georgy Girl (AAN) 66. *The Deadly Affair* 67. Stranger in the House 67. Duffy 68. Mayerling 68. Age of Consent 69. The Seagull 69. Spring and Port Wine 70. Kill! 70. Cold Sweat 70. Bad Man's River 71. A Dangerous Summer 72. Ivanhoe 72. Child's Play 72. The Last of Sheila 73. Frankenstein, the True Story (TV) 73. The Mackintosh Man 73. 11 Harrowhouse 74. The Marseilles Contract 74. Great Expectations (TV) 74. The Tempest 74. Nostro Nero in Casa Nichols 74. Centra di Respetto 75. La Città Sconvolta 75. Mandingo 75. Autobiography of a Princess 75. Voyage of the Damned 76. Inside Out 76. The Left Hand of the Law 76. Jesus of Nazareth (TV) 77. Cross of Iron 77. The Water Babies 78. Heaven Can Wait 78. The Boys from Brazil 78. *Murder by Decree* (as Dr Watson) 79. The Passage 79. Bloodline 79. North Sea Hijack 80. Evil Under the Sun 82. The Verdict (AAN) 82. Yellowbeard 83. The Shooting Party 84.
✪ For his incisive professionalism over a long period of gradually declining standards. *A Star Is Born*.

Mason, Marsha (1942–)
American leading actress, formerly married to Neil Simon (1973–83).
Hot Rod Hullaballoo 66. Blume in Love 73. Cinderella Liberty (AAN) 73. Audrey Rose 77. *The Goodbye Girl* (AAN) 77. The Cheap Detective 78. Promises in the Dark 79. Chapter Two (AAN) 79. Only When I Laugh (AAN) 81. Max Dugan Returns 83. Heartbreak Ridge 86. Trapped in Silence (TV) 86. Dinner at Eight (TV) 89. Stella 90. Drop Dead Fred 91. I Love Trouble 94. Nick of Time 95. Broken Trust (TV) 95. 2 Days in the Valley 96, etc.

Mason, Richard (1919–1997)
English novelist and screenwriter, of stories of inter-racial love affairs. Born in Hale, Cheshire, he used his own wartime experiences as the basis for his first novel, *The Wind Cannot Read* (1947), about a soldier falling in love with a Japanese woman who teaches him her language. He stopped writing in the early 60s and moved to Rome. Married three times.
■ A Town Like Alice (co-w) 56. Pacific Destiny (w) 56. The Wind Cannot Read (w, oa) 58. Passionate Summer (oa) 58. The World of Susie Wong (oa) 60.

Mason, Shirley (1900–1979) (Leona Flugrath)
American leading lady of the silent screen, sister of Viola Dana.
Vanity Fair 15. Goodbye Bill 18. Treasure Island 20. Merely Mary Ann 20. Lights of the Desert 22. What Fools Men 25. Don Juan's Three Nights 26. Sally in Our Alley 27. Show of Stars 29, etc.

Massaccesi, Aristide
see D'AMATO, Joe.

Massari, Lea (1933–) (Anna Maria Massatani)
French-Italian leading lady.
L'Avventura 58. The Colossus of Rhodes 61. Four Days of Naples 62. Made in Italy 65. Les Choses de la Vie 69. Le Souffle au Coeur 71. Impossible Object 73. Violette et François 77. Christ Stopped at Eboli 79. Vengeance 86. A Woman Destroyed 88. Journey of Love 91, etc.

Massen, Osa (1916–)
Danish-born actress in Hollywood from the late 30s.
Honeymoon in Bali 39. The Devil Pays Off 41. The Master Race 44. Tokyo Rose 44. Cry of the Werewolf 44. Deadline at Dawn 47. Rocketship XM 50, etc.

Massey, Anna (1937–)
British character actress, daughter of Raymond MASSEY. Married (1958-62) actor Jeremy BRETT.
Gideon's Day 58. Peeping Tom 59. Bunny Lake Is Missing 65. De Sade 69. The Looking Glass War 69. Frenzy 72. A Doll's House 73. Vault of Horror 73. Sweet William 80. Five Days One Summer 82. Another Country 84. The Chain 84. The Little Drummer Girl 84. Foreign Body 87. Impromptu 89. Killing Dad 89. The Tall Guy 89. Angels and Insects 95. Haunted 95. The Grotesque/Grave Indiscretions 96. Sweet Angel Mine 96. Déjà Vu (US) 97. Slab Boys 97. A Respectable Trade (TV) 98. Captain Jack 98. Mad Cows 99. Room to Rent 00, etc.
TV series: Rebecca (as Mrs Danvers) 79. Nice Day at the Office 94.

Massey, Daniel (1933–1998)
British actor, son of Raymond MASSEY, usually seen on stage or TV.
Girls at Sea 57. Upstairs and Downstairs 59. The Queen's Guard 61. Go to Blazes 62. Moll Flanders 65. The Jokers 66. *Star!* (as Noël Coward) (AAN) 68. Fragment of Fear 70. Mary Queen of Scots 72. Vault of Horror 73. The Incredible Sarah 76. The Cat and the Canary 77. Bad Timing 80. Escape to Victory 81. Love with a Perfect Stranger (TV) 86. Intimate Contact 87. Scandal 88. In the Name of the Father 93. Samson and Delilah (TV) 96, etc.

Massey, Ilona (1912–1974) (Ilona Hajmassy)
Hungarian-born actress and singer. Born in Budapest, she began her career in Vienna before moving to Hollywood in the mid-30s. The second of her four husbands was actor Alan CURTIS (1941-42).
■ Knox und die Lustigen Vagabunden 35. Der Himmel auf Erden 35. *Rosalie* 37. Balalaika 39. New Wine 41. International Lady 41. Invisible Agent 42. Frankenstein Meets the Wolf Man (as 'Frankenstein') 43. Holiday in Mexico 46. Northwest Outpost 47. The Plunderers 48. Love Happy 49. Jet over the Atlantic 58.

Massey, Raymond (1896–1983)
Canadian-born actor, on stage (in Britain) from 1922. In films, has played saturnine, benevolent or darkly villainous, with a penchant for impersonations of Abraham Lincoln.
Autobiography: 1976, *When I Was Young*. 1979, *A Hundred Lives*.
■ The Speckled Band (as Sherlock Holmes) 31. The Face at the Window 31. *The Old Dark House* 32. *The Scarlet Pimpernel* 34. *Things to Come* 36. Fire over England 36. Under the Red Robe 37. *The Prisoner of Zenda* 37. Dreaming Lips 37. The Hurricane 37. The Drum 38. Black Limelight 39. *Abe Lincoln in Illinois* (AAN) 40. Santa Fe Trail (as John Brown) 40. 49th Parallel 41. Dangerously They Live 41. Desperate Journey 42. Reap the

Wild Wind 42. Action in the North Atlantic 43. *Arsenic and Old Lace* 44. The Woman in the Window 44. Hotel Berlin 45. God Is My Co-Pilot 45. A Matter of Life and Death 46. Possessed 47. Mourning Becomes Electra 47. The Fountainhead 48. Roseanna McCoy 49. Chain Lightning 49. Barricade 50. Dallas 50. Sugarfoot 51. Come Fill the Cup 51. David and Bathsheba 51. Carson City 52. The Desert Song 53. Prince of Players 55. Battle Cry 55. *East of Eden* 55. Seven Angry Men 55. Omar Khayyam 57. The Naked and the Dead 58. The Great Impostor 60. The Fiercest Heart 61. The Queen's Guard 61. How the West Was Won 62. Mackenna's Gold 68. All My Darling Daughters (TV) 72. The President's Plane Is Missing (TV) 73.

TV series: I Spy 55. Dr Kildare (as Dr Gillespie) 61–66.

✪ For his leathery, reliable and highly intelligent presence during most of the cinema's most interesting years (though in few of its more interesting films). *Things to Come*.

❝ Famous line (*Things to Come*) 'It is this, or that – all the universe, or nothing. Which shall it be, Passworthy? Which shall it be?'

Massie, Paul (1932–)
Canadian-born actor, on British stage and screen.
High Tide at Noon 57. *Orders to Kill* 58. Sapphire 59. Libel 60. The Two Faces of Dr Jekyll 60. The Rebel 60. Raising the Wind 61. The Pot Carriers 62, many others.

Massine, Leonid (1896–1979)
Russian-born choreographer of international renown, best displayed on film in *The Red Shoes* 48.

Massingham, Richard (1898–1953)
British actor-producer-director: a qualified doctor who abandoned his medical career to make numerous short propaganda films for government departments during World War II and after, infusing them with quiet wit and sympathy. Gratefully remembered as the stout party bewildered by government restrictions: bathing in five inches of water, collecting salvage, avoiding colds, preventing rumours, wearing a gasmask, etc.

Masters, Anthony (1919–1990)
English art director and production designer.
The Bespoke Overcoat 55. The Story of Esther Costello 57. Corridors of Blood 58. Expresso Bongo 59. The Day the Earth Caught Fire 61. The Heroes of Telemark 65. 2001: A Space Odyssey (AAN) 68. ZPG/Zero Population Growth 70. Papillon 73. The Deep 77. Dune 84. The Clan of the Cave Bear 85, etc.

Masters, Quentin (1946–)
Australian director of international films.
■ Thumb Tripping (& w) 73. The Stud 78. The Psi Factor 81. A Dangerous Summer 82. Midnite Spares 83.

Masterson, Mary Stuart (1966–)
American leading actress.
The Stepford Wives 75. Heaven Help Us 85. At Close Range 86. My Little Girl 86. Gardens of Stone 87. Some Kind of Wonderful 87. Mr North 88. Chances Are 89. Immediate Family 89. Funny about Love 90. Fried Green Tomatoes at the Whistle Stop Café 91. Mad at the Moon 92. Married to It 92. Benny & Joon 93. Bad Girls 94. The Radioland Murders 94. Bed of Roses 95. Lily Dale (TV) 96, etc.

Masterson, Peter (1934–) (Carlos B. Masterson)
American actor and director, the father of Mary Stuart Masterson.
AS ACTOR: Ambush Bay 66. Counterpoint 68. Von Richthofen and Brown 71. The Exorcist 73. The Stepford Wives 75. A Question of Guilt (TV) 78. Gardens of Stone 87, etc.
AS DIRECTOR: The Trip to Bountiful 85. Blood Red 88. Full Moon in Blue Water 88. Night Game 89. Convicts 91. Arctic Blue 93. Lily Dale (TV) 96, etc.

Masterson, William Barclay 'Bat' (1855–1921)
American lawman, buffalo hunter, and friend and colleague of Wyatt EARP, who became sheriff of Dodge City at the age of 22. After he was voted out of office, he was involved with Earp and Doc HOLLIDAY in various dubious enterprises in Dodge City and Tombstone, was an army scout during the Apache uprising of 1886, a gambler, and, finally, a sports reporter and drama critic in New York. He was played by Albert DEKKER in *Woman of the Town* 43, Randolph SCOTT in *Trail Street* 47, Monte HALE in *Prince of the Plains* 49, Steve Darrell in *Winchester '73* 50, George MONTGOMERY in *Masterson of Kansas* 54, Keith LARSEN in *Wichita* 55, Kenneth TOBEY in *Gunfight at the O.K. Corral* 56, Gregory WALCOTT in *Badman's Country* 58, Joel McCREA in *The Gunfight at Dodge City* 58, and Tom SIZEMORE in *Wyatt Earp* 94.

❝ There are many in this old world of ours who hold that things break about even for all of us. I have observed for example that we all get the same amount of ice. The rich get it in the summertime and the poor get it in the winter. – B.M. *(discovered in his typewriter when he died of heart failure at his desk)*

Masterson was a bad man to cross; he had killed several hearties 'in self-defense'. This tight-lipped fellow had never been known to smile. – *Gene Fowler*

Mastrantonio, Mary Elizabeth (1958–)
American leading actress, with stage experience.
Scarface 83. The Color of Money (AAN) 86. Slamdance 87. The January Man 88. The Abyss 89. The January Man 89. Fools of Fortune 90. Class Action 91. Robin Hood: Prince of Thieves 91. White Sands 92. Consenting Adults 92. Three Wishes 95. Two Bits 96. My Life So Far 98. Limbo 99. The Perfect Storm 00, etc.

Mastroianni, Chiara (1972–)
French leading actress, the daughter of Catherine DENEUVE and Marcello MASTROIANNI.
My Favorite Season/Ma Saison Préférée 93. Under the Stars/à la Belle étoile) 93. Prêt-à-Porter 94. Don't Forget You're Going to Die/N'Oublie Pas que Tu Vas Mourir 95. Chameleon/Cameleone 96, etc.

Mastroianni, Marcello (1923–1996)
Italian leading man, a former clerk who broke into films with a bit part in *I Miserabili* 47. In his day Italy's most respected and sought-after lead. Married actress Flora Carabella (1927-1999) in 1948; they separated in 1970 but never divorced.
Sunday in August 49. Girls of the Spanish Steps 51. The Bigamist 55. *White Nights* 57. I Soliti Ignoti 58. La Dolce Vita 59. *Il Bell'Antonio* 60. La Notte 61. *Divorce Italian Style* (AAN, BFA) 62. Family Diary 62. Eight and a Half 63. *Yesterday, Today and Tomorrow* (BFA) 63. The Organizer 63. Marriage Italian Style 64. Casanova 70 65. The Tenth Victim 65. Shoot Loud, Louder, I Don't Understand 66. The Stranger 67. Diamonds for Breakfast (GB) 68. A Place for Lovers 69. Sunflower 70. What? 72. Blowout 73. The Slightly Pregnant Man 73. Massacre in Rome 74. The Priest's Wife 74. Down the Ancient Stairs 75. The Sunday Woman 76. A Special Day (AAN) 77. Traffic Jam 78. City of Women 80. Revenge 80. General of the Dead Army 83. Henry IV 84. The Two Lives of Mattia Pascal 85. Big Deal on Madonna Street – 20 Years Later 85. Macaroni 85. *Ginger and Fred* 85. The Bee Keeper 86. Dark Eyes/Oci Ciornie (AAN) 87. Miss Arizona 88. Splendor 89. Everybody's Fine/Stanno Tutti Bene 90. Sometime Tonight/Verso Sera 90. Le Voleur d'Enfants 91. Tchin-Tchin 91. The Suspended Step of the Stork/To Meteoro Vima to Pelargou 91. La Nonna 92. Used People 92. Viva i Bambini 92. Consenting Adults 92. 1, 2, 3, Soleil 93. We Don't Want to Talk about It/De Eso No Se Habla 93. How Long Till Daylight (TV) 94. Prêt-à-Porter/Ready to Wear 94. According to Pereira 95. Beyond the Clouds 95. Three Lives and Only One Death 96. Journey to the Beginning of the World 97, etc.

❝ I only really exist when I am working on a film. – M.M.

I don't like that Method thing: what sufferance to go into a role! I'm not going to enter a monastery so I can play a priest. An actor is a buffoon – this is the miracle, being a chameleon. – M.M.

Life has been generous to me. I come from a very modest family – my father was a cabinet-maker – and I'm in a profession I like. – M.M.

Masur, Richard (1948–)
Plump American supporting actor.
W.H.I.F.F.S. 75. Semi Tough 77. Who'll Stop the Rain? 78. Hanover Street 79. Scavenger Hunt 79. Walking through the Fire (TV) 79. Heaven's Gate 80. East of Eden (TV) 81. *Fallen Angel* (TV) 81. I'm Dancing as Fast as I Can 82. The Thing 82. Risky Business 83. Under Fire 83. The Mean Season 84. My Science Project 85. Heartburn 86. The Believers 86. Walker 87. License to Drive 88. Rent-a-Cop 88. Shoot to Kill 88. Far from Home 89. Flashback 90. My Girl 91. The Man without a Face 93. Six Degrees of Separation 93. My Girl 2 94. Les Patriotes (Fr.) 94. Forget Paris 95. Multiplicity 96. Fire Down Below 97. Play It To The Bone 99, etc.
TV series: One Day at a Time 75–76. Hot L Baltimore 75. Empire 84.

Mata Hari (1876–1917) (Margaret Gertrude Zelle)
Four films have been made about the French spy executed during World War I: by Friedrich Feher in 1927 with Magda Sonia; by George Fitzmaurice in 1931 with Greta Garbo; by Jean-Louis Richard in 1964 with Jeanne Moreau; by Curtis Harrington in 1984 with Sylvia Kristel. She was caricatured by Zsa Zsa Gabor in *Up the Front* 72. Her pseudonym, in Dutch, means 'eye of the dawn'.

Matarazzo, Heather (1982–)
American actress.
Welcome to the Dollhouse 95. The Devil's Advocate 97. 54 98. Scream 3 00. Company Man 01, etc.
TV series: The Adventures of Pete and Pete 93. Roseanne 97. Now and Again 99- .

Maté, Rudolph (1898–1964)
Austrian-born cameraman, later in Hollywood.
The Passion of Joan of Arc 28. *Vampyr* 31. Liliom 33. *Dante's Inferno* 35. Dodsworth 36. Love Affair 39. *Foreign Correspondent* 40. To Be or Not To Be 42. Cover Girl 44, etc.
■ LATER AS DIRECTOR: It Had to Be You (co-d) 47. The Dark Past 49. D.O.A. 50. No Sad Songs for Me 50. *Union Station* 50. Branded 50. The Prince Who Was a Thief 51. When Worlds Collide 51. The Green Glove 52. Paula 52. Sally and Saint Anne 52. Mississippi Gambler 53. Second Chance 53. Forbidden 53. The Siege At Red River 54. *The Black Shield of Falworth* 54. The Violent Men 55. The Far Horizons 55. Miracle in the Rain 56. The Rawhide Years 56. Port Afrique 56. Three Violent People 57. The Deep Six 58. For the First Time 59. The Immaculate Road 60. Revak the Rebel 60. The 300 Spartans 62. Aliki 63. Seven Seas to Calais 64.

Mather, Aubrey (1885–1958)
British character actor, on stage from 1905, films from 1931. Settled in Hollywood and became useful member of English contingent, playing butlers and beaming, bald-headed little men.
Young Woodley 31. As You Like It 36. When Knights Were Bold 36. Jane Eyre 44. The Keys of the Kingdom 44. The Forsyte Saga 49. The Importance of Being Earnest 52, many others.

Mathers, Jerry (1948–)
American actor whose career has been mainly confined to playing 'Beaver' Cleaver in the folksy US sitcom *Leave It to Beaver*. In television from the age of two, he was a child star of the 50s and enjoyed some later success playing Beaver as an adult.
This Is My Love 54. The Trouble with Harry 55. Bigger than Life 56. That Certain Feeling 56. Still the Beaver (TV) 83. Back to the Beach 87, etc.
TV series: Leave It to Beaver 57–63. Still the Beaver 85–86. The New Leave It to Beaver 86–89.

Matheson, Murray (1912–1985)
Soft-spoken Australian actor in Hollywood, mostly on TV.
Hurricane Smith 52. Botany Bay 53. Love Is a Many Splendored Thing 55. Assault On a Queen 66. How to Succeed in Business 67, etc.
TV series: Banacek 72–74.

Matheson, Richard (1926–)
American science-fiction novelist and screenwriter.
The Incredible Shrinking Man (oa, w) 57. The House of Usher (w) 60. The Pit and the Pendulum (w) 61. The Raven (w) 63. The Comedy of Terrors (w) 63. The Last Man on Earth (oa) 64. The Young Warriors (oaw) 68. The Devil Rides Out (w) 68. De Sade (w) 69. The Omega Man (oa) 71. The Legend of Hell House (w) 73. Dracula (TV) 73. Somewhere in Time 80. Jaws 3-D 83. Twilight Zone: The Movie 83. Loose Cannons 90. Trilogy of Terror 2 (co-w) (TV) 96. What Dreams May Come (oa) 98. Stir of Echoes (oa) 99, etc.

Matheson, Tim (1947–)
American leading man, in TV from childhood.
Yours Mine and Ours 65. Divorce American Style 68. Magnum Force 73. National Lampoon's Animal House 78. The Apple Dumpling Gang Rides Again 79. Dreamer 79. A Little Sex 82. To Be or Not To Be 83. Impulse 84. Fletch 85. Drop Dead Fred 91. Mortal Passion 91. Stephen King's Sometimes They Come Back 91. Starfire 92. Black Sheep 96. A Very Brady Sequel 96. Twilight Man 96. Buried Alive 2 97. The Story of Us 99. Jackie Bouvier Kennedy Onassis (TV) 00, etc.
TV series: Window on Main Street 61–62. Johnny Quest (voice) 64–65. The Virginian 69–70. Bonanza 72–73. The Quest 76. Tucker's Witch 82–83. Just in Time 88. Forever Love 98. The West Wing 99- .

Mathews, Kerwin (1926–)
American leading man, former teacher.
Five Against the House 55. The Seventh Voyage of Sinbad 58. Man on a String 60. The Three Worlds of Gulliver 60. Jack the Giant Killer 61. Pirates of Blood River 62. Maniac (GB) 63. Battle Beneath the Earth (GB) 68. Barquero 69. The Boy Who Cried Werewolf 73. Nightmare in Blood 78, etc.

Mathieson, Muir (1911–1975)
Influential Scottish musical director. Born in Stirling, he studied at the Royal College of Music and was in films from 1931 as assistant musical director to Alexander KORDA, later becoming musical director of London Films and musical director for Rank. He persuaded such British composers as Arthur BLISS, William WALTON, Ralph VAUGHAN WILLIAMS and Benjamin BRITTEN to write for films. He worked on more than 400 movies, and can be seen on screen, conducting the London Symphony Orchestra, in *The Seventh Veil* and *A Girl in a Million*.
Things to Come 36. Dangerous Moonlight 40. In Which We Serve 42. Brief Encounter 46. The Sound Barrier 52. The Swiss Family Robinson 60. Becket 64, many others.

Mathis, June (1892–1927)
American screenwriter.
An Eye for an Eye 18. *The Four Horsemen of the Apocalypse* 21. Blood and Sand 22. Three Wise Fools 23. *Greed* 23. *Ben Hur* 27, etc.

Mathis, Samantha (1970–)
American actress, daughter of actress Bibi BESCH.
Pump Up the Volume 90. This Is My Life 92. Ferngully: The Last Rainforest (voice) 92. The Music of Chance 93. The Thing Called Love 93. Super Mario Bros 93. Little Women 94. Jack and Sarah 95. The American President 95. Making an American Quilt 95. Broken Arrow 96. Sweet Jane 97, etc.
TV series: Aaron's Way 88. Knightwatch 88–89.

Mathison, Melissa (1949–)
American screenwriter. She married actor Harrison Ford in 1983.
The Black Stallion 79. The Escape Artist 82. E.T. – the Extraterrestrial (AAN) 82. Son of the Morning Star (TV) 91. Kundun 97, etc.

Matlin, Marlee (1965–)
American actress. She is deaf.
Children of a Lesser God (AA) 86. Walker 87. Bridge to Silence (TV) 89. The Linguini Incident 91. The Player 92. Hear No Evil 93. It's My Party 96, etc.

Matlock, Matty (1907–1978)
American jazz clarinettist and arranger. Born in Paducah, Kentucky, he worked with Ben Pollack's band and the Bob CROSBY Orchestra and Bobcats, becoming a studio musician and arranger in Los Angeles from the early 40s. He led the band and arranged the music for the film *Pete Kelly's Blues* 55, and the subsequent TV series 59.
Sis Hopkins 41. When You're Smiling 50. Rhythm Inn 51. Dragnet 54, etc.

Matras, Christian (1903–1977)
French cinematographer, in films from 1928.
La Grande Illusion 37. Boule de Suif 45. Les Jeux Sont Faits 47. La Ronde 50. Madame De 53. *Lola Montès* 55. Les Espions 57. Paris Blues 61. Les Fêtes Galantes 65. The Milky Way 68, many others.

Matray, Ernst (1891–1978)
Hungarian-born actor, director and choreographer. Born In Budapest, he was a leading actor with Max REINHARDT's company in Berlin, and acted in, and directed, comic two-reel silents from 1913. In the early 30s, he went to Hollywood, where he worked for MGM and others as a choreographer and stager of musical sequences. His wives included actress Greta Schroeder and actress and writer Maria Solveg.

As ACTOR: Die Insel der Seligen 13. Das Mirakel 13. Das Sportsmadel (&d) 15. Teufelchen (&d) 15. Zucker und Zimt (&co-d) 15. Weltbrand 20. Nathan der Weise 22. Adventure in Music (US, co-d only) 44. Musik, Musik-und Nur Musik (d only) 55, etc.

As CHOREOGRAPHER: Bitter Sweet 40. The Chocolate Soldier 41. Higher and Higher 44. Step Lively 44. George White's Scandals 1945, etc.

Mattes, Eva (1955–)
Leading German actress of that country's New Wave cinema, associated with the films of Fassbinder (whom she played in the biopic *A Man Like Eva*) and Werner Herzog.

Jailbait/Wildwechsel 72. The Bitter Tears of Petra von Kant/Die Bitteren Tränen der Petra von Kant 72. Supermarket/Supermarkt 74. Stroszek 77. Ravine Racer/Schluchtenflitzer 79. David 79. Germany Pale Mother/Deutschland Bleiche Mutter 79. Woyzeck 79. Celeste 81. Rita, Ritter 84. A Man Like Eva/Ein Mann Wie Eva 84. Felix 87. Herbstmilch 89. Der Kinoerzähler 93. The Promise 95, etc.

Matthau, Charles (c. 1965–)
American director, producer and actor, a graduate of the University of Southern California Film School; he is the son of actor Walter MATTHAU.

Charley Varrick (a) 73. The Bad News Bears (a) 76. House Calls (a) 78. Doin' Time on Planet Earth (a, d) 89. Number One Fan (a) 95. The Grass Harp (a, p, d) 95, etc.

Matthau, Walter (1920–2000) (Walter Matuschanskayasky)
American character actor with a penchant for wry comedy; his lugubrious features and sharp talent made him a star in the late 60s.

■ The Kentuckian 55. The Indian Fighter 55. Bigger Than Life 56. *A Face in the Crowd* 57. Slaughter on Tenth Avenue 57. King Creole 58. Ride a Crooked Trail 58. The Voice in the Mirror 58. Onionhead 58. Strangers When We Meet 60. Gangster Story (& d) 60. Lonely Are the Brave 62. Who's Got the Action? 62. Island of Love 63. *Charade* 63. Ensign Pulver 64. Fail Safe 64. Goodbye Charlie 64. *Mirage* 65. *The Fortune Cookie* (AA) 66. *A Guide for the Married Man* 67. *The Odd Couple* 68. The Secret Life of an American Wife 68. Candy 68. *Hello Dolly* 69. Cactus Flower 69. A New Leaf 71. Plaza Suite 71. *Kotch* (AAN) 71. Pete 'n' Tillie 72. Charley Varrick 73. The Laughing Policeman 73. Earthquake 74. The Taking of Pelham 123 74. The Front Page 75. The Sunshine Boys (AAN) 75. The Bad News Bears 76. Casey's Shadow 77. House Calls 78. California Suite 78. Funny Business (TV) 78. Little Miss Marker 80. *Hopscotch* 80. First Monday in October 81. Buddy Buddy 81. I Ought to Be in Pictures 82. The Survivors 83. Movers and Shakers 84. Pirates 85. The Couch Trip 88. The Incident (TV) 90. JFK 91. Dennis the Menace/Dennis 93. Grumpy Old Men 93. Incident in a Small Town (TV) 94. I.Q. 94. The Grass Harp 95. Grumpier Old Men 95. I'm Not Rappaport 96. My Fellow Americans 97. Out to Sea 97. The Odd Couple II 98.

TV series: Tallahassee 7000 59.

❝ Once seen, that antique-mapped face is never forgotten – a bloodhound with a head cold, a man who is simultaneously biting on a bad oyster and caught by the neck in lift-doors, a mad scientist's amalgam of Wallace Beery and Yogi Bear. – *Alan Brien, Sunday Times*

He's about as likely a candidate for stardom as the neighborhood delicatessen man. – *Time*

He looks like a half-melted rubber bulldog. – *John Simon*

Matthews, A. E. (1869–1960)
British actor, on stage from 1886, films from the mid-20s; in his youth a suave romantic lead, he was later famous for the crotchety cheerfulness of his extreme longevity.

Autobiography: 1953, *Matty*.

A Highwayman's Honour 14. The Lackey and the Lady 19. The Iron Duke 35. Men Are Not Gods 36. *Quiet Wedding* 40. The Life and Death of Colonel Blimp 43. Piccadilly Incident 46. Just William's Luck 48. *The Chiltern Hundreds* (in his stage role as Lord Lister) 49. The Galloping Major 51. Made in Heaven 52. The Million Pound Note 54. Three Men in a Boat 56. Inn for Trouble 60, many others.

❝ I always wait for *The Times* each morning. I look at the obituary column, and if I'm not in it, I go to work. – A.E.M.

Good God, doesn't he know I haven't got long to live? – *A.E.M., when he thought a long speech was ending, and it wasn't*

He bumbled through the play like a charming retriever who has buried a bone and can't quite remember where. – *Noël Coward*

Although he was always terribly funny, he never looked as if he thought what he said or did was even remotely amusing. He had become such a master at manipulating an audience that he had developed a habit of getting a good laugh with a line one night, then the next night, deliberately killing it, and trying for a different laugh. – *Rex Harrison*

He was hell to act with. He really could see no reason why anyone should get a laugh from an audience except himself. – *Roland Culver*

Matthews, Francis (1927–)
British leading man with TV and repertory experience.

Bhowani Junction 56. The Revenge of Frankenstein 58. The Lamp in Assassin Mews 62. Dracula, Prince of Darkness 65. That Riviera Touch 66. Just Like a Woman 66. Crossplot 69. The McGuffin (TV) 85. May We Borrow Your Husband? (TV) 86, etc.

TV series: Golden Girl 60. A Little Big Business 64. My Man Joe 67. Paul Temple 69–71. A Roof over My Head 77. Don't Forget to Write 77–79. Tears before Bedtime 83.

Matthews, Jessie (1907–1981)
Vivacious English singing and dancing star of light musicals in the 30s, on stage from 1917. Born in London, she first made her mark in the theatre in Charles B. Cochran's revues and the musical comedy *Evergreen*, which led to a contract with Gaumont-British to star in *The Good Companions* and, later, the screen version of *Evergreen*. For six years from the early 30s she quit the stage for films, becoming Britain's most popular musical star, under the careful direction of Victor SAVILLE. She turned down Hollywood offers because she did not want to be separated from Sonnie HALE, the second of her three husbands. He starred with her in several films, but her popularity waned when he took over as director for three movies. Her youthful appeal was fading, and she was having weight problems. Hale co-wrote and was to direct *Asking for Trouble*, which he intended as a lavish screen musical, but Gaumont-British were unable to raise the finance, and shooting was abandoned. Carol REED was brought in to direct a version with the musical numbers cut, retitled *Climbing High*; it also failed, though she and Reed briefly became lovers. She returned to the stage and variety performances before becoming a radio personality as Mrs Dale in the BBC soap opera *The Dales* 63–69.

Autobiography: 1974, *Over My Shoulder*.

Biography: 1974, *Jessie Matthews* by Michael Thornton.

■ The Beloved Vagabond 23. Straws in the Wind 24. Out of the Blue 31. There Goes the Bride 32. The Midshipmaid 32. The Man from Toronto 32. *The Good Companions* 32. Friday the Thirteenth 33. Waltzes from Vienna 33. *Evergreen* 34. First a Girl 35. It's Love Again 36. Head over Heels 37. Gangway 37. Sailing Along 38. Climbing High 39. Forever and a Day 43. Candles at Nine 44. Tom Thumb 58. The Hound of the Baskervilles 77. Edward and Mrs Simpson (TV) 79.

❝ Jessie had an engaging way with a song and, apart from her accent, which I guess they could have fixed, she was the equal of many Hollywood stars with the advantage of a big publicity machine behind them. And Jessie had something they did not have – a nymph-like sexuality. – *Ken Russell*

She had a heart. It photographed. – *Victor Saville*

Matthews, Lester (1900–1975)
Lofty English character actor, often in aristocratic roles, and in Hollywood from the mid-30s. Born in Nottingham, he was on stage from 1916. His second wife was actress Anne GREY.

Shivering Shocks 29. The Lame Duck 31. The Werewolf of London 35. The Raven 35. Thank You, Jeeves 36. Lloyd's of London 36. The Prince and the Pauper 37. The Adventures of Robin Hood 38. The Three Musketeers 39. The Sea Hawk 40. Northwest Passage 40. A Yank in the RAF 41. The Invisible Man's Revenge 44. Gaslight 44. Ministry of Fear 44. Bulldog Drummond at Bay 47. Rogues of Sherwood Forest 50. The Son of Dr Jekyll 51. Desert Fox 51. Lorna Doone 51. Les Misérables 52. Young Bess 53. King Richard and the Crusaders 54. The Seven Little Foys 55. Moonfleet 55. The Miracle 55. Song without End 60. Mary Poppins 64. Assault on a Queen 66. Star! 68, many others.

TV series: The Adventures of Fu Manchu (as Sir Dennis Nayland-Smith) 55–56.

Mattoli, Mario (1898–1980)
Italian producer and director, from the stage. Born in Tolentino, he began by running innovative and experimental theatrical companies, first working in cinema as a producer before turning to directing many commercial successes in various genres, but succeeding especially with comedies starring TOTO.

Tempo Massimo 34. Gli Ultimi Giorni di Pompeii 37. La Dama Bianca 38. Abbandono 40. *Ore Nove, Lezione di Chimica* 41. Catene Invisibli 42. La Vita Ricominicia 45. Assuntà Spina 47. Toto al Giro d'Italia 48. Adamo ed Eva 49. Tototarzan 50. Un Turco Napoletano 53. Toto Cerca Pace 54. Two Nights with Cleopatra/Due Notti con Cleopatra 54. L'Ultimo Amante 55. Peppino, le Modelle e Chella Llà 57. Toto, Peppino e le Fanatiche 58. Hercules in the Vale of Woe 62. For a Few Dollars Less/Per Qualche Dollaro in Meno 66, many others.

Mattsson, Arne (1919–1995)
Swedish director, in films from 1942.

She Only Danced One Summer 51. The Girl in Tails 56. Mannequin in Red 59. The Doll 62. Ann and Eve 69. Black Sun 78. Mask of Murder 85. The Girl 87. Sleep Well, My Love 87, etc.

Mature, Victor (1915–1999)
American leading man of the 40s, once known as 'The Hunk'. Born in Louisville, Kentucky, he had little education but gained free tuition at the Pasadena Playhouse Drama School in the mid 30s, and, after stage experience, was signed to a contract by Hal ROACH in 1940. He became best known for his roles in historical epics, beginning with Cecil B. DEMILLE's *Samson and Delilah*. He later happily mocked his image as a brawny, heavy-lidded star in Vittorio de Sica's *After The Fox*. Retired to become a successful businessman. Married and divorced five times.

■ The Housekeeper's Daughter 39. One Million BC 40. Captain Caution 40. No No Nanette 40. I Wake Up Screaming 41. The Shanghai Gesture 41. Song of the Islands 42. My Gal Sal 42. Footlight Serenade 42. Seven Days' Leave 42. *My Darling Clementine* (as Doc Holliday) 46. Moss Rose 47. *Kiss of Death* 47. Fury at Furnace Creek 48. Cry of the City 48. Red Hot and Blue 49. Easy Living 49. *Samson and Delilah* 49. Wabash Avenue 50. Stella 50. Gambling House 50. The Las Vegas Story 52. Androcles and the Lion 52. Something for the Birds 52. Million Dollar Mermaid 52. The Glory Brigade 53. Affair with a Stranger 53. *The Robe* 53. Veils of Baghdad 53. Dangerous Mission 54. Demetrius and the Gladiators 54. Betrayed 54. *The Egyptian* 54. Chief Crazy Horse 55. Violent Saturday 55. The Last Frontier 55. Safari (GB) 56. The Sharkfighters 56. Zarak (GB) 57. Interpol (GB) 57. The Long Haul (GB) 57. China Doll 57. No Time to Die (GB) 58. Escort West 59. The Bandit of Zhobe (GB) 59. The Big Circus 59. Timbuktu 59. Hannibal 60. The Tartars 60. The Mongols 60. *After the Fox* 66. Head 68. Every Little Crook and Nanny 72. Won Ton Ton 76. Firepower 79. Samson and Delilah (TV) 84.

❝ I'm no actor, and I've 64 pictures to prove it. – V.M.

I didn't care for *Samson and Delilah*. No picture can hold my interest when the leading man's bust is bigger than the leading lady's. – *Groucho Marx*

Matz, Peter (1928–)
American composer and conductor, mainly for TV.

Bye Bye Braverman 68. Marlowe 69. Rivals 72. Funny Lady (AAN) 75. The Prize Fighter 79. The Private Eyes 80. Lust in the Dust 85. Torch Song Trilogy 88. The Gumshoe Kid 89. Stepping Out 91, etc.

Mauch, Billy and Bobby (1925–)
American twins, boy actors who appeared in several films in the mid-30s, notably a 'Penrod' series and the Errol Flynn version of *The Prince and the Pauper* 37. Billy became a Hollywood sound editor, while Bob worked as a film editor.

Mauch, Thomas
German cinematographer, associated with the films of Werner Herzog.

Signs of Life/Lebenszeichen 68. Even Dwarfs Started Small/Auch Zwerge Haben Klein Angefangen 70. *Aguirre, Wrath of God*/Aguirre, Der Zorn Gottes 72. Stroszek 77. Signs of Life 81. *Fitzcarraldo* 82. War and Peace (co-ph) 83. The Blind Director 86. Deadline 87. i.d. 95. Sweety Barrett (Ire.) 98, etc.

Maude, Joan (1908–1998)
English actress, the daughter of Nancy PRICE. Born in Rickmansworth, Hertfordshire, she began her career as a solo dancer on the London stage at the age of 13, and worked in the theatre until the mid-30s, after which she appeared only in films and on television until the 50s. Married twice.

This Freedom 23. Chamber of Horrors 29. Hobson's Choice 31. The Wandering Jew 33. The Lash 34. Sabotage 34. Turn of the Tide 35. They Knew Mr Knight 45. The Rake's Progress 45. Night Boat to Dublin 46. A Matter of Life and Death 46. Corridor of Mirrors 48. Badger's Green 49. The Temptress 49. Life in Her Hands 51, etc.

Maugham, Robin (1916–1980)
British popular novelist, nephew of Somerset Maugham. *The Servant* and *The Intruder* have been filmed.

Maugham, W. Somerset (1874–1965)
Distinguished British novelist, short-story writer and playwright whose works have often been filmed.

Smith 17. A Man of Honour 19. The Circle 25 and 30 (as *Strictly Unconventional*). Rain 28 (as *Sadie Thompson*), 32 and 53 (as *Miss Sadie Thompson*). Our Betters 33. The Painted Veil 34 and 57 (as *The Seventh Sin*). Of Human Bondage 34, 46 and 64. Ashenden (as *Secret Agent*) 36. Vessel of Wrath 37 and 54 (as *The Beachcomber*). The Letter 40 (also very freely adapted as *The Unfaithful* 47). The Moon and Sixpence 42. Christmas Holiday 44. The Razor's Edge 46. Theatre (as *Adorable Julia*) 63, etc.

He also introduced three omnibus films of his stories: *Quartet* 48, *Trio* 50 and *Encore* 51; a film of his rather unhappy life is constantly promised.

❝ I'm all against pauses and silences. If the actors cannot give significance to their lines without these, they're not worth their salaries. – S.M.

He reminds me of an old Gladstone bag, covered with labels. God only knows what is inside. – *Christopher Isherwood*

Maunder, Wayne (1942–)
Canadian-born leading man of the 60s, who has been little heard from since.

Casino on Wheels (TV) 73. Porky's 81, etc.

TV series: *Custer* 67. Lancer 68–69. Chase 73–74.

Maura, Carmen (1945–)
Spanish leading actress from the stage, who gained national fame as a TV hostess. She has starred in several of Pedro Almodóvar's films.

El Hombre Oculto 70. La Petición 76. Los Ojos Vendados 78. La Mano Negra 80. Dark Habits/Entre Tinieblas 83. What Have I Done to Deserve This/Que He Hecho Yo para Merecer Esto? 84. Matador 86. Law of Desire/La Ley del Deseo 87. Women on the Verge of a Nervous Breakdown/Mujeres al Borde de un Ataque de Nervios 89. ¡Ay, Carmela! 90. Soleil Levant 91. How to Be a Woman and Not Die in the Attempt/Como Ser Mujer y No Morir en el Intento 91. In Heaven As on Earth/Sur la Terre, Comme au Ciel 92. La Reina Anónima 92. Sombras en una Batalla 93. Louis, Enfant Roi (Fr.) 93. How to Be Miserable and Enjoy It 94. King of the River/El Rey del Rio 95. Pareja de Tres 95. The Lame Pigeon/El Palomo Cojo 95. Love Kills/Amores que Matan 96. Elles (Lux.) 97. Alice and Martin (Fr.) 98. Superlove (Fr.) 98. Lisbon/Lisboa 99. Le Harem de Madame Osmane (Fr./Sp./Mor.) 00, etc.

Maureen, Mollie (1904–1987) (Elizabeth Mary Campfield)
Diminutive British stage actress, in a few films.
■ The Private Life of Sherlock Holmes (as Queen Victoria) 70. The Return of the Pink Panther 75. Jabberwocky 77. The Hound of the Baskervilles 78. The Wicked Lady 83. Little Dorrit 87.

Maurey, Nicole (1925–)
French leading lady.
Little Boy Lost (US) 51. The Secret of the Incas (US) 54. The Weapon (GB) 56. Me and the Colonel (US) 58. The House of the Seven Hawks (GB) 59. High Time (US) 60. The Day of the Triffids (GB) 62. Gloria 77. Chanel Solitaire 81, etc.

Maxwell, Edwin (1886–1948)
Stocky, balding American character actor, frequently cast as shady businessman.
The Jazz Singer 27. The Taming of the Shrew 29. Daddy Longlegs 31. Scarface 32. Cleopatra 34. Fury 36. Young Mr Lincoln 39. His Girl Friday 40. I Live on Danger 42. Holy Matrimony 43. Wilson 44. The Jolson Story 46. The Gangster 47, many others.

Maxwell, Elsa (1883–1963)
Dumpy, talkative American columnist and party-giver.
Autobiography: 1943, *My Last Fifty Years*. 1955, *I Married the World*. 1961, *Celebrity Circus*.
FILM APPEARANCES: Hotel for Women 39. Public Deb Number One 40. Stage Door Canteen 43, etc.
❝ Elsa Maxwell? She's just another pretty face. – *Hermione Gingold*

Maxwell, James (1929–1995)
American-born character actor, in Britain, often in avuncular roles. A founder member of Manchester's Royal Exchange Theatre Company from the mid-70s, he was also a theatre director and playwright.
Private Potter (TV) 61. Private Potter 62. Girl on Approval 62. One Day in the Life of Ivan Denisovich 71. Ransom 74, etc.

Maxwell, John (1875–1940)
Scottish lawyer who turned distributor and became co-founder of Associated British productions and the ABC cinema chain.

Maxwell, Lois (1927–) (Lois Hooker)
Canadian leading lady who had a brief Hollywood career (1946–48) before settling in England. She is best known for playing Miss Moneypenny in the James Bond films until *A View to a Kill* 85.
The Decision of Christopher Blake 47. Corridor of Mirrors 48. Women of Twilight 49. Domani è Troppo Tardi (It.) 50. The Woman's Angle 52. Aida (It.) 53. Passport to Treason 55. The High Terrace 56. Kill Me Tomorrow 57. Operation Kid Brother 67. Endless Night 72. Age of Innocence 77. Lost and Found 79. The Blue Man 87, etc.

Maxwell, Marilyn (1921–1972) (Marvel Maxwell)
Blond American radio singer and actress, formerly child dancer.
Stand By For Action 42. Swing Fever 42. Thousands Cheer 43. Lost in a Harem 44. Summer Holiday 47. The Lemon Drop Kid 51. Off Limits 53. New York Confidential 55. Rock-a-bye-Baby 58. Critic's Choice 62. Stagecoach to Hell 64, etc.

May, Brian (1934–1997)
Australian composer.
The True Story of Eskimo Nell 75. Barnaby and Me 78. Patrick 79. Mad Max 79. Harlequin 80. *The Survivor* 81. Gallipoli 81. Dangerous Summer 82. *Mad Max II*/The Road Warrior 82. Cloak and Dagger 84. Missing in Action II: The Beginning 84. Sky Pirates 86. Death before Dishonor 87. Steel Dawn 87. Hurricane Smith 90. Dead Sleep 90. Freddy's Dead: The Final Nightmare 91, etc.

May, Elaine (1932–)
American cabaret star of the 50s (with Mike NICHOLS); also screenwriter.
■ Luv (a) 67. Enter Laughing (a) 67. A New Leaf (a, wd) 71. Such Good Friends (w) 72. The Heartbreak Kid (d) 72. California Suite (a) 78. Mikey and Nickey (& w) 78. Heaven Can Wait (w, AAN) 78. Ishtar (d) 87. In the Spirit (a) 90. The Birdcage (w) 95. Primary Colors (w, AAN) 98. Small Time Crooks (a) 00.

May, Hans (1891–1959)
Viennese composer who settled in Britain in the early 30s.
The Stars Look Down 39. Thunder Rock 42. The Wicked Lady 45. Brighton Rock 46. The Gypsy and the Gentleman 57, etc.

May, Jodhi (1975–)
English juvenile actress.
A World Apart 87. Max and Helen (TV) 90. Eminent Domain 91. The Last of the Mohicans 92. Second Best 94. Sister, My Sister 94. The Gambler 97. The Woodlanders 97. Aristocrats (TV) 99. The House of Mirth 00, etc.

May, Joe (1880–1954) (Joseph Mandel)
German director of early serials and thrillers.
Stuart Webb 15. Veritas Vincit 16. The Hindu Tomb 21, etc.
Best German film probably *Asphalt* 29.
IN HOLLYWOOD: Music in the Air 34. The Invisible Man Returns 40. The House of Seven Gables 40. Hit the Road 41. Johnny Doesn't Live Here Any More 44, etc.

May, Karl (1842–1912)
German novelist whose output of pulp fiction included some 20 westerns, many of which were filmed, notably those about Winnetou, an Apache, and Shatterhand, a gentlemanly German-born adventurer. Shatterhand was played on screen by Lex Barker in a series of films mostly directed by Harald Reinl.
Der Schatz im Silbersee 52. Winnetou 64. Winnetou II 64. Shatterhand 64. Winnetou III 65. Winnetou und das Halbblut Apanatschi 67. Winnetou und Shatterhand im Tal der Toten 68, etc.

May, Mathilda (1965–)
French leading actress in international films.
Letters to an Unknown Lover 85. Lifeforce/Space Vampires (GB) 85. The Cry of the Owl/Le Cri du Hibou 87. Trois Places pour le 26 88. Naked Tango (Arg./US) 90. Isabel Eberhardt 91. Scream of Stone (Ger.) 91. Becoming Colette (Ger./US) 92. The Tit and the Moon (Sp.) 94. Grosse Fatigue 94. The Jackal (US) 97, etc.

Mayall, Rik (1958–)
Anarchic British actor, comedian and writer. He began writing comedy while at Manchester University and was a stand-up comedian before becoming a TV star in the 80s.
Shock Treatment 82. Whoops Apocalypse 86. Little Noises 91. Drop Dead Fred 91. Carry On Columbus 92. The Princess and the Goblin (voice) 92. The Wind in the Willows (voice, as Toad) 96. Bring Me the Head of Mavis Davis 97. Remember Me? 97. Guest House Paradiso (&co-w) 00, etc.
TV series: The Young Ones 82–84. A Kick up the Eighties 84. Filthy Rich and Catflap 87. The New Statesman 88–92. Bottom 90–92. Rick Mayall Presents 93.
❝ Just as long as I can do a bit of film, a bit of TV, a bit of live theatre, and a bit of sunbathing in Devon, that'll do me for as long as I've got. – *R.M.*

Maybury, John (1958–)
English director, mainly of experimental shorts. He made an appearance in the documentary *The Alternative Miss World* 80, as Miss Winscale Nuclear Reactor.
The Last of England (ed only) 87. Premonition of Absurd Perversion in Sexual Personae Part 1 (p, wd, ph, ed) 92. Man to Man (TV) 92. Remembrance of Things Fast: True Stories Visual Lies (wd) 94. *Love Is the Devil* (d) 98, etc.

Mayehoff, Eddie (1911–1992)
American comic actor, former dance bandleader.
That's My Boy 51. Off Limits 53. How to Murder Your Wife 65. Luv 67, etc.
TV series: Doc Corkle 52. That's My Boy 54.

Mayer, Arthur L. (1886–1981)
American author and commentator, a former cinema exhibitor who displayed his lively wit in *Merely Colossal* (1953) and as co-author of *The Movies*.

Mayer, Carl (1894–1944)
German screenwriter.
■ *The Cabinet of Dr Caligari* 19. Genuine 20. Die Hintertreppe 21. Scherben 21. Schloss Vogelod 21. Phantom 22. Vanina 22. Sylvester 23. Die Strasse 23. *The Last Laugh* 24. Tartuff 25. Berlin 27. *Sunrise* 27. Four Devils 28. Ariane 31. Träumende Mund 32. Dreaming Lips 37.

Mayer, Edwin Justus (1896–1960)
American screenwriter.
In Gay Madrid 30. Never the Twain Shall Meet 31. Merrily We Go to Hell 32. The Night Is Ours 33. I Am Suzanne 34. Thirty Day Princess 34. The Affairs of Cellini (original play) 34. So Red the Rose 35. Give Us This Night 36. *Desire* 36. Till We Meet Again 36. The Buccaneer 38. Rio 39. They Met in Bombay 41. *To Be or Not To Be* 42. A Royal Scandal 45. Masquerade in Mexico 45, etc.

Mayer, Gerald (1919–)
American director.
■ Dial 1119 50. Inside Straight 51. The Sellout 52. Holiday for Sinners 52. Bright Road 53. The Marauders 55. Diamond Safari 57.

Mayer, Louis B. (1885–1957)
American executive, former production head of MGM. Once a scrap merchant, he became a cinema manager and later switched to distribution. With Sam Goldwyn, formed Metro-Goldwyn-Mayer in 1924, and when Goldwyn bought himself out became one of Hollywood's most flamboyant and powerful tycoons until the 50s when he found himself less in touch and responsible to a board. Special Academy Award 1950 'for distinguished service to the motion picture industry'.
Biography: 1954, *Hollywood Rajah* by Bosley Crowther. 1975, *Mayer and Thalberg* by Sam Marx. 1993, *The Merchant of Dreams: Louis B. Mayer, MGM and the Secret Hollywood* by Charles Higham.
❝ This 'Hollywood rajah' was perhaps the archetypal movie mogul: sentimental, commonsensical, businesslike, unaesthetic, arrogant, illogical, naive, amoral, tasteless and physically unappealing. For twenty years he ran MGM splendidly in his own image, and became a legend of autocracy. He did not stint on his surroundings; Sam Goldwyn said of his office: 'You need an automobile to reach the desk.'
No detail escaped him. B. P. Schulberg gave him the title: 'Czar of all the rushes.'
Though he kept it well hidden, he did have a basic sense of humility: 'You know how I'm smart? I got people around me who know more than I do.'
His arguments were often irritatingly unanswerable. Arthur Freed recalls: 'If a writer complained of his work being changed, Mayer always said:
'The number one book of the ages was written by a committee, and it was called The Bible."
To Gottfried Reinhardt, who wanted to make a non-commercial picture, Mayer snapped: 'You want to be an artist, but you want other people to starve for your art.'
Mayer's idea of a good commercial movie was simple, homespun, warm, happy … in a phrase, the Hardy Family. That series, cheap to make, kept the studio in profit for many a year. Their success did not delude Mayer into thinking they were great movies: 'Don't make these pictures any better. Just keep them the way they are.'
This did not mean that he despised the American public, only that he knew what they liked. He even created and acted out for the producer a prayer that the son of the fictional family might speak when his mother was ill: 'Dear God, don't let my mom die, because she's the best mom in the world.'
He was similarly quick to correct a plot point: 'A boy may hate his father, but he will always respect him.'
As early as 1922 his credo in this vein was fully formed: 'I will only make pictures that I won't be ashamed to have my children see.'
His cry in later years, when permissiveness was creeping in, was: 'Don't show the natural functions!'
In argument Mayer was a great and exhausting opponent, violent, wheedling and pleading by turns. Robert Taylor remembered going in for more money. When he emerged, a friend asked him: 'Did you get the rise?
– No, but I gained a father.'
Taylor later remembered Mayer in a respectful light: 'He was kind, understanding, fatherly and protective, always there when I had problems.'
As Mayer himself said: 'Life without service isn't worth living.'
But he saw the dangers of life at the top: 'Look out for yourself or they'll pee on your grave.'
Herman J. Mankiewicz saw Mayer himself as a danger: 'He had the memory of an elephant and the hide of an elephant. The only difference is that elephants are vegetarians and Mayer's diet was his fellow man.'
Mayer was very proud of MGM's army of stars and technicians: 'We are the only kind of company whose assets all walk out of the gate at night.'
He needed their goodwill: 'I want to rule by love, not fear.'
But when he died, the usual caustic comments were heard: 'The only reason so many people attended his funeral was they wanted to make sure he was dead.'
He had then been for some years at odds with the MGM hierarchy, an unwilling exile from the boardroom. Said someone at the funeral: 'I see MGM got L.B. back at last.
– Yeah, but on its own terms.'
For some years people had been heard to remark: 'The old grey Mayer he ain't what he used to be.'
But Bob Hope, as so often, made the aptest wisecrack: 'Louis B. Mayer came out west with twenty-eight dollars, a box camera and an old lion. He built a monument to himself – the Bank of America.'

Mayersberg, Paul (1941–)
British screenwriter and director, a former critic who also worked in Paris and London as an assistant director for Roger Corman, Jean-Pierre Melville and Joseph Losey.
The Man Who Fell to Earth 76. The Disappearance 77. Merry Christmas, Mr Lawrence 83. Eureka 84. Captive (d) 86. Nightfall (& d) 88. Last Samurai (d) 89, etc.

Mayes, Wendell (1918–1992)
American screenwriter.
Spirit of St Louis 57. The Enemy Below 58. Anatomy of a Murder (AAN) 59. Advise and Consent 62. In Harm's Way 64. Hotel 67. The Poseidon Adventure (co-w) 72. Bank Shot 74. Death Wish 74. Go Tell the Spartans 78. Love and Bullets (co-w) 79. Monsignor (co-w) 82, etc.

Mayhew, Peter (1944–)
Tall (7 feet 2 inches) English actor, a former hospital porter, who played Chewbacca in the *Star Wars* trilogy.
Sinbad and the Eye of the Golden Tiger 77, etc.

Maylam, Tony (1943–)
British director.
Riddle of the Sands 78. The Burning 82. The Sins of Dorian Gray (TV) 83. Across the Lake 89. Split Second 92, etc.

Maynard, Bill (1928–) (Walter Williams)
Massive British comic actor familiar on TV as the accident-prone hero of *Oh No! It's Selwyn Froggitt* and as the rascally Claude Jeremiah Greengrass in the nostalgic TV series *Heartbeat*. Born in Farnham, Surrey, he was in music hall from childhood. Later a singer and a successful stand-up comedian, he quit to train as an actor in the early 60s.
Autobiography: 1975, *The Yo-Yo Man*. 1997, *Stand Up and Be Counted*.
Till Death Us Do Part 69. The Magnificent Six and a Half 69. Carry On Henry 71. The Four Dimensions of Greta 71. Steptoe and Son Ride Again 74. Carry On Dick 74. Confessions of a Pop Performer 75. Robin and Marian 76. All Things Bright and Beautiful (TV) 78. The Plague Dogs (voice) 82, etc.
TV series: Great Scott – It's Maynard 55–56. Mostly Maynard 57. Trinity Tales 75. The Life of Riley 75. Oh No! It's Selwyn Froggitt 76–77. Paradise Island 77. Selwyn 78. The Gaffer 81–83. Langley Bottom 86. Heartbeat 93– .

Maynard, Ken (1895–1973)
American cowboy star, mainly seen in low-budget features. Once a rodeo rider, he broke into films as a stuntman. Died of malnutrition.
Janice Meredith 24. Señor Daredevil 26. The Red Raiders 27. Branded Men 31. Texas Gunfighter 32. Come on, Tarzan 32. Wheels of Destiny 34. Mystery Mountain 34. Heir to Trouble 34. Wild Horse Stampede 45, many others.

Maynard, Kermit (1898–1971)
American action player, brother of Ken Maynard. Once doubled for George O'Brien, Victor McLaglen, Warner Baxter and Edmund Lowe.

The Fighting Trooper 34. Sandy of the Mounted 34. Wild Bill Hickok 38. Golden Girl 51, many others.
TV series: Saturday Roundup 51.

Mayne, Ferdy (1916–1998) (Ferdinand Mayer-Boerckel)
German-born actor, long in Britain; often seen as smooth villain.
Meet Sexton Blake 44. You Know What Sailors Are 53. Storm over the Nile 55. Ben Hur 59. Freud 62. Operation Crossbow 65. The Bobo 67. The Fearless Vampire Killers 68. Where Eagles Dare 69. When Eight Bells Toll 71. Innocent Bystanders 72. The Eagle Has Landed 76. The Pirate (TV) 78. A Man Called Intrepid (TV) 79. The Black Stallion Returns 83. Conan the Destroyer 84. Howling II 85. River of Diamonds 90, many others.

Mayo, Archie (1891–1968)
American director of very variable output. He began in films as an extra, after stage experience in musicals in America, Australia and Europe, then worked as a gag-man and a director of comedy shorts.
Money Talks 26. The College Widow 27. Beware of Married Men 28. Sonny Boy 29. Is Everybody Happy 29. The Sacred Flame 29. Doorway to Hell 30. Svengali 31. Under Eighteen 31. The Expert 32. Night after Night 32. Mayor of Hell 33. Convention City 33. Desirable 34. Bordertown 34. Go Into Your Dance 35. The Case of the Lucky Legs 35. The Petrified Forest 36. Give Me Your Heart 36. Black Legion 36. Call it a Day 37. It's Love I'm After 37. Youth Takes a Fling 38. They Shall Have Music 39. The House Across the Bay 40. Four Sons 40. The Great American Broadcast 41. Charley's Aunt 41. Confirm or Deny 41. Moontide 42. Orchestra Wives 42. Crash Dive 43. Sweet and Low Down 44. A Night in Casablanca 46. Angel on My Shoulder 46. The Beast of Budapest (p only) 57, etc.

Mayo, Virginia (1920–) (Virginia Jones)
American 'peaches and cream' leading lady of the 40s; played a few bit parts before being cast as decoration in colour extravaganzas.
The Adventures of Jack London 43. Up In Arms 44. The Princess and the Pirate 44. Wonder Man 45. The Best Years of Our Lives 46. Out of the Blue 47. The Secret Life of Walter Mitty 47. A Song Is Born 48. Smart Girls Don't Talk 48. The Girl from Jones Beach 49. White Heat 49. Backfire 50. The Flame and the Arrow 50. Along the Great Divide 51. Captain Horatio Hornblower 51. She's Working Her Way through College 52. South Sea Woman 53. King Richard and the Crusaders 54. Pearl of the South Pacific 55. Congo Crossing 56. The Story of Mankind 57. Fort Dobbs 58. Jet over the Atlantic 59. The Revolt of the Mercenaries (It.) 61. Young Fury 65. Castle of Evil 66. Fort Utah 67. Won Ton Ton 76. French Quarter 78. Evil Spirits 91. Midnight Witness 93, etc.

Maysles, David and Albert (1931–1987 and 1933–)
American film-making brothers, semi-professional and semi-underground.
Youth of Poland 57. Kenya 61. Safari Ya Gari 61. Showman 63. What's Happening 64. Marlon Brando 65. Truman Capote 66. Salesman 69. Gimme Shelter 71. Grey Gardens 75. Running Fence 77. When We Were Kings 97, etc.

Mazar, Debi
American actress.
Little Man Tate 91. Beethoven's 2nd 93. Money for Nothing 93. I Married an Axe Murderer 93. Empire Records 95. Girl 6 96. Space Truckers 96. Trees Lounge 96. Nowhere 96. Meet Wally Sparks 97. She's So Lovely 97. Hush 98. Frogs for Snakes 98. The Insider 99. Life in the Fast Lane 00, etc.
TV series: Civil Wars 91-93. LA Law 93-94. Temporarily Yours 97. Working 98-99. That's Life 00- .

Mazurki, Mike (1909–1990) (Mikhail Mazurwski)
Immense American character actor of Ukrainian descent; former heavyweight wrestler. Began in Hollywood as an extra.
The Shanghai Gesture (debut) 41. Farewell My Lovely 44. The French Key 46. Unconquered 47. Rope of Sand 49. Ten Tall Men 51. My Favorite Spy 52. Blood Alley 55. Davy Crockett 56. Donovan's Reef 63. Cheyenne Autumn 64. Seven Women 66. The Wild McCulloughs 75, many others.

TV series: It's About Time 66. Chicago Teddy Bears 71.

Mazursky, Paul (1930–) (Irwin Mazursky)
American writer-director and occasional actor.
I Love you Alice B. Toklas (co-w) 68. Bob and Carol and Ted and Alice (co-w, d) (AAN) 70. Alex in Wonderland (co-w, d, a) 70. Blume in Love (wd) 73. Harry and Tonto (co-w, p, d) (AAN) 74. Next Stop Greenwich Village (wd, p) 76. An Unmarried Woman (wd, co-p, a) (AAN) 78. Willie and Phil 80. Tempest 82. Moscow on the Hudson 84. Down and Out in Beverly Hills 85. Moon over Parador (a, wd) 88. Punchline (a) 88. Enemies, a Love Story (a, wd) (AANw) 89. Scenes from the Class Struggle in Beverly Hills (a) 89. Scenes from a Mall (a, co-w, d) 90. The Pickle (wd) 93. Love Affair (a) 94. Faithful (a, d) 95. 2 Days in the Valley (a) 96. Touch (a) 97. Weapons of Mass Distraction (a) (TV) 97. Why Do Fools Fall in Love (a) 98. Winchell (d) (TV) 98. Antz (voice) 98, etc.

Mazzacurati, Carlo (1956–)
Italian director and screenwriter.
Vagabondi 79. Notte Italiana 87. Il Prete Bello 89. Marrakech Express (w only) 89. Il Richiamo della Notte 91. Un 'Altra Vita 92. The Bull/Il Toro 93. Dear Diary/Caro Diario (a only) 94. Vesna Va Veloce 96, etc.

Mazzello, Joseph (1984–)
American child actor, in showbusiness from the age of five.
Unspeakable Acts (TV) 90. Presumed Innocent 90. Radio Flyer 92. Jurassic Park 93. Shadowlands 93. River Wild 94. The Cure 95. Three Wishes 95. Star Kid 97. Simon Birch 98, etc.

Mc
see MAC.

Meadows, Audrey (1926–1996)
American character actress, the sister of Jayne Meadows. Born in China to missionary parents, she began as a soprano before turning to acting, and is best known for playing Alice Kramden, wife to Jackie Gleason's bus driver Ralph, in the TV sitcom The Honeymooners 55–56.
That Touch of Mink 62. Take Her, She's Mine 63. Rosie 67, etc.
TV series: The Jackie Gleason Show 52–55, 56–57. Too Close for Comfort 82–83.

Meadows, Jayne (1920–) (Jayne Cotter)
American actress whose biggest role was in 1947 as the unsympathetic sister in Enchantment. She married Steve Allen in 1954.
Undercurrent 46. Song of the Thin Man 47. David and Bathsheba 51. Suspense 53. Hollywood Palace 68. The Ratings Game 84. Murder by Numbers 89. City Slickers 91, etc.
TV series: Medical Center 69–72. It's Not Easy 83.

Meadows, Shane (1973–)
British director, writer, actor and producer, so far of low-budget films. He was born in Nottingham, which has served as the setting for his films.
Small Time 96. 24/7 97. A Room for Romeo Brass 99, etc.

Meaney, Colm (1953–)
Irish character actor.
Nailed (TV) 81. The Dead 87. The Commitments 91. Far and Away 92. Into the West 92. Dr Quinn, Medicine Woman (TV) 92. The Snapper (TV) 93. The Road to Wellville 94. The War of the Buttons 94. The Englishman Who Went Up a Hill but Came Down a Mountain 95. The Van 96. The Last of the High Kings 96. Con Air 97. Claire Dolan 98, etc.
TV series: Star Trek: The Next Generation 87–93. Star Trek: Deep Space Nine 93–99.

Meara, Anne (1929–)
American comedienne who turned straight actress in a 1975 TV series, Kate McShane. Married actor Jerry Stiller in 1954. Mother of Ben Stiller.
Lovers and Other Strangers 69. Kate MacShane (TV) 75. Nasty Habits 76. The Boys from Brazil 78. The Other Woman (TV) 82. The Longshot 86. My Little Girl 86. That's Adequate 90. Awakenings 90. Kiss of Death 94. Heavyweights 94. The Search for One-Eyed Jimmy 96. The Daytrippers 96, etc.

TV series: The Paul Lynde Show 72–73. The Corner Bar 73. Kate McShane 75. Rhoda 76–77. Archie Bunker's Place 79–82.

Meat Loaf (1948–) (Marvin Lee Aday)
Bulky American character actor and rock singer.
Rocky Horror Picture Show 75. Americathon 79. Scavenger Hunt 79. Roadie 80. Feel the Motion 86. Out of Bounds 86. The Squeeze 87. Stand by Me (concert) 88. Wayne's World 92. Motorama 92. Leap of Faith 92. To Catch a Yeti 95. Spice World: The Movie 97. Black Dog 98. Everything that Rises (TV) 98. The Mighty 98. Gunshy 98. Outside Ozona 98. Fight Club 99. Crazy in Alabama 99, etc.

Medak, Peter (1937–)
Hungarian-born director, first in Britain, and later in the United States. Born in Budapest, he was in films from the mid-50s.
Negatives 68. A Day in the Death of Joe Egg 70. The Ruling Class 71. Third Girl from the Left (TV) 74. Ghost in the Noonday Sun (unreleased) 74. The Odd Job 78. The Changeling 80. Zorro the Gay Blade 81. Mistress of Paradise (TV) 82. The Men's Club 86. The Krays 90. Let Him Have It 91. Romeo Is Bleeding 93. Pontiac Moon 94. The Hunchback of Notre Dame (TV) 97. Species 2 98, etc.

Medem, Julio (1958–)
Spanish director. He studied medicine, intending to work as a psychiatrist, and was a film critic for the Basque newspaper La Voz de Euskadi before becoming a director.
Cows/Vacas 92. The Red Squirrel/La Ardilla Roja 93. Earth/Tierra 95. The Lovers of the Arctic Circle/Los Amantes del Círculo Polar 98, etc.

Medford, Don (1917–)
American director.
To Trap a Spy 64. Cosa Nostra, Arch Enemy of the FBI (TV) 66. Incident in San Francisco (TV) 71. The Hunting Party 71. The Organization 71. The November Plan 76. Sizzle (TV) 81. Hell Town (TV) 85, etc.

Medford, Kay (1914–1980)
American character actress.
The War Against Mrs Hadley 42. The Rat Race 60. Butterfield 8 60. Bye Bye Birdie 63. Funny Girl (AAN) 68. But I Don't Want to Get Married (TV) 70. No Place to Run (TV) 72. More Than Friends (TV) 78, etc.

Medina, Patricia (1921–)
British-born leading lady of the 40s and 50s, in routine international films. She married actor Joseph Cotten in 1960.
The Day Will Dawn 42. They Met in the Dark 42. The First of the Few 42. Don't Take It To Heart 44. Hotel Reserve 44. Waltz Time 45. The Secret Heart 46. Moss Rose 47. The Three Musketeers 48. The Fighting O'Flynn 49. Abbott and Costello in the Foreign Legion 50. The Magic Carpet 51. Lady in the Iron Mask 52. Siren of Baghdad 53. Phantom of the Rue Morgue 54. Pirates of Tripoli 55. Uranium Boom 56. Buckskin Lady 57. Count Your Blessings 59. The Killing of Sister George 68. The Big Push/Timber Tramps 77, etc.

Medoff, Mark (1940–)
American dramatist and screenwriter. Born in Mount Carmel, Illinois, he was educated at the University of Miami and at Stanford.
Good Guys Wear Black (co-w) 77. When You Comin' Back, Red Ryder (oa, w) 79. Off Beat (w) 86. Children of a Lesser God (co-w, oa) (AAN) 86. City of Joy (w) 92. Homage (p, w, oa) 95. Sante Fe (w) 97. Mighty Joe Young (w) 98, etc.

Medwin, Michael (1923–)
British light character comedian, usually seen as a cockney.
Piccadilly Incident 46. Boys in Brown 49. Top Secret 52. Above Us the Waves 55. A Hill in Korea 56. I Only Arsked 58. Night Must Fall 63. Rattle of a Simple Man 64. I've Gotta Horse 65. The Sandwich Man 66. Scrooge 70. The Jigsaw Man 84. Staggered 94, many others.
AS PRODUCER: Charlie Bubbles 67. If 68. Spring and Port Wine 69. Gumshoe 71. Alpha Beta 73. O Lucky Man 73. Law and Disorder 73.
TV series: The Army Game 57–62. Shoestring 79.

Meehan, John (1890–1954)
Canadian dramatist, screenwriter and actor. Born in Lindsay, Ontario, and educated at Harvard University, he began as an actor and worked as a director for George M. COHAN until his first play was produced in 1918. He went to Hollywood in 1929 to write the screen treatment of his play Gentleman of the Press.
The Lady Lies 29. The Divorcee (AAN) 30. A Lady's Morals 30. The Phantom of Paris 31. A Free Soul 31. Strangers May Kiss 31. The Miracle Woman 31. Washington Masquerade 32. Letty Lynton 32. Hell Below 33. Stage Mother 33. The Prizefighter and the Lady 33. When Ladies Meet 33. The Painted Veil 34. Sadie McKee 34. What Every Woman Knows 34. Peter Ibbetson 35. I've Been Around 35. His Brother's Wife 36. Stardust 37. Madame X 37. Boys Town (AA) 38. Seven Sinners 40. Kismet 44. The Valley of Decision 45. Three Daring Daughters 48, etc.

Meehan, John (1902–1963)
American art director who spent much of his career, from 1935 to 1950, at Paramount Studios. He studied architecture at the University of Southern California.
Bring on the Girls 45. The Virginian 46. The Bride Wore Boots 46. The Strange Love of Martha Ivers 46. The Heiress (AA) 49. Sunset Boulevard (AA) 50. Tarzan's Peril 51. Assignment Paris 52. The Marrying Kind 52. It Should Happen to You 53. Salome 53. Man in the Dark 53. 20,000 Leagues under the Sea (AA) 54. Cult of the Cobra 55, etc.

Meek, Donald (1880–1946)
Scottish-born character actor, long in Hollywood; a bald, worried and timidly respectable little man was his invariable role.
The Hole in the Wall (debut) 28. Mrs Wiggs of the Cabbage Patch 34. Barbary Coast 35. Captain Blood 35. Pennies from Heaven 36. The Adventures of Tom Sawyer 38. Stagecoach 39. Tortilla Flat 42. They Got Me Covered 43. State Fair 45. Magic Town 46, many others.

Meeker, George (1904–1984)
American character actor, frequently in smoothly sinister roles. Born in Brooklyn, he studied at the American Academy of Dramatic Arts and began on stage.
Chicken a la King 28. Four Sons 28. The Escape 28. Emma 31. Only Yesterday 33. Night of Terror 33. Broadway Bill 34. Hips, Hips, Hooray! 34. Melody in Spring 34. The Richest Girl in the World 34. Little Man, What Now? 34. The Wedding Night 35. Murder by Television 35. Remember Last Night? 35. Career Woman 36. Tango 36. Danger on the Air 38. Slander House 38. Tarzan's Revenge 38. Everything's on Ice 39. High Sierra 41. Love Crazy 41. Casablanca 42. Murder in the Big House 42. Secret Enemies 43. Up in Arms 44. Dead Man's Eyes 44. Seven Doors to Death 44. Crime Inc. 45. Mr Muggs Rides Again 45. The Red Dragon 45. The People's Choice 46. Her Sister's Secret 46. Apache Rose 47. Case of the Baby Sitter 47. Road to Rio 47. Superman 48. Omoo, Omoo/The Shark God 49. The Invisible Monster (serial) 50. Twilight in the Sierras 50. Wells Fargo Gunmaster 51, many others.

Meeker, Ralph (1920–1988) (Ralph Rathgeber)
American leading man of the Brando type, with Broadway experience.
Teresa (debut) 51. Four in a Jeep 51. Shadow in the Sky 51. Glory Alley 52. The Naked Spur 53. Jeopardy 53. Code Two 53. Big House USA 54. Kiss Me Deadly (as Mike Hammer) 55. Desert Sands 56. Paths of Glory 58. Ada 61. Something Wild 62. The Dirty Dozen 67. The St Valentine's Day Massacre 67. Gentle Giant 67. The Detective 68. I Walk the Line 70. The Anderson Tapes 71. The Happiness Cage 73. The Food of the Gods 76. Hi-Riders 78. Winter Kills 79. Without Warning 80, etc.

Meerson, Lazare (1900–1938)
Russian-born production designer. He worked in France 1924–36, where he influenced not only his contemporaries but a later generation of art directors, some of whom had been his assistants, before being brought to Britain by Sir Alexander Korda.
Gribiche 25. Carmen 26. An Italian Straw Hat 28. Sous les Toits de Paris 29. Le Million 31. à Nous la Liberté 32. La Kermesse Héroïque 35. As You

Morison, Patricia (1915–) (Eileen Morison)
Slightly sulky-looking American leading lady of the 40s; never quite made it but did well later on stage.
Persons in Hiding 39. I'm from Missouri 39. The Magnificent Fraud 39. Untamed 40. Rangers of Fortune 40. One Night in Lisbon 41. Romance of the Rio Grande 41. The Roundup 41. A Night in New Orleans 42. Beyond the Blue Horizon 42. Are Husbands Necessary? 42. Silver Skates 43. Hitler's Madman 43. Calling Dr Death 43. The Fallen Sparrow 43. The Song of Bernadette 43. Where are Your Children? 44. Without Love 45. Lady on a Train 45. Dressed to Kill 46. Danger Woman 46. Queen of the Amazons 47. Tarzan and the Huntress 47. Song of the Thin Man 47. Prince of Thieves 47. Walls of Jericho 48. The Return of Wildfire 48. Sofia 48. Song without End 60. Won Ton Ton, the Dog Who Saved Hollywood 75, etc.

Morita, Pat (1932–) (Noriyuki Morita)
Japanese-American character actor.
Thoroughly Modern Millie 64. Midway 76. When Time Ran Out 80. Full Moon High 81. Jimmy the Kid 82. *The Karate Kid* (AAN) 84. Karate Kid II 86. Captive Hearts (& co-w) 87. Collision Course 88. The Karate Kid Part III 89. Ice Runner 91. Lena's Holiday 91. Golden Chute ... Wings of Grey 92. Honeymoon in Vegas 92. The Next Karate Kid 94. Even Cowgirls Get the Blues 94. Time Master 95. Bloodsport 2 95. Bloodsport 3 95. Mulan (voice) 98. King Cobra 98, etc.
TV series: The Queen and I 69. Sanford and Son 74–75. Happy Days 75–76. Mr T and Tina 76. Blansky's Beauties 77. Happy Days 82–83.

Morita, Yoshimitsu (1950–)
Japanese director of comedies.
Something Like Yoshiwara/No Yo Na Mono 81. *The Family Game*/Kazoku Geemu 83. Sorekara 86. The Mercenaries 87, etc.

Moritzen, Henning (1928–)
Swedish leading actor, mainly in Danish films and best known internationally for the role of the abusive father in Thomas Vinterberg's The Celebration/Festen.
Kispus 56. Poeten Og Lillemor 59. Harry and the Butler/Harry Og Kammertjeneren 61. Diary of a Teenager/Stine Og Drengene 69. Your Money or Your Life/Pengene Elle Livet 82. Memories of a Marriage/Dansen Med Regitze 89. Sofie 92. The Celebration/Festen 98, etc.

Morlay, Gaby (1897–1964) (Blanche Fumoleau)
French character actress.
La Sandale Rouge 13. Les Nouveaux Messieurs 28. Derrière la Façade 38. Le Voile Bleu 42. Gigi 48. Le Plaisir 51. Mitsou 55. Ramuntcho 58, many others.

Morley, Karen (1905–) (Mildred Mabel Linton)
American leading lady of the 30s. Born in Ottumwa, Iowa, she was educated at the University of California. Her film career ended when she was blacklisted in the 50s, though she later appeared briefly on television. Married (1932-43) director Charles Vidor and actor Lloyd Gough.
Cuban Love Song 31. Daybreak 31. Mata Hari 31. Never the Twain Shall Meet 31. Politics 31. The Sin of Madelon Claudet 31. Are You Listening? 32. Arsène Lupin 32. Flesh 32. Man about Town 32. The Mask of Fu Manchu 32. Phantom of Crestwood 32. *Scarface* 32. Washington Masquerade 32. Dinner at Eight 33. Gabriel over the White House 33. Black Fury 34. Crime Doctor 34. Our Daily Bread 34. The Littlest Rebel 35. Thunder in the Night 35. Beloved Enemy 36. The Girl from Scotland Yard 37. The Last Train from Madrid 37. On Such a Night 37. Kentucky 38. Pride and Prejudice 40. Jealousy 45. The Unknown 46. M 51, etc.
TV series: Banyon 72-73.

Morley, Robert (1908–1992)
Portly British character actor (and playwright), on stage from 1929, films from 1938.
Autobiography: 1966, *Robert Morley, Responsible Gentleman*. Biography: 1993, *Robert My Father* by Sheridan Morley.
Marie Antoinette (US) (AAN) 38. *Major Barbara* 40. *The Young Mr Pitt* 42. I Live in Grosvenor Square 45. An Outcast of the Islands 51. The African Queen 51. *Gilbert and Sullivan* 53. *Beat the Devil* 53. Around the World in Eighty Days 56. The Doctor's Dilemma 59. *Oscar Wilde* 60. The Young Ones 61. Murder at the Gallop 63. Those Magnificent Men in Their Flying Machines 65. The Alphabet Murders 65. Genghis Khan 65. A Study in Terror 65. Hotel Paradiso 66. Way Way Out (US) 66. The Trygon Factor 67. Sinful Davey 69. When Eight Bells Toll 71. Theatre of Blood 73. The Blue Bird 76. *Who Is Killing the Great Chefs of Europe?* 78. Scavenger Hunt 79. The Human Factor 79. O Heavenly Dog 80. The Great Muppet Caper 81. High Road to China 82, etc.
❝ Anyone who works is a fool. I don't work: I merely inflict myself on the public. – *R.M.*
I believe there are two things necessary for salvation: money and gunpowder. – *R.M.*
It is a great help for a man to be in love with himself. For an actor it is absolutely essential. – *R.M.*
Fortunately, I'm not an actor who has ever got into the habit of refusing film roles, holding that if one doesn't read the script in advance, or see the finished product, there is nothing to prevent one accepting the money, and then spending it. – *R.M.*

Moroder, Giorgio (1940–)
Italian composer in America.
Midnight Express (AA) 78. Foxes 80. American Gigolo 80. Cat People 82. Flashdance (AA song) 83. Superman III 83. Scarface 83. The Neverending Story (co-m) 84. Electric Dreams 84. Metropolis (new m) 85. Top Gun (AAs) 86. Over the Top 87. Fair Game 88. Let It Ride 89. Cybereden (It.) 93, etc.

Moross, Jerome (1913–1983)
American composer.
When I Grow Up 51. The Sharkfighters 56. The Big Country 58. The Proud Rebel 58. The Jayhawkers 59. The Cardinal 63. The War Lord 65. Rachel Rachel 68, etc.

Morricone, Ennio (1928–)
Prolific Italian composer and arranger.
A Fistful of Dollars 64. El Greco 64. Fists in the Pockets 65. For a Few Dollars More 65. *The Good the Bad and the Ugly* 66. The Big Gundown 66. Matchless 67. Theorem 69. *Once Upon a Time in the West* 69. Investigation of a Citizen 69. Fraulein Doktor 69. The Bird with the Crystal Plumage 70. The Sicilian Clan 70. Two Mules for Sister Sara 70. Cat O'Nine Tails 71. The Red Tent 71. Four Flies in Grey Velvet 71. The Decameron 71. The Burglars 71. The Black Belly of the Tarantula 72. Bluebeard 72. The Serpent 72. A Fistful of Dynamite 72. 1900 76. Exorcist II: The Heretic 77. Orca 77. Days of Heaven 78. Blood line 79. The Island 80. La Cage aux Folles II 80. So Fine 81. Butterfly 82. White Dog 82. The Thing 82. Nana 83. Sahara 83. Once upon a Time in America 84. La Cage aux Folles III 85. *The Mission* (AAN) 86. *The Untouchables* (AAN) 87. A Time of Destiny 88. Frantic 88. Casualties of War 89. *Cinema Paradiso* 89. To Forget Palermo/Dimenticare Palermo 89. Everybody's Fine/Stanno Tutti Bene 90. Tie Me Up! Tie Me Down!/¡Atame! 90. State of Grace 90. Bugsy (AAN) 91. Husbands and Lovers 91. Especially on Sunday/La Domenica Specialmente 91. Jona che Visse nella Balena 93. La Scorta 93. In the Line of Fire 93. Il Lungo Silenzio 93. A Simple Formality/Una Pura Formalita 94. En Suivant la Comète 94. Love Affair 94. Wolf 94. Genesis: The Creation and the Flood/Genesi: La Creazione e il Diluvio 94. The Night and the Moment 94. According to Pereira 95. Pasolini, an Italian Crime/Pasolini, un Delitto Italiano 95. The Star Man/L'Uomo delle Stelle 95. The Stendhal Syndrome 96. La Lupa/The She-Wolf 96. Nostromo (TV) 97. Bulworth (US) 98 Malena (AAN) 00, etc.

Morris, Chester (1901–1970)
Jut-jawed American leading man of the 30s, an agreeable 'B' picture lead who later became a considerable stage and TV actor. Born in New York City, the son of actors, he was in silent films as a child, studied at the New York School of Fine Arts, and made his Broadway debut in 1918. His most familiar role was as Boston Blackie, a crook turned good guy in 13 films from 1941 to 1949. Married actress Suzanne Kilborne (1927–38) and model Lillian Barker. Died from an overdose of barbiturates.
Alibi (AAN) 29. She Couldn't Say No 30. The Divorce 30. *The Big House* 30. The Bat Whispers 31. The Miracle Man 32. Red Headed Woman 32. Blondie Johnson 33. The Gift of Gab 34. I've Been Around 35. Society Doctor 35. Moonlight Murder 36. They Met in a Taxi 36. Flight from Glory 37. Law of the Underworld 38. Smashing the Rackets 38. Blind Alibi 39. *Five Came Back* 39. The Marines Fly High 40. No Hands on the Clock 41. Meet Boston Blackie 41 (and subsequent series of 12 films until 1949). I Live on Danger 42. Wrecking Crew 43. Secret Command 44. Double Exposure 45. Unchained 55. The Great White Hope 70, etc.

Morris, Ernest (1915–1987)
British director, mainly of second features for the Danzigers.
Operation Murder 57. The Betrayal 58. Three Crooked Men 58. Night Train for Inverness 60. The Tell-Tale Heart 60. Striptease Murder 61. Three Spare Wives 62. What Every Woman Wants 62. Echo of Diana 63. Shadow of Fear 63. The Sicilians 64. The Return of Mr Moto 65, etc.

Morris, Errol (1948–)
American director and screenwriter, usually of quirky documentaries. His *The Thin Blue Line* helped release a man wrongly convicted of murder. *The Dark Wind* was his first fictional film.
Gates of Heaven 78. Vernon, Florida 81. The Thin Blue Line 88. A Brief History of Time (TV) 91. The Dark Wind 92. Fast, Cheap and Out of Control 97, etc.

Morris, Greg (1934–1996)
American supporting actor.
The Lively Set 64. The Doomsday Flight (TV) 66. Countdown at Kusini 76, etc.
TV series: Mission Impossible 66–73. Vegas 78–80.

Morris, Howard (1919–)
American comedy director.
Boys Night Out (a only) 62. Who's Minding the Mint? 67. With Six You Get Egg Roll 68. Don't Drink the Water 69. Goin' Coconuts 78, etc.

Morris, John (1926–)
American composer who has scored many of Mel Brooks' films.
The Producers 67. The Gamblers 69. The Twelve Chairs 70. Blazing Saddles (AAN title s) 74. Young Frankenstein 74. The Bank Shot 74. The Adventures of Sherlock Holmes' Smarter Brother 75. Silent Movie 76. The Last Remake of Beau Geste 77. The World's Greatest Lover 77. High Anxiety 77. The In-Laws 79. The Elephant Man (AAN) 80. In God We Trust 80. History of the World Part I 81. Table for Five 83. Yellowbeard 83. To Be or Not To Be 83. The Woman in Red 84. Johnny Dangerously 84. Clue 85. The Doctor and the Devils 85. Haunted Honeymoon 86. Ironweed 87. Dirty Dancing 87. Spaceballs 87. The Wash 88. Second Sight 89. Stella 90. Life Stinks 91, etc.

Morris, Lana (1930–1998)
British leading lady of the 50s.
Spring in Park Lane 47. The Weaker Sex 48. Trottie True 49. The Chiltern Hundreds 49. The Woman in Question 50. Trouble in Store 53. Man of the Moment 55. Home and Away 56. I Start Counting 70, many others.

Morris, Mary (1895–1970)
American stage actress who played her stage role of the evil old lady in *Double Door* 34.

Morris, Mary (1915–1988)
British character actress with dominant personality, on stage from 1925.
Prison without Bars (film debut) 38. The Spy in Black 39. The Thief of Baghdad 40. *Pimpernel Smith* 41. Undercover 43. The Man from Morocco 45. Train of Events 49. High Treason 51, many others.

Morris, Oswald (1915–)
British cinematographer, in films from 1932.
Green for Danger 46. *Moulin Rouge* 53. Knave of Hearts 53. Beat the Devil 53. Beau Brummell 54. Moby Dick 56. A Farewell to Arms 57. The Key 58. Roots of Heaven 59. Look Back in Anger 59. Our Man in Havana 59. The Entertainer 60. Lolita 62. Of Human Bondage 64. *The Pumpkin Eater* (BFA) 64. The Hill (BFA) 65. Life at the Top 65. The Spy Who Came In from the Cold 65. Stop the World I Want To Get Off 66. *The Taming of the Shrew* 67. Oliver! (AAN) 68. Goodbye Mr Chips 69. Scrooge 70. Fiddler on the Roof (AA) 71. Lady Caroline Lamb 72. The Mackintosh Man 73. The Odessa File 74. The Man Who Would Be King 75. Equus 77. The Wiz 78. Just Tell Me What You Want 80. The Great Muppet Caper 81. Dark Crystal 82, etc.

Morris, Wayne (1914–1959) (Bert de Wayne Morris)
Brawny American leading man with stage experience.
China Clipper (debut) 36. *Kid Galahad* 37. Brother Rat and a Baby 39. Bad Men of Missouri 40. The Smiling Ghost 41. Deep Valley 47. The Time of Your Life 47. The Tougher They Come 50. The Master Plan 55. The Crooked Sky 57. Paths of Glory 58, etc.

Morris, William (1873–1932) (Zelman Moses)
American agent who founded the company that bears his name, which remains one of the leading international showbusiness agencies. Born in Schwarzenau, Silesia, he came to the USA at the age of nine, and worked as a clerk and successfully sold advertising for a magazine publisher before working as an agent. He ran his company from its foundation in 1898 in New York to his death, when he was succeeded by his son, William Morris, Jnr, who headed it until 1952. Many successful agents began work in its mail room, and its former employees include Michael Ovitz.
Biography: 1995, *The Agency: William Morris and the Hidden History of Show Business* by Frank Rose.

Morrison, Ernie 'Sunshine Sammy' (1912–1989)
American child actor and vaudeville performer, one of the original kids in the Our Gang comedies of the early 20s, on screen from the age of three. In the early 40s, he appeared in films featuring the East Side Kids.

Morrison, James (1888–1974)
American leading actor in Vitagraph movies. He retired early to become a drama teacher.
A Tale of Two Cities 11. Beau Brummel 12. A Tale of Two Cities 17. Sacred Silence 19. The Midnight Bride 20. Black Beauty 21. The Little Minister 22. Captain Blood 24. Wreckage 25. The Count of Luxembourg 26. Twin Flappers 27, etc.

Morrison, Temuera
New Zealand leading actor, best known in his home country for his role as a doctor in the TV soap opera *Shortland Street*. He was an adviser on Jane Campion's *The Piano*.
Other Halves 84. Never Say Die 88. *Once Were Warriors* 94. Barb Wire (US) 96. Broken English 96. The Island of Dr Moreau (US) 96. Speed 2: Cruise Control (US) 97. Six Days, Seven Nights (US) 98. What Becomes of the Broken Hearted? 99. Vertical Limit (US) 00, etc.

Morriss, Frank
American editor, from television, who has worked on many of John Badham's films.
Duel (TV) 71. Charley Varrick 73. Ode to Billy Joe 76. First Love 77. I Wanna Hold Your Hand 78. Inside Moves 80. Whose Life Is It, Anyway? 81. Blue Thunder (AAN) 83. Romancing the Stone (AAN) 84. American Flyers 85. Short Circuit 86. Hot to Trot 88. Disorganized Crime 89. Bird on a Wire 90. Short Time 90. The Hard Way 91. Point of No Return 93. Another Stakeout 93. Drop Zone 94. Nick of Time 95. Incognito 97, etc.

Morrissey, Neil
English actor, best known for his role as Tony in the TV sitcom *Men Behaving Badly*. Born in Stafford, he studied at the Guildhall School of Music and Drama. He is also the voice of Bob the Builder in the children's TV series.
I Bought a Vampire Motorcycle 89. Kid Divine 92. My Summer with Des (TV) 98. Up 'N' Under 98. Hunting Venus (TV) 99. The Match 99, etc.
TV series: Boon 86-92. Men Behaving Badly 92-98. Paris 94.

Morrissey, Paul (1939–)
American 'underground' director associated with Andy Warhol.
Flesh 68. Trash 70. *Heat* 72. Women in Revolt 72. Andy Warhol's Frankenstein 73. Andy Warhol's Dracula 74. The Hound of the Baskervilles 77. Madame Wang's 81. Forty-Deuce 82. Mixed Blood 84. Beethoven's Nephew 85. Spike of Bensonhurst 88, etc.
❝ When you direct films you lose a lot of the qualities that Hollywood gave us, which were stars.

So we look for stars and let them do what they want. – *P.M.*

Morros, Boris (1891–1963) (Boris Milhailovitch)
Russian-born independent producer in America from the late 30s. Later revealed as an American agent via his 1957 book *Ten Years a Counterspy*, filmed in 1960 as *Man on a String*, with Ernest Borgnine as Morros.
The Flying Deuces 39. Second Chorus 41. Tales of Manhattan 42. Carnegie Hall 48.

Morrow, Doretta (1925–1968) (Doretta Marano)
American singing star who appeared in one film, *Because You're Mine* 52.

Morrow, Jeff (1913–1993)
Mature American leading man, former Broadway and TV actor, in Hollywood from 1953.
The Robe 53. Flight to Tangier 53. Siege of Red River 54. Tanganyika 54. Sign of the Pagan 54. *This Island Earth* 55. The Creature Walks Among Us 56. The Giant Claw 57. The Story of Ruth 60. Harbour Lights 63. Octaman 71, etc.
TV series: Union Pacific 58–59. Temperatures Rising 73–74.

Morrow, Jo (1940–)
American leading lady of the 60s.
Because They're Young 56. Brushfire 57. The Legend of Tom Dooley 59. Our Man in Havana 59. The Three Worlds of Gulliver 60. He Rides Tall 63. Sunday in New York 64. Doctor Death 73, etc.

Morrow, Rob (1962–)
American leading actor, best known for his role as Dr Joel Fleischman in the TV series *Northern Exposure*; he also turned to writing and directing in 2000.
Private Resort (a) 85. Quiz Show (a) 94. Last Dance (a) 96. Mother (a) 96. Into My Heart (a) 98. Maze (p, co-w,d, a) , etc.
TV series: Northern Exposure 90-95.

Morrow, Vic (1932–1982)
American actor formerly cast as a muttering juvenile delinquent. Stage experience. He died in an accident while filming *The Twilight Zone*. He is the father of actress Jennifer Jason Leigh.
The Blackboard Jungle (film debut) 55. Tribute to a Bad Man 56. Men in War 57. God's Little Acre 58. Cimarron 61. Portrait of a Mobster 61. Sledge (d only) 69. The Glass House (TV) 72. The Take 74. Captains and the Kings (TV) 76. Treasure of Matecumbe 76. The Bad News Bears 76. Roots (TV) 77. Funeral for an Assassin 77. The Hostage Heart (TV) 77. Wild and Wooly (TV) 78. Humanoids from the Deep 80. The Twilight Zone 83, etc.
TV series: Combat 62–66. B.A.D. Cats 80.

Morse, Barry (1919–)
British leading man who moved to Canada and became a star of stage and TV there.
The Goose Steps Out 42. When We Are Married 42. There's a Future in It 43. Late at Night 46. Daughter of Darkness 48. No Trace 50; then after long gap – Kings of the Sun 63. Justine 69. Asylum 72. Power Play 75. The Shape of Things to Come (TV) 79. The Changeling 80. The Winds of War (TV) 83. Sadat (as Begin) (TV) 83. Whoops Apocalypse 83. A Woman of Substance (TV) 84. Glory! Glory! 90, etc.
TV series: *The Fugitive* (as Lt Gerard) 63–66. The Adventurer 72. Zoo Gang 73. Space 1999 75–76.

Morse, David (1953–)
American actor, from theatre and television; best known for his role as Dr Jack Morrison in *St Elsewhere*. Born in Beverly, Massachusetts, he worked for the Boston Repertory Theatre from the early to mid-70s, when he moved to New York's Circle Repertory Company. He is co-founder of the Left Coast Repertory in Los Angeles. Married actress Susan Wheeler Duff.
Inside Moves 80. Max Dugan Returns 83. Prototype (TV) 83. Personal Foul 87. The Desperate Hours 90. Cry in the Wild 91. The Indian Runner 91. The Good Son 93. The Getaway 94. The Crossing Guard 95. Stephen King's The Langoliers 95. Twelve Monkeys 95. Extreme Measures 96. The Long Kiss Goodnight 96. The Rock 96. Contact 97. The Negotiator 98. The Green Mile 99. Crazy in Alabama 99. Bait 00. Proof of Life 00, etc.
TV series: St Elsewhere 82–88.

Morse, Helen (1948–)
Australian leading actress.
Jock Petersen 75. *Caddie* 78. Picnic at Hanging Rock 79. Agatha 79. *A Town Like Alice* (TV) 81. Far East 82. Iris 89, etc.

Morse, Robert (1931–)
American comedy actor who usually plays the befuddled innocent.
The Matchmaker 58. Honeymoon Hotel 64. Quick before It Melts 65. *The Loved One* 65. Oh Dad, Poor Dad 66. *How to Succeed in Business without Really Trying* 67. Where Were You When the Lights Went Out? 68. The Boatniks 69. The Emperor's New Clothes 87, etc.
TV series: That's Life 68. City of Angels 00- .

Morse, Susan E.
American film editor, mainly on Woody Allen's movies.
Manhattan 79. Stardust Memories 80. Arthur 81. A Midsummer Night's Sex Comedy 82. Zelig 83. Broadway Danny Rose 84. The Purple Rose of Cairo 85. Hannah and Her Sisters (AAN) 86. Radio Days 87. Another Woman 88. New York Stories 89. Crimes and Misdemeanors 89. Alice 90. Shadows and Fog 91. Manhattan Murder Mystery 93. Bullets over Broadway 94. Mighty Aphrodite 95. Everyone Says I Love You 96. Deconstructing Harry 97. Celebrity 98, etc.

Morse, Terry (1906–1984)
American second-feature director.
■ Jane Arden 39. On Trial 39. Waterfront 39. Smashing the Money Ring 39. No Place to Go 39. British Intelligence 40. Tear Gas Squad 40. Fog Island 45. Danny Boy 46. Shadows over Chinatown 46. Dangerous Money 46. Bells of San Fernando 47. Unknown World 51. Godzilla (US version) 56. Taffy and the Jungle Hunter 65. Young Dillinger 65.

Mortensen, Viggo
American leading actor.
Salvation! 87. Prison 88. The Reflecting Skin 91. The Indian Runner 91. American Yazuka 93. Boiling Point 93. Ruby Cairo 93. Young Americans 93. Carlito's Way 93. The Passion of Darkly Noon 95. Gimlet (Sp.) 95. Crimson Tide 95. God's Army 95. The Portrait of a Lady 96. Albino Alligator 96. Daylight 96. GI Jane 97. Kiss the Sky 98. A Perfect Murder 98. Psycho 98, etc.
❝ A lot of people want to get into acting because they want to be famous. I don't think much of that, but that's my perspective. It doesn't mean you'll be a bad actor if you're a shallow person. In fact, maybe it helps. – *V.M.*

Mortimer, John (1923–)
British playwright, novelist and barrister, who has occasionally worked in films, best known for his creation of the TV series *Rumpole of the Bailey*. He was originally a scriptwriter for the Crown Film Unit. Formerly married to novelist Penelope Mortimer.
Autobiography: 1982, *Clinging to the Wreckage*.
The Innocents 61. Guns of Darkness 62. The Dock Brief 62. Lunch Hour 62. The Running Man 63. Bunny Lake Is Missing 65. A Flea in Her Ear 68. John and Mary 69. Brideshead Revisited (TV) 81. Paradise Postponed (TV) 86. Tea with Mussolini 99, etc.
❝ For the old, the years flicker past like the briefest of afternoons. The playwright Christopher Fry, now 93, told me that after the age of 80 you seem to be having breakfast every five minutes. – *J.M., 2000*

Morton, Clive (1904–1975)
Straight-faced British character actor on stage from 1926, films from 1932, usually in slightly pompous roles.
The Blarney Stone 32. Dead Men Tell No Tales 39. While the Sun Shines 46. Scott of the Antarctic 48. The Blue Lamp 49. His Excellency 51. Carrington VC 54. Richard III 56. Shake Hands with the Devil 59. Lawrence of Arabia 62. Stranger in the House 67, many others.
TV series: Silk, Satin, Cotton, Rags 52. Our Man at St. Mark's 66.

Morton, Rocky
British director who works in collaboration with Annabel Jankel.
The Max Headroom Story (co-d) (TV) 85. D.O.A. (co-d) 88. Super Mario Bros (co-d) 93.

Morton, Samantha (1977–)
English actress, born in Nottingham, who began in television as a 13-year-old.
This Is the Sea 96. Under the Skin 97. Jane Eyre (TV) 97. Tom Jones (TV) 97. Emma (TV) 97. Dreaming of Joseph Lees 99. The Last Yellow 99. *Sweet and Lowdown* (US, AAN) 99. Jesus' Son 99. Pandaemonium 00, etc.
TV series: Band of Gold 95.

Moscovitch, Maurice (1871–1940) (Morris Maaskoff)
American character player, a Russian immigrant who spent many years starring in the Yiddish Theatre. Father of Noel Madison.
■ Winterset 36. Make Way for Tomorrow 37. Lancer Spy 37. Gateway 37. Suez 38. Love Affair 39. Susannah of the Mounties 39. In Name Only 39. Rio 39. The Great Commandment 39. Everything Happens at Night 39. South to Karanga 40. The Great Dictator 40. Dance Girl Dance 40.

Mosjoukine, Ivan (1889–1939)
Russian actor of the old school, who appeared in many international films.
The Defence of Sebastopol 11. Satan Triumphant 22. Tempest (Fr.) 22. Shadows That Mass (Fr.) 23. Casanova (Fr./It.) 27. Sergeant X (Fr.) 30. Nitchevo (Fr.) 36, etc.

Mosley, Roger E.
American character actor.
The New Centurions 72. Hit Man 72. Terminal Island 73. Leadbelly (title role) 76. The Greatest 77. Semi-Tough 77. Roots II (TV) 78. The Jericho Mile (TV) 79. Steel 80. Heart Condition 90. Unlawful Entry 92. Pentathlon 94. A Thin Line between Love and Hate 96. Letters from a Killer 98, etc.

Moss, Arnold (1910–1989)
American character actor often seen in sly or sinister roles.
Temptation 47. The Black Book (as Napoleon) 49. Kim 51. Viva Zapata 52. Casanova's Big Night 54. The Twenty-Seventh Day 57. The Fool Killer 64. Gambit 66. Caper of the Golden Bulls 67, many others.

Moss, Carrie-Anne (1967–)
Canadian actress. Born in Vancouver, she began as a model in Europe and Japan.
The Soft Kill 94. Sabotage 96. The Secret Life of Algernon 97. Lethal Tender 97. The Matrix 99. New Blood 99. The Crew 00. Memento 00. Chocolat 00. Red Planet 00, etc.
TV series: Dark Justice 91-93. Matrix 93. Models, Inc 94-95. FX: The Series 96-98.

Mostel, Josh (1957–)
American actor. Born in New York City, the son of Zero Mostel, he was educated at Brandeis University, and is a former boy soprano who sang at the Metropolitan Opera.
Zero Hour (TV) 67. Going Home 71. The King of Marvin Gardens 72. Jesus Christ, Superstar 73. Harry and Tonto 74. Sophie's Choice 82. Star 80 83. Animal Behavior 85. The Money Pit 86. Radio Days 87. Matewan 88. City Slickers 91. Little Man Tate 91. City Slickers II: The Legend of Curly's Gold 94. The Basketball Diaries 95. Billy Madison 95. Great Expectations 98. Big Daddy 99, etc.
TV series: Delta House 79. At Ease 83. Murphy's Law 88-89.

Mostel, Zero (1915–1977)
Heavyweight American comedian principally seen on Broadway stage.
Panic in the Streets 50. *The Enforcer* 51. A Funny Thing Happened on the Way to the Forum 66. Great Catherine 68. *The Producers* 68. The Great Bank Robbery 69. The Angel Levine 69. The Hot Rock 72. Marco 73. Rhinoceros 73. Journey into Fear 75. The Front 76. Mastermind 76, etc.
❝ Famous line (*The Producers*) 'Leo, he who hesitates is poor.'

Mostow, Jonathan
American screenwriter and director.
Beverly Hills Bodysnatchers (wd) 89. U571 (wd) 00, etc.

Mothersbaugh, Mark (1950–)
American composer, a former lead singer with rock group Devo.
The New Age 94. Bottle Rocket 96. Breaking Up 96. Happy Gilmore 96. The Last Supper 96. Best Men 97. Dead Man on Campus 98. Rushmore 98. The Rugrats Movie 99. Drop Dead Gorgeous 99. 200 Cigarettes 99. The Adventures of Rocky and Bullwinkle 00, etc.

Moulder Brown, John (1945–)
British actor, usually of intense roles.
Deep End 69. Vampire Circus 71. King Queen Knave 72. Ludwig 72. The Confessions of Felix Krull (TV) 82, Rumpelstiltskin 87, etc.

Moullet, Luc (1937–)
French director, screenwriter, producer and actor, usually of comic movies, a former film critic.
Brigitte et Brigitte 66. Une Aventure de Billy le Kid 71. La Comédie du Travail 87. Les Sièges de l'Alcazar 89. Cabale des Oursins 91. La Parpaillon 92. More and More/Toujours Plus 94. Foix 94, etc.

Mount, Peggy (1916–)
British character comedienne with long experience in repertory before starring as the termagant mother-in-law in *Sailor Beware*.
■ The Embezzler 54. *Sailor Beware* 56. Dry Rot 57. The Naked Truth 58. Inn for Trouble 59. Ladies Who Do 63. One Way Pendulum 64. Hotel Paradiso 65. Finders Keepers 66. Oliver! 68. The Princess and the Goblin (voice) 92.
TV series: The Larkins 58–60. George and the Dragon 66–67. Winning Widows. You're Only Young Twice 77.

Movita (1915–) (Movita Castenada)
Mexican leading lady, briefly in Hollywood. She was formerly married to Marlon Brando.
Mutiny on the Bounty 35. Paradise Isle 36. Wolf Call 39. Dream Wife 53. Apache Ambush 55. The Panic in Needle Park 71, etc.

Mowbray, Alan (1893–1969)
Imperious-mannered British character actor, in America from the early 1920s; appeared later in nearly 400 films, often as butler or pompous emissary.
Alexander Hamilton 31. Sherlock Holmes 32. Roman Scandals 33. Becky Sharp 35. Desire 36. *My Man Godfrey* 36. *Topper* 37. Stand In 37. *The Villain Still Pursued Her* 40. Lady Hamilton 41. That Uncertain Feeling 41. A Yank at Eton 42. His Butler's Sister 43. Holy Matrimony 43. Where Do We Go from Here? 45. *Terror by Night* 45. Merton of the Movies 46. *My Darling Clementine* 46. Prince of Thieves 47. The Jackpot 50. Wagonmaster 50. Dick Turpin's Ride 51. Androcles and the Lion 53. The King's Thief 55. The King and I 56, many others.
TV series: Colonel Flack 53. The Mickey Rooney Show 54. Dante 60.

Mowbray, Malcolm
British director who went to Hollywood after his first success.
A Private Function 84. Out Cold 88. Don't Tell Her It's Me 90. Clothes in the Wardrobe 92. Crocodile Shoes (TV) 94, etc.

Mower, Patrick (1940–)
British leading man, mainly in TV series *Callan*, *Special Branch*, *Target*.
The Devil Rides Out 68. The Smashing Bird I Used to Know 69. Cry of the Banshee 70. Incense for the Damned 70. Black Beauty 71. Catch Me a Spy 71. Carry On England 76. The Devil's Advocate 78. Marco Polo (TV) 81. The Asylum 00, etc.

Moxey, John (1920–)
British TV director who has made occasional films and many TV movies in America (as John Llewellyn Moxey).
City of the Dead 59. The £20,000 Kiss 63. Ricochet 63. Strangler's Web 65. Circus of Fear 67. San Francisco International (TV) 70. The House That Would Not Die (TV) 70. A Taste of Evil (TV) 71. The Night Stalker (TV) 72. The Death of Me Yet (TV) 72. The Bounty Man (TV) 72. The Strange and Deadly Occurrence (TV) 74. Where Have All the People Gone? (TV) 74. Charlie's Angels (TV) 76. Nightmare in Badham County (TV) 77. The President's Mistress (TV) 78. Sanctuary of Fear (TV) 79. The Power Within (TV) 79. The Children of An Lac (TV) 80. No Place to Hide (TV) 81. Killjoy (TV) 81. The Cradle Will Fall (TV) 83. Through Naked Eyes (TV) 83. Lady Mobster (TV) 88, etc.

Moyle, Allan (1947–)
Canadian screenwriter and director, a former actor, now in Hollywood.
Montreal Main (a, co-w, co-d) 78. The Rubber Gun (a, d) 78. Times Square (d) 80. Pump Up the Volume (wd) 90. Love Crimes (w) 91. The Gun in Betty Lou's Handbag (wd) 92. Empire Records (d) 95 New Waterford Girl (d) 99, etc.

Mudie, Leonard (1884–1965) (Leonard M. Cheetham)
British character actor in Hollywood.
The Mummy 32. The House of Rothschild 34. Clive of India 35. Lancer Spy 37. Dark Victory 39. Berlin Correspondent 42. My Name is Julia Ross 45. Song of My Heart 48. The Magnetic Monster 53. The Big Fisherman 59, many others.

Mueller, Elisabeth (1926–)
Swiss-German leading lady who made some Hollywood films.
The Power and the Prize 56. El Hakim 58. Confess Dr Corda 58. The Angry Hills 59, etc.

Mueller-Stahl, Armin (1930–)
German leading actor, from the theatre, now in international films. He was formerly a concert violinist.
The Secret Marriage/Heimliche Ehen 56. Königskinder 62. Naked among the Wolves/Nackt unter Wölfen 63. Wolf unter Wölfen 65. Der Dritte 72. Kit and Co. 74. Nelken in Aspik 76. Lola 82. Veronika Voss/Die Sehnsucht der Veronika 82. Glut 83. Love in Germany/Un Amour en Allemagne 83. A Thousand Eyes 84. Angry Harvest/Bittere Ernte 85. Forget Mozart 85. Colonel Redl 85. Momo 86. Midnight Cop 88. God Does Not Believe in Us Anymore 88. Music Box 89. Avalon 90. Kafka 91. The Power of One 91. Night on Earth 92. Utz 92. Red Hot 92. Der Kinoerzähler 93. The House of the Spirits 93. Holy Matrimony 94. Taxandria 94. Theodore Rex 95. A Pyromaniac's Love Story 95. *Shine* (AAN) 96. Conversation with the Beast (& d) 96. The Ogre 96. Twelve Angry Men (TV) 97. The Peacemaker 97. In the Presence of Mine Enemies 97. The Game 97. The X Files 98. Jakob the Liar 99. The Thirteenth Floor 99. The Third Miracle 99. Jesus (TV) 00, etc.

Muir, Esther (1895–1995)
American character actress usually seen as hard-faced blonde. Married Busby Berkeley and Sam Coslow. Her birthdate is also given as 1907.
A Dangerous Affair 31. So This is Africa 33. The Bowery 33. Fury 36. *A Day at the Races* (in which she suffered memorably at the hands of Groucho Marx) 37. The Law West of Tombstone 38. Stolen Paradise 41. X Marks the Spot 42, etc.

Muir, Gavin (1907–1972)
Quiet-spoken American actor with a British accent, usually a smooth villain.
Lloyds of London 36. Wee Willie Winkie 37. Eagle Squadron 41. *Nightmare* 42. The Master Race 44. Salome Where She Danced 45. California 46. Ivy 47. Abbott and Costello Meet the Invisible Man 51. King of the Khyber Rifles 54. The Sea Chase 55. The Abductors 57. Johnny Trouble 59, many others.
TV series: The Betty Hutton Show 59.

Muir, Jean (1911–1996) (J. M. Fullerton)
American leading lady of the 30s. Her refusal to conform to the studios' expectations hampered her career, which declined still further when she was blacklisted in the 50s, losing a role in the TV series *The Aldrich Family*; in the late 60s she became a drama teacher.
Female 34. A Midsummer Night's Dream 35. Jane Steps Out (GB) 37. And One Was Beautiful 40. The Lone Wolf Meets a Lady 40. The Constant Nymph 44, etc.

Mulcahy, Russell (1953–)
Australian director, now working in America.
Derek and Clive Get the Horn (TV) 81. Razorback 84. Highlander 86. Highlander II – the Quickening 90. Ricochet 91. Blue Ice 92. The Real McCoy 93. The Shadow 94. Silent Trigger 97, etc.

Mulcaster, G. H. (1891–1964)
British character actor, mainly on stage; played formal types.
The Dummy Talks 43. Bonnie Prince Charlie 47. Spring in Park Lane 48. Under Capricorn 50, etc.

Muldaur, Diana (1943–)
Sensitive-looking American leading lady, McCloud's girlfriend on TV; adept at nice sophisticated types; also on TV in 1974, played Joy Adamson in *Born Free*.
■ The Swimmer 68. Number One 69. The Lawyer 70. The Other 71. One More Train to Rob 72. McQ 73. The Chosen Survivors 74. Charlie's Angels (TV) 76. Pine Canyon Is Burning (TV) 77. Black Beauty (TV) 78. To Kill a Cop (TV) 78. Maneaters Are Loose (TV) 78. The Word (TV) 78. Beyond Reason 82. Master Ninja 3 83.
TV series: The Survivors 69–70. McCloud 70–77. Born Free 74. The Tony Randall Show 76–78. Hizzonner 79. Fitz and Bones 81.

Muldoon, Patrick (1969–)
American actor, a former model. He studied at the University of Southern California, and began on the TV soap opera *Days of Our Lives* 92–95.
Rage and Honor II: Hostile Takeover 93. Starship Troopers 97. Black Cat Run (TV) 98. The Second Arrival 98. Wicked 98, etc.
TV series: Days of Our Lives 92–95. Melrose Place 95–96.

Mulford, Clarence E. (1895–1970)
American western novelist, the creator of Hopalong Cassidy.

Mulhall, Jack (1888–1979)
American silent-screen leading man.
Sirens of the Sea 17. Mickey 18. All of a Sudden Peggy 20. Molly O' 21. The Bad Man 23. The Goldfish 24. Friendly Enemies 25. The Poor Nut 27. Just Another Blonde 28. Dark Streets 29, many others; appeared as an 'old-timer' in Hollywood Boulevard 36.

Mulhare, Edward (1923–1997)
Polished Irish leading actor. Born in Cork, he was on the British stage until he went to America to replace Rex Harrison in the musical *My Fair Lady*, after which he stayed there. Best known for his TV roles as Captain Daniel Gregg in *The Ghost and Mrs Miniver* 69–70, and Devon Miles in *Knightrider* 82–86.
Hill Twenty-Four Does Not Answer 55. Signpost to Murder 64. Von Ryan's Express 65. Our Man Flint 65. Eye of the Devil 67. *Caprice* 67. Gidget Grows Up (TV) 72. Megaforce 82, etc.

Mullan, Peter
Scottish actor, screenwriter and director.
Riff-Raff (a) 90. The Big Man (a) 90. Shallow Grave (a) 94. Ruffian Hearts (a) 95. Braveheart (a) 95. Trainspotting (a) 96. Fairytale: A True Story (a) 97. My Name Is Joe (a) 98. Orphans (wd) 98. Miss Julie (a) 99. The Escort (a) 99. Ordinary Decent Criminal (a) 00. The Claim (a) 00, etc.

Mullaney, Jack (1932–1982)
Easy-going light American actor.
The Young Stranger 57. Kiss Them for Me 58. The Absent Minded Professor 61. Seven Days in May 64. When the Legends Die 72. Where Does it Hurt? 72.
TV series: The Ann Sothern Show 58–60. Ensign O'Toole 62–63. My Living Doll 64–65. It's About Time 66–67.

Mullard, Arthur (1913–1995)
Big, bluff cockney character comedian who became a British television star of the 70s.
Autobiography: 1977, *Oh Yus, It's Arthur Mullard*.
Oliver Twist 48. The Lavender Hill Mob 51. Pickwick Papers 52. The Belles of St Trinian's 54. The Ladykillers 55. Brothers in Law 57. Two Way Stretch 60. Loneliness of the Long Distance Runner 62. Crooks Anonymous 62. The Wrong Arm of the Law 62. Sparrows Can't Sing 63. Morgan – a Suitable Case for Treatment 66. The Great St Trinian's Train Robbery 66. Casino Royale 67. Chitty Chitty Bang Bang 68. Lock Up Your Daughters! 69. On the Buses 71. Vault of Horror 73, etc.
TV series: The Arthur Askey Show 67. Vacant Lot 67. On the Rocks 69. Romany Jones 72–74. Yus My Dear 76–77.

Mullen, Barbara (1914–1979)
Irish-American actress, former dancer, who came to films as star of *Jeannie* 42.
Thunder Rock 42. A Place of One's Own 44. The Trojan Brothers 45. Corridor of Mirrors 48. So Little Time 52. The Challenge 60, etc.
TV series: Dr Finlay's Casebook 59–66.

Muller, Renate (1907–1937)
German leading lady best known abroad for *Sunshine Susie* 31.
Biography: 1944, *Queen of America?* by R. E. Clements.
Liebling der Götter 30. Viktor und Viktoria 34. Allotria 36.

Müller, Robby (1940–)
Dutch cinematographer, now in international films, who made his reputation working in Germany with Wim Wenders.
Summer in the City 70. The Goalkeeper's Fear of the Penalty Kick/Die Angst des Tormanns Beim Elfmeter 71. The Scarlet Letter/Der Scharlachrote Buchstabe 72. Alice in the Cities/Alice in den Städten 74. Falsche Bewegung/Wrong Move 75. Kings of the Road/Im Lauf der Zeit 76. The American Friend/Der Amerikanische Freund 77. Mysteries 79. Saint Jack 79. Honeysuckle Rose 80. They All Laughed 81. Paris, Texas 84. Repo Man 84. To Live and Die in L.A. 85. Down by Law 86. The Longshot 86. Barfly 87. The Believers 87. Mystery Train 89. Korczak 90. Until the End of the World/Bis ans Ende der Welt 91. Mad Dog and Glory 93. Beyond the Clouds 95. Breaking the Waves 96. The Tango Lesson 97. Shattered Image (US) 98, etc.

Mulligan, Gerry (1927–1996)
American jazz musician, arranger, composer and occasional actor. He was an influential baritone saxophonist and bandleader from the 50s, one of the creators of the cool approach to jazz, typified by his arrangements for the *Birth of the Cool* album made by Miles Davis. His early piano-less quartet included trumpeter Chet Baker. Lover of actress Judy Holliday, with whom he wrote songs in the late 50s and early 60s. Married actress Sandy Dennis (1965–76).
I Want to Live (soundtrack saxophone) 58. Jazz on a Summer's Day (doc) 60. The Bells Are Ringing (a) 60. The Rat Race (a) 60. The Subterraneans (a) 60. Luv (m) 67. The Hot Rock (soundtrack saxophone) 72. The Final Programme (soundtrack saxophone) 73. I'm Not Rappaport (m) 96.
❝ I think I managed to not be an adult in just about every imaginable area. – G.M.

Mulligan, Richard (1932–2000)
Lanky American character actor, the brother of director Richard Mulligan. Best known for his role as Burt Campbell in the TV sitcom Soap, he won an Emmy for his performances and another for his acting in the TV series *Empty Nest*. Born in New York, he planned to be a writer and became an actor by accident. The second of his four wives was actress Joan Hackett.
The Group 66. The Undefeated 69. Little Big Man 70. From the Mixed-Up Files of Mrs Basil E. Frankweiler 73. The Big Bus 76. Scavenger Hunt 79. S.O.B. 81. Trail of the Pink Panther 82. Micki and Maude 84. Teachers 84. Meatballs Part II 84. The Heavenly Kid 85. A Fine Mess 85. Oliver and Company (voice) 88, etc.
TV series: The Hero 66-67. Diana 73–74. *Soap* 77–81. Reggie 83. Empty Nest 88–95.

Mulligan, Robert (1925–)
American director, from TV.
■ Fear Strikes Out 57. The Rat Race 60. Come September 61. The Great Impostor 61. The Spiral Road 62. *To Kill a Mockingbird* (AAN) 62. Love with the Proper Stranger 64. Baby the Rain Must Fall 65. Inside Daisy Clover 65. Up the Down Staircase 67. The Stalking Moon 68. The Pursuit of Happiness 70. *Summer of '42* 71. The Other 73. The Nickel Ride 75. Bloodbrothers 78. Same Time Next Year 78. Kiss Me Goodbye 82. Clara's Heart 88. The Man in the Moon 91.

Mulock, Al (c. 1925–1970) (aka Al Mullach)
Canadian character actor, usually as a heavy, who worked in Britain in the mid-50s to mid-60s and then moved to Italy to appear in spaghetti westerns. Committed suicide.
Joe Macbeth 55. Kill Me Tomorrow 57. The Depraved 57. The Sheriff of Fractured Jaw 58. Tarzan's Greatest Adventure 59. Tarzan the Magnificent 60. The Hellions 61. The Longest Day 62. The Small World of Sammy Lee 62. Dr Terror's House of Horrors 64. The Good, the Bad and the Ugly 66. Reflections in a Golden Eye 67. Battle beneath the Earth 68, etc.

Mulroney, Dermot (1963–)
American actor. Married actress Catherine Keener.
Sunset 88. Young Guns 88. Staying Together 89. Survival Quest 89. Longtime Companion 90. Career Opportunities 91. Bright Angel 91. Where the Day Takes You 92. Samantha 92. Silent Tongue 93. Point of No Return 93. The Thing Called Love 93. Bad Girls 94. There Goes My Baby 94. Living in Oblivion 95. How to Make an American Quilt 95. Copycat 95. Kansas City 96. Bastard out of Carolina 96. The Trigger Effect 96. Box of Moonlight 96. My Best Friend's Wedding 97. Goodbye, Lover 98, etc.

Mumy, Billy (1954–)
American child actor of the 60s.
Palm Springs Weekend 63. A Ticklish Affair 63. *Dear Brigitte* 65. Rascal 69. Bless the Beasts and Children 71. Papillon 73. Twilight Zone – the Movie 83. Hard to Hold 84, etc.
TV series: Lost in Space 65–68. Sunshine 75.

Mundin, Herbert (1898–1939)
Short English character actor with expressive eyebrows, usually as comic relief. Born in St Helens, Lancashire, he began as a comedian in concert parties and revues. After working in British films in the 20s, he went to the US in search of work and was put under contract by Fox, remaining in Hollywood for the rest of his career, frequently in servile roles: as steward, publican or manservant. Died in a car crash. His best roles were as Barkis in *David Copperfield*, Much the Miller in *The Adventures of Robin Hood*, and Wilkins in *Another Dawn*.
The Devil's Lottery 31. Sherlock Holmes 32. Cavalcade 33. *David Copperfield* 34. Mutiny on the Bounty 35. Another Dawn 37. *The Adventures of Robin Hood* 38. Society Lawyer 39, etc.

Mune, Ian (1941–)
New Zealand director and screenwriter, a former actor.
Sleeping Dogs (a, co-w) 77. Goodbye, Pork Pie (co-w) 80. Came a Hot Friday (co-w, d) 84. Bridge to Nowhere (d) 85. The End of the Golden Weather (co-w, d) 91. The Piano (a) 93. Fallout (a) 93. The Whole of the Moon (co-w, d) 96. What Becomes of the Broken-Hearted (d) 99, etc.

Muni, Paul (1896–1967) (Muni Weisenfreund)
Distinguished American actor of Austrian parentage. Long stage experience.
Biography: 1974, *Actor* by Jerome Lawrence.
■ The Valiant (film debut) (AAN) 28. Seven Faces 29. *Scarface* 32. *I Am a Fugitive from a Chain Gang* (AAN) 32. The World Changes 33. Hi Nellie 33. Bordertown 34. Black Fury 35. Dr Socrates 35. *The Story of Louis Pasteur* (AA) 36. *The Good Earth* 37. *The Life of Emile Zola* (AAN) 37. The Woman I Love 38. Juarez 39. We Are Not Alone 39. Hudson's Bay 40. The Commandos Strike at Dawn 42. Stage Door Canteen 43. *A Song to Remember* 44. Counter Attack 45. Angel on My Shoulder 46. Stranger on the Prowl 51. The Last Angry Man (AAN) 59.
✪ For convincing world audiences of his day that heavy disguise made a great actor; and for his powerful early performances. *Scarface*.
❝ Every time Paul Muni parts his beard and looks down a microscope, this company loses two million dollars. – *Hal B. Wallis, as Warner head of production in the late 30s*
His voice is rich and pleasant, his personality is strong and virile, and if he is not pretty, neither is Lon Chaney. – *Variety, 1929*
He seemed intent on submerging himself so completely that he disappeared. – *Bette Davis*

Munk, Andrzej (1921–1961)
Polish director.
Men of the Blue Cross 55. Eroica 57. Bad Luck 60. The Passenger (incomplete) 61, etc.

Munro, Caroline (1951–)
British leading lady.
The Abominable Dr Phibes 71. Captain Kronos 72. The Golden Voyage of Sinbad 73. The Devil Within Her 73. At the Earth's Core 76. The Spy Who Loved Me 77. Maniac 80. Don't Open till Christmas 84. Slaughter High 86. Night Owl (as herself) 93, etc.

Munro, Janet (1934–1972)
British leading actress. Born in Blackpool, Lancashire, of Scottish parents, she was signed by Walt Disney a year after her screen debut and went

to Hollywood for a time before returning to Britain. Her later career was hampered by alcoholism. Married actors (1956-61) Tony Wright and (1963-71) Ian Hendry. Choked to death.

Small Hotel 57. The Trollenberg Terror 58. The Young and the Guilty 57. Darby O'Gill and the Little People 58. Third Man on the Mountain 59. Tommy the Toreador 59. The Swiss Family Robinson 60. The Day the Earth Caught Fire 61. Life for Ruth 62. Bitter Harvest 63. A Jolly Bad Fellow 64. Sebastian 68, etc.

Munsel, Patrice (1925–)
American operatic soprano who played the title role in *Melba* 53.

Munshin, Jules (1915–1970)
Lanky, rubber-limbed American comedian and dancer, in occasional films from the mid-40s. Born in New York City, he began in vaudeville and worked on Broadway before and after his brief stints in films. Died from a heart attack. He is at his best teamed with Gene Kelly and Frank Sinatra, as Nat Goldberg in *Take Me Out to the Ball Game* and as Ozzie in *On the Town*. Kelly tried to reunite the trio for a sequel to the latter, but Sinatra declined and the resulting film, *It's Always Fair Weather*, was rewritten for other stars.

Easter Parade 48. Take Me Out to the Ball Game 48. *On the Town* 49. Ten Thousand Bedrooms 56. Silk Stockings 57. Wild and Wonderful 64, etc.

Munson, Ona (1906–1955) (Ona Wolcott)
American character actress, former dancer. Born in Portland, Oregon, she trained as a ballet dancer, and was on stage from childhood as a dancer and singer, working in vaudeville as a teenager and becoming a Broadway success in *Hold Everything!* in the late 20s. Her film career faltered after a row with the studios, and she became depressed and put on weight. In the early 40s she became the first woman producer at CBS. Died from an overdose of sleeping pills, leaving a note that read, 'This is the only way I know to be free again.' She was married three times, including to actor and director Edward Buzzell (1926–30), and to Russian artist and designer Eugène Berman (1950–55). Among her lovers were director Ernst Lubitsch and Mercedes De Acosta.

Going Wild 30. Five Star Final 32. Gone with the Wind 39. Drums of the Congo 40. *The Shanghai Gesture* (as Mother Gin Sling) 41. The Cheaters 45. The Red House 47, etc.

Muraki, Yoshiro (1924–)
Japanese production designer, often for the films of Akira Kurosawa.

Throne of Blood 57. The Lower Depths 57. Yojimbo 61. Sanjuro 62. Red Beard/Akahige 65. Dodeska-den 70. Tora! Tora! Tora! 70. Tidal Wave/Nippon Shinbotsu 75. Kagemusha 80. *Ran* 85, etc.

Muratova, Kira G. (1934–)
Romanian-born film director and screenwriter, in Russia. Born in Soroca, she studied at VGIK, and began making short films in collaboration with her then husband, Alexander Muratov. Her feature films, often using experimental approaches, have run into censorship problems, having been rejected both for 'bourgeois realism' and for their bleak view of Russian society.

Brief Encounters/Korotkie Vstrechi (& a) 67. Long Goodbye/Dolgie Provody 71. Getting to Know the World/Poznavaya Belyi Svet 79. Among the Grey Stones/Sredi Serykh Kamnei (credited to 'Ivan Sidorov') 83. Change of Fate/Peremana Uchasti 87. *The Asthenic Syndrome*/Astenicheskij Sindrom 89. The Sensitive Policeman/Le Milicien Amoureux 92. Enthusiasms/Uvlechen'ia 94, etc.

Murch, Walter (1943–)
American film and sound editor, screenwriter and occasional director. He is a graduate of the University of Southern California film school.

THX 1138 (co-w) 70. American Graffiti 73. The Conversation (AAN) 74. Julia (AAN) 77. Apocalypse Now (AA) 79. Return to Oz (co-w, d) 85. The Unbearable Lightness of Being 88. The Godfather Part III (AAN) 90. Ghost (AAN) 90. House of Cards 93. First Knight 95. The English Patient (AA) 96, etc.

Murdoch, Richard 'Stinker' (1907–1990)
British radio entertainer, long partnered with Arthur Askey and Kenneth Horne.

Band Wagon 39. *The Ghost Train* 41. It Happened in Soho 48. Golden Arrow 52. Not a Hope in Hell 59. Strictly Confidential 61. Whoops Apocalypse 86, etc.

TV series: Silk, Satin, Cotton, Rags 52. Beside the Seaside 57. Living It Up 57-58. Doctors' Daughters 81.

Muren, Dennis
American special effects supervisor.

Equinox 71. Flesh Gordon 72. Close Encounters of the Third Kind 77. Star Wars 77. The Empire Strikes Back (AA) 80. Dragonslayer (AAN) 81. E.T. The Extra-Terrestrial (AA) 82. Return of the Jedi (AA) 83. Indiana Jones and the Temple of Doom (AA) 84. Young Sherlock Holmes (AAN) 85. Innerspace (AA) 87. Willow (AAN) 88. Ghostbusters II 89. The Abyss (AA) 89. Terminator 2: Judgment Day (AA) 91. Jurassic Park (AA) 93. Casper 95. Twister 96. The Lost World: Jurassic Park (AAN) 97. Deconstructing Harry 97. Star Wars Episode 1: The Phantom Menace (AAN) 99, etc.

Murer, Fredi M. (1940–)
Swiss director, screenwriter and novelist.

Swiss Made 69. The Grey Zones/Die Grauzone 78. Alpine Fire/Hohenfeuer 85. Green Mountain/Der Grune Berg (doc) 90. Full Moon/Vollmond 98, etc.

Muresan, Gheorghe (1971–)
Romanian-born athlete and occasional actor, best known as the lofty (7 ft 7 ins) centre with Washington Wizards basketball team.

My Giant 98. The Mask of Zorro 98, etc.

Murfin, Jane (1893–1955)
American screenwriter.

Miss Murfin's plays as co-author, usually with Jane Cowl, include *Daybreak* and *Smilin' Through*, both of which were filmed.

The Right to Lie 19. Flapper Wives 24. White Fang 25. Meet the Prince 26. Dance Hall 29. Leathernecking 30. Friends and Lovers 31. Our Betters 33. Ann Vickers 33. Spitfire 34. This Man Is Mine 34. Roberta 35. Alice Adams 35. Come and Get It 36. The Shining Hour 38. Stand Up and Fight 39. Pride and Prejudice 40. Andy Hardy's Private Secretary 41. Flight for Freedom 43. Dragon Seed 44, etc.

Murnau, F. W. (Friedrich) (1888–1931) (F. W. Plumpe)
German director in films from 1919; Hollywood from 1927. Died in a car crash. He was played by John Malkovich in *The Shadow of the Vampire* 00.

Satanas 19. Dr Jekyll and Mr Hyde 20. *Nosferatu*/Dracula 22. *The Last Laugh* 24. Tartuffe 24. *Faust* 26. *Sunrise* 27. Four Devils 28. Our Daily Bread/City Girl 30. Tabu (co-d) 31, etc.

✪ For unquestionable brilliance in showing what the camera can do. *The Last Laugh*.

Murphy, Audie (1924–1971)
Boyish American leading man of the 50s; came to films on the strength of his war record as America's most decorated soldier, but despite some talent was soon relegated to low-budget westerns. Killed in a plane crash.

■ Beyond Glory 48. Texas Brooklyn and Heaven 48. Bad Boy 49. Sierra 50. The Kid from Texas 50. Kansas Raiders 50. *The Red Badge of Courage* 51. The Cimarron Kid 51. The Duel at Silver Creek 52. Gunsmoke 52. Column South 53. Tumbleweed 53. Ride Clear of Diablo 54. Drums Across the River 54. *Destry* 55. *To Hell and Back* (based on his autobiography) 55. The World in My Corner 56. Walk the Proud Land 56. The Guns of Fort Petticoat 57. Joe Butterfly 57. Night Passage 57. *The Quiet American* 58. Ride a Crooked Trail 58. The Gun Runners 58. No Name on the Bullet 59. The Wild and the Innocent 59. Cast a Long Shadow 59. Hell Bent for Leather 60. The Unforgiven 60. Seven Ways from Sundown 60. Posse from Hell 61. The Battle at Bloody Beach 61. Six Black Horses 62. Showdown 63. Gunfight at Comanche Creek 63. The Quick Gun 64. Bullet for a Badman 64. Apache Rifles 64. Arizona Raiders 65. Gunpoint 66. Trunk to Cairo 66. The Texican 66. Forty Guns to Apache Pass 67. A Time for Dying (& p) 71.

TV series: Whispering Smith 58.

❝ I guess my face is still the same, and so is the dialogue. Only the horses have changed. – A.M. *at 40*

I am working with a handicap. I have no talent. – A.M.

Murphy, Ben (1942–)
Athletic American TV hero of many TV action series. Born in Jonesboro, Arkansas, he studied political science at the University of Illinois.

The One Thousand Plane Raid 69. The Letters (TV) 73. Runaway (TV) 73. Heatwave (TV) 74. This Was the West That Was (TV) 75. Sidecar Racers 75. Bridger (TV) 76. Time Walker 82. The Winds of War (TV) 83, etc.

TV series: The Name of the Game 68-71. Alias Smith and Jones 71-73. Griff 73-74. Gemini Man 76. The Chisholms 79-80. Lottery 83-84. Berrenger's 85. The Dirty Dozen 88.

Murphy, Brian (1933–)
English comic actor of stage and screen, also much on television and best known as the hen-pecked husband in the TV sitcoms *Man about the House* and *George and Mildred*. Born in Ventnor, Isle of Wight, he trained at RADA and was a member of Theatre Workshop from the mid-50s.

Sparrows Can't Sing 62. The Activist 69. The Devils 71. The Boy Friend 71. The Ragman's Daughter 72. Man about the House 74. I'm Not Feeling Myself Tonight 76. Black Jack 80. George and Mildred 80, etc.

TV series: Man about the House 73–76. George and Mildred 76–79. The Incredible Mr Tanner 81. L for Lester 82. Lame Ducks 84–85. Brookside 95.

Murphy, Brittany (1977–)
American actress, from television. Born in Atlanta, Georgia, she began in commercials as a child.

Family Prayers 93. Reporting Home (TV) 95. Clueless 95. Drive 96. Double Jeopardy (TV) 96. Freeway 96. The Prophecy 2: Ashtown 97. Drive 97. David and Lisa (TV) 98. Phoenix 98. Falling Sky 98. Bongwater 98. Girl, Interrupted 99. Drop Dead Gorgeous 99. Cherry Falls 99. Trixie 00, etc.

TV series: Drexells' Class 91–92. Sister, Sister 94–95. Almost Home 93. King of the Hill (voice) 97– .

Murphy, Dudley (1897–1968)
American journalist who was briefly in films as director in the 20s and 30s.

High Speed Lee 23. Alex the Great 28. The Sport Parade 32. *The Emperor Jones* 33. The Night Is Young 35. Don't Gamble with Love 36. One Third of a Nation 39. Main Street Lawyer 39. Alma del Bronce (Mex.) 44, etc.

Murphy, Eddie (1961–)
Aggressive American comedian and actor. His brash, fast-talking, guffawing style led to success with *48 Hours* and *Beverly Hills Cop*, but films that followed, in which he took greater control as producer and writer, and even director, were less profitable; he began remaking his earlier hits with diminishing returns until he found success again by refurbishing an old Jerry Lewis vehicle, *The Nutty Professor*, which took more than $100m at the US box-office.

48 Hours 82. Trading Places 83. Best Defense 84. *Beverly Hills Cop* 85. The Golden Child 86. Beverly Hills Cop II 87. Eddie Murphy Raw 87. Hollywood Shuffle 87. Coming to America 88. Harlem Nights (& wd) 89. Another 48 Hrs 90. Boomerang 92. The Distinguished Gentleman 92. Beverly Hills Cop III 94. Vampire in Brooklyn 95. The Nutty Professor 96. Metro 97. Dr Dolittle 98. Mulan (voice) 98. Bowfinger 98. Holy Man 98. Life 99. Nutty Professor II: The Klumps 00. Dr Dolittle 2 01, etc.

TV series: Saturday Night Live 81–84. The PJs (voice, p) 99.

❝ Wouldn't it be a helluva thing if this was burnt cork and you folk were being tolerant for nothing? – E.M.

Murphy, Fred
American cinematographer.

Girlfriends 78. Heartland 79. Q – The Winged Serpent 82. The State of Things 82. Eddie and the Cruisers 83. The Trip to Bountiful 85. Hoosiers 86. Best Seller 87. The Dead 87. Five Corners 88. Fresh Horses 88. Full Moon in Blue Water 88. Enemies, a Love Story 89. Funny about Love 90. Scenes from a Mall 90. Jack the Bear 93. The Pickle 93. Murder in the First 95. Faithful 96. A Family Thing 96. Metro 97. Dance with Me 98. October Sky 99. Stir of Echoes 99, etc.

Murphy, Geoff (1938–)
New Zealand director and musician, now working in America.

Wildman 77. Goodbye Pork Pie 80. Utu 83. The Quiet Earth 85. Never Say Die 88. Young Guns II 90. Freejack 92. The Last Outlaw (TV) 93. Blind Side (TV) 93. Under Siege 2: Dark Territory 95. Don't Look Back (TV) 96. Fortress 2: Re-entry 00, etc.

Murphy, George (1902–1992)
Amiable Irish-American actor and dancer, a pleasant light talent who left the screen for politics and became senator for California. Special Academy Award 1951 'for interpreting the film industry to the nation at large'.

Autobiography: 1970, *Say, Didn't You Used to Be George Murphy?*.

■ Kid Millions 34. Jealousy 34. Public Menace 35. I'll Love You Always 35. After the Dance 35. Woman Trap 36. Top of the Town 36. London by Night 37. You're a Sweetheart 37. Broadway Melody of 1938 38. Letter of Introduction 38. Little Miss Broadway 38. Hold that Co-Ed 38. Risky Business 39. Broadway Melody of 1940 40. *Little Nellie Kelly* 40. Public Deb. No. 1 40. A Girl a Guy and a Gob 40. Ringside Maisie 41. *Tom Dick and Harry* 41. Rise and Shine 41. The Mayor of 44th Street 41. For Me and My Gal 41. The Navy Comes Through 42. The Powers Girl 42. Bataan 43. This Is the Army 43. Broadway Rhythm 44. *Show Business* 44. *Step Lively* 44. Having a Wonderful Crime 44. Up Goes Maisie 46. The Arnelo Affair 47. Cynthia 47. Tenth Avenue Angel 48. Big City 48. Border Incident 49. Battleground 49. No Questions Asked 51. It's a Big Country 51. Walk East on Beacon 52. Talk about a Stranger 52.

Murphy, Mary (1931–)
American leading lady.

The Lemon Drop Kid (debut) 51. The Wild One 54. Beachhead 54. Hell's Island 55. The Desperate Hours 55. The Intimate Stranger (GB) 56. Crime and Punishment USA 59. Forty Pounds of Trouble 63. Junior Bonner 72, etc.

Murphy, Michael (1938–)
American general-purpose actor.

Countdown 67. The Arrangement 69. Brewster McCloud 70. What's Up Doc? 72. The Thief Who Came to Dinner 73. Nashville 75. An Unmarried Woman 77. Manhattan 79. The Year of Living Dangerously 82. Cloak and Dagger 84. Salvador 85. Shocker 89. Folks! 92. Batman Returns 92. Clean Slate 94. Kansas City 96. Private Parts 96, etc.

Murphy, Ralph (1895–1967)
American director, in Hollywood from silent days.

The Gay City 41. Hearts in Springtime 41. Mrs Wiggs of the Cabbage Patch 42. Rainbow Island 44. The Man in Half Moon Street 44. Red Stallion in the Rockies 49. Dick Turpin's Ride 51. Captain Blood, Fugitive 52. Desert Rats 53. The Lady in the Iron Mask 53. Three Stripes in the Sun (& w) 55, etc.

Murphy, Richard (1912–1993)
American writer, in Hollywood from 1937.

Boomerang (AAN) 47. Cry of the City 48. Panic in the Streets 50. Les Misérables 52. Desert Rats (AAN) 53. Broken Lance 54. Compulsion 58. The Wackiest Ship in the Army (& d) 60, etc.

Murphy, Rosemary (1925–)
American stage actress in occasional films.

That Night 57. The Young Doctors 61. To Kill a Mockingbird 62. Any Wednesday 66. Ben 72. You'll Like My Mother 72. Walking Tall 73. Forty Carats 73. Ace Eli and Rodger of the Skies 73. Julia (as Dorothy Parker) 77. September 87. For the Boys 91. The Tuskegee Airmen (TV) 95, etc.

Murray, Barbara (1929–)
British leading lady with stage experience.

Anna Karenina 48. Passport to Pimlico 48. Doctor at Large 56. Campbell's Kingdom 58. A Cry from the Streets 58. Girls in Arms 60. A Dandy in Aspic 68. Tales from the Crypt 72, many others.

TV series: The Power Game 66–68. The Bretts 87.

Murray, Bill (1950–)
Abrasive American leading actor, who first came to notice on TV's *Saturday Night Live*. Current asking price: around $10m a movie.

Meatballs 79. Caddyshack 80. Stripes 82. Tootsie (uncredited) 82. *Ghostbusters* 84. The Razor's Edge 84. Little Shop of Horrors 86. Scrooged 88. Ghostbusters II 89. Quick Change (& co-d) 90. What about Bob? 91. Mad Dog and Glory 93. *Groundhog Day* 93. Ed Wood 94. Kingpin 96. Larger than Life 96. Space Jam 96. The Man Who Knew Too Little 97. Wild Things 98. Rushmore 98, etc.

Murray, Charlie (1872–1941)
American vaudeville comedian long with Mack Sennett. In *Tillie's Punctured Romance* 15, and later played with George Sidney in a long series about the Cohens and Kellys.

Murray, Don (1929–)
Ambitious American actor who graduated from innocent to tough roles but does not seem to have received the attention he sought and merited.
■ Bus Stop (AAN) 56. *The Bachelor Party* 57. A Hatful of Rain 57. From Hell to Texas 58. These Thousand Hills 59. Shake Hands with the Devil 59. One Foot in Hell 60. *The Hoodlum Priest* (& co-p) 61. *Advise and Consent* 62. Escape from East Berlin 62. One Man's Way 64. Baby the Rain Must Fall 65. Kid Rodelo 66. The Plainsman 66. Sweet Love, Bitter 67. The Viking Queen 67. Tale of the Cock 67. The Borgia Stick (TV) 67. The Intruders (TV) 67. Daughter of the Mind (TV) 69. Childish Things (& wp) 70. Conquest of the Planet of the Apes 72. Happy Birthday Wanda June 72. Cotter 73. A Girl Named Sooner (TV) 74. The Sex Symbol (TV) 74. The Girl on the Late Late Show (TV) 75. Deadly Hero 76. Damien (w, d) 77. Rainbow (TV) 78. Crisis in Mid-air (TV) 79. The Far Turn (TV) 79. Endless Love 81. Peggy Sue Got Married 86. Scorpion 86. Made in Heaven 87. Stillwatch (TV) 87. Mistress (TV) 87. A Brand New Life: The Honeymoon (TV) 89. Ghosts Can't Do It 90. Kickboxer the Champion 91.
TV series: The Outcasts 68. Knots Landing 80–81. Sons and Daughters 91.

Murray, James (1901–1936)
American leading man, a former extra who was chosen by King Vidor to play the hero of *The Crowd* 28, but subsequently took to drink and died in obscurity.
The Big City 28. Thunder 29. Bright Lights 30. The Reckoning 32. Heroes for Sale 32. Skull and Crown 35, etc.

Murray, Jan (1917–) (Murray Janofsky)
American stand-up comedian and 50s TV game show host, in occasional films.
Who Killed Teddy Bear? 65. Thunder Alley 65. Tarzan and the Great River 67. The Angry Breed 68. Which Way to the Front? 70. Roll, Freddy, Roll (TV) 74. The Dream Merchants (TV) 80. Fear City 85, etc.
TV series: Songs for Sale 50–51. Sing It Again 51. Dollar a Second 53–57. Treasure Hunt 56–58.

Murray, Ken (1903–1988) (Don Court)
American comedy actor, radio and TV entertainer, especially as collector of old 'home movies' of the stars. Collected special Oscar for his 1947 bird fantasy *Bill and Coo*.
Autobiography: 1960, *Life on a Pogo Stick*.
Half Marriage 29. A Night at Earl Carroll's 41. The Man Who Shot Liberty Valance 62. Follow Me Boys 66. Power 68.

Murray, Lyn (1909–1989)
American composer.
Son of Paleface 52. The Bridges at Toko Ri 54. To Catch a Thief 55. Escape from Zahrain 61.

Promise Her Anything 66. Rosie 67. The Magic Carpet (TV) 71, etc.

Murray, Mae (1889–1965) (Marie Adrienne Koenig)
American leading lady of the silent screen; former dancer; usually in flashy roles. Retired to marry.
Biography: 1959, *The Self-Enchanted* by Jane Ardmore.
Sweet Kitty Bellairs 17. Her Body in Bond 18. The Mormon Maid 20. Jazz Mania 21. Fashion Row 23. The Merry Widow 25. Circe the Enchantress 27. Peacock Alley 31, etc.

Murray, Ruby (1935–1996)
Irish pop singer of the 50s, in occasional films. Born in Belfast, she toured Ireland as a child singer, and gained a wider fame on the BBC TV show *Quite Contrary*, having five records simultaneously in the Top Twenty. Alcoholism contributed to her later decline.
A Touch of the Sun 56. It's Great to Be Young 56, etc.

Murray, Stephen (1912–1983)
Under-used British character actor, on stage from 1933.
Pygmalion 38. *The Prime Minister* 41. *Next of Kin* 42. Undercover 43. *Master of Bankdam* 46. My Brother Jonathan 47. Silent Dust 48. *London Belongs to Me* 48. For Them That Trespass 49. Now Barabbas 50. The Magnet 50. 24 Hours of a Woman's Life 52. Four-Sided Triangle 53. The Stranger's Hand 54. The End of the Affair 55. Guilty 55. The Door in the Wall 56. At the Stroke of Nine 57. A Tale of Two Cities 58. The Nun's Story 59. Master Spy 63, etc.

Murray-Hill, Peter (1908–1957)
British leading man of stage and screen; was married to Phyllis Calvert.
A Yank at Oxford 38. The Outsider 39. Jane Steps Out 40. The Ghost Train 41. Madonna of the Seven Moons 44. They Were Sisters (last film) 45, etc.

Murton, Lionel (1915–)
Canadian character actor resident in Britain.
Meet the Navy 46. The Long Dark Hall 51. The Runaway Bus 54. The Battle of the River Plate 55. Up the Creek 58. Northwest Frontier 59. Confessions of a Window Cleaner 74. Twilight's Last Gleaming 77, etc.

Murton, Peter
English art director and production designer.
Billy Budd 62. The Ipcress File 65. Thunderball 65. Funeral in Berlin 66. *Half a Sixpence* 67. The Lion in Winter 68. The Ruling Class 72. The Man with the Golden Gun 74. The Eagle Has Landed 76. Death on the Nile 78. Dracula 79. Superman II 80. Superman III 83. Spies Like Us 85. King Kong Lives 86. Diamond's Edge 90. Popcorn 91. Stargate 94, etc.

Musante, Tony (1936–)
American character actor.
Once a Thief 65. The Detective 68. The Bird with the Crystal Plumage 70. The Grissom Gang 71, The Last Run 71. Eutanasia di un Amore 78. Rearview Mirror (TV) 84. Nutcracker: Money, Madness and Murder (TV) 87, etc.
TV series: Toma 72.

Muse, Clarence (1889–1979)
American character actor.
Hearts in Dixie 28. Cabin in the Cotton 32. Showboat 36. Tales of Manhattan 42. An Act of

Murder 48. So Bright the Flame 52. Car Wash 77. The Black Stallion 79, many others.

Musidora (1889–1957) (Jeanne Roques)
French actress, director and screenwriter of silent movies, best known as the star of Louis Feuillade's serials.
Fille d'Eve 15. Judex (serial) 16. Les Vampires (serial) 16. Le Spectre 16. La Vagabonde (1.) 17. Vicenta (& wd) 18. Pour Don Carlos 21. Soleil et Ombre 22. La Terre des Toros (& wd) 25. Le Berceau de Dieu 26, etc.

Mustin, Burt (1884–1977)
American comedy character actor who was 67 when he made his first film.
Detective Story 51. The Lusty Men 53. The Desperate Hours 55. The Big Country 57. Huckleberry Finn 61. The Thrill of It All 63. Cat Ballou 65. Speedway 68. Hail Hero 70. The Skin Game 71, etc.
TV series: A Date with the Angels 57. Ichabod 61–62. The Andy Griffith Show 61–66. All in the Family 73–76. Phyllis 76.

Musuraca, Nicholas (1895–1975)
American cinematographer.
Bride of the Storm 24. Lightning Lanats 25. Tyrant of Red Gulch 27. The Cuckoos 31. Cracked Nuts 33. Long Lost Father 34. Murder on a Bridle Path 36. Blind Alibi 38. Five Came Back 39. Golden Boy 39. The Swiss Family Robinson 40. Tom Brown's Schooldays 40. *Cat People* 42. The Seventh Victim 43. Curse of the Cat People 44. *The Spiral Staircase* 45. The Locket 46. The Bachelor and the Bobbysoxer 47. *Out of the Past* 47. Blood on the Moon 48. Where Danger Lives 51. Clash by Night 52. Devil's Canyon 53. The Story of Mankind 57. Too Much Too Soon 58, many others.

Muti, Ornella (1955–) (Francesca Romana Rivelli)
Sultry Italian leading actress who began her career at the age of 15.
Most Beautiful Wife/La Moglie Più Bella 70. Sensual Man/Paolo il Caldo 73. The Nun and the Devil 73. Italian Graffiti 74. First Love/Primo Amore 78. Flash Gordon 80. Love and Money 80. Tales of Ordinary Madness 81. Swann in Love/Un Amour de Swann 83. Chronicle of a Death Foretold/Cronaca di una Morte Annunciata 87. Wait until Spring, Bandini 89. Captain Fracassa's Journey/Il Viaggio di Capitan Fracassa 90. Oscar 91. Tonight at Alice's 91. Christmas Vacation '91/Vacanze di Natale '91 91. Especially on Sundays/La Domenica Specialmente 91. Once upon a Crime 92. El Amante Bilingüe 93. The Stranger from Strasbourg/L'Inconnu de Strasbourg (Fr.) 98. Jet Set 00, many others.

Mutrux, Floyd
American screenwriter and director.
The Christian Liquorice Store (w) 71. Dusty and Sweets McGhee (wd) 71. Freebie and the Bean 74. Aloha, Bobby and Rose (wd) 75. American Hot Wax (d) 78. The Hollywood Nights (wd) 80. Blood In Blood Out (co-w) 92. American Me (co-w) 93. There Goes My Baby (wd) 94, etc.

Muybridge, Eadweard (1830–1904) (Edward Muggeridge)
British photographer who, in America in 1877, succeeded in analysing motion with a camera by taking a series of pictures of a horse in motion. (He used 24 cameras attached to a tripwire.) Later he invented a form of projector which reassembled his pictures into the appearance of moving actuality, and called it the Zoopraxiscope; in 1877 he

published an influential book of his findings, *Animal Locomotion*.

Mycroft, Walter (1891–1959)
British director. Chief scriptwriter and director of productions at Elstree in the 30s.
Spring Meeting 40. My Wife's Family 41. Banana Ridge 41. The Woman's Angle (p only) 52, etc.

Myers, Carmel (1899–1980)
American leading lady of the 20s, in the 'vamp' tradition.
Sirens of the Sea 16. Intolerance 16. The Haunted Pyjamas 17. Mad Marriage 21. The Famous Mrs Fair 23. Beau Brummell 24. Ben Hur 25. Sorrell and Son 27. Svengali 31. Lady for a Night 42. Whistle Stop 45, etc.

Myers, Harry (1886–1938)
American character actor, in Hollywood from 1908.
Housekeeping 16. A *Connecticut Yankee* 21. The Beautiful and the Damned 26. *City Lights* (as the drunken millionaire) 31. Dangerous Lives 37, etc.

Myers, Mike (1963–)
Canadian comedian, actor and screenwriter, who first came to notice on the TV show *Saturday Night Live* in 1989 and turned his sketch 'Wayne's World' with Dana Carvey into an international success on film. He is best known for the role of secret agent Austin Powers, a send-up of 60s spy movies, the second of which earned him a reported $20m. Born in Toronto, he performed in commercials as a child. Married screenwriter Robin Ruzan.
Wayne's World (a, co-w) 92. So I Married an Axe Murderer (a) 93. Wayne's World 2 (a, co-w) 93. *Austin Powers: International Man of Mystery* (& w) 97. 54 98. Austin Powers: The Spy Who Shagged Me 99. Mystery, Alaska 99, etc.
66 Marriage can be viewed as the waiting room for death. – M.M.

Myers, Stanley (1930–1993)
British composer, from the theatre. His best-known work was *Cavatina*, originally written for The *Walking Stick* 76, but made famous by its use in The *Deerhunter*.
Kaleidoscope 66. Otley 68. Age of Consent 69. Raging Moon 71. Zee & Co 72. The Apprenticeship of Dudley Kravitz 74. The Greek Tycoon 78. The Deer Hunter 78. The Watcher in the Woods 80. Moonlighting 82. The Honorary Consul 83. The Lightship 85. My Beautiful Laundrette 85. Castaway 86. Prick Up Your Ears 87. Sammie and Rosie Get Laid 87. Wish You Were Here 87. Stars and Bars 88. The Boost 88. Scenes from the Class Struggle in Beverly Hills 89. The Witches 89. Torrents of Spring 90. Iron Maze 91. Voyager 91. Claude 92. Serafina! 92. Cold Heaven 92, many others.

Myrow, Fred (1939–1999)
American composer and pianist, associated with the films of director Don Coscarelli.
Leo the Last 70. Soylent Green 73. Kenny & Co 76. On the Nickel 79. Phantasm 79. Hour of the Assassin 87. Survival Quest/The Survival Game 87. Phantasm 2 88. What's Up, Hideous Sun Demon 89. Journey to Spirit Island 90. Phantasm III 94. Phantasm IV 98, etc.

Myrtil, Odette (1898–1978)
French character actress in Hollywood.
Dodsworth 36. Kitty Foyle 40. Yankee Doodle Dandy 42. Forever and a Day 43. Devotion 46. Here Comes the Groom 50. Lady Possessed 52, many others.

N

Nabokov, Vladimir (1899–1977)
Russian novelist and poet. Born in St Petersburg, he studied at Cambridge University, then lived in Europe, moving to the United States in 1940. He became an American citizen in 1945 and, in the late 40s, was appointed professor of Russian literature at Cornell University. From the early 40s he began to write in English, and caused controversy by the publication of *Lolita* in the mid-50s, which later flared up again when it was filmed, first by Stanley KUBRICK and then by Adrian LYNE.
Autobiography: 1967, *Speak Memory: An Autobiography Revisited.*
Biography: 1967, *Nabokov: His Life in Art* by Andrew Field.
Lolita (AANw) 62. Laughter in the Dark (oa) 69. King, Queen, Knave (oa) 72. Despair (oa) 78. Lolita (oa) 97. The Luzhin Defence (oa) 00, etc.

Nader, George (1921–)
American leading man who after TV experience starred in many Universal action films of the 50s but has lately been less active.
Monsoon (debut) 52. Four Guns to the Border 54. The Second Greatest Sex 55. Away All Boats 56. Congo Crossing 56. Four Girls in Town 57. Joe Butterfly 57. Nowhere to Go (GB) 58. The Human Duplicators 65. The Million Eyes of Su-Muru 66. Beyond Atlantis 73, etc.
TV series: Ellery Queen 54. The Man and the Challenge 59. Shannon 61.

Naderi, Amir (1945–)
Iranian director and screenwriter. Born in Abadan, and orphaned at the age of five, he survived by shining shoes and similar jobs before finding work as a messenger in a Teheran film studio; he became a still photographer and an assistant director before turning director. In the 90s, he moved to live in the USA. He is best known for his semi-autobiographical *The Runner*.
Goodbye My Friend 71. Elegy 75. Marsiyeh 79. The Search 81. The Runner/Dawandeh 85. Water, Wind, Dust/Ab, Bad, Khak 85. Manhattan by Numbers 93, etc.

Nagase, Masatoshi
Japanese leading actor.
Mystery Train (US) 89. Autumn Moon (HK) 92. The Most Terrible Time of My Life/Waga Jinsei Saisku No Toki 94. Cold Fever (US/Den./Ger./Ice.) 95. The Stairway to the Distant Past 95. Gojoe 00, etc.

Nagel, Anne (1912–1966) (Anne Dolan)
American supporting actress, the heroine's friend in countless movies of the 40s. Born in Boston, she was on screen from the early 30s. Married actor Ross ALEXANDER.
I Loved You Wednesday 33. Stand Up and Cheer 34. Hot Money 36. The Case of the Stuttering Bishop 37. Hoosier Schoolboy 37. Call a Messenger 39. Black Friday 40. Man Made Monster 40. The Green Hornet 40. Never Give a Sucker an Even Break 41. The Mad Monster 42. The Secret Code 42. Women in Bondage 43. Spirit of West Point 47, etc.

Nagel, Conrad (1896–1970)
American leading man of the 20s who came to Hollywood after stage experience; latterly ran acting school. Born in Keokuk, Iowa, he was on stage from 1914, and began his film career in 1919. He was one of Louis B. MAYER's three dinner guests who first discussed the idea of forming an Academy of Motion Picture Arts and Sciences in January 1927. The second of his three wives was actress Lynn Merrick. His lovers included actress Dolores COSTELLO.
Little Women 19. Fighting Chance 20. Three Weeks 24. The Exquisite Sinner 26. Slightly Used 27. Quality Street 27. One Romantic Night 30. Bad Sister 31. East Lynne 31. Dangerous Corner 34. Navy Spy 37. I Want a Divorce 40. The Woman in Brown 48. All that Heaven Allows 55. Stranger in My Arms 58. The Man Who Understood Women 59, many others.

Nagy, Ivan (1938–)
Hungarian-born director working in America, mainly as a director of TV movies.
Bad Charleston Charlie 73. Money, Marbles and Chalk 73. Five Minutes of Freedom 73. Deadly Hero 76. Captain America II: Death Too Soon (TV) 79. A Gun in the House (TV) 81. Jane Doe (TV) 83, etc.

Naha, Ed
American screenwriter.
Troll 86. Dolls 86. Honey, I Shrunk the Kids (co-w) 89. Chud II: Bud the Chud 89. Matinee (co-w) 92. Omega Doom 96, etc.

Nail, Jimmy (1954–) (James Bradford)
Lean English actor, singer, writer and songwriter, best known for his role as the violent, unpredictable Oz in the TV series *Auf Wiedersehen, Pet.* Born in Newcastle, he ran his own construction firm and was a rock singer before becoming an actor. His recording of 'Ain't No Doubt' topped the singles hit parade in the early 90s.
Morons from Outer Space 85. Blott on the Landscape (TV) 85. Howling II: Your Sister Is a Werewolf (US) 85. Dream Demon 88. Crocodile Shoes (& w) (TV) 94. Evita 96, etc.
TV series: Auf Wiedersehen, Pet 84. Spender (& co-w) 90.

Nair, Mira (1957–)
Indian director, producer and screenwriter who began as a documentary film-maker.
Salaam Bombay! 88 (p, d). Mississippi Masala (p, wd) 91. The Perez Family 95. Kama Sutra 96, etc.

Naish, J. Carrol (1900–1973)
American character actor with stage experience, in films from 1930. Born in New York City, he worked in Europe after the First World War, including a period on stage in Paris, and on his return to Hollywood established himself as an actor capable of portraying many nationalities, including Italians, Mexicans, Chinese, and American Indians.
The Hatchet Man 32. Lives of a Bengal Lancer 35. Anthony Adverse 36. King of Alcatraz 38. Persons in Hiding 39. *Beau Geste* 39. Birth of the Blues 41. Blood and Sand 41. The Corsican Brothers 41. The Pied Piper 42. Dr Renault's Secret 42. Batman (serial) 43. Behind the Rising Sun 43. Sahara (AAN) 43. Gung Ho! 44. *A Medal for Benny* (AAN) 45. House of Frankenstein 45. The Southerner 45. Enter Arsène Lupin 45. The Beast with Five Fingers 46. Joan of Arc 48. Black Hand 49. Annie Get Your Gun 50. Across the Wide Missouri 51. Sitting Bull 54. Violent Saturday 54. New York Confidential 54. The Young Don't Cry 57. The Hanged Man 64. Blood of Frankenstein 70, many others.
TV series: Life With Lugi 52. The New Adventures of Charlie Chan 57. Guestward Ho! 60.

Naismith, Laurence (1908–1992) (Lawrence Johnson)
Amiable British character actor with wide stage experience. Born in Thames Ditton, Surrey, he was on stage from 1927 after working as a merchant seaman, and in films from 1947.
Trouble in the Air 47. A Piece of Cake 48. I Believe in You 51. The Beggar's Opera 52. Mogambo 53. Carrington VC 55. *Richard III* 56. Boy on a Dolphin 57. Tempest 58. A Night to Remember 58. Sink the Bismarck 60. The Singer Not the Song 61. Jason and the Argonauts 63. The Three Lives of Thomasina 63. Sky West and Crooked 65. The Scorpio Letters 67. The Long Duel 67. Fitzwilly 67. *Camelot* 67. The Valley of Gwangi 68. Eye of the Cat 69. Scrooge 70. Diamonds Are Forever 71. *The Amazing Mr Blunden* 72, etc.
TV series: *The Persuaders* 71.

Najimy, Kathy (1957–)
American actress in comic roles. Married actor Dan Finnerty.
Soapdish 91. Sister Act 92. Hocus Pocus 93. Sister Act 2: Back in the Habit 93. It's Pat 94. Jeffrey 95. Bride of Chucky 98, etc.
TV series: Veronica's Closet 97– . King of the Hill (voice) 97– .

Nakadai, Tatsuya (1932–)
Japanese leading actor who was memorable in Kurosawa's *Yojimbo* and gained fame in Masaki Kobayashi's trilogy *The Human Condition*, appearing in many of the director's subsequent films.
Seven Samurai 54. Untamed/Arakure 57. Conflagration/Enjo 58. The Key/Kagi 59. The Human Condition Part I: No Greater Love/Ningen no Joken I-II 59. The Human Condition Part II: The Road to Eternity/Ningen no Joken III-IV 59. When a Woman Ascends the Stairs/Onna ga Kaidan o Agaru Toki 60. Yojimbo 61. The Other Woman/Tsuma Toshite Onna Toshite 61. The Human Condition Part III: A Soldier's Prayer/ Ningen no Joken V-VI 61. The Inheritance/ Karamiai 62. Sanjuro 62. Harakiri 62. High and Low/Tengokku to Jigoku 63. Kwaidan 64. A Woman's Story/Onna no Rekishi 63. Samurai Rebellion/Joiuchi 67. Inn of Evil/Inochi Bo ni Furo 71. I Am a Cat/Wagahai wa Neko de Aru 75. Kagemusha 80. Ran 85. Return to the River Kwai 89. Basara: The Princess Goh 92. After the Rain/ Ame Agaru 99, etc.

Nakano, Desmond
American screenwriter.
Boulevard Nights 79. Body Rock 84. Black Moon Rising (co-w) 86. Last Exit to Brooklyn 90. American Me (co-w) 92. White Man's Burden (d) 95, etc.

Naldi, Nita (1899–1961) (Anita Donna Dooley)
Italian-American leading lady of the 20s, formerly in the Ziegfeld Follies.
Dr Jekyll and Mr Hyde 20. The Unfair Sex 22. Blood and Sand 22. The Ten Commandments 23. Cobra 25. A Sainted Devil 25. The Marriage Whirl 26. The Lady Who Lied 27, etc.

Namath, Joe (1943–)
American professional sportsman who made a few films.
■ Norwood 69. C. C. and Company 70. The Last Rebel 71. Avalanche Express 78. Marriage Is Alive and Well (TV) 80. Chattanooga Choo Choo 84.

Nance, Jack (1943–1996) (John Nance)
American character actor, from the stage; associated with the films of David LYNCH and best known for playing the lead in that director's cult film *Eraserhead.* Died after a fight in a doughnut shop.
Fools 70. Eraserhead 76. Hammett 82. Ghoulies 85. Blue Velvet 86. Barfly 87. The Blob 88. Colors 88. Wild at Heart 90. The Hot Spot 90. Love and a .45 94. Voodoo 95. The Secret Agent Club 96, etc.
TV series: Twin Peaks 90–91.

Napier, Alan (1903–1988) (Alan Napier-Clavering)
Dignified British character actor, in Hollywood from 1940; usually played butlers or noble lords. Born in Harborne, Birmingham, he studied at RADA and was on stage from 1924, moving to Hollywood in the 40s. He was best known for playing Batman's manservant Alfred in the 60s TV series and feature film.
In a Monastery Garden 31. Loyalties 32. For Valour 37. The Four Just Men 39. The Invisible Man Returns 40. Random Harvest 42. Ministry of Fear 43. Lost Angel 44. *The Uninvited* 44. Forever Amber 47. Tarzan's Magic Fountain 50. Julius Caesar 53. The Court Jester 55. Journey to the Centre of the Earth 59. Marnie 64. Batman 66, many others.
TV series: Don't Call Me Charlie 62–63. Batman 66–68.

Napier, Charles (1936–)
American character actor, often in the films of Jonathan Demme.
Cherry, Harry and Raquel 69. Caged Heat 74. Beyond the Valley of the Dolls 70. Super Vixens 74. Citizens Band 77. The Last Emperor 79. The Blues Brothers 80. Swing Shift 84. Rambo: First Blood II 85. Something Wild 86. Deep Space 88. Married to the Mob 88. Future Zone 90. The Grifters 90. Miami Blues 90. The Silence of the Lambs 91. Soldier's Fortune 91. Center of the Web 92. Skeeter 93. Philadelphia 93. Jury Duty 95. Original Gangstas 96. Riot 96. The Cable Guy 96. Steel 97. Austin Powers: International Man of Mystery 97. The Big Tease 99 etc.
❝ I keep waiting for Chuck Napier to become a really big movie actor, but it seems so far it's been slightly out of his reach … I think he's one of America's finest actors. – *Jonathan Demme*

Napier, Diana (1905–1982) (Molly Ellis)
English leading lady of the 30s. Born in Bath, Somerset, she began on stage and, after several bit parts in silent films, was given a five-year contract, at £20 a week, by Alexander KORDA, who chose her to fit a female stereotype that he described as 'a high-class bitch'. She retired in the mid-30s, making a brief return to the screen in the late 40s. Her second husband was opera singer Richard TAUBER.
The Rat 25. The Farmer's Wife 28. Strange Evidence 32. Wedding Rehearsal 33. The Private Life of Henry VIII 33. Catherine the Great 34. The Private Life of Don Juan 34. Royal Cavalcade 35. Mimi 35. Heart's Desire 35. Land without Music 36. Pagliacci 36. *I Was a Dancer* 48. Bait 50, etc.

Napier, Russell (1910–1975)
Australian-born actor, long in Britain. Appeared in numerous small parts, usually as officials; also played the chief inspector in many of the 3-reel 'Scotland Yard' series.
End of the River 47. The Time Machine (TV) 49. Black Orchid 53. The Stranger Came Home 54. Little Red Monkey 54. The Brain Machine 54. The Narrowing Circle 55. A Town Like Alice 56. The Shiralee 57. Robbery under Arms 57. A Night to Remember 58. Hell Is a City 59. Sink the Bismarck! 60. Blood Beast Terror 67. The Black Windmill 74, etc.

Napoleon, Art (1923–)
American director.
Man on the Prowl (& w) 57. Too Much Too Soon 58. Ride the Wild Surf (w only) 64. The Activist 69, etc.

Napoleon Bonaparte
has been impersonated on screen by Charles Boyer in *Marie Walewska/Conquest*, Esmé Percy in *Invitation to the Waltz*, Emile Drain in *Madame sans Gêne* and *Les Perles de la Couronne*, Rollo Lloyd in *Anthony Adverse*, Julien Bertheau in *Madame*, Marlon Brando in *Désirée*, Arnold Moss in *The Black Book*, Pierre Mondy in *Austerlitz*, Herbert Lom in several films including *The Young Mr Pitt* and *War and Peace*, Eli Wallach in *The Adventures of Gerard*, Rod Steiger in *Waterloo*, and Kenneth Haigh in *Eagle in a Cage*.
Abel Gance's 1925 film *Napoleon* (with Albert Dieudonne) is noted for the first use of a triptych screen corresponding very closely to Cinerama. It

was revived with international success in 1980, in a version painstakingly reassembled by Kevin Brownlow, who in 1983 published a book about it.

Narcejac, Thomas (1908–1998) (Pierre Ayraud)
French thriller writer and screenwriter, in collaboration with Pierre Boileau. Born in Rochefort-sur-mer, he studied philosophy and literature at the Sorbonne, and worked as a teacher. After writing on his own, in 1951, he began working with Boileau, who devised the plots, while he wrote the stories, which, with their macabre suspense, appealed to many directors.
Autobiography: 1986, *Tandem* (with Pierre Boileau).
The Fiends/Les Diaboliques (from Celle Qui N'était Plus 55. The She-Wolves (from Les Louves) (& w) 57. *Vertigo* (from D'entre les Morts) 58. *Eyes without a Face*/Les Yeux sans Visage 60. Faces in the Dark (GB) 60. Frantic 60. Murder at 45 RPM 60. Where the Truth Lies 61. Crime Does Not Pay/Le Crime Ne Paie Pas (co-w only) 62. Letters to an Unknown Lover (GB/Fr.) 85. Body Parts (US) 91. Diabolique (oa) (US) 96, etc.

Nardini, Tom (1945–)
American character actor.
Cat Ballou 65. Africa Texas Style 67. The Young Animals 68. Siege/Self Defense 82, etc.
TV series: Cowboy in Africa 67.

Nares, Owen (1888–1943) (O. N. Ramsay)
British matinée idol and silent screen star. Born in Maiden Erleigh, Berkshire, he was on the London stage from 1908 and in films from 1913.
Autobiography: 1925, *Myself and Some Others. Pure Egotism.*
Dandy Donovan 14. The Sorrows of Satan 17. God Bless the Red, White and Blue 18. Indian Love Lyrics 23. Young Lochinvar 23. Milestones 28. The Middle Watch 30. Sunshine Susie 31. The Impassive Footman 32. The Private Life of Don Juan 34. The Show Goes On 37. The Prime Minister 41, etc.
❝ For an actor whose chief charm was his complete 'ease' and naturalness on the stage, almost in the du Maurier tradition, it was quite extraordinary to realize, when one played with Owen, how much he relied on sheer mechanics. Every gesture, every move was planned beforehand, and adhered to rigidly. – *Jean Webster-Brough*

Narizzano, Silvio (1927–)
Canadian-born director, of Italian-American parents, in British TV in the 50s and films from the 60s. Born in Montreal, he was educated at Bishop's University, Quebec. He began as an actor in Ottawa before working in Canadian television and, later, in Britain.
■ Under Ten Flags (co-d) 60. Fanatic 65. *Georgy Girl* 66. Blue (US) 68. Loot 70. Redneck 72. The Sky is Falling 76. *Why Shoot the Teacher* 78. The Class of Miss MacMichael 78. *Staying On* (TV) 80. Choices 81.

Naruse, Mikio (1905–1969)
Prolific Japanese director from 1930 onwards. His films often depicted drab working-class life. He began as a prop-man before becoming a scriptwriter and director's assistant. At least half of his films have been lost, including most of his earliest work.
Koshiben Gambare 31. Nasanu Naka 32. Kimi to Wakarete 33. Otomo-gokoro Sannin Shimai 35. Hataraku Ikka 39. Shanghai Moon/Shanhai no Tsuki 41. Uta Andon 41. Ginza Gesho 51. Meshi 51. Lightning/Inazuma 52. Fufu 53. Bangiku 54. Nagareru 56. Untamed/Arakure 57. Anzukko 58. The Other Woman/Tsuma Toshite Onna Toshite 61. Yearning/Midareru 64. Two in the Shadow/Midaregumo 67, many others.
❝ He was the most difficult director I ever worked for. He never said a word. A real nihilist. – *Tatsuya Nakadai*

Naschy, Paul (1936–) (Jacinto Molina Alvarez)
Spanish leading actor, writer and occasional producer and director of horror movies. His most notable and oft-repeated role is as werewolf Waldemar Daninsky. Born in Bilbao, he was a weightlifter and an architect before entering films in the mid-60s. He sometimes uses the pseudonym Jack Moll for his screenwriting.
Frankenstein's Bloody Terror/Hell's Creatures/La Marca del Hombre Lobo (& w) 67. Dracula vs Frankenstein/El Hombre que Vivo de Ummo (& w) 69. The Werewolf vs the Vampire Woman/Shadow of the Werewolf/La Noche de Walpurgis (& co-w) 70. Fury of the Wolfman/La Furia del Hombre Lobo (& w) 71. Dr Jekyll and the Wolfman/De Jeckill y el Hombre Lobo (& w) 71. Dracula's Great Love/aka Dracula's Virgin Lovers/El Gran Amor del Conde Dracula (& co-w) 72. Vengeance of the Zombies/La Rebellión de las Muertas (& w) 72. Horror Rises from the Tomb/El Espanto Surge de la Tumba (& w) 72. The Rue Morgue Massacres/Hunchback of the Morgue/El Jorobado de la Morgue (& co-w) 73. The Mummy's Revenge/La Vengenzia de la Momia (& w) 73. House of Psychotic Women/The Blue Eyes of the Broken Doll/Los Ojos Azules de la Muñeca Rota (& w) 73. Curse of the Devil/El Retorno de Walpurgis (& w) 74. Exorcism/Exorcismo (& co-w) 74. Night of the Howling Beast/The Werewolf and the Yeti/La Maldición de la Bestia (& w) 75. People Who Own the Dark 75. Inquisition/Inquisición (& wd) 76. The Craving/El Retorno del Hombre Lobo (& wd) 80. Human Beasts/El Carnaval de la Bestias (& p, wd) 80. Monster Island 81. The Beast and the Magic Sword (& p, wd) 83. Aqui Huele Muerto 90, etc.

Nascimbene, Mario (1916–)
Italian composer.
OK Nero 51. The Barefoot Contessa 54. Alexander the Great 55. A Farewell to Arms 57. *The Vikings* 58. Room at the Top 58. Solomon and Sheba 59. Sons and Lovers 60. Barabbas 61. Jessica 62. One Million Years BC 66. Dr Faustus 67. When Dinosaurs Ruled the Earth 70. Creatures the World Forgot 71. Year One/Anno Uno 74. The Messiah 78, many others.

Nash, Clarence (1904–1985)
American voice performer, the inimitable sound of Donald Duck for 40 years.

Nash, Marilyn (c. 1924–)
American leading lady selected by Chaplin to play in *Monsieur Verdoux* 47. Married writer-producer Philip Yordan.
Unknown World 51.

Nash, Mary (1885–1976) (Mary Ryan)
American stage actress in occasional films. Born in Troy, New York, she studied at the American Academy of Dramatic Art and was on stage from 1904.
■ Uncertain Lady 34. College Scandal 35. Come and Get It 36. The King and the Chorus Girl 37. Easy Living 37. Heidi 37. Wells Fargo 37. The Little Princess 39. The Rains Came 39. Charlie Chan in Panama 40. Sailor's Lady 40. Gold Rush Maisie 40. *The Philadelphia Story* 40. Men of Boys Town 41. Calling Dr Gillespie 42. The Human Comedy 43. In the Meantime Darling 44. Cobra Woman 44. The Lady and the Monster 44. Yolanda and the Thief 45. Monsieur Beaucaire 46. Swell Guy 46. Till the Clouds Roll By 46.

Nathan, Robert (1894–1985)
American novelist and screenwriter. His seventh wife (1970-85) was actress Anna Lee.
One More Spring (oa) 35. The Clock/Under the Clock (co-w) 45. Wake Up and Dream (oa) 46. The Bishop's Wife (oa) 47. Portrait of Jennie (oa) 48. Pagan Love Song (co-w) 50, etc.

Nation, Terry (1930–1997)
Welsh screenwriter, best known as the creator of the Daleks, the tinpot power-crazed villains of the *Dr Who* TV series and films. Born in Cardiff, he began as a stand-up comedian and comedy scriptwriter. He also created the science fiction TV series *Survivors* 75–77, and *Blake's Seven* 78–81. Moved to work in Hollywood in the late 70s.
What a Whopper! (w) 61. Dr Who and the Daleks (oa) 65. Daleks: Invasion Earth 2150 AD (oa) 66. And Soon the Darkness (co-w) 70. The House in Nightmare Park (co-w, p) 73, etc.

Natwick, Grim (1890–1990) (Myron Natwick)
Cartoonist and animator who created Betty Boop while working for Max Fleischer in 1930. He later worked for Disney on *Snow White and the Seven Dwarfs* 37, and animated the Sorcerer's Apprentice sequence in *Fantasia* 40.

Natwick, Mildred (1905–1994)
American character actress, at her best in eccentric roles. Born in Baltimore, Maryland, and educated at Bryn Mawr, she was on stage from 1932. Her best role, which she played first on Broadway, was as the harassed mother Mrs Banks in *Barefoot in the Park*.
■ The Long Voyage Home 40. The Enchanted Cottage 45. Yolanda and the Thief 45. The Late George Apley 47. A Woman's Vengeance 48. Three Godfathers 48. The Kissing Bandit 48. She Wore a Yellow Ribbon 49. Cheaper by the Dozen 50. The Quiet Man 52. Against All Flags 52. *The Trouble with Harry* 55. *The Court Jester* 55. Teenage Rebel 56. Tammy and the Bachelor 57. *Barefoot in the Park* (AAN) 67. If It's Tuesday This Must Be Belgium 69. The Maltese Bippy 69. Do Not Fold Spindle or Mutilate (TV) 71. The Snoop Sisters (TV) 72. Daisy Miller 74. At Long Last Love 75. Kiss Me Goodbye 82. Dangerous Liaisons 88.

Naughton, Bill (1910–1992)
Irish novelist, dramatist and screenwriter, a former lorry driver.
Autobiography: 1988, *Saintly Billy: A Catholic Boyhood.*
Alfie (AAN) 66. The Family Way 66. Spring and Port Wine 70. Alfie Darling (oa) 75.

Naughton, Charlie (1887–1976)
Chubby Scottish slapstick comedian, a former painter and decorator. Born in Glasgow, he formed a double act with Jimmy Gold, and was a member of the Crazy Gang in the 30s.
Highland Fling 36. Wise Guys 37. O-Kay for Sound 37. Alf's Button Afloat 38. The Frozen Limits 39. Gasbags 40. Down Melody Lane 43. Life Is a Circus 58.

Naughton, David (1951–)
American leading actor. Brother of James Naughton.
Separate Ways 79. Midnight Madness 80. An American Werewolf in London 81. Hot Dog – the Movie! 83. Not for Publication 84. Getting Physical (TV) 84. Separate Vacations 86. The Boy in Blue 86. Kidnapped 87. Private Affairs 89. Overexposed 90. The Sleeping Car 90. Wild Cactus 92. Body Bags (TV) 93. Desert Steel 94. Beanstalk 94. Ice Cream Man 95. Mirror, Mirror 3: The Voyeur 96, etc.
TV series: Making It 79. At Ease 83. My Sister Sam 86–88.

Naughton, James (1945–)
American leading man, mostly on television.
The Paper Chase 74. The Bunker (TV) 80. A Stranger Is Watching 82. The Glass Menagerie 87. The Good Mother 88. Second Wind 90. Birds II: Land's End (TV) 94. The First Wives Club 96. First Kid 96, etc.
TV series: Faraday and Company 72. Planet of the Apes 74. Making the Grade 82. Trauma Centre 83.

Nava, Gregory (1949–)
American director and screenwriter.
The Confessions of Amans (wd) 76. The End of August (co-w) 82. El Norte (wd) (AAN) 84. A Time of Destiny (wd) 88. My Family/Mi Familia (co-w, d) 95. Selena (wd) 97. Why Do Fools Fall in Love 98, etc.

Navarro, Guillermo
Mexican cinematographer.
Cabeza de Vaca 90. Cronos 92. Desperado 95. Four Rooms (co-ph) 95. From Dusk till Dawn 96. The Long Kiss Goodnight 96. Spawn 97. Jackie Brown 97, etc.

Nazarro, Ray (1902–1986)
American director and screenwriter of second features. Born in Boston, he worked mainly for Columbia, later moving into TV and making films in Europe.
Song of the Prairie 45. Cowboy Blues 46. Last Days of Boot Hill 47. Six-Gun Law 48. Quick on the Trigger 49. The Tougher They Come 50. Al Jennings of Oklahoma 50. China Corsair 51. Bandits of Corsica 51. Cripple Creek 52. Kansas Pacific 53. The Lone Gun 54. Top Gun 55. The Hired Gun 57. Apache Territory 58. Dog Eat Dog (Ger./It.) 64. Arrivederci Cowboy (It.) 67, etc.

Nazimova, Alla (1879–1945) (Alla Nazimoff)
Russian-born stage actress who made a number of films in America. Born in Yalta, she studied at the Moscow Academy and joined the Moscow Art Theatre under Stanislavsky. After appearing on the Broadway stage in the early 1900s she decided to remain in the United States. She was in films from 1916; in the mid-20s she went back to the stage, returning to Hollywood for a few appearances in the 40s. Married Russian actor Paul Orleneff and director Charles Bryant, who directed her in some of her early silents.
Biography: 1997, *Nazimova* by Gavin Lambert.
■ War Brides 16. Revelation 18. Toys of Fate 18. An Eye for an Eye 19. The Red Lantern 19. The Brat 19. Stronger than Death 20. Heart of a Child 20. Madame Peacock 20. Billions 20. Camille 21. A Doll's House 22. *Salome* 23. Madonna of the Streets 24. The Redeeming Sin 24. My Son 25. *Escape* 40. Blood and Sand 41. The Bridge of San Luis Rey 44. In Our Time 44. Since You Went Away 45.

Nazzari, Amedeo (1907–1979) (Salvatore Amedeo Buffa)
Italian leading actor, usually in dashing roles. Born in Cagliari, he was Italy's biggest male star in the late 30s, though his popularity had waned by the late 50s; he played character parts thereafter.
Ginevra degli Almieri 35. Cavalleria 36. Luciano Serra Pilota 38. Centomila Dollari 40. Scarpe Grosse 40. Caravaggio 41. L'Ultimo Ballo 41. Fedora 42. Harlem 43. Il Bandito 46. Malacarne 47. Don Juan de Serrallonga 48. Il Brigante Musolino 50. Bellissima 51. Il Tradimento 51. Altri Tempi 52. Il Brigante di Tacca del Lupo 52. We Are All Murderers/Nous Sommes Tous des Assassins 52. Angelo Bianco 55. Cabiria/Le Notti di Cabiria 57. Anna di Brooklyn 58. Labyrinth 59. The Naked Maja (US/It.) 59. The Best of Enemies (GB/It.) 62. Il Gaucho 64. The Column/Columna 68. The Sicilian Clan/Le Clan des Siciliens (Fr.) 69. The Valachi Papers/Cosa Nostra 72. A Matter of Time (US/GB/It.) 76, many others.

Neagle, Dame Anna (1904–1986) (Florence Marjorie Robertson)
British leading lady, a former chorus dancer who, in partnership with producer and, later, her husband Herbert Wilcox, built up a formidable film gallery of historical heroines. Born in Forest Gate, London, she was on stage from 1925, and also worked in cabaret as a dancer in the late 20s. Her success dated from the film of *Goodnight Vienna*, starring Jack Buchanan. After Evelyn Laye turned down the role opposite Buchanan, Wilcox went to call on him, saw Neagle performing with him on stage, and signed her for the film. When film roles grew hard to find, she returned successfully to the stage. She was made a Dame of the British Empire in 1969.
Autobiography: 1949, *It's Been Fun*. 1974, *There's Always Tomorrow*.
Produced three Frankie Vaughan films 58–61; returned to stage.
■ Those Who Love (as Marjorie Robertson) 29. The School for Scandal 30. Should a Doctor Tell? 30. The Chinese Bungalow 31. Goodnight Vienna 32. The Flag Lieutenant 32. The Little Damozel 33. *Bitter Sweet* 33. The Queen's Affair 33. *Nell Gwyn* 34. Peg of Old Drury 35. Limelight 36. The Three Maxims 36. London Melody 37. *Victoria the Great* 37. Sixty Glorious Years 38. *Nurse Edith Cavell* 39. Irene (US) 40. No No Nanette (US) 40. Sunny (US) 41. They Flew Alone (as Amy Johnson) 42. Forever and a Day 43. Yellow Canary 43. The Volunteer 43. I Live in Grosvenor Square 45. *Piccadilly Incident* 46. The Courtneys of Curzon Street 47. Royal Wedding (voice) 47. *Spring in Park Lane* 48. Elizabeth of Ladymead 49. Maytime in Mayfair 49. *Odette* 50. *The Lady with a Lamp* 51. Derby Day 52. Lilacs in the Spring 55. King's Rhapsody 56. My Teenage Daughter 56. No Time for Tears 57. The Man Who Wouldn't Talk 58. The Lady is a Square 58.
✪ For providing her faithful British admirers with the heroines they wanted her to be; and for her eagerness to please. *Victoria the Great.*
❝ I have seen few things more attractive than Miss Neagle in breeches. – *Graham Greene*
She moves rigidly on to the set, as if wheels were concealed under the stately skirt: she says her piece with flat dignity and trolleys out again, rather like a mechanical marvel from the World's Fair. – *Graham Greene on her performance as Edith Cavell*
I once joked that had she played Blance Dubois, the vehicle would have been re-titled *A Streetcar Named Respectability*. – *Hermione Gingold*

Neal, Patricia (1926–)
American leading actress who handled some interesting roles before illness caused her semi-retirement. Born in Packard, Kentucky, she studied drama at Northwestern University and first worked

as a model, making her Broadway debut in the mid-40s. A massive stroke in 1965 left her unable to speak or walk for a time; after three years of therapy, she resumed her career in *The Subject Was Roses*. She was married to writer Roald DAHL (1953–83) and romantically linked with actor Gary COOPER. She was played by Glenda JACKSON in the TV biopic *The Patricia Neal Story* 81.

Autobiography: *As I Am*.

■ John Loves Mary 49. *The Fountainhead* 49. It's a Great Feeling 49. *The Hasty Heart* (GB) 50. Bright Leaf 50. Three Secrets 50. The Breaking Point 50. Operation Pacific 51. Raton Pass 51. Diplomatic Courier 51. The Day the Earth Stood Still 51. Weekend with Father 51. Washington Story 52. Something for the Birds 52. Stranger from Venus (GB) 54. *A Face in the Crowd* 57. Breakfast at Tiffany's 61. *Hud* (AA, BFA) 63. Psyche 59 (GB) 64. In Harm's Way (BFA) 64. The Subject was Roses (AAN) 68. The Homecoming (TV) 71. The Night Digger 71. Baxter 72. Happy Mother's Day Love George 73. Run Stranger Run (TV) 74. Things in Their Season (TV) 75. Eric (TV) 77. Tail Gunner Joe (TV) 77. The Bastard (TV) 78. The Passage 79. All Quiet on the Western Front (TV) 80. Ghost Story 81. Glitter (TV) 84. Love Leads the Way (TV) 85. An Unremarkable Life 89. Caroline? 90. Heidi (TV) 93. A Mother's Right: The Elizabeth Morgan Story (TV) 93. Cookie's Fortune 99.

❝ I was one of those people born to be an actress. I remember being about 11 and going to church to give a monologue, and I said to myself, 'This is what I want to do.' – *P.N.*

Neal, Tom (1914–1972)
American leading man, mainly in second features; former athlete. Born in Evanston, Illinois, he studied at Northwestern University and was on stage from the mid-30s. He quit to take a law degree at Harvard and began making films in 1938. His career came to a spectacular end after he beat up actor Franchot TONE in a quarrel over actress Barbara Peyton, who then married Tone, divorced him within two months and returned to marry Neal. No studio would employ him thereafter and he worked as a landscape gardener. In 1965, he was charged with shooting his third wife and spent seven years in jail for her involuntary manslaughter. Shortly after his release he died from heart failure. His son, Tom Neal, Jnr (1957–) made his screen debut in 1990 in a remake of his father's *Detour*.

Four Girls in White 38. Within the Law 39. Another Thin Man 39. Jungle Girl 41. Bowery at Midnight 42. There's Something About a Soldier 43. She Has What It Takes 43. Detour 45. First Yank into Tokyo 45. Club Havana 46. The Brute Man 46. Bruce Gentry – Daredevil of the Skies 49. The Great Jesse James Raid 53, many others.

Neame, Ronald (1911–)
Outstanding British cinematographer who became a rather disappointing director. Born in London, the son of silent film actress Ivy Close, he began as an assistant cameraman on Hitchcock's *Blackmail* 29. In the 40s he became a producer at Cineguild, the independent company set up by Noël COWARD, David LEAN and Anthony HAVELOCK-ALLAN, and was cinematographer on some of Lean's best films.

SELECTED FILMS AS CINEMATOGRAPHER: Drake of England 34. The Gaunt Stranger 37. The Crimes of Stephen Hawke 39. Major Barbara 40. In Which We Serve 42. Blithe Spirit 45.

■ AS DIRECTOR: Take My Life 47. The Golden Salamander 50. *The Card* (& p) 52. The Million Pound Note 53. The Man Who Never Was 56. The Seventh Sin 57. Windom's Way 58. The Horse's Mouth 59. *Tunes of Glory* 60. Escape from Zahrain 61. I Could Go On Singing 62. The Chalk Garden 64. Mister Moses 65. A Man Could Get Killed (co-d) 66. Gambit 66. The Prime of Miss Jean Brodie 68. Scrooge 70. The Poseidon Adventure 72. The Odessa File 75. Meteor 79. Hopscotch 80. First Monday in October 81. Foreign Body 86.

Nebenzal, Seymour (1899–1961)
Distinguished German producer who had a disappointing career after going to Hollywood in the late 30s.

Westfront 30. M 31. Kameradschaft 32. The Testament of Dr Mabuse 33. Mayerling 36. We Who are Young 40. Summer Storm 44. Whistle Stop 46. Heaven Only Knows 47. Siren of Atlantis 48. M (remake) 51, etc.

Nedell, Bernard (1897–1972)
American character actor, often in villainous roles. Born in New York City, to parents in the theatre, and educated at Western Reserve University, Cleveland, he was on stage as a child. He trained as a violinist before deciding to become an actor, beginning in repertory and starting his film career as an extra. From the mid-20s to the late 30s he was on the London stage and appeared in British films. Married actress Olive Blakeney.

The Serpent 16. The Return of the Rat (GB) 29. Shadows (GB) 31. Lazybones (GB) 35. The Man Who could Work Miracles (GB) 36. Mr Moto's Gamble 38. Angels Wash Their Faces 39. Strange Cargo 40. The Desperadoes 43. One Body Too Many 44. Monsieur Verdoux 47. The Loves of Carmen 48. Heller in Pink Tights 60. Hickey and Boggs 72, many others.

Needham, Hal (1931–)
American director and screenwriter, associated with the films of Burt REYNOLDS. Born in Memphis, Tennessee, he worked in fairgrounds before going to Hollywood in the mid-50s as a stuntman and second-unit director. There he became friendly with Reynolds and directed the actor in movies that concentrated on high-spirited car chases.

■ *Smokey and the Bandit* 77. Hooper 78. The Villain 79. Death Car on the Freeway (TV) 79. Smokey and the Bandit II 80. The Cannonball Run 80. Stunts (TV) 81. Megaforce 82. Stroker Ace 83. Cannonball Run II 83. RAD 86. Body Slam 87.

Neeson, Liam (1952–)
Tall Irish leading actor, often in tough-guy roles. Born in Ballymena, Northern Ireland, he began acting on stage in 1976 and later joined the Abbey Theatre in Dublin, where he was spotted by director John BOORMAN, who cast him as Sir Gawain in *Excalibur*. Married actress Natasha RICHARDSON in 1994.

His best performance so far has been as Oskar Schindler in *Schindler's List*.

Excalibur 81. The Bounty 84. Lamb 86. Duet for One 86. The Mission 86. A Prayer for the Dying 87. Suspect 87. The Dead Pool 88. The Good Mother 88. High Spirits 88. Satisfaction 88. Next of Kin 89. The Big Man 90. Darkman 90. Under Suspicion 91. Husbands and Wives 92. Leap of Faith 92. Shining Through 92. Ruby Cairo 92. Ethan Frome 93. *Schindler's List* (AAN) 93. Nell 94. Rob Roy 95. Before and After 96. Michael Collins 96. Les Misérables 98. Star Wars Episode l: The Phantom Menace 99. The Haunting 99. Gun Shy 00, etc.

Neff, Hildegard (1925–) (Hildegard Knef)
German leading actress and cabaret artiste who spent some time in Hollywood. Born in Ulm, she studied art in Berlin and became a cartoonist for UFA before beginning her acting career in the theatre. After appearing in several German films, she was brought to Hollywood in the late 40s by David SELZNICK, but returned to Germany without making a film. In the early 50s she made a few American movies before returning to act in Europe. In the 60s she began a new career as a singer.

Autobiography: 1971, *The Gift Horse*. 1975, *The Verdict*.

The Murderers Are amongst Us 46. *Film without Title* 47. The Sinner 50. Decision before Dawn 51. *The Snows of Kilimanjaro* 52. Diplomatic Courier 52. Henriette 52. The Man Between 53. The Girl from Hamburg 57. And So to Bed 63. Landru 63. Mozambique 65. The Lost Continent (GB) 68. Fedora 78. Witchery 88, etc.

Negri, Pola (1897–1987) (Appolonia Chalupek)
Polish-born leading lady with experience on German stage and screen; went to Hollywood in the 20s and was popular until sound came in. Born in Janowa, she worked as a dancer and violinist before beginning on stage in Warsaw in 1913. After making films for director Ernst LUBITSCH in Germany, she went to the US in the early 20s. Married three times; her lovers included Charlie CHAPLIN and Rudolph VALENTINO, whose funeral she attended dressed in black, accompanied by a nurse and a doctor, all in white. In the 30s she moved back to Europe, made films in England, and was later allegedly romantically linked with Adolf Hitler. From the early 40s, she settled in the United States.

Autobiography: 1970, *Memoirs of a Star*.

Die Bestie 15. Madame du Barry 18. The Flame 20. Bella Donna (US) 23. *Forbidden Paradise* 24. Hotel Imperial 26. Three Sinners 28. A Woman Commands 31. Madame Bovary 35. Hi Diddle Diddle 43. The Moonspinners 64, etc.

Negulesco, Jean (1900–1993)
Rumanian-born director, in US from 1927. Born in Craiova and educated at Lyceul Carol University, he was first an artist and stage director. He went to America in the mid-20s and began to work in Hollywood as a technical director, assistant producer and second-unit director.

Autobiography: 1984, *Things I Did … and Things I Think I Did*.

■ Kiss and Make Up 34. Singapore Woman 41. *The Mask of Dimitrios* 44. The Conspirators 44. Three Strangers 46. Nobody Lives Forever 46. *Humoresque* 46. Deep Valley 47. *Roadhouse* 48. *Johnny Belinda* (AAN) 48. Britannia Mews 49. Under My Skin 50. *Three Came Home* 50. *The Mudlark* 51. Take Care of My Little Girl 51. Phone Call from a Stranger 52. Lydia Bailey 52. Lure of the Wilderness 52. Full House (part) 52. Scandal at Scourie 53. Titanic 53. *How to Marry a Millionaire* 53. *Three Coins in the Fountain* 54. *Woman's World* 54. Daddy Longlegs 55. The Rains of Ranchipur 55. Boy on a Dolphin 57. A Certain Smile 58. The Gift of Love 58. Count Your Blessings 59. The Best of Everything 59. Jessica 62. The Pleasure Seekers 65. The Invincible Six 68. Hello Goodbye 70. The Heroes 79.

❝ A director I had not expected to praise is Jean Negulesco, who has always reminded me of Michael Curtiz on toast. Mr Curtiz, in turn, has always seemed like Franz Murnau under onions. – *James Agee*

He had been an artist back in Rumania, and he had an artist's eye for excellent shots, but as far as people went he was hopeless. – *Paul Henreid*

Neil, Hildegarde (1939–)
South African leading lady.

The Man Who Haunted Himself 70. Antony and Cleopatra 71. England Made Me 72. A Touch of Class 73. The Legacy 78. The Mirror Crack'd 80. Seaview Knights 94, etc.

TV series: Diamonds 80.

Neilan, Marshall 'Mickey' (1891–1958)
Leading American director of silents who had a meteoric rise in the 20s. Born in San Bernardino, California, he acted from childhood and began in films after becoming chauffeur to D. W. GRIFFITH. He became a leading actor and occasional writer of silents, but from 1916 concentrated on directing. He was frequently Mary PICKFORD's leading man and directed some of her best films, but their collaboration came to an end in 1929 when she hired him to direct her in *Forever Yours*, and abandoned the film when it was two-thirds made. From the late 20s, his efficacy began to suffer as his alcoholism interfered with his directing; he was virtually unemployable by the late 30s. He later worked as a taxi driver and an extra, and in the mid-40s was hired as a writer by Twentieth Century-Fox. He left instructions that, on his death, no one should accompany his body to the cemetery; instead, 15 of his closest friends held a wake at a Hollywood hotel, where, on the chair he was accustomed to sit in, was a sign saying 'Reserved for Mickey Neilan' and, beside it, an empty glass and an open bottle of beer. Died of cancer. His second wife was actress Blanche SWEET (1922–29).

AS ACTOR: The Reward of Valor 12. A Busy Day in the Jungle 13. The Wall of Money (& w) 13. The Tattered Duke 14. Rags 15. A Girl of Yesterday 15. Madam Butterfly 15. The House of Discord 16. Calamity Anne 16. Daddy Long Legs 19. Broadway Gold 23. Souls for Sale 23. A Face in the Crowd 57, many others.

❝ Those were the days … We had fun, loved to go to the studio, and hated to go home. Today they hate to go to the studio, they have no laughs and are tickled to duck home. – *M.N., on his deathbed, to Mary Pickford*

Mickey was one of the most delightful, aggravating, gifted and charming human beings I have ever known. There were times when I could cheerfully have throttled him – especially at his frequent failures to make an appearance on the set until after luncheon, keeping a large company waiting at considerable expense. – *Mary Pickford*

Neill, Noel (1920–)
American actress, a former dancer, best known for playing Lois Lane in the 50s TV series *The Adventures of Superman*, after which she retired. She made a brief appearance as Lois Lane's mother in the *Superman* movie in 1978.

Henry Aldrich for President 41. Henry and Dizzy 42. Let's Face It 43. The Big Clock 47. Are You With It? 48. The Stork Club 48. Superman (serial) 48. The Adventures of Frank and Jesse James (serial) 48. Atom Man vs Superman (serial) 50. The James Brothers of Missouri (serial) 50, etc.

TV series: The Adventures of Superman 53–57.

Neill, Roy William (1890–1946) (Roland de Gostrie)
Irish-born director, long in Hollywood; never rose above low-budget thrillers but often did them well.

Love Letters 17. Good References 21. Toilers of the Sea 23. The Good Bad Girl 31. The Black Room 34. The Good Old Days (GB) 35. Dr Syn (GB) 37. Eyes of the Underworld 41. *Frankenstein Meets the Wolf Man* 43. Gypsy Wildcat 44. Black Angel 46, etc.; also produced and directed most of the *Sherlock Holmes* series starring Basil Rathbone 42–46.

Neill, Sam (1947–)
British leading actor in international films. Born in Northern Ireland, he grew up in New Zealand and was educated at the University of Canterbury.

Sleeping Dogs 77. My Brilliant Career 79. Attack Force Z 81. The Final Conflict 81. Possession 81. Enigma 82. Ivanhoe (TV) 82. From a Far Country (TV) 82. The Blood of Others (TV) 84. Robbery Under Arms 85. Plenty 85. For Love Alone 86. The Good Wife 87. Evil Angels 88. A Cry in the Dark 88. Dead Calm 88. The Hunt for Red October 90. Death in Brunswick 90. Until the End of the World/Bis ans Ende der Welt 91. Memoirs of an Invisible Man 92. Family Pictures (TV) 93. *The Piano* 93. Jurassic Park 93. Sirens 94. Country Life 94. Rudyard Kipling's Jungle Book 94. In the Mouth of Madness 95. Restoration (as Charles II) 96. Children of the Revolution 96. In Cold Blood (TV) 96. Forgotten Silver 96. Show White: A Tale of Terror 96. Revengers' Comedies 97. Event Horizon 97. The Horse Whisperer 97. Victory 98. Merlin (TV) 98. Bicentennial Man 99., etc.

TV series: Reilly Ace of Spies 83.

Neilson, James (1909–1979)
American director, former war photographer, who worked mostly for Walt Disney.

■ The Blackwell Story (TV) 57. Night Passage 57. The Country Husband (TV) 58. Moon Pilot 62. Bon Voyage 62. Summer Magic 63. Dr Syn 63. The Moon Spinners 63. Return of the Gunfighter (TV) 66. The Adventures of Bullwhip Griffin 67. The Gentle Giant 67. Where Angels Go 68. The First Time 69. Flare Up 69. Tom Sawyer (TV) 75.

Nell Gwyn
Charles II's orange-seller has appeared briefly in many films, but the two devoted to her story were both made in Britain by Herbert Wilcox: in 1927 with Dorothy Gish and in 1934 with Anna Neagle. Both caused censorship problems, the latter because of the lady's cleavage.

Nelligan, Kate (1951–)
Canadian actress first in Britain, now in Hollywood.

The Romantic Englishwoman 75. The Count of Monte Cristo (TV) 78. Dracula 79. Eye of the Needle 80. Without a Trace 83. Bethune: The Making of a Hero 84. Eleni 85. Kojak: The Price of Justice (TV) 87. Control (TV) 87. Il Giorno Prima 87. Love and Hate: A Marriage Made in Hell (TV) 90. The White Room 90. Frankie & Johnny 91. The Prince of Tides (AAN) 91. Shadows and Fog 92. Fatal Instinct 93. Spoils of War (TV) 94. Wolf 94. How to Make an American Quilt 95. Up Close and Personal 96. Romeo and Juliet 96. Calm at Sunset (TV) 96. US Marshals 98. Boy Meets Girl 98, etc.

Nelson, Barry (1920–) (Robert Neilson)
Stocky American leading man who makes films between stage shows.

China Caravan 42. A Guy Named Joe 43. Winged Victory 44. The Beginning of the End 45. The Man with My Face 51. The First Travelling Saleslady 56. Mary Mary 63. The Borgia Stick (TV) 68. Airport 69. Pete 'n' Tillie 72. The Shining 80, many others.

TV series: My Favorite Husband 53–54. Hudson's Bay 59.

Nelson, Billy (1904–1979)
Diminutive English music-hall comedian and character actor, who began in films as one of Duggie Wakefield's knockabout stooges; moved to the United States in the early 40s.
I'll Be Suing You 34. Look Up and Laugh 35. The Penny Pool 37. Calling All Crooks 38. I Live on Danger (US) 42. Wrecking Crew (US) 42. False Faces (US) 43. Minesweeper (US) 43. Hers to Hold (US) 43. Gambler's Choice (US) 44. Waterfront (US) 44. High-Powered (US) 45, etc.

Nelson, Craig T. (1946–)
Brawny American leading man.
And Justice for All 79. The Formula 80. Private Benjamin 80. Stir Crazy 80. Poltergeist 82. The Chicago Story (TV) 82. The Osterman Weekend 83. Silkwood 83. The Killing Fields 84. Call to Glory (TV) 84. Poltergeist II 86. Action Jackson 88. Troop Beverly Hills 89. Turner & Hooch 89. Me and Him 89. The Josephine Baker Story (TV) 91. The Fire Next Time (TV) 93. Probable Cause 95. I'm Not Rappaport 96. If These Walls Could Talk (TV) 96. Ghosts of Mississippi 96. The Devil's Advocate 97, etc.
TV series: Air Force 84. Coach 89–94. The District 00- .

Nelson, Ed (1928–)
American actor who played gangsters, brothers-in-law and boyfriends in innumerable 50s second features, then went into TV and found himself a secure niche as Dr Rossi in *Peyton Place* 64–68, and in *The Silent Force* 70.
Midway 76. Shining Star 77. Police Academy 3 85. The Boneyard 91. Cries of Silence 93, etc.

Nelson, Gary (1916–)
American director.
The Girl on the Late Late Show (TV) 74. Medical Story (TV) 75. Panache (TV) 76. *Washington: Behind Closed Doors* (TV) 77. To Kill a Cop (TV) 78. The Black Hole 79. Jimmy the Kid 82. Enigma 82. Allan Quatermain and the Lost City of Gold 86. Shooter (TV) 88. Get Smart, Again! (TV) 89. Ray Alexander: A Taste for Justice (TV) 94. Melanie Darrow (TV) 97, etc.

Nelson, Gene (1920–1996) (Leander Berg)
American actor-dancer, on stage from 1938, films from mid-40s. He began directing, mainly for TV, from the 60s.
I Wonder Who's Kissing Her Now 47. Gentleman's Agreement 48. The Daughter of Rosie O'Grady 50. Tea for Two 51. Lullaby of Broadway 52. She's Working Her Way through College 52. So This Is Paris 55. Oklahoma 55. 20,000 Eyes 62. The Purple Hills 63, etc.
AS DIRECTOR: Hand of Death 62. Hootenanny Hoot 63. Kissin' Cousins 64. Your Cheatin' Heart 64. Harum Scarum 65. The Cool Ones 67. Wake Me When the War Is Over (TV) 69. The Letters (TV) 73. The Baron and the Kid (TV) 84, etc.
TV series (as director): *Washington behind Closed Doors* 77.

Nelson, Lord Horatio (1758–1805)
the hero of Trafalgar, was portrayed in *Nelson* 19 by Donald Calthrop; in *Nelson* 26 by Cedric Hardwicke; in *The Divine Lady* 29 by Victor Varconi; in *Lady Hamilton* 42 by Laurence Olivier; in *Lady Hamilton* (Ger.) 68 by Richard Johnson; and in *Bequest to the Nation* 73 by Peter Finch.

Nelson, Judd (1959–)
American actor.
Making the Grade 84. The Breakfast Club 85. Fandango 85. St Elmo's Fire 85. Blue City 86. Transformers – the Movie 86. Dear America 87. From the Hip 87. Never on Tuesday 89. Relentless 89. Far Out Man 90. The Dark Backward 91. New Jack City 91. Primary Motive 92. Every Breath 93. Blackwater Trail 95. Steel 97, etc.
TV series: Suddenly Susan 96-99.

Nelson, Lori (1933–)
American light leading lady of the 50s.
Ma and Pa Kettle at the Fair 52. Bend of the River 52. Walking My Baby Back Home 53. Destry 55. Mohawk 56. Hot Rod Girl 56. The Day the World Ended 56. Untamed Youth 57, etc.
TV series: How to Marry a Millionaire 58.

Nelson, Oliver (1932–1975)
American composer, arranger, jazz saxophonist, and bandleader. Died of a heart attack.
Death of a Gunfighter 67. Skullduggery 70. Zigzag 70. Last Tango in Paris 73. Inside Job 73.

Nelson, Ozzie (1906–1975)
American bandleader whose genial, diffident personality became familiar in long-running domestic comedy series on TV.
Sweetheart of the Campus 41. Hi Good Lookin' 44. People are Funny 45. Here Come the Nelsons 52. Love and Kisses (& wpd) 65. The Impossible Years 68, etc.
TV series: *The Adventures of Ozzie and Harriet* 52–65. Ozzie's Girls 73.

Nelson, Ralph (1916–1987)
American director.
■ Requiem for a Heavyweight 62. *Lilies of the Field* 63. Soldier in the Rain 64. Fate is the Hunter 64. Father Goose 64. Once a Thief 65. Duel at Diablo 66. Counterpoint 67. Charly 68. Tick Tick Tick 70. Soldier Blue 70. Flight of the Doves 71. The Wrath of God 72. The Wilby Conspiracy 75. Embryo 76. A Hero Ain't Nothing But a Sandwich 77. Because He's My Friend (Aust.) 78. Lady of the House (TV) 78. You Can't Go Home Again (TV) 79. Christmas Lilies of the Field (TV) 79.

Nelson, Rick (1940–1985)
American singer and light actor, son of bandleader Ozzie Nelson and his wife Harriet (formerly Harriet Hilliard) with whom he appeared in the long-running TV series *The Adventures of Ozzie and Harriet* 52–65. He died in a plane crash.
Biography: 1992, *Teenage Idol, Travelin' Man* by Philip Bashe.
Here Come the Nelsons 52. Rio Bravo 59. The Wackiest Ship in the Army 60. Love and Kisses 65. The Over the Hill Gang (TV) 69, etc.

Nelson, Ruth (1905–1992)
American character actress, usually seen as sympathetic mother. She was married to actor-director John Cromwell.
Abe Lincoln in Illinois 40. Humoresque 46. The Late Show 77. 3 Women 77. The Haunting Passion (TV) 83. Awakenings 90, etc.

Nelson, Tim Blake (1965–)
American actor, screenwriter and director.
AS DIRECTOR: Eye of God (&w) 97. O 00, etc.
AS ACTOR: This Is My Life 92. Amateur 94. Joe's Apartment 96. Donnie Brasco 97. The Thin Red Line 98. Hamlet 00. O Brother, Where Art Thou? 00, etc.

Nelson, Willie (1933–)
American singer and character actor.
The Electric Horseman 79. Honeysuckle Rose 80. Thief 81. Barbarosa 81. Hells Angels Forever 83. Red Headed Stranger 84. Songwriter 85. Amazons 87. Once upon a Texas Train/Texas Guns (TV) 88. Pair of Aces (TV) 90. Wild Texas Wind 91. Starlight 96. Wag the Dog 97. Gone Fishin' 97. Half-Baked 97, etc.

Nemec, Jan (1936–)
Czech director.
Diamonds of the Night 64. The Party and the Guests 66. The Martyrs of Love 67. The Unbearable Lightness of Being (a) 88. In the Light of the King's Love (d) 91, etc.

Nero, Franco (1941–) (F. Spartanero)
Italian leading man in international films. He has a son by actress Vanessa Redgrave.
The Tramplers 66. The Bible 66. *Camelot* 67. The Day of the Owl 68. A Quiet Place in the Country 68. Tristana 70. The Virgin and the Gypsy 70. The Battle of Neretva 70. Pope Joan 72. The Monk 72. White Fang 74. Challenge to White Fang 75. Force Ten from Navarone 78. The Man with Bogart's Face 80. The Salamander 80. Enter the Ninja 81. The Last Days of Pompeii (TV) 84. Ten Days that Shook the World 84. Garibaldi 86. The Girl 86. Kamikaze 87. Silent Night 88. Die Hard 2 90. Di Ceria dell'Untore/The Plague Sower 92. Jonathan of the Bears 94. The King and Me 95. The Innocent Sleep 95. Painted Lady (TV) 97. David 97. Talk of Angels (US) 98, etc.

Nervig, Conrad A. (1895–)
American editor.
Bardelys the Magnificent 26. The Divine Woman 28. The Guardsman 31. Eskimo (AA) 34. A Tale of Two Cities 36. The Crowd Roars 38. Northwest Passage 40. The Human Comedy 43. High Barbaree 47. Side Street 49. King Solomon's Mines (AA) 50. The Bad and the Beautiful 52. Gypsy Colt 54, many others.

Nervo, Jimmy (1890–1975) (James Holloway)
Short, stocky English comedian and acrobat. A member of a circus family, he was a high-wire performer from childhood as one of the Four Holloways, then worked for Fred Karno, teaming up with Teddy Knox in a comedy act in 1919 and becoming part of the Crazy Gang in the 30s. The pair worked together for 44 years.
■ Nervo and Knox (short) 26. It's in the Bag 36. Skylarks 36. O-Kay for Sound 37. Alf's Button Afloat 38. Cavalcade of the Stars (short) 38. The Frozen Limits 39. Gasbags 40. Life Is a Circus 58.

Nesbit, Evelyn (1886–1967)
Notorious American beauty involved in a murder case of 1912; portrayed by Joan Collins in *The Girl in the Red Velvet Swing* and by Elizabeth McGivern in *Ragtime*.
■ Threads of Destiny 14. Redemption 17. The Hidden Woman 22.

Nesbitt, Cathleen (1888–1982)
British character actress, on stage from 1910; very occasional films, but active on stage and television into her nineties. Married actor Cecil Ramage.
Autobiography: 1973, *A Little Love and Good Companions*.
The Case of the Frightened Lady 32. The Passing of the Third Floor Back 36. Fanny by Gaslight 43. Nicholas Nickleby 47. Three Coins in the Fountain 54. Désirée 54. *An Affair to Remember* 57. Promise Her Anything 66. The Trygon Factor 67. Staircase 69. Villain 71. Family Plot 76. Julia 77, etc.
TV series: *The Farmer's Daughter* 65.

Nesbitt, Derren (c. 1932–)
British character actor, usually a smiling villain.
The Man in the Back Seat 60. *Victim* 62. Strongroom 62. *The Naked Runner* 67. Nobody Runs Forever 68. Where Eagles Dare 68. Innocent Bystanders 72. Ooh You Are Awful 72. The Amorous Milkman (wd) 74. Bullseye! 91. Double X 92, etc.

Nesbitt, James (1966–)
British actor, born in Coleraine, Northern Ireland.
Welcome to Sarajevo 97. Resurrection Man 98. Waking Ned 98, etc.

Nesbitt, John (1911–1960)
American producer of MGM's long-running *Passing Parade* series of informational one-reelers.

Nesmith, Michael (1942–)
American guitarist and songwriter who was a member of The Monkees pop group in the 60s. He became an influential director of rock videos and a producer of independent movies in the 70s and 80s.
Head 68. Elephant Parts (& wd) 81. An Evening with Sir William Martin 81. Timerider (& co-w) 83. Repo Man (p) 84. Square Dance (p) 87. Tapeheads (& p) 87. The Monkees: Heart and Soul (concert doc) 87, etc.
TV series: The Monkees 66–68. Television Parts 85.

Nettleton, John (1929–)
British character actor.
A Man for All Seasons 67. Some Will Some Won't 69. And Soon the Darkness 69. Black Beauty 70, etc.

Nettleton, Lois (1930–)
American character actress.
Period of Adjustment 62. Come Fly with Me 63. Mail Order Bride 63. Valley of Mystery 66. Bamboo Saucer 68. The Good Guys and the Bad Guys 69. Dirty Dingus Magee 70. Pigeons/Sidelong Glances of a Pigeon Kicker 70. The Forgotten Man (TV) 71. The Honkers 72. Echoes of a Summer 75. Fear on Trial (TV) 75. Washington: Behind Closed Doors (TV) 77. Centennial (TV) 78. Tourist (TV) 79. Soggy Bottom USA 80. Deadly Blessing 81. Butterfly 81. The Best Little Whorehouse in Texas 82. Brass (TV) 85. Manhunt for Claude Dallas (TV) 86. Mirror, Mirror 2: Raven Dance 94, etc.
TV series: Accidental Family 67.

Neumann, Kurt (1908–1958)
German director, in Hollywood from 1925.
My Pal the King 32. The Big Cage 33. Rainbow on the River 36. Island of Lost Men 39. Ellery Queen Master Detective 40. The Unknown Guest 43. Tarzan and the Leopard Woman 46. Bad Boy 49. Rocketship XM (& w, p) 50. Son of Ali Baba 53. Carnival Story 54. Mohawk 56. Kronos 57. *The Fly* 58. Watusi 58, etc.

Neumeier, Edward (1957–)
Austrian-born screenwriter in Hollywood. Born in Vienna, and brought up in San Francisco, he studied at UCLA Film School and first worked as a script reader and as a development executive at Universal Pictures.
Robocop (co-w) 87. Frankenstein Unbound (co-w) 90. Starship Troopers (w) 97, etc.

Neuwirth, Bebe (1958–) (Beatrice Neuwirth)
American actress, born in Princeton, New Jersey. She is best known for her role in the TV series *Cheers* as Dr Lilith Sternin, who became the lover and, later, wife of Dr Frasier Crane (played by Kelsey Grammer).
Say Anything 89. Green Card 90. Bugsy 91. Painted Heart 92. Malice 93. Wild Palms (TV) 93. Jumanji 95. The Adventures of Pinocchio 96. The Associate 96. All Dogs Go to Heaven 2 (voice) 96. Celebrity 98, etc.
TV series: Cheers 86–93. Deadline 00.

Neville, John (1925–)
British leading man, primarily on stage.
Oscar Wilde 60. Mr Topaze 61. Billy Budd 62. Unearthly Stranger 63. *A Study in Terror* (as Sherlock Holmes) 65. The Adventures of Gerard 70. The Adventures of Baron Munchausen 89. Stark (TV) 93. Baby's Day Out 94. The Road to Wellville 94. Little Women 94. Dangerous Minds 95. Swann 96. Regeneration 97. Goodbye, Lover 98. The X Files 98. Urban Legend 98. Sunshine 99, etc.

Newall, Guy (1885–1937)
British stage actor who became a popular leading man in silent sentimental dramas, especially with his wife Ivy Duke. Also directed most of his films.
Comradeship 18. The Garden of Resurrection 19. The Lure of Crooning Water 20. The Duke's Son 20. Beauty and the Beast 22. Boy Woodburn 22. The Starlit Garden 23. The Ghost Train 27. The Eternal Feminine 30. The Marriage Bond 30. Grand Finale 37, etc.

Newborn, Ira
American composer.
The Blues Brothers 80. All Night Long 81. Sixteen Candles 84. Weird Science 85. Ferris Bueller's Day Off 86. Wise Guys 86. Dragnet 87. Planes, Trains and Automobiles 87. The Naked Gun: From the Files of Police Squad 88. Uncle Buck 89. Short Time 90. My Blue Heaven 90. The Naked Gun $2\frac{1}{2}$: The Smell of Fear 91. Brain Donors 92. The Opposite Sex … And How to Live with Them 93. Ace Ventura, Pet Detective 94. Naked Gun $33\frac{1}{3}$: The Final Insult 94. Mallrats 95. The Late Shift (TV) 96. High School High 96. BASEketball 98, etc.

Newbrook, Peter (1916–)
British producer, former cinematographer.
The Yellow Teddy Bears 63. Black Torment 64. Gonks Go Beat 65. The Sandwich Man 66. Press for Time 66. Corruption 69. She'll Follow You Anywhere 70. The Asphyx 72, etc.

Newell, Mike (1942–)
British director, from TV.
The Man in the Iron Mask (TV) 77. The Awakening 80. Blood Feud (TV) 83. *Dance with a Stranger* 85. Amazing Grace and Chuck 87. *Soursweet* 88. Enchanted April 91. Into the West 92. *Four Weddings and a Funeral* 94. An Awfully Big Adventure 95. *Donnie Brasco* 97, etc.
❝ When you are dealing with the big stars, it's like being a tug that has to nudge a huge liner through a gap only just wide enough and you mustn't scrape the paint. So you don't direct them by telling them what to do, but by nudging them gently along. – *M.N.*

Newfeld, Sam (1900–1964)
American director of second features.
Reform Girl 33. Big Time or Bust 34. Northern Frontier 35. Timber War 36. Trail of Vengeance 37. Harlem on the Prairie 38. Secrets of a Model 40.

Billy the Kid's Fighting Pals 41. The Mad Monster 42. Nabonga 44. Ghost of Hidden Valley 46. The Counterfeiters 48. Motor Patrol 50. Three Desperate Men 51. Thunder Over Sangoland 55. Wolf Dog 58, many others.

Newhart, Bob (1929–)
American TV and record comedian who has appeared in a few movies.
Hell Is for Heroes 62. Hot Millions 68. On a Clear Day You Can See Forever 70. Catch 22 70. Cold Turkey 70. Thursday's Game (TV) 74. The First Family 80. Little Miss Marker 80. Marathon (TV) 80. The Rescuers Down Under (voice) 90. In & Out 97. Rudolph the Red-Nosed Reindeer: The Movie (voice) 98, etc.
TV series: The Bob Newhart Show 72–77. Newhart 82–86. George & Leo 97– .

Newland, John (1917–2000)
Tall, introverted American actor who turned to directing TV programmes from the 60s. Born in Cincinnati, Ohio, he began in vaudeville as a song-and-dance man. He was best known as the the host of the TV series *One Step Beyond*), and also played Algy in the Tom Conway *Bulldog Drummond* films 48–49. He directed episodes of such series as *Naked City*, *The Man From U.N.C.L.E.*, *Hawaii Five-O*, and *Fantasy Isalnd* and was executive producer of *The Man Who Never Was* 66-67.
That Night 57. The Violators 57. The Spy with My Face 65. Hush-a-Bye Murder 70. Don't Be Afraid of the Dark (TV) 73. The Legend of Hillbilly John (TV) 74. The Suicide's Wife (TV) 79, etc.
TV series: One Man's Family 50. Robert Montgomery Presents 52-54. The Kate Smith Hour 53-54. The Loretta Young Show 55-58. One Step Beyond 59-1961. The Next Step Beyond 78.

Newland, Mary
See Oldland, Lilian.

Newlands, Anthony (1926–)
British character actor, mainly on TV; usually plays schemers.
Beyond This Place 59. The Trials of Oscar Wilde 60. Hysteria 64. Theatre of Death 67. Universal Soldier 71. Mata Hari 84, etc.

Newley, Anthony (1931–1999)
Versatile but dislikeable British actor, composer, singer, comedian; former child star. The second of his three wives was actress Joan Collins.
Oliver Twist 48. Vice Versa 48. Those People Next Door 53. *Cockleshell Heroes* 56. X the Unknown 56. High Flight 57. *No Time to Die* 58. Idol on Parade 59. In the Nick 61. The Small World of Sammy Lee 63. Dr Dolittle (US) 67. Sweet November (US) 68. Can Hieronymus Merkin Ever Forget Mercy Humpe and Find True Happiness? (& wd) 69. Summertree (d only) 72. Mr Quilp 75. A Good Idea at the Time (Can.) 76. Malibu (TV) 83. The Garbage Pail Kids Movie 87. Boris and Natasha: The Movie (TV) 92. The Lakes (TV) 99, etc.
TV series: The Anthony Newley Show 60–61. The Strange World of Gurney Slade 60. EastEnders 98.

Newman, Alfred (1901–1970)
American composer, former child pianist; an eminent Hollywood musical director since early sound days, he composed over 250 film scores.
The Devil To Pay 30. Whoopee 31. *Arrowsmith* 31. Cynara 32. *The Bowery* 33. Nana 34. Dodsworth 36. *Dead End* 37. *Alexander's Ragtime Band* (AA) 38. *Gunga Din* 39. *Tin Pan Alley* (AA) 40. *The Grapes of Wrath* 40. Son of Fury 42. The Song of Bernadette (AA) 43. The Razor's Edge 46. *Mother Wore Tights* (AA) 47. Unfaithfully Yours 48. *With a Song in My Heart* (AA) 52. *Call Me Madam* (AA) 53. Love Is a Many Splendored Thing (AA) 55. *The King and I* (AA) 56. Flower Drum Song 61. The Counterfeit Traitor 62. How the West was Won 62. Nevada Smith 66, many others.
❝ Everybody here in Hollywood knows his business, plus music. – *A.N.*

Newman, Barry (1938–)
American leading actor.
Pretty Boy Floyd 60. The Moving Finger 63. *The Lawyer* 69. *Vanishing Point* 71. The Salzburg Connection 72. Fear is the Key 72. City on Fire 79. Amy 81. Fatal Vision (TV) 84. Daylight 96. Goodbye, Lover 98, etc.
TV series: Petrocelli 73–74. Nightingales 89.

Newman, David
American composer and conductor, the son of Alfred Newman.
Critters 86. The Brave Little Toaster 87. My Demon Lover 87. Throw Momma from the Train 87. Bill and Ted's Excellent Adventure 88. Disorganized Crime 89. Heathers 89. The War of the Roses 89. Madhouse 90. Fire Birds 90. The Freshman 90. Mr Destiny 90. The Marrying Man/Too Hot to Handle 91. Other People's Money 91. Bill & Ted's Bogus Journey 91. Don't Tell Mom the Babysitter's Dead 91. The Runestone 92. Honeymoon in Vegas 92. The Sandlot/The Sandlot Kids 93. Coneheads 93. Undercover Blues 93. My Father, the Hero 94. The Flintstones 94. The Air Up There 94. I Love Trouble 94. My Father, the Hero 94. Boys on the Side 95. Tommy Boy 95. Operation Dumbo Drop 95. The Phantom 96. The Nutty Professor 96. Matilda 96. Jingle All the Way 96. Out to Sea 97. Anastasia (AAN) 97. Never Been Kissed 98. Bowfinger 98. Galaxy Quest 99. Brokedown Palace 99. Duets 00. Bedazzled 00. 102 Dalmatians, etc.

Newman, David (1937–)
American screenwriter, in collaboration with Robert Benton until the early 70s, and occasionally with his wife, Leslie Newman.
■ *Bonnie and Clyde* (AAN) 67. There Was a Crooked Man 70. What's Up Doc? 72. Bad Company 72. Superman 78. Superman II 80. Jinxed 82. Superman III 83. Sheena 84. Santa Claus: The Movie 85.

Newman, Joseph M. (1909–)
American director, in films from 1931.
Jungle Patrol 48. 711 Ocean Drive 50. The Outcast of Poker Flats 52. Red Skies of Montana 52. Pony Soldier 53. The Human Jungle 54. Dangerous Crossing 54. Kiss of Fire 55. *This Island Earth* 55. Flight to Hong Kong (& p) 56. Gunfight at Dodge City 58. The Big Circus 59. Tarzan the Ape Man 59. King of the Roaring Twenties 61. A Thunder of Drums 61. The George Raft Story 61, etc.

Newman, Lionel (1916–1989)
American composer.
The Street with No Name 48. Cheaper by the Dozen 50. Diplomatic Courier 52. Dangerous Crossing 53. Gorilla at Large 54. How to Be Very Very Popular 55. A Kiss Before Dying 56. Mardi Gras 58. Compulsion 59. North to Alaska 60. Move Over Darling 63. Do Not Disturb 65. The Salzburg Connection 72. The Bluebird 76. Alien 79. Breaking Away 79. The Final Conflict 81. Cross Creek 83. Unfaithfully Yours 83, etc.

Newman, Nanette (1934–)
British leading lady, married to Bryan Forbes.
Personal Affair 53. House of Mystery 58. Faces in the Dark 59. The League of Gentlemen 59. Twice Round the Daffodils 62. The Wrong Arm of the Law 63. Of Human Bondage 64. Séance on a Wet Afternoon 64. The Wrong Box 66. The Whisperers 66. The Madwoman of Chaillot 69. *The Raging Moon* 70. The Love Ban 72. Man at the Top 73. The Stepford Wives 75. International Velvet 78. The Mystery of Edwin Drood 93, etc.

Newman, Paul (1925–)
American leading actor who suffered initially from a similarity to Marlon Brando but later developed a lithe impertinence which served him well in his better films. He was given a special Academy Award in 1986 for 'his many memorable and compelling screen performances'. He is married to actress Joanne Woodward.
Biography: 1975, *Paul Newman* by Charles Hamblett. 1997, *Paul Newman: A Celebration* by Eric Lax. 1998, *Paul Newman* by Lawrence J. Quirk.
The Silver Chalice 54. *Somebody Up There Likes Me* 56. The Rack 56. Until They Sail 57. The Helen Morgan Story 57. *The Long Hot Summer* 58. The Left Handed Gun 58. Rally Round the Flag Boys 58. Cat on a Hot Tin Roof (AAN) 58. The Young Philadelphians 59. From the Terrace 60. Exodus 60. *The Hustler* (AAN, BFA) 61. Paris Blues 61. Sweet Bird of Youth 62. Hemingway's Adventures of a Young Man 62. *Hud* (AAN) 63. A New Kind of Love 63. *The Prize* 63. What a Way to Go 64. The Outrage 64. Lady L 64. Torn Curtain 66. *Harper* 66. *Hombre* 67. *Cool Hand Luke* (AAN) 67. The Secret War of Harry Frigg 67. Rachel Rachel (d only) 68. Winning 69. *Butch Cassidy and the Sundance Kid* 69. W.U.S.A. 70. Sometimes a Great Notion (& d) 71. Pocket Money 72. The Effect of Gamma Rays on Man-in-the-Moon Marigolds (d only) 72. *Judge Roy Bean* 72. The Mackintosh Man 73. The Sting 73. The Towering Inferno 74. The Drowning Pool 75. Silent Movie 76. Buffalo Bill and the Indians 76. Slap Shot 77. Quintet 79. Fort Apache, the Bronx 80. When Time Ran Out 80. The Shadow Box (d only) 81. Absence of Malice (AAN) 82. *The Verdict* (AAN) 82. Harry and Son 84. The Color of Money (AA) 86. The Glass Menagerie (d only) 87. Fat Man and Little Boy/The Shadowmakers 89. Blaze 89. Mr & Mrs Bridge 90. The Hudsucker Proxy 94. Nobody's Fool (AAN) 94. Twilight 98, etc.
❝ You don't stop being a citizen just because you have a Screen Actors' Guild card. – *P.N.*
Acting is a question of absorbing other people's personalities and some of your own experience. – *P.N.*
Ever since *Slap Shot* I've been swearing more. I knew I had a problem one day when I turned to my daughter and said: 'Please pass the fucking salt.' – *P.N.*
I wasn't driven to acting by an inner compulsion. I was running away from the sporting goods business. – *P.N.*

Newman, Randy (1943–)
Witty American songwriter, musician and composer. He is the nephew of composers Lionel and Alfred Newman.
Performance (md) 70. Cold Turkey (m) 70. The Pursuit of Happiness (m) 71. Ragtime (m) (AAN) 81. The Natural (m) (AAN) 84. April Fool's Day (m) 86. Three Amigos! (a, co-w, s) 86. Huey Long (co-m) 86. Parenthood (m) 89. Avalon (m) 90. Awakenings (m) 90. The Paper (m) (AANs) 94. Maverick (m) 94. Toy Story (AANm, AANs) 95. James and the Giant Peach (AAN) 96. Michael 96. Cats Don't Dance 97. Pleasantville (AAN) 98. Babe: Pig in the City (AANs) 98. A Bug's Life (& voice, AANm) 98. Toy Story 2 (m, AANs) 99. Meet the Parents (AAN) 00, etc.

Newman, Thomas
American composer, the son of Alfred Newman, and the brother of David Newman.
Grandview, U.S.A. 84. Reckless 84. Revenge of the Nerds 84. Desperately Seeking Susan 85. The Man with One Red Shoe 85. Girls Just Want to Have Fun 85. Real Genius 85. Jumpin' Jack Flash 86. Gung Ho 86. Light of Day 87. The Lost Boys 87. Less than Zero 87. The Great Outdoors 88. The Prince of Pennsylvania 88. Cookie 89. Men Don't Leave 90. Naked Tango 90. Welcome Back, Roxy Carmichael 91. Fried Green Tomatoes at the Whistle Stop Café 91. Career Opportunities 91. Deceived 91. The Rapture 91. The Player 92. The Linguini Incident 92. Scent of a Woman 92. Whispers in the Dark 92. Flesh and Bone 93. Josh and S.A.M. 93. Threesome 94. The Favor 94. The Shawshank Redemption (AAN) 94. The War 94. Little Women (AAN) 94. Unstrung Heroes (AAN) 95. How to Make an American Quilt 95. American Buffalo 96. Phenomenon 96. Up Close and Personal 96. The People vs Larry Flynt 96. Oscar and Lucinda 97. Red Corner 97. Mad City 97. The Horse Whisperer 98. Meet Joe Black 98. American Beauty (AAN) 99. The Green Mile 99. Erin Brockovich 00, etc.

Newman, Walter (1916–1993)
American screenwriter.
Ace in the Hole (co-w) 51. Underwater 55. The Man with the Golden Arm (co-w) 56. The True Story of Jesse James 56. Crime and Punishment USA 59. The Interns (co-w) 62. Cat Ballou (co-w) (AAN) 65. Bloodbrothers (AAN) 78. The Champ 79. Saint Jack 79, etc.

Newmar, Julie (1930–) (Julia Newmeyer)
Tall American blonde actress.
Seven Brides for Seven Brothers 55. The Marriage Go Round 60. Mackenna's Gold 68. The Maltese Bippy 69. Hysterical 83. Streetwalkin' 85. Deep Space 87. Ghosts Can't Do It 90. Nudity Required 90. Oblivion 94, etc.
TV series: My Living Doll 64. Batman 65–67.

Newton, Robert (1905–1956)
British star character actor with a rolling eye and a voice to match; a ham, but a succulent one. Born in Shaftesbury, Dorset, he was on stage from 1920. His alcoholism hampered his career: when he made *This Happy Breed* it was written into his contract that his fee (£9,000) would be docked by £500 every time he was drunk on the set.
■ Reunion 32. Dark Journey 37. Fire Over England 37. *Farewell Again* 37. The Squeaker 37. The Green Cockatoo 37. Twenty One Days 38. Vessel of Wrath 38. Yellow Sands 38. Dead Men are Dangerous 39. Jamaica Inn 39. Poison Pen 39. Hell's Cargo 39. Bulldog Sees It Through 40. Gaslight 40. Busman's Honeymoon 40. *Major Barbara* 40. *Hatter's Castle* 41. They Flew Alone 42. *This Happy Breed* 44. *Henry V* (as Pistol) 45. Night Boat to Dublin 46. *Odd Man Out* 46. Temptation Harbour 47. Snowbound 48. *Oliver Twist* (as Bill Sikes) 48. Kiss the Blood off My Hands (US) 48. Obsession 49. *Treasure Island* (as Long John) 50. Waterfront 50. *Tom Brown's Schooldays* (as Dr Arnold) 51. Soldiers Three (US) 51. Les Misérables (US) 52. Blackbeard the Pirate (US) 52. *Androcles and the Lion* (US) 53. Desert Rats (US) 53. The High and the Mighty (US) 54. *The Beachcomber* 54. Long John Silver 55. Around the World in Eighty Days (US) 56.
TV series: *Long John Silver* 55.
✪ For being so enjoyably larger than life. *Treasure Island*.
❝ I had a great weakness for Bob Newton. He used to drink far too much, and when he had a couple of drinks, he would speak the absolute truth, which could be horrifying. – *David Lean*

Newton, Thandie
British leading actress. Born in Zambia to English and Zimbabwean parents, she began as a teenager in the films of director John Duigan, with whom she was romantically involved. She later studied archeology and anthropology at Cambridge University. Married screenwriter Oliver Parker in 1998.
Flirting 89. The Young Americans 93. Loaded 94. Interview with the Vampire 94. Jefferson in Paris 95. The Journey of August King 95. The Leading Man 96. Gridlock'd 97. In Your Dreams (TV) 97. Beloved 98. Besieged 98. Mission: Impossible 2 00. It Was An Accident 00, etc.

Newton, Wayne (1942–)
Actor and singer, performing from the age of six.
80 Steps to Jonah 69. Licence to Kill 89. The Adventures of Ford Fairlane 90. The Dark Backward 91. Best of the Best II 93. Vegas Vacation 96, etc.
TV series: North and South, Book II 89.

Newton-John, Olivia (1948–)
English singer and actress. Born in Cambridge, she moved to Australia when she was five, and is now resident in the USA. After being diagnosed with breast cancer in the early 90s, she spent much time involved in charitable work. Married actor Matt Lattanzi in 1985.
■ Toomorrow 70. *Grease* 78. Xanadu 80. Two of a Kind 83. A Mom for Christmas (TV) 90. It's My Party 96. Sordid Lives 00.

Ney, Marie (1895–1981)
British stage actress in occasional films.
Escape 30. The Wandering Jew 33. Scrooge 37. Jamaica Inn 39. Seven Days to Noon 50. Simba 55. Yield to the Night 56. Witchcraft 64, etc.

Ney, Richard (1917–)
American financier who almost accidentally went into acting but appears only occasionally. Married Greer Garson.
Mrs Miniver 42. The Late George Apley 47. Joan of Arc 48. Babes in Baghdad 52. The Premature Burial 62, etc.

Ngor, Haing S. (1950–1996)
Cambodian actor in America. He was a doctor when the Khmer Rouge invaded his country and was imprisoned and tortured before leaving for America in 1980. As his French medical qualifications were not recognized, he worked in other jobs until being unexpectedly offered a role in *The Killing Fields*. Died after being shot by an unknown gunman outside his home in Los Angeles.
Autobiography: 1988, *Haing Ngor: A Cambodian Odyssey*, with Roger Warner.
The Killing Fields (AA) 84. Eastern Condors 86. The Iron Triangle 89. Vietnam, Texas 90. Ambition 91. My Life 93. Heaven and Earth 93.

Ottiano, Rafaela (1894–1942)
Italian-born stage actress who went to Hollywood and played sinister housekeepers, etc.

As You Desire Me 32. Grand Hotel 32. She Done Him Wrong 33. Great Expectations 34. Maytime 37. Topper Returns 41, etc.

Otto, Barry
Australian leading actor. He is the father of actress Miranda OTTO.

Norman Loves Rose 82. *Bliss* 85. The Howling III: The Marsupials 87. The Last Voyage 88. The Punisher 89. Strictly Ballroom 92. The Custodian 93. Exile 94. Dad and Dave on Our Selection 95. Lilian's Story 95. *Cosi* 96. Mr Reliable: A True Story 96. Oscar and Lucinda 97. Kiss or Kill 97. Mr Nice Guy 97. Dead Letter Office 98, etc.

Otto, Miranda
Australian actress, mainly on the stage. She is the daughter of actor Barry OTTO.

Emma's War 85. Initiation 87. The 13th Floor 88. Daydream Believer 91. The Last Days of Chez Nous 92. The Nostradamus Kid 93. Sex Is a Four Letter Word 95. Love Serenade 96. The Well 97. Doing Time for Patsy Cline 97. In the Winter Dark 98. Dead Letter Office 98. The Thin Red Line (US) 98. What Lies Beneath (US) 00. Kin (SA/GB) 00, etc.

Ouédraogo, Idrissa (1954–)
African director and screenwriter, born in Burkina Faso. He studied film at the African Institute of Cinematography, and in Kiev and Paris.

The Choice/Yam Daabo 86. Yaaba 89. Tilai 90. Karim and Sala/A Karim Na Sala (TV) 91. Samba Traoré 93. Le Cri du Coeur 94.

Ouida (1839–1908) (Marie Louise de la Ramée)
Anglo-French novelist, born in Bury St Edmunds, Suffolk, who wrote more than forty fashionable and romantic novels, two of which have proved durable as sources of movie entertainment.

The Dog of Flanders 14. Under Two Flags 16. Two Little Wooden Shoes 20. Under Two Flags 22. A Boy of Flanders 24. In Maremma 24. A Dog of Flanders 35. Under Two Flags 36. A Dog of Flanders 59. A Dog of Flanders 99.

Oulton, Brian (1908–1992)
British stage and film comedy actor, usually in unctuous or prim roles.

Too Many Husbands 39. Miranda 48. Last Holiday 50. Castle in the Air 52. The Million Pound Note 54. Private's Progress 55. Happy is the Bride 57. The Thirty-Nine Steps 59. A French Mistress 60. Kiss of the Vampire 62. Carry on Cleo 64. The Intelligence Men 64. Carry on Camping 69. On the Buses 71. Ooh You are Awful 72.

Oury, Gérard (1919–) (Max-Gerald Tannenbaum)
Dapper French character actor, now director.

Antoine et Antoinette 46. La Belle que Voilà 49. Sea Devils (GB) 52. *Father Brown* (GB) 54.

House of Secrets (GB) 56. The Journey (US) 58. The Mirror Has Two Faces 59, etc.
■ AS DIRECTOR: La Main Chaude 60. *The Sucker/* Le Corniaud 64. The Big Spree 66. The Brain 69. Adventures of Rabbi Jacob 72. La Carapate 78. Le Coup de Parapluie 80/The Umbrella Coup 80. Ace of Aces 82. The Vengeance of the Winged Serpent 84. Levy and Goliath 86. Vanille Fraise 89. Le Grippe Sou 92. La Soif de l'Or 93. Ghost with Driver 96.

Ouspenskaya, Maria (1876–1949)
Distinguished, diminutive Russian character actress who enlivened some Hollywood films after the mid-30s.
■ Dodsworth (AAN) 36. Conquest 37. *Love Affair* (AAN) 39. *The Rains Came* 39. Judge Hardy and Son 39. Dr Ehrlich's Magic Bullet 40. Waterloo Bridge 40. The Mortal Storm 40. The Man I Married 40. Dance Girl Dance 40. Beyond Tomorrow 40. *The Wolf Man* 41. The Shanghai Gesture 41. *King's Row* 42. The Mystery of Marie Roget 42. Frankenstein Meets the Wolf Man 43. Tarzan and the Amazons 45. I've Always Loved You 46. Wyoming 47. A Kiss in the Dark 49.
66 Famous line (*The Wolf Man*): 'Even the man who is pure in heart
And says his prayers by night
May become a wolf when the wolf-bane blooms
And the moon is clear and bright.'

Overman, Lynne (1887–1943)
American character actor with stage experience. Memorable in cynical comedy roles for his relaxed manner and sing-song voice.
■ Midnight 34. Little Miss Marker 34. The Great Flirtation 34. She Loves Me Not 34. You Belong to Me 34. Broadway Bill 34. Enter Madame 34. Rumba 35. Paris in Spring 35. Men without Names 35. Two for Tonight 35. Collegiate 35. Poppy 36. Yours for the Asking 36. Three Married Men 36. The Jungle Princess 36. Blonde Trouble 37. Partners in Crime 37. Nobody's Baby 37. Don't Tell the Wife 37. Murder Goes to College 37. Wild Money 37. Hotel Haywire 37. Night Club Scandal 37. True Confession 37. The Big Broadcast of 1938. *Her Jungle Love* 38. Hunted Men 38. Spawn of the North 38. Sons of the Legion 38. Men with Wings 38. Ride a Crooked Mile 38. Persons in Hiding 39. *Death of a Champion* 39. Union Pacific 39. Edison the Man 40. Typhoon 40. Safari 40. Northwest Mounted Police 40. Aloma of the South Seas 41. Caught in the Draft 41. New York Town 41. The Hard Boiled Canary 41. *Roxie Hart* 42. Reap the Wild Wind 42. The Forest Rangers 42. The Silver Queen 42. Star Spangled Rhythm 42. *Dixie* 43. The Desert Song 43.

Ovitz, Michael (1946–)
American agent, former chairman of CAA (Creative Artists Agency) and frequently said to be the most influential person in Hollywood. He joined the Walt Disney Company in August 1995 as President, leaving 14 months later with a severance deal said to worth $125m. He set up

Artists Production Group, a new management and production company in 1998 and in 2000 signed a deal with Canal Plus to produce fifteen films in three years for the international market.
Biography: 1997, *Ovitz: The Inside Story of Hollywood's Most Controversial Power Broker* by Robert Slater.
66 A combination of barracuda and Mother Teresa – a crafty businessman, and I mean it in the best sense of the word. – *Paul Newman*

Owen, Bill (1914–) (Bill Rowbotham)
British character comedian, former dance-band musician and singer.
Autobiography: 1994, *Summer Wine and Vintage Years.*

The Way to the Stars (debut) 45. When the Bough Breaks 47. The Girl Who Couldn't Quite 49. Trottie True 49. Hotel Sahara 51. The Square Ring 53. The Rainbow Jacket 54. Davy 57. Carve Her Name with Pride 58. The Hellfire Club 61. The Secret of Blood Island 65. Georgy Girl 66. O Lucky Man 72. In Celebration 74. The Comeback 78. Laughterhouse/Singleton's Pluck 84, etc.
TV series: Last of the Summer Wine 74– .

Owen, Cliff (1919–)
British director, in films from 1937.
Offbeat 61. A Prize of Arms 62. The Wrong Arm of the Law 63. A Man Could Get Killed 66. That Riviera Touch 66. The Magnificent Two 67. Steptoe and Son 72. Ooh You Are Awful 72. No Sex Please We're British 73. The Bawdy Adventures of Tom Jones 76. Get Charlie Tully 76, etc.

Owen, Clive (1966–)
English leading actor. Married actress Sarah-Jane Fenton.
Lorna Doone (TV) 90. Close My Eyes 91. Century 94. Bad Boys (TV) 94. The Turnaround (TV) 95. The Rich Man's Wife (US) 96. Bad Boy Blues (TV) 96. Bent 97. Croupier 97. Split Second (TV) 99. Second Sight (TV) 00. Greenfingers 00, etc.
TV series: Chancer 90. Sharman 96.

Owen, Reginald (1887–1972)
British character actor, on stage from 1905, films (in Hollywood) from 1929.
The Letter (debut) 29. Platinum Blonde 32. Queen Christina 33. Call of the Wild 35. Anna Karenina 35. The Great Ziegfeld 36. A Tale of Two Cities 36. *Trouble for Two* 36. Conquest 37. The Earl of Chicago 39. Florian 40. Charley's Aunt 41. Tarzan's Secret Treasure 41. *Mrs Miniver* 42. Random Harvest 42. White Cargo 42. Madame Curie 43. Lassie Come Home 43. The Canterville Ghost 44. *Kitty* 45. The Diary of a Chambermaid 45. Cluny Brown 46. If Winter Comes 47. The Three Musketeers 48. The Miniver Story 50. Kim 51. Red Garters 54. The Young Invaders 58. Voice of the Hurricane (MRA film) 63. Mary Poppins 64. Rosie 68. Bedknobs and Broomsticks 71, many others.

Owen, Seena (1894–1966) (Signe Auen)
American silent-screen leading lady.
Intolerance 16. The Sheriff's Son 19. Victory 19. Shipwrecked 23. Flame of the Yukon 25. The Rush Hour 28. Marriage Playground 29, many others.

Owen, Yvonne (1923–)
British actress of the 40s, wife of Alan Badel.
The Seventh Veil 45. Girl in a Million 46. Holiday Camp 47. My Brother's Keeper 48. Quartet 48. Marry Me 49. Someone at the Door 50, etc.

Owens, Patricia (1925–2000)
Canadian leading lady who made films in Britain and America.
Miss London Ltd 43. While the Sun Shines 46. The Happiest Days of Your Life 49. Mystery Junction 52. The Good Die Young 53. Windfall 55. Island in the Sun 56. Sayonara (US) 57. *No Down Payment* (US) 57. The Fly (US) 58. Five Gates to Hell (US) 59. Hell to Eternity (US) 60. Seven Women from Hell 62. Black Spurs 65. The Destructors 67, etc.

Oxley, David (c. 1929–)
British actor.
Ill Met by Moonlight 57. Saint Joan 58. Yesterday's Enemy 58. The Hound of the Baskervilles 59. Life at the Top 64. House of the Living Dead 78, etc.

Oz, Frank (1944–) (Frank Oznowicz)
British-born director. He began as a puppeteer on the TV series *Sesame Street* and *The Muppet Show*, where he supplied the voices of Fozzie Bear, Miss Piggy and Sam the Eagle, among other characters, before becoming a director.
The Dark Crystal (co-d) 82. The Muppets Take Manhattan 84. Little Shop of Horrors 86. Dirty Rotten Scoundrels 88. What about Bob? 91. Housesitter 92. The Indian in the Cupboard 95. Muppet Treasure Island (a) 96. In & Out 97. Blues Brothers 2000 (a) 98. Bowfinger 98. Star Wars Episode I: The Phantom Menace (a) 99. Muppets from Space (voice) 99, etc.
TV series: The Muppet Show 76–81.

Ozep, Fedor (1893–1949)
Russian director. He was married to actress Anna Sten.
The Crime of Dmitri Karamazov 31. The Living Dead 33. Amok 34. Gibraltar 38. She Who Dares (US) 44. Whispering City (Can.) 48, etc.

Ozu, Yasujiro (1903–1963)
Japanese director, since 1927.
Biography: 1974, *Ozu* by Donald Ritchie.
A Story of Floating Weeds 34. Late Spring 49. Early Summer 51. Tokyo Story 53. Early Spring 56. Late Autumn 61. Early Autumn 62, etc.

P

Paar, Jack (1918–)
American actor and TV talk-show host. Born in Canton, Ohio, he began as a radio announcer in the 30s before gaining fame with his own TV show from the mid 50s.
Variety Time 48. Easy Living 49. Walk Softly, Stranger 50. Footlight Varieties 51. Love Nest 51. Down Among the Sheltering Palms 52, etc.
TV series: Up to Paar 52. Bank on the Stars 53. The Jack Paar Program 54. The Jack Paar Show 57-62. The Jack Paar Program 62-65. ABC late Night 73.
❝ I don't really do anything and have no talent. Having finally decided that, I decided to get out of showbusiness. But I can't, because I'm a star. – *J.P.*

Pabst, G. W. (1885–1967) (George Wilhelm)
Distinguished German director who usually tackled pessimistic themes. Born in Raudnitz, he studied engineering in Vienna, toured Europe and America as an actor, and went to Berlin in the early 20s to work in films, acting and writing, before turning to directing in the mid-20s. He made an enduring star of American actress Louise BROOKS in *Pandora's Box*. In the 30s, he worked in France, had an unhappy experience in Hollywood, and then returned to Germany for the remainder of his career.
■ Der Schatz 23. Gräfin Donelli 24. *Joyless Street* 25. *Secrets of a Soul* 26. Man Spielt Nicht mit der Liebe 26. *The Love of Jeanne Ney* 27. *Pandora's Box* 28. Abwege 28. *Diary of a Lost Girl* 29. The White Hell of Pitz Palu (co-d) 29. *Westfront 1918* 30. Skandal um Eva 30. *The Threepenny Opera/Die Dreigroschenoper* 31. *Kameradschaft* 31. L'Atlantide 32. Don Quixote 33. A Modern Hero (US) 34. De Haut en Bas 34. Mademoiselle Docteur 37. Le Drama de Shanghai 39. Mädchen in Uniform 39. Komödianten 41. Paracelsus 43. Der Fall Molander 45. Der Prozess 48. Geheimnisvolle Tiefen 49. The Voice of Silence 52. Cose da Pazzi 53. *Ten Days to Die* 54. Das Bekenntnis der Ina Kahr 54. Jackboot Mutiny 55. The Last Act 55. Roses for Bettina 56. Durch die Wälder 56.

Pace, Judy (1946–)
American leading actress of the 70s, born in Los Angeles.
13 Frightened Girls 63. The Thomas Crown Affair 68. Three in the Attic 68. Cotton Comes to Harlem 70. Up in the Cellar 70. The Fortune Cookie 66. Cool Breeze 72. Frogs 72. The Slams 73, etc.
TV series: The Young Lawyers 70–71.

Pacino, Al (1940–) (Alfredo Pacino)
American leading actor, of New York/Sicilian descent, from off-off-Broadway theatre. Over the years, his acting has changed from intense, tightly clenched performances to a more open, flamboyant style. Unlike many of his contemporaries, he continues to act in the theatre. He is romantically involved with actress Beverly D'ANGELO.
Biography: 1992, *Al Pacino: A Life on the Wire* by Andrew Yule.
■ Me Natalie 69. The Panic in Needle Park 71. *The Godfather* (AAN) 72. Scarecrow 73. Serpico (AAN) 73. The Godfather Part II (AAN) 74. *Dog Day Afternoon* (AAN) 75. Bobby Deerfield 77. And Justice for All (AAN) 79. Cruising 80. Author! Author! 82. Scarface 83. Revolution 85. Sea of Love 89. Dick Tracy (AAN) 90. The Godfather Part III 90. Frankie & Johnny 91. Scent of a Woman (AA) 92. Glengarry Glen Ross (AAN) 92. Carlito's Way 93. Two Bits 95. Heat 95. City Hall 96. Looking for Richard (& p, d) 96. *Donnie Brasco* 97. The Devil's Advocate 97. Any Given Sunday 99. The Insider 99. Chinese Coffee (&d) 00.

Pack, Charles Lloyd
See LLOYD PACK, Charles.

Pack, Roger Lloyd
See LLOYD PACK, Roger.

Pacula, Joanna (1957–)
Polish actress in international films.
Gorky Park 83. Not Quite Jerusalem/Not Quite Paradise 86. Death before Dishonor 87. Options 88. Sweet Lies 88. The Kiss 88. Marked for Death 90. Husbands and Lovers 91. Black Ice 92. Warlock: The Armageddon 93. Tombstone 94. Kim Novak Is on the Phone (It.) 94. The Silence of the Hams (It.) 94. Last Gasp 95. Captain Nuke and the Bomber Boys 95. Not Like Us 96. The Haunted Sea 97. Virus 98. My Giant 98. Sweet Deception 99. Virus 99, etc.

Paderewski, Ignace (1860–1941)
Polish prime minister and classical pianist. Appeared in a few films including the British *Moonlight Sonata* 37.

Padovani, Lea (1920–1991)
Italian leading actress, in films from 1945.
Give Us This Day (GB) 49. Three Steps North (US) 51. Tempi Nostri 53. Montparnasse 19 57. The Naked Maja (US) 58. Candy 68, etc.

Pagano, Bartolomeo (1888–1947)
Italian actor who originated the role of strongman MACISTE.

Page, Anita (1910–) (Anita Pomares)
American leading actress whose stardom lasted only a few years. Born in Long Island, she began as an extra in Rudolph VALENTINO's *Monsieur Beaucaire* in 1924, later being put under contract to MGM. She managed the transition to sound, starring in MGM's first all-talkie, the Oscar-winning *The Broadway Melody*, but retired on her marriage.
The Flying Fleet 28. Our Dancing Daughters 28. While the City Sleeps 28. Broadway Melody 29. Navy Blues 29. Caught Short 30. Little Accident 30. War Nurse 30. Free and Easy 30. Reducing 31. Sidewalks of New York 31. The Easiest Way 31. Gentleman's Fate 31. Are You Listening? 32. Prosperity 32. Night Court 32. Skyscraper Souls 32. I Have Lived 33. Soldiers of the Storm 33. The Big Cage 33. Hitch Hike to Heaven 35, etc.

Page, Anthony (1935–)
British director, with stage experience.
■ *Inadmissible Evidence* 68. Alpha Beta 73. Pueblo (TV) 73. *The Missiles of October* (TV) 74. Collision Course (TV) 76. F. Scott Fitzgerald in Hollywood (TV) 76. I Never Promised You a Rose Garden 77. The Lady Vanishes 79. The Patricia Neal Story (TV) 81. Grace Kelly (TV) 83. Forbidden (TV) 85. Second Serve (TV) 85. Monte Carlo (TV) 86. Pack of Lies (TV) 87. Absolution 88. Scandal in a Small Town (TV) 88. The Nightmare Years (TV) 89. Chernobyl: The Final Warning (TV) 91. Silent Cries (TV) 93. Middlemarch (TV) 94. Human Bomb (TV) 96.

Page, Gale (1911–1983) (Sally Rutter)
American leading actress, born in Spokane, Washington. Her career was spent mainly at Warner Brothers, and most successfully in the three films about the Lemp family that began with *Four Daughters*. Died of cancer.
Crime School 38. *Four Daughters* 38. Heart of the North 38. The Amazing Dr Clitterhouse 38. Naughty but Nice 39. You Can't Get Away with Murder 39. Indianapolis Speedway 39. Four Wives 39. A Child Is Born 39. Daughters Courageous 39. They Drive by Night 40. Knute Rockne, All American 40. Four Mothers 40. The Time of Your Life 48. Anna Lucasta 49. About Mrs Leslie 54, etc.

Page, Geneviève (1931–) (G. Bonjean)
French leading lady who has made American films.
Foreign Intrigue 56. Trapped in Tangiers 60. Song without End 60. El Cid 61. L'Honorable Stanislas 63. Youngblood Hawke 64. Les Corsaires 65. Belle de Jour 67. Decline and Fall 68. The Private Life of Sherlock Holmes 70. Beyond Therapy 87. Aria 88. Stranger in the House/L'Inconnu dans la Maison 92. Lovers (Fr.) 99, etc.

Page, Geraldine (1924–1987)
American leading actress, on stage from 1940. Her second husband was actor Rip TORN.
■ Taxi 53. Hondo (AAN) 54. *Summer and Smoke* (AAN) 61. Sweet Bird of Youth (AAN) 62. Toys in the Attic 63. *Dear Heart* 65. The Happiest Millionaire 67. You're a Big Boy Now (AAN) 67. Monday's Child (Arg.) 67. Trilogy (TV) 69. Whatever Happened to Aunt Alice? 69. The Beguiled 71. Pete 'n' Tillie (AAN) 72. J. W. Coop 73. The Day of the Locust 74. Nasty Habits 76. Something for Joey (TV) 77. Interiors (AAN, BFA) 78. Honky Tonk Freeway 81. Harry's War 81. I'm Dancing as Fast as I Can 82. The Pope of Greenwich Village (AAN) 84. White Nights 85. The Trip to Bountiful (AA) 85. The Bride 85. Nazi Hunter (TV) 86.

Page, Patti (1927–) (Clara Ann Fowler)
American TV singer.
■ Elmer Gantry 60. Dondi 61. Boys' Night Out 63.

Paget, Debra (1933–) (Debralee Griffin)
American leading lady with brief stage experience. The second of her three husbands was director Budd BOETTICHER.
Cry of the City 48. House of Strangers 49. Broken Arrow 50. Les Misérables 52. Prince Valiant 54. Love Me Tender 56. From the Earth to the Moon 58. Tales of Terror 62. The Haunted Palace 64, many others.

Pagett, Nicola (1945–) (Nicola Scott)
British leading lady of the 70s, much on TV. Born in Cairo, she studied at RADA. Her autobiography, *Diamonds Behind My Eyes* (with Graham Swannell), detailing her manic depression and breakdown in the mid-90s, was published in 1997. Married former actor and playwright Graham Swannell.
Frankenstein, the True Story (TV) 73. Operation Daybreak 76. Oliver's Story 79. Privates on Parade 83. All of You 86. Scoop (TV) 87. An Awfully Big Adventure 95, etc.
TV series: A Bit of a Do 89–90. Ain't Misbehavin' 94.

Pagnol, Marcel (1894–1974)
French writer-director noted for sprawling comedy dramas which strongly evoke country life without being very cinematic.
Autobiography: 1960, *The Days Were Too Short*. 1962, *The Time of Secrets*.
Marius (script only) 31. *Fanny* (script only) 32. *César* 34. Joffroi 34. Regain/Harvest 37. *La Femme du Boulanger* 38. *La Fille du Puisatier* 40. La Belle Meunière 48. Manon des Sources 53. Lettres de Mon Moulin 55. Jean de Florette (oa) 86. Manon des Sources (oa) 86. My Mother's Castle/Le Château de Ma Mère (oa) 90. My Father's Glory/La Gloire de Mon Père (oa) 90, etc.
❝ The cinema and I were born on the same day, in the same place. – M.P.

Paige, Janis (1922–) (Donna Mac Jaden)
American leading lady with operatic training.
Hollywood Canteen (debut) 44. Cheyenne 46. Romance on the High Seas 48. Mr Universe 51. Remains to be Seen 53. *Silk Stockings* 57. Please Don't Eat the Daisies 61. The Caretakers 63. Welcome to Hard Times 67. Gibbsville (TV) 75. Lanigan's Rabbi (TV) 76. Angel on My Shoulder (TV) 80. Love at the Top 86. Natural Causes 94, etc.
TV series: It's Always Jan 56. Lanigan's Rabbi 77. Gun Shy 83. Baby Makes Five 83. Trapper John MD 85–86.

Paige, Mabel (1880–1954)
American character actress.
My Heart Belongs to Daddy 42. *Lucky Jordan* 43. The Good Fellows 43. *Someone to Remember* (lead role) 43. If You Knew Susie 48. The Sniper 52. Houdini 53, etc.

Paige, Robert (1910–1987) (John Arthur Page)
American leading man, former radio announcer, in many films of the 40s, little thereafter.
Cain and Mabel 37. Hellzapoppin 41. Shady Lady 42. Son of Dracula 43. Can't Help Singing 44. Red Stallion 47. The Flame 48. Raging Waters 51. Abbott and Costello Go to Mars 53. The Big Payoff 58. The Marriage Go Round 61. Bye Bye Birdie 63, etc.
TV series: Run Buddy Run 66.

Pailhas, Geraldine (1971–)
French leading actress.
La Neige et le Feu 91. IP5: L'Ile aux Pachydermes 92. La Folie Douce 94. Don Juan de Marco 95. Le Garcu 95. Suite 16 95, etc.
❝ I am very shy. I am more the convent girl type. Characters in movies help you do stuff that you would never do in life. Like having a gun, or being a whore. – G.P.

Painlevé, Jean (1902–1989)
French documentarist, famous for short naturalist studies of sea horses, sea urchins, shrimps, etc.

Paiva, Nestor (1905–1966)
American character actor of assorted foreign peasant types.
Ride a Crooked Mile 38. The Marines Fly High 40. The Falcon in Mexico 44. Fear 46. Road to Rio 46. Five Fingers 52. The Creature from the Black Lagoon 54. The Deep Six 57. The Nine Lives of Elfego Baca 59. The Spirit Is Willing 66, many others.

Pakula, Alan J. (1928–1998)
American producer who turned director. Died in a car accident, after a metal bar flew up from the road and crashed through the windscreen of his car, hitting him on the head.
■ AS PRODUCER: Fear Strikes Out 57. To Kill a Mockingbird (AAN) 63. Love with the Proper Stranger 63. Baby the Rain Must Fall 65. Inside Daisy Clover 66. Up the Down Staircase 67. The Stalking Moon 68. The Nickel Ride 74. Kiss Me Goodbye 82.
■ AS PRODUCER -DIRECTOR: The Sterile Cuckoo 69. *Klute* 71. Love, Pain and the Whole Damn Thing 73. The Parallax View 74. *All The President's Men* (AAN) 76. Comes A Horseman 78. Starting Over 80. Rollover (d only) 81. Sophie's Choice (wd only) (AANw) 82. Dream Lover 85. Orphans 87. See You in the Morning (wd, p) 89. Presumed Innocent (d) 90. Consenting Adults 92. The Pelican Brief (wd) 93. The Devil's Own 97.

Pal, George (1908–1980)
Hungarian puppeteer whose short advertising films enlivened programmes in the late 30s; went to Hollywood 1940 and produced series of 'Puppetoons'; later produced many adventure films involving trick photography. Special Academy Award 1943 'for the development of novel methods and techniques'.
Destination Moon (AA) 50. *When Worlds Collide* (AA) 51. *The War of the Worlds* (AA) 53. The Naked Jungle 55. *Tom Thumb* (AA) (& d) 58. *The Time Machine* (AA) (& d) 60. The Wonderful World of the Brothers Grimm 63. The Power 68.

Palance, Jack (1920–) (Walter Palanuik)
Gaunt American leading man with stage experience; started in films playing villains.

Panic in the Streets 50. Halls of Montezuma 51. Sudden Fear (AAN) 52. *Shane* (AAN) 53. Sign of the Pagan 54. *The Big Knife* 55. I Died a Thousand Times 56. Attack 56. The Man Inside 57. The Lonely Man 57. House of Numbers 57. Ten Seconds to Hell 58. The Mongols 60. Barabbas 62. Warriors Five 62. Le Mépris 63. Once a Thief 65. The Professionals 66. The Torture Garden (GB) 67. Kill a Dragon 67. A Professional Gun 68. Che! 69. The Desperados 69. They Came to Rob Las Vegas 69. The Companeros 70. Monte Walsh 70. The McMasters 70. The Horsemen 72. Chato's Land 72. Oklahoma Crude 73. Dracula (TV) 73. Craze 73. The Four Deuces 75. God's Gun 77. Mr Scarface 77. One Man Jury 78. The Shape of Things to Come (TV) 79. Hawk the Slayer 80. Without Warning 80. Alone in the Dark 82. Gor 87. Bagdad Café 88. Young Guns 88. Outlaw of Gor 88. Batman 89. Tango & Cash 89. Solar Crisis 90. *City Slickers* (AA) 91. Cops and Robbersons 94. City Slickers II 94. Buffalo Girls (TV) 95, etc.

TV series: The Greatest Show on Earth 63. Bronk 75. Believe It or Not 82–86.

Palca, Alfred (1920–1998)
American producer and writer who made one film before blacklisting forced him to find other means of making a living. Part of the FBI evidence of his communism, he later said, was that he had hired a black actor, Sidney Poitier, for the film; he had to remove his name from the credits in order to get it distributed. He thereafter worked as a writer and journalist.

Go Man Go 54.

Palcy, Euzhan (1955–)
Martinique director and screenwriter, a former editor and camera operator.

La Rue Cases Nègres/Sugar Cane Alley 83. A Dry White Season 89. Simeon (co-w, d) 93.

Palin, Michael (1943–)
British light actor and screenwriter, a former member of the Monty Python team. His novel, *Hemingway's Chair*, was published in 1996.

Biography: 1998, *Michael Palin* by Jonathan Margolis.

And Now for Something Completely Different (& co-w) 72. Monty Python and the Holy Grail (& co-w) 74. Monty Python's Life of Brian (& co-w) 79. The Missionary (& w, p) 81. Time Bandits (& co-w) 81. Monty Python's The Meaning of Life (& co-w) 83. A Private Function 84. Brazil 85. Consuming Passions (oa) 88. A Fish Called Wanda (BFA) 88. American Friends (& co-w) 91. The Wind in the Willows (voice, as Rat) 96. Fierce Creatures 96. You've Got Mail 98, etc.

TV series: Pole to Pole 92. Palin's Column 94. Palin's Pacific 97. Full Circle with Michael Palin 97.

Pallette, Eugene (1889–1954)
Rotund, gravel-voiced American character actor, at his peak as an exasperated father or executive in the 30s and 40s.

Intolerance 16. Alias Jimmy Valentine 20. The Three Musketeers 21. To the Last Man 23. Light of the Western Stars 25. Lights of New York 28. The Canary Murder Case 29. The Sea God 30. It Pays to Advertise 31. Shanghai Express 32. The Kennel Murder Case 33. Bordertown 34. Steamboat Round the Bend 35. *The Ghost Goes West* 36. *My Man Godfrey* 36. One Hundred Men and a Girl 37. Topper 37. *The Adventures of Robin Hood* (as Friar Tuck) 38. Mr Smith Goes to Washington 39. The Mark of Zorro 40. The Lady Eve 41. Tales of Manhattan 42. It Ain't Hay 43. Heaven Can Wait 43. Step Lively 44. Lake Placid Serenade 45. In Old Sacramento 46, many others.

Pallos, Stephen (1902–)
Hungarian producer who worked with Korda in England from 1942, later as independent.

Call of the Blood 46. The Golden Madonna 48. Jet Storm 59. Foxhole in Cairo 60. A Jolly Bad Fellow 64. Where the Spies Are 65. Captain Nemo and the Underwater City 69. Catch Me a Spy 71, etc.

Palmer, Betsy (1929–) (Patricia Brumek)
American light actress and TV panellist.

The Long Gray Line 55. Queen Bee 55. The Tin Star 57. The Last Angry Man 59. It Happened to Jane 59. Friday the Thirteenth 80. Friday the Thirteenth Part II 81. Goddess of Love (TV) 88. Still Not Quite Human 92, etc.

TV series: Number 96 80–81. Knots Landing 89–90.

Palmer, Christopher (1946–1995)
English orchestrator and arranger of film music, rescuing many classic scores so that they could be re-recorded, and author of *The Composer in Hollywood*, a study of film music. Died of AIDS.

Palmer, Ernest (1885–1978)
American cinematographer.

Ivanhoe 12. Lothar 17. Ladies Must Live 21. The Wanters 23. The Kiss Barrier 25. The Palace of Pleasure 26. Seventh Heaven 27. The River 29. City Girl 30. A Connecticut Yankee 31. The Painted Woman 32. Cavalcade 33. Berkeley Square 33. Music in the Air 34. Charlie Chan in Paris 35. Banjo on My Knee 36. Slave Ship 37. Four Men and a Prayer 38. News is Made at Night 39. The Great Profile 40. Blood and Sand (AA) 41. Song of the Islands 42. Coney Island 43. Pin Up Girl 44. The Dolly Sisters 45. Centennial Summer 46. I Wonder Who's Kissing Her Now? 47. Broken Arrow 50, many others.

Palmer, Ernest (1901–1964)
British cinematographer who began as an office boy and a laboratory assistant. He worked at Elstree in the 30s and at Ealing Studios in the early 40s and later in television, shooting *The Adventures of Sir Lancelot* 56–57.

Kiss Me Sergeant 30. What a Night! 31. Innocents of Chicago 32. Old Spanish Customers 32. The River Wolves 33. Music Hall 34. Birds of a Feather 35. The Man behind the Mask 36. The Edge of the World 37. Save a Little Sunshine 38. The Spider 39. He Found a Star 41. The Goose Steps Out 42. San Demetrio London 43. Return of the Vikings 44. 29 Acacia Avenue 45. The Lisbon Story 46. The Ghosts of Berkeley Square 47. School for Randle 49. Over the Garden Wall 50. It's a Grand Life 53. The Heart Within 57. The Crowning Touch 58, etc.

Palmer, Geoffrey (1927–)
English light leading actor, much on television.

A Prize of Arms 61. Incident at Midnight 63. O Lucky Man! 73. The Outsider 80. Retribution 81. The Honorary Consul 83. Clockwise 85. A Zed and Two Noughts 85. A Fish Called Wanda 88. Hawks 88. Smack and Thistle 91. The Madness of King George 94. Mrs Brown 97. Tomorrow Never Does 97, etc.

TV series: The Fall and Rise of Reginald Perrin 76–79. Butterflies 78–82. The Last Song 81–83. Whoops Apocalypse 82. Fairly Secret Army 84–86. Executive Stress 86–88. Blackadder Goes Forth (as Field Marshal Haig) 89. As Time Goes By 92–98. The Legacy of Reginald Perrin 96.

Palmer, Gregg (1927–) (Palmer Lee)
American 'second lead', former disc jockey.

Son of Ali Baba 51. Veils of Baghdad 53. Magnificent Obsession 54. The Creature Walks among Us 56. Forty Pounds of Trouble 62. The Undefeated 69. Big Jake 71. The Shootist 76, etc.

Palmer, Lilli (1911–1986) (Lilli Peiser)
Austrian leading actress, on stage from childhood, in films from teenage years.

Autobiography: 1975, *Change Lobsters and Dance*.

Crime Unlimited (GB) 34. Good Morning, Boys (GB) 36. Secret Agent (GB) 36. A Girl Must Live (GB) 38. The Door with Seven Locks (GB) 40. *Thunder Rock* (GB) 42. The Gentle Sex (GB) 43. English without Tears (GB) 44. *The Rake's Progress* (GB) 45. Beware of Pity (GB) 46. Cloak and Dagger (US) 46. My *Girl Tisa* (US) 47. Body and Soul (US) 48. No Minor Vices (US) 48. The Long Dark Hall (GB) 51. The Fourposter (US) 52. Is Anna Anderson Anastasia? (Ger.) 56. La Vie à Deux (Fr.) 58. But Not for Me (US) 58. Conspiracy of Hearts (GB) 60. Rendezvous at Midnight (Fr.) 60. *The Pleasure of His Company* (US) 61. The Counterfeit Traitor (US) 62. Adorable Julia (Ger.) 63. The Flight of the White Stallions (US) 64. Operation Crossbow (GB) 65. Moll Flanders (GB) 65. Sebastian (GB) 67. Oedipus the King (GB) 67. Nobody Runs Forever (GB) 68. The Dance of Death (Swe.) 68. De Sade (US) 69. Hard Contract (US) 69. Murders in the Rue Morgue (GB) 71. Night Hair Child (GB) 71. The Boys from Brazil 78. The Holcroft Covenant 85. Peter the Great (TV) 86, many others.

TV series: Lilli Palmer Theatre 54. *Zoo Gang* 73.

Palmer, Maria (1924–1981)
Austrian leading lady. Wide stage experience at home, TV and films in America.

Mission to Moscow 42. Lady on a Train 44. Rendezvous 24 46. Slightly Dishonourable 51. Three for Jamie Dawn 56, many others.

Palmer, Peter (1931–)
American actor-singer who repeated his stage role as *Li'l Abner* 59.

Deep Space 87. A Time of Destiny 88. Edward Scissorhands 90, etc.

TV series: Custer 67. The Kallikaks 77.

Palminteri, Chazz (1951–) (Calogero Palminteri)
American actor and dramatist.

Oscar 91. *A Bronx Tale* (& w, from his play) 93. Bullets over Broadway (AAN) 94. The Perez Family 95. The Usual Suspects 95. Jade 95. Faithful (& w, from his play) 96. Diabolique 96. Mulholland Falls 96. Hurlyburly 98. Falcone 98. Down to Earth 01, etc.

Paltrow, Bruce (1943–)
American director. Married actress Blythe Danner. Their daughter is actress Gwyneth Paltrow.

A Little Sex 82. Ed McBain's 87th Precinct (TV) 85. Duets 00, etc.

Paltrow, Gwyneth (1973–)
American leading actress, the daughter of Blythe Danner and director Bruce Paltrow. She was engaged to actor Brad Pitt and has been romantically linked with actor Ben Affleck.

Shout 91. Flesh and Bone 93. Mrs Parker and the Vicious Circle 94. Jefferson in Paris 95. Moonlight and Valentino 95. Seven 95. Sydney/ Hard Eight 96. The Pallbearer 96. *Emma* (title role) 96. Sliding Doors 98. Great Expectations 98. A Perfect Murder 98. Hush 98. *Shakespeare in Love* (AA) 98. The Talented Mr Ripley 99. Duets 00. Bounce 00, etc.

Paluzzi, Luciana (1939–)
Italian leading lady in international films.

Three Coins in the Fountain 54. Sea Fury 58. Thunderball 65. The Venetian Affair 66. Chuka 67. 99 Women 69. The Green Slime 69. Black Gunn 72. War Goddess 74. The Klansman 74. The Greek Tycoon 78, etc.

TV series: Five Fingers 59.

Pampanini, Silvana (1927–)
Voluptuous Italian leading lady of the 50s, a former Miss Italy, who lent her charms to many frolics of the period; her appeal waned with the arrival of Sophia Loren and Gina Lollobrigida.

L'Apocalisse 47. Marechiaro 49. La Bisarca 50. Bellissima 51. Miracle at Viggiu/Miracolo a Viggiu 51. Scandal in the Roman Bath/OK Nerone 51. Dangerous Woman/Bufere 53. The Island Sinner/ La Peccatrice dell'Isola 53. L'Allegro Squadrone 54. Il Matrimonio 54. Orient Express 54. La Schiava del Peccato 54. Roman Signorina/La Bella di Roma 55. Thirst for Love/Sed de Amor 58. Napoleoncito 63. Il Gaucho 64. Mondo Pazzo, Gente Matta 66, many others.

Pan, Hermes (1905–1990) (H. Panagiotopolous)
American dance director.

Top Hat 35. Swing Time 36. Damsel in Distress (AA) 37. Let's Dance 50. Lovely to Look At 52. Silk Stockings 57. Can Can 59. Flower Drum Song 62. Cleopatra 63. My Fair Lady 64. Finian's Rainbow 68. Lost Horizon 73, many others.

Panahi, Jafar (1960–)
Iranian director. *The Circle* won the Gold Lion at the Venice film Festival in 2000.

■ The White Balloon 95. The Mirror 97. The Circle 00.

Panama, Norman (1914–)
Writer-producer-director who has long worked in collaboration with Melvin Frank (see entry for note on films). Now working solo.

Not with My Wife You Don't (wd, p) 66. How to Commit Marriage (d only) 69. The Maltese Bippy (wd) 69. Coffee, Tea or Me? (TV) 73. I Will, I Will ... For Now (co-w, d) 76. Barnaby and Me 77.

Panfilov, Gleb (1934–)
Russian film director and screenwriter. He trained as a chemical engineer before studying direction at Mosfilm. Married actress Inna Churikova.

Across the Stream and Fire/Vogne Broda Nyet 68. The Debut/Nachalo 70. May I Have the Floor?/ Proshu Slova 75. Valentina, Valentine 81. Vassa 83. The Theme 84. *The Mother* 88, etc.

Pangborn, Franklin (1894–1958)
American character comedian with long stage experience; in scores of films from the 20s, typically as flustered hotel clerk or organizer.

My Friend from India 27. My Man 30. International House 33. My Man Godfrey 36. Stage Door 37. Christmas in July 40. *The Bank Dick* 40. *The Palm Beach Story* 42. The Carter Case 42. Now Voyager 42. *Hail the Conquering Hero* 44. Mad Wednesday 47. Romance on the High Seas 48. The Story of Mankind 57, etc.

Panh, Rithy (1964–)
Cambodian director. Born in Phnom Penh, he now lives in France.

Rice People/Neak Sri 94. One Fine Evening after War 98, etc.

Pantoliano, Joe (1951–)
American actor, born in Hoboken, New Jersey.

The Idolmaker 80. Risky Business 83. The Final Terror 83. Eddie and the Cruisers 83. The Goonies 85. The Mean Season 85. Running Scared 86. La Bamba 87. The Squeeze 87. Empire of the Sun 87. Short Time 87. Midnight Run 88. Downtown 89. Backstreet Dreams 90. Blue Heat 90. The Last of the Finest 90. Short Time 90. Zandalee 90. Used People 92. Three of Hearts 92. Calendar Girl 93. The Fugitive 93. Three of Hearts 93. Baby's Day Out 94. Bad Boys 95. Steal Big, Steal Little 95. Bound 96. Top of the World 97. US Marshals 98. The Matrix 99. Black and White 99. New Blood (GB/Can.) 99. The Life Before This (Can.) 99. Memento 00. Ready to Rumble 00, etc.

TV series: Free Country 78. From Here to Eternity 79. The Fanelli Boys 90–91.

Panzer, Paul (1872–1958)
American silent screen villain, an extremely hissable specimen.

The Perils of Pauline 14. The Exploits of Elaine 15. The Mystery Mind 19. The Johnstown Flood 26. Under the Red Robe 36. Casablanca 42. The Perils of Pauline 47, many others.

Papamichael, Phedon
American cinematographer and production designer.

as cinematographer: After Midnight 89. Streets 90. Body Chemistry 90. Prayer of the Rollerboys 90. Poison Ivy 92. Cool Runnings 93. Wild Palms (TV) 93. Unstrung Heroes 95. While You Were Sleeping 95. Bio-Dome 96. Unhook the Stars 96. Phenomenon 96. The Locusts 97. Mouse Hunt 97. The Locusts 97. Patch Adams 98. The Million Dollar Hotel 99, etc.

Papas, Irene (1926–) (I. Lelekou)
Greek stage actress who has made films at home and abroad.

Necripolitia (debut) 51. Theodora Slave Empress 54. Attila the Hun 54. Tribute to a Bad Man (US) 55. The Power and the Prize (US) 56. The Guns of Navarone 61. Electra 62. *Zorba the Greek* 64. Beyond the Mountains 66. The Brotherhood (US) 68. 'Z' 68. A Dream of Kings (US) 69. Anne of the Thousand Days 70. The Trojan Women 71. The Fifth Offensive 73. Moses (TV) 76. The Message 76. Iphigenia 77. Bloodline 79. Into the Night 84. The Assisi Underground 85. High Season 87. Sweet Country 87. Pano Kato Ke Plagios 93. Jacob (TV) 94. Party 96. The Odyssey (TV) 98. Inquietude 98, etc.

Paquin, Anna (1982–)
New Zealand juvenile actress, in international films.

The Piano (AA) 93. Jane Eyre 96. Fly Away Home 96. The Member of the Wedding (TV) 97. Amistad 97. Kiss the Sky 98. Hurlyburly 98. A Walk on the Moon 98. She's All That 99. X-Men 00. Almost Famous 00. Finding Forrester 00, etc.

Paradis, Vanessa (1972–)
French pop singer and model whose film debut was much praised.

Noce Blanche 90. Elisa 95. Pleasure/Le Plaisir (voice) 98, etc.

Paradjanov, Sergei (1924–1990)
Georgian film director whose idiosyncratic films ran foul of Soviet authorities. His international reputation dates from 1968. He was imprisoned for four years in 1974 and forbidden to make films on his release. *The Bogeyman/Bobo*, a documentary on his life and work released in 1991, includes film of the heart attack that killed him when he was flying home from Paris, as well as extracts from his last, uncompleted film, *Confession*.
Andriesh 54. The First Lad/Perwyi Paren 58. Flower on the Stone/Zwetok na Kamne 63. The Ballad 64. Shadows of Our Forgotten Ancestors/Teni Zabytykh Predkov 64. *The Colour of Pomegranates*/Sayat Nova 68. The Legend of Suram Fortress (co-d) 84. Asahik Kerib 88, etc.

Paré, Michael (1959–)
American young leading actor. He trained as a chef before deciding to become an actor.
Eddie and the Cruisers 83. The Philadelphia Experiment 84. Streets of Fire 84. Undercover 84. Instant Justice 87. Space Rage 87. The Women's Club 87. World Gone Wild 88. Eddie and the Cruisers II: Eddie Lives 89. Moon 44 90. Empire City 91. The Closer 91. Into the Sun 92. Blink of an Eye 92. Dragonfight 92. Sunset Heat 92. Village of the Damned 95. Raging Angels 95. Bad Moon 96. Sworn Enemies 96. Carver's Gate 96. Strip Search 97. Hope Floats 97. The Virgin Suicides 98, etc.
TV series: The Greatest American Hero 81–83. Houston Knights 87–88.

Paredes, Marisa (1946–)
Spanish leading actress, known internationally for her roles in the films of Pedro ALMODOVAR.
Dark Habits 83. High Heels 91. The Flower of My Secret 95. Deep Crimson/Profundo Carmesi 96. Three Lives and Only One Death/Trois Vies et une Seule Mort 96. Life Is Beautiful (It.) 97. Preference 98. Talk of Angels (US) 98, etc.
❝ I am more sure of myself if I am risking everything. I tire of people who look too much at what they are doing. – *M.P.*

Parer, Damien (1912–1944)
Australian cameraman whose coverage of the war in New Guinea, *Kokoda Front Line* 42, won Australia's first Oscar for the best documentary.

Parfitt, Judy
English actress, from the stage. Born in Sheffield, she trained at RADA and was on-stage from 1954.
Hamlet 69. The Mind of Mr Soames 70. Galileo 74. Secret Orchards 80. Champions 83. Bloody Chamber 83. The Chain 84. The Jewel in the Crown (TV) 84. Maurice 87. Getting It Right 89. Diamond Skulls 89. King Ralph (US) 91. Midnight's Child (US) 92. Dolores Claiborne (US) 95. Element of Doubt 96. Wilde 97. Berkeley Square (TV) 98. Ever After 98, etc.
TV series: Diamond Crack Diamond 70. The Charmings 87-88.

Parillaud, Anne (1960–)
French leading actress. Married director Luc Besson.
Nikita/La Femme Nikita 91. Innocent Blood 92. Map of the Human Heart 93. Six Days, Six Nights/à la Folie 94. Frankie Starlight 95. The Man in the Iron Mask (US) 98. Shattered Image (US) 98. One 4 All/Une Pour Toutes 99, etc.

Paris, Jerry (1925–1986)
American supporting actor.
The Caine Mutiny 54. *Marty* 55. *Unchained* 55, many others; also played the neighbour in *The Dick Van Dyke Show* 61–66.
AS DIRECTOR: *Never a Dull Moment* 68. *Don't Raise the Bridge, Lower the River* 68. *Viva Max* 69. *The Grasshopper* 70.
Police Academy 2 84. Police Academy 3 85.

Park, Chul-Soo
South Korean director and screenwriter.
A Bell for Nirvana 83. Mother/Omi 85. Pillar of Mist/Angae Gidung 86. The Five Year Old Buddha 91. 301,302 95. Farewell My Darling 96, etc.

Park, Nick (1959–)
English animator whose shorts starring inventor Wallace and his dog Gromit have won three Oscars. In 2000, *Broadcast* magazine estimated his financial worth at £12m.
Creature Comforts (AA) 89. A Grand Day Out 91. The Wrong Trousers (AA) 93. A Close Shave (AA) 95. Chicken Run 00, etc.

Park, Ray
Scottish martial arts expert and actor, best known for playing Darth Maul in *Star Wars*.
Star Wars Episode I: The Phantom Menace 99. X-Men 00, etc.

Parker, Alan (1944–)
British director with enough self-assurance to make him an international talking point.
■ Melody (w only) 70. Footsteps (& w) 73. Our Cissy (& w) 73. No Hard Feelings 73. The Evacuees (TV) 74. *Bugsy Malone* (& w) 77. *Midnight Express* (AAN, BFA) 78. Fame (& w) 79. Shoot the Moon (& w) 82. Pink Floyd the Wall 82. Birdy 85. Angel Heart 87. Mississippi Burning (AAN) 88. Come See the Paradise 90. The Commitments 91. The Road to Wellville (wd) 94. Evita 96. Angela's Ashes 98.

Parker, Barnett (1890–1941)
British character actor in Hollywood, one of the perfect butlers of the 30s.
The President's Mystery 36. Espionage 37. Wake Up and Live 37. Listen Darling 38. At the Circus 39. Love Thy Neighbour 40. The Reluctant Dragon 41, etc.

Parker, Cecil (1897–1971) (Cecil Schwabe)
British character actor with upper-class personality which could be amiable or chill.
The Silver Spoon (film debut) 33. A Cuckoo in the Nest 33. Storm in a Teacup 37. Dark Journey 37. *The Lady Vanishes* 38. The Citadel 38. *Caesar and Cleopatra* 45. Hungry Hill 46. Captain Boycott 47. *The First Gentleman* (as the Prince Regent) 47. *Quartet* 48. Dear Mr Prohack 49. *The Chiltern Hundreds* 49. Tony Draws a Horse 51. The Man in the White Suit 51. His Excellency 52. I Believe in You 52. Isn't Life Wonderful? 54. *Father Brown* 54. The Constant Husband 55. The Ladykillers 55. *The Court Jester* (US) 55. It's Great to be Young 56. The Admirable Crichton 57. Indiscreet 58. I was Monty's Double 58. Happy is the Bride 58. A Tale of Two Cities 58. The Navy Lark 59. A French Mistress 60. On the Fiddle 61. Petticoat Pirates 62. Heavens Above 63. The Comedy Man 64. Guns at Batasi 64. Moll Flanders 65. A Study in Terror 65. Circus of Fear 67. Oh What a Lovely War 69, many others.

Parker, Cecilia (1905–1993)
Canadian leading lady who played many Hollywood roles but is best remembered as Andy's sister in the *Hardy Family* series 37–44.
Young as You Feel 31. The Painted Veil 34. Naughty Marietta 35. A Family Affair (first of the Hardy films) 37. Seven Sweethearts 42. Andy Hardy Comes Home 58, etc.

Parker, Charlie 'Bird' (1920–1955)
American jazz alto saxophonist, a seminal figure in the development of modern jazz. Born in Kansas City, he played in local bands before helping to create bebop in company with Dizzy Gillespie in the mid-40s. Drink and heroin addiction led to his early death. Archive footage of him was used in the 1979 jazz documentary *The Last of the Blue Devils*. He was played by Forest Whitaker in Clint Eastwood's biopic *Bird* 88.

Parker, Clifton (1905–1990)
British composer.
The Yellow Canary 43. Johnny Frenchman 45. Blanche Fury 48. The Blue Lagoon 49. Diamond City 49. The Wooden Horse 50. Treasure Island 50. The Story of Robin Hood and His Merrie Men 52. The Gift Horse 52. The Teckman Mystery 54. Hell below Zero 54. Passage Home 55. The Feminine Touch 56. Tarzan and the Lost Safari 57. The Birthday Present 57. Campbell's Kingdom 57. Night of the Demon 57. The Secret Place 57. Sea of Sand 58. Harry Black 58. The Thirty Nine Steps 59. The House of the Seven Hawks 59. Circle of Deception 60. The Hellfire Club 60. The Big Day 60. The Treasure of Monte Cristo 60. Snowball 60. Sink the Bismarck! 60. Taste of Fear 61. Girl on Approval 62. HMS Defiant 62. Mystery Submarine 62. The Informers/Underworld Informers 63, etc.

Parker, Dorothy (1893–1967)
American short-story writer, reviewer and wit who spent some years in Hollywood as an associate scriptwriter of mainly undistinguished films. Her second husband was actor and fellow screenwriter Alan Campbell (1933–47). (In 1933 they went to Hollywood at a joint salary of $5,000 a month.) She was played by Dolores Sutton in *F. Scott Fitzgerald in Hollywood* (TV) 76, Rosemary Harris in *Julia* 77, Jennifer Jason Leigh in *Mrs Parker and the Vicious Circle* 94 and Bebe Neuwirth in the TV biopic *Dash and Lilly* 99.
Biography: 1971, *You Might as Well Live* by John Keats.
Paris in Spring (co-s) 35. Suzy 36. Lady Be Careful 36. *A Star Is Born* (AAN) 37. Woman Chases Man 37. Sweethearts 38. Trade Winds 38. Weekend for Three 41. Saboteur 42. Smash-Up – The Story of a Woman (co-story) (AAN) 46. The Fan 49, etc.
See also: ALGONQUIN ROUND TABLE.
❝ Through the sweat and tears I shed over my first script, I saw a great truth – one of those eternal, universal truths that serve to make you feel much worse than you did when you started. And that is no writer, whether he writes from love or from money, can condescend to what he writes. – *D.P.*
Come grace this lotus-laden shore
The isle of Do-What's-Done-Before.
Come curb the new and watch the old win
Out where streets are paved with
Goldwyn. – *D.P.*
Scratch an actor and you'll find an actress. – *D.P.*
Hollywood money isn't money. It's congealed snow, melts in your hand. – *D.P.*
So odd a blend of Little Nell and Lady Macbeth. – *Alexander Woollcott*
The first modern American woman: she could out-talk, out-drink, out-fuck all the men. – *Alan Rudolph*

Parker, Eddie (1900–1960)
American stuntman who doubled for most of Universal's horror stars.

Parker, Eleanor (1922–)
American leading lady with brief stage experience before a Hollywood contract; her career followed a typical pattern, with increasingly good leading roles followed by a decline, with a later comeback in character parts.
Biography: 1989, *Eleanor Parker* by Doug McClelland.
■ They Died with Their Boots On (debut as extra) 41. Buses Roar 42. Mysterious Doctor 43. Mission to Moscow 43. The Very Thought of You 44. Crime by Night 44. Between Two Worlds 44. The Last Ride 44. Pride of the Marines 45. Of Human Bondage (as Mildred) 46. Never Say Goodbye 46. Escape Me Never 47. *The Voice of the Turtle* 47. The Woman in White 48. Chain Lightning 49. Three Secrets 50. *Caged* (AAN) 50. Valentino 51. A Millionaire for Christy 51. *Detective Story* (AAN) 51. Scaramouche 52. Above and Beyond 52. Escape from Fort Bravo 53. The Naked Jungle 54. Valley of the Kings 54. Many Rivers to Cross 54. *Interrupted Melody* (AAN) 55. The Man with the Golden Arm 56. The King and Four Queens 56. Lizzie 57. The Seventh Sin 57. A Hole in the Head 59. Home from the Hill 60. Return to Peyton Place 61. Madison Avenue 62. Panic Button 64. The Sound of Music 65. The Oscar 66. An American Dream 66. Warning Shot 66. The Tiger and the Pussycat 67. How to Steal the World 68. Eye of the Cat 69. Maybe I'll Come Home in the Spring 70. Vanished (TV) 71. Home for the Holidays (TV) 72. The Great American Beauty Contest (TV) 74. *She's Dressed to Kill* (TV) 79. Sunburn 79. Madame X (TV) 81.
TV series: Bracken's World 69.

Parker, Fess (1925–)
American leading man with some stage experience. He is now a vintner and hotelier in California.
Untamed Frontier 52. *Davy Crockett* 54 (and two sequels). The Great Locomotive Chase 56. Westward Ho the Wagons 56. Old Yeller 57. The Hangman 59. Hell is for Heroes 62. Smoky 66, etc.
TV series: Mr Smith Goes to Washington 62. Daniel Boone 64–68.

Parker, Jameson (1947–)
American leading man who first appeared on the daytime soap operas *Somerset* and *One Life to Live* in the 70s.
The Bell Jar 79. A Small Circle of Friends 80. Women at West Point (TV) 80. Anatomy of a Seduction (TV) 80. White Dog 82. Who Is Julia? (TV) 86. Prince of Darkness 87. Dead before Dawn 93, etc.
TV series: Simon and Simon 81–88.

Parker, Jean (1912–) (Luis Stephanie Zelinska)
Once-demure American leading lady, popular in the 30s; latterly playing hard-boiled roles.
Rasputin and the Empress 32. *Little Women* 33. *Sequoia* 34. The Ghost Goes West (GB) 36. Princess O'Hara 37. The Flying Deuces 39. Beyond Tomorrow 40. No Hands on the Clock 42. One Body Too Many 42. Minesweeper 43. Bluebeard 44. Detective Kitty O'Day 44. Lady in the Death House 44. The Gunfighter 50. Those Redheads from Seattle 53. Black Tuesday 54. A Lawless Street 55. Apache Uprising 65. The Morning After 72, etc.

Parker, Mary-Louise (1964–)
American actress.
Signs of Life 89. Longtime Companion 90. Fried Green Tomatoes 91. Grand Canyon 91. Naked in New York 93. Mr Wonderful 93. The Client 94. Bullets over Broadway 94. Boys on the Side 95. Reckless 95. Sugartime (TV) 95. The Portrait of a Lady 96. Murder in Mind 97. The Maker 97. Goodbye, Lover 98. Legalese (TV) 98. The Five Senses (Can) 99. Let the Devil Wear Black 98, etc.

Parker, Oliver
English director, screenwriter and actor. He studied at Cambridge University and began in the theatre.
Nightbreed (a) 90. Nuns on the Run (a) 90. Othello (wd) 95. An Ideal Husband (a,wd) 99, etc.
TV series: Casualty 93.

Parker, Sarah Jessica (1965–)
American actress, a former child star who played the title role in *Annie* on Broadway in the late 70s. Married actor Matthew BRODERICK in 1997.
Rich Kids 79. Somewhere Tomorrow 83. Firstborn 84. Footloose 84. Girls Just Want to Have Fun 85. Flight of the Navigator 86. L.A. Story 91. Honeymoon in Vegas 92. Hocus Pocus 93. Striking Distance 93. Ed Wood 94. Miami Rhapsody 95. If Lucy Fell 96. The Substance of Fire 96. The First Wives Club 96. Mars Attacks! 96. Extreme Measures 96. 'Til There Was You 97. Dudley Do-Right 99. State and Main 00, etc.
TV series: Square Pegs 82–83. A Year in the Life 87–88. Equal Justice 90–91. Sex and the City 98– .

Parker, Suzy (1932–) (Cecelia Parker)
Statuesque American leading lady, former model. She married actor Bradford Dillman, her third husband, in 1963.
Kiss Them for Me (debut) 57. *Ten North Frederick* 58. The Best of Everything 59. Circle of Deception 61. The Interns 62. Chamber of Horrors 66, etc.

Parker, Trey (1972–) (Donald McKay Parker III)
American actor, writer, director and songwriter, best known as the creator of the TV cartoon series *South Park* with Matt STONE. Born in Auburn, Alabama, he began acting as a teenager, with his family relocating to Los Angeles so that he could continue his career. He studied at the Berklee School of Music before transferring to Colorado University to study film. He has also performed and recorded as part of the hip-hop group EYC (Express Yourself Clearly).
Newsies (a) 92. A Christmas Story (short) 92. Cannibal! The Musical/Alfred Packer: The Musical (p, a, wd, s) 96. Orgazmo (wd, a) 97. BASEketball (a) 98. South Park: Bigger Longer & Uncut (p, co-w, d, voices, AANs) 99, etc.
TV series: Hull High 90. South Park 97– .

Parker, Willard (1912–1996) (Worster van Eps)
Tall American 'second lead', in films from 1938 after stage experience.
A Slight Case of Murder (debut) 38. The Fighting Guardsman 43. You Gotta Stay Happy 48. Sangaree 53. The Great Jesse James Raid 53. The Earth Dies Screaming 64. Waco 66, etc.
TV series: Tales of the Texas Rangers 55–57.

Parkins, Barbara (1942–)
Canadian leading lady whose major success was TV.
Valley of the Dolls 67. The Kremlin Letters 69. The Mephisto Waltz 71. Puppet on a Chain 72. Asylum 72. Captains and the Kings (TV) 76. Shout at the Devil 76. Ziegfeld: the Man and his Women (as Anna Held) (TV) 78. The Critical List (TV) 78. Bear Island 80, etc.
TV series: *Peyton Place* 64–68.

Parks, Gordon (1925–)
American director, former stills photographer, novelist and composer.
The Learning Tree 68. *Shaft* 71. Shaft's Big Score 72. Leadbelly 76. Moments without Proper Names 86, etc.

Parks Jnr, Gordon (1948–1979)
American director, son of Gordon Parks. Killed in a plane crash.
Superfly 72. Thomasine and Bushrod 74. Three the Hard Way 74. Aaron Loves Angela 75.

Parks, Larry (1914–1975) (Sam Kleusman Lawrence Parks)
American light leading man whose career in 'B' pictures was interrupted by his highly successful impersonation of Al Jolson. He subsequently proved difficult to cast, and was forced out of Hollywood after testifying to the UnAmerican Activities Committee.
■ You Belong to Me 41. Mystery Ship 41. Harmon of Michigan 41. Blondie Goes to College 42. Harvard Here I Come 42. The Boogie Man Will Get You 42. Atlantic Convoy 42. Canal Zone 42. Three Girls About Town 42. Sing for your Supper 42. Flight Lieutenant 42. Submarine Raiser 42. Honolulu Lu 42. Hello Annapolis 42. You were never Lovelier 42. A Man's World 42. North of the Rockies 42. Alias Boston Blackie 42. They All Kissed the Bride 42. Redhead from Manhattan 43. Is Everybody Happy? 43. First Comes Courage 43. Power of the Press 43. The Deerslayer 43. Destroyer 43. Reveille with Beverly 43. She's a Sweetheart 44. The Racket Man 44. The Black Parachute 44. Stars on Parade 44. Hey Rookie 44. Sergeant Mike 44. Counter Attack 45. Jealousy 45. Renegades 46. *The Jolson Story* (AAN) 46. Her Husband's Affairs 47. Down to Earth 47. The Swordsman 47. Gallant Blade 48. *Jolson Sings Again* 49. Emergency Wedding 50. Love is Better than Ever 52. Tiger by the Tail 55. *Freud* 62.

Parks, Michael (1938–)
Brooding American leading man.
Wild Seed 64. Bus Riley's Back in Town 65. The Bible (as Adam) 66. The Idol (GB) 66. The Happening 67. Can Ellen Be Saved? (TV) 73. The Last Hard Men 76. Sidewinder One 77. Love and the Midnight Auto Supply 77. The Private Files of J. Edgar Hoover 78. Breakthrough 79. Fast Friends (TV) 79. North Sea Hijack 80. Reward (TV) 81. Savannah Smiles 82. Chase (TV) 85. Club Life 86. Return of Josey Wales (& d) 86. Stamp of a Killer (TV) 87. Arizona Heat 88. Welcome to Spring Break 88. Gore Vidal's Billy the Kid 89. The Hitman 91. Storyville 92. Death Wish V: The Face of Death 94. From Dusk till Dawn 96. Julian Po 97. Niagra, Niagra 98, etc.
TV series: Then Came Bronson 69. The Colbys 87.

Parks, Van Dyke (1941–)
American composer and singer, a former child actor.
Goin' South 78. Popeye 80. Club Paradise 86. Rented Lips 88. Casual Sex? 88. The Two Jakes (& a) 90. Wild Bill 95. The Summer of Ben Tyler (TV) 96. Private Parts 96. Bastard out of Carolina (TV) 96, etc.

Parkyakarkus (1904–1958) (Harry Einstein)
American radio comedian formerly known as Harry Parke. He is the father of actor-director Albert Brooks.
Strike Me Pink 36. Night Spot 38. Glamour Boy 40. Earl Carroll's Vanities 45.

Parkyn, Leslie (–1983)
British executive producer, associated with *Sergei Nolbandov* 1951–57, subsequently with Julian Wintle.
The Kidnappers 53. Tiger Bay 59. The Waltz of the Toreadors 62. Father Came Too 64, many others.

Parlo, Dita (1906–1971) (Gerthe Kornstadt)
German star actress of the 30s.
Homecoming 28. Melody of the Heart 30. Secrets of the Orient 31. L'Atalante 34. The Mystic Mountain 36. Mademoiselle Docteur 37. La Grande Illusion 37. Ultimatum 39. Justice est Faite 50. Quand le Soleil Montera 56, etc.

Parnell, Emory (1894–1979)
American general-purpose character actor: could be villain, prison warden, weakling or kindly father.
King of Alcatraz 39. I Married a Witch 42. Mama Loves Papa 46. Words and Music 48. Call Me Madam 53. Man of the West 58, many others.

Parr-Davies, Harry (1914–1955)
Welsh composer and songwriter who contributed songs to many of Gracie Fields' films and other British musicals of the 30s and 40s. He had a big wartime hit with 'Pedro the Fisherman', from his stage show *The Lisbon Story*, which was subsequently filmed.
This Week of Grace 33. Sing as We Go 34. Queen of Hearts 36. We're Going to Be Rich 38. Keep Smiling/Smile as You Go 38. It's in the Air 38. Shipyard Sally 39. Maytime in Mayfair 49. The Lisbon Story 49, etc.

Parrish, Helen (1922–1959)
American leading lady, former baby model and child actress.
The Big Trail 31. A Dog of Flanders 34. Mad about Music 38. You'll Find Out 40. They All Kissed the Bride 42. The Mystery of the Thirteenth Guest 44. The Wolf Hunters 50, etc.

Parrish, Robert (1916–1995)
American director, former editor and child actor.
Autobiography: 1976, *Growing Up in Hollywood*. 1988, *Hollywood Doesn't Live Here Anymore*.
■ Cry Danger 51. The Mob 51. My Pal Gus 52. The San Francisco Story 52. Rough Shoot (GB) 52. Assignment Paris 52. The Purple Plain 54. Lucy Gallant 55. Fire Down Below 57. Saddle the Wind 58. The Wonderful Country 59. In the French Style (& p) 63. Up from the Beach 65. The Bobo 67. Casino Royale (part) 67. Duffy 68. Journey to the Far Side of the Sun 69. A Town Called Bastard 71. The Marseilles Contract 74. Mississippi Blues (co-d) 84.
❝ His films belong to a director who craves anonymity. – *Andrew Sarris, 1968*

Parrondo, Gil
American art director and production designer.
The 7th Voyage of Sinbad 58. The 3 Worlds of Gulliver 60. The Valley of Gwangi 69. The Battle of Britain 69. Patton (AA) 70. Nicholas and Alexandra (AA) 71. Travels with My Aunt (AAN) 72. Robin and Marian 76. The Boys from Brazil 78. Cuba 79. Lionheart 87. Farewell to the King 89. The Return of the Musketeers 89. Christopher Columbus: The Discovery 92. The Disappearance of Garcia Lorca 97, etc.

Parrott, James (1892–1939)
American director, mainly of two-reelers featuring Laurel and Hardy (*Blotto*, *The Music Box*, *County Hospital*, etc), Charlie Chase and Max Davidson. Features include *Jailbirds* 31, *Sing, Sister, Sing* 35.

Parry, Gordon (1908–1981)
British director of mainly secondary films: former actor, production manager, etc.
Bond Street 48. Third Time Lucky 48. Now Barabbas… 49. Midnight Episode 50. Tom Brown's Schooldays 51. Golden Arrow 52. Front Page Story 53. Innocents in Paris 53. Women of Twilight 53. Fast and Loose 54. A Yank in Ermine 55. Sailor Beware 56. A Touch of the Sun 56. Tread Softly Stranger 58, etc.

Parry, Natasha (1930–)
British leading lady who married Peter Brook. Appears occasionally on stage and screen.
Dance Hall 49. The Dark Man 50. Crow Hollow 52. Knave of Hearts 53. Windom's Way 57. The Rough and the Smooth 59. Midnight Lace 60. The Fourth Square 62. The Girl in the Headlines 64. Romeo and Juliet 68. Oh What a Lovely War 69. La Chambre Voisine 80, etc.

Parsons, Estelle (1927–)
American character actress with stage background.
Bonnie and Clyde (AA) 67. Rachel Rachel (AAN) 68. I Never Sang for My Father 69. Don't Drink the Water 69. I Walk the Line 70. Watermelon Man 71. Two People 73. For Pete's Sake 74. Foreplay 75. Open Admissions (TV) 88. The Lemon Sisters 89. Dick Tracy 90. A Private Matter (TV) 92. That Darn Cat 96. Looking for Richard 96, etc.

Parsons, Harriet (1906–1983)
American producer, daughter of Louella Parsons.
I Remember Mama 47. Clash by Night 51. Susan Slept Here 54, etc.

Parsons, Louella (1880–1972) (L. Oettinger)
Hollywood columnist whose gossip rivalled in readership that of Hedda Hopper. In occasional films as herself, e.g. *Hollywood Hotel* 37, *Starlift* 51.
Autobiography: 1944, *The Gay Illiterate*. 1962, *Tell It to Louella*.
Biography: 1973, *Hedda and Louella* by George Eels.
❝ Her friends always stand by her. When she prematurely published a claim that an actress was pregnant, the actress's husband hastened to prove her correct. – *Time Magazine*
Her writings stand out like an asthmatic's gasps. – *Nunnally Johnson*
Not a bad old slob. – *James Mason*

Parsons, Milton (1904–1980)
Lugubrious American character actor often seen as undertaker.
The Hidden Hand 42. Margie 44, many others.

Parsons, Nicholas (1928–)
English light actor, also a variety and cabaret performer and quiz-game chairman, much on radio. Born in Grantham, Lincolnshire, he studied engineering at Glasgow University before beginning on stage.
Autobiography: 1994, *The Straight Man: My Life in Comedy*.
Master of Bankdam 48. Brothers in Law 57. Too Many Crooks 59. Doctor in Love 62. Don't Raise the Bridge, Lower the River 68. Spy Story 76, etc.
TV series: The Eric Barker Half Hour 51–53. Look at It This Way 52. What's It All About? 55. Here and Now 55–56. Strike a New Note 56. Get Happy 56. Four Feather Falls (voice) 60. The Arthur Haynes Show 57–62, 63–65. The Ugliest Girl in Town (US) 68–69. Sale of the Century 78–83.

Parton, Dolly (1946–)
Voluptuous American country and western singer.
Nine to Five (AANs) 81. The Best Little Whorehouse in Texas 82. Rhinestone (& m) 84. Steel Magnolias 89. Wild Texas Wind 91. Straight Talk 92, etc.
TV series: Dixie Fixin's 94.
❝ I enjoy the way I look, but it's a joke. – *D.P.*
I'm on a seafood diet – I see food, I eat it. – *D.P.*

Pascal, Christine (1952–1996)
French actress, screenwriter and director. Born in Lyon, she studied acting at the local conservatoire. Committed suicide by throwing herself from the window of a psychiatric clinic in Paris.
AS ACTRESS: The Watchmaker of Saint-Paul/L'horloger de Saint-Paul 73. La Meilleure Façon de Marcher 76. Des Enfants Gâtés (& co-w) 77. On Efface Tout 78. Panny z Wilka (Pol.) 79. Coup de Foudre 83. Elsa, Elsa 85. Round Midnight/Autour de Minuit 86. La Travestie 88. Rien que des Mensonges 91. Les Patriotes 93, etc.
AS DIRECTOR: Felicité (& a, co-w) 77. La Garce (& co-w) 83. Zanzibar (& co-w) 88. Le Petit Prince a Dit (& co-w) 92. Adultery, a User's Manual/Adultère, Mode d'Emploi 96.

Pascal, Gabriel (1894–1954) (Gabor Lehöl)
Romanian-born producer and director, a former actor, of somewhat mysterious origins. After working in Germany and Italy, he came to Britain in the 30s, won the esteem of Bernard Shaw and persuaded him to part, for a token payment, with the film rights to his plays, which many had tried to do and failed. His version of *Caesar and Cleopatra* was the most expensive British film of its time, costing around £1.25m, more than twice its original budget, which did much to damage the reputation of the Rank Organization, and grounded his career. Failed projects included a version of Shaw's *St Joan* starring Katharine Hepburn, *The Devil's Disciple* with Clark Gable and Cary Grant, and a film of the life of Gandhi. He was also a prime mover in turning *Pygmalion* into the musical *My Fair Lady*.
Biography: 1971, *The Disciple and His Devil* by Valerie Pascal.
Populi Morituri (It.) (a, co-d) 28. The Living Dead/Friedricke, Unheimliche Geschichten (Ger.) (p) 32. Café Mascot (p) 36. Reasonable Doubt (p) 36. *Pygmalion* (p) 38. Major Barbara (p, co-d) 41. Caesar and Cleopatra (p, d) 45. Androcles and the Lion (US) (p) 53, etc.
❝ I give you my word of honor as a Hungarian Cavalry Officer and an English Farmer, you are the greatest crook unhung. – *G.P., in a telegram to a Hollywood agent*
Life is a divine poem, and it is our own fault if we recite it badly. – *G.P.*
Gabriel Pascal is one of those extraordinary men who turn up occasionally, say once in a century, and may be called godsends in the arts to which they are devoted. Pascal is doing for the films what Diaghileff did for the Russian Ballet. – *George Bernard Shaw*
A marvellous gypsy rogue with incredible panache and no guile, as open as a baby and as ruthless as a tiger. – *Rex Harrison*
A Rumanian who claimed to be Hungarian and looked like a Himalayan. Architecturally he was circular and his voice had the timbre of a 78 record played at 33. – *Alan Jay Lerner*
Gabby was a showman of some magnitude, but not a director. He knew as much about directing as a cow does about playing the piano. – *Michael Powell*

Pascal, Gisèle (1923–) (Gisèle Tallone)
French leading actress of stage and screen. Born in Cannes, she was in films from the early 40s. Romantically involved with actor Yves MONTAND and Prince Rainier of Monaco, she married actor Raymond PELLEGRIN.
L'Arlésienne 42. Mademoiselle S'Amuse 47. The Naked Woman/La Femme Nue 49. Bel Amour 51. Boum sur Paris 54. Mademoiselle de Paris 55. Sylviane de Mes Nuits 57. The Iron Mask/Le Masque de Fer 62. La Femme Publique 84. Juillet en Septembre 87, etc.

Pasco, Richard (1926–)
British character actor, mainly on stage and TV.
Room at the Top 59. Yesterday's Enemy 60. The Gorgon 64. Rasputin the Mad Monk 66. The Watcher in the Woods 80. Wagner 83. Mrs Brown 97, etc.

Pasdar, Adrian (1965–)
American leading actor.
Top Gun 86. Streets of Gold 86. Solarwarriors 87. Near Dark 87. Big Time 88. Cookie 89. Torn Apart 90. Vital Signs 90. Grand Isle 91. Just Like a Woman (GB) 92. The Killing Box 93. The Last Good Time 94. The Pompatus of Love 96, etc.

Paskaljevic, Goran (1947–)
Serbian (formerly Yugoslavian) film director.
The Beach Guard in Winter/Cuvar Plaze U Zimskom Periodu 76. The Dog Who Loved Trains/Pas Koji Je Voleo Vozove 77. Twilight Time/Suton 83. Varljivo Leto '68 84. Guardian Angel/Andjeo Cuvar 87. Time of Miracles/Vreme Cuda (& p, co-w) 90. Tango Argentino (& p) 92. Someone Else's America 95. The Powder Keg/Bure Baruta (co-p, co-w, d) 98, etc.

Pasolini, Pier Paolo (1922–1975)
Italian director, novelist, poet and critic. Born in Bologna, he was expelled from the Communist Party for homosexuality, but remained passionately proletarian in his attitudes. He started in films as a writer, before becoming an increasingly controversial director and social commentator. He was beaten and run over near the seaside town of Ostia, allegedly by a homosexual prostitute, though there is evidence that his murder was committed by right-wing thugs. A documentary, *Pasolini: An Italian Crime*, made by Marco Tullio Giordana in 1995, comes to the conclusion that more than one person was involved in his death.
Biography: 1987, *Pasolini* by Enzo Siciliano.
Accattone 61. Mamma Roma 62. The Witches (part) 63. *The Gospel According to St Matthew* 64. Oedipus Rex 67. *Theorem* 68. Pigsty 69. Medea 70. Decameron 70. The Canterbury Tales 71. The Arabian Nights 74. The 120 Days of Sodom 75, etc.
❝ Life is a heap of insignificant and ironic ruins. – *P.P.P.*

Passer, Ivan (1933–)
Czech director, latterly in Hollywood.
A Boring Afternoon 64. Intimate Lighting 66. Born to Win 71. Law and Disorder 74. Silver Bears 78. Ace Up My Sleeve 78. Cutter's Way 81. Creator 85. Haunted Summer 88. Stalin (TV) 92. Kidnapped (TV) 95, etc.

Pasternak, Boris (1890–1960)
Russian novelist, author of *Dr Zhivago*.

Pasternak, Joe (1901–1991)
Hungarian producer in Hollywood during the golden years; especially identified with cheerful light musicals.
Autobiography: 1956, *Easy the Hard Way*.
Three Smart Girls 36. One Hundred Men and a Girl 37. *Mad about Music* 38. Destry Rides Again 39. *Seven Sinners* 40. *It Started with Eve* 41. *Presenting Lily Mars* 42. *Song of Russia* 43. *Two Girls and a Sailor* 44. *Anchors Aweigh* 45. *Holiday in Mexico* 46. *The Unfinished Dance* 47. *On an Island with You* 48. *In the Good Old Summertime* 49. *The Duchess of Idaho* 50. The Great Caruso 51. *Skirts Ahoy* 52. *Latin Lovers* 53. *The Student Prince* 54. *Love Me or Leave Me* 55. *The Opposite Sex* 56. *Ten Thousand Bedrooms* 57. *Party Girl* 58. *Ask Any Girl* 59. *Please Don't Eat the Daisies* 60. *The Horizontal Lieutenant* 61. *Jumbo* 62. *The Courtship of Eddie's Father* 63. *Girl Happy* 65. *Penelope* 66. *The Sweet Ride* 68, *many others*.

Pastor, Rosana
Spanish leading actress.
Black Man with a Sax/Negro Con Un Saxo 88. Land and Freedom (GB) 95. In Praise of Older Women/En Brazos De La Mujer Madura 97. A Further Gesture (GB/Ger./Ire.) 97. The Commissioner (GB/Ger./Bel.) 98. Un Banco en el Parque 99. The Wheel of Fire 99. Leo 00, etc.

Pastorelli, Robert (1954–)
American actor.
Outrageous Fortune 87. Beverly Hills Cop II 87. Dances with Wolves 90. Folks! 92. FernGully: The Last Rainforest 92. Painted Heart 92. Sister Act II: Back in the Habit 93. Striking Distance 93. Michael 96. Eraser 96. A Simple Wish 97. Scotch and Milk 98. Bait 00, etc.
TV series: Murphy Brown 88–94. Cracker 97.

Pastrone, Giovanni (1883–1959)
Pioneer producer and director of Italian cinema, whose spectacular *Cabiria* was one of the first, and most influential, of epic movies. He abandoned cinema in the 20s.
Giordano Bruno 08. The Fall of Troy 10. Padre 12. Cabiria 14. Tigre Real 16. Hedda Gabler 19, etc.

Patch, Wally (1888–1970) (Walter Vinicombe)
Burly British cockney character actor, in films from 1920 after varied show-business experience.
Shadows 31. The Good Companions 32. Get Off My Foot 35. Not So Dusty 36. Bank Holiday 38. Quiet Wedding 40. Gasbags 40. The Common Touch 41. Old Mother Riley at Home 45. The Ghosts of Berkeley Square 47. The Guinea Pig 49. Will Any Gentleman? 53. Private's Progress 55. I'm All Right, Jack 59. Sparrows Can't Sing 63, many others.

Pate, Michael (1920–)
Australian actor in Hollywood in the 50s and 60s, often as Red Indian chief or second-string villain.
The Rugged O'Riordans 49. The Strange Door 51. Five Fingers 52. Houdini 53. The Silver Chalice 54. The Court Jester 56. Congo Crossing 56. The Oklahoman 57. Green Mansions 59. The Canadians 61. McLintock 63. Major Dundee 65. Tim (wd) 79. Return of Captain Invincible 83. Death of a Soldier 87. Howling III: The Marsupials 87. Official Denial 94, etc.
TV series: Matlock Police 71.

Paterson, Bill (1945–)
Scottish character actor, from the stage.
Licking Hitler (TV) 71. The Ploughman's Lunch 83. Comfort and Joy 84. The Killing Fields 84. A Private Function 84. Defence of the Realm 85. The Adventures of Baron Munchausen 88. Truly Madly Deeply 90. The Witches 90. The Object of Beauty 91. Chaplin 92. Spice World: The Movie 97. Melissa (TV) 97. Hilary and Jackie 98. Heart 98. The Match 99. Wives and Daughters (TV) 99. Sunshine 99. Complicity 99, etc.
TV series: The Writing on the Wall 96.

Paterson, Neil (1916–1995)
British screenwriter and novelist.
The Kidnappers 53. Devil on Horseback 54. The Woman for Joe 55. High Tide at Noon 57. Innocent Sinners 57. The Shiralee 57. *Room at the Top* (AA) 58. The Spiral Road 62. Mister Moses 65, etc.

Paterson, Pat (1911–1978)
English leading lady who went to Hollywood but gave up her career to marry Charles Boyer.
■ The Professional Guest 31. The Great Gay Road 31. Night Shadows 31. Murder on the Second Floor 32. Partners Please 32. Here's George 32. Bitter Sweet 33. Love Time 34. Bottoms Up 34. Call it Luck 34. Charlie Chan in Egypt 35. Lottery Lover 35. Spendthrift 36. 52nd Street 37. Idiot's Delight 39.

Pathé, Charles (1863–1957)
Pioneer French executive and producer, founder of Pathé Frères and later Pathé Gazette. Also credited with making the first 'long' film: *Les Misérables* (made in 1909, it ran four whole reels).

Patinkin, Mandy (1952–)
American actor.
The Big Fix 78. Ragtime 81. Daniel 83. Yentl 83. The Princess Bride 87. Alien Nation 88. The House on Carroll Street 88. Dick Tracy 90. Impromptu 91. True Colors 91. The Doctor 91. The Music of Chance 93. Broken Glass (TV) 96. The Hunchback of Notre Dame (title role, TV) 97. Lulu on the Bridge 98, etc.
TV series: Chicago Hope 94–95, 99.

Patric, Jason (1966–)
Young American leading actor, the son of playwright Jason Miller and the grandson of actor Jackie Gleason.
Toughlove (TV) 85. Solarbabies 86. The Lost Boys 87. The Beast 88. Frankenstein Unbound 90. After Dark, My Sweet 90. Rush 91. Geronimo: An American Legend 93. The Journey of August King 95. Sleepers 96. Incognito 97. Speed 2: Cruise Control 97. Your Friends & Neighbors 98, etc.

Patrick, Dorothy (1922–1987)
Blonde American actress of the 40s.
Boy's Ranch 45. Till the Clouds Roll By 46. The Mighty McGurk 46. High Wall 47. New Orleans 47. Alias a Gentleman 47. Follow Me Quietly 49. Come to the Stable 49. 711 Ocean Drive 50. Torch Song 53. Violent Saturday 55. The View from Pompey's Head 55, etc.

Patrick, Gail (1911–1980) (Margaret Fitzpatrick)
American leading lady in Hollywood from early 30s, usually in routine smart-woman roles. Retired from acting and became a TV producer, notably of the successful *Perry Mason* series.
The Phantom Broadcast 32. Cradle Song 33. No More Ladies 35. Artists and Models 37. Reno 40. Quiet, Please, Murder 43. Women in Bondage 44. Twice Blessed 45. The Plainsman and the Lady 46. Calendar Girl 47, many others.

Patrick, John (1905–1995) (John Patrick Goggan)
American playwright. Works filmed include *The Hasty Heart*, *The Teahouse of the August Moon*. Committed suicide.
SCREENPLAYS: Educating Father 36. One Mile from Heaven 37. International Settlement 38. Mr Moto Takes a Chance 38. Enchantment 48. The President's Lady 53. Three Coins in the Fountain 54. Love Is a Many Splendored Thing 55. High Society 56. Les Girls 57. Some Came Running 58. The World of Suzie Wong 61. The Main Attraction 63. The Shoes of the Fisherman 68, etc.

Patrick, Lee (1906–1982)
American character actress with stage experience, in Hollywood from 1937, usually as hard-bitten blondes.
Strange Cargo (debut) 29. *The Maltese Falcon* 41. Now Voyager 42. Mother Wore Tights 47. Caged 50. There's No Business Like Show Business 54. Vertigo 58. Summer and Smoke 61. The New Interns 64. *The Black Bird* 75, many others.
TV series: Topper 53–55. Mr Adams and Eve 56–57.

Patrick, Nigel (1913–1981) (Nigel Wemyss)
Debonair British leading actor, on stage from 1932.
■ Mrs Pym of Scotland Yard 39. Uneasy Terms 48. *Noose* 48. Spring in Park Lane 48. Silent Dust 49. Jack of Diamonds 49. The Perfect Woman 50. *Trio* 50. Morning Departure 50. Pandora and the Flying Dutchman 51. Encore 51. The Browning Version 51. Young Wives' Tale 51. Meet Me Tonight 52. *The Pickwick Papers* (as Mr Jingle) 52. Who Goes There 52. *The Sound Barrier* 52. Grand National Night 53. Forbidden Cargo 54. The Sea Shall Not Have Them 54. All for Mary 55. A Prize of Gold 55. Raintree County 57. How to Murder a Rich Uncle 57. Count Five and Die 58. The Man Inside 58. Sapphire 59. *The League of Gentlemen* 60. The Trials of Oscar Wilde 60. Johnny Nobody (& d) 61. The Informers 63. The Virgin Soldiers 69. The Battle of Britain 69. The Executioner 70. Tales from the Crypt 72. The Great Waltz 72. The Mackintosh Man 73.
TV series: Zero One 62.

Patrick, Robert (1959–)
American actor, often in action films.
Future Hunters 86. Equalizer 2000 87. Die Hard 2 90. Terminator II: Judgment Day (as the Terminator) 91. Fire in the Sky 93. Double Dragon 94. Striptease 96. Cop Land 97. Asylum 97. The Vivero Letter 98. The Faculty 98, etc.

Patten, Luana (1938–1996)
American teenage actress of the 50s. Died of respiratory failure after a long illness.
Song of the South 46. So Dear to My Heart 48. Johnny Tremain 57. The Little Shepherd of Kingdom Come 61. A Thunder of Drums 61. Follow Me Boys 66. Grotesque 88, etc.

Patterson, Elizabeth (1876–1966)
American character actress with stage experience; in Hollywood from the late 20s, usually as kindly or shrewish elderly ladies.
Daddy Longlegs 30. A Bill of Divorcement 32. Miss Pinkerton 32. Dinner at Eight 33. So Red the Rose 36. Sing You Sinners 38. *The Cat and the Canary* 39. *Tobacco Road* 41. Hail the Conquering Hero 44. Lady on a Train 45. *Intruder in the Dust* 48. Little Women 49. Bright Leaf 50. Pal Joey 57. The Oregon Trail 59, many others.

Patterson, Lee (1929–)
Sturdy Canadian leading man of minor British and American films who spent a decade in the 60s and 70s on the soap opera *One Life to Live*.
36 Hours 51. The Passing Stranger 54. Above Us the Waves 55. Soho Incident 56. Cat and Mouse 58. Jack the Ripper 60. The Ceremony 63. Valley of Mystery 67. Chato's Land 72. Bullseye! 90, etc.
TV series: Surfside Six 60–62.

Patterson, Neva (1925–)
American character actress.
Desk Set 57. Too Much Too Soon 58. The Domino Principle 77. Women of Valor (TV) 86, etc.
TV series: The Governor and JJ 69. Nichols 71.

Patton, Will (1954–)
American actor.
Silkwood 83. After Hours 85. Desperately Seeking Susan 85. No Way Out 86. Wildfire 88. A Shock to the System 90. Dillinger 91. In the Soup 92. Cold Heaven 92. Romeo Is Bleeding 93. Natural Causes 94. The Puppet Masters 94. Judicial Consent 94. Copycat 95. The Spitfire Grill 96. Fled 96. This World, Then the Fireworks 97. The Postman 97. Inventing the Abbots 97. Armageddon 98. OK Garage 98. I Woke Up Early the Day I Died 98. Entrapment 99. Breakfast of Champions 99. Jesus' Son 99. Gone In 60 Seconds 00. Remember the Titans 00, etc.

Paul, Robert (1869–1943)
Pioneer British movie camera inventor (1895). The following year he invented a projector, which he called a theatrograph. Later turned showman.

Paull, Lawrence G (1943–)
American production designer. He trained as an architect and a city planner.
Little Fauss and Big Halsy 70. The Hired Hand 71. The Naked Ape 73. The Bingo Long Traveling All-Stars and Motor Kings 76. Blue Collar 78. In God We Trust 80. Blade Runner (AAN) 82. Romancing the Stone 84. Back to the Future 85. Project X 87. Cocoon: The Return 88. Harlem Nights 89. The Last of the Finest 90. Predator 2 90. City Slickers 91. Memoirs of an Invisible Man 92. Another Stakeout 93. Naked Gun $33\frac{1}{3}$: The Final Insult 94. Man of the House 95. Escape from L.A. 96, etc.

Paulvé, André (1898–1982)
French producer.
La Comédie du Bonheur 39. Lumière d'Eté 42. L'Eternel Retour 43. Les Visiteurs du Soir 43. La Belle et la Bête 45. Ruy Blas 47. Orphée 49. Manèges 49. Casque d'Or 51, many others.

Pavan, Marisa (1932–) (Marisa Pierangeli)
Italian leading lady, sister of Pier Angeli. In Hollywood from 1950.
What Price Glory? (debut) 52. The Rose Tattoo (AAN) 55. The Man in the Grey Flannel Suit 56. Solomon and Sheba 59. John Paul Jones 59. The Slightly Pregnant Man (Fr.) 73. Johnny Monroe 87, etc.

Pavarotti, Luciano (1935–)
Italian tenor in international opera. Starred in one film in 1982, *Yes Giorgio*.

Pavlow, Muriel (1921–)
British leading lady, on stage and screen from 1936; her youthful appearance enabled her to continue in juvenile roles for many years.
A Romance in Flanders (debut) 36. Quiet Wedding 40. Night Boat to Dublin 45. The Shop at Sly Corner 47. Malta Story 53. Doctor in the House 54. *Reach for the Sky* 56. Tiger in the Smoke 57. Rooney 58. Murder She Said 62. Memento Mori (TV) 92. Daisies in December 95, etc.

Pawle, Lennox (1872–1936)
British character actor, mainly on stage.
The Admirable Crichton (GB) 18. The Great Adventure (GB) 21. Married in Hollywood (US) 29. The Sin of Madeleine Claudet (US) 32. *David Copperfield* (as Mr Dick) 34. Sylvia Scarlett (US) 35, etc.

Paxinou, Katina (1900–1973) (Katina Constantopoulos)
Greek actress with international experience; played in some Hollywood films.
For Whom the Bell Tolls (AA) 43. Confidential Agent 44. Uncle Silas (GB) 47. *Mourning Becomes Electra* 47. Confidential Report 55. Rocco and His Brothers 60. Zita 68, etc.

Paxton, Bill (1955–)
American leading actor. Born in Fort Worth, Texas, he studied at New York University and began as a set dresser on exploitation movies in the mid-70s.
Impulse 84. The Terminator 84. Weird Science 85. Aliens 86. Near Dark 87. Next of Kin 89. Brain Dead 89. The Last of the Finest 90. Navy SEALS 90. Predator 2 90. Hurricane 91. The Vagrant 91. One False Move 92. Monolith 93. Boxing Helena 93. Trespass 93. Indian Summer 93. Tombstone 94. True Lies 94. Apollo 13 95. The Last Supper 96. *Twister* 96. Evening Star 96. Traveller (& p) 97. Titanic 97. A Bright Shining Lie (TV) 98. A Simple Plan 98. Mighty Joe Young 98. U-571 00. Vertical Limit 00, etc.

Paxton, John (1911–1985)
American screenwriter.
■ *Murder My Sweet* 44. My Pal Wolf (co-w) 44. Cornered 46. Crack Up (co-w) 46. *Crossfire* (AAN) 47. So Well Remembered 47. Of Men and Music (co-w) 50. *Fourteen Hours* 51. The Wild One 54. A Prize of Gold (co-w) 55. The Cobweb 55. Interpol 57. How to Murder a Rich Uncle (& p) 59. On the Beach 59. Kotch 71.

Paymer, David (1954–)
American actor, born in Long Island, New York. He studied at the Professional Performing Arts School and the Lee Strasberg Theater Institute.
Airplane II: The Sequel 82. Best Defense 84. Perfect 85. Howard the Duck 86. No Way Out 87. Crazy People 90. City Slickers 91. Mr Saturday Night 92. Searching for Bobby Fischer/Innocent Moves 93. Heart and Souls 93. Quiz Show 94. Cagney & Lacey: The Return (TV) 94. Cagney & Lacey: Together Again (TV) 95. The American President 95. Get Shorty 95. Nixon 95. City Hall 96. Unforgettable 96. Carpool 96. Amistad 97. Gang Related 97. The Sixth Man 97. Mighty Joe Young 98. Outside Ozona 98. Chill Factor 99. Mumford 99. Payback 99. The Hurricane 99. State and Main 00. Bait 00, etc.
TV series: Downtown 86. The Commish 91–92.

Payne, Alexander (1961–)
American director and screenwriter. He studied history and Spanish literature at Stanford and film at UCLA.
Citizen Ruth 96. Precious 96. *Election* (co-wAAN, d) 99, etc.
❝ American films rely more on gimmicks, they don't trust real life enough. – A.P.
We must allow formal experimentation. If we filmmakers can keep our costs down, we can get

things made. Now's the time, and we have to recognize that. There's a window now – if we keep costs down. – *A.P.*

Payne, Jack (1899–1969)
British bandleader who appeared in two films: *Say it with Music* 32, *Sunshine Ahead* 36.

Payne, John (1912–1989)
General-purpose American leading man, mostly of 40s musicals and 50s westerns.
Dodsworth 36. Fair Warning 37. Love on Toast 38. Wings of the Navy 39. *Kid Nightingale* 39. Maryland 40. The Great Profile 40. *Tin Pan Alley* 40. *The Great American Broadcast* 41. Weekend in Havana 41. Remember the Day 41. Sun Valley Serenade 41. To the Shores of Tripoli 42. Springtime in the Rockies 42. Hello Frisco Hello 43. The Dolly Sisters 45. Sentimental Journey 46. The Razor's Edge 46. Miracle on 34th Street 47. The Saxon Charm 48. The Crooked Way 49. Captain China 49. Tripoli 50. Crosswinds 51. Caribbean 52. Kansas City Confidential 52. Raiders of the Seven Seas 53. 99 River Street 53. Rails into Laramie 54. Santa Fé Passage 55. Hell's Island 55. Slightly Scarlet 56. *The Boss* 56. Bailout at 43,000 57. Hidden Fear 57. Gift of the Nile 68, etc.
TV series: *The Restless Gun* 58–59.

Payne, Laurence (1919–)
British leading man, on stage and (occasionally) screen from 1945.
Train of Events 49. Ill Met by Moonlight 57. Ben Hur 59. The Tell Tale Heart 61. The Court Martial of Major Keller 61. Vampire Circus 72. One Deadly Owner 74, etc.

Payne, Sally (c. 1914–1999)
American actress of the 30s and early 40s, born in Chicago, Illinois. Most of her roles were in Westerns for Republic. After her second marriage in 1942, she retired from films to become an illustrator of children's books.
Hollywood Hobbies 34. The Big Show 36. Exiled to Shanghai 37. My Wife's Relatives 39. La Conga Nights 40. Rodeo Dough 40. Young Bill Hickok 40. Bad Man of Deadwood 41. Red River Valley 41. Robin Hood of the Pecos 41. Tuxedo Junction 41. Jessie James at Bay 41. Cooks and Crooks 42. Man from Cheyenne 42. Romance on the Range 42, etc.

Paynter, Robert (1928–)
British cinematographer who worked on many of Michael Winner's films in the 60s and 70s.
■ Hannibal Brooks 68. The Games 69. Lawman 70. The Nightcomers 71. Chato's Land 71. The Mechanic 72. Scorpio 72. High Velocity 76. The Big Sleep 78. Firepower 79. Saturn 3 80. Superman II 80. The Final Conflict 81. An American Werewolf in London 81. Curtains 82. Superman III 83. Trading Places 83. Scream for Help 84. The Muppets Take Manhattan 84. National Lampoon's European Vacation 85. Spies Like Us 85. Into the Night 85. Little Shop of Horrors 86. When the Whales Came 89. Strike It Rich 90. Get Back 91.

Pays, Amanda (1959–)
English actress. Married actor Corbin Bernsen.
Oxford Blues 84. Cold Room/The Prisoner (TV) 84. Off Limits 87. The Kindred 87. Leviathan 89. Dead on the Money (TV) 91. Exposure 91. Solitaire for 2 95, etc.
TV series: Max Headroom 87. The Flash 90–91. Thief Takers 96.

Payton, Barbara (1927–1967)
American leading lady.
Once More My Darling 49. Dallas 50. Kiss Tomorrow Goodbye 51. Drums in the Deep South 51. Bride of the Gorilla 52. The Great Jesse James Raid 53. Four-Sided Triangle (GB) 54. The Flanagan Boy (GB) 55, etc.

Peach, Mary (1934–)
British leading lady, in films from 1957.
Follow That Horse 59. Room at the Top 59. *No Love for Johnnie* 61. A Pair of Briefs 62. A Gathering of Eagles (US) 63. Ballad in Blue 65. The Projected Man 66. Scrooge 70. Cat on a Hot Tin Roof (TV) 76. The Far Pavilions (TV) 84. Grandma's House 89. Mothers and Daughters 92. CutThroat Island 95, etc.

Pearce, Alice (1913–1966)
American character comedienne, usually in adenoidal roles.
On the Town 49. The Opposite Sex 56. The Disorderly Orderly 64. Dear Brigitte 65. The Glass Bottom Boat 66, etc.
TV series: Bewitched 65–66.

Pearce, Guy (1967–)
Australian leading actor, from the soap operas *Neighbours* and *Home and Away*.
Hunting 92. My Forgotten Man (as Errol Flynn) 93. *The Adventures of Priscilla, Queen of the Desert* 94. Dating the Enemy 96. LA Confidential 97. Woundings (GB) 98. Ravenous 99. Memento 00, etc.

Pearl, Jack (1894–1982)
Jewish-American comic known on radio as Baron Munchausen and famous for his catchphrase. 'Vass you dere. Sharlie?' Film appearance: *Hollywood Party* 34.

Pearson, Beatrice (1920–)
American leading lady with a brief career.
■ Force of Evil 49. Lost Boundaries 49.

Pearson, George (1875–1973)
British writer-producer-director who came to films at the age of 37 after being a schoolmaster. Hundreds of films to his credit.
Autobiography: 1957, *Flashback*.
The Fool 12. A Study in Scarlet 14. Ultus the Man from the Dead 15. The Better Ole 18. The Old Curiosity Shop 20. *Squibs* 21. Squibs Wins the Calcutta Sweep 22. Satan's Sister 25. Huntingtower 27. The Silver King 28. Journey's End (p) 30. The Good Companions (p) 32. Four Marked Men 34. The Pointing Finger 38, many others.

Pearson, Lloyd (1897–1966)
Portly British character actor, usually of bluff Yorkshire types.
The Challenge 38. Tilly of Bloomsbury 40. Kipps 41. *When We Are Married* 42. Schweik's New Adventures (leading role) 43. My Learned Friend 44. Mr Perrin and Mr Traill 49. Hindle Wakes 52. The Good Companions 57. The Angry Silence 59, etc.

Pearson, Neil
English actor, much on television. He was born in Battersea, South London.
Eskimos Do It 81. Privates on Parade 83. The Secret Rapture (TV) 93. Fever Pitch 96. Rhodes (TV) 96. Bostock's Cup (TV) 99. The Mystery of Men (TV) 99, etc.
TV series: Chelmsford 123 88-90. That's Love 89-92. Drop the Dead Donkey 90-94. Between the Lines 92-94. See You Friday 97.

Pearson, Richard (1918–)
British stage character actor in occasional films.
Love Among the Ruins (TV) 75. The Bluebird 77. She Fell Among Thieves (TV) 78. The Mirror Crack'd 80. Water 85. Pirates 86. Whoops Apocalypse 87, etc.

Peary, Harold (1908–1985) (Harold José Pereira de Faria)
American character comedian who for years in the 40s played The Great Gildersleeve on radio and in a short-lived film series, also in *Coming Round the Mountain, County Fair, Clambake*.

Peck, Bob (1945–1999)
English character actor, from the stage, where he was a member of the Royal Shakespeare Company and later acted with the National Theatre Company. Died of cancer.
Edge of Darkness (TV) 85. The Kitchen Toto 87. *On the Black Hill* 88. Ladder of Swords 88. Slipstream 89. Lord of the Flies 90. Jurassic Park 93. Seasick 96. Surviving Picasso 96. Smilla's Sense of Snow/Smilla's Feeling for Snow 97. Fairytale: A True Story 97. Deadly Summer (TV) 97. The Scold's Bridle (TV) 98, etc.

Peck, Gregory (1916–)
Durable and likeable American leading actor, with stage experience before sudden success in Hollywood.
Biography: 1980, *Gregory Peck* by Michael Freedland.
Days of Glory 43. *The Keys of the Kingdom* (AAN) 44. The Valley of Decision 44. *Spellbound* 45. The Yearling (AAN) 46. *Duel in the Sun* 46. *The Macomber Affair* 47. *Gentleman's Agreement* (AAN) 47. The Paradine Case 47. Yellow Sky 48. The Great Sinner 49. *Twelve o'Clock High* (AAN) 49. *The Gunfighter* 50. David and Bathsheba 51. Captain Horatio Hornblower (GB) 51. Only the Valiant 52. The World in His Arms 52. The Snows of Kilimanjaro 52. Roman Holiday 53. Night People 54. The Million Pound Note (GB) 54. The Purple Plain (GB) 55. *The Man in the Grey Flannel Suit* 56. Moby Dick 56. Designing Woman 57. The Bravados 58. *The Big Country* 58. Pork Chop Hill 59. Beloved Infidel (as Scott Fitzgerald) 59. On the Beach 59. The Guns of Navarone (GB) 61. Cape Fear 62. How the West was Won 62. *To Kill a Mockingbird* (AA) 63. Captain Newman 63. Behold a Pale Horse 64. Mirage 65. Arabesque 66. Mackenna's Gold 68. The Stalking Moon 68. The Most Dangerous Man in the World 69. Marooned 69. I Walk the Line 70. Shootout 71. Billy Two Hats 73. The Dove (p only) 75. *The Omen* 76. MacArthur 77. The Boys from Brazil 78. The Sea Wolves 80. The Blue and the Gray (TV) (as Lincoln) 82. The Scarlet and the Black (TV) 82. Amazing Grace and Chuck 87. Old Gringo 89. Other People's Money 91. Cape Fear 91. The Portrait (TV) 93. Moby Dick (TV) 98, etc.

Peck, Raoul (1953–)
Haitian director and screenwriter. A former minister of culture for his country, he began by making documentaries and short films.
Haitian Corner 87. Lumumba: La Mort du Prophète (Swiss/Ger.) 91. The Man by the Shore 92. Falling Bodies/Corps Plongés 98, etc.

Peckinpah, Sam (1925–1984)
American director of tough westerns. Married actress Begona Palacios (1942-2000).
Biography: 1994, *'If They Move ... Kill 'Em': The Life and Times of Sam Peckinpah* by David Weddle.
■ The Deadly Companions 61. *Ride the High Country* 62. Major Dundee 65. *The Wild Bunch* (AANw) 69. The Ballad of Cable Hogue 69. Straw Dogs 71. Junior Bonner 72. The Getaway 72. Pat Garrett and Billy the Kid 73. Bring Me the Head of Alfredo Garcia 74. The Killer Elite 76. Cross of Iron 77. Convoy 78. The Osterman Weekend 83.
❝ I can shoot three people, put 'em on a cart, take 'em to the burial ground and bury 'em by the time he gets one person down to the ground. – *Howard Hawks, on Peckinpah's slow-motion approach to death*
Peckinpah was a working alcoholic, as he called himself. His genius would last about four hours a day. – *James Coburn*

Peerce, Jan (1904–1984)
American tenor who appeared in a few films. He began as a popular singer at Radio City Music Hall, and on radio, before turning to opera and becoming a star at the Metropolitan Opera House from the 40s to the mid-60s; later, he also appeared in Broadway musicals.
Carnegie Hall 47. Something in the Wind 47. Tonight We Sing 53, etc.

Peerce, Larry (1930–)
American writer-director, son of opera singer Jan Peerce.
One Potato Two Potato 66. Goodbye Columbus 69. A Separate Peace 73. Ash Wednesday 74. The Other Side of the Mountain 76. Two Minute Warning 76. The Other Side of the Mountain Part Two 78. The Bell Jar 79. Why Would I Lie? 80. Love Child 82. Hard to Hold 84. Elvis and Me (TV) 88. The Neon Empire 89. A Woman Named Jackie (TV) 91. Child of Rage (TV) 92, etc.

Peet, Amanda (1972–)
American actress, from the stage. Born in New York, she studied at Columbia University.
Animal Room 95. She's the One 96. Grind 96. One Fine Day 96. Grind 96. Touch Me 97. Ellen Foster (TV) 97. Southie 98. Playing By Heart 98. Simply Irresistible 99. Body Shots 99. Isn't She Great? 00. The Whole Nine Yards 00. Whipped 00, etc.
TV series: Pertners 99. Jack and Jill 99- .

Pelissier, Anthony (1912–1988)
British director with stage experience; son of Fay Compton.
The History of Mr Polly 49. The Rocking Horse Winner 50. Night without Stars 50. Meet Me Tonight 52. Meet Mr Lucifer 54, etc.

Pellegrin, Raymond (1925–)
French leading actor of stage, screen and television, also in international films. Born in Nice, of Italian parents, he specialized in brooding roles. Married actress Gisèle PASCAL.
Six Petites Filles en Blanc 41. Naïs 45. Un Flic 47. Topaze 51. Forbidden Fruit/Le Fruit Défendu 52. Manon des Sources 53. Napoléon 54. Woman of Rome/La Romana (It.) 54. Flesh and the Woman/Le Grand Jeu 54. Law of the Streets/La Loi des Rues 56. Bitter Victory 57. Le Chien de Pique 61. Horace 62 62. Venus Impériale 62. A View from the Bridge 62. Behold a Pale Horse (Fr./US) 64. Second Breath/Le Deuxième Souffle 64. Code Name Cobra/Le Saut de L'Ange 71. L'Onorata Famiglia (It.) 73. Le Rose et le Blanc 80. Louisiana (TV) 84. Maigret à New York (TV) 90, many others.

Pellonpaa, Matti (1951–1995)
Finnish leading actor, born in Helsinki, and a familiar, lugubrious presence in the films of Aki and Mika KAURISMAKI. Died of a heart attack.
Valehtelija 80. Crime and Punishment/Rikos ja Rangaistus 83. Calamari Union 85. Hamlet Goes Business/Hamlet Liikemaailmassa 87. Ariel 88. Leningrad Cowboys Go America 88. Cha Cha Cha 89. Night on Earth (US) 91. La Vie de Bohème 92. The Last Border 93. Leningrad Cowboys Meet Moses 94. Take Care of Your Scarf, Tatiana/Pida Huivista Kiini, Tatiana 94. Iron Horsemen 94, etc.

Peña, Elizabeth (1961–)
Cuban-born actress in Hollywood.
El Super 79. Times Square 80. They All Laughed 81. Crossover Dreams 85. Down and Out in Beverly Hills 86. Batteries Not Included 87. La Bamba 87. Vibes 88. Blue Steel 90. Jacob's Ladder 90. The Waterdance 92. Across the Moon 94. Dead Funny 95. Free Willy 2: The Adventure Home 95. The Invaders (TV) 95. Lone Star 96. Contagious 96. Rush Hour 98. Dee Snider's Strangeland 98, etc.

Pendleton, Austin (1940–)
Slightly built American character actor.
Skidoo 68. What's Up, Doc? 72. Every Little Crook and Nanny 72. The Thief Who Came to Dinner 73. *The Front Page* 74. The Great Smokey Roadblock 78. Starting Over 79. The First Family 80. Mr & Mrs Bridge 90. My Cousin Vinny 92. Mr Nanny 93. My Boyfriend's Back 93. Guarding Tess 94. Home for the Holidays 95. 2 Days in the Valley 96. The Proprietor 96. The Mirror Has Two Faces 96, etc.

Pendleton, Nat (1895–1967)
American character actor, formerly professional wrestler, usually seen in 'dumb ox' roles. In films from *c.* 1930.
You Said a Mouthful 32. The Sign of the Cross 32. *The Thin Man* 34. Manhattan Melodrama 34. The Great Ziegfeld 36. The Marx Brothers at the Circus 39. Young Dr Kildare (and series) 39. On Borrowed Time 39. Northwest Passage 40. Top Sergeant Mulligan 42. Rookies Come Home 45. Scared to Death 47. Death Valley 49, many others.

Pene Du Bois, Raoul (1914–1985)
American set and costume designer, mainly on Broadway but occasionally noticed on Hollywood credits.
Louisiana Purchase 41. Happy Go Lucky 43. Frenchman's Creek 44. Lady in the Dark 44. Kitty 45. New Faces 53, etc.

Penhaligon, Susan (1950–)
British leading lady of the late 70s.
Under Milk Wood 73. No Sex Please We're British 73. The Land that Time Forgot 75. Nasty Habits 77. The Uncanny 77. Patrick 78. Leopard in the Snow 78. The Masks of Death (TV) 84. The Ruth Rendell Mysteries: Thornapple (TV) 97. Junk (TV) 99, etc.
TV series: Bouquet of Barbed Wire 76. A Fine Romance 81–84. Trouble in Mind 91.

Penn, Arthur (1922–)
American director, a former actor, who was often at odds with Hollywood. Born in Philadelphia, Pennsylvania, he studied at the Black Mountain College, in Italy at the Universities of Perugia and Florence, and at the Actors' Studio in Los Angeles. He began in television, and directed on Broadway before breaking through to wider recognition with *Bonnie and Clyde*.

■ The Left Handed Gun 58. The Miracle Worker (AAN) 62. Mickey One 65. The Chase 66. *Bonnie and Clyde* (AAN) 67. Alice's Restaurant (AAN) 69. Little Big Man 70. Night Moves 75. The Missouri Breaks 76. Four Friends 81. Target 85. Dead of Winter 87. Penn & Teller Get Killed 89. The Portrait (TV) 93. Inside 96.

❝ There hasn't been that much of a market for what I can do. I'm not into outer space epics or youth pictures. – *A.P.*

Penn, Chris (1966–)
Burly American actor, the son of Leo PENN and brother of Sean PENN.

Rumble Fish 83. All the Right Moves 83. Footloose 84. At Close Range 86. Made in the USA 88. Best of the Best 89. Mobsters 91. Futurekick 91. Leather Jackets 91. Reservoir Dogs 92. The Music of Chance 93. Best of the Best II 93. True Romance 93. Short Cuts 93. Josh and S.A.M. 93. Beethoven's 2nd 94. Imaginary Crimes 94. Mulholland Falls 96. The Boys Club 96. The Funeral 96. Deceiver 97. One Tough Cop 98, etc.

Penn, Leo (1921–1998)
American actor and director, the father of Sean and Christopher PENN.

Undercover Man (a) 49. The Story on Page One (a) 60. A Man Called Adam (d) 66. Murder in Music City (d) (TV) 79. Hellinger's Law (d) (TV) 81. Judgement in Berlin (d) 88, etc.

TV series: The Gertrude Berg Show 61.

Penn, Sean (1960–)
Scrawny but tough-looking American actor who has turned to writing and directing. He is the son of director Leo PENN, and the brother of Chris PENN. He was formerly married to singer MADONNA (1985–89). Married actress Robin WRIGHT, the mother of his two children, in 1996.

Taps 81. Fast Times at Ridgemont High 82. Bad Boys 83. Racing with the Moon 83. Crackers 84. The Falcon and the Snowman 84. At Close Range 85. Shanghai Surprise 86. Colors 88. Casualties of War 89. We're No Angels 89. State of Grace 90. The Indian Runner (wd) 91. Carlito's Way 93. The Crossing Guard (wd) 95. Dead Man Walking (AAN) 95. Loved 96. U-Turn 97. The Game 97. Hugo Pool 97. She's So Lovely 97. Hurlyburly 98. The Thin Red Line 98. Sweet and Lowdown (AAN) 99. Up at the Villa 00. Before Night Falls 00. The Weight of Water 00, etc.

❝ I don't like any directors. I don't get along with any of them. Mostly I think they're a bunch of whiny people without any point of view. So I don't want to be around them at 6 o'clock in the morning with make-up and bells on. And I'm probably the same way for the actors on my set – but that's their problem. – *S.P.*

With the Academy Awards, if you're standing there and looking out, you're not going to see many people who can find their butt with their hand. – *S.P.*

Pennebaker, D. A. (1930–) (Don Alan Pennebaker)
American documentary film-maker.

Don't Look Back 67. Monterey Pop 67. Town Bloody Hall (co-d) 80. Jimi 86. The Music Tells You (co-d) 93, etc.

Penner, Joe (1904–1941) (J. Pinter)
Hungarian-American radio comedian who made a few films.

College Rhythm 33. Collegiate 36. Go Chase Yourself 38. Glamour Boy 40. The Boys from Syracuse 40, etc.

Pennick, Jack (1895–1964)
American small-part actor and horse trainer, often in John Ford westerns.

Four Sons 28. Under Two Flags 36. Stagecoach 39. Northwest Mounted Police 40. My Darling Clementine 46. Fort Apache 48. Rio Grande 50. The Alamo 60.

Pennington-Richards, C. M. (1911–)
British director, former photographer.

The Oracle 54. Inn for Trouble 60. Double Bunk 62. Ladies Who Do 63. A Challenge for Robin Hood 67. Headline Hunters (co-w only) 68. The Boy with Two Heads (co-w only) 74. Sky Pirates 76, etc.

Penrose, Charles (1876–1952)
Hearty comedian and writer who played a few character roles in 30s films. He is best remembered for his recording of 'The Laughing Policeman' and similar songs. He wrote and starred, as a policeman, in the radio comedy series *The Pig and Whistle* 38–44.

Dreams Come True 36. The Crimes of Stephen Hawke 36. Calling the Tune 36. Dark Eyes of London/The Human Monster 39, etc.

Peploe, Clare
British screenwriter and director. Married to Bernardo Bertolucci, she is the sister of writer Mark Peploe.

Zabriskie Point (co-w) 70. Luna (w) 79. High Season (co-w, d) 87. Rough Magic (co-w, d) 95. Besieged (co-w) (It.) 98, etc.

Peploe, Mark
British screenwriter and director.

The Pied Piper (w) 72. The Passenger (w) 75. The Last Emperor (w) (AAN) 87. High Season (w) 88. The Sheltering Sky (w) 90. Afraid of the Dark (wd) 91. Little Buddha (w) 93. Victory (d) 98, etc.

Peppard, George (1928–1994)
American leading man with Broadway experience; began interestingly, but developed into an acceptable tough lead of hokum adventures.

■ *The Strange One* 57. Pork Chop Hill 59. Home from the Hill 60. The Subterraneans 60. *Breakfast at Tiffany's* 61. How the West Was Won 62. The Victors 63. *The Carpetbaggers* 64. Operation Crossbow 65. The Third Day 65. *The Blue Max* 66. Tobruk 67. Rough Night in Jericho 67. P. J. 68. What's So Bad about Feeling Good? 68. House of Cards 68. Pendulum 68. The Executioner 69. Cannon for Cordoba 70. One More Train to Rob 70. The Bravos (TV) 71. The Groundstar Conspiracy 72. Newman's Law 74. One of Our Own (TV) 75. Guilty or Innocent: The Sam Sheppard Murder Case (TV) 75. Damnation Alley 77. Your Ticket Is No Longer Valid 79. From Hell to Victory 79. Torn between Two Lovers (TV) 79. Crisis in Mid Air (TV) 79. Battle beyond the Stars 80. Five Days from Home (& d) 80. Race For the Yankee Zephyr 81. The A-Team (TV) 83. Target Eagle 84. Man against the Mob (TV) 88. Man against the Mob: The Chinatown Murders (TV) 89. Night of the Fox (TV) 90.

TV series: *Banacek* 72–73. Doctors' Hospital 75. *The A-Team* 83–86.

Pepper, Barbara (1912–1969)
American second-lead actress who usually played tramps.

Our Daily Bread 33. Winterset 36. Lady in the Morgue 38. Brewster's Millions 45. Terror Trail 47. Inferno 53. The D.I. 57. A Child is Waiting 63. Kiss Me Stupid 64, many others.

TV series: Green Acres 65–69.

Pepper, Barry (1970–)
Canadian actor, born in Campbell River, British Columbia.

Titanic (TV) 96. Enemy of the State 98. Saving Private Ryan 98. The Green Mile 99. Battlefield Earth 00, etc.

Perabo, Piper
American actress. Born in Toms River, New Jersey, she studied acting at Ohio University and the LaMama Theater in New York .

White Boyz 99. Adventures of Rocky and Bullwinkle 00. Coyote Ugly 00. Lost and Delirious 01, etc.

Percival, Lance (1933–)
British light comedian.

Twice Round the Daffodils 62. The VIPs 63. Carry On Cruising 63. The Yellow Rolls-Royce 64. The Big Job 65. Darling Lili 69. Up Pompeii 71. Our Miss Fred 72. The Boy with Two Heads 74. The Water Babies (voice) 75. Confessions from a Holiday Camp 77. Rosie Dixon – Night Nurse 78, etc.

TV series: It's a Living 62. Lance at Large 64. Up the Workers 74–76. Bluebirds 89.

Percy, Esmé (1887–1957)
Distinguished English stage actor, noted for his performances in the plays of George Bernard SHAW. Born in London, of French origin, he studied drama at the Brussels Conservatoire, and was also trained by Sarah BERNHARDT, having told her he would throw himself into the Seine if she did not let him join her company. He was on stage in England from 1904. As a young actor he was noted for his looks: when actor-manager Herbert Beerbohm Tree invited him to an intimate supper, Lady Tree paused on her way out and said, 'The port is on the sideboard, Herbert, and remember it's adultery just the same.' But after a dog removed one of his eyes, and he substituted a glass one, and his nose was broken in an accident, his choice of screen roles was somewhat limited.

Murder 30. Bitter Sweet 33. On Secret Service 33. The Lucky Number 33. The Unfinished Symphony 34. Nell Gwyn 34. Love, Life and Laughter 34. Lord Edgware Dies 34. Abdul the Damned 35. Invitation to the Waltz 35. Royal Cavalcade 35. It Happened in Paris 35. *The Frog* 36. The Invader 36. Land without Music 36. Song of Freedom 36. The Amateur Gentleman 36. The Return of the Scarlet Pimpernel 37. Twenty-One Days 37. Our Fighting Navy 37. Pygmalion 38. Caesar and Cleopatra 45. Dead of Night 45. Lisbon Story 46. The Ghosts of Berkeley Square 47. Death in the Hand 48, etc.

Pereira, Hal (1905–1983)
American art director, supervisor at Paramount from the 50s.

Double Indemnity 44. *Carrie* (AAN) 51. Ace in the Hole 52. Roman Holiday (AAN) 53. Sabrina (AAN) 54. *The Rose Tattoo* (AA) 55. To Catch a Thief (AAN) 55. The Proud and the Profane (AAN) 56. The Ten Commandments (AAN) 56. Funny Face (AAN) 57. *Vertigo* (AAN) 58. Career (AAN) 59. Visit to a Small Planet (AAN) 60. It Started in Naples (AAN) 60. *Breakfast at Tiffany's* (AAN) 61. Summer and Smoke (AAN) 61. The Pigeon that Took Rome (AAN) 62. Hud (AAN) 64. The Slender Thread (AAN) 65. The Spy Who Came In from the Cold (AAN) 65. The Oscar (AAN) 66. Barefoot in the Park 67. Blue 68, many others.

Perelman, S. J. (1904–1979)
Renowned American humorist whose name appeared on a few films, mostly in collaboration.

Monkey Business 31. Horse Feathers 32. Ambush 39. The Golden Fleecing 40. Around the World in Eighty Days (AA) 56, etc.

Perez, Rosie (1964–)
American actress, dancer and choreographer, born in Brooklyn.

Do the Right Thing 89. Criminal Justice (TV) 90. Night on Earth 91. White Men Can't Jump 92. Untamed Heart 93. Fearless (AAN) 93. It Could Happen to You 94. Somebody to Love 94. A Brother's Kiss 97. Perdita Durango 97. The 24-Hour Woman 98. The Road to El Dorado (voice) 00, etc.

Perez, Vincent (1965–)
Swiss-born leading actor, of German and Spanish parents, from the French stage. He studied acting in Geneva, at the Paris Conservatoire and at L'école des Amandiers.

Hôtel de France 87. The House of Jade/La Maison de Jade 88. Cyrano de Bergerac 90. Capitaine Fracasse 91. Indochine 92. Fanfan 93. Queen Margot/La Reine Margot 94. Beyond the Clouds 95. The Crow: City of Angels 96. Amy Foster 97. Le Bossu 97. Talk of Angels 98. On Guard! 97. Those Who Love Me Can Take The Train 98/Ceux Qui M'Aiment Prendront le Train 98. Shot through the Heart (TV) 98, etc.

Périer, Etienne (1931–)
French director.

Bobosse 59. Murder at 45 RPM 60. Bridge to the Sun 61. Swordsman of Siena 63. When Eight Bells Toll 71. Zeppelin 71. Five against Capricorn 72. A Murder is a Murder 72. The Fire's Share 77. Venetian Red 89, etc.

Périer, François (1919–) (François Pilu)
Sturdy French actor, in films from mid-30s.

Hôtel du Nord 38. Un Revenant 46. Le Silence est d'Or 48. *Orphée* 49. The Bed 53. *Gervaise* 55. Nights of Cabiria 56. Charmants Garçons 57. Weekend at Dunkirk 65. The Samurai 67. The Red Circle 70. Just Before Nightfall 73. Le Bar du Téléphone 80. Le Tartuffe 84. La Pagaille 91. Voyage à Rome 92, etc.

Perinal, Georges (1897–1965)
French cinematographer, in films from 1913.

Les Nouveaux Messieurs 28. Sous les Toits de Paris 30. *Le Sang d'un Poète* 30. *Le Million* 31. *A Nous la Liberté* 32. The Private Life of Henry VIII 33. *Rembrandt* 36. *The Thief of Baghdad* (AA) 40. *The Life and Death of Colonel Blimp* 43. *Nicholas Nickleby* 47. An Ideal Husband 47. *The Fallen Idol* 48. Lady Chatterley's Lover 55. A King in New York 57. Saint Joan 57. Bonjour Tristesse 58. Oscar Wilde 60, many others.

Perkins, Anthony (1932–1992)
Gangly American leading actor who became forever associated with the role of Norman Bates in *Psycho*, directed by Alfred HITCHCOCK. Born in New York City, the son of actor Osgood PERKINS, he was acting in summer stock at the age of 15 and made his film debut five years later. He played with success young men, troubled and unsure of themselves, but found maturer roles scarce. Married photographer and occasional actress Berry Berenson, the sister of actress Marisa BERENSON. He was romantically involved with actor Tab HUNTER. Died of AIDS.

Biography: 1991, *Osgood and Anthony Perkins* by Laura Kay Palmer. 1995, *Anthony Perkins: A Haunted Life* by Ronald Bergan. 1996, *Split Image: The Life of Anthony Perkins* by Charles Winecoff.

■ *The Actress* 53. Friendly Persuasion (AAN) 56. The Lonely Man 57. *Desire Under the Elms* 57. *Fear Strikes Out* 57. The Tin Star 57. *This Angry Age* 58. The Matchmaker 58. Green Mansions 58. On the Beach 59. Tall Story 60. *Psycho* 60. Goodbye Again 61. Phaedra 62. Five Miles to Midnight 62. The Trial 62. Two are Guilty 64. The Fool Killer 64. A Ravishing Idiot 64. Is Paris Burning? 66. The Champagne Murders 68. Pretty Poison 68. Catch 22 70. *WUSA* 70. How Awful About Allan (TV) 70. Ten Days Wonder 71. Someone Behind the Door/Two Minds for Murder 71. Judge Roy Bean 72. Play It as It Lays 72. Lovin' Molly 73. Murder on the Orient Express 74. Mahogany 75. Remember My Name 78. First You Cry (TV) 78. Winter Kills 79. The Black Hole 79. Double Negative 79. North Sea Hijack 80. Twice a Woman 80. Les Misérables (TV) 80. For the Term of His Natural Life (TV) 82. *Psycho II* 83. Sins of Dorian Gray (TV) 83. Crimes of Passion 85. Psycho III (& d) 86. Destroyer 88. Edge of Sanity 89. I'm Dangerous Tonight (TV) 90. Psycho IV: The Beginning 90. The Naked Target 91. A Demon in My View 92. The Mummy Lives 92. In the Deep Woods (TV) 92.

❝ Famous line (*Psycho*) 'A boy's best friend is his mother.'

Perkins, Elizabeth (1960–)
American actress.

About Last Night 86. From the Hip 87. Big 88. Sweet Hearts Dance 88. Love at Large 90. Enid Is Sleeping 90. Avalon 90. He Said, She Said 91. Indian Summer 93. The Flintstones 94. Miracle on 34th Street 94. Moonlight and Valentino 95. I'm Losing You 98, etc.

Perkins, Millie (1938–)
American leading lady who went to Hollywood from dramatic school.

The Diary of Anne Frank 59. Wild in the Country 61. Wild in the Streets 68. Lady Cocoa 75. Table for Five 83. At Close Range 85. Jake Speed 86. Slam Dance 87. Pistol: The Birth of a Legend 91. Necronomicon 93. Bodily Harm 95. The Chamber 96, etc.

TV series: Knots Landing 83–84. Elvis 90.

Perkins, Osgood (1892–1937)
American character actor, mainly on the stage, the father of Anthony PERKINS. Born in West Newton, Massachusetts, he studied French at Harvard University and turned to acting in his late 20s, first in silent films, before making his reputation on the Broadway stage, often in psychologically disturbed roles. Died from a heart attack, following the first night's performance of a new play in Washington. His one great regret was that he was passed over in favour of Adolphe MENJOU for the role of newspaper editor Walter Burns in the film of *The Front Page*, which he had originated on the Broadway stage. His best screen performance was as the gangster Johnny Lovo in *Scarface*.

Biography: 1991, *Osgood and Anthony Perkins* by Laura Kay Palmer.

The Cradle Buster 22. Puritan Passions 23. Knockout Reilly 27. Mother's Boy 29. Tarnished Lady 31. Scarface 32. Kansas City Princess 34. I Dream Too Much 35, etc.

“ I always had the theory that heavies had beady eyes and Osgood certainly had them. – *Howard Hawks*

In every aspect of technical facility, he was peerless. – *Elia Kazan*

Perlberg, William (1899–1969)
American producer, often in conjunction with George Seaton; came from agency business, in Hollywood from mid-30s.

Golden Boy 39. The Song of Bernadette 43. Forever Amber 47. The Country Girl 54. Teacher's Pet 58. The Counterfeit Traitor 62. Thirty-Six Hours 64, many others.

Perlich, Max (1968–)
American actor. Born in Cleveland, Ohio, he was raised in Los Angeles.

Ferris Bueller's Day Off 86. Can't Buy Me Love 87. Gleaming the Cube 87. Drugstore Cowboy 89. The Butcher's Wife 91. Rush 92. Born Yesterday 93. Maverick 94. Georgia 95. Beautiful Girls 96. Homeward Bound II: Lost in San Francisco 96. Feeling Minnesota 96. Gummo 97. House on Haunted Hill 99, etc.

TV series: Homicide: Life On The Streets 95-97.

Perlman, Rhea (1948–)
American actress, best known for her role as Carla in the TV series *Cheers* 82–92. Married Danny DeVito.

Intimate Strangers (TV) 77. Love Child 82. The Ratings Game (TV) 84. My Little Pony (voice) 86. Stamp of a Killer (TV) 87. Class Act 91. Enid Is Sleeping/Over Her Dead Body 91. Ted & Venus 91. There Goes the Neighborhood/Paydirt 92. Class Act 92. Canadian Bacon 95. Sunset Park 96. Matilda 96. Carpool 96, etc.

TV series: Pearl 96– .

Perlman, Ron (1950–)
American character actor, often in menacing roles, and best known for playing the lion-faced Vincent in the TV series *Beauty and the Beast*.

Quest for Fire 81. The Ice Pirates 84. The Name of the Rose 86. Blind Man's Bluff (TV) 91. Sleepwalkers 92. Cronos (Mex.) 92. The Adventures of Huck Finn 93. Double Exposure 93. Romeo Is Bleeding 93. City of Lost Children (Fr.) 95. The Island of Dr Moreau 96. Prince Valiant 97. Body Armour 97. Alien: Resurrection 97. I Woke Up Early the Day I Died 98, etc.

TV series: Beauty and the Beast 87–90. The Magnificent Seven 98–99.

Perón, Eva (1919–1952) (Maria Eva Duarte)
Argentinian actress and politician. Born in Los Toldos, she worked as a radio and film actress in the 30s and 40s before becoming the influential wife of Juan Perón in 1945, a year before he was elected President of Argentina. Died of cancer. She was played by Faye DUNAWAY in the TV movie *Evita Peron* 81, and by MADONNA in the musical biopic *Evita* 96.

Autobiography: 1997, *Evita: In My Own Words*.
Biography: 1997, *Eva Peron* by Alicia Dujovne Ortiz.

■ Only the Valiant/La Carga de los Valientes 40. The Unhappiest Man in Town/El Más Infeliz del Pueblo 41. Una Novia en Apuros 42. Circus Cavalcade/La Cabalgata del Circo 45. The Prodigal Woman/La Prodiga 45.

Perreau, Gigi (1941–) (Ghislaine Perreau-Saussine)
American child actress of the 40s who seems not quite to have managed the transition to adult stardom.

Madame Curie 43. Song of Love 47. My Foolish Heart 49. Has Anybody Seen My Gal? 51. The Man in the Grey Flannel Suit 56. Wild Heritage 58. Look in Any Window 61. Journey to the Center of Time 67. Hell on Wheels 67, etc.

TV series: The Betty Hutton Show 59. Follow the Sun 69.

Perrine, Valerie (1944–)
American leading lady of the 70s.

Slaughterhouse Five 72. The Last American Hero 73. Lenny (AAN) 74. W. C. Fields and Me 76. Mr Billion 77. Ziegfeld: the Man and his Women (TV) 78. Superman 78. The Electric Horseman 79. Can't Stop the Music 80. Superman II 80. Agency 81. The Border 82. Water 85. When Your Lover Leaves (TV) 85. Maid to Order 87. Reflections in a Dark Sky/Riflessi in un Cielo Scuro 91. Bright Angel 91. Boiling Point 93. Girl in the Cadillac 95, etc.

Perrins, Leslie (1902–1962)
British character actor, often seen as a smooth crook. Born in Moseley, Birmingham, he studied at RADA and was on stage from 1922.

The Sleeping Cardinal 31. The Pointing Finger 34. Tudor Rose 36. Old Iron 39. The Woman's Angle 43. A Run for Your Money 49. Guilty 56, many others.

Perry, Eleanor (1925–1981)
American screenwriter; wrote all the scripts of her husband Frank Perry's films until their divorce in 1970, after which she continued on her own.

David and Lisa (AAN) 62. The Swimmer 68. The Lady in the Car with Glasses and a Gun 69. Last Summer 69. Diary of a Mad Housewife 70. The Deadly Trap 71. The Man Who Loved Cat Dancing 73, etc.

Perry, Frank (1930–1995)
American director, a pioneer in establishing independent film-making as commercially viable. In 1992 he made a TV documentary, *On the Bridge*, dealing with his reactions to the discovery that he had cancer of the prostate.

■ David and Lisa (AAN) 63. Ladybug, Ladybug 64. The Swimmer 68. Trilogy 68. Last Summer 69. Diary of a Mad Housewife 70. Doc 71. Play It as It Lays 72. Man on a Swing 74. Rancho de Luxe 76. Monsignor 82. Compromising Positions 85. Hello Again 87.

“ I never really felt happy being part of the system, but it's preferable to be eaten by it than not eat. – *F.P.*

Perry, Luke (1966–)
American leading actor from TV soap operas who gained fame as Dylan McKay in the TV series *Beverly Hills, 90210* 90–93.

Buffy, the Vampire Hunter 92. Terminal Bliss 92. Lane Frost 93. 8 Seconds 94. Vacanze di Natale '95 (as himself) 95. Normal Life 96. American Strays 96. The Fifth Element 97. Lifebreath 97, etc.

TV series: Loving 87–88.

“ I felt like I belonged on a screen. I don't know why. I guess because I related to the people up on that screen much more than the people around me. I always felt like I was one of them and in a matter of time I'd get there. – *L.P.*

Perry, Matthew (1969–)
American actor, best known for his role as Chandler in the 90s TV sitcom *Friends*. He was treated for an addiction to painkillers in 1997. In 2000, he signed a contract worth an estimated $40m to appear in *Friends* for the following two years.

A Night in the Life of Jimmy Reardon 88. She's Out of Control 89. Fools Rush In 97. Almost Heroes 97. Three to Tango 99. The Whole Nine Yards 00, etc.

Perry, Paul P. (1891–1963)
Pioneer American cinematographer who experimented with colour.

Rose of the Rancho 14. The Cheat 15. Hidden Pearls 17. The Sea Wolf 21. Rosita 23. Souls for Sables 26, many others.

Persoff, Nehemiah (1920–)
Israeli actor, long in America; trained at Actors' Studio.

On the Waterfront 54. The Harder They Fall 56. *This Angry Age* 57. The Badlanders 58. Never Steal Anything Small 58. Al Capone 59. Some Like It Hot 59. The Big Show 61. The Comancheros 62. The Hook 63. *Fate is the Hunter* 64. The Greatest Story Ever Told 65. Panic in the City 68. Red Sky at Morning 71. Psychic Killer 75. Voyage of the Damned 76. The Word (TV) 78. Yentl 83. The Last Temptation of Christ 88. An American Tail: Fievel Goes West (voice) 91, etc.

Persson, Essy (1941–)
Swedish leading lady.

I a Woman 67. Thérèse and Isabelle 68. Cry of the Banshee 70. Flourishing Times/Blomstrande Tider 80, etc.

Persson, Jörgen (1936–)
Swedish cinematographer, associated with the films of director Bille AUGUST.

The White Sport/Den Vita Sporten (co-d) 68. *Elvira Madigan* 67. Ådalen 31 69. The Ballad of Joe Hill (co-ph) 71. Visions of Eight 73. My Life as a Dog 85. The Serpent's Way/Ormens Väg På Hälleberget 86. Pelle the Conqueror/Pelle Erobreren 87. Black Jack 90. Sophie 92. The Best Intentions/Den Goda Viljan 92. House of the Spirits 93. Zorn 94. Smilla's Sense of Snow 97. Les Misérables 98, etc.

Pertwee, Jon (1919–1996)
British comic actor, brother of Michael Pertwee, son of playwright Roland.

Autobiography: 1996, *I Am the Doctor* (with David J. Howe).

Murder at the Windmill 48. Mr Drake's Duck 51. Will Any Gentleman? 53. A Yank in Ermine 56. Carry On Cleo 64. Carry On Screaming 66. The House that Dripped Blood 70. One of Our Dinosaurs is Missing 75. Adventures of a Private Eye 77, etc.

TV series: Doctor Who (title role) 70–74. Worzel Gummidge 79.

Pertwee, Michael (1916–1991)
British playwright who has been involved in many screenplays.

Autobiography: 1974, *Name Dropping*.

Silent Dust (from his play) 48. The Interrupted Journey 49. *Laughter in Paradise* 51. Top Secret 52. Now and Forever 54. *The Naked Truth* 58. In the Doghouse 62. The Mouse on the Moon 62. Ladies Who Do 63. A Funny Thing Happened on the Way to the Forum 66. Finders Keepers 66. The Magnificent Two 67. Salt and Pepper 68. One More Time 70. Digby 73, etc.

Pertwee, Roland (1885–1963)
English playwright, screenwriter, novelist and occasional director. Born in Brighton, he began as an actor, and was on-stage from 1902. He wrote his screenplays usually in collaboration with others, and was briefly contracted to Warner's in Hollywood (according to P. G. WODEHOUSE, 'he did a story for Marilyn Miller, and they slapped him on the back and said it was great. He returned to the studio as usual next morning, and was informed by the policeman at the gate that he could not be let in as he was fired.'). Married twice: he was the father of writer Michael PERTWEE and actor Jon PERTWEE.

The Ghoul 33. The Night of the Party (oa) 34. Man of the Moment 35. Without Regret (oa) 35. Non Stop New York 37. King Solomon's Mines 37. A Yank at Oxford 37. Dinner at the Ritz 37. The Ware Case 38. Kicking the Moon Around/The Playboy 38. Young Man's Fancy 39. The Four Just Men 39. The Proud Valley 39. They Came by Night 39. The Spy in Black 39. Return to Yesterday 40. Freedom Radio 41. *Pimpernel Smith/ The Fighting Pimpernel* (& a) 41. Breach of Promise/ Adventure in Blackmail (& d) 41. Jeannie 41. Talk about Jacqueline 42. The Lamp Still Burns 43. The Gentle Sex 43. The Night Invader 43. Madonna of the Seven Moons 44. Pink String and Sealing Wax (oa) 45. They Were Sisters (w) 45. The Magic Bow 46. Caravan (w) 46. Silent Dust (oa) 48. Night Beat 48. Diamond City 49. Not Wanted on Voyage 57, etc.

Pertwee, Sean (1965–)
English actor, the son of Jon PERTWEE. He is co-founder of the production company Natural Nylon, together with actors Sadie FROST, Jude LAW, Jonny Lee MILLER, and Ewan MCGREGOR.

Prick Up Your Ears 87. Swing Kids 93. Dirty Weekend 93. Leon the Pig Farmer 94. Shopping 94. Clockwork Mice 95. i.d. 95. Blue Juice 95. Bodyguards (TV) 96. Stiff Upper Lips 97. Event Horizon 97. Soldier (US) 98. Love, Honour and Obey 99, etc.

TV series: Bodyguards 97.

Perugorria, Jorge (1965–)
Cuban leading actor.

Strawberries and Chocolate/Fresa y Chocolate 93. Guantanamera 95. Cachito 95. Bámbola 96. Vertical Love/Amor Vertical 97. What I Left Behind in Havana (Sp.) 98, etc.

Pesci, Joe (1943–)
Short American character actor, on radio as a child.

Death Collector 76. *Raging Bull* (AAN) 80. Easy Money 83. Eureka 83. Once upon a Time in America 84. Man on Fire 87. Lethal Weapon 2 89. Catchfire 89. Betsy's Wedding 90. Home Alone 90. *GoodFellas* (AA) 90. JFK 91. My Cousin Vinny 92. Lethal Weapon 3 92. Home Alone 2: Lost in New York 92. The Public Eye 92. A Bronx Tale 94. Jimmy Hollywood 94. With Honors 94. Casino 95. 8 Heads in a Duffel Bag 96. Gone Fishin' 97. Lethal Weapon 4 98, etc.

TV series: Half Nelson 85.

Peterman, Donald
American cinematographer.

When a Stranger Calls 79. King of the Mountain 81. Rich and Famous 81. Young Doctors in Love 82. Kiss Me Goodbye 82. Flashdance (AAN) 83. Splash 84. Best Defence 84. Cocoon 85. American Flyers 85. Star Trek IV: The Voyage Home (AAN) 86. Planes, Trains and Automobiles 87. She's Having a Baby 88. She's Out of Control 89. Point Break 91. Mr Saturday Night 92. Addams Family Values 93. Speechless 94. Get Shorty 95. Men in Black 97. Mighty Joe Young 98, etc.

Peters, Bernadette (1948–) (B. Lazarro)
American leading lady.

Ace Eli and Rodger of the Skies 72. The Longest Yard 74. The Jerk 79. Pennies from Heaven 81. Heartbeeps 81. Annie 82. David (TV) 88. Pink Cadillac 89. Slaves of New York 89. Fall from Grace (TV) 90. Alice 90. Impromptu 92. The Odyssey (TV) 97. Anastasia (voice) 97. Snow Days 99, etc.

Peters, Brock (1927–)
American actor in international films.

To Kill a Mockingbird 62. The L-Shaped Room 62. *Heavens Above* (GB) 63. The Pawnbroker 64. Major Dundee 65. P. J. 67. The McMasters 70. Black Girl 73. Framed 75. Two Minute Warning 76. Star Trek IV: the Voyage Home 86. Star Trek VI: The Undiscovered Country 91. The Importance of Being Earnest 91. Alligator II: The Mutation 91. Ghosts of Mississippi 96. Two Weeks from Sunday 97, etc.

TV series: Star Trek: Deep Space Nine 93– .

Peters, House (1880–1967)
American silent screen leading man.

Leah Kleschna 12. The Pride of Jennico 14. The Great Divide 15. Mignon 15. The Storm 22. Held to Answer 23. Raffles 25. Head Winds 25, many others.

Peters, Jean (1926–2000) (Elizabeth J. Peters)
American leading actress of the late 40s and early 50s. Born in Canton, Ohio, she won the Miss Ohio State popularity contest in 1946, which took her to Hollywood. Retired after marrying reclusive millionaire and producer Howard HUGHES, her second husband, in 1955. After divorcing Hughes in 1971, she married 20th Century Fox executive Stanley Hough and appeared in occasional TV movies.

■ Captain from Castile 47. Deep Waters 48. It Happens Every Spring 49. Love That Brute 50. Take Care of My Little Girl 51. As Young as You Feel 51. Anne of the Indies 52. Viva Zapata 52. Wait Till the Sun Shines, Nellie 52. Lure of the Wilderness 52. Full House 52. Niagara 53. Pickup on South Street 53. Blueprint for Murder 53. Vicki 53. *Three Coins in the Fountain* 54. Apache 54. Broken Lance 54. *A Man Called Peter* 55. Winesburg, Ohio (TV) 73. The Moneychangers (TV) 74. Peter and Paul (TV) 81.

Peters, Jon (1947–)
American producer, former hairdresser. He formed the Guber-Peters company with Peter Guber in 1982 and went with Guber to run Columbia following its takeover by Sony in 1989, before leaving to become an independent producer once more.

Books: 1996, *Hit and Run: How Jon Peters and Peter Guber Took Sony for a Ride in Hollywood* by Nancy Griffin & Kim Masters.

A Star Is Born 76. Eyes of Laura Mars 78. The Main Event 79. Die Laughing 80. Missing 82. Six Weeks 82. Flashdance 83. Sheena 84. Clue 85. The Color Purple 85. Vision Quest 85. Innerspace 87. Rain Man 88. Batman 89. Tango & Cash 89. Bonfire of the Vanities 90. Money Train 95. My Fellow Americans 96. Rosewood 97. The Wild, Wild West 99, etc.

“ When I was in the hair business I produced huge spectacular shows. Film is just another form of production. – *J.P.*

Peters, Susan (1921–1952) (Suzanne Carnahan)
American leading lady of the 40s; badly injured in an accident, she continued her career from a wheelchair.
Santa Fé Trail 40. *Random Harvest* (AAN) 42. Assignment in Brittany 43. Song of Russia 44. Keep Your Powder Dry 45. The Sign of the Ram 48, etc.

Peters, Werner (1918–1971)
German character actor in occasional international films.
L'Affaire Blum 49. Der Untertan 51. The Girl Rosemarie 58. Scotland Yard vs. Dr Mabuse 63. The Corrupt Ones 66. Assignment K 68. Istanbul Express (TV) 68, etc.

Petersen, Colin (1946–)
British child actor of the 50s.
Smiley 56. The Scamp 57. A Cry from the Streets 57, etc.

Petersen, Paul (1945–)
American teen actor and singer who was unable to sustain his career as an adult. He began as a Mouseketeer on Disney's Mickey Mouse Club, had two hit records in the early 60s, and later became a novelist. He heads A Minor Consideration, set up to protect infant actors from exploitation.
Autobiography: 1977, *Walt, Mickey and Me.*
This Could Be the Night 57. The Monolith Monsters 57. Houseboat 58. The Happiest Millionaire 67. A Time for Killing 67. Journey to Shiloh 68, etc.
TV series: The Donna Reed Show 58–66.
❝ Fame is not a career. It's a sentence. – *P.P.*
What happens to ex-bubblegum stars? No room left for me. – *P.P.*

Petersen, William (1953–)
American actor, born in Evanston, Illinois.
To Live and Die in L.A. 85. Hard Travelling 86. Amazing Grace and Chuck 87. Manhunter 86. Cousins 89. The Kennedys of Massachusetts 90. Young Guns II 90. Hard Promises 91. Passed Away 92. Fear 96. 12 Angry Men (TV) 97. The Rat Pack (TV) 98. Gunshy 98. The Contender 00, etc.
TV series: CSI: Crime Scene Investigation 00- .

Petersen, Wolfgang (1941–)
German director and screenwriter, from television. His *The Boat/Das Boot* was an international hit.
Wolf 70. Einer von uns Beiden 73. The Consequence/Die Konsequenz (wd) 77. Black and White Like Night and Day/Schwarz und Weiss Wie Tage und Nächte (wd) 78. The Boat/Das Boot (wd) (AAN) 81. The Neverending Story 84. Enemy Mine 85. Shattered 91. In the Line of Fire 93. Outbreak 95. Air Force One 97. The Perfect Storm 00, etc.

Peterson, Dorothy (c. 1900–1979)
American supporting actress of the 30s, usually in maternal roles.
Cabin in the Cotton 32. I'm No Angel 33. Treasure Island 34. The Country Doctor 36. Dark Victory 39. Lillian Russell 40. The Moon Is Down 43. The Woman in the Window 45. That Hagen Girl 47, many others.

Petit, Chris (1949–)
English critic turned director, much influenced by the films of Wim Wenders.
Radio On 79. A Suitable Job for a Woman 82. Flight to Berlin 84. Chinese Boxes 84, etc.

Petit, Jean-Claude (1943–)
French composer.
Vive la Sociale! 83. Jean de Florette 87. Manon des Sources 87. Return of the Musketeers 89. Cyrano de Bergerac 90. Uranus 90. Mother/Mayrig 91. All Out 91. 588 Rue Paradis 92. The Playboys 92. Foreign Student 94. Beaumarchais the Scoundrel 96. Desire 96, etc.

Petit, Pascale (1938–) (Anne-Marie Petit)
French leading lady.
The Witches of Salem 57. Les Tricheurs 58. Girls for the Summer 59. L'Affaire d'Une Nuit 60. Demons at Midnight 62. The Spy Who Went into Hell 65. The Sweet Sins of Sexy Susan 67. Boccaccio 72. Le Dolci Zie (It.) 75. Aggression 87, etc.

Petri, Elio (1929–1982)
Italian director, a political satirist.
The Assassin 61. The Tenth Victim 65. We Still Kill the Old Way 68. A Quiet Place in the Country 68. Investigation of a Citizen above Suspicion (AA, AANw) 69. The Working Class Goes to Heaven 71. Property is No Longer Theft 73. Todo Modo 76, etc.

Petrie, Daniel (1920–)
Canadian-born director in Hollywood, from an academic background, with stage and TV experience.
The Bramble Bush 59. A Raisin in the Sun 61. The Main Attraction 62. Stolen Hours 63. The Idol 66. The Spy with a Cold Nose 67. Silent Night Lonely Night (TV) 69. The City (TV) 71. A Howling in the Woods (TV) 71. Moon of the Wolf (TV) 72. Trouble Comes to Town (TV) 72. The Neptune Factor 73. Buster and Billie 74. The Gun and the Pulpit (TV) 74. Eleanor and Franklin (TV) 76. Lifeguard 76. Sybil (TV) 77. The Betsy 78. Resurrection 80. Fort Apache, the Bronx 80. Six Pack 82. Bay Boy 84. Square Dance 86. Rocket Gibraltar 88. Cocoon: The Return 88. Mark Twain and Me (TV) 91. Grumpy Old Men 93. Lassie 94. Kissinger and Nixon (TV) 95. Calm at Sunset (TV) 96. The Assistant 97, etc.

Petrie Jnr, Daniel (1952–)
American screenwriter and director. A former literary agent, he is the son of Daniel Petrie.
Beverly Hills Cop (w) (AAN) 84. The Big Easy (w) 87. Shoot to Kill (w) 88. Turner & Hooch (w) 89. Toy Soldiers (wd) 91. In the Army Now (wd) 94. Dead Silence (d) (TV) 96. Maximum Risk/The Exchange (co-w) 96, etc.

Petrie, Hay (1895–1948)
Scots character actor of stage and screen, specializing in eccentrics.
Suspense 30. The Private Life of Henry VIII 33. Nell Gwyn 34. *The Old Curiosity Shop* (as Quilp) 34. The Ghost Goes West 36. *Twenty-One Days* 38. The Spy in Black 39. Q Planes 39. Jamaica Inn 39. Crimes at the Dark House 40. The Thief of Baghdad 40. One of Our Aircraft is Missing 42. A Canterbury Tale 44. Great Expectations 46. The Red Shoes 48. The Guinea Pig 48, etc.

Petrov, Vladimir (1896–1966)
Russian director.
Thunderstorm 34. *Peter the Great* 38, etc.

Petrova, Olga (1886–1977) (Muriel Harding)
British-born leading lady of Hollywood silents in which she played *femmes fatales.*
Autobiography: 1942, *Butter with My Bread.*
The Tigress 14. The Soul Market 16. The Undying Flame 17. Daughter of Destiny 18. The Panther Woman 18, etc.

Petrovic, Aleksander (1929–1994)
Yugoslavian director, a former film critic, and an influential figure in the 60s.
■ Two/Dvoje 61. The Days/Dani 63. Three/Tri (AAN) 65. I Even Met Happy Gypsies/Skuplijaci Perja (AAN) 67. The Master and Margarita 72. Group Portrait with Lady 77. Migrations 94.

Pettet, Joanna (1944–)
Anglo-American leading lady.
The Group 65. Night of the Generals 66. Robbery 67. Blue 68. The Weekend Nun (TV) 74. Welcome to Arrow Beach 75. Captains and the Kings (TV) 76. The Evil 78. The Return of Frank Cannon (TV) 80. Double Exposure 82, etc.

Pettingell, Frank (1891–1966)
British north-country character actor who dispensed rough good humour on stage from 1910; films from 1931.
Hobson's Choice (as Mossop) 31. Jealousy 31. *The Good Companions* 32. *Sing As We Go* 34. The Last Journey 36. Fame 36. Millions 36. Sailing Along 38. *Gaslight* 39. Busman's Honeymoon 40. The Seventh Survivor 41. This England 41. Kipps 41. Once a Crook 41. *When We are Married* 42. The Young Mr Pitt 42. Get Cracking 44. Gaiety George 46. The Magic Box 51. Meet Me Tonight 52. Value for Money 57. Becket 64, many others.

Petty, Lori (1965–)
American leading actress, a former graphic artist.
Cadillac Man 90. Point Break 91. A League of Their Own 92. Free Willy 93. Poetic Justice 93. In the Army Now 94. Tank Girl (title role) 95. The Glass Shield 95. Serial Bomber 96, etc.
TV series: The Thorns 88. Booker 89-90. Lush Life 96. Brimstone 98-99.

Pevney, Joseph (1920–)
American director, former stage actor.
Shakedown 50. Undercover Girl 50. Iron Man 51. The Strange Door 51. Meet Danny Wilson 51. Just across the Street 52. Because of You 54. Desert Legion 54. The Female on the Beach 55. Three Ring Circus 55. Away All Boats 56. Congo Crossing 56. Tammy 57. *Man of a Thousand Faces* 57. Twilight for the Gods 58. Cash McCall 60. Night of the Grizzly 66. Who Is the Black Dahlia? (TV) 75. Mysterious Island of Beautiful Women (TV) 77. Prisoners of the Sea 85, etc.

Pfeiffer, Dedee (1965–)
American actress, the sister of Michelle PFEIFFER.
Vamp 86. The Allnighter 87. Brothers in Arms 89. The Horror Show 89. Red Surf 90. Tune in Tomorrow/Aunt Julia and the Scriptwriter 90. Frankie & Johnny 91. Up Close and Personal 96, etc.
TV series: Cybill 95–98. For Your Love 98– .

Pfeiffer, Michelle (1957–)
Blonde American leading actress, a former beauty queen. Born in Midway City, California, she worked in a supermarket and began to train as a court stenographer before deciding to become an actress. Formerly married to actor Peter Horton (1982–88), she married TV producer and writer David Kelley in 1993. She has also been romantically linked with actors Michael KEATON, John MALKOVICH and Fisher STEVENS. Her current asking price: around $6m a film.
Her best roles so far have been as Madame de Tourvel in *Dangerous Liaisons*, Susie Diamond in *The Fabulous Baker Boys*, Catwoman in *Batman Returns*, and Countess Ellen Olenska in *The Age of Innocence*.
Biography: 1994, *Michelle Pfeiffer* by Bruce Crowther.
Charlie Chan and the Curse of the Dragon Queen 80. Grease 2 82. Scarface 83. Into the Night 85. Ladyhawke 85. Sweet Liberty 86. Amazon Women on the Moon 87. The Witches of Eastwick 87. Married to the Mob 88. Tequila Sunrise 88. Dangerous Liaisons (AAN) 88. The Fabulous Baker Boys (AAN) 89. The Russia House 90. Frankie and Johnny 91. Love Field (AAN) 92. Batman Returns 92. The Age of Innocence 93. Wolf 94. Dangerous Minds 95. Up Close and Personal 96. One Fine Day 96. To Gillian on Her 37th Birthday 96. A Thousand Acres 97. Prince of Egypt (voice) 98. William Shakespeare's A Midsummer Night's Dream 99. The Deep End of the Ocean 99. The Story of Us 99. What Lies Beneath 00, etc.
TV series: Delta House 79. B.A.D. Cats 80.
❝ Hollywood is filled with beautiful, unhappy women who have shut down. – M.P.

Phifer, Mekhi (1975–)
American actor.
Clockers 95. The Tuskegee Airmen (TV) 95. High School High 96. Soul Food 97. I Still Know What You Did Last Summer 98. Hell's Kitchen NYC (&co-m) 98. Shaft 00, etc.

Philbin, Mary (1903–1993)
American leading lady of the silent screen.
The Blazing Trail 21. Merry Go Round 23. Phantom of the Opera 25. The Man Who Laughs 28. After the Fog 30, etc.

Philipe, Gérard (1922–1959)
France's leading young actor of the 50s, who alternated stage and screen activities.
Biography: 1964, *No Longer than a Sigh* by Anne Philipe.
■ La Boîte aux Rêves 43. The Children of the Flower Quay 45. Land without Stars 46. *The Idiot* 46. *Le Diable au Corps* 47. La Chartreuse de Parme 47. *Une Si Jolie Petite Plage* 49. All Roads Lead to Rome 49. La Beauté du Diable 50. La Ronde 50. Juliette ou la Clef des Songes 51. *Fanfan la Tulipe* 51. The Seven Deadly Sins 51. *Les Belles de Nuit* 52. Les Orgueilleux 53. Versailles 53. Knave of Hearts (GB) 54. Villa Borghese 54. The Red and the Black 54. Les Grandes Manoeuvres 55. La Meilleure Part 55. Si Paris Nous était Conté 55. Till Eulenspiegel 57. Pot Bouille 57. Montparnasse 19 57. La Vie à Deux 58. The Gambler 58. Les Liaisons Dangereuses 59. La Fièvre Monte à El Pao 59.

Philips, Lee (1927–1999)
American leading man of the 50s, born in Brooklyn, New York. He became a director of TV series and movies from the late 50s, working on such shows as *The Andy Griffith Show*, *Mayberry RFD*, *The Dick Van Dyke Show* and *The Waltons*.
AS ACTOR: Marty (TV) 48. Peyton Place 57. The Hunters 58. Tess of the Storm Country 60. Violent Midnight/Psychomania 64. The Lollipop Cover 65, etc.
AS DIRECTOR: Getting Away From It All (TV) 71. The Red Badge of Courage (TV) 74. Louis Armstrong—Chicago Style (TV) 76. Valentine (& co-w, TV) 79. Mae West (TV) 82. Barnum (TV) 86. Silent Motive (TV) 91, many others.
TV series: The Adventures of Ellery Queen (title role) 59.

Philips, Mary (1900–1975)
American stage actress who made very occasional film appearances.
Life Begins 32. A Farewell To Arms 33. That Certain Woman 37. Lady in the Dark 44. Leave Her to Heaven 46. Dear Wife 47, etc.

Philliber, John (1872–1944)
Slightly-built American character actor in a few early 40s films; best remembered for *It Happened Tomorrow* 44.

Phillippe, Ryan (1974–)
American actor, brought up in New Castle, Delaware. He first came to attention playing a gay teenager on the TV soap opera *One Life to Live*. He married actress Reese WITHERSPOON in 1999.
White Squall 96. I Know What You Did Last Summer 97. Nowhere 97. 54 98. Homegrown 98. Playing By Heart 98. Cruel Intentions 99. The Way of the Gun 00. Antitrust 01. Company Man 01, etc.
TV series: One Life to Live 92–93.

Phillips, Alex (1901–1977)
Canadian cinematographer who worked in Hollywood in the 20s and then went to Mexico to shoot that country's first sound film, *Santa* 31. He remained based in Mexico for the rest of his career, photographing more than 200 films, though he also returned to work in Hollywood in the 50s and 60s.
The Carnation Kid (US) 29. Divorce Made Easy (US) 29. The Mad Empress (Mex./US) 39. Pancho Villa Returns (Mex.) 50. Subida al Cielo (Mex.) 51. Adventures of Robinson Crusoe (Mex.) 52. The Proud Ones/Les Orgueilleux (Fr./Mex.) 53. The Littlest Outlaw (US) 54. The Western Story (US) 57. Last of the Fast Guns (US) 58. Villa! (US) 58. Ten Days to Tulara (US) 58. Sierra Baron (US) 58. The Wonderful Country (US) 59. For the Love of Mike (US) 60. The Last Sunset (US) 61. Geronimo (Mex./US) 62. Of Love and Desire (US) 63. Robinson Crusoe and the Tiger (Mex.) 69, many others.

Phillips, Bijou (1980–)
American actress, singer and songwriter, the daughter of rock singer John Phillips and actress Genevieve WAITE, and half-sister of Mackenzie PHILLIPS.
Sugar Town 99. Black and White 00, etc.

Phillips, Conrad (1930–) (Conrad Philip Havord)
English leading man, best known for playing the title role in the TV series, *William Tell*. Born in London, he worked mostly in television and on the stage.
A Song For Tomorrow 48. The Temptress 49. The Last Page 52. The Secret Tent 56. Zarak 56. Strangers' Meeting 57. A Question Of Adultery 58. Witness In The Dark 59. The Desperate Man 59. The White Trap 59. Circus Of Horrors 60. Sons And Lovers 60. The Shadow Of The Cat 61. The Fourth Square 61. The Secret Partner 61. Murder She Said 61. Dead Man's Evidence 62. No Love for Johnnie 62. Don't Talk To Strange Men 62. A Guy Called Caesar 62. The Durant Affair 62. The Switch 63. Impact (& co-w) 63. Stopover Forever 64. Dateline Diamonds 65. The Murder Game 65. Who Killed The Cat? 66, etc.
TV series: *The Adventures of William Tell* 58-59.

Phillips, Frank (1912–1994)
American cinematographer.
The Island at the Top of the World 74. Escape to Witch Mountain 75. No Deposit No Return 76. The Shaggy D.A. 76. Pete's Dragon 77. Return from Witch Mountain 78. Hot Lead and Cold Feet

78. Goin' Coconuts 78. The Apple Dumpling Gang Rides Again 79. The Black Hole (AAN) 79. Midnight Madness 80. Herbie Goes Bananas 80. Going Ape! 81, etc.

Phillips, Julia and Michael (1945– and 1943–)
American husband-and-wife producers, now divorced, who hit the big time with *The Sting*, *Taxi Driver* and *Close Encounters of the Third Kind*.
Autobiography: Julia Phillips gained notoriety in 1991 with the publication of her acerbic, best-selling memoir, , detailing her drug-fuelled decline as a producer and notable for her low opinion of most of her former colleagues. A further volume of autobiography, *Driving under the Affluence*, appeared in 1995.

MICHAEL PHILLIPS AS SOLE PRODUCER: Cannery Row 81. Heartbeeps 81. The Flamingo Kid 84. Don't Tell Mom the Babysitter's Dead 91. Dick & Marge Save the World 91.
❝ From *You'll Never Eat Lunch in This Town Again*. On John Landis: 'That little megalomaniacal prick.'
On Steven Spielberg: 'I taught the little prick he deserved limos before he even knew what it was to travel in a first-class seat on a plane.'
On François Truffaut: 'Deep down I knew he was a prick.'
On Donald Sutherland: 'A top-ten brain fucker.'

Phillips, Leslie (1924–)
British light comedian, former child actor from 1935.
The Citadel 38. Train of Events 49. The Sound Barrier 52. Value for Money 57. *Carry On Nurse* 59. Carry On Constable 60. Doctor in Love 60. Watch Your Stern 60. *Very Important Person* 61. Raising the Wind 61. In the Doghouse 62. Crooks Anonymous 62. *The Fast Lady* 62. And Father Came Too 64. Doctor in Clover 66. Maroc 7 (& p) 66. Doctor in Trouble 70. The Magnificent Seven Deadly Sins 71. Not Now Darling 73. Don't Just Lie There Say Something 73. Spanish Fly 75. Not Now Comrade 77. Out of Africa 85. Empire of the Sun 87. Scandal 89. Mountains of the Moon 90. King Ralph 91. Love on a Branch Line (TV) 94. August 96. Caught in the Act 96. The Canterville Ghost (TV) 96. Saving Grace 99. Take a Girl Like You (TV) 00, etc.
TV series: My Wife Jacqueline 52. Tracey and Me 56. Our Man at St Mark's 63. Foreign Affairs 66. The Culture Vultures 70. Casanova '73 73. Honey for Tea 94. The House of Windsor 94.

Phillips, Lou Diamond (1962–)
American young leading actor. In 1996, he received rave reviews for his performance as the King of Siam in a Broadway revival of the musical *The King and I*.
Trespasses (& w) 83. Harley 85. La Bamba 87. Dakota 88. Stand and Deliver 88. Young Guns 88. Disorganized Crime 89. Renegades 89. The First Power 90. A Show of Force 90. Young Guns II 90. Harley 90. Ambition (& w) 91. Dark Wind 91. Shadow of the Wolf (& co-w) 93. Sioux City (& d) 94. Boulevard 94. Teresa's Tattoo 94. Courage under Fire 96. Brokedown Palace 99. Bats 99. Picking Up The Pieces 00. Supernova 00, etc.

Phillips, Mackenzie (1959–)
American second lead of the 70s.
American Graffiti 75. Eleanor and Franklin (TV) 76. More American Graffiti 79. Love Child 82, etc.
TV series: One Day at a Time 75–83.

Phillips, Robin (1942–)
British juvenile lead, later stage director in Canada.
Decline and Fall 68. David Copperfield 69. Two Gentlemen Sharing 70. Tales From the Crypt 72. Miss Julie (d) 73. The Wars (d) 82, etc.

Phillips, Sian (1934–)
Dignified British stage actress. She was married to actor Peter O'Toole (1959–79).
Autobiography: 1999, *Private Faces*.
Becket 64. Young Cassidy 64. Laughter in the Dark 69. Goodbye Mr Chips 69. Murphy's War 70. Under Milk Wood 72. I, Claudius (TV) 76. Tinker Tailor Soldier Spy (TV) 79. Nijinksy 80. Clash of the Titans 81. Dune 85. The Doctor and the Devils 85. The Two Mrs Grenvilles (TV) 86. Valmont 89. The Age of Innocence 93. Ivanhoe (TV) 97. House of America 97. The Scold's Bridle (TV) 98. Aristocrats (TV) 99, etc.

Philo Vance
see Van Dine, S. S.

Philpotts, Ambrosine (1912–1980)
British character actress, mainly on stage.
This Man is Mine 46. The Franchise Affair 51. The Captain's Paradise 53. Up in the World 56. Room at the Top 59. Doctor in Love 60. Life at the Top 65, etc.

Phipps, Nicholas (1913–1980)
British light comedian often seen in cameo roles. On stage from 1932. Has also scripted or co-scripted many films, in most of which he appeared.
Piccadilly Incident 46. Spring in Park Lane 48. Doctor in the House 53. Doctor in Love 60. The Wild and the Willing 62, many others.

Phoenix, Joaquin (1974–) (aka Leaf Phoenix)
American actor, the brother of River Phoenix. Brought up in Puerto Rico and a religious commune (the Children of God) in Venezuela, he began performing on the streets with his siblings. He is the brother of actresses Rain Phoenix and Summer Phoenix. He has been romantically linked with actress Liv Tyler.
Spacecamp 86. Russkies 87. Parenthood 89. Walking the Dog 91. To Die For 95. U-Turn 97. Inventing the Abbots 97. Return to Paradise 98. Clay Pigeons 98. 8mm 99. Gladiator (AAN) 00. Quills 00, etc.

Phoenix, Rain (1971–)
American actress, the sister of River and Joaquin Phoenix.
Even Cowgirls Get the Blues 93. The Thing Called Love 94. Interview with the Vampire 94. Spent 00, etc.

Phoenix, River (1970–1993)
American young leading actor. He also played guitar and sang with his own rock group, Aleka's Attic. Died outside a Hollywood night-club after overdosing on heroin and cocaine. His final performance was in *Dark Blood*, a film which was abandoned three weeks from completion.
Explorers 85. Mosquito Coast 86. Stand by Me 86. Little Nikita 88. A Night in the Life of Jimmy Reardon 88. Running on Empty (AAN) 88. Indiana Jones and the Last Crusade 89. I Love You to Death 90. Dogfight 91. My Own Private Idaho 91. Sneakers 92. Silent Tongue 93. The Thing Called Love 93, etc.
TV series: Seven Brides for Seven Brothers 82–83.
❝ I don't see any point or any good in drugs that are as disruptive as cocaine. – *R.P.*
There wasn't a false bone in his body. – *Sidney Lumet*

Pialat, Maurice (1925–)
French director.
L'Enfance Nue 68. We Will Not Grow Old Together 72. La Gueule Ouverte 73. Graduate First/Passe Ton Bac d'Abord 79. Loulou 79. A Nos Amours 83. Police 85. Under Satan's Sun 87. Van Gogh 91. Le Garcu 95, etc.

Piazza, Ben (1934–1991)
Canadian actor who went to Hollywood, but was little heard from.
A Dangerous Age (Can.) 58. The Hanging Tree 59. I Never Promised You a Rose Garden 77. Apocalypse Now 79. The Blues Brothers 80. Rocky V 90. Guilty by Suspicion 91, etc.
TV series: Ben Casey 65. Forever Fernwood 77. The Waverly Wonders 78. Dallas 82–83.

Picardo, Robert (1953–)
American actor, frequently hidden under elaborate make-up in horror movies.
The Howling 80. Explorers (as Wak) 85. Legend (as Meg Mucklebones) 85. Innerspace 87. Jack's Back 87. The 'burbs 88. 976-EVIL 88. Gremlins 2: The New Batch 90. Matinee 92. Wagons East 94. Revenge of the Nerds 4: Nerds in Love 94. Star Trek: First Contact 96, etc.
TV series: China Beach 88–91. Star Trek: Voyager (as the medical hologram) 95– .

Piccoli, Michel (1925–)
Franco-Italian leading man. The second of his three wives was singer Juliette Greco.
French Cancan 55. The Witches of Salem 56. Le Bal des Espions 60. Le Mépris 63. Diary of a Chambermaid 64. De L'Amour 65. Lady L. 65. La Curée 66. The Young Girls of Rochefort 67. Un Homme de Trop 67. Belle de Jour 67. Dillinger is Dead 68. The Milky Way 69. Topaz 69. Blowout 73. The Infernal Trio 74. Mado 76. The Savage State 78. Le Sucre 78. A City 80. La Chambre Voisine 80. Leap into the Void 81. General of the Dead Army 81. Dangerous Moves 84. Revenge 84. Departure. Return 85. The Nonentity 86. Bad Blood 86. La Rumba 86. Martha und Ich 90. May Fools/Milou en Mai 90. La Belle Noiseuse 91. Le Voleur d'Enfants 91. Le Bal des Casse-Pieds 91. Archipelago/Archipel 92. Ruptures 93. Le Souper 93. La Cavale des Fous 93. Les Cent et Une Nuits 95. Beaumarchais the Scoundrel 96. Travelling Companion 96. Alors Voilà (d only) 97, etc.

Picerni, Paul (1922–)
American leading man, usually in second features.
Saddle Tramp (debut) 50. Maru Maru 52. House of Wax 53. Drive a Crooked Road 54. Hell's Island 55. Omar Khayyam 57. Strangers When We Meet 60. The Scalphunters 68. The Land Raiders 69. Kotch 71. Capricorn One 77. Beyond the Poseidon Adventure 79. The Fearmaker 89, etc.
TV series: The Untouchables 59–62.

Pichel, Irving (1891–1954)
American actor-director, in Hollywood from 1930.
AS ACTOR: The Right to Love 30. The Miracle Man 31. Oliver Twist (as Fagin) 33. Cleopatra 34. Jezebel 38. Juarez 40. Sante Fé 51, many others.
■ AS DIRECTOR: *The Most Dangerous Game* (co-d) 32. Before Dawn 33. *She* (co-d) 35. The Gentleman from Louisiana 36. Beware of Ladies 37. Larceny of the Air 37. The Sheik Steps Out 37. The Duke Comes Back 37. The Great Commandment 39. Earthbound 40. The Man I Married 40. Hudson's Bay 40. Dance Hall 41. Secret Agent of Japan 42. The Pied Piper 42. Life Begins at 8.30 42. *The Moon is Down* 43. *Happy Land* 43. And Now Tomorrow 44. A Medal for Benny 45. Colonel Effingham's Raid 45. Tomorrow is Forever 46. The Bride Wore Boots 46. O.S.S. 46. Temptation 46. They Won't Believe Me 47. Something in the Wind 47. The Miracle of the Bells 48. Mr Peabody and the Mermaid 48. Without Honor 49. The Great Rupert 50. Quicksand 50. Destination Moon 50. Santa Fé 51. Martin Luther 53. Day of Triumph 54.

Pick, Lupu
See Lupu -Pick.

Pickens, Slim (1919–1983) (Louis Bert Lindley)
Slow-talking American character actor, in scores of low-budget westerns from mid-40s, latterly in bigger films.
The Sun Shines Bright 53. The Great Locomotive Chase 56. One-Eyed Jacks 61. *Dr Strangelove* 63. Major Dundee 65. Rough Night in Jericho 67. The Cowboys 72. Pat Garrett and Billy the Kid 73. Blazing Saddles 74. The Apple Dumpling Gang 75. Whiteline Fever 75. The White Buffalo 77. Mr Billion 77. Wishbone Cutter 78. Beyond the Poseidon Adventure 79. Honeysuckle Rose 80. The Howling 81. Pink Motel 82, etc.
TV series: Outlaws 61. Custer 67.

Pickering, Donald (1933–)
British actor who played Holmes in the little seen 1980 TV series *Sherlock Holmes and Dr Watson*.
A Bridge Too Far 76. The Thirty-Nine Steps 78. Half Moon Street 87, etc.

Pickford, Jack (1896–1933)
American light actor, brother of Mary Pickford. He was married to actresses Marilyn Miller and Olive Thomas.
Tom Sawyer 17. Sandy 18. Just Out of College 21. The Goose Woman 25. The Bat 26. Brown of Harvard 26. Exit Smiling 26. Gang War 28, etc.

Pickford, Mary (1893–1979) (Gladys Smith)
Canadian actress who in the heyday of silent films was known as 'the world's sweetheart'; became co-founder of United Artists Films and one of America's richest women. Acting on stage from five years old; was brought into films by D. W. Griffith. Married actors Owen Moore (1911–20), Douglas Fairbanks (1920–36), and Charles 'Buddy' Rogers in 1937.
Special Academy Award 1976.
Autobiography: 1955, *Sunshine and Shadow*.
Biography: 1974, *Sweetheart* by Robert Windeler. 1991, *Mary Pickford: America's Sweetheart* by Scott Eyman. 1997, *Pickford: The Woman Who Made Hollywood* by Eileen Whitfield.
Her First Biscuits 09. The Violin Maker of Cremona 10. The Paris Hat 13. Madame Butterfly 15. Less Than the Dust 16. The Little Princess 17. Rebecca of Sunnybrook Farm 17. Stella Maris 18. *Pollyanna* 19. Suds 20. *Little Lord Fauntleroy* 21. The Love Light 21. *Tess of the Storm Country* 22. Rosita 23. Dorothy Vernon of Haddon Hall 24. Little Annie Rooney 25. My Best Girl 27. The Taming of the Shrew 29. Secrets 29. *Coquette* (AA) 29. Kiki 31. Secrets 33, many others.
✪ For entrancing the world, and for knowing when to stop. *Little Lord Fauntleroy*.
❝ The appeal of the world's sweetheart is not well understood in the 80s. Her screen image was ever-childlike, sweet and demure, the antithesis of today's heroines. Alistair Cooke said: 'She was the girl every young man wanted to have – as his sister.'
Yet on first encounter D. W. Griffith told her: 'You're too little and too fat, but I might give you a job.'
Later, he ruefully recollected: 'She never stopped listening and learning.'
She was soon telling Adolph Zukor: 'I can't afford to work for only ten thousand dollars a week.'
And Sam Goldwyn reflected: 'It took longer to make one of Mary's contracts than it did to make one of Mary's pictures.'
Spoiled by success she may have been, but never blind to her own failings: 'I never liked one of my pictures in its entirety.'
By 1929 she was surprisingly intolerant of her screen image: 'I am sick of Cinderella parts, of wearing rags and tatters. I want to wear smart clothes and play the lover.'
Richard Griffith and Arthur Mayer thought the secret of her success was that: 'Her sweetness and light were tempered by a certain realism. In spite of her creed, the Glad Girl knew it was no cinch to make everything come out right. Nothing could have been more in tune with an era which combined limitless optimism with a belief that 'git up and git' was necessary to make optimism come true.'
But Mabel Normand at a press conference struck a sour note: 'Say anything you like, but don't say I want to work. That sounds like Mary Pickford, that prissy bitch.'

Pickles, Vivian (1933–)
British character actress.
Play Dirty 68. Nicholas and Alexandra 71. Harold and Maude 71. Sunday Bloody Sunday 72. O Lucky Man 73. Candleshoe 77. Britannia Hospital 82. Suspicion 87, etc.

Pickles, Wilfred (1904–1978)
British radio personality and latterly character actor; played Yorkshiremen.
Autobiography: 1949, *Between You and Me*.
The Gay Dog 53. Billy Liar 63. The Family Way 66. For the Love of Ada 72, etc.
TV series: For the Love of Ada 70–71.

Pickup, Ronald (1940–)
British character actor, mainly on stage.
Three Sisters 68. Day of the Jackal 73. Mahler 74. Jennie (TV) (as Randolph Churchill) 75. Joseph Andrews 76. The Thirty-Nine Steps 78. Zulu Dawn 79. Nijinsky 80. The Letter (TV) 82. Ivanhoe (TV) 82. Never Say Never Again 83. Eleni 85. The Mission 86. Fortunes of War (TV) 87. Bethune: The Making of a Hero 89. Journey of Honor 91. A Time to Dance (TV) 92. Scarlett (TV) 94. Ivanhoe (TV) 97, etc.
TV series: The Riff Raff Element 94. Black Hearts in Battersea 96.

Picon, Molly (1898–1992)
American stage actress; films very occasional.
Come Blow Your Horn 63. Fiddler on the Roof 71. For Pete's Sake 74, etc.

Pidgeon, Rebecca (1963–)
Scottish-born actress and singer in Hollywood. She studied at RADA. Married writer and director David Mamet.
The Dawning 88. She's Been Away (TV) 89. Homicide (US) 91. The Water Engine (TV) 92. Oleanna 94. The Spanish Prisoner (US) 97. The Winslow Boy 98. State and Main 00, etc.

Pidgeon, Walter (1897–1984)
Good-looking, quiet-spoken Canadian leading man in Hollywood; during the 30s and 40s he gave

gentlemanly support to several dominant leading ladies.

■ Mannequin 25. Old Loves and New 26. The Outsider 26. Miss Nobody 26. Marriage License 26. The Girl from Rio 27. The Heart of Salome 27. The Gorilla 27. The Thirteenth Juror 27. Gateway of the Moon 27. Clothes Make the Woman 28. Woman Wise 28. Turn Back the Hours 28. Melody of Love 28. A Most Immoral Lady 29. Her Private Life 29. Bride of the Regiment 30. Sweet Kitty Bellairs 30. Viennese Nights 30. Kiss Me Again 30. Going Wild 30. The Gorilla 31. The Hot Heiress 31. Rockabye 32. The Kiss Before the Mirror 33. Journal of a Crime 34. Big Brown Eyes 36. Fatal Lady 36. Girl Overboard 37. Saratoga 37. A Girl with Ideas 37. She's Dangerous 37. As Good as Married 37. My Dear Miss Aldrich 37. Man Proof 38. The Girl of the Golden West 38. Shopworn Angel 38. Too Hot to Handle 38. Listen Darling 38. *Society Lawyer* 39. Six Thousand Enemies 39. Stronger than Desire 39. Nick Carter Master Detective 39. The House across the Bay 40. It's a Date 40. Dark Command 40. Phantom Raiders 40. Sky Murder 40. Flight Command 40. *Man Hunt* 41. *Blossoms in the Dust* 41. *How Green was My Valley* 41. Design for Scandal 42. *Mrs Miniver* (AAN) 42. White Cargo 42. The Youngest Profession 43. *Madame Curie* (AAN) 43. Mrs Parkington 44. Weekend at the Waldorf 45. Holiday in Mexico 46. The Secret Heart 46. Cass Timberlane 47. If Winter Comes 47. Julia Misbehaves 48. Command Decision 48. *That Forsyte Woman* (as Young Jolyon) 49. The Red Danube 49. The Miniver Story 50. Soldiers Three 51. Calling Bulldog Drummond 51. The Unknown Man 51. The Sellout 52. Million Dollar Mermaid 52. The Bad and the Beautiful 52. Scandal at Scourie 53. Dream Wife 53. *Executive Suite* 54. Men of the Fighting Lady 54. The Last Time I Saw Paris 54. Deep in My Heart 54. Hit the Deck 55. The Glass Slipper 55. *Forbidden Planet* 56. These Wilder Years 56. The Rack 56. Voyage to the Bottom of the Sea 61. *Advise and Consent* 62. The Two Colonels 62. Big Red 62. The Shortest Day 63. Cosa Nostra (TV) 67. Warning Shot 67. Funny Girl (as Ziegfeld) 68. Rascal 69. The Mask of Sheba (TV) 69. The Vatican Affair 69. Skyjacked 72. The Neptune Factor 73. Harry in Your Pocket 73. Yellow Headed Summer 74. Live Again Die Again (TV) 75. You Lie So Deep My Love (TV) 75. The Lindbergh Kidnapping Case (TV) 76. Murder at 40,000 Feet (TV) 76. Two Minutes Warning 76. Sextette 77.

Pieraccioni, Leonardo
Italian comic actor, writer and director, whose *The Cyclone* and *Fireworks* are among the highest-grossing Italian features.

The Graduates/I Laureati (co-w, a, d) 95. The Cyclone/Il Ciclone (co-w, a, d) 86. Fireworks/Fuochi D'Artificio (co-w, a, d) 97. My West/Il Mio West (co-w, a) 98, etc.

Pierce, Charles B.
American horror film screenwriter and director.

The Legend of Boggy Creek (wd) 73. Bootleggers (d) 74. Winterhawk (wd) 75. The Winds of Autumn (wd) 76. The Town that Dreaded Sundown (d) 77. Greyeagle (wd) 77. The Norsemen (wd) 78. The Evictors (wd) 79. Sacred Ground (wd) 83. Boggy Creek II (wd) 85. Hawken's Breed (d) 89, etc.

Pierce, Jack (1889–1968)
American make-up artist who worked at Universal for many years and created the familiar images of Dracula, the Wolf Man, the Mummy and the Frankenstein monster.

Pierce, Justin (1975–2000)
American actor, born in Los Angeles. Hanged himself.

■ Kids 95. Next Friday 00. Pigeonholed 00.

Pierce-Roberts, Tony
British cinematographer.

Moonlighting 82. A Private Function 84. A Room with a View (AAN) 85. A Tiger's Tale 87. Out Cold 89. Slaves of New York 89. Mr & Mrs Bridge 90. White Fang 90. The Dark Half 91. *Howards End* 92. Splitting Heirs 93. The Remains of the Day 93. The Client 94. Haunted 95. Surviving Picasso 96. Jungle 2 Jungle 97. Paulie 98. The Trench 99. Asterix & Obelix Take on Caesar 99. The Golden Bowl 00, etc.

Pierlot, Francis (1876–1955)
American character actor, usually of mild professional types.

Night Angel 31. The Captain Is a Lady 40. Night Monster 42. The Doughgirls 44. Dragonwyck 46. The Late George Apley 47. That Wonderful Urge 48. My Friend Irma 49. Cyrano de Bergerac 50. The Robe 53, many others.

Pierson, Frank L. (1945–)
American director, from TV.

Cat Ballou (co-w) 65. Cool Hand Luke (co-w, AAN) 67. The Looking Glass War 69. The Anderson Tapes (w only) 71. Dog Day Afternoon (w only) (AA) 75. A Star Is Born (d only) 76. King of the Gypsies 78. In Country (w) 89. Presumed Innocent (w) 90. Somebody Has to Shoot the Picture 91. Truman (TV) 95, etc.

TV series: *Nichols* 71.

Piesiewicz, Krzysztof
Polish screenwriter who co-wrote the scripts of Krzysztof Kieslowski's later films, including *Decalogue*, and 10 films for television based on the Ten Commandments that included the powerful *A Short Film about Killing*.

No End/Bez Konca 84. Decalogue/Dekalog 88. The Double Life of Veronique/Podwojne Zycie Weroniki 91. Three Colours: White/Trzy Kolory: Bialy 93. Three Colours: Blue/Trzy Kolory: Niebieski 93. Three Colours: Red/Trzy Kolory: Czerwony 94, etc.

Piggott-Smith, Tim (1946–)
British character actor.

Sweet William 79. Richard's Things (TV) 80. Clash of the Titans 81. Victory 81. *The Jewel in the Crown* (TV) 82. A State of Emergency 86. The Bullion Boys (TV) 93. The Remains of the Day 93.

Pigott, Tempe (1884–1962)
British character actress in Hollywood, usually as garrulous cockney.

Seven Days Leave 30. Cavalcade 33. One More River 34. Limehouse Blues 35. Becky Sharp 35, etc.

Pike, Kelvin
Australian-born cinematographer, in Britain, from documentary films.

The Dresser 83. Gulag 84. Anna Karenina 84. Bad Medicine 85. Strong Medicine 86. Spot Marks the X 86. Apprentice to Murder 86. A New Life 87. A Dry White Season 88. Betsy's Wedding 90, etc.

Pike, Nicholas (1955–)
British-born composer and musician, in Hollywood. Born in Water Orton, Warwickshire, he was a chorister at Canterbury Choir School before studying at Boston's Berklee College of Music in the early 70s. He played flute with his own jazz group in New York before going to Hollywood.

Critters 2 88. The Prince and the Pauper 90. Stephen King's Sleepwalkers 92. Captain Ron 92. Blank Check 94. Attack of the 50 Foot Woman (TV) 94. The Sadness of Sex (co-m) 95. The Shining (TV) 97. Telling Lies in America 97. Star Kid 98, etc.

Pilbeam, Nova (1919–)
British teenage star of the 30s.

Little Friend 34. The Man Who Knew Too Much 34. *Tudor Rose* 35. *Young and Innocent* 37. Spring Meeting 40. Banana Ridge 41. This Man Is Mine 46. Counterblast 47. The Three Weird Sisters 48, etc.

Pillsbury, Sam (1946–)
American-born director, screenwriter and producer, in New Zealand from the 60s.

The Scarecrow (& co-w) 82. The Quiet Earth (p, w only) 85. Starlight Hotel 87. Zandalee 90. Into the Badlands (TV) 91. The President's Child (TV) 92. Free Willy 3: The Rescue 97, etc.

Pinchot, Bronson (1959–) (Bronson Poncharavsky)
American actor.

Risky Business 83. Beverly Hills Cop 84. The Flamingo Kid 84. Hot Resort 85. After Hours 85. Second Sight 89. Blame It on the Bellboy 92. True Romance 93. Beverly Hills Cop III 94. Courage under Fire 96. The First Wives Club 96. Courage Under Fire 96. Quest for Camelot 98. Out of the Cold 99, etc.

TV series: Sara 85–88. Perfect Strangers 86–92. Meego 97– .

Pine and Thomas (William H. Pine, 1896–1955, and William C. Thomas, 1903–1984)
An American production executive and an exhibitor-writer who banded together in the early 40s to make scores of second features for Paramount. *Power Dive*, *Wildcat*, *Midnight Manhunt*, *They Made Me a Killer*, *Wrecking Crew*, *Torpedo Boat*, *I Cover Big Town*, etc. Continued into the 50s with larger-scale adventures: *Sangaree*, *Jamaica Run*, *The Far Horizons*, etc., but never managed a top-notcher. Because of their economy they were known as 'the Dollar Bills'. Thomas was almost always the director of their joint productions.

Pinelli, Tullio (1908–)
Italian dramatist and screenwriter, a former lawyer, who has worked on many of Fellini's films.

Without Pity/Senza Pietà 47. The Mill on the Po 49. The White Sheik/Lo Sceicco Bianco 52. I Vitelloni 53. La Strada 54. The Nights of Cabiria/Le Notti di Cabiria 56. La Dolce Vita (AAN) 60. Boccaccio 70 62. Eight and a Half (AAN) 63. Juliet of the Spirits 65. Ginger and Fred 86. The Voice of the Moon 90, many others.

Pinero, Sir Arthur Wing (1855–1934)
British playwright who dealt mainly with the upper middle class. Many films were made of his work in silent days; the most popular later were *The Second Mrs Tanqueray* and *The Enchanted Cottage*, though his farce *The Magistrate* had several incarnations, notably as *Those Were the Days* 34.

Pineyro, Marcelo
Argentinian director.

Wild Tango 93. Wild Horses/Caballos Salvajes 95. Ashes from Paradise/Cenizas del Paraíso (AAN) 97. Plata Quemada 00., etc.

Ping, Yuen Woo
Hong Kong actor and director of martial arts movies.

AS DIRECTOR: Snake in the Eagle's Shadow 78. Drunken Master 78. Buddhist Fist 80. Legend of a Fighter 81. Shaolin Drunkard 82. Mismatched Couples 85. Tiger Cage 88. Tiger Cage 2 89. In the Line of Duty 4 90. Tiger Cage 3 91. Tai Chi Master 93. Fire Dragons 94. Fist of Legend 94, etc.

Pink, Sidney (1916–)
American director.

Journey to the Seventh Planet 61. Reptilicus 62. Finger on the Trigger 65. The Tall Women 66.

Pink, Steve
American screenwriter and actor, a founder of Chicago's New Crime Theater with John Cusack and Jeremy Piven.

AS WRITER: Grosse Point Blank 97. High Fidelity 99, etc.

AS ACTOR: Touch and Go 86. Dangerous Curves 88. Bob Roberts 92. Grosse Pointe Blank 97, etc.

Pinkett, Jada (1971–) (aka Jada Pinkett Smith)
American actress, born in Baltimore, Maryland. Married actor Will Smith in 1998.

Menace II Society 93. The Inkwell 94. A Low Down Dirty Shame 94. Tales from the Crypt: Demon Knight 95. The Nutty Professor 96. *Set It Off* 96. Scream 2 97. Woo 98. Return to Paradise 98. Princess Mononoke (voice) 99, etc.

Pinon, Dominique (1955–)
French leading actor.

Diva 81. The Return of Martin Guerre/Le Retour de Martin Guerre 82. Nemo 83. The Moon in the Gutter/La Lune Dans Le Caniveau 83. Ghostdance (GB) 84. Zina (GB) 86. The Devil's Paradise/Des Teufels Paradies (Ger) 87. The Legend of the Holy Drinker/La Leggenda del Santo Bevitore 88. Delicatessen 90. Je M'Appelle Victor 92. The City of Lost Children/Cite Des Enfants Perdus 95. Alien Resurrection (US) 97. Viletta The Motorcycle Queen/Violetta La Reine de la Moto 98. Like a Fish Out of Water/Comme Un Poisson Hors de L'Eau 99. Highway Melody/Sur Un Air D'Autoroute 00, etc.

Pinsent, Gordon (1933–)
Canadian leading actor, much on TV.

The Thomas Crown Affair 68. The Forbin Project 69. Quarantined (TV) 69. The Rowdy Man 72. Newman's Law 74. Silence of the North 81. John and the Missus (& wd, from his novel) 87. Two Men (d, TV) 88. In the Eyes of the Stranger (TV) 93, etc.

TV series: *Quentin Durgens MP* 66.

Pinter, Harold (1930–)
British playwright, of menace and obscure violence, and screenwriter. A former actor, he has also occasionally appeared on screen, usually in threatening roles. Married (1956–80) actress Vivien Merchant and author Lady Antonia Fraser.

Biography: 1996, *The Life and Work of Harold Pinter* by Michael Billington.

The Servant (w) 63. The Caretaker (oa, w) 64. The Pumpkin Eater (w) (BFA) 64. The Quiller Memorandum (w) 67. Accident (w) 67. The Birthday Party (woa) 69. The Go Between (w) 71. The Homecoming (oa) 73. Butley (d) 73. Rogue Male (TV) (a) 76. The Last Tycoon (w) 76. The French Lieutenant's Woman (AAN) 81. Betrayal (AAN) 83. Turtle Diary 85. Reunion/L'Ami Retrouvé 89. The Handmaid's Tale 90. The Comfort of Strangers 90. The Trial 93. Breaking the Code (a) (TV) 97. Mojo (a) 98. Mansfield Park (a) 99. Wit (a) 01, etc.

❝ What concerns me most is shape and structure. – *H.P.*

When Pinter turned 50 I was asked to say something and couldn't think of anything. Later I thought there should be a two-minute silence. – *Alan Bennett*

Pintoff, Ernest (1931–)
Modernist American cartoon maker:

Flebus 57. *The Violinist* 59. *The Interview* 60. *The Critic* 63, etc.

Also wrote and directed live-action features: Harvey Middleman, Fireman 64. Dynamite Chicken 69. Who Killed Mary What's Her Name? 70. Blade 75. Jaguar Lives 79. Lunch Wagon 81. St Helens 81, etc.

Pinza, Ezio (1893–1957) (Fortunato Pinza)
Italian-American opera singer who graced a few films. Born in Rome, he became a star with the Metropolitan Opera in New York and, in his mid-50s, on Broadway in *South Pacific* and *Fanny*.

■ Carnegie Hall 48. Mr Imperium 50. Slightly Dishonorable 51. Tonight We Sing 53.

TV series: The RCA Victor Show 51–52. Bonino 53.

❝ I didn't know Pinza was the greatest baritone in the world. To me he was a big, unattractive, over-sexed man, the most conceited egomaniac I'd ever met. – *Debbie Reynolds*.

Pious, Minerva (1909–1979)
American radio comedienne of the 40s, famous with Fred Allen as Mrs Nussbaum.

It's In the Bag 45. The Ambassador's Daughter 56. Love in the Afternoon 57, etc.

Piovani, Nicola (1946–)
Italian composer.

Nel Nome del Padre 70. The Rebel Nun 74. Hyena's Sun 77. Il Minestrone 81. The Night of the Shooting Stars/La Notte di San Lorenzo 81. La Trace (Fr.) 84. Ginger and Fred 86. Good Morning, Babylon 87. The Voice of the Moon 90. Fiorile 93. We Don't Want to Talk about It/De Eso No Se Habla (Arg.) 93. Amok 93. Il Giovane Mussolini 93. Per Amore, Solo per Amore 94. The Tit and the Moon 94. A Month by the Lake 95. Life is Beautiful (AA) 97, etc.

Piper, Frederick (1902–1979)
British character actor, mostly on stage: usually played the average man or police inspector. Born in London, he began as a tea merchant; from the late 30s he was frequently on TV.

Sabotage 36. Everything Is Thunder 36. Oh, Mr Porter! 37. Jamaica Inn 39. The Four Just Men/The Secret Four 39. East Of Piccadilly/The Strangler 40. 49th Parallel/The Invaders 41. San Demetrio London 43. Nine Men 43. Champagne Charlie 44. Return Of The Vikings 44. Johnny Frenchman 45. Hue And Cry 46. It Always Rains on Sunday 47. The Blue Lamp 49. It's Not Cricket 49. Brandy For The Parson 51. Escape Route 52. Hunted 52. Home at Seven 52. Cosh Boy 52. The Hideaway 54. The Rainbow Jacket 54. The Passionate Stranger/A Novel Affair 56. The Man In The Road 57. Barnacle Bill 57. Doctor At Large 57. Dead Lucky 60. The Frightened City 61. Return Of A Stranger 62. Only Two Can Play 62. Ricochet

63. One Way Pendulum 64. He Who Rides A Tiger 65, etc.

Pirès, Gérard
French director. A motorcycle accident in 1981, which resulted in a tracheostomy, brought a hiatus to his career, and he turned to directing commercials.
Erotissimo 69. Fantasia Chez Les Ploucs 70. Act of Aggresion/L'Agression 74. L'Entourloupe 79. Rends-Moi La Cle! 80. Taxi 98, etc.

Pirosh, Robert (1910–1989)
American writer-director.
The Winning Ticket (oa) 35. A Day at the Races (w) 37. I Married a Witch (w) 42. Rings on Her Fingers (w) 42. Up in Arms (w) 44. *Battleground* (w) (AA) 49. Go for Broke (wd) (AANw) 51. Washington Story (wd) 52. Valley of the Kings (wd) 54. The Girl Rush (wd) 55. Spring Reunion (wd) 57. Hell Is for Heroes (w) 62. A Gathering of Eagles (w) 63. What's So Bad about Feeling Good? (w) 68, etc.

Piscator, Erwin (1893–1966)
German director whose importance lies in his theatrical work and his theories of total theatre, a multi-media approach using newsreels, film clips and sound, which influenced Joan Littlewood's Theatre Workshop in Britain and Joseph Losey's Living Newspaper productions in New York. In the 40s, he ran a dramatic workshop at the New School for Social Research in New York, where the teachers included Lee Strasberg and Stella Adler. Marlon Brando, Maureen Stapleton, Montgomery Clift and Rod Steiger were among the students.
Hoppla! Wir Leben 28. *Revolt of the Fishermen*/ Vostaniye Rybakov 35.

Pisier, Marie-France (1944–)
French leading lady of the 70s.
French Provincial 76. Love at Twenty 76. Cousin Cousine 76. The Other Side of Midnight 76. Barocco 77. Sérail 77. Love on the Run 79. French Postcards 79. La Banquière 80. Miss Right 81. Hot Touch 82. Les Nanas 84. Parking 85. Le Bal du Gouverneur (wd) 90. Blue Note/La Note Bleue 91. Pourquoi Maman Est dans Mon Lit? 94. Tous les Jours Dimanche 94. The Ice Rink/La Patinoire 98, etc.

Pistilli, Luigi (1930–1996)
Italian leading actor on stage and in films. Committed suicide shortly before he was due to go on stage in Milan in a play that had been critically savaged. He studied at Milan's Piccolo Teatro acting school in the mid-50s and was noted for his performances in the plays of Bertolt Brecht.
For a Few Dollars More 65. The Good, the Bad and the Ugly 66. Texas Addio 66. Death Rides a Horse/Da Uomo a Uomo 67. Bandidos 67. To Each His Own/A Ciascuno il Suo 67. Number One 73. Illustrious Corpses/Cadaveri Eccellenti 75. La Moglie di Mio Padre 76, etc.

Pithey, Wensley (1914–1993)
Heavily built South African-born character actor of stage and screen, in Britain from 1947.
The October Man 47. Cardboard Cavalier 49. Brandy for the Parson 52. The Titfield Thunderbolt 53. The Belles of St Trinian's 54. Moby Dick 56. Doctor at Large 57. Hell Drivers 57. Blue Murder at St Trinian's 58. The Knack 65. Oliver! 68. Oh What a Lovely War 69. The Adventurers 70. One of Our Dinosaurs Is Missing 75. Ike (as Churchill) (TV) 79. Red Monarch (TV) 83. The English Week at Dallas Texas (as Churchill) (TV) 84. White Mischief 87. American Friends 91, etc.

Pitillo, Maria (1965–)
American actress, born in Elmira, New York.
Wise Guys 86. Bright Lights, Big City 88. She-Devil 89. White Palace 91. Chaplin (as Mary Pickford) 92. I'll Do Anything 94. Natural Born Killers 94. Bye Bye Love 95. Dear God 96. Something to Believe In 97. Godzilla 98, etc.
TV series: Ryan's Hope 87–89. Partners 95–96.

Pitt, Brad (1963–) (William Bradley Pitt)
American leading actor, from television. Raised in the Ozark Mountains, Oklahoma, he left his journalism studies at the University of Missouri to seek work as an actor in Los Angeles. He was paid a reported $17.5m plus 15 per cent of the first-dollar gross to star in *Meet Joe Black*. He was engaged to actress Gwyneth PALTROW, and was romantically involved with actress Juliette LEWIS. Married actress Jennifer ANISTON in 2000.
Biography: 1995, *Brad Pitt* by Chris Nickson. 1997, *Brad Pitt* by US Magazine.
Cutting Class 89. Happy Together 90. Across the Tracks 91. Thelma and Louise 91. Johnny Suede 91. A River Runs through It 92. Cool World 92. Kalifornia 93. *True Romance* 93. The Favor 94. Interview with the Vampire 94. Legends of the Fall 94. Seven 95. Twelve Monkeys (AAN) 95. Sleepers 96. The Devil's Own 96. Seven Years in Tibet 97. Meet Joe Black 98. Fight Club 99. Snatch 00, etc.
TV series: Glory Days 90.
❝The truth is, I don't want people to know me. I don't know a thing about my favourite actors. I don't think you should. Then they become personalities. – *B.P.*
Hollywood is characterised by an extreme asocial individualism not seen in any other industry or societal form in the West. In your everyday life here, you have to deal with self-idolizing, highly self-satisfied people. It numbs the spirit. – *B.P.*

Pitt, Ingrid (1944–) (Ingrid Petrov)
Polish-born leading lady in British films.
Books: 1998, *The Ingrid Pitt Bedside Companion for Vampire Lovers*.
Where Eagles Dare 69. The Vampire Lovers 70. The House that Dripped Blood 70. Countess Dracula 71. Nobody Ordered Love 72. The Wicker Man 73. Smiley's People (TV) 82. Who Dares Wins 82. Underworld 85.Wild Geese II 86. Parker 86. The Asylum 00, etc.

Pitts, ZaSu (1898–1963)
American actress, a heroine of the 20s and a tearful comedienne of the 30s.
ZaSu was originally cast as the mother in *All Quiet on the Western Front*. Her scenes were reshot after preview audiences laughed.
The Little Princess 17. Early to Wed 21. *Greed* 23. Twin Beds 27. The Wedding March 28. Seed 30. Bad Sister 31. The Guardsman 32. Back Street 32. Walking Down Broadway 32. Many two-reeler comedies with Thelma Todd (32–34): Dames 34, Mrs Wiggs of the Cabbage Patch 34. Ruggles of Red Gap 35. So's Your Aunt Emma 38. Buck Privates 39. Nurse Edith Cavell 40. Niagara Falls 41. Let's Face It 43. Life with Father 47. Francis 50. Francis Joins the WACS 55. This Could Be the Night 57. It's a Mad Mad Mad Mad World 63, many others.
TV series: Oh Susanna 56–59.

Piven, Jeremy (1965–)
American actor, from the stage. Born in New York and raised in Evanston, Illinois, he trained at the Piven Theatre Workshop established in Chicago by his parents, actors Byrne Piven and Joyce Hiller Piven, also studying at Drake University and New York University. He was a founder of the New Crime Theater in Chicago with John CUSACK and Steve PINK.
One Crazy Summer 86. Lucas 86. Say Anything 89. The Grifters 90. There Goes the Neighborhood 92. The Player 92. Singles 92. Bob Roberts 92. Judgment Night 93. PCU 94. Car 54, Where Are You? 94. Heat 95. Dr Jekyll and Ms Hyde 95. Miami Rhapsody 95. Larger than Life 96. Layin' Low 96. Kiss the Girls 97. Grosse Pointe Blank 97. Don King: Only in America (TV) 97. Very Bad Things 98. The Crew 00, etc.
TV series: Carol & Company 90–91. The Larry Sanders Show 92–94. Pride and Joy 95. Ellen 95–98. Cupid 98–99.

Pizer, Larry
British cinematographer.
The Party's Over 63. Four in the Morning 65. Morgan 65. Our Mother's House 66. Isadora 68. All Neat in Black Stockings 69. Phantom of the Paradise 74. The Fury 78. The Europeans 79. Cattle Annie and Little Britches 81. The Clairvoyant/The Killing Hour 83. Phantom of the Opera (TV) 83. Grace Quigley 84. Too Scared to Scream 84. Where Are the Children 86. Blind Witness (TV) 90. Mannequin on the Move 91. Folks! 92. In Custody 93. The Proprietor 96, etc.

Place, Mary Kay (1947–)
American actress, born in Tulsa, Oklahoma.
Bound for Glory 76. New York, New York 77. More American Graffiti 79. Starting Over 79. Private Benjamin 80. Waltz Across Texas 82. The Big Chill 83. Smooth Talk 85. Explorers 85. A New Life 88. Samantha 91. Captain Ron 92. Precious 96. John Grisham's The Rainmaker 97. Pecker 98. Being John Malkovich 99. Girl, Interrupted 99, etc.

Placido, Michele (1946–)
Italian actor turned director.
Till Marriage Do Us Part/Dio Mio, Come Sono Caduta in Basso! 74. Corelone 78. Ernesto 79. Lulu 80. Three Brothers/Tre Fratelli 81. The Art of Love/L'Art d'Aimer 83. The Sicilian Connection 85. Forever Mary/Mery per Sempre 88. Big Business (US) 88. Private Affairs 89. Pummaro (d) 89. Le Amiche del Cuore (a, d) 91. Drug Wars (US) (TV) 92. Lamerica 94. Un Eroe Borghese (a, d) 95. Of Lost Love/Del Perduto Amore (co-w, a, d) 98, etc.

Planchon, Roger (1931–)
Leading French theatre director, actor and playwright who makes occasional films. The company he created near Lyons in the 50s became the Théâtre National Populaire in 1972.
Dandin (wd) 88. Camille Claudel (a) 88. Louis, Enfant Roi (d) 93. Lautrec (d) 98, etc.

Planck, Robert (1894–1971)
American cinematographer.
Our Daily Bread 33. *Jane Eyre* 43. Cass Timberlane 47. The Three Musketeers 48. Little Women 49. Rhapsody 54. Moonfleet 55, etc.

Planer, Franz (1894–1963)
German cinematographer, in Hollywood from 1937.
Drei von Der Tankstelle 30. *Liebelei* 33. Maskerade 34. The Beloved Vagabond (GB) 36. Holiday 38. The Face Behind the Mask 41. The Adventures of Martin Eden 42. Once Upon a Time 44. The Chase 47. *Letter from an Unknown Woman* 48. Criss Cross 48. The Scarf 51. The Blue Veil 51. *Death of a Salesman* 52. Twenty Thousand Leagues under the Sea 54. Not as a Stranger 55. The Pride and the Passion 57. *The Big Country* 58. *The Nun's Story* 59. The Unforgiven 60. The Children's Hour (AAN) 62, etc.

Plaschkes, Otto (1931–)
Austrian producer, in Britain.
Georgy Girl 66. The Bofors Gun 68. The Homecoming 73. In Celebration 74. The Sailor's Return 78. The Hound of the Baskervilles 83. The Sign of Four 83. The Holcroft Covenant 85. Shadey 85, etc.

Plato, Dana (1964–1999)
American actress, who had success as a juvenile. Born in Maywood, California, she was best known for her role as Kimberly Drummond in the TV sitcom Diff'rent Strokes, but adult roles proved hard to find. She was placed on probation in 1991 for robbing a video store and in 1992 for forging prescriptions for Valium. Committed suicide with painkilling drugs.
Beyond the Bermuda Triangle (TV) 75. Return to Boggy Creek 77. Schoolboy Father (TV) 80. Prime Suspect/Trauma 89. Bikini Beach Race 92. Diff'rent Strokes: A Story of Jack and Jill... and Jill TV) 97, etc.
TV series: Diff'rent Strokes 1978-84.

Platt, Edward (1916–1974)
American character actor who usually plays generals, stern fathers and similar types.
The Shrike 55. Rebel Without a Cause 55. Serenade 56. The Great Man 56. Designing Woman 57. The Gift of Love 58. North by Northwest 59. Pollyanna 60. A Ticklish Affair 63, many others.
TV series: *Get Smart* 65–69.

Platt, Louise (1914–)
American leading lady who retired after a brief career. She was formerly married to producer Jed Harris.
Spawn of the North 38. *Stagecoach* 39. Forgotten Girls 40. Captain Caution 40. Street of Chance 41, etc.

Platt, Marc (1913–)
American dancer and lightweight actor: few appearances.
Tonight and Every Night 44. Tars and Spars 44. Down to Earth 47. Seven Brides for Seven Brothers 54. Oklahoma 55, etc.

Platt, Oliver (1963–)
American actor.
Married to the Mob 86. Working Girl 88. Flatliners 90. Beethoven 92. Indecent Proposal 93. The Three Musketeers (as Porthos) 93. Benny and Joon 93. Tall Tale: The Incredible Adventures of Pecos Bill 94. Funny Bones 95. A Time to Kill 96. Executive Decision 96. Dr Dolittle 98. Dangerous Beauty 98. Bulworth 98. The Imposters 98. Simon Birch 98. Bicentennial Man 99. Lake Placid 99, etc.
TV series: Deadline 00.

Platt, Polly (1941–)
American production designer who became a producer in the late 80s. Formerly married to director Peter BOGDANOVICH.
The Last Picture Show 71. What's Up, Doc? 72. Paper Moon 73. The Thief Who Came to Dinner 73. A Star Is Born 76. Pretty Baby 78. Young Doctors in Love 82. Terms of Endearment (AAN) 83. Between Two Women (TV) 86. The Witches of Eastwick 87. Broadcast News (p) 88. The War of the Roses (p) 89. Say Anything (p) 89. I'll Do Anything 94. The Evening Star (co-p) 96. A Map of the World (co-w only) 99, etc.

Platts-Mills, Barney (1944–)
British independent director of low-budget films.
■ Bronco Bullfrog 70. Private Road 71.

Pleasence, Donald (1919–1995)
Bald, pale-eyed British character actor usually seen in villainous or eccentric roles.
Manuela 57. A Tale of Two Cities 57. The Flesh and the Fiends 59. Hell Is a City 60. No Love for Johnnie 61. Dr Crippen 62. The Great Escape 63. *The Caretaker* 64. The Greatest Story Ever Told 65. The Hallelujah Trail 65. Fantastic Voyage 66. Cul de Sac 66. The Night of the Generals 66. Eye of the Devil 67. Will Penny 67. The Madwoman of Chaillot 69. Soldier Blue 70. Outback 71. The Jerusalem File 72. Henry VIII and His Six Wives 72. Innocent Bystanders 72. Tales That Witness Madness 73. The Mutations 73. The Black Windmill 74. Hearts of the West 75. Trial by Combat 76. The Last Tycoon 76. The Eagle has Landed (as Himmler) 76. Jesus of Nazareth (TV) 77. Oh God 77. Telefon 77. The Passover Plot 77. Halloween 78. Sergeant Pepper's Lonely Hearts Club Band 78. Dracula 79. All Quiet on the Western Front (TV) 80. Escape from New York 81. Halloween II 81. Alone in the Dark 82. The Devonsville Terror 83. Where is Parsifal? 84. Arch of Triumph (TV) 84. The Last Days of Pompeii (TV) 85. Scoop (TV) 87. Ground Zero 87. Phantom of Death 87. Deep Cover 88. Hannah's War 88. Halloween 4: The Return of Michael Myers 88. Halloween 5: The Revenge of Michael Myers 89. Casablanca Express 89. River of Death 89. Buried Alive 90. American Tiger 91. Dien Bien Phu 91. Shadows and Fog 92. The Hour of the Pig 93. Femme Fatale (TV) 93. Halloween: The Curse of Michael Myers 95. Signs and Wonders (TV) 95, etc.
TV series: Robin Hood (as Prince John) 55–57.

Pleshette, Suzanne (1937–)
Intelligent American leading actress whose roles have been generally disappointing. She was married to actor Troy Donahue for nine months in 1964.
The Geisha Boy 58. Rome Adventure 62. Forty Pounds of Trouble 63. The Birds 63. Wall of Noise 63. A Distant Trumpet 64. Fate is the Hunter 64. Youngblood Hawke 64. A Rage to Live 65. The Ugly Dachshund 66. Nevada Smith 66. Mister Buddwing 66. The Adventures of Bullwhip Griffin 67. Wings of Fire (TV) 67. Blackbeard's Ghost 68. The Power 68. If It's Tuesday This Must Be Belgium 69. Along Came a Spider 69. Suppose They Gave a War and Nobody Came 69. Support Your Local Gunfighter 71. In Broad Daylight (TV) 71. Beyond the Bermuda Triangle (TV) 75. The Legend of Valentino (TV) 75. Return of the Pink Panther 75. The Shaggy D.A. 76. Kate Bliss and the Tickertape Kid (TV) 78. *Flesh and Blood* (TV) 79. Hot Stuff 79. Oh God Book Two 80. Help Wanted: Male (TV) 82. One Cooks, the Other Doesn't (TV) 83. Dixie: Changing Habits (TV) 83. For Love or Money (TV) 84. Kojak: The Belarus File (TV) 85. A Stranger Waits (TV) 87. The Queen of Mean (TV) 90. Battling for Baby (TV) 92, etc.
TV series: The Bob Newhart Show 72. Maggie Briggs 84. Bridges to Cross 86. The Boys Are Back 94–95.

❝ I don't sit around and wait for great parts. I'm an actress, and I love being one, and I'll probably be doing it till I'm 72, standing around the backlot doing *Gunsmokes*. – *S.P.*

Plimpton, Martha (1970–) (Martha Carradine)
American actress, the daughter of Keith Carradine.
Rollover 81. The River Rat 84. The Goonies 85. The Mosquito Coast 86. Shy People 87. Running on Empty 88. Stars and Bars 88. Parenthood 89. Silence Like Glass 90. Stanley and Iris 90. Samantha 92. Josh and S.A.M. 93. Chantilly Lace (TV) 93. Mrs Parker and the Vicious Circle 94. Last Summer in the Hamptons 95. I Shot Andy Warhol 96. Beautiful Girls 96. I'm Not Rappaport 96. Eye of God 97. Colin Fitz 97. 200 Cigarettes 98. Pecker 98, etc.

Plowright, Joan (1929–)
Leading British stage actress, widow of Laurence Olivier.
Time without Pity 58. The Entertainer 60. Equus 77. The Diary of Anne Frank (TV) 81. Britannia Hospital 82. Brimstone and Treacle 82. Wagner 82. Drowning by Numbers 88. The Dressmaker 89. I Love You to Death 90. Avalon 90. Enchanted April (AAN) 91. The Clothes in the Wardrobe/The Summer House (TV) 93. Last Action Hero 93. Dennis the Menace/Dennis 93. Widows' Peak 94. On Promised Land (TV) 94. A Pin for the Butterfly 94. Hotel Sorrento 95. A Pyromaniac's Love Story 95. The Scarlet Letter 95. Mr Wrong 96. Jane Eyre 96. Surviving Picasso 96. 101 Dalmatians 96. Tom's Midnight Garden 98. Dance with Me 98. This Could Be the Last Time (TV) 98. Tea with Mussolini 99, etc.
TV series: Encore! Encore! 98-99.

Plummer, Amanda (1957–)
American actress. She is the daughter of Christopher Plummer and Tammy Grimes.
Cattle Annie and Little Britches 81. The World According to Garp 82. Daniel 83. The Hotel New Hampshire 84. Courtship 86. Static 86. Made in Heaven 87. Prisoners of Inertia 89. Joe versus the Volcano 90. The Fisher King 91. The Lounge People 91. Freejack 92. So I Married an Axe Murderer 93. Last Light 93. Needful Things 93. Pulp Fiction 94. Pax (Port.) 94. Nostradamus 94. Butterfly Kiss 95. God's Army 95. Drunks 95. Freeway 96. Don't Look Back 96. A Simple Wish 97. American Perfekt 97. You Can Thank Me Later 98. LA without a Map (GB/Fr./Fin.) 98. The Million Dollar Hotel 99. 8&fr12; Women 99, etc.

Plummer, Christopher (1927–)
Canadian leading man with stage experience including Shakespeare. His first wife was actress Tammy Grimes; their daughter is actress Amanda Plummer. In 1997 he won a Tony for his one-man show *Barrymore*, as John Barrymore.
Stage Struck 57. Wind Across the Everglades 58. *The Fall of the Roman Empire* 64. *The Sound of Music* 65. Inside Daisy Clover 65. The Night of the Generals 67. Triple Cross 67. Oedipus the King 67. Nobody Runs Forever 68. Lock Up Your Daughters 69. The Royal Hunt of the Sun 69. Battle of Britain 69. *Waterloo* (as the Duke of Wellington) 70. The Pyx 73. The Return of the Pink Panther 74. Conduct Unbecoming 75. The Spiral Staircase 75. The Man Who Would Be King 75. The Moneychangers (TV) 75. Aces High 76. Jesus of Nazareth (TV) 77. The Day that Shook the World 77. The Assignment 77. The Disappearance 77. The Silent Partner 78. Starcrash 78. International Velvet 78. Murder by Decree 78. Hanover Street 79. Starcrash 79. Somewhere in Time 80. Highpoint 80. Eyewitness 81. The Amateur 81. Little Gloria ... Happy at Last (TV) 82. Dreamscape 84. Highpoint 84. Lily in Love 85. Ordeal by Innocence 85. The Boss's Wife 86. An American Tail (voice) 86. The Boy in Blue 86. I Love N.Y. 87. Dragnet 87. Souvenir 87. Light Years 88. Vampires in Venice/Nosferatu a Venezia 88. Shadow Dancing 88. Kingsgate 89. Mind Field 89. Rock-a-Doodle (voice) 90. Where the Heart Is 90. Red Blooded American Girl 90. Star Trek VI: The Undiscovered Country 91. Firehead 91. Don't Tell Mom the Babysitter's Dead 91. Liars Edge 92. Wolf 94. Dolores Claiborne 95. 12 Monkeys 95. Skeletons 96. The Clown at Midnight 98. Winchell (TV) 98. The Insider 99. Nuremberg 00, etc.
TV series: Counterstrike 90.
❝ I'm bored with questions about acting. – *C.P.*
Unless you can surround yourself with as many beautiful things as you can afford, I don't think life has very much meaning. – *C.P.*

Plunkett, Patricia (1928–)
British leading lady of the early 50s.
It Always Rains on Sunday 47. Bond Street 48. For Them That Trespass 48. Landfall 50. Murder Without Crime 52. Mandy 53. The Crowded Day 55. Dunkirk 58, etc.

Plunkett, Walter (1902–1982)
American costume designer, at RKO 1926–39, then MGM 1947–65.
Hit the Deck 29. Rio Rita 29. Cimarron 31. *Little Women* 33. *The Gay Divorcee* 34. Of Human Bondage 34. Mary of Scotland 36. Quality Street 37. *Gone with the Wind* 39. *The Hunchback of Notre Dame* 39. Stagecoach 39. Ladies in Retirement 41. To Be or Not to Be 42. A Song to Remember 45. Duel in the Sun 46. The Three Musketeers 48. That Forsyte Woman 49. *An American in Paris* (AA) 51. *The Prisoner of Zenda* 52. *Kiss Me Kate* 53. Seven Brides for Seven Brothers 54. Lust for Life 56. Pollyanna 60. How the West was Won 63. Seven Women 66, many others.

Plympton, Bill (1946–)
Quirky American director, writer and animator. Born in Portland, Oregon, he studied at Portland State University and the School of Visual Arts in New York, beginning as a cartoonist and illustrator. He started working on animated shorts in the early 80s; *The Tune* was his first full-length animated film; he has since made live-action films, such as *J. Lyle* and *Guns on the Clackamas*. His short films have been issued on video as Plymptoons, and he is the author of the comic book *The Sleazy Cartoons of Bill Plympton*.
Your Face (AAN) 88. One of Those Days 88. How to Kiss 89. The Tune 92. J. Lyle 94. How to Make Love to a Woman 95. Guns on the Clackamas 95. Mondo Plympton 97. I Married a Strange Person 97, etc.

Podesta, Rossana (1934–)
Italian leading lady who has been in international films.
Cops and Robbers 51. La Red 53. Ulysses 54. Helen of Troy 56. Santiago 58. The Golden Arrow 65. Il Prete Sposato 70. The Sensual Man 75. Il Gatto Mammone 76. Secrets 85, etc.

Poe, Edgar Allan (1809–1849)
American poet, story-writer and manic depressive, whose tortured life as well as his strange tales have been eagerly seized upon by film-makers. Griffith made *The Life of Edgar Allan Poe* in 1909, and in 1912 another version was disguised as *The Raven*. In 1915 Charles Brabin made another film called *The Raven* with Henry B. Walthall as Poe; a few months earlier Griffith had released his own alternative version under the title *The Avenging Conscience*. The next film called *The Raven*, in 1935, starred Karloff and Lugosi and had nothing to do with Poe's life, being merely an amalgam of his stories; but in 1942 Fox brought out *The Loves of Edgar Allan Poe* starring Shepperd Strudwick; and in 1951 MGM made a curious melodrama called *Man with a Cloak*, in which the dark stranger who solved the mystery signed himself 'Dupin' and was played by Joseph Cotten in the Poe manner.
Of the stories, *The Mystery of Marie Roget* was filmed by Universal in 1931 and 1942; *The Tell-Tale Heart* was told as an MGM short directed by Jules Dassin in 1942, by a British company with Stanley Baker in 1950, by UPA as a cartoon narrated by James Mason in 1954, by an independent American company in a film known as both *Manfish* and *Calypso* in 1956 (the film also claimed to be partly based on *The Gold Bug*) and by the Danzigers in Britain in 1960. *The Fall of the House of Usher* was filmed in France by Jean Epstein in 1929, in Britain by semi-professionals in 1950, in Hollywood by Roger Corman in 1960, and in South Africa by Alan Birkinshaw in 1988. Universal released films called *The Black Cat* in 1934 and 1941, both claiming to be 'suggested' by Poe's tale; in fact, neither had anything at all to do with it, but the genuine story was told in a German film called *The Living Dead* in 1933, and in Corman's 1962 *Tales of Terror*. *The Pit and the Pendulum* was filmed in 1913 and 1961, and the central idea has been borrowed by many film-makers without credit, most recently by the 'Uncle' boys in *One Spy Too Many*. *The Premature Burial* was filmed straight in 1962, and around the same time TV's *Thriller* series presented a fairly faithful adaptation; the idea was also used in 1934 in *The Crime of Dr Crespi*, a low-budgeter starring Erich Von Stroheim. *The Murders in the Rue Morgue* was filmed in 1914 and 1932, turned up again in 3-D in 1954 under the title *Phantom of the Rue Morgue*, and was remade under the original title in 1971. Other Poe stories filmed once include *The Bells* 13, *The Facts in the Case of M. Valdemar* in *Tales of Terror* 62, *The Masque of the Red Death* 64 and 89, and *The Tomb of Ligeia* 64.

Poe, James (1918–1980)
American writer, from radio and TV.
■ Without Honor 49. Scandal Sheet (co-w) 52. Paula 52. The Big Knife 55. Around the World in 80 Days (co-w, AA) 56. *Attack!* 56. Hot Spell 58. Cat on a Hot Tin Roof (co-w) 58. Last Train from Gun Hill 59. Sanctuary 61. Summer and Smoke (co-w) 63. Toys in the Attic 63. Lilies of the Field (AAN) 63. The Bedford Incident 64. They Shoot Horses Don't They? (co-w) 69.

Pogostin, S. Lee (1926–)
American writer-director.
Pressure Point (co-w) 62. Synanon (co-w) 65. Hard Contract (wd) 69. Golden Needles (co-w) 74. High Road to China (co-w) 83, etc.

Pohlmann, Eric (1903–1979)
Viennese character actor, on British stage and radio from 1948; also a familiar bald, portly villain on screen.
The Constant Husband 55. House of Secrets 56. Expresso Bongo 59. The Kitchen 62. Carry on Spying 64. The Million Dollar Collar (US) 67. The Horsemen 71, many others.
TV series: Colonel March of Scotland Yard 53.

Poiret, Paul (1879–1944)
French fashion designer who created the costumes for Sarah Bernhardt in her film debut *Queen Elizabeth* as well as her *Adrienne Lecouvreur*. He influenced many subsequent movie designers.

Poitier, Sidney (1924–)
Handsome American leading actor; his success in the late 60s helped to break the race barrier.
Autobiography: 00, *The Measure of a Man: A Spiritual Biography*.
No Way Out 50. Cry the Beloved Country 52. Red Ball Express 52. Go Man Go 54. *The Blackboard Jungle* 55. Goodbye, My Lady 56. *Edge of the City* 57. Something of Value 57. Band of Angels 58. Mark of the Hawk 58. *The Defiant Ones* (AAN) 58. *Porgy and Bess* 59. Virgin Islands 60. All the Young Men 60. A Raisin in the Sun 61. Paris Blues 61. Pressure Point 62. *Lilies of the Field* (AA) 63. The Long Ships 64. The Greatest Story Ever Told 65. *The Bedford Incident* (for the first time his colour was not mentioned or relevant) 65. A Patch of Blue 65. The Slender Thread 65. Duel at Diablo 66. *In the Heat of the Night* 67. To Sir with Love 67. *Guess Who's Coming to Dinner* 67. For Love of Ivy 68. The Lost Man 69. They Call Me Mister Tibbs 70. The Organization 71. Brother John 71. Buck and the Preacher (& d) 72. A Warm December (& d) 73. Uptown Saturday Night (& d) 74. The Wilby Conspiracy 75. Let's Do It Again (& d) 76. A Piece of the Action (& d) 77. Stir Crazy (d only) 80. Hanky Panky (d only) 82. Fast Forward (d only) 84. Little Nikita 88. Shoot to Kill 88. Ghost Dad (d) 90. Separate but Equal (TV) 91. Sneakers 92. To Sir with Love II (TV) 96. The Jackal 97. Mandela and de Klerk (TV) 97, etc.
✪ For being the first black actor to be accepted in a romantic situation with a white girl. *Guess Who's Coming to Dinner*.

Polanski, Roman (1933–)
Polish director and screenwriter, former actor. Gained a reputation with shorts such as *Two Men and a Wardrobe* 58. He was married to actress Sharon Tate, who was murdered in 1969 by followers of Charles Manson. In 1979 he left America when awaiting sentencing on a charge of unlawful sexual intercourse, and has since worked in Europe.
Autobiography: 1984, *Roman*.
Biography: 1982, *Polanski, the Filmmaker as Voyeur* by Barbara Leaming. 1982, *Life and Times of Roman Polanski* by Thomas Kiernan. 1994, *Polanski* by John Parker.
■ *Knife in the Water* 61. *Repulsion* 65. Cul de Sac 66. The Fearless Vampire Killers 67. *Rosemary's Baby* (AANw) 68. Macbeth 71. What? 72. *Chinatown* (AAN) 74. The Tenant 76. Tess (AAN) 80. Pirates 85. Frantic 88. Back in the USSR (a) 92. Bitter Moon 92. A Simple Formality/Una Pura Formalita (a) 94. Death and the Maiden 95. The Ninth Gate (&p) 99.
❝ Nothing is too shocking for me. When you tell the story of a man who loses his head, you have to show the head being cut off. Otherwise it's just a dirty joke without a punchline. – *R.P.*
I know in my heart of hearts that the spirit of laughter has deserted me. – *R.P.*
The director is never wrong. – *R.P.*
His talent is as undeniable as his intentions are dubious. – *Andrew Sarris, 1968*
The four-foot Pole you wouldn't want to touch with a ten-foot pole. – *Kenneth Tynan*

Poledouris, Basil (1945–)
American composer.
Extreme Close-up 73. Big Wednesday 78. The Blue Lagoon 80. Conan the Barbarian 82. Summer Lovers 82. Conan the Destroyer 84. Red Dawn 84. Flesh and Blood 85. Iron Eagle 86. Cherry 2000 86. Robocop 87. No Man's Land 87. Split Decisions 88. Farewell to the King 89. Wired 89. Why Me? 89. The Hunt for Red October 90. Quigley Down Under 90. The Flight of the Intruder 90. Harley Davidson and the Marlboro Man 91. Wind 92. Hot Shots! Part Deux 93. Robocop 3 93. Free Willy 93. On Deadly Ground 94. Serial Mom 94. Lassie 94. Rudyard Kipling's Jungle Book 94. Free Willy 2: The Adventure Home 95. Under Siege 2: Dark Territory 95. It's My Party 96. Celtic Pride 96. Breakdown 97. Starship Troopers 97. Switchback 97. Les Misérables 98, etc.

Poletto, Piero
Italian art director who has worked on several of Antonioni's films.
L'Avventura 60. The Minotaur/Teseo contra il Minotauro 60. The Eclipse/L'Eclisse 62. Gladiators 62. *The Red Desert*/Il Deserto Rosso 64. *More than a Miracle*/C'Era una Volta 67. The Chastity Belt 67. A Place for Lovers/Amanti 68. Sunflower/I Girasoli 69. In Search of Gregory 69. *The Passenger* 75, etc.

Polglase, Van Nest (1898–1968)
American art director, a former architect, in films from 1919. He worked for several studios before being hired as supervising art director for RKO 1932–42, when his alcoholism led to his dismissal. He later worked for Columbia, and on several films for director Allan Dwan. Although individual credit for RKO's productions is hard to establish, he was probably responsible for the Art Deco look of the Astaire-Rogers musicals.
A Kiss in the Dark 25. Stage Struck 25. Flying Down to Rio 33. *The Gay Divorcee* (AAN) 34. *Top Hat* (AAN) 35. Follow the Fleet 36. Mary of Scotland 36. Stage Door 37. Carefree (AAN) 38. *The Hunchback of Notre Dame* 39. Gunga Din 39. Love Affair (AAN) 39. My Favorite Wife (AAN) 40. *Citizen Kane* (AAN 41. Gilda 46. Cattle Queen of Montana 54. Escape to Burma 55. Slightly Scarlet 56. The River's Edge 57, many others.

Poliakoff, Stephen (1952–)
British playwright, screenwriter and director.
Hidden City 87. Close My Eyes 92. Century 93. The Tribe (wd) (TV) 98, etc.

Polito, Gene (1918–)
American cinematographer.
Prime Cut 72. Westworld 73. Five on the Black Hand Side 73. Trackdown 76. The Bad News Bears Go to Japan 78, etc.

Polito, Jon (1950–)
American character actor.
Deadly Business 86. Fire with Fire 86. Highlander 86. Homeboy 88. The Freshman 90. Miller's Crossing 90. Leather Jackets 90. Barton Fink 91. The Crow 94. Blank Man 94. The Crow 94. Bushwhacked 95. Fluke 95. Homeward Bound II: Lost in San Francisco 96. Just Your Luck 96. Angel's Dance 99. The Adventures of Rocky and Bullwinkle 00, etc.
TV series: Homicide: Life on the Street 93-94.

Polito, Sol (1892–1960)
American cinematographer.
Treason 18. Hard-Boiled Haggerty 27. Five Star Final 31. *I Am a Fugitive from a Chain Gang* 32. *Forty-second Street* 33. G Men 35. *The Petrified Forest* 36. *The Charge of the Light Brigade* 36. *The Adventures of Robin Hood* 38. Confessions of a Nazi Spy 39. *The Sea Hawk* 40. The Sea Wolf 41. Now

Goopy and Bagha 68. The Adversary 71. Company Limited 72. Distant Thunder 74. The Middle Man 76. *The Chess Players* 77. The Elephant God 79. Deliverance 82. The Home and the World 84. An Enemy of the People/Ganashatru 89. The Branches of the Tree 90. The Stranger/Agantuk 91. Broken Journey/Jagoran (w) 94, etc.

Ray, Ted (1906–1977) (Charles Olden)
British music-hall comedian and violinist who was in occasional films. Born in Wigan, the son of a comedian, he first worked as a comic under the name Hugh Neek and later did a Gypsy violin act as Nedlo. He became a success on the halls from the early 30s, but his greatest success came on the radio in the comedy series *Ray's a Laugh*, which ran for twelve years from 1949, and also featured Kenneth CONNOR and Graham STARK. He was the father of actor Andrew RAY.
Autobiography: 1952, *Raising the Laughs*. 1963, *My Turn Next*.
Elstree Calling 30. Radio Parade of 1935. A Ray of Sunshine 47. Meet Me Tonight 50. Escape by Night 52. My Wife's Family 54. Carry On Teacher 59. Please Turn Over 60, etc.

Raye, Carol (1923–) (Kathleen Corkrey)
Australian leading lady of British films of the 40s. She began appearing in Australian films from the 70s.
Strawberry Roan 45. Spring Song 46. While I Live 48. The Journalist 79. Relatives (TV) 85. Business as Usual 86, etc.

Raye, Martha (1916–1994) (Maggie O'Reed)
Wide-mouthed American comedienne and vocalist, popular on radio and TV. The second of her six husbands was composer David Rose.
Rhythm on the Range (debut) 36. Waikiki Wedding 37. Artists and Models 38. The Boys from Syracuse 40. Keep 'Em Flying 41. *Hellzapoppin* 41. Pin-Up Girl 43. Four Jills in a Jeep 44. *Monsieur Verdoux* 47. Jumbo 62. *Pufnstuf* 70. The Concorde – Airport 79 79, etc.
TV series: The Martha Raye Show 59. The Bugaloos 70–71. McMillan 76. Alice 82–84.
❝ I didn't have to work till I was three. But after that, I never stopped. – *M.R.*

Rayfiel, David
American screenwriter and dramtist, formerly married to actress Maureen STAPLETON.
Castle Keep (co-w) 69. Valdez Is Coming (co-w) 70. Three Days of the Condor (co-w) 75. Lipstick 76. Death Watch (co-w) 80. Round Midnight (co-w) 86. The Firm (co-w) 93. Intersection (co-w) 94. Sabrina (co-w) 95, etc.

Raymond, Cyril (c. 1897–1973)
British stage and screen actor often seen as the dull husband or professional man.
The Shadow 32. Mixed Doubles 33. The Tunnel 35. Dreaming Lips 37. Come On George 39. Brief Encounter 46. This was a Woman 47. Jack of Diamonds 48. Angels One Five 51. Lease of Life 53. Charley Moon 56, etc.

Raymond, Gary (1935–)
British 'second lead'.
The Moonraker 58. *Look Back in Anger* 59. Suddenly Last Summer 59. The Millionairess 61. El Cid 61. Jason and the Argonauts 63. The Greatest Story Ever Told 65. Traitors' Gate 65. The Playboy of the Western World 66. The Two Faces of Evil 82. Scarlett (TV) 94, etc.
TV series: The Rat Patrol 65.

Raymond, Gene (1908–1998) (Raymond Guion)
American leading man of the 30s, and later a character actor. Born in New York, he was on stage from the age of five, making his Broadway debut in 1920 and going to Hollywood in the early 30s, where his successes came after he was contracted to RKO from the mid-30s. After the Second World War, his career faltered, and he appeared mainly on stage and TV. Married twice; his first wife was actress and singer Jeanette MACDONALD (1937–65), with whom he appeared in *Smilin' Through*. Directed one film, *Million Dollar Weekend* (& a) 48.
Personal Maid (debut) 31. *Zoo in Budapest* 33. Flying Down to Rio 33. I Am Suzanne 34. Seven Keys to Baldpate 34. That Girl from Paris 37. Stolen Heaven 38. Mr and Mrs Smith 41. Smilin' Through 41. The Locket 46. Assigned to Danger 49. Hit the Deck 55. The Best Man 64, etc.
TV series: Paris 7000 70.

Raymond, Jack (1886–1953) (John Caines)
English director and producer, mainly of lightweight comedies, in films as an actor from 1910.
Barbara Elopes (co-d) 21. French Leave 30. Up for the Cup 31. Just My Luck 33. Sorrell and Son 33. Girls Please! 34. Chick (p only) 36. The Frog 37. Blondes for Danger 38. The Mind of Mr Reeder 39. Shake Hands with Murder (a) 44. Take Me to Paris 50. Up for the Cup 50. Reluctant Heroes 51. Worm's Eye View 51. Little Big Shot 52, etc.

Raymond, Paula (1923–) (Paula Ramona Wright)
American leading lady, former model.
Devil's Doorway 49. Crisis 50. The Tall Target 51. The Beast from Twenty Thousand Fathoms 53. The Human Jungle 54. The Gun that Won the West 55. The Flight That Disappeared 62. Blood of Dracula's Castle 70. Mind Twister 94, etc.

Razatos, Spiros
American director of action films, a former stunt expert.
Fast Getaway 91. Class of 1999 II: The Substitute 93.

Rea, Stephen
Irish leading actor of stage, screen and television.
Angel/Danny Boy 83. Loose Connections 83. Company of Wolves 84. Four Days in July (TV) 84. The Doctor and the Devils 85. Life Is Sweet 91. *The Crying Game* (AAN) 92. Bad Behaviour 93. Angie 94. Princess Caraboo 94. Interview with the Vampire 94. The Shadow of a Gunman (TV) 95. Citizen X (TV) 95. All Men Are Mortal 95. Between the Devil and the Deep Blue Sea 95. Crime of the Century (TV) 96. Michael Collins 96. The Van 96. The Last of the High Kings 96. The Butcher Boy 97. Fever Pitch 97. Trojan Eddie 97. A Further Gesture 97. Still Crazy 98. In Dreams 99. The Life Before This (Can.) 99. The End of the Affair 99, etc.

Reader, Ralph (1903–1982)
English character actor, choreographer, composer, writer and producer, best known for staging his *The Gang Show* in more than 30 different productions from the 50s onwards. Born in Crewkerne, Somerset, he was on-stage in the United States from 1924 before returning to England, where he specialized in devising dance routines for revues and musicals and, later, in staging large-scale pageants.
Autobiography: 1954, *It's Been Terrific*. 1960, *This Is the Gang Show*.
The Red Robe 24. I Adore You (ch) 33. Over the Garden Wall (ch) 34. The Blue Squadron (a) 34. Squibs (ch) 35. First a Girl (ch) 35. Limelight/Backstage) (ch) 35. Hello Sweetheart (ch) 35. The Gang Show (co-w, a) 37. London Melody (ch) 37. Splinters in the Air (m, ch) 37. Derby Day (a) 52. Lilacs in the Spring (a) 54. These Dangerous Years (a) 57. All for the Boys (a) 68, etc.
TV series: It's a Great Life 54–55. This Is the West 61.

Reagan, Ronald (1911–)
American leading man of the 40s, former sports reporter. Went into politics and in 1966 was elected Governor of California; in 1976 narrowly missed the Republican presidential nomination; in 1980, elected US President.
Autobiography: 1965, *Where's the Rest of Me?*.
Biography: 1987, *Early Reagan: The Rise of an American Hero* by Anne Edwards. 1994, *Ronald Reagan in Hollywood: Movies and Politics* by Stephen Vaughn.
Love Is on the Air 37. Accidents Will Happen 38. Dark Victory 39. Hell's Kitchen 39. Brother Rat and a Baby 40. Santa Fé Trail 40. International Squadron 41. Nine Lives are Not Enough 41. *Kings Row* 41. Juke Girl 42. *Desperate Journey* 42. This is the Army 43. Stallion Road 47. That Hagen Girl 47. The Voice of the Turtle 47. Night unto Night 48. John Loves Mary 49. The Hasty Heart (GB) 49. Louisa 50. Storm Warning 51. Hong Kong 52. Prisoner of War 54. Law and Order 54. Tennessee's Partner 55. Hellcats of the Navy 57. The Killers 64, etc.
TV series: Death Valley Days 62–64.
❝ Famous line (*Kings Row*) 'Where's the rest of me?'
Famous line (*Knute Rockne, All American*) 'Win one for the Gipper!'

Reason, Rex (1928–) (formerly known as Bart Roberts)
American leading man, mainly in routine films.
Storm over Tibet 52. Salome 53. Yankee Pasha 54. This Island Earth 55. Raw Edge 56. Band of Angels 57. The Rawhide Trail 60, etc.
TV series: Man without a Gun 57–59. The Roaring Twenties 60–62.

Reason, Rhodes (1928–)
American leading man, mainly in second features. Twin of Rex Reason.
Crime against Joe 56. Jungle Heat 57. Yellowstone Kelly 59. King Kong Escapes (Jap.) 68. Cruisin' High 75, etc.
TV series: *White Hunter* 58.

Rebhorn, James
American actor.
Deadly Business (TV) 86. Heart of Midnight 88. White Sands 92. Lorenzo's Oil 92. Scent of a Woman 92. White Sands 92. Carlito's Way 93. Skylark (TV) 93. Lane Frost 93. 8 Seconds 94. Blank Check 94. Guarding Tess 94. I Love Trouble 94. If Lucy Fell 96. Independence Day 96. Up Close and Personal 96. My Fellow Americans 96. The Game 97. From the Earth to the Moon (TV) 98. A Bright Shining Lie 98. All of It 98. Snow Falling On Cedars 99. The Talented Mr Ripley 99. Meet the Parents 00. The Adventures of Rocky and Bullwinkle 00, etc.

Red, Eric (1961–)
American screenwriter and director.
The Hitcher (w) 86. Near Dark (co-w) 87. Cohen & Tate (wd) 88. Blue Steel (co-w) 90. Body Parts (d) 91. The Last Outlaw (w, TV) 93. Bad Moon (wd) 96. Undertow (wd) 96, etc.

Reddy, Helen (1942–)
Australian folk singer.
Airport 75 74. Pete's Dragon 77.

Redfield, William (1927–1976)
American general-purpose actor with long stage experience; former boy actor. Author of one of the best books about acting: 1966, *Letters from an Actor*.
I Married a Woman 58. Fantastic Voyage 66. Duel at Diablo 66. A New Leaf 70. Death Wish 74. For Pete's Sake 74. One Flew Over the Cuckoo's Nest 76, etc.
❝ Movie actors learn that they must fight hard when a fight is called for lest they wake up days later no longer movie stars. – *W.R.*
Genuine success in motion pictures has not so much to do with talent as with bone structure, personality and what is called 'career management'. – *W.R.*
Movies are the swellest way to make money that ever happened in the history of the world. – *W.R.*

Redford, Robert (1937–)
Engaging, blond American leading actor and director who, although working within the studio system, has encouraged independent film-makers. Born in Santa Monica, California, he went to the University of Colorado on a baseball scholarship, but dropped out and later studied art and architecture at the Pratt Institute, New York, and at the American Academy of Dramatic Art. He began working on television and in the theatre, becoming a star with *Butch Cassidy and the Sundance Kid* in 1969. His best roles so far have been as Johnny Hooker in *The Sting* and Bob Woodward in *All the President's Men*; as a director, he scored with *Ordinary People* and *Quiz Show*. He set up the Sundance Film Institute in Utah for independent film-makers and in 1997 announced the creation of Sundance Cinemas, a venture with a major distributor to set up a chain of cinemas for the screening of independent films. Married once and divorced, he has three children.
Redford is alleged to have turned down the leading roles in *Who's Afraid of Virginia Woolf?*, *The Graduate*, *Rosemary's Baby*, *Love Story* and *The Day of the Jackal*.
Biography: 1977, *Robert Redford* by Donald A. Reed.
■ War Hunt 61. Situation Hopeless but not Serious 65. Inside Daisy Clover 65. *The Chase* 66. This Property is Condemned 66. Barefoot in the Park 67. Tell Them Willie Boy is Here 69. *Butch Cassidy and the Sundance Kid* 69. Downhill Racer 69. Little Fauss and Big Halsy 70. The Hot Rock 72. Jeremiah Johnson 72. *The Candidate* 72. The Way We Were 73. *The Sting* (AAN) 73. The Great Gatsby 74. The Great Waldo Pepper 75. Three Days of the Condor 75. *All the President's Men* 76. A Bridge Too Far 77. The Electric Horseman 79. Brubaker 80. Ordinary People (d only) (AA) 80. The Natural 84. Out of Africa 85. Legal Eagles 86. The Milagro Beanfield War (d) 88. Havana 90. Indecent Proposal 92. A River Runs through It (d) 92. Sneakers 92. Indecent Proposal 93. Quiz Show (AANd) 94. Up Close and Personal 96. The Horse Whisperer (p, a, d) 98. A Civil Action (p) 98. The Legend of Bagger Vance (p, d) 00.
❝ Other people have analysis. I have Utah. – *R.R.*
I often feel I'll just opt out of this rat-race and buy another hunk of Utah. – *R.R.*
A lot of what acting is, is paying attention. – *R.R.*
All my life I've been dogged by guilt because I feel there is this difference between the way I look and the way I feel inside. – *R.R.*
There's always the promise you can penetrate his cool, that you can get through to him. But you can't. – *Paul Newman*

Redgrave, Corin (1939–)
British supporting actor, son of Sir Michael REDGRAVE. Gave up acting for a time to work in politics. In 1996, he published a biography of his father. His second wife was actress Kika MARKHAM.
A Man for All Seasons 66. Charge of the Light Brigade 68. Oh What a Lovely War 69. David Copperfield 69. Von Richthofen and Brown 71. When Eight Bells Toll 71. Serail 77. Sunday Too Far Away 77. Excalibur 81. Eureka 81. The Fool 91. In the Name of the Father 93. Four Weddings and a Funeral 94. Jane Austen's Persuasion (TV) 95. The Ice House (TV) 97. Honest 00, etc.
TV series: Circles of Deceit 95–96.

Redgrave, Jemma
English actress, the daughter of Corin REDGRAVE.
The Dream Demon 88. The Real Charlotte 89. Howards End 92. Diana: Her True Story (TV) 93. The Buddha of Suburbia (TV) 93. Mosley (TV) 98, etc.
TV series: Bramwell 95–98.

Redgrave, Lynn (1943–)
British actress, daughter of Sir Michael REDGRAVE; has tended to play gauche comedy roles.
■ Tom Jones 63. Girl with Green Eyes 64. *Georgy Girl* (AAN) 66. The Deadly Affair 67. Smashing Time 67. The Virgin Soldiers 69. Blood Kin 69. Killer from Yuma 71. Every Little Crook and Nanny 72. Everything You Always Wanted to Know about Sex 72. The National Health 73. The Happy Hooker 75. The Big Bus 76. Sunday Lovers 80. Gauguin the Savage (TV) 81. Rehearsal for Murder (TV) 82. The Shooting (TV) 82. Morgan Stewart's Coming Home 87. Midnight 89. Getting It Right 89. Whatever Happened to Baby Jane? (TV) 91. Shine 96. Toothless 97. Gods & Monsters (AAN) 98. Strike 98. The Annihilation of Fish 99. Touched (Can.) 99.The Next Best Thing 00.
TV series: House Calls 80–81. Teachers Only 82. Rude Awakening 98– .
❝ Looking up at my horrible ugly bulk on a huge screen was the turning point in my life. – *L.R.*
(she shed many pounds before making it big in Hollywood and on American TV game shows)

Redgrave, Sir Michael (1908–1985)
Tall, distinguished British actor, former schoolmaster, on stage from 1934. Married actress Rachel Kempson. Their children are all actors: Corin, Vanessa and Lynn REDGRAVE.
Autobiography: 1958, *Mask or Face*. 1983, *In My Mind's Eye*.
Biography: 1956, *Michael Redgrave, Actor* by Richard Findlater. 1996, *Michael Redgrave: My Father* by Corin Redgrave.
■ *The Lady Vanishes* 38. Climbing High 38. A Stolen Life 39. A Window in London 39. *The Stars Look Down* 39. *Kipps* 41. Atlantic Ferry 41. *Jeannie* 41. *Thunder Rock* 42. The Big Blockade 42. The Way to the Stars 45. *Dead of Night* 45. The Captive Heart 46. The Years Between 46. The Man Within 47. *Fame is the Spur* 47. Mourning Becomes Electra (US) (AAN) 47. The Secret beyond the Door (US) 48. *The Browning Version* 50. The Magic Box 51. *The Importance of Being Earnest* 52. The Sea Shall Not Have Them 54. The Green Scarf 54. Oh Rosalinda 55. Confidential Report 55. The Night my Number Came Up 55. *The Dam Busters* 55.

Nineteen Eighty-Four 56. Time Without Pity 57. *The Quiet American* 58. Law and Disorder 58. Behind the Mask 58. Shake Hands with the Devil 59. No My Darling Daughter 60. The Innocents 61. The Loneliness of the Long Distance Runner 63. Young Cassidy 64. The Hill 65. The Heroes of Telemark 65. Assignment K 67. Oh What a Lovely War 69. Goodbye Mr Chips 69. The Battle of Britain 69. David Copperfield 69. Connecting Rooms 69. Goodbye Gemini 70. Nicholas and Alexandra 71. The Go-Between 71.

Redgrave, Vanessa (1937–)
British leading lady, daughter of Sir Michael REDGRAVE; as well known for her espousal of causes as for her acting. She was married to director Tony RICHARDSON (1962–67) and has a son by actor Franco NERO.

Autobiography: 1991, *Vanessa Redgrave*.

Behind the Mask 58. *Morgan* (AAN) 66. Red and Blue 66. A Man for all Seasons (uncredited) 66. Blow Up 66. *Camelot* 67. Sailor from Gibraltar 67. The Charge of the Light Brigade 68. *Isadora* (AAN) 68.The Seagull 68. A Quiet Place in the Country (It.) 68. Dropout (It.) 69. Vacation (It.) 69. Oh What a Lovely War 69. The Devils 70. The Trojan Women 71. *Mary Queen of Scots* (AAN) 71. Murder on the Orient Express 74. Out of Season 75. The Seven Per Cent Solution 76. Julia (AA) 77. Agatha 79. Yanks 79. Bear Island 79. *Playing for Time* (TV) 81. Wagner 82. My Body My Child (TV) 83. The Bostonians (AAN) 84. Steaming 85. Wetherby 85. Three Sovereigns for Sarah (TV) 86. Peter the Great (TV) 86. Second Serve (TV) 86. Comrades 87. Prick Up Your Ears 87. Consuming Passions 88. The Ballad of the Sad Café 90. Whatever Happened to Baby Jane? (TV) 91. Howards End (AAN) 92. The Plague Sower/Di Ceria dell'Untore 92. Sparrow/Storia di una Capinera (It.) 93. Black Flowers/Un Muro de Silencio (Arg.) 93. The House of the Spirits 93. Mother's Boys 94. Little Odessa 94. Great Moments in Aviation 94. A Month by the Lake 94. Down Came a Blackbird (TV) 95. The Wind in the Willows (narrator) 96. Mission: Impossible 96. Vita and Virginia (TV) 97. Mrs Dalloway 97. Smilla's Feeling for Snow 97. Wilde 97. Déjà Vu 97. Deep Impact 98. Lulu on the Bridge 98. Celebrity 98. The Cradle Will Rock 99. Girl, Interrupted 00. The Three Kings 00, etc.

❝ America is gangsterism for the private profit of the few. – *V.R.*

I give myself to my parts as to a lover. – *V.R.*

I have a tremendous use for passionate statement. – *V.R.*

It's a kinky part of my nature – to meddle. – *V.R.*

I choose all my roles very carefully so that when my career is finished I will have covered all our recent history of oppression. – *V.R.*

The Ellen Terry of her time. – *Caryl Brahms*

Redman, Joyce (1918–)
Irish stage actress whose most memorable film role was in the eating scene in *Tom Jones* (AAN) 63.

Othello (AAN) 65. Prudence and the Pill 67. Les Misérables (TV) 77. A Different Kind of Love 85.

Redmond, Liam (1913–1989)
Irish character actor, an Abbey player.

I See a Dark Stranger 45. Captain Boycott 48. High Treason 51. The Gentle Gunman 52. The Divided Heart 54. Jacqueline 56. Night of the Demon 57. The Boy and the Bridge 59. The Ghost and Mr Chicken (US) 65. Tobruk (US) 66. The Twenty-Fifth Hour 66. The Last Safari 67. Barry Lyndon 75, etc.

Redmond, Moira
British actress, mainly on the stage.

Doctor in Love 58. *Nightmare* 62. Jigsaw 62. The Limbo Line 66, etc.

Reece, Brian (1913–1962)
British light actor whose success was mainly on stage.

A Case for PC 49 51. Fast and Loose 54. Orders are Orders 55. Carry on Admiral 58, etc.

Reed, Alan (1907–1977) (Edward Bergman)
Burly American character actor, TV's voice of Fred Flintstone.

Days of Glory 43. Nob Hill 44. Viva Zapata 52. The Desperate Hours 55. Breakfast at Tiffany's 62, etc.

Reed, Sir Carol (1906–1976)
Distinguished British director who after a peak in the late 40s seemed to lose his way; his infrequent later films, though always civilized, were generally disappointing. Born in London, the illegitimate son of actor Herbert Beerbohm Tree, he began as an actor in the theatre, where he also directed and formed a close working relationship with Edgar WALLACE, who stimulated his interest in films: he began as a dialogue director, working under Basil DEAN at Ealing Studios. He was at his best in collaborations with writer Graham Greene on *The Fallen Idol* and *The Third Man*. Married actresses Diana Wynyard (1943–47) and Penelope Ward. His lovers included actress Jessie MATTHEWS and novelist Daphne DU MAURIER.

Biography: 1991, *The Man Between* by Nicholas Wapshott.

■ Midshipman Easy 34. Laburnum Grove 36. Talk of the Devil 36. Who's Your Lady Friend? 37. *Bank Holiday* 38. Penny Paradise 38. Climbing High 38. A Girl Must Live 39. *The Stars Look Down* 39. *Night Train to Munich* 40. The Girl in the News 40. *Kipps* 41. The Young Mr Pitt 42. *The Way Ahead* 44. The True Glory (co-d) 45. *Odd Man Out* 46. *The Fallen Idol* (AAN) 48. *The Third Man* (AAN) 49. *An Outcast of the Islands* 51. The Man Between 53. A Kid for Two Farthings 55. Trapeze 56. The Key 58. Our Man in Havana 59. The Running Man 63. The Agony and the Ecstasy 65. *Oliver!* (AA) 68. Flap 70. Follow Me 72.

✪ For the sympathy and expertise which sadly left him after the early 50s. *Kipps*.

❝ To be any good to a director, an actor or actress must either be wonderful, or know absolutely nothing about acting. A little knowledge – that's what is bad! – *C.R.*

His career demonstrates that a director who limits himself to solving technical problems quickly lapses into the decadence of the inappropriate effect. – *Andrew Sarris, 1968*

Reed, Donna (1921–1986) (Donna Mullenger)
American leading lady of the 40s, later star of long-running TV series *The Donna Reed Show*. Won screen test after a beauty contest while still at college.

The Getaway (debut) 41. Shadow of the Thin Man 42. The Courtship of Andy Hardy 42. Calling Dr Gillespie 42. The Human Comedy 43. See Here, Private Hargrove 44. The Picture of Dorian Gray 44. It's a Wonderful Life 46. Green Dolphin Street 47. Chicago Deadline 49. *From Here to Eternity* (AA) 53. The Last Time I Saw Paris 55. Ransom 56. Backlash 56. The Benny Goodman Story 56. Beyond Mombasa 57. The Best Place to Be (TV) 79. Deadly Lessons (TV) 83, etc.

TV series: Dallas 84.

❝ Forty pictures I was in, and all I remember is 'What kind of bra will you be wearing today, honey?' That was always the area of big decision – from the neck to the navel. – *D.R.*

Reed, George (1867–1952)
American character actor.

The Birth of a Nation 14. The Green Pastures 36. So Red the Rose 36. Swanee River 39. Tales of Manhattan 42. Home in Indiana 44, many others.

Reed, Jerry (1937–) (Jerry Reed Hubbard)
American country singer and songwriter, guitarist, character actor and occasional director. Born in Atlanta, Georgia, he was a musician from his 'teens and moved to Nashville in the late 50s to work as a session guitarist and songwriter; from the mid-60s, he also made hit records.

WW and the Dixie Dancekings 75. Gator 76. Smokey and the Bandit 77. High-Ballin' 78. Hot Stuff 79. Smokey and the Bandit II 80. Smokey and the Bandit III 83. The Survivors 83. What Comes Around (& p, d) 87. Bat 21 (& ex-p) 88. The Waterboy 98., etc.

TV series: The Glen Campbell Goodtime Hour 70-72. The Jerry Reed When You're Hot You're Hot Hour 72. Dean Martin Presents Music Country 73. Nashville 99 77. Concrete Cowboys 81.

Reed, Joel M.
American director and screenwriter of exploitation movies.

GI Executioner 71. Blood Bath 75. Bloodsucking Freaks/The Incredible Torture Show 77. Night of the Zombies/Curse of the Ghoul Battalions 81, etc.

Reed, Les (1935–)
British composer and conductor. A former member of the John Barry Seven, he has written many popular hits and, occasionally, film scores and songs.

Girl on a Motorcycle (m) 68. Les Bicyclettes de Belsize (m) 69. One More Time (m) 69. The Lady Vanishes (s) 79. Play Misty for Me (s) 71. Creepshow 2 (m) 87, etc.

Reed, Maxwell (1919–1974)
Brooding Irish leading man in British films from 1946, after repertory experience. He was actress Joan COLLINS's first husband, and created a minor sensation by suing her for alimony.

The Years Between 46. Daybreak 47. *The Brothers* 48. The Dark Man 49. The Square Ring 53. Before I Wake 56. Notorious Landlady 62. Picture Mommy Dead 66, etc.

TV series: Captain David Grief 56.

❝ A star should always behave like a star. – *M.R.*

When he stopped posturing and posing and using a phony American accent he was a fairly good actor. – *Joan Collins*

Reed, Michael (1929–)
British cinematographer.

October Moth 60. Linda 61. The Gorgon 64. Dracula Prince of Darkness 66. On Her Majesty's Secret Service 69. The Mackenzie Break 71. The Groundstar Conspiracy 73. The Hireling 73. Galileo 75. Shout at the Devil 76. Loophole 80. Kim (TV) 84. Wild Geese 85, etc.

Reed, Oliver (1938–1999)
Burly British leading man, usually in sullen roles. He eschewed formal training, but was Britain's highest paid actor for a brief period in the late 60s. Notorious for his heavy drinking and barroom exploits, by the 80s he was reduced to appearing in dire European Z movies. Died after being taken ill in a bar in Malta, where he was appearing in *Gladiator*, which was to have been a role that re-established him as an actor. He was the nephew of director Carol REED.

The Rebel 60. His and Hers 60. The Curse of the Werewolf 61. Pirates of Blood River 61. Captain Clegg 62. *The Damned* 63. Paranoic 63. The Scarlet Blade 63. The Party's Over 63. *The System* 64. The Brigand of Kandahar 65. *The Trap* 66. The Shuttered Room 67. *The Jokers* 67. I'll Never Forget Whatshisname 67. The Assassination Bureau 68. Oliver! 68. Hannibal Brooks 68. *Women in Love* 69. The Lady in the Car with Glasses and a Gun 69. The Devils 70. Take a Girl Like You 70. The Hunting Party 71. Zero Population Growth 71. Sitting Target 72. Triple Echo 72. Days of Fury 73. Blue Blood 73. The Three Musketeers 73. The Four Musketeers 74. And Then There Were None 74. Royal Flash 75. Tommy 75. The Sellout 75. Great Scout and Cathouse Thursday 76. Burnt Offerings 76. The Prince and the Pauper 77. The Big Sleep 77. Tomorrow Never Comes 77. The Class of Miss MacMichael 78. The Brood 79. Lion of the Desert 80. Dr Heckyl and Mr Hype 80. Condorman 81. Venom 81. No Secrets 82. Masquerade (TV) 82. The Sting 2 83. Two of a Kind 83. Second Chance 84. Christopher Columbus (TV) 84. Black Arrow (TV) 85. Castaway 86. Adventures of Baron Munchausen 89. Return of the Musketeers 89. Hold My Hand I'm Dying 90. The Pit and the Pendulum 90. Treasure Island 90. Severed Ties 91. House of Usher 91. Prisoners of Honor (TV) 91. The Mummy Lives 92. Return to Lonesome Dove (TV) 93. Funny Bones 95. Parting Shots 98. *Gladiator* 00, etc.

❝ He was a saint. – *Ken Russell*

He could have been a very big star but, as you know, he was sick all over Steve McQueen. Americans can't take that. – *Michael Winner*

Reed, Pamela (1953–)
American leading actress.

The Long Riders 80. Melvin and Howard 80. Eyewitness/The Janitor 81. Young Doctors in Love 82. The Right Stuff 83. The Best of Times 86. Tanner '88 (TV) 88. Rachel River 89. Chattahoochee 89. Cadillac Man 90. Kindergarten Cop 90. Caroline? (TV) 90. Passed Away 92. The Best of Times 94. Junior 94. Santa Fe 97. Critical Choices 97. Bean 97. Proof of Life 00, etc.

TV series: Andros Targets 77.

Reed, Philip (1908–1996)
American leading man with long stage experience.

Female 34. Last of the Mohicans 36. Aloma of the South Seas 41. Old Acquaintance 44. I Cover Big Town 47. Unknown Island 50. The Tattered Dress 57. Harem Scarem 67, etc.

Reed, Rex (1938–)
American interviewer and showbiz gossip columnist. Collections published include *Valentines and Vitriol, Do You Really Sleep in the Nude?, Big Screen Little Screen* and *Conversations in the Raw*. Not a great success as an actor when he played the transsexual *Myra Breckinridge*.

Reed, Robert (1932–1992) (John Robert Reitz, Jnr)
American leading actor, mainly on TV and best known for playing the ever-tolerant father of *The Brady Bunch*. Died of AIDS.

Bloodlust 59. Hurry Sundown 67. Star! 68. The Love Bug 68. The Maltese Bippy 69. Haunts of the Very Rich (TV) 72. Snatched (TV) 72. Nightmare (TV) 76. The Boy in the Plastic Bubble (TV) 76. The Hunted Lady (TV) 77. Bud and Lou (TV) 78. The Seekers (TV) 79. Love's Savage Fury (TV) 79. Casino (TV) 80. Death of a Centerfold (TV) 81. A Very Brady Christmas (TV) 88. Prime Target 91, etc.

TV series: The Defenders 61–65. *The Brady Bunch* 69–74. Mannix 69–75. Rich Man, Poor Man Book I 76. The Brady Bunch Hour 77. Roots 77. The Runaways 78. Scruples 80. Nurse 81–82. The Bradys 90.

Rees, Angharad (1949–)
Welsh leading lady, best known for her role as Demelza in the TV series *Poldark* 75–77. Formerly married to actor Christopher Cazenove.

Hands of the Ripper 72. Under Milk Wood 72. The Love Ban 73. Moments 74. The Curse of King Tut's Tomb (TV) 80, etc.

Rees, Roger (1944–)
Introspective Welsh actor and theatre director. Born in Aberystwyth, he studied art at the Slade, made his stage debut at the age of 22, and was in films from 1983. A leading member of the Royal Shakespeare Company for eight years, he played the title role in its notable production of *Nicholas Nickleby*, which was also televised.

A Bouquet of Barbed Wire (TV) 76. Star 80 83. A Christmas Carol (TV) 84. Ebony Tower (TV) 86. Mountains of the Moon 90. If Looks Could Kill 91. Stop or My Mom Will Shoot 91. Robin Hood: Men in Tights 93. Sudden Manhattan 96. The Substance of Fire 96. Titanic (TV) 96, etc.

TV series: Cheers 89–91.

Reese, Tom (1930–)
American character actor, a notable 'heavy'.

Flaming Star 60. Marines Let's Go 61. Forty Pounds of Trouble 62. Murderers' Row 66. Vanishing Point 71. The Outfit 73. The Wild Party 74. Defiance 79, etc.

Reeve, Ada (1874–1966)
British character actress and singer whose career lasted more than 80 years. Born in Whitechapel, London, she appeared in pantomime at the age of four and made her music-hall debut when she was 12. She became a star of musicals in the 1890s, touring the world until the mid-30s when she turned to acting on stage and in films.

Autobiography: 1954, *Take It for a Fact*.

They Came to a City 44. When the Bough Breaks 47. Night and the City 50. Eye Witness 56. The Passionate Stranger/A Novel Affair 57, etc.

Reeve, Christopher (1952–)
Strapping American leading man who flew to fame. He was paralysed from the neck down in a riding accident in 1995. The Christopher Reeve Paralysis Foundation was set up in 1999.

Autobiography: 1997, *Still Me*.

Gray Lady Down 77. *Superman* 78. Superman II 80. Somewhere in Time 80. Death Trap 82. Monsignor 82. Superman III 83. The Aviator 84. The Bostonians 84. Anna Karenina (TV) 84. Street Smart 87. Superman IV 87. Switching Channels 88. The Great Escape II: The Untold Story (TV) 88. The Rose and the Jackal (TV) 90. Bump in the Night 90. Noises Off 92. The Sea Wolf (TV) 93. Black Fox 93. Morning Glory 93. The Remains of the Day 93. Above Suspicion 94. Village of the Damned 95. Rear Window (TV) 98, etc.

Reeve, Geoffrey (1932–)
British director and producer.
Puppet on a Chain (d) 70. Caravan to Vaccares (p, d) 74. The Shooting Party (p) 84. The Far Pavilions (p) (TV) 84. Half Moon Street (p) 86. The Whistle Blower (p) 86. Souvenir (d) (TV) 88, etc.

Reeves, George (1914–1959) (George Brewer)
American leading man. Typecast as Superman, he found no parts available for him and became a wrestler. Shot himself.
Biography: 1996, *Hollywood Kryptonite: The Bulldog, the Lady and the Death of Superman* by Sam Kashner and Nancy Schoenberger.
Gone with the Wind (debut) 39. Strawberry Blonde 41. Blood and Sand 42. Bar 20 44. Jungle Jim 49. Samson and Delilah 50. Sir Galahad (serial) 50. From Here to Eternity 53.
TV series: Superman 51–57.

Reeves, Keanu (1964–)
American leading actor. Born in Beirut, Lebanon, the son of a Hawaiian father, he began acting in Canada and first came to notice on TV. He also plays bass guitar in the rock group Dogstar, which toured Europe in 1996 to indifferent reviews. The success of the thriller *Speed*, for which he was reportedly paid $1.25m, put up his asking price to $7m a film, though he turned down a sequel, *Speed II*. He was paid $10m against ten per cent of the gross for *Matrix*, which earned him around $30m. His deal for two sequels–$39m against fifteen per cent of the gross–was expected to bring him as much as $100m.
Biography: 1996, *Keanu* by Sheila Johnston.
Flying 86. Youngblood 86. River's Edge 86. Dangerous Liaisons 88. The Night Before 88. Permanent Record 88. The Prince of Pennsylvania 88. Bill and Ted's Excellent Adventure 88. Parenthood 89. I Love You to Death 90. Tune in Tomorrow/Aunt Julia and the Scriptwriter 90. Point Break 91. Bill and Ted's Bogus Journey 91. My Own Private Idaho 91. Bram Stoker's Dracula 92. Much Ado about Nothing 93. Even Cowgirls Get the Blues 93. Little Buddha 93. *Speed* 94. Johnny Mnemonic 95. A Walk in the Clouds 95. Feeling Minnesota 96. Chain Reaction 96. The Devil's Advocate 97. The Last Time I Committed Suicide 97. *The Matrix* 99. The Replacements 00. The Watcher 00, etc.

Reeves, Kynaston (1893–1971)
British character actor of stage and screen, often seen as academic. In films from 1919.
The Lodger 32. The Housemaster 38. The Prime Minister 40. Vice Versa 48. The Guinea Pig 49. The Mudlark 50. Top of the Form 53. Brothers in Law 57. School for Scoundrels 60. The Private Life of Sherlock Holmes 70, many others.

Reeves, Michael (1944–1969)
British director whose promising career barely got started. Died from an overdose of drink and drugs.
■ Sister of Satan/Revenge of the Blood Beast (It.) 65. The Sorcerers 67. Witchfinder General 68.

Reeves, Saskia
British leading actress, from the stage.
December Bride 90. The Bridge 91. Close My Eyes 91. Antonia and Jane 91. Traps 94. Butterfly Kiss 95. i.d. 95. Different for Girls 96. LA without a Map 98. Heart 98. A Christmas Carol (TV) 99. Unknown Things 00, etc.
TV series: Plotlands 97.

Reeves, Steve (1926–2000)
American actor, formerly 'Mr World' and 'Mr Universe'; found stardom from 1953 in Italian muscleman spectacles. He retired to his Californian ranch in the late 60s.
■ Athena 54. The Labours of Hercules 57. Hercules and the Queen of Sheba/Hercules Unchained 58. The White Warrior 58. Goliath and the Barbarians 59. The Giant of Marathon 59. The White Devil 59. The Last Days of Pompeii 59. Thief of Baghdad 60. Morgan the Pirate 60. The Wooden Horse of Troy 61. Duel of the Titans/Romulus and Remus 61. Son of Spartacus 62. War of the Trojans 62. Sandokan the Great 63. The Pirates of Malaya 64. A Long Ride from Hell 68.
❝ I found acting very stressful. I never liked it. – *S.R.*

Refn, Anders (1944–)
Danish director and editor. He is the father of Nicolas Refn.
AS EDITOR: Dear Irene/Kaere Irene 71. With Love and Kisses/Med Kaerling Hilsen 71. Carl, My Childhood Symphony/Min Finske Barndom 94, etc.
AS DIRECTOR: Prins Piwi (co-d) 74. Stromer 76. The Heritage/Slaegten 78. The Flying Devils/De Flyvende Djaevle 85. I Familiens Skod 93. Black Harvest/Sort Host (& co-w) 93, etc.

Refn, Nicolas Winding (*c.* 1972–)
Danish director, the son of Anders Refn. He lived in New York as a child. He turned down an offer from Hollywood to remake *Pusher*.
Pusher (co-w,d) 97. Bleeder (wd) 99, etc.

Regan, Phil (1906–1996)
American singer and actor of the 30s and 40s, a former policeman, who was best known for singing 'Happy Days Are Here Again' at President Truman's inauguration; later involved in politics, he was imprisoned for a time for attempted bribery in the early 70s.
The Key 34. Dames 34. We're in the Money 35. Laughing Irish Eyes 36. Manhattan Merry-Go-Round 37. She Married a Cop 39. Sweet Rosie O'Grady 43. Swing Parade of 1946 46. Three Little Words 50, etc.

Reggiani, Serge (1922–)
Slightly-built French-Italian actor with stage experience.
Les Portes de la Nuit 46. Manon 48. Les Amants de Vérone 48. La Ronde 50. Secret People (GB) 51. *Casque d'Or* 51. The Wicked Go to Hell 55. Les Misérables 57. Marie Octobre 58. Paris Blues 60. The Leopard 63. The 25th Hour 67. Les Aventuriers 67. Day of the Owl (It.) 68. The Good and the Bad 76. Cat and Mouse 76. L'Empreinte des Géantes 80. Fantastica 80. I Hired a Contract Killer 90. Under the Stars 93. Le Petit Garçon 95, etc.

Reggio, Godfrey (1940–)
American director of unclassifiable films, usually featuring the music of Philip Glass. Born in New Orleans, he became a novitiate of the Christian Brothers before leaving the order in the late 60s.
Koyaanisquati 83. Powaqqatsi 88. Anima Mundi 92. Evidence (short) 94, etc.

Régnier, Natacha (1974–)
Belgian leading actress, born in Brussels.
Dis-moi oui... 95. Encore 96. *The Dreamlife of Angels/La Vie Rêvée Des Anges* 98. A Time To Love 99. Calino Maneige 99. Criminal Lovers/Les Amants Criminels 99. Everything's Fine, We're Leaving/Tout Va Bien, On S'En Va 00, etc.

Reichenbach, François (1922–1993)
French documentarist with an ironic viewpoint.
L'Amérique Insolite 59. Un Coeur Gros Comme ça 61. Les Amoureux du France 64. Hollywood through a Keyhole 66. Love of Life (co-d) 68. F for Fake (co-d) 75. Sex O'Clock 76. Pele 77. Houston, Texas 80. François Reichenbach's Japan 83. Visages Suisses (co-d) 91, etc.

Reicher, Frank (1875–1965)
German-born character actor, long in Hollywood.
Her Man O' War 26. Mata Hari 32. *King Kong* 33. Kind Lady 36. Anthony Adverse 36. Lancer Spy 38. They Dare Not Love 41. House of Frankenstein 45. The Mummy's Ghost 46. The Secret Life of Walter Mitty 47. Samson and Delilah 50, many others.
AS DIRECTOR: The Eternal Mother 17. Behind Masks 21. Wise Husbands 21, etc.

Reid, Alastair (1939–)
British director. From the mid-70s on, working in television.
■ Baby Love 69. The Night Digger 71. Something to Hide 72. Man on the Screen (TV) 83.

Reid, Beryl (1920–1996)
British comedienne and character actress, in variety from 1936, and known for her act as a Birmingham schoolgirl, Marlene.
Autobiography: 1984, *So Much Love*.
The Belles of St Trinian's 54. The Extra Day 56. The Dock Brief 62. Star! 68. Inspector Clouseau 68. The Assassination Bureau 68. *The Killing of Sister George* (her stage role) (US) 68. Entertaining Mr Sloane 70. The Beast in the Cellar 71. Dr Phibes Rises Again 72. Psychomania 72. Father Dear Father 73. No Sex Please We're British 73. Joseph Andrews 76. Smiley's People (TV) 82. Yellowbeard 83. The Doctor and the Devils 85, etc.
TV series: The Most Likely Girl 57. Bold as Brass 64. Beryl Reid Says Good Evening 68. Alcock and Gander 72. Beryl Reid 77, 79. The Secret Diary of Adrian Mole Aged 13¾ 85. The Growing Pains of Adrian Mole 87.

Reid, Carl Benton (1894–1973)
American character actor with stage career before settling in Hollywood.
The Little Foxes 41. In a Lonely Place 50. Convicted 50. The Great Caruso 51. Lorna Doone 51. Carbine Williams 52. The Egyptian 54. The Left Hand of God 55. The Gallant Hours 59, etc.
TV series: Amos Burke – Secret Agent 65.

Reid, Elliott (1920–)
American comedy actor who often played the dumb son of an executive.
The Story of Dr Wassell 44. Gentlemen Prefer Blondes 53. Woman's World 54. Inherit the Wind 60. Who's Been Sleeping in My Bed? 63. The Thrill of It All 63. Some Kind of a Nut 69, etc.

Reid, Kate (1930–1993)
Canadian actress.
This Property Is Condemned 66. The Andromeda Strain 71. Death Among Friends (TV) 75. Equus 77. Atlantic City USA 81. Fire with Fire 86. Sweethearts Dance 88. Bye Bye Blues 90. Deceived 91, etc.
TV series: The Whiteoaks of Jalna 72.

Reid, Tara (1975–)
American actress, born in New Jersey, and appearing in commercials from childhood.
The Big Lebowski. Urban Legend 98. Girl 98. American Pie 99. Body Shots 99. Dr T and the Women 00, etc.

Reid, Wallace (1891–1923)
American leading man of the silent screen. Addiction to morphine, following an accident in 1919, and heavy drinking led to his early death. Married actress Dorothy Davenport.
The Deerslayer 11. The Birth of a Nation 14. The Love Mask 16. House of Silence 18. The Dancing Fool 20. The Affairs of Anatol 21. Forever 21. The Ghost Breaker 22, many others.
❝ Wallace Reid was the stud of the studio, and whenever (Cecil B.) De Mille had a new sweet thing under contract, he sent Wally over to 'make her a woman' as they said in those days. – *Mitchell Leisen*

Reilly, John C. (1965–)
American actor, born in Chicago, Illinois.
Casualties of War 89. We're No Angels 89. Days of Thunder 90. State of Grace 90. Hoffa 92. Out on a Limb 92. The River Wild 94. Georgia 95. Dolores Claiborne 95. Boys 96. Hard Eight 96. Boogie Nights 97. Never Been Kissed 98. Nightwatch 98. The Thin Red Line 98. Magnolia 99. The Perfect Storm 00, etc.

Reiner, Carl (1922–)
Balding, genial American comedy writer and actor.
AS ACTOR: Happy Anniversary 59. The Gazebo 59. Gidget Goes Hawaiian 61. *It's a Mad Mad Mad Mad World* 63. The Art of Love 65. The Russians Are Coming, the Russians Are Coming 66. A Guide for the Married Man 67. The Comic 69. The End 78. Dead Men Don't Wear Plaid 82. Spirit of '76 91. The Right to Remain Silent (TV) 95. Slums of Beverly Hills 98. The Adventures of Rocky and Bullwinkle 00, etc.
AS WRITER: The Thrill of It All 63. The Art of Love 65. Enter Laughing 67. The Comic 69. The Jerk 79. Dead Men Don't Wear Plaid 82. The Man with Two Brains (co-w) 83.
AS DIRECTOR: Enter Laughing 67. The Comic 69. Where's Poppa? 70. Oh God 77. The Jerk 79. Dead Men Don't Wear Plaid 82. The Man with Two Brains 83. Summer School 87. Bert Rigby, You're a Fool (wd) 89. Triple Indemnity 93. Fatal Instinct 93. That Old Feeling 97, etc.
TV series: Good Heavens 76 (as actor). *The Dick Van Dyke Show* 61–65 (as writer).

Reiner, Rob (1945–)
American director, writer and former comic actor. He is the son of director Carl Reiner and was formerly married to actress and director Penny Marshall.
This Is Spinal Tap 85. The Sure Thing 85. Stand by Me 86. The Princess Bride 87. When Harry Met Sally 89. Postcards from the Edge 90. Misery 90. Spirit of '76 90. Sleepless in Seattle (a) 93. North 94. Bullets over Broadway (a) 94. Lifesavers (a) 94. Mixed Nuts (a) 94. Bye Bye, Love (a) 95. The American President 95. Ghosts of Mississippi 97. Primary Colors (a) 98, etc.
TV series: All in the Family (a) 71–78. Free Country (a) 78.

Reinhardt, Gottfried (1911–1994)
Austrian producer, son of theatrical producer Max Reinhardt. Went to US with his father and became assistant to Walter Wanger. Produced and occasionally directed.
The Great Waltz (script) 38. Comrade X (p) 40. Two-Faced Woman (p) 41. Command Decision (p) 48. The Red Badge of Courage (p) 51. Invitation (d) 52. The Story of Three Loves (d) 53. Betrayed (d) 54. The Good Soldier Schweik (p) 59. Town without Pity (p, d) 61. Situation Hopeless but Not Serious (p, d) 65, etc.

Reinhardt, Max (1873–1943) (Max Goldman)
Influential Austrian theatrical director and producer, a former actor. He studied drama in Vienna, became a leading actor in Berlin and went on to run theatres in Berlin and Salzburg. After the Nazis came to power in the early 30s he settled in America. He made three German silents between 1908 and 1914 that reveal little of his skills. But the style of his spectacular productions, influenced by the theories of Edward Gordon Craig, were captured in his one sound film of *A Midsummer Night's Dream*, 35, which was co-directed by William Dieterle; its failure at the box-office and with critics brought a sudden end to his seven-picture contract with Warners. In the late 30s he established a school for Hollywood hopefuls on Sunset Boulevard, where the teachers included Erich Wolfgang Korngold, Samson Raphaelson and John Huston, but it was not a success and he returned to work in the theatre. Those from his German companies who carried his influence into film included Ernst Lubitsch, Paul Wegener, Ernst Matray, William Dieterle and F.W. Murnau.

Reinhold, Judge (1956–)
American actor.
Running Scared 79. Stripes 81. Fast Times at Ridgemont High 82. The Lords of Discipline 83. Beverly Hills Cop 84. Gremlins 84. Head Office 86. Offbeat 86. Ruthless People 86. Beverly Hills Cop II 87. Vice Versa 88. Rosalie Goes Shopping 89. Daddy's Dyin', Who's Got the Will? 90. Zandalee 90. Baby on Board 92. Bank Robber 93. Beverly Hills Cop III 94. The Santa Clause 94. The Wharf Rat (TV) 95. The Right to Remain Silent (TV) 95. As Good as Dead 95. Hostage Train 97. Teen Monster 99, etc.
TV series: Secret Service Guy 96.

Reiniger, Lotte (1899–1981)
German animator, well known for her silhouette cartoons.
The Adventures of Prince Achmed 26. Dr Dolittle (series) 28. Carmen 33. Papageno 35. The Brave Little Tailor 55, etc.

Reinking, Ann (1949–)
American dancer, from Broadway.
■ Movie Movie 78. All That Jazz 79. Annie 82. Micki & Maude 84.

Reinl, Harald (1908–1986) (Karl Reiner)
German director of popular entertainments, including a series of European westerns based on the novels of Karl May and starring Lex Barker. He was killed by his wife.
Bergkristall 49. Der Schatz im Silbersee 52. The Return of Dr Mabuse/Im Stahinetz des Dr Mabuse 61. Forger of London 61. The Invisible Dr Mabuse/Die Unsichtbaren Krallen des Dr Mabuse 62. Winnetou 64. Winnetou II 64. Shatterhand 64. Winnetou III 65. Winnetou und das Halbblut Apanatschi 67. The Torture Chamber of Dr Sadism/Die Schlangengrube und das Pendel 67. Winnetou und Shatterhand im Tal der Toten 68, etc.

Reis, Irving (1906–1953)
American director, with radio experience.
■ One Crowded Night 40. I'm Still Alive 40. Weekend for Three 41. A Date with the Falcon 41. The Gay Falcon 41. The Falcon Takes Over 42. The Big Street 43. Hitler's Children 43. Crack Up 46. *The Bachelor and the Bobby-soxer* 47.

Enchantment 48. All My Sons 48. Roseanna McCoy 49. Dancing in the Dark 49. Three Husbands 50. New Mexico 51. The Fourposter 52.

Reisch, Walter (1903–1983)
Austrian writer who in the 30s came to Britain, then Hollywood.
Men Are Not Gods (& d) 36. Ninotchka (AAN) 39. Comrade X (AAN) 40. The Heavenly Body 43. Gaslight (co-w, AAN) 44. Song of Scheherezade (& d) 46. Titanic (AA) 52. The Girl in the Red Velvet Swing 55. Journey to the Centre of the Earth 59, etc.

Reiser, Paul (1957–)
American actor and comedian. In 1998 he was paid $1m an episode for his TV series *Mad about You*, which he co-created.
Diner 82. Sunset Limousine 83. Beverly Hills Cop 84. From Here to Maternity (TV) 85. Odd Jobs 85. Aliens 86. Beverly Hills Cop II 87. Cross My Heart 88. Crazy People 90. Family Prayers 91. The Marrying Man 91. Mr Write 94. Bye Bye, Love 95, etc.
TV series: My Two Dads 87–90. Mad about You 92–99.

Reisner, Allen
American director, from TV.
■ All Mine to Give 56. St Louis Blues 58. To Die in Paris (TV) (co-d) 68. Your Money or Your Wife (TV) 72. Captains and the Kings (TV) 86. Mary Jane Harper Cried Last Night (TV) 77. Cops and Robin (TV) 78. The Love Tapes (TV) 80.

Reisner, Charles (1887–1962)
American director.
The Man in the Box 25. Reducing 32. The Show-Off 34. Sophie Lang Goes West 37. *The Big Store* 41. Meet the People 44. Lost in a Harem 44. The Cobra Strikes 48. The Travelling Saleswoman 50, many others, mainly second features.

Reisz, Karel (1926–)
Czech director, in Britain from childhood. Former film critic. In recent years he has been working mainly as a theatre director.
■ We are the Lambeth Boys 58. *Saturday Night and Sunday Morning* 60. Night Must Fall 63. This Sporting Life (p only) 63. *Morgan: A Suitable Case for Treatment* 66. Isadora 68. The Gambler 74. Who'll Stop the Rain? 78. The French Lieutenant's Woman 81. Sweet Dreams 86. Everybody Wins 88.

Reitherman, Wolfgang (1909–1985)
American animator, director of Disney cartoon features from the mid-60s.

Reitman, Ivan (1946–)
Canadian director and producer.
Foxy Lady 71. Cannibal Girls 73. Meatballs 79. Stripes (p, d) 81. *Ghostbusters* 84. Legal Eagles 86. Twins 88. Ghostbusters II (p, d) 89. Kindergarten Cop (p, d) 90. Stop or My Mom Will Shoot (p) 91. Beethoven (p) 92. Dave 93. Junior 94. Space Jam (p) 96. Fathers' Day 97. Six Days, Seven Nights 98, etc.

Reitz, Edgar (1932–)
German director, best known for *Homeland/Heimat*, his epic film on the life of a family over three generations, which ran for more than 15 hours. Born in Moorbach, he studied at Munich University and was a member of the Oberhausen group that announced a new German cinema in 1962. He worked as a cameraman and editor with various companies and began making short films and documentaries in the mid-50s. With Alexander Kluge and others he set up the Institute of Film Composition in Ilum, where he taught.
Mealtimes/Mahlzeiten 67. Fussnoten 67. Cadillac 69. Stories of the Bucket Baby/Geschichten von Kubelkind (co-d) 70. Die Reise nach Wien 73. Zero Hour/Stunde Null 76. The Tailor from Ulm/Der Schneider von Ulm 78. Homeland/Heimat 84, etc.
❝ We don't believe in the 'new film' but rather in the 'new cinema'. The cinema is a place where 'film' happens. The dark room, the mystery that constitute the 'audience', a glowing screen, music, voices and sounds that fill the room, an event, a fluidity that sweeps up the audience, which needs it as an integral part of cinema ... that's 'cinema'. – *E.R.*
The filmmaker should develop a feeling for the fact that when he is filming, what he sees, what he hears, is being transported into the past. The sorrow we feel about the transitory nature of happiness can never be greater than in the moment of filming. – *E.R.*

Reizenstein, Franz (1911–1968)
German-born composer who scored British horror movies. In films from 1951.
The Mummy 59. The White Trap 59. Jessy 60. Circus of Horrors 60, etc.

Relph, George (1888–1960)
British character actor mainly seen on stage.
Nicholas Nickleby 47. I Believe in You 52. *The Titfield Thunderbolt* (leading role as the vicar) 53. Doctor at Large 57. Davy 57, etc.

Relph, Michael (1915–)
British producer-director, son of George Relph. Former art director and production designer; from 1947 to 1969 he worked almost exclusively with Basil Dearden, usually producing while Dearden directed.
The Captive Heart 46. Frieda 47. Saraband for Dead Lovers 48. *The Blue Lamp* 50. I Believe in You (& co-w) 52. The Rainbow Jacket 54. Davy (d) 57. Rockets Galore (d) 57. Violent Playground 58. Sapphire 59. *The League of Gentlemen* 59. *Victim* 61. Life for Ruth 62. The Mind Benders 63. Woman of Straw 63. Masquerade 65. The Assassination Bureau 68. An Unsuitable Job for a Woman 82, etc.

Relph, Simon (1940–)
English producer, the son of Michael Relph.
Reds 81. The Return of the Soldier 81. Privates on Parade 82. The Ploughman's Lunch 83. Laughterhouse 84. Secret Places 85. Wetherby 85. Comrades 87. Enchanted April 91. Damage 92. Camilla 94, etc.

Remar, James (1953–)
American actor, often as a heavy.
The Warriors 79. Cruising 80. The Long Riders 80. Windwalker 81. 48 Hours 82. The Cotton Club 84. Clan of the Cave Bear 85. Quiet Cool 86. Rent-a-Cop 88. The Dream Team 89. Drugstore Cowboy 89. White Fang 90. Wedlock 91. Tales from the Darkside: The Movie 90. The Tigress/Die Tigerin 92. Fatal Instinct 93. Renaissance Man 94. Blink 94. Across the Moon 94. Exquisite Tenderness 94. Miracle on 34th Street 94. Boys on the Side 95. Wild Bill 95. The Quest 96. The Phantom 96. Mortal Kombat 2: Annihilation 97. Psycho 98. What Lies Beneath 00, etc.
TV series: Total Security 97. The Huntress 00- .

Remarque, Erich Maria (1898–1970)
German novelist, born in Osnabrück. In the early 30s, as his pacifist views became unwelcome, he moved to Switzerland and, in 1939, to Hollywood, later becoming an American citizen. His second wife was actress Paulette Goddard; his lovers included Marlene Dietrich.
All Quiet on the Western Front 30. The Road Back 37. Three Comrades 38. So Ends Our Night 41. Arch of Triumph 48. A Time to Love and a Time to Die (& a) 57. All Quiet on the Western Front (TV) 79. Bobby Deerfield 77. Arch of Triumph (TV) 85, etc.

Remick, Lee (1935–1991)
American leading lady with stage and TV experience.
A Face in the Crowd (film debut) 57. The Long Hot Summer 58. *Anatomy of a Murder* 59. Sanctuary 61. Experiment in Terror 62. *Days of Wine and Roses* (AAN) 63. The Wheeler Dealers 64. Baby the Rain Must Fall 65. The Hallelujah Trail 65. No Way to Treat a Lady 68. A Severed Head 70. Loot 70. Sometimes a Great Notion 72. A Delicate Balance 73. QB VII 74. The Blue Knight (TV) 74. Hennessy 75. *Jennie* (TV) 75. The Omen 76. Telefon 77. The Medusa Touch 77. Ike (TV) 79. The Europeans 79. Torn between Two Lovers (TV) 79. The Competition 80. Tribute 80. The Women's Room (TV) 80. The Letter (TV) 82. Mistral's Daughter (TV) 84. Emma's War 85. The Vision 87, etc.
❝ It would be nice to make films for grown-ups again, and when they decide to start filming them, I'll start acting in them. – *L.R.*

Remsen, Bert (1925–1999)
American character actor. His career was interrupted in the mid-60s when he broke his back in an accident; for a time he worked as a casting director.
Pork Chop Hill 59. Dead Ringer 64. Brewster McCloud 70. McCabe and Mrs Miller 71. California Split 74. Thieves Like Us 74. Nashville 75. Buffalo Bill and the Indians 76. Harry and Walter Go to New York 76. Borderline 80. The Sting II 83. Eye of the Tiger 86. Daddy's Dying – Who's Got the Will? 90. Only the Lonely 91. The Bodyguard 92. The Player 92. Jack the Bear 93. Maverick 94. Dillinger and Capone 95. White Man's Burden 95. Hugo Pool 97. Conspiracy Theory 97. Lansky (TV) 99, many others.
TV series: Gibbsville 76. It's a Living 80-81. Dalls 87-88.

Renaldo, Duncan (1904–1980) (Renault Renaldo Duncan)
American actor and painter with varied experience. In many films from *Trader Horn* 30 to *For Whom the Bell Tolls* 43; later more famous as The Cisco Kid in a series of second-feature westerns (1945–50). Directed some films in the 20s. Also a screenwriter under the name Renault Duncan.

Renan, Sergio
Argentinian director, a former actor, from the stage. He went into exile in the mid-70s after receiving death threats following the release of *The Truce*.
AS ACTOR: Pasó en Mi Barrio 51. *Los Siete Locos* 72. Juan Manuel de Rosas 72, etc.
AS DIRECTOR: Growing Up Suddenly/Crecer de Golpe 70. *The Truce*/La Tregua (AAN) 73. Thanks for the Light 84. High Heels 85, etc.

Renaud, Madeleine (1903–1994)
Distinguished French stage actress, in occasional films. Married Jean-Louis Barrault, with whom she ran the post-war Compagnie Renaud-Barrault, acting in many of its notable productions.
Vent Debout 22. Jean de la Lune 31. La Maternelle 32. The Naked Heart/Maria Chapdelaine 34. Stormy Waters/Remorques 41. The Woman Who Dared/Le Ciel Est à Vous 44. Le Plaisir 52. The Longest Day 62. The Devil by the Tail/Le Diable par la Queue 69. La Mandarine 72, etc.

Rendell, Ruth
British crime novelist who also writes under the name Barbara Vine. Her stories featuring Inspector Wexford were the basis of a successful television series, starring George Baker.
A Judgement in Stone/La Cérémonie (oa) 86. Tree of Hands (oa) 88. Live Flesh/Carne Tremula (oa) 98, etc.
TV series: The Ruth Rendell Mysteries 87–92.

Rene, Norman (1951–1996)
American director whose films were written by Craig Lucas, with whom he also worked in the theatre. Died of AIDS.
■ Longtime Companion 90. Prelude to a Kiss 92. Reckless 95.

Renfro, Brad (1982–)
American teenage actor.
The Client 94. The Cure 95. Tom and Huck 96. Sleepers 96. Telling Lies in America 97. Apt Pupil 97. Skipped Parts 00, etc.

Rennahan, Ray (1896–1980)
American cinematographer, in Hollywood from 1917; an expert on colour.
Fanny Foley Herself 31. *The Mystery of the Wax Museum* 33. *Becky Sharp* 35. *Wings of the Morning* 37. *Gone with the Wind* (co-ph) (AA) 39. *The Blue Bird* 40. Down Argentine Way 40. *Blood and Sand* (co-ph) (AA) 42. *For Whom the Bell Tolls* 43. Belle of the Yukon 44. The Perils of Pauline 47. The Paleface 48. A Yankee at King Arthur's Court 49. Arrowhead 53. Terror in a Texas Town 58, many others.

Rennie, James (1890–1965)
American hero of the 20s.
Remodelling Her Husband 20. The Dust Flower 22. His Children's Children 23. Clothes Make the Pirate 25. The Girl of the Golden West 30. Illicit 31, etc.

Rennie, Michael (1909–1971)
Lean, good-looking British leading man best known as TV's *The Third Man*. Varied experience before going into repertory and film stand-in work.
Secret Agent 36. The Divorce of Lady X 38. Dangerous Moonlight 40. Ships with Wings 41. I'll be Your Sweetheart 45. *The Wicked Lady* 45. The Root of All Evil 47. Idol of Paris 48. The Black Rose 50; Then to US; Five Fingers 52. Les Misérables 52. *The Day the Earth Stood Still* 52. The Robe 53. Désirée 54. The Rains of Ranchipur 55. Island in the Sun 56. Omar Khayyam 57. Third Man on the Mountain 59. *The Lost World* 60. Mary, Mary 63. Ride beyond Vengeance 65. The Power 67. Hotel 67. The Devil's Brigade 68. The Battle of El Alamein (as Montgomery) 68. Subterfuge 69, etc.

Réno, Jean (1948–)
French leading actor, a constant presence in the films of Luc Besson. Born in Casablanca, of Spanish parents, he studied drama there and in Paris, first working in theatre and television. Married twice.
The Last Battle/Le Dernier Combat 83. The Big Blue/Le Grand Bleu 88. Nikita/La Femme Nikita 90. Operation Corned-Beef 91. L'Homme au Masque d'Or 91. Les Visiteurs 93. Leon/The Professional 94. Beyond the Clouds 95. French Kiss 95. Two Jerks and a Pig/Les Truffes 95. Mission: Impossible 96. Roseanna's Grave/For Roseanna 96. Le Jaguar 96. Godzilla (US) 98. Ronin (US) 98. The Corridors of Time 98, etc.

Renoir, Claude (1914–1993)
French cinematographer.
Toni 34. *Une Partie de Campagne* 36. La Règle du Jeu 39. Monsieur Vincent 47. *The River* 51. The Green Glove 52. *The Golden Coach* 53. *Eléna et les Hommes* 56. Crime and Punishment 56. The Witches of Salem 56. Les Tricheurs 58. *Blood and Roses* 60. Lafayette 61. Circus World 64. The Game is Over 66. Barbarella 68. The Madwoman of Chaillot (co-ph) 69. The Horsemen 71. Paul and Michelle 74. The Spy Who Loved Me 77. Le Toubib 79, many others.

Renoir, Jean (1894–1979)
Distinguished French director, son of painter Auguste Renoir, brother of Pierre Renoir. Stage experience in productions of his own plays.
Autobiography: 1973, *My Life and My Films*. *Letters by Jean Renoir* edited by Lorraine Lo Bianco and David Thompson.
Biography: 1977, *Jean Renoir, the World of His Films* by Len Brandy. 1991, *Jean Renoir – a Life in Pictures* by Célia Bertin.
La Fille de L'Eau 24. Nana 26. Charleston 27. The Little Match-Seller 28. *La Chienne* 31. *Boudu Sauvé des Eaux* 32. Toni 34. Madame Bovary 34. *Le Crime de Monsieur Lange* 35. *Les Bas Fonds* 36. *Une Partie de Campagne* 36. *La Grande Illusion* 37. *La Marseillaise* 38. *La Bête Humaine* 38. *La Règle du Jeu* (& a) 39; to US; Swamp Water 41. This Land Is Mine 43. *The Southerner* (AAN) 44. Diary of a Chambermaid 45. The Woman on the Beach 47. Back to Europe. The River 51. The Golden Coach 53. French Cancan 55. Eléna et les Hommes 56. Lunch on the Grass 59. The Vanishing Corporal 61. C'est la Révolution 67. Le Petit Théâtre de Jean Renoir 69, etc.
❝ Renoir has a lot of talent, but he isn't one of us. – *Darryl F. Zanuck*
Life was not so much the subject as the *stuff* of his movies, spilling over the edges of his frames. – *Newsweek*
Only when style is confused with meaningless flourishes does Renoir's economy of expression seem inadequate for textbook critics. – *Andrew Sarris, 1968*
My dream is of a craftsman's cinema in which the author can express himself as directly as the painter in his paintings or the writer in his books. – *J.R.*
A director makes only one film in his life. Then he breaks it into pieces and makes it again. – *J.R.*
The saving grace of the cinema is that with patience, and a little love, we may arrive at that wonderfully complex creature which is called man. – *J.R.*

Renoir, Pierre (1885–1952)
French character actor, brother of Jean Renoir.
Madame Bovary 34. La Marseillaise 38. Les Enfants du Paradis 44. Doctor Knock 50, many others.

Renzi, Eva (1944–)
German leading lady in international films.
Funeral in Berlin 66. The Pink Jungle 68. Beiss Mich Liebling 70. La Chambre Voisine 80, etc.

Rerberg, Georgy (1937–1999)
Influential Russian cinematographer, a graduate of Moscow's State film Institute. He was associated with the early films of Andrei Konchalovsky.
The First Teacher/Pervyi Uchitel 65. Asya's Happiness/Istoriya Asi Klyachinoj, Kotoraya Lyubila, Da Ne Vyshla Zamuzh 67. A Nest of Gentlefolk/Dvorianskoe Gnezdo 69. Uncle Vanya/Dyadya Vanya 71. Mirror/Zerkalo 74. Plumbum/Plumbum Ili Opasnaya Igra 86, etc

Rescher, Gayne
American cinematographer.
A Face in the Crowd 57. The Troublemaker 64. Rachel, Rachel 68. John and Mary 69. A New Leaf 71. Claudine 74. Olly, Olly Oxen Free 78. Star Trek II: The Wrath of Khan 82. Toughlove (TV) 85. Shooter (TV) 88. Single Women, Married Men (TV) 90, etc.

Resnais, Alain (1922–)
Controversial French director, former editor.
Statues Also Die 51. Nuit et Brouillard (short) 55. Toute la Mémoire du Monde 56. *Hiroshima Mon Amour* 59. *Last Year at Marienbad* 61. Muriel 62. The War Is Over 66. Je n'Aime, Je t'Aime 69. Stavisky 74. Providence 77. My American Uncle 80. La Vie est un Roman 83. Love unto Death 84. Mélo 86. I Want to Go Home 89. Smoking/No Smoking 93. Same Old Song/On Connaît la Chanson 97, etc.

Retford, Ella (1896–1962)
English actress, singer and dancer, from music hall, and best known as a principal boy in pantomime.
Poison Pen 39. Variety Jubilee 43. I'll Be Your Sweetheart 45. Noose 48. Paper Orchid 49. Shadow of the Past 50, etc.

Rettig, Tommy (1941–1996)
American boy actor of the 50s. Died of kidney failure.
Panic in the Streets 50. The Five Thousand Fingers of Dr T 53. The Egyptian 54. The Last Wagon 56. At Gunpoint 57, etc.
TV series: Lassie 54–57.

Reuben, Gloria (1964–)
Canadian actress, from television.
Time Cop 94. Nick of Time 95. Johnny's Girl (TV) 95, etc.
TV series: ER 94– .

Reubens, Paul (1952–)
American actor, best known for his role as Pee-Wee Herman.
The Blues Brothers 80. Cheech & Chong's Next Movie 80. Cheech & Chong's Nice Dreams 81. Meatballs Part II 84. Pee-Wee's Big Adventure 85. Flight of the Navigator 86. Big Top Pee-Wee 88. Batman Returns 92. Buffy, the Vampire Slayer 92. Tim Burton's The Nightmare before Christmas (voice) 93. Dunston Checks In 95. Mathilda 96. Buddy 97, etc.

Revel, Harry (1905–1958)
British composer in Hollywood, usually in association with Mack Gordon.
Scores: College Rhythm 34. The Gay Divorcee 34. We're Not Dressing 34. Stowaway 36. You Can't Have Everything 37. Are You with It? 48, etc.

Revell, Graeme (1955–)
New Zealand-born composer. He studied politics and economics at the University of Auckland and turned to composing after working as a psychiatric nurse in Australia. In the early 80s he formed the experimental London-based group SPK.
Dead Calm 89. Spontaneous Combustion 90. Until the End of the World 90. Child's Play 2 90. The Hand that Rocks the Cradle 91. Hear No Evil 93. Hard Target 93. Body of Evidence 93. Boxing Helena 93. The Crush 93. Ghost in the Machine 94. The Crow 94. No Escape 94. S.F.W. 94. The Basketball Diaries 95. Tank Girl 95. Mighty Morphin Power Rangers: The Movie 95. Strange Days 95. The Tie that Binds 95. Killer: A Journal of Murder 96. From Dusk till Dawn 96. Fled 96. The Crow: City of Angels 96. The Craft 96. The Saint 97. Chinese Box 97. Suicide Kings 98. The Big Hit 98. Lulu on the Bridge 98. The Negotiator 98. Strike 98. The Siege 98, etc.

Revere, Anne (1903–1990)
American character actress, mainly on stage. Her movie career was disrupted in the early 50s when she was blacklisted for refusing to testify before the House Un-American Activities Committee.
Double Door 34. The Devil Commands 41. The Gay Sisters 42. *The Song of Bernadette* (AAN) 43. The Keys of the Kingdom 44. *National Velvet* (AA) 44. Dragonwyck 46. Body and Soul 47. *Gentleman's Agreement* (AAN) 48. A Place in the Sun 51. Macho Callahan 70. Birch Interval 76, etc.

Revier, Dorothy (1904–1993) (Doris Velagra)
American leading lady of the silents, usually as a vamp; couldn't cope with sound. Her first husband was director Harry Revier.
Broadway Madonna 22. The Wild Party 23. The Virgin 24. When Husbands Flirt 25. When the Wife's Away 26. Poor Girls 27. Sinner's Parade 28. The Iron Mask 29. The Dance of Life 29. Call of the West 30. The Black Camel 31. Sally of the Subway 32. By Candlelight 33. Unknown Blonde 34. The Cowboy and the Kid 36, many others.

Revier, Harry J.
American director, a former cameraman. He was married for a time to actress Dorothy Revier, who starred in his *Broadway Madonna*.
A Grain of Dust 18. The Return of Tarzan 20. The Revenge of Tarzan 20. Broadway Madonna 22. What Price Love 27. The Mysterious Airman (serial) 28. The Convict's Code 30. The Lost City 35. Child Bride 38, etc.

Revill, Clive (1930–)
New Zealander in Britain playing mainly comic character roles.
Bunny Lake is Missing 65. Modesty Blaise 66. Kaleidoscope 66. A Fine Madness (US) 66. The Double Man 67. Fathom 67. Nobody Runs Forever 68. The Shoes of the Fisherman 68. The Private Life of Sherlock Holmes 70. A Severed Head 71. Avanti 72. The Legend of Hell House 73. The Black Windmill 74. Galileo 75. One of Our Dinosaurs Is Missing 75. Matilda 78. T. R. Sloane (TV) 79. Moviola (as Charlie Chaplin) (TV) 80. Zorro the Gay Blade 81. The Emperor's New Clothes 87. Rumpelstiltskin 87. Mack the Knife 89. The Sea Wolf (TV) 93. Dracula: Dead and Loving It 95. Possums 97, etc.

Reville, Alma (1900–1982)
British screenwriter, married to Alfred Hitchcock; worked on many of his films.
The Ring 27. Rich and Strange 32. The Thirty-Nine Steps 35. Secret Agent 36. Sabotage 37. Young and Innocent 37. The Lady Vanishes 38. Suspicion 41. Shadow of a Doubt 43. The Paradine Case 47. Stage Fright 50, etc.

Revueltas, Rosaura (1911–1996)
Mexican actress, best known for acting in *Salt of the Earth* 53, a film about a strike in Silver City, New Mexico, which resulted in her deportation from the United States. She worked with Bertolt Brecht in Germany in the late 50s, and later taught dance and yoga. (According to official sources she was 76 years old at the time of her death.)
Marias Islands 50. Girls in Uniform 50. Soledad/El Rebozo de Soledad 52. Das Lied über dem Tal 56. Mina, Wind of Freedom/Mina, Viento de Libertad 77, etc.

Rey, Alejandro (1930–1987)
Argentinian actor in American TV and films.
The Wild Pack 72. The Stepmother 73. Money to Burn 73. Mr Majestyk 74. Breakout 75. High Velocity 76. The Swarm 78. Cuba 79. Sunburn 79. The Ninth Configuration 80. Rita Hayworth the Love Goddess (TV) 83, many others.

Rey, Fernando (1915–1994) (Fernando Arambillet)
Suave Spanish actor in international films, a favourite of Luis Buñuel.
Welcome Mr Marshall 52. Viridiana 61. Villa Rides 68. The Adventures 70. A Town Called Bastard 71. Tristana 71. *The French Connection* 71. *The Discreet Charm of the Bourgeoisie* 72. French Connection II 75. La Grande Bourgeoise 76. Jesus of Nazareth (TV) 77. *That Obscure Object of Desire* 77. Quintet 79. Monsignor 82. The Hit 84. The Knight of the Dragon 85. Saving Grace 86. My General 87. Moon over Parador 88. Naked Tango 91. L'Atlantide 92. 1492 92. Di Ceria dell'Untore/The Plague Sower 92. After the Dream 92. El Cianuro Solo o con Leche? 93. Al Otro Lado del Tunel 94, many others.

Reynolds, Adeline de Walt (1862–1961)
American character actress with long stage experience; for many years Hollywood's oldest bit player.
Come Live with Me (film debut) 41. The Human Comedy 43. Going My Way 44. A Tree Grows in Brooklyn 45. The Girl from Manhattan 48. Lydia Bailey 52. Witness to Murder 54, etc.

Reynolds, Burt (1936–)
Lithe, virile American leading man who after years in television became a 'bankable' box-office star of the early 70s, but found his popular appeal declining from the 80s. He was married to actresses Judi Carne (1963–66) and Loni Anderson.
Angel Baby 61. Armored Command 61. Operation CIA 65. Navajo Joe 67. Shark 68. Impasse 68. Skullduggery 69. Sam Whiskey 69. 100 Rifles 69. Fuzz 72. *Deliverance* 72. Shamus 72. White Lightning 73. The Man Who Loved Cat Dancing 73. The Longest Yard 74. WW and the Dixie Dancekings 75. At Long Last Love 75. Hustle 76. Lucky Lady 76. Gator (& d) 76. Nickelodeon 76. *Smokey and the Bandit* 77. Semi-Tough 77. The End (& d) 78. Hooper 78. Starting Over 79. Smokey and the Bandit II 80. Rough Cut 80. The Cannonball Run 81. Sharkey's Machine (also d) 81. The Best Little Whorehouse in Texas 82. Best Friends 82. Stroker Ace 83. The Man Who Loved Women. 83. Cannonball Run II 84. City Heat 84. Stick (& d) 85. Heat 87. Malone 87. Rent-a-Cop 88. Switching Channels 88. Physical Evidence 88. Breaking In 89. All Dogs Go to Heaven (voice) 89. Modern Love 90. Cop and a Half 93. The Maddening 95. Precious 96. Striptease 96. Frankenstein and Me 96. Citizen Ruth 96. The Cherokee Kid (TV) 96. Trigger Happy/Mad Dog Time 96. Raven 97. Meet Wally Sparks 97. Bean 97. *Boogie Nights* (AAN) 97. Stringer (Fr.) 98. The Crew 00, etc.
TV series: Riverboat 59–60. Gunsmoke 65–67. Hawk 67. Dan August 70. Evening Shade 90–93.
❝ I think the most underrated thing in the world is a good hot bath. With bubbles. – *B.R.*
My movies were the kind they show in prisons and aeroplanes, because nobody can leave. – *B.R.*

Reynolds, Debbie (1932–) (Mary Frances Reynolds)
Petite, vivacious American leading lady of 50s musicals; later a pleasing comedienne. She now owns and performs in her own hotel in Las Vegas which also displays her collection of movie memorabilia, much of it bought when MGM sold off its warehouses of costumes and furniture. She was married to singer Eddie Fisher (1955–59) and is the mother of actress Carrie Fisher. In 1997 she and her Las Vegas hotel filed for Chapter 11 bankruptcy protection.
Autobiography: 1989, *Debbie – My Life* (with David Patrick Columba).
■ June Bride 48. The Daughter of Rosie O'Grady 50. Three Little Words 50. Two Weeks with Love 50. Mr Imperium 51. *Singin' in the Rain* 52. Skirts Ahoy 52. I Love Melvin 53. The Affairs of Dobie Gillis 53. Give a Girl a Break 53. *Susan Slept Here* 54. Athena 54. Hit the Deck 55. The Tender Trap 55. The Catered Affair 56. Bundle of Joy 56. Meet Me in Las Vegas 56. Tammy and the Bachelor 57. This Happy Feeling 58. The Mating Game 59. Say One for Me 59. It Started with a Kiss 59. The Gazebo 59. The Rat Race 60. Pépé 60. The Pleasure of His Company 61. The Second Time Around 61. How the West was Won 62. My Six Loves 63. Mary Mary 63. *The Unsinkable Molly Brown* (AAN) 64. Goodbye Charlie 64. The Singing Nun 66. Divorce American Style 67. How Sweet It Is 68. *What's the Matter with Helen?* 71. Charlotte's Web (voice only) 72. That's Entertainment! 74. Sadie and Son (TV) 87. Perry Mason: The Case of the Musical Murder (TV) 89. The Bodyguard 92. Heaven and Earth 93. Mother 96. Wedding Bell Blues (as herself) 96. In & Out 97. Rudolph the Red-Nosed Reindeer: The Movie (voice) 98.
TV series: *The Debbie Reynolds Show* 69. Aloha Paradise 81.
❝ I do twenty minutes every time the refrigerator door opens and the light comes on. – *D.R.*
I stopped making movies because I don't like taking my clothes off. – *D.R.*
When I die I'm going to have myself stuffed like Trigger. They'll put me in a museum, all stuffed. Just put a quarter in and I'll sing 'Tammy'. – *D.R.*
Some people, if they're looking for their mother, would go into the kitchen. I'd go to Vegas. – *Todd Fisher (D.R.'s son)*

Reynolds, Gene (1925–)
American boy actor who later became a producer of TV series including *The Ghost and Mrs Muir*, *Anna and the King* and *M*A*S*H*.
Thank You Jeeves 36. In Old Chicago 38. The Blue Bird 40. The Penalty 40. The Tuttles of Tahiti 42. Eagle Squadron 44. The Country Girl 54. Diane 55, many others.

Reynolds, Joyce (1924–)
Vivacious American leading lady of the 40s, usually in teenage roles.
George Washington Slept Here 42. Janie 44. Always Together 48. Dangerous Inheritance 50. Girls' School 50, etc.

Reynolds, Kevin (1952–)
American director and screenwriter whose *Robin Hood* was one of the box-office hits of 1991.
Red Dawn (co-w) 84. Fandango (wd) 85. Beast of War (d) 88. Robin Hood: Prince of Thieves (d) 91. Rapa Nui (co-w, d) 94. Waterworld 95. 187 97, etc.

Reynolds, Marjorie (1921–1997) (Marjorie Goodspeed)
American leading lady of the 40s. Former child actress.
Up in the Air 40. Holiday Inn 42. Star Spangled Rhythm 43. Ministry of Fear 43. Dixie 43. Three Is a Family 44. Bring on the Girls 45. Meet Me on Broadway 46. Heaven Only Knows 47. Home Town Story 51. The Great Jewel Robber 51. The Silent Witness 54, etc.
TV series: The Life of Riley 53–57. Our Man Higgins 62.

Reynolds, Norman
British production designer.
The Little Prince 74. Lucky Lady 75. Mr Quilp 75. The Incredible Sarah (AAN) 76. Star Wars (AA) 77. The Empire Strikes Back (AAN) 80. Raiders of the Lost Ark (AA) 81. Return of the Jedi (AAN) 83. Young Sherlock Holmes 85. Empire of the Sun (AAN) 87. Avalon 90. Mountains of the Moon 90. Alien ^{3} 92. Alive 93. Clean Slate 94. Mission: Impossible 96. Sphere 98, etc.

Reynolds, Peter (1926–1975) (Peter Horrocks)
British light character actor, given to shifty roles.
The Captive Heart 46. Guilt Is My Shadow 49. Smart Alec 50. Four Days 51. The Last Page 52. Devil Girl from Mars 54. You Can't Escape 55. The Delavine Affair 56. Shake Hands with the Devil 59. West Eleven 63. Nobody Runs Forever 68, etc.

Reynolds, Sheldon (1923–)
American radio and TV writer who wrote, produced and directed two films.
■ Foreign Intrigue 56. Assignment to Kill 68.
TV series: Sherlock Holmes 56. Sherlock Holmes and Dr Watson 81.

Reynolds, William (1931–) (William Regnolds)
American leading actor, born in Los Angeles.
Carrie 51. The Cimarron Kid 51. No Questions Asked 51. The Desert Fox 51. Francis Goes To West Point 52. Has Anybody Seen My Gal? 52. Riders of Vengeance 52. Gunsmoke 53. All That Heaven Allows 55. Cult of the Cobra 55. There's Always Tomorrow 56. The Land Unknown 57. The Big Beat 57. The Land Unknown 57. Mister Cory 57. The Thing That Couldn't Die 58. Compulsion 59. Chartroose Caboose 60. FBI Code 98 64. A Distant Trumpet 64. Follow Me Boys 66, etc.
TV series: Pete Kelly's Blues 59. The Islanders 60-61. The Gallant Men 62-63. The FBI 67-73.

Reynolds, William H. (1910–1997)
American editor.
So Ends Our Night 41. Moontide 42. Carnival in Costa Rica 47. Come to the Stable 49. The Day the Earth Stood Still 51. Red Skies of Montana 52. Three Coins in the Fountain 54. Bus Stop 56. South Pacific 58. Compulsion 59. Fanny (AAN) 61. Kings of the Sun 63. The Sound of Music (AA) 65. Star 68. The Great White Hope 70. *The Godfather* 72. *The Sting* (AA) 73. The Great Waldo Pepper 75. The Turning Point (AAN) 77. A Little Romance 77. Heaven's Gate 80. Nijinsky 80. Author! Author! 82. Making Love 82. Yellowbeard 83. The Little Drummer Girl 84. The Lonely Guy 84. Pirates 86. Dancers 87. Ishtar 87. A New Life

88. Rooftops 89. Taking Care of Business 90. Gypsy (TV) 93, etc.

Rhames, Ving (1961–) (Irving Rhames)
American actor of threatening appearance.
Go Tell It on the Mountain (TV) 84. Patty Hearst 88. Casualties of War 89. The Long Walk Home 89. Flight of the Intruder 90. Jacob's Ladder 90. Rising Son 90. Homicide 91. The People under the Stairs 91. Stop! Or My Mum Will Shoot 92. The Saint of Fort Washington 93. Dave 93. Pulp Fiction 94. Kiss of Death 95. Mission: Impossible 96. Striptease 96. Rosewood 97. Dangerous Ground 97. Body Count 97. Con Air 97. Don King: Only in America 97. Out of Sight 98, etc.
❝ Be careful: The toes you step on today may be connected to the ass you'll be kissing tomorrow. – *V.R.*

Rhoades, Barbara (1947–)
American character actress.
The Shakiest Gun in the West 68. There Was a Crooked Man 70. Up the Sandbox 72. Harry and Tonto 74. Conspiracy of Terror (TV) 75. The Choirboys 77. Serial 80, etc.
TV series: Busting Loose 77. Soap 80.

Rhodes, Betty Jane (1921–)
American singing second lead of the early 40s.
Stage Door 37. Sweater Girl 41. The Fleet's In 42. Salute for Three 43. You Can't Ration Love 44. Practically Yours 44, etc.

Rhodes, Erik (1906–1990)
American comic actor from the musical comedy stage, best remembered as the excitable Italian in two Astaire-Rogers films, *The Gay Divorcee* 34 and *Top Hat* 35 ('Your wife is safe with Tonetti – he prefers spaghetti').
■ *The Gay Divorcee* 34. A Night at the Ritz 35. Charlie Chan in Paris 35. The Nitwits 35. Old Man Rhythm 35. *Top Hat* 35. Another Face 35. Two in the Dark 35. Chatterbox 36. One Rainy Afternoon 36. Special Investigator 36. Second Wife 36. The Smartest Girl in Town 36. Criminal Lawyer 37. Woman Chases Man 37. Music for Madame 37. Fight for Your Lady 37. Beg Borrow or Steal 37. Dramatic School 38. Say It in French 38. Meet the Girls 38. Mysterious Mr Moto 38. On Your Toes 39.

Rhodes, Marjorie (1902–1979)
Homely British character actress, on stage from 1920; usually played warm-hearted mums, nosy neighbours, etc.
Poison Pen (debut) 39. *Love on the Dole* 40. World of Plenty 41. *When We are Married* 43. Uncle Silas 47. *The Cure for Love* 50. Those People Next Door 53. Hell Drivers 58. Watch It, Sailor 62. *The Family Way* 66. Mrs Brown, You've Got a Lovely Daughter 68. Hands of the Ripper 71, many others.

Rhue, Madlyn (1934–) (Madeleine Roche)
American supporting actress.
Operation Petticoat 59. Escape from Zahrain 62. It's a Mad Mad Mad Mad World 63. He Rides Tall 64. Stand Up and Be Counted 72. Crackle of Death 76. A Mother's Justice (TV) 91, etc.
TV series: Bracken's World 69. Executive Suite 76. Houston Knights 87–88.

Rhys, Matthew (1974–)
Welsh actor, born in Cardiff.
House of America 97. Heart 98. Whatever Happened To Harold Smith? 98. Titus 99. Sorted 00. Peaches 00. Shiners 00. The Testimony of Taliesin Jones 00, etc.

Rhys-Davies, John (1944–)
Heavyweight British character actor, a good roisterer.
Shogun (TV) 80. Sphinx 81. Raiders of the Lost Ark 81. Victor/Victoria 81. Ivanhoe (TV) 82. Sahara 83. Best Revenge 83. King Solomon's Mines 85. In the Shadow of Kilimanjaro 86. The Living Daylights 87. Nairobi Affair 88. Indiana Jones and the Last Crusade 89. Tusks 89. Rebel Storm 90. The Company 90. The Company II: Sacrifices 91. Canvas 92. The Unnameable Returns 92. Sunset Grill 92. Journey of Honor 92. The Seventh Coin 93. The High Crusade 94. Catherine the Great (TV) 95. The Great White Hype 96. Marquis de Sade 96. Bloodsport 3 96. Glory Daze 96. The Protector 97. Secret of the Andes 98, etc.

TV series: The Untouchables 93. Sliders 95–97. You Wish 97.

Riano, Renie (1899–1971)
American comedienne in small film roles, especially the *Jiggs and Maggie* series.
Tovarich 37. Adam Had Four Sons 41. The Time of Your Life 46. Three on a Couch 66, many others.

Ribisi, Giovanni (1976–)
American actor, born in Los Angeles. Married model and actress Mariah O'Brien.
Promised a Miracle (TV) 88. That Thing You Do! 96. Lost Highway 96. SubUrbia 97. The Postman 97. First Love, Last Rites 98. Saving Private Ryan 98. The Other Sister 98, etc.
TV series: My Two Dads 87. The Wonder Years 92–93. Davis Rules 92. Family Album 93.

Ricci, Christina (1980–)
American actress, in quirky roles. Born in Santa Monica, California, she began acting as a child and scored an early success with her performances as Wednesday in *The Addams Family*, before making a transition to parts as a troubled teenager.
Mermaids 90. *The Addams Family* 91. The Cemetery Club 93. *Addams Family Values* 93. Casper 95. Now and Then 95. Gold Diggers: The Secret of Bear Mountain 95. Bastard out of Carolina 96. The Last of the High Kings 96. The Ice Storm 97. That Darn Cat 97. Buffalo '66 98. Fear and Loathing in Las Vegas 98. Pecker 98. The Opposite of Sex 98. Small Soldiers (voice) 98. Sleepy Hollow 99. 200 Cigarettes 99. The Man Who Cried (GB/Fr.) 00, etc.
❝ I can't imagine what kids today would be like if violence on TV and in the movies hadn't prepared us for the violence that is out there in the real world. – *C.R.*
I have life rage. What am I going to do with it? I can't kick the shit out of someone. I can't yell or be constantly rude to people, because that's unacceptable. I have a therapist on each coast. I've had a problem with that, too, because I've had a different personality when I go to different ones. – *C.R., 1998*

Rice, Anne (1941–)
American writer of vampire novels. She also writes erotic novels under the names Anne Rampling and A. N. Roquelaure.
Interview with the Vampire 94. Exit to Eden 94.

Rice, Elmer (1892–1967) (Elmer Reizenstern)
American playwright. Works filmed include *Street Scene*, *The Adding Machine*, *Dream Girl* and *Counsellor at Law*.

Rice, Florence (1907–1974)
American leading lady of the late 30s, always in sweet-tempered roles.
The Best Man Wins 34. Sweethearts 39. Miracles for Sale 39. *At the Circus* 39. Fighting Marshal 41. The Ghost and the Guest 43, etc.

Rice, Grantland (1881–1954)
American sportscaster who made innumerable one-reelers under the title *Grantland Rice Sportslights*. Father of Florence Rice.

Rice, Jack (1893–1968)
American light actor who for many years played Edgar Kennedy's useless brother-in-law in RKO shorts. Last film: *Son of Flubber* 63.

Rice, Joan (1930–1997)
British leading lady, former waitress, briefly popular in the 50s. Retired in the 70s to run an estate agency in Maidenhead, Berkshire.
Blackmailed 50. One Wild Oat 51. The Story of Robin Hood and His Merrie Men 52. A Day to Remember 54. His Majesty O'Keefe (US) 55. One Good Turn 56. Payroll 61. Horror of Frankenstein 70, etc.

Rice, Sir Tim (1944–)
English lyricist, associated with Sir Andrew Lloyd WEBBER's early musicals. He was knighted 'for services to music' in 1994.
Autobiography: 1999, Oh, What a Circus.
Jesus Christ Superstar 73. Aladdin (AAs) 92. The Lion King (AAs, AANs) 94. Evita (AAs 'You Must Love Me').

Rich, David Lowell (1923–)
American director, from TV.
Senior Prom 58. Hey Boy, Hey Girl 59. Have Rocket Will Travel 59. Madame X 66. The Plainsman 66. Rosie 67. A Lovely Way to Die 68. *Eye of the Cat* 69. The Sex Symbol (TV) 74. The Concorde – Airport 79 79. Chu Chu and the Philly Flash 81. Thursday's Child (TV) 83. The Defiant Ones (TV) 86. Infidelity (TV) 87, etc.

Rich, Irene (1891–1988) (Irene Luther)
American silent-screen heroine, little seen after sound.
Stella Maris 18. Beau Brummell 24. Lady Windermere's Fan 25. So This is Paris 26. *Craig's Wife* 28. Shanghai Rose 29. That Certain Age 38. The Lady in Question 41. New Orleans 47. Joan of Arc 48, etc.

Rich, John (1925–)
American director. Since the 70s he has directed episodes of TV series, such as *All in the Family*, *Newhart* and *Murphy Brown*.
Wives and Lovers 63. The New Interns 64. Boeing Boeing 65. Easy Come Easy Go 67, etc.

Rich, Matty (1971–) (Matthew Richardson)
American director.
Straight out of Brooklyn 90. The Inkwell 94.

Rich, Roy (1909–1970)
British producer, director and executive, with widely varied experience including radio and TV.
My Brother's Keeper (d only) 47. It's Not Cricket (d only) 48. Double Profile (d only) 54. Phantom Caravan (d only) 54, etc.

Richard, Sir Cliff (1940–) (Harold Webb)
Boyish British pop singer who succeeded by restricting his film appearances. He was knighted in 1995 for services to charity. In 1998 the *Sunday Times* estimated his fortune at £25m.
Biography: 1993, *Cliff Richard* by Steve Turner.
■ Serious Charge 59. Expresso Bongo 60. *The Young Ones* 61. Summer Holiday 62. Wonderful Life 64. Finders Keepers 66. Two a Penny 68. Take Me High 73.

Richard, Pierre (1934–)
Leading French comic actor, director, producer and screenwriter.
Les Heures Chaudes 61. Agent 505 65. Le Distrait (& d) 70. The Tall Blond Man with One Black Shoe 72. Return of the Tall Blond 74. French Mustard (& co-w) 74. The Daydreamer 75. It's Not Me, It's Him (& d) 79. The Goat/Le Chevre 81. Les Compères 83. The Twin 84. The Fugitives 86. The Door on the Left As You Leave the Elevator 88. Nord 91. We Can Always Dream (& wd) 91. Old Rascal 92. Loonies at Large (& p, w) 93. The Chess Game 94, etc.

Richard III (1452–1485)
The best-known account of the life and crimes of the short-lived king of England is Laurence Olivier's version of Shakespeare's play, centring on his own performance as a charming, ruthless villain. The story was also dealt with in Rowland V. Lee's outrageous but amusing *Tower of London* 39, with Basil Rathbone as Richard and Boris Karloff as Mord the Executioner; this was remade in 1963 by Roger Corman with Vincent Price, who had played the Duke of Clarence in the earlier version, as Richard. In 1995, Ian McKellen starred in Shakespeare's play, set in a fascist Britain of the 1930s.

Richard the Lionheart (1157–1199) (Richard I of England)
was a king who has gone down into legend rather than history as a nearly wronged idealist. The truth may have been less inspiring. He was played by Wallace Beery in *Robin Hood* (1922), by Henry Wilcoxon in *The Crusades*, by Ian Hunter in *The Adventures of Robin Hood*, by Norman Wooland in *Ivanhoe*, by Patrick Barr in Disney's *Robin Hood*, by George Sanders in *King Richard and the Crusaders*, by Patrick Holt in *Men of Sherwood Forest*, by Anthony Hopkins (as a prince) in *The Lion in Winter*, by Richard Harris in *Robin and Marian*, and Sean Connery in *Robin Hood: Prince of Thieves*.

Richards, Addison (1887–1964)
American character actor with long stage experience; in Hollywood from early 30s, usually as professional man; later in TV series.
Riot Squad 34. Colleen 36. Black Legion 37. Boom Town 40. My Favorite Blonde 42. Since You Went Away 44. The Mummy's Curse 46. Indian Scout 50. Illegal 56. The Oregon Trail 59, many others.
TV series: Fibber McGee 59. Cimarron City 58–60.

Richards, Ann (1918–)
Australian leading lady.
Tall Timbers 38. The Rudd Family 39, etc. Then to Hollywood: Random Harvest 42. Dr Gillespie's New Assistant 43. An American Romance 44. Love Letters 45. The Searching Wind 46. Sorry, Wrong Number 48. Breakdown 52, etc.

Richards, Ariana (1979–)
American child actress, from commercials.
Into the Homeland (TV) 87. I'm Gonna Get You Sucka 88. Prancer 89. Tremors 90. Spaced Invaders 90. Switched at Birth (TV) 91. Jurassic Park 93. Come the Dawn 95. Angus 95, etc.

Richards, Beah (1926–2000)
American character actress and playwright, from the theatre. Born in Vicksburg, Mississippi, she was educated at Dillard University and studied at The Globe theatre in San Diego. She won an Emmy in 1988 for her role in the drama series *Frank's Place*, and another in 2000 for her acting in the series *The Practice*. She also made occasional appearances in the TV medical drama *ER* 94-95.
The Miracle Worker 62. In the Heat of the Night 67. *Guess Who's Coming to Dinner* (AAN) 67. Hurry Sundown 67. Mahogany 75. Inside Out 86. Drugstore Cowboy 89. Homer & Eddie 90. Capital News (TV) 90. Out of Darkness (TV) 94. Beloved 98, etc.
TV series: The Bill Cosby Show 70-71. Sandford and Son 72. Roots: The Next Generation 79-81. Hearts Afire 92.

Richards, Denise (1972–)
American actress. Born in Downer's Grove, Illinois, she moved to Los Angeles in the late 80s to continue working as a model. She began with a recurring role on the TV series *Doogie Howser M.D.* in the early 90s.
National Lampoon's Loaded Weapon 1 93. Tammy and the T-Rex 94. In the Blink of an Eye (TV) 96. Nowhere 97. Starship Troopers 97. Wild Things 98. Drop Dead Gorgeous 99. The World Is Not Enough 99, etc.
❝ I don't want to be, you know, the pin-up girl. I want to have a nice career where I'm taken seriously. – *D.R.*

Richards, Dick (1936–)
American director.
■ The Culpepper Cattle Company 72. *Farewell My Lovely* 75. Rafferty and the Gold Dust Twins 75. March or Die (& w, p) 77. Death Valley 82. Tootsie (co-p only) 82. Man, Woman and Child 83. Heat 87.

Richards, Jeff (1922–1989) (Richard Mansfield Taylor)
American general-purpose actor.
Johnny Belinda 48. Kill the Umpire 50. The Strip 51. Above and Beyond 52. Seven Brides for Seven Brothers 55, many others.
TV series: Jefferson Drum 58.

Richards, Michael (1949–)
American stand-up comedian and actor, best known for his role as Cosmo Kramer in the TV sitcom *Seinfeld*. Born in Los Angeles, he studied at the California Institute of the Arts.
Young Doctors in Love 82. Transylvania 6-5000 85. Whoops Apocalypse 86. UHF 89. Problem Child 90. So I Married an Axe Murderer 93. Coneheads 93. Airheads 94. Unstrung Heroes 95. London Suite (TV) 96. Trial and Error 97, etc.
TV series: Fridays 80–82. Seinfeld 90–98.

Richards, Paul (1924–1974)
American general-purpose actor.
The Black Whip 55. Tall Man Riding 56. Battle for the Planet of the Apes 71, etc.
TV series: Breaking Point 63.

Richards, Silvia (1916–)
American screenwriter, from radio. A former communist, she was called to testify during the HUAC investigations of Hollywood; soon after, as work became scarce, she quit to become a nursery teacher. Married screenwriter A. I. BEZZERIDES.
Possessed (co-w) 47. Secret beyond the Door (w) 48. Tomahawk/Battle of Powder River (co-w)

51. Ruby Gentry (w) 52. Rancho Notorious (story) 52, etc.

Richardson, Ian (1934–)
Scottish character actor whose precise playing of many varied roles is an increasing delight.
The Marat/Sade 68. Man of La Mancha 72. The Darwin Adventure 73. *Ike* (TV) (as Bernard Montgomery) 79. The Sign of Four (as Sherlock Holmes) (TV) 84. The Master of Ballantrae (TV) 84. Mistral's Daughter (TV) 84. Mountbatten (TV) 85. Brazil 85. The Fourth Protocol 87. Porterhouse Blue (TV) 87. Cry Freedom 87. Burning Secret 89. The Plot to Kill Hitler (TV) 90. Rosencrantz and Guildenstern Are Dead 90. Year of the Comet 92. House of Cards (TV) 92. To Play the King (TV) 93. Foreign Affairs (TV) 93. M. Butterfly 93. Dirty Weekend 93. Words upon the Window Pane 94. Catherine the Great (TV) 95. The Final Cut (TV) 95. BAPS 97. Incognito 97. Dark City 98. A Knight in Camelot (TV) 98. The King and I 99. Murder Rooms: The Dark Beginnings of Sherlock Holmes (TV) 00. Gormenghast (TV) 00. 102 Dalmatians 00, etc.

Richardson, Joely (1965–)
British actress, the daughter of Vanessa Redgrave and Tony Richardson. Formerly married to film producer Tim Bevan.
Hotel New Hampshire 84. Wetherby 85. Drowning by Numbers 88. Heading Home 91. King Ralph 91. Rebecca's Daughters 91. Shining Through 92. Lady Chatterley's Lover (TV) 92. I'll Do Anything 94. Sister, My Sister 94. Hollow Reed 95. Loch Ness 95. 101 Dalmatians 96. Event Horizon 97. The Tribe (TV) 98. Wrestling with Alligators 99. Maybe Baby 00, etc.

Richardson, John (1936–)
British leading man, mainly in fancy dress.
Bachelor of Hearts 58. She 65. One Million Years BC 66. The Vengeance of She 68. The Chastity Belt 68. On a Clear Day You Can See Forever 70. Duck in Orange Sauce (It.) 75. Eyeball 78. Frankenstein 80 80. The Church/La Chiesa (It.) 88. Pistol: The Birth of a Legend 91, etc.

Richardson, Miranda (1958–)
British actress.
Dance with a Stranger 84. The Innocent 85. Underworld 85. Blackadder (TV) 86. After Pilkington (TV) 87. Empire of the Sun 87. Ball-Trap on the Côte Sauvage 89. The Mad Monkey/El Mono Loco 89. My Dear Doctor Gräsler/Mio Caro Dottore Gräsler 89. The Fool 90. Twisted Obsession 90. The Bachelor 91. Enchanted April 91. The Crying Game 92. Damage (AAN) 92. Century 93. Tom and Viv (AAN) 94. The Night and the Moment 94. Kansas City 96. Evening Star 96. Swann 96. Saint-Ex 96. Designated Mourner 97. A Dance to the Music of Time (TV) 97. The Apostle 97. Merlin (TV) 98. The Scold's Bridle (TV) 98. All for Love 98. Jacob Two Two Meets the Hooded Fang (Can.) 98. The King and I 99. Sleepy Hollow 99. The Miracle Maker 99. Chicken Run (voice) 00, etc.

Richardson, Natasha (1963–)
British actress, the daughter of Vanessa Redgrave and Tony Richardson. She married Liam Neeson in 1994.
Every Picture Tells a Story 84. In the Secret State 85. Gothic 86. A Month in the Country 87. Patty Hearst 88. Fatman and Little Boy/Shadow Makers 89. The Comfort of Strangers 90. The Handmaid's Tale 90. The Favour, the Watch and the Very Big Fish/Rue Saint-Sulpice 91. Past Midnight 91. Suddenly Last Summer (TV) 93. Zelda (TV) 93. Widows' Peak 93. Nell 94. The Parent Trap 98. Blow Dry 00, etc.

Richardson, Peter
British comedy director.
■ The Supergrass 86. Eat the Rich 87. The Pope Must Die/The Pope Must Diet 91.
TV series: The Comic Strip Presents … (a, co-wd) 93.

Richardson, Sir Ralph (1902–1983)
Distinguished British stage actor, in occasional films. Despite his splendid theatrical voice and thespian mannerisms, he was at his best playing ordinary chaps, though his gallery included plenty of eccentrics. Born in Cheltenham, he was on stage from 1921, notably in productions at the Old Vic, in partnership with Laurence Olivier, at the Royal Court Theatre and the National Theatre, where first nights were marked by firing 'Ralph's Rocket', in memory of his love of fireworks. (He once destroyed Olivier's dining room with a misdirected rocket.) In private life, he was as eccentric as some of the characters he played: stopped by police late at night when walking very slowly along the gutter of an Oxford street, he explained that he was taking his pet mouse for a stroll.
Biography: 1958, *Ralph Richardson* by Harold Hobson. 1982, *Ralph Richardson: A Celebration* by Robert Tanitch. 1995, *Ralph Richardson: the Authorised Biography* by John Miller.
■ The Ghoul 33. Friday the Thirteenth 33. The Return of Bulldog Drummond 34. Java Head 34. King of Paris 34. *Bulldog Jack* 35. Things to Come 36. The Man Who Could Work Miracles 36. Thunder in the City 37. *South Riding* 38. The Divorce of Lady X 38. The Citadel 38. *Q Planes* 39. *The Four Feathers* 39. The Lion Has Wings 39. On the Night of the Fire 39. The Day Will Dawn 42. The Silver Fleet 43. The Volunteer 43. School for Secrets 46. *Anna Karenina* 48. *The Fallen Idol* 48. *The Heiress* (AAN) 49. An Outcast of the Islands 51. Home at Seven (& d) 52. The Sound Barrier 52. The Holly and the Ivy 53. *Richard III* (as Buckingham) 56. Smiley 57. The Passionate Stranger 57. Our Man in Havana 59. *Oscar Wilde* (as Sir Edward Carson) 60. Exodus 61. The 300 Spartans 62. *Long Day's Journey into Night* 62. Woman of Straw 64. Doctor Zhivago 66. *The Wrong Box* 66. Khartoum 67. Oh What a Lovely War 69. The Midas Run 69. The Bed Sitting Room 69. The Battle of Britain 69. The Looking Glass War 69. David Copperfield (as Micawber) 69. Eagle in a Cage 71. Who Slew Auntie Roo? 71. Tales from the Crypt 71. Lady Caroline Lamb 72. Alice's Adventures in Wonderland (as the Caterpillar) 72. A Doll's House 73. O Lucky Man 73. Frankenstein: The True Story (TV) 73. Rollerball 75. Jesus of Nazareth (TV) 77. The Man in the Iron Mask (TV) 77. Time Bandits 80. Dragonslayer 81. Wagner 83. Greystoke (AAN) 84. Witness for the Prosecution (TV) 84. Invitation to the Wedding 85.
TV series: Blandings Castle (as Lord Emsworth) 67.
✪ For casting his whimsical eye over a surprisingly large range of movies, and invariably walking off with the honours. *Q Planes*.
❝ I don't like my face at all. It's always been a great drawback to me. – *R.R.*
The art of acting lies in keeping people from coughing. – *R.R.*
Actors never retire; they just get offered fewer parts. – *R.R.*
Acting on the screen is like acting under a microscope. The slightest movement becomes a gesture and therefore the discipline has to be very severe. – *R.R.*
I've never been one of those stage chaps who scoff at films. I think they're a marvellous medium, and are to the stage what engravings are to paintings. – *R.R.*
Film is a wonderful medium and I love it, but I find that I cannot increase my talent by working in pictures, any more than a painter can do so by increasing the size of his brush. – *R.R.*
I have put on so many make-ups that sometimes I have feared that when I go to wipe it off there will be nobody left underneath. – *R.R.*

Richardson, Robert
American cinematographer, associated with the films of Oliver Stone.
Salvador 86. Platoon (AAN) 86. Dudes 87. Wall Street 87. Eight Men Out 88. Talk Radio 88. Born on the Fourth of July (AAN) 89. City of Hope 91. The Doors 91. *JFK* (AA) 91. A Few Good Men 92. Heaven and Earth 93. *Natural Born Killers* 94. Casino 95. Nixon 95. Fast, Cheap & Out of Control 97. U-Turn 97. Wag the Dog 97. The Horse Whisperer 98. Snow Falling On Cedars (AAN) 99. Bringing Out the Dead 99, etc.

Richardson, Tony (1928–1991) (Cecil Antonio Richardson)
Born in Shipley, Yorkshire, he was educated at Oxford University and worked in television before founding, with George Devine, the English Stage Company at London's Royal Court Theatre, which had a profound impact on British theatre through his production of John Osborne's *Look Back in Anger*. The collaboration with Osborne also resulted in the creation of Woodfall Films. From the mid-70s, he moved to America to work. Married Vanessa Redgrave; their daughters, Natasha and Joely Richardson, are actresses. Died of AIDS.
Autobiography: 1993, *Long Distance Runner*.
■ Momma Don't Allow (short, d) 56. Look Back in Anger (d) 59. *The Entertainer* (d) 60. A Subject of Scandal and Concern (d) (TV) 60. Saturday Night and Sunday Morning (p) 60. Sanctuary (d) 61. A Taste of Honey (p, co-w, d) 61. The Loneliness of the Long Distance Runner £ 62. *Tom Jones* (p, d) (AAp, AAd) 63. Girl with Green Eyes (p) 64. The Loved One (d) (US) 65. Mademoiselle (d) 66. The Sailor from Gibraltar (co-w, d) 67. Red and Blue (short, co-w, d) 67. *The Charge of the Light Brigade* (d) 68. Hamlet (d) 69. Laughter in the Dark (d) 69. Ned Kelly (co-w, d) 70. A Delicate Balance (d) 73. Dead Cert (co-w, d) 74. Joseph Andrews (story, d) 77. A Death in Canaan (d) 78. The Border (d) 82. Hotel New Hampshire (wd) 84. Penalty Phase (d) (TV) 88. Shadow on the Sun (d) (TV) 88. The Phantom of the Opera (d) (TV) 90. Hills Like White Elephants (d) (TV) 90. Blue Sky (d) (made 91) 94.
❝ The most prolific and the most prosperous of the *Sight and Sound* crop, and ultimately the least respected. – *Andrew Sarris, 1968*
He convinced me (wrongly, of course) that anyone can make a movie. All Tony Richardson did was come in and ask his cameraman what he should do … He was a useless, unpleasant creature. – *Robert Stephens*

Richelieu, Cardinal (1585–1642)
Louis XIII's chief minister, doubtless a clever and powerful chap, was used by the movies as a schemer and often a villain, seldom on the hero's side. George Arliss gave the fullest portrait, in *Cardinal Richelieu* 35. Others who have played him include Nigel de Brulier in *The Iron Mask*, the 1935 version of *The Three Musketeers*, and the 1939 version of *The Man in the Iron Mask*; Osgood Perkins in *Madame Dubarry*; Raymond Massey in *Under the Red Robe*; Miles Mander in the 1939 version of *The Three Musketeers*; Aimé Clairond in *Monsieur Vincent*; Vincent Price in the 1948 version of *The Three Musketeers*; Paul Cavanagh in *Sword of D'Artagnan*; Christopher Logue in *The Devils*; and Charlton Heston in the 1974 versions of *The Three Musketeers* and *The Four Musketeers*.

Richert, William
American screenwriter and director. He also played the role of a modern-day Falstaff in Gus Van Sant's *My Own Private Idaho*.
Law and Disorder (co-w) 74. The Happy Hooker (w) 75. Winter Kills (wd) 79. Success (co-w, d) 79. A Night in the Life of Jimmy Reardon (wd) 88. My Own Private Idaho (a) 91. Paradise Framed (a) 95. The Man in the Iron Mask (a, wd) 98, etc.

Richfield, Edwin (1922–1990)
English character actor, usually portraying bluff, dependable authority figures.
The Jack of Diamonds 49. The Blue Parrot 53. The Black Rider 54. X the Unknown 56. Quatermass II/Enemy from Space 57. Up the Creek 58. Further up the Creek 58. The Camp on Blood Island 58. Ben Hur 59. Tommy the Toreador 59. Sword of Sherwood Forest 60. Calculated Risk (w) 63. The Secret of Blood Island 65. Quatermass and the Pit/Five Million Miles to Earth 67. Diamonds on Wheels 72. The Champions 83, etc.
TV series: The Buccaneers 56–57. Interpol Calling 59–60. The Odd Man 62–63. 199 Park Lane 65. The Man in the Iron Mask (as D'Artagnan) 68.

Richler, Mordecai (1931–)
Canadian novelist and screenwriter on Jewish themes.
■ No Love for Johnnie (co-w) 60. Young and Willing (co-w) 62. Life at the Top 65. The Apprenticeship of Duddy Kravitz (w, oa) (AAN) 74. Fun with Dick and Jane (co-w) 77. Jacob Two-Two Meets the Hooded Fang 78. Joshua Then and Now (w, oa) 85.

Richman, Harry (1895–1972) (Harold Reichman)
American entertainer, in occasional films.
Autobiography: 1966, *A Hell of a Life*.
■ Putting on the Ritz 30. The Music Goes Round 36. Kicking the Moon Around 38.

Richman, Peter Mark (1927–)
American general-purpose actor, much on TV.
Friendly Persuasion 56. The Strange One 57. The Black Orchid 58. The Crime Busters 61. Dark Intruder 65. For Singles Only 68. Dandy in Aspic 68. The City Killer 87. Judgement Day 88. Friday the Thirteenth Part VIII: Jason Takes Manhattan 89. Naked Gun 2½: The Smell of Fear 91, etc.
TV series: *Cain's Hundred* 61–62. Longstreet 71–72. Dynasty 81–84.

Richmond, Anthony B. (1942–)
British cinematographer and occasional director, now in Hollywood.
Sympathy for the Devil 68. Only When I Larf 68. Let It Be 70. Madame Sin 72. Don't Look Now 73. Vampira 74. Stardust 74. The Man Who Fell to Earth 76. The Eagle Has Landed 76. Silver Bears 77. The Greek Tycoon 78. Love and Bullets 79. Improper Channels 79. Bad Timing 80. Nightkill 81. A Man Called Rage (d) 84. Déjà Vu (d) 85. Blake Edwards' That's Life 86. The In Crowd 88. Sunset 88. Cat Chaser 88. The Indian Runner 91. Timebomb 91. Kryo (co-w, d) 92. Candyman 92. The Sandlot 93. Heart of Darkness (TV) 94. Full Body Massage (TV) 95. Bastard out of Carolina 96. First Kid 96. Playing God 97. Ravenous 99. Agnes Browne 99. Men of Honor 00, etc.

Richmond, Kane (1906–1973) (Frederick W. Bowditch)
American leading man of second features.
The Leather Pushers (serial) 30. Nancy Steele is Missing 36. Hard Guy 41. Action in the North Atlantic 43. Tiger Woman 45. Black Gold 47, many others.

Richmond, Ted (1912–)
American producer, former writer.
So Dark the Night 46. The Milkman 50. The Strange Door 51. Desert Legion 53. Forbidden 54. Count Three and Pray 55. Seven Waves Away 57. Solomon and Sheba 59. Advance to the Rear 64. Return of the Seven 66. Villa Rides 68. Papillon 74, others.

Richter, Hans (1888–1976)
German Dadaist director of animated and surrealist films, most active in the 20s. His books include *The Struggle for the Film: Towards a Socially Responsible Cinema/Der Kampf um den Film*, 1976.
Prelude and Fugue 20. Film is Rhythm 20. Rhythm 23. Rhythm 25. Film Study 26. Inflation 26. Twopenny Magic 27. Vormittagspuk 28. Everything Revolves 30. Dreams That Money Can Buy 44. 8 8 57, etc.
❝ To varnish our lives with entertaining stories is too petty a task for this mighty technology, too petty if it is to grow to artistic maturity. Let it, on the contrary, be allowed to participate in the intellectual conflicts of the age, let us dare apply this technology to shape genuine emotions, thoughts and ideas: to shape social life; it will be stimulated as never before and manage to change from a tool for more or less elegant reproduction to an instrument of genuine imagination. – *H.R.*

Richter, Jason James (1980–)
American child actor. Born in Oregon, he was raised in Honolulu and began his career in Japanese television.
Free Willy 93. Cops and Robbersons 94. The Neverending Story III 94. Free Willy 2: The Adventure Home 95. Free Willy 3 97, etc.

Richter, W. D. (1945–)
American screenwriter and director, a former script analyst for Warner.
■ Slither 72. Peeper 75. Nickelodeon 76. Invasion of the Body Snatchers 78. Dracula 79. Brubaker (AAN) 80. All Night Long 81. Hang Tough 82. The Adventures of Buckaroo Banzai across the Eighth Dimension (d) 84. Big Trouble in Little China 86. Late for Dinner (d) 91. Needful Things (d) 93. Home for the Holidays (w) 95.

Rickert, Shirley Jean (1926–)
American actress who was on screen as a child from 1929, and appeared in the Our Gang shorts of the 30s. Later worked as a dancer and a stripper before quitting showbusiness.
How's My Baby 29. Follow Thru 30. Night Work 30. Everything's Rosie 31. Bargain Days 31. 'Neath the Arizona Skies 34, etc.

Rickles, Don (1926–)
American insult comedian.
Run Silent Run Deep 58. The Rabbit Trap 59. The Rat Race 60. Enter Laughing 67. The Money Jungle 68. Where It's At 69. Kelly's Heroes 70. Innocent Blood 92. *Casino* 95. Toy Story (voice) 95. Quest for Camelot (voice) 98, etc.

TV series: CPO Sharkey 77.

Rickman, Alan (1946–)
English classical actor from the stage, so far typecast by Hollywood as a villain, who became an actor in his mid-20s after a career as a graphic designer. He also directs plays.
Biography: 1996, *Alan Rickman* by Maureen Paton.
Shock! Shock! Shock! 87. Die Hard 88. The January Man 89. Truly Madly Deeply 90. Quigley Down Under 90. Robin Hood: Prince of Thieves 91. Close My Eyes 91. Closet Land 91. Bob Roberts 92. Mesmer 94. An Awfully Big Adventure 94. Sense and Sensibility 95. Michael Collins 96. Winter Guest (d) 96. Judas Kiss (US) 98. Dark Harbor (US) 98. Galaxy Quest 99. Dogma 99. Blow Dry 00, etc.
❝ I do take my work seriously and the way to do that is not to take yourself too seriously. – *A.R.*

Rickman, Thomas
American screenwriter and director.
Kansas City Bomber (co-w) 72. The Laughing Policeman (w) 73. W.W. and the Dixie Dancekings 75. The White Dawn (co-w) 76. Hooper (co-w) 78. Coal Miner's Daughter (AAN) 80. The River Rat (wd) 84. Everybody's All-American 88. Truman (TV) 95, etc.

Riddle, Nelson (1921–1985)
American composer.
A Kiss before Dying 55. St Louis Blues 58. Ocean's Eleven 60. Lolita 62. Robin and the Seven Hoods 64. Marriage on the Rocks 65. El Dorado 66. Paint Your Wagon 69. The Great Gatsby (AA) 74. Harper Valley PTA 78, etc.

Ridgeley, John (1909–1968) (John Huntingdon Rea)
American supporting actor generally cast as gangster.
Invisible Menace 38. They Made Me a Fugitive 39. Brother Orchid 40. The Big Shot 42. Destination Tokyo 44. My Reputation 46. The Big Sleep 46. Possessed 47. Command Decision 48. The Blue Veil 52, many others.

Ridges, Stanley (1892–1951)
Incisive, heavy-featured British character actor who appeared in many Hollywood films.
■ Success 23. Crime without Passion 34. The Scoundrel 35. Winterset 36. Sinner Take All 36. Internes Can't Take Money 37. Yellow Jack 38. The Mad Miss Manton 38. If I Were King 38. There's That Woman Again 38. Let Us Live 39. Confessions of a Nazi Spy 39. I Stole a Million 39. Silver on the Sage 39. Union Pacific 39. Each Dawn I Die 39. Espionage Agent 39. Dust Be My Destiny 39. Nick Carter Master Detective 39. *Black Friday* 40. The Sea Wolf 41. Mr District Attorney 41. Sergeant York 41. They Died with Their Boots On 41. The Lady Is Willing 42. The Big Shot 42. *To Be or Not to Be* 42. Eagle Squadron 42. Eyes in the Night 42. Tarzan Triumphs 43. Air Force 43. This Is the Army 43. The Master Race 44. The Story of Dr Wassell 44. Wilson 44. *The Suspect* 45. Captain Eddie 45. God Is My Co-Pilot 45. The Phantom Speaks 45. Because of Him 46. Mr Ace 46. Canyon Passage 46. Possessed 47. An Act of Murder 47. You're My Everything 49. Streets of Laredo 49. The File on Thelma Jordon 49. Task Force 49. There's a Song in My Heart 49. Paid in Full 50. No Way Out 50. The Groom Wore Spurs 51.

Ridley, Arnold (1896–1984)
English playwright, character actor and occasional director, best known for his role as the bumbling, incontinent Private Godfrey in the TV sitcom *Dad's Army* 68–77. His greatest achievement was writing the perennial comedy thriller *The Ghost Train*, which was filmed in 1927 and 1931 and was also the inspiration for Will Hay's *Oh Mr Porter* 37 and several other films, including *Back Room Boy* 42. Born in Bath, he was educated at Bristol University and made his stage debut in 1914, abandoning acting for many years from the early 20s because of wounds suffered while serving in the army during the First World War.
The Wrecker (oa) 28. The Flying Fool (oa) 31. Third Time Lucky (oa) 31. Keepers of Youth (oa) 31. Blind Justice (oa) 34. The Warren Case (oa) 34. Royal Eagle (co-d, story) 36. Seven Sinners (oa) 36. East of Ludgate Hill (story) 37. Shadowed Eyes (story) 39. Stolen Face (a) 52. Meet Mr Lucifer (oa) 53. Wings of Mystery (a) 63. Crooks in Cloisters (a) 64. Who Killed the Cat? (oa) 66. Dad's Army (a) 71. Carry On Girls (a) 73. The Amorous Milkman (a) 74, etc.

Ridley, Philip (1960–)
British director, screenwriter, dramatist, author and artist.
The Krays (w) 90. The Reflecting Skin (wd) 90. The Passion of Darkly Noon 96.

Riefenstahl, Leni (1902–)
German director, former dancer, who made brilliant propaganda films for Hitler.
Autobiography: 1993, *The Sieve of Time*.
Biography: 1976, *Leni Riefenstahl* by Glenn B. Infield. 1998, *A Portrait of Leni Riefenstahl* by Audrey Salkeld.
The White Hell of Pitz Palu (a) 29. The Blue Light (a, d) 32. S.O.S. Iceberg (a) 33. *Triumph of the Will* (the Nuremberg Rally) (d) 34. *Olympische Spiele* 36. Tiefland 45, etc.

Riegert, Peter (1947–)
American character lead, in the George Segal tradition.
National Lampoon's Animal House 78. Head over Heels 80. National Lampoon's Movie Madness 81. *Local Hero* 83. Ellis Island (TV) 85. Man in Love/Un Homme Amoureux (Fr./It.) 87. The Stranger 87. Crossing Delancey 88. That's Adequate 89. Beyond the Ocean 90. A Shock to the System 90. Oscar 91. Object of Beauty 91. Utz (TV) 92. The Runestone 92. Passed Away 92. Gypsy (TV) 93. The Mask 94. White Man's Burden 94. Coldblooded 95. Pie in the Sky 95. The Infiltrator (TV) 95. Infinity 96. North Shore Fish 97. Face Down 97. The Baby Dance (TV) 98. Hi-Life 98. Jerry and Tom 98. In the Weeds 00. Traffic 00, etc.

Riesner, Dean (1918–)
American screenwriter, a former child actor under the name Dinky Dean. He also directed the curious *Bill and Coo*, with its cast of birds in hats and neckties, which won a special Oscar for 'artistry and patience'.
Bill and Coo (d) 47. The Helen Morgan Story (co-w) 57. Coogan's Bluff (co-w) 69. Dirty Harry (co-w) 71. Charlie Varrick (co-w) 73. The Enforcer (co-w) 76. Fatal Beauty (co-w) 87, etc.

Rifkin, Adam
American director and screenwriter.
Never on Tuesday (d) 88. Tale of Two Sisters (d) 89. Invisible Maniac (d, as Rif Coogan) 90. The Dark Backward (wd) 91. The Nutt House (d) 92. Psycho Cop 2 (d, as Rif Coogan) 93. The Chase (wd) 94. Mouse Hunt (w) 97. Small Soldiers (w) 98, etc.

Rigby, Arthur (1900–1970)
Burly English character actor, mainly on stage and television. Born in London, he was on stage from 1919 and in films from 1927. He is best known for his role as Station Sergeant Flint in the long-running TV series *Dixon of Dock Green*, a role he first played on stage in a version of *The Blue Lamp*.
Q Ships 27. The Deputy Drummer 35. The Marriage of Corbal 36. Cheer Up! 36. Dangerous Cargo 54. Crossroads to Crime 60, etc.

Rigby, Edward (1879–1951)
British stage character actor; became a familiar figure in endearingly doddery roles. On stage from 1900, he appeared in two silent films in 1907 and 1910.
Lorna Doone 35. Mr Smith Carries On 37. The Proud Valley 39. *Kipps* 41. The Common Touch 41. *Let the People Sing* 42. *Salute John Citizen* 42. Get Cracking 43. *Don't Take It to Heart* 44. Quiet Weekend 47. *Easy Money* 48. It's Hard to be Good 49. *The Happiest Days of Your Life* 49. *The Mudlark* 50, many others.

Rigby, Terence (1937–)
British character actor, mostly on stage.
The Little Ones 61. West Eleven 63. Accident 67. Get Carter 71. The Homecoming 73. The Dogs of War 80. The Hound of the Baskervilles (TV) 83. Lace (TV) 84. Lace II (TV) 85. Young Americans 93. Funny Bones 95. England My England 95. Our Friends in the North (TV) 96. Tomorrow Never Dies 97. Elizabeth 98. Great Expectations (TV) 99. Plunkett & Macleane 99. Essex Boys 00, etc.
TV series: Softly Softly 66–76. Airline 82. Crossroads 86–88. Common as Muck 97– .

Rigg, Dame Diana (1938–)
British leading actress who came to fame in *The Avengers* TV series 65–67. She won a Tony award as best actress on Broadway in *Medea* in 1994.
The Assassination Bureau 68. A Midsummer Night's Dream 68. On Her Majesty's Secret Service 69. Julius Caesar 70. The Hospital 71. Theatre of Blood 73. In This House of Brede (TV) 75. A Little Night Music 77. Evil Under the Sun 81. The Great Muppet Caper 81. Witness for the Prosecution (TV) 84. Bleak House (TV) 85. Genghis Cohen (TV) 93. A Good Man in Africa 94. Moll Flanders (TV) 96. Samson and Delilah (TV) 96. Rebecca (TV) 97. Parting Shots 98, etc.
TV series: The Diana Rigg Show 73. The Mrs Bradley Mysteries 00.

Rilla, Walter (1895–1980)
German actor on stage from 1921; to Britain in mid-30s.
Der Geiger von Florenz 26. The Scarlet Pimpernel 34. Victoria the Great 37. At the Villa Rose 39. The Adventures of Tartu 43. The Lisbon Story 46. State Secret 50. Behold the Man £ 51. Cairo 61. The Thousand Eyes of Dr Mabuse 63. The Face of Fu Manchu 65, etc.

Rilla, Wolf (1920–)
British director, son of Walter Rilla.
Noose for a Lady 53. The End of the Road 54. Pacific Destiny 56. The Scamp 57. Bachelor of Hearts 58. Witness in the Dark 59. Piccadilly Third Stop 60. *Village of the Damned* 62. Cairo 63. The World Ten Times Over (& w) 63. Secrets of a Door to Door Salesman 73, etc.

Rimmer, Shane
American supporting actor.
S*P*Y*S 74. Twilight's Last Gleaming 77. The People That Time Forgot 77. Silver Bears 79. Arabian Adventure 79. Hanover Street 79. Gandhi 82. Crusoe 88. A Kiss before Dying 91. The Year of the Comet 92. Lipstick on Your Collar (TV) 93. A Kid in King Arthur's Court 95. Space Truckers 97, etc.

Rin Tin Tin (1916–1932)
American dog star of silent films who kept Warner Brothers solvent in its early days. He was one of five German shepherd puppies found in a trench during the First World War by Lee Duncan, then a lieutenant, who brought him back to California and earned more than $5m from his escapades. According to Jack Warner, he died with Jean Harlow cradling his head in her lap. His son Rin Tin Tin Jnr also starred in several films from the late 20s to the mid-30s.
The Man from Hell's River 22. Where the North Begins 23. Below the Line 25. A Hero of the Big Snows 26. A Dog of the Regiment 27. Jaws of Steel 27. Land of the Silver Fox 28. The Man Hunter 30. Lightning Warrior (serial) 31, etc.
❝ The dog faced one hazard after another and was grateful to get an extra hamburger for a reward. He didn't ask for a raise, or a new press agent, or an air-conditioned dressing room, or more close-ups. – *Jack Warner*

Rinehart, Mary Roberts (1876–1958)
American mystery novelist, whose plots usually involve heroines in frightening situations. *The Bat* and *Miss Pinkerton* were each filmed more than once.

Ringwald, Molly (1968–)
American teenage actress of the 80s.
P.K. and the Kid 82. Tempest 82. Spacehunter: Adventures in the Forbidden Zone 83. Sixteen Candles 85. The Breakfast Club 85. Pretty in Pink 86. King Lear 87. The Pick-Up Artist 87. For Keeps 88. Fresh Horses 88. Maybe Baby 88. Strike It Rich 90. Betsy's Wedding 90. Loser Takes All 90. Face the Music 92. Seven Sundays/Tous les Jours Dimanche (Fr./It.) 94. The Stand (TV) 94. Bastard Brood/Enfants de Salaud (Fr.) 96. Office Killer 97. Teaching Mrs Tingle 99. In the Weeds 00, etc.
TV series: The Facts of Life 79–80. Townies 96.

Rintoul, David (1948–)
Scottish leading actor, much on television and best known for his role as Dr Finlay in the TV series of the same name 92–96. Born in Aberdeen, he was educated at Edinburgh University and studied at RADA.
Legend of the Werewolf 74. The Flight of the Heron (TV) 76. Scotch Myths – the Movie 82, etc.

Ripley, Arthur (1895–1961)
American director whose films are oddly sparse.
■ I Met My Love Again 38. Prisoner of Japan 42. *A Voice in the Wind* 44. The Chase 47. Thunder Road 58.

Ripper, Michael (1913–2000)
British character actor, often in comic roles.
Captain Boycott 48. Treasure Hunt 52. The Belles of St Trinian's 54. Richard III 56. Quatermass II 57. The Revenge of Frankenstein 58. Brides of Dracula 60. Captain Clegg 62. The Secret of Blood Island 65. The Reptile 66. The Plague of the Zombies 66. Where the Bullets Fly 66. Scars of Dracula 70. Legend of the Werewolf 75. The Prince and the Pauper 78. No Surrender 85. Revenge of Billy the Kid 91, etc.
TV series: Butterflies 78–82.

Ripstein, Arturo (1943–)
Mexican director, influenced by Buñuel, for whom he worked as a production assistant on *The Exterminating Angel*.
A Time to Die/Tiempo de Morir 65. Children's Hour/La Hora de los Niños 69. Castle of Purity/El Castillo de la Pureza 73. The Holy Office/El Santo Oficio 73. The Black Widow/La Viuda Negra 77. Vicious Circle/Cadena Perpétua 79. Seduction/La Seducción 80. The Other/El Otro 84. Realm of Fortune/El Imperio de la Fortuna 87. White Lies/Mentiras Piadosas 88. La Mujer del Puerto 91. The Beginning and the End/Principio y Fin 93. The Queen of the Night/La Reina de la Noche 94. Profundo Carmesi 96. Divine 98, etc.
❝ In Mexico there is no such thing as a cinematic career. – *A.R.*

Riscoe, Arthur (1896–1954)
British stage comedian with rare film appearances.
Going Gay 34. Paradise for Two 38. *Kipps* (as Chitterlow) 41, etc.

Risdon, Elizabeth (1887–1958) (E. Evans)
English leading actress of early silents who in 1915 was voted the most popular British film star. On stage from 1910, she moved to America to work in the theatre in 1917 and went to Hollywood in the mid-30s, becoming a character actress. Married to director George Loane Tucker and actor Brandon Evans (1903–78).
Maria Marten 13. Idol of Paris 14. Florence Nightingale 15. A Mother of Dartmoor 16. Guard That Girl 35. Crime and Punishment 36. Tom Sawyer 38. Huckleberry Finn 39. The Roaring Twenties 39. Mexican Spitfire 40. High Sierra 41. Random Harvest 42. Mexican Spitfire at Sea 42. Reap the Wild Wind 42. The Canterville Ghost 44. The Egg and I 47. Life with Father 47. Secret Fury 50. Bannerline 51. Scaramouche 52, etc.

Risi, Dino (1917–)
Italian director.
The Sign of Venus 55. Poveri ma Belli 56. Il Sorpasso 62. Scent of a Woman 75. How Funny Can Sex Be 76. Viva Italia 78. Primo Amore 78. Caro Papa 79. Sunday Lovers 80. Ghost of Love 81. Le Bon Roi Dagobert 84. Teresa 87. Two Women (TV) 89. A Love for Living (TV) 89. Mission of Love 91, etc.

Risi, Marco (1951–)
Italian director, the son of Dino Risi.
Vado a Vivere da Solo 81. Un Ragazzo, una Ragazza 83. Soldati 86. Forever Mary 89. Ragazzi Fuori 90. The Italians/Nel Continente Nero 93. The Pack 94, etc.

Riskin, Robert (1897–1955)
Distinguished American screenwriter.
Illicit 31. The Miracle Woman 31. *Lady for a Day* (AAN) 33. *It Happened One Night* (AA) 34. Broadway Bill 34. The Whole Town's Talking 35. *Mr Deeds Goes to Town* (AAN) 36. *Lost Horizon* 37. *You Can't Take It with You* (AAN) 38. The Real Glory 39. *Meet John Doe* 41. The Thin Man Goes Home 44. Magic Town 46. Riding High 50. Mister 880 50. The Groom Wore Spurs 51. Here Comes the Groom (co-w, AAN) 51, etc.

Ritchard, Cyril (1896–1977)
Australian dancer and light comedian, mainly on stage; latterly in US.
Piccadilly 29. Blackmail 30. I See Ice 38. Half a Sixpence 67.

Ritchie, Guy
English director and screenwriter who spearheaded a British cycle of gangster movies in the late 90s following the success of his first, *Lock, Stock and Two Smoking Barrels*. Married singer and actress MADONNA in 2000.
Lock, Stock and Two Smoking Barrels (wd) 98. Snatch (wd) 00, etc.

Ritchie, June (1939–)
British leading lady, mainly in 'realist' films.
A Kind of Loving 61. Live Now Pay Later 63. The Mouse on the Moon 63. The World Ten Times Over 63. This is My Street 64. The Syndicate (GB) 67, etc.

Ritchie, Michael (1938–2001)
American director. Born in Waukesha, Wisconsin, he graduated from Harvard University and worked in television, directing episodes of TV dramas, before turning to directing features in the late 60s. After an incisive beginning, his work became increasingly routine.
The Outsider (TV) 67. The Sound of Anger (TV) 69. Downhill Racer 69. Prime Cut 72. *The Candidate* 72. *Smile* 75. The Bad News Bears 76. Semi-Tough 77. An Almost Perfect Affair 79. Divine Madness 80. The Island 80. The Survivors 83. Fletch 85. Wildcats 86. The Golden Child 86. The Couch Trip 88. Fletch Lives 89. Diggstown 92. The Positively True Adventures of the Alleged Texas Cheerleader-Murdering Mom (TV) 93. Cops and Robbersons 94. A Simple Wish 97, The Fantasticks (made 95) 00, etc.

Ritt, Martin (1914–1990)
American director, a former actor. Born in New York City, and educated at St John's University, Brooklyn, he worked at the Group Theatre in the late 30s and early 40s, and, after war service with the US Army Air Force, directed and acted in plays and TV dramas. During the first half of the 50s he was blacklisted by the TV industry and taught at the ACTORS' STUDIO, where his pupils included Paul NEWMAN and Rod STEIGER.
Books: 1972, *The Films of Martin Ritt* by Sheila Whitaker.
■ *Edge of the City* 56. *No Down Payment* 57. *The Long Hot Summer* 58. The Sound and the Fury 59. The Black Orchid 59. Five Branded Women 60. Paris Blues 61. Hemingway's Adventures of a Young Man 62. *Hud* (AAN) 63. The Outrage 64. *The Spy Who Came in from the Cold* 65. Hombre 67. The Brotherhood 68. The Molly Maguires 69. The Great White Hope 71. Sounder 72. Pete 'n' Tillie 72. Conrack 74. The Front 76. The End of the Game (a only) 76. Casey's Shadow 77. Norma Rae 79. Cross Creek 83. Murphy's Romance 85. The Slugger's Wife (a only) 85. Stanley & Iris 90.
❝ I don't need a final cut. I only cut the thing once. If they're dumb enough to fool around with it, let 'em do it. – M.R.
As far as a Martin Ritt Production is concerned, I wouldn't embarrass myself to take that credit. What about the Ravetches? They wrote it. What about the actors who appear in it? If ever I write one, direct it and appear in it, then you can call it a Martin Ritt Production. – *M.R.*

Ritter, John (1948–) (Jonathan Ritter)
American actor, in comic or light romantic roles, from TV. He is the son of country singer and cowboy star Tex RITTER.
The Barefoot Executive 70. Scandalous John 71. The Other 72. Nickelodeon 76. Americathon 79. Hero at Large 80. Wholly Moses! 80. The Flight of the Dragon 82. They All Laughed 82. Letting Go 85. The Last Fling 86. Real Men 87. Skin Deep 89. Problem Child 90. Stephen King's IT 90. Problem Child 2 91. Noises Off 92. Stay Tuned 92. North 94. Sling Blade 96. Mercenary 96. A Gun, a Car, a Blonde 97. I Woke Up Early the Day I Died 98. Bride of Chucky 98. Panic 00, etc.
TV series: The Waltons 72–77. Three's Company 77–84. Three's a Crowd 84–85. Hearts Afire 92.

Ritter, Tex (1905–1974) (Woodward Ritter)
American singing cowboy star of innumerable second features, from the stage and radio. He sang the title song for the film *High Noon*.
Song of the Gringo 36. Sing, Cowboy, Sing 38. The Old Chisholm Trail 43. Marshal of Gunsmoke 46. Apache Ambush 55. Girl from Tobacco Road 66. What Am I Bid 67, etc.

Ritter, Thelma (1905–1969)
Wry-faced American character actress and comedienne; she provided a sardonic commentary on the antics of the principals in many 50s comedies.
■ Miracle on 34th Street 47. Call Northside 777 48. A Letter to Three Wives 49. City across the River 49. Father was a Fullback 49. Perfect Strangers 50. *All About Eve* (AAN) 50. I'll Get By 50. The Mating Season 51. As Young as You Feel 51. *The Model and the Marriage Broker* 51. With a Song in My Heart (AAN) 52. Titanic 53. The Farmer Takes a Wife 53. *Pickup on South Street* (AAN) 53. Rear Window 54. Daddy Longlegs 55. Lucy Gallant 55. The Proud and Profane 56. A Hole in the Head 59. Pillow Talk (AAN) 59. The Misfits 61. The Second Time Around 61. Birdman of Alcatraz (AAN) 62. How the West was Won 62. For Love or Money 63. A New Kind of Love 63. Move Over Darling 63. Boeing Boeing 65. The Incident 67. What's So Bad about Feeling Good? 68.
❝ Famous line (*All About Eve*) 'What a story. Everything but the bloodhounds snapping at her rear end.'
Famous line (*Pillow Talk*) 'If there's anything worse than a woman living alone, it's a woman saying she likes it.'

The Ritz Brothers (1901–1965) (*Al*, 1901–1965, *Jim*, 1903–1985, and *Harry* (the leader), 1906–1986)
Zany American nightclub comedians who made many enjoyable appearances in musicals of the 30s. Their real surname was Joachim.
■ Hotel Anchovy (short) 34. Sing Baby Sing 36. One in a Million 37. *On the Avenue* 37. You Can't Have Everything 37. Life Begins at College 37. *The Goldwyn Follies* 38. Kentucky Moonshine 38. Straight Place and Show 38. *The Three Musketeers* 39. The Gorilla 39. Pack Up Your Troubles 39. Argentine Nights 40. Behind the Eight Ball 42. Hi Ya Chum 43. Never a Dull Moment 43. Won Ton Ton (guest appearance by Harry and Jim) 76.

Riva, Emmanuele (1927–)
French leading actress, a former dressmaker.
Hiroshima Mon Amour 59. Adua et Sa Compagnie/Hungry for Love 60. Kapo 60. Leon Morin Priest 61. Climats 61. Thérèse Desqueyroux 63. Soledad 66. The Eyes, the Mouth 83. Three Colours: Blue/Trois Couleurs: Bleu 93. God, My Mother's Lover, and the Butcher's Son 95, etc.

Riva, Juan Antonio de la (1953–)
Mexican director.
Wandering Lives/Vidas Errantes 83. Pueblo de Madera 91. La Ultima Batalla 93. Una Maestra con Angel 94, etc.

Rivera, Chita (1933–) (Dolores Conchita Figueroa del Rivero)
Dynamic American dancer and singer.
Sweet Charity 69. Pippin 81. That's Singing 84. The Mayflower Madam (TV) 87, etc.

Rivers, Joan (1933–)
American cabaret comedienne with a strong line in smut.
Rabbit Test 78. The Muppets Take Manhattan 84.Tears and Laughter: The Joan and Melissa Rivers Story (TV) 94. Whispers: An Elephant's Tale (voice) 00, etc.
❝ I'm Jewish. I don't work out. If God had intended me to bend over he'd have put diamonds on the floor. – *J.R.*

Rivette, Jacques (1928–)
French director and screenwriter, former critic.
Le Coup du Berger 56. Paris Nous Appartient 60. La Religieuse (& w) 65. L'Amour Fou (& w) 68. Celine and Julie Go Boating 74. La Vengeresse 76. Merry Go Round 83. Love on the Ground/L'Amour par Terre 84. Hurlevent 85. The Gang of Four/La Bande des Quatre 89. *La Belle Noiseuse* 91. Jeanne la Pucelle 94. Up Down Fragile/Haut Bas Fragile 95. Secret Defence 98, etc.

Rivkin, Allen (1903–1990)
American screenwriter and novelist. Born in Hayward, Wisconsin, and educated at the University of Minnesota, he worked as a journalist and publicist and in advertising before going to Hollywood in the early 30s. He later worked in television, and produced the series *Troubleshooters* 59–60. He also wrote (with Laura Kerr) *Hello Hollywood*, an anthology of reminiscences about film.
70,000 Witness 32. Meet the Baron 33. The Picture Snatcher 33. Dancing Lady 33. Cheating Cheaters 34. Our Little Girl 35. This Is My Affair 37. Love under Fire 37. Let Us Live 37. Straight, Place and Show 38. It Could Happen to You 39. Typhoon 40. Kid Glove Killer 42. Joe Smith American 42. The Guilt of Janet Ames 47. The Farmer's Daughter 47. Tension 50. Grounds for Marriage 50. Gambling House 50. The Strip 51. It's a Big Country 52. Timberjack 54. Prisoner of War 54. The Eternal Sea 55. Road to Denver 55. Live Fast, Die Young 58. The Big Operator 59, many others.

Rix, Brian (Lord Rix) (1924–)
English leading actor and producer of farce. Born in Cottingham, Yorkshire, he was on stage from 1942 and actor-manager at London's Whitehall and Garrick theatres for 30 years from 1950. He then became Secretary-General and, later, Chairman of MENCAP (The Royal Society for Mentally Handicapped Children and Adults). He was knighted in 1986 and made a life peer in 1992. Married actress Elspet Gray in 1949.
Books: 1989, *Farce about Face*. 1992, *Tour de Farce*.
Reluctant Heroes 51. What Every Woman Wants 54. Up to His Neck 54. Dry Rot 55. The Night We Dropped a Clanger 59. And the Same to You 60. Nothing Barred 61. Don't Just Lie There, Say Something 73, etc.
TV series: Dial Rix 62–63. Laughter from Whitehall 63–64. Laughter from the Whitehall 65. Men of Affairs 73. A Roof over My Head 77.

Roach, Bert (1891–1971)
American silent screen actor.
The Millionaire 21. The Rowdy 21. The Flirt 22. Excitement 24. Don't 25. Money Talks 26. The Taxi Dancer 27. The Desert Rider 29. No No Nanette 30. Viennese Nights 30. Hallelujah I'm a Bum 33. San Francisco 36. Algiers 38. Hi Diddle Diddle 43. The Perils of Pauline 47, etc.

Roach, Hal (1892–1992)
American producer chiefly associated with gag comedies. Varied early experience before he teamed with Harold Lloyd 1916; later made films with Our Gang, Laurel and Hardy, etc.
AA 1983 'in recognition of his distinguished contributions to the motion picture art form'.
SOUND FILMS: Sons of the Desert 33. *Way Out West* 36. *Topper* 37. *Of Mice and Men* 39. *Turnabout* 40. One Million BC 40. *Topper Returns* 41, many others.
❝ One of the few producers who knew talent when he saw it, and gave his stars, writers and directors the freedom to create great comedy. – *Leonard Maltin*

Roach, Jay (1958?–)
American director. Born in New Mexico, he graduated from Stanford University and studied for a master's degree in film production at the University of Southern California. Married singer Susanna Hoffs.
Lifepod (co-w) (TV) 93. Blown Away (story) 94. The Empty Mirror (co-w) 96. Austin Powers: International Man of Mystery 97. Austin Powers II 99, etc.

Roache, Linus (1964–)
English leading actor, the son of William Roache (1932–), who plays Ken Barlow in the ITV soap opera *Coronation Street*.
Priest 94. The Wings of the Dove 97. Shot through the Heart (TV) 98. Siam Sunset 99. Best 99. Shot Through the Heart (TV) 99. The Venice Project 99. Pandaemonium (as Samuel Taylor Coleridge) 00, etc.
TV series: Seaforth 94.

Roarke, Adam (1938–1996)
American actor and occasional director. A regular in biker movies of the 60s, he is said to have turned down a leading role in *Easy Rider*. He later became an acting coach. Died of a heart attack.
Women of the Prehistoric Planet 66. Hell's Angels on Wheels 67. Psych-Out 68. The Savage Seven 68. The Losers 70. Play It as It Lays 72. How Come Nobody's on Our Side? 73. Dirty Mary, Crazy Larry 74. Four Deuces 75. The Stunt Man 80. Beach Girls 82. Trespasses (& co-d) 83, etc.

Rob Roy (1671–1734) (Robert Roy McGregor)
Scottish outlaw, a drover whose clan had been proscribed by the English as Jacobite sympathizers; like many outlaws, he became famous for his kindness to the oppressed. Sir Walter Scott immortalized him in his novel *Rob Roy*, published in 1817, and he was played by Liam Neeson in the Hollywood film *Rob Roy* 95, directed by Michael Caton-Jones.

Robards, Jason, Snr (1892–1963)
American stage actor, who made character appearances in films.
The Cohens and the Kellys 26. On Trial 28. Abraham Lincoln 30. The Crusades 35. I Stole a Million 39. Isle of the Dead 45. Bedlam 46. Riff Raff 47. Wild in the Country 61, many others.
TV series: Acapulco 61.

Robards, Jason (1922–2000)
American stage actor, son of Jason ROBARDS. Born in Chicago, he came to notice in the 50s for his performances in the plays of Eugene O'NEILL. The third of his four wives was actress Lauren BACALL (1961–69).
The Journey 58. By Love Possessed 59. *Tender is the Night* 61. Long Day's Journey into Night 62. A Thousand Clowns 65. A Big Hand for the Little Lady 66. Any Wednesday 66. Divorce American Style 67. *The Hour of the Gun* 67. The St Valentine's Day Massacre 67. The Night They Raided Minsky's 68. Isadora 68. Once Upon a Time in the West 69. Tora! Tora! Tora! 70. Julius Caesar 70. The Ballad of Cable Hogue 70. Murders in the Rue Morgue 71. Johnny Got His Gun 71. The War Between Men and Women 72. Pat Garrett and Billy the Kid 73. Play It as It Lays 73. All The President's Men (AA) 76. Washington behind Closed Doors (TV) 77. Julia (as Dashiell Hammett) (AA) 77. Comes a Horseman 78. Hurricane 79. Melvin and Howard (as Howard Hughes) (AAN) 80. Raise the Titanic 80. Caboblanco 81. The Legend of the Lone Ranger 81. Max Dugan Returns 83. The Day After (TV) 83. Something Wicked This Way Comes 83. Sakharov (TV) 84. The Last Frontier (TV) 86. Square Dance 86. Bright Lights, Big City 88. The Good Mother 88. Black Rainbow 89. Dream a Little Dream 89. Reunion 89. Parenthood 89. Quick Change 90. Gettysburg 90. Chernobyl: The Final Warning (TV) 91. Storyville 92. The Trial 93. The Adventures of Huck Finn 93. Philadelphia 93. The Paper 94. Little Big League 94. The Enemy Within (TV) 94. My Antonia (TV) 95. Journey 95. A Thousand Acres 97. Beloved 98. The Real Macaw (Aus.) 98. Enemy of the State (uncredited) 98. Heartwood (TV) 98. Magnolia 99. Going Home (TV) 00, etc.
❝ I've always played disintegrated characters. – *J.R.*
I don't want actors reasoning with me about motivation and all that bull. All I want them to do is learn the goddamn lines and don't bump into each other. – *J.R.*
His view of acting was just do it. Learn it. Serve it. Jason didn't spend his time trying to figure it all out. He was too busy working. Not taking it all too seriously. – *Kevin Spacey*

Robbe-Grillet, Alain (1922–)
French writer and director.
Last Year at Marienbad (AAN) 61. *L'Immortelle* 62. *Trans-Europe Express* 66. Glissements Progressifs du Plaisir 73. Le Jeu avec le Feu 74. La Belle Captive 83. Un Bruit Qui Rend Fou 94. The Blue Villa 95, etc.

Robbins, Brian (1964–)
American director, writer and producer, a former actor, born in Brooklyn, New York.
AS ACTOR: Crime of Innocence (TV) 85. The Gladiator (TV) 86. One Terrific Guy (TV) 86. Cellar Dweller 87. BUD/CHUD II 88. Camp Cucamonga (TV) 90, etc.
AS DIRECTOR: The Show 95. Good Burger 97.
TV series: Head of the Class 86–91.

Robbins, Gale (1922–1980)
American leading lady and singer.
In the Meantime Darling 44. My Girl Tisa 48. The Barkleys of Broadway 49. Oh You Beautiful Doll 49. Three Little Words 50. Strictly Dishonourable 51. The Belle of New York 52. Calamity Jane 53. Double Jeopardy 55. Stand Up and Be Counted 72, etc.

Robbins, Harold (1916–1997) (Francis Kane)
Best-selling American novelist and occasional screenwriter and producer. His 23 books, often based on actual events including film-world

scandals, found favour for a time in Hollywood: *The Carpetbaggers*, which sold 6m copies, drew on the life of Howard HUGHES, and *Where Love Has Gone*, which was inspired by the killing of Lana TURNER's gangster lover, was filmed as *Stiletto*. Born in New York, he was a foundling, first given the name of Francis Kane and then called Harold Rubin when he was adopted at the age of 11. After a variety of jobs, and making and losing a fortune on the stock exchange, he went to work for Universal Pictures in the 40s, where he took charge of budgets and planning and began writing. Married three times.

■ Never Love a Stranger (co-w, oa) 58. King Creole (oa) 58. The Pusher (w) 59. The Carpetbaggers (oa) 63. Where Love Has Gone (oa) 64. Nevada Smith (oa) 65. Stiletto (oa) 69. The Adventurers (oa) 70. The Betsy (oa) 78. Harold Robbins' The Pirate (TV) 78. 79 Park Avenue (oa) (TV) 79. The Dream Merchants (oa) (TV) 80. The Lonely Lady (oa) 82.

TV series: The Survivors 69–70.

❝ All my characters are real. They are written as fiction to protect the guilty. – *H.R.*

Hemingway was a jerk. – *H.R.*

I'm the world's best novelist – there's nothing more to say. – *H.R.*

At best, he ranks as another King of Pulp, alongside Edgar Wallace or Mickey Spillane. – *John Sutherland*

Robbins, Jerome (1918–1998) (Jerome Rabinowitz)

American dancer and ballet-master who has choreographed several films. Born in New York, he studied briefly at New York University and at the Dance Center in Manhattan, beginning as a dancer in the chorus of Broadway musicals. The first ballet he created, *Fancy Free*, became the basis for the musical and the movie *On the Town*. After co-directing the screen version of *West Side Story*, he turned down other offers to direct.

The King and I 56. *West Side Story* (& co-d) (AA) 61, etc.

Robbins, Matthew

American director and screenwriter.

The Sugarland Express (co-w) 74. The Bingo Long Traveling All-Stars and Motor Kings (co-w) 76. MacArthur (co-w) 77. Corvette Summer (co-w, d) 78. Dragonslayer (co-w, d) 81. Warning Sign (co-w) 85. The Legend of Billy Jean (d) 85. Batteries Not Included (co-w, d) 87. Bingo (d) 91. Mimic (co-w) 97, etc.

Robbins, Richard

American composer, usually for Merchant-Ivory films. His association with the company dates from 1976, when he made a short film, *Sweet Sounds*, about the children and teaching methods at the Mannes College of Music Preparatory School in New York, where he was then the director.

The Europeans 79. Jane Austen in Manhattan 80. Quartet 81. Heat and Dust 82. The Bostonians 84. Room with a View 85. My Little Girl 86. Maurice 87. Sweet Lorraine 87. The Perfect Murder 88. Slaves of New York 89. The Ballad of the Sad Café 90. Mr & Mrs Bridge 90. Howards End (AAN) 92. The Remains of the Day (AAN) 93. Jefferson in Paris 95. The Proprietor 96. Surviving Picasso 96. A Soldier's Daughter Never Cries 98. Place Vendôme (Fr.) 98. Cotton Mary 99. The Golden Bowl 00, etc.

Robbins, Tim (1958–)

American leading actor, singer and songwriter who has recently turned to screenwriting and directing.

No Small Affair 84. The Sure Thing 85. Howard the Duck 86. Top Gun 86. Bull Durham 88. Erik the Viking 89. Miss Firecracker 89. Cadillac Man 90. Jacob's Ladder 90. The Player 92. Bob Roberts (& wd, s) 92. The Hudsucker Proxy 94. The Shawshank Redemption 94. Prêt-à-Porter/Ready to Wear 94. I.Q. 94. Dead Man Walking (wd, AANd) 95. Nothing to Lose 96. Arlington Road 98. The Cradle Will Rock (p, wd) 99. Mission to Mars 00. High Fidelity 00. Antitrust 01, etc.

❝ Whether a movie is going to be a success or a failure, and consequently whether you're going to be a success or failure yourself, is always a crapshoot. – *T.R.*

Rober, Richard (1906–1952)

American general-purpose actor with stage experience.

Smart Girls Don't Talk 48. Deported 50. The Well 52. The Devil Makes Three 52, etc.

Robert, Yves (1920–)

French director, former actor.

The War of the Buttons 61. *Bébert et l'Omnibus* 63. *Copains* 64. *Follow the Guy with One Black Shoe* 72. Pardon Mon Affaire 76. We All Shall Go to Paradise 77. Courage Fuyons 79. Le Jumeau 84. My Father's Glory/La Gloire de Mon Père 90. My Mother's Castle/Le Château de Ma Mère 90. Le Bal des Casse-Pieds 92. Montparnasse Pondichery 94, etc.

Roberti, Lyda (1910–1938)

German-Polish leading lady, former child café singer, in several Hollywood films of the 30s.

■ Million Dollar Legs 32. The Kid from Spain 32. Dancers in the Dark 32. Torch Singers 33. Three-Cornered Moon 33. College Rhythm 34. The Big Broadcast of 1936 35. George White's Scandals 35. Pick a Star 37. Nobody's Baby 37. Wide Open Faces 37.

Roberts, Ben (1916–1984) (Benjamin Eisenberg)

American writer, almost always with Ivan GOFF. Born in New York, he was educated at NYU and, after a time in public relations, began by working on Broadway shows.

Backfire 49. White Heat 49. Goodbe My Fancy 51. Captain Horatio Hornblower RN 51. Come Fill the Cup 51. White Witch Doctor 53. King of the Khyber Rifles 53. Green Fire 54. Serenade 56. Man of a Thousand Faces (AAN) 57. Band of Angels 57. Shake Hands With the Devil 59. Portrait in Black 60. Midnight Lace 60. The Legend of the Lone Ranger 61, etc.

TV series: The Rogues 64-65. Mannix (p) 67-75. Charlie's Angels 76-87. Time Express 79.

Roberts, Eric (1956–)

American leading man. He is the brother of actress Julia ROBERTS.

King of the Gypsies 78. Raggedy Man 81. Star 80 83. The Pope of Greenwich Village 84. The Coca Cola Kid 85. Runaway Train (AAN) 85. Nobody's Fool 86. Dear America 87. Blood Red 87. Best of the Best 89. Options 89. Rude Awakening 89. The Ambulance 90. Descending Angel 91. Lonely Hearts 91. By the Sword 91. Final Analysis 92. Best of the Best II 93. The Hard Truth 94. Love, Cheat & Steal 94. The Specialist 94. The Grave 96. It's My Party 96. Dr Who (TV) 96. Heaven's Prisoners 96. Power 98 96. American Strays 96. The Cable Guy 96. The Glass Cage 96. In Cold Blood (TV) 96. Saved by the Light (TV) 97. The Odyssey (TV) 97. Most Wanted (TV) 97. Past Perfect 98, etc.

TV series: C16: FBI 97– .

Roberts, Ewan (1914–1983) (Thomas McEwan Hutchinson)

Scottish character actor of stage and screen.

Castle in the Air 52. The Lady Killers 55. Night of the Demon 57. The Day of the Triffids 61. The Traitors 62. Five to One 63. Hostile Witness 67. Bedevilled 71. Endless Night 72, etc.

Roberts, Florence (1860–1940)

American character actress best remembered as Granny in the Jones Family series 1936–40.

Westward Passage 32. Make Me a Star 32. Dangerously Yours 33. Torch Singer 33. Babes in Toyland 34. Les Misérables 35. Next Time We Love 36. The Life of Emile Zola 37, etc.

Roberts, Julia (1967–)

American actress, a former model who rapidly established herself as the most sought-after actress of the 90s. She is the sister of actor Eric ROBERTS. Current asking price: $20m a movie. At one time engaged to actor Kiefer SUTHERLAND, she was briefly married (1993-1995) to singer Lyle LOVETT. She has been romantically linked with actor Benjamin Bratt.

Blood Red 87. Satisfaction 88. Baja Oklahoma (TV) 88. Mystic Pizza 88. Steel Magnolias (AAN) 89. Pretty Woman (AAN) 90. Flatliners 90. Sleeping with the Enemy 90. Dying Young 91. Hook 91. The Pelican Brief 93. I Love Trouble 94. Prêt-à-Porter/Ready to Wear 94. Something to Talk About 95. Mary Reilly 96. Michael Collins 96. Everyone Says I Love You 96. *My Best Friend's Wedding* 97. Conspiracy Theory 98. Stepmom 98. Notting Hill 99. Runaway Bride 99. *Erin Brockovich* (AA, BFA) 00. America's Sweethearts 01, etc.

❝ I never really made it to acting school. I went to acting classes a few times, but it never seemed very conducive to what I wanted to do. – *J.R.*

I live a privileged life–hugely privileged. I'm rich. I'm happy. I have a great job. It would be absurd to pretend it's anything different. I'm like a pig in shit. – *J.R.*

Roberts, Kenneth (1885–1957)

American adventure novelist. The filming of *Northwest Passage* was never completed; the title on King Vidor's film reads *Northwest Passage, Part One: Rogers' Rangers*. *Lydia Bailey* fared better.

Roberts, Lynne (1919–1978) (Mary Hart)

American leading lady of 40s second features.

Dangerous Holiday 37. Winter Wonderland 39. Call of the Klondike 41. Quiet Please Murder 42. The Great Plane Robbery 47. The Blazing Forest 52. Port Sinister 53, many others.

Roberts, Marguerite (1908–1989)

American screenwriter of tough, masculine films, specializing in westerns. Born in Nebraska and brought up in Greeley, Colorado, she began as a journalist and then went to work at Fox in 1927 as secretary to studio head Winfield Sheehan, before becoming a script reader. She later worked for Paramount and MGM. A prominent member of the Screen Writers Guild, she was blacklisted for a decade from the early 50s and her name was removed from the credits of *Ivanhoe*, on which she was working at the time. Her second husband was novelist and occasional screenwriter John Sanford.

Sailor's Luck (w) 33. Peck's Bad Boy (w) 34. Hollywood Boulevard (w) 36. Turn of the Moon (co-w) 37. Escape (co-w) 40. Honky Tonk (co-w) 41. Ziegfeld Girl (co-w) 41. Somewhere I'll Find You (w) 42. Dragon Seed (w) 44. Desire Me (co-w) 46. If Winter Comes (co-w) 47. Sea of Grass (co-w) 47. Ambush (w) 49. The Bribe (story) 49. Soldiers Three (co-w) 51. Rampage (co-w) 62. Diamond Head (w) 63. Love Has Many Faces (w) 64. Five Card Stud (w) 68. Norwood (w) 69. *True Grit* (w) 69. Red Sky at Morning (w) 70. Shoot Out (w) 71, etc.

❝ I was weaned on stories about gunfighters and their doings, and I know all the lingo too. My grandfather came West as far as Colorado by covered wagon. He was a sheriff in the state's wildest days. – *M.R.*

She writes men with more balls than any other guy on this lot. – *Clark Gable at MGM*

Roberts, Pernell (1930–)

American general-purpose actor; became famous as one of the brothers in TV's *Bonanza*, but left after four years and never regained the limelight until 1979, when he played the title role in the series *Trapper John MD*.

Ride Lonesome 58. The Silent Gun (TV) 69. The Magic of Lassie 78. Night Train to Kathmandu (TV) 88, etc.

Roberts, Rachel (1927–1980)

Welsh character actress in leading roles. Born in Llanelli, she studied at the University of Wales and RADA and, in 1950, began working with a repertory company in Swansea (where her fellow players included Kenneth Williams and Richard Burton) and was in films from the mid-50s, coming into her own with *Saturday Night and Sunday Morning* 60 and *This Sporting Life*. Insecurity, the breakdown of her marriage to Rex Harrison (1962–71) and alcoholism bedevilled her later career and she committed suicide. Her first husband was actor Alan Dobie (1955–61).

Autobiography: *No Bells on Sunday* (edited by Alexander Walker).

Valley of Song 52. The Good Companions 57. Our Man in Havana 59. *Saturday Night and Sunday Morning* (BFA) 60. *This Sporting Life* (AAN, BFA) 63. A Flea in Her Ear 68. Doctors' Wives 71. Wild Rovers 71. *O Lucky Man* 73. The Belstone Fox 73. Murder on the Orient Express 74. Great Expectations (TV) 75. Picnic at Hanging Rock 76. Foul Play 78. When a Stranger Calls 79. Yanks (BFA) 79. Charlie Chan and the Curse of the Dragon Queen 81, etc.

TV series: The Tony Randall Show 76.

❝ Whenever I act well, my head clears. Always a bit frail I was personally, but never professionally. – *R.R.*

Day after day and night after night, I'm in this shaking fear. What am I so terribly frightened of? Life itself, I think. – *R.R.'s last entry in her journal*

She was like a ball of fire: the only trouble was, so often she had no material worthy of setting alight with her combustible energy. – *Pamela Mason*

She had good legs. How do I know? Because she was forever throwing her dress up over her head. – *Richard Gere*

That big, carnal, sensuous stage personality of hers is damn hard to find nowadays. – *Hal Prince*

Roberts, Roy (1900–1975)

American character actor who once played cops but graduated to senior executives.

Guadalcanal Diary 43. My Darling Clementine 46. Flaming Fury 49. The Big Trees 52. The Glory Brigade 53. The Boss 56, many others.

TV series: Petticoat Junction 64–68.

Roberts, Stephen (1895–1936)

American director, a former pilot and trick and exhibition flyer, in films from 1922.

■ Sky Bride 32. Lady and Gent 32. The Night of June 13th 32. If I Had a Million (part) 32. The Story of Temple Drake 33. *One Sunday Afternoon* 33. The Trumpet Blows 34. Romance in Manhattan 34. *Star of Midnight* 35. The Man Who Broke the Bank at Monte Carlo 35. The Lady Consents 36. The Ex Mrs Bradford 36.

Roberts, Tanya (1954–) (Tanya Leigh)

American actress and model, born in the Bronx, New York. She studied acting under Lee Strasberg and Uta Hagen.

The Last Victim 75. The Yum-Yum Girls 76. Fingers 78. Racquet 79. The Beastmaster 82. Sheena, Queen of the Jungle 84. A View to a Kill 85. Body Slam 87. Ladies' Game 90. Night Eyes 90. Inner Sanctum 91. Almost Pregnant 92. Sins of Desire 92. Deep Down 93, etc.

TV series: Charlie's Angels 80–81. That '70s Show 98– .

Roberts, Theodore (1861–1928)

American character actor, the grand old man of the silent screen.

Where the Trail Divides 14. The Trail of the Lonesome Pine 16. Male and Female 19. The Affairs of Anatol 21. Our Leading Citizen 22. *The Ten Commandments* (as Moses) 23. Grumpy 23. Locked Doors 25. Masks of the Devil 28, many others.

Roberts, Tony (1939–)

American light leading man.

The Beach Girls and the Monster 70. Star Spangled Girl 71. Play It Again Sam 72. Serpico 73. Le Sauvage 75. Annie Hall 77. Just Tell Me What You Want 80. A Midsummer Night's Sex Comedy 82. Amityville 3-D 83. Key Exchange 85. Hannah and Her Sisters 85. Radio Days 87. Switch 91. Popcorn 91, etc.

Robertshaw, Jerrold (1866–1941)

Gaunt British stage actor who made several film appearances.

Dombey and Son 18. She 25. Downhill 27. Kitty 29. Don Quixote (title role) 33, etc.

Robertson, Cliff (1925–)

Ambitious American leading man with long stage experience before being spotted for films. His second wife was actress Dina Merrill (1966–89).

In 1979 Robertson's career suffered unfairly when he accused executive David Begelman of having falsely signed a cheque in his name. The incident became a major scandal and is covered in the book *Indecent Exposure* by David McClintick.

■ *Picnic* (debut) 55. Autumn Leaves 56. The Girl Most Likely 57. The Naked and the Dead 58. Gidget 59. Battle of the Coral Sea 59. As the Sea Rages 60. All in a Night's Work 61. The Big Show 61. Underworld USA 61. The Interns 62. My Six Loves 63. *PT 109* (as President Kennedy) 63. Sunday in New York 64. *The Best Man* 64. 633 Squadron 64. Love Has Many Faces 65. Masquerade (GB) 65. Up from the Beach 65. *The Honey Pot* 67. The Devil's Brigade 68. *Charly* (AA) 68. Too Late the Hero 69. The Great Northfield Minnesota Raid 72. J. W. Coop (& p, d) 72. Ace Eli and Rodger of the Skies 73. Man on a Swing 74. My Father's House (TV) 75. Out of Season 75. Three Days of the Condor 76. Midway 76. Shoot 76. Obsession 76. *Washington behind Closed Doors* (TV) 77. Fraternity Row (narrator) 77. Dominique 78. The Pilot (& wd) 80. Two of a Kind (TV) 82. Class 83. Brainstorm 83. Star 80 83. The Key to Rebecca (TV) 85. Shaker Run 85. Wild Hearts Can't Be Broken 91. Wind 92. Renaissance Man 94. Escape from L.A. 96.

TV series: Rod Brown of the Rocket Rangers 53. Falcon Crest 83–84.

❝ As long as I get phone calls from the Museum of Modern Art, that all the film buffs love it, that's a residual. It isn't a financial residual and it isn't an artistic residual, but it's an ego residual. – *C.R.*

Robertson, Dale (1923–)
American western star, former schoolteacher.
Fighting Man of the Plains (debut) 49. Two Flags West 50. Lydia Bailey 52. The Silver Whip 53. Sitting Bull 54. A Day of Fury 56. Law of the Lawless 63. Blood on the Arrow 65. Coast of Skeletons 65, etc.
TV series: Tales of Wells Fargo 57–61. The Iron Horse 66. Dynasty 80–81.

Robertson, John S. (1878–1964)
Canadian director in Hollywood, a former actor, on stage from 1890.
The Money Mill 17. Let's Elope 19. Dr Jekyll and Mr Hyde 20. Sentimental Tommy 21. Tess of the Storm Country 22. The Enchanted Cottage 24. Shore Leave 25. Annie Laurie 27. Shanghai Lady 29. Madonna of the Streets 30. One Man's Journey 33. Wednesday's Child 34. Captain Hurricane 35. Our Little Girl 35, many others.

Robertson, Michael
Australian director and screenwriter.
The Best of Friends 82. Going Sane 85. Back of Beyond 95, etc.

Robertson, Robbie (1943–) (Jaime Robertson)
Canadian composer, songwriter, and guitarist, a member of the leading 70s rock group The Band.
The Last Waltz (doc) 78. Carny (a, co-w) 80. The King of Comedy 83. The Color of Money 86. Jimmy Hollywood 94, etc.

Robertson, Willard (1886–1948)
American character actor, often seen as lawyer or prison governor.
Skippy 31. Sky Devils 32. I Am a Fugitive from a Chain Gang 32. Doctor X 32. Tugboat Annie 33. Death on the Diamond 34. Here Comes the Navy 34. Black Fury 35. The Gorgeous Hussy 36. Exclusive 37. Men with Wings 38. Jesse James 39. Each Dawn I Die 39. My Little Chickadee 40. The Monster and the Girl 41. Juke Girl 42. Nine Girls 44. The Virginian 46. To Each His Own 46. Sitting Pretty 48, many others.

Robeson, Paul (1898–1976)
American actor and singer, on stage including concerts from mid-20s.
Biography: all entitled *Paul Robeson*. 1958, by Marie Seton. 1968, by Edwin P. Hoyt. 1974, by Virginia Hamilton.
■ Body and Soul 24. The Emperor Jones 33. *Sanders of the River* 35. *Showboat* 36. *Song of Freedom* 36. Jericho 38. Big Fella 38. *King Solomon's Mines* 38. *The Proud Valley* 39. Tales of Manhattan 42. Native Land 42. Il Canto dei Grandi Fiumi 55.

Robey, Sir George (1869–1954) (George Edward Wade)
British music-hall comedian, 'the prime minister of mirth'. Appeared in silent farcical comedies, later in character roles.
Autobiography: 1933, *Looking Back on Life*.
Biography: 1972, *George Robey, the Darling of the Halls* by Peter Cotes; 1991, *George Robey* by James Harding.
The Rest Cure 23. Don Quixote (as Sancho Panza) 23 and 33. Her Prehistoric Man 24. Chu Chin Chow 33. Marry Me 33. Birds of a Feather 36. A Girl Must Live 39. Variety Jubilee 40. Salute John Citizen 42. Henry V 44. The Trojan Brothers 45. The Pickwick Papers 52, etc.

Robin, Dany (1927–1995)
French leading lady who trained as a ballet dancer. Married French actor George Marchel and, from 1969, producer Michael Sullivan, who died with her in a fire.
Le Silence Est d'Or 46. Histoire d'Amour 52. Act of Love 54. In Six Easy Lessons 60. The Waltz of the Toreadors 62. Topaz 69, etc.

Robin, Leo (1899–1984)
American lyricist. Songs include 'Louise', 'Beyond the Blue Horizon', 'June in January', 'No Love No Nothing'.
Innocents of Paris 29. Monte Carlo 30. One Hour with You 32. Little Miss Marker 34. The Big Broadcast of 1938 (AA for 'Thanks for the Memory'). Gulliver's Travels 39. My Gal Sal 43. Meet Me after the Show 50. My Sister Eileen 55, etc.

Robinson, Andrew
Baby-faced American character actor who has played a couple of memorable villains.
Dirty Harry 71. Charley Varrick 73. The Drowning Pool 75. Cobra 86. Shoot to Kill 88. Prime Target 91. Child's Play 3 91. Trancers III: Deth Lives 92. Pumpkinhead II 93. There Goes My Baby 94, etc.

Robinson, Bernard (1912–1970)
English art director and production designer, latterly with Hammer Films.
Tony Draws a Horse 50. Old Mother Riley Meets the Vampire 52. Albert R.N. 53. The Sea Shall Not Have Them 54. Reach for the Sky 56. Quatermass II 57. Carve Her Name with Pride 58. *Dracula* 58. The Revenge of Frankenstein 58. The Sheriff of Fractured Jaw 58. The Hound of the Baskervilles 59. The Mummy 59. Brides of Dracula 60. Watch It Sailor! 61. *The Damned* 61. Curse of the Werewolf 64. Curse of the Mummy's Tomb 64. Dracula – Prince of Darkness 65. Frankenstein Created Woman 66. The Devil Rides Out 67. Quatermass and the Pit 67, etc.

Robinson, Bill (1878–1949)
American tap-dancer and entertainer, famous for his stairway dance.
The Little Colonel 35. In Old Kentucky 36. Rebecca of Sunnybrook Farm 38. *Stormy Weather* 43, etc.

Robinson, Bruce (1946–)
English actor, screenwriter, director and novelist. Born in London, he studied at the Central School of Speech and Drama. He was romantically involved with actress Leslie-Anne Down.
Biography: 2000, *Smoking in Bed, Conversations with Bruce Robinson*, ed Alistair Owen.
Romeo and Juliet (a) 68. Private Road (a) 71. Los Viajes Escolares (a) 74. The Brute (a) 75. The Story of Adèle H (a) 75.The Killing Fields (w, AAN) 84. *Withnail and I* (wd) 87. How to Get Ahead in Advertising (wd) 89. Fat Man and Little Boy/The Shadow Makers (co-w) 89. Jennifer Eight (wd) 92. Return to Paradise (co-w) 98. Still Crazy (a) 98. In Dreams (co-w) 99, etc.
❝ I can't think of anything more fundamentally nasty than the film industry. – *B.R.*
There are two types of animals roaming the Hollywood jungle. Those who do the screwing, those who get screwed. You have to try to ensure you're one of the former. – *B.R.*

Robinson, Cardew (1917–1992) (Douglas Robinson)
Lanky English comic actor, best known for his act as delinquent schoolboy 'Cardew the Cad, the Bad Boy of St Fanny's', from variety and radio.
Knight without Armour 37. A Piece of Cake 48. Fun at St Fanny's 56. Happy Is the Bride 58. I'm All Right, Jack 59. The Navy Lark 59. Waltz of the Toreadors 62. Heavens Above 63. Father Came Too 64. Alfie 66. Carry On up the Khyber 67. Where's Jack 69. The Magnificent 7 Deadly Sins 71. What's Up Nurse? 75. Guess Who's Coming to Dinner? 85. Pirates 86, etc.

Robinson, Casey (1903–1979)
American screenwriter, in Hollywood from 1921.
I Love That Man 33. Captain Blood 35. Call it a Day 37. It's Love I'm After 37. Four's a Crowd 39. *Kings Row* 42. Passage to Marseilles 44. Days of Glory 44. *The Macomber Affair* 47. Under My Skin (& p) 50. Two Flags West (& p) 50. Diplomatic Courier (& p) 52. The Snows of Kilimanjaro 52. While the City Sleeps 56. This Earth is Mine (& p) 59, etc.

Robinson, David (1930–)
English critic and author, notably as the biographer of Charlie Chaplin in *Chaplin: His Life and Art* (1985). He was film critic for the *Financial Times* and *The Times*. His books include *World Cinema*, *The Great Funnies*, *Buster Keaton*.

Robinson, Dewey (1898–1950)
Burly, bristling-eyebrowed American character actor, usually in tough or gangster roles. Died of a heart attack.
Enemies of the Law 31. Blonde Venus 32. *She Done Him Wrong* (as Spider Kane) 33. A Midsummer Night's Dream (as Snug) 35. New Faces of 1937 37. The Great McGinty 40. Tin Pan Alley 40. The Big Store 41. Palm Beach Story 42. Scarlet Street 45. Dillinger 45. The Gangster 46. The Beautiful Blonde from Bashful Bend 49. My Friend Irma 49. Father of the Bride 50. Jim Thorpe – American 51, etc.

Robinson, Edward G. (1893–1973) (Emanuel Goldenberg)
Dynamic American star actor of Rumanian origin. On stage from 1913; later settled in Hollywood. Special Academy Award 1972.
Autobiography: 1973, *All My Yesterdays*.
■ The Bright Shawl 23. The Hole in the Wall 29. Night Ride 30. A Lady to Love 30. Outside the Law 30. East is West 30. Widow from Chicago 30. *Little Caesar* (which made him a star) 30. *Five Star Final* 31. Smart Money 31. The Hatchet Man 31. Two Seconds 32. Tiger Shark 32. Silver Dollar 32. The Little Giant 33. I Loved a Woman 33. Dark Hazard 34. The Man with Two Faces 34. *The Whole Town's Talking* 34. Barbary Coast 35. Bullets or Ballots 36. Thunder in the City (GB) 37. Kid Galahad 37. The Last Gangster 38. *A Slight Case of Murder* 38. *The Amazing Dr Clitterhouse* 38. I Am the Law 38. Confessions of a Nazi Spy 39. Blackmail 39. *Dr Ehrlich's Magic Bullet* 40. *Brother Orchid* 40. A Dispatch from Reuters 41. *The Sea Wolf* 41. Manpower 41. Unholy Partners 41. Larceny Inc. 42. Tales of Manhattan 42. Destroyer 43. Flesh and Fantasy 43. Tampico 44. *Double Indemnity* 44. Mr Winkle Goes to War 44. *The Woman in the Window* 44. Our Vines Have Tender Grapes 45. *Scarlet Street* 45. Journey Together (GB) 45. The Stranger 46. The Red House 47. *All My Sons* 48. *Key Largo* 48. Night Has a Thousand Eyes 48. *House of Strangers* 49. My Daughter Joy (GB) 50. Actors and Sin 52. Vice Squad 53. Big Leaguer 53. The Glass Web 53. Black Tuesday 54. The Violent Men 55. Tight Spot 55. A Bullet for Joey 55. Illegal 55. Hell on Frisco Bay 56. Nightmare 56. The Ten Commandments 56. A Hole in the Head 59. Seven Thieves 59. Pépé 60. My Geisha 62. *Two Weeks in Another Town* 62. Sammy Going South (GB) 62. The Prize 63. Good Neighbour Sam 64. Robin and the Seven Hoods 64. Cheyenne Autumn 64. The Outrage 64. *The Cincinnati Kid* 65. Who Has Seen the Wind? 65. The Biggest Bundle of Them All 66. Never a Dull Moment 67. Grand Slam 67. Mackenna's Gold 68. It's Your Move 68. Operation St Peter's 68. Blonde from Peking 68. Song of Norway 69. Operation Heartbeat (TV) 69. The Old Man Who Cried Wolf (TV) 71. Soylent Green 73.
✪ For the dynamic personality which turned many a dubious script into dramatic gold. *Double Indemnity*.
❝ Some people have youth, some have beauty – I have menace. – *E.G.R.*
Famous line (*Little Caesar*) 'Mother of mercy, is this the end of Rico?'

Robinson, Frances (1916–1971)
American supporting actress, usually in smart roles.
Forbidden Valley 25. The Last Warning 28. Tim Tyler's Luck 35. The Lone Wolf Keeps a Date 37. The Invisible Man Returns 39. Tower of London 39. Smilin' Through 41. Suddenly It's Spring 46. Keeper of the Bees 47. Backfire 50, many others.

Robinson, George (c. 1895–1958)
American cinematographer.
No Defense 21. Back to God's Country 27. Hell's Heroes 30. Her First Mate 33. The Mystery of Edwin Drood 35. Diamond Jim 35. The Invisible Ray 36. Sutter's Gold 36. Dracula's Daughter 36. The Road Back 37. *Son of Frankenstein* 39. Tower of London 39. Son of Monte Cristo 40. Frankenstein Meets the Wolf Man 43. Son of Dracula 43. *The Scarlet Claw* 44. House of Frankenstein 45. The Naughty Nineties 45. Slave Girl 47. The Creeper 48. Abbott and Costello Meet Dr Jekyll and Mr Hyde 53. Tarantula 55. Joe Dakota 57, many others.

Robinson, Jay (1930–)
American stage actor of eccentric roles.
The Robe 53. Demetrius and the Gladiators 54. The Virgin Queen 55. My Man Godfrey 57. Bunny O'Hare 71. Shampoo 75. Partners 82. The Malibu Bikini Shop 86. Transylvania Twist 89. Sinatra (TV) 92. Bram Stoker's Dracula 92. Skeeter 93. Murder between Friends (TV) 94, etc.

Robinson, Joe (1929–)
British actor and professional boxer.
Master of Bankdam 48. Daughter of Darkness 49. *A Kid for Two Farthings* 55. The Flesh Is Weak 57. The Two Faces of Dr Jekyll 58. Barabbas 62. Diamonds Are Forever 71, etc.

Robinson, John (1908–1979)
British stage actor, familiar in heavy father or tough executive roles.
The Scarab Murder Case 36. The Lion Has Wings 40. Uneasy Terms 49. Hammer the Toff 51. The Constant Husband 55. Fortune is a Woman 58. The Doctor's Dilemma 58. And the Same to You 61, etc.

Robinson, Madeleine (1916–) (Madeleine Svoboda)
French stage and film actress.
Soldats sans Uniformes 43. Douce 43. Une Si Jolie Petite Plage 48. Dieu a Besoin des Hommes 50. Le Garçon Sauvage 51. The She Wolves 57. A Double Tour 59. The Trial 64. A Trap for Cinderella 65. A New World 66. Le Voyage du Père 66. Le Petit Matin 70. Camille Claudel 88, etc.

Robinson, Phil Alden (1950–)
American director and screenwriter.
All of Me (w) 84. Rhinestone (co-w) 84. In the Mood (wd) 87. Field of Dreams (wd) (AAN) 89. Sneakers (co-w, d) 92, etc.

Robison, Arthur (1888–1935)
Chicago-born director of German films.
Warning Shadows 24. The Informer (GB) 29. The Student of Prague 35, etc.

Robson, Dame Flora (1902–1984)
Distinguished British stage actress.
Biography: 1981, *Flora: The Life of Dame Flora Robson* by Kenneth Barrow.
■ Dance Pretty Lady 31. One Precious Year 33. Catherine the Great 34. *Fire over England* 36. Farewell Again 37. Wuthering Heights 39. Poison Pen 39. We Are Not Alone 39. Invisible Stripes 39. The Sea Hawk 40. Banana Passage 41. Saratoga Trunk 43. 2000 Women 44. Great Day 45. Caesar and Cleopatra 45. The Years Between 46. *Black Narcissus* 46. Saratoga Trunk (AAN) 46. Good Time Girl 47. Frieda 47. Holiday Camp 47. Saraband for Dead Lovers 48. The Tall Headlines 52. The Malta Story 53. Romeo and Juliet 54. *Innocent Sinners* 57. High Tide at Noon 57. No Time for Tears 57. The Gypsy and the Gentleman 58. 55 Days at Peking 62. Murder at the Gallop 63. Guns at Batasi 64. Those Magnificent Men in Their Flying Machines 64. Young Cassidy 65. Seven Women 65. The Shuttered Room 66. A Cry in the Wind 66. Eye of the Devil 67. Fragment of Fear 69. The Beloved 70. The Beast in the Cellar 71. Alice's Adventures in Wonderland 72. Comedy, Tragedy and All That 72. Dominique 78. A Man Called Intrepid (TV) 79. Les Misérables (TV) 80. A Tale of Two Cities (TV) 80. Clash of the Titans 81.

Robson, Mark (1913–1978)
Canadian-born director, former editor: began with Lewton and Kramer but progressed to more solidly commercial subjects. Born in Montreal, he studied political science and economics at the University of California at Los Angeles and law at Pacific Coast University before beginning work as a prop boy at Fox.
■ *The Seventh Victim* 43. The Ghost Ship 43. Youth Runs Wild 44. Isle of the Dead 45. Bedlam 46. *Champion* 49. Home of the Brave 49. Roughshod 49. My Foolish Heart 49. Edge of Doom 50. Bright Victory 51. I Want You 51. Return to Paradise 53. Hell Below Zero (GB) 54. The Bridges at Toko-Ri 54. Phffft 54. A Prize of Gold 55. Trial 55. The Harder They Fall 56. The Little Hut (& p) 57. Peyton Place (AAN) 58. The Inn of the Sixth Happiness (GB) (AAN) 58. From the Terrace (& p) 59. Lisa/The Inspector (p only) 62. Nine Hours to Rama (GB) (& p) 63. The Prize 63. *Von Ryan's Express* (& p) 65. Lost Command (& p) 66. Valley of the Dolls (& p) 67. Daddy's Gone A-Hunting (& p) 69. Happy Birthday Wanda June 71. Limbo 73. Earthquake 74. Avalanche Express 79.

Robson, May (1858–1942) (Mary Robison)
Australian actress, in America from childhood. Long experience on stage tours before coming to Hollywood, where she played domineering but kindly old ladies.
■ How Molly Made Good 15. A Night Out 16. His Bridal Night 19. A Broadway Saint 19. The Lost Battalion 19. Pals in Paradise 26. Angel of

Broadway 27. Chicago 27. A Harp in Hock 27. King of Kings 27. The Rejuvenation of Aunt Mary 27. Rubber Tires 27. Turkish Delight 27. The Blue Danube 28. Mother's Millions 31. Letty Lynton 32. Strange Interlude 32. Two against the World 32. Red Headed Woman 32. Little Orphan Annie 32. *If I Had a Million* 32. Reunion in Vienna 33. Dinner at Eight 33. Beauty for Sale 33. Broadway to Hollywood 33. Solitaire Man 33. Dancing Lady 33. *Lady for a Day* (AAN) 33. One Man's Journey 33. Alice in Wonderland 33. The White Sister 33. Men Must Fight 33. You Can't Buy Everything 34. Straight Is the Way 34. Lady by Choice 34. Vanessa, Her Love Story 35. Reckless 35. Grand Old Girl 35. Age of Indiscretion 35. Anna Karenina 35. Strangers All 35. Mills of the Gods 35. Three Kids and a Queen 36. Wife vs Secretary 36. The Captain's Kid 36. Rainbow on the River 36. Woman in Distress 37. *A Star Is Born* 37. The Perfect Specimen 37. Top of the Town 37. *The Adventures of Tom Sawyer* 38. *Bringing Up Baby* 38. The Texans 38. *Four Daughters* 38. They Made Me a Criminal 39. Yes My Darling Daughter 39. Daughters Courageous 39. Four Wives 39. The Kid from Kokomo 39. Nurse Edith Cavell 39. That's Right You're Wrong 39. Irene 39. The Texas Rangers Ride Again 40. *Granny Get Your Gun* 40. Four Mothers 41. Million Dollar Baby 41. Playmates 42. Joan of Paris 42.

Roc, Patricia (1915–) (Felicia Miriam Ursula Herold)
British leading lady of the 40s, signed for films after brief stage experience.

The Rebel Son/Taras Bulba 38. The Gaunt Stranger 39. The Mind of Mr Reeder 39. Three Silent Men 40. Let the People Sing 42. Millions Like Us 43. 2000 Women 44. Love Story 44. Madonna of the Seven Moons 44. The Wicked Lady 45. Johnny Frenchman 45. Canyon Passage (US) 46. *The Brothers* 47. Jassy 47. When the Bough Breaks 48. One Night with You 48. The Perfect Woman 49. Circle of Danger 50. The Man on the Eiffel Tower 51. Something Money Can't Buy 53. The Hypnotist 55. Bluebeard's Ten Honeymoons 60, etc.

Rocca, Daniela (1937–1995)
Voluptuous Italian actress of the early 60s, a former model who was a beauty queen (Miss Catania) at the age of 15. Her career ended after the break-up of her relationship with director Pietro GERMI, which resulted in a suicide attempt and was followed by spells in mental hospitals. She later released an album of her poetry and also featured in an Italian documentary, *The Cinema Machine* 81.

Mercanti di Donne 57. The Giant of Marathon/La Battaglia di Maratona 60. Queen of the Amazons/Colossus and the Amazon Queen/La Regina delle Amazzoni 60. *Esther and the King* 60. Head of a Tyrant/Giuditta e Oloferne 60. Revenge of the Barbarians/La Vendetta dei Barbari 61. *Divorce Italian Style*/Divorzio all'Italiana 61. The Empty Canvas 64. Behold a Pale Horse 64, etc.

Rocha, Glauber (1938–1981)
Brazilian director and screenwriter, a leader of his country's 'new cinema' movement. He went into exile 1970–76, making films in Europe, and died of pulmonary disease.

Barravento/The Turning Wind 62. Deus e o Diabo na Terra do Sol/Black God, White Devil 64. Terra em Transe/Earth Entranced 67. Antônio das Mortes 69. Le Vent d'Est/East Wind 69. O Leão Have Sete Cabeças/The Lion Has Seven Heads 70. Cabeças Cortadas/Severed Heads 71. Claro 75. A Idade da Terra/The Age of the Earth 80, etc.

Rochant, Eric (1961–)
French director and screenwriter.

Tough Life 89. Love without Pity/Un Monde sans Pitié 91. Autobus/Aux Yeux du Monde 91. Les Patriotes 94, etc.

Roche, Eugene (1928–)
American character actor with a slightly bewildered look; much on TV.

They Might Be Giants 71. Newman's Law 74. The Late Show 76. Corvette Summer 78. Foul Play 78. Oh God You Devil 84. Eternity 90. When a Man Loves a Woman 94. Roswell (TV) 94. Liz: The Elizabeth Taylor Story (TV) 95. Executive Decision 96, etc.

TV series: Lenny 90–91. Julie 92.

Roché, Henri-Pierre
French author and diarist, whose two autobiographical novels were turned into memorable films by François TRUFFAUT.
■ Jules et Jim 62. Anne and Muriel/Two English Girls/Les Deux Anglaises et Le Continent 71.

Rochefort, Jean (1930–)
French leading actor, often in comic roles.

Swords of Blood/Cartouche 61. Angélique 64. Angélique et le Roi 65. The Devil by the Tail/Le Diable par la Queue 69. The Tall Blond Man with One Black Shoe/Le Grand Blond avec une Chaussure Noire 72. Salut l'Artiste 74. A Happy Divorce 75. Pardon Mon Affaire/Un Eléphant ça Trompe Enormément 76. The Clockmaker 76. Pardon Mon Affaire Too 77. Who Is Killing the Great Chefs of Europe?/Too Many Chefs 78. Till Marriage Us Do Part 79. French Postcards 79. I Hate Blondes/Odio le Bionde 83. Birgit Haas Must Be Killed/Il Faut Tuer Birgit Haas 83. My First Forty Years/I Miei Primi Quarant'anni 89. The Hairdresser's Husband/Le Mari de la Coiffeuse 91. Dien Bien Phu 91. Le Bal des Casse-Pieds 91. L'Atlantide 92. The Long Winter/El Largo Invierno 92. *Tango* 93. Wild Target/Cible émouvante 93. Tombés du Ciel 93. La Prossima Volta il Fuoco 93. Tom Est Tout Seul 94. Palace (Sp.) 95. Ridicule 96. Wind with the Gone/El Viento Se Llevó lo Que 98, etc.

Rock, Chris (1966–)
Fast-talking American stand-up comedian, actor and screenwriter. Born in Jamestown, South Carolina, and brought up in Brooklyn, New York, he was discovered performing in a New York club as an 18-year-old by Eddie MURPHY, and first came to notice on NBC's *Saturday Night Live* from 1990.

Books: 1998, *Rock This!*

I'm Gonna Git You Sucka (a) 88. New Jack City (a) 91. Boomerang (a) 92. Coneheads (a) 93. CB4: The Movie (a, co-w) 93. Panther 95. The Immortals (a) 95. Sgt Bilko (a) 96. Beverly Hills Ninja (a) 97. Doctor Dolittle (voice) 98. Lethal Weapon 4 (a) 98. Nurse Betty 00. Down to Earth 01, etc.

TV series: In Living Color 93–94. The Chris Rock Show 97– .

❝ Why do famous people die of drug overdoses when they have everything in the world anyone could want? Because they have everything in the world anyone could want. And then they want more of it. And when that doesn't make them happy, they get high … And then next thing you know they get dead. – *C.R*

Rock, Crissy (1958–)
English actress and comedian.

Ladybird, Ladybird 94. Butterfly Collectors (TV) 99. Dockers (TV) 99, etc.

Rock, Joe (1891–1984)
American independent producer who, after experience in vaudeville and a brief spell in Hollywood, worked in Britain from the mid-30s, turning out quota quickies, several featuring Leslie Fuller, and also backed Michael Powell's *The Edge of the World*. He expanded his studios at Elstree to increase production but became bankrupt in 1937.

Krakatoa (US) 33. Captain Bill 35. The Stoker 35. Strictly Illegal 35. Everything Is Rhythm 36. One Good Turn 36. The Man behind the Mask 36. Boys Will Be Girls 37. Cotton Queen 37. The Edge of the World 37. Swing as You Swing 37. Reverse Be My Lot 38, etc.

Rockwell, Alexandre (1956–)
American director. He is married to actress Jennifer Beals.

Lenz 81. Hero 83. Sons 89. In the Soup 92. Somebody to Love 94. Four Rooms (co-d) 95, etc.

Rockwell, Sam (1968–)
American actor who made a breakthrough to notable starring roles with *Box of Moonlight* and *Lawn Dogs*. Educated at the High School for the Performing Arts in San Francisco, he began acting in the theatre from the age of 10.

Clown House (TV) 88. Last Exit to Brooklyn 89. Teenage Mutant Ninja Turtles 90. Light Sleeper 92. Jack and His Friends 92. In the Soup 92. Last Call 95. Mercy 95. The Search for One-Eyed Jimmy 96. Box of Moonlight 96. *Lawn Dogs* 97. Safe Men 98. Jerry and Tom 98. Galaxy Quest 99. The Green Mile 99. William Shakespeare's A Midsummer Night's Dream 99. Charlie's Angels 00, etc.

❝ I actually think that no-one should be allowed to be famous until they're 30. – *S.R.*

Roddam, Franc (1946–)
British director.

Quadrophenia 79. The Lords of Discipline 82. The Bride 85. Aria (co-d) 87. War Party 89. K2 91. Moby Dick (co-w, d) (TV) 98, etc.

Roddenberry, Gene (1921–1991)
American TV producer and writer, creator of *Star Trek* and *Star Trek: The Next Generation* and executive producer of the *Star Trek* films. Wrote and produced *Pretty Maids All in a Row* 70.

Biography: 1994, *Gene Roddenberry: The Myth and the Man behind Star Trek* by Joel Engel.

Rodgers, Anton (1933–)
British comic character actor.

Rotten to the Core 65. Scrooge 70. The Day of the Jackal 73. The Fourth Protocol 87. Dirty Rotten Scoundrels 88. Impromptu 89. Son of the Pink Panther 93, etc.

TV series: Fresh Fields 83–86. May to December 92–94. Noah's Ark 97– .

Rodgers, Richard (1902–1979)
American composer who worked variously with lyricists Lorenz Hart and Oscar Hammerstein II.

Love Me Tonight 32. *Hallelujah I'm a Bum* 33. On Your Toes 38. Babes in Arms 39. The Boys from Syracuse 40. *State Fair* 45. *Oklahoma!* 55. *The King and I* 56. *Pal Joey* 57. *South Pacific* 58. *The Sound of Music* 65, many other complete scores and single songs.

Rodney, Red (1928–1994) (Robert Chudnik)
American jazz trumpeter and bandleader, best known for his association with alto saxophonist Charlie Parker. He was an adviser on Clint Eastwood's biopic of Parker, *Bird*, in which he was played by Michael Zelniker.

Rodrigues, Percy (1924–)
Canadian character actor.

The Plainsman 67. The Sweet Ride 68. The Heart is a Lonely Hunter 68. Genesis II (TV) 73. Brainwaves 82, etc.

Rodriguez, Estelita (1913–1966)
Pert Cuban-born actress and singer, mainly in Republic's musicals and westerns as a Mexican. Performing on radio in Havana from the age of nine, she went to the US in the late 20s, beginning by working in nightclubs and theatre. She was sometimes billed as Estelita. Married actor Grant WITHERS.

Along the Navajo Trail 45. Mexicana 45. Old Los Angeles 48. The Golden Stallion 49. Belle of Old Mexico 50. Federal Agent at Large 50. California Passage 50. Hit Parade of 1951 50. Cuban Fireball 51. In Old Amarillo 51. Havana Rose 51. Pals of the Old West 51. The Fabulous Senorita 52. Tropical Heat Wave 52. South Pacific Trail 52. Tropic Zone 53. Sweethearts on Parade 53. Rio Bravo 59. Jesse James Meets Frankenstein's Daughter 56, etc.

Rodriguez, Robert (1968–)
American director, screenwriter, and editor, born in San Antonio, Texas, whose first film was made in Mexico at a reported cost of $7,000 and picked up by Columbia Pictures for distribution.

Autobiography: 1995, *Rebel without a Crew*.

El Mariachi 92. Roadracers (TV) 94. Desperado 95. Four Rooms (co-d) 95. From Dusk till Dawn 95. The Faculty 98, etc.

Roeg, Nicolas (1928–)
British cinematographer and director. Married actress Theresa Russell.

AS CINEMATOGRAPHER: The System 63. Nothing but the Best 64. The Caretaker 66. Petulia 67. A Funny Thing Happened on the Way to the Forum 68. *Far from the Madding Crowd* 68, etc.

AS DIRECTOR: Performance (co-d) 72. *Walkabout* 72. *Don't Look Now* 73. The Man Who Fell to Earth 76. Bad Timing 79. Eureka 83. Insignificance 85. Castaway 87. Aria (co-d) 87. Track 29 87. The Witches 90. Cold Heaven 92. Heart of Darkness (TV) 94. Two Deaths 95. Full Body Massage (TV) 95. Samson and Delilah (TV) 96, etc.

❝ They said, even the bath water's dirty. – *N.R. on Warner's reaction to Performance*

Roemer, Michael (1928–)
German-born independent film director and academic, in America. His feature *The Plot against Harry* 69 was released to good reviews after 20 years on the shelf.

A Touch of the Times (d) 49. The Inferno (co-d) 62. *Nothing but a Man* (co-d) 65. The Plot against Harry (wd) 69 (released 89). Pilgrim Farewell (wd) 80. Haunted (d) (TV) 84, etc.

Roemheld, Heinz (1901–1985)
German musical director, long in Hollywood.

Golden Harvest 33. The Invisible Man 33. Imitation of Life 34. Dracula's Daughter 36. A Child Is Born 40. The Strawberry Blonde (AAN) 41. Blues in the Night 41. Yankee Doodle Dandy (AA) 42. Shine On, Harvest Moon 44. Heaven Only Knows 47. The Lady from Shanghai 48. Rogues of Sherwood Forest 50. Ruby Gentry 53. The 5,000 Fingers of Dr T. (co-m) 53. The Creature Walks among Us 56. The Monster that Challenged the World 57. Ride Lonesome 59. Lad: A Dog 61, many others.

Roëves, Maurice (1937–)
English character actor, stage director and television writer. Born in Sunderland, Tyne and Wear, he studied at the Royal College of Drama, Glasgow.

The Fighting Prince of Donegal 66. Ulysses 67. Oh What a Lovely War 69. A Day at the Beach 70. When Eight Bells Toll 71. Young Winston 72. The Eagle Has Landed 76. SOS Titanic 79. Escape to Victory/Victory 81. Who Dares Wins 82. North and South Book II (TV) 86. The Big Man 90. Hidden Agenda 90. The Last of the Mohicans (US) 92. Judge Dredd (US) 95. Moses (TV) 96. Acid House 98. Forgive and Forget 00. Beautiful Creatures 00, etc.

TV series: Tutti Frutti 87. Danger UXB 87. Rab C. Nesbitt 92.

Rogell, Albert S. (1901–1988)
American producer and director of second features. Born in Oklahoma City, Oklahoma, he worked as a stage electrician and carpenter, and as an editor and cameraman, and was in Hollywood from 1917.

Señor Daredevil 26. Mamba 30. Riders of Death Valley 32. The Last Warning 38. Start Cheering 38. Argentine Nights 40. Private Affairs 40. The Black Cat 41. Tight Shoes 41. Priorities on Parade 42. Hit Parade of 1943 43. War of the Wildcats 43. Earl Carroll Sketchbook 46. Heaven Only Knows 47. Northwest Stampede 48. Song of India 49. The Admiral Was a Lady (&p) 50. Before I Wake (GB) 54. Men Against Speed 58, many others.

Rogers, Charles (c. 1890–1960)
Diminutive English music-hall comedian who had a long association with Laurel and Hardy as gag-man, screenwriter, and director. He played bit parts in several of their films, and also co-starred with Harry Langdon in a couple of comedies.

Two Tars (a) 28. Habeas Corpus (a) 28. The Devil's Brother (co-d) 33. Me and My Pal (co-d) 33. Going Bye-Bye! (d) 34. Them Thar Hills (d) 34. Babes in Toyland (co-d) 34. The Bohemian Girl (co-d) 36. Way out West (co-w) 37. Blockheads (co-w) 38. The Flying Deuces (co-w) 39. A Chump at Oxford (co-w) 40. Saps at Sea (co-w) 40. Misbehaving Husbands (a) 40. Double Trouble (a) 41. The Dancing Masters (a) 43, etc.

Rogers, Charles 'Buddy' (1904–1999)
American light leading man of the 20s and 30s; married actress Mary PICKFORD in 1936.

Fascinating Youth 26. Wings 27. Abie's Irish Rose 29. Paramount on Parade 30. Varsity 30. Young Eagles 31. This Reckless Age 32. Old Man Rhythm 35. Once in a Million 36. This Way Please 38. Golden Hooves 41. Mexican Spitfire's Baby 43. Don't Trust Your Husband 48, many others.

Rogers, Eric (–1981)
English composer who scored many of the Carry On movies.

The Iron Maiden 62. Carry On Regardless (co-m) 62. Carry On Cabby 63. Carry On Spying 64. Carry On Cleo 64. Carry On Cowboy 65. Carry On Screaming 66. Carry On – Don't Lose Your Head 66. Carry On Doctor 68. Carry On up the Khyber 68. Carry On Again Doctor 69. Assault/In the Devil's Garden 70. Quest for Love 71. Carry On Abroad 72. Carry On Behind 75. Carry On Emmannuelle 78, etc.

Rogers, Ginger (1911–1995) (Virginia McMath)
American leading actress, comedienne and dancer, affectionately remembered for her 30s musicals with Fred ASTAIRE. Former band singer; then brief Broadway experience before being taken to Hollywood.

Autobiography: 1991, *Ginger, My Story*.

Biography: 1996, *Shall We Dance: The Life of Ginger Rogers* by Sheridan Morley.

■ Young Man of Manhattan 30. Queen High 30. The Sap from Syracuse 30. Follow the Leader 30. Honor among Lovers 31. The Tip Off 31. Suicide Fleet 31. Carnival Boat 32. The Tenderfoot 32. The Thirteenth Guest 32. Hat Check Girl 32. You Said a Mouthful 32. *42nd Street* (as Anytime Annie) 33. Broadway Bad 33. Gold Diggers of 1933. Professional Sweetheart 33. A Shriek in the Night 33. Don't Bet on Love 33. Sitting Pretty 33. *Flying Down to Rio* 33. Chance at Heaven 33. Rafter Romance 34. Finishing School 34. Twenty Million Sweethearts 34. Change of Heart 34. Upperworld 34. *The Gay Divorcee* 34. Romance in Manhattan 34. Roberta 35. Star of Midnight 35. *Top Hat* 35. In Person 35. *Follow the Fleet* 36. Swing Time 36. Shall We Dance 36. *Stage Door* 37. Having Wonderful Time 38. Vivacious Lady 38. Carefree 38. The Story of Vernon and Irene Castle 39. *Bachelor Mother* 39. Fifth Avenue Girl 39. The Primrose Path 40. Lucky Partners 40. *Kitty Foyle* (AA) 40. Tom Dick and Harry 41. *Roxie Hart* 42. Tales of Manhattan 42. The Major and the Minor 42. Once Upon a Honeymoon 42. Tender Comrade 43. Lady in the Dark 44. I'll Be Seeing You 44. Weekend at the Waldorf 45. Heartbeat 46. Magnificent Doll 46. It Had to Be You 47. The Barkleys of Broadway 49. Perfect Strangers 50. Storm Warning 50. The Groom Wore Spurs 51. We're Not Married 52. Monkey Business 52. Dreamboat 52. Forever Female 53. Black Widow 54. Twist of Fate/Beautiful Stranger 54. Tight Spot 55. The First Travelling Saleslady 56. Teenage Rebel 56. Oh Men Oh Women 57. The Confession 64. Harlow (electronovision) 64.

✪ For being everybody's favorite working girl of the 30s; and for being so unarguably right with Fred Astaire. *The Gay Divorcee*.

❝ He gives her class and she gives him sex. – *Katharine Hepburn of Astaire and Rogers*

They're not going to get my money to see the junk that's made today. – *G.R., 1983*

Famous line (*Young Man of Manhattan*) 'Cigarette me, big boy.'

Rogers, Jean (1916–1991) (Eleanor Lovegren)
American light leading lady of the 30s and 40s. Born in Belmont, Massachusetts, she was a former New England beauty queen.

Eight Girls in a Boat 34. Flash Gordon 36. My Man Godfrey 36. Night Key 37. Flash Gordon's Trip to Mars 38. Hotel for Women 39. Heaven with a Barbed Wire Fence 40. Charlie Chan in Panama 40. Dr Kildare's Victory 42. Whistling in Brooklyn 43. Hot Cargo 46. Backlash 47. The Second Woman 51, etc.

Rogers, Maclean (1899–1962)
British director, mainly of low-budget features for which he often wrote his own unambitious scripts.

The Third Eye 29. Busman's Holiday 36. Old Mother Riley Joins Up 39. Gert and Daisy's Weekend 42. Variety Jubilee 43. The Trojan Brothers 45. Calling Paul Temple 48. The Story of Shirley Yorke 49. Johnny on the Spot 54. Not So Dusty 56. Not Wanted on Voyage 57. Not a Hope in Hell 60, many others.

Rogers, Mimi (1956–)
American leading actress. She was formerly married to actor Tom CRUISE.

Blue Skies Again 83. Gung Ho 86. Someone to Watch Over Me 87. Street Smart 87. Hider in the House 89. The Mighty Quinn 89. Desperate Hours 90. The Doors 91. Wedlock 91. The Rapture 92. White Sands 92. Dark Horse 92. Shooting Elizabeth 92. Monkey Trouble 94. Killer 94. Reflections on a Crime 94. Far from Home: The Adventures of Yellow Dog 95. Full Body Massage (TV) 95. Wild Bill 95. Bulletproof Heart 95. Trees Lounge 96. The Mirror Has Two Faces 96. Tricks 97. Weapons of Mass Distraction (TV) 97. Austin Powers: International Man of Mystery 97. Lost in Space 98, etc.

TV series: The Rousters 83–84. Paper Dolls 84.

Rogers, Paul (1917–)
British character actor, on stage from 1938, occasional films from 1932.

Beau Brummell 53. Our Man in Havana 59. The Trials of Oscar Wilde 60. No Love for Johnnie 61. Billy Budd 62. Life for Ruth 62. The Prince and the Pauper 62. The Wild and the Willing 63. The Third Secret 64. He Who Rides a Tiger 65. A Midsummer Night's Dream 68. The Looking Glass War 69. Three into Two Won't Go 69. The Reckoning 69. I Want What I Want 72. The Homecoming 73. The Abdication 75. Mr Quilp 75. Nothing Lasts Forever 83. The Tenth Man (TV) 88, etc.

Rogers, Peter (1916–)
British producer in films from 1942; wrote and co-produced many comedies during 40s and early 50s; conceived and produced the *Carry On* series.

Rogers, Roy (1912–1998) (Leonard Slye)
American singing cowboy star, usually seen with horse Trigger (1932–65). Varied early experience; formed 'Sons of the Pioneers' singing group; in small film roles from 1935, a star from 1938 till 1953. Married actress Dale EVANS, his second wife, in 1947.

Autobiography: 1994, *Happy Trails*.

Under Western Skies 38. The Carson City Kid 40. Dark Command 40. Robin Hood of the Pecos 42. The Man from Music Mountain 44. Brazil 44. Hollywood Canteen 44. Along the Navajo Trail 46. Roll On Texas Moon 47. My Pal Trigger 46. Bells of St Angelo 47. Hit Parade of 1947 47. Under California Stars 48. Night Time in Nevada 49. Trail of Robin Hood 51. Son of Paleface 52. Pals of the Golden West 53. Mackintosh and T.J. 75. Roy Rogers, King of the Cowboys (doc) 91, etc.

TV series: The Roy Rogers Show 51–56.

❝ When my time comes, just skin me and put me right up there on Trigger, just as though nothing had ever changed. – *R.R.*

Nowadays, Roy Rogers seems almost too good. I find myself being moved by his common decency. – *Quentin Tarantino, 2000*

Rogers, Wayne (1933–)
American light actor.

Once in Paris 78. The Top of the Hill (TV) 80. He's Fired, She's Hired (TV) 84. The Gig 85. The Lady from Yesterday (TV) 85. American Harvest (TV) 87. The Killing Time 87. Drop-Out Mother (TV) 88. Bluegrass (TV) 88. The Goodbye Bird 93. Ghosts of Mississippi 96, etc.

TV series: Stagecoach West 60–61. M*A*S*H 72–75. City of Angels 76. House Calls 79–82. Chiefs 83. High Risk 88.

Rogers, Will (1879–1935)
American rustic comedian, ex-Ziegfeld Follies, whose crackerbarrel philosophy almost moved nations. His home in Los Angeles is the centrepiece of the Will Rogers State Park.

When he was killed, Rogers had signed to play Dr Dafoe, who delivered the Dionne Quins, in *The Country Doctor*.

Autobiography: 1927, *There's Not a Bathing Suit in Russia*.

Biography: 1953, *Our Will Rogers* by Homer Croy. 1974, *Will Rogers, the Man and His Times* by Richard M. Ketchum. 1996, *American Original: A Life of Will Rogers* by Ray Robinson.

Biopic: 1952, *The Story of Will Rogers* (starring his son).

■ Laughing Bill Hyde 18. Almost a Husband 19. Water Water Everywhere 19. *Jubilo* 19. Jes' Call Me Jim 20. The Strange Boarder 20. Scratch My Back 20. A Poor Relation 20. Cupid the Cowpuncher 20. Honest Hutch 20. Guile of Women 21. Boys Will Be Boys 21. An Unwilling Hero 21. Doubling for Romeo 21. One Glorious Day 21. The Headless Horseman 22. The Ropin' Fool 22. One Day in 365 22. Hustling Hank 22. Uncensored Movies 22. Fruits of Faith 22. Just Passing Through 23. Gee Whiz Genevieve 23. Highbrow Stuff 23. Family Fits 23. The Cake Eater 24. Big Moments from Little Pictures 24. Don't Park There 24. The Cowboy Sheik 24. Going to Congress 24. Our Congressman 24. A Truthful Liar 24. Two Wagons 24. A Texas Steer 27. Tiptoes 27. They Had to See Paris 29. Happy Days 30. So This is London 30. Lightnin' 30. A Connecticut Yankee 31. Young as You Feel 31. Ambassador Bill 31. Business and Pleasure 32. Too Busy to Work 32. *State Fair* 33. Doctor Bull 33. Mister Skitch 33. *David Harum* 34. *Handy Andy* 34. *Judge Priest* 34. County Chairman 35. *Life Begins at Forty* 35. Doubting Thomas 35. In Old Kentucky 35. *Steamboat round the Bend* 35.

✪ For establishing the wisdom of the common man. *Judge Priest*.

❝ There's only one thing that can kill the movies, and that's education. – *W.R.*

When you put down the good things you ought to have done, and leave out the bad things you did do – that's Memoirs. – *W.R.*

Rogosin, Lionel (1924–2000)
American documentarist. Born in new York, he studied at Yale and worked as a chemical engineer before producing and directing films on social themes. He also ran the influential Bleecker Street cinema in Greenwich Village in the 60s, which showed independent and experimental films..

On the Bowery (AAN) 56. *Come Back Africa* 59. Good Times Wonderful Times 66. Black Roots 70. Black Fantasy 72. Woodcutters of the Deep South 73. The Long Walk of Nelson Mandela (TV) 99, etc.

Rohmer, Eric (1920–) (Jean Maurice Scherer)
French director of rarefied conversation pieces.

Le Signe du Lion 59. La Boulangère de Monceau 63. La Carrière de Suzanne 64. La Collectionneuse 67. Ma Nuit chez Maud (AAN) 69. Le Genou de Claire 70. Love in the Afternoon 72. The Marquise of O 76. Perceval 78. The Aviator's Wife 81. Pauline at the Beach 83. Full Moon in Paris 84. Summer 86. Girlfriends and Boyfriends/L'Ami de Mon Amie 87. Four Adventures of Reinette and Mirabelle/Quatre Aventures de Reinette et Mirabelle 87. Springtime/Conte de Printemps 90. A Winter's Tale/Conte d'Hiver 92. L'Arbre, Le Maire et La Médiathèque 93. Les Rendez-Vous de Paris 95. A Summer's Tale/Conte d'été 96. An Autumn Tale/Conte d'Automne 98, etc.

Rohmer, Sax (1883–1959) (Arthur Sarsfield Ward)
British novelist, the creator of the much-filmed Dr Fu Manchu. A former journalist, he also wrote the lyrics for music-hall songs and the book of a musical, *Round in Fifty*, starring George ROBEY. In 1955 he sold the film, radio and TV rights in his Fu Manchu books for $4m.

Rohrig, Walter (1893–1945)
German art director whose expressionist style was influential.

Cabinet of Dr Caligari/Das Cabinet des Dr Caligari 19. The Golem/Der Golem 20. Destiny/Der Müde Tod 21. The Last Laugh/Der Letzte Mann 24. Faust 26. Luther 27. Looping the Loop/Die Todesschleife 28. The Wonderful Lie of Nina Petrowna/Die Wunderbare Lüge der Nina Petrowna 29. Manolescu 29. Congress Dances/Der Kongress Tanzt 31. Refugees/Flüchtlinge 33. Capriccio 38. Rembrandt 42, etc.

Roizman, Owen (1936–)
American cinematographer.

The French Connection (AAN) 71. Play It Again Sam 72. The Exorcist (AAN) 73. The Taking of Pelham One Two Three 74. The Stepford Wives 75. Network (AAN) 76. Straight Time 78. The Electric Horseman 79. The Black Marble 80. True Confessions 81. Absence of Malice 81. Taps 81. Tootsie (AAN) 82. Vision Quest 85. I Love You to Death 90. Havana 90. The Addams Family 91. Grand Canyon 92. Wyatt Earp (AAN) 94. French Kiss 95, etc.

Roland, Gilbert (1905–1994) (Luis Antonio Damaso de Alonso)
Mexican leading man, trained as bullfighter, who gatecrashed Hollywood in the mid-20s and became immediately popular.

The Plastic Age (debut) 25. Camille 27. Men of the North 29. Call Her Savage 32. *She Done Him Wrong* 33. Last Train from Madrid 37. Juarez 39. The Sea Hawk 40. My Life with Caroline 41. Isle of Missing Men 42. Captain Kidd 45. Pirates of Monterey 47. Riding the California Trail 48. *We Were Strangers* 49. The Furies 50. The Bullfighter and the Lady 51. The Bad and the Beautiful 52. Beyond the Twelve Mile Reef 53. The Racers 54. Treasure of Pancho Villa 56. Guns of the Timberland 58. The Big Circus 59. Cheyenne Autumn 64. The Reward 65. The Poppy is also a Flower (TV) 66. Johnny Hamlet 72. Running Wild 73. Islands in the Stream 77. The Black Pearl 77. Deadly Sunday 82. Barbarosa 82, many others.

Roland, Ruth (1893–1937)
American leading lady, a silent serial queen.

The Red Circle 15. The Neglected Wife 17. Hands Up 18. Tiger's Trail 19, etc.

FEATURES: While Father Telephoned 13. The Masked Woman 26. Reno 30. From Nine to Nine 36, many others.

Rolfe, Guy (1915–)
Lean British leading man and character actor, former racing driver and boxer. Married actress Jane Aird.

Hungry Hill (debut) 46. Nicholas Nickleby 47. Uncle Silas 47. Broken Journey 47. Portrait from Life 49. *The Spider and the Fly* 50. Prelude to Fame 51. Ivanhoe 52. King of the Khyber Rifles 54. It's Never Too Late 56. Snow White and the Three Stooges 62. Taras Bulba 62. Mr Sardonicus 62. The Fall of the Roman Empire 64. The Alphabet Murders 65. The Land Raiders 69. Nicholas and Alexandra 71. And Now the Screaming Starts 73. Dolls 87. Puppet Master III: Toulon's Revenge 91, etc.

Rolfe, Sam (1924–1993)
American screenwriter and television producer, best known for creating the TV series *Have Gun Will Travel* 57–63 and *The Man from U.N.C.L.E.* 64–68.

The Naked Spur (AAN) 53. Target Zero 55. The McConnell Story 55. Bombers B-52 57, etc.

Features edited from episodes of The Man from U.N.C.L.E.: To Trap a Spy 66. The Spy with My Face 66. One Spy Too Many 66. The Karate Killers 67. The Spy in the Green Hat 67. One of Our Spies Is Missing 67. The Helicopter Spies 67. How to Steal the World 68.

Rollin, Jean (1940–)
French screenwriter and director, mainly of horror and exploitation movies containing scenes of sex and sadism, tinged with surrealism.

Vampire Women/Les Femmes Vampires 67. The Naked Vampire/La Vampire Nue 69. Terror of the Vampires/Les Frissons des Vampires 70. Requiem for a Vampire/Virgins and Vampires/Requiem pour une Vampire 71. La Rose de Fer 73. Lèvres de Sang 75. Once upon a Virgin/Phantasmes 76. Pesticide/Les Raisins de la Mort 78. Fascination 78. Zombie Lake/Lake of the Living Dead/El Lago de los Muertos Vivientes 80. The Living Dead Girl/La Morte Vivante 82. Les Meurtrières 83, etc.

Rollins Jnr, Howard (1951–1996)
American leading actor.

Ragtime (AAN) 81. A Soldier's Story 84. The Children of Times Square (TV) 86. Dear America: Letters Home from Vietnam 87. Johnnie Gibson F.B.I. (TV) 87. For Us, the Living (TV) 88. On the Block 89, etc.

TV series: In the Heat of the Night 88–89.

Romain, Yvonne (1938–) (Yvonne Warren)
British leading lady.

The Baby and the Battleship 56. Seven Thunders 57. Corridors of Blood 58. Chamber of Horrors 60. Curse of the Werewolf 61. Village of Daughters 61. Devil Doll 63. The Brigand of Kandahar 65. The Swinger (US) 66. Double Trouble (US) 67. The Last of Sheila 73, etc.

Roman, Leticia (1939–)
American leading lady of the 60s.

Pirates of Tortuga 61. Gold of the Seven Saints 61. The Evil Eye (It.) 62. Fanny Hill 64, etc.

Roman, Ruth (1924–1999)
American actress; leading lady of the 50s, then a plumpish character player.

Ladies Courageous 44. Jungle Queen 45. You Came Along 45. A Night in Casablanca 45. The Big Clock 48. Good Sam 48. *The Window* 49. Champion 49. Barricade 50. Three Secrets 50. Lightning Strikes Twice 51. *Strangers On a Train* 51. Maru Maru 52. Blowing Wild 53. Down Three Dark Streets 54. The Far Country 55. Joe Macbeth 56. Five Steps to Danger 57. Bitter Victory 58. Desert Desperadoes 59. Look in Any Window 61. Love Has Many Faces 65. The Baby 73. Go Ask Alice (TV) 73. Day of the Animals 77. Echoes 83, etc.

TV series: *The Long Hot Summer* 65–66. Knots Landing 86.

Romance, Viviane (1912–1991) (Pauline Ortmans)
French leading lady of the 30s and 40s.

La Belle Equipe 35. Gibraltar 37. The White Slave 38. Blind Venus 39. Box of Dreams 39. Carmen 42. Panique 46. Maya 50. Flesh and Desire

53. Pleasures and Vices 56. Mélodie en Sous-Sol 63, etc.

Romanoff, Mike (1890–1972) (Harry Gerguson)
Amiable American con man who posed as a Russian prince (but 'renounced' his title in 1958). Best known as proprietor of Hollywood's most famous and expensive restaurant. Played occasional bit parts.

Arch of Triumph 48. Do Not Disturb 65. Tony Rome 67, etc.

❝ No one has ever discovered the truth about me – not even myself. – *M.R.*

A rogue of uncertain nationality. – *Scotland Yard*

Romberg, Sigmund (1887–1951)
Hungarian composer of light music. Scores include *The Desert Song* 29 and 43, *New Moon* 31 and 40, *Maytime* 37, *Balalaika* 39, *The Student Prince* 54. (Most of these began as stage operettas.) José Ferrer played him in a biopic, *Deep in My Heart* 54.

Rome, Stewart (1886–1965) (Septimus William Ryott)
British stage matinée idol who made several romantic films in the 20s and later appeared in character roles.

The Prodigal Son 25. Sweet Lavender 26. The Gentleman Rider 27. Thou Fool 28. Dark Red Roses 29. The Man Who Changed His Name 30. Designing Women 33. Men of Yesterday 34, Wings of the Morning 37. Banana Ridge 41. The White Unicorn 47. Woman Hater 48, etc.

Romero, Cesar (1907–1994)
Handsome Latin-American leading man, former dancer and Broadway actor. Also on TV.

The Thin Man 34. Metropolitan 35. Wee Willie Winkie 37. The Return of the Cisco Kid (and others in this series) 39. The Gay Caballero 40. Weekend in Havana 41. Tales of Manhattan 42. Orchestra Wives 42. Coney Island 43. Carnival in Costa Rica 47. That Lady in Ermine 48. Happy Go Lovely 51. Prisoners of the Casbah 53. Vera Cruz 54. The Racers 55. The Leather Saint 56. Villa 58. Two on a Guillotine 64. Marriage on the Rocks 65. Batman 66. Hot Millions 68. Crooks and Coronets (GB) 69. The Midas Run (GB) 69. A Talent for Loving 69. Now You See Him Now You Don't 72. The Strongest Man in the World 74. The Big Push 77. Mission to Glory 80. Judgement Day 88. Simple Justice 90, etc.

TV series: Passport to Danger 56. *Batman* (as the Joker) 65–67.

Romero, Eddie (1924–)
Filipino director of low-budget exploitation movies.

The Day of the Trumpet 57. Moro Witch Doctor 64. Mad Doctor of Blood Island 68. Best of the Yellow Night 70. Twilight People 72. Beyond Atlantis 73. The Woman Hunt 75. Sudden Death 77. Desire 83. The White Force 88. A Case of Honor 88, etc.

Romero, George (1940–)
American director of exploitation pictures.

Night of the Living Dead 68. The Crazies 73. Hungry Wives 73. Zombies 78. Martin 79. Knightriders 81. Creepshow 82. Day of the Dead 85. Creepshow 2 (w) 87. Monkey Shines (wd) 88. Two Evil Eyes/Due Occhi Diabolici (co-d) 89. Tales from the Darkside: The Movie (co-w) 90. Night of the Living Dead (w, p) 90. The Dark Half 91. Tales from the Darkside: The Movie II (co-w) 92, etc.

❝ Just because I'm showing somebody being disembowelled doesn't mean I have to get heavy and put a message round it. – *G.R.*

Romero, Manuel (1891–1954)
Prolific Argentinian director, playwright and lyricist. A former journalist, he began his career in the 30s in Paris. He was notable for his output, which included some 150 plays and as many songs, as well as more than 50 films. He made the first Argentinian gangster movie, *Outlaw*/Fuera de la Ley, in 1937.

Romm, Mikhail (1901–1971)
Russian director.

Boule de Suif 34. *Lenin in October* 37. Thirteen 37. Lenin in 1918 39. Dream/Mechta 43. The Russian Question 48. Nine Days of One Year 61. Ordinary Fascism 64, etc.

Rommel, Field Marshal Erwin (1891–1944)
German soldier, a worthy adversary for the Eighth Army in World War II. He killed himself in 1944 after being accused of complicity in the plot against Hitler. In films he was melodramatically impersonated by Erich Von Stroheim in 1943 in *Five Graves to Cairo*, and more soberly in 1951 by James Mason in *The Desert Fox* (also in 1953 in *The Desert Rats*). Other minor portrayals were by Albert Lieven in *Foxhole in Cairo*, by Gregory Gaye in *Hitler*, by Werner Hinz in *The Longest Day*, by Christopher Plummer in *The Night of the Generals*, by Karl Michael Vogler in *Patton*, and by Wolfgang Preiss in *Raid on Rommel*.

Romney, Edana (1919–) (E. Rubenstein)
South African-born leading lady, in three British films of the 40s.

■ East of Piccadilly 41. Alibi 42. Corridor of Mirrors 48.

Ronet, Maurice (1927–1983)
French leading man.

Rendezvous de Juillet 49. La Sorcière 56. He Who Must Die 56. Lift to the Scaffold 57. Carve Her Name with Pride (GB) 58. Plein Soleil 59. Rendezvous de Minuit 61. *Le Feu Follet* 63. Enough Rope 63. The Victors 63. La Ronde 64. Three Weeks in Manhattan 65. Lost Command 66. The Champagne Murders/La Scandale 67. The Road to Corinth 68. How Sweet It Is (US) 68. L'Infidèle 69. Qui? 73. The Marseilles Contract 74. Bloodline 79. La Balance 83, etc.

Roodt, Darrell (1962–)
South African director and screenwriter.

Place of Weeping 86. City of Blood 87. Jobman (& co-w) 90. Sarafina 92. Father Hood (US) 93. Cry the Beloved Country 95. Dangerous Ground (US) 97, etc.

Rooker, Michael (1955–)
American character actor, usually as a heavy.

Eight Men Out 88. Mississippi Burning 88. Sea of Love 89. Music Box 89. Henry: Portrait of a Serial Killer 90. Days of Thunder 90. The Dark Half 91. JFK 91. Cliffhanger 93. The Hard Truth 94. Tombstone 94. Bastard out of Carolina (TV) 96. The Trigger Effect 96. Rosewood 96. Keys to Tulsa 96. Back to Back 96. Deceiver 97. The Replacement Killers 98. Brown's Requiem 98, etc.

Rooks, Conrad (1934–)
American experimental director.

■ Chappaqua 66. Siddhartha 72.

Room, Abram (1894–1976)
Russian director, former journalist, with stage experience.

In Pursuit of Moonshine 24. The Haven of Death 26. Bed and Sofa 27. The Ghost that Never Returns 29. The Five Year Plan 30. Invasion 44. Silver Dust 53, etc.

Rooney, Mickey (1920–) (Joe Yule Jnr)
Diminutive, aggressively talented American performer, on stage from the age of two (in parents' vaudeville act). In films from 1926 (short comedies) as Mickey McGuire, then returned to vaudeville; came back as Mickey Rooney in 1932. By the late 30s and early 40s he was the most popular film star in the world, later developing into an accomplished character actor. Married eight times, his wives include actresses Ava Gardner and Martha Vickers. He was given an honorary Oscar in 1938 for 'bringing to the screen the spirit and personification of youth', and in 1982 'in recognition of his 60 years of versatility in a variety of memorable film performances'.

Autobiography: 1965, *I.E.* 1991, *Life Is Too Short*.

My Pal the King 32. The Hide-Out 34. *A Midsummer Night's Dream* (as Puck) 35. *Ah Wilderness* 35. Little Lord Fauntleroy (not in title role) 36. Captains Courageous 37. *A Family Affair* (as Andy Hardy) 37. *Judge Hardy's Children* 38. Love Finds Andy Hardy 38. *Boys' Town* (special AA) 38. The Adventures of Huckleberry Finn 39. *Babes in Arms* (AAN) 39. Young Tom Edison 40. Strike Up the Band 40. Men of Boys' Town 41. Babes on Broadway 41. A Yank at Eton 42. Andy Hardy's Double Life 42. *The Human Comedy* (AAN) 43. Girl Crazy 43. Andy Hardy's Blonde Trouble 44. National Velvet 44. Love Laughs at Andy Hardy 46. Summer Holiday 47. The Fireball 50. A Slight Case of Larceny 53. *The Bold and the Brave* (AAN) 56. Andy Hardy Comes Home 58. Baby Face Nelson 58. The Big Operator 59. Breakfast at Tiffany's 61. It's a Mad Mad Mad Mad World 63. Twenty-Four Hours to Kill 65. Ambush Bay 66. The Extraordinary Seaman 68. Skidoo 68. The Comic 69. Pulp 72. The Domino Principle 77. Pete's Dragon 77. The Magic of Lassie 78. Arabian Adventure 79. The Black Stallion (AAN) 79. *Leave 'em Laughing* (TV) 80. *Bill* (TV) 81. The Fox and the Hound (voice) 81. La Traversée de la Pacifique 82. The Care Bears Movie (voice) 85. Lightning – the White Stallion 86. Rudolph and Frosty's Christmas in July 86. Erik the Viking 89. My Heroes Have Always Been Cowboys 91. Silent Night Deadly Night 5: The Toymaker 91. The Milky Way/La Via Lactea 92. Sweet Justice 92. The Legend of O.B. Taggart (& w) 94. Revenge of the Red Baron 94, many others.

TV series: The Mickey Rooney Show/Hey Mulligan 54. Mickey 64. One of the Boys 81, etc.

✪ For never being counted out. *Babes in Arms*.

❝ I was a fourteen-year-old boy for thirty years. – *M.R.*

I've been through four publics. I've been coming back like a rubber ball for years. – *M.R.*

I just want to be a professional. I couldn't live without acting. – *M.R.*

There may be a little snow on the mountain, but there's a lot of fire in the furnace. – *M.R.*

All the muddy waters of my life cleared up when I gave myself to Christ. – *M.R.*

I didn't ask to be short. I didn't want to be short. I've tried to pretend that being a short guy didn't matter. – *M.R.*

The guys with the power in Hollywood today, the guys with their names above the title, are thieves. They don't make movies, they make deals. Their major function is to cut themselves in for 10 per cent of the gross – off the top, of course – which is why they make movies that cost $50 million. – *M.R.*

His favourite exercise is climbing tall people. – *Phyllis Diller*

A rope-haired, kazoo-voiced kid with a comic strip face. – *James Agee*

Tennessee Williams once told me that he considered Rooney the best actor in the history of the movies. – *Gore Vidal*

Roope, Fay (1893–1961)
American character actress, usually as a tough old lady.

You're in the Navy Now 51. The Day the Earth Stood Still 51. Washington Story 52. Viva Zapata! 52. From Here to Eternity 53. The System 53. Naked Alibi 54. Ma and Pa Kettle at Waikiki 55. The Proud Ones 56. The F.B.I. Story 59, etc.

Roos, Don
American screenwriter and director.

Love Field 92. Single White Female 92. Boys on the Side 95. Diabolique 96. The Opposite of Sex (& d) 98. Bounce (& d) 00, etc.

Roosevelt, Franklin Delano (1882–1945)
American President 1933–45, exponent of the 'New Deal'. He was played by Ralph Bellamy in Dore Schary's play and film of his life, *Sunrise at Campobello* 60, by Capt. Jack Young in *Yankee Doodle Dandy* and by Godfrey Tearle in *The Beginning of the End*. In TV's *Eleanor and Franklin* (1976) he was played by Edward Herrmann, and in *Ike* (1979) by Stephen Roberts.

Roosevelt, Theodore (Teddy) (1858–1919)
American President 1901–1909. His extrovert personality and cheerful bullish manners have been captured several times on screen, notably by John Alexander in *Arsenic and Old Lace* (a parody) and *Fancy Pants*, by Wallis Clark in *Yankee Doodle Dandy*, by John Merton in *I Wonder Who's Kissing Her Now*, by Sidney Blackmer in *My Girl Tisa*, *This is My Affair* and *Buffalo Bill*; and by Brian Keith in *The Wind and the Lion*. In *The Private Files of J. Edgar Hoover* (1978) it was Howard da Silva's turn; Ralph Bellamy had a revised go in *The Winds of War* (1982), and Edward Herrmann again in *Annie* (1982).

Root, Wells (1900–1993)
American screenwriter, a former journalist, who later wrote for television and then taught writing at UCLA.

The Storm 30. Politics (co-w) 31. The Prodigal (co-w) 31. Tiger Shark 32. I Cover the Waterfront (co-w) 33. Black Moon 34. Paris Interlude 34. Pursuit 35. Sworn Enemy 36. The Prisoner of Zenda (co-w) 37. Sergeant Madden 39. Thunder Afloat (co-w) 39. Flight Command (co-w) 40. The Bad Man 41. Mokey (co-w) 42. Tennessee Johnson 42. Salute to the Marines 43. The Man from Down Under 43. Magnificent Obsession 54. Texas across the River 66, etc.

Roquevert, Noël (1894–1973) (N. Benevent)
French character actor, usually as mean-spirited bourgeois.

The Three Must-Get-Theres 22. Cartouche 34. Entrée des Artistes 38. Les Inconnus dans la Maison 42. Le Corbeau 43. Antoine et Antoinette 47. Justice Est Faite 50. Fanfan la Tulipe 52. Les Compagnes de la Nuit 53. The Sheep Has Five Legs 54. Marie Octobre 59. A Monkey in Winter 62, many others.

Rosay, Françoise (1891–1974) (Françoise de Naleche)
Distinguished French actress in films from the mid-20s.

Autobiography: 1974, *La Traversée d'une Vie*.

Gribiche 25. *Le Grand Jeu* 33. *La Kermesse Héroïque* 35. Jenny 36. *Un Carnet de Bal* 37. Les Gens du Voyage 38. *Une Femme Disparait* 41. Johnny Frenchman (GB) 45. Macadam 46. September Affair 50. *The Red Inn* 51. The Thirteenth Letter (US) 51. That Lady (GB) 54. The Seventh Sin (US) 57. Le Joueur 58. The Sound and the Fury (US) 58. The Full Treatment (GB) 60. Up from the Beach (US) 65. Le Piétou 72, etc.

Rose, Bernard
English director and screenwriter.

The Paperhouse 88. Chicago Joe and the Showgirl 89. Candyman 92. Immortal Beloved 94. Leo Tolstoy's Anna Karenina 97. Ivansxtc (To Live and Die in Hollywood) 00, etc.

Rose, Billy (1899–1966)
American nightclub owner and songwriter, husband of Fanny Brice. He was played in *Funny Lady* by James Caan.

Biography: 1968, *Manhattan Primitive* by Earl Rogers.

Rose, David (1910–1990)
London-born composer and pianist, in America from 1914. From the 50s he also worked in television, writing the themes for the series *Bonanza*, *The High Chaparral* and *The Little House on the Prairie*, and in the 70s and 80s scored several TV movies. He was married to Judy Garland (1941–45).

Never a Dull Moment 43. The Princess and the Pirate (AAN) 44. Winged Victory 44. The Underworld Story 50. The Clown 53. Jupiter's Darling 55. Operation Petticoat 59. Please Don't Eat the Daisies 60. Hombre 67. Sam's Son 84, etc.

Rose, David E. (1896–1992)
American producer, in films from 1930, long in charge of United Artists productions. More recently in Britain.

The End of the Affair 55. The Safecracker 58. The House of the Seven Hawks 59, etc.

Rose, George (1920–1988)
British stage and screen character actor, who worked mainly in the US from the mid-60s. Born in Bicester, Oxfordshire, he worked as a secretary and a farmer before studying at the Central School of Speech and Drama. He was on stage, with the Old Vic Company, from 1944, and in films from 1952. He won Tonys for his Broadway performances in the musicals *My Fair Lady* 75 and *Drood* 85. He was beaten to death at his holiday home in the Dominican Republic by four men, including his adopted son and the youth's biological father.

Pickwick Papers 52. Grand National Night 53. The Sea Shall Not Have Them 54. The Night My Number Came Up 54. Brothers in Law 57. Barnacle Bill 57. The Shiralee 57. Cat and Mouse 58. A Night to Remember 58. Jack the Ripper 59. The Devil's Disciple 59. Jet Storm 59. The Flesh and the Fiends 59. Jet Storm 59. Hamlet 64. Hawaii (US) 66. The Pink Jungle 68. A New Leaf 70. From the Mixed-Up Files of Mrs Basil E. Frankweiler 73. Holocaust (TV) 78. The Pirates of Penzance 82, etc.

TV series: Beacon Hill 75.

Rose, Helen (1904–1985)
American costume designer, heading MGM's department from 1942 to 1966.

Coney Island 43. Stormy Weather 43. Hello Frisco, Hello 43. The Harvey Girls 46. Two Sisters from Boston 46. Ziegfeld Follies 46. Till the Clouds Roll By 46. Take Me out to the Ball Game 48. Luxury Liner 48. Words and Music 48. East Side, West Side 49. On the Town 49. Pagan Love Song 50. Father of the Bride 50. Three Little Words 50. The Belle of New York 51. The Great Caruso (AAN) 51. The Bad and the Beautiful (AA) 52. The Merry Widow (AAN) 52. Mogambo 53. Dangerous When Wet 53. Dream Wife (AAN) 53. The Glass Slipper 54. Executive Suite (AAN) 54. It's Always Fair Weather 55. Interrupted Melody (AAN) 55. I'll Cry Tomorrow (AA) 55. Forbidden Planet 56. High Society 56. The Swan 56. The Power and the Prize (AAN) 56. Designing Woman 57. Tip on a Dead Jockey 57. Cat on a Hot Tin Roof 58. The Tunnel of Love 58. Ask Any Girl 59. The Gazebo (AAN) 59. Go Naked in the World 60. Butterfield 8 60. All the Fine Young Cannibals 60. Ada 61. Bachelor in Paradise 61. The Honeymoon Machine 61. The Courtship of Eddie's Father 63. Made in Paris 65. Mister Buddwing (AAN) 65. Made in Paris 66. How Sweet It Is! 68, many others.

Rose, Jack
See Shavelson, Melville.

Rose, Reginald (1921–)
American writer who has created numerous TV plays, also a series, *The Defenders*.
Crime in the Streets 56. *Twelve Angry Men* (AAN) 57. The Man in the Net 58. Man of the West 58. The Wild Geese 78. Somebody Killed Her Husband 78. The Sea Wolves 80. Who Dares Wins 82. Wild Geese II 85, etc.

Rose, William (1918–1987)
American screenwriter who spent some years in Britain.
Once a Jolly Swagman (co-w) 48. The Gift Horse 51. I'll Get You for This 52. *Genevieve* (AAN) 53. *The Maggie* 54. The Lady Killers (AAN) 55. Touch and Go 55. Man in the Sky 56. The Smallest Show on Earth 57. *It's a Mad Mad Mad Mad World* 63. The Russians Are Coming, the Russians Are Coming (AAN) 66. The Flim Flam Man 67. *Guess Who's Coming to Dinner* (AA) 67. The Secret of Santa Vittoria 69, etc.

Rosen, Phil (1888–1951)
Russian-born American director of second features. In films from 1912 as a cameraman with Edison.
The Single Sin 21. The Young Rajah 22. Abraham Lincoln 25. Burning Up Broadway 28. Two-Gun Man 31. Beggars in Ermine 34. Two Wise Maids 37. Double Alibi 40. Forgotten Girls 40. Spooks Run Wild 41. Prison Mutiny 43. Step by Step 46. The Secret of St Ives 49, many others.

Rosenberg, Aaron (1912–1979)
American producer, in Hollywood from 1934; working for Universal from 1946.
Johnny Stool Pigeon 47. Winchester 73 50. The Glenn Miller Story 54. To Hell and Back 55. The Great Man 57. Morituri 65. The Reward 65. Tony Rome 67, many others.

Rosenberg, Philip
American production designer, from the theatre.
The Owl and the Pussycat 70. The Anderson Tapes 71. Child's Play 72. The Gambler 74. The Sentinel 77. The Wiz (AAN) 78. All That Jazz (AA) 79. Eyewitness 80. Daniel 83. The Manhattan Project 86. Moonstruck 87. The January Man 88. Running on Empty 88. Family Business 89. Q & A 90. Other People's Money 91. A Stranger among Us 92. Guilty as Sin 93. The Pelican Brief 93. Night Falls on Manhattan 97. Critical Care 97. A Perfect Murder 98, etc.

Rosenberg, Scott
American screenwriter, closely associated with director Gary Fleder.
Things to Do in Denver When You're Dead 95. Beautiful Girls 96. Con Air 97. Disturbing Behavior 98. Gone In 60 Seconds 00. High Fidelity 00, etc.

Rosenberg, Stuart (1928–)
American director with long TV experience.
■ Murder Inc. 60. Question 7 61. Fame Is the Name of the Game (TV) 66. Asylum for a Spy (TV) 67. *Cool Hand Luke* 67. The April Fools 69. Move 70. W.U.S.A. 70. Pocket Money 72. The Laughing Policeman 73. The Drowning Pool 75. Voyage of the Damned 76. Love and Bullets 78. The Amityville Horror 79. Brubaker 80. The Pope of Greenwich Village 84. Let's Get Harry 86. My Heroes Have Always Been Cowboys 91.

Rosenbloom, David
American editor.
Best Seller 87. Fresh Horses 88. Rudy 93. Blue Chips 94. Moonlight and Valentino 95. A Pyromaniac's Love Story 95. Primal Fear 96. The Peacemaker 97. Deep Impact 98. The Insider (AAN) 99, etc.

Rosenbloom, 'Slapsie' Maxie (1906–1976)
American 'roughneck' comedian, ex-boxer, in occasional comedy films as gangster or punch-drunk type.
Mr Broadway 33. Nothing Sacred 37. Louisiana Purchase 41. Hazard 48. Mr Universe 51. Abbott and Costello Meet the Keystone Kops 55. The Beat Generation 59, etc.

Rosenblum, Ralph (1925–1995)
American editor.
Mad Dog Coll 61. *Fail Safe* 64. The Pawnbroker 65. The Group 66. The Night They Raided Minsky's 67. Goodbye Columbus 69. Bananas 71. Sleeper 73. Love and Death 75. *Annie Hall* 77. The Great Bank Hoax 78. Interiors 78. Stuck on You 83. Forever Lulu 87, etc.

Rosenman, Leonard (1924–)
American composer.
The Cobweb 55. East of Eden 55. Rebel without a Cause 55. Lafayette Escadrille 58. The Chapman Report 62. Fantastic Voyage 66. Hellfighters 68. Beneath the Planet of the Apes 71. Phantom of Hollywood (TV) 74. Race with the Devil 75. *Barry Lyndon* (AAmd) 75. Bound for Glory (AAmd) 76. The Car 77. Lord of the Rings 78. Promises in the Dark 79. Hide in Plain Sight 80. Cross Creek (AAN) 83. Miss Lonelyhearts 83. Heart of the Stag 84. Sylvia 85. Star Trek IV: The Voyage Home (AAN) 86. Robocop 2 90. Ambition 91. Mrs Munck 95, etc.

Rosenthal, Jack (1931–)
British scriptwriter, mainly for television, in which medium he has won many awards.
The Lovers 72. *The Chain* 85. Captain Jack 98, etc.

Rosenthal, Laurence (1926–)
American composer and conductor who now scores TV movies and mini-series.
Yellowneck 55. Naked in the Sun 57. A Raisin in the Sun 61. The Miracle Worker 62. Becket (AAN) 64. Hotel Paradiso 66. The Comedians 67. A Gunfight 70. Man of La Mancha (AAN) 72. The Wild Party 74. Rooster Cogburn 75. The Return of a Man Called Horse 76. Who'll Stop the Rain/Dog Soldiers 78. Meteor 79. Clash of the Titans 81. Heart Like a Wheel 83. Easy Money 83, etc.

Rosher Jnr, Charles
American cinematographer.
■ Pretty Maids All in a Row 71. Semi Tough 77. Three Women 77. A Wedding 78. The Muppet Movie 79. The Onion Field 79. Heartbeeps 81. Independence Day 83. Police Academy 6: City under Siege 89.

Rosher, Charles (1885–1974)
Distinguished American cinematographer.
The Clown 16. The Love Night 20. Smilin' Through 22. *Sparrows* 26. *Sunrise* (AA) 27. *Tempest* 28. What Price Hollywood? 32. Our Betters 33. The Affairs of Cellini 34. Little Lord Fauntleroy 36. White Banners 38. A Child Is Born 40. Kismet 44. *The Yearling* (co-ph) (AA) 46. *Show Boat* 51. Scaramouche 52. Kiss Me Kate 53. Young Bess 54. Jupiter's Darling 55, many others.

Rosi, Francesco (1922–)
Italian director.
La Sfida 57. Salvatore Giuliano (& w) 61. Hands over the City 63. The Moment of Truth 64. More than a Miracle 68. Three Brothers (& w) 82. Christ Stopped at Eboli 82. I Tre Fratelli 80. Bizet's Carmen 84. Chronicle of a Death Foretold/ Crònaca di una Morte Annunciata 87. To Forget Palermo/Dimenticare Palermo 90. The Truce 97, etc.

Rosmer, Milton (1881–1971) (Arthur Milton Lunt)
British stage actor, in many films from 1913.
General John Regan 21. The Passionate Friends 22. The Phantom Light 35. South Riding 38. Goodbye Mr Chips 39. Atlantic Ferry 41. Fame Is the Spur 47. The Monkey's Paw 48. The Small Back Room 49, etc.
AS DIRECTOR: Dreyfus 31. Channel Crossing 32. The Guvnor 36. The Challenge 37, etc.

Ross, Annie (1930–) (Annabelle Short Lynch)
British jazz singer and character actress. Brought up in America, she was a juvenile actress in Hollywood, studied drama in New York, and became a singer in England in the 50s before returning to America to form a jazz vocal trio, Lambert, Hendricks and Ross. From the 70s, she began to act on stage and TV.
Presenting Lily Mars 43. Alfie Darling 75. Superman III 83. Throw Momma from the Train 87. Witchery 88. Basket Case 2 90. Pump Up the Volume 90. Short Cuts 93. Blue Sky (made 91) 94, etc.

Ross, Benjamin (1964–)
English director and screenwriter who studied at the Columbia Film School.
The Young Poisoner's Handbook (co-w, d) 95.
❝ So often you come out of the cinema feeling soothed, patronised, morphined up to the eyeballs or given a jerk-off. It's important that people should take a journey they'd rather not take, and leave with a firecracker up their arse. – *B.R.*

Ross, Betsy King (1923–1989)
American juvenile actress, popular in western series of the 30s opposite such stars as Ken Maynard and Gene Autry. An award-winning trick rider, she later became an anthropologist and writer.
Smoke Lightning 33. Fighting with Kit Carson (serial) 33. In Old Sante Fe 34. Phantom Empire (serial) 35. Radio Ranch 35, etc.

Ross, Diana (1944–)
American singer and actress.
■ *Lady Sings the Blues* (as Billie Holiday) (AAN) 72. Mahogany 75. The Wiz 78. Out of Darkness (TV) 94.

Ross, Frank (1904–1990)
American producer, in Hollywood from early 30s.
Of Mice and Men 39. The Devil and Miss Jones 41. The Robe 53. The Rains of Ranchipur 55. Kings Go Forth 58. Mister Moses 65. Where It's At 70, etc.

Ross, Gary
American screenwriter, director and producer.
Big (co-w) 86. Dave (w) 93. Lassie (co-w) 94. Pleasantville (p, wd) 98, etc.

Ross, Herbert (1927–)
American director and choreographer.
Doctor Dolittle 67. Funny Girl 69, etc.
AS DIRECTOR: Goodbye Mr Chips 69. The Owl and the Pussycat 70. T. R. Baskin 71. Play It Again Sam 72. The Last of Sheila (& p) 73. Funny Lady 75. The Sunshine Boys 75. The Seven Per Cent Solution 76. The Turning Point (AAN) 77. The Goodbye Girl 77. Nijinsky 80. Pennies from Heaven 81. I Ought to Be in Pictures 82. Max Dugan Returns 83. Flashdance 83. Footloose 84. Protocol 84. Dancers 87. The Secret of My Success 87. Steel Magnolias 89. My Blue Heaven 90. True Colors 91. Undercover Blues 93. Boys on the Side 95, etc.

Ross, Joe E. (1905–1982)
Short, fat American comedian with a frazzled manner, mostly on TV.
TV series: Bilko 56–59. Car 54 Where Are You? 61–62. It's about Time 64.

Ross, Katharine (1943–)
American leading lady. Married actor Sam Elliott.
■ Shenandoah 65. Mr Buddwing 66. The Longest Hundred Miles (TV) 66. The Singing Nun 66. Games 67. *The Graduate* (AAN) 67. Hellfighters 68. Tell Them Willie Boy is Here 69. Butch Cassidy and the Sundance Kid 69. Fools 70. Get to Know Your Rabbit 72. They Only Kill Their Masters 72. Le Hasard et la Violence 74. The Stepford Wives 75. Voyage of the Damned 76. Wanted, the Sundance Woman (TV) 77. The Legacy 78. The Betsy 78. The Swarm 78. Murder by Natural Causes (TV) 79. The Final Countdown 80. Murder in Texas (TV) 81. Wrong Is Right 82. The Shadow Riders (TV) 82. Travis McGee (TV) 82. Red-Headed Stranger 86. A Row of Crows 90.

Ross, Lillian (1926–)
American journalist who wrote *Picture*, a fascinating account of the production of *The Red Badge of Courage*.

Ross, Shirley (1909–1975) (Bernice Gaunt)
American pianist and singer who appeared as leading lady in a few films.
The Age of Indiscretion 35. San Francisco 36. *Thanks for the Memory* 38. Paris Honeymoon 39. Kisses for Breakfast 41. A Song for Miss Julie 45, etc.

Ross, Steven (1927–1992) (Steven Rechnitz)
American studio executive, head of Warner from 1967 and the man who masterminded the merger of Warner and Time Inc. in 1989 to create the world's largest media and entertainment group. According to Steven Spielberg, he was the model for the portrayal of Schindler in *Schindler's List*.
Biography: 1992, *Master of the Game* by Connie Bruck.

Ross, William
American composer and orchestrator.
One Good Cop 91. Look Who's Talking Now 93. Cops and Robbersons 94. Little Rascals 94. Thumbelina 94. The Amazing Panda Adventure 95. Black Sheep 96. The Evening Star 96. Tin Cup 96. My Fellow Americans 96. A Smile Like Yours 97. My Dog Skip 00, etc.

Rossellini, Isabella (1952–)
Italian actress, daughter of Ingrid Bergman and director Roberto Rossellini.
Autobiography: 1997, *Some of Me*.
White Nights 85. Blue Velvet 86. Tough Guys Don't Dance 87. Zelly and Me 88. Cousins 89. Dames Galantes 90. Wild at Heart 90. Ivory Hunters (TV) 90. Death Becomes Her 92. The Pickle 93. The Innocent 93. Fearless 93. Wyatt Earp 94. Immortal Beloved 94. Crime of the Century 96. Big Night 96. The Funeral 96. The Odyssey (TV) 97. Left Luggage (Hol.) 98. Merlin (TV) 98. The Imposters 98. The Sky Will Fall/Il Cielo Cade 00, etc.

Rossellini, Roberto (1906–1977)
Italian director, in films from 1938. Started as writer; co-scripted his own films.
Autobiography: 1993, *My Method: Writings and Interviews*.
Biography: 1987, *Roberto Rossellini* by Peter Brunette.
Open City 45. *Paisa* (co-w, AAN) 46. Germany Year Zero 48. Stromboli 49. Europa 51. General Della Rovere 59. Louis XIV Seizes Power 66. Il Messia 76, many others.

Rossen, Robert (1908–1966)
American writer-producer-director, in Hollywood from 1936 after stage experience.
■ Marked Woman (w) 37. They Won't Forget (w) 37. Racket Busters (w) 38. Dust be My Destiny (w) 39. *The Roaring Twenties* (w) 39. A Child is Born (w) 39. The Sea Wolf (w) 41. Out of the Fog (w) 41. Blues in the Night (w) 41. Edge of Darkness (w) 42. *A Walk in the Sun* (w) 45. The Strange Love of Martha Ivers (w) 46. Desert Fury (w) 47. Johnny O'Clock (wd) 47. *Body and Soul* (d) 47. Treasure of the Sierra Madre (co-w, uncredited) 47. *All the King's Men* (wpd) (AAp, AANw, AANd) 49. The Brave Bulls (pd) 50. Mambo (wd) 54. Alexander the Great (wpd) 56. Island in the Sun (d) 57. They Came to Cordura (wd) 59. *The Hustler* (wpd) (AAN) 61. Billy Budd (co-w) 62. Lilith (wpd) 64.
❝ In retrospect, the dreariness of his direction is remarkably consistent. – *Andrew Sarris, 1968*

Rossi, Franco (1919–2000)
Italian director and screenwriter, who began in the neo-realist tradition. Born in Florence, he studied philosophy and worked in radio before beginning in films as an assistant to Mario Camerini and Renato Castellani. From the early 60s he turned to directing in television.
I Falsari 52. Il Seduttore 54. *Amici per la Pelle*/ Friends for Life 55. Morte di un Amico 60. Smog 62. Quo Vadis (TV) 85, etc.

Rossi-Drago, Eleonora (1925–) (Palmina Omiccioli)
Italian leading lady.
Pirates of Capri 48. Persiane Chiuse 50. Three Forbidden Stories 51. The White Slave 53. Le Amiche 55. Maledetto Imbroglio 59. David and Goliath 59. Under Ten Flags 60. Uncle Tom's Cabin (Ger.) 65. Camille 2000 69, etc.

Rossif, Frédéric (1922–1990)
French documentarist.
Le Temps du Ghetto 61. Mourir à Madrid 62. The Fall of Berlin 65, etc.

Rossington, Norman (1928–1999)
Burly, dependable English character actor of stage and screen. Born in Liverpool, he left school at the age of 14 to become an office boy, and was later a carpenter and a draughtsman. He began in amateur dramatics before training at the Bristol Old Vic theatre school. In the late 50s, when his role as Private 'Cupcake' Cook in the sitcom *The Army Game* was taken over by another actor, there was such a public outcry that he was reinstated in the role. He later acted with the Royal National Theatre and the Royal Shakespeare Company. Married twice. Died of cancer.
A Night to Remember 58. Carry On Sergeant 58. *Saturday Night and Sunday Morning* 60. Go to Blazes 61. The Comedy Man 64. A Hard Day's Night 64. Tobruk (US) 67. Negatives 68. The Charge of the Light Brigade 68. The Adventures of Gerard 70. Casanova (TV) 71. The Search for the Nile (TV) 71. Deathline 72. Go for a Take 72. The Prisoner of Zenda 79. SOS Titanic (TV) 79. Let Him Have It 91. Sharpe's Regiment (TV) 96, etc.
TV series: The Army Game 57-61. Our House 60. The Big Noise 64. Curry and Chips 69. Follow That Dog 74. Spooner's Patch 79-80. Big Jim and the Figaro Club 81.The Nineteenth Hole 89.

Rossio, Terry
American scriptwriter and director, usually in collaboration with Ted Elliott.
Little Monsters 89. Aladdin (& co-d) 92. Puppet Masters 94. Godzilla (story) 98. Small Soldiers 98. The Mask of Zorro (story) 98. Antz (story consultant) 98, etc.

Rossiter, Leonard (1926–1984)
British comic actor.
Billy Liar 62. King Rat 65. Hotel Paradiso 66. The Wrong Box 66. The Whisperers 67. 2001: A Space Odyssey 68. Oliver 68. Otley 68. Barry Lyndon 75. The Pink Panther Strikes Again 77. Rising Damp 79. Britannia Hospital 82. Trail of the Pink Panther 82, etc.
TV series: Rising Damp 77–80. The Fall and Rise of Reginald Perrin 78–80. Tripper's Day 83.

Rosson, Hal (Harold) (1895–1988)
Distinguished American cinematographer. He was married to Jean HARLOW (1933–35).
The Cinema Murder 19. Manhandled 24. Gentlemen Prefer Blondes 28. *Tarzan of the Apes* 32. *The Scarlet Pimpernel* 34. The Ghost Goes West 36. The Garden of Allah (AA) 36. *The Wizard of Oz* 39. Johnny Eager 42. The Hucksters 47. *On the Town* 49. *The Red Badge of Courage* 51. *Singin' in the Rain* 52. The Bad Seed 56. No Time for Sergeants 58. El Dorado 67, many others.

Rossovich, Rick (1958–)
American actor.
The Lords of Discipline 83. Streets of Fire 84. The Terminator 84. Warning Sign 85. Morning After 86. Top Gun 86. Roxanne 87. Let's Get Harry 87. Secret Ingredient 88. The Spellbinder 88. Paint It Black 89. Navy SEALS 90. Tropical Heat 93. New Crime City: Los Angeles 2020 94. Fatally Yours 95. Cover Me 95. Black Scorpion 95. Legend of the Lost Tomb (TV) 97, etc.
TV series: MacGruder & Loud 85. Sons & Daughters 91.

Rota, Nino (1911–1979) (Nino Rinalde)
Italian composer, responsible for innumerable film scores (including all of FELLINI's) as well as operas. He studied at the Milan Conservatory, the Santa Cecilia Academy, and the Curtis Institute of the United States, and for many years was director of the Bari Conservatory.
The Popular Train 33. Zaza 43. Open City 46. My Son the Professor 46. Flight into France 48. *The Glass Mountain* 48. To Live in Peace 48. E Primavera 49. Anna 52. I Vitelloni 53. La Strada 54. Amici per la Pelle 56. *War and Peace* 56. Il Bidone 56. Cabiria 58. La Dolce Vita 59. Plein Soleil 60. Rocco and His Brothers 60. Boccaccio 70 62. Eight and a Half 63. Juliet of the Spirits 65. Shoot Loud, Louder, I Don't Understand 66. Romeo and Juliet 68. Satyricon 69. Waterloo 70. *The Godfather* 72. The Abdication 74. The Godfather Part II (co-m, AA) 74. Casanova 77. Death on the Nile 78. Hurricane 79, many others.

Roth, Ann
American costume designer.
The World of Henry Orient 64. A Fine Madness 66. Up the Down Staircase 67. Midnight Cowboy 69. The Owl and the Pussycat 70. They Might Be Giants 71. Klute 71. The Day of the Locust 74. Mandingo 75. Burnt Offerings 76. The Goodbye Girl 77. Coming Home 78. California Suite 78. Hair 79. Dressed to Kill 80. Nine to Five 80. Only When I Laugh 81. Honky Tonk Freeway 81. The World According to Garp 82. Silkwood 83. Places in the Heart (AA) 84. Heartburn 86. The Unbearable Lightness of Being 87. Working Girl 88. Biloxi Blues 88. January Man 89. Family Business 89. Postcards from the Edge 90. The Bonfire of the Vanities 90. Regarding Henry 91. The Mambo Kings 92. Dave 93. Guarding Tess 94. Wolf 94. Sabrina 95. The Birdcage 96. The English Patient 96. Primary Colors 98. The Talented Mr Ripley (AAN) 99, etc.

Roth, Cecilia (1956–)
Argentinian leading actress, mainly in Spanish films, and most familiar to international audiences in three films directed by Pedro ALMODÓVAR.
The Semester We Loved Kim Novak/El Curso en Que Amamos a Kim Novak 80. Pepi, Luci, Bom and other Girls 80. Tragala, Perro 81. Best Seller 82. Labyrinth of Passions/Laberinto de Pasiones 82. The Secret Garden/El Jardin Secreto 84. The Stranger/Mortifero 87. The Loves of Kafka/Los Amores De Kafka 89. A Place in the World/Un Lugar En El Mundo 92. Ashes From Paradise/Cenizas del Paraiso 97. All About My Mother/Todo Sobre Mi Madre 99, etc.

Roth, Eric
American screenwriter.
The Nickel Ride 75. The Concorde: Airport '79 79. Suspect 87. Memories of Me (co-w) 88. *Forrest Gump* (AA) 94. The Postman 97. The Horse Whisperer 98. The Insider (AAN) 99, etc.

Roth, Gene (1903–1976) (Gene Stuttenroth)
Heavy-set American character actor.
A Game of Death 46. The Baron of Arizona 50. Pirates of the High Seas 50. Red Planet Mars 52. The Farmer Takes a Wife 53. Attack of the Giant Leeches 59, etc.

Roth, Joe (1948–)
American producer and director, former chairman of Twentieth Century-Fox. He was co-founder of the production company Morgan's Creek. In 1994 he became chairman of the Walt Disney Company, leaving in 2000 to head his own production company, Revolution Studios.
■ AS DIRECTOR: Streets of Gold 86. Revenge of the Nerds II 87. Coupe de Ville 90.

Roth, Lillian (1910–1980) (Lillian Rutstein)
American leading lady who began her professional career as the baby in the Educational Pictures trademark. After a few films in the early 30s, personal problems caused her retirement. Her story was filmed in 1955 as *I'll Cry Tomorrow*, with Susan Hayward.
The Love Parade 20. The Vagabond King 30. *Madame Satan* 30. Animal Crackers 30. Sea Legs 31. Ladies They Talk About 33. Take a Chance 33. Communion/Alice, Sweet Alice 77, etc.

Roth, Philip (1933–)
American novelist, somewhat excessively concerned with Jewish guilt and masturbation. *Portnoy's Complaint* and *Goodbye Columbus* were filmed. Formerly married to actress Claire BLOOM.

Roth, Tim (1961–)
British character actor, from the stage.
The Hit 84. A World Apart 87. To Kill a Priest 89. The Cook, the Thief, His Wife and Her Lover 89. Rosencrantz and Guildenstern Are Dead 90. Farendj 90. Vincent and Theo 90. Backsliding 91. Jumpin' at the Boneyard 91. *Reservoir Dogs* 92. The Perfect Husband/La Mujer de Ed Medio 92. Murder in the Heartland (TV) 93. Bodies, Rest & Motion 93. Heart of Darkness (TV) 94. Pulp Fiction 94. Captives 94. Little Odessa 94. Rob Roy (AAN) 95. Four Rooms 95. No Way Home 96. Everyone Says I Love You 96. Gridlock'd 97. Deceiver 98. The Legend of 1900/The Legend of the Pianist on the Ocean (It.) 98. Lucky Numbers 00. Planet of the Apes 01, etc.

Rotha, Paul (1903–1984)
British documentarist and film theorist. With GPO Film Unit in the 30s, later independent. Author of *The Film till Now*, *Documentary Film*, etc.
Shipyard 30. Contact 33. The Rising Tide 33. The Face of Britain 34. The Fourth Estate 40. *World of Plenty* 42. Land of Promise 46. The World Is Rich 48. No Resting Place 50. World without End (co-d) 52. Cat and Mouse 57. *The Life of Adolf Hitler* 62. The Silent Raid 62, etc.

Rothafel, Samuel 'Roxy' (1882–1936) (Samuel Rothapfel)
American showman and movie exhibitor, who was among those responsible for raising the image of cinemas so that they appealed to a middle-class audience in the early 1900s. He insisted on opulence, excellent service and full-scale musical accompaniment to the films shown, as well as providing ballet and orchestral concerts for his patrons. He ran his first movie house in Forest City, Pennsylvania, and by 1914 was managing the 4,000-seater Strand Theater on Broadway, then America's largest, and, later, the Capitol, which had 26 million patrons in its first five years. In 1926, he opened the biggest movie theatre in the world, the Roxy in New York, which seated 6,000 and was built at a cost of $6m. In 1932, he left the Roxy to control the even larger Radio City Music Hall; but he was ill, its opening was a disaster, and his career never had time to recover. Died of a heart attack.
❝ My ancestors were peasants. Not one of them played the violin or eloped with a beautiful Russian opera singer. They just never did anything. – *S.R.*

Rothrock, Cynthia (1961–)
American exponent of martial arts whose mainly Hong Kong-made films tend to be released direct to video, except in Hong Kong.
No Retreat, No Surrender 2 89. China O'Brien 89. Martial Law 90. Karate Cop 91. Lady Dragon 91. Triple Cross 91. Tiger Claws 91. Fast Getaway 91. Rage and Honor 92. Angel of Fury 92. Guardian Angel 93. Fast Getaway II 94. Night Vision 97, etc.

Rothwell, Talbot (1916–1981)
English screenwriter who scripted 20 of the Carry On comedies. He also created the television series *Up Pompeii!* and wrote for TV comedies, including *Before Your Very Eyes*, *Friends and Neighbours*, *Dear Dotty*, and *The Army Game*.
Is Your Honeymoon Really Necessary 53. The Crowded Day 54. Look Before You Laugh 56. Tommy the Toreador (co-w) 59. Make Mine a Million (co-w) 59. Friends and Neighbours 60. Carry On Cabby 63. Carry On Jack 64. Carry On Spying (co-w) 64. Carry On Cleo 64. Carry On Cowboy 65. Carry On Screaming 66. Carry On – Don't Lose Your Head 66. Carry On – Follow That Camel 66. Carry On Doctor 68. Carry On up the Khyber 68. Carry On Again Doctor 69. Carry On Camping 69. Carry On up the Jungle 70. Carry On Loving 70. Carry On Henry 71. Carry On at Your Convenience 71. Carry On Abroad 72. Carry On Matron 72. Carry On Girls 73. Carry On Dick 74, etc.

Rotunno, Giuseppe (1923–)
Italian cinematographer.
Scandal in Sorrento 55. White Nights 57. Anna of Brooklyn 58. The Naked Maja 59. On the Beach 59. The Angel Wore Red 60. Rocco and His Brothers 60. The Best of Enemies 61. The Leopard 62. Yesterday, Today and Tomorrow 63. Anzio 68. The Secret of Santa Vittoria 69. Satyricon 69. Sunflower 70. Carnal Knowledge 71. Man of La Mancha 72. Amarcord 74. Casanova 77. The End of the World 78. All That Jazz (AAN, BFA) 79. Popeye 81. Five Days One Summer 82. And the Ship Sails On 84. China 9, Liberty 37 84. American Dreamer 84. The Assisi Underground 85. Red Sonja 85. Hotel Colonial 87. Julia and Julia 88. Rent-a-Cop 88. Haunted Summer 88. The Adventures of Baron Munchausen 89. Regarding Henry 91. Once upon a Crime 92. Wolf 94. Night and the Moment 94. The Stendhal Syndrome 96, etc.

Rouch, Jean (1917–)
French documentary director, cinematographer, and ethnographer who has used cinéma vérité techniques and non-professional actors, much in the style of Flaherty, to recreate the lives of ordinary people. Apart from his features, he has also made many shorts, from 1946, some of which were compiled to form *Les Fils de L'Eau* 55.
Moi, un Noir 58. Chronicle of a Summer/Chronique d'un été (co-d) 61. Paris Vu par (co-d) 64. Jaguar 67. Petit à Petit 70. Cocorico Monsieur Poulet 77. Dionysos 84. Enigma 87. Boulevards d'Afrique 88. Cantate pour Deux Généraux 90, etc.

Roundtree, Richard (1937–)
American leading man of the 70s.
Shaft 71. Embassy 72. Charley One Eye 72. Shaft's Big Score 72. Earthquake 74. Man Friday 75. Escape to Athena 79. Game for Vultures 79. The Winged Serpent 82. One Down Two to Go 82. The Big Score 83. City Heat 84. Killpoint 84. Opposing Forces 87. Maniac Cop 88. Angel III – the Final Chapter 88. Bad Jim 89. Night Visitor 89. Cry Devil 89. Crack House 89. Bloodfist III: Forced to Fight 91. Black Heart/Nero come il Cuore 91. Deadly Rivals 92. Seven 95. Theodore Rex 95. Once upon a Time … When We Were Colored 96. Original Gangstas 96. Steel 97. Any Place But Home (TV) 97. George of the Jungle 97. Steel 97. Shaft 00, etc.
TV series: Shaft 73. 413 Hope Street 97. Rescue 77 99.

Rounseville, Robert (1914–1974)
American opera singer.
■ Tales of Hoffman 51. Carousel 56.

Rouquier, Georges (1909–1989)
French documentarist.
Le Tonnelier 42. Farrebique 46. Salt of the Earth 50. Lourdes and Its Miracles 56, etc.

Rourke, Mickey (1950–)
Tough, abrasive American actor.
■ 1941 79. Fade to Black 80. Heaven's Gate 80. Body Heat 81. Diner 81. Rumble Fish 83. Eureka 83. The Pope of Greenwich Village 84. *The Year of the Dragon* 85. Nine and a Half Weeks 86. Angel Heart 87. Barfly 87. A Prayer for the Dying 87. Homeboy 88. Johnny Handsome 89. Wild Orchid 90. Desperate Hours 90. Harley Davidson and the Marlboro Man 91. White Sands 92. F.T.W. 94. Fall Time 95. Saints and Sinners 95. Bullet 95. John Grisham's The Rainmaker 97. Buffalo '66 97. Exit in Red 97. Double Team 97. Thursday 98. Shades (Bel.) 99. Out in Fifty 99. Shergar 00. Animal Factory 00. Get Carter 00.
❝ I always knew I'd accomplish something very special – like robbing a bank perhaps. – *M.R.*

Rouse, Russell (1916–1987)
American director and co-writer, usually in partnership with Clarence GREENE.
D.O.A. 50. The Well (AANw) 51. The Thief 52. New York Confidential 55. The Fastest Gun Alive 56. Thunder in the Sun 59. A House Is Not a Home 64. The Oscar 66. Caper of the Golden Bulls 67, etc.

Rousselot, Philippe (1945–)
French cinematographer, now in international films.
Absences Répétées 72. Adam ou le Sang d'Abel 77. Peppermint Soda/Diabolo Menthe 77. Pour Clemence 77. La Drôlesse 79. Diva 82. The Moon in the Gutter/La Lune dans le Caniveau 83. Emerald Forest 85. Thérèse 86. Hope and Glory (AAN) 87. The Bear 89. Dangerous Liaisons 89. Too Beautiful for You/Trop Belle pour Toi 89. We're No Angels 89. Henry and June (AAN) 90. The Miracle 90. Merci la Vie 91. A River Runs through It (AA) 92. Sommersby 93. Queen Margot/La Reine Margot 94. Interview with the Vampire 94. Mary Reilly 96. The People vs. Larry Flynt 96. The Serpent's Kiss (d) 97. Instinct 99. Random Hearts 99, etc.

Routledge, Patricia (1929–)
English character actress and singer, best known for her role as the fearsome social climber Hyacinth Bucket ('pronounced Bouquet') in the TV sitcom *Keeping Up Appearances* 90–95. Born in Birkenhead, she studied at the University of Liverpool and the Bristol Old Vic Theatre School and made her stage debut in 1952, subsequently appearing in dramas, musicals and revues. Won a

Tony for best musical actress on the Broadway stage in 1967.

Victoria Regina (TV) 64. To Sir with Love 67. 30 Is a Dangerous Age, Cynthia 67. The Bliss of Mrs Blossom 68. If It's Tuesday, This Must Be Belgium 69. Lock Up Your Daughters 69. Girl Stroke Boy 71. Doris and Doreen (TV) 78. Talking Heads (TV) 88, etc.

TV series: Victoria Regina (as Queen Victoria) 64. Marjorie and Men 85. Victoria Wood – As Seen on TV 85–86. Hetty Wainthropp Investigates 96–.

❝ My ambition was to be a Go-Ahead headmistress. – *P.R.*

Rowan, Dan (1922–1987)
American comedian, one-half of Rowan and Martin, the other being Dick Martin (1922–). Belatedly successful on TV with *Laugh In* 1968–72, they have not been popular in films.

■ Once upon a Horse 57. The Maltese Bippy 69.

Rowland, Bruce
Australian composer.

The Man from Snowy River 82. Phar Lap 83. Rebel 85. Les Patterson Saves the World 87. Return to Snowy River 88. Cheetah 89. Fast Getaway 91. Lightning Jack 94. Andre 94. Zeus and Roxanne 96. North Star 96, etc.

Rowland, Roy (1910–1995)
American director, mainly of routine features, in Hollywood from the mid-30s. Many shorts, including *Benchley, Pete Smith, Crime Does Not Pay*.

Lost Angel 44. Our Vines Have Tender Grapes 45. *Killer McCoy* 48. *Tenth Avenue Angel* 48. *Scene of the Crime* 49. *Two Weeks with Love* 50. *Bugles in the Afternoon* 53. *The Moonlighter* 53. *Rogue Cop* 53. *The 5,000 Fingers of Doctor T* 53. *Affair with a Stranger* 53. *Many Rivers to Cross* 55. *Hit the Deck* 55. *Meet Me in Las Vegas* 56. *These Wilder Years* 56. *Gun Glory* 57. *Seven Hills of Rome* 58. *The Girl Hunters* 64. *Gunfighters of Casa Grande* 66. *They Called Him Gringo* 68, *many others*.

Rowlands, Gena (1930–) (Virginia Rowlands)
American leading actress, mostly on stage. Married actor-director John CASSAVETES.

The High Cost of Loving 58. A Child is Waiting 62. Lonely are the Brave 62. Tony Rome 67. Faces 68. Minnie and Moskowitz 71. A Woman under the Influence (AAN) 75. Two Minute Warning 76. Opening Night 77. The Brink's Job 78. Gloria (AAN) 80. Love Streams 85. Light of Day 87. Another Woman 88. Montana (TV) 90. Once Around 91. Night on Earth 91. Crazy in Love 92. Silent Cries (TV) 93. Parallel Lives (TV) 94. The Neon Bible 95. Something to Talk About 95. Unhook the Stars 96. She's So Lovely 97. Paulie 98. The Mighty 98. Hope Floats 98. Playing By Heart 98, etc.

TV series: 87th Precinct 61.

Rowlands, Patsy (1934–)
British character comedienne.

In the Doghouse 61. Dateline Diamonds 65. Carry on Loving 70. Carry on Girls 73. Joseph Andrews 76. Tess 79. The Fiendish Plot of Dr Fu Manchu 80, etc.

Roxburgh, Richard
Australian leading actor.

The Riddle of the Stinson (TV) 87. Dead to the World 90. Tracks of Glory 91. Talk 93. Billy's Holiday 95. Doing Time for Patsy Cline 97. Oscar and Lucinda 97. Passion: The Story of Percy Grainger 99, etc.

Roy, Harry (1900–1971)
British bandleader who made two films: *Everything is Rhythm* 36. *Rhythm Racketeer* 37.

Royle, Selena (1904–1983)
American character actress.

The Misleading Lady 32. Mrs Parkington 44. The Fighting Sullivans 44. Gallant Journey 47. Cass Timberlane 47. Joan of Arc 48. Branded 50. Robot Monster 53. Murder Is My Beat 55, etc.

Rozema, Patricia (1958–)
Canadian director and screenwriter.

I've Heard the Mermaids Singing 87. White Room 91. Montreal Sextet (co-d) 91. The Case of the Missing Mother 92. When Night Is Falling 95. Mansfield Park 99, etc.

Rozsa, Miklos (1907–1995)
Hungarian composer, in Hollywood from 1940.

Autobiography: 1982, *A Double Life*.

Knight without Armour 37. *The Four Feathers* 39. *The Thief of Baghdad* (AAN) 40. Lady Hamilton 41. Five Graves to Cairo 43. Double Indemnity (AAN) 44. A Song to Remember 44. The Lost Weekend 45. *Spellbound* (AA) 45. *The Killers* (AAN) 46. Brute Force 47. *A Double Life* (AA) 47. Naked City 48. Adam's Rib 49. The Asphalt Jungle 50. Quo Vadis (AAN) 51. Ivanhoe (AAN) 52. Julius Caesar 53. Moonfleet 55. Lust for Life 56. *Ben Hur* (AA) 59. King of Kings 61. El Cid (AAN) 61. Sodom and Gomorrah 62. The VIPs 63. The Power 67. The Green Berets 68. The Private Life of Sherlock Holmes 70. Providence 77. Fedora 78. The Private Files of J. Edgar Hoover 78. Time after Time 79. Last Embrace 79. Dead Men Don't Wear Plaid 82, many others.

Ruane, John (1952–)
Australian director and screenwriter, from television commercials.

Death in Brunswick 91. That Eye, the Sky 94. Dead Letter Office 98, etc.

Rub, Christian (1887–1956)
Austrian character actor, long in Hollywood. Was the model and voice for Gepetto the wood-carver in Disney's *Pinocchio*.

The Trial of Vivienne Ware 32. The Kiss behind the Mirror 33. A Dog of Flanders 35. Dracula's Daughter 36. Heidi 37. Mad about Music 38. The Great Waltz 38. The Swiss Family Robinson 40. Tales of Manhattan 42. Fall Guy 48. Something for the Birds 52, many others.

Rubell, Paul
American editor.

The Island of Dr Moreau 96. Blade 98. The Insider (AAN) 99, etc.

Ruben, Joseph (1951–)
American director and screenwriter.

The Sister-in-Law (wd) 75. The Pom-Pom Girls (wd) 76. Joyride (wd) 76. Our Winning Season (wd) 78. Gorp (d) 80. Dreamscape (wd) 84. The Stepfather (d) 87. True Believer (d) 89. Sleeping with the Enemy (d) 90. The Good Son (d) 93. Money Train (d) 95. Return to Paradise (d) 98, etc.

Rubens, Alma (1897–1931) (Alma Smith)
American leading lady of the silent screen; her career was prematurely ended by drug addiction.

Intolerance 15. The Firefly of Tough Luck 17. Humoresque 20. Cytherea 24. Fine Clothes 25. Siberia 26. Masks of the Devil 28. Showboat 29, etc.

Rubens, Percival
South African director and screenwriter.

The Foster Gang 64. Three Days of Fire (It.) 67. Mister Kingstreet's War (US) 70. Saboteurs 74. Survival Zone 81. Raw Terror 85. Sweet Murder 90, etc.

Rubin, Bruce Joel (1944–)
American screenwriter and director.

Brainstorm 83. Deadly Friend 86. Ghost (co-w, AA) 90. Jacob's Ladder 90. My Life (& d) 93. Deep Impact (co-w) 98, etc.

Rubinstein, Arthur B.
American composer who also scores many TV movies and series.

Whose Life Is It Anyway? 81. Blue Thunder 83. Wargames 83. Deal of the Century 83. Lost in America 85. Stakeout 87. The Hard Way 91. Another Stakeout 93. Nick of Time 95, etc.

Rubinstein, Artur (1887–1982)
Internationally renowned classical pianist who made guest appearances in occasional films, e.g. *Carnegie Hall*.

Biography: 1996, *Artur Rubinstein: A Life* by Harvey Sachs.

Rubinstein, John (1946–)
American character actor, and occasional composer. Son of Artur Rubinstein.

Getting Straight 70. Zachariah 70. The Wild Pack 72. All Together Now (TV) 75. The Car 77. The Boys from Brazil 78. She's Dressed to Kill (TV) 79. Killjoy (TV) 81. Daniel 83. Someone to Watch over Me 87. Shadow on the Sun (TV) 88. Liberace (TV) 88. Another Stakeout 93. Mercy 95, etc.

TV series: Crazy Like a Fox 84–85.

Ruby, Harry (1895–1974)
American songwriter (with Bert Kalmar). See KALMAR, Bert.

Rudd, Paul (1940–)
American actor, born in Boston, Massachusetts.

Johnny We Hardly Knew Ye (TV) 77. The Betsy 78. Beulah Land (TV) 80. Kung Fu – the Movie (TV) 86, etc.

TV series: Beacon Hill 75. Knots Landing 80–81.

Rudd, Paul (1969–) (aka Paul Stephen Rudd)
American actor. Born in Passaic, New Jersey, to an American father and an English mother, and raised in Overland Park, Kansas, he studied at the University of Kansas and the American Academy of Dramatic Arts in Los Angeles before working in the theatre in Britain.

Halloween: The Curse of Michael Myers 95. Clueless 95. William Shakespeare's Romeo and Juliet 96. The Size of Watermelons 97. The Locusts 97. Overnight Delivery 98. The Object of My Affection 98. Twelfth Night (TV) 98, etc.

TV series: Sisters 91. Wild Oats 94.

Rudd, Steele (1868–1935) (Arthur Hoey Davis)
Australian author whose tales of outback farm and family life in Queensland have enjoyed long-lasting success on stage and screen in Australia. They were first dramatized by actor Bert Bailey, who starred as Dad Rudd in the early films. Theatre director George Whaley also adapted them for the stage and directed a film version in 1995, featuring Leo McKern as Dad Rudd and Joan Sutherland as Mother Rudd.

On Our Selection 20. Rudd's New Selection 21. On Our Selection 32. Grandad Rudd 35. Dad and Dave Come to Town 38. Dave Rudd MP 40. Dad and Dave on Our Selection 95, etc.

Ruddy, Albert S. (1934–)
American producer.

The Godfather 72. The Longest Yard 74. The Mcahans (TV) 76. Matilda 78. Death Hunt 81. The Cannonball Run 81. Megaforce 82. Cannonball Run II 83. Lassiter 83. Farewell to the King 89. Speed Zone 89. Impulse 90. Bad Girls 94. The Scout 94, etc.

❝ Show me a relaxed producer and I'll show you a failure. – *A.S.R.*

Rudin, Scott (1958–)
American producer.

Mrs Soffel 84. Reckless 84. Pacific Heights 90. The Addams Family 91. Regarding Henry 91. Little Man Tate 91. Jennifer 8 92. Sister Act 92. White Sands 92. Addams Family Values 93. Sister Act 2: Back in the Habit 93. Searching for Bobby Fischer/Innocent Moves 93. Life with Mikey 93. The Firm 93. IQ 94. Nobody's Fool 94. Sabrina 95. Clueless 95. Marvin's Room 96. Ransom 96. Up Close and Personal 96. In & Out 97. The Truman Show 98. A Civil Action 98. Bringing Out the Dead 99. Sleepy Hollow 99. Angela's Ashes 99. Rules of Engagement 00. Shaft 00. Wonder Boys 00, etc.

❝ The thing that Scott taught me was that almost everyone in Hollywood–almost everyone on the planet but most importantly in Hollywood–is afraid. They're afraid of failure, they're afraid of making their own decisions and having to stick by them. – *Barry Sonnenfeld*

Rudkin, David (1936–)
English dramatist and occasional screenwriter, a former music teacher. Educated at Oxford University, he made his reputation in the early 60s with his play *Afore Night Come* for the Royal Shakespeare Company.

Fahrenheit 451 (dialogue) 66. Artemis 81 (TV) 81. Testimony (co-w) 87. December Bride 90. The Woodlanders 98, etc.

Rudley, Herbert (1911–)
American supporting actor.

Abe Lincoln in Illinois 39. The Seventh Cross 44. *Rhapsody in Blue* (as Ira Gershwin) 45. A Walk in the Sun 46. Joan of Arc 48. The Silver Chalice 55. The Black Sleep 56. Beloved Infidel 59. The Great Imposter 61. Falling in Love Again 80, etc.

TV series: The Californians 57. Michael Shayne 60. Meet Mona McCluskey 65. The Mothers-in-Law 67–68.

Rudnick, Paul
American screenwriter and dramatist. He writes a witty film column for *Premiere* magazine under the pseudonym Libby Waxman-Gellner.

Addams Family Values 93. Jeffrey (w, from his play) 95. In & Out 97, etc.

❝ Movie actors are the planet's sex-education instructors: they show us how to do it right. – *P.R.*

Rudolph, Alan (1943–)
American director and screenwriter.

Premonition (wd) 72. Buffalo Bill and the Indians, or Sitting Bull's History Lesson (w) 76. Welcome to L.A. (wd) 76. Remember My Name (wd) 78. Roadie (d) 80. Endangered Species (wd) 82. Return Engagement (d) 83. Choose Me (d) 84. Songwriter (d) 84. Trouble in Mind (wd) 85. Made in Heaven (d) 87. The Moderns (co-w, d) 88. Love at Large (d) 89. Mortal Thoughts (d) 91. Equinox (d) 92. Mrs Parker and the Vicious Circle (co-w, d) 94. Afterglow (wd) 97, etc.

❝ (Robert) Altman always says that he makes hats and Hollywood makes shoes, but for me it's like Hollywood makes shoes and I grow asparagus. You know? I'm not even in the same simile. – *A.R.*

Ruehl, Mercedes (1954–)
American actress, from the stage.

The Warriors 79. Four Friends 81. 84 Charing Cross Road 86. Heartburn 86. Leader of the Band 87. Radio Days 87. The Secret of My Success 87. Big 88. Married to the Mob 88. Slaves of New York 89. Crazy People 90. Another You 91. The Fisher King (AA) 91. Lost in Yonkers 93. The Last Action Hero 93. Indictment: The McMartin Trial (TV) 95. Roseanna's Grave/For Roseanna 96. North Shore Fish 97. Gia 98. Out of the Cold 99, etc.

Ruggles, Charles (1886–1970)
American character comedian, brother of Wesley Ruggles. In films regularly from 1928 after stage experience; quickly became popular for his inimitably diffident manner.

■ Peer Gynt 15. The Majesty of the Law 15. The Reform Candidate 15. The Heart Raider 23. Gentlemen of the Press 29. The Lady Lies 29. The Battle of Paris 29. Roadhouse Nights 30. Young Man of Manhattan 30. Queen High 30. Her Wedding Night 30. *Charley's Aunt* 30. Honor among Lovers 31. The Girl Habit 31. The Smiling Lieutenant 31. Beloved Bachelor 31. Husband's Holiday 31. This Reckless Age 32. One Hour with You 32. This is the Night 32. Make Me a Star 32. *Love Me Tonight* 32. 70,000 Witnesses 32. The Night of June 13th 32. *Trouble in Paradise* 32. Evenings for Sale 32. If I Had a Million 32. Madame Buttlerfly 32. Murders in the Zoo 33. Terror Aboard 33. Melody Cruise 33. Mama Loves Papa 33. Girl without a Room 33. Alice in Wonderland 33. Six of a Kind 34. Goodbye Love 34. Melody in Spring 34. Murder in the Private Car 34. Friends of Mr Sweeney 34. The Pursuit of Happiness 34. *Ruggles of Red Gap* 35. People will Talk 35. No More Ladies 35. The Big Broadcast of 1936 35. Anything Goes 36. *Early to Bed* 36. Hearts Divided 36. Wives Never Know 36. Mind Your Own Business 36. Turn Off the Moon 37. Exclusive 37. *Bringing Up Baby* 38. Breaking the Ice 38. Service De Luxe 38. His Exciting Night 38. Boy Trouble 39. Sudden Money 39. Invitation to Happiness 39. Night Work 39. Balalaika 39. The Farmer's Daughter 40. Opened by Mistake 40. Maryland 40. Public Deb Number One 40. No Time for Comedy 40. Invisible Woman 41. Honeymoon for Three 41. Model Wife 41. The Parson of Panamint 41. Go West Young Lady 41. The Perfect Snob 41. Friendly Enemies 42. Dixie Dugan 43. Our Hearts Were Young and Gay 44. The Doughgirls 44. Three Is a Family 44. Bedside Manner 45. Incendiary Blonde 45. A Stolen Life 46. Gallant Journey 46. The Perfect Marriage 46. My Brother Talks to Horses 46. *It Happened on Fifth Avenue* 47. Ramrod 47. Give My Regards to Broadway 48. The Loveable Cheat 49. *Look for the Silver Lining* 49. Girl on the Subway (TV) 58. All in a Night's Work 61. *The Pleasure of His Company* 61. The Parent Trap 61. Son of Flubber 63. Papa's Delicate Condition 63. *I'd Rather Be Rich* 64. The Ugly Dachshund 66. Follow Me Boys 66.

TV series: The World of Mr Sweeney 53.

✪ For devoting a lifetime of professional experience to the presentation of dapper optimism, and for helping to cheer up several generations of filmgoers. *Trouble in Paradise*.

Ruggles, Wesley (1889–1972)
American director, in Hollywood from 1914. One of the original Keystone Kops: brother of Charles Ruggles.

Wild Honey 22. The Plastic Age 26. Silk Stockings 27. Are These Our Children? 30. *Cimarron* (AAN) 31. No Man of Her Own 32. College Humour 33. *I'm No Angel* 33. Bolero 34. The Gilded Lily 35. Valiant is the Word for Carrie 36. *I Met Him in Paris* 37. True Confession 37. *Sing You Sinners* (& p) 38. Invitation to Happiness 39. My Two Husbands 40. Arizona (& p) 40. Good Morning Doctor 41. Somewhere I'll Find You 42. See Here Private Hargrove 44. London Town (GB) 46, etc.

Rugolo, Pete (1915–)
American composer. Born in Sicily, he was first noted for his jazz arrangements for the Stan Kenton orchestra; he also wrote the music for the 60s TV series *The Fugitive*, and for TV movies.

The Sweet Ride 68. The Story of Pretty Boy Floyd (TV) 74. Chu Chu and the Philly Flash 81. This World, Then the Fireworks 97, etc.

Rühmann, Heinz (1902–1994)
German actor whose films have rarely been seen abroad.

Das Deutsche Mutterherz 26. Drei von der Tankstelle 30. Bomben auf Monte Carlo 31. The Man Who Was Sherlock Holmes 37. Die Feuerzangenbowle 44. The Captain from Kopenick 56. Menschen im Hotel 59. The Good Soldier Schweik 59. Das Schwarze Schaf (as Father Brown) 60. *Ship of Fools* (US) 65. La Bourse et la Vie (Fr.) 65. Maigret und Sein Grosster Fall 66. So Far Away, So Close/In Weiter Ferne, So Nah! 93, etc.

Ruick, Barbara (1932–1974)
American leading actress and singer of the 50s, the daughter of Lurene Tuttle. Her husbands included actor Robert Horton and composer John Williams.

I Love Melvin 51. Invitation 52. Carousel 56. California Split 75, etc.

TV series: The College Bowl 50–51. The Jerry Colonna Show 51. The RCA Victor Show 53–54. The Johnny Carson Show 55–56.

Ruiz, Raúl (1941–)
Chilean director and screenwriter who began as a dramatist. Noted for his innovative approach, he went into exile in 1973 and is now based in Paris.

Three Sad Tigers/Tres Tristes Tigres 68. The Penal Colony/La Colonia Penal 71. The Suspended Vocation/La Vocation Suspendue 77. Games/Jeux 79. L'Or Gris 80. On Top of the Whale/Het Dak van de Walvis 82. Bérénice 84. Treasure Island 86. Richard III 86. Life Is a Dream/La Mémoire des Apparances: La Vie Est un Songe 87. The Golden Boat 90. Dark at Noon 92. The Man Who Was Thursday 92. Palomita Blanca 93. The Secret Journey: Lives of Saints and Sinners/Il Viaggio Clandestino: Vite di Santi e Peccatori (wd) 94. Fado, Major and Minor 94. Three Lives and Only One Death 96. Shattered Image (US) 98. The Stranger from Strasbourg/L'Inconnu de Strasbourg (Fr.) (co-w only) 98. Son of Two Mothers/Fils De Deux Meres ou Comedie De L'Innocence 00, many others.

Ruiz-Anchia, Juan (1949–)
Spanish cinematographer, in Hollywood.

Reborn 82. Miss Lonely Hearts 83. Valentina 83. The Stone Boy 83. Maria's Lovers 84. That Was Then ... This Is Now 85. At Close Range 86. Where the River Runs Black 86. Surrender 87. House of Games 87. The Seventh Sign 88. Things Change 88. The Road Home 89. Lost Angels 89. The Last of the Finest 90. Naked Tango 90. Liebestraum 91. Dying Young 91. Glengarry Glen Ross 92. A Far Off Place 93. Mr Jones 93. Rudyard Kipling's Jungle Book 94. Two Bits 95. The Adventures of Pinocchio 96. The Disappearance of Garcia Lorca 97. The Corruptor 99. The Crew 00, etc.

Rule, Janice (1931–)
American leading lady with stage and TV experience. Now a psychoanalyst. Formerly married to actor Ben Gazzara.

Goodbye My Fancy 51. Holiday for Sinners 52. Rogues' March 53. Gun for a Coward 57. Bell, Book and Candle 58. The Subterraneans 60. Invitation to a Gunfighter 64. *The Chase* 66. Alvarez Kelly 66. The Ambushers 67. The Swimmer 68. Doctors' Wives 71. Gumshoe 71. Welcome to Hard Times 72. Kid Blue 73. Three Women 77. Missing 82, etc.

Ruman, Sig (1884–1967) (Siegfried Rumann)
German character actor, usually of explosive roles, in Hollywood from 1934.

The Wedding Night 35. *A Night at the Opera* 35. *A Day at the Races* 37. *Ninotchka* 39. Bitter Sweet 41. *To Be or Not To Be* 42. The Hitler Gang 44. *A Night in Casablanca* 45. On The Riviera 49. *Stalag 17* 53. The Glenn Miller Story 54. Three-Ring Circus 56. The Wings of Eagles 57. Robin and the Seven Hoods 64. Last of the Secret Agents 66, many others.

❝ Famous line (*To Be or Not To Be*) 'So they call me Concentration Camp Erhardt!'

Runacre, Jenny (1943–)
South African character actress in Britain.

Goodbye Mr Chips 69. Dyn Amo 71. The Creeping Flesh 72. The Final Programme 73. The Mackintosh Man 73. Passenger 75. All Creatures Great and Small 75. Joseph Andrews 77. The Duellists 78. Spectre (TV) 78. The Lady Vanishes 79. The Final Programme 81. That Englishwoman 90, etc.

Runyon, Damon (1884–1946)
Inimitable American chronicler of the ways of a never-never New York inhabited by good-hearted and weirdly-named guys and dolls who speak a highly imaginative brand of English. Among the films based on his stories are *Lady for a Day* 33 (and its remake *Pocketful of Miracles* 61), *The Lemon Drop Kid* 34 and 51, *A Slight Case of Murder* 38 (and *Stop You're Killing Me* 52), *The Big Street* 42, *Guys and Dolls* 55, and *The Bloodhounds of Broadway* 52 and 89.

❝ I am frankly a hired Hessian on the typewriter and have never pretended to be anything else and when I write something I want to know in advance how much I am going to be paid for it and when. – *D.R.*

It is my observation that the rich have all the best of it in this nation and my studies of American History fail to disclose any time when this same situation did not prevail. – *D.R.*

When Damon Runyon died, Broadway wept. It had lost its first citizen, its chronicler and its glorifier. – *Don Iddon*

RuPaul (1967–)
Tall American drag performer and singer, who also became a spokesperson for the cosmetics company M.A.C.

Autobiography: 1995, *Lettin' It All Hang Out*.

The Brady Bunch Movie 95. Red Ribbon Blues 95. But I'm a Cheerleader 00, etc.

TV series: The RuPaul Show 96.

Rush, Barbara (1927–)
American leading lady who came to Hollywood from college. Born in Denver, Colorado and educated at the University of California, she was on-stage at the age of ten. Married (1950-55) actor Jeffrey Hunter.

The First Legion 51. When Worlds Collide 51. Flaming Feather 52. It Came from Outer Space 53. Magnificent Obsession 54. The Black Shield of Falworth 54. Captain Lightfoot 55. The World in My Corner 56. Bigger Than Life 57. Oh Men! Oh Women! 58. Harry Black 58. The Young Philadelphians/The City Jungle 59. The Bramble Bush 60. Strangers When We Meet 60. *Come Blow Your Horn* 63. Robin and the Seven Hoods 64. Hombre 67. The Eyes of Charles Sand (TV) 72. Superdad 74. The Last Day (TV) 75. Can't Stop the Music 80. Summer Lovers 82. Between Friends 83, many others.

TV series: Flamingo Road 80–81.

Rush, Geoffrey (1951–)
Australian actor, mainly on the stage, where he also works as a director. Born in Toowoomba, Queensland, he studied at the University of Queensland, and began his acting career with the Queensland Theatre Company in Brisbane. Married actress Jane Menelaus.

Starstruck 82. Twelfth Night 86. Children of the Revolution 96. On Our Selection 96. Call Me Sal 96. *Shine* (AA) 96. Oscar and Lucinda (narrator) 97. Les Misérables 98. Elizabeth 98. Shakespeare in Love (AAN) 98. House on Haunted Hill 99. Mystery Men 99. Quills (as the Marquis de Sade) (AAN) 00, etc.

Rush, Richard (1930–)
American director.

■ Too Soon to Love (w, p) 60. Of Love and Desire 63. The Fickle Finger of Fate 67. Hell's Angels on Wheels 67. Thunder Alley 67. A Man Called Dagger 68. Psych-Out 68. The Savage Seven 68. Getting Straight 70. Freebie and the Bean (& p) 74. The Stunt Man (& p) (AAN) 80. Color of Night (d) 94.

Rushing, Jimmy (1902–1972)
Short, rotund American blues and jazz singer, pianist and occasional actor, nicknamed, after one of his songs, 'Mr Five by Five'. Born in Oklahoma, he gained fame working in Kansas City with the orchestras of Bennie Moten and Count Basie, making several soundies and shorts in the 40s with the latter.

Crazy House 43. Top Man 43. The Sound of Jazz (TV) 57. The Learning Tree 69. Monterey Jazz 73, etc.

Rushton, Jared (1974–)
Young American actor.

Overboard 87. Big 88. The Lady in White 88. Honey, I Shrunk the Kids 89. A Cry in the Wild 90. Pet Sematary 2 92, etc.

Rushton, William (1937–1996)
English comic actor, writer, novelist and cartoonist, one of the founders of the satirical magazine *Private Eye* in 1961. Died after complications arising from heart surgery.

As actor: Nothing but the Best 64. Those Magnificent Men in Their Flying Machines 65. The Best House in London 68. The Bliss of Mrs Blossom 68. Monte Carlo or Bust 69. Flight of the Doves 71. The Adventures of Barry McKenzie 72. Keep It Up Downstairs 76. The Adventures of a Private Eye 77. The Adventures of a Plumber's Mate 78. Consuming Passions 88, etc.

TV series: That Was the Week That Was 63. Up Pompeii 70.

Russell, Billy (1893–1971) (Adam George Brown)
English music-hall comedian and character actor, on stage from the age of seven. His music-hall experience as a tumbler led to his being hired to teach Charles Laughton how to fall down a chute in *Hobson's Choice*.

Catchphrase: On behalf of the working classes.

Take Off That Hat 38. For Freedom 40. The Man in the White Suit 51. Judgement Deferred 52. Negatives 68. I Start Counting 69. Leo the Last 70, etc.

Russell, Chuck
American screenwriter and director.

■ Dreamscape (co-w) 84. A Nightmare on Elm Street Part 3: Dream Warriors (co-w, d) 87. The Blob (co-w, d) 88. The Mask (d) 94. Eraser 96.

Russell, Clive
Scottish leading actor, a former teacher, from the theatre.

Tumbledown (TV) 89. The Grass Arena (TV) 91. Hancock (TV) 91. The Power of One (US) 92. Tell Tale Hearts (TV) 92. Soft Top, Hard Shoulder 92. The Hawk 93. Fatherland (TV) 94. Margaret's Museum (Can.) 95. NeverWhere (TV) 96. Oscar and Lucinda 97. Bodywork 98. The 13th Warrior 99. Hope and Glory (TV) 99. Oliver Twist (TV) 99. The Railway Children (TV) 00, etc.

Russell, Craig (1948–1990)
Canadian actor and female impersonator who had a big hit with his low-budget semi-autobiographical film *Outrageous* 77, featuring his nightclub act. Died of AIDS.

Too Outrageous 86.

Russell, David O(wen) (1958–)
American screenwriter and director. He studied political science and literature at Amherst College. He worked as a teacher and in community politics before turning to film-making in his late 20s.

Spanking the Monkey (&p) 95. Flirting with Disaster 96. Three Kings 99, etc.

Russell, Gail (1924–1961)
American leading lady of the 40s; came to Hollywood straight from dramatic training. Died from alcoholism. Married (1949-54) actor Guy Madison.

Henry Aldrich Gets Glamour (debut) 43. Lady in the Dark 43. *The Uninvited* 44. Our Hearts Were Young and Gay 44. Salty O'Rourke 45. Night Has a Thousand Eyes 47. Moonrise 48. Wake of the Red Witch 49. Air Cadet 51. The Tattered Dress 57. The Silent Call 61, etc.

Russell, Harold (1914–)
Canadian paratroop sergeant who lost both hands in an explosion during World War II and demonstrated his ability not only to use hooks in their place but to act as well in *The Best Years of Our Lives* 46, for which he won two Oscars. Became a public relations executive. Appeared again 1980 in *Inside Moves*.

Autobiography: 1949, *Victory in My Hands*. 1981, *The Best Years of My Life*.

Russell, Jane (1921–)
American leading lady who came to Hollywood when an agent sent her photo to producer Howard Hughes; he starred her in *The Outlaw* 43 but it was held up for three years by censor trouble. The publicity campaign emphasized the star's physical attributes.

Autobiography: 1985, *Jane Russell*.

■ The Young Widow 47. *The Paleface* 48. Double Dynamite 50. Macao 51. Montana Belle 51. His Kind of Woman 51. Son of Paleface 52. The Las Vegas Story 52. Gentlemen Prefer Blondes 53. The French Line 54. Underwater 55. Gentlemen Marry Brunettes 55. Foxfire 55. Hot Blood 56. The Tall Men 56. The Revolt of Mamie Stover 57. The Fuzzy Pink Nightgown 57. Fate is the Hunter (guest appearance) 64. Waco 66. Johnny Reno 66. Born Losers 67. Darker than Amber 70. The Yellow Rose (TV) 84.

❝ There are two good reasons why men will go to see her. – *Howard Hughes*

The first time I saw Jane Russell I wondered how she got her kneecaps up in her sweater. – *Fred Allen*

Russell, John (1921–1991)
American 'second lead'.

A Bell for Adano 45. The Fat Man 51. The Sun Shines Bright 53. The Last Command 55. Rio Bravo 59. Fort Utah 66. Cannon for Cordoba 70. Blood Legacy 73. The Changeling 80. The Runaways 84. Under the Gun 88, many others.

TV series: Soldiers of Fortune 55. Lawman 58–62.

Russell, Ken (1927–)
British director and novelist, a middle-aged *enfant terrible* of the 70s who after a rigorous training in BBC art films turned out to want to shock people, and did so with flair but no subtlety. Born in Southampton, he worked as a ballet dancer, actor and photographer before joining the BBC. Married three times, he has eight children.

Autobiography: 1989, *A British Picture*. 1994, *Fire Over England*.

■ French Dressing 64. Billion Dollar Brain 67. *Women In Love* (AAN) 69. *The Music Lovers* 70. The Devils 71. The Boy Friend 71. Savage Messiah 72. Mahler 74. Tommy 75. Lisztomania 75. Valentino 77. Clouds of Glory (TV) 78. Altered States 80. Crimes of Passion 84. Gothic 87. Aria (co-d) 87. The Lair of the White Worm 88. Salome's Last Dance 88. The Rainbow 89. The Russia House (a) 90. Whore 91. Prisoner of Honor (TV) 92. Lady Chatterley (a, d) (TV) 93. Erotic Tales (co-d) 94. Ken Russell's Treasure Island (TV) 95.

❝ This is not the age of manners. This is the age of kicking people in the crotch and telling them something and getting a reaction. I want to shock people into awareness. I don't believe there's any virtue in understatement. – *K.R.*

I know my films upset people. I *want* to upset people. – *K.R.*

Life is too short to make destructive films about people one doesn't like. My films are meant to be constructive and illuminating. – *K.R.*

Mr Ken Russell, the film director who now specializes in vulgar travesties of the lives of dead composers ... – *Nicholas de Jongh, Guardian*

His originality these days seems to consist of disguising the banal behind a barrage of garish, distorted, noisy and fleeting images looted from every juvenile fantasy from Rider Haggard to *Superman*, with nods to Dali and Bosch, and strong tincture of Kubrick. – *Sunday Times, 1981*

Russell, Kurt (1951–)
American leading man, often in tough-guy roles, and former child actor, frequently in Disney films. He was married to actress Season Hubley and has

a son by Goldie HAWN. Current asking price: around $15m a film.

The Absent-Minded Professor 60. Follow Me Boys 66. The Horse in the Grey Flannel Suit 68. Charley and the Angel 73. Superdad 74. *Elvis* (TV) 79. Used Cars 80. Escape from New York 81. The Fox and the Hound (voice) 81. The Thing 82. Silkwood 83. Swing Shift 84. The Mean Season 84. The Best of Times 85. Big Trouble in Little China 86. Overboard 87. Tequila Sunrise 88. Tango & Cash 89. Winter People 89. Backdraft 91. Unlawful Entry 92. Captain Ron 92. Tombstone 93. Stargate 94. Executive Decision 96. Escape from LA 96. Breakdown 97. Soldier 98, etc.

TV series: The Travels of Jamie McPheeters 63–64. The New Land 74. The Quest 76.

Russell, Lillian (1861–1922) (Helen Louise Leonard)
Statuesque American singer-entertainer, highly popular around the turn of the century. Only one film, *Wildfire* (1914); was played by Alice Faye in a 1940 biopic, by Ruth Gillette in *The Great Ziegfeld*, by Andrea King in *My Wild Irish Rose*, and by Binnie Barnes in *Diamond Jim*.

Russell, Reb (1905–1978) (Fay Russell)
American star of 30s westerns, after success as a football full-back. He quit acting at the end of the 30s to become a rancher.

All-American 32. Man From Hell 34. Border Vengeance 35. Lightning Triggers 35. Rough and Tough 36. Outlaw Rule 36. Arizona Badman 42, etc.

Russell, Rosalind (1908–1976)
Dominant American leading lady of the 30s and 40s, usually as career women; later attempted character roles, but her choice was sometimes unwise.

Autobiography: 1977, *Life Is a Banquet*.

■ Evelyn Prentice 34. The President Vanishes 34. West Point of the Air 35. The Casino Murder Case 35. Reckless 35. China Seas 35. Rendezvous 35. Forsaking All Others 35. The Night is Young 35. It Had to Happen 36. Under Two Flags 36. Trouble for Two 36. Craig's Wife 36. *Night Must Fall* 37. Live Love and Learn 37. Manproof 38. *The Citadel* 38. Four's a Crowd 38. Fast and Loose 39. *The Women* 39. *His Girl Friday* 40. No Time for Comedy 40. Hired Wife 40. This Thing Called Love 41. They Met in Bombay 41. The Feminine Touch 41. Design for Scandal 41. Take a Letter Darling 42. *My Sister Eileen* (AAN) 42. Flight for Freedom 43. What a Woman 43. Roughly Speaking 45. She Wouldn't Say Yes 45. Sister Kenny (AAN) 46. The Guilt of Janet Ames 47. Mourning Becomes Electra (AAN) 48. The Velvet Touch 48. Tell it to the Judge 49. A Woman of Distinction 50. Never Wave at a WAC 52. The Girl Rush 55. Picnic 56. *Auntie Mame* (AAN) 58. A Majority of One 61. Gypsy 62. Five-Finger Exercise 62. The Trouble with Angels 66. Oh Dad, Poor Dad 67. Where Angels Go Trouble Follows 68. Rosie 68. The Unexpected Mrs Pollifax 70. The Crooked Hearts (TV) 72.

❝ At MGM there was a first wave of top stars, and a second wave to replace them in case they got difficult. I was in the second line of defence, behind Myrna Loy. – *R.R.*

Success is a public affair. Failure is a private funeral. – *R.R.*

Acting is standing up naked and turning around very slowly. – *R.R.*

Russell, Shirley (1935–)
English costume designer.

Women in Love 69. The Music Lovers 70. The Devils 71. The Boyfriend 71. Savage Messiah 72. Inserts 75. Valentino 77. Yanks 79. Agatha (AAN) 79. Reds (AAN) 81. The Razor's Edge 84. The Bride 85. Hope and Glory 87. Gulliver's Travels (TV) 96. Fairytale: A True Story 97, etc.

Russell, Theresa (1957–)
American leading lady who settled in the UK. She is married to director Nicolas ROEG.

The Last Tycoon 77. Straight Time 78. Bad Timing 80. Eureka 83. The Razor's Edge 84. Insignificance 86. Black Widow 87. Aria 87. Track 29 87. Physical Evidence 88. Impulse 90. Whore 91. Kafka 91. Cold Heaven 92. A Woman's Guide to Adultery (TV) 93. Being Human 94. The Grotesque/Gentlemen Don't Eat Poets/Grave Indiscretions 96. A Young Connecticut Yankee in King Arthur's Court 95. Public Enemies 96. The Proposition 96. Wild Things 98, etc.

Russell, William D. (1908–1968)
American director.

■ Our Hearts Were Growing Up 46. Ladies' Man 47. *Dear Ruth* 47. The Sainted Sisters 48. The Green Promise 49. Bride for Sale 49. Best of the Badmen 51.

Russell, Willy (1947–)
British dramatist and composer who has adapted his own plays for the screen.

■ *Educating Rita* (AAN) 83. Mr Love (m) 85. *Shirley Valentine* (& m) 89. Dancin' thru the Dark (& m) 91.

Russo, James (1953–)
American actor.

Vortex 81. Fast Times at Ridgemont High 82. Beverly Hills Cop 84. Extremities 86. China Girl 87. Blue Iguana 88. Freeway 88. We're No Angels 89. Illicit Behavior 91. Intimate Stranger 91. A Kiss before Dying 91. My Own Private Idaho 91. Cold Heaven 92. Bad Girls 94. Panther 95. Livers Ain't Cheap 96. American Strays 96. No Way Home 96. The Real Thing 97. The Postman 97. Love to Kill 97. Donnie Brasco 97. The Postman 97. The Ninth Gate 99, etc.

Russo, Rene (1954–)
American leading actress, a former model. Married screenwriter Dan Gilroy.

Major League 89. Mr Destiny 90. One Good Cop 91. Lethal Weapon 3 92. Freejack 92. In the Line of Fire 93. Outbreak 95. Get Shorty 95. Ransom 96. Tin Cup 96. Buddy 97. Lethal Weapon 4 98. The Thomas Crown Affair 99. The Adventures of Rocky and Bullwinkle 00. Big Trouble 01, etc.

TV series: Sable 87–88.

Rustichelli, Carlo (1916–)
Italian composer.

Gran Premio 43. Gioventu Perduta 47. In the Name of the Law 48. Behind Closed Shutters 50. The Road to Hope 50. Black 13 (GB) 53. Il Ferroviere 55. Maledetto Imbroglio 59. Queen of the Nile 61. Mamma Roma 62. Torpedo Bay 63. Blood and Black Lace 64. The Secret War of Harry Frigg 67. Alfredo, Alfredo 71. The Black Hand 73. Le Gang 76. Le Beaujolais Nouveau Est Arrivé 78. Claretta and Ben 83. Heads or Tails 83, many others.

Ruth, Babe (1895–1948)
Legendary big-hitting American baseball player who has been the subject of two biopics, *The Babe Ruth Story*, directed by Roy del Ruth in 1948, starring William Bendix, and *The Babe*, made by Arthur Hiller in 1992, starring John Goodman. He was the model for the character of Roy Hobbs in Bernard Malamud's novel *The Natural*, filmed by Barry Levinson in 1984 with Robert Redford in the role, and appears as a minor character in *The Sandlot/The Sandlot Kids*. He also appeared as himself in a few movies.

Babe Comes Home 26. Speedy 27. The Pride of the Yankees 42, etc.

Rutherford, Ann (1917–)
American leading lady of the 40s, former child stage star.

Love Finds Andy Hardy 38. The Hardys Ride High 39. Gone with the Wind 39. Pride and Prejudice 40. Happy Land 43. Two O'Clock Courage 45. *The Secret Life of Walter Mitty* 47. The Adventures of Don Juan 48. They Only Kill Their Masters 72, etc.

Rutherford, Dame Margaret (1892–1972)
Inimitable, garrulous, shapeless, endearing British comedy character actress, who usually seemed to be playing somebody's slightly dotty spinster aunt. Born in London, she studied at the Royal Academy of Music, and worked as a piano teacher; she was 33 when she began her professional career, studying at the Old Vic School and acting in various repertory theatres. The daughter of a man who had spent seven years in Broadmoor criminal asylum, for killing his father, and a mother who committed suicide, she suffered from several nervous breakdowns, fearing that she, too, might go mad. Married actor Stringer DAVIS in 1945. Her best roles were as Miss Prism in *The Importance of Being Earnest*, Madame Arcati in *Blithe Spirit*, Headmistress Miss Evelyn Whitchurch in *The Happiest Days of Your Life*, and the Duchess of Brighton in *The VIPS*, though her most popular role was probably as Agatha Christie's detective Miss Marple in four films.

Autobiography: 1972, *An Autobiography*.

Biography: 1983, *Margaret Rutherford: A Blithe Spirit* by Dawn Langley Simmons.

■ Talk of the Devil 36. Dusty Ermine 38. Beauty and the Barge 38. Catch as Catch Can 38. Missing Believed Married 38. Quiet Wedding 40. Spring Meeting 41. *The Demi Paradise* 43. Yellow Canary 43. English without Tears 44. *Blithe Spirit* (as Madame Arcati) 45. While the Sun Shines 46. Meet Me at Dawn 47. *Miranda* 47. Passport to Pimlico 48. *The Happiest Days of Your Life* 50. Her Favourite Husband 51. The Magic Box 51. Castle in the Air 51. *The Importance of Being Earnest* 52. Curtain Up 52. Miss Robin Hood 53. Innocents in Paris 53. Trouble in Store 53. The Runaway Bus 54. Mad about Men 55. Aunt Clara 55. An Alligator Named Daisy 56. The Smallest Show on Earth 57. I'm All Right Jack 59. Just My Luck 59. On the Double 61. *Murder She Said* (as Miss Marple) 62. Mouse on the Moon 63. Murder at the Gallop 63. *The VIPs* (AA) 63. Murder Most Foul 63. Murder Ahoy 64. The Alphabet Murders 65. Chimes at Midnight 66. A Countess from Hong Kong 67. Arabella 68.

✪ For being her splendidly eccentric self. *Blithe Spirit*.

❝ You never have a comedian who hasn't got a very deep strain of sadness within him or her. One thing is incidental on the other. Every great clown has been very near to tragedy. – *M.R.*

Ruttenberg, Joseph (1889–1983)
Russian cinematographer, in Hollywood from 1915.

Over the Hill 28. Fury 36. *The Great Waltz* (AA) 38. *Dr Jekyll and Mr Hyde* 41. *Mrs Miniver* (AA) 42. Madame Curie 43. Adventure 46. BF's Daughter 48. Side Street 49. The Forsyte Saga 49. The Great Caruso 51. Julius Caesar 53. The Last Time I Saw Paris 54. The Swan 56. *Somebody Up There Likes Me* (AA) 56. *Gigi* (AA) 58. The Reluctant Debutante 58. Butterfield 8 60. Bachelor in Paradise 61. Who's Been Sleeping in My Bed? 63. Sylvia 63. Harlow 65. Love Has Many Faces 65. The Oscar 66. Speedway 68, many others.

Ruttman, Walter (1887–1941)
German director most famous for his experimental film *Berlin* 27.

Weekend 30. Mannesmann 37. Deutsche Panzer 40, etc.

Ruven, Paul (1958–)
Dutch director and screenwriter, a former actor.

Naughty Boys 83. Max and Laura and Henk and Willie (co-d) 89. Let the Music Dance (w) 90. The Night of the Wild Donkeys (w) 91. How to Survive a Broken Heart (co-w, d) 91. Sur Place (wd) 96, etc.

Ruysdael, Basil (1888–1960)
Authoritative Russian-American character actor, former opera singer.

The Coconuts 29. Come to the Stable 49. Broken Arrow 50. My Forbidden Past 51. Carrie 52. The Blackboard Jungle 56. The Last Hurrah 58. The Story of Ruth 60, many others.

Ryan, Frank (1907–1947)
American director.

Hers to Hold 43. Can't Help Singing 44. Patrick the Great 45. A Genius in the Family 46, etc.

Ryan, Irene (1903–1973) (Irene Riordan)
Wiry American comedienne, was famous as Granny in TV's *The Beverly Hillbillies*.

Melody for Three 41. San Diego I Love You 44. Diary of a Chambermaid 45. Meet Me after the Show 51. Blackbeard the Pirate 52. Spring Reunion 57, etc.

Ryan, John P. (1938–)
American leading man.

The Tiger Makes Out 65. Five Easy Pieces 70. The King of Marvin Gardens 72. Shamus 72. Dillinger 73. Cops and Robbers 73. It's Alive 75. The Missouri Breaks 76. Futureworld 76. It Lives Again 79. The Cotton Club 84. The Runaway Train 85. Avenging Force 86. Rent-a-Cop 88. Class of 1999 89. Best of the Best 89. Delta Force 2: Operation Stranglehold 90. Eternity 90. The Inner Circle 91. Hoffa 92. Young Goodman Brown 93. CIA 2: Target Alexa 94. Bound 96, etc.

Ryan, Kathleen (1922–1985)
Irish leading lady with stage experience.

Odd Man Out (debut) 47. Captain Boycott 47. Esther Waters 48. Give Us This Day 50. The Yellow Balloon 52. Captain Lightfoot 53. Laxdale Hall 53. *Jacqueline* 56. Sail into Danger 58, etc.

Ryan, Madge (1919–1994)
Australian character actress of stage and screen, in Britain from the mid-50s. She was a member of the National Theatre in the 60s, where her roles included *Mother Courage*.

The Strange Affair 68. I Start Counting 69. A Clockwork Orange 71. Endless Night 71. Frenzy 72. Who Is Killing the Great Chefs of Europe?/Too Many Chefs 78. The Lady Vanishes 80, etc.

Ryan, Meg (1961–)
American leading actress who began acting to help pay for her university studies in journalism. She married actor Dennis QUAID in 1991, and announced in mid-2000 that they were living apart. She was romantically involved with actor Russell CROWE. She was reportedly paid $15 to appear in *Proof of Life*.

Rich and Famous 81. Amityville 3-D 83. Armed and Dangerous 86. Top Gun 86. Innerspace 87. Promised Land 88. DOA 88. Presidio 88. *When Harry Met Sally* 89. Joe versus the Volcano 90. The Doors 91. Prelude to a Kiss 92. *Sleepless in Seattle* 93. Flesh and Bone 93. When a Man Loves a Woman 94. I.Q. 94. French Kiss 95. Restoration 95. Courage under Fire 96. Addicted to Love 97. City of Angels 98. Hurlyburly 98. You've Got Mail 98. Hanging Up 00. Proof of Life 00, etc.

TV series: One of the Boys 82. Wildside 85.

Ryan, Mitchell (Mitch) (1928–)
Stalwart American character actor, mostly on TV.

Robert Kennedy & His Times (TV) 85. Northstar 86. Lethal Weapon 87. Winter People 89. Aces: Iron Eagle III 92. Dirty Work 92. Hot Shots! Part Deux 93. Speechless 94. Blue Sky 94. Halloween: The Curse of Michael Myers 95. Judge Dredd 95. Ed 96. The Devil's Own 97. Liar Liar 97. Grosse Pointe Blank 97, etc.

TV series: Chase 73–74. Executive Suite 76–77. Having Babies 78–79. The Chisholms 80. High Performance 83. All My Children 85–87. Santa Barbara 89. Dharma & Greg 97.

Ryan, Peggy (1924–)
American teenage comedienne of the early 40s, often teamed with Donald O'Connor. In vaudeville from childhood.

Top of the Town 37. Give Out Sisters 42. Top Man 43. The Merry Monahans 44. Bowery to Broadway 44. That's the Spirit 43. On Stage Everybody 45. All Ashore 52, etc.

TV series: Hawaii Five-O 69–76.

Ryan, Robert (1909–1973)
Strong-featured American leading actor who never seemed to get the roles he deserved.

Biography: 1990, *Robert Ryan* by Franklin Jarlet.

■ Golden Gloves 40. Queen of the Mob 40. Northwest Mounted Police 40. Texas Rangers Ride Again 41. The Feminine Touch 41. Bombardier 43. *Gangway for Tomorrow* 43. The Sky's the Limit 43. Behind the Rising Sun 43. The Iron Major 43. Tender Comrade 43. The Hitler Gang 44. Marine Raiders 44. The Walls Came Tumbling Down 46. Trail Street 47. The Woman on the Beach 47. *Crossfire* (AAN) 47. Berlin Express 48. Return of the Badmen 48. The Boy with Green Hair 48. Act of Violence 49. Caught 49. *The Set-Up* 49. The Woman on Pier 13 49. The Secret Fury 50. Born to be Bad 50. Best of the Badmen 51. Flying Leathernecks 51. The Racket 51. On Dangerous Ground 51. Hard Fast and Beautiful 51. *Clash by Night* 52. Beware My Lovely 52. Horizons West 52. City beneath the Sea 53. The Naked Spur 53. Inferno 53. Alaska Seas 54. About Mrs Leslie 54. Her Twelve Men 54. Bad Day at Black Rock 55. Escape to Burma 55. House of Bamboo 55. The Tall Men 55. The Proud Ones 56. Back from Eternity 56. Men in War 57. *God's Little Acre* 58. Lonelyhearts 58. Day of the Outlaw 59. *Odds against Tomorrow* 59. Ice Palace 60. The Canadians 61. King of Kings 61. The Longest Day 62. *Billy Budd* 62. The Crooked Road 65. Battle of the Bulge 65. The Dirty Game 66. The Professionals 66. The Busy Body 67. The Dirty Dozen 67. Hour of the Gun 67. Custer of the West 67. Dead or Alive 67. Anzio 68. Captain Nemo and the Underwater City 68. The Wild Bunch 69. Lawman 71. The Love Machine 71. The Man Without a

Beverly Hills Brats 89. Cold Front 89. Beyond the Stars 89. The Maid 91. Cadence (& d) 89. Original Intent 91. Reason to Believe 93. Queen (TV) 93. Hear No Evil 93. Gettysburg 93. Guns of Honor (TV) 94. Roswell (TV) 94. Boca 94. The American President 95. The War at Home 96. Truth or Consequences, N.M. 97. Hostile Waters 97. Spawn 97. A Stranger in the Kingdom 98. A Letter from Death Row 98. Snitch 98. Ninth Street 99, etc.

TV series: The West Wing 99- .

❝ I'm a recovering alcoholic. I've been struggling with demons for about two-thirds of my life. The bottom line is surrendering to the will of God. – *M.S., 1997*

A lot of what we do has very little to do with art. It has to do with sleaze and gratuitous sex and unnecessary violence. – *M.S., 2000*

Sheen, Michael (1969–)
Welsh leading actor, from the theatre. He trained at RADA and acted with the National Theatre and Royal Shakespeare Company.
Gallowglass (TV) 93. Othello 95. Mary Reilly 96. Wilde 97, etc.

Sheffer, Craig (1960–)
American leading actor.
That Was Then ... This Is Now 85. Fire with Fire 86. Some Kind of Wonderful 87. Babycakes (TV) 89. Night Breed 90. Instant Karma 90. Fire on the Amazon 91. Blue Desert 91. Eye of the Storm 91. A River Runs through It 92. Fire in the Sky 93. Sleep with Me 94. Roadflower 94. In Pursuit of Honor (TV) 95. Wings of Courage 95. The Grave 96. Head above Water 96. Bliss 97. Miss Evers' Boys (TV) 97. Double Take 97. Executive Power 97. Shadow of Doubt 98. The Fall 98. Maze 00, etc.
TV series: The Hamptons 83.

Sheffield, Johnny (1931–)
American boy actor of the 30s, especially in the *Tarzan* and later the *Bomba* series.
Babes in Arms 39. Roughly Speaking 45, etc.

Sheffield, Reginald (1901–1957)
British actor in Hollywood, father of Johnny Sheffield; formerly a child star.
David Copperfield 23. White Mice 26. The Green Goddess 30. Old English 30. Of Human Bondage 34. Cardinal Richelieu 35. Another Dawn 57. Earthbound 40. Eyes in the Night 42. Wilson 44. Kiss the Blood Off My Hands 48. The Buccaneer 58, etc.

Shefter, Bert (1904–)
Russian-born composer in Hollywood.
Danger Zone 51. M 51. No Escape 53. Kronos 57. Cattle Empire 58. The Big Circus 59. The Lost World 60. Jack the Giant Killer 62. Curse of the Fly 65. The Last Shot You Hear 69. The Christine Jorgensen Story 70, many others.

Sheldon, Gene (1909–1982)
American comedy actor.
A Thousand and One Nights 45. Where Do We Go from Here? 45. Golden Girl 52. Three Ring Circus 55. Babes in Toyland 60, etc.

Sheldon, Sidney (1917–)
American writer-director.
The Bachelor and the Bobbysoxer (w) (AA) 47. Dream Wife (co-w, d) 53. You're Never Too Young (w) 55. Pardners (w) 56. The Buster Keaton Story (wpd) 57. Jumbo (w) 62. The Other Side of Midnight (oa) 77. Bloodline (oa) 79. Rage of Angels (TV) (oa) 83. Master of the Game (TV) 84. The Naked Face (oa) TV 84. Windmills of the Gods (oa) (TV) 88. Memories of Midnight (oa) (TV) 91. Sidney Sheldon's The Sands of Time (oa) (TV) 92. Sidney Sheldon's A Stranger in the Mirror (oa) (TV) 93. Nothing Lasts Forever (oa) (TV) 95, etc.

Shelley, Barbara (1933–)
British leading lady who has filmed in Italy; latterly associated with horror films.
Cat Girl 57. Blood of the Vampire 59. Village of the Damned 61. Shadow of the Cat 62. Postman's Knock 62. The Gorgon 64. The Secret of Blood Island 65. Rasputin the Mad Monk 65. Dracula, Prince of Darkness 65. *Quatermass and the Pit* 67. Ghost Story 74, etc.

Shelley, Mary Wollstonecraft (1797–1851)
British writer (wife of the poet) who somewhat unexpectedly is remembered as the creator of *Frankenstein*, which she composed to pass the time during a wet summer. She was played in *Bride of Frankenstein* by Elsa Lanchester. Three films have dealt with the creation of her novel: Ken Russell's *Gothic* 86, in which she was played by Natasha Richardson, Ivan Passer's *Haunted Summer* 88, with Alice Krige, and Roger Corman's *Frankenstein Unbound* 90, with Bridget Fonda.

Shelly, Adrienne (1966–)
American leading actress, often in independent films.
The Unbelievable Truth 90. Trust 91. Big Girls Don't Cry ... They Get Even/Stepkids 92. Hold Me, Thrill Me, Kiss Me 93. Hexed 93. Roadflower 94. Sleep with Me 94. Teresa's Tattoo 94. Grind 96. Sudden Manhattan (& wd) 96, etc.

Shelton, John (1917–1972) (John Price)
Rather colourless American second lead.
The Smartest Girl in Town 36. Navy Blue and Gold 37. I Take This Woman 40. Blonde Inspiration 41. Whispering Ghosts 42. The Time of Their Lives 46. Siren of Atlantis 48. Sins of Jezebel 51, etc.

Shelton, Joy (1922–2000)
British leading lady.
Millions like Us 43. Waterloo Road 44. No Room at the Inn 48. Uneasy Terms 48. A Case for P.C. 49 50. Midnight Episode 50. Once a Sinner 50. Emergency Call 52. Impulse 54. No Kidding 60. HMS Defiant 62, etc.

Shelton, Ron (1945–)
American screenwriter and director, a former basketball player.
Under Fire (co-w) 83. The Best of Times (w) 85. Bull Durham (d, AANw) 88. Blaze (wd) 89. White Men Can't Jump (wd) 92. Blue Chips (w) 94. Cobb (wd) 94. The Great White Hype (co-w only) 96. Tin Cup (co-w, d) 96. Play it to the Bone (wd) 99, etc.

Shengeleya, Georgy (1937–)
Russian director whose *Pirosmani* 71 was widely praised.

Shenson, Walter (1919–2000)
American producer, best known for his work with the Beatles on *A Hard Day's Night* and *Help!*. Born in San Francisco, he studied at Stanford University and first worked as publicist for Paramount and Clumbia, settling in Britain in the mid-50s.
Korea Patrol 53. The Mouse That Roared 59. A Matter of Who 61. *A Hard Day's Night* 64. Help! 65. A Talent for Loving 69. Welcome to the Club (d) 70. Digby 73. The Chicken Chronicles 77. Reuben Reuben 83, etc.

Shentall, Susan (1934–)
British leading lady who made a solitary appearance in *Romeo and Juliet* 54.

Shepard, Jewel (1962–)
American actress, a former stripper; a star of 'B' and sexploitation movies, she is probably best known for her self-deprecating autobiography: 1996, *If I'm So Famous, How Come Nobody's Ever Heard of Me?*
My Tutor 82. Christina 84. Hollywood Hot Tubs 84. Return of the Living Dead 84. Party Camp 87. Scenes from the Goldmine 87. Hollywood Hot Tubs II: Educating Crystal 89. Roots of Evil 91. Caged Heat II: Stripped of Freedom 94. Scanner Cop II 95, etc.

❝ There are times in this world when one must make the supreme sacrifice for one's art. – *J.S.*

Shy people do not dream of becoming movie stars. – *J.S.*

Shepard, Sam (1943–) (Samuel Shepard Rogers)
American leading man; also screenwriter and playwright. He has two children by actress Jessica Lange.
Biography: 1986: *Sam Shepard: The Life and Work of an American Dreamer* by Ellen Oumano.
■ Zabriskie Point 70. Renaldo and Clara 78. Days of Heaven 78. Resurrection 80. Raggedy Man 81. Frances 82. The Right Stuff (AAN) 83. Paris, Texas (w only) 84. Country 84. Fool for Love (& w) 85. Crimes of the Heart 86. Baby Boom 87. Far North (wd) 88. Steel Magnolias 89. Bright Angel 91. Voyager 91. Defenseless 91. Thunderheart 92. Silent Tongue (wd) 93. The Pelican Brief 93. Curse of the Starving Class (oa) 94. Safe Passage 94. The Good Old Boys (TV) 95. Lily Dale (TV) 96. Snow Falling On Cedars 99. Dash and Lilly (TV) 99. Simpatico (oa) 99. Hamlet 00.

❝ I didn't go out of my way to get into this movie stuff. I think of myself as a writer. – *S.S.*

The most complete Renaissance Man since Sir Philip Sidney. – *Professor John Sutherland*

Shepherd, Cybill (1950–)
American leading actress and singer. Born in Memphis, she won a contest for Miss Congeniality at 16 and was a model before becoming an actress.
Autobiography: 00, *Cybill Disobedience*.
■ The Last Picture Show 71. The Heartbreak Kid 72. Daisy Miller 74. At Long Last Love 75. Taxi Driver 76. Special Delivery 76. Silver Bears 77. The Lady Vanishes 79. The Return 80. Chances Are 89. Alice 90. Texasville 90. Once upon a Crime 92. Married to It 93. There Was a Little Boy (TV) 93. Telling Secrets (TV) 93. The Muse (as herself) 99.
TV series: The Yellow Rose 83. Moonlighting 85–89. Cybill 95–98.

❝ I've grown in spirtuality and as a human being since I began to relate to Mother Earth. – *C.S.*

Shepherd, Elizabeth
British actress.
The Queen's Guards 61. Blind Corner 63. *The Tomb of Ligeia* 64. Hell Boats 69. Damien: Omen II 78. Double Negative 80. The Kidnapping of the President 80. Invitation to the Wedding 85. Criminal Law 89. Mustard Bath 93. Let Me Call You Sweetheart (TV) 97, etc.
TV series: Side Effects 94. The Adventures of Shirley Holmes 96.

Shepherd, Jack (1940–)
British actor, in character roles in films and leads on stage and TV. He is also a dramatist and theatre director.
The Virgin Soldiers 69. The Bed Sitting Room 69. Ready When You Are Mr McGill (TV) 76. Count Dracula (TV) 77. The Big Man 90. Twenty-One 91. The Object of Beauty 91. Blue Ice 92. Wycliffe (TV) 93. No Escape 94. Over Here (TV) 96, etc.
TV series: Bill Brand 76. Wycliffe 94– .

Shepitko, Larissa (1938–1979)
Russian director and screenwriter. She was married to director Elem Klimov, who took over the direction of *Farewell* following her death in a car accident. He also made a documentary, *Larissa*, about her in 1980.
Heat/Znoi 63. Wings/Krylia 66. At One O'Clock/V Trinadtsatom Chasu 68. You and I/Ty i Ia 72. The Ascent/Voskhozhdenie (co-w, d) 76. Farewell/Proshchanie (co-w) 81.

Shepley, Michael (1907–1961) (Michael Shepley-Smith)
British stage actor who usually played amiable buffoons.
Black Coffee 30. Goodbye Mr Chips 39. Quiet Wedding 40. The Demi Paradise 43. Maytime in Mayfair 49. An Alligator Named Daisy 56. Don't Bother to Knock 61, etc.

Shepperd, John (1907–1983) (also known under his real name, Shepperd Strudwick)
American leading man and latterly character actor, usually in gentle, understanding roles.
Congo Maisie (debut) 40. *Remember the Day* 41. *The Loves of Edgar Allan Poe* 42. Enchantment 47. Joan of Arc 48. All the King's Men 49. A Place in the Sun 51. Autumn Leaves 56. The Sad Sack 57. The Unkillables 67. Cops and Robbers 73, etc.

Sher, Sir Antony (1949–)
South African-born Shakespearean actor and novelist, mainly on stage in Britain. Born in Capetown, he came to Britain in the late 60s and studied acting at the Webber-Douglas Academy. He was knighted for services to the arts in 2000.
Yanks 79. Superman II 80. Shadey 84. Erik the Viking 89. The Young Poisoner's Handbook 95. Indian Summer 96. The Wind in the Willows 96. *Mrs Brown* (as Disraeli) 97. Hornblower (TV) 98. Shakespeare in Love 98, etc.

Sher, Jack (1913–1988)
American writer-director, former columnist.
My Favorite Spy (w) 51. Off Limits (w) 53. Four Girls in Town (wd) 56. Kathy O' (wd) 58. The Wild and the Innocent (wd) 59. The Three Worlds of Gulliver (wd) 60. Paris Blues (co-w) 61. Critic's Choice (w) 63. Move Over Darling (co-w) 63, etc.

Sheridan, Ann (1915–1967) (Clara Lou Sheridan)
American leading lady at her peak in the early 40s; a cheerful beauty contest winner who developed a tough style and became known as the 'oomph' girl.
■ Search for Beauty 34. Bolero 34. Come on Marines 34. Murder at the Vanities 34. Kiss and Make Up 34. Shoot the Works 34. The Notorious Sophie Lang 34. Ladies Should Listen 34. Wagon Wheels 34. Mrs Wiggs of the Cabbage Patch 34. College Rhythm 34. You Belong to Me 34. Limehouse Blues 34. Enter Madame 35. Home on the Range 35. Rumba 35. Behold My Wife 35. Car 99 35. Rocky Mountain Mystery 35. Mississippi 35. The Glass Key 35. The Crusades 35. The Red Blood of Courage 35. Fighting Youth 35. Sing Me a Love Song 35. Black Legion 36. The Great O'Malley 37. San Quentin 37. Wine, Women and Horses 37. The Footloose Heiress 37. Alcatraz Island 37. She Loves a Fireman 38. The Patient in Room 18 38. Mystery House 38. Cowboy from Brooklyn 38. Little Miss Thoroughbred 38. Letter of Introduction 38. Broadway Musketeers 38. *Angels with Dirty Faces* 38. They Made Me a Criminal 39. Dodge City 39. Naughty but Nice 39. Winter Carnival 39. Indianapolis Speedway 39. Angels Wash Their Faces 39. Castle on the Hudson 40. It All Came True 40. *Torrid Zone* 40. *They Drive by Night* 40. City for Conquest 40. Honeymoon for Three 41. Navy Blues 41. *Kings Row* 41. *The Man Who Came to Dinner* 41. Juke Girl 42. Wings for the Eagle 42. George Washington Slept Here 42. Edge of Darkness 43. *Thank Your Lucky Stars* 43. *Shine on Harvest Moon* 44. The Doughgirls 44. One More Tomorrow 46. Nora Prentiss 47. *The Unfaithful* 47. Silver River 48. Good Sam 48. *I Was a Male War Bride* 49. Stella 50. Woman on the Run 50. Steel Town 52. Just Across the Street 52. Take Me to Town 53. Appointment in Honduras 53. *Come Next Spring* 56. The Opposite Sex 56. Woman and the Hunter 57.
TV series: Pistols and Petticoats 67.

Sheridan, Dinah (1920–) (Dinah Mec)
British leading lady. She was married to actor Jimmy Hanley and Rank chairman Sir John Davis.
Irish and Proud of It 36. Full Speed Ahead 39. Salute John Citizen 42. For You Alone 44. Hills of Donegal 47. Calling Paul Temple 48. The Story of Shirley Yorke 48. Paul Temple's Triumph 50. Where No Vultures Fly 51. *Genevieve* 53. The Railway Children 71. The Mirror Crack'd 80, etc.
TV series: All Night Long 94.

Sheridan, Jim (1949–)
Irish director, screenwriter and dramatist, from the theatre.
■ My Left Foot (AAN) 89. The Field 90. Into the West (w) 92. In the Name of the Father (p, co-w, d) (AANd, AANw) 93. Words upon the Window Pane (a) 94. Some Mother's Son (co-w) 96. The Boxer (co-w, d) 97.

Sheriff, Paul (1903–1961) (Paul Schouvaloff)
Russian art director in Britain from the mid-30s.
French without Tears 39. Quiet Wedding 40. The Gentle Sex 43. *Henry V* 44. The Way to the Stars 45. Vice Versa 48. Flesh and Blood 51. Moulin Rouge (AA) 53. Gentlemen Marry Brunettes 55. Interpol 57. The Doctor's Dilemma 58. The Grass Is Greener 60, etc.

Sherin, Edwin (1930–)
American director.
Valdez Is Coming 70. Glory Boy 71. Lena: My 100 Children (TV) 87. Daughter of the Streets (TV) 90, etc.

Sherman, Cindy (1956?–)
American photographer and director. Her best-known photographic work was called *Untitled Film Stills*, a set of 69 black-and-white photographs showing her posed in a series of ambiguous narrative situations, which was sold to New York's Museum of Modern Art for $1m. Married French video artist Michel Auder.
Office Killer 96.

Sherman, Gary A.
American director.

Death Line/Raw Meat 73. Dead and Buried 81. Vice Squad 82. Wanted Dead or Alive 86. Poltergeist III 88. Lisa 90. After the Shock (TV) 90, etc.

Sherman, George (1908–1991)
American director who graduated slowly from second-feature westerns.
Wild Horse Rodeo 37. Death Valley Outlaws 41. Outside the Law 41. Mantrap 43. Mystery Broadcast 44. The Lady and the Monster 44. *The Bandit of Sherwood Forest* 46. Renegades 46. Last of the Redskins 48. Sword in the Desert 49. Panther's Moon 50. The Golden Horde 51. Against All Flags 52. War Arrow 54. Dawn at Socorro 54. Count Three and Pray 55. Comanche 56. Son of Robin Hood 58. The Enemy General 60. Panic Button 64. Smoky 66. Big Jake 71, many others.

Sherman, Harry (1884–1952)
American producer of westerns.

Sherman, Lowell (1885–1934)
American leading man with stage experience. He was married to actress Helen Costello.
Way Down East 20. Monsieur Beaucaire 24. The Divine Woman 27. Mammy 30. The Greeks Had a Word for Them 32. False Faces 32. She Done Him Wrong (d only) 33. Morning Glory 33. Broadway Through a Keyhole 33, etc.

Sherman, Richard and Robert (1928– and 1925–)
American songwriting brothers who have worked mainly for Disney.
Mary Poppins (AA) 64. The Happiest Millionaire 67. The One and Only Genuine Original Family Band 68. Bedknobs and Broomsticks 71. Huckleberry Finn (& w) 74. The Slipper and the Rose (& w) 76, etc.

Sherman, Vincent (1906–) (Abram Orovitz)
American director, formerly stage actor.
The Return of Doctor X 39. *All Through the Night* 41. The Hard Way 42. Old Acquaintance 43. In Our Time 44. Mr Skeffington 45. The Unfaithful 47. The New Adventures of Don Juan 48. The Hasty Heart 49. Lone Star 51. Affair in Trinidad 52. The Garment Jungle 57. Naked Earth 57. The Young Philadelphians 59. Ice Palace 60. The Second Time Around 61. Cervantes 66. The Last Hurrah (TV) 77. Women at West Point (TV) 79. Trouble in High Timber Country (TV) 82, etc.

Sherriff, R. C. (1896–1975)
Prolific British playwright and screenwriter.
Autobiography: 1969, *No Leading Lady*.
AS PLAYWRIGHT: Journey's End 30. Badger's Green 47. Home at Seven 52.
AS SCREENWRITER: *The Invisible Man* 33. *Goodbye Mr Chips* (AAN) 39. Lady Hamilton 41. *Odd Man Out* 47. *Quartet* 48. No Highway 50. The Dam Busters 55, many others.

Sherrin, Ned (1931–)
British ex-barrister who became a BBC producer and performer, then turned to producing movies for a time, before going on to work in radio and the theatre.
Autobiography: 1983, *A Small Thing – Like an Earthquake*.
The Virgin Soldiers 69. Every Home Should Have One 70. Girl Stroke Boy 71. Up Pompeii 71. Rentadick 72. Up the Chastity Belt 72. The Alf Garnett Saga 72. Up the Front 72. The National Health 73, etc.

Sherwin, David
English scriptwriter, associated with the films of Lindsay Anderson, who later went to Hollywood and regretted it.
Autobiography: 1996, *Going Mad in Hollywood*.
If … 68. *O Lucky Man!* 73. Britannia Hospital 82, etc.

Sherwin, Manning (1903–1974)
American composer, working for Paramount during the 30s; at the end of the decade he came to Britain to write for films and theatre, including many London musicals and revues. His best-known song, to Eric Maschwitz's lyrics, was 'A Nightingale Sang in Berkeley Square'.
Stolen Holiday 37. Blossoms on Broadway 37. Vogues of 1938 37. College Swing/Swing, Teacher, Swing 38. A Girl Must Live 39. He Found a Star 41. Hi, Gang! 41. King Arthur Was a Gentleman 42. Miss London Limited 43. Bees in Paradise 43. I'll Be Your Sweetheart 45, etc.

Sherwood, Bill (1952–1990)
American director. Died of AIDS.
Parting Glances 86.

Sherwood, Madeleine (1922–) (Madeleine Thornton)
Canadian character actress.
Cat on a Hot Tin Roof 58. Parrish 61. Sweet Bird of Youth 62. Hurry Sundown 67. Pendulum 69. Wicked Wicked 73, etc.
TV series: The Flying Nun 67–68.

Sherwood, Robert (1896–1955)
American dramatist. Plays filmed:
Reunion in Vienna 32. The Petrified Forest 36. Tovarich 38. Idiot's Delight 39. Abe Lincoln in Illinois 39, etc.
OTHER SCRIPTS: Waterloo Bridge 32. The Adventures of Marco Polo 38. *Rebecca* (AAN) 40. *The Best Years of Our Lives* (AA) 45. The Bishop's Wife 48. Jupiter's Darling/The Road to Rome 54.

Sheybal, Vladek (1923–1992)
Intense-looking Polish character actor in Britain.
Kanal 56. Women in Love 69. The Music Lovers 70. The Boy Friend 71. QB VII 74. The Wind and the Lion 75. Memed My Hawk 87. Strike It Rich 90, etc.

Shields, Arthur (1895–1970)
Irish character actor, an Abbey player, long in Hollywood; brother of Barry FITZGERALD. Born in Dublin, he was on stage from the age of 13.
The Plough and the Stars 37. *Drums along the Mohawk* 39. *The Long Voyage Home* 40. The Keys of the Kingdom 44. The Corn is Green 45. The River 51. The Quiet Man 52. The King and Four Queens 56. Night of the Quarter Moon 59. The Pigeon That Took Rome 62, etc.

Shields, Brooke (1965–)
American juvenile actress of the late 70s, a former model. Married tennis player Andre Agassi (1997-1999).
Alice Sweet Alice 78. King of the Gypsies 78. Pretty Baby 79. Just You and Me Kid 79. Tilt 79. Two of a Kind 79. Wanda Nevada 80. The Blue Lagoon 80. Endless Love 81. Sahara 82. The Muppets Take Manhattan 84. The Diamond Trap (TV) 88. Brenda Starr 89. Speed Zone 89. Backstreet Dreams 90. Brenda Starr 92. Freaked 93. Freeway 96. The Misadventures of Margaret 98. The Bachelor 99. Black and White 99, etc.
TV series: Suddenly Susan 96-99.
❝ Baudelaire incited in me a desire never to settle for mediocrity. – *Brooke Shields*

Shields, Ella (1880–1952)
British music-hall performer, as a top-hatted male impersonator, associated with the song 'Burlington Bertie'; in films as herself.
Men of Yesterday 36. Ella Shields (short) 36. Cavalcade of the Stars (short) 38, etc.

Shigeta, James (1933–)
Hawaiian leading man who usually plays Japanese in Hollywood films.
The Crimson Kimono 59. Cry for Happy 60. Walk Like a Dragon 60. Bridge to the Sun 61. Flower Drum Song 61. Cry for Happy 61. Paradise Hawaiian Style 65. Nobody's Perfect 68. Lost Horizon 73. Midway 76. Tomorrow's Child 82. Die Hard 88. Cage 89. China Cry 91. Blood for Blood 95. Space Marines (TV) 96. Drive 97. Mulan (voice) 98. Brother (GB/Jap.) 00, etc.

Shilkret, Nathaniel (1895–1982)
American arranger and conductor.
The Plough and the Stars 36. Mary of Scotland 36. The Toast of New York 37. She Went to the Races 45. The Hoodlum Saint 46, many others.

Shilling, Marion (1910–)
American actress, from the stage.
Wise Girls 29. Lord Byron of Broadway 30. Forgotten Women 31. Heart Punch 32. A Parisian Romance 32. The Westerner 34. The Red Rider 34. Thunder Over Texas 34. Blazing Guns 35. The Clutching Hand 36. The Idaho Kid 36. Romance Rides the Range 36, etc.

Shimkus, Joanna (1943–)
Canadian leading lady in American and European films. She is married to actor Sidney POITIER.
Paris Vu Par 66. Les Aventuriers 67. Zita 68. Ho! 68. Boom 68. The Lost Man 69. *The Virgin and the Gypsy* 70. The Marriage of a Young Stockbroker 71. A Time for Loving 71, etc.

Shimoda, Yuki (1924–1981)
Japanese-American character actor.
Auntie Mame 59. A Majority of One 61. Midway 75. Farewell to Manzanar (TV) 76. MacArthur 77. The Last Flight of Noah's Ark 79, many others.

Shimura, Takashi (1905–1982) (Shoji Shiazaki)
Japanese leading actor, in films from 1935. He is to be seen most frequently in the films of Kurosawa.
Stray Dog 49. *Rashomon* 50. Seven Samurai 54. Godzilla 54. *Ikuru* 55. Throne of Blood 57. The Hidden Fortress 58. Yojimbo 62. Kwaidan 64. Red Beard/Akahige 65. Frankenstein Conquers the World 65. The Bullet Train/Shinkansen Daiakuha 75. Oginsama 79. Kagemusha 80. Fifth Movement/ Honoo No Daigo Gakusho 81, etc.

Shindo, Kaneto (1912–)
Japanese director. Began as assistant art director and successful screenwriter, particularly in collaboration with YOSHIMURA, before concentrating on directing.
Children of Hiroshima 53. The Wolf 56. *The Island* 62. Ningen 63. *Onibaba* 64. Kuroncko 67. Iron Ring 72. Heart 73. Life of Chikuzan 77. The Horizon 84. Eiga Joyu 87. The Strange Story of Oyuki/Bokuto Kidan 93. Faraway Sunset/Tooki Rakujitsu (w) 93. A Last Note 95, etc.

Shine, Bill (1911–1997)
Amiable British small-part actor often seen as vacuous dandy.
The Scarlet Pimpernel 34. Farewell Again 37. Let George Do It 40. Perfect Strangers 45. Melba 53. Father Brown 54. Jack the Ripper 58. Double Bunk 61. The Pure Hell of St Trinian's 61. Left Right and Center 61. Burke and Hare 71. The Jigsaw Man 83, many others.

Shiner, Ronald (1903–1966)
British comedy actor, on stage from 1928, films from 1934, at first in bit parts, later as star.
King Arthur Was a Gentleman 42. The Way to the Stars 45. *Worm's Eye View* 50. *Reluctant Heroes* 51. Laughing Anne 53. Top of the Form 54. Up to His Neck 55. Keep It Clean 56. Dry Rot 56. Girls at Sea 58. Operation Bullshine 59. The Night We Got the Bird 60, etc.

Shingleton, Wilfrid (1914–1983)
British art director who won an Oscar for *Great Expectations* 46.

Shinoda, Masahiro (1931–)
Japanese director, part of the so-called 'New Wave' movement with Oshima. He studied drama at university before becoming an assistant director.
One Ticket for Love/Koi no Katamichi Kippu 60. Epitaph to My Love/Waga Koi no Tabiji 61. Our Marriage/Watakushi-tachi no Kekkon 62. Pale Flower/Kawaita Hana 63. Assassination/Ansatsu 64. Captive's Island/Shokei no Shima 66. Double Suicide/Shinju Ten no Amijima 69. Silence/ Chinomoku 71. Sapporo Winter Olympic Games 72. Hanare Goze Orin 77. MacArthur's Children 84. Gonza the Spearman 86. The Dancer 89. Boyhood/Shonen Jidai 91. Sharaku 95, etc.

Shire, David (1937–)
American composer.
One More Train to Rob 71. Drive He Said 71. Showdown 73. The Conversation 74. Farewell My Lovely 75. The Hindenburg 75. All the President's Men 76. Saturday Night Fever 77. Norma Rae (AA, s) 79. Only When I Laugh 81. Paternity 81. Max Dugan Returns 82. The World According to Garp 82. Oh God! You Devil 84. Return to Oz 85. Night, Mother 86. Short Circuit 86. Backfire 87. Monkey Shines 88. Vice Versa 88. The Women of Brewster Place (TV) 89. Bed and Breakfast 92. Sidekicks 93. Lily in Winter (TV) 94. One Night Stand 95. Larry McMurtry's Streets of Laredo (TV) 96. Last Stand at Saber River (TV) 96. Rear Window (TV) 98, etc.

Shire, Talia (1946–) (Talia Coppola)
American leading lady, sister of Francis COPPOLA. She is the mother of actor Jason Schwartzman.
The Wild Races 68. The Dunwich Horror 70. Un Homme Est Mort 72. *The Godfather* 72. The Outside Man 72. The Godfather Part II (AAN) 74. Rocky (AAN) 76. Old Boyfriends 78. Rocky II 79. Prophecy 79. Rocky III 82. Rocky IV 85. RAD 86. From Another Star 87. New York Stories 89. The Godfather Part III 90. Rocky V 90. Bed and Breakfast 92. Cold Heaven 92. Chantilly Lace (TV) 93. Deadfall 93. One Night Stand (d) 94. The Visit 00, etc.

Shirley, Anne (1918–1993) (Dawn Paris)
American child star of the 20s (under the name Dawn O'Day) who later graduated to leading lady roles. She retired in 1944. Married to actor John Payne (1937–43), producer Adrian Scott (1945–49), and screenwriter Charles Lederer.
So Big 32. *Anne of Green Gables* 34. Stella Dallas (AAN) 37. Vigil in the Night 39. Anne of Windy Poplars 40. West Point Widow 41. All that Money Can Buy 41. *Farewell My Lovely* 44. Murder My Sweet 45, etc.

Shoemaker, Ann (1891–1978)
American character actress with stage experience.
A Dog of Flanders 35. Alice Adams 35. Stella Dallas 37. Babes in Arms 39. Conflict 45. A Woman's Secret 49. Sunrise at Campobello 60. The Fortune Cookie 66, many others.

Sholem, Lee (c. 1900–2000)
Efficient American director of B movies of the 40s and 50s, a former editor, who was known as 'Roll'em Sholem' for his fast working methods. Later, he worked in TV, directing episodes of series such as *The Adventures of Superman*, *Maverick* and *The Lawman*.
Tarzan's Magic Fountain 49. Tarzan and the Slave Girl 50. The Stand at Apache River 53. Redhead from Wyoming 53. Tobor the Great 53. Jungle Man-Eaters 54. Cannibal Attack 54. Emergency Hospital 56. Pharaoh's Curse 56. Sierra Stranger 57. The Doomsday Machine 72, etc.

Shore, Dinah (1917–1994) (Frances Rose Shore)
American cabaret singer, in very occasional films. Later she ran a daily TV chat show for women. As a child singer, she was known as Fanny Rose. Married actor George MONTGOMERY (1943–62).
■ Thank Your Lucky Stars 43. Up in Arms 44. Follow the Boys 44. Belle of the Yukon 45. Till the Clouds Roll By 46. Aaron Slick from Punkin Crick 52. Oh God 77. Health 80.

Shore, Howard (1946–)
Canadian composer, from TV.
The Brood 79. Scanners 80. Videodrome 82. Nothing Lasts Forever 84. After Hours 85. Fire with Fire 86. The Fly 86. Heaven 87. Nadine 87. Big 88. Dead Ringers 88. Moving 88. An Innocent Man 89. She-Devil 89. Silence of the Lambs 90. A Kiss before Dying 91. Naked Lunch 91. Prelude to a Kiss 92. Single White Female 92. Guilty as Sin 93. M. Butterfly 93. Mrs Doubtfire 93. Philadelphia 93. The Client 94. Ed Wood 94. Nobody's Fool 94. Moonlight and Valentino 95. Seven 95. White Man's Burden 95. Before and After 96. Crash 96. Looking for Richard 96. Striptease 96. That Thing You Do! 96. The Truth about Cats & Dogs 96. Cop Land 97. The Game 97. Gloria 98. Analyze This 99. eXistenZ 99. Dogma 99. The Cell 00. High Fidelity 00. The Yards 00, etc.

Shore, Pauly (1968–)
American comic actor, from television.
Encino Man/California Man 92. Son-in-Law 93. Dream Date 93. In the Army Now 94. Jury Duty 95. Bio-Dome 96. Casper: A Spirited Beginning (voice) 97, etc.
TV series: Pauly 96.

Short, Martin (1950–)
Canadian comic actor and writer. He first gained recognition with Toronto's Second City Troupe. Born in Hamilton, Ontario, he studied medicine at McMaster University.
Lost and Found 79. The Outsider 79. The Canadian Conspiracy 86. Three Amigos! 86. Cross My Heart 87. Innerspace 87. The Big Picture 88. Three Fugitives 89. Pure Luck 91. Father of the Bride 92. Captain Ron 92. We're Back! A Dinosaur's Story (voice) 93. Clifford 94. The Pebble and the Penguin (voice) 95. Father of the Bride Part II 95. Mars Attacks! 96. Jungle 2 Jungle 96. A Simple Wish 97. Merlin (TV) 98. Prince of Egypt (voice) 98. Mumford 99, etc.
TV series: The Associates 79–80. I'm a Big Girl Now 80–81. SCTV Network 90 82–83. Saturday Night Live 84–85. The Martin Short Show 95.

The Show Formerly Known as the Martin Short Show 95. The Martin Short Show 99-00.

Shostakovich, Dmitri (1906–1975)
Russian composer.
The New Babylon 28. The Youth of Maxim 35. The Fall of Berlin 47. Hamlet 64. War and Peace 64.

Shotter, Winifred (1904–1996)
British leading lady of the 30s, chiefly remembered in the Aldwych farces beginning with *Rookery Nook* 30. Born in Maidenhead, she was on stage from 1918.
Rookery Nook 30. Plunder 30. Jack's the Boy 32. A Night Like This 32. Night of the Garter 33. Sorrell and Son 33. D'Ye Ken John Peel? 35. Petticoat Fever 36. Candles at Nine 44. John and Julie 55, etc.

Showalter, Max (1917–2000) (formerly known as Casey Adams)
American supporting actor and composer, often seen as reporter, newscaster or good-guy friend. He was also noted for playing the role of Horace Vandergelder in the stage musical *Hello Dolly*. Born in Caldwell, Kansas, he is credited with having written the first TV musical, *Time for Love*, which was broadcast in 1939.
Always Leave Them Laughing 50. With a Song in My Heart 52. My Wife's Best Friend 52. Niagara 52. Destination Gobi 53. Vicki 53. Dangerous Crossing 53. Down Three Dark Streets 54. Naked Alibi 54. Bus Stop 56. Indestructible Man 56.The Naked and the Dead 58. It Happened to Jane 59. Elmer Gantry 60. Summer and Smoke 61. Bon Voyage 62. Fate Is the Hunter 64. Lord Love a Duck 66. The Moonshine War 70. The Anderson Tapes 71. Sergeant Pepper's Lonely Hearts Club Band 78. 10 79. Racing with the Moon 84. Sixteen Candles 84, etc.
TV series: The Swift Show 49. The Stockard Channing Show 80.

Shue, Elisabeth (1963–)
American leading actress., who began in commercials. She studied political science at Harvard. Married director Davis Guggenheim.
The Karate Kid 84. Link 86. Adventures in Babysitting 87. Cocktail 88. Back to the Future Part II 89. Back to the Future Part III 90. The Marrying Man/Too Hot to Handle 91. Soapdish 91. Twenty Bucks 93. Heart and Souls 93. Radio Inside (TV) 94. *Leaving Las Vegas* (AAN) 95. The Underneath 95. The Trigger Effect 96. The Saint 97. Deconstructing Harry 97. Palmetto 98. Cousin Bette 98. Hollow Man 00, etc.
TV series: Call to Glory 84–85.

Shuken, Leo (1906–1976)
American orchestrator.
Waikiki Wedding 37. The Flying Deuces 39. *Stagecoach* (AA) 39. The Lady Eve 41. *Sullivan's Travels* 41. The Miracle of Morgan's Creek 43. The Fabulous Dorseys 47. The Greatest Story Ever Told 64, etc.

Shuler Donner, Lauren
American producer. Married director Richard Donner.
Mr Mom 83. St Elmo's Fire 85. Ladyhawke 85. Pretty in Pink 86. Three Fugitives 89. Radio flyer 92. Dave 93. Free Willy 93. Free Willy 2 95. Free Willy 3 97. Volcano 97. Bulworth 98. You've Got Mail 98. Any Given Sunday 99. X-Men 00, etc.

Shull, Richard B. (1929–1999)
Craggy American character actor, mainly on the stage; born in Evanston, Illinois.
B.S. I Love You 71. Klute 71. The Anderson Tapes 71. Cockfighter 74. Hearts of the West 75. The Fortune 75. The Pack 77. Wholly Moses 80. Unfaithfully Yours 83. Garbo Talks 84. Splash! 84. Tune in Tomorrow/Aunt Julia and the Scriptwriter 90. Housesitter 92. Trapped in Paradise 94. Private Parts 97, etc.
TV series: Diana 73-74. Holmes and Yoyo 75.

Shulman, Irving (1913–1995)
American novelist, biographer and screenwriter who introduced the theme of juvenile delinquency into 40s novels and 50s films. Born in Brooklyn, he studied at Ohio and Columbia Universities, and was a teacher before working as a contract writer at Warner's. He turned his version of the script for *Rebel without a Cause* into a novel, *Children of the Dark* 56.
City across the River (from his novel The Amboy Dukes) 49. Journey into Light (co-w) 51. The Ring (w, oa) 52. Champ for a Day (w) 53. *Rebel without a Cause* (adaptation) 55. Terror at Midnight (co-w) 56. Baby Face Nelson (co-w) 57. Cry Tough (oa) 59. College Confidential (w) 60. Harlow (oa) 65, etc.

Shumlin, Herman (1898–1979)
American stage producer who directed two films in the 40s.
■ Watch on the Rhine 43. Confidential Agent 45.

Shurlock, Geoffrey (1895–1976)
Film administrator, an Englishman who became the power behind the MPEA Production Code 1954–68.

Shusett, Ronald
American screenwriter.
Alien (story) 79. Dead and Buried 81. Phobia 81. The Final Terror 83. King Kong Lives 86. Above the Law 88. Total Recall 90. Freejack 92, etc.

Shute, Nevil (1899–1960)
English best-selling novelist.
The Pied Piper 43. No Highway 52. Landfall 54. A Town Like Alice 56. On the Beach 59, etc.

Shyamalan, M(anoj) Night (1971–)
American screenwriter, director and producer, born in Philadelphia. He studied film at New York University. Following the success of *The Sixth Sense*, which made the list of Top 20 top-grossing films, Disney paid him $5m for his script for his supernatural thriller *Unbreakable*, and $5m to produce and direct it.
Praying With Anger (a, d) 93. Wide Awake (wd) 98. *The Sixth Sense* (AANw, AANd) 99. Stuart Little (co-w) 00. Unbreakable (wd) 00, etc.

Shyer, Charles (1941–)
American director and screenwriter. Married writer and producer Nancy Myers.
Smokey and the Bandit (co-w) 77. Goin' South (co-w) 78. House Calls (co-w) 78. Private Benjamin (co-w, AAN) 80. Irreconcilable Differences (co-w, d) 84. Baby Boom (co-w, d) 87. Father of the Bride (co-w, d) 91. I Love Trouble (co-w, d) 94. Father of the Bride 2 95. The Parent Trap (p, co-w) 98, etc.

Siao, Josephine (1947–) (Siao Fong-fong)
Chinese leading actress, a former child star. Born in Shanghai, she moved to Hong Kong as a child and became a star of family pictures and musicals from the early 50s. In 1968, after making 200 features, she stopped acting to study for a degree in communications in the US before returning to Hong Kong to act and, from the mid-70s and early 80s, to set up her own production company. She again quit acting when she moved to Australia with her second husband. On their return to Hong Kong, she scored a success as the kung-fu fighting mother of Jet Li in *Fong Sai Yuk* and its sequel. Deaf in one ear from childhood, she has lost much of her hearing in the other as an adult.
Mai Goo 55. A Purple Stormy Night 68. The True Story of a Rebellious Girl 69. Jumping Ash (& p, co-d) 76. The Spooky Bunch (& p) 80. The Wrong Couples 87. Fong Sai Yuk 93. Fong Sai Yuk II 93. Summer Snow 95. Hu-Du-Men 96. Mahjong Dragon 97, many others.

Sidney, George (1878–1945) (Sammy Greenfield)
American comedian, once popular in vaudeville.
Potash and Perlmutter 23. Millionaires 26. Clancy's Kosher Wedding 27. The Cohens and Kellys in Paris 28. Manhattan Melodrama 34. Good Old Soak 37, many others.

Sidney, George (1916–)
American director, former musician and MGM shorts director.
Free and Easy 41. Thousands Cheer 43. Bathing Beauty 44. Anchors Aweigh 45. *The Harvey Girls* 46. Cass Timberlane 47. *The Three Musketeers* 48. The Red Danube 49. Annie Get Your Gun 50. *Showboat* 51. Scaramouche 52. Young Bess 53. *Kiss Me Kate* 53. Jupiter's Darling 54. The Eddy Duchin Story 56. *Jeanne Eagels* 57. Pal Joey 57. Who Was That Lady? 59. Pepe 60. Bye Bye Birdie 62. Viva Las Vegas 63. The Swinger 66. Half a Sixpence 67, etc.

Sidney, Sylvia (1910–1999) (Sophia Kosow)
Fragile, dark-eyed American heroine of the 30s. Born in the Bronx, she trained at the Theatre Guild School, and was on-stage from the age of 16, making her Broadway debut in 1927. Soon after, she was signed by Paramount, became a star with her first film, and was typecast as a victim. From the 40s, she turned more to the theatre, which offered a greater variety of roles, before returning to the screen in the early 70s. She wrote two books on needlepoint. Married publisher Bennett A Cerf, actor Luther Adler and producer Carleton W. Alsop. Her lovers included producer B.P. Schulberg.
■ Thru Different Eyes 29. *City Streets* 31. Confessions of a Co-Ed 31. An American Tragedy 31. *Street Scene* 31. Ladies of the Big House 32. The Miracle Man 32. Merrily We Go to Hell 33. Madame Butterfly 33. Pick Up 33. Jennie Gerhardt 33. Good Dame 34. Thirty Day Princess 34. Behold My Wife 34. Accent on Youth 35. Mary Burns Fugitive 35. Trail of the Lonesome Pine 36. Fury 36. Sabotage (GB) 37. *You Only Live Once* 37. Dead End 37. You and Me 37. One Third of a Nation 39. The Wagons Roll at Night 41. Blood on the Sun 45. The Searching Wind 46. Mr Ace 46. Love from a Stranger 47. Les Misérables 53. Violent Saturday 55. Behind the High Wall 56. Do Not Fold Spindle or Mutilate (TV) 71. Summer Wishes, Winter Dreams (AAN) 73. Death at Love House (TV) 76. God Told Me To 76. Raid on Entebbe (TV) 77. I Never Promised You a Rose Garden 77. WKRP in Cincinnati (TV) 78. Siege (TV) 78. Damien: Omen II 79. The Shadow Box (TV) 80. Hammett 82. Corrupt 83. Finnegan Begin Again (TV) 85. An Early Frost (TV) 85. Pals (TV) 87. Beetlejuice 88. Mars Attacks! 96.
TV series: Morningstar/Eveningstar 86. Fantasy Island 98-99.
❝ I'd be the girl of the gangster … then the sister who was bringing up the gangster … then the mother of the gangster … and they always had me ironing somebody's shirt. – *S.S.*
What did Hitchcock teach me? To be a puppet and not try to be creative. – *S.S.*
Paramount paid me by the tear. – *S.S.*

Siegel, Don (1912–1991)
American director, former editor; an expert at crime thrillers, he latterly attracted the attention of highbrow critics.
Autobiography: 1993, *A Siegel Film: An Autobiography*.
■ *Hitler Lives* (short) (AA) 45. Star in the Night (short) (AA) 45. The Verdict 46. Night Unto Night 48. The Big Steal 49. Duel at Silver Creek 52. No Time for Flowers 52. Count the Hours 53. China Venture 54. *Riot in Cell Block 11* 54. Private Hell 36 55. An Annapolis Story 55. *Invasion of the Body Snatchers* 56. Crime in the Streets 57. Spanish Affair 57. *Baby Face Nelson* 57. The Line Up 58. The Gun Runners 58. The Hound Dog Man 59. Edge of Eternity 59. Flaming Star 60. Hell Is for Heroes 62. The Killers 64. The Hanged Man 64. Madigan 67. Stranger on the Run (TV) 68. *Coogan's Bluff* 68. Two Mules for Sister Sara 69. Death of a Gunfighter (co-d) 69. The Beguiled 71. Play Misty for Me (a only) 71. *Dirty Harry* 72. *Charley Varrick* 73. The Black Windmill 74. *The Shootist* 76. Telefon 77. Escape from Alcatraz 79. Rough Cut 80. Jinxed 82. Into the Night (a) 85.
❝ I once told Godard that he had something I wanted – freedom. He said: 'You have something I want – money.' – *D.S.*
Most of my pictures, I'm sorry to say, are about nothing. Because I'm a whore. I work for money. It's the American way. – *D.S.*

Siegel, Sol C. (1903–1982)
American producer, in films from 1929.
Kiss and Tell 44. Blue Skies 46. House of Strangers 49. A Letter to Three Wives 49. I Was a Male War Bride 49. Fourteen Hours 51. Monkey Business 52. Gentlemen Prefer Blondes 52. Call Me Madam 53. Three Coins in the Fountain 54. High Society 56. Les Girls 57. Home from the Hill 59. Walk Don't Run 66. Alvarez Kelly 66. No Way to Treat a Lady 68, etc.

Siemaszko, Casey (1961–) (Kazimierz Siemaszko)
American actor.
Class 83. Back to the Future 85. Secret Admirer 85. Stand by Me 86. Gardens of Stone 87. Three o'Clock High 87. Biloxi Blues 88. Young Guns 88. Back to the Future II 89. Breaking In 89. The Big Slice 91. Near Mrs 91. Of Mice and Men 92. Painted Heart 92. Milk Money 94. Teresa's Tattoo 94. The Phantom 95. Black Scorpion 95. Bliss 97. Limbo 99. The Crew 00, etc.

Sienkiewicz, Henryk (1846–1916)
Polish novelist, author of the much-filmed *Quo Vadis?* (published 1895). Polish director Jerzy Hoffman has filmed, in reverse order, his trilogy of novels dealing with life in 17th century Poland: *Colonel Wolodyjowski*, *The Deluge* and *With Fire and Sword*.

Sierra, Gregory
American supporting actor.
The Wrath of God 72. Papillon 72. The Towering Inferno 74. The Prisoner of Zenda 79. Something Is Out There (TV) 88. Honey I Blew Up The Kid 92. Deep Cover 92. Hot Shots! Part Deux 93. The Wonderful Ice Cream Suit 98, etc.
TV series: Sanford and Son 72–75. Barney Miller 75–76. Soap 80–81. Zorro and Son 83.

Siffredi, Rocco (1964–)
Italian actor and director of erotic and pornographic films, who became better known to a wider public for displaying his erection in the controversial French feminist film *Romance*, directed by Catherine Breillat.
Una Ragazza Molto Viziosa 89. Steamy Windows (US) 89. Curse of the Cat Woman (US) 91. Grand Prix Australia (US) 93. Rocco e Le Storie Verre, Part I (&d) 93. Rocco e Le Storie Verre, Part 2 (&d) 93. Anal Princess (US) 96. Romance 99, many others.

Sigel, Newton Thomas (aka Tom Sigel)
American cinematographer.
Latino 85. Rude Awakening 89. Salmonberries (Ger.) 91. Into the West 92. Indian Summer 93. The Usual Suspects 95. Foxfire 96. The Trigger Effect 96. Blood & Wine 96. Fallen 98. Apt Pupil 97. Fallen 98. Three Kings 99. Brokedown Palace 99. X-Men 00, etc.

Signoret, Simone (1921–1985) (Simone Kaminker)
Distinguished French leading actress, married to Yves Montand.
Autobiography: 1976, *Nostalgia Isn't What It Used to Be*.
Biography: 1992, *Simone Signoret* by Catherine David.
■ Le Prince Charmant 42. Bolero 42. Les Visiteurs du Soir 42. Adieu Léonard 43. Beatrice 43. La Boîte aux Rêves 45. The Ideal Couple 45. Les Démons de l'Aube 45. Macadam 45. Fantomas 47. Against the Wind (GB) 47. *Dédée d'Anvers* 48. L'Impasse des Deux Anges 49. *Manèges* 49. Four Days' Leave 50. *La Ronde* 50. Gunman in the Streets 50. Ombre et Lumière 51. *Casque d'Or* 52. Thérèse Raquin 53. *Les Diaboliques* 54. Le Mort en ce Jardin 56. The Witches of Salem 57. *Room at the Top* (GB) (AA) 58. Adua and Company 60. Les Mauvais Coups 61. Les Amours Célèbres 61. Term of Trial (GB) 62. The Day and the Hour 63. Dragées au Poivre 63. *Ship of Fools* (US) (AAN) 65. The Sleeping Car Murders 65. Is Paris Burning? 66. The Deadly Affair (GB) 67. Games (US) 67. The Seagull 68. L'Armée des Ombres 69. The American 69. The Confession 70. Comptes à Rebours 71. *Le Chat* 72. La Veuve Couderc 73. Rude Journée pour la Reine 73. Défense de Savoir 74. The Investigator 74. Flesh of the Orchid 74. Police Python 357 76. Madame Rosa 78. L'Adolescente 79. I Sent a Letter to My Love 81.

Sikes, Cynthia (1951–)
American actress, best known for her role as Dr Annie Cavanero in the TV series *St Elsewhere*. Born in Coffeyville, Kansas, she was a former Miss Kansas and began her career on Bob Hope's tour of Southeast Asia in 1972.
Goodbye Cruel World 82. That's Life! 86. The Man Who Loved Women 83. Arthur 2: On the Rocks 88. Love Hurts 90. Possums 98, etc.
TV series: Captains and the Kings 76-77. Big Shamus, Little Shamus 79. Flamingo Road 81-82. St Elsewhere 82-85.

Sikking, James B. (1934–)
American actor, usually in authoritative roles. Born in Los Angeles, he was best known as Lt. Howard Hunt in the TV series *Hill Street Blues*.
The Strangler 64. Point Blank 67. The New Centurions 72. Scorpio 72. Capricorn One 78. The Electric Horseman 79. Ordinary People 80. Outland 81. The Star Chamber 83. Star Trek III:

The Search for Spock 84. Morons from Outer Space 85. Soul Man 86. Narrow Margin 90. The Pelican Brief 93. Mutiny (TV) 99, etc.

TV series: General Hospital 73–76. Turnabout 79. Hill Street Blues 81–87. Invasion America (voice) 98.

Siliotto, Carlo
Italian composer.

Flight of the Innocent 94. Snowball/Palla di Neve 95, etc.

Silliphant, Sterling (1918–1996)
American writer-producer with much TV experience (*Naked City*, *Route 66*, etc.). Former advertising executive. Also a novelist, he became a Buddhist and went to live in Thailand.

The Joe Louis Story (w) 53. Five Against the House (w, co-p) 55. Nightfall (w) 56. Damn Citizen (w) 57. Village of the Damned 60. The Slender Thread (w) 66. In The Heat of the Night (w) (AA) 67. Charly 68. A Walk in the Spring Rain 69. The Liberation of L.B. Jones 70. The Poseidon Adventure 72. The Towering Inferno 74. The Killer Elite (w) 75. Telefon (co-w) 77. The Swarm (w) 78. Pearl (TV) 79. When Time Ran Out (co-w) 80. Space (TV) 85. Catch the Heat 87. Over the Top 87. The Grass Harp (co-w) 95, etc.

Sillitoe, Alan (1928–)
British north-country novelist best known to filmgoers for *Saturday Night and Sunday Morning* and *The Loneliness of the Long Distance Runner*. His less successful novel *The General* was filmed as *Counterpoint*.

Sills, Milton (1882–1930)
Stalwart American leading man of the silent screen.

The Rack 15. The Claw 17. Eyes of Youth 19. The Weekend 20. Burning Sands 22. Adam's Rib 23. Madonna of the Streets 24. The Sea Hawk 24. Paradise 26. Valley of the Giants 27. His Captive Woman 29. The Sea Wolf 30, many others.

Silva, Henry (1928–)
Pale-eyed American actor of Italian and Basque descent, often seen as sadistic villain or assorted Latin types.

Viva Zapata 52. Crowded Paradise 56. A Hatful of Rain 57. The Bravados 58. Green Mansions 59. Cinderfella 60. *The Manchurian Candidate* 62. *Johnny Cool* (leading role) 63. The Return of Mr Moto 65. The Reward 65. The Plainsman 66. The Hills Ran Red (It.) 66. Never a Dull Moment 68. Five Savage Men 70. The Kidnap of Mary Lou 75. Shoot 76. Cry of a Prostitute 76. Thirst 79. Buck Rogers 79. Alligator 80. Sharkey's Machine 81. Wrong Is Right 82. Allan Quatermain and the Lost City of Gold 86. Bulletproof 87. Above the Law 88. Dick Tracy 90. South Beach 92. The Harvest 92. Possessed by the Night 93. Trigger Happy/Mad Dog Time 96, etc.

Silver, Joan Micklin (1935–)
American director.
■ Limbo (w) 72. *Hester Street* (& w) 74. Bernice Bobs Her Hair (& w) (TV) 76. Between the Lines 78. Head over Heels (& w) 79. Crossing Delancey 88. Loverboy 89. Big Girls Don't Cry … They Get Even/Stepkids 92. In the Presence of Mine Enemies (TV) 97. A Fish in the Bathtub 98.

Silver, Joel (1952–)
American producer, mainly of high-budget action films.

48 Hours 82. Streets of Fire 84. Brewster's Millions 85. Commando 85. Weird Science 85. Jumpin' Jack Flash 86. Lethal Weapon 87. Predator 87. Action Jackson 88. Die Hard 88. Road House 89. Lethal Weapon 2 89. The Adventures of Ford Fairlane 90. Predator 2 90. Die Hard II 90. Hudson Hawk 91. Ricochet 91. The Last Boy Scout 92. Lethal Weapon 3 92. Demolition Man 93. Executive Decision 96. Tales from the Crypt Presents: Bordello of Blood 96. Fathers' Day 97. Conspiracy Theory 97. Lethal Weapon 4 98. House on Haunted Hill 99, etc.

Silver, Marisa (1960–)
American director and screenwriter.
Old Enough (wd) 84. Permanent Record (d) 88. Vital Signs (d) 90.

Silver, Ron (1946–)
American leading actor.

The French Connection 71. Tunnel Vision 76. Semi-Tough 77. Best Friends 82. Silent Rage 82. The Entity 82. Silkwood 83. Betrayal 83. Garbo Talks 84. Oh, God! You Devil 84. Eat and Run 86. Enemies, a Love Story 89. Fellow Traveller 89. Blue Steel 90. Reversal of Fortune 90. Trapped in Silence (TV) 90. Live Wire 92. Mr Saturday Night 92. Married to It 93. Timecop 94. A Woman of Independent Means (TV) 95. Kissinger and Nixon (TV, as Kissinger) 95. The Arrival 96. Rhapsody in Bloom 98, etc.

TV series: Rhoda 76–78. Dear Detective 79. The Stockard Channing Show 80. Baker's Dozen 82.

Silvera, Frank (1914–1970)
American general-purpose actor with stage experience. Electrocuted while repairing a kitchen appliance.

Viva Zapata 52. Killer's Kiss 55. Crowded Paradise 56. The Mountain Road 60. Mutiny on the Bounty 62. The Appaloosa 66. Che! 69. Valdez Is Coming 71, etc.

TV series: The High Chaparral 67–70.

Silverheels, Jay (1919–1980)
Canadian Red Indian actor, mainly in western films.

The Prairie 47. Fury at Furnace Creek 48. Broken Arrow 50. War Arrow 53. The Lone Ranger 55. Indian Paint 65. The Phynx 70. Santee 73, many others.

TV series: The Lone Ranger (as Tonto) 52–56.

Silvers, Louis (1889–1954)
American composer.

The Jazz Singer 27. Dancing Lady 33. It Happened One Night 34. One Night of Love (AA) 35. Lloyds of London 36. Heidi 37. In Old Chicago (AAN) 38. Suez (AAN) 38. Jesse James 39. Swanee River (AAN) 39. The Powers Girl 42, many others.

Silvers, Phil (1912–1985) (Philip Silver)
American vaudeville star comedian in occasional films from 1941.

Autobiography: 1974, *The Laugh Is on Me*.

Tom, Dick and Harry (debut) 41. *You're in the Army Now* 42. Roxie Hart 42. My Gal Sal 42. Coney Island 43. *Cover Girl* 44. A Thousand and One Nights 45. Where Do We Go from Here? 45. Summer Stock 50. Lucky Me 54. Forty Pounds of Trouble 63. *It's a Mad Mad Mad Mad World* 63. A Funny Thing Happened on the Way to the Forum 66. Follow That Camel (GB) 67. Buona Sera, Mrs Campbell 68. Deadly Tide (TV) 75. Won Ton Ton 76. The Chicken Chronicles 77. The New Love Boat (TV) 77. The Night They Took Miss Beautiful (TV) 78. There Goes the Bride 80, etc.

TV series: You'll Never Get Rich (as Bilko) 55–58. *The New Phil Silvers Show* 64.

Silverstein, Elliot (1927–)
American director, from TV.
■ Belle Sommers (TV) 62. Cat Ballou 65. The Happening 67. A Man Called Horse 69. The Car 77. Betrayed by Innocence (TV) 86. Night of Courage (TV) 87. Fight for Life (TV) 87. Rich Men, Single Women (TV) 90. Flashfire 94.

Silverstone, Alicia (1976–)
Young American leading actress, from the stage. Born in San Francisco to British parents, she attracted a teen following by appearing in Aerosmith's rock videos and, after the success of *Clueless*, signed a $10m three-picture deal with Columbia-TriStar; but the first film she produced and starred in, *Excess Baggage*, flopped at the box-office.

The Crush 93. True Crime 95. The Babysitter 95. Hideaway 95. The New World/Le Nouveau Monde 95. *Clueless* (as Cher Horowitz) 95. Excess Baggage 96. Batman and Robin (as Batgirl) 97. Excess Baggage 97. Blast from the Past 99. Love's Labours Lost 00, etc.

Silvestri, Alan
American composer.

The Doberman Gang 72. The Amazing Dobermans 77. Fandango 84. Romancing the Stone 84. Cat's Eye 85. Back to the Future 85. Clan of the Cave Bear 85. Summer Rental 85. Critical Condition 86. Delta Force 86. Flight of the Navigator 86. No Mercy 86. Outrageous Fortune 87. Predator 87. Overboard 87. Who Framed Roger Rabbit? 88. Mac and Me 88. My Stepmother Is an Alien 88. The Abyss 89. She's Out of Control 89. Back to the Future II 89. Downtown 90. Back to

the Future III 90. Predator 2 90. Young Guns II 90. Soapdish 91. Ricochet 91. Shattered 91. Father of the Bride 91. Dutch/Driving Me Crazy 91. The Bodyguard 92. Death Becomes Her 92. FernGully: The Last Rainforest 92. Stop! Or My Mom Will Shoot 92. Super Mario Bros 93. Cop and a Half 93. Sidekicks 93. Judgment Night 93. Grumpy Old Men 93. Clean Slate 94. Blown Away 94. Forrest Gump (AAN) 94. Richie Rich 95. The Quick and the Dead 95. The Perez Family 95. Judge Dredd 95. Grumpier Old Men 95. Father of the Bride 2 95. Sgt Bilko 96. The Long Kiss Goodnight 96. Eraser 96. Volcano 97. Mouse Hunt 97. Contact 97. Fools Rush In 97. The Parent Trap 98. Holy Man 98. Practical Magic 98. The Odd Couple II 98. Stuart Little 99. What Lies Beneath 00, etc.

Sim, Alastair (1900–1976)
Lugubrious Scottish comedy actor of stage and screen; his diction and gestures were inimitable. Married actress and writer Naomi Sim (1913-1999).

Biography: 1987, *Dance and Skylark. 50 years with Alastair Sim* by Naomi Sim.
■ Riverside Murder 35. The Private Secretary 35. A Fire Has Been Arranged 35. Late Extra 35. The Case of Gabriel Perry 35. Troubled Waters 36. Wedding Group 36. The Big Noise 36. Keep Your Seats Please 36. The Man in the Mirror 36. The Mysterious Mr Davis 36. Strange Experiment 37. Clothes and the Woman 37. Gangway 37. The Squeaker 37. A Romance in Flanders 37. Melody and Romance 37. Sailing Along 38. *The Terror* 38. Alf's Button Afloat 38. This Man is News 38. Climbing High 38. Inspector Hornleigh 39. This Man in Paris 39. Inspector Hornleigh on Holiday 39. Law and Disorder 40. Inspector Hornleigh Goes to It 41. *Cottage to Let* 41. *Let the People Sing* 42. Waterloo Road 44. *Green for Danger* 46. Hue and Cry 47. Captain Boycott 47. *London Belongs to Me* 48. *The Happiest Days of Your Life* 50. Stage Fright 50. *Laughter in Paradise* 51. Scrooge 51. Lady Godiva Rides Again 51. Folly to be Wise 52. Innocents in Paris 53. An Inspector Calls 54. *The Belles of St Trinian's* 54. Escapade 55. Geordie 55. The Green Man 56. Blue Murder at St Trinian's 57. The Doctor's Dilemma 58. Left, Right and Centre 59. School for Scoundrels 60. The Millionairess 60. The Ruling Class 71. Royal Flash 75. Escape from the Dark 76. Rogue Male (TV) 76.
☼ For marvellous moments of high comedy and for the lasting comic image of his unique physiognomy. *Green for Danger.*

Sim, Gerald (1925–)
British supporting actor, often in well-bred and slightly prissy roles.

Fame is the Spur 47. The Wrong Arm of the Law 63. The Pumpkin Eater 64. King Rat 64. The Whisperers 66. Oh What a Lovely War 68. Dr Jekyll and Sister Hyde 71. No Sex Please We're British 73. The Slipper and the Rose 76. Gandhi 82. Cry Freedom 87, many others.

TV series: To the Manor Born (as the rector) 79–81.

Sim, Sheila (1922–)
English leading actress, in occasional films. Married to Lord (Richard) Attenborough.

A Canterbury Tale 43. Great Day 45. The Guinea Pig 48. Dear Mr Prohack 49. Pandora and the Flying Dutchman 51. The Magic Box 51. The Night My Number Came Up 55, etc.

Simenon, Georges (1903–1989)
Prolific French novelist, the creator of Inspector Maigret. More than 50 of his 220 novels (he wrote some 200 more under pseudonyms) have been filmed, and in the 50s his sales reached 3 million a year. He also wrote 21 volumes of memoirs. As president of the jury at the Cannes Film Festival in 1960, he ensured that Fellini's *La Dolce Vita* won the prize for best film. Years later, during an interview with Fellini to publicize the director's *Casanova*, he claimed to have had sexual relationships with 10,000 women, who included dancer and cabaret performer Josephine Baker. In the 40s, he had moved to America for a time, though, apart from a couple of films, he was unable to interest Hollywood in his stories. He was then taking no more than 10 days to write a novel: when Alfred Hitchcock rang and was told Simenon was busy, having just started another book, he replied: 'All right. I'll wait.'

Biography: 1992, *The Man Who Wasn't Maigret* by Patrick Marnham. 1997, *Simenon* by Pierre Assouline.

Les Inconnus dans la Maison 43. Panique 46. Temptation Harbour (GB) 46. La Marie du Port 50. The Man on the Eiffel Tower (US) 50. Le Fruit Défendu 52. The Brothers Rico (US) 57. Maigret Sets a Trap 58, etc.

TV series: Maigret 63. Thirteen against Fate 67.
❝ Can there be a more intimate communication between two beings than copulation? – G.S.

The artist is above all else a sick person, in any case an unstable one, if the doctors are to be believed. Why see in that some form of superiority? I would do better to ask people's forgiveness. – G.S.

Simmons, Anthony (c. 1924–)
British writer-director, known for short films.

Sunday by the Sea 53. Bow Bells 54. The Gentle Corsican 56. Your Money or Your Wife 59. Four in the Morning 65. *The Optimists of Nine Elms* 73. Black Joy 78. Little Sweetheart 88, etc.

Simmons, Jean (1929–)
Self-possessed and beautiful British leading lady who settled in Hollywood to make films which have generally been unworthy of her talents. Married (1950–60) actor Stewart Granger and (1961–77) writer-director Richard Brooks.

Give Us the Moon 43. Mr Emmanuel 44. Meet Sexton Blake 44. Kiss the Bride Goodbye 44. The Way to the Stars 45. Caesar and Cleopatra 45. Hungry Hill 45. The Woman in the Hall 45. *Great Expectations* 46. *Black Narcissus* 46. Uncle Silas 47. *Hamlet* (AAN) 48. The Blue Lagoon 48. Adam and Evelyne 49. Trio 50. Cage of Gold 50. So Long at the Fair 50. The Clouded Yellow 50. Angel Face 52. Androcles and the Lion 53. Young Bess 53. Affair with a Stranger 53. The Robe 53. The Actress 53. She Couldn't Say No 54. The Egyptian 54. A Bullet is Waiting 54. Désirée 54. Footsteps in the Fog 55. Guys and Dolls 56. Hilda Crane 56. This Could be the Night 57. Until They Sail 57. *The Big Country* 58. Home Before Dark 58. This Earth is Mine 59. *Elmer Gantry* 60. Spartacus 60. *The Grass is Greener* 61. All the Way Home 63. Life at the Top 65. Mister Buddwing 66. Rough Night in Jericho 67. Divorce American Style 67. The Happy Ending (AAN) 69. Say Hello to Yesterday 71. Mr Sycamore 75. The Dain Curse (TV) 78. Dominique 79. Beggarman Thief (TV) 79. Golden Gate (TV) 80. The Thorn Birds (TV) 82. Midas Valley (TV) 84. Perry Mason: The Case of the Lost Love (TV) 87. The Dawning 88. Great Expectations (TV) 89. Sense and Sensibility (TV) 90. Laker Girls (TV) 90. How to Make an American Quilt 95. Daisies in December (TV) 95, etc.

TV series: Dark Shadows 91.

Simms, Ginny (1916–1994) (Virginia Sims)
Glamorous American vocalist, with Kay Kyser's band.

That's Right You're Wrong 39. You'll Find Out 40. Playmates 42. Hit the Ice 43. Broadway Rhythm 44. Shady Lady 45. Night and Day 46. Disc Jockey 51, etc.

Simms, Larry (1934–)
American boy actor, notably in the *Blondie* series 1938–48. (He was Baby Dumpling.)

The Last Gangster 37. Mr Smith Goes to Washington 39. Madame Bovary 49, etc.

Simon, Adam
American director.

Brain Dead 90. Body Chemistry II: The Voice of a Stranger 92. Carnosaur 93.

Simon, Carly (1945–)
American composer and singer.
■ Perfect (a) 85. Heartburn (m) 86. Postcards from the Edge (m) 90. This Is My Life (m) 92.

Simon, Melvin (1925–)
American independent producer, former shopping-plaza developer.

Love at First Bite 79. Scavenger Hunt 79. The Runner Stumbles 79. When a Stranger Calls 79. Cloud Dancer 80. My Bodyguard 80. The Man with Bogart's Face 80. The Stunt Man 80. Porky's 82, etc.

Simon, Michel (1895–1975) (François Simon)
Heavyweight French character actor, in films from the 20s after music-hall experience.

Feu Mathias Pascal 25. The Passion of Joan of Arc 28. La Chienne 31. *Boudu Sauvé des Eaux* 32. Lac aux Dames 34. *L'Atalante* 34. Jeunes Filles de

Paris 36. Drôle de Drame 37. Les Disparus de Saint-Agil 38. Quai des Brumes 38. Fric Frac 39. *La Fin du Jour* 39. Circonstances Atténuantes 39. Vautrin 43. Un Ami Viendra Ce Soir 45. *Panique* 46. Fabiola 48. *La Beauté du Diable* 49. The Strange Desire of Monsieur Bard 53. Saadia 53. La Joyeuse Prison 56. It Happened in Broad Daylight 58. The Head 59. Austerlitz 59. Candide 60. The Devil and Ten Commandments 62. The Train 64. Two Hours to Kill 65. *The Two of Us* 67. La Maison 70. Blanche 71, many others.

Simon, Neil (1927–)
American comedy playwright whose Broadway success has been remarkable and his Hollywood follow-up diligent, either as scenarist or as original author with a watching brief.
Autobiography: 1996, *Rewrites: A Memoir*.
Come Blow Your Horn 63. After the Fox (oa) 66. Barefoot in the Park 67. The Odd Couple (AAN) 68. Sweet Charity 68. The Out of Towners 70. Plaza Suite 71. Last of the Red Hot Lovers 72. The Sunshine Boys (AAN) 75. Murder by Death 76. The Goodbye Girl (AAN) 78. California Suite (AAN) 78. Chapter Two 79. I Ought to Be in Pictures 82. Max Dugan Returns 83. The Lonely Guy 84. The Slugger's Wife 85. Brighton Beach Memoirs 87. Biloxi Blues 88. The Marrying Man 91. Lost in Yonkers 93. The Odd Couple II (& co-p) 98, etc.

Simon, Paul (1942–)
American lyricist and singer, long a team element as Simon and Garfunkel. Primarily known to the non-pop public for the music backing *The Graduate*, Simon also appeared in an unsuccessful 1980 movie, *One Trick Pony*, and can be glimpsed in *Annie Hall* 77. Married actress Carrie Fisher (1983–84).
Biography: 1995, *Simon and Garfunkel* by Victoria Kingston.

Simon, S. Sylvan (1910–1951)
American director with radio experience.
A Girl with Ideas 37. Four Girls in White 39. Whistling in the Dark 41. Rio Rita 42. Song of the Open Road 44. Son of Lassie 45. Her Husband's Affairs 47. I Love Trouble 48. The Lust for Gold 49. Born Yesterday (p) 50, etc.

Simon, Simone (1910–)
Pert French leading lady with brief stage experience.
Le Chanteur Inconnu (debut) 31. Lac aux Dames 34; to US: Girls' Dormitory 36. *Seventh Heaven* 37. Josette 38. *La Bête Humaine* 38. *All That Money Can Buy* 41. *Cat People* 42. Tahiti Honey 43. Mademoiselle Fifi 44. Temptation Harbour (GB) 47. Donna Senza Nome (It.) 49. La Ronde 50. Olivia 50. Le Plaisir 51. Double Destin 54. The Extra Day (GB) 56. The Woman in Blue 73, etc.

Simoneau, Yves (1955–)
French-Canadian director.
Les Célébrations 79. Pouvoir Intime 86. In the Shadow of the Wind 87. Perfectly Normal 90. Cruel Doubt (TV) 92. Mother's Boys 94. Amelia Earhart: The Final Flight (TV) 94. Larry McMurty's 'Dead Man's Walk' (TV) 96. Nuremberg (TV) 00, etc.

Simpson, Alan (1929–)
British TV and film comedy writer, with Ray Galton.

Simpson, Don (1945–1996)
American producer, in partnership with Jerry Bruckheimer; also famous for his excessive life-style. Died of a drug overdose.
Biography: 1998, *High Concept: Don Simpson and the Hollywood Culture of Excess* by Charles Fleming.
Flashdance 83. Beverly Hills Cop 84. Thief of Hearts 84. Top Gun 86. Beverly Hills Cop II 87. The Big Bang 89. Days of Thunder 90. Young Guns II 90. The Ref 94. Bad Boys 95. The Rock 96, etc.
❝ In another industry, Simpson's behaviour would have made him an outcast and ensured his expulsion from the club of the powerful. – *Charles Fleming*

Simpson, Geoffrey
Australian cinematographer in international films, from television documentaries.
Call Me Mr Brown (TV) 85. Riddle of the Stinson (TV) 88. Celia 88. *The Navigator: A Medieval Odyssey* 88. Till There Was You 90. Green Card (US) 90. Deadly 91. Fried Green Tomatoes at the Whistle Stop Café (US) 91. The Last Days of Chez Nous 92. Mr Wonderful (US) 92. The War (US) 94. Little Women (US) 94. *Shine* 96. Some Mother's Son (Ire.) 96. Oscar and Lucinda 97, etc.

Simpson, Ivan (1875–1951)
Scottish character actor in Hollywood.
The Dictator 15. The Green Goddess 23 and 30. The Man Who Played God 32. Phantom of Cresswood 33. David Copperfield 34. Maid of Salem 37. The Hour before the Dawn 43, many others.

Simpson, O. J. (1947–) (Orenthal James Simpson)
American actor and TV sportscaster, a former football star with the Buffalo Bills in the 70s, nicknamed 'The Juice'. In 1994, his arrest for the murder of his wife and a young man became headline news. The police chase of him, at a stately 45 mph along the San Diego Freeway, as he sat in a car pointing a gun at his own head, was broadcast live on television and watched by an estimated 95 million viewers; it was later released on video. Simpson was acquitted of murdering his former wife and her friend Ron Goldman, but was later found liable for the deaths by a civil court jury and ordered to pay the survivors $35.5 million in damages.He was played by Bobby Hosea in the TV movie *The O. J. Simpson Story* 95.
■ The Klansman 74. The Towering Inferno 74. The Diamond Mercenaries 75. The Cassandra Crossing 77. Roots (TV) 77. A Killing Affair (TV) 77. Capricorn One 78. Firepower 79. Detour (TV) 79. Goldie and the Boxer (TV) 79. Goldie and the Boxer Go to Hollywood (TV) 80. Hambone and Hillie 84. The Naked Gun: From the Files of Police Squad 88. The Naked Gun 2&fr12;: The Smell of Fear 91. Naked Gun 33&fr13;: The Final Insult 94.
TV series: Roots 77–78.

Simpson, Russell (1878–1959)
American character actor, in Hollywood from silent days.
Billy the Kid 31. Way Down East 36. Ramona 37. Dodge City 39. The Grapes of Wrath 40. Outside the Law 41. They Were Expendable 45. My Darling Clementine 46. The Beautiful Blonde from Bashful Bend 49. Seven Brides for Seven Brothers 54. Friendly Persuasion 56. The Horse Soldiers 59, many others.

Sims, Joan (1930–)
British stage, TV and film comedienne, often in cameo roles.
Trouble in Store 53. Will Any Gentleman? 53. The Belles of St Trinian's 54. Lost 55. Dry Rot 56. Carry On Admiral 57. The Captain's Table 58. Life in Emergency Ward 10 58. Carry On Nurse 59. Carry On Teacher 59. Please Turn Over 59. Upstairs and Downstairs 59. Carry On Constable 60. Doctor in Love 60. His and Hers 60. Watch Your Stern 60. Carry On Regardless 61. Mr Topaze 61. No, My Darling Daughter 61. Twice round the Daffodils 62. Nurse on Wheels 63. Carry On Cleo 64. The Big Job 65. Carry On Cowboy 65. Carry On – Don't Lose Your Head 66. Carry On – Follow That Camel 66. Carry On Screaming 66. Doctor in Clover 66. Carry On Doctor 68. Carry On up the Khyber 68. Carry On Again Doctor 69. Carry On Camping 69. Carry On Loving 70. Carry On up the Jungle 70. Doctor in Trouble 70. Carry On at Your Convenience 71. Carry On Henry 71. The Magnificent Seven Deadly Sins 71. The Alf Garnett Saga 72. Carry On Abroad 72. Carry On Matron 72. Not Now, Darling 72. Carry On Girls 73. Don't Just Lie There, Say Something! 73. Carry On Dick 74. Carry On Behind 75. One of Our Dinosaurs Is Missing 75. Carry On England 76. Carry On Emmannuelle 78. Martin Chuzzlewit (TV) 94. Last of the Blonde Bombshells (TV) 00, etc.
TV series: Here and Now 55-56. Our House 60. The Stanley Baxter Show 63. The Dick Emery Show 63. Sam and Janet 67. The Kenneth Williams Show 70. Lord Tramp 77. Born and Bred 78-80. Farrington of the FO 86-87. On the Up 90-92.

Sinatra, Frank (1915–1998)
American leading actor and vocalist, former band singer. A teenage rave in the 40s, he later became respected as an actor and a powerful producer. His four wives included actress Ava Gardner (1951–54) and actress Mia Farrow (1966–68). He was the father of singer and actress Nancy Sinatra. He was played by Ray Liotta in the TV biopic *The Rat Pack* 98.
Biography: 1962, *Sinatra* by Robin Douglas-Home. 1978, *Sinatra, an Unauthorized Biography* by Earl Wilson. 1980, *Frank Sinatra* by John Howlett. 1984, *Sinatra: An American Classic* by John Rockwell. 1985, *Frank Sinatra, a Celebration* by Derek Jewell. 1985, *Frank Sinatra, My Father* by Nancy Sinatra. 1986, *His Way: The Unauthorized Biography* by Kitty Kelley. 1995, *Completely Frank* by Deborah Hill. 1997, *All or Nothing at All: A Life of Frank Sinatra* by Donald Clarke.
Other books: 1997, *Frank Sinatra at the Movies* by Roy Pickard.
■ Las Vegas Nights 41. Ship Ahoy 42. Reveille with Beverly 43. Higher and Higher (acting debut) 43. *Step Lively* 44. *Anchors Aweigh* 45. Till the Clouds Roll By 46. It Happened in Brooklyn 46. The Kissing Bandit 47. The Miracle of the Bells 48. *Take Me out to the Ball Game* 48. *On the Town* 49. Double Dynamite 50. Meet Danny Wilson 51. *From Here to Eternity* (AA) 53. Suddenly 54. Young at Heart 54. The Tender Trap 55. Not as a Stranger 55. *The Man with the Golden Arm* (AAN) 56. Johnny Concho 56. The Pride and the Passion 56. Around the World in Eighty Days 56. Guys and Dolls 56. *High Society* 56. *Pal Joey* 57. The Joker is Wild 57. Kings Go Forth 58. Some Came Running 58. A Hole in the Head 59. Can Can 59. Never So Few 59. Pepe 60. Ocean's Eleven 60. The Devil at Four O'Clock 61. Sergeants Three 62. *The Manchurian Candidate* 62. Four for Texas 63. The List of Adrian Messenger 63. Come Blow Your Horn 63. Robin and the Seven Hoods 64. None But the Brave (& d) 65. Von Ryan's Express 65. Marriage on the Rocks 65. Cast a Giant Shadow 66. Assault on a Queen 66. The Naked Runner (GB) 67. Tony Rome 67. *The Detective* 68. Lady in Cement 68. Dirty Dingus Magee 70. Contract on Cherry Street (TV) 77. The First Deadly Sin 80. Cannonball Run II 84.
See also: Rat Pack.
❝ Don't tell me. Suggest. But don't tell me. – *F.S.*
I detest bad manners. If people are polite, I am. They shouldn't try to get away with not being polite to me. – *F.S.*
He's the kind of guy that, when he dies, he's going up to heaven and give God a bad time for making him bald. – *Marlon Brando*
When he dies, they're giving his zipper to the Smithsonian. – *Dean Martin*
The charm that once made him irresistible was lost in the unpredictable whims of a spoiled child. – *Roger Vadim*
I was not impressed by the creeps and Mafia types he kept about him. – *Prince Charles*
Age has softened his sinister aura. – *Newsweek, 1982*

Sinatra, Nancy (1940–)
American leading lady and singer, daughter of Frank Sinatra. She was formerly married to singer Tommy Sands.
For Those Who Think Young 64. The Last of the Secret Agents 66. Speedway 68, etc.

Sinclair, Andrew (1935–)
British director.
Before Winter Comes (w only) 69. The Breaking of Bumbo 70. Under Milk Wood 72. Blue Blood 73.

Sinclair, Arthur (1883–1951) (Arthur McDonnell)
Irish actor, often in comic roles. Born in Dublin, he was a member of the Abbey Theatre company for its first 12 years. In the 20s, he also worked in variety. Married actress Maire O'Neill.
M'Blimey 31. Evensong 34. Irish Hearts 34. Sing as We Go 34. Wild Boy 34. Charing Cross Road 35. Peg of Old Drury 35. King Solomon's Mines 37. The Show Goes On 37. Welcome Mr Washington 44, etc.

Sinclair, Hugh (1903–1962)
British stage leading man, in occasional films.
Our Betters 33. Escape Me Never 35. A Girl Must Live 39. Alibi 42. They Were Sisters 45. Corridor of Mirrors 48. The Rocking Horse Winner 50. The Second Mrs Tanqueray 52, etc.

Sinclair, John Gordon (1962–)
Scottish actor, a former electrician, who began as the star of Bill Forsyth's comedy *Gregory's Girl*.
That Sinking Feeling 79. *Gregory's Girl* 80. Britannia Hospital 82. Local Hero 83. The Girl in the Picture 86. Erik the Viking 89. The Brylcreem Boys (TV) 96. Gregory's Two Girls 99, etc.
TV series: Hot Metal 86–88. Nelson's Column 94. Loved by You 97.

Sinclair, Madge (1940–1995)
Jamaican actress, a former teacher, who spent most of her working life in the US. Died of leukaemia.
Conrack 74. Cornbread, Earl and Me 75. Leadbelly 76. Convoy 78. Coming to America 88. Lion King (voice of Sarabi) 94.
TV series: Roots (as Belle) 77.

Sinclair, Robert (1905–1970)
American director. Married to Heather Angel.
Woman against Woman 38. Dramatic School 38. Mr and Mrs North 41. Mr District Attorney 46. That Wonderful Urge 48, etc.

Sinden, Sir Donald (1923–)
British leading man, on stage from mid-30s. Knighted 1997.
Autobiography: 1982, *A Touch of the Memoirs*.
The Cruel Sea (film debut) 53. Doctor in the House 54. Simba 55. Eyewitness 56. Doctor at Large 58. Operation Bullshine 59. Twice Round the Daffodils 62. Decline and Fall 68. Villain 71. Rentadick 72. The National Health 73. The Day of the Jackal 73. The Island at the Top of the World 74. That Lucky Touch 75, etc.
TV series: Our Man at St Mark's 58. Two's Company 77–80. Never the Twain 81–83.

Singer, Alexander (1932–)
American director.
■ *A Cold Wind in August* 62. Psyche 59 64. Love Has Many Faces 65. Captain Apache 71. The First 36 Hours of Dr Durant (TV) 75. The Million Dollar Rip-Off (TV) 76. Hunters of the Reef (TV) 78. The Return of Marcus Welby, MD (TV) 84.

Singer, Bryan (1967–)
American director.
Public Access 93. *The Usual Suspects* 95. Apt Pupil 97. X-Men 00, etc.

Singer, Campbell (1909–1976)
British character actor, often seen as heavy father, commissionaire, sergeant-major or policeman.
Premiere 37. Take My Life 47. The Ringer 52. Simba 55. The Square Peg 58. The Pot Carriers 63, many others.

Singer, Lori (1962–)
Lissom leading American actress, the sister of Marc Singer.
Born Beautiful (TV) 82. Footloose 84. The Falcon and the Snowman 85. The Man with One Red Shoe 85. Trouble in Mind 86. Summer Heat 87. Warlock 91. Short Cuts 93. F.T.W. 94, etc.
TV series: Fame 82–83.

Singer, Marc (1948–)
American leading actor, frequently in bare-chested roles.
Things in Their Season 74. Journey from Darkness 75. Go Tell the Spartans 78. For Ladies Only (TV) 81. The Beastmaster 82. If You Could See What I Hear 82. Her Life as a Man (TV) 83. Born to Race 88. Body Chemistry 90. High Desert Kill (TV) 90. A Man Called Sarge 90. The Raven Red Kiss-Off 90. Watchers II 90. In the Cold of the Night 91. Dead Space 91. Beastmaster 2: Through the Portal of Time 91. Sweet Justice 92. The Sea Wolf (TV) 93, etc.
TV series: The Contender 80. Roots: The Next Generation 79–81. V 84–85. Dallas 86.

Singleton, John (1968–)
American screenwriter and director.
Boyz N the Hood (AAN) 91. Poetic Justice 93. Higher Learning 94. Rosewood 97, etc.

Singleton, Penny (1908–) (Mariana McNulty)
American leading lady who made her greatest hit as *Blondie*.
Good News 30. After the Thin Man 36. *Swing Your Lady* 38. The Mad Miss Manton 38. *Blondie* 38 (then two films in the series every year, more or less, until 1950). The Best Man 64, etc.

Sinise, Gary (1955–)
American director and actor, on stage and screen. He was a founder of Chicago's Steppenwolf Theatre.
Miles from Home (d) 88. Of Mice and Men (a, d) 92. A Midnight Clear (a) 92. Jack the Bear (a)

93. The Stand (a) (TV) 94. Forrest Gump (a) (AAN) 94. The Quick and the Dead 95. Truman (TV, title role) 95. Ransom 96. Albino Alligator 96. George Wallace (TV) 97. Snake Eyes 98. The Green Mile 99. Mission to Mars 00. Reindeer Games 00, etc.

Sinyor, Gary
British director.
Leon the Pig Farmer (co-d) 92. Solitaire for 2 95. Stiff Upper Lips 97.

Siodmak, Curt (1902–2000)
German writer-director, in films from 1929, Hollywood from 1937. Brother of Robert Siodmak.
People on Sunday (co-w) 29. The Tunnel (co-w) 34. Her Jungle Love (co-w) 38. Frankenstein Meets the Wolf Man (w) 42. Son of Dracula (w) 43. The Beast with Five Fingers (w) 47. Bride of the Gorilla (wd) 51. *The Magnetic Monster* (d) 51. Donovan's Brain (oa) 53. Love Slaves of the Amazon (w, d) 57. Ski Fever (w, d) 66, etc.

Siodmak, Robert (1900–1973)
American director with early experience in Germany and France.
People on Sunday 29. The Weaker Sex 32. La Vie Parisienne 35. *Pièges* 39. West Point Widow 41. Son of Dracula 43. *Phantom Lady* 44. *The Suspect* 44. Christmas Holiday 44. *The Spiral Staircase* 45. The Strange Affair of Uncle Harry 45. *The Killers* (AAN) 46. *The Dark Mirror* 46. Cry of the City 48. Criss Cross 48. The File on Thelma Jordon 49. The Great Sinner 49. Deported 50. The Whistle at Eaton Falls 51. The Crimson Pirate 52. Le Grand Jeu 53. Mein Vater der Schauspieler 56. Jatja 59. The Rough and the Smooth 59. Tunnel 28/Escape from East Berlin 62. Custer of the West 67, many others.
66 He manipulated Hollywood's fantasy apparatus with taste and intelligence. – *Andrew Sarris, 1968*

Sirk, Douglas (1900–1987) (Detlef Sierck)
Danish director, with stage experience; in America from early 40s. Born in Hamburg, he was a theatre director before turning to film in Germany. His Hollywood films take an opulent, stylized approach to melodramatic subjects.
Books: 1994, *History, Culture and the Films of Douglas Sirk* by Barbara Klinger. 1998, *Sirk on Sirk*, ed. Jon Halliday.
SELECTED EUROPEAN FILMS: April April 35. Das Hofkonzert 36. La Habanera 37. Home Is Calling 37.
■ AMERICAN FILMS: Hitler's Madman 43. Summer Storm 44. A Scandal in Paris 46. *Lured* 47. *Sleep My Love* 48. Shockproof 49. Slightly French 49. Mystery Submarine 50. The First Legion 51. Thunder on the Hill 51. The Lady Pays Off 51. Weekend with Father 51. No Room for the Groom 52. *Has Anybody Seen My Gal?* 52. Meet Me at the Fair 52. Take Me to Town 53. All I Desire 53. Taza Son of Cochise 54. *Magnificent Obsession* 54. Sign of the Pagan 54. Captain Lightfoot 55. There's Always Tomorrow 56. All That Heaven Allows 56. *Written on the Wind* 57. Battle Hymn 57. Interlude 57. The Tarnished Angels 58. A Time to Love and a Time to Die 58. Imitation of Life 59.

Sisto, Jeremy (1974–)
American actor, from the stage. Born in Grass Valley, California, he studied at the University of California in Los Angeles.
Grand Canyon 91. The Crew 94. The Shaggy Dog (TV) 94. Hideaway 95. Clueless 95. Moonlight & Valentino 95. White Squall 96. Without Limits 98. This Space Between Us 99. The Auteur Theory 99. Jesus (title role) (TV) 00, etc.

Sitting Bull (1831–1890)
Chief of the Sioux at the time General Custer and his Seventh Cavalry were wiped out at the Little Big Horn, he later joined Buffalo Bill's Wild West. He was killed by Indian police in a raid during an uprising in which he was not a participant. On film, he is almost always on the warpath, the villain of countless westerns. He was played twice by J. Carrol Naish, in *Annie Get Your Gun* 50 and *Sitting Bull* 54. Also played by Chief Thunder Bird in *Annie Oakley* 35, Michael Granger in *Fort Vengeance* 53, John War Eagle in *Tonka* 58, Michael Pate in *The Great Sioux Massacre* 55, and Frank Kaquitts in *Buffalo Bill and the Indians* 76.
66 Most of what he earned went into the pockets of small, ragged boys. He could not understand why all the wealth he saw in the cities wasn't divided up among the poor. Among the Indians, a man who had plenty of food shared it with those who had none. – *Annie Oakley*

Sizemore, Tom (1964–)
American leading actor.
Born on the Fourth of July 89. Lock Up 89. Where Sleeping Dogs Lie 91. Flight of the Intruder 91. Guilty by Suspicion 91. Harley Davidson & the Marlboro Man 91. Striking Distance 93. Watch It 93. Heart and Souls 93. True Romance 93. Wyatt Earp 94. Natural Born Killers 94. Strange Days 95. Devil in a Blue Dress 95. Heat 95. The Relic 96. Saving Private Ryan 98. Enemy of the State 98. Bringing Out the Dead 99. The Match 99. Play It To The Bone 99. Red Planet 00. Big Trouble 01, etc.

Sjoberg, Alf (1903–1980)
Swedish director, former stage actor and director.
The Road to Heaven 42. *Frenzy* 44. Only a Mother 49. *Miss Julie* 51. Barabbas 53. Karin Mansdotter 54. Wild Birds 55. The Judge 60. The Island 66, many others.

Sjoman, Vilgot (1924–)
Swedish director, chiefly famous (and notorious) for '*491*' 66. *I Am Curious: Blue* 67, *I Am Curious: Yellow* 67, and *Blushing Charlie* 71.
Also: Troll 73. A Handful of Love 74. The Garage 74. Tabu 77. Linus Eller Tegelhusets Hemlighet 79. Malacca 86. Fallgropen 89. Alfred 95, etc.

Sjostrom, Victor
See Seastrom, Victor.

Skaaren, Warren (1947–1991)
American screenwriter and producer. Previously he was first commissioner of the Texas Film Commission and then ran a production services company.
Fire with Fire/Captive Hearts (co-w) 86. Top Gun (p) 86. Beverly Hills Cop II (co-w) 87. Beetlejuice (co-w) 88. Batman (co-w) 89, etc.

Skala, Lilia (1896–1994)
Austrian actress in America.
Lilies of the Field (AAN) 64. Deadly Hero 76. Roseland 77. Heartland 80. The End of August 82. Flashdance 83. House of Games 87, etc.

Skall, William V. (1898–1976)
American cinematographer.
Victoria the Great 37. The Mikado 39. Northwest Passage 40. Life with Father 47. *Joan of Arc* (AA) 48. Quo Vadis 51. The Silver Chalice 55, many others.

Skarsgard, Stellan (1951–)
Swedish actor, in international films. Born in Gothenburg, he came to notice as a teenager in Sweden in the TV series *Bombi Bitt and Me* 68. From the early 70s to the mid-80s, he acted at the Royal Dramatic Theatre in Stockholm.
Anita 73. Inkraktarna 74. Yon Sylissa 77. Den Enfaldige Mördaren 82. Bakom Jalousin 83. P&B 83. Ake and His World 84. Noon Wine (TV) 85. Hip, Hip, Hurra! 87. The Unbearable Lightness of Being (US) 87. Friends 88. The Perfect Murder (Ind.) 88. The Woman on the Roof/Kvinnorna Pa Teket 89. The Hunt for Red October (US) 90. Wind (US) 92. The Ox/Oxen 92. The Slingshot/Kadisbellan 93. Harry & Sonja 96. Breaking the Waves 96. Riget II/Kingdom II (TV) 97. Amistad (US) 97. *Insomnia* 97. Good Will Hunting (US) 97. My Son the Fanatic (GB) 98. Ronin (US) 98. Savior (US) 98. Deep Blue Sea (US) 99. Timecode (US) 00. Aberdeen (GB/Nor.) 00, etc.

Skeggs, Roy
British production executive, a former accountant. He worked for Hammer in the 60s and bought the company in 1985 after it went into official receivership. He announced plans to remake old Hammer features in 1994 in partnership with producer Lauren Shuler-Donner and director Richard Donner.
Frankenstein and the Monster from Hell 73. Satanic Rites of Dracula 73. To the Devil a Daughter 76, etc.
66 Hammer was Walt Disney with a bit of blood. – *R.S.*

Skelly, Hal (1891–1934) (Joseph Harold Skelly)
American character actor from Broadway and vaudeville. Born in Allegheny, Pennsylvania, he left home at the age of 15 to work as a circus acrobat. He made his screen debut in a re-titled version of his Broadway hit, *Burlesque*. Died in a car accident.
■ *The Dance of Life* 29. Woman Trap 29. Behind the Make Up 30. Men Are Like That 30. The Struggle 31. Hotel Variety 31. Shadow Laughs 31.

Skelton, Red (1910–1997) (Richard Bernard Skelton)
American comedian of radio, film and television. Born in Vincennes, Indiana, the son of a circus clown, he began in vaudeville as a child. In the early 40s, he signed a long-term contract with MGM, but in the 50s he switched to performing on television, retiring in the early 70s. Married three times.
■ Having Wonderful Time 38. Flight Command 40. The People Versus Dr Kildare 41. Lady Be Good 41. *Whistling in the Dark* 41. Dr Kildare's Wedding Day 41. Ship Ahoy 42. Maisie Gets Her Man 42. Panama Hattie 42. Whistling in Dixie 42. *Dubarry Was a Lady* 43. I Dood It 43. Whistling in Brooklyn 43. Thousands Cheer 43. Bathing Beauty 44. Ziegfeld Follies 46. The Show Off 46. *Merton of the Movies* 47. The Fuller Brush Man 48. A Southern Yankee 48. Neptune's Daughter 49. The Yellow Cab Man 50. The Fuller Brush Girl (gag) 50. Three Little Words 50. Duchess of Idaho (gag) 50. Watch the Birdie 50. Excuse My Dust 51. Texas Carnival 51. Lovely to Look at 52. The Clown 52. Half a Hero 53. The Great Diamond Robbery 53. Susan Slept Here (gag) 54. Around the World in Eighty Days 56. Public Pigeon Number One 57. Ocean's Eleven (gag) 60. Those Magnificent Men in Their Flying Machines 65. Rudolph's Shiny New Year (voice) 79.
TV series: The Red Skelton Show 51–71.
66 I'm nuts and I know it. But so long as I make 'em laugh, they ain't going to lock me up. – *R.S.*
I always believed God puts each one of us here for a purpose ... and mine is to try to make people happy. – *R.S.*

Skerritt, Tom (1933–)
American actor.
War Hunt 62. One Man's Way 64. Those Callaways 65. M*A*S*H 70. Wild Rovers 71. Fuzz 72. Thieves Like Us 74. Big Bad Mama 74. The Devil's Rain 75. The Turning Point 77. Up in Smoke 78. Alien 79. Ice Castles 79. Savage Harvest 81. A Dangerous Summer 81. Silence of the North 81. Fighting Back 82. The Dead Zone 83. Top Gun 86. Wisdom 86. Opposing Force 87. Maid to Order 87. The Big Town 87. Poltergeist III 88. Big Man on Campus 89. The Heist (TV) 89. Red King, White Knight (TV) 89. Steel Magnolias 89. Child in the Night (TV) 90. The Rookie 90. Wild Orchid II: Two Shades of Blue 92. Poison Ivy 92. A River Runs Through It 92. Knight Moves 93. Divided by Hate (TV) 93. Contact 97. Two for Texas (TV) 98. Jackie Bouvier Kennedy Onassis (TV) 00, etc.
TV series: Run, Run, Joe 74. Picket Fences 92–96.

Skiles, Marlin (1906–)
American composer.
The Impatient Years 44. Gilda 46. Dead Reckoning 47. Callaway Went Thataway 51. The Maze 53. Bowery to Baghdad 55. Fort Massacre 58. The Hypnotic Eye 60. The Strangler 64. The Resurrection of Zachary Wheeler 71, many others.

Skinner, Claire (1965–)
British actress, from the stage and TV.
Life Is Sweet 91. Naked 93. The Return of the Native (TV) 94. I.D. 95. Clockwork Mice 95. Smilla's Sense of Snow/Smilla's Feeling for Snow 97, etc.
TV series: Chef! 94.

Skinner, Cornelia Otis (1901–1979)
American stage actress, daughter of Otis Skinner the tragedian. Toyed with Hollywood occasionally. Her autobiographical book *Our Hearts Were Young and Gay* (co-written with Emily Kimbrough) was filmed with Gail Russell.
The Uninvited 44. The Girl in the Red Velvet Swing 55. The Swimmer 67.

Skinner, Frank (1898–1968)
American composer.
Son of Frankenstein 39. Destry Rides Again 39. Hellzapoppin 41. Back Street 41. Saboteur 42. Gung Ho 43. The Suspect 44. The Egg and I 47. Abbott and Costello Meet Frankenstein 48. Francis 49. Harvey 50. The World in His Arms 52. Thunder Bay 53. Battle Hymn 56. Imitation of Life 58. Back Street 61. Shenandoah 65. Madame X 66, many others.

Skinner, Otis (1858–1942)
American stage actor who appeared in films only in two versions of *Kismet* 20 & 30. Charles Ruggles played him in *Our Hearts Were Young and Gay* 44.

Skipworth, Alison (1875–1952) (Alison Groom)
Chubby British character actress, long in Hollywood; a favourite foil for W. C. Fields.
Raffles 30. Outward Bound 30. Devotion 31. Night After Night 32. *If I Had a Million* 32. Song of Songs 33. *Tillie and Gus* 33. Six of a Kind 34. The Captain Hates the Sea 34. Becky Sharp 35. Shanghai 35. Satan Met a Lady 36. Stolen Holiday 37. Wide Open Faces 38, many others.
66 *A.S., concerned that Mae West was stealing her scene:* I'll have you know I'm an actress.
Mae West: It's all right, dearie. I'll keep your secret.

Skirball, Jack H. (1896–1985)
American independent producer, former salesman.
Miracle on Main Street 38. Lady from Cheyenne 41. Saboteur 42. Shadow of a Doubt 43. It's in the Bag/The Fifth Chair 45. Guest Wife 46. Payment on Demand 51, etc.

Skjoldbjaerg, Erik (1965–)
Norwegian director.
Insomnia 97.

Skolimowski, Jerzy (1938–)
Polish director.
The Barrier 66. The Departure 67. Hands Up 67. Dialogue 69. The Adventures of Gerard 70. Deep End 71. King, Queen, Knave 72. The Shout 78. Circle of Deceit (a only) 81. Moonlighting (& w) 82. Success Is the Best Revenge 84. The Lightship 85. Torrents of Spring 89. The Hollow Men (p) 93. Mars Attacks! (a) 96. LA without a Map (a) (GB/Fr./Fin.) 98. Before Night Falls (a) 00, etc.

Skouras, Spyros (1893–1971)
Greek-American executive, former hotelier. President of Twentieth Century-Fox 1943–62; instigator of CinemaScope.
66 The only Greek tragedy I know is Spyros Skouras. – *Billy Wilder*

Skye, Ione (1971–) (Ione Skye Leitch)
British actress, working in America. She is the daughter of 60s folk singer Donovan.
The River's Edge 87. Stranded 87. A Night in the Life of Jimmy Reardon 88. Carmilla 89. The Rachel Papers 89. Say Anything 89. Mindwalk 90. Samantha 91. Gas, Food, Lodging 92. Guncrazy 92. Wayne's World 92. Four Rooms 95. Dream of an Insomniac 96. The Size of Watermelons 96. One Night Stand 97. Went to Coney Island on a Mission From God ... Be Back by Five 98. Mascara 98, etc.
TV series: Covington Cross 92.

Slaney, Ivor (1921–)
English composer.
The Gambler and the Lady 53. Spaceways 53. The Saint's Return/The Saint's Girl Friday 53. Face the Music/The Black Glove 54. The House across the Lake/Heat Wave 54. The Stranger Came Home/The Unholy Four 54. Five Days/Paid to Kill 54. Murder by Proxy/Blackout 55. Terror 79, etc.

Slate, Jeremy (1935–)
American general-purpose actor.
Wives and Lovers 63. I'll Take Sweden 65. The Sons of Katie Elder 66. The Devil's Brigade 68. Hells Angels '69 69. The Centerfold Girls 74. Stranger in Our House (TV) 78. Mr Horn (TV) 79. Dead Pit 89. Dream Machine 91. The Lawnmower Man 92, etc.

Slater, Christian (1969–) (Christian Hawkins)
Saturnine young American leading actor. Born in New York City, the son of an actor and a casting director, he acted from childhood and was in films as a teenager. In 1997 he was jailed for 90 days after pleading no contest to charges of battery and

being under the influence of a controlled substance.

The Legend of Billie Jean 85. The Name of the Rose 86. Heathers 88. Tucker: The Man and His Dream 88. Gleaming the Cube 88. The Wizard 89. Beyond the Stars 89. Tales from the Darkside: The Movie 90. Young Guns II 90. Pump Up the Volume 90. Robin Hood: Prince of Thieves 91. Mobsters 91. Star Trek VI: The Undiscovered Country 91. Where the Day Takes You (uncredited) 92. Ferngully: The Last Rainforest (voice) 92. Kuffs 92. Untamed Heart 93. True Romance 93. Interview with the Vampire: The Vampire Chronicles 94. Jimmy Hollywood 94. Murder in the First 95. Bed of Roses 95. Broken Arrow 96. Julian Po 97. Hard Rain 98. Very Bad Things 98. The Contender 00, etc.

❝ I have been acting since the age of eight and have been a celebrity for a long time. And when you're a celebrity, you start believing you can act off the screen any way you want without consequence. – C.S.

Slater, Helen (1963–)
Blonde American actress who made her debut in the title role of *Supergirl* but has since tended to play supporting roles.

Supergirl 84. The Legend of Billie Jean 85. Ruthless People 86. The Secret of My Success 87. Sticky Fingers 88. Happy Together 89. City Slickers 91. A House in the Hills 93. Chantilly Lace (TV) 93. Lassie 94. Parallel Lives (TV) 94. No Way Back 96. Toothless 97, etc.

Slater, John (1916–1975)
British cockney character actor and comedian of stage and TV, occasionally in films.

Love on the Dole (debut) 40. Went the Day Well? 42. A Canterbury Tale 44. Passport to Pimlico 48. Johnny You're Wanted 54. Violent Playground 58. Three on a Spree 61. A Place to Go 63, many others.

Slater, Ryan (1984–)
American child actor, the brother of Christian Slater.

The Amazing Panda Adventure 95.

Slattery, Tony (1959–)
British actor, TV presenter, and comedian, from television and the stage. Born in London, he studied at Cambridge University, where he was a member of Footlights. He suffered from clinical depression in the late-90s and stopped working for two years.

How to Get a Head in Advertising 89. Peter's Friends 92. The Crying Game 92. To Die For 94. Up 'n' Under 98. The Wedding Tackle 99, etc.

TV series: David Harper 91. Just a Gigolo 93.

❝ Words are loaded pistols. You use them at your peril. – *T.S.*

Slaughter, Tod (1885–1956) (N. Carter Slaughter)
Barnstorming British actor who toured the provinces with chop-licking revivals of outrageous old melodramas, all of which he filmed after a fashion.

■ Maria Marten 35. Sweeney Todd 36. The Crimes of Stephen Hawke 36. Song of the Road 37. Darby and Joan 37. It's Never Too Late to Mend 37. The Ticket of Leave Man 37. Sexton Blake and the Hooded Terror 38. *The Face at the Window* 39. Crimes at the Dark House 40. The Curse of the Wraydons 43. The Greed of William Hart 48. King of the Underworld 52. Murder at Scotland Yard 52.

Sletaune, Pal
Norwegian director.

Junk Mail/Budbringeren 97. Blood, Guts, Bullets and Octane 98, etc.

Slezak, Walter (1902–1983)
Austrian character actor, of theatrical family; in America from 1930. Committed suicide.

Autobiography: 1962, *What Time's the Next Swan?*.

Once upon a Honeymoon (English-speaking debut) 42. *Lifeboat* 44. Step Lively 44. The Spanish Main 45. Cornered 45. Sinbad the Sailor 47. The Pirate 48. *The Inspector General* 49. Call Me Madam 53. White Witch Doctor 54. The Steel Cage 54. Come September 61. Emil and the Detectives 64. Wonderful Life (GB) 64. Twenty-Four Hours to Kill 65. A Very Special Favor 65. Caper of the Golden Bulls 67. Dr Coppelius 68. Black Beauty 71, etc.

Sloan, Holly Goldberg (1958–)
American screenwriter, director and producer.

Indecency (co-w) 92. Made in America (w) 93. Angels in the Outfield (w) 94. The Big Green (wd) 95. The Secret Life of Girls (wd) 99, etc.

Sloane, Everett (1909–1965)
Incisive American character actor, brought to Hollywood by Orson Welles.

■ *Citizen Kane* 41. *Journey into Fear* 42. *The Lady from Shanghai* 48. Prince of Foxes 49. *The Men* 50. Bird of Paradise 51. The Enforcer 51. Sirocco 51. The Prince Who Was a Thief 51. The Blue Veil 51. The Desert Fox 51. The Sellout 51. Way of a Gaucho 52. *The Big Knife* 55. *Patterns* 56. *Somebody Up There Likes Me* 56. Lust for Life 56. Marjorie Morningstar 58. The Gun Runners 58. Home from the Hill 60. By Love Possessed 61. Brushfire 62. The Man from the Diners Club 63. The Patsy 64. Ready for the People 64. The Disorderly Orderly 64.

TV series: Official Detective 58.

❝ Famous line (*Citizen Kane*) 'Old age, Mr Thompson: it's the only disease you don't look forward to being cured of.'

Sloane, Olive (1896–1963)
British character actress of stage and screen whose best role was in *Seven Days to Noon* 50. Countless other small roles since film debut in *Greatheart* 21.

Sloane, Paul (1893–1963)
American director, in films as a screenwriter from 1914, moving to direction for Paramount in 1925 with movies starring Richard Dix. Moved to Japan in the early 50s.

A Man Must Live 25. The Shock Punch 25. Too Many Kisses 25. The Coming of Amos 25. The Woman Accused 33. Terror Aboard 33. Lone Cowboy 34. The Texans (co-w only) 38. *Geronimo* (& w) 39. The Sun Sets at Dawn (& p, w) 50. Forever My Love/Itsu Itsu Made Mo 52, etc.

Slocombe, Douglas (1913–)
British cinematographer, former journalist.

Dead of Night 45. The Captive Heart 46. Hue and Cry 46. The Loves of Joanna Godden 47. *It Always Rains on Sunday* 47. *Saraband for Dead Lovers* 48. Kind Hearts and Coronets 49. Cage of Gold 50. The Lavender Hill Mob 51. Mandy 52. The Man in the White Suit 52. *The Titfield Thunderbolt* 53. Man in the Sky 56. The Smallest Show on Earth 57. Tread Softly Stranger 58. Circus of Horrors 59. The Young Ones 61. The L-Shaped Room 62. *Freud* 63. The Servant 63. Guns at Batasi 64. A High Wind in Jamaica 65. The Blue Max 66. Promise Her Anything 66. The Vampire Killers 67. Fathom 67. Robbery 67. Boom 68. The Lion in Winter 68. The Italian Job 69. *The Music Lovers* 70. Murphy's War 70. The Buttercup Chain 70. Travels with My Aunt (AAN) 73. The Great Gatsby 74. Love Among the Ruins (TV) 75. Rollerball 75. Hedda 76. Julia (AAN, BFA) 77. Nasty Habits 77. Caravans 78. Lost and Found 79. The Lady Vanishes 79. Nijinsky 80. Lost and Found 80. Raiders of the Lost Ark (AAN) 81. The Pirates of Penzance 83. Never Say Never Again 83. Indiana Jones and the Temple of Doom 84. Lady Jane 85. Indiana Jones and the Last Crusade 89, etc.

Sloman, Edward (1887–1972)
English director in Hollywood, mainly of silents, a former actor.

Lying Lips 16. The Eagle's Feather 23. The Foreign Legion 28. The Lost Zeppelin 29. Hell's Island 30. Puttin' on the Ritz 30. His Woman 31. There's Always Tomorrow 34. A Dog of Flanders 35. The Jury's Secret 38, etc.

Sluizer, George (1932–)
Dutch director and screenwriter, a former documentary film-maker.

Twice a Woman 79. Red Desert Penitentiary 87. The Vanishing/Spoorloos 88. Utz (GB) 91. The Vanishing (US) 93. Dark Blood (uncompleted) 94. Crimetime 96. The Commissioner 99, etc.

Small, Edward (1891–1977)
Veteran American independent producer, former actor and agent, in Hollywood from 1924.

I Cover the Waterfront 35. The Man in the Iron Mask 39. The Corsican Brothers 41. Brewster's Millions 45. Down Three Dark Streets 55. Witness for the Prosecution 57. Jack the Giant Killer 62. I'll Take Sweden 65. Forty Guns to Apache Pass 66, many others; also TV series.

Small, Michael (1939–)
American composer.

Puzzle of a Downfall Child 70. Klute 71. Child's Play 72. The Parallax View 74. Night Moves 75. Marathon Man 76. Comes a Horseman 78. Those Lips Those Eyes 80. The Postman Always Rings Twice 81. Continental Divide 81. Rollover 81. The Star Chamber 83. Firstborn 84. Target 85. Dream Lover 86. Brighton Beach Memoirs 86. Black Widow 87. Orphans 87. Jaws – the Revenge 87. 1969 88. See You in the Morning 89. Mountains of the Moon 90, etc.

Smalley, Phillips (1875–1939)
American leading actor and director of silents. He was married to director Lois Weber and was involved in some of her films as actor and co-director. From the 20s, he continued as a character actor.

The Armorer's Daughter (a) 10. The Chorus Girl (d) 12. The Jew's Christmas (a, co-d) 13. The Merchant of Venice (a, co-d) 14. Scandal (a, co-d) 15. The Dumb Girl of Portici (co-d) 15. Where Are My Children? (co-d) 15. The Flirt (co-d) 16. Flaming Youth (a) 23. Charley's Aunt (a) 25. Man Crazy (a) 27. True Heaven 29. Charley's Aunt 30. Cocktail Hour 33. A Night at the Opera 35, etc.

Smart, J. Scott (1903–1950)
Heavyweight radio actor who took his *Fat Man* character to Hollywood for one 50s film of that name.

Smart, Ralph (1908–)
British producer-director, latterly of TV series *The Invisible Man*, *Danger Man*, etc. Former editor and writer.

AS DIRECTOR: Bush Christmas 46. A Boy, a Girl and a Bike 48. Bitter Springs 50. Never Take No for an Answer (co-d) 51. Curtain Up 52. Always a Bride 54, etc.

Smeaton, Bruce
Australian composer.

The Cars that Ate Paris 74. Picnic at Hanging Rock 75. The Devil's Playground 76. Eliza Fraser 76. The Chant of Jimmie Blacksmith 78. The Last of the Knucklemen 78. Circle of Iron 79. Double Deal 81. Barbarosa 81. Undercover 83. The Naked Country 84. Iceman 84. Plenty 85. Eleni 85. Roxanne 87. A Cry in the Dark 88, etc.

Smedley-Aston, E. M. (1912–)
British producer.

The Extra Day 56. Two-Way Stretch 60. Offbeat 61. The Wrong Arm of the Law 63. Ooh You Are Awful 72, etc.

Smethurst, Jack (1932–)
English character actor, born in Collyhurst, Manchester, and much on television.

A Kind of Loving 62. The Main Chance 64. The Agony and the Ecstasy 65. Run with the Wind 66. Night after Night after Night 70. For the Love of Ada 72. Love Thy Neighbour 73. Man about the House 74. King Ralph 91, etc.

TV series: For the Love of Ada 70–71. Love Thy Neighbour 72–76. Hilary 84.

Smight, Jack (1926–)
American director, from TV.

■ I'd Rather Be Rich 64. The Third Day 65. *Harper* 66. Kaleidoscope 66. The Secret War of Harry Frigg 67. No Way to Treat a Lady 68. The Illustrated Man 69. Strategy of Terror (TV) 69. Rabbit Run (TV) 69. The Travelling Executioner 70. The Screaming Woman (TV) 72. Detour to Nowhere (TV) 72. The Longest Night (TV) 72. Linda (TV) 73. Double Indemnity (TV) 73. Frankenstein: The True Story (TV) 73. Airport 75 74. Midway 76. Damnation Alley 77. Roll of Thunder (TV) 78. Fast Break 78. Loving Couples 80. Number One with a Bullet 87. The Favorite 89.

Smith, Albert E. (1875–1958)
British pioneer producer in America, one of the founders of the Vitagraph Company.

Smith, Alexis (1921–1993) (Gladys Smith)
American leading lady of the 40s who won an acting contest from Hollywood high school. Married to Craig Stevens.

Lady with Red Hair 41. Dive Bomber 41. The Smiling Ghost 41. Gentleman Jim 42. The Constant Nymph 42. The Doughgirls 44. Conflict 45. Rhapsody in Blue 45. San Antonio 45. Night and Day 46. Of Human Bondage 46. Stallion Road 47. The Woman in White 47. The Decision of Christopher Blake 48. Any Number Can Play 50. Undercover Girl 52. Split Second 53. The Sleeping Tiger (GB) 55. The Eternal Sea 56. The Young Philadelphians/The City Jungle 59. Once is Not Enough 75. The Little Girl Who Lives Down the Lane 77. Casey's Shadow 78. A Death in California (TV) 85. Tough Guys 86. The Age of Innocence 93, etc.

TV series: Dallas 84. Hothouse 88.

❝ When they tell me one of my old movies is on TV, I don't look at it. – *A.S.*

Those films weren't very good at the time, and they haven't improved with age. – *A.S.*

There are so many more interesting things to think about than whether Ida Lupino or Jane Wyman got the roles I should have gotten. – *A.S.*

Smith, Art (1899–1973)
Bland, avuncular American character actor.

A Tree Grows in Brooklyn 44. Letter from an Unknown Woman 47. Cover Up 50. In a Lonely Place 51, etc.

Smith, Bernard (c. 1905–)
American producer, ex-publisher and story editor.

Elmer Gantry (AA) 60. How the West Was Won 62. Seven Women 65. Alfred the Great 69, etc.

Smith, Bessie (1894–1937)
America's greatest singer of classic blues, known as 'The Empress of the Blues', who made one short in 1929, singing 'St Louis Blues', which has been re-issued on video-cassette. The highest-paid black star in the 20s, she hit hard times in the 30s and died following a car crash. There are plans to make a biopic of her life.

Biography: 1972, *Bessie* by Chris Albertson.

Smith, Betty (1904–1972)
American novelist.

Works filmed include *A Tree Grows in Brooklyn*, *Joy in the Morning*.

Smith, Bubba (1945–) (Charles Smith)
Tall American actor, a former football star.

Stroker Ace 83. Police Academy 84. Police Academy 2 85. Police Academy 3 86. Police Academy 4 87. The Wild Pair 87. Police Academy 5 88. Police Academy 6 89. Gremlins 2: The New Batch 90. My Samurai 92, etc.

Smith, Sir C. Aubrey (1863–1948)
Distinguished English leading actor on stage who went to Hollywood in his 60s to play crusty, benevolent, or authoritarian old gentlemen. Born in London, he was a first-class sportsman, playing soccer for the Corinthians and cricket for Cambridge University. Nicknamed 'Round the Corner Smith' for his unusual bowling style, he captained Sussex County Cricket Club for four years, an English team that went to Australia in 1887, and the first English team to tour South Africa. A teacher and a stockbroker before becoming an actor, he was on stage from 1892, including a notable Professor Higgins in George Bernard Shaw's *Pygmalion* in 1914. He was in films from 1915 and was one of the founders of a short-lived English company, Minerva Films. Success came when he repeated for MGM his stage hit *The Bachelor Father*. A founder-member of the Hollywood Cricket Club, he was knighted in 1944. The characters of Sir Ambrose Abercrombie and, to a lesser extent, Sir Francis Hinsley in Evelyn Waugh's novel *The Loved One* are modelled on him.

Biography: 1982, *Sir Aubrey* by David Rayvern Allen.

SELECTED SILENT FILMS: The Witching Hour 16. The Bohemian Girl 23. The Rejected Woman 24.

■ SOUND FILMS: Birds of Prey (GB) 30. Such Is the Law (GB) 30. Contraband Love (GB) 31. Trader Horn 31. Never the Twain Shall Meet 31. Bachelor Father 31. Daybreak 31. Just a Gigolo 31. Son of India 31. The Man in Possession 31. Phantom of Paris 31. Guilty Hands 31. Surrender 31. Polly of the Circus 31. Tarzan the Ape Man 32. But the Flesh Is Weak 32. *Love Me Tonight* 32. Trouble in Paradise 32. No More Orchids 32. They Just Had to Get Married 32. Luxury Liner 33. Secrets 33. The Barbarian 33. Adorable 33. The Monkey's Paw 33. *Morning Glory* 33. Bombshell 33. Queen Christina 33. The House of Rothschild 34. The Scarlet Empress 34. Gambling Lady 34.

Curtain at Eight 34. The Tunnel (GB) 34. Bulldog Drummond Strikes Back 34. Cleopatra 34. Madame du Barry 34. One More River 34. Caravan 34. The Firebird 34. The Right to Live 35. *Lives of a Bengal Lancer* 35. The Florentine Dagger 35. The Gilded Lily 35. Clive of India 35. China Seas 35. Jalna 35. The Crusades 35. Little Lord Fauntleroy 36. Romeo and Juliet 36. The Garden of Allah 36. Lloyds of London 36. Wee Willie Winkie 36. *The Prisoner of Zenda* 37. Thoroughbreds Don't Cry 37. The Hurricane 37. Four Men and a Prayer 38. Kidnapped 38. Sixty Glorious Years (GB) 38. East Side of Heaven 39. Five Came Back 39. *The Four Feathers* (GB) 39. The Sun Never Sets 39. Eternally Yours 39. Another Thin Man 39. The Underpup 39. Balalaika 39. *Rebecca* 40. City of Chance 40. A Bill of Divorcement 40. Waterloo Bridge 40. Beyond Tomorrow 40. A Little Bit of Heaven 40. Free and Easy 41. Maisie was a Lady 41. Dr Jekyll and Mr Hyde 41. Forever and a Day 43. Two Tickets to London 43. Flesh and Fantasy 43. Madame Curie 43. The White Cliffs of Dover 44. The Adventures of Mark Twain 44. Secrets of Scotland Yard 44. Sensations of 1945 44. They Shall Have Faith 44. *And Then There Were None* 45. Scotland Yard Investigator 45. Cluny Brown 46. Rendezvous with Annie 46. High Conquest 47. Unconquered 47. *An Ideal Husband* (GB) 47. Little Women 49.

✪ For relishing and perpetuating the stereotype of the fine old English gentleman. *The Four Feathers*.

❝ Mr Aubrey Smith has few equals in the delineation of the polished, straightforward, simple-minded English gentleman. – *The Graphic*

He was born to smell of tobacco and Harris tweeds, and to wave portentous eyebrows … He stands for all that is most essentially British: that queer admixture of sportsmanship, dunderheadedness and sentiment which has rendered the inhabitants of these islands the most exasperating enigma with which any other nation has ever had to cope. – *Theatre World*

The Bank of England, the cliffs of Dover, the Rock of Gibraltar and several super-dreadnoughts rolled into one. – *New York Times*

He *was* England, to a great many – perhaps an older England, but an England rich in dignity, graciousness and good will. Certainly no one could ever have known him, either in life or on the screen, without liking England better afterwards. – *James Hilton*

My God! I can't possibly act with a cricket bat! – *Mrs Patrick Campbell, objecting to appearing with him in Pygmalion*

Aubrey, Aubrey, don't go on the stage, think of what will become of your two sisters if their brother is an actor. – *His mother*

Smith, Charles (1920–1988)
American character actor who in the 40s played Dizzy in the *Henry Aldrich* series and other amiably doltish roles.

The Shop around the Corner 40. Tom Brown's Schooldays 40. Three Little Girls in Blue 45. Two Weeks with Love 50. City of Bad Men 53, many others.

Smith, Charles Martin (1953–)
American leading actor and occasional director.

Culpepper Cattle Co. 72. Fuzz 72. American Graffiti 73. Pat Garrett and Billy the Kid 73. Law of the Land 76. The Campus Corpse 77. The Buddy Holly Story 78. More American Graffiti 79. Herbie Goes Bananas 80. Cotton Candy 82. Starman 84. Trick or Treat (& d) 86. The Untouchables 87. The Hot Spot 90. Boris & Natasha (& d) 92. Deep Cover 92. Fifty/Fifty (& d) 93. And the Band Played On (TV) 93. I Love Trouble 94. Speechless 94. Larry McMurtry's Streets of Laredo (TV) 95. Peter Benchley's The Beast (TV) 96. Dead Silence (TV) 96. The Final Cut 96. Air Bud (d only) 97. Deep Impact 98, etc.

Smith, Constance (1929–)
British leading lady.

Brighton Rock 47. Don't Say Die 50. The Thirteenth Letter (US) 51. Red Skies of Montana (US) 52. Treasure of the Golden Condor (US) 53. Tiger by the Tail 55. Cross Up 58, etc.

Smith, Cyril (1892–1963)
British character actor of stage and screen, often a hen-pecked husband but equally likely to be a grocer, dustman or policeman. On stage from 1900, films from 1908, and was in over 500 of the latter.

Friday the Thirteenth 33. School for Secrets 46. It's Hard to Be Good 48. Mother Riley Meets the Vampire 52. John and Julie 54. *Sailor Beware* (his stage role) 56, etc.

Smith, Dick (1922–)
Influential American make-up artist, noted for his work on special effects, from television.

Misty 59. The World of Henry Orient 64. Little Big Man 70. House of Dark Shadows 70. The Godfather 72. The Exorcist 73. The Godfather Part II 74. The Stepford Wives 74. Burnt Offerings 76. Exorcist II: The Heretic 77. The Sentinel 77. The Fury 78. Altered States 80. Ghost Story 81. Scanners 81. Amadeus (AA) 84. Poltergeist III 88. Tales from the Darkside: The Movie 90. Death Becomes Her 92, etc.

Smith, Dodie (1896–1990)
English dramatist and novelist, a former actress, whose children's book *The Hundred and One Dalmatians* was turned into a classic animated feature by Walt Disney in 1961. Disney made a live-action version in 1996, starring Glenn Close.

Biography: 1996, *Dear Dodie* by Valerie Grove.

Looking Forward (oa) 33. Autumn Crocus (oa) 34. Dear Octopus (oa) 43. 101 Dalmatians (oa) 96, etc.

❝ What people won't realize is that if you're separated from your dog for more than five hours, you become absolutely miserable. Five hours is the absolute maximum. – *D.S.*

Smith, G. A. (1864–1959)
British pioneer cinematographer who invented a cine-camera in 1896 and made some trick films.

The Corsican Brothers 97. The Fairy Godmother 98. Faust 98, etc.

Smith, Jack Martin (c. 1910–1993)
American art director who worked for MGM, specializing in musicals, from the late 30s to the early 50s, when he joined Twentieth Century-Fox, becoming supervising art director in 1961.

One Hundred Men and a Girl 37. Meet Me in St Louis 44. Yolanda and the Thief 45. Easter Parade 48. Madame Bovary 49. Show Boat 51. Carousel 56. Teenage Rebel (AAN) 56. An Affair to Remember 57. Voyage to the Bottom of the Sea 61. Cleopatra (AA) 63. Move Over, Darling 63. What a Way to Go (AAN) 64. The Agony and the Ecstasy 65. Fantastic Voyage (AA) 66. Batman 66. Doctor Dolittle (AAN) 67. The Detective 68. The Boston Strangler 68. Planet of the Apes 68. Hello Dolly (AA) 69. Butch Cassidy and the Sundance Kid 69. M*A*S*H 69. Justine 69. Tora! Tora! Tora! (AAN) 70. Beyond the Valley of the Dolls 70. Emperor of the North 73. Lost in the Stars 74. Pete's Dragon 77, etc.

Smith, Jaclyn (1947–)
American leading actress, mainly on television.

Goodbye Columbus 69. The Adventurers 70. Bootleggers 74. The Users 74. Nightkill 80. Jacqueline Bouvier Kennedy (TV) 81. George Washington (TV) 84. Déjà Vu 84. Rage of Angels (TV) 85. The Night They Saved Christmas (TV) 87. The Bourne Identity (TV) 88. Lies Before Kisses (TV) 92. My Very Best Friend (TV) 96, etc.

TV series: Charlie's Angels 76–81.

Smith, Jada Pinkett
See PINKETT, Jada.

Smith, Joe (1884–1981) (Joseph Sultzer)
American vaudeville comedian in partnership with Charles DALE for 73 years and the inspiration for the play and movie *The Sunshine Boys*.

Manhattan Parade 31. The Heart of New York 32. Two Tickets to Broadway 51.

Smith, John (1931–1995) (Robert Van Orden)
Boyish American leading man.

The High and the Mighty 54. Ghost Town 56. The Bold and the Brave 57. Circus World 64. Waco 66, etc.

TV series: Cimarron City 58. Laramie 59–62.

Smith, Kate (1909–1986)
Heavyweight American singer who was popular on radio in the 30s and 40s. Made one film in 1933 (*Hello, Everybody*) and another in 1943 (*This Is the Army*).

Smith, Kent (1907–1985)
Smooth, quiet American leading man of the 40s; latterly a useful character actor.

Cat People 42. Hitler's Children 43. This Land Is Mine 43. *The Spiral Staircase* 46. *Nora Prentiss* 47. The Decision of Christopher Blake 48. The Fountainhead 49. The Damned Don't Cry 50. Paul 52. Comanche 56. Party Girl 58. Strangers When We Meet 60. Moon Pilot 62. A Distant Trumpet 64. The Trouble with Angels 66. Assignment to Kill 68. Death of a Gunfighter 69. Pete 'n' Tillie 72. Cops and Robbers 73, many others.

TV series: *Peyton Place* 64–67.

Smith, Kevin (1966–)
American director and screenwriter. His first film was made on a budget of $27,000. He runs his own production company, View Askew, from Red Bank, New Jersey, where he also owns a comic store, Jay and Silent Bob's Secret Stash.

Clerks 94. Mallrats 95. Chasing Amy 97. Dogma 99. Scream 3 (a only) 00, etc.

❝ We need more killer shark movies. – *K.S.*

If that guy is the voice of my generation, I'll kill myself. – *Harmony Korine*

Smith, Kurtwood (1943–)
American character actor, often in sadistic roles.

Roadie 80. Staying Alive 83. Flashpoint 84. Robocop 87. Rambo III 88. Dead Poets Society 89. Heart of Dixie 89. True Believer 89. Quick Change 90. Oscar 91. Company Business 91. Star Trek VI: The Undiscovered Country 91. Shadows and Fog 92. Fortress 93. Boxing Helena 93. The Crush 93. Under Siege 2: Dark Territory 95. Last of the Dogmen 95. Time to Kill 96. Citizen Ruth 96. Prefontaine 97. Shelter 97. Deep Impact 98, etc.

TV series: That '70s Show 98- .

Smith, Liz
British character actress.

A Private Function (BFA) 84. We Think the World of You 88. High Spirits 88. Apartment Zero 88. The Cook, the Thief, His Wife and Her Lover 89. Bert Rigby, You're a Fool 89. Dakota Road 92. Pretty Princess (It.) 93. Haunted 95. Karaoke (TV) 96. Keep the Aspidistra Flying 97. The Revengers' Comedies 97. Tom's Midnight Garden 98. A Christmas Carol (TV) 00, etc.

TV series: The Royle Family 98- .

Smith, Lois (1930–)
American character actress.

Five Easy Pieces 70. Resurrection 80. Reckless 84. Black Widow 87. Green Card 90. Fried Green Tomatoes 91. Hard Promises 92. Falling Down 92. Skylark (TV) 93. Holy Matrimony 94. How to Make an American Quilt 95. Twister 96. Larger than Life 96, etc.

Smith, Dame Maggie (1934–)
Leading British actress with a taste for eccentric comedy. Married to actor Robert STEPHENS (1967–74) and writer Beverley Cross.

Biography: 1992, *Maggie: A Bright Particular Star* by Michael Coveney.

Nowhere to Go 58. Go to Blazes 62. *The VIPs* 63. The Pumpkin Eater 64. Young Cassidy 65. Othello (AAN) 66. *The Honey Pot* 67. Hot Millions 68. Oh What a Lovely War 69. *The Prime of Miss Jean Brodie* (AA) 69. Love Pain and the Whole Damn Thing 73. Travels with My Aunt (AAN) 73. Murder by Death 76. California Suite (AA) 78. Death on the Nile 78. Clash of the Titans 81. Quartet 81. Evil under the Sun 82. Better Late than Never 82. The Missionary 83. A Private Function (BFA) 84. A Room with a View (AAN) 85. The Lonely Passion of Judith Hearne 87. Hook 91. Memento Mori (TV) 92. Sister Act 92. The Secret Garden 93. Suddenly Last Summer (TV) 93. Sister Act 2: Back in the Habit 93. Richard III 95. The First Wives Club 96. Washington Square 97. Tea with Mussolini 99, etc.

❝ I said, 'Periods in life are sometimes like a dark tunnel but you come out into the light eventually.' She said, 'I think I'm on the Inner Circle.' – *Kenneth Williams*

Smith, Mel (1952–)
British comic actor and director. He is partner with his frequent collaborator Griff Rhys JONES in the production company Talkback. In 2000, *Broadcast* magazine estimated that he was worth £20m.

Bullshot 83. Slayground 84. Morons from Outer Space 85. The Princess Bride 87. The Wolves of Willoughby Chase 88. The Tall Guy (d) 89. Wilt/The Misadventures of Mr Wilt 89. Brain Donors 92. Art Deco Detective 94. The Radioland Murders (d) 94. Romeo, Romeo (d) 97. Bean (d) 97, etc.

TV series: Not the Nine O'Clock News 79–81. Alas Smith and Jones 84–86. Smith and Jones 95, 97– .

Smith, Oliver (1918–1994)
American production designer, mainly for the Broadway stage and the American Ballet Theatre.

Oklahoma! 55. Guys and Dolls 55. Porgy and Bess 59, etc.

Smith, Paul (1939–)
Towering American character actor who played the guard in *Midnight Express* and Bluto in *Popeye*.

Retreat, Hell! 52. Madron 70. Raiders in Action 71. Midnight Express 78. Popeye 80. Dune 84. Red Sonja 85. Crimewave 86. Haunted Honeymoon 86. Death Chase 87. Caged Fury 90. Crossing the Line 90, etc.

Smith, Paul J. (1906–1985)
American composer, almost exclusively for Disney.

Snow White and the Seven Dwarfs (AAN) 37. Pinocchio (AA) 40. Victory through Air Power (AAN) 43. The Three Caballeros (AAN) 44. Song of the South (AAN) 46. Cinderella (AAN) 50. Twenty Thousand Leagues Under the Sea 54. Perri (AAN) 57. Pollyanna 60. The Parent Trap 61. The Three Lives of Thomasina 64, etc.

Smith, Pete (1892–1979) (Peter Schmidt)
American producer of punchy one-reel shorts on any and every subject from 1935 to the 50s, all narrated by 'a Smith named Pete'. Born in New York City, he became a press agent and publicity director at MGM. He was given a special Academy Award in 1953 'for his witty and pungent observations on the American scene'. Committed suicide by jumping from the roof of a nursing home.

Smith, Roger (1932–)
American leading man. Formerly married to actress Victoria SHAW, he married actress ANN-MARGRET in 1967. Retired owing to a muscle disorder.

The Young Rebels 56. Operation Mad Ball 57. Man of a Thousand Faces (as Lon Chaney Jnr) 57. Never Steal Anything Small 59. Auntie Mame 59. Rogues' Gallery 68. The First Time (wp) 70.

TV series: 77 Sunset Strip 58–64. Mr Roberts 65.

Smith, Roy Forge
British production designer, now working in America.

Far from the Madding Crowd 67. The Amazing Mr Blunden 72. Monty Python and the Holy Grail 74. Jabberwocky 77. The Hound of the Baskervilles 79. Running 79. Mrs Soffel 84. The Kiss 88. Bill & Ted's Excellent Adventure 88. Teenage Mutant Ninja Turtles 90. Warlock 91. Teenage Mutant Ninja Turtles II 93. Teenage Mutant Ninja Turtles III 93. Robin Hood: Men in Tights 93. The Pagemaster 94. Born to Be Wild 95. Dracula: Dead and Loving It 95. Rocket Man 97, etc.

Smith, Thorne (1892–1934)
American humorous novelist. Works filmed include *Topper*, *Turnabout*, *I Married a Witch*.

Smith, Will (1968–)
American leading actor and rap performer. Born in Philadelphia, Pennsylvania, he began as the rapper Fresh Prince, performing with DJ Jazzy Jeff, before becoming a star of his own TV sitcom. His current asking price: around $15m a movie. Married his second wife, actress Jada PINKETT, in 1997.

Where the Day Takes You 92. Made in America 93. *Six Degrees of Separation* 93. Bad Boys 95. Independence Day 96. *Men in Black* 97. Enemy of the State 98. Wild Wild West 99. The Legend of Bagger Vance 00, etc.

TV series: Fresh Prince of Bel Air 91–96.

❝ It's great to be black in Hollywood. When a black actor does something, it seems new and different just by virtue of the fact that he's black. I've got it so much easier than Brad Pitt or Tom Cruise. – *W.S.*

I feel like I could run for President. People often laugh, but if I set my mind to it, within the next 15 years I could be in the White House. – *W.S., 1998*

I'd be happy to just make Will Smith moves the rest of my career. – *Barry Sonnenfeld*

Smithee, Alan (1967–) (aka Allen Smithee)
Pseudonym used by members of the Director's Circle when the actual director wants his name removed from the credits. *An Alan Smithee Film: Burn, Hollywood, Burn* 97, a satire produced and scripted by Joe ESZTERHAS about a director named Smithee who disowns his own film, was in turn disowned by its actual director, Arthur HILLER, after it was recut. An earlier satirical movie, *Only in America*, featured a film director named Alan Smithee, played by Raphael Perry. It is possible that Smithee is now dead: when Walter HILL had his name removed from the credits of *Supernova*, the film was credited to Thomas Lee.
Death of a Gunfighter (d Don Siegel, Robert Totten) 67. Fade In (d Jud Taylor) 68. City in Fear (d Jud Taylor) (TV) 80. Fun and Games (d Paul Bogart) (TV) 80. Moonlight (d Jackie Cooper, Rod Holcomb) (TV) 82. Stitches (d Rod Holcomb) 82. Appointment with Fear (d Ramzi Thomas) 85. Let's Get Harry (d Stuart Rosenberg) 86. Morgan Stewart's Coming Home (d Terry Winsor, Paul Aaron) 87. Ghost Fever (d Lee Madden) 87. I Love NY (d Gianni Bozzachi) 87. Catchfire/Backtrack (d Dennis Hopper) 89. Boyfriend from Hell/The Shrimp on the Barbie (d Martin Gottlieb) 90. Starfire (d Richard Sarafian) 92. Call of the Wild (d Michael Uno, TV) 93. The Birds II: Land's End (TV) (d Rick Rosenthal) 94. Raging Angels 95. Hellraiser: Bloodline (d Kevin Yeager) 96 An Alan Smithee Film: Burn, Hollywood, Burn! (Arthur Hiller) 97, etc.

Smitrovich, Bill (1948–)
American actor.
Without a Trace 83. Maria's Lovers 84. Splash 84. Silver Bullet 85. Key Exchange 85. Manhunter 86. Her Alibi 89. Renegades 89. Crazy People 90. Nick of Time 95. Independence Day 96. The Great White Hype 96. Trigger Effect 96. Air Force One 97. Fail Safe (TV) 00, etc.
TV series: Crime Story 86–88. Life Goes On 89–91.

Smits, Jimmy (1955–)
American leading actor.
Running Scared 86. The Believers 87. Old Gringo 89. Vital Signs 90. Fires Within 91. Switch 91. Gross Misconduct 93. The Tommyknockers (TV) 93. The Cisco Kid (title role) (TV) 94. My Family/Mi Familia 95. Murder in Mind 96. The Million Dollar Hotel 99. Bless the Child 00, etc.
TV series: L.A. Law 86–92. NYPD Blue 95–98.

Smoktunovsky, Innokenti (1925–1994)
Leading Russian stage actor, seen in a few films including *Nine Days of One Year* 60. *Hamlet* 64. *Tchaikovsky* 69. Crime and Punishment 75.

Smothers, Tom (1937–)
American light leading man and comedian who with his brother Dick (1939–) was popular on American TV in the 60s. Tom himself went on to appear in a few films:
■ Get to Know Your Rabbit 74. Silver Bears 78. The Kids Are Alright 78. Serial 80. There Goes the Bride 80. Pandemonium 82. Speed Zone 88.

Snell, David
American composer.
Madame X 37. Young Dr Kildare 38. Twenty Mule Team 40. Love Crazy 41. Pacific Rendezvous 42. The Man from Down Under 43. Keep Your Powder Dry 45. Merton of the Movies 47. The Lady in the Lake 47. Alias a Gentleman 48, etc.

Snipes, Wesley (1962–)
American leading actor.
Streets of Gold 86. Wild Cats 86. Critical Condition 87. Major League 89. Mo' Better Blues 90. King of New York 90. Jungle Fever 91. New Jack City 91. The Waterdance 92. White Men Can't Jump 92. Passenger 57 92. Rising Sun 93. Boiling Point 93. Sugar Hill 93. Demolition Man 93. Drop Zone 94. To Wong Foo, Thanks for Everything, Julie Newmar 95. Money Train 95. The Fan 96. One Night Stand 97. Murder at 1600 97. US Marshals 98. Blade 98. Down in the Delta 98. Disappearing Acts 00, etc.
TV series: H.E.L.P. 90.

Snodgress, Carrie (1945–)
American leading actress.
The Forty-Eight Hour Mile (TV) 68. Silent Night Lonely Night (TV) 69. Rabbit Run 71. *Diary of a Mad Housewife* (AAN) 72. The Fury 78. Homework 82. Trick or Treats 82. A Night in Heaven 83. Pale Rider 85. Murphy's Law 86. Blueberry Hill 88. The Chill Factor 89. Across the Tracks 90. Mission of the Shark 91. The Ballad of Little Joe 93. 8 Seconds 94. Blue Sky (made 91) 94. White Man's Burden 95. Death Benefit (TV) 96. Wild Things 98. A Stranger in the Kingdom 98, etc.

Snyder, David L.
American production designer.
In God We Trust 80. The Idolmaker 80. Blade Runner (co-pd, AAN) 82. Brainstorm 83. The Woman in Red 84. Pee-Wee's Big Adventure 85. Armed and Dangerous 86. Summer School 87. She's out of Control 89. Cold Dog Soup 90. Bill & Ted's Bogus Journey 91. Demolition Man 93. Terminal Velocity 94. Vegas Vacation 97. An Alan Smithee Film: Burn, Hollywood, Burn 97. Soldier 98, etc.

Snyder, William (1901–1984)
American cinematographer. Noted for his colour photography in the 40s, he worked for Disney during the 60s.
Aloma of the South Seas (AAN) 41. The Bandit of Sherwood Forest 45. The Swordsman 47. The Loves of Carmen (AAN) 48. The Younger Brothers 49. Jolson Sings Again (AAN) 49. Flying Leathernecks 51. Blackbeard the Pirate 52. Second Chance 53. Creature from the Black Lagoon 54. Son of Sinbad 55. Tarzan's Fight for Life 58. Bon Voyage 62. Guns of Wyoming 63. The Tenderfoot 64. Rascal 69. Million Dollar Duck 71. Menace on the Mountain 72, etc.

Soavi, Michele (1958–)
Italian director of horror movies, a former actor, much influenced by the work of Dario Argento, for whom he worked as an assistant.
Creepers (a) 85. Demons/Demoni (a) 86. Dario Argento's World of Horror (doc) (d) 86. Stagefright/Deliria (a, d) 87. The Church/La Chiesa (a, d) 89. The Sect/La Setta (co-w, d) 91. Dellamorte Dellamore (d) 94, etc.

Sobieski, Leelee (1982–)
American actress, born in New York, who began in films as a teenager. Current asking price: $1m a movie.
Never Been Kissed 98. Deep Impact 98. A Soldier's Daughter Never Cries 98. Eyes Wide Shut 99. Joan of Arc (TV) 99. Here on Earth 00, etc.
TV series: Charlie Grace 95.

Sobocinski, Piotr (1958–2001)
Polish cinematographer, in international films. He studied at the Lodz Film School, and began in documentaries.
Draw 83. The Magnate 86. Lava 87. Three Colours: Red 94. Ransom (US) 96. Marvin's Room (US) 96, etc.

Soderbergh, Steven (1963–)
American director and screenwriter.
sex, lies and videotape (wd, AANw) 89. Kafka (d) 91. King of the Hill (wd) 93. The Underneath (d) 95. Schizopolis (a, wd, ph) 96. Gray's Anatomy (d) 97. Out of Sight (d) 98. The Limey (d) 99. *Erin Brockovich* (d) (AAN) 00. Traffic (d) (AA) 00, etc.

Soeteman, Gerard
Dutch screenwriter, associated with the pre-Hollywood films of Paul Verhoeven.
Max Havelaar 76. Soldier of Orange 77. Spetters 80. The Fourth Man/De Vierde Man 83. Flesh and Blood 85. The Assault 86. The Bunker (& d) 92, etc.

Sofaer, Abraham (1896–1988)
Burmese actor, on British stage from 1921.
Dreyfus (debut) 31. Rembrandt 36. *A Matter of Life and Death* 46. Judgment Deferred 51. *Elephant Walk* (US) 54. The Naked Jungle (US) 54. Bhowani Junction 56. King of Kings 61. Captain Sinbad (US) 63. Head 68. Che! 69, etc.

Soffici, Mario (1900–1977)
Italian-born director who became one of the leading figures in Argentinian cinema in the 30s and 40s; his best films dealt with the effects of change on rural areas. He began as a circus clown and actor, and returned to acting late in his life. In 1974 he replaced Hugo DEL CARRIL as head of the National Film Institute.
Muñequitas Porteñas (a) 31. El Alma del Bandoneón (d) 34. Viente Norte (d) 37. *Kilómetre 111* (d) 38. *Prisoners of the Earth*/Prisioneros de la Tierra (d) 39. Besos Perdidos (d) 43. Kreutzer Sonata 46. Tierra del Fuego 48. El Hombre y la Bestia (d) 50. La Dama del Mar (d) 53. Barrio Gris (d) 54. Oro Bajo (d) 56. *Rosaura at Ten o'Clock*/Rosaura a las Diez (d) 57. This Land Is Mine (a) 61. Maternidad sin Hombres (a) 68, etc.

Softley, Iain
English director. Educated at Cambridge University, he began in TV documentaries and music videos.
Backbeat 94. Hackers 95. Wings of a Dove 97, etc.

Sojin (1884–1954)
Japanese actor most memorable in western films as Douglas Fairbanks' antagonist in the 1924 *Thief of Bagdad*. Back in Japan after 1930.

Sokoloff, Vladimir (1889–1962)
Russian character actor, in Hollywood from 1936.
The Loves of Jeanne Ney 27. West Front 1918 30. Die Dreigroschenoper 31. L'Atlantide 32. Mayerling 35. The Life of Emile Zola 37. Spawn of the North 38. Juarez 39. Road to Morocco 42. For Whom the Bell Tolls 43. Cloak and Dagger 46. Back to Bataan 46. Istanbul 56. Confessions of a Counterspy 60. Sardonicus 62, many others.

Sokurov, Alexander (1951–)
Russian director and screenwriter, who began as a documentary filmmaker.
Skorbnoe Bescuvstvie 86. Dni Zatmenija 88. Second Circle/Krug Vtoroj 90. The Stone/Kamen 92. Tikhie Stranicy 93. *Mother and Son/Mat I Syn* 97. Moloch 99, etc.

Solanas, Fernando (1936–)
Argentinian director and screenwriter, of revolutionary intentions. He began as a documentary film-maker, and was in exile during the late 70s and early 80s, making films in France. He was shot in the legs in 1991 after accusing the government of corruption.
The Hour of the Furnaces/La Hora de los Hornos 68. Los Hijos de Fierro 76. Tangos: The Exile of Gardel 86. Sur 88. The Voyage/El Viaje 93. The Cloud/La Nube (wd) 98, etc.

Solás, Humberto (1942–)
Cuban director.
Lucia 68. A Day in November/Un Día de Noviembre 72. Simparele 74. Cantata de Chile 75. Cecilia Valdés 82. A Successful Man/Un Hombre de Exito 87, etc.

Soldati, Mario (1906–1999)
Italian director.
Her Favourite Husband 50. Scandal in the Roman Bath 51. The Wayward Wife 53. The Stranger's Hand 53. Woman of the River 55. War and Peace 56. Il Maestro 89, many others.

Sologne, Madeleine (1912–1995) (Madeleine Vouillon)
French leading actress, a former milliner who turned to acting after marrying cinematographer Jean Douarinou. Retired in the late 60s.
La Vie Est à Nous 36. Adrienne Lecouvreur 38. Tattooed Raphael/Raphael Le Tatoué 40. Fever/Fièvres 41. The Eternal Return/L'Eternel Retour 43. Mademoiselle X 44. The Devil and the Angel/La Foire aux Chimères 46. Bernadette of Lourdes/Il Suffit d'Aimer 60. Les Temps de Loups 69, etc.

Solon, Ewen (c. 1923–1985)
New Zealand character actor in Britain, especially on TV in *Maigret* series (as Lucas).
The Sundowners 59. Jack the Ripper 60. The Hound of the Baskervilles 60. The Terror of the Tongs 61. The Wicked Lady 83, etc.

Solondz, Todd (1960–)
American director and screenwriter, born in Newark, New Jersey. *Happiness* won the International Critics' Prize at the 1998 Cannes Film Festival, but its financiers, October Films, a subsidiary of Universal, decided not to distribute it because of its content, which included scenes of paedophilia and violence.
Fear, Anxiety and Depression (& a) 89. Welcome to the Dollhouse 95. Happiness 98, etc.

Solzhenitsyn, Alexander (1918–)
Russian novelist, expelled from his own country in 1974 for too much free thought. *One Day in the Life of Ivan Denisovitch* was filmed.

Somers, Suzanne (1946–) (S. Mahoney)
American leading lady of the late 70s, especially on TV in the series *Three's Company*.
American Graffiti 73. It Happened at Lakewood Manor (TV) 77. Nothing Personal 80. Happily Ever After (TV) 82. Rich Men, Single Women (TV) 90, etc.

Somlo, Josef (1885–1974)
Hungarian producer with long experience at UFA; in Britain from 1933.
Dark Journey 37. The Mikado 39. Old Bill and Son 40. Uncle Silas 47. The Man Who Loved Redheads 55. Behind the Mask 59, etc.

Sommer, Elke (1940–) (Elke Schletz)
German leading lady now in international films.
Don't Bother to Knock (GB) 60. The Victors (GB) 63. *The Prize* (US) 63. A Shot in the Dark (US) 64. The Art of Love (US) 65. Four Kinds of Love (It.) 65. The Money Trap (US) 65. The Oscar (US) 66. Boy, Did I Get a Wrong Number (US) 66. Deadlier than the Male (GB) 66. The Venetian Affair (US) 66. The Corrupt Ones 67. The Wicked Dreams of Paula Schultz (US) 68. Zeppelin (US) 71. Percy (GB) 71. Carry On Behind (GB) 76. Lily in Love 84. Adventures beyond Belief 87. Severed Ties 91. Patch Adams 98, etc.

Sommer, Josef (1934–)
American character actor.
The Stepford Wives 75. Too Far to Go (TV) 78. Hide in Plain Sight 80. Still of the Night 82. Sophie's Choice 82. Hanky Panky 82. Witness 84. Dracula's Widow 88. Chances Are 89. The Bloodhounds of Broadway 89. Money, Power, Murder (TV) 89. Shadows and Fog 92. Malice 93. Hidden in America (TV) 96. The Proposition 97, etc.
TV series: Hothouse 88. Under Cover 91.

Sommers, Stephen
American director and screenwriter.
Terroreyes (co-d) 88. Catch Me If You Can (wd) 89. Gunmen (w) 92. The Adventures of Huck Finn (wd) 93. Rudyard Kipling's The Jungle Book (wd) 94. Tom and Huck (co-w) 96. Deep Rising (wd) 98. The Mummy (wd) 99, etc.

Sondergaard, Gale (1899–1985) (Edith Sondergaard)
Tall, dark American character actress with a sinister smile. Born in Litchfield, Minnesota, and educated at the University of Minnesota, she began on stage. She went to Hollywood after marrying director Herbert BIBERMAN, her second husband and one of the 'Hollywood Ten'; as a result her career also suffered because of the anti-communist witchhunt of the early 50s.
■ *Anthony Adverse* (AA) 36. Maid of Salem 37. Seventh Heaven 37. The Life of Emile Zola 37. Lord Jeff 38. Dramatic School 38. Never Say Die 38. Juarez 38. *The Cat and the Canary* 39. The Llano Kid 40. *The Bluebird* 40. The Mark of Zorro 40. The Letter 40. The Black Cat 41. Paris Calling 41. My Favourite Blonde 42. Enemy Agent Meets Ellery Queen 42. A Night to Remember 43. Appointment in Berlin 43. Isle of Forgotten Sins 43. The Strange Death of Adolf Hitler 43. *Spider Woman* 44. Follow the Boys 44. Christmas Holiday 44. The Invisible Man's Revenge 44. Gypsy Wildcat 44. The Climax 44. Enter Arsène Lupin 44. Spider Woman Strikes Back 46. A Night in Paradise 46. Anna and the King of Siam (AAN) 46. The Time of Their Lives 46. *Road to Rio* 47. Pirates of Monterey 47. East Side West Side 49. Slaves 69. The Cat Creature (TV) 74. The Return of A Man Called Horse 76. Pleasantville 76. Echoes 83.

Sondheim, Stephen (1930–)
Celebrated American composer, lyricist and occasional screenwriter. Born in New York to an upper-middle-class family, he learned much from Oscar HAMMERSTEIN, a family friend, and, after graduating from Williams College, studied for two years with composer Milton Babbitt. He began by working on the TV series *Topper* as a writer and, after some projects collapsed, wrote the lyrics for *West Side Story*, which opened on Broadway in 1957 and later became a greater success as a film. He went on to write a dozen Broadway musicals, though few have been filmed. His love of puzzles and word-games was reflected in *The Last of Sheila*, his one screenplay, written with actor Anthony PERKINS.

Biography: 1974, *Sondheim & Co* by Craig Zadan. 1998, *Stephen Sondheim: A Life* by Meryle Secrest.

West Side Story (ly) 61. Gypsy (ly) 62. A Funny Thing Happened on the Way to the Forum (m/ly) 66. Evening Primrose (m/ly) (TV) 66. The Last of Sheila (co-w) 73. Stavisky (m) (Fr.) 74. The Seven Percent Solution (s) 76. A Little Night Music (m/ly) 77. Reds (m) 81, etc.

❝ I'm a lazy writer. My idea of heaven is not writing. On the other hand, I'm obviously compulsive about it. – S.S.

Without question, Steve is the best Broadway lyricist, past or present. – *Arthur Laurents*

Sonego, Rodolfo (1921–2000)
Italian screenwriter, closely associated with Alberto SORDI, with whom he worked on most of the actor's features from the mid-50s.

Anna 51. Crimen 60. *A Difficult Life/Una Vita Difficile* 61. The Flying Saucer/Il Disco Volante 64. Un Italiano in America 67. Contestazione Generale 70. The Scientific Cardplayer/Lo Scopone Scientifico 72. Cara Sposa (&co-d) 78. The Cat/Il Gatto 78. Tutti Dentro 84. Too Strong/Troppo Forte 85. Once Upon a Crime (story, US) 92. Forbidden Encounters/Incontri Proibiti 98, many others.

Sonnenfeld, Barry (1953–)
American director, a former cinematographer. Born in New York, he studied political science at New York University and at the NYU film school.

Blood Simple 83. Compromising Positions 85. Raising Arizona 87. Three o'Clock High 87. Throw Momma from the Train 87. Big 88. When Harry Met Sally 89. Miller's Crossing 90. Misery 90. The Addams Family (d) 91. Addams Family Values (d) 93. For Love or Money/The Concierge (d) 94. Get Shorty (d) 95. Men in Black (d) 97. Wild, Wild West (d) 99. Big Trouble (d) 01, etc.

Soo, Jack (1916–1979) (Goro Suzuki)
Japanese character actor in America, best remembered in *Flower Drum Song* 60, and as one of the gang in TV's *Barney Miller* series.

Soon-Tek, Oh (1943–)
Korean-born actor in the United States. He studied at the University of Southern California and trained at New York's Neighborhood Playhouse.

Charlie Chan (TV) 71. One More Train To Rob 71. The Man With the Golden Gun 74. Good Guys Wear Black 78. The Final Countdown 79. Missing in Action 2: The Beginning 85. Steele Justice 87. Death Wish 4: The Crackdown 87. Sour Sweet 89. A Home Of Our Own 93. Street Corner Justice 96. Beverly Hills Ninja 97. Yellow 97. Mulan (voice), etc.

Sorbo, Kevin (1958–)
American leading actor, a former model, best known for his role as Hercules in the TV series *Hercules: The Legendary Journeys* 94–97. Born in Minneapolis, he studied at the University of Minnesota. Married actress Sam Jenkins (1964–) in 1998.

Slaughter of the Innocents 94. Hercules and the Amazon Women (TV) 94. Hercules and the Circles of Fire (TV) 94. Kull the Conqueror 97, etc.

TV series: Hercules: The Legendary Journeys 94-99.

Sordi, Alberto (1919–)
Italian leading actor, usually in comic roles; also directed and wrote many of his films from the mid-60s.

I Vitelloni 53. The Sign of Venus 55. A Farewell to Arms 57. The Best of Enemies 60. Those Magnificent Men in Their Flying Machines 65. To Bed or Not To Bed 65. Le Streghe 67. Polvere di Stelle 73. Viva Italia 77. Le Témoin 78. Il Marchese del Grillo (& w) 81. Bertoldo, Bertoldino e Cacasenno 84. Tutti Dentro (a, wd) 84. The Miser/L'Avaro (& co-w) 89. Christmas Vacation '91/Vacanze di Natale '91 91. Assolto per Aver Commesso Il Fatto (& co-w, d) 92. Nestore l'Ultima Corsa (& co-w, d) 94. The Story of a Poor Young Man 95. Forbidden Encounters/Incontri Proibiti (& co-w, d) 98, etc.

Sorel, Jean (1934–) (Jean de Rochbrune)
French-Canadian leading man.

The Four Days of Naples 62. A View from the Bridge 62. Vaghe Stella dell'Orsa 65. Le Bambole 66. Belle de Jour 67. A Quiet Place to Kill 70. Mil Millones para una Rubia 78, etc.

Sorel, Louise (1944–)
American leading lady of occasional films.

The Party's Over 65. B.S. I Love You 70. Plaza Suite 71. Every Little Crook and Nanny 72. When Every Day Was the Fourth of July (TV) 78. Mazes and Monsters (TV) 82, etc.

TV series: The Survivors 69–70. The Don Rickles Show 72. Curse of Dracula 79. Ladies' Man 80–81.

Sorkin, Aaron
American screenwriter, from the theatre. He was also an executive producer and a writer of the TV series *Sports Night* 98, and *The West Wing* 99- .

A Few Good Men 92. Malice 93. The American President 95, etc.

Sorvino, Mira
American actress, the daughter of actor Paul SORVINO. She took a degree in East Asian studies from Harvard and worked as an assistant director before becoming an actress.

Amongst Friends 93. Barcelona 94. Parallel Lives (TV) 94. Quiz Show 94. Mighty Aphrodite (AA) 95. Sweet Nothing 95. Blue in the Face 95. Beautiful Girls 96. Romy and Michele's High School Reunion 97. Mimic 97. The Replacement Killers 98. Lulu on the Bridge 98. At First Sight 99. Summer of Sam 99. The Great Gatsby (TV) 01, etc.

Sorvino, Paul (1939–)
Chubby American actor.

Where's Poppa? 70. Cry Uncle 72. A Touch of Class 73. The Day of the Dolphin 73. The Gambler 75. I Will, I Will … For Now 75. Oh God 77. Slow Dancing in the Big City 78. The Brink's Job 78. Bloodbrothers 78. Slow Dancing in the Big City 78. Lost and Found 79. Cruising 80. Reds 81. I the Jury 82. That Championship Season 82. Turk 182 85. The Stuff 85. A Fine Mess 85. Vasectomy, a Delicate Matter 86. Dick Tracy 90. GoodFellas 90. The Rocketeer 91. Parallel Lives (TV) 94. Nixon 95. Escape Clause (TV) 96. Love Is All There Is 96. William Shakespeare's Romeo and Juliet 96. Most Wanted 97. American Perfekt 97. Money Talks 97. Dogwatch (TV) 97. Knock Off 98. Bulworth 98. Houdini (TV) 99. That Championship Season (TV) 99. The Prince of Central Park 00, etc.

TV series: We'll Get By 75. Bert Angelo/Superstar 76. The Oldest Rookie 87–88. Law and Order 90–92. That's Life 00- .

Sothern, Ann (1909–2001) (Harriette Lake)
Pert American comedienne and leading lady with stage experience.

Let's Fall in Love (debut) 34. Kid Millions 35. Trade Winds 38. Hotel for Women 39. *Maisie* 39. Brother Orchid 40. Congo Maisie 40. Gold Rush Maisie 41 (and seven others in series before 1947). Lady Be Good 41. Panama Hattie 42. Cry Havoc 43. The Judge Steps Out 47. *A Letter to Three Wives* 49. Nancy Goes to Rio 50. Lady in a Cage 63. The Best Man 64. Sylvia 65. Chubasco 67. The Great Man's Whiskers (TV) 71. Golden Needles 74. Crazy Mama 75. Captains and the Kings (TV) 76. The Manitou 78. The Whales of August (AAN) 87, etc.

TV series: *Private Secretary* 52–53. The Ann Sothern Show 58–61.

Soto, Talisa (1967–) (Miriam Soto)
American actress and model.

Spike of Bensonhurst 88. Licence to Kill 89. Silhouette (TV) 91. Hostage (TV) 92. The Mambo Kings 92. Don Juan DeMarco 95. Mortal Kombat 95. The Sunchaser 96. Mortal Kombat 2: Annihilation 97, etc.

Soul, David (1943–) (David Solberg)
American leading man who made a killing in TV but never found the right movie; nor was singing a wise choice as a second career.

Johnny Got His Gun 71. Magnum Force 73. Dogpound Shuffle 74. The Stick Up 77. Little Ladies of the Night (TV) 77. Salem's Lot (TV) 79. Swan Song (TV) 79. Rage (TV) 80. The Hanoi Hilton 87. The Bride in Black 90. In the Cold of the Night 90. Pentathlon 94, etc.

TV series: Here Come the Brides 68–70. Owen Marshall, Counsellor at Law 74. *Starsky and Hutch* 75–80. Casablanca 83. The Yellow Rose 83.

Sousa, John Philip (1854–1932)
American composer, most notably of rousing marches. His 1928 biography, *Marching Along*, was filmed in 1953 as *Stars and Stripes Forever*.

Soutendijk, Renée (1957–)
Dutch leading actress, in international films. She is a former Olympic athlete.

Pastorale 43 76. Spetters 80. The Girl with Red Hair/Het Meisje met Rode Haar 81. Inside the Third Reich (TV) 82. The Fourth Man/De Vierde Man 83. The Cold Room 84. Out of Order/Abwarts 85. The Second Victory 87. Der Madonna-Man 87. Wherever You Are 88. Forced March 89. Grave Secrets 89. Murderers Among Us: The Simon Wiesenthal Story (TV) 90. Eve of Destruction 90. Keeper of the City 91. Heatwave/Hittegolf 93. The Betrayed/Op Afbetaling 93. House Call 94, etc.

Southern, Terry (1924–1995)
American satirist and black-comedy writer.

■ *Dr Strangelove* (co-w) (AAN) 64. The Cincinnati Kid (co-w) 65. The Loved One (co-w) 65. Barbarella 68. Easy Rider (co-w) (AAN) 69. End of the Road (co-w) 70. The Magic Christian (co-w) 70. The Telephone (co-w) 88.

Spaak, Catherine (1945–)
Belgian leading lady, daughter of Charles SPAAK.

Le Trou 60. The Empty Canvas 64. Weekend at Dunkirk 65. Hotel 67. Libertine 68. Cat o' Nine Tails 71. Take a Hard Ride 75. Honey 81. Secret Scandal 89, etc.

Spaak, Charles (1903–1975)
Leading Belgian-born screenwriter of many French films. Born in Brussels, he went to Paris in the late 20s to work as secretary to director Jacques FEYDER and soon began collaborating on scripts. Among the directors he worked with were Julien DUVIVIER, Jean RENOIR and André Cayatte. His daughters, Agnès and Catherine SPAAK, were both actresses.

Les Nouveaux Messieurs 28. Le Grand Jeu 34. Carnival in Flanders/*La Kermesse Héroïque* 35. They Were Five/La Belle équipe 36. The Lower Depths/Les Bas-Fonds 36. *La Grande Illusion* 37. *La Fin du Jour* 39. The Postman Always Rings Twice/Le Dernier Tournant 39. Heart of a Nation/Untel Père et Fils 40. L'Homme au Chapeau Rond 46. Panique 46. Le Mystère Barton (& d) 49. Justice Est Faite 50. The Seven Deadly Sins 52. Are We All Murderers?/Nous Sommes Tous les Assassins 52. Adorable Creatures 52. Captain Blackjack 52. The Adulteress/Thérèse Raquin 53. Too Many Lovers/Charmants Garçons 58. The Vanishing Corporal 61. Cartouche 62. Germinal 62. Two Are Guilty/Le Glaire et la Balance 73, etc.

Space, Arthur (1908–1983)
American character actor, in many film roles and such TV series as *National Velvet* and *Lassie*.

Tortilla Flat 42. Wilson 44. Leave Her to Heaven 45. The Barefoot Mailman 52. Spirit of St Louis 57. The Shakiest Gun in the West 68. On the Nickel 80, etc.

Spacek, Sissy (1949–)
Tomboy-ish American leading lady. She is married to director Jack FISK.

Prime Cut 71. Ginger in the Morning 72. *Badlands* 73. Katherine (TV) 75. Carrie (AAN) 76. Three Women 77. Welcome to L.A. 77. Heart Beat 79. *Coal Miner's Daughter* (AA) 80. Raggedy Man 81. Missing (AAN) 82. Country 84. The River (AAN) 84. Marie 85. Violets Are Blue 85. 'Night, Mother 86. Crimes of the Heart (AAN) 86. The Long Walk Home 90. JFK 91. Hard Promises 92. Trading Mom 94. The Good Old Boys (TV) 95. The Grass Harp 95. If These Walls Could Talk (TV) 96. Affliction 98. Blast from the Past 99. The Straight Story 99, etc.

Spacey, Kevin (1959–) (Kevin Fowler)
Versatile American leading man. Born in South Orange, New Jersey, he studied drama at the Juilliard School and began acting with the New York Shakespeare Festival. In the mid-90s he began to emerge as one of the best actors of his generation, though, unlike many stars, he is one that submerges his own personality in the parts he plays.

Heartburn 86. Rocket Gibraltar 88. Working Girl 88. See No Evil, Hear No Evil 89. Dad 89. A Show of Force 90. Henry and June 90. Glengarry Glen Ross 92. Consenting Adults 92. Iron Will 94. The Ref 94. The Buddy Factor (& p) 94. Outbreak 95. *The Usual Suspects* (AA) 95. *Seven* 95. A Time to Kill 96. Albino Alligator (d) 96. *LA Confidential* 97. Midnight in the Garden of Good and Evil 97. The Negotiator 98. Hurlyburly 98. A Bug's Life (voice) 98. *American Beauty* (AA) 99. Ordinary Decent Criminal 00. Pay It Forward 00, etc.

TV series: Wiseguy 88.

Spade, David
American actor and comedian, from TV's *Saturday Night Live*.

Police Academy 4: Citizens on Patrol 87. Light Sleeper 91. Coneheads 93. PCU 94. Tommy Boy 95. Black Sheep 96. Beavis and Butthead Do America (voice) 96. 8 Heads in a Duffel Bag 97. Jerome (ex p only) 98. The Rugrats Movie (voice) 99. Loser 00. The Emperor's New Groove (voice) 00, etc.

TV series: Saturday Night Live 91-96. Just Shoot Me 97. Sammy (ex-p, voices) 2000.

Spader, James (1960–)
Youthful-appearing American actor.

Endless Love 81. Family Secrets 84. The New Kids 85. Tuff Turf 85. Pretty in Pink 86. Baby Boom 87. Jack's Back 87. Less than Zero 87. Mannequin 87. Wall Street 87. The Rachel Papers 89. sex, lies and videotape 89. Bad Influence 90. White Palace 90. True Colors 91. Bob Roberts 92. Chicago Loop 92. Storyville 92. The Music of Chance 93. Wolf 94. Dream Lover 94. Stargate 94. Crash 96. Driftwood 96. 2 Days in the Valley 96. Keys to Tulsa 96. Critical Care 97. Keys to Tulsa 97. Supernova 00. The Watcher 00, etc.

TV series: The Family Tree 83.

Spall, Timothy (1957–)
British character actor, often in grotesque roles.

Quadrophenia 79. Remembrance 82. The Missionary 83. The Bride 85. Gothic 86. Dutch Girls 87. To Kill a Priest 88. Dream Demon 88. 1871 89. The Sheltering Sky 90. White Hunter, Black Heart 90. *Life Is Sweet* 90. For One Night Only (as Margaret Rutherford) (TV) 93. Secrets and Lies 95. Hamlet 96. The Wisdom of Crocodiles 98. Still Crazy 98. Clandestine Marriage 99. Topsy-Turvy 99. Love's Labours Lost 00. Chicken Run (voice) 00, etc.

TV series: Auf Wiedersehen Pet 83–84. Frank Stubbs Presents 93. Frank Stubbs 94. Outside Edge 94. Nice Day at the Office 94.

Spano, Vincent (1962–)
American leading actor.

The Double McGuffin 79. Over the Edge 79. Baby, It's You 83. The Black Stallion Returns 83. Rumble Fish 83. Alphabet City 84. Creator 85. Maria's Lovers 85. Good Morning Babylon 86. And God Created Woman 88. High-Frequency 88. The Heart of the Deal 90. Oscar 91. City of Hope 91. Alive 93. Indian Summer 93. The Ascent 94. The Tie that Binds 95. Downdraft 96. A Brooklyn State of Mind 97, etc.

Spark, Dame Muriel (1918–)
British novelist feted by the intelligentsia. Two films of her work, *The Prime of Miss Jean Brodie* and *The Driver's Seat*, have both been unsatisfactory.

Nasty Habits (oa) 76. Memento Mori (oa) (TV) 92.

Sparks, Ned (1883–1957) (Edward Sparkman)
Hard-boiled, cigar-chewing Canadian comic actor often seen in Hollywood films of the 30s as grouchy reporter or agent.

The Big Noise 27. The Miracle Man 30. Forty-Second Street 33. Two's Company (GB) 37. The Star Maker 39. For Beauty's Sake 40. Magic Town 46, etc.

Sparkuhl, Theodor (1891–1945)
German cinematographer in Hollywood from the early 30s.

Carmen 18. Manon Lescaut 26. La Chienne 31. Too Much Harmony 33. Enter Madame 35. *Beau Geste* 39. *The Glass Key* 42. Star Spangled Rhythm 43. Blood on the Sun 46. Bachelor Girls 46, many others.

Sparv, Camilla (1943–)
Swedish-born leading lady in Hollywood films. She was formerly married to producer Robert Evans.

The Trouble with Angels 66. Murderers' Row 66. Dead Heat on a Merry-Go-Round 66. Department K 67. Mackenna's Gold 68. Downhill

Racer 69. The Italian Job 69. Survival Zone 84, etc.

Speakman, Jeff (1957–)
American karate expert in action movies.
The Perfect Weapon 91. A.W.O.L./Lionheart 91. Street Knight 93. Deadly Takeover 95. Timelock 96. Escape from Atlantis (TV) 97. Scorpio 97, etc.

Spence, Bruce (1945–)
Lanky Australian character actor.
Stork 71. The Cars that Ate Paris 74. Newsfront 78. Dimboola 79. Mad Max 2/The Road Warrior 81. Midnight Spares 82. Buddies 83. Where the Green Ants Dream 84. Mad Max beyond Thunderdrome 85. Rikky and Pete 88. The Year My Voice Broke 88.... Almost 90. Boyfriend from Hell/The Shrimp on the Barbie 90. Wendy Cracked a Walnut 90. Sweet Talker 91. Ace Ventura: When Nature Calls 95. Dark City 98, etc.

Spencer, Bud (1929–) (Carlo Pedersoli)
Italian character actor in many spaghetti westerns.
Blood River 67. Beyond the Law 68. Boot Hill 69. They Call Me Trinity 70. Four Flies on Grey Velvet 71. Watch Out We're Mad 74. Trinity Is Still My Name 75. The Knock Out Cop 78. Crime Busters 80. Aladdin 86, etc.

Spencer, Dorothy (1909–)
American editor.
The Moon's Our Home 36. Blockade 38. *Stagecoach* 39. *Foreign Correspondent* 40. To Be or Not To Be 42. Heaven Can Wait 43. Lifeboat 43. My Darling Clementine 46. The Snake Pit 48. Three Came Home 50. Fourteen Hours 51. Black Widow 54. The Man in the Grey Flannel Suit 56. The Young Lions 58. North to Alaska 60. Cleopatra (AAN) 63. Von Ryan's Express 65. Valley of the Dolls 67. Limbo 71. *Earthquake* (AAN) 74. The Concorde – Airport 79 79, many others.

Spencer, Kenneth (1912–1964)
American singer who appeared in a few 40s films including *Cabin in the Sky* and *Bataan*, both 43.

Spenser, Jeremy (1937–)
British leading man, former child actor, also on stage. He has not acted since the mid-60s and has sunk into obscurity.
Portrait of Clare 48. *Prelude to Fame* 50. Appointment with Venus 51. Summer Madness 55. The Prince and the Showgirl 57. Wonderful Things 58. Ferry to Hong Kong 58. *The Roman Spring of Mrs Stone* 61. King and Country 64. He Who Rides a Tiger 65. Fahrenheit 451 66, etc.

Sperling, Milton (1912–1988)
American producer.
Cloak and Dagger 46. Three Secrets 50. The Enforcer 51. Blowing Wild 54. The Court Martial of Billy Mitchell (& co-w) (AAN) 55. The Bramble Bush (& co-w) 59. The Battle of the Bulge 65. Captain Apache (w, p) 71, etc.

Spewack, Sam (1899–1971)
American playwright who with his wife Bella turned out several scripts for Hollywood.
The Secret Witness 31. Rendezvous 35. *Boy Meets Girl* 38. Three Loves Has Nancy 38. My Favorite Wife (AAN) 40. Weekend at the Waldorf 45. Kiss Me Kate 53. Move Over Darling 63, etc.

Spheeris, Penelope (1945–)
American director and screenwriter, concentrating mainly on themes of disaffected youth. She had her first commercial hit in 1992 with the rock-oriented comedy *Wayne's World*.
The Decline of Western Civilization (wd) 80. Suburbia (wd) 83. The Boys Next Door (d) 85. Summer Camp Nightmare (w) 86. Hollywood Vice Squad (d) 86. Dudes (d) 87. The Decline of Western Civilization Part II: The Metal Years (d) 88. Thunder & Mud (d) 89. Wayne's World (d) 92. The Beverly Hillbillies (p, d) 93. The Little Rascals (co-w, d) 94. Black Sheep 96. Senseless 98, etc.

Spiegel, Sam (1903–1985) (aka S. P. Eagle)
Polish-born producer, in Hollywood from 1941.
Biography: 1988, *Spiegel* by Andrew Sinclair.
Tales of Manhattan 42. *The Stranger* 45. *We Were Strangers* 48. *The African Queen* 51. *On the Waterfront* (AA) 54. The Strange One 57. *The Bridge on the River Kwai* (AA) 57. *Lawrence of Arabia* (AA) 62. The Chase 66. *The Night of the Generals* 66. The Happening 67. The Swimmer 68. Nicholas and Alexandra 71. The Last Tycoon 76. Betrayal 82, etc.

Spielberg, David (1939–)
American character actor.
The Effect of Gamma Rays 72. Newman's Law 74. Hustle 75. The Choirboys 77. The End 78. Stone (TV) 79. Sworn to Silence (TV) 87. Alice 90, etc.
TV series: Bob and Carol and Ted and Alice 73. The Practice 76.

Spielberg, Steven (1946–)
American director, the most commercially successful in the history of cinema so far, who in 1994 founded his own studio, DreamWorks SKG, with Jeffery Katzenberg and David Geffen. Born in Cincinnati, Ohio, he was fascinated by film from childhood, studied it at California State College, and began in television. His box-office successes, which began with *Jaws*, gave semi-adult treatment to what would once have been considered comic-strip material for children; although, with *Schindler's List* and *Saving Private Ryan*, he demonstrated that he could comprehend more serious subject-matter. With yearly earnings that have reached $335m, according to *Forbes* magazine (*Jurassic Park* alone brought him $200m), he is in a position to do precisely what he wants: judging by DreamWorks' output so far, that is to make genre movies that do not break the usual conventions of Hollywood. He was awarded a Golden Lion for Lifetime Achievement at the Venice Film Festival in 1993, and the British government awarded him an honorary knighthood in 2001. Married actresses Amy Irving and Kate Capshaw.
Biography: 1992, *Steven Spielberg* by Philip M. Taylor. 1996, *Steven Spielberg: The Unauthorized Biography* by John Baxter. 1997, *Steven Spielberg* by Joseph McBride.
■ Amblin' (short) 69. Something Evil (TV) 71. Savage (TV) 72. *Duel* (TV) 72. Sugarland Express 73. *Jaws* 75. 1941 75. Close Encounters of the Third Kind (AAN) 77. Raiders of the Lost Ark (AAN) 81. Poltergeist (p only) 82. *E.T. – the Extraterrestrial* (AAN) 82. Twilight Zone (co-d) 83. Indiana Jones and the Temple of Doom 84. Gremlins (p) 85. Back to the Future (p) 85. The Goonies (p) 85. The Color Purple 85. An American Tail (p) 86. Empire of the Sun (& p) 87. Innerspace (p) 87. The Land before Time (p) 88. Who Framed Roger Rabbit? (p) 88. Always (p, d) 89. Back to the Future II (p) 89. Dad (p) 89. Indiana Jones and the Last Crusade (d) 89. Arachnophobia (p) 90. Back to the Future III (p) 90. Gremlins 2: The New Batch (p) 90. Joe versus the Volcano (p) 90. Hook (p, d) 91. Jurassic Park (p, d) 93. Schindler's List (AAp, AAd) 93. The Lost World: Jurassic Park 97. Amistad 97. Deep Impact (ex p only) 98. *Saving Private Ryan* (AAp, AAd) 98.
❝ I've never been through psychoanalysis. I solve my problems with the pictures I make. – S.S.
Rosebud will go over my typewriter to remind me that quality in movies comes first. – S.S. *after buying (for $55,000) the sled used in Citizen Kane*
Stories don't have a middle and an end any more. They usually have a beginning that never stops beginning. – S.S.
I'd rather direct than produce. Any day. And twice on Sunday. – S.S.
What binds my films together is the concept of loneliness and isolation and being pursued by all the forces of character and nature. – S.S.
The next time you scan the movie listings only to find the neighborhood multiplex stuffed with footling Spielbergers – cartoonish action pictures, over-produced B-movie monster pictures and saccharine family fare – you're witnessing his legacy. – *Joel E. Siegel*
In many ways Spielberg is the Puccini of cinema, one of the highest compliments I can pay. He may be a little too sweet for some tastes, but what melodies, what orchestrations, what cathedrals of emotion ... – *J. G. Ballard*

Spillane, Mickey (1918–) (Frank Morrison)
Best-selling American crime novelist of the love-'em and kill-'em variety: I the Jury 53. The Long Wait 54. Kiss Me Deadly 55. *I The Jury* was remade in 1981, with Armand Assante.
as actor: Ring of Fear 54. The Girl Hunters (as Mike Hammer) (& w) 64.
TV series: Darren McGavin played Hammer in a 1960 TV series, as did Stacy Keach in 1983 and Rob Estes in the TV film *Deader than Ever* 96.

Spilsbury, Klinton (1955–)
Mexican-born actor who played the title role in *The Legend of the Lone Ranger* 81, which was a box-office disaster, and then dropped out of sight.

Spinetti, Victor (1933–)
Italo-Welsh comic actor with stage experience.
A Hard Day's Night 64. The Wild Affair 64. Help! 65. The Taming of the Shrew 66. Hieronymus Merkin 69. The Return of the Pink Panther 76. Voyage of the Damned 76. The Krays 90. The Princess and the Goblin (voice) 92. Julie and the Cadillacs 97, etc.

Spinotti, Dante (1943–)
American cinematographer.
Sotto, Sotto 84. Manhunter 86. Crimes of the Heart 87. Beaches 88. Torrents of Spring 89. The Comfort of Strangers 90. True Colors 91. The Last of the Mohicans 92. La Fine è Nota 93. Blink 94. The Quick and the Dead 95. The Star Man 95. Heat 95. The Mirror Has Two Faces 96. LA Confidential (AAN) 97. Goodbye, Lover 98. The Insider (AAN) 99. The Other Sister 99. Wonder Boys 00, etc.

Spoliansky, Mischa (1898–1985)
Russian composer, in Germany from 1930, Britain from 1934.
Don Juan 34. *Sanders of the River* 35. The Ghost Goes West 36. *King Solomon's Mines* 37. Jeannie 42. Don't Take It To Heart 44. Mr Emmanuel 44. Wanted for Murder 46. *The Happiest Days of Your Life* 50. Trouble in Store 53. Saint Joan 57. Northwest Frontier 59. The Battle of the Villa Fiorita 65. Hitler: The Last Ten Days 73, many others.

Spottiswoode, Roger (1947–)
English director and screenwriter now active in Hollywood, a former editor in television and film.
Terror Train 80. The Pursuit of D. B. Cooper 81. 48 Hours (co-w) 82. Under Fire 83. The Best of Times 86. The Last Innocent Man (TV) 87. Shoot to Kill 88. 3rd Degree Burn (TV) 89. Time Flies When You're Alive (TV) 89. Turner & Hooch 89. Air America 90. Stop! or My Mom Will Shoot 92. And the Band Played On (TV) 93. Mesmer 94. Hiroshima (co-d, TV) 95. Tomorrow Never Dies 97. Noriega: God's Favorite (TV) 99. The 6th Day 00, etc.

Spradlin, G. D. (1926–)
American character actor.
Will Penny 67. Zabriskie Point 68. Hell's Angels '69 69. Monte Walsh 70. The Only Way Home (& d) 72. The Godfather, Part II 74. One on One 77. MacArthur 77. North Dallas Forty 79. Apocalypse Now 79. The Formula 80. The Lord of Discipline 82. Tank 84. The War of the Roses 89. Ed Wood 94. Clifford 94. Nick of Time 95. Riders of the Purple Sage (TV) 96. The Long Kiss Goodnight 96, etc.

Spriggs, Elizabeth (1929–)
English character actress, from the stage, usually in dominant or eccentric roles.
Work Is a Four Letter Word 68. Three into Two Won't Go 69. The Glittering Prizes (TV) 76. An Unsuitable Job for a Woman 82. Impromptu 89. Oranges Are Not the Only Fruit (TV) 90. Hour of the Pig 93. *Martin Chuzzlewit* (as Mrs Gamp) (TV) 94. The Secret Agent 97. Paradise Road 97, etc.
TV series: Fox 80. Shine On Harvey Moon 82, 95. A Kind of Living 88. Jeeves and Wooster (as Aunt Agatha) 92–93. Taking Over the Asylum 94.

Spring, Howard (1889–1965)
British novelist. Works filmed include *Fame Is the Spur* and *My Son My Son*.

Springer, Jerry (1944–)
American talk-show host, noted for concentrating on outrageous subject-matter. Born in London to German-Jewish parents who fled to England in 1939 and then moved to the US in 1945, he has degrees in political science and law. In films as himself.
Meet Wally Sparks 97. Ringmaster 98. Austin Powers: The Spy Who Shagged Me 99. The 24 Hour Woman 99 etc.
TV series: The Jerry Springer Show 91- .
❝ When people call me despicable and loathsome, my answer is, 'I love flattery.' – J.S.
My hope is that nobody remembers me. – J.S.

Springsteen, R. G. (1904–1989)
American director who made efficient low-budget westerns from 1930.
Honeychile 48. Hellfire 49. The Enemy Within 49. The Toughest Man in Arizona 53. Track the Man Down 53. Come Next Spring 56. Cole Younger, Gunfighter 58. Battle Flame 59. Black Spurs 64. Taggart 65. Waco 66. Johnny Reno 66. Red Tomahawk 66, many others.

Squire, Ronald (1886–1958) (Ronald Squirl)
British character actor of stage and screen, usually in hearty roles. Born in Tiverton, Devon, he first worked as a journalist, and was on stage from 1909 and in films from the mid 30s. Married twice.
Come Out of the Pantry 35. Love in Exile 36. Action for Slander 37. Dusty Ermine 38. Don't Take it to Heart 44. While the Sun Shines 46. The First Gentleman 48. Woman Hater 48. The Rocking Horse Winner 49. Encore 51. No Highway 51. It Started in Paradise 52. Laxdale Hall 52. My Cousin Rachel 52. The Million Pound Note 53. Footsteps in the Fog 55. Josephine and Men 55. Now and Forever 55. Raising a Riot 55. Around the World in Eighty Days 56. The Silken Affair 56. Island in the Sun 57. The Inn of the Sixth Happiness 58. Law and Disorder 58. The Sheriff of Fractured Jaw 58. Count Your Blessings 59, etc.
❝ A jovial British character actor of some talent, as long as his parts didn't stray too far from playing the captain of a suburban golf club. – *Bernard Braden*

Stack, Robert (1919–) (Robert Modini)
Personable, cold-eyed American leading man of the 50s, later successful in television.
■ First Love 39. The Mortal Storm 40. A Little Bit of Heaven 40. *Nice Girl* (in which he gave Deanna Durbin her first screen kiss) 41. Badlands of Dakota 41. To Be or Not To Be 42. Eagle Squadron 42. Men of Texas 42. A Date with Judy 48. Miss Tatlock's Millions 48. Fighter Squadron 48. My Music 50. My Outlaw Brother 51. The Bullfighter and the Lady 52. Bwana Devil 53. War Paint 53. Conquest of Cochise 53. Sabre Jet 53. The High and the Mighty 54. The Iron Glove 54. House of Bamboo 55. Good Morning Miss Dove 55. Great Day in the Morning 56. *Written on the Wind* (AAN) 56. *The Tarnished Angels* 57. The Gift of Love 58. *John Paul Jones* 59. The Last Voyage 60. The Caretakers 63. Is Paris Burning? 66. The Corrupt Ones 67. Le Soleil des Voyous 68. The Story of a Woman 70. The Action Man 70. The Strange and Deadly Occurrence (TV) 75. 1941 75. Adventures of the Queen (TV) 76. Murder on Flight 502 (TV) 76. Airplane 80. Uncommon Valour 83. Big Trouble 84. The Transformers (voice) 86. Perry Mason: The Case of the Sinister Spirit (TV) 87. Caddyshack II 88. Joe versus the Volcano 90. The Return of Eliot Ness (TV) 91. Beavis and Butthead Do America 96. BASEketball 98. Mumford 99. Totally Irresponsible 99.
TV series: *The Untouchables* 59–62. *The Name of the Game* 68–70. Most Wanted 76. Strike Force 81–82. Falcon Crest 88.

Staenberg, Zach
American editor.
Nowhere to Run 92. Bound 96. The Matrix (AA) 99. Antitrust 01, etc.

Stafford, Frederick (1928–1979) (F. Strobl von Stein)
Austrian leading man who after many he-man roles in European movies imitating James Bond was signed by Alfred Hitchcock to play the lead in *Topaz* 69. Died in a plane crash.
Agent 505—Todesfalle Beirut (It./Fr./Ger.) 65. OSS 117—Mission for a Killer/Furia A Bahia Pour OSS 117 (It/Fr.) 65. Terror in Tokyo/A Tout Coeur A Tokyo Pour OSS 117 (It./Fr.) 66. Dirty Heroes/Dalle Ardenne All'Inferno (It./Fr./Ger.) 67. Million Dollar Man/L' Homme Qui Valait Des Milliards (Fr./It.) 67. Desert Tanks/La Battaglia Di El Alamein (It./Fr.) 68. Topaz (US) 69. Werewolf Woman/La Lupa Mannara (It.) 76, etc.

Stafford, John
English producer and occasional director. Born in London, he worked in various capacities in Hollywood from 1918-1927 before returning to

England. He produced English-language versions of foreign, mainly German, movies, produced ten films for RKO-Radio British, and set up Premier-Stafford productions, which made mainly second features, often directed by Victor Hanbury. In the mid-40s, he produced some films in Italy, and then continued as an independent producer in Britain.

The Inseperables (& co-d) 29. The Beggar Student 31. Where is This Lady? 32. Dick Turpin (& co-d) 33. No Funny Business (& co-d) 33. Spring in the Air 34. There Goes Susie/Scandals in Paris (& co-d) 34. Admirals All 35. The Crouching Beast 35. The Avenging Hand 36. Ball at Savoy 36. Beloved Imposter 36. Second Bureau 36. Wings Over Africa 36. Return of a Stranger 37. Wake Up Famous 37. The Wife of General Ling 37. Candleight in Algeria 43. Teheran/The Plot to Kill Roosevelt 47. Call of the Blood 48. The Golden Madonna 49. The Planter's Wife/Outpost in Malaya 52. Loser Takes All 56. Across the Bridge 57. Nor the Moon By Night/Elephant Gun 58, etc.

Stahl, Jerry (c. 1954–)
American writer who worked on such TV series as *Twin Peaks*, *thirtysomething* and *Moonlighting* and became a heroin addict. He was played by Ben Stiller in the biopic *Permanent Midnight* 98.

Dr Caligari (co-w) 89.

Stahl, John M. (1886–1950)
American director, former stage actor; in films from 1914.

Wives of Men 18. Husbands and Lovers 23. The Child Thou Gavest Me 24. The Naughty Duchess 28. Seed 31. *Back Street* 32. *Imitation of Life* 34. *Magnificent Obsession* 35. Parnell 37. Letter of Introduction 38. *When Tomorrow Comes* 39. Our Wife 41. *Holy Matrimony* 43. The Immortal Sergeant 43. The Eve of St Mark 44. *The Keys of the Kingdom* 44. Leave Her to Heaven 45. The Foxes of Harrow 47. The Walls of Jericho 47. Oh You Beautiful Doll 49, many others.

Stahl, Nick (1980–)
American child actor.

Stranger at My Door (TV) 92. The Man without a Face 93. Safe Passage (TV) 94. Tall Tale: The Unbelievable Adventures of Pecos Bill 95. Blue River 95. Eye of God 97. Disturbing Behavior 98, etc.

Stainton, Philip (1908–1961)
Rotund British actor with surprised expression; often played policemen.

Scott of the Antarctic 47. Passport to Pimlico 48. The Quiet Man 52. Angels One Five 52. Hobson's Choice 54. The Woman for Joe 56, many others.

Stalinska, Dorota (1953–)
Polish leading actress, often in the films of Barbara Sass.

Without Love/Bez Milosci 80. The Outsider/Debiutantka 82. The Scream/Krzyk 82. The Sex Mission/Saksmisja 84. An Immoral Story/Historia Niemoralna 90. Ferdydurke 91, etc.

Stalling, Carl (1888–1972)
American composer and arranger, scoring cartoons. A silent-movie pianist and conductor, he became Disney's musical director in 1928, moving to Ub Iwerks' studio and then to Warner in 1936, retiring in 1958. His scores enlivened many cartoons from *Steamboat Willie* 28 to *To Itch His Own* 58.

Stallings, Laurence (1894–1968)
American screenwriter and playwright. Born in Macon, Georgia, he lost a leg serving in the Marines in the First World War, and, after studying at Georgetown University, worked for New York newspapers while writing plays and musicals. His first play, *What Price Glory?*, was filmed, but after further success eluded him in the theatre, he turned to writing for Hollywood. He also edited and wrote the captions to a best-selling book, *The First World War: A Pictorial History* 33.

The Big Parade 25. *What Price Glory?* (co-w) 26. So Red the Rose (co-w) 35. Northwest Passage (co-w) 39. Jungle Book 42. Salome Where She Danced 45. *She Wore a Yellow Ribbon* (co-w) 49. The Sun Shines Bright 52, etc.

Stallone, Sylvester (1946–)
Beefy, solemn-looking American star who shot to the top in a modest film he wrote himself, and then became a hero of action films. He is now pondering the problem of what action stars do as they grow older. His second wife was actress Brigitte Nielsen (1985–88). Married former model Jennifer Flavin in 1997.

Biography: 1991, *Sylvester Stallone* by Adrian Wright.

A Party at Kitty and Stud's/The Italian Stallion 70. Bananas 71. The Lords of Flatbush 73. Capone 73. The Prisoner of Second Avenue 75. Death Race 2000 75. Farewell My Lovely 75. Carquake 75. *Rocky* (AANw, AANa) 76. F.I.S.T. (& w) 78. Paradise Alley (& wd) 78. Rocky II (& wd) 79. Nighthawks 81. Victory 81. Rocky III 82. First Blood 82. Staying Alive (co-w, co-p, d) 83. Rhinestone 84. Rambo 85. Rocky IV (& d) 85. Cobra 85. Over the Top 87. Rambo III 88. Lock Up 89. Tango & Cash 89. Rocky V 90. Oscar 91. Stop! or My Mom Will Shoot 92. Demolition Man 93. Cliffhanger (& co-w) 93. The Specialist 94. Judge Dredd 95. Assassins 95. Daylight 96. Cop Land 97. Antz (voice) 98. Get Carter 00, etc.

❝ I'll just go on playing Rambo and Rocky. Both are money-making machines that can't be switched off. – *S.S.*

I'm not handsome in the classical sense. The eyes droop, the mouth is crooked, the teeth aren't straight, the voice sounds like a Mafioso pallbearer, but somehow it all works. – *S.S.*

I'd say between 3 p.m. and 8 p.m. I look great. After that it's all downhill. Don't photograph me in the morning or you're gonna get Walter Brennan. – *S.S.*

I'm not a genetically superior person. I built my body. – *S.S.*

I'm a very physical person. People don't credit me with much of a brain, so why should I disillusion them? – *S.S.*

I really am a manifestation of my own fantasy. – *S.S.*

Once in a man's life, for one mortal moment, he must make a grab for immortality. If not, he has not lived. – *S.S.*

All art, in this business, is an act of compromise. It's not one man's vision unless he takes very weak actors. – *S.S.*

Both warrior and bard, he is the author of his own myth, one of the best examples yet of how Hollywood artefacts are in the main line of Western culture and how, amid the collapse of modernism, they have inherited the traditional unifying role of high art. – *Camille Paglia*

Stamp, Terence (1939–)
British leading man.

Autobiography: 1987, *Stamp Album*, 1988, *Coming Attractions*, 1989, *Double Feature*.

Billy Budd (AAN) 62. Term of Trial 62. The Collector 65. Modesty Blaise 66. Far from the Madding Crowd 67. Poor Cow 67. Blue 68. Theorem (It.) 68. The Mind of Mr Soames 69. Superman 78. Meetings with Remarkable Men 78. The Thief of Bagdad 79. Superman II 81. The Hit 84. Company of Wolves 85. Link 86. The Sicilian 87. Wall Street 87. Young Guns 88. Alien Nation 88. Genuine Risk 90. Prince of Shadows/Beltenebros 92. The Real McCoy 93. The Adventures of Priscilla Queen of the Desert 94. Limited Edition/Tire à Part 96. Love Walked In 97. Bliss 97. Bowfinger 98. Star Wars Episode l: The Phantom Menace 99. The Limey 99. Red Planet 00, etc.

❝ I would have liked to be James Bond. – *T.S.*

Stamp-Taylor, Enid (1904–1946)
British character actress with stage experience.

Feather Your Nest 37. Action for Slander 37. The Lambeth Walk 38. Hatter's Castle 41. The Wicked Lady 45. Caravan 46, etc.

Stander, Lionel (1908–1994)
Gravel-voiced American character actor, on stage and screen from the early 30s. His career was harmed by the communist witch-hunts of the late 40s.

The Scoundrel 34. Mr Deeds Goes to Town 36. *A Star is Born* 37. Guadalcanal Diary 42. The Spectre of the Rose 46. Unfaithfully Yours 48. St Benny the Dip 51. *Cul de Sac* (GB) 66. Promise Her Anything (GB) 66. A Dandy in Aspic (GB) 68. The Gang that Couldn't Shoot Straight 72. The Con Men 73. The Black Bird 75. New York New York 77. The Cassandra Crossing 77. Matilda 78. Hart to Hart (TV) 79. The Transformers (voice) 86. Wicked Stepmother 88. Cookie 89, etc.

TV series: Hart to Hart 79.

Standing, Sir Guy (1873–1937)
British stage actor, father of Kay Hammond, in some Hollywood films.

■ The Story of Temple Drake 33. Midnight Club 33. Hell and High Water 33. The Cradle Song 33. A Bedtime Story 33. The Eagle and the Hawk 33. Death Takes a Holiday 34. Now and Forever 34. The Witching Hour 34. Double Door 34. *The Lives of a Bengal Lancer* 35. Car 99 35. Annapolis Farewell 35. The Big Broadcast of 1936 35. The Return of Sophie Lang 36. Palm Springs 36. I'd Give My Life 36. Lloyds of London 36. Bulldog Drummond Escapes 37.

Standing, John (1934–) (Sir John Leon)
British character actor, son of Kay Hammond.

The Wild and the Willing 62. A Pair of Briefs 63. King Rat 65. Walk Don't Run 66. The Psychopath 66. Torture Garden 67. Zee and Co. 71. Rogue Male (TV) 76. The Eagle Has Landed 76. The Elephant Man 80. The Sea Wolves 80. Night Flyers 87. Gulliver's Travels (TV) 96. A Dance to the Music of Time (TV) 97. Mrs Dalloway 97. The Man Who Knew Too Little 97. Mrs Dalloway 97. Rogue Trader 98. Mad Cows 99. 81/2 Women 99, etc.

TV series: Lime Street 86.

Stanley, Kim (1925–) (Patricia Reid)
American stage actress.

■ The Goddess 58. Seance on a Wet Afternoon (AAN) 64. Three Sisters 67. Frances (AAN) 82. The Right Stuff 83.

❝ Directing Kim was as if you'd been given a piano and suddenly found you could play as well as Glenn Gould. – *Tony Richardson*

Stanley, Richard (1964–)
South-African born director and screenwriter of fantasy movies.

Hardware (wd) 90. Dust Devil (wd) 92. The Island of Dr Moreau (co-w) 96, etc.

Stannard, Don (1916–1949)
British light leading man who played Dick Barton in three serial-like melodramas 1948–49.

Stanton, Harry Dean (1926–)
American character actor.

The Proud Rebel 58. Ride in the Whirlwind 65. Rebel Rousers 69. Cisco Pike 71. Dillinger 73. Cockfighter 74. Where the Lilies Bloom 74. Zandy's Bride 74. 92 in the Shade 75. Rafferty and the Gold Dust Twins 75. The Missouri Breaks 76. Straight Time 78. Alien 79. The Rose 79. Wise Blood 79. The Black Marble 80. Deathwatch 80. Private Benjamin 80. Escape from New York 81. One from the Heart 82. Young Doctors in Love 82. Christine 83. Paris, Texas 84. Red Dawn 84. Repo Man 84. The Care Bears Movie 85. Fool for Love 85. One Magic Christmas 85. Pretty in Pink 86. Slamdance 87. The Last Temptation of Christ 88. Mr North 88. Stars and Bars 88. The Fourth War 90. Wild at Heart 90. Man Trouble 92. Twin Peaks: Fire Walk with Me 92. Hotel Room (TV) 93. Against the Wall (TV) 94. Blue Tiger 94. Never Talk to Strangers 95. Down Periscope 96. She's So Lovely 97. Fire Down Below 97. The Mighty 98. Fear and Loathing in Las Vegas 98. The Green Mile 99. The Straight Story 99. The Man Who Cried (GB/Fr.) 00, etc.

Stanwyck, Barbara (1907–1990) (Ruby Stevens)
Durable American star actress, a sultry lady usually playing roles in which she is just as good as a man, if not better. Married comedian Frank Fay (1928–32) and actor Robert Taylor (1939–51). Her lovers included director Frank Capra and actor William Holden. She was awarded an honorary Oscar in 1981 'for superlative creativity and unique contribution to the art of screen acting'.

Biography: 1994, *Stanwyck* by Alex Madsen.

■ Broadway Nights 27. The Locked Door 29. Mexicali Rose 29. Ladies of Leisure 30. Ten Cents a Dance 31. Illicit 31. *Miracle Woman* 31. *Night Nurse* 31. Forbidden 32. Shopworn 32. *So Big* 32. The Purchase Price 32. *The Bitter Tea of General Yen* 33. Ladies They Talk About 33. *Baby Face* 33. Ever in My Heart 33. A Lost Lady 34. Gambling Lady 34. The Secret Bride 35. The Woman in Red 35. Red Salute 35. *Annie Oakley* 35. A Message to Garcia 36. The Bride Walks Out 36. His Brother's Wife 36. Banjo on My Knee 36. The Plough and the Stars 36. Internes Can't Take Money 37. This Is My Affair 37. *Stella Dallas* (AAN) 37. Breakfast for Two 38. The Mad Miss Manton 38. Always Goodbye 38. Union Pacific 39. Golden Boy 39. Remember the Night 40. *The Lady Eve* 41. *Meet John Doe* 41. You Belong to Me 41. *Ball of Fire* (AAN) 41. The Great Man's Lady 42. The Gay Sisters 42. Lady of Burlesque 42. Flesh and Fantasy 43. *Double Indemnity* (AAN) 44. Hollywood Canteen 44. Christmas in Connecticut 45. My Reputation 45. The Bride Wore Boots 46. *The Strange Love of Martha Ivers* 46. California 46. The Other Love 47. The Two Mrs Carrolls 47. Cry Wolf 47. BF's Daughter 48. *Sorry Wrong Number* (AAN) 48. The Lady Gambles 49. East Side West Side 49. Thelma Jordon 50. No Man of Her Own 50. *The Furies* 50. To Please a Lady 50. Man with a Cloak 51. Clash by Night 52. Jeopardy 53. Titanic 53. All I Desire 53. The Moonlighter 53. Blowing Wild 53. *Executive Suite* 54. Witness to Murder 54. Cattle Queen of Montana 54. The Violent Men 55. Escape to Burma 55. There's Always Tomorrow 56. The Maverick Queen 56. These Wilder Years 56. Crime of Passion 57. Trooper Hook 57. Forty Guns 57. Walk on the Wild Side 62. Roustabout 64. The Night Walker 65. The House That Would Not Die (TV) 70. A Taste of Evil (TV) 71. The Letters (TV) 73. The Thorn Birds (TV) 83.

TV series: *The Big Valley* 65–68.

✪ For holding more than her own in comedy or melodrama, and being a match for any man. *The Lady Eve*.

❝ I want to go on until they have to shoot me. – *B.S.*

Put me in the last fifteen minutes of a picture and I don't care what happened before. I don't even care if I was IN the rest of the damned thing – I'll take it in those fifteen minutes. – *B.S.*

Attention embarrasses me. I don't like to be on display. – *B.S.*

Career is too pompous a word. It was a job, and I have always felt privileged to be paid for doing what I love doing. – *B.S.*

Stapleton, Jean (1923–) (Jeanne Murray)
American actress familiar from TV's *All in the Family*.

Damn Yankees 58. Bells are Ringing 60. Something Wild 61. Up the Down Staircase 67. Cold Turkey 70. Klute 71. The Trial 93. Michael 96. Pocahontas II: Journey to a New World (voice) 98, etc.

Stapleton, Maureen (1925–)
American character actress, from the stage. Born in Troy, New York, she came to fame on Broadway in the early 50s. Her second husband was playwright and screenwriter David Rayfiel.

Lonelyhearts (AAN) 58. The Fugitive Kind 60. A View from the Bridge 61. Bye Bye Birdie 63. Airport (AAN) 70. Plaza Suite 71. Tell Me Where It Hurts 74. *Queen of the Stardust Ballroom* 75. The Gathering (TV) 77. Interiors (AAN) 78. Lost and Found 79. The Runner Stumbles 79. Reds (AA, BFA) 81. The Fan 81. Johnny Dangerously 84. Cocoon 85. The Cosmic Eye 85. The Money Pit 86. Heartburn 86. Sweet Lorraine 87. Nuts 87. Made in Heaven 87. Cocoon: The Return 88. Passed Away 92. Trading Mom 94. The Last Good Time 94. Addicted to Love 97, etc.

Stapleton, Oliver
British cinematographer.

Restless Natives 85. My Beautiful Laundrette 86. Absolute Beginners 86. Sammy and Rosie Get Laid 87. Prick Up Your Ears 87. Chuck Berry: Hail! Hail! Rock 'n' Roll 87. Aria 88. Earth Girls Are Easy 88. Danny, the Champion of the World (TV) 89. Cookie 89. She-Devil 89. The Grifters 90. Let Him Have It 91. Hero/Accidental Hero 92. Look Who's Talking Now 93. Kansas City 96. The Van 96. Restoration 96. One Fine Day 96. The Designated Mourner 97. The Object of My Affection 98. The Hi-Lo Country 99. The Cider House Rules 99. William Shakespeare's A Midsummer Night's Dream 99. Birthday Girl 00. State and Main 00, etc.

Stapley, Richard (1922–)
English leading man who went to Hollywood after wartime service in the RAF. Also known, from the late 60s, as Richard Wyler.

The Three Musketeers 48. Little Women 49. The Strange Door 51. King of the Khyber Rifles 53. Target Zero 55. The Ugly Ones 68, etc.

Stark, Graham (1922–)
British comedy actor of films and TV, mostly in cameo roles.

The Millionairess 61. Watch It, Sailor 62. A Shot in the Dark 64. Becket 64. Alfie 66. Finders Keepers 66. Salt and Pepper 68. Doctor in Trouble 70. Return of the Pink Panther 75. The Prince and the Pauper 77. Revenge of the Pink Panther 78. Hawk the Slayer 80. Trail of the Pink Panther 82. Blind Date 87. Son of the Pink Panther 93, etc.

Stark, Ray (c. 1909–)
American producer.
The World of Suzie Wong 60. Oh Dad, Poor Dad 66. This Property is Condemned 66. Funny Girl (AAN) 67. Reflections in a Golden Eye 68. The Way We Were 73. Funny Lady 75. California Suite 78. The Goodbye Girl 78. Chapter Two 79. The Electric Horseman 79. Seems Like Old Times 80. Annie 82. The Slugger's Wife 85. Brighton Beach Memoirs 86. Biloxi Blues 88. Steel Magnolias 89. Lost in Yonkers 93, etc.

Stark, Richard
American thriller writer, one of the pen-names used by Donald WESTLAKE.
Point Blank 67. The Split 68. The Outfit 74. Slayground 83. Payback 99.

Starke, Pauline (1901–1977)
American silent screen actress.
Intolerance 16. Salvation Nell 19. A Connecticut Yankee 21. Shanghai 24. Twenty Cents a Dance 26, etc.

Starr, Belle (1848–1889)
American female outlaw of the wild west period. On screen she has been glamorized by Gene Tierney in the film of that name, by Jane Russell in *Montana Belle* and by Isabel Jewell in *Badman's Territory*. Elizabeth Montgomery had an odd view of her in a 1980 TV movie.

Starr, Irving (1906–1982)
American producer, former agent.
The Crimson Trail 34. Music in My Heart 40. Swing Fever 42. Four Jills in a Jeep 44. Johnny Allegro 47. Slightly French 49, etc.

Starr, Ringo (1940–)
See THE BEATLES.

Starrett, Charles (1904–1986)
American cowboy star of innumerable second features in the 30s and 40s. Inactive after 1952. Born in Athol, Massachusetts, he was educated at Dartmouth College and studied acting at the Academy of Dramatic Arts, beginning in theatre with various stock companies. In the 30s he was contracted to Paramount; success came when he began making westerns for Columbia from the mid-30s.
The Quarterback (debut) (playing himself, a professional footballer) 26. Fast and Loose 30. Sky Bride 32. Green Eyes 34. So Red the Rose 35. Mysterious Avenger 36. Two Gun Law 37. The Colorado Trail 38. Spoilers of the Range 39. Blazing Six Shooters 40. Thunder Over the Plains 41. Pardon My Gun 42. Fighting Buckaroo 43. Sundown Valley 44. Sagebrush Heroes 45. Gunning for Vengeance 46. Riders of the Lone Star 47. Last Days of Boot Hill 48. The Blazing Trail 49. Texas Dynamo 50. The Kid from Amarillo 51. Rough Tough West 52, many others.

Starrett, Jack (1936–1989)
American director, mainly of low-budget action pieces.
Run Angel Run 69. Cry Blood Apache 70. The Strange Vengeance of Rosalie 72. Slaughter 72. Nowhere to Hide (TV) 73. Cleopatra Jones 73. Race with the Devil 75. A Small Town in Texas 76. Final Chapter Walking Tall 77. Big Bob Johnson and His Fantastic Speed Circus (TV) 78. Mr Horn (TV) 79. First Blood (a only) 82.
❝ I jump in with both feet. I figure if you ain't got balls you're in the wrong business. – *J.S., 1975*

Staudte, Wolfgang (1906–1984)
German director of socially conscious films.
The Murderers Are amongst Us (& w) 46. Der Untertan (& w) 51. Rose Bernd 56. Roses for the Prosecutor 59. Die Dreigroschenoper 63. Herrenpartie 64. Heimlichkeiten 68. Die Herren mit die Weissen Weste 70. Wolf of the Seven Seas 73. Zwischengleis (TV) 78, etc.

Staunton, Imelda (1958–)
English actress, from the stage. Trained at RADA, she has worked for the Royal Shakespeare Company and the National Theatre.
Comrades 87. Peter's Friends 92. Much Ado about Nothing 93. Terminus (TV) 94. Deadly Advice 94. Sense and Sensibility 95. Twelfth Night 96. Remember Me? 97. Shakespeare in Love 98. Rat 00. Another Life 00. Chicken Run (voice) 00. Rat 00, etc.
TV series: Up the Garden Path 90–93. If You See God, Tell Him 93.

Stawinksi, Jerzy Stefan (1921–)
Polish screenwriter, novelist and director. In the mid-50s he was literary head of the Kamera production unit, which also included directors Roman Polanski, Jerzy Skolimowski and Andrzej Wajda.
Kanal (& oa) 56. Man on the Track/Czlowiek Na Torze 57. *Eroica* (& oa) 57. Bad Luck/Zezowate Szczescie 60. *The Teutonic Knights*/Krzyzacy 60. Love at Twenty/L'Amour à Vingt Ans (Fr.) 61. Pingwin/Penguin (d) 65. Christmas Eve/ Przedswiateczny Wieczor (co-d) 66. Who Believes in Storks/Kto Wierzy W Bociany (co-d) 71. Chasing Adam/Pogon Za Adamem (co-d) 71. Matilda's Birthday/Urodziny Matyldy (d) 74. Colonel Kwiatkowski 96, etc.

Steadman, Alison (1946–)
English actress, mainly on the stage and television. Formerly married to director Mike LEIGH.
Nuts in May (TV) 76. Abigail's Party (TV) 77. Ptang, Bang, Kipperbang 82. Number One 84. Champions 84. A Private Function 84. The Singing Detective (TV) 86. Clockwise 86. Stormy Monday 87. The Adventures of Baron Munchausen 89. Shirley Valentine 89. Wilt/The Misadventures of Mr Wilt 90. Life Is Sweet 91. Blame It on the Bellboy 92. Pride and Prejudice (TV) 95. Chunky Monkey 00. Fat Friends (TV) 00, etc.
TV series: The Wackers 75. Gone to Seed 92. No Bananas 96. Let Them Eat Cake 99. Fat Friends 00.

Steckler, Ray Dennis (1939–)
American director of low-budget exploitation movies that are most notable for their titles. He also acts in them under the pseudonym of Cash Flagg.
Drivers in Hell/Wild Ones on Wheels 61. Wild Guitar 62. The Incredibly Strange Creatures Who Stopped Living and Became Mixed-up Zombies 62. Rat Pfink a-Boo-Boo 62. Scream of the Butterfly 65. Lemon Grove Kids Meet the Monsters 66. Body Fever 72. The Hollywood Strangler Meets the Skid Row Slasher 79, etc.

Steege, Johanna Ter
Dutch leading actress.
The Vanishing 77. Vincent and Theo 90. Meeting Venus 91. La Naissance de l'Amour (Fr.) 93. Goodbye 95. Paradise Road 97, etc.

Steel, Anthony (1919–2001)
Athletic British leading man with slight stage experience.
Saraband for Dead Lovers (film debut) 48. Marry Me 49. *The Wooden Horse* 50. Laughter in Paradise 51. The Malta Story 52. *Albert RN* 53. The Sea Shall Not Have Them 55. Storm over the Nile 56. The Black Tent 56. Checkpoint 56. A Question of Adultery 57. Harry Black 58. Honeymoon 60. The Switch 63. Hell Is Empty 67. Anzio 68. Massacre in Rome 74. The World Is Full of Married Men 79. The Mirror Crack'd 80. The Monster Club 81, etc.

Steel, Dawn (1947–1997) (Dawn Spielberg)
American production executive. She worked first for Paramount and became president of Columbia Pictures in 1987, leaving in 1990 when Sony took over the company. She then ran an independent production company, Atlas Entertainment, with her husband Charles Roven and Robert Cavallo. Died from a brain tumour.
Autobiography: 1992, *They Can Kill You ... But They Can't Eat You*.
Flashdance 83. Footloose 84. Top Gun 86. Fatal Attraction 87. The Untouchables 87. Casualties of War 90. Cool Runnings 93. Sister Act 2: Back in the Habit 93. Angus 95. Fallen 98. City of Angels 98, etc.
❝ I was trained to be loud, passionate, direct. I didn't realise for the longest time I was intimidating. – *D.S.*

Steele, Barbara (1938–)
British leading lady who has appeared mainly in Italian horror films.
Bachelor of Hearts 58. Sapphire 59. Black Sunday/The Devil's Mask 60. The Pit and the Pendulum (US) 61. The Terror of Dr Hitchcock 62. Eight and a Half 63. The Spectre 64. Sister of Satan/The Revenge of the Blood Beast 65. Nightmare Castle 66. Renegade Girls 74. Pretty Baby 78. Silent Scream 80. Winds of War (TV) 83, etc.
TV series: Dark Shadows 91.

Steele, Bob (1907–1988) (Robert Bradbury)
American character actor, on stage from the age of two and in more than 400 second-feature westerns, appearing as Billy the Kid in a series in the early 40s. One of the 'Three Mesquiteers', he was the son of Robert N. Bradbury, who directed many westerns for Monogram and Republic Pictures and starred him and his twin brother William in his first film, *The Adventures of Bob and Bill* 14. Also played Curley in *Of Mice and Men* 39, and the villainous Canino in *The Big Sleep* 46.
Davy Crockett at the Fall of the Alamo 26. The Bandit's Son 27. Texas Cowboy 30. South of Santa Fe 32. Kid Courageous 35. Riders of the Sage 39. The Carson City Kid 40. Billy the Kid in Texas 40. Westward Ho! 42. Wildfire 45. South of St Louis 49. The Savage Horde 50. Island in the Sky 53. Drums across the River 54. Band of Angels 57. Giant from the Unknown 58. The Bonnie Parker Story 58. Atomic Submarine 59. Pork Chop Hill 59. Rio Bravo 59. McClintock! 63. Taggart 64. Requiem for a Gunfighter 65. The Great Bank Robbery 69. Rio Lobo 70. The Skin Game 71. Charley Varrick 73, many others.
TV series: F Troop 65–66.

Steele, Tom (1909–1990)
American stuntman in serials of the 40s and 50s. He was head of Republic's stunt team during its serial heyday, working as a double for the heroes and villains and also for the studio's western stars, and playing minor roles. He played the uncredited title role in *The Masked Marvel* 43.
Bound for Glory 76. The Cat from Outer Space 78. Alligator 80. The Blues Brothers 80. Scarface 83, etc.

Steele, Tommy (1936–) (Tommy Hicks)
Energetic British cockney performer and pop singer.
Kill Me Tomorrow 55. The Tommy Steele Story 57. The Duke Wore Jeans 59. Light Up The Sky 59. Tommy the Toreador 60. It's All Happening 62. *The Happiest Millionaire* (US) 67. *Half a Sixpence* 67. Finian's Rainbow (US) 68. Where's Jack? 69.

Steenburgen, Mary (1953–)
American leading actress. Married actors Malcolm MCDOWELL (1980–90) and Ted DANSON.
Going South 78. Time after Time 79. Melvin and Howard (AA) 80. Ragtime 81. A Midsummer Night's Sex Comedy 82. Cross Creek 83. Romantic Comedy 83. One Magic Christmas 85. Dead of Center 87. The Whales of August 87. End of the Line 88. Miss Firecracker 89. Parenthood 89. Back to the Future Part III 90. The Butcher's Wife 91. Gilbert Grape 93. Philadelphia 93. Clifford 94. It Runs in the Family 94. Pontiac Moon 94. Nixon 95. The Grass Harp 95. Powder 95. Gulliver's Travels (TV) 96, etc.
TV series: Ink 96–97.

Steiger, Rod (1925–)
Burly American leading character actor who became known on stage and TV after training at New York's Theatre Workshop. His four wives included actresses Sally Grace (1952–58) and Claire BLOOM (1959–69).
Biography: 1998, *Rod Steiger: Memoirs of a Friendship* by Tom Hutchinson.
Teresa 51. *On the Waterfront* (AAN) 54. The Big Knife 55. Oklahoma 55. *The Court Martial of Billy Mitchell* 55. The Unholy Wife 56. Jubal 56. *The Harder They Fall* 56. Back from Eternity 57. Run of the Arrow 57. Across the Bridge (GB) 57. *Al Capone* 58. Cry Terror 58. Seven Thieves 59. The Mark 61. 13 West Street 61. On Friday at Eleven 61. The Longest Day 62. Convicts Four 62. Time of Indifference 63. Hands Over the City (It.) 63. *The Pawnbroker* (BFA, AAN) 64. A Man Called John 64. The Loved One 65. Doctor Zhivago 65. The Girl and the General 66. *In the Heat of the Night* (AA, BFA) 67. No Way to Treat a Lady 68. The Sergeant 68. The Illustrated Man 69. Three into Two Won't Go 69. Waterloo (as Napoleon) 71. A Fistful of Dynamite 71. The Heroes (It.) 72. Happy Birthday Wanda June 72. Lolly Madonna XXX 72. Lucky Luciano 73. Hennessy 74. Innocents With Dirty Hands 75. W.C. Fields and Me 76. Jesus of Nazareth (TV) 77. Jimbuck 77. The Last Four Days (as Mussolini) 77. Wolf Lake 78. Love and Bullets 78. F.I.S.T. 78. Breakthrough 79. The Amityville Horror 79. Lucky Star 80. Klondike Fever 80. Lion of the Desert (as Mussolini) 81. Cattle Annie and Little Britches 81. The Chosen 82. The Magic Mountain 82. The Glory Boys (TV) 84. Hollywood Wives (TV) 84. The Naked Face 84. The Kindred 86. Feel the Heat 87. American Gothic 87. The January Man 89. Tennessee Waltz 89. The Ballad of the Sad Café 90. Men of Respect 91. Guilty as Charged 92. That Summer of White Roses 92. The Neighbor 93. Seven Sundays/Tous les Jours Dimanche (Fr.) 94. The Specialist 94. Tom Clancy's Op Center (TV) 95. In Pursuit of Honor 95. Out There (TV) 95. Carpool 96. Mars Attacks! 96. Livers Ain't Cheap 96. Shiloh 96. Mars Attacks! 96. Incognito 97. Modern Vampires/Revenant 98, etc.

Stein, Herman (1915–)
American composer, prolific co-writer of scores at Universal in the 50s.
Back at the Front 52. Has Anybody Seen My Gal? 52. Meet Me at the Fair 52. Abbott & Costello Meet Dr Jekyll and Mr Hyde 53. Girls in the Night 53. Gunsmoke 53. The Black Shield of Falworth 54. The Creature from the Black Lagoon 54. Destry 54. Drums across the River 54. The Glenn Miller Story 54. So This Is Paris 54. The Far Country 55. This Island Earth 55. I've Lived Before 56. The Incredible Shrinking Man 57. Mister Cory 57. Slim Carter 57. Last of the Fast Guns 58. No Name on the Bullet 59. The Intruder 61, many others.

Stein, Paul (1892–1952)
Austrian director who made films in America and Britain.
Ich Liebe Dich 23. My Official Wife (US) 26. Forbidden Woman (US) 27. Sin Takes a Holiday (US) 30. One Romantic Night 30. Born to Love 31. A Woman Commands (US) 31. Lily Christine (GB) 32. The Outsider (GB) 38. The Saint Meets the Tiger (GB) 41. Talk about Jacqueline (GB) 42. Kiss the Bride Goodbye (GB) 43. Twilight Hour (GB) 44. The Lisbon Story (GB) 46. Counterblast (GB) 48. The Twenty Questions Murder Mystery (GB) 49, etc.

Stein, Ronald (1930–1988)
American composer, conductor and pianist, mainly of B features, including many for American International Pictures. Born in St Louis, Missouri, he was educated at Washington , St. Louis, and Yale Universities, and combined composing with working as a teacher, becoming professor of music at the University of Colorado in 1980, and as a theatrical musical director. He composed the music for many of Roger CORMAN's movies, and wrote more than 80 scores. He was also a documentary film director, writer, editor and photographer.
Day the World Ended 55. Apache Woman 55. Attack of the Crab Monsters 56. It Conquered the World 56. The Oklahoma Woman 56. The She Creature 56. The Undead 56. Dragstrip Girl 57. Invasion of the Saucermen 57. Not of This Earth 57. Sorority Girl 57. The Attack of the 50-Foot Woman 58. The Bonnie Parker Story 58. The Legend of Tom Dooley 59. Tank Commandos 59. Dinosaurus! 60. The Premature Burial 61. Dementia 13 63. The Haunted Palace 63. Of Love and Desire 63. The Terror 63. Spider Baby 64. The Rain People 69. Getting Straight 70, etc.

Steinbeck, John (1902–1968)
American novelist.
Of Mice and Men 39, 81 (TV) and 92. The Grapes of Wrath 40. Tortilla Flat 42. The Moon Is Down 43. Lifeboat (AAN) 44. A Medal for Benny (AAN) 45. The Red Pony 49. Viva Zapata! (AAN) 52. East of Eden 54. The Wayward Bus 57, etc.
❝ We bought *The Moon Is Down*, which was on the stage in New York, and when I said, 'Look, have you got any suggestions?' he said, 'Yeah, tamper with it.' – *Nunnally Johnson*

Steinberg, Michael (1959–)
American director and screenwriter.
The Waterdance (co-d) 92. Bodies, Rest and Motion 93.

Steinberg, Norman
American screenwriter.
Blazing Saddles 73. Yes, Giorgio 82. My Favorite Year 82. Johnny Dangerously 84. Funny about Love 90, etc.

Steiner, Fred (1923–)
American composer who also scores TV movies.
Run for the Sun 56. The Man from Del Rio 56. Time Limit 57. Robinson Crusoe on Mars 64. The St Valentine's Day Massacre 67. The Sea Gypsies 78. The Color Purple (AAN) 85, etc.

Steiner, Max (1888–1971)
Austrian composer, in America from 1924; became one of Hollywood's most reliable and prolific writers of film music.
Cimarron 31. A Bill of Divorcement 32. *King Kong* 33. The Lost Patrol 34. *The Informer* (AA) 35. *She* 35. The Charge of the Light Brigade 36. A Star Is Born 37. *Gone with the Wind* 39. *The Letter* 40. *The Great Lie* 41. *Now Voyager* (AA) 42. *Casablanca* 42. *Since You Went Away* (AA) 44. Rhapsody in Blue 45. The Big Sleep 46. The Treasure of the Sierra Madre 47. Johnny Belinda 48. The Fountainhead 49. The Glass Menagerie 50. Room for One More 52. The Charge at Feather River 53. The Caine Mutiny 54. Battle Cry 55. Come Next Spring 56. Band of Angels 57. The FBI Story 59. The Dark at the Top of the Stairs 60. Parrish 61. Youngblood Hawke 64, many others.

Steinhoff, Hans (1882–1945)
German director, from the theatre. Directed features containing Nazi propaganda from the early 30s. Died in a plane crash.
Angst 28. The Alley Cat (GB) 29. The Three Kings (GB) 29. Chacun Sa Chance (Fr.) 30. Hitlerjunge Quex 33. Robert Koch, der Bekämpfer des Todes 39. Die Geierwally 40. Ohm Krüger 41. Rembrandt 42. Gabriele Dambrone 43. Shiva und die Galgenblume 45, etc.

Steinkamp, Frederic
American editor.
Two Loves 61. Sunday in New York 64. Grand Prix (co-ed) (AA) 66. Charly 68. A New Leaf 71. Haunts of the Very Rich (TV) 72. Freebie and the Bean 74. Three Days of the Condor 75. Bobby Deerfield 77. Tootsie (AAN) 82. Against All Odds 84. White Nights 85. Out of Africa (AAN) 85. Adventures in Babysitting 87. Burglar 87. Scrooged 87. Havana 90. The Firm 93. Sabrina 95, etc.

Stembridge, Gerard
Irish writer and director, born in Limerick.
Guiltrip (d) 95. Ordinary Decent Criminal (w) 00. Nora (co-w) 00. About Adam (wd) 00, etc.

Sten, Anna (1908–1993) (Anjuschka Stenski Sujakevitch)
Russian leading actress imported to Hollywood by Goldwyn in 1933 in the hope of rivalling Garbo; but somehow she didn't click. The first of her two husbands was director Feder Ozep.
SELECTED EUROPEAN FILMS: The Yellow Ticket 27. Storm Over Asia 28. The White Eagle 28. The Murder of Dimitri Karamazov 31. Bombs in Monte Carlo 31.
■ ENGLISH -SPEAKING FILMS: *Nana* 34. We Live Again 34. The Wedding Night 35. A Woman Alone 36. Exile Express 39. The Man I Married 40. So Ends Our Night 41. Chetniks 43. They Came To Blow Up America 43. Three Russian Girls 43. Let's Live a Little 48. Soldier of Fortune 55. Heaven Knows Mr Allison 57. The Nun and the Sergeant 62.

Steno (1915–1988) (Stefano Vanzina)
Italian screenwriter and director, mainly of comedies. Born in Rome, he began as a satirical writer and cartoonist, before working as an assistant to directors Mario MATTOLI, Carlo Ludovico BRAGAGLIA and Riccardo FREDA, and writing screenplays for Mario SOLDATI and Alessandro BLASETTI. His first films were made in collaboration with Mario MONICELLI, and some of his most successful starred the comedian TOTO and, later, Bud SPENCER (Carlo Pedersoli).
AS DIRECTOR: Al Diavoli la Celebrità (co-d) 49. Cops and Robbers/Guardie e Ladri (co-d) 51. Toto a Colori (co-d) 52. Le Avventure di Giacomo Casanova 54. Piccola Pasta (co-d) 56. Toto nella Luna 58. Copacabana Palace 62. Toto Diabolicus 62. Gli Eroi del West 63. Love Italian Style/Amore all'Italiana 66. Transplant/Il Trapianto 70. Flatfoot/Piedone lo Sbirro 73. Piedone a Hong Kong 75. Doppio Delitto 77. Piedone l'Africano 78. Jekyll Junior/Dottor Jekyll e Gentile Signora 79. Piedone d'Egitto 80. Banana Joe 82. Il Professore – Boomerang 89. Il Professore – Polizzia Inferno 89, many others.

Stepanek, Karel (1899–1980)
Czech character actor, in Britain from 1940. Usually played Nazis or other villains.
They Met in the Dark 43. *The Captive Heart* 46. The Fallen Idol 48. State Secret 50. Cockleshell Heroes 55. *Sink the Bismarck* 60. Operation Crossbow 65. Before Winter Comes 69, many others.

Stephen, Susan (1931–2001)
British leading lady of the 50s. She was formerly married to director Nicolas ROEG.
His Excellency 51. The Red Beret 53. For Better For Worse 54. Golden Ivory 54. The Barretts of Wimpole Street 57. Carry On Nurse 59. Return of a Stranger 61. The Court Martial of Major Keller 63, etc.

Stephens, Ann (1931–)
British juvenile actress of the 40s.
In Which We Serve 42. Dear Octopus 43. The Upturned Glass 47. The Franchise Affair 51. Intent to Kill 58, many others.

Stephens, Martin (1949–)
British juvenile player. Later became an architect.
The Hellfire Club 61. *Village of the Damned* 62. *The Innocents* 62. Battle of the Villa Fiorita 65. The Witches 66, etc.

Stephens, Sir Robert (1931–1995)
Distinguished English classical actor, in occasional films. Born in Bristol, he studied at the Bradford Civic Theatre School and began in repertory theatre. He was a founding member of the English Stage Company at the Royal Court Theatre and of the National Theatre. In the mid-70s his career faltered through his heavy drinking, but he made a triumphant return at the Royal Shakespeare Company in the 90s as Falstaff and King Lear. Married four times: his third wife was actress Maggie SMITH and his fourth actress Patricia Quinn. He was romantically involved with actresses Margaret LEIGHTON and Tammy GRIMES and writer Lady Antonia Fraser. He was knighted in 1992. His film career began when he signed a three-year contract with Twentieth Century-Fox ('the most terrible mistake') and came unstuck while he played the title role in Billy WILDER's *The Private Life of Sherlock Holmes*, an experience that led him to attempt suicide. He later replaced Peter FINCH to play opposite Elizabeth TAYLOR in the film of *A Little Night Music*, but was fired during rehearsals by director Harold PRINCE. After Taylor claimed that the 'chemistry' wasn't right between them, he replied, 'Chemistry? Chemistry? We're actors, not bloody pharmacists.'
Autobiography: 1995, *Knight Errant* (with Michael Coveney).
Circle of Deception 60. Pirates of Tortuga (US) 61. A Taste of Honey 61. The Inspector 62. Cleopatra 62. The Small World of Sammy Lee 63. Morgan 66. Romeo and Juliet 68. The Prime of Miss Jean Brodie 69. *The Private Life of Sherlock Holmes* 69. The Asphyx 72. Travels with My Aunt 73. Luther 73. QB VII (TV) 73. Holocaust (TV) 78. The Shout 78. Fortunes of War (TV) 87. War and Remembrance (TV) 87. High Season 87. Testimony 87. Henry V 89. Wings of Fame 90. The Pope Must Die/The Pope Must Diet 91. Afraid of the Dark 91. Adam Bede (TV) 91. Searching for Bobby Fischer/Innocent Moves 93. Century 93. The Secret Rapture 93. England, My England (as John Dryden) (TV) 95, etc.
❝ One reason I've never chased after films is that once you become a film star, you really can't stop, because you have to be before the public's eye all the time. I wouldn't care for that. Also, in films the material can't be that good all the time. You have to make mostly bad films, or films that aren't frightfully good. That wouldn't interest me – not that I've ever been offered the opportunity. – *R.S.*
Film acting is difficult to do properly. I remember I once said to George Cukor that I think it's as difficult to be Spencer Tracy as it is to be Laurence Olivier. He said, wrong, it's much more difficult to be Spencer Tracy. – *R.S.*

Stephens, Toby (1969–)
English actor, the son of actors Robert STEPHENS and Maggie SMITH, who made his reputation acting with the Royal Shakespeare Company in the mid-90s.
Orlando 92. The Camomile Lawn (TV) 92. Twelfth Night 96. The Tenant of Wildfell Hall (TV) 96. Sunset Heights 97. Photographing Fairies 97. Cousin Bette 98. Onegin 98. The Great Gatsby (TV) 01, etc.

Stephenson, Henry (1871–1956) (H. S. Garroway)
British stage actor who came to Hollywood films in his 60s and remained to play scores of kindly old men.
■ The Spreading Dawn 17. The Black Panther's Cub 21. Men and Women 25. Wild Wild Susan 25. *Cynara* 32. Red Headed Woman 32. Guilty as Hell 32. A Bill of Divorcement 32. The Animal Kingdom 32. Little Women 33. Queen Christina 33. Tomorrow at Seven 33. Double Harness 33. My Lips Betray 33. If I Were Free 33. Blind Adventure 33. Man of Two Worlds 34. The Richest Girl in the World 34. Thirty Day Princess 34. Stingaree 34. The Mystery of Mr X 34. What Every Woman Knows 34. One More River 34. Outcast Lady 34. She Loves Me Not 34. All Men Are Enemies 34. Mutiny on the Bounty 35. Vanessa, Her Love Story 35. Reckless 35. The Flame Within 35. O'Shaughnessy's Boy 35. The Night Is Young 35. Rendezvous 35. The Perfect Gentleman 35. Captain Blood 35. Beloved Enemy 36. Half Angel 36. Hearts Divided 36. Give Me Your Heart 36. Walking on Air 36. Little Lord Fauntleroy 36. *The Charge of the Light Brigade* 36. When You're in Love 37. The Prince and the Pauper 37. The Emperor's Candlesticks 37. Conquest 37. Wise Girl 37. *The Young in Heart* 38. The Baroness and the Butler 38. Suez 38. Marie Antoinette 38. Dramatic School 38. Tarzan Finds a Son 39. The Private Lives of Elizabeth and Essex 39. The Adventures of Sherlock Holmes 39. It's a Date 40. Little Old New York 40. Spring Parade 40. Down Argentine Way 41. The Man Who Lost Himself 41. The Lady from Louisiana 41. This Above All 42. Rings on Her Fingers 42. Half Way to Shanghai 42. Mr Lucky 43. *Mantrap* 43. The Hour Before the Dawn 44. Secrets of Scotland Yard 44. The Reckless Age 44. Two Girls and a Sailor 44. Tarzan and the Amazons 45. The Green Years 46. Her Sister's Secret 46. The Locket 46. Heartbeat 46. Night and Day 46. Of Human Bondage 46. The Return of Monte Cristo 46. Dark Delusion 47. The Homestretch 47. Time Out of Mind 47. Ivy 47. Song of Love 47. Julia Misbehaves 48. Enchantment 48. *Oliver Twist* (as Mr Brownlow) 48. Challenge to Lassie 48.

Stephenson, James (1888–1941)
Suave British-born stage actor, in Hollywood from 1938.
When Were You Born? (debut) 38. Boy Meets Girl 38. Confessions of a Nazi Spy 38. Beau Geste 39. Calling Philo Vance 40. The Sea Hawk 40. *The Letter* (AAN) 40. Shining Victory 41. International Squadron 41, etc.

Stephenson, Pamela (1951–)
New Zealand leading lady who has done a variety of light work on British stage and TV (especially *Not the Nine o'Clock News*).
History of the World Part One 81. Scandalous 83. Superman III 83. Bloodbath at the House of Death 83. Finders Keepers 84. Les Patterson Saves the World 87, etc.

Steppat, Ilse (1917–1969)
German character actress.
Marriage in the Shadow 47. The Bridge 51. The Confessions of Felix Krull 62. On Her Majesty's Secret Service 69, etc.

Sterling, Ford (1883–1939) (George F. Stitch)
American comic actor, a leading Keystone Kop and slapstick heavy.
Drums of the Desert 26. Gentlemen Prefer Blondes 28. Kismet 30. Alice in Wonderland 33. The Black Sheep 35, etc.

Sterling, Jan (1923–) (Jane Sterling Adriance)
Blonde American leading lady with slight stage experience.
Johnny Belinda 48. Rhubarb 51. *Ace in the Hole* 51. Split Second 52. Pony Express 53. Alaska Seas 54. The High and the Mighty (AAN) 54. Women's Prison 55. The Female on the Beach 55. 1984 56. The Harder They Fall 56. Kathy O 58. Love in a Goldfish Bowl 61. Having Babies (TV) 76. Backstairs at the White House (TV) 79. First Monday in October 81, etc.
❝ Famous line (*Ace in the Hole*) 'I don't go to church. Kneeling bags my nylons.'
Famous line (*Ace in the Hole*) 'I've met some hard-boiled eggs in my time, but you – you're twenty minutes!'

Sterling, Robert (1917–) (William John Hart)
American leading man of the 40s, mainly in second features. Married actresses Ann Sothern and Anne Jeffreys.
Only Angels Have Wings 39. I'll Wait for You 41. Somewhere I'll Find You 42. The Secret Heart 46. Bunco Squad 48. Roughshod 50. Thunder in the Dust 51. Column South 53. Return to Peyton Place 61. Voyage to the Bottom of the Sea 62, etc.
TV series: Topper 53–54. Love That Jill 58. Ichabod and Me 61–62.

Stern, Daniel (1957–)
American leading actor and director.
Breaking Away 79. Starting Over 79. Stardust Memories 80. One Trick Pony 80. Diner 82. Blue Thunder 83. C.H.U.D. 84. Frankenweenie 84. Key Exchange 85. Hannah and Her Sisters 86. D.O.A. 88. The Milagro Beanfield War 88. Friends, Lovers and Lunatics 89. Leviathan 89. Little Monsters 89. My Blue Heaven 90. Home Alone 90. City Slickers 91. Home Alone 2: Lost in New York 92. Rookie of the Year (& d) 93. City Slickers II: The Legend of Curly's Gold 94. Bushwhacked 95. Celtic Pride 96. Very Bad Things 98, etc.
TV series: Hometown 85. The Wonder Years (voice) 88– .

Sternhagen, Frances (1930–)
American actress, from stage and television.
Up the Down Staircase 67. The Tiger Makes Out 67. The Hospital 71. Fedora 78. Starting Over 79. Outland 81. Prototype (TV) 83. Romantic Comedy 83. Bright Lights, Big City 88. Communion 89. See You in the Morning 89. Sibling Rivalry 90. Misery 90. Doc Hollywood 91. Raising Cain 92, etc.
TV series: Spencer 84–85. Stephen King's Golden Years 91.

Stevenin, Jean-François (1944–)
French leading actor and occasional director, associated with the films of François TRUFFAUT and other directors of the New Wave.
Wild Child 70. Day for Night 73. Si Je Cherche, Je Me Trouve 74. Small Change 76. Barocco 76. Merry-Go-Round 78. Le Passe Montagne (& d) 79. The Dogs of War (GB) 80. Neige 81. Passion 82. Le Pont du Nord 82. Notre Histoire 84. Tenue de Soirée 86. Double Messieurs (& p, wd) 86. Lune Froide 89. Olivier, Olivier 91. 23:58 93. Les Patriotes 93. Fast 95. Noir comme le Souvenir 95. à Vendre 98, etc.

Stevens, Andrew (1955–)
American actor, producer and director, latterly of direct-to-video thrillers. Born in Memphis, Tennessee, he is the son of actress Stella STEVENS.
Shampoo 75. Massacre at Central High 76. Day of the Animals 77. Secrets 77. The Boys in Company C 78. The Fury 78. Topper (TV) 79. Death Hunt 81. Forbidden Love (TV) 82. Ten to Midnight 83. Hollywood Wives (TV) 85. Tusks (GB) 87. The Ranch 88. The Terror Within 89. Night Eyes 90. Night Eyes 2 91. Munchie 92. The Terror Within II (& d) 92. Night Eyes 3 (& d) 93. Scorned (& d) 93. Body Chemistry 4 95. Virtual Combat (d only) 95. Grid Runners (d only) 95. Scorned 2 96. Crash Dive (d only) 96. The Corporation (& d) (TV) 96, etc.
TV series: The Oregon Trail 77. Code Red 81–82. Emerald Point NAS 83–84.

Stevens, Connie (1938–) (Concetta Ingolia)
American leading lady with mixed Italian, English, Irish and Mohican blood. She was formerly married to singer Eddie FISHER.
Young and Dangerous 57. Rockabye Baby 58. Parrish 61. Susan Slade 61. Palm Springs Weekend 63. Two on a Guillotine 65. Never Too Late 65. Way Way Out 66. Mr Jericho (TV) 70. The Grissom Gang 71. The Sex Symbol (TV) 73. Scorchy 76. Grease 2 82. Back to the Beach 87. Tapeheads 89. Love Is All There Is 96. Becoming Dick (TV) 00, etc.
TV series: Hawaiian Eye 59–62.

Stevens, Craig (1918–2000) (Gail Shikles Jnr)
American leading man, best known for his role of the cool detective Peter Gunn on TV. Born in

Montana, he gave up his dentistry studies at the University of Kansas to become an actor. Married actress Alexis SMITH in 1944.

Affectionately Yours 41. The Body Disappears 41. Dive Bomber 41. Law of the Tropics 41. The Hidden Hand 42. Since You Went Away 44. The Doughgirls 44. God Is My Co-Pilot 45. Humoresque 46. That Way with Women 47. The Lady Takes a Sailor 47. Night unto Night 49. Where the Sidewalk Ends 50. Drums in the Deep South 51. Katie Did It 51. The Lady from Texas 51. Phone Call from a Stranger 52. Abbott and Costello Meet Dr Jekyll and Mr Hyde 53. Duel on the Mississippi 55. The Deadly Mantis 57. Buchanan Rides Alone 58. The French Line 54. Gunn 67. The Limbo Line 68. The Snoop Sisters (TV) 72. Rich Man Poor Man (TV) 76. S.O.B. 81, etc.

TV series: *Peter Gunn* 58–60. Man of the World 62. Mr Broadway 64. The Invisible Man 75-76. Dallas 81.

Stevens, Fisher (1963–) (Steven Fisher)
American actor of stage, screen and television, born in Chicago, Illinois.

The Burning 81. Baby It's You 83. The Brother from Another Planet 84. The Flamingo Kid 84. My Science Project 85. Short Circuit 86. Short Circuit 2 88. Bloodhounds of Broadway 89. Reversal of Fortune 90. The Marrying Kind 91. Bob Roberts 92. Super Mario Bros 93. Nina Takes a Lover 94. Only You 94. Hackers 95. Cold Fever 95. The Pompatus of Love 96, etc.

Stevens, George (1904–1975)
American director, in Hollywood from 1923. In the late 30s and early 40s he made smooth and lively entertainments, but his infrequent later productions tended towards elephantiasis.

■ The Cohens and Kellys in Trouble 33. Bachelor Bait 34. Kentucky Kernels 34. Laddie 34. The Nitwits 34. Alice Adams 34. Annie Oakley 35. Swing Time 36. A Damsel in Distress 37. *Quality Street* 37. Vivacious Lady 38. *Gunga Din* 39. Vigil in the Night 40. Penny Serenade 40. *Woman of the Year* 41. *Talk of the Town* 42. *The More the Merrier* (AAN) 43. *I Remember Mama* 47. *A Place in the Sun* (AA) 51. Something to Live For 52. *Shane* (AAN) 53. *Giant* (AA) 56. The Diary of Anne Frank (AAN) 59. The Greatest Story Ever Told 65. The Only Game in Town 69.

❝ He was a minor director with major virtues before *A Place in the Sun*, and a major director with minor virtues after. – *Andrew Sarris, 1968*

Stevens Jnr, George (1932–)
American producer, son of George Stevens, who in 1977 became head of the American Film Institute.

Stevens, Inger (1935–1970) (Inger Stensland)
Pert and pretty Swedish leading lady, in America from childhood. Died of a drug overdose.

Man on Fire (film debut) 57. Cry Terror 58. The World, the Flesh and the Devil 58. The Buccaneer 59. The New Interns 64. *A Guide for the Married Man* 67. Firecreek 67. Madigan 68. Five Card Stud 68. Hang 'Em High 68. House of Cards 68. The Borgia Stick (TV) 68. A Dream of Kings 69. Run Simon Run (TV) 70, etc.

TV series: *The Farmer's Daughter* 63–65.

Stevens, K. T. (1919–1994) (Gloria Wood)
American leading lady of a few 40s films; daughter of director Sam Wood.

Kitty Foyle 40. The Great Man's Lady 41. Address Unknown 44. Vice Squad 53. Tumbleweed 53. Missile to the Moon 58, etc.

Stevens, Leith (1909–1970)
American musical arranger and composer.

The Wild One 52. Julie 56. The Five Pennies 59. A New Kind of Love 63, many others for Fox and Paramount, including TV series.

Stevens, Leslie (1924–1998)
American screenwriter.

The Left-Handed Gun 58. Private Property (& p, d) 59. The Marriage-Go-Round (from his play) 60. Hero's Island (& p, d) 62. Buck Rogers 79. Sheena (story) 84. Three Kinds of Heat (w, d) 87, etc.

TV series (as creator-producer-director): Stony Burke. The Outer Limits. Battlestar Galactica.

Stevens, Mark (1915–1994) (aka Stephen Richards)
American leading man with varied early experience; usually in routine roles.

Objective Burma 45. *From This Day Forward* 45. The Dark Corner 46. I Wonder Who's Kissing Her Now 47. The Snake Pit 48. The Street with No Name 48. Sand 49. Mutiny 53. Cry Vengeance (also pd) 54. Timetable (also pd) 55. September Storm 60. Fate is the Hunter 64. Frozen Alive 66. Sunscorched 66.

TV series: Big Town 52–57.

Stevens, Onslow (1902–1977) (Onslow Ford Stevenson)
American stage actor occasionally seen in film character roles. Son of Houseley Stevenson. He was murdered.

Heroes of the West (debut) 32. Counsellor at Law 33. The Three Musketeers 36. Under Two Flags 36. When Tomorrow Comes 39. Mystery Sea Raider 40. *House of Dracula* 45. O.S.S. 46. Night Has a Thousand Eyes 48. The Creeper 48. State Penitentiary 50. Them 54. Tarawa Beachhead 58. All the Fine Young Cannibals 60. Geronimo's Revenge 63, etc.

Stevens, Rise (1913–)
American opera singer, seen in a few films.

■ The Chocolate Soldier 41. Going My Way 44. Carnegie Hall 47.

Stevens, Robert (c. 1925–1989)
American director, from TV.

■ The Big Caper 57. Never Love a Stranger 58. I Thank a Fool 62. In the Cool of the Day 63. Change of Mind 69.

Stevens, Ronnie (1925–)
British comic actor with stage and TV experience.

Made in Heaven 52. An Alligator Named Daisy 55. I Was Monty's Double 58. I'm All Right, Jack 59. Dentist in the Chair 60. San Ferry Ann 65. Give a Dog a Bone 66. Some Girls Do 68. Morons from Outer Space 85. The Parent Trap 98, etc.

Stevens, Stella (1936–) (Estelle Eggleston)
American leading lady, mother of actor Andrew STEVENS.

Say One for Me (debut) 58. Li'l Abner 59. Too Late Blues 61. The Courtship of Eddie's Father 63. The Nutty Professor 63. Synanon 65. The Secret of My Success 65. The Silencers 66. How to Save a Marriage 67. The Mad Room 69. The Ballad of Cable Hogue 70. A Town Called Bastard 71. Stand Up and Be Counted 71. The Poseidon Adventure 72. Arnold 74. Cleopatra Jones and the Casino of Gold 74. Las Vegas Lady 74. Nickelodeon 76. The Night They Took Miss Beautiful (TV) 77. Cruise into Terror (TV) 78. The Manitou 78. The Terror Within II 91. Exiled 91. Mom 91. South Beach 92. The Night Caller 92. Molly & Gina 94. In Cold Blood (TV) 96. The Corporation 96, etc.

TV series: Ben Casey 65. Flamingo Road 80–81.

Stevens, Warren (1919–)
American general-purpose actor.

The Frogmen 51. The Barefoot Contessa 54. Forbidden Planet 56. Hot Spell 58. No Name on the Bullet 59. Forty Pounds of Trouble 62. An American Dream 66. Madigan 68. The Sweet Ride 68. Stroker Ace 83. Stormy Nights 96, many others.

TV series: 77th Bengal Lancers 56–57. The Richard Boone Show 63–64. Bracken's World (voice) 69–70. Behind the Screen 81–82.

Stevenson, Edward (1906–1968)
American costume designer, in Hollywood from 1922. He was chief designer at RKO from 1936–49. From the mid-50s he designed Lucille Ball's costumes for her TV series *I Love Lucy*.

The Joy of Living 38. They Knew What They Wanted 40. Citizen Kane 41. The Magnificent Ambersons 42. Journey into Fear 42, etc.

Stevenson, Houseley (1879–1953)
American character actor, latterly familiar as a gaunt, usually unshaven, old man.

Native Land 42. Somewhere in the Night 46. Dark Passage 47. Casbah 48. Moonrise 49. All the King's Men 49. The Sun Sets at Dawn 51. The Wild North 52, etc.

Stevenson, Juliet (1956–) (Juliet Stevens)
British leading actress, from classical theatre.

Drowning by Numbers 88. Ladder of Swords 88. Truly Madly Deeply 91. The Trial 93. The Secret Rapture 93. The Politician's Wife (TV) 95. Emma 96. Cider with Rosie (TV) 98, etc.

❝ I'm hardly Hollywood material – they're interested in youth and perfection and I lay no claims to either. It's not a place that's particularly interested in talent. – *J.S.*

Stevenson, Robert (1905–1986)
British director, a former journalist, in Hollywood from 1939. There he achieved his greatest success making live-action movies for Disney, including *Mary Poppins*. Born in London, and educated at Cambridge University, he began in films in 1929 as a screenwriter. Formerly married (1933-1944) to actress Anna LEE.

As WRITER: Michael and Mary 31. Sunshine Susie 31. Love on Wheels 32. F.P.I. 33. The Battle (Fr.) 34. Paradise for Two/Gaiety Girls 37, etc.

■ Happy Ever After (co-d) 32. Falling for You (co-w, co-d) 33. Tudor Rose (& co-w) 36. The Man Who Changed His Mind 36. Jack of all Trades (co-d) 36. *King Solomon's Mines* 37. Non Stop New York 37. Owd Bob 38. The Ware Case 38. Young Man's Fancy 39. Return to Yesterday (& co-w) 40. *Tom Brown's Schooldays* 40. *Back Street* 41. Joan of Paris 42. Forever and a Day (co-d) 43. *Jane Eyre* 43. Dishonored Lady 47. *To the Ends of the Earth* 48. The Woman on Pier 13 49. Walk Softly Stranger 50. My Forbidden Past 51. The Las Vegas Story 52. Johnny Tremain 57. Old Yeller 57. Darby O'Gill and the Little People 59. Kidnapped 59. The Absent-Minded Professor 61. In Search of the Castaways 61. Son of Flubber 63. The Misadventures of Merlin Jones 64. *Mary Poppins* (AAN) 64. The Monkey's Uncle 65. That Darn Cat 65. The Gnome-Mobile 67. Blackbeard's Ghost 67. The Love Bug 68. My Dog the Thief 70. Bedknobs and Broomsticks 71. Herbie Rides Again 74. The Island at the Top of the World 74. One of Our Dinosaurs Is Missing 75. The Shaggy D.A. 76.

Stevenson, Robert Louis (1850–1894)
British novelist and short-story writer. Works filmed include *Dr Jekyll and Mr Hyde* (many versions), *Treasure Island* (many versions), *The Body Snatcher*, *The Suicide Club*, *Kidnapped*, *The Master of Ballantrae*, *Ebb Tide*, *The Wrong Box*.

Steward, Ernest (–1990)
British cinematographer.

Appointment with Venus 51. Trouble in Store 53. Doctor in the House 54. Simon and Laura 55. Above Us the Waves 55. Doctor at Sea 55. The Secret Place 57. A Tale of Two Cities 58. The Wind Cannot Read 58. No Love for Johnnie 61. A Pair of Briefs 61. Crooks Anonymous 62. The Wild and the Willing 62. The Face of Fu Manchu 65. Circus of Fear 66. Doctor in Clover 66. Carry On Up the Khyber 68. Carry On Again Doctor 69. Carry On Camping 69. Carry On at Your Convenience 71. Percy 71. Steptoe and Son Ride Again 73. Callan 74. Carry On Dick 74. Carry On Behind 75. Hennessy 75. Carry On England 76. The Wild Cats of St Trinian's 80, etc.

Stewart, Alexandra (1939–)
Canadian leading lady who has filmed mainly in Europe.

Exodus 60. Le Feu Follet 63. Dragées au Poivre 65. Maroc 7 67. The Bride Wore Black 67. The Man Who Had Power Over Women 70. Day for Night 73. Marseilles Contract 74. In Praise of Older Women 78. Phobia 80. Chanel Solitaire 81. Your Ticket Is No Longer Valid 84. Kemek 88. Seven Servants (Ger.) 96, etc.

Stewart, Anita (1895–1961) (Anna May Stewart)
American silent screen leading lady.

A Million Bid 13. The Goddess 15. Mary Regan 19. Her Kingdom of Dreams 20. Never the Twain Shall Meet 25. Sisters of Eve 28, many others.

Stewart, Athole (1879–1940)
British stage character actor.

The Speckled Band 31. The Clairvoyant 34. Dusty Ermine 37. The Spy in Black 39. Tilly of Bloomsbury 40, etc.

Stewart, Donald (1930–1999)
American screenwriter, a former journalist and advertising copywriter. He moved to Hollywood in the mid-70s.

Jackson County Jail 76. Deathsport 78. Missing (AA) 82. The Hunt for Red October 90. Patriot Games (co-w) 92. Clear and Present Danger (co-w) 94. Dead Silence (TV) 97, etc.

Stewart, Donald Ogden (1894–1980)
American playwright and screenwriter.

Autobiography: 1974, *By a Stroke of Luck*.

■ Brown of Harvard 26. Laughter 30. Finn and Hattie (oa) 30. Rebound (oa) 31. Tarnished Lady (& oa) 31. Smilin' Through 32. The White Sister 33. Another Language 33. Dinner at Eight 33. The Barretts of Wimpole Street 34. No More Ladies 35. *The Prisoner of Zenda* 37. Holiday 38. Marie Antoinette 38. Love Affair 39. The Night of Nights 39. Kitty Foyle 40. *The Philadelphia Story* (AA) 40. That Uncertain Feeling 41. A Woman's Face 41. Smilin' Through 41. Tales of Manhattan 42. Without Love 45. Life with Father 47. Cass Timberlane 47. Edward My Son 49. Escapade 55. Moment of Danger 60.

NB: Some of the above were in collaboration with other writers.

Stewart, Elaine (1929–) (Elsy Steinberg)
American leading lady of a few 50s films; former usherette.

Sailor Beware 51. The Bad and the Beautiful 52. Young Bess 53. Brigadoon 54. The Tattered Dress 56. The Adventures of Hajji Baba 57. The Rise and Fall of Legs Diamond 60. The Most Dangerous Man Alive 61. The Seven Revenges 63, etc.

Stewart, Eve
British production designer, associated with the films of Mike LEIGH.

Career Girls 97. Topsy-Turvy (AAN) 99, etc.

Stewart, Hugh (1910–)
British producer, former editor.

Trottie True 49. The Long Memory 52. Man of the Moment 55 (and all subsequent Norman Wisdom comedies). The Intelligence Men 65, etc.

Stewart, James (1908–1997)
American leading actor of inimitable slow drawl and gangly walk; portrayed slow-speaking, honest heroes for thirty-five years.

Special AA 1984 'for 50 years of meaningful performances, for his high ideals, both on and off the screen, with the respect and affection of his colleagues'.

Biography: 1984, *James Stewart* by Allen Eyles. 1994, *James Stewart: Leading Man* by Jonathan Coe. 1997, *James Stewart* by Donald Dewey. 1998, *Pieces of Time: The Life of James Stewart* by Gary Fishgall and Lisa Drew. 1998, *A Wonderful Life: The Films and Career of James Stewart* by Tony Thomas.

■ Murder Man 35. Rose Marie 36. Next Time We Love 36. Wife versus Secretary 36. Small Town Girl 36. Speed 36. The Gorgeous Hussy 36. Born to Dance 36. After the Thin Man 36. *Seventh Heaven* 37. The Last Gangster 37. Navy Blue and Gold 37. Of Human Hearts 38. Vivacious Lady 38. Shopworn Angel 38. *You Can't Take It with You* 38. Made for Each Other 38. Ice Follies of 1939. It's a Wonderful World 39. *Mr Smith Goes to Washington* (AAN) 39. *Destry Rides Again* 39. *The Shop around the Corner* 40. The Mortal Storm 40. No Time for Comedy 40. *The Philadelphia Story* (AA) 40. Come Live with Me 40. Pot O' Gold 41. Ziegfeld Girl 41; war service; *It's a Wonderful Life* (AAN) 46. Magic Town 46. *Call Northside 777* 47. On Our Merry Way 48. Rope 48. You Gotta Stay Happy 48. The Stratton Story 49. Malaya 49. *Winchester 73* 50. *Broken Arrow* 50. The Jackpot 50. *Harvey* (AAN) 50. No Highway (GB) 51. The Greatest Show on Earth 51. Bend of the River 52. Carbine Williams 52. The Naked Spur 53. Thunder Bay 53. *The Glenn Miller Story* 53. *Rear Window* 54. The Far Country 54. Strategic Air Command 55. *The Man from Laramie* 55. The Man Who Knew Too Much 56. The Spirit of St Louis 57. Night Passage 57. Vertigo 58. Bell, Book and Candle 58. *Anatomy of a Murder* (AAN) 59. The FBI Story 59. The Mountain Road 60. Two Rode Together 61. The Man Who Shot Liberty Valance 62. *Mr Hobbs Takes a Vacation* 62. How the West Was Won 62. Take Her She's Mine 63. Cheyenne Autumn 64. Dear Brigitte 65. *Shenandoah* 65. The Flight of the Phoenix 65. The Rare Breed 66. Firecreek 67. Bandolero 68. The Cheyenne Social Club 70. Fool's Parade 71. The Shootist 76. The Big Sleep 77. Airport 77 77. The Magic of Lassie 78. Right of Way (TV) 83. North and South II (TV) 86. An American Tail: Fievel Goes West (voice) 91.

TV series: The Jimmy Stewart Show 71. Hawkins on Murder 73.

✪ For becoming one of everybody's family even when playing a tough westerner. *The Philadelphia Story*.

❝ I don't act. I react. – *J.S.*

I'm the inarticulate man who tries. I don't really have all the answers, but for some reason, somehow, I make it. – *J.S.*

The big studios were an ideal way to make films – because they were a home base for people. When you were under contract, you had a chance to relax. – *J.S.*

If I had my career over again? Maybe I'd say to myself, speed it up a little. – *J.S.*

He has so many of his pictures being shown on the late show, he keeps more people up than Mexican food. – *Hal Kanter*

Famous line (*The Philadelphia Story*) 'The prettiest sight in this fine pretty world is the privileged class enjoying its privileges.'

Famous line (*Harvey*) 'I wrestled with reality for 35 years, doctor, and I'm happy. I finally won out over it.'

Famous line (*It's a Wonderful Life*) 'Well, you look about the kind of angel I'd get. Sort of a fallen angel, aren't you? What happened to your wings'

Stewart, Martha (1922–) (Martha Haworth)
American actress and singer. Married comedian Joe E. Lewis (1946–48). She was played by Mitzi Gaynor in the biopic *The Joker Is Wild*.

Daisy Kenyon 47. Are You With It? 48. I Wonder Who's Kissing Her Now 47. In a Lonely Place 50. Aaron Crick from Punkin Crick 52. Surf Party 63, etc.

Stewart, Patrick (1940–)
Balding British leading actor, from classical theatre. He is now best known for his role as Captain Jean-Luc Picard in the TV series *Star Trek: The Next Generation* (1987–94). Born in Mirfield, Yorkshire, he began as a journalist.

Antony and Cleopatra 72. Hennessy 75. Hedda 75. Hamlet (TV) 79. Excalibur 81. Dune 84. Lifeforce 85. Lady Jane 86. L.A. Story 91. Gunmen 92. Robin Hood: Men in Tights 93. The Pagemaster (voice) 94. Star Trek: Generations 94. Jeffrey 95. Star Trek: First Contact 96. The Canterville Ghost (TV) 96. Conspiracy Theory 97. Dad Savage 97. Moby Dick (TV) 98. Star Trek: Insurrection 98. Prince of Egypt (voice) 98. Animal Farm (voice, TV) 99. A Christmas Carol (TV) 99. X-Men 00, etc.

TV series: Maybury 81.

Stewart, Paul (1908–1986) (P. Sternberg)
American character actor, often in clipped, sinister roles.

Citizen Kane 41. Johnny Eager 42. Government Girl 43. Mr Lucky 43. Appointment with Danger 49. *Champion* 49. *The Window* 49. Easy Living 49. Illegal Entry 49. Twelve O'Clock High 49. Walk Softly Stranger 50. Edge of Doom 50. The Bad and the Beautiful 52. Carbine Williams 52. Deadline USA 52. Loan Shark 52. The Juggler 53. Deep in My Heart 54. Prisoner of War 54. The Cobweb 55. Chicago Syndicate 55. Hell on Frisco Bay 55. Kiss Me Deadly 55. Top Secret Affair 56. The Wild Party 56. King Creole 58. A Child Is Waiting 63. The Greatest Story Ever Told 65. In Cold Blood 67. How to Commit Marriage 69. City beneath the Sea 70. Live a Little, Steal a Lot 74.The Day of the Locust 74. Bite the Bullet 75. W. C. Fields and Me 76. Opening Night 78. The Dain Curse (TV) 78. The Revenge of the Pink Panther 78. S.O.B. 81. Tempest 82, etc.

Stewart, Sophie (1909–1977)
British stage and radio actress, in occasional films.

Maria Marten 35. As You Like It 36. The Return of the Scarlet Pimpernel 37. Nurse Edith Cavell 39. The Lamp Still Burns 43. Uncle Silas 47. Yangtse Incident 56, etc.

Stiers, David Ogden (1942–)
Tall, balding American comedy actor.

Drive He Said 70. Charlie's Angels (TV) 76. Oh God 77. The Cheap Detective 78. Magic 78. Better Off Dead 85. Another Woman 88. The Accidental Tourist 88. Doc Hollywood 91. Beauty and the Beast (voice) 91. Shadows and Fog 92. Iron Will 94. Bad Company 95. Mighty Aphrodite 95. Pocahontas (voice) 95. Steal Big, Steal Little 95. The Hunchback of Notre Dame (voice) 96. Everyone Says I Love You 96. Meet Wally Sparks 97. Krippendorf's Tribe 98. Pocahontas II: Journey to the New World (voice) 98, etc.

TV series: Doc 75–76. M*A*S*H 77–83.

Stigwood, Robert (1934–)
International impresario whose dominance of the pop-music field led him to produce *Saturday Night Fever* and *Grease*. In 1998, the *Sunday Times* estimated his fortune at £175m.

Stiles, Julia (1981–)
American actress. She studied at the Professional Children's School in New York City and was acting from her early 'teens.

The Devil's Own 97. Wicked 98. Wide Awake 98. The '60s (TV) 99. 10 Things I Hate about You 99. Down to You 00. O 00. Hamlet 00. State and Main 00. Save the Last Dance 01, etc.

Stiller, Ben (1965–)
American actor and director, the son of television comedians and actors Jerry Stiller and Anne Meara. Married actress Christine Taylor in 2000.

Empire of the Sun (a) 87. Elvis Stories (a) 89. Reality Bites (a, d) 94. A Simple Plan (a, d) 95. If Lucy Fell 96. The Cable Guy (& d) 96. Happy Gilmore 96. Zero Effect 98. There's Something about Mary 98. Your Friends & Neighbors 98. Permanent Midnight 98. Mystery Men 99. Black and White 99. Meet the Parents 00. Keeping the Faith 00, etc.

TV series: The Ben Stiller Show.

Stiller, Mauritz (1883–1928) (Mowscha Stiller)
Russian-Swedish director who went to Hollywood in the 20s with Garbo, but died shortly after.

Vampyren 12. *Sir Arne's Treasure* 19. Erotikon 20. *The Atonement of Gosta Berling* 24. The Blizzard (US) 26. Hotel Imperial 27. Street of Sin 28, etc.

Stillman, Whit (1952–)
American independent director, screenwriter and producer.

Metropolitan (AANw) 90. Barcelona 94. Last Days of Disco 98, etc.

Sting (1951–) (Gordon Sumner)
British musician and composer, founder-member of the rock band Police. In 1997, *Business Age* estimated his personal fortune at £97m. Married actress Frances Tomelty and actress and producer Trudie Styler.

Biography: 1998, *Sting: Demolition Man* by Christopher Sandford.

■ Quadrophenia 78. Radio On 79. The Secret Policeman's Other Ball 81. Brimstone and Treacle 82. Dune 84. The Bride 85. Plenty 85. Bring on the Night 86. Julia and Julia 87. Stormy Monday 88. The Adventures of Baron Munchausen 89. Resident Alien 90. The Grotesque/Gentlemen Don't Eat Poets/Grave Indiscretions 96. Lock, Stock and Two Smoking Barrels 98. The Emperor's New Groove (m) (AANs) 00.

Stock, Nigel (1919–1986)
British character actor, former boy performer.

Lancashire Luck 38. Brighton Rock 46. Derby Day 51. The Dam Busters 55. Eye Witness 56. Victim 61. HMS Defiant 62. The Great Escape 63. The Lost Continent 68. The Lion in Winter 68. A Bequest to the Nation 73. Russian Roulette 75. A Man Called Intrepid (TV) (as Winston Churchill) 79, many others.

TV series: *Sherlock Holmes* 65 (as Dr Watson).

Stockfeld, Betty (1905–1966)
Australian-born stage actress, in occasional films.

City of Song 30. The Impassive Footman 32. The Beloved Vagabond 36. Derrière la Façade (Fr.) 40. Flying Fortress 42. Edouard et Caroline (Fr.) 50. The Lovers of Lisbon 55. True As a Turtle 57, etc.

Stockwell, Dean (1935–)
American boy actor of the 40s, later leading man.

The Valley of Decision 45. Anchors Aweigh 45. Abbott and Costello in Hollywood 45. *The Green Years* 46. Home Sweet Homicide 46. The Mighty McGurk 47. The Arnelo Affair 47. Song of the Thin Man 47. The Romance of Rosy Ridge 47. Gentleman's Agreement 48. *The Boy with Green Hair* 48. Deep Waters 48. Down to the Sea in Ships 49. The Secret Garden 49. Stars in My Crown 50. The Happy Years 50. Kim 50. Cattle Drive 51. Gun for a Coward 57. The Careless Years 57. *Compulsion* 59. *Sons and Lovers* 60. Long Day's Journey into Night 62. Rapture 65. Psych-Out 68. The Dunwich Horror 70. Ecstasy 70. The Failing of Raymond (TV) 71. The Last Movie 71. The Loners 72. Another Day at the Races 73. Werewolf of Washington 73. Won Ton Ton 75. Win, Place or Steal 75. Tracks 77. Wrong Is Right 82. Human Highway 82. Paris, Texas 84. Dune 84. The Legend of Billie Jean 85. To Live and Die in L.A. 85. Blue Velvet 86. Gardens of Stone 87. The Gambler III: The Legend Continues (TV) 87. The Blue Iguana 88. Tucker: The Man and His Dream 88. Married to the Mob (AAN) 88. Limit Up 89. Backtrack/Catchfire 89. Son of the Morning Star (TV) 91. The Player 92. Chasers 94. Stephen King's The Langoliers (TV) 95. Mr Wrong 96. Twilight Man 96. Midnight Blue 96. Living in Peril 97. McHale's Navy 97. Air Force One 97. The Shadow Men 97. Rites of Passage 99, etc.

TV series: Quantum Leap 89–93.

Stockwell, Guy (1936–)
American leading actor. He is the brother of Dean Stockwell.

The War Lord 65. *Blindfold* 65. And Now Miguel 66. *Beau Geste* 66. The Plainsman 66. Tobruk 66. The King's Pirate 67. The Million Dollar Collar 67. In Enemy Country 68. The Gatling Gun 72. Airport 75 74. It's Alive 76. Grotesque 87. Santa Sangre 90, etc.

TV series: Adventures in Paradise 60. The Richard Boone Show 64.

Stoker, Bram (1847–1912)
Irish novelist, the creator of *Dracula*. Was also Henry Irving's manager.

Stokowski, Leopold (1882–1977) (Leopold Stokes or Boleslowowicz)
British-born orchestral conductor.

■ *One Hundred Men and a Girl* 37. The Big Broadcast of 1937 37. *Fantasia* 40. Carnegie Hall 47.

Stoler, Shirley (1929–1999)
Overweight American character actress, usually in unsympathetic roles and notable as the murderous nurse in *The Honeymoon Killers*.

The Honeymoon Killers 69. The Displaced Person 76. Seven Beauties 76. The Deer Hunter 78. Below the Belt 80. Splitz 84. Sticky Fingers 88. Miami Blues 90. Frankenhooker 90, etc.

Stoll, George (1905–1985)
American musical director, with MGM from 1945.

Anchors Aweigh (AA) 45. Neptune's Daughter 49. I Love Melvin 53. The Student Prince 54. Hit the Deck 55. Meet Me in Las Vegas 56, many others.

Stoloff, Ben (1895–1960)
American director. He began in comedy shorts, making his first feature for Fox in 1926.

The Canyon of Light 26. Fox Movietone Follies of 1930 30. Destry Rides Again 32. The Night Mayor 32. Palooka/The Great Schnozzle 34. Sea Devils 37. Radio City Revels 38. The Lady and the Mob 39. The Marines Fly High 40. Secret Enemies 42. Take It or Leave It 44. Johnny Comes Flying Home 46. It's a Joke, Son! 47, etc.

Stoloff, Morris (1894–1980)
American musical director, in Hollywood from 1936.

Lost Horizon 37. You Can't Take It with You 38. Cover Girl (AA) 44. A Song to Remember 45. The Jolson Story (AA) 46. The 5000 Fingers of Dr T 53. Picnic 55, many others.

Stoltz, Eric (1961–)
American leading actor.

The Grass Is Always Greener over the Septic Tank (TV) 78. Fast Times at Ridgemont High 82. Running Hot 84. The Wild Life 84. Code Name: Emerald 85. Mask 85. The New Kids 85. Lionheart 87. Sister, Sister 87. Some Kind of Wonderful 87. Haunted Summer 88. Manifesto 88. The Fly II 89. Say Anything 89. Memphis Belle 90. The Waterdance 91. Singles 92. Bodies, Rest and Motion (& p) 93. Foreign Affairs (TV) 93. Naked in New York 93. Killing Zoe 93. Pulp Fiction 94. Sleep with Me (& p) 94. Little Women 94. Fluke 95. Kicking and Screaming 95. The Prophecy 95. Rob Roy 95. God's Army 95. Kicking and Screaming 95. Inside 96. Grace of My Heart 96. 2 Days in the Valley 96. Anaconda 97. Keys to Tulsa 97. Hi-Life 98. The House of Mirth 00, etc.

TV series: Chicago Hope 98-99.

Stone, Andrew L(ysander) (1902–1999)
American producer-director (for a time with his first wife Virginia, who was also a film editor) who made it a rule from the mid-40s not to shoot his melodramas in a studio, but always on location, and with real trains, liners, airplanes, etc. Born in Oakland, California, he made his first, silent, film in 1926 and his first full-length feature in 1928. Formed Andrew Stone Productions 1943.

The Elegy 26. Dreary House 28. The Great Victor Herbert 39. *Stormy Weather* (d only) 42. Hi Diddle Diddle 43. Sensations of 1945 45. Highway 301 51. The Steel Trap 52. The Night Holds Terror 54. Julie (AANw) 56. *Cry Terror* 58. The Decks Ran Red 59. The Last Voyage 60. Ring of Fire 61. The Password Is Courage 62. Never Put It in Writing 64. The Secret of My Success 65. *Song of Norway* 69. *The Great Waltz* 72, etc.

❝ If the Stones had made *On the Beach*, none of us would be around now to review it. – *Andrew Sarris, 1968*

Stone, Dee Wallace (1948–) (aka Dee Wallace)
American actress who first made an impression as the mother in *E.T. – the Extraterrestrial*. She changed her name after marrying actor Christopher Stone.

The Stepford Wives 75. The Hills Have Eyes 77. 10 79. The Howling 80. E.T. – the Extraterrestrial 82. Jimmy the Kid 82. Cujo 83. Club Life 84. Secret Admirer 85. Critters 86. Shadow Play 86. Popcorn 91. Witness to the Execution (TV) 94. The Frighteners 96. Nevada 97. Black Circle Boys 97. Love's Deadly Triangle: The Texas Cadet Murder (TV) 97. Bad as I Wanna Be: The Dennis Rodman Story (TV) 98, etc.

Stone, George E. (1903–1967) (George Stein)
Short (5ft 3in) Polish-born character actor, who in Hollywood films played oppressed little men. Born in Lodz, he began as a child performer in vaudeville and silent films, first as an extra. He was best known as The Runt, the loquacious, dim-witted friend of Boston Blackie in the 'B' features of the 40s.

The Front Page 30. Little Caesar 30. Cimarron 31. Anthony Adverse 36. *The Housekeeper's Daughter* 38. His Girl Friday 40. The Boston Blackie series 41–9. Dancing in the Dark 50. The Robe 53. Guys and Dolls 55. The Man with the Golden Arm 56. Babyface Nelson 57. Some Like It Hot 59. Pocketful of Miracles 61, many others.

Stone, Harold J. (1911–)
American character actor.

The Harder They Fall 56. Garment Center 57. Man Afraid 57. Spartacus 60. The Chapman Report 62. The Man with X-Ray Eyes 63. Which Way to the Front? 70. Mitchell 75, etc.

TV series: My World and Welcome To It 68. Bridget Loves Bernie 74.

Stone, Irving (1903–1989)
American novelist whose *Lust for Life*, *The Agony and the Ecstasy* and *The President's Lady* were filmed.

Stone, Lewis (1879–1953)
Distinguished American stage actor, a leading man of silent films and later a respected character actor.

Honour's Altar (debut) 15. *The Prisoner of Zenda* 22. Scaramouche 23. *The Lost World* 24. The Patriot (AAN) 28. Madame X 30. The Mask of Fu Manchu 32. Mata Hari 32. Grand Hotel 33. Queen Christina 33. *David Copperfield* 34. *Treasure Island* 35. The Thirteenth Chair 37. *You're Only Young Once* 37. Judge Hardy's Children 38. Love Finds Andy Hardy 38. Out West with the Hardys 39 (and ten further episodes of this series, ending in 1947). Yellow Jack 39. The Bugle Sounds 41. Three Wise Fools 46. The State of the Union 48. Key to the City 50. Scaramouche 52. The Prisoner of Zenda 52. All the Brothers Were Valiant 53, many others.

Stone, Marianne (1923–)
British character actress, usually in bit parts. Innumerable appearances.

Angels One Five 51. The Pickwick Papers 54. The Runaway Bus 54. Yield to the Night 56. Heavens Above 63. Ladies Who Do 65. Here We Go Round the Mulberry Bush 67. The Wicked Lady 83, many others.

Stone, Matt (1971–)
American actor and writer, best known as the creator of the TV cartoon series *South Park* with Trey PARKER. Born in Houston, Texas.
Cannibal: The Musical 96. BASEketball 98. Orgazmo 98, etc.

Stone, Milburn (1904–1980)
American character actor, in Hollywood from the mid-30s; was in hundreds of low-budget action features, usually as villain or tough hero; more recently became famous as 'Doc' in the *Gunsmoke* TV series.
Ladies Crave Excitement 35. Port of Missing Girls 37. King of the Turf 39. Enemy Agent 40. The Phantom Cowboy 41. Rubber Racketeers 42. Sherlock Holmes Faces Death 43. Hat Check Honey 44. On Stage Everybody 45. Spider Woman Strikes Back 46. Train to Alcatraz 48. Snow Dog 50. The Sun Shines Bright 53. Black Tuesday 54. Drango 57, many others.

Stone, Oliver (1946–)
Combative American director, screenwriter and producer. Born in New York City, he studied film at New York University and began as a writer. His films tend to be controversial and bombastic in their re-examination of the events of America's recent past, particularly the experience of Vietnam, and how they have shaped present-day attitudes.
Biography: 1996, *Stone* by James Riordan.
Other books: 1996, *The Films of Oliver Stone* by Don Kunz.
Seizure (wd) 74. The Hand (wd) 81. Midnight Express (AAw) 78. Scarface (w) 83. The Year of the Dragon (co-w) 85. *Platoon* (wd) (AAd, AANw) 86. Salvador (wd) 86. Wall Street (wd) 87. Talk Radio (wd) 88. *Born on the Fourth of July* (wd) (AAd, AANw) 89. The Doors (wd) 91. *JFK* (wd) (AANd, AANw) 91. Heaven and Earth (wd) 93. The New Age (p) 93. Natural Born Killers (co-w, d) 94. *Nixon* (co-w, d) (AANw) 95. U-Turn 97, etc.
❝ The film business? I love film, but the film business is shit. – O.S.
I think you are really acknowledging the Vietnam veteran, and for the first time you really understand what happened out there. – O.S. *(receiving his award for Platoon)*
I do my films to take me out of where I am. The questions the movies ask – those are the questions I'm asking myself at that point in time. – O.S.
Anybody who's been through a divorce will tell you that at one point in their life they've thought of murder. No one's innocent. – O.S.
If it sometimes seems that all Hollywood is striving for the Op-Ed-page prominence that Stone has so quickly achieved, he is not necessarily the representative it would have picked. For the off-camera Stone is given to tirades and bad language, to strenuous womanizing and long, intoxicated journeys into the night. – *Stephen Schiff, New Yorker*
A Saturday night with Oliver after a long week is basically pagan Rome, 26 A.D. – *Robert Downey Jnr*

Stone, Peter (1930–) (aka Pierre Marton)
American screenwriter.
■ *Charade* 63. Father Goose (AA) 64. *Mirage* 65. Arabesque 66. The Secret War of Harry Frigg 67. The Mercenaries (as Quentin Werty) 68. Sweet Charity 69. Skin Game 71. 1776 (from his own stage musical) 72. The Taking of Pelham 123 74. Silver Bears 77. Someone Is Killing the Great Chefs of Europe 78. Why Would I Lie? 80. Just Cause 95.

Stone, Sharon (1958–)
American leading actress in sexy roles, a former model who became a star after baring all in *Basic Instinct*, with its notorious crotch shot. With *Casino*, she received critical plaudits as well. Her current asking price: around $10m a movie (less if working for Scorsese).
Biography: 1994, *Sharon Stone: Basic Ambition* by Douglas Thompson. 1997, *The Sharon Stone Story* by Michael Munn.
Deadly Blessing 81. The Vegas Strip Wars (TV) 84. Irreconcilable Differences 84. King Solomon's Mines 85. Allan Quatermain and the Lost City of Gold 86. Cold Steel 87. Above the Law 88. Action Jackson 88. Beyond the Stars 89. Scissors 90. Total Recall 90. Year of the Gun 91. He Said, She Said 91. Where Sleeping Dogs Lie 91. Basic Instinct 92. Diary of a Hit Man 92. Sliver 93. Intersection 94. The Specialist 94. The Quick and the Dead 95. *Casino* (AAN) 95. Diabolique 96. Last Dance 96. Sphere 97. Antz (voice) 98. The Mighty 98. The Muse 99. Simpatico 99. Picking Up The Pieces 00. If These Walls could Talk II (TV) 00, etc.
TV series: Bay City Blues 83.
❝ I've been at this so long that I knew everyone in the business long before I became famous, and I didn't have value to many of them. Now, suddenly, the people who were coarse and rude to me before treat me as though we've never met, and now I'm fabulous, they're fabulous and isn't it fabulous we're chatting. – S.S.
In this business there is Plan A, in which you become successful by living and acting with a lot of integrity. Then there's Plan B, where you sell your soul to the devil. I still find it hard to distinguish one from the other. – S.S.
I've really given up my life to God, and I know that's why I'm OK and at peace. I've never had a conflict when I'm praying on a set. – S.S.
She is incredibly stylish and sophisticated in a somewhat self-conscious way, as if she has watched a catalogue of Grace Kelly movies a little too closely. – *Richard E. Grant*
When I suggest that Ireland is also a country of depressed and brooding writers, she is prompted to gush about one of her favorite 'Irish' authors. 'I have to say, Dylan Thomas just cuts me to the bone!' – *Lloyd Grove, Vanity Fair*

The Stooges
A trio of American knockabout comics specializing in a peculiarly violent form of slapstick. They originally went from vaudeville to Hollywood with Ted Healy (as Ted Healy and his Stooges) but broke away to become world-famous in hundreds of two-reelers throughout the 30s, 40s and 50s. The original trio were *Larry Fine* (1911–1975), *Moe Howard* (1895–1975) and his brother *Jerry (Curly) Howard* (1906–1952). In 1947 Curly was replaced by yet another brother, *Shemp Howard (Samuel Howard)* (1891–1955). On Shemp's death he was replaced by *Joe Besser*, who in 1959 was replaced by *Joe de Rita* (1910–1993). Towards the end of their popularity the Stooges appeared in a few features. Although during their career the rights to the Three Stooges were vested in Moe Howard, a court hearing in 1996 decided that the rights were now owned by the heirs of Larry Fine and Joe de Rita. As a result, there were plans for Columbia to make a feature film on the trio's lives.
Stop Look and Laugh 61. Snow White and the Three Stooges 61. The Three Stooges Meet Hercules 63. The Outlaws Is Coming 64. The Three Stooges Go around the World in a Daze 65, etc.

Stoppa, Paolo (1906–1988)
Italian character actor, in films from 1932.
La Beauté du Diable 49. Miracle in Milan 50. The Seven Deadly Sins 52. Love Soldiers and Women 55. La Loi 59. The Leopard 63. Becket 64. After the Fox 66. Once upon a Time in the West 67, etc.

Stoppard, Sir Tom (1937–) (Thomas Strausler)
Czechoslovakian-born playwright and occasional screenwriter, in England. Born in Zlin, he arrived in England via Singapore in the mid-40s and worked as a journalist until the early 60s, when he began writing plays for radio and television. His *Rosencrantz and Guildenstern Are Dead* in the mid-60s brought him theatrical success, as did later plays produced at the National Theatre and the Royal Shakespeare Company, notable for their verbal wit, wordplay and teasing of theatrical conventions. His screenwriting has been less original. He was knighted in 1997.
Despair 78. The Human Factor 79. Brazil (AAN) 85. Empire of the Sun 87. Rosencrantz and Guildenstern Are Dead (wd) 90. The Russia House (w) 90. Billy Bathgate (w) 91. Poodle Springs (w) (TV) 98. Shakespeare in Love (AAw) 98, etc.

Storaro, Vittorio (1946–)
Italian cinematographer.
The Spider's Stratagem 70. The Conformist 71. Last Tango in Paris 72. 1900 77. Agatha 79. *Apocalypse Now* (AA) 79. *Reds* (AA) 81. One from the Heart 82. Ladyhawke 85. Ishtar 87. *The Last Emperor* (AA) 87. Tucker: The Man and His Dream 88. New York Stories 89. Dick Tracy 90. *The Sheltering Sky* 90. Little Buddha 93. Taxi (Sp.) 96. Bulworth (US) 98. Tango 98. Goya in Bordeaux 99. Picking Up The Pieces (US) 00, etc.

Storch, Larry (1923–)
American comic actor.
Captain Newman MD 63. Wild and Wonderful 64. The Monitors 69. The Couple Takes a Wife (TV) 72. The Adventures of Huckleberry Finn (TV) 78. Better Late than Never 79. S.O.B. 81. Adventures beyond Belief 87, etc.
TV series: F Troop.

Storck, Henri (1907–1999)
Belgian documentarist.
Pour Vos Beaux Yeux 29. The Story of the Unknown Soldier 32. Symphonie Paysanne 42. Au Carrefour de la Vie 49. Les Belges de la Mer 54. Les Gestes du Silence 61. Le Musée Vivant 65, etc.

Storm, Gale (1922–) (Josephine Cottle)
American leading lady of the 40s.
Autobiography: 1981, *I Ain't Down Yet.*
Tom Brown's Schooldays 40. Foreign Agent 42. Nearly Eighteen 43. The Right to Live 45. Sunbonnet Sue 46. It Happened on Fifth Avenue 47. Abandoned 49. Underworld Story 50. The Texas Rangers 51. Woman of the North 53, etc.
TV series: My Little Margie 52–54. The Gale Storm Show 56–59.

Stormare, Peter (1953–)
Swedish actor, from the theatre, where he also works as a director and playwright, notably for the National Theatre of Sweden. Now based in America.
Fanny and Alexander 82. Awakenings 90. Damage 92. *Fargo* (as Gaer Grimsrud) 96. The Lost World: Jurassic Park 97. Playing God 97. The Big Lebowski 98. Hamilton 98. Armageddon 98. Mercury Rising 98. 8mm 99. The Million Dollar Hotel 99. Circus 00, etc.

Stossel, Ludwig (1883–1973)
Austrian character actor in Hollywood from the mid-30s.
Four Sons 39. Man Hunt 41. Woman of the Year 42. Hilter's Madman 43. Cloak and Dagger 46. A Song Is Born 48. Call Me Madam 53. Me and the Colonel 58. G.I. Blues 60, many others.

Stothart, Herbert (1885–1949)
American composer, long with MGM, and responsible for the scores of many of the studio's most prestigious films.
Madame Satan 30. Rasputin and the Empress 33. Queen Christina 33. David Copperfield 35. Mutiny on the Bounty 35. A Night at the Opera 35. San Francisco 36. Camille 37. The Good Earth 37. Marie Antoinette 38. Idiot's Delight 39. Waterloo Bridge 40. Mrs Miniver 42. Random Harvest 42. Madame Curie 44. The Green Years 46. The Yearling 47. The Three Musketeers 48, many others.

Stott, Ken (1955–)
Scottish leading actor, born in Edinburgh.
The Singing Detective (TV) 86. Shallow Grave 94. Fever Pitch 96. Rhodes (TV) 96. Saint-Ex 96. The Boxer 97. Plunkett & Macleane 99. Dockers (TV) 99. The Debt Collector 99. The Vice (TV) 99. The Miracle Maker (voice) 99, etc.

Stout, Archie (1886–1973)
American cinematographer in Hollywood from 1914.
Young Eagles 30. Gun Smoke 31. The Lucky Texan 33. Riders of Destiny 33. Sagebrush Trail 33. West of the Divide 33. Blue Steel 34. The Lawless Frontier 34. The Man from Utah 34. 'Neath the Arizona Skies 34. Randy Rides Alone 34. The Star Packer 34. The Trail Beyond 34. The Dawn Rider 35. The Desert Trail 35. Paradise Canyon 35. Professor Beware 38. Beau Geste 39. Rulers of the Sea 39. It Happened Tomorrow 44. Summer Storm 44. Captain Kidd 45. Tarzan and the Amazons 45. Angel and the Badman 46. Tarzan and the Huntress 47. Fort Apache 48. Lust for Gold 49. Outrage 50. Hard Fast and Beautiful 51. *The Quiet Man* (AA) 52. Big Jim McLain 52. Hondo 53. Island in the Sky 53. The Sun Shines Bright 53. Trouble along the Way 53. The High and the Mighty 54. Goodbye My Lady 56, etc.

Stout, Rex (1886–1975)
American detective story writer, creator of Nero Wolfe, who appeared in two minor films of the 30s (played by Edward Arnold and Walter Connolly) and in a 70s TV movie (played by Thayer David).

Stowe, Harriet Beecher (1811–1896)
American novelist, author of the much-filmed *Uncle Tom's Cabin*.

Stowe, Madeleine (1958–)
American leading actress.
Nativity (TV) 78. The Amazons (TV) 83. Stakeout 87. Worth Winning 89. Revenge 90. The Two Jakes 90. Closet Land 91. The Last of the Mohicans 92. Unlawful Entry 92. Short Cuts 93. Another Stakeout 93. Blink 94. Bad Girls 94. China Moon 94. 12 Monkeys 95. Playing by Heart 98. The Proposition 98. Playing By Heart 98. The General's Daughter 99, etc.
TV series: The Gangster Chronicles 81.

Stradling, Harry (1901–1970)
British-born cinematographer, long in US.
La Kermesse Héroïque 35. *Knight without Armour* 37. *Pygmalion* 38. The Citadel 38. Jamaica Inn 39. Suspicion 41. *The Picture of Dorian Gray* (AA) 44. The Pirate 48. The Barkleys of Broadway (AAN) 49. *A Streetcar Named Desire* 51. Valentino 51. Hans Christian Andersen 52. Helen of Troy 55. Guys and Dolls 55. The Eddy Duchin Story 56. The Pajama Game 57. A Face in the Crowd 57. The Dark at the Top of the Stairs 60. *My Fair Lady* (AA) 64. How to Murder Your Wife 65. Moment to Moment 65. Walk, Don't Run 66. Funny Girl (AAN) 68. *Hello Dolly* 69, many others.

Stradling Jnr, Harry (1925–)
American cinematographer, son of Harry Stradling.
Welcome to Hard Times 67. Support Your Local Sheriff 69. The Mad Room 69. Hello Dolly (AAN) 69. Something Big 71. Fools Parade 71. The Way We Were 73. McQ 74. Bite the Bullet 75. Midway 76. The Big Bus 76. Airport 77 77. Damnation Alley 77. Convoy 78. Go Tell the Spartans 78. Prophecy 79. Carny 80. S.O.B. 81. The Pursuit of D.B. Cooper 81. Buddy Buddy 81. O'Hara's Wife 82. Micki and Maude 84. A Fine Mess 86. Blind Date 87. Caddyshack II 88, etc.

Stradner, Rose (1913–1958)
Austrian actress who made a few Hollywood films.
The Last Gangster 38. Blind Alley 39. The Keys of the Kingdom 44, etc.

Straight, Beatrice (1916–)
American character actress.
Network (AA) 76. Bloodline 79. The Promise 79. Poltergeist 82. Two of a Kind 83. Power 85. Deceived 91, etc.

Strange, Glenn (1899–1973)
Giant-size American character actor, in Hollywood from 1937, mainly in cowboy roles. Also played the monster in *House of Frankenstein* 45, *Abbott and Costello meet Frankenstein* 48, etc.
TV series: Gunsmoke 56–73.

Strasberg, Lee (1899–1982)
American drama teacher; founded the Actors' Studio which in the 50s taught The Method.
■ *The Godfather Part Two* (AAN) 74. The Cassandra Crossing 77. Boardwalk 79. And Justice for All 79. Going in Style 79.
❝ I never felt Lee Strasberg could act, and I fail to see how someone who can't act can teach acting. – *Paul Henreid*

Strasberg, Susan (1938–1999)
American leading lady, daughter of Lee *Strasberg*, founder of the New York Actors' Studio. Born in New York City, she made her stage debut at the age of 14 and appeared on TV as a teenager. Formerly married to actor Christopher JONES. Died of cancer.
Autobiography: 1980, *Bittersweet.*
Picnic (film debut) 55. Stage Struck 57. Taste of Fear 59. Kapo 60. Hemingway's Adventures of a Young Man 62. The High Bright Sun 65. Psych-Out 68. The Brotherhood 68. Rollercoaster 77. In Praise of Older Women 78. The Returning 83. The Delta Force 85. Lambarene 90. Trauma 92, etc.
TV series: The Marriage 54. Toma 73-74.

Strathairn, David (1949–)
American general-purpose actor, often in the films of John SAYLES.
Return of the Secaucus 7 80. Enormous Changes at the Last Minute 83. Silkwood 83. The Brother from Another Planet 84. Iceman 84. Matewan 87. Eight Men Out 88. The Feud 90. Memphis Belle 90. Judgment (TV) 90. City of Hope 91. Big Girls

Don't Cry ... They Get Even/Stepkids 92. A League of Their Own 92. Passion Fish 92. Sneakers 92. Lost in Yonkers 93. The Firm 93. River Wild 94. Losing Isaiah 95. Dolores Claiborne 95. Home for the Holidays 95. Mother Night 96. LA Confidential 97. In the Gloaming (TV) 97. Simon Birch 98. William Shakespeare's A Midsummer Night's Dream 99. Limbo 99. A Map of the World 99, etc.

TV series: The Days and Nights of Molly Dodd 87–88.

Stratten, Dorothy (1960–1980) (Dorothy Hoogstraten)
Canadian actress and *Playboy* pin-up whose short life, which ended when she was shot by her estranged husband, was retold in the biopic *Star* 80, starring Mariel Hemingway. She was also the subject of a TV movie, *Death of a Centrefold: The Dorothy Stratten Story* 81. At the time of her death she was the lover of director Peter Bogdanovich.

Biography: 1984, *Death of a Unicorn* by Peter Bogdanovich.

Americathon 79. Skatetown USA 79. Galaxina 80. They All Laughed 81.

Stratton, John (1925–)
British general-purpose actor.

The Cure for Love 49. Appointment with Venus 52. The Cruel Sea 54. The Long Arm 55. Frankenstein and the Monster from Hell 74, etc.

Stratton-Porter, Gene (1863–1924)
American author of sentimental stories for girls.

A Girl of the Limberlost 34. Keeper of the Bees 35. Laddie 35. The Harvester 36. Michael O'Halloran 37 and 49. Her Father's Daughter 40. Freckles 60.

Straub, Jean-Marie (1933–)
French director in German films, in collaboration with his wife Danielle Huillet (1936–).

Machorka Muff 63. Nicht Versohnt 65. *The Chronicle of Anna-Magdalena Bach* 67. Othon 72. History Lessons 73. Moses and Aaron 75. Dalla Nube alla Resistenza 79. Too Early, Too Late 81. Class Relations/Klassenverhältnisse 84. The Death of Empedocles/Der Tod des Empedokles 86. Schwarze Sunde 89. Sicily!/Sicilia! 99, etc.

Straus, Oscar (1870–1954)
Austrian operetta composer who also occasionally provided film music.

The Smiling Lieutenant 31. One Hour with You 32. Land Without Music 36. La Ronde 50. Madame De 52, etc.

Strauss, Helen (1909–1987)
American literary agent (for Michener and others) who became an occasional film producer: *Tom Sawyer, Huckleberry Finn, The Incredible Sarah.*

Autobiography: 1979, *A Talent for Luck.*

Strauss, Peter (1947–)
American leading man who became well known in *Rich Man Poor Man* (TV) 76.

Soldier Blue 71. The Last Tycoon 76. Young Joe the Forgotten Kennedy (TV) 77. The Jericho Mile (TV) 79. Masada (TV) 80. Spacehunter 83. Tender Is the Night (TV) 85. Kane and Abel (TV) 85. Peter Gunn (TV) 90. Nick of Time 95. Keys to Tulsa 96, etc.

Strauss, Robert (1913–1975)
American comedy actor (occasionally in menacing roles); former salesman.

Sailor Beware 52. *Stalag 17* (AAN) 53. The Seven Year Itch 54. Attack 56. The Last Time I Saw Archie 61. The Family Jewels 65, etc.

Strayer, Frank (1891–1964)
American director of second features.

Rough House Rosie 27. Enemy of Men 30. The Monster Walks 32. The Vampire Bat 33. The Ghost Walks 35. Blondie (and many others in this series) 38. The Daring Young Man 42. Messenger of Peace 50, etc.

Streep, Meryl (1949–) (Mary Louise Streep)
American leading lady of the late 70s and star actress of the 80s. Born in Summit, New Jersey, she studied drama at Vassar, Dartmouth and Yale, and began in the New York theatre. She became remarkable for the number of foreign and regional accents she displayed in her roles, and for the virtuosity of her contrasting performances. In the 90s, she has appeared in less demanding films, though once again she showed her mastery of an Irish accent in *Dancing at Lughnasa.* Married sculptor Donald Gummer.

Biography: 1988, *Meryl Streep* by Eugene E. Pfaff Jnr and Mark Emerson.

The Deadliest Season (TV) 77. Julia 77. The Deer Hunter (AAN) 78. *Holocaust* (TV) 78. Manhattan 79. The Seduction of Joe Tynan 79. *Kramer vs Kramer* (AA) 79. The French Lieutenant's Woman (BFA) 81. Sophie's Choice (AA) 82. Still of the Night 82. Silkwood (AAN) 83. Falling in Love 84. Plenty 85. Out of Africa (AAN) 85. Heartburn 86. Ironweed (AAN) 87. A Cry in the Dark (AAN) 88. She-Devil 89. Postcards from the Edge (AAN) 90. Defending Your Life 91. Death Becomes Her 92. The House of the Spirits 93. The River Wild 94. *The Bridges of Madison County* (AAN) 95. Before and After 96. Marvin's Room 96. One True Thing (AAN) 98. Dancing at Lughnasa 98. Music of the Heart (AAN) 99, etc.

❝ You can't get spoiled if you do your own ironing. – M.S.

The danger I'm talking about here is that she tends to sound boring because she's so perfect. – *Sydney Pollack*

Streeter, Edward (1892–1976)
American humorous novelist: *Father of the Bride* and *Mr Hobbs Takes a Vacation* were filmed.

Streisand, Barbra (1942–)
Ambitious American singer, actress, producer and director, who made a virtue of her unusual looks. Born in Brooklyn, New York, she began in the theatre and opened her movie career by repeating her show-stopping role in the Broadway musical *Funny Girl.* From the mid-70s she started to take greater control of her career by producing and directing her own films; but her choice of material has been erratic and she sometimes concentrates on her own performance to the detriment of the film as a whole. Married actor Elliott Gould (1963–71) and, in 1998, actor James Brolin; she was romantically involved with producer Jon Peters. She is the mother of actor Jason Gould.

Biography: 1982, *Streisand: The Woman and the Legend* by James Spada with Christopher Nickens. 1994, *Her Name Is Barbra* by Randall Riese. 1995, *Streisand: The Intimate Biography* by James Spada. 1996, *Streisand: It Only Happens Once* by Anne Edwards.

Funny Girl (as Fanny Brice) (AA) 68. Hello Dolly 69. On a Clear Day You Can See Forever 70. The Owl and the Pussycat 70. What's Up, Doc? 72. Up the Sandbox 72. The Way We Were (AAN) 73. For Pete's Sake 74. Funny Lady 75. A Star Is Born (AAs) 76. The Main Event 79. All Night Long 81. Yentl (& co-w, co-p, d) 83. Nuts 87. The Prince of Tides (& d) 91. The Mirror Has Two Faces (& p, d) (AANs 'I've Finally Found Someone') 96, etc.

❝ When I sing, people shut up. – B.S.

Success to me is having ten honeydew melons and eating only the top half of each one. – B.S.

Nobody really knows me: I'm a mixture of self-confidence and insecurity. One thing's for sure – I hate talking about myself. – B.S.

This is for posterity. Everything I do will be on film for ever. – *B.S. on Funny Girl*

It's kind of a wonderful thing, to appreciate my own career. – *B.S. in 1994*

Streisand embodies everything that is tacky and cheap and hopelessly corny and unsophisticated about Middle America. – *Joe Queenan*

She really ought to be called Barbra Strident. – *Stanley Kaufmann*

To know her is not necessarily to love her. – *Rex Reed*

The most pretentious woman the cinema has ever known. – *Ryan O'Neal*

I'd love to work with her again, in something appropriate. Perhaps *Macbeth.* – *Walter Matthau*

It is given to few actresses to start out as Cinderella, pass through the fairy godmother stage and finish up as one of the ugly sisters by the time they are 50, but Streisand has managed that. – *Sheridan Morley*

Stribling, Melissa (1927–1992)
Scottish actress. Married director Basil Dearden.

The First Gentleman 48. Crow Hollow 52. Noose for a Lady 52. Wide Boy 52. Thought to Kill 53. The Safecracker 57. Dracula 58. League of Gentlemen 59. The Secret Partner 61. Only When I Larf 68. Crucible of Terror 71. Confessions of a Window Cleaner 74, etc.

Strick, Joseph (1923–)
American director.

The Savage Eye 59. The Balcony 64. *Ulysses* (AANw) 67. Ring of Bright Water (GB) (p only) 69. Tropic of Cancer 69. The Darwin Adventure (p only) 71. Janice 73. Road Movie 74. A Portrait of the Artist as a Young Man 79. Criminals (doc) 95, etc.

Strick, Wesley
American screenwriter.

True Believer 89. Arachnophobia (co-w) 90. Cape Fear 91. Final Analysis 92. Wolf (co-w) 94. The Tie that Binds (d) 95. The Saint 97. Return to Paradise 98, etc.

Stricklyn, Ray (1930–)
American 'second lead' with stage experience.

The Proud and the Profane 56. The Last Wagon 57. Ten North Frederick 58. Young Jesse James 60. Arizona Raiders 65. Track of Thunder 68, etc.

Stride, John (1936–)
British supporting actor, much on TV.

Bitter Harvest 63. Macbeth 72. Juggernaut 74. Brannigan 75. The Omen 76. A Bridge Too Far 77, etc.

TV series: The Main Chance 69–75. The Wilde Alliance 78.

Strindberg, Johan August (1849–1912)
Prolific and influential Swedish dramatist, poet, and novelist, a former teacher and journalist. Born in Stockholm, he spent long periods living in France, Germany and elsewhere in Europe and often wrote of the conflict between the sexes, drawing on his own three unhappy marriages. Died of cancer.

Hemsöborna 44. The Dance of Death/La Danse de Mort (Fr./It.) 46. Miss Julie/Pecador Julie (Arg.) 47. Miss Julie/Froken Julie 51. Erik XIV/Karin Mansdotter 54. Ett Dockhem 55. Hemsöborna 55. Of Love and Lust/Giftas 57. Dance of Death/ Paarungen (Ger.) 67. The Dance of Death (GB) 69. The Father/Fadren 69. Miss Julie (GB) 72. Miss Julie (GB) 99, etc.

Stritch, Elaine (1925–)
Sharp, lanky American character comedienne, mainly on stage; a popular London resident during the mid-70s.

The Scarlet Hour 55. Three Violent People 57. A Farewell to Arms 57. The Perfect Furlough 58. Who Killed Teddy Bear? 65. Sidelong Glances of a Pigeon Kicker 70. The Spiral Staircase 75. Providence 77. September 87. Cocoon: The Return 88. Cadillac Man 90. Out to Sea 97. Krippendorf's Tribe 98. Small Time Crooks 00, etc.

TV series: The Growing Paynes 49. *My Sister Eileen* 60. The Trials of O'Brien 65. Two's Company 76–78. The Ellen Burstyn Show 86–87.

Strock, Herbert L. (1918–)
American director, former publicist and editor.

The Magnetic Monster 52. Riders to the Stars 54. Battle Taxi 55. Teenage Frankenstein 57. How to Make a Monster 58. Rider on a Dead Horse 62. The Crawling Hand 63. Man on the Run 74. Monster 78. Witches' Brew (co-d) 79, etc.

Strode, Woody (Woodrow) (1914–1994)
Tall American actor.

The Lion Hunters 51. The Ten Commandments 56. *Sergeant Rutledge* 60. Spartacus 60. Two Rode Together 62. The Man Who Shot Liberty Valance 62. Genghis Khan 65. *The Professionals* 66. Shalako 68. Che! 69. The Revengers 72. The Gatling Gun 72. Winterhawk 76. Loaded Guns 76. The Black Stallion Returns 83. Vigilante 83. The Cotton Club 84. Lust in the Dust 84. Storyville 92. Posse 93, etc.

Stromberg, Hunt (1894–1968)
American producer, long with MGM, who went independent in the 40s.

Breaking into Society (as d) 24. Fire Patrol (as d) 26. Torrent 27. Our Dancing Daughters 28. Red Dust 32. *The Thin Man* 34. *The Great Ziegfeld* (AA) 36. Maytime 38. Marie Antoinette 38. Idiot's Delight 39. *The Women* 39. Northwest Passage 40. *Pride and Prejudice* 41. Guest in the House 44. Lured 47. Too Late for Tears 49. Between Midnight and Dawn 50. Mask of the Avenger 51, many others.

❝ Boys, I've an idea. Let's fill the screen with tits. – *H.S. on taking over White Shadows in the South Seas in 1928*

Stross, Raymond (1916–1988)
British producer, in films from 1933; married to Anne Heywood.

As Long as They're Happy 52. An Alligator Named Daisy 56. The Flesh is Weak 56. A Question of Adultery 58. A Terrible Beauty 59. The Very Edge 62. The Leather Boys 63. Ninety Degrees in the Shade 65. The Midas Run 69. I Want What I Want 72, etc.

Stroud, Don (1937–)
American leading man.

Madigan 68. Games 68. What's So Bad about Feeling Good 68. Coogan's Bluff 69. Bloody Mama 70. Explosion 70. Von Richthofen and Brown 70. Tick Tick Tick 70. Joe Kidd 72. Scalawag 73. The Choirboys 77. The Buddy Holly Story 78. The Amityville Horror 79. Armed and Dangerous 86. Down the Drain 89. Prime Target 91. Frogtown II 92. Sawbones (TV) 95. Dillinger and Capone 95. Hyper Space 97. The Haunted Sea 97, etc.

TV series: Kate Loves a Mystery 79. Mickey Spillane's Mike Hammer 84–87. Dragnet 89–90.

Strouse, Charles (1928–)
American composer, mainly for Broadway musicals.

The Mating Game (s) 59. Bonnie and Clyde 67. The Night They Raided Minsky's 68. There Was a Crooked Man 70. Just Tell Me What You Want 80. Annie (from musical) 82.

Strudwick, Shepperd
See Shepperd, John.

Strummer, Joe (1952–) (John Mellors)
British composer, musician and occasional actor. He was a founder-member of the late-70s punk band The Clash.

Rude Boy (co-m) 80. Sid and Nancy (co-m) 86. Love Kills (co-m) 86. Straight to Hell (a) 87. Walker (m) 87. Permanent Record (m) 88. Candy Mountain (a) 88. Mystery Train (a) 89. I Hired a Contract Killer (a, s) 90. When Pigs Fly (m) 93, etc.

Struss, Karl (1891–1981)
American cinematographer.

Ben Hur 26. *Sunrise* (AA) 27. Abraham Lincoln 30. The Sign of the Cross 32. *Dr Jekyll and Mr Hyde* 32. The Great Dictator 40. Bring on the Girls 44. Suspense 46. The Macomber Affair 47. Rocketship XM 50. *Limelight* 52. Tarzan and the She-Devil 53, many others.

Struthers, Sally (1948–)
American young character actress, a hit as the daughter in TV's *All in the Family* 71–74.

Five Easy Pieces 70. The Getaway 72. Aloha Means Goodbye (TV) 76. A Gun in the House (TV) 81, etc.

❝ Acting is cheap group therapy, being a schizo fifty different ways. And we're paid! – S.S.

Stuart, Binkie (c. 1932–)
British child actress of the 30s.

Moonlight Sonata 37. Little Dolly Daydream 38. My Irish Molly 39, etc.

Stuart, Gloria (1910–) (Gloria Stuart Finch)
American leading lady of the 30s, who became busy again in the 90s.

Autobiography: 1999, *I Just Keep Hoping.*

Air Mail 32. The All-American 32. The Old Dark House 32. Street of Women 32. Beloved 33. The Invisible Man 33. The Kiss before the Mirror 33. Roman Scandals 33. The Secret of the Blue Room 33. Sweepings 33. The Gift of Gab 34. Gold Diggers of 1935 34. Here Comes the Navy 34. Laddie 35. The Crime of Dr Forbes 36. The Girl on the Front Page 36. Poor Little Rich Girl 36. The Prisoner of Shark Island 36. Professional Soldier 36. Wanted: Jane Turner 36. Change of Heart 37. Life Begins in College 37. Keep Smiling 38. Rebecca of Sunnybrook Farm 38. It Could Happen to You 39. The Three Musketeers 39. She Wrote the Book 46. My Favorite Year 82. Titanic (AAN) 97. The Love Letter 99. The Million Dollar Hotel 99, etc.

Stuart, Jeb
American screenwriter.

Die Hard 88. Leviathan 89. Lock Up 89. Vital Signs 90. Another 48 Hrs 90. The Fugitive (co-w) 93. Outbreak (co-w) 95. Going West (wd) 97. Fire Down Below (co-w) 97. Switchback (& d) 97, etc.

Stuart, John (1898–1979) (John Croall)
British leading man of the 20s, character actor of the 40s and after. Born in Edinburgh, Scotland, he was on stage from 1919. The first of his two wives was actress Muriel ANGELUS.
Autobiography: 1971, *Caught in the Act.*
Her Son (debut) 20. We Women 25. The Pleasure Garden 26. Blackmail 29. Elstree Calling 30. Atlantic 30. Number Seventeen 31. Taxi for Two 32. The Pointing Finger 34. Abdul the Damned 35. Old Mother Riley's Ghost 41. The Phantom Shot 46. Mine Own Executioner 47. The Magic Box 51. Quatermass II 57. Blood of the Vampire 58. Sink the Bismarck 60. Superman 78, etc.

Stuart, Leslie (1864–1928) (Thomas Barrett)
British songwriter ('Tell Me Pretty Maiden', 'Florodora', etc.) played by Robert Morley in the 1940 biopic *You Will Remember.*

Stuart, Mel (1928–)
American director.
If It's Tuesday This Must Be Belgium 69. I Love My Wife 70. Willie Wonka and the Chocolate Factory 71. One Is a Lonely Number 72. Mean Dog Blues 78. The Chisholms (TV) 79. The White Lions 79, etc.

Stubbs, Imogen (1961–)
English leading actress, from the stage. Married director Trevor Nunn in 1994.
Privileged 82. Nanou 86. A Summer Story 88. Erik the Viking 89. Fellow Traveller 89. True Colors 91. Jack & Sarah 95. Sense and Sensibility 95. Twelfth Night 96, etc.

Studi, Wes
American actor, usually playing an Indian. A Cherokee, he was born in Oklahoma and was formerly a teacher.
Dances with Wolves 90. The Doors 91. Last of the Mohicans 92. Geronimo: An American Legend (title role) 93. The Broken Chain (TV) 93. Street Fighter 95. Heat 95. The Killing Jar 96. Crazy Horse (TV) 96. Deep Rising 97. Soundman 98, etc.

Stuhr, Jerzy (1947–)
Polish leading actor, most closely associated with the films of Krzysztof KIESLOWSKI. Born in Cracow, he began in the theatre and turned to directing in the mid-90s.
Top Dog/Wodzirej 78. Camera Buff/Amator 79. Decalogue 88. Three Colours: White 93. Love Stories (& d) 97. A Week in the Life of a Man/ Tydzien Z Zycua Mezczyzny (wd, a) 99. The Big Animal/Duxe Zwierze (&d) 00 etc.

Sturges, John (1911–1992)
American director of smooth if increasingly pretentious action films, former editor and documentarist.
■ The Man Who Dared 46. Shadowed 46. Alias Mr Twilight 47. For the Love of Rusty 47. Keeper of the Bees 48. The Best Man Wins 48. The Sign of the Ram 48. The Walking Hills 49. The Capture 49. Mystery Street 50. The Magnificent Yankee 50. Right Cross 50. Kind Lady 51. The People Against O'Hara 51. It's a Big Country (part) 51. The Girl in White 52. Fast Company 52. Jeopardy 53. Escape from Fort Bravo 53. *Bad Day at Black Rock* (AAN) 54. Underwater 55. The Scarlet Coat 55. Backlash 56. *Gunfight at the OK Corral* 57. The Law and Jake Wade 58. The Old Man and the Sea 58. Last Train from Gun Hill 58. Never So Few 59. *The Magnificent Seven* 60. By Love Possessed 61. Sergeants Three 62. A Girl Named Tamiko 63. *The Great Escape* 63. The Satan Bug 65. The Hallelujah Trail 65. The Hour of the Gun 67. Ice Station Zebra 68. Marooned 69. Joe Kidd 72. Valdez the Halfbreed (Sp.) 73. McQ 74. The Eagle Has Landed 76.
❝ It is hard to remember why his career was ever considered meaningful. – *Andrew Sarris, 1968*

Sturges, Preston (1898–1959) (Edmund P. Biden)
American writer-director who in the early 40s was Hollywood's wonder boy who never lost the common touch despite his free-wheeling witty style and subject matter. By 1950 his talent had disappeared, and he retired unhappily to France.
Books: 1991, *Preston Sturges on Preston Sturges* edited by Sandy Sturges.
AS WRITER: *The Power and the Glory* 33. We Live Again 34. The Good Fairy 35. Diamond Jim 35. Easy Living 37. Port of Seven Seas 38. If I Were King 39. Never Say Die 39. Remember the Night 40, etc.
■ AS WRITER-DIRECTOR: *The Great McGinty* (AA) 40. *Christmas in July* 40. *Sullivan's Travels* 41. The Lady Eve 41. *The Palm Beach Story* 42. *The Great Moment* 43. *The Miracle of Morgan's Creek* (AANw) 43. *Hail the Conquering Hero* (AANw) 44. Mad Wednesday 46. Unfaithfully Yours 48. The Beautiful Blonde from Bashful Bend 49. The Diary of Major Thompson 56.
✪ For being the wonder boy of the early 40s, with his unique blend of sophisticated comedy and pratfall farce. *Sullivan's Travels.*
❝ The Breughel of American comedy directors … the absurdity of the American success story was matched by the ferocity of the battle of the sexes … Lubitsch treated sex as the dessert of a civilized meal of manners. Sturges, more in the American style, served sex with all the courses. – *Andrew Sarris, 1968*
Jesus, he was a strange guy. Carried his own hill with him, I tell you. – *Frank Capra*
There was a desperate, hectic quality to all his films – an intense desire to believe all the Horatio Alger ideals often associated with America, intermingled with a cynical 'European' view of those ideals. – *James Ursini*
He has restored to the art of the cinema a certain graphic velocity it has missed since the turmoil of Mack Sennett's zanies. – *Bosley Crowther*
Preston is like a man from the Italian Renaissance – he wants to do everything at once. – *James Agee*
He was too large for this smelly resort, and the big studios were scared to death of him. A man who was a triple threat kept them awake nights, and I'm positive they were waiting for him to fall on his face so they could pounce and devour this terrible threat to their stingy talents. They pounced, and they got him, good. But he knew the great days when his can glowed like a port light from their kissing it. – *Earl Felton*
When the last dime is gone, I'll sit on the curb outside with a pencil and a ten-cent notebook, and start the whole thing over again. – *P.S., 1957*

Sturridge, Charles (1951–)
English director, from TV.
Runners 83. Aria (co-d) 87. A Handful of Dust 88. Where Angels Fear to Tread 91. A Foreign Field (TV) 93. Gulliver's Travels (TV) 96. Illumination 97. Fairy Tale: A True Story 97, etc.
TV series: Brideshead Revisited 81.

Styne, Jule (1905–1994) (Jules Styne)
British-born composer, in US from childhood. Former pianist and conductor. Film songs include 'There Goes That Song Again', 'Give Me Five Minutes More', 'It's Magic', 'Three Coins in the Fountain'. Shows filmed include *Gentlemen Prefer Blondes, Bells Are Ringing, Gypsy, Funny Girl.*

Subiela, Eliseo (1944–)
Argentinian director.
La Conquista del Paraiso 81. Man Facing Southeast 87. Ultimas Imágenes del Naúfragio 89. El Lado Oscuro del Corazón 92. Don't You Die without Telling Me Where You Go 95. Little Miracles/Pequeños Milagros (wd) 98, etc.

Sublett, John
See BUBBLES, John.

Subotsky, Milton (1921–1991)
American independent producer and writer.
Rock Rock Rock 56. The Last Mile 58. City of the Dead (GB) 60. It's Trad Dad (GB) 63. Dr Terror's House of Horrors (GB) 64. Dr Who and the Daleks (GB) 65. The Skull (GB) 66. The Psychopath (GB) 66. Daleks Invasion Earth 2150 AD (GB) 66. Torture Garden (GB) 67. The House That Dripped Blood (GB) 70. Tales from the Crypt (GB) 71. Asylum (GB) 72. Madhouse (GB) 73. The Land that Time Forgot (GB) 75. At the Earth's Core (GB) 76. The Monster Club 80. Cat's Eye 84. The Lawnmower Man 92, etc.

Suchet, David (1946–)
English character actor, much on stage and television. He acted with the Royal Shakespeare Company from the late 70s.
Hunchback of Notre Dame (TV) 82. Trenchcoat 82. The Missionary 83. Red Monarch (TV) 83. Greystoke: The Legend of Tarzan, Lord of the Apes 84. Little Drummer Girl 84. The Falcon and the Snowman 85. Harry and the Hendersons 87. Blott on the Landscape (TV) 85. A World Apart 87. To Kill a Priest 88. When the Whales Came 89. Secret Agent (TV) 92. Executive Decision 96. Sunday 97. Seesaw (TV) 98. A Perfect Murder 98, etc.
TV series: Poirot (title role) 88–93.

Sucksdorff, Arne (1917–)
Swedish documentarist who has normally written and photographed his own films, which vary from six minutes to feature length.
The West Wind 42. Shadows on the Snow 45. *Rhythm of a City* 47. *A Divided World* 48. The Road 48. The Wind and the River 51. *The Great Adventure* 53. The Flute and the Arrow 57. The Boy in the Tree 60. My Home is Copacabana 65. Forbush and the Penguins 71, etc.

Suhrstedt, Tim
American cinematographer.
Forbidden World/Mutant 82. Android 82. The House on Sorority Row 82. Suburbia 84. Teen Wolf 85. Critters 86. Mystic Pizza 88. Bill & Ted's Excellent Adventure 88. Men at Work 90. Don't Tell Mom the Babysitter's Dead 91. Traces of Red/ Beyond Suspicion 92. Noises Off 92. The Favor 94. Getting Even with Dad 94. To Gillian on Her 37th Birthday 96. The Wedding Singer 98, etc.

Sukowa, Barbara (1950–)
German leading actress.
Berlin Alexanderplatz (TV) 80. Lola 81. Deadly Game 83. Rosa Luxemburg 86. The Sicilian 87. Voyager 91. Europea/Zentropa 92. Johnny Mnemonic (US) 95. Office Killer (US) 97. The Cradle Will Rock (US) 99. The Third Miracle 99, etc.

Sullavan, Margaret (1911–1960) (Margaret Brooke)
American leading actress in light films of the 30s and 40s; she had a special whimsical quality which was unique. The first three of her four husbands were actor Henry FONDA (1931–33), director William WYLER (1934–36), and agent Leland HAYWARD (1936–48). Her lovers included producer Jed HARRIS. Committed suicide.
Biography: 1977, *Haywire* by Brooke Hayward (her daughter).
■ Only Yesterday 33. Little Man What Now? 34. So Red the Rose 35. *The Good Fairy* 35. Next Time We Love 36. The Moon's Our Home 36. *Three Comrades* (AAN) 38. Shopworn Angel 38. The Shining Hour 39. *The Shop around the Corner* 39. *The Mortal Storm* 40. So Ends Our Night 40. Back Street 41. Appointment for Love 41. Cry Havoc 43. No Sad Songs for Me 50.

Sullivan, Barry (1912–1994) (Patrick Barry)
American leading man with stage experience.
Lady in the Dark 43. Two Years before the Mast 44. And Now Tomorrow 44. Suspense 46. The Gangster 47. Tension 49. The Great Gatsby 49. The Outriders 50. Three Guys Named Mike 51. *The Bad and the Beautiful* 52. Jeopardy 54. Queen Bee 55. Forty Guns 57. Wolf Larsen 57. Seven Ways from Sundown 60. The Light in the Piazza 62. Stagecoach to Hell 64. My Blood Runs Cold 64. Harlow (electronovision version) 65. An American Dream/See You in Hell, Darling 66. Intimacy 66. Buckskin 68. Willie Boy 69. Earthquake 74. The Human Factor 75. Oh God 77. Casino 80, etc.
TV series: The Man Called X 55–56. Harbourmaster 57–58. The Tall Man 60–62. The Road West 67. Rich Man, Poor Man Book II 76–77.

Sullivan, C. Gardner (1885–1965)
American screenwriter.
The Battle of Gettysburg 14. The Wrath of the Gods 15. Civilization 16. The Aryan 16. The Zeppelin's Last Raid 17. Carmen of the Klondike 18. Sahara 19. Human Wreckage 23. Sparrows 26. Tempest 27. Sequoia 34. The Buccaneer 38, many others.

Sullivan, Francis L. (1903–1956)
Heavyweight British character actor, often seen as advocate. On stage from 1921, films from 1933.
The Missing Rembrandt (debut) 33. Chu Chin Chow 33. Great Expectations (US) 35. *The Mystery of Edwin Drood* (US) 35. Sabotage 36. Action for Slander 37. Dinner at the Ritz 37. Twenty-one Days 38. The Citadel 38. The Four Just Men 39. *Pimpernel Smith* 41. *Fiddlers Three* 44. Caesar and Cleopatra 45. *Great Expectations* 46. *Oliver Twist* 48. Night and the City 51. Plunder of the Sun (US) 51. The Prodigal (US) 55. Hell's Island (US) 55, many others.
TV series: Destiny (host) 57–58.

Sullivan, Pat (1887–1933)
Australian newspaper cartoonist who settled in the US and invented Felix the Cat, the most popular character in film cartoons of the 20s.

Sully, Frank (1910–1975)
American small-part actor often seen as farmer or dumb crook.
Mary Burns Fugitive 35. The Grapes of Wrath 40. Escape to Glory 41. Thousands Cheer 43. Renegades 46. With a Song in My Heart 52. The Naked Street 56, many others.

Sumac, Yma (1928–) (Emparatriz Chavarri)
Peruvian singer with five-octave range.
■ The Secret of the Incas 54. Omar Khayyam 57.

Summerfield, Eleanor (1921–)
British character comedienne, on stage from 1939.
London Belongs to Me (film debut) 47. Scrooge 51. It's Great To Be Young 56. Dentist in the Chair 59. On the Beat 62. Guns of Darkness 63. Some Will Some Won't 70. The Watcher in the Woods 80, many others.

Summers, Jeremy (1931–)
British director, from TV.
The Punch and Judy Man 62. Crooks in Cloisters 64. Ferry Cross the Mersey 64. House of a Thousand Dolls 67. Vengeance of Fu Manchu 67. Strangers and Brothers (TV) 83, etc.

Summers, Walter (1896–1973)
British director of the 20s and 30s.
Ypres 25. Mons 26. The Battle of the Coronel and Falkland Islands 31. Deeds Men Do 32. The Return of Bulldog Drummond 33. Mutiny on the Elsinore 36. Music Hath Charms (co-d) 36. At the Villa Rose 38. Dark Eyes of London 38. Traitor Spy 40, etc.

Summerville, Slim (1892–1946) (George J. Summerville)
Lanky, mournful-looking American character comedian, former gagman and director for Mack Sennett.
The Beloved Rogue 27. *All Quiet on the Western Front* 30. The Front Page 31. Life Begins at Forty 35. White Fang 36. The Road Back 37. Rebecca of Sunnybrook Farm 38. Jesse James 39. *Tobacco Road* 41. Miss Polly 41. Niagara Falls 42. The Hoodlum Saint 46, many others.

Sumner, Geoffrey (1908–1989)
British comic actor of silly-ass types.
Helter Skelter 49. The Dark Man 52. A Tale of Five Cities 53. Traveller's Joy 55, etc.

Sundberg, Clinton (1906–1987)
American character actor, former teacher; usually played flustered clerk or head-waiter.
Undercurrent 46. Living in a Big Way 47. Annie Get Your Gun 50. Main Street to Broadway 52. The Caddy 53. The Birds and the Bees 56. The Wonderful World of the Brothers Grimm 63. Hotel 67, many others.

Suo, Masayuki (1956–)
Japanese director and screenwriter. Born in Tokyo and brought up in Kawasaki, he studied French at university and began his career as an assistant director and, later, director of PINK MOVIES. *Shall We Dance?* was the sixth-most successful foreign-language film at the American box-office. Married actress and former dancer Tamiyo Kusakari, who starred in the film.
My Brother's Wife 84. A Fancy Dance/Manic Zen 89. Sumo Do, Sumo Don't/Shiko Funjatta 92. *Shall We Dance?* 97, etc.

Surtees, Bruce (1937–)
American cinematographer. He is the son of Robert L. SURTEES.
The Beguiled 71. Play Misty for Me 71. Dirty Harry 72. The Great Northfield Minnesota Raid 72. Blume in Love 73. High Plains Drifter 73. Lenny (AAN) 74. Night Moves 75. The Outlaw Josey Wales 76. Movie Movie 78. Big Wednesday 78. Escape from Alcatraz 79. Inchon 81. White Dog 82. Firefox 82. Tightrope 84. Beverly Hills Cop 84. Pale Rider 85. Out of Bounds 86. Psycho III 86. Ratboy 86. Back to the Beach 87. License to

Drive 88. Men Don't Leave 90. The Super 91. Run 91. The Crush 93. The Birds II: Land's End (TV) 94. The Stars Fell on Henrietta 95. The Substitute 96. Just a Little Harmless Sex 99, etc.

Surtees, Robert L. (1906–1985)
Distinguished American cinematographer, in Hollywood from 1927.
Thirty Seconds over Tokyo (AAN) 44. Our Vines Have Tender Grapes 45. The Unfinished Dance 47. Act of Violence 48. *Intruder in the Dust* 49. *King Solomon's Mines* (AA) 50. Quo Vadis (AAN) 51. *The Bad and the Beautiful* (AA) 52. Escape from Fort Bravo 53. Trial 55. *Oklahoma!* (AAN) 55. The Swan 56. Raintree County 57. Merry Andrew 58. *Ben Hur* (AA) 59. Mutiny on the Bounty (AAN) 62. The Hallelujah Trail 65. The Collector 65. The Satan Bug 65. Lost Command 66. Doctor Dolittle (AAN) 67. *The Graduate* (AAN) 67. *Sweet Charity* 68. The Arrangement 69. Summer of 42 (AAN) 71. The Last Picture Show (AAN) 71. The Cowboys 72. The Other 72. Oklahoma Crude 73. The Sting (AAN) 73. The Great Waldo Pepper 75. The Hindenberg (AAN) 75. A Star Is Born (AAN) 76. The Turning Point (AAN) 77. Bloodbrothers 78. Same Time Next Year (AAN) 78, etc.

Susann, Jacqueline (1921–1974)
American best-selling novelist, a former unsuccessful actress and model. Her lovers included actors Eddie CANTOR and Joe E. LEWIS, and actresses Carol LANDIS and Ethel MERMAN. Died of cancer. She was played by Michele Lee in the TV movie *Scandalous Me: The Jacqueline Susann Story* 98, and by Bette MIDLER in the biopic *Isn't She Great*, 00, with Nathan LANE as her husband, agent Irving Mansfield.
Biography: 1988, *Lovely Me* by Barbara Seaman.
Valley of the Dolls (oa) 67. The Love Machine (oa) 71. Once Is Not Enough (oa) 75.
❝ I write for women who read me in the goddam subways on the way home from work. I know who they are, because that's who I used to be ... But here's the catch. All the people they envy in my books, the ones who are glamorous, or beautiful, or rich, or talented – they have to suffer, see, because that way the people who read me can get off the subway and go home feeling better about their own crappy lives. – *J.S.*
The 1960s will be remembered for three people: me, Andy Warhol and the Beatles. – *J.S.*
She had a miserable life. But she was determined to be famous. She willed herself to be famous. That's what she wanted. She was a failed actress, a failed gameshow host. She was a sort of a joke until the novels. – *Andrew Bergman*

Suschitzky, Peter (1941–)
British cinematographer.
It Happened Here 65. Privilege 66. Charlie Bubbles 67. A Midsummer Night's Dream 68. Lock Up Your Daughters 68. Leo the Last 70. Lisztomania 76. Valentino 77. The Empire Strikes Back 80. Krull 83. Falling in Love 84. Dead Ringers 88. Where the Heart Is 90. Naked Lunch 91. M. Butterfly 93. The Vanishing 93. Crash 96. Mars Attacks! 96, etc.

Suschitzky, Wolfgang (1912–)
Austrian cinematographer in Britain.
No Resting Place 51. Cat and Mouse 57. The Small World of Sammy Lee 63. Ulysses 67. Theatre of Blood 73. Something to Hide 74, etc.

Susskind, David (1920–1987)
American TV and theatre personality and producer who also produced a few films.
Edge of the City 57. A Raisin in the Sun 61. Requiem for a Heavyweight 62. All the Way Home 63. Lovers and Other Strangers 70. Alice Doesn't Live Here Any More 74. Buffalo Bill and the Indians 76. Loving Couples 80, etc.

Sutherland, A. Edward (1895–1974)
American director, in Hollywood from 1914.
Wild Wild Susan 25. Dance of Life 29. Palmy Days 31. Mississippi 35. Diamond Jim 35. Champagne Waltz 37. Every Day's a Holiday 38. The Flying Deuces 39. *The Boys from Syracuse* 40. Beyond Tomorrow 41. Invisible Woman 41. Nine Lives Are Not Enough 42. Dixie 43. Follow the Boys 44. Abie's Irish Rose 46. Having Wonderful Crime 46. Bermuda Affair 56, many others.

Sutherland, Donald (1935–)
Gaunt Canadian actor who became very fashionable at the end of the 60s. He is the father of Kiefer SUTHERLAND.
The World Ten Times Over 63. Castle of the Living Dead 64. Dr Terror's House of Horrors 65. Fanatic 65. The Bedford Incident 65. Promise Her Anything 66. The Dirty Dozen 67. Billion Dollar Brain 67. Sebastian 68. Oedipus the King 68. Interlude 68. Joanna 68. The Split 68. Start the Revolution without Me 69. Act of the Heart 70. M*A*S*H 70. Kelly's Heroes 70. Alex in Wonderland 70. Little Murders 70. *Klute* 71. Johnny Got His Gun (as Christ) 71. Steelyard Blues 72. Lady Ice 73. Alien Thunder 73. Don't Look Now 73. S*P*Y*S 74. The Day of the Locust 74. End of the Game 76. 1900 76. Casanova 76. The Eagle Has Landed 76. The Disappearance 77. Blood Relations 77. The Kentucky Fried Movie 78. Invasion of the Body Snatchers 78. National Lampoon's Animal House 78. The First Great Train Robbery 78. Murder by Decree 78. Bear Island 79. A Man, a Woman and a Bank 79. Nothing Personal 80. Ordinary People 80. Eye of the Needle 81. Threshold 81. Gas 81. Max Dugan Returns 83. The Winter of Our Discontent (TV) 84. Crackers 84. Ordeal by Innocence 85. Heaven Help Us 85. Revolution 85. The Wolf at the Door 86. The Rosary Murders 87. Apprentice to Murder 88. Lost Angels 89. A Dry White Season 89. Bethune: The Making of a Hero 89. Lock Up 89. The Road Home 89. Backdraft 91. JFK 91. Scream of Stone 91. Buster's Bedroom 91. The Railway Station Man 92. Buffy the Vampire Slayer 92. Benefit of the Doubt 93. Six Degrees of Separation 93. Shadow of the Wolf (co-w) 93. Younger and Younger 93. The Puppet Masters 94. Younger & Younger 94. The Lifeforce Experiment (TV) 94. Oldest Living Confederate Widow Tells All (TV) 94. Disclosure 94. Citizen X (TV) 95. Outbreak 95. A Time to Kill 96. Hollow Point 96. Natural Enemy (TV) 96. Shadow Conspiracy 97. Without Limits 97. Fallen 97. The Assignment 97. Fallen 98. Without Limits 98. Instinct 99. Virus 99. Panic 00, etc.
❝ Unbridled criticism affects your life. Forever. It becomes a part of the pattern that designs the fabric of your suffering. The torturer and the tortured, married in painful redemption, marking indelibly the way you live and die, the way you perform your art. – *D.S.*

Sutherland, Dame Joan (1926–)
Distinguished Australian soprano who retired in 1990 and made her feature film debut as Mother Rudd in an adaptation of the Australian stories of outback life by Steele RUDD.
Dad and Dave on Our Selection 95.

Sutherland, Kiefer (1966–)
American leading actor (born in London), the son of Donald SUTHERLAND.
The Bay Boy 85. Stand by Me 86. Crazy Moon 87. The Killing Time 87. The Lost Boys 87. Bright Lights, Big City 88. Promised Land 88. Renegades 89. Flashback 89. 1969 89. Young Guns 90. Flatliners 90. Trapped in Silence 90. Young Guns II 90. Flashback 91. Article 99 92. A Few Good Men 92. Twin Peaks: Fire Walk with Me 92. The Vanishing 93. Last Light (& d) (TV) 93. The Three Musketeers 93. The Cowboy Way 94. Eye for an Eye 95. Freeway 96. A Time to Kill 96. Truth or Consequences, N.M. 97. Dark City 97. A Soldier's Sweetheart 98, etc.

Sutton, Dudley (1933–)
British character actor.
The Leather Boys 63. Rotten to the Core 65. Crossplot 69. The Walking Stick 70. The Devils 71. The Pink Panther Strikes Again 76. Casanova 76. Valentino 77. The Big Sleep 78. Trail of the Pink Panther 82. Lamb 86. The Rainbow 88. Edward II 91. Orlando 92. Moses (TV) 96. The Tichborne Claimant 98, etc.
TV series: Lovejoy 86, 90–95.

Sutton, Grady (1908–1995)
American character comedian usually seen as vacuous country cousin; in Hollywood from 1926.
The Story of Temple Drake 32. Alice Adams 35. Stage Door 37. Alexander's Ragtime Band 38. *The Bank Dick* 40. The Great Moment 44. My Wild Irish Rose 48. White Christmas 54. The Birds and the Bees 56. My Fair Lady 64. Paradise Hawaiian Style 66. The Great Bank Robbery 69. Myra Breckinridge 70. Support Your Local Gunfighter 71. Rock 'n' Roll High School 79, many others.
TV series: The Pruitts of Southampton 66.

Sutton, John (1908–1963)
British actor with stage experience; in Hollywood from 1937, usually as second lead or smooth swashbuckling villain.
Bulldog Drummond Comes Back 37. The Adventures of Robin Hood 38. The Invisible Man Returns 40. A Yank in the RAF 41. *Ten Gentlemen from West Point* 42. Jane Eyre 43. Claudia and David 46. The Three Musketeers 48. The Golden Hawk 52. East of Sumatra 54. The Bat 59, many others.

Suvari, Mena (1979–)
American actress, a former teenage model, born in Newport, Rhode Island. Married cinematographer Robert Brinkman.
Nowhere 97. Kiss the Girls 97. Snide and Prejudice 97. American Pie 99. American Beauty 99. Loser 00. American Virgin 00. Sugar and Spice 01, etc.

Suzman, Janet (1939–)
South African stage actress in Britain.
■ A Day in the Death of Joe Egg 70. *Nicholas and Alexandra* (AAN) 72. The Black Windmill 74. Voyage of the Damned 76. The House on Garibaldi Street (TV) 79. Nijinsky 80. The Priest of Love 81. The Draughtsman's Contract 82. And the Ship Sailed On 84. Mountbatten (as Edwina) (TV) 85. A Dry White Season 89. Nuns on the Run 90. Leon the Pig Farmer 93.

Svankmajer, Jan (1934–)
Czechoslovakian director with a disturbing and surreal turn of mind. His reputation has been made by a series of short films that mix live action with stop-motion animation.
Alice/Neco z Alenky 88. Faust 94. The Conspirators of Pleasure 96.

Svenson, Bo (1941–)
American action lead.
The Great Waldo Pepper 75. Part Two Walking Tall 75. Special Delivery 76. Breaking Point 76. Final Chapter – Walking Tall 77. North Dallas Forty 79. Counterfeit Commandos 81. Heartbreak Ridge 86. The Delta Force 86. The Last Contract 86. Deep Space 87. Curse II: The Bite 88. The Kill Reflex 89. Soda Cracker 89. Primal Rage 90. Killer Mania 92. Three Days to a Kill 92. Savage Land 94. Private Obsession 94, etc.

Sverák, Jan (1965–)
Czech director and screenwriter who studied at FAMU (Film Academy of Music and Drama) in Prague and began as a maker of documentaries. He is the son of screenwriter and actor Zdenák Sverák. *Accumulator 1* was the most expensive Czech film so far made at a cost of $3m; he followed it with a road movie shot in two weeks at a cost of $20,000.
Elementary School/Obecná Skola (AAN) 91. Accumulator 1 94. The Ride 95. *Kolya* (AA) 96, etc.
❝ It is a mistake to fall into the view that Europe is only the ante-room of the place where the real party is. There has to be a way to do films in Europe and compete with America. Half the box-office takings come from the rest of the world. – *J.S.*

Sverák, Zdenák (1936–)
Czech screenwriter and actor, notably associated with the films of Jiri Menzel. He also wrote the semi-autobiographical script for the feature film debut of his son, director Jan SVERAK, and starred in his second film.
The Hit/Trhak (a) 80. Like Hares/Jako Zajici (a) 82. My *Sweet Little Village* (w) 85. *Elementary School*/Obecná Skola 91. The Life and Extraordinary Adventures of Private Chonkin (w) 94. *Accumulator 1* (a, co-w) 94, etc.

Swaim, Bob (1943–)
American director and screenwriter, based in France.
La Nuit de Saint-Germain-des-Prés 77. La Balance 82. Half Moon Street 86. Masquerade 88. L'Atlantide (w) 91, etc.

Swain, Dominique (1980–)
American schoolgirl actress who made her screen debut in the title role of *Lolita*.
Lolita 97. Face/Off 97, etc.

Swain, Mack (1876–1935)
American silent actor, a Mack Sennett heavy from 1914; most memorable in *The Gold Rush* 24. Last part, *Midnight Patrol* 32.

Swank, Hilary (1975–)
American actress, from television. Born in Lincoln, Nebraska, she began acting in her mid-teens. Married actor Chad LOWE.
Buffy the Vampire Slayer 92. The Next Karate Kid 94. Sometimes They Come Back ... Again 96. Kounterfeit 96. Quiet Days in Hollywood 97. Boys Don't Cry (AA) 99. The Gift 00, etc.
TV series: Beverly Hills 90110 97-98.

Swanson, Gloria (1897–1983) (G. Svensson)
American leading lady of the silent screen who started as a Mack SENNETT bathing beauty and made many comebacks. The first of her six husbands was actor Wallace BEERY (1916–18).
Biography: 1988, *Gloria and Joe: The Star-Crossed Love Affair of Gloria Swanson and Joe Kennedy* by Axel Madsen.
Other books: 1981, *Swanson on Swanson*. 1988, *The Films of Gloria Swanson* by Lawrence J. Quirk.
The Meal Ticket 15. Teddy at the Throttle 17. The Pullman Bride 17. Shifting Sands 18. Don't Change Your Husband 18. *Male and Female* 19. Why Change Your Wife? 19. *The Affairs of Anatol* 21. Adam's Rib 23. Prodigal Daughters 23. Madame Sans Gêne 25. Untamed Lady 26. *Sadie Thompson* (AAN) 28. *Queen Kelly* (unfinished) 28. The Trespasser (AAN) 29. Indiscreet 31. Perfect Understanding 33. Music in the Air 34. Father Takes a Wife 41. *Sunset Boulevard* (AAN) 50. Three for Bedroom C 52. Nero's Mistress (It.) 56. Killer Bees (TV) 73. Airport 75 74, many others.
❝ I acquired my expensive tastes from Mr De Mille. – *G.S.*
When I die, my epitaph should read: she paid the bills. – *G.S.*
Dietrich's legs may be longer, but I have seven grandchildren. – *G.S.*
Famous line (*Sunset Boulevard*, when told she used to be a big star) 'I *am* big. It's the pictures that got small.'

Swanson, Kristy (1969–)
American leading actress. In 2000, she was put on probation and ordered to attend ten Alcoholics Anonymous meetings after pleading no contest to drunken driving.
Deadly Friend 86. Flowers in the Attic 87. Diving In 90. Dream Trap 90. Mannequin 2: On the Move 91. Hot Shots! 91. Highway to Hell 92. Buffy the Vampire Slayer 92. The Program 93. The Ref 94. The Chase 94. Higher Learning 94. The Phantom 96. Marshal Law 96. 8 Heads in a Duffel Bag 96. Lover Girl 97. Self Storage 97. Meeting Daddy 98. Big Daddy 99. Dude, Where's My Car? 00, etc.
TV series: Knots Landing 87–88. Nightingales 89. Early Edition 98-99.

Swanson, Maureen (1932–)
British leading lady who retired to marry after a brief career.
Moulin Rouge 53. A Town Like Alice 56. The Spanish Gardener 56. Robbery under Arms 57. The Malpas Mystery 63, etc.

Swarthout, Gladys (1904–1969)
American opera singer who acted in a few films.
Rose of the Rancho 35. Give Us This Night 36. Champagne Waltz 37. Romance in the Dark 38. Ambush 39, etc.

Swayze, Patrick (1952–)
American leading man, a former dancer.
Skatetown USA 79. The Outsiders 83. Uncommon Valor 83. Grandview USA 84. Red Dawn 84. Youngblood 85. *North and South* (TV) 86. Dirty Dancing 87. Steel Dawn 87. Tiger Warsaw 88. Road House 89. Next of Kin 89. Ghost 90. Point Break 91. City of Joy 92. Father Hood 93. To Wong Foo, Thanks for Everything, Julie Newmar 95. Tall Tale: The Unbelievable Adventures of Pecos Bill 95. Three Wishes 95. Black Dog 98. Letters from a Killer 98, etc.
TV series: Renegades 83.

Sweeney, Birdy (1931–1999) (Edmund Sweeney, aka Birdie Sweeney)
Irish character actor, best known for his role as Eamon Byrne in the TV series *Ballykissangel*. Born in Dungannon, he began as a bird impersonator as a child, and also worked as a comic, record-shop

proprietor and furniture salesmen before turning to acting in his mid-50s.

Reefer and the Model 88. The Crying Game 92. The Snapper (TV) 93. Moll Flanders (US) 96. Downtime 97. The Butcher Boy 97. The Nephew 98. Divorcing Jack 98. Angela's Ashes 99, etc.

TV series: Ballykissangel 96-99.

Sweeney, D. B. (1961–) (Daniel Bernard Sweeney)
American leading actor.

Fire with Fire 86. Gardens of Stone 87. No Man's Land 87. Eight Men Out 88. Memphis Belle 90. A Day in October/En Dag i Oktober 91. Blue Desert 91. Heaven Is a Playground 91. Cutting Edge 92. Miss Rose White (TV) 92. Fire in the Sky 93. Hear No Evil 93. Roommates 95. Pawn 97, etc.

TV series: Strange Luck 95. C16: FBI 97.

Sweet, Blanche (1895–1986) (Daphne Wayne)
American silent heroine.

The Lonedale Operator 11. Judith of Bethulia 13. The Secret Sin 15. The Deadliest Sex 20. In the Palace of the King 23. Anna Christie 23. Tess of the D'Urbervilles 24. Bluebeard's Seven Wives 26. Singed 27. The Woman Racket 30. The Silver Horde 30, etc.

Sweet, Dolph (1921–1985)
Barrel-chested American character actor.

The Young Doctors 61. The Lost Man 69. Fear Is the Key 72. The Lords of Flatbush 74. Go Tell the Spartans 77. Reds 81, etc.

TV series: The Trials of O'Brien 65–66. *Gimme a Break* 81–85.

Swenson, Inga (1932–)
American actress.

Advise and Consent 61. The Miracle Worker 62. Earth II (TV) 71. The Betsy 78.

TV series: Soap 78. Benson 79–86. Doctor, Doctor 89–91.

Swerling, Jo (1893–1964) (Joseph Swerling)
Russian-American writer, long in Hollywood. His son Jo Swerling Jnr (1931–) writes and produces for TV.

Ladies of Leisure 30. Rain or Shine 30. Dirigible 31. The Miracle Woman 31. Ten Cents a Dance 31. Attorney for the Defense 32. Behind the Mask 32. Forbidden 32. Platinum Blonde 32. Hollywood Speaks 32. Love Affair 32. Washington Merry-go-round 32. The Circus Queen Murder 33. Man's Castle 33. Lady By Choice 34. No Greater Glory 34. Once to Every Woman 34. Sisters under the Skin 34. Love Me Forever 35. The Whole Town's Talking 35. Pennies from Heaven 36. Double Wedding 37. Dr Rhythm 38. I Am the Law 38. Made for Each Other 38. The Real Glory 39. *The Westerner* 40. Blood and Sand 41. Confirm or Deny 41. The Pride of the Yankees (co-w, AAN) 42. Crash Dive 43. *Lifeboat* 44. Leave Her to Heaven 46. Thunder in the East 51. Guys and Dolls 55. King of the Roaring Twenties 61, etc.

Swicord, Robin
American screenwriter. Married Nicholas Kazan in 1984.

Shag (co-w) 88. Little Women 94. The Perez Family 95. Roald Dahl's Matilda 96. Practical Magic 98, etc.

Swift, David (1919–)
American radio and TV writer-producer-director (TV series include *Mr Peepers, Grindl*).

Pollyanna 60. The Parent Trap 61. Love is a Ball 63. The Interns 63. Under the Yum Yum Tree 64. Good Neighbour Sam 64. How to Succeed in

Business without Really Trying (wd, p) 67. Candleshoe (co-w) 77, etc.

Swift, Jonathan (1667–1745)
Irish satirist best known for the much-filmed *Gulliver's Travels*, which is not a children's book.

Swinburne, Nora (1902–2000) (Elinore Johnson)
British leading actress, usually in upper-class roles. Born in Bath, Somerset, she trained at RADA and was on the London stage from the age of 14, making her name in drawing-room comedies. She retired in the mid-70s. The first of her three husbands was actor Francis LISTER, and the third actor Esmond KNIGHT.

Branded 20. Hornet's Nest 23. The Unwanted 24. A Girl of London 25. Caste 30. Alf's Button 30. Alibi 30. Potiphar's Wife 31. Perfect Understanding 33. Jury's Evidence 35. Dinner at the Ritz 37. The Farmer's Wife 40. They Flew Alone 41. Dear Octopus 43. The Man in Grey 43. Fanny by Gaslight 43. They Knew Mr Knight 45. The Blind Goddess 47. Jassy 47. *Quartet* 48. Marry Me 49. My Daughter Joy 50. Quo Vadis 51. The River 51. The End of the Affair 54. Betrayed 54. Helen of Troy 55. Third Man on the Mountain 59. Conspiracy of Hearts 60. Forsyte Saga (TV) 67. Interlude 68. Anne of the Thousand Days 69. Up the Chastity Belt 71, many others.

Swink, Robert E. (1918–2000)
American editor and second unit director associated with the films of William WYLER. Born in Colorado, he moved to Hollywood as a child and began as an apprentice film editor with RKO; later, he worked for Paramount.

Passport to Destiny 43. Action in Arabia 44. Criminal Court 46. I Remember Mama 48. Riders of the Range 49. Adventure in Baltimore 49. Storm Over Wyoming 50. Rider From Tucson 50. The Company She Keeps 50. Detective Story 51. The Narrow Margin 52. The Captive City 52. Roman Holiday (AAN) 53. Witness To Murder 54. The Desperate Hours 55. Friendly Persuasion 56. The Young Stranger 57. The Diary Of Anne Frank 59. The Young Doctors 61. The Children's Hour 61. Captain Sindbad 63. The Best Man 64. The Collector 65. How To Steal A Million 66. The Flim-Flam Man 67. *Funny Girl* (AAN) 68. The Liberation Of L.B. Jones 70. The Cowboys 72. Papillon 73. Rooster Cogburn 75. Midway 76. Islands In The Stream 77. Gray Lady Down 78. *The Boys From Brazil* (AAN) 78. Going In Style 79. Sphinx 81. Welcome Home 89, etc.

Swinton, Tilda (1961–)
British actress in experimental and low-budget movies, most often to be seen in the films of Derek JARMAN.

Caravaggio 86. Aria 87. Friendship's Death 87. The Last of England 87. War Requiem 88. Play Me Something 89. The Garden 90. Edward II 91. The Party/Nature Morte 91. Man to Man 92. Orlando 92. Wittgenstein 93. Female Perversions 96. Love Is the Devil 98, etc.

Swit, Loretta (1937–)
American comedy actress of the 70s, familiar as Hot Lips Houlihan from TV's M*A*S*H.

Stand Up and Be Counted 72. Shirts/Skins (TV) 73. Freebie and the Bean 74. The Last Day (TV) 75. Race with the Devil 75. The Hostage Heart (TV) 77. The Love Tapes (TV) 79. Cagney and Lacey (TV pilot) 81. S.O.B. 81. The Kid from Nowhere (TV) 82. First Affair (TV) 83. The Execution (TV) 85. Beer 85. Whoops Apocalypse 86.

Switzer, Carl ('Alfalfa') (1926–1959)
American boy actor of the 30s, a graduate of 'Our Gang'; later in character roles. Died from a gunshot wound in an argument over a $50 debt.

General Spanky 37. The War Against Mrs Hadley 42. State of the Union 48. Track of the Cat 54. The Defiant Ones 58, many others.

Swofford, Ken
Burly American character actor.

Father Goose 64. The Lawyer 69. One Little Indian 73. Crisis at Sun Valley (TV) 78. Black Roses 88. The Taking of Beverly Hills 91, etc.

TV series: Switch 75–76. Fame 83–85.

Syberberg, Hans-Jurgen (1935–)
German producer-director, mainly of documentaries.

Scarabea 68. Ludwig – Requiem for a Virgin King 72. Ludwig's Cook 72. Karl May 74. Confessions of Winifred Wagner 75. Our Hitler 76–77. Parsifal 82. The Night/Die Nacht 85, etc.

Sydney, Basil (1894–1968) (Basil Nugent)
British actor of heavy roles, on stage from 1911.

Romance (film debut) 20. The Midshipmaid 32. The Tunnel 35. Rhodes of Africa 36. The Four Just Men 39. Ships with Wings 41. Went the Day Well? 42. *Caesar and Cleopatra* 45. The Man Within 47. *Hamlet* 48. Treasure Island 50. Ivanhoe 52. Hell below Zero 54. The Dam Busters 55. The Three Worlds of Gulliver 60, etc.

Sykes, Eric (1923–)
British TV comedian.

Invasion Quartet 61. Village of Daughters 62. Kill or Cure 63. Heavens Above 63. The Bargee 63. One-Way Pendulum 64. Those Magnificent Men in Their Flying Machines 65. Rotten to the Core 65. The Liquidator 65. The Spy with a Cold Nose 67. The Plank (& d) 67. Shalako 68. Monte Carlo or Bust 69. Rhubarb (& d) 70. Theatre of Blood 73. The Boys in Blue 83. Splitting Heirs 93. Gormenghast (TV) 00, etc.

TV series: Dinnerladies 98.

Sylbert, Paul
American production designer, occasional director and writer, from television.

Riot 69. The Steagle (wd) 71. Bad Company 72. The Drowning Pool 75. One Flew over the Cuckoo's Nest 76. Heaven Can Wait (AA) 78. Kramer vs Kramer 79. Resurrection 80. Wolfen 81. Gorky Park 83. The Pope of Greenwich Village 84. First Born 84. The Journey of Natty Gann 85. The Pick-Up Artist 87. Ishtar 87. Biloxi Blues 88. Fresh Horses 88. Rush 91. Career Opportunities 91. The Prince of Tides (AAN) 91. Sliver 93. Milk Money 94. The Grass Harp 95. Free Willy 2: The Adventure Home 95, etc.

Sylbert, Richard (1928–)
American art director.

Baby Doll 56. Splendor in the Grass 61. Walk on the Wild Side 62. The Manchurian Candidate 62. How to Murder Your Wife 64. Long Day's Journey into Night 64. The Pawnbroker 64. Who's Afraid of Virginia Woolf? (AA) 66. The Graduate 67. Rosemary's Baby 68. Catch 22 70. Carnal Knowledge 71. The Day of the Dolphin 73. The Fortune 75. Players 79. Reds (AAN) 81. Partners 82. Frances 82. The Cotton Club (AAN) 84. Under the Cherry Moon 86. Shoot to Kill 88. Tequila Sunrise 88. The Bonfire of the Vanities 90. Dick Tracy (AA) 90. Mobsters 91. Ruby Cairo 93. Milk Money 94. Mulholland Falls 96, etc.

Sylvester, William (1922–1995)
American leading man, in British films from 1949, later back in US.

Give Us This Day 50. Appointment in London 52. The Yellow Balloon 52. Albert RN 53. The Stranger Came Home 54. Portrait of Alison 55. High Tide at Noon 57. Gorgo 59. Offbeat 60. Ring of Spies 63. Devil Doll 64. Devils of Darkness 64. The Hand of Night 66. The Syndicate 67. 2001: A Space Odyssey 68. Heaven Can Wait 78, many others.

TV series: Gemini Man 76.

Sylvie (1883–1970) (Louise Sylvain)
French character actress.

Un Carnet de Bal 37. Le Corbeau 43. Le Diable au Corps 46. Dieu a Besoin des Hommes 51. Nous Sommes Tous des Assassins 56. *The Shameless Old Lady* 64.

Syms, Sylvia (1934–)
British leading lady with brief stage and TV experience.

My Teenage Daughter 56. The Birthday Present 57. The House for Tears 57. Woman in a Dressing Gown 57. Bachelor of Hearts 58. Ferry to Hong Kong 58. No Trees in the Street 58. Expresso Bongo 59. Conspiracy of Hearts 60. The World of Suzie Wong 60. Flame in the Streets 61. Victim 61. The Punch and Judy Man 62. The Quare Fellow 62. The World Ten Times Over 63. East of Sudan 64. The Big Job 65. Danger Route 67. The Desperados 68. Run Wild, Run Free 69. Asylum 72. The Tamarind Seed 74. There Goes the Bride 80. Shining Through 92. Food of Love 97, etc.

TV series: At Home With The Braithwaites 00.

Szabó, Ildikó (1951–)
Hungarian director, screenwriter, and costume designer, a former leading actress.

Love Emilia (a) 70. The Old Time Soccer/Régi Idök Focija (a) 73. Hótréal (wd) 87. Child Murders/Gyerekgyilkosságok (wd, cost.) 93. Bitches 96, etc.

Szabó, István (1938–)
Hungarian director.

Age of Illusion 65. Father 66. A Film about Love 70. 25 Firemen's Street 74. Tales of Budapest 77. The Hungarians 78. Bizalom 79. *Mephisto* 81. *Colonel Redl* 84. Hanussen 88. Meeting Venus 91. Sweet Emma, Dear Bob/Edes Emma, Draga Bobe 92. Sunshine 99 (co-w, d) 99, etc.

Szasz, Janos (1958–)
Hungarian director and screenwriter; he began as a documentary film-maker in the early 50s.

Wozzeck 93. The Witman Boys/Witman Fiuk (AAN) 97, etc.

Szubanski, Magda
Australian comedian and actress, much on television in her homeland.

The Search for Christmas (TV) 95. Babe 95. Babe: Pig in the City 98, etc.

TV series: The D Generation 86. Fast Forward 89. Bligh 92. Big Girl's Blouse 94. Something Stupid 98, etc.

Szwarc, Jeannot (1936–)
French director in America.

Extreme Close Up 74. Bug 75. Jaws 2 78. Somewhere in Time 80. Enigma 82. Supergirl 84. Santa Claus 85. Honor Bound 91, etc.

Biography: 1993, *It Ain't So Easy as It Looks: Ted Turner's Amazing Story* by Porter Bibb.

Turner, Tina (1938–) (Annie Mae Bullock)
American rhythm and blues and soul singer and actress. A biopic of her life, *What's Love Got to Do with It*, was made in 1993 starring Angela Bassett.
■ Gimme Shelter (doc) 70. Taking Off 71. Soul to Soul (concert) 71. Tommy 75. Mad Max beyond Thunderdome 85. The Last Action Hero 93.

Turney, Catherine (1906–1998)
American screenwriter, novelist and playwright, mainly for Warner Bros, who created vehicles for Barbara STANWYCK, Bette DAVIS and the studio's other female stars of the 40s. She later worked in television.
Mildred Pierce 45. Of Human Bondage 45. One More Tomorrow 46. A Stolen Life 46. My Reputation 46. The Man I Love 47. Cry Wolf 47. Winter Meeting 48. No Man of Her Own 50. Japanese War Bride 52. Back from the Dead (from her novel The Other One) 57, etc.

Turpin, Ben (1874–1940)
Cross-eyed American silent comedian, mainly popular in short slapstick skits of the 20s. In films from 1915 after vaudeville experience.
Uncle Tom's Cabin 19. Small Town Idol 21. Show of Shows 29. The Love Parade 30, many others.

Turpin, Dick (1706–1739)
was a seasoned criminal without too many obvious redeeming characteristics. Film-makers have seized on his ride to York and his affection for his horse as an excuse to view him through rose-tinted glasses. So he was played as a hero by Matheson Lang in 1922, Tom Mix in 1925, Victor McLaglen in 1933, Louis Hayward in 1951, and David Weston (for Walt Disney) in 1965. In the late 70s Richard O'Sullivan appeared in an ITV series, again featuring the highwayman as a kind of Robin Hood.

Turpin, Gerry (c. 1930–1997)
British cinematographer.
The Queen's Guards 61. Seance on a Wet Afternoon 64. The Whisperers 67. Deadfall 68. Oh What a Lovely War 69. The Man Who Had Power over Women 70. I Want What I Want 71. The Last of Sheila 73. The Doctor and the Devils 85, etc.

Turteltaub, Jon
American director.
Think Big 90. Driving Me Crazy 91. 3 Ninjas 92. Cool Runnings 93. While You Were Sleeping 95. Phenomenon 96. Instinct 99. Disney's The Kid 00, etc.

Turturro, John (1957–)
American leading actor, from the stage. Married actress Katherine Borowitz.
Raging Bull 80. Exterminator 2 84. The Flamingo Kid 84. Desperately Seeking Susan 85. To Live and Die In L.A. 85. The Color of Money 86. Gung Ho 86. Hannah and Her Sisters 86. Off Beat 86. Five Corners 88. The Sicilian 87. Do the Right Thing 89. Catchfire/Backtrack 89. Men of Respect 90. Miller's Crossing 90. Mo' Better Blues 90. State of Grace 90. Jungle Fever 91. Barton Fink 91. Brain Donors 92. Mac (& d) 92. Fearless 93. Being Human 94. Quiz Show 94. Clockers 95. Search and Destroy 95. Unstrung Heroes 95. Sugartime (TV) 95. Girl 6 96. The Search for One-Eyed Jimmy (made 93) 96. Box of Moonlight 96. Grace of My Heart 96. The Truce 97. The Big Lebowski 98. He Got Game 98. Animals 98.

Illuminata (& d) 98. Rounders 98. OK Garage 98. The Cradle Will Rock 99. Two Thousand and None (Can.) 00. The Luzhin Defence (GB) 00. O, Brother Where Art Thou? 00. The Man Who Cried (GB/Fr.) 00. Company Man 01, etc.

Tushingham, Rita (1940–)
British leading character actress with stage experience.
A Taste of Honey 61. The Leather Boys 63. A Place to Go 63. Girl with Green Eyes 64. *The Knack* 65. Dr Zhivago 65. The Trap 66. Smashing Time 67. Diamonds for Breakfast 68. The Guru 69. The Bed-Sitting Room 69. Straight On till Morning 72. The Human Factor 75. Rachel's Man 75. Mysteries 79. Confessions of Felix Krull (TV) 81. Judgment in Stone 86. Hem 87. Resurrected 88. Hard Days, Hard Nights 88. Paper Marriage 93. An Awfully Big Adventure 95. The Boy from Mercury 96. Under the Skin 97, etc.

Tutin, Dame Dorothy (1930–)
Leading British actress. Occasional films. She was made a Dame in the New Year's Honours of 1999.
The Importance of Being Earnest 52. The Beggar's Opera 53. A Tale of Two Cities 57. Cromwell 69. The Spy's Wife 70. *Savage Messiah* 72. The Shooting Party 85. Murder with Mirrors (TV) 85. Great Moments in Aviation 94. Alive and Kicking/Indian Summer 96. This Could Be the Last Time (TV) 98, etc.
TV series: Body and Soul 93. Jake's Progress 95.

Tuttle, Frank (1892–1963)
American director of mainly routine films; in Hollywood from the 20s.
Kid Boots 27. Roman Scandals 33. The Glass Key 35. Waikiki Wedding 37. I Stole a Million 39. *This Gun For Hire* 42. Lucky Jordan 43. Hostages 43. The Hour Before the Dawn 43. A Man Called Sullivan 45. Suspense 46. Swell Guy 47. The Magic Face 51. Gunman in the Streets 51. Hell on Frisco Bay 55. A Cry in the Night 56, etc.

Tuttle, Lurene (1906–1986)
American character actress, from radio. Married radio and stage actor Melville Ruick (1898–1972); their daughter was actress Barbara RUICK.
Mr Blandings Builds His Dream House 46. Montana Mike 47. Macbeth 48. The Whip Hand 51. The Affairs of Dobie Gillis 53. Niagara 53. The Sweet Smell of Success 57. Psycho 60. The Fortune Cookie 66. Walking Tall 73. Part Two Walking Tall/Legend of the Lawman 75. Walking Tall: Final Chapter 77. The Adventures of Huckleberry Finn 81, etc.
TV series: Life with Father 53–55. Father of the Bride 61–62. Julia 68–70.

Twain, Mark (1835–1910) (Samuel Langhorne Clemens)
Beloved American humorist and travel writer; was played by Fredric March in *The Adventures of Mark Twain* 44. Works filmed include *Tom Sawyer*, *Huckleberry Finn*. A Connecticut Yankee, *The Prince and the Pauper*, *The Celebrated Jumping Frog* (as *The Best Man Wins*), *The Million-Pound Banknote*.

Twelvetrees, Helen (1907–1958) (Helen Jurgens)
American leading lady of the 30s; films fairly unmemorable. Born in Brooklyn, New York, she trained at the American Academy of Dramatic Arts. Died from an overdose of sleeping pills.
The Ghost Talks 29. The Cat Creeps 30. Her Man 30. The Painted Desert 31. Is My Face Red? 32. State's Attorney 32. King for a Night 33. All Men Are Enemies 34. Now I'll Tell 34. Times

Square Lady 35. Hollywood Round Up 37. Persons in Hiding 39. Unmarried 39, etc.

Twiggy (1948–) (Lesley Hornby)
British fashion model of the 60s. Married actor Leigh LAWSON, her second husband.
Autobiography: 1997, *Twiggy in Black and White* (with Penelope Dening).
The Boy Friend 71. 'W' 74. There Goes the Bride 80. The Doctor and the Devils 85. Club Paradise 86. The Little Match Girl (TV) 87. Madame Sousatzka 88. The Diamond Trap (TV) 88. Young Charlie Chaplin (TV) 88. Istanbul 89. Woundings 98, etc.

Twist, Derek (1905–1979)
British director, former editor and associate producer.
The End of the River 47. All over the Town 48. Green Grow the Rushes 51. Police Dog 55. Family Doctor 57, etc.

Twist, John (1895–1976)
American screenwriter.
The Toast of New York 36. The Great Man Votes 39. So Big 53. Helen of Troy 55. The FBI Story 56. Esther and the King 60. None But the Brave 64, etc.

Twitty, Conway (1934–1993) (Harold Lloyd Jenkins)
American rock singer and songwriter who appeared in a couple of films as himself and from the mid-60s became a successful country and western performer and businessman, owner of the Twitty City theme park just outside Nashville.
College Confidential 59. Platinum High School/ Trouble at 16/Rich Young and Deadly 60, etc.

Twohy, David T.
American screenwriter.
Critters 2 88. Warlock 90. The Fugitive (co-w) 93. Terminal Velocity (w) 94. Waterworld (co-w) 95. The Arrival (wd) 96. GI Jane (w) 97, etc.

Tykwer, Tom (c. 1965–)
German director, screenwriter and composer. Born in Berlin, he began working as a projectionist in his early teens and was later a cinema manager before beginning by making short films. He is co-founder of the production company X-Filme.
Deadly Maria/Die Todliche Maria 94. Winterschlafer/Wintersleepers (co-w, d, co-m) 97. Life Is a Construction Site (co-w only) 97. Run Lola Run/Lola Rennt (wd, co-m) 98. The Princess and the Warrior (wd, co-m) 00, etc.

Tyler, Beverly (1924–)
American leading lady of routine 40s films.
Best Foot Forward 43. The Green Years 46. The Beginning or the End 47. The Fireball 50. Chicago Confidential 47. The Toughest Gun in Tombstone 58, etc.

Tyler, Judy (1933–1957) (Judith Mae Hess)
American actress who began as a child and starred opposite Elvis Presley in *Jailhouse Rock*.
Bob Girl Goes Calypso 57. Jailhouse Rock 57.

Tyler, Liv (1977–)
American actress and model, the daughter of rock guitarist Steven Tyler. She has been romantically linked with actor Joaquin PHOENIX.
Silent Fall 94. Heavy 95. Empire Records 95. *Stealing Beauty* 95. That Thing You Do 96. U-Turn 97. Inventing the Abbotts 97. Armageddon 98. Onegin 98. Plunkett & Macleane 99. Cookie's Fortune 99. Dr T & the Women 00, etc.

Tyler, Parker (1904–974)
American highbrow film critic. Author of *The Hollywood Hallucination*, *Magic and Myth of the Movies*, *The Shadow of an Airplane Climbs the Empire State Building*, etc.

Tyler, Tom (1903–1954) (Vincent Markowsky)
American cowboy star of innumerable second features in the 30s: *The Cowboy Cop* 26. *The Sorcerer* 29. *Riding the Lonesome Trail* 34. *Pinto Rustlers* 38. Roamin' Wild 39, etc. Also played small roles in such films as *Gone with the Wind* 39. *Stagecoach* 39. The Mummy's Hand (as the mummy) 40; and had the title role in *The Adventures of Captain Marvel* (serial) 41.

Tynan, Kenneth (1927–1980)
British journalist and critic who was briefly a script editor at Ealing in the mid-50s. The character of Professor Marcus, played by Alec Guinness in *The Ladykillers*, is said to have been based on his physical appearance (though Guinness has denied it). He was film critic of the *Observer* in 1964.
Nowhere to Go (co-w) 58. Macbeth (co-w) 71.

Tyrrell, Susan (1946–)
American leading lady.
Fat City (AAN) 72. Shootout 72. Catch My Soul 73. The Killer inside Me 76. I Never Promised You a Rose Garden 77. Islands in the Stream 77. Another Man, Another Chance 77. Andy Warhol's Bad 77. September 30, 1955 77. Lady of the House 78. Forbidden Zone 80. Loose Shoes 80. Night Warning 81. Fast-Walking 82. Tales of Ordinary Madness 83. Angel 84. Flesh and Blood 85. Avenging Angel 85. Big-Top Pee-Wee 88. Far from Home 89. Tapeheads 89. Cry-Baby 90. Rockula 90. Motorama 92. Powder 95, etc.

Tyson, Cathy (1966–)
British actress, from the stage.
Mona Lisa 86. The Serpent and the Rainbow 88. Business as Usual 88. Rules of Engagement (TV) 89. The Lost Language of Cranes (TV) 91. Priest (TV) 94, etc.
TV series: Band of Gold 95–96. Gold 97.

Tyson, Cicely (1933–)
American leading actress. Married jazz musician Miles DAVIS.
A Man Called Adam 66. The Comedians 67. The Heart Is a Lonely Hunter 68. *Sounder* (AAN) 72. *The Autobiography of Miss Jane Pittman* (TV) 74. Roots (TV) 77. A Hero Ain't Nothin' but a Sandwich 77. The Concorde – Airport '79 79. Bustin' Loose 81. Fried Green Tomatoes at the Whistle Stop Café 91. Duplicates (TV) 92. Oldest Living Confederate Widow Tells All (TV) 94. The Road to Galveston (TV) 96. Riot (TV) 97. Hoodlum 97, etc.
TV series: East Side West Side 63.

Tyzack, Margaret (1933–)
British character actress, familiar on TV in *The First Churchills* and *The Forsyte Saga*.
Ring of Spies 64. The Whisperers 67. A Clockwork Orange 71. The Legacy 79. Mr Love 86. The King's Whore 90. Mrs Dalloway 97. Our Mutual Friend (TV) 98, etc.
TV series: The Young Indiana Jones Chronicles 92–93. Family Money 97.

Tzelniker, Meier (1894–1982)
British character actor well known in the Yiddish theatre.
Mr Emmanuel 44. It Always Rains on Sunday 48. Last Holiday 50. The Teckman Mystery 54. Make Me an Offer 54. A Night to Remember 58. *Expresso Bongo* 60. The Sorcerers 67, etc.

U

Uchida, Tomu (1898–1970)
Japanese director, a former comic actor. He began as an assistant, working with Mizoguchi and others, and first directed comedies before turning to realistic subjects. During the Second World War, he left Japan for Manchuria and China, not returning until the mid-50s, when he specialized in period films, often remakes. His best film, *Earth*, was made in secret over a period of a year.
A Living Doll/Ikeru Ningyo 29. Hot Wind 34. *Earth*/Tsuchi 39. Outsiders/Mori To Mizuumi No Matsuri 58. Zen and Sword/Miyamoto Musashi – Ichijoji No Ketto 62. Swords of Death/Shinken Shobu 72, etc.

Uchida, Yuya
Japanese actor and screenwriter, a former rock performer.
A Pool without Water/Mizu No Nai Puuru 82. Merry Christmas, Mr Lawrence 82. The Mosquito on the Tenth Floor/Jukai No Mosukiito 83. *Comic Magazine*/Komikku Zasshi Nanika Irani (& w) 86. Black Rain 89, etc.

Uggams, Leslie (1943–)
American revue actress.
Skyjacked 72. Roots (TV) 77. Backstairs at the White House (TV) 79. Sizzle 81. Sugar Hill 93, etc.
TV series: The Leslie Uggams Show 69. Roots 77–78.

Uhry, Alfred H. (1937–)
American dramatist and screenwriter.
Mystic Pizza 88. Driving Miss Daisy (AA) 89. Rich in Love 92.

Ullman, Daniel (1918–1979)
American scriptwriter.
The Maze 53. Seven Angry Men 54. Wichita 55. Good Day for a Hanging 59. Face of a Fugitive 59. Mysterious Island 61, etc.

Ullman, Tracey (1959–)
British actress and singer, often in comic roles, who moved to America in the mid-80s. She began her career in British theatre and television and has recorded a hit single, 'They Don't Know', and some pop albums.
Give My Regards to Broad Street 84. The Young Visitors (TV) 84. Plenty 85. Jumpin' Jack Flash 86. I Love You to Death 90. Death Becomes Her 92. Household Saints 93. Robin Hood: Men in Tights 93. I'll Do Anything 94. Bullets over Broadway 94. Prêt-à-Porter 94. Panic 00. Small Time Crooks 00, etc.
TV series: Three of a Kind 81. Kick Up the Eighties 81–82. Girls on Top 85–86. The Tracey Ullman Show 87–90. Tracey Takes On ... 96.

Ullmann, Liv (1939–)
Norwegian leading actress in international films. She turned to writing and directing in the 90s.
Autobiography: 1977, *Changing*.
The Wayward Girl 59. Persona 66. Hour of the Wolf 67. Shame 68. A Passion 70. The Night Visitor 70. Pope Joan 71. The Emigrants (AAN) 72. Lost Horizon 73. Forty Carats 73. The Abdication 74. Face to Face (AAN) 76. A Bridge Too Far 77. The Serpent's Egg 77. Leonor 77. *Autumn Sonata* 78. Players 79. Richard's Things (TV) 80. The Wild Duck 82. Bay Boy 84. Dangerous Moves 84. Ingrid 85. Let's Hope It's a Girl 85. Gaby – a True Story 87. La Amiga 88. The Rose Garden 89. Mindwalk 90. The Ox/Oxen 91. The Long Shadow 92. Sofie (co-w, d) 92. Dreamplay/Dromspel 94. Kristin Lavransdatter (wd) 95. Private Confessions (d) (TV) 96. Faithless (d) 00, etc.

Ulmer, Edgar G. (1900–1972)
Austrian-born director long in Hollywood specializing in second features and exploitation subjects. In his later years somewhat mysteriously revered by French critics.
The Black Cat 34. The Singing Blacksmith 38. Isle of Forgotten Sins 43. Blueboard 44. The Wife of Monte Cristo 46. Detour 46. Her Sister's Secret 47. Ruthless 48. The Man from Planet X 53. The Naked Dawn 55. Daughter of Dr Jekyll 57. The Amazing Transparent Man 60. Beyond the Time Barrier 61. Atlantis, the Lost Kingdom/L'Atlantide 62. The Cavern 65, many others.

Ulric, Lenore (1892–1970) (Lenore Ulrich)
American stage actress.
Tiger Rose 23. Frozen Justice 29. Camille 36. Temptation 46. Northwest Outpost 47, etc.

Ulrich, Skeet (1969–) (Brian Ulrich)
American actor. Born in Concord, he studied marine biology at the University of North Carolina, and acting under David MAMET at New York University. Married actress Georgina CATES.
Last Dance 96. The Craft 96. Boys 96. Albino Alligator 96. Touch 97. Scream 96. As Good as It Gets 97. The Newton Boys 98. Ride with the Devil 99. Chill Factor 99, etc.

Ultra Violet (1934–) (Isabelle Collin-Dufresne)
French-born actress who became part of the entourage that surrounded Andy Warhol and appeared in some of his films.
Autobiography: 1988, *Famous for 15 Minutes*.
I, a Man 67. Midnight Cowboy 69. Maidstone 70. Dinah East 70. Taking Off 71. Simon, King of the Witches 71. Believe in Me 71. An Unmarried Woman 78. Blackout 92, etc.
❝ Nearly all of us at the Factory have had our moments of anger at Andy. He's promised us fame, money, Superstardom, and only given us walk-on parts in his home-made movies. When a film has succeeded, he's kept the profits and seized the headlines. – *U.V.*
She was popular with the press because she had a freak name, purple hair, an incredibly long tongue, and a mini-rap about the intellectual meaning of underground films – *Andy Warhol*

Umeki, Miyoshi (1929–)
Japanese leading lady who won an Academy Award for her performance in *Sayonara* 57.
Cry for Happy 61. Flower Drum Song 61. A Girl Named Tamiko 63, etc.
TV series: The Courtship of Eddie's Father 69.

Underdown, Edward (1908–1989)
British actor on stage from 1932; once a jockey. Often cast as a dull Englishman.
The Warren Case 33 (debut). Wings of the Morning 37. They Were Not Divided 50. The Voice of Merrill 52. Beat the Devil 54. The Camp on Blood Island 58. The Day the Earth Caught Fire 61. Khartoum 66. The Hand of Night 67. Running Scared 72. Digby, the Biggest Dog in the World 73. The Abdication 74, etc.

Underwood, Blair (1964–)
American actor, born in Tacoma, Washington.
Krush Groove 85. Heat Wave (TV) 90. Dangerous Relations (TV) 92. Posse 93. Just Cause 95. Set It Off 96. Gattaca 97. Deep Impact 98. Rules of Engagement 00, etc.
TV series: One Life to Live 85-86. Downtown 86-87. LA Law 87-94. High Incident 96-97. City of Angels 00- .

Underwood, Ron
American director.
Tremors 90. City Slickers 91. Heart and Souls 93. Speechless 94. Mighty Joe Young 98, etc.

Unger, Deborah Kara (1966–)
Canadian actress, born in Vancouver. She studied philosophy and economics at the University of Victoria, and acting at the Australian National Institute of Dramatic Art.
Bangkok Hilton (TV) 89. Prisoners of the Sun 90. Till There Was You 90. Breakaway 90. Blood Oath 90. Whispers in the Dark 92. Highlander III: The Sorcerer 94. Crash 96. No Way Home 97. The Game 97. Luminous Motion 98. The Rat Pack (as Ava Gardner) (TV) 98. Payback 99. The Hurricane 99. Sunshine 99, etc.

Unsworth, Geoffrey (1914–1978)
British cinematographer.
The Million Pound Note 53. Hell Drivers 57. *A Night to Remember* 58. Northwest Frontier 59. The 300 Spartans 62. *Becket* (BFA) 64. Genghis Khan 65. Half a Sixpence 67. *2001: A Space Odyssey* 68. The Bliss of Mrs Blossom 68. The Assassination Bureau 68. The Reckoning 69. Three Sisters 70. *Cabaret* (AA) 72. Alice's Adventures in Wonderland 72. Zardoz 73. Murder on the Orient Express 74. Lucky Lady 75. A Matter of Time 76. The Great Train Robbery 78. Superman 78. Tess (AA, BFA) 79, etc.

Urban, Charles (1871–1942)
American pioneer of British films. He left Edison to found his own production company in London, and developed commercial non-fiction films.

Urban, Joseph (1872–1933)
Austrian-born art director, architect, illustrator, and noted stage designer. Most famous for designing the sets for the Ziegfeld Follies on Broadway from 1915–32, he worked in films at the invitation of William Randolph Hearst to add distinction to the movies of Hearst's mistress Marion Davies.
Humoresque 20. Passionate Pilgrim 21. Enchantment 21. Beauty's Worth 22. When Knighthood Was in Flower 22. Adam and Eve 23. The Great White Way 24. Zander the Great 25. The Man Who Came Back 31. East Lynne 31, etc.

Ure, Mary (1933–1975)
British leading actress of stage and (occasionally) screen. She was married to dramatist John Osborne and later actor Robert Shaw.
■ Storm over the Nile 55. Windom's Way 59. Look Back in Anger 59. *Sons and Lovers* (AAN) 60. The Mind Benders 63. The Luck of Ginger Coffey 64. Custer of the West 67. Where Eagles Dare 68. Reflection of Fear 71.

Urecal, Minerva (1896–1966)
American character actress.
Oh Doctor 37. Boys of the City 40. The Bridge of San Luis Rey 44. Who's Guilty? 47. The Lost Moment 48. Harem Girl 52. Miracle in the Rain 56. The Seven Faces of Dr Lao 64, etc.
TV series: Tugboat Annie.

Urich, Robert (1946–)
American TV actor who has made a few films.
■ Endangered Species 82. The Ice Pirates 83. Turk 182 84. Murder by Night (TV) 89. Survive the Savage Sea 91.
TV series: S.W.A.T. 75–76. Soap 77. Tabitha 77–78. Vega$ 78–81. Gavilan 82–83. Spencer: For Hire 85–88. Crossroads 92. The Lazarus Man 96. Love Boat, the Next Wave 98– .

Urioste, Frank J.
American film editor.
Whatever Happened to Aunt Alice 69. The Grissom Gang 71. Midway 76. Damnation Alley 77. The Boys in Company C 78. Fast Break 79. Loving Couples 80. The Jazz Singer 80. The Entity 83. Trenchcoat 83. Amityville 3-D 83. Conan the Destroyer 84. Red Sonja 85. The Hitcher 86. Robocop (AAN) 87. Die Hard (AA) 88. Road House 89. Total Recall 90. Basic Instinct 92. Cliffhanger 93. Tombstone 94. CutThroat Island 95, etc.

Urquhart, Robert (1922–1995)
Scottish character actor, in films since 1951 after stage experience. He also ran a notable hotel in the Highlands of Scotland. The first of his two wives was actress Zena Walker.
You're Only Young Twice (debut) 51. Knights of the Round Table 54. You Can't Escape 56. The Curse of Frankenstein 56. Dunkirk 58. 55 Days at Peking 62. Murder at the Gallop 64. Country Dance 70. The Dogs of War 80. Restless Natives 85. The Kitchen Toto 87, etc.
TV series: The Pathfinders 72. The Amazing Mr Goodall 74.

Ustinov, Sir Peter (1921–)
Garrulous, hirsute, multi-talented British actor-director-playwright-screenwriter-raconteur.
Autobiography: 1978, *Dear Me*.
■ AS ACTOR: Hullo Fame 40. Mein Kampf 40. The Goose Steps Out 41. One of Our Aircraft is Missing 42. Let the People Sing 42. The Way Ahead 44. *Private Angelo* 49. Odette 50. *Hotel Sahara* 51. The Magic Box 51. *Quo Vadis* (as Nero) (AAN) 51. *Beau Brummell* (as George IV) 54. The Egyptian 54. We're No Angels 55. Lola Montez 55. The Man Who Wagged His Tail 57. The Spies 57. *The Sundowners* 60. *Spartacus* (AA) 60. *Romanoff and Juliet* 61. Billy Budd 62. Topkapi (AA) 64. John Goldfarb Please Come Home 65. Lady L 65. The Comedians 67. Blackbeard's Ghost 68. Hot Millions 68. Viva Max 69. Hammersmith Is Out (& d) 72. One of Our Dinosaurs Is Missing 75. Logan's Run 76. Treasure of Matecumbe 76. The Purple Taxi 77. The Last Remake of Beau Geste 77. Jesus of Nazareth (TV) 77. *Death on the Nile* (as Hercule Poirot) 78. Ashanti 78. The Thief of Baghdad (TV) 79. Charlie Chan and the Curse of the Dragon Queen 81. Evil Under the Sun 82. Memed My Hawk (& w, d) 83. Murder with Mirrors (TV) 85. Thirteen at Dinner (TV) 85. Dead Man's Folly (TV) 86. Appointment with Death 88. La Révolution Française 89. C'era un Castello con 40 Cani 90. Lorenzo's Oil 92. The Dancer 93. The Old Curiosity Shop (TV) 95. Stiff Upper Lips 97. Animal Farm (voice, TV) 99. the Bachelor 99, etc.
■ AS DIRECTOR -WRITER: School for Secrets 46. *Vice Versa* 48. *Private Angelo* 49. Romanoff and Juliet 61. Billy Budd 62. Lady L 65.
TV series: Planet Ustinov 98.

Uys, Jamie (1921–1996)
South African producer, writer and director, the first from his country to gain an international reputation, achieved with his comedy *The Gods Must Be Crazy*, the success of which he tried, but failed, to duplicate in a sequel. An Afrikaner, born in Boksburg, he studied mathematics at the University of Pretoria and worked as a teacher and farmer before becoming a film-maker, financing all his own films to retain his independence.
Rip Van Winkle 60. *Dingaka* 64. The Professor and the Beauty Queen 67. Dirkie 69. Lost in the Desert 70. *The Gods Must Be Crazy* 81. Beautiful People II 83. The Gods Must Be Crazy II 89, etc.

V

Vacano, Jost (1934–)
German cinematographer, noted for his work with director Paul Verhoeven.
The Lost Honour of Katharina Blum/Die Verlorene Ehre der Katharina Blum 75. Soldier of Orange/Soldaat van Oranje 77. Spetters 80. The Boat/Das Boot (AAN) 82. The Neverending Story 84. 52 Pick-Up 86. Robocop 87. Rocket Gibraltar 88. Total Recall 90. Untamed Heart 93. Showgirls 95. Starship Troopers 97, etc.

Vaccaro, Brenda (1939–)
American character actress.
Midnight Cowboy 69. Where It's At 69. I Love My Wife 70. Summertree 71. What's a Nice Girl Like You … (TV) 72. Honor Thy Father 73. Sunshine (TV) 74. Once Is Not Enough (AAN) 76. The House by the Lake 77. Airport 77 77. Capricorn One 78. Fast Charlie the Moonbeam Rider 78. Supergirl 84. Water 84. Cookie 89. Heart of Midnight 89. Masque of the Red Death 90. Lethal Games 90. Love Affair 94. The Mirror Has Two Faces 96, etc.
TV series: Sara 76. Dear Detective 79.

Vachon, Christine (1962–)
American producer of independent films.
Swoon 92. Go Fish 94. Kids 95. Safe 95. I Shot Andy Warhol 96. Office Killer 97. Kiss Me Guido 97. Velvet Goldmine 98. Happiness 98. I'm Losing You 98, etc.

Vadim, Roger (1928–2000) (Roger Vadim Plemiannikow)
French writer-director. His wives included Brigitte BARDOT (1952–57) and Jane FONDA (1965–73). He had a son by actress Catherine DENEUVE.
Autobiography: 1986, *Bardot, Deneuve and Fonda: The Memoirs of Roger Vadim*.
Futures Vedettes (w) 54. *And God Created Woman* (wd) 56. Heaven Fell That Night (wd) 57. *Les Liaisons Dangereuses* (wd) 59. Warrior's Rest (wd) 62. Vice and Virtue (wd) 62. La Ronde (wd) 64. Nutty Naughty Château/Château en Suède 64. The Game Is Over (wd) 66. Histoires Extraordinaires (part) 68. Barbarella 68. Pretty Maids All in a Row 71. Don Juan 73. Night Games 79. Rich and Famous (a) 81. Hot Touch 81. Surprise Party 82. Come Back 83. Into the Night (a) 85. And God Created Woman 88. Mad Love/Amour Fou 94, etc.

Vague, Vera
See ALLEN, Barbara Jo.

Vajna, Andrew
Hungarian-born production executive, a co-founder of Carolco in 1976 and, following his departure, chief executive of Cinergi Pictures until that company went out of business in 1997. In 1998, following the liquidation of the company, he formed a new partnership with his former partner Mario KASSAR.
First Blood 82. Rambo 85. Angel Heart 86. Red Heat 88. Total Recall 90. Tombstone 93. Renaissance Man 94. Color of Night 94. Die Hard with a Vengeance 95. Judge Dredd 95. The Scarlet Letter 95. Nixon 95. Evita 97, etc.

Valdez, Luis (1940–)
American director, screenwriter and dramatist. Of Mexican ancestry, he first worked in the theatre, and his first film was based on his own play.
Zoot Suit 81. La Bamba 87. The Cisco Kid (TV) 94.

Vale, Virginia (1920–) (Dorothy Howe)
Blonde American actress who was credited as 'the most beautiful woman in Westerns'. Born in Dallas, Texas, she began as a Paramount starlet under her real name before winning a 'Gateway to Hollywood' talent contest run by Jesse L. Lasky, which gave her a three year contract with RKO. Retired in the early 40s to become a secretary.
Cocoanut Grove 38. Her Jungle Love 38. King of Alcatraz 38. The Marshal of Mesa City 39. Legion of the Lawless 40. Bullet Code 40. Triple Justice 40. Prairie Law 40. Millionaires in Prison 40. Robbers of the Range 41. Crime Incorporated 45. The Fired Man 45, etc.

Valens, Ritchie (1941–1959) (Ritchie Valenzuela)
American rock singer and songwriter who appeared as himself in one movie before being killed in the same plane crash as singer Buddy HOLLY. He was played by Lou Diamond Phillips in the biopic *La Bamba* 87.
Go Johnny Go 58. Rock and Roll – The Early Days (doc) 84.

Valenti, Jack (1921–)
American executive, dynamic president of the Motion Picture Association of America.

Valentine, Joseph (1900–1949) (Giuseppe Valentino)
Italian-American cinematographer, long in Hollywood.
Curlytop 24. Speakeasy 29. Soup to Nuts 30. Night of Terror 33. Remember Last Night 35. The Moon's Our Home 36. Three Smart Girls 36. One Hundred Men and a Girl 37. Mad About Music 38. That Certain Age 38. First Love 39. My Little Chickadee 40. Spring Parade 40. *The Wolf Man* 41. *Saboteur* 42. *Shadow of a Doubt* 43. Guest Wife 45. Tomorrow Is Forever 46. Magnificent Doll 46. Possessed 47. *Sleep My Love* 48. *Rope* 48. Joan of Arc (AA) 48. Bride for Sale 49, etc.

Valentine, Karen (1948–)
American light actress who has had most success on television.
Gidget Grows Up (TV) 69. The Daughters of Joshua Cabe (TV) 72. Coffee, Tea or Me? (TV) 73. The Girl Who Came Gift Wrapped (TV) 74. Having Babies (TV) 76. Murder at the World Series (TV) 77. Go West Young Girl (TV) 78. The North Avenue Irregulars 78. Muggable Mary: Street Cop (TV) 82. Children in the Crossfire (TV) 84. Perfect People (TV) 88. The Power Within 95, etc.
TV series: *Room 222* 69–72. Karen 75. Our Time 85.

Valentino, Rudolph (1895–1926) (Rodolpho d'Antonguolla)
Italian-American leading man, the great romantic idol of the 20s; his personality still shows. His sudden death caused several suicides and his funeral was a national event.
There have been two films called *Valentino*. Anthony Dexter played him in 1951, Rudolf Nureyev in 1977. A TV movie, *The Legend of Valentino*, appeared in 1975 with Franco Nero.
Biography: 1926, *Rudy* by his wife, Natacha Rambova. 1927, *The Real Valentino* by George S. Ullman. 1952, *Valentino* by Alan Arnold. *Rudolph Valentino* by Robert Oberfirst. 1962, *The Man behind the Myth*. 1967, *Valentino* by Irving Shulman. 1976, *Valentino the Love God* by Noel Botham and Peter Donnelly.
■ My Official Wife 14. Patria 16. Alimony 18. A Society Sensation 18. All Night 18. The Delicious Little Devil 19. A Rogue's Romance 19. The Homebreaker 19. Virtuous Sinners 19. The Big Little Person 19. Out of Luck 19. Eyes of Youth 19. The Married Virgin 20. An Adventuress 20. The Cheater 20. Passion's Playground 20. Once to Every Woman 20. Stolen Moments 20. The Wonderful Chance 20. *The Four Horseman of the Apocalypse* (the part that made him a super-star) 21. Unchained Seas 21. Camille 21. The Conquering Power 21. *The Sheik* 21. Moran of the Lady Letty 21. Beyond the Rocks 22. The Young Rajah 22. *Blood and Sand* 22. *Monsieur Beaucaire* 24. A Sainted Devil 24. Cobra 24. *The Eagle* 25. *Son of the Sheik* 26.
✪ For turning animal magnetism into at least the semblance of talent. *The Eagle*.
❝ His acting is largely confined to protruding his large, almost occult eyes until the vast areas of white are visible, drawing back the lips of his wide, sensuous mouth to bare his gleaming teeth, and flaring his nostrils. –
Thus Adolph Zukor's famous put-down; but Valentino's simple technique was very effective on female audiences the world over. Yet in the year of his death, 1926, he wrote: 'A man should control his life. Mine is controlling me.'
And H. L. Mencken summed him up: 'He was essentially a highly respectable young man; his predicament touched me. Here was one who was catnip to women … he had youth and fame … and yet he was very unhappy.'

Valk, Frederick (1901–1956)
Heavyweight Czech stage actor, in Britain from 1939.
Gasbags 40. *Thunder Rock* 42. *Dead of Night* 45. Latin Quarter 46. An Outcast of the Islands 51. Top Secret 52. The Colditz Story 53. Zarak 55, etc.

Vallee, Rudy (1901–1986) (Hubert Vallee)
American character comedian, the former crooning idol of the late 20s; in the early 40s Preston Sturges gave him a new lease of life.
Autobiography: 1976, *Let the Chips Fall*.
Biography: 1997, My *Vagabond Lover* by Eleanor Vallee (with Jill Amadio).
The Vagabond Lover 29. Sweet Music 34. Gold Diggers in Paris 38. Second Fiddle 39. Too Many Blondes 41. *The Palm Beach Story* 42. Happy Go Lucky 43. It's in the Bag 45. *The Bachelor and the Bobbysoxer* 47. Unfaithfully Yours 48. The Beautiful Blonde from Bashful Bend 49. Ricochet Romance 54. Gentlemen Marry Brunettes 55. The Helen Morgan Story 57. *How to Succeed in Business Without Really Trying* (his stage role) 67. Live a Little, Love a Little 68. Won Ton Ton 76, etc.
❝ People called me the guy with the cock in his voice. Maybe that's why in 84 years of life I've been with over 145 women and girls. – *R.V. in the RKO Story*
Famous line (*The Palm Beach Story*) 'That's one of the tragedies of life – that the men most in need of a beating-up are always enormous.'

Vallejo, Gerardo (1942–)
Argentinian director of documentaries of country life, a member of the radical collective CINE LIBERACION. He went into exile in the mid-70s, working in Panama and Spain before returning home in the mid-80s.
El Camino hacia la Muerte del Viejo Reales 69. Reflexiones de un Salvaje (Sp.) 78. El Rigor del Destino 84. Otra Historia de Amor de Buenos Aires 87, etc.

Valli, Alida (1921–) (Alida Maria Altenburger)
Beautiful Italian actress.
I Due Sergenti 36. Manon Lescaut 39. Piccolo Mondo Antico 41. Eugénie Grandet 46. The Paradine Case (US) 47. The Miracle of the Bells 48. *The Third Man* 49. Walk Softly Stranger 49. The White Tower 50. The Lovers of Toledo 52. *Senso* 53. The Stranger's Hand 53. Heaven Fell That Night 57. The Sea Wall/This Angry Age 57. Le Dialogue des Carmélites 59. Ophelia 61. Une Aussi Longue Absence 61. The Spider's Stratagem 71. 1900 76. The Cassandra Crossing 77. Suspiria 77. Aspern 82. Il Lungo Silenzio 93. A Month by the Lake 94. The Sweet Noise of Life/Il Dolce Rumore Della Vita 99, etc.

Valli, Virginia (1898–1968) (Virginia McSweeney)
American silent screen heroine who retired in 1932 to marry Charles Farrell.
Efficiency Edgar's Courtship 17. The Storm 22. A Lady of Quality 23. Paid to Love 27. Isle of Lost Ships 32, etc.

Vallone, Raf (1916–)
Italian leading man, former journalist.
Bitter Rice 48. Vendetta 49. Il Cristo Proibito 50. Anna 51. Thérèse Raquin 53. The Beach 53. The Sign of Venus 55. El Cid 61. *A View from the Bridge* (US) 61. Phaedra 62. The Cardinal 63. Harlow 65. Beyond the Mountains 66. The Italian Job 69. Cannon for Cordoba 70. A Gunfight 71. Rosebud 75. The Human Factor 75. The Other Side of Midnight 77. The Greek Tycoon 78. An Almost Perfect Affair 79. A Time to Die 79. Lion of the Desert 80. The Scarlet and the Black (TV) 83. Power of Evil 85. The Godfather Part III 90, etc.

Vampira (1921–) (Maila Nurmi)
Finnish-born actress in America, a former chorus girl best known as a presenter of late-night horror movies on TV, and for her role as a Ghoul Girl in Ed WOOD's *Plan Nine from Outer Space*. She was played by Lisa Marie in the biopic *Ed Wood*.
The Beat Generation 59. The Big Operator 59. Plan Nine from Outer Space 59. Night of the Ghouls 59. Sex Kittens Go to College 60. The Magic Sword/Saint George and the Seven Curses 61. Vampira: About Sex, Death, and Taxes (doc) 96, etc.

Van, Bobby (1930–1980) (Robert Stein King)
American song-and-dance man who went out of fashion with musicals but found a new audience in his 40s and became a TV personality.
■ Because You're Mine 52. Small Town Girl 52. Kiss Me Kate 53. The Navy Versus the Night Monsters 66. *Lost Horizon* 73. Lost Flight (TV) 73.

Van Cleef, Lee (1925–1989)
American character actor who after years as a sneaky western villain found fame and fortune as the hero of tough Italian westerns.
High Noon 52. Arena 53. Yellow Tomahawk 54. A Man Alone 55. Joe Dakota 57. Guns Girls and Gangsters 58. The Man Who Shot Liberty Valance 62. *For a Few Dollars More* 65. Day of Anger 66. *The Good the Bad and the Ugly* 67. Death Rides a Horse 67. Sabata 69. Barquero 70. El Condor 70. Captain Apache 71. Bad Man's River 71. The Magnificent Seven Ride 72. Take a Hard Ride 75. Vendetta 76. God's Gun 77. Kid Vengeance 77. The Octagon 80. Escape from New York 81. The Squeeze 82. Jungle Raiders 84. Armed Response 86. Speed Zone 88. Thieves of Fortune 89, etc.
❝ Being born with a beady-eyed sneer was the luckiest thing that ever happened to me. – *L.V.C.*

Van Damme, Jean-Claude (1960–) (Jean-Claude Van Varenberg)
Belgian actor in Hollywood action films. A former kickboxing champion, he is sometimes known as 'The Muscles from Brussels'. He married for the sixth time in 1999, when he wed again his third wife.
No Retreat, No Surrender 86. Black Eagle 88. Bloodsport 88. Kickboxer 89. Cyborg 89. Death Warrant 90. Double Impact (& co-w) 91. Universal Soldier 92. Nowhere to Run 93. Timecop 94. Streetfighter 95. Sudden Death 95. Maximum Risk 96. The Quest (& d) 96. The Exchange 96. The Colony 97. Knock Off 98. Universal Soldier: The Return 99, etc.
❝ He does what he does very well – kick boxing and stuff – but acting is not his forte. Neither is being humble. – *Rosanna Arquette*

Van de Sande, Theo (1947–)
Dutch cinematographer, in international films.
The Girl with the Red Hair 83. The Assault 86. Crossing Delancey 88. Rooftops 89. Once Around 91. Wayne's World 92. Erotic Tales 94. Bushwhacked 95. Volcano 97. Blade 98. Cruel Intentions 99. Big Daddy 99. Little Nicky 00, etc.

Van de Ven, Monique (1952–)
Dutch leading actress, best known internationally for her role in Paul Verhoeven's *Turkish Delight*, in

which she appeared after leaving acting school. Moved briefly to the United States with her then husband, cinematographer Jan De Bont.

Turkish Delight/Turks Fruit 73. Dakota 74. A Girl Called Keetje Tippel 75. A Woman Like Eve/Een Vrouw Als Eva 79. *Dreamland*/Ademloos 82. Burning Love/Brendende Liefde 83. *The Scorpion*/De Schorpiden 84. The Assault/De Aanslag 86. Iris 87. Amsterdamned 88. *Romeo* 90. The Man Inside 90. Paint It Black (US) 90. Eline Vere 91, etc.

Van den Ende, Walther
Belgian cinematographer.

Wedding in Galilee/Noce En Galilee 87. The Music Teacher/Le Maitre De Musique 88. Toto Le Héros 91. Farinelli Il Castrato 94. The Eighth Day/Le Huitième Jour 96. Left Luggage 98. A Dog of Flanders (US) 99, etc.

Van Der Beek, James (1977–)
American actor, best known for his role as Dawson Leery in the TV teenage soap opera *Dawson's Creek*. Born in Chesire, Connecticut, he began acting in his early 'teens and was working off-Broadway at the age of 17.

Angus 95. I Love You, I Love You Not 96. Varsity Blues 99. Harvest 99. Texas Rangers 01, etc.

TV series: Dawson's Creek 98- .

Van Devere, Trish (1943–) (Patricia Dressel)
American leading lady of the 70s. She married actor George C. Scott in 1972.

Where's Poppa? 70. The Last Run 71. One Is a Lonely Number 72. The Day of the Dolphins 73. Beauty and the Beast (TV) 76. Movie Movie 78. The Hearse 80. The Changeling 80. Uphill All the Way (TV) 85. Hollywood Vice Squad 86. Messenger of Death 88. Deadly Currents 93, etc.

❝ Barely more than a smiling hole in the air. – *Sunday Times*

Van Dien, Caspar (1968–)
Square-jawed American actor, from television, who took over the role of Tarzan in 1998. Born in Ridgefield, New Jersey, he studied at the Admiral Farragut Military Academy, and at Florida State University, where he intended to study medicine; instead he began acting and moved to Los Angeles. Formerly married to actress Carrie Mitchum, granddaughter of actor Robert Mitchum.

Night Eyes 4: Fatal Passion 95. Beastmaster 3: The Eye of Braxus 95. James Dean: Race with Destiny 95. Starship Troopers 97. On the Border 97. Tarzan and the Lost City 98. Modern Vampires/Revenant 98. Sleepy Hollow 99, etc.

TV series: Titans 00.

Van Dine, S. S. (1888–1939) (Willard Huntingdon Wright)
American author who created the wealthy man-about-town detective Philo Vance, personified on screen by several actors. William Powell played him in *The Canary Murder Case* 29, *The Greene Murder Case* 29, *The Benson Murder Case* 30, and *The Kennel Murder Case* 33. Basil Rathbone had one attempt, *The Bishop Murder Case* 30. Warren William took over for *The Dragon Murder Case* 34 and *The Gracie Allen Murder Case* 39. Meanwhile there were Paul Lukas in *The Casino Murder Case* 35, Edmund Lowe in *The Garden Murder Case* 36, and Grant Richards in *Night of Mystery* 37. 1940 brought James Stephenson in *Calling Philo Vance*; in 1947 there was William Wright in *Philo Vance Returns*; and Alan Curtis in 1948 appeared in two poor attempts, *Philo Vance's Gamble* and *Philo Vance's Secret Mission*.

Van Doren, Mamie (1933–) (Joan Lucille Olander)
American leading lady, the blonde bombshell of the second feature, in Hollywood from 1954.

Autobiography: 1987, *Playing the Field*.

Forbidden (debut) 54. Yankee Pasha 54. The Second Greatest Sex 55. Running Wild 55. The Girl in Black Stockings 56. Teacher's Pet 58. The Navy versus the Night Monsters 66. Free Ride 85, etc.

Van Dormael, Jaco (1957–)
Belgian director and screenwriter.

In Heaven as on Earth (co-w) 91. Toto the Hero (wd) 91. The Eighth Day (wd) 96.

Van Druten, John (1901–1957)
Prolific English playwright, novelist and theatre director. Born in London, of Dutch parents, he studied law at London University, and achieved success as a writer in America, emigrating in 1938 and becoming an American citizen in 1944. His successful play, *I Am a Camera*, an adaptation of Christopher Isherwood's *Goodbye to Berlin*, has been filmed twice, the second time as the musical *Cabaret*. His long-time companion was actor and theatrical producer Walter Starke.

Autobiography: 1957, *The Widening Circle*.

■ Young Woodley 30. After Office Hours/London Wall 31. New Morals for Old/After All 32. If I Were Free/Behold We Live 33. One Night in Lisbon/There's Always Juliet 41. Old Acquaintance 43 and 81 (as Rich and Famous). Gaslight (co-w, AAN) 44. Voice of the Turtle 47. I Remember Mama 48. I Am a Camera 55. Bell, Book and Candle 58. Cabaret 72.

Van Dyke, Dick (1925–)
Lanky American TV comedian who never quite made it in movies.

■ Bye Bye Birdie 63. What a Way to Go 64. *Mary Poppins* 64. The Art of Love 65. Lt Robin Crusoe 65. Never a Dull Moment 67. Divorce American Style 67. Fitzwilly 67. Chitty Chitty Bang Bang 68. *The Comic* 69. Some Kind of a Nut 70. Cold Turkey 71. The Morning After (TV) 74. The Runner Stumbles 79. Dropout Father (TV) 82. Found Money (TV) 84. The Wrong Way Kid (TV) 84. Strong Medicine (TV) 86. Ghost of a Chance (TV) 87. Dick Tracy 90.

TV series: *The Dick Van Dyke Show* 61–66. The New Dick Van Dyke Show 71–72. Diagnosis Murder 93-00.

❝ I never wanted to be an actor, and to this day I don't. I can't get a handle on it. An actor wants to become someone else. I am a song-and-dance man and I enjoy being myself, which is all I can do. – *D.V.D.*

Van Dyke, W(oodbridge) S(trong) (1889–1943)
Competent, adaptable American director, at his peak in the 30s. Born in San Diego, California, he was on stage for 25 years from childhood before becoming an assistant to D. W. Griffith on *Intolerance*, and soon after turned to directing. Noted for his speed in finishing films ahead of time, he was nicknamed 'One-Take Woody'. His exploits filming *Trader Horn* in Africa made him the model for film director Carl Denham in *King Kong*.

■ Men of the Desert 18. Gift of Gab 18. Land of Long Shadows 18. Open Spaces 18. Lady of the Dugout 19. Our Little Nell 20. According to Hoyle 22. Boss of Camp 4 22. Forget Me Not 22. Little Girl Next Door 23. Miracle Makers 23. Loving Lies 23. You Are In Danger 23. The Destroying Angel 23. The Battling Fool 24. Winner Take All 24. Barriers Burned Away 24. Half Dollar Bill 24. The Beautiful Sinner 25. Gold Heels 25. Hearts and Spurs 25. The Trail Rider 25. Ranger of the Big Pines 25. The Timber Wolf 25. The Desert's Price 25. The Gentle Cyclone 26. War Paint 26. Winners of the Wilderness 27. Heart of the Yukon 27. Eyes of the Totem 27. Foreign Devils 27. California 27. Spoilers of the West 27. Wyoming 28. Under the Black Eagle 28. *White Shadows in the South Seas* 28. The Pagan 29. *Trader Horn* 30. Never the Twain Shall Meet 31. Guilty Hands 31. Cuban Love Song 32. *Tarzan the Ape Man* 32. Night World 32. Penthouse 33. Eskimo 33. The Prizefighter and the Lady 33. Laughing Boy 34. Hideout 34. *Manhattan Melodrama* 34. *The Thin Man* (AAN) 34. Forsaking all Others 35. Naughty Marietta 35. I Live My Life 35. Rose Marie 36. *San Francisco* (AAN) 36. His Brother's Wife 36. The Devil is a Sissy 36. Love on the Run 36. After the Thin Man 36. Personal Property 37. They Gave Him a Gun 37. Rosalie 37. Marie Antoinette 38. *Sweethearts* 38. Stand Up and Fight 39. It's a Wonderful World 39. Andy Hardy Gets Spring Fever 39. Another Thin Man 39. I Take This Woman 40. I Love You Again 40. Bitter Sweet 40. Rage in Heaven 41. The Feminine Touch 41. Shadow of the Thin Man 41. Dr Kildare's Victory 41. I Married an Angel 42. Cairo 42. Journey for Margaret 42.

❝ Woody cut as he shot. He used his camera as though it were a six-shooter and he was the fastest gun in Hollywood. Actors rarely got more than one take on any scene, then the camera was moved rapidly to another set-up. – *Robert Taylor*

Van Enger, Charles (1890–1980)
American cinematographer.

Treasure Island 20. A Doll's House 22. The Famous Mrs Fair 23. The Marriage Circle 24. Forbidden Paradise 24. *Phantom of the Opera* 25. Kiss Me Again 25. Puppets 26. Easy Pickings 27. Port of Missing Girls 28. Fox Movietone Follies 29. High Society Blues 30. Mad Parade 31. I Was a Spy 33. The Case of Gabriel Perry 34. Seven Sinners 36. Wife Doctor and Nurse 37. Miracle on Main Street 40. Never Give a Sucker an Even Break 41. Night Monster 42. Sherlock Holmes Faces Death 43. The Merry Monahans 44. That Night with You 45. The Time of Their Lives 46. The Wistful Widow 47. Abbott and Costello Meet Frankenstein 48. Africa Screams 49. Ma and Pa Kettle Back on the Farm 51. The Magnetic Monster 53. Sitting Bull 54. Time Table 56. Gun Fever 58, many others.

Van Eyck, Peter (1911–1969)
Blond German actor, in America from mid-30s, later international.

The Moon is Down 42. Five Graves to Cairo 43. Rommel, Desert Fox 51. *The Wages of Fear* 53. Retour de Manivelle 57. The Girl Rosemarie 58. The Snorkel 58. Foxhole in Cairo 60. Station Six Sahara 63. The Spy Who Came in from the Cold 65. Million Dollar Man 67. Shalako 68. Assignment to Kill 69, many others.

Van Eyssen, John (1922–1995)
South African actor who appeared in a number of British films before turning agent. Chief production executive in Britain for Columbia 1969–73.

Quatermass II 56. Dracula 57. I'm All Right Jack 59. The Criminal 60. Exodus 60, etc.

Van Fleet, Jo (1919–1996)
American character actress who usually played older than her real age.

■ *East of Eden* (AA) 55. The Rose Tattoo 55. I'll Cry Tomorrow 55. The King and Four Queens 56. Gunfight at the OK Corral 57. This Angry Age 58. *Wild River* 60. Cool Hand Luke 67. I Love You Alice B. Toklas 67. 80 Steps to Jonah 69. The Gang that Couldn't Shoot Straight 72. The Tenant 76.

Van Gogh, Vincent (1853–1890)
The tormented Dutch post-Impressionist artist who went mad and shot himself has attracted the attention of several film-makers. In 1956 Vincente Minnelli made the big-budget biopic *Lust for Life* starring Kirk Douglas, which garnered Anthony Quinn an Oscar for his brief supporting role as Gauguin, and since then there have been several art films: Paul Cox's documentary *Vincent: The Life and Death of Vincent van Gogh* 87, with the voice of John Hurt reading from the painter's letters; Robert Altman's *Vincent and Theo* 90, starring Tim Roth and Paul Rhys, which concentrated on his relationship with his brother; and Maurice Pialat's *Van Gogh* 91, starring Jacques Dutronc, which dealt with the final three months of the artist's life.

Van Heusen, Jimmy (1913–1990)
American songwriter, usually with lyrics by Johnny Burke: 'Swinging on a Star' (AA 1944), 'Sunday, Monday or Always', 'Sunshine Cake', many others. His later partner was lyricist Sammy Cahn, with whom he wrote such songs as 'All the Way', 'High Hopes' and 'Call Me Irresponsible'.

The Tender Trap 55. The Joker Is Wild 57. Some Came Running 58. A Hole in the Head 59. The World of Suzie Wong 60. The Road to Hong Kong 62. A Walk on the Wild Side 62. Papa's Delicate Condition 63. Robin and the Seven Hoods 64 (s 'My Kind of Town'). Thoroughly Modern Millie 67. Love and Marriage 69.

Van Horn, Buddy
American director.

Any Which Way You Can 80. Date with an Angel 87. The Dead Pool 88. Pink Cadillac 91, etc.

Van Pallandt, Nina (1932–)
Danish actress, a former singer.

The Long Goodbye 73. Guilty or Innocent (TV) 75. Quintet 78. A Wedding 79. American Gigolo 80. Cloud Dancer 80. Cutter's Way 81. Jungle Warriors 85, etc.

Van Parys, Georges (1902–1971)
French composer.

Le Million 31. Jeunesse 34. Café de Paris 38. Le Silence Est d'Or 46. Fanfan la Tulipe 51. Adorables Créatures 52. Les Diaboliques 55. French Cancan 55. Charmants Garçons 57, many others.

Van Patten, Dick (1928–)
Chubby American character actor usually in comedy roles; brother of Joyce Van Patten.

Joe Kidd 72. Westworld 73. The Strongest Man in the World 75. Gus 76. Freaky Friday 77. High Anxiety 77. The New Adventures of Pippi Longstocking 88. Robin Hood: Men in Tights 93. Love Is All There Is 96. Demolition High 96. Love Is All There Is 96, etc.

TV series: Mama 49–57. The Partners 71–72. The New Dick Van Dyke Show 73–74. When Things Were Rotten 75. Eight Is Enough 77–81.

Van Patten, Joyce (1934–)
American leading lady of the 70s. Sister of Dick Van Patten. Married actors Martin Balsam and Dennis Dugan.

The Goddess 58. I Love You Alice B. Toklas 68. Something Big 71. The Bravos (TV) 72. Thumb Tripping 72. The Manchu Eagle Murder Caper Mystery 75. The Bad News Bears 76. Mikey and Nicky 76. Billy Galvin 86. Monkey Shines 88. Breathing Lessons (TV) 94, etc.

TV series: The Good Guys 68–70. The Don Rickles Show 72. The Mary Tyler Moore Hour 79.

Van Peebles, Mario (1957–)
American director, screenwriter and actor. He is the son of Melvin Van Peebles.

Sweet Sweetback's Baadasss Song (a) 71. Cotton Club (a) 84. Exterminator II (a) 84. Rappin' (a, s) 85. South Bronx Heroes (a) 86. Hot Shot (a) 86. Last Resort (a) 86. Heartbreak Ridge (a) 86. Jaws 4 – the Revenge (a) 87. Identity Crisis (w) 89. New Jack City (wd) 91. Gunmen (a) 93. Posse (a, d) 93. Erotic Tales (co-d) 94. Panther (d) 95. Solo (a) 97. Gang in Blue (co-d, TV) 97. Riot (a) 97. Stag (a) 97. Los Locos (a, co-p, w) 97. Love Kills (a, wd) 98, etc.

Van Peebles, Melvin (1932–)
American director.

The Story of a Three-Day Pass 67. Watermelon Man 69. *Sweet Sweetback's Baadasss Song* 71. Identity Crisis 89. Panther (w) 95. Gang in Blue (co-d, TV) 97. Bellyful/Le Conte Du Ventre Plein (wd, m) (Fr./Neth.) 00, etc.

Van Rooten, Luis (1906–1973)
Mexican-born American character actor.

The Hitler Gang (as Himmler) 44. Two Years before the Mast 44. To the Ends of the Earth 48. Champion 49. Detective Story 51. The Sea Chase 55, etc.

Van Runkle, Theadora
American costume designer.

Bonnie and Clyde (AAN) 67. The Thomas Crown Affair 68. Mame 74. The Godfather Part II (AAN) 74. New York, New York 77. S.O.B. 81. The Best Little Whorehouse in Texas 82. Peggy Sue Got Married (AAN) 86. Stella 90. Butcher's Wife 91. Leap of Faith 92. Kiss of Death 95. The Last Don (TV) 97. Goodbye, Lover 98, etc.

Van Sant, Gus (1952–)
American director, screenwriter and musician, a former ad-man and assistant to Roger Corman.

Mala Noche 85. Drugstore Cowboy 89. My Own Private Idaho 91. Even Cowgirls Get the Blues (wd) 93. To Die For 95. *Good Will Hunting* (AAN) 97. Psycho 98. Finding Forrester 00, etc.

❝ I guess I'm a post-modernist. – G.V.S.

Van Sloan, Edward (1882–1964)
American character actor with stage experience; often seen as elderly professor.

Dracula 30. *Frankenstein* 31. The Mummy 33. Death Takes a Holiday 34. The Last Days of Pompeii 35. *Dracula's Daughter* 36. The Phantom Creeps 39. The Doctor Takes a Wife 40. The Conspirators 44. The Mask of Dijon 47. A Foreign Affair 47, etc.

Van Upp, Virginia (1912–1970)
American executive producer, at Columbia in the late 40s. Former writer.

Young and Willing 40. The Crystal Ball 42. Cover Girl 44. The Impatient Years (& p) 44. Together Again (& p) 45, etc.

Van Vorhees, Westbrook (1904–1968)
American commentator whose familiar stentorian voice as narrator of *The March of Time* was widely imitated.

Van Warmerdam, Alex (1952–)
Dutch director, screenwriter, and actor, an art school graduate who began as a theatre designer and writer.
Abel (a, wd) 85. *The Northerners*/De Noorderlingen (a, wd) 92. The Dress/De Jurk (wd) 96. Little Tony/Kleine Teun (a, p, wd) 98, etc.

Van Zandt, Philip (1904–1958)
Dutch character actor, in Hollywood films. Born in Amsterdam, he was in Hollywood from the late 30s. Died from an overdose of sleeping pills.
Citizen Kane 41. House of Frankenstein 45. April Showers 48. The Vicious Circle 48. Viva Zapata 52. Knock on Wood 54. Gog 54. The Pride and the Passion 57, etc.

Vanbrugh, Irene (1872–1949) (Irene Barnes)
Distinguished British stage actress. Films rare.
Autobiography: 1978, *To Tell My Story*.
The Gay Lord Quex 27. Moonlight Sonata 37.

Vance, Courtney B. (1960–)
American actor of stage and screen, born in Detroit, Michigan.
Hamburger Hill 87. The Hunt for Red October 90. Fixing the Shadow 92. The Adventures of Huck Finn 93. Holy Matrimony 94. Dangerous Minds 95. Panther 95. The Tuskagee Airmen (TV) 95. The Last Supper 96. The Preacher's Wife 96. 12 Angry Men (TV) 97. Cookie's Fortune 99. Space Cowboys 00, etc.

Vance, Danitra (1959–1994)
American actress, from the stage, and a regular on TV's *Saturday Night Live*. Died of cancer.
Sticky Fingers 88. Limit Up 89. Little Man Tate 91. Jumpin' at the Boneyard 92, etc.

Vance, Vivian (1911–1979)
Cheerful American character comedienne, long a partner of Lucille Ball in various TV series.
The Secret Fury 50. The Blue Veil 51. The Great Race 65, etc.

Vance-Straker, Marilyn
American costume designer.
Fast Times at Ridgemont High 82. 48 Hrs 82. Romancing the Stone 84. Pretty in Pink 86. Predator 87. The Untouchables (AAN) 87. Die Hard 88. Road House 89. Pretty Woman 90. Die Hard 2 90. Predator 2 90. Hudson Hawk 91. The Rocketeer 91. Ricochet 91. The Last Boy Scout 91. Medicine Man 92. Sommersby 93. Judgment Night 93. Street Fighter 94. The Getaway 94. Jade 95. GI Jane 97, etc.

Vanel, Charles (1892–1989)
French character actor, with stage experience.
Les Misérables 33. Le Grand Jeu 34. La Belle Equipe 36. Légion d'Honneur 38. Carrefour 39. *La Ferme du Pendu* 45. In Nome della Legge 49. *The Wages of Fear* 53. Maddalena 54. *Les Diaboliques* 55. Rafles sur la Ville 57. Le Dialogue des Carmélites 59. La Vérité 60. Un Homme de Trop 67. La Puce et le Privé 79, many others.

Vangelis (1943–) (Vangelis Papathanassiou)
Greek composer.
Chariots of Fire (AA) 81. Missing 82. Blade Runner 82. The Bounty 84. Nosferatu a Venezia 87. Francesco 89. Bitter Moon 92, etc.

Vanity (1958–) (aka D. D. Winters, born Denise Matthews)
American leading actress and singer, in action movies.
Terror Train 80. Tanya's Island 81. The Last Dragon 85. 52 Pickup 86. Never Too Young to Die 86. Deadly Illusion/Love You to Death 87. Action Jackson 88. Memories of Murder 90. Neon City 91. DaVinci's War 92. South Beach 92, etc.

Vanna, Nina (1902–) (Nina Yarsikova)
Beautiful Russian leading actress who fled the revolution and had a brief career in English and European films.
Guy Fawkes (GB) 23. *The Man without Desire* (GB) 23. The Cost of Beauty (GB) 24. In the Night Watch/Veille d'Armes 24. We Women (GB) 25. The Woman Tempted (GB) 26. The Triumph of the Rat (GB) 27. Café Electric (Aus.) 27. Manner vor der Ehe (Ger.) 27, etc.

Varconi, Victor (1896–1976) (Mihaly Varkonyi)
Hungarian actor long in Hollywood.
Autobiography: 1976, *It's Not Enough to Be Hungarian*.
The Volga Boatmen 26. King of Kings 27. The Divine Lady (as Nelson) 29. The Doomed Battalion 31. Roberta 34. The Plainsman 36. Disputed Passage 39. Reap the Wild Wind 42. For Whom the Bell Tolls 43. Samson and Delilah 49, etc.

Varda, Agnès (1928–)
Belgian-born writer-director of the 'left bank' school. She was married to director Jacques DEMY.
La Pointe Courte 56. Cléo de 5 à 7 62. Le Bonheur 65. Les Créatures 66. Lions Love 69. One Sings, the Other Doesn't/L'Une Chante, l'Autre Pas 77. Vagabond/Sans Toit ni Loi 85. Kung Fu Master!/Le Petit Amour 87. Jane B. par Agnes V. 88. Jacquot de Nantes 91. Les Cent et Une Nuits/A Hundred and One Nights 95. The World of Jacques Demy (doc) 95. The Gleaners and I (doc) 00, etc.

Varden, Evelyn (1895–1958)
American stage character actress who made several films.
Pinky 49. Cheaper by the Dozen 50. Phone Call from a Stranger 52. The Student Prince 54. Night of the Hunter 55. The Bad Seed 56, etc.

Varden, Norma (1899–1989)
British character actress, usually as haughty aristocrat in comedies; went to Hollywood in the 40s.
A Night Like This 32. The Iron Duke 35. Foreign Affairs 36. Shipyard Sally 39. Random Harvest 42. The Green Years 46. Strangers on a Train 51. Gentlemen Prefer Blondes 53. *Witness for the Prosecution* 58. The Sound of Music 65. Doctor Dolittle 67, many others.

Varley, Beatrice (1896–1969)
British character actress who played worried little elderly ladies for thirty years.
Hatter's Castle 41. So Well Remembered 47. No Room at the Inn 49. Hindle Wakes 53. The Feminine Touch 55, many others.
TV series: Dick and the Duchess 57–58.

Varnel, Marcel (1894–1947)
French-born director, in Hollywood from 1924; came to England in the 30s and made some of the best comedies of Will Hay and the Crazy Gang. Died in a car crash.
The Silent Witness 32. Chandu the Magician 32. Girls will be Boys 34. No Monkey Business 35. Good Morning Boys 36. OK for Sound 37. *Oh Mr Porter* 38. Convict 99 38. *Alf's Button Afloat* 38. *Old Bones of the River* 38. *Ask a Policeman* 39. *The Frozen Limits* 39. Where's That Fire? 39. Let George Do It 40. Gasbags 40. I Thank You 41. Hi Gang 41. *The Ghost of St Michaels* 41. Much Too Shy 42. King Arthur Was a Gentleman 42. Get Cracking 43. He Snoops to Conquer 44. I Didn't Do It 45. George in Civvy Street 46. This Man is Mine 46. The First Gentleman 47, etc.
❝ The only pure comedy director we've ever had in this country. – *Basil Wright*

Varnel, Max (1925–)
British second feature director, son of Marcel Varnel.
A Woman Possessed 58. The Great Van Robbery 49. A Taste of Money 60. Return of a Stranger 61. Enter Inspector Duval 62. The Silent Invasion 63, etc.

Varney, Jim (1949–2000)
American comic actor, from commercials, who was best known as the dimwitted Ernest in a series of low-budget comedies. Died from lung cancer.
Ernest Goes to Camp 87. Ernest Saves Christmas 88. Ernest Goes to Jail 90. Ernest Scared Stupid 91. Wilder Napalm 93. Beverly Hillbillies 93. Ernest Rides Again 93. Toy Story (voice) 95. Toy Story 2 (voice) 99. Daddy and Them 01, etc.

Varney, Reg (1922–)
Chirpy British comedian who after years of availability found fame in the 60s in TV series *The Rag Trade* and *On the Buses*.
The Great St Trinian's Train Robbery 66. On the Buses 71. Mutiny on the Buses 72. Go for a Take 72. The Best Pair of Legs in the Business 72. Holiday on the Buses 73, etc.

Varsi, Diane (1938–1992)
Slightly-built American leading lady who had a brief career in the 50s, with sporadic appearances later.
■ *Peyton Place* (AAN) 57. *Ten North Frederick* 58. From Hell to Texas 59. Compulsion 59. Sweet Love, Bitter 66. Wild in the Streets 68. Killers Three 69. Bloody Mama 70. Johnny Got His Gun 71. I Never Promised You a Rose Garden 77.

Vaughan, Frankie (1928–) (Frank Abelsohn)
Flamboyant British song-and-dance man who never really made it in movies despite a sojourn in Hollywood.
■ Ramsbottom Rides Again 56. *These Dangerous Years* 57. The Lady is a Square 58. Wonderful Things 58. Heart of a Man 59. Let's Make Love 60. The Right Approach 62. It's All Over Town 64.

Vaughan, Peter (1923–) (Peter Ohm)
British character actor of solid presence, good or evil.
Sapphire 59. Village of the Damned 60. The Devil's Agent 62. The Punch and Judy Man 63. Smokescreen 64. Fanatic 65. The Naked Runner 67. Hammerhead 68. A Taste of Excitement 68. A Twist of Sand 68. The Bofors Gun 68. Alfred the Great 69. Eye Witness 70. Straw Dogs 71. The Pied Piper 72. The Mackintosh Man 73. Massacre in Rome 73. 11 Harrowhouse 74. Symptoms 74. Porridge 79. Zulu Dawn 79. Fox (TV) 80. Time Bandits 81. The French Lieutenant's Woman 81. Jamaica Inn (TV) 83. The Razor's Edge 84. Brazil 85. Haunted Honeymoon 86. Monte Carlo (TV) 86. War and Remembrance (TV) 87. The Bourne Identity (TV) 88. King of the Wind 89. Mountains of the Moon 89. Prisoners of Honor (TV) 91. The Remains of the Day 93. The Crucible 96. Joseph Conrad's Secret Agent 96. Face 97. Our Mutual Friend (TV) 98. Les Misérables (US) 98. The Legend of 1900/The Legend of the Pianist on the Ocean (It.) 98. An Ideal Husband 99. Hotel Splendide 99, etc.

Vaughan, Stevie Ray (1956–1990)
American blues guitarist. Born in Dallas, Texas, he worked with local bands before forming his own groups from the mid-70s. Died in a plane crash. A biopic of his life was announced in 1996, to be written and directed by Robert Rodriguez.
Biography: *Stevie Ray Vaughan: Caught in the Crossfire* by Joe Nick Patoski and Bill Crawford.
Gung Ho 86. Back to the Beach 87, etc.

Vaughan Williams, Ralph (1872–1958)
Distinguished English composer who scored some 40s films.
■ The 49th Parallel/The Invaders 41. Coastal Command 42. The People's Land 42. The Flemish Farm 43. Stricken Peninsula 44. The Loves of Joanna Godden 48. Scott of the Antarctic 48. Dim Little Island 49.

Vaughn, Robert (1932–)
Slight, intense American actor who didn't quite make the front rank. He is the author of *Only Victims*, 1972, a study of the effect of the HUAC investigations on Hollywood in the late 40s and the subsequent blacklisting of actors, directors and writers.
Teenage Caveman 58. No Time to Be Young 58. The Young Philadelphians (AAN) 59. *The Magnificent Seven* 60. The Big Show 61. The Caretakers 63. One Spy Too Many 66. The Venetian Affair 67. The Helicopter Spies 68. Bullitt 68. The Mind of Mr Soames 69. The Bridge at Remagen 69. The Statue 71. The Towering Inferno 74. *Washington Behind Closed Doors* (TV) 76. Brass Target 78. Good Luck Miss Wyckoff 79. Battle beyond the Stars 80. Inside the Third Reich (TV) 82. The Return of the Man from UNCLE (TV) 83. Superman III 83. Private Sessions (TV) 85. International Airport (TV) 85. The Delta Force 85. Hour of the Assassin 87. River of Death 89. Nobody's Perfect 90. Joe's Apartment 96. Milk & Money 96. BASEketball 98, etc.
TV series: The Lieutenant 63. *The Man from UNCLE* 64–67. The Protectors 72–73. Centennial 78–79. Emerald Point N.A.S. 83–84. The A-Team 86–87.

Vaughn, Vince (1970–)
American actor. Born in Minneapolis, Illinois, he began in commercials before moving to Los Angeles, where he first played small parts in TV series.
Rudy 93. At Risk 94. Swingers 96. The Lost World: Jurassic Park 97. The Locusts 97. Return to Paradise 98. Clay Pigeons 98. Psycho (as Norman Bates) 98. The Cell 00, etc.

Veber, Francis (1937–)
French director, screenwriter and dramatist. He remade his local success as the Hollywood film *Three Fugitives*.
The Tall Blond Man with One Black Shoe/Le Grand Blond avec une Chaussure Noire (co-w) 72. A Pain in the A--/L'Emmerdeur (co-w) 73. Le Magnifique 73. Return of the Tall Blond Man with One Black Shoe/Le Retour du Grand Blond (w) 74. Peur sur la Ville (w) 75. The Toy/Le Jouet (d) 76. La Cage aux Folles (co-w) (AAN) 79. Hothead/Coup de Tête (w) 80. Sunday Lovers (co-w) 81. The Goat/La Chèvre (wd) 81. La Cage aux Folles II (w) 81. Partners (w) 82. Les Compères (wd) 83. Les Fugitifs (wd) 86. The Lover (w) 86. Three Fugitives (wd) 89. Out on a Limb (d) 92. My Father, the Hero (co-w) 94. Ghost with Driver (w) 96. Le Jaguar (wd) 96. Father's Day (oa) 97. Le Diner de Cons (wd) 98, etc.

Védrès, Nicole (1911–1965)
French director, mainly of probing documentaries.
Paris 1900 47. *La Vie Commence Demain* 50. Aux Frontières de l'Homme 53, etc.

Vee, Bobby (1943–) (Robert Velline)
American pop singer of the 60s.
Swingin' Along/Double Trouble 62. Play It Cool 62. Just for Fun 63. C'mon Let's Live a Little 67.

Veidt, Conrad (1893–1943)
Distinguished German character actor who also filmed in Britain and Hollywood.
The Cabinet of Dr Caligari 19. *Waxworks* 24. Lucrezia Borgia 25. *The Student of Prague* 26. *The Hands of Orlac* 26. The Beloved Rogue (US) 27. The Man Who Laughs 27. Rasputin 30. *Congress Dances* 31. *Rome Express* (GB) 32. I Was a Spy (GB) 33. F.P.I. 33. The Wandering Jew (GB) 33. Jew Süss (GB) 34. Bella Donna (GB) 34. *The Passing of the Third Floor Back* (GB) 35. King of the Damned (GB) 35. *Under the Red Robe* (GB) 36. *Dark Journey* (GB) 37. *The Spy in Black* (GB) 39. Contraband (GB) 40. *The Thief of Baghdad* (GB) 40. Escape (US) 40. A Woman's Face (US) 41. Whistling in the Dark (US) 41. All through the Night (US) 41. The Men in Her Life (US) 42. Nazi Agent (US) 42. Casablanca (US) 42. Above Suspicion (US) 43, etc.
✪ For his almost liquid villainy, and for a score of authentic star performances. *The Thief of Baghdad*.
❝ Women fight for Conrad Veidt! – *30s publicity*
No matter what roles I play, I can't get Caligari out of my system. – *C.V.*

Veiller, Anthony (1903–1965)
American scriptwriter, in Hollywood from 1930. Born in New York City, the son of playwright Bayard Veiller, he worked as a journalist and in theatre management before joining RKO; later he worked for Paramount and MGM.
Menace 34. The Notorious Sophie Lang 34. The Witching Hour 34. Break of Hearts 35. Jalna 35. Star of Midnight 35. The Ex-Mrs Bradford 36. The Lady Consents 36. Winterset 36. A Woman Rebels 36. Let Us Live 37. The Soldier and the Lady 37. Stage Door (AAN) 37. Radio City Revels 38. Disputed Passage 39. Her Cardboard Lover 42. Assignment in Brittany 43. Battle for Russia 43. The Killers (AAN) 46. The Stranger 46. State of the Union 48. Moulin Rouge 52. Red Planet Mars (&p) 52. That Lady 55. Safari 56. Monkey on My Back 57. Timbuktu 58. Solomon and Sheba 59. The List of Adrian Messenger 63. The Night of the Iguana 64, etc.

Velez, Lupe (1908–1944) (Guadeloupe Velez de Villalobos)
Temperamental Mexican leading lady of the 30s; best remembered with Leon ERROL in the Mexican Spitfire series. She was married (1933–38) to actor Johnny WEISSMULLER. Committed suicide when pregnant after a love affair went wrong.
The Gaucho 27. Wolf Song 29. East is West 30. The Squaw Man 31. Kongo 32. Hot Pepper 33. Palooka 34. The Morals of Marcus (GB) 36. Gypsy Melody (GB) 37. *The Girl from Mexico* 39. *Mexican Spitfire* 39. Six Lessons from Madame La Zonga 41. Playmates 42. Mexican Spitfire's Elephant 42. Mexican Spitfire's Blessed Event 43, many others.

❝ The first time you buy a house you think how pretty it is and sign the cheque. The second time you look to see if the basement has termites. It's the same with men. – *L.V.*

Venable, Evelyn (1913–1993)
American leading lady of the 30s, usually in demure roles. She was the original model for Columbia Pictures' logo of a woman holding aloft a lamp. Married cinematographer Hal Mohr in 1934.
Cradle Song 33. Mrs Wiggs of the Cabbage Patch 34. Alice Adams 35. The Frontiersman 38. He Hired the Boss 43, etc.

Veness, Amy (1876–1960)
British character actress who latterly played cheerful old souls.
My Wife's Family 31. Hobson's Choice 31. Lorna Doone 35. Aren't Men Beasts? 37. Yellow Sands 39. The Man in Grey 43. This Happy Breed 44. Here Come the Huggetts 49. Doctor in the House 54, etc.

Venora, Diane (1952–)
American leading actress.
Wolfen 81. Terminal Choice 82. The Cotton Club 84. F/X 85. Ironweed Bird 88. Heat 96. Surviving Picasso 96. Romeo and Juliet 97. The Jackal 97. True Crime 99. The 13th Warrior 99. The Insider 99. Hamlet 00, etc.
TV series: Chicago Hope 94-95.

Ventham, Wanda (1938–)
British leading lady.
My Teenage Daughter 56. The Navy Lark 59. Solo for Sparrow 62. The Cracksman 63. The Big Job 65. The Knack 65. The Spy with a Cold Nose 67. Carry On Up the Khyber 68. Captain Kronos 73. Lost Empires (TV) 86, etc.

Ventura, Lino (1919–1987) (Angelino Borrini)
Italian leading man, former boxer.
Touchez Pas au Grisbi 53. Marie Octobre 57. Crooks in Clover 63. Les Aventuriers 67. The Valachi Papers 72. Wild Horses (US) 72. La Bonne Année 73. The Pink Telephone 75. Le Silencieux 76. Sunday Lovers 80. Les Misérables 82, many others.

Venuti, Joe (1903–1978) (Giuseppe Venuti)
American jazz violinist and bandleader, in films as himself. Born on the ship taking his parents from Italy to America, and brought up in Philadelphia, he played in symphony orchestras in his early teens before joining Paul Whiteman's orchestra in the 30s and later forming a long association with Bing Crosby. He was played by Emile Levisetti in the biopic *Bix*, about Bix Beiderbecke. His recordings with his school-friend, guitarist Eddie Lang, formed the basis for the soundtrack of *The Fortune* 74.
King of Jazz 30. Garden of the Moon 38. Syncopation 42. Two Guys from Texas 48. Riding High 49. Disc Jockey 51. Sarge Goes to College 66, etc.
❝ I don't think my father spoke to me for seven years after he found out I was a jazz player. – *J.V.*

Vera-Ellen (1920–1981) (Vera-Ellen Westmeyr Rohe)
American dancer and songstress of 40s musicals, a former Rockette.
■ *Wonder Man* 45. The Kid from Brooklyn 46. Three Little Girls in Blue 46. Carnival in Costa Rica 47. Words and Music 48. Love Happy 49. *On the Town* 49. Three Little Words 50. Happy Go Lovely (GB) 51. The Belle of New York 52. *Call Me Madam* 53. The Big Leaguer 53. White Christmas 54. Let's Be Happy (GB) 56.

Verbong, Ben (1949–)
Dutch director.
The Girl with the Red Hair 81. De Schorpioen 84. Lily Was Here 89. De Onfatoenlijke Vrouw 91. House Call 94, etc.

Verdon, Gwen (1925–2000)
American dancer and choreographer, mainly on Broadway. Born in Culver City, California, she began as a journalist before working with choreographers Jack Cole and Michael Kidd. She won 4 Tonys for her performances in Broadway musicals, including *Damn Yankees*, in which she also appeared on film. From the 80s she had character roles in several movies. Her second husband was dancer and director Bob Fosse, whom she married in1960.
On the Riviera 51. Meet Me After the Show 51. David and Bathsheba 51. The Merry Widow 52. The I Don't Care Girl 53. The Farmer Takes a Wife 53. *Damn Yankees* 58. Legs (TV) 83. The Cotton Club 84. Cocoon 85. Nadine 87. Cocoon: The Return 88. Alice 90. In Cold Blood (TV) 96. Marvin's Room 96, etc.

Verdu, Maribel (1970–) (Maria Isabel Verdu Rollan)
Spanish leading actress, usually in sensuous roles. Born in Madrid, she was in films from her early 'teens.
Captain Sanchez's Crime/El Crimen del Capitain Sanchez (TV) 84. 27 Hours/27 Horas 85. The Year Of Awakening/El Año De Las Luces 86. Sinatra 88. Barcelona Connection 88. Scent Of A Crime/El Aire De Un Crimen 88. Soldadito Español 88. Manolo 89. The Days Of The Comet/ Los Dias Del Cometa 89. Badis (Mor.) 90. Black Sheep/Ovejas Negras 90. Lovers/Amantes 91. Belle Epoque 92. The Kiss Of Sleep/El Beso Del Sueno 93. Golden Balls/Huevos De Oro 93. Tres Palabras 94. Lullaby/Cancion De Cuna 95. The Year of Awakening/El Año de las Luces 96. La Celestina 96. Lucky Star/La Buena Estrella 97. Neighborhood 98. Goya in Bordeaux 99, etc.

Verdugo, Elena (1926–)
Spanish-American leading lady.
Down Argentine Way 40. The Moon and Sixpence 42. House of Frankenstein 45. Song of Scheherazade 47. Cyrano de Bergerac 50. Thief of Damascus 52. How Sweet It Is 68, etc.
TV series: Meet Millie 52. The New Phil Silvers Show 63. *Marcus Welby M.D.* 69–75.

Vereen, Ben (1946–)
American dancer.
Funny Lady 75. *Roots* (TV) 77. All That Jazz 79. Breakin' Through 84. The Zoo Gang 85. Buy and Cell 89. Once upon a Forest 93. Why Do Fools Fall in Love 98, etc.
TV series: Tenspeed and Brown Shoe 80.

Verhoeven, Michael (1938–)
German director and screenwriter, a former doctor.
Danse Macabre/Paarungen 67. Mitgift 75. Gutenbach 78. White Rose/Die Weisse Rose 82. The Nasty Girl 90. New Germany (co-d) 90. Lilli Lottofee 91. My Mother's Courage 95, etc.

Verhoeven, Paul (1938–)
Dutch director, in America from 1985. Born in Amsterdam, he studied at the University of Leiden, obtaining a doctorate in mathematics and physics, then serving with the Royal Dutch Navy as a documentary film-maker before working in television as a director of documentaries.
Biography: 1998, *Paul Verhoeven* by Rob van Scheer.
Business Is Business/Wat Zien Ik 71. *Turkish Delight*/Turks Fruit (AAN) 73. Katie's Passion/ Keetje Tippel 75. Soldier of Orange/Soldaat van Oranje 77. *Spetters* 80. The Fourth Man/De Vierde Man 83. Flesh and Blood 85. *Robocop* 87. Total Recall 90. Basic Instinct 92. Showgirls 95. Starship Troopers 97, etc.
❝ My resistance to violence is less than other people's, perhaps due to my upbringing in Holland where we were occupied by the Germans and saw violence in front of our eyes. It's possible that I have more problems judging what is over the top and what is not. – *P.V.*
People seem to have this strange idea that films can influence people to be violent, but in my sincere opinion film only reflects the violence of society. – *P.V.*
It's the antagonism of American society that makes me feel alive. – *P.V.*

Vermilyea, Harold (1889–1958)
Russian-American character actor, former operatic singer.
O.S.S. 46. The Big Clock 48. Edge of Doom 50. Born to Be Bad 51, etc.

Verne, Jules (1828–1905)
French adventure novelist whose inventive science-fiction themes have latterly endeared him to Hollywood. Films of his works since 1954 include *Twenty Thousand Leagues Under the Sea, Around the World in Eighty Days, From Earth to the Moon, Journey to the Center of the Earth, Five Weeks in a Balloon, Master of the World, The Children of Captain Grant (In Search of the Castaways), Rocket to the Moon, The Light at the Edge of the World, The Southern Star* and *Michael Strogoff*.

Verne, Karen (1915–1967) (Ingabor Katrine Klinckerfuss)
German leading lady who made a number of Hollywood films.
Ten Days in Paris (GB) 39. All Through the Night 41. Kings Row 42. The Seventh Cross 44. A Bullet for Joey 55. Ship of Fools 65. Torn Curtain 67, etc.

Verneuil, Henri (1920–) (Achod Malakin)
French director, former journalist.
La Table aux Crevés 50. Forbidden Fruit 52. Public Enemy Number One 53. Paris Palace Hotel 56. The Cow and I 59. L'Affaire d'une Nuit 61. The Big Snatch/Mélodie en Sous-Sol 63. Guns for San Sebastian 68. The Burglars 71. The Serpent 72. The Night Caller 72. Le Corps de Mon Ennemi 76. Mille Milliards de Dollars 82. Les Morfalous 84. Mother/Mayrig 91. 588 rue Paradis 92, etc.

Verno, Jerry (1895–1975)
British cockney character actor.
His Lordship 32. The Thirty-Nine Steps 35. Farewell Again 37. Old Mother Riley in Paris 38. The Common Touch 41. The Red Shoes 48. The Belles of St Trinian's 54. After the Ball 57, many others.

Vernon, Anne (1925–) (Edith Vignaud)
Vivacious French leading lady who has also filmed in Britain and Hollywood.
Le Mannequin Assassiné 48. Warning to Wantons (GB) 48. Shakedown (US) 49. *Edward and Caroline* 50. Rue de l'Estrapade 52. The Love Lottery (GB) 54. Time Bomb (GB) 54. Le Long des Trottoirs 56. Les Lavandières de Portugal 57. *The Umbrellas of Cherbourg* 64. Patate 64. La Démoniaque 67. Therese and Isabelle 68, etc.

Vernon, Bobby (1897–1939)
Boyish American star comedian of the silents, usually in shorts.

Vernon, Howard (1914–1996) (Mario Lippert)
Swiss actor, in films of many nationalities, frequently as a villain. His career dipped in the 60s and 70s, when he became a regular in the mediocre films of Jesús Franco, though this gained him a cult following. Born in Baden, of a Swiss father and an American mother, he studied acting in Berlin and Paris and was on stage from the 40s.
Le Silence de Mer (Fr.) 41. Boule de Suif (Fr.) 45. Bob le Flambeur (Fr.) 46. Le Diable Boiteaux (Fr.) 48. The Elusive Pimpernel (GB) 50. Black Jack (Fr.) 50. The Thousand Eyes of Dr Mabuse (Ger.) 60. The Secret Ways (US) 61. The Awful Dr Orloff (Sp.) 62. Léon Morin, Priest/Léon Morin, Prêtre (Fr.) 62. The Train (US) 64. *Alphaville* (Fr.) 65. Danger Grows Wild (US) 66. Triple Cross (GB) 66. Night of the Generals (GB) 67. Mayerling (GB) 68. Le Silence de la Mer (Fr.) 68. Virgin among the Living Dead (Fr.) 71. Dracula – Prisoner of Frankenstein (Sp.) 72. The Demons (Port.) 72. La Malédiction de Frankenstein (Sp.) 73. Love and Death (US) 75. L'Assassin Musicien (Fr.) 76. Le Théâtre des Matières (Fr.) 77. Blood Bath of Dr Jekyll (Fr.) 81. The Boy Who Had Everything (Aus.) 84. Fauborg Saint-Martin (Fr.) 86. Faceless (Fr.) 88. Le Complexe de Toulon (Fr.) 91, many others.

Vernon, John (1932–)
Canadian character actor.
Point Blank 67. Topaz 69. Dirty Harry 71. One More Train to Rob 71. The Black Windmill 74. The Outlaw Josey Wales 76. A Special Day 76. National Lampoon's Animal House 78. Herbie Goes Bananas 80. Airplane II: The Sequel 82. Chained Heat 83. Jungle Warriors 85. Blue Monkey 87. Killer Klowns from Outer Space 87. Border Heat 88. Deadly Stranger 88. I'm Gonna Git You Sucka 89. Bail Out 90. Mob Story 90, etc.
TV series: Delta House 79. Hail to the Chief 85. Acapulco H.E.A.T. 93-94.

Vernon, Richard (1925–1997)
British character actor of stage and TV, usually in soft-spoken aristocratic roles.
Accidental Death 63. A Hard Day's Night 64. Goldfinger 64. The Secret of My Success 65. The Satanic Rites of Dracula 73. The Pink Panther Strikes Again 76. The Human Factor 79. O Heavenly Dog 80. Evil Under the Sun 82. Gandhi 82. A Month in the Country 87, many others.
TV series: The Man in Room 17 65–66. The Lions 66. The Fellows 67. The Sandbaggers 78–80. L for Lester 82. Legacy of Murder 82. Roll Over Beethoven 85. A Gentleman's Club 88. Class Act 94–95.

Vernon, Wally (1904–1970)
American eccentric comedian.
Mountain Music 37. Alexander's Ragtime Band 38. The Gorilla 39. Tahiti Honey 43. Always Leave Them Laughing 49. What Price Glory? 52. What a Way to Go 64, many others.

Verrill, Virginia (1916–1999)
America singer who dubbed Jean Harlow and other film actresses. She was on-stage from childhood in her mother's vaudeville act, and at the age of 15 sang the title song in the movie *Ten Cents a Dance*. From the mid-30s she worked on radio and recorded with the Isham Jones orchestra.
Reckless (singing for Jean Harlow) 35. Suzy (singing for Jean Harlow) 36. 52nd Street (singing for Pat Paterson) 37. The Goldwyn Follies (singing for Andrea Leeds) 38, etc.

Versois, Odile (1930–1980) (Militza de Poliakoff-Baidarov)
French leading lady, sister of Marina Vlady.
Les Dernières Vacances 46. Into the Blue (GB) 48. Bel Amour 51. A Day to Remember (GB) 53. *The Young Lovers*/Chance Meeting (GB) 55. To Paris with Love (GB) 55. Passport to Shame (GB) 58. Cartouche/Swords of Blood 62. Benjamin 68, etc.

Vertov, Dziga (1896–1954) (Dennis Kaufman)
Russian director and film theorist. Many documentaries.
One-Sixth of the World 27. The Man with the Movie Camera 28. Three Songs of Lenin 34. In the Line of Fire 41, etc.

Vetri, Victoria (1944–) (Angela Dorian)
Australian leading lady.
Chuka 67. Rosemary's Baby 68. When Dinosaurs Ruled the Earth 69. Invasion of the Bee Girls 73, etc.

Veysset, Sandrine
French screenwriter and director. She studied art before working for director Leos Carax as a set decorator and driver.
Will It Snow for Christmas? 96.
❝ People have the strangest ideas about cinema. There are so many other more complicated things – I find carpenters and sculptors a lot more impressive than film-makers. – *S.V.*

Vicas, Victor (1918–1985)
Franco-Russian director. Later in French TV.
No Way Back 53. Double Destiny 54. Back to Kandara 57. The Wayward Bus 57. Count Five and Die (GB) 58. Les Disparus 60, etc.

Vickers, Martha (1925–1971) (M. MacVicar)
American leading lady of the 40s.
The Falcon in Mexico 44. *The Big Sleep* 46. Love and Learn 47. Ruthless 48. Bad Boy 49. Daughter of the West 51. The Burglar 57. Four Fast Guns 60, etc.

Victor, Charles (1896–1965)
British character actor with long stage experience: in films from 1938, usually in cockney roles.
The 39 Steps 35. Old Mother Riley in Society 40. Love on the Dole 41. Major Barbara 41. The Foreman Went to France 42. When We Are Married 43. San Demetrio – London 43. The Rake's Progress 45. Caesar and Cleopatra 45. The Way to the Stars 45. Gaiety George 46. The Magic Bow 47. The Cure for Love 49. The Elusive Pimpernel 50. The Magic Box 51. The Frightened Man 52. The Ringer 52. Meet Mr Lucifer 53. An Alligator Named Daisy 55. Charley Moon 56. Tiger in the Smoke 56. The Prince and the Showgirl 57. The Pit and the Pendulum 61, etc.

Victor, Henry (1898–1945)
British character actor, a silent screen star who went to Hollywood in the 30s and played villainous bit roles.
She 25. The Guns of Loos 28. The Fourth Commandment 28. The Mummy 33. Our Fighting Navy 37. Confessions of a Nazi Spy 39. Zanzibar 40. King of the Zombies 41. To Be or Not to Be 42.

Sherlock Holmes and the Secret Weapon 42. They Got Me Covered 43, etc.

Victoria
Queen of England 1837–1901, was born in 1819. Her full-length screen portraits were by Anna Neagle in *Victoria the Great* and *Sixty Glorious Years*, and by Irene Dunne, who failed rather badly, in *The Mudlark*. She was also played by Fay Compton in *The Prime Minister*, by Helena Pickard in *The Lady with the Lamp*, by Muriel Aked in *The Story of Gilbert and Sullivan*, by Sybil Thorndike in *Melba*, and by Mollie Maureen in *The Private Life of Sherlock Holmes*.

Vidal, Gore (1925–)
Elegant American novelist, essayist, dramatist, screenwriter, and occasional actor, an intellectual gadfly. In 1996, he angered Charlton Heston by claiming that there was a homosexual subtext to the film of *Ben-Hur*.
Autobiography: 1992, *Screening History*. 1995, *Palimpsest: A Memoir*.
Biography: 1999, *Gore Vidal: A Biography* by Fred Kaplan.
The Catered Affair (w) 56. I Accuse (w) 58. The Left-Handed Gun (oa) 58. The Scapegoat (co-w) 59. Visit to a Small Planet (oa) 60. Suddenly Last Summer 60. The Best Man (w, from his play) 64. Is Paris Burning? (co-w) 66. Last of the Mobile Hot-Shots (w) 70. Myra Breckinridge (oa) 70. Caligula (co-w) 79. Dress Gray (TV) 86. Gore Vidal's Lincoln (oa) (TV) 88. Gore Vidal's Billy the Kid (& a) (TV) 89. Bob Roberts (a) 92. With Honors (a) 94. The Eighth Day (a) 97. Shadow Conspiracy (a) 97, etc.
❝ As I now move, graciously, I hope, toward the door marked Exit, it occurs to me that the only thing I ever really liked to do was go to the movies. Naturally, Sex and Art always took precedence over the cinema. Unfortunately, neither ever proved to be as dependable as the filtering of present light through that moving strip of celluloid which projects past images and voices onto a screen. – *G.V.*
To write a script today means working for a committee of people who know nothing about movies, as opposed, say, to real estate or the higher art of bookkeeping. – *G.V., 1996*

Vidal, Henri (1919–1959)
Tough-looking French leading man, in films from 1940.
Les Maudits 46. Quai de Grenelle 50. Port du Désir 54. The Wicked Go to Hell 55. Porte des Lilas 56. Come Dance with Me 59, etc.

Vidgeon, Robin (1939–)
British cinematographer. He began as a second assistant cameraman in 1955 and previously worked on many films with cinematographer Douglas Slocombe and cameraman Chic Waterson.
Mr Corbett's Ghost 86. Hellraiser 87. Mr North 88. The Penitent 88. Hellbound: Hellraiser II 88. Parents 89. The Fly II 89. Nightbreed 90. Highway to Hell 92. Lady Chatterley (TV) 93. August 96, etc.

Vidor, Charles (1900–1959)
Hungarian-American director, in Hollywood from 1932. Married (1932-43) actress Karen Morley.
Double Door 34. Sensation Hunters 34. The Great Gambini 37. *Blind Alley* 39. My Son My Son 40. The Lady in Question 40. Ladies in Retirement 41. The Tuttles of Tahiti 42. The Desperadoes 43. *Cover Girl* 44. Together Again 44. A Song to Remember 45. Over 21 45. *Gilda* 46. The Guilt of Janet Ames 48. Hans Christian Andersen 52. Love Me or Leave Me 55. The Swan 56. The Joker Is Wild 57. A Farewell to Arms 58. Song without End (part) 59, many others.

Vidor, Florence (1895–1977) (Florence Arto)
American leading lady of the silent screen.
Lying Lips 21. Barbara Frietchie 24. The Grand Duchess and the Waiter 26. Are Parents People? 26. The Patriot 28. Chinatown Nights 29, etc.

Vidor, King (1894–1982)
American director, formerly journalist; high style alternates with disappointing banality. Special AA 1979 'for his incomparable achievements as a cinematic creator and innovator'.
In the last year of his life he acted a role in *Love and Money*.
Autobiography: 1953, *A Tree Is a Tree*.
■ The Turn in the Road 18. Better Times 19. The Other Half 19. Poor Relations 19. The Jack Knife Man 19. The Family Honour 20. The Sky Pilot 21. Love Never Dies 21. Conquering the Woman 21. Woman Wake Up 21. The Real Adventure 22. Dusk to Dawn 22. Alice Adams 22. Peg O' My Heart 23. The Woman of Bronze 23. Three Wise Fools 23. Wild Oranges 23. Happiness 23. Wine of Youth 24. His Hour 24. Wife of the Centaur 24. Proud Flesh 25. *The Big Parade* 25. La Bohème 25. Bardelys the Magnificent 26. *The Crowd* (AAN) 28. *Show People* 28. *Hallelujah* (AAN) 29. Not So Dumb 30. *Billy the Kid* 30. *Street Scene* 31. *The Champ* (AAN) 31. Bird of Paradise 32. Cynara 32. The Stranger's Return 33. *Our Daily Bread* 34. The Wedding Night 34. So Red the Rose 35. The Texas Rangers 36. Stella Dallas 37. The Citadel (GB) (AAN) 38. *Northwest Passage* 39. Comrade X 40. H. M. Pulham Esq 41. An American Romance 44. Duel in the Sun 46. On Our Merry Way 47. *The Fountainhead* 49. Beyond the Forest 49. Lightning Strikes Twice 51. Japanese War Bride 52. Ruby Gentry 52. The Man without a Star 55. *War and Peace* (AAN) 56. Solomon and Sheba 59.

Vierny, Sacha (1919–)
French cinematographer, associated with the films of Peter Greenaway.
Night and Fog 55. *Hiroshima Mon Amour* 59. *Last Year in Marienbad* 61. Muriel 63. Do You Like Women? 64. La Guerre Est Finie 66. *Belle de Jour* 67. The Monk 72. My American Uncle 80. Beau-Père 81. L'Amour à Mort 84. A Zed and Two Noughts 85. The Belly of an Architect 87. Drowning by Numbers 88. The Cook, the Thief, His Wife and Her Lover 89. *Prospero's Books* 91. Rosa 92. The Baby of Macon 93. *The Pillow Book* 95. 8&fr12; Women 99. The Man Who Cried 00, etc.

Viertel, Berthold (1885–1953)
Austrian director of stage and screen, playwright and poet. Born in Vienna, he began as an actor and stage director, then made films in Germany from the 20s. He settled in California in the late 20s, but continued for a time working in England and elsewhere in Europe. In the 50s he returned to Europe to direct plays. The first of his two wives was Salka Viertel, and he is the father of Peter Viertel. He is the model for Friedrich Bergmann in Christopher Isherwood's novel *Prater Violet*.
The Wise Sex 31. The Man from Yesterday 32. Little Friend 34. The Passing of the Third Floor Back 35. Rhodes of Africa 36, etc.

Viertel, Peter (1920–)
German-born novelist and screenwriter in Hollywood, the son of Berthold and Salka Viertel. Born in Dresden and raised in California, he wrote his first novel at the age of 18. Married (1944–59) Virginia Ray, one-time dancer in the Paramount chorus and former wife of writer Budd Schulberg, and, in 1960, actress Deborah Kerr. He later moved back to live in Europe, dividing his time between Switzerland and Spain.
Autobiography: 1992, *Dangeous Friends*.
Saboteur (co-w) 42. Roughshow (oa) 49. We Were Strangers (co-w) 49. Decision before Dawn (co-w) 51. The Sun Also Rises (w) 57. The Old Man and the Sea (w) 58. Heaven Fell That Night (Fr./It.) 58. Blood and Roses (Fr./It.) (co-w) 60. Five Miles to Midnight (Fr./It.) 62. White Hunter, Black Heart (co-w, oa) 90, etc.

Viertel, Salka (1889–1978)
Polish-born actress and screenwriter, in Hollywood from the 30s and an American citizen from 1939. After acting in the Viennese theatre, she became a friend of Greta Garbo, and worked on some of the actress's films for MGM. She married director Berthold Viertel, and in the 30s and 40s their home was a refuge for European writers and actors; later she was the lover of Gottfried Reinhardt. In the 50s, she was blacklisted and moved back to Europe to find work. She was the mother of Peter Viertel.
Autobiography: 1969, *The Kindness of Strangers*.
Anna Christie (a) 30. Queen Christina (co-w) 31. The Painted Veil (co-w) 34. Anna Karenina (co-w) 35. Two-Faced Woman (co-w) 41. Deep Valley (co-w) 47. Il Battellieri del Volga (w) 58, etc.

Vigne, Daniel (1942–)
French director and screenwriter.
Les Hommes 73. The Return of Martin Guerre/Le Retour de Martin Guerre 83. One Woman or Two/Une Femme ou Deux 85. Comédie d'Eté 89. The King's Whore (co-w) 90, etc.

Vigo, Jean (1905–1934) (Jean Almereyda)
Influential French director on the strength of three semi-experimental, dream-like films.
■ *A Propos de Nice* 30. *Zéro de Conduite* 32. *L'Atalante* 34.

Vigoda, Abe (1921–)
American character actor, popular on TV in the 70s series *Barney Miller* and *Fish*.
The Godfather 71. The Don Is Dead 73. Newman's Law 74. Having Babies (TV) 76. The Cheap Detective 78. The Comedy Company (TV) 78. Vasectomy – a Delicate Matter 86. Plain Clothes 88. Look Who's Talking 89. Prancer 89. Joe versus the Volcano 90. Sugar Hill 93. Batman: Mask of the Phantasm (voice) 94. North 94. Jury Duty 95. Underworld 96. Love Is All There Is 96. A Brooklyn State of Mind 97. Underworld 97. Good Burger 97, etc.

Villa-Lobos, Heitor (1887–1959)
Brazilian composer who worked in Hollywood on *Green Mansions* 59.

Villalobos, Reynaldo
American cinematographer.
Urban Cowboy 80. Nine to Five 80. Blame It on Rio 84. Lucas 86. Punchline 88. Major League 89. Coup de Ville 90. American Me 92. A Bronx Tale 93. Roosters 95. Romy and Michelle's High School Reunion 97. Telling Lies in America 97. Loved 97. An Alan Smithee film: Burn, Hollywood, Burn 97. Return to Paradise 98, etc.

Villard, Frank (1917–1980) (François Drouineau)
French leading man, often in shifty roles.
Le Dernier des Six 41. Gigi 48. Manèges/The Wanton 49. L'Ingénue Libertine 50. Le Garçon Sauvage 51. Huis Clos 54. Crime Passionnel 55. Mystères de Paris 57. Le Cave se Rebiffe 61. Gigot 62. Mata Hari 64, etc.

Villaverde, Teresa (1966–)
Portuguese director and screenwriter, born in Lisbon.
Alex/A Idade Maior 91. Two Brothers, My Sisters/Tres Irmaos 94. The Mutants 98, etc.

Villechaize, Hervé (1943–1993)
French dwarf actor in international films. His health deteriorating, he committed suicide.
The Man with the Golden Gun 74. The One and Only 78. Forbidden Zone 80, etc.
TV series: Fantasy Island 77–82.
❝ He looked like a miniature Edward G. Robinson, and had the vigour of six, with the promiscuity of six for that matter, as if he wanted to make the most of every second of a life that would not be very long. – *Christopher Lee*

Villeret, Jacques (1951–)
Chubby French comic actor.
RAS 73. Second Chance/Si C'Etait a Refaire 75. The Good and the Bad/Les Bons et Les Méchants 76. Bete Mais Discipline 78. Mon Premier Amour 78. Robert et Robert 78. An Adventure for Two/A Nous Deux 79. Malevil 81. The Ins and Outs/Les Uns et Les Autres 81. Garçon! 83. Edith and Marcel 84. Hold-Up 86. Watch Your Right/Soigne Ta Droite 87. 588 Rue Paradis 90. The Favour, The Watch and the Very Big Fish 91. Parano 93. *The Dinner Game/Le Diner de Cons* 98, etc

Villiers, James (1933–1998)
British actor, usually in snooty or villainous roles.
The Entertainer 60. Eva 62. The Damned 63. Murder at the Gallop 63. King and Country 64. The Nanny 65. The Alphabet Murders 65. You Must Be Joking 65. Half a Sixpence 67. Otley 68. Some Girls Do 69. A Nice Girl Like Me 69. Blood from the Mummy's Tomb 71. The Ruling Class 71. The Amazing Mr Blunden 72. Asylum 72. Seven Nights in Japan 76. Joseph Andrews 77. Saint Jack 79. The Scarlet Pimpernel (TV) 82. Under the Volcano 84. Fortunes of War (TV) 87. Mountains of the Moon 89. King Ralph 91. Let Him Have It 91. The Tichborne Claimant 98, etc.
TV series: Marty Back Together Again 74. The Other 'Arf 80-82. Emery Presents 83.

Villon, François (c. 1431–1470) (François de Loges)
French poet who led the life of a Robin Hood and was romanticized in *If I Were King* (in which he was played by Ronald Colman) and its musical version *The Vagabond King* (Dennis King, Oreste Kirkop).

Vilsmaier, Joseph (1939–)
German director, producer, screenwriter and cinematographer, born in Munich.
Herbstmilch 89. Rama Dama (& co-w) 91. Stalingrad (& co-w) 93. Charlie & Louise 94. Brother of Sleep/Schalfes Bruder (& co-w) 94. Comedian Harmonists 98, etc.

Vince, Pruitt Taylor (1960–)
American character actor, born in Baton Rouge, Louisiana.
Shy People 87. Angel Heart 87. Barfly 87. Mississippi Burning 88. Red Heat 88. K-9 88. Fear 89. Jacob's Ladder 90. Come See the Paradise 90. Wild at Heart 91. JFK 91. China Moon 94. City Slickers II: The Legend of Curly's Gold 94. Nobody's Fool 94. Natural Born Killers 94. Heavy 95. Under the Hula Moon 95. Beautiful Girls 96. A Further Gesture/The Break 97. The End of Violence 97. Cold around the Heart 97. A Further Gesture 97. The Legend of 1900 98. Mumford 99. Nurse Betty 00. The Cell 00, etc.

Vincent, Alex (1982–)
American child actor of the 80s, best known as Andy, the owner of the Chucky doll in two *Child's Play* horror movies.
Child's Play 88. Wait until Spring, Bandini 89. Child's Play 2 90. My Family Treasure 93, etc.

Vincent, Jan-Michael (1944–)
Boyish American leading man, usually in forgettable films, who first came to notice in the TV soap opera *The Survivors* 69–70. He was sentenced to 60 days in jail in 2000 for violating probation, which resulted from a drunken driving crash in 1996 that left him with a broken neck.
The Undefeated 68. Tribes (TV) 70. The Mechanic 72. The World's Greatest Athlete 73. Buster and Billie 74. Bite the Bullet 74. White Line Fever 75. Baby Blue Marine 76. Damnation Alley 77. Hooper 78. Big Wednesday 78. Defiance 80. Hard Country 81. *The Winds of War* (TV) 83. Last Plane Out 83. Born in East L.A. 87. Deadly Embrace 88. Hit List 89. Hangfire 90. Raw Nerve 91. Animal Instincts 92. Xtro II 92. Indecent Behaviour 94. Red Line 96. Orbit 96. Body Count 97. Buffalo '66 98, etc.
TV series: Airwolf 84–86.

Vincent, June (1919–)
Blond American leading lady of some 40s 'B's.
Ladies Courageous 44. The Climax 44. Can't Help Singing 44. Here Come the Co-eds 45. That's the Spirit 45. Black Angel 46. Shed No Tears 48. The Lone Wolf and His Lady 49. Mary Ryan, Detective 50. Secrets of Monte Carlo 51. Clipped Wings 53. City of Shadows 55. The Miracle of the Hills 59, etc.

Vincent, Robbie (1896–1966)
English comedian who appeared in some low-budget farces starring Frank Randle. Best known for his role as Enoch alongside Harry Korris and Cecil Frederick in the 40s radio show *Happidrome*.
Somewhere in England 40. Somewhere in Camp 42. Somewhere on Leave 42. Happidrome 43, etc.

Vincze, Ernest (1942–)
British cinematographer.
Jane Austen in Manhattan 81. A Woman of Substance (TV) 84. Biggles 85. Shanghai Surprise 85. Escape from Sobibor (TV) 86. The Nightmare Years (TV) 89. Cream in My Coffee (TV) 90. The Camomile Lawn (TV) 92. The Dance 98, etc.

Vinson, Helen (1907–1999) (Helen Rulfs)
Cool, aristocratic leading lady of Hollywood films of the 30s and 40s. Born in Beaumont, Texas, she was educated at the University of Texas. The second of her three husbands was the English (later naturalised American) tennis champion Fred Perry.
I Am a Fugitive from a Chain Gang 32. Jewel Robbery 32. Lawyer Man 32. Grand Slam 33. The Kennel Murder Case 33. The Little Giant 33. Midnight Club 33. The Power and the Glory 33. As Husbands Go 34. Broadway Bill 34. The Captain Hates the Sea 34. Let's Try Again 34. The Life of Vergie Winters 34. Age of Indiscretion 35.

King of the Damned 35. A Notorious Gentleman 35. Private Worlds 35. The Tunnel 35. The Wedding Night 35. Love in Exile 36. Reunion 36. Live, Love and Learn 37. Vogues of 1938 37. In Name Only 39. Curtain Call 40. Enemy Agent 40. Torrid Zone 40. Nothing but the Truth 41. Are These Our Parents? 44. Chip off the Old Block 44. The Lady and the Monster 44, etc.

Visconti, Luchino (1906–1976) (L. V. de Modrone)
Italian writer-director, former art director.
Biography: 1982, *Luchino Visconti* by Gaia Servadio.
Other books: 1998, *Visconti: Explorations of Beauty and Decay* by Henry Bacon.
Ossessione 42. *La Terra Trema* 48. Bellissima 51. Siamo Donne (part) 52. *Senso* 53. White Nights 57. *Rocco and His Brothers* 60. Boccaccio 70 62. *The Leopard* 63. *The Damned* 69. Death in Venice 71. Ludwig 72. Conversation Piece 74. The Innocent 76, etc.

Visnjic, Goran (c. 1972–)
Croatian leading actor, born in Sibenik. He is best known for playing the role of Dr Luka Kovac in the TV drama series *ER*.
See You/Vidimo Se 96. Recognition/Prepoznavanje 97. Welcome to Sarajevo (GB/US) 97. The Peacemaker (US) 97. Practical Magic (US) 98. Committed (US) 00, etc.
TV series: ER 99- .

Vitale, Milly (1928–)
Italian leading lady in American films.
The Juggler 53. The Seven Little Foys 55. A Breath of Scandal 60.

Viterelli, Joe
Tubby American character actor, frequently in gangster roles.
State of Grace 90. Ruby 92. Bullets over Broadway 94. Black Rose of Harlem 95. American Strays 96. Heaven's Prisoners 96. Eraser 96. Mafia!/Jane Austen's Mafia 98. Analyze This 99. Mickey Blue Eyes 99, etc.

Vitti, Monica (1931–) (Monica Luisa Ceciarelli)
Italian leading lady in international demand in the 60s.
L'Avventura 59. La Notte 60. *L'Eclisse* 62. Dragées au Poivre 63. Nutty Naughty Château 64. *The Red Desert* 64. Modesty Blaise (GB) 65. The Chastity Belt 67. Girl with a Pistol 69. The Pacifist 71. Duck in Orange Sauce 75. An Almost Perfect Affair 79. The Mystery of Oberwald 80. Tango della Gelosia 81. When Veronica Calls 83. Secret Scandal/Scandalo Segreto (& co-w, d) 89, etc.

Viva (1941–) (Janet Sue Hoffman)
Witty, skinny American star of Andy Warhol's films, originally a painter and also a novelist. She was played by Tahnee Welch in the bio-pic *I Shot Andy Warhol* 96.
The Loves of Ondine 67. Bikeboy 67. Nude Restaurant 67. *Lonesome Cowboys* 68. Blue Movie 69. Lion's Love 69. Play It Again, Sam 72. Forbidden Zone 80. State of Things 82, etc.

Vlacil, Frantisek (1924–1999)
Czechoslovakian director. He began in puppet animation and as a director of educational, army and documentary films. For much of the 1970s, he was banned from making feature films by the government. His medieval drama *Marketa Lazarova* was voted the best-ever Czech film in 1998 in a poll of Czech critics and film industry leaders.
The White Dove/Holubice 60. The Devil's Trap/Dablova Past 61. Marketa Lazarova 67. The Valley of the Bees/Udoli Vcel 67. Adelheid 69. The Magician/Mag 87, etc.

Vlad, Roman (1919–)
Romanian composer.
La Beauté du Diable 49. Sunday in August 50. Three Steps North 51. Romeo and Juliet 54. Knave of Hearts 54. The Law 60. The Mighty Ursus 62. The Young Toscanini 88, etc.

Vlady, Marina (1938–) (Marina de Poliakoff-Baidarov)
French leading lady, sister of Odile Versois.
Orage d'Eté 49. Avant le Déluge 53. The Wicked Go to Hell 55. Crime and Punishment 56. Toi le Venin 59. La Steppa 61. Climats 62. Enough Rope 63. Dragées au Poivre 63. Queen Bee 64. Chimes at Midnight 66. Sapho 70. Les Jeux de la Comtesse 80. Bordello 85. Twist Again à Moscou 86. Migrations 88. Follow Me 89. Splendor 89. The Dream of Russia/Kodayu 91. The Son of Gascogne/Le Fils de Gascogne 95, etc.

Vogel, Paul C. (1899–1975)
American cinematographer.
The Lady in the Lake 46. Black Hand 49. *Battleground* (AA) 49. Rose Marie 54. High Society 56. The Wings of Eagles 56. The Time Machine 60. The Rounders 64, etc.

Vogel, Virgil (1919–1996)
American director, from TV.
The Mole People 56. Terror in the Midnight Sun 58. Son of Ali Baba 64. The Return of Joe Forrester (TV) 75. Law of the Land (TV) 76. Centennial (part) (TV) 78. Beulah Land (TV) 80. Longarm (TV) 88. Mario and the Mob (TV) 92, etc.

Vogler, Karl Michael (1928–)
German stage actor who has appeared in a few international films.
Those Magnificent Men in Their Flying Machines 65. The Blue Max 67. How I Won the War 67. Patton 69. Downhill Racer 69. Deep End 70, etc.

Voight, Jon (1938–)
American leading actor of the 70s.
The Hour of the Gun 67. Fearless Frank 68. Out of It 69. *Midnight Cowboy* (AAN) 69. The Revolutionary 70. The All American Boy 70. Catch 22 70. *Deliverance* 72. Conrack 74. The Odessa File 74. End of the Game 75. Coming Home (AA) 78. The Champ 79. Lookin' to Get Out 82. Table for Five 83. Runaway Train (AAN) 85. Desert Bloom 86. Eternity 90. Chernobyl: The Final Warning (TV) 91. Return to Lonesome Dove (TV) 93. Heat 95. Mission: Impossible 96. Anaconda 96. U-Turn 97. Most Wanted 97. Boys Will Be Boys 97. John Grisham's The Rainmaker 97. The General 98. Enemy of the State 98. The General 98. Varsity Blues 99. A Dog of Flanders 99, etc.
❝ Famous line (*Midnight Cowboy*) 'I'll tell you the truth now. I ain't a real cowboy, but I am one hell of a stud.'

Volk, Stephen
British screenwriter and dramatist specializing in horror stories.
Gothic 86. The Kiss (co-w) 88. The Guardian (co-w) 90.

Volonté, Gian Maria (1933–1994)
Italian leading man of the 60s.
A Fistful of Dollars 64. For a Few Dollars More 65. We Still Kill the Old Way 68. *Investigation of a Citizen above Suspicion* 69. Sacco and Vanzetti 71. The Working Class Go to Heaven 72. Lucky Luciano 73. Christ Stopped at Eboli 79. Chronicle of a Death Foretold/Cronaca di una Morte Annunciata 87. Tre Colonne in Cronaca 89. Open Doors/Porte Aperte 90. A Simple Story/Una Storia Semplice 91. Funes, un Gran Amor (Arg.) 93. Tirano Banderas 94, etc.

Von Bargen, Daniel
American actor, from the stage.
Silence of the Lambs 91. Company Business 91. Shadows and Fog 92. Basic Instinct 92. Six Degrees of Separation 93. The Saint of Fort Washington 93. Philadelphia 93. Rising Sun 93. IQ 94. Crimson Tide 95. Lord of Illusions 95. Before and After 96. Looking for Richard 96. Broken Arrow 96. The Real Blonde 97. Amistad 97. GI Jane 97. The Postman 97. The Faculty 98. The General's Daughter 99. Universal Soldier: The Return 99. O Brother, Where Art Thou? 00. Disney's The Kid 00, etc.

Von Brandenstein, Patrizia (1943–)
American production designer.
Heartland 79. Tell Me a Riddle 80. Silkwood 83. Touched 83. Amadeus (AA) 84. A Chorus Line 85. The Money Pit 86. No Mercy 87. The Untouchables (AAN) 87. Betrayed 88. Working Girl 88. The Lemon Sisters 90. State of Grace 90. Postcards from the Edge 90. Billy Bathgate 91. Sneakers 92. Leap of Faith 92. Six Degrees of Separation 93. The Quick and the Dead 95. Mercury Rising 98. A Simple Plan 98, etc.

Von Dassanowsky, Elfi (1924–)
Austrian-born actress, producer, singer and musician, now resident in the USA. She trained as a pianist and opera singer at Vienna's Academy of Music, but turned down a contract as an actress from UFA in Berlin because of its associations with the Nazi Party. She taught Curt JURGENS to play piano for his first major role in *Wen die Götter Lieben* 42. In the mid-40s, with producer Emmerich Hanus, she founded Belvedere Film, which helped kick-start the revival of the German film industry, and later worked as a casting director.
AS PRODUCER: Symphonie in Salzburg 46. Die Glücksmühle (& a) 47. Kunstschätze des Klosterneuburger Stiftes 47. The Freckle/Der Leberfleck 48. Doktor Rosin 49. Märchen vom Glück 49. Walzer von Strauss/Waltz by Strauss 52, etc.

Von Harbou, Thea (1888–1954)
German screenwriter, mainly associated with Fritz Lang's silent films.
Der Müde Tod 21. *Dr Mabuse* 22. *Nibelungen Saga* 24. Chronicles of the Grey House 25. *Metropolis* 26. The Spy 28. The Woman in the Moon 29. *The Testament of Dr Mabuse* 32. The Old and the Young King 35. Annélie 41. Fahrt ins Gluck 45. The Affairs of Dr Holl 51, many others.

Von Praunheim, Rosa (1942–) (Holger Mischwitzsky)
German experimental and independent film director, producer, actor and screenwriter. Born in Riga, Latvia, he studied at the School of Applied Arts in Offenbach and in Berlin. He began by collaborating with Werner SCHROETER and as an assistant director to the American avant garde filmmaker Gregory MARKOPOULOS in the late 60s. His often satirical films reflect his militant homosexuality.
Schwestern Der Revolution (short) 69. Rosy Worker On A Golden Street (short) 69. Nicht Der Homosexuelle Ist Pervers, Sondern Die Situation 71. Leidenschaften 72. Macbeth 72. Berliner Bettwurst 73. Axel Von Auersperg 74. Underground And Emigrants 76. Ich Bin Ein Antistar 77. Todesmagazin Oder: Wie Werde Ich Ein Blumentopf? (&a) 79. Tally Brown, N.Y. (doc) 79. Unsere Leichen Leben Noch (&a) 81. Stadt Der Verlorenen Seelen 83. Horror Vacui 84. A Virus Knows No Morals/Ein Virus Kennt Keine Moral (&a) 86. Anita – Tänze Des Lasters 87. Dolly, Lotte Und Maria 88. Schweigen = Tod (&w) 89. Überleben In New York (doc) 89. Positiv 89. Ich Bin Meine Eigene Frau 92. Affengeil (&p,w,a) 92. Neurosia: Fifty Years of Perversity (doc) 96. The Einstein of Sex (&p) 99, etc.

Von Seyffertitz, Gustav (1863–1943)
Dignified German character actor in Hollywood films; during World War I was known as G. Butler Clonblough.
Old Wives for New 18. Moriarty (title role) 22. Sparrows 26. The Wizard 27. Docks of New York 28. The Bat Whispers 30. Shanghai Express 32. Queen Christiana 33. She 35. In Old Chicago 38. Nurse Edith Cavell 39, many others.

Von Sternberg, Josef (1894–1969) (Jonas Sternberg)
Austrian-American director, a great pictorial stylist and the creator of Marlene Dietrich's American image. He was played by Hans-Werner Mayer in the German biopic *Marlene*, 99.
Autobiography: 1965, *Fun in a Chinese Laundry*. A critical study by Herman G. Weinberg was published in 1967.
■ *The Salvation Hunters* 25. The Seagull (unreleased) 26. *Underworld* 27. The Last Command 28. The Dragnet 28. *Docks of New York* 28. The Case of Lena Smith 29. Thunderbolt 29. *The Blue Angel* (Ger.) 30. *Morocco* (AAN) 30. Dishonoured 31. An American Tragedy 31. *Shanghai Express* (AAN) 32. Blonde Venus 32. *The Scarlet Empress* 34. *The Devil is a Woman* 35. The King Steps Out 36. Crime and Punishment 36. I Claudius (unfinished) 37. Sergeant Madden 39. *The Shanghai Gesture* 41. Jet Pilot 50. Macao 51. The Saga of Anatahan (Jap.) 53.
✪ For being the kind of director who, if he didn't exist, publicists would have to invent. *The Scarlet Empress*.
❝ I care nothing about the story, only how it is photographed and presented. – *J.V.S.*
The only way to succeed is to make people hate you. That way they remember you. – *J.V.S.*
A lyricist of light and shadow rather than a master of montage. – *Andrew Sarris, 1968*
He brought to the screen new horizons in the art of lighting, to the photography of shadowed and broken rays … His scenes seem almost always to be seen through streamers and feathers, through loose gauze, through slatted shutters or an intricate lattice wall. – *Ivan Butler*

Von Stroheim, Erich (1885–1957) (Hans Erich Maria Stroheim Von Nordenwall)
Austrian actor and director whose ruthless extravagance in Hollywood in the 20s harmed his later career. Usually played despotic villains or stiff-necked Prussians.
Biography: 1954, *Hollywood Scapegoat* by Peter Noble. 1972, *Erich Von Stroheim* by Tom Curtis.
AS ACTOR: The Heart of Humanity 18. Blind Husbands 19. *Foolish Wives* 21. The Wedding March 27. The Great Gabbo 29. Three Faces East 30. Friends and Lovers 30. The Lost Squadron 32. As You Desire Me 32. Walking Down Broadway 32. Crimson Romance 35. The Crime of Dr Crespi 35. *La Grande Illusion* 37. Mademoiselle Docteur 37. Alibi 38. Boys' School 39. I Was an Adventuress 40. Thunder Over Pariéges 40. So Ends Our Night 41. *Five Graves to Cairo* (as Rommel) 43. North Star 43. The Lady and the Monster 44. Storm Over Lisbon 44. 32 Rue de Montmartre 44. The Great Flamarion 45. La Danse de Mort 47. *Sunset Boulevard* (AAN) 50. La Maison du Crime 52. Napoleon 54. L'Homme aux Cents Visages 56, etc.
■ AS DIRECTOR: *Blind Husbands* 19. *The Devil's Passkey* 19. *Foolish Wives* 21. Merry Go Round 22. *Greed* 23. The Merry Widow 25. *The Wedding March* 27. *Queen Kelly* 28.
✪ For taking Hollywood on and winning – for a while. *Greed*.
❝ The difference between me and Lubitsch is that he shows you the king on the throne and then he shows you the king in his bedroom. I show you the king in his bedroom first. Then when you see him on the throne you have no illusions about him. – *E.V.S.*
When I first saw Von Stroheim at the wardrobe tests, I clicked my heels and said, 'Isn't it ridiculous, little me directing you, when you were always ten years ahead of your time?' And he replied, 'Twenty.' – *Billy Wilder, 1942*
As to directing his own performance, Von always had an assistant to give him an opinion of his acting. Whether he listened to it or not was another matter. – *William Daniels*
One of the cinema's great enigmas … he conjured up a world very much in its infancy psychologically. It was a grotesque and brutal world, and the bleakness and callousness of his characters' lives were revealed with a meticulous realism. – *Claire Johnston*
He was a short man, almost squat, with a vulpine smirk that told you, as soon as his image flashed on to the screen, that no wife or bankroll must be left unguarded. – *S.J. Perelman*

Von Sydow, Max (1929–) (Carl Adolf Von Sydow)
Leading Swedish actor, a member of Ingmar BERGMAN's company.
Miss Julie 51. *The Seventh Seal* 57. Wild Strawberries 57. So Close to Life 58. *The Face* 58. The Virgin Spring 59. *Through a Glass Darkly* 61. Winter Light 62. The Mistress 62. *The Greatest Story Ever Told* (as Jesus) (US) 65. The Reward (US) 65. *Hawaii* (US) 66. The Quiller Memorandum (GB) 66. *Hour of the Wolf* 68. The Shame 68. The Kremlin Letter (US) 70. *The Emigrants* 70. The Touch 70. The Night Visitor 71. Embassy 72. The Exorcist (US) 73. The New Land 75. Illustrious Corpses 75. Three Days of the Condor (US) 75. The Ultimate Warrior 75. Voyage of the Damned 76. Exorcist II: The Heretic 77. Foxtrot 77. March or Die 77. Brass Target 78. Hurricane 79. Deathwatch 80. Flash Gordon 80. Conan the Barbarian 81. Victory 81. Never Say Never Again 83. Strange Brew 83. Dreamscape 84. Dune 84. Kojak: The Belarus File (TV) 85. Christopher Columbus (TV) 85. Code Name: Emerald 85. The Second Victory 86. The Wolf at the Door 86. Hannah and Her Sisters 86. Duet for One 87. *Pelle the Conqueror* (AAN) 87. Katinka (d) 88. My Dear Doctor Grasler/Mio Caro Dottor Gräsler 89. Father 89. Awakenings 90. Father 90. Europa 91. A Kiss before Dying 91. Until the End of the World/Bis ans Ende der Welt 91. The Bachelor 91. The Ox/Oxen 92. The Touch 92. The Best Intentions 92. Morfars Resa 93. Needful

Things 93. Time Is Money 94. Judge Dredd 95. Hamsun (title role) 95. Citizen X (TV) 95. Jerusalem 96. Hostile Waters 97. What Dreams May Come 98. Private Confessions 98. Snow Falling on Cedars 99. Nuremberg (TV) 00, etc.

Von Trier, Lars (1956–)

Danish director, screenwriter and producer. Born in Copenhagen, he studied film at the University of Copenhagen and began making short films in the mid-70s before graduating from the National Film School in the early 80s. His *Breaking the Waves* won the Grand Jury Prize at the Cannes Film Festival in 1996. In 1998 his production company Zentropa launched a new division, Pussy Power, to produce erotic films. *The Humiliated/De Ydmyygede*, a documentary by Jasper Jargil on the making of *The Idiots*, was released in 99. He is one of the founders of the DOGME movement for a simpler cinema.

Element of Crime 84. Epidemic 89. *Europa/ Zentropa* 91. The Kingdom/Riget 94. Breaking the Waves 96. Idiots/Idioterne 98. Dancer in the Dark (AANs) 00, etc.

Von Trotta, Margarethe (1942–)

German director who married Volker Schlöndorff.

The Lost Honour of Katerina Blum (co-d) 75. The Second Awakening of Krista Clarges 77. Sisters 79. The German Sisters 81. Friends and Husbands 83. Rosa Luxemburg 85. Felix 87. The Return/Die Rückkehr 90. Three Sisters/Paura e Amore 90. The African/L'Africana 91. Anni del Muro 93. Il Lungo Silenzio (It.) 94. The Promise 95, etc.

Vonnegut, Kurt (1922–)

American novelist, often of science fiction, who gained a cult following from the 60s.

Slaughterhouse Five (oa) 72. Harrison Bergeron (TV) (oa) 95. Mother Night (oa) 96, etc.
66 I tell you, we are here on Earth to fart around, and don't let anybody tell you any different. – K.V.

Vorhaus, Bernard (1904–2000)

American director, who moved to work in Britain in the 20s and 30s. Born in New York City, the son of Austrian immigrants, he studied law at Harvard and began as a writer with Columbia and MGM. His career ended when he was named to HUAC as a Communist by director Edward DMYTRYK and blacklisted. He later became a British citizen and a property developer.

AS WRITER: Steppin' Out (story) 25. No Other Woman (co-w) 28, etc.

AS DIRECTOR: Money for Speed (GB) 33. The Ghost Camera (GB) 33. Broken Melody (GB) 35. The Last Journey (GB) 35. Cotton Queen (GB) 37. Dusty Ermine (GB) 38. Fisherman's Wharf 39. Meet Dr Christian 39.Three Faces West 40. Lady from Louisiana 41. Ice-Capades Revue 42. Bury Me Dead (US) 47. The Amazing Dr X 48. So Young So Bad 50. The Lady from Boston 51. Pardon My French 51, etc.

Vorkapich, Slavko (1892–1976)

Yugoslavian writer who came to Hollywood in 1922, did a little screenwriting, tried direction in 1931 (*I Take This Woman*), then settled as a montage expert.

Viva Villa 34. *Crime without Passion* 34. San Francisco 36. Maytime 37. The Last Gangster 38. Shopworn Angel 38. Mr Smith Goes to Washington 39, etc.

Voskovec, George (1905–1981) (Jiri Voskovec)

Czech stage actor, long in US.

Anything Can Happen 52. *Twelve Angry Men* 57. The Bravados 58. Butterfield 8 60. The Spy Who Came in from the Cold 65. Mister Buddwing 66. The Boston Strangler 68. Skag (TV) 80. Somewhere in Time 80. Barbarossa 82, etc.

Vosloo, Arnold (1962–)

South African actor, frequently in in Hollywood horror movies.

Gor (US) 87. Steel Dawn (US) 87. Circles in a Forest 88. A Reason to Die 89. Act of Piracy 90. The Finishing Touch (US) 91. Hard Target (US) 93. Darkman III: Die, Darkman, Die (US) 95. Diary of a Serial Killer (US) 95. Zeus and Roxanne (US) 97. Progeny (US) 98. The Mummy (US) 99, etc.

Vosper, Frank (1899–1937)

Bulky English stage actor, playwright and screenwriter, who appeared in a few films. Born in London, he was on stage from 1919, often as a smooth villain. Fell overboard from a transatlantic liner and drowned.

Blinkeyes 26. Rome Express 32. Strange Evidence 32. Murder on the Second Floor (oa) 32. Dick Turpin 33. No Funny Business (co-w) 33. Waltzes from Vienna 33. Jew Suss 34. The Man Who Knew Too Much 34. Heart's Desire 35. Love from a Stranger (oa) 36. The Secret of Stamboul 36. Spy of Napoleon 36. Shadows on the Stairs (from his play *Murder on the Second Floor*) 41, etc.
66 A kind, funny, sweet-natured and generous man of considerable talent. I suppose that now he is forgotten, except by a very few. – *Alec Guinness, 1999*

Voulgaris, Pantelis (1940–)

Greek director and screenwriter. Born in Athens and a former film critic, he worked as an assistant director in the 60s.

The Engagement of Anna/To Proxenio tis Annas 72. O Megalos Erotikos 73. Happy Day 75. Venizelos 80. Stone Years/Petrina Chronia 85. The Striker with the No. 9/I Fanella Me To Ennia 88. Quiet Days in August 91. Acropole 95. It's a Long Road/Ola Ine Dromos 98, etc.

Vye, Murvyn (1913–1976)

Burly American character actor who usually played heavies.

Golden Earrings 48. A Connecticut Yankee at King Arthur's Court 49. Pick-Up 51. Road to Bali 52. Green Fire 54. Pearl of the South Pacific 55. Al Capone 58. Pay or Die 60. Andy 64, etc.

TV series: Lots of half-hours and hours, especially *Rawhide* and *The Beverly Hillbillies*.

Wickes, David
British director and producer, working mainly in television.
Sweeney! 76. Silver Dream Racer (& p, w) 80. Jack the Ripper (TV) 88. Jekyll and Hyde (TV) 90. Frankenstein (TV) 93.

Wickes, Mary (1910–1995) (Mary Wickenhauser)
American character comedienne.
The Man Who Came to Dinner (as the nurse) 41. Now Voyager 42. Higher and Higher 43. June Bride 48. Young Man with Ideas 52. The Actress 54. Good Morning, Miss Dove 56. It Happened to Jane 59. The Music Man 62. How to Murder Your Wife 64. The Trouble with Angels 66. Where Angels Go Trouble Follows 68. Snowball Express 73. Postcards from the Edge 90. Sister Act 92. Sister Act 2: Back in the Habit 93. Little Women 94. The Hunchback of Notre Dame (voice) 96, etc.
TV series: The Peter Lind Hayes Show 50. Bonino 50. Halls of Ivy 54. Dennis the Menace 59–61. The Gertrude Berg Show 61–62. Julia 68–71. Doc 75.
❝ Famous line (*The Man Who Came to Dinner*) 'If Florence Nightingale had ever nursed you, Mr Whiteside, she would have married Jack the Ripper instead of founding the Red Cross!'

Wicki, Bernhard (1919–2000)
Austrian actor-director, from the stage. He grew up in Vienna and studied at the Reinhardt drama school and the Berlin state drama school. He spent some months in a concentration camp in the early 40s because of his membership of a communist organisation.
AS ACTOR: Der Fallende Stern 50. The Last Bridge 53. Kinder, Mütter und ein General 54. Jackboot Mutiny 55. The Face of the Cat 57. La Notte 60. Despair 78. Spring Symphony 83. Paris, Texas 84. Killing Cars 85. Marie Ward 85. Das Geheimnis 92, etc.
AS DIRECTOR: *The Bridge* 59. The Miracle of Malachias 61. The Longest Day (co-d) 62. The Visit (US) 64. The Saboteur, Code Name Morituri (US) 65. Karpfs Karriere 72. Die Eroberung der Zitadelle 77. Die Grunstein-Variante 85. The Spider's Web/Das Spinnennetz 89. Success/Erfolg 91, etc.

Wicking, Christopher (1943–)
English screenwriter, mainly of horror movies. Born in London, he studied at St Martin's School of Art.
Scream and Scream Again 69. The Oblong Box 69. Cry of the Banshee 70. Blood from the Mummy's Tomb 71. Murders in the Rue Morgue 71. Venom 71. To the Devil a Daughter 76. Lady Chatterley's Lover 81. Absolute Beginners 86. Dream Demon 88, etc.

Widdoes, Kathleen (1939–)
American actress with stage experience.
The Group 66. Petulia 68. The Seagull 68. The Mephisto Waltz 71. Savages 72. Mafia Princess (TV) 86. Courage under Fire 96, etc.

Widerberg, Bo (1930–1997)
Swedish writer-director and editor, much influenced by the French New Wave. Born in Malmö, he began as a journalist, short-story writer, novelist and film critic, first making a local reputation with a 1962 pamphlet, *Visions of Swedish Film*, attacking postwar Swedish cinema and the work of Ingmar BERGMAN. In films dealing with Sweden's past, intended to throw light on contemporary life, he often worked with non-professional actors, though his best-known films starred Thommy BERGGREN.
Raven's End (AAN) 63. Karlek 63. Thirty Times Your Money 66. *Elvira Madigan* 67. *Adalen 31* (AAN) 69. The Ballad of Joe Hill 69. The Man on the Roof 75. Victoria 79. The Man from Majorca 85. The Serpent's Way 87. Up the Naked Rock 88. *End All Things Fair* (AAN) 95, etc.

Widerberg, Johan (1974–)
Swedish actor, the son of Bo WIDERBERG.
Tango in August/Augustitango 93. Love Lessons/All Things Fair/Lust och Fägring Stor 95. Svart, Vitt 96. Under the Sun/Under Solen 99, etc.

Widmark, Richard (1914–)
American leading actor; once typed as cold-eyed killer, he fought successfully for more varied roles. Born in Sunrise, Minnesota, he taught drama at Lake Forest College, where he graduated in Speech and Political Science, and worked in radio and theatre in the early 40s. Married former actress and occasional screenwriter Jean Hazelwood in 1942.
■ *Kiss of Death* (AAN) 47. Road House 48. The Street with No Name 48. Yellow Sky 49. Down to the Sea in Ships 49. Slattery's Hurricane 49. Night and the City 50. Panic in the Streets 50. No Way Out 50. Halls of Montezuma 50. The Frogmen 51. Full House 52. Don't Bother to Knock 52. Red Skies of Montana 52. My Pal Gus 52. Destination Gobi 53. Pickup on South Street 53. Take the High Ground 53. Hell and High Water 54. Garden of Evil 54. Broken Lance 54. The Cobweb 55. A Prize of Gold 55. Backlash 56. Run for the Sun 56. The Last Wagon 56. Saint Joan 57. Time Limit 57. The Law and Jake Wade 58. The Tunnel of Love 58. The Trap 59. Warlock 59. The Alamo 60. The Secret Ways 61. Two Rode Together 61. Judgment at Nuremberg 61. How the West Was Won 63. Flight from Ashiya 64. The Long Ships 64. Cheyenne Autumn 64. *The Bedford Incident* 65. Alvarez Kelly 66. The Way West 67. *Madigan* 68. Death of a Gunfighter 69. A Talent for Loving 69. The Moonshine War 70. Brock's Last Case (TV) 71. Vanished (TV) 71. When the Legends Die 72. Murder on the Orient Express 74. To the Devil a Daughter 75. The Sellout 76. Twilight's Last Gleaming 76. Rollercoaster 77. The Domino Principle 77. Mr Horn (TV) 78. Coma 78. The Swarm 78. Bear Island 79. All God's Children (TV) 80. A Whale for the Killing (TV) 81. Who Dares Wins 82. Hanky Panky 82. National Lampoon's Movie Madness 82. The Final Option 82. Against All Odds 83. Blackout 85. A Gathering of Old Men (TV) 87. Once upon a Texas Train/Texas Guns (TV) 88. Cold Sassy Tree (TV) 89. True Colors 91.
TV series: *Madigan* 72.
❝ It is clear that murder is one of the kindest things he is capable of. – *James Agee*

Wieck, Dorothea (1908–1986)
Swiss-born character actress, in German and American films. Born in Davos, she studied acting under Max REINHARDT and began on the German stage. The success of *Madchen in Uniform* took her to Hollywood, with Paramount hoping that she would prove a rival to Marlene DIETRICH, but her two films failed at the box-office and she returned to Germany.
Mädchen in Uniform 31. Cradle Song (US) 33. Miss Fane's Baby Is Stolen 33. The Student of Prague 35. Der Vierte Kommt Nicht 39. Man on a Tightrope (US) 53, etc.

Wiene, Robert (1881–1938)
German director of expressionist films.
The Cabinet of Dr Caligari 19. Genuine 20. Raskolnikov 23. The Hands of Orlac 24, etc.

The Wiere Brothers
German eccentric comedians, long in America: *Harry* (1908–1992), *Herbert* (1909–), *Sylvester* (1910–1970). Films very occasional.
The Great American Broadcast 41. Swing Shift Maisie 44. *Road to Rio* 47. Double Trouble 68, etc.
TV series: *Oh Those Bells* 62.

Wiest, Dianne (1948–)
American character actress.
Footloose 84. Falling in Love 84. The Purple Rose of Cairo 85. *Hannah and Her Sisters* (AA) 86. Radio Days 87. September 87. The Lost Boys 87. Bright Lights, Big City 88. Cookie 89. Parenthood (AAN) 89. Edward Scissorhands 90. Little Man Tate 91. Cops and Robbersons 94. Bullets over Broadway (AA) 94. The Scout 94. Drunks 95. The Bird Cage 96. The Associate 96. The Horse Whisperer 98. Practical Magic 98, etc.

Wilbur, Crane (1887–1973)
American writer-director.
Canon City 48. The Story of Molly X 49. Outside the Wall 49. Inside the Walls of Folsom Prison 50. House of Wax (script only) 53. The Bat 59. Solomon and Sheba (script only) 59, etc.

Wilby, James (1958–)
Elegant British actor (born in Burma), from the stage.
Privileged 82. Dreamchild 85. A Room with a View 85. Maurice 87. A Handful of Dust 88. A Summer Story 88. Conspiracy 90. Adam Bede (TV) 91. Immaculate Conception 91. Howards End 92. Lady Chatterley (TV) 93. Regeneration 97. Tom's Midnight Garden 98. Cotton Mary 99. Trial and Retibution IV (TV) 00, etc.

Wilcox, Frank (1907–1974)
Tall American character actor, a bit player who was always seen in Warner films of the 40s – sometimes in two parts in the same film.
The Fighting 69th 39. River's End 40. Highway West 41. Across the Pacific 42. Juke Girl 43. The Adventures of Mark Twain 44. Conflict 45. Gentleman's Agreement 47. Samson and Delilah 49. Those Redheads from Seattle 53. Dance with Me Henry 56. A Majority of One 61, many others.

Wilcox, Fred M. (1905–1964)
American director, former publicist; films mainly routine.
Lassie Come Home 43. Blue Sierra 46. Courage of Lassie 46. Hills of Home 48. Three Daring Daughters 48. The Secret Garden 49. Shadow in the Sky 50. Code Two 53, Tennessee Champ 54. *Forbidden Planet* 56. I Passed for White 60.

Wilcox, Herbert (1892–1977)
British independent producer-director in films from 1919 (as salesman); married to Anna Neagle.
The Wonderful Story 20. The Dawn of the World 21. Chu Chin Chow 23. *Nell Gwyn* 24. *Dawn* 26. Wolves 28. Rookery Nook 30. Good Night Vienna 32. Carnival 32. *Bitter Sweet* 33. *Nell Gwyn* 34. Peg of Old Drury 35. Limelight 36. The Three Maxims 36. The Frog 37. *Victoria the Great* 37. Sixty Glorious Years 38. Our Fighting Navy 38. *Nurse Edith Cavell* (US) 39. Sunny (US) 39. *No No Nanette* (US) 40. Irene (US) 40. They Flew Alone 42. Yellow Canary 43. I Live in Grosvenor Square 45. *Piccadilly Incident* 46. The Courtneys of Curzon Street 47. *Spring in Park Lane* 48. Elizabeth of Ladymead 49. Maytime in Mayfair 49. *Odette* 50. The Lady with a Lamp 51. Trent's Last Case 52. Laughing Anne 53. Lilacs in the Spring 55. King's Rhapsody 56. Yangtse Incident 56. My Teenage Daughter 56. Those Dangerous Years 57. The Lady Is a Square 58. Heart of a Man 59. To See Such Fun (ex p only) 77, etc.
❝ Mr Herbert Wilcox proceeds on his appointed course. As slow and ponderous and well protected as a steamroller, he irons out opposition. We get from his films almost everything except life, character, truth. – *Graham Greene reviewing Nurse Edith Cavell*

Wilcox, Jack (John) (1905–1984)
British cinematographer.
Mr Topaz 61. Where's Jack? 68. The Chairman 68. The Last Valley 70. Legend of the Werewolf 75, etc.

Wilcox, Larry (1946–)
American actor and producer, best known for his role as Officer Jon Baker in the TV series *CHiPS* 77–82. A former professional rodeo roper, he also runs his own network marketing company.
Sky Hei$t (TV) 75. The Last Hard Men 76. The Last Ride of the Dalton Gang (TV) 79. The Love Tapes (TV) 80. Death of a Centerfold: The Dorothy Stratten Story (p) (TV) 81. Deadly Lessons (TV) 83. The Dirty Dozen: The Next Mission (TV) 85. National Lampoon's Loaded Weapon 93, etc.

Wilcoxon, Henry (1905–1984)
British leading man with stage experience, in Hollywood from early 30s, latterly as executive for Cecil B. de Mille.
The Perfect Lady 31. The Flying Squad 32. Cleopatra 34. The Crusades 35. The Last of the Mohicans 36. Mrs Miniver 42. Samson and Delilah 49. Scaramouche 52. The Greatest Show on Earth 53. The Ten Commandments (& co-p) 56. The Buccaneer (& p) 59. The Private Navy of Sergeant O'Farrell 69. Man in the Wilderness 71. Against a Crooked Sky 75. Pony Express Rider 76. F.I.S.T. 78. Caddyshack 80. Sweet Sixteen 81, etc.

Wild, Jack (1952–)
British juvenile, popular around 1970.
Oliver (AAN) 68. Melody 70. Flight of the Doves 71. The Pied Piper 72. The Fourteen 73. Robin Hood: Prince of Thieves 91, etc.
TV series: *H. R. Pufnstuf* 69.

Wilde, Cornel (1915–1989)
American leading man of the 40s; later produced and directed some interesting films, but never equalled his 1944 impact as Chopin. His second wife was actress Jean Wallace (1951–81).
■ Lady with Red Hair 40. Kisses for Breakfast 41. High Sierra 41. Right to the Heart 41. The Perfect Snob 42. Life Begins at 8.30 42. Manila Calling 42. Wintertime 43. *A Song to Remember* (AAN) 45. A Thousand and One Nights 45. Leave Her to Heaven 45. *The Bandit of Sherwood Forest* 46. Centennial Summer 46. The Homestretch 46. Forever Amber 47. It Had to be You 47. Roadhouse 48. The Walls of Jericho 48. Shockproof 49. Four Days' Leave 50. Two Flags West 50. At Sword's Point 52. Operation Secret 52. The Greatest Show on Earth 52. California Conquest 52. Treasure of the Golden Condor 53. Main Street to Broadway 53. Saadia 53. Passion 54. *Woman's World* 54. The Scarlet Coat 55. Storm Fear (& d) 55. The Big Combo 55. Star of India 55. Hot Blood 56. The Devil's Hairpin (& w) 57. Omar Khayyam 57. Beyond Mombasa 57. Maracaibo (& d) 58. Edge of Eternity 59. Constantine and the Cross 60. Sword of Lancelot (& d) 63. *The Naked Prey* (& d) 66. Beach Red (& d) 67. The Comic 69. No Blade of Grass (& d) 71. Gargoyles (TV) 72. Shark's Treasure (& d) 75. The Fifth Musketeer 78. The Norseman 78.

Wilde, Hagar (1904–1971)
American screenwriter.
Bringing Up Baby 38. Carefree 39. Fired Wife 43. Guest in the House 44. The Unseen 45. I Was a Male War Bride 49. This is My Love 54, etc.

Wilde, Marty (1939–) (Reginald Smith)
British pop singer who appeared in a film or two.
Jetstorm 59. The Hellions 61. What a Crazy World 63. Stardust 74, etc.

Wilde, Oscar (1854–1900)
British playwright, poet and wit, the subject in 1960 of two film biographies: *Oscar Wilde* starring Robert Morley and *The Trials of Oscar Wilde* starring Peter Finch. The former was directed by Gregory Ratoff from a script by Jo Eisinger, and had Ralph Richardson as Carson, John Neville as Lord Alfred, and Edward Chapman as the Marquess of Queensberry. The latter, written and directed by Ken Hughes, had James Mason, John Fraser and Lionel Jeffries respectively in these roles. Films have been made of several of Wilde's works including *The Importance of Being Earnest*, *An Ideal Husband*, *Lady Windermere's Fan*, *The Picture of Dorian Gray*, *Lord Arthur Savile's Crime* (in *Flesh and Fantasy*) and *The Canterville Ghost*. In 1997, the biopic *Wilde*, which put much emphasis on him as a married man and father, was directed by Brian Gilbert and starred Stephen Fry in the title role, Jude Law as his nemesis Lord Alfred Douglas, and Tom Wilkinson as the Marquess of Queensberry.
❝ One needs misfortunes to live happily. – *O.W.*

Wilder, Billy (1906–) (Samuel Wilder)
Austro-Hungarian writer-director, in Hollywood from 1934. A specialist for years in bitter comedy and drama torn from the world's headlines, he has lately concentrated on rather heavy-going bawdy farce.
Biography: 1970, *The Brighter Side of Billy Wilder, Primarily* by Tom Wood. 1976, *Billy Wilder in Hollywood* by Maurice Zolotow. 1996, *Wilder Times* by Kevin Lally. 1999, *Conversations with Wilder* by Cameron Crowe.
■ AS WRITER: People on Sunday 30; followed by ten other German films; Adorable (Fr.) 34. Music in the Air (co-w) 34. Lottery Lover (co-w) 35. Bluebeard's Eighth Wife (co-w) 38. *Midnight* (co-w) 39. What a Life (co-w) 39. *Ninotchka* (co-w, AAN) 39. *Arise My Love* (co-w) 40. Ball of Fire (co-w, AAN) 41. Hold Back the Dawn (co-w, AAN) 41.
■ AS WRITER -DIRECTOR (script always in collaboration): Mauvaise Graine (Fr.) 33. *The Major and the Minor* 42. *Five Graves to Cairo* 43. *Double Indemnity* (AAN) 44. *The Lost Weekend* (AA) 45. The Emperor Waltz 47. *A Foreign Affair* (co-w, AAN) 48. *Sunset Boulevard* (AAN) 50. *Ace in the Hole* 51. *Stalag 17* (AAN) 53. Sabrina (AAN) 54. *The Seven Year Itch* 55. The Spirit of St Louis 57. Love in the Afternoon 57. *Witness for the Prosecution* (AAN) 57. *Some Like It Hot* (AAN) 59. *The Apartment* (AA) 60. *One Two Three* 61. Irma La Douce 63. Kiss Me Stupid 64. The Fortune Cookie 66. *The Private Life of Sherlock Holmes* 70.

Avanti 72. The Front Page 74. Fedora 78. Buddy Buddy 81.
✪ For being Hollywood's most mischievous immigrant. *Sunset Boulevard.*
❝ The pixie wit of this Hollywood Viennese has sporadically brightened the film scene for more than thirty years. Nor does he save all his wit for his scripts; he is the most quotable of film-makers: 'I have ten commandments. The first nine are, thou shalt not bore. The tenth is, thou shalt have right of final cut.'

On critical prejudice: 'What critics call dirty in our movies, they call lusty in foreign films.'

On fashion: 'You watch, the new wave will discover the slow dissolve in ten years or so.'

On messages: 'In certain pictures I do hope they will leave the cinema a little enriched, but I don't make them pay a buck and a half and then ram a lecture down their throats.'

On direction: 'The best director is the one you don't see.'

On technique: 'The close-up is such a valuable thing – like a trump at bridge.'

On finances: 'No one says, "Boy I must see that film – I hear it came in under budget."'

A man with such waspish wit naturally invites retaliation, even from his wife: 'Long before Billy Wilder was Billy Wilder, he thought he was Billy Wilder.'

That may have been in response to a cable he sent her from Paris just after the war. She had requested him to buy and send a bidet. After a vain search he sent the message: 'Unable obtain bidet. Suggest handstand in shower.'

Wilder is the kind of man who can scarcely observe anything without being funny about it. For instance: 'France is a country where the money falls apart in your hands and you can't tear the toilet paper.'

But he could be just as ornery as anybody else. As Harry Kurnitz said: 'Billy Wilder at work is two people: Mr Hyde and Mr Hyde.'

Andrew Sarris summed up accurately: 'Wilder is a curdled Lubitsch, romanticism gone sour, 78rpm played at 45 an old-worldling from Vienna perpetually sneering at Hollywood as it engulfs him.'

Wilder wouldn't be listening – too busy constructing scenarios: 'An actor enters through a door, you've got nothing. But if he enters through a window, you've got a situation.'

Wilder, Gene (1934–) (Jerry Silberman)
American comic actor. Married actress Gilda Radner.

Bonnie and Clyde 67. *The Producers* (AAN) 68. Start the Revolution Without Me 69. Quackser Fortune has a Cousin in the Bronx 70. Willy Wonka and the Chocolate Factory 71. Everything You Always Wanted to Know about Sex 72. Rhinoceros 73. The Little Prince 73. Blazing Saddles 74. Young Frankenstein (AANw) 74. The Adventure of Sherlock Holmes' Smarter Brother (& p, d) 75. Silver Streak 76. The World's Greatest Lover (& wd, p) 77. The Frisco Kid 79. Stir Crazy 80. Sunday Lovers 80. Hanky Panky 82. The Woman in Red (& d) 84. Haunted Honeymoon (& d) 86. See No Evil, Hear No Evil 89. Funny about Love 90. Another You 91. Murder in a Small Town (&w) (TV) 99, etc.

Wilder, Robert (1901–1974)
American novelist and screenwriter.

Flamingo Road (& oa) 48. *Written on the Wind* (& oa) 56. The Big Country 58. Sol Madrid 66, etc.

Wilder, Thornton (1897–1975)
American playwright and novelist. Works filmed include *Our Town*, *The Bridge of San Luis Rey* (several times), *The Matchmaker*; also wrote screenplay of Hitchcock's *Shadow of a Doubt*.

Wilder, W. Lee (1904–)
Austro-Hungarian producer in America, brother of Billy Wilder. Films mainly low-budget oddities.

The Great Flamarion 44. Phantom from Space 53. The Snow Creature 54. Bluebeard's Ten Honeymoons 60, etc.

Wilding, Michael (1912–1979)
British leading man of the 40s. His four wives included actresses Elizabeth Taylor and Margaret Leighton.

Autobiography: 1982, *Apple Sauce* (published posthumously).

Wedding Group 35. Tilly of Bloomsbury 40. *Sailors Three* 40. Kipps 41. Cottage To Let 41. *In Which We Serve* 42. Dear Octopus 43. *English Without Tears* 44. Carnival 46. *Piccadilly Incident* 46. The Courtneys of Curzon Street 47. An Ideal Husband 47. *Spring in Park Lane* 48. Maytime in Mayfair 50. Under Capricorn 50. Stage Fright 50. Into the Blue 51. The Law and the Lady (US) 52. Derby Day 52. Trent's Last Case 53. The Egyptian 54. The Glass Slipper 55. Zarak 56. Danger Within 57. The World of Suzie Wong 60. The Naked Edge 61. The Best of Enemies 61. A Girl Named Tamiko 63. The Sweet Ride 68. Waterloo 69. Lady Caroline Lamb 72. Frankenstein: The True Story (TV) 73, etc.

❝ I was the worst actor I ever came across. – *M.W.*

He was a man who should never have become an actor because his nerves were so terrible that every appearance was an ordeal. – *Hermione Baddeley*

Wildman, John (1961–)
Canadian actor. Won a Genie (the Canadian equivalent of an Oscar) for his performance in My *American Cousin*.

Humongous 81. My *American Cousin* 85. Sorority Babes in the Slimeball Bowl-A-Rama 87. Lethal Pursuit 88. American Boyfriends 89, etc.

Wilke, Robert J. (1911–1989)
American character actor, usually in mean, shifty or villainous roles.

San Francisco 36. Sheriff of Sundown 44. The Last Days of Boot Hill 47. Kill the Umpire 50. Twenty Thousand Leagues under the Sea 54. Night Passage 57. The Gun Hawk 63. The Hallelujah Trail 65. Tony Rome 67. A Gunfight 71. Days of Heaven 78. Stripes 81, etc.

Wilkinson, Tom (1948–)
English character actor.

Wetherby 85. Sylvia 85. Paper Mask 90. A Business Affair 93. Martin Chuzzlewit (as Pecksniff) (TV) 94. *Priest* 94. A Very Open Prison (TV) 95. The Ghost and the Darkness 96. Crossing the Floor (TV) 96. Smilla's Sense of Snow/Smilla's Feeling for Snow 97. *The Full Monty* 97. Wilde 97. Oscar and Lucinda 97. The Governess 97. Rush Hour 98. Shakespeare in Love 98. Molokai 98. Ride With The Devil 99. Essex Boys 00. Another Life 00, etc.

William, Warren (1895–1948) (Warren Krech)
Suave American leading man with stage experience.

The Perils of Pauline 14. The Woman from Monte Carlo 32. The Mouthpiece 33. *Lady for a Day* 33. *Imitation of Life* 34. Cleopatra (as Julius Caesar) 34. The Case of the Lucky Legs 35. Satan Met a Lady 36. The Firefly 37. *The Lone Wolf's Spy Hunt* 39 (and others in this series). The Man in the Iron Mask 39. Lillian Russell 40. The Wolf Man 41. Counter Espionage 42. One Dangerous Night 43. Fear 46. Bel Ami 47, etc.

Williams, Adam (1929–)
American 'second lead'.

Queen for a Day 50. Without Warning 52. Crashout 55. Garment Centre 57. Darby's Rangers 58. North by Northwest 59. The Last Sunset 61. The Glory Guys 67, etc.

Williams, Bill (1916–1992) (William Katt)
American leading man, an innocent-type hero of the 40s. Former professional swimmer and singer.

Murder in the Blue Room (debut) 44. Those Endearing Young Charms 45. Till the End of Time 46. Deadline at Dawn 47. The Great Missouri Raid 51. The Outlaw's Daughter 53. Wiretapper 56. A Dog's Best Friend 61. Tickle Me 65, etc.

TV series: Kit Carson 52–54. Assignment Underwater 61.

Williams, Billy (1929–)
British cinematographer.

Just Like a Woman 66. Billion Dollar Brain 67. *Women in Love* 69. Two Gentlemen Sharing 70. Tam Lin 70. *Sunday Bloody Sunday* 72. Night Watch 73. The Wind and the Lion 75. Eagle's Wing 79. Saturn Three 80. *On Golden Pond* 81. *Gandhi* (AA) 82. Monsignor 82. The Survivors 83. Dreamchild 85. Eleni 85. The Manhattan Project 86. Suspect 87. The Rainbow 89. Stella 90. Diamond's Edge 90. Shadow of the Wolf 92. Reunion (TV) 94. Driftwood 95, etc.

Williams, Billy Dee (1937–)
American leading man.

Brian's Song (TV) 71. Lady Sings the Blues 72. Hit! 73. The Take 74. Mahogany 75. Bingo Long and the Travelling All Stars 76. *Scott Joplin* 78. The Empire Strikes Back 80. Nighthawks 81. Marvin and Tige 83. Return of the Jedi 83. Fear City 85. Number One with a Bullet 87. Deadly Illusion 87. The Impostor 88. Batman 89. Dangerous Passion (TV) 90. Alien Intruder 93. TripleCross 95. Dangerous Passion 95. Moving Target 96. Steel Sharks 97. Mask of Death 97. The Visit 00, etc.

Williams, Bransby (1870–1961) (Bransby William Pharez)
British actor and mimic, a former clerk. Born in Hackney, London, he was on stage from the 1890s and in silent films from 1911, but was best known for his music-hall performances from the mid-1890s which made him a star, imitating popular actors of the time, including Henry Irving and Beerbohm Tree, reciting monologues to music, including 'The Green Eye of the Yellow God', and presenting characters from Dickens. In later life, he was much on radio and also appeared on television. He made an early talkie appearance in an experimental Lee de Forest Phonofilm.

Royal England 11. Grimaldi 14. Hard Times 15. Adam Bede 18. The Adventures of Mr Pickwick 21. The Cold Cure 25. Jungle Woman 26. Scrooge 28. Troublesome Wives 28. Hearts of Humanity 36. *Song of the Road* 37. The Common Touch 41. Tomorrow We Live 42. The Trojan Brothers 46. Judgment Deferred 52, etc.

Williams, Cara (1925–) (Bernice Kamiat)
American TV and radio comedienne. She was formerly married to John Drew Barrymore.

Happy Land 43. Don Juan Quilligan 45. Sitting Pretty 48. The Girl Next Door 53. The Defiant Ones (AAN) 58. The Man from the Diners Club 63. The White Buffalo 77.

TV series: Pete and Gladys 60–61. The Cara Williams Show 64. Rhoda 74–75.

Williams, Charles (1893– *)
English composer and musical director. Born in London, he studied at the Royal Academy of Music and began by composing scores for silent pictures. He worked for Gaumont-British for much of the 30s. His best-known composition was 'The Dream of Olwyn', the theme for *While I Live*, which became so popular that the film was later reissued under the tune's title.

Kipps 41. The Night Has Eyes/Terror House 42. The Young Mr Pitt 42. The Life and Death of Colonel Blimp (md) 43. Twilight Hour (md) 44. Quiet Weekend 46. While I Live/The Dream of Olwen 47. Noose 48. The Romantic Age 49, etc.

Williams, Cindy (1948–)
American leading lady.

Drive He Said 71. American Graffiti 73. Travels with My Aunt 73. The Conversation 74. Mr Ricco 75. More American Graffiti 79. The Creature Wasn't Nice 81. Rude Awakening 89. Bingo! 91. Meet Wally Sparks 97, etc.

TV series: Laverne and Shirley 76–82. Normal Life 90. Getting By 93–94.

Williams, Derick (1906–)
English cinematographer and producer. Born in Nottingham, he studied at Nottingham University and began his career as assistant cameraman on Alfred Hitchcock's *Blackmail* 29. In the early 30s he became head of Gainsborough's camera department, then spent a year in Hollywood before returning to Britain. He set up his own production company in the 50s.

The Lucky Number (co-ph) 33. Inspector Hornleigh 38. Ask a Policeman 38. Ghost of St Michael's 41. The Way Ahead (co-ph) 44. The Way to the Stars/Johnny in the Clouds 45. Beware of Pity 46. White Cradle Inn/High Fury 47. My Brother Jonathan 47. For Them that Trespass 48. Don't Talk to Strange Men (p) 62. Seventy Deadly Pills (p) 63. On the Run (p) 69, etc.

Williams, Elmo (1913–)
American editor and producer. Produced, edited and directed *The Cowboy* 54; worked as editor on several major productions; became head of Twentieth Century-Fox British productions.

Williams, Emlyn (1905–1987)
Welsh leading actor, dramatist, screenwriter and director. Born in Mostyn, he was a poor boy from a mining village who, encouraged by his teacher, won a scholarship to Oxford, a subject that formed the basis of his most successful play, *The Corn Is Green*. On stage from 1927, and a prolific playwright in the 30s and 40s, he began in films repeating one of his stage successes, later becoming an occasional screenwriter and director. Two projects that never came to fruition were the role of Caligula in Alexander Korda's abandoned *I, Claudius* and a screenplay, *Gala Night*, based on Arthur Machen's *The Terror*. From the early 50s, he gained a new fame for his one-man shows based on the work of Charles Dickens, Dylan Thomas and Saki. His best film roles were as Lord Lebanon in *The Frightened Lady*, Shorty Matthews in *They Drive by Night*, Dennis in *Hatter's Castle*, Maxwell Bard in *Three Husbands*, and William Collyer in *The Deep Blue Sea*. He is the father of actor Brook Williams (1938–).

Autobiography: 1972, *George*. 1974, *Emlyn*.

Biography: 1992, *Emlyn Williams* by James Harding.

The Frightened Lady 32. Sally Bishop 32. Men of Tomorrow 32. Friday the Thirteenth (& w) 34. My Song for You 34. Evensong 34. The Iron Duke 34. Evergreen (co-w only) 34. The Man Who Knew Too Much (co-w only) 34. The Love Affair of a Dictator 35. Roadhouse 35. The Divine Spark (co-w only) 35. The City of Beautiful Nonsense 35. Broken Blossoms (& w) 36. Night Must Fall (oa) 37. Night Alone 38. Dead Men Tell No Tales 39. The Citadel 39. *They Drive by Night* 39. Jamaica Inn 39. The Stars Look Down 40. You Will Remember 41. The Girl in the News 41. Major Barbara 41. This England (& w) 41. *Hatter's Castle* 42. The Corn Is Green (oa) 45. *The Last Days of Dolwyn* (& wd) 49. *Three Husbands* (US) 51. Another Man's Poison 51. The Scarf (US) 51. The Magic Box 52. Ivanhoe 52. *The Deep Blue Sea* 55. I Accuse 57. Time without Pity (oa) 57. Beyond This Place 59. The Wreck of the Mary Deare 59. The L-Shaped Room 62. Night Must Fall (oa) 64. The Eye of the Devil 66. David Copperfield (TV) 69. The Walking Stick 70. The Corn Is Green (oa) (TV) 78. The Deadly Game (TV) 82. Past Caring (TV) 85. King Ralph (oa) 91, etc.

Williams, Esther (1923–)
Aquatic American leading lady, former swimming champion. Her four husbands included actor Fernando Lamas. Her lovers included actor Jeff Chandler.

Autobiography: 1999, *Million Dollar Mermaid* (with Digby Diehl.)

■ Andy Hardy's Double Life (debut) 42. A Guy Named Joe 43. *Bathing Beauty* 44. Ziegfeld Follies 44. Thrill of a Romance 45. Easy to Wed 45. This Time for Keeps 46. Till the Clouds Roll By 46. Fiesta 47. On an Island with You 48. *Take Me Out to the Ball Game* 48. Neptune's Daughter 49. Pagan Love Song 50. Duchess of Idaho 51. Callaway Went Thataway 51. Texas Carnival 52. Skirts Ahoy 52. Million Dollar Mermaid 52. *Dangerous When Wet* 53. Easy to Love 54. Jupiter's Darling 54. The Unguarded Moment 56. Raw Wind in Eden 57. The Big Show 61. The Magic Fountain (Sp.) 61.

❝ All they ever did for me at MGM was change my leading men and the water in my pool. – *E.W.*

Wet she was a star. – *Joe Pasternak*

Williams, Grant (1930–1985)
American leading man who never quite made the big time.

Written on the Wind 56. *The Incredible Shrinking Man* 57. The Monolith Monsters 58. PT 109 63. Doomsday 72, etc.

TV series: Hawaiian Eye 59–63.

Williams, Guinn 'Big Boy' (1900–1962)
American character actor, usually in amiably tough roles. In Hollywood 1919 as an extra.

Noah's Ark 29. Dodge City 39. Mr Wise Guy 42. The Desperadoes 43. Thirty Seconds Over Tokyo 44. Bad Men of Tombstone 49. Hangman's Knot 53. The Outlaw's Daughter 55. The Comancheros 62, many others.

TV series: Circus Boy 56–57.

Williams, Guy (1924–1989) (Armand Catalano)
American leading man, the 'Zorro' of Walt Disney's TV series and films.

The Prince and the Pauper 62. Captain Sinbad 63, etc.

TV series: Lost in Space 65–68.

Williams, Hank (1923–1953)
Influential American country singer and songwriter who had a short, unruly life. In the biopic *Your Cheatin' Heart* 64, he was played by George Hamilton, with his songs dubbed by his son, Hank Williams Jnr.

Williams, Harcourt (1880–1957)
Distinguished British stage actor.
Henry V 44. *Brighton Rock* 47. Hamlet 48. Third Time Lucky 48. *The Late Edwina Black* 51. Roman Holiday 53. Around the World in Eighty Days 56.

Williams, Heathcote (1941–)
English poet, dramatist and actor.
Maltesta (Ger) 69. Dreams of Thirteen/Wet Dreams (Ger) (& co-wd) 74. The Tempest (as Prospero) 79. Wish You Were Here 87. Little Dorrit 87. Stormy Monday 88. Orlando 92. The Browning Version 94. The Steal 94. Blue Juice 95. The Cold Light of Day 95. The Tango Lesson 97. Cousin Bette (US/GB) 98. Alegria (Can/Fr/Neth) 99. Miss Julie 99, etc.
66 Fame is the perversion of the natural human instinct for validation and attention. – *H.W.*

Williams, Hugh (1904–1969) (Brian Williams)
British leading man and playwright on stage from 1921.
Charley's Aunt (film debut) 30. In a Monastery Garden 31. Rome Express 33. Sorrell and Son 34. *David Copperfield* (US) 34. The Amateur Gentleman 36. Dark Eyes of London 38. Wuthering Heights (US) 39. A Girl in a Million 46. *An Ideal Husband* 47. Take My Life 47. The Blind Goddess 48. Elizabeth of Ladymead 49. The Gift Horse 52. The Fake 53. Twice Upon a Time 53. Khartoum 66, etc.

Williams, Jo Beth (1953–)
American leading lady.
Kramer vs Kramer 79. The Dogs of War 80. Stir Crazy 80. Poltergeist 82. Endangered Species 82. The Big Chill 83. American Dreamer 84. Teachers 84. Desert Bloom 85. Poltergeist II 86. Memories of Me 88. Welcome Home 89. Victim of Love 91. Switch 91. Dutch/Driving Me Crazy 91. Stop! or My Mom Will Shoot 92. Chantilly Lace (TV) 93. Wyatt Earp 94. Parallel Lives (TV) 94. Ruby Jean and Joe 96. Jungle 2 Jungle 96. When Danger Follows You Home 97. Just Write 98, etc.
TV series: The Client 95–96.

Williams, John (1903–1983)
Suave British stage actor, usually in polished comedy roles.
Emil and the Detectives 35. Next of Kin 42. A Woman's Vengeance 48. Dick Turpin's Ride 51. *Dial M for Murder* 54. Sabrina Fair 54. To Catch a Thief 55. *The Solid Gold Cadillac* 56. Island in the Sun 56. Witness for the Prosecution 57. Visit to a Small Planet 60. Last of the Secret Agents 66. The Secret War of Harry Frigg 67. A Flea in Her Ear 68. The Hound of the Baskervilles (TV) 72. No Deposit No Return 76. Hot Lead and Cold Feet 78, etc.

Williams, John (1932–)
Prolific American composer and pianist, the creator of sweeping scores, and best known for the music to the *Star Wars* films. Born in Floral Park, New York, the son of a musician, he studied at the Juilliard School and worked as a studio musician and arranger before turning to composition. During the 80s and early 90s he was also conductor of the Boston Pops Orchestra.
The Secret Ways 61. Diamond Head 62. None but the Brave 65. How to Steal a Million 66. Valley of the Dolls (AAN) 67. Goodbye Mr Chips (AAN) 69. The Reivers (AAN) 69. The Cowboys 71. *Fiddler on the Roof* (AA) 71. The Poseidon Adventure (AAN) 72. Images (AAN) 72. Tom Sawyer (AAN) 73. Cinderella Liberty (AANm, AANs) 73. Earthquake 74. The Towering Inferno (AAN) 74. *Jaws* (AA) 75. The Eiger Sanction 75. *Star Wars* (AA) 77. Close Encounters of the Third Kind (AAN) 77. Jaws 2 78. Superman (AAN) 78. The Fury 78. 1941 79. Dracula 79. Superman 2 80. The Empire Strikes Back (AAN, BFA) 80. Raiders of the Lost Ark (AAN) 81. E.T. – the Extraterrestrial (AA, BFA) 82. Yes, Giorgio (AANs) 82. Return of the Jedi (AAN) 83. Monsignor 83. Indiana Jones and the Temple of Doom (AAN) 84. The River (AAN) 84. Spacecamp 85. The Witches of Eastwick (AAN) 87. Empire of the Sun (AAN) 87. Jaws: The Revenge 87. Superman IV: The Quest for Peace 87. The Accidental Tourist (AAN) 88. Always 89. Born on the Fourth of July (AAN) 89. Indiana Jones and the Last Crusade (AAN) 89. *Home Alone* (AANm, AANs) 90. Stanley and Iris 90. JFK (AAN) 91. Hook (AAN) 91. Far and Away 92. Jurassic Park 93. Schindler's List (AA) 93. Nixon (AAN) 95. Sabrina (AANm, AANs) 95. Sleepers (AAN) 96. Seven Years in Tibet 97. Amistad (AAN) 97. Stepmom 98. Saving Private Ryan (AAN) 98. Star Wars Episode l: The Phantom Menace 99. Angela's Ashes (AAN) 99. The Patriot (AAN) 00, etc.

Williams, Kathlyn (1888–1960)
American leading lady of silent films: one of the first serial queens.
Witch of the Everglades 11. Driftwood 12. The Adventures of Kathlyn 13. Sweet Alyssum 15. The Highway of Hope 17. Just a Wife 20. Morals 23. The Enemy Sex 24. Our Dancing Daughters 28. Blood Money 33, many others.

Williams, Kenneth (1926–1988)
British comic actor adept at 'small boy' characters and a variety of outrageous voices. Also on stage, radio and TV. He starred in 22 'Carry On' films.
Autobiography: 1985, *Just Williams*. Also: 1993, *The Diaries of Kenneth Williams*, edited by Russell Davies. 1994, *The Letters of Kenneth Williams*, edited by Russell Davies.
The Beggar's Opera 52. The Seekers 54. *Carry On Sergeant* 58 (and most other 'Carry Ons'). Raising the Wind 61. Twice Round the Daffodils 62. Don't Lose Your Head 67. Follow That Camel 68. Carry On Dick 74, etc.
66 The thing to do, in any circumstance, is to appear to know exactly what you are doing and at the same time convey casual doubts about the abilities of everybody else and undermine their confidence. – *K.W.*
It is not as an actor that he will be remembered, but as a voice veering between posh and rough-trade and all of it laced with camp. And as a look too: beady eyes, cavernous nostrils and pursed mouth. – *George Melly*

Williams, Lia
English leading actress, mainly on stage and TV.
Dirty Weekend 92. Mr Wroe's Virgins (TV) 93. Different for Girls 96. Flowers of the Forest (TV) 96. The Fifth Province 97. The Uninvited (TV) 97. Firelight 97. Shot Through the Heart (TV) 98. Bad Blood (TV) 99. The King is Alive 00, etc.
TV series: Seaforth 94.

Williams, Michelle (1980–)
American teenaged actress, born in Kalispell, Montana, who began appearing in commercials at the age of 10, when her family moved to San Diego. She is best known for her role as Jennifer in the TV series *Dawson's Creek*.
Lassie 94. Species 95. A Thousand Acres 97. Halloween H20: Twenty Years Later 98. Dick 99, etc.
TV series: Dawson's Creek 98– .

Williams, Olivia (c. 1969–)
English actress, from the theatre. Born in London, she studied English at Cambridge University and acting at the Bristol Old Vic school.
The Postman (US) 97. Emma (TV) 97. Rushmore (US) 98. The Sixth Sense (US) 99. Jason and the Argonauts (TV) 00. Four Dogs Playing Poker (US) 00. Born Romantic 00, etc.

Williams, Patrick (1939–)
American composer who has also scored many TV movies and series.
How Sweet It Is! 68. Don't Drink the Water 69. Evel Knievel 72. Framed 74. The Cheap Detective 78. The One and Only 78. Casey's Shadow 78. Breaking Away (AAN) 79. Butch and Sundance: The Early Days 79. Cuba 79. Hot Stuff 79. Charlie Chan and the Curse of the Dragon Queen 80. Hero at Large 80. It's My Turn 80. Used Cars 80. Wholly Moses 80. Some Kind of Hero 81. The Best Little Whorehouse in Texas 82. The Toy 83. Two of a Kind 83. All of Me 84. Swing Shift 84. Best Defense 84. Just Between Friends 86. Fresh Horses 88. Worth Winning 89. Cry-Baby 90. In the Spirit 90. Big Girls Don't Cry... They Get Even 92. The Cutting Edge 92. Geronimo (TV) 94. Kingfish (TV) 95. The Grass Harp 95. That Old Feeling 97. Julian Po 97. Jeus (TV) 00, etc.

Williams, Paul (1940–)
Diminutive American singer, composer and actor.
The Chase (a) 65. Phantom of the Paradise (a, m) (AANm) 74. Bugsy Malone (m) 76. A Star Is Born (AAs) 76. Smokey and the Bandit (a) 77. The End (m) 78. The Muppet Movie (a, m) (AANm) 79. The Wild Wild West Revisited (a) (TV) 79. Rooster (a) (TV) 82. Smokey and the Bandit III 83. Headless Body in a Topless Bar 95, etc.

Williams, Paul (1943–)
American director of quirky films.
Out of It 69. The Revolutionary 70. Dealing: Or the Berkeley-to-Boston Forty-Brick Lost-Bag Blues 72. A Light in the Afternoon 86. The November Men 93. Mirage 95, etc.

Williams, Rhys (1892–1969)
Welsh character actor, long in Hollywood; former technical adviser.
How Green Was My Valley 40. The Spiral Staircase 45. Scandal at Scourie 53. There's No Business Like Show Business 54. The Kentuckian 55. The Fastest Gun Alive 56. The Sons of Katie Elder 65. Skullduggery 69, many others.

Williams, Richard (1933–)
Canadian animator in England who has been working on his animated feature *The Thief and the Cobbler* for more than 20 years. After he lost control of it, it was finally released in 1995 as *Arabian Knight*.
The Little Island 58. *The Charge of the Light Brigade* (titles) 67. *A Christmas Carol* 73, etc.
Designed title sequences for *What's New Pussycat*, *The Liquidator*, *Casino Royale*, *Sebastian*, etc.

Williams, Robert (1899–1931)
Slow-speaking American leading man of the early 30s.
The Common Law 31. Rebound 31. Devotion 31. *Platinum Blonde* 31, etc.

Williams, Robin (1952–)
Eccentric American nightclub comedian who became a TV star as Mork from Ork in *Mork and Mindy*. He has a claim as the biggest box-office attraction from the mid-80s: since 1986, he has starred in seven films that have each taken more than $100m at the US box-office, putting him ahead of Tom Hanks, who has appeared in five $100m films, and Tom Cruise, who has appeared in six. Current asking price: around $15m. In 1998 *Fortune* magazine estimated his personal wealth at $100m.
Popeye 80. The World According to Garp 82. The Survivors 83. Moscow on the Hudson 84. The Best of Times 85. Club Paradise 86. Good Morning Vietnam (AAN) 87. Dear America: Letters Home from Vietnam 88. The Adventures of Baron Munchausen (uncredited) 89. Dead Poets Society (AAN) 89. Cadillac Man 90. Awakenings 90. Dead Again (uncredited) 91. The Fisher King (AAN) 91. Shakes the Clown (uncredited) 91. Hook 91. Ferngully ... the Last Rainforest (voice) 92. *Aladdin* (voice) 92. Toys 92. Mrs Doubtfire 93. Being Human 94. Nine Months 95. Jumanji 95. The Bird Cage 96. Jack 96. Hamlet 96. Father's Day 96. Joseph Conrad's Secret Agent 96. Flubber 97. *Good Will Hunting* (AA) 97. Deconstructing Harry 97. What Dreams May Come 98. Patch Adams 98, etc.
66 Cocaine is God's way of saying you're making too much money. – *R.W.*
You're only given a little madness. You mustn't lose it. – *R.W.*

Williams, Simon (1946–)
British light leading man, son of Hugh Williams, who became a TV star in *Upstairs Downstairs*.
The Incredible Sarah 75. Jabberwocky 76. The Odd Job 77. The Prisoner of Zenda 79. The Fiendish Plot of Fu Manchu 80. The Return of the Man from UNCLE (TV) 83.

Williams, Tennessee (1911–1983) (Thomas Lanier Williams)
Popular American playwright whose work, usually concerned with strong sexual emotions, has often been translated to the screen, despite the fact that in the process it has been so watered down as to lose much of its power. Born in Columbus, Mississippi, the son of a shoe salesman, he studied at the University of Iowa and found success with his autobiographical *The Glass Menagerie* 45, the only one of his plays not to have been distorted by the film studios. The Broadway production of *A Streetcar Named Desire* 47 made a star of Marlon Brando, who repeated his role in the film directed by Elia Kazan. Williams was not often happy with the films of his work: he thought *Baby Doll* lacked the right wanton hilarity; that *Suddenly, Last Summer* ('It made me throw up,' he said) suffered from the miscasting of Elizabeth Taylor in the part of a woman used by her homosexual cousin to attract youths. He was no happier with her performance in *Boom*, based on *The Milk Train Doesn't Stop Here Anymore*, thinking her too young for her role, and Richard Burton too old for his, though he thought the result 'an artistic success'. His later plays, which were written under the stimulus of alcohol and drugs, have not attracted film-makers. He died choking on a bottle-cap in a New York hotel room.
Autobiography: 1976, *Memoirs*.
Biography: 1993, *Tennessee Williams: Everyone Else Is an Audience* by Ronald Hayman.
■ *The Glass Menagerie* 50. *A Streetcar Named Desire* (AAN) 52. The Rose Tattoo 56. Baby Doll (AAN) 56. Cat on a Hot Tin Roof 58. Suddenly Last Summer 59. The Fugitive Kind 60. Summer and Smoke 61. The Roman Spring of Mrs Stone 61. Period of Adjustment 62. Sweet Bird of Youth 63. *The Night of the Iguana* 64. This Property Is Condemned 66. Boom 68. Blood Kin 70.
66 Why did I write? Because I found life unsatisfactory. – *T.W.*

Williams, Treat (1952–) (Richard Williams)
American leading actor of heavy presence, from Broadway.
The Ritz 76. The Eagle Has Landed 76. *Hair* 79. 1941 79. Why Would I Lie? 80. The Pursuit of D. B. Cooper 81. Prince of the City 81. Flashpoint 84. Once upon a Time in America 84. Dempsey (TV) 85. Smooth Talk 85. The Men's Club 86. Russicum 87. Dead Heat 88. Heart of Dixie 89. Sweet Lies 89. Beyond the Ocean/Oltre l'Oceano (a, co-w, d) 89. Max and Helen (TV) 90. Bonds of Love (TV) 93. Where the Rivers Flow North 93. Handgun 94. Parallel Lives (TV) 94. Things to Do in Denver When You're Dead 95. Mulholland Falls 96. The Phantom 96. The Late Shift 96. The Devil's Own 97. Deep Rising 98, etc.
TV series: Eddie Dodd 91.

Williams, Vanessa (1963–)
American actress and singer. Born in Tarrytown, New York, she studied at Syracuse University.
New Jack City 91. Harley Davidson and the Marlboro Man 91. Another You 91. Candyman 92. DROP Squad 94. Hoodlum 96, etc.
TV series: Melrose Place 92–93. Murder One 95. Chicago Hope 96– .

Williamson, David (1942–)
Australian dramatist and screenwriter.
Stork 71. Petersen 74. The Removalists 75. Don's Party 76. Eliza Fraser 76. The Club 80. Gallipoli 81. Duet for Four 82. The Year of Living Dangerously 82. Phar Lap 83. Sanctuary 95. Brilliant Lies 96, etc.

Williamson, Fred (1938–)
American action hero.
M*A*S*H 70. The Legend of Nigger Charley 72. Hammer 72. Black Caesar 72. Crazy Joe 73. That Man Bolt 74. Boss Nigger 75. Darktown 75. Take a Hard Ride 75. Mr Mean (& p, d) 77. Fist of Fear, Touch of Death 80. Vigilante 83. The Big Score (& d) 83. Foxtrap (& d) 86. The Messenger (& d) 87. Soda Cracker (& d) 89. Black Cobra 3: Manila Connection 91. Three Days to a Kill (& story, p, d) 92. South Beach (& p, d) 92. The Night Caller (& p, d) 92. From Dusk till Dawn (a) 95. Original Gangstas (a) 96. Night Vision (a) 97. Blackjack (a) 97, etc.
TV series: Julia 70–71. Wheels 79. Half Nelson 85.

Williamson, James A. (1855–1933)
British production pioneer.
The Big Swallow 01. Fire! 01, etc.

Williamson, Kevin (1965–)
American screenwriter of horror movies, born in Oriental, North Carolina. He is the creator of the TV series *Dawson's Creek*.
Scream 96. I Know What You Did Last Summer 97. Scream 2 97. The Faculty 98. Teaching Mrs Tingle (&d) 99, etc.

Williamson, Lambert (1907–)
British composer.

Edge of the World 38. End of the River 48. One Night With You 48. Cosh Boy 53. The Spaniard's Curse 58, etc.

Williamson, Malcolm (1931–)
Australian-born composer, pianist, and organist, in Britain from 1953. Composer of operas, ballets, choral and orchestral music, he was made Master of the Queen's Music in 1975.
The Brides of Dracula 60. The Horror of Frankenstein 70. Crescendo 72. Nothing but the Night 75. Watership Down (co-m) 76, etc.

Williamson, Nicol (1938–)
British leading actor of stage and screen; tends to play bulls in china shops. In 1994 he starred in a one-man play on the life of actor John Barrymore.
Six Sided Triangle 64. *Inadmissible Evidence* 67. *The Bofors Gun* 68. Laughter in the Dark 68. *The Reckoning* 69. Hamlet 69. The Jerusalem File 72. The Wilby Conspiracy 75. Robin and Marian 76. The Seven Per Cent Solution 76. The Word (TV) 78. The Cheap Detective 78. The Human Factor 79. Venom 81. Excalibur 81. I'm Dancing as Fast as I Can 82. Sakharov (TV) 85. Return to Oz 85. Black Widow 87. The Exorcist III 90. The Hour of the Pig 93. The Wind in the Willows 96. Spawn 97, etc.
❝ I don't even notice competition. I'm a centre-forward. I don't watch them. Let them watch me. – *N.W.*
I can understand people's pain, passion, fear, hurt, and I can mirror it and set it up for them to look at. – *N.W.*
The greatest actor since Marlon Brando. – *John Osborne*

Willingham, Calder (1922–1995)
American novelist and screenwriter.
The Strange One/End as a Man (w, oa) 57. Paths of Glory (co-w) 57. The Bridge on the River Kwai (co-w, uncredited) 57. The Vikings 58. One-Eyed Jacks (co-w) 61. *The Graduate* (co-w) (AAN) 67. Little Big Man (w) 70. Thieves Like Us (co-w) 74. *Rambling Rose* (w, oa) 91, etc.

Willis, Bruce (1955–)
American leading man. He was formerly married to actress Demi Moore (1987-2000).
Biography: 1997, *Bruce Willis: The Unauthorised Biography* by John Parker.
Blind Date 87. Sunset 88. *Die Hard* 88. In Country 89. That's Adequate 89. Look Who's Talking (voice) 90. Die Hard 2 90. The Bonfire of the Vanities 90. Look Who's Talking Too (voice) 90. Hudson Hawk (& co-story) 91. Mortal Thoughts 91. Billy Bathgate 91. Last Boy Scout 91. Death Becomes Her 92. The Player 92. Striking Distance 93. Pulp Fiction 94. North 94. Color of Night 94. Nobody's Fool 94. Die Hard with a Vengeance 95. Four Rooms 95. 12 Monkeys 95. Last Man Standing 96. The Jackal 97. The Fifth Element 97. Armageddon 98. Mercury Rising 98. The Siege 98. *The Sixth Sense* 99. The Story of Us 99. Breakfast of Champions 99. The Whole Nine Yards 00. Unbreakable 00. Bandits 01, etc.
TV series: Moonlighting 85–89.

Willis, Gordon
American cinematographer.
Loving 70. The Landlord 70. The People Next Door 70. Klute 71. Little Murders 71. Bad Company 72. *The Godfather* 72. Up the Sandbox 72. The Paper Chase 73. The Godfather Part Two 74. The Parallax View 74. The Drowning Pool 75. All the President's Men 76. Annie Hall 77. Comes a Horseman 78. Manhattan 79. Stardust Memories 80. Windows 80. Pennies from Heaven 81. A Midsummer Night's Sex Comedy 82. Zelig (AAN) 83. Broadway Danny Rose 84. The Purple Rose of Cairo 85. Perfect 85. The Money Pit 86. The Pick-Up Artist 87. Bright Lights, Big City 88. Presumed Innocent 90. The Godfather Part III (AAN) 90. Malice 93. The Devil's Own 97, etc.

Willis, Ted (1918–1992) (Lord Willis)
Influential British writer who set the scene for television's preoccupation with low life via such items as *Dixon of Dock Green* and *Woman in a Dressing Gown*. Dixon was derived from his filmscript *The Blue Lamp*; *Hot Summer Night* was later filmed as *Flame in the Streets*.

Willman, Noel (1918–1988)
British actor and stage director whose film roles were often coldly villainous.
Pickwick Papers 52. The Net 53. Beau Brummell 54. Cone of Silence 60. The Girl on the Boat 62. *Kiss of the Vampire* 63. The Reptile 65. Doctor Zhivago 65. The Vengeance of She 68, etc.

Willock, Dave (1909–1990)
American light actor, usually the hero's friend.
Legion of Lost Flyers 39. Let's Face It 43. Pin Up Girl 44. The Runaround 46. Chicago Deadline 49. Call Me Mister 51. It Came from Outer Space 53. The Buster Keaton Story 57. Wives and Lovers 63. Send Me No Flowers 64, many others.
TV series: Boots and Saddles 57. Margie 61.

Wills, Brember (1883–1948)
Slightly built British character actor best remembered for playing the mad arsonist Saul Femm in *The Old Dark House* (1932).

Wills, Chill (1903–1978)
Gravel-voiced American character actor, in films from 1934, mainly low-budget westerns. Also the voice of the talking mule in the 'Francis' series.
Boom Town 40. Best Foot Forward 43. The Harvey Girls 46. Raw Deal 48. High Lonesome 50. Bronco Buster 52. City That Never Sleeps 53. Timberjack 55. Giant 56. The Alamo (AAN) 60. The Deadly Companions 62. The Cardinal 63. The Over the Hill Gang Rides Again (TV) 71. Mr Billion 77, etc.
TV series: Frontier Circus 61. The Rounders 67.

Wills, J. Elder (1900– *)
English director, art director, screenwriter, and producer. Born in London and educated at London University, he was a scenic artist in Drury Lane before entering films in 1927 and working as an art director on more than 200 movies. He began directing in the early 30s, including two films for Hammer (of which he was then a director), and, after serving in the Second World War, worked as a producer and production designer for Rank before returning to art directing for Hammer. The Ealing spy thriller *Against the Wind* 47 was based on his own war experiences.
Biography: *Sabotage* by Leslie Bell.
AS DIRECTOR: Tiger Bay (& ad, co-story) 33. Song of Freedom 36. Everything in Life 36. Sporting Love 36. Big Fella 37.
AS ART DIRECTOR: The Informer 29. Alf's Carpet 29. Holiday Lovers 32. Money Mad 34. Sing as We Go 34. Honeymoon for Three 35. It Happened in Paris 35. No Limit 35. Look Up and Laugh 35. The Stoker 35. Queen of Hearts 36. Against the Wind 47. Mantrap 52. Spaceways 53. Blood Orange/Three Stops to Murder 53. Face the Music/The Black Glove 54. Break in the Circle 55. The Quatermass Experiment/The Creeping Unknown 55, etc.

Wills, Mary (1914–1997)
American costume designer, often in collaboration with Charles LeMaire at Twentieth Century-Fox in the 50s.
Song of the South 46. Hans Christian Anderson (AAN) 52. The Virgin Queen (AAN) 55. Carousel 56. Teenage Rebel (AAN) 56. A Certain Smile (AAN) 58. The Diary of Anne Frank (AAN) 59. The Wonderful World of the Brothers Grimm (AA) 62. Cape Fear 62. Camelot 67. The Passover Plot (AAN) 76, etc.

Willson, Meredith (1902–1984) (Robert Meredith Reiniger)
American song composer and lyricist whose chief bequests to the cinema are *The Music Man* and *The Unsinkable Molly Brown*.

Wilmer, Douglas (1920–)
British character actor of stage, screen and TV.
Richard III 56. An Honourable Murder 60. El Cid 61. Cleopatra 62. The Fall of the Roman Empire 64. One Way Pendulum 65. Brides of Fu Manchu 66. Unman Wittering and Zigo 71. The Golden Voyage of Sinbad 73. The Adventure of Sherlock Holmes' Smarter Brother 75. Sarah 76. The Revenge of the Pink Panther 78. Rough Cut 80. Octopussy 83, many others.

Wilson, Andy
English film director, from television. Born in London, he studied drama at Birmingham University and also worked with Circus Lumière and Archaos as a clown.
Dread Poets Society (TV) 92. An Evening with Gary Lineker (TV) 94. Playing God (US) 97, etc.
❝ Films should be iconic, mythic and have a moral. – *A.W.*

Wilson, Bridgette (1973–)
American actress and singer, born in Gold Beach, Oregon. She was Miss Teen USA 1990, and began on the daytime TV soap opera *Santa Barbara* 92–93.
Last Action Hero 93. Higher Learning 94. Billy Madison 95. Mortal Kombat 95. Nixon 95. Unhook the Stars 96. I Know What You Did Last Summer 97. The Real Blonde 97. Starf*cker 98. House on Haunted Hill 99. Beautiful 00, etc.

Wilson, Carey (1889–1962)
American screenwriter of the 20s and 30s, for Goldwyn and MGM, who wrote more than 80 films, usually in collaboration. He was said to be Louis B. Mayer's favourite writer. In the 40s, he turned to producing for MGM, and was executive producer of films in the Dr Kildare and Andy Hardy series. Born in Philadelphia, Pennsylvania, he studied at the city's Industrial Art School.
AS WRITER: He Who Gets Slapped 24. Wine of Youth 24. The Masked Bride 25. Monte Carlo 26. Ben-Hur 27. Oh Kay! 28. The Cardboard Lover 28. Diamond Handcuffs 28. Footlights and Fools 29. Gabriel over the White House 33. Murder at the Vanities 34. Mutiny on the Bounty 35. Dangerous Number 36. Between Two Women 37. Judge Hardy and Son 39, many more.
AS PRODUCER: The Postman Always Rings Twice 46. Dark Delusion 47. Green Dolphin Street 47. The Red Danube 49. The Happy Years 50. Scaramouche 52. This Is Russia (narrator) 57, etc.
❝ Wilson was a catch-all of information, a gusher of trivia and some profundity, an unstoppable chatterbox who was described by a friend, 'Ask him what time it is and he'll tell you how they make a watch.' – *Samuel Marx*

Wilson, Don 'The Dragon'
American leading actor in martial arts and action movies, a former kick-boxing champion.
Bloodfist 89. Bloodfist 2 90. Bloodfist 3: Forced to Fight 91. Ring of Fire 91. Futurekick 91. Ninja Dragons 92. Ring of Fire 2: Blood and Steel 92. Cyber-Tracker 93. Bloodfist 7: Manhunt 95. Manhunt: Bloodfist 8 96, etc.

Wilson, Dooley (1894–1953)
American character actor.
It is alleged that Elliot Carpenter played the piano for Wilson in *Casablanca* … and some say Wilson didn't sing either.
Casablanca (as Sam, who played it again) 42. Stormy Weather 43. Come to the Stable 49. Passage West 51, etc.

Wilson, Flip (1932–1998) (Clerow Wilson)
American actor and entertainer.
Uptown Saturday Night 74. Pinocchio (TV) 76. Skatetown USA 79.

Wilson, Georges
French leading actor and occasional director, the father of actor Lambert Wilson.
The Green Mare/La Jument Verte 59. The Joker/Le Farceur 60. Une Aussi Longue Absence 61. The Longest Day 62. The Stranger (It.) 67. Beatrice Cenci (It.) 69. Blanche 71. The Three Musketeers/The Queen's Diamonds 73. Tendre Poulet 77. La Vouivre (wd) 89. Cache-Cash 94. Marquise 97. From the Earth to the Moon (TV) 98, etc.

Wilson, Harry Leon (1867–1939)
American comedy novelist; chief works filmed are *Ruggles of Red Gap* and *Merton of the Movies*.

Wilson, Hugh (1943–)
American director and screenwriter.
Stroker Ace (co-w) 83. Police Academy (co-w, d) 84. Rustler's Rhapsody (wd) 85. Burglar (cow, d) 87. Guarding Tess (co-w, d) 94. Down Periscope (co-w) 96. The First Wives Club (d) 96. Rough Riders (w) (TV) 97. Blast from the Past (wd) 98. Dudley Do-Right (wd) 99, etc.

Wilson, Ian
British cinematographer.
Tell Me Lies 67. Bartelby 70. Up Pompeii 71. Captain Kronos Vampire Hunter 72. The House in Nightmare Park 73. Privates on Parade 84. Wish You Were Here 87. Dream Demon 88. Checking Out 89. Erik the Viking 89. Edward II 91. The Crying Game 92. The Secret Rapture 93. Backbeat 94. Emma 96. A Midsummer Night's Dream 96. Savior 98, etc.

Wilson, Janis
American child actress, long retired, who made an impressive debut in *Now Voyager*.
Now Voyager 42. Watch on the Rhine 43. Snafu/Welcome Home 45. The Strange Love of Martha Ivers 46, etc.

Wilson, Lambert (1956–)
French leading actor, the son of actor and director Georges Wilson.
From Hell to Victory 79. Chanel Solitaire 81. Five Days One Summer 82. Sahara (US) 84. The Blood of Others 84. Red Kiss/Rouge Baiser 85. Rendez-Vous 85. The Possessed 87. The Belly of an Architect 87. El Dorado 88. A Man and Two Women/Un Homme et Deux Femmes 91. Frankenstein: The Real Story (TV) 92. Jefferson in Paris (US) 95. The Leading Man (US) 96. Same Old Song/On Connaît la Chanson 97. Marquise 97. The Last September 99. Jet Set 00, etc.

Wilson, Lois (1895–1988)
American leading lady of the silent screen.
The Dumb Girl of Potici 16. Why Smith Left Home 19. The Covered Wagon 23. Miss Lulu Bett 24. Monsieur Beaucaire 24. What Every Woman Knows 24. Icebound 24. The Show Off 26. Seed 28. Manslaughter 28. The Crash 32. Laughing at Life 33. Bright Eyes 34. The Girl from Jones Beach 49, etc.

Wilson, Mara (1987–)
American child actress.
Mrs Doubtfire 93. A Time to Heal (TV) 94. Miracle on 34th Street 94. Matilda 96. A Simple Wish 97. Thomas and the Magic Railroad 00 etc.
TV series: Melrose Place 93.

Wilson, Margery (1896–1986)
American star of silent films, and occasional director. With the coming of sound, she turned to writing self-help books, including *Get the Most out of Life* and *The Woman You Want to Be*.
Bred in the Bone 15. *Intolerance* 16. The Clodhopper 17. The Gun Fighter 17. The Hand at the Window 18. Venus in the East 19. That Something (& d) 21. Insinuation (& d) 22. The Offenders 24, etc.

Wilson, Marie (1916–1972) (Katherine Elizabeth White)
American leading lady often seen as 'dumb blonde'.
Satan Met a Lady 36. Fools for Scandal 38. *Boy Meets Girl* 40. Broadway 42. The Young Widow 47. Linda Be Good 48. *My Friend Irma* (title role) 49. A Girl in Every Port 51. Marry Me Again 54. Mr Hobbs Takes a Vacation 62, etc.
TV series: My Friend Irma 52.

Wilson, Michael (1914–1978)
American screenwriter whose career was interrupted by the communist witch-hunt of the late 40s.
The Men in Her Life 42. It's a Wonderful Life (co-w) 46. Salt of the Earth 51. Five Fingers (AAN) 52. *A Place in the Sun* (AA) 52. Friendly Persuasion (uncredited) 56. *The Bridge on the River Kwai* (uncredited) 57. Lawrence of Arabia 62. The Sandpiper 65. *Planet of the Apes* 67. Che! 69, etc.

Wilson, Owen
American actor and screenwriter, often in collaboration with Wes Anderson. Born in Austin, Texas, he studied at the University of Texas.
Bottle Rocket (& w) 96. The Cable Guy 96. Anaconda 97. Armageddon 98. Rushmore (co-w only) 98. Permanent Midnight 98. The Haunting 99. Breakfast of Champions 99. Meet the Parents 00. Shanghai Noon 00. Behind Enemy Lines 01, etc.

Wilson, Richard (1915–1991)
American producer and director, former radio actor.
The Golden Blade (p) 54. Man with a Gun (wd, p) 55. Raw Wind in Eden (d) 58. Al Capone (d) 59. Pay or Die (p, d) 60. Invitation to a Gunfighter (p, d) 64. Three in an Attic (p, d) 68, etc.

Wilson, Richard (1936–)
Sardonic Scottish actor and director, mainly on stage and television, best known for his role as

Victor Meldrew in the TV series *One Foot in the Grave*. Born in Greenock, he was a research scientist before deciding to become an actor at the age of 27. He studied at RADA and first worked in repertory theatre. As a director he has been associated with the Oxford Playhouse and the Stables Theatre, Manchester.

Biography: 1996, *One Foot on the Stage* by James Roose Evans.

A Sharp Intake of Breath (TV) 77. Virginia Fly Is Drowning (TV) 82. A Passage to India 84. Whoops Apocalypse 86. Prick Up Your Ears 87. A Dry White Season 89. Fellow Traveller 89. How to Get Ahead in Advertising 89. Carry On Columbus 92. Soft Top, Hard Shoulder 92. The Vision Thing (TV) 93. One Foot in the Algarve (TV) 93. Gulliver's Travels (TV) 96. The Man Who Knew Too Little 97. Women Talking Dirty 00, etc.

TV series: My Good Woman 72. A Sharp Intake of Breath 78–80. Only When I Laugh 79–82. Room at the Bottom 86–88. Tutti Frutti 87. High and Dry 87. Hot Metal 88. One Foot in the Grave 90–95, 00. Under the Hammer 94. Duck Patrol 98. Life Support 99.

Wilson, Rita (1958–) (Margarita Ibrahimoff)
American actress, who trained in London at LAMDA. Married actor Tom Hanks in 1988.

The Day It Came to Earth 79. Volunteers 85. Sleepless in Seattle 93. Mixed Nuts 94. Now and Then 95. Jingle All the Way 96. Runaway Bride 99. The Story of Us 99, etc.

Wilson, Sandy (1924–)
British songwriter and lyricist whose best show, *The Boy Friend*, reached the screen in mangled form through the intervention of Ken Russell.

Wilson, Sandy (1947–)
Canadian director.

My American Cousin 85. Mama's Going to Buy You a Mocking Bird 88. American Boyfriends 89. Harmony Cats 93, etc.

Wilson, Scott (1942–)
American general-purpose actor, usually in tough roles.

In Cold Blood 67. Castle Keep 69. The Gypsy Moths 69. The Grissom Gang 71. The New Centurions 72. Lolly Madonna XXX 73. The Great Gatsby 74. The Passover Plot 77. The Ninth Configuration 80. On the Line 83. The Right Stuff 83. A Year of the Quiet Sun 84. The Aviator 85. Blue City 86. Malone 87. The Tracker 88. Johnny Handsome 89. The Exorcist III 90. Femme Fatale 91. Pure Luck 91. Lethal Weapon 3 92. Teenage Mutant Ninja Turtles 3 93. Flesh and Bone 93. Judge Dredd 95. Dead Man Walking 95. Shiloh 96. GI Jane 97. Pride/Unmei No Toki (Jap.) 98. Clay Pigeons 98. The Way of the Gun 00, etc.

Wilson, Stuart (1934–)
English character actor.

Dulcima 71. The Strauss Family (TV) 72. I, Claudius (TV) 76. The Prisoner of Zenda 79. The Highest Honour 82. The Old Men at the Zoo (TV) 83. Wetherby 85. Wallenberg: A Hero's Story (TV) 85. Nonni (Nor.) 88. Lionheart/AWOL (US) 91. Lethal Weapon 3 (US) 92. Teenage Mutant Ninja Turtles III (US) 92. The Age of Innocence (US) 93. No Escape (US) 94. Exit to Eden (US) 94. Death and the Maiden 95. Edie and Pen (US) 95. Crosswords (US) 96. The Mask of Zorro (US) 98. Enemy of the State (US) 98. Second Sight (TV) 99. The Luzhin Defence 00. Vertical Limit (US) 00, etc.

Wilson, Trey (1949–1989)
American character actor. Died of a cerebral haemorrhage.

A Soldier's Story 84. F/X 85. Raising Arizona 87. The House on Carroll Street 88. Bull Durham 88. Married to the Mob 88. Twins 88. Miss Firecracker 89. Great Balls of Fire 89. Welcome Home 89, etc.

Wilson, Whip (1915–1964) (Charles Meyer)
American cowboy actor who appeared in a great number of second features in the 30s and 40s.

Wilton, Penelope (1946–)
British actress, mainly on stage and TV. Married actor Ian Holm in 1990.

Joseph Andrews 77. The French Lieutenant's Woman 81. Othello 82. Laughterhouse/Singleton's Pluck 84. Clockwise 86. Cry Freedom 87. Blame It on the Bellboy 92. The Secret Rapture 93. Carrington 95. This Could Be the Last Time (TV) 98. Wives and Daughters (TV) 99. Tom's Midnight Garden 00, etc.

TV series: Ever Decreasing Circles 84.

Wilton, Robb (1882–1957) (Robert Wilton Smith)
Much admired English music-hall and radio comedian and character actor. His act, notably as a muddled policeman, fireman, or member of the Home Guard, has been preserved in several films. Born in Liverpool, he began as an engineer before working first as an actor in a local repertory theatre specialising in melodramas. Married actress Florence Palmer, who appeared with him on stage. Catchphrase: 'The day war broke out …'

The Fire Brigade 28. Stars on Parade 35. Don't Rush Me 36. Servants All 36. Chips 38. Pathé Radio Music Hall 45. The Love Match 55, etc.

❝ We have many grave responsibilities, but at the moment I cannot think of any. – *R.W. as his best-known character, Mr Muddlecombe J.P.*

–

Wimperis, Arthur (1874–1953)
British librettist and screenwriter, usually in collaboration.

The Private Life of Henry VIII 33. Sanders of the River 35. The Four Feathers 39. Mrs Miniver (AA) 42. Random Harvest (AAN) 43. The Red Danube 48. Calling Bulldog Drummond 51. Young Bess 53, many others.

Wincer, Simon (1943–)
Australian director, from TV.

The Day after Halloween 79. Harlequin 79. Phar Lap 83. D.A.R.Y.L 85. The Lighthorsemen 87. Blue Grass (TV) 88. Lonesome Dove (TV) 89. Quigley Down Under 90. Harley Davidson and the Marlboro Man 91. Free Willy 93. Lightning Jack 94. Operation Dumbo Drop 95. The Phantom 96, etc.

Winchell, Walter (1897–1972)
Fast-talking American newspaper columnist with a keen eye for crime and showbusiness, in movies as himself. A vaudeville song-and-dance performer from the age of 15, he became the highest-paid and most widely read gossip columnist of his time from the mid-20s, and also had a vast radio audience in the 30s and 40s, doing much to create a public appetite for celebrity-led journalism. His film performances in the 30s are said to have influenced the urban tough-guy approach of such actors as James Cagney and George Raft. He was the model for J. J. Hunsecker, the Broadway columnist played by Burt Lancaster in *Sweet Smell of Success* 57, and was played by Michael T. Wright in the TV biopic *The Rat Pack* 98, and by Stanley Tucci in the TV biopic *Winchell* 98.

Autobiography: 1975, *Winchell Exclusive: 'Things that Happened to Me – And Me to Them'*.

Biography: 1971, *Winchell* by Bob Thomas. 1976, *Winchell, His Life and Times* by Herman Klurfeld. 1994, *Walter Winchell: Gossip, Power and the Culture of Celebrity* by Neal Gabler.

Broadway through a Keyhole (story) 33. Wake Up and Live 37. Love and Kisses 37. The Private Lives of Adam and Eve 59. College Confidential 60. Dondi 61. Wild in the Streets 68, etc.

TV series: The Walter Winchell Show 52–56. The Walter Winchell File 57–58. The Untouchables (as narrator) 59–63. The Walter Winchell Show 60.

❝ He wore a hat because he was embarrassed about being bald, and he was a little ratlike figure, with a megalomaniac meanness and insecurity. – *Alexander Mackendrick*

Wincott, Jeff (1957–)
Canadian leading man of action movies.

Happy Birthday, Gemini 80. Prom Night 80. Deadly Bet 91. Martial Law 2: Undercover 91. Mission of Justice 92. Martial Outlaw 93. The Killing Man 94. Last Man Standing 95. When the Bullet Hits the Bone 96. Fatal Combat 96. The Undertaker's Wedding 97. Future Fear 97, etc.

TV series: Night Heat 85–91.

Windom, William (1923–)
American leading man, usually in minor film roles.

To Kill a Mockingbird 62. For Love or Money 63. One Man's Way 64. The Americanization of Emily 64. The Detective 68. Brewster McCloud 70. Fool's Parade 71. Now You See Him Now You Don't 72. Echoes of a Summer 75. Mean Dog Blues 78. Grandview USA 84. Planes, Trains and Automobiles 87. She's Having a Baby 88. Funland 89. Sommersby 93. Miracle on 34th Street 94. Fugitive X 96. Children of the Corn 4: The Gathering 96, etc.

TV series: The Farmer's Daughter 63–66. My World and Welcome to It 69. The Girl with Something Extra 73–74. Brothers and Sisters 79. Murder She Wrote 85–91.

Windsor, Barbara (1937–) (Barbara Deeks)
British cockney actress specializing in dumb blondes.

Autobiography: 2000, *All of Me*.

Lost 55. Too Hot to Handle 59. Sparrows Can't Sing 62. Crooks in Cloisters 63. Carry On Spying 64. A Study in Terror 65. Carry On Doctor 68. Carry On Again Doctor 69. Carry On Camping 69. The Boy Friend 71. Carry On Henry 71. Carry On Abroad 72. Carry On Matron 72. Not Now, Darling 72. Carry On Girls 73. Carry On Dick 74. Comrades 87, etc.

TV series: Worzel Gummidge 78–81. EastEnders 94– .

Windsor, Claire (1898–1972) (Olga Cronk)
American leading lady of the silent screen. Her second husband was actor Bert Lytell (1925–27).

To Please a Woman 20. Rich Men's Wives 22. Nellie the Beautiful Cloak Model 24. Money Talks 26. Captain Lash 29, etc.

Windsor, Marie (1919–2000) (Emily Marie Bertelson)
Tall, large-eyed American leading actress with stage and radio experience; films mainly routine. She was at her best in *film noir*, as a *femme fatale*, though she has retained a cult following for her appearance in monster and science-fiction movies. Born in Marysvale, Utah, she studied at Brigham Young University and first went to Hollywood after winning a Miss Utah contest. There she trained with Maria Ouspenskaya. Married twice.

All American Co-Ed 41. Call Out the Marines 42. Lets' Face It 43. The Hucksters 47. Song of the Thin Man 47. Force of Evil 48. The Fighting Kentuckian 49. Outpost in Morocco 49. Frenchie 50. The Showdown 50. Hurricane Island 51. Little Big Horn 51. Japanese War Bride 52. *The Narrow Margin* 52. The Sniper 52. Cat Women of the Moon 53. City that Never Sleeps 53. Trouble along the Way 53. The Bounty Hunter 54. Abbott and Costello Meet the Mummy 55. *The Killing* 56. The Girl in Black Stockings 57. The Unholy Wife 57. Critic's Choice 63. Mail Order Bride 63. The Day Mars Invaded Earth 64. Bedtime Story 64. Chamber of Horrors 66. The Good Guys and the Bad Guys 69. Support Your Local Gunfighter 71. Cahill, US Marshal 73. The Apple Dumpling Gang 74. Hearts of the West 75. Freaky Friday 76. Salem's Lot (TV) 79. Lovely … but Deadly 81. Commando Squad 87, etc.

❝ I wasn't that particular, shall I say. I never asked who the costars were or anything like that. I just asked when it was and how much money. – M.W.

Windust, Bretaigne (1906–1960)
American director, from the New York stage.

Winter Meeting 47. June Bride 48. Pretty Baby 50. *The Enforcer* 51. Face to Face 52. The Pied Piper of Hamelin 59, etc.

Winfield, Paul (1941–)
American leading actor.

The Lost Man 69. RPM 70. Brother John 71. *Sounder* (AAN) 72. Gordon's War 73. Conrack 74. Hustle 75. Damnation Alley 77. Twilight's Last Gleaming 77. The Greatest 77. Backstairs at the White House (TV) 79. King (TV) 80. Angel City (TV) 81. Star Trek II: The Wrath of Khan 82. On the Run 82. Mike's Murder 82. Go Tell It on the Mountain 84. The Terminator 84. Blue City 85. The Serpent and the Rainbow 88. Presumed Innocent 90. Dennis the Menace/Dennis 93. Cliffhanger 93. Scarlett (TV) 94. Breathing Lessons (TV) 94. Tyson (TV) 95. Original Gangstas 96. The Legend of Gator Face 96. The Assassination File 96. Mars Attacks! 96. Relax... It's Just Sex 98. Catfish in Black Bean Sauce 99, etc.

Winfrey, Oprah (1954–)
American actress, a former newsreader who became rich, successful and powerful airing topical problems on her syndicated TV talk show from 1986. In the 90s she donated $2m to Atlanta's Morehouse College.

The Color Purple (AAN) 85. Native Son 86. Throw Momma from the Train 87. The Women of Brewster Place (TV) 89. There Are No Children Here (TV) 93. Beloved (& p) 98, etc.

❝ Arguably has more influence in the culture than any university president, politician, or religious leader, except perhaps the Pope. – *Vanity Fair*

Winger, Debra (1955–)
American leading lady of the early 80s, in increasingly strong roles. Married actors Timothy Hutton (1986–89), and Arliss Howard.

Thank God It's Friday 78. French Postcards 79. Urban Cowboy 80. Cannery Row 82. An Officer and a Gentleman (AAN) 82. Terms of Endearment (AAN) 83. Mike's Murder 84. Legal Eagles 85. Black Widow 87. Made in Heaven 87. Betrayed 88. Everybody Wins 90. The Sheltering Sky 90. Wilder Napalm 93. Shadowlands (AAN) 93. A Dangerous Woman 93. Forget Paris 95, etc.

Winkler, Henry (1945–)
Extrovert American actor best known as Fonz in TV's *Happy Days* .He began directing in the mid-80s.

The Lords of Flatbush 72. Heroes 77. The One and Only 78. Night Shift 82. A Smokey Mountain Christmas (d) 86. Memories of Me (d) 88. Absolute Strangers (TV) 91. Cop and a Half (d) 93. Scream (a) 96. National Lampoon's Dad's Week Off (a) 97. The Waterboy (a) 98, etc.

TV series: Happy Days 74-83. Monty 94.

Winkler, Irwin (1931–)
American producer who began directing in the 90s.

The Split 68. They Shoot Horses Don't They? 69. The Strawberry Statement 70. The Mechanic 72. Up the Sandbox 72. Peeper 75. The Gambler 75. Nickelodeon 76. Rocky (AA) 76. New York New York 77. Comes a Horseman 78. Rocky II 79. Raging Bull (AAN) 81. True Confessions 81. Author! Author! 82. Rocky III 82. The Right Stuff (AAN) 83. Revolution 85. Rocky IV 85. Round Midnight 86. Betrayed 88. Music Box 90. GoodFellas (AAN) 90. Rocky V 90. Guilty by Suspicion (wd) 90. Night and the City (d) 92. The Net (d) 95. At First Sight (d) 99, etc.

Winn, Godfrey (1908–1971)
British journalist who made rare film appearances.

Blighty 27. Very Important Person 61. Billy Liar 63. The Great St Trinian's Train Robbery 66. Up the Chastity Belt 71, etc.

Winner, Michael (1935–)
Ebullient British director who never shoots in a studio. His own best publicist. Also a restaurant columnist.

Climb Up the Wall 57. The Clock Strikes Eight 57. Man with a Gun 58. Shoot to Kill 59. Some Like It Cool 61. Haunted England 61. Play It Cool 62. The Cool Mikado 63. West Eleven 63. *The System* 64. You Must be Joking 65. *The Jokers* 66. *I'll Never Forget Whatshisname* 67. Hannibal Brooks 69. The Games 69. *Lawman* 70. The Night Comers 71. Chato's Land 72. The Mechanic 72. Scorpio 72. The Stone Killer 73. *Death Wish* 74. Won Ton Ton 76. The Sentinel 77. The Big Sleep 78. Firepower 79. Death Wish II 81. The Wicked Lady 83. Scream for Help 84. Death Wish 3 85. Appointment with Death 87. A Chorus of Disapproval (p, wd) 89. Bullseye! (story, d, ed) 91. Dirty Weekend (wd) 93. Decadence (a) 94. Parting Shots (p, d) 98, etc.

TV series: Michael Winner's True Murders 92–93. Michael Winner's True Crimes 93–94.

❝ In a time when diffidence is fashionable, it is refreshing to find a British director who seems deliberately to court comparison with Erich Von Stroheim: 'A team effort is a lot of people doing what I say.'

Original? It seems so. It is also true; and unlike Von Stroheim Mr Winner does get his films out on time and below budget, facts which tend to atone for his arrogance. He knows that: 'In this business, disaster is always just around the corner.'

And that: 'Every film is a great success until it is released.'

He remembers the days when: 'You could make a film for £100,000 and get your money back from people sheltering from the rain.'

He won't make the mistake of imagining that those days are still here. He enjoys the big money: 'Success has gone to my stomach.'

And he finds that: 'The hardest part of directing is staying awake for nine weeks at a stretch.'

He has no qualms about what he purveys: 'There's no moralistic side to *Death Wish*: it's a pleasant romp.'

And he is proud of his prowess: 'Being in the movie business is like being a tennis player. You have to keep your total concentration and your mind on the ball. The minute you fall in love with Tatum O'Neal or get flabby, you've had it.'

Winninger, Charles (1884–1969) (Karl Winninger)
Chubby, lovable American character actor, in films from 1916 as vaudeville appearances permitted. His catchphrase: '*Happ-y* new year …'
■ Pied Piper Malone 24. The Canadian 24. Summer Bachelors 26. Soup to Nuts 30. Bad Sister 31. Night Nurse 31. Flying High 31. God's Gift to Women 31. Fighting Caravans 31. Gun Smoke 31. Children of Dreams 31. The Sin of Madelon Claudet 31. Husband's Holiday 31. Social Register 34. *Show Boat* (as Captain Andy) 36. White Fang 36. *Three Smart Girls* 36. You're a Sweetheart 37. Woman Chases Man 37. *Nothing Sacred* 37. Café Metropole 37. You Can't Have Everything 37. The Go-Getter 37. Every Day's a Holiday 37. Goodbye Broadway 38. Hard to Get 38. Three Smart Girls Grow Up 39. *Destry Rides Again* 39. *Babes in Arms* 39. Barricade 39. If I Had My Way 40. My Love Came Back 40. Beyond Tomorrow 40. Little Nellie Kelly 40. When Ladies Meet 41. *Ziegfeld Girl* 41. The Getaway 41. My Life with Caroline 41. Pot o' Gold 41. Friendly Enemies 42. Coney Island 43. A Lady Takes a Chance 43. Flesh and Fantasy 43. Hers to Hold 43. Broadway Rhythm 44. Belle of the Yukon 44. Sunday Dinner for a Soldier 44. She Wouldn't Say Yes 45. *State Fair* 45. Lover Come Back 46. Living in a Big Way 47. Something in the Wind 47. The Inside Story 48. *Give My Regards to Broadway* 48. Father Is a Bachelor 50. *The Sun Shines Bright* 53. Torpedo Alley 53. A Perilous Journey 53. Champ for a Day 53. Las Vegas Shakedown 55. Raymie 60.

TV series: The Charlie Farrell Show 56.

Winningham, Mare (1959–) (Mary Winningham)
American actress.

One-Trick Pony 80. Threshold 81. Single Bars, Single Women (TV) 84. St Elmo's Fire 85. Nobody's Fool 86. Shy People 87. Made in Heaven 87. Miracle Mile 89. Turner & Hooch 89. Eye on the Sparrow (TV) 91. Fatal Exposure (TV) 91. Hard Promises 92. Wyatt Earp 94. Georgia (AAN) 95. The Boys Next Door (TV) 96. George Wallace (TV) 97. Everything that Rises (TV) 98, etc.

Winslet, Kate (1975–)
English leading actress whose rise to stardom benefited from being the love of Leonardo DiCaprio in James Cameron's record-breaking *Titanic*. Born in Reading, Berkshire, she studied from the age of 11 at Redroofs Theatre School, Maidenhead, and began appearing in commercials when she was 16. Married assistant director James Threapleton in 1998.

Heavenly Creatures 94. *Sense and Sensibility* (AAN) 95. A Kid in King Arthur's Court 95. Jude 96. Hamlet (as Ophelia) 96. *Titanic* (AAN) (US) 97. Hideous Kinky 98. Holy Smoke 99. Quills 00, etc.

TV series: Get Back 92.

Winslow, George (1946–) (George Wenzlaff)
American boy actor whose throaty voice earned him the nickname 'Foghorn'.

Room for One More 52. My Pal Gus 52. Mr Scoutmaster 53. Gentlemen Prefer Blondes 53. Artists and Models 55. Wild Heritage 58, etc.

Winston, Stan (1946–)
American make-up special effects and creature creator, and occasional director.

Blacula 72. The Wiz 78. The Exterminator 80. Heartbeeps 81. Parasite 82. The Terminator 84. Aliens (AA) 86. Predator 87. The Monster Squad 87. Pumpkinhead (co-story, d) 88. Leviathan 89. Predator 2 90. Edward Scissorhands (AAN) 90. Terminator 2: Judgment Day (AA) 91. Batman Returns (AAN) 92. Jurassic Park (AA) 93. Interview with the Vampire 94. The Island of Dr Moreau 96. *The Lost World: Jurassic Park* (AAN) 97. Mouse Hunt 97. Paulie 98. Creature (TV) 98. Small Soldiers 98, etc.

Winstone, Ray (1957–)
Burly English character actor, born in Hackney, London, often in violent or criminal roles.

Scum 79. That Summer! 79. Quadrophenia 79. Ladies and Gentlemen, the Fabulous Stains (US) 82. Tank Malling 88. Underbelly (TV) 91. Black and Blue (TV) 92. Ladybird Ladybird 94. *Nil by Mouth* 97. Face 97. Final Cut 97. Darkness Falls 98. Woundings 98. The Sea Change 98. Martha, Meet Frank, Daniel & Laurence 98. The War Zone 98. Final Cut 98. Agnes Browne (US) 99. Love, Honour and Obey 99. Five Seconds To Spare 99. Sexy Beast 99. There's Only One Jimmy Gribble 00. Tough Love (TV) 00, etc.

TV series: Fox 80. Fairly Secret Army 84. Robin of Sherwood 84–86. Get Back 92–93. Ghostbusters of East Finchley 95.

Winter, Alex (1965–)
English-born leading actor, in America from the early 70s, from the stage.

Death Wish 3 85. The Lost Boys 87. Haunted Summer 88. Rosalie Goes Shopping 89. Bill and Ted's Excellent Adventure 88. Bill and Ted's Bogus Journey 91. Freaked (& co-w, co-d) 93, etc.

Winter, Donovan
British director of eccentric low-budgeters.

The Trunk 60. A Penny for Your Thoughts 65. Promenade 68. Come Back Peter 69. Give Us Tomorrow 77, etc.

Winter, Vincent (1947–1998)
Scottish juvenile actor, born in Aberdeen, who gave a remarkable performance at the age of five in *The Kidnappers*. He became unhappy with the roles offered him as he grew up, and later worked as an assistant director, production manager and production supervisor on various films.

The Dark Avenger 55. Time Lock 56. Beyond This Place 59. Gorgo 60. Greyfriars Bobby 61. Almost Angels 63. The Three Lives of Thomasina 63. The Horse Without a Head 64, etc.

Winterbottom, Michael (1961–)
English director and screenwriter. Born in Blackburn, he studied English at Oxford University before working in television as a documentary director.

Forget about Me 90. Under the Sun 92. Love Lies Bleeding (TV) 92. Cracker: The Mad Woman in the Attic (TV) 93. Family (TV) 94. Butterfly Kiss (& co-w) 95. Go Now (TV) 95. Jude 96. Welcome to Sarajevo 97. I Want You 98. Wonderland 99. With or Without You 99. The Claim 00, etc.

Winters, Jonathan (1925–)
American comedian with TV and nightclub experience.

It's a Mad Mad Mad Mad World 63. *The Loved One* 65. The Russians Are Coming, the Russians Are Coming 66. Eight on the Lam 66. Oh Dad, Poor Dad, Mamma's Hung You in the Closet and I'm Feelin' So Sad 66. Penelope 66. Viva Max 69. The Fish that Saved Pittsburgh 79. The Longshot 86. Moon over Parador 88. The Flintstones 94. The Shadow 94. The Adventures of Rocky and Bullwinkle 00, etc.

TV series: The Jonathan Winters Show 56–57, 67–69. The Wacky World of Jonathan Winters 72–74. Mork & Mindy 81–82. Hee Haw 83–84. Davis Rules 91–92.

Winters, Ralph
American film editor. He was on the staff of MGM for more than 30 years and edited 13 of Blake Edwards' films.

Mr and Mrs North 41. Eyes in the Night 42. Cry Havoc 43. Gaslight 44. Boy's Ranch 46. Tenth Avenue Angel 47. Hills of Home 48. Any Number Can Play 49. Little Women 49. On the Town 49. King Solomon's Mines (AA) 50. Quo Vadis? (AAN) 51. Kiss Me Kate 53. Young Bess 53. Executive Suite 54. Seven Brides for Seven Brothers (AAN) 54. Love Me or Leave Me 55. High Society 56. Jailhouse Rock 57. The Sheepman 58. Ben Hur (AA) 59. Butterfield 8 60. Soldier in the Rain 63. The Pink Panther 64. The Great Race (AAN) 65. What Did You Do in the War, Daddy? 66. How to Succeed in Business without Really Trying 67. The Party 68. The Thomas Crown Affair 68. Gaily Gaily 69. Kotch (AAN) 71. Avanti 72. The Outfit 73. The Front Page 74. Mr Majestyk 74. King Kong 75. Orca 77. 10 79. S.O.B. 81. Victor/Victoria 82. The Curse of the Pink Panther 83. Micki and Maude 84. Let's Get Harry 87. Moving 88. CutThroat Island 95, etc.

❝ The general public doesn't understand a thing about editing and I don't think they should. – *R.W.*

Winters, Roland (1904–1989)
Heavily built American character actor with stage and radio experience, in Hollywood from 1946; played Charlie Chan in six Monogram features 1948–52.

13 rue Madeleine 46. Inside Straight 52. So Big 53. Loving 70, etc.

TV series: Meet Millie 52–55. The Smothers Brothers Show 65.

Winters, Shelley (1920–) (Shirley Schrift)
American leading character actress with vaudeville and stage experience, in Hollywood from 1943.

Autobiography: 1980, *Shelley*. 1987, *Also Known as Shirley*. 1989, *The Middle of My Century/The Best of Times, the Worst of Times*.
■ What a Woman 43. Sailor's Holiday 44. The Racket Man 44. Two Man Submarine 44. She's a Soldier Too 44. Nine Girls 44. Cover Girl 44. Knickerbocker Holiday 44. 1001 Nights 45. Tonight and Every Night 45. Living in a Big Way 47. The Gangster 48. Red River 48. Larceny 48. *A Double Life* 48. Cry of the City 48. Take One False Step 49. Johnny Stool Pigeon 49. The Great Gatsby 49. Winchester 73 50. East of Java 51. He Ran All The Way 51. Frenchie 51. Behave Yourself 51. The Raging Tide 51. A Place in the Sun (AAN) 51. My Man and I 52. Phone Call from a Stranger 52. Meet Danny Wilson 52. Untamed Frontier 52. Tennessee Champ 54. Saskatchewan 54. Playgirl 54. Executive Suite 54. To Dorothy a Son 54. *The Big Knife* 55. *The Night of the Hunter* 55. Mambo 55. I Am a Camera 55. I Died a Thousand Times 56. Treasure of Pancho Villa 56. Odds Against Tomorrow 58. *The Diary of Anne Frank* (AA) 59. Let No Man Write My Epitaph 60. The Young Savages 61. Lolita 62. Wives and Lovers 63. The Chapman Report 63. The Balcony 63. A House is Not a Home 64. Time of Indifference 64. The Greatest Story Ever Told 65. *A Patch of Blue* (AA) 65. Alfie (GB) 66. Harper 66. Enter Laughing 67. The Scalp Hunters 67. Wild in the Streets 68. Buona Sera Mrs Campbell 68. The Mad Room 69. Arthur! Arthur! 69. Flap 70. Bloody Mama 70. How Do I Love Thee 70. What's the Matter with Helen? 70. Who Slew Auntie Roo? 71. Revenge! (TV) 71. The Poseidon Adventure (AAN) 72. Something to Hide 72. The Devil's Daughter (TV) 72. Blume in Love 73. Cleopatra Jones 73. Big Rose (TV) 74. Diamonds 75. That Lucky Touch 75. Journey Into Fear 75. Next Stop Greenwich Village 76. The Tenant 76. Pete's Dragon 77. Tentacles 77. Black Journey 77. King of the Gypsies 78. City on Fire 79. The Magician of Lublin 79. Redneck County Rape 79. The Visitor 79. Elvis (TV) 79. S.O.B. 81. Over the Brooklyn Bridge 83. Déjà Vu 84. Delta Force 85. Purple People Eater 88. Rudolph & Frosty's Christmas in July 88. An Unremarkable Life 89. Touch of a Stranger 90. Stepping Out 91. The Pickle 93. Heavy 95. Jury Duty 95. Mrs Munck 95. Raging Angels 95. The Portrait of a Lady 96. Gideon 99. Once Upon a Time in Little Italy/La Bomba (It.) 99.
❝ I did a picture in England one winter and it was so cold I almost got married. – *S.W.*

I'm more comfortable playing victims. I feel ashamed to reveal nasty aspects of myself. I was afraid to play an unsympathetic character in *A Patch of Blue*. I thought I was lousy, and I won the Oscar. – *S.W.*

Wintle, Julian (1913–1980)
British producer, former editor, in films from 1934. Co-founder of Independent Artists 1958.

Hunted 51. High Tide at Noon 57. Tiger Bay 59. Very Important Person 61. This Sporting Life 63. And Father Came Too 64, many others.

Winwood, Estelle (1882–1984) (Estelle Goodwin)
British stage character actress who played in many American films, usually as eccentric ladylike flutterers. Married actor Arthur Chesney, the brother of Edmund Gwenn.

The House of Trent 34. Quality Street 37. The Glass Slipper 55. *The Swan* 56. Twenty-three Paces to Baker Street 56. *Alive and Kicking* (GB) 58. Darby O'Gill and the Little People 59. Notorious Landlady 62. Dead Ringer 64. Camelot 67. Games 67. The Producers 68. Murder by Death 76, etc.

Wisbar, Frank (1899–1967) (aka Frank Wysbar)
German screenwriter, producer and director. Born in Tilsit, he worked as a writer and producer for UFA in the early 30s, associated with directors Carl Boese and Carl Froelich. His first films met with disapproval from the Nazi party, so that he emigrated to the United States in 1939, where he was restricted to making low-budget movies for Poverty Row studios. He then worked in US TV as a prolific producer-director from the late 40s before returning to Germany in the mid-50s.

Im Banne des Eulenspiegels 32. Anna and Elizabeth 33. *Ferryboat Pilot Maria/Führmann Maria* (co-w, d) 36. Women in Bondage (co-w) (US) 43. *Strangler of the Swamp* (co-w, d)(US) 46. Devil Bat's Daughter (co-w, d) (US) 46. Lighthouse (US) 46. The Prairie (US) 47. U Boat 55/Haie Und Kleine Fische 57. Fabrik Der Offiziere 60. Barbara 61. The Breakthrough/Durchbruch Lok 234 63, etc.

Wisberg, Aubrey (1909–1990)
British-born writer-producer of Hollywood films, mainly second features.

So Dark the Night (w) 41. The Man from Planet X (wp) 51. The Neanderthal Man (wp) 53. Captain Kidd and the Slave Girl (wp) 54. Son of Sinbad (w) 55, many others.

Wisdom, Sir Norman (1920–)
British slapstick comedian, also on stage and TV. He received a knighthood in the New Year's Honours of 1999.

Biography: 1991, *Trouble in Store* by Richard Dacre.
■ *Trouble in Store* (film debut) 53. One Good Turn 54. Man of the Moment 55. Up in the World 56. Just My Luck 58. The Square Peg 58. Follow a Star 59. There Was a Crooked Man 60. The Bulldog Breed 61. The Girl on the Boat 61. On the Beat 62. A Stitch in Time 63. The Early Bird 65. Press for Time 66. The Sandwich Man 66. The Night They Raided Minsky's (US) 68. What's Good for the Goose 69. Going Gently (TV) 81. Double X 92.

Wise, Ernie
See Morecambe, Eric.

Wise, Robert (1914–)
American director, former editor (worked on *Citizen Kane*, *All That Money Can Buy*, *The Magnificent Ambersons*).
■ Mademoiselle Fifi 44. Curse of the Cat People 44. *The Body Snatcher* 45. A Game of Death 46. Criminal Court 46. Born to Kill 47. Mystery in Mexico 47. Blood on the Moon 48. *The Set-Up* 49. Three Secrets 50. Two Flags West 50. The House on Telegraph Hill 51. *The Day the Earth Stood Still* 51. Captive City 52. Destination Gobi 52. Something for the Birds 52. Desert Rats 52. So Big 53. *Executive Suite* 54. Helen of Troy 55. Tribute to a Bad Man 56. Somebody Up There Likes Me 56. Until They Sail 57. This Could Be the Night 57. Run Silent Run Deep 58. I Want to Live (AAN) 58. Odds Against Tomorrow 59. *West Side Story* (AA) 61. Two for the Seesaw 62. The Haunting (GB) 63. *The Sound of Music* (AA) 65. The Sand Pebbles 66. Star! 68. The Andromeda Strain 70. Two People 73. The Hindenberg 75. Audrey Rose 77. Star Trek 79. Rooftops 89.

Wiseman, Debbie (1963–)
British composer, pianist and conductor. Born in London, she is a graduate of the Guildhall School of Music and Drama.

Tom and Viv 94. Haunted 95. Female Perversions 96. Wilde 97. Resurrection (TV) 99. Deep In My Heart (TV) 99. Warriors (TV) 99. Tom's Midnight Garden 00. Lighthouse 00. The Guilty 00 etc.

Wiseman, Frederick (1931–)
American documentarist, former law professor.

Titicut Follies 67. High School 68. Law and Order 69. Hospital 70. Basic Training 71. Essene 72. Juvenile Court 73. Primate 74. Welfare 75. Meat 76. Model 80. Racetrack 85. Blind 87. Near Death 89. Aspen 91. Zoo 93. La Comédie Française, ou l'Amour Joue 96. Public Housing 97. Belfast, Maine 99, etc.

Wiseman, Joseph (1918–)
American stage actor who has made several film appearances.

Detective Story 51. Viva Zapata 52. Les Misérables 52. The Prodigal 55. The Garment

Jungle 57. The Unforgiven 60. *Dr No* (title role) 62. *The Night They Raided Minsky's* 68. Bye Bye Braverman 68. Stiletto 69. The Valachi Papers 72. The Apprenticeship of Duddy Kravitz 74. Buck Rogers 79. Rage of Angels (TV) 83. The Ghost Writer 84. Seize the Day 86, etc.

Wister, Owen (1860–1938)
American western novelist whose *The Virginian*, published in 1902, was the basis of several films and a television series.

Withers, Googie (1917–) (Georgette Withers)
English leading actress of stage, screen and television. Born in Karachi, of English and Dutch parents, she trained at the Italia Conti School, studied dancing with Buddy Bradley, and was on stage from the age of 13, beginning in the chorus. Given a small part in her first film, *Girl in the Crowd*, she took over the star role when the leading lady walked out, going on to make more than 60 films. Married actor-producer John McCallum, and moved to Australia, though she returned to Britain to appear on stage and television.

Biography: 1979, *Life with Googie* by John McCallum.

Girl in the Crowd 34. Accused 36. Strange Boarders 37. The Lady Vanishes 38. Trouble Brewing 39. Back Room Boy 41. *One of Our Aircraft Is Missing* 42. *On Approval* 44. They Came to a City 44. Dead of Night 45. The Loves of Joanna Godden 46. Pink String and Sealing Wax 46. *It Always Rains on Sunday* 47. Miranda 48. Once Upon a Dream 49. Traveller's Joy 50. Night and the City 50. *White Corridors* 51. Derby Day 52. Devil on Horseback 54. Port of Escape 55. The Nickel Queen 70. Time after Time 85. Country Life 94. Shine 96, etc.

TV series: Within These Walls 74–77.

Withers, Grant (1904–1959)
Rugged American general-purpose actor, a former salesman and reporter who began in silent films as an extra. Born in Pueblo, Colorado, he found success first as a leading man in the 20s, then as an action hero of low-budget movies and serials of the 30s, and later as a character actor. Married actresses Loretta Young (1930–31) and Estelita Rodriguez. Committed suicide.

The Gentle Cyclone 26. Tiger Rose 29. Red Haired Alibi 32. The Red Rider (serial) 34. Tailspin Tommy (serial) 34. Fighting Marines (serial) 35. Society Fever 35. Jungle Jim (serial) 37. Radio Patrol (serial) 37. The Secret of a Treasure Island 38. Mr Wong, Detective 38. Mexican Spitfire 39. Billy the Kid 41. Woman of the Year 42. The Fighting Seabees 44. The Yellow Rose of Texas 44. Bring On the Girls 45. My Darling Clementine 46. Fort Apache 48. Rio Grande 50. Springfield Rifle 52. Fair Winds to Java 53. Lady Godiva 55. The Hired Gun 57. I, Mobster 58, many others.

Withers, Jane (1926–)
American child star of the 30s, more mischievous and less pretty than Shirley Temple.

Bright Eyes 34. Ginger 35. The Farmer Takes a Wife 35. The Mad Martindales 42. North Star 43. Faces in the Fog 44. Affairs of Geraldine 46. Giant 56. The Right Approach 62. Captain Newman 63, etc.

Witherspoon, Cora (1890–1957)
American character comedienne often seen as shrewish wife; on stage from 1910.

Libeled Lady 36. Madame X 38. The Bank Dick 40. This Love of Ours 45. The Mating Season 50. The First Time 52, etc.

Witherspoon, John
American character actor.

Ratboy 86. Hollywood Shuffle 87. Bird 88. I'm Gonna Git You, Sucka 88. House Party 90. Killer Tomatoes Strike Back 90. The Five Heartbeats 91. Talkin' Dirty after Dark 91. Boomerang 92. Friday 95. Vampire in Brooklyn 95. Fakin' Da Funk 97. Sprung 97. Ride 98. Next Friday 00, etc.

Witherspoon, Reese (1976–)
American leading actress. She married actor Ryan Philippe in 1999.

Wildflower (TV) 91. The Man in the Moon 91. The Crush 93. A Far Off Place 93. Jack the Bear 93. Return to Lonesome Dove (TV) 93. SFW 94. Fear 96. Freeway 96. Overnight Delivery 97. Twilight 98. Pleasantville 98. Election 99. Best Laid Plans 99. Cruel Intentions 99. American Psycho 00. Little Nicky 00, etc.

Witney, William (1910–)
American director of fast-moving B movies. He moved from serials and westerns for Republic, including many starring Roy Rogers, and on to crime and juvenile delinquent movies.

The Painted Stallion (co-d, serial) 37. SOS Coast Guard (co-d, serial) 37. Zorro Rides Again (co-d, serial) 37. Dick Tracy Returns (co-d, serial) 38. Fighting Devil Dogs (co-d, serial) 38. Hawk of the Wilderness (co-d) 38. The Lone Ranger (co-d) 38. Daredevils of the Red Circle (co-d, serial) 39. Dick Tracy's G-Men (co-d, serial) 39. The Lone Ranger Rides Again (co-d, serial) 39. Zorro's Fighting Legion (co-d, serial) 39. Adventures of Red Ryder (co-d, serial) 40. Drums of Fu Manchu (co-d, serial) 40. King of the Royal Mounted (co-d, serial) 40. The Mysterious Dr Satan (co-d, serial) 40. Adventures of Captain Marvel (co-d, serial) 41. Dick Tracy vs Crime Inc (co-d, serial) 41. Jungle Girl (co-d, serial) 41. King of the Texas Rangers (co-d, serial) 41. King of the Mounties (serial) 42. Perils of Nyoka (serial) 42. Spy Smasher (serial) 42. G-Men vs The Black Dragon (serial) 43. The Crimson Ghost (co-d, serial) 46. Bells of St Angelo 47. Under California Stars 48. The Outcast 54. Santa Fe Passage 55. Stranger at My Door 56. The Bonnie Parker Story 58. The Cool and the Crazy 58. Master of the World 61. Arizona Raiders 65. Forty Guns to Apache Pass 66. I Escaped from Devil's Island 73. Darktown Strutters 75, etc.

❝ I've found directors who I'm really into, but Witney is ahead of them all, the one whose movies I can show to anyone and they are just blown away. – *Quentin Tarantino*

Wixted, Michael James (1961–)
American child actor of the 70s.

Lost in the Stars 74. Where Have All the People Gone? (TV) 74. Islands in the Stream 77, etc.

TV series: The Smith Family 71. The Swiss Family Robinson 75.

Wizan, Joe (1935–)
American producer.

Jeremiah Johnson 72. Junior Bonner 72. Prime Cut 72. The Last American Hero 73. Audrey Rose 77. And Justice for All 79. Voices 79. Best Friends 82. Unfaithfully Yours 83. Iron Eagle 85. Tough Guys 86. Spellbinder 88. Split Decisions 88. Short Time 90. The Nanny 90. Stop, or My Mom Will Shoot 91. Wrestling Ernest Hemingway 93. Fire in the Sky 93. Dunston Checks In 96. Kiss the Girls 97, etc.

Wodehouse, Sir P(elham) G(ranville) (1881–1975)
Prolific English comic novelist, lyricist and screenwriter. Born in Guildford, Surrey, he was educated at Dulwich College, published his first novel in 1902, and wrote some 120 books. He also worked as a journalist and moved to America to become drama critic of *Vanity Fair*. He adapted his work as plays and musicals, often in collaboration with Guy Bolton, and spent a year in Hollywood from 1929, under contract to MGM at $2,000, where he also gained a reputation as Beverly Hills' only pedestrian, always walking the six miles from his home to the studio. He returned to the studio in 1936, at $2,500 a week for six months, and, as previously, found that he was given little work to do. His best-known lyrics, to Jerome Kern's music, were 'Bill' for the three-times-filmed musical *Showboat*, which also featured in *The Man I Love* 47 and *The Helen Morgan Story/Both Ends of the Candle* 57, and the title song for a biopic of Kern, *Till the Clouds Roll By* 46. His broadcasts to America during the Second World War from Germany, where he had been detained, caused a scandal in Britain, which resulted in him returning to live in America and becoming an American citizen in 1955. He was knighted in 1975, shortly before his death. His work has been somewhat neglected by the cinema, though it has proved more popular on television, with the series *Blandings Castle* 67, starring Ralph Richardson as the pig-obsessed Lord Emsworth; *Ukridge* 68, starring Anton Rodgers; and *Wodehouse Playhouse* 75–78, based on his short stories, with John Alderton and Pauline Collins. Two American films were made about the perfect manservant Jeeves, starring Arthur Treacher, though neither bore much resemblance to the original. In the 30s, MGM considered buying the rights to the character, but Irving Thalberg decided against it when he asked his chauffeur if he had ever heard of anyone called Jeeves, and the driver replied that he thought it was the name of his wife's butcher. Faithful to the spirit of the stories were two British TV series about the ineffectual, upper-class Bertie Wooster and his impeccable valet: *The World of Wooster* 65–67, starring Ian Carmichael and Dennis Price, and *Jeeves and Wooster* 90–93, with Stephen Fry and Hugh Laurie.

Autobiography: 1953, *Bring On the Girls* (with Guy Bolton). 1953, *Performing Flea/Author! Author!*. 1957, *America, I Like You/Over Seventy*.

Biography: 1975, *P. G. Wodehouse: A Portrait of a Master* by David Jasen. 1982, *P. G. Wodehouse* by Frances Donaldson.

Oh Lady, Lady! (oa) 20. A Gentleman of Leisure (oa) 23. Those Three French Girls (co-w) 30. The Man in Possession (co-w) 31. Piccadilly Jim (oa) 36. Thank You Jeeves (oa) 36. Anything Goes (co-w) 36. Step Lively, Jeeves (oa) 37. A Damsel in Distress (co-w) 37, etc.

❝ I suppose the secret of writing is to go through your stuff until you come on something you think is particularly good, and then cut it out. – *P.G.W.*

I get much more kick out of a place like Droitwich, which has no real merits, than out of something like the Taj Mahal. – *P.G.W.*

As a rule pictures are a bore. – *P.G.W.*

Wolfe, Ian (1896–1992)
American character actor who usually played worried, grasping or officious roles. He appeared in more than 150 films.

The Barretts of Wimpole Street 33. Clive of India 35. Hudson's Bay 40. The Moon is Down 43. The Invisible Man's Revenge 44. Mr Blandings Builds His Dream House 48. The Great Caruso 50. Gaby 56. The Lost World 60. Games 67. The Fortune 74. Jinxed 82, many others.

TV series: Soap 78–80.

Wolff, Lothar (1909–1988)
German producer-director, former editor; with 'The March of Time' for many years, and still associated with Louis de Rochemont.

Lost Boundaries (p) 45. Martin Luther (co-wp) 53. Windjammer (p) 57. Question Seven (pd) 61. Fortress of Peace (p) 63, etc.

Wolfit, Sir Donald (1902–1968)
Distinguished British thespian who, having brought Shakespeare to the provinces, gave some enjoyably hammy performances in films.

Autobiography: 1954, *First Interval*.

Biography: 1971, *The Knight Has Been Unruly* by Ronald Harwood.

■ Death at Broadcasting House 34. Drake of England 35. The Silent Passenger 35. Sexton Blake and the Bearded Doctor 35. Checkmate 35. Late Extra 35. Hyde Park Corner 35. Calling the Tune 36. *The Ringer* 52. Pickwick Papers 53. Isn't Life Wonderful? 53. Svengali 54. A Prize of Gold 55. Guilty 56. The Man in the Road 56. The Man on the Beach 56. Satellite in the Sky 56. The Traitor 57. I Accuse 57. Blood of the Vampire 58. *Room at the Top* 59. The House of Seven Hawks 59. The Angry Hills 59. The Rough and the Smooth 59. The Hands of Orlac 60. The Mark 61. Lawrence of Arabia 62. Dr Crippen 63. Becket 64. Ninety Degrees in the Shade 65. Life at the Top 65. The Sandwich Man 66. *Decline and Fall* 68. The Charge of the Light Brigade 68.

Wolfman, Jack (1938–1995) (Robert Smith)
American rock disc jockey, noted for his extrovert style, who gained national fame after playing himself in *American Graffiti*.

Autobiography: 1995, *Have Mercy: The Confession of the Original Party Animal*.

The Committee 68. The Seven Minutes 71. American Graffiti 73. Deadman's Curve (TV) 78. Hanging on a Star 78. Motel Hell 80. Midnight 89. Mortuary Academy 91, etc.

Wolfson, P. J. (1903–1979)
American screenwriter.

Madison Square Garden 31. The Picture Snatcher 33. Mad Love 35. Public Enemy's Wife 37. Shall We Dance? (co-w) 37. Vivacious Lady (co-w) 38. Allegheny Uprising (& p) 39. They All Kissed the Bride (co-w) 42. Saigon (co-w & p) 48, many others.

Wolheim, Louis (1880–1931)
German-born character actor, often of semi-brutish roles, with American stage experience; in Hollywood from 1919. He was a former mathematics teacher at Cornell University.

Dr Jekyll and Mr Hyde 20. Little Old New York 22. America 24. *Two Arabian Knights* 27. The Racket 28. Tempest 28. Frozen Justice 29. *All Quiet on the Western Front* 31. Sin Ship (& d) 31, etc.

Wolper, David L. (1928–)
American documentarist who turned feature film producer and TV executive.

If It's Tuesday This Must Be Belgium 69. The Bridge at Remagen 69. The Hellstrom Chronicle 71. Roots (TV) 77. The Man Who Saw Tomorrow 80. This Is Elvis 81. Imagine: John Lennon 88. Murder in Mississippi (TV) 90. Murder in the First 95. Surviving Picasso 96. LA Confidential 97, etc.

Wolski, Dariusz
Polish-born cinematographer, in America.

Heart 87. The Land of Little Rain 88. Nightfall 88. Romeo Is Bleeding 94. The Crow 94. Crimson Tide 95. The Fan 96. Dark City 98. A Perfect Murder 98, etc.

Wolsky, Albert (1930–)
American costume designer.

The Turning Point 77. An Unmarried Woman 78. Grease 78. All That Jazz (AA) 79. Manhattan 79. The Jazz Singer 80. Sophie's Choice (AAN) 82. Star 80 83. The Journey of Natty Gan (AAN) 85. Moon over Parador 88. Scenes from a Mall 91. Bugsy (AA) 91. Toys (AAN) 92. The Pickle 93. Striptease 96. Red Corner 97. The Jackal 97. You've Got Mail 98, etc.

Wong, Anna May (1907–1961) (Wong Liu Tsong)
Chinese-American actress popular in the 30s.

Red Lantern 19. The Thief of Bagdad 24. *Piccadilly* (GB) 29. On the Spot 30. Shanghai Express 32. *Chu Chin Chow* (GB) 33. *Java Head* (GB) 34. Limehouse Blues 36. Bombs Over Burma 42. Impact 49. Portrait in Black 60, etc.

Wong, Faye (1969–) (Wong Fei)
Beijing-born, Hong Kong-based Chinese singer and actress.

Chungking Express 94. Summer in Beijing 98.

Wong, Kirk (aka Che-Kirk Wong, Kirk Wong Chi-keung)
Hong Kong director, best known for his trio of police procedural thrillers based on actual cases.

The Club 81. True Colours 86. Gunmen 90. Crime Story/Chung On Tsou 92. Organized Crime and Triad Bureau 94. Rock'n'Roll Cop/Sang Gong Yatho Tungchap Fan 95. *The Big Hit* (US) 98, etc.

Wong, Victor
Affable Chinese-American character actor.

Dim Sum: A Little Bit of Heart 85. Big Trouble in Little China 86. Shanghai Surprise 86. The Golden Child 86. The Last Emperor 87. Prince of Darkness 87. Eat a Bowl of Tea 89. 3 Ninjas 92. The Joy Luck Club 93. 3 Ninjas Kick Back 94. 3 Ninjas Knuckle Up 95. The Stars Fell on Henrietta 95. Jade 95. Paper Dragons 96. The Devil Takes a Holiday 96. Search 97. Seven Years in Tibet 97. 3 Ninjas: High Noon at Mega Mountain 98, etc.

Wontner, Arthur (1875–1960)
Gaunt British character actor of stage and screen; a splendid, if elderly, Sherlock Holmes.

Frailty 16. Bonnie Prince Charlie 23. Eugene Aram 24. The Infamous Lady 28. The Sleeping Cardinal 31. *The Sign of Four* 32. *The Triumph of Sherlock Holmes* 35. Dishonour Bright 36. Silver Blaze 36. Storm in a Teacup 37. Kate Plus Ten 38. The Terror 38. The Life and Death of Colonel Blimp 43. Blanche Fury 47. Brandy for the Parson 52. *Genevieve* 53, etc.

Woo, John (1946–) (Ng Ya-sum)
Chinese director, screenwriter and occasional actor who moved to the USA in the early 90s. Born in China, he lived in Hong Kong as a child. He began as script supervisor at Cathay Studios in the late 60s, then became an assistant director at Shaw Brothers studios in the early 70s, later becoming a production manager. International recognition came with *The Killer*, with its violent, elaborately choreographed action sequences.

The Young Dragons 73. Money Crazy 77. Last Hurrah for Chivalry 78. Laughing Times 81. The Time You Need a Friend 84. Run Tiger, Run 85. A

Better Tomorrow 86. The Killer 89. Bullet in the Head 90. Once a Thief 91. Hard Boiled 92. Hard Target (US) 93. Broken Arrow (US) 96. *Face/Off* (US) 97. Replacement Killers (ex p) (US) 98. The Big Hit (ex p) (US) 98. Blackjack (TV) 98, etc.

AS ACTOR: Starry Is the Night 88. Rebel from China 90. Twin Dragons 92, etc.

❝ I hate violence. – *J.W.*

The most exciting director to emerge in action cinema since Sergio Leone. – *Quentin Tarantino*

Wood, Charles (1932–)
British playwright with a penchant for military matters.

Help 65. The Knack 65. How I Won the War 67. The Charge of the Light Brigade 68. The Long Day's Dying 68. The Bed Sitting Room 69. Cuba 79. The Red Monarch (TV) 83. Wagner 83. Sharpe's Company (TV) 94. An Awfully Big Adventure 95, etc.

Wood Jnr, Edward D. (1924–1978)
American film director and screenwriter generally regarded as making the worst films in the history of the cinema. Most starred Bela Lugosi, at the sad and drug-addicted end of his career, and the bulky Tor Johnson. A cult has grown around the worst of his worst, *Plan 9 from Outer Space*, which was even the inspiration for a computer game in 1992. A biopic, *Ed Wood*, directed by Tim Burton and starring Johnny Depp in the title role, was released in 1994. A documentary, *The Haunted World of Edward J. Wood Jnr*, directed by Brett Thompson, was released in 1995. A restored and re-edited version of his first 20-minute western, *Crossroads at Laredo*, which was made in 1948, was also released in 1995.

Biography: 1992, *Nightmare of Ecstasy: The Life and Art of Edward D. Wood Jnr* by Rudolph Grey.

■ Glen or Glenda (a, wd) 53. Jail Bait (a, wd) 54. Bride of the Monster (wd) 55. The Violent Years (w) 56. The Bride and the Beast (w) 58. Plan 9 from Outer space (a, wd) 59. The Sinister Urge (a, wd) 60. Night of the Ghouls/Revenge of the Dead (wd) 60. Shotgun Wedding (w) 63. Orgy of the Dead (w) 65. 1,000,000 AC/DC (w) 69. Take It Out in Trade (a, wd) 71. Class Reunion (w) 73. Fugitive Girls (a, w) 74. The Cocktail Hostess (w) 74. Necromancy/Necromania (wd) 75. I Woke Up Early the Day I Died (oa) 98.

Wood, Elijah (1981–)
American child actor, a former model.

Avalon 90. Radio Flyer 92. Forever Young 92. The Adventures of Huck Finn 93. The Good Son 93. North 94. Flipper 96. Oliver Twist 97. The Ice Storm 97. Deep Impact 98. The Faculty 98. The Bumblebee Flies Anyway 98. Black and White 99, etc.

Wood, Mrs Henry (1814–1887)
British Victorian novelist whose *East Lynne* has been filmed several times.

Wood, John (1937–)
British stage actor usually seen in intellectual roles.

The Rebel 60. Nicholas and Alexandra 72. Slaughterhouse Five 72. Somebody Killed Her Husband 77. War Games 83. Ladyhawke 85. The Purple Rose of Cairo 85. Jumpin' Jack Flash 86. Memento Mori (TV) 92. Orlando 92. Young Americans 93. Shadowlands 93. Uncovered 94. Citizen X (TV) (US) 95. Sabrina 95. Richard III 95. Jane Eyre 96. Family Money (TV) 97. The Gambler 97. Metroland 97. Revengers' Comedies 97. The Avengers 98. An Ideal Husband 99. The Venice Project 99. The Little Vampire 00, etc.

Wood, Lawson (1878–1957)
British artist and illustrator, noted for his humorous drawings of animals. He was the creator of *Gran' Pop Monkey*, a short-lived cartoon series about an artful chimpanzee, animated by Ub Iwerks.

A Busy Day 40. Beauty Shoppe 40. Baby Checkers 40.

Wood, Natalie (1938–1981) (Natasha Gurdin)
Former American child actress who became a top star of the 60s. Born in San Francisco, she began to dance almost before she could walk and was on screen from the age of five. Married actor Robert WAGNER (1957–62, 1972–81) and British producer Richard Gregson (1969–71). Drowned after falling from a yacht. Mother of actress Natasha Gregson WAGNER.

Happy Land 43. Tomorrow Is Forever 45. The Bride Wore Boots 46. Miracle on 34th Street 47. No Sad Songs for Me 50. The Blue Veil 52. Rebel without a Cause (AAN) 55. A Cry in the Night 56. The Searchers 56. *Marjorie Morningstar* 58. Kings Go Forth 59. Cash McCall 60. *Splendor in the Grass* (AAN) 61. *West Side Story* 61. Gypsy 62. *Love with the Proper Stranger* (AAN) 64. Sex and the Single Girl 64. *The Great Race* 65. Inside Daisy Clover 66. This Property is Condemned 66. Penelope 66. *Bob and Carol and Ted and Alice* 69. The Affair (TV) 73. Peeper 74. *From Here to Eternity* (TV) 79. Meteor 79. Brainstorm 83 (release), etc.

TV series: Pride of the Family 53.

Wood, Oliver
American cinematographer.

The Honeymoon Killers 69. Don't Go in the House 79. Q the Winged Serpent/The Winged Serpent 82. Maya 82. Alphabet City 84. Body Rock 84. Joey 85. Hoosiers/Best Shot 86. The Adventures of Ford Fairlane 90. Die Hard 2 90. Rudy 93. Sister Act 2: Back in the Habit 93. Terminal Velocity 94. Mr Holland's Opus 95. 2 Days in the Valley 96. Celtic Pride 96. SwitchBack 97. Face/Off 97. Mighty Joe Young 98. U-571 00, etc.

Wood, Peggy (1894–1978)
American character actress, former opera singer.

Almost a Husband 19. Handy Andy 34. The Housekeeper's Daughter 39. The Story of Ruth 60. *The Sound of Music* (AAN) 65, etc.

TV series: Mama 49–56.

Wood, Sam (1883–1949)
American director, in business before becoming assistant to Cecil B. De Mille *c.* 1915; directing from 1920.

The Beloved Villain 20. Under the Lash 22. Bluebeard's Eighth Wife 23. One Minute to Play 26. The Latest from Paris 28. Within the Law 30. Stamboul Quest 32. The Late Christopher Bean 33. Get-Rich-Quick Wallingford 34. *A Night at the Opera* 35. The Unguarded Hour 36. *A Day at the Races* 37. Madame X 37. Lord Jeff 38. *Goodbye Mr Chips* (AAN) 39. Raffles 39. *Our Town* 40. Kitty Foyle (AAN) 40. *The Devil and Miss Jones* 41. The Pride of the Yankees 42. *Kings Row* (AAN) 42. Saratoga Trunk 43 (released 46). *For Whom the Bell Tolls* (& p) 43. Casanova Brown 44. Guest Wife 45. Heartbeat 46. Ivy 47. Command Decision 48. Ambush 49, etc.

Wood, 'Wee Georgie' (1895–1979)
Diminutive, squeaky-voiced English music-hall comedian, on stage from the age of five.

Convict 99 19. Two Little Drummer Boys 28. The Black Hand Gang 30. Stepping Toes 38. The Visit 61, etc.

Woodard, Alfre (1953–)
American actress.

Remember My Name 78. Health 80. Cross Creek (AAN) 83. Go Tell It on the Mountain 84. Extremities 86. Scrooged 88. Miss Firecracker 89. Grand Canyon 91. Passion Fish 92. Rich in Love 93. Heart and Souls 93. Bopha! 93. Crooklyn 94. Blue Chips 94. How to Make an American Quilt 95. Primal Fear 96. Star Trek: First Contact 96. Miss Evers' Boys (TV) 97. The Member of the Wedding (TV) 97. Down in the Delta (& co-p) 98. Mumford 99. Dinosaur (voice) 00. Love & Basketball 00, etc.

TV series: Tucker's Witch 82–83. St Elsewhere 85–87. Sara 85–88.

Woodbridge, George (1907–1973)
Portly British character actor, often seen as tavern-keeper or jovial policeman.

Tower of Terror 42. Green for Danger 46. Bonnie Prince Charlie 48. The Story of Gilbert and Sullivan 53. The Constant Husband 55. Dracula 58. Two-Way Stretch 60. Dracula Prince of Darkness 65, many others.

Woodbury, Joan (1915–1989)
American leading lady of 40s second features.

Without Children 35. Forty Naughty Girls 38. The Mystery of the White Room 39. The Desperadoes 43. Flame of the West 46. Here Comes Trouble 49. The Ten Commandments 56, many others.

Woodlawn, Holly (1947–) (Harold Ajzenberg)
Puerto Rico-born transvestite star of Andy Warhol's movies.

Trash 69. Scarecrow in a Garden of Cucumbers 72. Women in Revolt 72. Night Owl 93, etc.

❝ We tried to be women so much. I think that basically Andy loved glamorous women and around that time he just didn't know any. – *H.W.*

Woods, Arthur B. (1904–1942)
British director.

On Secret Service 34. Radio Parade 35. Drake of England 35. The Dark Stairway 37. The Return of Carol Deane 38. *They Drive by Night* 38. The Nursemaid Who Disappeared 39. Busman's Honeymoon 40, etc.

Woods, Aubrey (1928–)
British character actor.

Nicholas Nickleby 47. Queen of Spades 48. Father Brown 54. School for Scoundrels 59. Spare the Rod 61. Just Like a Woman 66. The Abominable Dr Phibes 71. The Darwin Adventure 72. That Lucky Touch 75, etc.

Woods, Donald (1906–1998) (Ralph L. Zink)
Canadian leading man of the 30s and 40s.

Sweet Adeline 33. *A Tale of Two Cities* 35. *Anthony Adverse* 36. Forgotten Girls 40. Love, Honour and Oh Baby 41. I Was a Prisoner on Devil's Island 41. Watch on the Rhine 43. Roughly Speaking 45. Wonder Man 45. Barbary Pirate 49. Undercover Agent 54. Thirteen Ghosts 60. Kissing Cousins 64. Moment to Moment 65. True Grit 69, many others.

TV series: Craig Kennedy, Criminologist 52. Damon Runyon Theatre (host) 55–56. Tammy 65–66.

Woods, Eddie (1905–1989)
American leading man of the early 30s. He seemed to lose heart after swapping roles with Cagney for *The Public Enemy* (he was originally cast for the top role and elected to take the less interesting role of the brother).

Woods, Harry Macgregor (1896–1970)
American songwriter. Educated at Harvard, he lacked any fingers on his left hand and played the piano one-handed. He came to Britain in the 30s to work for Gaumont British Pictures and wrote, among other hits, 'Over My Shoulder' and 'When You've Got a Little Springtime in Your Heart' for Jessie Matthews to sing in *Evergreen*. He returned to America in the 40s and wrote no more.

Aunt Sally 33. Jack Ahoy! 34. Evergreen 35. It's Love Again 36.

Woods, James (1947–)
Lean American actor, in roles of increasing stature. Born in Vernal, Utah, he studied politcal science at the Massachusetts Institute of Technology and began as an actor on the stage.

The Way We Were 72. Alex and the Gypsy 76. The Choirboys 78. The Onion Field 79. The Black Marble 80. Eyewitness 80. Split Image 82. Videodrome 83. Against All Odds 83. Once upon a Time in America 84. Cat's Eye 84. *Salvador* (AAN) 85. Joshua Then and Now 87. Best Seller 87. Cop 88. The Boost 88. True Believer 89. Immediate Family 89. The Hard Way 91. Straight Talk 92. Chaplin 92. Diggstown/Midnight Sting 92. The Getaway 94. Curse of the Starving Class 94. Next Door (TV) 94. The Specialist 94. Casino 95. Nixon 95. Indictment: The McMartin Trial (TV) 95. Killer: A Journal of Murder 96. The Summer of Ben Tyler (TV) 97. *Ghosts of Mississippi* (AAN) 97. Kicked in the Head 97. Contact 97. John Carpenter's Vampires 98. Another Day in Paradise 98. True Crime 99. The General's Daughter 99. Any Given Sunday 99. Virgin Suicides 99, etc.

Woodward, Edward (1930–)
British stage actor who achieved popularity on TV as the tough secret agent Callan. Born in Croydon, Surrey, he studied at RADA and was on stage from 1946. He is the father of actor Tim Woodward. Married actresses Venetia Barratt and Michele DOTRICE.

Where There's a Will 54. Becket 64. The File of the Golden Goose 69. Incense for the Damned 70. Sitting Target 72. Young Winston 72. The Wicker Man 73. Callan 74. Stand Up Virgin Soldiers 77. Breaker Morant 80. Winston Churchill, the Wilderness Years (TV) 81. Who Dares Wins 82. A Christmas Carol (TV) 84. Champions 83. King David 85. Mr Johnson 90. Deadly Advice 94. Gulliver's Travels (TV) 96, etc.

TV series: Callan 67-72. 1990 77-78. The Equalizer 85–89. Over My Dead Body 90–91. Common as Muck 94–97.

Woodward, Joanne (1930–)
American leading actress, from the stage. Born in Thomasville, Georgia, she studied at Louisiana State University and at the Neighborhood Playhouse in New York. In 1955, Twentieth Century-Fox signed her and she became a star two years later with *The Three Faces of Eve*. Married in 1958 actor Paul NEWMAN, with whom she has often co-starred. She won Emmys for her performances in *See How They Run* and *Do You Remember Love*.

Eve in *The Three Faces of Eve*, playing a woman with multiple personalities; as Leola Boone, an abused wife, in *No Down Payment*; as Mary Meredith, a demure wife forced to play high-stakes poker, in *A Big Hand for the Little Lady*; as Rachel Cameron, an unhappy spinster, in *Rachel, Rachel*; and as India Bridge, a conventional upper middle class wife, in *Mr and Mrs Bridge*.

■ Count Three and Pray 55. A Kiss before Dying 56. *The Three Faces of Eve* (AA) 57. *No Down Payment* 57. The Long Hot Summer 58. Rally round the Flag Boys 58. The Sound and the Fury 59. The Fugitive Kind 59. From the Terrace 60. Paris Blues 61. The Stripper 63. A New Kind of Love 63. Signpost to Murder 64. *A Big Hand for the Little Lady* 66. A Fine Madness 66. *Rachel Rachel* (AAN) 68. Winning 69. W.U.S.A. 70. They Might Be Giants 71. The Effect of Gamma Rays on Man-in-the-Moon Marigolds 72. Summer Wishes, Winter Dreams (AAN) 73. The Drowning Pool 75. Sybil (TV) 77. The End 78. See How She Runs (TV) 78. A Christmas to Remember (TV) 78. The Shadow Box (TV) 80. Harry and Son 84. Passions (TV) 84. Do You Remember Love (TV) 85. The Glass Menagerie 87. *Mr & Mrs Bridge* (AAN) 90. Foreign Affairs (TV) 93. Blind Spot (TV) 93. The Age of Innocence (narrator) 93. Philadelphia 93. Breathing Lessons (TV) 94.

Woof, Emily (1970–)
British leading actress, from the stage. Born in Newcastle, she studied English at Oxford University and first came to notice writing and performing experimental one-woman shows.

The Full Monty 97. Photographing Fairies 97. The Woodlanders 97. Killer Net (TV) 98. Velvet Goldmine 98. Fast Food 98. Passion: The Story of Percy Grainger 99. This Year's Love 99. Daylight Robbery (TV) 99. Oliver Twist (TV) 99. Pandaemonium 00. Daylight Robbery (TV) 00, etc.

Wooland, Norman (1905–1989)
British actor, former radio announcer.

Hamlet (film debut) 48. All over the Town 48. Escape 49. Romeo and Juliet 53. The Master Plan 55. Richard III 56. Guilty 56. The Rough and the Smooth 59. The Fall of the Roman Empire 64. Saul and David 65. The Projected Man 66, etc.

Wooldridge, Susan
English leading actress, from the stage and television, daughter of actress Margaretta SCOTT.

Butley 74. The Shout 78. The Jewel in the Crown (TV) 84. Loyalties 85. Hope and Glory 87. Bye Bye Blues 89. How to Get Ahead in Advertising 89. Twenty-One 91. Afraid of the Dark 92. Just Like a Woman 92. Bad Company (TV) 93, etc.

TV series: Underworld 97.

Wooley, Sheb (1921–)
American character actor and country singer-songwriter. Born in Erick, Oklahoma, he was best known for the role of scout Pete Nolan in the TV series *Rawhide*. In Western films, he was often a bad guy, while maintaining a parallel stage career as a singer of comedy songs. His recording of his song *The Purple People Eater* was a hit in 1958 and later formed the basis of a movie in which he also appeared.

Rocky Mountain 50. Little Big Horn 51. High Noon 52. Bugles in the Afternoon 52. Texas Badman 53. Giant 56. Ride a Violent Mile 57. Terror in a Texas Town 58. The Outlaw Josey Wales 76. Silverado 85. Hoosiers 86. Purple People Eater 88, etc.

TV series: Rawhide 59-65. Hee Haw 69.

Woolf, James (1919–1966)
British producer. With brother, Sir John WOOLF (1913–1999), founded Romulus Films 1949. Both

are sons of leading producer-distributor C. M. Woolf, who died in 1942.

Pandora and the Flying Dutchman 51. The African Queen 52. Moulin Rouge 53. Three Men in a Boat 56. Room at the Top 59, etc.

JAMES ONLY: The L-Shaped Room 62. The Pumpkin Eater 64. Life at the Top 65. King Rat 65.

JOHN ONLY: Oliver! (AA) 68. Day of the Jackal 73. No Sex Please We're British 73. The Odessa File 74.

Woolf, Virginia (1882–1941)
British novelist whose introspection and sensitivity, rather than her themes, were used as symbols in the title *Who's Afraid of Virginia Woolf? Orlando* was successfully filmed by Sally Potter in 1992. *Mrs Dalloway* followed in 1998.

Woolfe, H. Bruce (1880–1965)
British producer, best known for his war reconstructions of the 20s (*Armageddon*, *Ypres*, *The Battle of the Somme*, etc.) and for the *Secrets of Nature* series begun in 1919. Head of British Instructional Films from 1926; later in charge of production for children.

Woollcott, Alexander (1887–1943)
Waspish American columnist and critic, the original inspiration for Kaufman and Hart's *The Man Who Came to Dinner*. He was played by Tom McGowan in *Mrs Parker and the Vicious Circle* 94.

Biography: 1976, *Smart Aleck* by Howard Teichmann.

■ Gift of Gab 34. *The Scoundrel* 35. Babes on Broadway 41.

See also: ALGONQUIN ROUND TABLE.

❝ He spoke the English language with all the style of a prose writer; his wit was devastating and original; he was a man of great but deviating loyalty to his friends; and, if he chose, could make an evening come brightly to light. – *George Oppenheimer*

He was petty, shockingly vindictive in a feminine fashion, given to excesses when expressing his preferences or his prejudices. He probably endorsed more second-rate books than any man of his time. – *Tallulah Bankhead*

Woolley, Monty (1888–1963) (Edgar Montillion Woolley)
American comedy character actor of ebullient personality, a former Yale professor who came to movie stardom via a big hit as Alexander Woollcott on the Broadway stage.

Live, Love and Learn 37. Nothing Sacred 37. Arsène Lupin Returns 38. Girl of the Golden West 38. Everybody Sing 38. Three Comrades 38. Lord Jeff 38. Artists and Models Abroad 38. Young Dr Kildare 38. Vacation from Love 38. Never Say Die 39. Midnight 39. Zaza 39. Man about Town 39. Dancing Co-Ed 39. *The Man Who Came to Dinner* 41. The Pied Piper (AAN) 42. Life Begins at 8.30 42. *Holy Matrimony* 43. Since You Went Away (AAN) 44. Irish Eyes Are Smiling 44. Molly and Me 45. *Night and Day* 46. The Bishop's Wife 47. *Miss Tatlock's Millions* 48. As Young as You Feel 51. Kismet 55, etc.

❝ Famous line (*The Man Who Came to Dinner*) 'Gentlemen, will you all now leave quietly, or must I ask Miss Cutler to pass among you with a baseball bat?'

Famous line (*The Man Who Came to Dinner*) (to his nurse who has reproved him for eating chocolates) 'My great aunt Elizabeth ate a box of chocolates every day of her life. She lived to be a hundred and two, and when she had been dead three days, she looked healthier than you do now.'

Woolley, Stephen (1956–)
British producer. With Nik POWELL, he was a co-founder of Palace Pictures, a distribution and production company.

Books: 1996, *The Egos Have Landed: The Rise and Fall of Palace Pictures* by Angus Finney.

The Company of Wolves 85. A Letter to Brezhnev 85. Absolute Beginners 86. Mona Lisa 86. The Courier 87. High Spirits 88. Shag 88. Scandal 89. The Big Man 90. The Miracle 91. The Pope Must Die/The Pope Must Diet 91. A Rage in Harlem 91. Interview with the Vampire 94. Michael Collins 96. Hollow Reed 96. Welcome to Woop-Woop 97. Downtime 97. TwentyFourSeven 97. Fever Pitch 97. The Lost Son 98. Little Voice 98. *The Butcher Boy* 98. B. Monkey 98. Divorcing Jack 98, etc.

Woolrich, Cornell (1903–1968)
American mystery writer also known as William Irish. A recluse, he handed some interesting ideas to Hollywood, but most were ineptly handled.

Street of Chance (from The Black Curtain) 42. The Leopard Man (from Black Alibi) 43. Phantom Lady 44. Deadline at Dawn 46. Black Angel 46. Fear in the Night 47. Night Has a Thousand Eyes 48. The Window 49. No Man of Her Own 50. Rear Window 54. The Bride Wore Black 67. Union City 79. Cloak and Dagger 84. Mrs Winterbourne (from I Married a Dead Man) 96, etc.

Woolsey, Ralph
American cinematographer.

The Culpeper Cattle Company 72. The New Centurions 72. The Mack 73. The Iceman Cometh 73. Black Eye 74. 99 44/100 Per Cent Dead 74. Rafferty and the Gold Dust Twins 75. Mother, Jugs and Speed 76. The Promise 79. The Great Santini 80. The Last Married Couple in America 80. Oh God! Book II 80, etc.

Woolsey, Robert
See WHEELER, Bert.

Woolvett, Jaimz (1967–)
Canadian actor. In 1996, he was awarded a $3.2m settlement against a producer in a contractual dispute that had kept him from appearing on television.

The Prom 92. Unforgiven 92. The Dark 93. Dead Presidents 95. The Assistant 97. Reluctant Angel 97. Y2K 99. Rites of Passage 99. The Guilty 99, etc.

Woo-ping, Yuen (1945–)
Chinese director of martial arts movies, whose early work helped make a star of Jackie CHAN. He is better known in the West as the choreographer of the fight sequences in the US film *The Matrix*, 99, and its sequels, and in Ang Lee's *Crouching Tiger, Hidden Dragon*, 00.

Drunken Master 78. Dance Of The Drunken Mantis 79. Buddhist Fist 80. Dreadnaught 81. Shaolin Drunkard 82. Drunken Tai-Chi 83.Tiger Cage 1 88. Tiger Cage 2 89. In The Line Of Duty 4 90. Tiger Cage 3 91. Iron Monkey 93. Hero Among Heroes 94. Fist Of Legends 95. Iron Monkey 2 95, many others.

Worden, Hank (1901–1992) (Norton Earl Worden)
American western character actor.

The Plainsman 36. Northwest Passage 40. The Bullfighters 45. The Secret Life of Walter Mitty 47. Yellow Sky 48. Fort Apache 48. Red River 48. Wagon Master 50. The Searchers 56. McLintock 63. Scream 82, many others.

Wordsworth, Richard (1915–1993)
Lanky English character actor, on stage, frequently in Shakespearian roles, from 1938. Also a director of plays and the great-great-grandson of the poet William Wordsworth, whom he impersonated in his one-man show, *The Bliss of Solitude*. His most memorable screen role was as the astronaut who turned to fungus in *The Quatermass Experiment/The Creeping Unknown* 55.

The Man Who Knew Too Much 56. Time without Pity 57. The Camp on Blood Island 58. Revenge of Frankenstein 58. Curse of the Werewolf 61. The Moving Toyshop (as detective Professor Gervase Fen) 64. Lock Up Your Daughters! 69. Song of Norway 70, etc.

TV series: R3 64. The Regiment 72.

Worlock, Frederick (1886–1973)
British character actor in Hollywood after long stage career.

Miracles for Sale 39. The Sea Hawk 40. Rage in Heaven 41. The Black Swan 43. Sherlock Holmes Faces Death 44. Terror by Night 46. Joan of Arc 48. Notorious Landlady 62. Spinout 66, etc.

Woronov, Mary (1942–)
American actress and novelist, who was one of Andy WARHOL's Superstars. Under the name of Mary Might she was a dancer with the Exploding Plastic Inevitable, the troupe that accompanied the rock group the Velvet Underground.

Autobiography: 2000, *Swimming Underground: My Years in the Warhol Factory*.

Hedy 65. The Chelsea Girls 66. Death Race 2000 75. Hollywood Boulevard 77. Rock 'n' Roll High School 79. Eating Raoul 82. Night of the Comet 84. Warlock 88. Let It Ride 89. Scenes from the Class Struggle in Beverly Hills 89. Where Sleeping Dogs Lie 91. The Living End 92, etc.

Worsley, Wallace (1880–1944)
American director of the 20s.

Honor's Cross 18. The Little Shepherd of Kingdom Come 19. *The Penalty* 20. A Blind Bargain 21. Rags to Riches 22. *The Hunchback of Notre Dame* 23. The Man Who Fights Alone 24. The Shadow of Law 26. The Power of Silence 28, etc.

Worth, Brian (1914–1978)
British light leading man.

The Lion Has Wings 39. One Night with You 48. Hindle Wakes 52. An Inspector Calls 54. Ill Met by Moonlight 57. Peeping Tom 60. On Her Majesty's Secret Service 69, etc.

Worth, Irene (1916–)
American leading actress, in recent years mainly on British stage.

■ One Night with You 48. Another Shore 48. Secret People 51. *Orders to Kill* (BFA) 58. The Scapegoat 59. Seven Seas to Calais (as Elizabeth I) 63. King Lear 69. Nicholas and Alexandra 71. Rich Kids 79. Deathtrap 82. Forbidden 85. Lost in Yonkers 93.

Worth, Marvin (1925–1998)
American producer and screenwriter. Born in Brooklyn, he began as a jazz promoter while still in his teens, then becoming a writer for TV shows, and of special material for comedians, and manager of Lenny BRUCE.

AS WRITER: Boys Night Out 62. Three on a Couch (co-w) 66. Promise Her Anything 66. Malcolm X (& d) (doc) 72, etc.

AS PRODUCER: Where's Poppa? 70. Lenny 74. The Rose 79. Up the Academy 80. Soup for One 82. Unfaithfully Yours 83. Rhinestone 84. Falling in Love 84. Less than Zero 87. Patty Hearst 88. Flashback 90. Diabolique 96. Norman Jean & Marilyn (TV) 96. Goa (TV) 98, etc.

Wotruba, Michael
see D'AMATO, Joe.

Wouk, Herman (1915–)
American best-selling novelist.

The Caine Mutiny 54. Marjorie Morningstar 58. Youngblood Hawke 64. The Winds of War (TV) 83. The Caine Mutiny Court-Martial (TV) 88. War and Remembrance (TV) 89, etc.

TV series: Troubleshooters 59–60. Dallas 79–80. Call to Glory 84–85. The Last Precinct 86.

Wray, Fay (1907–)
American leading lady of the 30s, a great screamer. Born in Canada, she moved to America as a child. The first and second of her three husbands were screenwriters John Monk Saunders (1928–40) and Robert Riskin.

Autobiography: 1989, *On the Other Hand*.

Street of Sin 28. The Wedding March 28. The Four Feathers 29. The Texan 30. Dirigible 30. Doctor X 31. *The Most Dangerous Game* 32. The Vampire Bat 33. The Mystery of the Wax Museum 33. *King Kong* 33. The Bowery 33. Madame Spy 34. The Affairs of Cellini 34. The Clairvoyant 35. They Met in a Taxi 36. Murder in Greenwich Village 37. The Jury's Secret 38. Adam Had Four Sons 41. Small Town Girl 53. Queen Bee 55. Crime of Passion 56. Tammy and the Bachelor 57. Gideon's Trumpet (TV) 80, etc.

TV series: Pride of the Family 53.

❝ At the premiere of *King Kong* I wasn't too impressed. I thought there was too much screaming ... I didn't realize then that King Kong and I were going to be together for the rest of our lives, and longer ... – *F.W.*

Wray, John (1890–1940) (John Malloy)
American general-purpose actor.

All Quiet on the Western Front 30. Doctor X 32. I Am a Fugitive from a Chain Gang 32. The Defence Rests 34. The Whole Town's Talking 35. Valiant is the Word for Carrie 36. You Only Live Once 37. The Cat and the Canary 39. The Man from Dakota 40, etc.

Wrede, Caspar (1929–1998)
Finnish director, in British TV.

■ The Barber of Stamford Hill 62. Private Potter 64. One Day in the Life of Ivan Denisovich 71. Ransom 74.

Wren, P. C. (1885–1941) (Percival Christopher Wren)
British adventure novelist who after a military life wrote the much filmed *Beau Geste*, followed by *Beau Sabreur* and *Beau Ideal*.

Wright, Basil (1907–1987)
British producer-director. In films from 1929; worked with John Grierson in creation of 'documentary'.

Books: 1975, *The Long View*.

Windmill in Barbados (d) 30. Song of Ceylon (p, d) 34. Night Mail (co-d) 36. Waters of Time (p, d) 51. World without End (d) 53. The Immortal Land (p, d) 58. A Place for Gold (p, d) 61, etc.

Wright Jnr, Cobina (1921–)
American actress of the 40s, a slinky blonde.

Charlie Chan in Rio 41. Weekend in Havana 41. Moon over Miami 41. Footlight Serenade 42. Something to Shout About 43, etc.

Wright, Geoffrey
Australian director and screenwriter, a former journalist.

Romper Stomper 92. Metal Skin 94.

Wright, Robin (1966–) (aka Robin Wright Penn)
American leading actress. Married actor Sean PENN, by whom she has a son and a daughter, in 1996.

Hollywood Vice Squad 86. The Princess Bride 87. State of Grace 90. The Playboys 92. Toys 92. Forrest Gump 94. The Crossing Guard 95. Moll Flanders 96. Loved 96. She's So Lovely 97. Hurlyburly 98, etc.

Wright, Teresa (1918–)
American leading actress with stage experience.

■ *The Little Foxes* (debut) (AAN) 41. *Mrs Miniver* (AA) 42. The Pride of the Yankees (AAN) 42. *Shadow of a Doubt* 43. Casanova Brown 44. *The Best Years of Our Lives* 46. Pursued 47. The Imperfect Lady 47. The Trouble with Women 47. Enchantment 48. *The Men* 50. The Captive 50. The Steel Trap 52. Something to Live For 52. Count the Hours 53. The Actress 53. Track of the Cat 54. *The Search for Bridey Murphy* 56. Escapade in Japan 57. The Wonderful Years 58. Hail Hero 69. The Happy Ending 69. Crawlspace (TV) 71. The Elevator (TV) 73. Flood (TV) 76. *Roseland* 77. Somewhere in Time 80. Bill: On His Own (TV) 83. The Good Mother 88.

Wright, Tony (1925–1986)
British light leading man, with stage experience.

The Flanagan Boy (film debut) 51. Jumping for Joy 54. Jacqueline 56. Seven Thunders 57. Faces in the Dark 60. Journey to Nowhere 62. All Coppers Are 72, etc.

Wright, Will (1894–1962)
Lugubrious American character actor.

China Clipper 36. World Première 41. Bewitched 45. *The Blue Dahlia* (his best role, as the murderer) 46. Adam's Rib 49. Excuse My Dust 51. The Wild One 52. The Deadly Companions 62. Cape Fear 62. Fail Safe 64, many others.

Wrightsman, Stan (1910–1975)
American jazz pianist. Born in Gotebo, Oklahoma, he worked in New Orleans before settling in the late 30s in Los Angeles, where he often played for films and television. He dubbed the piano playing of Richard WHORF in *Blues in the Night* 41, and of Bonita GRANVILLE in *Syncopation* 42. He is seen on-screen backing guitarist Tony Romano in *The Man I Love* 46. He also played on the soundtracks of *The Time, the Place and the Girl* 46, *Young Man with a Horn* 49, *Picnic* 55, and *The Five Pennies* 59.

Wrixon, Maris (1917–)
American light leading lady of the 30s.

Broadway Musketeers 38. The Ape 41. The Man Who Talked Too Much 42. Bullets for O'Hara 43. As You Were 51, etc.

Wrubel, Allie (1905–1973)
American composer. A big-band saxophonist and bandleader, he went to Hollywood in the 30s to write songs for Warner's movies.

Dames 34. Housewife 34. Flirtation Walk 34. Happiness Ahead 34. The Key 34. Sweet Music 35. Broadway Hostess 35. I Live for Love 35. In Caliente 35. Bright Lights 35. Life of the Party 37. Radio City Revels 38. Sing Your Way Home 45.

Song of the South (AA for song 'Zip-a-Dee-Doo-Dah') 46. Never Steal Anything Small 58, etc.

Wu, Vivian (1966–) (Wu Jun Mei)
Chinese actress, now based in Los Angeles. Married to producer-director Oscar Costo.

The Last Emperor 87. Iron and Silk 90. Shadow of China 91. The Guyver 91. Teenage Mutant Turtles III 92. Man Tseung (HK) 93. Heaven and Earth 93. The Joy Luck Club 93. Vanishing Son (TV) 94. The Pillow Book 95. Blindness 98. A Bright Shining Lie (TV) 98. 8 ½ Women 99. Dinner Rush 01, etc.

Wuhl, Robert (1951–)
American comedian and actor.

The Hollywood Knights 80. Good Morning, Vietnam 87. Bull Durham 88. Tales from the Crypt (TV) 89. Wedding Band 89. Blaze 89. Batman 89. Mistress 92. The Bodyguard 92. Blue Chips 94. Cobb 94. Open Season (& wd) 95. The Last Don (TV) 97. Good Burger 97. The Last Don II (TV) 98, etc.

Wurlitzer, Rudy
American screenwriter and occasional director, often of quirky, individualistic road movies.

Glen and Randa 71. Two Lane Blacktop (co-w) 71. Pat Garrett and Billy the Kid 73. Walker 87. Candy Mountain (& co-d) 87. Voyager 91. Little Buddha (co-w) 93. Shadow of the Wolf (co-w) 93. Fearless 94, etc.

Wurtzel, Sol M. (1881–1958)
American producer, mainly of B features for Fox and Twentieth Century Fox.

Bright Eyes 34. Judge Priest 34. Paddy O'Day 35. Life Begins at 40 35. Steamboat 'Round the Bend 35. Thank You, Jeeves 36. Can This Be Dixie? 36. Ramona 36. Change of Heart 37. Dangerously Yours 37. Dante's Inferno 35. Frontier Marshall 39. Heaven with a Barbed Wire Fence 39. Twenty Thousand Men a Year 39. Earthbound 40. Great Guns 41. Scotland Yard 41. A-Haunting We Will Go 42. Whispering Ghosts 42. Jitterbugs 43. The Big Noise 44. Deadline for Murder 46. Rendevous 24 46, many others.
66 An unbenevolent tyrant saved by his lack of humor. – *Oscar Levant*

Wyatt, Jane (1912–)
Pleasing American leading lady of the 30s and 40s, with stage experience.

One More River 34. The Luckiest Girl in the World 36. *Lost Horizon* 37. Kisses for Breakfast 41. The Kansan 42. The Iron Road 43. None but the Lonely Heart 44. Boomerang 47. Gentleman's Agreement 47. Pitfall 48. Bad Boy 49. Task Force 49. Our Very Own 50. The Man Who Cheated Himself 51. Never Too Late 65. Tom Sawyer (TV) 73. Treasure of Matecumbe 76. Star Trek IV: The Journey Home 86. Amityville 4: The Evil Escapes (TV) 89, many others.

TV series: Father Knows Best 54–59 (reunion show 77).

Wycherly, Margaret (1881–1956)
British-born character actress with American stage experience.

The Thirteenth Chair 29. Sergeant York (AAN) 41. Keeper of the Flame 43. The Yearling 46. *White Heat* 49. Man with a Cloak 51. That Man from Tangier 53, many others.

Wyler, Richard
See STAPLEY, Richard.

Wyler, William (1902–1981)
Distinguished German-American director, former film publicist, in Hollywood from 1920. Director from 1925, starting with low-budget silent westerns.

Biography: 1996, *A Talent for Trouble: The Life of Hollywood's Most Acclaimed Director, William Wyler* by Jan Herman.
■ TALKIES: Hell's Heroes 30. The Storm 30. A House Divided 31. Tom Brown of Culver 32. Her First Mate 33. Counsellor at Law 33. Glamour 34. *The Good Fairy* 35. The Gay Deception 35. These Three 36. Come and Get It (co-d) 36. *Dodsworth* (AAN) 36. Dead End 37. Jezebel 38. *Wuthering Heights* (AAN) 39. *The Letter* (AAN) 40. *The Westerner* 40. *The Little Foxes* (AAN) 41. *Mrs Miniver* (AA) 42. The Memphis Belle (doc) 44. The Fighting Lady (doc) 44. *The Best Years of Our Lives* (AA) 46. *The Heiress* (AAN) 49. *Detective Story* (AAN) 51. Carrie 52. Roman Holiday (AAN) 53. The Desperate Hours 55. The Friendly Persuasion (AAN) 56. *The Big Country* 58. *Ben Hur* (AA) 59. The Children's Hour 62. The Collector (AAN) 65. How to Steal a Million 66. Funny Girl 68. The Liberation of L.B. Jones 70.
66 Doing a picture with Willie is like getting the works at a Turkish bath. You damn near drown, but you come out smelling like a rose. – *Charlton Heston*

Wyman, Jane (1914–) (Sarah Jane Faulks)
American leading lady of the 40s, at first in dumb blonde roles, later as serious actress. The second of her three husbands was Ronald Reagan (1940–48).

When asked why she divorced Ronald Reagan, she said: 'He talked too much.'

My Man Godfrey 36. Brother Rat 38. Flight Angels 40. Bad Men of Missouri 41. The Body Disappears 41. You're in the Army Now 41. My Favourite Spy 42. Princess O'Rourke 43. Crime by Night 44. The Doughgirls 44. Make Your Own Bed 44. *The Lost Weekend* 45. Night and Day 46. Magic Town 46. The Yearling (AAN) 46. *Johnny Belinda* (AA) 48. Three Guys Named Mike 49. Here Comes the Groom 51. The Blue Veil (AAN) 52. Just for You 53. So Big 53. *Magnificent Obsession* (AAN) 54. All that Heaven Allows 55. Miracle in the Rain 56. Pollyanna 60. Bon Voyage 63. How to Commit Marriage 69. The Failing of Raymond (TV) 71. The Incredible Journey of Dr Meg Laurel (TV) 79, etc.

TV series: The Jane Wyman Theater 56–60. Falcon Crest 81– .

Wymark, Patrick (1920–1970) (Patrick Cheesman)
British TV actor, in occasional films. The voice of Churchill in *The Finest Hours* 64, *A King's Story* 65.

The Criminal 60. Repulsion 65. The Secret of Blood Island 65. The Psychopath 66. Where Eagles Dare 68. Cromwell 69. Satan's Skin 70, etc.

Wymore, Patrice (1926–)
American leading lady. She married Errol Flynn in 1953.

Tea for Two 50. Rocky Mountain 50. The Big Trees 52. She's Working Her Way through College 52. She's Back on Broadway 53. Chamber of Horrors 66, etc.

Wyndham, John (1903–1969) (John Wyndham Harris)
British science fiction novelist. Works filmed include *Village of the Damned/The Midwich Cuckoos* and *The Day of the Triffids*.

Wynn, Ed (1886–1966) (Isaiah Edwin Leopold)
American vaudeville, radio and TV comic who after initial film failure returned to Hollywood in the 50s as a character actor of fey old gentlemen.
■ Rubber Heels 27. Follow the Leader 30. Manhattan Mary 30. The Chief 33. Stage Door Canteen 43. *The Great Man* 56. Marjorie Morningstar 58. *The Diary of Anne Frank* (AAN) 59. The Absent Minded Professor 60. Cinderfella 60. Babes in Toyland 61. Son of Flubber 63. Those Calloways 64. *Mary Poppins* 64. That Darn Cat 65. Dear Brigitte 65. The Greatest Story Ever Told 65. The Gnome-Mobile 67.

TV series: The Ed Wynn Show 58.

Wynn, Keenan (1916–1986)
American character actor, son of Ed Wynn. In Hollywood from early 40s after stage experience.

Autobiography: 1960, *Ed Wynn's Son*.

See Here Private Hargrove 44. Under the Clock 45. Weekend at the Waldorf 45. The Hucksters 47. Annie Get Your Gun 50. Kiss Me Kate 53. The Glass Slipper 55. The Great Man 57. A Hole in the Head 59. The Absent-Minded Professor 60. Man in the Middle 63. Dr Strangelove 63. The Americanization of Emily 65. The Great Race 65. The War Wagon 67. Mackenna's Gold 68. Smith 69. Once upon a Time in the West 69. Five Savage Men 70. Pretty Maids all in a Row 71. Herbie Rides Again 73. Hit Lady (TV) 75. Nashville 75. The Devil's Rain 76. Orca 77. High Velocity 77. Coach 78. Piranha 78. Sunburn 79. Just Tell Me What You Want 80. The Glove 81. Best Friends 82, many others.

TV series: The Trouble Shooters 59.
66 He's the fellow who, when Esther Williams jumps into the pool, gets splashed. – *Ed Wynn of Keenan Wynn*

Wynn, May (1931–) (Donna Lee Hickey)
American leading lady of the 50s.
■ 3 The Caine Mutiny 54. The Violent Men 54. They Rode West 55. Hong Kong Affair 59.

Wynn, Tracy Keenan (1945–)
American screenwriter, son of Keenan Wynn.

The Glass House (TV) 70. Tribes (TV) 71. *The Autobiography of Miss Jane Pittman* (TV) 73. The Longest Yard 74. The Drowning Pool (co-w) 75. The Deep (co-w) 77, etc.

Wynorski, Jim (1950–)
American director and screenwriter of exploitation movies. He began as a writer for Roger CORMAN's productions.

Sorceress (w) 83. Screwballs (co-w) 83. The Lost Empire (wd) 84. Chopping Mall/Killbots (co-w, d) 86. Deathstalker II: Duel of the Titans (d) 87. Big Bad Mama 2 (co-w, d) 87. Not of This Earth (d) 88. The Return of the Swamp Thing (d) 89. Transylvania Twist (d) 89. The Haunting of Maurella (wd) 90. 976 Evil: The Return (d) 91. Sins of the Flesh (d) 92. Tough Cookies (co-w, d) 93. Munchie Strikes Back 94. Attack of the 60 Foot Centerfold (a) 94. Body Chemistry 4: Full Exposure (d) 95. Demolition High (d) 96. Wasp Woman (d) (TV) 96. Vampirella (d) (TV) 96, etc.
66 I got into this business for two reasons – chicks and money. Art has nothing to do with it. – *J.W.*

Wynter, Dana (1927–) (Dagmar Wynter)
British leading lady.

White Corridors 51. Colonel March Investigates 53. *Invasion of the Body Snatchers* (US) 56. D Day Sixth of June 56. Value 57. Shake Hands with the Devil 59. *Sink the Bismarck* 60. The List of Adrian Messenger 63. If He Hollers Let Him Go 68. Airport 69. Santee 73. Backstairs at the White House (TV) 79. The Royal Romance of Charles and Diana (TV) 82. The People from Another Star 86. Dead Right 88, etc.

TV series: The Man Who Never Was 66.

Wynter, Sarah (1973–)
Australian-born actress in Hollywood.

Let It Be Me 95. Species II 98. Molly 99. Farewell My Love 99. Lost Souls 00. The 6th Day 00, etc.

Wynyard, Diana (1906–1964) (Dorothy Isobel Cox)
Distinguished British stage actress who began her film career with MGM in Hollywood, returning to Britain to act on the stage. Married to director Carol Reed.
■ Rasputin and the Empress 32. *Cavalcade* (AAN) 33. Men Must Fight 33. Reunion in Vienna 33. Where Sinners Meet 34. Let's Try Again 34. One More River 34. On the Night of the Fire 39. Freedom Radio 40. *Gaslight* 40. The Prime Minister 40. *Kipps* 41. An Ideal Husband 47. Tom Brown's Schooldays 51. The Feminine Touch 56. Island in the Sun 57.

Xiaowen, Zhou (1954–)
Chinese director. Born in Beijing, he studied at the
Film Academy there and then worked at the Xi'an
Film Studio.
   In Their Prime (co-d) 86. Desperation 87.
Obsession 89. No Regrets about Youth 92. Ermo
94. The Emperor's Shadow 96, etc.

Y

Yablans, Frank (1935–)
American independent producer.
The Other Side of Midnight 77. The Silver Streak 77. The Fury 78. North Dallas Forty (& w) 80. Mommie Dearest 81. Monsignor 82. The Star Chamber 83. Buy & Cell 89. Lisa 90. Congo 95, etc.

Yablans, Irwin (1934–)
American independent producer.
Badge 373 73. Halloween 78. Roller Boogie 79. Fade to Black 80. The Seduction 82. Parasite 82. Halloween III: Season of the Witch 83. Tank 84. Prison 88. Men at Work 90. Arena 91, etc.

Yagher, Kevin
American special effects and make-up expert; also an occasional director.
A Nightmare on Elm Street 3: Dream Warriors 87. A Nightmare on Elm Street 4: The Dream Master 88. Child's Play 88. Child's Play 3 91. The Borrower 91. Hellraiser III: Hell on Earth (d credited to Allan Smithee) 92. Radio Flyer 92. Honey, I Blew Up the Kid 92. Dr Jekyll and Ms Hyde 96. The Fan 96. Starship Troopers 97. Face/Off 97. Bride of Chucky 98. Sleepy Hollow 99, etc.

Yakin, Boaz (1966–)
American director and screenwriter.
The Punisher (w) 89. Rookie (w) 90. *Fresh* (wd) 94. A Price above Rubies (wd) 98. Remember the Titans 00, etc.

Yakusho, Koji (1956–) (Koji Hashimoto)
Japanese leading actor, from the theatre. After working in an office for four years, he began acting in 1981.
Tampopo 86. Kamikaze Taxi 95. The Eel 96. Shall We Dance? 96. Cure/Kyua 97. Shitsurakuen 97, etc.

Yamada, Isuzu (1917–) (Mitsu Yamada)
Japanese leading actress, best known for her role as Lady Washizu (an oriental Lady Macbeth) in Kurosawa's *Throne of Blood*. She began her career at the age of 14 and married director Teinosuke Kinusaga, with whom she set up a short-lived production company in the 50s.
Osaka Elegy/Niniwa Hika 36. Sisters of the Gion/Gion No Shimai 36. Throne of Blood/Kumonosu-jo 57. Buddha/Shaka 61. Yojimbo 61, etc.

Yamada, Yoji (1931–)
Japanese director of working-class comedies. He is best known for the popular series of *Tora-san* movies, about the adventures of an itinerant pedlar. So far, he has directed more than 40 of them at the rate of two a year since 1969.

Yamamoto, Satsuo (1910–1983)
Japanese director, a former actor, in films as an assistant director from 1933. His own anti-authoritarian films were influenced by his wartime experiences, fighting in Manchuria. In the 50s, when he was one of the many sacked by Toho in trade union disputes, he ran his own independent production company.
La Symphonie Pastorale 37. Street of Violence/Boryoku No Machi 50. Storm Clouds over Mount Hakone/Hakone Fuun Roku 51. *Vacuum Zone*/Shinku Chitai 52. End of the Sun/Hi No Hate 54. Duckweed Story/Ukigusa Nikki 55. Tycoon/Kizu Darake No Sanga 64. Hyoten 66. The Bride from Hades/Botandoro 68. *The Family*/Kareinaru Ichizoku 74. Solar Eclipse/Kinkanshoku 75. The Barren Zone/Fumo Chitai 76, etc.

Yamanaka, Sadeo (1909–1938)
Japanese director whose promising career, which began in 1932, was cut short by his early death. He was sent to fight on the Chinese front by a government unhappy with his depiction of samurai as less than heroic, and died there. Only two of his 12 films survive.
The Pot Worth a Million Ryo/Hyaku-Man Ryono Tsubo 35. *Humanity and Paper Balloons*/Ninjo Kai Fusen 37.

Yanagimachi, Mitsuo (1944–)
Japanese director.
Farewell to the Land 82. Himatsuri 85. Shadow of China 91. About Love, Tokyo 92, etc.

Yang, Edward (1947–) (Yang Dechang)
Chinese-born director, working in Taiwan.
In Our Time (co-d) 82. That Day on the Beach 83. Taipei Story 85. The Terrorizers 86. A Brighter Summer Day 91. A Confucian Confusion/Duli Shidai 94. Mahjong 96, etc.

Yanne, Jean (1933–) (J. Gouye)
Heavy-set French actor.
Life Upside Down 65. Weekend 67. *Le Boucher* 69. Cobra 73. The Accuser 75. The Pink Telephone 76. Hanna K 83. Quicker than the Eye 88. Madame Bovary 91. Indochine 92. Chacun pour Toi 93. Fausto 93. Pétain 93. Regarde les Hommes Tomber 94. The Horseman on the Roof 95. News from the Good Lord 96. Desire 96. Des Nouvelles du Bon Dieu 96. La Belle Verte 96. Tenue Correcte Exigée 97, etc.

Yarbrough, Jean (1900–1975)
American director of second features, former prop man.
Devil Bat 41. Lure of the Islands 42. Good Morning Judge 43. In Society 44. The Naughty Nineties 45. The Brute Man 46. Curse of the Allenbys 47. The Creeper 48. Abbott and Costello Lost in Alaska 52. Jack and the Beanstalk 52. Women of Pitcairn Island 57. Saintly Sinners 61. Hillbillies in a Haunted House 67. The Over-the-Hill Gang (TV) 69, many others.

Yared, Gabriel (1949–)
Lebanese-born composer, resident in Paris.
Every Man for Himself/Sauve Qui Peut (La Vie) 80. Invitation au Voyage 82. Hanna K. 83. The Moon in the Gutter 83. Dream One 84. Dangerous Moves 85. Red Zone/Zone Rouge 86. Betty Blue/37.2 Degrés le Matin 86. Beyond Therapy 86. Clean and Sober 88. Camille Claudel 88. Romero 89. The King's Whore 90. Tatie Danielle 90. Vincent and Theo 90. The Lover/L'Amant 92. La Fille de l'Air 92. IP5 92. Map of the Human Heart 92. Des Feux Mal éteints 94. Profil Bas 94. Black for Remembrance 96. *The English Patient* (AA) 96. City of Angels 98. Message in a Bottle 99. The Talented Mr Ripley (AAN) 99. The Next Best Thing 00, etc.

Yates, Herbert (1880–1966)
American executive, ex-president of Republic Pictures, where his word was law in the 40s. Many of his productions starred his wife, Vera Hruba Ralston.

Yates, Marjorie (1941–)
English character actress, mainly in theatre and TV.
The Optimists of Nine Elms 73. Stardust 74. The Black Panther 77. Priest of Love 81. Wetherby 85. The Long Day Closes 92, etc.

Yates, Peter (1929–)
British director. He trained at the Royal Academy of Dramatic Arts and was an actor with repertory companies, then worked at the Royal Court Theatre.
Summer Holiday 62. One Way Pendulum 64. *Robbery* 67. *Bullitt* (US) 68. John and Mary (US) 69. Murphy's War 70. The Hot Rock (US) 72. *The Friends of Eddie Coyle* 73. For Pete's Sake 74. Mother Jugs and Speed 76. The Deep 77. Breaking Away (AAN) 79. Eyewitness 81. Krull 83. *The Dresser* (& p) (AAN) 83. Eleni 85. Suspect 87. The House on Carroll Street 88. Hard Rain 89. Year of the Comet 92. Roommates 95. The Run of the Country 95, etc.
❝ I've given American culture the car chase and the wet T-shirt. – *P.Y.*

Yen, Donnie (1966–) (Yan Chi Tan)
American-born star of Hong Kong action movies. He spent three years in China from the age of 16 studying martial arts.
Drunken Tai-Chi 85. Mismatched Couples 87. Tiger Cage 88. Tiger Cage 2 90. Holy Virgin versus the Evil Dead 90. Once upon a Time in China 91. Butterfly and Sword 93. Iron Monkey 93. Circus Kid 94. High Voltage 94, etc.

Yeoh, Michelle (1963–) (Yeo Chu-Kheng)
Leading Malaysian-born actress, in action films, also known as Michelle Khan earlier in her career. Born in Ipoh, she trained as a ballet dancer and studied at the Royal Academy of Dance in London. She was Miss Malaysia of 1983 and then moved to Hong Kong, where she began making films. Formerly married to producer Dickson Poon, she heads her own production company Mythical Films.
Yes, Madam 85. Royal Warriors 86. Twinkle Twinkle Lucky Stars 86. In the Line of Duty 87. In the Line of Duty II 87. Police Assassins II 87. Police Story III: Super Cop 92. The Heroic Trio 92. Police Story V 93. Tai Chi Master 93. Wing Chun 93. Ah Kam 96. Tomorrow Never Dies 97. Crouching Tiger, Hidden Dragon 00, etc.
❝ The young *grande dame* of Hong Kong films. – *Oliver Stone*

Yeung, Bolo (Yang Sze)
Hong Kong martial arts actor, often as a villain.
Enter the Dragon 73. Young Dragon 77. Bolo 78. Bloodsport 88. Bloodfight 90. Tiger Claws 91. Double Impact 91. Iron Heart 92. TC 2000 93. Shootfighter: Fight to the Death 93. Fearless Tiger 94. Shootfighter 2: Kill or Be Killed 96, etc.

Yimou, Zhang (1950–)
Chinese director of the so-called Fifth Generation, a former cinematographer and actor. His more recent films have been banned in China. In 1994, the authorities forbade him from making films in China for five years.The Story of *Qiu Ju* won the Golden Lion in 1992. *Not One Less* won the Golden Lion at the 1999 Venice film Festival.
AS ACTOR: Old Well 87. The Terra-Cotta Warrior 90.
AS CINEMATOGRAPHER: Yellow Earth 83. The Big Parade 85.
AS DIRECTOR: Red Sorghum/Hong Gaoliang 87. Operation Cougar 89. Jou Dou 90. Raise the Red Lantern/Dahong Denglong Gaogao Gua 91. *The Story of Qiu Jou* 92. To Live 94. The Great Conqueror's Concubine/Xi Chu Bawang (p) 94. Shanghai Triad 95. Breaking Up Is Hard to Do 97. Not One Less 99. The Road Home 00, etc.
❝ To survive is to win. – Z.Y.

Yoda, Yoshikata (1909–)
Japanese screenwriter who collaborated with Kenji Mizoguchi on the scripts of many of the director's films from the mid-30s.
Osaka Elegy/Niniwa Hika 36. Sisters of the Gion/Gion No Shimai 36. Roei No Uta 38. Zangiku Monogatari 39. The Woman of Osaka/Naniwa Onna 40. The Loyal 47 Ronin I and II 41. Woman of the Night/Yoru No Onnatachi 48. The Life of Oharu/Saikaki Ichidai Onna 52. Ugetsu 53. Sansho the Bailiff/Sansho Dayu 54. A Story from Chikamatsu/Chikamatsu Monogatari 54. Shin Heike Monogatari 55, etc.

Yordan, Philip (1913–)
Prolific American writer-producer.
SCREENPLAYS: Syncopation 42. Dillinger (AAN) 45. House of Strangers 49. Detective Story (AAN) 51. Johnny Guitar 54. Broken Lance (AA story) 54. El Cid 61. 55 Days at Peking 62. The Fall of the Roman Empire 64, many others.
WROTE AND PRODUCED: The Harder They Fall 56. Men in War 57. God's Little Acre 58. Day of the Outlaw 59. Studs Lonigan 60. The Thin Red Line 64. The Battle of the Bulge 65. Captain Apache 71. Savage Journey 83. Night Train to Terror 85. Bloody Wednesday 87. Cry Wilderness 87. The Unholy 88, etc.
❝ People would rather go and see a big bad picture than a good small one. – *P.Y.*

Yorick, John (1969–)
Polish actor, director, and screenwriter, the son of Jerzy Skolimowski. He co-wrote, co-directed and co-starred in *The Hollow Men* with his brother Joseph Kay (1971–).
Success Is the Best Revenge (as Michael Lyndon) 84. The Lightship (as Michael Lyndon) 85. The Hollow Men (a, co-w, co-d) 93.

York, Dick (1928–1992)
American actor.
My Sister Eileen 55. Operation Mad Ball 57. They Came to Cordura 58. Inherit the Wind 60, etc.
TV series: Going My Way 62–63. Bewitched 64–69.

York, Michael (1942–) (Michael Hugh Johnson)
English leading actor, often in sensible, clean-cut roles. Born in Fulmer, Buckinghamshire, he began acting as a schoolboy with Michael Croft's Youth Theatre and continued at Oxford University, where he studied English. He began his professional career with the Dundee Repertory before joining the National Theatre, where he worked with ZEFFIRELLI, who gave him his first screen role.
Autobiography: 1991, *Travelling Player*.
The Taming of the Shrew 67. *Accident* 67. Red and Blue 67. Smashing Time 67. Romeo and Juliet 68. The Strange Affair 68. The Guru 69. Alfred the Great 69. Justine 69. Something for Everyone 70. Zeppelin 71. *Cabaret* 72. England Made Me 72. *Lost Horizon* 73. The Three Musketeers 73. The Four Musketeers 74. Murder on the Orient Express 74. Conduct Unbecoming 75. Great Expectations 75. Logan's Run 76. *Jesus of Nazareth* (TV) 77. The Last Remake of Beau Geste 77. Seven Nights in Japan 77. The Island of Dr Moreau 77. Fedora 78. The Riddle of the Sands 79. A Man Called Intrepid (TV) 79. The White Lions 80. Final Arrangement 80. Phantom of the Opera (TV) 82. The Master of Ballantrae (TV) 83. Success Is the Best Revenge 84. Space (TV) 85. The Dawn 85. The Far Country (TV) 86. Sword of Gideon (TV) 86. Phantom of Death 87. Midnight Cop 88. Till We Meet Again (TV) 89. The Lady and the Highwayman (TV) 89. The Return of the Musketeers 89. Eline Vere 91. The Heat of the Day (TV) 91. Duel of Hearts (TV) 92. Wide Sargasso Sea 93. Our Lady/Gospa 94. Fall from Grace 94. A Young Connecticut Yankee in King Arthur's Court 95. Not of This Earth 96. True Women 97. The Ripper (TV) 97. Dark Planet 97. Austin Powers: International Man of Mystery 97. Wrongfully Accused 98. 54 98. Merchants of Venus 98. A Knight in Camelot (TV) 98. Austin Powers: The Spy Who Shagged Me 99, etc.
❝ Cinema, it has always seemed to me, is essentially filmed thought. – M.Y.

York, Susannah (1941–) (Susannah Yolande Fletcher)
British leading lady of stage and screen.
■ *Tunes of Glory* (debut) 60. There Was a Crooked Man 60. *The Greengage Summer* 61. Freud 62. Tom Jones 63. The Seventh Dawn 64. Scene Nun Take One. 64. Scruggs 64. Sands of the Kalahari 65. Kaleidoscope 66. A Man For All Seasons 66. Sebastian 67. The Killing of Sister George 68. Duffy 68. Oh What a Lovely War 69. The Battle of Britain 69. Lock Up Your Daughters 69. *They Shoot*

Horses Don't They? (US) (AAN) 69. Country Dance 70. Jane Eyre 70. Zee and Co. 71. Happy Birthday Wanda June (US) 71. *Images* 72. The Maids 73. Gold 74. Conduct Unbecoming 75. That Lucky Touch 75. Sky Riders 76. Eliza Frazer 76. Superman 78. The Golden Gate Murders (TV) 79. The Silent Partner 79. The Shout 79. Falling in Love Again 80. Superman II 80. The Awakening 80. Loophole 81. Yellowbeard 83. A Christmas Carol (TV) 84. Prettykill 87. Superman IV: The Quest for Peace (voice) 87. The Land of Faraway 87. American Roulette 88. A Summer Story 88. Just Ask for Diamond 88. Bluebeard Bluebeard/Barbablu Barbablu 89. Melancholia 89. A Handful of Time/En Handfull Tid 90. Fate 90. Pretty Princess (It.) 93.

TV series: Second Chance 80. We'll Meet Again 81.

Yorkin, Bud (1926–) (Alan Yorkin)
American director, from TV.

Come Blow Your Horn 63. Never Too Late 65. Divorce American Style 67. Inspector Clouseau 68. Start the Revolution without Me 69. The Thief Who Came to Dinner 73. Twice in a Lifetime 85. Arthur 2: On the Rocks 88. Love Hurts 90. Intersection (p) 93, etc.

Yoshida, Yoshishige (1933–)
Japanese director and screenwriter, a member of the 'New Wave' of the 60s. He studied French literature at Tokyo University before becoming an assistant director. In the 70s, he was in Europe making TV documentaries.

Good for Nothing/Rokudenashi 60. Blood Is Dry/Chi Wa Kawaite Iru 60. Akitsu Onsen 62. 18 Roughs/Arashi o Yobu Juhachinim 63. Woman of the Lake/Onna no Mizumi 66. Honoo To Onna 67. Affair in the Snow/Juhyo no Yorumeki 68. Eros and Massacre/Eros Purasu Gyakusatsu 69. Rengoku Eroica 70. Coup d'Etat/Kaigenre 73. Wuthering Heights/Arashi ga Oka 89, etc.

Yoshimura, Kozaburo (1911–)
Japanese director. Many of his most successful films were scripted by Kaneto Shindo, with whom he set up his own production company in the 50s.

Tomorrow's Dancers 39. Blossom 41. Temptation 48. Spring Snow 50. A Tale of Genji 51. Before Dawn 53. Beauty and the Dragon 55. Undercurrent 56. Design for Dying 61. The Bamboo Doll 63. A Fallen Woman 67. A Hot Night/Atsui Yoru 68. A Ragged Flag 74, etc.

Youmans, Vincent (1898–1946)
American song composer of the 20s. Shows filmed include *No No Nanette* and *Hit the Deck.*

Young, Aden
Australian leading actor.

The Great Pretender 91. Black Robe 91. Over the Hill 92. Sniper (US) 92. Broken Highway 93. Shotgun Wedding 93. Love in Limbo 93. Metal Skin 94. Exile 94. *River Street* 96. Hotel de Love 97. Cousin Bette 97. The Girl of Your Dreams/La Niña de Tus Ojos 98, etc.

Young, Alan (1919–) (Angus Young)
British-born comic actor, in Canada since childhood.

Margie (debut) 46. Mr Belvedere Goes to College 49. Aaron Slick from Punkin Crick 52. *Androcles and the Lion* 53. Gentlemen Marry Brunettes 55. Tom Thumb 58. The Time Machine 60. The Cat from Outer Space 78. Duck Tales: The Movie (voice) 90. Beverly Hills Cop 3 94. Twin Falls Idaho 99, etc.

TV series: Mister Ed 60–65.

Young, Arthur (1898–1959)
Portly British stage actor; film appearances usually in self-important roles.

No Limit 35. Victoria the Great 37. My Brother Jonathan 48. The Lady with a Lamp 51. An Inspector Calls 54. The Gelignite Gang 56, etc.

Young, Burt (1940–)
American supporting actor.

The Gambler 75. The Killer Elite 75. Rocky (AAN) 76. The Choirboys 77. Twilight's Last Gleaming 77. Convoy 78. Rocky II 79. Murder Can Hurt You (TV) 79. All the Marbles... 81. Blood Beach 80. Amityville II: The Possession 82. Lookin' to Get Out 82. Rocky III 82. Over the Brooklyn Bridge 83. Once Upon a Time in America 84. The Pope of Greenwich Village 84. Rocky IV 85. Back to School 86. Blood Red 88. Beverly Hills Brats 89. Last Exit to Brooklyn 89. Betsy's Wedding 90. Backstreet Dreams 90. Diving In 90. Rocky V 90. Vendetta 90. Red American/Americano Rosso 91. Club Fed 91. Bright Angel 91. Excessive Force 93. North Star 96. The Mouse 96. The Undertaker's Wedding 97. Kicked in the Head 97. Mickey Blue Eyes 99. The Day the Ponies Come Back (Fr.) 00, etc.

Young, Carleton (1906–1971)
American character actor, from radio; father of Tony Young.

The Glory Brigade 53. The Court Martial of Billy Mitchell 55. The Horse Soldiers 59. Sergeant Rutledge 60, many others.

Young, Christopher (1958–)
American composer, born in Redbank, New Jersey; often scoring horror movies and dark thrillers.

The Dorm that Dripped Blood 81. Barbarian Queen 85. Wizards of the Lost Kingdom 85. A Nightmare on Elm Street Part 2: Freddy's Revenge 85. Trick or Treat 86. Invaders from Mars 86. Flowers in the Attic 87. Hellraiser 87. Hellbound: Hellraiser II 88. The Fly II 89. The Dark Half 91. Jennifer Eight 92. Rapid Fire 92. Vagrant 92. Sliver 93. Judicial Consent 94. Dream Lover 94. Virtuosity 95. Species 95. Murder in the First 95. Copycat 95. Unforgettable 96. Set It Off 96. Head above Water 96. The Man Who Knew Too Little 97. Hard Rain 98. Judas Kiss 98. Hush 98. Rounders 98. Urban Legend 98. The Hurricane 99. Entrapment 99. In Too Deep 99. The Big Kahuna 00. Wonder Boys 00, etc.

Young, Clara Kimball (1890–1960)
Popular American heroine of the silent screen.

Cardinal Wolsey (debut) 12. Beau Brummell 13. Goodness Gracious 16. Eyes of Youth 19. Cheating Cheaters 19. Forbidden Woman 20. Hush 21. Charge It 21. Lying Wives 25. Kept Husbands 31. Love Bound 33. Romance in the Rain 34. The Frontiersman 39. Mr Celebrity 42, etc.

Young, Collier (1908–1980)
American writer-producer.

The Hitch-Hiker 53. The Bigamist 54. Mad at the World 55. Huk! 56, etc.

TV series: One Step Beyond 58–60. Ironside 67, etc.

Young, Dan
British character actor, from music hall, most often seen supporting comedian Frank RANDLE.

The New Hotel 32. Off the Dole 35. Dodging the Dole 36. Calling All Crooks 38. Somewhere in England 40. Somewhere in Camp 42. Somewhere on Leave 42. Demobbed 44. Under New Management 46. Cup-Tie Honeymoon 48. Holidays with Pay 48. School for Randle 49. Over the Garden Wall 50. It's a Grand Life 53, etc.

Young, Freddie (1902–1998)
Distinguished British cinematographer, best known for his work on David LEAN's epic films. He was in movies from silents and received his first credit as an assistant cameraman on *Rob Roy* 22.

In 1985, at the age of 82, he directed his first film, *Arthur's Hallowed Ground.*

Bitter Sweet 33. Nell Gwyn 34. When Knights Were Bold 36. Victoria the Great 37. Sixty Glorious Years 38. Goodbye Mr Chips 39. The Young Mr Pitt 41. 49th Parallel 41; war service; Bedelia 46. So Well Remembered 47. Edward My Son 49. Treasure Island 50. *Ivanhoe* (AAN) 52. *Lust for Life* 56. *Invitation to the Dance* 56. Bhowani Junction 56. Island in the Sun 56. *Lawrence of Arabia* (AA) 62. The Seventh Dawn 64. Lord Jim 65. Rotten to the Core 65. *Doctor Zhivago* (AA) 65. The Deadly Affair 67. You Only Live Twice 67. The Battle of Britain 69. *Ryan's Daughter* (AA) 70. Nicholas and Alexandra (AAN) 71. The Tamarind Seed 74. The Blue Bird 76. Seven Nights in Japan 77. Stevie 78. Bloodline 79. Rough Cut 80. Richard's Things 81. Sword of the Valiant 84. Invitation to the Wedding 85, etc.

Young, Gig (1913–1978) (Byron Barr; aka Bryant Fleming)
American light comedy leading man with a pleasantly bemused air. Committed suicide after killing his fifth wife. He was previously married to actress Elizabeth Montgomery.

Misbehaving Husbands 40. They Died With Their Boots On 41. Dive Bomber 41. The Gay Sisters (in which he played a character called Gig Young and thereafter used the name) 41. Old Acquaintance 43. Air Force 43; war service; Escape Me Never 46. The Woman in White 47. Wake of the Red Witch 48. The Three Musketeers 49. *Come Fill the Cup* (AAN) 51. City That Never Sleeps 54. Young at Heart 55. Desk Set 57. Teachers Pet (AAN) 58. The Story on Page One 59. Ask Any Girl 59. *That Touch of Mink* 62. For Love or Money 63. Strange Bedfellows 65. The Shuttered Room 67. *They Shoot Horses, Don't They?* (AA) 69. *Lovers and Other Strangers* 70. The Neon Ceiling (TV) 71. A Son-in-Law for Charlie McReady 73. Bring Me the Head of Alfredo Garcia 74. The Hindenburg 75. The Killer Elite 75. Sherlock Holmes in New York (TV) 77. Spectre (TV) 78.

TV series: *The Rogues* 64. *Gibbsville* 76.

❝ Famous line (*They Shoot Horses, Don't They?*) 'There can only be one winner, folks, but isn't that the American way?'

Young, Harold (1897–1970)
American director, a former editor, who made distinguished British films for KORDA but was little heard from on his return to Hollywood. Educated at Columbia University, he worked as an editor for Warner and MGM, then became supervising editor with Paramount in Paris before working in a similar capacity for Korda.

AS EDITOR: Service for Ladies 32. Wedding Rehearsal 32. Counsel's Opinion 33. The Girl from Maxim's 33. Catherine the Great 34, etc.

AS DIRECTOR: *The Scarlet Pimpernel* 34. 52nd Street 37. Let Them Live 37. Little Tough Guy 38. The Storm 38. Forgotten Woman 39. Newsboys' Home 39. Bachelor Daddy 41. The Mummy's Tomb 42. Hi Buddy 43. Hi Ya Chum 43. I Escaped from the Gestapo 43. The Frozen Ghost 45. Jungle Captive 45, etc.

Young, Loretta (1913–2000) (Gretchen Young)
American leading lady whose career in films began when she accidentally, at 15, answered a studio call meant for her elder sister, Polly Ann Young. Her three husbands included actor Grant WITHERS (1930–31) and costume designer Jean LOUIS (1993–97).

Autobiography: 1962, *The Things I Had to Learn.*

Laugh Clown Laugh (debut) 28. Loose Ankles 29. The Squall 30. Kismet 30. *The Devil to Pay* 30. I Like Your Nerve 31. Platinum Blonde 32. The Hatchet Man 32. Big Business Girl 32. Life Begins 32. Zoo in Budapest 33. *Man's Castle* 33. The House of Rothschild 34. Midnight Mary 35. The Crusaders 35. Clive of India 35. Call of the Wild 35. Shanghai 36. *Ramona* 36. Ladies in Love 37. Wife, Doctor and Nurse 37. Second Honeymoon 38. Four Men and a Prayer 38. Suez 38. Kentucky 38. Three Blind Mice 38. The Story of Alexander Graham Bell 39. The Doctor Takes a Wife 39. He Stayed for Breakfast 40. Lady from Cheyenne 41. The Men in Her Life 41. *A Night to Remember* 42. China 43. Ladies Courageous 44. And Now Tomorrow 44. The Stranger 45. Along Came Jones 46. The Perfect Marriage 46. *The Farmer's Daughter* (AA) 47. The Bishop's Wife 48. Rachel and the Stranger 48. Come to the Stable (AAN) 49. Cause for Alarm 51. Half Angel 51. Paula 52. Because of You 52. It Happens Every Thursday 53. Christmas Eve (TV) 86, many others.

TV series: anthology dramas 53–60.

Young, Ned (1914–1968)
American actor and screenwriter.

AS ACTOR: The Devil's Playground 46. Border Incident 49. Gun Crazy 49. Captain Scarlett 52. House of Wax 53. Terror in a Texas Town 58. Seconds 66, etc.

AS WRITER: Joe Palooka in the Knockout (w) 47. Passage West (story) 51. Jailhouse Rock (story) 57. *The Defiant Ones* (co-w) 58. Inherit the Wind (co-w) 60, etc.

Young, Otis (1932–)
American actor.

The Last Detail 73. The Capture of Bigfoot 79. Blood Beach 81, etc.

TV series: The Outcasts 68.

Young, Robert (1907–1998)
American leading actor invariably cast in amiable, dependable roles, at his best on television, in the title roles of *Father Knows Best* and *Marcus Welby, MD.* Born in Chicago, he was brought up in Los Angeles and worked in various jobs as well as acting at the Pasadena Community Playhouse, before beginning in small roles in silents. He was contracted to MGM in the early 30s, staying with the studio until the mid-40s. He appeared in 125 movies: his best roles were out of his usual range, as the spy Robert Marvin in *Secret Agent* and in the title role in *H. M. Pulham Esq.* For much of his career he suffered from alcoholism and also depression, attempting suicide in 1991. He was married for 61 years to his high-school sweetheart Elizabeth Henderson (d. 1994); they had four daughters.

The Sin of Madelon Claudet 31. Strange Interlude 31. The Kid from Spain 32. Hell Below 32. Tugboat Annie 33. Lazy River 34. The House of Rothschild 34. Spitfire 34. Whom the Gods Destroy 35. West Point of the Air 35. It's Love Again (GB) 36. *Secret Agent* (GB) 36. Stowaway 36. The Emperor's Candlesticks 37. I Met Him in Paris 37. The Bride Wore Red 37. Josette 38. Frou Frou 38. Three Comrades 39. Rich Man, Poor Girl 39. Honolulu 39. Miracles for Sale 39. Maisie 39. Northwest Passage 40. The Mortal Storm 40. Florian 40. Western Union 41. The Trial of Mary Dugan 41. Lady Be Good 41. *H. M. Pulham Esq.* 41. Joe Smith American 42. Cairo 42. Journey for Margaret 42. Sweet Rosie O'Grady 43. *Claudia* 43. The Canterville Ghost 44. The Enchanted Cottage 44. Those Endearing Young Charms 45. Lady Luck 46. Claudia and David 46. The Searching Wind 46. They Won't Believe Me 47. *Crossfire* 47. Sitting Pretty 48. The Forsyte Woman 49. And Baby Makes Three 50. The Second Woman 51. Goodbye My Fancy 51. The Half-Breed 52. The Secret of the Incas 54. Vanished (TV) 71. All My Darling Daughters (TV) 72. My Darling Daughters' Anniversary (TV) 73. Little Women (TV) 78. The Return of Marcus Welby MD 84. Mercy or Murder (TV) 86. Conspiracy of Love (TV) 87. A Holiday Affair (TV) 88. Talent for the Game 91, etc.

TV series: Father Knows Best 54–60. Window on Main Street 61. Marcus Welby MD 69–75.

❝ I was an introvert in an extrovert profession. – *R.Y.*

Young, Robert M. (1924–)
American director.

Nothing but a Man (co-d) 65. Alambrista! 77. Short Eyes 78. Rich Kids 79. One-Trick Pony 80. The Ballad of Gregorio Cortez (& co-w) 83. Saving Grace 86. Extremities 86. Dominick and Eugene 88. Triumph of the Spirit 89. Talent for the Game 91. Roosters 93. Solomon & Sheba (TV) 95. Slave of Dreams (TV) 95. Caught 96, etc.

Young, Roland (1887–1953)
British character actor with stage experience; made a screen career in Hollywood and is affectionately remembered for a gallery of whimsical or ineffectual types.

Sherlock Holmes (debut) 22. Moriarty 22. The Unholy Night 29. Madame Satan 30. New Moon 30. *One Hour with You* 32. Wedding Rehearsal (GB) 32. The Guardsman 32. His Double Life 33. *David Copperfield* (as Uriah Heep) 34. Ruggles of Red Gap 34. One Rainy Afternoon 36. *The Man Who Could Work Miracles* (GB) 36. Call It a Day 37. King Solomon's Mines (GB) 37. *Topper* (title role) (AAN) 37. Ali Baba Goes to Town 38. Sailing Along (GB) 38. *The Young in Heart* 39. Topper Takes a Trip 39. No No Nanette 40. *The Philadelphia Story* 40. Flame of New Orleans 41. Topper Returns 41. The Lady Has Plans 42. They All Kissed the Bride 42. Tales of Manhattan 42. Forever and a Day 43. Standing Room Only 44. And Then There Were None 45. Bond Street (GB) 47. The Great Lover 49. Let's Dance 50. St Benny the Dip 51. That Man from Tangier 53, many others.

✪ For his inimitable diffidence; and for becoming quite a character actor whenever he shaved off his moustache. *The Young in Heart.*

❝ Famous line (*The Philadelphia Story*) 'Oh, this is one of those days that the pages of history teach us are best spent lying in bed.'

Young, Sean (1959–)
American leading actress, a former model.

Jane Austen in Manhattan 80. Stripes 81. Blade Runner 82. Young Doctors in Love 82. Baby: The Secret of the Lost Legend 85. Dune 85. Under the Biltmore Clock (TV) 85. No Way Out 87. Wall Street 87. The Boost 88. Cousins 89. Fire Birds 90. Wings of the Apache 90. A Kiss before Dying 91. Love Crimes 91. Once upon a Crime 92. Hold Me, Thrill Me, Kiss Me 92. Blue Ice 92. Sketch Artist 92. Even Cowgirls Get the Blues 93. Fatal Instinct 93. Ace Ventura, Pet Detective 94. Witness to the Execution (TV) 94. Dr Jekyll and Ms Hyde 95.

Saturday night performance; and in *Targets* a killer was apprehended by Boris Karloff at a drive-in. A drive-in was used as a rendezvous in *White Heat* and a 42nd Street cinema was a homosexual rendezvous in *Midnight Cowboy*. *Cinema Paradiso* was a love-letter to a small-town cinema and its projectionist. Home movies figured most notably in *Rebecca* and *Adam's Rib*.
See also: EXCERPTS, THEATRES.

circuses,
according to the cinema, are full of drama and passion behind the scenes. So you would think if you judged from *Variety*, *Freaks*, *The Wagons Roll at Night*, *The Greatest Show on Earth*, *The Big Show*, *The Big Circus*, *Sawdust and Tinsel*, *Circus of Horrors*, *Tromba*, *Four Devils*, *The Three Maxims*, *Trapeze*, *Captive Wild Woman*, *Ring of Fear*, *Charlie Chan at the Circus*, *A Tiger Walks*, *Circus World*, *The Trojan Brothers*, *Circus of Fear*, *Berserk*, *The Dark Tower*, *He Who Gets Slapped*, *Flesh and Fantasy*, *Man on a Tightrope*, *Chad Hanna*, *Pagliacci*, *Far From the Madding Crowd*, and *Vampire Circus*. But there is a lighter side, as evidenced by *Doctor Dolittle*, *Yo Yo*, *Jumbo*, *High Wide and Handsome*, *Lady in the Dark*, *Life is a Circus*, *The Marx Brothers at the Circus*, *Three Rings Circus*, Chaplin's *The Circus*, *The Great Profile*, *You Can't Cheat an Honest Man*, *Road Show*, *Merry Andrew*, and *Toby Tyler*.

TV series have included *Circus Boy*, *Frontier Circus* and *The Greatest Show on Earth*.

The Cisco Kid
was a Mexican outlaw of the 1890s, created by O. Henry in a short story, *The Caballero's Way*. The character died in his first, silent-screen appearance in 1914, and owed his later longevity to the early talkie *In Old Arizona* 29, in which he was played as a dashing rogue by Warner BAXTER. The role made Baxter a star and earned him an Oscar, after he took over the part from an injured Raoul WALSH; he followed it with three lesser sequels. Cesar ROMERO played the role in seven 'B' features from 1939, and was followed by Duncan RENALDO, who appeared in eight films from 1945, and Gilbert ROLAND, who clocked up six appearances in the late 40s. Renaldo also starred in a popular TV series, *The Cisco Kid* 50-56, with Leo CARRILLO as his sidekick, Pancho. A TV film, *The Cisco Kid* 94, starred Jimmy SMITS, with Cheech MARIN as Pancho.

clairvoyance
on the screen seems to have caused a remarkable amount of suffering to Edward G. Robinson: he was haunted by the effects of a prophecy in *Flesh and Fantasy*, *Nightmare* and *Night Has a Thousand Eyes*. Other frightened men for similar reasons were Claude Rains in *The Clairvoyant*, Dick Powell in *It Happened Tomorrow*, George Macready in *I Love a Mystery*, Mervyn Johns in *Dead of Night*, and Michael Hordern in *The Night My Number Came Up*. Rosanna Arquette suffers more than most as a medium able to foretell the violent deaths of those around her in *Black Rainbow* 89.

coal mines
and the bravery of the men who work in them formed a theme which commanded the respect of cinema audiences for many years. Apart from *Kameradschaft* (the French-German border), *Black Fury* (US), and *The Molly Maguires* (US), all the major films on this subject have been about Britain: *The Proud Valley*, *The Stars Look Down*, *How Green Was My Valley*, *The Citadel*, *The Corn is Green*, *The Brave Don't Cry*, *Sons and Lovers*, *Women in Love*.

Cobra (1986):
see FAIR GAME.

the Cold War
has occupied the cinema right from Churchill's Fulton speech in 1948. For three years diehard Nazis had been the international villains par excellence, but a change was required, and Russians have been fair game ever since, in films like *The Iron Curtain*, *Diplomatic Courier*, *I Was a Communist for the FBI*, *I Married a Communist*, *The Big Lift*, *Red Snow*, *The Red Danube*, *Red Menace*, *Red Planet Mars*, *The Journey*, *From Russia With Love* and innumerable pulp spy thrillers, as well as such classier productions as *The Third Man*, *The Man Between* and *The Spy Who Came in from the Cold*. Rather surprisingly none of these caused much escalation of tension between the nations, and cooler feelings have permitted comedies like *One Two Three*, *Dr Strangelove* and *The Russians are Coming, The Russians are Coming*; while such terrifying panic-button melodramas as *Fail Safe* and *The Bedford Incident* are probably our best guarantee that the dangers are realized on both sides.

colleges:
see UNIVERSITIES.

comedy:
see COMEDY TEAMS; CRAZY COMEDY; LIGHT COMEDIANS; SATIRE; SEX; SOCIAL COMEDY; SLAPSTICK.

comedy teams
in the accepted sense began in vaudeville, but, depending so much on the spoken word, could make little headway in films until the advent of the talkies. Then they all tried, and many (Amos 'n Andy, Gallagher and Shean, Olsen and Johnson) didn't quite make it, at least not immediately. Laurel and Hardy, who had been successful in silents by the use of mime, adapted their methods very little and remained popular; during the 30s they were really only challenged by Wheeler and Woolsey, whose style was more frenetic, and briefly by Burns and Allen. From 1940 the cross-talking Abbott and Costello reigned supreme, with an occasional challenge from Hope and Crosby and the splendid *Hellzapoppin* from Olsen and Johnson. Then came Martin and Lewis, who didn't appeal to everybody, Rowan and Martin, who in 1957 didn't appeal to anybody, and sporadic attempts to popularize such teams as Brown and Carney and Allen and Rossi. In Britain, comedy teams were popular even in poor films: the best of them were Jack Hulbert and Cicely Courtneidge, Tom Walls and Ralph Lynn, Lucan and MacShane ('Old Mother Riley'), Arthur Askey and Richard Murdoch, and the Crazy Gang, a bumper fun bundle composed of Flanagan and Allen, Naughton and Gold, and Nervo and Knox. One should also mention Basil Radford and Naunton Wayne, not cross-talkers but inimitable caricaturists of the Englishman abroad; and others, not strictly comedians, who raised a lot of laughs together: Edmund Lowe and Victor McLaglen, Slim Summerville and ZaSu Pitts, Joan Blondell and Glenda Farrell, George Sidney and Charlie Murray, Marie Dressler and Polly Moran, Wallace Beery and Raymond Hatton, James Cagney and Pat O'Brien, Jack Lemmon and Walter Matthau. Recent teams include Morecambe and Wise and Cannon and Ball.

See: 1970, *Movie Comedy Teams* by Leonard Maltin.

Of larger groups, among the most outstanding are Our Gang, the Keystone Kops, the Marx Brothers, the Three Stooges, the Ritz Brothers, Will Hay with Moore Marriott and Graham Moffat, the 'Carry On' team, the Beatles and the Monty Python team.
See also: ROMANTIC TEAMS.
❝ Nobody should try to play comedy unless they have a circus going on inside. – *Ernst Lubitsch*

comic strips
in newspapers have always been avidly watched by film producers with an eye on the popular market. Among films and series so deriving are the following:

Gertie the Dinosaur (cartoon series) 19; The Gumps (two-reelers) 23-28; *Bringing Up Father* 16 (drawn), 20 (two-reeler), 28 (feature with J. Farrell MacDonald and Marie Dressler), 45 (series of 'Jiggs and Maggie' features with Joe Yule and Renée Riano); *The Katzenjammer Kids* (cartoon series) 17 and 38, *Krazy Kat* (various cartoons 16-38); *Ella Cinders* (with Colleen Moore) 22; *Tillie the Toiler* (with Marion Davies) 27; *Skippy* (with Jackie Cooper) 30; *Little Orphan Annie* 32 (with Mitzi Green) and 38 (with Ann Gillis); *Joe Palooka* 34 (with Stu Erwin) and 47-51 (with Joe Kirkwood); *Blondie* (with Penny Singleton) 38-48; *Gasoline Alley* (with James Lydon) 51; *L'il Abner*; *Popeye*; *Jungle Jim* 49-54; Prince Valiant 54; *Up Front* 51-53; *Felix the Cat*; *Old Bill* (GB) 40; *Dick Barton* (GB) in various personifications; *Jane* (GB) in an abysmal 1949 second feature; and, of course, *Modesty Blaise* 66, *Batman* 66, *Barbarella* 68, and *Fritz the Cat* 71.

Strip characters whose adventures were turned into Hollywood serials during the 30s and 40s include *Tailspin Tommy*, *Mandrake the Magician*, *Don Winslow of the Navy*, *Jet Jackson Flying Commando*, *Flash Gordon*, *Batman*, *Buck Rogers in the 25th century*, *Brick Bradford* ('in the centre of the earth'), *Chandu*, *Superman*, *Dick Tracy* (also in 40s features), *The Lone Ranger* and *Red Ryder*. The re-emergence of Superman and Batman as heroes of big-budget films from the late 70s led to a search for similar fantastic figures to appeal to a mass audience. The Shadow and The Phantom both made unsuccessful appearances in the 90s, together with such recent and ambivalent comic-book creations as Judge Dredd and Tank Girl, where the distinctions between good and evil are more blurred. With the successful marketing on video of Japanese ANIME, derived from their comic books, and MANGA, featuring fantastic heroes, came an attempt to turn Crying Freeman, a Chinese hitman, into an action movie hero.

In the late 70s comic strip characters became popular TV action heroes, and until the balloon burst audiences were overwhelmed by the antics of *The Incredible Hulk*, *Wonder Woman*, *Buck Rogers in the 25th Century*, etc., following on the success of TV's own creations in this vein, *The Six Million Dollar Man*, *Bionic Woman* and *The Man from Atlantis*.

communism
has always been treated by Hollywood as a menace. In the 30s one could laugh at it, in *Ninotchka* and *He Stayed for Breakfast*. Then in World War II there was a respite during which the virtues of the Russian peasantry were extolled in such films as *Song of Russia* and *North Star*. But with the Cold War, every international villain became a Commie instead of a Nazi, and our screens were suddenly full of dour dramas about the deadliness of 'red' infiltration: *I Married a Communist*, *I Was a Communist for the FBI*, *The Red Menace*, *The Iron Curtain*, *Trial*, *My Son John*, *Walk East on Beacon*, *The Red Danube*, *Red Snow*, *Red Planet Mars*, *Blood Alley*, *Big Jim McLain*, *The Manchurian Candidate*. In the early 60s a documentary compilation of red aggression was released under the title *We'll Bury You*. The British never seemed to take the peril seriously, though the agitator in *The Angry Silence* was clearly labelled red.

Famous line: 'Communism,' said the butler in *Soak the Rich*, 'is the growing pains of the young.'

compilation films
became commonplace on TV through such series as *Twentieth Century*, *Men of Our Time* and *The Valiant Years*, all using library material to evoke a pattern of the past. Thanks to the careful preservation of original documentary material, film-makers have been able, over the last thirty years or so, to give us such films on a wide variety of subjects and to develop an exciting extra dimension of film entertainment which also serves a historical need.

The first outstanding efforts in this direction were made by H. Bruce WOOLFE in his 20s documentaries of World War I, mixing newsreel footage with reconstructed scenes. In 1940 CAVALCANTI assembled his study of Mussolini, *Yellow Caesar*; and in 1942 Frank CAPRA, working for the US Signal Corps, gave a tremendous fillip to the art of the compilation film with his 'Why We Fight' series. Paul ROTHA's *World of Plenty* 43 was a clever study of world food shortages using all kinds of film material including animated diagrams and acted sequences. In 1945 Carol REED and Garson KANIN, in *The True Glory*, gave the story of D-Day to Berlin an unexpected poetry, and in 1946 Don SIEGEL in his short *Hitler Lives* showed all too clearly what a frightening potential the compilation form had as propaganda. Nicole VÉDRÈS in 1947 turned to the more distant past and in *Paris 1900* produced an affectionate portrait of a bygone age; Peter Baylis followed this with *The Peaceful Years*, covering the period between the two wars. In 1950 Stuart LEGG's *Powered Flight* traced the history of aviation.

The THORNDIKES, working in East Germany, started in 1956 their powerful series *The Archives Testify*, attributing war crimes to West German officials; this aggressive mood was followed in their *Du und Mancher Kamerad* ('The German Story') and *The Russian Miracle*, though in the latter case they seemed somewhat less happy in praising than in blaming. In 1959 George Morrison's *Mise Eire* graphically presented the truth of the much-fictionalized Irish troubles; and in 1960 came the first of the films about Hitler, Erwin LEISER's *Mein Kampf*, to be sharply followed by Rotha's *The Life of Adolf Hitler* and Louis Clyde Stoumen's rather fanciful *Black Fox*. Jack Le Vien, producer of the last-named, went on to make successful films about Churchill (*The Finest Hours*) and the Duke of Windsor (*A King's Story*). Now every year the compilations come thick and fast. From France, *Fourteen-Eighteen*; from BBC TV, twenty-six half-hours of *The Great War*; from Granada TV, *The Fanatics* (suffragettes), *The World of Mr Wells* (H. G., that is) and a long-running weekly series, *All Our Yesterdays*, which consisted entirely of old newsreels; from Associated-British, *Time to Remember*, a series devoting half an hour to each year of the century; from Italy, *Allarmi Siam' Fascisti*, a history of the fascist movement; from Japan, *Kamikaze*, about the suicide pilots; from France, ROSSIF's *Mourir à Madrid* and *The Fall of Berlin*. The list will be endless, because even though every foot of old newsreel were used up, one could begin again, using different editing, juxtapositions and commentary to achieve different effects.

Best book on the subject: Jay Leyda's *Films Beget Films*.

In the late 50s there began a pleasing fashion for compilations of scenes from fictional films on a theme. This began with Robert YOUNGSON's masterly evocations of silent slapstick: *The Golden Age of Comedy*, *When Comedy Was King*, etc. TV series such as *Silents Please* and *Hollywood and the Stars* followed suit. In the 70s MGM had an immense success with *That's Entertainment*, and two sequels, compiled from its past successes, and also brought out *The Big Parade of Comedy*. Twentieth-Century-Fox turned its backlog into a television series, *That's Hollywood*; and for a while wherever one looked in Hollywood there was at least one studio cutting room devoted to turning over and reassembling highlights of the past.
See also: DOCUMENTARY (Section 5).

composers
have frequently been lauded on cinema screens, usually in storylines which bore little relation to their real lives, and the films were not often box-office successes. Here are some of the subjects of musical biopics:
•George Frederick Handel (1685-1759): Wilfred Lawson, *The Great Mr Handel* 42.
•Wolfgang Amadeus Mozart (1756-91): Stephen Haggard, *Whom the Gods Love* 36; Hannes Steltzer, *Die Kleine Nachtmusik* 39; Gino Cervi, *Eternal Melody* 39; Oskar Werner, *The Life of Mozart* 56; Tom Hulce, *Amadeus* (84).
•Ludwig van Beethoven (1770-1827): Albert Basserman, *New Wine* 41; Ewald Balser, *Eroica* 49; Karl Boehm, *The Magnificent Rebel* 60; Gary Oldman, *Immortal Beloved* 95.
•Niccolò Paganini (1782-1840): Stewart Granger, *The Magic Bow* 47.
•Franz Schubert (1797-1828): Nils Asther, *Love Time* 34; Richard Tauber, *Blossom Time* 34; Hans Jaray, *Unfinished Symphony* 35; Alan Curtis *New Wine* 41; Tino Rossi, *La Belle Meunière* 47; Claude Laydu, *Symphony of Love* 54; Karl Boehm, *Das Dreimaederlhaus* 58.
•Vincenzo Bellini (1801-35): Phillips Holmes, *The Divine Spark* 35.
•Hector Berlioz (1803-69): Jean-Louis Barrault, *La Symphonie Fantastique* 40.
•Frederic Chopin (1810-49): Jean Servais, *Adieu* 35; Cornel Wilde, *A Song to Remember* 44; Czeslaw Wollejko, *The Young Chopin* 52; Alexander Davion, *Song Without End* 60; Hugh Grant, *Impromptu* 89; Janusz Olejniczak, *La Note Bleue* 91.
•Robert Schumann (1810-56): Paul Henreid, *Song of Love* 47.
•Franz Liszt (1811-86): Stephen Bekassy, *A Song to Remember* 44; Henry Daniell, *Song of Love* 47; Will Quadflieg, *Lola Montez* 55; Dirk Bogarde, *Song Without End* 60; Henry Gilbert, *Song of Norway* 70; Roger Daltrey, *Lisztomania* 75.
•Richard Wagner (1813-83): Alan Badel, *Magic Fire* 56; Trevor Howard, *Ludwig* 73; Richard Burton, *Wagner* 83.
•Johann Strauss Jnr (1825-99): Esmond Knight, *Waltzes from Vienna* 33; Anton Walbrook, *Vienna Waltzes* 34. Fernand Gravey, *The Great Waltz* 38; Kerwin Matthews, *The Waltz King* 60; Horst Buchholz, *The Great Waltz* 72.
•Stephen Foster (1826-64): Don Ameche, *Swanee River* 39; Bill Shirley, *I Dream of Jeannie* 52.
•Johannes Brahms (1833-97): Robert Walker, *Song of Love* 47.
•W. S. Gilbert (1836-1911) and Arthur Sullivan (1842-1900): Nigel Bruce and Claud Allister, *Lillian Russell* 41; Robert Morley and Maurice Evans, *The Story of Gilbert and Sullivan* 53.

•Peter Ilich Tchaikovsky (1840-93): Frank Sundstrom, *Song of My Heart* 47; Innokenti Smoktunovsky, *Tchaikovsky* 69; Richard Chamberlain, *The Music Lovers* 70.
•Edvard Grieg (1843-1907): Toralv Maurstad, *Song of Norway* 70.
•Nikolai Rimsky-Korsakov (1844-1908): Jean-Pierre Aumont, *Song of Scheherezade* 47.
•John Philip Sousa (1854-1932): Clifton Webb, *Stars and Stripes Forever* 52.
•Victor Herbert (1859-1924): Walter Connolly, *The Great Victor Herbert* 39; Paul Maxey, *Till the Clouds Roll By* 46.
•Gustav Mahler (1860-1911): Robert Powell, *Mahler* 74.
•Leslie Stuart (1866-1928): Robert Morley, *You Will Remember* 40.
•W. C. Handy (1873-1948): Nat King Cole, *St Louis Blues* 58.
•Jerome Kern (1885-1945): Robert Walker, *Till the Clouds Roll By* 46.
•Sigmund Romberg (1887-1951): Jose Ferrer, *Deep in My Heart* 54.
•Irving Berlin (1888-1989): Tyrone Power, *Alexander's Ragtime Band* 38.
•Cole Porter (1892-1964): Cary Grant, *Night and Day* 45.
•George Gershwin (1898-1937): Robert Alda, *Rhapsody in Blue* 45.

The list of biopics of lesser modern composers would be long indeed.

computers

from the mid-70s became so commonplace as barely to rate a mention, forming the basis of such films as *Rollover* and *War Games* and TV series such as *Knight Rider* and *Whiz Kids*. Some of their earlier uses in film, however, were in Disney's *The Computer Wore Tennis Shoes*; in the unpleasant *Demon Seed*; in space fiction such as *The Forbin Project*, *2001* and *Dark Star*; in *Billion Dollar Brain*; and in a rather advanced TV movie of 1971 called *Paper Man*. In the beginning, computers tended to be regarded as evil, machines that wanted to control people, as in *Superman III* or *Electric Dreams*. But as computers became familiar objects in many homes, and computer and video games grew in popularity, and in turn were often based on hit movies, attitudes changed. Disney's *Tron* tried to capitalize on computer games, as did *Interface*, in which a game turned into reality. The appeal of *The Lawnmower Man* depended on its stunning computer graphics and its simulation of the latest technology of 'virtual reality', a computer-generated world with which people can interact. Androids – half-men, half-computers – emerged as popular heroes in such films as *Robocop* and *The Terminator 2*. By 1992, the tail was beginning to wag the dog, with computer games on compact disk incorporating film clips, and the Nintendo game *Super Mario Brothers* being turned into a movie starring Bob Hoskins. Computers continued to be seen as dangerous devices in *Sneakers* 92, *Hackers* 95, *Strange Days* 95, *Lawnmower Man 2: Beyond Cyberspace* 95, and *The Net* 95. In *Virtuosity* 95, a computerized composite of the world's worst serial killers was let loose in real life. It was not until *You've Got Mail* 98, in which Tom Hanks and Meg Ryan conducted a romance via e-mail, that computers became cuddly.

Conan the Barbarian.

A warrior from the land of Cimmeria in the Hyborian Age who was created in the 30s by pulp writer Robert E. HOWARD for the magazine *Weird Tales*. The stories were later re-edited and rewritten by other hands, and the thick-headed hero gained an increasing popularity from his appearance in Marvel comic-books in the 70s, which culminated in two films, *Conan the Barbarian* 82 and *Conan the Destroyer* 84, both starring Arnold SCHWARZENEGGER in the title role. A TV series, starring Ralf Moeller, followed in 1997. Many of the SWORD AND SORCERY films of the 70s and 80s unfortunately show the influence of Howard's hero.

concentration camps,

until long after World War II, were thought too harrowing a subject for film treatment; but a few serious reconstructions have emerged, notably *The Last Stage* (Poland) 48, *Kapo* (Italy) 60, *Passenger* (Poland) 61, and *One Day in the Life of Ivan Denisovich* 71, while the shadow of Auschwitz hangs over *The Diary of Anne Frank* 59 and *The Pawnbroker* 64. An alleged British concentration camp in South Africa was depicted in the Nazi film *Ohm Krüger* 42. The best documentary on the subject was probably RESNAIS' *Night and Fog*. In 1978 TV included much footage on the subject in *Holocaust*, which was quickly followed by *Playing for Time*. *Shoah* (1986) used no archive footage at all, but spent its nine hours in long interviews with survivors. *Triumph of the Spirit* told the true story of a boxer's survival in Auschwitz. Steven SPIELBERG's stirring *Schindler's List* 93 told the true story of how one man saved many Jews from the camps, while *Paradise Road* 97 showed how women imprisoned by the Japanese kept their spirits high by forming a choir. Robert BENIGNI's *Life Is Beautiful* 98 was a tragi-comedy in a concentration camp setting.

concerts

of serious music naturally figure largely in films about the lives of COMPOSERS, and also in those concerned to show off living musicians: *They Shall Have Music*, *Music for Millions*, *Battle for Music*, *Tonight We Sing*, *Carnegie Hall*, *A Hundred Men and a Girl*, *Rhapsody in Blue*. In the 40s a string of romantic films were centred on classical musicians and had concert climaxes: *Dangerous Moonlight*, *Love Story*, *The Seventh Veil*, *Intermezzo*, *The Great Lie*; this style later returned in *Interlude*. Other dramatic and comic concerts were featured in *Unfaithfully Yours*, *Tales of Manhattan*, *The Man Who Knew Too Much*, *The World of Henry Orient*, *The Bride Wore Black*, *Counterpoint* and *Deadfall*. The most influential film concert was certainly *Fantasia*, and the most poignant probably Myra Hess's recital in the blitz-beset National Gallery in *Listen to Britain*.

confidence tricksters

have figured as minor characters in hundreds of films, but full-length portraits of the breed are few and choice. Harry Baur in *Volpone* and Rex Harrison in *The Honey Pot*; Roland Young, Billie Burke, Janet Gaynor and Douglas Fairbanks Jnr in *The Young in Heart*; Gene Tierney, Laird Cregar and Spring Byington in *Rings on Her Fingers*; Tyrone Power in *Nightmare Alley* and *Mississippi Gambler*; Mai Zetterling in *Quartet*; Paul Newman in *The Hustler*; Charles Coburn and Barbara Stanwyck in *The Lady Eve*; David Niven and Marlon Brando in *Bedtime Story*; George C. Scott in *The Flim Flam Man*; Richard Attenborough and David Hemmings in *Only When I Larf*; James Garner in *The Skin Game*; Newman and Robert Redford in *The Sting*; Ryan and Tatum O'Neal in *Paper Moon*; James Coburn in *Dead Heat on a Merry-go-Round*; Joe Mantegna in *House of Games*, demonstrating how to do it to a bemused Lindsay Crouse; Steve Martin and Michael Caine in *Dirty Rotten Scoundrels*; John Cusack, Annette Bening and Angelica Huston in *The Grifters*.

continuity errors and boo-boos

occur even in the best-regulated movies; sometimes they pass the eagle eye of editor and director and find their way into the release version. Here are a few which have delighted me.
•In *Carmen Jones*, the camera tracks with Dorothy Dandridge down a shopping street, and the entire crew is reflected in the windows she passes.
•In *The Invisible Man*, when the naked but invisible hero runs from the police but is given away by his footprints in the snow, the footprints are of shoes, not feet.
•In *The Wrong Box*, the roofs of Victorian London are disfigured by TV aerials.
•In *The Viking Queen*, one character is plainly wearing a wrist watch.
•In *One Million Years BC*, all the girls wear false eyelashes.
•In *The Group*, set in the 30s, there are several shots of the Pan Am building in New York, built in the 60s.
•In *Stagecoach*, during the Indian chase across the salt flats one can see the tracks of rubber tyres.
•In *Decameron Nights*, Louis Jourdan as Paganino the Pirate stands on the deck of his fourteenth-century ship ... and down a hill in the distance trundles a large white truck.
•In *Camelot*, the character played by Lionel Jeffries first meets King Arthur about an hour into the movie; yet twenty minutes earlier he is plainly visible at the king's wedding.
•In *Son of Frankenstein*, Basil Rathbone during a train journey draws attention to the weirdly stunted trees ... one of which passes by three times during the conversation.
•In *Castle of Fu Manchu*, one of the leading characters is referred to in the film as Ingrid, in the synopsis as Anna, and in the end credits as Maria.
•In *Tea and Sympathy*, a pair of china dogs are back to back in a general view of the scene, but face to face in the close-ups.
•In *Dracula*, Bela Lugosi refers to Whitby as 'so close to London'. It is in fact 243 miles away.
•In *The Yellow Mountain* and *A Man Alone*, both westerns set in the last century, aeroplane vapour trails can be seen in the sky.
•In *The King and I*, while Yul Brynner is singing 'Puzzlement' he is wearing an earring in some shots but not in others.
•In *Emma Hamilton* (1969) Big Ben is heard to strike in 1804, fifty years before it was built.
•In *The Lodger* (1944) London's Tower Bridge is shown, ten years before it was built.
•In *Hello Dolly*, set at the turn of the century, a modern car lies derelict by the side of the railway track.
•In *Anatomy of a Murder*, Lee Remick in the café scene wears a dress, but when she walks outside she is wearing slacks.
•In *Hangover Square*, the introductory title gives the date of the action as 1899, but shortly thereafter a theatre programme shows 1903.
•In *Queen Christina*, the famous final close-up apparently has the wind blowing in two directions at once, one to get the boat under way and the other to arrange Garbo's hair to the best advantage.
•In *The Desk Set*, Katharine Hepburn leaves her office carrying a bunch of white flowers. By the time she reaches the pavement they are pink.
•In *Knock on Wood*, Danny Kaye turns a corner in London's Oxford Street, and finds himself in Ludgate Hill, three miles away.
•In *23 Paces to Baker Street*, Van Johnson has an apartment in Portman Square, with a river view which seems to be that of the Savoy Hotel two miles away.
•In *Triple Cross*, a World War II newspaper bears a headline about the cost of Concorde going up again.
•In *The Lady Vanishes*, Miss Froy writes her name in the steam on a train window, but two or three shots later the writing is quite different and in another place.
•In *The Eddie Cantor Story*, the scene is set in 1904, but Eddie sings 'Meet Me Tonight in Dreamland' which was not written till 1909.
•Similarly, in *Thoroughly Modern Millie*, clearly set in 1922 per the song title, one of the big numbers is 'Baby Face', written in 1926.
•In *Miracle on 34th Street*, a camera shadow follows Edmund Gwenn and John Payne as they walk across a square.
•In *Broken Lance*, Katy Jurado's dress changes colour in alternate shots as she stands in a doorway talking to Spencer Tracy at the gate.
•In *North by Northwest*, Cary Grant's only suit during his stay in Chicago is a different colour out in the prairie from back at the hotel. Hitchcock said this was because of different kinds of lighting which were used.
•In *Mysterious Island*, set in 1860, an air balloon rises above a nest of TV aerials.
•In *The Alamo*, mobile trailers are clearly seen in the battle sequences, and a falling stuntman lands on a mattress.
•In *North to Alaska* during a fistfight, John Wayne loses his toupee and then regains it.
•In *The Green Berets*, the sun sets in the east during the final shot.
•In *The Scalphunters*, set in the 1800s, Ossie Davis mentions the planet Pluto, which was not discovered until 1930.
•In *Annie*, set in 1933, characters go to Radio City Music Hall and see *Camille*, which was not made until 1937.
•In *Yankee Doodle Dandy*, the *Lusitania* is sunk and there is a newspaper picture showing a ship with two funnels. The *Lusitania* had four funnels.
•In the same film a luggage label with a picture of Nelson's Column bears the legend 'Nelson Square Hotel'.
•In *Brief Encounter*, Celia Johnson runs through a downpour but remains dry.
•In *National Lampoon's Animal House*, the word Satan written on a blackboard looks totally different in adjacent shots.
•In *Quadrophenia*, clearly set in 1964, a cinema is showing Warren Beatty in *Heaven Can Wait*, made fourteen years later.
•In *Carrie*, the final dream was projected backwards to achieve the right effect. But in the background a car is also moving backwards...
•In *Halloween*, which is set in Illinois, all the cars have California number plates.
•In *The Birds*, the creatures which pursue the children cast no shadows.
•In *Cain and Mabel*, a workman walks across a sound stage during a production number.
•In *The Band Wagon*, during the train ride to Baltimore, the scenery is dark on one side and light on the other.
•In *Knock on Wood*, a policeman rushes upstairs wearing a helmet, and into a room wearing a peaked cap.
•In *Silk Stockings*, a typewriter shown on a table vanishes in the reverse shot taken from the balcony.
•In *Fire Maidens from Outer Space*, Sidney Tafler in a T-shirt glances down at his watch, and we get an insert of a watch on a fully-sleeved arm.
•In *Genevieve*, Kenneth More comes out of a pub carrying a pint of beer, which has become a half pint by the time he reaches his table.
•In *The Band Wagon*, a theatre is shown on its canopy as the Alcott; but on the programme it says the Stratton.
•In *Meet Me In St Louis*, during the Trolley Song, one of the extras calls 'Hi, Judy!' Judy Garland's character name is Esther.
•In *The Adventures of Robin Hood*, Errol Flynn takes a bite at a complete leg of mutton. In the next shot, only a bone is left.
•In *Round Midnight*, which is set in the 50s, there is a shot of New York's World Trade Center towers, which were built much later.
•In *Camelot*, Richard Harris plays one scene with a Band-Aid on his neck.
•In *North by Northwest*, a small boy (who has obviously been to rehearsal) puts his fingers in his ears *before* Eva Marie Saint picks up a gun to shoot Cary Grant.
•In *Mysterious Island*, during the air balloon sequence, it is raining *above* the clouds.
•In *The Smallest Show on Earth*, although the cinema is supposedly in the north of England, a taxi arriving at it stops outside Hammersmith station.
•In *The Corn Is Green*, the villagers are all said to be illiterate, but they cluster round to read a poster.
•In *The Bridges of Madison County*, as Clint Eastwood drives Meryl Streep to Roseman Bridge, they twice pass the same house and a field containing some black cows.
•In *Conspiracy Theory*, Mel Gibson plays a paranoid taxi driver called Jerry Fletcher. But his identity card displayed in the cab shows the name Raffi Paloulian.
•In James Cameron's *Titanic*, when the officer of the watch orders 'full starboard rudder' on sighting the iceberg, the helmsman puts the wheel smartly to port. Perhaps (as Rear Admiral J. F. Perowne pointed out) the confusion was caused by the officers wearing their shoulder boards back to front, which is known in the Royal Navy as 'going astern'.

courtesans

have always been viewed by the cinema through rose-coloured glasses. There have been innumerable films about Madame du Barry, Madame Sans Gêne and Nell Gwyn; Garbo played Camille and Marie Walewska as well as Anna Christie; even Jean Simmons had a shot at Napoleon's *Désirée*, and Vivien Leigh was a decorative Lady Hamilton. Martine Carol played Lola Montes in the Max Ophüls film, Yvonne de Carlo in *Black Bart* (in which she became involved in western villainy during an American tour).
See also: PROSTITUTES.

courtroom scenes

have been the suspenseful saving grace of more films than can be counted; and they also figure in some of the best films ever made.

British courts best preserve the ancient aura of the law; among the films they have figured in are *London Belongs to Me*, *The Paradine Case*, *Eight O'Clock Walk*, *Life for Ruth*, *Twenty-one Days*, *Brothers in Law*, *The Winslow Boy*, *Witness for the Prosecution*, *The Blind Goddess* and *The Dock Brief*. The last four are based on stage plays, as are the American *Madame X*, *Counsellor at Law*, and *The Trial of Mary Dugan*. Other American films depending heavily on courtroom denouements include *They Won't Believe Me*, *The Unholy Three*, *The Mouthpiece*, *Boomerang*, *They Won't Forget*, *The Missing Juror*, *Trial*, *The Young Savages*, *The Criminal Code*, *To Kill a Mockingbird*, *Criminal Lawyer*, *Fury*, *The Lawyer*, *A Free Soul*, *The Seven Minutes*, *The People Against O'Hara*, *The Lady from Shanghai*, *Twilight of Honour*, *An American Tragedy* (and its remake *A Place in the Sun*), the several Perry Mason films, *Young Mr Lincoln*, *Philadelphia, The Accused, Class Action, The Crucible, A Few Good Men, Presumed Innocent* and *The People vs Larry Flynt*. These, even the last-named, were fictional: genuine cases were reconstructed in *I Want to Live, Cell 2455 Death Row, Compulsion, Inherit the Wind, Dr Ehrlich's Magic Bullet, The Witches of Salem, The Trials of Oscar Wilde, Judgment at Nuremberg, The Life of Emile Zola, Dr Crippen, Captain Kidd, Landru* and *The Case of Charles Peace*. Comedy courtroom scenes have appeared in *I'm No Angel, Mr Deeds Goes to Town, You Can't Take It With You, Roxie Hart, My Learned Friend, Adam's Rib, Pickwick Papers, Brothers in Law, What's Up Doc?, Star!, A Pair of Briefs* and *Cousin Vinny*.

Films in which special interest has centred on the jury include *Twelve Angry Men, Murder/Enter Sir John, Perfect Strangers/Too Dangerous to Love, Justice est Faite* and *The Monster and the Girl* in which the criminal brain inside the gorilla murders the jurors at his trial one by one). Ghostly juries figured in *All That Money Can Buy* and *The Remarkable Andrew*. The judge has been the key figure in *The Judge Steps Out, Talk of the Town, The Bachelor and the Bobbysoxer*, and *Destry Rides Again*; and we are constantly being promised a film of Henry Cecil's *No Bail for the Judge*. *Anatomy of a Murder* remains the only film in which a real judge (Joseph E. Welch) has played a fictional one. A lady barrister (Anna Neagle) had the leading role in *The Man Who Wouldn't Talk*.

Specialized courts were seen in *M* (convened by criminals), *Saint Joan* and *The Hunchback of Notre Dame* (church courts), *Black Legion* (Ku Klux Klan), *The Devil's Disciple* (18th-century military court), *Kind Hearts and Coronets* (a court of the House of Lords), *The Wreck of the Mary Deare* (mercantile), *Cone of Silence* (civil aviation), *A Tale of Two Cities* and *The Scarlet Pimpernel* (French Revolutionary courts). Courts in other countries were shown in *The Lady in Question, The Count of Monte Cristo, Crack in the Mirror, A Flea in Her Ear, La Vérité*, and *Can Can* (French); *The Purple Heart* (Japanese); *The Fall of the Roman Empire* (ancient Roman); *The Spy Who Came in from the Cold* (East German); and *Shoeshine* (Italian). Coroners' courts were featured in *Inquest, My Learned Friend* and *Rebecca*.

Courts martial figured largely in *The Caine Mutiny, Time Limit, The Man in the Middle, Across the Pacific, The Rack, Carrington VC, The Court Martial of Billy Mitchell, A Few Good Men* and *Rules of Engagement*. There was also a TV series called *Court Martial/Counsellors at War*.

Heavenly courts were convened in *A Matter of Life and Death, Outward Bound* and *The Flight That Disappeared*; while other fantasy courts appeared in *Rashomon, Morgan, One Way Pendulum, Alice in Wonderland, The Balcony, The Wonderful World of the Brothers Grimm, The Trial, All That Money Can Buy*, and *The Remarkable Andrew*. The court in *Planet of the Apes* is perhaps best classed as prophetic, along with that in *1984*.

TV series based on trials and lawyers include *The Law and Mr Jones, Harrigan and Son, Sam Benedict, The Trials of O'Brien, Perry Mason, Arrest and Trial, The Defenders, The D.A., The Verdict is Yours, Judd for the Defense, Owen Marshall, Petrocelli, Adam's Rib* and *L.A. Law*.

crazy comedy

has two distinct meanings in the cinema. On one hand it encompasses the Marx Brothers, *Hellzapoppin* and custard pies; for this see *Slapstick*. On the other it means the new kind of comedy which came in during the 30s, with seemingly adult people behaving in what society at the time thought was a completely irresponsible way. The Capra comedies, for instance, are vaguely 'agin' the government', upholding Mr Deeds' right to give away his money and play the tuba, the Vanderhofs' right not to work, and Mr Smith's right to be utterly honest. This endearing eccentricity permeated many of the funniest and most modern comedies of the period. William Powell and Myrna Loy in *The Thin Man* were a married couple who upheld none of the domestic virtues. In *Libeled Lady* four top stars behaved like low comedians. In *My Man Godfrey* a rich man pretended to be a tramp and so reformed a party of the idle rich who found him during a 'scavenger hunt'. *Theodora Goes Wild, I Met Him in Paris* and *Easy Living* had what we would now call 'kooky' heroines. In *True Confession* Carole Lombard confessed to a murder she hadn't done, and was told by John Barrymore

that she would 'fry'; in *Nothing Sacred* she pretended to be dying of an obscure disease and was socked on the jaw by Fredric March. Hal Roach introduced comedy ghosts, played by two of Hollywood's most sophisticated stars, in *Topper*, and followed it up with two sequels as well as three individual and endearingly lunatic comedies called *The Housekeeper's Daughter* (a battle of fireworks), *Turnabout* (a husband and wife exchange bodies) and *Road Show* (an asylum escapee runs a travelling circus). *The Awful Truth* had no respect for marriage; *You Can't Take It With You* had no respect for law, business, or the American way of life. A film called *Bringing Up Baby* turned out to be about a leopard and a brontosaurus bone; *Boy Meets Girl* was a farcical send-up of Hollywood; and *A Slight Case of Murder* had more corpses than characters. *The Women* had its all-female cast fighting like tiger-cats. *Road to Singapore* began as a romantic comedy but degenerated into snippets from Joe Miller's gag-book; and any Preston Sturges film was likely to have pauses while the smart and witty hero and heroine fell into a pool. In *Here Comes Mr Jordan* the hero was dead after five minutes or so and spent the rest of the film trying to get his body back.

The genre was by this time well established, and although America's entry into the war modified it somewhat it has remained fashionable and popular ever since. A 1966 film like *Morgan* may seem rather startling, but in fact it goes little further in its genial anarchy than *You Can't Take It With You*; only the method of expression is different. What modern crazy comedies lack is the clear pattern which produced so many little masterpieces within a few years: even direct imitations like *What's Up Doc?* fail to produce the same results.

Crime Doctor

was a series of 'B' features, based on a popular CBS radio show created by Max Marcin, and made by Columbia. They starred Warner BAXTER as Dr Robert Ordway, a former gangster who, after a blow on the head caused amnesia, became a criminologist and psychiatrist specializing in solving mysteries.

Crime Doctor 43. Crime Doctor's Strangest Case 43. Shadows in the Night 44. The Crime Doctor's Courage 45. Crime Doctor's Warning 45. Crime Doctor's Man Hunt 46. Just Before Dawn 46. The Millerson Case/The Crime Doctor's Vacation 47. The Crime Doctor's Gamble 47. Crime Doctor's Diary 49.

criminals

– real-life ones – whose careers have been featured in films include Burke and Hare (*The Flesh and the Fiends, Burke and Hare*), Cagliostro (*Black Magic*), Al Capone (*Little Caesar, The Scarface Mob, Al Capone*), Caryl Chessman (*Cell 2455 Death Row*), Crippen (*Dr Crippen*), John Wilkes Booth (*Prince of Players*), Jack the Ripper (*The Lodger, A Study in Terror, Jack the Ripper*, many others), Landru (*Landru, Bluebeard, Monsieur Verdoux, Bluebeard's Ten Honeymoons*), Leopold and Loeb (*Rope, Compulsion* and *Swoon*), Christie (*10 Rillington Place*), Charles Peace (*The Case of Charles Peace*), Dick TURPIN, Jesse James, Vidocq (*A Scandal in Paris*), Robert Stroud (*Birdman of Alcatraz*), Barbara Graham (*I Want to Live*), RASPUTIN, Eddie Chapman (*Triple Cross*), the Kray brothers (*The Krays*), Phoolan Devi (*The Bandit Queen*), Graham Young (*The Young Poisoner's Handbook*) and the various American public enemies of the 30s: *Bonnie and Clyde, Dillinger, Baby Face Nelson, Bloody Mama* (Barker), *A Bullet for Pretty Boy* (Floyd), etc. The clinical 60s also brought accounts of the motiveless murderers of *In Cold Blood* and of *The Boston Strangler*. Criminal movements have been very well explored in fictional films, especially the Mafia, the Thugs, Murder Inc. and the racketeers and bootleggers of the 20s.

critics

Very little film criticism is quotable: at its best it is an expression of personality rather than wit. The reviews one remembers tend to be the scathing ones, especially those dismissive one-liners which are really unforgivable but linger over the arch of years:

❝ *No Leave, No Love*. No comment.
I Am a Camera. Me no Leica.
Lost in a Harem. But with Abbott and Costello.
Aimez-vous Brahms? Brahms, oui.
Ben Hur. Loved Ben, hated Hur.
Samson and Delilah. A movie for de Millions.

Bill and Coo. By conservative estimate, one of the God-damnedest things ever seen.

The authors of these pearls are now, by me, forgotten, with the exception of the last, which came from the pen of James Agee, a lamented American writer whose economical, literate reviews delighted all film enthusiasts in the 40s and established a few Hollywood reputations. His collected reviews should all be read with affection; here we can spare room for five of his more waspish put-downs:

Random Harvest. I would like to recommend this film to those who can stay interested in Ronald Colman's amnesia for two hours and who could with pleasure eat a bowl of Yardley's shaving soap for breakfast.

During the making of *Pin Up Girl* Betty Grable was in an early stage of pregnancy – and everyone else was evidently in a late stage of paresis.

Tycoon. Several tons of dynamite are set off in this picture – none of it under the right people.

You Were Meant For Me. That's what you think.

Star Spangled Rhythm. A variety show including everyone at Paramount who was not overseas, in hiding or out to lunch.

A few more moments of invective. First, *Variety* on Hedy Lamarr's independent production *The Strange Woman*:

Hedy bit off more than she could chew, so the chewing was done by the rest of the cast, and what was chewed was the scenery.

And Pamela Kellino on *The Egyptian*:

One of those great big rotten pictures Hollywood keeps on turning out.

And Stanley Kauffmann on *Isadora*:

This long but tiny film...

And the *New Statesman* (Frank Hauser) on *Another Man's Poison*:

Like reading Ethel M. Dell by flashes of lightning.

And the *Saturday Evening Post* on *Macabre*:

It plods along from its opening scene in a funeral parlor to its dénouement in a graveyard, unimpeded by the faintest intrusion of good taste, literacy, or sense.

And Don Herold on *The Bride Walks Out*:

You've seen this a million times on the screen, but they keep on making it, and folks keep asking me why I am so dyspeptic regarding the cinema. Because I have judgment, is the answer.

And John Simon on *Camelot*:

This film is the Platonic idea of boredom, roughly comparable to reading a three-volume novel in a language of which one knows only the alphabet.

And David Lardner on *Panama Hattie*:

This film needs a certain something. Possibly burial.

And Judith Crist on *Five Card Stud*:

So mediocre that you can't get mad at it.

And Charles Champlin on *The Missouri Breaks*:

A pair of million dollar babies in a five and ten cent flick.

Now for some self-criticism. Joseph L. Mankiewicz on his own movie *Cleopatra*:

This picture was conceived in a state of emergency, shot in confusion, and wound up in blind panic.

He also called it:

The toughest three pictures I ever made.

Ethel Barrymore, when asked her opinion of *Rasputin and the Empress*, in which she co-starred with her brothers Lionel and John, replied:

I thought I was pretty good, but what those two boys were up to I'll never know.

Erich Von Stroheim, reminiscing on his own much-mutilated picture *Greed*:

When ten years later I saw the film myself, it was like seeing a corpse in a graveyard.

Otto Preminger on *Saint Joan*:

My most distinguished flop. I've had much less distinguished ones.

And Victor Fleming, director of *Gone with the Wind*, refusing David O. Selznick's offer of a percentage of the profits instead of salary:

Don't be a damn fool, David. This picture is going to be one of the biggest white elephants of all time.

Philip French on *Carry on Emmanuelle*:

Put together with an almost palpable contempt for its audience, this relentless sequence of badly written, badly timed dirty jokes is surely one of the most morally and aesthetically offensive pictures to emerge from a British studio.

Similarly misguided was Adolph Zukor when he first read the script of *Broken Blossoms*:

You bring me a picture like this and want money for it? You may as well put your hand in my pocket and steal it. It isn't commercial. Everyone in it dies.

I can recall only three memorable items of praise. Cecilia Ager on *Citizen Kane*:

It's as though you had never seen a movie before.

Terry Ramsaye on *Intolerance*:

The only film fugue.

And Woodrow Wilson on *The Birth of a Nation*:

Like writing history with lightning. And it's all true.

My own favourite critiques also include Sarah Bernhardt's enthusiastic remark when she saw her 1912 version of *Queen Elizabeth*:

Mr Zukor, you have put the best of me in pickle for all time.

And the comment of macabre New Yorker cartoonist Charles Addams, when asked his opinion after the première of *Cleopatra*:

I only came to see the asp.

And the anonymous reviewer of a Jack Benny violin concert:

Jack Benny played Mendelssohn last night. Mendelssohn lost.

Come to that, another anonymous gentleman had a pretty good definition of critics:

Yawning as a profession.

Channing Pollock defined a critic as:

A legless man who teaches running.

To Whitney Balkett he was:

A bundle of biases held together by a sense of taste.

And to Ken Tynan:

A man who knows the way but can't drive a car.

Mel Brooks was scathing:

Critics can't even make music by rubbing their back legs together.

R. W. Emerson was dismissive:

Taking to pieces is the trade of those who cannot construct.

Perhaps the wisest reflection on the critics was made by Rouben Mamoulian:

The most important critic is Time.

Cry the Beloved Country.

Alan Paton's novel of racial tension in South Africa, as a Zulu Christian pastor searches Johannesburg for his missing son, has been filmed twice: in 1951, directed by Zoltan KORDA, starring Canada LEE, and in 1995, starring James Earl JONES and Richard HARRIS and directed by South African Darrell James ROODT.

Crying Freeman.

Heroic and lachrymose hitman of Japanese MANGA and ANIME, created by Kazuo Koike and Ryoichi Ikegami, the basis of two live-action movies made in Hong Kong, in which the character was played by Simon Yam and Sam Hui, and a European production in 1995 in which the role was taken by Mark DACASCOS. Three animated Japanese films of the early 90s, which have been released on video dubbed into English, retain the narrative of the original comic books.

Killers Romance 89. Dragon from Russia 90. Crying Freeman Chapter One: Portrait of a Killer 92. Crying Freeman Chapter Two: The Enemy Within 92. Crying Freeman Chapter Three: Retribution 92. Crying Freeman 95.

custard pies

as a comic weapon were evolved in music hall by Fred Karno and at the Keystone studio around 1915, and most silent comedians relied heavily on them. In the 30s Mack Sennett staged a splendid one for a nostalgic farce called *Keystone Hotel*. Other notable pie fighters have included Laurel and Hardy in *The Battle of the Century* 28; the whole cast of *Beach Party* 63; and most of the cast of *The Great Race* 64 and *Smashing Time* 65.

Daffy Duck.

Witty, manic duck who was a star of Warner Looney Tunes and Merrie Melodies cartoons from 1937 and evolved into a mischief-making foil to Bugs Bunny and Porky Pig. He is said to have been modelled on Harpo MARX, although he was far more loquacious and developed a spluttering speech impediment in the 50s. He was voiced by Mel BLANC.

Porky's Duck Hunt 37. The Daffy Doc 38. A Coy Decoy 41. To Duck or Not to Duck 43. The Stupid Cupid 44. Ain't That Ducky 45. Birth of a Notion 47. Wise Quackers 49. Rabbit Fire 51. Rabbit Seasoning 52. Duck Dodgers in the 24½th Century 53. A Star Is Bored 56. Robin Hood Daffy

58. The Abominable Snow-Rabbit 61. The Iceman Ducketh 64. Moby Duck 65. Daffy's Diner 67. The Duckorcist 87. Night of the Living Duck 88, etc.

dance bands.
in the 30s and 40s were so popular as to be stars in their own films: Henry Hall's in *Music Hath Charms*, Kay Kyser's in half a dozen films including *That's Right You're Wrong*, Paul Whiteman's in *King of Jazz*, Tommy and Jimmy Dorsey's in *The Fabulous Dorseys*. Also frequently on hand to assist the stars were the bands of Glenn Miller, Xavier Cugat, Woody Herman and Harry James, to name but a few. In the 50s bands became too expensive to maintain, but *The Glenn Miller Story* and *The Benny Goodman Story* reawakened interest.

The Dead End Kids
were Gabriel Dell, Huntz Hall, Billy Halop, Bobby Jordan, Leo Gorcey and Bernard Punsley, a group of young actors who appeared in Sidney Kingsley's Broadway play of slum life, *Dead End*, and were hired by Sam Goldwyn to repeat their roles on film in 1937. They went on to make six other gangster films for Warner, and some also appeared in a series for Universal, *The Dead End Kids and Little Tough Guys*. The group reformed in various combinations as the EAST SIDE KIDS and THE BOWERY BOYS, turning out 'B' features that soon emphasized comedy rather than crime.

Angels with Dirty Faces 38. Crime School 38. They Made Me a Criminal 39. Hell's Kitchen 39. The Angels Wash Their Faces 39. On Dress Parade 39.

deaf mutes
have been movingly portrayed by Jane WYMAN in *Johnny Belinda*, Mandy MILLER in *Mandy*, Harry BELLAVER in *No Way Out*, and Alan ARKIN in *The Heart Is a Lonely Hunter*. Dorothy MCGUIRE in *The Spiral Staircase* was mute but not deaf, as was Samantha MORTON in Sweet and Lowdown; Patty DUKE in *The Miracle Worker* was deaf but could make sounds.

death
has always fascinated film-makers, though the results have often appeared undergraduate-ish, as fantasy tends to look when brought down to a mass-appeal level. Death has been personified in *Death Takes a Holiday* by Fredric MARCH, in the 1971 TV remake by Monte Markham and Martin BREST's 1998 remake *Meet Joe Black*, in *On Borrowed Time* by Cedric HARDWICKE, in *Here Comes Mr Jordan* by Claude RAINS, in *Orphée* by Maria CASARÈS, in *The Seventh Seal* by Bengt Ekerot, by Richard BURTON in *Boom*, by George JESSEL in *Hieronymous Merkin* and by several actors in *The Masque of the Red Death*. In *Devotion*, Ida LUPINO as Emily Brontë dreamed of death on horseback coming to sweep her away; in *The Bluebird* Shirley TEMPLE ventured into the land of the dead to see her grandparents. Most of the characters in *Thunder Rock*, and all in *Outward Bound* (remade as *Between Two Worlds* and later varied for TV as *Haunts of the Very Rich*) were already dead at the start of the story. Other films to involve serious thought about death include *Dark Victory*, *Jeux Interdits*, *All the Way Home*, *Sentimental Journey*, *No Sad Songs for Me*, *One Way Passage*, *Paths of Glory*, *Wild Strawberries*, and *Ikuru*. *Flatliners* and *The Rapture* both dealt with experiences after death.

Comedies taking death lightly included *A Slight Case of Murder*, *Kind Hearts and Coronets*, *The Trouble with Harry*, *Too Many Crooks*, *The Criminal Life of Archibaldo de la Cruz*, *Send Me No Flowers*, *The Assassination Bureau*, *The Loved One*, *The Wrong Box*, *Arrivederci Baby*, *Kiss the Girls and Make Them Die*, *Arsenic and Old Lace*, *Une Journée Bien Remplie*, and *Weekend at Bernie's*.

dentists
are seldom popular chaps, but Preston STURGES made a film about one of them, the inventor of laughing gas: *The Great Moment*. *The Counterfeit Traitor* had a spy dentist. Sinister dentists were found in *The Man Who Knew Too Much* (original version), *The Secret Partner*, and *Footsteps in the Dark*, and comic ones, in the person of Bob HOPE, in *The Paleface* . Dentistry is the subject of two British farces: *Dentist in the Chair* and *Dentist on the Job*. W. C. FIELDS once made a film of his sketch *The Dentist*; and LAUREL and HARDY in *Leave 'Em Laughing* were overcome by laughing gas. The most notable dentist hero was in the twice remade *One Sunday Afternoon*; and the most villainous dentist is certainly Laurence Olivier in *Marathon Man*, though Corbin BERNSEN in Brian YUZNA's horror movie *The Dentist* and its sequel will leave audiences squirming. The dentist with the most hectic private life was Walter MATTHAU in *Cactus Flower*. The oddest were Daniel Day-Lewis as a motorcycling enthusiast for dental hygiene in *Eversmile, New Jersey* and Kirstie ALLEY in the TV movie *Toothless*, as a dentist who dies and becomes the Tooth Fairy.

department stores
have usually been a background for comedy. New York store backgrounds have often shown the native superiority of the working girl to snobbish shopwalkers and obtuse management, as in *Bachelor Mother* and its remake *Bundle of Joy*, *The Devil and Miss Jones* and *Manhandled* 24. Broader comedy elements were to the fore in *Miracle on 34th Street*, *Modern Times*, *The Big Store*, *Who's Minding the Store?*, *Fitzwilly* and *How to Save a Marriage*. British comedies with store settings include *Kipps*, *The Crowded Day*, *Laughter in Paradise*, *Keep Fit*, and *Trouble in Store*.

desert islands
have provided the locale of many a film adventure. *Robinson Crusoe* has been filmed several times, with two variations in *Robinson Crusoe on Mars* and *Lt Robin Crusoe USN*. *Treasure Island* too has survived three or four versions, to say nothing of imitations like *Blackbeard the Pirate* and parodies such as *Abbott and Costello Meet Captain Kidd* and *Old Mother Riley's Jungle Treasure*. *The Admirable Crichton* is perhaps the next most overworked desert island story, with *The Swiss Family Robinson* following on. Dorothy LAMOUR found a few desert islands in films like *Typhoon* and *Aloma of the South Seas*; the inhabitants of *The Little Hut* had one nearly to themselves; Joan GREENWOOD and co. were marooned on a rather special one in *Mysterious Island*. *Our Girl Friday* played the theme for sex; *Dr Dolittle* found educated natives on one; Cary GRANT lived on one as a reluctant spy in *Father Goose*; *Sea Wife*, *Lord of the Flies* and *The Day the Fish Came Out* were three recent but not very successful attempts to take the theme seriously: *Hell in the Pacific* was one that did work. *The Blue Lagoon* was treated decorously in the 50s and sexily in the 80s. In 2000, Tom HANKS became *Cast Away* on one for more than four years, reduced to talking to a football.

A comic TV series on the subject was *Gilligan's Island* 64-66; a serious one, *The New People* 69.

deserts
have figured in many a western, from *Tumbleweed* to *Mackenna's Gold*. Other films which have paid particularly respectful attention to the dangers that too much sand can provide include *The Sheik* and *Son of the Sheik*, *Greed*, *The Lost Patrol*, *The Garden of Allah*, *Sahara*, *Five Graves to Cairo*, *Ice Cold in Alex*, *Sea of Sand*, *Desert Rats*, *Play Dirty*, *An Eye for an Eye*, *Inferno*, *Zabriskie Point*, *The Sabre and the Arrow*, *Legend of the Lost*, *The Ten Commandments*, *She*, *Lawrence of Arabia*, *The Black Tent*, *Oasis*, *Sands of The Kalahari*, *The Flight of the Phoenix*, *Garden of Evil* and *The Professionals*.

the devil
has made frequent appearances in movies. There were versions of *Faust* in 1900, 1903, 1904, 1907, 1909, 1911, 1921 and 1925, the last of these featuring Emil JANNINGS as Mephistopheles. Later variations on this theme include *The Sorrows of Satan* 27, with Adolphe Menjou; *All That Money Can Buy* 41, with Walter HUSTON as Mr Scratch; *Alias Nick Beal* 49, with Ray MILLAND; *La Beauté du Diable* 50 with Gérard PHILIPE; *Damn Yankees* 58 with Ray WALSTON; *Bedazzled* 67 with Peter COOK, remade in 00 with Elizabeth HURLEY; and *Doctor Faustus* 68 with Andreas Teuber. In other stories, Satan was played by Helge Nissen in *Leaves From Satan's Book* 20, Jules BERRY in *Les Visiteurs du Soir* 42, Alan MOWBRAY in *The Devil with Hitler* 42, Rex INGRAM in *Cabin in the Sky* 43, Laird CREGAR in *Heaven Can Wait* 43, Claude RAINS in *Angel on My Shoulder* 46, Stanley HOLLOWAY in *Meet Mr Lucifer* 53, Richard Devon in *The Undead* 56, Vincent PRICE in *The Story of Mankind* 57, Cedric HARDWICKE in *Bait* 54, Vittorio GASSMAN in *The Devil in Love* 67, Stig Järrel in *The Devil's Eye* 60, Donald PLEASENCE in *The Greatest Story Ever Told* 65, Burgess MEREDITH in *Torture Garden* 68, Pierre CLEMENTI in *The Milky Way* 68, Ralph RICHARDSON in *Tales From the Crypt* 71, Rod Dumont in the erotic-horror *The Devil Inside Her* 76, John RITTER in *Wholly Moses* 80, Robert HELPMANN in *Second Time Lucky* 84, Leo Marks in *The Last Temptation of Christ* 88, Bruce Payne in *Switch* 91, Barry Gerdsen in the horror movie *The Good Book* 97, Jeroen KRABBÉ in the TV movie *Jesus* 99, Colin Fox in the TV movie *Angels in the Infield* 00 and Harvey KEITEL in *Little Nicky* 00. In the Swedish *Witchcraft through the Ages* 21, the devil was played by the director, Benjamin Christensen. Devil worship has been the subject of *The Black Cat* 34, *The Seventh Victim* 43, *Night of the Demon* 57, *Back from the Dead* 57, *The Witches* 66, *Eye of the Devil* 66, *The Devil Rides Out* 68, *Rosemary's Baby* 68; while the last-named presaged a rash of diabolically-inspired children in *The Exorcist*, *I Don't Want to be Born*, *It's Alive*, *Devil Within Her* and *The Omen*.

Devil's Island,
the French Guianan penal colony, has intermittently fascinated film-makers. Apart from the versions of the Dreyfus case (*Dreyfus*, *The Life of Emile Zola*, *I Accuse*), there have been Ronald Colman in *Condemned to Devil's Island*, Donald Woods in *I Was a Prisoner on Devil's Island*, Boris Karloff in *Devil's Island*, Clark Gable in *Strange Cargo*, Humphrey Bogart in *Passage to Marseilles*, Bogart and company in *We're No Angels*, Eartha Kitt in *Saint of Devil's Island*, Steve McQueen in *Papillon*, and Jim Brown in *I Escaped From Devil's Island*. The prison colony opened in 1852 and closed in 1946.

Dick Barton.
Tough British special agent, created by Edward J. Mason, who was the hero of a popular radio programme 1946-51, and three low-budget films starring Don Stannard. In 1978, Tony Vogel played him in an unsuccessful television series.

Dick Barton, Special Agent 48. Dick Barton Strikes Back 49. Dick Barton at Bay 50.

Dick Tracy.
The lantern-jawed detective of the comic strips made sporadic film appearances, notably when impersonated by Ralph Byrd or Morgan Conway in a number of 40s second features and serials. In 1951 Byrd starred in a TV series. Tracy also appeared in a TV cartoon series in the 50s, in *TV Funnies* in 1971, and in the big-budget film of 1990, starring Warren BEATTY.

Die Hard.
The film starring Bruce WILLIS as a tough cop outwitting a group of terrorists who had taken his wife and others hostage in a skyscraper was followed by two sequels that repeated the formula, first in an airport and then in various New York locations. The popularity of the series led to similar movies of lone heroes battling against overwhelming odds in claustrophobic situations, which were usually defined in terms of the original: *Passenger 57* ('Die Hard on a plane'), *Under Siege* ('Die Hard on a boat'), *On Lonely Ground* ('Die Hard on ice'), *Speed* ('Die Hard on a bus'), etc. In similar fashion, the *Die Hard* sequels were adapted from already existing scripts. The addition of Samuel L. JACKSON as Willis's sidekick in the third film seemed an attempt to emulate the *Lethal Weapon* series which coupled Mel GIBSON with Danny GLOVER. The first and third films were directed by John MCTIERNAN, the second by Renny HARLIN. A fourth film in the series is likely.

Die Hard 88. Die Hard 2/Die Hard: Die Harder 90. Die Hard with a Vengeance 95.

dinosaurs
have been a cinematic favourite since the earliest days of cinema, when Winsor MCCAY appeared with his cartoon creation Gertie in 1909. But it was *The Lost World* 25 which proved to be the template for virtually all the succeeding dinosaur films. This silent movie adaptation of CONAN DOYLE's novel of an isolated plateau where prehistoric monsters survived improved on the original. Where that had a pterodactyl loose in London, the film sent a brontosaurus rampaging through the streets, attacking Tower Bridge (special effects by Willis O'BRIEN). It was a scene that became a standard in most subsequent movies, from the Japanese series that began with *Godzilla, King of the Monsters!* 54, in which Tokyo was flattened, to *Gorgo*, which brought a monster swimming up the Thames to rescue its offspring; *Behemoth the Sea Monster* 58, which was just another *Beast from Twenty Thousand Fathoms*, also gave London a going-over. The GODZILLA movies, in which the beast progressed from ravening monster to a saviour of mankind, also drew on the dinosaur battles from *King Kong* 33, in which O'Brien refined the stop-motion techniques he used in *The Lost World*. The problem of getting man and dinosaur into the same setting was solved in many ways: *One Million BC* simply ignored the anachronism, using lizards optically enlarged and a stuntman in a suit for its creatures, and covering elephants with fur to pass as mastodons; its footage was to turn up in later, low-budget efforts, such as Bert I. Gordon's *King Dinosaur* 55. *Unknown Island* 48, *The Land that Time Forgot* and its sequel *The People that Time Forgot* used a similar amnesiac low-budget approach. Hammer's remake *One Million Years BC* used stop-motion for the beasts, although the film is remembered, if at all, for Raquel WELCH in a fur bikini. Hammer also made *When Dinosaurs Ruled the Earth* 70, which again relied on the sex appeal of its leading lady. Others used nuclear power to revive the long-dead creatures, including *The Beast from Twenty Thousand Fathoms*, with special effects by Ray HARRYHAUSEN. *The Land Unknown* 57 put them in a lost, underground world beneath the Pole, as did *Journey to the Center of the Earth* 59, which again used real lizards (ignoring modern thinking which believes that dinosaurs are related to birds rather than reptiles), and *The Last Dinosaur* 77. Lizards again turn up in the 60s remake of *The Lost World*. *Jurassic Park* was scientifically more advanced, using modern techniques of DNA cloning to bring the creatures back; it and its sequel *The Lost World: Jurassic Park* once again made dinosaurs monster box-office (special effects by Stan WINSTON and others), although the mutated creatures of *Super Mario Bros* proved that special effects were not enough on their own to make a successful film, and Roger CORMAN's attempt to cash in on the craze with *Carnosaur* proved to be no more than a throwback to 50s monster films. There have been two dinosaur westerns, *The Beast of Hollow Mountain* 56 and *The Valley of the Gwangi* 68. Walt DISNEY has used dinosaurs to good effect in two animated films: *Fantasia* 40 and *Dinosaur* 00, which had dazzling computer-generated animation married to a fossilised story. They were also to be found in Steven Spielberg's jokey *We're Back: A Dinosaur's Story*, and *The Land before Time*.

Books: 1988, *Beasts and Behemoths: Prehistoric Creatures in the Movies* by Roy Kinnard. 1992, *When Dinosaurs Ruled the Screen* by Marc Shapiro. 1993, *The Illustrated Dinosaur Movie Guide* by Stephen Jones.

directors' appearances
in films are comparatively few. HITCHCOCK remains the unchallengeable winner, with moments in over thirty of his fifty-odd films, including the confined *Rope* (in which his outline appears on a neon sign) and *Lifeboat* (in which he can be seen in a reducing ad. in a newspaper). Preston STURGES can be glimpsed in *Sullivan's Travels*, and in *Paris Holiday*, as a French resident, gets a whole scene to himself. John HUSTON, uncredited, plays a tourist in *The Treasure of the Sierra Madre* and a master of foxhounds in *The List of Adrian Messenger*; he later began to take sizeable credited roles, e.g. in *The Cardinal* and *The Bible*. The Paramount lot became a familiar scene in many 40s pictures, with notable guest appearances by Mitchell LEISEN in *Hold Back the Dawn* and Cecil B. DE MILLE in *Sunset Boulevard*, *The Buster Keaton Story*, *Star-Spangled Rhythm*, *Variety Girl*, *Son of Paleface* and others. Jean COCTEAU played an old woman in *Orphée* and appeared throughout *The Testament of Orphée*. Nicholas RAY was the American ambassador in *55 Days in Peking*. Jules DASSIN played major roles in *Rififi* (as Perlo Vita) and *Never on Sunday*, as did Jean RENOIR in *La Règle du Jeu*. Hugo FREGONESE was a messenger in *Decameron Nights*, Samuel Fuller a Japanese cop in *House of Bamboo* and as himself in *Pierrot le Fou* and other films. Others who can be glimpsed in their own work include Tony RICHARDSON in *Tom Jones*, Michael WINNER in *You Must Be Joking*, George MARSHALL in *The Crime of Dr Forbes*, Frank BORZAGE in *Jeanne Eagels*, Robert ALDRICH in *The Big Knife*, Ingmar BERGMAN in *Waiting Women*, King VIDOR in *Our Daily Bread*, William CASTLE (producer) in *Rosemary's Baby*, Claude CHABROL in *Les Biches* and *The Road to Corinth*, and Joseph LOSEY in *The Intimate Stranger* (which he made under the name of Joseph Walton). Huston, POLANSKI, Truffaut, and BONDARCHUK are among those who have played major roles in

their own and other films. Woody ALLEN and Clint EASTWOOD are among the busiest of actor-directors.

Dirty Harry:
see HARRY CALLAHAN.

disaster films
have always been popular. In the 30s large crowds flocked to see *Tidal Wave, San Francisco, The Last Days of Pompeii, In Old Chicago* and *The Rains Came*. World War II was disaster enough for the 40s, but the 50s brought *Titanic, A Night to Remember,* and *Invasion USA,* and the 60s *The Devil at Four O'Clock* and *Krakatoa East of Java*. It was the 70s, however, that found the killing of large numbers of people to be really top box office. *Earthquake* and *The Towering Inferno* were giants of their kind, and even though *The Hindenburg* was not clever enough to attract, there were plenty of successful imitators: *The Swarm, Avalanche, Meteor,* etc. A new cycle began in the mid-90s, featuring such large-scale natural disasters as hurricanes (*Twister*), erupting volcanoes (*Dante's Peak; Volcano*) and looming asteroids (*Deep Impact; Armageddon*). TV contributions include *Smash-up on Interstate Five, Hanging by a Thread, The Death of Ocean View Park* and *Disaster on the Coastliner*.

disguise
has featured in many hundreds of films, and was in the 20s the perquisite of Lon CHANEY, all of whose later films featured it. Lon CHANEY JNR has also had a tendency to it, as had John BARRYMORE; while most of the Sherlock Holmes films involved it. Other notable examples include Henry HULL in *Miracles for Sale;* Donald WOLFIT in *The Ringer;* Marlene DIETRICH in *Witness for the Prosecution;* Jack LEMMON and Tony CURTIS in *Some Like It Hot;* Alec GUINNESS in *Kind Hearts and Coronets;* Peter SELLERS in *The Naked Truth* and *After the Fox;* Rod STEIGER in *No Way to Treat a Lady;* Tony RANDALL in *Seven Faces of Dr Lao;* John BARRYMORE in *Bulldog Drummond Comes Back;* Michael CAINE in *Sleuth;* Dustin HOFFMAN in *Tootsie;* and practically the entire cast of *The List of Adrian Messenger*. It was taken to extremes by Nicolas CAGE and John TRAVOLTA in *Face/Off,* where each was surgically altered to resemble the other, and by Tom CRUISE and Dougray SCOTT in *Mission: Impossible 2*. Extensions of disguise are the split personality films: *Dr Jekyll and Mr Hyde, Lizzie, The Three Faces of Eve, Sybil, Darkman*.
See also: TRANSVESTISM; MULTIPLE ROLES.

Django.
Eponymous machinegun-toting hero of a spaghetti western that spawned many sequels, including several that had no connection with the original, but were simply renamed outside Italy in order to cash in on the international success of a film that was banned for many years in Britain. The ploy worked because the genre so often featured a dark, morose, lone gunfighter. The first in the series, directed by Sergio CORBUCCI in 1966, starred Franco NERO, who also appeared in a sequel, *Django 2: The Big Comeback,* in 1987.

Dr Christian
was the kindly country doctor hero, played by Jean HERSHOLT, of a number of unambitious little films which came out between 1938 and 1940, based on a radio series and inspired by the publicity surrounding Dr Dafoe, who delivered the DIONNE QUINS in 1934. In 1956 Macdonald CAREY featured in a TV series of the same name, but he played the nephew of the original Dr Christian.

Dr Mabuse.
The criminal mastermind was created by novelist Norbert Jacques and first filmed in 1922 by Fritz LANG in the two-part *Doctor Mabuse, the Gambler/Doktor Mabuse, der Spieler,* starring Rudolf KLEIN-ROGGE, who repeated the role in Lang's 1933 sound film *The Testament of Dr Mabuse/Das Testament des Dr Mabuse,* which was banned by the Nazis and led to Lang fleeing to America. He returned to West Germany in 1960 to make the less successful *The Thousand Eyes of Dr Mabuse/Die Tausend Augen des Dr Mabuse* with Wolfgang PREISS in the role. In 1990, Claude CHABROL updated Jacques' original novel in *Docteur M/Club Extinction,* starring Alan BATES, but the story no longer seemed plausible.

Dr Who.
Ageless time traveller with a time machine, the Tardis, disguised as a police box. Created by producer Sydney Newman as a science-fiction TV series in 1963, its mixture of fantasy, adventure and comedy captured the imagination of the nation and became almost required viewing in the 60s, especially in adventures involving the Daleks, aliens encased in what looked like mobile pepperpots, whose conversation consisted mainly of 'Exterminate! Exterminate!' Also featuring men in rubber suits as aliens, its popularity waned as some odd choices were made in casting the title role, and its run of 695 episodes ended in 1989. It gave rise to a stage play and two dull films starring Peter CUSHING as the Doctor. On TV the role was played by William HARTNELL (with Richard HURNDALL substituting for him after his death in one episode featuring five incarnations of the Doctor), Patrick TROUGHTON, Jon PERTWEE, Tom BAKER, Peter Davison, Colin Baker, and Sylvester McCoy. A pilot for a television series produced by Steven Spielberg was shown in 1996, starring Paul McGANN in the title role, but it lacked the charm of the original.
Dr Who and the Daleks 65. Daleks: Invasion Earth 2150 AD 66.

doctors
(in the medical sense) have been crusading heroes of many movies: fictional epics that come readily to mind include *Arrowsmith, The Citadel, Magnificent Obsession, Private Worlds, Men in White, The Green Light, Disputed Passage, Yellow Jack, The Last Angry Man, Not as a Stranger, Johnny Belinda, The Girl in White, The Doctor and the Girl, Green Fingers, The Outsider, The Crime of Dr Forbes, The Interns, The New Interns, The Young Doctors, Behind the Mask, Doctor Zhivago,* and *White Corridors*. A few have even commanded whole series to themselves: *Dr Kildare, Dr Christian, Dr Gillespie, The Crime Doctor*. Once-living doctors have received the accolade of a Hollywood biopic: *The Story of Louis Pasteur, Dr Ehrlich's Magic Bullet, Prisoner of Shark Island (Dr Mudd), L'Enfant Sauvage (Dr Jean Retard), The Story of Dr Wassell, Il Est Minuit Dr Schweitzer*. Many less single-minded films have had a background of medicine and doctors as leading figures: *The Nun's Story, Kings Row, No Way Out, People Will Talk, The Hospital*. More or less villainous doctors were found in *The Flesh and the Fiends, Frankenstein, Dr Socrates, Dr Jekyll and Mr Hyde, Green for Danger, Dr Cyclops, The Hands of Orlac, Dr Goldfoot, The Amazing Dr Clitterhouse,* and *Malice*.
TV series on medical subjects have included *Medic* 54-55. *Ben Casey* 60-65. *Dr Kildare* 61-66. *Dr Christian* 56. *Dr Hudson's Secret Journal* 55-56. *The Nurses* 62-63. *The Doctors and the Nurses* 64. *Marcus Welby MD* 69. *The Bold Ones* 68-72. *Police Surgeon* 72. *St Elsewhere* 82-88. *Ryan's Four* 83. And, in the 90s, *Casualty* and *ER*.
See also: HOSPITALS.

A Dog of Flanders,
a novel written by Ouida in 1872 about a stray dog who finds a runaway boy, has been filmed five times: as a silent in 1914; and in 1924, under the title *Boy of Flanders,* by Victor SCHERTZINGER and starring Jackie COOGAN; in 1935 by Edward SLOMAN, starring Frankie Thomas; in 1959 by James B. CLARK, starring David LADD, and in 1999 by Kevin Brodie, starring Jesse James and Jeremy James Kissner as the boy.

Don Juan.
The amorous adventures of this legendary rascal, a heartless seducer created in stories by Gabriel Tellez (1571-1641), have been filmed several times, notably with John BARRYMORE in 1927, Douglas FAIRBANKS Snr in 1934, Errol FLYNN in 1948 and (of all people) FERNANDEL in 1955. Versions of the opera, *Don Giovanni,* are legion: the most elaborate was directed by Joseph LOSEY in 1979.

Don Quixote.
There have been many screen versions of Cervantes' picaresque novel about the adventures of the addled knight and his slow but faithful lieutenant Sancho Panza ... but none have been entirely successful because the genius of the book is a purely literary one. There was a French production in 1909; an American one in 1916 directed by Edward Dillon; a British one in 1923 directed by Maurice Elvey and starring Jerrold

Robertshaw with George Robey. In 1933 Pabst made a British film of the story with Chaliapin and (again) George Robey; meanwhile a Danish director, Lau Lauritzen, had done one in 1926. The next batch of Quixotes began in 1947 with Rafael Gil's Spanish version; but the Russian production of 1957, directed by Kozintsev with Cherkassov in the title role, was probably the best of all. Orson Welles filmed sections of his own version, which it looks as though we may never see, though edited versions are being screened at festivals; a Jugoslavian cartoon version appeared in 1961; in 1962 Finland, of all nations, contributed its own Quixote, directed by Eino Ruutsalo; and in 1972 the BBC and Universal made a TV film with Rex Harrison. The popular stage musical *Man of la Mancha,* filmed in 1972, is based on the life of author Miguel de Cervantes (1547-1616) and its correlation with that of his hero. There followed in 1973 a ballet version with Rudolph Nureyev.

Donald Duck.
Belligerent Disney cartoon character who was introduced in 1934 in *The Wise Little Hen,* was quickly streamlined and became more popular than Mickey Mouse. Still going strong.

Dracula.
The Transylvanian vampire count created by Bram Stoker in his novel published 1897 has been on the screen in many manifestations. Max Schreck played him in MURNAU's German silent *Nosferatu* 23. Bela LUGOSI first donned the cloak for Universal's *Dracula* 31, was not in *Dracula's Daughter* 36 but reappeared as one of Dracula's relations in *Return of the Vampire* 44 and played the Count in *Abbott and Costello Meet Frankenstein* 48. Lon CHANEY JNR starred in *Son of Dracula* 43; John CARRADINE took over in *House of Frankenstein* 45 and *House of Dracula* 45; Francis LEDERER had a go in *The Return of Dracula* 58. Also in 1958 came the British remake of the original *Dracula (Horror of Dracula)* with Christopher LEE; David Peel was one of the Count's disciples in *Brides of Dracula* 60 and Noel Willman another in *Kiss of the Vampire* 63; while Lee ingeniously reappeared in 1965 as *Dracula Prince of Darkness,* in 1968 in *Dracula Has Risen from the Grave,* in 1969 in *Taste the Blood of Dracula,* and in 1970 in *Scars of Dracula*. In the same year Ingrid PITT was *Countess Dracula* and 1972 brought *Vampire Circus*. Meanwhile the Count had American rivals in Count Yorga, in *The House of Dark Shadows* and in *Blacula*. (Hollywood in 1957 had produced a lady vampire in *Blood of Dracula,* and in 1965 *Billy the Kid Meets Dracula*. Polanski's failed satire of 1967, *The Fearless Vampire Killers,* had Ferdy MAYNE as Von Krolock, who was Dracula in all but name.) *Dracula AD 1972* and *The Satanic Rites of Dracula* were further variations on the main theme, both with Mr Lee; while Jack PALANCE in 1973 did a TV film version of the original story for Dan Curtis. It seemed that the Count, though officially dead, was unlikely ever to lie down for long; but no one could have been prepared for the profusion of Dracula variations of the late 70s, by which time Hammer had given up participating. Klaus KINSKI aped Schreck in a remake of *Nosferatu*. George HAMILTON appeared in a sexy spoof, *Love at First Bite*. Laurence OLIVIER played Van Helsing to Frank LANGELLA's *Dracula*. Would it never end? No, it wouldn't. Francis Ford COPPOLA's *Bram Stoker's Dracula* in 1992 began another frenzied cycle of vampire movies. The cycle came full circle with *Shadow of the Vampire* 00, in which Willem DAFOE played Max Schreck as a real vampire in a movie about the making of *Nosferatu*.
Books: 1987, *The Dracula Scrapbook* by Peter Haining. 1990, *Hollywood Gothic* by David J. Skal.
See also: VAMPIRES.

drag:
see TRANSVESTISM.

dreams,
with their opportunities for camera magic and mystery, are dear to Hollywood's heart. The first film with dream sequences followed by a psychological explanation was probably PABST's *Secrets of a Soul:* the trick caught on very firmly in such later pictures as *Lady in the Dark, A Matter of Life and Death, Spellbound, Dead of Night, Fear in the Night, Farewell My Lovely, The Secret Life of Walter Mitty, Possessed, Dream Girl, Three Cases of Murder* and *The Night Walker*. In *Vampyr* and *Wild Strawberries* the hero dreamed of his own funeral;

and in *Devotion* Ida Lupino dreamed of death as a man on horseback coming across the moor to sweep her away. Stories were also told as in a series of daydreams by the main character, the past mingling with the present, as in *Death of a Salesman* and *I Was Happy Here*. *Roman Scandals, A Connecticut Yankee at the Court of King Arthur, Ali Baba Goes to Town, Fiddlers Three* and *Dreaming* are but five examples of the many comedies in which a character has been knocked on the head and dreams himself back in some distant time.
In the mid-40s such films as *The Woman in the Window, The Strange Affair of Uncle Harry* and *The Horn Blows at Midnight* set the fashion for getting the hero out of some impossible situation by having him wake up and find he'd been dreaming. This was scarcely fair in adult films, though it had honourable origins in *Alice in Wonderland* and *The Wizard of Oz*. Nor is there much excuse for the other favourite script trick of having one's cake and eating it, as in *Portrait of Jennie* and *Miracle in the Rain,* when some ghostly occurrence to the hero is passed off as a dream until he finds some tangible evidence – a scarf, a coin or some other memento – that it was real.
The closest a film dream came to coming true was in *The Night My Number Came Up,* when the foreseen air crash was narrowly averted. In the brilliantly clever frame story of *Dead of Night,* the hero dreams he will commit a murder, and does, only to wake up and find the whole sequence of events beginning again: he is caught in an endless series of recurring nightmares. *A Nightmare on Elm Street* developed the idea of dreams becoming real, with its sadistic child murderer haunting the horrific dreams of a group of teenagers who burned him to death, only to find that the power of their emotions brings him back to life. Its many sequels continued the nightmare until it became quite soporific. The notion was developed with more subtlety in *Paperhouse,* in which a young girl dreams her drawings into existence. In *In Dreams,* a woman found that she could communicate with a serial killer in her dreams, while THE CELL had a psychiatrist exploring the hallucinatory-like mind of another killer.
See also: FANTASY.

Droopy.
Stony-faced, lugubrious bloodhound star of MGM cartoons. Created by Tex Avery, he was inspired by Wallace Wimple, of the popular radio comedy *The Fibber McGee and Molly Show,* played by Bill Thompson, who first supplied the voice for Droopy.
Dumb Hounded 43. The Shooting of Dan McScrew 45. Señor Droopy 49. Caballero Droopy 52. Dixieland Droopy 54. Millionaire Droopy 56. One Droopy Knight (AAN) 57. Sheep Wrecked 58, etc.

drug addiction,
long forbidden by the Hays Code, even in Sherlock Holmes films (though it featured in Chaplin's *Easy Street* in 1917), has recently been the subject of many intense reforming movies such as *The Man with the Golden Arm, A Hatful of Rain, Bigger than Life, Monkey on My Back* and *Synanon. Confessions of an Opium Eater,* on the other hand, is a throwback to the Hollywood films of the 20s, when almost every adventure involved a chase through a Chinatown opium den. The addiction has provided plots for many thrillers about the tireless efforts of agents of the US Narcotics Bureau: *Johnny Stool Pigeon, To the Ends of the Earth, Sol Madrid, The Poppy is Also a Flower, The French Connection,* etc. In the late 60s drugs began to be advocated as a permissible opting out, or to be freely and seriously discussed, in such films as *The Trip, Chappaqua* and *Beyond the Valley of the Dolls; Panic in Needle Park; Born to Win; Believe in Me; Jennifer on my Mind;* and *Lenny*.

drunk scenes
have been the delight of many actors as well as audiences. Who can judge between the charms of the following? Greta Garbo in *Ninotchka;* Robert Montgomery in *June Bride;* Jean Arthur in *Mr Smith Goes to Washington;* Laurel and Hardy in *The Bohemian Girl* and *Scram;* Lionel Barrymore in *A Free Soul;* Eva Marie Saint in *That Certain Feeling;* Errol Flynn in *The Sun Also Rises;* Katharine Hepburn in *The Desk Set;* Leslie Caron in *Father Goose;* Fredric March in *There Goes My Heart;* Lee Marvin in *Cat Ballou* (accompanied by a drunken horse); Albert Finney in *Saturday Night and Sunday Morning;* Alan Bates in *A Kind of Loving;* Bette Davis in *Dark Victory;* Claudia Cardinale in *The*

Pink Panther; Charles Laughton in *Hobson's Choice;* Katharine Hepburn in *The Philadelphia Story* and *State of the Union;* Lucille Ball in *Yours Mine and Ours;* Arthur Askey in *The Love Match;* Dan Dailey in *It's Always Fair Weather;* Vanessa Redgrave in *Isadora;* Julie Andrews in *Star!;* Dudley Moore in *Arthur;* Dean Martin and Tony Curtis in *Who Was That Lady?* Martin indeed deliberately built himself an off-screen alcoholic reputation, as did W. C. Fields.
See also: ALCOHOLICS.

Dudley Do-Right,
a dim-witted, good-hearted Mountie, was a regular on the TV cartoon series *Rocky and His Friends* 59-61, *The Bullwinkle Show*, which was originally shown 61-63 and re-broadcast frequently, and *The Dudley Do-Right Show* 69-70. A live-action movie of his exploits, starring Brendan FRASER and written and directed by Hugh WILSON, was released in 1999.

duels
are fought in hundreds of low-budget action dramas, but the well-staged ones are rare enough to be recounted. Basil Rathbone fought Errol Flynn in *The Adventures of Robin Hood* (and later spoofed the occasion in *The Court Jester*). He also lost to Tyrone Power in *The Mark of Zorro;* Flynn also encountered Rathbone in *Captain Blood* and Henry Daniell in *The Sea Hawk*. Douglas Fairbanks Snr fought duels in *The Mark of Zorro*, *The Black Pirate* and others; Douglas Fairbanks Jnr was a memorable opponent for Ronald Colman in *The Prisoner of Zenda* (later restaged for James Mason and Stewart Granger and mimicked by Tony Curtis and Ross Martin in *The Great Race*) and duelled again in *The Corsican Brothers*. Granger also duelled with Mason in *Fanny by Gaslight*, but used pistols this time; it was back to foils again for *Scaramouche* and *Swordsman of Siena*. John Barrymore fought splendid duels in his silent films, notably *Don Juan* and *General Crack*, later opposing Rathbone in *Romeo and Juliet*. In the 40s Cornel Wilde became fencer in chief, in such films as *Bandit of Sherwood Forest*, *Forever Amber* and *Sons of the Musketeers*. All the versions of *The Three Musketeers* involved duelling, but Gene Kelly turned it into a splendid series of acrobatic feats. Paul Henreid duelled in *The Spanish Main*, Larry Parks in *The Swordsman*, Fredric March in *The Buccaneer*, Charlton Heston in *El Cid*, Louis Hayward in half a dozen low-budgeters. In more serious films Ferrer duelled in *Cyrano de Bergerac* and Olivier in *Hamlet*, and there was a pistol duel in the Russian *War and Peace* and the Italian *Colpi di Pistola*. The most recent major films to feature duels are *Barry Lyndon*, *Royal Flash* and the ultimate *The Duellists*.

The East Side Kids.
Set up in 1939 by Monogram as a Poverty Row challenge to the Dead End Kids, the original team consisted of Hally Chester, Harris Berger, Frankie Burke, Donald Hines, Eddie Brian and Sam Edwards. They were later joined by Bobby Jordan and Leo Gorcey from Dead End, and within a few years elements of both rival gangs were absorbed into the Bowery Boys.

El Santo.
Silver-masked Mexican wrestler who was a star of the ring and of more than 50 cheap, popular and profitable adventure movies in which he defeated crooks, monsters, vampires, werewolves and extra-terrestrials. He first appeared in films in *Santo – El Enmascarado de Plata* 52, but the series proper began in 1961 with *Santo versus the Diabolic Brain* and ended in 1982 with *Santo versus the Television Assassin*. It was probably not always the same actor behind the mask. Most often, it was Rodolfo Guzmán HUERTA, but Eric del Castillo may have taken the role in some of the films. Occasionally El Santo was paired with a rival masked wrestler, Blue Demon (El Demonio Azul), played by Alejandro Cruz. In versions of the films dubbed into English, the character is sometimes renamed Samson.

the electric chair
has figured prominently in innumerable gangster and prison movies, notably *Two Seconds*, *Twenty Thousand Years in Sing Sing*, *Angels with Dirty Faces* and *The Last Mile*. *Front Page Woman* concentrated on the reporters ushered in to watch. The death cell scenes in *Double Indemnity* were deleted before the film's release. The most horrific sequence of this kind was the gas chamber climax of *I Want To Live*.

elephants
have come closest to starring roles in *Zenobia*, *Elephant Boy* and *Hannibal Brooks;* but they were the subject of concern in *Chang*, *Where No Vultures Fly*, *Elephant Walk*, *Maya*, and *Roots of Heaven*, and Tarzan and Dorothy Lamour (in her jungle days) usually had one around as a pet. (*Tarzan Goes to India* had a splendid elephant stampede.) Circus elephants were stars of *Jumbo*, and above all of *Dumbo*.

elevators:
see LIFTS.

Ellery Queen.
The fictional American detective was played by four actors between 1935 and 1943: Donald Cook, Eddie Quillan, Ralph Bellamy and William Gargan. The name is a pseudonym for two authors: Frederick Dannay (1905-82) and Manfred Lee (1905-71). In 1971 Peter Lawford turned up in a TV movie, *Don't Look Behind You*, and in 1975 there was a TV series with Jim Hutton, following a 1954 one with George Nader.

Elmer Fudd.
Warner Brother's cartoon star. An adversary of Bugs Bunny, Elmer is a constantly frustrated wabbit-hunter noted for his deer-stalker hat, double-barrelled shotgun, and his inability to pronounce the letter 'r'. He made his debut in 1939 in a Tex Avery cartoon.

Dangerous Dan McFoo 39. Wabbit Twouble 41. An Itch in Time 43. Hare Remover 46. Hare Do 49. Rabbit Fire 51. Rabbit Seasoning 52. Robot Rabbit 53. Hare Brush 55. Pre-Hysterical Hare 58. What's My Lion? 61, etc.

the end of the world
has been fairly frequently considered in movies, and not only in panic button dramas like *Dr Strangelove*, *The Bedford Incident* and *Fail Safe*. Movement of the earth was threatened in *The Day the Earth Stood Still* and stopped (by Roland Young) in *The Man Who Could Work Miracles*. Plague very nearly ended everything in *Things to Come*. Danger from other planets looming perilously close was only narrowly averted in *Red Planet Mars*, while in *When Worlds Collide* and *The Day the Earth Caught Fire* the worst happened. Another kind of danger was met in *Crack in the World*. The Martians nearly got us in *The War of the Worlds*. In *Five* there were only five people left alive, in *The World, the Flesh and the Devil* only three, and in *On the Beach* none at all. The world was saved at the last moment from being pulverized by huge asteroids in two disaster movies of 1998, *Deep Impact* and *Armageddon*.

Enoch Arden
was a character in a Tennyson poem who came back to his family after having been long supposed dead. Films with an 'Enoch Arden' theme include *Tomorrow Is Forever* (with Orson Welles), *The Years Between* (with Michael Redgrave), *My Two Husbands* (with Fred MacMurray) and its remake *Three for the Show* (with Jack Lemmon), *My Favourite Wife* (with Irene Dunne) and its remake *Move Over Darling* (with Doris Day), *Piccadilly Incident* (with Anna Neagle), *Return from the Ashes* (with Ingrid Thulin), *Desire Me* (with Robert Mitchum), *Laura* (with Gene Tierney), *Man Alive* (with Pat O'Brien), and *The Man from Yesterday* (with Clive Brook). D. W. Griffith in 1910 and 1911 made short versions of the original story.

entertainers,
including actors and impresarios, have frequently been the subject of biopics, and if all their stories have seemed much the same, that is Hollywood's fault rather than theirs. Here is a reasonably comprehensive list:

Always Leave Them Laughing Milton Berle, *After the Ball* Pat Kirkwood as Vesta Tilley, *Bound for Glory* David Carradine as Woody Guthrie, *The Buddy Holly Story* Gary Busey, *The Buster Keaton Story* Donald O'Connor, *Champagne Charlie* Tommy Trinder as George Leybourne and Stanley Holloway as the Great Vance, *Chaplin* Robert Downey Jnr as Charlie Chaplin, *The Dolly Sisters* Betty Grable & June Haver, *The Doors* Val Kilmer as Jim Morrison, *The Eddie Cantor Story* Keefe Brasselle, *The Fabulous Dorseys* Tommy and Jimmy Dorsey, *W. C. Fields and Me* Rod Steiger as W. C. Fields, *The Five Pennies* Danny Kaye as Red Nichols, *Frances* Jessica Lange as Frances Farmer, *Funny Girl* Barbra Streisand as Fanny Brice, *Gable and Lombard* James Brolin and Jill Clayburgh, *The Gene Krupa Story* Sal Mineo, *The Glenn Miller Story* James Stewart, *Great Balls of Fire* Dennis Quaid as Jerry Lee Lewis, *The Great Caruso* Mario Lanza, *The Great Ziegfeld* William Powell, *Gypsy* Natalie Wood as Gypsy Rose Lee, *Harlow* Carroll Baker/Carol Lynley, *The Helen Morgan Story* Ann Blyth, *Houdini* Tony Curtis, *The I Don't Care Girl* Mitzi Gaynor as Eva Tanguay, *Incendiary Blonde* Betty Hutton as Texas Guinan, *Interrupted Melody* Eleanor Parker as Marjorie Lawrence, *Jeanne Eagels* Kim Novak, *The Joker is Wild* Frank Sinatra as Joe E. Lewis, *The Jolson Story* Larry Parks, *La Bamba* Lou Diamond Phillips as Richie Valens, *A Lady's Morals* Grace Moore as Jenny Lind, *Lady Sings the Blues* Diana Ross as Billie Holiday, *Lady With Red Hair* Miriam Hopkins as Mrs Leslie Carter and Claude Rains as David Belasco, *Leadbelly* Roger E. Mosley, *Lenny* Dustin Hoffman as Lenny Bruce, *Lillian Russell* Alice Faye, *Look for the Silver Lining* June Haver as Marilyn Miller, *Love Me or Leave Me* Doris Day as Ruth Etting, *Man of a Thousand Faces* James Cagney as Lon Chaney, *Melba* Patrice Munsel, *Peg of Old Drury* Anna Neagle as Peg Woffington, *Prince of Players* Richard Burton as Edwin Booth, *The Seven Little Foys* Bob Hope as Eddie Foy, *Shine on Harvest Moon* Ann Sheridan as Nora Bayes, *Somebody Loves Me* Betty Hutton as Blossom Seeley, *So This Is Love* Kathryn Grayson as Grace Moore, *Star!* Julie Andrews as Gertrude Lawrence and Daniel Massey as Noël Coward, *The Story of Vernon and Irene Castle* Fred Astaire and Ginger Rogers, *The Story of Will Rogers* Will Rogers Jnr, *Tonight We Sing* David Wayne as Sol Hurok, *Too Much Too Soon* Dorothy Malone as Diana Barrymore and Errol Flynn as John Barrymore, *With a Song in My Heart* Susan Hayward as Jane Froman, *Yankee Doodle Dandy* James Cagney as George M. Cohan, *Young Man With a Horn* Kirk Douglas as Bix Beiderbecke, *Your Cheatin' Heart* George Hamilton as Hank Williams.

Movies made for TV include: *Bud and Lou* Buddy Hackett and Harvey Korman as Abbott and Costello, *Elvis* Kurt Russell as Presley, *Elvis and Me* Dale Midkiff as Elvis, *James Dean* Stephen McHattie, *The Jayne Mansfield Story* Loni Anderson with Arnold Schwarzenegger as Mickey Hargitay, *The Legend of Valentino* Franco Nero, *Liberace* Andrew Robinson, *Liberace: Behind the Music* Victor Garber, *Marilyn: The Untold Story* Catherine Hicks as Monroe, *Rainbow* Andrea McArdle as the young Judy Garland, *Rita Hayworth: The Love Goddess* Lynda Carter, *Sophia Loren: Her Own Story* Sophia Loren as herself and her mother, John Gavin as Cary Grant, Edmund Purdom as Vittorio De Sica.

epidemics
featured memorably in *Jezebel*, *Yellow Jack*, *Arrowsmith*, *The Rains Came*, *Forever Amber*, *Panic in the Streets*, *The Killer that Stalked New York*, *Elephant Walk No Blade of Grass*, *The Andromeda Strain*, *Eighty Thousand Suspects*, *The Omega Man*, *Things to Come*, *Isle of the Dead*, *The Satan Bug*, *The Seventh Seal* and *Outbreak*.

episodic films
in a sense have always been with us – *If I Had a Million*, after all, came out in 1932, and *Intolerance* in 1916 – but it was in the 40s, possibly spurred by the all-star variety films intended to help the war effort, that they achieved their greatest popularity. Julien Duvivier, who had made *Un Carnet de Bal* in Paris, remade it in Hollywood as *Lydia* and followed it with *Tales of Manhattan* which was linked by a tailcoat and *Flesh and Fantasy* which was linked by the ramblings of a club bore. The stories in *Forever and a Day* were held together by a house, *Easy Money* by football pools, *Train of Events* by a railway accident, *Meet Mr Lucifer* by television. Then came the author complex: *Quartet* (Somerset Maugham), *Le Plaisir* (Maupassant), *Meet Me Tonight* (Noël Coward). The French took over with films like *The Seven Deadly Sins*, *The Devil and Ten Commandments*, *Life Together;* and the Italians were at it with *Four Kinds of Love*, *Made in Italy* and *The Queens*. For English-speaking markets the form was killed in the mid-50s by the advent of the half-hour TV play, but the 60s saw a brief revival with *How the West Was Won* and *The Yellow Rolls-Royce*. The 80s showed signs: the Italians were at it again with *Sunday Lovers* and Hollywood assigned four directors to one story each for *Twilight Zone*.

epitaphs
Over the years, a few stars have been nudged by the press into composing their own epitaphs. Herewith a selection of this grave humour.
• *W. C. Fields:* On the whole, I'd rather be in Philadelphia.
• *Cary Grant:* He was lucky – and he knew it.
• *Edward Everett Horton:* A nice part – only four 'sides', but good company and in for a long run.
• *Lionel Barrymore:* Well, I've played everything but a harp.
• *Hedy Lamarr:* This is too deep for me.
• *Dorothy Parker:* Excuse my dust.
• *Warner Baxter:* Did you hear about my operation?
• *William Haines:* Here's something I want to get off my chest.
• *Lewis Stone:* A gentleman farmer goes back to the soil.
• *Constance Bennett:* Do not disturb.
• *Wallace Ford:* At last I get top billing.
• *Preston Sturges:*
Now I've laid me down to die
I pray my neighbours not to pry
Too deeply into sins that I
Not only cannot here deny
But much enjoyed as time flew by...

Eskimos
have seldom been seriously tackled by the cinema. Documentaries abound, from *Nanook of the North* to *Eskimo*, and *Ukaliq* is a charming cartoon of Eskimo folklore, but the fictional stuff such as *Savage Innocents* and *The White Dawn* has been dull and unsympathetic. The most authentic was probably *Igloo* 32, starring CHEEAK, but it failed to attract audiences, as did the more recent *Shadows of the Wolf/Agaguk* 93.

excerpts
from films are sometimes incorporated into other films in which characters go to a cinema or watch television. So in *Hollywood Cavalcade* Don Ameche watched a rough-cut of *The Jazz Singer*, just as ten years later Larry Parks in *Jolson Sings Again* watched a rough-cut of himself in *The Jolson Story;* an unidentified silent comedy was being played in the room below when the first murder took place in *The Spiral Staircase;* Linda Christian and Louis Jourdan saw *Son of the Sheik* at their local in *The Happy Time*, and Fredric March and his son watched a William S. Hart film in *One Foot in Heaven*. Prisoners watched *Wings of the Navy* during *Each Dawn I Die* and *The Egg and I* during *Brute Force;* and the chain gang in *Sullivan's Travels* roared with laughter at a Mickey Mouse cartoon. Footage from *Phantom of the Opera* was shown in *Hollywood Story*, from *Comin' thru' the Rye* in *The Smallest Show on Earth*, from *Tol'able David* in *The Tingler*, from *Queen Kelly* in *Sunset Boulevard*, from *Camille* in *Bridge to the Sun*, from *Destination Tokyo* in *Operation Pacific*, and from *Boom Town* in *Watch the Birdie*. Other movies shown in 'cinemas' in later films include: *Uncle Tom's Cabin* in *Abbott and Costello Meet the Keystone Kops; Gold Diggers of 1933* in *Bonnie and Clyde; Crossroads* in *The Youngest Profession; Casablanca* in *First to Fight; Red River* in *The Last Picture Show; Hell Divers* in *The Wings of Eagles; Task Force* in *White Heat; The Walking Dead* in *Ensign Pulver; Tin Pan Alley* in *Wing and a Prayer; Now Voyager* in *Summer of '42; Red Dust* in *Heavy Traffic;* various Bogart films in *Play It Again Sam; Caprice* in *Caprice* (Doris Day went to the movies, saw herself on the screen, and didn't like it). In *Two Weeks in Another Town*, which had a plot pretty close to that of *The Bad and the Beautiful*, Kirk Douglas watched himself in – *The Bad and the Beautiful!* The Bette Davis character in *Whatever Happened to Baby Jane?* was criticized as a bad actress on the strength of clips from early Bette Davis movies, *Ex-Lady* and *Parachute Jumper*. In the same film Joan Crawford watched herself on TV in *Sadie McKee;* and in *Walk Don't Run* there was a flash of James Stewart dubbed in Japanese in *Two Rode Together*. Finally the cosmonauts on their space station in *Conquest of Space* were entertained by a showing of *Here Come the Girls* ... thus showing, as one critic remarked, that in 50 years' time TV will still be relying on old movies!

Other uses for old footage in new films include such gags as Bob Hope in *Road to Bali* meeting up with Humphrey Bogart in *The African Queen;* and economy dictates such measures as the ten-minute chunk of *The Mummy* at the beginning of *The Mummy's Hand* and the use in *Singin' in the Rain*, as part of a 'new' picture in production, of sequences from Gene Kelly's version of *The Three Musketeers*.

Similarly bits of *The Sheik* were in *Son of the Sheik*, and *Topper* in *Topper Takes a Trip*. Great chunks of the *Joan of Arc* battles turned up in *Thief of Damascus*, as did *The Black Knight* in *Siege of the Saxons* and *The Four Feathers* in *Storm Over the Nile* and *East of Sudan*. Universal's *Sword of Ali Baba* used so much footage from their *Ali Baba and the Forty Thieves* that one actor had to be engaged to replay his original part! It was, however, wit rather than economy that persuaded Preston Sturges to open *Mad Wednesday* with the last reel of *The Freshman* and the Boris Karloff clips were central to the concept of *Targets*. As for *Dead Men Don't Wear Plaid*, the new footage was constructed entirely to fit in with clips from old movies, so that the hero appeared to be taking part in 40s scenes with the likes of Dorothy Lamour and Alan Ladd.

explorers

have inspired many documentaries but surprisingly few features except wholly fictitious ones like *Trader Horn*, *She* and *The Lost World*. *Marco Polo* has thrice been dealt with, and *Christopher Columbus* got the full Rank treatment as well as featuring in the satirical *Where Do We Go from Here?* The Pilgrim Fathers were the heroes of *Plymouth Adventure*, and Drake of *Seven Seas to Calais*. Lewis and Clark in *The Far Horizons* were played by Fred MacMurray and Charlton Heston. *Scott of the Antarctic* was played by John Mills, and Amundsen in *The Red Tent* by Sean Connery; Pierre Radisson in *Hudson's Bay* by Paul Muni; Cortez in *Captain from Castile* by César Romero; Pizarro in *The Royal Hunt of the Sun* by Robert Shaw; Junipero Serra in *Seven Cities of Gold* by Michael Rennie. *Penn of Pennsylvania* and *Stanley and Livingstone* were in the practical sense explorers, though driven by other motives; *Aguirre Wrath of God* seemed to be driven chiefly by greed.

Fair Game.

Paula Gosling's thriller about a cop who uses a female witness as bait to catch a serial killer was filmed as *Cobra* in 1986, directed by George Pan Cosmatos and starring Sylvester Stallone. The emphasis was on the cop. In 1995 it was remade under its original title, the emphasis now being on the woman, who was played by leading model Cindy Crawford in her first film role. Neither movie enjoyed much critical or commercial success.

fairy tales:

see FANTASY.

The Fall of the House of Usher.

This grisly tale by Edgar Allan Poe was filmed by Jean Epstein in 1928, by Americans Melville Webber and James Watson in the same year, by British semi-professionals in 1950, by Roger Corman in 1960, and by Allan Burkinshaw in 1988.

falling

is, of all man's inherited fears, the one most spectacularly played on by Hollywood, where the shot of the villain's hand slipping away from the hero's frenzied grasp, followed by a quick-fading scream, has become a screen stereotype. Harold Lloyd's skyscraper comedies played on this fear, as have the films of many comedians since; in *The Horn Blows at Midnight*, for instance, Jack Benny is only one of six people hanging on to each other's coat-tails from the top of a high building. All circus films, and that includes *The Marx Brothers at the Circus*, base one or two of their thrills on trapeze acts that might go wrong. And whenever a villain starts climbing upwards, as Ted de Corsia did in *Naked City*, or along a ledge, as the same accident-prone Ted de Corsia did in *The Enforcer*, the audience grits its teeth and waits for the inevitable. The whole action of *Fourteen Hours* was based on the question whether a potential suicide would or would not jump from a ledge.

Some of the screen's most spectacular falls include Walter Abel's in *Mirage*, the key to the whole action; Agnes Moorehead's (through a window) in *Dark Passage*; Charlotte Henry's in *Alice in Wonderland*; Cedric Hardwicke's in *Hunchback of Notre Dame*; W. C. Fields' (from an aeroplane) in *Never Give a Sucker an Even Break*; Alan Ladd's (through a roof) in *The Glass Key*; Slim Pickens' (on the bomb) in *Dr Strangelove*; Eleanor Parker's in *An American Dream*; *King Kong's* (from the top of the Empire State Building); William Bendix's from a skyscraper in *The Dark Corner*. To Alfred Hitchcock, falls are a speciality: Edmund Gwenn fell from Westminister Cathedral in *Foreign Correspondent*, Norman Lloyd from the torch of the Statue of Liberty in *Saboteur*, while *Vertigo* not only boasted three falls but based its entire plot on the hero's fear of heights. Falls under trains and buses are legion, but in *The Well* a little girl fell down an old wellshaft, in *The List of Adrian Messenger* a victim fell to his death in a lift (as did characters in *Hotel* and *House of Wax*, while in *Ivy* Joan Fontaine fell down a lift shaft), in Somerset Maugham's *Encore* an acrobat hoped to fall safely into a water tank; and an unnamed gentleman was pushed out of *The High Window* by Florence Bates.

the family

is the centre of most people's lives, so naturally there have been many memorable film families. Those popular enough to have warranted a series include the Joneses, the Hardys, the Huggetts, the Wilkinses of *Dear Ruth*, *The Cohens and the Kellys*, the Bumsteads of *Blondie* and the *Four Daughters* saga. World War II brought a sentimental attachment to the family which in Hollywood expressed itself in *Happy Land*, *The Human Comedy*, *Our Town*, *The Happy Time*, *Since You Went Away*, *Meet Me in St Louis*, *A Genius in the Family*, *The Sullivans* and *The Best Years of Our Lives*; in Britain, *Salute John Citizen*, *The Holly and the Ivy*, *Dear Octopus*, *Quiet Wedding*, *This Man is Mine*. Semi-classical treatments of the theme include *Cavalcade*, *The Swiss Family Robinson*, *Pride and Prejudice*, *Little Women*, *Scrooge* and *Whiteoaks*. Odd families, ranging from the merely sophisticated to the downright bizarre, were seen in *Three Cornered Moon*, *The Old Dark House*, *The Royal Family of Broadway*, *My Man Godfrey*, *You Can't Take It With You*, *The Young in Heart*, *The Little Foxes*, *Tobacco Road*, *The Bank Dick*, *House of Strangers*, *An Inspector Calls*, *Sweethearts*, *Treasure Hunt*, *Holiday*, *The Philadelphia Story*, *The Anniversary*, and *The Lion in Winter*. Vaudeville families were seen in *Yankee Doodle Dandy*, *The Merry Monahans*, *The Seven Little Foys*, *The Buster Keaton Story* and *There's No Business Like Show Business*. There has been a fashion for the large family, started by *Cheaper by the Dozen* and *Chicken Every Sunday* in 1949 and reprised by *With Six You Get Egg Roll* and *Yours Mine and Ours* in 1968 and a TV series *The Brady Bunch* in 1969. Other charming families have included those in *Our Vines Have Tender Grapes*, *Background*, *The Happy Family*, *Four Sons*, *The Holly and the Ivy*, *Made in Heaven*, *29 Acacia Avenue*, *Little Murders*, *Never Too Late*, *This Happy Breed* and *My Wife's Family*; but the most memorable family of all is likely to remain the Joads in *The Grapes of Wrath*, unless it is one of the real families put under the microscope by American and British TV.

Fanny.

Originally one of Marcel PAGNOL's 1932-34 trilogy (the others: *Marius* and *César*) about the Marseilles waterfront, this tale of a girl left pregnant by a sailor was almost unrecognizable in the MGM version *Port of Seven Seas* 38. The film was subsequently turned into a stage musical, and in 1960 Joshua LOGAN filmed this – but deleted the songs. The stars were Leslie CARON, Maurice CHEVALIER, and Charles BOYER.

fans

have been with us as long as the star system. One way of describing them is as people who adore an actor whatever he's doing and whether he's good or not. Another definition is: 'People who tell an actor he's not alone in the way he feels about himself.' Judy Garland once played a fan when she sang 'Dear Mr Gable'; and MGM made a whole movie about them, called *The Youngest Profession*. *The Fan* who pursued Lauren Bacall was quite another matter, a homicidal lunatic; and Eve in *All About Eve* was another fan who didn't do her star any good. The baseball fan in *The Fan* 96 became so upset that he kidnapped a player's son and threatened to murder him.

fantasy

has always been a popular form of cinema entertainment because the camera can lie so well, and trick work is most easily used in an unrealistic or fanciful story. The early films of Méliès and his innumerable imitators set a high standard and were still popular when the sombre German classics of the 20s – *The Golem*, *Nosferatu*, *Faust*, *Warning Shadows*, *The Niebelungen Saga*, *Metropolis* – awakened filmgoers to the possibilities of the medium for sustaining impossible situations throughout a whole serious feature.

Although Ince's *Civilisation* showed Christ on the battlefields, and the 20s brought such films as *The Four Horsemen of the Apocalypse*, *The Lost World* and *The Sorrows of Satan*, Hollywood did not fully explore the possibilities of fantasy until sound. Then in quick succession picturegoers were startled by *Outward Bound*, *Dracula*, *Frankenstein*, *Berkeley Square*, *King Kong* and *The Invisible Man*. *The Scoundrel*, with Noël Coward, was the forerunner of the few serious ghost films: *The Uninvited*, *The Return of Peter Grimm*, *Earthbound*, *The Ghost and Mrs Muir*, *Portrait of Jennie*, *The Haunting*, etc. Comic ghosts have, of course, been legion, notably in the *Topper* films, *The Ghost Breakers*, *I Married a Witch*, *The Canterville Ghost*, *The Man in the Trunk*, *The Remarkable Andrew*, *Thirteen Ghosts*, *The Spirit Is Willing*, *Blackbeard's Ghost*, *Wonder Man*, and so on. There were even singing ghosts in *Maytime*, *Bitter Sweet* and *Carousel*. Britain's contributions to the genre were few but choice: *The Ghost Goes West*, *Blithe Spirit*, *Things to Come*, *The Man Who Could Work Miracles*, *A Matter of Life and Death*, *Dead of Night*.

In 1936 *Green Pastures* showed the Negro view of heaven, and *On Borrowed Time* three years later paved the way for the heavenly comedies of the 40s: *Here Comes Mr Jordan*, *That's the Spirit*, *A Guy Named Joe*, *Heaven Can Wait*, *Down to Earth*, *The Horn Blows at Midnight*, *You Never Can Tell*, even *Ziegfeld Follies* (in which Ziegfeld's shade wrote in his diary 'Another *heavenly* day...'). For many years the last in this vein was *Carousel* 56; but 1968 brought *Barbarella* with its slightly tarnished angel, and *The Adding Machine* had its own perverse view of the hereafter. Meanwhile objects with magical properties were well served in *Alf's Button Afloat*, *A Thousand and One Nights*, *The Thief of Baghdad*, *Turnabout* and *The Picture of Dorian Gray*.

Among the many fairy tales filmed are *The Bluebird*, *The Wizard of Oz*, *Alice in Wonderland*, *The Glass Slipper*, *Tom Thumb*, *Mary Poppins* and a selection in *Hans Christian Andersen* and *The Wonderful World of the Brothers Grimm*. Disney's cartoon versions included *Pinocchio*, *Dumbo*, *The Sleeping Beauty*, *Cinderella*, *Peter Pan*, and, of course, *Snow White and the Seven Dwarfs*, which was cannily adapted for grown-ups by Billy Wilder as *Ball of Fire*. *Lost Horizon* was a kind of grown-up fairy tale too; and *The Red Shoes* as shown was certainly not for children. Original fairy tales for both categories were *The Luck of the Irish*, with Cecil Kellaway as a leprechaun, and *Miracle on 34th Street*, with Edmund Gwenn as Santa Claus. Modern fairy tales adapted for the screen include: *Chitty Chitty Bang Bang*, *Mary Poppins*, *Bedknobs and Broomsticks* and *Willy Wonka and the Chocolate Factory*.

In France during the occupation Marcel Carné made *Les Visiteurs du Soir*, a medieval fantasy with allegorical overtones, and after the war poet Jean Cocteau once again turned his attention to the cinema with such results as *La Belle et la Bête*, *Love Eternal*, *Orphée*, and *The Testament of Orphée*. More recently Albert Lamorisse has produced fantasies like *Crin Blanc* and *The Red Balloon*. Japan electrified the world with *Rashomon* and other strange, fanciful, stylized entertainments; Russia contributed many solidly-staged versions of old legends like *Sadko* and *Epic Hero and the Beast/Ilya Muromets*.

Since 1950, when in Hollywood Dick Powell played an Alsatian dog in *You Never Can Tell* and James Stewart in *Harvey* had a white rabbit six feet high which the script could never quite categorize as fact or hallucination, fantastic elements have been infiltrating into supposedly realistic films to such an extent that it is now difficult to separate them, especially in the films of Fellini, Antonioni, Tony Richardson, Richard Lester and Robert Altman.

See also: DREAMS; HORROR; PROPHECY; SPACE EXPLORATION.

farce

was once called 'tragedy with its trousers down'. Like melodrama, it presents exaggerated accounts of things that might happen in life. Comedy is more plausible than farce, but farce is often more enjoyable, involving more happenings, more chases, more doors slamming, more misunderstandings and mistaken identities. Good farce must be played with great style, and no lapses are permitted until the curtain comes down. Major exponents in Britain have been the Aldwych team of Tom Walls, Ralph Lynn and Robertson Hare and the Whitehall team headed by Brian Rix. In Hollywood good farce has been more occasional, but one might highlight *Nothing Sacred*, *To Be or Not to Be*, *Topper Returns*, *Love Crazy* and *The Palm Beach Story* (or almost anything else by Preston Sturges, who so delighted in controlled disorder). France gave us Fernandel and Pierre Etaix. The real trouble with farce on film is that it needs an audience: watched cold, it can often seem merely silly, and great stage farces such as Feydeau's *Hotel Paradiso* don't really translate.

Farewell, My Lovely.

Raymond CHANDLER's thriller of private eye Philip Marlowe searching for the girlfriend of an ex-convict was first filmed as vehicle for George SANDERS' suave detective The Falcon (based on a character created by Michael Arlen) in *The Falcon Takes Over* 42. It was more faithfully and successfully remade two years later as *Murder, My Sweet/Farewell, My Lovely*, starring Dick POWELL. In 1975, Dick RICHARDS made another good version with Robert MITCHUM in the lead.

A Farewell to Arms.

Hemingway's tough-romantic anti-war novel has been filmed twice: in 1932 by Frank BORZAGE, with Gary COOPER and Helen HAYES, and in 1957 by Charles VIDOR, with Rock HUDSON and Jennifer JONES. Neither version was a triumph artistically, but the first proved more popular than the second, which was badly inflated by David O. SELZNICK into a pseudo-epic.

fashions

were the basis of many a woman's film of the 30s: *Roberta*, *Fashions of 1934*, *Vogues of 1938*. Later attempts to recapture this interest had an air of *déjà vu*: *Maytime in Mayfair*, *It Started in Paradise*, *Lucy Gallant*, *Designing Woman*. But the wheel turns, and the 70s brought *Mahogany*, the 80s *Chanel Solitaire* and the 90s *Ready to Wear/Prêt-à-Porter*.

fastest money-making movies:

Independence Day holds the record, taking $104m at the US box-office in six days in 1996. It beat *Jurassic Park*, which took $100m in nine days in 1993. *Independence Day* reached $200m in 20 days, while *Jurassic Park* took 23. In 1989, *Batman* took 10 days to reach that mark, while *Batman Returns* took 11 days in 1992.

Father Brown.

The only British attempt to film the adventures of G. K. CHESTERTON's tubby detective in 1958 was a civilized comedy with all concerned on the same wavelength. A quietly witty script by Thelma Schnee, polished direction by Robert HAMER, and high-comedy acting by Alec GUINNESS, Peter FINCH, Joan GREENWOOD, and Ernest THESIGER made it a film with a rare flavour. On television, Kenneth MORE played the role in a 1974 series. In 1934 Walter CONNOLLY played the role in a Hollywood second feature, *Father Brown Detective*. In West Germany, Heinz Ruhmann played the role in two 60s films, and Josef Meinrad in a 1969 TV series. In 1980 Barnard Hughes played the priest on TV in *The Girl in the Park*.

FBI.

The US governmental crime-fighting agency was set up in 1924 by J. Edgar Hoover and became famous for its heroic stand against the public enemies of the 30s, when its agents became known as G-Men. Surface glamour concealed an immensely painstaking organization relying heavily on science, but only the glamour was shown in such films as *Show 'Em No Mercy*, *G-Men*, *Persons in Hiding*, *Let 'Em Have It*, *The FBI Story*, *FBI Girl*, *Parole Fixer*, *Confessions of a Nazi Spy*, *FBI Code 98*, *Walk East on Beacon* and *Queen of the Mob*. *The House on 92nd Street* in 1945 gave the best impression of the FBI at work, but its sequel *The Street with No Name* reverted to stereotype, which was maintained by Quinn Martin's nine-year TV series. In 1978, *The Private Files of J. Edgar Hoover* provided a rather superficial exposé.

Felix (the Cat).

Cartoon creation of Pat Sullivan, a perky and indestructible character highly popular in the 20s; in the 50s revived for TV by other hands in more streamlined style. An unsuccessful full-length feature, directed by Tibor Hernadi, was released in 89.

female impersonation:
see TRANSVESTISM.

fights
provide the climax to many a film, but only the outstandingly staged ones remain in the mind. The slugging match between the two heroes of *The Spoilers* became a tradition, as each of the five versions tried to outdo the previous one. John Wayne had many fighting triumphs, notably against Victor McLaglen in *The Quiet Man; McLintock* and *North to Alaska* seemed at times to have more brawling than dialogue. Spoof fights were probably topped by the saloon brawl in *The Great Race;* serious ones by the solemn allegorical punch-up in *The Big Country*. Other good western fights are found in *Shane*, *The Sheepman*, and (between Dietrich and Una Merkel) in *Destry Rides Again*. For viciousness within a serious picture the waterfront fights in *Edge of the City* and *On the Waterfront* take some beating. Bruce LEE, Jackie CHAN and other athletic Chinese actors introduced some spectacular fighting techniques to the West in their films. By the 1990s these influenced fight sequences in such movies as *The Matrix*, choreographed by Yuen WOO-PING, who also choreographed the spectacular hig-flying fights in Ang LEE's *Crouching Tiger, Hidden Dragon* 00.

film-making
is not too frequently used as a background for movies, as movies about movies are thought to be bad box office. Certainly not too many of the following were big hits: *OK for Sound*, *The Best Pair of Legs in the Business*, *Go for a Take*, *The Comedy Man*, *The Bad and the Beautiful*, *Two Weeks in Another Town*, *It's a Great Feeling*, *Shooting Stars*, *Pick a Star*, *A Star is Born*, *The Carpetbaggers*, *Eight and a Half*, *Hellzapoppin*, *Day for Night*, *Stand In*, *Singin' In The Rain*, *Abbott and Costello Meet the Keystone Kops*, *Gable and Lombard*, *Harlow*, *W.C. Fields and Me*, *The Big Knife*, *Once in a Lifetime*, *Wonderful Life*, *Hollywood Cavalcade*, *Hollywood Boulevard*, *Hollywood Story*, *Nickelodeon*, *The Last Tycoon*, *Everything for Sale*, *The Stunt Man*, *Crimes and Misdemeanors*, *The Big Picture*, *The Player*, *Living in Oblivion*, *Swimming with Sharks*, *Cecil B. Demented*, *State and Main*.

films à clef
are those which appear to be fiction but are really based on factual cases with the names changed. The obvious example is *Citizen Kane*, which parallels the career of William Randolph Hearst. Others are *The Great Dictator*, in which Hynkel is obviously Hitler; *Compulsion*, *Rope*, and *Swoon*, based on the Leopold and Loeb murder; *Inherit the Wind*, about the Scopes monkey trial; *The Moon and Sixpence*, in which Charles Strickland stands in for Paul Gauguin; *The Man Who Came to Dinner*, in which Sheridan Whiteside is Alexander Woollcott, Banjo is Harpo Marx, and Beverly Carlton is Noël Coward; *Young Cassidy*, drawn from the early life of Sean O'Casey; *All About Eve*, in which Margo Channing was said to be Tallulah Bankhead and Addison de Witt George Jean Nathan; *Twentieth Century*, in which Oscar Jaffe is an amalgam of Jed Harris and David Belasco; *All the King's Men* and *A Lion is in the Streets*, both essentially about Huey Long; *The Lost Moment*, in which the old lady is allegedly Claire Clairemont, the aged mistress of Byron; *The Adventurers*, in which the characters are supposedly based on Porfirio Rubirosa, Barbara Hutton, Aristotle Onassis and Maria Callas; *The Carpetbaggers*, plainly about Howard Hughes; *Little Caesar*, who was clearly Al Capone; *Major Barbara*, in which Adolphus Cusins was Gilbert Murray; *Call Me Madam*, based on the exploits of Perle Mesta; *The Winslow Boy*, based on the Archer-Shee case, with Sir Robert Morton standing in for Sir Edward Carson; *An American Tragedy*, from the real life Chester Gillette murder case; *Monsieur Verdoux*, who was Landru; *Death of a Scoundrel*, from the career of Charles Rubenstein; *The Prisoner*, inspired by the sufferings of Cardinal Mindzenty; *Fame is the Spur*, in which Homer Radshaw was Ramsay MacDonald; and if you like, *Dr Jekyll and Mr Hyde*, whose story was inspired by the burglarious second life of Deacon William Brodie; or even any Sherlock Holmes story, as Holmes was modelled on Dr Joseph Bell. *Where Love Has Gone* was modelled on the Lana Turner case in which her daughter murdered her lover; and *Imitation of Life* also reflected the Turner career, as *Dancing Lady* and *Torch Song* reflected Joan Crawford's. *The Barefoot Contessa* was vaguely drawn from Rita Hayworth's international goings-on, though the star who played her, Ava Gardner, was also no slouch in the fun department. *Bombshell* was an obvious echo of Jean Harlow's own troubles with hangers-on. *I Could Go on Singing* featured Judy Garland clearly playing herself; *The Devil Is a Woman* can be seen as Sternberg's farewell to Dietrich (with Lionel Atwill playing himself), just as Orson Welles cast himself as bedevilled by his then wife Rita Hayworth in *The Lady from Shanghai*. The leading roles in *Will Success Spoil Rock Hunter?*, *After the Fox*, *The Band Wagon*, *Blondie of the Follies* and *Kiss Me Stupid* were clearly based on those who played them: Jayne Mansfield, Victor Mature, Fred Astaire, Marion Davies and Dean Martin. The same can be said of Gloria Swanson in *Sunset Boulevard*, Bette Davis in *The Star*, Errol Flynn in *The Sun Also Rises*, Hedy Lamarr in *The Female Animal*, Marlene Dietrich in *No Highway*, John Wayne in *The Shootist*, John Barrymore in *The Great Profile* and Zero Mostel in *The Front*. *The Goddess* reflected Marilyn Monroe's marriage with Joe Di Maggio. *Flight for Freedom*, though not using Amelia Earhart's name, gave a fictional solution to the aviatrix's real-life disappearance. *Funny Girl* was the official biography of Fanny Brice, but *Rose of Washington Square* also had lots of similarities. *All About Eve's* leading character, Margo Channing, according to its creator, was based on Elisabeth Bergner. *New York New York* seemed to be taken from Doris Day's autobiography. *Smash-Up* was allegedly based on the drinking problems of Bing Crosby's first wife Dixie Lee, just as *Written on the Wind* had connections with the suicide of Libby Holman's first husband. Evangelist Aimee Semple McPherson was clearly impersonated by Barbara Stanwyck in *The Miracle Woman* and by Jean Simmons in *Elmer Gantry*. Columnist Walter Winchell was parodied in several Lee Tracy vehicles – Tracy even looked like him – and also by Burt Lancaster in *Sweet Smell of Success*. The Robert Ryan character in *Caught* was allegedly based on Howard Hughes. Bette Midler in *The Rose* is obviously Janis Joplin. *The Greek Tycoon* is clearly inspired by Aristotle Onassis and Jackie Kennedy. In *It's Tough to Be Famous*, Douglas Fairbanks Jnr could only be Charles Lindbergh. James Cagney and Pat O'Brien in *Boy Meets Girl* were inspired by Charles MacArthur and Ben Hecht. In *The Last Tycoon*, Robert de Niro was Irving Thalberg. Anne Baxter in *You're My Everything* was Clara Bow. The sliding marriage in *A Star Is Born* could have been based on Al Jolson and Ruby Keeler, or on John Gilbert and Greta Garbo. Patty Duke in *Valley of the Dolls* was Judy Garland. And so on.

fire
is a standard part of the melodramatist's equipment, whether it be used for disposing of country houses with too many memories (*Dragonwyck*, *Rebecca*, *The Lost Moment*, *The Fall of the House of Usher*, *The Tomb of Ligeia*, *Gone with the Wind*) or whole cities (*Forever Amber*, *In Old Chicago*, *Quo Vadis*, *City on Fire*). Sometimes, as in *House of Wax*, it makes a splendid starting point; though to judge from *She* one can't rely on its life-prolonging qualities. Its use in realistic films is rare, though cases of arson were seriously studied in *On the Night of the Fire* and *Violent Playground*. The fires of hell were most spectacularly recreated in the 1935 version of *Dante's Inferno*. Comedies about firemen include *Where's That Fire?* (Will Hay), *Fireman Save My Child*, *Harvey Middleman Fireman*, and *Go to Blazes* (Dave King); and firemen who start fires instead of putting them out are prophesied in *Fahrenheit 451*. Oil fires were spectacularly depicted in *Tulsa*, *Wildcat*, and *Hellfighters*. The classic study of conventional firemen remains *Fires Were Started*; TV series which took up the theme include *Emergency*, *Firehouse* and *London's Burning*. For many, the greatest screen fire will be the burning of Atlanta in *Gone with the Wind*, but *The Towering Inferno* was probably the most spectacular. *Backdraft* is another where the flames stole the picture. *Endless Love* was brought to an end by a pyromaniac, *Firestarter* dealt with a psychic who could set anything ablaze, while *Quest for Fire* dealt with a Stone Age tribe who weren't able to set anything alight after their fire went out. Finally, fire was always a splendid aid for serial producers, as the oft-used title 'Next Week: Through the Flames' may suggest.

See also: FOREST FIRES.

firing squads
have figured chiefly in films about World War I (*Paths of Glory*, *King and Country*) or those telling the lives of spies (*Mata Hari*, *Nurse Edith Cavell*, *Carve Her Name With Pride*). Other uses have been in *Dishonoured*, *The Fugitive*, *Custer of the West*, *The Victors*, *The Long Ride Home*, *Reach for Glory*, *The Counterfeit Traitor* and *The Ceremony*; and firing squads were given a comic effect in *The Captain's Paradise*, *Casino Royale*, *Morgan* and *The Ambushers*.

The Flag Lieutenant.
The stiff-upper-lip stage melodrama by W. P. Drury and Lee Trevor, about the intrepid exploits of a naval officer in an outpost of empire, was filmed as a silent in 1919 with George Wynn, and in 1926 with Henry Edwards. In 1932 Edwards appeared in a sound remake with Anna Neagle as his leading lady.

Flash Gordon.
American newspaper strip hero whose exploits were featured in three famous Hollywood serials starring Buster Crabbe. In the original *Flash Gordon* 36 our hero and his friends saved the Earth from collision with another planet at the cost of being stranded there at the mercy of the wicked Emperor Ming. *Flash Gordon's Trip to Mars* 38 and *Flash Gordon Conquers the Universe* 40 were compounded of similar elements. The directors respectively were Frederick Stephani; Ford Beebe and Robert Hill; and Ray Taylor. A softcore spoof, *Flesh Gordon*, appeared in 1974. In 1980 Dino de Laurentiis presented a lavish but empty remake of the original, and in the following year came a cartoon remake from Filmation.

The Flintstones.
An animated TV suburban situation comedy set in the Stone Age, created by Bill Hanna and Joe Barbera, was turned into a feature film using actors in 1994. In the cartoon version, Fred Flintstone was voiced by Alan Reed, his wife Wilma by Jean Vanderpyl, and their pet dinosaur, Dino, by Mel BLANC, who also supplied the voice for their neighbour Barney Rubble. Broadcast from 1960-66 and often repeated, it owed much to an earlier TV sitcom, *The Honeymooners*, starring Jackie GLEASON, and became the longest-running animated show on television; its spin-offs included *The Flintstone Kids*, broadcast in the late 80s. In the feature film, John GOODMAN appeared as Fred, Rosie O'DONNELL as Wilma, and Rick MORANIS as Barney. Its sequel, *The Flintstones in Viva Rock Vegas* had Mark ADDY as Fred, Kristen Johnson as Wilma, and Stephen BALDWIN as Barney.

fog
has been a godsend to many a cinematic entertainment, whether it's the genuine pea-souper inseparable from Hollywood's idea of London, or the ankle-high white mist which used to distinguish heaven and dream sequences. Fog can provide a splendid dramatic background, especially in horror-thrillers like *Dracula*, *The Wolf Man* and *The Cat and the Canary*; but too often it is simply imposed on a film to force a particular atmosphere, as in *Footsteps in the Fog*, *Fog over Frisco*, *Fog Island*, *Winterset*, *Out of the Fog* and *The Notorious Landlady*. *Barbary Coast* seemed to be permanently enveloped in fog, as did the village in *Sherlock Holmes and the Scarlet Claw:* while in *The Adventures of Sherlock Holmes* London had fog in May! Fog was dramatically used in *The VIPs* and *The Divorce of Lady X* (for bringing people together in a hotel); in *The Runaway Bus* (for bringing people together in an abandoned village); in *Midnight Lace* (for masking the identity of the voice threatening Doris Day); in *Twenty-Three Paces to Baker Street* (for hampering the villain but not the blind hero); in *Alias Nick Beal* (as a background for the devil's materialization); in *The Lost Continent* (as a nauseous yellow background for the weird community); in *Random Harvest* (as a means for the hero's escape); and in the various versions of *The Sea Wolf* (for causing the accident that brings hero and heroine together on Wolf Larsen's boat). Even comedies find it useful: the chase through fog in *After the Fox* results in happy confusion. Oddly enough John Carpenter's film *Fog* made insufficient use of its titular commodity.

Foghorn Leghorn.
Boastful rooster from the Deep South, a star of Warner Brothers' Merrie Melodies and Looney Tunes cartoons. His voice was supplied by Mel BLANC.

Walky Talky Hawky (AAN) 46. The Foghorn Leghorn 48. Leghorn Swoggled 51. All Fowled Up 55. The High and the Flighty 56. Fox Terror 57. A Broken Leghorn 59. Strangled Eggs 61. Banty Raids 63, etc.

Folies Bergère.
This innocuous 1935 musical comedy was written by Bess MEREDYTH and Hal Long as a vehicle for Maurice CHEVALIER, who played a dual role; at the climax his double had to masquerade to his wife as himself. It was too good an idea not to be used again. In 1941 came *That Night in Rio* with Don AMECHE; in 1951, there was *On the Riviera* with Danny KAYE. Kaye apparently liked it so much that he had it altered a little and it served for *On the Double* 61 as well.

the Foreign Legion
has been taken reasonably seriously in the three versions of *Beau Geste*, the two versions of *Le Grand Jeu*, *Beau Sabreur*, *China Gate*, *Rogue's Regiment*, *Ten Tall Men*, and *The Legion's Last Patrol*. It was sent up something wicked by LAUREL and HARDY in *Beau Hunks* and *The Flying Deuces;* by ABBOTT and COSTELLO *In the Foreign Legion;* and by the CARRY ON gang in *Follow That Camel*, and treated very seriously by Claire Denis in the obsessive *Beau Travail* 99.

forest fires
have made a roaring climax for many films including *The Blazing Forest*, *Red Skies of Montana*, *Guns of the Timberland*, *The Bluebird*, *The Big Trees* and *Ring of Fire*. None was more dramatic than the cartoon version in *Bambi*.

The Fox.
Name of an actor-detective played by Red SKELTON in three films directed by S. Sylvan SIMON. He plays an actor who plays The Fox, hero of a radio series, and finds himself called upon to solve crimes in the real world. The character Skelton plays resembles that projected by Bob HOPE in many of his films of the period – a wisecracking coward who nevertheless comes good and gets the girl (played in Skelton's films by Ann SOTHERN).

Whistling in the Dark 41. Whistling in Dixie 42. Whistling in Brooklyn 43.

Fox and the Crow.
Stars of Columbia Pictures' (1941-47) and UPA's (1948-50) cartoons. Created by Frank Tashlin, Fox was voiced by Frank Graham and Crow by Paul Frees.

The Fox and the Grapes 41. Woodman Spare That Tree 42. Slay It with Flowers 43. The Dream Kids 44. Treasure Jest 45. Tooth or Consequences 47. Robin Hoodlum (AAN) 48. Magic Fluke (AAN) 49. Punchy De Leon 50, etc.

Francis.
The talking mule of several Universal comedies (1950-56) was the direct ancestor of TV's talking palomino *Mister Ed*, also produced by Arthur Lubin. Francis' first master was Donald O'CONNOR, but later Mickey ROONEY took over the reins. Francis was 'voiced' by Chill WILLS, Ed by Allan LANE.

Frankenstein.
The man/monster theme was explored in American movies of 1908 (with Charles Ogle) and 1916 (*Life Without Soul*); also in Italy in 1920 (*Master of Frankenstein*). The 1931 Hollywood film, written by Robert Florey and directed by James WHALE, borrowed as much from Wegener's *The Golem* 22 as from Mary Shelley's early 19th-century novel; but despite censorship problems the elements jelled, with Boris KARLOFF a great success as the monster composed from dead bits and pieces, and a legend was born. Sequels included *Bride of Frankenstein* 35. *Son of Frankenstein* 39. *Ghost of Frankenstein* 41. *Frankenstein Meets the Wolf Man* 43. *House of Frankenstein* 45. *House of Dracula* 45. *Abbott and Costello Meet Frankenstein* 48; among those who took over from Karloff were Lon CHANEY, Bela LUGOSI and Glenn STRANGE. In 1956 the original story was remade in Britain's Hammer Studios under the title *The Curse of Frankenstein;* colour

and gore were added, and sequels, with various monsters, came thick and fast: *The Revenge of Frankenstein* 58. *The Evil of Frankenstein* 63. *Frankenstein Created Woman* 67. *Frankenstein Must Be Destroyed* 69. *Horror of Frankenstein* 70. *Frankenstein and the Monster from Hell* 73. A variation on the original monster make-up was used by Fred Gwynne in the TV comedy series, *The Munsters* 64-65. There have also been several recent American, Japanese and Italian attempts to cash in on the name of Frankenstein in cheap exploitation pictures: *I Was a Teenage Frankenstein* 57. *Frankenstein 1970* 58. *Frankenstein Versus the Space Monsters* 65. *Frankenstein Conquers the World* 68. *Lady Frankenstein* 70, etc. In 1973 a four-hour TV version called *Frankenstein: The True Story* (which it could scarcely be) was co-authored by Christopher Isherwood but proved merely a laborious reworking of the earlier films, with occasional references back to the book, but no humour. Films about Mary Shelley's creation of Frankenstein appeared towards the end of the 80s: *Haunted Summer, Gothic* and *Frankenstein Unbound*, and *Mary Shelley's Frankenstein*, directed by Kenneth Branagh with Robert De Niro as the monster, appeared in 1994.

Book: 1994, *The Illustrated Frankenstein Movie Guide* by Stephen Jones.

Friday the 13th.
A series of low-budget horror movies about serial killer Jason Vorhees, who wears a hockey mask and, in the style of such films, murders teenagers. The first, produced and directed by Sean S. Cunningham, became a cult hit among young audiences and was turned into a computer game. The later films were low on quality and inspiration. In 1995 there were plans to team Jason and New Line's other horror creation, Freddy Kruger (of *Nightmare on Elm Street*), together in a film.

Fritz the Cat.
Randy feline, created by cartoonist Robert Crumb, who appeared in various magazines of the 60s and was the star of two animated adult features: *Fritz the Cat* 72. *The Nine Lives of Fritz the Cat* 74.

The Front Page.
Ben Hecht and Charles MacArthur's indestructible, fast-moving, witty and cynical play about journalists and politicians has been filmed four times: in 1931, directed by Lewis Milestone with Pat O'Brien as reporter Hildy Johnson and Adolphe Menjou as editor Walter Burns; in 1940, as the superlative *His Girl Friday*, directed by Howard Hawks, with Rosalind Russell as Hildy and Cary Grant as Burns; in 1974, directed by Billy Wilder, with Jack Lemmon as Hildy and Walter Matthau as Burns; and in 1988, as *Switching Channels*, directed by Ted Kotcheff, with Kathleen Turner and Burt Reynolds. Hecht thought the best performance of Hildy was by Lee Tracy in the original 1928 Broadway production, in which Osgood Perkins also triumphed as Walter Burns.

Fu Manchu.
Sax Rohmer's oriental master-criminal was played by Harry Agar Lyons in a series of British two-reelers in the 20s. Warner Oland played him in *The Mysterious Fu Manchu* 29, *The Return of Fu Manchu* 30 and *Daughter of the Dragon* 31; Boris Karloff in *Mask of Fu Manchu* 32, and Henry Brandon in *Drums of Fu Manchu* 41. Otherwise he was oddly neglected until the 60s series starring Christopher Lee, beginning with *The Face of Fu Manchu* 65 and *Brides of Fu Manchu* 66: it degenerated into shambling nonsense. Peter Sellers took the role in a lamentable spoof, The Fiendish Plot of Dr Fu Manchu, 79.

funerals
provided a starting point for *The Third Man, Frankenstein, The Great Man, Death of a Salesman, The Bad and the Beautiful, Citizen Kane,* and *Keeper of the Flame*; figured largely in *The Premature Burial, The Mummy, The Egyptian, The Fall of the House of Usher, The Counterfeit Traitor, Funeral in Berlin, The Godfather, The Glass Key, I Bury the Living, Miracle in Milan, Doctor Zhivago* and *Hamlet*; and formed a climax for *Our Town* and *Four Weddings and a Funeral*. In *Vampyr* and *Wild Strawberries* the hero dreamed of his own funeral; and in *Holy Matrimony* Monty Woolley attended his own funeral, having arranged to have his valet's body mistaken for his. Funerals were taken lightly

in *I See a Dark Stranger, Little Caesar, Kind Hearts and Coronets, Too Many Crooks, A Comedy of Terrors, Charade, The Wrong Box, I Love You Alice B. Toklas, Robin and the Seven Hoods, Monsieur Hulot's Holiday, Entr'acte, Ocean's Eleven, Comrade X, What a Way to Go, The Private Life of Sherlock Holmes,* and above all *The Loved One*. One of the funniest, and touching, moments came in *Orphans* 99, with Gary Lewis bent ever-more double as he insists on carrying his mother's coffin on his own.

funfairs
have provided fascinating settings for many a bravura film sequence. *The Wagons Roll at Night, Nightmare Alley, Dante's Inferno, Rollercoaster* and *The Ring* were set almost entirely on fairgrounds. Tawdry or 'realistic' funfairs were shown in *Jeanne Eagels, Saturday Night and Sunday Morning, East of Eden, Picnic,* and *Inside Daisy Clover*; glamorized or sentimentalized ones cropped up in *The Wolf Man, My Girl Tisa, State Fair, Roseanna McCoy, The Great Ziegfeld* and *Mr and Mrs Smith*. Musicals like *On the Town, On the Avenue, Coney Island, Centennial Summer, State Fair* and *Down to Earth* had funfair sequences and they are also used to excellent advantage in thrillers:

Brighton Rock, Spider Woman, Horrors of the Black Museum, Gorilla at Large, The Third Man, Lady from Shanghai, Strangers on a Train. Naturally funfairs are also marvellous places for fun: though not for Eddie Cantor in *Strike Me Pink*, Tony Curtis in *Forty Pounds of Trouble*, Laurel and Hardy in *The Dancing Masters*, or Bob Hope (fired from a cannon) in *Road to Zanzibar*. *The Beast from 20,000 Fathoms* was finally cornered in a funfair; *Dr Caligari* kept his cabinet in one. The star who made the most of a funfair sequence was undoubtedly Mae West as the carnival dancer in *I'm No Angel*, in which she delivered her famous line: 'Suckers!'

gambling,
in the indoor sport sense, is quite a preoccupation of film-makers. Gregory Peck in *The Great Sinner* played a man who made a great career of it, as did James Caan in *The Gambler* and George Segal in *California Split*; while in *The Queen of Spades* Edith Evans learnt the secret of winning at cards from the devil himself. Other suspenseful card games were played in *The Cincinnati Kid, Lucky Jordan, The Lady Eve, Hazard, Big Hand for a Little Lady, The Music of Chance* and *Lock, Stock and Two Smoking Barrels*; snooker pool was the game in *The Hustler* and *The Color of Money*; old-time Mississippi river-boats were the setting for *Mississippi Gambler, The Naughty Nineties, Frankie and Johnny* and a sequence in *The Secret Life of Walter Mitty*. Roulette, however, is the most spectacular and oft-used film gambling game, seen in *The Shanghai Gesture, Robin and the Seven Hoods, Ocean's Eleven, The Big Snatch, Doctor No, La Baie des Anges, Quartet* (the 'Facts of Life' sequence), *Seven Thieves, The Las Vegas Story, The Only Game in Town, The Big Sleep, Gilda, Kaleidoscope,* and many others. Second features with such titles as *Gambling House, Gambling Ship* and *Gambling on the High Seas* were especially popular in the 40s. Musically, the filmic high-point was undoubtedly the 'oldest established permanent floating crap game in New York' number in *Guys and Dolls*. This stemmed from the writings of Damon Runyon, also adapted in such films as *Sorrowful Jones* and *The Lemon Drop Kid*. The most comic game on film was perhaps the hand of poker played between Judy Holliday and Broderick Crawford in *Born Yesterday*.

gangsters,
a real-life American menace of the 20s, provided a new kind of excitement for early talkies like *Little Caesar* and *Public Enemy*, which told how their heroes got into criminal activities but didn't rub in the moral very hard. The pace of the action, however, made them excellent movies, and critics defended them against religious pressure groups. *Quick Millions, Scarface, Lady Killer, The Little Giant* and *Public Enemy's Wife* were among the titles which followed; then Warner Brothers cleverly devised a way of keeping their thrills while mollifying the protesters: they made the policeman into the hero, in films like *G-Men, I Am the Law, Bullets or Ballots*. By 1938 it seemed time to send up the whole genre in *A Slight Case of Murder*, with its cast of corpses, and in the later *Brother Orchid* the gangster-in-chief became a monk; yet in 1939 the heat had cooled off sufficiently to allow production of *The Roaring Twenties*, one of the most violent gangster movies of them all. The war

made gangsters old-fashioned, but in the late 40s Cagney starred in two real psychopathic toughies, *White Heat* and *Kiss Tomorrow Goodbye*. After that the fashion was to parody gangsterism, in *Party Girl, Some Like It Hot*, and a couple of Runyon movies; but the success of a French film called *Rififi* and a TV series called *The Untouchables* left the field wide open for redevelopment. Successes in the 60s included *Bonnie and Clyde, The St Valentine's Day Massacre, Pay or Die, The Rise and Fall of Legs Diamond, King of the Roaring Twenties,* and from the French *Borsalino* and various *Rififi* sequels. The 70s brought British gang violence in *Get Carter, Villain, The Squeeze* and *Sweeney*, and in 1972 the gigantic success of *The Godfather* spawned sequels, rivals (*The Valachi Papers*) and parodies (*The Gang That Couldn't Shoot Straight*). Britain showed that it could make gangster movies in the American style with *The Long Good Friday*, but there were few successors, although *The Krays* followed the fortunes of its most notorious criminals. Alan Parker's *Bugsy Malone* parodied the Chicago gangster movies by having one acted by kids armed with pop guns, but the era continued to fascinate film-makers. Sergio Leone's epic *Once Upon a Time in America*, hacked about by its producers on its first release, became available on video-cassette in an uncut version. Brian De Palma remade *Scarface* as a film about Hispanic gangsters and turned *The Untouchables* into a big-screen success. Coppola's examination of the Mafia was extended into *The Godfather II* and *III*, while Marlon Brando parodied his title role in *The Freshman*. Martin Scorsese had a hit with *GoodFellas* while Shakespeare's *Macbeth* was turned into a gangland movie in *Men of Respect*. Jonathan Demme found some humour in the subject of a Mafia widow fleeing the gangs in *Married to the Mob*. In the 90s, the hot subject became the gangs' involvement in drug-dealing. Abel Ferrera's *The King of New York* traced the rise of a white drug baron and his black confederates taking over from the Mafia, while *New Jack City* showed a gang turning an apartment block into a fortified drug factory. It was almost a relief to return to the simpler antics of the 50s in Bill Duke's *A Rage in Harlem*. In the late 90s British directors turned to crime in numbers, led by Guy Ritchie with *Lock, Stock and Two Smoking Barrels* and *Snatch*. But there was also *The Criminal, Gangster No 1, Essex Boys, Sexy Beast, Love, Honour and Obey, Circus,* and *Going Off Big Time*. The best was John Boorman's *The General*, based on the life of Dublin gangster Martin Cahill, who also inspired *Ordinary Decent Criminal*. In America, the Mafia found itself the subject of psychoanalysis in *Analyse This* and, especially, the much-praised TV series *The Sopranos*.

The Garden of Allah.
Robert Hichen's novel, about a sophisticated woman whose husband turns out to be an escaped Trappist monk, was filmed as a silent in 1917, with Tom Santschi and Helen Ware, and again in 1927 with Ivan Petrovich and Alice Terry. The 1936 sound remake had excellent early colour, elegant direction by Richard Boleslawski, and exotic performances from Charles Boyer and Marlene Dietrich.

Gaslight.
Patrick Hamilton's stage suspense thriller, about a Victorian wife deliberately being driven insane by her murderous husband, was perfectly filmed in Britain in 1940 by Thorold Dickinson with Anton Walbrook, Diana Wynyard, and Frank Pettingell. MGM promptly bought and destroyed the negative, and in 1944 produced an opulent and inferior remake with Charles Boyer, Ingrid Bergman (AA), and Joseph Cotten, directed by George Cukor. In Britain this version was known as *The Murder in Thornton Square*; prints of the original did survive and have been shown in America as *Angel Street*.

Gentlemen Prefer Blondes.
Anita Loos's comic novel about a gold-digging 20s chorus girl on the make in the millionaire set was filmed in 1928 by Mal St Clair, with Ruth Taylor and Alice White, then in 1953 by Howard Hawks with Marilyn Monroe and Jane Russell. Hawks's film was followed in 1955 by a sequel of sorts, *Gentlemen Marry Brunettes*, directed by Richard Sale and starring Jane Russell and Jeanne Crain.

George of the Jungle
was a blundering apeman created by Jay Ward, which ran as a TV cartoon series 67-70. It lost money for its creator, but the character was turned into a successful live-action film in 1997, starring Brendan Fraser in the title-role. Fraser went on to play another character created by Ward in *Dudley Do-Right* 99.

Gerald McBoing Boing.
A smiling little boy who could only make sounds, created by author Dr Seuss and the hero of four UPA cartoons. The spareness of line and sharpness of wit, particularly in the first of the series, contrasted happily with Disney's chocolate-box period.

Gerald McBoing Boing (AA) 51. *Gerald McBoing Boing's Symphony* 53. *How Now Boing Boing* 54. *Gerald McBoing Boing on the Planet Moo* (AA) 56.

Gertie the Dinosaur.
Early American cartoon character created by Winsor McKay in 1909.

The Ghost Breaker.
This American stage thriller by Paul Dickey and Charles W. Goddard, about an heiress's voodoo-haunted castle, was filmed in 1915 with H. B. Warner and in 1922, directed by Alfred E. Green, with Wallace Reid. In 1940 George Marshall directed a talkie version as a vehicle for Bob Hope, and the result was an oddly successful combination of laughs and horror, with contributions from Willie Best, Paulette Goddard and Paul Lukas. (The title, incidentally, was made plural.) In 1953 Marshall remade it, with remarkable fidelity to the 1940 script, as a vehicle for Dean Martin and Jerry Lewis under the title *Scared Stiff*, with Lizabeth Scott and Carmen Miranda; the results were hardly stimulating.

The Ghost Train.
This hugely successful British stage comedy-thriller by Arnold Ridley (also an actor best known for playing Private Godfrey in the long-running television series *Dad's Army*), about stranded passengers at a lonely Cornish station being used by gun-runners, was first filmed in 1928, directed by Geza Bolvary, with Guy Newall as the silly-ass hero who turns out to be a policeman. A talkie version followed in 1931 with Jack Hulbert, directed by Walter Forde, who also directed the 1941 remake in which the leading role was split between Arthur Askey and Richard Murdoch.

ghosts:
see FANTASY.

giants
are infrequently encountered in films, but Harold Lloyd met one in *Why Worry?*, as did Abbott and Costello in *Lost in a Harem*. Costello also met *The Thirty Foot Bride of Candy Rock*, not to be confused with *The Attack of the Fifty Foot Woman*. Then there was *The Giant of Marathon*, and Glenn Langan played *The Amazing Colossal Man* in two films. Back to Abbott and Costello again: it was they who appeared with Buddy Baer in *Jack and the Beanstalk*. The lofty Romanian-born basketball player Gheorghe Muresan played the the title role in *My Giant* 98.

Gidget.
An American teenager of the early 60s, a kind of female Andy Hardy. The first film was released in 1959 and starred Sandra Dee. Then in 1961 came *Gidget Goes Hawaiian* with Deborah Walley, and in 1963 *Gidget Goes to Rome* with Cindy Carol. In 1969 and 1971 there were TV movies called *Gidget Grows Up* with Karen Valentine, and *Gidget Gets Married* with Monie Ellis; in 1972 came a cartoon version, *Gidget Makes the Wrong Connection*. In 1965 there was also a TV series with Sally Field.

gigolos
are figures from another age, when women could be imposed on, but they were memorably played by David Niven in *Dodsworth*, Montgomery Clift in *The Heiress*, Fred MacMurray in *The Lady is Willing*, Burt Lancaster in *Sorry Wrong Number*, William Holden in *Sunset Boulevard*, Van Johnson in *Invitation*, Bekim Fehmiu in *The Adventurers*, Jon Voight in *Midnight Cowboy*, Charles Grodin in *The Heartbreak Kid*, Helmut Berger in *Ash Wednesday*, David Bowie in *Just a Gigolo* and Richard Gere in *American Gigolo*. The

was turned into a Broadway musical, and *Aladdin* 92, and, with various songwriters, *The Lion King* 94 and *Pocahontas* 95. Whether there is any long-term future for the musical other than as an accompaniment to animation may depend on the success or otherwise of Andrew Lloyd Webber's *Evita*, directed by Alan Parker, which has taken 19 years from its first stage performance in 1978 to reach the cinema.

Books: *Gotta Sing Gotta Dance* by John Kobal. *The Hollywood Musical* by John Russell Taylor. *All Singing, All Dancing* by John Springer. 1987, *The American Film Musical* by Rick Altman.
See also: ENTERTAINERS.

Mutiny on the Bounty.
Three films have been made of this semi-historical account of how Captain Bligh was cast adrift in an open boat in 1787: the first was directed in 1935 by Frank Lloyd with Clark Gable and Charles Laughton, in a performance that launched a thousand impersonations; the second, in 1962, was directed by Carol Reed (who resigned) and Lewis Milestone, with Marlon Brando and Trevor Howard; the most recent, *The Bounty*, was directed by Roger Donaldson in Australia in 1984, with Anthony Hopkins and Mel Gibson.

My Man Godfrey.
The crazy comedy about a family of bored millionaires brought to heel by a butler they pick up in the gutter has been filmed twice: in 1936 by Gregory La Cava with William Powell and Carole Lombard; and in 1957 by Kenry Koster with David Niven and June Allyson.

My Sister Eileen.
The stories by Ruth McKenney about two sisters on the hunt for fame and men in New York was turned first into a play and then a film by Joseph Fields and Jerome Chodorov; directed by Alexander Hall, it starred Rosalind Russell and Janet Sherwood as the sisters; Richard Quine remade it in 1955 as a semi-musical with Betty Garrett and Janet Leigh. A Broadway musical of 1953, *Wonderful Town*, was also based on the stories, and there was a TV series with Elaine Stritch and Shirley Bonne, 1960-61. (In real life, Eileen McKenney married writer Nathanael West and died with him in a car crash.)

mystery
has always been a popular element of motion picture entertainment. Always providing scope for sinister goings-on and sudden revelations, mystery films divide themselves into two basic genres: who done it, and how will the hero get out of it? Silent melodramas like *The Perils of Pauline* were full of clutching hands and villainous masterminds, devices adopted by the German post-war cinema for its own purposes: *The Cabinet of Dr Caligari*, *Dr Mabuse* and *Warning Shadows* are all mysteries, peopled by eccentrics and madmen. American silent who-done-its like *The Cat and the Canary*, *The Thirteenth Chair* and *One Exciting Night* set a pattern for thrillers which could not come fully into their own until music and sound were added. In the 30s the 'thunderstorm mystery', with its spooky house and mysterious servants (the butler usually did it) quickly became a cliché; but this is not to denigrate the entertainment value of such movies as *The Bat*, *The Terror*, *Murder by the Clock*, *The Gorilla*, *Seven Keys to Baldpate*, *Double Door*, *You'll Find Out*, *Topper Returns*, *The House on Haunted Hill*, and the Bob HOPE remakes of *The Cat and the Canary* and *The Ghost Breakers*.

The 30s also saw a movement to relegate the puzzle film to the detective series, a genre later taken over eagerly by TV. These films were built around such protagonists as Charlie Chan, Sherlock Holmes, Hercule Poirot, Inspector Hanaud, Ellery Queen, Perry Mason, Inspector Hornleigh, Nero Wolfe, Philo Vance, Nick Carter, The Crime Doctor, The Saint, The Falcon, Bulldog Drummond, Mrs Pym, the 'Thin Man' (the thin man was actually the victim of the first story, but the tag stuck to William Powell), Mr Moto, Michael Shayne, Hildegarde Withers, Mr Wong, Arsène Lupin, Dick Barton, The Baron, The Toff, Gideon, Slim Callaghan, Lemmy Caution and Maigret ... all soundly spoofed by Groucho MARX as Wolf J. Flywheel in *The Big Store*. The best of these fictional detectives were the creations of Dashiell HAMMETT (Sam Spade in *The Maltese Falcon*) and Raymond CHANDLER (Philip Marlowe in *The Big Sleep*, *Farewell My Lovely* and *The High Window*); and after a twenty-year hiatus the threads were picked up by Ross MACDONALD's *Harper*, Craig STEVENS as Gunn, Frank SINATRA as *Tony Rome*, films of Chandler's *Marlowe* and J.D. MACDONALD's *Darker Than Amber*, and Richard ROUNDTREE, and much later Samuel L. JACKSON, as *Shaft*. Single who-done-its of great merit were *Gaslight*, *Laura*, *Green for Danger* (one ached for a whole series starring Alastair SIM as Inspector Cockrill), *The Spiral Staircase*, *Crossfire*, *Boomerang*, *Bad Day at Black Rock*, *Les Diaboliques*, *Charade*, *Mirage*, *Taste of Fear*, *The List of Adrian Messenger*, and *Ten Little Indians/And then There Were None*. Two gentler detectives were provided by Alec GUINNESS' *Father Brown* and Margaret RUTHERFORD's Miss Marple.

The other type of mystery, with a hero on the run, usually suspected of murder, finally uncovering the real villain after many narrow escapes from death, was developed by Alfred HITCHCOCK in such films as *The Thirty-Nine Steps*, *The Lady Vanishes*, *Saboteur*, *Spellbound*, *Strangers on a Train*, *North by Northwest* and *Torn Curtain*. But stars as various as Alan LADD, Bob HOPE, Danny KAYE, Robert MITCHUM, Paul NEWMAN and Harrison FORD have also found the device useful.

More recently, the emphasis has shifted, to the cleverness of the criminals with the detectives blundering along behind. They are outsmarted most, or all, of the time in such movies as *The Silence of the Lambs*, *Seven*, *The Usual Suspects*, *The Bone Collector*, *The Watcher* and *Hannibal*.

The 60s vogue for tongue-in-cheek spy thrillers is to all intents and purposes a reversion to the Pearl White school, with the hero menaced at every turn but, of course, finally triumphant. It still finds an audience in Mike MYERS' *Austin Powers* spoofs of the late 90s.

Books: 1974, *The Detective in Film* by William K. Everson. 1984, *Dark Cinema* by Jon Tuska; 1990, *The Great Detective Pictures* by James Robert Parish; 1996, *Raymond Chandler in Hollywood* by Al Clark; 1997, *The BFI Companion to Crime*, ed Phil Hardy.
See also: SPIES; PRIVATE EYES.

The Mystery of the Wax Museum.
This badly structured but interesting shocker in two-colour Technicolor, with sets by Anton Grot and direction by Michael Curtiz, survives as a milestone of its era, with Lionel Atwill as a mad sculptor who uses a wax face to disguise his hideously burned features. In 1953, the story was remade in 3-D as *House of Wax*, starring Vincent Price, and in 1966 most of it turned up again in *Chamber of Horrors*.

Nana.
Zola's novel of the Paris demi-monde in the 1860s has been filmed at least a dozen times, and can be seen in five major film versions: a silent French film directed by Jean RENOIR in 1926, with Catherine Hessling and Werner Krauss; an American version, sometimes known as *The Lady of the Boulevards*, directed by Dorothy ARZNER in 1934, with Anna STEN, Lionel ATWILL, and Phillips HOLMES; a second French version, directed by CHRISTIAN-JAQUE in 1955, with Martine CAROL and Charles BOYER; a Franco-Swedish version, *Take Me, Love Me*, directed by Mac AHLBERG, with Anna GAEL; a Franco-German version made in 1982, directed by Dan WOLMAN, with Katya BERGER and Jean-Pierre AUMONT.

Nancy Drew.
The teenage heroine, created by Carolyn Keene (one of many pseudonyms used by the team of Edward Stratemeyer and Harriet Adams), appeared in a series of second features made by Warner, directed by William Clemens and starring Bonita Granville: *Nancy Drew, Detective* 38; *Nancy Drew – Reporter* 39; *Nancy Drew – Troubleshooter* 39; *Nancy Drew and the Hidden Staircase* 39. A television series, *The Nancy Drew Mysteries*, ran from 1977-78, starring Pamela Sue Martin.

narrators
are heard at the beginning of many important movies. Well-known actors are normally used, but sometimes take no credit. Here is a selected checklist to silence nagging doubts:

Arizona Bushwhackers: James Cagney.
Barry Lyndon: Michael Hordern.
The Big Knife: Richard Boone.
Casablanca: Lou Marcelle.
The Curse of King Tutankhamun's Tomb: Paul Scofield.
Desert Rats: Michael Rennie.
Dragon Seed: Lionel Barrymore.
Duel in the Sun: Orson Welles.
The Hallelujah Trail: John Dehner.
How Green Was My Valley: Irving Pichel.
How the West Was Won: Spencer Tracy.
The Human Comedy: Ray Collins.
An Ideal Husband: Ralph Richardson.
It's a Big Country: Louis Calhern.
Khartoum: Leo Genn.
King of Kings: Orson Welles.
Kings of the Sun: James Coburn.
A Letter to 3 Wives: Celeste Holm.
Mackenna's Gold: Victor Jory.
The Master of Ballantrae: Robert Beatty.
Mother Wore Tights: Anne Baxter.
The Mummy's Shroud: Peter Cushing.
The Night They Raided Minsky's: Rudy Vallee.
The Picture of Dorian Gray: Cedric Hardwicke.
Quo Vadis: Walter Pidgeon.
The Red Badge of Courage: James Whitmore.
The Reivers: Burgess Meredith.
Repeat Performance: John Ireland.
Romeo and Juliet (1968): Laurence Olivier.
The Secret Heart: Hume Cronyn.
The Solid Gold Cadillac: George Burns.
The Story of Jacob and Joseph: Alan Bates.
Summer of 42: Robert Mulligan.
The Swiss Family Robinson: Orson Welles.
The Third Man: Wilfrid Thomas.
Those Magnificent Men in Their Flying Machines: James Robertson Justice.
To Hell and Back: John McIntire.
To Kill a Mockingbird: Kim Stanley.
Tom Jones: Micheal MacLiammoir.
The Unseen: Ray Collins.
The Vikings: Orson Welles.
The Wild Heart: Joseph Cotten.
The War of the Worlds: Cedric Hardwicke.
Zulu: Richard Burton.

naval comedy
in British movies usually has a 30s look about it, may well be written by Ian Hay, and almost always concerns the officers; as in *The Middle Watch*, *Carry On Admiral*, *The Midshipmaid*, *The Flag Lieutenant* and *Up the Creek* (though the other ranks had their look in with *The Bulldog Breed*, *The Baby and the Battleship* and *Jack Ahoy*). In Hollywood movies the focus of interest is set firmly among the other ranks: *Follow the Fleet*, *Abbott and Costello in the Navy*, *Anchors Aweigh*, *Operation Petticoat*, *Mr Roberts*, *South Pacific*, *Ensign Pulver*, *On the Town*, *You're in the Navy Now*, *The Fleet's In*, *Onion-Head*, *Don't Go Near the Water*, *Don't Give Up the Ship*, *The Honeymoon Machine*, *Down Periscope*.

nepotism.
Hollywood moguls were at one time well known for promoting within the family. Hence the quip: the son-in-law also rises. Hence the rhyme:
"Uncle Carl Laemmle
Has a very large faemmle."

Of an untalented Warner relative, Julius Epstein once commented that he had set the son-in-law business back twenty years. And when another gentleman of similar ilk taunted Oscar Levant with 'Oscar, play us a medley of your hit', Oscar came back with 'Okay, play us a medley of your father-in-law.' Of Louis B. Mayer's brother, Irving Brecher remarked: 'Jerry has a very important job and he has to have that big corner office. He's supposed to watch Washington Boulevard and warn everybody to evacuate the studio if icebergs are spotted coming down the street.' Similarly in London, after Alexander Korda's rise to fame and power, it was said that in order to get a job in British films you had to be Hungarian. These days, nepotism seems limited to directors giving their children roles in their films, sometimes with disastrous results.

New York
has provided a vivid backcloth for films of many types, and its skyscrapers allegedly gave Fritz Lang the inspiration for *Metropolis*. Studio re-creations provided the period flavour of *Little Old New York*, *New York Town*, *One Sunday Afternoon*, *A Tree Grows in Brooklyn*, *Incendiary Blonde*, *My Girl Tisa*, and *The Bowery*; and it was a studio city which was wrecked by *King Kong*. But the camera has also explored the real article, notably in thrillers like *Saboteur*, *Naked City*, *Union Station*, *The FBI Story* and *North by Northwest*; in realistic comedy dramas like *From This Day Forward*, *So This is New York*, *Miracle on 34th Street*, *Lovers and Lollipops*, *Marty*, *It Should Happen to You*, *Sunday in New York*, *Breakfast at Tiffany's*, *The Lost Weekend*, *The Bachelor Party*, *A Man Ten Feet Tall*, *A Fine Madness*, *Love with the Proper Stranger*, *The World of Henry Orient*, *Midnight Cowboy*, *The Pawnbroker*, *Barefoot in the Park*, *Beau James*, *The French Connection*, *Cotton Comes to Harlem*, *Shaft*, *The Out-of-Towners*, *Any Wednesday*, *Serpico*, *Bye Bye Braverman*, *Sweet Charity*, *The Seven-Ups*, *The Taking of Pelham One Two Three*, *The Prisoner of Second Avenue*, *Mean Streets*, *Taxi Driver*, *Death Wish* and *Three Days of the Condor*; in hard-hitting social melodramas like *On the Waterfront*, *Sweet Smell of Success*, and *The Young Savages*; and in musicals like *On the Town* and *West Side Story*. Other films which concern the effect of New York without showing much of the actuality include *Mr Deeds Goes to Town*, *Bachelor Mother*, *Lady on a Train*, *Bell, Book and Candle*, *Portrait of Jennie*, *Kid Millions*, *Dead End*, *The Apartment*, *Patterns of Power*, *The Garment Jungle*, *Mr Blandings Builds His Dream House* and *America, America*. Finally Manhattan Island was bought from the Indians by Groucho Marx in *The Story of Mankind*, *Knickerbocker Holiday* pictured the city in its Dutch colonial days as New Amsterdam and *Godspell* used it as a novel background for its revised version of the Life of Christ. Television series with authentic New York locations include *Naked City*, *The Defenders*, *East Side West Side*, *N.Y.P.D.*, *Madigan*, *McCloud*, *Kojak*, *Eischied*.

Nick and Nora Charles.
Married detectives created by Dashiell Hammett in his novel *The Thin Man* 34. In the book, the thin man is the murderer's first victim. Oddly enough, the tag stuck to William Powell (not all that thin), who played Nick Charles and starred in five sequels: *After the Thin Man* 37, *Another Thin Man* 38, *Shadow of the Thin Man* 42, *The Thin Man Goes Home* 44, *Song of the Thin Man* 46. Myrna Loy played Nora in all the features, and it was said that her domestic scenes with Powell in the original film marked the first time a sophisticated, affectionate marriage had been realistically portrayed on the screen. A later TV series, 57-59, starred Peter Lawford and Phyllis Kirk.

Nick Carter.
The tough young American detective, the occidental answer to Sexton Blake, was created in 1886 by Ormond G. Smith (1860-1933) and John Russell Coryell (1848-1924) for the *New York Weekly*. Dozens of hack writers later authored the stories under pseudonyms. Four French films starring André Liabel were made in 1912; Thomas Carrigan appeared in some shorts in 1920; Edmund Lowe had a series in 1924; Walter Pidgeon was in three in 1940; Eddie Constantine in two (French) in 1963 and 1965. From 1943 the character was very popular on radio, but television has made one poorish attempt in 1972, *The Adventures of Nick Carter* starring Robert Conrad.

Nightmare on Elm Street.
A series of low-budget horror movies starring Robert Englund as Freddy Kruger, a child killer who returns from the dead through dreams to kill again. The first, written and directed by Wes Craven, was made for $1.3m and took more than $26m at the American box-office. The sequels were of diminishing interest, although a TV series was spun off from the films. The series seemingly came to an end with the sixth film, *Freddy's Dead: The Final Nightmare* 91, but was revived by the self-referential *Wes Craven's New Nightmare* 94. There are plans, yet to come to fruition, to team Freddy with another killer-hero, the hockey-masked Jason, from the Friday the 13th series.

No Man of Her Own
was the film, starring Barbara STANWYCK, of Cornell WOOLRICH's novel *I Married a Dead Man*. It was also filmed by the French as *I Married a Shadow*, and as *Mrs Winterbourne* by Richard BENJAMIN in 1996, starring Ricki LAKE.

Norman Bates.
The mother-obsessed killer, based on the real-life murderer Ed GEIN, was memorably portrayed by Anthony PERKINS in Alfred HITCHCOCK's *Psycho* and three sequels. Although in the first film his sexual orientation seemed ambiguous, he became more heterosexual in outlook with each sequel. In a 1998 remake of Hitchcock's original, directed by

Gus VAN SANT, the role was played by Vince VAUGHN.

Nothing but the Truth.

James Montgomery's Broadway comedy about a man who takes a bet that he can tell the absolute truth for 24 hours was filmed in 1920, with Taylor HOLMES; in 1929, with Richard DIX; and in 1941, with Bob HOPE. In 1996, a similar notion was used in *Liar, Liar*, starring Jim CARREY.

numbered sequels.

This rather offhand practice probably began in 1956 with *Quatermass II*, but did not really become fashionable until the 70s. Among the successes to label their sequels so casually are *The French Connection*, *Jaws*, *The Sting*, *Mad Max*, *Walking Tall*, *Superman*, *Halloween*, *Death Wish*, *Grease*, *That's Entertainment*, *Piranha*, *Friday the 13th*, *La Cage aux Folles*, *The Amityville Horror*, *Porky's*, *Rocky*, *Airplane*, *The Howling*, *Die Hard*, *The Terminator*, *Predator* and *The Naked Gun*, which spoofed the process, going to 2½ and 33⅓.

nuns

have been popular figures on the screen, though only in *The Nun's Story* and the Polish *The Devil and the Nun* has any real sense of dedication been achieved; the French *Dialogue des Carmélites* tried hard but failed. Sentimentalized nuns were seen in *The Cradle Song*, *Bonaventure*, *The White Sister*, *Conspiracy of Hearts*, *The Bells of St Mary's*, *Come to the Stable*, *Portrait of Jennie*, *Heaven Knows Mr Allison*, *Black Narcissus*, *Lilies of the Field*, *The Miracle*, *The Song of Bernadette* and *The Sound of Music;* while nuns who combined modern sophistication with sweetness and light afflicted us in *The Singing Nun* and *The Trouble with Angels*, and in *Two Mules for Sister Sara* Shirley Maclaine played a prostitute disguised as a nun. A nun was raped in *Five Gates to Hell*. The most sinister nun was perhaps Catherine Lacey, with her high heels, in *The Lady Vanishes*, but the nuns in *The Trygon Factor* also count. The most agonized nuns were in *The Devils*, *La Religieuse*, and *The Awful Story of the Nun of Monza*. The weirdest was TV's *The Flying Nun*. More recently, they have been a source of amusement: *Dark Habits/Entre Tinieblas*, *Nuns on the Run* and *Sister Act*.

nurses

have inspired biopics (*Sister Kenny*, *The White Angel*, *The Lady with a Lamp*, *Nurse Edith Cavell*); sentimental low-key studies of the profession (*The Lamp Still Burns*, *The Feminine Touch*, *Vigil in the Night*, *No Time for Tears*, *White Corridors*, *Prison Nurse*, *Private Nurse*, *Night Nurse*); even comedies (*Carry On Nurse*, *Twice Round the Daffodils*, *Nurse on Wheels*). *Green for Danger* is probably still the only thriller in which both victim and murderer were nurses. The best satire has been *The National Health* (or *Nurse Norton's Affair*). There was a popular TV series called *Janet Dean Registered Nurse* 53, and later *The Nurses* 62-64.
See also HOSPITALS; DOCTORS.

nymphomaniacs

are still fairly rare in normal commercial movies. The fullest studies have been by Suzanne Pleshette in *A Rage to Live*, Françoise Arnoul in *La Rage au Corps*, Claire Bloom in *The Chapman Report*, Merle Oberon in *Of Love and Desire*, Sue Lyon in *Night of the Iguana*, Lee Remick in *The Detective*, Melina Mercouri in *Topkapi*, Maureen Stapleton in *Lonelyhearts*, Jean Seberg in *Road to Corinth*, Elizabeth Taylor in *Butterfield 8*, and Sandra Jullien in *I Am a Nymphomaniac;* but one should not forget Myrna Loy's comic nympho in *Love Me Tonight*.

Of Mice and Men.

John Steinbeck's spare little morality tale about a gentle but homicidal giant who has to be killed by his best friend has been filmed twice: in 1939, directed by Lewis MILESTONE with Lon CHANEY JNR, Burgess MEREDITH, and Betty FIELD; and in 1992, directed by Gary SINISE, starring himself, John MALKOVICH, and Sherilyn FENN. A TV movie, released on video, starred Robert BLAKE and Randy QUAID.

offices

have provided the setting for many a film. *The Crowd* in 1926 and *The Rebel* in 1961 chose pretty much the same way of stressing the dreariness of daily routine; but *Sunshine Susie* in 1931 and *How to Succeed in Business without Really Trying* in 1967 both saw the office as a gay place full of laughter and song. Satyajit RAY in *Company Limited* and Ermanno OLMI in *Il Posto* and *One Fine Day* took a realistic look at office life. Billy WILDER took a jaundiced view of it in *The Apartment*, as did the makers of *Patterns of Power*, *Executive Suite*, *Bartleby* and *The Power and the Prize*. More modern problems were explored in *Office Killer* 97, an experimental film about a copy editor who discovers she enjoys murder, and *Office Space* 99, about a rebellious computer programmer. Romantic comedies of the 30s like *Wife versus Secretary*, *After Office Hours* and *Take a Letter Darling* saw it as ideal for amorous intrigue, and in 1964 *The Wild Affair* took pretty much the same attitude. Orson WELLES in *The Trial* made it nightmarish; Preston STURGES in *Christmas in July* made it friendly; *The Desk Set* made it computerized; *The Bachelor Party* made it frustrating; *The Hudsucker Proxy* 94, a throwback to the style of Sturges, made it fun. Perhaps the best film office is that of Philip Marlowe in the Raymond CHANDLER films: there's seldom anyone in it but himself. The most spectacular was that of Alfred ABEL in *Metropolis*.

Oh God!

Avery Corman's novel of God coming to Earth to ask a supermarket manager for help in promulgating his message was filmed in 1977 by Carl REINER with the veteran comedian George BURNS as the deity and was followed by two lacklustre sequels: *Oh God! Book II*, directed by Gilbert CATES in 1980, and *Oh God! You Devil*, directed by Paul BOGART from Andrew BERGMAN's script.

oil

and its procurement from the earth have been the subjects of a number of films including *High Wide and Handsome* 38, *Boom Town* 40, *The Big Gusher* 51, *Tulsa* 49, *Thunder Bay* 53, *Lucy Gallant* 55, *Giant* 56, *The Houston Story* 56, *Maracaibo* 58, *Black Gold* 60, *Hellfighters* 68, *Oklahoma Crude* 73, *Waltz Across Texas* 82 and *The Stars Fell on Henrietta* 95.

old age

on the screen has seldom been explored, and the commercial reasons for this are obvious. Among the serious studies are *The Whisperers*, with Edith EVANS; *Umberto D*, with Carlo Battisti; *The Shameless Old Lady*, with SYLVIE; *Ikuru*, with Takashi SHIMURA; *The End of the Road*, with Finlay CURRIE; *I Never Sang for My Father*, with Melvyn DOUGLAS; *Make Way for Tomorrow*, with Beulah BONDI; *Alive and Kicking*, with Sybil THORNDIKE and Estelle WINWOOD; *Kotch* with Walter MATTHAU; *Harry and Tonto* with Art CARNEY; *Tokyo Story* with Chishu Ryu and Chieko Higashiyama; *On Golden Pond* with Henry FONDA and Katharine HEPBURN; *The Gin Game* with Jessica TANDY and Hume CRONYN (a video version of their stage hit); *The Whales of August* with Bette DAVIS and Lillian GISH; and *Driving Miss Daisy* with Jessica TANDY and Morgan FREEMAN. Sentimentality crept in in *Mr Belvedere Rings the Bell*; and *The Old Man and the Sea* was merely pretentious.

There was an element of black comedy in the attitudes expressed towards the old people in *Grapes of Wrath*, *Tobacco Road* and *Nights of the Iguana*; and more melodramatic caricatures were presented in *The Lost Moment* (Agnes MOOREHEAD), *The Queen of Spades* (Edith EVANS), *Little Big Man* (Dustin HOFFMAN), and *The Old Dark House* (John DUDGEON). Fantasy crept in with *Lost Horizon*, in which the lamas grew incredibly old by natural processes, and *The Man in Half Moon Street*, in which Nils ASTHER was assisted by science. *Cocoon* used alien methods to rejuvenate the elderly. Other actors who have specialized in geriatric portraits include A. E. MATTHEWS, Edie MARTIN, Clem BEVANS, Andy CLYDE, Maria OUSPENSKAYA, Jessie RALPH, Nancy PRICE and Adeline de Walt REYNOLDS, who did not become an actress until she was eighty. Perhaps the Screen's most delightful senior citizens were the capering Harbottle, played by Moore MARRIOTT in Will Hay comedies, and Barry FITZGERALD in *Broth of a Boy;* the most horrific was Cathleen NESBITT in *Staircase;* the most commercially successful were George BURNS and Walter MATTHAU in *The Sunshine Boys*. Katie JOHNSON became a star at 78 in *The Lady Killers:* Ruth GORDON played capering old dames well into her 80s, and in *Harold and Maude*, when she was 75, played an 80-year-old who had an affair with an immature young boy.

Stars who donned ageing make-up include HOPE, CROSBY and LAMOUR in *Road to Utopia;* Barbara STANWYCK in *The Great Man's Lady;* Tyrone POWER in *The Long Gray Line;* Anna NEAGLE in *Victoria the Great;* Madeleine CARROLL in *The Fan;* GABLE and SHEARER in *Strange Interlude;* Rosalind RUSSELL and Alexander KNOX in *Sister Kenny;* Joel McCREA in *Buffalo Bill;* Fredric MARCH in *The Adventures of Mark Twain;* Dustin HOFFMAN in *Little Big Man*. The most tasteless treatment of old age was surely that offered in *The Ultimate Solution of Grace Quigley;* the most graceful that of *Going in Style*.

Old Mother Riley.

The vociferous, anarchic Irish washerwoman was created by Arthur LUCAN on the music halls and in many films, with daughter Kitty played by the resistible Kitty McSHANE, Lucan's wife. Most of the films were atrociously made but all of them made a sizeable profit from British provincial showings.

For a complete list, see LUCAN, Arthur.

Oliver Twist.

Dickens's novel was filmed many times in the early silent period: in 1909 by Pathé, in 1910 by Vitagraph, in 1912 by an independent company with Nat C. Goodwin as Fagin. A famous American version of 1916 had Tully Marshall as Fagin and Marie Doro as Oliver; in 1922 the roles were played by Lon Chaney and Jackie Coogan, and in 1933 by Irving Pichel and Dickie Moore. The definitive version so far, however, is the British one directed by David Lean in 1948, with John Howard Davies in the title role. Alec Guinness's brilliant performance as Fagin caused a hold-up in American distribution as it was accused of anti-Semitism. *Oliver!*, a 1968 musical version directed by Carol Reed, with Ron Moody as Fagin and Mark Lester as Oliver, won six Oscars. *Twisted*, an updated version, set among New York's homosexuals, was made in 1996 by Seth Michael Donsky, with William Hickey in the role of a Fagin-like pimp.

One Million B.C.

This highly unscientific account of the tribulations of primitive man has been filmed several times. The 1939 version featured Carole Landis and Victor Mature and was produced and directed by Hal Roach with assistance from D. W. Griffith, upon whose 1912 *Man's Genesis* it was based. The dialogue consisted largely of grunts and there were a variety of prehistoric monsters which were rather obviously normal reptiles crudely decorated and magnified. Hammer remade it in 1960 with Don Chaffey directing Raquel Welch and John Richardson; this time the monsters were plastic animations. A kind of sequel, *When Dinosaurs Ruled the Earth*, directed by Val Guest, came out in 1970, and *Creatures the World Forgot* followed in 1971. Another all-grunting caveman epic followed in 1981, with *Quest for Fire*, directed by Jean-Jacques Annaud. This, however, aimed for accuracy, with the cast using a prehistoric language created by novelist Anthony Burgess and gestures devised by zoologist Desmond Morris, and was consequently much less fun.

One Way Passage.

A popular tear-jerker of 1932, written and directed by Tay Garnett, about a dying beauty (Kay Francis) and a convicted murderer (William Powell) who meet on an ocean liner and fall in love while keeping their secrets, it was remade in 1940 by Edmund Goulding as *Till We Meet Again*, with Merle Oberon and George Brent.

opera

has never been a successful commodity on the screen, although many operas have been filmed as from the stalls, and appear to have succeeded with minority audiences. The occasional big opera production such as *Porgy and Bess*, *Pagliacci* or *Carmen Jones*, however, can expect to meet with only moderate success. Opera does, however, make an excellent background for thrillers (*Charlie Chan at the Opera*), farces (*A Night at the Opera*) and melodramas (*Metropolitan*). Opera singers who have succeeded as film stars include Grace Moore, Lily Pons, Mario Lanza, Tito Gobbi, Richard Tauber, Lauritz Melchior, Ezio Pinza and Gladys Swarthout. Oddly enough the singer Mary Garden was a big hit in *silent* films.

In a comprehensive reference guide, *Opera on Screen*, published in 1997, Ken Wlaschin lists the best operas on film as Francesco Rosi's *Carmen* 84, Ingmar Bergman's *The Magic Flute* 74, Franco Zeffirelli's *La Traviata* 82, Joseph Losey's *Don Giovanni* 78, Max Ophuls' *The Bartered Bride* 32, Michael Powell and Emeric Pressburger's *The Tales of Hoffman* 51, and Gian Carlo Menotti's *The Medium* 51. The title of best operetta goes to Ernst Lubitsch's *The Merry Widow* 32. The worst opera on film is said to be Albert Hopkins's version of *Faust* 36, made in Britain and starring Anne Ziegler and Webster Booth.

orchestral conductors

have figured as leading men in *Intermezzo*, *Interlude*, *Once More with Feeling*, *Unfaithfully Yours*, *Song of Russia*, *Break of Hearts*, *Prelude to Fame*, *Counterpoint;* Charles Laughton cut a tragi-comic figure in *Tales of Manhattan*. Real conductors who have played dramatic roles in movies include Leopold Stokowski, José Iturbi and many swing and jazz figures such as Paul Whiteman, Tommy Dorsey, Henry Hall, Glenn Miller, Benny Goodman, Xavier Cugat.

oriental roles.

It never seems a good idea, but occidental actors have often been tempted by the wish to play Eastern. Among the less fortunate results are Lee J. Cobb in *Anna and the King of Siam;* John Wayne in *The Conqueror;* Katharine Hepburn in *Dragon Seed;* Alec Guinness in *A Majority of One;* Mickey Rooney in *Breakfast at Tiffany's;* George Raft in *Limehouse Blues;* Edward G. Robinson in *The Hatchet Man*. Those who more or less got away with it include Robert Donat in *Inn of the Sixth Happiness;* Boris Karloff in *The Mask of Fu Manchu;* and Luise Rainer and Paul Muni in *The Good Earth*.

Oswald the Rabbit.

Cute cartoon star who survived the transition from silent to talking pictures. Originated by Walt Disney, he was taken over by Universal Pictures and animator Walter Lantz from 1929 and appeared in many cartoons until 1938. He was voiced by Mickey Rooney and Bernice Hansen. His finest moment was an appearance in 1930 in *The King of Jazz* with bandleader Paul Whiteman.

Othello.

Shakespeare's tragedy of a jealous lover was filmed many times as a silent and on three notable occasions in more recent times. Orson WELLES starred in and directed an uneven version in 1952, which was beset by financial problems and inspired a hilarious account of its travails, *Put Money in Thy Purse*, by Michael MACLIAMMOIR, who played Iago. Sergei Yutkevich made a Russian version in 1955, starring Sergei BONDARCHUK, and Laurence OLIVIER's astonishing National Theatre performance as a West Indian Othello, with Maggie SMITH as Desdemona and Frank FINLAY as Iago, was preserved in Stuart BURGE's unsatisfactory screen version in 1965. Laurence FISHBURNE played the role in a much-cut and rewritten version in 1995, with Kenneth BRANAGH as Iago and Irene JACOB as Desdemona. A musical version, *Catch My Soul*, was filmed in 1972, and murderous actors playing the role of Othello have also turned up in *Men Are Not Gods* 36, directed by Walter REISCH and starring Sebastian SHAW, and *A Double Life* 47, directed by George CUKOR and starring Ronald COLMAN. Basil DEARDEN's *All Night Long* 61 updated the play as a tale of a jealous jazz musician (Patrick McGOOHAN), and a western, *Jubal* 56, had Ernest BORGNINE as a jealous rancher being urged to commit murder by Rod STEIGER.

'Our Gang'.

A collection of child actors first gathered together in short slapstick comedies by producer Hal Roach in the mid-20s. They remained popular through the 30s and 40s, though the personnel of the team naturally changed. The originals included 'Fat' Joe Cobb, Jackie Condon, Mickey Daniels, Mary Kornman and Ernie 'Sunshine Sammy' Morrison, said to be the highest-paid member at $12 a week in 1927. Later cast members, joining in the late 20s, were Matthew 'Stymie' Beard, Norman 'Chubby' Chaney, Jackie Cooper, Johnny Downs and Bobby 'Wheezer' Hutchins, who were followed by, among others, Scotty Beckett, Tommy 'Butch' Bond, Dorothy De Borba, Mary Anne Jackson, Darla Hood, Dickie Moore, Carl 'Alfalfa' Switzer,

Billy 'Buckwheat' Thomas and Spanky McFarland, who became leader of the gang in the early 30s. Roach sold the series to MGM in 1938 and production continued until 1944. Many of Roach's Our Gang shorts have appeared on television and have been released on video under the title 'The Little Rascals', since MGM hold copyright in the original name. One, *Bored of Education*, won an Oscar in 1936 and a feature, *General Spanky*, directed by Fred Newmeyer, was made in 1938. More than 90 of their short films were restored for television showing in the 90s, and Steven Spielberg produced a new feature film, *The Little Rascals*, based on the series, in 1994, directed by Penelope Spheeris.

Book 1977: *Our Gang* by Leonard Maltin.

painters

have frequently had their lives glamorized to provide film-makers with drama to counterpoint art. Among the most notable are Charles LAUGHTON as *Rembrandt*, George SANDERS as Gauguin in *The Moon and Sixpence*, José FERRER as Toulouse-Lautrec in *Moulin Rouge*, Régis ROYER as Toulouse-Lautrec in *Lautrec*, Anthony FRANCIOSA as Goya in *The Naked Maja*, Kirk DOUGLAS as Van Gogh and Anthony QUINN as Gauguin in *Lust for Life*, Tim ROTH as Van Gogh in *Vincent and Theo*, Jacques DUTRONC as the dying artist in *Van Gogh*, Gérard PHILIPE as Modigliani in *Montparnasse 19*, Cecil KELLAWAY as Gainsborough in *Kitty*, Charlton HESTON as Michelangelo in *The Agony and the Ecstasy*, and Mel FERRER as *El Greco*.

The Paleface.

Bob Hope's western romp with Jane Russell as Calamity Jane, directed by Norman Z. McLeod in 1948, was followed by an even crazier extravaganza, *Son of Paleface*, which also featured Roy Rogers. In 1968 the original was revamped for Don Knotts as *The Shakiest Gun in the West*.

Paris

has usually figured in films as the centre of sophistication, romance and luxury: thus *Ninotchka*, *I Met Him in Paris*, *The Last Time I Saw Paris*, *Innocents in Paris*, *April in Paris*, *How to Steal a Million*, *To Paris with Love*, *Paris When It Sizzles*, *A Certain Smile*, *Funny Face*, *Paris Holiday*, *Can Can*, *Parisienne*, *Paris Palace Hotel*, *Two for the Road* and innumerable others. The bohemian aspect is another favourite, as depicted in *An American in Paris*, *Latin Quarter*, *Paris Blues*, *What's New, Pussycat?*, *Svengali*, *French Cancan*, *Moulin Rouge*, *What a Way to Go*, *The Moon and Sixpence*, etc. The tourists' Paris has provided a splendid backcloth for films as diverse as *The Great Race*, *The Man on the Eiffel Tower*, *Charade*, *Those Magnificent Men in Their Flying Machines*, *Zazie dans le Métro*, *Pig Across Paris*, *The Red Balloon*, *Father Brown*, *Take Her She's Mine*, *Dear Brigitte*, *Bon Voyage*, and *Paris Nous Appartient*. French film-makers seem particularly fond of showing the city's seamy side in thrillers about vice, murder and prostitution: *Quai de Grenelle*, *Quai des Orfèvres*, *Les Compagnes de la Nuit*, *Le Long des Trottoirs*, *Rififi*, etc. René Clair has always had his own slightly fantastic view of Paris, from *Paris Qui Dort* through *Sous les Toits de Paris*, *A Nous la Liberté*, *Le Million*, *Le Quatorze Juillet*, and *Porte des Lilas*. Rouben Mamoulian recreated this vision in *Love Me Tonight*, and *The Mad Woman of Chaillot* lived in a city of similar nuances. Historical Paris has been recreated for *The Hunchback of Notre Dame*, *The Scarlet Pimpernel*, *The Three Musketeers*, *Camille*, *A Tale of Two Cities*, *Marie Antoinette*, *So Long at the Fair* and *Les Enfants du Paradis*; while Paris under fire in World War II was depicted in *Is Paris Burning?* As for *Last Tango in Paris*, its emphasis was hardly on the city.

parody

without satire was never prominent among film genres until the 70s, when the easy-going talents of such as Mel BROOKS and Gene WILDER produced films such as *Blazing Saddles*, *Sherlock Holmes' Smarter Brother*, *Young Frankenstein*, *Murder by Death*, *The Black Bird*, *The Big Bus*, *Phantom of the Paradise*, *High Anxiety* and *The Cheap Detective*. The ZUCKER brothers and Jim ABRAHAMS have made a speciality of the form with *Kentucky Fried Movie*, *Airplane*, *The Naked Gun* and their sequels, and *Hot Shots!* (Abrahams only). The WAYANS brothers have made fun of rap-flavoured movies in *Don't Be a Menace to South Central While Drinking Your Juice in the Hood*, and horror in *Scary Movie* and its sequel. Short films in this vein are headed by *Six-Sided Triangle*, *The Dove* and *Cry Wolf*.

parties

in movies have often been wild, as for instance in *The Wild Party*, also *The Party's Over*, *I'll Never Forget What's 'is Name*, *Breakfast at Tiffany's*, *I Love You Alice B. Toklas*, *The Impossible Years*, *Skidoo*, *Beyond the Valley of the Dolls*, *Camille 2000*, *The Pursuit of Happiness*, *The Party Crashers*, and *The Party* itself, which started out sedately but finished with an elephant in the swimming pool. Some of the more amusing film parties, however, were better behaved, as in *The Apartment*, *Only Two Can Play*, *All About Eve* and *Citizen Kane*.

The Passing of the Third Floor Back.

Jerome K. Jerome's popular novel and play, about a Christ-like stranger who has a benign influence on the down-at-heel inhabitants of a boarding house, has been filmed twice. Sir Johnston Forbes-Robertson, who had a lasting success on stage in the role from 1908 ('Chr-r-rist! Will they never let me give up this *bloody* part?' he once exclaimed before going on as the saintly figure), starred in a silent film in 1918, two years after he had retired from the stage, and Conrad Veidt appeared in a version, also British, in 1935.

The Passing Parade.

A series of one-reel films, mostly historical cameos enacted in corners of MGM's great sets, devised and produced by John Nesbitt in the 30s and 40s.

Penrod.

Booth Tarkington's American boy character, in his mid-west small-town setting, was for many years a favourite Hollywood subject. Marshall Neilan directed Gordon Griffith in a 1922 version. In 1923 William Beaudine directed Ben Alexander in the role in *Penrod and Sam*, which was remade by Beaudine in 1931 with Leon Janney, and again by William McGann in 1937 with Billy Mauch. Mauch and his twin brother Bobby appeared in two sequels: *Penrod's Double Trouble* 38, directed by Lewis Seiler, and *Penrod and His Twin Brother* 38, directed by McGann. Two Doris Day musicals, *On Moonlight Bay* 51 and *By the Light of the Silvery Moon* 53, were also lightly based on the Tarkington stories: Penrod, unaccountably disguised as 'Wesley', was played by Billy Gray.

Pepe Le Pew.

Smooth, romantic French skunk, the star of 14 Warner Brothers cartoons. Based on Charles Boyer's Pepe Le Moko in *Algiers*, he was created by writer Michael Maltese and animator Chuck Jones and voiced by Mel Blanc.

Scent-Imental over You 47. For Scent-Imental Reasons (AA) 49. Scent-Imental Romeo 51. Cat's Bah 54. Heaven Scent 56. Really Scent 59. Who Scent You? 60. Louvre Come Back to Me 62, etc.

The Perils of Pauline.

Pearl White's famous 1914 serial was directed by Donald Mackenzie, co-starred Crane Wilbur, and concerned the heroine's evasion of attempts on her life by her dastardly guardian. The 1947 film of the same name was a lightly fictionalized biography of Pearl White, directed by George Marshall, with Betty Hutton in the title role. The 1967 film was vaguely based on the original serial, with Pamela Austin as the heroine, directed by Herbert Leonard and Joshua Shelley.

Perry Mason,

a crime-solving lawyer who wins all his cases, usually during a court-room cross-examination, was created by Erle Stanley Gardner in *The Case of the Velvet Claws* 33, the first of more than 80 novels in which he was the hero. On film, he has been played by Warren WILLIAM, Ricardo CORTEZ and Donald WOODS, but it was Raymond BURR who became closely identified with the character in the TV series of 245 hour-long episodes that ran 1957-66. Monte MARKHAM took over the part in the unsuccessful *The New Adventures of Perry Mason* 73-74; then in 1985 Burr returned to the role in a continuing series of TV movies.

The Case of the Howling Dog 34. The Case of the Curious Bride 35. The Case of the Lucky Legs 35. The Case of the Velvet Claws 36. The Case of the Black Cat 36. The Case of the Stuttering Bishop 37. Perry Mason Returns (TV) 85. Perry Mason: The Case of the Notorious Nun (TV) 86. Perry Mason: The Case of the Lost Love (TV) 87. Perry Mason: The Case of the Lady in the Lake (TV) 88. Perry Mason: The Case of the All-Star Assassin (TV) 89. Perry Mason: The Case of the Ruthless Reporter (TV) 91. Oerry Mason: The Case of the Telltale Talk Show Host 93, etc.

Peyton Place.

The 1957 film version of Grace Metalious's novel started a fashion for small-town sex exposés on the screen, and was followed by a sequel, *Return to Peyton Place*, in 1961. A TV series of two half-hours a week followed in 1964 and proved so popular that in 1965 it was given three half-hours and lasted until 1969, bringing to public notice Mia Farrow and Ryan O'Neal.

The Phantom of the Opera.

Gaston Leroux's melodramatic tale of the embittered, disfigured composer who haunts the sewers beneath the Paris Opéra and takes a pretty young singer as his protégée has been filmed several times: in 1925 Rupert Julian directed a version with Lon Chaney and Mary Philbin; in 1943 Arthur Lubin directed Claude Rains and Susanna Foster; in 1962 came a British version, directed by Terence Fisher, with Herbert Lom and Heather Sears; in 1989 Dwight H. Little directed Robert Englund, better known as Freddy from *A Nightmare on Elm Street*, in a version set in London. Italian director Dario Argento filmed it in 1998, with an original touch: Julian Sands in the title role is neither masked or disfigured, though he was raised in the sewers by rats. In 1977 Brian DePalma made a rock version, *Phantom of the Paradise*, and there have been two TV movies, one in 1983 starring Maximilian Schell and Jane Seymour, and another in 1990, directed by Tony Richardson from a script by Arthur Kopit, with Charles Dance and Teri Polo. Andrew Lloyd-Webber's highly successful stage musical, premiered in 1986, will no doubt be filmed in the future.

Philip Marlowe

was the weary but incorruptible private-eye creation of Raymond Chandler, treading the seamier streets of Los Angeles in a dogged hunt for suspects. On television he was played in a poor series by Phil Carey, on screen by Humphrey Bogart, Robert Montgomery, George Montgomery, Dick Powell, James Garner, Robert Mitchum and (very badly) by Elliott Gould. In 1983 he was portrayed in a British television series, *Chandlertown*, by Powers Boothe. He was played by James Caan in *Poodle Springs* (TV) 98.

The Pink Panther.

Blake Edwards' 1964 film of an unequal battle of wits between an aristocratic jewel thief (David Niven) and an accident-prone French policeman, Inspector Clouseau (Peter Sellers), spawned several sequels: *A Shot in the Dark* 64; *Inspector Clouseau* 68, in which Alan Arkin took the title role; *The Return of the Pink Panther* 74, which brought back Sellers; *The Pink Panther Strikes Again* 76; and *Revenge of the Pink Panther* 78. Sellers' widow, Lynne Frederick, objected to *The Trail of the Pink Panther* 82, which cobbled together outtakes of Sellers from earlier films and new linking material. It was followed by *Curse of the Pink Panther* 83, in which Ted Wass starred as the world's worst detective, and *Son of the Pink Panther* 93, with Italian comedian Robert Benigni in the title role, but neither was a success. The animated credits of the original film, featuring a pink panther and Henry Mancini's catchy title song, inspired a long-running cartoon series, beginning with the Oscar-winning *The Pink Phink* 64, and a comic book that was published from 1971-84.

pirates

have regularly appeared on the screen. Stories with some claim to historical authenticity, or at least based on the exploits of a pirate who once lived, include *Captain Blood* (and its various sequels), *The Black Swan*, *Morgan the Pirate*, *Seven Seas to Calais*, *Blackbeard the Pirate*, *Captain Kidd*, *The Buccaneer*, and *Anne of the Indies* (a rare female pirate: one other was depicted in *The Pirate Queen*). Totally fictitious stories are of course headed by *Treasure Island* in its various versions; other swashbuckling yarns included *The Sea Hawk*, *The Black Pirate*, *The Crimson Pirate*, *The Golden Hawk*, *Fair Wind to Java*, *A High Wind in Jamaica*, *Pirates of Tortuga*, *Yankee Buccaneer*, *The Spanish Main*, *Pirates of Tripoli*, *Devil Ship Pirates*, *Pirates of Blood River*, *Prince of Pirates*, and *Raiders of the Seven Seas*. The only notable musical pirate was Gene Kelly in *The Pirate*; comic pirates are also rare, but they do include *The Princess and the Pirate*, *Blackbeard's Ghost*, *Double Crossbones*, *The Dancing Pirate* and *Old Mother Riley's Jungle Treasure*. 1983's *Yellowbeard* was a sad spoof of the genre. *Pirates* in 1985 didn't even seem to know whether it was a spoof or not. *Hook* 91 put the pirate captain of *Peter Pan* centre-galleon.

The Plainsman.

Cecil B. De Mille's 1937 western starred Gary Cooper as Wild Bill Hickok, James Ellison as Buffalo Bill, and Jean Arthur as Calamity Jane. It was poorly remade in 1966 with Don Murray, Guy Stockwell, and Abby Dalton.

Planet of the Apes.

Pierre Boulle's novel of an astronaut who lands on a planet where the humans have degenerated and the apes rule with wisdom was adapted by Paul DEHN and stylishly directed by Franklin SCHAFFNER in 1967; Charlton HESTON played the hero who discovers, in a twist at the end, that the planet is Earth, and John CHAMBERS provided the splendidly flexible ape make-up. It spawned four sequels of increasing violence and decreasing interest: *Beneath the Planet of the Apes* 69; *Escape from the Planet of the Apes* 70; *Conquest of the Planet of the Apes* 72; and *Battle for the Planet of the Apes* 73. They were followed by a short-lived television series in 1974, and an animated series, *Beyond the Planet of the Apes*, in 1975-76. A big-budget remake came in 2001, directed by Tim BURTON, with ape-specialist Rick BAKER in charge of make-up.

plastic surgery

was long a staple of horror films, but improved techniques have made it a subject for 'woman's pictures' such as *Ash Wednesday* and *Once is not Enough*. *Arsenic and Old Lace* made a comedy point of it, and *Seconds* took it seriously. Other examples: *Dark Passage*, *False Faces*, *A Woman's Face*, *Eyes without a Face*, *Johnny Handsome*.

police

in the 40s and earlier were offered in British films only for our admiration; in the 50s they began to have human frailties; in the 60s began a trend that continued into the present century: many of them were shown, truthfully or not, to be corrupt. *The Blue Lamp*, *The Long Arm* and *Gideon of Scotland Yard* are only three of many of the first kind; *Violent Playground* one of the second; and *The Strange Affair* a corking example of the last. But the *Z Cars* series on British TV will long uphold the best traditions of the force ... as will *Maigret* for France.

American cops have always been tougher, but even so a gradual change can be traced through *Naked City*, *The Big Heat*, *Detective Story*, *Shield for Murder*, *Experiment in Terror*, *Madigan*, *The Detective*, *The French Connection*, *Fuzz* and *The New Centurions*.

TV series which have been influential include *Dragnet* 52-59 and 67-69, *Naked City* 58-62, *87th Precinct* 61, *M Squad* 57-60, *The Detectives* 60-61, *The Line-up* 54-59, *Hawk* 66, *The New Breed* 61, *Adam 12* 68-75, *Hawaii Five O* 68-80, *The Rookies* 72, *Police Story* 73-77, *Police Woman* 74-76, *Starsky and Hutch* 75-78, *Miami Vice* 84-88, *Hill Street Blues* 81-87, *NYPD Blue* 93-, *Homicide: Life on the Streets* 93-99.

Comic policemen go right back to the Keystone Kops. Other examples: Will HAY in *Ask a Policeman*, George FORMBY in *Spare a Copper*, Norman WISDOM in *On the Beat*, Alastair SIM in *Green for Danger*, Peter SELLERS in *The Pink Panther*, Lionel JEFFRIES in *The Wrong Arm of the Law*, 'Officer Krupke' in *West Side Story*, Donald MCBRIDE in *Topper Returns*, Dennis HOEY as Inspector Lestrade in the Sherlock Holmes films, Sidney JAMES and crew in *Carry On Constable*, LAUREL and HARDY in *Midnight Patrol*, Buster KEATON's cast in *Cops*, Charles CHAPLIN in *Easy Street*, the cast of *Police Academy* and, on TV, *Car 54 Where are You?*

politics,

as any exhibitor will tell you, is the kiss of death to a film as far as box office is concerned. Nevertheless many films with serious political themes have been made. Among those presenting biographies of actual political figures, the American ones include *Young Mr Lincoln*, *Abe Lincoln in Illinois*, *Tennessee Johnson*, *The Man with Thirty Sons* (Oliver Wendell Holmes), *Magnificent Doll* (Dolly Madison and Aaron Burr), *The President's Lady* (Andrew Jackson), *Wilson*, Teddy Roosevelt (in My Girl Tisa and others), Franklin

Roosevelt (in *Sunrise at Campobello*), *Beau James* (Jimmy Walker) and John Kennedy (*PT 109*), *JFK* (Kennedy again), *Thirteen Days* (Kennedy and the Cuban missile crisis) and *Nixon*, while *All the King's Men* and *A Lion Is in the Streets* are clearly based on Huey Long, and there was a real-life original for the idealistic young senator from Wisconsin in *Mr Smith Goes to Washington*. Fictional presidencies have been involved in *Gabriel over the White House*, *First Lady*, *The Tree of Liberty* (*The Howards of Virginia*), *Advise and Consent*, *The Manchurian Candidate*, *Seven Days in May*, *Dr Strangelove*, *Kisses for My President*, and *Fail Safe*. Among the many films alleging political graft and corruption in the US are *Mr Smith Goes to Washington*, *Confessions of a Nazi Spy*, *Louisiana Purchase*, *Alias Nick Beal*, *State of the Union*, *Li'l Abner*, *The Great McGinty*, *The Glass Key*, *Citizen Kane*, *All the King's Men*, *Bullets or Ballots*, *A Lion Is in the Streets*, *The Last Hurrah*, *The Best Man*, *The Senator was Indiscreet*, *The Candidate* and *The Contender*, while *Bulworth* offered Warren Beatty as a senator who told the truth, however unpalatable. The witch-hunts of 1948 produced a series of right-wing melodramas like *I Was a Communist for the FBI*, *I Married a Communist* and *My Son John* ... a striking contrast to 1942, when *Mission to Moscow* could be made. In 1971 TV produced a four-hour thriller called *Vanished* about a president with doubtful motives. The mid-70s brought a number of TV drama-documentaries about political matters: *Eleanor and Franklin*, *Collision Course* (Truman and MacArthur), *The Missiles of October*, *Fear On Trial*, *Tail Gunner Joe* (McCarthy), *Meeting at Potsdam*.

The British House of Commons and its characters have been involved in many a film with DISRAELI coming out as favourite. Pitt the Younger was impersonated by Robert DONAT, and Charles James Fox by Robert MORLEY, in *The Young Mr Pitt*; Gladstone was played by Ralph RICHARDSON in *Khartoum*, Malcolm KEEN in *Sixty Glorious Years* and Stephen MURRAY in *The Prime Minister*; Cromwell by Richard HARRIS; Canning by John MILLS and William Lamb by Jon FINCH in *Lady Caroline Lamb*; while Ramsay MACDONALD was allegedly pictured in *Fame is the Spur*. MPs were also the leading figures of the fictional *No Love for Johnnie*, *Three Cases of Murder* and *The Rise and Rise of Michael Rimmer*.

Political films from other countries abound; one might almost say that every Soviet film is political. But politics do not export well, so that for the life of Villa, Zapata, Juarez and Che Guevara we have to turn to glamorized Hollywood versions of the truth; ditto for Parnell, Richelieu and even Hitler. Lenin has been pictured in innumerable Soviet films, and Richard BURTON starred in *The Assassination of Trotsky*.

That politics is not entirely a serious matter can be seen from the number of comedies about it. The best of them is the already mentioned *State of the Union*, but one can also instance the *Don Camillo* series, *Old Mother Riley MP*, *Angelina MP*, *Dad Rudd MP*, *Louisiana Purchase*, *Kisses for My President*, *The Great Man Votes*, *Left Right and Centre*, *Vote for Huggett*, *The American President*, *Election* and *Dick*.

Popeye.
Tough sailorman hero of over 250 cartoon shorts produced by Max Fleischer *c.* 1933-50. Other characters involved were girlfriend Olive Oyl and tough villain Bluto, against whose wiles Popeye fortified himself with tins of spinach. The films were so popular on TV that a newly-drawn series was produced *c.* 1959 by King Features – but the old vulgar panache was missing.

In 1980 Robert Altman directed a live-action version, but it was a sad affair.

Porky Pig.
Stammering, nervous pig whose cry of 'Th-th-th-th-that's all, folks' brought to an end many Warner Brothers cartoons. Created by Bob Clampett, for the first two years he was voiced by Joe Dougherty (who did stutter), after which Mel Blanc took over.

I Haven't Got a Hat 35. *Gold Diggers of '49* 36. *Porky's Pet* 36. *Porky's Duck Hunt* 37. *The Case of the Stuttering Pig* 37. *Porky and Daffy* 38. *The Lone Stranger and Porky* 39. *Prehistoric Porky* 40. *Porky's Ant* 41. *My Favorite Duck* 42. *Swooner Crooner* (AAN) 44. *The Pest that Came to Dinner* 48. *Porky's Chops* 49. *Cracked Quack* 52. *Deduce, You Say* 56. *China Jones* 59. *Daffy's Inn Trouble* 61, many others.

poverty
in America and Britain is rare enough now to be little discussed, but in the days when film-makers began to have a social conscience a number of films memorably examined the problem in different milieux. American hoboes and shanty-town dwellers were revealed in *Sullivan's Travels*, *Hallelujah I'm a Bum*, *Man's Castle*, *My Man Godfrey*, *One More Spring*; the rural poor were the subject of *Our Daily Bread*, *The Grapes of Wrath*, *Tobacco Road*. Hollywood's regretful gaze wandered to China for *The Good Earth* and for *Tortilla Flat* to Mexico, which was more memorably covered by Buñuel in *Los Olvidados*. Poverty in Italy was the subject of *Bicycle Thieves*, and in England of *Love on the Dole*, *Doss House* and *The Whisperers*.

priests
have been a godsend to film-makers. Most male stars have played them occasionally: the combination of masculine attractiveness and non-availability apparently works at the box office. Thus Frank Sinatra in *The Miracle of the Bells*; William Holden and Clifton Webb in *Satan Never Sleeps*; Bing Crosby in *Going My Way*, *The Bells of St Mary's* and *Say One for Me*; Richard Dix in *The Christian*; Pat O'Brien in a dozen films including *Angels with Dirty Faces*, *The Fighting 69th* and *Fighting Father Dunne*; ditto Spencer Tracy, in *Boys' Town*, *San Francisco*, *The Devil at Four O'Clock*, and others; George Arliss in *Cardinal Richelieu*; Don Murray in *The Hoodlum Priest*; Karl Malden in *On the Waterfront* and *The Great Impostor*; Pierre Fresnay in *Monsieur Vincent*; Claude Laydu in *Diary of a Country Priest*; Jean-Paul Belmondo in *Leon Morin Priest*; John Mills in *The Singer Not the Song*; Tom Tryon in *The Cardinal*; Gregory Peck in *The Keys of the Kingdom*; Geoffrey Bayldon in *Sky West and Crooked*; Richard Burton in *Becket*; David Warner in *The Ballad of Cable Hogue*; Ward Bond in *The Quiet Man*; Mickey Rooney in *The Twinkle in God's Eye*; Montgomery Clift in *I Confess*; Alec Guinness in *Father Brown* and *The Prisoner*; Trevor Howard in *Ryan's Daughter*; Donald Sutherland in *Act of the Heart*; and Marcello Mastroianni in *The Priest's Wife*.

Protestant priests included Anthony Quayle in *Serious Charge*; Richard Burton in *The Sandpiper*; Robert Donat in *Lease of Life*; Wilfred Lawson in *Pastor Hall*; Peter Sellers in *Heavens Above*; Richard Todd in *A Man Called Peter*; Fredric March in *One Foot in Heaven*; David Niven in *The Bishop's Wife*. Actors who have got to play pope include Anthony Quinn and John Gielgud in *The Shoes of the Fisherman*, Rod Steiger in *A Man Called John*, Paolo Stoppa in *Becket* and Rex Harrison in *The Agony and the Ecstasy*.

False priests were Humphrey Bogart in *The Left Hand of God*, Rod Steiger in *No Way to Treat a Lady*, Dennis Price in *Kind Hearts and Coronets*, and Peter Sellers in *After the Fox*; while priestly villains were Ralph Richardson in *The Ghoul*, George Arliss in *Dr Syn* (followed by Peter Cushing in *Captain Clegg*), Keenan Wynn in *Johnny Concho*, Cedric Hardwicke in *The Hunchback of Notre Dame* and Robert Mitchum in *Night of the Hunter*. Classifiable as fallen priests were Henry Fonda in *The Fugitive*, Richard Burton in *Night of the Iguana*, Max Von Sydow in *Hawaii*, Burt Lancaster in *Elmer Gantry*, Lars Hanson in *The Scarlet Letter*, and Pierre Fresnay in *Le Défroqué* and *Dieu a Besoin des Hommes*.

Priests came into their own again in a spate of diabolical thrillers: Max Von Sydow and Jason Miller in *The Exorcist*, Patrick Troughton in *The Omen*, Oliver Reed in *The Devils*. Other troubled priests have included Rod Steiger (and various successors) in *The Amityville Horror* series Christopher Reeve in *Monsignor*, and the protagonists of *True Confessions*.

The Prince and the Pauper.
Mark Twain's novel, about the young King Edward VI changing places with a street urchin who happens to be his double, has been a favourite with film-makers, though it has transferred unsatisfactorily to the screen so far. There were at least five silent versions before William Keighley made it into a moderate swashbuckler in 1937, starring Errol Flynn and with twins Billy and Bobby Mauch as the prince and the beggar-boy. Don Chaffey directed a dull television version for Disney in 1962 which was released in cinemas elsewhere with a cast headed by TV's Zorro, Guy Williams, and young Sean Scully in the title roles. (Disney also turned the tale into an animated short with Mickey Mouse and Donald Duck.) In 1977,

Richard Fleischer directed a lacklustre version in the US retitled *Crossed Swords*, starring Oliver Reed and Raquel Welch, and with Mark Lester taking both roles. It was then updated and given a sex change in 1995 as *It Takes Two*, starring twins Mary-Kate and Ashley Olsen, Steve Guttenberg and Kirstie Alley. A British TV version, with Keith Michell as Henry VIII and Philip Sarson in the two roles, was shown in 1996.

prison films
have always had an audience, but did not reach their full potential until sound. Then and through the 30s, film-makers took us on a conducted tour of American prisons. *The Big House*, *The Last Mile*, *I Was a Fugitive from a Chain Gang*, *Twenty Thousand Years in Sing Sing*, *Front Page Woman* (with its gas chamber scene), *Angels with Dirty Faces*, *San Quentin*, *Blackwell's Island*, *Each Dawn I Die*, *Invisible Stripes*, *King of Alcatraz*, *Prison Ship*, *Prison Doctor*, *Mutiny in the Big House* and many others. During the war prison films were surpassed in excitement, but they came back with a bang in *Brute Force*, the toughest of them all, and *White Heat*. The 50s brought *Behind the High Wall*, *Duffy of San Quentin*, *Riot in Cell Block Eleven*, *Inside the Walls of Folsom Prison*, *Black Tuesday*, *I Want to Live*, *Cell 2455 Death Row*, and a remake of *The Last Mile*. Burt LANCASTER appeared in the factual *Bird Man of Alcatraz*; and in the second half of the 60s the subject became popular again with *The Brig*, *The Ceremony*, *Reprieve*, *Point Blank*, *The Dirty Dozen*, *Triple Cross*, *Riot*, *There was a Crooked Man*, *A Clockwork Orange* and *Fortune and Men's Eyes*. It continued in the 80s and 90s with forgettable action movies, but also with such dramas as *The Shawshank Redemption* and *The Green Mile*.

British studios have produced few prison films until the realist wave of the 60s which brought with it *The Criminal*, *The Pot Carriers*, and the army prison film *The Hill*.

Unusual prisons were shown in *Sullivan's Travels*, *Devil's Canyon*, *One Day in the Life of Ivan Denisovich*, and *Nevada Smith*; while among the films poking fun at prison life are *Up the River*, *Pardon Us* (LAUREL and HARDY), *Convict 99* (Will HAY), *Jailhouse Rock* and *Two-Way Stretch*.

Prisons for women crop up quite regularly in such films as *Prison without Bars*, *Caged* (US), *Caged* (It.), *Au Royaume des Cieux*, *Women's Prison*, *Girls behind Bars*, *So Evil So Young*, *The Weak and the Wicked*, *Yield to the Night*, *The Smashing Bird I Used to Know* and *Women in Chains* (TV).

The Prisoner of Zenda.
At least four versions have been made of Anthony Hope's classic Ruritanian romance about a great impersonation, all in Hollywood: Rex Ingram directed a version in 1922 with Lewis Stone and Ramon Novarro; in 1937 John Cromwell directed Ronald Colman and Douglas Fairbanks Jnr in a version that was a model of its kind; Richard Thorpe made a mechanical scene-by-scene remake in 1952 with Stewart Granger and James Mason; in 1979 Peter Sellers appeared in an unsatisfactory half-humorous version by Dick Clement and Ian La Frenais. Comic variations on the story were included in *The Great Race* 65 and *Royal Flash* 75.

prisoners of war
were featured in many films after World War II. The British examples often made the camps seem almost too comfortable, despite the possibility of being shot while attempting to escape; this was perhaps because they were all filled with the same familiar faces. *Albert RN*, *The Captive Heart*, *The Colditz Story*, *The Betrayal*, *Danger Within*, *Reach for the Sky* and *The Password is Courage* all found humour in the situation at any rate; whereas the American counterparts, *The Purple Heart*, *Prisoner of War*, *Stalag 17* and *The Mackenzie Break* saw the harsher side which doubtless existed. The co-production, *The Bridge on the River Kwai*, gave a mixed picture of a Japanese camp; Britain's Hammer horror studio then produced *The Camp on Blood Island*, a fictitious record of atrocity, followed some years later by *The Secret of Blood Island*. Meanwhile the British in *The One That Got Away* paid tribute to the one German to escape from a British camp; and more recently *The Great Escape* showed the Americans coming some way towards the British idea of how jolly life in a camp can be. The ultimate absurdity was reached by an American TV series, *Hogan's Heroes*, which has a camp almost entirely controlled by the prisoners.

The best serious film about prisoners of war remains undoubtedly Renoir's *La Grande Illusion*, made in 1937; though *King Rat* in 1965 made a fair bid to reveal the squalor and futility of the life, as did *The Empire of the Sun* 87, from the perspective of a young boy. Comic adventure stories about the escape of POWs have included *Very Important Person*, *The Secret War of Harry Frigg*, *Where Eagles Dare*, *Hannibal Brooks* and *Situation Hopeless but Not Serious*.

Women's camps were shown in *Two Thousand Women* (GB 1944), *Three Came Home* (US 1950), *A Town Like Alice* (GB 1956) and *Kapo* (It. 1960).

Vietnam made a horrifying start to its quota of prisoner-of-war films with *The Deer Hunter*, and brought it to its nadir with *Rambo: First Blood Part II*.

private eyes:
see MYSTERY.

prizefighting:
see BOXING.

prophecy
has interested film-makers only occasionally, but at least two outstanding films have resulted: *Metropolis* and *Things to Come*. *Just Imagine* painted a light-hearted picture, and *Seven Days in May* was not too frightening about what might be happening politically a few years from now; but one hopes not to take too seriously the predictions in *1984*, *The Time Machine*, *Fahrenheit 451*, *Alphaville*, *When Worlds Collide*, *The World*, *the Flesh and the Devil*, *The War Game*, *Dr Strangelove*, *Punishment Park*, *Beyond the Time Barrier*, *No Blade of Grass*, *Barbarella*, *A Clockwork Orange*, *Planet of the Apes*, *Westworld*, *Futureworld*, *Logan's Run*, *Star Wars*, *The Final Programme*, *Death Race 2000*, *Soylent Green*, *The Ultimate Warrior*, *Robocop*, *Terminator 2*, *Strange Days* (though that is already set in the past), *The Fifth Element* and *2001*.

prostitutes
for many years could not be so labelled in Hollywood films, which featured a surprising number of 'café hostesses'. It was however fairly easy to spot the real profession of the various ladies who played Sadie Thompson in *Rain*, of Marlene Dietrich in *Dishonoured* and *Shanghai Express*, of Clara Bow in *Call Her Savage*, of Greta Garbo in *Anna Christie*, of Miriam Hopkins in *Dr Jekyll and Mr Hyde*, of Tallulah Bankhead in *Faithless*, of Bette Davis in *Of Human Bondage*, of Vivien Leigh in *Waterloo Bridge*, and of Joan Bennett in *Man Hunt*, to name but a few. The French, who have always called a spade a spade, flaunted the calling in hundreds of films including *Dedée D'Anvers*, *La Ronde*, *Le Plaisir*, *Boule de Suif*, *Le Long des Trottoirs*, *La Bonne Soupe*, *Adua et sa Compagnie* and *Les Compagnons de la Nuit*; Italy chipped in with *Mamma Roma* and Japan with *Street of Shame*. In the 50s Britain moved into the field with surprising eagerness – every other movie seemed to feature Dora Bryan in a plastic mac – and there were several alleged exposés of Soho corruption under such titles as *The Flesh is Weak*, *Passport to Shame* and *The World Ten Times Over*. Hollywood half-heartedly followed with some double-talking second features about call girls – *Why Girls Leave Home*, *Call Girl*, *Girls in the Night* – and some 'medical case histories' such as *The Three Faces of Eve*, *Girl of the Night*. Around 1960 the floodgates opened, eased by the sensationally successful Greek comedy *Never on Sunday* (and some continental imitators like *Always on Saturday* and *Every Night of the Week*). Among English-speaking stars who have played prostitutes are Shirley Maclaine in *Some Came Running* and *Irma La Douce*, Sophia Loren in *Lady L*, *Yesterday*, *Today and Tomorrow*, *Marriage Italian Style*, *Boccaccio 70* and *Man of La Mancha*, Anna Karina in *Vivre sa Vie*, Lee Grant in *Divorce American Style* and *The Balcony*, Catherine Deneuve in *Belle de Jour*, Carroll Baker in *Sylvia*, Shirley Jones in *Elmer Gantry*, Nancy Kwan in *The World of Suzie Wong*, Elizabeth Taylor in *Butterfield 8*, Diane Cilento in *Rattle of a Simple Man*, Carol White in *Poor Cow*, Inger Stevens in *Five Card Stud*, Margot Kidder in *Gaily*, *Gaily*, Kitty Wynn in *Panic in Needle Park*, Jane Fonda in *Klute*, Julia Roberts in *Pretty Woman*. Brothels have been shown in *Lady L*, *A Walk on the Wild Side*, *The Revolt of Mamie Stover*, *A House is not a Home*, *Ulysses*, *The Balcony*, *A Funny Thing Happened on the Way to the Forum*, *The Assassination Bureau*, *The Best House in London*, *Games That Lovers Play*, *The Reivers*, *Gaily*, *Gaily*, and an increasing

number of westerns. In *Our Man Flint*, girls were described as 'pleasure units'...
See also: COURTESANS.

psychology

is featured most prominently in American films – quite naturally since the United States is the home of the psychiatrist. However, one of the best serious psychological films, *Mine Own Executioner*, did come from Britain and showed the doctor to be more in need of help than the patient; while two other notable British films, *Thunder Rock* and *Dead of Night*, centred on the depiction of psychological states.

Although films about psychology can be firmly traced back to *The Cabinet of Dr Caligari* and *Secrets of a Soul*, the subject took its firmest hold in the middle of World War II, when so many people needed reassurance; the recounting of dreams to an analyst could even take the place of musical numbers in a romantic trifle like *Lady in the Dark*. Soon we were inundated with melodramas like *Spellbound*, *The Dark Mirror* and *Possessed*, in which the question to be answered was not so much who or how but why; and it wasn't until about 1950, with *Harvey*, that analysts could be laughed at; they were still being analysed in the 70s in such films as *Taking Off*. In the 50s the schizophrenic drama took on a new lease of life (*The Three Faces of Eve*, *Lizzie*, *Vertigo*), as did the tendency to guy individual psychiatrists while still claiming to respect the profession (*Oh Men Oh Women*, *Mirage*, *A Fine Madness*, *The Group*, *What a Way to Go*, *Marriage of a Young Stockbroker*, *The Couch Trip*). Of course, films were still made which took the whole matter with deadly seriousness, as in *The Cobweb*, *The Mark*, *Captain Newman MD*, *The Third Secret* and *Pressure Point*. John HUSTON's underrated film on the life of *Freud* may have been unlucky to arrive at a time of change: the fashion is now for case histories in which no solution is offered (*Repulsion*, *Morgan*, *Cul-de-Sac*) or psychological horror comics such as *Psycho*, *Homicidal*, and *The Night Walker*, while in *Promise Her Anything* we were finally shown a psychiatrist (Robert CUMMINGS) who doesn't believe in psychiatry. The subject turned romantic in 1991 with Barbra STREISAND as an analyst who falls in love with her patient's brother in *The Prince of Tides*, and sinister in *What about Bob?*, in which the patient drives the analyst crazy, the same year. In 1998 came *Analyze This* in which a psychiatrist is faced with a patient he'd rather avoid: a Mafia boss.
See also DREAMS; FANTASY; AMNESIA; CASE HISTORIES.

publicity.

No right minded film-maker believes his own publicity ... but he surely hopes it works. The tag-line devised for a film can have a make-or-break effect on its box-office record. Seldom can such lines be claimed as an honest distillation of truth, and very often they hint at more sensations than can be found in the film to which they are attached. But for sheer ingenuity some are unbeatable, and a few have even passed into the language.

NB: In 1972 a New York magazine ran a competition, inviting readers to invent way-out and hilarious tag-lines for non-existent movies. The results were indeed hilarious, but not so way-out that one can't imagine them being used. Here are some of the winners:

Makes Myra Breckinridge look like Snow White!

It took guts to film. Have you the guts to see it?

There were four men in her life. One to love her. One to marry her. One to take care of her. And one to kill her...

They lived a lifetime in 24 crowded hours!

The picture that could change your life – or save it!

If you scoff at the powers of darkness, do not see this film alone!

The book they said could never be written has become the movie they said could never be filmed!

❝ *The Twenties:*

The dangerous age for women is from three to seventy! – *Adam's Rib (1922)*

A photoplay of tempestuous love between a madcap English beauty and a bronzed Arab chief! – *The Sheik*

A cast of 125,000! – *Ben Hur*

The mightiest dramatic spectacle of all the ages! – *The Ten Commandments (1923)*

The epic of the American doughboy! – *The Big Parade*

A thrill a minute! A laugh a second! A comedy cyclone! – *Feet First*

Love of tender girlhood! Passionate deeds of heroes! A rushing, leaping drama of charm and excitement! – *America*

A thing of beauty is a joy forever... – *Street Angel*

The Thirties:

The knockout picture of the year! – *The Champ*

The most startling drama ever produced! – *Strange Interlude*

Mothered by an ape – he knew only the law of the jungle – to seize what he wanted! – *Tarzan of the Apes*

Strange Desires! Loves and hates and secret yearnings ... hidden in the shadows of a man's mind. – *Dr Jekyll and Mr Hyde*

The picture that will make 1933 famous! – *Gabriel over the White House*

The dance-mad musical triumph of two continents! – *The Gay Divorcee*

The love affair that shook the world! – *Cleopatra*

The most glorious musical romance of all time! – *One Night of Love*

His love challenged the flames of revolution! – *A Tale of Two Cities*

Love as burning as Sahara's sands! – *Under Two Flags*

The march of time measured by a human heart – a mother's heart! – *Cavalcade*

Romance aflame through dangerous days and nights of terror! In a land where anything can happen – most of all to a beautiful girl alone! – *Gunga Din*
(in which the girl was very dispensable indeed)

The picture made behind locked doors! – *Dr Cyclops*

The strangest love a man has ever known! – *Dracula*

More sensational than her unforgettable father! – *Dracula's Daughter*

A love story that lived for three thousand years! – *The Mummy*

He's just as funny as his old man was fierce! – *Son of Kong*

Three centuries in the making! – *A Midsummer Night's Dream*

He plucked from the gutter a faded rose and made an immortal masterpiece! – *The Life of Emile Zola*

135 women – with men on their minds! – *The Women*

He treated her rough – and she loved it! – *Red Dust*

A story so momentous it required six Academy Award stars and a cast of 1,186 players! – *Juarez*

Only the rainbow can duplicate its brilliance! – *The Adventures of Robin Hood*

Don't pronounce it – see it! – *Ninotchka*

A monster in form but human in his desire for love! – *Bride of Frankenstein*

Boiling passions in the burning sands! – *The Lost Patrol*

Six sticks of dynamite that blasted his way to freedom – and awoke America's conscience! – *I Am a Fugitive from a Chain Gang*

The Forties:

No one is as good as Bette when she's bad! – *In This Our Life*

If she were yours, would you forgive? – *The Unfaithful*

The relentless drama of a woman driven to the depths of emotion by a craving beyond control! – *The Lady Gambles*

The thousands who have read the book will know why WE WILL NOT SELL ANY CHILDREN TICKETS to see this picture! – *The Grapes of Wrath*

Half men, half demons, warriors such as the world has never known – they lived with death and danger for the women who hungered for their love! – *Northwest Passage*

You can't keep a good monster down! – *The Ghost of Frankenstein*

A romantic gentleman by day – a love-mad beast by night! – *Dr Jekyll and Mr Hyde*

The minx in mink with a yen for men! – *Lady in the Dark*

The immortal thriller... – *Orpheus*

How'd you like to tussle with Russell? – *The Outlaw*

Gable's back and Garson's got him! – *Adventure*

There never was a woman like... – *Gilda*

It tells ALL about those Brontë sisters! – *Devotion*

More thrilling than the deeds of man ... more beautiful than the love of woman ... more wonderful than the dreams of children! – *The Jungle Book*

The picture they were born for! – *The Big Sleep*

The picture that helped to win the war! – *Mrs Miniver (reissue)*

He's as fast on the draw as he is in the drawing room! – *The Maltese Falcon*

We're going to see Jennifer Jones AGAIN in... – *The Song of Bernadette*

The sum total of all human emotion! – *Leave Her to Heaven*

The truth about the Nazis from the cradle to the battlefront! – *Hitler's Children*

A peek into the other woman's male! – *A Letter to Three Wives*

She knows all about love potions and lovely motions! – *I Married a Witch*

Paramount proudly brings to the screens of America one of the three great love stories of all time! – *To Each His Own*
(which were the others?)

'I bought this woman for my own ... and I'll kill the man who touches her!' – *Unconquered*

A thousand miles of danger with a thousand thrills a mile! – *Santa Fé Trail*

168 minutes of breathless thrills and romance! – *For Whom the Bell Tolls*

The girl of the moment in the wonderful picture of America's hey! hey! day! – *Margie*

The kind of woman most men want – but shouldn't have! – *Mildred Pierce*

They had a date with fate in... – *Casablanca*

The flaming drama of a high-born beauty who blindly loved the most icy-hearted big shot gangland ever knew! – *Johnny Eager*

Whisper her name! – *The Strange Love of Martha Ivers*

A mouth like hers is just for kissing ... not for telling! – *Nora Prentiss*

She insulted her soul! – *Dishonored Lady*

She's got the biggest six-shooters in the west! – *The Beautiful Blonde from Bashful Bend*

The private lady of a public enemy! – *The Damned Don't Cry*

It was the look in her eyes that did it! How could he know it meant murder? – *The Woman in the Window*

A love story every woman would die a thousand deaths to live! – *Jane Eyre*

'The men in her life sometimes lived to regret it!' – *Temptation*

The Fifties:

Greater than IVANHOE! – *Julius Caesar*

First they moved (1895)! Then they talked (1927)! Now they smell! – *Scent of Mystery*

The butler did it! He made every lady in the house oh so very happy! – *My Man Godfrey*

Sing, Judy! Dance, Judy! The world is waiting for your sunshine! – *A Star Is Born*

Even in the first wild joy of her arms, he realized that she would be ... an unfit mother! – *Because of You*

A lion in your lap! – *Bwana Devil*
(the first 3-D film)

In making this film, MGM feel privileged to add something of permanent value to the cultural treasure house of mankind... – *Quo Vadis*

Ancient Rome is going to the dogs, Robert Taylor is going to the lions, and Peter Ustinov is going crazy! – *Quo Vadis (revived for TV in the 70s)*

You have never really seen Gregory Peck until you see him in CinemaScope! – *Night People*

We didn't say nice people, we said – *Night People*

Their story is not in the history books. It has never been seen on the screen – until now! – *Désirée*

A hard cop and a soft dame! – *The Big Heat*

A completely new experience between men and women! – *The Men*
(about paraplegics)

He faced a decision that someday may be yours to make! – *Ransom*
(the hero's son was kidnapped)

The colossus who conquered the world!

The most colossal motion picture of all time! – *Alexander the Great*

When the hands point straight up ... the excitement starts! – *High Noon*

That streetcar man has a new desire! – *The Wild One*

Her treachery stained every stone of the pyramid! – *Land of the Pharaohs*

The supreme screen achievement of our time! – *Salome*

Of what a girl did ... what a boy did ... of ecstasy and revenge! – *East of Eden*

If a woman answers ... hang on for dear life! – *Dial M For Murder*

Body of a boy! Mind of a monster! Soul of an unearthly thing! – *I Was a Teenage Frankenstein*

The story of a family's ugly secret and the stark moment that thrust their private lives into public view! – *Written on the Wind*

'She was too hungry for love to care where she found it!' – *The Female on the Beach*

The Sixties:

If you miss the first five minutes you miss one suicide, two executions, one seduction and the key to the plot! – *The Kremlin Letter*

The motion picture with something to offend everybody! – *The Loved One*

Beware the beat of the cloth-wrapped feet! – *The Mummy's Shroud*

The world's most uncovered undercover agent! – *Fathom*

Don't give away the ending – it's the only one we have! – *Psycho*

The birds is coming! – *The Birds*

Every time a woman turns her face away because she's tired or unwilling, there's someone waiting like me... – *The Dark at the Top of the Stairs*

The hot line suspense comedy! – *Dr Strangelove*

A thousand thrills ... and Hayley Mills! – *In Search of the Castaways*

A picture that goes beyond what men think about – because no man ever thought about it in quite this way! – *Eight and a Half*

You may not believe in ghosts, but you cannot deny terror... – *The Haunting*

There are many kinds of love, but are there any without guilt? – *Five Finger Exercise*

You can expect the unexpected! – *Charade*

Now ... add a motion picture to the wonders of the world! – *Taras Bulba*

One man ... three women ... one night! – *The Night of the Iguana*

You'll laugh your pants off! – *Laurel and Hardy's Laughing Twenties*

£10,000 if you die of fright! – *Macabre*

The picture with the fear flasher and the horror horn! – *Chamber of Horrors*

Meet the girls with the thermo-nuclear navels! The most titillating time bombs you've ever been tempted to trigger! – *Dr Goldfoot and the Girl Bombs*

Keep the children home! And if you're squeamish, stay home with them! – *Witchfinder General*

A side of life you never expected to see on the screen! – *Walk on the Wild Side*

You are cordially invited to George and Martha's for an evening of fun and games! – *Who's Afraid of Virginia Woolf?*

Why the crazy title? If we told you, you'd only laugh! – *The Russians are Coming, The Russians are Coming*

Every father's daughter is a virgin! – *Goodbye Columbus*

They're young ... they're in love ... and they kill people. – *Bonnie and Clyde*

'What we've got here is a failure to communicate.' – *Cool Hand Luke*

The big comedy of nineteen-sexty-sex! – *Boeing Boeing*

He is a shy schoolmaster. She is a music hall star. They marry and immediately have 283 children ... all boys! – *Goodbye Mr Chips*

The Seventies:

Love means never having to say you're sorry... – *Love Story*

Hope never dies for a man with a good dirty mind! – *Hoffman*

The story of a homosexual who married a nymphomaniac! – *The Music Lovers*

Like the act of love, this film must be experienced from beginning to end... – *The Sailor Who Fell from Grace with the Sea*

They stand side by side. Young and old. Rich and poor. They gather together for a single purpose. Survival. – *The Seagull*

We don't love – we just make love. And damn little of that! – *The Happy Ending*

She gave away secrets to one side and her heart to the other! – *Darling Lili*

For the price of a movie you'll feel like a million! – *The Sunshine Boys*

The damnedest thing you ever saw. – *Nashville*

1953 was a good year for leaving home. – *Next Stop Greenwich Village*

The epic love story in which everybody has a great role and a big part. – *Joseph Andrews*

You have nothing to lose but your mind. – *Asylum*

A degenerate film with dignity! – *Inserts*

In space no one can hear you scream. – *Alien*

We are not alone. – *Close Encounters of the Third Kind*

Just when you thought it was safe to go back into the water. – *Jaws 2*

It was a line which spawned such imitations as:

Now you're not safe OUT of the water. – *Piranha II – Flying Killers*

Just when you thought it was safe to go back into the departure lounge. – *Airplane II*

Just when he thought it was safe to go back into the water. – *10*

The Eighties:

He was D. H. Lawrence. She was his Lady Chatterley. Their extraordinary romance was more tempestuous than any he wrote. – *Priest of Love*

The film where you hiss the villain and cheer the hero. – *The Legend of the Lone Ranger*

As brutal, beautiful, vicious and vast as America itself! – *Heaven's Gate*

Breaking out is impossible. Breaking in is insane! – *Escape from New York*

The most exciting pair in the jungle! – *Tarzan the Ape-Man (starring Bo Derek)*

From the very beginning, they knew they'd be friends to the very end. What they didn't count on was everything in between. – *Rich and Famous*

The last word about the first time. – *Losin' It*

To the valley of beauty came the shadow of death! – *Deadly Blessing*

Every great love leaves its mark. – *Tattoo*

The third dimension is terror. – *Jaws 3-D*

It's 22 years later. And Norman Bates is coming home. – *Psycho II*

Trust me, I'm a doctor. – *Shock Treatment* (a line that turned up a decade later for *Paper Mask*)

The good news is Jonathan's having his first affair. The bad news is she's his roommate's mother. – *Class*

I'd been shot so many times you could use my shirt as a tea strainer. – *Dead Men Don't Wear Plaid*

Forged by a god. Foretold by a wizard. Found by a King. – *Excalibur*

What they wanted most wasn't on the menu. – *Diner*

He is afraid. He is totally alone. He is 3 million light years from home. – *E.T. – the Extraterrestrial*

She was the woman of Allen's dreams. She had large dark eyes, a beautiful smile and a great pair of fins. – *Splash*

When the going gets tough, the tough get going! – *Jewel of the Nile*

They left for war as boys, never to return as men. – *All Quiet on the Western Front*

The tenant in room seven is very small, very twisted and very mad. – *Basket Case*

Be afraid. Be very afraid. – *The Fly*

When he pours, he reigns. – *Cocktail*

Just when he was ready for mid-life crisis, something unexpected came up. Puberty. – *Vice Versa*

Dying is easy. Comedy is hard. – *Punchline*

Somewhere under the sea and beyond your imagination is an adventure in fantasy. – *The Little Mermaid*

Can two friends sleep together and still love each other in the morning? – *When Harry Met Sally*

The Nineties:

Their love was as dangerous as the secrets they kept. – *The Russia House*

Paul Sheldon used to write for a living ... Now he's writing to stay alive. – *Misery*

There was a time when the only way to uphold justice was to break the law. – *Robin Hood: Prince of Thieves*

He's coming to town with a few days to kill. – *Predator 2*

Having a wonderful time. Wish I were here. – *Postcards from the Edge*

Eight legs, two fangs and an attitude. – *Arachnophobia*

Once in a lifetime comes a motion picture that makes you feel like falling in love all over again. This is not that picture. – *The War of the Roses*

How many times can you die for love? – *Dead Again*

There is nothing in the dark that isn't there in the light. Except fear. – *Cape Fear*

He'd be the perfect criminal if he wasn't the perfect cop. – *Deep Cover*

He was a man who couldn't care less ... until he met a man who couldn't care more. – *City of Joy*

The fountain of youth. The secret of eternal life. The power of an ancient potion. Sometimes it works ... Sometimes it doesn't. – *Death Becomes Her*

An adventure 65 million years in the making – *Jurassic Park*

63 million years ago they ruled the Earth. They're back, and it's no theme park! – *Carnosaur*

No one would take on his case ... until one man was willing to take on the system – *Philadelphia*

Just your average Girl meets Girl, Girl loses Girl, Girl hires Boy to get Girl back story. With a twist. – *Three of Hearts*

Stealing ... Cheating ... Killing ... Who says romance is dead? – *True Romance*

Houston, we have a problem. – *Apollo 13*

When intimacy is forbidden and passion is a sin, love is the most defiant crime of all – *The Scarlet Letter*

Leave your inhibitions at the door – *Showgirls*

Paul Edgecomb didn't believe in miracles. Until the day he met one. – *The Green Mile*

Warning: Exposing the Truth May Be Hazardous – *The Insider*

Not every gift is a blessing – *The Sixth Sense*

The Naughties:

What We Do In Life Echoes In Eternity. – *Gladiator*

No mercy. No shame. No sequel. – *Scary Movie*

We lied. – *Scary Movie II*

Killer Looks – *American Psycho*

There's a new reason to be afraid of the dark. – *Pitch Black*

He was the perfect husband until his one mistake followed them home – *What Lies Beneath*

He is the target of the most merciless family in New York. His own. – *The Yards*

put-downs.

Waspish comments about other people always make good reading. Here are a few for starters:

❝ Let's face it, Billy Wilder at work is two people – Mr Hyde and Mr Hyde. – *Harry Kurnitz*

I loved it – particularly the ideas he took from me. – *D.W. Griffith on Citizen Kane*

Jack Lemmon's Hildy Johnson is like a mortuary assistant having a wild fling. – *New Yorker review of The Front Page*

Mae West, playing a ghastly travesty of the travesty of womanhood she once played, has a Mae West face painted on the front of her head and moves to and fro like the Imperial Hotel during the 1923 Tokyo earthquake. – *Joseph Morgenstern reviewing Myra Breckinridge*

As a pompous middle-European intellectual Kenneth Mars mugs and drools in a manner that Jerry Lewis might find excessive. – *Jay Cocks reviewing What's Up, Doc?*

To insinuate that Leslie Bricusse's plodding score is merely dreadful would be an act of charity. – *Rex Reed on Goodbye Mr Chips*

Miss Martin, I notice, is playing Jean Arthur, a tendency which even Miss Arthur should learn to curb. – *James Agee on True To Life*

Mr Muni seemed intent on submerging himself so completely in make-up that he disappeared. – *Bette Davis on Juarez*

Which is he playing now? – *W. Somerset Maugham while watching Spencer Tracy on the set of Dr Jekyll and Mr Hyde*

Ryan O'Neal is so stiff and clumsy that he can't even manage a part requiring him to be stiff and clumsy. – *Jay Cocks on What's Up Doc?*

He has a gift for butchering good parts while managing to look intelligent, thus constituting Hollywood's abiding answer to the theatre. – *Wilfred Sheed of Jack Lemmon*

Just how garish her commonplace accent, squeakily shrill voice, and the childish petulance with which she delivers her lines are, my pen is neither scratchy nor leaky enough to convey. – *John Simon of Elizabeth Taylor in The Taming of the Shrew*

George Raft and Gary Cooper once played a scene in front of a cigar store, and it looked like the wooden Indian was overacting. – *George Burns*

Quiller.

Code name of a tough British secret agent, able to take any amount of torture, who is the hero of a series of novels by Adam Hall (Elleston Trevor). United Artists acquired the film rights to them in 1993 with the intention of producing a series of movies featuring what the company called 'the thinking man's James Bond'. A film of the first novel, *The Quiller Memorandum*, was directed by Michael Anderson in 1966 starring George Segal, and Michael Jayston played the role in a BBC TV series, *Quiller*, in 1975.

Quo Vadis?

The biblical epic by Henryk Sienkiewicz has been filmed three times: in Italy in 1912 and 1924, and in America in 1951. The third version, though less impressive as a product of its period than the others, was certainly the most spectacular. Robert Taylor and Deborah Kerr suffered under Peter Ustinov's *Nero*; Mervyn Le Roy directed.

radio,

being a competitor, was largely ignored by serious movies in the 30s, but radio stars featured in a number of musicals, especially the *Big Broadcast* series and the British *Radio Parade*, *Music Hath Charms*, etc.; in the 40s, a number of low-budgeters such as *Reveille with Beverly* had a radio background. Popular radio series to be filmed included *Dr Christian*, *Fibber McGee and Molly*, *Charlie McCarthy Detective*, *The Great Gildersleeve*, *Hi Gang*, *Band Waggon* and *It's That Man Again*. Mysteries set in radio stations included *Who Done It* and *Death at Broadcasting House*; *Helter Skelter* was a slapstick comedy set at the BBC. In the 70s, *Play Misty for Me* revolved around a disc jockey, as did the TV movie *A Cry for Help*; while *WUSA* was undoubtedly the most serious drama on the subject unless one counts the sharply satirical *A Face in the Crowd* and *Talk Radio*, highlighting the potential dangers of chat shows.

Raffles.

The sophisticated burglar who returns to crime to help an old friend was created by E. W. Hornung and has attracted the attentions of several suave leading men. There were half a dozen silent Raffles, including one from House Peters in 1925, directed by King Baggot; Ronald Colman played the role in 1930, and a shot-by-shot remake in 1939 starred David Niven.

railway stations

have provided a major setting for some memorable films including *The Ghost Train*, *Doctor Zhivago*, *Knight without Armour*, *I'll Never Forget Whatshisname* (with its white 'dream' station), *Union Station*, *3.10 to Yuma*, *Last Train from Madrid*, *Bhowani Junction*, *Northwest Frontier*, *100 Rifles*, *The Mercenaries*, *Waterloo Road*, *Anna Karenina*, *Grand Central Station*, *Under the Clock*, *Brief Encounter*, *Oh Mr Porter*, *The Titfield Thunderbolt*, *High Noon*, *In the Heat of the Night* and *The Train* ... while Orson Welles made *The Trial* almost entirely within a deserted station, and de Sica made *Indiscretion* among the crowds of Rome's Stazione Termini.

See also: TRAINS.

rain

has been put to many uses by film scenarists. It was the direct cause of dramatic situations in *Rebecca* (a shower flattened Joan Fontaine's hair-do just as she arrived at Manderley); in *The Loneliness of the Long Distance Runner* (it revealed evidence which the hero was trying to conceal); in *Floods of Fear* (it permitted the escape of three convicts, one of whom then rescued the heroine); in *The African Queen* (it raised the water level and so released the boat from the reeds which held it captive); in *Desk Set* (it persuaded Spencer Tracy to accept Katharine Hepburn's offer of hospitality); in *Pygmalion* (it caused the meeting of Higgins and Eliza); in *Sands of the Kalahari* (it flooded a pit in which Stuart Whitman was imprisoned and permitted his escape); in *When Tomorrow Comes* (it stranded Charles Boyer and Irene Dunne in a remote church for the night); and in many others. Two splendid symbolic uses were in *Saraband for Dead Lovers* (a raindrop made a stained-glass madonna appear to weep at the ill-fated wedding) and *The Stars Look Down* (as the hero and heroine make love, two raindrops intertwine on the window-pane).

Rain has often been used symbolically as a relief from tension and heat, in films as diverse as *Night of the Iguana*, *Passport to Pimlico*, *The Long Hot Summer*, *Key Largo*, *Twelve Angry Men*, *Black Narcissus*, *The Good Earth* and *Rain* itself. It has provided a solemn or ominous background in *Psycho*, *Term of Trial*, *Rashomon*, *It Always Rains on Sunday*, *Room at the Top*, *The Robe*, *Fires on the Plain*, *The Collector* and many others. It has a particularly depressing effect at a funeral, as was shown in *The Glass Key* and *Our Town*; or at an assassination (*Foreign Correspondent*). But it can also be used for farcical purposes: in *Three Men in a Boat*, *The Silencers*, *Fraternally Yours*, *Oh Mr Porter*, etc. And it can provide a comedy twist, as at the end of *The Lady Vanishes*, when the English travellers so eager to get back to the test match find that rain has stopped play.

It can produce a decorative effect (*Les Parapluies de Cherbourg*, *Miracle in the Rain*, *Breakfast at Tiffany's*). It can be spectacular (the climax of *Journey into Fear*, the glistening streets in *The Third Man*, the downpours in *The Rains Came*, and *Pather Panchali*, the battles in the rain in *Tower of London* and *Seven Samurai*). And it can provide a cue for song: 'Isn't it a Lovely Day to be Caught in the Rain' in *Top Hat*, the title songs of *Singin' in the Rain* and *Stormy Weather*, 'The Rain in Spain' in *My Fair Lady*, 'April Showers' in *The Jolson Story*, 'Little April Shower' in *Bambi*. In fact, it seems to be by far the most versatile of all the film-maker's effects. It has even featured as the subject of a disaster movie, *Hard Rain* 98, in which a town was flooded, and its cast, wet, no longer seemed stars.

Rain.

Somerset Maugham's story of the conflict between a missionary and a woman of highly doubtful character has been filmed three times in Hollywood: in 1928 with Gloria Swanson and Lionel Barrymore; in 1932 with Joan Crawford and Walter Huston; and in 1957 (as *Miss Sadie Thompson*) with Rita Hayworth and José Ferrer. In each case the Production Code made you guess what the lady's actual profession was.

The Rains Came.

Louis Bromfield's novel of the high days of British India was filmed in 1939 with Myrna Loy and Tyrone Power, and, as *The Rains of Ranchipur*, in 1955 with Lana Turner and Richard Burton.

Rambo.

The disgruntled former Green Beret has been played by Sylvester STALLONE in three increasingly violent films: *First Blood* 82, directed by Ted KOTCHEFF; *Rambo: First Blood Part II* 85, directed by George P. COSMATOS, in which he had become a comic-strip hero, destroying enemies in Vietnam; and *Rambo III* 88, directed by Peter MACDONALD, in which he continued as a one-man army, this time defeating the Russians in Afghanistan, most of which he blew up. The series was spoofed in *Hot Shots! Part Deux* 93, with Charlie SHEEN as a dim mercenary with big muscles and bigger guns.

Ramona.

Helen Hunt Jackson's novel about an Indian girl was filmed four times: by D. W. Griffith in 1910, with Mary Pickford and Henry B. Walthall; by Donald Crisp in 1916, with Adda Gleason and Monroe Salisbury; by Edwin Carewe in 1928, with Dolores del Rio and Warner Baxter; and by Henry King in 1936, with Loretta Young and Don Ameche.

The Range Busters.

A series of 'B' westerns produced for seven years from 1940 by Monogram Pictures in imitation of Republic's THREE MESQUITEERS series. It starred two of the Mesquiteers, Ray 'Crash' CORRIGAN and Mex TERHUNE, together with John 'Dusty' KING. Many were directed by S. Roy Luby, who churned out dozens of westerns from the mid-30s to the late 40s.

rape

was virtually unmentionable in English-speaking films until Warner's got away with it in *Johnny Belinda* in 1947. Then it became the centre of attention in *Outrage*, *Peyton Place*, *Wicked as They Come*, *A Streetcar Named Desire*, *Last Train from Gun Hill*, *Two Women*, *To Kill a Mockingbird*, *Satan Never Sleeps*, *Shock Corridor*, *Assault*, *Trial*, *Five Gates to Hell*, *The Chapman Report*, *The Mark*, *Anatomy of a Murder*, *Town without Pity*, *The Party's Over* (in which the victim proved to be dead), and *The Penthouse*. In *Waterhole Three* James Coburn, accused of the crime, shrugged it off as 'assault with a friendly weapon'. There was much talk of rape in *The Knack* and *Lock Up Your Daughters*, threat of rape in *Experiment in Terror* and *Cape Fear*, and an accusation of rape in *Term of Trial*. Foreign language films on the subject have included *Rashomon*, *The Virgin Spring*, *Two Women*, *Viridiana* and the Greek *Amok*. In 70s films it became too commonplace to be worth mentioning, outstanding fictional instances being *Straw Dogs*, *A Clockwork Orange*, *Lipstick*, and *Death Wish*, with *Cry Rape* and *A Case of Rape* adopting a documentary treatment. *The Accused* 88 caused controversy with its depiction of the gang-rape of a provocative woman and subsequent court-room trial – it also brought an Oscar for Jodie Foster as best actress. And some cheered in *Thelma & Louise* 91 when a would-be rapist was shot and killed.

Rashomon.

Akira Kurosawa's 1951 masterpiece, featuring the different accounts by four people concerned in a moment of violence, re-opened Western cinemas to Japanese films and established his international reputation. It was remade by Martin Ritt in 1964 and given a western setting, starring Paul Newman as a Mexican bandit.

The Rat

began as a film script written by Ivor NOVELLO for director Adrian BRUNEL, following their success in the film *The Man without Desire*. When Brunel was unable to finance it, Novello collaborated with actress Constance COLLIER to turn it into a lurid melodrama, which they wrote under the pseudonym of David L'Estrange and subtitled 'The Story of an Apache'. It starred Novello as Pierre Boucheron, a French crook who is reformed by the love of a poor but honest woman. It was a surprising success on the stage, as was the subsequent film in 1925, which was followed by two sequels: *The Triumph of the Rat* 26, in which he goes from riches to rags, and *The Return of the Rat* 28, in which he is suspected of murdering his philandering wife. In 1937, Herbert WILCOX directed a remake of the original, starring Anton WALBROOK, but it failed to repeat its earlier success.

Rebecca of Sunnybrook Farm.

The American children's classic by Kate Douglas Wiggin was filmed in 1917 by Marshall Neilan, with Mary Pickford; in 1932 by Alfred Santell, with Marian Nixon; and in 1938, much changed, by Allan Dwan, with Shirley Temple.

Red Dust.

This rubber-plantation drama by Wilson Collinson is remembered for the electric teaming of Clark Gable and Jean Harlow in the 1932 version, directed by Victor Fleming, and for the scene in which Harlow takes a primitive shower. It was remade in 1939 as *Congo Maisie*, with Ann Sothern and John Carroll; and in 1954 Gable himself appeared opposite Ava Gardner in a lavish restyling under the title *Mogambo*, directed by John Ford.

Red Indians (native Americans),

it is generally thought, were always portrayed as villains on screen until *Broken Arrow* in 1950, when Jeff Chandler played Cochise. But in fact there were many silent films in which Indians were not only on the side of right but the leading figures in the story. In 1911 one finds titles like *An Indian Wife's Devotion*, *A Squaw's Love*, *Red-Wing's Gratitude*; *Ramona* had already been made once and was to survive three remakes; 1913 brought *Heart of an Indian* and *The Squaw Man*. Later there were versions of *In the Days of Buffalo Bill* 21, *The Vanishing American* 25, and *Redskin* 28. It seems to have been sound that made the Indians villainous, and kept them that way for twenty-two years.

After *Broken Arrow* there was a deluge of pro-Indian films. *Devil's Doorway*, *Across the Wide Missouri*, *The Savage*, *Arrowhead*, *The Big Sky*, *Apache*, *Taza – Son of Cochise*, *Chief Crazy Horse*, *Sitting Bull*, *White Feather*, *Navajo*, *Hiawatha*, all came within four years. There were even biopics of modern Indians: *The Outsider* (Ira Hayes) and *Jim Thorpe*, *All American*. In recent years the Indians have been slipping back into villainy: but the 60s brought *Flaming Star*, *Cheyenne Autumn*, *Tell them Willie Boy is Here*, *A Man called Horse*, *Flap*, *Little Big Man*, *The Stalking Moon*; and TV in 1966 boasted a series based on a Red Indian cop in New York (the name is *Hawk*) as well as comic Indians in *F Troop*; and Elvis Presley played a Red Indian hero in *Stay Away Joe*. In the 90s, *Dances with Wolves* established the Indians as heroes and the American cavalry as the villains.

Other whites who have played red include Boris Karloff in *Tap Roots*; Victor Mature in *Chief Crazy Horse*; Charlton Heston in *The Savage*; Burt Lancaster in *Apache*; Paul Newman in *Hombre*; Robert Taylor in *Devil's Doorway*; Don Ameche in *Ramona*.

- The Jacarillo tribe financed *A Gunfight* in 1971.

reincarnation

has seldom been seriously tackled in the cinema: *The Search for Bridey Murphy*, *I've Lived Before* and *The Reincarnation of Peter Proud* are almost the only examples. Many characters of farce and melodrama have *thought* they were reincarnated, including the hero of *She* and heroine of *The Vengeance of She*. The real thing happened to Oliver Hardy in *The Flying Deuces* (he came back as a horse); to a dog in *You Never Can Tell* (he came back as Dick Powell); and to the luckless heroine of *The Bride and the Beast*, who found that in a former existence she had been a gorilla. Reincarnation was also the basis of *Here Comes Mr Jordan*, and of *The Mummy*. A man came back as Debbie Reynolds in *Goodbye Charlie*, and in *Quest for Love* there were parallel love stories two centuries apart. In 1968 a version was made of Elmer Rice's *The Adding Machine*, with its celestial laundry for souls; and in 1970 there was even a musical on the subject, *On a Clear Day You Can See Forever*.

rejuvenation

is not a theme the cinema has frequently explored. *She* tried it several times with unhappy results, as did Laurel and Hardy in *Dirty Work* (Olly came back as a chimpanzee). *The Man in Half Moon Street* and *Countess Dracula* both kept young on the blood of others; *Dorian Gray* did it by keeping a picture of himself in the attic. Most successful were *Lost Horizon*'s inhabitants of Shangri-La, but once the cold winds of the outside world blew they were done for. Rock Hudson had worse luck in *Seconds*. *Cocoon* introduced alien aid to staying young, although *Cocoon: The Return* showed that there was no permanent solution to the problems of age.

religion

has inspired film-makers from the beginning – as a commercial trump card. In the early years of the century it was the Italians who produced vast semi-biblical spectacles like *Quo Vadis* and *Cabiria*, but Hollywood was not slow to catch on, and producers soon found that religious shorts gave them extra prestige. There were several versions of *From the Manger to the Cross*; Griffith, in *Judith of Bethulia* and *Intolerance*, contributed his share; *Ben Hur* was the biggest spectacular of all; but it was Cecil B. de Mille in the 20s who brought the Bible to full commercial flower with *The Ten Commandments* and *King of Kings*. (His 1932 *The Sign of the Cross*, 1950 *Samson and Delilah* and 1956 remake of *The Ten Commandments* show that for him at least time continued to stand still.) In 1929, though *Noah's Ark* was spectacle pure and simple, Vidor's *Hallelujah* at least partially transmitted Negro religious fervour. In the 30s Hollywood was seeking fresh ways to combine religion with sentiment or spectacle, in *The Cradle Song*, *Dante's Inferno*, *The Garden of Allah*, *The Green Light* and *Boys' Town*. One result was a new characterization of PRIESTS as jolly good fellows: stars like Spencer Tracy and Pat O'Brien were eager to play them. Yet none had the quiet dignity of Rex Ingram as De Lawd in *Green Pastures*, a Negro version of the Scriptures.

The war naturally brought a religious revival. Every film set in England seemed to end with a service in a bombed church, and religious figures became big time in films like *The Song of Bernadette*, *Going My Way*, *The Keys of the Kingdom* and *The Bells of St Mary's*. Savage war films masqueraded under such titles as *God Is My Co-Pilot* and *A Wing and a Prayer*. And heaven was used as a background for light-hearted fantasy films about death and judgement day, such as *Here Comes Mr Jordan*, *Heaven Can Wait*, and *The Horn Blows at Midnight*. The only film of this period to question religion at all was the British *Major Barbara*: 'What price salvation now?'

In the cynical post-war years religion was at a low ebb. An expensive *Joan of Arc* in 1948 failed disastrously, and an attempt to bring God into our everyday life, *The Next Voice You Hear*, fared no better. A sincere performance by Robert Donat could not bring people to see *Lease of Life*. Indeed, the only religious films to break even at the box office were those with a direct Roman Catholic appeal, such as *Monsieur Vincent* and *The Miracle of Fatima*. True religion, to Hollywood, was out, and the Bible became once more a source book for a string of tawdry commercial epics: *Quo Vadis*, *Salome*, *The Prodigal*, *The Robe*, a remake of *Ben Hur*, *Barabbas*, *The Silver Chalice*, *Sodom and Gomorrah* and many cut-rate dubbed Italian spectacles of a similar kind (most with Hollywood stars). Occasionally a spark of sincerity would flash through, as in the otherwise dull *David and Bathsheba*; while small independent companies could produce interesting films like *The First Legion*. Towards the end of the 50s there were occasional attempts to see religion afresh: *A Man Called Peter*, *The Nun's Story*, *Inn of the Sixth Happiness*, *Whistle Down the Wind*. Otto Preminger, despite a 1957 failure with *Saint Joan*, tried again in 1963 with *The Cardinal*. In 1965 George Stevens unveiled *The Greatest Story Ever Told*, a tepid life of Jesus which found little box-office favour, being overtaken in some quarters by Pasolini's *The Gospel According to St Matthew*. 1966 brought the long-promised Italian-American epic known as *The Bible*: in fact it dealt only with the Book of Genesis, and that at such a dull pace and inordinate length that it is doubtful whether sequels will be called for. 1969 offered a drama of modern popes, *The Shoes of the Fisherman*, but it died. The most fashionable film interpretations of religion in the early 70s were the pop operas exemplified by *Godspell* and *Jesus Christ Superstar*; but in 1977 Lew Grade's mammoth six-hour *Jesus of Nazareth*, directed by Franco Zeffirelli, achieved record viewing figures and pointed to a benighted world's requirement to believe in *something*.

Martin Scorsese's *The Last Temptation of Christ* 88 focused on Jesus's self-doubts as he faced his crucifixion, while Michael Tolkin's *The Rapture* 91 dealt in fundamentalist terms with the end of the world, complete with the Four Horsemen of the Apocalypse.

remakes in disguise.

Hollywood studios were famous for squeezing every drop of value from a literary property, even if it meant changing the locale, switching the sexes and generally bamboozling the audience, which hopefully would not get that I-have-been-here-before feeling until they were half-way home. Here are just a few movies which went through a change of title but used up the same old plot:

- *Sentimental Journey*; *The Gift of Love*
- *Libelled Lady*; *Easy to Wed*
- *Here Comes Mr Jordan*; *Heaven Can Wait*
- *Love Is News*; *Sweet Rosie O'Grady*; *That Wonderful Urge*
- *The Bowery*; *Coney Island*; *Wabash Avenue*
- *The Greeks Had a Word for Them*; *Ladies in Love*; *Three Blind Mice*; *Moon over Miami*; *Three Little Girls in Blue*; *How to Marry a Millionaire*; *Three Coins in the Fountain*; *The Pleasure Seekers*
- *Kentucky*; *Down Argentine Way*
- *Folies Bergère*; *That Night in Rio*; *On the Riviera*; *On the Double*
- *The Front Page*; *His Girl Friday*; *Torrid Zone*; *Switching Channels*
- *Gunga Din*; *Sergeants Three*
- *My Favorite Wife*; *Move Over Darling*
- *Grand Hotel*; *Weekend at the Waldorf*
- *It Happened One Night*; *You Can't Run Away From It*
- *Tiger Shark*; *Slim*; *Manpower*
- *House of Strangers*; *Broken Lance*
- *High Sierra*; *I Died a Thousand Times*
- *20,000 Years in Sing Sing*; *Castle on the Hudson*
- *Mystery of the Wax Museum*; *House of Wax*
- *One Way Passage*; *Till We Meet Again*
- *Bordertown*; *They Drive by Night*
- *Dangerous*; *Singapore Woman*
- *The Petrified Forest*; *Escape in the Desert*
- *Four Daughters*; *Young at Heart*
- *Dr Socrates*; *King of the Underworld*
- *The Butter and Egg Man*; *The Tenderfoot*; *Dance Charlie Dance*; *An Angel from Texas*
- *The Most Dangerous Game*; *A Game of Death*; *Run for the Sun*
- *The Kennel Murder Case*; *Calling Philo Vance*
- *The Letter*; *The Unfaithful*
- *The Mouthpiece*; *The Man Who Talked Too Much*; *Illegal*
- *Oil for the Lamps of China*; *Law of the Tropics*
- *The Sea Wolf*; *Wolf Larsen*; *Barricade*; *Wolf of the Seven Seas*
- *Kid Galahad*; *The Wagons Roll at Night*
- *Casablanca*; *Far East*
- *The Man Who Played God*; *Sincerely Yours*
- *The Millionaire*; *That Way with Women*
- *The Miracle of Morgan's Creek*; *Rock-a-bye Baby*
- *Anna and the King of Siam*; *The King and I*
- *London After Midnight*; *Mark of the Vampire*
- *Love Affair*; *An Affair to Remember*
- *Morning Glory*; *Stage Struck*
- *The Lady Eve*; *The Birds and the Bees*
- *The Marriage Circle*; *One Hour with You*
- *Nothing Sacred*; *Living It Up*
- *Dark Victory*; *Stolen Hours*
- *One Sunday Afternoon*; *The Strawberry Blonde*
- *A Slight Case of Murder*; *Stop! You're Killing Me*
- *The Paleface*; *The Shakiest Gun in the West*
- *Le Jour Se Lève*; *The Long Night*
- *The Women*; *The Opposite Sex*
- *The Asphalt Jungle*; *The Badlanders*; *Cairo*; *Cool Breeze*
- *The Four Feathers*; *Storm over the Nile*
- *It Started with Eve*; *I'd Rather Be Rich*
- *Rome Express*; *Sleeping Car to Trieste*
- *This Gun for Hire*; *Short Cut to Hell*
- *The Informer*; *Uptight*
- *Against All Flags*; *The King's Pirate*
- *Red Dust*; *Congo Maisie*; *Mogambo*
- *An American Tragedy*; *A Place in the Sun*
- *Outward Bound*; *Between Two Worlds*
- *Ebb Tide*; *Adventure Island*
- *Ah, Wilderness*; *Summer Holiday*

reporters

in American films have since the beginning of the sound era been pictured as trench-coated, trilby-hatted, good-looking guys with a smart line in wisecracks. Among the outstanding examples of this tradition are Pat O'Brien in *The Front Page*, Robert Williams in *Platinum Blonde*, Clark Gable in *It Happened One Night* and *Teacher's Pet*, Fredric March in *Nothing Sacred*, Lee Tracy in *Doctor X*, Joel McCrea in *Foreign Correspondent*, David Janssen in *The Green Berets*, James Stewart in *The Philadelphia Story*, Lynne Overman in *Roxie Hart*, Gene Kelly in *Inherit the Wind*; while on the distaff side one can't overlook Glenda Farrell in *The Mystery of the Wax Museum*, Bette Davis in *Front Page Woman*, Jean Arthur in *Mr Deeds Goes to Town*, Rosalind Russell in *His Girl Friday* or Barbara Stanwyck in *Meet John Doe*. Presented somewhat more realistically were William Alland in *Citizen Kane*, James Stewart in *Call Northside 777*, Burgess Meredith as Ernie Pyle in *The Story of G.I. Joe*, Kirk Douglas in *Ace in the Hole*, and Arthur Kennedy in *Lawrence of Arabia*. The apotheosis of the reporter as hero was *All the President's Men*, with Robert Redford and Dustin Hoffman as Bob Woodward and Carl Bernstein of *The Washington Post* investigating Watergate.

British films have used their newshawks more flippantly, especially in the case of *This Man Is News* with Barry K. Barnes and *A Run for Your Money* with Alec Guinness. Just as well; for Edward Judd in *The Day the Earth Caught Fire*, Jack Hawkins in *Front Page Story*, Sidney James in *Quatermass II* and Norman Wooland in *All Over the Town* were a pretty dull lot, and Colin Gordon's imitation of the American model in *Escapade* was hardly convincing. Television series, of course, have found the reporter a convenient peg, as in the British *Deadline Midnight* and the American *Saints and Sinners* and *The Reporter*.

The Ringer.

Edgar Wallace's thriller about a vengeful master of disguise has been filmed three times in Britain: as a silent directed by Arthur Maude in 1928, starring Leslie Faber and Lawson Butt; and two versions directed by Walter Forde: the first with Gordon Harker and Franklin Dyall in 1931; and, under the title *The Gaunt Stranger*, with Sonnie Hale and Wilfred Lawson in 1938.

road movie.

A genre in which the main characters are on the move, usually in a car. The journey is more important than the destination, and puts its protagonists among unfamiliar people and situations. The form was best defined in a novel, Jack Kerouac's *On the Road* (1957), which, with its travellers looking for some kind of fulfilment, has influenced many subsequent movies. The form, in which cars often seem to be the main characters and the emphasis is on action, had an immediate appeal to the young of America and, to an extent, replaced the western as popular entertainment. Sub-genres that grew out of road movies include car race movies, such as *The Cannonball Run* and *Deathrace 2000*, the biker movies of the 60s, which reached a peak with *Easy Rider* 69, and the young outlaw movies, such as *Badlands*, *Natural Born Killers*, *Love and a.45*. The emphasis was on male bonding until the 90s, when *Thelma and Louise* and *The Adventures of Priscilla, Queen of the Desert* added feminist and gay interest.

Book: 1982, *Road Movies* by Mark Williams.

Road Runner.
Long-necked bird who whizzes along Arizona desert roads with a cry of 'Beep! Beep!' and gets the better of its pursuer Wile E. Coyote in Warner Brothers' Looney Tunes and Merrie Melodies cartoons. Its creators were Chuck Jones and writer Michael Maltese and its beep was supplied by the ubiquitous Mel Blanc.

Fast and Furry-Ous 49. Beep, Beep 52. There They Go-Go-Go 56. Fastest with the Mostest 60. Beep Prepared (AAN) 61. Tired and Feathered 65. Shot and Bothered 66. Run, Run, Sweet Road Runner 65. Out and Out Rout 66, etc.

robberies
have been a commonplace of film action fare since *The Great Train Robbery* itself; but of late there has been a fashion for showing the planning and execution of robberies through the eyes of the participants. Perhaps this started in 1950 with *The Asphalt Jungle* (and its two remakes *The Badlanders* and *Cairo*); anyway, some of the films built in this mould are *Rififi*, *Five against the House*, *Seven Thieves*, *The Killing*, *Payroll*, *Piccadilly Third Stop*, *The Day They Robbed the Bank of England*, *A Prize of Gold*, *On Friday at Eleven*, *Once a Thief*, *He Who Rides a Tiger*, *Robbery*, *Charley Varrick*, *Cops and Robbers*, *The Taking of Pelham One Two Three*, *The Getaway*, *11 Harrowhouse*, *The Bank Shot*, *Gambit*, *Dog Day Afternoon* and *Inside Out*; while films treating the same subject less seriously included *The Lavender Hill Mob*, *The Lady Killers*, *Ocean's Eleven*, *Persons Unknown*, *The League of Gentlemen*, *Topkapi*, *The Big Job*, *Assault on a Queen*, *The Biggest Bundle of Them All*, *Grand Slam*, *They Came to Rob Las Vegas*, *The Italian Job*, *The Hot Rock* and *The Anderson Tapes*. The biggest attempted robbery of all was probably the raid on Fort Knox in *Goldfinger*. Sometimes one longs for a return to the days of the dapper jewel thieves: Ronald Colman or David Niven in *Raffles*, Herbert Marshall in *Trouble in Paradise*, John Barrymore or even Charles Korvin as Arsène Lupin, Cary Grant in *To Catch a Thief*. The closest we have come to this style for many years, apart from William Wyler's *How to Steal a Million*, is 1973's *The Thief Who Came to Dinner* with Ryan O'Neal. In 1964 TV made a gallant effort with *The Rogues*.

Robin Hood.
The legendary outlaw leader of Plantagenet England is one of literature's most oft-filmed characters. There were film versions in 1909 (GB), 1912 (GB), 1912 (US), 1913 (US), and 1913 (GB). Douglas Fairbanks made his big-scale *Robin Hood* in 1922, with Wallace Beery as King Richard. In 1938 came *The Adventures of Robin Hood*, one of Hollywood's most satisfying action adventures, with Errol Flynn as Robin, Claude Rains as Prince John and Basil Rathbone as Guy of Gisbourne; directed by William Keighley and Michael Curtiz, from a script by Norman Reilly Raine and Seton I. Miller. Its exhilaration has not diminished with time. In 1946 (US) Cornel Wilde played Robin's son in *Bandit of Sherwood Forest;* in 1948 (US) Jon Hall was Robin in *Prince of Thieves;* in 1950 (US) John Derek was Robin's son in *Rogues of Sherwood Forest;* Robert Clarke played Robin in an odd concoction called *Tales of Robin Hood* (US 1952). Also in 1952, in Britain, Disney filmed Richard Todd in *The Story of Robin Hood and His Merrie Men*, with only fair success, though the real Sherwood Forest was used for the first time. Robin also appeared briefly (played by Harold Warrender) in *Ivanhoe* 52. *Men of Sherwood Forest* (GB 1956) had Don Taylor as Robin; *Son of Robin Hood* (GB 1959) turned out to be a daughter, played by June Laverick. Most durable Robin is Richard Greene, who played the role not only in 165 half-hour TV films but in a feature, *Sword of Sherwood Forest* (GB 1961). In 1967 Barrie Ingham took over in *A Challenge for Robin Hood*, in 1973 the Disney studios produced a cartoon version, and in 1976 came *Robin and Marian*, which traced the sad fortunes of the protagonists twenty years later. A new television series, *Robin of Sherwood*, appeared in 1984. Patrick Bergin played the role, with Uma Thurman as a petulant Maid Marian, in the downbeat *Robin Hood* 91. It was swiftly eclipsed by the dour Kevin Costner in *Robin Hood: Prince of Thieves* which was, surprisingly, one of the box-office successes of 1991 – though the acting honours went to Alan Rickman as a dastardly Sheriff of Nottingham.

Robinson Crusoe.
There have been many film variations on Defoe's novel. The closest to the original have been Luis Buñuel's *The Adventures of Robinson Crusoe* (Mexico, 1953), with Dan O'Herlihy, and oddly enough Byron Haskin's *Robinson Crusoe on Mars* (US, 1954), with Paul Mantee. *Lt Robin Crusoe, U.S.N.* (US, 1966) had a shipwrecked mariner teaming up with a chimpanzee and a Girl Wednesday. *Man Friday* (GB, 1975), with Peter O'Toole and Richard Roundtree, tried to be satirical by showing the situation from Friday's viewpoint. *Crusoe* (US, 1988), with Aidan Quinn, turned him into a slave trader.

Robocop.
A cyborg created from the remains of a cop shot by drug-dealers in a future Detroit, and turned into an invincible upholder of law and order, who has been the hero of three films so far. The first, directed by Paul VERHOEVEN, is by far the best. Peter WELLER played the role in the first two films. In *Robocop 3*, Robert BURKE took over. Richard Eden played the role in a 1994 television series.

robots
have been sparingly used in movies. Brigitte Helm memorably played one in *Metropolis;* so did Patricia Roc in *The Perfect Woman*. Robby the Robot featured sympathetically in *Forbidden Planet* and *Invisible Boy;* then there was *Kronos*, and Gort in *The Day the Earth Stood Still*. *Westworld*, *Futureworld* and *Star Wars* brought in a whole race of robots, one of whom looked like Yul Brynner; while in TV, *The Avengers* have frequently encountered the Cybernauts and *Dr Who* the Daleks.

Rocky Balboa.
Dim but enduring, and even endearing, boxer created by Sylvester STALLONE, as actor and screenwriter, in the Oscar-winning film *Rocky* 75, directed by John AVILDSEN, and four sequels (1979-90), in which he wins and loses championships and ends up brain-damaged, but training a protégé to succeed him.

Roger Rabbit.
Madcap rabbit with a sexy human wife and the troublesome Baby Herman to look after. Following the success of the Walt Disney feature *Who Framed Roger Rabbit*, combining animated characters and live actors, he has appeared in shorts noted for their fast, slapstick action. Created by novelist Gary Wolf, he is voiced by Charles Fleischer and his wife Jessica by Kathleen Turner.

Who Framed Roger Rabbit 88. Tummy Trouble 89. Rollercoaster Rabbit 90.

Rogue Male.
Geoffrey Household's adventure melodrama about a big-game hunter stalking Hitler has been filmed twice: by Fritz Lang as *Manhunt* 41, with Walter Pidgeon and George Sanders in hilariously foggy London settings, and as a TV movie in 1976 under its original title, starring Peter O'Toole.

romantic teams
who have been popular enough to make several films together are headed by William Powell and Myrna Loy, who made 12 joint appearances. Runners-up include Janet Gaynor and Charles Farrell (11 appearances); Dick Powell and Joan Blondell (10); Fred Astaire and Ginger Rogers (10); Spencer Tracy and Katharine Hepburn (9); Richard Burton and Elizabeth Taylor (9); Judy Garland and Mickey Rooney (8); Clark Gable and Joan Crawford (8); Nelson Eddy and Jeanette Macdonald (8); Greer Garson and Walter Pidgeon (8); Errol Flynn and Olivia de Havilland (8); Bette Davis and George Brent (7); Clark Gable and Jean Harlow (6); James Cagney and Joan Blondell (6). Even though most of these teamings began because both stars happened to be under contract to the same studio, they would not have continued had they not been felicitous. Other teams who struck notable sparks off each other but have fewer films to their credit include Humphrey Bogart and Lauren Bacall; Ronald Colman and Greer Garson; Cary Grant and Irene Dunne; Greta Garbo and John Gilbert; Greta Garbo and Melvyn Douglas; Bob Hope and Paulette Goddard; Danny Kaye and Virginia Mayo; Alan Ladd and Veronica Lake; Donald O'Connor and Peggy Ryan; Marie Dressler and Wallace Beery; Rita Hayworth and Glenn Ford; John Barrymore and Carole Lombard; Charlie Ruggles and Mary Boland; Rock Hudson and Doris Day; Jack Hulbert and Cicely Courtneidge; John Payne and Betty Grable; James Dunn and Sally Eilers; David Niven and Loretta Young; Van Johnson and June Allyson; Louis Hayward and Patricia Medina; Bob Hope and Dorothy Lamour; John Wayne and Maureen O'Hara; Tom Hanks and Meg Ryan.

Rome
in its ancient days was reconstructed for *Quo Vadis*, *The Sign of the Cross*, *Ben Hur*, *The Last Days of Pompeii*, *Androcles and the Lion*, *The Fall of the Roman Empire*, *The Robe*, *I Claudius*, *Julius Caesar*, *Cleopatra*, *Spartacus* and *The Gladiator*. The funny side of its life was depicted in *Roman Scandals*, *Fiddlers Three*, *Carry On Cleo*, *Scandal in the Roman Bath* and *A Funny Thing Happened on the Way to the Forum*. Modern Rome has been seen hundreds of times in Italian movies, notably *Bicycle Thieves*, *Paisa*, *La Dolce Vita*, *The Girls of the Spanish Steps*, *Sunday in August*, *Rome Eleven o'Clock* and the American co-production *Indiscretion* which was shot entirely within Rome's railway station. American views of Rome include *Three Coins in the Fountain*, *Seven Hills of Rome*, *Roman Holiday*, *Two Weeks in Another Town*, *The Pigeon That Took Rome* and *The Roman Spring of Mrs Stone;* while the Colosseum was used for the finale of films as various as *House of Cards* and *Twenty Million Miles to Earth*. The Vatican was well shown in *Never Take No for an Answer*, about the small boy who persists in getting an audience with the Pope.

Romeo and Juliet.
Shakespeare's tragedy of star-crossed lovers has been a director's favourite ever since it was first filmed in 1900, and many more silent versions followed. There have been three major straight versions since sound: in 1936 George Cukor directed Leslie Howard and Norma Shearer in a lavish, genteel, studio-bound, semi-pop version for MGM; in 1953 Renato Castellani came to Britain and made for Rank a more sober, but duller film in colour, with Laurence Harvey and Susan Shentall; and in 1968 came Franco Zeffirelli's youthful version with Leonard Whiting and Olivia Hussey. In the late 40s, a French film noir, *Les Amants de Verone*, transposed the story to a modern setting. The musical *West Side Story* 61 is a violent modernization of Shakespeare's tale, and Peter Ustinov's *Romanoff and Juliet* 61 a satirical rendering. The oddest so far is Armando Acosta's 1990 Belgian version played by a cast of cats (Juliet is a white Angora, Romeo a grey Persian), dubbed with the voices of, among others, Robert Powell, Francesca Annis, Ben Kingsley, Vanessa Redgrave, and Maggie Smith. A grunge version, *Tromeo and Juliet*, was released in 1996 by Troma Films, directed by Lloyd Kaufman and written by James Gunn. Set in the future ('What light from yonder Plexiglas breaks?' asked Tromeo), it featured Tromeo proposing to Juliet while seated on the toilet. A more conventional contemporary adaptation, set in a US resort called Verona Beach, also appeared in 1996, starring Leonardo DiCaprio and Claire Danes and directed by Baz Luhrmann.

Rose Marie.
The Rudolph Friml/Oscar Hammerstein operetta about the Mounties getting their man was first filmed in 1928 by Lucien Hubbard as a silent; Joan Crawford has the title role. In 1936 W. S. Van Dyke made the well-remembered version with Jeanette MacDonald and Nelson Eddy, and in 1954 Mervyn LeRoy directed a remake with Ann Blyth and Howard Keel.

Rosebud.
The enigmatic last word of *Citizen Kane*, referring back to Kane's childhood sled. It is also said to be the pet name William Randolph Hearst gave to his mistress Marion Davies's private parts, which may help explain that tycoon's implacable hostility to the film. Several sleds were said to have been used in the film, in addition to the one burned at the end. One of them was bought at auction for $55,000 by Steven Spielberg in 1982, although its authenticity has since been questioned.

Ruggles of Red Gap.
The story by Harry Leon Wilson, about a British butler exported to the American midwest, was filmed with Edward Everett Horton in 1923 and with Charles Laughton in 1935. Bob Hope's *Fancy Pants* 50 bore more than a passing resemblance to it.

Sabrina.
Billy WILDER's romantic comedy, made in 1954, from Samuel Taylor's play about an up-tight businessman who falls in love with his chauffeur's daughter, who, in turn, is attracted by his high-living brother, starred Humphrey BOGART, Audrey HEPBURN and William HOLDEN. Sydney POLLACK's less successful remake in 1995 starred Harrison FORD in the Bogart role, Julia ORMOND and Greg KINNEAR.

Sahara:
see LOST PATROL.

sailors
of whom screen accounts have been given include Christopher Columbus (1446-1506), by Fredric MARCH in *Christopher Columbus* 49, Gérard DEPARDIEU in *1492: Discovery of Paradise* 92, and George CORRAFACE in *Christopher Columbus: The Discovery* 92; Horatio NELSON; Captain Bligh, by Charles LAUGHTON, and later by Trevor HOWARD, in *Mutiny on the Bounty;* John Paul Jones (1747-92), by Robert STACK in *John Paul Jones* 59; Francis Drake (1540-96), by Matheson LANG in *Drake of England* 35 and by Rod TAYLOR in *Seven Seas to Calais* 62; Walter Raleigh by Richard TODD in *The Virgin Queen* 55; and Admiral Halsey, by James CAGNEY in *The Gallant Hours* 61 and by Robert MITCHUM in *Midway*. A less successful sailor, and his amateur crew, featured in Captain Jack 98, with Bob HOSKINS in the title role.

The Saint.
Among the actors who have played Leslie Charteris' 'Robin Hood of crime' in both British and American films since 1937 are Louis HAYWARD, Hugh SINCLAIR and George SANDERS. One feels that 'the Falcon', a series character played in the 40s by George Sanders and later Tom CONWAY, was heavily indebted to the Saint, who made a strong comeback on television in the person of Roger MOORE in the 60s. In France, a barely recognizable 'Saint' has been played in several films by Jean MARAIS. In 1995, Val KILMER was signed for the role, which prevented him from continuing to play Batman; he was replaced by George CLOONEY. Other actors approached for the role of the Saint included Ralph FIENNES, Mel GIBSON, Hugh GRANT and Arnold SCHWARZENEGGER.

Saint Johnson
W.R. BURNETT's novel, based on Wyatt Earp's exploits in cleaning up Tombstone, has been filmed four times. Walter HUSTON starred in a lively version in 1932, scripted by his son John and directed by Edward L. CAHN under the title *Law and Order*. In 1937, it was turned into *Wild West Days*, a 13-episode serial, starring Johnny Mack BROWN. Brown also starred in another version in 1940, again entitled *Law and Order*. Finally Ronald REAGAN played the lawman in a 1953 version, directed by Nathan JURAN.

St Trinian's.
This school full of little female horrors was originally conceived by cartoonist Ronald Searle. From his formula Frank LAUNDER and Sidney GILLIAT made four commercially successful if disappointing farces: *The Belles of St Trinian's* 54, *Blue Murder at St Trinian's* 57, *The Pure Hell of St Trinian's* 60, *The Great St Trinian's Train Robbery* 66. In 1980 Launder alone produced yet another, *The Wildcats of St. Trinian's*.

Salome.
Oscar Wilde's play of Salome's Dance of the Seven Veils before King Herod for the head of John the Baptist was filmed at least seven times in silent days, notably by Nazimova in 1923 against backgrounds inspired by the drawings of Aubrey Beardsley. It was remade in 1953 with Rita Hayworth as Salome and Charles Laughton as Herod, while Ken Russell's *Salome's Last Dance* 87 had Wilde watching a performance of his play in a brothel.

San Francisco,
replete with cable cars, steep streets, Golden Gate Bridge and Alcatraz out there in the bay, has

provided a picturesque location for innumerable movies, outstandingly *Vertigo*, *What's Up Doc?*, *The Glenn Miller Story*, *The Well Groomed Bride*, *Bullitt*, *Guess Who's Coming to Dinner*, *Point Blank*, *Yours Mine and Ours*, *The House on Telegraph Hill*, *Sudden Fear*, *Experiment in Terror*, *Flower Drum Song*, *The Maltese Falcon*, *The Conversation*, *Daddy's Gone a-Hunting*, *Dirty Harry*, *Pete 'n' Tillie*, *The Laughing Policeman*, *Dark Passage*, *Foul Play* and *Petulia*. The Barbary Coast days were well caught in *San Francisco*, *Nob Hill*, *Barbary Coast*, *Flame of the Barbary Coast*, and many other movies.

TV series have also used it *ad nauseam*: *The Line Up*, *Sam Benedict*, *Ironside*, *McMillan and Wife*, *Streets of San Francisco*, *Phyllis*.

satire,
being defined in theatrical circles as 'what closes Saturday night', has seldom been encouraged by Hollywood, and the few genuinely satirical films have not been commercially successful, from *A Nous la Liberté* through *American Madness*, *Nothing Sacred* and *Roxie Hart* to *The Loved One*. However, the odd lampoon in the middle of an otherwise straightforward comedy has often brought critical enthusiasm for films as diverse as *Modern Times*, *Boy Meets Girl*, *I'm All Right, Jack*, *The President's Analyst* and *The Groove Tube*; and in future it looks as though one can at least expect that the range of permissible targets will become even wider. The spotty but considerable success in 1976 of *Network*, the screen's most hysterical satire of all, was at least partly due to its sexy scenes and uninhibited language.

Scarface.
Armitage Trail's novel, about the rise of a thinly disguised Al Capone, made an exciting gangster movie under the direction of Howard Hawks in 1932, with Paul Muni in the title role and George Raft flipping a coin at moments of stress. Brian DePalma remade it as an exercise in excess in 1983, starring Al Pacino as a modern-day Latin American thug, thriving in Miami.

The Scarlet Letter.
Nathaniel Hawthorne's story of puritanical 18th-century New England was filmed in 1917 with Mary Martin as the adulteress and Stuart Holmes as her priest-lover forced to accuse her. In 1926 came Victor Sjostrom's more famous version with Lillian Gish and Lars Hanson; 1934 brought a talkie remake with Colleen Moore and Hardie Albright; and Wim Wenders made a German version in 1973, starring Senta Berger. Demi Moore starred in a version directed by Roland Jaffe which took many liberties with the original, but even so flopped at the box-office in 1995.

The Scarlet Pimpernel.
Baroness Orczy's foppish hero of the French Revolution has been filmed three times in Britain since sound: in 1935, directed by Harold YOUNG, with Leslie HOWARD opposing Raymond MASSEY as Chauvelin; in 1938, directed by Hans SCHWARZ, with Barry K. BARNES winning out over Francis LISTER; in 1950, directed by Michael POWELL and Emeric PRESSBURGER, with David NIVEN as Sir Percy. There has also been a TV series starring Marius GORING. Silent versions included one in 1917 starring Dustin FARNUM and one in 1929 starring Matheson LANG. The idea was modernized in Leslie HOWARD's *Pimpernel Smith* 41. In 1982, the original was remade for television with Anthony ANDREWS, Jane SEYMOUR, and Ian MCKELLEN, and again in 2000 with Richard E. GRANT in the title role.

Scattergood Baines,
an amiable small-town busybody created by Clarence Buddington Kelland, was personified by Guy Kibbee in six second features (41-42), all directed by Christy Cabanne.

schooldays
have often been depicted in films with a thick sentimental veneer, as in *Goodbye Mr Chips*, *Good Morning Miss Dove* and *Blossoms in the Dust*. But more usually the pupils have serious problems to worry about, as in *Young Woodley*, *The Guinea Pig*, *Friends for Life*, *Tea and Sympathy* and *Tom Brown's Schooldays*; while with at least equal frequency our sympathies are elicited on behalf of the staff: *The Housemaster*, *Bright Road*, *The Blackboard Jungle*, *The Browning Version*, *Spare the Rod*, *Edward My Son*, *The Blue Angel*, *The Children's Hour*, *The Corn Is Green*, *Term of Trial*, *To Sir with Love*, *Spinster*, *The Prime of Miss Jean Brodie*, *Please Sir*, *Unman Wittering and Zigo*. More light-hearted treatment of the whole business is evident in *The Trouble with Angels* and *Margie*, and in some cases the treatment has undeniably been farcical: *Boys Will Be Boys*, *The Ghost of St Michael's*, *Good Morning Boys*, *A Yank at Eton*, *Vice Versa*, *Bottoms Up* and *The Happiest Days of Your Life*; with the St Trinian's saga wildest of all. The strangest schools on film are those depicted in *Zéro de Conduite* and its semi-remake *If...* while very special schools were seen in *Battement de Coeur* (for pickpockets), *School for Secrets* (for 'boffins'), *Old Bones of the River* (for African tiny tots), *The Goose Steps Out* (for young Nazis), *Orders to Kill*, *The House on 92nd Street*, *13 rue Madeleine*, *Carve Her Name with Pride* and *From Russia with Love* (for spies).

science fiction,
a term incapable of precise definition, may perhaps be taken as that kind of fantasy which depends not on legend only, like *Dracula*, but involves the work of man. Thus *King Kong* and 'natural' monsters would not qualify, but *Frankenstein* and *The Invisible Man* would. Space exploration and prophecy, considered elsewhere, are branches of it, as are all the films about mad doctors and colliding worlds.

scientists
have been the subject of many films, though few real-life ones have led sufficiently dramatic lives to warrant filming. Warners led the way in the 30s with *The Story of Louis Pasteur* and *Dr Ehrlich's Magic Bullet*. In 1939 Mickey Rooney played *Young Tom Edison*, followed by Spencer Tracy as *Edison the Man*. Then, in 1943, Greer Garson played *Madame Curie*. At this point the movie fan's thirst for scientific knowledge died out, and John Huston's *Freud* in 1962 did not revive it. In the 80s, the lives of Oppenheimer and Sakharov have been filmed.
See also: INVENTORS.

The Sea Wolf.
Jack London's stark psychological novel of an obsessed sea captain, Wolf Larsen, has been filmed at least seven times: in 1913 it starred Hobart Bosworth, in 1920 Noah Beery, in 1925 Ralph Ince, in 1930 Milton Sills, and in 1941 Edward G. Robinson. A disguised western version, *Barricade*, with Raymond Massey, appeared in 1950, and in 1957 yet another straight version, under the title *Wolf Larsen*, was made with Barry Sullivan. In 1974 Chuck Connors starred in a European version, *Wolf of the Seven Seas*.

seances
on the screen have often been shown to be fake, as in *Seance on a Wet Afternoon*, *Bunco Squad*, *Palmy Days*, *The Spiritualist*, *Houdini*, and *The Medium*. But just occasionally they do result in something being called up from over there. It happened in *Blithe Spirit*, *The Haunting*, *The Uninvited*, *Night of the Demon*, *Thirteen Ghosts*, *Hands of the Ripper*, and *The Legend of Hell House*.

seaside resorts
have provided lively settings for many British comedies: Douglas in *No Limit*, Brighton in *Bank Holiday*, Blackpool in *Sing As We Go*, and a variety of south coast resorts in *The Punch and Judy Man*, *French Dressing*, *All Over the Town*, *Barnacle Bill*. Sometimes the resort has provided a contrast to more serious goings-on, as in *The Entertainer*, *Brighton Rock*, *Room at the Top*, *The Dark Man*, *A Taste of Honey*, *I Was Happy Here*, *Family Doctor*, *The System*, *The Damned*. Hollywood usually comes a cropper when depicting British resorts, either comically as in *The Gay Divorcee* or seriously as in *Separate Tables*; its own resorts have a monotonous look, whether viewed romantically in *Moon Over Miami* and *Fun in Acapulco*, nostalgically in *Some Like It Hot*, trendily in *Beach Party* and its many sequels, or morosely in *Tony Rome*. The French Riviera has never been notably well captured on film since Vigo's *A Propos de Nice*, but among the movies to have a go with the aid of back projection are *On the Riviera*, *That Riviera Touch* and *Moment to Moment*. Hitchcock got some picture-postcard views but little else out of *To Catch a Thief*, while the French had a go for themselves in *St Tropez Blues* and others. A Mediterranean resort was the setting of the climax of *Suddenly Last Summer*; other European watering-places featured memorably in *Une Si Jolie Petite Plage*, *Sunday in August* and *The Lady with the Little Dog*. The most ingenious use of the seaside for purposes of film fantasy was certainly in *Oh What a Lovely War*.

Seaside settings of the 70s and 80s have included *Out of Season*, *Atlantic City USA* and *The King of Marvin Gardens*.

Sergeant Ernie Bilko.
Wisecracking, loquacious, conniving army sergeant played by Phil SILVERS in his TV show from 1955 to 1959. Stationed at Fort Baxter, Kansas, Bilko tried to get rich quick, aided and also hindered by his platoon, and at war with his superior officer, Colonel Hall (Paul FORD). A feature film version, directed by Jonathan LYNN and starring Steve MARTIN as Bilko and Dan AYKROYD as Colonel Hall, appeared in 1996. It contained the credit: 'The filmmakers gratefully acknowledge the total lack of cooperation from the US Army.'

serial killers.
Mass murderers have long held a fascination for film-makers and audiences alike, as is demonstrated by Charlie CHAPLIN's *Monsieur Verdoux* 47, and the many *Bluebeard* films from the 40s onwards, based on the activities of the French murderer Henri LANDRU, and such comedies as *Kind Hearts and Coronets* 49 and *No Way to Treat a Lady* 68. But a specific genre emerged after the term serial killer was coined by the FBI in the 60s and following the success of Alfred HITCHCOCK's *Psycho*, from Robert Bloch's novel based on Ed GEIN. A succession of slasher movies ensued featuring fictional murderers, including *Halloween* and its successors, and two long-drawn-out series featuring killers returning from the dead: Jason in *Friday the Thirteenth* (eight films so far) and Freddy in *Nightmare on Elm Street*. Terrence MALICK's *Badlands*, based on teenagers Charley Starkweather and Caril Fugate's killing spree which left 10 dead, was followed by a series of murderous road movies which includes *True Romance* 93, *Kalifornia* 93, and *Natural Born Killers* 94. The latter two made much of public fascination with serial killers, as did John MCNAUGHTON's chilling *Henry: Portrait of a Serial Killer* 90, the Belgian film *Man Bites Dog* 92, in which a film crew begin to record a murderer at work and end by helping him with his crimes, and David FINCHER's *Seven* 95, with a killer working his way through victims guilty of one of the deadly sins. Certainly Thomas Harris's fictional creation, the cannibalistic Hannibal Lecter, has become a favourite ogre following the performances of Brian Cox in *Manhunter* 86 and Anthony HOPKINS in *The Silence of the Lambs* 90 and *Hannibal* 01. Real-life serial killers on film include the Boston Strangler, Peter Kurten (M and *The Vampire of Dusseldorf*), and Fritz Haarman (*The Tenderness of Wolves*).

❝ The serial killer has become our debased, condemned, yet eerily glorified Noble Savage, the vestiges of the frontier spirit. – *Joyce Carol Oates*

serials
demand a book to themselves. They began in the early years of the century and continued until the early 50s, their plethora of adventurous and melodramatic incident being usually divided into fifteen or twenty chapters of about twenty minutes each. They were the domain of mad doctors, space explorers, clutching hands, mysterious strangers, diabolical villains and dewy-eyed heroines. Each chapter ended with a 'cliffhanger' in which the hero or heroine was left in some deadly danger from which it was plain he could not escape; but at the beginning of the next chapter, escape he did. A few favourite serials are *Fantomas*, *The Perils of Pauline*, *Batman*, *Flash Gordon's Trip to Mars* and *Captain Marvel*. Almost all of them were American. They were finally killed by the advent of TV and by the increasing length of the double-feature programme.

Books on the subject include *To Be Continued* by Weiss and Goodgold; *Days of Thrills and Adventure* by Alan Barbour; and *The Great Movie Serials* by Harmon and Glut.

series
of feature films used to be popular enough, and many are individually noted in this book; in recent years the series concept has been taken over by TV, and in any case low-budget movies featuring cut-to-pattern characters could no longer be made to pay their way in theatres. When one looks back over these old heroes, who flourished chiefly in the 30s and 40s, most of them turn out to be sleuths of one kind or another. They included *Sherlock Holmes*, *The Saint*, *The Lone Wolf*, *Father Brown*, *Nero Wolfe*, *Duncan McLain*, *The Crime Doctor*, *Sexton Blake*, *Mr Moto*, *Perry Mason*, *Bulldog Drummond*, *Nancy Drew*, *Mr Wong*, *Charlie Chan*, *Ellery Queen*, *Boston Blackie*, *The Falcon*, *Hildegarde Withers*, *Hercule Poirot*, *Dick Tracy*, *Torchy Blane*, *Michael Shayne*, *Philip Marlowe* and, more recently, *Inspector Clouseau*, *Tony Rome*, *Virgil Tibbs*, *Coffin Ed Johnson* and *Shaft*. Nor should one forget crime anthologies like *Inner Sanctum* and *The Whistler*. The spy vogue, a recent happening, is naturally headed by *James Bond*: in his wake you may discern *Counterspy*, *Coplan*, *Flint*, *The Tiger*, *The Man from UNCLE*, *Harry Palmer*, and *Superdragon*. Among the more muscular outdoor heroes may be counted *Hopalong Cassidy*, *The Three Mesquiteers*, *The Lone Ranger*, *Captain Blood*, *Zorro*, *Robin Hood*, *Tarzan*, *Jungle Jim*, *The Cisco Kid*, *Bomba*, *The Man with No Name* and the Italian giants who go under such names as *Maciste*, *Goliath*, *Hercules* and *Ursus*. The longest surviving series villain is certainly *Fu Manchu*. As for monsters, take your pick from *Frankenstein*, *Dracula*, *The Mummy*, *The Creature from the Black Lagoon*, *The Invisible Man*, *The Wolf Man*, *Dr X*; while if you prefer comedy freaks there are *Topper* and *Francis*. There have been a goodly number of domestic comedies and dramas, including *Squibs*, *The Jones Family*, *The Hardy Family*, *The Cohens and the Kellys*, *Blondie*, *Ma and Pa Kettle*, *Maisie*, *Henry Aldrich*, *Scattergood Baines*, *Lum and Abner*, *Jeeves*, *Mr Belvedere*, *Gidget* and the *Four Daughters* saga. Other comedy series have ranged from the subtleties of *Don Camillo* to the pratfalls of *Old Mother Riley*, *Mexican Spitfire*, the *Doctor* series, *Carry On* films, the *Police Academy* series, and the *Naked Gun* movies. Animals have had series to themselves, as for instance *Rin Tin Tin*, *Flicka*, *Lassie*, *Rusty* and *Flipper*. So have children of various ages: *Our Gang*, *Gasoline Alley*, *The Dead End Kids*, *The East Side Kids*, *The Bowery Boys*. The best-established musical series were *Broadway Melody* and *The Big Broadcast*. And three cheers for *Dr Kildare*, *Dr Christian*, *Dr Mabuse* and *Dr Goldfoot* ... to say nothing of Professor *Quatermass*.

servants
in movies have provided great pleasure, mainly because the vast majority of the audience has been unlikely to encounter the breed in person. Actors who spent their lives playing stately butlers include Eric Blore, Charles Coleman, Robert Greig, Barnett Parker, Halliwell Hobbes and Arthur Treacher. Louise Beavers and Hattie McDaniel were the leading coloured maids, and many black comedians played frightened valets: Mantan Moreland, Stepin Fetchit, Willie Best. Sinister housekeepers are led by Gale Sondergaard and Judith Anderson. Even more eccentric servants were played by Edward Rigby in *Don't Take it to Heart*, Cantinflas in *Around the World in Eighty Days*, Seymour Hicks in *Busman's Honeymoon*, Edward Brophy in the Falcon series; and downright villainous ones by Dirk Bogarde in *The Servant*, Philip Latham in *Dracula Prince of Darkness*, Boris Karloff in *The Old Dark House* and Bela Lugosi in *The Body Snatcher*. Romantic comedies in which servants have had liaisons with their masters (or mistresses) include *History is Made at Night*, *When Tomorrow Comes*, *Common Clay*, *What Price Hollywood?*, *The Farmer's Daughter*, *If You Could Only Cook*, *Lord Richard in the Pantry* and *Upstairs Downstairs*; while 30s comedies in which Russian exiles and new poor took jobs as servants are exemplified by *Tovarich* and *My Man Godfrey*. One should not forget *The Admirable Crichton* in any of his forms; but other servants less admirable were James Mason in *Five Fingers*, and Glenda Jackson and Susannah York in *The Maids*. Anthony Hopkins in *The Remains of the Day* was a butler whose loyalty to his master is his undoing.

Seven Keys to Baldpate.
The famous stage comedy-thriller by Earl Derr Biggers and George M. Cohan has been filmed five times: with Cohan himself in 1917, Douglas MacLean in 1926, Richard Dix in 1929, Gene Raymond in 1935, and Philip Terry in 1947. The most recent version, in 1983, was *House of Long Shadows*, with Christopher Lee and Peter Cushing.

Seventh Heaven.
Austin Strong's play, a simple garret love story set in Paris at the time of World War I, from which the hero returns blinded, was successfully filmed by Frank Borzage, with Janet Gaynor and Charles Farrell; Henry King remade it in 1937 with Simone Simon and James Stewart.

sewers
have figured in several thrillers, most notably *The Third Man* with its exciting final chase; its sewer complex was recently spoofed in *Carry On Spying*. In 1948 in *He Walked by Night* Richard Basehart played a criminal who invariably escaped through the sewers; and our old friend *The Phantom of the Opera* was similarly skilled, as was Lee Marvin in *Point Blank*. As recently as the British thriller *Invasion* a sewer detour was used; while the Frankenstein monster was saved from the burning windmill by falling through to the sewer, where he was found at the beginning of *Bride of Frankenstein*. As for more serious films, sewers are of course featured in the many versions of *Les Misérables*, while the Polish resistance film *Kanal* takes place entirely – and nauseatingly – in the sewers of Warsaw. Fred MacMurray had a comic sewer escape in *Bon Voyage*, and the giant ants of *Them!* were cornered in the sewers of Los Angeles, while the mutant beast of *Alligator* and *Alligator II* emerged from the sewers and the pizza-loving *Teenage Mutant Ninja Turtles* lived in them.

sex.
This was once called 'romance': the beginnings of corruption set in with DE MILLE's silent comedies such as *Why Change Your Wife?* and LUBITSCH's classics *Forbidden Paradise* and *The Marriage Circle*. These gentlemen carried their sophistication into the early sound period, assisted by such stars as VALENTINO, HARLOW, DIETRICH, Clara Bow and Ginger ROGERS; and there was considerable help from a film called *The Private Life of Henry VIII*, a lady named Mae WEST and a director named Josef VON STERNBERG; but around 1934 the Hays Code and the Legion of Decency forced innocence upon Hollywood to such an extent that the smart hero and heroine of 1934's *It Happened One Night* just wouldn't dream of sharing a bedroom without a curtain between them. The later 30s, perforce, were the heyday of the boy-next-door and the *ingénue*: nice people all, personified by such stars as Gary COOPER, Dick POWELL, Ray MILLAND, David NIVEN, Ruby KEELER, Janet GAYNOR, Deanna DURBIN and Irene DUNNE. Meanwhile a strong rearguard action was being fought by actors like William POWELL, Myrna LOY, Melvyn DOUGLAS, Ann SHERIDAN and Cary GRANT, but usually the blue pencil had been wielded so heavily on their scripts that it was difficult to tell what was really being implied. The best way out was found in such comedies as *The Philadelphia Story*, which were basically earthy but gave every appearance of keeping it all in the mind. The war years produced a certain slackening of restrictions; for instance, the pin-up girl became not only permissible but desirable as a way of building up military morale. Preston STURGES brought sex out into the open in *The Palm Beach Story* and *The Miracle of Morgan's Creek*; Spencer TRACY and Katharine HEPBURN started (in *Woman of the Year*) a series of films portraying the battle of the sexes in a recognizably human way. The 'love goddesses' became progressively more blatant in their appeal: Jane RUSSELL, Marilyn MONROE, Jayne MANSFIELD. (But in the 50s it turned out that one of the earthiest of them, Sophia LOREN, was also the best actress.) By now the production code had been broken down to the extent of permitting words like 'virgin' and 'mistress'(*The Moon is Blue*), the recognition of adultery and prostitution as human facts (*Wives and Lovers*, *Kiss Me Stupid*), depiction of the lustfulness of males (*Tom Jones*, *Alfie*), 'realistic' dramas like *Room at the Top*, erotic romances like *Les Amants*, and the presentation, albeit in a fantasy, of girls as 'pleasure units' (*Our Man Flint*). Indeed, after *Georgy Girl*, *Night Games* and *Who's Afraid of Virginia Woolf?*, it seemed that public frankness could go very little further; but along came *Blow Up*, *Midnight Cowboy*, *Satyricon*, *Flesh*, *The Music Lovers*, *Percy*, *Last Tango in Paris* and *Deep Throat* to prove the opposite. There even emerged an X-rated cartoon *Fritz the Cat*; and by the mid-70s pornographic films on view in most cities outnumbered the other kind. Ironically, perhaps, in 1999 the first film containing explicit sexual activity to be given an '18' certificate in Britain was Catherine Breillat's *Romance*.

sex changes
have not been a profitable line of inquiry for the cinema, though the gimmick thriller *Homicidal* depended on one, as did *Myra Breckinridge*. *The Christine Jorgenson Story* was an account of a genuine case, and *I Want What I Want* presented a fictitious case history. The most amusing film on the subject is certainly *Turnabout*. In Blake Edwards' *Switch*, a male chauvinist is reincarnated as a woman.

Sexton Blake.
The lean, ascetic detective hero of several generations of British boys was the creation of Harry Blyth ('Hal Meredith') (1852-98). On screen he was first portrayed in 1914 in *The Clue of the Wax Vesta*. He was played in the 20s by Langhorne Burton, in the 30s by George Curzon, in the 40s by David Farrar and in the 50s by Geoffrey Toone; while 1962's *Mix Me a Person* was taken from a Blake story but cast Anne Baxter in the role.

Shaft.
Ernest TIDYMAN's tough Harlem private eye was played by Richard ROUNDTREE in three films: *Shaft* 71; *Shaft in Africa* 73; and *Shaft's Big Score* 73. In 2000 came a remake *Shaft*, starring Samuel L. JACKSON as Shaft's nephew, with Roundtree making a brief appearance in his old role.

She.
Seven silent versions were made of Rider Haggard's adventure fantasy about a lost tribe, an ageless queen, and a flame of eternal life in darkest Africa. Only the last remains, made in London and Berlin by G. B. SAMUELSON, with Betty BLYTHE and Carlyle BLACKWELL. In 1934 in Hollywood, Merian COOPER and Ernest SCHOEDSACK remade the story in a North Pole setting, with Helen GAHAGAN and Randolph SCOTT. In 1965 came a lifeless Hammer version directed by Robert DAY, with Ursula ANDRESS and John RICHARDSON; this was followed in 1968 by a sequel, *The Vengeance of She*, which was more than slightly daft.

She Loves Me Not.
The story of a night-club singer taking refuge in a men's college and disguising herself as an undergraduate after witnessing a murder has been filmed three times: in 1934, directed by Elliott Nugent, with Bing Crosby and Miriam Hopkins; in 1942, as *True to the Army*, in which Judy Canova pretends to be a soldier; in 1955, as *How to Be Very, Very Popular*, in which strippers Betty Grable and Sheree North hide in a college. The notion also served Whoopi Goldberg well in *Sister Act* 92, as a singer fleeing from the Mob who takes refuge in a convent and disguises herself as a nun.

The Sheik.
Rudolph Valentino first appeared as a romantic Arab in 1922, with Agnes Ayres as his willing co-star, in an adaptation of E. M. Hull's novelette. It was one of his most successful roles, and *Son of the Sheik* came out in 1926, with Vilma Banky partnering him. His death prevented further episodes, but in 1937 Ramon Novarro made fun of the idea in *The Sheik Steps Out*, and in 1962 came an Italian spoof called *The Return of the Son of the Sheik*, with Gordon Scott.

Sherlock Holmes,
Conan Doyle's classic fictional detective, around whom a detailed legend has been created by ardent followers, has a long screen history. There were American one-reel films featuring him in 1903, 1905 and 1908. Also in 1908 there began a series of twelve Danish one-reelers starring Forrest Holger-Madsen. In 1910 there were two German films and in 1912 six French. A second French series began in 1913; also in this year an American two-reel version of *The Sign of Four* featured Harry Benham. British six-reelers were made of *A Study in Scarlet* 14, and *Valley of Fear* 16; also in 1916 the famous stage actor William Gillette put his impersonation of Holmes on film for Essanay. In 1917 came a German version of *The Hound of the Baskervilles*; then nothing till 1922, when John Barrymore played Holmes and Roland Young was Watson in Goldwyn's *Sherlock Holmes*, based on Gillette's stage play. In Britain in the same year Maurice Elvey directed a full-length version of *The Hound of the Baskervilles* and followed it with over 25 two-reelers starring Eille Norwood, remaining faithful to the original stories. In 1929 Carlyle Blackwell played Holmes in a German remake of *The Hound of the Baskervilles*; and in the same year Clive Brook played in a talkie, *The Return of Sherlock Holmes*, with H. Reeves-Smith as Watson. Arthur Wontner, a perfect Holmes, first played the role in *Sherlock Holmes' Final Hour* (GB) 31, later appearing in *The Sign of Four* 32, *The Missing Rembrandt* 33, *The Triumph of Sherlock Holmes* 35, and *The Silver Blaze* 36 (Ian Fleming was Watson). Raymond Massey was Holmes in *The Speckled Band* (GB) 31, with Athole Stewart as Watson; in 1932 Robert Rendel was in *The Hound of the Baskervilles* (GB). Clive Brook again appeared in *Sherlock Holmes* (US) 32, with Reginald Owen as Watson; Owen then played Holmes in *A Study in Scarlet* (US) 33. The Germans made three more Holmes films in the mid-30s, including yet another remake of *The Hound*, which in 1939 was again tackled by Fox in Hollywood, this time with Basil Rathbone as the detective and Nigel Bruce as Watson. Its success led to a hurried remake of the Gillette play under the title *The Adventures of Sherlock Holmes* 39; two years later the same two actors began a series of twelve films in which the settings were modernized and most of the stories unrecognizable, although the acting and much of the writing were well in character. The titles were *Sherlock Holmes and the Voice of Terror* 41, *Sherlock Holmes and the Secret Weapon* 42, *Sherlock Holmes in Washington* 42, *Sherlock Holmes Faces Death* 43, *Spider Woman* 44, *The Scarlet Claw* 44, *Pearl of Death* 44, *House of Fear* 45, *Woman in Green* 45, *Pursuit to Algiers* 45, *Terror by Night* 46, *Dressed to Kill/Sherlock Holmes and the Secret Code* 46. Then a long silence was broken by Peter Cushing and André Morell in the leads of a British remake of *The Hound of the Baskervilles* 59. In 1962 Christopher Lee and Thorley Walters played Holmes and Watson in a German film, *Sherlock Holmes and the Deadly Necklace*; and in 1965 John Neville and Donald Houston appeared in an original story involving the famous pair with Jack the Ripper: *A Study in Terror*. Also in 1965 a BBC TV series featured Douglas Wilmer and Nigel Stock, with Peter Cushing later taking over as Holmes; the period atmosphere was carefully sought but the stories suffered from being padded out to the standard TV length. (There was also a Franco-American TV series in 1954 with Ronald Howard and Howard Marion-Crawford.) In 1969 Billy Wilder made *The Private Life of Sherlock Holmes* with Robert Stephens, apparently intending a send-up but producing only a further pleasant variation. In 1970 George C. Scott thought he was Sherlock Holmes in *They Might Be Giants*, so did Larry Hagman in a 1976 TV movie, *The Return of the World's Greatest Detective*. Nicol Williamson as Holmes was treated by Sigmund Freud in 1976's *The Seven Per Cent Solution*, and in the same year Gene Wilder tried a spoof, *The Adventure of Sherlock Holmes' Smarter Brother*. The same year brought a TV movie called *Sherlock Holmes in New York*, with Roger Moore and Patrick MacNee. In 1978 there was a perfectly ghastly, supposedly comic *Hound of the Baskervilles* with Peter Cook and Dudley Moore, while Christopher Plummer starred in a TV half-hour of *Silver Blaze* and a feature called *Murder by Decree*, which again linked Holmes with Jack the Ripper. A stage revival of the William Gillette version was followed by other adaptations. 1979 brought another TV series with Geoffrey Whitehead and Donald Pickering; but *Sherlock Holmes and Doctor Watson* was barely seen outside Poland, where it was shot. In 1983 Sy Weintraub made TV movies of *The Sign of Four* and *The Hound of the Baskervilles*, with Ian Richardson an excellent Holmes; and Tom Baker starred in a BBC serial of *The Hound of the Baskervilles*. In 1984 Granada TV had a 13-hour series starring Jeremy Brett and David Burke, and this continues. Brett also starred in a full-length 1987 version of *The Sign of Four*. Christopher Lee played the role in TV versions made in South Africa in the 90s.

ships,
of the modern passenger kind, have provided a useful setting for many films, most recently in *Ship of Fools*. Four notable versions of the *Titanic* disaster were *Atlantic* 30, *Titanic* 53, *A Night to Remember* 58 and *Titanic* 97; while sinking ships also figured in *We're Not Dressing* 34, *Souls at Sea* 37, *History Is Made at Night* 37, *The Blue Lagoon* 48, *Our Girl Friday* 52, *The Admirable Crichton* 57 (and earlier versions), *The Last Voyage* 60 and *The Poseidon Adventure* 72. A sinister time was had on board ship in *Journey into Fear*, *Across the Pacific*, *King Kong*, *My Favorite Blonde*, *The Ghost Ship*, *The Mystery of the Marie Celeste*, *The Sea Wolf*, *The Hairy Ape*, *Dangerous Crossing*, *Ghost Breakers*, *The Wreck of the Mary Deare*, *Juggernaut*, and *Voyage of the Damned*; laughter, however, was to the fore in *Monkey Business* 31, *The Lady Eve* 41, *Luxury Liner* 48, *Doctor at Sea* 55, *The Captain's Table* 58, *A Countess from Hong Kong* 66, and *A Night at the Opera* 35 with its famous cabin scene. The romance of a cruise was stressed in *Dodsworth* 36, *The Big Broadcast of 1938*, *Now Voyager* 42, and the two versions of *Love Affair* 39 (the second being *An Affair to Remember* 56); while in the 'Winter Cruise' section of *Encore* 51, it was almost forced on Kay Walsh. In *Assault on a Queen* 66 the leading characters plan to hijack the *Queen Mary*. The weirdest ship was the ship of the dead in *Outward Bound* 30, and its remake *Between Two Worlds* 44.

Mississippi riverboats have featured in *Mississippi*, *Rhythm on the River*, *Mississippi Gambler*, *The Secret Life of Walter Mitty*, *The Naughty Nineties*, *The Adventures of Mark Twain*, *Four for Texas*, *Frankie and Johnny*, and the several versions of *Showboat*; also in the TV series *Riverboat*.

Sailing ships of olden days are too numerous to detail.

The Shop around the Corner.
Nikolaus Laszlo's play about two Budapest shop assistants who are unaware that they are pen pals was filmed by Ernst Lubitsch in 1940, with Margaret Sullavan and James Stewart, as a charming piece of Hollywood schmaltz. In 1949 Robert Z. Leonard remade it as a musical, *In the Good Old Summertime*, with Judy Garland and Van Johnson.

The Shopworn Angel.
This comedy-drama about a Hollywood gold-digger who gives up her rich provider for a poor soldier has been filmed four times: as *Pettigrew's Girl*, a silent in 1919, with Ethel Clayton and Monte Blue; in 1929, with Nancy Carroll, Paul Lukas, and Gary Cooper; in 1938, with Margaret Sullavan, Walter Pidgeon, and James Stewart; and in 1959, as *That Kind of Woman*, with Sidney Lumet directing Sophia Loren, George Sanders, and Tab Hunter.

Show Boat.
Jerome Kern and Oscar Hammerstein II's operetta from Edna Ferber's novel was filmed by Harry Pollard in 1929 with Laura La Plante and Joseph Schildkraut; by James Whale in 1936 with Irene Dunne, Allan Jones, and Paul Robeson; and by George Sidney in 1951 with Kathryn Grayson, Howard Keel, and William Warfield.

Silly Symphony.
The name given by Walt Disney to all his short cartoon fables of the 30s which did not feature Mickey Mouse, Pluto or Donald Duck.

A Sister to Assist'er.
George Dewhurst wrote, from John le Breton's play, and directed three versions of this comedy about a poor tenant who pretends to be her rich sister in order to trick her landlady into giving her back her possessions: in 1930, starring Barbara Gott; in 1938, starring Muriel George; and again in 1948, with Muriel George. The definitive performance as the hard-up Mrs May, though, was given on the stage by Fred Emney (1866-1917), father of the film and stage comic actor Fred Emney.

Sitting Pretty.
The 1947 comedy starring Clifton Webb as Lynn Belvedere, babysitter extraordinary, brought two sequels: *Mr Belvedere Goes to College* 49, and *Mr Belvedere Rings the Bell* 51. The title was also used for a 1933 comedy featuring Jack Oakie and Jack Haley as two songwriters hitch-hiking their way to Hollywood.

skiing
has formed a pleasant background in many romantic comedies including *I Met Him in Paris* and *Two-Faced Woman*; in farces including *The Pink Panther* and *Snowball Express*; dramas including *Last of the Ski Bums*, *Ski Fever* and *Downhill Racer*; and in a plethora of spy stories, including *Caprice*, *The Double Man* and a couple of Bonds. The most musical ski sequence was provided by The Beatles in *Help!*

slapstick.
One of the earliest (1895) Lumière shorts, *L'Arroseur Arrosé*, was a knockabout farce, and in 1966 *A Funny Thing Happened on the Way to the Forum* was keeping the tradition going. Out of simple slapstick developed the great silent clowns, each with his own brand of pathos: Harold Lloyd,

Charlie Chaplin, Buster Keaton, Fatty Arbuckle, Harry Langdon, Mabel Normand, Larry Semon, Laurel and Hardy. Pure destructive slapstick without humanity was superbly dispensed by Mack Sennett, especially in his Keystone Kops shorts. France had produced Max Linder; Britain lagged behind, but in the 20s Betty Balfour, Monty Banks and Lupino Lane kept the flag flying. Many of these names survived in some degree when sound came, but cross-talk was an added factor in the success of Wheeler and Woolsey, Charlie Chase, Edgar Kennedy, Leon Errol, Hugh Herbert, Joe E. Brown, W. C. Fields, Eddie Cantor, Abbott and Costello and above all the Marx Brothers. Similarly in Britain there was an influx of stage comics with firm music-hall traditions: George Formby, Will Hay, Max Miller, Gracie Fields, Leslie Fuller, the Crazy Gang, Arthur Askey, Gordon Harker, Sandy Powell, Frank Randle and Old Mother Riley. The 40s in Hollywood brought the more sophisticated slapstick of Danny Kaye, writer-director Preston Sturges, and the Bob Hope gag factory, with extreme simplicity keeping its end up via Olsen and Johnson and Jerry Lewis. In the 50s, TV finally brought a female clown, Lucille Ball, to the top; though competition was thin. France since the war has had Fernandel, Louis de Funes, Jacques Tati and Pierre Etaix; Britain, Norman Wisdom and Morecambe and Wise; Italy, Toto and Walter Chiari. In Hollywood the fashion over more than thirty years was for epic comedies of violence and destruction, such as *It's a Mad Mad Mad Mad World*, *The Great Race*, *Those Magnificent Men in Their Flying Machines* and *The Blues Brothers*.

Slaughter.
A Vietnam veteran out for revenge on those who killed his parents and friend was played by Jim Brown in two films: *Slaughter* 72 and *Slaughter's Big Rip-Off* 73.

slogans
All kinds of claims have been made over the years for all kinds of products. Here are a few of the most memorable.

❝ Famous Players in Famous Plays
is certainly the longest lasting, all the way from 1912. The films hardly lived up to it, any more than it was true that:

Selznick Pictures Create Happy Homes
Or that Warners fooled anybody by linking:
Good Films – Good Citizenship
Or MGM by claiming that their spur was:
Ars Gratia Artis (art for its own sake)
MGM's secondary claim:
More Stars than there are in Heaven
was simply a slight exaggeration. When talkies came in, two favourite lines were:
All Talking, All Singing, All Dancing
And, from Vitaphone:
Pictures that Talk Like Living People!
The whole industry sometimes gets together on a propaganda campaign. In the 30s, it was:
Go to a Motion Picture – and Let Yourself Go!
In the 40s, simply:
Let's go to a movie!
In the 50s, in face of the arch-enemy television:
Don't be a Living Room Captive! Go Out and See a Great Movie!
And a few years later:
Movies are Your Best Entertainment!
The one I like best was concocted by the proprietors of CinemaScope in the face of 3-D. Originally it ran:
You see it without the use of glasses!
This not unnaturally brought a few complaints from bespectacled patrons who thought they were being guaranteed a new freedom, so hurriedly and rather lamely it was changed to:
You see it without the use of special glasses!

small towns
were for many years the staple of the American cinema. Most audiences were small-town folk, and wanted to see slightly idealized versions of themselves. Thus the popularity of the happy families, the Hardys and the Joneses; thus *Our Town*, *The Human Comedy*, *Ah Wilderness*, *The Music Man* and *The Dark at the Top of the Stairs*. The darker side of small-town life was shown in *The Chase*, *Kings Row*, *Peyton Place* and *Invasion of the Body Snatchers*. British small towns did not have the same aura; most of the comparable stories were set against industrial backgrounds.

Smilin' Through.
The popular sentimental stage play by Jane Cowl and June Murfin, about a tragedy affecting the romances of two generations, was filmed in 1922 by Sidney Franklin, with Norma Talmadge, Wyndham Standing, and Harrison Ford; in 1932, again by Sidney Franklin, with Norma Shearer, Leslie Howard, and Fredric March. In 1941 Frank Borzage remade it with Jeanette MacDonald, Brian Aherne, and Gene Raymond.

smoking
has served as the springboard of a few plots. *No Smoking* and *Cold Turkey* concerned cures for it, and one also figured in *Taking Off*. In *On a Clear Day You Can See Forever* Barbra Streisand launched the plot by taking psychiatric advice about it. The most fashionable smoking habit was Paul Henreid's in *Now Voyager*, lighting two cigarettes and passing one to Bette Davis; this was mimicked with eight cigarettes by Bob Hope in *Let's Face It*. The longest cigarette holder was sported by Harpo Marx in *A Night in Casablanca*. In the 90s there was a concerted campaign to stop stars smoking on-screen, on the grounds that it encouraged the young and impressionable to take up the habit. Perhaps as a reaction came *Smoke* and *Blue in the Face* 95, two films set in a Brooklyn cigar store. *The Insider* 99, dealt with a former tobacco company scientist exposing official denials that cigarettes harm health.

smugglers
of the old-fashioned type are almost entirely a British concern, figuring in *Fury at Smugglers' Bay*, *Jamaica Inn*, *The Ghost Train*, *Oh Mr Porter*, *Ask a Policeman*, *I See a Dark Stranger*, *Moonfleet*, and others. Smuggling in American films has been a much more modern and less picturesque affair.

social comedy.
Silent romantic comedies were completely unrealistic, though they sometimes found it prudent to pretend satirical intent to cloak their lowbrow commercialism. Social comedy really came in as a substitute for sex comedy when the Hays Office axe fell in 1934. Frank Capra took by far the best advantage of it, with his series of films showing an America filled to bursting point with good guys who only wanted a simple and comfortable home life in some small town where corruption never raised its ugly head. The best of these films were *Mr Deeds Goes to Town*, *You Can't Take It with You* and *Mr Smith Goes to Washington*; by the time *Meet John Doe* came along in 1941 war had soured the mood again. There was no British equivalent to Capra, unless one counts a few attempts by Priestley (*The Good Companions*, *Let the People Sing*) and such amusing depictions of the middle class as *Quiet Wedding* and *Dear Octopus*; but in the late 40s came the Ealing comedies, delightful and apparently realistic, but presenting a picture of England just as false as Capra's America. In both countries the 50s saw the development of an affluent society in which cynicism was fashionable and few reforms seemed worth urging except in bitterly serious fashion.

social conscience
has long been a feature of Hollywood film production. Other countries have presented the odd feature pointing to flaws in their national make-up, but America has seemed particularly keen to wash its own dirty linen on screen, perhaps because this is rather easier than actually cleaning up the abuses.

The evolution of this attitude can be traced back as far as 1912 and Griffith's *The Musketeers of Pig Alley*, showing slum conditions, a theme developed in *Intolerance* 16; and, of course, Chaplin was a master at devising humour and pathos out of the unpleasant realities of poverty, a fact which endeared him to poor people all over the world. But it was not till the late 20s that the flood of socially conscious films began in earnest. Vidor's *The Crowd* investigated the drabness of everyday life for a city clerk. John Baxter's British *Dosshouse* was a lone entry on the lines of *The Lower Depths*. *City Streets* and *One-Third of a Nation* treated slum conditions; Vidor's *Our Daily Bread* concerned a young couple driven out of the city by poverty only to find farming just as precarious. *Little Caesar* and the gangster dramas which followed always assumed a crusading moral tone deploring the lives of vice and crime which they depicted; there was a somewhat more honest ring to *I Was a Fugitive from a Chain Gang*, which showed how circumstance can drive an honest man into anti-social behaviour. Capra sugared his pill with comedy: *American Madness* (the madness was money) and the popular comedies which followed all pitted common-man philosophy against urban sophistication and corruption.

In the mid-30s there were certainly many abuses worth fighting. *Black Legion* began Hollywood's campaign against the Ku Klux Klan, later followed up in *The Flaming Cross*, *Storm Warning* and *The Cardinal*. Lynch law, first tackled in *Fury*, was subsequently the subject of *They Won't Forget*, *The Ox Bow Incident* and *The Sound of Fury*. Juvenile delinquency was probed in *Dead End*, *Angels with Dirty Faces* and *They Made Me a Criminal*, but the 'Dead End Kids' were later played for comedy. Prison reform was advocated in *Each Dawn I Die*, *Castle on the Hudson*, and many other melodramas of questionable integrity. *The Good Earth* invited concern for the poor of other nations; *Mr Smith Goes to Washington* and *The Glass Key* were among many dramas showing that politicians are not incorruptible; *Love on the Dole* depicted the poverty of industrial Britain; *The Grapes of Wrath* and *Tobacco Road* pondered the plight of farming people deprived of a living by geographical chance and thoughtless government. In *Sullivan's Travels*, Preston Sturges came to the curious conclusion that the best thing you can do for the poor is make them laugh.

During World War II the nations were too busy removing the abuse of Nazidom to look inward, and indeed much poverty was alleviated by conscription and a fresh national awareness which, together with the increased need for industrial manpower, greatly improved the lot of the lower classes. But with victory came a whole crop of films, led by *The Best Years of Our Lives* and *Till the End of Time*, about the rehabilitation of war veterans. Concern about mental illness was shown in *The Snake Pit*, about paraplegia in *The Men*, and about labour relations in *The Whistle at Eaton Falls*. Alcoholism was treated in *The Lost Weekend* and *Smash-Up*, and the racial issues were thoroughly aired in *Lost Boundaries*, *Crossfire*, *Home of the Brave*, *No Way Out*, *Gentleman's Agreement* and *Pinky*. A plea for nations to help and understand each other was made in the French *Race for Life*.

With the development in the 50s of the affluent society, the number of reforms worth urging was drastically reduced. Teenage hoodlums figured largely in a score of films of which the best were *The Wild One* and *Rebel without a Cause*. Mentally handicapped children were sympathetically portrayed in *A Child is Waiting*. In the 1960s, however, it was one world issue which dominated the film-makers' social consciousness, that of the panic button; and this manifested itself in films as diverse as *On the Beach*, *Dr Strangelove*, *Fail Safe* and *The Bedford Incident*.

Social consciousness was apparent in almost every drama of the 70s, but used as a top dressing, sometimes to permit the exploitation of violence.

soldiers
depicted at length in films include Alexander the Great (by Richard Burton), Hannibal (by Victor Mature), Genghis Khan (by John Wayne and Omar Sharif), Alexander Nevsky (by Cherkassov), Clive of India (by Ronald Colman), Napoleon (by Charles Boyer, Marlon Brando, Herbert Lom, and others), Bonnie Prince Charlie (by David Niven), Wellington (by George Arliss), General Gordon (by Charlton Heston), Custer (by Errol Flynn and Robert Shaw), La Fayette (by Michel le Royer), Davy Crockett (by Fess Parker and others), Sergeant York (by Gary Cooper), Audie Murphy (by Audie Murphy), Rommel (by Erich von Stroheim and James Mason), Che Guevara (by Omar Sharif), General Patton (by George C. Scott), and General Macarthur (by Gregory Peck).

space exploration
on screen began in 1899 with Méliès; in the 20s Fritz Lang made *The Woman in the Moon* and in the 30s there was *Buck Rogers in the Twenty-Fifth Century*, but not until 1950 did the subject seem acceptable as anything but fantasy. In that year an adventure of the comic-strip type, *Rocketship XM*, competed for box-office attention with George Pal's semi-documentary *Destination Moon*, and suddenly the floodgates were opened. During the years that followed we were offered such titles as *Riders to the Stars*, *Fire Maidens from Outer Space*, *Satellite in the Sky*, *From the Earth to the Moon*, *Conquest of Space*, *Forbidden Planet*, *It!*, *The Terror from Beyond Space*, *Robinson Crusoe on Mars*, *The First Men in the Moon*, *2001: A Space Odyssey*, *Saturn Three*, *Outland*, the *Star Wars* sagas, and *Mission to Mars*. Nor was the traffic all one way: Earth had many strange visitors from other planets, notably in *The Thing From Another World*, *The Day the Earth Stood Still*, *Devil Girl from Mars*, *Stranger from Venus*, *It Came from Outer Space*, *Invasion of the Body Snatchers* (the best and subtlest of them all), *The War of the Worlds*, *The Quatermass Experiment*, *Quatermass II*, *Visit to a Small Planet*, *This Island Earth*, and *The Man Who Fell to Earth*. On television, the most imaginative exploits have been in *Star Trek*, *Space 1999*, *Buck Rogers* and *Galactica*.

spaghetti westerns.
A dismissive name for the blood-spattered Italian imitations of American westerns which became popular in the 60s, using such actors as Lee Van Cleef and Clint Eastwood. They gained an international reputation, and incidentally made Eastwood into a star, through the work of Sergio Leone in the mid-60s, beginning with his *A Fistful of Dollars*. Leone orchestrated the action around dramatic close-ups, with a slow build to moments of extreme action, to the accompaniment of Ennio Morricone's plangent, percussive music. Eastwood set the pattern for the protagonist: a taciturn, laconic wanderer who was deadly with a gun. While he was 'the man with no name', other recurring heroes of the genre were Sartana, Django and Ringo. Other US actors who found employment in the films included Charles Bronson. Italian actors also found a role, including Franco Nero as Django, Tomas Milian and, as the genre encompassed more comedy, Bud Spencer and Terence Hill. By the beginning of the 70s, the genre has lost most of its impetus, though it influenced later westerns such as Sam Peckinpah's *The Wild Bunch*.

Books: 1975, *Italian Western: The Opera of Violence* by Laurence Staig and Tony Williams; 1998, *Spaghetti Westerns: Cowboys and Europeans from Karl May to Sergio Leone* by Christopher Frayling.

The Spanish Civil War
featured in a few Hemingway picturizations, notably *For Whom the Bell Tolls* and *The Snows of Kilimanjaro*; in *The Fallen Sparrow*, *Blockade*, *The Angel Wore Red*, *Love under Fire*, *Last Train from Madrid*, *Arise My Love*, *Confidential Agent* and (remotely) *The Prime of Miss Jean Brodie*. In more documentary style were *L'Espoir*, *Spanish Earth*, *Guernica*, *To Die in Madrid*, *¡Ay, Carmela!* and *Land and Freedom*, while British television has produced two extended assemblies of newsreel footage.

speeches
of any length are the antithesis of good film-making, but sometimes a long monologue has been not only an actor's dream but absolutely right, memorable and hypnotic in its context. The record (20 minutes) is probably held by Edwige Feuillère in *The Eagle Has Two Heads*, but more effective, and somewhat shorter, were Sam Jaffe in *Lost Horizon*, Alec Guinness in *The Mudlark*, Orson Welles in *Compulsion*, Spencer Tracy in *Inherit the Wind*, Anne Baxter in *The Walls of Jericho*, James Stewart in *Mr Smith Goes to Washington*, Paul Muni in *The Life of Emile Zola*, Don Murray in *One Man's Way*, Orson Welles in *Moby Dick*, and Charles Chaplin in *The Great Dictator*.

Speedy Gonzales.
Fast-moving Mexican mouse who was the hero of Warner Brothers cartoons. Created by Friz Freleng and animator Hawley Pratt, he was voiced by Mel Blanc.

Speedy Gonzales (AA) 55. Tabasco Road (AAN) 57. The Pied Piper of Guadalupe (AAN) 61. Mexican Cat Dance 63. Chili Corn Corny 66. Speedy Ghost to Town 67. See Ya Later, Gladiator 67, etc.

spies
enjoyed enormous popularity as the heroes of over-sexed, gimmick-ridden melodramas. Real-life spies have been less frequently depicted, the world of James Bond being much livelier than those of Moyzich (*Five Fingers*), Odette Churchill (*Odette V.C.*), *Nurse Edith Cavell*, Violette Szabo (*Carve Her Name with Pride*), *Mata Hari*, or the gangs in *The House on 92nd Street*, *13 Rue Madeleine*, and *Ring of Spies*.

Fictional spy films first became popular during and after World War I: they added a touch of glamour to an otherwise depressing subject, even though the hero often faced the firing squad in the last reel. Right up to 1939 romantic melodramas on this theme were being made: *I Was a Spy*, *The Man Who Knew Too Much*, *The Thirty-Nine Steps*, *Lancer Spy*, *The Spy in Black*, *Dark Journey*, *British Agent*, *Secret Agent*, *The Lady Vanishes*, *Espionage Agent*, *Confessions of a Nazi Spy*. The last-named brought the subject roughly up to date, and with the renewed outbreak of hostilities new possibilities were hastily seized in *Foreign Correspondent*, *Night Train to Munich*, *Casablanca*, *The Conspirators*, *They Came to Blow Up America*, *Berlin Correspondent*, *Across the Pacific*, *Escape to Danger*, *Ministry of Fear*, *Confidential Agent*, *Sherlock Holmes and the Secret Weapon*, *Hotel Reserve*, and innumerable others. (It was fashionable during this period to reveal that the villains of comedy-thrillers and who-done-its were really enemy agents.) During the post-war years two fashions in film spying became evident: the downbeat melodrama showing spies as frightened men and women doing a dangerous job (*Notorious*, *Cloak and Dagger*, *Hotel Berlin*, *Orders to Kill*) and the 'now it can be told' semi-documentary revelation (*O.S.S.*, *Diplomatic Courier*, *The Man Who Never Was*, *The Two-Headed Spy*, *The Counterfeit Traitor*, *Operation Crossbow*). In the late 40s Nazis and Japs were replaced by reds, and we had a spate of melodramas under such titles as *I Married a Communist*, *I Was a Communist for the FBI*, *I Was an American Spy*, *Red Snow* and *The Red Danube*.

There had always been spy comedies. Every comedian made one or two: the Crazy Gang in *Gasbags*, Duggie Wakefield in *Spy for a Day*, Jack Benny in *To Be or Not To Be*, Bob Hope in *They Got Me Covered*, Radford and Wayne in *It's Not Cricket*, George Cole in *Top Secret*, right up to the *Carry On* Team in *Carry On Spying* and Morecambe and Wise in *The Intelligence Men*. There were also occasional burlesques like *All Through the Night* and sardonic comedies like *Our Man in Havana*. But it was not until the late 50s that the spy reasserted himself as a romantic figure who could be taken lightly; and not until 1962 was the right box-office combination of sex and suspense found in *Dr No*. Since then we have been deluged with pale imitations of James Bond to such an extent that almost every leading man worth his salt has had a go. Cary Grant in *Charade*, David Niven in *Where the Spies Are*, Rod Taylor and Trevor Howard in *The Liquidator*, Dirk Bogarde in *Hot Enough for June*, Michael Caine in *The Ipcress File*, Paul Newman in *Torn Curtain*, James Coburn in *Our Man Flint*, Gregory Peck in *Arabesque*, Yul Brynner in *The Double Man*, George Peppard in *The Executioner*, Stephen Boyd in *Assignment K*, Frank Sinatra in *The Naked Runner*, Anthony Hopkins in *When Eight Bells Toll*, Kirk Douglas in *Catch Me a Spy*, Tom Adams in *Licensed to Kill*. There have also been elaborations such as the extreme sophistication of *The Manchurian Candidate*, the cold realism of *The Spy Who Came in from the Cold*, the op-art spoofing of *Modesty Blaise*, even the canine agent of *The Spy with a Cold Nose* and spies from outer space in *This Island Earth*. And the TV screens of 1970 were filled with such tricky heroes as those in *Danger Man* (Secret Agent), *The Man from U.N.C.L.E.*, *Amos Burke Secret Agent*, *The Baron*, *I Spy* and *The Avengers*. The trend of the 70s was towards sour and disenchanted looks at the whole business, such as *Callan*, *The Killer Elite*, *Permission to Kill* and *Three Days of the Condor*.

The Spoilers.

Rex Beach's action novel has been filmed five times, with interest centring on its climactic fight scene between the two male leads, who were as follows: 1914, William Farnum and Tom Santschi; 1922, Milton Sills and Noah Beery; 1930, William Boyd and Gary Cooper; 1942, John Wayne and Randolph Scott; 1956, Jeff Chandler and Rory Calhoun.

sportsmen

who have been the subject of biopics include Babe Ruth (William Bendix) in *The Babe Ruth Story* and *Babe* (John Goodman); Grover Cleveland Alexander (Ronald Reagan) in *The Winning Team*; Lou Gehrig (Gary Cooper) in *The Pride of the Yankees*; Monty Stratton (James Stewart) in *The Stratton Story*; Jim Piersall (Anthony Perkins) in *Fear Strikes Out*; Jim Corbett (Errol Flynn) in *Gentleman Jim*; John L. Sullivan (Greg McClure) in *The Great John L.*; Knute Rockne (Pat O'Brien) in *Knute Rockne All-American*; Jim Thorpe (Burt Lancaster) in *Jim Thorpe All-American/Man of Bronze*; Ben Hogan (Glenn Ford) in *Follow the Sun*; Annette Kellerman (Esther Williams) in *Million Dollar Mermaid*. American athlete Steve Prefontaine, who died young, was the subject of two competing biopics in 1997: *Prefontaine*, starring Jared Leto, and *Without Limits*, starring Billy Crudup. He was also the subject of a 1995 TV documentary, *Fire on the Track*.

Squibs.

The cockney flower-seller heroine of George Pearson's silent comedy put in her first successful appearance in 1921. Public acclaim produced three sequels: *Squibs Wins the Calcutta Sweep* 22, *Squibs MP* 23, *Squibs' Honeymoon* 23. Pearson then grew tired of the tomboyish character and cast Betty Balfour in other roles, but she reappeared in a not-too-successful talkie version in 1936, with Gordon Harker and Stanley Holloway.

staircases

have provided dramatic backgrounds for many films. Martin Balsam was murdered on one in *Psycho*; the climax of *The Spiral Staircase* took place just there; Vivien Leigh was carried up one by a lustful Clark Gable in *Gone with the Wind*; Jerry Lewis danced down one in *Cinderfella*; Errol Flynn and Basil Rathbone duelled on one in *The Adventures of Robin Hood*; Ann Todd rode a horse up one in *South Riding*; Joan Fontaine in *Rebecca* descended one in delight and ascended it in tears; Raymond Massey ascended a particularly shadowy one in *The Old Dark House*, and later a very sinister character came down it; the entire cast of *Ship of Fools* came down one at the end, like a musical finale; a severed head bumped down one in *Hush Hush Sweet Charlotte*; Gene Tierney threw herself down one in *Leave Her to Heaven*; an old lady was tossed down one in a wheelchair in *Kiss of Death*; Bela Lugosi in *Dracula* passed through the cobwebs on one without breaking them; Laurel and Hardy in *Blockheads* had to descend and ascend innumerable flights of stairs in pursuit of a lost ball; Anna Sten was killed on one in *The Wedding Night*; the lighthouse staircase was a dramatic feature of *Thunder Rock*; James Cagney danced down the White House staircase in *Yankee Doodle Dandy*; and the main feature of *A Matter of Life and Death* was a moving stairway to heaven. In his last film, *Greystoke*, Ralph Richardson slid down a staircase on a tea-tray. Universal and Paramount both had very striking and oft-used staircase sets in the 40s; the latter was most dramatically used for Kirk Douglas' death in *The Strange Love of Martha Ivers*. Oddly enough in the film called *Staircase* the staircase was not an essential feature.

A Star Is Born.

Dorothy Parker, Alan Campbell, and Robert Carson's screenplay for the 1937 film has become a Hollywood legend and in some cases a reality: the marriage of two stars goes on the rocks because one of them is on the way up and the other on the way down. It was first tailored for Janet Gaynor and Fredric March and directed by William Wellman. In 1954 George Cukor directed Judy Garland and James Mason in the star roles. In 1976 it was revamped for Barbra Streisand and Kris Kristofferson. The theme can be traced back to a 1930 film, *What Price Hollywood?*, from a story by Adela Rogers St Johns.

Star Wars.

George LUCAS's immensely popular science-fiction romp of 1977 was swiftly followed by two sequels: *The Empire Strikes Back* 80 and *The Return of the Jedi* 83. In 1999 came *Star Wars Episode 1: The Phantom Menace*, the first of a projected trilogy of prequels to the original three films, detailing the earlier history of the protagonists. It was preceded, in 1997, by a re-release of *Star Wars* and its two sequels, featuring enhanced special effects. The films proved as popular the second time around.

State Fair.

Philip Strong's novel of small-town virtues, champion hogs, and bucolic romance has been filmed three times: in 1933, directed by Henry King, with Will Rogers and Janet Gaynor; in 1945, as a musical, directed by Walter Lang, with Jeanne Crain, Dana Andrews, Dick Haymes, Vivian Blane, and songs by Oscar Hammerstein II; and in 1962, directed by José Ferrer, with Pat Boone, Bobby Darin, Pamela Tiffin, and Ann-Margret, and new songs added by Richard Rodgers.

statesmen

who have frequently been depicted in films include Disraeli (most often), Gladstone, Melbourne, Ramsay Macdonald (disguised in *Fame is the Spur*), Woodrow Wilson, Churchill, Roosevelt (notably in *Sunrise at Campobello*), LINCOLN, Parnell, John F. Kennedy and Richard Nixon. Fleeting glimpses of famous leaders were also given in *Mission to Moscow* and some Russian wartime films.
See also: POLITICS

statues

have come to life in *Night Life of the Gods*, *Animal Crackers*, *Turnabout*, *One Touch of Venus*, and *Mannequin*. They were central to the plots of *The Light that Failed*, *Latin Quarter*, *Song of Songs* and *Mad Love*, while *A Taste of Honey* involved them in an attractive title sequence. In horror films, they came murderously alive in *Night of the Eagle*, *The Norliss Tapes* (TV) and that grand-daddy of them all, *The Golem*.

Stella Dallas.

The weepy novel of frustrated mother love, written by Olive Higgins Prouty, was filmed by Henry King in 1925, with Belle Bennett and Ronald Colman; by King Vidor in 1937, with Barbara Stanwyck and John Boles; and by John Erman in 1990, as *Stella*, with Bette Midler and John Goodman.

storms

of one kind or another have been brilliantly staged in *The Hurricane*, *The Wizard of Oz*, *When Tomorrow Comes*, *Reap the Wild Wind*, *Typhoon*, *Lord Jim*, *A High Wind in Jamaica*, *The Blue Lagoon*, *Sunrise*, *Key Largo*, *Ryan's Daughter*, *Portrait of Jennie*, *Noah's Ark* and *The Bible*, to name but a handful; they have also been essential situation-builders in such films as *Five Came Back*, *Hatter's Castle*, *Our Man Flint*, *The Card*, *Storm Fear* and *The Blue Lagoon*. A whole genre of films, known as the 'thunderstorm mystery', grew up in the 30s when every screen murder took place in a desolate mansion during a terrifying storm with no means of communication with the outside world; typical of these are *The Black Cat*, *The Cat and the Canary*, *The Ghost Breakers*, *Night Monster*, *Hold That Ghost*, *You'll Find Out* and *The Spiral Staircase*. Finally there is nothing like a good electrical storm for breathing life into a monster, as evidenced in a score of films from *Frankenstein* to *The Electric Man* and after.

strikes:

see LABOUR RELATIONS.

striptease.

The staple of burlesque and Las Vegas finally made it to the screen with no holds barred and no breasts bra'ed in Paul VERHOEVEN's *Showgirls* 95, a film about the lives of two 'lap dancers'. It also brought Demi MOORE $12m, the most money ever paid to a Hollywood actress, to play the role of a stripper in *Striptease* 96, based on Carl Hiassen's thriller. Strippers also featured in Atom EGOYAN's award-winning art film *Exotica* 94. The first known stripper was Lady Godiva, whose legend formed the basis for the updated British movie *Lady Godiva Rides Again* 51, and *Lady Godiva* 55, a US historical recreation set in Saxon times. The most famous artiste remains Gypsy Rose LEE whose autobiography of her early life was filmed as *Gypsy* 62; she was played by Natalie WOOD, a guarantee that proceedings remained genteel. Gypsy Rose Lee's novel *G-String Murders* was filmed as *Lady of Burlesque/Striptease Lady* 43, featuring Barbara STANWYCK as a stripper who solves a number of backstage murders, and her play *Doll Face/Come Back to Me*, about a burlesque queen who goes to Broadway, was filmed in 1945. From the 30s onwards, she also appeared in Hollywood films, including *The Stripper* 63, but that had little to do with taking off clothes to music. Roger CORMAN produced a couple of exploitation movies on the theme, with *Stripped to Kill* 87 and *Stripped to Kill II* 89. Other strippers have included Britt EKLAND in *The Night They Raided Minsky's* 68; Melanie GRIFFITH in *Fear City* 84; Lolita DAVIDOVITCH, bringing about politician Earl Long's downfall in *Blaze* 89; Sherilyn FENN in *Ruby* 92; Goldie HAWN as a hard-working mother in *CrissCross* 92; and Demi Moore in *Striptease* 96. Male strippers have been less popular so far, though Christopher ATKINS appeared as one in *A Night in Heaven* 83, and Mel CHIONGLO's *Midnight Dancers* 94 was set in a nightclub featuring little else. *The Full Monty* 97 focused on a group of unemployed men who try stripping to earn some cash.

The Student of Prague.

The old German legend, about a man who sold his soul to the devil and bought it back only at the expense of his life, was filmed in 1913 by Stellan Rye, with Paul Wegener; in 1926 by Henrik Galeen, with Conrad Veidt; and in 1936 by Arthur Robison, with Anton Walbrook.

The Student Prince.

The Sigmund Romberg/Dorothy Donnelly operetta about a Ruritanian prince who loves a barmaid was filmed by Lubitsch in 1927 with Ramon Novarro and Norma Shearer. There was no sound version until 1954, when Richard Thorpe directed Ann Blyth and Edmund Purdom (the latter using Mario Lanza's voice).

student protest

was a feature of a few films of the late 60s. They were not successful, with the exception of *If*. For the record the other main titles were *Flick*, *The Strawberry Statement*, *Getting Straight*, *R.P.M.* and *The Revolutionary*.

stuntmen,

who risk their lives doubling for the stars when the action gets too rough, have been featured in remarkably few movies: *Hollywood Stunt Men*, *Lucky Devils*, *The Lost Squadron*, *Sons of Adventure*, *Callaway Went Thataway*, *Singin' in the Rain* and *Hooper*, *Hell's Angels* was said to be the film on which most stuntmen were killed; more recently Paul Mantz lost his life while stunt-flying for *The Flight of the Phoenix*, which was subsequently dedicated to him. Most famous stuntmen are probably Yakima Canutt, who later became a famous second-unit director; Richard Talmadge, who doubled for Douglas Fairbanks and also directed a few films himself; and Cliff Lyons, who stood in for most of the western stars. Stuntmen who became famous in their own right include George O'Brien, Jock Mahoney, Rod Cameron and George Montgomery. In the early 80s a film called *The Stunt Man* took a wry view of the matter and a TV series called *The Fall Guy* was popular for a while.

submarines

have been the setting for so many war action films that only a few can be noted. Pure entertainment was the object of *Submarine Patrol*, *Submarine Command*, *Torpedo Run*, *Destination Tokyo*, *Run Silent Run Deep*, *Crash Dive*, *The Deep Six* and *Ice Station Zebra*. Somewhat deeper thoughts were permitted in *Morning Departure*, *The Silent Enemy*, *Les Maudits*, *We Dive at Dawn*, *Crimson Tide* and, best of all *The Boat/Das Boot*. Submarines became objects of farce in *Jack Ahoy*, *Let's Face It*, and *Operation Petticoat*.

More unusual submarine vehicles appeared in *Voyage to the Bottom of the Sea*, *Around the World Under the Sea*, *Twenty Thousand Leagues Under the Sea*, *Thunderball*, *You Only Live Twice*, *Above Us the Waves* and *The Beast from 20,000 Fathoms*.

subways:

see UNDERGROUND RAILWAYS.

suicide

became the central subject of two 60s films, *Le Feu Follet* and *The Slender Thread*, in which the motives for it in two particular cases are examined. It has, of course, been part of countless other plots, including factual or legendary ones such as *Cleopatra*, *Romeo and Juliet* and *Scott of the Antarctic*. Innumerable melodramas have begun with apparent suicides which have been proved by the disbelieving hero to be murder; the least likely of these may be *The Third Secret*. In *An Inspector Calls* a girl's suicide caused guilt complexes in an entire family for different reasons. In *An American Dream* the hero virtually commits suicide by walking into a room full of gangsters out to kill him. In *Leave Her to Heaven* the leading character commits suicide in such a way that her husband will be blamed for her murder. Several Japanese films have been based on the suicide pilots or kamikaze, and there has also been a graphic account of the principles of *hara kiri*. Suicide has often been the way out for villains in mystery pictures: drowning for Herbert Marshall in *Foreign Correspondent*, shooting for Leo G. Carroll in *Spellbound*, poison for Rosamund John in *Green for Danger* and Barry Fitzgerald in *And Then There*

Were None. And one could not begin to count the films in which characters have been narrowly saved from suicide, like Ray Milland in *The Lost Weekend*. Attempted suicide was even played for comedy by Laurel and Hardy in *The Flying Deuces*, by Graham Chapman in *The Odd Job*, by Jack Lemmon in *Buddy Buddy* and *Luv*, by Burt Reynolds in *The End*, while in *It's a Wonderful Life* James Stewart was dissuaded from suicide by a friendly angel. In *The Long Goodbye*, Elliott Gould finds a presumed suicide alive, and shoots him.

Superman.
A comic strip character of the 30s, a being of giant powers from the planet Krypton; until they are needed he masquerades as Clark Kent, a timid newspaperman. Superman has never been out of fashion – 1978 brought a multi-million-dollar live version to follow the various cartoons and serials which have been popular over the years – and along the way he has inspired Batman, Spiderman, Doc Savage, the Six Million Dollar Man, the Bionic Woman, etc, etc. In 1984, after two further sequels, *Superman* gave way to *Supergirl*. The role has been played by Kirk ALYN in two serials, George REEVES, who took over for one serial before playing the part on television, Christopher REEVE in the big-budget films of the 70s and 80s, and Dean Cain in a 90s TV series.

Superman (serial) 48. Atom Man vs Superman (serial) 50. Superman and the Mole Men (serial) 51. Superman 78. Superman II 80. Superman III 83. Superman IV: The Quest for Peace 87.

TV series: Superman (with George Reeves) 53-57. Lois and Clark: The New Adventures of Superman 93-97.

Svengali,
the evil genius of George du Maurier's Victorian romance *Trilby*, has been seen at least five times on-screen. In 1915 Wilton Lackaye and Clara Kimball Young appeared in a version under the title *Trilby*. There was a British one-reeler in 1922 in the 'Tense Moments with Great Authors' series, and in 1923 James Young directed a second Hollywood version with Arthur Edmund Carewe and Andrée Lafayette. In 1931, under the title *Svengali*, Archie Mayo directed a sound remake with John Barrymore as the hypnotist to Marian Marsh's heroine, and in 1954 Donald Wolfit and Hildegarde Neff appeared in a British version directed by Noel Langley. (Robert Newton had proved incapable of playing the lead.) In 1982 Peter O'Toole and Jodie Foster were in a dismal TV modernization set in New York.

swashbucklers
are films of period adventure in which the hero and villain usually settle the issue by a duel to the death. The greatest screen swashbucklers of all are probably Douglas FAIRBANKS Snr and Errol FLYNN, but one should also be grateful for the efforts of Tyrone POWER (*The Mark of Zorro*), Douglas FAIRBANKS Jnr (*Sinbad the Sailor*), Ronald COLMAN (*The Prisoner of Zenda*), Stewart GRANGER (*Scaramouche*), Rudolph VALENTINO (*The Eagle*), Gene KELLY (*The Three Musketeers*), Robert DONAT (*The Count of Monte Cristo*), Louis HAYWARD (*The Man in the Iron Mask*), Cornel WILDE (*The Bandit of Sherwood Forest*), Tony CURTIS (*The Purple Mask*) and their numerous imitators. The 1976 attempt to revive (or spoof) the genre in *Swashbuckler* was a sorry failure; but *The Mask of Zorro* 98, with Antonio BANDERAS, showed that there was some life left in the genre after all.

swinging London
was a myth, a creation of *Time* Magazine which rebounded through the world's press and lasted for several silly seasons from 1965. It also helped British production finances by persuading American impresarios that London was where the action was, and its influence was felt in scores of trendy and increasingly boring films, including *Georgy Girl, Alfie, The Jokers, Kaleidoscope, Smashing Time, Help!, The Knack, Blow Up, Casino Royale, I'll Never Forget Whatshisname, To Sir with Love, Up the Junction, Bedazzled, Poor Cow, The Strange Affair, Salt and Pepper, Joanna, Darling* and *Otley*.

The Swiss Family Robinson.
The classic children's novel by Johann Wyss was filmed in Hollywood in 1940 by Edward Ludwig, with Thomas Mitchell, Edna Best, Freddie Bartholomew, and Terry Kilburn. In 1960 Ken Annakin remade it as a Disney spectacular, with John Mills, Dorothy McGuire, James Macarthur, and Tommy Kirk as the desert island castaways.

sword and sorcery
is the term used to describe stories set in mythic fantasy worlds, where muscular heroes cleave their way through a landscape filled with monsters and magic. The most influential author in the genre has been Robert E. HOWARD, creator of Conan the Barbarian. In the mid-90s, the genre found its home on television in the series *Hercules: the Legendary Journeys*, starring Kevin Sorbo, and *Xena: Warrior Princess*, starring Lucy Lawless, which put the emphasis on spectacle and camp humour.

Hawk the Slayer 80. Conan the Barbarian 81. Fire and Ice 82. The Beastmaster 82. Sword and the Sorcerer 82. Ator the Fighting Eagle 83. Deathstalker 83. Krull 83. Blade Master/Ator the Invincible 84. Conan the Destroyer 84. Red Sonja 85. Wizards of the Lost Kingdom 85. Highlander 86. Deathstalker 2: Duel of the Titans 87. Deathstalker 3: The Warriors from Hell 89. Wizards of the Lost Kingdom 2 89. Highlander II: The Quickening 90. Beastmaster 2: Through the Portals of Time 91. Deathstalker 4: Match of the Titans 92. Highlander III: The Sorcerer 94. Wizards of the Demon Sword 94. Beastmaster 3: The Eye of Braxus 95. Kull the Conqueror 97, etc.

Sylvester.
The celebrated cartoon cat with the lisping Bronx accent, always in pursuit of Tweetie Pie but never quite managing to win, appeared from the 40s to the 60s in Warner shorts, voiced by the inimitable Mel BLANC.

Life with Feathers (AAN) 45. Tweetie Pie (AA) 47. Little Red Rodent Hood 52. Claws for Alarm 54. Speedy Gonzales (AA) 55. Tabasco Road (AAN) 57. Mouse-Taken Identity 57. Birds Anonymous (AA) 57. Trip for Tat 60. The Pied Piper of Guadalupe (AAN) 61. Freudy Cat 64, etc.

A Tale of Two Cities.
Apart from three very early one-reel versions, Dickens's novel of the French Revolution was filmed in 1917, with William Farnum, in 1926 with Maurice Costello and (as *The Only Way*) with Sir John Martin-Harvey, in 1935, with Ronald Colman, and in 1958, with Dirk Bogarde.

Tales of Manhattan.
Julien Duvivier's 1942 film, a string of anecdotes linked by the travels of one tail-coat, can be credited with starting or revivifying the short-story compendium form, later developed in such movies as *Flesh and Fantasy, Quartet, Full House, The Story of Three Loves, It's a Great Country*, and many others. The film's inspiration was Duvivier's own *Un Carnet de Bal*, made in 1937, which gave him his ticket to Hollywood.

talkies
caused the biggest revolution the film industry has known, and provoked critical resentment difficult to understand until one sees a very early talkie and realizes what a raucous and unpleasant experience it must have been until Hollywood caught up with itself. The main steps of development were as follows. In 1923 Lee DE FORREST made primitive shorts. In 1926 Warners created Vitaphone, a disc process, and Fox pioneered sound on film with Movietone. Also in 1926 came *Don Juan*, the first film with synchronized music and effects. The first speaking and singing came in 1927 with Al Jolson in *The Jazz Singer*. In 1928 the first all-talking film, *Lights of New York*, set the seal of popular success on the new medium.

“The addition of sound to the movies was ridiculed and frantically opposed; but the industry needed the fresh impetus and at great expense the revolution was achieved.

No closer approach to resurrection has ever been made by science,

said Professor M. Pupin of the American Institute of Electrical Engineers. But it was years before he could claim perfect reproduction.

The tinkle of a glass, the shot of a revolver, a footfall on a hardwood floor, and the noise of a pack of cards being shuffled, all sounded about alike,

said Gilbert Seldes in 1929. And Tallulah Bankhead complained:

They made me sound as if I'd been castrated.

E.V. Lucas complained:

They are doing away with the greatest boon that has ever been offered to the deaf.

The distinguished documentarist Paul Rotha joined in the dismay:

A film in which the speech and sound effects are perfectly synchronized and coincide with their visual images on screen is absolutely contrary to the aims of the cinema. It is a degenerate and misguided attempt to destroy the real use of the film.

Nor was the prestige of the industry helped by claims of mathematical impossibility such as:

100% talking! 100% singing! 100% dancing!

But the public forgave all: the novelty value was tremendous, even though they missed a number of favourite stars whose voices proved unsuitable. As Jack Warner said:

Men and women whose names were known throughout the land disappeared as though they had been lost at sea.

And *Variety* summed up:

Talkies didn't do more to the industry than turn it upside down, shake the entire bag of tricks from its pocket, and advance Warner Brothers from last place to first in the league.

But Ernst Lubitsch took a more cynical view:

You could name the great stars of the silent screen who were finished; the great directors, gone; the great title writers who were washed up. But remember this, as long as you live: the producers didn't lose a man. They all made the switch. That's where the great talent is.

Tammy.
Cid Ricketts Sumner's romantic novel of a cheerful country girl was filmed in 1957 with Debbie Reynolds in the title role; two sequels, *Tammy Tell Me True* and *Tammy and the Doctor*, followed in 1961 and 1963 starring Sandra Dee; they were followed by a fourth film, *Tammy and the Millionaire*, in 1967, starring Debbie Watson.

Tarzan.
The brawny jungle hero, an English milord lost in Africa as a child and who grew up with the apes, was a creation of novelist Edgar Rice Burroughs (1875-1950); the first Tarzan story was published in 1913. The films quickly followed. *Tarzan of the Apes* 18 starred Elmo Lincoln with Enid Markey as Jane; so did *Romance of Tarzan* 18. *The Return of Tarzan* 20 had Gene Pollar and Karla Schramm. *Son of Tarzan* 20 was a serial with Kamuela C. Searle in the title role; Tarzan was P. Dempsey Tabler, Elmo Lincoln returned in another serial, *The Adventures of Tarzan* 21, with Louise Lorraine. *Tarzan and the Golden Lion* 27 starred James Pierce and Dorothy Dunbar. Another serial, *Tarzan the Mighty* 28, had Frank Merrill and no Jane; a runner-up, *Tarzan the Tiger* 30, had the same crew. In 1932 came Johnny WEISSMULLER in the first of MGM's long line of Tarzan pictures: *Tarzan the Ape Man*, with Maureen O'SULLIVAN as Jane. There followed *Tarzan and His Mate* 34, *Tarzan Escapes* 36, *Tarzan Finds a Son* 39, *Tarzan's Secret Treasure* 41, and *Tarzan's New York Adventure* 42. Meanwhile in 1935 an independent company had made a serial starring Herman Brix which was later released as two features, *Tarzan and the Green Goddess* and *New Adventures of Tarzan*; and in 1933 producer Sol Lesser had started his Tarzan series with *Tarzan the Fearless*, starring Buster Crabbe; he followed this up with *Tarzan's Revenge* 38 starring Glenn Morris. In 1943 Lesser took over Weissmuller (but not O'Sullivan or any other Jane) for *Tarzan Triumphs*, followed by *Tarzan's Desert Mystery* 44, *Tarzan and the Amazons* (reintroducing Jane in the shape of Brenda Joyce) 45, *Tarzan and the Leopard Woman* 46, *Tarzan and the Huntress* 47, and *Tarzan and the Mermaids* 48. Then Weissmuller was replaced by Lex BARKER for *Tarzan's Magic Fountain* 48, *Tarzan and the Slave Girl* 49, *Tarzan's Peril* 50, *Tarzan's Savage Fury* 51, and *Tarzan and the She-Devil* 52. Gordon SCOTT next undertook the chore in *Tarzan's Hidden Jungle* 55, *Tarzan and the Lost Safari* 57, *Tarzan's Fight for Life* 58, *Tarzan's Greatest Adventure* 59 and *Tarzan the Magnificent* 60. MGM now remade *Tarzan the Ape Man* 60 starring Denny Miller; and, with Jock Mahoney, *Tarzan Goes to India* 62 and National General presented *Tarzan's Three Challenges* 64. There followed *Tarzan and the Valley of Gold* 66, *Tarzan and the Great River* 67, and *Tarzan and the Jungle Boy* 68, all with Mike Henry. A 1982 remake of *Tarzan the Ape Man* had Miles O'Keeffe in the role but concentrated on the charms of Bo DEREK as Jane; however, in 1984 *Greystoke* set the record straight by remaining slightly more faithful to Burroughs' original legend. A 1966-67 TV series starred Ron Ely. Joe Lara played him in a TV movie, *Tarzan in Manhattan* 89, and a subsequent TV series, *Tarzan – The Epic Adventures*. Casper Van Dien was a live-action ape-man in *Tarzan and the Lost City* 98, but failed to interest a new generation in his antics. More successful, and certainly more animated, was Disney's cartoon version *Tarzan* 99.

teachers
have been notably played by Robert Donat in *Goodbye Mr Chips*; Jennifer Jones in *Good Morning Miss Dove*; Greer Garson in *Her Twelve Men*; Michael Redgrave and Albert Finney in *The Browning Version*; Aline MacMahon in *Back Door to Heaven*; Claudette Colbert in *Remember the Day*; Bette Davis in *The Corn Is Green*; Jack Hawkins in *Mandy*; Judy Garland in *A Child Is Waiting*; Anne Bancroft in *The Miracle Worker*; Shirley Maclaine in *Spinster*; Glenn Ford in *The Blackboard Jungle*; Sidney Poitier in *To Sir With Love*; Sandy Dennis in *Up the Down Staircase*; Dorothy Dandridge in *Bright Road*; Max Bygraves in *Spare the Rod*; Otto Kruger in *The Housemaster*; Cecil Trouncer in *The Guinea Pig*; Maggie Smith in *The Prime of Miss Jean Brodie*; Joanne Woodward in *Rachel, Rachel*; Robert Mitchum in *Ryan's Daughter*; Laurence Olivier in *Term of Trial*; Richard Todd in *The Love-Ins*; James Whitmore in *The Harrad Experiment*; David Hemmings in *Unman, Wittering and Zigo*; Per Oscarsson in *Who Saw Him Die?* James Mason in *Child's Play*; Glenda Jackson in *The Class of Miss MacMichael*; Michael Ontkean in *Willie and Phil*; Perry King in *Class of 1984*, harassed by his pupils; Robin Williams in *Dead Poets Society*; Danny DeVito in *Renaissance Man*; and Michelle Pfeiffer in *Dangerous Minds*. In *Class of 1999*, the teachers got their revenge – they turned out to be androids equipped with military hardware. J. Eddie Peck taught by day and danced all night in *Lambada* so he could teach maths to his slum students. In the more inspiring *Stand and Deliver*, based on a true story, Edward James Olmos forced his pupils to succeed against the odds. So did Danny De Vito in *Renaissance Man* 94, Michelle Pfeiffer in *Dangerous Minds* 95, Richard Dreyfuss in the tear-jerking *Mr Holland's Opus* 95, and Meryl Streep, as another music teacher, in *Hearts and Minds* 99. The genre was mocked in *High School High* 96.

Comic teachers were to the fore in *Boys Will Be Boys* (Will Hay, the best of them all); the *St Trinian's* films; *Carry On Teacher; Old Mother Riley Headmistress; Bottoms Up* (Jimmy Edwards); *Fun at St Fanny's* (Fred Emney); *The Happiest Days of Your Lives; Please Sir*; and *Vice Versa* (James Robertson Justice).

See also: SCHOOLDAYS.

teams:
see ROMANTIC TEAMS.

Teenage Mutant Ninja Turtles.
Comic-book heroes created by Kevin Eastman and Peter Laird in 1984. There are four, each named after a European artist – Leonardo, Raphael, Donatello and Michelangelo – because their creators thought that Japanese names would sound silly. Their transformation into humanoids came about in the way of 50s movie monsters: they were contaminated by radioactivity while babies. They were featured in animated TV cartoons (rechristened by BBC-TV *Teenage Mutant Hero Turtles*) in 1988, and a live-action film, directed by Steve Barron in 1990, became the most successful independent movie so far released. Sequels followed in 1991 and 1993.

the telephone
has been a very useful instrument to film scenarists. The saga of its invention was told in *The Story of Alexander Graham Bell*. It brought sinister, menacing and threatening calls in *Sorry – Wrong Number, The Small World of Sammy Lee, Midnight Lace, I Saw What You Did, Experiment in Terror, Sudden Fear, Strangers on a Train*, and *Dirty Harry*. *Chicago Calling* and *The Slender Thread* were among the films based entirely on someone trying to contact another character by telephone. *Bells Are Ringing, The Glenn Miller Story* and *Bye Bye Birdie* had musical numbers based on telephones. Shelly Berman, Jeanne de Casalis and Billy de Wolfe are among the revue artists famous for telephone sketches. Single phone calls were of high dramatic significance in *The Spiral Staircase, Little Caesar, Fail Safe, Dr Strangelove, Murder Inc., Dial M for Murder, The Silencers, 2001: A Space Odyssey, No*

4

Movie Studios and Production Companies, etc.

Abbey Theatre.
Significant Irish theatre, founded in Dublin in 1904, which presented the first performances of plays by W. B. Yeats, J. M. Synge and Sean O'Casey. Over the years, many of its actors went on to film careers, though the theatre discouraged them and often refused to ever employ them again as a result. They included J. M. Kerrigan, who also directed some now-lost silent films, Fred O'Donovan, also a director of some silents, Sara ALLGOOD, Maire O'NEILL, Arthur SINCLAIR, W. G. FAY, F. J. MCCORMICK, Dudley DIGGES, Barry FITZGERALD, Cyril CUSACK, Liam REDMOND, Dan O'HERLIHY, Denis O'DEA, Jack MACGOWRAN, Niall TOIBIN, T. P. MCKENNA, and Ray MCANALLY. John FORD drew on Abbey actors for his two Irish films, *The Informer* 35 and *The Plough and the Stars* 36, and some, like Arthur SHIELDS and Una O'CONNOR, became familiar players in Hollywood. In the 50s, six Abbey plays were filmed at the newly opened Ardmore Studios, including *Broth of a Boy* 58, directed by George POLLOCK from the play by Hugh LEONARD, and *This Other Eden* 60, directed by Muriel Box from Louis D'Alton's play, but they were not commercially successful.

Books: 1958, *The Abbey Theatre* by Gerard Fay; 1967, *The Story of the Abbey Theatre*, ed. Sean McCann.

The Actors' Studio.
Drama school established in 1947 by Elia KAZAN, Cheryl CRAWFORD and Robert LEWIS at West 48th Street, Manhattan (later West 44th Street). It is currently under the leadership of Al PACINO, Ellen BURSTYN and Harvey KEITEL, with Arthur Penn as its president emeritus. It is especially associated with Lee STRASBERG, who ran it for 30 years from 1949, and The Method, a style of acting that owed much to the teachings of Stanislavsky and which revolutionized American acting, becoming the predominant film style, from Marlon BRANDO to Robert DE NIRO and Al PACINO. In its earlier days, the Studio gained much publicity through Marilyn MONROE's involvement. Among those who studied there were Brando (though he credits Stella Adler with teaching him how to act), Rod STEIGER, James DEAN, Geraldine PAGE, Karl MALDEN, Shelley WINTERS, Steve MCQUEEN and Paul NEWMAN.

Books: 1980, *A Player's Place: The Story of the Actors Studio* by David Garfield; 1984, *A Method to Their Madness* by Foster Hirsch.

Documentary: 1981, *Lee Strasberg and The Actors' Studio* (d. Herbert Kline).

Allied Artists Corporation.
An American production company, more recently involved in TV, which flourished throughout the 30s and 40s as a purveyor of routine crime and comedy second features. Its policy was to put out the poorer product under the banner of its subsidiary, *Monogram Pictures Corporation*; the 'quality' AA product was little in evidence until the 50s, when films like *Love in the Afternoon*, *Friendly Persuasion* and *Al Capone* came from this stable. Meanwhile the Monogram films, boasting such attractions as Frankie Darro, the East Side Kids, the Bowery Boys, Bela Lugosi and Charlie Chan, had their faithful following, and in France attracted highbrow cinéastes to such an extent that Jean-Luc Godard dedicated his film *A Bout de Souffle* to Monogram.

Amalgamated Dynamics, Inc.
Visual effects and creature design company established in 1988 by Tom Woodruff, Jnr, and Alec Gillis, who formerly worked with Stan WINSTON. Woodruff played a monster in *Monster Squad* 87, and the title role in *Pumpkinhead* 88.

Tremors 90. Death Becomes Her (AA) 92. Alien 3 (AAN) 92. Demolition Man 93. Wolf 94. The Santa Clause 94. Tremors 2: Aftershocks 95. Mortal Kombat 95. Jumanji 95. Michael 96. Alien: Resurrection 97. Starship Troopers 97. The X Files Movie 98, etc.

American International Pictures.
Independent production company founded in 1955 by Samuel Z. ARKOFF and James H. NICHOLSON. After a profitable splurge of Z pictures churned out mainly by Roger CORMAN the company began to set its sights on the big time. In 1980 the ailing company was taken over by Filmways, which in 1982 was in its turn taken over by Orion.

Amicus
British production company specialising in low budget exploitation movies, mainly of horror and science-fiction. It was founded by American screenwriter and producer Milton SUBOTSKY and American producer Max J. Rosenberg. Casts often included HAMMER favourites Peter CUSHING and Christopher LEE, and writer Robert BLOCH was involved in six of their productions. It specialised in horror compendiums, with several stories combined in one feature.

Book: 2000, *Amicus: The Studio that Dripped Blood*, ed Alan Bryce.

Dr. Terror's House of Horrors 65. The Skull 65. Dr Who and the Daleks/Daleks' Invasion Earth: 2150 A.D 66 The Deadly Bees 66. The Psychopath 66. Terrornauts 67. They Came From Beyond Space 67. Torture Garden 67. Danger Route 68. The House That Dripped Blood 70. The Mind of Mr. Soames 70. I, Monster 71. Asylum/House of Crazies 72. Tales from the Crypt 72. What Became of Jack and Jill? 72. And Now the Screaming Starts! 73. The Vault of Horror 73. From Beyond the Grave 73. Tales That Witness Madness 73. The Beast Must Die/Black Werewolf 74. The Land That Time Forgot 75. At the Earth's Core 76. The People That Time Forgot 77, etc.

The Archers.
British production company set up in 1943 by Michael POWELL and Emeric PRESSBURGER. Its films were produced, directed and written by the pair. The partnership lasted until 1956.

Book: 1985, *Arrows of Desire* by Ian Christie.

■ The Silver Fleet 43. *The Life and Death of Colonel Blimp* 43. The Volunteer 43. A Canterbury Tale 44. I Know Where I'm Going 45. *A Matter of Life and Death* 46. *Black Narcissus* 47. The End of the River 47. *The Red Shoes* 48. The Small Back Room 49. Gone to Earth 50. The Elusive Pimpernel 50. The Tales of Hoffman 51. Oh Rosalinda! 55. The Battle of the River Plate 56. Ill Met by Moonlight 56.

Artists Management Group
(AMG) is an organisation formed in 1998 by former agent and Disney executive Mike OVITZ. Its activities caused controversy in Hollywood, with CAA (Creative Artists Association), which was also founded by Ovitz, claiming that it was raiding its agents and clients.

Associated British
was the only British complex of companies which had power comparable to that of the RANK Organization. Its history is tied up with Elstree Studios, originally owned by British International Pictures, which after many mergers emerged as Associated British in 1933. The men involved in the story are producer Herbert Wilcox, John Maxwell, a lawyer who turned film distributor and later founded the ABC cinema chain, and J. D. Williams, a wealthy exhibitor. Distribution was arranged through Pathé Pictures, which became a powerful partner. Elstree was the first British studio to wire for sound (*Blackmail*) and the first to produce a bilingual talkie (*Atlantic*). Throughout the thirties it turned out fifteen films a year, usually unambitious but competent; and unmistakably British. In 1940 a great number of shares were sold to Warner Brothers, and in 1956 the distribution arm became known as Warner-Pathé. Other associated companies include Pathé News, Pathé Laboratories, Pathé Equipment, and ABC Television. In 1969, after several years of comparative inactivity, the complex was taken over by EMI. In the 80s Cannon took over all the companies, but promptly sold the library to Jerry Weintraub.

Boreham Wood.
A British studio fourteen miles north of London, a site originally chosen by John M. East (1860-1924), a stage and silent screen actor. It opened in 1914 as Neptune Films, which folded in 1921; the stages were later taken over by Ideal, Rock, British National, and Associated Television. MGM and ABPC also had studios in nearby Elstree.

Bray Studios
became the home of Hammer Films in the late 40s, with many of its horror movies being shot in the grounds and in its mansion, Down Place, which dated from the 17th century. After Hammer ceased production in the late 60s, the studios continued to provide facilities for various films and television series.

British Lion Film Corporation.
A film production company of the 20s which, in the 30s, became mainly a distributor of cheap American product but was revived after World War II by the control of Alexander Korda, then by Michael Balcon, the Boulting Brothers and Frank Launder and Sidney Gilliat. It merged in 1976 with EMI.

Carolco.
American production company founded by Mario Kassar and Andrew Vajna in 1982 and noted for its big-budget approach to film-making. Vajna left later to found another production company, Cinergi. Carolco filed for bankruptcy in 1995 and its assets were sold to Twentieth Century- Fox.

First Blood 82. Rambo: First Blood Part Two 85. Angel Heart 87. Red Heat 88. Total Recall 90. Terminator 2: Judgment Day 91. Basic Instinct 91. Cliffhanger 93. CutThroat Island 95, etc.

Castle Rock Entertainment.
Hollywood production company co-founded by director Rob Reiner. Now a subsidiary of the Turner Broadcasting System, it has plans to become a distributor also.

Children's Film Foundation.
British company formed in 1951 to produce and distribute specially devised entertainment films for children's Saturday matinées. Sponsored by trade organizations.

Cine Liberación
was a radical film collective founded in Argentina in the late 60s by Fernando SOLANAS and Octavio GETINO. Its manifesto, *Toward a Third Cinema*, argued for a cinema based on collective, and even clandestine, production, distribution that involved its audience in discussion of the film and the issues raised, and opposition to the country's military dictatorship. (The first two cinemas were defined as the Hollywood studio system and the *auteur* approach.) The two founders put their theories into practice in *The Hour of the Furnaces* 68, a revolutionary documentary clandestinely distributed in Argentina, while a third member of the group, Gerardo Vallejo, made *El Camino hacia la Muerte del Viejo Reales* 70, about three years he spent with a rural family.

Cinecittà.
Large film studios in Rome, built in 1935, that have been at the centre of the Italian film industry and have also housed such international blockbusters as *Ben Hur* 59 and *Cleopatra* 63.

Cineguild.
A short-lived British production company set up in 1943 by David LEAN, Ronald NEAME and Anthony HAVELOCK-ALLAN following their success working together on Noël COWARD's *In Which We Serve*. After filming versions of Coward's plays, the trio moved on to create classic adaptations of two of DICKENS's novels. Associated with the Rank Organization, the company came to an end when Rank cut back on its production plans in 1949.

This Happy Breed 44. Blithe Spirit 45. *Brief Encounter* 45. *Great Expectations* 46. *Oliver Twist* 48. The Passionate Friends 49. Madeleine 50, etc.

Columbia Pictures.
American production and distribution company long considered one of the 'little two' (the other being Universal) against the 'big five' (MGM, RKO, Fox, Warner and Paramount). Columbia originated with one man, Harry Cohn, who founded it in 1924 after a career as a salesman and shorts producer. Throughout the 30s and 40s he turned out competent co-features and second features, apart from prestige pictures such as the CAPRA comedies and an ill-fated KRAMER deal; he was also prepared to spend big money on certainties such as Rita HAYWORTH and *The Jolson Story*. From the late 40s, with films like *All the King's Men*, *Born Yesterday* and *From Here to Eternity*, the company began to pull itself into the big-time, and when Cohn died in 1958 it was one of the leaders of international co-production, with such major films to its credit as *On the Waterfront* and *The Bridge on the River Kwai*, with *Lawrence of Arabia* and *A Man For All Seasons* to come. It also produces and distributes TV films through its subsidiary Screen Gems (Columbia Television). In 1990, the Japanese company Sony paid $3.4 billion for the company. Peter Guber and Jon Peters were installed to run the organization, but Peters soon left to resume life as an independent producer. Since then, the studio has had mixed fortunes. It has had moderate successes, such as *A League of Their Own*, *A Few Good Men*, *In The Line of Fire* and *Philadelphia*, but it also had many misses, culminating in the disaster of *The Last Action Hero* starring Arnold SCHWARZENEGGER, which turned out to be not the expected blockbuster but a dismal flop. In 1994 Peter Guber followed Jon Peters' example and quit to become an independent producer. Many of its recent films were less successful than expected, including *City Hall*, with Al PACINO, *Cable Guy*, with the seemingly impregnable Jim CARREY, *Striptease* with Demi MOORE, and *Multiplicity* with Michael KEATON in several roles. Lisa Henson, president of Columbia, and Marc Platt, president of TriStar, were among the executives who left the company in 1996. Under John CALLEY, who joined the studio from MGM in 1996, it has enjoyed better times. In 1997, Sony announced box-office revenues of $1.3 billion, a figure reached in record time. The company absorbed its sister company TriStar in 1998. Its recent hits have included *Jerry Maguire*, *Anaconda*, *The Fifth Element*, *My Best Friend's Wedding*, *Men in Black*, *Airforce One*, *Starship Troopers*, and *As Good as It Gets*, *The Patriot*, *Charlie's Angels* and *Stuart Little*.

Books: 1967, *King Cohn* by Bob Thomas; *Hail Columbia* by Rochelle Larkin; 1989, *The Columbia Story* by Clive Hirschhorn; 1991, *The Columbia Checklist* by Leo D. Martin; 1996, *Hit & Run: How Jon Peters and Peter Guber Took Sony for a Ride in Hollywood* by Nancy Griffin & Kim Masters.

DEFA (Deutsche Film Aktiengesellschaft).
The East German party line film production company which absorbed UFA in 1946.

Denham.
An English village north of London where in 1936 Korda opened a huge film studio which was later

taken over by the Rank Organisation but closed in the 50s so that production could be concentrated at Pinewood a few miles away. The studio was designed by American art director Jack OKEY. Originally intended to be relatively small, with three sound stages, it grew under construction to have seven sound stages and to be the best-equipped studio in Europe; but it was too large to be profitable in the long term.

Dogme 95
is a declaration on filmmaking made by a collective of Danish directors: Lars VON TRIER, Thomass Vinterberg, Soren Kragh-Jacobsen and Kristian Levring. Its manifesto states that 'To DOGME 95 the movie is not illusion! Today a technological storm is raging of which the result is the elevation of cosmetics to God. By using new technology anyone at any time can wash the last grains of truth away in the deadly embrace of sensation. The illusions are everything the movie can hide behind. DOGME 95 counters the film of illusion by the presentation of an indisputable set of rules known as THE VOW OF CHASTITY.'

The vow, signed in Copenhagen on March 13, 1995, lays down ten commandments:

1. Shooting must be done on location. Props and sets must not be brought in (if a particular prop is necessary for the story, a location must be chosen where this prop is to be found).
2. The sound must never be produced apart from the images or vice versa. (Music must not be used unless it occurs where the scene is being shot.)
3. The camera must be hand-held. Any movement or immobility attainable in the hand is permitted. (The film must not take place where the camera is standing; shooting must take place where the film takes place.)
4. The film must be in colour. Special lighting is not acceptable. (If there is too little light for exposure the scene must be cut or a single lamp be attached to the camera.)
5. Optical work and filters are forbidden.
6. The film must not contain superficial action. (Murders, weapons, etc. must not occur.)
7. Temporal and geographical alienation are forbidden. (That is to say that the film takes place here and now.)
8. Genre movies are not acceptable.
9. The film format must be Academy 35 mm.
10. The director must not be credited.

It also states: 'Furthermore I swear as a director to refrain from personal taste! I am no longer an artist. I swear to refrain from creating a "work", as I regard the instant as more important than the whole. My supreme goal is to force the truth out of my characters and settings. I swear to do so by all the means available and at the cost of any good taste and any aesthetic considerations.'

Directors from other countries have begun to make Dogme films, though no one seems to adhere to all the rules.

The Celebration/Festen (*d* Vinterberg) 98. The Idiots/Idioterne (*wd* von Trier) 98. Mifune/Mifunes Sidste Sang (*co-w, d* Kragh-Jacobsen) 99. The King is Alive (*wd* Kristian Levring) 99. Lovers (Fr., *d* Jean-Marc Barr) Julien Donkey-Boy (US, *wd* Harmony Korine) 00. Interview (Kor., *d* Daniel H. Byun). Fuckland 00 (Arg., *d* Jose Luis Marques). Babylon 00 (Swe. *d* Vladan Zdravkovic). Chetzemoka's Curse 00 (US, *d* Rick Schmidt, Maya Berthoud). Diapason 00 (It. *d* Antonio Domenici). Italiensk For Begyndere 00 (*d* Lone Scherfig). Joy Ride 00 (Swi. *d* Martin Rengel). Camera 00 (US, *d* Rich Martini). Bad Actors 00 (US, *d* Shaun Monson) 00. Reunion 01 (US, *d* Leif Tilden). Et Rigtigt Menneske 01 (*wd* Ake Sandgren) 01. Når Nettene Blir 01 (Nor., *d* Mona J. Hoel), etc.

URL: www.dogme95.dk/

DreamWorks SKG.
Hollywood studio set up in 1994 by Steven SPIELBERG, Jeffrey KATZENBERG and David GEFFEN. Its plans to set up the first fully electronic studios have been held up by an environmental dispute. Its first releases were lacklustre, and it was not until 1998 that it enjoyed hits, with Spielberg's *Saving Private Ryan* and the computer-animated feature *Antz*; the following year came the Oscar-winning *American Beauty*, a critical and popular success.The studio has stuck to offering familiar Hollywood fare, and most of its ambitions appear to be channelled into challenging Disney's dominance of animated features with such films as *Chicken Run*.

Ealing Studios
In its heyday in the 40s and 50s this famous little studio in suburban west London was the independent home of scores of well-paced comedies featuring the likes of Will Hay and George Formby, and from 1948 on aspired a little higher, to quiet comedies of the English character, usually featuring a downtrodden group who rebelled against authority. The resulting films, including *The Lavender Hill Mob, Whisky Galore!* and *The Titfield Thunderbolt*, became known the world over. The credit for these films is largely due to Michael BALCON as impresario, and often to T. E. B. CLARKE as writer and Alec GUINNESS as actor; but the results were less happy when the studio tackled epic themes such as *Scott of the Antarctic* and *The Cruel Sea*, though it certainly brought off non-comic subjects like *Dead of Night* and *Mandy*. The studios were bought by the BBC in 1955, when Balcon put up a plaque: 'Here films were made projecting Britain and the British character.' The BBC sold them in 1992 to a film company which went into receivership, and the studios were acquired as a home for the National Film and Television School, though continuing to provide production facilities. In 1998 the School decided it needed premises near London and put the studio up for sale.

Books: 1977 (revised 1995), *Ealing Studios* by Charles Barr; 1981, *Forever Ealing* by George Perry; 1983, *Projecting Britain* edited by David Wilson was a collection of Ealing posters.

Come On George 39. Let George Do It 40. Convoy 40. Sailors Three 40. The Ghost of St Michael's 41. The Black Sheep of Whitehall 42. The Foreman Went to France 42. The Goose Steps Out 42. Went the Day Well? 43. They Came to a City 44. Champagne Charlie 44. *Dead of Night* 45. The Captive Heart 46. The Overlanders 46. Nicholas Nickleby 47. *It Always Rains on Sunday* 47. Scott of the Antarctic 48. Passport to Pimlico 49. *Whisky Galore!* 49. *Kind Hearts and Coronets* 49. The Blue Lamp 50. *The Lavender Hill Mob* 51. *The Man in The White Suit* 51. Mandy 52. The Cruel Sea 53. *The Ladykillers* 55. Dunkirk 58, etc.

Elstree Studios.
Production complex at Borehamwood, north of London, started in the 20s by British International, which later became ASSOCIATED BRITISH. After many vicissitudes the facilities and library passed into the hands of Thorn-EMI, who sold out in the 80s to Cannon, who sold off the library to Weintraub. The studio was deemed unprofitable and shut down in 1993, but went back into production in 1996 after it was bought by Hertsmere Council.

Book: 1982, *Elstree, the British Hollywood* by Patricia Warren.

Essanay.
A production company formed in 1907 by G. K. Spoor and G. M. Anderson (S and A). Mainly remembered for enormous output of early westerns and for Chaplin's first comedies.

Famous Players.
A production company founded by Adolph Zukor in New York in 1912, following his success in distributing Sarah Bernhardt in *Queen Elizabeth*. The motif was 'famous players in famous plays' which could not work too well as the films were silent; but the tag caught on and the company did well enough. It was later absorbed into Paramount.

First National
was a Hollywood company founded in 1917. During the next 12 years it was very active, with films featuring Chaplin, Pickford, Milton Sills and Richard Barthelmess. In 1929 it was taken over by Warner Brothers, who however kept the name going for certain product until the mid-30s.

Free Cinema.
A term applied to their own output by a group of British documentarists of the 50s, e.g. Lindsay Anderson, Karel Reisz. Their aim was to make 'committed' films which cared about the individual and the significance of the everyday. The resulting films were not always better than those produced by professional units with more commercial intent. The most notable were *O Dreamland, Momma Don't Allow, The March to Aldermaston, Every Day Except Christmas* and *We Are the Lambeth Boys*, the two latter films being sponsored by commercial firms.

Gainsborough.
A British film company of the 30s, associated with costume drama and Aldwych farces. Subsequently merged with Rank. Its trademark showed actress Glennis Lorrimer as Mrs Siddons in Thomas Gainsborough's portrait, turning to smile at the audience. She was the daughter of Harry Ostrer, co-founder of the company.

Group 3.
A British production company set up in 1951 by the National Film Finance Corporation. In charge were John Baxter, John Grierson and Michael Balcon, and their aim was to make low-budget films employing young talent. The venture was regarded with suspicion by the trade, and the results were not encouraging – a string of mildly eccentric comedies and thrillers lucky to get second-feature circuit bookings. Some of the titles: *Judgement Deferred, Brandy for the Parson, The Brave Don't Cry, You're Only Young Twice, The Oracle, Laxdale Hall, Time Gentlemen Please*.

Group Theatre.
A left-wing company founded in New York in 1931 by Harold Clurman, Cheryl Crawford and Lee Strasberg, it fostered and encouraged many talents who went on to have careers in Hollywood, though some were later damaged by blacklisting in the 50s. Those involved included writer Clifford Odets, and Luther Adler, Lee J. Cobb, Morris Carnovsky, Frances Farmer, John Garfield, Elia Kazan, Robert Lewis, Ruth Nelson, Franchot Tone, and Sylvia Sidney. Two other members, Stella ADLER and Sanford MEISNER, both became influential teachers from the 40s. The Group Theatre was disbanded in 1940.

Book: 1945, *The Fervent Years* by Harold Clurman.

See also: The ACTORS' STUDIO.

Hammer Films.
British production company set up in 1947 which gained fame and fortune from its cycle of horror films, beginning in 1955 with *The Quatermass Experiment/The Creeping Unknown*. It revived the Frankenstein myth with *The Curse of Frankenstein* 56, and followed it with the first of its Dracula series a year later, making stars of Christopher LEE and Peter CUSHING. The company grew out of Exclusive Films, a distribution company formed by Will Hammer and Enrique Carreras, a Spaniard who had opened cinemas in London in 1913. Enrique's son, Sir James CARRERAS, and his grandson Michael, were the main forces behind Hammer's success, together with Hammer's son Tony HINDS, who produced and wrote scripts under the name of John Elder, and director Terence FISHER. Hammer announced its return to film production in 1994, planning to remake some of its previous successes. Among the films in development were said to be *The Day the Earth Caught Fire*, to be directed by Renny Harlin, *The Devil Rides Out, The Quatermass Xperiment* and *Vlad the Impaler*, though none appeared. In 1997, British investors, including Charles Saatchi, bought a 50 per cent stake in the company for $9m, with plans to use the brand name in theme parks, restaurants and video games, and to remake old movies, including *Quatermass and the Pit*. A series of short animated horror films for children's television, *Hammer Horror Zone*, appeared in 1998.

Book: 1973, *The House of Horror* edited by Allen Eyles, Robert Adkinson and Nicholas Fry. 1996, *Hammer, House of Horror: Behind the Screams* by Howard Maxford.

HandMade Films.
British production company formed by Denis O'Brien and former Beatle George Harrison. Among its successes have been *Monty Python's Life of Brian* 79, *The Long Good Friday* 80, *Time Bandits* 81, *A Private Function* 84, *Mona Lisa* 86, and *Withnail and I* 87.

Hecht-Hill-Lancaster:
see HECHT-LANCASTER.

Hecht-Lancaster
was an independent production company set up by former agent Harold HECHT and actor Burt LANCASTER. They had earlier formed Hecht-Norma (named after Lancaster's wife) to make films with Warner's. When that arrangement came to an end, Hecht-Lancaster was formed in 1954, to make films in partnership with United Artists, a studio then in decline which, anxious to secure Lancaster's services, agreed a deal that offered the two full financing and 75 per cent of the profits as well as other sweeteners. In 1956, it became Hecht-Hill-Lancaster with the addition, at Lancaster's insistence, of writer James HILL. The company was wound up in 1960, when the partners began to disagree more often and it was overspending after too rapid an expansion.

AS HECHT-NORMA: Kiss the Blood Off My Hands 48. The Flame and the Arrow 50. Ten Tall Men 51. The Crimson Pirate 52. His Majesty O'Keefe 54, etc.

AS HECHT-LANCASTER: Apache 54. Vera Cruz 54. The Kentuckian 55. Trapeze 56, etc.

AS HECHT-HILL-LANCASTER: *Marty* (AA) 55. *Sweet Smell of Success* 57. Run Silent, Run Deep 58. Separate Tables 58. The Devil's Disciple 59. The Unforgiven 60, etc.

Hecht-Norma:
see HECHT-LANCASTER.

IDHEC,
Institut des Hautes Études Cinématographiques, the leading French film school founded in Paris in the early 40s by Marcel L'HERBIER, where many French and foreign directors, producers, cinematographers and other production staff have studied. It closed in 1968, reopening two years later.

Industrial Light and Magic.
Special effects company formed by producer-director George LUCAS when making *Star Wars*. It was headed by John DYKSTRA, who later left to form his own special effects company. It is part of Lucas's production company Lucasfilm, which also includes a software company that produces computer games which are often based on the company's movies. Since its beginnings working on Lucas's own projects, it has established itself as the leading special effects company, employed by many other producers and directors, including Steven SPIELBERG.

Book: 1996, *Industrial Light and Magic: Into the Digital Realm* by Mark Cotta Vaz and Patricia Rose Duignan.

Star Wars (AA) 77. The Empire Strikes Back (AA) 80. Raiders of the Lost Ark (AA) 81. Dragonslayer (AAN) 81. Poltergeist 82. Star Trek II: The Wrath of Khan 82. E.T. – the Extra-Terrestrial (AA) 82. Return of the Jedi (AA) 83. Indiana Jones and the Temple of Doom (AA) 84. Star Trek III: The Search for Spock 84. The Neverending Story 84. Starman 84. The Goonies 85. Cocoon (AA) 85. Back to the Future 85. Explorers 85. Mishima 85. Young Sherlock Holmes (AAN) 85. Enemy Mine 85. Out of Africa 85. Howard the Duck 86. Star Trek IV: The Voyage Home 86. The Golden Child 86. The Witches of Eastwick 87. Innerspace 87. Batteries Not Included 87. Star Trek: The Next Generation 87. Empire of the Sun 87. Willow (AAN) 88. Who Framed Roger Rabbit? (AA) 88. Caddyshack II 88. Cocoon: The Return 88. The Last Temptation of Christ 88. The Burbs 89. Field of Dreams 89. Indiana Jones and the Last Crusade 89. Ghostbusters II 89. The Abyss (AA) 89. Back to the Future, Part II (AAN) 89. Always 89. Joe versus the Volcano 90. The Hunt for Red October 90. Back to the Future, Part III 90. Die Hard 2 90. Ghost 90. Switch 91. The Doors 91. Hudson Hawk 91. Backdraft (AAN) 91. The Rocketeer 91. Terminator 2: Judgement Day (AA) 91. Hook (AAN) 91. Memoirs of an Invisible Man 92. Death Becomes Her 92. Alive 92. The Meteor Man 93. Jurassic Park (AA) 93. Schindler's List 93. Rising Sun 93. Manhattan Murder Mystery 93. Baby's Day Out 94. Star Trek VII: Generations 94. Disclosure 94. The Flintstones 94. Forrest Gump (AA) 94. The Mask (AAN) 94. Congo 95. In the Mouth of Madness 95. Casper 95. Jumanji 95. Dragonheart (AAN) 96. Star Trek: First Contact 96. 101 Dalmatians 96. Mars Attacks! 96. Daylight 96. Twister 96. Mission: Impossible 96. Eraser 96. The Lost World: Jurassic Park (AAN) 97. Men in Black 97. Titanic 97. Speed 2: Cruise Control 97. Contact 97. Spawn 97. Starship Troopers 97. Flubber 97. Saving Private Ryan 98. Deep Impact 98. Small Soldiers 98. Meet Joe Black 98. Mercury Rising 98. Deep Rising 98. Mighty Joe Young 98. Jack Frost 98. Star Wars Episode 1: The Phantom Empire 99. Deep Blue Sea 99. Galaxy Quest 99. The Green Mile 99. The Perfect Storm 00. Mission to Mars 00. The Adventures of Rocky & Bullwinkle 00, etc.

International Pictures.
Independent production company set up by Nunnally JOHNSON, William Goetz and Leo Spitz, formerly head of RKO, to distribute their films. In 1946 it was merged with Universal, which became Universal-International, and Goetz and Spitz took over the new company's production duties for a time.

Casanova Brown 44. The Woman in the Window 44. It's a Pleasure 45. Along Came Jones 45. Tomorrow Is Forever 46. The Stranger 46, etc.

Kalem.
An early American production company founded in 1907, taking its name from the initials of its three principals, George Klein, Sam Long and Frank Marion (K-L-M). Its most famous production is *From the Manger to the Cross* 12.

Keystone.
A company established in 1912 to produce comedies. Run by Mack Sennett, who also directed and edited most of the films, the company's early films featured Mabel Normand and created a fast and furious slapstick comedy. Its star performers included Fatty Arbuckle, Charlie Chaplin, Chester Conklin and Mack Swain. Sennett's second innovation came in 1915 when he introduced his Bathing Beauties to add some glamour. Sennett left Keystone in 1917 to work for Paramount and the company soon foundered without him.

Leavesden.
English studio complex sited on an aerodrome formerly owned by Rolls-Royce. It was first used in 1994 to house the James Bond movie *GoldenEye* and then bought, at a cost of £42.75m, by Third Millennium Studios, a Malaysian-owned company.

Lexington.
Production company set up in 1996 by producer-director Don BOYD to make distinctive British films.

Lucia 98.

Liberty Films.
Independent production company set up in 1946 by Frank CAPRA, William WYLER, George STEVENS and Sam Briskin. It made only one feature, *It's a Wonderful Life*, directed by Capra in 1946, before it ran into financial problems and was taken over by Paramount in 1947.

London Films.
Production company founded by Alexander KORDA and associated with his own major films of the 30s and later with other leading names operating under his banner. Others associated with the company included the Hungarian screenwriter Lajos BIRO and actor George GROSSMITH, who was its first chairman.

Mancunian Films.
A small but dauntless little British studio which throughout the 40s and early 50s earned its keep locally with a stream of wild farces starring home-grown music-hall talent: Frank Randle, Harry Korris, Sandy Powell, Tessie O'Shea, Betty Jumel, Nat Jackley, Josef Locke, Jewel and Warriss, Suzette Tarri and Norman Evans. Neither art nor craft entered into the matter.

Merton Park.
A small, independent south London studio. Founded in 1930 to make advertising films, it later housed Radio Luxembourg. Training films were made there during the war, and in the 50s it turned to the production of Edgar Lustgarten's *Scotland Yard* shorts, the Edgar Wallace supports, and *Scales of Justice*. It closed in the mid-60s.

Metro-Goldwyn-Mayer.
For many years the undoubted leader of the industry, this famous American production company has lately suffered most from the lack of 'front office' control and the proliferation of independent productions: now that it doesn't own the racecourse, it can't seem to pick the winners. The company stems from Loew's Inc., an exhibiting concern which in 1920 bought into Metro Pictures, which then produced two enormous money-spinners, *The Four Horsemen of the Apocalypse* and *The Prisoner of Zenda*. In 1924 Metro was merged with the Goldwyn production company (though Samuel Goldwyn himself promptly opted out and set up independently); and the next year Louis B. Mayer Pictures joined the flourishing group to add further power. Mayer himself became studio head and remained the dominant production force for over twenty-five years. Ideas man and executive producer in the early years was young Irving Thalberg, whose artistic flair provided a necessary corrective to Mayer's proletarian tastes, and who, before his death in 1936, had established a lofty pattern with such successes as *Ben Hur, The Big Parade, Anna Christie, Grand Hotel, The Thin Man, David Copperfield* and *Mutiny on the Bounty*, and stars like Garbo, Gable, Beery, Lionel Barrymore, Joan Crawford, John Gilbert, Lon Chaney, William Powell, Jean Harlow, Spencer Tracy, Lewis Stone, Nelson Eddy, Jeanette MacDonald, Laurel and Hardy and the Marx Brothers. (MGM's motto was in fact 'more stars than there are in heaven...') The success story continued through the 40s with *Goodbye Mr Chips*, Greer Garson, *The Wizard Of Oz*, Judy Garland, the Hardy Family, Gene Kelly and Esther Williams. Such continuity of product is a thing of the past, but MGM keep its end up in the 60s and 70s with occasional big guns like *Dr Zhivago, Where Eagles Dare* and *Network*; while reissues of *Gone with the Wind*, which it did not produce, kept the image of Leo the Lion fresh on cinema screens. In the 70s MGM gave up movie-making to concentrate on its huge Las Vegas hotel. A comeback attempt failed, and it was taken over by United Artists and Ted Turner. The 80s were a troubled time for the new MGM-UA; production fell and many of the films were lacklustre. There were some successes: *My Favorite Year, Moonstruck, A Fish Called Wanda* (MGM), *Rainman* (UA) and *Rocky III* (UA) and its sequels, as well as some failures: *Yes Giorgio*, an attempt to make a star of opera singer Luciano Pavarotti, and *2010*, a poor sequel to *2001: A Space Odyssey*. At the beginning of the 90s, the situation worsened as MGM was taken over by Italian Giancarlo Paretti, of Pathé Communications, to become MGM-Pathé. But Paretti turned out to lack the necessary financial resources, and legal complications between him and his bankers were not sorted out until mid-1992, when the company was auctioned off to its biggest creditor, Crédit Lyonnais of Paris. The dispute had held up production plans, but the future looked brighter as Alan Ladd Jnr, former president of Twentieth Century-Fox, became MGM's chairman and CEO. Ladd left in mid-1993, to be replaced by Frank Mancuso, former chairman and CEO of Paramount. Under him, its fortunes revived with such hits as *GoldenEye* and *The Birdcage*. Credit Lyonnais, the French bank, put it up for sale in mid-1996, when the studio was bought for $1.3 billion by a group headed by Mancuso, with finance coming from Kirk Kerkorian and the Australian television company Seven Network. Its progress has remained unpredictable; the long-term aim seems to be a merger with, or takeover of, a distribution company. In 1997 few films were in production; those that were released included the dull family film *Zeus and Roxanne*, about dolphins, and *Turbulence*, a disaster movie that did poor business. Its one critical success was *Ulee's Gold*, with Peter Fonda, but that earned little more than $4m at the US box-office. In 1998 it scored with its James Bond movie, *Tomorrow Never Dies*, but its flops included *Disturbing Behavior, Species 2* and *Dirty Work*. It had ambitious plans for 1999, including the release of around a dozen films, involving such stars as Arnold Schwarzenegger, Richard Gere and Robert De Niro.

Books: 1991, *Fade Out* by Peter Bart details MGM's collapse in the 80s. 1992, *When the Lion Roars* by Peter Hay. *The MGM Story* by John Douglas Eames is an excellent illustrated film-by-film history of the studio 1924-89.

Minerva Films.
A British production company set up in 1920 by Leslie Howard, C. Aubrey Smith, Adrian Brunel, A. A. Milne, and Nigel Playfair. Its shareholders included H. G. Wells. It made four comedy shorts, directed by Brunel from Milne's stories, before running out of money.

Miramax Films
is a distribution and production company founded in 1979 by Bob and Harvey Weinstein. It first became noted for its ability to attract audiences to foreign art-house and American independent films such as *Pelle the Conqueror, Cinema Paradiso, sex, lies and videotape*, and *The Crying Game*. After a decade of success as a distributor, in 1989 it also began to produce films. In 1993 the Disney company acquired it for $100m. Recent successes have included *Good Will Hunting*, the horror movies *Scream* and *Scream 2*, and *Sliding Doors*.

Monogram Pictures:
see ALLIED ARTISTS.

New Line Cinema Corporation
was founded in 1967 by Robert SHAYE and began as a distributor of movies for college audiences. It moved into production later, and had its greatest hits with two film series, *A Nightmare on Elm Street*, which began in 1984, and *Teenage Mutant Ninja Turtles*, which became one of the most commercially successful independent movies following its release in 1990, and spawned two sequels. In 1991, Fine Line Features was formed, catering for more adult tastes, and also had critical successes with *My Own Private Idaho* 92, *The Player* 92, *Menace II Society* 93, and *Short Cuts* 93. In 1993 the companies were taken over by Ted TURNER. Since then, major hits have been scored with *The Mask* 94, *Dumb and Dumber* 94, *Seven* 95 (which took more than $320m around the world), and *Mortal Kombat* 95, which took around $120m. But in 1996 the companies had a series of flops, including *Long Kiss Goodnight*, which earned not much more than the $25m spent on marketing it, *The Island of Dr Moreau* (cost: $50m; US earnings: $28m), and *Last Man Standing*, which took less than half of its $57m cost. More recently, it has done better with such hits as the Jackie Chan film *Rush Hour* and the vampire movie *Blade*.

Oberhausen Group
was a collection of 26 young West German film-makers who, at the Short Film Festival at Oberhausen in 1962, announced the birth of a new German cinema: 'We declare our intention of creating the new German feature film. This new film needs new freedoms: freedom from influence by commercial partners, freedom from domination by special interest groups. We have concrete artistic, formal, and economic conceptions about the production of the new German film. We are collectively prepared to bear the economic risks. The old film is dead. We believe in the new.' The signatories included Alexander KLUGE and Edgar REITZ. It was followed in 1967 by the Mannheim Declaration, also signed by Kluge and Reitz, among others, which noted 'Six years have passed since the Oberhausen Declaration. The renewal of German film has not yet taken place', and called again for that renewal.

Paramount Pictures Corporation
was basically the creation of Adolph ZUKOR, a nickelodeon showman who in 1912 founded Famous Players, with the intention of presenting photographed versions of stage successes. In 1914 W. W. Hodkinson's Paramount Pictures took over distribution of Famous Players and Lasky products, and in the complex mergers which resulted, Zukor came out top man. Through the years his studio more than any other gave a family atmosphere, seldom producing films of depth but providing agreeable light entertainment with stars like Valentino, Maurice Chevalier, the Marx Brothers, Mary Pickford, Claudette Colbert, Bob Hope, Bing Crosby, Dorothy Lamour, Alan Ladd, and directors like Lubitsch, de Mille and Wilder. Notable films include *The Sheik, The Covered Wagon, The Ten Commandments* (both versions), *Trouble in Paradise, The Crusades, Union Pacific*, the Road films, *Going My Way, The Greatest Show on Earth*, etc. In recent years, since Zukor's retirement, the company had many difficulties, but was helped by a takeover by Gulf and Western Industries which spurred the commercial instinct, and produced two enormous winners in *Love Story* and *The Godfather*, followed in 1977 by *Saturday Night Fever*, in 1978 by *Grease*, in 1979 by *Star Trek* and in 1981 by *Raiders of the Lost Ark*. The latter's two sequels, *Indiana Jones and the Temple of Doom* and *Indiana Jones and the Last Crusade*, were box-office successes in 1984 and 1989 respectively. *Beverly Hills Cop* 84 and its sequel in 1987 also brought box-office rewards and established Eddie Murphy as a star, while *Top Gun* was among the top films of 1986, as were, in their respective years, *The Hunt for Red October* 90, *The Addams Family* 91 and *Wayne's World* 92. But all that paled besides the phenomenal success of *Forrest Gump* in 1994, a film that became the company's biggest box-office success and among the top ten grossing films so far produced. In mid-1994 the studio was taken over by Viacom, an entertainment conglomerate that includes MTV, Nickelodeon and Showtime television channels. The company enjoyed great success with *Forrest Gump*, but its following films were less popular; while *Mission: Impossible* was a hit, the studio had to write off some $30m when *The Phantom* flopped at the box-office. The studio, along with Twentieth Century-Fox, enjoyed a spectacular success with *Titanic*, a film that went wildly over budget before becoming a worldwide success, taking more than $1 billion at box-offices. The thriller *Face/Off* was also one of the hits of 1997, and, in 1998, *The Truman Show* was a critical and financial success.

Pinewood Studios,
seventeen miles northwest of London, was built in 1935 and opened in 1936 by a millionaire named Charles Boot as Britain's reply to Hollywood. It rapidly came under the control of the Rank Organisation, and its fortunes have fluctuated, but on the whole it has been fairly well used.

History published 1976: *Movies from the Mansion* by George Perry.

Pixar.
Computer animation company that created *Toy Story*, the first feature-length computer-generated film, and plans to make more. Founded by George LUCAS, it was bought by Steve Jobs, former head, and co-founder, of Apple Computers. *Toy Story* was directed by John LASSETER, and distributed by Walt Disney.

Polygram.
A subsidiary of the electronics company Philips, Polygram Filmed Entertainment was established in 1991, producing films through Propaganda, Interscope and the British company Working Title. In 1995, it acquired ITC Entertainment and set up an American distribution company. It also owns half of Gramercy Pictures with Universal. It was acquired in 1998, together with the remainder of the Polygram Group, by Seagram, whose interests include Universal Studios, and put up for sale. When no buyer for the company was forthcoming, Polygram Filmed Entertainment was absorbed by Universal.

Republic Pictures Corporation.
A small Hollywood production and distribution company founded in 1935 by a former tobacco executive named Herbert J. YATES, who had spent some years building up a film laboratory. Republic continued as a one-man concern, producing innumerable competently-made second-feature westerns and melodramas with such stars as Roy Rogers, Vera Hruba Ralston (Yates' wife), John Carroll, Constance Moore. The studio also churned out the majority of Hollywood's serials. Very occasionally there would be a major production such as *Rio Grande* or *The Quiet Man*. Production stopped in the mid-50s, when 'bread and butter' pictures were no longer needed, and the company's interests moved into TV.

RKO Radio Pictures Inc.
was for many years one of Hollywood's 'big five' production companies, with its own distribution arm. It started in 1921 as a joint enterprise of the Radio Corporation of America and the Keith-Orpheum cinema circuit. Despite severe financial vicissitudes, it struggled on for twenty-seven years, buoyed by a generally decent production standard; stars like Cary Grant, Katharine Hepburn, Wheeler and Woolsey, Leon Errol; individual films such as *Cimarron, King Kong, The Informer, Suspicion, Mr Blandings Builds His Dream House* and *Fort Apache*; and the participation of Goldwyn, Disney and Selznick, all released through RKO at its peak. In 1948 Howard HUGHES acquired a large share of the stock; but after a period of uncertainty RKO ceased production in 1953 and the studio was sold to Desilu TV.

A glossy book by Richard B. Jewell and Vernon Harbin, *The RKO Story*, came out in 1982 and was a valuable research tool.

Saturday Night Live.
The late-night US TV comedy series that began in 1975 has spawned several films based on the programme's characters, though only two so far have been successful. It has also provided a showcase for many comic talents who have gone on to movie careers, including Chevy CHASE, John BELUSHI, Dan AYKROYD, Bill MURRAY, Eddie MURPHY, Billy CRYSTAL, Martin SHORT, Jon LOVITZ, Damon WAYANS, Chris FARLEY, David SPADE and Chris ROCK.

The Blues Brothers 80. Wayne's World 92. Wayne's World 2 93. Coneheads 93. It's Pat 94. Stuart Saves His Family 95. Blues Brothers 2000 98, etc.

Silicon Graphics Inc.
is a computer company whose workstations are used extensively in the film industry to provide special effects in movies. *Toy Story*, the first computer-generated animated feature, was created on SGI computers. Other films such as *Men in Black*, *Jurassic Park*, *The Peacemaker*, *Starship Troopers*, *Alien: Resurrection* and the remake of *Flubber* also relied on SGI equipment.

Sony Pictures Entertainment
was formed in 1991, after the Japanese electronics company had bought Columbia Pictures and TriStar Pictures from Coca-Cola in 1989. At the time, SPE's executives believed that it was an advantage to have two studios because it was difficult for any one company to produce and market more than a dozen or so movies a year. But in 1998, TriStar was merged into Columbia Pictures.

Tempean Films.
British production company founded by Monty Berman and Robert S. Baker, who were active in the 40s and 50s making second features, mainly low-budget thrillers and horror movies.

Theatre Workshop
was a co-operative, populist, left-wing company formed in 1945, with Joan Littlewood as its director. After years of touring, in 1953 the company took over and transformed the derelict Theatre Royal in Stratford, East London, doing much to revolutionize British theatre in the process. Littlewood left the company for a time in the early 60s, and it had a sporadic existence thereafter, finally breaking up in 1974. Its plays dealing with working-class experience influenced the mood of British films of the 60s. Actors associated with the company included Avis Bunnage, Harry H. Corbett, Howard Goorney, Stephen Lewis, Murray Melvin, Brian Murphy and Maxwell Shaw. Among the writers it introduced to cinema were Brendan Behan and Shelagh Delaney. Plays filmed, though few resembled the stage productions, included *A Taste of Honey* 61, *The Quare Fellow* 62, *Sparrows Can't Sing* 62, and *Oh, What a Lovely War* 69.

Book: 1981, *The Theatre Workshop Story* by Howard Goorney.

Triangle Film Corporation.
Company formed by D. W. Griffith, Thomas Ince, and Mack Sennett in 1915 to produce and release films made by the three directors, who left the company in 1917.

TriStar Pictures
was a movie production and distribution company founded in 1982 by CBS, the cable TV company Home Box Office, and Columbia Pictures. Columbia bought out CBS in 1985, and HBO also reduced its stake in the company. In 1987 TriStar was merged with Columbia to become Columbia Pictures Entertainment, although it retained its separate identity. In 1998 it was absorbed into Columbia Pictures.

Troma.
Company specializing in the production and distribution of low-budget exploitation movies, usually combining kitsch and gore, many produced and directed by the company's president, Lloyd Kaufman, and vice-president, Michael Herz. It is best known for its *Toxic Avenger* series, which has spawned dolls and other novelty merchandising.

Squeeze Play! 80. Waitress! 82. Stuck on You 83. The First Turn-On! 84. The Toxic Avenger 84. Nuke 'em High 85. The Toxic Avenger: Part II 88. Troma's War 88. The Toxic Avenger III: The Last Temptation of Toxie 90. Def by Temptation 90. Class of Nuke 'em High II: Subhumanoid Meltdown 91. Sgt Kabukiman N.Y.P.D. 94, etc.

Twentieth Century-Fox Film Corporation.
An American production and distribution company formed in 1935 by a merger of Joseph Schenck's Twentieth Century Pictures with William Fox's Fox Film Corporation. Fox had started in nickelodeon days as a showman, then a distributor.

Putting his profits into production, he started the careers of several useful stars including Theda Bara, and pioneered the Movietone sound-on-film process; but in the early 30s, after a series of bad deals, he lost power. The new company had Darryl F. Zanuck as production head from 1935 to 1952; he returned in 1962 as president after the resignation of Spyros Skouras, who had reigned from 1942. These two men are therefore largely responsible for the Fox image, which usually gave the impression of more careful budget-trimming and production-processing than did the films of the rest of the 'big five'. Fox's successful personality stars include Shirley Temple, Alice Faye, Don Ameche, Betty Grable and Marilyn Monroe; its best westerns include *The Big Trail*, *Drums along the Mohawk*, *My Darling Clementine* and *The Gunfighter*; in drama it can claim *What Price Glory?*, *Dante's Inferno*, *The Grapes of Wrath*, *How Green Was My Valley*, *The Ox Bow Incident*, *The Song of Bernadette*, *Wilson*, *The Snake Pit*, and *Gentlemen's Agreement*. In 1953 Spyros Skouras successfully foisted the new screen shape, CinemaScope, on to world markets, but Fox have not used it with greater success than anyone else, their most elaborate 'spectaculars' being *The Robe*, *There's No Business Like Show Business*, *The King and I*, *South Pacific*, *The Diary of Anne Frank*, *The Longest Day*, *Cleopatra*, *Those Magnificent Men in Their Flying Machines*, *The Sound of Music*, *Star!*, *Hello Dolly*, and *Tora! Tora! Tora!*

On his return, Darryl Zanuck appointed his son Richard as vice-president in charge of production and, in 1965, the company enjoyed one of its greatest successes with the musical *The Sound of Music*. Darryl and Richard Zanuck, who went on to become a successful independent producer, left at the beginning of the 70s after a succession of big-budget flops (*Hello Dolly* and *Tora! Tora! Tora!* among them). The fashion for disaster films brought the company successes with *The Towering Inferno* (made with Warners) and *The Poseidon Adventure*. Alan Ladd Jnr became President in the mid-70s, leaving in 1979 to become an independent producer; during his time Fox hit the jackpot in 1977 with *Star Wars* and its sequels. In 1981, the company was bought by oil billionaire Marvin Davis; he in turn sold it in 1985 to publishing tycoon Rupert Murdoch, who took over personal control following the resignation of its chairman and CEO Barry Diller in 1992. In recent years, the company has enjoyed hits with *Big*, *Aliens*, *Die Hard* and *Die Hard 2*, *Sleeping with the Enemy* and *Home Alone*, the most financially successful of comedies. In 1996, in a summer of blockbuster movies, it produced the biggest hit of the year: *Independence Day*, which took more than $286m at the US box-office and more than $435m worldwide. The company had a poor 1997: two blockbusters, *Volcano* and *Speed 2: Cruise Control*, did not do as well as expected, and James Cameron was going way over budget with *Titanic*; its greatest success came with the re-release of the 20-year-old *Star Wars*, which went on to become the fifth most popular film at the box-office, auguring well for its prequel, *Star Wars: The Phantom Empire*, which was among the most eagerly awaited releases of 1999. *Titanic* proved to be a massive hit, and the company had surprise hits in 1998 with the comedies *Doctor Dolittle* and *There's Something about Mary*.

Two Cities Films.
A British company set up in the early days of World War II by the expatriate Italian Filippo del Giudice. It was responsible for many of Britain's most famous films, including *In Which We Serve*, *The Way Ahead*, *Henry V*, *Blithe Spirit* and *Odd Man Out*.

UFA.
Universum Film Aktien Gesellschaft: the main German film production company since 1917, owning its studio and linked in the 20s with Paramount and MGM. In the 30s it was brought under state control and in the 40s, with the end of the war, it ceased to exist.

United Artists Corporation
was founded in 1919 by Mary Pickford, Douglas Fairbanks, Charlie Chaplin and D. W. Griffith, the object being to make and distribute their own and other people's quality product. Among the company's early successes were *His Majesty the American*, *Pollyanna* (the first film sold on a percentage basis), *Broken Blossoms*, *Way Down East*, and *A Woman of Paris*. In the mid-20s Joe Schenck was brought in to run the company, and he in turn gained Valentino, Goldwyn, Keaton and Swanson; but later all were bought out by various syndicates. Howard Hughes contributed *Hell's Angels* and *Scarface*, but in the 30s the UA product began to thin out, partly because the company was purely a distributor and financer of independent producers, without any studio of its own or any large roster of stars under contract. The hardest times, with only inferior product to sell, were between 1948 and 1953; but after that a new board of directors, through careful choice of product, fought its way back to the top; despite the defection of half its executives to Orion, UA was again riding high with *The Magnificent Seven*, *The Battle of Britain*, *Tom Jones*, *One Flew Over the Cuckoo's Nest*, *Rocky* and the James Bond films. The 80s however brought the 40-million-dollar calamity of *Heaven's Gate* (book: *Final Cut* by Steven Bach) and a takeover by MGM to become MGM-UA. Once MGM's problems were sorted out and the company was sold in a management buyout in 1996, studio executives began planning to spend more money than in the past, intending to make expensive films, such as the volcano disaster movie *Dante's Peak*, budgeted at more than $110m, and a costly remake of *King Kong*, to be produced, written and directed by Peter Jackson. The company, like its parent MGM, has been suffering from uncertainty and lack of direction. But its *The Man in the Iron Mask* gained from the backwash of the success of *Titanic*, since, like that massive hit, it also starred the hottest actor in Hollywood, Leonardo DiCaprio.

Book: 1986, *The United Artists Story* by Ronald Bergen.

Universal Pictures
was founded in 1912 by Carl Laemmle, an exhibitor turned producer. Universal City grew steadily and included among its output many of the most famous titles of Von Stroheim, Valentino and Lon Chaney. In 1930 came *All Quiet on the Western Front*, and soon after *Dracula* and *Frankenstein*, the precursors of a long line of horror pictures. Laemmle lost power in the mid-30s and the studio settled down to be one of Hollywood's 'little two', producing mainly modest, low-budget co-features without too many intellectual pretensions. The Deanna Durbin series saved it from receivership, and there were occasional notable pictures: *Destry Rides Again*, *Hellzapoppin*, *Flesh and Fantasy*. The stars under contract were durable: Boris Karloff, Lon Chaney Jnr, Donald O'Connor, Abbott and Costello, Jeff Chandler, Audie Murphy. More ambition was noted in the 50s, when the era of the bread-and-butter picture was ended by TV. Decca Records gained a large measure of control, but in 1962 a merger gave the ultimate power to the Music Corporation of America, ex-agents and TV producers. The 1960s saw a steady resumption of prestige, with films like *Spartacus*, the Doris Day – Rock Hudson sex comedies, *Charade*, *The War Lord*, Ross Hunter's soapily sentimental but glossy remakes of Hollywood's choicest weepies, *Thoroughly Modern Millie*, *The Day of the Jackal*, *Earthquake*, *Airport* and *The Seven Per Cent Solution*. The company, now a division of MCA Inc. is currently one of Hollywood's most powerful sources of box-office films and television series, though its venture into 'enlightened' European production was fairly disastrous. In the 80s the company enjoyed its biggest-ever hit, *E.T. – the Extraterrestrial*, courtesy of Steven Spielberg, who had also scored for them in the mid-70s with *Jaws*. Spielberg also produced Universal's other big winners, *Back to the Future* and its sequels, while it enjoyed Oscar successes with *Out of Africa*. His contribution remained important to the company when his *Jurassic Park* was a monster hit around the world. Science fact also met with approval in *Apollo 13*, a story of a space flight that went wrong. The studio found success by recycling familiar subject-matter, such as the TV favourites *The Flintstones* and *Casper*, and an updating of the old Jerry Lewis comedy *The Nutty Professor*, which brought Eddie Murphy a much-needed hit. Its only box-office successes in 1997 were the disaster movie *Dante's Peak* and, especially, the comedy *Liar Liar*, starring Jim Carrey. The studio's more recent record has been poor. It announced a $65m loss for the third quarter of 1998, owing to the failure of its $100m-budgeted *Meet Joe Black*, starring Brad Pitt, *Babe: Pig in the City*, and Gus van Sant's remake of Alfred Hitchcock's *Psycho*. As a result, several top executives left the company.

Clive Hirschhorn's splendidly illustrated book *The Universal Story* (1983) is an excellent critical history. Also: 1991, *The Best of Universal* by Tony Thomas.

UPA
(United Productions of America)

was a cartoon factory which in the early 50s received generous critical plaudits for a hundred or so shorts and even pushed the Disney studio into a more sophisticated style. Its creations included Mr Magoo, Gerald McBoing Boing and Pete Hothead, and it specialized in a stylish economy of line and in an appeal to a much higher intelligence bracket than any cartoon had aspired to in the past.

VGIK
is the acronym for the All-Union State Cinema Institute (Vsesoyuznyi Gosudarstvennyi Institut Kinematografii), the leading film school in Russia. Its founders in 1919 included Vladimir Gardin and Lev Kuleshov.

Vitagraph.
An early American production company which had great success but was taken over in the 20s by Warner's.

Walt Disney Productions,
the studio founded and controlled by Walt Disney, has dominated animated features since the release of the first, *Snow White and the Seven Dwarfs*, in 1937. The company began in Kansas City as Laugh-O-Gram films, with Disney in partnership with Ub Iwerks. Disney moved to Hollywood in the early 20s, and set up a studio with his brother Roy. After his death, its features declined in quality for a time, and many leading animators, including Don Bluth, quit the studio in the late 70s over the issue of deteriorating standards. In the 90s, under the chairmanship of Michael Eisner, its animated films improved and the company had deserved hits with *Beauty and the Beast* 91, *Aladdin* 92, *The Lion King* 94, and *Toy Story* 95, which was the first computer-animated feature. Both *Beauty and the Beast* and *The Lion King* were turned into successful stage musicals. The studio's live-action films have continued to be bland family entertainment, many of them remakes of earlier movies, including *That Darn Cat*, *Flubber* and *The Parent Trap*, although it did have an unexpected success with the comic *George of the Jungle* in 1997. Other studios have challenged Disney's domination of animated features, including Don Bluth's, but so far without success. The strongest challenge has come from Jeffrey Katzenberg, who left Disney to become a co-founder of the new Hollywood studio DreamWorks skg. DreamWorks' computer-generated feature *Antz* was a hit in 1998, taking around $90m at the US box-office, but it had little effect on the success of Disney's similarly themed *A Bug's Life*, which was released later.

Warner Brothers Pictures Inc.
is a family affair started in 1923 by four American exhibitor brothers. After a very shaky start it soared to pre-eminence through their gamble on talking pictures in the shape of *The Jazz Singer* and *The Singing Fool*. Through the 30s and 40s the company kept its popularity through tough gangster films starring James Cagney, Edward G. Robinson and Humphrey Bogart, and musicals with Dick Powell and Ruby Keeler; and its prestige by exposés like *Confessions of a Nazi Spy* and *Mission to Moscow* and biographies of Zola, Pasteur, Ehrlich and Reuter. Other Warner stars included Bette Davis and Errol Flynn, both enormously popular with all classes. Warner films were not usually over-budgeted but contrived to look immaculate through solid production values and star performances. Since 1950 the company's product has been more variable, as deals have had to be done with independent producers, and there has been a patchy flirtation with TV; yet on the serious side directors like Kazan have been encouraged, popular taste is taken care of by spectaculars like *My Fair Lady* and *The Great Race*, and the company took a calculated risk (which paid off in spades) with *Who's Afraid of Virginia Woolf?* In the mid-60s came a merger with Seven Arts, and in 1969 the company was taken over by a conglomerate. In 1989 the company merged with the publishing group Time Inc. to become Time-Warner.

During the 80s the famous production company seemed to be kept solvent by Clint Eastwood toughies, although it had a success with the fast-paced action film *Lethal Weapon* and immediately repeated the process with satisfying results: the movie had reached its second sequel by 1992. *Gremlins*, a hit in 1984, begat *Gremlins II: The New Batch*, which did less well. Its dark fantasy *Batman* was the top box-office attraction of 1989, and *Batman Returns* became a hit in 1992. *Robin Hood: Prince of Thieves* was a surprise success in 1991. Fortunately, there has so far been no attempt to repeat it. The company also had a monumental flop with the costly *Hudson Hawk*, which brought Bruce Willis's career to a temporary halt. But the company was soon enjoying great success, with a succession of hit films, including *Batman Returns*, *Lethal Weapon 3*, *The Bodyguard*, *Sommersby* and *The Fugitive*. Time Warner is the world's largest media company, a title it briefly lost to the Walt Disney organization, and then regained when it took over Turner Broadcasting Systems for $7.3 billion in 1996. Its hits that year included *Twister* and *A Time to Kill*. Its blockbuster for 1997, *Batman and Robin*, was a disappointment, although it took more than $100m at the box-office and was the ninth most successful film of the year. But its thriller *LA Confidential* was among the critically acclaimed films of the year. *Lethal Weapon 4*, the latest instalment of the thriller series, was its biggest hit in 1998.

Various books have been published about its glory days, including: 1986, *Inside Warner Brothers 1935-51* by Rudy Behlmer (a collection of memos).

Woodfall Films.

British production company set up in the late 50s by director Tony Richardson and playwright John Osborne together with financier Harry Saltzman (though it turned out he didn't actually have any money). They first produced a screen version of Osborne's *Look Back in Anger* 59. Productions that helped change the nature of British films included *The Entertainer* 60, *Saturday Night and Sunday Morning* 60,

A *Taste of Honey* 61, *The Loneliness of the Long Distance Runner* 62, *Tom Jones* 63, *Girl with Green Eyes* 64, *The Knack* 65. Other productions included *One Way Pendulum* 65, *Mademoiselle* 66, *The Sailor from Gibraltar* 67, *Red and Blue* (short) 67, *Hamlet* 69, *Laughter in the Dark* 69, *Ned Kelly* 70, *Dead Cert* 74, *Joseph Andrews* 77.

5
Movie Talk –
An A–Z of Technical and Critical terms

'A' picture.
A term used to indicate the most important film in the days of double-feature programmes, one that used the talents of a studio's top actors, directors and technicians. The distinction between 'A' pictures and supporting films, or 'B' pictures, disappeared with the demise of double features in the 1950s.

above the title.
Credits that appear on posters or the screen before the title of a film. At one time, such billing was an indication of star status, though that no longer necessarily holds; these days it is more to do with deal-making and the massaging of egos than with the ability to draw an audience to a film. Only a few producers and directors, such as Cecil B. De Mille, Alfred Hitchcock and Steven Spielberg, have achieved above the title billing, and even fewer writers have managed it, of whom the most prominent is Stephen King.

above-the-line costs
refer to the expenses contracted before filming begins: on obtaining film rights, where necessary, and accounting for the cost of the principal talents involved, such as producer, screenwriter, director and actors.

abstract film.
One in which the images are not representational but fall into visually interesting or significant patterns: e.g. Disney's *Fantasia*, Norman McLaren's hand-drawn sound films, etc.

Academy Awards.
Merit prizes given annually since 1927 by the American Academy of Motion Picture Arts and Sciences. The award is in the form of a statuette known in the trade – for reasons variously explained – as Oscar, and each April the ABC network televises the award ceremonies as an increasingly pretentious spectacular: Johnny Carson in 1979 called it 'two hours of sparkling entertainment spread out over a four-hour show'. See Appendix for full list of awards.
Books: *The Academy Awards* by Paul Michael (1968), *Inside Oscar* by Mason Wiley and Damien Bona (1985), *60 Years of the Oscar* by Robert Osborne (1989), *The Oscars: The Secret History of Hollywood's Academy Awards* by Anthony Holden (1993), *The Academy Awards Handbook* by John Harkness (1994).

Academy Frame.
The standard film frame in a ratio of 4 to 3, more usually referred to as 1.33 to 1.

Academy Leader.
Regulation length of film attached to the front of a reel about to be projected, bearing a 'countdown' and various standard images to facilitate focusing.

accelerated motion.
An effect obtained by running the camera more slowly than usual: when the resulting film is projected at normal speed, the movements seem faster because they occupy fewer frames than would normally be the case. The opposite of SLOW MOTION.

ACE.
Initials that indicate membership of the American Cinema Editors, a professional society for film and TV editors.

acetate.
Another word for safety base, which replaced nitrate stock in the 50s and is much slower to burn.

acting
A short selection of attitudes.
See also: THE METHOD.

action film
is one where movement and events, usually of a violent nature such as explosions, fist- and gunfights, take precedence over characterization and, increasingly, intelligible narrative.

action still.
A photograph of a scene as it actually appears in the film as opposed to one specially posed for publicity purposes. Sometimes called a frame blow-up. In TV, an 'action stills' programme has come to mean one consisting of still photographs given a semblance of life by camera movement.

ACTT.
The Association of Cinematograph, Television and Allied Technicians, a British trade union, founded 1931. Now renamed BECTU.

ADR
stands for Automatic Dialogue Replacement, the term used to describe the re-recording of dialogue to improve the quality of a soundtrack.
See also: LOOPING.

agent.
An intermediate who acts on behalf of talent and takes a percentage of the rewards. Agents played little part in the early years of Hollywood when studios controlled the system and signed actors to long-term contracts. With the decline of the studios, agents became more powerful by acting as packagers, putting together director, stars and script and selling the result to the studios. A few, such as Irving 'Swifty' LAZAR, became almost as famous as the stars they represented; the power became concentrated not with individuals but with the large agencies who were able to put together deals in which they represented all the major talent involved. William Morris founded the talent agency named after him in 1898, and in the 50s and 60s, as the studios relinquished control, represented many of Hollywood's leading stars and directors. Its later rivals include International Creative Management (ICM), founded in 1975 from a merger of Creative Management Associates and International Famous Agency, and Creative Artists Agency (CAA), also founded in 1975. Michael OVITZ, until 1995 head of CAA, was said to be the most important man in Hollywood, and agents have even moved on to run studios. Agents were partly blamed for the rising cost of Hollywood movies because many were too concerned with increasing their client's income, and therefore their own, at the expense of sound economic film-making. Some also became producers, though few succeeded.

Agfacolor.
German multilayer colour process, widely used in Europe and basically the same as Russian Sovcolor and American Anscocolor (which became Metrocolor). Noted for softness and often lack of sharpness.

aka.
A 70s abbreviation for 'also known as'.

'also known as':
see AKA.

American Film Institute.
Government-sponsored body rather belatedly founded in 1967. Based in Washington, its comprehensive catalogue will provide full detail on every American film ever made. Its first director was George Stevens, Jnr.
See Section 7 for its choice of best American films.

American Society of Cinematographers:
see ASC.

anaglyph.
A simple system for making three-dimensional films. The two slightly differing images are printed in different colours, usually red and green, and viewed through similarly coloured lenses to sort them out into a single image. (The alternative is to use polaroid, which distinguishes the two images through lenses invisibly stripped in different directions.)

anamorphic lens.
One which, in a camera, 'squeezes' a wide picture on to standard film; in a projector, 'unsqueezes' the image to fill a wide screen (usually of a 2.45:1 aspect ratio); e.g. CinemaScope, Panavision, TohoScope, HammerScope, WarnerScope, DyaliScope, which are not essentially different from each other.
See also: ASPECT RATIO.

animation.
The filming of static drawings, puppets or other objects in sequence so that they give an illusion of movement. Sometimes called 'stop-frame animation' because only one frame of film is exposed at a time.
Leading figures in the history of animation include Winsor McKAY, who in 1909 introduced Gertie the Dinosaur, Emile COHL, Len LYE, Max FLEISCHER, Walt DISNEY, the UPA Group, Norman McLAREN, William HANNA and Joe BARBERA, HALAS AND BATCHELOR, Ralph BAKSHI and Richard WILLIAMS.
Best books on the subject are *The Technique of Film Animation* by John Halas and Roger Manvell; *The Art of Walt Disney* by Christopher Finch; *The Animated Film* by Ralph Stephenson.

Anime.
A Japanese term for animated films, applied particularly to its own tradition, which differs from the American style, as exemplified in the work of the Walt Disney studios. Japanese animation is often based on comic books and features more adult fantasies, often marked by an excess of sex and violence and drawing on local legends and myths. The graphic techniques are often stylized: the heroes and heroines tend to cuteness, with large round eyes. The best film so far is Otomo Katsuhiro's *Akira* 87, though many others are gaining a cult following in the West owing to their release on video and there are several magazines devoted to Anime. The Anime style has influenced some action films, such as *Gunhed*, and other live-action films are being based on animated originals, such as the gangster epic *Crying Freeman*. The process is likely to quicken with the trend for computer games inspiring movies, since these also are influenced by Japanese comic-book styles.
Books: 1993, *Anime! A Beginner's Guide to Japanese Animation* by Helen McCarthy; 1996, *The Anime! Movie Guide* by Helen McCarthy.

See also: MANGA.

Anscocolor.
American process derived from AGFACOLOR.

answer print.
The first complete combined print supplied by the laboratory, usually with no very careful attempt to grade colour or contrast.

arc.
A high-powered lamp used in projectors and studio lighting, its illumination consisting of an electrical discharge between two carbon rods.

archive.
A vault, usually government-sponsored, containing a selection of films to be preserved for research and for posterity.

Aromarama.
A process that linked smells to sequences in a movie, the perfume being pumped through the air-conditioning system into the auditorium. It was first used for the screening of a documentary, *The Great Wall of China* 59, but, like the similar SMELL-O-VISION, was never more than a short-lived gimmick.

art director.
Technician responsible for designing sets, sometimes also costumes and graphics. 'Production designer' is a more pretentious way of saying much the same thing. The importance of this work to the finished product first became noticeable in *Intolerance* and the German expressionist films of the 20s, then in such diverse talking films as *The Old Dark House*, *Things to Come*, *The Cat and the Canary* (both versions), *Citizen Kane*, *Trouble in Paradise*, *The Mystery of the Wax Museum*, *A Matter of Life and Death*, *Les Enfants du Paradis*, and *Kings Row*. Important figures include William Cameron MENZIES, Anton GROT, Cedric GIBBONS, Ken ADAM, Vincent KORDA, Hans DREIER, Alfred JUNGE, Carmen DILLON.

art house.
American term (now displacing 'specialized hall' in GB) for cinema showing classic revivals and highbrow or off-beat new films of limited commercial appeal.

ASC.
Often seen on credit titles after the names of cinematographers, these initials stand for the American Society of Cinematographers, a professional association, membership of which is by invitation only. Its aims since its foundation in 1918 have been 'to advance the art and science of cinematography'. The Society publishes a monthly periodical, *American Cinematographer*.

aspect ratio.
Relative breadth and height of screen. Before 1953 this was 4:3 or 1.33:1. 'Standard' wide screen varies from 1.66:1 to 1.85:1. Anamorphic processes are wider: SuperScope 2:1, CinemaScope and most others 2.35:1 (or 2.55:1 with magnetic stereophonic sound). Vista-Vision, a printing process, was shot in 1.33:1 but recommended for screening at up to 2:1, i.e. with top and bottom cut off and the rest magnified. The TV screen is fixed at 1.33:1, therefore all wide-screen films lose something when played on it.

assistant director.
More properly 'assistant to the director', being concerned with details of administration rather than creation.

associate producer.
Usually the actual producer or supervisor of the film, the title of 'executive producer' having been taken by the head of the studio.

Association of Cinematograph, Television and Allied Technicians:
see ACTT.

auteur.
A term used in the 60s and 70s by egghead critics to denote directors whom they judge to have a discernible message or attitude which runs throughout their work. Oddly enough the term is not applied to authors.

authenticator.
Studio researcher responsible for establishing accuracy of all script details, ensuring use of 'clear' telephone numbers, etc.

avant-garde.
An adjective generally used to describe artists 'in advance of their time'; especially used of French surrealists in the 20s, e.g. Kirsanoff, Buñuel, Germaine Dulac.

Avid Media Composer
is a digital editing system, based on the Apple Macintosh computer. It was first used in film in 1992 by Steve Cohen when editing *Lost in Yonkers*. His success led other editors to adopt the method. The advantage of digital editing is that it is non-linear, providing swift access to all raw film footage and allowing multiple versions of each edited sequence. Some editors prefer a rival system, LIGHTWORKS.

'B' picture.
A low-budget production usually designed as part of a double bill or to support a more important feature. There are four excellent books on the subject: *B Movies* by Don Miller, *The Wonderful World of B Films* by Alan G. Barbour, *Kings of the Bs* by Todd McCarthy and Charles Flynn and *The Big Book of B Movies* by Robin Cross.

back projection.
A method of producing 'location' sequences in the studio: the players act in front of a translucent screen on which the scenic background is projected.

ballyhoo.
An expressive term, allegedly Irish in origin, used in show business to denote the kind of publicity that has nothing to do with the merits, or indeed the actual contents, of the film in question.

barring clause.
The part of an exhibitor's contract with a renter preventing him from showing new films before other specified cinemas in the area. The showing of a film in London may thus prevent its exhibition elsewhere within a radius of fifty miles or more.

BECTU
is the Broadcasting, Entertainment, Cinematograph and Theatre Union, which replaced the ACTT.

below-the-line costs
are the expenses that cover the cost of filming and post-production work.

best boy.
Term used to describe the assistant to the chief electrician, or gaffer, on a film set.

bicycling.
A trade term for the sharing, usually illegally, of one print between two theatres: the manager had to make frequent bicycle trips!

billing.
The official credits for a film, usually stating the relative sizes of type to be accorded to title, stars, character actors, etc.

biograph.
(1) An old name for a cinema projector. (2) The name of Britain's first public cinema, near Victoria Station, London, opened 1905. (3) The name of D. W. Griffith's New York studios, 1903–10.

biopic.
A contraction of 'biographical picture', i.e. a film about the life of a real person. For examples see under COMPOSERS, COURTESANS, ENTERTAINERS, EXPLORERS, INVENTORS, KINGS AND QUEENS, PAINTERS, POLITICIANS, SCIENTISTS, SOLDIERS, SPIES, SPORTSMEN, WRITERS.

Black Maria.
In the history of film this evocative phrase for a police van has a secondary meaning, being the nickname given to Edison's first portable studio.

blackface.
A vaudeville adjective for comedians or singers who found their best appeal in 'Negro' disguise, i.e. with faces entirely blacked save for thick lips. Among the singers Al Jolson was perhaps the most famous exponent of this art, with Eddie Cantor a close second; the style derived from the minstrel shows which toured America from the mid-nineteenth century and which are clearly depicted in Jolson's *Mammy* and *Swanee River*. Dockstader's minstrels are recreated in *The Jolson Story*, and Dan Emmet's in *Dixie*; while Judy Garland and Mickey Rooney created their own blackface troupe in *Babes in Arms*. Among blackface comics there were Moran and Mack, the 'two black crows'; and others who made themselves black for comic effect were Betty Grable and June Haver in *The Dolly Sisters*, Myrna Loy in *Ham and Eggs at the Front*, Gene Wilder in *Silver Streak*, Buster Keaton in *College*, Marion Davies in *Going Hollywood*, Fred Astaire in *Swing Time*, Dan Dailey in *You're My Everything*, and Chick Chandler in *The Big Shot*. In *Watermelon Man*, on the other hand, Godfrey Cambridge appeared in whiteface, as did Lenny Henry in *True Identity*.

blacklisting:
see THE HOLLYWOOD TEN.

blimp.
A soundproof cover fixed over a camera during shooting to absorb running noise.

block booking.
A system supposedly illegal but still practised, whereby a renter forces an exhibitor to book a whole group of mainly mediocre films in order to get the one or two he wants.

bloop.
To cover a splice in the sound track, usually with thick 'blooping ink'.

blow up.
To magnify an image, either a photograph for background purposes, or a piece of film (e.g. from 16mm to 35mm).

boom.
A 'long arm' extending from the camera unit and carrying a microphone to be balanced over the actors so that sound can be picked up in a semi-distant shot. A 'camera boom' is a high movable platform strong enough to support the entire camera unit.

break figure.
A specified amount of takings after which an exhibitor pays a greater percentage to the renter. For the protection of both parties many contracts are on a sliding scale, with the exhibitor paying anything from 25% to 50% of the gross according to the business he does.

breakaway furniture
is specially constructed from balsa wood for those spectacular saloon brawls in which so much damage is apparently done to stars and stunt men.

British Film Academy.
An organization founded in 1946 'for the advancement of the film'. Since 1959 it has been amalgamated with the Society of Film and Television Arts. Its award statuette is noted in this book by the letters BFA. See Section 8 for full listing.

British Film Commission.
An organization set up in 1992 and funded by the British government to provide information and services to international film and television companies to encourage the use of British technicians, artists, facilities and locations. The first British Film Commissioner was Sir Sydney Samuelson, who began working in the cinema industry in 1939.

British Film Institute.
Partly government-subsidized organization founded in 1933 'to encourage the use and development of cinema as a means of entertainment and instruction'. Includes the National Film Archive (founded 1935) and the National Film Theatre (founded after the 1951 Festival of Britain). Also library, information section, stills collection, film distribution agency, lecture courses, etc. Chief publication: *Sight and Sound*.

B.S.C.
British Society of Cinematographers, a professional society founded in the 50s, similar in aims to the A.S.C.

burned out.
Cinematographer's jargon for 'over-exposed'.

cable.
A method of disseminating television programmes by underground cable whose fibres can accommodate a great many channels, none of them subject to interference from the others. From the mid-70s it became highly popular in America because of poor airwave reception in many areas; as a subscription service it also screened fewer commercials and most of its movies were uncut. These advantages however did not apply in most other countries, where it had a slower start.

cameo.
A word coined (in its cinematic sense) by Mike Todd when persuading famous stars to accept walk-on parts for *Around the World in Eighty Days*.

cartoon:
a film composed of animated drawings, carefully varied to give the appearance of motion. Gertie the Dinosaur, who appeared in 1909, is thought to be the first cartoon character; Mutt and Jeff followed soon after. In the 20s, Pat Sullivan's Felix the Cat and Max Fleischer's Out of the Inkwell series vied for popularity until both were ousted by Walt Disney, who with Ub Iwerks created Mickey Mouse and his familiar friends. In the 30s, Disney went on to Silly Symphonies, Fleischer to Popeye. Other creations were Woody Woodpecker (Walter Lantz), Mighty Mouse, Heckle and Jeckle, Tom and Jerry (Hanna-Barbera for MGM) and Bugs Bunny. Disney's Donald Duck became more popular than Mickey. In the 40s, David Hand made British cartoons for the Rank Organisation, but they were not commercially successful. The 50s brought U.P.A. with their new refined lines, intellectual conceptions and sophisticated jokes; Mr Magoo and Gerald McBoing Boing led the new characters but quickly palled. Then the needs of television led to innumerable cartoon series which for the sake of economy had to be only semi-animated and had little vitality; the best of them were The Flintstones and Yogi Bear. These series proliferated into hundreds and not until 1972 did anyone try an adult cartoon series, Hanna-Barbera's *Wait Till Your Father Gets Home*.
■ Feature-length cartoons were started by Disney in 1937 with *Snow White and the Seven Dwarfs*; Fleischer responded in 1939 with *Gulliver's Travels*. Disney's outstanding serious cartoon was *Fantasia* 40, an interpretation of classical music. Later, French and Japanese cartoons flooded the market, but inspiration was lacking in most of them. Halas and Batchelor's British *Animal Farm* was a fair summation of Orwell's fable, but their later attempts to interpret Gilbert and Sullivan failed. In recent years the cartoon has been put to every kind of serious and comic purpose, including propaganda and advertising, and many prizewinners have come from Europe. Ralph Bakshi's ruderies of Fritz the Cat were startling, but he atoned with his careful rendering of *Lord of the Rings*.

cast.
The actors in a movie.

casting.
To the old Hollywood, casting usually meant type-casting, or bending the character to suit the star. In the 70s, stars became less important, and leading actors became more chameleon-like. Even so, many best-remembered performances have been given by actors who were second or third choice. The original requirement for *Dracula* was Paul Muni, not Bela Lugosi. Clark Gable was thought of for Tarzan. Greta Garbo was asked to play Dorian Gray as a woman. Gloria Swanson's role in *Sunset Boulevard* was first offered to Mae West. Humphrey Bogart got *High Sierra* and *The Maltese Falcon* only because George Raft turned them down. Robert Montgomery, Fredric March, Carole Lombard and Myrna Loy all turned down *It Happened One Night* before Gable and Colbert accepted. Carole Lombard however benefited when Miriam Hopkins turned down *Twentieth Century*. Olivier's role as Maxim de Winter in *Rebecca* was first offered to William Powell and Ronald Colman. Doris Day was offered Mrs Robinson in *The Graduate*. Lana Turner gave way to Lee Remick on *Anatomy of a Murder*. Bette Davis would have been Scarlett O'Hara if she hadn't thought Errol Flynn was to play Rhett. George Jessel would have starred in *The Jazz Singer* if his demands had been less outrageous. Danny Thomas would have starred in *The Jolson Story* if he had agreed to have his nose shortened. Marlon Brando, Montgomery Clift and Paul Newman were all sought for *East of Eden* before James Dean got the role. Bette Davis played Margo in *All About Eve* only because Claudette Colbert gave it up. Ingrid Bergman was second choice to Vera Zorina for *For Whom the Bell Tolls*. Jack Nicholson took over from Rip Torn in *Easy Rider*, Marlon Brando from Montgomery Clift in *On The Waterfront*. Bette Davis turned down *Mildred Pierce* and Joan Crawford grabbed it. Olivia de Havilland, not Vivien Leigh, was first choice for *A Streetcar named Desire*. Ingrid Bergman won Oscars for *Gaslight*, first offered to Hedy Lamarr, and *Anastasia*, intended for Jennifer Jones; but she turned down *The Farmer's Daughter* and *To Each His Own*, which won Oscars for Loretta Young and Olivia de Havilland. If Grace Kelly hadn't become Princess of Monaco, she would have played in *Cat on a Hot Tin Roof* and *Designing Woman*, not Elizabeth Taylor or Lauren Bacall. William Holden got *Sunset Boulevard* after Montgomery Clift said no. Frank Sinatra walked out of *Carousel*: Gordon MacRae took over. Ginger Rogers replaced the ailing Judy Garland in *The Barkleys of Broadway*. Deborah Kerr got *From Here to Eternity* when Joan Crawford withdrew. Vivien Leigh thought herself too young to play the role in *Suddenly Last Summer* which went to Katharine Hepburn. Shirley Temple was wanted for Judy Garland's role in *The Wizard of Oz*; W. C. Fields was to have been the wizard, but argued over money. Fields himself only got Micawber in *David Copperfield* because Charles Laughton walked out after two days of filming.

CD-ROM
stands for Compact Disc – Read Only Memory. It is a computer-compatible means of storing a mass of information (up to 630 megabytes of data, enough to hold an entire encyclopedia) on one compact disc. It has been used as an alternative method to video cassette and laser disc for making films available at home, but has so far failed to gain a large consumer base and is likely to be superseded by DVD. As it can contain high-quality sound, animation and text, CD-ROM is now the preferred method of distributing computer programs, including games, many of which are derived from successful films. It has also been used as a method of publishing film guides: see Section 10.

cel.
The sheet of celluloid on which cartoon animators draw their foreground actions, one cel per film frame.

censorship.
Each country has found it necessary to apply its own rules for film producers; in Britain and America at least these rules were drawn up and enforced at the request of the industry itself. The British Board of Film Censors was founded in 1912. It has now changed its name to the British Board of Film Classification and covers material released on video-cassette as well as films. For many years films were classified as 'U' (for universal exhibition), 'A' (adults and accompanied children only) or (from 1933) 'H' (horrific; prohibited for persons under 16). In 1951, with the growing emphasis on sex, 'H' was replaced by 'X', which includes sex *and* horror. In the 60s 'X' came to mean over 18, 'AA' no one under 14, and 'A' was simply a warning to parents (children could still

get in unaccompanied). The current ratings system is 'U', suitable for children; 'PG', parental guidance advised; '12', suitable for persons over the age of 12; '15', only suitable for persons over the age of 15; and '18', only suitable for adults. In America, the Arbuckle scandal of 1921 precipitated the founding of the 'Hays Office' (named after its first paid president) by the Motion Picture Producers and Distributors of America. The first Production Code was issued in 1930 and has undergone constant amendment especially since *The Moon is Blue* 53, and very rapidly indeed since *Room at the Top* 59; in 1966 *Who's Afraid of Virginia Woolf?* almost swamped it completely and a revised, broadened code was issued. In 1968 this was replaced by a new rating system: 'X', 'R' (restricted), 'PG' (parental guidance advised) and 'G' (general audience). In the 90s the 'X' rating was replaced by an 'NC-17' rating. The independent and very strict Catholic Legion of Decency was founded in 1934 and issues its own classifications; it recently changed its name to the National Catholic Office for Motion Pictures.

Best books: Murray Schumach's *The Face on the Cutting Room Floor*, Doug McClelland's *The Unkindest Cuts*, Leonard J. Leff and Jerold L. Simmons's *The Dame in the Kimono: Hollywood's Censorship and the Production Code* (1990), and Tom Dewe Mathews' *Censored* (1994).

Central Casting.
The talent agency through whose doors passed many unknowns who stayed that way. In the 30s the Hollywood office had a sign above the door: DON'T TRY TO BECOME AN ACTOR. FOR EVERY ONE WE EMPLOY, WE TURN AWAY THOUSANDS.

chambara
is the term for a genre of samurai films, which could be described as the Japanese equivalent of westerns.

chanchada.
Term used to describe a genre of popular Brazilian films that mixes love stories with comedy and colourfully staged musical numbers, usually involving the samba. The form was created by Watson Macedo (1918-81), a Brazilian director, screenwriter and art director, in his musicals of the 40s and 50s, particularly *Carnaval No Fogo* 49. It includes parodies of Hollywood movies, such as Carlos Manga's *Matar ou Correr*, based on *High Noon*.

change-over.
Transition from one reel of film to another during projection. A reel originally lasted ten minutes but most 35mm projectors now take 20 or 30 minutes. Change-over cues are given in the form of dots which appear on the top right-hand corner of the screen a standard number of seconds before the end of the reel.

character actor.
Usually thought of as one who does not play romantic leads.

Cinecolor.
A two-colour process that was a cheaper alternative to Technicolor and so was used on many 'B' pictures in the 30s and 40s. The film had an orange-red emulsion on one side and a blue-green emulsion on the other.

cinéma vérité
A fashionable term of the 60s for what used to be called candid camera. A TV-style technique of recording life and people as they are, in the raw, using handheld cameras, natural sound and the minimum of rehearsal and editing. Chiefly applied to *Chronique d'un Eté* 61, *Le Joli Mai* 62, and the documentaries of Richard Leacock and the Maysles brothers.

CinemaScope
Wide-screen process copyrighted by Fox in 1953 and first used in *The Robe*; invented many years earlier by Henri Chrétien. Other companies either adopted it or produced their own trade name: WarnerScope, SuperScope, etc. Basically, the camera contains an anamorphic lens which 'squeezes' a wide picture on to a standard 35mm frame (which has a breadth/height ratio of 4:3 or 1.33:1). This, when projected through a complementary lens, gives a picture ratio on screen of 2.55:1 with stereophonic magnetic sound, or 2.35:1 with optical sound. Directors found the new shape awkward to compose for, the easiest way of handling it being to park the camera and let the actors move, a reversion to early silent methods. Although wide screens are said to have helped the box office, they have effectively prevented the full use of cinematic techniques. Oddly enough Fox in the mid-60s quietly dropped their own system and moved over to Panavision. The last word belongs to writer Nunnally Johnson, who, when asked how he would cope with the demands of CinemaScope, replied: 'Easy. What I'm going to do from now on is put the paper in my typewriter sideways.'

cinematographer.
Lighting cameraman or chief photographer.

Cinemobile.
A massive truck into which everything necessary for location shooting, including dressing rooms and toilets, can be packed.

Cinerama.
Extra-wide-screen system, invented by Fred Waller. Three projectors, electronically synchronized, were used to put the picture on the screen in three sections: this gave a disturbing wobble at the joins, though the range of vision was sometimes magnificently wide, as in the aerial shots and roller coaster sequence in *This is Cinerama* 52. After ten years of scenic but cinematically unremarkable travelogues (*Cinerama Holiday*, *Seven Wonders of the World*, *Search for Paradise*, etc.), the first story film in the process, *How the West Was Won*, was made in 1962. Shortly afterwards the three-camera system was abandoned in favour of 'single-lens Cinerama' which is virtually indistinguishable from CinemaScope except for the higher definition resulting from using wider film. 'Cinemiracle', a similar process, was short-lived. In 1997 the Cinerama Preservations Society was set up in the US to save the films made using the process. At that time, there were two cinemas in the world still capable of showing the films, one in the United States – the New Neon in Dayton, Ohio – and the other in England, at the National Museum of Photography, Film and Television in Bradford.

The released Cinerama features were:

This is Cinerama 52. Cinerama Holiday 55. Seven Wonders of the World 56. Search for Paradise 57. South Seas Adventure 58. The Wonderful World of the Brothers Grimm 62. How the West Was Won 62. It's a Mad Mad Mad Mad World (single lens) 63. Circus World 64. The Best of Cinerama 64. Battle of the Bulge 65. Grand Prix 66. Cinerama's Russian Adventure 66. Ice Station Zebra 68. Custer of the West 68. 2001: A Space Odyssey 68. Krakatoa – East of Java 69.

circuit.
A chain of cinemas under the same ownership, often playing the same release programme.

clapperboard.
A hinged board recording film details. At the beginning of each 'take' it is held before the camera for identification and then 'clapped' to make a starting point in the sound track. This point is then synchronized with the image of the closed board.

cliffhanger.
Trade name for a serial, especially an episode ending in an unresolved situation which keeps one in suspense till next time.

close-up.
Generally applied to a head-and-shoulders shot of a person or any close shot of an object. The first close-up is said to be that of Fred Ott sneezing in an Edison experimental film of 1900.
See: LONG SHOT.

co-feature.
A moderate-budget production designed (or fated) to form equal half of a double bill.

cokuloris.
A palette with random irregular holes, placed between lights and camera to prevent glare and give a better illusion of real-life light and shadow.

colour
prints of a primitive kind were made as long ago as 1898. During the next few years many films were hand-coloured by stencil, and two unsatisfactory processes. KinemaColor and Gaumont colour, were tried out. D. W. Griffith in *The Birth of a Nation* 14 developed the French practice of tinting scenes for dramatic effect: blue for night, orange for sunshine, etc. In 1918 red-and-green Technicolor was tried out along with half a dozen other processes. 1921: Prizmacolour was used for the British historical film *The Great Adventure*. 1923: de Mille used a colour sequence in *The Ten Commandments*. 1926: *The Black Pirate* was shot in two-colour Technicolor. 1932: first three-colour Technicolor film, Disney cartoon *Flowers and Trees* (AA). 1934: colour used in dramatic sequences of *La Cucaracha* and *The House of Rothschild*. 1935: first feature film entirely in three-strip colour, *Becky Sharp*. 1937: first British Technicolor feature, *Wings of the Morning*. 1939: two-colour Cinecolor, very cheap, became popular for low-budget westerns. 1942: Technicolor introduced monopack process, using one negative instead of three and making equipment less cumbersome and more flexible. 1948: Republic adopted Trucolor. 1949: Anscocolor, later to become Metrocolor, used on *The Man on the Eiffel Tower*. 1951: Supercinecolor (3 colours) adopted by Columbia in *Sword of Monte Cristo*. 1952: Eastmancolor used in *Royal Journey*; Warners adopted it as Warnercolor. 1954: Fox adopted De Luxe Color.

Today, with new colours springing up all the time, effectiveness seems to depend not on the trademark but on how well the film is shot, processed and printed.

colour sequences
in otherwise black-and-white movies were used at first experimentally (see above) but have also been employed for dramatic effect. Early examples include *The Ten Commandments* 23, *Ben Hur* 26, *The Wedding March* 28, *Chasing Rainbows* 30; many of the early sound musicals went into colour for their final number, and this went on as late as *Kid Millions* 35. *Victoria the Great* 37 had colour for the final 'Empress of India' scenes. *The Wizard of Oz* 39 had the Oz scenes in colour and the Kansas scenes in sepia. *Irene* 40 went into colour for the 'Alice Blue Gown' number – which made the second half of the film anti-climactic. *The Moon and Sixpence* 42 blazed into colour for the fire at the end ... and the same director, Albert Lewin, used a similar trick whenever the picture was shown in *The Picture of Dorian Gray* 44. *A Matter of Life and Death* 45 had earth in colour, heaven in a rather metallic monochrome. *Task Force* 49 went into colour for its final battle reels, most of which consisted of blown-up 16mm war footage. *The Secret Garden* 49 played the same trick as *The Wizard of Oz*. *The Solid Gold Cadillac* 56 had a few final feet of colour to show off the irrelevant car of the title. In 1958 *I Was a Teenage Frankenstein* revived the old dodge of colour for the final conflagration. In *Cleo de 5 à 7* only the ominous tarot cards were in colour; in *The House of Rothschild* only the court finale. In *If*, nobody was ever able to work out why black-and-white alternated with colour until someone guessed that the producers kept on running out of money as shooting progressed. And *Is Paris Burning?* 66 used colour for the climactic victory sequence, having been forced into black-and-white for the rest of the movie by the necessity of using old newsreel footage. In few of the above cases has reissue printing maintained the original intention: printing short sequences in colour is time-consuming.
See also: TINTING.

combined print.
One on which both sound and picture (always produced separately) have been 'married', i.e. a standard print as shown in cinemas.
See also: DOUBLE-HEADED PRINT.

composite print:
see COMBINED PRINT for which it is an alternative term.

continuity.
The development of cinematic narrative from beginning to end of a film. If continuity is good the audience will be carried smoothly from one scene to another without disturbing breaks or lapses of detail.

contrast.
The tone range in a print. Heavy contrast results in 'soot and whitewash', i.e. blurry blacks and burnt-out whites.

copyright.
British law relating to film copyright is notably vague, but in practice the owner of a film is protected against piracy for fifty years. In America copyright must be renewed in the 28th year, which has resulted in some fatal errors: e.g. MGM now have no control over *Till the Clouds Roll By* because they forgot to renew it, and Chaplin renewed only the version of *The Gold Rush* including his specially composed 40s music track.

coverage.
All the shots that comprise the photography from various angles of a particular scene in a film.

crane shot.
A high-angle shot in which the camera travels up, down or laterally while mounted on a travelling crane.

credits.
Titles at beginning or end of film (nowadays very often five minutes *after* the beginning) listing the names of the creative talents concerned.

creeping title.
One which moves up (or sometimes across) the screen at reading pace. Also known as *roller title*.

cross cutting.
Interlinking fragments of two or more separate sequences so that they appear to be taking place at the same time. One of the most famous examples is the climax of *Intolerance* which intertwines four stories; and in more modern times *The Godfather* crosscut a murder with a baptism.

cut.
Noun: abrupt transition from one shot to another, the first being instantaneously replaced by the second (as opposed to a wipe or a dissolve). Verb: to edit a film, or (during production) to stop the camera running on a scene.

cutaway.
An intervening shot allowing an editor to change the focus of action, e.g. clouds or a clock face.

cutting copy.
The first print assembled from the 'rushes'. When this is deemed satisfactory, the negative will be cut to match it, and release prints made.

cyclorama.
A smooth, curved giant screen at the back of the set, cunningly lit to give the impression of daylight.

dailies:
see RUSHES.

day for night,
which is often abbreviated to D/N, is the technique of shooting in daylight but making the result look as if it was shot at night. This can be achieved by using filters, underexposing the film, or by printing. Its advantage is that it is both easier and cheaper to film during daylight hours.

DeLuxe Color
is the Twentieth Century-Fox version of Eastmancolor but usually comes out decidedly blue.

deep focus.
Dramatic camera technique which brings both foreground and background objects into equal focus and clarity; notably used in *Citizen Kane* and *Hamlet*.

definitions
A selection, chosen for entertainment rather than instruction.

Agent: A guy who is sore because an actor gets ninety per cent of what he makes.

Casting: Deciding which of two faces the public is least tired of.

Disneyland: The biggest people trap ever built by a mouse.

Double feature: A show that enables you to sit through a picture you don't care to see, so you can see one you don't like. *-Henry Morgan*

Epic: The easiest kind of picture to make badly. *-Charlton Heston*

It: The indefinable something. *-Elinor Glyn*, creator of 'It'

Musicals: A series of catastrophes ending with a floor show. *-Oscar Levant*

Oomph: The sound a fat man makes when he bends over to tie his laces in a phone booth. *-Ann Sheridan*

Romanoff's Restaurant: A place where a man can take his wife and family and have a lovely seven-course meal for $3,400. *-George Jessel*

Starlet: Any woman under thirty not actively employed in a brothel.

Television: A medium, so called because it is neither rare nor well done. *-Ernie Kovacs*

digital distribution
is a method of distributing and projecting on a screen an image transmitted from elsewhere, either by cable or from a satellite. Technically, it is possible to provide instant distribution of a film simultaneously to hundreds of individual cinemas, by digitally transmitting a movie from one central computer. All that is holding back such developments at the moment is the very high cost of the necessary equipment. The long-term effect of such technology may be the disappearance of independent or art movies and the cinemas that show such films.

director.
Normally the most influential creator of a film, who may not only shoot scenes on the studio floor but also supervise script, casting, editing, etc., according to his standing. In more routine films these functions are separately controlled.

dissolve (or mix).
A change of scene accomplished by gradually exposing a second image over the first while fading the first away.

distributor (or renter).
A company which, for a percentage of the profits or a flat fee, undertakes to rent a film to exhibitors on the producing company's behalf. Originally major producers like MGM, Warner and Paramount distributed their own films exclusively, but with the rise of independent producers the situation has become much more fluid, with distributors bidding for the films they consider most likely to succeed at the box office and tying up successful producers to long-term contracts.

documentary
was not coined as a word until 1929, but several famous films, including Ponting's *With Scott to the Antarctic*, Lowell Thomas' *With Allenby in Palestine*, and Flaherty's *Nanook of the North*, had before 1921 brought an attitude to their reportage which made them more than mere travel films. In Britain during the 20s, H. Bruce Woolfe made a series of painstaking and still evocative reconstructions of the battles of World War I; while Cooper and Schoedsack went even further afield for the exciting material in *Grass* and *Chang*. 1928 brought Eisenstein's *The General Line*, a brilliant piece of farming propaganda, and Turin's *Turksib*, a showy account of the building of the Turko-Siberian railway. John Grierson, who invented the term 'documentary', made in 1929 a quiet little two-reeler about Britain's herring fleet, and called it *Drifters*; for the next ten years Britain's official and sponsored film units produced such brilliant results as *Shipyard*, *Coalface*, *Housing Problems*, *Song of Ceylon*, *North Sea* and *Night Mail*. In 1931 Vigo made his satirical documentary *A Propos de Nice*, and shortly afterwards Eisenstein was at work on his never-finished *Thunder over Mexico*, brilliant fragments of which survive as *Time in the Sun*. Travel films by explorers like the Martin Johnsons proliferated during the 30s; Flaherty spent two uncomfortable years off the Irish coast to make his *Man of Aran*, and later produced in India the semi-fictional *Elephant Boy*. Pare Lorenz produced cinematic poetry out of America's geographical problems in *The Plow that Broke the Plains* and *The River*.

World War II stimulated documentarists to new urgency and new techniques, brilliantly exemplified by Frank Capra's *Why We Fight* series for the US Signal Corps, turning unpleasant facts into breathtaking entertainment. With a predictably understated approach the British units produced a more sober but equally stirring series of reports on the war (*Western Approaches*, *Desert Victory*, *Target for Tonight*) and the home front (*Listen to Britain*, *Fires Were Started*, *A Diary for Timothy*), many of them directed by Britain's first documentary poet, Humphrey Jennings. The two countries combined resources to present a brilliant,

high-flying compilation film about the last year of war, *The True Glory*.

Since 1945 the use of documentary for advertising (often very subtly) and teaching has so proliferated that no simple line of development can be shown. Television has relentlessly explored and elaborated every technique of the pioneers, with special attention to 'action stills', compilation films, and hard-hitting popular journalist approaches such as NBC's White Paper series and Granada's *World in Action*. Entertainment films devised a popular blend of fact and fiction in such neo-classics as *Boomerang*, *The House on 92nd Street* and *Naked City*. At last documentary was accepted as an agreeable blend of instruction and pleasure; and in the changed environment Flaherty's lyrical *Louisiana Story* seemed slow and solemn.

Book: *Documentary, a History of the Non-fiction film*, by E. Barnouw, was published by OUP in 1974.

Dolby system.
A method of improving the sound quality of optical sound tracks by reducing background noise and hiss, first used for tape recordings. The Dolby stereo system creates four sound tracks.

dolly.
A trolley on which a camera unit can be soundlessly moved about during shooting: can usually be mounted on rails. A 'crab dolly' will move in any direction.

dope sheet.
A list of the contents of a piece of film, usually applied to newsreel libraries.

double exposure.
This occurs when two or more images are recorded on the same piece of film. Used for trick shots when two characters played by the same actor have to meet; also for dissolves, dream sequences, etc.

double take.
A form of comic reaction to a piece of news or situation. The subject at first fails to take it in, and after a few moments the penny drops with a start. Cary Grant and Oliver Hardy were among the prime exponents of the device, but the comedian who really brought it to the point of art was James Finlayson, who not only had the most pronounced reactions but added a slow withdrawal of the head, calling the entire effect a 'double take and fade away'.

double-headed print.
One in which sound and picture are recorded on separate pieces of film, usually at cutting copy stage or before OK is received to make combined negative.

drive-in.
A cinema in the open air, with loudspeakers relaying the sound track into your car.

dry ice.
A chemical substance which in water produces carbon dioxide gas and gives the effect of a low-hanging white ground mist, very effective in fantasy sequences.

DTS
stands for Digital Theatre Systems, a new sound recording and playback system launched by Universal Pictures and used first for *Jurassic Park* in 1993. The sound is stored on a compact disk which is synchronized with the film.

dubbing
has several shades of meaning within the general one of adding sound (effects, music, song, dialogue) to pictures already shot. It can mean re-recording; or replacing original language dialogue by a translation; or having someone else provide top notes for a star who can't sing. Here is an incomplete list of singers who provided uncredited voice-overs for actors who couldn't quite measure up.

Band Wagon India Adams for Cyd Charisse, *The Belle of New York* Anita Ellis for Vera-Ellen, *Brigadoon* Carole Richards for Cyd Charisse, *Call Me Madam* Carole Richards for Vera-Ellen, *Cover Girl* Nan Wynn for Rita Hayworth, *Down to Earth* Anita Ellis for Rita Hayworth, *Gigi* Betty Wand for Leslie Caron, *Gilda* Nan Wynn for Rita Hayworth, *The Great Ziegfeld* Allan Jones for Dennis Morgan,

Gypsy Lisa Kirk for Rosalind Russell, *Happy Go Lovely* Eve Boswell for Vera-Ellen, *The Helen Morgan Story* Gogi Grant for Ann Blyth, *Interrupted Melody* Eileen Farrell for Eleanor Parker, *The Jolson Story* Al Jolson for Larry Parks, *The King and I* Marni Nixon for Deborah Kerr, *Meet Me in St Louis* Arthur Freed for Leon Ames, *The Merry Widow* Trudy Erwin for Lana Turner, *My Fair Lady* Marni Nixon for Audrey Hepburn, *Orchestra Wives* Pat Friday for Lynn Bari, *Pal Joey* Jo Ann Greer for Rita Hayworth, *South Pacific* Muriel Smith for Juanita Hall, *South Pacific* Giorgio Tozzi for Rossano Brazzi, *Showboat* Annette Warren for Ava Gardner, *A Song Is Born* Jeri Sullivan for Virginia Mayo, *The Sound of Music* Bill Lee for Christopher Plummer, *State Fair* (1945) Lorraine Hogan for Jeanne Crain, *To Have and Have Not* (believe it or not) Andy Williams for Lauren Bacall, *Torch Song* India Adams for Joan Crawford, *West Side Story* Marni Nixon for Natalie Wood, *West Side Story* Jim Bryant for Richard Beymer, *West Side Story* Betty Wand for Rita Moreno, *White Christmas* Trudy Stevens for Vera-Ellen, *With a Song in My Heart* Jane Froman for Susan Hayward.

Dubbing of speaking parts is comparatively rare, but note Joan Barry for Anny Ondra in *Blackmail* and Angela Lansbury for Ingrid Thulin in *The Four Horsemen of the Apocalypse*.

dupe negative.
One made from the original negative (via a lavender print) to protect it from wear by producing too many copies.

duping (lavender) print.
A high-quality print made from the original negative. From it dupe negatives can be made.

DVD
stands for digital video disc, a compact disc format that is capable of containing on a single disc a feature film in several different formats and languages, with stereo sound. Movies released on DVD became generally available in 1996/97, though some film companies were initially reluctant to release their productions in this format because of the problems of piracy, and of films becoming available on disc before they reached cinemas, because of their staggered release around the world. These problems have been overcome, from the studios' point of view, by dividing the world into six areas and making DVD releases in one area incompatible with DVD players in another area. Despite DVD's improvement in picture quality and sound over videocassettes, sales of discs and players were initially lower than anticipated. It remains to be seen whether DVD will gain mass acceptance.

dynamic frame.
A concept invented in 1955 by an American, Glenn Alvey: the screen was maximum size, i.e. CinemaScope, but individual scenes were to be masked down to whatever ratio suited them best, e.g. rather narrow for a corridor. Only one experimental British film, a version of H. G. Wells' *The Hole in the Wall*, was made in dynamic frame, which proved distracting and has in any case been overtaken by multiscreen experiments of the 60s.

edge numbers.
Serial numbers printed along the edge of all film material to assist identification when re-ordering sections.

editor.
Technician who assembles final print of film from various scenes and tracks available; works closely under director's control except in routine pictures. Conventional editing involved cutting scenes of the film in sequence to produce first a rough cut, and then the final result. Technical developments have led to the use of digital or non-linear editing with computer-based systems such as the AVID MEDIA COMPOSER and LIGHTWORKS.

8mm.
A substandard gauge introduced in 1932 and used mostly by amateurs, though from the early 60s, often with sounded recorded on an added magnetic strip, it also found use in schools and similar institutions. From the mid-60s, Super-8 was introduced which allowed a larger area to be used for film and provided better soundtrack reproduction. Both have now been superseded by the advent of cam-corders using video-cassettes or

digital means for recording, and providing an instant playback, of sound and images.

electronovision.
A much-touted form of transfer from videotape to film, thought likely to save money in putting great stage performances on to the big screen.

Unfortunately it proved technically and aesthetically unacceptable, and the two features shot in it in 1965 are only interesting if one can ignore the technical shortcomings. They are *Harlow* with Carol Lynley and *Hamlet* with Richard Burton.

Elektrotachyscope.
A device for displaying motion pictures, patented in 1887 by the Polish inventor Ottomar Anschutz, who also took the photographs of the movement of people and animals it showed.

epic film.
Term used to describe a film directed and designed on a spectacular scale, focusing on the actions of a great hero and featuring a cast of thousands. The style has fallen out of favour in recent times, mainly due to the fiasco of *Cleopatra* 63 and the increasing cost of elaborate sets and large casts, so that the continuing appetite for spectacle is now supplied by movies that concentrate on violent action, such as car chases and crashes, and special effects. Favourite settings for epic films have included Rome (*Ben Hur*, *Spartacus* and dozens of movies from Italian directors) and Biblical times, in the productions of Cecil B. De Mille. More modern history featured in D. W. Griffith's *Birth of a Nation* 15 and in the work of the last master of the epic form, David Lean's, *Lawrence of Arabia* 62 and *Dr Zhivago* 65.

Books: 1984, *The Epic Film* by Derek Elley. 1992, *Epic Films: Casts, Credits and Commentary on over 250 Historical Spectacle Movies* by Gary A. Smith.

establishing shot.
Opening shot of sequence, showing location of scene or juxtaposition of characters in action to follow.

exchange.
An American enterprise: a middleman business which for a commission deals with the small exhibitors of an area on behalf of major renters.

exploitation.
A trade word covering all phases of publicity, public relations and promotion.

exploitation film.
A term used to describe low-budget movies of a sensational kind that either focus on some headline-making social phenomenon or attempt to cash in on a current box-office success. Sex, horror and fantasy are the predominant subject matters. Sometimes the title or the poster comes first, and the movie is made to match it. Such films flourished from the early 60s when drive-in cinemas provided double-bills and there was a new youthful audience for rock 'n' roll and biker movies. One of the most successful companies in the field was AIP, run by Samuel Arkoff and Jack Nicholson. The most notable exponent of the form has been producer and director Roger Corman, who began by supplying films for AIP to distribute before setting up his own production companies. Many of today's most successful directors, writers and cinematographers began by making films for Corman. That may, in part, be the reason why in recent years Hollywood studios have been turning out what are in effect big-budget exploitation movies, such as *Terminator 2*, and have also followed the exploitation movie-makers' habit of recycling their successes, as witness the seemingly endless succession of sequels to *A Nightmare on Elm Street*, *Halloween*, etc. As the subject matter of exploitation movies is now part of mainstream cinema, and there are fewer cinemas in which to show such movies, the likelihood is that the day of the exploitation film is nearly over. Its main market is now video, with films bypassing the cinema entirely, or being given very restricted releases in the hope of garnering publicity for their video-release. It is possible, however, that the growth in soft-core pornography for satellite and cable TV will provide its practitioners with a continuing market.

expressionism.

A term indicating the fullest utilization of cinematic resources to give dramatic larger-than-life effect, as in *Citizen Kane* or, in a different way, *The Cabinet of Dr Caligari*. In a secondary sense it also allows the fullest expression to be given, by the above means, to states of emotion.

exterior.

A shot taken in normal lighting outside the studio.

extra.

A crowd player with no lines to speak.

fade in.

Gradual emergence of a scene from blackness to full definition; opposite of *fade out*.

FAMU

stands for Film Faculty of the Academy of Music and Drama, the Prague Film School that was established in 1947 and where the majority of Czech and Slovak film-makers trained. Graduates of the school include Agnieszka HOLLAND, Vojtech JASNY and Emir KUSTURICA.

fast motion.

see ACCELERATED MOTION.

feature film.

Normally accepted to mean a (fictional) entertainment film of more than 3000 feet in length (approx. 34 minutes). Anything less than this is technically a 'short'. *NB*: In journalism and television a 'feature' usually means a *non-fiction* article or documentary.

featured players.

Those next in importance to the stars: usually billed after the title.

Federation of Film Societies.

British organization which issues information and arranges screening for film societies; also publishes magazine *Film*.

festivals.

Since World War II a great many cities round the world have derived excellent publicity from annual film festivals. Producers, distributors and actors in search of accolades now diligently trek each year to Cannes, Venice, Berlin, Mar del Plata, Cork, Edinburgh, Karlovy Vary, San Sebastian, Moscow, etc., while London and New York offer résumés in October.

F.I.D.O.

The Film Industry Defence Organization, a body formed by British renters and exhibitors to prevent old feature films being sold to television. It collapsed in 1964 after five years during which no renter dared sell his product for fear of reprisals.

film noir.

A French phrase meaning *dark film*. It was probably first applied to the moody, downbeat character melodramas of the late 30s, such as *Quai des Brumes* and *Le Jour se Lève*, but it soon came to be thought of as applying chiefly to the American urban crime film of the 40s, for instance *Double Indemnity*, *Laura*, *Scarlet Street* (based on a French original) and the versions of Raymond Chandler novels.

Books: 1980 (revised 1988), *Film Noir: An Encyclopedic Reference Guide*, edited by Alain Silver and Elizabeth Ward. 1984, *Dark City: The Film Noir* by Spencer Selby.

Films include:

The Maltese Falcon 41. Johnny Eager 42. The Glass Key 42. Double Indemnity 44. Laura 44. Murder, My Sweet/Farewell My Lovely 44. Ministry of Fear 44. Mildred Pierce 45. Scarlet Street 45. Gilda 46. The Big Sleep 46. The Blue Dahlia 46. The Chase 46. Notorious 46. The Postman Always Rings Twice 46. Crossfire 47. Lady in the Lake 47. He Walked by Night 48. The Big Clock 48. Key Largo 48. The Naked City 48. White Heat 49. Follow Me Quietly 49. The Asphalt Jungle 50. D.O.A. 50. Gun Crazy 50. Ace in the Hole 51. M 51. The Prowler 51. Beware, My Lovely 52. Clash by Night 52. Angel Face 53. The Big Heat 53. The Hitch-Hiker 53. Drive a Crooked Road 54. Witness to Murder 54. The Big Knife 55. Kiss Me Deadly 55. The Killing 56. Sweet Smell of Success 57. Touch of Evil 58. The Crimson Kimono 59. Odds against Tomorrow 59. Underworld USA 61. Cape Fear 62. The

Manchurian Candidate 62. The Servant 63. Marlowe 69. The Friends of Eddie Coyle 73. Chinatown 74. Farewell My Lovely 75. Taxi Driver 76. The Driver 78. Body Heat 81. The Postman Always Rings Twice 81. Blood Simple 84. Backfire 88. Miller's Crossing 90. The Grifters 90. The Two Jakes 90. Cape Fear 91. The Last Seduction 94.

film society.

A club formed to show high-quality revivals and new films not normally found in public cinemas.

fine grain print.

One of high quality stock (avoiding the coarseness of silver salt deposit); used for making dupe negatives.

first dollar-gross

is a contractual agreement in which the participants receive a percentage of a film's gross receipts without any deductions for distribution fees or production costs. It was once limited to a few top stars, but these days there are also producers, directors and writers who command it. As a result, studios complain that they can make little profit on films involving several such talents, and as a result more films will be made featuring no more than one star name. According to the studios, the system also means that producers and directors do not care whether they bring a movie in on budget as their payment depends not on the film's profitability but on box-office receipts. Around 15 producers, including Arnold KOPELSON, Jerry Bruckheimer, Brian GRAZIER and Scott RUDIN, directors such as Steven SPIELBERG, Chris Columbus and Sydney POLLACK, and writers such as Michael CRICHTON and Tom CLANCY are among those who can command first dollar-gross.

flashback.

A break in chronological narrative during which we are shown events of past time which bear on the present situation. The device is as old as the cinema: you could say that *Intolerance* was composed of four flashbacks. As applied to more commonplace yarns, however, with the flashback narrated by one of the story's leading characters, the convention soared into popularity in the 30s until by 1945 or so a film looked very dated indeed if it was not told in retrospect. In the 50s flashbacks fell into absolute disuse, but are now creeping back into fashion again. Some notable uses are:

The Power and the Glory 33, which was advertised as being in 'Narratage' because Ralph Morgan spoke a commentary over the action. *Bride of Frankenstein* 35, which was narrated by Elsa Lanchester as Mary Shelley; the gag was that she also played the monster's mate. *The Great McGinty* 40, in which the flashback construction revealed the somewhat corrupt leading figures finally as penniless, thus mollifying the Hays Office. *Rebecca* 40, in which the introductory narrative, while revealing that Manderley was to go up in flames, also comforted in the knowledge that the hero and heroine would be saved. *Citizen Kane* 41, the complex structure of which was so influential that a whole host of pictures followed in which we tried to get at the truth about a character already dead, by questioning those who knew him: cf. *The Killers*, *The Rake's Progress*, *The Moon and Sixpence*, *The Bridge of San Luis Rey*, *The Woman in Question*, *Letter from an Unknown Woman*, *Rashomon*, *The Great Man*, even *Doctor Zhivago*. *Hold Back the Dawn* 41, in which Charles Boyer as a penniless refugee visited Paramount Studios and sold his story to Mitchell Leisen. *The Mummy's Hand* 41, in which the ten-minute chunk telling how the mummy came to be buried alive was lifted straight from the 1932 film *The Mummy*. (Such economies have become commonplace.) *Roxie Hart* 42, in which George Montgomery told a twenty-year-old tale about a notorious lady who at the end of the film was revealed as the mother of his large family. *Ruthless* 48, a tortuous Zachary Scott melodrama, reviewed as follows by the British critic C. A. Lejeune:

Beginning pictures at the end
Is, I'm afraid, a modern trend;
But I'd find *Ruthless* much more winning
If it could end at the beginning.

Road to Utopia 45, in which Hope and Lamour appeared as old folks telling the story; as a pay-off their 'son' appeared, looking just like Crosby, and Hope told the audience: 'We adopted him.' *Passage to Marseilles* 44, a complex melodrama ranging

from Devil's Island to war-torn Britain; it has flashbacks within flashbacks *within flashbacks*. In *Dead of Night* 45, all the characters told supernatural experiences to a psychiatrist, who was then murdered by one of them; the murderer then woke up with no recollection of his nightmare, and proceeded to meet all the other characters again as though for the first time, being caught in an endless series of recurring dreams. *Enchantment* 47, and later *Death of a Salesman* 52, and many films up to *I Was Happy Here* 66, in which characters walk straight out of the present into the past, dispensing with the boring 'I remember' bit. *Edward My Son* 49 and *Teahouse of the August Moon* 56, in which characters step out of the play to tell the story to the audience. *Dead Reckoning* 47, in which Humphrey Bogart confesses the entire plot to a priest. *Kind Hearts and Coronets* 49, in which the story springs from the memoirs of a murderer being written on the night before his execution. *Sunset Boulevard* 50, in which the story is told by the dead hero. *An Inspector Calls* 54, in which a supernatural figure visits a family to make them remember their harsh treatment of a girl who has committed suicide. *Repeat Performance* 47, in which a desperate husband relives the events of the year, leading up to his predicament, and gets a chance to change the outcome. *A Woman's Face* 41, in which the story was based on the recollections of eight courtroom witnesses. *The Locket* and *Lust for Gold*, in which complex flashbacks framed and divided the action.

If the format is to catch on again it will have to be more deftly used than in two 60s films: *Ride Beyond Vengeance*, with its completely irrelevant framing story about a census-taking, and *Lady L*, in which the framing story with the characters as old folks is only marginally less inept than the basic one. Two big-scale musicals, *Star!* and *Funny Girl*, have flashbacks with style but little purpose, and *Little Big Man* barely used its framework except to show that Dustin Hoffman can play a 121-year-old.

fleapit.

An affectionate British term for the kind of tatty little cinema in which, it was sometimes alleged, the management loaned a hammer with each ticket.

floor effects

is the term used to describe special effects that occur live, in-camera, during filming rather than being added later; it covers such effects as explosions, bullet impacts, and many types of mechanical effect.

Foley artist.

A sound effects specialist, named after Jack Foley, who is credited for creating the techniques for adding post-production sound effects to enhance the action on the screen.

footage.

Length of a film expressed in feet.

foyer cards.

Elaborate, oversized stills with coloured borders bearing credits, all designed for lobby display. A collection of them by John Kobal was published in 1983: it bore the wince-making title *Foyer Pleasure*.

frame.

A single picture on a strip of film. At normal sound projection speed, 24 frames are shown each second.

franchise.

A term used to describe a film that provides opportunities for more of the same: that lends itself to sequels or features a character who can appear in several more films, often virtually indistinguishable from the original. There are low-rent franchises, such as *Nightmare on Elm Street* or *Friday the 13th*, and big-budget ones such as *James Bond*, *Superman*, *Batman* and *Lethal Weapon*. Such series have been around since the early days of films, beginning with serials like *The Perils of Pauline* and such series as *Tarzan*, but they used to be largely confined to the low-budget end of film-making; these days creating a franchise seems to be the main preoccupation of mainstream Hollywood producers and directors. Apart from the films themselves, franchises also lend themselves to MERCHANDISING. The term derives from business, and results from films being seen as the artistic equivalent of fast food.

freeze frame.

A printing device whereby the action appears to 'freeze' into a still, this being accomplished by printing one frame many times.

frost

on movie windows is usually produced from a mixture of Epsom salts and stale beer.

Fujicolor.

Japanese colour film first used in 1955. Fuji's ultra-high-speed colour negative film was given an Academy Award of Merit in 1981, and was used to film the international success *Das Boot*, directed by Wolfgang Petersen.

gaffer.

The chief electrician on a film, responsible for operating the lights under the instructions of the cinematographer or director of photography.

gaffer tape.

is a heavy-duty adhesive tape, backed with canvas, which is used to secure objects on film sets.

genny

is a mobile electric generator used to supply power while working on location.

ghosting.

Another word for dubbing, especially when a star apparently singing is actually miming to the voice of the real artist.
See also: DUBBING.

glass shot.

Usually a scenic shot in which part of the background is actually painted on a glass slide held in front of the camera and carefully blended with the action. In this way castles, towns, etc. may be shown on a location where none exist, without the expense of building them.

grading:

the laboratory process of matching the density and brightness of each shot to the next.

grip.

A technician who builds or arranges the film set; a specialized labourer. The chief grip on a picture is usually credited as 'Key Grip'.
Book: 1997, *Grip Book: How to Become a Motion Picture Film Technician* by Michael G. and Sabrina Uva.

Hale's Tours.

In 1902 at the St Louis Exposition, George C. Hale, ex-chief of the Kansas City Fire Department, had the bright idea of shooting a film from the back of a moving train and screening the result in a small theatre decorated like an observation car. During the screening bells clanged, train whistles sounded, and the 'coach' rocked slightly. The idea was so successful that it toured for several years in the United States.

hard ticket.

A phrase used in the 60s to describe film exhibition of the type once called 'road show': separate performances, reserved seats, long runs and high prices.

HDTV,

High Definition Television, the latest development in television technology, which provides a better picture by increasing the resolution to 1,125 lines and having a screen with a similar ratio to the cinema. Future development may be held up by the failure of interested parties to agree on a standard; it seems likely that Europe will set a standard that differs from America and Japan in order to protect European manufacturers of electronic equipment. Japan began HDTV broadcasts in 1991, using an analog system. In the long term, as computers grow in importance in entertainment, it is more likely that the HDTV of the future will be digital. It has already attracted the attention of film-makers: Peter Greenaway used HDTV editing facilities to create the rich imagery of *Prospero's Books* 91, his version of Shakespeare's *The Tempest*, and Wim Wenders used it for his *Until the End of the World/ Bis ans Ende der Welt* 92.

hokum.

A word allegedly derived from an Indian word for a stodgy food, it came to mean pure entertainment of a routine kind, usually involving fast action. From it came the adjective 'hokey'. It was not always applied in the pejorative sense: many of most people's favourite films are basically hokum, in that they do not advance the art, but they may show it at its professional best.

The Hollywood Ten.
Alvah Bessie, Herbert Biberman, Lester Cole, Edward Dmytryk, Ring Lardner Jnr, John Howard Lawson, Albert Maltz, Sam Ornitz, Adrian Scott and Dalton Trumbo were the famous band of writers, producers and directors who in 1947 refused to tell the Unamerican Activities Committee whether or not they were communists. All served short prison sentences and had difficulty getting work in Hollywood for several years.

Imax.
A large-screen technology, developed in Canada, that provides an image three times bigger than 70mm systems, and which uses six magnetic soundtracks to drive loudspeakers surrounding its audience. So far there are some 80 cinemas in the world capable of utilizing the system. There is one in Britain, at the National Museum of Photography, Film and Television in Bradford, with a screen 52 x 64 feet, and the British Film Institute plans to open another in London in the near future. Imax was first shown at Expo '70 in Japan, but attracted wider interest following the release in 1992 of a concert film, *At the Max*, directed by Julien Temple and featuring the rock band The Rolling Stones. The system's name is derived from a combination of the words Image and Maximum.

impressionism.
Generally understood to mean contriving an effect or making a point by building up a sequence from short disconnected shots or scenes.

independent film
is the term applied to a film made outside the Hollywood studio system. It can be used of uncommercial films intended for a specialized audience, or of films made by talent that wishes to keep creative control of the project, though many such productions do tend to involve the financial participation of studio-distributors, so that the term is often used indiscriminately to describe small-scale movies. With the breakdown of the old studio system in the late 40s, following the US Supreme Court decision that forced the major studios to get rid of their cinema chains, there has been a plethora of independent producers, though many work within the system. Some directors, such as Hal HARTLEY, Jim JARMUSCH and Shane MEADOWS, have preferred to work outside the mainstream, and others have done so when major studios have rejected them: Orson Welles raised the finance for his later films, and, in 1997, Robert Duvall used his own money to direct and star in *The Apostle* after many years of trying to obtain studio backing.

Independent Frame
was a technique devised in the mid-40s for the Rank Organization by art director David RAWNSLEY to save costs on location shooting by using back and front projection and a stylized, mass production approach to film-making. Rawnsley believed that it would also increase production and free directors' imaginations from literal representations. It was championed by Michael POWELL, but in practice its factory methods proved constricting, and involved working out a production in every detail, including camera placements, before filming began. Hailed by *Kinematograph Weekly* as 'one of the greatest technical advances since the advent of commercial colour photography', it was abandoned when films made by the method were critical and box-office failures. They included *Warning to Wantons* 49, *Floodtide* 49, *Stop Press Girl* 49, and *Poet's Pub* 49.

independent producer.
One not employed by a studio or distributor, who raises his own finance and makes his own deals. For many years independent productions tended to lack big studio expertise, and Tallulah Bankhead is said to have remarked, after viewing one of them, 'I don't see what that producer has got to be so independent about.' Since the breakup of the big studios in the 50s, however, most productions have been 'independent', and as Billy Wilder remarked, 'You now spend eighty per cent of your time making deals and only twenty per cent making pictures.'

insert shot.
One inserted into a dramatic scene, usually for the purpose of giving the audience a closer look at what the character on screen is seeing, e.g. a letter or a newspaper headline.

interactive films
are a goal towards which many seem to be working, though few agree on what is exactly meant by the term. At the moment, it is used to describe computer games on CD-ROM which incorporate filmed sequences using actors, who usually do little more than set the scene or tell the player what to do next. Interaction by the player is usually limited to choosing between one of several alternative actions. In the future, as technology progresses, it may be possible for an audience to interact more directly with what is happening, by altering the outcome of the story to suit its own tastes or by taking over the role of director to give instructions to the participants.

iris.
An adjustable diaphragm in the camera which opens or closes from black like an expanding or contracting circle, giving a similar effect on the screen. So called because it resembles the iris of the human eye.

jump-cutting.
Moving abruptly from one scene to another to make a dramatic point, e.g. from cause to effect.

Kaiju eiga
is the term used by the Japanese to describe its genre of monster movies, of which the best known are the GODZILLA series.

Kinematograph Renters' Society (KRS).
This British organization was founded by film distributors in 1915 for their own protection and collective bargaining power, chiefly against exhibitors.

Kinescope.
American term for what the British call a telerecording, i.e. a live or tape show transferred for convenience on to tape. The technical quality is seldom satisfactory, and the process was gradually discontinued in favour of electronic tape conversion from one line standard to another.

Kinetoscope.
An early film viewing apparatus (1893) in which a continuous loop of film could be viewed by one person only.

lavender print.
A high-quality fine-grain master positive film, struck from the original negative for the purpose of making duplicates, so called because the emulsion was coated with a lavender-tinted base to reduce halation and scatter in the image.

leader.
Length of blank film joined to the beginning of a reel for lacing up in projector. 'Academy' leaders give a numbered countdown to the start of action.

library shot:
see STOCK SHOT.

Lightwave 3D
is a relatively low-cost computer graphics program, originally developed by NewTek for the Amiga computer in conjunction with the Video Toaster hardware, which is used to create animation and special effects in TV programmes and movies. It has been used in *Men in Black* (for the opening sequence of the dragonfly), *Contact*, *The Jackal*, *Titanic*, *The Fifth Element*, *Mortal Kombat II*, *Spawn*, and *Tomorrow Never Dies*.

Lightworks
is a computer-based digital editing system, one of the two, with AVID MEDIA COMPOSER, that is rapidly becoming the preferred method of editing film. It was first used in 1992 by David Brenner and Sally MENKE on *Heaven and Earth*, directed by Oliver STONE.

The Lion's Share,
by Bosley Crowther. A lively history of the Metro-Goldwyn-Mayer company, written in 1957 by the critic of the *New York Times*.

location.
A shooting site away from the studio, not encouraged in the days of the moguls, but considered essential in the cause of realism as soon as the studio system broke up.

long shot.
One taken from a distance, usually to establish a scene or a situation but sometimes for dramatic effect. Opposite of close-up.

looping
is the term used to describe the process of dubbing dialogue onto the soundtrack of a film, usually because the original sound was not of sufficiently good quality, owing to extraneous noises caused by shooting on location. The scene to be dubbed is contained on a short loop of film joined together so that it can be projected continuously in order that the actors can match exactly their speaking of the new dialogue with the old. The method is also used for adding dialogue in another language to a foreign film. The process is also known as DUBBING, POST-SYNCHRONIZATION or post-synching and, more recently, as ADR, a recent technical improvement that does away with the need for actual looping.

losing the light.
What happens during outdoor shooting when the natural light of the sun is obscured and filming comes to a stop.

lot.
A term used to cover all areas of a studio where filming takes place, and also where sets are built and stored.

m and e track.
A sound track giving music and effects but not dialogue, necessary in dubbing stages.

Macguffin
(aka McGuffin).
Term invented by writer Angus MacPhail, and associated with the films of Alfred HITCHCOCK, to describe a plot device of little intrinsic interest, such as stolen papers, that triggers the action.

make-up.
A general term for the cosmetic application to the body of materials intended to enhance or change the appearance, from glamorization to the creation of monsters.

Manga.
Japanese term for comics, which translates as 'irresponsible pictures'. The word has come to be applied in the West to Japanese animated films owing to the release of such films on the Manga video label and the appearance of fan magazines devoted to the style. Many of the best-selling comic books have been turned into animated films, which are more properly known as ANIME.

mask.
A technical device for blocking out part of the image. *Masking* is the black cloth which surrounds the actual cinema screen: these days it has to be electrically adjustable to encompass the various screen sizes.

matt or matte.
A technique (sometimes known as *travelling matt*) for blending actors in the studio with location or trick scenes. The actor is photographed against a non-reflective background (e.g. black velvet) and a high-contrast negative of this image is combined with the desired background. Thus men can move among animated monsters, and ghosts can slowly disappear.

medium shot.
One taking in the full body of the actor, not so close as a close-up, not so far off as a long shot.

merchandising.
The means of exploiting films and personalities through souvenirs, toys and other consumable items has always brought in considerable revenue to canny film-makers, often more than the film itself. Film editions of novels, illustrated with stills from the movie, and novelizations of film scripts were being published from the early 20s onwards, but Walt Disney was among the first to realize the commercial possibilities of exploiting his animated characters, with such goods as a Mickey Mouse

watch, a trend culminating in the opening of an international chain of shops selling Disney goods from the mid-80s onwards. Television accelerated the process, with such personalities as Hopalong Cassidy appearing on everything from lunch boxes to pillow cases. Disney's shops were followed in the 90s by Warner opening a store merchandising Bugs Bunny and other cartoon heroes. But it is only in comparatively recent times that films have been primarily designed to sell a range of toys or to advertise particular products. Product placement, in which cameras linger on a particular range of footwear or obtrusively feature a certain type of soft drink, has become a means of gaining as much income as possible from a film. It was no accident that E.T. munched on M&Ms rather than, say, jelly-babies. E.T. still remains one of the most successful merchandising operations – in Britain alone, the wholesaler of E.T. merchandise guaranteed sales of £1 million – together with the *Star Wars* movies, which shifted around $2 billion of toys and other paraphernalia now gathering dust in cupboards. Occasionally, merchandisers do get caught short. The makers of *Forrest Gump* did not believe that the film lent itself to merchandising opportunities. Once it was a runaway hit in America, they changed their minds and began producing Forrest Gump goods, including a book of Gump sayings. In 1995, the toy company Mattel sold $450m of Disney products. The amount of money involved was revealed in a proposed deal in 1996 between the fast-food chain McDonald's and Disney, in which McDonald's would pay Disney $100m a year for the rights to 14 to 17 film and television features, a sponsorship of Disney's projected Animal Kingdom theme park, and video promotions. It was estimated that the cost of the deal, including promotional advertising, would amount to $2 billion over a 10-year period.

The Method
is a style of acting derived initially from the teachings and writings of the Russian actor and director Konstantin Stanislavsky, as refracted through the Actors' Studio in New York, which was co-founded by director Elia KAZAN and later dominated by the teaching of Lee STRASBERG. See also: The ACTORS' STUDIO.

moguls.
The name given half-affectionately to the men who ran Hollywood in the golden days of the studios: Mayer, Thalberg, Selznick, Goldwyn, Warner, Zanuck, Zukor, Cohn, etc. The best capsule guide to them is Philip French's *The Movie Moguls* (1970).

montage.
In the most general sense, the whole art of editing or assembling scenes into the finished film. Specifically, 'a montage' is understood as an impressionistic sequence of short dissolve-shots either bridging a time gap, setting a situation or showing the background to the main story. Classic montages which come to mind are in *The Battleship Potemkin*, *The Roaring Twenties* and *Citizen Kane*.

MOS
Mysterious Hollywood script abbreviation indicating a silent shot. Allegedly it derived from the early 30s, when one of the many immigrant German directors called for a scene 'mit out sound'.

motion capture
is a method of capturing in real time the actual movements of a person and transferring them to a computer-generated character, from a rabbit to Godzilla.

Motion Picture Alliance for the Preservation of American Ideals
was an organization set up in 1943 in opposition to the unionization of the film industry and the promulgation of left-wing opinions. Its founding members included directors Sam WOOD, Clarence Brown and King VIDOR, actors Clark GABLE, Gary COOPER, Adolphe MENJOU, Charles COBURN, Barbara STANWYCK, Robert TAYLOR and Ward BOND, and writers Hedda HOPPER and Ayn RAND, who wrote for it *A Screen Guide for Americans*. Later members included Irene DUNNE and Ginger ROGERS, and it had the support of the anti-union Walt DISNEY and the newspaper tycoon William Randolph HEARST. Its statement of principles was: 'we resent the growing impression that this industry is made up of, and

dominated, by communists, radicals and crackpots'. The Alliance asked for a congressional investigation of communism in Hollywood and also invited HUAC (the House Un-American Activities Committee) to come to Hollywood, which resulted in the interrogation of many film-makers, the imprisonment of what became known as The HOLLYWOOD TEN, and the blacklisting by the studios of those suspected of left-wing opinions. It had lost all influence and ceased to exist by the mid-50s.

Motion Picture Association of America
A trade guild in which distributors meet to set tariffs and deal with complaints, also set a censorship code.

Moviola.
A portable editing machine which enables the user to run film backwards and forwards at various speeds and to examine it frame by frame while viewing it on a small screen.

MOW.
Acronym for a movie made for television, deriving from ABC's Movie of the Week, consisting of 90-minute dramas, which ran from 1968 to 1975. The first TV movie was probably *See How They Run*, made by Universal TV and aired on NBC in October 1964, directed by David Lowell Rich and starring John Forsythe, Leslie Nielsen, George Kennedy, Franchot Tone and Jane Wyatt. Some earlier TV dramas from the 50s, when television was live, were later remade as films, the most notable example being *Marty*.

MPEG
stands for the Motion Picture Experts Group and is a standard for the digital compression of images. The method compares and saves only the changes between one frame of a film or animation and another, thus enabling 72 minutes of film to be recorded on a five-inch compact disk. A refinement of the system, MPEG II, is being prepared.

multiplane.
A word introduced by Walt Disney to explain his new animation process for *The Old Mill* 37. Instead of building up a drawing by laying 'cells' directly on top of each other, a slight illusion of depth was obtained by leaving space between the celluloid images of foreground, background, principal figure, etc. Special Academy Award 1938.

mute print.
One with only the picture, no sound track.

National Film Archive.
A government-financed museum of films of artistic and historical value. Operated by the British Film Institute.

The National Film Board of Canada
was set up in 1939, with John Grierson at its head, to show Canada's face to the world. Many excellent documentaries ensued, not to mention the brilliant animation films of Norman McLaren, but by the end of the 60s the Board's fortunes were at a lower ebb and its reputation declined.

The National Film Finance Corporation
was founded in 1949 to provide loans for film production, but began to withdraw its facilities in the early 70s, at a time when financial encouragement had never been more needed for British production.

The National Film Theatre
on London's South Bank is an extension of the British Film Institute; founded in 1951, it runs a daily repertory in three theatres of films of all nationalities and types.

neo-realism
is a term mainly applied to the Italian post-war films which seemed to present a fresh and vivid kind of social realism. The essentials were real locations and at least a proportion of amateur actors. The most famous neo-realist film is *Bicycle Thieves*.

'new wave'/'nouvelle vague'.
Term used (by themselves) for a group of new, exploring young French directors towards the end of the 50s: François Truffaut, Jean-Luc Godard, Louis Malle, Alain Resnais, etc. As their talents

were widely divergent, the term meant very little. It was coined by Françoise Giroud.

newsreels
were part of the very earliest cinema programme, and the nine-minute round up of topical events filmed by roving cameramen was a feature of programmes in cinemas throughout the world until the mid-60s, when it was clear that the newsreel had been replaced by television. Most newsreel companies have looked after their libraries, and the result is a vivid history of the twentieth century, frequently plundered by producers of compilation films.

nickelodeon.
A humorous term applied to early American cinemas once they had become slightly grander than the converted stores which were used for the purpose at the turn of the century.

The Nine Old Men
was the name Walt Disney gave to his most trusted animators, who had joined the studio by the mid-30s, before it began feature film production. They were: Les Clark, Marc Davis, Ollie Johnson, Milt Kahl, Ward Kimball, Eric Larson, John Lounsbery, Wolfgang Reitherman, Frank Thomas.

nitrate.
Until 1950 film stock had a nitrate base, which helped give a splendid sheen, but was very inflammable. The change was made to safety stock, which burns much more slowly, but black-and-white films at least never looked so good again.

non-theatrical.
A descriptive adjective usually applied to film showings at which there is no paid admission on entrance, e.g. schools, clubs, etc. Some distributors apply the term to all 16mm showings.

opticals.
A general term indicating all the visual tricks such as wipes, dissolves, invisibility, mattes, etc., which involve laboratory work.

original version.
In European countries, this indicates a foreign language film which is sub-titled and not dubbed.

'Oscar'.
An affectionate name given to the Academy Award statuette; reputedly because when the figure was first struck in 1927 a secretary said: 'It reminds me of my Uncle Oscar.'

pan.
A shot in which the camera rotates horizontally. Also used as a verb.

Panavision.
A wide-screen system which outdistanced CinemaScope because of its improved anamorphic lens. Super-Panavision and Panavision 70 are 'road show' processes involving projection on wide film: in the first case the film is shot on 65mm, in the second blown up after photography. Great confusion was caused in the 70s by the company insisting on the credit 'filmed with Panavision equipment' even on non-anamorphic films.

paparazzi
is the term used to describe freelance photographers who stalk celebrities to take unposed photographs of them. It is derived from the character of the photographer Paparazzo in Fellini's *La Dolce Vita*, who was based on the Italian photographer Tazio Secchiaroli.

paper prints
were made of most films between 1895 and 1912 because the US Copyright Act did not allow for celluloid. This quirk of the law meant the preservation of hundreds of early titles which could otherwise have been lost, and in the 60s they were all copied for the archives of the Motion Picture Academy on to 16mm film.

Patsy Awards
are annual awards given to the top animal performers in movies and, from 1958, television by the American Humane Association, in co-operation with the Hollywood studios. The title is an acronym for Picture Animal Top Star of the Year. The first winner, in 1951 at a ceremony with Ronald Reagan as the master of ceremonies, was

FRANCIS the mule, who also won awards in 1952, 1954, 1955, 1956 and 1957.

peplum.
Term to describe Italian historical epics, which are also known as 'sword and sandal'. Both expressions relate to the costumes of the participants, 'peplum' referring to the short skirts worn by both the men and the women. Such films were at their height in the early 60s, sparked off by the success in the US of *Ben-Hur* and of *Hercules*, made in 1957 by Pietro Francisci and starring Steve Reeves, which was promoted heavily by Joseph E. Levine. The genre in Italy goes back to *Cabiria*, made in 1914, starring Bartolomeo Pagano as MACISTE. The 60s cycle was notable for using mainly American muscle-men to play its heroes and for employing many talents, such as Sergio Leone, who went on to make the even more popular spaghetti westerns. See also: EPIC FILM.

persistence of vision.
The medical explanation for our being able to see moving pictures. Twenty-four ordered still pictures are shown to us successively each second, and our sense of sight is slow enough to merge them into one continuous action. The retina of the eye retains each still picture just long enough for it to be replaced by another only slightly different.

pilot:
in television terminology, a film which is made as a trial, to see whether a series on the same premise will be ordered.

pin screen animation:
a curious and short-lived means of animation by photographing pins pushed through a rubber sheet. The shadows caused by the varying height of the pins gives the single picture. The best example is Alexieff's *Night on Bald Mountain* 33.

pink movies
– *pinku eiga* – was the name given to the genre of low-budget erotic films that emerged in Japan during the mid-60s and became extremely popular, accounting for as much as half the studios' output. The most controversial director was Tetsuji Takechi, whose *Black Snow/Kuroi Yuki* in 1965 was the subject of a failed prosecution for public indecency. Other directors included Seijun Suzuki and Koji Wakamatsu. The films were notable for scenes of rape, torture and voyeurism. See also: ROMAN PORNO.

Pixelvision.
Title given to films made by a group of experimental film-makers using a Fisher-Price PXL 2000 video camera. Made of moulded plastic, with a fixed lens or 'image receptor', and recording on standard audio cassettes, the camera produces images that tend to fade rapidly, are composed of easily visible pixels, like an over-enlarged computer image, and blur if the camera is moved. It was made as a toy for Christmas 1987 and discontinued soon after; working cameras are now much sought after. So far, Michael ALMEREYDA has made a 56-minute feature, *Another Girl Another Planet*, using the camera; shorts made with it include *Glass Jaw* 91, directed by Michael O'Reilly, *Don from Lakewood* 91, directed by Pat Tierney and Eric Saks, *Elegy* 91, directed by Joe Gibbons, *It Wasn't Love* 91, directed by Sadie Benning, and *Black and White/Grain* 93, directed by Stuart Sherman.

Pixilation.
A method of stop-motion animation applied to real objects or people. The shots are taken in a camera that exposes one frame at a time, with the person moving slightly between each shot. Animating people frame by frame can be a simple way of achieving special effects, such as flying, or to produce jerky, comic results. It was used to good effect in *The Secret Adventures of Tom Thumb* 93, a feature-length film by Dave Borthwick which combined animated and human figures, and by Japanese director Shinya Tsukamoto in his fantasies *Tetsuo: The Iron Man* 91 and *Tetsuo II: Bodyhammer* 91. The effect can also be achieved by editing normally photographed action.

Possessory credit
is the term used for the director's credit that gives him sole credit for the film, usually in the form 'A Film By ', as in 'A Film By Alan Smithee', or, sometimes, 'An Alan Smithee Film'. It has caused resentment and protests among screenwriters that

directors should claim sole credit, encapsulated in a remark by writer William BOWERS, who was once out for a walk with a friend when he pointed out, 'That's Otto Preminger's house. Or, as we say in Hollywood, "A House by Otto Preminger".' The view of most directors reflects the AUTEUR approach, and was best expressed by David LEAN: 'We directors who have possessory credits have hard earned them over many years for good reason. We are paid big money because we can bring audience-pulling star quality to our films... We bring it by our personal influence over all, including the writer.'

post-synchronization.
Adding sound, by dubbing, to visuals already shot. Sound can only rarely be recorded at the time of shooting because of extraneous noise and requirements of volume, pitch, etc.; actors must usually repeat their lines in accordance with their image on screen.

pratfall.
Something in which all silent comedians were skilled: the art of falling on one's fundament without getting hurt.

pre-credits sequence.
It has recently become fashionable to start films with an explosive opening scene, sometimes running seven or eight minutes, before the titles appear. This now over-worked device, used by almost all American TV series, is generally traced back to *Rommel, Desert Fox* 51, which had a long pre-credits sequence showing a commando raid; but the titles come quite late in *The Egg and I* 47, and even in *Destry Rides Again* 39 there is nearly a minute of shooting before they appear; while in *The Magnificent Ambersons* 42 they are not seen at all, only spoken at the end of the picture.
    More recently, *Cruising* and *Papillon* are among the movies to place all their credits at the end.

prequel.
The opposite of a sequel, i.e. a film showing events which happened *before* one already known. The first film prequel may have been *Another Part of the Forest*, which came after *The Little Foxes* but described events before it. The word came into being in the late 70s with the production of *Butch and Sundance: The Early Days*. A game rapidly sprang up in which one had to supply prequel titles for famous films. Among them were *Mr Blandings Applies for Planning Permission; The Boy Who Would Be Prince; Friday Night Slight Temperature; Destry Dismounts;* and *Hello Mr Chips*.

preview:
see SNEAK PREVIEW.

Prizmacolour.
An early American colour process used for *The Glorious Adventure* 21. Crude in effect, in using orange and turquoise filters, it anticipated Cinecolor.

Producer.
On the stage this term may be equivalent to 'director', i.e. the man who actually marshals the actors and whose conception of the show is supreme. In the film world it almost always indicates the man in control of the budget, whether an independent or working for a big studio. He controls all personnel including the director, and though the film may originally be his overall conception, he normally delegates his artistic responsibilities, remaining responsible chiefly for the film's ultimate commercial success or failure.

production designer.
Technician responsible for the overall 'look' of a film, ranging from actual set design to photographic style.

production manager.
The person responsible for administrative details of a production, e.g. salaries, transport, departmental expenditure.

programmer.
Trade term for a routine feature of only moderate appeal, likely to form half a bill; similar to 'co-feature'.

B. De Mille; Jean Hersholt; *The Bicycle Thief* (foreign film)

1950
Picture: *All About Eve*
Director: Joseph L. Mankiewicz (*All About Eve*)
Actor: José Ferrer (*Cyrano de Bergerac*)
Actress: Judy Holliday (*Born Yesterday*)
Supporting Actor: George Sanders (*All About Eve*)
Supporting Actress: Josephine Hull (*Harvey*)
Motion Picture Story: Edna Anhalt, Edward Anhalt (*Panic in the Streets*)
Screenplay: Joseph L. Mankiewicz (*All About Eve*)
Story & Screenplay: Charles Brackett, Billy Wilder, D. M. Marshman Jnr (*Sunset Boulevard*)
B/w Cinematography: Robert Krasker (*The Third Man*)
Colour Cinematography: Robert Surtees (*King Solomon's Mines*)
B/w Art Direction: Hans Dreier, John Meehan (*Sunset Boulevard*)
Colour Art Direction: Hans Dreier, Walter Tyler (*Samson and Delilah*)
B/w Costume Design: Edith Head, Charles LeMaire (*All About Eve*)
Colour Costume Design: Edith Head, Dorothy Jeakins, Elois Jenssen, Gile Steele, Gwen Wakeling (*Samson and Delilah*)
Sound: TCF Sound Dept (*All About Eve*)
Editing: Ralph E. Winters, Conrad A. Nervig (*King Solomon's Mines*)
Special Effects: *Destination Moon*
Song: 'Mona Lisa' from *Captain Carey* (m/ly Ray Evans, Jay Livingston)
Scoring of a Drama or Comedy: Franz Waxman (*Sunset Boulevard*)
Scoring of a Musical: Adolph Deutsch, Roger Edens (*Annie Get Your Gun*)
Documentary Short: *Why Korea?*
Documentary Feature: *The Titan: Story of Michelangelo*
Cartoon: *Gerald McBoing Boing*
One-Reel Short: *Grandad of Races*
Two-Reel Short: *Beaver Valley*
Honorary Awards: George Murphy; Louis B. Mayer; *The Walls of Malapaga* (foreign film)
Irving Thalberg Memorial Award: Darryl F. Zanuck

1951
Picture: *An American in Paris*
Director: George Stevens (*A Place in the Sun*)
Actor: Humphrey Bogart (*The African Queen*)
Actress: Vivien Leigh (*A Streetcar Named Desire*)
Supporting Actor: Karl Malden (*A Streetcar Named Desire*)
Supporting Actress: Kim Hunter (*A Streetcar Named Desire*)
Motion Picture Story: Paul Dehn, James Bernard (*Seven Days to Noon*)
Screenplay: Michael Wilson, Harry Brown (*A Place in the Sun*)
Story & Screenplay: Alan Jay Lerner (*An American in Paris*)
B/w Cinematography: William C. Mellor (*A Place in the Sun*)
Colour Cinematography: Alfred Gilks, John Alton (*An American in Paris*)
B/w Art Direction: Richard Day (*A Streetcar Named Desire*)
Colour Art Direction: Cedric Gibbons, Preston Ames (*An American in Paris*)
B/w Costume Design: Edith Head (*A Place in the Sun*)
Colour Costume Design: Orry-Kelly, Walter Plunkett, Irene Sharaff (*An American in Paris*)
Sound: Douglas Shearer (*The Great Caruso*)
Editing: William Hornbeck (*A Place in the Sun*)
Special Effects: *When Worlds Collide*
Song: 'In the Cool, Cool, Cool of the Evening' from *Here Comes the Groom* (m Hoagy Carmichael, ly Johnny Mercer)
Scoring of a Drama or Comedy: Franz Waxman (*A Place in the Sun*)
Scoring of a Musical: Johnny Green, Saul Chaplin (*An American in Paris*)
Documentary Short: *Benjy*
Documentary Feature: *Kon-Tiki*
Cartoon: *Two Mouseketeers*
One-Reel Short: *World of Kids*
Two-Reel Short: *Nature's Half Acre*
Honorary Awards: Gene Kelly; *Rashomon* (foreign film)
Irving Thalberg Memorial Award: Arthur Freed

1952
Picture: *The Greatest Show on Earth*
Director: John Ford (*The Quiet Man*)

Actor: Gary Cooper (*High Noon*)
Actress: Shirley Booth (*Come Back, Little Sheba*)
Supporting Actor: Anthony Quinn (*Viva Zapata!*)
Supporting Actress: Gloria Grahame (*The Bad and the Beautiful*)
Motion Picture Story: Frederic M. Frank, Theodore St John, Frank Cavett (*The Greatest Show on Earth*)
Screenplay: Charles Schnee (*The Bad and the Beautiful*)
Story & Screenplay: T. E. B. Clarke (*The Lavender Hill Mob*)
B/w Cinematography: Robert Surtees (*The Bad and the Beautiful*)
Colour Cinematography: Winton C. Hoch, Archie Stout (*The Quiet Man*)
B/w Art Direction: Cedric Gibbons, Edward Carfagno (*The Bad and the Beautiful*)
Colour Art Direction: Paul Sheriff (*Moulin Rouge*)
B/w Costume Design: Helen Rose (*The Bad and the Beautiful*)
Colour Costume Design: Marcel Vertes (*Moulin Rouge*)
Sound: London Film Sound Dept (*Breaking the Sound Barrier*)
Editing: Elmo Williams, Harry Gerstad (*High Noon*)
Special Effects: *Plymouth Adventure*
Song: 'High Noon' from *High Noon* (m Dimitri Tiomkin, ly Ned Washington)
Scoring of a Drama or Comedy: Dimitri Tiomkin (*High Noon*)
Scoring of a Musical: Alfred Newman (*With a Song in My Heart*)
Documentary Short: *Neighbors*
Documentary Feature: *The Sea around Us*
Cartoon: *Johann Mouse*
One-Reel Short: *Light in the Window*
Two-Reel Short: *Water Birds*
Honorary Awards: George Alfred Mitchell; Joseph M. Schenck; Merian C. Cooper; Harold Lloyd; Bob Hope; *Forbidden Games* (foreign film)
Irving Thalberg Memorial Award: Cecil B. De Mille

1953
Picture: *From Here to Eternity*
Director: Fred Zinnemann (*From Here to Eternity*)
Actor: William Holden (*Stalag 17*)
Actress: Audrey Hepburn (*Roman Holiday*)
Supporting Actor: Frank Sinatra (*From Here to Eternity*)
Supporting Actress: Donna Reed (*From Here to Eternity*)
Motion Picture Story: Ian McLellan Hunter, fronting for the blacklisted Dalton Trumbo (*Roman Holiday*)
Screenplay: Daniel Taradash (*From Here to Eternity*)
Story & Screenplay: Charles Brackett, Walter Reisch, Richard Breen (*Titanic*)
B/w Cinematography: Burnett Guffey (*From Here to Eternity*)
Colour Cinematography: Loyal Griggs (*Shane*)
B/w Art Direction: Cedric Gibbons, Edward Carfagno (*Julius Caesar*)
Colour Art Direction: Lyle Wheeler, George W. Davis (*The Robe*)
B/w Costume Design: Edith Head (*Roman Holiday*)
Colour Costume Design: Charles LeMaire, Emile Santiago (*The Robe*)
Sound: J. P. Livadary and Columbia Sound Dept (*From Here to Eternity*)
Editing: William Lyon (*From Here to Eternity*)
Special Effects: *The War of the Worlds*
Song: 'Secret Love' from *Calamity Jane* (m Sammy Fain, ly Paul Francis Webster)
Scoring of a Drama or Comedy: Bronislau Kaper (*Lili*)
Scoring of a Musical: Alfred Newman (*Call Me Madam*)
Documentary Short: *The Alaskan Eskimo*
Documentary Feature: *The Living Desert*
Cartoon: *Toot, Whistle, Plunk and Boom*
One-Reel Short: *The Merry Wives of Windsor Overture*
Two-Reel Short: *Bear Country*
Honorary Awards: Pete Smith; Joseph I. Breen; Twentieth Century-Fox for Cinemascope
Irving Thalberg Memorial Award: George Stevens

1954
Picture: *On the Waterfront*
Director: Elia Kazan (*On the Waterfront*)
Actor: Marlon Brando (*On the Waterfront*)
Actress: Grace Kelly (*The Country Girl*)

Supporting Actor: Edmond O'Brien (*The Barefoot Contessa*)
Supporting Actress: Eva Marie Saint (*On the Waterfront*)
Motion Picture Story: Philip Yordan (*Broken Lance*)
Screenplay: George Seaton (*The Country Girl*)
Story & Screenplay: Budd Schulberg (*On the Waterfront*)
B/w Cinematography: Boris Kaufman (*On the Waterfront*)
Colour Cinematography: Milton Krasner (*Three Coins in the Fountain*)
B/w Art Direction: Richard Day (*On the Waterfront*)
Colour Art Direction: John Meehan (*20,000 Leagues under the Sea*)
B/w Costume Design: Edith Head (*Sabrina*)
Colour Costume Design: Sanzo Wada (*Gate of Hell*)
Sound: Leslie I. Carey (*The Glenn Miller Story*)
Editing: Gene Milford (*On the Waterfront*)
Special Effects: *20,000 Leagues under the Sea*
Song: 'Three Coins in the Fountain' from *Three Coins in the Fountain* (m Jule Styne, ly Sammy Cahn)
Scoring of a Drama or Comedy: Dimitri Tiomkin (*The High and the Mighty*)
Scoring of a Musical: Adolph Deutsch, Saul Chaplin (*Seven Brides for Seven Brothers*)
Documentary Short: *Thursday's Children*
Documentary Feature: *The Vanishing Prairie*
Cartoon: *When Magoo Flew*
One-Reel Short: *This Mechanical Age*
Two-Reel Short: *A Time out of War*
Honorary Awards: Greta Garbo; Danny Kaye; Jon Whiteley; Vincent Winter; *Gate of Hell* (foreign film)

1955
Picture: *Marty*
Director: Delbert Mann (*Marty*)
Actor: Ernest Borgnine (*Marty*)
Actress: Anna Magnani (*The Rose Tattoo*)
Supporting Actor: Jack Lemmon (*Mister Roberts*)
Supporting Actress: Jo Van Fleet (*East of Eden*)
Motion Picture Story: Daniel Fuchs (*Love Me or Leave Me*)
Screenplay: Paddy Chayevsky (*Marty*)
Story & Screenplay: William Ludwig, Sonya Levien (*Interrupted Melody*)
B/w Cinematography: James Wong Howe (*The Rose Tattoo*)
Colour Cinematography: Robert Burks (*To Catch a Wife*)
B/w Art Direction: Hal Pereira, Tambi Larsen (*The Rose Tattoo*)
Colour Art Direction: William Flannery, Jo Mielziner (*Picnic*)
B/w Costume Design: Helen Rose (*I'll Cry Tomorrow*)
Colour Costume Design: Charles LeMaire (*Love Is a Many-Splendored Thing*)
Sound: Fred Hynes and Todd-AO Sound Dept (*Oklahoma!*)
Editing: Charles Nelson, William A. Lyon (*Picnic*)
Special Effects: *The Bridges at Toko-Ri*
Song: 'Love Is a Many-Splendored Thing' from *Love Is a Many-Splendored Thing* (m Sammy Fain, ly Paul Francis Webster)
Scoring of a Drama or Comedy: Alfred Newman (*Love Is a Many-Splendored Thing*)
Scoring of a Musical: Robert Russell Bennett, Jay Blackton, Adolph Deutsch (*Oklahoma!*)
Documentary Short: *Men against the Arctic*
Documentary Feature: *Helen Keller in Her Story*
Cartoon: *Speedy Gonzales*
One-Reel Short: *Survival City*
Two-Reel Short: *The Face of Lincoln*
Honorary Awards: *Samurai, the Legend of Musashi* (foreign film)

1956
Picture: *Around the World in Eighty Days*
Foreign-Language Film: *La Strada* (Federico Fellini)
Director: George Stevens (*Giant*)
Actor: Yul Brynner (*The King and I*)
Actress: Ingrid Bergman (*Anastasia*)
Supporting Actor: Anthony Quinn (*Lust for Life*)
Supporting Actress: Dorothy Malone (*Written on the Wind*)
Motion Picture Story: Dalton Trumbo (as Robert Rich) (*The Brave One*)
Original Screenplay: Albert Lamorisse (*The Red Balloon*)
Adapted Screenplay: James Poe, John Farrow, S. J.

Perelman (*Around the World in Eighty Days*)
B/w Cinematography: Joseph Ruttenberg (*Somebody Up There Likes Me*)
Colour Cinematography: Lionel Lindon (*Around the World in Eighty Days*)
B/w Art Direction: Cedric Gibbons, Malcolm F. Brown (*Somebody Up There Likes Me*)
Colour Art Direction: Lyle Wheeler, John DeCuir (*The King and I*)
B/w Costume Design: Jean Louis (*The Solid Gold Cadillac*)
Colour Costume Design: Irene Sharaff (*The King and I*)
Sound: Carl Faulkner and TCF Sound Dept (*The King and I*)
Editing: Gene Ruggiero, Paul Weatherwax (*Around the World in Eighty Days*)
Special Effects: John Fulton (*The Ten Commandments*)
Song: 'Whatever Will Be, Will Be' from *The Man Who Knew Too Much* (m/ly Jay Livingston, Ray Evans)
Scoring of a Drama or Comedy: Victor Young (*Around the World in Eighty Days*)
Scoring of a Musical: Alfred Newman, Ken Darby (*The King and I*)
Documentary Short: *The True Story of the Civil War*
Documentary Feature: *The Silent World*
Cartoon: *Mister Magoo's Puddle Jumper*
One-Reel Short: *Crashing the Water Barrier*
Two-Reel Short: *The Bespoke Overcoat*
Honorary Award: Eddie Cantor
Irving Thalberg Memorial Award: Buddy Adler

1957
Picture: *The Bridge on the River Kwai*
Foreign-Language Film: *The Nights of Cabiria* (Federico Fellini)
Director: David Lean (*The Bridge on the River Kwai*)
Actor: Alec Guinness (*The Bridge on the River Kwai*)
Actress: Joanne Woodward (*The Three Faces of Eve*)
Supporting Actor: Red Buttons (*Sayonara*)
Supporting Actress: Miyoshi Umeki (*Sayonara*)
Original Story & Screenplay: George Wells (*Designing Woman*)
Adapted Screenplay: Pierre Boulle, Michael Wilson, Carl Foreman (*The Bridge on the River Kwai*)
Cinematography: Jack Hildyard (*The Bridge on the River Kwai*)
Art Direction: Ted Hayworth (*Sayonara*)
Costume Design: Orry-Kelly (*Les Girls*)
Sound: George Groves and Warner Sound Dept (*Sayonara*)
Editing: Peter Taylor (*The Bridge on the River Kwai*)
Special Effects: Walter Rossi (*The Enemy Below*)
Song: 'All the Way' from *The Joker Is Wild* (m James van Heusen, ly Sammy Cahn)
Music Scoring: Malcolm Arnold (*The Bridge on the River Kwai*)
Documentary Feature: *Albert Schweitzer*
Cartoon: *Birds Anonymous*
Live-Action Short: *The Wetback Hound*
Honorary Awards: Charles Brackett; B. B. Kahane; Gilbert 'Bronco Billy' Anderson

1958
Picture: *Gigi*
Foreign-Language Film: *My Uncle* (Jacques Tati)
Director: Vincente Minnelli (*Gigi*)
Actor: David Niven (*Separate Tables*)
Actress: Susan Hayward (*I Want to Live!*)
Supporting Actor: Burl Ives (*The Big Country*)
Supporting Actress: Wendy Hiller (*Separate Tables*)
Original Story & Screenplay: Nathan E. Douglas (the blacklisted Ned Young), Harold Jacob Smith (*The Defiant Ones*)
Adapted Screenplay: Alan Jay Lerner (*Gigi*)
B/w Cinematography: Sam Leavitt (*The Defiant Ones*)
Colour Cinematography: Joseph Ruttenberg (*Gigi*)
Art Direction: William A. Horning, Preston Ames (*Gigi*)
Costume Design: Cecil Beaton (*Gigi*)
Sound: Fred Hynes and the Todd-AO Sound Dept (*South Pacific*)
Editing: Adrienne Fazan (*Gigi*)
Special Effects: Tom Howard (*Tom Thumb*)
Song: 'Gigi' from *Gigi* (m Frederick Loewe, ly Alan Jay Lerner)
Scoring of a Drama or Comedy: Dimitri Tiomkin (*The Old Man and the Sea*)

Scoring of a Musical: André Previn (*Gigi*)
Documentary Short: *Ama Girls*
Documentary Feature: *White Wilderness*
Cartoon: *Knighty Knight Bugs*
Live-Action Short: *Grand Canyon*
Honorary Award: Maurice Chevalier
Irving Thalberg Memorial Award: Jack L. Warner

1959
Picture: *Ben-Hur*
Foreign-Language Film: *Black Orpheus* (Marcel Camus)
Director: William Wyler (*Ben-Hur*)
Actor: Charlton Heston (*Ben-Hur*)
Actress: Simone Signoret (*Room at the Top*)
Supporting Actor: Hugh Griffith (*Ben-Hur*)
Supporting Actress: Shelley Winters (*The Diary of Anne Frank*)
Original Story & Screenplay: Russell Rouse, Clarence Greene, Stanley Shapiro, Maurice Richlin (*Pillow Talk*)
Adapted Screenplay: Neil Paterson (*Room at the Top*)
B/w Cinematography: William C. Mellor (*The Diary of Anne Frank*)
Colour Cinematography: Robert L. Surtees (*Ben-Hur*)
B/w Art Direction: Lyle R. Wheeler, George W. Davis (*The Diary of Anne Frank*)
Colour Art Direction: William A. Horning, Edward Carfagno (*Ben-Hur*)
B/w Costume Design: Orry-Kelly (*Some Like It Hot*)
Colour Costume Design: Elizabeth Haffenden (*Ben-Hur*)
Sound: Franklin E. Milton and MGM Sound Dept (*Ben-Hur*)
Editing: Ralph E. Winters, John D. Dunning (*Ben-Hur*)
Special Effects: Arnold Gillespie, Robert MacDonald, Milo Lory (*Ben-Hur*)
Song: 'High Hopes' from *A Hole in the Head* (*m* James Van Heusen, *ly* Sammy Cahn)
Scoring of a Drama or Comedy: Miklos Rosza (*Ben-Hur*)
Scoring of a Musical: André Previn, Kim Darby (*Porgy and Bess*)
Documentary Short: *Glass*
Documentary Feature: *Serengeti Shall Not Die*
Cartoon: *Moonbird*
Live-Action Short: *The Golden Fish*
Honorary Awards: Lee De Forest; Buster Keaton

1960
Picture: *The Apartment*
Foreign-Language Film: *The Virgin Spring* (Ingmar Bergman)
Director: Billy Wilder (*The Apartment*)
Actor: Burt Lancaster (*Elmer Gantry*)
Actress: Elizabeth Taylor (*Butterfield 8*)
Supporting Actor: Peter Ustinov (*Spartacus*)
Supporting Actress: Shirley Jones (*Elmer Gantry*)
Original Story & Screenplay: Billy Wilder, I. A. L. Diamond (*The Apartment*)
Adapted Screenplay: Richard Brooks (*Elmer Gantry*)
B/w Cinematography: Freddie Francis (*Sons and Lovers*)
Colour Cinematography: Russell Metty (*Spartacus*)
B/w Art Direction: Alexander Trauner (*The Apartment*)
Colour Art Direction: Alexander Golitzen, Eric Orbom (*Spartacus*)
B/w Costume Design: Edith Head, Edward Stevenson (*The Facts of Life*)
Colour Costume Design: Valles, Bill Thomas (*Spartacus*)
Sound: Gordon E. Sawyer and Samuel Goldwyn Sound Dept (*The Alamo*)
Editing: Daniel Mandell (*The Apartment*)
Special Effects: Gene Warren, Tim Baar (MGM) (*The Time Machine*)
Song: 'Never on Sunday' from *Never on Sunday* (*m/ly* Manos Hadjidakis)
Scoring of a Drama or Comedy: Ernest Gold (*Exodus*)
Scoring of a Musical: Morris Stoloff, Harry Sikman (*Song without End*)
Documentary Short: *Giuseppina*
Documentary Feature: *The Horse with the Flying Tail*
Cartoon: *Munro*
Live-Action Short: *Day of the Panther*
Honorary Awards: Gary Cooper; Stan Laurel; Hayley Mills

1961
Picture: *West Side Story*
Foreign-Language Picture: *Through a Glass Darkly* (Ingmar Bergman)
Director: Jerome Robbins, Robert Wise (*West Side Story*)
Actor: Maximilian Schell (*Judgment at Nuremberg*)
Actress: Sophia Loren (*Two Women*)
Supporting Actor: George Chakiris (*West Side Story*)
Supporting Actress: Rita Moreno (*West Side Story*)
Original Story & Screenplay: William Inge (*Splendor in the Grass*)
Adapted Screenplay: Abby Mann (*Judgment at Nuremberg*)
B/w Cinematography: Eugene Schufftan (*The Hustler*)
Colour Cinematography: Daniel L. Fapp (*West Side Story*)
B/w Art Direction: Harry Horner (*The Hustler*)
Colour Art Direction: Boris Leven (*West Side Story*)
B/w Costume Design: Piero Gherardi (*La Dolce Vita*)
Colour Costume Design: Irene Sharaff (*West Side Story*)
Sound: Fred Hynes and Samuel Goldwyn Sound Dept, Gordon E. Sawyer (*West Side Story*)
Editing: Thomas Stanford (*West Side Story*)
Special Effects: Bill Warrington, Vivian C. Greenham (*The Guns of Navarone*)
Song: 'Moon River' from *Breakfast at Tiffany's* (*m* Henry Mancini, *ly* Johnny Mercer)
Scoring of a Drama or Comedy: Henry Mancini (*Breakfast at Tiffany's*)
Scoring of a Musical: Saul Chaplin, Johnny Green, Sid Ramin, Irwin Kostal (*West Side Story*)
Documentary Short: *Project Hope*
Documentary Feature: *Le Ciel et la Boue*
Cartoon: *Ersatz*
Live-Action Short: *Seawards the Great Ships*
Honorary Awards: William L. Hendricks; Fred L. Metzler; Jerome Robbins
Irving Thalberg Memorial Award: Stanley Kramer

1962
Picture: *Lawrence of Arabia*
Foreign-Language Film: *Sundays and Cybele* (Serge Bourgignon)
Director: David Lean (*Lawrence of Arabia*)
Actor: Gregory Peck (*To Kill a Mockingbird*)
Actress: Anne Bancroft (*The Miracle Worker*)
Supporting Actor: Ed Begley (*Sweet Bird of Youth*)
Supporting Actress: Patty Duke (*The Miracle Worker*)
Original Story & Screenplay: Ennio De Concini, Alfredo Gianetti, Pietro Germi (*Divorce Italian Style*)
Adapted Screenplay: Horton Foote (*To Kill a Mockingbird*)
B/w Cinematography: Jean Bourgoin, Walter Wottitz (*The Longest Day*)
Colour Cinematography: Fred A. Young (*Lawrence of Arabia*)
B/w Art Direction: Alexander Golitzen, Henry Bumstead (*To Kill a Mockingbird*)
Colour Art Direction: John Box, John Stoll (*Lawrence of Arabia*)
B/w Costume Design: Norma Koch (*What Ever Happened to Baby Jane?*)
Colour Costume Design: Mary Wills (*The Wonderful World of the Brothers Grimm*)
Sound: John Cox, Shepperton Studio Sound Dept (*Lawrence of Arabia*)
Editing: Anne Coates (*Lawrence of Arabia*)
Special Effects: Robert MacDonald, Jacques Maumont (*The Longest Day*)
Song: 'Days of Wine and Roses' from *Days of Wine and Roses* (*m* Henry Mancini, *ly* Johnny Mercer)
Original Score: Maurice Jarre (*Lawrence of Arabia*)
Adapted Score: Ray Heindorf (*The Music Man*)
Documentary Short: *Dylan Thomas*
Documentary Feature: *Black Fox*
Cartoon: *The Hole*
Live-Action Short: *Happy Anniversary*

1963
Picture: *Tom Jones*
Foreign-Language Film: *8_* (Federico Fellini)
Director: Tony Richardson (*Tom Jones*)
Actor: Sidney Poitier (*Lilies of the Field*)
Actress: Patricia Neal (*Hud*)
Supporting Actor: Melvyn Douglas (*Hud*)
Supporting Actress: Margaret Rutherford (*The VIPs*)
Original Story & Screenplay: James R. Webb (*How the West Was Won*)
Adapted Screenplay: John Osborne (*Tom Jones*)
B/w Cinematography: James Wong Howe (*Hud*)
Colour Cinematography: Leon Shamroy (*Cleopatra*)
B/w Art Direction: Gene Callahan (*America America*)
Colour Art Direction: John DeCuir, Jack Martin Smith, Hilyard Brown, Herman Blumenthal, Elven Webb, Maurice Pelling, Boris Juraga (*Cleopatra*)
B/w Costume Design: Piero Gherardi (*8_*)
Colour Costume Design: Irene Sharaff, Vittorio Nino Novarese, Renie (*Cleopatra*)
Visual Effects: Emil Kosa Jnr (*Cleopatra*)
Sound Effects: Walter G. Elliott (*It's a Mad, Mad, Mad, Mad World*)
Sound: Franklin E. Milton, MGM Sound Dept (*How the West Was Won*)
Editing: Harold F. Cress (*How the West Was Won*)
Song: 'Call Me Irresponsible' from *Papa's Delicate Condition* (*m* James Van Heusen, *ly* Sammy Cahn)
Original Score: John Addison (*Tom Jones*)
Adapted Score: André Previn (*Irma La Douce*)
Documentary Short: *Chagall*
Documentary Feature: *Robert Frost: A Lover's Quarrel with the World*
Cartoon: *The Critic*
Live-Action Short: *An Occurrence at Owl Creek Bridge*
Irving Thalberg Memorial Award: Sam Spiegel

1964
Picture: *My Fair Lady*
Foreign-Language Film: *Yesterday, Today and Tomorrow* (Vittorio De Sica)
Director: George Cukor (*My Fair Lady*)
Actor: Rex Harrison (*My Fair Lady*)
Actress: Julie Andrews (*Mary Poppins*)
Supporting Actor: Peter Ustinov (*Topkapi*)
Supporting Actress: Lila Kedrova (*Zorba the Greek*)
Original Story & Screenplay: S. H. Barnett, Peter Stone, Frank Tarloff (*Father Goose*)
Adapted Screenplay: Edward Anhalt (*Becket*)
B/w Cinematography: Walter Lassally (*Zorba the Greek*)
Colour Cinematography: Harry Stradling (*My Fair Lady*)
B/w Art Direction: Vassilis Fotopoulos (*Zorba the Greek*)
Colour Art Direction: Gene Allen, Cecil Beaton (*My Fair Lady*)
B/w Costume Design: Dorothy Jeakins (*The Night of the Iguana*)
Colour Costume Design: Cecil Beaton (*My Fair Lady*)
Visual Effects: Peter Ellenshaw, Hamilton Luske, Eustace Lycett (*Mary Poppins*)
Sound Effects: Norman Wanstall (*Goldfinger*)
Sound: George R. Groves, Warner Sound Dept (*My Fair Lady*)
Editing: Cotton Warburton (*Mary Poppins*)
Song: 'Chim Chim Cheree' from *Mary Poppins* (*m/ly* Richard M. Sherman, Robert B. Sherman)
Original Score: Richard M. Sherman, Robert B. Sherman (*Mary Poppins*)
Adapted Score: André Previn (*My Fair Lady*)
Documentary Short: *Nine from Little Rock*
Documentary Feature: *Jacques-Yves Cousteau's World without Sun*
Cartoon: *The Pink Phink*
Live-Action Short: *Casals Conducts: 1964*
Honorary Award: William Tuttle (for make-up on *Seven Faces of Dr Lao*)

1965
Picture: *The Sound of Music*
Foreign-Language Film: *The Shop on Main Street* (Jan Kadar)
Director: Robert Wise (*The Sound of Music*)
Actor: Lee Marvin (*Cat Ballou*)
Actress: Julie Christie (*Darling*)
Supporting Actor: Martin Balsam (*A Thousand Clowns*)
Supporting Actress: Shelley Winters (*A Patch of Blue*)
Original Story & Screenplay: Frederic Raphael (*Darling*)
Adapted Screenplay: Robert Bolt (*Dr Zhivago*)
B/w Cinematography: Ernest Laszlo (*Ship of Fools*)
Colour Cinematography: Freddie Young (*Dr Zhivago*)
B/w Art Direction: Robert Clatworthy (*Ship of Fools*)
Colour Art Direction: John Box, Terry Marsh (*Dr Zhivago*)
B/w Costume Design: Julie Harris (*Darling*)
Colour Costume Design: Phyllis Dalton (*Dr Zhivago*)
Visual Effects: John Stears (*Thunderball*)
Sound Effects: Tregoweth Brown (*The Great Race*)
Sound: James P. Corcoran, TCF Sound Dept, Fred Hynes, Todd-AO Sound Dept (*The Sound of Music*)
Editing: William Reynolds (*The Sound of Music*)
Song: 'The Shadow of Your Smile' from *The Sandpiper* (*m* Johnny Mandel, *ly* Paul Francis Webster)
Original Score: Maurice Jarre (*Dr Zhivago*)
Adapted Score: Irwin Kostal (*The Sound of Music*)
Documentary Short: *To Be Alive!*
Documentary Feature: *The Eleanor Roosevelt Story*
Cartoon: *The Dot and the Line*
Live-Action Short: *The Chicken*
Honorary Award: Bob Hope
Irving Thalberg Memorial Award: William Wyler

1966
Picture: *A Man for All Seasons*
Foreign-Language Film: *A Man and a Woman* (Claude Lelouch)
Director: Fred Zinnemann (*A Man for All Seasons*)
Actor: Paul Scofield (*A Man for All Seasons*)
Actress: Elizabeth Taylor (*Who's Afraid of Virginia Woolf?*)
Supporting Actor: Walter Matthau (*The Fortune Cookie*)
Supporting Actress: Sandy Dennis (*Who's Afraid of Virginia Woolf?*)
Original Story & Screenplay: Claude Lelouch, Pierre Uytterhoeven (*A Man and a Woman*)
Adapted Screenplay: Robert Bolt (*A Man for All Seasons*)
B/w Cinematography: Haskell Wexler (*Who's Afraid of Virginia Woolf?*)
Colour Cinematography: Ted Moore (*A Man for All Seasons*)
B/w Art Direction: Richard Sylbert (*Who's Afraid of Virginia Woolf?*)
Colour Art Direction: Jack Martin Smith, Dale Hennesy (*Fantastic Voyage*)
B/w Costume Design: Irene Sharaff (*Who's Afraid of Virginia Woolf?*)
Colour Costume Design: Elizabeth Haffenden, Joan Bridge (*A Man for All Seasons*)
Visual Effects: Art Cruickshank (*Fantastic Voyage*)
Sound Effects: Gordon Daniel (*Grand Prix*)
Sound: Franklin E. Milton, MGM Sound Dept (*Grand Prix*)
Editing: Frederic Steinkamp, Henry Berman, Stewart Linder, Frank Santillo (*Grand Prix*)
Song: 'Born Free' from *Born Free* (*m* John Barry, *ly* Don Black)
Original Score: John Barry (*Born Free*)
Adapted Score: Ken Thorne (*A Funny Thing Happened on the Way to the Forum*)
Documentary Short: *A Year toward Tomorrow*
Documentary Feature: *The War Game*
Cartoon: *Herb Alpert and the Tijuana Brass Double Feature*
Live-Action Short: *Wild Wings*
Honorary Award: Yakima Canutt
Irving Thalberg Memorial Award: Robert Wise

1967
Picture: *In the Heat of the Night*
Foreign-Language Film: *Closely Observed Trains* (Jiri Menzel)
Director: Mike Nichols (*The Graduate*)
Actor: Rod Steiger (*In the Heat of the Night*)
Actress: Katharine Hepburn (*Guess Who's Coming to Dinner*); Barbra Streisand (*Funny Girl*)
Supporting Actor: George Kennedy (*Cool Hand Luke*)
Supporting Actress: Estelle Parsons (*Bonnie and Clyde*)
Original Story & Screenplay: William Rose (*Guess Who's Coming to Dinner*)
Adapted Screenplay: Sterling Silliphant (*In the Heat of the Night*)
Cinematography: Burnett Guffey (*Bonnie and Clyde*)
Art Direction: John Truscott, Edward Carrere (*Camelot*)
Costume Design: John Truscott (*Camelot*)
Special Effects: L. B. Abbott (*Doctor Dolittle*)
Sound Effects: John Poyner (*The Dirty Dozen*)
Sound: Samuel Goldwyn Studio Dept (*In the Heat of the Night*)
Editing: Hal Ashby (*In the Heat of the Night*)
Song: 'Talk to the Animals' from *Doctor Dolittle* (*m/ly* Leslie Bricusse)
Original Score: Elmer Bernstein (*Thoroughly Modern Millie*)
Adapted Score: Alfred Newman, Ken Darby (*Camelot*)

Documentary Short: *The Redwoods*
Documentary Feature: *The Anderson Platoon*
Cartoon: *The Box*
Live-Action Short: *A Place to Stand*
Honorary Award: Arthur Freed
Irving Thalberg Memorial Award: Alfred Hitchcock

1968
Picture: *Oliver!*
Director: Carol Reed (*Oliver!*)
Actor: Cliff Robertson (*Charly*)
Actress: Katharine Hepburn (*The Lion in Winter*)
Supporting Actor: Jack Albertson (*The Subject Was Roses*)
Supporting Actress: Ruth Gordon (*Rosemary's Baby*)
Original Story & Screenplay: Mel Brooks (*The Producers*)
Adapted Screenplay: James Goldman (*The Lion in Winter*)
Cinematography: Pasqualino De Santis (*Romeo and Juliet*)
Art Direction: John Box, Terence Marsh (*Oliver!*)
Costume Design: Danilo Donati (*Romeo and Juliet*)
Sound: Shepperton Sound Dept (*Oliver!*)
Editing: Frank P. Keller (*Bullitt*)
Special Effects: Stanley Kubrick (*2001: A Space Odyssey*)
Song: 'The Windmills of Your Mind' from *The Thomas Crown Affair* (*m* Michel Legrand, *ly* Alan and Marilyn Bergman)
Original Score: John Barry (*The Lion in Winter*)
Scoring of a Musical: John Green (*Oliver!*)
Documentary Short: *Why Man Creates*
Documentary Feature: *Journey into Self*
Cartoon: *Winnie the Pooh and the Blustery Day*
Live-Action Short: *Robert Kennedy Remembered*
Honorary Awards: John Chambers (make-up for *Planet of the Apes*); Onna White (choreography for *Oliver!*)

1969
Picture: *Midnight Cowboy*
Foreign-Language Film: *Z* (Costa-Gavras)
Director: John Schlesinger (*Midnight Cowboy*)
Actor: John Wayne (*True Grit*)
Actress: Maggie Smith (*The Prime of Miss Jean Brodie*)
Supporting Actor: Gig Young (*They Shoot Horses, Don't They?*)
Supporting Actress: Goldie Hawn (*Cactus Flower*)
Original Story & Screenplay: William Goldman (*Butch Cassidy and the Sundance Kid*)
Adapted Screenplay: Waldo Salt (*Midnight Cowboy*)
Cinematography: Arthur Ibbetson (*Anne of the Thousand Days*)
Art Direction: John DeCuir, Jack Martin Smith, Herman Blumenthal (*Hello, Dolly!*)
Costume Design: Margaret Furse (*Anne of the Thousand Days*)
Sound: Jack Solomon, Murray Spivack (*Hello, Dolly!*)
Editing: Françoise Bonnot (*Z*)
Special Effects: Robbie Robertson (*Marooned*)
Song: 'Raindrops Keep Fallin' on My Head' from *Butch Cassidy and the Sundance Kid* (*m* Burt Bacharach, *ly* Hal David)
Original Score: Burt Bacharach (*Butch Cassidy and the Sundance Kid*)
Scoring of a Musical: Lennie Hayton, Lionel Newman (*Hello, Dolly!*)
Documentary Short: *Czechoslovakia 1968*
Documentary Feature: *Arthur Rubinstein – the Love of Life*
Cartoon: *It's Tough to Be a Bird*
Live-Action Short: *The Magic Machines*
Honorary Award: Cary Grant

1970
Picture: *Patton*
Foreign-Language Film: *Investigation of a Citizen above Suspicion* (Elio Petri)
Director: Franklin J. Schaffner (*Patton*)
Actor: George C. Scott (*Patton*)
Actress: Glenda Jackson (*Women in Love*)
Supporting Actor: John Mills (*Ryan's Daughter*)
Supporting Actress: Helen Hayes (*Airport*)
Original Story & Screenplay: Francis Ford Coppola, Edmund H. North (*Patton*)
Adapted Screenplay: Ring Lardner Jnr (*M*A*S*H*)
Cinematography: Freddie Young (*Ryan's Daughter*)
Art Direction: Urie McCleary, Gil Parrondo (*Patton*)
Costume Design: Nino Novarese (*Cromwell*)
Sound: Douglas Williams, Don Bassman (*Patton*)
Editing: Hugh S. Fowler (*Patton*)
Special Effects: A. D. Flowers, L. B. Abbott (*Tora! Tora! Tora!*)
Song: 'For All We Know' from *Lovers and Other Strangers* (*m* Fred Karlin, *ly* Robb Royer, James Griffin)
Original Score: Francis Lai (*Love Story*)
Original Song Score: The Beatles (*Let It Be*)
Documentary Short: *Interviews with My Lai Veterans*
Documentary Feature: *Woodstock*
Cartoon: *Is It Always Right to Be Right*
Live-Action Short: *The Resurrection of Bronco Billy*
Honorary Awards: Lillian Gish; Orson Welles
Irving Thalberg Memorial Award: Ingmar Bergman

1971
Picture: *The French Connection*
Foreign-Language Film: *The Garden of the Finzi-Continis* (Vittorio De Sica)
Director: William Friedkin (*The French Connection*)
Actor: Gene Hackman (*The French Connection*)
Actress: Jane Fonda (*Klute*)
Supporting Actor: Ben Johnson (*The Last Picture Show*)
Supporting Actress: Cloris Leachman (*The Last Picture Show*)
Original Story & Screenplay: Paddy Chayevsky (*The Hospital*)
Adapted Screenplay: Ernest Tidyman (*The French Connection*)
Cinematography: Oswald Morris (*Fiddler on the Roof*)
Art Direction: John Box, Ernest Archer, Jack Maxsted, Gil Parrondo (*Nicholas and Alexandra*)
Costume Design: Yvonne Blake, Antonio Castillo (*Nicholas and Alexandra*)
Sound: Gordon K. McCallum, David Hildyard (*Fiddler on the Roof*)
Editing: Jerry Greenberg (*The French Connection*)
Special Effects: Alan Maley, Eustace Lycett, Danny Lee (*Bedknobs and Broomsticks*)
Song: Theme from *Shaft* (*m/ly* Isaac Hayes)
Original Dramatic Score: Michel Legrand (*Summer of '42*)
Adaptation and Original Song Score: John Williams (*Fiddler on the Roof*)
Documentary Short: *Sentinels of Silence*
Documentary Feature: *The Hellstrom Chronicle*
Animated Film: *The Crunch Bird*
Live-Action Short: *Sentinels of Silence*
Honorary Award: Charles Chaplin

1972
Picture: *The Godfather*
Foreign-Language Film: *The Discreet Charm of the Bourgeoisie* (Luis Buñuel)
Director: Bob Fosse (*Cabaret*)
Actor: Marlon Brando (*The Godfather*)
Actress: Liza Minnelli (*Cabaret*)
Supporting Actor: Joel Grey (*Cabaret*)
Supporting Actress: Eileen Heckart (*Butterflies Are Free*)
Original Story & Screenplay: Jeremy Larner (*The Candidate*)
Adapted Screenplay: Mario Puzo, Francis Ford Coppola (*The Godfather*)
Cinematography: Geoffrey Unsworth (*Cabaret*)
Art Direction: Rolf Zehetbauer, Jurgen Kiebach (*Cabaret*)
Costume Design: Anthony Powell (*Travels with My Aunt*)
Sound: Robert Knudson, David Hildyard (*Cabaret*)
Editing: David Bretherton (*Cabaret*)
Song: 'The Morning After' from *The Poseidon Adventure* (*m/ly* Al Kasha, Joel Hirschhorn)
Original Dramatic Score: Charles Chaplin, Raymond Rasch, Larry Russell (*Limelight*)
Adaptation and Original Song Score: Ralph Burns (*Cabaret*)
Documentary Short: *This Tiny World*
Documentary Feature: *Marjoe*
Animated Film: *A Christmas Carol*
Live-Action Short: *Norman Rockwell's World ... An American Dream*
Special Achievement Award: L. B. Abbott, A. D. Flowers (for visual effects, *The Poseidon Adventure*)
Honorary Award: Edward G. Robinson

1973
Picture: *The Sting*
Foreign-Language Film: *Day for Night* (François Truffaut)
Director: George Roy Hill (*The Sting*)
Actor: Jack Lemmon (*Save the Tiger*)
Actress: Glenda Jackson (*A Touch of Class*)
Supporting Actor: John Houseman (*The Paper Chase*)
Supporting Actress: Tatum O'Neal (*Paper Moon*)
Original Story & Screenplay: David S. Ward (*The Sting*)
Adapted Screenplay: William Peter Blatty (*The Exorcist*)
Cinematography: Sven Nykvist (*Cries and Whispers*)
Art Direction: Henry Bumstead (*The Sting*)
Costume Design: Edith Head (*The Sting*)
Sound: Robert Knudson, Chris Newman (*The Exorcist*)
Editing: William Reynolds (*The Sting*)
Song: 'The Way We Were' from *The Way We Were* (*m* Marvin Hamlisch, *ly* Alan and Marilyn Bergman)
Original Dramatic Score: Marvin Hamlisch (*The Way We Were*)
Adaptation and Original Song Score: Marvin Hamlisch (*The Sting*)
Documentary Short: *Princeton: A Search for Answers*
Documentary Feature: *The Great American Cowboy*
Animated Film: *Frank Film*
Live-Action Short: *The Bolero*
Honorary Awards: Henri Langlois; Groucho Marx
Irving Thalberg Memorial Award: Lawrence Weingarten

1974
Picture: *The Godfather Part II*
Foreign-Language Film: *Amarcord* (Federico Fellini)
Director: Francis Ford Coppola (*The Godfather Part II*)
Actor: Art Carney (*Harry and Tonto*)
Actress: Ellen Burstyn (*Alice Doesn't Live Here Any More*)
Supporting Actor: Robert De Niro (*The Godfather Part II*)
Supporting Actress: Ingrid Bergman (*Murder on the Orient Express*)
Original Story & Screenplay: Robert Towne (*Chinatown*)
Adapted Screenplay: Francis Ford Coppola, Mario Puzo (*The Godfather Part II*)
Cinematography: Fred Koenekamp, Joseph Biroc (*The Towering Inferno*)
Art Direction: Dean Tavoularis, Angelo Graham (*The Godfather Part II*)
Costume Design: Theoni V. Aldredge (*The Great Gatsby*)
Sound: Ronald Pierce, Melvin Metcalfe Snr (*Earthquake*)
Editing: Harold F. Kress, Carl Kress (*The Towering Inferno*)
Song: 'We May Never Love Like This Again' from *The Towering Inferno* (*m/ly* Al Kasha, Joel Hirshhorn)
Original Dramatic Score: Nino Rota, Carmine Coppola (*The Godfather Part II*)
Adaptation and Original Song Score: Nelson Riddle (*The Great Gatsby*)
Documentary Short: *Don't*
Documentary Feature: *Hearts and Minds*
Animated Film: *Closed Mondays*
Live-Action Short: *One-Eyed Men Are Kings*
Honorary Awards: Howard Hawks; Jean Renoir
Special Achievement Award: Frank Brendel, Glen Robinson, Albert Whitlock (for visual effects, *Earthquake*)

1975
Picture: *One Flew over the Cuckoo's Nest*
Foreign-Language Film: *Dersu Uzala* (Akira Kurosawa)
Director: Milos Forman (*One Flew over the Cuckoo's Nest*)
Actor: Jack Nicholson (*One Flew over the Cuckoo's Nest*)
Actress: Louise Fletcher (*One Flew over the Cuckoo's Nest*)
Supporting Actor: George Burns (*The Sunshine Boys*)
Supporting Actress: Lee Grant (*Shampoo*)
Original Screenplay: Frank Pierson (*Dog Day Afternoon*)
Adapted Screenplay: Lawrence Hauben, Bo Goldman (*One Flew over the Cuckoo's Nest*)
Cinematography: John Alcott (*Barry Lyndon*)
Art Direction: Ken Adam, Roy Walker (*Barry Lyndon*)
Costume Design: Britt Soderland, Milena Canonero (*Barry Lyndon*)
Sound: Robert L. Hoyt, Roger Heman, Earl Madery, John Carter (*Jaws*)
Editing: Verna Fields (*Jaws*)
Song: 'I'm Easy' from *Nashville* (*m/ly* Keith Carradine)
Original Score: John Williams (*Jaws*)
Adaptation and Original Song Score: Leonard Rosenman (*Barry Lyndon*)
Documentary Short: *The End of the Game*
Documentary Feature: *The Man Who Skied Down Everest*
Animated Film: *Great*
Live-Action Short: *Angel and Big Joe*
Honorary Award: Mary Pickford
Special Achievement Awards: Peter Berkos (sound effects, *The Hindenburg*); Albert Whitlock and Glen Robinson (visual effects, *The Hindenburg*)
Irving Thalberg Memorial Award: Mervyn Le Roy

1976
Picture: *Rocky*
Foreign-Language Film: *Black and White in Colour* (Jean-Jacques Annaud)
Director: John G. Avildsen (*Rocky*)
Actor: Peter Finch (*Network*)
Actress: Faye Dunaway (*Network*)
Supporting Actor: Jason Robards (*All the President's Men*)
Supporting Actress: Beatrice Straight (*Network*)
Original Screenplay: Paddy Chayevsky (*Network*)
Adapted Screenplay: William Goldman (*All the President's Men*)
Cinematography: Haskell Wexler (*Bound for Glory*)
Art Direction: George Jenkins (*All the President's Men*)
Costume Design: Danilo Donati (*Fellini's Casanova*)
Sound: Arthur Piantadosi, Les Fresholtz, Dick Alexander, Jim Webb (*All the President's Men*)
Editing: Richard Halsey, Scott Conrad (*Rocky*)
Song: 'Evergreen' from *A Star Is Born* (*m* Barbra Streisand, *ly* Paul Williams)
Original Score: Jerry Goldsmith (*The Omen*)
Adaptation and Original Song Score: Leonard Rosenman (*Bound for Glory*)
Documentary Short: *Number Our Days*
Documentary Feature: *Harlan County, USA*
Animated Film: *Leisure*
Live-Action Short: *In the Region of Ice*
Special Achievement Awards: Carlo Rambaldi, Glen Robinson, Frank Van Der Veer (visual effects, *King Kong*); L. B. Abbott, Glen Robinson, Matthew Yuricich (visual effects, *Logan's Run*)
Irving Thalberg Memorial Award: Pandro S. Berman

1977
Picture: *Annie Hall*
Foreign-Language Film: *Madame Rosa* (Moshe Mizrahi)
Director: Woody Allen (*Annie Hall*)
Actor: Richard Dreyfuss (*The Goodbye Girl*)
Actress: Diane Keaton (*Annie Hall*)
Supporting Actor: Jason Robards (*Julia*)
Supporting Actress: Vanessa Redgrave (*Julia*)
Original Screenplay: Woody Allen, Marshall Brickman (*Annie Hall*)
Adapted Screenplay: Alvin Sargent (*Julia*)
Cinematography: Vilmos Zsigmond (*Close Encounters of the Third Kind*)
Art Direction: John Barry, Norman Reynolds, Leslie Dilley (*Star Wars*)
Costume Design: John Mollo (*Star Wars*)
Sound: Don MacDougall, Ray West, Bob Minkler, Derek Ball (*Star Wars*)
Editing: Marcia Lucas, Richard Chew (*Star Wars*)
Visual Effects: John Stears, John Dystra, Richard Edlund, Grant McCune, Robert Black (*Star Wars*)
Song: 'You Light Up My Life' from *You Light Up My Life* (*m/ly* Joseph Brooks)
Adaptation and Original Song Score: Jonathan Tunick (*A Little Night Music*)
Documentary Short: *Gravity Is My Enemy*
Documentary Feature: *Who Are the DeBolts? And Where Did They Get Nineteen Kids?*
Animated Film: *Sand Castle*
Live-Action Short: *I'll Find a Way*
Honorary Award: Margaret Booth (for contribution to the art of film editing)
Special Achievement Awards: Frank Warner (sound effects editing, *Close Encounters of the Third Kind*); Benjamin Burtt Jnr (sound effects, *Star Wars*)
Irving Thalberg Memorial Award: Walter Mirisch

1978
Picture: *The Deer Hunter*
Foreign-Language Film: *Get Out Your Handkerchiefs* (Bertrand Blier)
Director: Michael Cimino (*The Deer Hunter*)
Actor: Jon Voight (*Coming Home*)
Actress: Jane Fonda (*Coming Home*)
Supporting Actor: Christopher Walken (*The Deer Hunter*)
Supporting Actress: Maggie Smith (*California Suite*)
Original Screenplay: Nancy Dowd, Waldo Salt, Robert C. Jones (*Coming Home*)
Adapted Screenplay: Oliver Stone (*Midnight Express*)
Cinematography: Nestor Almendros (*Days of Heaven*)
Art Direction: Paul Sylbert, Edwin O'Donovan (*Heaven Can Wait*)
Costume Design: Anthony Powell (*Death on the Nile*)
Sound: Richard Portman, William McCaughey, Aaron Rochin, Darrin Knight (*The Deer Hunter*)
Editing: Peter Zinner (*The Deer Hunter*)
Song: 'Last Dance' from *Thank God It's Friday* (*m/ly* Paul Jabara)
Original Score: Giorgio Moroder (*Midnight Express*)
Adaptation and Original Song Score: Joe Renzetti (*The Buddy Holly Story*)
Documentary Short: *The Flight of the Gossamer Condor*
Documentary Feature: *Scared Straight*
Animated Film: *Special Delivery*
Live-Action Short: *Teenage Father*
Honorary Awards: Walter Lantz (for his animated pictures); Laurence Olivier (for the full body of his work); King Vidor (for his incomparable achievements)
Special Achievement Award: Les Bowie, Colin Chilvers, Denys Coop, Roy Field, Derek Meddings, Zoran Perisic (visual effects, *Superman*)

1979
Picture: *Kramer vs Kramer*
Foreign-Language Film: *The Tin Drum* (Volker Schlöndorff)
Director: Robert Benton (*Kramer vs Kramer*)
Actor: Dustin Hoffman (*Kramer vs Kramer*)
Actress: Sally Field (*Norma Rae*)
Supporting Actor: Melvyn Douglas (*Being There*)
Supporting Actress: Meryl Streep (*Kramer vs Kramer*)
Original Screenplay: Steve Tesich (*Breaking Away*)
Adapted Screenplay: Robert Benton (*Kramer vs Kramer*)
Cinematography: Vittorio Storaro (*Apocalypse Now*)
Art Direction: Philip Rosenberg, Tony Walton (*All That Jazz*)
Costume Design: Albert Wolsky (*All That Jazz*)
Sound: Walter Murch, Mark Berger, Richard Beggs, Nat Boxer (*Apocalypse Now*)
Editing: Alan Heim (*All That Jazz*)
Visual Effects: H. R. Giger, Carlo Rambaldi, Brian Johnson, Nick Allder, Denys Ayling (*Alien*)
Song: 'It Goes Like It Goes' from *Norma Rae* (*m* David Shire, *ly* Norman Gimbel)
Original Score: Georges Delerue (*A Little Romance*)
Adaptation and Original Song Score: Ralph Burns (*All That Jazz*)
Documentary Short: *Paul Robeson: Tribute to an Artist*
Documentary Feature: *Best Boy*
Animated Film: *Every Child*
Live-Action Short: *Board and Care*
Honorary Award: Alec Guinness (for advancing the art of screen acting)
Special Achievement Award: Alan Splet (sound editing, *The Black Stallion*)
Irving Thalberg Memorial Award: Ray Stark

1980
Picture: *Ordinary People*
Foreign-Language Film: *Moscow Does Not Believe in Tears* (Vladimir Menshov)
Director: Robert Redford (*Ordinary People*)
Actor: Robert De Niro (*Raging Bull*)
Actress: Sissy Spacek (*Coal Miner's Daughter*)
Supporting Actor: Timothy Hutton (*Ordinary People*)
Supporting Actress: Mary Steenburgen (*Melvin and Howard*)
Original Screenplay: Bo Goldman (*Melvin and Howard*)
Adapted Screenplay: Alvin Sargent (*Ordinary People*)
Cinematography: Geoffrey Unsworth, Ghislain Cloquet (*Tess*)
Art Direction: Pierre Guffroy, Jack Stephens (*Tess*)
Costume Design: Anthony Powell (*Tess*)
Sound: Bill Varney, Steve Maslow, Gregg Landacker, Peter Sutton (*The Empire Strikes Back*)
Editing: Thelma Schoonmaker (*Raging Bull*)
Song: 'Fame' from *Fame* (*m* Michael Gore, *ly* Dean Pitchford)
Original Score: Michael Gore (*Fame*)
Documentary Short: *Karl Hess: Towards Liberty*
Documentary Feature: *From Mao to Mozart: Isaac Stern in China*
Animated Film: *The Fly*
Live-Action Short: *The Dollar Bottom*
Honorary Award: Henry Fonda (in recognition of his brilliant accomplishments)
Special Achievement Award: Brian Johnson, Richard Edlund, Dennis Muren, Bruce Nicholson (visual effects, *The Empire Strikes Back*)

1981
Picture: *Chariots of Fire*
Foreign-Language Film: *Mephisto* (Istvan Szabo)
Director: Warren Beatty (*Reds*)
Actor: Henry Fonda (*On Golden Pond*)
Actress: Katharine Hepburn (*On Golden Pond*)
Supporting Actor: John Gielgud (*Arthur*)
Supporting Actress: Maureen Stapleton (*Reds*)
Original Screenplay: Colin Welland (*Chariots of Fire*)
Adapted Screenplay: Ernest Thompson (*On Golden Pond*)
Cinematography: Vittorio Storaro (*Reds*)
Art Direction: Norman Reynolds, Leslie Dilley (*Raiders of the Lost Ark*)
Costume Design: Milena Canonero (*Chariots of Fire*)
Make-Up: Rick Baker (*An American Werewolf in London*)
Sound: Bill Varney, Steve Maslow, Gregg Landaker, Roy Charman (*Raiders of the Lost Ark*)
Editing: Michael Kahn (*Raiders of the Lost Ark*)
Song: 'Arthur's Theme' from *Arthur* (*m/ly* Burt Bacharach, Carole Bayer Sager, Christopher Cross, Peter Allen)
Original Score: Vangelis (*Chariots of Fire*)
Documentary Short: *Close Harmony*
Documentary Feature: *Genocide*
Animated Film: *Crac*
Live-Action Short: *Violet*
Honorary Award: Barbara Stanwyck
Special Achievement Awards: Ben Burtt, Richard L. Anderson (sound effects editing, *Raiders of the Lost Ark*)
Irving Thalberg Memorial Award: Albert R. Broccoli

1982
Picture: *Gandhi*
Foreign-Language Picture: *To Begin Again* (José Luis Garci)
Director: Richard Attenborough (*Gandhi*)
Actor: Ben Kingsley (*Gandhi*)
Actress: Meryl Streep (*Sophie's Choice*)
Supporting Actor: Louis Gossett Jnr (*An Officer and a Gentleman*)
Supporting Actress: Jessica Lange (*Tootsie*)
Original Screenplay: John Briley (*Gandhi*)
Adapted Screenplay: Costa-Gavras, Donald Stewart (*Missing*)
Cinematography: Billy Williams, Ronnie Taylor (*Gandhi*)
Art Direction: Stuart Craig, Bob Lang (*Gandhi*)
Costume Design: John Mollo, Bhanu Athaiya (*Gandhi*)
Make-Up: Sarah Monzani, Michele Burke (*Quest for Fire*)
Sound: Robert Knudson, Robert Glass, Don Digirolamo, Gene Cantemassa (*ET*)
Sound Effects Editing: Charles L. Campbell, Ben Burtt (*ET*)
Editing: John Bloom (*Gandhi*)
Visual Effects: Carlo Rambaldi, Dennis Muren, Kenneth F. Smith (*ET*)
Song: 'Up Where We Belong' from *An Officer and a Gentleman* (*m* Jack Nitzsche, Buffy Sainte-Marie, *ly* Will Jennings)
Original Score: John Williams (*ET*)
Original Song Score or Adaptation: Henry Mancini, Leslie Bricusse (*Victor/Victoria*)
Documentary Short: *If You Love This Planet*
Documentary Feature: *Just Another Missing Kid*
Animated Film: *Tango*
Live-Action Short: *A Shocking Accident*
Honorary Award: Mickey Rooney

1983
Picture: *Terms of Endearment*
Foreign-Language Film: *Fanny and Alexander* (Ingmar Bergman)
Director: James L. Brooks (*Terms of Endearment*)
Actor: Robert Duvall (*Tender Mercies*)
Actress: Shirley MacLaine (*Terms of Endearment*)
Supporting Actor: Jack Nicholson (*Terms of Endearment*)
Supporting Actress: Linda Hunt (*The Year of Living Dangerously*)
Original Screenplay: Horton Foote (*Tender Mercies*)
Adapted Screenplay: James L. Brooks (*Terms of Endearment*)
Cinematography: Sven Nykvist (*Fanny and Alexander*)
Art Direction: Anna Asp (*Fanny and Alexander*)
Costume Design: Marik Vos (*Fanny and Alexander*)
Sound: Mark Berger, Tom Scott, Randy Thom, David MacMillan (*The Right Stuff*)
Sound Effects Editing: Jay Boekelheide (*The Right Stuff*)
Editing: Glenn Farr, Lisa Fruchtman, Stephen A. Rotter, Douglas Stewart, Tom Rolf (*The Right Stuff*)
Song: 'Flashdance' from *Flashdance* (*m* Giorgio Moroder, *ly* Keith Forsey, Irene Cara)
Original Score: Bill Conti (*The Right Stuff*)
Original Song Score or Adaptation: Michel Legrand, Alan and Marilyn Bergman (*Yentl*)
Documentary Short: *Flamenco at 5:15*
Documentary Feature: *He Makes Me Feel Like Dancin'*
Animated Film: *Sundae in New York*
Live-Action Short: *Boys and Girls*
Honorary Award: Hal Roach
Special Achievement Awards: Richard Edlund, Dennis Muren, Ken Ralston, Phil Tippett (visual effects, *Return of the Jedi*)

1984
Picture: *Amadeus*
Foreign-Language Film: *Dangerous Moves* (Richard Dembo)
Director: Milos Forman (*Amadeus*)
Actor: F. Murray Abraham (*Amadeus*)
Actress: Sally Field (*Places in the Heart*)
Supporting Actor: Haing S. Ngor (*The Killing Fields*)
Supporting Actress: Peggy Ashcroft (*A Passage to India*)
Original Screenplay: Robert Benton (*Places in the Heart*)
Adapted Screenplay: Peter Shaffer (*Amadeus*)
Cinematography: Chris Menges (*The Killing Fields*)
Art Direction: Patrizia Von Brandenstein (*Amadeus*)
Costume Design: Theodor Pistek (*Amadeus*)
Make-Up: Paul LeBlanc, Dick Smith (*Amadeus*)
Sound: Mark Berger, Tom Scott, Todd Boekelheide, Chris Newman (*Amadeus*)
Editing: Jim Clark (*The Killing Fields*)
Visual Effects: Dennis Muren, Michael McAlister, Lorne Petersen, George Gibbs (*Ghostbusters*)
Song: 'I Just Called to Say I Love You' from *The Woman in Red* (*m/ly* Stevie Wonder)
Original Score: Maurice Jarre (*A Passage to India*)
Original Song Score or Adaptation: Prince (*Purple Rain*)
Documentary Short: *The Stone Carvers*
Documentary Feature: *The Times of Harvey Milk*
Animated Film: *Charade*
Live-Action Short: *Up*
Honorary Award: James Stewart
Special Achievement Award: Kay Rose (sound effects editing, *The River*)

1985
Picture: *Out of Africa*
Foreign-Language Film: *The Official Story* (Luis Puenzo)
Director: Sydney Pollack (*Out of Africa*)
Actor: William Hurt (*Kiss of the Spider Woman*)
Actress: Geraldine Page (*The Trip to Bountiful*)
Supporting Actor: Don Ameche (*Cocoon*)
Supporting Actress: Anjelica Huston (*Prizzi's Honor*)
Original Screenplay: William Kelley, Pamela Wallace, Earl W. Wallace (*Witness*)
Adapted Screenplay: Kurt Luedtke (*Out of Africa*)
Cinematography: David Watkin (*Out of Africa*)
Art Direction: Stephen Grimes (*Out of Africa*)
Costume Design: Emi Wada (*Ran*)
Make-Up: Michael Westmore, Zoltan Elek (*Mask*)
Sound: Chris Jenkins, Gary Alexander, Larry Stensvold, Peter Handford (*Out of Africa*)
Sound Effects Editing: Charles L. Campbell, Robert Rutledge (*Back to the Future*)
Editing: Thom Noble (*Witness*)
Visual Effects: Ken Ralston, Ralph McQuarrie, Scott Farrar, David Berry (*Cocoon*)
Song: 'Say You, Say Me' from *White Nights* (*m/ly* Lionel Richie)
Original Score: John Barry (*Out of Africa*)
Documentary Short: *Witness to War*
Documentary Feature: *Broken Rainbow*
Animated Film: *Anna & Bella*
Live-Action Short: *Molly's Pilgrim*
Honorary Awards: Paul Newman; Alex North

1986
Picture: *Platoon*
Foreign-Language Film: *The Assault* (Fons Rademakers)
Director: Oliver Stone (*Platoon*)
Actor: Paul Newman (*The Color of Money*)
Actress: Marlee Matlin (*Children of a Lesser God*)
Supporting Actor: Michael Caine (*Hannah and Her Sisters*)
Supporting Actress: Dianne Wiest (*Hannah and Her Sisters*)
Original Screenplay: Woody Allen (*Hannah and Her Sisters*)
Adapted Screenplay: Ruth Prawer Jhabvala (*A Room with a View*)
Cinematography: Chris Menges (*The Mission*)
Art Direction: Gianni Quaranta, Brian Ackland-Snow (*A Room with a View*)
Costume Design: Jenny Beavan, John Bright (*A Room with a View*)
Make-Up: Chris Walas, Stephan Dupuis (*The Fly*)
Sound: John K. Wilkinson, Richard Rogers, Charles Grenzbach, Simon Kaye (*Platoon*)
Sound Effects Editing: Don Sharpe (*Aliens*)
Editing: Claire Simpson (*Platoon*)
Visual Effects: Robert Skotak, Stan Winston, John Richardson, Suzanne Benson (*Aliens*)
Song: 'Take My Breath Away' from *Top Gun* (*m* Giorgio Moroder, *ly* Tom Whitlock)
Original Score: Herbie Hancock (*Round Midnight*)
Documentary Short: *Women – For America, For the World*
Documentary Feature: *Artie Shaw: Time Is All You've Got*
Animated Film: *A Greek Tragedy*
Live-Action Short: *Precious Images*
Honorary Award: Ralph Bellamy
Irving Thalberg Memorial Award: Steven Spielberg

1987
Picture: *The Last Emperor*
Foreign-Language Film: *Babette's Feast* (Gabriel Axel)
Director: Bernardo Bertolucci (*The Last Emperor*)
Actor: Michael Douglas (*Wall Street*)
Actress: Cher (*Moonstruck*)
Supporting Actor: Sean Connery (*The Untouchables*)
Supporting Actress: Olympia Dukakis (*Moonstruck*)
Original Screenplay: John Patrick Shanley (*Moonstruck*)
Adapted Screenplay: Mark Peploe, Bernardo Bertolucci (*The Last Emperor*)
Cinematography: Vittorio Storaro (*The Last Emperor*)
Art Direction: Ferdinando Scarfiotti (*The Last Emperor*)
Costume Design: James Acheson (*The Last Emperor*)
Make-Up: Rick Bajer (*Harry and the Hendersons*)
Sound: Bill Rowe, Ivan Sharrock (*The Last Emperor*)
Editing: Gabriella Cristiani (*The Last Emperor*)
Visual Effects: Dennis Muren, William George, Harley Jessup, Kenneth Smith (*Innerspace*)
Song: 'The Time of My Life' from *Dirty Dancing* (*m* Franke Previte, John DeNicola, Donald Markowitz, *ly* Franke Previte)
Original Score: Ryuichi Sakamoto, David Byrne, Cong Su (*The Last Emperor*)
Documentary Short: *Young at Heart*
Documentary Feature: *The Ten-Year Lunch: The Wit and Legend of the Algonquin Round Table*
Animated Film: *The Man Who Planted Trees*
Live-Action Short: *Ray's Male Heterosexual Dance Hall*
Special Achievement Awards: Stephen Flick, John

Pospisil (sound effects, *Robocop*)
Irving Thalberg Memorial Award: Billy Wilder

1988

Picture: *Rain Man*
Foreign-Language Film: *Pelle the Conqueror* (Bille August)
Director: Barry Levinson (*Rain Man*)
Actor: Dustin Hoffman (*Rain Man*)
Actress: Jodie Foster (*The Accused*)
Supporting Actor: Kevin Kline (*A Fish Called Wanda*)
Supporting Actress: Geena Davis (*The Accidental Tourist*)
Original Screenplay: Ronald Bass, Barry Morrow (*Rain Man*)
Adapted Screenplay: Christopher Hampton (*Dangerous Liaisons*)
Cinematography: Peter Biziou (*Mississippi Burning*)
Art Direction: Stuart Craig (*Dangerous Liaisons*)
Costume Design: James Acheson (*Dangerous Liaisons*)
Make-Up: Ve Neill, Steve LaPorte, Robert Short (*Beetlejuice*)
Sound: Les Fresholtz, Dick Alexander, Vern Poore, Willie D. Burton (*Bird*)
Sound Effects Editing: Charles L. Campbell, Louis L. Edelman (*Who Framed Roger Rabbit?*)
Editing: Arthur Schimdt (*Who Framed Roger Rabbit?*)
Visual Effects: Ken Ralston, Richard Williams, Edward Jones, George Gibbs (*Who Framed Roger Rabbit?*)
Song: 'Let the River Run' from *Working Girl* (m/ly Carly Simon)
Original Score: Dave Grusin (*The Milagro Beanfield War*)
Documentary Short: *You Don't Have to Die*
Documentary Feature: *Hotel Terminus: The Life and Times of Klaus Barbie*
Animated Film: *Tin Toy*
Live-Action Short: *The Appointments of Dennis Jennings*
Special Achievement Award: Richard Williams (animation direction, *Who Framed Roger Rabbit?*)

1989

Picture: *Driving Miss Daisy*
Foreign-Language Film: *Cinema Paradiso* (Giuseppe Tornatore)
Director: Oliver Stone (*Born on the Fourth of July*)
Actor: Daniel Day-Lewis (*My Left Foot*)
Actress: Jessica Tandy (*Driving Miss Daisy*)
Supporting Actor: Denzel Washington (*Glory*)
Supporting Actress: Brenda Fricker (*My Left Foot*)
Original Screenplay: Tom Schulman (*Dead Poets Society*)
Adapted Screenplay: Alfred Uhry (*Driving Miss Daisy*)
Cinematography: Freddie Francis (*Glory*)
Art Direction: Anton Furst (*Batman*)
Costume Design: Phyllis Dalton (*Henry V*)
Make-Up: Manlio Rocchetti, Lynn Barber, Kevin Haney (*Driving Miss Daisy*)
Sound: Donald O. Mitchell, Kevin O'Connell, Greg P. Russell, Keith A. Wester (*Black Rain*)
Sound Effects Editing: Ben Burtt, Richard Hymns (*Indiana Jones and the Last Crusade*)
Editing: David Brenner, Joe Hutshing (*Born on the Fourth of July*)
Visual Effects: John Bruno, Dennis Muren, Hoyt Yeatman, Dennis Skotak (*The Abyss*)
Song: 'Under the Sea' from *The Little Mermaid* (m Alan Menken, ly Howard Ashman)
Original Score: Alan Menken (*The Little Mermaid*)
Documentary Short: *The Johnstown Flood*
Documentary Feature: *Common Threads: Stories from the Quilt*
Animated Film: *Balance*
Live-Action Short: *Work Experience*
Honorary Award: Akira Kurosawa

1990

Picture: *Dances with Wolves*
Foreign-Language Film: *Journey of Hope* (Xavier Koller)
Director: Kevin Costner (*Dances with Wolves*)
Actor: Jeremy Irons (*Reversal of Fortune*)
Actress: Kathy Bates (*Misery*)
Supporting Actor: Joe Pesci (*GoodFellas*)
Supporting Actress: Whoopi Goldberg (*Ghost*)
Original Screenplay: Bruce Joel Rubin (*Ghost*)
Adapted Screenplay: Michael Blake (*Dances with Wolves*)
Cinematography: Dean Semler (*Dances with Wolves*)

Art Direction: Richard Sylbert (*Dick Tracy*)
Costume Design: Franca Squarciapino (*Cyrano de Bergerac*)
Make-Up: John Caglione Jnr, Doug Drexler (*Dick Tracy*)
Sound: Russell Williams II, Jeffrey Perkins, Bill W. Benton, Greg Watkins (*Dances with Wolves*)
Sound Effects Editing: Cecelia Hall, George Watters II (*The Hunt for Red October*)
Editing: Neil Travis (*Dances with Wolves*)
Song: 'Sooner or Later' from *Dick Tracy* (m/ly Stephen Sondheim)
Original Score: John Barry (*Dances with Wolves*)
Documentary Short: *Days of Waiting*
Documentary Feature: *American Dream*
Animated Film: *Creature Comforts*
Live-Action Short: *The Lunch Date*
Honorary Awards: Sophia Loren; Myrna Loy
Special Achievement Awards: Eric Brevig, Rob Bottin, Tim McGovern, Alex Funke (visual effects, *Total Recall*)
Irving Thalberg Memorial Award: Richard Zanuck and David Brown

1991

Picture: *Silence of the Lambs*
Foreign-Language Film: *Mediterraneo* (Gabriele Salvatores)
Director: Jonathan Demme (*Silence of the Lambs*)
Actor: Anthony Hopkins (*Silence of the Lambs*)
Actress: Jodie Foster (*Silence of the Lambs*)
Supporting Actor: Jack Palance (*City Slickers*)
Supporting Actress: Mercedes Ruehl (*The Fisher King*)
Original Screenplay: Callie Khouri (*Thelma and Louise*)
Adapted Screenplay: Ted Tally (*Silence of the Lambs*)
Cinematography: Robert Richardson (*JFK*)
Art Direction: Dennis Gassner (*Bugsy*)
Costume Design: Albert Wolsky (*Bugsy*)
Make-Up: Stan Winston, Jeff Dawn (*Terminator 2*)
Sound: Tom Johnson, Gary Rydstrom, Gary Summers, Lee Orloff (*Terminator 2*)
Sound Effects Editing: Gary Rydstrom, Gloria S. Borders (*Terminator 2*)
Editing: Joe Hutshing, Pietro Scalia (*JFK*)
Visual Effects: Dennis Muren, Stan Winston, Gene Warren Jnr, Robert Skotak (*Terminator 2*)
Song: 'Beauty and the Beast' from *Beauty and the Beast* (m Alan Menken, ly Howard Ashman)
Original Score: Alan Menken (*Beauty and the Beast*)
Documentary Short: *Deadly Deception*
Documentary Feature: *In the Shadow of the Stars*
Animated Film: *Manipulation*
Live-Action Short: *Session Man*
Honorary Award: Satyajit Ray
Irving Thalberg Memorial Award: George Lucas

1992

Picture: *Unforgiven*
Foreign-Language Film: *Indochine* (Régis Wargnier)
Director: Clint Eastwood (*Unforgiven*)
Actor: Al Pacino (*Scent of a Woman*)
Actress: Emma Thompson (*Howards End*)
Supporting Actor: Gene Hackman (*Unforgiven*)
Supporting Actress: Marisa Tomei (*My Cousin Vinny*)
Original Screenplay: Neil Jordan (*The Crying Game*)
Adapted Screenplay: Ruth Prawer Jhabvala (*Howards End*)
Cinematography: Philippe Rousselot (*A River Runs through It*)
Art Direction: Luciana Arrighi (*Howards End*)
Costume Design: Eiko Ishioka (*Bram Stoker's Dracula*)
Make-Up: Greg Cannom, Michele Burke, Matthew W. Mungle (*Bram Stoker's Dracula*)
Sound: Chris Jenkins, Doug Hemphill, Mark Smith, Simon Kaye (*The Last of the Mohicans*)
Sound Effects Editing: Tom C. McCarthy, David E. Stone (*Bram Stoker's Dracula*)
Editing: Joel Cox (*Unforgiven*)
Visual Effects: Ken Ralston, Doug Chiang, Doug Smythe, Tom Woodruff (*Death Becomes Her*)
Song: 'A Whole New World' from *Aladdin* (m Alan Menken, ly Tim Rice)
Original Score: Alan Menken (*Aladdin*)
Documentary Short: *Educating Peter*
Documentary Feature: *The Panama Deception*
Animated Film: *Mona Lisa Descending a Staircase*
Live-Action Short: *Omnibus*
Honorary Award: Federico Fellini

1993

Picture: *Schindler's List*
Foreign-Language Film: *Belle Époque* (Fernando Trueba)
Director: Steven Spielberg (*Schindler's List*)
Actor: Tom Hanks (*Philadelphia*)
Actress: Holly Hunter (*The Piano*)
Supporting Actor: Tommy Lee Jones (*The Fugitive*)
Supporting Actress: Anna Paquin (*The Piano*)
Original Screenplay: Jane Campion (*The Piano*)
Adapted Screenplay: Steve Zaillian (*Schindler's List*)
Cinematography: Janusz Kaminski (*Schindler's List*)
Art Direction: Allan Starski (*Schindler's List*)
Costume Design: Gabriella Pescucci (*The Age of Innocence*)
Make-Up: Greg Cannom, Ve Neill, Yolanda Toussieng (*Mrs Doubtfire*)
Sound: Gary Summers, Gary Rydstrom, Shawn Murphy, Rod Judkins (*Jurassic Park*)
Sound Effects Editing: Gary Rydstrom, Richard Hymns (*Jurassic Park*)
Editing: Michael Kahn (*Schindler's List*)
Visual Effects: Dennis Muren, Stan Winston, Phil Tippett, Michael Lantieri (*Jurassic Park*)
Song: 'Streets of Philadelphia' from *Philadelphia* (m/ly Bruce Springsteen)
Original Score: John Williams (*Schindler's List*)
Documentary Short: *Defending Our Lives*
Documentary Feature: *I Am a Promise*
Animated Film: *The Wrong Trousers*
Live-Action Short: *Black Rider*
Honorary Award: Deborah Kerr

1994

Picture: *Forrest Gump*
Foreign-Language Film: *Burnt By the Sun* (Nikita Mikhalkov)
Director: Robert Zemeckis (*Forrest Gump*)
Actor: Tom Hanks (*Forrest Gump*)
Actress: Jessica Lange (*Blue Sky*)
Supporting Actor: Martin Landau (*Ed Wood*)
Supporting Actress: Dianne Wiest (*Bullets Over Broadway*)
Original Screenplay: Quentin Tarantino, Roger Avary (*Pulp Fiction*)
Adapted Screenplay: Eric Roth (*Forrest Gump*)
Cinematography: John Toll (*Legends of the Fall*)
Art Direction: Ken Adam, Carolyn Scott (*The Madness of King George*)
Costume Design: Lizzy Gardiner, Tim Chappel (*The Adventures of Priscilla, Queen of the Desert*)
Make-up: Rick Baker, Ve Neill, Yolanda Toussieng (*Ed Wood*)
Sound: Gregg Landaker, Steve Maslow, Bob Beemer, David R.B. MacMillan (*Speed*)
Sound Effects Editing: Stephen Hunter Flick (*Speed*)
Editing: Arthur Schmidt (*Forrest Gump*)
Visual Effects: Ken Ralston, George Murphy, Stephen Rosenbaum, Allen Hall (*Forrest Gump*)
Song: 'Can You Feel the Love Tonight' from *The Lion King* (m Elton John, ly Tim Rice)
Original Score: Hans Zimmer (*The Lion King*)
Documentary Short: *A Time For Justice*
Documentary Feature: *Maya Lin: A Strong Clear Vision*
Animated film: *Bob's Birthday*
Live-Action Short: *Franz Kafka's It's A Wonderful Life*
Honorary Award: Michelangelo Antonioni
Irving G. Thalberg Memorial Award: Clint Eastwood

1995

Picture: *Braveheart*
Foreign-Language Film: *Antonia's Line* (Marleen Gorris)
Director: Mel Gibson (*Braveheart*)
Actor: Nicolas Cage (*Leaving Las Vegas*)
Actress: Susan Sarandon (*Dead Man Walking*)
Supporting Actor: Kevin Spacey (*The Usual Suspects*)
Supporting Actress: Mira Sorvino (*Mighty Aphrodite*)
Original Screenplay: Christopher McQuarrie (*The Usual Suspects*)
Adapted Screenplay: Emma Thompson (*Sense and Sensibility*)
Cinematography: John Toll (*Braveheart*)
Art Direction: Eugenio Zanetti (*Restoration*)
Costume Design: James Acheson (*Restoration*)
Make-up: Peter Frampton, Paul Pattison, Lois Burwell (*Braveheart*)
Sound: Rick Dior, Steve Pederson, Scott Millan, David MacMillan (*Apollo 13*)
Sound Effects Editing: Lon Bender, Per Hallberg (*Braveheart*)

Editing: Michael J. Hill, Daniel P. Hanley (*Apollo 13*)
Visual Effects: Scott E. Anderson, Charles Gibson, Neal Scanlan, John Cox (*Babe*)
Song: 'Colours of the Wind' from *Pocahontas* (m Alan Menken, ly Stephen Schwartz)
Original Dramatic Score: Luis Enriquez Bacalov (*Il Postino*)
Original Musical or Comedy Score: *Pocahontas* (Alan Menken, Stephen Schwartz)
Documentary Short: *One Survivor Remembers*
Documentary Feature: *Anne Frank Remembered*
Animated film: *A Close Shave*
Live-Action Short: *Lieberman in Love*
Honorary Awards: Kirk Douglas, Chuck Jones

1996

Picture: *The English Patient* (Saul Zaentz)
Foreign-Language Film: *Kolya* (Jan Sverák)
Director: Anthony Minghella (*The English Patient*)
Actor: Geoffrey Rush (*Shine*)
Actress: Frances McDormand (*Fargo*)
Supporting Actor: Cuba Gooding, Jnr (*Jerry Maguire*)
Supporting Actress: Juliette Binoche (*The English Patient*)
Original Screenplay: *Fargo* (Ethan Coen, Joel Coen)
Adapted Screenplay: *Sling Blade* (Billy Bob Thornton)
Cinematography: John Seale (*The English Patient*)
Art Direction: Stuart Craig (*The English Patient*)
Costume Design: Ann Roth (*The English Patient*)
Make-up: David Leroy Anderson, Rick Baker (*The Nutty Professor*)
Sound: Mark Berger, Walter Murch, Chris Newman, David Parker (*The English Patient*)
Sound Effects Editing: Bruce Stambler (*The Ghost and the Darkness*)
Editing: Walter Murch (*The English Patient*)
Visual Effects: Volker Engel, Clay Pinney, Douglas Smith, Joseph Viskocil (*Independence Day*)
Song: 'You Must Love Me' from *Evita* (m Andrew Lloyd Webber, ly Tim Rice)
Original Dramatic Score: Gabriel Yared (*The English Patient*)
Original Musical or Comedy Score: Rachel Portman (*Emma*)
Documentary Short: *Breathing Lessons: The Life And Work of Mark O'Brien* (Jessica Yu)
Documentary Feature: *When We Were Kings* (Leon Gast, David Sonenberg)
Animated Film: *Quest* (Tyron Montgomery, Thomas Stellmach)
Live-Action Short: *Dear Diary* (David Frankel, Barry Jossen)
Honorary Award: Michael Kidd
Irving G. Thalberg Memorial Award: Saul Zaentz

1997

Picture: *Titanic* (James Cameron, Jon Landau)
Foreign-Language Film: *Character* (Mike Van Diem)
Director: James Cameron (*Titanic*)
Actor: Jack Nicholson (*As Good as It Gets*)
Actress: Helen Hunt (*As Good as It Gets*)
Supporting Actor: Robin Williams (*Good Will Hunting*)
Supporting Actress: Kim Basinger (*LA Confidential*)
Original Screenplay: Ben Affleck, Matt Damon (*Good Will Hunting*)
Adapted Screenplay: Curtis Hanson, Brian Helgeland (*LA Confidential*)
Cinematography: Russell Carpenter (*Titanic*)
Art Direction: Peter Lamont (*Titanic*)
Costume Design: Deborah L. Scott (*Titanic*)
Make-up: David Leroy Anderson, Rick Baker (*Men in Black*)
Sound: Tom Johnson, Gary Rydstrom, Gary Summers, Mark Ulano (*Titanic*)
Sound Effects Editing: Tom Bellfort, Christopher Boyes (*Titanic*)
Editing: Conrad Buff, James Cameron, Richard A. Harris (*Titanic*)
Visual Effects: Thomas L. Fisher, Michael Kanfer, Mark Lasoff, Robert Legato (*Titanic*)
Song: 'My Heart Will Go On' from *Titanic* (m James Horner, ly Will Jennings)
Original Dramatic Score: James Horner (*Titanic*)
Original Musical or Comedy Score: Anne Dudley (*The Full Monty*)
Documentary Short: *A Story of Healing* (Donna Dewey, Carol Pasternak)
Documentary Feature: *The Long Way Home* (Rabbi Marvin Hier, Richard Trank)
Animated Film: *Geri's Game* (Jan Pinkava)

Live-Action Short: *Visas and Virtue* (Chris Donahue, Chris Tashima)
Honorary Award: Stanley Donen

1998
Picture: *Shakespeare in Love*
Foreign Language Film: *Life is Beautiful* (Roberto Benigni)
Director: Steven Spielberg (*Saving Private Ryan*)
Actor: Roberto Benigni (*Life is Beautiful*)
Actress: Gwyneth Paltrow (*Shakespeare in Love*)
Supporting Actor: James Coburn (*Affliction*)
Supporting Actress: Judi Dench (*Shakespeare in Love*)
Original Screenplay: *Shakespeare in Love* (Marc Norman, Tom Stoppard)
Adapted Screenplay: Bill Condon (*Gods and Monsters*)
Cinematography: Janusz Kaminski (*Saving Private Ryan*)
Art Direction: Martin Childs (*Shakespeare in Love*)
Costume Design: Sandy Powell (*Shakespeare in Love*)
Make-up: Jenny Shircore (*Elizabeth*)
Sound: Gary Rydstrom, Gary Summers, Andy Nelson, Ronald Judkins (*Saving Private Ryan*)
Sound Effects Editing: Gary Rydstrom, Richard Hymns (*Saving Private Ryan*)
Editing: Michael Kahn (*Saving Private Ryan*)
Visual Effects: Joel Hynek, Nicholas Brooks, Stuart Robertson, Kevin Mack (*What Dreams May Come*)
Song: 'When You Believe' from *The Prince of Egypt* (m/l Stephen Schwartz)
Original Score: Nicola Piovani (*Life is Beautiful*)
Original Musical or Comedy Score: Stephen Warbeck (*Shakespeare in Love*)
Documentary Short: *The Personals: Improvisation on Romance in the Golden Years* (Keiko Ibi)
Documentary Feature: *The Last Days* (James Moll, Ken Lipper)
Animated film: *Bunny* (Chris Wedge)
Live-Action Short: *Election Night/Valgaften* (Kim Magnusson, Anders Thomas Jensen)
Honorary Award: Elia Kazan
Irving G.Thalberg Memorial Award: Norman Jewison

1999
Picture: *American Beauty*
Foreign Language Film: *All about My Mother* (Pedro Almodóvar)
Director: Sam Mendes (*American Beauty*)
Actor: Kevin Spacey (*American Beauty*)
Actress: Hilary Swank (*Boys Don't Cry*)
Supporting Actor: Michael Caine (*The Cider House Rules*)
Supporting Actress: Angelina Jolie (*Girl, Interrupted*)
Original Screenplay: Alan Ball (*American Beauty*)
Adapted Screenplay: John Irving (*The Cider House Rules*)
Cinematography: Conrad L. Hall (*American Beauty*)
Art Direction: Rick Heinrichs (*Sleepy Hollow*)
Costume Design: Lindy Hemming (*Topsy-Turvy*)
Make-up: Christine Blundell, Trefor Proud(*Topsy-Turvy*)
Sound: John Reitz, Gregg Rudloff, David Campbell, David Lee (*The Matrix*)
Sound Effects Editing: Dane A. Davis (*The Matrix*)
Editing: Zach Staenberg (*The Matrix*)
Visual Effects: John Gaeta, Janek Sirrs, Steve Courtley, Jon Thum (*The Matrix*)
Song: 'You'll Be in My Heart' from *Tarzan* (m/l Phil Collins)
Original Score: John Corigliano (*The Red Violin*)
Documentary Short: *King Gimp* (Susan Hannah Hadary, William A. Whiteford)
Documentary Feature: *One Day in September* (Arthur Cohn, Kevin MacDonald)
Animated film: *The Old Man and the Sea* (Alexandre Petrov)
Live-Action Short: *My Mother Dreams The Satan's Disciples in New York* (Barbara Schock, Tammy Tiehel)
Honorary Award: Andrzej Wajda
Irving Thalberg Memorial Award: Warren Beatty

2000
Picture: *Gladiator*
Foreign-Language Film: *Crouching Tiger, Hidden Dragon* (Ang Lee)
Director: Stephen Soderbergh (*Traffic*)
Actor: Russell Crowe (*Gladiator*)
Actress: Julia Roberts (*Erin Brockovich*)
Supporting Actor: Benicio Del Toro (*Traffic*)
Supporting Actress: Marcia Gay Harden (*Pollock*)
Original Screenplay: Alan Ball (*American Beauty*)
Adapted Screenplay: Stephen Gaghan (*Traffic*)
Cinematography: Peter Paul (*Crouching Tiger, Hidden Dragon*)
Art Direction: Tim Yip (*Crouching Tiger, Hidden Dragon*)
Costume Design: Janty Yates (*Gladiator*)
Make-up: Rick Baker, Gail Ryan (*Dr Seuss' How the Grinch Stole Christmas*)
Sound: Scott Millan, Bob Beemer, Ken Weston (*Gladiator*)
Sound Effects Editing: Jon Johnson (*U-571*)
Editing: Stephen Mirrione (*Traffic*)
Visual Effects: John Nelson, Neil Corbould, Tim Burke, Rob Harvey (*Gladiator*)
Song: Things Have Changed from *Wonder Boys* (m/l Bob Dylan)
Original Score: Tan Dan (*Crouching Tiger, Hidden Dragon*)
Documentary Short: *Big Mama* (Tracy Seretean)
Documentary Feature: *Into the Arms of Strangers: Stories of the Kindertransport* (Mark Jonathan Harris, Deborah Oppenheimer)
Animated film: *Father and Daughter* (Michael Dudok de Wit)
Live-Action Short: *Quiero Ser (I Want to Be...)* (Florian Gallenberger)
Honorary Award: Jack Cardiff
Irving Thalberg Memorial Award: Dino de Laurentiis

Books
60 Years of The Oscar: The Official History of the Academy Awards, Robert Osborne (Abbeville Press, 1989).
The Oscars: The Secret History of Hollywood's Academy Awards, Anthony Holden (Little, Brown, 1993).

BAFTA Awards
The British Academy of Film and Television Arts began in 1947 as the British Film Academy, becoming the Society of Film and Television Arts in 1959, and changing its name to its present title in 1975. The BAFTA award, a bronze theatrical mask, was originally nicknamed a Stella. At the beginning, there were two awards for feature films – one for the best film from any source and one for the best British film. Over the years, the awards have widened. The film winners in the major categories are listed below.

1947
Film: *The Best Years of Our Lives* (William Wyler)
British Film: *Odd Man Out* (Carol Reed)

1948
Film: *Hamlet* (Laurence Olivier)
British Film: *The Fallen Idol* (Carol Reed)

1949
Film: *The Bicycle Thief* (Vittorio De Sica)
British Film: *The Third Man* (Carol Reed)

1950
Film: *All About Eve* (Joseph L. Mankiewicz)
British Film: *The Blue Lamp* (Basil Dearden)

1951
Film: *La Ronde* (Max Ophuls)
British Film: *The Lavender Hill Mob* (Charles Crichton)

1952
Film: *The Sound Barrier* (US: *Breaking the Sound Barrier*) (David Lean)
British Film: *The Sound Barrier* (David Lean)
Actor: Ralph Richardson (*The Sound Barrier*)
Actress: Vivien Leigh (*A Streetcar Named Desire*)
Foreign Actor: Marlon Brando (*Viva Zapata!*)
Foreign Actress: Simone Signoret (*Casque d'Or*)
Newcomer: Claire Bloom (*Limelight*)

1953
Film: *Forbidden Games* (René Clément)
British Film: *Genevieve* (Henry Cornelius)
Actor: John Gielgud (*Julius Caesar*)
Actress: Audrey Hepburn (*Roman Holiday*)

Foreign Actor: Marlon Brando (*Julius Caesar*)
Foreign Actress: Leslie Caron (*Lili*)
Newcomer: Norman Wisdom (*Trouble in Store*)

1954
Film: *The Wages of Fear* (Henri-Georges Clouzot)
British Film: *Hobson's Choice* (David Lean)
Actor: Kenneth More (*Doctor in the House*)
Actress: Yvonne Mitchell (*The Divided Heart*)
Foreign Actor: Marlon Brando (*On the Waterfront*)
Foreign Actress: Cornell Borchers (*The Divided Heart*)
Newcomer: David Kossoff (*Chance Meeting*)
Screenplay: Robin Estridge, George Tabori (*Young Lovers aka Chance Meeting*)

1955
Film: *Richard III* (Laurence Olivier)
British Film: *Richard III* (Laurence Olivier)
Actor: Laurence Olivier (*Richard III*)
Actress: Katie Johnson (*The Ladykillers*)
Foreign Actor: Ernest Borgnine (*Marty*)
Foreign Actress: Betsy Blair (*Marty*)
Newcomer: Paul Scofield (*That Lady*)
Screenplay: William Rose (*The Ladykillers*)

1956
Film: *Gervaise* (René Clément)
British Film: *Reach for the Sky* (Lewis Gilbert)
Actor: Peter Finch (*A Town Like Alice aka The Rape of Malaya*)
Actress: Virginia McKenna (*A Town Like Alice aka The Rape of Malaya*)
Foreign Actor: François Périer (*Gervaise*)
Foreign Actress: Anna Magnani (*The Rose Tattoo*)
Newcomer: Eli Wallach (*Baby Doll*)
Screenplay: Nigel Balchin (*The Man Who Never Was*)

1957
Film: *The Bridge on the River Kwai* (David Lean)
British Film: *The Bridge on the River Kwai* (David Lean)
Actor: Alec Guinness (*The Bridge on the River Kwai*)
Actress: Heather Sears (*The Story of Esther Costello*)
Foreign Actor: Henry Fonda (*Twelve Angry Men*)
Foreign Actress: Simone Signoret (*The Witches of Salem*)
Newcomer: Eric Barker (*Brothers in Law*)
Screenplay: Pierre Boulle (*The Bridge on the River Kwai*)

1958
Film: *Room at the Top* (Jack Clayton)
British Film: *Room at the Top* (Jack Clayton)
Actor: Trevor Howard (*The Key*)
Actress: Irene Worth (*Orders to Kill*)
Foreign Actor: Sidney Poitier (*The Defiant Ones*)
Foreign Actress: Simone Signoret (*Room at the Top*)
Newcomer: Paul Massie (*Orders to Kill*)
Screenplay: Paul Dehn (*Orders to Kill*)

1959
Film: *Ben-Hur* (William Wyler)
British Film: *Sapphire* (Basil Dearden)
Actor: Peter Sellers (*I'm All Right Jack*)
Actress: Audrey Hepburn (*The Nun's Story*)
Foreign Actor: Jack Lemmon (*Some Like It Hot*)
Foreign Actress: Shirley MacLaine (*Ask Any Girl*)
Newcomer: Hayley Mills (*Tiger Bay*)
Screenplay: John Boulting, Frank Harvey, Alan Hackney (*I'm All Right Jack*)

1960
Film: *The Apartment* (Billy Wilder)
British Film: *Saturday Night and Sunday Morning* (Karel Reisz)
Actor: Peter Finch (*The Trials of Oscar Wilde*)
Actress: Rachel Roberts (*Saturday Night and Sunday Morning*)
Foreign Actor: Jack Lemmon (*The Apartment*)
Foreign Actress: Shirley MacLaine (*The Apartment*)
Newcomer: Albert Finney (*Saturday Night and Sunday Morning*)
Screenplay: Bryan Forbes (*The Angry Silence*)

1961
Film: *Ballad of a Soldier* (Grigori Chukrai); *The Hustler* (Robert Rossen)
British Film: *A Taste of Honey* (Tony Richardson)
Actor: Peter Finch (*No Love for Johnnie*)
Actress: Dora Bryan (*A Taste of Honey*)
Foreign Actor: Paul Newman (*The Hustler*)
Foreign Actress: Sophia Loren (*Two Women*)

Newcomer: Rita Tushingham (*A Taste of Honey*)
Screenplay: Shelagh Delaney, Tony Richardson (*A Taste of Honey*); Val Guest, Wolf Mankowitz (*The Day the Earth Caught Fire*)

1962
Film: *Lawrence of Arabia* (David Lean)
British Film: *Lawrence of Arabia* (David Lean)
Actor: Peter O'Toole (*Lawrence of Arabia*)
Actress: Leslie Caron (*The L-Shaped Room*)
Foreign Actor: Burt Lancaster (*Birdman of Alcatraz*)
Foreign Actress: Anne Bancroft (*The Miracle Worker*)
Newcomer: Tom Courtenay (*The Loneliness of the Long Distance Runner*)
Screenplay: Robert Bolt (*Lawrence of Arabia*)

1963
Film: *Tom Jones* (Tony Richardson)
British Film: *Tom Jones* (Tony Richardson)
Actor: Dirk Bogarde (*The Servant*)
Actress: Rachel Roberts (*This Sporting Life*)
Foreign Actor: Marcello Mastroianni (*Divorce Italian Style*)
Foreign Actress: Patricia Neal (*Hud*)
Newcomer: James Fox (*The Servant*)
Screenplay: John Osborne (*Tom Jones*)
Cinematography: b/w Douglas Slocombe (*The Servant*); colour Ted Moore (*From Russia with Love*)

1964
Film: *Dr Strangelove* (Stanley Kubrick)
British Film: *Dr Strangelove* (Stanley Kubrick)
Actor: Richard Attenborough (*Séance on a Wet Afternoon; Guns at Batasi*)
Actress: Audrey Hepburn (*Charade*)
Foreign Actor: Marcello Mastroianni (*Yesterday, Today and Tomorrow*)
Foreign Actress: Anne Bancroft (*The Pumpkin Eater*)
Newcomer: Julie Andrews (*Mary Poppins*)
Screenplay: Harold Pinter (*The Pumpkin Eater*)
Cinematography: b/w Oswald Morris (*The Pumpkin Eater*); colour Geoffrey Unsworth (*Becket*)
Production Design: b/w Ken Adam (*Dr Strangelove*); colour John Bryan (*Becket*)

1965
Film: *My Fair Lady* (George Cukor)
British Film: *The Ipcress File* (Sidney J. Furie)
Actor: Dirk Bogarde (*Darling*)
Actress: Julie Christie (*Darling*)
Foreign Actor: Lee Marvin (*Cat Ballou; The Killers*)
Foreign Actress: Patricia Neal (*In Harm's Way*)
Newcomer: Judi Dench (*Four in the Morning*)
Screenplay: Frederic Raphael (*Darling*)
Cinematography: b/w Oswald Morris (*The Hill*); colour Otto Heller (*The Ipcress File*)
Production Design: b/w Ray Simm (*Darling*); colour Ken Adam (*The Ipcress File*)

1966
Film: *Who's Afraid of Virginia Woolf?* (Mike Nichols)
British Film: *The Spy Who Came in from the Cold* (Martin Ritt)
Actor: Richard Burton (*Who's Afraid of Virginia Woolf?*; *The Spy Who Came in from the Cold*)
Actress: Elizabeth Taylor (*Who's Afraid of Virginia Woolf?*)
Foreign Actor: Rod Steiger (*The Pawnbroker*)
Foreign Actress: Jeanne Moreau (*Viva Maria!*)
Newcomer: Vivien Merchant (*Alfie*)
Screenplay: David Mercer (*Morgan – A Suitable Case for Treatment*)
Cinematography: b/w Oswald Morris (*The Spy Who Came in from the Cold*); colour Christopher Challis (*Arabesque*)
Production Design: b/w Tambi Larsen (*The Spy Who Came in from the Cold*); colour Wilfred Shingleton (*The Blue Max*)

1967
Film: *A Man for All Seasons* (Fred Zinnemann)
British Film: *A Man for All Seasons* (Fred Zinnemann)
Actor: Paul Scofield (*A Man for All Seasons*)
Actress: Edith Evans (*The Whisperers*)
Foreign Actor: Rod Steiger (*In the Heat of the Night*)
Foreign Actress: Anouk Aimée (*A Man and a Woman*)
Newcomer: Faye Dunaway (*Bonnie and Clyde*)
Screenplay: Robert Bolt (*A Man for All Seasons*)
Cinematography: b/w Gerry Turpin (*The*

Whisperers); colour Ted Moore (*A Man for All Seasons*)
Production Design: John Box (*A Man for All Seasons*)

1968
Film: *The Graduate* (Mike Nichols)
Director: Mike Nichols (*The Graduate*)
Actor: Spencer Tracy (*Guess Who's Coming to Dinner?*)
Actress: Katharine Hepburn (*Guess Who's Coming to Dinner?*)
Supporting Actor: Ian Holm (*The Bofors Gun*)
Supporting Actress: Billie Whitelaw (*The Twisted Nerve; Charlie Bubbles*)
Newcomer: Dustin Hoffman (*The Graduate*)
Screenplay: Buck Henry, Calder Willingham (*The Graduate*)
Cinematography: Geoffrey Unsworth (*2001: A Space Odyssey*)
Music: John Barry (*The Lion in Winter*)
Production Design: Tony Masters, Harry Lange, Ernie Archer (*2001: A Space Odyssey*)

1969
Film: *Midnight Cowboy* (John Schlesinger)
Director: John Schlesinger (*Midnight Cowboy*)
Actor: Dustin Hoffman (*Midnight Cowboy; John and Mary*)
Actress: Maggie Smith (*The Prime of Miss Jean Brodie*)
Supporting Actor: Laurence Olivier (*Oh! What a Lovely War*)
Supporting Actress: Celia Johnson (*The Prime of Miss Jean Brodie*)
Newcomer: Jon Voight (*Midnight Cowboy*)
Screenplay: Waldo Salt (*Midnight Cowboy*)
Cinematography: Gerry Turpin (*Oh! What a Lovely War*)
Music: Mikis Theodorakis (*Z*)
Production Design: Don Ashton (*Oh! What a Lovely War*)

1970
Film: *Butch Cassidy and the Sundance Kid* (George Roy Hill)
Director: George Roy Hill (*Butch Cassidy and the Sundance Kid*)
Actor: Robert Redford (*Butch Cassidy and the Sundance Kid; Tell Them Willie Boy Is Here; Downhill Racer*)
Actress: Katharine Ross (*Butch Cassidy and the Sundance Kid; Tell Them Willie Boy Is Here*)
Supporting Actor: Colin Welland (*Kes*)
Supporting Actress: Susannah York (*They Shoot Horses, Don't They?*)
Newcomer: David Bradley (*Kes*)
Screenplay: William Goldman (*Butch Cassidy and the Sundance Kid*)
Cinematography: Conrad Hall (*Butch Cassidy and the Sundance Kid*)
Music: Burt Bacharach (*Butch Cassidy and the Sundance Kid*)
Production Design: Mario Garbuglia (*Waterloo*)

1971
Film: *Sunday, Bloody Sunday* (John Schlesinger)
Director: John Schlesinger (*Sunday, Bloody Sunday*)
Actor: Peter Finch (*Sunday, Bloody Sunday*)
Actress: Glenda Jackson (*Sunday, Bloody Sunday*)
Supporting Actor: Edward Fox (*The Go-Between*)
Supporting Actress: Margaret Leighton (*The Go-Between*)
Newcomer: Dominic Guard (*The Go-Between*)
Screenplay: Harold Pinter (*The Go-Between*)
Cinematography: Pasqualino De Santis (*Death in Venice*)
Music: Michel Legrand (*Summer of '42*)
Production Design: Ferdinando Scarfiotti (*Death in Venice*)

1972
Film: *Cabaret* (Bob Fosse)
Director: Bob Fosse (*Cabaret*)
Actor: Gene Hackman (*The French Connection; The Poseidon Adventure*)
Actress: Liza Minnelli (*Cabaret*)
Supporting Actor: Ben Johnson (*The Last Picture Show*)
Supporting Actress: Cloris Leachman (*The Last Picture Show*)
Newcomer: Joel Grey (*Cabaret*)
Screenplay: Peter Bogdanovich, Larry McMurtry (*The Last Picture Show*)
Cinematography: Geoffrey Unsworth (*Cabaret; Alice's Adventures in Wonderland*)
Music: Nina Rota (*The Godfather*)

Production Design: Rolf Zehetbauer (*Cabaret*)

1973
Film: *Day for Night* (François Truffaut)
Director: François Truffaut (*Day for Night*)
Actor: Walter Matthau (*Pete 'n' Tillie; Charley Varrick*)
Actress: Stéphane Audran (*The Discreet Charm of the Bourgeoisie; Just before Nightfall*)
Supporting Actor: Arthur Lowe (*O Lucky Man!*)
Supporting Actress: Valentina Cortese (*Day for Night*)
Newcomer: Peter Egan (*The Hireling*)
Screenplay: Luis Buñuel, Jean-Claude Carrière (*The Discreet Charm of the Bourgeoisie*)
Cinematography: Anthony Richmond (*Don't Look Now*)
Music: Alan Price (*O Lucky Man!*)
Production Design: Natasha Kroll (*The Hireling*)

1974
Film: *Lacombe Lucien* (Louis Malle)
Director: Roman Polanski (*Chinatown*)
Actor: Jack Nicholson (*Chinatown; The Last Detail*)
Actress: Joanne Woodward (*Summer Wishes, Winter Dreams*)
Supporting Actor: John Gielgud (*Murder on the Orient Express*)
Supporting Actress: Ingrid Bergman (*Murder on the Orient Express*)
Newcomer: Georgina Hale (*Mahler*)
Screenplay: Robert Towne (*Chinatown; The Last Detail*)
Cinematography: Douglas Slocombe (*The Great Gatsby*)
Music: Richard Rodney Bennett (*Murder on the Orient Express*)
Production Design: John Box (*The Great Gatsby*)

1975
Film: *Alice Doesn't Live Here Any More* (Martin Scorsese)
Director: Stanley Kubrick (*Barry Lyndon*)
Actor: Al Pacino (*The Godfather Part II; Dog Day Afternoon*)
Actress: Ellen Burstyn (*Alice Doesn't Live Here Any More*)
Supporting Actor: Fred Astaire (*The Towering Inferno*)
Supporting Actress: Diane Ladd (*Alice Doesn't Live Here Any More*)
Newcomer: Valerie Perrine (*Lenny*)
Screenplay: Robert Getchell (*Alice Doesn't Live Here Any More*)
Cinematography: John Alcott (*Barry Lyndon*)
Music: John Williams (*Jaws; The Towering Inferno*)
Production Design: John Box (*Rollerball*)

1976
Film: *One Flew over the Cuckoo's Nest* (Milos Forman)
Director: Milos Forman (*One Flew over the Cuckoo's Nest*)
Actor: Jack Nicholson (*One Flew over the Cuckoo's Nest*)
Actress: Louise Fletcher (*One Flew over the Cuckoo's Nest*)
Supporting Actor: Brad Dourif (*One Flew over the Cuckoo's Nest*)
Supporting Actress: Jodie Foster (*Taxi Driver; Bugsy Malone*)
Newcomer: Jodie Foster (*Taxi Driver; Bugsy Malone*)
Screenplay: Alan Parker (*Bugsy Malone*)
Cinematography: Russell Boyd (*Picnic at Hanging Rock*)
Music: Bernard Herrmann (*Taxi Driver*)
Production Design: Geoffrey Kirkland (*Bugsy Malone*)

1977
Film: *Annie Hall* (Woody Allen)
Director: Woody Allen (*Annie Hall*)
Actor: Peter Finch (*Network*)
Actress: Diane Keaton (*Annie Hall*)
Supporting Actor: Edward Fox (*A Bridge Too Far*)
Supporting Actress: Jenny Agutter (*Equus*)
Newcomer: Isabelle Huppert (*The Lacemaker*)
Screenplay: Woody Allen, Marshall Brickman (*Annie Hall*)
Cinematography: Geoffrey Unsworth (*A Bridge Too Far*)
Music: John Addison (*A Bridge Too Far*)
Production Design: Danilo Donati (*Fellini's Casanova*)

1978

Film: *Julia* (Fred Zinnemann)
Director: Alan Parker (*Midnight Express*)
Actor: Richard Dreyfuss (*The Goodbye Girl*)
Actress: Jane Fonda (*Julia*)
Supporting Actor: John Hurt (*Midnight Express*)
Supporting Actress: Geraldine Page (*Interiors*)
Newcomer: Christopher Reeve (*Superman*)
Screenplay: Alvin Sargent (*Julia*)
Cinematography: Douglas Slocombe (*Julia*)
Music: John Williams (*Star Wars*)
Production Design: Joe Alves (*Close Encounters of the Third Kind*)

1979
Film: *Manhattan* (Woody Allen)
Director: Francis Ford Coppola (*Apocalypse Now*)
Actor: Jack Lemmon (*The China Syndrome*)
Actress: Jane Fonda (*The China Syndrome*)
Supporting Actor: Robert Duvall (*Apocalypse Now*)
Supporting Actress: Rachel Roberts (*Yanks*)
Newcomer: Dennis Christopher (*Breaking Away*)
Screenplay: Woody Allen, Marshall Brickman (*Manhattan*)
Cinematography: Vilmos Zsigmond (*The Deer Hunter*)
Music: Ennio Morricone (*Days of Heaven*)
Production Design: Michael Seymour (*Alien*)

1980
Film: *The Elephant Man* (David Lynch)
Director: Akira Kurosawa (*Kagemusha*)
Actor: John Hurt (*The Elephant Man*)
Actress: Judy Davis (*My Brilliant Career*)
Newcomer: Judy Davis (*My Brilliant Career*)
Screenplay: Jerzy Kozinski (*Being There*)
Cinematography: Giuseppe Rotunno (*All That Jazz*)
Music: John Williams (*The Empire Strikes Back*)
Production Design: Stuart Craig (*The Elephant Man*)

1981
Film: *Chariots of Fire* (Hugh Hudson)
Director: Louis Malle (*Atlantic City*)
Actor: Burt Lancaster (*Atlantic City*)
Actress: Meryl Streep (*The French Lieutenant's Woman*)
Supporting Artist: Ian Holm (*Chariots of Fire*)
Newcomer: Joe Pesci (*Raging Bull*)
Screenplay: Bill Forsyth (*Gregory's Girl*)
Cinematography: Geoffrey Unsworth, Ghislain Cloquet (*Tess*)
Music: Carl Davis (*The French Lieutenant's Woman*)
Production Design: Norman Reynolds (*Raiders of the Lost Ark*)

1982
Film: *Gandhi* (Richard Attenborough)
Foreign-Language Film: *Christ Stopped at Eboli* (Francesco Rosi)
Director: Richard Attenborough (*Gandhi*)
Actor: Ben Kingsley (*Gandhi*)
Actress: Katharine Hepburn (*On Golden Pond*)
Supporting Actor: Jack Nicholson (*Reds*)
Supporting Actress: Maureen Stapleton (*Reds*); Rohini Hattangadi (*Gandhi*)
Newcomer: Ben Kingsley (*Gandhi*)
Screenplay: Costa-Gavras, Donald Stewart (*Missing*)
Cinematography: Jordan Cronenweth (*Blade Runner*)
Music: John Williams (*ET*)
Production Design: Lawrence G. Paull (*Blade Runner*)

1983
Film: *Educating Rita* (Lewis Gilbert)
Foreign-Language Film: *Danton* (Andrzej Wajda)
Director: Bill Forsyth (*Local Hero*)
Actor: Michael Caine (*Educating Rita*)
Actress: Julie Walters (*Educating Rita*)
Supporting Actor: Denholm Elliott (*Trading Places*)
Supporting Actress: Jamie Lee Curtis (*Trading Places*)
Newcomer: Phyllis Logan (*Another Time, Another Place*)
Adapted Screenplay: Ruth Prawer Jhabvala (*Heat and Dust*)
Original Screenplay: Paul D. Zimmerman (*King of Comedy*)
Cinematography: Sven Nykvist (*Fanny and Alexander*)
Music: Ryuichi Sakamoto (*Merry Christmas, Mr Lawrence*)
Production Design: Franco Zeffirelli, Gianni Quaranta (*La Traviata*)

1984
Film: *The Killing Fields* (Roland Joffe)
Foreign-Language Film: *Carmen* (Carlos Saura)
Director: Wim Wenders (*Paris, Texas*)
Actor: Haing S. Ngor (*The Killing Fields*)
Actress: Maggie Smith (*A Private Function*)
Supporting Actor: Denholm Elliott (*A Private Function*)
Supporting Actress: Liz Smith (*A Private Function*)
Newcomer: Haing S. Ngor (*The Killing Fields*)
Adapted Screenplay: Bruce Robinson (*The Killing Fields*)
Original Screenplay: Woody Allen (*Broadway Danny Rose*)
Cinematography: Chris Menges (*The Killing Fields*)
Music: Ennio Morricone (*Once Upon a Time in America*)
Production Design: Roy Walker (*The Killing Fields*)

1985
Film: *The Purple Rose of Cairo* (Woody Allen)
Foreign-Language Film: *Colonel Redl* (Istvá Szabó)
Actor: William Hurt (*Kiss of the Spider Woman*)
Actress: Peggy Ashcroft (*A Passage to India*)
Supporting Actor: Denholm Elliott (*Defence of the Realm*)
Supporting Actress: Rosanna Arquette (*Desperately Seeking Susan*)
Adapted Screenplay: Richard Condon, Janet Roach (*Prizzi's Honor*)
Original Screenplay: Woody Allen (*The Purple Rose of Cairo*)
Cinematography: Miroslav Ondricek (*Amadeus*)
Music: Maurice Jarre (*Witness*)
Production Design: Norman Garwood (*Brazil*)

1986
Film: *A Room with a View* (James Ivory)
Foreign-Language Film: *Ran* (Akira Kurosawa)
Director: Woody Allen (*Hannah and Her Sisters*)
Actor: Bob Hoskins (*Mona Lisa*)
Actress: Maggie Smith (*A Room with a View*)
Supporting Actor: Ray McAnally (*The Mission*)
Supporting Actress: Judi Dench (*A Room with a View*)
Adapted Screenplay: Kurt Luedtke (*Out of Africa*)
Original Screenplay: Woody Allen (*Hannah and Her Sisters*)
Cinematography: David Watkin (*Out of Africa*)
Music: Ennio Morricone (*The Mission*)
Production Design: Gianni Quaranta, Brian Ackland-Snow (*A Room with a View*)

1987
Film: *Jean de Florette* (Claude Berri)
Foreign-Language Film: *The Sacrifice* (Andrei Tarkovsky)
Director: Oliver Stone (*Platoon*)
Actor: Sean Connery (*The Name of the Rose*)
Actress: Anne Bancroft (*84 Charing Cross Road*)
Supporting Actor: Daniel Auteuil (*Jean de Florette*)
Supporting Actress: Susan Wooldridge (*Hope and Glory*)
Adapted Screenplay: Gérard Brach, Claude Berri (*Jean de Florette*)
Original Screenplay: David Leland (*Wish You Were Here*)
Cinematography: Bruno Nuytten (*Jean de Florette*)
Music: Ennio Morricone (*The Untouchables*)
Production Design: Santo Loquasto (*Radio Days*)

1988
Film: *The Last Emperor* (Bernardo Bertolucci)
Foreign-Language Film: *Babette's Feast* (Gabriel Axel)
Director: Louis Malle (*Au Revoir les Enfants*)
Actor: John Cleese (*A Fish Called Wanda*)
Actress: Maggie Smith (*The Lonely Passion of Judith Hearne*)
Supporting Actor: Michael Palin (*A Fish Called Wanda*)
Supporting Actress: Judi Dench (*A Handful of Dust*)
Adapted Screenplay: Jean-Claude Carrière, Philip Kaufman (*The Unbearable Lightness of Being*)
Original Screenplay: Shawn Slovo (*A World Apart*)
Cinematography: Allen Daviau (*Empire of the Sun*)
Music: John Williams (*Empire of the Sun*)
Production Design: Dean Tavoularis (*Tucker: The Man and His Dream*)

1989
Film: *Dead Poets Society* (Peter Weir)
Foreign-Language Film: *Life and Nothing But* (Bertrand Tavernier)
Director: Kenneth Branagh (*Henry V*)
Actor: Daniel Day-Lewis (*My Left Foot*)

Actress: Pauline Collins (*Shirley Valentine*)
Supporting Actor: Ray McAnally (*My Left Foot*)
Supporting Actress: Michelle Pfeiffer (*Dangerous Liaisons*)
Adapted Screenplay: Christopher Hampton (*Dangerous Liaisons*)
Original Screenplay: Nora Ephron (*When Harry Met Sally*)
Cinematography: Peter Biziou (*Mississippi Burning*)
Music: Maurice Jarre (*Dead Poets Society*)
Production Design: Dante Ferretti (*Adventures of Baron Munchausen*)

1990
Film: *GoodFellas* (Martin Scorsese)
Foreign-Language Film: *Nuovo Cinema Paradiso* (Giuseppe Tornatore)
Director: Martin Scorsese (*GoodFellas*)
Actor: Philippe Noiret (*Nuovo Cinema Paradiso*)
Actress: Jessica Tandy (*Driving Miss Daisy*)
Supporting Actor: Salvatore Cascio (*Nuovo Cinema Paradiso*)
Supporting Actress: Whoopi Goldberg (*Ghost*)
Adapted Screenplay: Nicholas Pileggi, Martin Scorsese (*GoodFellas*)
Original Screenplay: Giuseppe Tornatore (*Nuovo Cinema Paradiso*)
Cinematography: Vittorio Storaro (*The Sheltering Sky*)
Music: Ennio and Andrea Morricone (*Nuovo Cinema Paradiso*)
Production Design: Richard Sylbert (*Dick Tracy*)

1991
Film: *The Commitments* (Alan Parker)
Foreign-Language Film: *The Nasty Girl* (*Das Schreckliche Mädchen*) (Michael Verhoeven)
Director: Alan Parker (*The Commitments*)
Actor: Anthony Hopkins (*The Silence of the Lambs*)
Actress: Jodie Foster (*The Silence of the Lambs*)
Supporting Actor: Alan Rickman (*Robin Hood: Prince of Thieves*)
Supporting Actress: Kate Nelligan (*Frankie and Johnnie*)
Adapted Screenplay: Dick Clement, Ian La Frenais, Roddy Doyle (*The Commitments*)
Original Screenplay: Anthony Minghella (*Truly Madly Deeply*)
Cinematography: Pierre Lhomme (*Cyrano de Bergerac*)
Music: Jean-Claude Petit (*Cyrano de Bergerac*)
Production Design: Bo Welch (*Edward Scissorhands*)

1992
Film: *Howards End* (James Ivory)
Foreign-Language Film: *Raise the Red Lantern* (Zhang Zimou)
Director: Robert Altman (*The Player*)
Actor: Robert Downey Jnr (*Chaplin*)
Actress: Emma Thompson (*Howards End*)
Supporting Actor: Gene Hackman (*Unforgiven*)
Supporting Actress: Miranda Richardson (*Damage*)
Adapted Screenplay: Michael Tolkin (*The Player*)
Original Screenplay: Woody Allen (*Husbands and Wives*)
Cinematography: Dante Spinotti (*The Last of the Mohicans*)
Music: David Hirschfelder (*Strictly Ballroom*)
Production Design: Catherine Martin (*Strictly Ballroom*)

1993
Film: *Schindler's List* (Steven Spielberg)
Foreign-Language Film: *Farewell My Concubine* (Chen Kaige)
British Film: *Shadowlands* (Richard Attenborough)
Director: Steven Spielberg (*Schindler's List*)
Actor: Anthony Hopkins (*The Remains of the Day*)
Actress: Holly Hunter (*The Piano*)
Supporting Actor: Ralph Fiennes (*Schindler's List*)
Supporting Actress: Miriam Margolyes (*The Age of Innocence*)
Adapted Screenplay: Steven Zaillian (*Schindler's List*)
Original Screenplay: Danny Rubin, Harold Ramis (*Groundhog Day*)
Cinematography: Janusz Kaminski (*Schindler's List*)
Music: John Williams (*Schindler's List*)
Production Design: Andrew McAlpine (*The Piano*)

1994
Film: *Four Weddings and a Funeral* (Mike Newell)
Foreign-Language Film: *To Live* (Zhang Yimou)
British Film: *Shallow Grave* (Danny Boyle)
Director: Mike Newell (*Four Weddings and a Funeral*)
Actor: Hugh Grant (*Four Weddings and a Funeral*)
Actress: Susan Sarandon (*The Client*)
Supporting Actor: Samuel L. Jackson (*Pulp Fiction*)
Supporting Actress: Kristin Scott Thomas (*Four Weddings and a Funeral*)
Adapted Screenplay: Paul Attanasio (*Quiz Show*)
Original Screenplay: Quentin Tarantino and Roger Avary (*Pulp Fiction*)
Cinematography: Philippe Rousselot (*Interview with the Vampire*)
Music: Don Was (*Backbeat*)
Production Design: Dante Ferretti (*Interview with the Vampire*)

1995
Film: *Sense and Sensibility* (Ang Lee)
Foreign-Language Film: *The Postman/Il Postino* (Michael Radford)
British Film: *The Madness of King George* (Nicholas Hytner)
Director: Michael Radford (*The Postman/Il Postino*)
Actor: Nigel Hawthorne (*The Madness of King George*)
Actress: Emma Thompson (*Sense and Sensibility*)
Supporting Actor: Tim Roth (*Rob Roy*)
Supporting Actress: Kate Winslet (*Sense and Sensibility*)
Adapted Screenplay: John Hodge (*Trainspotting*)
Original Screenplay: Christopher McQuarrie (*The Usual Suspects*)
Cinematography: John Toll (*Braveheart*)
Music: Luis Bacalov (*Il Postino*)
Production Design: Michael Corenblith (*Apollo 13*)

1996
Film: *The English Patient* (Anthony Minghella)
Foreign-Language Film: *Ridicule* (Patrice Leconte)
British Film: *Secrets and Lies* (Mike Leigh)
Director: Joel Coen (*Fargo*)
Actor: Geoffrey Rush (*Shine*)
Actress: Brenda Blethyn (*Secrets and Lies*)
Supporting Actor: Paul Scofield (*The Crucible*)
Supporting Actress: Juliette Binoche (*The English Patient*)
Adapted Screenplay: Anthony Minghella (*The English Patient*)
Original Screenplay: Mike Leigh (*Secrets and Lies*)
Cinematography: John Seale (*The English Patient*)
Music: Gabriel Yard (*The English Patient*)
Production Design: Tony Burrough (*Richard III*)

1997
Film: *The Full Monty* (Peter Cattaneo)
Foreign-Language Film: *L'Appartement* (Gilles Mimouni)
British Film: *Nil by Mouth* (Gary Oldman)
Director: Baz Luhrmann (*William Shakespeare's Romeo & Juliet*)
Actor: Robert Carlyle (*The Full Monty*)
Actress: Judi Dench (*Mrs Brown*)
Supporting Actor: Tom Wilkinson (*The Full Monty*)
Supporting Actress: Sigourney Weaver (*The Ice Storm*)
Adapted Screenplay: Baz Luhrmann, Craig Pearce (*William Shakespeare's Romeo & Juliet*)
Original Screenplay: Gary Oldman (*Nil by Mouth*)
Audience Award: *The Full Monty* (Peter Cattaneo)
Cinematography: Eduardo Serra (*The Wings of the Dove*)
Music: Nellee Hooper (*William Shakespeare's Romeo & Juliet*)
Production Design: Catherine Martin (*William Shakespeare's Romeo & Juliet*)

1998
Film: *Shakespeare in Love* (John Madden)
Foreign Language Film: *Central Station Brazil/Central Do Brasil* (Walter Salles)
British Film: *Elizabeth* (Shekhar Kapur)
Director: Peter Weir (The Truman Show)
Actor: Robert Begnini (*Life is Beautiful*)
Actress: Cate Blanchett (*Elizabeth*)
Supporting Actor: Geoffrey Rush (*Shakespeare in Love*)
Supporting Actress: Judi Dench (*Shakespeare in Love*)
Adapted Screenplay: Elaine May (*Primary Colors*)
Original Screenplay: Andrew Niccol (*The Truman Show*)
Audience Award: *Lock, Stock and Two Smoking Barrels* (Guy Ritchie)
Cinematography: Remi Adefarasin (*Elizabeth*)
Music: David Hirschfelder (*Elizabeth*)
Production Design: Dennis Gassner (*The Truman Show*)
Editing: David Gamble (*Shakespeare in Love*)

1999
Film: *American Beauty* (Sam Mendes)
Foreign Language Film: *All About My Mother* (Pedro Almodóvar)
British Film: *East is East* (Damien O'Donnell)
Director: Pedro Almodóvar (*All About My Mother*)
Actor: Kevin Spacey (*American Beauty*)
Actress: Annette Bening (*American Beauty*)
Supporting Actor: Jude Law (*The Talented Mr Ripley*)
Supporting Actress: Maggie Smith (*Tea with Mussolini*)
Adapted Screenplay: Neil Jordan (*The End of the Affair*)
Original Screenplay: Charlie Kaufman (*Being John Malkovich*)
Audience Award: *Notting Hill* (Roger Michell)
Cinematography: Conrad L. Hall (*American Beauty*)
Music: Thomas Newman (*American Beauty*)
Production Design: Rick Heinrichs (*Sleepy Hollow*)
Editing: Tariq Anwar, Christopher Greenbury (*American Beauty*)
Costume Design: Colleen Atwood (*Sleepy Hollow*)
Most Promising Newcomer: Richard Kwietniowksi (*Love and Death on Long Island*)

2000
Film: *Gladiator* (Ridley Scott)
Foreign-Language Film: *Crouching Tiger, Hidden Dragon* (Ang Lee)
British Film: *Billy Elliot* (Stephen Daldry)
Director: Ang Lee (*Crouching Tiger, Hidden Dragon*)
Actor: Jamie Bell (*Billy Elliot*)
Actress: Julia Roberts (*Erin Brockovich*)
Supporting Actor: Benicio Del Toro (*Traffic*)
Supporting Actress: Julie Walters (*Billy Elliot*)
Adapted Screenplay: Stephen Gaghan (*Traffic*)
Original Screenplay: Cameron Crowe (*Almost Famous*)
Audience Award: *Gladiator* (Ridley Scott)
Cinematography: John Mathieson (*Gladiator*)
Music: Tan Dun (*Crouching Tiger, Hidden Dragon*)
Production Design: Arthur Max (*Gladiator*)
Editing: Pietro Scalia (*Gladiator*)
Costume Design: Tim Yip (*Crouching Tiger, Hidden Dragon*)
Most Promising Newcomer: Pawel Pawlikowski (*Last Resort*)

Cannes Film Festival Awards

The Cannes Film Festival, held each year in May, has established itself as the world's leading festival. The first, in 1939, was abandoned when Hitler invaded Poland and it resumed in 1946. There was no festival in 1948 and 1950, and the one in 1968 was disrupted by the nationwide demonstrations. In 1946, there was a multitude of prizes, one for each participating nation, although there was an International Jury Prize, which went to *The Battle of the Rails* (*La Bataille du Rail*), directed by René Clément. In 1947, six prizes were given for various vague genres of film. In 1949, a Grand Prize was given to the best film, together with other prizes for direction, acting, writing, composing, and set design. A special Jury Prize was added in 1951, and the Palme d'Or (Golden Palm) for best film was inaugurated in 1955. Over the years the juries have varied the nature of the awards, according to whim, although always retaining a prize for the best film. The main prizewinners since 1949 are:

1949
Grand Prix: *The Third Man* (Carol Reed)
Director: René Clément (*The Walls of Malapaga* (*Le Mura di Malapaga*))*Malapaga/Le Mura di Malapaga*)
Actor: Edward G. Robinson (*House of Strangers*)
Actress: Isa Miranda (*The Walls of Malapaga* (*Le Mura di Malapaga*))*Malapaga/Le Mura di Malapaga*)

1951
Grand Prix: *Miracle in Milan* (*Miracolo a Milano*)*Milan/Miracolo a Milano* (Vittoria De Sica); *Miss Julie* (Alf Sjöberg)
Director: Luis Buñuel (*Los Olvidados*)
Actor: Michael Redgrave (*The Browning Version*)
Actress: Bette Davis (*All About Eve*)

1952
Grand Prix: *Two Pennyworth of Hope* (*Due Soldi di Speranza*)*Hope/Due Soldi di Speranza* (Renato Castellani); *Othello* (Orson Welles)
Director: Christian-Jaque (*Fanfan la Tulipe*)
Actor: Marlon Brando (*Viva Zapata*)
Actress: Lee Grant (*Detective Story*)

1953
Grand Prix: *The Wages of Fear* (Henri-Georges Clouzot)
Actor: Charles Vanel (*The Wages of Fear*)

1954
Grand Prix: *Gate of Hell* (*Jigoku-Mon*)*Hell/Jigoku-Mon* (Teinosuke Kinugasa)

1955
Palme d'Or: *Marty* (Delbert Mann)
Director: Sergei Vasiliev (*The Heroes of Shipka* (*Geroite Na Shipka*));*Shipka/Geroite Na Shipka*); Jules Dassin (*Rififi*)
Performance: Spencer Tracy

1956
Palme d'Or: *The Silent World* (*Le Monde du Silence*)*World/Le Monde du Silence* (Jacques Yves Cousteau, Louis Malle)
Director: Sergei Yutkevich (*Othello*)
Performance: Susan Hayward (*I'll Cry Tomorrow*)

1957
Palme d'Or: *Friendly Persuasion* (William Wyler)
Director: Robert Bresson (*A Man Escaped* (*UnEscaped/Un Condamné à Mort S'Est Échappé*))
Actor: John Kitzmiller (*Valley of Peace* (*Dolina Miru*))*Peace/Dolina Miru*)
Actress: Giulietta Masina (*Cabiria* (*Nights of Cabiria*))(*Cabiria/Nights of Cabiria*)

1958
Palme d'Or: *The Cranes Are Flying* (*Letiat Zhuravli*)*Flying/Letiat Zhuravli* (Mikhail Kalatozov)
Director: Ingmar Bergman (*So Close to Life* (*Nara Livet*))*Life/Nara Livet*)
Actor: Paul Newman (*The Long Hot Summer*)
Actress: Bibi Andersson, Eva Dahlbeck, Barbro Hiortas-Ornas, Ingrid Thulin (*So Close to Life* (*Nara Livet*))*Life/Nara Livet*)

1959
Palme d'Or: *Black Orpheus* (*Orfeu Negro*)*Orpheus/Orfeu Negro* (Marcel Camus)
Director: François Truffaut (*The 400 Blows* (*LesBlows/Les Quatre Cents Coups*))
Actor: Dean Stockwell, Bradford Dillman, Orson Welles (*Compulsion*)
Actress: Simone Signoret (*Room at the Top*)

1960
Palme d'Or: *La Dolce Vita* (Federico Fellini)
Actress: Melina Mercouri (*Never on Sunday*); Jeanne Moreau (*Moderato Cantabile*)

1961
Palme d'Or: *Viridiana* (Luis Buñuel); *Une Aussi Longue Absence* (Henri Colpi)
Director: Julia Solntseva (*The Flaming Years* (*Povest'Years/Povest' Plamennykh Ket*))
Actor: Anthony Perkins (*Goodbye Again*)
Actress: Sophia Loren (*Two Women* (*La Ciociara*))*Women/La Ciociara*)

1962
Palme d'Or: *The Given Word* (*OWord/O Pagador de Promessas*) (Anselmo Duarte)
Actor: Ralph Richardson, Jason Robards Jnr, Dean Stockwell (*Long Day's Journey into Night*); Murray Melvin (*A Taste of Honey*)
Actress: Katharine Hepburn (*Long Day's Journey into Night*); Rita Tushingham (*A Taste of Honey*)

1963
Palme d'Or: *The Leopard* (*Il Gattopardo*)*Leopard/Il Gattopardo* (Luchino Visconti)
Actor: Richard Harris (*This Sporting Life*)
Actress: Marina Vlady (*Queen Bee*, aka *The Conjugal Bed* (*UnaBed/Una Storia Moderna: L'Ape Regina*))

1964
Palme d'Or: *The Umbrellas of Cherbourg* (*LesCherbourg/Les Parapluies de Cherbourg*) (Jacques Demy)
Actor: Saro Urzi (*Seduced and Abandoned* (*Sedotta e Abbandonata*));*Abandoned/Sedotta e Abbandonata*); Antal Pager (*The Lark* (*Pacsirta*))*Lark/Pacsirta*)
Actress: Anne Bancroft (*The Pumpkin Eater*); Barbara Barrie (*One Potato, Two Potato*)

1965
Palme d'Or: *The Knack … And How to Get It* (Richard Lester)
Director: Liviu Ciulei (*The Forest of the Hanged* (*Padurea Spinzuratilor*))*Hanged/Padurea Spinzuratilor*)
Actor: Terence Stamp (*The Collector*)
Actress: Samantha Eggar (*The Collector*)

1966
Palme d'Or: *A Man and a Woman* (*UnWoman/Un Homme et une Femme*) (Claude Lelouch); *The Birds, the Bees, and the Italians* (*Signore et Signori*)*Italians/Signore et Signori* (Pietro Germi)
Director: Sergei Yutkevich (*Lenin in Poland* (*Lenin en Poland*))*Poland/Lenin en Poland*)
Actor: Per Oscarsson (*Hunger* (*Sult*))(*Hunger/Sult*)
Actress: Vanessa Redgrave (*Morgan!*)

1967
Palme d'Or: *Blow Up* (Michelangelo Antonioni)
Director: Ferenc Kósa (*Ten Thousand Suns* (*Tízezer Nap*))*Suns/Tízezer Nap*)
Actor: Odded Kotier (*Three Days and a Child*)
Actress: Pia Degermark (*Elvira Madigan*)

1969
Palme d'Or: *If...* (Lindsay Anderson)
Director: Glauber Rocha (*Antonio das Mortes*); Vojtech Jasn (*All My Good Countrymen* (*Vsichni Dobri Rodaci*))*Countrymen/Vsichni Dobri Rodaci*)
Actor: Jean-Louis Trintignant (*Z*)
Actress: Vanessa Redgrave (*Isadora*)

1970
Palme d'Or: *M*A*S*H* (Robert Altman)
Director: John Boorman (*Leo the Last*)
Actor: Marcello Mastroianni (*Jealousy, Italian Style* (*DrammaStyle/Dramma della Gelosia … Tutti i Particolari in Cronaca*))
Actress: Ottavia Piccolo (*Metello*)

1971
Palme d'Or: *The Go-Between* (Joseph Losey)
Actor: Riccardo Cucciolla (*Sacco e Vanzetti*)
Actress: Kitty Winn (*Panic in Needle Park*)

1972
Palme d'Or: *The Mattei Affair* (*Il Caso Mattei*)*Affair/Il Caso Mattei* (Francesco Rossi); *The Working Class Go to Heaven, aka Lulu the Tool* (*LaTool/La Classe Operaia Va in Paradiso*) (Elio Petri)
Director: Miklós Jancsó (*Red Psalm* (*Még Kér A Nép*))*Psalm/Még Kér A Nép*)
Actor: Jean Yanne (*We Will Not Grow Old Together* (*NousTogether/Nous Ne Vieillirons Pas Ensemble*))
Actress: Susannah York (*Images*)

1973
Palme d'Or: *Scarecrow* (Jerry Schatzberg); *The Hireling* (Alan Bridges)
Actor: Giancarlo Giannini (*Love and Anarchy* (*Film d'Amore e d'Anarchia*))*Anarchy/Film d'Amore e d'Anarchia*)
Actress: Joanne Woodward (*The Effect of Gamma Rays on Man-in-the-Moon Marigolds*)

1974
Palme d'Or: *The Conversation* (Francis Ford Coppola)
Actor: Jack Nicholson (*The Last Detail*)
Actress: Marie-José Nat (*Les Violons du Bal*)

1975
Palme d'Or: *Chronicle of the Burning Years* (*AhdatYears/Ahdat Sanawouach Eldjamr*) (Mohammed Lakhdar Hamina)
Director: Michel Brault (*The Orders* (*Les Ordres*))*Orders/Les Ordres*); Costa-Gavras (*Special Section* (*Section Spéciale*))*Section/Section Spéciale*)
Actor: Vittorio Gassman (*Scent of a Woman* (*Profumo di Donna*))*Woman/Profumo di Donna*)
Actress: Valerie Perrine (*Lenny*)

1976
Palme d'Or: *Taxi Driver* (Martin Scorsese)
Director: Ettore Scola (*Down and Dirty* (*Brutti, Dirty/Brutti, Sporchi e Cattivi*))
Actor: José Luis Gomez (*Pascual Duarte*)
Actress: Mari Töröcsic (*Where Are You, Mrs Dery?* (*Deryne, Hol Van?*))*Dery?/Deryne, Hol Van?*); Dominique Sanda (*The Inheritance* (*L'Eredità Ferramonti*))*Inheritance/L'Eredità Ferramonti*)

1977
Palme d'Or: *Padre Padrone* (Paolo and Vittorio Taviani)

Actor: Fernando Rey (*Elisa, My Life* (*Elisa, Vida Mia*))*Life/Elisa, Vida Mia*)
Actress: Shelley Duvall (*Three Women*); Monique Mercure (*J. A. Martin Photographe*)

1978
Palme d'Or: *The Tree of Wooden Clogs* (*L'Albero degli Zoccoli*)*Clogs/L'Albero degli Zoccoli* (Ermanno Olmi)
Director: Nagisa Oshima (*The Empire of Passion* (*Ai No Borei*))*Passion/Ai No Borei*)
Actor: Jon Voight (*Coming Home*)
Actress: Jill Clayburgh (*An Unmarried Woman*); Isabelle Huppert (*Violette* (*Violette Nozière*))(*Violette/Violette Nozière*)

1979
Palme d'Or: *The Tin Drum* (*Die Blechtrommel*)*Drum/Die Blechtrommel* (Volker Schlöndorff); *Apocalypse Now* (Francis Ford Coppola)
Director: Terrence Malick (*Days of Heaven*)
Actor: Jack Lemmon (*The China Syndrome*)
Actress: Sally Field (*Norma Rae*)

1980
Palme d'Or: *Kagemusha* (Akira Kurosawa); *All That Jazz* (Bob Fosse)
Actor: Michel Piccoli (*Leap into the Void* (*Salto nel Vuoto*))*Void/Salto nel Vuoto*)
Actress: Anouk Aimée (*Leap into the Void* (*Salto nel Vuoto*))*Void/Salto nel Vuoto*)

1981
Palme d'Or: *Man of Iron* (*Czolowieck z Zelaza*)*Iron/Czolowieck z Zelaza* (Andrzej Wajda)
Actor: Ugo Tognazzi (*Tragedy of a Ridiculous Man* (*LaMan/La Tragedia di un Uomo Ridicolo*))
Actress: Isabelle Adjani (*Quartet*; *Possession*)

1982
Palme d'Or: *Missing* (Costa-Gavras); *Yol* (Yilmaz Güney, Serif Gören)
Director: Werner Herzog (*Fitzcarraldo*)
Actor: Jack Lemmon (*Missing*)
Actress: Jadwiga Jankowska-Cieslak (*Another Way* (*Egymásra Nézve*))*Way/Egymásra Nézve*)

1983
Palme d'Or: *The Ballad of Narayama* (*Narayama Bushi Ko*)*Narayama/Narayama Bushi Ko* (Shohei Imamura)
Actor: Gian Maria Volonte (*The Death of Mario Ricci* (*LaRicci/La Mort de Mario Ricci*))
Actress: Hanna Schygulla (*Story of Piera* (*Storia di Piera*))*Piera/Storia di Piera*)

1984
Palme d'Or: *Paris, Texas* (Wim Wenders)
Director: Bertrand Tavernier (*A Sunday in the Country* (*Un Dimanche à la Campagne*))
Actor: Alfredo Landa, Francisco Rabal (*The Holy Innocents* (*Los Santos Innocentes*))*Innocents/Los Santos Innocentes*)
Actress: Helen Mirren (*Cal*)

1985
Palme d'Or: *When Father Was Away on Business* (*OtakBusiness/Otak Na Sluzbenom Putu*) (Emir Kusturica)
Director: André Téchiné (*Rendezvous*)
Actor: William Hurt (*Kiss of the Spider Woman*)
Actress: Cher (*Mask*); Norma Aleandro (*The Official Story* (*LaStory/La Historia Oficial*))

1986
Palme d'Or: *The Mission* (Roland Joffe)
Director: Martin Scorsese (*After Hours*)
Actor: Michel Blanc (*Menage* (*Tenue de Soirée*)); Bob Hoskins (*Mona Lisa*)
Actress: Barbara Sukowa (*Rosa Luxemburg*); Fernanda Torres (*I Love You* (*EuYou/Eu Sei Que Vou Te Amar*))

1987
Palme d'Or: *Under Satan's Sun* (*SousSun/Sous le Soleil de Satan*) (Maurice Pialat)
Director: Wim Wenders (*Wings of Desire* (*DerDesire/Der Himmel über Berlin*))
Actor: Marcello Mastroianni (*Dark Eyes* (*Ocie Ciornie*))*Eyes/Ocie Ciornie*)
Actress: Barbara Hershey (*Shy People*)

1988
Palme d'Or: *Pelle the Conqueror* (*Pell Erobreren*)*Conqueror/Pell Erobreren* (Bille August)

Director: Fernando E. Solanas (*South* (*Sur*))(*South/Sur*)
Actor: Forest Whitaker (*Bird*)
Actress: Barbara Hershey, Johdi May, Linda Mvusi (*A World Apart*)

1989
Palme d'Or: *sex, lies and videotape* (Steven Soderbergh)
Director: Emir Kusturica (*The Time of the Gypsies*)
Actor: James Spader (*sex, lies and videotape*)
Actress: Meryl Streep (*A Cry in the Dark*, aka *Evil Angels*)

1990
Palme d'Or: *Wild at Heart* (David Lynch)
Director: Pavel Lounguine (*Taxi Blues*)
Actor: Gérard Depardieu (*Cyrano de Bergerac*)
Actress: Krystyna Janda (*Interrogation* (*Przesluchanie*))(*Interrogation/Przesluchanie*)

1991
Palme d'Or: *Barton Fink* (Joel and Ethan Coen)
Director: Joel Coen (*Barton Fink*)
Actor: John Turturro (*Barton Fink*)
Actress: Irene Jacob (*The Double Life of Veronique* (*LaVeronique/La Double Vie de Véronique*))

1992
Palme d'Or: *Best Intentions* (*Den Goda Vilijan*) (Bille August)
Director: Robert Altman (*The Player*)
Actor: Tim Robbins (*The Player*)
Actress: Pernilla August (*Best Intentions* (*Den Goda Vilijan*))*Intentions/Den Goda Vilijan*)

1993
Palme d'Or: *Farewell My Concubine* (Chen Kaige); *The Piano* (Jane Campion)
Director: Mike Leigh (*Naked*)
Actor: David Thewlis (*Naked*)
Actress: Holly Hunter (*The Piano*)

1994
Palme d'Or: *Pulp Fiction* (Quentin Tarantino)
Director: Nanni Moretti (*Dear Diary*)
Actor: Ge You (*To Live*)
Actress: Virna Lisi (*Queen Margaret* (*La Reine Margot*))*Margaret/La Reine Margot*)

1995
Palme d'Or: *Underground* (Emir Kusturica)
Director: Mathieu Kassovitz (*La Haine*)
Actor: Jonathan Pryce (*Carrington*)
Actress: Helen Mirren (*The Madness of King George*)

1996
Palme d'Or: *Secrets and Lies* (Mike Leigh)
Director: Joel Coen (*Fargo*)
Actor: Daniel Auteuil, Pascal Duquenne (*The Eighth Day*)
Actress: Brenda Blethyn (*Secrets and Lies*)

1997
Palme d'Or: *The Eel* (Shohei Imamura); *The Taste of Cherries* (Abbas Kiorostami)
Director: Wong Kar-Wai (*Happy Together*)
Actor: Sean Penn (*She's So Lovely*)
Actress: Kathy Burke (*Nil by Mouth*)

1998
Palme d'Or: *Eternity and a Day* (Theo Angelopoulos)
Director: John Boorman (*The General*)
Actor: Peter Mullen (*My Name Is Joe*)
Actress: Élodie Bouchez, Natacha Régnier (*Dream Life of Angels/Vie Rêve des Anges*))*Angels/Vie Rêve des Anges*)

1999
Palme d'Or: *Rosetta* (Jean-Pierre Dardenne, Luc Dardenne)
Director: Pedro Almodóvar (*All About My Mother*)
Actor: Emil Schotté (*L'Humanité*)
Actress: Séverine Caneele (*L'Humanité*), Emilie Dequenne (*Rosetta*)

2000
Palme d'Or: *Dancer in the Dark* (Lars von Trier)
Director: Edward Yang (*A One and a Two/Yi yi*)
Actor: Tony Leung Chiu Wai (*In the Mood for Love*)
Actress: Björk (*Dancer in the Dark*)

Books
Hollywood on the Riviera: The Inside Story of the

Cannes Film Festival, Cari Beauchamp and Henri Béhar (1992).
Hype and Glory, William Goldman (Macdonald, 1990).

Golden Bear Awards
The Berlin Film Festival began in 1951. Its main prize is the Golden Bear for best feature, which was inaugurated in 1956. The Golden Bear winners are:

1956
Invitation to the Dance (Gene Kelly)

1957
Twelve Angry Men (Sidney Lumet)

1958
Wild Strawberries/Smultonstället (Ingmar Bergman)

1959
The Cousins/Les Cousins (Claude Chabrol)

1960
Lazarillo/El Lazarillo de Tormes (Cesar Ardavin)

1961
The Night/La Notte (Michelangelo Antonioni)

1962
A Kind of Loving (John Schlesinger)

1963
Bushido/Bushido Zankoku Monogatari (Tadashi Imai); *The Devil/Il Diavolo* (US: *To Bed … Or Not to Bed*) (Gian Luigi Polidoro)

1964
Dry Summer aka *I Had My Brother's Wife/Süsuz Yaz* (Ismail Metin)

1965
Alphaville (Jean-Luc Godard)

1966
Cul-de-Sac (Roman Polanski)

1967
Le Départ (Jerzy Skolimowski)

1968
Ole Dole Doff (Jan Troell)

1969
Early Years/Rani Radovi (Zelimir Zilnik)

1970
No prize awarded

1971
The Garden of the Finzi Contini (Vittorio de Sica)

1972
The Canterbury Tales (Pier Paolo Pasolini)

1973
Distant Thunder (Satyajit Ray)

1974
The Apprenticeship of Duddy Kravitz (Ted Kotcheff)

1975
Adoption/Örökbefogadás (Márta Mészáros)

1976
Buffalo Bill and the Indians (Robert Altman)

1977
The Ascent/Voskhozhdenie (Larisa Sheptiko)

1978
The Trout/Las Truchas (José Luis Garcia Sánchez); *The Words of Max/Las Palabras de Max* (Emilio Martinez-Lazaro)

1979
David (Peter Lilienthal)

1980
Heartland (Richard Pearce); *Palermo Oder Wolfsberg* (Werner Schroeter)

1981
Fast, Fast/Depiesa, Deprisa (Carlos Saura)

1982
Veronika Voss/Die Sehnsucht der Veronica Voss (Rainer Werner Fassbinder)

1983
Ascendancy (Edward Bennett); *The Beehive/La Colmena* (Mario Camus)

1984
Love Streams (John Cassavetes)

1985
Wetherby (David Hare); *The Woman and the Stranger/ Die Frau und Der Fremde* (Rainer Simon)

1986
Stammheim (Reinhard Hauff)

1987
The Theme/Thema (Gleb Panfilov)

1988
Red Sorghum/Hong Gao Liang (Zhang Yimou)

1989
Rain Man (Barry Levinson)

1990
Music Box (Costa-Gavras); *Larks on a String* (Jiri Menzel)

1991
House of Smiles (Marco Ferreri)

1992
Grand Canyon (Lawrence Kasdan)

1993
The Woman from the Lake of Scented Souls/Xiang Hun N (Xei Fei); *The Wedding Banquet/Xiyan* (Ang Lee)

1994
In The Name of the Father (Jim Sheridan)

1995
Fresh Bait/L'Appat (Bertrand Tavernier)

1996
Sense and Sensibility (Ang Lee)

1997
The People vs Larry Flynt (Milos Forman)

1998
Central Station (Walter Salles)

1999
The Thin Red Line (Terence Malick)

2000
Magnolia (Paul Thomas Anderson)

Golden Lion Awards

The Venice Film Festival, held every September, began in 1934, was suspended in 1942, and started again in 1946. Its main award is the Golden Lion of St Mark, which since 1980 has been given to the best feature film. The Golden Lion winners are:

1980
Gloria (John Cassavetes); *Atlantic City* (Louis Malle)

1981
The German Sisters/Die Bleierne Zeit (Margarethe Von Trotta)

1982
The State of Things (Wim Wenders)

1983
First Name Carmen/Prénom: Carmen (Jean-Luc Godard)

1984
The Year of the Quiet Sun/Rok Spokojnego Slonca (Krzysztof Zanussi)

1985
Vagabonde/aka Sans Toit Ni Loi (Agnès Varda)

1986
The Green Ray US: Summer/Le Rayon Vert (Eric Rohmer)

1987
Au Revoir les Enfants (Louis Malle)

1988
The Legend of the Holy Drinker/La Leggenda del Santo Bevitore (Ermanno Olmi)

1989
A City of Sadness/Beiqing Chengshi (Hou Hsiao-hsien)

1990
Rosencrantz and Guildenstern Are Dead (Tom Stoppard)

1991
Urga (Nikita Mikhalkov)

1992
The Story of Qiu Ju/Qiu Ju de Guansi (Yang Zimou)

1993
Short Cuts (Robert Altman); *Three Colours: Blue/Trois Couleurs: Bleu* (Krzysztof Kiéslowski)

1994
Before the Rain (Milcho Manchevski); *Vive l'Amour/Aiqing Wansui* (Tsai Ming-liang)

1995
Cyclo (Tran Anh Hung)

1996
Michael Collins (Neil Jordan)

1997
Fireworks/Hana-Bi (Takeshi Kitano)

1998
They All Laughed/Cosi Ridevano (Gianni Amelio)

1999
Not One Less/Yi Ge Dou Bu Neng Shao (Zhang Yimou)

2000
The Circle/Dayereh (Jafar Panahi)

European Film Awards

The European Film Awards, known until 1997 as Felixes, were inaugurated in 1988. The European Film Academy announced in 1995 that it would no longer administer the award, partly because of financial problems, but also because it was impossible 'to put a single name on something as multifaceted and complicated as European cinema'. However, after a rethink and new sources of finance, the awards are continuing, though they were privatized from 1997. The main prizewinners were:

1988
Film: *A Short Film about Killing* (Krzysztof Kiéslowski)
Director: Wim Wenders (*Wings of Desire*)
Actor: Max Von Sydow (*Pelle the Conqueror*)
Actress: Carmen Maura (*Women on the Verge of a Nervous Breakdown*)
Supporting Actor: Curt Bois (*Wings of Desire*)
Supporting Actress: Johnna Ter Steege (*The Vanishing*)
Screenplay: Louis Malle (*Au Revoir, les Enfants*)

1989
Film: *Landscape in the Mist* (Theo Angelopoulos)
Director: Géza Bereményi (*The Midas Touch*)
Actor: Philippe Noiret (*Life and Nothing But; Cinema Paradiso*)
Actress: Ruth Sheen (*High Hopes*)
Supporting Performance: Edna Doré (*High Hopes*)
Screenplay: Maria Khmelik (*Little Vera*)

1990
Film: *Open Doors* (*Porte Aperte*) (Gianni Amelio)
Actor: Kenneth Branagh (*Henry V*)
Actress: Carmen Maura (*Ay! Carmela*)
Supporting Actor: Dimitri Pevsov (*Mother* (*Matj*))
Supporting Actress: Malin Ek (*The Guardian Angel* (*Skyddsanglen*))
Screenplay: Vitaly Kanevsky (*Don't Move, Die and Rise Again* (*Zamri Umi Voskresni*))

1991
Film: *Riff-Raff* (Ken Loach)
Actor: Michel Bouquet (*Toto le Héros*)
Actress: Clotilde Courau (*Le Petit Criminel*)
Supporting Actor: Ricky Memphis (*Ultrè*)
Supporting Actress: Marta Keler (*Virginia*)
Screenplay: Jaco Van Dormael (*Toto le Héros*)

1992
Film: *Il Ladro di Bambini* (Gianni Amelio)
Actor: Matti Pellonpää (*La Vie de Bohème*)
Actress: Juliette Binoche (*Les Amants du Pont-Neuf*)

Supporting Actor: André Wilms (*La Vie de Bohème*)
Supporting Actress: Ghita Norby (*Freud Flyttar Hemifran*)
Screenplay: István Szabó (*Edes Emma, Draga Böbe*)

1993
Film: *Urga* (Nikita Mikhalkov)
Actor: Daniel Auteuil (*Un Coeur en Hiver*)
Actress: Maia Morgenstern (*Balanta*)

1994
Film: *Lamerica* (Gianni Amelio)
Lifetime achievement: Robert Bresson

1995
Film: *Land and Freedom* (Ken Loach)

1996
Film: *Breaking the Waves* (Lars von Trier)
Young Film: *Some Mother's Son* (Terry George)
Actress: Emily Watson (*Breaking the Waves*)
Actor: Ian McKellen (*Richard III*)
Screenwriter: Arief Aliev, Sergai Bodrov, Boris Giler (*The Prisoner of the Mountains*)

1997
Film: *The Full Monty* (Peter Cattaneo)
Actor: Bob Hoskins (*TwentyFourSeven*)
Actress: Juliette Binoche (*The English Patient*)
Screenwriter: Chris Vander Stappen, Alain Berline (*Ma Vie en Rose*)

1998
Film: *Life Is Beautiful* (Roberto Begnini)
Actor: Roberto Begnini (*Life Is Beautiful*)
Actress: Élodie Bouchez, Natacha Régnier (*Dream Life of Angels/Vie Rêve des Anges*)
Screenwriter: Peter Howitt (*Sliding Doors*)
Cinematographer: Adrian Biddle (*The Butcher Boy*)
Oustanding European Achievement in World Cinema: Stellan Skarsgard (*Amistad, Good Will Hunting*)
Special Achievement: Jeremy Irons
Audience Awards: actor: Antonio Banderas (*Godzilla*);(*Mask of Zorro*); actress: Kate Winslet (*Titanic*); director: Roland Emmerich (*Godzilla*)

1999
Film: *All About My Mother* (Pedro Almodóvar)
Actor: Ralph Fiennes (*Sunshine*)
Actress: Cecilia Roth (*All About My Mother*)
Screenwriter: Istvan Szabo (*Sunshine*)
Cinematographer: Lajos Koltai (*The Legend of 1900/La Leggenda Del Pianista Sull'Oceano; Sunshine*)
Oustanding European Achievement in World Cinema: Antonio Banderas (*Crazy in Alabama*); Roman Polanski (*The Ninth Gate*)
Audience Awards: actor: Sean Connery (*Entrapment*); actress Catherine Zeta-Jones (*Entrapment*); director: Pedro Almodóvar (*All About My Mother*)
Lifetime Achievement: Ennio Morricone

2000
Film: *Dancer in the Dark* (Lars von Trier)
Actor: Sergi López (*Harry, He's Here to Help/Harry, Un Ami Qui Vous Vent Du Bien*)
Actress: Björk (*Dancer in the Dark*)
Screenwriter: Agnès Jaoui, Jean-Pierre Bacri (*It Takes All Kinds/Le Goût Des Autres*)
Cinematographer: Vittorio Storaro (*Goya in Bodeaux/Goya En Burdeos*)
Oustanding European Achievement in World Cinema: Roberto Benigni; Jean Réno
Audience Awards: actor: Ingvar Eggert Sigurdsson (*Angels of the Universe/Englar Alheimsins*); actress: Björk (*Dancer in the Dark*); director: Lars von Trier (*Dancer in the Dark*)
Lifetime Achievement: Richard Harris

American Society of Cinematographers' Annual Awards

This professional association gives an award for the best cinematography of the year. Its winners are:
1986   Jordan Cronenweth (*Peggy Sue Got Married*)
1987   Allen Daviau (*Empire of the Sun*)
1988   Conrad L. Hall (*Tequila Sunrise*)
1989   Haskell Wexler (*Blaze*)
1990   Dean Semler (*Dances with Wolves*)
1991   Allen Daviau (*Bugsy*)
1992   Stephen H. Burum (*Hoffa*)
1993   Conrad L. Hall (*Searching for Bobby Fischer*)
1994   Roger Deakins (*The Shawshank Redemption*)
1995   John Toll (*Braveheart*)

1996   John Seale (*The English Patient*)
1997   Russell Carpenter (*Titanic*)
1998   John Toll (*The Thin Red Line*)
1999   Conrad L. Hall (*American Beauty*)
2000   Caleb Deschanel (*The Patriot*)

The Directors Guild of America Awards

The national union of directors presents annual awards for feature film direction, which also usually provide an indication of the likely Oscar winner for best direction. Its winners are:
1948   Joseph Mankiewicz (*A Letter to Three Wives*)
1949   Robert Rossen (*All the King's Men*)
1950   Joseph Mankiewicz (*All About Eve*)
1951   George Stevens (*A Place in the Sun*)
1952   John Ford (*The Quiet Man*)
1953   Fred Zinnemann (*From Here to Eternity*)
1954   Elia Kazan (*On the Waterfront*)
1955   Delbert Mann (*Marty*)
1956   George Stevens (*Giant*)
1957   David Lean (*Bridge on the River Kwai*)
1958   Vincente Minnelli (*Gigi*)
1959   William Wyler (*Ben-Hur*)
1960   Billy Wilder (*The Apartment*)
1961   Robert Wise, Jerome Robbins (*West Side Story*)
1962   David Lean (*Lawrence of Arabia*)
1963   Tony Richardson (*Tom Jones*)
1964   George Cukor (*My Fair Lady*)
1965   Robert Wise (*The Sound of Music*)
1966   Fred Zinnemann (*A Man for All Seasons*)
1967   Mike Nichols (*The Graduate*)
1968   Anthony Harvey (*The Lion in Winter*)
1969   John Schlesinger (*Midnight Cowboy*)
1970   Franklin J. Schaffner (*Patton*)
1971   William Friedkin (*The French Connection*)
1972   Francis Ford Coppola (*The Godfather*)
1973   George Roy Hill (*The Sting*)
1974   Francis Ford Coppola (*The Godfather, Part II*)
1975   Milos Forman (*One Flew over the Cuckoo's Nest*)
1976   John G. Avildsen (*Rocky*)
1977   Woody Allen (*Annie Hall*)
1978   Michael Cimino (*The Deer Hunter*)
1979   Robert Benton (*Kramer vs Kramer*)
1980   Robert Redford (*Ordinary People*)
1981   Warren Beatty (*Reds*)
1982   Richard Attenborough (*Gandhi*)
1983   James L. Brooks (*Terms of Endearment*)
1984   Milos Forman (*Amadeus*)
1985   Steven Spielberg (*The Color Purple*)
1986   Oliver Stone (*Platoon*)
1987   Bernardo Bertolucci (*The Last Emperor*)
1988   Barry Levinson (*Rain Man*)
1989   Oliver Stone (*Born on the Fourth of July*)
1990   Kevin Costner (*Dances with Wolves*)
1991   Jonathan Demme (*Silence of the Lambs*)
1992   Clint Eastwood (*Unforgiven*)
1993   Steven Spielberg (*Schindler's List*)
1994   Robert Zemeckis (*Forrest Gump*)
1995   Ron Howard (*Apollo 13*)
1996   Anthony Minghella (*The English Patient*)
1997   James Cameron (*Titanic*)
1998   Steven Spielberg (*Saving Private Ryan*)
1999   Sam Mendes (*American Beauty*)
2000   Ang Lee (*Crouching Tiger, Hidden Dragon*)

London Critics' Circle Awards (ALFS)

The Critics' Circle was founded in 1913. The Film Critics' Circle, based in London, has more than 80 members, and began presenting awards, known as ALFS (Awards of the London Film Critics' Circle), in 1980. Its prizes include the Dilys Powell Award for lifetime achievement. Until 1991, there was no separate award for actress of the year; the term 'actor' applied to men and women.

1980
Film: *Apocalypse Now* (Francis Ford Coppola)
Foreign Film: *Agni Vera* (Pal Gabor); *The Marriage of Maria Braun* (Rainer Werner Fassbinder)
Director: Nicolas Roeg (*Bad Timing*)
Screenwriter: Steve Tesich (*Breaking Away*)
Special Award: Gillian Armstrong (*My Brilliant Career*); Peter Sellers (*Being There*)

1981
Film: *Chariots of Fire* (Hugh Hudson)
Foreign Film: *Man of Iron* (Andrzej Wajda)
Director: Andrzej Wajda (*Man of Iron*)
Screenwriter: Colin Welland (*Chariots of Fire*)
Special Award: Freddie Francis (*The Elephant Man*); Bill Forsyth (*Gregory's Girl; That Sinking Feeling*)

Pederson (Collins, 1939). A small-town furniture salesman, together with his wife and dog, leaves Idaho to try, and fail, to become a screenwriter in Hollywood.

A Voyage to Puerilia, Elmer Rice (1930). A satire on Hollywood.

What Makes Sammy Run, Budd Schulberg (1961). Classic story of a producer (who resembles Jerry Wald) on the make.

White Hunter, Black Heart, Peter Viertel (W. H. Allen, 1954). A film director (who resembles John Huston) is more interested in shooting big game than his movie in Africa; filmed in 1990 by Clint Eastwood.

Film Periodicals

American Cinematographer: The International Journal of Film and Electronic Production Techniques, established 1920. Covers current cinema from the point of view of the cinematographer. Published monthly in Hollywood.

American Film: Film, Video and Television Arts. News and features on current cinema. Published bi-monthly, six times a year, from New York.

The Dark Side: The Magazine of the Macabre and Fantastic. British magazine covering horror films, video, and books. Published monthly.

Empire. British magazine, with news and features on current cinema, and reviews of new cinema, video, laser disc, and soundtrack releases. Published monthly.

Entertainment Weekly. American magazine covering all aspects of show-business: movies, television, books, music, and video.

Fangoria. Long-established American magazine covering horror, including films and books. Published monthly, except February and December.

Film Comment. Magazine covering current and past cinema. Published bi-monthly, six times a year, by the Film Society of Lincoln Center, New York.

Film Dope. British magazine providing biographical information and credits of actors, directors, and others involved in films. Published at irregular intervals, two or three times a year.

Film Review. British magazine with features and reviews of current cinema and video releases. Published monthly with special extra issues, including a video movie guide and a yearbook.

Films in Review. American magazine with reviews of new releases and features on past and current cinema. Published bi-monthly.

The Hollywood Reporter. US trade daily and weekly.

Impact. British magazine covering action movies and stars from around the world. Published monthly.

The Independent Film & Video Monthly. US magazine published by the Foundation for Independent Video and Film, covering all aspects of independent film-making. Published monthly except February and September.

Monthly Film Bulletin 1934–91. Monthly magazine containing reviews and complete credits for all feature films released in Britain. From May 1991, it was incorporated into *Sight and Sound*.

Movieline. Los Angeles-based magazine, with news and features on current cinema. Published monthly except February.

Moving Pictures International. Trade publication covering the business of movies, television and the new media. Published ten times a year.

Premiere. US magazine, with news and features on current cinema. Published monthly.

Premiere (UK edition). Magazine containing a mix of original features and material originating in the US edition. Published monthly.

Screen International. British trade weekly.

Shivers. British magazine covering horror films, videos, and personalities. Published monthly.

Sight and Sound. Magazine with an academic approach to current and past films, published by the British Film Institute. Quarterly from 1935 until May 1991, when it became a monthly, incorporating the *Monthly Film Bulletin*. Now includes reviews and complete credits of all current cinema releases, and short reviews of new videos.

Starburst. British magazine covering science fiction in all its forms, including film and television. Published monthly.

Total Film. British magazine, with news and features on current cinema, and reviews of new cinema, video, laser disc, and soundtrack releases. Published monthly.

US. American magazine featuring interviews and news on current show-business stars. Published monthly.

Variety. US trade daily and weekly.

10
Movie Guides on CD-ROM

General Guides
• *Blockbuster Entertainment Guide to Movies and Videos*, 2nd Edition (Creative Multimedia, £27.99).

Minimum system requirements: IBM-compatible PC 486DX2/66, Windows 3.1, 8 Mb of RAM, 7 Mb available hard drive space, double-speed CD-ROM drive, 256-colour display, Sound Blaster or compatible sound card.

Now that many rivals have ceased publication, including Microsoft's *Cinemania* (the 1997 edition was, unfortunately, the last), *VideoHound Multimedia* and the *Mega Movie Guide*, this is the best general-purpose CD-ROM-based guide available, and a great improvement on the first edition. It gives cast and credits for more than 23,000 films and includes 5,500 photographs. There are brief clips from 30 or so classic films, such as *Casablanca*, *Chinatown*, *Lawrence of Arabia* and *Psycho*. Films are given star ratings, and there are 11,000 reviews taken from the *Time Out Film Guide*, and biographies of stars and directors from David Thomson's *Biographical Dictionary of Film*. You can click on the names of many stars and directors and get a list of their films, though not of other talents, such as composers and cinematographers. Free monthly updates to the guide can be downloaded via the Internet.
• *The Cannes Film Festival* (EMME Interactive, £30 or $24.95).

Minimum system requirements: IBM-compatible PC 386 or 486 with Windows 3.1 with 4 Mb of RAM, SVGA display.

A history of the first 50 years of the Cannes Film Festival from 1939 to 1990, providing details of all award-winners, together with 2,000 film stills, and some grainy and not very interesting newsreel footage of past festivals.
• *Corel/AMG All-Movie Guide 2.0* (Corel, £20 or $19.95).

Minimum system requirements: IBM-compatible PC 486SX 66 MHz, Windows 3.x, MS-DOS 5.0, with 8 Mb RAM and 6 Mb (9 Mb for Windows 95) hard drive space, SVGA display. Macintosh LCIII, System 7.1, with 8 Mb RAM, and 19.5 Mb hard drive space.

This remains potentially an excellent guide, with details of 100,000 movies and some 170,000 filmographies/biographies. You can annotate entries, and there's a useful glossary of film terms. But, like the first edition, it has many inaccuracies and the same films are included under different titles. More information at AMG's Web site (www.allmusic.com/AMGCorel.htm).

• *Halliwell's Film & Video Guide* (Palmtop, £40). Minimum system requirements: Psion series 5 with 8 Mb RAM and a computer with a CD-ROM drive that can transfer files to the Psion.

Our companion volume, the comprehensive *Halliwell's Film & Video Guide*, a bulky book of 918 pages, fits happily into a hand-held Psion computer, providing plot synopses, critical evaluations and credits for more than 20,000 films, filmographies for more than 36,300 actors, directors and writers, and information on video, laser disc and soundtrack availability. The computer version adds sophisticated search facilities and the ability to annotate the entries. More information can be found at Palmtop's Web site (www.palmtop.nl/).

Specialist Guides
• *The Complete Index to World Film* by Alan Goble (Bowker Saur, £495).

Minimum system requirements: IBM-compatible PC 486 with a VGA or SVGA colour monitor with 4 Mb RAM.

The second edition of Alan Goble's guide is even more comprehensive than the first and almost half the price. It covers films from 1895 to 1998, includes 300,154 titles from 173 countries, including more than 100,000 silent films, 13,000 animated films and 8,000 TV films. There are filmographies for 45,075 directors, and credits for 1,085,827 actors. There are 63,850 films with cinematographer credits, 27,906 with composer credits, 91,757 with production credits, and 17,137 with their literary source.
• *Film Index International* (British Film Institute/Chadwyck-Healey, £1,295 with annual updates costing £350; £1,095 plus updates at £295 for universities and public libraries).

Minimum system requirements: IBM-compatible PC 386 with MS-DOS 3.1 or Windows 3.1, with 4 Mb of RAM.

Based on SIFT (Summary of Information on Film and Television), a database compiled by the Library and Information Services Department of the British Film Institute, it provides detailed production details on 98,000 films, with basic biographical information on more than 41,000 personalities, as well as references to articles on films and people from various periodicals. It now includes details of Oscars and other awards. For more information see Chadwyck-Healey's Web site (www.chadwyck.co.uk).

11
Movie Resources on the Internet

The Internet is a great source of movie information, gossip and reviews. More than other media, it is also in a constant state of flux, with publications appearing and disappearing with great speed. For that reason, I have listed just the most useful websites, ones that are likely to stay around, and which also provide the best starting points, by classifying current sources of information.

The World Wide Web

The World Wide Web often seems more of a maze, in which you can easily become lost in a series of dead ends. Search engines can save a lot of wasted effort. These days simple search engines are built into the latest operating systems of both Windows and Macintosh computers. Also available are some excellent commercial search engines that reside on your computer's hard disk; there are at least two useful free ones that can be downloaded to your computer from the Internet: Webferret (at http:www.ferretsoft.com) and Copernic (http:www.copernic.com). If you are searching for information on a new movie, particularly if it's a blockbuster, then frequently you'll be able to reach it by typing: 'http://www.nameofthemovie.com'. *Godzilla*, for instance, could be found at 'http://www.godzilla.com'. The addresses (or Universal Resource Locators) below are not given in full. You'll need to add 'http://' to the beginning of each one.

Fan Pages

These range from those originated by enthusiastic and usually uncritical fans of a particular personality to official fan clubs and pages organized by the actors and actresses themselves – everyone from yesterday's sex symbol Mamie Van Doren to today's hottest stars, such as Leonardo DiCaprio, have their own official sites. The best places to begin a search for a favourite is at sites that provide alphabetical lists of fan sites:

- Celebsite (www.celebsite.com) has links to celebrity sites for actors, actresses, directors, comedians, producers and musicians.
- Cinema Confidential (www.cinecon.com) has news, interviews and gossip on new and upcoming releases.
- Fan Links (www.tnef.com/stars/) provides links to actors and actresses.
- Fan Sites (www.fansites.com) provides links to more than 2,500 sites for actors and actresses. Oddly, it indexes them by first names.
- Star Seeker (www.starseeker.com/index.com) is a collection of links to fan pages, news, and movies.

Film Reference

- All Movie Guide (www.allmovie.com/) provides casts and production information for many movies.
- Internet Movie Database (uk.imdb.com or us.imdb.com) details more than 170,479 films with some 2.4m filmography entries, and includes links to other sites of interest.
- Motion Picture Guide (www.tvgen.com/movies/) has full production details, cast credits and reviews for 35,000 movies, with biographical information from Ephraim Katz's *Movie Encyclopedia*.

Movie Publications

- 6 Degrees (www.6degrees.co.uk/en/2/index.html) is a monthly on-line film magazine with features and reviews, and news updated weekly.
- Boxoffice Magazine (www.boxoff.com/) is a monthly trade publication with an on-line site featuring news stories and interviews with directors and stars.
- Bright Lights Film Journal (www.slip.net/gmm/bright.html) is a quarterly magazine of movie analysis, history and commentary.
- Cinescape (www.cinescape.com/) has news and features on science-fiction and fantasy movies.
- The Dark Side (www.ebony.co.uk/darkside/) is an on-line site for the British monthly horror magazine.
- Entertainment Weekly (cgi.pathfinder.com/ew) has star interviews, reviews and celebrity gossip.
- Empire Magazine (www.futurenet.com) is the on-line version of the best-selling British film monthly.
- Film Comment (www.interactive.line.com/film/cover.html) is an on-line version of the bimonthly publication of the Film Society of Lincoln Center.
- Film Review (www.visimag.com) is designed to persuade people to buy the monthly British film magazine, but includes a few features.
- FilmScore Monthly (www.filmscoremonthly.com) covers film music and composers.
- Film Threat (www.filmthreat.com) has information on independent film-makers.
- Hollywood Reporter (www.hollywoodreporter.com) is a trade publication providing free news and a subscription service for those who want to know more.
- Movieline (www.movieline.mag.com) is the on-line version of the American movie monthly.
- Motion Picture (www.motionpicture.com) offers news and gossip, as well as reviews of movies currently in cinemas, and on video and television.
- People (cgi.pathfinder.com/people) has celebrity gossip and interviews.
- Premiere Magazine (www.premieremag.com/) is the on-line version of the American movie monthly.
- Total Film (www.futurenet.com) is the on-line version of the British movie monthly.
- Variety (www.variety.com): the showbusiness trade paper provides news and has a subscription service for those who want *Daily Variety* on-line.

Movie News and Features

- Ain't It Cool News (www.aint-it-cool-news.com) has gossip and advance information on audiences' reactions to previews of new films. The film studios don't like it, but they're doing their best to co-opt it.
- E! Online (www.eonline.com/) for celebrity gossip and features.
- Film.com (www.film.com) is an independent voice of film criticism on the Internet, providing news, reviews, features and previews, and bringing together critics, writers and movie buffs everywhere.
- Hollywood Online (www.hollywood.com) for trailers, photos and information.
- Jam! (www.canoe.ca/JamMovies/home.html) for news, interviews and reviews on current movies and personalities.
- Movie Snapshot (www.moviesnapshot.com/) has news-service reviews, features, interviews and photographs on Hollywood.
- Movieweb (www.movieweb.com/) has previews of, and information on, current and upcoming movies.
- Film Scouts (www.filmscouts.com/) has news about film and leading festivals, including Cannes, Sundance and Toronto.
- Rough Cut (www.roughcut.com) has movie news, reviews and features.
- Mr Showbiz (www.mrshowbiz.com/) provides news, features, interviews on current movies and personalities.
- Showbizwire (www.showbizwire.com) is an entertainment news resource.

Search Engines and Links

- About.com(home.about.com/movies/index.html) includes twenty sites covering many aspects of film, from action and adventure movies to world film.
- Cinema Sites (www.cinema-sites.com/) has links to reviews, previews, screenings, fan pages, magazines, journals, festivals and more.
- Excite (www.excite.com.entertainment/movies) has the latest entertainment news.
- Filmworld (www.filmworld.co.uk), a DVD and video sales site, contains news and reviews and links to many other film sites in the UK, US and other countries, and to film festival sites.
- Intertainment Cybercenter (hollywoodnetwork.com/hn/directory/hec/index.html) provides links to film studios, TV networks and news sources.
- Movie Review Query Engine (www.mrqe.com/lookup?) will search the Web for reviews of particular films.
- Movies Net (www.movies.net/index.html) has links to stars and celebrities, studios, films, festivals, reviews, gossip, databases, archives, and movie memorabilia.
- Rotten Tomatoes (www.rottentomatoes.com) has quotes from, and links to, movie reviews.
- Yahoo! (www.yahoo.com/entertainment/movies_and_films/) provides links to everything from actors and actresses, awards, box-office reports to news, reviews, screenplays and more, classified under 40 headings.

Specialist Sites

- Absolute Horror (www.smackem.com/horror/horror.htm) provides information on, and reviews of, many horror movies.
- American Movie Classics Company (www.amctv.com/home.html) has features on classic movies and video releases.
- Cyber Film School (www.cyberfilmschool.com/) is an on-line film learning environment to assist student and professional film-makers to improve their craft.
- Film Festivals (www.filmfestivals.com) has information on the world's leading film festivals.
- The Film 100 (www.film100.com) gives a ranking of the 100 most influential people in the history of the cinema, with biographies, interactive demos and links to other websites.
- Films: Research and Resources (www.gen.umn.edu/faculty_staff/yahnke/film/Default.htm), compiled by Professor Robert E. Yahnke, includes a work-in-progress, *Cinema History*, an on-line book beginning with silents and, when last viewed, discussing 60s films.
- Greatest Films (www.filmsite.org/) contains plot summaries, commentary and film posters of classic films, compiled by Tim Dirks.
- Horror Movies (www.horrormovies.com/) provides a classified guide.
- The Movie Times (www.the-movie-times.com/) provides movie box-office information, movie release schedules, reviews, and information on actors and actresses.
- Red Flower Society (www.geocities.com/Tokyo/9667/) for links to Hong Kong movies, actors and actresses, film companies and picture archives.
- Roger Ebert on Movies (www.suntimes.com/ebert/) has reviews by an influential critic.
- The Silents Majority (www.mdle.com/ClassicFilms/) is devoted to silent films.
- Silver Screen Legends (www.cowboypal.com/cowboy2.html) links to old-time cowboy film stars, such as Rex Allen, Monte Hale and Tex Ritter.
- The Ultimate Science Fiction Web Guide (magicdragon.com/UltimateSF/SF-index.html) has information on sf movies and links to associated sites.
- Women in Cinema (www.people.virginia.edu/pm9k/libsci/womFilm.html) is just what it says it is.
- The World of Bollywood (www.indopak.com/bolly/home.htm) has information on Indian movies.

Professional Organizations

- Academy of Motion Picture Arts and Sciences (www.oscars.org/ampas/) for everything you want to know about the Oscars and AMPAS's other activities.
- American Film Institute (www.afionline.org/home.html) includes the AFI OnLine Cinema (www.afionline.org/cinema/archive/lobby.html) showing classic movies.
- The British Film Institute (www.bfi.org.uk/) is a dull site about BFI activities, although improvements are promised.for information on its activities and what's on at the National Film Theatre..
- The Bill Douglas Centre at the University of Exeter (www.ex.ac.uk/bill.douglas/) has information on the beginnings of cinema.
- Directors Guild of America (www.dga.org/) includes interviews with its distinguished members.
- US National Film Registry (www.cs.cmu.edu/afs/cs.cmu.edu/user/clamen/misc/movies/NFR-Titles.html) lists the 'culturally, historically, or esthetically important' films selected by the Library of Congress for preservation.

Studios and Production Companies

- Aardman Animations (bchannel.avonibp.co.uk/productioncos/aardman/aardman.html) is the home of Wallace and Gromit.
- Buena Vista (bvp.wdp.com/BVI/) has information on upcoming and current releases.
- Disney Pictures (www.disney.com/DisneyPictures/index.html) has information on upcoming and current releases, and merchandise to buy.
- Fine Line Features (www.flf.com) details its current and upcoming releases.
- Fox Searchlight (www.foxsearchlight) has information on upcoming and current releases.
- Jim Henson Company (www.henson.com) has movie information and Muppets galore.
- MCA/Universal Studios (www.mca.com) has information on upcoming and current releases.
- MGM/UA Pictures (www.mgmua.com) has information on upcoming and current releases.
- Miramax Films (www.miramax.com) has information on upcoming and current releases.
- New Line Cinema (www.newline.com/) has details of its releases.
- October Films (www.octoberfilms.com) details its art-house releases (like *Hilary and Jackie* and *Touch of Evil*).
- Paramount Pictures (www.paramount.com/BronsonGate.htm) has information on upcoming and current releases.
- Sony (www.music.sony.com/index.alternate.html) has information on upcoming and current releases.
- Star Wars (www.starwars.com) has information on the current and upcoming films in the series.
- Troma (www.troma.com/) has information about the studio responsible for the Toxic Avenger.
- Twentieth Century-Fox (www.fox.com) has information on upcoming and current releases.
- UIP (www.uip.com/lingos/uk/uk_index.html) has information on the films it distributes in English, Dutch, French, German and Spanish.
- Universal (www.universalstudios.com) has information on upcoming and current releases.
- View Askew (www.viewaskew.com/) for information on the films of director Kevin Smith.
- Warner's (www.warnerbros.com) has information on upcoming and current releases.

Usenet

Newsgroups provide the opportunity to share news, gossip and information with like-minded people. You can subscribe directly to groups, or access them through the World Wide Web by way of Deja News (http:www.dejanews.com). There are newsgroups devoted to individuals, such as Woody Allen, Alfred Hitchcock and Stanley Kubrick. But the more general discussion groups include:

- alt.celebrities has gossip about the famous, though curiosity is often focused on the sexual proclivities of the stars.
- alt.fan.actors has discussion of the current favourite male performers.
- alt.fan.actors.dead deals with stars of the past.
- alt.fan.british-actors discusses British actors.
- alt.fan-james.bond discusses in minute detail

every aspect of the films.
- alt.movies discusses all aspects of movies and movie-going.
- alt.asian-movies deals mainly with Hong Kong movies and their stars.
- alt.movies.cinematography holds discussions of techniques and equipment.
- alt.cult-movies deals with a wide variety of movies, some seemingly with a cult of only one fan.
- alt.movies.monster finds Godzilla endlessly fascinating.
- alt.movies.independent discusses movies that you might otherwise miss, or never hear of.
- alt.movies.silent has often erudite discussions on the silent era.
- alt.movies.uk deals with British films and releases.

- alt.showbiz.gossip is similar in style to alt.celebrities.
- alt.movies.visual-effects discusses how film-makers achieve their spectacular effects.
- rec.arts.movies.announce has birthday lists and box-office grosses.
- rec.arts.movies.current-films has opinions and discussions on the latest films, and the critical response to them.
- rec.arts.movies.international discusses and reviews foreign films.
- rec.arts.movies.misc discusses all aspects of movies, much as does alt.movies.
- rec.arts.movies.movie-going discusses the physical pleasures and discomforts of cinemas and their audiences.
- rec.arts.movies.past-films deals with classic

genres.
- rec.arts.movies.people has discussion and opinion on those in front of, and behind, the camera.
- rec.arts.movies.production deals with technical matters, and questions and discussions on movie-making equipment.
- rec.arts.movies.reviews has reviews and often heated discussions on the worth of particular movies.
- rec.arts.sf.movies deals with sf and fantasy movies and their stars.
- rec.music.movies concerns itself with movie music, composers and soundtrack releases.
- uk.media.films discusses British films and personalities.

12
A Brief History of the Cinema

1873
America: Eadweard Muybridge, an English photographer, uses cameras spaced along a race-track to capture the movement of a galloping horse.

1878
America: Muybridge improves his method of taking photographs of animals in motion. He begins work on a projector.

1881
America: Muybridge perfects his Zoopraxiscope, which uses rotating glass disks containing painted images based on his photographs. He lectures on his work in America and, from 1892, in Europe, inspiring others.
1884
America: American artist Thomas Eakins, one of Muybridge's assistants, creates a single-motion picture camera.
Britain: John Rudge, an inventor living in Bath, patents a means of showing animations with a magic lantern. William Friese-Greene later demonstrates it as his own invention.
Germany: Ottomar Anschütz photographs animals and men in motion which can be viewed on his Tachyscope.

1885
America: George Eastman markets film on a roll, made of sensitized paper.
Britain: William Friese-Greene, a Bath photographer, exhibits the results of his experiments in film: an image of a girl moving her eyes.

1887
Germany: Ottomar Anschütz demonstrates his Electro-Tachyscope, which uses a sequence of still photographs fitted on a large wheel and viewed through a small hole to produce the effect of motion. His machines are shown around the world, as penny-in-the-slot novelties.

1888
Britain: French inventor Louis Augustin Le Prince patents a machine to film and project a sequence of images.

1889
America: Eastman's company, now named Eastman Kodak, begins to manufacture roll-film on celluloid.
Thomas Edison takes out a patent on perforated film.
Britain: William Friese-Greene obtains a patent for a moving picture camera.

1890
France: Louis Augustin Le Prince boards a train for Paris at Dijon and vanishes. He is never seen again.

1891
America: Edison applies for a patent on the Kinetoscope, a cabinet for displaying film to one spectator at a time, designed by his assistant William Dickson.

1892
France: Émile Renaud exhibits his Praxinoscope, which projects brief animations of hand-drawn images onto a screen.

1893
Britain: Friese-Greene patents a rapid-sequence camera.

1894
America: Fred Ott, one of Edison's workers, is recorded sneezing on film shot in the inventor's 'Black Maria' studio. Edison's assistant Dickson makes films to show in the Kinetoscope. They

last around 20 seconds and feature vaudeville acts and famous personalities, including Buffalo Bill Cody.
Edison begins to manufacture Kinetoscopes but doubts whether 'there is any commercial future in it'. The first Kinetoscope parlour opens in New York. More follow in other cities, although the glimpse of a Spanish dancer's ankle upsets some.
Britain: In October, Edison's Kinetoscope goes on show in Oxford Street, London.
Robert W. Paul, a London scientific instrument maker, is asked to copy Edison's Kinetoscope and discovers that Edison has not patented his invention in England. He works on improving it, by projecting images on a screen and by incorporating a wheel shaped like a Maltese cross to stop each frame of film for a moment in order to make the image seem less jerky.
Germany: Ottomar Anschütz demonstrates a projection system in Berlin.

1895
Films average between 40 to 80 feet in length, running for little more than a minute at most.
America: The American Mutoscope Company is set up to manufacture peep-show machines. It soon goes into film production proper and is renamed the Biograph Company.
Britain: Robert W. Paul and photographer Birt Acres begin to collaborate on designing a motion picture camera. Acres films sporting events, including the Derby.
France: Louis and Auguste Lumière, partners in a photographic business, patent the Cinématographe, a camera and projector, in February. In March, they demonstrate the system with a film of their workers leaving the factory and go on to hold other demonstrations. The brothers open Le Cinématographe, the first-ever public film show, in the basement of the Grand Café in Paris on 28 December. Twelve films are shown during the half-hour show.
Germany: In Berlin, Max Skladanowsky patents his Bioskop projector and gives a public show of films in November.

1896
America: Edison demonstrates the new Vitascope, a projector designed by Thomas Armat. The first public show is held in a New York music hall on 23 April.
In June, the Lumière show opens in New York.
Britain: In January, Birt Acres demonstrates motion picture projection in London and founds the Northern Photographic Works.
On 20 February, the Lumière show opens in London. It transfers in March to the Empire Music Hall, Leicester Square.
On 21 February, Robert W. Paul demonstrates his method of motion picture projection, the Theatrograph. Shortly after, his films open at Olympia and become a special attraction at music halls, including the Alhambra, Leicester Square.
Paul makes the first British fiction film, *The Soldier's Courtship*, on the roof of the Alhambra in April. He films the Derby winners and screens it the next day to appreciative audiences. The Derby is later shown in colour, with the tints added by hand.
In Kingston-upon-Thames, the first cinema opens in a converted shop. It fails. But film flourishes as an attraction at fairground sideshows.
Denmark: Peter Elfelt shoots the first Danish film, a fake short of huskies pulling a sledge in the snows of Greenland.
France: Charles and Émile Pathé found the Pathé Frères, mainly to sell phonographs, but soon become involved in film production.
In Paris, George Méliès begins to make films with trick effects.
Auguste Baron begins working on a process of adding sound to film. He also invents a system of

multi-screen cinema, Cinématorama, without attracting much interest.
Germany: Oskar Messter develops a motion picture camera and projection system.
India: The Lumière show opens in Bombay.
South Africa: Carl Hertz, a magician, shows as part of his stage act films bought, together with a projector, from Paul. He then takes them to Australia.
Spain: The first public film show of Lumière's films takes place in Madrid to an audience mainly of schoolgirls.

1897
France: In Paris, Alexander Rapoutat opens the first cinema devoted to newsreels.
One hundred and fifty people die in a Paris cinema fire caused by a burning projector, creating widespread concern about the safety of cinemas and equipment.
Spain: Fructuoso Gelabert makes the country's first fictional film, *Riña en un Café*.

1898
America: Biograph cameramen film war in Cuba.
Britain: Cecil M. Hepworth, son of a magic-lantern lecturer, writes *Animated Photography*, the first handbook on cinema.
In Brighton, G. A. Smith becomes the first Englishman to use double exposure for trick effects in *Cinderella and the Fairy Godmother* and other films.
The French Gaumont company opens a London office and begins making films at Dulwich.
American Charles Urban forms the Warwick Trading Company, which soon becomes a major producer and distributor.

1899
Films average around 70 feet in length, running for just over a minute.
Britain: Supply of American films dries up as Edison tries to combat what he regards as piracy. R. W. Paul opens one of Britain's earliest studios at New Southgate, North London, consisting of a stage, similar to that of a theatre, with a camera platform running on wheels in front of it. Among the first films produced is Dickens's *A Christmas Carol*.
Cecil M. Hepworth begins film production.
France: Auguste Baron perfects his system of sound cinema, but can find no one interested in exploiting his method.
Méliès' *Cinderella* is one of the first films to approach a narrative style.

1900
Australia: Joseph Perry directs films for the Salvation Army, including *Soldiers of the Cross*, mixing brief movies, lantern slides, and music.
Britain: The Warwick Trading Company's Joseph Rosenthal becomes the most celebrated of war cameramen with his film of the Boer War, which he follows with action from the Boxer Rebellion in China.
France: Léon Gaumont demonstrates synchronized sound and pictures.

1901
Britain: Will Barker founds the Autoscope Company and erects a rudimentary open-air studio at Stamford Hill, London.
G. H. Cricks and H. M. Sharp open a studio at Mitcham, Surrey, and make *Saved from the Burning Wreck* and a series of shorts featuring music-hall comedian Fred Evans.

1902
Films begin to reach a length of 250 feet or so, running for around four minutes.
Britain: Gaumont's Chronophone, by which gramophone recordings are synchronized to films of music-hall performers, is installed at the London Pavilion.

France: Charles Pathé opens a studio and begins turning out a film a day.
Méliès makes *A Trip to the Moon*, the first science-fiction film.
Germany: Oskar Messter establishes a production company in Berlin and begins to make films using cabaret artists and actors.
Spain: Segundo de Chomón begins to make films full of trick effects, but finds it hard to attract finance. He is later to work in Italy on *Cabiria* and in France on *Napoleon*.

1903
America: Edwin S. Porter makes *Life of an American Fireman*, mixing real-life and staged action to tell a story. He follows it with *Uncle Tom's Cabin* and *The Great Train Robbery*, an exciting western drama which causes a sensation and influences future directors.
Britain: Cecil Hepworth builds an indoor studio at Walton-on-Thames and films scenes from *Alice in Wonderland*.
Denmark: Peter Elfelt makes the country's first fiction film, *Capital Punishment* (*Henrettelsen*).
France: Méliès makes another science-fiction film full of trick effects, *Impossible Voyage*.

1904
America: At the St Louis Exhibition, George C. Hale presents Hale's Tours: travelogues shown in a mock-up of a railway carriage with train sound-effects and a swinging floor to simulate movement. Similar shows open in other American cities.
Cinema owner William Fox founds a distribution company.
German inventor Oskar Messter demonstrates sound films at the St Louis World Exposition.
Britain: The Clarendon Film Company opens a studio in Croydon.

1905
America: The first nickelodeon, a simple cinema where the price of admission is five cents, opens in Pittsburgh.
Vitagraph, which will become the most successful production company of its day, opens its own studio in Brooklyn. Its stars include Florence Turner and plump comedian John Bunny.
Variety begins publication.
Britain: Cecil Hepworth, using his family as actors, makes *Rescued by Rover* at the cost of £7 and sells 400 copies of it at £8 a time. Actors who are to begin their careers at his studio include Chrissie White, Alma Taylor, Helen Mathers, and Ronald Colman.
The first purpose-built cinemas open in London: the New Gallery in Regent Street and the Rialto in Coventry Street.
Italy: *La Presa di Roma* is the country's first feature film.

1906
Films are reaching 850 feet in length, running for around 14 minutes.
America: Cartoonist Winsor McCay incorporates an animated cartoon into his vaudeville act.
Carl Laemmle opens a nickelodeon in Chicago.
Pennsylvania cinema owner S. L. Rothafel adds the scent of roses to the showing of the Pasadena Rose Bowl game, the first use of smells in the cinema.
Australia: Charles Tait makes *The Story of the Kelly Gang*, one of the longest narrative films so far, running for more than 40 minutes.
Britain: In Ealing, Will Barker opens the Barker Motion Picture Company, which amalgamates with the Warwick Trading Company. He shoots a film of Shakespeare's *Hamlet* in a day.
Hale's Tours opens in Oxford Street, London.
The first news cinema, the Daily Bioscope, opens in London.
G. A. Smith patents his Kinemacolor colour process.

Denmark: Ole Olsen, a former fairground operator, establishes Nordisk Films, which soon becomes one of Europe's biggest production companies.

France: Charles Pathé signs music-hall performer André Deed to make comic films.

Sweden: Inventor Sven Berglund works on a system of recording sound on film by an optical process.

1907

America: Gilbert M. Anderson and George K. Spoor form Essanay production company in Chicago.

Finland: Apollo Studios release the first Finnish feature, *The Moonshiners.*

France: Actor Charles Le Bargy and other people from the Comédie Française form Film d'Art to make artistic films. Camille Saint-Saëns is to write the scores for its first production, *The Assassination of the Duke de Guise.*

1908

America: Anderson moves Essanay to California, away from Edison's law suits, and begins starring as 'Bronco Billy' in more than 300 westerns in eight years, despite the fact that he can hardly sit on a horse.

D. W. Griffith, an actor and writer, directs his first film, *The Adventures of Dollie,* for Biograph.

Hale's Tours goes into liquidation.

Argentina: Mario Gallo makes *El Fusilamiento de Dorrego,* the country's first feature film using professional actors.

Brazil: Portuguese-born director and cinematographer Antonio Leal makes *Os Estranguladores* and *Os Guaranis.*

Britain: The Gaumont Company hold the first Trade Show. Sir Geoffrey Tearle plays Romeo for Gaumont's version of *Romeo and Juliet.*

Colour films are shown for the first time at London's Palace Theatre.

The British Cinephone system of recorded sound synchronized to pictures begins to be installed in cinemas.

Electric Theatres becomes the first British cinema chain.

France: Max Linder becomes Pathé's leading comedian when André Deed leaves to make films in Italy.

1909

America: Edison, with seven leading film production companies and France's Pathé and Méliès, forms the Motion Picture Patents Company, claiming a monopoly on film production, and attempting to control distribution and license exhibition.

Distributors William Fox and Carl Laemmle decide to fight the monopoly by making their own films.

In December, D. W. Griffith directs his 100th one-reel film for Biograph. His films for the year include *The Violin Maker of Cremona,* starring Mary Pickford, who had begun her career months earlier as an extra. She becomes known as 'The Biograph Girl with the Curls'.

Australia: A 4,000-seater cinema opens in Melbourne. In Sydney, the Colonial cinema shows films non-stop from 11 a.m. to 11 p.m.

Ireland: Irish novelist James Joyce opens Dublin's first cinema, with the aid of Swiss financiers.

1910

America: *Pathé's Weekly* becomes the first newsreel.

Britain: Montague Pyke opens a cinema chain offering greater comfort and luxury.

Paul closes his studio and returns to making scientific instruments.

Denmark: Actress Asta Nielsen creates a sensation in *The Abyss,* as a man-hungry circus performer.

1911

America: *Photoplay* and *Motion Picture Story Magazine* are the world's first fan magazines.

Britain: London's Scala Theatre begins a two-year run of showing colour films.

France: The lavish Gaumont Palace opens in Paris as the world's biggest and best cinema.

Italy: Giovanni Pastrone's *The Fall of Troy,* with its cast of thousands, is the first epic movie.

1912

America: Dorothy and Lillian Gish begin their careers in films by Griffith.

Mack Sennett forms Keystone with two partners and begins making slapstick comedies.

Carl Laemmle founds Universal Pictures.

Adolph Zukor founds the Famous Players Film Company and begins by importing the French *Queen Elizabeth,* starring Sarah Bernhardt.

Britain: The British Board of Film Censors is established.

Fred Karno decides to make a second tour of America's music halls. Among his troupe are Charlie Chaplin and Stan Laurel, who will not return.

France: Film d'Art releases Louis Mercanton's *Les Amours de la Reine Élizabeth,* starring an ageing Sarah Bernhardt, thus helping cinema gain respectability.

Auguste Baron invents a new multi-screen process, Multirama, but can find no backers.

Gaumont gives the first public show in Paris of its Chronophone, synchronizing sound and pictures.

Germany: Shooting begins at Babelsberg studios of Asta Nielsen in *The Death Dance.*

Italy: Enrico Guazzoni's *Quo Vadis?,* a 12-reel epic of Roman life with a spectacular chariot race, is a box-office hit around the world.

Sweden: Inventor Sven Berglund claims to be the first to perfect a system of recording sound on film by an optical process.

1913

America: Mary Pickford signs a five-year contract with Adolph Zukor to become one of the first female film stars.

Fatty Arbuckle signs to make comedies for Mack Sennett.

Charlie Chaplin is spotted by Mack Sennett and goes to Hollywood.

The Adventures of Kathlyn, starring Kathlyn Williams, is the first serial, in 13 parts, to reach the cinemas.

Edison demonstrates his Kinetophone for synchronizing sound and pictures.

Orlando Kellum develops his system of synchronizing sound and pictures.

Vitagraph opens a studio in Santa Monica, California.

Jesse Lasky sets up the Jesse Lasky Feature Play Company.

Britain: Cinema attendance in Britain reaches an average of 10 visits a year.

Will Barker films *Jane Shore.*

Hepworth makes Dickens's *Barnaby Rudge,* restaging the Gordon Riots.

Eugene Lauste invents a method of recording sound on film, but fails to arouse any interest as war approaches. He emigrates to America.

India: Dadasaheb Phalke makes the first feature, *Raja Harishchandra.*

Sweden: Actor Victor Sjöström turns director with *Ingeborg Holm.*

Mauritz Stiller's *The Vampire* runs into censorship problems.

Venezuela: Lucas Manzano and Enrique Zimmerman direct the country's first feature film, *La Dama de las Cayenas,* based on Alexandre Dumas's *Camille.*

1914

America: Cecil B. De Mille shoots *The Squaw Man* in Los Angeles, converting a barn into a studio.

Mack Sennett makes the first comedy feature, *Tillie's Punctured Romance,* starring Chaplin, Mabel Normand, and Marie Dressler.

Pearl White stars in the serial *The Perils of Pauline.*

Winsor McCay creates the cartoon *Gertie the Dinosaur.*

William Fox produces his first feature.

Paramount Pictures is formed as a distribution company.

Poet Vachel Lindsay writes *Art of the Moving Picture,* one of the first critical studies of the new medium.

Britain: George Pearson directs *A Study in Scarlet,* the first major screen treatment of Sherlock Holmes.

Gaumont opens its new studio at Lime Grove, Shepherd's Bush.

France: Méliès runs out of money. His films are sold and many are destroyed to recover the celluloid.

Germany: Oskar Messter begins a weekly newsreel which is distributed around the world.

Italy: Giovanni Pastrone finishes the influential epic *Cabiria.*

1915

America: D. W. Griffith's *The Birth of a Nation,* 12 reels long and photographed by Bill Bitzer, causes a sensation when it opens in New York. It becomes the first film to be screened at the White House.

Cecil B. De Mille makes *The Cheat,* influential for its style and sexually suggestive content.

Chaplin goes to work for Essanay at $1,000 a week.

Douglas Fairbanks makes his film debut.

Triangle Films is set up by D. W. Griffith, Thomas Ince, and Mack Sennett.

Metro Pictures is founded and soon becomes a leading, though not particularly profitable, production company.

Edwin S. Porter retires from films.

Britain: A million people vote the six most popular British film stars as Alma Taylor, Elizabeth Risdon, Charlie Chaplin, Stewart Rome, Chrissie White, and Fred Evans.

Denmark: Nordisk releases more than 140 films during the year.

1916

America: D. W. Griffith releases the spectacular epic *Intolerance,* but audiences stay away.

Chaplin signs with Mutual for $10,000 a week. Mary Pickford demands and gets more from Zukor.

Zukor and Lasky acquire an interest in Paramount Pictures and merge their production companies.

Samuel Goldfish and his partners Archibald and Edgar Selwyn found Goldwyn Pictures. Goldfish soon takes the name as his own.

Britain: Hepworth's *Coming through the Rye* is seen by Queen Alexandra as the first film to have a Royal Command Performance.

Italy: Leading stage actress Eleanora Duse makes her only film, *Cenere,* but is disappointed with the result.

1917

America: Charlie Chaplin makes the first of his two-reel comedies, *The Cure* and *Easy Street.*

Fatty Arbuckle founds his own studio. Vaudeville performer Buster Keaton appears in many of his films.

After beginning as a Chaplin imitator, Harold Lloyd begins to define his own distinctive personality as a bespectacled, shy young man.

Erich Von Stroheim makes the first of his many appearances as a vicious Prussian officer in *For France.*

Douglas Fairbanks's earnings are more than $750,000 a year.

Britain: Cinema attendances reach 20 million a week.

Germany: The German High Command forms UFA to make propaganda films. It absorbs many other production companies, as well as controlling the largest chain of cinemas in the country.

1918

America: Chaplin makes his first film, *A Dog's Life,* in his own studio, which resembles a British village. His *Shoulder Arms,* parodying war films, is a success.

Oscar Micheaux makes *The Homesteader,* from his novel, establishing the best-known production company making films for black audiences.

Warner Bros releases its first major feature, *My Four Years in Germany.*

1919

America: Lon Chaney becomes a star with *The Miracle Man.*

D. W. Griffith shoots *Broken Blossoms* with Richard Barthelmess and Lillian Gish.

Charlie Chaplin, D. W. Griffith, Mary Pickford, and Douglas Fairbanks form United Artists. Hollywood quips, 'The lunatics have taken charge of the asylum.'

Hal Roach opens his own studio and begins to make comedy films with such stars as Harold Lloyd, Laurel and Hardy, and Charley Chase.

Australia: Raymond Longford makes *The Sentimental Bloke,* the country's best-regarded silent.

Germany: Ernst Lubitsch establishes himself as a leading director with *Madame Dubarry,* starring Pola Negri and Emil Jannings as Louis XV.

Sweden: Yearly attendances reach eight million.

USSR: The film industry is nationalized.

1920

America: Douglas Fairbanks marries Mary Pickford. He begins his swashbuckling career with *The Mark of Zorro.*

Fatty Arbuckle is arrested on charges of rape and manslaughter following the death of Virginia Rappe at a party. His films are withdrawn from cinemas and the scandal ends his Hollywood career, despite his acquittal.

Britain: Paramount opens a London studio, but it soon folds.

Denmark: Nordisk's output falls to eight films a year.

Germany: Robert Weine directs the expressionist *The Cabinet of Dr Caligari.*

Paul Wegner directs *The Golem,* an influential monster movie.

Norway

Rasmus Breistein makes the first feature, *Anna, the Gypsy Girl.*

Sweden

Mauritz Stiller's comedy *Erotikon* excites audiences with its sexual innuendo.

1921

America: Charlie Chaplin's feature *The Kid* makes Jackie Coogan a star at the age of six.

Rudolph Valentino stars in *The Four Horsemen of the Apocalypse* and creates a sensation. His appeal to women is increased by his next film, *The Sheik.*

Max Linder makes two features, *Seven Years Bad Luck* and *Be My Wife.*

D. W. Griffith makes *Dream Street,* with sound synchronized on disk at the film's beginning, using Orlando Kellum's system. It is a hit, but exhibitors remain unconvinced that talking pictures have a future.

Britain: *The Glorious Adventure* is the first feature in colour to be made in England.

At a meeting called to save the British film industry, William Friese-Greene makes a passionate speech in favour of the continuance of British production, sits down, and dies, penniless. A monument erected over his grave in Highgate Cemetery reads, 'The Inventor of Kinematography. His Genius Bestowed Upon Humanity The Boon of Commercial Cinematography Of Which He Was The First Inventor And Patentee.'

Germany: UFA is privatized and soon becomes a leading company with large studios, laboratories, and cinemas.

Japan: Actor Teinosuke Kinugasa turns director with *The Death of My Sister* and soon exerts a powerful influence on the development of Japanese cinema.

Sweden: Benjamin Christensen directs the sexually explicit *Witchcraft through the Ages.*

Greta Garbo makes her debut as an extra in *A Fortune Hunter.*

Sven Berglund demonstrates his sound system in Stockholm.

1922

America: Harold Lloyd's *Grandma's Boy* establishes him as a gifted and original comedian.

Robert Flaherty makes *Nanook of the North.*

The Toll of the Sea, with Anna May Wong, is the first feature to be made using Technicolor's two-colour process.

The Power of Love, with Noah Beery, is the first feature to be made in 3-D.

Rin Tin Tin makes his debut in *The Man from Hell's River* and becomes the greatest dog star, saving Warner from bankruptcy during the 20s.

Irving Thalberg fires Erich Von Stroheim as director of *Merry Go Round* at Universal.

Director William Desmond Taylor is murdered and scandal follows with revelations of his involvement with Mabel Normand and others. Producers and distributors get together to form an association to 'maintain the highest possible moral and artistic standards'. The righteous Will Hays is chosen to head it.

The Cohn Brothers start C. B. C. Film Sales Corporation, which is to become Columbia Pictures in 1924.

Walt Disney founds Laugh-O-Gram Films in Kansas City with Ub Iwerks.

Samuel Goldwyn is forced out of Goldwyn Pictures.

Britain: The first British serial is released: *The Great London Mystery,* in 16 episodes, starring Lady Doris Stapleton and David Devant, the magician.

Germany: Fritz Lang makes *Dr Mabuse the Gambler,* about a master criminal.

F. W. Murnau directs the vampire film *Nosferatu.*

Ernst Lubitsch leaves to work in Hollywood.
Sven Berglund demonstrates his sound system in Berlin.

1923

America: Lon Chaney stars in *The Hunchback of Notre Dame*.
Harold Lloyd makes *Safety Last*, performing its dangerous stunts.
Cecil B. De Mille turns from sex to religion with *The Ten Commandments*. James Cruze makes an epic western, *The Covered Wagon*, for Paramount.
Eric Von Stroheim turns Frank Norris's novel *McTeague* into an eight-hour epic which he cuts to four hours. Thalberg orders it reduced to two hours and finally releases it as *Greed*, a flawed masterpiece. Stroheim hardly works in Hollywood again.
The high-living Mabel Normand survives the scandal of William Desmond Taylor's death but her career falters when her chauffeur kills a millionaire at a party with her pistol.
Wallace Reid, Paramount's leading actor, dies of drug addiction at the age of 30. Mrs Wallace Reid stars in the anti-drug film *Human Wreckage*, as part of Hollywood's new moral crusade.
Disney goes to Hollywood to start his own studio.
Britain: The British National Film League is formed to promote local movies with 'British Film Week', in which exhibitors are urged to show British films. The audiences stay away.
Victor McLaglen and others campaign for protection of British films.
After becoming a star in America in *The White Rose*, directed by D. W. Griffith, Ivor Novello offers a solution to the problem of English films in America: 'What we must do is establish our stars in the States. It is to see certain actors that the people in America go to the pictures.'
Germany: The government attempts to protect its film industry by allowing only German producers to import foreign films. American companies open German production offices to overcome the problem.
Hans Dreier leaves UFA for Hollywood where he joins Paramount to become head of its art department.
Italy: Guazzoni's epic *Messalina* captures the imagination with its climactic chariot race.
Sweden: Victor Sjöström leaves for Hollywood, where he will be known as Seastrom and direct for MGM.

1924

America: Buster Keaton's comic skills show to advantage in *Sherlock Jr and the Navigator*.
Douglas Fairbanks stars in *The Thief of Bagdad*.
English romantic novelist Elinor Glyn supervises the filming of her *Three Weeks*, about love on a tiger-skin rug. Two years later she will proclaim Clara Bow the 'It' girl.
Metro-Goldwyn-Mayer is formed from Metro Pictures, Louis B. Mayer's production company, and the Goldwyn Company. In charge of production is Irving Thalberg.
Scandal and rumours of murder follow the sudden death of producer and director Thomas Ince aboard William Randolph Hearst's yacht.
Britain: British film-making falters: Ideal Studios, British and Colonial, Stoll and Samuelson close. Broadwest and Hepworth cut production. But Michael Balcon and partners found Gainsborough Pictures at Islington Studios.
Germany: F. W. Murnau directs *The Last Laugh*, starring Emil Jannings.
Fritz Lang makes the epic *Die Nibelungen*.
Sweden: Mauritz Stiller directs *The Atonement of Gösta Berling* with Greta Garbo.

1925

America: Charlie Chaplin makes *The Gold Rush*.
Lon Chaney stars in *The Phantom of the Opera*.
MGM release *Ben Hur*, directed by Fred Niblo, after production problems.
Willis O'Brien creates the special effects for *The Lost World*, which include a dinosaur rampaging through London.
Joan Crawford makes her screen debut.
Stiller and Garbo sign contracts with MGM.
Warner Bros buys Vitagraph.
Britain: *The Lost World* becomes the world's first in-flight movie when it is shown on an Imperial Airways flight from London to France, but it is not until the 60s that in-flight movies become routine.
Lee De Forest Phonofilms opens a studio in Clapham, London to make films with integral sound, which are shown in music halls.
The British Empire Exhibition cinema at Wembley is the first in the UK to be equipped for showing talkies.
France: Leading comedian Max Linder and his wife are found dead in their hotel rooms, apparent suicides.
Germany: Ewald-André Dupont directs *Variety* starring Emil Jannings and English actor Warwick Ward.
Sweden: Mauritz Stiller and Greta Garbo leave for Hollywood, as does Benjamin Christensen.
USSR: Eisenstein makes *Strike* and *The Battleship Potemkin*, which are to influence all film-makers who see them.

1926

America: Buster Keaton makes his comic masterpiece, *The General*.
Ronald Colman stars in *Beau Geste*.
Stiller leaves MGM without making a film. He makes *Hotel Imperial* for Paramount.
The first all-sound film programme is shown at the Warner in New York in August using the Vitaphone method, with music recorded on heavy disks played at $33^1/_3$ rpm.
Rudolph Valentino dies.
Britain: Alfred Hitchcock directs *The Lodger*, about Jack the Ripper.
France: Jean Renoir makes *Nana*.
Germany: During a period of national financial problems, UFA gets a cash injection from the US studios Universal, Paramount and MGM in return for forming a releasing organization, Parafamet, which will distribute ten films from each of the partners and guarantee that three quarters of UFA's cinemas will show Parafamet productions. In return Paramount and MGM agree to distribute ten UFA films of their choice in the USA.
Japan: Kinugasa's *A Page of Madness* almost does away with the need for titles.
USSR: Pudovkin's *Mother* is a brilliantly edited social melodrama.

1927

America: On 6 October *The Jazz Singer* opens at the Warner, and Al Jolson's cry of 'you ain't heard nothin' yet' ushers in the era of sound. It takes $3.5m at the box-office.
On 28 October, the first Fox Movietone newsreel with sound is shown at the Roxy, New York.
Cecil B. De Mille makes *The King of Kings*, on the life of Christ.
Garbo and John Gilbert are a romantic pair in *Flesh and the Devil*.
New York's lavish Roxy Theater, dubbed 'The Cathedral of the Motion Picture', opens, seating nearly 6,000.
William Fox shows his first sound-on-film short in January and in May shows *Seventh Heaven* with a synchronized musical accompaniment.
Will Hays draws up a production code for the industry, emphasizing morality.
Britain: Alfred Hitchcock directs the boxing drama *The Ring*.
The Cinematograph Films Act makes it compulsory for British cinemas to show seven and a half per cent local films, rising to 20 per cent by 1936. British studios begin to turn out 'quota quickies', low-budget films made with little finesse to satisfy the law.
Victor McLaglen decides to go to Hollywood.
British Lion Film Corporation opens studios at Beaconsfield.
George Tootell, organist of London's Stoll Theatre, publishes *How to Play the Cinema Organ*.
France: Abel Gance's epic five-hour *Napoleon* uses three screens to cinematic effect. It will be shown in the US in a 70-minute version in 1929.
Germany: Fritz Lang directs his futuristic, spectacular *Metropolis*.
F. W. Murnau leaves for Hollywood, where he makes *Sunrise*.
Sweden: Mauritz Stiller leaves Hollywood and returns to Stockholm to direct for the theatre.

1928

America: King Vidor's *The Crowd* tackles the impersonal nature of modern life.
Victor Sjöström directs *The Wind*, starring Lillian Gish.
Warner produce the first all-talking film, *The Lights of New York*.
Walt Disney makes the first Mickey Mouse cartoon and follows it with the first sound cartoon, *Steamboat Willie*, again starring Mickey Mouse.
RKO Radio Pictures is founded.
Frank Capra is hired by Columbia. His involvement, together with the acumen of Harry Cohn, is to take the studio from poverty row to the status of a major.
Britain: *The Jazz Singer* causes a sensation when it opens in London in September.
Alfred Hitchcock makes *Blackmail*, Britain's first all-talking feature film. Joan Barry speaks the dialogue for its Polish-born star Anny Ondra.
Herbert Wilcox directs *Dawn*, with Sybil Thorndike as Nurse Edith Cavell.
Opposition to sound remains strong. Edward Wood, editor of *Picture Show* annual, writes: 'True progress in picture plays must be based on maintaining the silence of the screen.' British distributors predict failure for the development.
In a poll for *Picturegoer*, the public vote Ivor Novello the most popular male actor, followed by Ronald Colman, Ramon Novarro, Matheson Lang, Harold Lloyd and Milton Sills.
France: Carl Theodor Dreyer's *The Passion of Joan of Arc* stars Maria Falconetti in her only screen role. It will be banned by the British censors.
Luis Buñuel makes *Le Chien Andalou* with Salvador Dali.
Germany: The Germans try to set up a European union to compete with Hollywood on equal terms. It fails.
Sweden: Mauritz Stiller dies.
USSR: Eisenstein makes a propaganda masterpiece, *October*.
Pudovkin makes *Storm over Asia*, about a Mongolian trapper who becomes a puppet emperor.
Dovzhenko makes *Arsenal*, set in World War I.
Dziga Vertov makes the abstract documentary *The Man with the Movie Camera*.
Kinugasa travels to Moscow from Japan to meet Eisenstein and Pudovkin.

1929

America: Cinema attendances reach 95 million in the second year of talkies, an increase of 38 million since 1927.
King Vidor makes *Hallelujah* with an all-black cast.
MGM's *Broadway Melody* is the first film musical with an original score.
The Marx Brothers make their debut in *The Cocoanuts*.
Douglas Fairbanks and Mary Pickford make their first sound film, Shakespeare's *The Taming of the Shrew*, 'with additional dialogue by Sam Taylor'.
The coming of sound ends many careers; Constance and Norma Talmadge retire. Those soon to return to Europe include Emil Jannings, Pola Negri, and Vilma Banky.
Warner Bros buy First National Pictures.
Fox develop a wide-screen system, Fox Grandeur, but it fails to catch on.
The first Academy Awards ceremony is held.
The Reverend William H. Short, head of the Motion Picture Research Council, recruits a team of social psychologists to investigate the effect of films on children, hoping to prove that they are damaging.
Britain: New studios, occupied by producer Archibald Nettlefold, open at Walton-on-Thames on the site of Hepworth's original studio.
France: Charles Pathé retires.
Méliès is found running a sweet-stall at a Paris station and is belatedly honoured for his contribution to cinema.
Germany: G. W. Pabst makes *Pandora's Box*, aka *Lulu*, with American actress Louise Brooks.
Karl Freund, leading German cinematographer, moves to Hollywood, as does director William Dieterle.

1930

America: Lewis Milestone makes the anti-war *All Quiet on the Western Front*.
Romantic star John Gilbert disappoints in his sound film *Redemption*.
The Marx Brothers star in *Animal Crackers*.
MGM publicize Anna Christie with the line 'Garbo Talks!'
The Motion Picture Producers and Distributors of America agree to a production code largely drawn up by the Reverend Daniel A. Lord, a Jesuit moralist. Its central principle is that 'no picture shall be produced which will lower the moral standards of those who see it'.
William Fox loses control of his company. Upton Sinclair, in his biography published in 1933, is to charge that Fox was forced out 'by a criminal conspiracy of Wall Street bankers'.
Monogram Productions opens, and will become one of the more successful 'Poverty Row' companies, turning out low-budget genre movies.
Britain: Tom Walls directs and stars in Ben Travers's Aldwych farce *Rookery Nook*, with most of its original cast, including Ralph Lynn and Robertson Hare.
Basil Dean founds the New Ealing Studios.
Denmark: George Schéevoigt makes the first talkie, *Eskimo*.
France: Demonstrators wreck a Paris cinema showing Luis Buñuel's surrealist *L'Age d'Or*, made in collaboration with Salvador Dali.
Germany: Joseph Von Sternberg makes *The Blue Angel*, starring Emil Jannings and Marlene Dietrich. Von Sternberg and Dietrich leave for Hollywood.
USSR: Alexander Dovzhenko makes the lyrical *Earth*.

1931

America: Chaplin stars in his sentimental comedy *City Lights*.
Cimarron, about the Oklahoma land rush, is a rugged epic.
Warner begins its gritty gangster films with *The Public Enemy* and *Little Caesar*, a cycle which is to make stars of Edward G. Robinson, James Cagney, and Humphrey Bogart.
Horror movies also catch the public imagination: Tod Browning makes *Dracula*, starring Bela Lugosi, and James Whale directs *Frankenstein*, starring Boris Karloff, for Universal, beginning that studio's long involvement with horror.
David O. Selznick becomes production chief at RKO.
Britain: Basil Dean produces Gracie Fields' first film, *Sally in Our Alley*.
Top films at the box-office include Ben Travers's farce *Plunder* and the American films *Hell's Angels*, *One Heavenly Night*, and *Trader Horn*.
Alexander Korda founds London Films.
The British Board of Film Censors report that its examiners took exception to 284 films and totally rejected 34, with action on another eight outstanding. The report added: 'There has unquestionably been a tendency of late for films to become more and more daring, the result probably of the large number of stage plays which are now presented on the screen, and of the licence which is today allowed in current fiction.'
France: René Clair makes the satirical *À Nous la Liberté*, which is to inspire Chaplin's *Modern Times* and the equally influential *Le Million*, an example of the possibilities of the film musical.
Jean Cocteau's experimental *The Blood of a Poet* excites admiration and derision.
Maurice Pagnol founds a film company and writes and produces film versions of his stage hit *Marius* and its successor *Fanny*, starring Raimu.
Germany: Fritz Lang directs M, starring Peter Lorre as a child murderer.
Leontine Sagan's all-female *Mädchen in Uniform*, about a schoolgirl's love for her female teacher, causes a sensation. The Nazis will ban it as an attack on authoritarianism.
India: *Alam Ara*, the first Indian talking picture, includes six songs and sets a lasting fashion.
Japan: Heinosuke Gosho's *The Neighbour's Wife and Mine* is the first talkie.
Norway: Tancred Ibsen makes the first talkie, *The Big Baptism*.

1932

America: MGM's star-studded *Grand Hotel* is the hit of the year.
Mervyn Le Roy's *I Am a Fugitive from a Chain Gang*, starring Paul Muni, epitomizes the Depression.
Howard Hawks directs *Scarface*, inspired by Al Capone.
Mae West makes her screen debut at the age of 40 in *Night after Night*.
Rouben Mamoulian directs Frederic March in *Dr Jekyll and Mr Hyde* for Paramount.
Johnny Weismuller as *Tarzan the Ape Man* provides escapist fare in the first of a series that will keep him occupied until the late 40s.
Marie Dressler tops the first *Motion Picture Herald-Fame* poll of US distributors for the top money-making stars, followed by Janet Gaynor, Joan

Crawford, Charles Farrell, and Greta Garbo.
Australia: Ken G. Hall makes the first talkie, *On Our Selection*, which becomes the most successful Australian film of the 30s and 40s.
Britain: Walter Forde directs an exciting and influential train thriller, *Rome Express*.
The Sunday Entertainments Act allows cinemas to open on Sundays.
Gaumont opens a bigger and better studio at Lime Grove, one that will be able to handle the production of four films at the same time.
Britain produces 141 features, which is a little less than France (143) and Germany (164).
France: Jean Renoir makes *Boudu Saved from Drowning*.
Danish director Carl Dreyer makes his first sound movie, *Vampyr*.
Germany: Leni Riefenstahl directs and stars in *The Blue Light*.
Spain: José Buchs makes the first talkie, *Carceleras*.

1933

America: The average time for making a film is now 22 days. The average cost is $70,000. Production rises to 547 films.
Roman Scandals and *42nd Street* are the big hits of the year.
King Kong is the sensation of the year.
Fred Astaire dances for the first time with Ginger Rogers in *Flying Down to Rio*. They are to make nine more films together.
The Marx Brothers reach new heights of delirium in *Duck Soup*.
Garbo insists on John Gilbert as her co-star in *Queen Christina*. It is his last film.
Frank Capra directs *Lady for a Day* for Columbia.
James Whale makes *The Invisible Man* for Universal.
Selznick leaves RKO to join MGM. Merian C. Cooper takes over, following the success of his *King Kong* (co-director) for the studio. He lasts only a year.
Warner's production chief, Darryl F. Zanuck, leaves the studio.
Mae West has two box-office hits with *She Done Him Wrong* and *I'm No Angel*.
Mary Pickford retires and refuses to let her films be seen. She is to become ever more reclusive until her death in 1979.
Marie Dressler tops the box-office poll, followed by Will Rogers, Janet Gaynor, Eddie Cantor, and Wallace Beery.
The Reverend William Short's team reports, in *Our Movie Made Children*, that films are 'extremely likely to create a haphazard, promiscuous and undesirable national consciousness', though the research findings, on closer examination, prove to be much more inconclusive, and are ignored.
Australia: Errol Flynn makes his film debut as Fletcher Christian in Charles Chauvel's *In the Wake of the Bounty*.
Britain: Average cost of a British film is £20,000. Production reaches 169 films.
Alexander Korda directs *The Private Life of Henry VIII* with Charles Laughton. Its success brings him financial backing.
Victor Savile's *The Good Companions*, starring Jessie Matthews, brings J. B. Priestley's bestselling novel to the screen.
Czechoslovakia: Gustav Machaty's *Ecstasy* becomes notorious for a scene with its star, Hedy Kiesler, naked. Five years later she goes to Hollywood, where she is renamed Hedy Lamarr.
France: Erich Von Stroheim stars in Jean Renoir's *La Grande Illusion* and makes his home in Paris.
Raymond Bernard directs an epic version of *Les Misérables* starring Harry Baur.
Jean Vigo makes his rebellious *Zero for Conduct*, which is immediately banned.
Germany: As the Nazis come to power, Dr Joseph Goebbels assumes control of the arts. He bans Fritz Lang's *The Testament of Dr Mabuse*, but offers to make him head of film production. Lang leaves for France and then goes to Hollywood. Many other producers, directors, and actors are to follow him into exile.

1934

America: Frank Capra directs *It Happened One Night* with Clark Gable and Claudette Colbert, and helps create a genre of screwball comedies.
W. C. Fields establishes himself in five films, including *Six of a Kind*.
Bette Davis seizes her opportunity in *Of Human Bondage*, from Somerset Maugham's novel.
Astaire and Rogers are together again in *The Gay Divorcée*.

The Production Code Administration is established under Joseph Breen to clean up films. Producers put the emphasis on family films and turn to Dickens and Victorian authors.
Will Rogers is voted America's top money-making star, followed by Clark Gable, Janet Gaynor, Wallace Beery, and Mae West.
Britain: Hitchcock directs the spy drama *The Man Who Knew Too Much*.
Anna Neagle flirts in *Nell Gwynn*, directed by future husband Herbert Wilcox.
Jessie Matthews stars in one of the few successful local musicals, *Evergreen*.
Basil Dean directs *Sings as We Go*, starring Gracie Fields.
J. Arthur Rank, heir to a flour and milling fortune, founds the Religious Film Society to make evangelical films and also the commercial British National Films. Its first film is *Turn of the Tide*, about Yorkshire fishing families.
France: Jean Vigo makes his masterpiece, *L'Atalante*. Its producers recut it and it flops at the box-office. Vigo dies at the age of 29 shortly after.

1935

America: George Cukor's *David Copperfield*, with W. C. Fields as Mr Micawber, is perfect family entertainment.
Charles Laughton's Captain Bligh in *Mutiny on the Bounty*, directed by Frank Lloyd, becomes the most memorable, and most often imitated, of screen villains.
Jeanette MacDonald and Nelson Eddy are together for the first of many times in *Naughty Marietta*.
Victor McLaglen stars in John Ford's *The Informer*.
Max Reinhardt transfers Shakespeare to the screen in *A Midsummer Night's Dream*, with James Cagney as Bottom and Mickey Rooney as Puck.
James Whale makes *The Bride of Frankenstein* for Universal, with the electric-haired Elsa Lanchester in the title role.
Becky Sharp, based on Thackeray's *Vanity Fair*, is the first feature to be made in three-colour Technicolor.
Fox merges with Twentieth Century Pictures to become Twentieth Century-Fox, with Darryl F. Zanuck in charge of production and Joseph Schenck as chairman.
Herbert Yates founds Republic Studios, which is to become the most successful producer of 'B' movies.
David O. Selznick forms Selznick Independent Pictures, his own production company.
Shirley Temple tops the list of America's money-making stars, followed by Will Rogers, Clark Gable, Fred Astaire and Ginger Rogers, and Joan Crawford.
Britain: Alfred Hitchcock makes the comedy thriller *The Thirty-Nine Steps* with Robert Donat and Madeleine Carroll.
Harold Young directs *The Scarlet Pimpernel*, starring Leslie Howard and Merle Oberon.
France: Jacques Feyder directs *Carnival in Flanders*, inspired by Old Master paintings.
Germany: Leni Riefenstahl directs *Triumph of the Will*, a documentary about Hitler's 1934 Nuremberg Rally.
The government sets up a censorship board, which is to ban many European and American films. It will also ban film criticism in the coming year.

1936

America: *San Francisco*, with Clark Gable, Spencer Tracy, Jeanette MacDonald, and a spectacular earthquake, is the box-office hit of the year.
Frank Capra directs for Columbia *Mr Deeds Goes to Town*, starring Gary Cooper.
Chaplin mocks the mechanical aspects of society in *Modern Times*.
Fritz Lang makes his first Hollywood film, *Fury*, about a lynch mob.
Douglas Fairbanks retires.
Irving Thalberg dies.
Carl Laemmle is ousted from Universal. But the company does well with Deanna Durbin's *Three Smart Girls*.
Selznick's first independent production is *Little Lord Fauntleroy*.
Shirley Temple remains America's top money-making star, followed by Clark Gable, Fred Astaire and Ginger Rogers, Robert Taylor, and Joe E. Brown.
Britain: Charles Laughton is at his best as *Rembrandt*, directed by Alexander Korda.
Korda produces H. G. Wells's futuristic *Things to*

Come, directed by William Cameron Menzies, and the intriguing *The Man Who Could Work Miracles*.
René Clair makes *The Ghost Goes West*, starring Robert Donat.
Alfred Hitchcock directs the brooding *Sabotage*.
Basil Wright and Harry Watt make *Night Mail*, a documentary about a mail train with music by Benjamin Britten and words by W. H. Auden.
J. Arthur Rank opens the company's new Pinewood studios in Buckinghamshire.
Vigo's *Zero for Conduct* gets a British release and is disliked by critics. 'Nought for direction. Nought for acting,' writes the *Observer*'s C. A. Lejeune.
France: Pagnol directs *César*, the last of his Marius trilogy.
Jean Renoir makes the charming 40-minute *A Day in the Country*, although it is not seen until 1946.
Anatole Litvak, who left Germany when the Nazis came to power, directs the romantic *Mayerling*. He is invited to Hollywood.
Sweden: Ingrid Bergman stars in Gustaf Molander's *Intermezzo*, which she will remake in Hollywood for David O. Selznick three years later, bringing her international stardom.

1937

America: Garbo stars as *Camille*, directed by George Cukor.
Roland Colman and Douglas Fairbanks Jnr add distinction to the romantic, swashbuckling fantasy *The Prisoner of Zenda*.
Frank Capra provides more escapism in *Lost Horizon* for Columbia.
Laurel and Hardy reach comic perfection in *Way Out West*.
Disney's first animated feature, *Snow White and the Seven Dwarfs*, is a huge success.
America's top five money-making stars are Shirley Temple, Clark Gable, Robert Taylor, Bing Crosby, and Joan Withers.
Britain: Will Hay stars in his best comedy, *Oh, Mr Porter*, with help from Moore Marriott and Graham Moffat.
Flora Robson stars as Elizabeth I in *Fire over England*.
Anna Neagle takes the title role in Herbert Wilcox's successful *Victoria the Great*.
Wings of the Morning is the first British film to be made in Technicolor.
MGM open a British offshoot at Denham Studios.
France: Jean Renoir directs a prison-camp drama, *La Grande Illusion*, with Jean Gabin and Erich Von Stroheim, promoting tolerance between nations. It is banned in Nazi Germany and Fascist Italy.
Jean Gabin stars as the romantic gangster in Julien Duvivier's *Pépé Le Moko*. At Von Stroheim's suggestion, MGM acquire the rights to remake it. Duvivier and his female star Mireille Balin leave for Hollywood, but Gabin turns down the trip. Balin is back in France without making a film within a year.
Germany: Director Detlef Sierck makes *La Habanera*, attacking US colonialism, and leaves for Hollywood, where he becomes Douglas Sirk.
Goebbels puts film production under state control.
USSR: Eisenstein's *Bezhin Meadow* is banned.

1938

America: Errol Flynn brings new panache to swashbucklers in *The Adventures of Robin Hood*.
James Cagney stars as the doomed gangster in *Angels with Dirty Faces*, directed by Michael Curtiz.
Walter Wanger acquires the rights to *Pépé Le Moko* and remakes it as *Algiers*, with Charles Boyer and Hedy Lamarr.
Mickey Rooney and Judy Garland star in *Love Finds Andy Hardy*, the first of a wholesome series.
Shirley Temple still has the public enthralled, again topping the list of America's money-making stars, followed by Clark Gable, Sonja Henie, Mickey Rooney, and Spencer Tracy.
Britain: Hitchcock makes *The Lady Vanishes* with its very English chorus of Caldicott and Charters, played by Naughton Wayne and Basil Radford.
Bernard Shaw's *Pygmalion* is filmed with Wendy Hillier in the role of Eliza and earns the author a shared Oscar for best screenplay.
Michael Balcon becomes head of production at Ealing Studios.
France: Marcel Pagnol writes and directs *The Baker's Wife* with Raimu.
Marcel Carné's *Port of Shadows*, starring Jean

Gabin and Michèle Morgan, establishes him as a leading director.
Méliès dies.
Germany: Leni Riefenstahl's *Olympia*, a film of the 1936 Olympic Games in Berlin, is released.
USSR: Eisenstein makes *Alexander Nevsky*, a patriotic epic about a German defeat, with a score by Prokoviev.

1939

America: David O. Selznick's *Gone with the Wind*, despite its production problems, swiftly becomes a Hollywood classic and a box-office phenomenon.
Judy Garland stars in *The Wizard of Oz* with Ray Bolger, Bert Lahr, and Jack Haley.
Garbo stars in *Ninotchka*, directed by Ernst Lubitsch and with Billy Wilder among the contributors to its witty script.
John Ford makes *Stagecoach*, giving John Wayne a boost to stardom and reviving the western.
Marlene Dietrich mocks western conventions in *Destry Rides Again*.
Charles Laughton stars as Quasimodo in *The Hunchback of Notre Dame*.
Laurence Olivier scores as Heathcliff in *Wuthering Heights*, directed by William Wyler.
Frank Capra makes the populist *Mr Smith Goes to Washington*, with James Stewart.
In a national poll, 22 million people vote Jeanette MacDonald America's most popular actress. But the professionals' poll of top money-makers is headed by Mickey Rooney, followed by Tyrone Power, Spencer Tracy, Clark Gable, and Shirley Temple, whose appeal is slipping as she grows older.
Britain: As the Second World War begins, cinemas are closed, briefly. Directors are urged to make films to raise morale – and to encourage America to enter the war. Pinewood Studios is used for food storage.
Zoltan Korda makes the rousing *The Four Feathers* with John Clements, Ralph Richardson, and C. Aubrey Smith.
Robert Donat and Greer Garson star in *Goodbye Mr Chips*, directed by Sam Wood at MGM's British studio.
Hitchcock directs the dull *Jamaica Inn* and then heads for Hollywood.
France: Marcel Carné's *Le Jour Se Lève* consolidates his reputation. Hollywood is to remake it eight years later with a happy ending as *The Long Night*.
Jean Renoir's *The Rules of the Game* is banned by the government soon after its release. He leaves for Italy.
Spain: As Franco is triumphant in the civil war, Luis Buñuel moves to New York.

1940

America: Walt Disney's *Pinocchio* builds on the success of *Snow White*; the studio's ambitious *Fantasia* marries animations to classical music and is the first feature to use stereo sound.
Rebecca, Hitchcock's first Hollywood film for David O. Selznick, combines mystery and romance with an impeccable cast headed by Laurence Olivier and Joan Fontaine.
Hitchcock also makes the suspenseful *Foreign Correspondent*, which encourages the US to enter the war.
George Cukor directs the sparkling *The Philadelphia Story*, teaming Katharine Hepburn, Cary Grant, and James Stewart.
Howard Hawks scores with the snappy newspaper comedy *His Girl Friday*.
Chaplin mocks Hitler and Mussolini, but also becomes sententious in *The Great Dictator*.
John Ford makes the sombre, populist *The Grapes of Wrath*.
Writer Preston Sturges turns director with *The Great McGinty*, the first of his exuberant comedies.
W. C. Fields writes (as Mahatma Kane Jeeves) and stars in his best comedy, *The Bank Dick*.
Mickey Rooney heads the list of top money-making stars, followed by Spencer Tracy, Clark Gable, singing cowboy Gene Autry, and Tyrone Power.
Australia: Charles Chauvel's First World War film *Forty Thousand Horsemen* is the first movie to attract attention outside the country for more than a decade.
Britain: Korda produces, Michael Powell and others direct, the great fantasy *The Thief of Bagdad*, pitting Sabu against the wicked Conrad Veidt.

Thorold Dickinson makes the suspenseful *Gaslight* with Anton Walbrook and Diana Wynyard.

Carol Reed directs the comedy thriller *Night Train to Munich*.

Quentin Reynolds narrates the documentary *London Can Take It*, directed by Harry Watt, designed to persuade the US to take up arms.

1941

America: Howard Hawks's *Sergeant York*, about a hero of the First World War, is the hit of the year.

Orson Welles, playing with 'the biggest electric train set a boy ever had', directs and stars in *Citizen Kane*. The film is attacked by the newspapers of William Randolph Hearst, the model for Kane.

Preston Sturges's *Sullivan's Travels* emphasizes the value of comedy.

Laurence Olivier and Vivien Leigh star in Alexander Korda's *That Hamilton Woman*, a mixture of sex and patriotism.

Writer John Huston turns director with the thriller *The Maltese Falcon*, with Humphrey Bogart, Mary Astor, Sidney Greenstreet, and Peter Lorre.

William Dieterle remakes the Faust story as *All that Money Can Buy*, with Walter Huston as the Devil.

Walt Disney releases another classic animated feature, *Dumbo*.

After starring in George Cukor's *Two-Faced Woman*, Garbo retires.

Jean Renoir makes his home in Hollywood.

Mickey Rooney remains America's top money-making star, testifying to the enduring appeal of the sentimental small-town Andy Hardy series, followed by Clark Gable, Abbott and Costello, Bob Hope, and Spencer Tracy.

Britain: Michael Powell's *The Forty-Ninth Parallel* stars Eric Portman as a German trying to escape from Canada to the US.

Dangerous Moonlight combines romance and the war with the music of Richard Addinsell's 'Warsaw Concerto' to provide some welcome escapism.

Leslie Howard brings *The Scarlet Pimpernel* up to date by directing and starring in *Pimpernel Smith*.

Humphrey Jennings directs the documentary *Listen to Britain*, about the effects of the war.

Harry Watt's *Target for Tonight* effectively tells the story of an RAF raid over Germany.

J. Arthur Rank acquires the Odeon cinema chain.

USSR: *Land of Youth* is a 3-D film that does away with the requirement for the audience to wear glasses.

1942

America: Michael Curtiz overcomes severe production problems to deliver, surprisingly, a Hollywood classic, *Casablanca*, with Humphrey Bogart and Ingrid Bergman.

Mervyn Le Roy's *Random Harvest*, with Ronald Colman and Greer Garson, is the weepie of the year, though running it close is *Now, Voyager*, with Bette Davis and Paul Henreid.

Orson Welles's *The Magnificent Ambersons* is re-edited without his approval.

Walt Disney scores again with the animated feature *Bambi*.

Ernst Lubitsch's *To Be or Not to Be*, starring Jack Benny, is fun at the expense of the Nazis.

Sam Wood's *Kings Row*, with Ann Sheridan and Robert Cummings, is gripping melodrama.

Jacques Tourneur's *Cat People* begins another cycle of horror movies, under producer Val Lewton.

Olsen and Johnson star in the anarchic comedy *Hellzapoppin*.

William Wyler's *Mrs Miniver* shows the plucky British coping with the war and scores heavily at the box-office.

Abbott and Costello head the poll of top money-making stars, followed by Clark Gable, Gary Cooper, Mickey Rooney, and Bob Hope.

Britain: David Lean and Noël Coward direct *In Which We Serve*, the archetypal British war film.

Went the Day Well?, directed by Alberto Cavalcanti from a Graham Greene story, shows German paratroopers invading an English village.

Thorold Dickinson's propaganda film *The Next of Kin* is a popular success.

Robert Donat as *Young Mr Pitt*, directed by Carol Reed, provides more wartime propaganda.

Italy: Luchino Visconti's first film, *Ossessione*, based on James M. Cain's *The Postman Always Rings Twice*, begins the flowering of neo-realist films.

1943

America: Howard Hughes's aerodynamic bra lifts Jane Russell to stardom in *The Outlaw*.

The Warner production of Irving Berlin's musical *This Is the Army* and Sam Wood's ponderous version of Ernest Hemingway's *For Whom the Bell Tolls* are the hits of the year.

Stormy Weather, a black musical with Bill Robinson, Lena Horne, and Fats Waller, is the liveliest film of the year.

The forces' pin-up Betty Grable heads the list of top money-making stars, followed by Bob Hope, Abbott and Costello, Bing Crosby, and Gary Cooper.

Britain: Frank Launder and Sidney Gilliat's *Millions Like Us* deals effectively with a family's wartime difficulties.

Gainsborough Films hit on what was to be a successful formula of historical romances with *The Man in Grey*, directed by Leslie Arliss and starring James Mason and Margaret Lockwood.

Michael Powell and Emeric Pressburger make *The Life and Death of Colonel Blimp*.

David MacDonald's *Desert Victory* is a classic war documentary.

Leslie Howard dies when his plane is shot down by Nazis.

R. W. Paul dies.

Denmark: Carl Theodor Dreyer makes the spellbinding melodrama with a message, *Day of Wrath*.

Germany: Josef Von Baky directs *Münchausen*, commemorating the 25th anniversary of UFA.

1944

America: Leo McCarey's *Going My Way*, with Bing Crosby, is the hit of the year.

Billy Wilder's *Double Indemnity*, with Fred MacMurray and Barbara Stanwyck, is a classic film noir.

Otto Preminger's *Laura*, with Dana Andrews and Clifton Webb, is another early example of film noir.

Preston Sturges's *Hail the Conquering Hero* is a deft comedy of small-town attitudes to returning heroes.

Producer Arthur Freed makes MGM the home of the lavish musical, beginning with Vincente Minnelli's *Meet Me in St Louis*, with Judy Garland.

Luis Buñuel heads for Mexico to make films.

Bing Crosby is the top money-making star in America, followed by Gary Cooper, Bob Hope, Betty Grable, and Spencer Tracy.

Britain: Laurence Olivier makes Shakespeare's *Henry V* into a rousing patriotic boost to wartime spirits.

Carol Reed's semi-documentary *The Way Ahead*, with David Niven and Stanley Holloway, is a hit with audiences.

Sidney Gilliat's wartime story of romance and revenge, *Waterloo Road*, catches the mood of the moment.

Sweden: Alf Sjöberg makes *Frenzy*, scripted by Ingmar Bergman, and starring Mai Zetterling and Alf Kjellin.

1945

America: *The Bells of St Mary's* and Hitchcock's *Spellbound*, both starring Ingrid Bergman, are the hits of the year.

Billy Wilder makes an alcoholic classic, *The Lost Weekend*, starring Ray Milland.

Bing Crosby remains the top money-making star, followed by Van Johnson, Greer Garson, Betty Grable, and Spencer Tracy.

Britain: The documentary *True Glory* provides an uplifting account of the last years of the war.

David Lean has audiences laughing and weeping with *Brief Encounter* and *Blithe Spirit*, both written by Noël Coward.

Anthony Asquith's *The Way to the Stars*, written by Terence Rattigan, successfully recreates the wartime mood.

Robert Hamer makes a classic compendium of spooky stories, *Dead of Night*.

Leslie Arliss directs another successful piece of period hokum for Gainsborough, *The Wicked Lady*, with Margaret Lockwood and James Mason.

France: Marcel Carné makes his masterpiece *Les Enfants du Paradis* with Arletty and Jean-Louis Barrault.

Vigo's 12-year-old *Zero for Conduct* is seen for the first time.

Italy: Roberto Rossellini's *Rome, Open City*, using mainly amateur actors, electrifies audiences with its realistic approach.

USSR: Eisenstein makes *Ivan the Terrible, Part II*.

1946

America: Film audiences reach 100 million a week.

William Wyler's *The Best Years of Our Lives*, produced by Sam Goldwyn, is the box-office hit of the year with its stories of servicemen returning to civilian life.

Larry Parks stars as Al Jolson in *The Jolson Story*, another of the year's hits.

Duel in the Sun, produced by David O. Selznik and directed mainly by King Vidor, brings passion and profit back to the western.

Hitchcock does some of his best work in *Notorious*, with Cary Grant and Ingrid Bergman.

Howard Hawks's *The Big Sleep*, with Humphrey Bogart and Lauren Bacall, is a classic tough thriller.

Frank Capra's optimistic *It's a Wonderful Life* is received coolly, although it goes on to become a Christmas-time classic.

Universal merge with International Pictures to become Universal-International.

Bing Crosby is the American box-office favourite, followed by Ingrid Bergman, Van Johnson, Gary Cooper, and Bob Hope.

Australia: Harry Watt's *The Overlanders*, starring Chips Rafferty, is the first and best result of Ealing Studio's involvement in Australian film.

Britain: 25 million Britons go to the cinema each week.

Humphrey Jennings's documentary *A Diary for Timothy* encapsulates feelings about the war and the future.

David Lean makes a superb adaptation of Dickens's *Great Expectations*.

Michael Powell and Emeric Pressburger's *A Matter of Life and Death* (aka *Stairway to Heaven*) is a witty, stylish fantasy.

Caesar and Cleopatra, with Claude Rains and Vivien Leigh, is, at more than £1m, the most expensive British film so far, but no one cares for it.

Margaret Lockwood becomes Britain's favourite female star.

Feature-film production resumes at Pinewood.

Sir Alexander Korda says that discussions about the British film industry 'succeed only in betraying the sad fact that we have not got one – as yet.'

France: Jean Cocteau's austere and poetic *Beauty and the Beast* is an artistic success.

Italy: Roberto Rossellini consolidates his reputation with his war film *Paisa*.

Vittorio de Sica's *Shoeshine* is another key film in the neo-realist movement, with its story of two boys trying to survive in Nazi-occupied Rome.

1947

America: Edward Dmytryk's tense thriller *Crossfire* confronts racial bigotry.

The House Un-American Activities Committee, chaired by J. Parnell Thomas, holds its first hearings in Los Angeles, at which friendly witnesses condemn Communist subversion in Hollywood. HUAC subpoenas witnesses to appear at further hearings. Writers, directors, and producers who refuse to answer HUAC's questions on their political affiliations, known as the Hollywood Ten, are sentenced to prison (where some find as a fellow inmate J. Parnell Thomas, sentenced for misappropriation of funds). Blacklisting by the studios of those with left-wing sympathies begins and is to continue throughout the 50s. Carl Foreman, Joseph Losey, and Jules Dassin are among those who are to leave the US for Britain.

The top five money-making stars are the bland Bing Crosby, Betty Grable, Ingrid Bergman, Gary Cooper, and Humphrey Bogart.

Britain: Ronald Hamer's *It Always Rains on Sunday*, starring Googie Withers and John McCallum, is a sensational low-life melodrama.

Carol Reed directs *Odd Man Out*, starring James Mason, a performance that takes him to Hollywood.

The Boulting Brothers film *Brighton Rock*, Graham Greene's tale of a petty criminal, starring Richard Attenborough.

Michael Powell and Emeric Pressburger's heady *Black Narcissus* is one of the cinema's most beautiful films.

American studios embargo their films being shown, following a tax imposed on export. As Rank gears up to fill the cinemas with British films, the embargo is lifted, causing Rank financial problems. Managing director John Davis, who regards producers and directors as extravagant, wields the axe.

France: Claude Autant-Lara's *Devil in the Flesh* makes Gérard Philipe a star.

1948

America: Jules Dassin's *The Naked City* adopts a semi-documentary approach to a murder mystery.

Fred Astaire returns to dancing in *Easter Parade*, with Judy Garland.

The melodramatic *Johnny Belinda*, directed by Jean Negulesco, makes Jane Wyman a star.

The Supreme Court rules that the five major studios can no longer own cinemas, so breaking their monopoly of the industry.

Millionaire Howard Hughes buys RKO.

America's top five money-making stars are Bing Crosby, Betty Grable, Abbott and Costello, Gary Cooper, and Bob Hope.

The big studios threaten to cease funding the Academy of Motion Picture Arts and Sciences when they discover that the British movie *Hamlet* is a favourite to win the Oscar for best picture.

Britain: David Lean's *Oliver Twist* is another successful Dickens adaptation, notable for Alec Guinness's performance as Fagin.

Michael Powell and Emeric Pressburger's *The Red Shoes*, with Moira Shearer, makes ballet box-office.

Carol Reed's *The Fallen Idol*, with Ralph Richardson, is a near-perfect piece of small-scale cinema.

Iceland: Loftur Gudmundsson makes the first talkie, *Between the Mountains and the Sea*.

Italy: Vittorio De Sica's *The Bicycle Thief* is hailed as a neo-realist classic.

Luchino Visconti takes neo-realism to its limits with *La Terra Trema*, about a Sicilian fisherman and his family.

Giuseppe De Santis's *Bitter Rice* attacks American corruption of Italian culture, but it is Silvano Mangano at work in the rice fields who attracts international attention.

USSR: Eisenstein dies less than three weeks after his 50th birthday.

1949

America: William Dieterle's glossy *Portrait of Jennie*, with Jennifer Jones and Joseph Cotten, is David O. Selznick's last production with his company, which he folds soon after.

James Cagney is back at his energetic best as a brutal gangster in the searing *White Heat*.

Cecil B. De Mille's *Samson and Delilah*, with Victor Mature and Hedy Lamarr in the title roles, is a hit despite derisive reviews.

Gene Kelly and Stanley Donen's *On the Town*, produced by Arthur Freed and with a cast that includes Kelly, Frank Sinatra, and Vera-Ellen, is one of the best-ever musicals.

Larry Parks scores another hit with *Jolson Sings Again*.

The top five money-making stars are Bob Hope, Bing Crosby, Abbott and Costello, John Wayne, and Gary Cooper.

Britain: Carol Reed directs the thrilling *The Third Man*, starring Orson Welles and with Anton Karas's haunting zither music.

Three Ealing comedies make the studio's reputation: Henry Cornelius's *Passport to Pimlico*, Alexander Mackendrick's *Whisky Galore*, and Robert Hamer's *Kind Hearts and Coronets*.

Rank sells its Shepherd's Bush studios to BBC-TV.

France: Jacques Tati's *Jour de Fête* introduces his gentle humour to the world.

1950

America: Billy Wilder's *Sunset Boulevard* is a tart classic, with William Holden as the innocent who becomes involved with ageing star Gloria Swanson.

Joseph Mankiewicz's *All about Eve* gives Bette Davis the best role of her career as a bitchy actress.

Delmer Daves's *Broken Arrow* is the first revisionist western, on the side of the Indians.

Judy Holliday scores as the not-so-dumb chorus girl in *Born Yesterday*, directed by George Cukor.

Disney's live-action film *Treasure Island* provides Robert Newton with the opportunity for an eye-rolling, lip-smacking performance as Long John Silver.

The top five money-making stars are John Wayne, Bob Hope, Bing Crosby, Betty Grable, and James Stewart.

Britain: Basil Dearden directs the crime drama *The Blue Lamp*, starring Dirk Bogarde and Jack Warner, which is to inspire the long-running television series *Dixon of Dock Green*.

The Boulting Brothers make a tense and influential thriller, *Seven Days to Noon*.

Frank Launder's *The Happiest Days of Your Life* is a sprightly comedy, sparked by the performances of Alastair Sim and Margaret Rutherford.

The prison-camp drama, *The Wooden Horse*, is a success, as nostalgia for recent heroics continues.

France: Jean Cocteau's *Orpheus* is a fantastic success and a successful fantasy.

Max Ophuls makes the stylish and sexy *La Ronde*. Its banning in New York leads to a court case that eventually frees films from local censorship.

Robert Bresson directs the austere *The Diary of a Country Priest*.

Italy: Ingrid Bergman stars in *Stromboli*, directed by Roberto Rossellini, and scandalizes many when she has a child by him, an event that is to keep her away from Hollywood for much of the decade.

Mexico: Luis Buñuel signals his re-emergence with *The Young and the Damned*.

Sweden: Alf Sjöberg directs Anita Björk and Ulf Palme in an exemplary version of Strindberg's *Miss Julie*.

1951

America: Vincente Minnelli scores with *An American in Paris*, culminating in a ballet sequence for Gene Kelly and Leslie Caron.

Marlon Brando makes his film debut in the role that brought him fame on Broadway: Stanley Kowalski in *A Streetcar Named Desire*, directed by Elia Kazan.

Montgomery Clift is at his best in the steamy *A Place in the Sun*, also starring Elizabeth Taylor and directed by George Stevens.

Hitchcock makes the quirky *Strangers on a Train*, with Farley Granger and Robert Walker.

Dean Martin and Jerry Lewis star in *Sailor, Beware* to become the top comedy act.

Howard Hawks's *The Thing* begins a cycle of monster movies, based on fear of the atom bomb.

Larry Parks admits to having been a Communist at the HUAC hearings. His contract with Columbia, and his film career, ends.

Louis B. Mayer is forced out of MGM, to be replaced by Dore Schary.

The box-office favourites are John Wayne, Dean Martin and Jerry Lewis, Betty Grable, Abbott and Costello, and Bing Crosby.

Britain: Ealing comedies keep audiences happy with Charles Crichton's *The Lavender Hill Mob* and Alexander Mackendrick's *The Man in the White Suit*, starring Alec Guinness.

John Huston's *The African Queen* delights, with the antagonistic Humphrey Bogart and Katharine Hepburn.

Michael Powell and Emeric Pressburger's *The Tales of Hoffman* combines operetta and ballet in a remarkable way.

John Boulting directs the pageant-like *The Magic Box*, on the life of William Friese-Greene, as part of the Festival of Britain celebrations.

France: Robert Bresson's *Diary of a Country Priest* gains him international fame.

Japan: Kurosawa's *Rashomon* opens Western eyes to Japanese cinema.

Yashujiro Ozu makes the complex family drama *Early Summer*.

1952

America: Cecil B. De Mille's circus film, *The Greatest Show on Earth*, is a smash hit.

This Is Cinerama, a film using stereo sound and a wide-screen process that requires three projectors, causes a sensation with its opening roller-coaster ride, but the system is cumbersome and there are no more than 40 cinemas equipped to show its films by the early 60s.

Fred Zinnemann makes a classic western, *High Noon*, with Gary Cooper, which can be read as a condemnation of blacklisting in Hollywood.

Gene Kelly stars in *Singin' in the Rain*, a brilliant musical about Hollywood at the time the talkies arrived.

Charlie Chaplin's *Limelight* seems a sentimental farewell to his own past.

Arch Oboler's *Bwana Devil* revives interest in 3-D films.

Charlie Chaplin leaves to visit Britain and is told by the Attorney-General not to return.

John Garfield dies of a heart attack. Friends claim it was caused by the stress of his appearance as an unfriendly witness before HUAC and his subsequent blacklisting.

Decca Records takes over Universal.

Dean Martin and Jerry Lewis are tops at the box-office, followed by Gary Cooper, John Wayne, Bing Crosby, and Bob Hope.

Britain: David Lean directs the topical *The Sound Barrier*, with Ralph Richardson and Nigel Patrick.

Anthony Asquith's version of Oscar Wilde's *The Importance of Being Earnest* captures Edith Evans's definitive performance as Lady Bracknell.

The National Film Theatre is created from a cinema built for the Festival of Britain.

France: René Clément directs *Forbidden Games*, a sombre film of childhood trauma.

Jacques Becker's *Casque d'Or*, with Simone Signoret and Serge Reggiani, is an impeccable piece of film-making.

Brigitte Bardot lands her first significant role in *The Lighthouse Keeper's Daughter* and marries her mentor, Roger Vadim.

Fernandel becomes an international star in *The Little World of Don Camillo*.

Italy: Vittorio De Sica makes the deeply pessimistic *Umberto D*, a study of neglected old age.

Federico Fellini directs the satirical *The White Sheik*.

Japan: Kenji Mizoguchi directs *The Life of Oharu*, about a samurai's daughter's ill-fated love for a servant.

1953

America: In an attempt to combat falling audiences and the influence of television, Twentieth Century-Fox shows off CinemaScope, its new wide-screen process, with *The Robe*, which becomes the most successful film of the year and one of the big hits of the decade.

From Here to Eternity, with Burt Lancaster and Deborah Kerr rolling in the sand and sea, is also a box-office success.

Vincente Minnelli makes another classic musical for MGM, *The Band Wagon*, with Fred Astaire and his English equivalent, Jack Buchanan.

George Stevens's western *Shane* pits Alan Ladd against Jack Palance.

Joseph Mankiewicz's *Julius Caesar* combines the classical English acting of John Gielgud and the Method of Marlon Brando.

The horror film *The House of Wax*, starring Vincent Price, gives 3-D films a further fillip. It is directed by the one-eyed André de Toth.

Chaplin sells his Hollywood studio and settles in Switzerland.

Gary Cooper is the top money-making star followed by Dean Martin and Jerry Lewis, John Wayne, Alan Ladd, and Bing Crosby.

Britain: Cosy comedy predominates, exemplified by Henry Cornelius's *Genevieve*, with Kenneth More.

The Cruel Sea, with its stiff-upper-lipped officers still fighting the war, is a good representative of the alternative, and audiences flock to it.

Cecil Hepworth dies.

France: Jacques Tati's *Monsieur Hulot's Holiday* develops his concept of comedy without stars.

Henri-Georges Clouzot's thriller *The Wages of Fear* electrifies audiences and provides Yves Montand with his first serious role.

Italy: Federico Fellini's *I Vitelloni*, in the neo-realist tradition, focuses on the aimless young.

Jean Renoir, having left the US, makes the unsuccessful *The Golden Coach* with Anna Magnani.

Japan: Yashujiro Ozu's *Tokyo Story* is an austere and moving drama of disappointments.

Teinosuke Kinugasa's 12th-century saga *Gate of Hell* wins the top prize at Cannes and an Oscar.

Kenji Mizoguchi's 16th-century story *Ugetsu Monogatari* is hailed at the Venice Film Festival.

Mexico: Luis Buñuel makes a brilliantly faithful version of *The Adventures of Robinson Crusoe* with Dan O'Herlihy.

1954

America: Elia Kazan's *On the Waterfront*, with Marlon Brando and Rod Steiger at their best, can be read as his apologia for naming names to HUAC; it is powerfully convincing on its own terms.

Brando also plays a somewhat elderly rebel in *The Wild One*, a biker movie that causes controversy.

Hitchcock's teasing thriller *Rear Window* stars Grace Kelly and James Stewart as a voyeuristic photographer.

Judy Garland and James Mason bring passion to the remake of *A Star Is Born*, but it at first fails to find an audience and is drastically cut.

Gordon Douglas's *Them!*, with its giant ants, is the first of a cycle of post-atomic monster movies.

Paramount's VistaVision wide-screen process makes its debut in *White Christmas*, a cosy musical with Bing Crosby. The process fades by the end of the 50s.

Samuel Z. Arkoff and James H. Nicholson found American International Pictures (AIP), the low-budget film company that includes Roger Corman among its producers.

John Wayne is America's top money-making star, followed by Dean Martin and Jerry Lewis, Gary Cooper, James Stewart, and Marilyn Monroe.

Britain: David Lean's *Hobson's Choice* features Charles Laughton at his best.

Alexander Mackendrick's Ealing comedy *The Maggie* comes perilously close to *Whisky Galore* but manages to amuse.

Frank Launder's *The Belles of St Trinian's*, with Alastair Sim in drag, is a commercial success and brings three sequels.

Ralph Thomas's *Doctor in the House*, with Dirk Bogarde and James Robertson Justice, is a comic success, but unfortunately results in several sequels.

The BBFC bans *The Wild One*, which will not be seen in Britain until 1968.

Italy: Vittorio De Sica makes Sophia Loren a star in *The Gold of Naples*, the first of their six collaborations.

Federico Fellini's *La Strada*, with Giulietta Masina and Anthony Quinn, infuses neo-realism with poetry in its story of an ill-used simpleton.

Japan: Akira Kurosawa directs the exciting and action-filled epic *The Seven Samurai* with Toshiro Mifune.

Poland: Andrzej Wajda directs *A Generation* starring Zbigniew Cybulski.

1955

America: A new star is born, and quickly dies: James Dean makes *East of Eden* and *Rebel without a Cause* – before crashing his sports car and becoming an enduring screen icon.

Spencer Tracy stars with Robert Ryan in John Sturges's seminal suspense thriller, *Bad Day at Black Rock*.

Paddy Chayevsky's TV play *Marty* transfers successfully to the screen, bringing stardom to Ernest Borgnine.

Billy Wilder's *The Seven Year Itch* makes the most of Marilyn Monroe's comic talents.

Charles Laughton directs *The Night of the Hunter*; its reputation is to grow with the years.

Rock 'n' roll arrives with Bill Haley and the Comets singing 'Rock around the Clock' behind the credits of *The Blackboard Jungle*, about life in a slum school. Within months, Haley and others will be starring in cheap exploitation movies, such as *Rock around the Clock* and *Don't Knock the Rock*, and popular music will never be the same.

Robert Aldrich's *Kiss Me Deadly* announces the arrival of an overwrought talent.

Oklahoma is shown in Todd-AO, a new wide-screen process promoted by showman Mike Todd.

Disney opens the first Disneyland, extending the appeal of its films and characters.

Hitchcock luminaries James Stewart and Grace Kelly head America's money-making stars, followed by John Wayne, William Holden, and Gary Cooper.

Britain: Yet another war film, Michael Anderson's *The Dam Busters*, does well, thanks to R. C. Sherriff's script and the acting of Michael Redgrave and others.

Alexander Mackendrick's *The Ladykillers* is almost the last of the Ealing comedies.

John Halas and Joy Batchelor direct Britain's first animated feature, George Orwell's *Animal Farm*.

Brigitte Bardot stars with Dirk Bogarde in *Doctor at Sea*.

Hammer Films, a small production company recycling TV programmes, strikes it rich with *The Quatermass Experiment*, a horror movie based on a BBC serial written by Nigel Kneale.

France: Jean Renoir makes a frothy musical, *French Cancan*, with Jean Gabin.

Henri-Georges Clouzot's *Les Diaboliques* is a grim suspense story.

Henri Verneuil's *The Sheep Has Five Legs* gives comedian Fernandel the six roles of his life.

Jules Dassin's film *Rififi*, with its tense safe-cracking sequence, captures audiences' imaginations around the world.

Max Ophuls directs the sumptuous *Lola Montes*.

India: Satyajit Ray's *Pather Panchali* is an art-house hit in the West.

Sweden: Bergman's comedy *Smiles of a Summer Night* brings him international recognition.

1956

America: Cecil B. De Mille's *The Ten Commandments* tops the box-office.

George Stevens's family saga *Giant* also does well, owing in part to the growing cult around James Dean.

Mike Todd's star-packed *Around the World in Eighty Days*, in Todd-AO, is a hit.

John Ford's *The Searchers* provides John Wayne with his best, most complex role.

Forbidden Planet, starring Leslie Nielsen, gives a science-fiction twist to Shakespeare's *The Tempest*.

The blacklisted Dalton Trumbo, writing under a pseudonym, wins an Oscar for *The Brave One*.

Fox experiment with CinemaScope 55, using 55mm film, for *Carousel*, but the process is not a success.

Dore Schary is sacked from MGM.

Darryl F. Zanuck leaves Twentieth Century-Fox.

Dean Martin and Jerry Lewis split.

Fritz Lang decides he has had enough of Hollywood.

William Holden is the top money-making star, followed by John Wayne, James Stewart, Burt Lancaster, and Glenn Ford.

Britain: Jack Lee's war film *A Town Like Alice*, with Virginia McKenna and Peter Finch, is a hit.

Hammer Films switches its attention to horror, reviving a Universal favourite with *The Curse of Frankenstein*, starring Christopher Lee and Peter Cushing and directed by Terence Fisher.

Lindsay Anderson, Karel Reisz, and others issue the Free Cinema manifesto.

The BBC buys Ealing Studios.

France: Robert Bresson's *A Man Escaped* details an escape by a Resistance fighter imprisoned by the Nazis.

India: Satyajit Ray makes *Aparajito*, a sequel to *Pather Panchali*.

Italy: Fellini's *Cabiria* (aka *The Nights of Cabiria*) is a life-enhancing look at Roman low-life.

Japan: Kon Ichikawa directs the horrifying war film *The Burmese Harp*.

Poland: Andrzej Wajda directs *Kanal*, starring Zbigniew Cybulski as one of the Polish partisans trapped in the sewers of Warsaw by the Nazis.

1957

America: Stanley Kubrick directs the overpowering *Paths of Glory*, set in the First World War.

Don Siegel's *The Invasion of the Body Snatchers* is a brilliantly effective paranoid parable.

Sidney Lumet makes *Twelve Angry Men*, a TV play that transfers successfully to the screen.

Alexander Mackendrick makes the moody, brilliant *Sweet Smell of Success*, with Burt Lancaster and Tony Curtis.

Mark Robson's *Peyton Place*, from a bestselling novel, is a hit; in the 60s it will become a long-running TV soap opera.

William Hanna and Joseph Barbera found Hanna-Barbera Productions to make family entertainment for television, including such animated series as *The Flintstones*.

Rock Hudson becomes America's top star at the box-office, followed by John Wayne, Pat Boone, Elvis Presley, and Frank Sinatra.

Argentina: Leopold Torre Nilsson gains international recognition with *The House of the Angel*.

Britain: David Lean's *The Bridge on the River Kwai*, produced by Sam Spiegel and starring William Holden and Alec Guinness, is the box-office success of the year.

Hammer Films remake *Dracula*, with Christopher Lee in the title role, and *The Revenge of Frankenstein*, with Peter Cushing.

France: Brigitte Bardot becomes an international star as Roger Vadim's *And God Created Woman* is released around the world.

Japan: Akira Kurosawa's *Throne of Blood* re-invents Shakespeare's *Macbeth*.

Sweden: Ingmar Bergman's reputation is made with *The Seventh Seal*, with the gaunt Max Von Sydow as a knight returning from the Crusades,

and the gentler *Wild Strawberries*, starring Victor Sjöström.
USSR: Mikhail Kalatozov makes the sleek love story *The Cranes Are Flying*.

1958
America: Rodgers and Hammerstein's musical *South Pacific*, despite its old-fashioned air and airs, is the hit of the year.
Orson Welles stars in, and directs, the brooding thriller *Touch of Evil*.
Hitchcock's dizzying thriller *Vertigo* stars James Stewart as a man trying to remake the past.
Harry Cohn, head of Columbia, dies.
Mike Todd is killed in a plane crash.
The top five money-making stars are Glenn Ford, Elizabeth Taylor, Jerry Lewis, Marlon Brando, and Rock Hudson.
Britain: Gerald Thomas's *Carry On Sergeant*, an army farce produced by Peter Rogers, is a surprising hit; it begins a sequence of low-budget Carry On comedies that are to become a profitable staple of British cinema.
Mark Robson directs *The Inn of the Sixth Happiness* starring Ingrid Bergman, with Wales standing in for its Chinese locations.
France: Louis Malle's *Lift to the Scaffold* (aka *Frantic*) and *The Lovers*, both starring Jeanne Moreau, announce the arrival of the French 'New Wave'.
Mexico: Luis Buñuel directs *Nazarin*, about a priest who tries to follow Christ's example.
Poland: Andrzej Wajda makes the compelling *Ashes and Diamonds*, starring Zbigniew Cybulski as a man confused about killing after the end of war.
Sweden: Ingmar Bergman's startling *The Face* stars Max Von Sydow as a 19th-century magician.

1959
America: William Wyler's *Ben Hur* takes epic amounts of money at the box-office.
Hitchcock makes his chase thriller *North by Northwest*, with Cary Grant doing the running.
Billy Wilder directs his comic masterpiece *Some Like It Hot*.
Behind the Great Wall is the first film to be shown in Aromarama. It is also the last.
Joseph E. Levine buys US rights to *Hercules*, a cheap Italian film, and spends $1.2m on promoting it; it becomes a hit, making body-builder Steve Reeves a star and starting a cycle of muscle-man movies.
Herbert Yates resigns as president of Republic Pictures and production ceases.
Cecil B. De Mille dies.
Rock Hudson is America's top money-making star, along with Cary Grant, James Stewart, Doris Day, and Debbie Reynolds.
Brazil: French director Marcel Camus's *Black Orpheus* uses myth and carnival to impressive effect.
Britain: Jack Cardiff's *Room at the Top* claims to bring sex and the industrial north into British films.
Tony Richard and John Osborne form Woodfall Films with producer Harry Saltzman to film Osborne's *Look Back in Anger*, a play that helped bring a new realism to British theatre.
Young Hayley Mills becomes a star in *Tiger Bay*, directed by J. Lee-Thompson.
Peter Cushing and Christopher Lee star in *The Mummy* for Hammer, directed by Terence Fisher.
Rank backs Richard Attenborough, Bryan Forbes, and others in founding Allied Film Makers.
France: Claude Chabrol's *The Cousins* rides the New Wave.
Cocteau's final masterpiece is *Testament of Orpheus*.
François Truffaut's *The 400 Blows* is the first of his semi-autobiographical films to track the life of Antoine Doinel, played by Jean-Pierre Léaud.
Alain Resnais directs *Hiroshima, Mon Amour*, written by Marguerite Duras.
Germany: Bernard Wicki directs *The Bridge*, about boy soldiers in the last days of the war.
Greece: Jules Dassin makes *Never on Sunday*, with Melina Mercouri and a hummable score by Monos Hadjidakis.
India: Satyajit Ray makes *The World of Apu*, the third film in his trilogy.
USSR: Grigori Chukrai's *Ballad of a Soldier* focuses on the detail of everyday life.

1960
America: Alfred Hitchcock's creepy *Psycho*, with a twitchy Anthony Perkins, scores at the box-office.

John Sturges remakes *The Seven Samurai* as a western, *The Magnificent Seven*. It results in three sequels.
Roger Corman's *The House of Usher* for AIP, starring Vincent Price, starts a new horror cycle.
John Cassavetes makes the semi-improvised *Shadows*, which is to influence many independent film-makers.
Scent of Mystery is the first feature to be shown in Smell-o-Vision. It is also the last.
Joseph E. Levine repeats his success with *Hercules Unchained*, again starring Steve Reeves.
New York's Roxy Theater, once the largest and grandest cinema in the world, is demolished 33 years after it was opened.
Doris Day and Rock Hudson, a double act in innocuous comedies, are America's top stars at the box-office, followed by Cary Grant, Elizabeth Taylor, and Debbie Reynolds.
Australia: Fred Zinnemann makes *The Sundowners*, with Robert Mitchum, Deborah Kerr, and the ubiquitous Chips Rafferty.
Britain: Karel Reisz's gritty, anti-authoritarian *Saturday Night and Sunday Morning*, with Albert Finney, is to transform British cinema, for a time.
Michael Powell's voyeuristic *Peeping Tom* upsets audiences and critics.
Richard Attenborough and Bryan Forbes produce, and Guy Green directs, the topical *The Angry Silence*.
Jack Cardiff directs D. H. Lawrence's *Sons and Lovers*, with Dean Stockwell and Trevor Howard.
France: Jean-Luc Godard's *Breathless* is a New Wave hit in art cinemas and makes a star of Jean-Paul Belmondo.
Louis Malle directs the inventive comedy *Zazie dans le Métro*.
François Truffaut makes *Shoot the Pianist*, starring Charles Aznavour.
Italy: Fellini's *La Dolce Vita*, starring Marcello Mastroianni and Anita Ekberg, is a worldwide hit, with its depiction of the wasted lives of the rich in Rome.
Visconti directs *Rocco and His Brothers*, with Alain Delon, about a peasant family in Milan.
Michelangelo's *L'Avventura*, with Monica Vitti, and *La Notte*, starring Marcello Mastroianni, Jeanne Moreau, and Monica Vitti, make the emptiness of life seem attractive.
Vittorio De Sica's *Two Women* gives Sophia Loren her best screen role.

1961
America: Robert Wise and Jerome Robbins make a successful film of the stage hit *West Side Story*.
Robert Rossen directs the brilliantly handled *The Hustler*, with Paul Newman and Jackie Gleason.
Disney releases *One Hundred and One Dalmatians*, which is to be its last splendid animated feature for 30 years.
Elizabeth Taylor becomes the top money-making star, followed by Rock Hudson, Doris Day, John Wayne, and Cary Grant.
Britain: Tony Richardson directs another 'kitchen sink' drama, *A Taste of Honey*, with Rita Tushingham, Dora Bryan, and Murray Melvin.
Basil Dearden's *Victim*, starring Dirk Bogarde, is one of the first films to deal sympathetically with homosexuality.
Joseph Losey directs the science-fiction *The Damned* for Hammer Films.
Pop singer Cliff Richard stars in the innocuous musical *The Young Ones*, directed by Sidney J. Furie.
France: Alain Resnais directs the enigmatic *Last Year at Marienbad*.
Italy: Poet and novelist Pier Paolo Pasolini directs his first film, the low-life *Accatone*.
Francesco Rosi makes *Salvatore Giuliano*, about a Sicilian bandit.
Pietro Germi's *Divorce Italian Style* mocks the country's divorce laws.
Ermanno Olmi makes the social comedy *The Job*.
Japan: Kurosawa directs *Yojimbo*, with Toshiro Mifune as a wandering samurai.
Spain: Luis Buñuel returns to Spain at the government's invitation and makes the sacrilegious *Viridiana*; it is promptly banned.
Sweden: Max Von Sydow goes to Hollywood to play Christ in *The Greatest Story Ever Told*.

1962
America: John Frankenheimer directs the brilliantly plotted thriller *The Manchurian Candidate*.

Robert Aldrich shocks by casting Bette Davis and Joan Crawford as two ageing, homicidal harridans in *Whatever Happened to Baby Jane?*
Darryl F. Zanuck returns to Twentieth Century-Fox as president with his son Richard as head of production as the company runs into difficulties over the out-of-control *Cleopatra*, starring Richard Burton and Elizabeth Taylor. His production of *The Longest Day*, about the Allied landings at Normandy, is a hit.
MCA acquire Universal.
Doris Day and Rock Hudson bounce back as the top money-makers, followed by Cary Grant, John Wayne, and Elvis Presley.
Britain: Tony Richardson directs the anti-authoritarian *The Loneliness of the Long Distance Runner*, starring Tom Courtenay.
John Schlesinger makes *A Kind of Loving*, with Alan Bates, June Ritchie, and Thora Hird.
David Lean's painstaking epic *Lawrence of Arabia* brings stardom to the lanky Peter O'Toole in the title role as the short, enigmatic hero.
Sean Connery plays James Bond in *Dr No*, a role that elevates him to stardom and begins a profitable cycle of films.
France: François Truffaut directs *Jules and Jim*, starring Jeanne Moreau as the woman shared by two friends.
Germany: 26 film-makers issue a manifesto for a new German feature film.
Japan: Yashujiro Ozu makes his last film, *An Autumn Afternoon*, on the loneliness of old age.
Mexico: Luis Buñuel directs *The Exterminating Angel*, about dinner guests who find themselves unable to leave the room.
Poland: Roman Polanski's *Knife in the Water* is attacked by the authorities and he soon leaves to work elsewhere.
USSR: Andrei Tarkovsky makes the tragic *Ivan's Childhood*, about a boy who joins the partisans.

1963
America: Martin Ritt directs the incisive character drama *Hud*, well acted by Paul Newman, Patricia Neal, and Melvyn Douglas.
Cleopatra is released but fails to make a profit.
Andy Warhol and his entourage begin making films at his Factory.
AIP's *Beach Party*, with Annette Funicello and Frankie Avalon, begins a cycle of beach movies.
Doris Day remains the top money-making star, followed by John Wayne, Rock Hudson, Jack Lemmon, and Cary Grant.
Brazil: Glauber Rocha gains an international reputation with his grim and violent *Black God, White Devil*.
Britain: Joseph Losey directs *The Servant*, scripted by Harold Pinter and starring Dirk Bogarde and James Fox.
Lindsay Anderson makes the tough *This Sporting Life*, written by David Storey and starring Richard Harris and Rachel Roberts.
Tony Richardson and John Osborne bring sex and exuberance to the cinema in *Tom Jones*, portrayed by Albert Finney.
John Schlesinger's *Billy Liar*, starring Tom Courtenay and Julie Christie, is another seminal film in the revival of British cinema, taken from Keith Waterhouse's novel of adolescent fantasy.
Italy: Fellini's brilliantly self-indulgent *8½*, with Marcello Mastroianni, depicts an artist suffering from a creative block.
Visconti makes a perfect adaptation of Giuseppe de Lampedusa's *The Leopard*, about the decline of the Sicilian aristocracy.

1964
America: Disney's *Mary Poppins*, with Julie Andrews, is the hit of the year.
Franklin Schaffner's *The Best Man*, starring Henry Fonda, is a brilliant political melodrama, as is John Frankenheimer's *Seven Days in May*, with Kirk Douglas.
Sidney Lumet's *Fail Safe* deals frighteningly with the threat of nuclear war.
Doris Day is still the most bankable star, followed by Jack Lemmon, Rock Hudson, John Wayne, and Cary Grant.
Britain: Stanley Kubrick makes the blackly comic *Dr Strangelove*, with Peter Sellers and George C. Scott.
Richard Lester finds a way to make the Beatles funny in *A Hard Day's Night*.
Guy Hamilton directs the Bond film *Goldfinger*.
Michael Winner makes *The System*, about sex at the seaside.
France: Jacques Demy's musical *The Umbrellas of*

Cherbourg, written by Michel Legrand, charms audiences everywhere.
Greece: Michael Cacoyannis's *Zorba the Greek*, with Anthony Quinn and the music of Mikis Theodorakis, is an international hit.
Italy: Sergio Leone borrows the plot of Kurosawa's *Yojimbo* for his western *A Fistful of Dollars*, starring a young American television actor, Clint Eastwood. Its success is helped by the evocative music of Ennio Morricone.
Antonioni's *The Red Desert*, with Monica Vitti and Richard Harris, revels in the possibilities for colour in film.
Bernardo Bertolucci's *Before the Revolution* heralds the arrival of a new, politicized talent.
Japan: Masaki Kobayashi's *Kwaidan* is a collection of perfectly composed ghost stories.
USSR: Innokenti Smoktunovsky is an impressive Hamlet in a version of Shakespeare's tragedy directed by Grigori Kozintsev.

1965
America: Robert Wise's *The Sound of Music*, starring Julie Andrews, is a massive hit.
Daniel Mann directs *Our Man Flint*, starring James Coburn, in an attempt to duplicate the success of the Bond movies. It fails.
David Lean's romantic *Dr Zhivago*, starring Omar Sharif and Julie Christie, is a worldwide box-office hit.
The Bond movies take British actor Sean Connery to the top of the list of money-making stars, followed by John Wayne, Doris Day, Julie Andrews, and Jack Lemmon.
Britain: The new Bond movie, *Thunderball*, is another big hit.
Sidney J. Furie's *The Ipcress File*, with Michael Caine as a shabby agent, attempts to cash in on the Bond phenomenon.
Richard Lester's comic *The Knack* gives impetus to the image of what is soon to be called 'Swinging London'.
John Schlesinger's *Darling*, with Julie Christie, catches the mood of the moment.
Roman Polanski makes the psychological horror film *Repulsion*, with Catherine Deneuve.
Czechoslovakia: Milos Forman directs *A Blonde in Love* (aka *Loves of a Blonde*).
France: Jean-Luc Godard directs the futuristic *Alphaville*, starring Eddie Constantine.
Hungary: Miklós Jancsó's *The Round-Up* gains him international recognition.
Italy: Fellini makes his first film in colour, the exuberant *Juliet of the Spirits*.
Sergio Leone's *For a Few Dollars More* establishes spaghetti westerns and Clint Eastwood as forces to be reckoned with.

1966
America: Sidney Lumet's *The Group*, from Mary McCarthy's novel, is the most talked-about film of the year with its cast of unknowns, who mostly remain so.
Mike Nichols films Edward Albee's *Who's Afraid of Virginia Woolf?* with Hollywood's most famous couple, Richard Burton and Elizabeth Taylor, as the embattled husband and wife.
Roger Corman's *The Wild Angels* for AIP begins a cycle of biker and youthful-protest movies.
Charles Bluhdorn's Gulf Western acquire Paramount Pictures.
Seven Arts Productions acquires Warner Bros.
Two British talents, Julie Andrews and Sean Connery, head the poll of money-making stars, followed by Elizabeth Taylor, Jack Lemmon, and Richard Burton.
Britain: Fred Zinnemann directs an impeccable version of Robert Bolt's play *A Man for All Seasons*, finely performed by Paul Scofield and Robert Shaw.
Michael Caine becomes an international star as the raffish *Alfie*, directed by Lewis Gilbert from Bill Naughton's play.
Antonioni comes to London to make *Blow-Up* with David Hemmings as a fashionable fashion photographer.
Karel Reisz directs the anarchic *Morgan*, which gives David Warner his best role before he goes to Hollywood to become a fixture in horror movies.
Silvio Narrizano's *Georgy Girl*, with James Mason and Lynn Redgrave, gives further impetus to the image of London as the place to be.
Universal Pictures establish a London office and other American companies step up local productions.
Czechoslovakia: Vera Chytilova makes the lively